New Venture Creation

ENTREPRENEURSHIP FOR THE 21st CENTURY

EIGHTH EDITION

New Venture Creation

ENTREPRENEURSHIP FOR THE 21st CENTURY

Jeffry A. Timmons, AB, MBA, DBA

Franklin W. Olin Distinguished Professor of Entrepreneurship
Director, Price Babson College Fellows Program
Babson College
Babson Park, Massachusetts

and

Stephen Spinelli, Jr., BA, MBA, PhD

John H. Muller, Jr. Chair, Entrepreneurship
Director, Arthur M. Blank Center for Entrepreneurship
Chairman, Entrepreneurship Division
Philadelphia University
Philadelphia, Pennsylvania

McGraw-Hill
Irwin

Boston   Burr Ridge, IL   Dubuque, IA   New York   San Francisco   St. Louis
Bangkok   Bogotá   Caracas   Kuala Lumpur   Lisbon   London   Madrid   Mexico City
Milan   Montreal   New Delhi   Santiago   Seoul   Singapore   Sydney   Taipei   Toronto

NEW VENTURE CREATION: ENTREPRENEURSHIP FOR THE 21st CENTURY

Published by McGraw-Hill/Irwin, a business unit of The McGraw-Hill Companies, Inc., 1221 Avenue of the Americas, New York, NY, 10020. Copyright © 2009, 2007, 2004, 1999, 1994, 1990, 1985, 1977 by Jeffry Timmons. All rights reserved. No part of this publication may be reproduced or distributed in any form or by any means, or stored in a database or retrieval system, without the prior written consent of Jeffry Timmons, including, but not limited to, in any network or other electronic storage or transmission, or broadcast for distance learning.

Some ancillaries, including electronic and print components, may not be available to customers outside the United States.

This book is printed on acid-free paper.

1 2 3 4 5 6 7 8 9 0 QPD/QPD 0 9 8

ISBN-13: 978-0-07-338155-8
ISBN-10: 0-07-338155-1

Editorial director: *Brent Gordon*
Publisher: *Paul Ducham*
Managing developmental editor: *Laura Hurst Spell*
Editorial assistant: *Sara Knox Hunter*
Editorial assistant: *Jane Beck*
Marketing manager: *Natalie Zook*
Project manager: *Bruce Gin*
Full service project manager: *Deb Darr, Aptara®, Inc.*
Lead production supervisor: *Michael R. McCormick*
Lead designer: *Joanne Mennemeier*
Senior media project manager: *Susan Lombardi*
Cover design: *Joanne Schapler*
Typeface: *10.5/12 New Caledonia*
Compositor: *Aptara®, Inc.*
Printer: *Quebecor World Dubuque Inc.*

Library of Congress Cataloging-in-Publication Data

Timmons, Jeffry A.
    New venture creation: entrepreneurship for the 21st century / Jeffry A. Timmons and Stephen Spinelli, Jr.—8th ed.
        p. cm.
    Includes index.
    ISBN-13: 978-0-07-338155-8 (alk. paper)
    ISBN-10: 0-07-338155-1 (alk. paper)
    1. New business enterprises–Handbooks, manuals, etc. 2. Entrepreneurship–Handhooks, manuals, etc. I. Spinelli, Stephen. II. Title.
HD62.5.T55 2009
658.1'141–dc22

2008008608

DEDICATION

To William F. Glavin, ninth president of Babson College, 1989–1995. Our hero, our mentor, our leader extraordinaire, and our dear friend. You are to Babson College, to us, and to university presidencies what Tom Brady, Wayne Gretzky, and Michael Jordan are to football, hockey, and basketball . . . simply the greatest! Thank you, Bill, for supporting and propelling entrepreneurship toward our dreams.

Jeffry A. Timmons (December 7, 1941-April 8, 2008): **In Memoriam**

Franklin W. Olin Distinguished Professor of Entrepreneurship and Director, Price-Babson College Fellows Program at Babson College AB, Colgate University; MBA, DBA, Harvard University Graduate School of Business.

Days before he died Jeff submitted the last few revisions for this text. He was never more engaged intellectually then when he was translating research and experiences into coursework. He worked on the belief that deep thinking could motivate decisive action and provide dedicated students of entrepreneurship a competitive advantage.

Jeff's commitment to higher education and to entrepreneurship was a statement of his belief in humanity...striving for the betterment of the human condition. He believed goodness and achievement were inherent in everyone. Jeff also believed that entrepreneurship classes were a perfect vehicle to refine and amplify purposeful study and action that would lead to a better life and a better world.

Beginning his career in the 1960's, Jeffry A. Timmons was one of the pioneers in the development of entrepreneurship education and research in America. He is recognized as a leading authority internationally for his research, innovative curriculum development, and teaching in entrepreneurship, new ventures, entrepreneurial finance, and venture capital.

Professor Timmons was also an enigma in academia—having resigned tenure twice, as well as resigning two endowed chairs. In 1994, he resigned the Harvard endowed professorship he had held since 1989 to return to Babson College, which he had joined in 1982, and in 1995 was named the first Franklin W. Olin Distinguished Professor of Entrepreneurship. Earlier he had been the first to hold the Paul T. Babson professorship for two years, and subsequently became the first named to the Frederic C. Hamilton Professorship in Free Enterprise Studies, from which he resigned in 1989 to accept the Harvard chair. Earlier at Northeastern University in 1973, he launched what is believed to be the first undergraduate major in new ventures and entrepreneurship in the country, and later created and led the Executive MBA program. Both of these programs exist today. *Business Week's 1995 Guide to Graduate Business Schools* rated Timmons as the "best bet" and among the top 10 professors at Harvard Business School. *Success* magazine (September, 1995) in a feature article called him "one of the two most powerful minds in entrepreneurship in the nation." Michie P. Slaughter, former president of the Kauffman Center for Entrepreneurial Leadership at the Ewing Marion Kauffman Foundation, calls him "the premier entrepreneurship educator in America." Before her death in January 2001, Gloria Appel, as president of the Price Institute for Entrepreneurial Studies noted, "he has done more to advance entrepreneurship education than any other educator in America." In 1995, the Price Institute and Babson College faculty and friends chose to honor Dr. Timmons by endowing The Jeffry A. Timmons Professorship in recognition of his contributions to Babson and to the field. In 2007, Forbes Small Business called Dr. Timmons one of the country's best entrepreneurship educators.

In 1985, he designed and launched the Price-Babson College Symposium for Entrepreneurship Educators, aimed at improving teaching and research by teaming highly successful entrepreneurship with "an itch to teach" with experienced faculty. This unique initiative was in response to a need to create a mechanism enabling colleges and universities to attract and support entrepreneurship educators and entrepreneurs and help them create lasting collaborations that would enhance the classroom experience for their students. There is now a core group of over 1400 entrepreneurship educators and entrepreneurs from over 300 colleges and universities in the US and

38 foreign countries, who are alumni of the Price-Babson College Fellows Program. In May 1995, *INC.* magazine's "Who's Who" special edition on entrepreneurship called him "the Johnny Appleseed of entrepreneurship education" and concluded that this program had "changed the terrain of entrepreneurship education." The program was the winner of two national awards, has been replicated outside the USA, and has now been expanded to eight countries outside of the United States and continues to grow. In 1998, Dr. Timmons led an initiative now funded by the Kauffman Center for Entrepreneurial Leadership to create Lifelong Learning for Entrepreneurship Education Professionals (LLEEP) offering a series of training clinics for entrepreneurship educators.

In 2003 Timmons worked with Professor Steve Spinelli to conceive a sister program to the SEE program which would be available for engineering schools with an interest in entrepreneurship. They partnered with colleagues at the new Olin College of Engineering on the Babson campus; President Rick Miller, Provost David Kerns, Dean Michael Moody and Professors John Bourne, Ben Linder, Heidi Neck, and Stephen Schiffman to win a three-year National Science Foundation grant to design, develop and deliver such a program. The first pilot was done in June 2005 with significant success, and offered on the Babson/Olin Campus in 2006 and 2007.

During the past decades, Dr. Timmons helped launch several new initiatives at Babson, including the Babson-Kauffman Entrepreneurship Research Conference, the Kauffman Foundation/CEL Challenge Grant, the Price Challenge Grant, business plan competitions, and a president's seminar. In 1997 he led an initiative to create the first need-based full-tuition scholarship for MBA students with a $900,000 matching grant from the Price Institute for Entrepreneurial Studies. Each year one of the recipients of this Price-Babson Alumni Scholarship is named the Gloria Appel Memorial Scholar in honor of this longtime benefactor, colleague and friend. In addition to teaching, Professor Timmons devoted a major portion of his efforts at Babson to the Price-Babson programs and to joint initiatives funded by the Kauffman Center for Entrepreneurial Leadership and Babson, including new research and curriculum development activities. He provided leadership in developing and teaching in initiatives that assist Native Americans seeking economic self-determination and community development most notably through entrepreneurship education programs at the nation's several Tribal Colleges. In April 2001, Professor Timmons was recognized for these efforts in a citation voted by the legislature of the State of Oklahoma naming him Ambassador for Entrepreneurship.

Since 1999, he served as special advisor to the National Commission on Entrepreneurship. The work of the Commission culminated in a national conference held in April 2001 that was jointly sponsored by the John F. Kennedy School of Government at Harvard University, the National Commission of Entrepreneurship, and the Kauffman Center for Entrepreneurial Leadership. Professor Timmons served as a lead moderator at conference sessions.

A prolific researcher and writer, he wrote nine books, including this textbook first published in 1974. *New Venture Creation* has been rated by *INC.*, *Success*, and the *Wall Street Journal* as a "classic" in entrepreneurship, and has been translated into both Japanese and Chinese. In 1996 and 1998, *INC.* featured the book's fourth edition as one of the top eight "must read" books for entrepreneurs. *Venture Capital at the Crossroads* written with Babson colleague William Bygrave (1992) is considered the seminal work on the venture capital industry and is also translated into Japanese. Earlier, Dr. Timmons wrote *The Entrepreneurial Mind* (1989), *New Business Opportunities* (1990), *The Insider's Guide to Small Business Resources* (1984), *The Encyclopedia of Small Business Resources* (1984), and his contributed chapters to other books including The Portable MBA in Entrepreneurship (1994, 1997, 2003). More recently, he has co-authored How to Raise Capital with Babson Professor Andrew Zacharakis (2005), and Business Plans that Work, with Steve Spinelli (2004). Timmons authored over 100 articles and papers, which appeared in numerous leading publications, such as *Harvard Business Review* and *Journal of Business Venturing*, along with numerous teaching case studies. In 1995, he began to develop a new audiotape series on entrepreneurship, working with Sam Tyler, producer of the *In Search of Excellence series* for PBS with Tom Peters. He has also appeared in the national media in the United States and numerous other countries and has been quoted in *INC.*, *Success, The Wall Street Journal, The New York Times, The Los Angeles Times, Business Week, Working Woman, Money, USA Today*, and has had feature articles written about him in *The Rolling Stone* (1997), *The Boston Globe* (1997), and *Success* (1994).

Dr. Timmons earned a reputation for "practicing what he teaches." One former graduate and software entrepreneur interviewed for the *Rolling Stone* article put it succinctly: "When going to his classes I couldn't wait to get there; and when I got there I didn't ever want to leave!" For over 35 years he has been immersed in the world of entrepreneurship as an investor, director, and/or advisor in private companies and investment funds including Cellular One in

Boston, and New Hampshire and Maine, the Boston Communications Group, BCI Advisors, Inc., Spectrum Equity Investors, Internet Securities, Inc., Chase Capital Partners, Color Kinetics, Inc., Flat World Knowledge and others. He also served since 1991 as founding member of the Board of Directors of the Kauffman Center for Entrepreneurial Leadership at the Ewing Marion Kauffman Foundation. For the next 10 years he served as a special advisor to the President and Board of Directors of the Kauffman Center, where he conceived of the Kauffman Fellows Program and served as its dean of faculty. In 2003 he worked closely with the President and alumni of the Kauffman Fellows Program to successfully spin the program out of the Kauffman Foundation into an independent entity as the Center for Venture Management, and continues as Dean, Chairman of the Educational Advisory Committee, and on the Board of Directors. The aim of this innovative program is to create for aspiring venture capitalists and entrepreneurs what the Rhodes scholarship and White House Fellows programs are to politics and public affairs. In 2001, Jeff joined the President's Council at the newly formed Franklin W. Olin College of Engineering. In 1994 and 1996, he served as a National Judge for the Ernst & Young Entrepreneur of the Year Awards.

Dr. Timmons received his MBA and DBA from Harvard Business School, where he was a National Defense Education Act fellow and is a graduate of Colgate University, where he was a Scott Paper Foundation Scholar. He served as a trustee of Colgate from 1991 to 2000. He lived on his 500+ acre farm in New Hampshire with his wife of over 40 years, Sara, and winters at Brays Island Plantation near Savannah, Georgia. He loved the outdoors: fly-fishing; hunting and golf. He is one of the founders of the Wapack Highlands Greenway Initiative in New Hampshire, was an active in the Henry's Fork Foundation and Wildlife Conservation Trust of New Hampshire, and served as a director of Timber Owners of New England. He was a member of numerous other wildlife and nature organizations, including The Monadnock Conservancy, The Harris Center, The Nature Conservancy, The Moosehead Region Futures Committee, Atlantic Salmon Federation, and Ruffed Grouse Society.

Stephen Spinelli, Jr.

President, Philadelphia University

Formerly Babson College, Vice Provost for Entrepreneurship and Global Management; Director Arthur M. Blank Center for Entrepreneurship and Chairman, Entrepreneurship Division , Paul T. Babson Chair in Entrepreneurship

B.A., McDaniel College (formerly Western Maryland College); MBA, Babson Graduate School of Business; and PhD (Economics), Imperial College, University of London

The majority of Dr. Spinelli's professional experience has been in entrepreneurship. He was a founding shareholder, director and manager of Jiffy Lube International. He was also founder, chairman and CEO of American Oil Change Corporation. In 1991, he completed a sale of Jiffy Lube to Pennzoil Company. Dr. Spinelli led the Entrepreneurship Division at Babson and taught full-time, he has not abandoned his business roots. He continues to consult with regional, national, and international companies; serves as a Director at several corporations and participates as an angel investor with investments in more than a dozen startups.

Dr. Spinelli is the quintessential "pracademic"—a business practitioner turned academic. Having successfully harvested Jiffy Lube, Dr. Spinelli was invited to attend the Price Babson College Fellows Program and his career in academia was launched. After several years of part-time teaching, he joined the ranks of full-time faculty after receiving his PhD in October 1995 from Imperial College, University of London. Dr. Spinelli's expertise is in startup and growth management. His research has focused on an understanding of strategic entrepreneurial relationships. He is the author of more than two-dozen journal articles, book chapters, academic papers, and teaching case studies. He is also the author of six books including *Franchising: Pathway to Entrepreneurship*, (Prentice-Hall; 2003). *His latest book Never Bet the Farm, is co-authored with* Anthony Iaquinto. A superb educator, he served as a key member of the faculty of the Price Babson College Fellows Program's Symposium for Entrepreneurship Educators (SEE) for 12 years, in addition to his teaching in the undergraduate, graduate, and executive education programs, and is a shining example of the many contributions that entrepreneurs can make to an academic institution. Dr. Spinelli led the internationalization of SEE to Chile, Argentina, Costa Rica, China and Europe. In 2003 Dr. Spinelli founded the Babson-Historically Black Colleges and Universities case writing consortium. This group is dedicated to writing entrepreneurship teaching cases focused on African American entrepreneurs.

He was a leading force in curriculum innovation at Babson, and with his colleagues in Entrepreneurship Division continually defines and delivers new initiatives. In 1999, he led the design and implementation of an Entrepreneurship Intensity Track for MBAs seeking to launch new business ventures upon graduation. Building on this highly successful initiative, he led the design and development of ACE—an accelerated honors curriculum for aspiring entrepreneurs in Babson's undergraduate program. Dr. Spinelli's presentation to the United States Association for Small Business and Entrepreneurship (USASBE) resulted in the naming the F.W. Olin Graduate School of Business the 2002 National Model MBA program

Dr. Spinelli has been a strong voice for entrepreneurship. He has been a keynote speaker for Advent International's CEO Conference, the MCAA National Convention and Allied Domecq International's Retailing Conference, the Entrepreneur's Organization at MIT and many others; has been called to testify before the US Senate Subcommitee on Small Business and Entrepreneurship; and is often quoted as an expert in the field in such leading publications as the *Wall Street Journal, Forbes magazine, The Financial Times, Success Magazine and Inc. magazine.*

President Stephen Spinelli was touted as a new model of college president in a front page story in the May 17, 2008 <u>Philadelphia Inquirer</u>.

He also serves as a director for several local, regional and national not-for-profits or community based associations.

Stephen Spinelli, Jr., Ph.D.
President
Philadelphia University
Henry Avenue and School House Lane
Philadelphia, PA 19144
SpinelliS@Philau.edu
215 951 2727 office

PREFACE

A Book for a New Generation of Entrepreneurial Leaders—Worldwide

The entrepreneurship revolution in America over the past 40 years has had an extraordinary impact on the cultural and economic landscape in the United States. While there will always be opportunities for improvement and innovation, America's opportunity-driven style of entrepreneurship has sparked an entrepreneurial revolution around the globe.

Technology has certainly played a major role in this global phenomenon. In 2007 there were over 1.1 billion Internet users in the world, with over 900 million of them outside the United States. Even in tiny Iceland, 86 percent of the homes are connected. In the United States an iPod is sold *every eight seconds*. Entrepreneurship and the Internet continue to flatten the world at a staggering pace. In the process, they are spawning fertile fields of opportunities that are being tilled and seized on every continent.

In our roles as students, teachers, researchers, observers, and participants in this stunning revolution, we see that global adoption of the entrepreneurial mind-set is growing exponentially larger and faster. That new venture mind-set, which increasingly places a premium on sustainable models, is now affecting strategies at global corporations and in the not-for-profit world as well. The golden age of entrepreneurial reasoning, value creation and capture, and philanthropy has arrived; and we can only guess at the positive impact it will have in the coming years.

An Edition for an Era of Uncertainty and Extraordinary Opportunity

The new millennium is being defined as much by worldwide challenges and uncertainty as it is by the enormous opportunities afforded by technology, global communications, and the increasing drive to develop socially, economically, and environmentally sane and sensible new ventures. As with past generations, entrepreneurs in this arena face the ultimate and most demanding juggling act: how to simultaneously balance the insatiable requirements of marriage, family, new venture, and community service, and still have time for personal pleasure and peace.

A Book about the Entrepreneurial Process: The Basis for a Curriculum as Well as a Course!

New Venture Creation is about the actual process of getting a new venture started, growing the venture, successfully harvesting it, and starting again.

There is a substantial body of knowledge, concepts, and tools that entrepreneurs need to know—before, during, and after taking the start-up plunge—if they are to get the odds in their favor. Accompanying the explosion in entrepreneurship has been a significant increase in research and knowledge about the entrepreneurial process. Much of what was known previously has been reinforced and refined, whereas some has been challenged. Numerous new insights have emerged. *New Venture Creation* continues to be the product of experience and considerable research in this field—rooted in real-world application and refined in the classroom.

As with previous editions, the design and flow of this book are aimed at creating knowledge, skills, and awareness. In a pragmatic way—through text, case studies, and hands-on exercises—students are drawn in to discover critical aspects of entrepreneurship, and what levels of competencies, know-how, experience, attitudes, resources, and networks are required to pursue different entrepreneurial opportunities.

There is no substitute for the real thing—actually starting a company. But short of that, it is possible to expose students to many of the vital issues and immerse them in key learning experiences, such as critical self-assessment and the development of a business plan.

The exciting news is that you can learn from other people's experiences, know-how, and wisdom; you don't have to learn it all by doing it yourself. If that were the case, wouldn't everyone succeed as an entrepreneur? Besides, insisting on learning everything from scratch would take far too much time and money! By fully engaging the material in this book—the required analysis, thinking, and practice with the cases, exercises, assignments, and discussions both in and out of the classroom—you can significantly compress your learning curve, reduce your ultimate risk and pain, and gain a lot more from your subsequent hands-on experiences.

This book is divided into five parts. Parts I through IV detail the driving forces of entrepreneurship: opportunity recognition, the business plan, the founder and the team, and resource requirements. Part I describes the global entrepreneurial revolution and addresses the mind-set required to tackle this tremendously challenging and rewarding pursuit. Part II lays out the process by which real opportunities—not just ideas—can be discovered and selected. This section examines the type of opportunity around which higher-potential ventures can be built (with acceptable risks and trade-offs), sustainable enterprising, and opportunities for social entrepreneurship. Part III concerns entrepreneurial leadership, team creation, and personal ethics. Part IV addresses franchising as an entrepreneurial vehicle, marshaling resources, entrepreneurial finance, and fund-raising. The book concludes with a section dealing with strategies for success, managing rapid growth, and harvest issues.

Once you understand how winning entrepreneurs think, act, and perform, you can establish goals to emulate those actions, attitudes, habits, and strategies. *New Venture Creation* challenges you to think about the process of becoming an entrepreneur and seeks to enable you to immerse yourself in the dynamics of launching and growing a company. The book addresses practical issues such as the following:

What are my real talents, strengths, and weaknesses? How can I exploit my talents and strengths and minimize my weaknesses? How can I recognize when an opportunity is more than just another good idea, and whether it's one that fits with my personal mind-set, capabilities, and life goals? Why do some firms grow quickly

to several million dollars in sales but then stumble, never growing beyond a single product? What are the critical tasks and hurdles in seizing an opportunity and building the business? How much money do I need, and when, where, and how can I get it on acceptable terms? What financing sources, strategies, and mechanisms can I bring to bear throughout the process—from pre-start, through the early growth stage, to the harvest of my venture?

What are the minimum resources I need to gain control over the opportunity, and how can I do this? Is a business plan needed? If so, what kind is required, and how and when should I develop one? For what constituents must I create or add value to achieve a positive cash flow and to develop harvest options? What is my venture worth, and how do I negotiate what to give up? What are the critical transitions in entrepreneurial management as a firm grows from $1 million, to $5 million, to over $25 million in sales?

What are some of the pitfalls, minefields, and hazards I need to anticipate, prepare for, and respond to? What contacts and networks do I need to access and develop?

Do I know what I do and do not know, and do I know what to do about this? How can I develop a personal entrepreneurial game plan to acquire the experience I need to succeed? How critical and sensitive is the timing in each of these areas? Why do entrepreneurship and entrepreneurial leadership seem surrounded by paradoxes, well-known to entrepreneurs, such as these:

- Ambiguity and uncertainty versus planning and rigor.
- Creativity versus disciplined analysis.
- Patience and perseverance versus urgency.
- Organization and management versus flexibility.
- Innovation and responsiveness versus systemization.
- Risk avoidance versus risk management.
- Current profits versus long-term equity.

The *New Venture Creation* models are useful not only as a comprehensive textbook for a course in entrepreneurship, but also as a road map for a curriculum or departmental major in entrepreneurship. Since the late 1990s, for example, Babson College has been setting the standard for management education with an approach based on the model of the entrepreneurial process in this text. This integrative program has been a major factor in keeping Babson College in the top spot among entrepreneurship schools in America and around the world.

A Summary of Changes in the Eighth Edition: New Cases, New Chapters, New Data, and Major Revisions

This edition is a significant update from the seventh edition. New cases and exercises, updated Web sites, and text material have been added to capture the current financial, economic, technological, and globally competitive environment of this first decade of the new century. A special effort has been made to include cases that capture the dynamic ups and downs new firms experience over an extended time. By grappling with decisions faced by entrepreneurs—from start-up to harvest—this text offers a broad and rich perspective on the often turbulent and unpredictable nature of the entrepreneurial process.

We have updated our real-world application of the Timmons Model of the entrepreneurial process with a look at Google's amazing trajectory. For those concerned about our environment and wide-ranging social issues and how these present enormous opportunities for your generation of entrepreneurs to solve these problems, we have included two new chapters, "Clean Commerce: Seeing Opportunity through a Sustainability Lens" and "Opportunities for Social Entrepreneurship," which you will find thought-provoking and worthwhile.

This edition features important changes and additions. As with the previous edition, we have undertaken a major restructuring and reordering of the flow of the book, which now begins with a focus on the worldwide impact of entrepreneurship. Six new cases have been added, as well as a series of three vignettes to spark discussion and learning in the difficult realm of business ethics.

This eighth edition contains the latest updates, including examples of entrepreneurs in action coping with the post-Internet bubble era and the mortgage loan crisis in 2007. This edition features refined exercises and five new ones: Venturekipedia, a tool for enhancing research; Virtual Brain Trust, a complementary exercise to the Brain Trust exercise; and in the final chapter, a new interview exercise titled Wisdom from the Harvest—a visit with successful, harvested entrepreneurs that could connect you to the most insightful discussions you have ever had. Slicing the Equity Pie is a new tool for resolving ownership participating and ethical caselettes is a new set of challenging ethical decisions.

Chapter 1, "The Global Entrepreneurial Revolution for a Flatter World": A Major Rewrite with a New Exercise and a New Case

Chapter 1, derived from the second chapter of the previous edition, looks at entrepreneurship as a 40-year transformational force in America that is now driving economic opportunity and prosperity worldwide. We have substantially updated the material in this edition, which now includes a discussion of the state of entrepreneurship education, how nonprofits are adopting entrepreneurial methods, and how the creation and liberation of human energy through entrepreneurship have become the single largest transformational force on the planet. This chapter includes the Visit with an Entrepreneur exercise that will help to establish important benchmarks, role models, and comparisons that are referenced throughout the text.

The new Venturekipedia exercise is a tool to assist students in making frugal use of their time while doing research, due diligence, and other investigations, regardless of the topic. In this exercise, students utilize Wikipedia to identify new Web sites and resources closely related to their original set of keywords. The result is a valuable bank of new insights and Web site links.

The new ImageCafé case discusses Clarence Wooten, who has been bent on becoming an entrepreneur since childhood. Following his academic and technical interests, after college he founded Envision Design, an award-winning 3D animation company targeting architects. His second start-up, Metamorphosis Studios, morphed into his third: ImageCafé, a business offering Web site templates that appeared to have been designed by high-end professionals. We follow Clarence's efforts to raise capital and grow the company when he receives advances by an industry leader to buy his company.

This case can be used in the first third of the course to address issues around opportunity assessment and reinvention. ImageCafé is a third iteration by this tenacious and thoughtful entrepreneur. The effect his first two ventures had on shaping the new venture is a great example of how entrepreneurial failure can be a vital learning experience. Opportunities for discussion include scalability, burn rate, OOC (out of cash), and valuation.

Chapter 2, "The Entrepreneurial Mind": A Significant Rewrite with a New Case

Chapter 2 is a major revision of Chapter 1 from the previous edition; it presents the strategies, habits, attitudes, and behaviors that work for entrepreneurs who build higher-potential ventures. This chapter outlines exciting new research that supports the authors' long-standing assertion that effective entrepreneurs are internally motivated, high-energy leaders with a unique tolerance for ambiguity, a keen eye toward mitigating risk, and a passion for discovery and innovation. Still here is the popular exercise Crafting a Personal Entrepreneurial Strategy—the personal equivalent of developing a business plan.

The new Lakota Hills case follows Laura Ryan, a Native American who has taken her family's special recipe for frybread from the kitchen to supermarkets all over the Midwest. But is their current strategy the best way to build their specialty foods venture? This case provides an excellent overview of the entrepreneurial process, including creating value, channel marketing, and fund-raising. The case includes metrics that will work for MBA-level discussions and analysis as well.

Chapter 3, "The Entrepreneurial Process": New and Updated Material

This chapter develops the Timmons Model framework for the entrepreneurial process and offers a real-world illustration of this conceptual model with an examination of Google's rise from a garage venture to a multifaceted international powerhouse. This edition emphasizes how building a sustainable venture means achieving economic, environmental, and social goals without compromising the same opportunity for future generations.

The Roxanne Quimby case tells the remarkable story of a young woman, living at a subsistence level in the backwoods of Maine, who sees an opportunity and grows it in a few years into a multimillion-dollar venture.

Chapter 4, "Clean Commerce: Seeing Opportunity through a Sustainability Lens": New Chapter by Andrea Larson and Karen O'Brien

This new chapter was developed by Professors Andrea Larson and Karen O'Brien from the University of Virginia. They have built on their pioneering work on clean commerce and sustainable enterprising to prepare this exciting new material. This chapter demonstrates how clean commerce is spawning what may be the greatest flow of new entrepreneurial opportunities that will occur this century: in energy conservation and independence, pollution control, green materials and construction, and saving the environment of the planet. This dramatic sea change is linked to the Timmons Model and shows how its

principles and methodologies can be applied to this new arena. Your thinking and imagination about big ideas and big opportunities will be stimulated and enlightened by this chapter—it's a must-read.

The Jim Poss case describes Jim's enterprise, Seahorse Power Company, which is an engineering start-up that encourages the adoption of environmentally friendly methods of power generation by designing products that are cheaper and more efficient than 20th-century technologies. Jim is sure that his first product, a patent-pending, solar-powered trash compactor, could make a real difference. This case chronicles the evolution of this green venture and places the entrepreneur at the critical point of deciding how best to deal with potential investors and funding alternatives.

Chapter 5, "The Opportunity: Creating, Shaping, Recognizing, Seizing": Updated Material

An important precursor to the next chapter on screening venture opportunities, this chapter introduces opportunity assessment and due diligence strategies. The authors challenge budding entrepreneurs to "think big enough" as they examine opportunities using criteria favored by successful entrepreneurs, angels, and venture capital investors in evaluating potential ventures.

The Burt's Bees case follows the Roxanne Quimby story explored in Chapter 3. Roxanne is a remarkable entrepreneur whose creative ideas and entrepreneurial spirit led her to create a new business around beeswax products and derivatives. With her company experiencing profitable growth, Roxanne faces a major issue of relocation to North Carolina and the offer of a significant strategic sale.

In the Next Sea Changes exercise students are challenged to research, brainstorm, and identify new technologies and discoveries that will drive the next growth industries, just as the integrated circuit drove the evolution from mainframe computers to personal computers to iPhones.

Chapter 6, "Screening Venture Opportunities": Revised Material with a New Case

This chapter builds on the drivers and criteria in Chapter 5, utilizing two screening methodologies that can help students determine whether their ideas are potential opportunities. By applying the opportunity criteria from the previous chapter, students begin to assess the probable fit of their ideas with their own lives, their teams, the required resources, and the balance of risk and reward.

The QuickScreen and Venture Opportunity Screening exercises provide valuable formats to guide the initial evaluation of an idea and the due diligence needed to determine its profit potential, probable risk and reward, and sustainability. The QuickScreen is a dehydrated version of the core exercise that helps students to quickly cut through to the core characteristics of an opportunity. These exercises may be used separately or together, allowing maximum flexibility in the syllabus, when counseling individual students, and with mentoring field study projects.

The new Globant case discusses a four-year-old venture making business headlines in Argentina as the largest independent information technology (IT) outsourcer in that country. From the beginning, Martin Migoya and cofounder Guibert Englebienne have fueled sales by tapping their personal networks and by successfully following up on every lead and referral coming their way. Their sustained push for wins, however, has resulted in such a broadly diversified portfolio of clients and service offerings that they risk being marginalized by larger, more focused competitors. This case lets students examine opportunity criteria such as skill sets, geography, industry segments, and client needs with the aim of determining a best-fit growth strategy—on the fly.

Chapter 7, "Opportunities for Social Entrepreneurship": New Chapter and a New Case

This chapter by Heidi Neck, assistant professor of entrepreneurship at Babson College, presents new research and a framework for identifying and executing opportunities that intrinsically have important societal outcomes and benefits. The field of social entrepreneurship is an exciting convergence of *doing good* and *doing well*, and this chapter shows that the principles, ways of thinking and reasoning, and methodologies in the Timmons Model can be used effectively to identify opportunities for, develop, and build for-profit and nonprofit enterprises with social missions.

The new Northwest Community Venture Fund case describes Michelle Foster, general partner of NVC, a for-profit equity fund with a socially responsible mission to invest in rural communities in Oregon and Washington State. As with most venture funds, NVC is raising a follow-on fund long before performance results are in for the current effort. Michelle wonders whether institutional investors can be attracted to the fund's unique brand of socially responsible venture capital—especially if better returns are available elsewhere at lower risk. Michelle's immediate challenge, however, is Eileen O'Brien, the passionate founder of NCV's staunchly nonprofit parent organization. At first their vastly different business philosophies had been a source of respect, philosophical curiosity, and even amusement. Increasingly, though, that relationship has become strained by the pressures that both leaders face to satisfy their respective—and highly disparate—mandates.

Chapter 8, "The Business Plan": Updated Material and a New Exercise

This chapter, including the classic and detailed Business Plan Guide, offers in this edition a comprehensive list of the benefits of writing a business plan—especially for the first-timer. The authors stress that embarking on the perilous journey of starting a new venture without some serious planning defies sensibility. At the same time they discuss the sorts of businesses and entrepreneurs that can move forward with a "dehydrated business plan"—backed by experience or necessitated by a closing window of opportunity.

The new Virtual Brain Trust exercise discusses how today's social networking Web sites and the worldwide connectivity of the Internet have opened up vast new opportunities to identify and build the most important part of the external team—the venture's brain trust. This exercise, a precursor to the Brain Trust exercise in Chapter 11, uses online resources to attract brain trust members who are direct and honest and have the entrepreneur's best interests at heart.

The Newland Medical Technologies case describes what seemed like a perfect plan. With two assertive angel investors guiding her medical device company on what looked like an acquisition fast track, young entrepreneur Sarah Foster and her husband decided that the time was right to start a family. However, by the middle of her first trimester, everything had changed. As cofounder and president, Sarah was now compelled to reconsider the course she'd set for her medical device venture. In doing so, she was going to have to make some tough choices to strike a balance between motherhood and her professional passions.

Chapter 9, "The Entrepreneurial Leader and the Team": Major Rewrite with Two New Exercises

Recognizing that in high-potential ventures the entrepreneurial leader(s) and the team are inseparable, this edition combines Chapters 7 and 8 of the previous edition. Note also that throughout this chapter (and the book) the term *manager* has been replaced with *leader* as a far more accurate reflection of what it takes to grow a venture. In the process of merging these critical chapters, we have replaced some sections and exhibits with new material, including discussion and exercises relating to the important issue of rewards and equity.

The Leadership Skills and Know-How Assessment exercise offers an organized inventory of leadership skills, enabling students to obtain feedback and to assess their skills, know-how, competencies—now including ethics—and other relevant experience and attributes necessary to pursue the opportunities they are developing.

The new Slicing the Equity Pie exercise begins the process of enabling the lead entrepreneur to think through tricky and delicate compensation and equity allocations.

The new Founder's Assignment exercise has the lead entrepreneur draft a one-page summary of what he or she believes the salaries and stock ownership will look like at the time of launch—in dollars and shares. To test his or her thinking, assumptions, and assessment of the potential contributions of the team, the entrepreneur shares the document with brain trust members who have experience in a company that has gone public.

The Maclean Palmer case discusses an African American founder of a new private equity fund in 2000. The case details his meticulous and thoughtful approach to putting a team together from scratch for a potential lifelong partnership.

Chapter 10, "Ethical Decision Making and the Entrepreneur": Updated Material and a New Exercise

With help from Professors James Klingler and William Bregman at the Center for Entrepreneurship at Villanova University, we have been able to considerably enhance this chapter about the complex and thorny issues of ethics and integrity for the entrepreneur. New sections and examples and three caselettes have been added.

In the new exercise called Ethical Decisions— What Would You Do? we present three interesting real-life ethical decision situations that will spark group discussion and foster an understanding of the critical importance of high ethical standards and awareness in the team and the company.

The Ethics exercise compels students to make various ethical choices and utilizes their answers to focus discussion on the issues raised by the assignment and in the chapter.

Chapter 11, "Resource Requirements": Updated Material

Chapter 11 examines the third element of the Timmons Model—managing resources. Successful strategies and techniques used by entrepreneurs to gain control over and minimize resources are discussed, including bootstrapping, using other people's resources, and decisions and issues related to setting up informal and formal boards.

The Build Your Brain Trust exercise complements the Virtual Brain Trust exercise in Chapter 8. This exercise is modeled after the Babson Brain Trust, a program at Babson College designed to create collisions and networking opportunities for student entrepreneurs as they seek to identify significant venture opportunities.

The exercise called How Entrepreneurs Turn Less into More is a short field project requiring students to identify and interview in depth entrepreneurs who have created companies with sales over $3 million, having started with less than $50,000 of seed capital. This can be a powerful and revealing exercise for students.

The Quick Lube Franchise Corporation case examines how one of the original founders of the Jiffy Lube franchise becomes a leading franchisee and then faces harvesting issues. The complex valuation, timing, deal structuring, and negotiating issues are an important aspect of the case.

Chapter 12, "Franchising": Updated Material

Chapter 12 examines franchising as an opportunity and as a risk–reward management strategy. It examines the entrepreneurial aspects of franchising, including structural and strategic alternatives available to entrepreneurs, selection criteria, resource and experience requirements, and the building and managing of the franchise system, as well as the complex relationships that can evolve.

The Mike Bellobuono case follows the story of an undergraduate who becomes enamored with a bagel shop concept and chooses franchising to grow his concept.

Chapter 13, "Entrepreneurial Finance": Updated Material

This chapter discusses what entrepreneurs need to know about entrepreneurial finance, such as determining capital requirements, the free cash flow format, and developing financial and fund-raising strategies.

The Midwest Lighting case is always a favorite; it's a classic partners-in-conflict case. The valuation, the future estimates of the business's potential, and a mechanism for getting one of the partners out are embedded in the case. The teaching note shares the methodology that breaks the logjam and the subsequent success stories of each. This is the 2005 version with updated numbers that bring it into the current period. The fundamental content, issues, and lessons from the case are timeless.

Chapter 14, "Obtaining Venture and Growth Capital": Updated Material

Chapter 14 discusses sources of informal angel equity and venture capital, how angels and venture capital investors evaluate deals, and how to deal with investors. Included are significant new and updated materials such as data and exhibits on capital markets, Web resources, and a discussion of the venture capital environment in down markets, such as the one that the followed the dot-com mania of the late 1990s. The concept and framework for a capital markets food chain remain a chapter anchor.

The Forte Ventures case chronicles the development and fund-raising challenges of Maclean Palmer (see Chapter 9) as he attempts to create his own private equity firm during the worst period in the history of the U.S. venture capital industry: 2000–2001.

Chapter 15, "The Deal: Valuation, Structure, and Negotiation": Updated Material

This chapter lays out in detail the various valuation methodologies used by entrepreneurs and venture capitalists, pre- and post-money, deal structuring principles, and negotiation issues faced by entrepreneurs. It also discusses the pitfalls and traps encountered by entrepreneurs.

The Lightwave Technology case is set in the mid-1990s, when seasoned entrepreneurs George Kinson and Dr. Schyler Weiss shocked the staid lighting industry with their full-spectrum digital lighting prototypes. After taking the award for product of the year at a major trade show, their company rapidly evolved from a fledgling start-up to one of the most talked-about companies in the industry. Then the Internet bubble burst, and Lightwave was forced to abandon its plans for going public. By 2003, however, the company was back on track. The question for the team now was whether to move ahead with an additional round of financing in anticipation of an IPO, and how to price and structure that deal.

Chapter 16, "Obtaining Debt Capital": Updated Material

Here the various sources of debt capital are discussed in detail, including managing and orchestrating the banking relationship before and after the loan. The chapter examines how a bank looks at a loan proposal, including criteria, covenants, and personal guarantees, and what to do when a bank declines a loan. The traps awaiting the unwary borrower are also covered.

In the case called Bank Documents: "The Devil Is in the Details," students are treated to an intimate journey through an actual bank loan and review by a lending institution, including the financial statements and money flows of the company. This case examines how and why the bank considers such a loan, the issues of whether to renew the credit line, and the thinking and perspective of both the company and the bank. Developed by Professor Leslie Charm at Babson College, this is the best case we have ever seen on the subject.

Chapter 17, "Leading Rapid Growth, Crises, and Recovery": A Major Rewrite and a New Case

This chapter combines Chapters 16 and 18 from the previous edition. The roles of leadership, culture, and current climate are discussed in relation to the unique issues, demands, and crises entrepreneurs can expect to encounter in a rapid-growth environment. This chapter also addresses the signs and symptoms of companies heading for trouble, what turnaround experts look for, and the strategies and approaches of resuscitating stalled or disintegrating ventures.

A new case called Telephony Translations, Inc. (TTI), discusses Dave Santolli's entrepreneurial career embodying the notion that life is about the journey rather than the destination. At 42 he'd experienced the glow of venture success and the sting of business failure—to the tune of over $280 million. He'd withstood the shock of learning his wife was facing an uphill battle with cancer, and he felt waves of relief when she pulled through. But in early 2005 it seemed as if all he'd been through was a preseason practice. Not only was he being sued by investors from his previous venture; his new investors at TTI—concerned that after five years the complex technology company was still in the red—had brought in a new CEO to comanage the operation. Although the business seemed to be on the right track, this was an enormously critical time in the development of the opportunity. And now Dave had to tell his stunned staff that he had a particularly vicious form of cancer.

Chapter 18, "The Family as Entrepreneur": Updated Material

Chapter 18, which is based on Professor Tim Habbershon's model and extensive research, outlines the significant economic and entrepreneurial contribution families make to communities and countries worldwide, and examines the different roles families play in the entrepreneurial process. The chapter describes the six dimensions of family enterprising, provides a model to assess a family's relative mind-set for enterprising, and identifies key issues for family dialogue.

The Mind-Set and Methods Continua exercises establish a family's financial risk and return expectations and their competitive posture in relation to the marketplace, as well as the organization's entrepreneurial orientation and actions. The aim of these assessments is to surface family members' beliefs and fuel family dialogue. Plotting these scores into the Family Enterprising Model provides a visual tool for constructive family dialogue.

The Indulgence Spa Products case discusses how Robert and Ulissa Dawson had become role models in the African American community. Their family enterprise, Dawson Products, was one of the last remaining privately held black enterprises in the personal care products industry. They had taught their daughters to be self-sufficient. Bright, energetic, and independent, the talented young women have become key figures in the growth trajectory of this family enterprise. Now Jimella, the younger daughter, wants to strike out on her own rather than stay and grow the core family business. This case is loaded with classic issues facing a family firm.

Chapter 19, "The Harvest and Beyond": Revised Material, a New Exercise, and a New Case

New Venture Creation concludes by looking at the entrepreneurial process as a journey and not a destination, harvest options and their consequences, and beyond the harvest. We challenge students to think far ahead and beyond merely financial success and consider deeper issues such as these: What distinguishes wealthy families who create legacies of community renewal and philanthropy from those who seem to become obsessed with consumption and material symbols? What if you had all the money you ever dreamed of? And what if all that money was suddenly gone?

A new exercise, Wisdom from the Harvest, provides a framework for dialogue with highly successful and wealthy entrepreneurs, exploring with them critical issues, lessons, pain, and trade-offs they have faced, conquered, and been beaten up by. It will enable you to ask and explore questions about not just creating and realizing wealth, but the realities and challenges of coping with it and utilizing it to create a healthy family legacy through renewal and philanthropy. In the process you are likely to discover some of the most important insights of your career—and gain a valuable mentor or two.

The new Optitech case describes Jim Harris, who at age 36 had spent his years since college building Optitech, a $45 million toner cartridge refurbishing business he started in his parents' garage. He and his father—who joined to help oversee their relationships with Asian manufacturers—were scoring wins against some industry giants. Jim had engaged an investment banker to investigate options, particularly fueling growth with acquisitions. Although that was an option, the banker produced another: a $40 million harvest to a private equity group. Jim was torn, and he knew it was time to make some major life decisions.

OF SPECIAL INTEREST TO ENTREPRENEURSHIP EDUCATORS

We believe that we can positively change the world through entrepreneurship education. In 1984 we launched the Symposia for Entrepreneurship Educators (SEE) to teach educators from institutions around the globe. Since then we have trained over 1,640 academics and entrepreneurs from 477 different academic institutions, government organizations, and foundations in 49 countries to teach entrepreneurship in a way that combines theory and practice to tens of thousands of students each year. We are committed to helping colleges and universities develop creative and innovative entrepreneurship curricula, increase teaching effectiveness, and develop the teaching skills of entrepreneurs who are interested in engaging in full- or part-time teaching.

Our Symposia for Entrepreneurship Educators program include the following:

Price-Babson Symposium for Entrepreneurship Educators: Our flagship program, created in partnership with the Price Institute for Entrepreneurial Studies, is held each spring on our campus to build an international cadre of educators who understand the importance of combining entrepreneurship theory and practice in teaching. Cross-disciplinary educators from around the world attend Price-Babson SEE.

Babson-Olin Symposium for Engineering Entrepreneurship Educators (SyE3): Designed and delivered in partnership with Olin College of Engineering and funded through a grant from the NSF Partnerships for Innovation program, this special-focus program is offered to engineering educators who want to incorporate entrepreneurship content and pedagogy into their engineering courses and curricula. Babson-Olin SyE3 alumni will develop engineering graduates who can successfully transform innovations into the products, systems, services, and companies that drive economic growth.

Babson Symposium for Entrepreneurship Educators: Our customized programs are hosted on multiple occasions throughout the year at institutions around the world. Babson SEE programs foster global entrepreneurial growth and economic development through entrepreneurship education. We have recently completed programs in China, Argentina, Chile, Venezuela, Mexico, Costa Rica, and Puerto Rico. Upcoming programs are scheduled for Switzerland, Ecuador, Peru, Colombia, and Russia.

SEE +: Our reunion program is hosted for all SEE alumni. REFLECT provides half-day "deep dives" on content and techniques, presentations from alumni on successful course and classroom strategies, and valuable networking.

For more information about any of these SEE programs, go to http://www3.babson.edu/ESHIP/outreach-events/symposia.

ACKNOWLEDGMENTS

The eighth edition of this book celebrates over 40 years of intellectual capital acquired through research, case development, course development, teaching, and practice. The latter has included risking both reputations and wallets in a wide range of ventures, involving former students and others. All of this was possible because of Jeff's wife, Sara, and their grown daughters, and Steve's wife, Carol, and their grown son and daughter. It has also been made possible by the support, encouragement, thinking, and achievements of many people: colleagues at Babson and Harvard, former professors and mentors, associates, entrepreneurs, former students, and our many friends who till this soil.

Once again this new edition is possible because of the tremendous effort of our colleague, friend, and former MBA student, Carl Hedberg, who took complete charge of the editing, project management, and much of the research, writing, and revising of various cases and revision of other material. All of this was accomplished on schedule with the most cheerful mind-set. We are extremely grateful for your herculean effort, Carl, and for all your work and contributions to Babson and the Arthur M. Blank Center for Entrepreneurship. The major upgrades in earlier editions were made possible in large part by the superb assistance of Jeff's research assistants, Christy Remey Chin and Rebecca Voorheis—both of whom have since gone on to complete MBAs at Harvard Business School and Duke, respectively.

The original book (1977) stemmed from research and concepts developed in Jeff's doctoral dissertation at Harvard. Later work with various coauthors from earlier editions, his course development work and research in new ventures at Northeastern University in the 1970s, and his work in new ventures and financing entrepreneurial ventures at Babson College in the 1980s contributed heavily to the evolution of this text. From 1989 to 1995 Jeff's research in venture capital and his course development work in the elec-tives at Harvard enabled him to make major additions and improvements in many of the chapters.

Once again Jeff has found it an absolute delight and a rewarding experience to work with Steve Spinelli; this is the second edition he has coauthored. His ideas and insights, disciplined work style, and great collegial approach to everything make him a world-class colleague. Since the last edition, Steve has been selected as the new president of Philadelphia University. Although this is a huge loss for Babson College, we are all extremely proud of Steve's innumerable and significant contributions to Babson, and we wish him the best in his new role. True to the inherent beliefs in this text that focus on the integration of thought and action, Steve was a cofounder of Jiffy Lube International and the largest franchisee in the nation, and he is a franchising expert. He has invested in more than a dozen start-ups and serves on the boards of small, midsize, and large enterprises.

We have drawn on intellectual capital from many roots and we contributors, and we have received support and encouragement, as well as inspiration. To list them all might take a full chapter by itself, but we wish to offer special thanks to those who have been so helpful in recent years, especially Jeff's former colleagues from Harvard Business School, who have been a constant source of encouragement, inspiration, and friendship. Thanks to William Sahlman for his superb work in entrepreneurial finance, much of which is evident in this text, and Howard Stevenson for his tremendous support and encouragement over many years.

A special thanks goes to Helen Coates, who joined our team as head of our Price-Babson Fellows and SEE programs (see on the preceding page of Special Interest to Entrepreneurship Educators) in the midst of working on this new edition. She has been a great asset in coordinating our new geographies and normally packed schedules and facilitating our work. Thank you, Helen! Her predecessor, Janet Strimaitis, now associate director of the Arthur M. Blank Center for Entrepreneurship, was also quite helpful in supporting this effort throughout the project.

This eighth edition was made possible by the tremendous support of Babson College and the wonderful $30 million gift by the Franklin W. Olin Foundation to build the F.W. Olin Graduate School of Business and to fund the chair now held by Jeff Timmons. Special thanks to William F. Glavin, to whom we dedicate this edition, for convincing Jeff to return to Babson College full-time and for always providing complete support for his work. Other key supporters at Babson include our president, Brian Barefoot; Michael Fetters, former provost; Mark P. Rice, the former Murata Dean of the MBA program and the first Jeffry A. Timmons professor of entrepreneurial studies; Patti Greene, provost and a huge champion for entrepreneurship; and Fritz Fleischman, dean of faculty, for his support of entrepreneurship at Babson College and this project.

We are most appreciative of the support of our new division chair, Candy Brush, and of Professor Tim Habbershon for his chapter on family enterprising. Tim has done groundbreaking work on family enterprises at Babson College, and readers will find this chapter the most useful material on the subject that they have seen. Tim has since joined Fidelity Investments to work directly with the Johnson family.

Thanks to our other colleagues in Babson's Entrepreneurship Division, especially longtime partner Bill Bygrave, for their continuing friendship and support. And a special thank-you to Arthur M. Blank for his generous support and the gift that provided our wonderful facility, the Arthur M. Blank Center for Entrepreneurship. Thanks to Julian E. Lange for his ongoing counsel and advice on Internet-related issues. The adjunct faculty members at Babson College—whom we call our entrepreneur faculty—continually share their expertise with their academic colleagues and our students. Leslie Charm and Edward Marram have each contributed significantly to the chapters on debt equity, managing rapid growth, and managing troubled companies. They are fabulous teachers and colleagues while still remaining active in the business world. We are also grateful to colleagues and friends Fred Alper, Michael Gordon, Elizabeth Riley, and Ernie Parizeau for sharing their insights with this edition of *New Venture Creation*. All these colleagues continue to be immensely valuable resources.

Special thanks also to Ada Chen, a second-year undergraduate at Babson, who began as Steve's assistant but who has quickly branched into other areas of service at the Arthur M. Blank Center for Entrepreneurship.

The cases in this and previous editions would not be possible without the collaboration and support of sharing entrepreneurs. We wish to thank Mike Healey; Gary and George Mueller; Roxanne Quimby; Doug Ranalli and Shae Plimley; Carl Youngman; Clarence Wooten; Lisa Little Chief Bryan; Todd, David, and Sally Snyder; Paul Tobin; Mike Bellobuono; Thomas Darden, Jr.; Jim Poss; Gloria Ro Kolb; and Joe, Eunice, and Ursula Dudley. In addition to sharing their stories for the cases, these entrepreneurs continue to make class visits at Babson as well as other academic institutions across the country, enriching the educational experience of our students. Thanks also to case writers Sandra Sowell-Scott (in memoriam), Professor Sylvia Carbonelli, and MIT Sloan School MBA candidates Shingo Murakami, Roger Premo, Ina Trantcheva, and Erik Yeager, who have all given their time and talent.

We are also extremely appreciative of two groundbreaking new chapters in this edition. We believe these are the first on these topics in an entrepreneurship or new ventures text. Professors Andrea Larson of the University of Virginia and Karen O'Brien of the Green Chemistry Institute have contributed "Clean Commerce: Seeing Opportunity through a Sustainability Lens" from their pioneering work in this field. Our tremendously valued colleague Professor Heidi Neck of Babson College has contributed "Opportunities for Social Entrepreneurship," an important new chapter based on her insightful work and research in this exciting area.

One of the most inspiring and rewarding sources of our energy for this project and the entire entrepreneurial mission is the nearly 1,640 alumni (from over 477 institutions and 49 countries) who are our partners and colleagues in the Price-Babson Fellows program. In 2008 we will celebrate the 24th year of our annual Symposium for Entrepreneurship Educators (SEE). Gloria Appel, the late president of the Price Institute for Entrepreneurial Studies, was a phenomenal partner, friend, mentor, and supporter from the beginning and, despite her passing, continues to be an inspiration for our work.

In 2004 we partnered with our neighbors at Olin College of Engineering on the Babson College campus to create a sister program to SEE for engineering colleges, and we received a three-year National Science Foundation grant to design, develop, and deliver this program. The first highly successful pilot program was held in June 2005, and the program was repeated annually at Babson and Olin Colleges through 2007. This program is aimed at increasing the entrepreneurship literacy of engineering faculty and students, as well as the technology literacy of business faculty and students, thereby improving prosperity in America.

From 1991 to 2001 Jeff's colleagues and dear friends at the Ewing Marion Kauffman Foundation in Kansas City have continued to be a source of both support and inspiration. Their important work in accelerating entrepreneurship in America has made important strides in so many arenas. It is a joy to have colleagues who share our passion for entrepreneurship: the late Mr. K (Ewing Marion Kauffman), Michie Slaughter (retired), Kurt Mueller, Bob Rogers, Bert Berkeley, Pat Cloherty, Bob Compton, Willie Davis, Jeff's fishing buddy Mike Herman, Tony Maier, Judith Cone, and Jim McGraw. We can think of no other foundation in America that has done more to advance education, research, public policy, entrepreneurial thinking, and practice than the Kauffman Center.

We continue to derive great inspiration from our Native American colleagues who were the first to create entrepreneurship curricula and centers in America's tribal colleges and institutions. Michele Lansdowne at Salish Kootenai College and Lisa Little Chief Bryan from Rosebud Reservation, now teaching at Black Hills State University, have both worked tirelessly to write and produce two sets of case studies and case videos based on Native American entrepreneurs. With support from the Kauffman Center and the Theodore R. and Vivian M. Johnson Scholarship Foundation, they have worked to build a Native American entrepreneurship curriculum. The Johnson Foundation has also provided ongoing support of training for tribal college faculty in this curriculum to ensure its continued use. Florence Stickney from San Francisco State University has led groundbreaking efforts at Pine Ridge Reservation. For the Cherokee Nation, Charles Gourd continues his strong efforts to bring entrepreneurship education to rural Oklahoma. In 2004 Jeff worked closely with Dwight Gorneau, a founder and past president of the American Indian Society for Engineers and Scientists, to present a day-long workshop on entrepreneurship at their annual meeting in Anchorage, Alaska, along with Charlie Gourd and Lisa Little Chief Bryan.

The relevance and richness of the cases and materials in this text can be traced in considerable measure to Jeff's involvement with both ventures and venture funds. His colleagues at BCI Growth Capital (Don Remey, Hoyt Goodrich, Steve Ely, and Ted Horton) have contributed ideas and cases, and Brion Applegate, Bill Collatos, and Bob Nicholson and their associates at Spectrum Equity Investors have been generous with their time and ideas in contributing to cases and in coming to Jeff's classes.

In addition to all those acknowledged and thanked in previous editions, a special thanks and debt of appreciation is due to all our current and former students from whom we learn—and by whom we are inspired with each encounter. We marvel at your accomplishments, and we sigh in great relief at how little damage we have usually imparted.

We would like to extend a special thanks to the professors who have reviewed previous editions of *New Venture Creation*; they have helped to shape the direction of the text.

Finally, we want to express a very special thank-you to Laura Spell, Sara Hunter, and Meg Beamer at Irwin/McGraw-Hill for their highly competent and professional efforts in advancing this revision.

J.A.T. and S.S.

BRIEF CONTENTS

TABLE OF CONTENTS

PART II

The Opportunity

PART III

The Founder and Team

PART IV

Financing Entrepreneurial Ventures

PART V

Startup and Beyond

I

PART ONE

The Entrepreneurial Mind for an Entrepreneurial World

At the heart of the entrepreneurial process is the founder: the opportunity seeker, the creator and initiator; the leader, problem solver, and motivator; the strategizer and guardian of the mission, values, and culture of the venture. Without this human energy, drive, and vitality, the greatest ideas—even when they are backed by an overabundance of resources and staff—will fail, grossly underperform, or simply never get off the ground. Brilliant musical, scientific, or athletic aptitude and potential do not equal the great musician, the great scientist, or the great athlete. The difference lies in the intangibles: creativity and ingenuity, commitment, tenacity and determination, a passion to win and excel, and leadership and team-building skills.

Think of the number of first-round draft picks who never made the grade in professional sports—even without suffering career-ending injuries. Then consider the many later-round picks who became superstars, like Tom Brady, the 199th pick in the 12th round by the New England Patriots, who has quarterbacked the team to three Super Bowl Championships—in his first four years!

So what is it that an aspiring young entrepreneur needs to know, and what habits, attitudes, and mind-sets can be learned, practiced, and developed in order to improve the odds of success? We begin this eighth edition with a focus on you—the lead entrepreneur. We examine the mind-sets, the learnable and acquirable attitudes and habits that lead to entrepreneurial success—and failure. By examining patterns and practices of entrepreneurial thinking and reasoning, and the entrepreneurial mind in action, you can begin your own assessment and planning process to get you headed where you want to go. This personal entrepreneurial strategy will evolve into your personal business plan—a blueprint to help you learn, grow, attract mentors who can change your life and your ventures, and pursue the opportunities that best suit you.

1

Survival odds for a venture go up once you reach the benchmark of $1 million in sales and 20 employees. Launching or acquiring and then building a business that will exceed these levels is more fun and more challenging than being involved in the vast majority of small one- or two-person operations. But perhaps most important, a business of this magnitude achieves the critical mass necessary to attract good people and, as a result, significantly enhances the prospects of realizing a harvest. An entrepreneur isn't simply creating a job; he or she can build a business that can lift a community.

A leader who thinks and acts with an "entrepreneurial mind" can make a critical difference as to whether a business is destined to be a traditional, very small lifestyle firm, a stagnant or declining large one, or a higher-potential venture. Practicing certain mental attitudes and actions can stimulate, motivate, and reinforce the kind of zest and entrepreneurial culture whose self-fulfilling prophecy is success.

It is almost impossible to take a number of people, give them a single test, and determine who possess entrepreneurial minds and who do not. Rather, it is useful for would-be entrepreneurs and others involved in entrepreneurship to study how successful entrepreneurs think, feel, and respond and how significant factors can be developed and strengthened—as a decathlete develops and strengthens certain muscles to compete at a certain level.

Entrepreneurs who create or recognize opportunities and then seize and shape them into higher-potential ventures think and do things differently. They operate in an entrepreneurial domain, a place governed by certain modes of action and dominated by certain driving forces.

Take for example, Rick Adam, who by the late 1990s had made his fortune as a software entrepreneur. He had also spotted a compelling opportunity in the general aviation industry. As an avid pilot, Adam knew firsthand how few new aircraft designs were available—at any price. The reason was that the cost to design, engineer, and bring to market an FAA-certified general aviation product was estimated by industry veterans to be in the neighborhood of $250 million,

requiring a minimum of 10 years. Despite having no previous experience in manufacturing, Adam put up tens of millions of his own money (and raised tens of millions more) to start up Adam Aircraft. Using sophisticated model fabrication technology, and by applying design and engineering practices Adam had mastered in software development, his company spent under $60 million to develop the A-500—a sleek, pressurized twin-engine design that achieved FAA certification in just five years. Their A-700 prototype—a personal jet that utilized the same airframe structure—was flying for another $20 million. By the fall of 2007, the A-700 was nearing FAA certification, and the company was reporting an order backlog for the jet of just under $800 million. Rick Adam commented on the endeavor:

> I've done a lot of entrepreneurial things, and when you think there is a big opportunity, you look at it thoughtfully and you say, well, if this is such a big opportunity, why isn't anybody taking it? What do I know, or what do I see that nobody else is seeing? So, very often, entrepreneurial opportunities occur because a series of events come together—particularly with technology—and you suddenly have all the ingredients you need to be successful at something that just moments ago was impossible. Then, assuming you are a good business person and a good executer, you can get there if you focus, and keep at it.

It makes a lot of sense for entrepreneurs to pay particular attention to picking partners, key business associates, and managers with an eye for complementing the entrepreneurs' own weaknesses and strengths and the needs of the venture. As will be seen, they seek people who fit. Not only can an entrepreneur's weakness be an Achilles' heel for new ventures, but also the whole is almost always greater than the sum of its parts.

Finally, ethics are terribly important in entrepreneurship. In highly unpredictable and fragile situations, ethical issues cannot be handled according to such simplistic notions as "always tell the truth." It is critical that an entrepreneur understand, develop, and implement an effective integrity strategy for the business.

Chapter One

The Global Entrepreneurial Revolution for a Flatter World

When I was growing up, my parents told me, "Finish your dinner. People in China and India are starving." I tell my daughters, "Finish your homework. People in India and China are starving for your job."

Tom Friedman
American author, journalist, and a
three-time winner of the Pulitzer Prize

Results Expected

Upon completion of this chapter, you will be able to

1. Explain how the entrepreneurial revolution in the United States has helped "flatten the world."

2. Assess why this revolution is driving future economic prosperity worldwide.

3. Discuss how entrepreneurs, innovators, and their growing companies are the engine of wealth and job creation, innovation, and new industries, and how venture and risk capital fuels that engine.

4. Describe how entrepreneurship is the principal source of philanthropy in the world.

5. Share your views on the ImageCafé case study.

Entrepreneurship Flattens the World

In 2007 there were over 1.1 billion Internet users in the world with over 900 million of them outside the United States; even in tiny Iceland 86 percent of the homes were connected. In the United States an iPod was sold every eight seconds. Entrepreneurship and the Internet continue to flatten the world at a staggering pace and in the process are spawning fertile fields of opportunities that are being tilled and seized on every continent. How is this global revolution manifesting itself?

For starters, Exhibit 1.1 shows just how far international Web entrepreneurs have penetrated the world.

This remarkable array of 39 Web clone knockoffs of leading Web sites represents just a tiny tip of the worldwide iceberg of Internet entrepreneuring. While the Internet alone is reshaping the world in staggering ways, the spread of global entrepreneurship reaches far beyond. Take, for example, some recent descriptions in the August 2007 edition of *Business 2.0*:

- In 2006, 10 billion Indian emigrants worldwide sent over $275 billion back to their families in India. Sahara House Care, a firm in India, has tapped into that market by providing 60 products and services immigrants can buy for their families. These include such

EXHIBIT 1.1

Send in the Clones

	digg	Facebook	LinkedIn	YouTube
Brazil	Linkk linkk.com.br	—	—	Videolog videolog.uol.com.br
China	Verydig verydig.com	Xiaoneiwang xiaonei.com	Wealink wealink.com	56.com 56.com
France	Scoopeo scoopeo.com	Skyrock skyrock.com	Viadeo viadeo.com	Dailymotion dailymotion.com
Germany	Yigg yigg.de	StudiVZ Studivz.net	Xing xing.com	MyVideo myvideo.de
India	Best of Indya bestofindya.com	Minglebox minglebox.com	Rediff Connexions connexions.rediff.com	Rajshri rajshri.com
Israel	Hadash Hot hadash-hot.co.il	Mekusharim mekusharim.co.il	Hook hook.co.il	Flix flix.co.il
Mexico	Enchilame enchilame.com	Vostu vostu.com	InfoJobs infoJobs.com.mx	BuscaTube buscatube.com
Netherlands	eKudos ekudos.nl	Hyves hyves.net	—	Skoeps skoeps.nl
Russia	News2 news2.ru	V Kontakte vkontakte.ru	MoiKrug moiKrug.ru	Rutube rutube.ru
South Africa	Muti muti.co.za	—	—	MyVideo myvideo.co.za
Turkey	Nooluyo nooluyo.com	Qiraz qiraz.com	Cember cember.net	Resim ve Video resimvideo.org

Source: *Business 2.0.* ©2007 Time Inc. All rights reserved.

services as delivering flowers, finding buyers for real estate, offering exhaustive online catalogs of just about anything, and even accompanying loved ones to a hospital.

- Consider a new supersize RV built on an 18-wheeler chassis turned into a mobile hotel facility that can sleep as many as 44 people. As American as apple pie, as the saying goes? Wrong! A 36-year-old Spaniard, Fernando Saenz de Tejada, has created Hotelmovil. The first five units will roll out of a factory in Italy and will sell for $500,000 a unit or rent for $8,000 per week.

- In Norway entrepreneur Jan-Olaf Willums, already wealthy from his investment in REC, a solar energy company, is leading the development of a Web-enabled, carbon-free electric car he calls Think. He has teamed with Segway creator Dean Kamen and Google founders Larry Page and Sergey Brin, and with Silicon Valley and European investors, to raise $78 million. His vision: Upend the century-old fossil fuel-based automotive paradigm by changing how cars are made, sold, owned, and driven.

- "Anything seems possible in Rwanda," asserts former San Francisco resident Josh Ruxin, who,

with his wife Alissa, has invested life savings of $100,000 to build the Heaven Café in the capital city of Kigali. The African nation of 8 million—ravaged by the genocide of 1 million people in 1994—is now attracting foreign entrepreneurs in tourism, telecom, mining, farming, and real estate.

- Everyone is now aware of just how dynamic and entrepreneurial the Chinese economy has become in recent years. Consider the following examples of explosive growth in this country of 1.3 billion people. Computer usage increased from 2.1 million in 1999 to 68 million in 2004—a 34-fold increase! According to Volkswagen, automotive production in 2003 was 4.44 million and is expected to grow to over 10 million by 2010. In 2006, 80 percent of BMW's global sales increase came from China. Phone installations totaled just 100 million in 1998 but grew to 650 million in 2004, with mobile phones exploding in the same six-year period from around 10 million to over 350 million.

Sensing this huge growth in opportunities, numerous leading U.S. venture capital firms—including IDG Ventures, Venrock, and Kleiner, Perkins, Caufield & Byers—have established relationships and operations in China and made many successful (and some not so successful) investments. These are but a few examples of the entrepreneurial surge in China. A similar pattern is now emerging in India and other southeast Asian nations. In India and Vietnam, for example, IDG has dedicated venture capital funds, and other firms are getting established as well.

Finally, imagine that you are owed US$100,000 by a business in another country, founded by one of your close friends in graduate school, which is due next week. The borrower's business has done well, and you are assured that the note will be repaid in full. The next day the government of that nation announces a three-to-one devaluation of its currency; so you will receive just one-third of the note. That is exactly what happened in Argentina in January 2002, causing financial chaos and an economic recession. Nevertheless, a young Argentine entrepreneur was convinced that major opportunities still existed for a global information technology outsourcing business based in Buenos Aires. In 2008 his business will exceed US$40 million in revenue.

Two Nobel Prizes Recognize Entrepreneurship

The front page of *The Wall Street Journal* on October 10, 2006, had the following stunning headline: "The New Nobel Prize Winner Makes a Case for Entrepreneurship." The accompanying article by Professor Edmund S. Phelps of Columbia University, New York, the prize recipient, was full of wonderful commentary and arguments for entrepreneurship. The awarding of this prize in economics to Professor Phelps is the most important academic recognition of the field and subject in our lifetime. One of Phelps's main arguments is that "entrepreneurship is lucrative—and just." This is an important point; we will see later in this chapter how entrepreneurs are the leading philanthropists of our time. He further made his case: "Instituting a high level of dynamism, so that the economy is fired by the new ideas of entrepreneurs, serves to transform the workplace in the firms developing an innovation and also the firms dealing with the innovation."

The ink was barely dry on this announcement when the Nobel Peace Prize was announced for another economist championing micro-enterprise. Farid Hossain of the Associated Press wrote the story in the Manchester, New Hampshire, *Union Leader* on October 14, 2006: "A simple yet revolutionary idea—in the form of a $90 loan—changed her life, putting the Bangladeshi villager out of a devastating cycle of poverty. Yesterday, that idea—lending tiny sums to poor people looking to escape poverty by starting a business—won the Nobel Peace Prize for economist Muhammad Yunus and the Grameen Bank he founded." Hossain noted the Nobel Committee's rationale at the citation: "Lasting peace cannot be achieved unless large population groups find ways in which to break out of poverty. Micro-credit is one such means. Development from below also serves to advance democracy and human rights."

In just four days these two Nobel Prizes changed forever the academic and practical significance of entrepreneurship as a fertile ground for education and research. This should stimulate even more and wider interest in entrepreneurship as a field of study and research. For those of us who have been creating and building the field since our doctoral student days, this was an especially gratifying occasion and recognition.

A Macro Phenomenon

The work of Phelps and Yunus, along with our earlier examples, illustrates at a tangible level how dynamic entrepreneurs and their firms are altering the landscape in this entrepreneurial explosion globally. These represent a much broader, more pervasive, but also varied pattern of entrepreneurial activity. We are fortunate to have the latest version of Babson's Global Entrepreneurship Monitor (GEM) for 2006, as well as the Praeger Perspectives series *Engine of Growth*, which carefully track this phenomenon. We draw here on both of these 2007 publications to augment and enrich your understanding and perspective on the global entrepreneurial revolution.

The accumulation of several years of adult population survey data from the Global Entrepreneurship Monitor (GEM) has enabled an international comparative study of high-expectation entrepreneurs (defined as all early-stage businesses that expect to employ at least 20 workers within five years). In the GEM comparison published in 2006, North America (United States and Canada) stood out as having the highest prevalence of high-growth potential entrepreneurial activity, with an approximately 1.5 percent participation rate. As regions, Oceana (Australia and New Zealand) and Latin America (Argentina, Brazil, Chile, Ecuador, Mexico, Peru, and Venezuela) came next, with participation rates of 1.1 percent and 1 percent, respectively.

Entrepreneurship is exploding in countries like India, China, and the former Soviet bloc—and effecting positive social and economic change in such diverse countries as Korea, Mexico, South Africa, and Ireland. According to the 2006 GEM study, countries exhibiting very high rates of individuals participating in early-stage entrepreneurial activity included Venezuela (25 percent), Thailand (20.7 percent), and New Zealand (17.6 percent). The highest rates of established business owners (owner–managers who have paid wages or salaries for more than three months) were found in Thailand (14.1 percent), followed by China (13.5 percent), New Zealand (10.8 percent), Greece (10.5 percent), and Brazil (10.1 percent).

Although many might not consider international expansion as part of the new venture process, in his contribution to the Praeger Perspectives series, *Going Global*, Pat Dickson reviews research that shows just how prevalent it is. For example, 80 percent of all small- to medium-sized enterprises are affected by or involved with international trade, and advances in technology, manufacturing, and logistics have created opportunities where firms of all sizes can compete internationally. Dickson notes that this view of an emerging world market accessible to even the most resource-constrained and remote nations and organizations is described by Thomas Friedman in *The World Is Flat*, which traces the convergence of technology and world events and its role in bringing about significant changes in traditional value chains.

It is clear that the mainstreaming of entrepreneurship in America has not merely had an extraordinary impact on the cultural and economic landscape in the United States. America's entrepreneurial revolution has become a model for business people, educators, and policy makers around the globe. For example, as part of a goal to "make the EU the most competitive economy in the world by 2010," in 2000 an action plan was derived with the following broad objectives:

1. Fueling entrepreneurial mind-sets.
2. Encouraging more people to become entrepreneurs.
3. Gearing entrepreneurs for growth and competitiveness.
4. Improving the flow of finance.
5. Creating a more entrepreneurial-friendly regulatory and administrative framework.

These goals mirror the factors that have been critical in advancing entrepreneurship in the United States. In July 2004 an EU commission followed up on these goals with recommendations for fostering entrepreneurial mind-sets through school education. These too reflect the American experience:

- Introduce entrepreneurship into the national (or regional) curriculum at all levels of formal education (from primary school to university), either as a horizontal aspect or as a specific topic.

- Train and motivate teachers to engage in entrepreneurial education.
- Promote the application of programs based on "learning by doing," such as by means of project work, virtual firms, and minicompanies.
- Involve entrepreneurs and local companies in the design and running of entrepreneurship courses and activities.
- Increase the teaching of entrepreneurship within higher education outside economic and business courses, notably at scientific and technical universities, and place emphasis on setting up companies in the curricula of business-type studies at universities.

In our roles as students, researchers, observers, and participants in this revolution, we can honestly say that global adoption of the entrepreneurial mind-set appears to be growing exponentially larger and faster. In our assessment, we are at the dawn of a new age of entrepreneurial reasoning, equity creation, and philanthropy, whose impact in the coming years will dwarf what we experienced over the last century.

Entrepreneurship: 40 Years as a Transformational Force

Who could have imagined 40 years ago that the world would see so many revolutions ascend and vanish in so many arenas by today? Technology and science. Sex, drugs, music, telecommunications, iPod, Blackberry, media. The explosive rise of entrepreneurship, first in America and now the world. The demise of centrally planned economies in both totalitarian communist states and socialist states, giving way to entrepreneurship, open and free markets, and struggling democracies. The entrepreneurial revolution has transformed and will continue to transform the world.

The impact of entrepreneurship as an emerging academic field and as a life option—highly admired, respected, and sought after by youth around the world—has been profound and continues to expand worldwide in places hard to imagine just a few years ago: China, India, Vietnam, former Eastern bloc countries, and the Middle East; the Catholic Church; historically black colleges and universities in America, Native American reservations, and grades K–12.

Why is this so? What does it mean? Why is the field of entrepreneurship gaining attention, resources, and community credibility? Where is this leading us? What are the next great opportunities and challenges for you to consider? These are some of the questions we will attempt to address in this section.

Four Entrepreneurial Transformations That Are Changing the World

During the past 40 years, the evidence and trends point to at least four entrepreneurial transformations that profoundly impact how the world lives, works, learns, and enjoys leisure. Consider the following:

1. Entrepreneurship is the new management paradigm: Entrepreneurial thinking and reasoning—so common in dynamic, higher-potential, and robust new and emerging firms—are now becoming infused and embedded into the strategies and practices of corporate America.
2. Entrepreneurship has spawned a new education paradigm for learning and teaching.
3. Entrepreneurship is becoming a dominant management model for running nonprofit businesses and in the emerging field of social ventures.
4. Entrepreneurship is rapidly transcending business schools: Engineering, life sciences, architecture, medicine, music, liberal arts, and K–12 are new academic grounds that are exploring and embracing entrepreneurship in their curricula.

Entrepreneurship as the New Management Paradigm

Virtually every management model in vogue today can find its roots in great entrepreneurial companies and organizations founded within the past 40 years. Progressive researchers of new and different ways of conceptualizing and practicing management found those dynamic and creative founders and leaders at new ventures and at high-growth businesses—and rarely at large, established firms.

Nevertheless, virtually all mainstream research and case development until the 1970s dwelled on large companies; new and smaller ventures were mostly ignored. In contrast to what had prevailed in large companies—hierarchical, top-down, centralized, and militarylike ways of organizing and managing—new research was uncovering refreshing, at times radically different, modes: flat organizations (many without organization charts or detailed operating manuals), a passion for innovation, comfort with change and even chaos, team-driven efforts, significant performance-based equity incentives, and consensual decision making. Researchers also found cultures and value systems where people, integrity, honesty and ethics, a sense of responsibility to one's environment and community, and even fair play were common. Much of what is sought after and emulated by companies trying to rein-

vent themselves and to compete globally today embodies many of these principles, characteristics, and concepts of entrepreneurship, entrepreneurial leadership, and management. Think of the keywords used to describe these new ventures and concepts: flat, fast, flexible, fluid; innovation-driven; principle-based management; values-based management; opportunity- and customer-focused; resource parsimonious; living with and managing chaos and change; people and team-centered management (we could go on).

Our favorite early example of a great entrepreneurial leader is Ewing Marion Kauffman—founder, in 1950, of Marion Laboratories of Kansas City, Missouri, and also of America's leading foundation devoted to fostering entrepreneurship: the Ewing Marion Kauffman Foundation. He was 30–40 years ahead of the present emphasis on values and principle-based management, responsibility to community, and ethical high ground. His three core principles were treat people as you would want to be treated, share the wealth with the people who help create it, and give back to the community. These principles were the foundation upon which Marion Laboratories attracted and motivated a high-performing team and grew to $1 billion in revenue with market capitalization of $6.5 billion. It is no wonder today that corporate recruiters are coming to have high regard for the graduates of quality entrepreneurship programs.

It is also remarkable that some of the leading business schools in America now require courses in entrepreneurship. At Harvard in the late 1990s, all MBAs began taking a required course in entrepreneurial management—an astonishing event given the history and nature of the institution. Harvard's entrepreneurship electives are now perpetually oversubscribed. Even the national college accrediting agencies have come to see the importance of entrepreneurship and innovation as a vital part of any future business leader's education.

Across the curriculum, business school faculty are including more topics and issues relating to entrepreneurship—from accounting and finance to marketing and information technology. New courses are emerging from finance, marketing, and accounting faculty that focus on the entrepreneurial perspective. As a unit of analysis, few things are more exciting to study than the birth, growth, and adaptation of new companies and the complex issues they face from initial conceptualization to start-up financing, managing rapid growth, and an initial public offering. Doctoral students are increasingly finding rich veins here for research, database development, and theory building and testing. The more global entrepreneurship becomes, the more this type of research will grow. And other disciplines (economics, sociology, geography, and subfields of science) are now discovering the same opportunities. Thus our knowledge about entrepreneurship will continue to grow and expand to all fields. In many ways we can liken this progress to the field of leadership 100–150 years ago. Back then it was believed that leaders were born, not made: You either were a leader or you weren't. Fortunately for the world, that notion has long since been debunked. The same will happen in the field of entrepreneurship.

Entrepreneurship as a New Education Paradigm

Antidote for Academic Arrogance   Here is a true story that reveals much about the education and teaching philosophies, underlying assumptions, and beliefs of faculty at some business schools. It gets at the heart of what some educators believe and practice about what and how we teach in order to prepare future entrepreneurs and business leaders. A few years ago a notable Harvard faculty colleague was invited to meet with faculty at a distinguished midwestern university's business school to discuss entrepreneurship and the role of cases. He shared how real cases about real entrepreneurs facing real opportunities, crises, decisions, and time crunches could be powerful learning and pedagogical vehicles. One senior faculty member could hardly conceal his indifference. He made his views and philosophy of educating future business leaders clear: "I have never worked in business. I have never been near or inside a business. I have absolutely no intention of ever doing either. And I cannot see why anyone who teaches business would need to or want to, and the use of such cases is totally irrelevant!"

Imagine a medical school professor who never saw a patient, never saw or performed an operation or procedure, and never went to a hospital for any reason—and never wanted to. As preposterous as that may seem, it is the equivalent of what this business professor was exhorting. This is the epitome of academic arrogance. For some of us, this is what you hope the competition thinks and believes!

At a large southwestern state university, a new faculty member aggressively launched an entrepreneurship program that quickly became successful, attracting large enrollments. Key to his strategy was a long-proven strategy we have used to build Babson College: the use of "pracademics." These are highly successful founders and builders of companies with a real itch and talent for teaching. Besides being multimillionaires, in many cases they have earned advanced degrees. Students raved about their exciting classes and quality of teaching. The young professor spearheading the program simply told his pracademics that unless they were in the top quarter in teaching evaluations among all professors universitywide, they would not be invited back the following year. They won teaching awards, and it did not take long for these entrepreneurship pracademics to be disproportionately represented in the universitywide ranking of best professors. This so infuriated the general faculty that the faculty senate voted to have these entrepreneur faculty members eliminated from all teaching. So the young faculty champion for entrepreneurship joined a smaller private university nearby and is now building a successful entrepreneurship program there.

If we look at what transpires in general in college and university classrooms in America (and around the world), it is predominantly lectures. A few years ago a retired, distinguished university president joined a leading foundation concerned with the quality of teaching and learning. He visited many classrooms to observe what and how students were being taught. Even at a top Ivy League university he observed that "Ninety-nine percent of what goes on in the classroom is passive: students sitting taking notes, professors lecturing."

Transformation of What and How Business Leaders Learn   This pattern leads us to believe that entrepreneurship education has created a new educating/teaching/learning paradigm that can transform what and how students learn and that may eventually permeate the rest of the university. The preceding illustrations show how differently entrepreneurship educators think. Their fundamental philosophies and beliefs about learning and teaching, their attitudes toward students, and their views of the role of the student versus instructor and effective pedagogies all differ radically from the faculty noted previously.

Some prime examples can be shared. For one thing, most entrepreneurship educators are not facultycentric; they are student- and opportunity-centric. They do not believe that expertise, wisdom, and knowledge are housed solely in the faculty brain or in the library or accessed through Google. They reject the traditional lecture model: Students sit with pens ready, open craniums, pour in facts, memorize facts, regurgitate facts to achieve top grades, and begin again. Rather, there is a more student-centered, work-in-progress philosophy that is more hands-on and treats the learning process as not occurring solely in the classroom but as more of an apprenticeship, much like the medical model of "see one—do one— teach one." There is a far greater belief in students' capacities for self-evaluation, self-development, and devising personal entrepreneurial strategies that enable them to see if entrepreneurship is for them.

Entrepreneurship faculty are more likely to see their role as mentors, coaches, and advocates for students.

As we like to put it, we see our job as helping to get the genie of the entrepreneurial spirit out of the bottle. We are enablers rather than judges, evaluators, or disciplinarians (though these roles are necessary from time to time) in the process of helping students to discover and to liberate their entrepreneurial potential, and equally important, to decide whether it is right for them. We are notoriously inaccurate in predicting who will be the next Bill Gates, Steve Jobs, or Tom Stemberg, so we don't even try. It is nearly impossible to say in advance, here are the students who will be the best entrepreneurs, and here are the ideas that will win. These are educated guesses at best. Getting students to see that they often start with an unanswerable and thus irrelevant question—Will I be a good entrepreneur? Will my idea be a winner?—leads to a critical learning transformation for them. They come to ask more relevant questions: Is this a good opportunity worth pursuing or just another idea? How do I know, and who does know? What are the risks and rewards here, and what can I do to improve them? Whom can I get to enable me to do that? How can I improve the fit among the opportunity, resources, and team? What are the things that can go right and wrong here, and how can I change that? Whom do I need on my brain trust to make this happen?

By getting students to think of the team as not just the founders, but a broad coalition of people who know better than anyone the revenue and cost model; sales, distribution, and marketing; financial requirements and realities; competition, and so forth and who want to help the entrepreneur succeed, students' grasp and mind-set can be altered permanently. This is not just a process that is classroom and professor dependent; it is a much more complex, dynamic, and engaging learning experience. Such learning experiences are far more compelling, fun, enduring, and even addictive. This is why entrepreneurship is enticing so many students. These questions and issues capture the essence of inquiry underlying the Timmons Model of Entrepreneurial Process, which we will examine in Chapter 3.

A third dimension that is a central part of the new paradigm is the richness and creativity of many entrepreneurship faculty, courses, and curricula. We have seen far more quality, creativity, and inventiveness among entrepreneurship faculty over these 40 years than in most other parts of academia. The concept of "the clashroom" as a place for the intellectual and practical collisions of theory, practice, ideas, and strategies has been a major anchor at Babson College for decades. Each year at the reunion of our Price-Babson Fellows Program we are amazed at the impressive innovations and creative ideas that entrepreneurship faculty continue to develop, refine, and

create anew. Their teaching methods are more interactive and far more diverse and eclectic in strategies, approaches, and pedagogies than is common in lecture-based courses. We have seen the creative use of improvisation; the use of classical music (did you know that listening to baroque music can enhance creativity?); of film clips that appear to have nothing to do with entrepreneurship or business—for instance, *Dead Poets Society* and *Octapussy*! Others have used historic figures whose feats seem totally unrelated to entrepreneurship, such as Joshua Chamberlain, a college classics and theology professor who became the single most important leader in the turning point at Little Round Top at the Battle of Gettysburg in America's Civil War. And of course the hands-on, field- and reality-based nature of designing and creating new products and concepts, exploring opportunities, developing business plans, and raising capital is both engaging and mind-expanding for students.

Another important aspect of this new paradigm is the highly integrative and multidisciplinary nature of the courses and curricula. A more balanced, holistic approach to education has been one of the most elusive goals of higher education over the past 40 years. There is no question that entrepreneurship, for educating entrepreneurs and business leaders at least, is by far the most holistic, integrative, and multidisciplined field in business schools. MBA students over the years, typically with significant experience and accomplishments, put it this way: "This is the first and only course (New Venture Creation) where I have learned about the total business, not just the stand-alone silos of accounting, marketing, finance, IT, and so on."

Today around the world we are seeing some amazing curricular innovations that are derivatives of the entrepreneurship education model and philosophy. Two examples we are most familiar with are at Babson College at both the graduate and undergraduate levels. All first-year undergraduates take a required course, Foundation in Management Experience, which is a highly integrated approach to learning the underlying bodies of business knowledge while engaging teams in actually starting and operating a small business, fueled with a $3,000 start-up loan from the college. The profits, incidentally, are donated to a community service project, such as Habitat for Humanity. At the MBA level, the entire traditional structure of the first year of the program being centered around core disciplines was abandoned over 15 years ago in favor of a modular, integrated design that took students through the entrepreneurial process from idea inception through opportunity recognition and development, to business plan development, fund-raising, managing growth, and crises.

Since 1999 second-year MBAs have been able to opt for a dedicated entrepreneurship intensity track devoted to helping them identify a compelling higher-potential opportunity and actually launching the business; several students have done so. The faculty proposes to them, Have at it; we'll give up when you give up! A third unprecedented example is the new Olin College of Engineering on the Babson campus. This is the first undergraduate engineering college in America in over 75 years. A central part of the mission and strategy of the Olin Foundation trustees in creating the college was to infuse the best of what is done in entrepreneurship at Babson into the Olin curriculum for engineers. It is based on a deep conviction, supported by endless evidence, that engineering education in America has regressed toward the underlying disciplines to the detriment of aspiring engineers and eventually the nation. Its first class of exceptional students, who turned down acceptances at the top engineering schools in the nation to come to Olin, graduated in 2006. Numerous creative new approaches to teaching entrepreneurship to engineering students have been and are being developed. A major grant by the National Science Foundation enabled us in January 2006 to launch a joint Babson-Olin Program, modeled after the Price-Babson Fellows Symposium for Entrepreneurship Educators, for faculty of engineering and life science schools.

Entrepreneurship as the New Not-for-Profit and Philanthropy Management Paradigm

During the past 15 years hundreds of new philanthropic foundations and other not-for-profit organizations have been created from scratch using the entrepreneurship and new venture development model. From the beginning they have employed many of the concepts and principles for conceptualizing an idea, transforming it into an opportunity, building a brain trust, raising funds, and growing the management team and organization as if it was a new entrepreneurial venture. My chief example of this is the Ewing Marion Kauffman Foundation of Kansas City, America's leading foundation dedicated to fostering entrepreneurship. It was Jeff Timmons's great privilege to have known and worked with Mr. Kauffman prior to his death in 1993 to help create and shape the foundation's initiative in entrepreneurship. Other derivatives in the not-for-profit world include the Kauffman Fellows Program, the leading program in the world for aspiring venture capitalists. Endeavor is another such program founded, organized, and run as an entrepreneurial venture to foster the

development of young entrepreneurs throughout Latin America initially, and now around the world.

At the kindergarten–12th grade level, the National Foundation for Teaching Entrepreneurship (NFTE) is another wonderful example of how this can work. Boston's Center for Women and Enterprise (CWE) has similar roots anchored in entrepreneurial leadership and management principles.

Perhaps the most innovative and entrepreneurial foundation is the Franklin W. Olin Foundation. First, in the 1990s the trustees decided to end the foundation's life by giving away its assets in one final project that could have lasting impact in a manner true and consistent to Olin's intentions as a donor. They were vehemently opposed to letting those assets be perpetuated in the hands of future trustees who never knew the founder, thus risking violation of the founder's intent, as has happened in so many large, old foundations that have outlived their founders. Rather, they sought to do exhaustive research, engage other leaders, and define and create a breakthrough concept worthy of Mr. Olin's dreams for his foundation, just as the original leaders of the Ewing Marion Kauffman Foundation, who knew and loved Mr. K., as he was affectionately known, did for him.

In the early 1990s the Olin Foundation helped fund, along with the National Science Foundation and in cooperation with the National Academy of Engineering and six leading undergraduate engineering schools, an examination of undergraduate engineering education. The conclusions were discouraging to some and surprising to others: Undergraduate engineering education at America's top schools had lost its compass and its focus on engineering application and commercialization as it regressed toward its underlying disciplines of math, physics, and chemistry. As a result U.S. undergraduate engineering education was failing to meet America's needs for engineers and was being vigorously challenged by schools in Japan, Europe, India, China, and elsewhere.

President Larry Milas and his fellow trustees took these conclusions seriously and conceived of a bold (many would say revolutionary) idea to create from scratch the first new undergraduate engineering school in America in over 75 years. At first they sought to collaborate with and fund one of the leading schools in the original study to undertake this formidable task. However, in a few months of discussions and negotiations they realized that this institution was not interested in the highly innovative direction the Olin Foundation was proposing. They concluded they needed not a makeover but an entirely new curriculum that was boldly innovative in both subjects and methods. Unique to this concept was the inclusion of entrepreneurship principles, concepts, and modes of thinking and reasoning throughout the engineering curriculum. Further, they wanted to have uniquely tailored courses and learning experiences for every student directly in entrepreneurship. Having given up on one of the top schools in the nation, they decided to approach Babson College, which they knew well. Earlier the Olin Foundation had made major capital gifts to build the new Olin Graduate School of Management and fund the author's Franklin W. Olin Distinguished Professorship. They proposed to acquire nearly 50 acres of land on Babson's 500-acre campus and then work closely with Babson and its entrepreneurship faculty to "bring the best of what Babson does in entrepreneurship to the new Olin College curriculum" as they built the new college. Its first few classes had numerous students who turned down acceptances at MIT, Cal Tech, Harvard, and other leading schools to come to Olin College as part of this bold experiment. The first entering class graduated in May 2006, and the new college is winning awards and setting a new standard for what is possible in engineering and entrepreneurship. The entrepreneurial appreciation of the Olin trustees, and their entrepreneurial approach to this enormous challenge, made this new venture possible.

Entrepreneurship beyond Business Schools

It is often said that none are more zealous than the converted. It would appear that this may be true of academic institutions and faculty who are converted to entrepreneurship as well. One of the most surprising and robust trends in the past two to three years has been major universities deciding to infuse entrepreneurship across most schools in their universities, not just business and engineering schools. Quite frankly, this is something we never expected to live long enough to see! In America the Kauffman Foundation led the charge by making major gifts ($25 million in total) to a dozen national universities to infuse entrepreneurship into their life sciences programs. The two national universities in Singapore decided to require entrepreneurship as part of the curricula across the campuses, including their schools of engineering, architecture, medicine, and life sciences. In Mexico, ITESM, the 36-campus national university, has launched a similar initiative. Even staid Cambridge University has made great progress with the inclusion of innovation and entrepreneurship programs along with its technology transfer initiatives and innovation center.

Throughout Europe and the world we are seeing more and more interest in this direction. In New Zealand at the University of Auckland, the first universitywide professorship was created in entrepreneurship to help facilitate its inclusion. In Latin America leading universities in Argentina, Ecuador, Peru, Mexico, and Puerto Rico, to mention a few, are creating entrepreneurship curricula in their business schools and across the universities. In China the current five-year plan includes education and research in entrepreneurship and innovation—a quite astonishing fact.

At the K–12 level and in online programs for adults, entrepreneurship education is plowing new ground. The genie is out of the bottle.

The Energy Creation Effect

Several "energy creators and liberators" are driving the successful expansion of entrepreneurship education and research as we've just discussed. This energizing process for faculty and students alike is also driving the rapid explosion of entrepreneurship education worldwide: China, India, Japan, Russia, South America, the old Eastern bloc, and developing countries, to name a few. First, the field seems to attract, by its substance and nature, highly entrepreneurial people. Historically entrepreneurial thinkers and doers have been few and far between in the vast majority of schools in the United States and abroad. These creative, can-do, resilient, and passionate people bring their entrepreneurial ways of thinking, acting, doing, and building to their courses, their research, and their institutions. They are the change agents—the movers and shakers.

Second, their entrepreneurial bent brings a new mind-set to universities and schools: They think and act like owners! They are creative, courageous, and determined to make it work and happen; they build teams, practice what they preach, are institution builders, and don't let myopic allegiance to their disciplines impede becoming better educators. Such thinking has been uncommon among faculty in the vast majority of universities. Their links to the world of practice build in relevance and excitement to their courses and research. They do not operate in traditional ivory-tower isolation. Students, deans, and colleagues can be energized by the leading-by-example pace they establish.

Third, entrepreneurship faculty constantly think in terms of opportunity. This is in sharp contrast to the typical mentality: We don't have the resources; it will cost too much; if they would only give us the money we'd create a great program; the curriculum committee will never approve this; and so on. Entrepreneurial faculty know that money follows superior teams and superior opportunities—so they create them! They find ways to innovate, raise money, and implement curricula and programs with entrepreneurial, bootstrapping methods, which, in resource-strapped universities, is a critical strategic advantage. They are ingenious at matching their innovative ideas with wealthy entrepreneurs and their foundations to raise seed money and to launch programs. There are thousands of examples of this. As a result of their entrepreneurial thinking and behavior, they become powerful role models for their students. The coupling of theory and knowledge with actual accomplishments that demonstrate how these principles, strategies, and concepts can work in the private sector and within the university is not lost on students.

Fourth, they create powerful strategic alliances with others—colleagues, alumni, and CEO/entrepreneurs—by practicing the teamwork principles of entrepreneurship they teach. As high-energy types they rub off on those around them. There is something exciting and compelling about being around highly intelligent and creative entrepreneurs as the centerpiece of your subject matter. They invariably inspire other faculty and students as well.

Finally, they often themselves experience personal career and life transformations. Entrepreneurs with an itch to teach find the pastures of entrepreneurship among the richest they have ever grazed. Time and again they make major career changes to include more teaching because they find it so energizing and rewarding. They usually report that their businesses improve even though they are there less! Many become significant benefactors to their universities, funding new endowed chairs and centers. To teach is to learn. Many of their students experience and report the same. The compelling nature of the entrepreneurial journey may not be for everyone, but many youths and adults today are anxious to find out. The journey can be addictive for faculty and students alike.

The Road Ahead

A number of years ago the famous Texas real estate entrepreneur Trammel Crow was inducted into Babson's Academy of Distinguished Entrepreneurs. This hulk of a man both physically and by reputation put his arm around my shoulder and asked the dreaded question: "Preefessor Timmons" (the tone revealed he knew his own answer), "can you really teach someone to be an entreeepreeeneur [our phonetic emphasis]?" "Mr. Crow," I replied, "what I think you may be asking me is this: Are you so preposterous and optimistic that you believe you can take average undergraduate students and in 15 weeks, and 35–40 hours of classroom time, turn them into the economic equivalent of a Beethoven or Picasso? I think you and

I both know the answer to that question, Mr. Crow." He laughed and smiled and simply said, "I see what you mean."

As time has gone on we have realized the question isn't a very good one, and it doesn't matter. Can you teach someone to have the basketball moves of a Michael Jordan, the creative flair on ice of a Wayne Gretzky, the unparalleled determination and will of a Lance Armstrong, the ball control of a Beckham, the grit and composure under the most intense competition of a Tom Brady? If you apply such an exceptional standard of genius, most will say probably not. But if you ask, "Could we create the environment to provide people with the opportunity to learn, build, test, discover, and reshape their aptitudes and talent as entrepreneurs?" our answer has been for decades a resounding yes, and we have in fact been doing just that at Babson College since its founding in 1919.

In essence, the cumulative programmatic experiences of students engaging in courses, field projects, and business plan competitions, actually starting new businesses, and having numerous interactions with faculty, outside entrepreneurs, and other students puts them in collisions and competition that enable them to see far more clearly what is possible—and to have the courage to try. In this book we will urge you to think big enough. You will see failure as part of the learning process: There is no such thing as an entrepreneur failing. Businesses fail; strategies may not work; a product may be flawed. The key for beginners is to keep the tuition (i.e., investment) low and learn as fast and as much as they can. As in sports, if you create the equivalent of the Little League and junior, high school, and then college teams, you will eventually have a flow-through of individuals who will fill the normal curve of performance as entrepreneurs. They will figure out for themselves in this Darwinian competition at what level they can perform, or not, and decide if it is right for them. Further, the very best, just as with world-class athletes, will not simply settle for one victory: thus the pattern of repeat entrepreneurs and entrepreneurs who are already wealthy who risk millions to start other businesses. Perhaps one of the most striking recent examples is Dan Neeleman, founder of the U.S. discount airline JetBlue.

It is increasingly clear that beyond learning the knowledge-based nuts and bolts of accounting, finance, cash flow, business plans, and the like, there are teachable and learnable mind-sets—ways of thinking and reasoning, skills, concepts, and principles that when translated into strategies, tactics, and practices can significantly improve the chances for success. These are at the heart of the content and process you will engage in with *New Venture Creation*. Among the most important things you can learn are how to think about the difference between a good idea and a good opportunity; the development and molding of the idea into an opportunity; the minimizing and control of resources; and resource parsimony and bootstrapping. (The latter may be uniquely American. At a recent Price-Babson program tailored for a group of Japanese educators, the translator had a difficult time with "bootstrapping." There was no direct word in Japanese. It seemed to convey more a notion of hardscrabble existence, even socially undesirable behavior in the down-and-out sense.) All of these areas are learnable and teachable. Yet one of the most important areas of the entrepreneurial mind-set deals with the role of and attitude toward risk, failure, and even bankruptcy. In Japan and Germany, for instance, once you bankrupt a firm it is basically legally impossible to start another company.

For the entrepreneur, the mind-set when 1,000 experiments fail is just like that of Thomas Edison: "Those weren't 1,000 failures; those were just 1,000 ways that didn't work!" The new venture is nothing more than a huge, perpetual learning puzzle; it is at least three-dimensional, highly dynamic, chaotic, and not very predictable. The process is characterized by enormous contradiction: It requires careful thought and planning, but much of it is an unplannable event, much like a battle plan's obsolescence once the battle starts.

The Genie Is out of the Bottle

More than ever we are convinced that the creation and liberation of human energy through entrepreneurship is the single largest transformational force on the planet today. The power of a single person is so profound, and nowhere is that more true and relevant than in entrepreneurship. Perhaps the best news of all is that it is not confined to business and the private sector alone. Fortunately, the genie is out of the bottle and is wielding her magic in every conceivable arena: education, religious organizations, the military, not-for-profits, and even government. How can one not be bullish about the next four decades?

Entrepreneurship: Innovation + Entrepreneurship = Prosperity and Philanthropy

Surely one of the most promising recent developments in the entrepreneurial revolution is entrepreneurship becoming a central, nonpartisan cornerstone in America's policy debates. As the debates among candidates for the 2008 U.S. presidential election accelerate, the significance of policies affecting the potential fruits of an entrepreneurial economy are ever present. Political rhetoric aside, the relevance and economic importance of the entrepreneurial phenomenon have legitimized entrepreneurship as vital to any debate about our social economic policies. The creation of the National Commission on Entrepreneurship in 1999 launched an awareness of building educational initiative to help legislators, governors, and policy makers understand the contributions and potential of the entrepreneurial economy.

In June 2001 the long-standing U.S. Senate Committee on Small Business changed its name to Small Business and Entrepreneurship, sending a significant message. The National Governor's Association is also including entrepreneurship in its meetings and policy discussions.

The formidable link between public policy and entrepreneurial activity in the United States has become increasingly important. Politicians are now aware of this link and have begun to emphasize the ways entrepreneurship leads to greater national and global prosperity.

> In every neighborhood in my hometown of Memphis, and all across America, I see young people tutoring and mentoring, building homes, caring for seniors, and feeding the hungry. I also see them using their entrepreneurial spirit to build companies, start non-profits, and drive our new economy.
>
> Harold Ford, Jr., United States Representative
> 2000 Democratic National Convention Speech

Job Creation   Twenty years ago, MIT researcher David Birch began to report his landmark findings that defied all previous notions that large established businesses were the backbone of the economy and the generator of new jobs. In fact, one Nobel Prize–winning economist gained his award by "proving" that any enterprise with fewer than 100 employees was irrelevant to the study of economics and policy making! Birch stunned researchers, politicians, and the business world with just the opposite conclusion: New and growing smaller firms created 81.5 percent of the net new jobs in the economy from 1969 to 1976.[1] This general pattern has been repeated ever since.

Entrepreneurial firms account for a significant amount of employment growth (defined by at least 20 percent a year for four years, from a base of at least $100,000 in revenues). These "gazelles," as David Birch calls them, made up only 3 percent of all firms but added 5 million jobs from 1994 to 1998. According to the U.S. Small Business Administration's

---

[1] D. L. Birch, 1979, *The Job Creation Process*, unpublished report, MIT Program on Neighborhood and Regional Change prepared for the Economic Development Administration, U.S. Department of Commerce, Washington, DC.

Office of Advocacy, in 2004 small firms with fewer than 500 employees represented 99.9 percent of the 26.8 million businesses in the United States. Over the past decade, small businesses created 60–80 percent of the net new jobs. In the most recent year with data (2004), small firms accounted for *all* of the net new jobs. Small firms had a net gain of 1.86 million new jobs, while firms with 500 or more employees lost more jobs than they created, for a net loss of 181,122 jobs.[2] When one considers the history of Microsoft, a start-up in the late 1970s, these job creation findings are not so surprising. In 1980, for instance, Microsoft had just $8 million in revenue and 38 employees. By the end of 2006, its sales were nearly $50 billion, it had over 71,000 employees, and the total market value of its stock was over $255 billion.

We can readily see the far-reaching change in employment patterns caused by this explosion of new companies. In the 1960s about one in four persons worked for a Fortune 500 company. As recently as 1980, the Fortune 500 employed 20 percent of the workforce. By 2006 that figure had dropped to less than 9 percent! This same pattern tells the story of the explosive growth of new regions and centers of technology and entrepreneurship throughout the country. It is impossible to name a new high-growth area—starting with Silicon Valley and Boston and extending to the Research Triangle of North Carolina; Austin, Texas; Denver/Boulder, Colorado; Indianapolis, Columbus, and Ann Arbor; or Atlanta, Georgia—without observing this same job creation phenomenon from new and growing smaller companies.

New Venture Formation

Classical entrepreneurship means new venture creation. But it is much more, as you will discover throughout this chapter and book. It is arguably the single most powerful force to create economic and social mobility. Because it is opportunity-centered and rewards only talent and performance—and could not care less about religion, gender, skin color, social class, national origin, and the like—it enables people to pursue and realize their dreams, to falter and to try again, and to seek opportunities that match who they are, what they want to be, and how and where they want to live. No other employer can make this claim.

The role of women in entrepreneurship is particularly noteworthy. Consider what has happened in just a single generation. In 1970 women-owned businesses were limited mainly to small service businesses and employed fewer than 1 million persons nationwide. They represented only 4 percent of all businesses. Analyzing recent data provided by the U.S. Bureau of

the Census, the Center for Women's Business Research (www.nfwbo.org) projected that as of the end of 2005, there were an estimated 10.1 million privately held, majority-women-owned firms in the United States. These firms employed 18.2 million people and generated $2.32 trillion in sales. Women-owned businesses account for 28 percent of all U.S. businesses and represent about 775,000 new start-ups per year, or about 55 percent of all new start-ups. Because a growing portion of these new ventures founded by women are high-potential, higher-growth businesses, women entrepreneurs are without a doubt crucial to continued economic expansion.

At a time when the average growth for U.S. firms was 7 percent (between 1997 and 2002), women-owned firms grew by 19.8 percent. Employment at these firms increased by 30 percent (1½ times the U.S. rate) and sales grew by 40 percent—the same rate as all firms in the United States. Between 1997 and 2004, the number of privately held firms owned by women of color grew by 54.6 percent (as opposed to the average growth of only 9 percent). Women's business ownership is up among all groups, but the number of Hispanic-owned (up 63.9 percent) and Asian-owned (up 69.3 percent) firms has grown especially fast. An estimated one in five (21 percent) women-owned businesses are owned by women of color.

A similar pattern can be seen for a variety of ethnic and racial groups (Exhibit 1.2). According to the 2002 U.S. Census statistics, black-owned businesses were the fastest-growing segment of new businesses, growing 45 percent between 1997 and 2002, with revenue growth of 25 percent. The 1.2 million black-owned businesses in the United States in 2002 (5.2 percent of nonfarm businesses) employed more than 756,000 people and generated nearly $89 billion in business revenues. In 2002 Hispanic-owned businesses in the United States totaled 1.6 million firms (6.8 percent of nonfarm businesses)—an increase of 31 percent from 1997. Those businesses employed 1.5 million people and generated $222 billion in revenue. In 2002, 1.1 million Asian/Pacific Islander–owned businesses (4.8 percent of nonfarm businesses) generated more than $326 billion in revenue—up 8 percent from 1997. There were 201,387 Native American–owned businesses with receipts of over $26 billion. Since 1997 the number of Native American–owned businesses in the United States has jumped by 84 percent to 197,300 (just under 1 percent of nonfarm businesses). Eighty percent of these firms would be classified as micro-enterprises.

American Dream: For the Young at Start!
Aspiring to work for oneself is deeply embedded in American culture and has never been stronger. In

[2] For information on employment dynamics by firm size from 1989 to 2004, see www.sba.gov/advo/research/data.html#us.

EXHIBIT 1.2

Growth of Entrepreneurship among Ethnic and Racial Groups

Ownership	Number of Firms Owned		% Change	Sales and Receipts ($ billion)		% Change	Number of Employees (Millions)		% Change
	1997	2002		1997	2002		1997	2002	
African American	780,770	1,197,567	53	42.7	88.6	107	0.7	0.8	6
Hispanic	1,120,000	1,573,600	41	114.0	221.9	95	1.3	1.5	18
Asian/Pacific Islander	785,480	1,133,137	44	161.0	331.0	106	2.2	2.24	2
Native American	187,921	201,387	7	22.0	26.8	22	0.3	0.19	−37

a 2004 Gallup Poll, 90 percent of American parents said they would approve if one or more of their children pursued entrepreneurship. In a 2006 poll of 1,474 middle and high school students, the youth entrepreneurship organization Junior Achievement found that 70.9 percent would like to be self-employed at some point in their lives. That's up from 68.6 percent in 2005 and 64 percent in 2004. The National Association for the Self-Employed projected that its ranks would increase to about 250,000 members by the end of 2006, up from 100,000 in 1988. In 2004 *USA Today* asked a national sample of men and women if for one year they could take any job they wanted, what would that job be? The results reveal how ingrained the entrepreneurial persona has become in society: 47 percent of the women and 38 percent of the men said they would want to run their own companies. Surprisingly, for the men, this was a higher percentage than those who said "professional athlete"!

Among corporate managers laid off as a result of downsizing, 70 percent are over 40 years of age, and one-fifth of them are starting their own companies. Other recent studies show that at any one time about 10 percent of the adult population is attempting to start a business of some kind.

A 2006 study showed that young people with entrepreneurs as role models were more likely to achieve a broad range of success in business, school, and in life.[3] Uniformly, the self-employed report the highest levels of personal satisfaction, challenge, pride, and remuneration. They seem to love the entrepreneurial game for its own sake. They love their work because it is invigorating, energizing, and meaningful. Entrepreneurs, as they invent, mold, recognize, and pursue opportunities, are the genius and energy behind this extraordinary value and wealth creation phenomenon: *the entrepreneurial process.*

Sir Winston Churchill probably was not thinking about the coming entrepreneurial generation when he wrote in his epic book *While England Slept,* "The world was meant to be wooed and won by youth." Yet this could describe perfectly what has transpired over the past 30 years as young entrepreneurs in their 20s conceived of, launched, and grew new companies that, in turn, spawned entirely new industries. Consider just a few of these 20-something entrepreneurs (see Exhibit 1.3).

EXHIBIT 1.3

Mega-Entrepreneurs Who Started in Their 20s

Entrepreneurial Company	Founder(s)
Microsoft	Bill Gates and Paul Allen
Netscape	Marc Andressen
Dell Computer	Michael Dell
Gateway 2000	Ted Waitt
McCaw Cellular	Craig McCaw
Apple Computer	Steve Jobs and Steve Wozniak
Digital Equipment Corporation	Ken and Stan Olsen
Federal Express	Fred Smith
Google	Larry Page and Sergey Brin
Genentech	Robert Swanson
Polaroid	Edward Land
Nike	Phil Knight
Lotus Development Corporation	Mitch Kapor
Ipix.com	Kevin McCurdy
Yahoo!	David Filo and Jerry Yang
PayPal	Max Levchin
Skype	Janus Friis
Facebook	Mark Zuckerberg (at 19)
YouTube	Chad Hurley
MySpace	Tom Anderson

---

[3] H. Van Auken, F. L. Fry, and P. Stephens, "The Influence of Role Models on Entrepreneurial Intentions," *Journal of Developmental Entrepreneurship,* June 2006.

There are many more, lesser known, but just as integral a part of the entrepreneurial revolution as these exceptional founders. You will come to know and appreciate some of them in this book, for example, Martin Migoya, founder of Globant, an IT outsourcing company based in Buenos Aires, Argentina. In four years he and his team have built a company with more than 240 employees, sales approaching $12 million, and clients in Europe and the Americas. Their goal: build an offshore IT services business that can go head to head with major players such as Infosys, IBM, and Accenture.

Roxanne Quimby is a very different but extraordinary entrepreneur. Enjoying basic subsistence living on a small farm in the woods of Maine, she conceived of an idea to develop natural products from beeswax and other natural components. Her new business began slowly and was fragile. She thrived, relocated the business to North Carolina, and eventually sold her company for nearly $200 million. Roxanne returned to Maine and is using a significant portion of her fortune to buy up huge parcels of undeveloped land in northern Maine—over 28,000 acres so far—that she hopes will one day be part of a federal preserve.

Jack Stack had worked his way up, after dropping out of school, to the mailroom and the factory floor at an International Harvester Plant in Springfield, Missouri, in the early 1980s, when it was announced that the plant would likely close. He and a handful of colleagues pooled $100,000 of their own money and borrowed $8.9 million from a local bank—note the 89 to 1 leverage!—and bought the plant for 10 cents a share to try to save the business and their jobs. The plant was failing, with $10 million in revenues. Starting as a rebuilder of engines shipped to the United States by Mercedes, the business expanded to include over 20 businesses. The outcome is an organization that moved from near death to a current revenue of nearly $200 million. Stack's book, *The Great Game of Business*, is a business classic.

Brian Scudamore started his company 1-800-GOT-JUNK? in 1989 straight out of high school with $700 and a beat-up old pickup truck. In 2006 the company posted sales of more than $112 million, up from just $2 million in 2000. Over the past two years its corporate staff has burgeoned from 43 to 116 employees. Their plan to double again by 2008 will be partly fueled by their first international offices in Australia (2005) and in England (2006). With 330 locations and 250 franchisees, 1-800-GOT-JUNK? is the world's largest junk removal service.

Back in 1982, Patricia Gallup and David Hall decided there must be a better way to buy information technology products, so they established PC Connection. Seeing a significant business opportunity in the emerging personal computer industry, the two entrepreneurs launched their direct computer supply business with the philosophy that providing technical advice and focusing on customer service was as important as low prices. PC Connection went public in 1998 and has grown into a Fortune 1000 company, with revenues of $1.7 billion and more than 1,600 employees.

While still an MBA candidate at Babson College, Ann Stockbridge Sullivan developed a business plan to build a retirement community in Kennebunk, Maine. She succeeded in raising $6 million of capital, achieved a 97 percent occupancy rate in the first year, and has had a two-year wait-list since 1993!

Wayne Postoak, a Native American, was a young professor and a highly successful basketball coach at Haskell Indian Nations University, in Lawrence, Kansas, in the 1970s. Haskell is the only national four-year university for Native Americans, enrolling students from nearly 200 tribes throughout North America. Haskell also launched the first Center for Tribal Entrepreneurial Studies in 1995. Postoak's children had aspirations for a college education and medical school, which he knew he could not afford on his coaching and teaching salary. He decided to launch his own construction firm, which today employs nearly 100 people and has sales above $10 million. (Note that fewer than 4 percent of all businesses in the country exceed $10 million in annual sales.)

In 2001, at age 14, Sean Belnick invested $500 to start up a direct shipping company for office furniture—out of his bedroom. The Georgia-based company, which had 2006 revenues of $24 million, has branched out into home furniture, medical equipment, and school furniture. Notable clients include Microsoft, the *American Idol* television show, and the Pentagon.

Babson graduate Matt Coffin founded LowerMyBills.com in 1999. The company partnered with service providers across more than 20 categories, including home mortgage, home equity loans, purchase loans, debt consolidation loans, credit cards, auto loans, insurance, and cell phones. The company devised a wide range of creative online advertising to attract customers to the free service that matched them with the companies that best met their needs, making money on commissions from participating vendors. In 2007 LowerMyBills.com was one of the top five Internet advertisers, and ranked number one among financial advertisers. Matt, a high-energy motivational leader, bootstrapped, scrimped, and managed by the numbers to such an extent that he was able to raise $13 million in venture capital while retaining over 25 percent ownership—quite a feat. In May 2005 he sold the company to Experian for approximately $400 million.

EXHIBIT 1.4

New Industries Launched by the E-Generation

Personal computers	Cellular phone services
Biotechnology	CD-ROM
Wireless cable TV	Internet publishing and shopping
Fast oil changes	Desktop computing
PC software	Virtual imaging
Desktop information	Convenience foods superstores
Wireless communications/ handheld devices/PDAs	Digital media and entertainment
	Pet care services
Healthful living products	Voice over Internet applications
Electronic paging	Green buildings
CAD/CAM	Large, scalable wind and solar
Voice mail information technology services	power systems
	Biofuels and biomaterials

Formation of New Industries

This generation of economic revolutionaries has become the creators and leaders of entire new industries, not just a few outstanding new companies. From among the staggering raw number of start-ups emerge the lead innovators and creators that often become the dominant firms in new industries. This is evident from the 20-something list (Exhibit 1.3). Exhibit 1.4 is a partial list of entirely new industries, not in existence a generation ago, that are today major sectors in the economy.

These new industries have transformed the economy. In the true creative birth and destruction process first articulated by Joseph Schumpeter, these new industries replace and displace older ones. David Birch has reported how this pace has accelerated. In the 1960s to the 1990s, it took 20 years to replace 35 percent of the companies then on the list of Fortune 500 companies. By the late 1980s, that replacement took place every five years (e.g., nearly 30 new faces each year); and in the 1990s, it occurred in three to four years. This outcome is the downsizing and rightsizing of large companies we commonly hear about today. A generation earlier virtually no one predicted such a dramatic change. How could this happen so quickly? How could huge, cash-rich, dominant firms of the 1960s and 1970s get toppled from their perch by newcomers?

Consider the following example of a new industry in the making. Skype began as a software program in the early 2000s. Developed by Swedish entrepreneurs Niklas Zennström and Janus Friis, Skype allowed users to make telephone calls from their computers to other Skype users free of charge, or to landlines and cell phones for a fee. Additional features included instant messaging, file transfer, short message service, video conferencing, and the ability to circumvent firewalls. The main difference between Skype and voice over Internet protocol (VoIP) clients was that Skype was devised as a peer-to-peer model rather than the more traditional server–client model. As a decentralized system, the Skype user directory was able to scale easily without a complex and costly infrastructure.

This unique concept was quickly embraced by consumers around the world. In late 2005 the Skype Group was acquired by eBay for $2.6 billion, plus a performance earn-out of another $1.5 billion. In 2007 the company introduced SkypeOut, a system to allow Skype users to call traditional telephone numbers, including mobile telephones, for a fee. By the second quarter of that year, Skype reported that nearly 220 million active user accounts had logged 7.1 billion Skype-to-Skype minutes and 1.3 billion minutes using SkypeOut—for total Q2 revenues of $90 million.

Time and again, in industry after industry, the vision, drive, and innovations of entrepreneurial ventures demolish the old Fortune 500 group. The capital markets note the future value of these up-and-comers, compared to the old giants. Take, for instance, the Big Three automakers, giants of the prior generation of the 1950s and 1960s. By year-end 2006 they had combined sales of $568 billion, employed 923,000, but had a year-ending market capitalization (total value of all shares of the company) of $92.9 billion, or just 16 cents per dollar of revenue. Intel, Microsoft, and Google had 2006 total sales of $96.2 billion, employed just 215,000, but enjoyed a market capitalization of $517.7 billion. That's 5.6 times the value of the Big Three, and $5.38 per dollar of revenue—34 times the Big Three!

This pattern of high market value characterizes virtually every new industry that has been—and continues to be—created. This is also the case when entrepreneurs compete directly with industry stalwarts. Airlines Delta, American, and Continental employed 181,600 employees and had combined sales in 2006 of $54.1 billion. Their market capitalization was $15.4 billion, about 28 cents per dollar of revenue. In contrast, with a total of 45,400 employees, JetBlue, Southwest, and Frontier had 2006 sales of $13.1 billion and a combined market capitalization of $14.8 billion—over $1 per dollar of revenue. Exhibit 1.5 shows these relationships.

Innovation

At the heart of the entrepreneurial process is the innovative spirit. After all, from Ben Franklin to Thomas Edison to Steve Jobs and Bill Gates, the history of the country shows a steady stream of brilliant entrepreneurs and innovators. For years it was believed by the press, the public, and policy makers that research and development occurring

EXHIBIT 1.5

The Impact of Entrepreneurship on American Giants Old and New

Firm	Sales in 2006 ($ billion)	Employees in 2006 (000s)	Market Capitalization in Late December 2006 ($ billion)
Ford	162.4	283.0	14.0
GM	198.9	280.0	17.1
DaimlerChrysler	206.7	360.4	61.7
Total	**568.0**	**923.4**	**92.9**
Intel	36.0	94.1	116.4
Microsoft	49.6	71.0	255.1
Google	10.6	10.7	146.1
Total	**96.2**	**175.8**	**517.7**
Delta	17.9	51.3	4.1
American	22.6	86.6	7.3
Continental	13.6	43.7	4.0
Total	**54.1**	**181.6**	**15.4**
JetBlue	2.5	8.4	2.5
Southwest	9.4	32.7	12.0
Frontier	1.2	4.3	0.3
Total	**13.1**	**45.4**	**14.8**

in large companies after World War II and driven by the birth of the space age after Sputnik in 1957 were the main drivers of innovation in the nation.

This belief was shown to be a myth—similar to the earlier beliefs about job creation—as the National Science Foundation, U.S. Department of Commerce, and others began to report research in the 1980s and 1990s that surprised many. They found that since World War II, *small entrepreneurial firms have been responsible for half of all innovation and 95 percent of all radical innovation in the United States!* Other studies showed that research and development at smaller entrepreneurial firms were more productive and robust than at large firms: Smaller firms generated twice as many innovations per R&D dollar spent as the giants; twice as many innovations per R&D scientist as the giants; and 24 times as many innovations per R&D dollar versus those megafirms with more than 10,000 employees!

Clearly smaller entrepreneurial firms do things differently when it comes to research and development activities. This innovative environment accounted for the development of the transistor and then the semiconductor. Today Moore's law—the power of the computer chip will double every 18 months at constant price—is actually being exceeded by modern chip technology. Combine this with man-

agement guru Peter Drucker's postulate: A 10-fold increase in the productivity of any technology results in economic discontinuity. Thus every five years there will be a 10-fold increase in productivity. Author George Gilder recently argued that communications bandwidth doubles every 12 months, creating an economic discontinuity every three to four years.[4] It does not take a lot of imagination to see the profound economic impact of such galloping productivity on every product use and application one can envision. The explosion in a vast array of opportunities is imminent.

This innovation cylinder of the entrepreneurial engine of America's economy has led to the creation of major new inventions and technologies. Exhibit 1.6 summarizes some of these major innovations.

Today the fast pace of innovation is actually accelerating. New scientific breakthroughs in biotechnology and nanotechnology are driving the next great waves of innovation. *Nano* means one-billionth, so a nanometer is one-billionth of a meter or 1/80,000 the diameter of a human hair. A new class of nano-size products in drugs, optical network devices, and bulk materials is attracting substantial research funding and private equity.[5] The next generation of entrepreneurs will create leading ventures and wealth in these and other applications of nanotechnology.

---

[4] Jeffry Timmons is indebted to Robert Compton, a colleague on the board of directors of the Kauffman Center for Entrepreneurial Leadership, for bringing his attention to these economic discontinuities arguments.

[5] *Red Herring*, "Nanotech Grows Up," June 15 and July 1, 2001, pp. 47–58.

EXHIBIT 1.6

Major Inventions by U.S. Small Firms

Acoustical suspension speakers	Aerosol can	Air conditioning
Airplane	Artificial skin	Assembly line
Audiotape recorder	Automatic fabric cutting	Automatic transfer equipment
Bakelite	Biosynthetic insulin	Catalytic petroleum cracking
Continuous casting	Cotton picker	Fluid flow meter
Fosin fire extinguisher	Geodesic dome	Gyrocompass
Heart valve	Heat sensor	Helicopter
Heterodyne radio	High-capacity computer	Hydraulic brake
Leaning machine	Link trainer	Nuclear magnetic resonance
Pacemaker	Personal computer	Prefabricated housing
Piezo electrical devices	Polaroid camera	Pressure-sensitive cellophane
Quick-frozen foods	Rotary oil drilling bit	Safety razor
Six-axis robot arm	Soft contact lens	Sonar fish monitoring
Spectrographic grid	Stereographic image sensoring	Zipper

Source: Office of Advocacy of the U.S. Small Business Administration.

Venture and Growth Capital   Venture capital has deep roots in our history, and the evolution to today's industry is uniquely American. This private risk capital is the rocket fuel of America's entrepreneurial engine. Classic venture capitalists work as coaches and partners with entrepreneurs and innovators at a very early stage to help shape and accelerate the development of the company.[6] The fast-growth, highly successful companies backed by venture capital investors read like a "Who's Who of the Economy": Apple Computer, Intuit, Compaq Computer, Staples, Intel, Federal Express, Cisco, e-Bay, Starbucks Coffee, Nextel Communication, Juniper Networks, Yahoo!, Sun Microsystems, Amazon.com, Genetech, Google, Blackberry, Microsoft, and thousands of others. Typical of these legendary investments that both created companies and lead their new industry are the following:

- In 1957 General George Doriot, father of modern American venture capital, and his young associate Bill Congelton at American Research & Development (ARD) invested $70,000 for 77 percent of the founding stock of a new company created by four MIT graduate students, led by Kenneth Olsen. By the time their investment was sold in 1971, it was worth $355 million. The company was Digital Equipment Corporation and became the world leader in microcomputers by the 1980s.
- In 1968 Gordon Moore and Robert Noyce teamed with Arthur Rock to launch Intel Corporation with $2.5 million, and $25,000 from each of the founders. Intel is the leader in semiconductors today.

- In 1975 Arthur Rock, in search of concepts "that change the way people live and work," invested $1.5 million in the start-up of Apple Computer. The investment was valued at $100 million at Apple's first public stock offering in 1978.
- After monthly losses of $1 million and more for 29 consecutive months, a new company that launched the overnight delivery of small packages turned the corner. The $25 million invested in Federal Express was worth $1.2 billion when the company issued stock to the public.

A good depiction of the long gestation period for upstart companies like these, whose collective expansions blossom into entire new industries, is reflected in the nearly ancient interest in harnessing the sun's energy as a power source. The movement began when French inventor Auguste Mouchout patented the world's first solar-powered motor—an innovation he touted as an alternative to the industrializing world's dangerous dependence on coal. The year? 1861.

For a century and a half, innovation in solar energy sources has never managed to yield a cost-competitive model relative to fossil fuels. Venture capitalists have been placing modest bets on solar for years, but in 2006 things changed (see Exhibit 1.7). In 2006 venture capitalists invested $590 million into 49 solar technology and/or photovoltaics ventures, up from $254 million in 41 solar-related ventures a year earlier—a two-year total that exceeded the previous five years. Consulting firm Clean Edge forecasts that the solar

[6] W. D. Bygrave and J. A. Timmons, *Venture Capital at the Crossroads* (Boston, MA: Harvard Business School, 1992), Chapter 1.

industry will grow from $15.6 billion in 2006 to $69.3 billion by 2016.[7] So can we conclude that a great leap forward in solar energy ventures is imminent now that the industry is gaining traction and the "smart money" is getting on board? On the contrary, the ultimate vision fueling these investments—that solar will be able to compete on cost with other power sources—is still a long way off.

The recent surge in venture capital interest in biofuels also reflects this investment profile. Biofuel ventures—business models focused on creating cheap alternatives to fossil fuels using plant and waste materials—are expensive propositions. Intrastructure heavy, these ventures typically require $100 million in risk capital—about 10 times what would be required for an average software start-up. Biofuel businesses also require up to $100 million more in follow-on money in the form of debt and project financing.[8] The upside, of course, is that sooner or later, an Exxon/Mobil of biofuels will emerge to change the entire energy use and production landscape. Virtually every other new industry, from biotechnology to PC software to wireless communications to the Internet, has involved entrepreneurial visionaries and patient venture investors.

Thousands of companies exist today because of venture capital support. Clearly the technology start-up has benefited from venture capital—companies like Apple Computer, Cisco, Genentech, Google, eBay, and Yahoo! But countless others like Federal Express, Staples, Outback Steakhouse, and Starbucks are examples of traditional companies that were launched with venture backing.

Studies suggest that more than one out of three Americans will use a medical product or service generated by a venture-backed life sciences company.[9] According to Global Insight (www.globalinsight.com), in 2006 U.S.-based, venture-backed companies accounted for more than 10.4 million jobs and generated over $2.3 trillion in revenue. Nearly 1 out of every 10 private sector jobs is at a company that was originally venture-backed. Almost 18 percent of U.S. GDP comes from venture-backed companies. What is particularly important is that these are new jobs and, in fact, often new industries, as depicted in Exhibit 1.6.

In addition to the $20+ billion of venture capital, moderately wealthy to very wealthy individuals represent a total annual pool of about $120 billion, which they invest in new ventures. So-called angel investors represent a seasoned subset of this investor pool. The angel investor market showed signs of steady growth in 2006, with total investments of $25.6 billion, an increase of 10.8 percent over 2005, according to the Center for Venture Research at the University of New Hampshire. A total of 51,000 entrepreneurial ventures received angel funding in 2006, a 3 percent increase from 2005. In 2006 there were 234,000 active investors. The sharp increase in total investment dollars was matched by a more modest increase in total deals, resulting in an increase in the average deal size of 7.5 percent compared to 2005. This continued rise in total investments points to a healthy angel market.

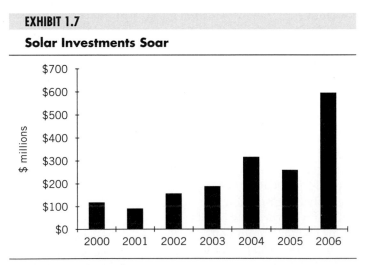

EXHIBIT 1.7

Solar Investments Soar

Source: Thomson Financial.

Note: Data are for totals invested by U.S.-based venture capitalists in solar and/or photovoltaic companies.

[7] *Thomson Venture Capital Journal*, May 2007, pp. 21, 22.
[8] *Thomson Venture Capital Journal*, June 2007, pp. 24, 25.
[9] House of Representatives Committee on Ways and Means, September 6, 2007, "Hearing on Fair and Equitable Tax Policy for America's Working Families." Testimony of Jonathan Silver, founder and managing director, Core Capital Partners.

Similar to the venture capitalists, these angels bring far more than money to the entrepreneurial process. As successful entrepreneurs themselves, they bring experience, learning curves, networks, wisdom, and maturity to the fledgling companies in which they invest. As directors and advisors, they function as coaches, confidants, mentors, and cheerleaders. Given the explosion of the entrepreneurial economy in the past 30 years, there is now a cadre of harvested entrepreneurs in the nation that is 20 to 30 times larger than that of the past generation. This pool of talent, know-how, and money continues to play an enormously important role in cultivating and accelerating e-generation capabilities.

Philanthropy and Leadership: Giving Back to the Community

Another lesser known and largely ignored role of American entrepreneurs is that of philanthropists and creative community leaders. A majority of new buildings, classrooms, athletic facilities, and endowed professorships at universities across the nation have been funded by a harvested company founder who wants to give back. The largest gifts and the greatest proportion of donors among any groups giving to university capital campaigns are successful entrepreneurs. At one time, half of the total MIT endowment was attributed to gifts of founders' stock.

This same pattern also characterizes local churches, hospitals, museums, orchestras, and schools. Most financial gifts to these institutions are from successful entrepreneurs. According to the *Chronicle of Philanthropy*, the number of individual donations of $100 million or more hit a record in 2006. These 21 donations were principally made by individual entrepreneurs to universities, hospitals, and charities. The time and creative leadership that entrepreneurs devote to these community institutions are as important as their money. Talk with any person from another country who has spent enough time in America to see these entrepreneurial leaders active in their communities, and they will convince you just how truly unique this is. America's leading foundations were all created by gifts of the founders of great companies: Ford, Carnegie, Kellogg, Mellon, Kauffman, Gates.

As we might imagine, when a successful entrepreneur gets involved in the nonprofit sector, those efforts often involve what has become known as "high-engagement" philanthropy, an approach in which the funder is directly and personally engaged with the organization. This engagement often involves strategic assistance like long-term planning, board and executive recruitment, coaching, and leveraging relationships to identify additional resources and facilitate partnerships. These high-engagement philanthropists have a stronger focus and deeper investments in a smaller, more select number of investment partners, and a healthy ambition for the long-term reach and ripple of their efforts.[10]

One example of this type of nonprofit is the Robin Hood Foundation, which was started in 1988 by three Wall Street executives. This foundation is an engaged grant maker, applying investment principles to philanthropy. Since its founding, Robin Hood has provided about $175 million in grants and an additional $95 million in donated goods and strategic support services. In the wake of the 9/11 attacks, this organization established a relief fund and by 2004 had provided $54 million in funds to those affected by the attacks.

The Kauffman Center for Entrepreneurial Leadership in Kansas City, at the Ewing Marion Kauffman Foundation, is now among the 15 largest foundations in the country with approximately $2 billion in assets. Their vision is clear: self-sufficient people in healthy communities. The Kauffman Center's mission is at the core of the entrepreneurial revolution: *accelerating entrepreneurship in America.*

Mr. K. was probably best known outside Kansas City as owner of the Kansas City Royals (which he later gave to the city). His entrepreneurial genius created Marion Laboratories, Inc., which grew to $1 billion in revenues and $6.5 billion in market capitalization. You will hear more about the remarkable success of Mr. K. in subsequent chapters, but the following quotes best sum Mr. K.'s entrepreneurial spirit and life philosophy:

> Live what you talk, make your actions match your words. You must live what you preach and do it right and do it often. Day after day.
>
> As an entrepreneur, you really need to develop a code of ethics, a code of relationships with your people, because it's the people who come and join you. They have dreams of their own. You have your dream of the company. They must mesh somewhat.

These sentiments are mirrored time and again by highly successful mega-entrepreneurs who have created America's leading foundations: Carnegie, Olin, Ford, Kellogg, Lilly, Gates, and Blank, to name a few. What is much less known and appreciated by the general public is the extent to which this giving-back-to-the-community ethic of philanthropy is repeated by entrepreneurs at the local community level. Take, for example, the Varney family of Antrim, New Hampshire. Their Monadnock Paper Mills company, a multigenerational firm, is the largest employer in the area. They have been industry leaders in environmentally clean papermaking. In fact, the major river for miles downstream from their mill has some of the best

---

[10] Venture Philanthropy Partners (www.vppartners.org), "High-Engagement Philanthropy: The Bridge to a More Effective Social Sector," 2004.

catch-and-release trophy trout water in the state. They also support many community causes, from the local hospital, to the arts center, to the leading conservation organizations, and many more, to which the family has generously contributed time and money. The extent of this volunteerism and generosity in communities across America often surprises European visitors.

One cannot find a building, stadium, science or arts center at either private or public universities in America that has not come from the wealth creation and gift of a highly successful entrepreneur.

One great example of a philanthropic entrepreneur is Babson alumnus Arthur M. Blank, cofounder of The Home Depot and owner of the Atlanta Falcons. As a way of giving back to the community, he funded the Arthur M. Blank Center for Entrepreneurship at Babson College, which opened in 1998, and created the Arthur Blank Family Foundation to support innovative endeavors leading to better circumstances for low-income youth and their families.

At colleges and universities, hospitals, churches and synagogues, private schools, museums, and the like, the boards of directors and trustees who lead, fund, and help perpetuate these institutions are, more often than not, entrepreneurs. As in their own companies, their creative, entrepreneurial leadership is their most valuable contribution.

The Entrepreneurial Revolution: A Decade of Acceleration and Boom

A "revolution" in higher education has played a critical role in the steady growth of entrepreneurship. Today well over 2,000 colleges, universities, and community colleges offer such courses, and many of them offer majors in entrepreneurship or entrepreneurial studies. In the past 10 years alone, American universities have invested over $1 billion in creating entrepreneurship education and research capacity. There are over 44 academic journals and over 200 entrepreneurship centers. The number of endowed professorships has grown from the very first (the Paul T. Babson Professorship at Babson College in 1980) to nearly 400 today in the United States and almost 200 in the rest of the world. Here is a sampling of the many indicators—including innumerable entrepreneurial initiatives among not-for-profit foundations and organizations—that point to an ever-expanding culture of entrepreneurship.

Education

- Charitable contributions to colleges and universities in the United States grew by 9.4 percent in 2006, reaching $28 billion, finds a new study from the New York City–based Council for Aid to Education. The organization's annual Voluntary Support of Education survey, which has tracked giving to higher education for more than 50 years, found that of the $28 billion raised by institutions of higher education in 2006, just over half came directly from individuals, while alumni giving grew by 18.3 percent and foundation giving increased by 1.4 percent.

- In 2005 the National Science Foundation awarded a three-year grant to Babson College to partner with the new Olin College of Engineering to create a new program for engineering faculty. The Babson-Olin Program—sister program of the longtime successful Price-Babson Program—will educate engineering faculty to bring entrepreneurship into their curricula, to build their own teaching capacities, and thereby improve prosperity in America.

- In 2004 the Ewing Marion Kauffman Foundation of Kansas City—America's leading foundation in entrepreneurship—made $25 million in grants to eight major universities to create entrepreneurship education across life sciences, medicine, and engineering.

- The Kauffman Foundation has been joined by other new and established foundations in supporting entrepreneurship, including the Franklin W. Olin Foundation, the Donald W. Reynolds Foundation, the Theodore R. M. Vivian Johnson Scholarship Foundation, the Charles G. Koch Foundation, the Manchester Craftsmen's Guild in Pittsburgh, and others.

- Haskell Indian Nations University in Lawrence, Kansas, created the first Center for Tribal Entrepreneurial Studies and is now partnering with numerous tribal colleges around the nation to develop appropriate entrepreneurship curricula.

- In Salt Lake City the University of Utah began a venture fund in 2002 with a $500,000 gift from local businessman James Sorenson and his son Jim. The fund is supported by the university but is not part of the university. The fund had raised $18 million by March 2006 and is a joint venture with Brigham Young University, Westminster Stanford, and Wharton. The universities partner with venture funds to do research on investments. In return, the universities are entitled to coinvest. The university of Utah students are mainly undergrates, although Wharton's program is composed of MBAs.

Policy

- To credit the entrepreneurs who create more than 75 percent of the net new jobs nationwide and generate more than 50 percent of the nation's gross domestic product, President Bush declared May 6–12, 2001, to be Small Business Week.

- The National Commission on Entrepreneurship (NCOE) was launched in February 1999. As a nonpartisan organization, the goal of NCOE is to serve as a necessary bridge between entrepreneurs and lawmakers. In April 2001 the Center for Business and Government, John F. Kennedy School of Government, and the NCOE hosted a conference on Entrepreneurship and Public Policy in the 21st Century. Conference attendees consisted of policy makers, academics, and entrepreneurs from around the country.

Women

- Between 1997 and 2004, the number of privately held firms owned by women of color in the United States grew 54.6 percent, while the overall number of firms in the United States grew by only 9 percent over the same period. These firms appear to be prospering as both employment (up 61.8 percent) and sales (up 73.6 percent) also grew during this period. Women's business ownership is up among all groups, but the number of Hispanic (up 63.9 percent) and Asian-owned firms (up 69.3 percent) has grown especially fast.
- A 2003 Babson College/MassMutual report on women in family-owned businesses found that female-owned family firms are nearly twice as productive as male-owned family enterprises. With average revenues of $26.9 million, firms run by women were somewhat smaller compared to their male-owned counterparts ($30.4 million average revenues). Allowing for that, however, the women generated their sales with far fewer median employees—26 individuals compared with 50 at male-owned firms. Conclusion: Women in business typically do more with less.

Minority Groups

- In 2003 African American self-employment reached its highest levels in both number, at 710,000, and rate, at 5.2 percent (calculated as the number of African American self-employed divided by the number of African Americans in the labor force).
- The 2002 *Panel Study of Entrepreneurial Dynamics* (Babson College, Ewing Marion Kauffman Foundation) reported that African Americans are 50 percent more likely to start a business than whites. This difference is even more noticeable among populations with advanced degrees: African American males with graduate degrees are 2.6 times more likely to start a business than their white counterparts.
- Latino self-employment increased significantly, from 241,000 in 1979 to 1 million in 2003. The Latino self-employment rate was 7 percent (calculated as the number of Latino self-employed divided by the number of Latinos in the labor force) in 2003.
- Data from the 2000 census show that since 1997 the number of Native American–owned businesses has risen by 84 percent to 197,300, and that their gross incomes have increased by 179 percent to $34.3 billion. Asian Americans and Pacific Islanders constitute a little more than 3 percent of the population and own nearly 4.5 percent of businesses.
- While efforts to promote entrepreneurship among low-income communities have expanded over the years, only recently have Native American communities begun to benefit from these programs and services. The Corporation for Enterprise Development and Native American Entrepreneurship Development has been created to strengthen the support for Native American entrepreneurship across the country.

Youth Entrepreneurship

- Entrepreneurship education is now gaining a foothold in elementary through high schools in at least 30 states. At least eight states have passed legislation requiring such education, and the federal Department of Education has approved the first curriculum, YESS/Mini-Society, created by the Kauffman Center.
- The National Foundation for Teaching Entrepreneurship (NFTE) has significantly expanded its out-of-school educational programs in the inner cities to help youths seeking self-sufficiency and self-respect through entrepreneurship. NFTE now teaches 10,000 students per year.
- The national Girls Scouts and Boys Scouts in 1997 created, with the help and support of the Kauffman Center, the very first Scout merit badges in entrepreneurship. The badge symbol: a hand reaching for a star!

Entrepreneurs: America's Self-Made Millionaires

The founders of great companies such as Apple Computer, Federal Express, Staples, Intuit, and Lotus Development Corporation become millionaires when their companies become publicly traded. But the vast majority of the new generation of millionaires are invisible to most Americans, and do not at all fit the stereotype one derives from the press and media. The authors of *The Millionaire Next Door*, Thomas J. Stanley and William D. Danko, share some new insights into this group:

> the television image of wealthy Americans is false: The truly wealthy are not by and large ostentatious but, rather, are very persistent and disciplined people running ordinary businesses.[11]

The profile of these 3.1 million—out of 100 million households in the nation—millionaires (defined as having a net worth of $1 million or more) is revealing: They accumulated their wealth through hard work, self-discipline, planning, and frugality—all very entrepreneurial virtues. Two-thirds of them still working are self-employed. They are not descendants of the Rockefellers or Vanderbilts. Instead they are truly self-made: More than 80 percent are ordinary people who have accumulated their wealth in one generation. They live below their means, would rather be financially independent than display high social status, and don't look like most people's stereotype of millionaires. They get rich slowly: The average millionaire is 57 years old. Their businesses are not the sexy, high-tech, Silicon Valley variety; rather they have created and own such businesses as ambulance services, citrus farming, cafeteria services, diesel engine rebuilding, consulting services, janitorial services, job training schools, meat processors, mobile home parks, pest controllers, newsletter publishers, rice farmers, and sandblasting contractors![12]

The implications of this new study are quite significant and encouraging for the vast majority of entrepreneurs. Clearly the American dream is more alive and well than ever—and more accessible than ever. One does not have to be born to wealth, attend prep school, and go to an elite Ivy League school to become successful. Further, the study seems to confirm what has been articulated in all editions of *New Venture Creation:* A combination of talent and skills plus opportunity matched with the needed resources and applied with the entrepreneurial mind-set is key. And there have never been more opportunities to pursue an entrepreneurial dream.

A New Era of Equity Creation

Value creation is not a linear process; it requires a long-term perspective. While the U.S. investment and capital markets have been an integral part of this revolution in entrepreneurship, it is more important to recognize the long-term resilience of the system. Despite a recession in the late 1980s, and a downturn in the first years of the new century (precipitated by the tragic events of 9/11), the capital markets have continued to trend upward.

The venture capital industry has closely mirrored these overall economics. During the late 1990s the venture capital industry nearly quadrupled in size, with a staggering surge to $103 billion in 2000 alone. Between 1998 and 2002, $223 billion was committed by limited partners to the U.S. venture capital industry. Predictably, this spike in the supply of venture capital resulted in extremely disappointing returns, with substantial losses, and a major shakeout in the industry beginning in 2001—similar to what had occurred between 1988 and 1993.

This most recent downturn in the venture capital industry culminated in 2003 with a six-year aggregate investment low of $18.9 billion. According to the National Venture Capital Association, the industry had rebounded by 2006 with aggregate investments of $26.3 billion into 3,553 deals (Exhibit 1.8). Although this increase was largely related to later-stage investments, there were 897 early-stage deals that year—accounting for just under $4 billion, or 25 percent of all investments.

In 2001 the Dow Jones Industrial Average—the nation's oldest and most recognizable stock barometer—set a bear market low of 7,286. By the end of 2003 the Dow had recovered to 10,454—just about 9 percent less than what the Dow was at the height of the stock market bubble. By 2006 it was above 12,463 (Exhibit 1.9), and on October 1, 2007, it exceeded 14,000. Average daily trading in shares increased between 2003 and 2006, but the value of the NASDAQ issues—many of which were associated with the Internet boom—was still well below the level in 2000 (Exhibit 1.10). After a dip in 2003, initial public offerings (IPOs) and all equity values in 2006 were rising again but were below the highs in 2000 (Exhibit 1.11). What is important to note is that by 2006, total underwritings had recovered, and that in 2003, IPOs and all equity had gained over 400 and 600 percent in value, respectively, since 1990.

The implications of all this are profound for aspiring entrepreneurs and the nation. The overall wealth of the nation, expressed as a U.S. household balance

---

[11] "The Millionaire Next Door," *Success,* March 1997, pp. 45–51.
[12] Ibid., pp. 46–48.

EXHIBIT 1.8

U.S. Venture Capital Investment by Year (1990–2006)

Year	Number of Companies	Average per Company ($ million)	Sum Investment ($ million)
1990	1,433	1.9	2,767.1
1991	1,231	1.8	2,241.7
1992	1,345	2.6	3,511.1
1993	1,161	3.2	3,708.1
1994	1,197	3.4	4,120.6
1995	1,776	4.4	7,853.5
1996	2,464	4.5	10,992.9
1997	3,084	4.8	14,646.9
1998	3,557	5.9	20,899.8
1999	5,403	9.9	53,579.6
2000	7,832	13.4	104,827.4
2001	4,451	9.2	40,798.4
2002	3,042	7.1	21,579.3
2003	2,825	6.7	18,911.0
2004	2,873	7.3	21,004.4
2005	3,128	7.4	23,048.6
2006	3,553	7.4	26,295.6

Source: PricewaterhouseCoopers/National Venture Capital Association MoneyTree™ Report. Data: Thomson Financial—updated August 2007.

EXHIBIT 1.9

The Stock Market Metrics

	1985	1990	1999	2003	2006
Dow Jones Industrial Average (at Year-End)	1,546.67	2,633.66	11,497.12	10,453.92	12,463.15
Equity Mutual Fund Assets	$116.9 billion	$245.6 billion	$4,041.9 billion	$3,684.8 billion	$5,909.6 billion
Net Cash Flows into Mutual Funds	$68.2 billion	$44.4 billion	$363.4 billion	−$42.5 billion	$476.1 billion

Source: *Security Industries Fact Book: 2007*, Securities Industry Association.

EXHIBIT 1.10

U.S. Stock Markets Average Daily Trading

	Number of Shares (in Millions)					Dollar Value (in Billions)				
	1980	1990	2000	2003	2006	1980	1990	2000	2003	2006
NYSE	44.9	156.8	1,041.6	1,398.4	1,826.7	$ 1.5	$ 5.2	$ 43.9	$ 35.5	$ 69.1
NASDAQ	26.4	131.9	1,757	1,685.5	2,001.9	$ 0.3	$ 1.8	$ 80.9	$ 28.0	$ 46.7

Source: SIA Research Reports, vol. V, no. 6 (June 2007).

EXHIBIT 1.11

U.S. Stock Markets Total Value

	1980 (in Billions)	1990 (in Billions)	2000 (in Billions)	2003 (in Billions)	2004 (in Billions)
IPOs	1.4	4.5	75.8	15.9	45.9
Total Underwritings	57.6	192.7	1,280.7	1,949.6	333.7
All Equity	16	23.9	204.5	156.3	188

Source: *Securities Industry Fact Book: 2007*.

sheet, grew from $550 billion in 1970 to about $9 trillion by the end of 1997. What may astonish some is that over 95 percent of the nation's wealth has been created since 1980, a direct result of this entrepreneurial revolution. We are now beginning to see this result culminate in the rest of the world.

Building an Enterprising Society

The Poorer Get Richer One of the most durable debates in American society is our love–hate relationship with wealth and income distribution. Our immigrant heritage as a land of opportunity came to be known as "Horatio Alger stories" as these 120 novels after the Civil War portrayed ordinary boys rising from rags to riches in a generation. All too often, however, we hear the notion that "the rich get richer" and, by implication, the poor must be getting poorer.

Many traditional sociologists and economists support this notion by talking about socioeconomic classes in America as if they are permanent castes. Although moving up from an impoverished urban existence requires persistence, self-direction, and a strong work ethic, it is by no means a rare occurrence in the United States. In her book *Chutes and Ladders*, Katherine Newman describes the economic and personal trajectories of a number of black and Latino workers from Harlem, a New York neighborhood with high poverty rates and low expectations.[13] Nevertheless, over 20 percent of the workers she tracked over a decade are no longer poor. Their persistence paid off in the form of educational degrees, better living standards, and well-paying jobs with benefits and pensions. In doing so, they were able to break free and move themselves and their families up and out of a seemingly hopeless social and economic environment. Here are three that made that journey.

Adam: The Union Path. Adam is the classic embodiment of a character from Horatio Alger. He grew up black and poor in Brooklyn, and his mother went on welfare after his father left her. His mom took low-paying jobs and put in long hours to work her way up and out of welfare. Adam has applied the same work ethic in his own life. He dropped out of high school in the 10th grade, and at age 27 he was rejected for an entry-level position at a local Burger Barn. He persisted, survived on meager wages, and eventually landed an entry-level job with a unionized express delivery firm in New York City. He took whatever shifts they offered, secured his commercial driver's license, and worked his way up the union ladder.

At 36 Adam is now a well-respected and reliable driver for the firm, earning $70,000 a year with full benefits. Over the years he has turned down opportunities to move into management: "Supervisors are often fired, and I prefer the protection of the union." Inspired by a delivery client with a screenprinting business, Adam created a second job for himself running a T-shirt printing company out of his home. He and his wife are bringing in another $30,000 a year with that venture. The extra money is critical because he now has custody of his two children from previous marriages—a 13-year-old girl and a 6-year-old boy. They rent in the Bronx, but they are in the process of building a home of their own in North Carolina, near where Adam's family lives, and where the schools are superior to the ones his children attend in the city. Although transferring to a new post down south with the same delivery firm is proving to be a challenge (comparable wage rates but no benefits), Adam is confident that he can figure out a way to make it work.[14]

Helena: The Corporate Ladder. Ten years ago Helena, a 21-year-old of Dominican descent, was married and the mother of a 2-year-old son. Her first experience in the corporate sector had been in high school as an intern at a large insurance company. Although she interspersed her unpaid internship time with stints at a Burger Barn in her Harlem neighborhood, she was able to land a "real job" as an entry-level administrative assistant at the insurance firm. Helena immediately understood that she had grabbed onto the lower rung of an internal ladder that promised increasing wages and more responsibility on the job.

While racking up seniority, security, and skills, she took full advantage of the educational allowances and programs offered by the firm. While raising two young boys and creatively juggling parenting duties and schedules with her husband and extended family members, she completed her associate's degree at a City University of New York junior college, and then advanced to the City College of New York for her bachelor's in public administration. The arrangement worked for both parties; her employer got a more skilled and educated worker who could be promoted, and Helena ended up with a much better résumé than she could ever have hoped for if she had had to cover the educational costs herself. She is married with two children, and her full-time job at the insurance company as the call center manager pays more than $60,000 a year with benefits.[15]

Lanice: The Enterprising Route. As a teen African American in Harlem, Lanice struggled to find

[13] K. S. Newman, *Chutes and Ladders* (Cambridge, MA: Harvard University Press, 2006).
[14] Ibid., pp. 95, 184, 218.
[15] Ibid., pp. 91–92.

steady employment. Burger Barn wouldn't hire her, and the few companies she had worked for had gone out of business or moved away. Lanice wasn't picky: She said she'd work for any kind of company, so long as she had an opportunity to advance. She finished high school and took some adult education classes. In one year she applied for more than 20 jobs, mostly at retail stores. When she did find work, the pay was paltry and the job never seemed to last very long.

With almost reckless confidence in herself, Lanice landed a job in the entertainment industry. Her boss, a demanding taskmaster, had cycled through 17 administrative assistants in the previous year. He took an immediate liking to Lanice, who was personable, a quick learner, and a tolerant subordinate—someone who didn't take offense at the stream of Post-it notes left on her desk, with things not done written in big letters and underlined. She has been there for two years, makes a $42,000 salary, and is loving every minute of it.

Experience and success have made Lanice more ambitious. At the age of 26, she has found a job she likes, but she is clear that she doesn't want to stay there for the rest of her life. Now she has bigger plans. Lanice is starting her own business: a consulting firm that will help individuals, schools, and small businesses with fund-raising and networking. She has already hooked up with an accounting firm and a legal service and is intent on working (and networking) her way into the big leagues.[16]

Create Equal Opportunities, Not Equal Incomes

What has been lost historically in this debate is that equal incomes are neither desirable nor possible. Most important is that opportunities are available for anyone who wants to prepare and to compete. The entrepreneurial process will take over and result in economic expansion and accompanying social mobility. A recent study at the Federal Reserve Bank of Dallas sheds valuable insight.[17] In one exper-

iment in the 1970s, for instance, three groups of Canadians, all in their 20s, all with at least 12 years of schooling, volunteered to work in a simulated economy where the only employment was making woolen belts on small hand looms. They could work as much or as little as they liked, earning $2.50 for each belt. After 98 days, the results were anything but equal: 37.2 percent of the economy's income went to the 20 percent with the highest earnings. The bottom 20 percent received only 6.6 percent.[18]

Entrepreneurship = Economic and Social Mobility

The authors of the Federal Reserve study would agree with the earlier case presented here showing the radical transformation of the American economy as a result of the entrepreneurial revolution. Their data also show this is still the land of opportunity. Income mobility in America from 1975 to 1991 shows that a significant portion of those in the lowest quintile in 1975 had moved up, including 29 percent all the way to the top quintile (see Exhibit 1.12). In terms of absolute gain, the data, adjusted for inflation, showed the poor are getting richer faster (see Exhibit 1.13). The study concluded with this important summation:

> Striving to better oneself isn't just private virtue. It sows the seeds of economic growth and technical

EXHIBIT 1.12

Moving Up

Income Quintile in 1975	Percentage in Each Quintile in 1991				
	1st	2nd	3rd	4th	5th
5th (highest)	.9%	2.8%	10.2%	23.6%	62.5%
4th	1.9	9.3	18.8	32.6	37.4
3rd (middle)	3.3	19.3	28.3	30.1	19.0
2nd	4.2	23.5	20.3	25.2	26.8
1st (lowest)	5.1	14.6	21.0	30.0	29.0

EXHIBIT 1.13

The Poor Are Getting Richer Faster

Income Quintile in 1975	Average Income in 1975*	Average Income in 1991*	Absolute Gain
5th (highest)	$45,704	$49,678	$ 3,974
4th	22,423	31,292	8,869
3rd (middle)	13,030	22,304	9,274
2nd	6,291	28,373	22,082
1st (lowest)	1,153	26,475	25,322

*Figures are in 1993 dollars.

[16] Ibid., pp. 245–46.
[17] W. M. Cox and R. Aim, "By Our Own Bootstraps: Economic Opportunity and the Dynamics of Income Distribution," *1995 Annual Report* (Dallas, TX: Federal Reserve Bank), pp. 2–23.
[18] Ibid., p. 5.

advancement. There's no denying that the system allows some Americans to become richer than others. We must accept that. Equality of income is not what has made the U.S. economy grow and prosper. It's opportunity. . . . Our proper cultural icon is not the common man. It's the *self-made* man or woman.[19]

In another comparison, the standard of living of the bottom 10 percent of American families in 1995 was actually higher than the average family in 1970. It is clear that America's success is becoming a global success story. Just as this nation has created and encouraged policies and priorities to support the entrepreneurial process, countries around the world are following that lead, and in doing so, they are fostering and ensuring the mobility of opportunity just described.

Chapter Summary

- Entrepreneurship is a truly global phenomenon, and, coupled with the Internet, is flattening and democratizing the world.

- Entrepreneurs are the creators, the innovators, and the leaders who give back to society as philanthropists, directors, and trustees, and who, more than any others, change how people live, work, learn, play, and lead.

- Entrepreneurs create new technologies, products, processes, and services that become the next wave of new industries, and these in turn drive the economy.

- Entrepreneurs create value with high-potential, high-growth companies, which are the job creation engines of the U.S. economy.

- Venture capital provides the fuel for high-potential, high-growth companies.

- America and the world are at the dawn of a new age of equity creation as evidenced by a 10- to 30-fold increase in our capital markets in just 20 years.

- Entrepreneurs are realizing the value they have created; more than 95 percent of the wealth America has today has been created since 1980.

- North America's 3.1 million millionaires are mostly self-made entrepreneurs.

- In America, the poor get richer as a result of the entrepreneurial process.

- Building an entrepreneurial society for the 21st century and beyond is the highest priority for the new and global e-generation.

Study Questions

1. How has the economy changed in your region and country over the past generation?

2. How has the number of new venture formations in the United States changed in the past 30 years? Why has this happened? Why will this pattern continue?

3. From where do the new jobs in America derive? Why?

4. Explain the extent to which large versus new and emerging companies contribute to all innovations and to radical innovations.

5. When was the vast majority of wealth created in America, and by whom? (*a*) Carnegies, Vanderbilts, and Rockefellers before 1990. (*b*) Automobile, food, and real estate magnates after 1900 but before 1970. (*c*) Founders of companies since 1970.

6. Who are the millionaires today?

7. Name some exceptional companies whose founders were in their 20s when they launched their companies.

8. What role has venture capital played in this economic transformation?

9. It is often argued that "the rich get richer and the poor get poorer." How and why has the entrepreneurial revolution affected this stereotype? What are its implications?

10. What has happened to large and established companies as a result of this surge by entrepreneurial upstarts?

Internet Resources for Chapter 1

www.gemconsortium.org *The Global Entrepreneurship Monitor (GEM) is a not-for-profit academic research consortium that has as its goal making high-quality international research data on entrepreneurial activity readily available to as wide an audience as possible. GEM is the largest single study of entrepreneurial activity in the world.*

---

[19]Ibid., p. 18.

www.babson.edu/eship *Arthur M. Blank Center for Entrepreneurship, Babson College.*

www.olin.edu *Franklin W. Olin College of Engineering.*

www.cfwbr.org *The Center for Women's Business Research is a comprehensive source for the trends, characteristics, achievements, and challenges of women business owners and their enterprises.*

www.ncaied.org *Founded in 1969, the National Center for American Indian Enterprise Development (NCAIED) is the first national nonprofit 501(c)3 corporation created and directed by Native Americans, solely dedicated to developing Native Americans economic self-sufficiency through business ownership.*

https://www.venturesource.com *A Dow Jones company database of research focused on the venture capital industry.*

www.nfte.org *Through entrepreneurship education, NFTE, which is also referred to as Network for Teaching Entrepreneurship, helps young people from low-income communities build skills and unlock their entrepreneurial creativity.*

www.nvca.org *The National Venture Capital Association (NVCA) is a trade association that represents the U.S. venture capital industry. It is a member-based organization, which consists of venture capital firms that manage pools of risk equity capital designated to be invested in high-growth companies.*

MIND STRETCHERS

Have You Considered?

1. As a citizen, what policies are needed to encourage and build an entrepreneurial society?

2. How will opportunities and the availability of capital change in this new century as a result of this economic and social revolution? How can one be best prepared for this?

3. Many, if not most, people prefer predictability to unpredictability. Yet the entrepreneurial process is inherently chaotic, unpredictable, and unplannable. Who will succeed and who will falter in this dynamic process? What skills and mind-sets are required?

4. If this revolution continues at its pace of the past 30 years (e.g., a 10- to 15-fold increase), at your 25th college or graduate school reunion what averages might you see in the Dow Jones Industrial, the NASDAQ, and the FTSI, CAC, German, and Asian indexes? How many businesses and jobs will there be? How many new industries that no one has thought of today? What if this pace is 50 percent faster or slower?

5. Which countries offer the greatest entrepreneurial opportunities in the next decade? What do you need to do about this?

Visit with an Entrepreneur and Create a Lifelong Learning Log

By interviewing entrepreneurs who have, within the past 5 to 10 years, started firms whose sales now exceed $2 million to $3 million and are profitable, you can gain insight into an entrepreneur's reasons, strategies, approaches, and motivations for starting and owning a business. Gathering information with interviews is a valuable skill to practice. You can learn a great deal in a short time through interviewing if you prepare thoughtfully and thoroughly.

This exercise ("Visit with an Entrepreneur") has helped students interview successful entrepreneurs. While there is no right way to structure an interview, the format in this exercise has been tested successfully on many occasions. A breakfast, lunch, or dinner meeting is often an excellent vehicle.

Select two entrepreneurs and businesses about which you would like to learn. This could be someone you see as

an example or role model to which you aspire, or which you know the least about but are eager to learn. Interview at least two entrepreneurs with differing experiences, such as a high-potential (i.e., $5+ million revenue) and a lifestyle business (usually much smaller, but not necessarily).

Create a Lifelong Learning Log

Create a computer file or acquire a notebook or binder in which you record your goals, triumphs, disappointments, and lessons learned. This can be done as key events happen or on some other frequent basis. You might make entries during times of crisis and at year's end to sum up what you accomplished and your new goals. The record of personal insights, observations, and lessons learned can provide valuable anchors during difficult decisions as well as interesting reading—for you at least.

A Visit with an Entrepreneur

STEP 1

Contact the Person You Have Selected and Make an Appointment.
Be sure to explain why you want the appointment and to give a realistic estimate of how much time you will need.

STEP 2

Identify Specific Questions You Would Like to Have Answered and the General Areas about Which You Would Like Information. (See the Interview In Step 3.)
Using a combination of open-end questions, such as general questions about how the entrepreneur got started, what happened next, and so forth, and closed-end questions, such as specific questions about what his or her goals were, if he or she had to find partners, and so forth, will help keep the interview focused and yet allow for unexpected comments and insights.

STEP 3

Conduct the Interview.
Recording this interview can be helpful and is recommended unless you or the person being interviewed objects. Remember, too, that you most likely will learn more if you are an interested listener.

The Interview

Questions for Gathering Information

- Would you tell me about yourself before you started your first venture?

  Whom else did you know while you were growing up who had started or owned a business, and how did they influence you? Anyone later, after you were 21 years old?

  Were your parents, relatives, or close friends entrepreneurial? How so?

  Did you have role models?

  What was your education/military experience? In hindsight, was it helpful? In what specific ways?

  Did you have a business or self-employment during your youth?

  In particular, did you have any sales or marketing experience? How important was it, or a lack of it, to starting your company?

When, under what circumstances, and from whom did you become interested in entrepreneurship and learn some of the critical lessons?

- Describe how you decided to create a job by starting your venture instead of taking a job with someone else.

  How did you spot the opportunity? How did it surface?

  What were your goals? What were your lifestyle needs or other personal requirements? How did you fit these together?

  How did you evaluate the opportunity in terms of the critical elements for success? The competition? The market? Did you have specific criteria you wanted to meet?

  Did you find or have partners? What kind of planning did you do? What kind of financing did you have?

  Did you have a start-up business plan of any kind? Please tell me about it.

  How much time did it take from conception to the first day of business? How many hours a day did you spend working on it?

  How much capital did it take? How long did it take to reach a positive cash flow and break-even sales volume? If you did not have enough money at the time, what were some ways in which you bootstrapped the venture (bartering, borrowing, and the like)? Tell me about the pressures and crises during that early survival period.

  What outside help did you get? Did you have experienced advisors? Lawyers? Accountants? Tax experts? Patent experts? How did you develop these networks and how long did it take?

  How did any outside advisors make a difference in your company?

  What was your family situation at the time?

  What did you perceive to be the strengths of your venture? Weaknesses?

  What was your most triumphant moment? Your worst moment?

  Did you want to have partners or do it solo? Why?

- Once you got going:

  What were the most difficult gaps to fill and problems to solve as you began to grow rapidly?

  When you looked for key people as partners, advisors, or managers, were there any personal attributes or attitudes you were particularly seeking because you knew they would fit with you and were important to success? How did you find them?

  Are there any attributes among partners and advisors that you would definitely try to avoid?

  Have things become more predictable? Or less?

Do you spend more time, the same amount of time, or less time with your business now than in the early years?

Do you feel more managerial and less entrepreneurial now?

In terms of the future, do you plan to harvest? To maintain? To expand?

In your ideal world, how many days a year would you want to work? Please explain.

Do you plan ever to retire? Would you explain?

Have your goals changed? Have you met them?

Has your family situation changed?

What do you learn from both success and failure?

What were/are the most demanding conflicts or trade-offs you face (the business versus personal hobbies or a relationship, children, etc.)?

Describe a time you ran out of cash, what pressures this created for you, the business, your family, and what you did about it. What lessons were learned?

Can you describe a venture that did not work out for you and how this prepared you for your next venture?

Questions for Concluding

- What do you consider your most valuable asset, the thing that enabled you to make it?

- If you had it to do over again, would you do it again, in the same way?

- As you look back, what do you believe are the most critical concepts, skills, attitudes, and know-how you needed to get your company started and grown to where it is today? What will be needed for the next five years? To what extent can any of these be learned?

- Some people say there is a lot of stress being an entrepreneur. What have you experienced? How would you say it compares with other "hot seat" jobs, such as the head of a big company, or a partner in a large law or accounting firm?

- What things do you find personally rewarding and satisfying as an entrepreneur? What have been the rewards, risks, and trade-offs?

- Who should try to be an entrepreneur? And who should not?

- What advice would you give an aspiring entrepreneur? Could you suggest the three most important lessons you have learned? How can I learn them while minimizing the tuition?

- Would you suggest any other entrepreneur I should talk to?

- Are there any other questions you wish I had asked, from which you think I could learn valuable lessons?

STEP 4
Evaluate What You Have Learned.
Summarize the most important observations and insights you have gathered from these interviews. Contrast especially what patterns, differences, and similarities exist between lifestyle and high-potential entrepreneurs. Who can be an entrepreneur? What surprised you the most? What was confirmed about entrepreneurship? What new insights emerged? What are the implications for you personally, your goals, and your career aspirations?

STEP 5
Write a Thank-You Note.
This is more than a courtesy; it will also help the entrepreneur remember you favorably should you want to follow up on the interview.

Exercise 2

The Venturekipedia Exercise—Time Is Everything!
Doing Frugal and Parsimonious Research and Due Diligence

One great and durable value of a college education is that you are totally overloaded with course workload, sports, and other extracurricular activities, not to mention social opportunities. This forced march in time management teaches you to prioritize and triage: the *must dos*, the *should dos*, and the *can waits*. Couple this with the "80-20 rule" (the Pareto principle: you get 80 percent of the creative work done in the first 20 percent of the effort; 20 percent of your sales force will account for 80 percent of your sales, etc.) and you can develop some effective ways of setting goals, establishing priorities, and managing your limited time; there never seems to be enough!

Here is a tool to help you make frugal and parsimonious use of your time while doing research, due diligence, and other investigations, regardless of the topic. It will assist you beyond doing a simple Google search, which, while useful, can often generate so many potential entries and site links that you go off on an endless trek that may not yield what you really need.

Create Your Own "Venturekipedia"

STEP 1

Think Keywords and Phrases.
Throughout your entrepreneurship education, in the classroom and especially outside the classroom, you will face different tasks, hurdles, and opportunities requiring research. Whatever the assignment, you can quickly focus on some key words. These can be both generic, such as creativity or new ventures, and more focused: entrepreneurial mind, opportunity identification, opportunity assessment, bootstrapping, team formation, green products, sustainable business opportunities, mentors, business plan, solar opportunities, spreadsheet cash flow templates, or social ventures, to name a few popular searches. Be especially sensitive to the words that inspire, excite, and challenge you to action.

STEP 2

Deepen the Search.
For illustration, let's say you have the interest and opportunity to join a family business after college—yours or someone else's. Once you've zeroed in on the key words related to family business and the particular industry, conduct a search for these and closely related words and phrases in http://en.wikipedia.

STEP 3

Share and Discuss.
Locate and read at least one article in Wikipedia about family business (see http://en.wikipedia.org/wiki/Family_business), and share what you learned with other classmates and colleagues interested in this topic. Highlighted within the article you will find a list of links to additional information on your subject. Find, read, and share insights from at least two additional sources about family business. Identify and discuss the critical issues and challenges associated with family businesses. Would you start or join one? Why, and under what conditions, why not? What did you discover in reading these pieces that reinforced what you already knew, informed you in new ways, or raised new questions you hadn't really considered before.

STEP 4

Create an Insites Log.
Note the double meaning here: the new insights you gain, and the new Web sites you discover. Be sure to continue to seek and include the information, insights, and valuable Web sites your classmates have uncovered.

Limitless Applications

You can quickly envision limitless other applications and uses for this simple but powerful exercise. Think, for instance, about the new venture opportunity you're working on this semester or quarter. All the research and due diligence concerning competitors, new entrants, substitutes and alternative solutions or products, channels of distribution, typical margins and cost structures in the value chain, outsourcing suppliers in China, India, and Vietnam . . . all such research can now be done with this method. Try it! It will save you a great deal of time and significantly raise the quality and efficiency of your due diligence.

Case

ImageCafé

Preparation Questions

1. Evaluate Clarence Wooten's strengths and weaknesses.
2. What do you think about Wooten's product versus service conclusion? What are the strengths and weaknesses of his argument?
3. Analyze and assess the ImageCafé opportunity.
4. What do you think of Wooten's fund-raising strategy?
5. Should he have taken Dwayne Walker's offer?
6. Does he need to raise $3 million?
7. How would you respond to the Network Solutions offer?
8. How would you go about valuing ImageCafé?
9. What are the personal implications for Wooten if he sells or not?

Staying Afloat

With his company, ImageCafé, struggling with financial uncertainty, Clarence Wooten, Jr., faced some difficult decisions. With a current burn rate[1] of nearly $50,000 per month, the bridge loans[2] and angel investments[3] of $710,000 would not be enough capital to carry the company to breakeven. While he was struggling to close a $3 million financing round, a Virginia-based Internet services company, Network Solutions Inc., approached Wooten about selling ImageCafé. Time seemed to be running out, and closing the $3 million on acceptable terms was proving to be more difficult than Wooten had anticipated.

Should he sell ImageCafé to Network Solutions, or risk losing it all for the potential of a greater gain, if and when the financing materialized? And if he did decide to sell, what was the right price? Time was clearly not on his side.

Source: This case is written by Kathryn F. Spinelli under the direction of Professor Stephen Spinelli, Jr. © Copyright Babson College, 2004. Funding provided by the HBCU Consortium. All rights reserved.
[1] *Burn rate* is the amount of cash consumed by a new venture. The burn rate is usually stated in terms of cash used on a monthly basis but sometimes is stated on a quarterly or annual basis.
[2] A *bridge loan*, or *swing loan*, is short-term financing that is expected to be repaid quickly, such as by a subsequent longer-term loan.
[3] *Angel investors* are individuals who provide capital to one or more start up companies. These individual are usually affluent or have a personal stake in the success of the venture. High levels of risk and a potentially large return on investment characterize such investments.

Clarence Wooten, Jr.

Clarence Wooten, Jr., had a typical childhood dream: to get rich. His early childhood, however, was less typical. At an early age, Wooten was fascinated by television-based video games; for Christmas one year, he convinced his parents to buy him an Atari game system. Wooten soon discovered that the game cartridges were too expensive for him to purchase by himself. One day a friend told him that home computers such as the Commodore 64 did not require cartridges to play games, but used program diskettes instead. One advantage of this new medium was that diskettes could be copied from the original, effectively eliminating the expense of paying for game cartridges. Wooten also learned that with a computer, games could be transferred, or downloaded, between computers through conventional telephone lines using a modem and what was called bulletin board software (BBS). A bulletin board was a computer that would run 24 hours a day so that people could log in and download files from that host computer. The following Christmas, Wooten persuaded his parents to buy him a Commodore 64 home computer equipped with a modem.

It wasn't long before his computer gave him access to a world he found more exciting than noncomputer reality. Wooten reflected fondly, "It was like the wild, wild West." This was clearly a discovery filled with adventure and challenge. From the age of 12, Wooten was on his computer from the minute he came home from school until well after midnight, when his parents would finally make him go to sleep. He became so immersed in this computer-based world, so obsessed with downloading the latest games, that by age 14 his parents decided it was necessary to intervene. They banned him from using the computer; it spent more than three months on a shelf locked in a closet. And Wooten did not have the key. He remembers, "It was like going cold turkey, like sending a hacker to jail. But I was always computer savvy because of that background." Although the rest of his high school career was dominated by his involvement in athletics, particularly basketball, Wooten never lost interest in his first love, the computer.

Growing Up

Wooten saw good times and bad during his childhood, moving between the city and the suburbs in and around Baltimore, Maryland. Wooten was an only child; by the time he was a teenager, both of his parents had become self-employed. As such, the family's income fluctuated depending on the success of his parents' small businesses. His father, Clarence Wooten, Sr., formerly a steel mill laborer, gradually accumulated rental properties in Baltimore. His mother, Cecilia, formerly a seamstress, ran a 24-bed assisted living home with her sisters. The Wootens owned a house in the city, and when times were good, they would rent that out while renting a house in the suburbs for themselves. When times were not as good, they would move back into the city.

These frequent moves meant that Wooten had to transfer in and out of different school systems—eight times in all. The constant transitioning between homes, school systems, and friends was difficult for Wooten; however, this lifestyle enabled him to become comfortable adapting quickly to different situations. Wooten recalls, "Looking back, it really helped me in terms of being able to be comfortable around all people. I can deal with, literally, thugs and hardened criminals as well as people raised in a pampered suburban lifestyle." Wooten also credits his tumultuous lifestyle as his motivation to create wealth that would sustain himself and eventually his entire family. He did not want his adult life to be dictated by small fluctuations in income, as it had for his parents. He was serious about his ambitions. Wooten joked that he was the only high school kid with a business card.

An Underworld Introduction to Entrepreneurship

It was in the suburbs of Baltimore that he became a member of a "cracking group."[4] Under the alias of "King Kaoz," Wooten and fellow group members used their computers to crack anticopying features enabling electronic games to be duplicated. Unknown to his parents, Wooten had become well known as part of a competitive and elite computer underworld. The term "elite" meant that within 24 hours of a new game's release, you either cracked it or had access to a cracked version. "I was more interested in getting the games than actually playing them; it was the competition." With his computer and his intellect, he began to feel nothing was unobtainable; nothing was out of his reach.

Wooten's days as a software pirate started with his love of video games. After acquiring his first home computer and receiving copies of cracked games from friends, Wooten became obsessed with acquiring more and more games as quickly as possible. Diskettes could easily be copied, but the software companies became more savvy and started writing code onto the disks for copyright protection. This is where Wooten and his cracking group came in. The group was a team: Each had a task to perform in the duplication process. The rich kid bought the software as soon as it was released; the cracker removed the copy protection and added the group's intro screen into the game; and then Wooten, the distributor, used his computer to post the games on

virtual bulletin boards. The software was distributed to pirates and crackers around the world. The bulletin board distribution method also involved getting around the phone bill incurred from the dial-up connection necessary to distribute and download software. It would have been difficult for a preteen such as Wooten to explain to his parents why there were international long distance calls on the phone bill, let alone afford the charges. One of the "entry exams" to becoming "elite" was learning all of this on your own. Crackers never divulged their dodging techniques. Wooten explained,

> I eventually ran my own bulletin board, Kastle Kaoz, with my computer which went all day and night, connected to the phone line so that people could log in, and if you were "elite," I would give you access so you could download all the latest games. There were only about 15–20 people in the world that had access to my bulletin board; if you had access, you were like a "made" guy. Our group was the biggest in the world on the Commodore 64 for 6–7 months. So it's like being an entrepreneur, it's like being part of the Fortune 500, when you think of it.

They were spurred on by the love of competition: which groups could crack the latest software first, and who could crack the most overall. There was a sense of pride from accomplishing something new. The reward was in a job well done and the title of being elite, albeit pirate, members of the computer-cracking underworld. Wooten noted, "We'd add our own intro screens to games that we cracked so that any kid in the world who received a copy of the game knew who we were. We were the celebrities of the computer underworld."

College Years: From Architecture to Computer Graphics

In 1990 Wooten, then 18, wanted to attend college to study architecture. He had a small list of schools that were not only offering him a basketball scholarship, but also had well-known architectural programs. Wooten believed that the study of architecture would satisfy all of his creative instincts. Unfortunately he felt he had to compromise his choice of academic programs to those offering him money. After Wooten's best scholarship offer fell through, he decided to attend Catonsville Community College in Maryland. There he decided to balance his time between basketball and architecture classes, all the while deciding into which other college program he would eventually transfer.

The recession of the late 1980s and early 1990s left many professionals out of work; many of these professionals returned to school to gain more marketable skills. Wooten met many such professional architects in his college classes who had returned to the classroom to learn about the newest computer-based architectural design programs, known simply as CAD.[5] Wooten

---

[4] Crackers are groups of individuals that "crack" software protection codes for copying purposes.

[5] CAD is the acronym for computer-aided design software.

learned from these seasoned professionals that architects generally did not start making significant incomes until they had reached their 40s and had started their own firms. This notion raised doubts about architecture as his career choice—Wooten's intention was to achieve above-average financial success in a less-than-average amount of time. He remembered an event from his childhood when he attended a catered party at a friend's house. The reality of what "catered" meant came to him as a shock; he had not previously known such things existed. In that seemingly wealthy neighborhood everyone's father was an entrepreneur of sorts, and no one's mother had to work. He recalled someone at that party telling him that a disproportionately large amount of the country's wealth was controlled by a relatively small percentage of the population.[6] That was one conversation Wooten never forgot.

Wooten was anxious to seek out opportunity and determined not to let his age or lack of experience deter him. While still enrolled in architecture classes, he submitted a prototype of one of his computer programs to a competition held by *CADalyst* magazine. He came in first place, winning an AutoDesk Caddie Image Award for his production of 3-D architectural walk-through animation.[7] More impressively, the prototype that won the contest used information that was self-taught. Considering Wooten's affinity for computers and programming, it came as no surprise that he was a natural with CAD. In fact, his skill with CAD and animation began to surpass that of his professors. As a result, the college asked him to teach a course in animation while still a student. He accepted the offer without hesitation.

Start-Up #1: Envision Design

At the age of 20, while still enrolled at Catonsville Community College, Wooten started his first company. Spurred by the desire to create and to make money, he founded Envision Design, a company based on his CAD and animation prowess. Wooten's idea was to produce 3-D walk-through animation for architects using software similar to that which won Wooten the *CADalyst* magazine contest.

Wooten identified his competition as the scale model business; architects still made elaborate scale models of proposed buildings out of foam and cardboard. Some architectural companies were willing to pay between $10,000 and $50,000 for such scale models. He decided to price his service in line with scale models, under the assumption that if customers were willing to pay a certain amount of money for a model, they would be willing to pay the same amount for his higher-quality product. He charged between $10,000 and $20,000 for a complete walk-through animation sequence. Intuitively it made sense to the 20-year-old Wooten that a

young college student starting a small business should target other small firms as clients. He attempted to attract clients by sending letters to every small architectural firm in the telephone directory from Baltimore to Washington, D.C. The letters were on Envision Design letterhead, describing the service he offered and asking for a meeting to make a sales presentation. Envision Design was ultimately unsuccessful. After one paying contract with a small firm, Envision fizzled.

Failure and Restart: Lessons Learned

Wooten decided that even though Envision Design had not been a success, he wanted to continue working with animation. To further his understanding and education in the field of animation, Wooten wanted to learn more about special effects and film animation. He discovered that he would need to learn how to use the latest high-end computer animation software that ran on Silicon Graphics Computers (SGI). He found that the University of Maryland–Baltimore County was building a state-of-the-art computer science building equipped with SGI computers. He quickly decided to transfer there. At UMBC, Peggy Southerland, herself a three-time Emmy-winning computer animator, ran the university's imaging researching center. Wooten was constantly talking to Peggy, asking her countless questions and soliciting advice for his career. Eventually she offered him an internship, which meant that Wooten would gain the necessary knowledge to work with SGIs and have a well-known animator as his mentor.

Start-Up #2: Metamorphosis Studios

Constantly on the lookout for an opportunity, Wooten saw a way to use his new knowledge of SGI animation software to start his second company; Metamorphosis Studios was developed with a partner, Andre Forde. Wooten and Forde had met at a party when Wooten overheard a group of college students (including Forde) talking about SGI software. Wooten was surprised to hear this topic of conversation because as far as he knew not many people, let alone young people, even knew about SGI. After meeting and engaging in the conversation, both men knew they wanted to work together. A chance encounter had become a major milestone for both Wooten and Forde.

Metamorphosis Studios focused on special effects and multimedia presentations. These were achieved using PC-based animation and authoring software packages. As yet, the two young men could not afford to purchase high-end Silicon Graphics Computers. The company developed presentations and electronic brochures for any kind of medium, including diskettes, CD-ROMs, and touch screens. The first Metamorphosis customer, Bingwa, was an educational software company that made an offer for a yearlong contract. The

[6] http://research.aarp.org/econ/dd44_wealth.html.
[7] *Fast Company*, July 2000.

contract required the Metamorphosis team to develop one software product per month for a year, a total of 12 products, one for each grade (1–12). Metamorphosis was to be paid $30,000 per product, a total of $360,000 by the year's end. Both Wooten and Forde considered this an enormous amount of money; the pair was elated. After paying $60,000 in two months for the software programs for grades 1 and 2, Bingwa asked Metamorphosis Studios to relocate to Princeton, New Jersey, and to become employees of Bingwa. Although both Wooten and Forde were offered salaries of $80,000 per year, they rejected the offer. They knew they were headed for bigger things.

Shifting Gears

After his experience with Bingwa and other various business customers, Wooten decided to shift his business model from a service-oriented focus to a product-oriented focus. He wanted to bypass payment and commitment problems that had arisen in dealing with customers such as Bingwa. Wooten saw service customers as unreliable.

As Wooten and Forde contemplated their next move, they concluded that one of their largest failings was their lack of focus and dedication to a specific task or goal. Their multimedia skills gave them too many options to pursue. They had dabbled in products ranging from CD-ROM educational titles and games, to Afrocentric Web site portals, to virtual tours for online real estate brokers. Wooten had so many ideas and so much energy that before he had fully thought out one idea, he had another, and the first idea was pushed off to the side while the subsequent new idea began to take shape. It was a problematic cycle that was impeding their success. To succeed, they would have to pick the "most" right product idea and develop it from start to finish without distraction.

Besides the issues of focus and idea selection, another problem Wooten and Forde encountered was that Metamorphosis Studios was not generating revenue during its new product development cycle. There seemed to be a dearth of capital available for the right deal, especially for young African American entrepreneurs such as him.[8] Traditionally, African American entrepreneurs tended to be trapped in small-scale ventures more often than their Caucasian counterparts because it was more difficult to obtain growth capital. Wooten believed that social, cultural, and racial hierarchies and biases were to blame for the disproportionately large number of Caucasian investors—and for the disproportionately small amount of growth capital available to the African American business community. Although he could empathize with the risk perspective of such investors, he felt the result to be unfortunate. (See Notes 1 and 2 at the end of this case.) Despite this belief, Wooten remained undeterred. Once they had identified the idea and target market for their next venture, ImageCafé, Wooten and Forde sold the assets of Metamorphosis Studios for $20,000.[9] It was time to move on.

Back to School Again

Fascinated by entrepreneurs and their roads to success, Wooten read everything he possibly could about their lives and their experiences, good and bad. He found the stories of Fred Smith, Reginald Lewis, and Bill Gates particularly inspirational. Wooten realized that the common thread connecting these entrepreneurs was that they all understood finance. Based on this conclusion, he changed his major to business administration and finance and enrolled at Johns Hopkins University. Wooten knew that he needed a much deeper understanding of finance if he wanted to be a successful entrepreneur, regardless of how creative with a computer he was. He finally understood that the value of being fluent in finance would be reflected by his success in raising capital to build a high-potential venture. In addition to finance, Wooten was intensely interested in understanding exactly how to scale and grow a business—the two kernels essential for success as Wooten envisioned it. Wooten received his business degree in 1998 with great personal satisfaction.

In 1995 the Internet began to grow with exponential speed. Companies were flocking to the Internet in droves. Even small companies that lacked the resources to hire professional Web design firms were experiencing a growing need to be on the World Wide Web. When Wooten thought about it, creating Web sites seemed like a natural transition for Wooten and Forde given their background. They had extensive knowledge in the field and the creative design skills. In fact, it was what Wooten and Forde did best. And most important, to fulfill their personal goals, Wooten had an idea of how they could make creating Web sites for companies a product, not a service. This time he believed they had the knowledge and the focus to succeed.

Launching ImageCafé

Wooten became obsessed with Web sites. At this time there were about 4.1 million active commercial online service users and a forecast 9 million online service customers worldwide. The number of online customers worldwide was expected to increase by 6 million in the next year.[10] Online observers also forecast that in 1996 there would be nearly 80,000 Web sites worldwide,

---

[8]"Small Business, The Racial Ravine: Minority Entrepreneurs Who Want a Piece of the Internet Gold Rush Face a Formidable Barrier: The Clubby, White-Male Universe of Venture Capitalists," *The Wall Street Journal*, May 22, 2000.

[9] Wooten had two other smaller start-ups that are not included to compress the storyline. See http://www.startupjournal.com/howto/minorityissues/20011224-tannenbaum.html for more information.

[10] "Computer Industry Forecasts: Communications," First Quarter 1996, p. 59.

and in 2001 approximately 50 million.[11] Wooten surmised that many of these computer users and companies would need Web sites.

Wooten saw that there were two ways for a company to obtain a Web site. The first was to hire a dedicated, full-time Web design firm. The cost of such a service was typically $3,000–$6,000.[12] The second option was more of a do-it-yourself (DIY) method with relatively inexpensive software programs that gave businesses the basic tools to design a Web site independently. Wooten perceived problems with both options. His experience with Metamorphosis Studios had shown him that small businesses could not afford to hire a full-service Web design company. And the problem with the DIY software was that there was a steep learning curve for its appropriate use, not to mention the sheer necessity of pure creativity. Without technical skill and artistic ability, the results were often Web sites that seemed cheap and unprofessional. The Web was becoming an extension of a company's image; firms could not afford to erode their images. Wooten saw a clear demand by small businesses for his innovative product.

Times were changing fast. Small businesses were beginning to understand that a Web site was a necessary cost of doing business. They generally did not have the resources big businesses had to invest in costly professionally designed Web sites.[13] Wooten knew he could meet some of this demand, and in early 1998 Image-Café was founded. His vision was to create the world's first online superstore of prefabricated Web sites for small businesses. Using their extensive knowledge of high-end software, HTML, Web programming, and artistic ability for developing graphical user interfaces, Image-Café would design high-end Web sites. The interesting angle of ImageCafé was that it would develop Web site templates created to imitate the premium and costly custom sites designed by fully dedicated Web design firms. Wooten referred to the templates as "customizable Web site masters," a term he felt was marketable. By prefabricating the Web site masters, ImageCafé lowered its costs without sacrificing the premium appearance of the Web sites. The template business model also took the service aspect out of the business by providing a product that was ready to be deployed quickly. The array of Web site templates was offered through ImageCafé's online superstore. Customers would create an account, log in, and shop for a Web site, which could then be customized easily to specific needs using ImageCafé's online Web site manager tools. Wooten remarked,

> Small businesses are tough clients because they want the world, but they are not willing to pay for it. Business owners started to see a Web site like they did their telephones. They couldn't imagine not having a telephone, and they started to think the same about a Web site.

By prefabricating the templates, ImageCafé could charge under $500 for what would have cost many times that amount as a custom design. This model seemed an incredible value for the world of small business. Wooten's slogan was "look like the Fortune 500 for under $500." ImageCafé addressed and solved the pitfalls that had been the downfall of his two previous companies. He knew this market, he focused on what he knew he could do best, and he transitioned from the service industry to the product industry as planned.

The Search for Capital

Once Wooten had thoroughly thought through the concept and model of ImageCafé, the next critical step was to secure enough capital for its launch. Wooten had recently read *The Burn Rate*,[14] which mentioned the law firm Wilson, Sonsini, Goodrich & Rosati (WSGR), one of the most powerful law firms in Silicon Valley. Wooten believed that if he could become a client of WSGR, it would help give him the credibility needed to raise capital.

WSGR practiced in the areas of antitrust, corporate and securities, employee benefits, employment law, fund services, intellectual property, litigation, real estate/environmental, tax, and wealth management; it was known for its technology practice. On the firm's Web site, Wooten began reading the alphabetical profiles of its attorneys. He quickly picked out four young associates close in age to himself who he hoped might be able to relate to him and his goals. He sent e-mail messages to these associates, saying that he had founded an East Coast–based e-commerce Internet start-up and was looking for not only Silicon Valley–based legal representation but also venture capital funding.

Wooten's plan worked—he managed to catch the attention of attorney Mike Arrington. After reading ImageCafé's executive summary and viewing the Web-based prototype, Arrington was intrigued by the unique idea; he believed that Wooten and Forde would be able to obtain funding. Within a few short days of that initial meeting, Wooten and Forde had WSGR representation. Wooten had negotiated a package of legal services totaling $40,000, which would be written off if Image-Café failed to receive sufficient funding.

The Relentless Pursuit of Capital

Now began ImageCafé's quest for capital. Wooten decided he needed to meet other entrepreneurs or individuals who might be interested in supporting his vision. One such individual was Dwayne Walker, a well-known ex-Microsoft employee who left with stock options, great technical knowledge, and a thirst to start his own company—Techwave. As Wooten put it, "He was a

---

[11] "Computer Industry Forecasts: Communications," Third Quarter 1996, p. 81.

[12] *Fast Company*, July 2000.

[13] *Washington Techway*, August 28, 2000.

[14] M. Wolff, *The Burn Rate: How I Survived the Gold Rush Years on the Internet* (New York: Simon & Schuster, 1998).

black man who raised $10 million. That qualified him as a man I needed to meet." After calling Walker daily, Wooten eventually spoke with him to set up a meeting in Seattle, where Walker was based. The meeting went well. As the meeting ended, Walker declared that he wanted to be ImageCafé's first angel investor.

But there was a catch. Walker wanted to be able to incubate[15] the new company in the Seattle area, which meant that Wooten and Forde would have to relocate to the West Coast. At the time Wooten and Forde had a small team of two programmers working on the back-end programming as part-time moonlighters. The programmers had agreed to be paid $30,000 in stock or cash once capital had been raised. When Walker made his offer the ImageCafé superstore was 60 percent finished; Wooten could not possibly relocate his whole team at the crucial last hour.

After hearing the second catch—that the half million dollars would be paid to ImageCafé in $20,000 increments based on milestones—Wooten and Forde said no thank you and goodbye to Walker.

Still Going

WSGR set up several meetings for Wooten with venture capital firms in Silicon Valley. While waiting for the flight to the West Coast, he remembered reading about an African American, Earl Graves (see Note 3 at the end of this case), who had obtained his Pepsi bottling franchise in part by sitting next to one of the Pepsi executives on a plane in first class. Wooten said to himself, "Maybe it does pay to fly first class." Wooten convinced a flight attendant friend to move him up from coach. With luck apparently on his wing, Wooten found himself seated next to Bill Daniels, a principal at Bank Boston Robertson Stevenson. Wooten recalled, "I had a captive audience for literally six hours. I talked about why I was going to Silicon Valley and whom I was going to see. I showed him the business plan." By the end of the flight Daniels had become Wooten's first realistically interested angel investor. Wooten walked off the plane with a list of people to see in Silicon Valley. This was a good way to start off his trip.

Shortly after returning from his trip to Silicon Valley, Wooten decided to speak to his family and friends to raise a few hundred thousand dollars. Closing the "friends and family round" proved to be challenging. However, his girlfriend (now wife) at the time passed the business plan on to her cousin, who worked for Sonny Stern, a New Jersey doctor who had been involved with venture capital for many years. As luck would have it, Stern turned out to be a client of the same Bill Daniels that Wooten had met on his trip to Silicon Valley a month earlier. Upon conferring with Daniels and send-

ing Wooten to meet with other potential investors in New York, Stern and Daniels decided to lead an angel round. Wooten was also able to get WSGR to invest in the financing. This was big!

Wooten wanted $300,000 in capital, based on a $3,000,000 valuation; for this he was willing to give up 10 percent of the company. In total, ImageCafé received $110,000 from 10 angel investors, for which he relinquished 11 percent of ImageCafé's equity. And to think this chain of events had all started with a "chance" encounter on an airplane! This was good news; still, Wooten was a bit disappointed—he had been expecting more.

It was December 1998, the software was 70 percent finished, and the $110,000 would not be nearly enough. With a touch of sour grapes, Wooten remembered, "During that time, everybody was throwing out $5,000,000 valuations before they had anything. I had a functional prototype, as well as a plan. I went from Silicon Valley to Silicon Alley, raising money. I thought a $3,000,000 valuation was fair, but I couldn't get a bite."

Four months later, in April 1999, the ImageCafé Web site was finished and ready for launch—but Wooten and Forde were out of cash. Upon launch, ImageCafé received enough press attention that additional investors seemingly came out of nowhere to invest in the company. Armed with additional interest from new potential investors, Wooten was able to negotiate an additional $150,000 in the form of a bridge loan from the existing investors. The loan would be convertible at a small discount at the close of the first venture capital round. Wooten expected to raise $3,000,000 at a $10,000,000 valuation from one or more venture capitalist firms.

Just before the $150,000 came through, Wooten was able to secure a big customer, Mindspring, one of the largest Internet service providers (ISPs). Mindspring agreed to commit to ImageCafé's products before Wooten and Forde had even finished the products! They had only a prototype and knew they would need millions of dollars to execute their plan. Wooten recalls,

> We wanted to leverage the existing channel, and that was the Internet service providers. They had a lot of small business customers. We basically would allow them to co-brand and create their own, what I call, virtual franchise, their own ImageCafé superstore—ImageCafé at Mindspring, ImageCafé at Earthlink, ImageCafé at AOL . . . and it was good for them because it allowed them to pick up more hosting business. They wanted to host the Web site; we wanted to sell the Web site as well as subscriptions to our Web site manager tool. I made sure we didn't go into the hosting business because I didn't want to cannibalize our channel. It was a beautiful business model.

Still, this required cash that ImageCafé did not have. Although Wooten and Forde had burned through the $260,000 (the initial $110,000 equity investment plus the $150,000 bridge loan), they had managed to launch the product and attract a large customer.

---

[15] An *incubator* is a company or facility designed to foster entrepreneurship and help start-up companies, usually technology-related, to grow through the use of shared resources, management expertise, and intellectual capital.

At the same time as the Mindspring deal, Wooten was also courting Network Solutions, Inc., a company that nearly had a monopoly on dot-com (domain) names. Wooten believed that Network Solutions would be a perfect channel to deliver the ImageCafé product line. Millions of people went to Network Solutions "credit card in hand" to buy a domain name; the next natural step after obtaining a domain name was to build (or buy) a Web site. Because ImageCafé was a shopping experience and not a building experience, Network Solutions could attach ImageCafé to its purchase flow. As soon as a small business customer bought a domain name, the new company could also buy an ImageCafé Web site. The phrase "one-stop shopping" certainly came to mind. Wooten recalls, "It didn't hurt their channel because most of their resellers of domain names were ISPs. So here we could help them to reward their top resellers, by sending them hosting business from customers who had purchased ImageCafé Web sites."

Wooten finally set a meeting with Network Solutions and quickly moved up the ranks to the company's new CEO, Jim Rutt. Rutt loved ImageCafé and believed it was the perfect product extension for Network Solutions' business.

Product on Track, But Out of Cash (OOC)

By June 1999 ImageCafé was again out of cash. Wooten had been working to arrange what he perceived as the perfect financing round for several months: He had three major investors who were interested in investing, two venture capital firms, and Network Solutions. Wooten was looking for a total investment of $3,000,000; he wanted $1,000,000 from each investor, on a $10,000,000 valuation. One investor felt a $10,000,000 valuation was too high. As the negotiations dragged on, another of the three agreed to lend ImageCafé $150,000. Negotiations continued to drag because of the valuation. Wooten was even willing to sweeten the deal with $500,000 in warrants, split three ways.

In the middle of the valuation discussions, Network Solutions made a buyout offer. After brief but intense discussions with Rutt, Wooten found himself with an offer that was potentially worth $21 million: one third in cash, one third in Network Solutions stock, and one third in an earn-out.[16] Wooten owned a majority of ImageCafé, and this offer would clearly mean a big payday. But there was a hitch. The last bridge loan Wooten had received from the venture capitalists had a 90-day "no shop" clause attached. Running out of cash, and unable to sell the company until September, Wooten went to a company called Mid-Atlantic Venture Association, which had been interested in investing all along.

With now more than 20 employees to pay and a burn rate of $50,000 per month, the cash was going fast. Although very interested, Mid Atlantic Ventures (MAV) would not be able to invest until it had performed its required due diligence. In the meantime, understanding Wooten's immediate cash needs, MAV referred him to two new angel investors who agreed to extend him a $300,000 bridge loan with warrant coverage on a $6,000,000 valuation; this would at least hold ImageCafé over through the summer. Wooten remembered intensely, "I had worked so long and hard to put together the perfect financing round that never went through because I wanted a $10,000,000 valuation—and on a Sunday afternoon, I ended up giving that away out of necessity."

It was September; and again out of cash, Wooten had a difficult decision to make. ImageCafé hung in the balance. Should he sell now or secure more capital to continue the fight?

Additional Case Information

Note 1 African American applicants for small business financing are denied credit twice as often as Caucasians with similar creditworthiness, according to the latest research. One key study by the National Bureau of Economic Research found raw loan denial rates of 27 percent for Caucasians and 66 percent for African Americans. "There's evidence that the market isn't working properly," says lead author David G. Blanchflower, chairman of the economics department at Dartmouth College in Hanover, New Hampshire.

Note 2 A new study from the Ewing Marion Kauffman Foundation provides the most detailed look to date at the connections between minority entrepreneurs and the venture capital industry. The report examines funds operated by members of the National Association of Investment Companies (NAIC), an association of investment firms with interest in backing minority business enterprises (MBEs). A few interesting findings stand out. First, the growth in minority enterprise venture financing has been rapid. In the early 1990s, only several million dollars had been invested in MBEs. Today the industry has more than $1 billion under management. The researchers, Wayne State's Timothy Bates and University of Washington's William Bradford, also found that this sector is quite profitable. The average investment per firm was $562,000; the average net return on this investment exceeded $1 million. The average rate of return exceeded 20 percent—compared to a 17 percent return for the S&P 500 over the same period. These funds also tend to invest in a wider mix of industrial sectors, thus cushioning the industry from some effects of the technology downturn. Overall, the authors conclude

---

[16] An *earn-out* is an arrangement in which sellers of a business receive additional future payment, usually based on future earnings.

that the minority venture capital investment sector is poised for further expansion.[17]

Note 3[18]   Earl G. Graves is considered the preeminent authority in America on African American business. The locus of that authority is *Black Enterprise*, the magazine he founded in 1970, which now has a circulation of nearly 300,000 and revenues of $24 million. Graves is the magazine's publisher as well as both the president and chief executive officer of the parent company, Earl G. Graves Ltd. He is also co-owner with Erving "Magic" Johnson of a Washington, D.C.–based Pepsi Cola distributorship, a firm that happens to be the largest minority-controlled Pepsi franchise in the nation. Johnson serves as chief executive officer of the Pepsi franchise. These two business ventures have propelled Graves into the ranks of elected board members of prestigious businesses and trustees of well-known foundations. He has become a leading spokesperson on issues that affect the well-being and economic success of African Americans. He has also used his expertise to educate others about trends and opportunities in African American entrepreneurship.

[17] Please see the following for more information: "Minorities and Venture Capital: A New Wave in American Business" by Timothy Bates and William Bradford, http://www.kauffman.org/pages/371.cfm.

[18] Biography Resource Center, Gale Group Inc., 2001.

Chapter Two

The Entrepreneurial Mind: Crafting a Personal Entrepreneurial Strategy

The secret of those who amaze the world is that they regard nothing to be impossible.

Henry David Thoreau
American philosopher, 1817–1862

Results Expected

Upon completion of this chapter, you will be able to

1. Determine whether being an entrepreneur would enhance your life and feed your creative energies.

2. Discuss the critical aspects of the entrepreneurial mind—the strategies, habits, attitudes, and behaviors that work for entrepreneurs who build higher-potential ventures.[1]

3. Describe the characteristics of various entrepreneurial groups.

4. Develop concepts for evaluating a personal entrepreneurial strategy and an apprenticeship, and be able to discuss the entrepreneur's creed.

5. Utilize a framework for self-assessment, and develop a personal entrepreneurial strategy.

6. Initiate a self-assessment and goal-setting process that can become a lifelong habit of entrepreneurial thinking and action.

7. Assess the Lakota Frybread case study.

8. Describe the entrepreneurial aspects depicted in the film *October Sky*.

Entrepreneurs Are Leaders

Until quite recently, a distinction was often made between the individual with the vision, skill, and mindset to start up a high-potential venture (the entrepreneur) and the typically more seasoned, risk-averse professional with the ability to scale the enterprise (the manager).

This old notion has given way to what we have sensed all along: Effective entrepreneurs are internally motivated, high-energy leaders with a unique tolerance for ambiguity, a keen eye toward mitigating

The authors would like to thank Frederic M. Alper, a longtime friend and colleague and adjunct professor at Babson College, for his insights and contributions to this chapter, in particular the graphic representation of entrepreneurial attributes and the development of the QuickLook exercise to develop a personal entrepreneurial strategy.

[1] J. A. Timmons, *The Entrepreneurial Mind* (Acton, MA: Brick House, 1989).

risk, and a passion for discovery and innovation. These leaders create or identify and pursue opportunities by marshalling the diverse resources required to develop new markets and engage the inevitable competition. More than ever, we are convinced that the creation and liberation of human energy resulting from entrepreneurial leadership are the largest transformational force on the planet today.

The power of a single leader can be profound, and nowhere is this more true and relevant than in entrepreneurship. Perhaps what is most exciting about entrepreneurial leaders is that in the aggregate, their alert actions have fueled a worldwide revolution that continues to define and shape our social, economic, and environmental frontiers.

Three Principles for Entrepreneurial Leadership

People don't want to be managed, they want to be led.
                                    Ewing Marion Kauffman

One of the most extraordinary entrepreneurial leadership stories of our time is that of the late Ewing Marion Kauffman, who founded and built Marion Labs, a company with over $1 billion in sales, and then founded the Ewing Marion Kauffman Foundation. Kauffman started his pharmaceutical company, now one of the leading companies in the world, in 1950 with $5,000 in the basement of his Kansas City home. Previously he had been very successful at another company. Kauffman (or "Mr. K." as he preferred) recalled, "The president first cut back my sales commission, then he cut back my territory. So I quit and created Marion Labs."

With the acquisition of the company by Merrell-Dow in 1989 (becoming Marion, Merrell Dow, Inc.), more than 300 people became millionaires. Thirteen foundations have been created by former Marion associates, and the Ewing Marion Kauffman Foundation is one of only a dozen or so foundations in America with assets of over $1 billion. The two-pronged mission of the foundation is to make a lasting difference in helping youths at risk and encouraging leadership in all areas of American life.

The following are the core leadership principles that are the cornerstone of the values, philosophy, and culture of Marion Labs and now of the Kauffman Foundation:

- Treat others as you would want to be treated.

- Share the wealth that is created with all those who have contributed to it at all levels.
- Give back to the community.

There are many legendary examples of Mr. K. practicing these principles while growing Marion Labs. There was the time when he had sent his young chief financial officer to Europe to negotiate a supply contract with a major German company. When the CFO returned, he proudly showed Mr. K. the incredibly favorable terms he had extracted from the supplier—who he had determined badly needed the business. From his point of view, he had "cleverly won" the contract by being a sharp and tough negotiator.

After reviewing the situation and the agreement, Mr. K. blasted the CFO: "This is a totally one-sided contract—in our favor—and it is terribly unfair. They won't be able to make any money on this, and that's not how we treat our suppliers, or our customers. You get back on that plane tomorrow, apologize to them, and then create a deal that works for us—and lets them make a reasonable return as well."

Stunned, the CFO sheepishly returned to Germany to work out a contract that met with Mr. K.'s approval. Less than two years later, a worldwide supply crisis forced that German supplier to reduce its customer shipments by over 90 percent. Mr. K.'s fairness principle had not been forgotten: Marion Labs was the only American company that continued to have its requirements filled.

As simple as these principles may be, few organizations truly, sincerely, and consistently practice them. It takes a lot more than lip service or a stand-alone profit-sharing plan to create an entrepreneurial culture like this. Consider the following unique characteristics at Marion Labs and the Ewing Marion Kauffman Foundation:

- No one is an employee; everyone is an associate.
- Even at $1 billion in sales, there are no formal organizational charts.
- Everyone who meets or exceeds high performance goals participates in a companywide bonus, profit-sharing, and stock option plan.
- Benefit programs treat all associates the same, even top management.
- Managers who attempt to develop a new product and fail are not punished with lateral promotions or geographic relocation, nor are they ostracized. Failures are gateways to learning and continual improvement.
- Those who will not or cannot practice these core principles are not tolerated.

EXHIBIT 2.1

Comparing Management and Leadership

	Management	Leadership
Creating an Agenda	Planning and budgeting—establishing detailed steps and timetables for achieving needed results, and then allocating the resources necessary to achieve these results	Establishing direction—developing a vision of the future, often the distant future, and strategies for producing the changes needed to achieve that vision
Developing a Human Network for Achieving the Agenda	Organizing and staffing—establishing some structure for accomplishing plan requirements, staffing that structure with individuals, delegating responsibility and authority for carrying out the plan, providing policies and procedures to help guide people, and creating methods or systems to monitor implementation	Aligning people—communicating the direction by words and deeds to all those whose cooperation may be needed to influence the creation of teams and coalitions that understand the vision and strategies, and accept their validity
Execution	Controlling and problem solving—monitoring results versus plans in some detail, identifying deviations, and then planning and organizing to solve these problems	Motivating and inspiring—energizing people to overcome major political, bureaucratic, and resource barriers to change by satisfying very basic, often unfulfilled human needs
Outcomes	Producing a degree of predictability and order, and having the potential of consistently producing key results expected by various stakeholders	Producing change, often to a dramatic degree, and having the potential of producing extremely useful change

Source: Reprinted with the permission of The Free Press, a Division of Simon & Schuster Adult Publishing Group, from *A Force for Change: How Leadership Differs from Management* by John P. Kotter. Copyright © 1990 by John P. Kotter, Inc. All rights reserved.

The ultimate message is clear: Great companies can be built upon simple but elegant principles; and all the capital, technology, service management, and latest information available cannot substitute for these principles, nor will they cause such a culture to happen. These ideals are at the heart of the difference between good and great companies.

Timeless Research

A single psychological model of entrepreneurship has not been supported by research. However, behavioral scientists, venture capitalists, investors, and entrepreneurs share the opinion that the eventual success of a new venture will depend a great deal upon the talent and behavior of the lead entrepreneur and of his or her team.

A number of myths still persist about entrepreneurs. Foremost among these myths is the belief that leaders are born, not made. The roots of much of this thinking reflect the assumptions and biases of an earlier era, when rulers were royal and leadership was the prerogative of the aristocracy. Fortunately, such notions have not withstood the tests of time or the inquisitiveness of researchers of leadership and management. Consider recent research, which distinguishes managers from leaders, as summarized in Exhibit 2.1. It is widely accepted today that leadership is an extraordinarily complex subject, depending more on the interconnections among the leader, the task, the situation, and those being led than on inborn or inherited characteristics.

Numerous ways of analyzing human behavior have implications in the study of entrepreneurship. For example, for over 40 years Dr. David C. McClelland of Harvard University and Dr. John W. Atkinson of the University of Michigan and their colleagues sought to understand individual motivation.[2] Their theory of psychological motivation is a generally accepted part of the literature on entrepreneurial behavior. The theory states that people are motivated by three principal needs: (1) the need for achievement, (2) the need for power, and (3) the need for affiliation. The *need for achievement* is the need to excel and for measurable personal accomplishment. A person competes against a self-imposed standard that does not involve competition with others. The individual sets realistic and challenging goals and likes to get feedback on how well he or she is doing in order to improve performance. The *need for power* is the need to influence others and to achieve an "influence goal." The *need for affiliation* is the need to attain an "affiliation

[2] See J. W. Atkinson, *An Introduction to Motivation* (Princeton, NJ: Van Nostrand, 1964); J. W. Atkinson, *Motives in Fantasy, Action and Society* (Princeton, NJ: Van Nostrand, 1958); D. C. McClelland, *The Achieving Society* (Princeton, NJ: Van Nostrand, 1961); J. W. Atkinson and N. T. Feather, eds., *A Theory of Achievement Motivation* (New York: John Wiley & Sons, 1966); and D. C. McClelland and D. G. Winter, *Motivating Economic Achievement* (New York: Free Press, 1969).

EXHIBIT 2.2

Characteristics of Entrepreneurs

Date	Authors	Characteristics
1848	Mill	Risk bearing
1917	Weber	Source of formal authority
1934	Schumpeter	Innovation; initiative
1954	Sutton	Desire for responsibility
1959	Hartman	Source of formal authority
1961	McClelland	Risk taking; need for achievement
1963	Davids	Ambition; desire for independence, responsibility, self-confidence
1964	Pickle	Drive/mental; human relations; communication ability; technical knowledge
1971	Palmer	Risk measurement
1971	Hornaday and Aboud	Need for achievement; autonomy; aggression; power; recognition; innovative/independent
1973	Winter	Need for power
1974	Borland	Internal locus of power
1982	Casson	Risk; innovation; power; authority
1985	Gartner	Change and ambiguity
1987	Begley and Boyd	Risk taking; tolerance of ambiguity
1988	Caird	Drive
1998	Roper	Power and authority
2000	Thomas and Mueller	Risk; power; internal locus of control; innovation
2001	Lee and Tsang	Internal locus of control

goal"—the goal to build a warm relationship with someone else and/or to enjoy mutual friendship.

Other research focused on the common attitudes and behaviors of entrepreneurs. A 1983 study found a relationship between attitudes and behaviors of successful entrepreneurs and various stages of company development.[3] A year later, another study found that entrepreneurs were unique individuals; for instance, this study found that "what is characteristic is not so much an overall type as a successful, growth-oriented entrepreneurial type. . . . It is the company builders who are distinctive."[4] A study of 118 entrepreneurs revealed that "those who like to plan are much more likely to be in the survival group than those who do not."[5] Clearly the get-rich-quick entrepreneurs are not the company builders; nor are they the planners of successful ventures. Rather it is the visionary who participates in the day-to-day routine to achieve a long-term objective and

who is generally passionate and not exclusively profit-oriented.

Academics have continued to characterize the special qualities of entrepreneurs. (See Exhibit 2.2 for a summary of this early research.) As participants in this quest to understand the entrepreneurial mind, in January 1983 Howard H. Stevenson and Jeffry Timmons spoke with 60 practicing entrepreneurs.[6] One finding was that entrepreneurs felt they had to concentrate on certain fundamentals: responsiveness, resiliency, and adaptiveness in seizing new opportunities. These entrepreneurs spoke of other attitudes, including an ability "to activate vision" and a willingness to learn about and invest in new techniques, to be adaptable, to have a professional attitude, and to have patience. They talked about the importance of "enjoying and being interested in business," as well as the business as "a way of life." Other attitudes they spoke of included a willingness

[3] N. Churchill, "Entrepreneurs and Their Enterprises: A Stage Model," *Frontiers of Entrepreneurship Research: 1983*, ed. J. A. Hornaday et al. (Babson Park, MA: Babson College, 1983), pp. 1–22.

[4] N. R. Smith and John B. Miner, "Motivational Considerations in the Success of Technologically Innovative Entrepreneurs," in *Frontiers of Entrepreneurship Research: 1984*, ed. J. A. Hornaday et al. (Babson Park, MA: Babson College, 1984), pp. 448–95.

[5] J. B. Miller, N. R. Smith, and J. S. Bracker, "Entrepreneur Motivation and Firm Survival among Technologically Innovative Companies," ed. N. C. Churchill et al., *Frontiers of Entrepreneurship Research: 1991* (Babson Park, MA: Babson College, 1992), p. 31.

[6] J. A. Timmons and H. H. Stevenson, "Entrepreneurship Education in the 80s: What Entrepreneurs Say," in *Entrepreneurship: What It Is and How to Teach It*, ed. J. Kao and H. H. Stevenson (Boston: Harvard Business School Press, 1985), pp. 115–34.

to learn about and invest in new techniques, to be adaptable, to have a professional attitude, and to have patience.

Many of the respondents recognized and endorsed the importance of human resource management; one entrepreneur said that one of the most challenging tasks was playing "a leadership role in attracting high-quality people, imparting your vision to them, and holding and motivating them." Other entrepreneurs focused on the importance of building an organization and teamwork. For example, the head of a manufacturing firm with $10 million in sales said, "Understanding people and how to pull them together toward a basic goal will be my main challenge in five years." The head of a clothing manufacturing business with 225 employees and $6 million in sales shared a view of many that one of the most critical areas where an entrepreneur has leverage and long-term impact is in managing employees. He said, "Treating people honestly and letting them know when they do well goes a long way."

A number of respondents believed that the ability to conceptualize their business and do strategic planning would be of growing importance, particularly when thinking five years ahead. Similarly, the ageless importance of sensitivity to and respect for employees was stressed by a chief executive officer of a firm with $40 million in sales and 400 employees: "It is essential that the separation between management and the average employee should be eliminated. Students should be taught to respect employees all the way down to the janitor and accept them as knowledgeable and able persons." One company that has taken this concept to heart is Stonyfield. For the past 25 years, Gary Hirshberg and founder Samuel Kaymen (now retired) have overseen Stonyfield Farm's phenomenal growth, from its infancy as a seven-cow organic farming school in 1983 to its current $300 million in annual sales. Their passionately green, employee-centric business has enjoyed a compounded annual growth rate of 27.4 percent for more than 18 years. In 2001 Stonyfield Farm entered a partnership with Groupe Danone, and in 2005 Hirshberg was named managing director of Stonyfield Europe, a joint venture between the two firms to build an entire industry around organics—a value chain that will stretch from the green farmer to the health-conscious consumer. Throughout its history, the company has never faltered in its commitment to its growing family of workers by offering great training and development opportunities, competitive pay, and strong benefits, as well as by perpetuating a fun, impassioned work environment.

A consulting study by McKinsey & Co. of medium-sized growth companies (i.e., companies with sales between $25 million and $1 billion and with sales or profit growth of more than 15 percent annually over five years) confirms that the chief executive officers of winning companies were notable for three common traits: perseverance, a builder's mentality, and a strong propensity for taking calculated risks.[7]

Converging on the Entrepreneurial Mind

The entrepreneur is one of the most intriguing and at the same time most elusive characters in the cast that constitutes the subject of economic analysis.

Professor William Baumol
Department of Economics, NYU

Desirable and Acquirable Attitudes, Habits, and Behaviors

Many successful entrepreneurs have emphasized that while their colleagues have initiative and a take-charge attitude, are determined to persevere, and are resilient and able to adapt, it is not just a matter of personality. It is what they *do* that matters most.[8]

Although there is an undeniable core of such inborn characteristics as energy and raw intelligence, which an entrepreneur either has or does not, it is becoming apparent that possession of these characteristics does not necessarily an entrepreneur make. There is also a good deal of evidence that entrepreneurs are born and made better and that certain attitudes and behaviors can be acquired, developed, practiced, and refined through a combination of experience and study.[9] In addition, although not all attitudes, habits, and behaviors can be acquired by everyone at the same pace and with the same proficiency, entrepreneurs are able to significantly improve their odds of success by concentrating on those that work, by nurturing and practicing them, and by eliminating, or at least mitigating, the rest. Painstaking effort may be required, and much will depend on the motivation of an individual to grow; but it seems

---

[7] D. K. Clifford, Jr., and R. E. Cavanagh, *The Winning Performance* (New York: Bantam Books, 1985), p. 3.

[8] Determining the attitudes and behaviors in entrepreneurs that are "acquirable and desirable" represents the synthesis of over 50 research studies compiled for the first and second editions of this book. See extensive references in J. A. Timmons, L. E. Smollen, and A. L. M. Dingee, Jr., *New Venture Creation*, 2nd ed. (Homewood, IL.: Richard D. Irwin, 1985), pp. 139–69.

[9] D. C. McClelland, "Achievement Motivation Can Be Developed," *Harvard Business Review*, November–December 1965; D. C. McClelland and David G. Winter, *Motivating Economic Achievement* (New York: Free Press, 1969); and J. A. Timmons, "Black Is Beautiful—Is It Bountiful?" *Harvard Business Review*, November–December 1971, p. 81.

people have an astounding capacity to change and learn if they are motivated and committed to do so.

Testimony given by successful entrepreneurs also confirms attitudes and behaviors that successful entrepreneurs have in common. Take, for instance, the first 21 inductees into Babson College's Academy of Distinguished Entrepreneurs,[10] including such well-known entrepreneurs as Ken Olsen of DEC, An Wang of Wang Computers, Wally Amos of Famous Amos Chocolate Chip Cookies, Bill Norris of Control Data, Sochiro Honda of Honda Motors, and the late Ray Kroc of McDonald's. All 21 of the inductees mentioned the possession of three attributes as the principal reasons for their successes: (1) the ability to respond positively to challenges and learn from mistakes, (2) personal initiative, and (3) great perseverance and determination.[11]

New Research. While Baumol's observation will resonate far into the future, we are fortunate to have the Praeger Perspectives series, a 2007 three-volume set of research that focuses on entrepreneurship from three angles: people, process, and place. This series brings together insights into the field of entrepreneurship by some of the leading scholars in the world and adds validation, new perspectives, and further debate to the complex questions that surround the entrepreneurial mind and entrepreneurial process. We have drawn on this work liberally in this edition of *New Venture Creation*.

The first volume, *people*, takes a broad view of entrepreneurship as a form of human action, pulling together the current state of the art in academic research with respect to cognitive, economic, social, and institutional factors that influence entrepreneurial behavior. Why do people start new businesses? How do people make entrepreneurial decisions? What is the role played by the social and economic environment in individuals' decisions about entrepreneurship? Do institutions matter? Do some groups of people such as immigrants and women face particular issues when deciding to start a business?

The second volume *process*, proceeds through the life cycle of a new venture start-up by tackling several key steps in the process: idea, opportunity, team building, resource acquisition, managing growth, and entering global markets. It is clear from the work in this volume that we have (as we alluded to earlier) learned a tremendous amount about the entrepreneurial process over the years.

The third volume, in the series examines *place*, which refers to a wide and diverse range of contextual factors that influence the entrepreneur and the entrepreneurial process. Chapters in this volume address entrepreneurship in the context of the corporation, family, and franchise. The research examines the impact of public policy and entrepreneurship support systems at the country and community level and from an economic and social perspective. In addition, the volume looks at the technology environment and financing support structures for entrepreneurship as context issues.

We will also be referring to the exciting and provocative work of Professors Stefan Kwiatkowski and Nawaz Sharif, editors of the *Knowledge Café* series on "Intellectual Entrepreneurship and Courage to Act." This text, the fifth in Kwiatkowski's series, provides further insight into the entrepreneurial mind-set involved in creating new intellectual property and knowledge creation ventures. We are especially swayed by their work and valuable insight on *courage* as a vital aspect of entrepreneurial behavior, and we have incorporated that into our dominant themes.

Undoubtedly many attitudes and behaviors characterize the entrepreneurial mind, and there is no single set of attitudes and behaviors that every entrepreneur must have for every venture opportunity. Further, the fit concept argues that what is required in each situation depends on the mix and match of the key players and how promising and forgiving the opportunity is, given the founders' strengths and shortcomings. A team might collectively show many desired strengths, but even then there is no such thing as a perfect entrepreneur—yet.

Seven Dominant Themes

Nothing that sends you to the grave with a smile on your face comes easy. Work hard doing what you love. Find out what gives you energy and improve on it.

Betty Coster, Entrepreneur

A consensus has emerged around seven dominant themes, shown in Exhibits 2.3 and 2.4.

Commitment and Determination   Commitment and determination are seen as more important than any other factor. With commitment and determination, an entrepreneur can overcome incredible obstacles and also compensate enormously for other weaknesses. For 16 long years following his graduation from Babson College, Mario Ricciardelli worked to create a travel agency that catered to students. He endured lean personal finances and countless setbacks, including several near bankruptcies, the sudden failure of a charter airline that left his young

---

[10] By 2008 a total of 90 inductees had joined the Academy of Distinguished Entrepreneurs, including founders Arthur M. Blank of Home Depot; Richard Branson of Virgin Group; Magic Johnson; Robert Kraft of the Kraft Group; and the Molson and Forbes families.

[11] J. A. Hornaday and N. B. Tieken, "Capturing Twenty-One Heffalumps," in *Frontiers of Entrepreneurship Research: 1983*, ed. J. A. Hornaday et al. (Babson Park, MA: Babson College, 1983), pp. 23–50.

EXHIBIT 2.3

Seven Themes of Desirable and Acquirable Attitudes and Behaviors

Theme	Attitude or Behavior
Commitment and determination	Tenacious and decisive, able to recommit/commit quickly
	Intensely competitive in achieving goals
	Persistent in solving problems, disciplined
	Willing to undertake personal sacrifice
	Immersed in the mission
Courage	Moral strength
	Fearless experimentation
	Not afraid of conflicts, failure
	Intense curiosity in the face of risk
Leadership	Self-starter; high standards but not perfectionist
	Team builder and hero maker; inspires others
	Treats others as you want to be treated
	Shares the wealth with all the people who helped create it
	Honest and reliable; builds trust; practices fairness
	Not a lone wolf
	Superior learner and teacher; courage
	Patient and urgent
Opportunity obsession	Leadership in shaping the opportunity
	Has intimate knowledge of customers' needs and wants
	Market driven
	Obsessed with value creation and enhancement
Tolerance of risk, ambiguity, and uncertainty	Calculated risk taker
	Risk minimizer
	Risk sharer
	Manages paradoxes and contradictions
	Tolerates uncertainty and lack of structure
	Tolerates stress and conflict
	Able to resolve problems and integrate solutions
Creativity, self-reliance, and adaptability	Nonconventional, open-minded, lateral thinker (helicopter mind)
	Restless with status quo
	Able to adapt and change; creative problem solver
	Quick learner
	No fear of failure
	Able to conceptualize and "sweat details"
Motivation to excel	Goal and results oriented; high but realistic goals
	Drive to achieve and grow
	Low need for status and power
	Interpersonally supporting (versus competitive)
	Aware of weaknesses and strengths
	Has perspective and sense of humor

clients stranded in Mexico, and a stock swap deal with a high-profile Internet venture that fell to earth after two difficult years when the bubble burst. Mario and Jacqui Lewis, his partner acquired in a subsequent acquisition, convinced the troubled parent company to let them turn in their shares in exchange for their cash-strapped online travel portal. Having

no money to expand into other markets, in 2003 the team refocused its efforts on building the most comprehensive and exciting online spring break travel program anywhere. By pouring all of its attention into that narrow space, the company was able to dramatically increase bookings and profitability. In its first season as a newly independent venture, it generated

EXHIBIT 2.4

Core and Desirable Entrepreneurial Attributes

The Nonentrepreneurial Attributes

Outer control

Invulnerability

DESIRABLE ATTRIBUTES

Intelligence

Being "macho"

Perfectionist

Capacity to inspire

CORE ATTRIBUTES
Courage
Commitment and
determination
Leadership
Opportunity obsession
Tolerance of risk,
ambiguity, and uncertainty
Creativity, self-reliance,
and adaptability
Motivation to excel

Knows it all

Creativity and
innovativeness

Values

Impulsiveness

Energy, health, and
emotional stability

Counter-dependency

Being antiauthoritarian

just under $1 million in free cash flow. In early 2004, with year-over-year growth in bookings of 100 percent, the partners decided to look for a buyer. Ninety days later, Mario and Jacqui joined the ranks of American millionaires when their company, StudentCity.com, was acquired by First Choice Holidays, a $5 billion tour operator in Europe. Today Mario operates a division of the acquiring company that generates nine figures in revenue.

Total commitment is required in nearly all entrepreneurial ventures. Almost without exception, entrepreneurs live under huge, constant pressures—first for their firms to survive start-up, then for them to stay alive, and finally for them to grow. A new venture demands top priority for the entrepreneur's time, emotions, and loyalty. Thus commitment and determination usually require personal sacrifice. An entrepreneur's commitment can be measured in several ways—through a willingness to invest a substantial portion of his or her net worth in the venture, through a willingness to take a cut in pay because he or she will own a major piece of the venture, and through other major sacrifices in lifestyle and family circumstances.

The desire to win does not equal the will to never give up. This is a critically important distinction. Countless would-be entrepreneurs (and lots of other types of people for that matter) say that they really want to win. But few have the dogged tenacity and

unflinching perseverance to make it happen. Take a young entrepreneur we will call Stephen. One of the authors introduced him to a potentially invaluable lead—a brain trust prospect and mega-angel investor. Stephen placed several phone calls to the investor, but none were returned. He made a few more calls, each time leaving a message with the referral information. Still no response.

Over the next week the young entrepreneur made yet another series of over two dozen calls that once again received no response. At that point, what would you have done? Have you ever called anyone that many times and not gotten any sort of reply? Would you keep trying, or decide to move on and not waste any more time? Feeling that this individual was a potentially invaluable contact, Stephen refused to give up. He would make 12 more calls before finally getting a response. In the luncheon meeting that followed soon after, the mega-angel agreed to invest $1 million in Stephen's start-up and serve as chairman of the board. The company became successful and was sold four years later for $55 million.

Entrepreneurs are intensely competitive: They love to win and love to compete—at anything! The best of them direct all this competitive energy toward the goal and toward their external competitors. This is critical; founders who get caught up in competing with peers in the company invariably destroy team cohesion and spirit and, ultimately, the team.

Entrepreneurs who successfully build new enterprises seek to overcome hurdles, solve problems, and complete the job; they are disciplined, tenacious, and persistent. They are able to commit and recommit quickly. They are not intimidated by difficult situations; in fact, they seem to think that the impossible just takes a little longer. However, they are neither aimless nor foolhardy in their relentless attack on a problem or obstacle that can impede their business. If a task is unsolvable, an entrepreneur will actually give up sooner than others. Most researchers share the opinion that while entrepreneurs are extremely persistent, they are also realistic in recognizing what they can and cannot do, and where they can get help to solve a very difficult but necessary task.

Courage   As we noted earlier, we are indebted to Stefan Kwiatkowski and Nawaz Sharif for their insightful and thoughtful work on *Courage* as an important dimension of the entrepreneurial mindset. Although we added *courage* as a subcategory in the previous edition of this text, we did not do it justice.

In his research essay titled "What the Hell, Let's Give It a Try," Kwiatkowski asserts that courage is not simple bravery resulting from deficient information about a given situation, nor pluck anchored in feelings of invulnerability. Courage rather has its source in broadly understood knowledge, experience, and integrity of the courageous individual. To prove his point, Kwiatkowski Googled "core and desirable entrepreneurial attributes" combined with "entrepreneurship." Results of that search, and two other searches also conducted in March 2005, are depicted in Exhibit 2.5.

EXHIBIT 2.5

Online Search for Desirable Attributes of Entrepreneurship

Timmons/ Spinelli Theme	Google	EBSCO	Proquest
Commitment	534,000	151	7,042
Leadership	1,200,000	377	7,230
Opportunity obsession	9,010	1	0
Opportunity immersion*	14,000	0	0
Risk tolerance	57,600	4	53
Adaptability	50,400	21	688
Achievement	370,000	192	4,169
Courage	81,000	10	647

*A non-Timmons/Spinelli theme.

Source: S. Kwiatkowski and N. M. Sharif, *Knowledge Café for Intellectual Entrepreneurship and Courage to Act* (Warsaw, Poland: Publishing house of Leon Kozminsky Academy of Entrepreneurship and Management, 2005), p. 231.

Hence, as we continue to converge on the entrepreneurial mind, we have included and elevated courage to the second of what are now seven themes. We see courage having at least three important aspects: first, *moral strength and principles*. This means the character and the personal integrity to know right from wrong, and the will and commitment to act accordingly (to do the right thing). The second is *being a fearless experimenter*. This is not to be confused with simply assessing and weighing risk and reward, upside and downside, and one's comfort with a certain level of risk and uncertainty. Fearless experimentation suggests a restlessness with convention and a rejection of the status quo. It is the innovator's passion to create, invent, and improve. This relentless experimentation is enhanced by a third aspect of courage: *a lack of fear of failing at the experiment—* and most undertakings for that matter—*and a lack of fear of conflicts that may arise.* In other words, there is a mental toughness that is quite impervious to fears but is not ignorant or oblivious to possible consequences. Consider the following examples of courage to help elucidate this important concept.

In 1961 the Cuban Missile Crisis was one of the most dangerous and frightening moments in American history, and especially in the Cold War between the old USSR and the United States. Many historians and military observers believe the two nations came within hours, even minutes, of hostilities that would have led to a nuclear holocaust. A few years earlier a young U.S. Navy ensign was on a ship in these same waters off Cuba, but he was not on watch at the time. A senior officer, by error, had charted a course that the young ensign, through his own sextant and map calculations (this was long before GPS), had concluded was incorrect and would run the ship aground. Such a calamity would end the careers of the navy ship's commander and officer in charge. The young ensign, if wrong, would be demoted and court-marshalled. All of his senior officers were certain that the ensign's much more experienced and senior officer was correct, and the young man was urged not to pursue his belief in his own calculations. Nonetheless, he showed enormous courage, fearlessness, and confidence that he was doing the right thing, and he insisted on making his case to the captain of the ship. The captain listened. Fortunately for all, the young ensign had carefully and accurately done his readings and calculations—and *was* correct. This avoided a near disaster. This young ensign went on to be a highly successful entrepreneur. His name was Ewing Marion Kauffman.

Another example involves an undergraduate student whom we will call Mike, who was working at a popular restaurant in a large northeastern city. He had worked there as a coop student during his college years, first as a dishwasher, and all the way up to manager by the time he graduated. He shared a story about an incident that happened to him at the restaurant that might have cost him his job, as well as other potential retribution. One early December day at a particularly quiet time of the late afternoon shift, a uniformed city policeman came to the restaurant and asked for the owner, who was there. Mike asked the officer what the call was about. The officer shoved a good-sized brown paper bag at Mike and simply said, "Here, give this to him. He'll know what it's for." Mike promptly gave the bag back to the officer and said, "No thanks. We don't do that here." And he escorted the officer out of the restaurant. The apparent solicitation of a bribe did not sway Mike, who had the courage and the principles to just say no. This young man was later admitted to Harvard Business School, graduated, and has had an outstanding career.

Leadership   Successful entrepreneurs are experienced, possessing intimate knowledge of the technology and marketplace in which they will compete, sound general management skills, and a proven track

record. They are self-starters and have an internal locus of control with high standards. They are patient leaders, capable of installing tangible visions and managing for the longer haul. The entrepreneur is at once a learner and a teacher, a doer and a visionary. The vision of building a substantial enterprise that will contribute something lasting and relevant to the world while realizing a capital gain requires the patience to stick to the task for 5 to 10 years or more.

Work by Dr. Alan Grant lends significant support to the fundamental "driving forces" theory of entrepreneurship that will be explored in Chapter 5. Grant surveyed 25 senior venture capitalists to develop an entrepreneurial leadership paradigm. Three clear areas evolved from his study: the lead entrepreneur, the venture team, and the external environment influences, which are outlined in further detail in Exhibit 2.6. Furthermore, Grant suggested that to truly understand this paradigm, it should be "metaphorically associated with a *troika*, a Russian vehicle pulled by three horses of *equal* strength. Each horse represents a cluster of the success factors. The troika was driven toward success by the visions and *dreams* of

EXHIBIT 2.6

The Entrepreneurial Leadership Paradigm

The Lead Entrepreneur

Self-concept	Has a realist's attitude rather than one of invincibility.
Intellectually honest	Trustworthy: his/her word is his/her contract.
	Admits what and when he/she does not know.
Pacemaker	Displays a high energy level and a sense of urgency.
Courage	Capable of making hard decisions: setting and beating high goals.
Communication skills	Maintains an effective dialogue with the venture team, in the marketplace, and with other venture constituents.
Team player	Competent in people management and team-building skills.

The Venture Team

Organizational style	The lead entrepreneur and the venture team blend their skills to operate in a participative environment.
Ethical behavior	Practices strong adherence to ethical business practices.
Faithfulness	Stretched commitments are consistently met or bettered.
Focus	Long-term venture strategies are kept in focus, but tactics are varied to achieve them.
Performance/reward	High standards of performance are created, and superior performance is rewarded fairly and equitably.
Adaptability	Responsive to rapid changes in product/technological cycles.

External Environmental Influences

Constituent needs	Organization needs are satisfied, in parallel with those of the other publics the enterprise serves.
Prior experience	Extensive prior experiences are effectively applied.
Mentoring	The competencies of others are sought and used.
Problem resolution	New problems are immediately solved or prioritized.
Value creation	High commitment is placed on long-term value creation for backers, customers, employees, and other stakeholders.
Skill emphasis	Marketing skills are stressed over technical ones.

Source: Adapted from A. J. Grant, "The Development of an Entrepreneurial Leadership Paradigm for Enhancing Venture Capital Success," *Frontiers of Entrepreneurship Research: 1992*, ed. J. A. Hornaday et al. (Babson Park, MA: Babson College, 1992).

the founding entrepreneurs."[12] Grant's work is supported by a later study by Nigel Nicholson in his 1998 *European Management* journal article, reporting on the personality and entrepreneurial leadership of the heads of the U.K.'s most successful independent companies.

Successful entrepreneurs possess a well-developed capacity to exert influence *without* formal power. These people are adept at conflict resolution. They know when to use logic and when to persuade, when to make a concession, and when to exact one. To run a successful venture, an entrepreneur learns to get along with many different constituencies—the customer, the supplier, the financial backer, and the creditor, as well as the partners and others on the inside—often with conflicting aims. Success comes when the entrepreneur is a mediator—a negotiator rather than a dictator.

Successful entrepreneurs are interpersonally supporting and nurturing—not interpersonally competitive. When a strong need to control, influence, and gain power over others characterizes the lead entrepreneur, or where he or she has an insatiable appetite for putting an associate down, the venture usually gets into trouble. Entrepreneurs should treat others as they want to be treated; they should share the wealth with those who contributed. A dictatorial, adversarial, and domineering management style makes it difficult to attract and keep people who thrive on a thirst for achievement, responsibility, and results. Compliant partners and managers often are chosen. Destructive conflicts often erupt over who has the final say, who is right, and whose prerogatives are what.

Entrepreneurs who create and build substantial enterprises are not lone wolves and superindependent. They do not need to collect all the credit for the effort. They not only recognize the reality that it is rarely possible to build a substantial business working alone, but also actively build a team. They have an uncanny ability to make heroes out of the people they attract to the venture by giving responsibility and sharing credit for accomplishments.

In the corporate setting, this "hero-making" ability is identified as an essential attribute of successful entrepreneurial managers.[13] These hero makers, of both the independent and corporate varieties, try to make the pie bigger and better, rather than jealously clutching and hoarding a tiny pie that is all theirs. They have a capacity for objective interpersonal relationships as well, which enables them to smooth out individual differences of opinion by keeping attention focused on the common goal to be achieved.[14]

Opportunity Obsession   Successful entrepreneurs are obsessed first with opportunity—not with the money, the resources, the contacts and networking, and not with image or appearances. Although some of these latter items have a place and time in the entrepreneurial process, they are not the source and driver for new ventures. Entrepreneurs, in their best creative mode, are constantly thinking of new ideas for businesses by watching trends, spotting patterns, and connecting the dots to shape and mold a unique enterprise.

Take Tom Stemberg, for example. After business school—and after over 15 years in the supermarket business—he began to look for major new opportunities. He researched and rejected many decent ideas that were either not good "big" opportunities or not the right fit for him. He then noted a recurring pattern with profound economic implications; every Main Street shop in America was selling ballpoint pens (wholesale cost about 30 cents) for $2, $3, and more. He soon learned that these very large gross margins were common for a wide range of products used by small businesses and the self-employed: copy paper, writing and clerical supplies, calculators, and other electronics. Stemberg believed there was a new business model underlying this opportunity pattern—which, if well-developed and executed, could revolutionize the office supply business and become a major enterprise. He and Leo Kahn founded Staples, and they were certainly right.

> Sternberg is now a managing general partner of the Highland Consumer Fund and focuses on retail and consumer services companies. He is also interested in ways technology can be applied to further impact existing businesses. Sternberg brings to bear his deep understanding of entrepreneurs, new markets, and product innovation in assisting portfolio companies in building successful and enduring companies. He also founded ZOOTS, one of the country's leading dry cleaning companies, as well as Olly Shoes, a leading children's shoe retailer.

Entrepreneurs realize good ideas are a dime a dozen, but good opportunities are few and far between. Fortunately, a great deal is now known about the criteria, the patterns, and the requirements that differentiate the good idea from the good opportunity. Entrepreneurs rely heavily on their own previous experiences (or their frustrations as customers) to come up with their breakthrough opportunities. Kurt Bauer, for instance, had no prior business training or experience before he headed for Eastern Europe in 1990 on a Fulbright Scholarship to work on privatization in Poland and Russia. In fact, he postponed his

[12] A. Grant, "The Development of an Entrepreneurial Leadership Paradigm for Enhancing New Venture Success," *Frontiers of Entrepreneurship Research: 1992,* ed. J. A. Hornaday et al. (Babson Park, MA: Babson College, 1992).

[13] D. L. Bradford and A. R. Cohen, *Managing for Excellence: The Guide to Developing High Performance in Contemporary Organizations* (New York: John Wiley & Sons, 1984).

[14] Churchill, "Entrepreneurs and Their Enterprises: A Stage Model," pp. 1–22.

acceptances to top medical schools in order to go east. He was so impressed with the seemingly endless stream of new business opportunities in the old eastern bloc countries that upon his return two years later, he decided to go to business school and try to figure out how to recognize and pursue the best of these opportunities. We will study his venture here from its roots and conception, to business plan development, to fund-raising and launch. Kurt and his brother John, and their venture, are a classic example of a pattern of opportunity obsession.

Throughout this text, we will examine in great detail how entrepreneurs and investors are "opportunity obsessed." We will see their ingenious, as well as straightforward, ways and patterns of creating, shaping, molding, and recognizing opportunities that are not just good ideas, and then transforming these "caterpillars into butterflies." These practices, strategies, and habits are part of the entrepreneurial mind-set and are skills and know-how that are learnable and acquirable.

The entrepreneur's credo is to think opportunity first and cash last. Time and again—even after harvesting a highly successful venture—lead entrepreneurs will start up another company. They possess all the money and material wealth anyone would ever hope for, yet it is not enough. Like the artist, scientist, athlete, or musician who, at great personal sacrifice, strives for yet another breakthrough discovery, new record, or masterpiece, the greatest entrepreneurs are similarly obsessed with what they believe is the next breakthrough opportunity.

An excellent example of this pattern is David Neeleman, founder of discount airline JetBlue. Having created the first electronic airline ticket a few years earlier while at Morris Air (later sold to Southwest Airlines), he was a wealthy man. And yet along the way he had developed a unique vision for a new airline. In 1998 he was having dinner with his longtime backer and friend Michael Lazarus, founding partner of Weston-Presidio Capital Partners. Lazarus asked, "Why do you want to start a new airline—what is the big opportunity you see?" Neeleman replied, "I'm going to fly people where they want to go!" This simple but brilliant concept saw an opportunity in what all other would-be airline entrepreneurs saw as a barrier to entry: the entrenched, massive hub system of large, established airlines.

Entrepreneurs like Stemberg and Neeleman think big enough about opportunities. They know that a mom-and-pop business can often be more exhausting and stressful, and much less rewarding, than a high-potential business. Their opportunity mind-set is how to create it, shape it mold it, or fix it so that the cus-

tomer/end user will respond, Wow! Their thinking habits focus on what can go right here—what and how can we change the product or service to make it go right? What do we have to offer to become the superior, dominant product or service?

Tolerance of Risk, Ambiguity, and Uncertainty

Because high rates of change and high levels of risk, ambiguity, and uncertainty are almost a given, successful entrepreneurs tolerate risk, ambiguity, and uncertainty. They manage paradoxes and contradictions.

Entrepreneurs risk money, but they also risk reputation. Successful entrepreneurs are not gamblers; they take calculated risks. Like the parachutist, they are willing to take a risk; however, in deciding to do so, they calculate the risk carefully and thoroughly and do everything possible to get the odds in their favor. Entrepreneurs get others to share inherent financial and business risks with them. Partners put up money and put their reputations on the line, and investors do likewise. Creditors also join the party, as do customers who advance payments and suppliers who advance credit. For example, one researcher studied three very successful entrepreneurs in California who initiated and orchestrated actions that had risk consequences.[15] It was found that while they shunned risk, they sustained their courage by the clarity and optimism with which they saw the future. They limited the risks they initiated by carefully defining and strategizing their ends and by controlling and monitoring their means—and by tailoring them both to what they saw the future to be. Further, they managed risk by transferring it to others.

In 1990 John B. Miner proposed his concept of motivation–organizational fit, within which he contrasted a hierarchic (managerial) role with a task (entrepreneurial) role.[16] This study of motivational patterns showed that those who are task oriented (i.e., entrepreneurs) opt for the following roles because of the corresponding motivations:

Role	Motivation
1. Individual achievement.	A desire to achieve through one's own efforts and to attribute success to personal causation.
2. Risk avoidance.	A desire to avoid risk and leave little to chance.
3. Seeking results of behavior.	A desire for feedback.
4. Personal innovation.	A desire to introduce innovative solutions.
5. Planning and setting goals.	A desire to think about the future and anticipate future possibilities.

[15] D. Mitton, "No Money, Know-How, Know-Who: Formula for Managing Venture Success and Personal Wealth," *Frontiers of Entrepreneurship Research: 1984*, ed. J. A. Hornaday et al. (Babson Park, MA: Babson College, 1984), p. 427.
[16] J. B. Miner, "Entrepreneurs, High-Growth Entrepreneurs, and Managers: Contrasting and Overlapping Motivational Patterns," *Journal of Business Venturing* 5, p. 224.

Entrepreneurs also tolerate ambiguity and uncertainty and are comfortable with conflict. Ask someone working in a large company how sure they are about receiving a paycheck this month, in two months, in six months, and next year. Invariably they will say that it is virtually certain and will muse at the question. Start-up entrepreneurs face just the opposite situation: There may be no revenue at the beginning, and if there is, a 90-day backlog in orders would be quite an exception. To make matters worse, lack of organization, structure, and order is a way of life. Constant changes introduce ambiguity and stress into every part of the enterprise. Jobs are undefined and changing continually, customers are new, coworkers are new, and setbacks and surprises are inevitable. And there never seems to be enough time.

Successful entrepreneurs maximize the good "higher-performance" results of stress and minimize the negative reactions of exhaustion and frustration. Two surveys have suggested that very high levels of both satisfaction and stress characterize founders, to a greater degree than managers, regardless of the success of their ventures.[17]

Creativity, Self-Reliance, and Adaptability

The high levels of uncertainty and very rapid rates of change that characterize new ventures require fluid and highly adaptive forms of organization that can respond quickly and effectively.

Successful entrepreneurs believe in themselves. They believe that their accomplishments (and setbacks) lie within their own control and influence and that they can affect the outcome. Successful entrepreneurs have the ability to see and "sweat the details" and also to conceptualize (i.e., they have "helicopter minds"). They are dissatisfied with the status quo and are restless initiators.

The entrepreneur has historically been viewed as an independent, highly self-reliant innovator and the champion (and occasional villain) of the free enterprise economy. More modern research and investigation have refined the agreement among researchers and practitioners alike that effective entrepreneurs actively seek and take initiative. They willingly put themselves in situations where they are personally responsible for the success or failure of the operation. They like to take the initiative to solve a problem or fill a vacuum where no leadership exists. They also like situations where personal impact on problems can be measured. Again, this is the action-oriented nature of the entrepreneur expressing itself.

Successful entrepreneurs are adaptive and resilient. They have an insatiable desire to know how well they are performing. They realize that to know how well they are doing and how to improve their performance, they need to actively seek and use feedback. Seeking and using feedback is also central to the habit of learning from mistakes and setbacks, and of responding to the unexpected. For the same reasons, these entrepreneurs often are described as excellent listeners and quick learners.

Entrepreneurs are not afraid of failing; rather, they are more intent on succeeding, counting on the fact that "success covers a multitude of blunders,"[18] as George Bernard Shaw eloquently stated. People who fear failure will neutralize whatever achievement motivation they may possess. They will tend to engage in a very easy task, where there is little chance of failure, or in a very difficult situation, where they cannot be held personally responsible if they do not succeed.

Further, successful entrepreneurs learn from failure experiences. They better understand not only their roles but also the roles of others in causing the failure, and thus they are able to avoid similar problems in the future. There is an old saying to the effect that the cowboy who has never been thrown from a horse undoubtedly has not ridden too many! The iterative, trial-and-error nature of becoming a successful entrepreneur makes serious setbacks and disappointments an integral part of the learning process.

Motivation to Excel   Successful entrepreneurs are motivated to excel. Entrepreneurs are self-starters who appear driven internally by a strong desire to compete against their own self-imposed standards and to pursue and attain challenging goals. This need to achieve has been well established in the literature on entrepreneurs since the pioneering work of McClelland and Atkinson on motivation in the 1950s and 1960s. Seeking out the challenge inherent in a start-up and responding in a positive way, noted by the distinguished entrepreneurs mentioned earlier, is achievement motivation in action.

Conversely, these entrepreneurs have a low need for status and power, and they derive personal motivation from the challenge and excitement of creating and building enterprises. They are driven by a thirst for achievement, rather than by status and power. Ironically, their accomplishments, especially if they are very successful, give them power. But it is important to recognize that power and status are a result of their activities. Setting high but attainable goals enables entrepreneurs to focus their energies, be selective in sorting out opportunities, and know what to say no to. Having goals and direction also helps define priorities and provides measures of how well they are performing. Possessing an objective way of keeping score, such as changes in profits, sales, or

---

[17] E. A. Fagonson, "Personal Value Systems of Men and Women Entrepreneurs versus Managers," *Journal of Business Venturing*, 1993.
[18] Cited in R. Little, *How to Lose $100,000,000 and Other Valuable Advice* (Boston: Little, Brown, 1979), p. 72.

stock price, is also important. Thus money is seen as a tool and a way of keeping score, rather than the object of the game by itself.

Successful entrepreneurs insist on the highest personal standards of integrity and reliability. They do what they say they are going to do, and they pull for the long haul. These high personal standards are the glue and fiber that bind successful personal and business relationships and make them endure.

A study involving 130 members of the Small Company Management Program at Harvard Business School confirmed how important this issue is. Most simply said it was the single most important factor in their long-term success.[19]

The best entrepreneurs have a keen awareness of their own strengths and weaknesses and those of their partners and of the competitive and other environments surrounding and influencing them. They are coldly realistic about what they can and cannot do and do not delude themselves; that is, they have "veridical awareness" or "optimistic realism." It also is worth noting that successful entrepreneurs believe in themselves. They do not believe that fate, luck, or other powerful, external forces will govern the success or failure of their ventures. They believe they personally can affect the outcome. This attribute is also consistent with achievement motivation, which is the desire to take personal responsibility, and self-confidence.

This veridical awareness often is accompanied by other valuable entrepreneurial traits—perspective and a sense of humor. The ability to retain a sense of perspective, and to "know thyself" in both strengths and weaknesses, makes it possible for an entrepreneur to laugh, to ease tensions, and to get an unfavorable situation set in a more profitable direction.

Entrepreneurial Reasoning: The Entrepreneurial Mind in Action

How do successful entrepreneurs think, what actions do they initiate, and how do they start and build businesses? By understanding the attitudes, behaviors, management competencies, experience, and know-how that contribute to entrepreneurial success, one has some useful benchmarks for gauging what to do. Exhibit 2.7 examines the role of opportunity in entrepreneurship.

EXHIBIT 2.7

Opportunity Knocks—Or Does It Hide? An Examination of the Role of Opportunity Recognition in Entrepreneurship

Number (and Proportion) of Opportunities of Various Sources and Types

Sources of Opportunities	Entrepreneurs	Nonentrepreneurs
Prior work	67 (58.3%)	13 (48.2%)
Prior employment	36	6
Prior consulting work	11	4
Prior business	20	2
Network	25 (21.7%)	8 (29.6%)
Social contact	7	6
Business contact	18	2
Thinking by analogy	13 (11.3%)	6 (22.2%)
Partner	10 (8.7%)	—

Types of Opportunities	Entrepreneurs	Nonentrepreneurs
Niche expansion/ underserved niche	29 (25.2%)	7 (29.2%)
Customer need	34 (29.6%)	6 (25.0%)
Own firm's need	6 (5.2%)	1 (4.2%)
Better technology	46 (40.0%)	10 (41.7%)

Source: Charlene, Zeitsma, "Opportunity Knocks—Or Does it Hide? An Examination of the *Role of Opportunity Recognition in Entrepreneurship*." In P. D. Reynolds, et al., eds., *Frontiers of Entrepreneurship Research: 1999*, Babson Park, MA: Babson College. Used by permission of the author.

Note: Numbers equal total people in the sample allocated to each category. Numbers in parentheses equal percentage of total surveyed.

---

[19] W. H. Stewart, Jr., W. E. Watson, J. C. Carland, and J. W. Carland, "A Comparison of Entrepreneurs, Small Business Owners, and Corporate Managers," *Journal of Business Venturing* 14, no. 2 (1999).

EXHIBIT 2.8

Who Is the Entrepreneur?

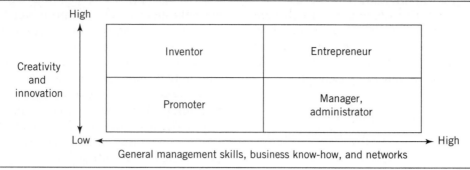

Successful entrepreneurs have a wide range of personality types. Most research about entrepreneurs has focused on the influences of genes, family, education, career experience, and so forth, but no psychological model has been supported. Studies have shown that an entrepreneur does not need specific inherent traits, but rather a set of acquired skills.[20] Perhaps one Price-Babson College fellow phrased it best when he said, "One does not want to overdo the personality stuff, but there is a certain ring to it."[21]

"There is no evidence of an ideal entrepreneurial personality. Great entrepreneurs can be either gregarious or low-key, analytical or intuitive, charismatic or boring, good with details or terrible, delegators or control freaks. What you need is a capacity to execute in certain key ways."[22] Successful entrepreneurs share common attitudes and behaviors. They work hard and are driven by an intense commitment and determined perseverance; they see the cup half full, rather than half empty; they strive for integrity; they thrive on the competitive desire to excel and win; they are dissatisfied with the status quo and seek opportunities to improve almost any situation they encounter; they use failure as a tool for learning and eschew perfection in favor of effectiveness; and they believe they can personally make an enormous difference in the final outcome of their ventures and their lives.

Those who have succeeded speak of these attitudes and behaviors time and again.[23] For example, two famous entrepreneurs have captured the intense commitment and perseverance of entrepreneurs. Wally Amos, famous for his chocolate chip cookies,

said, "You can do anything you want to do."[24] John Johnson of Johnson Publishing Company (publisher of *Ebony*) expressed it this way: "You need to think yourself out of a corner, meet needs, and never, never accept no for an answer."[25]

Successful entrepreneurs possess not only a creative and innovative flair, but also solid management skills, business know-how, and sufficient contacts. Exhibit 2.8 demonstrates this relationship.

Inventors, noted for their creativity, often lack the necessary management skills and business know-how. Promoters usually lack serious general management and business skills and true creativity. Managers govern, police, and ensure the smooth operation of the status quo; their management skills, while high, are tuned to efficiency as well, and creativity is usually not required. Although the management skills of the manager and the entrepreneur overlap, the manager is more driven by conservation of resources and the entrepreneur is more opportunity-driven.[26]

The Concept of Apprenticeship

Shaping and Managing an Apprenticeship

When one looks at successful entrepreneurs, one sees profiles of careers rich in experience. Time and again there is a pattern among successful entrepreneurs. They have all acquired 10 or more years of substantial experience, built contacts, garnered the know-how, and established a track record

---

[20] W. Lee, "What Successful Entrepreneurs *Really* Do," Lee Communications, 2001.

[21] Comment made during a presentation at the June 1987 Price-Babson College Fellows Program by Jerry W. Gustafson, Coleman-Fannie May Candies Professor of Entrepreneurship, Beloit College, at Babson College.

[22] Lee, "What Successful Entrepreneurs *Really* Do," Lee Communications, 2001.

[23] See the excellent summary of a study of the first 21 inductees into Babson College's Academy of Distinguished Entrepreneurs by J. A. Hornaday and N. Tieken, "Capturing Twenty-One Heffalumps," in *Frontiers of Entrepreneurship Research: 1983*, pp. 23, 50.

[24] Made during a speech at his induction in 1982 into the Academy of Distinguished Entrepreneurs, Babson College.

[25] Made during a speech at his induction in 1979 into the Academy of Distinguished Entrepreneurs, Babson College.

[26] Timmons, Muzyka, Stevenson, and Bygrave, "Opportunity Recognition: The Core of Entrepreneurship," pp. 42–49.

in the industry, market, and technology niche within which they eventually launch, acquire, or build a business. Frequently they have acquired intimate knowledge of the customer, distribution channels, and market through direct sales and marketing experience. The more successful ones have made money for their employer before doing it for themselves. Consider the following examples:

- Apple Computer founders Steve Jobs and Steve Wozniak were computer enthusiasts as preteens and had accumulated a relatively lengthy amount of experience by the time they started the company in their mid-20s. In entirely new industries such as PCs, a few years can be a large amount of experience.

- Paul Tobin had no prior cellular phone experience when he was picked up by John Kluge to launch Cellular One of eastern Massachusetts—but neither did anyone else! He had had six years of experience at Satellite Business Systems in marketing and had previously spent over five years launching and building his own company in a nontechnology business. His learning curves as an entrepreneur were invaluable in the next start-up.

- Jeff Parker had worked for 10 years in the bond-trading business at three major investment banks; he had sold, managed, and built a substantial trading business at one of the investment banks. His technical and computer background enabled him to write programs to assist bond traders on the first Apple computers. He launched Technical Data Corporation with $100,000, and built the first online computer system for bond traders. A few years later, his company was sold to Telerate for more than $20 million.[27]

Tens of thousands of similar examples exist. There are always exceptions to any such pattern, but if you want the odds in your favor, get the experience first. Successful entrepreneurs are likely to be older and to have at least 8 to 10 years of experience. They are likely to have accumulated enough net worth to contribute to funding the venture or to have a track record impressive enough to give investors and creditors the necessary confidence. Finally, they usually have found and nurtured relevant business and other contacts and networks that ultimately contribute to the success of their ventures.

The first 10 or so years after leaving school can make or break an entrepreneur's career in terms of how well he or she is prepared for serious entrepreneuring. Evidence suggests that the most durable entrepreneurial careers, those found to last 25 years or more, were begun across a broad age spectrum, but after the person selected prior work or a career to prepare specifically for an entrepreneurial career.

Having relevant experience, know-how, attitudes, behaviors, and skills appropriate for a particular venture opportunity can dramatically improve the odds for success. The other side of the coin is that if an entrepreneur does not have these, then he or she will have to learn them while launching and growing the business. The tuition for such an approach is often greater than most entrepreneurs can afford.

Since entrepreneurs frequently evolve from an entrepreneurial heritage or are shaped and nurtured by their closeness to entrepreneurs and others, the concept of an apprenticeship can be a useful one. Much of what an entrepreneur needs to know about entrepreneuring comes from learning by doing. Knowing what to prepare for, where the windows for acquiring the relevant exposure lie, how to anticipate these, where to position oneself, and when to move on can be quite useful.

As Howard Stevenson of the Harvard Business School has often reminded us when teaching in the Price-Babson College Fellows Program, and elsewhere:

> You have to approach the world as an equal. There is no such thing as being supplicant. You are trying to work and create a better solution by creating action among a series of people who are relatively equal. We destroy potential entrepreneurs by putting them in a velvet-lined rut, by giving them jobs that pay too much, and by telling them they are too good, before they get adequate intelligence, experience, and responsibility.

Windows of Apprenticeship

Exhibit 2.9 summarizes the key elements of an apprenticeship and experience curve and relates these to age windows.[28] Age windows are especially important because of the inevitable time it takes to create and build a successful activity, whether it is a new venture or within another organization.

There is a saying in the venture capital business that the "lemons," or losers, in a portfolio ripen in about two and one-half years and that the "pearls," or winners, usually take seven or eight years to come to fruition. Therefore, seven years is a realistic time frame to expect to grow a higher-potential business to a point where a capital gain can be realized. Interestingly, presidents of large corporations, presidents of

[27] This example is drawn from "Technical Data Corporation," HBS Cases 283-072, 283-073, Harvard Business School, 198-1.
[28] The authors wish to acknowledge the contributions to this thinking by Harvey "Chet" Krentzman, entrepreneur, lecturer, author, and nurturer of at least three dozen growth-minded ventures over the past 20 years.

EXHIBIT 2.9

Windows of Entrepreneurial Apprenticeship

Elements of the Apprenticeship and Experience Curve	Age			
	20s	*30s*	*40s*	*50s*
1. **Relevant business experience**	Low	Moderate to high	Higher	Highest
2. **Management skills and know-how**	Low to moderate	Moderate to high	High	High
3. **Entrepreneurial goals and commitment**	Varies widely	Focused high	High	High
4. **Drive and energy**	Highest	High	Moderate	Lowest
5. **Wisdom and judgment**	Lowest	Higher	Higher	Highest
6. **Focus of apprenticeship**	Discussing what you enjoy; key is learning business, sales, marketing; profit and loss responsibility	General management Division management Founder	Growing and harvesting	Reinvesting
7. **Dominant life-stage issues***	Realizing your dream of adolescence and young adulthood	Personal growth and new directions and ventures	Renewal, regeneration, reinvesting in the system	

*From *The Seasons of a Man's Life* by Daniel Levinson, copyright © 1978 by Daniel J. Levinson. Used by permission of Alfred A. Knopf, a division of Random House, Inc.

colleges, and self-employed professionals often describe years as the time it takes to do something significant.

The implications of this are quite provocative. First, time is precious. Assume an entrepreneur spends the first five years after college or graduate school gaining relevant experience. He or she will be 25 to 30 years of age (or maybe as old as 35) when launching a new venture. By the age of 50, there will have been time for starting, at most, three successful new ventures. What's more, entrepreneurs commonly go through false starts or even a failure at first in the trial-and-error process of learning the entrepreneurial ropes. As a result, the first venture may not be launched until later (i.e., in the entrepreneur's mid- to late 30s). This would leave time to grow the current venture and maybe one more. (There is always the possibility of staying with a venture and growing it to a larger company of $50 million or more in sales.)

Reflecting on Exhibit 2.9 will reveal some other paradoxes and dilemmas. For one thing, just when an entrepreneur's drive, energy, and ambition are at a peak, the necessary relevant business experience and management skills are least developed, and those critical elements, wisdom and judgment, are in their infancy. Later, when an entrepreneur has gained the necessary experience in the "deep, dark canyons of uncertainty" and has thereby gained wisdom and judgment, age begins to take its toll. Also, patience and perseverance to relentlessly pursue a long-term vision need to be balanced with the urgency and realism to make it happen. Flexibility to stick with the moving opportunity targets and to abandon some and shift to others is also required. However, flexibility and the ability to act with urgency disappear as the other commitments of life are assumed.

The Concept of Apprenticeship: Acquiring the 50,000 Chunks

During the past several years, studies about entrepreneurs have tended to confirm what practitioners have known all along: that some attitudes, behaviors, and know-how can be acquired and that some of these attributes are more desirable than others. It is also clear that apprenticeship is a vital aspect of entrepreneurial education.

Increasingly, research studies on the career paths of entrepreneurs and the self-employed suggest that the role of experience and know-how is central in successful venture creation. Many successful entrepreneurs do not have prior industry experience. More critical to the entrepreneur is the ability to gain information and act on it.[29] Evidence also suggests that success is linked to preparation and planning.[30] This is what getting 50,000 chunks of experience is all about.

[29] K. H. Vesper, "New Venture Ideas: Don't Overlook the Experience Factor," *Harvard Business Review*, reprinted in *Growing Concerns: Building and Managing the Smaller Business*, ed. D. E. Gumpert (New York: John Wiley & Sons, 1984), pp. 28–55.
[30] See R. Ronstadt's and H. Stevenson's studies reported in *Frontiers of Entrepreneurship Research: 1983.*

Although formal market research may provide useful information, it is also important to recognize the entrepreneur's collective, qualitative judgment must be weighted most heavily in evaluating opportunities. One study found that entrepreneurs view believing in the idea, and experimenting with new venture ideas that result in both failures and successes, as the most important components of opportunity recognition.[31]

Most successful entrepreneurs follow a pattern of apprenticeship, where they prepare for becoming entrepreneurs by gaining the relevant business experiences from parents who are self-employed or through job experiences. They do not leave acquisition of experience to accident or osmosis. As entrepreneur Harvey "Chet" Krentzman has said, "Know what you know and what you *don't* know."

Role Models

Numerous studies show a strong connection between the presence of role models and the emergence of entrepreneurs. For instance, an early study showed that more than half of those starting new businesses had parents who owned businesses.[32] Likewise, 70 percent of MIT graduates who started technology businesses had entrepreneurial parents.[33] The authors summarized it this way:

> Family firms spawn entrepreneurs. Older generations provide leadership and role modeling. This phenomenon cuts across industries, firm size and gender.

The Babson College Historically Black Colleges and Universities Case Writing Consortium write teaching cases featuring African American entrepreneurs. The experiences of these black entrepreneurs are exactly the role modeling that inspires students.

Myths and Realities

Folklore and stereotypes about entrepreneurs and entrepreneurial success are remarkably durable, even in these informed and sophisticated times. More is known about the founders and the process of entrepreneurship than ever before.

However, certain myths enjoy recurring attention and popularity, in part because while generalities may apply to certain types of entrepreneurs and particular situations, the great variety of founders tends to defy generalization. Exhibit 2.10 lists myths about entrepreneurs that have persisted and realities that are supported by research.

Studies have indicated that 90 percent or more of founders start their companies in the same marketplace, technology, or industry they have been working in.[34] Others have found that entrepreneurs are likely to have role models, have 8 to 10 years of experience, and be well educated. It also appears that successful entrepreneurs have a wide range of experiences in products/markets and across functional areas.[35] Studies also have shown that most successful entrepreneurs start companies in their 30s. One study of founders of high-tech companies on Route 128 in Boston showed that the average age of the founders was 40.

It has been found that entrepreneurs work both more and less than their counterparts in large organizations, that they have high degrees of satisfaction with their jobs, and that they are healthier.[36] Another study showed that nearly 21 percent of the founders were over 40 when they embarked on their entrepreneurial career, the majority were in their 30s, and just over one-fourth did so by the time they were 25.

What Can Be Learned?

For over 30 years, the authors have been engaged as educators, cofounders, investors, advisors, and directors of new, higher-potential ventures. Throughout the text are multipart cases about real, young entrepreneurs, including some of our former college and graduate students. You will face the same situations these aspiring entrepreneurs faced as they sought to turn dreams into reality. The cases and text, combined with other online resources, will enable you to grapple with all of the conceptual, practical, financial, and personal issues entrepreneurs encounter. This book will help you get the odds of success in your favor. It will focus your attention on developing answers for the most important of these questions, including these:

- What does an entrepreneurial career take?
- What is the difference between a good opportunity and just another idea?
- Is the opportunity I am considering the right opportunity for me now?

[31] "Successful Entrepreneurs' Insights into Opportunity Recognition," G. Hills and R. Shrader, University of Illinois, Chicago, 2000.
[32] A. Cooper and W. Dunkelberg, *A New Look at Business Entry* (San Mateo, CA: National Federation of Independent Businesses, March 1984).
[33] *Fortune,* June 7, 1999.
[34] A good summary of some of these studies is provided by R. H. Brockhaus, "The Psychology of the Entrepreneur," in *Encyclopedia of Entrepreneurship,* ed. C. Kent, D. Sexton, and K. Vesper (Englewood Cliffs, NJ: Prentice-Hall, 1982), pp. 50, 55.
[35] Over 80 studies in this area have been reported in *Frontiers of Entrepreneurship Research* (Babson Park, MA: Babson College) for the years 1981 through 1997.
[36] Stevenson, "Who Are the Harvard Self-Employed?" p. 233.

EXHIBIT 2.10

Myths and Realities about Entrepreneurs

Myth 1—Entrepreneurs are born, not made.

Reality—While entrepreneurs are born with certain native intelligence, a flair for creating, and energy, these talents by themselves are like unmolded clay or an unpainted canvas. The making of an entrepreneur occurs by accumulating the relevant skills, know-how, experiences, and contacts over a period of years and includes large doses of self-development. The creative capacity to envision and then pursue an opportunity is a direct descendant of at least 10 or more years of experience that lead to pattern recognition.

Myth 2—Anyone can start a business.

Reality—Entrepreneurs who recognize the difference between an idea and an opportunity, and who think big enough, start businesses that have a better chance of succeeding. Luck, to the extent it is involved, requires good preparation. And the easiest part is starting. What is hardest is surviving, sustaining, and building a venture so its founders can realize a harvest. Perhaps only one in 10 to 20 new businesses that survive five years or more results in a capital gain for the founders.

Myth 3—Entrepreneurs are gamblers.

Reality—Successful entrepreneurs take very careful, calculated risks. They try to influence the odds, often by getting others to share risk with them and by avoiding or minimizing risks if they have the choice. Often they slice up the risk into smaller, quite digestible pieces; only then do they commit the time or resources to determine if that piece will work. They do not deliberately seek to take more risk or to take unnecessary risk, nor do they shy away from unavoidable risk.

Myth 4—Entrepreneurs want the whole show to themselves.

Reality—Owning and running the whole show effectively puts a ceiling on growth. Solo entrepreneurs usually make a living. It is extremely difficult to grow a higher-potential venture by working single-handedly. Higher potential entrepreneurs build a team, an organization, and a company. Besides, 100 percent of nothing is nothing, so rather than taking a large piece of the pie, they work to make the pie bigger.

Myth 5—Entrepreneurs are their own bosses and completely independent.

Reality—Entrepreneurs are far from independent and have to serve many masters and constituencies, including partners, investors, customers, suppliers, creditors, employees, families, and those involved in social and community obligations. Entrepreneurs, however, can make free choices of whether, when, and what they care to respond to. Moreover, It Is extremely difficult, and rare, to build a business beyond $1 million to $2 million in sales single-handedly.

Myth 6—Entrepreneurs work longer and harder than managers in big companies.

Reality—There is no evidence that all entrepreneurs work more than their corporate counterparts. Some do, some do not. Some actually report that they work less.

Myth 7—Entrepreneurs experience a great deal of stress and pay a high price.

Reality—Being an entrepreneur is stressful and demanding. But there is no evidence that it is any more stressful than numerous other highly demanding professional roles, and entrepreneurs find their jobs very satisfying. They have a high sense of accomplishment, are healthier, and are much less likely to retire than those who work for others. Three times as many entrepreneurs as corporate managers say they plan to never retire.

Myth 8—Start a business and fail and you'll never raise money again.

Reality—Talented and experienced entrepreneurs—because they pursue attractive opportunities and are able to attract the right people and necessary financial and other resources to make the venture work—often head successful ventures. Further, businesses fail, but entrepreneurs do not. Failure is often the fire that tempers the steel of an entrepreneur's learning experience and street savvy.

Myth 9—Money is the most important start-up ingredient.

Reality—If the other pieces and talents are there, the money will follow, but it does not follow that an entrepreneur will succeed if he or she has enough money. Money is one of the least important ingredients in new venture success. Money is to the entrepreneur what the paint and brush are to the artist—an inert tool that in the right hands can create marvels.

Myth 10—Entrepreneurs should be young and energetic.

Reality—While these qualities may help, age is no barrier. The average age of entrepreneurs starting high-potential businesses is in the mid-30s, and there are numerous examples of entrepreneurs starting businesses in their 60s. What is critical is possessing the relevant know-how, experience, and contacts that greatly facilitate recognizing and pursuing an opportunity.

Myth 11—Entrepreneurs are motivated solely by the quest for the almighty dollar.

Reality—Entrepreneurs seeking high-potential ventures are more driven by building enterprises and realizing long-term capital gains than by instant gratification through high salaries and perks. A sense of personal achievement and accomplishment, feeling in control of their own destinies, and realizing their vision and dreams are also powerful motivators. Money is viewed as a tool and a way of keeping score, rather than an end in itself. Entrepreneurs thrive on the thrill of the chase; and, time and again, even after an entrepreneur has made a few million dollars or more, he or she will work on a new vision to build another company.

(continued)

EXHIBIT 2.10   (concluded)

Myths and Realities about Entrepreneurs

Myth 12—Entrepreneurs seek power and control over others.

Reality—Successful entrepreneurs are driven by the quest for responsibility, achievement, and results, rather than for power for its own sake. They thrive on a sense of accomplishment and of outperforming the competition, rather than a personal need for power expressed by dominating and controlling others. By virtue of their accomplishments, they may be powerful and influential, but these are more the by-products of the entrepreneurial process than a driving force behind it.

Myth 13—If an entrepreneur is talented, success will happen in a year or two.

Reality—An old maxim among venture capitalists says it all: The lemons ripen in two and a half years, but the pearls take seven or eight. Rarely is a new business established solidly in less than three or four years.

Myth 14—Any entrepreneur with a good idea can raise venture capital.

Reality—Of the ventures of entrepreneurs with good ideas who seek out venture capital, only 1 to 3 out of 100 are funded.

Myth 15—If an entrepreneur has enough start-up capital, he or she can't miss.

Reality—The opposite is often true; that is, too much money at the outset often creates euphoria and a spoiled-child syndrome. The accompanying lack of discipline and impulsive spending usually lead to serious problems and failure.

Myth 16—Entrepreneurs are lone wolves and cannot work with others.

Reality—The most successful entrepreneurs are leaders who build great teams and effective relationships working with peers, directors, investors, key customers, key suppliers, and the like.

Myth 17—Unless you attained 600+ on your SATs or GMATs, you'll never be a successful entrepreneur.

Reality—Entrepreneurial IQ is a unique combination of creativity, motivation, integrity, leadership, team building, analytical ability, and ability to deal with ambiguity and adversity.

- Why do some firms grow quickly to several million dollars in sales but then stumble, never growing beyond a single-product firm?

- What are the critical tasks and hurdles in seizing an opportunity and building the business?

- How much money do I need and when, where, and how can I get it—on acceptable terms?

- What financing sources, strategies, and mechanisms can I use from prestart, through meaningful careers in new and growing firms, and in the early growth stage to the harvest of my venture?

- What are the minimum resources I need to gain control over the opportunity, and how can I do this?

- Is a business plan needed? If so, what kind is needed and how and when should I develop one?

- Who are the constituents for whom I must create or add value to achieve a positive cash flow and to develop harvest options?

- What is my venture worth and how do I negotiate what to give up?

- What are the critical transitions in entrepreneurial management as a firm grows from $1 million to $5 million to $25 million in sales?

- What is it that entrepreneurial leaders do differently that enables them to achieve such competitive breakthroughs and advantages, particularly over conventional practices, but also so-called best practices?

- What are the opportunities and implications for 21st century entrepreneurs and the Internet, clean tech, and nanosciences? How can these be seized and financed?

- What do I need to know and practice in entrepreneurial reasoning and thinking to have a competitive edge?

- What are some of the pitfalls, minefields, and hazards I need to anticipate, prepare for, and respond to?

- What are the contacts and networks I need to access and to develop?

- Do I know what I do and do not know, and do I know what to do about it?

- How can I develop a personal "entrepreneurial game plan" to acquire the experience I need to succeed?

- How critical and sensitive is the timing in each of these areas?

- Why do entrepreneurs who succeed in the long term seek to maintain reputations for integrity and ethical business practices?

We believe that we can significantly improve the quality of decisions students make about entrepreneurship and thereby also improve the fit between what they aspire to do and the requirements of the particular opportunity. In many cases, those choices lead to self-employment or meaningful careers in new and growing firms and, increasingly, in large firms that "get it." In other cases, students join larger firms whose customer base and/or suppliers are principally the entrepreneurial sector. Still others seek careers in the financial institutions and professional services firms that are at the vortex of the entrepreneurial economy: venture capital, private equity, investment banks, commercial banks, consulting, accounting, and the like.

Our view of entrepreneurship is that it need not be an end in itself. Rather, it is a pathway that leads to innumerable ideas and opportunities, and opens visions of what young people can become. You will learn skills, and how to use those skills appropriately. You will learn how to tap your own and others' creativity, and to apply your new energy. You will learn the difference between another good idea and a serious opportunity. You will learn the power and potential of the entrepreneurial team. You will learn how entrepreneurs finance and grow their companies, often with ingenious bootstrapping strategies that get big results with minimal resources. You will learn the joy of self-sufficiency and independence. You will learn how entrepreneurial leaders make this happen, and give back to society. You will discover anew what it is about entrepreneurship that gives you sustaining entrepreneurial reasoning and thinking in order to fuel your dreams. One of the best perspectives on this comes from Jerry Gustafson, Coleman-Fannie May Candies Professor of Entrepreneurship and Chair, Beloit College, Beloit, Wisconsin, who was probably the first professor at a liberal arts college to create an entrepreneurship course:

> Entrepreneurship is important for its own sake. The subject frames an ideal context for students to address perennial questions concerning their identity, objectives, hopes, relation to society, and the tension between thought and action. Entrepreneurship concerns thinking of what we are as persons. . . . Furthermore, of its nature, entrepreneurship is about process. One cannot discuss entrepreneurship without encountering the importance of goal setting, information gathering, persistence, resourcefulness, and resiliency. It is not lost on students that the behaviors and styles of entrepreneurs tend to be socially rewarded, and these are precisely the behaviors we wish to see the students exhibit in the classroom.[37]

A Word of Caution: What SATs, IQ Tests, GMATs, and Others Don't Measure

Nothing in the world can take the place of persistence. Talent will not; nothing is more common than unsuccessful men with talent. Genius will not; unrewarded genius is almost a proverb. Education will not; the world is full of educated derelicts. Persistence and determination alone

are omnipotent. The slogan "Press on" has solved and solved and always will solve the problems of the human race.

President Calvin Coolidge

The following data about alumni whose careers were followed for nearly 25 years has always shocked second-year Harvard MBA students. Regardless of the measure one applies, among the very top of the class were graduates who were both highly successful and not very successful. At the bottom of the class were alumni who became outrageously successful, and others who accomplished little with their lives and exceptional education. The middle of the class achieved all points on the continuum of success. How could this be?

America's brightest fared poorly in the Third International Mathematics and Science Study comparing high school seniors from 20 nations, according to *The New York Times.* In a competition between the world's most precocious seniors, those taking physics and advanced math, the Americans performed at the bottom. The article noted,

> After decades of agonizing over the fairness of SAT scores, the differences between male and female mathematical skills, and gaps in IQ between various racial and ethnic groups, the notion of intelligence and how to measure it remains more political than scientific, and as maddenly elusive as ever.[38]

In short, there are many different kinds of intelligence—a much greater bandwidth than most researchers and test architects ever imagined. The dynamic and subtle complexities of the entrepreneurial task require its own special intelligences. How else would one explain the enormous contradiction inherent in business and financially failed geniuses?

One only need consider the critical skills and capacities that are at the heart of entrepreneurial leadership and achievement, yet are not measured by the IQ tests, SATs, GMATs, and the like that grade and sort young applicants with such imprecision. Consider the skills and capacities not measured by these tests:

✓ Leadership skills.
✓ Interpersonal skills.
✓ Team building and team playing.
✓ Creativity and ingenuity.
✓ Motivation.
✓ Learning skills (versus knowledge).
✓ Persistence and determination.
✓ Values, ethics, honesty, and integrity.

---

[37] J. Gustafson, "SEEing Is Not Only about Business," *PULSE,* 1988 (Babson Park, MA: Price-Babson College Fellows Program).
[38] "Tests Show Nobody's Smart about Intelligence," *The New York Times,* March 1, 1998, p. 4–1.

✓ Goal-setting orientation.
✓ Self-discipline.
✓ Frugality.
✓ Resourcefulness.
✓ Resiliency and capacity to handle adversity.
✓ Ability to seek, listen, and use feedback.
✓ Reliability.
✓ Dependability.
✓ Sense of humor.

It is no wonder that a number of excellent colleges and universities eliminated these measures or placed them in a proper perspective. Obviously this should not be construed to mean entrepreneurship is for dummies. Quite the opposite is true. Indeed, intelligence is a very valuable and important asset for entrepreneurs, but by itself is woefully inadequate.

Clearly just being very smart won't help much if one doesn't possess numerous other qualities (see Chapter 8, The Entrepreneurial Manager and the Team and Chapter 10, Ethical Decision Making, for an elaboration on these other qualities). A fascinating article by Chris Argyris, "Teaching Smart People How to Learn," is well worth reading to get some powerful insights into why it is often *not* the class genius who becomes most successful.[39]

A Personal Strategy

An apprenticeship can be an integral part of the process of shaping an entrepreneurial career. One principal task is to determine what kind of entrepreneur a person is likely to become, based on background, experience, and drive. Through an apprenticeship, an entrepreneur can shape a strategy and action plan to make it happen. The Crafting a Personal Entrepreneurship Strategy exercise at the end of this chapter addresses this issue more fully. For a quick inventory of your entrepreneurial attributes, do the second exercise, Personal Entrepreneurial Strategy.

Despite all the work involved in becoming an entrepreneur, the bottom line is revealing. Evidence about careers and job satisfaction of entrepreneurs all points to the same conclusion: If they had to do it over again, not only would more of them become entrepreneurs again, but also they would do it sooner.[40]

They report higher personal satisfaction with their lives and their careers than their managerial counterparts. Nearly three times as many say they plan never to retire, according to Stevenson. Numerous other studies show that the satisfaction from independence and living and working where and how they want to is a source of great satisfaction.[41] Financially, successful entrepreneurs enjoy higher incomes and a higher net worth than career managers in large companies. In addition, the successful harvest of a company usually means a capital gain of several million dollars or more and, with it, a new array of very attractive options and opportunities to do whatever they choose to do with the rest of their lives.

Entrepreneur's Creed

So much time and space would not be spent on the entrepreneurial mind if it were just of academic interest. But they are, entrepreneurs themselves believe, in large part responsible for success. When asked an open-ended question about what entrepreneurs believed are the most critical concepts, skills, and know-how for running a business—today and five years hence—their answers were very revealing. Most mentioned mental attitudes and philosophies based on entrepreneurial attributes, rather than specific skills or organizational concepts. These answers are gathered together in what might be called an entrepreneur's creed:

- Do what gives you energy—have fun.
- Figure out what can go right and make it.
- Say "can do" rather than "cannot" or "maybe."
- *Illegitimi non carborundum:* tenacity and creativity will triumph.
- Anything is possible if you believe you can do it.
- If you don't know it can't be done, then you'll go ahead and do it.
- The cup is half-full, not half-empty.
- Be dissatisfied with the way things are—and look for improvement.
- Do things differently.
- Don't take a risk if you don't have to—but take a calculated risk if it's the right opportunity for *you.*

[39] C. Argyris, "Teaching Smart People How to Learn," *Harvard Business Review,* May–June 1991.
[40] Stevenson, "Who Are the Harvard Self-Employed?" pp. 233–54.
[41] R. C. Ronstadt, "The Decision Not to Become an Entrepreneur," in *Frontiers of Entrepreneurship Research: 1983,* ed. J. A. Hornaday et al. (Babson Park, MA: Babson College, 1983), pp. 192–212; and R. C. Ronstadt, "Ex-Entrepreneurs and the Decision to Start an Entrepreneurial Career," in *Frontiers of Entrepreneurship Research: 1983,* pp. 437–60.

- Businesses fail; successful entrepreneurs learn—but keep the tuition low.
- It is easier to beg for forgiveness than to ask for permission in the first place.
- Make opportunity and results your obsession—not money.
- Money is a tool and a scorecard available to the right people with the right opportunity at the right time.
- Making money is even more fun than spending it.
- Make heroes out of others—a team builds a business; an individual makes a living.
- Take pride in your accomplishments—it's contagious!
- Sweat the details that are critical to success.

- Integrity and reliability equal long-run oil and glue.
- Accept the responsibility, less than half the credit, and more than half the blame.
- Make the pie bigger—don't waste time trying to cut smaller slices.
- Play for the long haul—it is rarely possible to get rich quickly.
- Don't pay too much—but don't lose it!
- Only the lead dog gets a change of view.
- Success is getting what you want: Happiness is wanting what you get.
- Give back.
- Embrace sustainability.
- Never give up.

Chapter Summary

- Entrepreneurs are men and women of all sizes, ages, shapes, religions, colors, and backgrounds. There is no single profile or psychological template.
- Successful entrepreneurs share seven common themes that describe their attitudes and ways of thinking and acting.
- Rather than being inborn, the behaviors inherent in these seven attributes can be nurtured, learned, and encouraged, which successful entrepreneurs model for themselves and those with whom they work.
- Entrepreneurs love competition and actually avoid risks when they can, preferring carefully calculated risks.
- Entrepreneurship can be learned; it requires an apprenticeship.
- Most entrepreneurs gain the apprenticeship over 10 years or more after the age of 21 and acquire networks, skills, and the ability to recognize business patterns.

- The entrepreneurial mind-set can benefit large, established companies today just as much as smaller firms.
- Many myths and realities about entrepreneurship provide insights for aspiring entrepreneurs.
- A word of caution: IQ tests, SATs, GMATs, LSATs, and others do not measure some of the most important entrepreneurial abilities and aptitudes.
- Most successful entrepreneurs have had a personal strategy to help them achieve their dreams and goals, both implicitly and explicitly.
- The principal task for the entrepreneur is to determine what kind of entrepreneur he or she wants to become based on his or her attitudes, behaviors, management competencies, experience, and so forth.
- Self-assessment is the hardest thing for entrepreneurs to do; but if you don't do it, you will really get into trouble. If you don't do it, who will?

Study Questions

1. Who was Ewing Marion Kauffman, what did he do, and what was his philosophy of entrepreneurial leadership?
2. What is the difference between a manager and a leader?
3. Define the seven major themes that characterize the mind-sets, attitudes, and actions of a successful entrepreneur. Which are most important, and why? How can they be encouraged and developed?
4. Entrepreneurs are made, not born. Why is this so? Do you agree, and why or why not?

5. Explain what is meant by the apprenticeship concept. Why is it so important to young entrepreneurs?
6. What is your personal entrepreneurial strategy? How should it change?
7. "What is one person's ham is another person's poison." What does this mean?
8. Can you evaluate thoroughly your attraction to entrepreneurship?
9. Who should be an entrepreneur and who should not?

Internet Resources for Chapter 2

www.benlore.com *The Entrepreneur's Mind is a Web resource that presents an array of real-life stories and advice from successful entrepreneurs and industry experts on the many different facets of entrepreneurship and emerging business.*

www.entrepreneurs.about.com *Comprehensive media-sponsored Web sites on small business and entrepreneurs.*
www.blackenterprise.com *Black Enterprise is a business news and investment resource aimed at African American entrepreneurs and business owners.*

MIND STRETCHERS

Have You Considered?

1. Who can be an entrepreneur, and who cannot? Why?

2. Why has there been a 30-year brain drain of the best entrepreneurial talent in America away from the largest established companies? Can this be reversed? How?

3. How do you personally stack up against the seven entrepreneurial mind-sets? What do you need to develop and improve?

4. If you work for a larger company, what is it doing to attract and keep the best entrepreneurial talent?

5. How would you describe and evaluate your own apprenticeship? What else has to happen?

6. Is Bill Gates an entrepreneur, a leader, a manager? How can we know?

7. How will you personally define success in 5, 10, and 25 years? Why?

8. Assume that at age 40 to 50 years, you have achieved a net worth of $25 million to $50 million in today's dollars. So what? Then what?

9. David Neeleman, founder of JetBlue, recently stepped down as CEO and chairman of the board. Why did he start JetBlue, (he was already wealthy from his success at Moms Air and Southwest Air). What might he revolutionize next?

10. Great athletic talent is not equal to a great athlete. Why? How does this apply to entrepreneurship?

Exercise 1

Crafting a Personal Entrepreneurial Strategy

If you don't know where you're going, any path will take you there.
From *The Wizard of Oz*

Crafting a personal entrepreneurial strategy can be viewed as the personal equivalent of developing a business plan. As with planning in other situations, the process itself is more important than the plan.

The key is the process and discipline that put an individual in charge of evaluating and shaping choices and initiating action that makes sense, rather than letting things just happen. Having a longer-term sense of direction can be highly motivating. It also can be extremely helpful in determining when to say no (which is much harder than saying yes) and can temper impulsive hunches with a more thoughtful strategic purpose. This is important because today's choices, whether or not they are thought out, become tomorrow's track record. They may end up shaping an entrepreneur in ways that he or she may not find so attractive 10 years hence and, worse, may also result in failure to obtain just those experiences needed in order to have high-quality opportunities later on.

Therefore, a personal strategy can be invaluable, but it need not be a prison sentence. It is a point of departure, rather than a contract of indenture, and it can and will change over time. This process of developing a personal strategy for an entrepreneurial career is a very individual one and, in a sense, one of self-selection.

Reasons for planning are similar to those for developing a business plan (see Chapter 7). Planning helps an entrepreneur to manage the risks and uncertainties of the future; helps him or her to work smarter, rather than simply harder; keeps him or her in a future-oriented frame of mind; helps him or her to develop and update a keener strategy by testing the sensibility of his or her ideas and approaches with others; helps motivate; gives him or her a "results orientation"; helps make him or her effective in managing and coping with what is by nature a stressful role; and so forth.

Rationalizations and reasons given for not planning, like those that will be covered in Chapter 7, are that plans are out of date as soon as they are finished and that no one knows what tomorrow will bring and, therefore, it is dangerous to commit to uncertainty. Further, the cautious, anxious person may find that setting personal goals creates a further source of tension and pressure and a heightened fear of failure. There is also the possibility that future or yet unknown options, which actually might be more attractive than the one chosen, may become lost or be excluded.

Commitment to a career-oriented goal, particularly for an entrepreneur who is younger and lacks much real-world experience, can be premature. For the person who is inclined to be a compulsive and obsessive competitor and achiever, goal setting may add gasoline to the fire. And, invariably, some events and environmental factors beyond one's control may boost or sink the best-laid plans.

Personal plans fail for the same reasons as business plans, including frustration when the plan appears not to work immediately and problems of changing behavior from an activity-oriented routine to one that is goal-oriented. Other problems are developing plans that are based on admirable missions, such as improving performance, rather than goals, and developing plans that fail to anticipate obstacles, and those that lack progress milestones, reviews, and so forth.

A Conceptual Scheme for Self-Assessment

Exhibit 2.11 shows one conceptual scheme for thinking about the self-assessment process called the Johari Window. According to this scheme, there are two sources of information about the self: the individual and others. According to the Johari Window, there are three areas in which individuals can learn about themselves.

There are two potential obstacles to self-assessment efforts. First, it is hard to obtain feedback; second, it is hard to receive and benefit from it. Everyone possesses a personal frame of reference, values, and so forth, which influence first impressions. It is, therefore, almost impossible for an individual to obtain an unbiased view of himself or herself from someone else. Further, in most social situations, people usually present self-images that they want to preserve, protect, and defend; and behavioral norms usually exist that prohibit people from telling a person that he or she is presenting a face or impression that differs from what

the person thinks is being presented. For example, most people will not point out to a stranger during a conversation that a piece of spinach is prominently dangling from between his or her front teeth.

The first step for an individual in self-assessment is to generate data through observation of his or her thoughts and actions and by getting feedback from others for the purposes of (1) becoming aware of blind spots and (2) reinforcing or changing existing perceptions of both strengths and weaknesses.

Once an individual has generated the necessary data, the next steps in the self-assessment process are to study the data generated, develop insights, and then establish apprenticeship goals to gain any learning, experience, and so forth.

Finally, choices can be made in terms of goals and opportunities to be created or seized.

Crafting an Entrepreneurial Strategy

Profiling the Past

One useful way to begin the process of self-assessment and planning is for an individual to think about his or her entrepreneurial roots (what he or she has done, his or her preferences in terms of lifestyle and work style, etc.) and couple this with a look into the future and what he or she would like most to be doing and how he or she would like to live.

In this regard, everyone has a personal history that has played and will continue to play a significant role in influencing his or her values, motivations, attitudes, and behaviors. Some of this history may provide useful insight into prior entrepreneurial inclinations, as well as into his or her future potential fit with an entrepreneurial role. Unless an entrepreneur is enjoying what he or she is doing for work most of the time, when in his or her 30s, 40s, or 50s, having a great deal of money without enjoying the journey will be a very hollow success.

Profiling the Present

It is useful to profile the present. Possession of certain personal entrepreneurial attitudes and behaviors (i.e., an "entrepreneurial mind") has been linked to successful careers

---

EXHIBIT 2.11

Peeling the Onion

	Known to Entrepreneur and Team	Not Known to Entrepreneur and Team
Known to Prospective Investors and Stakeholders	Area 1 *Known area:* (what you see is what you get)	Area 2 *Blind area:* (we do not know what we do not know, but you do)
Not Known to Prospective Investors and Stakeholders	Area 3 *Hidden area:* (unshared—you do not know what we do, but the deal does not get done until we find out)	Area 4 *Unknown area:* (no venture is certain or risk free)

Source: J. McIntyre, I. M. Rubin, and D. A. Kolb, *Organizational Psychology: Experiential Approach*, 2nd ed., © 1974. Adapted by permission of Pearson Education, Inc., Upper Saddle River, NJ.

in entrepreneurship. These attitudes and behaviors deal with such factors as commitment, determination, and perseverance; the drive to achieve and grow; an orientation toward goals; the taking of initiative and personal responsibility; and so forth.

In addition, various role demands result from the pursuit of opportunities. These role demands are external in the sense that they are imposed upon every entrepreneur by the nature of entrepreneurship. As will be discussed in Chapter 7, the external business environment is given, the demands of a higher-potential business in terms of stress and commitment are given, and the ethical values and integrity of key actors are given. Required as a result of the demands, pressures, and realities of starting, owning, and operating a substantial business are such factors as accommodation to the venture, toleration of stress, and so forth. A realistic appraisal of entrepreneurial attitudes and behaviors in light of the requirements of the entrepreneurial role is useful as part of the self-assessment process.

Also, part of any self-assessment is an assessment of management competencies and what "chunks" of experience, know-how, and contacts need to be developed.

Getting Constructive Feedback

A Scottish proverb says, "The greatest gift that God hath given us is to see ourselves as others see us." One common denominator among successful entrepreneurs is a desire to know how they are doing and where they stand. They have an uncanny knack for asking the right questions about their performance at the right time. This thirst to know is driven by a keen awareness that such feedback is vital to improving their performance and their odds for success.

Receiving feedback from others can be a most demanding experience. The following list of guidelines in receiving feedback can help:

- Feedback needs to be solicited, ideally, from those who know the individual well (e.g., someone he or she has worked with or for) and who can be trusted. The context in which the person is known needs to be considered. For example, a business colleague may be better able to comment upon an individual's managerial skills than a friend. Or a personal friend may be able to comment on motivation or on the possible effects on the family situation. It is helpful to chat with the person before asking him or her to provide any specific written impressions and to indicate the specific areas he or she can best comment upon. One way to do this is to formulate questions first. For example, the person could be told, "I've been asking myself the following question . . . and I would really like your impressions in that regard."

- Specific comments in areas that are particularly important either personally or to the success of the venture need to be solicited and more detail probed if the person giving feedback is not clear. A good way to check if a statement is being understood correctly is to paraphrase the statement. The person needs to be encouraged to describe and give examples of specific situations or behaviors that have influenced the impressions he or she has developed.

- Feedback is most helpful if it is neither all positive nor all negative, but it should be actionable.

- Feedback needs to be obtained in writing so that the person can take some time to think about the issues, and so feedback from various sources can be pulled together.

- The person asking for feedback needs to be honest and straightforward with himself or herself and with others.

- Time is too precious and the road to new venture success too treacherous to clutter this activity with game playing or hidden agendas. The person receiving feedback needs to avoid becoming defensive and taking negative comments personally.

- It is important to listen carefully to what is being said and think about it. Answering, debating, or rationalizing should be avoided.

- An assessment of whether the person soliciting feedback has considered all important information and has been realistic in his or her inferences and conclusions needs to be made.

- Help needs to be requested in identifying common threads or patterns, possible implications of self-assessment data and certain weaknesses (including alternative inferences or conclusions), and other relevant information that is missing.

- Additional feedback from others needs to be sought to verify feedback and to supplement the data.

- Reaching final conclusions or decisions needs to be left until a later time.

Putting It All Together

Exhibit 2.12 shows the relative fit of an entrepreneur with a venture opportunity, given his or her relevant attitudes and behaviors and relevant general management skills, experience, know-how, and contacts, and given the role demands of the venture opportunity. A clean appraisal is almost impossible. Self-assessment just is not that simple. The process is cumulative, and what an entrepreneur does about weaknesses, for example, is far more important than what the particular weaknesses might be. After all, everyone has weaknesses.

Thinking Ahead

As it is in developing business plans, goal setting is important in personal planning. Few people are effective goal setters. Perhaps fewer than 5 percent have ever committed their goals to writing, and perhaps fewer than 25 percent of adults even set goals mentally.

Again, goal setting is a process, a way of dealing with the world. Effective goal setting demands time, self-discipline, commitment and dedication, and practice. Goals, once set, do not become static targets.

EXHIBIT 2.12

Fit of the Entrepreneur and the Venture Opportunity

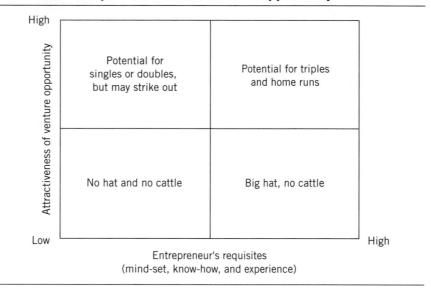

A number of distinct steps are involved in goal setting, steps that are repeated over and over as conditions change:

- Establishment of goals that are specific and concrete (rather than abstract and out of focus), measurable, related to time (i.e., specific about what will be accomplished over a certain time period), realistic, and attainable.

- Establishment of priorities, including the identification of conflicts and trade-offs and how these can be resolved.

- Identification of potential problems and obstacles that could prevent goals from being attained.

- Specification of action steps that are to be performed to accomplish the goal.

- Indication of how results will be measured.

- Establishment of milestones for reviewing progress and tying these to specific dates on a calendar.

- Identification of risks involved in meeting the goals.

- Identification of help and other resources that may be needed to obtain goals.

- Periodic review of progress and revision of goals.

Exercise 2
Personal Entrepreneurial Strategy

The exercise that follows will help you gather data, both from yourself and from others; evaluate the data you have collected; and craft a personal entrepreneurial strategy.

The exercise requires active participation on your part. The estimated time to complete the exercise is 1.5 to 3 hours. Those who have completed the exercise—students, practicing entrepreneurs, and others—report that the self-assessment process was worthwhile and it was also demanding. Issues addressed will require a great deal of thought, and there are, of course, no wrong answers.

Although this is a self-assessment exercise, it is useful to receive feedback. Whether you choose to solicit feedback and how much, if any, of the data you have collected you

choose to share with others is your decision. The exercise will be of value only to the extent that you are honest and realistic in your approach.

A complex set of factors clearly goes into making someone a successful entrepreneur. No individual has all the personal qualities, managerial skills, and the like, indicated in the exercise. And, even if an individual did possess most of these, his or her values, preferences, and such may make him or her a very poor risk to succeed as an entrepreneur.

The presence or absence of any single factor does not guarantee success or failure as an entrepreneur. Before proceeding, remember, it is no embarrassment to reach for the stars and fail to reach them. It is a failure not to reach for the stars.

Part I: Profile of the Past: Tear Out and Complete

Name:

Date:

STEP 1
Examine Your Personal Preferences.
What gives you energy, and why? These are things from either work or leisure, or both, that give you the greatest amount of personal satisfaction, sense of enjoyment, and energy.

Activities/Situations That Give You Energy	Reasons for Your Joy and Satisfaction

What takes away your energy, and why? These create for you the greatest amount of personal dissatisfaction, anxiety, or discontent and take away your energy and motivation.

Activities/Situations That Sap Your Energy	Reasons for This

Rank (from the most to the least) the items you have just listed:

Gives Energy	Takes Energy

In 20 to 30 years, how would you like to spend an ideal month? Include in your description your desired lifestyle, work style, income, friends, and so forth, and a comment about what attracts you to, and what repels you about, this ideal existence.

Complete the idea generation guide in Chapter 5 and list the common attributes of the 10 businesses you wanted to enter and the 10 businesses you did not:

Attributes—Would Energize	Attributes—Would Turn Off

Which of these attributes would give you energy and which would take it away, and why?

Attribute	Give or Take Energy	Reason

Complete this sentence: "I would/would not like to start/acquire my own business someday because . . ."

Discuss any patterns, issues, insights, and conclusions that have emerged:

Rank the following in terms of importance to you:

	Important	←	———	→	Irrelevant
Location	5	4	3	2	1
Geography (particular area)	5	4	3	2	1
Community size and nature	5	4	3	2	1
Community involvement	5	4	3	2	1
Commuting distance (one way):					
20 minutes or less	5	4	3	2	1
30 minutes or less	5	4	3	2	1
60 minutes or less	5	4	3	2	1
More than 60 minutes	5	4	3	2	1
Lifestyle and Work Style					
Size of business:					
Less than $2 million sales or under 5–10 employees	5	4	3	2	1
More than $2 million sales or 5–10 employees	5	4	3	2	1
More than $10 million sales and 40–50 employees	5	4	3	2	1
Rate of real growth:					
Fast (over 25%/year)	5	4	3	2	1
Moderate (10% to 15%/year)	5	4	3	2	1
Slow (less than 5%/year)	5	4	3	2	1
Workload (weekly):					
Over 70 hours	5	4	3	2	1
55 to 60 hours	5	4	3	2	1
40 hours or less	5	4	3	2	1
Marriage	5	4	3	2	1
Family	5	4	3	2	1
Travel away from home:					
More than 60%	5	4	3	2	1
30% to 60%	5	4	3	2	1
Less than 30%	5	4	3	2	1
None	5	4	3	2	1
Standard of Living					
Tight belt/later capital gains	5	4	3	2	1
Average/limited capital gains	5	4	3	2	1
High/no capital gains	5	4	3	2	1
Become very rich	5	4	3	2	1
Personal Development					
Utilization of skill and education	5	4	3	2	1
Opportunity for personal growth	5	4	3	2	1
Contribution to society	5	4	3	2	1
Positioning for opportunities	5	4	3	2	1
Generation of significant contacts, experience, and know-how	5	4	3	2	1
Status and Prestige	5	4	3	2	1
Impact on Ecology and Environment: Sustainability	5	4	3	2	1
Capital Required					
From you	5	4	3	2	1
From others	5	4	3	2	1
Other Considerations	5	4	3	2	1

Imagine you had $1,000 with which to buy the items you ranked on the previous page. Indicate below how you would allocate the money. For example, the item that is most important should receive the greatest amount. You may spend nothing on some items, you may spend equal amounts on some, and so forth. Once you have allocated the $1,000, rank the items in order of importance, the most important being number 1.

Item	Share of $1,000	Rank
Location		
Lifestyle and work style		
Standard of living		
Personal development		
Status and prestige		
Ecology and environment		
Capital required		
Other considerations		

What are the implications of these rankings?

STEP 2
Examine Your Personal History.
List activities (1) that have provided you financial support in the past (e.g., a part-time or full-time job or your own business), (2) that have contributed to your well-being (e.g., financing your education or a hobby), and (3) that you have done on your own (e.g., building something).

Discuss why you became involved in each of the activities just listed and what specifically influenced each of your decisions. Which were driven by financial necessity and which by opportunity?

Discuss what you learned about yourself, about self-employment, about managing people, and about working for money and someone else, versus creating or seizing an opportunity, and building something from scratch.

List and discuss your full-time work experience, including descriptions of specific tasks in which you innovated and led something, the number of people you led, whether you were successful, and so forth.

Discuss why you became involved in each of the employment situations just listed and what specifically influenced each of your decisions.

Discuss what you learned about yourself; about creating, innovating, or originating a project, club, or business; and about making money.

List and discuss other activities, such as sports, in which you have participated; indicate whether each activity was individual (e.g., chess or tennis) or team (e.g., football). Did you have a leadership role?

What lessons and insights emerged, and how will these apply to life as an entrepreneur?

If you have ever been fired from or quit either a full-time or part-time job, indicate the job, why you were fired or quit, the circumstances, and what you have learned and what difference this has made regarding working for yourself or someone else.

If you changed jobs or relocated, indicate the job, why the change occurred, the circumstances, and what you have learned from those experiences.

Among those individuals who have mentored and influenced you most, do any own and operate their own businesses or engage independently in a profession (e.g., certified public accountant)? How have these people influenced you? How do you view them and their roles? What have you learned from them about self-employment? Include a discussion of the things that attract or repel you, the trade-offs they have had to consider, the risks they have faced and rewards they have enjoyed, and entry strategies that have worked for them.

If you have ever started a business of any kind or worked in a small company, list the things you liked most and those you liked least, and why:

Like Most	Reason	Like Least	Reason

If you have ever worked for a larger company (over 500 employees or over $50 million in sales), list the things you liked most and those you liked least about your work, and why.

Like Most	Reason	Like Least	Reason

Part II: Profile of the Present: Where You Are

STEP 1
Examine Your "Entrepreneurial Mind."
Examine your attitudes, behaviors, and know-how. Rank yourself (on a scale of 5 to 1).

	Strongest	←	———	→	Weakest
Commitment and Determination					
Decisiveness	5	4	3	2	1
Tenacity	5	4	3	2	1
Discipline	5	4	3	2	1
Persistence in solving problems	5	4	3	2	1
Willingness to sacrifice	5	4	3	2	1
Total immersion in the mission	5	4	3	2	1
Courage					
Moral strength	5	4	3	2	1
Fearless experimentation	5	4	3	2	1
Not afraid of conflicts, failure	5	4	3	2	1
Intense curiosity in the face of risk	5	4	3	2	1
Opportunity Obsession					
Leadership in shaping the opportunity					
Having knowledge of customers' needs	5	4	3	2	1
Being market driven	5	4	3	2	1
Obsession with value creation and enhancement	5	4	3	2	1
Tolerance of Risk, Ambiguity, and Uncertainty					
Calculated risk taker	5	4	3	2	1
Risk minimizer	5	4	3	2	1
Risk sharer					
Tolerance of uncertainty and lack of structure	5	4	3	2	1
Tolerance of stress and conflict	5	4	3	2	1
Ability to resolve problems and integrate solutions	5	4	3	2	1
Creativity, Self-Reliance, and Ability to Adapt					
Nonconventional, open-minded, lateral thinker (helicopter mind)	5	4	3	2	1
Restlessness with status quo	5	4	3	2	1
Ability to adapt	5	4	3	2	1
Lack of fear of failure	5	4	3	2	1
Ability to conceptualize and to "sweat details"	5	4	3	2	1

	Strongest	←	——	→	Weakest
Motivation to Excel					
Goal and results orientation	5	4	3	2	1
Drive to achieve and grow (self-imposed)	5	4	3	2	1
Low need for status and power	5	4	3	2	1
Ability to be interpersonally supporting (versus competitive)	5	4	3	2	1
Awareness of weaknesses (and strengths)	5	4	3	2	1
Having perspective and sense of humor	5	4	3	2	1
Leadership					
Being self-starter	5	4	3	2	1
Having internal locus of control	5	4	3	2	1
Having integrity and reliability	5	4	3	2	1
Having patience	5	4	3	2	1
Being team builder and hero maker	5	4	3	2	1

Summarize your entrepreneurial strengths.

Summarize your entrepreneurial weaknesses.

STEP 2

Examine Entrepreneurial Role Requirements.

Rank where you fit in the following roles:

	Strongest	←	——	→	Weakest
Accommodation to Venture					
Extent to which career and venture are no. 1 priority	5	4	3	2	1
Stress					
The cost of accommodation	5	4	3	2	1
Values					
Extent to which conventional values are held	5	4	3	2	1
Ethics and Integrity	5	4	3	2	1

Summarize your strengths and weaknesses.

STEP 3
Examine Your Management Competencies.
Rank your skills and competencies below:

	Strongest	←	———	→	Weakest
Marketing					
Market research and evaluation	5	4	3	2	1
Marketing planning	5	4	3	2	1
Product pricing	5	4	3	2	1
Sales management	5	4	3	2	1
Direct mail/catalog selling	5	4	3	2	1
Telemarketing	5	4	3	2	1
Search engine optimization	5	4	3	2	1
Customer service	5	4	3	2	1
Distribution management	5	4	3	2	1
Product management	5	4	3	2	1
New product planning	5	4	3	2	1
Operations/Production					
Manufacturing management	5	4	3	2	1
Inventory control	5	4	3	2	1
Cost analysis and control	5	4	3	2	1
Quality control	5	4	3	2	1
Production scheduling and flow	5	4	3	2	1
Purchasing	5	4	3	2	1
Job evaluation	5	4	3	2	1
Finance					
Accounting	5	4	3	2	1
Capital budgeting	5	4	3	2	1
Cash flow management	5	4	3	2	1
Credit and collection management	5	4	3	2	1
Managing relations with financial sources	5	4	3	2	1
Short-term financing	5	4	3	2	1
Public and private offerings	5	4	3	2	1
Administration					
Problem solving	5	4	3	2	1
Communications	5	4	3	2	1
Planning	5	4	3	2	1
Decision making	5	4	3	2	1
Project management	5	4	3	2	1
Negotiating	5	4	3	2	1
Personnel administration	5	4	3	2	1
Management information systems	5	4	3	2	1
Computer/IT/Internet	5	4	3	2	1

	Strongest	←	——	→	Weakest
Interpersonal/Team					
Leadership/vision/influence	5	4	3	2	1
Helping and coaching	5	4	3	2	1
Feedback	5	4	3	2	1
Conflict management	5	4	3	2	1
Teamwork and people management	5	4	3	2	1
Law					
Corporations and LLCs	5	4	3	2	1
Contracts	5	4	3	2	1
Taxes	5	4	3	2	1
Securities and private placements	5	4	3	2	1
Intellectual property rights and patents	5	4	3	2	1
Real estate law	5	4	3	2	1
Bankruptcy	5	4	3	2	1
Unique Skills	5	4	3	2	1

STEP 4

Based on an Analysis of the Information Given in Steps 1–3, Indicate the Items You Would Add to a "Do" List, Including (1) Need for External Brain Trust Advisors; (2) Board Composition; (3) Additional Team Members; and (4) Additional Knowledge/Skills/Experience.

Part III: Getting Constructive Feedback

Part III is an organized way for you to gather constructive feedback.

STEP 1
(Optional) Give a Copy of Your Answers to Parts I and II to the Person Designated to Evaluate Your Responses. Ask Him or Her to Answer the Following:
Have you been honest, objective, hard-nosed, and complete in evaluating your skills?

Are there any strengths and weaknesses you have inventoried incorrectly?

Are there other events or past actions that might affect this analysis and that have not been addressed?

STEP 2
Solicit Feedback.
Give one copy of the feedback form (begins on the next page) to each person who has been asked to evaluate your responses.

Feedback Form

Feedback for:

Prepared by:

STEP 1
Please Check the Appropriate Column Next to the Statements about the Entrepreneurial Attributes, and Add Any Additional Comments You May Have.

	Strong	Adequate	Weak	No Comment
Commitment and Determination				
Decisiveness	S	A	W	NC
Tenacity	S	A	W	NC
Discipline	S	A	W	NC
Persistence in solving problems	S	A	W	NC
Willingness to sacrifice	S	A	W	NC
Total immersion in the mission	S	A	W	NC
Courage				
Moral strength	S	A	W	NC
Fearless experimentation	S	A	W	NC
Not afraid of conflicts, failure	S	A	W	NC
Intense curiosity in the face of risk	S	A	W	NC
Opportunity Obsession				
Leadership in shaping the opportunity				
Having knowledge of customers' needs	S	A	W	NC
Being market driven	S	A	W	NC
Obsession with value creation and enhancement	S	A	W	NC
Tolerance of Risk, Ambiguity, and Uncertainty				
Calculated risk taker	S	A	W	NC
Risk minimizer	S	A	W	NC
Risk sharer	S	A	W	NC
Tolerance of uncertainty and lack of structure	S	A	W	NC
Tolerance of stress and conflict	S	A	W	NC
Ability to resolve problems and integrate solutions	S	A	W	NC
Creativity, Self-Reliance, and Ability to Adapt				
Nonconventional, open-minded, lateral thinker (helicopter mind)	S	A	W	NC
Restlessness with status quo	S	A	W	NC
Ability to adapt	S	A	W	NC
Lack of fear of failure	S	A	W	NC
Ability to conceptualize and to "sweat details"	S	A	W	NC
Motivation to Excel				
Goal and results orientation	S	A	W	NC
Drive to achieve and grow (self-imposed standards)	S	A	W	NC
Low need for status and power	S	A	W	NC
Ability to be interpersonally supportive (versus competitive)	S	A	W	NC
Awareness of weaknesses (and strengths)	S	A	W	NC
Having perspective and sense of humor	S	A	W	NC
Leadership				
Being self-starter	S	A	W	NC
Having internal locus of control	S	A	W	NC
Having integrity and reliability	S	A	W	NC
Having patience	S	A	W	NC
Being team builder and hero maker	S	A	W	NC

Please make any comments that you can on such additional matters as my energy, health, and emotional stability; my creativity and innovativeness; my intelligence; my capacity to inspire; my values; and so forth.

STEP 2

Please Check the Appropriate Column Next to the Statements about Entrepreneurial Role Requirements to Indicate My Fit and Add Any Additional Comments You May Have.

	Strong	Adequate	Weak	No Comment
Accommodation to venture	S	A	W	NC
Stress (cost of accommodation)	S	A	W	NC
Values (conventional economic and professional values of free enterprise system)	S	A	W	NC
Ethics and integrity	S	A	W	NC

Additional Comments:

STEP 3

Please Check the Appropriate Column Next to the Statements about Management Competencies, and Add Any Additional Comments You May Have.

	Strong	Adequate	Weak	No Comment
Marketing				
Market research and evaluation	S	A	W	NC
Marketing planning	S	A	W	NC
Product pricing	S	A	W	NC
Sales management	S	A	W	NC
Direct mail/catalog selling	S	A	W	NC
Telemarketing	S	A	W	NC
Search engine optimization				
Customer service	S	A	W	NC
Distribution management	S	A	W	NC
Product management	S	A	W	NC
New product planning	S	A	W	NC
Operations/Production				
Manufacturing management	S	A	W	NC
Inventory control	S	A	W	NC
Cost analysis and control	S	A	W	NC
Quality control	S	A	W	NC
Production scheduling and flow	S	A	W	NC
Purchasing	S	A	W	NC
Job evaluation	S	A	W	NC
Finance				
Accounting	S	A	W	NC
Capital budgeting	S	A	W	NC
Cash flow management	S	A	W	NC
Credit and collection management	S	A	W	NC
Managing relations with financial sources	S	A	W	NC
Short-term financing	S	A	W	NC
Public and private offerings	S	A	W	NC
Administration				
Problem solving	S	A	W	NC
Communications	S	A	W	NC
Planning	S	A	W	NC
Decision making	S	A	W	NC
Project management	S	A	W	NC
Negotiating	S	A	W	NC
Personnel administration	S	A	W	NC
Management information systems	S	A	W	NC
Computer/IT/Internet	S	A	W	NC

	Strong	Adequate	Weak	No Comment
Interpersonal/Team				
Leadership/vision/influence	S	A	W	NC
Helping and coaching	S	A	W	NC
Feedback	S	A	W	NC
Conflict management	S	A	W	NC
Teamwork and people management	S	A	W	NC
Law				
Corporations and LLCs	S	A	W	NC
Contracts	S	A	W	NC
Taxes	S	A	W	NC
Securities and private placements	S	A	W	NC
Intellectual property rights and patents	S	A	W	NC
Real estate law	S	A	W	NC
Bankruptcy	S	A	W	NC
Unique Skills	S	A	W	NC

Additional Comments:

STEP 4
Please Evaluate My Strengths and Weaknesses.
In what area or areas do you see my greatest potential or existing strengths in terms of the venture opportunity we have discussed, and why?

Area of Strength	Reason

In what area or areas do you see my greatest potential or existing weaknesses in terms of the venture opportunity we have discussed, and why?

Area of Weakness	Reason

If you know my partners and the venture opportunity, what is your evaluation of their fit with me and the fit among them?

Given the venture opportunity, what you know of my partners, and your evaluation of my weaknesses, should I consider any additional members for my management team, my board, and my brain trust of advisors? If so, what should be their strengths and relevant experience? Can you suggest someone?

Please make any other suggestions that would be helpful for me to consider (e.g., comments about what you see that I like to do, my lifestyle, work style, patterns evident in my skills inventory, the implications of my particular constellation of management strengths and weaknesses and background, the time implications of an apprenticeship, or key people you think I should meet).

Part IV: Putting It All Together

STEP 1
Reflect on Your Previous Responses and the Feedback You Have Solicited or Have Received Informally (from Class Discussion or from Discussions with Friends, Parents, Etc.).

STEP 2
Assess Your Entrepreneurial Strategy.
What have you concluded at this point about entrepreneurship and you?

How do the requirements of entrepreneurship—especially the sacrifices, total immersion, heavy workload, and long-term commitment—fit with your own aims, values, and motivations?

What specific conflicts do you anticipate between your aims and values, and the demands of entrepreneurship?

How would you compare your entrepreneurial mind, your fit with entrepreneurial role demands, your management competencies, and so forth, with those of other people you know who have pursued or are pursuing an entrepreneurial career?

Think ahead 5 to 10 years or more, and assume that you would want to launch or acquire a higher-potential venture. What "chunks" of experience and know-how do you need to accumulate?

What are the implications of this assessment of your entrepreneurial strategy in terms of whether you should proceed with your current venture opportunity?

What is it about the specific opportunity you want to pursue that will provide you with sustained energy and motivation? How do you know this?

At this time, given your major entrepreneurial strengths and weaknesses and your specific venture opportunity, are there other "chunks" of experience and know-how you need to acquire or attract to your team? (Be specific!)

Who are the people you need to get involved with you?

What other issues or questions have been raised for you at this point that you would like answered?

What opportunities would you most want to be in a position to create/pursue in 5 to 10 years? What are the implications for new skills, know-how, mentors, team members, and resources?

Part V: Thinking Ahead

Part V considers the crafting of your personal entrepreneurial strategy. Remember, goals should be specific and concrete, measurable, and, except where indicated below, realistic and attainable.

STEP 1

List, in Three Minutes, Your Goals to Be Accomplished by the Time You Are 70.

STEP 2

List, in Three Minutes, Your Goals to Be Accomplished over the Next Seven Years. (If You Are an Undergraduate, Use the Next Four Years.)

STEP 3

List, in Three Minutes, the Goals You Would Like to Accomplish If You Have Exactly One Year from Today to Live. Assume You Would Enjoy Good Health in the Interim but Would Not Be Able to Acquire Any More Life Insurance or Borrow an Additional Large Sum of Money for a "Final Fling." Assume Further That You Could Spend That Last Year of Your Life Doing Whatever You Want to Do.

STEP 4

List, in Six Minutes, Your Real Goals and the Goals You Would Like to Accomplish over Your Lifetime.

STEP 5
Discuss the List from Step 4 with Another Person and Then Refine and Clarify Your Goal Statements.

STEP 6
Rank Your Goals According to Priority.

STEP 7
Concentrate on the Top Three Goals and Make a List of Problems, Obstacles, Inconsistencies, and So Forth That You Will Encounter in Trying to Reach Each of These Goals.

STEP 8
Decide and State How You Will Eliminate Any Important Problems, Obstacles, Inconsistencies, and So Forth.

STEP 9
For Your Top Three Goals, Write Down All the Tasks or Action Steps You Need to Take to Help You Attain Each Goal and Indicate How Results Will Be Measured.
It is helpful to organize the goals in order of priority.

Goal	Task/Action Step	Measurement	Rank

STEP 10
Rank Tasks/Action Steps in Terms of Priority.
To identify high-priority items, it is helpful to make a copy of your list and cross off any activities or task that cannot be completed, or at least begun, in the next seven days, and then identify the single most important goal, the next most important, and so forth.

STEP 11
Establish Dates and Durations (and, If Possible, a Place) for Tasks/Action Steps to Begin.
Organize tasks/action steps according to priority. If possible, the date should be during the next seven days.

Goal	Task/Action Step	Measurement	Rank

STEP 12
Make a List of Problems, Obstacles, Inconsistencies, and So Forth.

STEP 13
Decide How You Will Eliminate Any Important Problems, Obstacles, Inconsistencies, and So Forth, and Adjust the List in Step 12.

STEP 14
Identify Risks Involved and Resources and Other Help Needed.

Note on setting goals: Tear out Part V, keep a copy on file, and repeat the exercise at least once a year, or when a critical event occurs (job change, marriage, child, death in the family).

Case

Lakota Hills

Preparation Questions

1. Discuss the challenges and advantages of developing a specialty food business.
2. Is their current strategy the best way to build Lakota Hills?
3. How might they integrate other channels into their overall selling model?
4. How will Lakota Hills make money?
5. As an angel investor, would you participate in the round this venture is seeking?

In August 2007 Laura Ryan and her son Michael were flying back home to Wyoming following a four-day specialty food trade show in Houston, Texas. The event had generated a lot of interest for their growing enterprise, Lakota Hills. Their flagship product, a retail bag of traditional Native American fry bread, was currently on the shelves in over 350 midwestern supermarkets.

While they had made encouraging progress, they were nowhere near the critical mass of stores they would need to spark any sort of buyer momentum in the industry. Those decision makers were not an adventurous lot when it came to committing time and shelf space to new brands; but at the same time, they were always on the lookout for proven moneymakers. So until more stores said yes, the vast majority of buyers and brokers would continue to smile, nod, and say maybe. As she settled in for the flight, Laura pursed a grim smile as she considered the realities:

> The specialty food business is a lot harder than it looks—maybe because almost anyone with a kitchen, a family recipe, and some drive can get product packaged and out to their local stores. Going national is a very different story!

It was clear that getting to profitability in the hypercompetitive retail channel was going to require many more expense-laden trips like this one, and hundreds more in-store demonstrations. While other sales channels were open for discussion, gaining a foothold in this marketplace was their first priority. Their investors agreed, but with the need for a follow-on round of funding in the near term, everyone involved wanted to be sure that Lakota Hills was indeed on the best path to profits.

An Early Start

The daughter of a successful hog farmer and an enterprising elementary school teacher, Laura Ryan was an industrious adolescent:

This case was prepared by Carl Hedberg under the direction of Professor Jeffry Timmons. © Copyright Jeffry Timmons, 2008. All rights reserved.

> I was entrepreneurial ever since I was very young. I raised and sold little pigs, and my mother—who had always had sideline businesses like Avon and Mary Kay—taught me how to sew and bead. I was always making things, and being a member of 4-H[1] gave me the ability to talk to people, make presentations, and work with basic business concepts.
>
> I skipped a couple of grades in school, so I was just 13 in junior high. By that time I was sewing and selling clothes and thinking that down the road maybe I would be a designer.

Those early aspirations fell away when, at 16, Laura married Jim Cooper, the 18-year-old son of a local cattle rancher. Laura recalled the inevitable clash of cultures:

> My father was German and Russian and my mother was almost full-blood Lakota[2] with a little bit of French. So I'm actually 7/16th Native American. That was very hard for Jim's family—the idea that he would marry an Indian. Family gatherings were civil but very strained. Still, we knew we could make it work.

Within three years they were both in college and raising two young sons, Michael and Matt. Jim had started a cattle ranch, and Laura did double duty as a mother and part-time college student. Her first inclination had been to pursue a business degree, but when those classes proved dry and mundane, she chose to major in psychology. That began to change in 1987 when, at the age of 21, she met an enterprising uncle:

> For a class project, I had to interview a family member about our personal history. I found an uncle I had never met, and he was quite a character. He had never worked for anyone his entire life—lots of great dreams and great ideas, but he'd never had a successful venture. He was living in a motel and writing business plans for a living. He was the most fascinating person I'd ever met, and we talked for several hours about all sorts of business ideas. He really inspired me to the point where I was thinking, I've got to start my own business.

Quilting for the Stars

Laura's uncle had suggested that because Laura and her mother had a talent for sewing, materials, and color, producing traditional Native American star quilts

[1] 4-H was a rural youth organization in the United States centered in rural farm communities. The pledge: I pledge my Head to clearer thinking, my Heart to greater loyalty, my Hands to better service, and my Health to better living for my club, my community, my country, and my world.
[2] The Lakota form one of a group of seven Native American tribes (the Great Sioux Nation) and speak Lakota, one of the three major dialects of the Sioux language.

might be an excellent fit. After hand-crafting a couple of stunning samples, they figured on producing a range of sizes priced from $500 to over $5,000. Her uncle guided them through the process of writing a business plan that qualified for a Small Business Administration (SBA) loan of just over $27,000.[3] Laura recalled that their early momentum had obscured a few important details:

> We got the money and thought, "Now we're big-time entrepreneurs in the quilting business!" This was 1987, before the Internet was widely available for research. We didn't think much about cash flow, margins, or costs, and we had a hard time trying to figure out the demographics; like, who was really going to buy a $5,000 quilt? We went through the funding in about eight months, so it quickly became a word-of-mouth business.

They found a couple of galleries in Santa Fe, New Mexico, that catered to quilt collectors. A prominent U.S. state senator bought two, and the Smithsonian Institute put a particularly intricate quilt on display and offered smaller versions through its catalog.

Their efforts got a boost in the summer of 1992 when Laura took a short-term assignment as an assistant wardrobe designer for a Hollywood production shooting on location:

> I worked on the movie *Thunderheart*, which featured Val Kilmer, Sam Sheppard, and singer David Crosby. After two weeks, I was promoted to work as Val Kilmer's personal wardrobe assistant. They all purchased our quilts, and that opened up a really neat market for us.

While they had managed to make enough to pay off the SBA loan, Laura said that after a while it became clear that the business wasn't scalable:

> It took forever to make these handmade quilts. My mom, myself, some local artists, and a couple of other ladies in the community just couldn't make them fast enough to make much money at it. We considered machine-made quilts, but our cost per quilt would still have been over $200—compared with foreign manufacturers that could make them for about $40. It never really failed; we just transitioned to other ideas.

Fry Bread Feeds

Laura's life as mother and as the driver of the quilting business had limited her school sessions to a few classes per semester. In 1993, during what would be her final year in college, she served as vice president of a Native American club on campus. Her primary responsibility was to organize fund-raising venues, and one such event hinted at a new venture opportunity:

Every Friday at lunchtime we sold Indian tacos—deep-fried dough we call fry bread. It was a huge event. The students loved it, and we would sell between 350 and 500 in two hours. Our bread is very soft, and what makes it so popular is that you can actually cut it with a plastic fork. The students were all saying, "Wow, this is the best fry bread ever."

> We decided to go a step further and try a couple of county fairs that summer. We attended a festival with 6,000 people. We were the only Indian taco vendor, and we sold around 5,000 in one day. Once again, everyone was commenting that our bread was the best they'd ever tasted.

Laura's mom Sheila, who helped with the operation, wasn't a bit surprised by the accolades:

> I've been involved with this fry bread for over 70 years. It is my grandmother's recipe. She handed it down to my mom, and when she gave me the recipe, I added some new ingredients to it. And then my daughter took over. We really like the recipe because we can do so many things with it: muffins, cinnamon balls, pancakes, and waffles using milk—with or without eggs—and you can just bake it like bread. Our main meal growing up was bean soup and fry bread. I just loved that. My mom liked to make large flat pieces and cut them up like a pizza. At Christmas time I would bake a small loaf with candied cherries—that needs to be set out to rise a bit before it goes in the oven.

> The traditional way is to serve the fry bread with wasabi, an Indian pudding with blueberries or wild chokeberries or wild plums. My sons are ranchers, and after branding week each year, they put on a great feast of fry bread and mountain oysters for all the ranch hands and wranglers.

At a family gathering that summer, Laura's husband Jim had an idea:

> I figured that if festival goers like the product, why not try selling it to tourists? Government annuities[4] include bulk flour sacks that are simply stamped *FLOUR* with the net weight at the bottom. Why not create hand-tied muslin-lined burlap bags that would look like a miniversion of a flour sack—stamped in the same printing?

---

[3] Details of the SBA loan: rate and terms.

[4] For centuries the Indians of the Plains had lived a far-ranging nomadic existence. By the late 1800s the Western Expansion had decimated wild game populations and annexed most of the land. Reservation lands were established in the area of the Black Hills and the Badlands of South Dakota. To prevent starvation while the tribes of the Sioux Nation transitioned to an agricultural lifestyle, the U.S. government agreed to deliver monthly rations—also known as annuities. The treaty of 1877 provided the head of each separate household with "a pound and a half of beef (or in lieu thereof, one half pound of bacon), one-half pound of flour, and one-half pound of corn; and for every one hundred rations, four pounds of coffee, eight pounds of sugar, and three pounds of beans, or in lieu of said articles the equivalent thereof, in the discretion of the Commissioner of Indian Affairs."

Laura was soon calling various bag makers, but she found no one willing to produce anything less than 5,000 per run:

> We couldn't buy that many—this was just a concept—we didn't know how well the product would sell. As I've said, my mother is a really good seamstress. We bought some burlap and muslin, used rubber stamps, and made the bags ourselves. They were stamped "Lakota Hills Fry Bread Mix" and "Net Wt. 24 oz." There was nothing else on the bags, so we made little tags that we strung as we hand-tied the bags.

Laura found two tourist centers between the Devil's Tower in Wyoming and Deadwood, South Dakota. The product sold so well for the remainder of the season that they spent many hours in their ranch kitchen sewing, stamping, hand-mixing ingredients, and filling bags. By the time demand trailed off at the end of the season in October, Laura and her family were confident they had found a reasonably simple seasonal enterprise. Meanwhile, 23 and fresh out of college, Laura was thinking about how best to advance her career.

Entrepreneurship Educator

Laura's first inclination was to pursue a PhD in clinical psychology, but she didn't get into either program she'd applied to. In early 1994 she got a most unexpected call from Gene Taylor, the tribal college president at a nearby university:

> Gene had heard that I'd finished up my undergrad degree, and he knew that my mom and I were pretty entrepreneurial. The chair of his entrepreneurship department was leaving to start her own business, so he asked me if I would like to be the new department chair and a business teacher. I reminded him my degree was in psychology, and that I had only taken a couple of business courses. But he said, "You're an entrepreneur, and that's awesome; I think you can teach." So I accepted.

When she arrived for work in May, she learned that one of her first duties would be to attend the Symposium for Entrepreneurship Educators (SEE) at Babson College in Wellesley, Massachusetts. SEE's mission was to further entrepreneurship education by teaching motivated entrepreneurs how to teach at their respective institutions. Laura's predecessor had already been accepted as a faculty sponsor, so Laura had only about a month to locate an entrepreneur with an interest in spending time in the classroom. She found a woman who made a living as an independent seamstress and quilter. Laura began the four-day seminar in a state of severe overwhelm:

> I'll never forget the fear I had when I walked into a room filled with experienced instructors and successful entrepreneurs who were speaking in a language of business that I'd never heard. The businesses these people were talking about were huge—as big as some of the egos in the room. I felt totally lost and out of place. I wanted to just sneak away and sit in the back so I'd never get called on.
>
> But there were a couple of other Native American colleges there, and slowly I became more comfortable with the group. I discovered that they did care about what we had to say—about our culture, our values, and the tiny businesses we were working on. By the end of the week, I was certain I needed to take some more classes so that I could follow through.

Laura enrolled in an 18-month distance learning program in Southern New Hampshire for a degree in community economic development. Students came together once a month for three days of classroom work and then used e-mail to stay in touch on projects until the next month.

That summer, her studies had to be balanced with the fry bread business when their sales got an unexpected boost from a two-day appearance Laura made on the QVC selling show—live from Mt. Rushmore:

> As a one-time event, QVC had selected 20 specialty companies from around the country. It was a bit of a risk to go on, since the way they operate is they place their order based on their estimate of what will sell. You ship them the product, and then whatever doesn't sell they ship back at our expense. Anyway, that wasn't a concern, since we sold out in three minutes—twice. That was 6,000 bags in two days.

By the time she received her degree from the New Hampshire program in the spring of 1998, Laura was feeling far more confident in her roles as a teacher and department chair. In 2000 she decided to pursue a PhD in education—a decision concurrent with the arrival of her third child:

> Our boys were teenagers by this time. We had never had the intention of having another child, but the neat thing was, our daughter changed my entire outlook on life. I was gearing up to be entirely focused on my career, and now I was taking a step back. It was a good balance. Lisa was six months old when I started the [PhD] program. I took her with me to class; everyone called her the PhD baby.

For the next four years, Laura worked on her dissertation, taught entrepreneurship, and spent lots of time with her daughter. All the while, the family fry bread business supported itself as a seasonal operation:

> The business was always there, but we never grew it. Every year was the same. We began in March. We mixed and packed everything in our kitchen at the ranch. It was quite a process. We added maybe a couple of gift shops a year, but our volume never changed significantly. We would make enough inventory to carry us through October, and then we'd have a smaller mixing and packing session to cover holiday season orders. It was a very small, very manageable operation.

New Opportunities

In the early 2000s actor Kevin Costner developed Tatanka, a tourist destination near Deadwood, South Dakota, that told the story of the bison in relation to the Plains Indians.[5] In 2004, when Costner and his local investor group decided to bring in a Native American to run the operations, Laura got a call:

> I was still teaching entrepreneurship at a university not far from Tatanka. I went down there and was really intrigued. This was an interpretive center built around an authentic mid-1800s Native American camp. It was a living museum with everyone in period dress and in character—much like Plimoth Plantation in Massachusetts. I decided to take the job, and set up a leave of absence from my teaching duties.

The gift shop, of course, sold bags of their fry bread mix, and the restaurant offered Lakota Hills luncheon tacos.[6] The spike in sales that summer caused some grumblings from her two boys, who by their late teens had grown very tired of the kitchen production and packaging drill. Laura explained that on balance, her sons had a wondrous summer as one of the main attractions at Tatanka:

> Michael and Matt, who have been riding horses almost before they could walk, were our painted warriors on the hill: shirtless with buckskin pants, riding bareback and hollering war cries. By the end of that summer they were able to throw spears and shoot a bow and arrow while racing by the viewing area. They had quite a fun time with it.

In the summer of 2004 fry bread sales topped $58,000—a somewhat modest figure that Laura knew reflected their in-home manufacturing setup and their limited market reach.[7] In early 2005 Laura decided it was time to move out of the kitchen:

> We could see that the coming summer was going to be our best year yet for fry bread sales, and that was going to create a major disruption at home. I also wasn't sure whether our credit line with a bank in Laramie would cover increases to our preseason production costs.

Laura turned to Mark Wills, the Tatanka investor who had recommended her for the job:

> Mark had founded Greenhill, a small venture capital firm in Spearfish [South Dakota] that works with Native American entrepreneurs. They are willing to go out there on the edge to help businesses that might not usually attract venture capital.

Although Laura worked up a three-page outline of the business, Mark's decision to invest was largely based on what he saw in the lead entrepreneur:

> I was familiar with Laura's long-time involvement with entrepreneurship, and I knew how popular their fry bread mix was becoming. As manager at Tatanka, she had done a great job building on our vision. We gave her a credit line of $80,000 to cover raw materials and rent a more appropriate manufacturing space. We wanted to see how she'd do, and we left the door open for more funding down the road.

That season, fry bread sales and customer feedback were encouraging to the point where Laura was sure they could scale the business into a year-round operation. At the end of the summer, she resigned from Tatanka with the aim of discovering the best path for Lakota Hills. Her first iteration proved to be more trouble than it was worth:

> Our rented manufacturing space in Spearfish had a real rustic look, so in October we set up a small shop in front and started selling gift baskets for the holidays. Our baskets featured 100 percent Native American specialty foods: teas, jams, sweets, and our fry bread mix.
>
> We actually did really well with the business through the holiday season, but I knew at that point I was not going to stay in the gift basket industry. We spent hours upon hours designing and setting up elaborate baskets—only to have them arrive in terrible condition after being shipped across the country.

Laura had also begun making contact with specialty food stores in the hope of expanding their retail distribution. Those efforts came up short as well:

> I approached chain stores like Cabella's and Crackerbarrel because they sell lots of specialty food products. They seemed interested in the concept, but said our muslin bags were just not very professional. They also felt it was too specific of a product, and that there was not enough consumer awareness. They said, "We don't know what fry bread is, so how are our consumers going to know?"
>
> At that point I thought that it was time to raise enough money to cover the design of some proper packaging, find a professional co-packer, and really go for it.

A Plan to Expand

Although her PhD had opened up a number of academic career options, Laura decided to focus her energies on developing the fry bread business. In January 2006 she presented her plan to the partners at Greenhill Venture (see Exhibit 1). Mark Wills said that they agreed to invest $470,000 for 15 percent of the business:

> We suggested that she target grocery chains. To do that, she was going to need a new package, supermarket floor displays, sell sheets, and other marketing collateral.

---

[5] *Tatanka:* Lakota for a bull bison.

[6] The restaurant staff prepared a batch of measured dough balls. These were fried on order in the same oil used to fry the onion rings and French fries. A tent card was displayed on every table describing the history of fry bread and the story of the Lakota Hills family business.

[7] In 2005 the Lakota Hills mix was sold in eight tourist destination gift shops in Wyoming and in South Dakota.

EXHIBIT 1

Excerpts from the Lakota Hills Executive Summary

The Opportunity

This business promises to be successful because of the increased demand for specialty food products, and the interest in Native American products in particular. Based on current market trends and statistical data, bread and dessert mixes have been on a steady growth curve since 2004. Lakota Hills has been selling its fry bread since 1993, and positive consumer, distributor, and food broker feedback demonstrates that it has a quality product in the marketplace.

Competitive Advantage

Our primary competitors are Wooden Knife Fry Bread Mix, Crow Fry Bread Mix, and the Oklahoma Fry Bread Company. Wooden Knife Fry Bread has been in operation for over 15 years, while the other two companies were started less than 2 years ago. None of the three companies have improved their packaging design or have been aggressive in their marketing approach to meet the consumer's needs. Wooden Knife Fry Bread is the only company selling their product outside of their local area. Since 2004, they have been aggressively marketing their product throughout the Midwest, and primarily in supermarkets and tourism-related outlets.

Lakota Hills has a competitive advantage in the taste of our product versus the taste and texture of our competitors. Wooden Knife Fry Bread Mix adds a traditional Native American root called "timsula" that is very bitter in taste. The other two competitors are both powdered milk and yeast recipes, which impart a different taste and a tougher texture to the product.

Pricing

Wooden Knife Fry Bread Mix sells their 1.5-pound box of fry bread mix on the retail shelf in the range of $3.50–$7.00. The Oklahoma Fry Bread is priced for an 8-ounce bag of fry bread mix for approximately $3.20 retail. A 1-pound bag of the Crow Fry Bread Mix is priced at $6.00–$7.50. The key to success for Lakota Hills is to keep our pricing consistent in the marketplace. Our 16-ounce retail package will have a suggested retail price of $3.69.

Wooden Knife Fry Bread Mix is our only competitor in food service. They have frozen fry bread patties: 25 per case. They also have a 5-pound bulk dry fry bread mix. Both products are priced at $1.90–$2.25 per pound. Lakota Hills offers a 25-pound bulk pack at $1.40 per pound.

When that was ready to go, she was going to need to find a co-packer with the machinery and capacity to serve that channel.

Working with a local photographer, and using feedback from friends and family, Laura spent the spring and summer designing a new look and feel for Lakota Hills. The retail unit weight was trimmed by a third to 16 ounces, and the package—now a full-color poly bag designed to work on a high-volume heat-crimp production line—featured recipe suggestions and a history lesson (see Exhibit 2). Sell sheets, a basic Web site, and other collateral were color and concept coordinated. Laura said they also found a co-packer with a willingness to invest:

> John Gower has a pretty big kosher-certified dry mix operation in Laramie. He has lots of equipment like huge rotary mixers, augers, and bulk storage systems. He believed in our company and believed that we were going to have enough volume to justify his purchase of automatic bagging machinery that he tweaked into his system.[8]
>
> We talked a lot about where we had to be with our pricing, and his delivered price was based on our ramping up sales pretty quickly. The minimum order run for our poly bags was 500,000, and we also or-

dered printed shipping boxes to match that inventory at 6 units per box.

To introduce their product to major grocers, Laura participated in a very focused and intense trade show in Atlanta, Georgia:

> I had found some info about a show called ECRM [Efficient Collaborative Retail Marketing]. They facilitate sourcing reviews called Efficient Program Planning Sessions for retailers all over the country.[9] We were in their specialty/Hispanic/ethnic food show in August.
>
> It was very expensive—over $13,000 for the event. It starts with an evening reception where you mingle with the buyers. Over the next two days—from eight in the morning to six at night—you have 20-minute appointments with major supermarkets. It was very rigorous. They loved our packaging, our story, and our fry bread. It was very exciting to make so many great connections with so many significant buyers and brokers.

---

[8] The cost of the fill and heat-sealing additions to the plant equipment was approximately $42,000.

[9] In 2007 ECRM held more than 45 EPPS events. Planning sessions included every major supermarket category: hair care; pharmacy; personal care; cosmetics, fragrance, and bath; cough and cold/analgesics; private-label health and beauty care and food; general merchandise; sun care; grocery; snack, and beverage; cosmetics; vitamin, nutrition, and diet; school and office products; household products; health care; candy; photo; frozen foods; and international.

EXHIBIT 2

Selected copy from the Retail Poly Bag

Directions

Fry Bread is incredibly easy to prepare. First, place the entire contents of the bag into a large mixing bowl. Add ¾ cups of warm water and stir until the dough becomes sticky. Then add all-purpose flour a little at a time until the dough is no longer sticky.

Heat 3 cups of oil or shortening in a skillet or deep fryer to 375 degrees. Form your dough into the desired shape on a well-floured surface and roll or pat to about ½ inch in thickness. Lower the fry bread carefully into the hot oil and cook approximately 2 minutes on each side until golden in color. If you have made the fry bread into balls, no turning is required; just remove them from the oil when they are golden brown in color.

Place the hot fry bread on a paper towel and allow it to cool slightly before handling. Any leftover dough can be covered and held in a refrigerator for up to 24 hours.

Fry Bread History

At the turn of the century the Lakota people were given the ingredients to make bread. In their creative nature, the women developed a fry bread recipe from those ingredients. These recipes became closely guarded secrets passed from one generation to the next.

Laura Ryan was given this recipe by her great-grandmother to share with future generations. Please enjoy this traditional Native American family recipe. We hope it becomes a tradition for your family too!

Recipes

Indian Taco Meat Sauce

2 lbs. ground beef or bison

2 cans kidney beans

1 packet taco seasoning

½ cup water

Brown meat over medium heat until thoroughly cooked. Add taco seasoning, beans, and water. Stir and simmer for 15 minutes. Spoon meat mixture onto fry bread and add cheese, lettuce, tomatoes, onions, taco sauce, and sour cream.

Fry Bread Nuggets

Prepare fry bread mix as directed. Drop teaspoon-size balls into 375 degree oil until fry bread is golden brown on each side. Serve with whipped honey butter, maple syrup, or your favorite jelly. For a donutlike treat, roll the hot bread in powdered sugar and cinnamon or plain sugar.

Hearing how well the show had gone, Laura said their co-packer took it upon himself to see what the new equipment could do:

> John's a really nice guy, and I think he just wants to see our business make it. In late August he filled 300,000 bags, boxed them all up, palletized them, and then said, "I hope you can sell these" . . . *Oh my gosh!*

Knowing that they were not going to move close to 2,600 pallets of product in short order, they shipped the inventory to a dry storage warehouse in Chicago—a professional facility that was accustomed to working with large-scale overland transport. With their date stamp giving them just 18 months to clear out the inventory, the clock was ticking.

Buyer Education and Reeducation

The ECRM event generated a long list of intrigued buyers and an immediate performance-based agreement with a food broker in the Chicago area.[10] By the late fall of 2006, Laura's eldest son Michael had come on full-time as general manager. As he began to follow up on leads from the show, he could see that "getting to yes" with the supermarket buyers was going to be a real challenge:

[10] Food brokers typically received between 10 and 15 percent of sales on the grocery chain accounts they sold and managed.

> In school, and in football, there was always a clear and concise learning environment. The professor or coach would lay out their expectations, and let you know what you can expect in return.
>
> Working with buyers is a very different experience. They don't call back, they aren't there to take your call when they say they will be, samples get lost, samples get eaten. . . . After many calls to people who seem almost ready to buy, suddenly they're not even sure if they can use the product.
>
> I have an undergraduate business degree, and I've just enrolled in a one-year MBA program—and I can tell you, nowhere in all of that education is there anything about the food industry—and more importantly, the grocery industry. There is a lot of terminology you have to learn, and it takes experience to know how to work with buyers and brokers.
>
> For example, you don't hear no very much in this business. Instead you get a lot of "I'll get back to you" and "we're getting close." In some ways that's harder to deal with than straight rejection because there is a lot of running around chasing leads that ultimately won't pan out. You have to be very persistent.

Laura, who was still working leads as well, offered her assessment of the challenge:

> At the food shows, you get a lot of interest when they try the product, and you collect tons of cards. They get home to their regular work where they are sampling dozens of products a week, and they push it off and

EXHIBIT 3
Channel Costs and Pricing Snapshot

Retail units: 16-ounce bags

Unit cost: $1.17

Delivered cost per pallet (115 cases per pallet/6 bags per case): $807.30

Distributors

Price per case/unit: $9.60/1.60

Pop-up floor display (36 units): $57.60/$1.60

Supermarkets

Price per case/unit: $10.80/1.80

Pop-up floor display (36 units): $64.80/$1.80

Estimated retail price per unit: $3.59

Specialty food stores

Price per case/unit: $13.50/$2.25

Estimated retail price per unit: $4.29

Tourist destination shops

Price per case/unit: $18.00/$3.00

Estimated retail price per unit: $6.49

Wholesale bulk: 25-pound bags

Delivered cost per pallet (50 bulk bags): $600

Distributors: $30.00 per bag

Wholesale (food service): $35.00 per bag

Terms: Minimum order: 1 pallet

Payment: 2% 10, net 30

*Unit cost includes the following: ingredients, packaging, utilities, labor, and delivery.

---

push it off until they forget how good it was and what it tasted like.

Even worse, it seems that in the supermarket industry, hardly anyone stays in their position very long; lots of lateral moves to different divisions or product categories. So we're constantly having to educate and reeducate buyers about who we are. It can get pretty frustrating.

Lines of Entry

The Lakota Hills team and their investors were in agreement that because the story behind the product was so compelling, grocery retailing represented their best entry into high-volume sales. Laura explained that they were already working on direct line extensions to gain strength within that channel:

It's hard for the supermarkets to justify bringing in one product to see if it will sell—especially since for many chains fry bread represents a whole new subcategory under bread mixes. Creating a line of products will give us more credibility, and those additional SKUs[11] will translate into better visibility and more sales.

Right now we are looking at a range of related products: chokecherry- and buffaloberry-flavored fry bread mixes, a Dutch oven fry bread mix, blueberry and buttermilk pancake mix, and an Indian taco kit. From there, we can build on the brand by formulating or acquiring other Native American products like jellies, syrups, traditional snacks, and maybe a line of flavored protein sports drinks.

Steve Foster, a partner at Greenhill Ventures, said that once Lakota Hills built up a reputation in retail, the company would be ready to branch into other channels:

As a minority-certified business, they are exempt from upfront slotting fees—which at a top-tier supermarket

chain can run $25,000 per SKU. That advantage can also be carried over into packaging mixes for volume government contracts. They have a 25-pound bag ready to go for wholesale food service accounts, but it is harder to leverage the product and family story in those channels.

Another wholesale possibility would be setting up a national program with restaurant chains like Denny's or Pizza Hut, although it's not clearly the best way to enter that market. Retailing is where they ought to start out because that's a more straightforward effort involving advertising, promotion, and building a consumer connection.

Michael described the various channels for their fry bread mix:

Specialty food outlets like the gift shop at Mt. Rushmore represent the best margins because they will pay the most and still double the price on the shelf. The grocery store chains will want a lower delivered price, and their markup will be around 50 percent. Food service has the highest volume and the easiest pack, ship, and support profile, but they are going to want it as cheap as they can get it because they would be ordering truckloads.

We are a little cautious about the food service segment. In terms of volume, I think bulk wholesale has far more potential, but the margins are very small (see Exhibit 3). Our current production setup, and having a large amount of date-stamped retail packs in inventory, sort of forces us to pursue specialty food chains and supermarkets right now.

Laura said they were targeting the retail segment with a consumer education plan:

To draw people in, we are going to build on our human interest themes: a Native American woman entrepreneur and her family going national with a traditional family favorite. We are looking for all the free publicity we can get, like having newspapers we advertise in

[11] Pronounced "skews": stock keeping units.

write up stories about what we're doing. We will also be sending our press clippings and information to a few major East Coast newspapers like the *Washington Post* and *The New York Times*, and samples to food critics in New York, and to celebrity hosts like Martha Stewart, Oprah, and Letterman.

At the local level, we'll be running coupons in the Sunday papers and in the store flyers. We need to make sure that wherever we do run coupons, we're in the area that week to put on in-store demos. We could also build awareness by selling tacos and handing out store coupons at motorcycle rallies, state fairs, and festivals.

On the Road

In late November, a 280-store chain in the Midwest (a lead from the ECRM show) agreed to carry the product. The team soon discovered that selling the buyer in corporate didn't necessarily mean that the individual stores would be given a heads-up on the incoming SKU. Laura explained that this first big account was a real eye-opener:

We put a very specific store placement sheet in every case, and a trifold brochure is attached to every bag explaining the product. But the teenagers working in the stockroom don't care about that stuff. A few hadn't even bothered to bring it out from the receiving area. When it did get put out, it was all over the stores. I found it in the Oriental section, the breakfast food aisle, and the Hispanic section. A couple of managers thought it looked like a fish coating and put it in the meat department.

My mom had designed a nice floor display with a full-color topper. Lots of those toppers were missing—I suppose people were taking them home for decoration. At a dollar eighty per topper, that's going to cut our margins if we have to keep replacing them. And worse, if we didn't fix this, we'd be right back out the door. In this business, if you lose an account, it's virtually impossible to get back in. It's a good thing we have family that can help with the demos.

Their in-store tastings—conducted at various times by Laura, Michael, his brother Matt, and their grandmother—put a personal face on the business for store workers and enticed shoppers to try a bag. Michael noted that customer feedback suggested that loyal users would be regular, as opposed to frequent, buyers:

This is not like macaroni and cheese, where every time you go grocery shopping you get several boxes. Kids love to eat fry bread too, but it's a matter of the parents being willing to mix the dough, heat the oil, cook the bread, and then clean everything up.

A typical family would not prepare this a few times a week. More likely once a month, or even once every two or three months in place of taco shells. That said, we feel that if we can get our product into enough stores and get consumers using it at that level of regularity, we can do very well.

The good news was that when the bags were on the right shelf (with the bread mixes), and customers got a chance to try warm samples at an in-store tasting, the product moved. In July 2007 they landed an even larger grocery chain with nearly 800 stores from South Dakota to Colorado. Unlike the previous force-out, the team would be required to personally introduce the buyer-approved product to each store manager. Laura said that they were making excellent progress:

We are able to visit about 20 stores a day, and we have gotten into about 100 stores so far. We're hardly ever turned down when we make our presentation. So that's great, but it's a lot of expense up front to get out to every one of those stores. Michael is doing most of that work right now until we can bring on a food broker to represent us in that territory. But of course, selling a broker is just as difficult as selling a [supermarket] buyer. They are very selective about whom they'll represent. They love our product, the packaging, and our story, but many brokers have said they can't make enough money selling our product because it's so new and the volume isn't there.

Buy One, Get One Free

With over 1,300 pallets of retail product still on hand and barely six months left before the product would be too dated to distribute to supermarkets, the team was now offering a free pallet with every pallet sold. Laura said the promotion was helping to clear the backlog, but the increase in sales was bringing a new concern:

Right now we have a small enough number of accounts that if we see that the product isn't moving, we can go in and do damage control like tastings and making sure the product is displayed correctly. As we add new large accounts, we are going to have to find ways to educate consumers and in-store workers about our fry bread without having to visit each and every store personally.

Right now we are working with our investors to lay out how much we're spending in advertising, demo expenses, and store visits. Our costs are so crazy because when Michael is on the road selling, he has hotels, meals, mileage . . . that adds up. We've set up some projections (see Exhibits 4a–c) and estimate we are going to need an additional $500,000 to fund another year of this type of direct selling while we can build up a broker network.

When Michael road-tripped to a few stores to see how the product was being handled, suddenly visiting the rest became a top priority:

This was what they call a force-out, meaning they required all of their stores to take a case of our product, and some of the busier locations would receive our floor display that holds 24 bags. Well, that was great, but the downside was we didn't have the people out there to go to every store that week to educate the managers about what exactly it was that they had just received.

EXHIBIT 4A

Income Statement and Projections

	Actuals					Projected						
Sales Made	Q1 2007	Q2 2007	Q3 2007	Q4 2007	2007 Total	Q1 2008	Q2 2008	Q3 2008	Q4 2008	2008 Total	2009 Total	2010 Total
1.5-lb cases muslin	560	10,560	1,440	1,440	14,000	480	480	480	480	1,920	2,208	2,517
1.5-lb cases—world link	0	720	1,200	1,200	3,120	1,200	1,200	1,200	1,200	4,800	5,520	6,293
25-lb bags	375	2,910	6,480	12,960	22,725	12,960	12,960	25,920	25,920	77,760	89,424	101,943
Online sales	12	75	150	150	387	150	150	150	150	600	690	787
Future product line	0	0	0	0	0	0	0	0	0	0	0	0
Future product line	0	0	0	0	0	0	0	0	0	0	0	0
1-lb cases paper	0	8,400	39,200	50,400	98,000	67,200	84,000	100,800	117,600	369,600	425,040	484,546
Revenue												
1.5-lb cases muslin	16,800	316,800	43,200	43,200	420,000	14,400	14,400	14,400	14,400	57,600	66,240	75,514
1.5-lb cases—world link	0	22,810	38,016	38,016	98,842	38,016	38,016	38,016	38,016	152,064	174,874	199,356
5-lb cases	8,438	65,475	145,800	291,600	511,313	291,600	291,600	583,200	583,200	1,749,600	2,012,040	2,293,726
Online sales	216	1,350	2,700	2,700	6,966	2,700	2,700	2,700	2,700	10,800	12,420	14,159
Future product line	0	0	0	0	0	0	0	0	0	0	0	0
Future product line	0	0	0	0	0	0	0	0	0	0	0	0
Shipping charges	1,621	25,111	10,747	17,357	54,836	15,398	15,398	28,618	28,618	88,032	101,237	115,410
Discounts	0	(1,140)	(1,901)	(1,901)	(4,942)	0	0	0	0	0	0	0
1-lb cases paper	0	151,200	705,600	907,200	1,764,000	1,209,600	1,512,600	1,814,400	2,116,800	6,652,800	12,902,400	14,708,736
Total Revenue	27,074	581,605	944,162	1,298,172	2,851,014	1,571,714	1,874,114	2,481,334	2,783,734	8,710,896	15,269,210	17,406,900
Cost of Goods Sold												
Raw material	8,196	166,780	237,831	331,963	744,770	393,302	464,030	628,718	699,446	2,185,498	2,513,322	2,865,187
Labor	1,348	32,135	29,901	36,621	100,004	44,397	54,477	64,557	74,637	238,068	273,778	312,107
Total COGS	9,543	198,914	267,732	368,584	844,774	437,699	518,507	693,275	774,083	2,423,566	2,787,100	3,177,295
Gross Profit	17,531	382,690	676,430	929,588	2,006,240	1,134,015	1,355,607	1,788,058	2,009,650	6,287,330	12,482,110	14,229,605
Operating Expenses												
Sales and marketing	56,010	26,202	26,034	26,432	134,678	58,779	23,728	33,348	49,612	165,467	904,127	1,030,705
Production/distribution	3,153	47,659	34,181	44,968	129,961	46,086	50,385	69,225	73,374	239,070	279,809	318,982
Administration	45,388	69,501	77,291	80,517	272,698	122,010	121,969	111,897	111,766	467,642	502,678	573,053
Total Operating Expense	104,551	143,362	137,507	151,917	537,336	226,875	196,083	214,470	234,752	872,179	1,686,614	1,922,739
Net Income	(87,019)	239,329	538,923	777,671	1,468,904	907,140	1,159,524	1,573,588	1,774,899	5,415,151	10,795,496	12,306,866

EXHIBIT 4B

Cash Flow Actuals and Projections 2007

| | Actuals | | | | Projected | | | | | | | | 2007 |
	Jan-07	Feb-07	Mar-07	Apr-07	May-07	Jun-07	Jul-07	Aug-07	Sep-07	Oct-07	Nov-07	Dec-07	Total
Revenue collected	2,190	6,582	11,348	164,984	175,442	132,774	255,921	281,121	331,521	407,322	432,724	432,724	2,634,652
Increase in debt	12,500	25,000	25,000	25,000									87,500
Total cash sources	14,690	31,582	36,348	189,984	175,442	132,774	255,921	281,121	331,521	407,322	432,724	432,724	2,722,152
Purchase raw materials	2,652	4,217	96,540	10,609	59,630	71,418	71,418	94,994	110,654	110,654	110,564	131,101	874,545
Production labor	193	386	770	23,426	1,542	7,167	8,847	8,847	12,207	12,207	12,207	12,207	100,004
Operating expenses	14,930	22,835	64,381	55,578	37,380	47,270	48,829	47,104	38,787	48,530	47,805	54,953	528,383
Less non cash items:													
Depreciation	0	0	0	0	0	0	0	0	0	0	0	0	0
Debt payments:								0					
Principal				0	3,000	3,000	3,000	3,000	53,000	53,000	53,000	53,000	224,000
Interest				75	75	75	75	75	3,075	3,075	3,075	3,075	12,675
Capital investments													0
Total cash uses	17,775	27,438	161,691	89,688	101,627	128,931	132,170	154,021	217,723	227,467	226,742	254,336	1,739,607
Net cash increase/decrease	(3,085)	4,144	(125,344)	100,296	73,815	3,843	123,751	127,100	113,797	179,856	205,982	178,388	982,545
Cash beginning of month	0	(3,085)	1,059	(124,284)	(23,988)	49,827	53,670	177,421	304,522	418,319	598,174	804,157	982,545
Cash end of month	(3,085)	1,059	(124,284)	(23,988)	49,827	53,670	177,421	304,522	418,319	598,174	804,157	982,545	982,545

EXHIBIT 4C

Cash Flow Projections 2008–2010

	Q1 2008	Q2 2008	Q3 2008	Q4 2008	2008 Total	2009 Total	2010 Total
			Projected				
Revenue collected	1,526,124	1,823,714	2,380,130	2,733,334	8,463,302	15,096,949	17,361,491
Increase in debt					0	0	0
Total cash sources	1,526,124	1,823,714	2,380,130	2,733,334	8,463,302	15,096,949	17,361,491
Purchase raw materials	416,878	518,926	652,294	675,741	2,263,840	2,303,879	2,649,461
Production labor	44,391	54,477	64,557	74,637	238,068	273,778	314,845
Operating expenses	227,134	196,479	215,036	235,545	874,194	1,690,063	1,943,572
Less noncash items:							
Depreciation	0	0	0	0	0	0	0
Debt payments:							
Principal	9,000	9,000	13,000	15,000	46,000	0	0
Interest	225	225	375	450	1,275	0	0
Capital investments					0	0	0
Total cash uses	697,634	779,107	945,262	1,001,374	3,423,377	4,267,720	4,907,878
Net cash increase/decrease	828,490	1,044,607	1,434,868	1,731,960	5,039,925	10,829,229	12,453,613
Cash beginning of period	982,545	1,811,034	2,855,642	4,290,510		6,022,470	16,851,699
Cash end of period	1,811,034	2,855,642	4,290,510	6,022,470	6,022,470	16,851,699	29,305,312

Michael added that the moment the 2006 inventory was out the door, they would begin to consider expanding into other areas:

My mom and I are always trying to think about what market channels we should be in. At the food shows you get lots of advice, but there is no consensus. Right now we are geared up for and focused on the supermarket industry. That may change once we get a chance to think this through and get a bit deeper into the trade-offs, the logistics, and the numbers.

PART TWO

The Opportunity

One often hears, especially from younger, newer entrepreneurs, this exhortation: "Go for it! You have nothing to lose now. So what if it doesn't work out. You can do it again. Why wait?" While the spirit this reflects is commendable and there can be no substitute for doing, such itchiness can be a mistake unless it is focused on a solid opportunity.

Most entrepreneurs launching businesses, particularly the first time, run out of cash quicker than they bring in customers and profitable sales. While there are many reasons for this, the first is that they have not focused on the *right* opportunities. Unsuccessful entrepreneurs usually equate an idea with an opportunity; successful entrepreneurs know the difference!

Successful entrepreneurs know that it is important to "think big enough." They understand that they aren't simply creating a job for themselves and a few employees; they are building a business that can create value for themselves and their community.

While there are boundless opportunities for those with entrepreneurial zest, a single entrepreneur will likely be able to launch and build only a few good businesses—probably no more than three or four—during his or her energetic and productive years. (Fortunately, all you need to do is grow and harvest one quite profitable venture whose sales have exceeded several million dollars. The result will be a most satisfying professional life, as well as a financially rewarding one.)

How important is it, then, that you screen and choose an opportunity with great care? Very important! It is no accident that venture capital investors have consistently invested in no more than 1 or 2 percent of all the ventures they review.

As important as it is to find a good opportunity, even good opportunities have risks and problems. The perfect deal has yet to be seen. Identifying risks and problems before the launch while steps can be taken to eliminate them or reduce any negative effect early is another dimension of opportunity screening.

3

Chapter Three

The Entrepreneurial Process

"I don't make movies to make money. I make money to make movies."

—Walt Disney

Results Expected

Upon completion of this chapter, you will be able to

1. Articulate a definition of entrepreneurship and the entrepreneurial process—from lifestyle ventures to high-potential enterprises.

2. Describe the practical issues you will address and explore throughout the book.

3. Discuss how entrepreneurs and their financial backers get the odds for success in their favor by defying the familiar pattern of disappointment and failure.

4. Articulate the Timmons Model of the entrepreneurial process; describe how it can be applied to your entrepreneurial career aspirations and ideas for businesses; and describe how recent research confirms its validity.

5. Provide insights into and analysis of the Roxanne Quimby case study.

Demystifying Entrepreneurship

Entrepreneurship is a way of thinking, reasoning, and acting that is opportunity obsessed, holistic in approach, and leadership balanced for the purpose of value creation and capture.[1] Entrepreneurship results in the creation, enhancement, realization, and renewal of value, not just for owners, but for all participants and stakeholders. At the heart of the process is the creation and/or recognition of opportunities,[2] followed by the will and initiative to seize these opportunities. It requires a willingness to take risks—both personal and financial—but in a very calculated fashion in order to constantly shift the odds of success, balancing the risk with the potential reward.

Typically entrepreneurs devise ingenious strategies to marshall their limited resources.

Today entrepreneurship has evolved beyond the classic start-up notion to include companies and organizations of all types, in all stages. Thus *entrepreneurship can occur—and fail to occur—in firms that are old and new; small and large; fast and slow-growing; in the private, not-for-profit, and public sectors; in all geographic points; and in all stages of a nation's development, regardless of politics.*

Entrepreneurial leaders inject imagination, motivation, commitment, passion, tenacity, integrity, teamwork, and vision into their companies. They face dilemmas and must make decisions despite ambiguity and contradictions. Very rarely is entrepreneurship a get-

---

[1] This definition of entrepreneurship has evolved over the past three decades from research by Jeffry A. Timmons, Babson College and the Harvard Business School, and has recently been enhanced by Stephen Spinelli, Jr., former vice provost for entrepreneurship and global management at Babson College, and current president of Philadelphia University.

[2] J. A. Timmons, D. F. Muzyka, H. H. Stevenson, and W. D. Bygrave, "Opportunity Recognition: The Core of Entrepreneurship," in *Frontiers of Entrepreneurship Research* (Babson Park, MA: Babson College, 1987), p. 409.

rich-quick proposition. On the contrary, it is one of continuous renewal because entrepreneurs are never satisfied with the nature of their opportunity. The result of this value creation process, as we saw earlier, is that the total economic pie grows larger and society benefits.

Classic Entrepreneurship: The Start-Up

The classic expression of entrepreneurship is the raw start-up company, an innovative idea that develops into a high-growth company. The best of these become entrepreneurial legends: Microsoft, Netscape, Amazon.com, Sun Microsystems, Home Depot, McDonald's, Intuit, Staples, and hundreds of others are now household names. Success, in addition to the strong leadership from the main entrepreneur, almost always involves building a team with complementary talents. The ability to work as a team and sense an opportunity where others see contradiction, chaos, and confusion are critical elements of success. Entrepreneurship also requires the skill and ingenuity to find and control resources, often owned by others, in order to pursue the opportunity. It means making sure the upstart venture does not run out of money when it needs it the most. Most highly successful entrepreneurs have held together a team and acquired financial backing in order to chase an opportunity others may not recognize.

Entrepreneurship in Post-Brontosaurus Capitalism: Beyond Start-Ups

As we've seen, the upstart companies of the 1970s and 1980s have had a profound impact on the competitive structure of the United States and world industries. Giant firms, such as IBM (knocked off by Apple Computer and then Microsoft), Digital Equipment Corporation (another victim of Apple Computer and acquired by Compaq Computer Corporation), Sears (demolished by upstart Wal-Mart and recently merged with Kmart), and AT&T (knocked from its perch first by MCI, and then by cellular upstarts McCaw Communications, CellularOne, and others), once thought invincible, have been dismembered by the new wave of entrepreneurial ventures. *The New York Times, LA Times*, and most major city newspapers have been losing market share to Internet start-ups for the past 10 years. While large companies shrank payrolls, new ventures added jobs. Between 2003 and 2005, employ-

ment at venture-backed companies grew at an annual rate of 4.1 percent, compared to just 1.3 percent for the U.S. economy as a whole. Venture investment is particularly important in the software and computers and peripherals industries, where nearly 90 percent of all jobs are within venture-backed companies.[3] As autopsy after autopsy was performed on failing large companies, a fascinating pattern emerged, showing, at worst, a total disregard for the winning entrepreneurial approaches of their new rivals and, at best, a glacial pace in recognizing the impending demise and the changing course.

"People Don't Want to Be Managed. They Want to Be Led!"[4]

These giant firms can be characterized, during their highly vulnerable periods, as hierarchical in structure with many layers of reviews, approvals, and vetoes. Their tired executive blood conceived of leadership as *managing and administering* from the top down, in stark contrast to Ewing M. Kauffman's powerful insight: "People don't want to be managed. They want to be led!" These stagnating giants tended to reward people who accumulated the largest assets, budgets, number of plants, products, and head count, rather than rewarding those who created or found new business opportunities, took calculated risks, and occasionally made mistakes, all with bootstrap resources. While very cognizant of the importance of corporate culture and strategy, the corporate giants' pace was glacial: It typically takes six years for a large firm to change its strategy and 10 to 30 years to change its culture. Meanwhile, the median time it took start-ups to accumulate the necessary capital was one month but averaged six months.[5]

To make matters worse, these corporate giants had many bureaucratic tendencies, particularly arrogance. They shared a blind belief that if they followed the almost sacred best management practices of the day, they could not help but prevail. During the 1970s and 1980s, these best management practices did not include entrepreneurship, entrepreneurial leadership, and entrepreneurial reasoning. If anything, these were considered dirty words in corporate America. Chief among these sacred cows was staying close to your customer. What may shock you is the conclusion of two Harvard Business School professors:

> One of the most consistent patterns in business is the failure of leading companies to stay at the top of their industries when technologies or markets change. . . . But

---

[3] National Venture Capital Association, *Venture Impact: The Economic Importance of Venture Capital Backed Companies to the U.S. Economy,* 2007.
[4] The authors' favorite quote from Ewing M. Kauffman, founder of Marion Laboratories, Inc., the Ewing Marion Kauffman Foundation, Kansas City, Missouri.
[5] W. J. Dennis, Jr., "Wells Fargo/NFIB Series on Business Starts and Stops," November 1999.

a more fundamental reason lies at the heart of the paradox: Leading companies succumb to one of the most popular, valuable management dogmas. They stay close to their customers.[6]

When they do attack, the [new] entrant companies find the established players to be easy and unprepared opponents because the opponents have been looking up markets themselves, discounting the threat from below.[7]

One gets further insight into just how vulnerable and fragile the larger, so-called well-managed companies can become, and why it is the newcomers who pose the greatest threats. This pattern also explains why there are tremendous opportunities for the coming e-generation even in markets that are currently dominated by large players. Professors Bower and Christensen summarize it this way:

> The problem is that managers keep doing what has worked in the past: serving the rapidly growing needs of their current customers. The processes that successful, well-managed companies have developed to allocate resources among proposed investments are incapable of funneling resources in programs that current customers explicitly don't want and whose profit margins seem unattractive.[8]

Given how many new innovations, firms, and industries have been created in the past 30 years, it is no wonder that brontosaurus capitalism has found its ice age.

Signs of Hope in a Corporate Ice Age

Fortunately, for many giant firms, the entrepreneurial revolution may spare them from their own ice age. One of the most exciting developments of the decade is the response of some large, established U.S. corporations to the revolution in entrepreneurial leadership. After nearly three decades of experiencing the demise of giant after giant, corporate leadership, in unprecedented numbers, is launching experiments and strategies to recapture entrepreneurial spirit and to instill the culture and practices we would characterize as entrepreneurial reasoning. The e-generation has too many attractive opportunities in truly entrepreneurial environments. They do not need to work for a brontosaurus that lacks spirit.

Increasingly, we see examples of large companies adopting principles of entrepreneurship and entrepreneurial leadership in order to survive and to renew. Researchers document how large firms are applying entrepreneurial thinking, in pioneering ways,

to invent their futures, including companies such as GE, Corning, and Motorola,[9] Harley-Davidson ($1.35 billion in revenue), Marshall Industries ($2.2 billion), and Science Applications International Corporation (SAIC) in San Diego. Most large brontosaurus firms could learn valuable lessons on how to apply entrepreneurial thinking from companies such as these.

Metaphors

Improvisational, quick, clever, resourceful, and inventive all describe good entrepreneurs. Likewise, innumerable metaphors from other parts of life can describe the complex world of the entrepreneur and the entrepreneurial process. From music it is jazz, with its uniquely American impromptu flair. From sports many metaphors exist: LeBron James's agility, the broken-field running of Curtis Martin, the wizardry on ice of Wayne Gretzky, or the competitiveness of Tiger Woods. Even more fascinating are the unprecedented comebacks of athletic greats such as Michael Jordan, Picabo Street, and Lance Armstrong.

Perhaps the game of golf, more than any other, replicates the complex and dynamic nature of managing risk and reward, including all the intricate mental challenges faced in entrepreneuring. No other sport, at one time, demands so much physically, is so complex, intricate, and delicate, and is simultaneously so rewarding and punishing; and none tests one's will, patience, self-discipline, and self-control like golf. Entrepreneurs face these challenges and remunerations as well. If you think that the team concept isn't important in golf, remember the 2004 American Ryder Cup team, which failed to work together and lost to the Europeans. And what about the relationship between the caddy and golfer?

An entrepreneur also faces challenges like a symphony conductor or a coach, who must blend and balance a group of diverse people with different skills, talents, and personalities into a superb team. On many occasions it demands all the talents and agility of a juggler who must, under great stress, keep many balls in the air at once, making sure if one comes down it belongs to someone else.

The complex decisions and numerous alternatives facing the entrepreneur also have many parallels with the game of chess. As in chess, the victory goes to the most creative player, who can imagine several alternative moves in advance and anticipate possible defenses.

[6] J. L. Bower and C. M. Christensen, "Disruptive Technologies: Catching the Wave," *Harvard Business Review*, January–February 1995, p. 43.
[7] Ibid., p. 47.
[8] Ibid.
[9] *Fast Company*, June–July 1997, pp. 32, 79, 104; and U. S. Rangan, "Alliances Power Corporate Renewal," Babson College, 2001.

This kind of mental agility is frequently demanded in entrepreneurial decision making.

Still another parallel can be drawn from the book *The Right Stuff* by Tom Wolfe, later made into a movie. The first pilot to break the sound barrier, Chuck Yeager, describes what it was like to be at the edge of both the atmosphere and his plane's performance capability, a zone never before entered— a vivid metaphor for the experience of a first-time entrepreneur:

> In the thin air at the edge of space, where the stars and the moon came out at noon, in an atmosphere so thin that the ordinary laws of aerodynamics no longer applied and a plane could skid into a flat spin like a cereal bowl on a waxed Formica counter and then start tumbling, end over end like a brick . . . you had to be "afraid to panic." In the skids, the tumbles, the spins, there was only one thing you could let yourself think about: what do I do next?[10]

This feeling is frequently the reality on earth for entrepreneurs who run out of cash! Regardless of the metaphor or analogy you choose for entrepreneurship, each is likely to describe a creative, even artistic, improvised act. The outcomes are often either highly rewarding successes or painfully visible misses. Always urgency is on the doorstep.

Entrepreneurship = Paradoxes

One of the most confounding aspects of the entrepreneurial process is its contradictions. Because of its highly dynamic, fluid, ambiguous, and chaotic character, the process's constant changes frequently pose paradoxes. A sampling of entrepreneurial paradoxes follows. Can you think of other paradoxes that you have observed or heard about?

> *An opportunity with no or very low potential can be an enormously big opportunity.* One of the most famous examples of this paradox is Apple Computer. Founders Steve Jobs and Steve Wozniak approached their employer, Hewlett-Packard Corporation (HP), with the idea for a desktop, personal computer and were told this was not an opportunity for HP. Hence Jobs and Wozniak started their own company. Frequently business plans rejected by some venture capitalists become legendary successes when backed by another investor. Intuit, maker of Quicken software, for example, was rejected by 20 venture capitalists before securing backing.

> *To make money you have to first lose money.* It is commonly said in the venture capital business that the lemons, or losers, ripen in two and a half years, while the plums take seven or eight years. A start-up, venture-backed company typically loses money, often $10 million to $25 million or more, before sustaining profitability and going public, usually at least five to seven years later.

> *To create and build wealth one must relinquish wealth.* Among the most successful and growing companies in the United States, the founders aggressively dilute their ownership to create ownership throughout the company. By rewarding and sharing the wealth with the people who contribute significantly to its creation, owners motivate stakeholders to make the pie bigger.

> *To succeed, one first has to experience failure.* It is a common pattern that the first venture fails, yet the entrepreneur learns and goes on to create a highly successful company. Jerry Kaplan teamed with Lotus Development Corporation founder Mitch Kapor to start the first pen-based computer. After $80 million of venture capital investment, the company was shut down. Kaplan went on to launch On-Sale, Inc., an Internet Dutch auction, which experienced explosive growth and went public in 1996.

> *Entrepreneurship requires considerable thought, preparation, and planning, yet is basically an unplannable event.* The highly dynamic, changing character of technology, markets, and competition makes it impossible to know all your competitors today, let alone five years from now. Yet great effort is invested in attempting to model and envision the future. The resulting business plan is inevitably obsolete when it comes off the printer. This is a creative process—like molding clay. You need to make a habit of planning and reacting as you constantly reevaluate your options, blending the messages from your head and your gut, until this process becomes second nature.

> *For creativity and innovativeness to prosper, rigor and discipline must accompany the process.* For years, hundreds of thousands of patents for new products and technologies lay fallow in government and university research labs because there was no commercial discipline.

> *Entrepreneurship requires a bias toward action and a sense of urgency, but also demands patience and perseverance.* While his competitors were acquiring and expanding rapidly, one entrepreneur's management team became nearly

---

[10] T. Wolfe, *The Right Stuff* (New York: Bantam Books, 1980), pp. 51–52.

outraged at his inaction. This entrepreneur reported he saved the company at least $50 million to $100 million during the prior year by just sitting tight. He learned this lesson from the Jiffy Lube case series from *New Venture Creation,* which he studied during a weeklong program for the Young Presidents Organization (YPO), at Harvard Business School in 1991.

The greater the organization, orderliness, discipline, and control, the less you will control your ultimate destiny. Entrepreneurship requires great flexibility and nimbleness in strategy and tactics. One has to play with the knees bent. Overcontrol and an obsession with orderliness are impediments to the entrepreneurial approach. As the great race car driver Mario Andretti said, "If I am in total control, I know I am going too slow!"

Adhering to management best practice, especially staying close to the customer that created industry leaders in the 1980s, became a seed of self-destruction and loss of leadership to upstart competitors. We discussed earlier the study of "disruptive technologies."

To realize long-term equity value, you have to forgo the temptations of short-term profitability. Building long-term equity requires large, continuous reinvestment in new people, products, services, and support systems, usually at the expense of immediate profits.

The world of entrepreneurship is not neat, tidy, linear, consistent, and predictable, no matter how much we might like it to be that way.[11] In fact, it is from the collisions inherent in these paradoxes that value is created, as illustrated in Exhibit 3.1. These paradoxes illustrate just how contradictory and chaotic this world can be. To thrive in this environment, one needs to be very adept at coping with ambiguity, chaos, and uncertainty, and at building management skills that create predictability. Exhibit 3.2 exemplifies this ambiguity and need for patience. For example, Apple shipped the first iPod in November 2001. Eighteen months later Apple sold the one millionth unit and six months later sold another million units. In 2005 Apple shipped 13 million units. A Merrill Lynch analyst predicts iPod sales could eventually reach 300 million.

The Higher-Potential Venture: Think Big Enough

One of the biggest mistakes aspiring entrepreneurs make is strategic. They think too small. Sensible as it

EXHIBIT 3.1
Entrepreneurship IS a Contact Sport

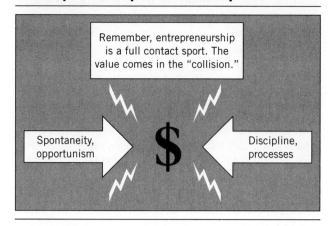

EXHIBIT 3.2
Time for New Technologies to Reach 25% of the U.S. Population

Household electricity (1873)	46 years
Telephone (1875)	35 years
Automobile (1885)	55 years
Airplane travel (1903)	54 years
Radio (1906)	22 years
Television (1925)	26 years
Videocassette recorder (1952)	34 years
Personal computer (1975)	15 years
Cellular phone	13 years
Internet	**7 years**
iPod	**5 years**

Source: *The Wall Street Journal,* 1997. Used by permission of Dow Jones & Co. Inc. via The Copyright Clearance Center with adaption for the inclusion of Internet and iPod.

may be to think in terms of a very small, simple business as being more affordable, more manageable, less demanding, and less risky, the opposite is true. The chances of survival and success are lower in these small, job-substitute businesses, and even if they do survive, they are less financially rewarding. As one founder of numerous businesses put it, unless this business can pay you at least five times your present salary, the risk and wear and tear won't be worth it.

Consider one of the most successful venture capital investors ever, Arthur Rock. His criterion for searching for opportunities is very simple: *Look for business concepts that will change the way people live or work.* His home-run investments are legendary, including Intel, Apple Computer, Teledyne, and

---

[11] See H. H. Stevenson, *Do Lunch or Be Lunch* (Boston, MA: Harvard Business School Press, 1998) for a provocative argument for predictability as one of the most powerful of management tools.

dozens of others. Clearly his philosophy is to think big. Today an extraordinary variety of people, opportunities, and strategies characterize the approximately 30 million proprietorships, partnerships, and corporations in the country. Remember, high-potential ventures become high-impact firms that often make the world a better place!

Nearly 11 percent of the U.S. population is actively working toward starting a new venture.[12] More than 90 percent of start-ups have revenues of less than $1 million annually, while 863,505 reported revenues of $1 million to $25 million—just over 9 percent of the total. Of these, only 296,695 grew at a compounded annual growth rate of 30 percent or more for the prior three years, or about 3 percent. Similarly, just 3 percent—1 in 33—exceeded $10 million in revenues, and only 0.3 percent exceeded $100 million in revenues.

Not only can nearly anyone start a business, but also a great many can succeed. While it certainly might help, a person does not have to be a genius to create a successful business. As Nolan Bushnell, founder of Atari, one of the first desktop computer games in the early 1980s, and Pizza Time Theater, said, "If you are not a millionaire or bankrupt by the time you are 30, you are not really trying!"[13] It is an entrepreneur's preparedness for the entrepreneurial process that is important. Being an entrepreneur has moved from cult status in the 1980s to rock star infamy in the 1990s to become de rigueur at the turn of the century. Amateur entrepreneurship is over. The professionals have arrived.[14]

A stunning number of mega-entrepreneurs launched their ventures during their 20s. While the rigors of new ventures may favor the "young at start," age is *not* a barrier to entry. One study showed that nearly 21 percent of founders were over 40 when they embarked on their entrepreneurial careers, the majority were in their 30s, and just over one-fourth did so by the time they were 25. Further, numerous examples exist of founders who were over 60 at the time of launch, including one of the most famous seniors, Colonel Harland Sanders, who started Kentucky Fried Chicken with his first Social Security check.

Smaller Means Higher Failure Odds

Unfortunately, the record of survival is not good among all firms started. One of the most optimistic research firms estimates the failure rate for start-ups is 46.4 percent. While government data, research, and business mortality statisticians may not agree on the precise failure and survival figures for new businesses, they do agree that failure is the rule, not the exception.

Complicating efforts to obtain precise figures is the fact that it is not easy to define and identify failures, and reliable statistics and databases are not available. However, the Small Business Administration determined that in 1999 there were 588,900 start-ups, while 528,600 firms closed their doors.[15]

Failure rates also vary widely across industries. In 1991, for instance, retail and services accounted for 61 percent of all failures and bankruptcies in that year.[16]

The following discussion provides a distillation of a number of failure rate studies over the past 50 years.[17] These studies illustrate that (1) failure rates are high, and (2) although the majority of the failures occur in the first two to five years, it may take considerably longer for some to fail.[18]

Government data, research, and business mortality statisticians agree that start-ups run a high risk of failure. Another study, outlined in Exhibit 3.3, found that of 565,812 firms one year old or less in the first quarter of 1998 only 303,517 were still alive by the first quarter of 2001. This is an average failure rate of 46.4 percent.

Failure rates across industries vary as seen in Exhibit 3.3. The real estate industry, with a 36.8 percent rate of start-up failure, is the lowest. The technology sector has a high rate of failure at 53.9 percent. The software and services segment of the technology industry has an even higher failure rate; 55.2 percent of start-ups tracked closed their doors. Unfortunately the record of survival is not good among all firms started.

To make matters worse, most people think the failure rates are actually much higher. Since actions

[12] *The Global Entrepreneurship Monitor,* Babson College and the London Business School, May 2007.

[13] In response to a student question at Founder's Day, Babson College, April 1983.

[14] Bob Davis, Partner, Highland Capital, June 2007.

[15] *The State of Small Business: A Report of the President, Transmitted to the Congress,* 1999 (Washington, DC: Small Business Administration, 1999).

[16] *The State of Small Business,* 1992, p. 128.

[17] Information has been culled from the following studies: D. L. Birch, MIT Studies, 1979–1980; M. B. Teitz et al., "Small Business and Employment Growth in California," Working Paper No. 348, University of California at Berkeley, March 1981, table 5, p. 22; U.S. Small Business Administration, August 29, 1988; B. D. Phillips and B. A. Kirchhoff, "An Analysis of New Firm Survival and Growth," *Frontiers in Entrepreneurship Research: 1988,* ed. B. A. Kirchhoff et al. (Babson Park, MA: Babson College, 1988), pp. 266–67; and *BizMiner 2002 Startup Business Risk Index: Major Industry Report,* Brandow Co., Inc., 2002.

[18] Summaries of these are reported by A. N. Shapero and J. Gigherano, "Exits and Entries: A Study in Yellow Pages Journalism," in *Frontiers of Entrepreneurship Research: 1982,* ed. K. Vesper et al. (Babson Park, MA: Babson College, 1982), pp. 113–41, and A. C. Cooper and C. Y. Woo, "Survival and Failure: A Longitudinal Study," in *Frontiers of Entrepreneurship Research: 1988,* ed. B. A. Kirchhoff et al. (Babson Park, MA: Babson College, 1988), pp. 225–37.

EXHIBIT 3.3

Starts and Closures of Employer Firms, 2002–2006

Category	2002	2003	2004	2005	2006
New Firms	569,750	612,296	628,917	653,100*	649,700*
Closures	586,890	540,658	541,047	543,700*	564,900*
Bankruptcies	38,540	35,037	39,317	39,201	19,695

*Estimate.

Sources: U.S. Dept. of Commerce, Bureau of the Census; Administrative Office of the U.S. Courts; U.S. Dept. of Labor, Employment and Training Administration.

often are governed by perceptions rather than facts, this perception of failure, in addition to the dismal record, can be a serious obstacle to aspiring entrepreneurs.

Still other studies have shown significant differences in survival rates among Bradstreet industry categories: retail trade, construction, and small service businesses accounted for 70 percent of all failures and bankruptcies. One study calculates a risk factor or index for start-ups by industry, which sends a clear warning signal to the would-be entrepreneur.[19] At the high end of risk is tobacco products, and at the low end you find the affinity and membership organizations such as AAA or Welcome Wagon. "The fishing is better in some streams versus others," is a favorite saying of the authors. Further, 99 percent of these failed companies had fewer than 100 employees. Through observation and practical experience one would not be surprised by such reports. The implications for would-be entrepreneurs are important: Knowing the difference between a good idea and a real opportunity is vital. This will be addressed in detail in Chapter 5.

A certain level of failure is part of the "creative self-destruction" described by Joseph Schumpeter in his numerous writings, including *Business Cycles* (1939) and *Capitalism*. It is part of the dynamics of innovation and economic renewal, a process that requires both births and deaths. More important, it is also part of the learning process inherent in gaining an entrepreneurial apprenticeship. If a business fails, no other country in the world has laws, institutions, and social norms that are more forgiving. Firms go out of existence, but entrepreneurs survive and learn.

The daunting evidence of failure poses two important questions for aspiring entrepreneurs. First, are there any exceptions to this general rule of failure, or are we faced with a punishing game of entrepreneurial roulette? Second, if there is an exception, how does one get the odds for success in one's favor?

Getting the Odds in Your Favor

Fortunately, there is a decided pattern of exceptions to the overall rate of failure among the vast majority of small, marginal firms created each year. Most smaller enterprises that cease operation simply do not meet our notion of entrepreneurship. They do not create, enhance, or pursue opportunities that realize value. They tend to be job substitutes in many instances. Undercapitalized, undermanaged, and often poorly located, they soon fail.

Threshold Concept

Who are the survivors? The odds for survival and a higher level of success change dramatically if the venture reaches a critical mass of at least 10 to 20 people with $2 million to $3 million in revenues and is currently pursuing opportunities with growth potential. Exhibit 3.4 shows that based on a cross-section of all new firms, one-year survival rates for new firms increase steadily as the firm size increases. The rates jump from approximately 54 percent for firms having up to 24 employees to approximately 73 percent for firms with between 100 and 249 employees.

One study found that empirical evidence supports the liability of newness and liability of smallness arguments and suggests that newness and small size make survival problematic. The authors inferred, "Perceived satisfaction, cooperation, and trust between

EXHIBIT 3.4

One-Year Survival Rates by Firm Size

Firm Size (Employees)	Survival Percentage
1–24	53.6%
25–49	68.0
50–99	69.0
100–249	73.2

Source: *BizMiner 2002 Startup Business Risk Index: Major Industry Report*, © 2002 BizMiner. Reprinted by permission.

[19] *BizMiner 2002 Startup Business Risk Index.*

the customer and the organization [are] important for the continuation of the relationship. High levels of satisfaction, cooperation, and trust represent a stock of goodwill and positive beliefs which are critical assets that influence the commitment of the two parties to the relationship."[20] The authors of this study noted, "Smaller organizations are found to be more responsive, while larger organizations are found to provide greater depth of service. . . . The entrepreneurial task is to find a way to either direct the arena of competition away from the areas where you are at a competitive disadvantage, or find some creative way to develop the required competency."[21]

After four years, the survival rate jumps from approximately 35 to 40 percent for firms with fewer than 19 employees to about 55 percent for firms with 20 to 49 employees. Although any estimates based on sales per employee vary considerably from industry to industry, this minimum translates roughly to a threshold of $50,000 to $100,000 of sales per employee annually. But highly successful firms can generate much higher sales per employee. According to several reports, the service (38.6 percent), distribution (28.7 percent), and production (17.8 percent) industries have the most closed businesses after four to five years.

Promise of Growth

The definition of entrepreneurship implies the promise of expansion and the building of long-term value and durable cash flow streams as well.

However, as will be discussed later, it takes a long time for companies to become established and grow. Historically, two of every five small firms founded survive six or more years, but few achieve growth during the first four years.[22] The study also found that survival rates more than double for firms that grow, and the earlier in the life of the business that growth occurs, the higher the chance of survival.[23] The 2007 INC. 500 exemplify this, with a three-year growth rate of 939 percent.[24]

Some of the true excitement of entrepreneurship lies in conceiving, launching, and building firms such as these.

Venture Capital Backing

Another notable pattern of exception to the failure rule is found for businesses that attract start-up financing from successful private venture capital companies. While venture-backed firms account for a very small percentage of new firms each year, in 2000, 238 of 414 IPOs, or 57 percent, had venture backing.[25]

Venture capital is not essential to a start-up, nor is it a guarantee of success. Of the companies making the 2007 INC. 500, about 18 percent raised venture capital and only 3 percent had venture funding at start-up.[26] Consider, for instance, that in 2000 only 5,557 companies received venture capital.[27] However, companies with venture capital support fare better overall. Only 46 companies with venture capital declared bankruptcy or became defunct in 2000.[28] This is less than 1 percent of companies that received venture capital in 2000.

These compelling data have led some to conclude that a threshold core of 10 to 15 percent of new companies will become the winners in terms of size, job creation, profitability, innovation, and potential for harvesting (and thereby realize a capital gain).

Private Investors Join Venture Capitalists

As noted previously, harvested entrepreneurs by the tens of thousands have become "angels" as private investors in the next generation of entrepreneurs. Many of the more successful entrepreneurs have created their own investment pools and are competing directly with venture capitalists for deals. Their operating experiences and successful track records provide a compelling case for adding value to an upstart company. Take, for example, highly successful Boston entrepreneur Jeff Parker. His first venture, Technical Data Corporation, enabled Wall Street bond traders to conduct daily trading with a desktop computer. Parker's software on the Apple II created a new industry in the early 1980s.

After harvesting this and other ventures, he created his own private investment pool in the 1990s. As the Internet explosion occurred, he was one of the early investors to spot opportunities in start-up

---

[20] S. Venkataraman and M. B. Low, "On the Nature of Critical Relationships: A Test of the Liabilities and Size Hypothesis," in *Frontiers in Entrepreneurship Research: 1991* (Babson Park, MA: Babson College, 1991), p. 97.

[21] Ibid., pp. 105–6.

[22] B. D. Phillips and B. A. Kirchhoff, "An Analysis of New Firm Survival and Growth," in *Frontiers in Entrepreneurship Research: 1988* (Babson Park, MA: Babson College, 1988), pp. 266–67.

[23] This reaffirms the exception to the failure rule noted above and in the original edition of this book in 1977.

[24] S. Greco, "The INC. 500 Almanac," *INC.*, October 2001, p. 80.

[25] "Aftermarket at a Glance," *IPO Reporter*, December 10, 2001; and "IPO Aftermarket," *Venture Capital Journal*, December 2001.

[26] www.inc.com/inc5000

[27] Venture Economics, http://www.ventureeconomics.com/vec/stats/2001q2/us.html, July 30, 2001.

[28] *VentureXpert*, Thompson Financial Data Services, 2001.

ventures. In one case, he persuaded the founders of a new Internet firm to select him as lead investor instead of accepting offers from some of the most prestigious venture capital firms in the nation. According to the founders, it was clear that Parker's unique entrepreneurial track record and his understanding of their business would add more value than the venture capitalists at start-up.

Private investors and entrepreneurs such as Parker have similar selection criteria to the venture capitalists: They are in search of the high-potential, higher-growth ventures. Unlike the venture capitalists, however, they are not constrained by having to invest so much money in a relatively short period that they must invest it in minimum chunks of $3 million to $5 million or more. Private investors, therefore, are prime sources for less capital-intensive start-ups and early-stage businesses. Bob Davis (Lycos) and Tom Stemberg (Staples) followed a similar path with Highland Capital.

This overall search for higher-potential ventures has become more evident in recent years. The new e-generation appears to be learning the lessons of these survivors, venture capitalists, private investors, and founders of higher-potential firms. Hundreds of thousands of college students now have been exposed to these concepts for more than two decades, and their strategies for identifying potential businesses are mindful of and disciplined about the ingredients for success. Unlike 20 years ago, it is now nearly impossible not to hear and read about these principles whether on television, in books, on the Internet, or in a multitude of seminars, courses, and programs for would-be entrepreneurs of all types.

Find Financial Backers and Associates Who Add Value

One of the most distinguishing disciplines of these higher-potential ventures is how the founders identify financial partners and key team members. They insist on backers and partners who do more than bring just money, friendship, commitment, and motivation to the venture. They surround themselves with backers who can add value to the venture through their experience, know-how, networks, and wisdom. Key associates are selected because they are smarter and better at what they do than the founder, and they raise the overall average of the entire company. This theme will be examined in detail in later chapters.

Option: The Lifestyle Venture

For many aspiring entrepreneurs, issues of family roots and location take precedence. Accessibility to a preferred way of life, whether it is access to fishing, skiing, hunting, hiking, music, surfing, rock climbing, canoeing, a rural setting, or the mountains, can be more important than how large a business one has or the size of one's net worth. Others vastly prefer to be with and work with their family or spouse. They want to live in a nonurban area that they consider very attractive. Take Jake and Diana Bishop, for instance. Both have advanced degrees in accounting. They gave up six-figure jobs they both found rewarding and satisfying on the beautiful coast of Maine to return to their home state of Michigan for several important lifestyle reasons. They wanted to work together again in a business, which they had done successfully earlier in their marriage. It was important to be much closer than the 14-hour drive to Diana's aging parents. They also wanted to have their children—then in their 20s—join them in the business. Finally, they wanted to live in one of their favorite areas of the country, Harbor Spring on Lake Michigan in the northwest tip of the state. They report never to have worked harder in their 50 years, nor have they been any happier. They are growing their rental business more than 20 percent a year, making an excellent living, and creating equity value. If done right, one can have a lifestyle business and actually realize higher potential.

Yet couples who give up successful careers in New York City to buy an inn in Vermont to avoid the rat race generally last only six to seven years. They discover the joys of self-employment, including seven-day, 70- to 90-hour workweeks, chefs and day help that do not show up, roofs that leak when least expected, and the occasional guests from hell. The grass is always greener, so they say.

The Timmons Model: Where Theory and Practice Collide in the Real World

How can aspiring entrepreneurs—and the investors and associates who join the venture—get the odds of success on their side? What do these talented and successful high-potential entrepreneurs, their venture capitalists, and their private backers do differently? What is accounting for their exceptional record? Are there general lessons and principles underlying their successes that can benefit aspiring entrepreneurs, investors, and those who would join a venture? If so, can these lessons be learned?

These are the central questions of our lifetime work. We have been immersed as students, researchers, teachers, and practitioners of the *entrepreneurial process*. As founding shareholders and investors of several high-potential ventures (some of which are now public), directors and advisors to ventures and venture capital funds, a charter director and advisor to the Kauffman Center for Entrepreneurial Leadership at the Ewing Marion Kauffman Foundation, and as director of the Arthur M. Blank Center for Entrepreneurship at Babson College, we have each applied, tested, refined, and tempered academic theory as fire tempers iron into steel: in the fire of practice.

Intellectual and Practical Collisions with the Real World

Throughout this period of evolution and revolution, *New Venture Creation* has adhered to one core principle: In every quest for greater knowledge of the entrepreneurial process and more effective learning, there must be intellectual and practical collisions between academic theory and the real world of practice. The standard academic notion of something being all right in practice but not in theory is unacceptable. This integrated, holistic balance is at the heart of what we know about the entrepreneurial process and getting the odds in your favor.

Value Creation: The Driving Forces

A core, fundamental entrepreneurial process accounts for the substantially greater success pattern among higher-potential ventures. Despite the great variety of businesses, entrepreneurs, geographies, and technologies, central themes or driving forces dominate this highly dynamic entrepreneurial process.

- It is *opportunity* driven.
- It is driven by a *lead entrepreneur* and an *entrepreneurial team*.
- It is *resource parsimonious and creative*.
- It depends on the *fit and balance* among these.
- It is *integrated and holistic*.
- It is *sustainable*.

These are the controllable components of the entrepreneurial process that can be assessed, influenced, and altered. Founders and investors focus on these forces during their careful due diligence to analyze the risks and determine what changes can be made to improve a venture's chances of success.

First, we will elaborate on each of these forces to provide a blueprint and a definition of what each means. Then using Google as an example, we will illustrate how the holistic, balance, and fit concepts pertain to a start-up.

Change the Odds: Fix It, Shape It, Mold It, Make It

The driving forces underlying successful new venture creation are illustrated in Exhibit 3.5. The process starts with opportunity, not money, strategy, networks, team, or the business plan. Most genuine opportunities are much bigger than either the talent

EXHIBIT 3.5

The Timmons Model of the Entrepreneurial Process

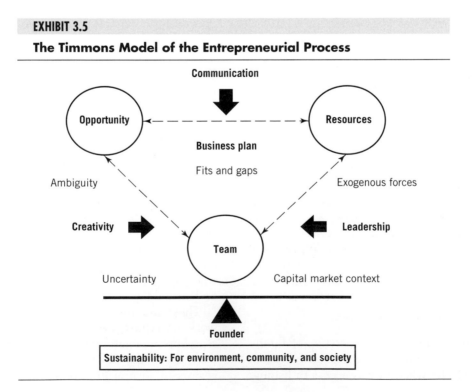

and capacity of the team or the initial resources available to the team. The role of the lead entrepreneur and the team is to juggle all these key elements in a changing environment. Think of a juggler bouncing up and down on a trampoline that is moving on a conveyor belt at unpredictable speeds and directions, while trying to keep all three balls in the air. That is the dynamic nature of an early-stage start-up. The business plan provides the language and code for communicating the quality of the three driving forces of the Timmons Model and of their fit and balance.

In the entrepreneurial process depicted in the Timmons Model, the shape, size, and depth of the opportunity establish the required shape, size, and depth of both the resources and the team. We have found that many people are a bit uncomfortable viewing the opportunity and resources somewhat precariously balanced by the team. It is especially disconcerting to some because we show the three key elements of the entrepreneurial process as circles, and thus the balance appears tenuous. These reactions are justified, accurate, and realistic. The entrepreneurial process is dynamic. Those who recognize the risks better manage the process and garner more return.

The lead entrepreneur's job is simple enough. He or she must carry the deal by *taking charge of the success equation*. In this dynamic context, ambiguity and risk are actually your friends. Central to the homework, creative problem solving and strategizing, and due diligence that lie ahead is analyzing the fits and gaps that exist in the venture. What is wrong with this opportunity? What is missing? What good news and favorable events can happen, as well as the adverse? What has to happen to make it attractive and a fit for me? What market, technology, competitive, management, and financial risks can be reduced or eliminated? What can be changed to make this happen? Who can change it? What are the least resources necessary to grow the business the farthest? Is this the right team? By implication, if you can determine these answers and make the necessary changes by figuring out how to fill the gaps and improve the fit and attract key players who can add such value, then the odds for success rise significantly. In essence, the entrepreneur's role is to manage and redefine the risk–reward equation—all with an eye toward *sustainability*. Because part of the entrepreneur's legacy is to create positive impact without harming the environment, the community, or society, the concept of sustainability appears as the underlying foundation in the model.

The Opportunity   At the heart of the process is the opportunity. Successful entrepreneurs and investors know that a good idea is not necessarily a good opportunity. For every 100 ideas presented to investors in the form of a business plan or proposal, usually fewer than 4 get funded. More than 80 percent of those rejections occur in the first few hours; another 10 to 15 percent are rejected after investors have read the business plan carefully. Fewer than 10 percent attract enough interest to merit a more due diligence thorough review that can take several weeks or months. These are very slim odds. Countless hours and days have been wasted by would-be entrepreneurs chasing ideas that are going nowhere. An important skill for an entrepreneur or an investor is to be able to quickly evaluate whether serious potential exists, and to decide how much time and effort to invest.

John Doerr is a senior partner at one of the most famous and successful venture capital funds ever, Kleiner, Perkins, Caulfield & Byers, and is considered by some to be the most influential venture capitalist of his generation. During his career, he has been the epitome of the revolutionaries described earlier, who have created new industries as lead investors in such legends as Sun Microsystems, Compaq Computer, Lotus Development Corporation, Intuit, Genentech, Millennium, Netscape, and Amazon.com. Regardless of these past home runs, Doerr insists, "There's never been a better time than now to start a company. In the past, entrepreneurs started businesses. Today they invent new business models. That's a big difference, and it creates huge opportunities."[29]

Another venture capitalist recently stated, "Cycles of irrational exuberance are not new in venture investing. The Internet bubble burst, we came back to earth, and then we began another period of excessive valuation that is subsiding in late 2007 with a credit squeeze."[30]

Exhibit 3.6 summarizes the most important characteristics of good opportunities. Underlying market demand—because of the value-added properties of the product or service, the market's size and 20-plus percent growth potential, the economics of the business, particularly robust margins (40 percent or more), and free cash flow characteristics—drives the value creation potential.

We build our understanding of opportunity by first focusing on market readiness: the consumer trends and behaviors that seek new products or services. Once these emerging patterns are identified, the aspiring entrepreneur develops a service or product concept, and finally the service or product delivery

---

[29] "John Doerr's Start-Up Manual," *Fast Company,* February–March 1997, pp. 82–84.
[30] Ernie Parizeau, Partner, Norwest Venture Partners, June 2007.

EXHIBIT 3.6

The Entrepreneurial Process Is Opportunity Driven*

Market demand is a key ingredient to measuring an opportunity:
- Is customer payback less than one year?
- Do market share and growth potential equal 20 percent annual growth and is it durable?
- Is the customer reachable?

Market structure and size help define an opportunity:
- Emerging and/or fragmented?
- $50 million or more, with a $1 billion potential?
- Proprietary barriers to entry?

Margin analysis helps differentiate an opportunity from an idea:
- Low-cost provider (40 percent gross margin)?
- Low capital requirement versus the competition?
- Break even in 1–2 years?
- Value added increase of overall corporate P/E ratio?

*Durability of an opportunity is a widely misunderstood concept. In entrepreneurship, durability exists when the investor gets her money back plus a market or better return on investment.

EXHIBIT 3.7

Understand and Marshall Resources, Don't Be Driven by Them

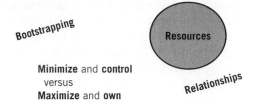

Minimize and control
versus
Maximize and own

Unleashing creativity

Financial resources
Assets
People   Think cash last!
Your business plan

---

system is conceived. We then ask the questions articulated in the exhibit.

These criteria will be described in great detail in Chapter 5 and can be applied to the search and evaluation of any opportunity. In short, the greater the growth, size, durability, and robustness of the gross and net margins and free cash flow, the greater the opportunity. The more *imperfect* the market, the greater the opportunity. The greater the rate of change, the discontinuities, and the chaos, the greater is the opportunity. The greater the inconsistencies in existing service and quality, in lead times and lag times, and the greater the vacuums and gaps in information and knowledge, the greater is the opportunity.

Resources: Creative and Parsimonious

One of the most common misconceptions among untried entrepreneurs is that you first need to have all the resources in place, especially the money, to succeed with a venture. Thinking money first is a big mistake. Money follows high-potential opportunities conceived of and led by a strong management team. Investors have bemoaned for years that there is too much money chasing too few deals. In other words, there is a shortage of quality entrepreneurs and opportunities, not money. Successful entrepreneurs devise ingeniously creative and stingy strategies to marshal and gain control of resources (Exhibit 3.7). Surprising as it may sound, investors and successful entrepreneurs often say one of the worst things that can happen to an entrepreneur is to have *too much money too early.*

Howard Head is a wonderful, classic example of succeeding with few resources. He developed the first metal ski, which became the market leader, and then the oversize Prince tennis racket; developing two totally unrelated technologies is a rare feat. Head left his job at a large aircraft manufacturer during World War II and worked in his garage on a shoestring budget to create his metal ski. It took more than 40 versions before he developed a ski that worked and could be marketed. He insisted that one of the biggest reasons he finally succeeded is that he had so little money. He argued that if he had complete financing he would have blown it all long before he evolved the workable metal ski.

Bootstrapping is a way of life in entrepreneurial companies and can create a significant competitive advantage. Doing more with less is a powerful competitive weapon. Effective new ventures strive to minimize and control the resources, but not necessarily own them. Whether it is assets for the business, key people, the business plan, or start-up and growth capital, successful entrepreneurs *think cash last.* Such strategies encourage a discipline of leanness, where everyone knows that every dollar counts, and the principle "conserve your equity" (CYE) becomes a way of maximizing shareholder value.

The Entrepreneurial Team   There is little dispute today that the entrepreneurial team is a key ingredient in the higher-potential venture. Investors are captivated "by the creative brilliance of a company's head entrepreneur: A Mitch Kapor, a Steve

Jobs, a Fred Smith . . . and bet on the superb track records of the management team working as a group."[31] Venture capitalist John Doerr reaffirms General George Doriot's dictum: I prefer a Grade A entrepreneur and team with a Grade B idea, over a Grade B team with a Grade A idea. Doerr stated, "In the world today, there's plenty of technology, plenty of entrepreneurs, plenty of money, plenty of venture capital. What's in short supply is great teams. Your biggest challenge will be building a great team."[32]

Famous investor Arthur Rock articulated the importance of the team more than a decade ago. He put it this way: "If you can find good people, they can always change the product. Nearly every mistake I've made has been I picked the wrong people, not the wrong idea."[33] Finally, as we saw earlier, the ventures with more than 20 employees and $2 million to $3 million in sales were much more likely to survive and prosper than smaller ventures. In the vast majority of cases, it is very difficult to grow beyond this without a team of two or more key contributors.

Clearly a new venture requires a lead entrepreneur that has personal characteristics described in Exhibit 3.8. But the high-potential venture also requires interpersonal skills to foster communications and, therefore, team building.

Exhibit 3.8 summarizes the important aspects of the team. These teams invariably are formed and led by a very capable entrepreneurial leader whose track record exhibits both accomplishments and several qualities that the team must possess. A pacesetter and culture creator, the lead entrepreneur is central to the team as both a player and a coach. The ability and skill in attracting other key management members and then building the team is one of the most valued capabilities investors look for. The founder who becomes the leader does so by building heroes in the team. A leader adapts a philosophy that rewards success and supports honest failure, shares the wealth with those who help create it, and sets high standards for both performance and conduct. We will examine in detail the entrepreneurial leader and the new venture team in Chapter 8.

Importance of Fit and Balance Rounding out the model of the three driving forces is the concept of fit and balance between and among these forces. Note that the team is positioned at the bottom of the triangle in the Timmons Model (Exhibit 3.5). Imagine the founder, the entrepreneurial leader of the venture, standing on a large ball, balancing the

---

EXHIBIT 3.8

An Entrepreneurial Team Is a Critical Ingredient for Success

An entrepreneurial leader
- Learns and teaches—faster, better
- Deals with adversity, is resilient
- Exhibits integrity, dependability, honesty
- Builds entrepreneurial culture and organization

Quality of the team
- Relevant experience and track record
- Motivation to excel
- Commitment, determination, and persistence
- Tolerance of risk, ambiguity, and uncertainty
- Creativity
- Team locus of control
- Adaptability
- Opportunity obsession
- Leadership and courage
- Communication

---

triangle over her head. This imagery is helpful in appreciating the constant balancing act because opportunity, team, and resources rarely match. When envisioning a company's future, the entrepreneur can ask, What pitfalls will I encounter to get to the next boundary of success? Will my current team be large enough, or will we be over our heads if the company grows 30 percent over the next two years? Are my resources sufficient (or too abundant)? Vivid examples of the failure to maintain a balance are everywhere, such as when large companies throw too many resources at a weak, poorly defined opportunity. For example, Lucent Technologies' misplaced assumption of slowness to react to bandwidth demand resulted in an almost 90 percent reduction in market capitalization.

Sustainability as a Base Building a sustainable venture means achieving economic, environmental, and social goals without compromising the same opportunity for future generations. The sea change in entrepreneurship regarding environment, community, and society is driven by many factors. We are seeing an elevated social awareness concerning a wide range of sustainability-related issues, including human rights, food quality, energy resources, pollution, global warming, and the like. By understanding these factors, the entrepreneur builds a firmer base, girding the venture for the long term.

---

[31] W. D. Bygrave and J. A. Timmons, *Venture Capital at the Crossroads* (Boston: Harvard Business School Press, 1992), p. 8.
[32] *Fast Company*, February–March 1997, p. 84.
[33] A. Rock, "Strategy vs. Tactics from a Venture Capitalist," *Harvard Business Review*, November–December 1987, pp. 63–67.

While the drawings oversimplify these incredibly complex events, they help us to think conceptually—an important entrepreneurial talent—about the company-building process, including the strategic and management implications of striving to achieve balance, and the inevitable fragility of the process. Visually, the process can be appreciated as a constant balancing act, requiring continual assessment, revised strategies and tactics, and an experimental approach. By addressing the types of questions necessary to shape the opportunity, the resources, and the team, the founder begins to mold the idea into an opportunity, and the opportunity into a business, just as you would mold clay from a shapeless form into a piece of art.

Exhibit 3.9 shows how this balancing act evolved for Google from inception through its initial public and secondary offerings. Back in 1996, online search was a huge, rapidly growing, but elusive opportunity. There were plenty of early entrants in the search space, but none had yet broken out of the pack. Stanford graduate students Larry Page and Sergey Brin began to collaborate on a search engine called BackRub, named for its unique ability to analyze the "back links" pointing to a given Web site. Within a year, their unique approach to link analysis was earning their dorm-room search engine a growing reputation as word spread around campus. Still, they had no team and no capital, and their server architecture was running on computers they borrowed from their computer science department.

Such a mismatch of ideas, resources, and talent could quickly topple out of the founders' control and fall into the hands of someone who could turn it into a real opportunity. At this tenuous point, the founders would have seen something like the first figure, Exhibit 3.9(a), with the huge search engine opportunity far outweighing the team and resources. The gaps were major.

Enter entrepreneur and angel investor Andy Bechtolsheim, one of the founders of Sun Microsystems. The partners of the search engine (now named Google, a variant of *googol,* an immense number), met Bechtolsheim very early one morning on the porch of a Stanford faculty member's home in Palo Alto. Impressed, but without the time to hear the details, Bechtolsheim wrote them a check for $100,000. From there, Page and Brin went on to raise a first round of $1 million. The partners were now in a position to fill the resource gaps and build the team.

In September 1998 they set up shop in a garage in Menlo Park, California, and hired their first employee: technology expert Craig Silverstein. Less than a year later, they moved to a new location, which quickly became a crush of desks and servers. In June 1999 the firm secured a round of funding that included $25 million from Sequoia Capital and Kleiner, Perkins, Caufield & Byers—two of the leading venture capital firms in Silicon Valley. The terrible office gridlock was alleviated with a move to Google's current headquarters in Mountain View, California.

This new balance in Exhibit 3.9(b) created a justifiable investment. The opportunity was still huge and growing, and some competitors were gaining market acceptance as well. To fully exploit this opportunity,

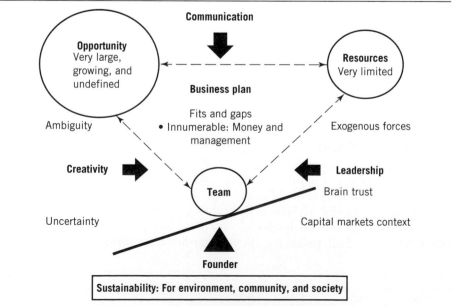

EXHIBIT 3.9(a)

Google—Classic Resource Parsimony, Bootstrapping—Journey through the Entrepreneurial Process: At Start-Up, a Huge Imbalance

EXHIBIT 3.9(b)

Google—Marshaling of Team and Resources to Pursue Opportunity—Journey through the Entrepreneurial Process: At Venture Capital Funding, toward New Balance

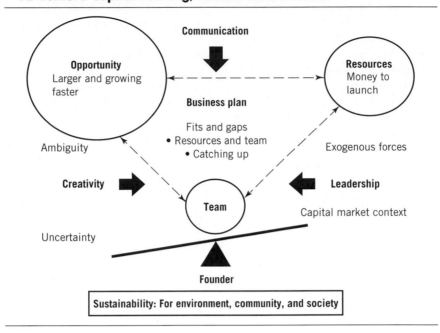

EXHIBIT 3.9(c)

Google—Building and Sustaining the Enterprise; Rebalancing—Journey through the Entrepreneurial Process: At IPO, a New Balance

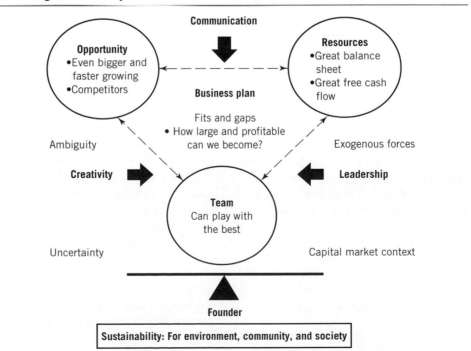

attract a large and highly talented group of managers and professionals, and create even greater financial strength than competitors like Yahoo!, the company had to complete an initial public stock offering (IPO). Following the close of that IPO in the summer of 2004, Google was worth more than $25 billion, giving it a first-day market capitalization greater than that of Amazon.com, Lockheed Martin, or General Motors. Within a year the company had raised another $4 billion in a secondary public offering.

By 2007 Google (see Exhibit 3.9(c)) had a share price in the range of $500 and was larger and stronger in people and resources than any direct competitor. The company was *the* place to work and employed over 10,000 of the best and brightest in the industry. Could such an unstoppable force as Google be blindsided and eclipsed by a new disruptive technology, just as Apple Computer and Microsoft bludgeoned IBM and Digital Equipment? While right now such a prospect might seem impossible given Google's momentum, scale, and ability to attract talent, history is quite clear on this: The answer is not whether, but when, Google will be overtaken.

This iterative entrepreneurial process is based on both logic and trial and error. It is both intuitive and consciously planned. It is a process not unlike what the Wright brothers originally engaged in while creating the first self-propelled airplane. They conducted more than 1,000 glider flights before succeeding. These trial-and-error experiments led to the new knowledge, skills, and insights needed to actually fly. Entrepreneurs have similar learning curves.

The fit issue can be appreciated in terms of a question: This is a fabulous opportunity, but for whom? Some of the most successful investments ever were turned down by numerous investors before the founders received backing. Intuit received 20 rejections for start-up funding by sophisticated investors. One former student, Ann Southworth, was turned down by 24 banks and investors before receiving funding for an elderly extended care facility. Ten years later, the company was sold for an eight-figure profit. Time and again, there can be a mismatch between the type of business and investors, the chemistry between founders and backers, or a multitude of other factors that can cause a rejection. Thus how the unique combination of people, opportunity, and resources come together at a particular time may determine a venture's ultimate chance for success.

The potential for attracting outside funding for a proposed venture depends on this overall fit and how the investor believes he or she can add value to this fit and improve the fit, risk–reward ratio, and odds for success. Exhibit 2.12 in the previous chapter shows the possible outcome.

Importance of Timing   Equally important is the timing of the entrepreneurial process. Each of these unique combinations occurs in real time, where the hourglass drains continually and may be friend, foe, or both. Decisiveness in recognizing and seizing the opportunity can make all the difference. Don't wait for the perfect time to take advantage of an opportunity: There is no perfect time. Most new businesses run out of money before they can find enough customers and the right teams for their great ideas. Opportunity is a moving target.

Recent Research Supports the Model

The Timmons Model originally evolved from doctoral dissertation research at the Harvard Business School, about new and growing ventures. Over nearly three decades, the model has evolved and been enhanced by ongoing research, case development, teaching, and experience in high-potential ventures and venture capital funds. The fundamental components of the model have not changed, but their richness and the relationships of each to the whole have been steadily enhanced as they have become better understood. Numerous other researchers have examined a wide range of topics in entrepreneurship and new venture creation. The bottom line is that the model, in its simple elegance and dynamic richness, harnesses what you need to know about the entrepreneurial process to get the odds in your favor. As each of the chapters and accompanying cases, exercises, and issues expand on the process, addressing individual dimensions, a detailed framework with explicit criteria will emerge. If you engage this material fully, you cannot help but improve your chances of success.

Similar to the INC. 500 companies mentioned earlier, the Ernst & Young LLP Entrepreneur of the Year winners were the basis of a major research effort conducted by the National Center for Entrepreneurship Research at the Kauffman Center for Entrepreneurial Leadership, with a specific focus on 906 high-growth companies.[34] These findings provide important benchmarks of the practices in a diverse group of industries among a high-performing group of companies.

Most significantly, these results reconfirm the importance of the model and its principles: the team, the market opportunity, the resource strategies, most of the individual criteria, the concept of fit and balance, and the holistic approach to entrepreneurship.

Exhibit 3.10 summarizes the 26 leading practices identified in four key areas: marketing, finances, management, and planning. (A complete version of the study is available from the National Center for Entrepreneurship Research, http://www.kauffman.org.)

---

[34] D. L. Sexton and F. I. Seale, *Leading Practices of Fast Growth Entrepreneurs: Pathways to High Performance* (Kansas City, MO: Kauffman Center for Entrepreneurial Leadership, 1997).

EXHIBIT 3.10

Leading Practices

Leading marketing practices of fast-growth firms
- Deliver products and services that are perceived as highest quality to expanding segments.
- Cultivate pacesetting new products and services that stand out in the market as best of the breed.
- Deliver product and service benefits that demand average or higher market pricing.
- Generate revenue flows from existing products and services that typically sustain approximately 90% of the present revenue base, while achieving flows from new products and services that typically expand revenue approximately 20% annually.
- Generate revenue flows from existing customers that typically sustain approximately 80% of the ongoing revenue base, while achieving flows from new customers that typically expand revenue flows by about 30% annually.
- Create high-impact, new product and service improvements with development expenditures that typically account for no more than approximately 6% of revenues.
- Utilize a high-yield sales force that typically accounts for approximately 60% of marketing expenditures.
- Rapidly develop broad product and service platforms with complementary channels to help expand a firm's geographic marketing area.

Leading financial practices of fast-growth firms
- Anticipate multiple rounds of financing (on average every 2.5 years).
- Secure funding sources capable of significantly expanding their participation amounts.
- Utilize financing vehicles that retain the entrepreneur's voting control.
- Maintain control of the firm by selectively granting employee stock ownership.
- Link the entrepreneur's long-term objectives to a defined exit strategy in the business plan.

Leading management practices of fast-growth firms
- Use a collaborative decision-making style with the top management team.
- Accelerate organizational development by assembling a balanced top management team with or without prior experience of working together.
- Develop a top management team of three to six individuals with the capacity to become the entrepreneur's entrepreneurs. Align the number of management levels with the number of individuals in top management.
- Establish entrepreneurial competency first in the functional areas of finance, marketing, and operations. Assemble a balanced board of directors composed of both internal and external directors.
- Repeatedly calibrate strategies with regular board of directors meetings.
- Involve the board of directors heavily at strategic inflection points.

Leading planning practices of fast-growth firms
- Prepare detailed written monthly plans for each of the next 12 to 24 months and annual plans for three or more years.
- Establish functional planning and control systems that tie planned achievements to actual performance and adjust management compensation accordingly.
- Periodically share with employees the planned versus actual performance data directly linked to the business plan.
- Link job performance standards that have been jointly set by management and employees to the business plan.
- Prospectively model the firm based on benchmarks that exceed industry norms, competitors, and the industry leader.

Chapter Summary

- We began to demystify entrepreneurship by examining its classic start-up definition and a broader, holistic way of thinking, reasoning, and acting that is opportunity obsessed and leadership balanced.
- Entrepreneurship has many metaphors and poses many paradoxes.
- Getting the odds in your favor is the entrepreneur's perpetual challenge, and the smaller the business, the poorer are the odds of survival.

- Thinking big enough can improve the odds significantly. Higher-potential ventures are sought by successful entrepreneurs, venture capitalists, and private investors.
- The Timmons Model is at the heart of spotting and building the higher-potential venture and understanding its three driving forces: opportunity, the team, and resources. The concept of fit and balance is crucial.
- Recent research on CEOs of fast-growth ventures nationwide adds new validity to the model.

Study Questions

1. Can you define what is meant by classic entrepreneurship and the high-potential venture? Why and how are threshold concepts, covering your equity, bootstrapping of resources, fit, and balance important?

2. How many additional metaphors and paradoxes about entrepreneurship can you write down?

3. "People don't want to be managed, they want to be led." Explain what this means and its importance and implications for developing your own style and leadership philosophy.

4. What are the most important determinants of success and failure in new businesses? Who has the best and worst chances for success, and why?

5. What are the most important things you can do to get the odds in your favor?

6. What criteria and characteristics do high-growth entrepreneurs, venture capitalists, and private investors seek in evaluating business opportunities? How can these make a difference?

7. Define and explain the Timmons Model. Apply it and graphically depict, as in the Google example, the first five years or so of a new company with which you are familiar.

8. What are the most important skills, values, talents, abilities, and mind-sets one needs to cultivate as an entrepreneur?

Internet Resources for Chapter 3

www.sba.gov/advo/research *The Office of Advocacy of the U.S. Small Business Administration (SBA) is an independent voice for small business within the federal government. This site is a useful resource for small business research and statistics on a wide range of topics.*

www.ypo.org/ *More that 11,000 young global leaders in 90 nations rely on one exclusive peer network that*

connects them to exchange ideas, pursue learning, and share strategies to achieve personal and professional growth and success.

www.inc.com/inc5000/ *The magazine has increased its database to include 5,00 private businesses. As in previous years, the top 500 fastest growing firms are ranked.*

MIND STRETCHERS

Have You Considered?

1. Who can be an entrepreneur? When?

2. More than 80 percent of entrepreneurs learn the critical skills they need after age 21. What does this mean for you?

3. In your lifetime, the odds are that leading firms today such as Microsoft, Google, Dell Computer, American Airlines, McDonald's, and American Express will be

knocked off by upstarts. How can this happen? Why does it present an opportunity, and for whom?

4. What do you need to be doing now, and in the next 12 months, to get the odds in your favor?

5. List 100 ideas and then pick out the best 5 that might be opportunities. How can these become opportunities? Who can make them opportunities?

Roxanne Quimby

Preparation Questions

1. Who can be an entrepreneur?
2. What are the risks, rewards, and trade-offs of a lifestyle business versus a high-potential business—one that will exceed $5 million in sales and grow substantially?
3. What is the difference between an idea and an opportunity? For whom? What can be learned from Exhibits C and D?
4. Why has the company succeeded so far?
5. What should Roxanne and Burt do, and why?

> *Our goal for the first year was $10,000 in total sales. I figured if I could take home half of that, it would be more money than I'd ever seen.*
>
> Roxanne Quimby

Introduction

Roxanne Quimby sat in the president's office of Burt's Bees' newly relocated manufacturing facility in Raleigh, North Carolina. She was surrounded by unpacked boxes and silence from the unmoving machines with no one there to operate them. Quimby looked around and asked herself, "Why did I do this?" She felt lonely and missed Maine, Burt's Bees' previous home. Quimby had founded and built Burt's Bees, a manufacturer of beeswax-based personal care products and handmade crafts, in central Maine and was not convinced she shouldn't move it back there. She explained,

> When we got to North Carolina, we were totally alone. I realized how much of the business existed in the minds of the Maine employees. There, everyone had their mark on the process. That was all lost when we left Maine in 1994. I just kept thinking, "Why did I move Burt's Bees?" I thought I would pick the company up and move it and everything would be the same. Nothing was the same except that I was still working 20-hour days.

Quimby had profound doubts about this move to North Carolina and was seriously considering moving back to Maine. She needed to make a decision quickly because Burt's Bees was in the process of hiring new employees and purchasing a great deal of manufacturing equipment. If she pulled out now, losses could be minimized and she could hire back each of the 44 employees she had left back in Maine, since none of them had found new jobs yet. On the other hand, it would be hard to ignore all the reasons she had decided to leave

Maine in the first place. If she moved Burt's Bees back, she would face the same problems that inspired this move. In Maine, Burt's Bees would probably never grow over $3 million in sales, and Quimby felt it had potential for much more.

Roxanne Quimby

The Black Sheep

"I was a real black sheep in my family," Quimby said. She had one sister who worked for AMEX and another sister who worked for Charles Schwab, and her father worked for Merrill Lynch. She was not interested in business at all, though, and considered it dull. Quimby attended the San Francisco Art Institute in the late 1960s and "got radicalized out there," she explained. "I studied, oil painted, and graduated without any job prospects. I basically dropped out of life. I moved to central Maine where land was really cheap—$100 an acre—and I could live removed from society."

Personal politics wasn't the only thing that pushed Quimby below the poverty line. While she was in college, Roxanne's father discovered she was living with her boyfriend and disowned her, severing all financial and familial ties. Her father, a Harvard Business School graduate and failed entrepreneur, did give her one gift—an early entrepreneurial education. At the age of 5, Roxanne Quimby's father told her he wouldn't give her a cent for college but would match every dollar she earned herself. By her high school graduation Quimby had banked $5,000 by working on her father's numerous entrepreneurial projects and selling her own handmade crafts.

In 1975 Quimby and her boyfriend married and moved to Guilford, Maine—an hour northwest of Bangor. They bought 30 acres of land at $100 an acre and built a two-room house with no electricity, running water, or phone. In 1977 Quimby had twins, and her lifestyle became a burden. She washed diapers in pots of boiling water on a wood-burning stove and struggled constantly to make ends meet with minimum wage jobs. Her marriage broke apart when the twins were 4. Quimby packed up everything she owned on a toboggan and pulled the load across the snow to a friend's house.

The moneymaking skills her father forced her to develop allowed Quimby to survive. She and her children

© Copyright Jeffry A. Timmons, 1997. This case was written by Rebecca Voorheis, under the direction of Jeffry A. Timmons, Franklin W. Olin Distinguished Professor of Entrepreneurship, Babson College. Funding provided by the Ewing Marion Kauffman Foundation. All rights reserved.

lived in a small tent, and Quimby made almost $150 a week by working local flea markets—buying low and selling high. She also held jobs waitressing. Quimby described, "I always felt I had an entrepreneurial spirit. Even as a waitress I felt entrepreneurial because I had control. I couldn't stand it when other people controlled my destiny or performance. Other jobs didn't inspire me to do my best, but waitressing did because I was accountable to myself. Eventually I got fired from these jobs because I didn't hesitate to tell the owners what I thought. I had a bit of an attitude."

In 1984 Quimby began to question her lifestyle and realized she had to make a change. She explained, "I decided I had to make a real income. I started to feel the responsibility of having kids. I had waitressing jobs but there were only three restaurants in town and I had been fired from all three. That's when I hooked up with Burt."

A Kindred Spirit

Like Roxanne Quimby, Burt Shavitz had also dropped out of life in the early 1970s. A New York native and ex-photographer for *Life* and *New York* magazines, Shavitz lived in an 8' by 8' house (previously a turkey coop) on a 20-acre farm in Dexter, Maine, which he purchased in 1973. Shavitz, a beekeeper with 30 hives, sold honey off the back of his truck during hunting season. He earned maybe $3,000 a year, which was exactly enough to pay property taxes and buy gas for his pickup truck.

When Roxanne first saw Burt, whom she described as a "good-looker," she knew she had to meet him. In an article in *Lear's* magazine Quimby said, "I pretended I was interested in the bees, but I was really interested in Burt. Here was this lone beekeeper. I wanted to fix him, to tame the wild man."[1] When Quimby and Shavitz met in 1984, the bond was immediate. Quimby talked about Shavitz's role at Burt's Bees:

> I convinced Burt into this enterprise. He has always believed in my vision, but unlike me he's emotionally detached and uninvolved. Therefore, he has some great ideas and is more likely to take risks. He's my main sounding board and gives me a lot of moral and psychological support. I never could have done this without him. In all this time, there's never been a conflict between us. The chemistry has always been there. We're just really on the same wavelength. We've been through a lot together that would have broken other relationships. I've always been the motivator and the one involved in day-to-day operations, but very rarely does he disagree with me. He's kind of my guru.

In the beginning of their fast friendship, Burt taught Roxanne about beekeeping and Roxanne discovered Burt's large stockpile of beeswax. Quimby suggested making candles with the beeswax. She took her hand-dipped and

[1] J. Bentham, "Enterprise," *Lear's*, March 1994, pp. 20–21.

sculpted candles to a crafts fair at a local high school and brought home $200. She remembers, "I had never held that much money in my hand." Burt's Bees was born.

Quimby and Shavitz pooled $400 from their savings to launch a honey and beeswax business. They purchased some household kitchen appliances for mixing, pouring, and dipping. A friend rented them an abandoned one-room schoolhouse with no heat, running water, windows, or electricity for $150 a year—the cost of the fire insurance. Neither of them had a phone, so they convinced the local health food store to take messages for Burt's Bees. Quimby traveled to fair after fair around the region, sleeping in the back of a pickup truck and making a few hundred dollars a day. She set what seemed like an impossible goal for the first year's sales—$10,000. That year, 1987, Burt's Bees made $81,000 in sales.

Burt's Bees' Early Success

Burt's Bees' big break came in 1989 at a wholesale show in Springfield, Massachusetts. The owner of an upscale boutique in Manhattan bought a teddy bear candle and put it in the window of his store. The candle was a hit, and the boutique owner barraged the health food store with messages asking for new shipments. Quimby began hiring employees to help with production and expanded the product line to include other handmade crafts and beeswax-based products like lip balm. In 1993 Burt's Bees had 44 employees.

Quimby explained her transformation into a businessperson:

> After a while, I realized I just liked it. I liked buying and selling things well, adding value. I had no security issues because I'd been living at the bottom for so many years. I knew if worse came to worse and the business failed, I could survive. I'd seen the worst and knew I could handle it. I'd never been trapped by the need for security or a regular paycheck. I loved the freedom of starting a business, of not knowing how it would turn out. It was this big experiment and whether it succeeded or failed totally depended on me. I realized the goal was not the most interesting part; the problems along the way were. I found business was the most incredibly liberating thing. I never would have thought that before. The only rule is that you have to make a little bit more than you spend. As long as you can do that, anything else you do is OK. There are no other opportunities that have as few rules.

Not only did Roxanne Quimby have a passion for business, but she also had a talent. Since the beginning of Burt's Bees in 1987, the company had never once dipped into the red, it had always turned a profit, and its profits had always increased (see Exhibit A). A number of large national retailers stocked Burt's Bees' products including L.L. Bean, Macy's, and Whole Foods Market Company. By 1993 Burt's Bees had sales representatives across the country and sold its products in

EXHIBIT A

Burt's Bees Sales, 1987–1993

Year	Sales
1987	$81,000
1988	$137,779
1989	$180,000
1990	$500,000
1991	$1,500,000
1992	$2,500,000
1993	$3,000,000

every state. By all accounts, Burt's Bees' products were a success. Quimby explained their appeal:

> We sell really well in urban areas. People in urban areas need us more because they can't step out the front door and get freshness or simplicity. Our products aren't sophisticated or sleek. They're down-home and basic. Everyone has an unconscious desire for more simplicity and our products speak to that need.

The company was not only profitable, it was totally debt-free. Burt's Bees had never taken out a loan. Quimby didn't even have a credit card. When she applied for one in 1993, by then a millionaire, she had to get her sister to cosign because she had no credit history. She was strongly averse to going into debt. Quimby explained,

> I've never taken on debt because I don't ever want to feel like I can't walk away from it this afternoon. That's important to me. A monthly payment would trap me into having to explain my actions. I love being on the edge with no predictability, no one to report to. Anyway, there was no way a bank would have given me the money to start Burt's Bees. I could just see myself with some banker trying to explain, "I've never had a job or anything but could you give me some money because I have this idea about beeswax."

Quimby was so debt-averse and cash-aware, she refused to sell products to any retailer that didn't pay its bill within the required 30 days. This meant turning down orders from retailing powerhouses like I. Magnin and Dean & Deluca. In 1993, with about $3 million in sales, the company wrote off only $2,500 in uncollected debts. In the same year, Burt's Bees had $800,000 in the bank, and pretax profits were 35 percent of sales.

The Move

The Costs of Doing Business in Maine

The main impetus for the move was the excessive costs associated with Burt's Bees' location in northern Maine:

1. *High transport costs:* "Our transport costs were ridiculously high," said Quimby. Because of its vast distance from any metropolitan areas, shipping products to distributors and receiving materials were astronomically expensive. Burt's Bees was almost always the last stop on truckers' routes.

2. *High payroll taxes:* Burt's Bees was being taxed about 10 percent of its payroll by the state of Maine. Payroll taxes were so high because unemployment in Maine hovered around 20 percent.

3. *Lack of expertise:* In 1993 Burt's Bees had 44 employees who were all "welfare moms." Quimby said, "They brought a set of hands and a good attitude to work, but no skills." Everything was made by hand. Burt's Bees' most popular product, lip balm, was mixed with a household blender, then poured from teapots into metal tins. "When we received a shipment of containers or labels, we had to break down the pallets inside the truck because no one knew how to operate a forklift. Everything was inefficient and costly. There weren't any people with expertise in Maine," Quimby explained. For a while, Quimby aggressively recruited managers from around New England. When they came up to Guilford to interview and realized how isolated the town was, though, they would turn down any offer Quimby made.

Roxanne Quimby moved the company to free Burt's Bees from these constraints and liberate it to grow. Since beginning operations in 1987, Burt's Bees had struggled to keep up with demand. Quimby had no time to focus on broad management issues because she spent most of her time pouring beeswax along with the other 44 employees in order to fill distributors' unceasing orders. She explained,

> The business had developed a life of its own and it was telling me it wanted to grow. But it was growing beyond me, my expertise, my goals, and definitely beyond Maine. If I kept it in northern Maine, I would have stunted its growth. But the business was my child in a way, and as its mother I wanted to enable it to grow. The business provided a great income and I could have gone on like that for a while. But I knew it had a lot more potential than $3 million. At the same time, I knew $3 million was the most I could do on my own. I was working all of the time and there was no one to lean on or delegate to. My lack of formal business training really began to bite me. I didn't even know about payroll taxes. We would get fined for missing tax deadlines we didn't even know existed.

Why North Carolina?

Roxanne Quimby felt she had to move the company away from Maine. But to where? She didn't want to live in a big, bustling city, but the new location had to be central. Quimby explained how she finally chose North Carolina as Burt's Bees' new home:

> I had a map of the United States in my office with pins where all of our sales reps were. I used to always look at that map—when I was on the phone, doing paperwork, or just sitting at my desk—until one day I noticed North Carolina. It just seemed central, well placed. And, it turned out, a large percentage of the country's population lives within a 12-hour drive of North Carolina. One of my biggest worries about moving was telling Burt. I said to Burt one day, "We need to move and it looks like North Carolina is the place to go." Burt said, "OK, Roxy" and I thought to myself, "Thank God Burt is always on my wavelength."

Burt got on the phone with a representative at the North Carolina Department of Commerce and told him about Burt's Bees. Burt and Roxanne were pleasantly surprised to learn North Carolina was extremely aggressive about recruiting new companies to the state and was eager to attract Burt's Bees, even though it was quite a bit smaller than other companies locating in the "Triangle."[2] The North Carolina Department of Commerce sent Burt's Bees a software program that Quimby used to plug in financial information and calculate the estimated taxes Burt's Bees would pay in North Carolina. The estimated taxes were significantly less than those they were paying in Maine.

Perhaps more compelling, though, was the large supply of skilled labor in North Carolina. If Burt's Bees moved, it would be able to hire an ex-Revlon plant engineer to establish and operate its manufacturing processes. Quimby also had a lead on a marketing manager in North Carolina with experience at Lancome, Vogue, and Victoria's Secret's personal care products division.

As a next step, the North Carolina Department of Commerce invited Roxanne and Burt to visit North Carolina for a three-day tour of the Triangle area and available manufacturing facilities. "You should have seen the look on the representative's face when he picked us up from the airport," Quimby laughed. "Burt has this deep, gruff voice, so he must have sounded very different on the phone than he looks. Burt is 62, has crazy white hair to his shoulders and a long white beard, is really tall, and pretty much looks like he just walked out of the woods of Maine." She continued to say, "The representative recovered really well, though, and took us around the whole area for three days. He showed us tons of plants and real estate. He made us a great offer and we were impressed."

When they got back to Maine, Quimby called the Maine Department of Commerce to give it a chance to keep Burt's Bees in the state. "If they had offered us half the deal North Carolina did," Quimby said, "I would have taken it." The Maine Department of Commerce asked Roxanne to call back in a couple of months because the person in charge of business recruiting was out on maternity leave. Quimby marveled, "We were the second largest employer in the town and they didn't respond to us at all. We finally heard from the governor of Maine when he read an article about us in *Forbes*[3] that mentioned we were leaving the state. By then it was too late. The move was only a few days away and we had already signed a lease on the new manufacturing facility."

Trimming the Azalea Bush: The Economics of the Move

Roxanne Quimby likened Burt's Bees' move to transplanting an azalea bush in full bloom. She said, "I realized I had to trim and prune radically to allow it to survive." In Maine, Burt's Bees biggest resource was cheap labor—people on the production line were paid $5 an hour. Therefore, most of Burt's Bees products were very labor-intensive and production was totally unautomated. All of its products, from birdhouses to candles to baby clothes, were handmade.

In North Carolina, though, the company's biggest resource was skilled labor. But skilled labor is expensive, and Burt's Bees wouldn't be able to keep making its labor-intensive handmade items. Quimby would have to automate everything and change Burt's Bees' whole product line to focus on skin care products (see Exhibit B for industry employment statistics). She explained, "Our products in Maine were totally unrelated production-wise, but they were related in the sense that each product communicated down-home values and simplicity. In North Carolina, though, we would have to get rid of all the handmade products, and that was pretty much everything. We had to automate."

When Quimby arrived in North Carolina she sat down to evaluate the product line and decided to focus on skin care (for general industry statistics, see Exhibits C and D). Skin care products require only blending and filling, which is very straightforward, and machinery can do almost everything. "To justify the move to North Carolina from a cost and manufacturing perspective, we would have to make more 'goop,'" Quimby stated. "I looked at my list of prospective new products, and there wasn't anything on the list that we made in 1988."

Quimby planned on retaining Burt's Bees environmental ethic by excluding any chemical preservatives and using primarily all-natural ingredients in its skin

---

[2] The "Triangle" area in North Carolina includes Chapel Hill, Raleigh, and Durham and is the home of Research Triangle Park, a large high-tech business park similar to Silicon Valley in California or Route 128 in Massachusetts.

[3] D. W. Linder, "Dear Dad," *Forbes*, December 6, 1993, pp. 98–99.

EXHIBIT B

Occupations Employed by Standard Industrial Classification (SIC) 284: Soap, Cleaners, and Toilet Goods

Occupation	% of Industry Total, 1994	% Change to 2005 (Projected)
Packaging & filling machine operators	8.5	−30.1
Hand packers & packagers	6.3	−20.1
Assemblers, fabricators, & hand workers	5.7	16.5
Sales & related workers	4.9	16.5
Freight, stock & material movers, hand	3.6	−6.8
Secretaries, executive, legal & medical	3.5	6.0
Chemical equipment controllers, operators	3.0	4.8
Industrial machinery mechanics	2.7	28.1
Machine operators	2.6	2.6
Industrial truck & tractor operators	2.6	16.5
Chemists	2.5	28.1
Crushing & mixing machine operators	2.5	16.4
General managers & top executives	2.5	10.5
Traffic, shipping, & receiving clerks	2.2	12.1
Marketing, advertising, & PR managers	2.0	16.5
Science & mathematics technicians	1.8	16.5
Bookkeeping, accounting, & auditing clerks	1.8	16.5
Maintenance repairers, general utility	1.7	4.8
Inspectors, testers & graders, precision	1.6	16.5
General office clerks	1.6	−.7
Order clerks, materials, merchandise & service	1.5	13.9
Machine feeders & offbearers	1.5	4.8
Clerical supervisors & managers	1.5	19.1
Professional workers	1.4	39.7
Industrial production managers	1.4	16.4
Stock clerks	1.4	−5.3
Managers & administrators	1.3	16.4
Adjustment clerks	1.2	39.8
Accountants & auditors	1.2	16.5
Management support workers	1.1	16.4
Engineering, mathematical, & science managers	1.1	32.2
Truck drivers, light & heavy	1.0	20.1

Source: *Manufacturing USA: Industry Analyses, Statistics, and Leading Companies*, 5th ed., vol. 1, ed. A. J. Darnay, Gale Research Inc. (1996), p. 837.

care products. Still, though, Burt's Bees would have to become an entirely new company and abandon the product line responsible for the company's early success.

Not only would the product line have to be overhauled, but Roxanne realized she and Burt couldn't remain the sole owners of the company if she wanted it to grow. Since the inception of Burt's Bees, Roxanne and Burt held 70 percent and 30 percent of its stock,

respectively. The truly talented employees Quimby hoped to attract would want shared ownership of the company and would be highly motivated by stock rewards. Quimby knew sharing ownership would mean feeling accountable to others and having to justify her sometimes unorthodox decisions. Accountability was exactly what she had fought so hard to avoid her whole life, and Quimby's autonomy was partly a cause of her success.

EXHIBIT C

General Industry Statistics for SIC 2844: Toilet Preparations*

	Establishments		Employment			Compensation		Production ($million)			
Year	Total	With ≤ 20 Employees	Total (00s)	Production Workers (00s)	Production Hours (mil)	Payroll ($mil)	Wages ($/hour)	Cost of Materials	Value Added by Manufacture	Value of Shipments	Capital Investment
1988	687	277	64.9	40.5	78.1	1,551.3	9.08	4,445.1	12,053.2	16,293.6	292.6
1989	676	282	63.6	39.4	75.4	1,615.5	9.69	4,758.2	11,979.2	16,641.9	313.7
1990	682	284	63.6	38.1	74.3	1,620.6	10.14	4,904.6	12,104.2	17,048.4	280.4
1991	674	271	57.4	35.6	69.8	1,616.3	10.81	5,046.3	12,047.4	18,753.5	299.5
1992	756	305	60.1	37.2	75.6	1,783.3	10.82	5,611.3	13,167.2	19,706.4	507.3
1993	778	299	61.7	38.6	79.7	1,857.8	10.59	6,152.6	13,588.8	19,736.0	472.6

*Manufacturing USA: Industry Analyses, Statistics, and Leading Companies, 5th ed., vol. 1, ed. A. J. Darnay, Gale Research Inc. (1996), p. 833.
Sources: 1982, 1987, 1992 Economic Census; Annual Survey of Manufactures, pp. 83–86, 88–91, 93–94. Establishment counts for noncensus years are from County Business Patterns.

EXHIBIT D

Comparison of Toilet Preparations Industry (SIC 2844) to the Average of All U.S. Manufacturing Sectors, 1994*

Selected Measurement	All Manufacturing Sectors Average	SIC 2844 Average	Index
Employees per establishment	49	77	157
Payroll per establishment	$1,500,273	$ 2,397,065	160
Payroll per employee	$ 30,620	$ 31,191	102
Production workers per establishment	34	47	137
Wages per establishment	$ 853,319	$ 1,061,646	124
Wages per production worker	$ 24,861	$ 22,541	91
Hours per production worker	2,056	2,062	100
Wages per hour	$ 12.09	$ 10.93	90
Value added per establishment	$4,602,255	$17,781,454	386
Value added per employee	$ 93,930	$ 231,375	246
Value added per production worker	$ 134,084	$ 377,541	282
Cost per establishment	$5,045,178	$ 8,648,566	171
Cost per employee	$ 102,970	$ 112,536	109
Cost per production worker	$ 146,988	$ 183,629	125
Shipments per establishment	9,576,895	26,332,221	275
Shipments per employee	195,460	342,639	175
Shipments per production worker	279,017	559,093	200
Investment per establishment	$ 321,011	$ 654,570	204
Investment per employee	$ 6,552	$ 8,517	130
Investment per production worker	$ 9,352	$ 13,898	149

*Manufacturing USA: Industry Analyses, Statistics, and Leading Companies, 5th ed., vol. 1, ed. A. J. Darnay, Gale Research Inc. (1996), p. 833.

Conclusion

Quimby walked around the empty North Carolina factory. She tried to imagine the empty space filled with machinery and workers, humming with activity and production. Her mind kept reflecting back to the old schoolhouse in Maine, though. Was her ambiguity about this move merely a temporary sentimentality or should she listen to her instinct, which hadn't failed her to date? She had to make a decision soon. As she saw it, Quimby had three choices:

1. *Stay in North Carolina:* Quimby could mentally and financially commit to the North Carolina move and try to get over her doubts. Burt's Bees had promising leads in North Carolina on a plant manager from Revlon and a sales and marketing manager with experience at Lancome, Vogue, and Victoria's Secret. Quimby's expertise deficit could largely be solved with these two experts.

2. *Move back to Maine:* Quimby could halt all purchasing and hiring and move back to Maine, where most of her ex-employees could be hired back. There would be some sunk costs involved, but they could be minimized if she acted quickly. Additionally, Burt's Bees could keep its original product line that made the company so successful in the first place. The governor of Maine had said to call him if she changed her mind about North Carolina. She could pursue a deal with the state of Maine to mitigate Burt's Bees' tax, transport, and employment costs.

3. *Sell the company:* Although it might be difficult to attract a buyer at only $3 million in sales, Burt's Bees had received quite a bit of attention in the industry and would be an enticing purchase to many prospective buyers. Quimby knew she didn't want to be at Burt's Bees forever and said, "I feel like at some point, this business isn't going to need me anymore. My child will grow up and want to move away from its mother. There are other things I want to do that are next on my list." Quimby dreamed about living in India and working with rural women on product design, production, and marketing of their handmade crafts. If she sold Burt's Bees, this dream could become an immediate reality.

Chapter Four

Clean Commerce: Seeing Opportunity Through a Sustainability Lens[1]

We believe that there's a cure for resource waste that is profitable, creative, and practical. We must create a company that addresses the needs of society and the environment by developing a system of industrial production that decreases our costs and dramatically reduces the burdens placed upon living systems.

Ray Anderson, Founder
Interface, Inc.

Greentech could be the largest economic opportunity of the 21st century.

John Doerr
Kleiner, Perkins, Caufield & Byers

Results Expected

Upon completion of this chapter, you will be able to

1. Discuss the pressures and demands in the marketplace that are driving opportunities for entrepreneurs with an eye toward sustainability.

2. Explain ways that entrepreneurial companies can gain competitive advantage by orienting products and processes that take environmental issues into account.

3. Describe the role that sustainability plays in building dynamic and profitable ventures.

4. Discuss the five facets of looking through a sustainability lens, and describe their impact on opportunity assessment, resources, and the team.

5. Provide insights into and analysis of the Jim Poss case study.

Clean Commerce Is an Opportunity Sea Change

As noted by perhaps the most famous modern venture capitalist in the world, John Doerr, the clean commerce and sustainable enterprise movement is one of the most exciting and promising opportunity sea changes of this century. Everyone is going green. Each week brings a new announcement of a company embracing sustainability and environmental issues. Those ahead of the pack have grasped that the environment is a growing source of strategic opportunity for companies. It is now clear that there is a revolution

[1] We are extremely appreciative of Associate Professor Andrea Larson of the Darden Graduate School of Business Administration, University of Virginia, and Dr. Karen O'Brien of Advancing Green Chemistry for the contribution of their pioneering work in this chapter. Leaders in this emerging field, the authors have shared a very insightful look at what the clean commerce and sustainability movement means and how that translates into enormous opportunities for the next generation of global entrepreneurs.

under way in business as entrepreneurial companies gain competitive advantage by orienting products and processes to take environmental issues into account. But if "green" is the new "black" (and if everyone is doing it), what new opportunities are being spawned by this seismic shift? How can entrepreneurs create and seize the opportunities? How can a company differentiate itself in this rapidly greening market space? What are the risks associated with ignoring the green imperative?

One is hard-pressed to point to an industry or manufacturer able to ignore the trends. Businesses now experience increased global regulatory pressure, demand for heightened transparency, and growing public concern about the environment and health. Government procurement and business buyers increasingly use environmental criteria in purchasing. Markets and taxes on carbon emissions now factor into corporate strategy. The cost of a barrel of oil has now risen sufficiently to make biofuels and other clean(er) energy technologies more economically attractive. Company brand names and stock prices are increasingly influenced by environmental records. Companies face environmental performance pressures from the investment sector, including stockholder petitions and unprecedented growth in screened investment funds that rank corporate behavior on environmental issues. Combined, these forces have created a much more complex and challenging business climate.

From General Electric to Wal-Mart, the names of companies announcing new sustainability strategies include big and small players alike. Growing numbers of firms working in areas as diverse as building construction, furnishings, food, energy, transportation, and materials design (to name a few) are bringing new "green" designs to market. So how can an entrepreneurial company in good faith—and in its own self-interest—differentiate itself and gain competitive advantage?

Clean Commerce and the Sustainability Lens: Seeing and Acting on New Opportunities and Strategies

Clean commerce has become the new norm of business; "dirty industry" is no longer tolerated, and pollution is not accepted as the price of progress. *Clean* here means more than just nontoxic; it refers to the net balance of costs and benefits to shareholders, to stakeholders, and to the planet. This is not a zero-sum game—the benefits are shared across sectors.

Sustainability Defined

Sustainability means that resource utilization should not deplete existing [natural] capital . . . that is, resources should not be used at a rate faster than the rate of replenishment, and waste generation should not exceed the carrying capacity of the surrounding ecosystem. . .

Dr. Karl-Henrik Robèrt, 1997
Oncologist and founder,
The Natural Step
www.naturalstep.org

As indicated in the Timmons Model of Entrepreneurial Process in Chapter 3, sustainability ought to be the bedrock of new ventures. This fundamental place reflects awareness that the conditions for global competition have changed, and environmental issues are now a primary source of new business growth and opportunity. Entrepreneurs can identify new opportunities—or even create new opportunities—and translate them into strategic advantage. But entrepreneurs need to see the world in a newly strategic way, looking at their industries through a *sustainability lens* to identify new opportunities and devise means of acting on them.

Sustainability includes the concept of economic viability. Revenues and earnings must sustain ongoing business success, and profits must be reinvested into product and service improvements to drive future growth. But sustainability also refers to the role new ventures play in supporting communities, improving human health, protecting ecological systems, and thus truly delivering on the promise of prosperity.

Looking through a sustainability lens requires that entrepreneurs radically rethink their place in the market and in the world. You can gain an entirely new vantage point to appreciate opportunities inherent in the current points of collision between business and natural systems. Some of the most fertile opportunities lie in the areas of greatest tension. If you can see them and act on them, you will differentiate your company and set the industry standard to best suit *your* venture's capabilities.

This is not trite "turn your problems into opportunities" talk. This approach uses the realities of today's competitive circumstances to see new competitive space for bottom-line growth and innovation. Keep in mind that most innovation is not high-tech. A reliable and powerful stimulus for innovation comes from changes in the conditions of people's lives. This can result from demographic shifts, new knowledge, technology impacts, and even shifts in people's perception and meaning. In a way, that's all we are talking about.

Critical changes have already occurred: in global demographics, in our knowledge of economic impacts, and in the fact that environmental issues have become more urgent. Likewise, entrepreneurial strategy is adapting and evolving.

Defining the Concept: How to Look through a Sustainability Lens

Consistent with the Timmons Model emphasis on opportunity and the resources a visionary entrepreneurial team brings to bear, today a subset of entrepreneurial leaders are looking through a sustainability lens and creating new competitive market space. They are successfully mobilizing resources and offering new products and alternative business models. These leaders integrating sustainability principles into their operations and strategies offer a distinct entrepreneurial and innovative business model for the future.

There are three strategic facets of looking through a sustainability lens:

- Weak ties.
- Systems thinking.
- Thinking like a molecule.

We will explore each of these aspects next. By appreciating each you will see your business environment anew and will begin to perceive untapped opportunities that your venture (new or otherwise) can seize upon. But how to proceed? The sustainability lens also illuminates new tactics:

- Value-added networks.
- Radical incrementalism.

All five of these facets together add up to a new strategic lens on the opportunities, the resources available to you, and the team you will need to assemble to act.

Weak Ties

Looking through a sustainability lens will show you new potential opportunities, but to access this lens you will need to borrow others' eyes and ears. You will need new partners to help you see and analyze issues and opportunities anew. This requires that you establish *weak ties* to individuals and organizations previously off your radar screen.[2] They are called *weak* not because they lack substance or will let you down, but because they lie outside your traditional network of relationships. Weak ties can provide critical information

because through them you can gain access to fresh ideas, emergent perspectives, and new scientific data that make what used to be peripheral issues (as many environmental issues have been and sustainability concerns continue to be) now salient to new venture success. The resources and strategic perspectives gained from weak ties enable discerning entrepreneurs and their companies to move faster and more effectively, to differentiate themselves, and to gain relative to their competitors. Weak ties and new partners are important resources for new ventures. In addition, the perspective they bring also allows you to see the bigger system of which your ideas are a part. Remember that your harshest critic can sometimes offer you the most important information on how to turn your problems into business opportunities. Good ideas can come from the least expected sources.

Systems Thinking

A sustainability lens by definition requires systems thinking. Companies generally design their strategy while implicitly assuming narrowly defined system boundaries: the firm, the market, or the industry. But the reality, of course, is that we all work in a complex and interconnected world. Those who grasp this and seek to leverage this understanding can discover new, previously unappreciated, and potentially lucrative areas in which to act. A sustainability lens requires that you expand your parameters. Using a wider systems perspective enables a powerful view of new opportunity.

Thinking Like a Molecule

In systems thinking we ask you to think big; here we are also asking you to think small. *Thinking like a molecule* opens up the micro-level possibilities inherent in product and process design that can be extended throughout the supply chain. Employing green chemistry techniques, for example, can not only save your company significant cost outlays for waste and potential liabilities, but can generate new products and open new markets.

Green chemistry is the utilization of a set of principles that embrace the reduction and elimination of hazardous substances in the design, manufacture, and application of chemical products. These principles can be applied to organic chemistry, inorganic chemistry, biochemistry, analytical chemistry, and even physical chemistry—with the focus being on minimizing the risks and maximizing the efficiency of any chemical reaction. Thinking like a molecule is a

---

[2] M. Granovetter, "The Strength of Weak Ties," *American Journal of Sociology* 6 (1973), pp. 1360–80.

mind-set that can be used to reengineer entire systems to discover ways of meeting market needs without being limited by traditional chemical choices or processes. Good things come in small packages; taking a strategic approach to greening the inherent nature of new venture products and processes can bring differentiation and profits.

Thinking like a molecule asks entrepreneurial leaders to examine not only a product's immediate functionality but also the product's entire molecular life cycle from raw material, through manufacture, to end of life and disposal. Smart leaders will ask, Where do we get our feedstocks? Are they renewable or limited? Are they vulnerable to price and supply fluctuations? Are they vulnerable to emerging regulations? Are they inherently benign, or does the management of risk incur costs in handling, processing, and disposal? Do chemicals in our products accumulate in human tissue? Do they biodegrade harmlessly? Where do the materials go when thrown away? Do they sit in landfills for eternity, create toxins when incinerated, or break down to pollute water? Can they be carried by air currents and influence the healthy functioning of natural systems far from the source?

Until recently these questions were not business concerns. Increasingly, however, business strategy, and perhaps even viability, demands that we think small in order to think big. As we learn to detect and understand chemical impacts, corporate tracking of product ingredients at the molecular level is becoming an imperative and a key to new areas of business growth.

This entire concept has some direct parallels to the ways entrepreneurs think. Two principles are especially useful to entrepreneurs. First, the devil is in the details. Successful entrepreneurs know they have to sweat the details at the bottom of the abstraction ladder (the helicopter mind we discussed earlier). It is hard to recall an entrepreneur who has not personally read and studied with care his or her own loan agreement, franchise agreement, or other contract, rather than just leaving it to the lawyers. Entrepreneurs know their perspectives and insights are an important test of the subtle but critical implications agreements like these can have. This attention to detail applies equally to supply chain processes and components that enable your venture to launch. The benefits of a sustainability lens and systems thinking can be leveraged or even extended throughout a value chain.

The 12 Principles of Green Chemistry

1. *Prevent waste:* Design chemical syntheses to prevent waste, leaving no waste to treat or clean up.

2. *Design safer chemicals and products:* Design chemical products to be fully effective yet have little or no toxicity.

3. *Design less hazardous chemical syntheses:* Design syntheses to use and generate substances with little or no toxicity to humans and the environment.

4. *Use renewable feedstocks:* Use raw materials and feedstocks that are renewable rather than depleting. Renewable feedstocks are often made from agricultural products or are the wastes of other processes; depleting feedstocks are made from fossil fuels (petroleum, natural gas, or coal) or are mined.

5. *Use catalysts, not stoichiometric reagents:* Minimize waste by using catalytic reactions. Catalysts are used in small amounts and can carry out a single reaction many times. They are preferable to stoichiometric reagents, which are used in excess and work only once.

6. *Avoid chemical derivatives:* Avoid using blocking or protecting groups or any temporary modifications if possible. Derivatives use additional reagents and generate waste.

7. *Maximize atom economy:* Design syntheses so that the final product contains the maximum proportion of the starting materials. There should be few, if any, wasted atoms.

8. *Use safer solvents and reaction conditions:* Avoid using solvents, separation agents, or other auxiliary chemicals. If these chemicals are necessary, use innocuous chemicals. If a solvent is necessary, water is a good medium, as well as certain ecofriendly solvents that do not contribute to smog formation or destroy the ozone.

9. *Increase energy efficiency:* Run chemical reactions at ambient temperature and pressure whenever possible.

10. *Design chemicals and products to degrade after use:* Design chemical products to break down to innocuous substances after use so that they do not accumulate in the environment.

11. *Analyze in real time to prevent pollution:* Include in-process, real-time monitoring and control during syntheses to minimize or eliminate the formation of by-products.

12. *Minimize the potential for accidents:* Design chemicals and their forms (solid, liquid, or gas) to minimize the potential for chemical accidents, including explosions, fires, and releases to the environment.

Source: P. T. Anastas and J. C. Warner, *Green Chemistry: Theory and Practice* (New York: Oxford University Press, 1998).

Second, entrepreneurial leaders know that even the most complex and difficult issues and challenges they face are reducible to a series of tenacious, relentless assaults on small, solvable pieces. In the compelling film *October Sky,* this is exactly how the main characters Homer and Quentin went about proving their rocket did not start the fire in a nearby town. This sequence in the film is a perfect example of how entrepreneurs think like molecules to break a problem or obstacle down into its smallest part—one that is solvable—and then move on. In a similar way, tracking materials through their respective life cycles breaks those processes down to essential constituent parts for effective analysis and redesign.

Thus far we have discussed new ways of thinking and seeing through a sustainability lens; to implement these ideas we must call on untapped sources of creativity as well as marshal dormant resources.

Value-Added Network

Your *value-added network* is the web within which you already work. Some of these colleagues will intuitively understand that a sustainability lens can offer inspiration and new pathways forward. Sometimes asking an old partner or colleague a new question can reveal unsuspected depths of knowledge and expertise. Find the mechanisms appropriate for your venture or entrepreneurial network and employ them for this purpose. In moving forward, your value-added network can function as a whole greater than the sum of its parts.

Be Radically Incremental

Once you have activated your value-added network, draw a map appropriate to scale, and be ready to adjust your pace as needed. Be *radically incremental.* Yes, this is an oxymoron; we use this terminology deliberately. It is counterintuitive to suggest that radical results can be gained by taking small steps, but this is possible. Set ambitious goals, but be flexible in how you get there. Taking small steps in a radical direction can be powerful. Zero emissions and zero toxicity may be radical goals; but by establishing them as strategic objectives, the entrepreneur focuses his or her network of stakeholders on the promise that constant improvement will ultimately lead to radical, systemwide innovations. Evaluate and measure everything you can to feed success back into the process, and gain the support of your less bold stakeholders. Most of all, be flexible; adaptation and learning determine the process and can help you adjust your goals.

Looking through a sustainability lens allows you to step back and view your entire business system; it gives you a wider perspective on the many ways in which your venture interacts with the world around it. Embrace the larger contextual challenges—therein lie the opportunities.

Sustainability is new territory for many of us. But exploring new territory is not new; we have many successful examples to follow. Imagine, for example, that you will be accompanying the early 19th-century explorers, Lewis and Clark, through the unfamiliar territory of the American West—the first European Americans to chart a course from the Eastern Seaboard to the Pacific Ocean. The year is 1803; there are very few maps of the American interior. The ones that exist are sketchy at best. How would you prepare for such a journey? You might talk to friends and acquaintances to learn what they know about the terrain you will be covering. But to get strategic information vitally necessary to surviving this foray into the unknown, you would go outside your immediate circle to talk with trappers, Native Americans, French traders, natural scientists, and other voyagers—people from diverse walks of life. You would need to build weak ties[3] to a wide range of people to gain the necessary data.

Similarly, creating and executing a new venture into unknown territory requires that you leave your familiar circle of advisors and seek information from diverse sources. This is particularly true to move successfully in the unfamiliar territory where environmental entrepreneurship and sustainability intersect. Remember that the weak ties in your world are new sources of information and resources that allow you to reach beyond the normal boundaries of strategic information. Sacagawea, the Shoshone teenage girl who traveled with the Lewis and Clark expedition, is a perfect example of a weak tie.

The partnership Lewis formed with Sacagawea as the party searched for a mountain passage through dangerous Shoshone territory in the Pacific Northwest was of life-sustaining importance. Her negotiation and translation skills and her knowledge of the geography contributed critically to the expedition's success. Her skills were not recognized initially, but her courage and fast thinking turned out to be pivotal in overcoming challenges along the way. Without her knowledge the group would never have made it to the shores of the Pacific Ocean.

Anybody can look through a sustainability lens and discover new opportunities. Entrepreneurial startups have an important role to play by setting the innovation bar high. They can rock the market with their flexibility and speed. And because experienced

---

[3] Ibid.

investors and committed multinationals have the power to fundamentally shift the playing field, their lean to green will certainly accelerate the pace of change, discovery, and entrepreneurial opportunities across a vast range of industries.

Illustrating the Concept: Green Cleaning

The entrepreneurial firm Method (methodhome.com), a relative newcomer to the retail home cleaning products market, is moving into the new environmental market space and redefining the rules of the game. The company was listed as the seventh fastest-growing company in the United States in 2006 (3,391 percent growth in three years). Method's founders, Adam Lowry and Eric Ryan (who started Method when they were in their twenties), have continued to drive sustainability principles through the company and its supply chains. Doing what they were told could not be done, these entrepreneurs have reinvented a mature product category that for decades had been characterized by thin margins, low innovation, and pitched big-company battles for market share. As the first company to deliver aesthetically appealing, ecologically friendly home cleaning products

to mainstream retailers (as opposed to just natural products stores), Method has changed the rules of that game to such an extent that major consumer packaged goods (CPG) global companies are following the lead of these upstart entrepreneurs.

Method has taken green to the mainstream with goods available at major retailers like Target. Consumers, who are getting on board with the green movement, are buying Method products because they are reasonably priced, are remarkably nontoxic, and work. Stylishly packaged in recyclable packaging and marketed as "clean," Method's products are designed to be displayed on countertops. From the inception of the company, environmental and health considerations were assumed to be part of the product design and operating principles. At Method, clean means not only getting dirt off surfaces in your home, but doing so without exposing children and adults to powerful and potentially toxic cleaning chemicals. There is no need to lock these products inside cabinets. They contain no toxins; and having been designed according to green chemistry principles, Method's products are exempt from the REACH regulatory requirements for chemicals enacted by the European Union (EU) in 2006.[4] Method is committed to finding more such competitive and differentiating

Greentech Alliance

Feeling that scientific breakthroughs in biology and materials technology mean there's never been a better time to start and grow a great green venture, the legendary Silicon Valley–based venture capitalist Kleiner, Perkins, Caufield & Byers (KPCB) is actively investing in greentech innovation and entrepreneurs.

To further these aims, in November 2007 KPCB announced a global collaboration with Generation Investment Management (Generation), a firm cofounded by Al Gore, former vice president of the United States and a leading advocate for climate change initiatives. The collaboration will find, fund, and accelerate green business, technology, and policy solutions with the greatest potential to help solve the current climate crisis. The partnership will provide funding and global business-building expertise to a range of businesses, both public and private, and to entrepreneurs. As a result of the collaboration, Gore will join KPCB as a partner; KPCB will co-locate their European operations at Generation's offices in London; and KPCB partner John Doerr will join Generation's advisory board. Gore commented,

> This alliance brings together world-class business talent to focus on solving the climate crisis. Together, we have a working understanding of this urgent, multidimensional challenge and are resolved to help business and government leaders accelerate the development of sustainable solutions.

This alliance represents a landmark alignment of resources to effect global change to protect the environment. It combines the research expertise of both organizations with a track record of successful investments in public and private companies, from early-stage to large-capitalization business. It aligns the convening power of Gore, the KPCB Greentech Innovation Network, and the Generation Advisory Board toward a common goal. In addition, KPCB's presence in Asia and the United States, combined with Generation's presence in the United States, Europe, and Australia, will support global-scale solutions.

Source: www.kpcb.com.

---

[4] See http://ec.europa.eu/enterprise/reach/index_en.htm.

advantages as they move forward to, in the words of founder Adam Lowry, "reinvent the category again."

Consider cleaning wipes, a product traditionally made from petroleum-derived plastics. Eighty-three tons of cleaning wipes are thrown away every year in the United States, and U.S. plastics manufacturers told Adam Lowry that single-use, nonwoven cleaning cloths could not be made from PLA (polylactic acid), a plant-based biomaterial recently commercialized by Cargill's NatureWorks subsidiary (discussed next). Undeterred, Lowry found innovative Chinese subcontractors to formulate biomass-based, microfiber plastic wipes that are both compostable and biodegradable. It wasn't long before those U.S. subcontractors (now wanting a piece of the business) were calling Adam back to say they had figured out how to do it. Working with domestic manufacturers is a sourcing strategy more consistent with the sustainability concept of reducing transportation fuel use and facilitating supplier management.

At every turn, Method seeks to be a catalyst for broader systemic change. The company uses biodiesel-fueled trucks, has developed solar-powered forklifts for its main Chicago warehouse, and is already carbon-neutral through offsets. Adam Lowry wants to implement onsite power generation wherever possible to become a net exporter of energy. Unable to recover packaging directly, the company has led the industry move to 2X and 3X ultra condensed laundry detergent, which reduces packaging materials, shipping cost, and water use. To positively influence packaging recovery, in California the company invests to improve municipal waste recycling technologies and methods.

Codevelopment of innovations with suppliers drives Method's capacity to remain on the competitive edge. Most early suppliers were small firms that wanted to be innovative and to learn new processes and designs. Many of these have scaled up successfully with Method's tremendous growth, continuing to provide creative input. The competitive picture emerges of a David-esque network of suppliers taking on the Goliaths of P&G, Johnson & Johnson, and Unilever.

"Find it, don't build it," guides the company's strategy. Method keeps R&D inside, holding onto a talented internal team. Manufacturing is outsourced. To stay innovative, Method will partner with anyone who can help it deliver "healthy, happy home revolution"— a phrase that places interestingly wide boundaries around the brand. Lowry also comments that rigid environmental rhetoric always frustrated him; he advises, "Don't let perfection be the enemy of progress" in the environmental and sustainability markets. He also recommends that entrepreneurs get people involved who have nothing to do with the business.

"Get people involved who design other cool stuff" was his comment to a classroom of Stanford MBA students in 2007.

The sustainability lens is sharpened by using weak ties, systems thinking, and thinking like a molecule and will clearly guide this upstart successful venture. As ecological, health, and community concerns grow more important in society, Method may represent a window onto the immediate future, showing a business model that fully integrates ecological and sustainability principles into product and strategy design. This is what entrepreneurs do: They create a better future.

Illustrating the Concepts: NatureWorks

How would it feel to show up Monday morning, check your e-mail, and learn that Wal-Mart—the ultimate supply chain captain—was going to begin sourcing your product? Not a bad start to the week. All the more so if you are CEO of a relatively small subsidiary struggling to make a profit by producing a relatively unknown commodity: plastic made from corn.

This Monday morning scenario actually happened at NatureWorks LLC, an entrepreneurial venture under the technical and managerial direction of Patrick Gruber. Born of a joint venture between agricultural processing giant Cargill and Dow Chemical, NatureWorks had been struggling to realize the vision of its original founders for 10 years: replacing oil-based plastics (for packaging, films, and fabrics) with plant-based (biomass) plastics. Employing 230 people and carrying some $750 million of capital investment by Cargill, in 2005 the company was operating at a lower capacity than expected. NatureWorks was not yet profitable, and the refrain "make the bleeding stop" was beginning to sound like a broken record. And then Wal-Mart called. As part of the megaretailer's new strategy to source environmentally sustainable products, Wal-Mart would begin purchasing deli containers made from NatureWork's corn-based plastic. By the end of 2007 NatureWorks was operating at capacity with more orders than it could fill.

NatureWorks' new plastic is the result of an entrepreneurial process where materials engineers and industrial chemists designed a product that has health, environmental attributes, and functional performance built in. Consequently the company has assumed leadership in the emerging market for greener plastics. NatureWorks' product is another excellent example of what happens when you think like a molecule and employ green chemistry techniques. This strategic approach has you question the nature and value of material inputs to your products, the efficiency of your manufacturing and formulation processes, and the ultimate fate of your outputs and products. Cradle to cradle is a concept of sustainability: At the end of a product's useful life, its constituent materials (understood as assets, not waste) become inputs for new products or return safely to the earth. Thinking like a molecule allows you to understand the complete cradle-to-cradle life cycle of your products and manufacturing processes—not just the visible outcomes, but the microscopic ones as well.

This knowledge gives you valuable strategic insights. Ironically, thinking like a molecule gives you a view of emerging market opportunities for green materials and processes and helps you design a strategy to seize these opportunities. At a minimum, this molecular review will reveal new opportunities for efficiency and cost savings. At a maximum, this strategic review will result in new products, expanding market share, and enhanced profitability.

The E-Factor

Included in green chemistry tools is the idea of the "atom economy," which would have manufacturers make as full use as possible of every input molecule in the final output product. If you consider that on average 94 percent of the resources that go into making a product are discarded as waste, this principle has profound systemwide ramifications.[5]

The pharmaceutical industry, an early adopter of green chemistry principles in industrial processing, uses a metric called *E-factor* to measure the ratio of inputs to outputs in any given product. In essence, an E-factor measurement tells you how many weight units of output one gets per weight unit of input. This figure gives companies a sense of process efficiency and inherent costs associated with waste, energy, and other resources' rates of use. Applying green chemistry principles to pharmaceutical production processes has enabled pharmaceutical companies to dramatically lower their E-factors—and significantly raise profits.

Merck and Co., for example, "discovered a highly innovative and efficient catalytic synthesis for sitagliptin, the active ingredient in Januvia™, their new treatment for type 2 diabetes. This revolutionary synthesis creates 220 pounds less waste for each pound of sitagliptin manufactured, and increases the overall yield by nearly 50 percent. Over the lifetime of Januvia™, Merck expects to eliminate the formation of at least 330 million pounds of waste, including nearly 110 million pounds of aqueous waste."[6]

This is a great example of how green chemistry places human and ecological health at the heart of profitable product design and manufacturing. It uses the creativity of nature's biological processes to create molecules, materials, and processes that are safe and high-performing. Moreover, because it calls for increased reliance on renewable inputs, at a macro level green chemistry provides the means of shifting away from a petrochemical-based economy to a biobased economy. This has profound consequences for a wide range of issues, from environmental health, to worker safety, to national security and the farm economy. While no single science supplies all the answers, green chemistry plays a foundational role in enabling companies to see concrete benefits from greener design.

Drivers of New Entrepreneurial Opportunities

As we pointed out earlier, the Timmons Model of Entrepreneurial Process has sustainability as the bedrock of new ventures. Granted, not all ventures currently include explicit environmental and sustainability considerations, but this reflects a past in which these issues did not have to be part of the business model. We live now in a world constrained by the capacities of natural systems to adapt to our activity.

The major challenge of this century is how to create prosperity for more people worldwide given climate change, water shortages, urban air pollution, energy supply challenges, and the necessity of feeding and providing decent lifestyles for a world population that is expected to double by 2050. Economic models that served as the foundation of the Industrial Revolution assumed limitless natural resources and infinite capacity for nature to absorb waste streams from commercial and industrial activity. Feedback from natural systems, communicated by the scientific communities that monitor pollution and ecological health, tell us that this growth model can no longer guide us.

We are inundated by media reports on the mounting challenges from environmental constraints. In fact, the revolution in communications is a major contributor to the opening of new opportunities for entrepreneurs in this field. Because information is now widely distributed and universally accessible, consumers can access new scientific findings and

---

[5] The definition of E-factor is evolving at this writing. Pharmaceutical companies engaged in green chemistry are still debating whether to include input factors such as energy, water, and other nontraditional inputs.
[6] http://www.epa.gov/greenchemistry/pubs/pgcc/winners/gspa06.html.

perspectives well in advance of government action and regulations. With climate change, for example, U.S. companies began to take action to protect their shareholders well in advance of governmental acceptance that climate change was even happening. Similarly, caution is beginning to prevail in the arena of consumer goods and environmental health. When a material in a common product comes under increasing scrutiny as a hazard, such as in imported children's toys, the consumer is increasingly disinclined to wait for the U.S. Environmental Protection Agency (EPA) to test, assess, and ban the substance. Instead end users now have the means and motivation to search out alternative products. Thus the entrepreneur who reads these trends and gets ahead of them can be ready when the market begins to shift— and indeed can help shift the market just by offering safe alternatives.

As with the REACH regulations in the European Union mentioned earlier, changing global standards and international regulations are shifting the playing field as well. "Why is this substance banned in Europe and Japan but sold in the United States?" an American consumer may wonder. It is becoming increasingly difficult to manufacture different qualities of goods for diverse regulatory regimes, so it is best to meet the highest global standard—not only to simplify supply chains but to avoid being caught selling "substandard" or even contaminated products in one country and "clean" products in another.

Europe and Japan are setting a high bar for international manufacturing standards. The Directive on the Restriction of the Use of Certain Hazardous Substances in Electrical and Electronic Equipment (commonly referred to as the Restriction of Hazardous Substances Directive or RoHS) was adopted in February 2003 by the European Union. RoHS took effect in July 2006 and is mandated to become law in each member state. This directive restricts the use of six hazardous (and commonly used) materials in the manufacture of various types of electronic and electrical equipment. RoHS is closely linked with the EU's Waste Electrical and Electronic Equipment Directive (WEEE), which sets collection, recycling, and recovery targets for electronics. Under WEEE, responsibility for the disposal of waste electrical and electronic equipment is placed on manufacturers. Both of these directives are part of an EU legislative initiative to solve the problem of increasing amounts of toxic e-waste.

There are other powerful drivers behind entrepreneurs using a sustainability lens. For example, green building design and construction are mainstream in this first decade of the 21st century. The LEED (Leadership in Energy and Environmental Design) standards provide green building rating systems under the U.S. Green Building Council. Being awarded silver, gold, or platinum levels of design and material use is a way companies now differentiate themselves and recoup costs through greater efficiency over time. Buildings with LEED certification realize benefits such as operating cost reductions due to energy and water savings, employee productivity gains, better recruitment and retention, and higher resale value.

The 21st-century entrepreneur must anticipate upcoming environmental laws and process regulations, and must view such measures as potential opportunities. Although old-school business leaders may be inclined to fight against such measures, entrepreneurs will instead spend their time coming up with new processes and products ahead of those regulations—and by doing so will ultimately lead the market.

Another area of rapid market growth is clean energy technology including wind, solar photovoltaics, fuel cells, and biofuels. Debate over climate change has shifted from whether it is happening to what to do about it. Venture investments in energy technologies were estimated to have tripled in 2006 to $2.4 billion.[7] The growing number of stock indexes tracking the North American clean energy sector (up to six in 2006) is another indicator of clean technology going mainstream. Close to 40 percent growth across the wind, solar, fuel cell, and biofuel markets indicates that opportunity abounds.

As ecological and economic pressures grow worldwide, the true entrepreneurial leader will be viewed as someone with a vision from which he or she creates new ventures that protect the integrity of natural systems, whether we are referring to atmospheric systems, watersheds and streams, urban housing/job/health systems, or human immune systems. Entrepreneurial visions that allow successful co-evolution of business with natural systems will have more durability and be better grounded in the new realities.

Consistent with the Timmons Model, today a growing number of entrepreneurs are creating this new competitive market space by effectively mobilizing resources, offering successful products, and devising alternative business models. These leaders are integrating sustainability principles into their operations and strategies and offer a distinct entrepreneurial and innovative business model for the future. It is an evolving model for positive and creative business adaptation to the increasingly problematic impact humans have on natural systems.

---

[7] J. Makower, R. Pernick, and C. Wilder, "Clean Energy Trends," March 2007, www.cleanedge.com.

Implications for 21st-Century Entrepreneurs

The implications of these trends for 21st-century entrepreneurs are profound. The opportunities exist today and are growing worldwide as people adapt and evolve in response to more complex social, economic, and environmental pressures. Resource constraints and the limits of ecological systems to absorb our waste are not transitory challenges. Green is not a fad. Clean commerce is a necessity given global population growth, rising economic aspirations in emerging economies, and a growing appreciation of our role in affecting the intricate balance of the earth's natural systems. Because climate change will directly influence our lives and those of our children, movement away from fossil fuel dependence has, in many countries, become a national strategy—and indeed a national security concern. These issues are among the most fundamental challenges of the 21st century.

Whether major change is desired or forced upon us, it is the entrepreneurially minded who respond creatively with alternatives. Entrepreneurs see opportunities, not obstacles. Unlike those caught in existing modes of thinking about business design, entrepreneurs focus on desired future outcomes and creatively craft pathways to get there. This is how entrepreneurs lead; and the most important tool for the 21st century entrepreneur is likely the sustainability lens.

A wave of entrepreneurial creativity and innovation is already under way, inspired by the sustainability lens. As Jeff Timmons has stated, "The force of one generation's entrepreneurs becomes the next generation's business paradigm." This is happening as new businesses and technologies emerge to address environmental and human health concerns. As the entrepreneurs behind Method and NatureWorks illustrate, by driving change in consumer product design and materials innovation, entrepreneurship trends in environmental sustainability are the leading indicators of business and social change.

Entrepreneurs have important opportunities to supply midsized and larger firms with newly designed products that meet environmental and sustainability criteria. Larger firms can move the market, but often they must buy innovations from smaller, more nimble entrepreneurial firms. Given the creative skill set required in this transition, entrepreneurial leaders—less limited by historical ideas of the possible—will be the ones to offer new solutions to large firms and to consumers. The transition to sustainability and clean commerce requires new technology, new products, and new markets. Providing these has historically been, and remains today, the role of the entrepreneur.

Chapter Summary

- Some of the most fertile opportunities lie in the areas of greatest tension. If you can see them and act on them, you will differentiate your company and set the industry standard to best suit your venture's capabilities.
- The five strategic facets of looking through a sustainability lens are weak ties, systems thinking, thinking like a molecule, value-added networks, and radical incrementalism.
- Employing green chemistry techniques can not only reduce process costs and the risk of production and product liability, but can generate new products and open new markets.
- Green chemistry places human and ecological health at the heart of profitable product design and manufacturing. It uses the creativity of nature's biological processes to create molecules, materials, and processes that are safe and high-performing.
- Consistent with the Timmons Model emphasis on opportunity and the resources a visionary entrepreneurial team brings to bear, today many entrepreneurial leaders are looking through a sustainability lens and creating new competitive market spaces.
- The entrepreneur who reads these trends and gets ahead of them can be ready when the market begins to shift—and indeed can help shift the market just by offering safe alternatives.
- Because it is becoming increasingly difficult to manufacture different qualities of goods for diverse regulatory regimes, it is best to meet the highest global standard—not only to simplify supply chains but to avoid being caught selling "substandard" or even contaminated products in one country and "clean" products in another.
- Although old-school business leaders may be inclined to fight against sustainability measures, entrepreneurs will instead spend their time coming up with new processes and products ahead of such regulations—and by doing so will ultimately lead the market.
- Entrepreneurial opportunities exist today and are growing worldwide as creative business leaders adapt and evolve in response to more complex social, economic, and environmental pressures.

Study Questions

1. In what ways does looking through a sustainability lens change how an entrepreneur approaches a new venture opportunity?
2. Explain how thinking like a molecule is related to the entrepreneurial process.
3. Why has the clean commerce domain become one of the hottest for venture capital investors?

4. How has the communications revolution become a major driver of entrepreneurial thinking and opportunities in sustainable, green business models?
5. How can entrepreneurs use the increasingly stringent product, raw material, and manufacturing process laws (particularly in Japan and in Europe) to their advantage?

Internet Resources for Chapter 4

www.sustainablebusiness.com *SustainableBusiness.com provides global news and networking services to help green business grow, covering all sectors: renewable energy, green building, sustainable investing, and organics.*

www.greenbiz.com *GreenBiz is a free information resource on how to align environmental responsibility with business success. It includes news and resources for large and small businesses through a combination of Web sites, workshops, daily news feeds, electronic newsletters, and briefing papers.*

www.cleanedge.com *Clean Edge is a leading research and publishing firm helping companies, investors, and*

governments understand and profit from clean technologies.

www.cleantech.com *The Cleantech Network founded cleantech as a viable investment category in 2002 and has played an influential role in the development of this fast-growth investment category. The network brings capital and innovation together through Cleantech Forums and membership services.*

www.environmentalhealthnews.org *Environmental Health Sciences is a not-for-profit organization founded in 2002 to help increase public understanding of emerging scientific links between environmental exposures and human health.*

MIND STRETCHERS

Have You Considered?

1. In the next decade hundreds of millions (if not billions) of dollars of value will be created with opportunities in clean commerce. What will you have to do to help make that happen?
2. How can you convert opportunities for energy independence and clean commerce into your next business?
3. What will be one of the next significant regulatory initiatives with a product or process that is not yet in the green domain, and how might this represent a sea change opportunity?

4. Which leading clean commerce companies will be the best to work for in your first three to five years out of college?
5. You believe you've spotted a massive market opportunity involving green chemistry techniques, but you have no background in the hard science needed to explore this concept further. What next?
6. If you are currently writing a business plan or currently operating a business, name three actions you can take as dictated by the sustainability lens.

Case

Jim Poss

Preparation Questions

1. Apply the Timmons entrepreneurship framework (entrepreneur–opportunity–resources) to analyze this case. Pay particular attention to the entrepreneur's traits and how he gathered resources for his venture.

2. Discuss Jim's fund-raising strategies. What other options might be considered for raising the funds SPC needs? Is this a good investment?

3. Discuss the growth strategy. What additional market(s) would you recommend pursuing as they move ahead?

On his way through Logan Airport, Jim Poss stopped at a newsstand to flip through the June 2004 *National Geographic* cover story that declared, "The End of Cheap Oil." Inside was a two-page spread of an American family sitting among a vast array of household possessions that were derived, at least in part, from petroleum-based products: laptops, cell phones, clothing, footwear, sports equipment, cookware, and containers of all shapes and sizes. Without oil, the world will be a very different place. Jim shook his head.

and here we are burning this finite, imported, irreplaceable resource to power three-ton suburban gas guzzlers with "these colors don't run" bumper stickers!

Jim's enterprise, Seahorse Power Company (SPC), was an engineering start-up that encouraged the adoption of environmentally friendly methods of power generation by designing products that were cheaper and more efficient than 20th-century technologies. Jim was sure that his first product, a patent-pending solar-powered trash compactor, could make a real difference.

In the United States alone, 180 million garbage trucks consume over a billion gallons of diesel fuel a year. . . .

By compacting trash on-site and off-grid, the mailbox-sized "BigBelly" could cut pickups by 400 percent. The prototype—designed on the fly at a cost of $10,000—had been sold to Vail Ski Resorts in Colorado for $5,500. The green technology had been working as promised since February, saving the resort lots of time and money on round trips to a remote lodge accessible only by snow machine.

Jim viewed the $4,500 loss on the sale as an extremely worthwhile marketing and proof-of-concept expense. Now that they were taking the business to the next level with a run of 20 machines, Jim and his SPC team had to find a way to reduce component costs and increase production efficiencies.

Jim returned the magazine to the rack and made his way to the New York Shuttle gate. An investor group in the city had called another meeting, and Jim felt that it

was time for him to start asking the hard questions about the deal they were proposing. These investors in socially responsible businesses had to be given a choice: Either write him the check they've been promising—and let him run SPC the way he saw fit—or decline to invest altogether so he could concentrate on locating other sources of funding to close this $250,000 seed round. So far, all Jim had received from this group were voices of concern and requests for better terms—it was time to do the deal or move on.

Green Roots

As a kid, Jim Poss was always playing with motors, batteries, and other electronics. He especially enjoyed fashioning new gadgets from components he had amassed by dismantling all manner of appliances and electronic devices. He also spent a lot of time out of doors cross-country skiing with his father. Jim said that by his senior year in high school, he knew where he was headed:

I had read *Silent Spring*[1] and that got me thinking about the damage we are doing to the earth. And once I started learning about the severity of our problems—that was it. By the end of my first semester at Duke University, I had taken enough environmental science to see that helping businesses to go green was going to be a huge growth industry.

Jim felt that the best way to get businesses to invest in superior energy systems was to make it profitable for them to do so. In order to prepare himself for this path, Jim set up a double major in environmental science and policy, and geology—with a minor in engineering. He graduated in 1996 and found work as a hydrologist, analyzing soil and rock samples for a company that engineered stable parking lots for shopping malls. He didn't stay long:

That certainly wasn't my higher calling. I poked around, and within six months I found a fun job redesigning the

This case was prepared by Carl Hedberg under the direction of Professor William Bygrave. © Copyright Babson College, 2004. Funding provided by the Franklin W. Olin Graduate School and a gift from the class of 2003.

[1] *Silent Spring*, written in 1962 by Rachel Carson, exposed the hazards of the pesticide DDT, eloquently questioned humanity's faith in technological progress, and helped set the stage for the environmental movement. Appearing on a CBS documentary shortly before her death from breast cancer in 1964, the author remarked, "Man's attitude toward nature is today critically important simply because we have now acquired a fateful power to alter and destroy nature. But man is a part of nature, and his war against nature is inevitably a war against himself . . . . [We are] challenged as mankind has never been challenged before to prove our maturity and our mastery, not of nature, but of ourselves."

production capabilities at a small electronics firm. Soon after that, I started working for this company called Solectria; that was right up my alley.

As a sales engineer at Solectria—a Massachusetts-based designer and manufacturer of sustainable transportation and energy solutions—Jim helped clients configure electric drive systems for a wide range of vehicles. He loved the work and developed an expertise in using spreadsheets to calculate the most efficient layout of motors, controllers, power converters, and other hardware. By 1999, though, he decided that it was once again time to move on:

> Solectria had a great group of people, but my boss was a micromanager and I wasn't going to be able to grow. I found an interesting job in San Francisco as a production manager for a boat manufacturing company—coordinating the flow of parts from seven or eight subcontractors. When the [Internet] bubble burst, the boat company wasn't able to raise capital to expand. My work soon became relatively mundane, so I left.

This time, though, Jim decided to head back to school:

> I had now worked for a bunch of different businesses and I had seen some things done well, but a lot of things done wrong. I knew that I could run a good company—something in renewable energy, and maybe something with gadgets. I still had a lot to learn, so I applied to the MBA program at Babson College. I figured that I could use the second-year EIT[2] module to incubate something.

Opportunity Exploration

Between his first and second years at Babson, Jim applied for a summer internship through the Kauffman Program. He sent a proposal to the Spire Corporation—a publicly traded manufacturer of highly engineered solar electric equipment—about investigating the market and feasibility of solar-powered trash compactors. Jim had discussed his idea with someone he knew on the board, and the same week that the HR department informed him that there were no openings, he got a call from the president of the company:

> Roger Little had talked with the board member I knew and said that while they weren't interested in having me write a case study on some solar whatever-it-was, he

said they'd like me to write some business plans for Spire—based on their existing opportunities and existing operations. I said sure, I'll take it.

That summer, Jim worked with the executive team to complete three business plans. When they asked him to stay on, Jim agreed to work 15 hours per week—on top of his full-time MBA classes. Every month or so he would bring up his idea for a solar-powered trash compactor with the Spire executives, but their answer was always the same:

> I was trying to get them to invest in my idea or partner with me in some way, and these guys kept saying, "It'll never work." So I just kept working on them. I did the calculations to show them that with solar we could do 10 compactions a day and have plenty [of electric charge] on reserve for a run of cloudy weather. Finally, they just said that they don't get into end-user applications.

Early in his second year, Jim attended a product design fair featuring young engineers from Babson's new sister school, the Franklin W. Olin School of Engineering. He connected with Jeff Satwicz, an engineering student with extensive experience in remote vehicle testing for the Department of Defense. When Jim got involved with a project that required engineering capabilities, he knew whom to call:

> I went up the hill to Olin to ask Jeff if he'd like to help design a folding grill for tailgating—he said sure. It's funny, the two schools are always talking about working together like that, but it doesn't happen until the students sit in the café together and exchange ideas. That's how it works; the faculty wasn't involved—and they didn't really need to be.

Although Jim didn't stay with the grill team, the project had forged a link with an engineer with a penchant for entrepreneurship. Now certain of his trajectory, Jim incorporated the Seahorse Power Company (SPC)—a nod to his ultimate aspiration of developing power systems that could harness the enormous energy of ocean waves and currents.

Understanding that sea-powered generators were a long way off, Jim began to investigate ways to serve well-capitalized ventures that were developing alternative-energy solutions. One idea was to lease abandoned oil wells in California for the purpose of collecting and selling deep-well data to geothermal energy businesses that were prospecting in the area. When Jim sought feedback, he found that even people who liked his concept invariably pointed him in a different direction:

> Everybody kept telling me that wind was where it's at—and they were right; it's the fastest-growing energy source in the world. All the venture capitalists are looking at wind power. I realized, though, that if I was going to make wind plants, I'd have to raise $200 million to $500 million—with no industry experience. Impossible. So instead, I started looking at what these [wind-plant ventures] needed.

---

[2] The Entrepreneurship Intensity Track (EIT) was a compressed and highly focused entrepreneurial curriculum for graduate students at Babson College. The program provided a select group of MBAs with the necessary skills to take a business idea through the critical stages of exploration, investigation, and refinement. The program's individual flexibility tailored each student's education to best fit their perceived market opportunity, and enabled them to fund and launch their business during the spring of their second year.

The DAQ Buoy

Jim discovered that The Cape Wind Project, a company working to build a wind farm on Nantucket Sound, had erected a $2.5 million, 200-foot monitoring tower to collect wind and weather data in the targeted area. Jim felt that there was a better way:

> Meteorological testing is a critical first step for these wind businesses. I thought, whoa, they've just spent a lot of money to construct a static tower that probably won't accurately portray the wind activity in that 25-square-mile area. And without good data, it's going to be really hard for them to get funding.
>
> My idea was to deploy data buoys that could be moved around a site to capture a full range of data points. I spent about six months writing a business plan on my data acquisition buoy—the DAQ. I figured that to get to the prototype stage I'd need between $5 million and $10 million. This would be a pretty sophisticated piece of equipment, and a lot of people worried that if a storm came up and did what storms typically do to buoys, we'd be all done. I was having a hard time getting much traction with investors.

Finding the Waste

Even while he was casting about for a big-concept opportunity, Jim had never lost sight of his solar compactor idea. With the spring semester upon him, he decided to see if that business would work as an EIT endeavor. Although he was sure that such a device would be feasible—even easy—to produce, he didn't start to get excited about the project until he took a closer look at the industry:

> I did an independent study to examine the trash industry. I was about a week into that when I looked at the market size and realized that I had been messing around with expensive, sophisticated business models that didn't offer close to the payback this compactor would.
>
> U.S. companies spent $12 billion on trash receptacles in 2000, and $1.2 billion on compaction equipment in 2001. The average trash truck gets less than three miles to the gallon and costs over $100 an hour to operate. There are lots of off-grid sites[3] that have high trash volumes—resorts, amusement parks, and beaches—and many are getting multiple pickups a day. That's a tremendous waste of labor and energy resources.

Joining him in the EIT module was first-year MBA candidate Alexander Perera. Alex had an undergraduate degree in environmental science from Boston University, as well as industry experience in renewable energy use

Copyright © The McGraw-Hill Companies, Inc.

EXHIBIT 1
Target Customers

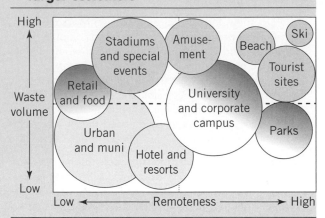

and energy efficiency measures. The pair reasoned that if a solar compactor could offer significant savings as a trash collection device, then the market could extend beyond the off-grid adopters to include retail and food establishments, city sidewalks, and hotels (see Exhibit 1).

Gearing Up

By the time the spring semester drew to a close, they had a clear sense of the market and the nature of the opportunity—in addition to seed funding of $22,500: $10,000 from Jim's savings, and $12,500 through the hatchery program at Babson College. Since solar power was widely perceived as a more expensive, more complex, and less efficient energy source than grid power, it was not surprising to discover that the competition—dumpster and compaction equipment manufacturers—had never introduced a system like this. Nevertheless, Jim and Alex were certain that if they could devise a reliable solar-powered compactor that could offer end users significant cost savings, established industry players could be counted on to aggressively seek to replicate or acquire that technology.

Understanding that patent protections were often only as good as the legal minds that drafted them, Jim had sought out the best. The challenge was that most of the talented patent attorneys he met with were far outside of his meager budget. In May 2003 Jim got a break when he presented his idea at an investor forum:

> I won $1,500 in patent services from Brown and Rudnick.[4] That might not have taken me too far, but they have a very entrepreneurial mind-set. They gave me a flat rate for the patent—which is not something many firms will do. I paid the $7,800 up front, we filed a provisional patent in June, and they agreed to work with me as I continued to develop and modify the machine.

---

[3] Sites without electrical power.

[4] Brown Rudnick Berlack Israels, LLP, Boston, Massachusetts.

Jim's efforts had again attracted the interest of Olin engineer Jeff Satwicz, who in turn brought in Bret Richmond, a fellow student with experience in product design, welding, and fabrication. When the team conducted some reverse engineering to see if the vision was even feasible, Jim said they were pleasantly surprised:

> I found a couple of kitchen trash compactors in the want ads and bought them both for about 125 bucks. We took them apart, and that's when I realized how easy this was going to be . . . of course, nothing is ever as easy as you think it's going to be.

Pitching without Product

Figuring that it was time to conduct some hard field research, they decided to call on businesses that would be the most likely early adopters of an off-grid compactor. Alex smiled as he described an unexpected turn of events:

> We had a pretty simple client-targeting formula: remoteness, trash volume, financial stability, and an appreciation for the environmental cachet that could come with a product like this. Literally the first place I called was the ski resort in Vail, Colorado. Some eco-terrorists had recently burned down one of their lodges to protest their expansion on the mountain, and they were also dealing with four environmental lawsuits related to some kind of noncompliance.
>
> This guy Luke Cartin at the resort just jumped at the solar compactor concept. He said, "Oh, this is cool. We have a lodge at Blue Sky Basin that is an hour and a half round trip on a snow cat. We pick up the trash out there three or four times a week, sometimes every day. We could really use a product like that . . ." That's when you put the phone to your chest and think, *oh my gosh . . .*

Jim added that after a couple of conference calls, they were suddenly in business without a product:

> I explained that we were students and that we had not actually built one of these things yet (sort of). Luke asked me to work up a quote for three machines. They had been very open about their costs for trash pickup, and I figured that they'd be willing to pay six grand apiece. I also had a rough idea that our cost of materials would fall somewhat less than that.
>
> Luke called back and said that they didn't have the budget for three, but they'd take one. I was actually really happy about that, because I knew by then that making just one of these was going to be a real challenge.

In September, SPC received a purchase order from Vail Resorts. When Jim called the company to work out a payment plan with 25 percent up front, Luke surprised them again:

> He said, "We'll just send you a check for the full amount, minus shipping, and you get the machine here by Christmas." That was great, but now we were in real

trouble because we had to figure out how to build this thing quickly, from scratch—and on a tight budget.

Learning by Doing

The team set out to design the system and develop the engineering plans for the machine that SPC had now trademarked as the "BigBelly Solar-Powered Trash Compactor." Although his Olin team was not yet versant with computer-aided design (CAD) software, Jim saw that as an opportunity:

> These guys were doing engineering diagrams on paper with pens and pencils—but now we were going to need professional stuff. I said that we could all learn CAD together, and if they made mistakes, great, that's fine; we'd work through it.

Concurrent to this effort was the task of crunching the numbers to design a machine that would work as promised. As they began to source out the internal components, they searched for a design, fabrication, and manufacturing subcontractor that could produce the steel cabinet on a tight schedule. Although the team had explained that SPC would be overseeing the entire process from design to assembly, quotes for the first box still ranged from $80,000 to $400,000. Jim noted that SPC had an even bigger problem to deal with:

> On top of the price, the lead times that they were giving me were not going to cut it; I had to get this thing to Colorado for the ski season!
>
> So we decided to build it ourselves. I went to a local fabricator trade show and discovered that although they all have internal engineering groups, some were willing to take a loss on the research and development side in order to get the manufacturing contract.
>
> We chose Boston Engineering since they are very interested in developing a relationship with Olin engineers. They gave me a hard quote of $2,400 for the engineering assistance, and $2,400 for the cabinet. By this time we had sourced all the components we needed, and we began working with their engineer to size everything up. Bob Treiber, the president, was great. He made us do the work ourselves out at his facility in Hudson (Massachusetts), but he also mentored us, and his firm did a ton of work pro bono.

Fulfillment and Feedback

As the Christmas season deadline came and went, the days grew longer. By late January 2004, Jim was working through both of the shifts they had set up, from four in the morning to nearly eleven at night. In February, they fired up the device, tested it for three hours, and shipped it off to Colorado (see Exhibit 2). Jim met the device at their shipping dock, helped unwrap it, met the staff, and

EXHIBIT 2

The BigBelly Arrives in Vail

put a few finishing touches on the machine. Although it worked, even at zero degree temperatures, it had never been tested in the field. Jim left after a few days, and for two weeks, he endured a deafening silence.

Jim wrestled with how he could check in with SPC's first customer without betraying his acute inventor's angst about whether the machine was still working, and if it was, what Vail thought about it. Finally, when he could stand it no longer, he placed the call under the guise of soliciting satisfied-customer feedback. The news from Vail nearly stopped his heart:

> They said that they had dropped the machine off a forklift and it fell on its face. Oh man, I thought; if it had fallen on its back, that would have been okay, but this was bad—real bad. And then Luke tells me that it was a bit scratched—but it worked fine. He told me how happy they were that we had made it so robust. When I asked how heavy the bags were that they were pulling out of the thing, he said, "I don't know; we haven't emptied it yet . . ." I was astounded.

As it turned out, the Vail crew discovered that the single collection bag was indeed too heavy—a two-bin system would be more user-friendly. The resort also suggested that the inside cart be on wheels, that the access door be in the back, and that there be some sort of wireless notification when the compactor was full.

As the SPC team got to work incorporating these ideas into their next generation of "SunPack" compactors, they were also engineering a second product that they hoped would expand their market reach to include manufacturers of standard compaction dumpsters. The "SunPack Hippo" would be a solar generator designed to replace the 220-volt AC-power units that were used to run industrial compactors. The waste hauling industry had estimated that among commercial customers that would benefit from compaction, between 5 and 20 percent were dissuaded

from adopting such systems because of the setup cost of electrical wiring. SPC planned to market the system through manufacturing and/or distribution partnerships.

Protecting the Property

While the interstate shipment of the BigBelly had given SPC a legal claim to the name and the technology, Jim made sure to keep his able patent attorneys apprised of new developments and modifications. SPC had applied for a provisional patent in June 2003, and they had one year to broaden and strengthen those protections prior to the formal filing. As that date approached, the attorneys worked to craft a document that protected the inventors from infringement, without being so broad that it could be successfully challenged in court.

The SPC patents covered as many aspects of SunPack products as possible, including energy storage, battery charging, energy draw cycle time, sensor controls, and wireless communication. The filing also specified other off-grid power sources for trash compaction such as foot pedals, windmills, and water wheels.

Even without these intellectual property protections, though, Jim felt that they had a good head start in an industry segment that SPC had created. Now they had to prove the business model.

The Next Generation

While the first machine had cost far more to build than the selling price, the unit had proven the concept and been a conduit for useful feedback. A production run of 20 machines, however, would have to demonstrate that the business opportunity was as robust as the prototype appeared to be. That would mean cutting the cost of materials by more than 75 percent to around $2,500 per unit. SPC estimated that although the delivered price of $5,000 was far more expensive than the cost of a traditional trash receptacle, the system could pay for itself by trimming the ongoing cost of collection (see Exhibit 3).

The team had determined that developing a lease option for the BigBelly would alleviate new-buyer jitters by having SPC retain the risk of machine ownership—a move that could increase margins by 10 percent. Over the next five years SPC expected to expand its potential customer pool by reducing the selling price to around $3,000—along with a corresponding drop in materials costs (see Exhibit 4).

With steel prices escalating, the SPC team designed their new machines with 30 percent fewer steel parts. They also cut the size of the solar panel and the two-week battery storage capacity in half, and replaced the expensive screw system of compaction with a simpler, cheaper, and more efficient sprocket and chain mechanism (see Exhibit 5).

EXHIBIT 3

Customer Economics

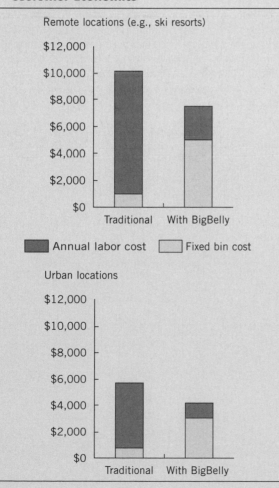

Remote locations (e.g., ski resorts)

Annual labor cost   Fixed bin cost

Urban locations

EXHIBIT 4

BigBelly Economics

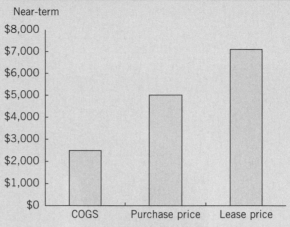

Near-term

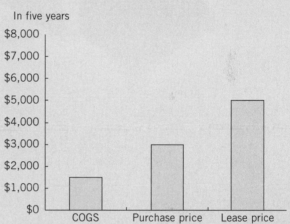

In five years

To offer an effective service response capability, the team tried to restrict their selling efforts to the New England area, although "a sale was a sale." One concern that kept cropping up was that this unique device would be a tempting target for vandals. Team members explained that the solar panel on top was protected by a replaceable sheet of Lexan,[5] that all mechanical parts were entirely out of reach, and that the unit had already proven to be quite solid. The general feeling, Jim noted, was that if the machine could be messed with, people would find a way:

> One state park ranger was worried that it would get tossed into the lake, so I assured him that the units would be very heavy. He said, "So they'll sink really fast . . ."

Jim added that the overall response had been very favorable—so much so that once again, there was a real need for speed:

> We have pre-sold nearly half of our next run to places like Acadia National Park in Maine, Six Flags Amusement Park in Massachusetts, Harbor Lights in Boston,

[5] A clear, high-impact-strength plastic used in many security applications.

EXHIBIT 5
BigBelly CAD Schematic

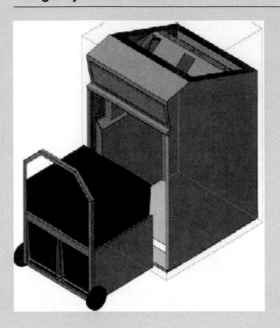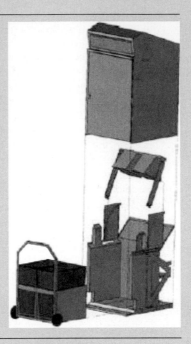

beaches on Nantucket, and Harvard University. Fifty percent down payment deposits should be coming in soon, but that won't cover what we'll need to get this done.

Projections and Funding

During this "early commercialization period," Jim was committed to moderating investor risk by leveraging on-campus and contractor facilities as much as possible.

The company was hoping to close on an A-round of $250,000[6] by early summer to pay for cost reduction engineering, sales and marketing, and working capital. The following year the company expected to raise a B-round of between $700,000 and $1 million.

SPC was projecting a positive cash flow in 2006 on total revenues of just over $4.7 million (see Exhibit 6).

[6] Based on a pre-money valuation of $2.5 million. The principal and interest on this seed-round note would convert into equity at the A-round with an additional 30 percent discount to A-round investors. Seed-round investors would have the right to reinvest in the A-round to offset dilution.

EXHIBIT 6
SPC Financial Projections

	2004	2005	2006	2007	2008
BigBelly unit sales	50	300	1,200	3,600	9,000
BigBelly revenues	$225,000	$1,200,000	$4,200,000	$10,800,000	$22,500,000
Hippo royalty revenues	0	120,000	525,000	1,620,000	3,937,500
Total income	225,000	1,320,000	4,725,000	12,420,000	26,437,500
COGS	146,250	660,000	2,100,000	4,860,000	9,000,000
Gross income	78,750	660,000	2,625,000	7,560,000	17,437,500
SG&A	400,000	1,600,000	2,600,000	5,000,000	11,000,000
EBIT	($321,250)	($940,000)	$25,000	$2,560,000	$6,437,500

EXHIBIT 7

Market Size and Penetration

	2004	2005	2006	2007	2008
Top-Down					
SunPack market* ($ billions)	$1.0	$1.0	$1.0	$1.0	$1.0
SunPack % penetration	0.0%	0.1%	0.5%	1.2%	2.6%
Bottom-Up					
Total potential customers**	30,000	30,000	30,000	30,000	30,000
Potential units/customer	20	20	20	20	20
Total potential units	600,000	600,000	600,000	600,000	600,000
Cumulative units sold	50	350	1,550	5,150	14,150
Cumulative % penetration	0.0%	0.1%	0.3%	0.9%	2.4%

*Assume $600,000 BigBelly market (5% of $12 billion waste receptacles sold to target segments) plus a $400,000 power unit market ($1.2 billion compacting dumpsters sold/$12,000 average price × $4,000 per power unit).

**Assume 400 resorts, 600 amusement parks, 2,000 university campuses, 5,000 commercial campuses, 2,200 hotels, 4,000 municipalities, 57 national parks, 2,500 state parks and forests, 3,700 RV parks and campgrounds, and 17,000 fast-food and retail outlets.

The team felt that if their products continued to perform well, their market penetration estimates would be highly achievable (see Exhibit 7). Jim estimated that by 2008, SPC would become an attractive merger or acquisition candidate.

In January 2004, as Jim began work on drafting an SBIR[7] grant proposal, his parents helped out by investing $12,500 in the venture. That same month, while attending a wind energy conference sponsored by Brown and Rudnick, Jim overheard an investor saying that he was interested in putting a recent entrepreneurial windfall to work in socially responsible ventures. Jim decided it was worth a try:

I gave him my three-minute spiel on the compactor. He said that it sounded interesting, but that he was into wind power—after all, this *was* a wind power conference. "Well then," I said, "have I got a business plan for you!"

That afternoon Jim sent the investor the most recent version of the data acquisition buoy business plan. That led to a three-hour meeting where the investor ended up explaining to Jim why the DAQ was such a good idea. Jim said that the investor also understood how difficult it would be to get the venture fully funded:

[The investor] said, "Well, I sure wish you were doing the data acquisition buoy, but I can also see why you're not." I assured him that my passion was, of

course, offshore wind, and that it was something I was planning to do in the future. So he agreed to invest $12,500 in the compactor—but only because he wanted to keep his foot in the door for what SPC was going to do later on.

In February, after the folks at Vail had come back with their favorable review, Jim called on his former internship boss at the Spire Corporation. Roger Little was impressed with Jim's progress, and his company was in for $25,000. In April the team earned top honors in the 2004 Douglas Foundation Graduate Business Plan Competition at Babson College. The prize—$20,000 cash plus $40,000 worth of services—came with a good deal of favorable press as well. The cash, which Jim distributed evenly among the team members, was their first monetary compensation since they had begun working on the project.

Although SPC could now begin to move ahead on the construction of the next 20 cabinets, Jim was still focused on the search for a rather uncommon breed of investor:

This is not a venture capital deal, and selling this idea to angels can be a challenge because many are not sophisticated enough to understand what we are doing. I had one group, for example, saying that this wouldn't work because most trash receptacles are located in alleys—out of the sun.

Here we have a practical, commonsense business, but since it is a new technology, many investors are unsure of how to value it. How scalable is it? Will our patent filings hold up? Who will fix them when they break?

[7] The Small Business Innovation Research (SBIR) Program was a source of government grant funding driven by 10 federal departments and agencies that allocated a portion of their research and development capital for awards to innovative small businesses in the United States.

Earlier that spring Jim had presented his case in Boston to a gathering of angels interested in socially responsible enterprises. Of the six presenters that day, SPC was the only one offering products that were designed to lower direct costs. During the networking session that followed, Jim said that one group in particular seemed eager to move ahead:

> They liked that Spire had invested, and they seemed satisfied with our projections. When I told them that we had a $25,000 minimum, they said not to worry—they were interested in putting in $50,000 now and $200,000 later. In fact, they started talking about setting up funding milestones so that they could be our primary backers as we grew. They wanted me to stop fundraising, focus on the business, and depend on them for all my near-term financing needs.
>
> At this point I felt like I needed to play hardball with these guys, show them where the line was. My answer was that I wasn't at all comfortable with that, and that I would be comfortable when I had $200,000 in the bank—my bank. They backed off that idea, and by the end of the meeting, they agreed to put in the $50,000; but first they said they had to perform some more due diligence.

Momentum

By May 2004 the Seahorse Power Company had a total of six team members.[8] All SPC workers had been given an equity stake in exchange for their part-time services. The investor group expressed deep concern with this arrangement, saying that the team could walk away when the going got tough—and maybe right when SPC needed them most. Jim explained that it wasn't a negotiable point:

> They wanted my people to have "skin in the game" because they might get cold feet and choose to get regular jobs. I told them that SPC workers are putting in 20 hours a week for free when they could be out charging consulting rates of $200 an hour. They have plenty of skin in this game, and I'm not going to ask them for cash. Besides, if we could put up the cash, we wouldn't need investors, right?

As Jim settled into his seat for the flight to New York, he thought some more about the investors' other primary contention: his pre-money valuation was high by a million:

> These investors—who still haven't given us a dime—are saying they can give me as much early-stage capital as SPC would need, but at a pre-money of $1.5 million and dependent on us hitting our milestones. With an immediate funding gap of about $50,000, it's tempting to move forward with these guys so we can fill current orders on time and maintain our momentum. On the other hand, I've already raised some money on the higher valuation, and maybe we can find the rest before the need becomes really critical.

---

[8] Three of the most recent equity partners were Richard Kennelly, a former director at Conservation Law Foundation where he concentrated on electric utility deregulation, renewable energy, energy efficiency, air quality, and global warming; Kevin Dutt, an MBA in operations management and quantitative methods from Boston University with extensive work experience in improving manufacturing and operational practices in a range of companies; and Steve Delaney, an MBA from Tuck School of Business at Dartmouth College with a successful track record in fund-raising, business development, market strategy, finance, and operations.

Chapter Five

The Opportunity: Creating, Shaping, Recognizing, Seizing

I was seldom able to see an opportunity, until it ceased to be one.

Mark Twain

Results Expected

Upon completion of this chapter, you will be able to

1. Discuss the importance of "think big enough" and the realities that accompany most new ventures.

2. Describe how the most successful higher-potential ventures track a "circle of ecstasy" and match investors' appetites in the "food chain" for ventures.

3. Define the differences between an idea and an opportunity.

4. Assess opportunity via a zoom lens on the criteria used by successful entrepreneurs, angels, and venture capital investors in evaluating potential ventures.

5. Explain the roles that ideas, pattern recognition, and the creative process play in entrepreneurship.

6. Identify sources of information for finding and screening venture opportunities.

7. Generate some new venture ideas and your personal criteria using the three idea generation exercises.

8. Conceive of the next sea changes related to recent advances in technology and societal, demographic, and environmental trends.

9. Provide insights into and analysis of the Burt's Bees case study.

Think Big Enough

Since its inception, *New Venture Creation* has attempted to inspire aspiring entrepreneurs to "think big enough." Time and again the authors have observed the classic small business owner who, almost like a dairy farmer, is enslaved by and wedded to the business. Extremely long hours of 70, 80, or even 100 hours a week, and rare vacations, are often the rule rather than the exception. And these hardworking owners rarely build equity, other than in the real estate they may own for the business. One of the big differences between the growth- and equity-minded entrepreneur and the traditional small business owner is that the entrepreneur thinks *bigger.* Longtime good friend Patricia Cloherty puts it this way: "It is critical to think big enough. If you want to start and build a company, you are going to end up exhausted. So you might as well think about creating a BIG company. At least you will end up exhausted and *rich,* not just exhausted!"

Pat has a wealth of experience as a venture capitalist and is past president of Patrioff & Company in

New York City. She also served as the first female president of the National Venture Capital Association. In these capacities, she has been a lead investor, board member, and creator of many highly successful high-technology and biotechnology ventures, many of which were acquired or achieved an initial public offering (IPO). Her theme of thinking bigger is embedded throughout this book. How can you engage in a "think big" process that takes you on a journey treading the fine line between high ambitions and being totally out of your mind? How do you know whether the idea you are chasing is just another rainbow or has a bona fide pot of gold at the end? You can never know which side of the line you are on—and can stay on—until you try and until you undertake the journey.

Opportunity through a Zoom Lens

The original proposal by founder Scott Cook to launch a new software company called Intuit was turned down by many venture capital investors before it was funded! Thousands of similar examples illustrate just how complex, subtle, and situational (at the time, in the market space, the investor's other alternatives, etc.) is the opportunity recognition process. If the brightest, most knowledgeable, and most sophisticated investors in the world miss opportunities such as Intuit, we can conclude that the journey from idea to high-potential opportunity is illusive, contradictory, and perilous. Think of this journey as a sort of road trip through varied terrain and weather conditions. At times the journey consists of full sunshine and straight, smooth superhighways, as well as twisting, turning, narrow one-lane passages that can lead to breathtaking views. Along the way you also will unexpectedly encounter tornadoes, dust storms, hurricanes, and volcanoes. All too often you seem to run out of gas with none in sight, and flat tires come when you least expect them. This is the entrepreneur's journey.

Transforming Caterpillars into Butterflies

This chapter is dedicated to making that journey friendlier by focusing a zoom lens on the opportunity. It shares the road maps and benchmarks used by successful entrepreneurs, venture capitalists, angels, and other private equity investors in their quest to transform the often shapeless caterpillar of an idea into a spectacularly handsome butterfly of a venture. These criteria comprise the core of their due diligence to ascertain the viability and profit potential of the proposed business, and therefore the balance of risk and reward. We will examine the role of ideas and pattern recognition in the creative process of entrepreneurship.

You will come to see the criteria used to identify higher-potential ventures as jumping-off points at this rarefied end of the opportunity continuum, rather than mere end points. Only about 5 percent of entrepreneurs create ventures that emerge from the pack. Examined through a zoom lens, these ventures reveal a highly dynamic, constantly molding, shaping, and changing work of art, rather than a product of a formula or a meeting of certain items on a checklist. This highly organic and situational character of the entrepreneurial process underscores the criticality of determining *fit* and balancing *risk and reward*. As the authors have argued for three decades: The business plan is obsolete as soon as it comes off the printer! It is in this shaping process that the best entrepreneurial leaders and investors add the greatest value to the enterprise and creatively transform an idea into a venture.

New Venture Realities

It is useful to put the realities faced by Scott Cook and millions of others in perspective. Consider the following fundamental realities as normal as you seek to convert your caterpillar into a gorgeous butterfly:

New Ventures: Fundamental Realities

Most new ventures are works in process and works of art. What you start out to do is not what you end up doing.

Most business plans are obsolete at the printer.

Onset Venture Partners found that 91 percent of portfolio companies that rigidly followed their business plans failed!

Speed, adroitness of reflex, and adaptability are crucial. Keep the knees bent! Stay on your toes!

The key to succeeding is failing quickly and recouping quickly, and keeping the tuition low.

Success is highly situational, depending on time, space, context, and stakeholders.

The best entrepreneurs specialize in making "new mistakes" only.

Starting a company is a lot harder than it looks, or you think it will be; but you can last a lot longer and do more than you think if you do not try to do it solo, and you don't give up prematurely.

These realities are intended to convey the highly dynamic, at times chaotic nature of this beast, and the highly dynamic context within which most new ventures evolve. Such realities present so much room for the unexpected and the contradictory that it places a premium on thinking big enough and doing everything you can to make sure your idea becomes an opportunity. Therefore, how can the aspiring entrepreneur think about this complex, even daunting challenge?

The Circle of Ecstasy and the Food Chain for Ventures

What most small businesses do not know, but what is a way of life in the world of high-potential ventures, is what we will call the "circle of venture capital ecstasy"

EXHIBIT 5.1

Circle of Venture Capital Ecstasy

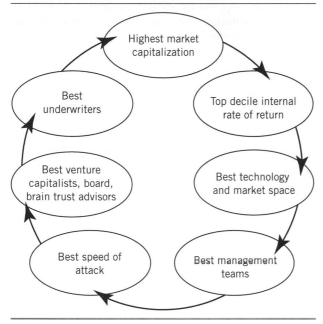

(Exhibit 5.1) and the "food chain for entrepreneurial ventures" (Exhibit 5.2). These concepts enable the entrepreneur to visualize how the company building–investing–harvesting cycle works. Understanding this cycle and the appetites of different suppliers in the capital markets food chain enables you to answer these questions: For *what* reason does this venture exist and for *whom?* Knowing the answers to these questions has profound implications for fundraising, team building, and growing and harvesting the company—or coming up short in any of these critical entrepreneurial tasks.

Exhibit 4.1 shows that the key to creating a company with the highest value (e.g., market capitalization) begins with identifying an opportunity in the "best technology and market space," which creates the attraction for the "best management team." Speed and agility to move quickly attract the "best venture capitalists, board members, and other mentors and advisers" who can add value to the venture.

Exhibit 4.2 captures the food chain concept, which will be discussed again in greater detail in Chapter 13. Different players in the food chain have very different capacities and preferences for the kind of venture in which they want to invest. The vast majority of start-up entrepreneurs spend inordinate amounts of time chasing the wrong sources with the wrong venture. One goal in this chapter, and again in Chapter 13, is to provide a clear picture of what those criteria are and

EXHIBIT 5.2

The Capital Markets Food Chain for Entrepreneurial Ventures

Stage of Venture	R&D	Seed	Launch	High Growth
Company enterprise Value at stage	Less than $1 million	$1 million–$5 million	> $1–$50 +million	More than $100 million
Sources	Founders High net worth individuals FFF* SBIR**	FFF* Angel funds Seed funds SBIR	Venture capital series A, B, C . . .† Strategic partners Very high net worth individuals Private equity	IPOs Strategic acquirers Private equity
Amount of capital invested	Up to $200,000	$10,000–$500,000	$500,000–$20 million	$10–$50 +million
% company owned at IPO	10%–25%	5%–15%	40%–60% by prior investors	15%–25% by public
Share price and number‡	$.01–$.50 1–5 million	$.50–$1.00 1–3 million	$1.00–$8.00+/− 5–10 million	$12–$18+ 3–5 million

* Friends, families, and fools.

† Venture capital series A, B, C . . . (average size of round)

		A	@ $5.1 million—startup
Round		B	@ $8.1 million—product development
(Q4 2004)		C+	@ $11.3 million—shipping product

Valuations vary markedly by industry (e.g., 2x^s).

Valuations vary by region and VC cycle.

‡ At post–IPO.

**Small Business Innovation Research, a N&F Program. The SBA provides a number of financial assistance programs for small businesses, including 7(a) loan guarantees, 504 long-term finance loans, and disaster assistance loans.

to grasp what "think big enough" means to the players in the food chain. This is a critical early step to avoid wasting time chasing venture capitalists, angels, and others when there is a misfit from the outset. As one CEO put it, "There are so many investors out there that you could spend the rest of your career meeting with them and still not get to all of them." In fact, the problem is compounded when seeking angel or informal investors because there are a hundred times more of them than there are venture capitalists.

Why waste time thinking too small and on ventures for which there is no appetite in the financial marketplace? Knowing how capital suppliers and entrepreneurs think about the opportunity creation and recognition process, their search and evaluation strategies, and what they look for is a key frame of reference.

When Is an Idea an Opportunity?

The Essence: Four Anchors
If an idea is not an opportunity, what is an opportunity? Superior business opportunities have the following four fundamental anchors:

1. They create or add significant value to a customer or end user.
2. They do so by solving a significant problem, removing a serious pain point, or meeting a significant want or need—for which someone is willing to pay a premium.
3. They have robust market, margin, and money-making characteristics that will allow the entrepreneur to estimate and communicate sustainable value to potential stakeholders: large enough ($50 million −), high growth (20 percent +), high gross margins (40 percent +), strong and early free cash flow (recurring revenue, low assets, and working capital), high profit potential (10 to 15 percent + after tax), and attractive, realizable returns for investors (25 to 30 percent + IRR).
4. They are a good *fit* with the founder(s) and management team at the time and marketplace—along with an attractive *risk–reward* balance.

For an opportunity to have these qualities, the "window of opportunity"[1] is opening and will remain open long enough. Further, entry into a market with the right characteristics is feasible, and the management team is able to achieve it. The venture has or is able to achieve a competitive advantage (i.e., to achieve leverage). Finally, the economics of the venture are rewarding and forgiving enough to allow for significant profit and growth potential.

To summarize: *A superior opportunity has the qualities of being attractive, durable, and timely and is anchored in a product or service that creates or adds value for its buyer or end user—usually by solving a very painful, serious problem.*[2] The most successful entrepreneurs, venture capitalists, and private investors are opportunity-focused; that is, they start with what customers and the marketplace want, and they do not lose sight of this.

The Real World

Opportunities are created, or built, using ideas and entrepreneurial creativity. Yet while the image of a carpenter or mason at work is useful, in reality the process is more like the collision of particles in a nuclear reaction or like the spawning of hurricanes over the ocean. Ideas interact with real-world conditions and entrepreneurial creativity at a point in time. The product of this interaction is an opportunity around which a new venture can be created.

The business environment in which an entrepreneur launches his or her venture cannot be altered significantly. Despite assumptions often made concerning social and nonprofit organizations, they also are subject to market forces and economic constraints. Consider, for instance, what would happen to donations if it were perceived that a nonprofit organization was not reinvesting its surplus returns, but instead was paying management excessive salaries. Or what if a socially oriented organization concentrated all its efforts on the social mission while neglecting revenues? Clearly dealing with suppliers, production costs, labor, and distribution is critical to the health of these social corporations. Thus social and nonprofit organizations are just as concerned with positive cash flow and generating sufficient cash flows, even though they operate in a different type of market than for-profit organizations. For-profit businesses operate in a free enterprise system characterized by private ownership and profits.

Spawners and Drivers of Opportunities

In a free enterprise system, changing circumstances, chaos, confusion, inconsistencies, lags or leads, knowledge and information gaps, and a variety of

---

[1] The window of opportunity is defined as the period of revenue growth in the life cycle of the target industry when the slope of the revenue curve is increasing. The window of opportunity begins to close as that revenue curve levels off.

[2] See J. A. Timmons, *New Business Opportunities* (Acton, MA: Brick House, 1989).

other vacuums in an industry or market spawn opportunities.

Changes in the business environment and the ability to anticipate these changes are so critical in entrepreneurship that constant vigilance for changes is a valuable habit. An entrepreneur with credibility, creativity, and decisiveness can seize an opportunity while others study it.

Opportunities are situational. Some conditions under which opportunities are spawned are idiosyncratic, while at other times they are generalizable and can be applied to other industries, products, or services. In this way, cross-association can trigger in the entrepreneurial mind the crude recognition of existing or impending opportunities. It is often assumed that a marketplace dominated by large, multibillion-dollar players is impenetrable by smaller, entrepreneurial companies. You can't possibly compete with entrenched, resource-rich, established companies. The opposite can be true for several reasons. A number of research projects have shown that it can take years or more for a large company to change its strategy and even longer to implement the new strategy because it can take 10 years or more to change the culture enough to operate differently. For a new or small company, 10 or more years is forever. When Cellular One was launched in Boston, giant NYNEX was the sole competitor. It is estimated NYNEX built twice as many towers (at $400,000 each), spent two to three times as much on advertising and marketing, and had a larger head count. Yet Cellular One grew from scratch to $100 million in sales in five years and won three customers for every one that NYNEX won. What made this substantial difference? It was an entrepreneurial management team at Cellular One.

Some of the most exciting opportunities have come from fields the conventional wisdom said are the domain of big business: technological innovation. The performance of smaller firms in technological innovation is remarkable—95 percent of the radical innovations since World War II have come from new and small firms, not the giants. A National Science Foundation study found that smaller firms generated 24 times as many innovations per research and development dollar as did firms with 10,000 or more employees.[3]

There can be exciting opportunities in plain vanilla businesses that might never get the attention of venture capital investors. For example, the lawn care industry is undergoing massive changes spurred by popular acceptance of organic fertilizers like Cock-a-Doodle Do. Dentistry is changing rapidly with innovations in cosmetic approaches and with new approaches to market segments. Alex Faigel, a young dental entrepreneur in Boston, caters to walk-in traffic by locating his five dental offices near subway stops. Keystone Automotive, an auto parts warehouse and distribution company, grew rapidly to become a national firm by utilizing sophisticated enterprise resource planning systems.

Technology and regulatory changes have profoundly altered and will continue to alter the way we conceive of opportunities. Cable television with its hundreds of channels came of age in the 1990s and brought with it new opportunities in the sale and distribution of goods from infomercials to shopping networks to pay-per-view. The Internet has created an even more diverse set of opportunities in sales and distribution, most notably Amazon.com, Priceline, eBay, and YouTube.

Consider the following broad range of examples that illustrate the phenomenon of vacuums in which opportunities are spawned:

- Deregulation of telecommunications and the airlines led to the formation of tens of thousands of new firms in the 1980s, including Cellular One (now Cingular) and Federal Express.
- Microcomputer hardware in the early 1980s far outpaced software development. The industry was highly dependent on the development of software, leading to aggressive efforts by IBM, Apple, and others to encourage software entrepreneurs to close this gap.
- Fragmented, traditional industries that have a craft or mom-and-pop character may have little appreciation or know-how in marketing and finance. Such possibilities can range from fishing lodges, inns, and hotels to cleaners/laundries, hardware stores, pharmacies, waste management plants, flower shops, nurseries, tents, and auto repairs.
- In our service-dominated economy (70 percent of businesses are service businesses, versus 30 percent just 30 years ago), customer service, rather than the product itself, can be the critical success factor. One study by the Forum Corporation in Boston showed that 70 percent of customers leave because of poor service and only 15 percent because of price or product quality. Can you think of your last "wow" experience with exceptional customer service?
- The tremendous shift to offshore manufacturing of labor-intensive and transportation-intensive products in Asia, Eastern Europe, and Mexico, such as computer-related and

---

[3] Leifer, McDermott, O'Connor, Peters, Rice, and Veryzer, *Radical Innovation: How Mature Companies Can Outsmart Upstarts* (Boston: Harvard Business School Press, 2000).

EXHIBIT 5.3

Summary of Opportunity Spawners and Drivers

Root of Change/Chaos/Discontinuity	Opportunity Creation
Regulatory changes	Cellular, airlines, insurance, telecommunications, medical, pension fund management, financial services, banking, tax and SEC laws, new societal and/or environmental standards and expectations
10-fold change in 10 years or less	Moore's law—computer chips double productivity every 18 months: financial services, private equity, consulting, Internet, biotech, information age, publishing
Reconstruction of value chain and channels of distribution	Superstores—Staples, Home Depot; all publishing; autos; Internet sales and distribution of all services
Proprietary or contractual advantage	Technological innovation: patent, license, contract, franchise, copyrights, distributorship
Existing management/investors burned out/undermanaged	Turnaround, new capital structure, new breakeven, new free cash flow, new team, new strategy; owners' desires for liquidity, exit; telecom, waste management service, retail businesses
Entrepreneurial leadership	New vision and strategy, new team equals secret weapon; organization thinks, acts like owners
Market leaders are customer obsessed or customer blind	New, small customers are low priority or ignored: hard disk drives, paper, chemicals, mainframe computers, centralized data processing, desktop computers, corporate venturing, office superstores, automobiles, software, most services

microprocessor-driven consumer products, is an excellent example.

- In a wide variety of industries, entrepreneurs sometimes find that they are the only ones who can perform. Such fields as consulting, software design, financial services, process engineering, and technical and medical products and services abound with examples of know-how monopolies. Sometimes a management team is simply the best in an industry and irreplaceable in the near term, just as is seen with great coaches with winning records.

Exhibit 5.3 summarizes the major types of discontinuities, asymmetries, and changes that can result in high-potential opportunities. Creating such changes through technical innovation (PCs, wireless telecommunications, Internet servers, software), influencing and creating the new rules of the game (airlines, telecommunications, financial services and banking, medical products, music and video), and anticipating the various impacts of such changes are central to recognizing opportunities.

Search for Sea Changes

A simple criterion for the highest-potential ventures comes from famed venture capitalist Arthur Rock: "We look for ideas that will change the way people live or work." As a lead investor in Apple Computer and a host of other world-class start-ups, he knows of what he speaks. The best place to start in seeking to identify such ideas in a macro sense is to identify significant sea changes that are occurring or will occur. Think of the profound impact that personal computing, biotechnology, and the Internet have had on the past generation. The great new ventures of the next generation will come about by the same process and will define these next great sea changes. Exhibit 5.4 summarizes some categories for thinking about such changes. These include technology, market and societal shifts, and even opportunities spawned from the excesses produced by the Internet boom. Moore's law (the computing power of a chip doubles every 18 months) has been a gigantic driver of much of our technological revolution over the past 30 years. Breakthroughs in gene mapping and cloning, biotechnology, and nanotechnology and changes brought about by the Internet will continue to create huge opportunities for the next generation. Beyond the macro view of sea changes, how can one think about opportunities in a more practical, less abstract sense? What are some parameters of business/revenue models that increase the odds of thinking big enough and therefore appeal to the food chain? At the end of this chapter is the sea change exercise, which will challenge you to think creatively and expansively about how new technology discoveries will drive the next new industries. This pattern continues to this day.

Desirable Business/Revenue Model Metrics

We will emphasize time and again in *New Venture Creation* that *happiness is a positive cash flow!—but think cash last.* You don't have an entry strategy until

EXHIBIT 5.4

Ideas versus Opportunities: Search for Sea Changes

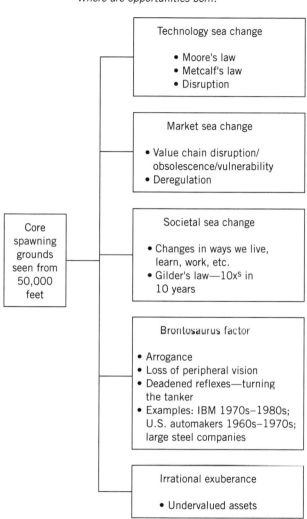

Where are opportunities born?

The importance of the idea is often overrated at the expense of underemphasizing the need for products or services, or both, that can be sold in enough quantity to real customers.

Further, the new business that simply bursts from a flash of brilliance is rare. Usually a series of trial-and-error iterations, or repetitions, is necessary before a crude and promising product or service fits with what the customer is willing to pay for. Howard Head made 40 different metal skis before he finally made the model that worked consistently. With surprising frequency, major businesses are built around totally different products than those originally envisioned. Consider these examples:

> When 3-M chemist Spence Silver invented a new adhesive that would not dry or permanently bond to things, he had no idea what to do with it. It wasn't until another 3-M chemist, Arthur Fry, needed a bookmark for his choir book that the idea for applying the glue to small pieces of paper was found, and Post-it Notes were born.[4] Polaroid Corporation was founded with a product based on the principle of polarized light. It was thought that polarized lamps would prevent head-on collisions between cars by preventing the "blinding" glare of oncoming headlights. But the company grew to its present size based on another application of the same technology: instant photography.
>
> William Steere, CEO of Pfizer, described the discovery of Viagra, the fastest-selling drug in history, as having "a certain serendipity" behind it. The drug was originally developed by Pfizer to treat angina; its real potency was discovered as a side effect.[5]

As one entrepreneur expressed it,

> Perhaps the existence of business plans and the language of business give a misleading impression of business building as a rational process. But as any entrepreneur can confirm, starting a business is very much a series of fits and starts, brainstorms and barriers. Creating a business is a round of chance encounters that leads to new opportunities and ideas, mistakes that turn into miracles.[6]

you have said no to lots of ideas; ideas that just come to you aren't usually opportunities; and the numbers don't matter but the economics really do matter.

The Role of Ideas

Ideas as Tools

A good idea is nothing more than a tool in the hands of an entrepreneur. Finding a good idea is the *first* of many steps in the process of converting an entrepreneur's creativity into an opportunity.

The Great Mousetrap Fallacy

Perhaps no one did a greater disservice to generations of would-be entrepreneurs than Ralph Waldo Emerson in his oft-quoted line, "If a man can make a

---

[4] P. R. Nayak and J. M. Ketterman, *Breakthroughs: How the Vision and Drive of Innovators in Sixteen Companies Created Commercial Breakthroughs That Swept the World* (New York: Rawson Associates, 1986), chapter 3.
[5] T. Corrigan, "Far More Than the Viagra Company: Essential Guide to William Steere," *Financial Times* (London), August 31, 1998, p. 7.
[6] J. Godfrey, *Our Wildest Dreams: Women Entrepreneurs, Making Money, Having Fun, Doing Good* (New York: Harper Business, 1992), p. 27.

better mousetrap than his neighbor, though he builds his house in the woods the world will make a beaten path to his door."

What can be called the great mousetrap fallacy was thus spawned. It is often assumed that success is possible if an entrepreneur can just come up with a new idea. In today's changing world, if the idea has anything to do with technology, success is certain—or so it would seem.

But the truth is that ideas are inert and, for all practical purposes, worthless. Further, the flow of ideas is phenomenal. Venture capital investors, for instance, receive as many as 100 to 200 proposals and business plans each month. Only 1 percent to 3 percent of these actually received financing, however.

Yet the fallacy persists despite the lessons of practical experience noted long ago in the insightful reply to Emerson by O. B. Winters: "The manufacturer who waits for the world to beat a path to his door is a great optimist. But the manufacturer who shows this 'mousetrap' to the world keeps the smoke coming out his chimney."

Contributors to the Fallacy

One cannot blame it all on Ralph Waldo Emerson. There are several reasons for the perpetuation of the fallacy. One is the portrayal in oversimplified accounts of the ease and genius with which such ventures as Xerox, IBM, and Polaroid made their founders wealthy. Unfortunately, these exceptions do not provide a useful rule to guide aspiring entrepreneurs.

Investors seem particularly prone to mousetrap myopia. Perhaps, like Emerson, they are substantially sheltered in viewpoint and experience from the tough, competitive realities of the business world. Consequently, they may underestimate, if not seriously downgrade, the importance of what it takes to make a business succeed. Frankly, inventing and brainstorming may be a lot more fun than the diligent observation, investigation, and nurturing of customers that are often required to sell a product or service.

Contributing also to the great mousetrap fallacy is the tremendous psychological ownership attached to an invention or to a new product. This attachment is different from attachment to a business. While an intense level of psychological ownership and involvement is certainly a prerequisite for creating a new business, the fatal flaw in attachment to an invention or product is the narrowness of its focus. The focal point needs to be the building of the business, rather than just one aspect of the idea.

Another source of mousetrap fallacy myopia lies in a technical and scientific orientation—that is, a desire to do it better. A good illustration of this is the experience of a Canadian entrepreneur who with his brother founded a company to manufacture truck seats. The entrepreneur's brother had developed a new seat for trucks that was a definite improvement over other seats. The entrepreneur knew he could profitably sell the seat his brother had designed, and they did so. When they needed more manufacturing capacity, one brother had several ideas on how to improve the seat. The first brother stated, "If I had listened to him, we probably would be a small custom shop today, or out of business. Instead, we concentrated on making seats that would sell at a profit, rather than just making a better and better seat. Our company has several million dollars of sales today and is profitable."

Related to "doing it better" is the idea of doing it first. Having the best idea first is by no means a guarantee of success. Just ask the creators of the first spreadsheet software, VisiCalc, what being first did for them. They would describe a painful downside to being first. Sometimes the first ones merely prove to the competition that a market exists to be snared. Therefore, unless having the best idea also includes the capacity to preempt other competitors by capturing a significant share of the market or by erecting insurmountable barriers to entry, first does not necessarily mean most viable.

Spotting an opportunity within an existing market was a key aspect in the development of a mass-produced rotary electric toothbrush. The founding entrepreneur had noted a large pricing spread among retail products. At the low end were devices in the range of $5. There was then a jump to the $60 to $80 range, and then another jump to products that were selling for well over $100. His research showed that new battery technology, plus outsourcing and a new rotary design, could result in a disposable product that would fill the gaps, steal market share, and yield substantial profits. His $1.75 million business turned into $475 million when his company was sold to Procter & Gamble. This is an excellent example of a clear pricing pattern that can be applied elsewhere.[7]

Pattern Recognition

The Experience Factor

One cannot build a successful business without ideas, just as one could not build a house without a hammer. In this regard, experience is vital in looking at new venture ideas.

---

[7] This example was provided by Harvard Business School professor William A. Sahlman during a session of the 2004 Symposium for Entrepreneurship Educators (SEE) at Babson College.

Time after time, experienced entrepreneurs exhibit an ability to recognize quickly a pattern—and an opportunity—while it is still taking shape. The late Herbert Simon, Nobel laureate and Richard King, Mellon University Professor of Computer Science and Psychology at Carnegie-Mellon University, wrote extensively about pattern recognition. He described the recognition of patterns as a creative process that is not simply logical, linear, and additive but intuitive and inductive as well. It involves, he said, the creative linking, or cross-association, of two or more in-depth "chunks" of experience, know-how, and contacts.[8] Simon contended that it takes 10 years or more for people to accumulate what he called the "50,000 chunks" of experience that enable them to be highly creative and recognize patterns—familiar circumstances that can be translated from one place to another.

Thus the process of sorting through ideas and recognizing a pattern can also be compared to the process of fitting pieces into a three-dimensional jigsaw puzzle. It is impossible to assemble such a puzzle by looking at it as a whole unit. Rather, one needs to see the relationships between the pieces and be able to fit together some that are seemingly unrelated before the whole is visible.

Recognizing ideas that can become entrepreneurial opportunities stems from a capacity to see what others do not—that one plus one equals three. Consider the following examples of the common thread of pattern recognition and new business creation by linking knowledge in one field or marketplace with quite different technical, business, or market know-how:

> In 1973 Thomas Stemberg worked for Star Market in Boston, where he became known for launching the first line of low-priced generic foods. Twelve years later, he applied the same low-cost, large-volume supermarket business model to office supplies. The result was Staples, the first office superstore and today a multi-billion-dollar company.[9]
>
> During travel throughout Europe, the eventual founders of Crate & Barrel frequently saw stylish and innovative products for the kitchen and home that were not yet available in the United States. When they returned home, the founders created Crate & Barrel to offer these products for which market research had, in a sense, already been done. In Crate & Barrel, the knowledge of consumer buying habits in one geographical region, Europe, was transferred successfully to another, the United States.

When Sycamore Systems went public in October 1999 its founders, Desh Deshpande and Daniel Smith, became multibillionaires—on paper, at least. But the success of Sycamore and its founders did not come about by chance. The pair had prior experience founding Cascade Communications Corp., one of the most touted telecommunications start-ups in the 1990s. That company delivered switches and accompanying software to handle the increasing demand for data over conventional phone lines. In Sycamore, Deshpande and Smith used their experience at Cascade to anticipate the need for similar switches and software that would increase the data-carrying efficiency of the nation's new fiber optic networks. One idea led to the birth of two giant telecommunications companies.[10] Sycamore survived the collapse of the telecommunications sector in 2000, and today the company has a market capitalization of approximately $1.7 billion.

Enhancing Creative Thinking

The creative thinking just described is of great value in recognizing opportunities, as well as other aspects of entrepreneurship. The notion that creativity can be learned or enhanced holds important implications for entrepreneurs who need to be creative in their thinking. Most people can certainly spot creative flair. Children seem to have it, and many seem to lose it. Several studies suggest that creativity actually peaks around the first grade because a person's life tends to become increasingly structured and defined by others and by institutions. Further, the development of intellectual discipline and rigor in thinking takes on greater importance in school than during the formative years, and most of our education beyond grade school stresses a logical, rational mode of orderly reasoning and thinking. Finally, social pressures may tend to be a taming influence on creativity.

Evidence suggests that one can enhance creative thinking in later years. The Eureka! Ranch (www.eurekaranch.com) business was founded on the principle that creativity is inherent in most people and can be unleashed by freeing them from convention. Often executives will be doused with water as they step out of their vehicles onto the ranch.

---

[8] H. A. Simon, "What We Know about the Creative Process" in *Frontiers in Creative and Innovative Management* ed. R. L. Kuhn, (Cambridge, MA: Ballinger, 1985), pp. 3–20.

[9] J. Pereira, "Focus, Drive and an Eye for Discounts: Staples of Stemberg's Business Success," *The Wall Street Journal*, September 6, 1996, p. A9B. Used by permission of Dow Jones & Co. Inc. via The Copyright Clearance Center.

[10] P. C. Judge, "Can Even a Proven Team Deliver on This Switchmaker's Astonishing IPO?" *BusinessWeek*, December 20, 1999, pp. 150–56.

One of the authors participated in one of these training sessions, and it became evident during the sessions that the methods did unlock the thinking process and yielded very imaginative solutions.

Approaches to Unleashing Creativity

Since the 1950s, much has been learned about the workings of the human brain. Today there is general agreement that the two sides of the brain process information in different ways. The left side performs rational, logical functions, while the right side operates the intuitive and nonrational modes of thought. A person uses both sides, actually shifting from one mode to the other (see Exhibit 5.5). Approaching ideas creatively and maximizing the control of these modes of thought can be of value to the entrepreneur.

More recently, professors have focused on the creativity process. For instance, Michael Gordon stressed the importance of creativity and the need for brainstorming in a presentation on the elements of personal power. He suggested that using the following 10 brainstorming rules could enhance creative visualization:

1. Define your purpose.
2. Choose participants.
3. Choose a facilitator.
4. Brainstorm spontaneously, copiously.
5. No criticisms, no negatives.
6. Record ideas in full view.
7. Invent to the "void."
8. Resist becoming committed to one idea.
9. Identify the most promising ideas.
10. Refine and prioritize.

Team Creativity

Teams of people can generate creativity that may not exist in a single individual. The creativity of a team of people is impressive, and comparable or better creative solutions to problems evolving from the collective interaction of a small group of people have been observed.

A good example of the creativity generated by using more than one head is that of a company founded by a Babson College graduate with little technical training. He teamed up with a talented inventor, and the entrepreneurial and business know-how of the founder complemented the creative and technical skills of the inventor. The result has been a rapidly growing multimillion-dollar venture in the field of video-based surgical equipment.

Students interested in exploring this further may want to do the creative squares exercise at the end of the chapter.

Big Opportunities with Little Capital

Within the dynamic free enterprise system, opportunities are apparent to a limited number of individuals—and not just to the individuals with financial resources. Ironically, successful entrepreneurs such as Howard Head attribute their success to the discipline

---

EXHIBIT 5.5

Comparison of Left-Mode and Right-Mode Brain Characteristics

L-Mode	R-Mode
Verbal: Using words to name, describe, and define.	*Nonverbal:* Awareness of things, but minimal connection with words.
Analytic: Figuring things out step-by-step and part-by-part.	*Synthetic:* Putting things together to form wholes.
Symbolic: Using a symbol to *stand for* something. For example, the sign + stands for the process of addition.	*Concrete:* Relating to things as they are at the present moment.
Abstract: Taking out a small bit of information and using it to represent the whole thing.	*Analogic:* Seeing likenesses between things; understanding metaphoric relationships.
Temporal: Keeping track of time, sequencing one thing after another, doing first things first, second things second, etc.	*Nontemporal:* Without a sense of time.
Rational: Drawing conclusions based on *reason* and *facts*.	*Nonrational:* Not requiring a basis of reason or facts; willingness to suspend judgment.
Digital: Using numbers as in counting.	*Spatial:* Seeing where things are in relation to other things, and how parts go together to form a whole.
Logical: Drawing conclusions based on logic, one thing following another in logical order—for example, a mathematical theorem or a well-stated argument.	*Intuitive:* Making leaps of insight, often based on incomplete patterns, hunches, feelings, or visual images.
Linear: Thinking in terms of linked ideas, one thought directly following another, often leading to a convergent conclusion.	*Holistic:* Seeing whole things all at once; perceiving the overall patterns and structures, often leading to divergent conclusions.

Source: "A Comparison of Left-Mode and Right-Mode Characteristics," from *Drawing on the Right Side of the Brain* by Betty Edwards, copyright © 1979, 1989, 1999 by Betty Edwards. Used by permission of Jeremy P. Tarcher, an imprint of Penguin Group (USA) Inc.

of limited capital resources. Thus, in the 1990s, many entrepreneurs learned the key to success is in the art of bootstrapping, which "in a start-up is like zero inventory in a just-in-time system: it reveals hidden problems and forces the company to solve them."[11] Consider the following:

- A 1991 study revealed that of the 110 start-ups researched, 77 had been launched with $50,000 or less; 46 percent were started with $10,000 or less as seed capital. Further, the primary source of capital was overwhelmingly personal savings (74 percent) rather than outside investors with deep pockets.[12] This pattern of frugality in start-ups is as true today as it was then.

- In the 1930s Josephine Esther Mentzer assisted her uncle by selling skin care balm and quickly created her own products with $100 initial investment. After convincing the department stores rather than the drugstores to carry her products, Estee Lauder was on its way to becoming a $4 billion corporation.[13]

- Putting their talents (cartooning and finance) together, Roy and Walt Disney moved to California and started their own film studio—with $290 in 1923. By mid-2007, the Walt Disney Co. had a market capitalization exceeding $67.5 billion.[14]

- While working for a Chicago insurance company, a 24-year-old sent out 20,000 inquiries for a black newsletter. With 3,000 positive responses and $500, John Harold Johnson published *Jet* for the first time in 1942. In the 1990s, Johnson Publishing publishes various magazines, including *Ebony*.[15]

- With $100 Nicholas Graham, age 24, went to a local fabric store, picked out some fabrics, and made $100 worth of ties. Having sold the ties to specialty shops, Graham was approached by Macy's to place his patterns on men's underwear. So Joe Boxer Corporation was born, and "six months into Joe Boxer's second year, sales had already topped $1 million."[16]

- Cabletron founders Craig Benson and Bob Levine literally started their company in a garage and grew it to over $1.4 billion in revenue in under 10 years.

- Vineyard Vines is a creative necktie company that was started on Martha's Vineyard with $40,000 of credit card debt.

Real Time

Opportunities exist or are created in real time and have what we call a window of opportunity. For an entrepreneur to seize an opportunity, the window must be open and remain open long enough to achieve market-required returns.

Exhibit 5.6 illustrates a window of opportunity for a generalized market. Markets grow at different rates over time, and as a market quickly becomes larger, more and more opportunities are possible. As the market becomes established, conditions are not as favorable. Thus at the point where a market starts to become sufficiently large and structured (e.g., at five years in Exhibit 5.6), the window opens; the window begins to close as the market matures (e.g., at 12–13 years in the exhibit).

The curve shown describes the rapid growth pattern typical of such new industries as microcomputers and software, cellular phones, quick oil changes, and biotechnology. For example, in the cellular phone industry, most major cities began service between 1983 and 1984. By 1989, there were more than 2 million subscribers in the United States, and the industry continued to experience significant growth. In other industries where growth is not so rapid, the slope of a curve would be less steep and the possibilities for opportunities fewer.

In considering the window of opportunity, the length of time the window will be open is important. It takes a considerable length of time to determine whether a new venture is a success or a failure. And if it is to be a success, the benefits of that success need to be harvested.

Exhibit 5.7 shows that for venture-capital-backed firms, the lemons (i.e., the losers) ripen in about two and a half years, while the pearls (i.e., the winners) take seven or eight years. An extreme example of the length of time it can take for a pearl to be harvested is the experience of a Silicon Valley venture capital firm that invested in a new firm in 1966 and was finally able to realize a capital gain in early 1984.

Another way to think of the process of creating and seizing an opportunity in real time is to think of it as a process of selecting objects (opportunities) from a conveyor belt moving through an open window—the window of opportunity. The speed of the conveyor belt changes, and the window through which it moves is constantly opening and closing. The continually opening and closing window and the constantly changing speed of the conveyor belt represent the

---

[11] A. Bhide, "Bootstrap Finance," *Harvard Business Review*, November–December 1992, p. 112.

[12] E. B. Roberts, *Entrepreneurs in High Technology: Lessons from MIT and Beyond* (New York: Oxford University Press, 1991), p. 144, table 5–2.

[13] T. Lammers and A. Longsworth, "Guess Who? Ten Big-Timers Launched from Scratch," *INC.*, September 1991, p. 69.

[14] Financial data from Dow Jones Interactive, http://www.djnr.com.

[15] Ibid.

[16] R. A. Mamis, "The Secrets of Bootstrapping," *INC.*, September 1991, p. 54.

EXHIBIT 5.6

Changes in the Placement of the Window of Opportunity

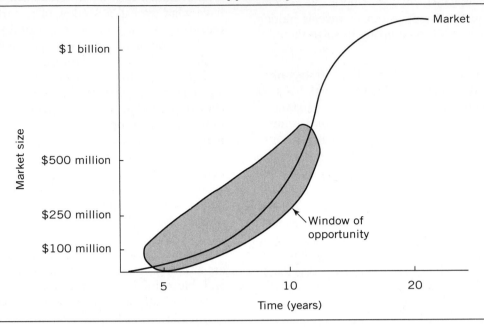

EXHIBIT 5.7

Lemons and Pearls

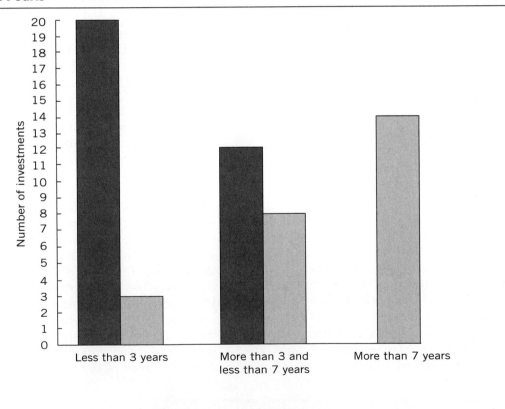

Number of years to appear

 Losers   Winners

volatile nature of the marketplace and the importance of timing. For an opportunity to be created and seized, it needs to be selected from the conveyor belt before the window closes.

The ability to recognize a potential opportunity when it appears and the sense of timing to seize that opportunity as the window is opening, rather than slamming shut, are critical. That opportunities are a function of real time is illustrated in a statement made by Ken Olsen, then president and founder of Digital Equipment Corporation, in 1977: "There is no reason for any individual to have a computer in their home." It is not easy for even the world's leading experts to predict just which innovative ideas and concepts for new business will evolve into the major industries of tomorrow. This is vividly illustrated by several quotations from very famous innovators. In 1901, two years before the famous flight, Wilbert Wright said, "Man will not fly for 50 years." In 1910 Thomas Edison said, "The nickel-iron battery will put the gasoline buggy . . . out of existence in no time." And in 1932 Albert Einstein made it clear: "[There] is not the slightest indication that nuclear energy will ever be obtainable. It would mean that the atom would have to be shattered at will."

Relation to the Framework of Analysis

Successful opportunities, once recognized, fit with the other forces of new venture creation. This iterative process of assessing and reassessing the fit among the central driving forces in the creation of a new venture was shown in Chapter 3. Of utmost importance is the fit of the lead entrepreneur and the management team with an opportunity. Good opportunities are both desirable to and attainable by those on the team using the resources that are available.

To understand how the entrepreneurial vision relates to the analytical framework, it may be useful to look at an opportunity as a three-dimensional relief map with its valleys, mountains, and so on, all represented. Each opportunity has three or four critical factors (e.g., proprietary license, patented innovation, sole distribution rights, an all-star management team, breakthrough technology). These elements pop out at the observer; they indicate huge possibilities where others might see obstacles. Thus it is easy to see why there are thousands of exceptional opportunities that will fit with a wide variety of entrepreneurs but that might not fit neatly into the framework outlines in Exhibit 5.8.

Screening Opportunities

Opportunity Focus

Opportunity focus is the most fruitful point of departure for screening opportunities. The screening process should not begin with strategy (which derives from the nature of the opportunity), nor with financial and spreadsheet analysis (which flow from the former), nor with estimations of how much the company is worth and who will own what shares.[17]

These starting points, and others, usually place the cart before the horse. Perhaps the best evidence of this phenomenon comes from the tens of thousands of tax-sheltered investments that turned sour in the mid-1980s. Also, many entrepreneurs who start businesses—particularly those for whom the ventures are their first—run out of cash faster than they bring in customers and profitable sales. There are lots of reasons why this happens, but one thing is certain: These entrepreneurs have not focused on the right opportunity.

Over the years, those with experience in business and in specific market areas have developed rules to guide them in screening opportunities. For example, during the initial stages of the irrational exuberance about the dot.com phenomenon, number of "clicks" changed to attracting "eyeballs," which changed to page view. Many investors got caught up in false metrics. Those who survived the NASDAQ crash of 2000–2001 understood that dot.com survivors would be the ones who executed transactions. Number of customers, amounts of the transactions, and repeat transactions became the recognized standards.[18]

Screening Criteria: The Characteristics of High-Potential Ventures

Venture capitalists, savvy entrepreneurs, and investors also use this concept of boundaries in screening ventures. Exhibit 5.8 summarizes criteria used by venture capitalists to evaluate opportunities, many of which tend to have a high-technology bias. As will be seen later, venture capital investors reject 60 percent to 70 percent of the new ventures presented to them very early in the review process, based on how the entrepreneurs satisfy these criteria.

However, these criteria are not the exclusive domain of venture capitalists. The criteria are based on good business sense that is used by successful entrepreneurs, angels, private investors, and venture capitalists. Consider the following examples of great

[17] See J. A. Timmons, D. F. Muzyka, H. H. Stevenson, and W. D. Bygrave, "Opportunity Recognition: The Core of Entrepreneurship" in *Frontiers of Entrepreneurship Research: 1987*, ed. Neil Churchill et al. (Babson Park, MA: Babson College, 1987), p. 409.
[18] E. Parizeau, partner, Norwest Venture Partners, in a speech to Babson College MBAs, December 2000.

EXHIBIT 5.8

Criteria for Evaluating Venture Opportunities

	Attractiveness	
Criteria	**Highest Potential**	**Lowest Potential**
Industry and Market	Changes way people live, work, learn, etc.	Incremental improvement only
Market:	Market driven; identified; recurring revenue niche	Unfocused; onetime revenue
Customers	Reachable; purchase orders Remove serious pain point	Loyal to others or unreachable
User benefits	Less than one-year payback Solves a very important problem/need	Three years plus payback
Value added	High; advance payments	Low; minimal impact on market
Product life	Durable	Perishable
Market structure	Imperfect, fragmented competition or emerging industry	Highly concentrated or mature or declining industry
Market size	$100+ million to $1+ billion sales potential	Unknown, less than $20 million or multibillion-dollar sales
Growth rate	Growth at 30%–50% or more	Contracting or less than 10%
Market capacity	At or near full capacity	Undercapacity
Market share attainable (Year 5)	20% or more; leader	Less than 5%
Cost structure	Low-cost provider; cost advantages	Declining cost
Economics		
Time to breakeven/positive cash flow	Under 1½–2 years	More than 4 years
ROI potential	25% or more; high value	Less than 15%–20%; low value
Capital requirements	Low to moderate; fundable/bankable	Very high; unfundable or unbankable
Internal rate of return potential	25% or more per year	Less than 15% per year
Free cash flow characteristics:	Favorable; sustainable; 20%–30% or more of sales	Less than 10% of sales
Sales growth	Moderate to high (+15% to +20%)	Less than 10%
Asset intensity	Low/sales $	High
Spontaneous working capital	Low, incremental requirements	High requirements
R&D/capital expenditures	Low requirements	High requirements
Gross margins	Exceeding 40% and durable	Under 20%
After-tax profits	High; greater than 10%; durable	Low
Time to break-even profit and loss	Less than two years; breakeven not creeping or leaping	Greater than four years; breakeven creeping or leaping up
Harvest Issues		
Value-added potential	High strategic value	Low strategic value
Valuation multiples and comparables	Price/earnings = +20x; +8−10x EBIT; +1.5−2x revenue: Free cash flow +8−10x	Price/earnings ≤ 5x, EBIT ≤ 3−4x; revenue ≤ .4
Exit mechanism and strategy	Present or envisioned options	Undefined; illiquid investment
Capital market context	Favorable valuations, timing, capital available; realizable liquidity	Unfavorable; credit crunch
Competitive Advantage Issues		
Fixed and variable costs	Lowest; high operating leverage	Highest
Control over costs, prices, and distribution	Moderate to strong	Weak
Barriers to entry:	Knowledge to overcome	
Proprietary protection	Have or can gain	None
Response/lead time	Competition slow; napping	Unable to gain edge
Legal, contractual advantage	Proprietary or exclusivity	None
Contracts and networks	Well-developed; accessible	Crude; limited
Key people	Top talent; an A team	B or C team
Sustainability	Low social and environmental impact	High social and/or environmental costs and consequences

(continued)

EXHIBIT 5.8 (concluded)

Criteria for Evaluating Venture Opportunities

Criteria	Attractiveness	
	Highest Potential	**Lowest Potential**
Management Team		
Entrepreneurial team	All-star combination; free agents	Weak or solo entrepreneur; not free agents
Industry and technical experience	Top of the field; super track record	Underdeveloped
Integrity	Highest standards	Questionable
Intellectual honesty	Know what they do not know	Do not want to know what they do not know
Fatal Flaw Issue	Nonexistent	One or more
Personal Criteria		
Goals and fit	Getting what you want; but wanting what you get	Surprises; only making money
Upside/downside issues	Attainable success/limited risks	Linear; on same continuum
Opportunity costs	Acceptable cuts in salary, etc.	Comfortable with status quo
Desirability	Fits with lifestyle	Simply pursuing big money
Risk/reward tolerance	Calculated risk; low risk/reward ratio	Risk averse or gambler
Stress tolerance	Thrives under pressure	Cracks under pressure
Strategic Differentiation		
Degree of fit	High	Low
Team	Best in class; excellent free agents	B team; no free agents
Service management	Superior service concept	Perceived as unimportant
Timing	Rowing with the tide	Rowing against the tide
Technology	Groundbreaking; one of a kind	Many substitutes or competitors
Flexibility	Able to adapt; commit and decommit quickly	Slow; stubborn
Opportunity orientation	Always searching for opportunities	Operating in a vacuum; napping
Pricing	At or near leader	Undercut competitor; low prices
Distribution channels	Accessible; networks in place	Unknown; inaccessible
Room for error	Forgiving and resilient strategy	Unforgiving, rigid strategy

small companies built without a dime of professional venture capital:

- Paul Tobin, who built Cellular One in eastern Massachusetts from the ground up to $100 million in revenue in five years, started Roamer Plus with less than $300,000 of internally generated funds from other ventures. Within two years, it grew to a $15 million annual sales rate and was very profitable.

- Entrepreneur and educator Ed Marram founded Geo-Systems without any money but with one paying customer. He sold the company in 2005 after 29 years of double-digit revenue growth.

- In 1986 Pleasant Rowland founded the Pleasant Company as a mail-order catalog company selling the American Girls Collection of historical dolls. She had begun the company with the modest royalties she received from writing children's books and did not have enough

capital to compete in stores with the likes of Mattel's Barbie.[19] By 1992 she had grown the company to $65 million in sales. Mattel acquired it in 1998 for $700 million, and under Rowland's continued management, the company had sales of $300 million in 1999 and 2000.[20]

- At age 66, Charlie Butcher had to decide whether to buy out an equal partner in his 100-year-old industrial polish and wax business (Butcher Polish) with less than $10 million in sales. This niche business had high gross margins, very low working capital and fixed-asset requirements for increased sales, substantial steady growth of more than 18 percent per year, and excellent products. The result was a business with very high free cash flow and potential for growth. He acquired the company with a bank loan and seller financing, and then

---

[19] M. Neal, "Cataloger Gets Pleasant Results," *Direct Marketing*, May 1992, p. 33.
[20] B. Dumaine, "How to Compete with a Champ," *Fortune*, January 10, 1994, p. 106.

he increased sales to over $50 million by 1993. The company continues to be highly profitable. Butcher vows never to utilize venture capital money or to take the company public.

The point of departure here is opportunity and, implicitly, the customer, the marketplace, and the industry. Exhibit 5.8 shows how higher- and lower-potential opportunities can be placed along an attractiveness scale. The criteria provide some quantitative ways in which an entrepreneur can make judgments about industry and market issues, competitive advantage issues, economic and harvest issues, management team issues, and fatal flaw issues and whether these add up to a compelling opportunity. For example, *dominant* strength in any one of these criteria can readily translate into a winning entry, whereas a flaw in any one can be fatal.

Entrepreneurs contemplating opportunities that will yield attractive companies, not high-potential ventures, can also benefit from paying attention to these criteria. These entrepreneurs will then be in a better position to decide how these criteria can be compromised. As outlined in Exhibit 5.8, business opportunities with the greatest potential will possess many of the following, or they will dominate in one or a few for which the competition cannot come close.

Industry and Market Issues

Market. *Higher-potential* businesses can identify a market niche for a product of service that meets an important customer need and provides high value-added or value-created benefits to customers. This invariably means the product or service eliminates or drastically reduces a major pain point for a customer or end user or solves a major problem/bottleneck for which the customer is willing to pay a premium. Customers are reachable and receptive to the product or service, with no brand or other loyalties. The potential payback to the user or customer of a given product or service through cost savings or other value-added or valued-created properties is one year or less and is identifiable, repeatable, and verifiable. Further, the life of the product or service exists beyond the time needed to recover the investment, plus a profit. And the company is able to expand beyond a one-product company. Take, for example, the growing success of cellular phone service. At prevailing rates, one can talk for about $25 an hour, and many providers of professional services can readily bill more than the $25 an hour for what would otherwise be unused time. If benefits to customers cannot be calculated in such dollar terms, then the market potential is far more difficult and risky to ascertain.

Lower-potential opportunities are unfocused regarding customer need, and customers are unreachable and/or have brand or other loyalties to others. A payback to the user of more than three years and low value-added or value-created properties also make an opportunity unattractive. Being unable to expand beyond a one-product company can make for a lower-potential opportunity. The failure of one of the first portable computer companies, Osborne Computer, is a prime example of this.

Market Structures. Market structure, such as evidenced by the number of sellers, size distribution of sellers, whether products are differentiated, conditions of entry and exit, number of buyers, cost conditions, and sensitivity of demand to changes in price, is significant.

A fragmented, imperfect market or emerging industry often contains vacuums and asymmetries that create unfilled market niches—for example, markets where resource ownership, cost advantages, and the like can be achieved. In addition, those where information or knowledge gaps exist and where competition is profitable, but not so strong as to be overwhelming, are attractive. An example of a market with an information gap is that experienced by a Boston entrepreneur who encountered a large New York company that wanted to dispose of a small, old office building in downtown Boston. This office building, with a book value of about $200,000, was viewed by the financially oriented firm as a low-value asset, and the company wanted to dispose of it so the resulting cash could be put to work for a higher return. The buyer, who had done more homework than the out-of-town sellers, bought the building for $200,000 and resold it in less than six months for more than $8 million.

Industries that are highly concentrated, that are perfectly competitive, or that are mature or declining are typically unattractive. The capital requirements and costs to achieve distribution and marketing presence can be prohibitive, and price-cutting and other competitive strategies in highly concentrated markets can be a significant barrier to entry. (The most blatant example is organized crime and its life-threatening actions when territories are invaded.) Revenge by normal competitors who are well positioned through product strategy, legal tactics, and supplier pressure also can be punishing to the pocketbook.

The airline industry, after deregulation, is an example of a perfectly competitive market and one where many of the recent entrants will have difficulty. The unattractiveness of perfectly competitive industries is captured by the comment of prominent Boston venture capitalist William Egan, who put it this way: "I want to be in a nonauction market."[21]

---

[21] Comment made during a presentation at Babson College, May 1985.

Market Size.   An attractive new venture sells to a market that is large and growing (i.e., one where capturing a small market share can represent significant and increasing sales volume). A minimum market size of more than $100 million in sales is attractive. In the medical and life sciences today, this target boundary is more like $500 million. Such a market size means it is possible to achieve significant sales by capturing roughly 5 percent or less and thus not threatening competitors. For example, to achieve a sales level of $1 million in a $100 million market requires only 1 percent of the market. Thus a recreational equipment manufacturer entered a $60 million market that was expected to grow at 20 percent per year to over $100 million by the third year. The founders were able to create a substantial smaller company without obtaining a major market share and possibly incurring the wrath of existing companies.

However, such a market can be too large. A multibillion-dollar market may be too mature and stable, and such a level of certainty can translate into competition from Fortune 500 firms and, if highly competitive, into lower margins and profitability. Further, an unknown market or one that is less than $10 million in sales also is unattractive. To understand the disadvantages of a large, more mature market, consider the entry of a firm into the microcomputer industry today versus the entry of Apple Computer into that market in 1975.

Growth Rate.   An attractive market is large and growing (i.e., one where capturing a good share of the increase is less threatening to competitors and where a small market share can represent significant and increasing sales volume). An annual growth rate of 30 percent to 50 percent creates niches for new entrants, and such a market is a thriving and expansive one, rather than a stable or contracting one, where competitors are scrambling for the same niches. Thus, for example, a $100 million market growing at 50 percent per year has the potential to become a $1 billion industry in a few years, and if a new venture can capture just 2 percent of sales in the first year, it can attain sales in the first year of $1 million. If it just maintains its market share over the next few years, sales will grow significantly.

Market Capacity.   Another signal of the existence of an opportunity in a market is a market at full capacity in a growth situation—in other words, a demand that the existing suppliers cannot meet. Timing is of vital concern in such a situation, which means the entrepreneur should be asking, Can a new entrant fill that demand before the other players can decide to and then actually increase capacity?

Market Share Attainable.   The potential to be a leader in the market and capture at least a 20 percent share can create a very high value for a company that might otherwise be worth not much more than book value. For example, one such firm, with less than $15 million in sales, became dominant in its small market niche with a 70 percent market share. The company was acquired for $23 million in cash.

A firm that will be able to capture less than 5 percent of a market is unattractive in the eyes of most investors seeking a higher-potential company.

Cost Structure.   A firm that can become the low-cost provider is attractive, but a firm that continually faces declining cost conditions is less so. Attractive opportunities exist in industries where economies of scale are insignificant (or work to the advantage of the new venture). Attractive opportunities boast of low costs of learning by doing. Where costs per unit are high when small amounts of the product are sold, existing firms that have low promotion costs can face attractive market opportunities.

For instance, consider the operating leverage of Johnsonville Sausage. Its variable costs were 6 percent labor and 94 percent materials. What aggressive incentives could management put in place for the 6 percent to manage and to control the 94 percent? Imagine the disasters that would occur if the scenario were reversed!

A word of caution from Scott W. Kunkel and Charles W. Hofer, who observed,

> Overall, industry structure . . . had a much smaller impact on new venture performance than has previously been suggested in the literature. This finding could be the result of one of several possibilities:
>
> 1. Industry structure impacts the performance of established firms, but does not have a significant impact on new venture performance.
> 2. The most important industry structural variables influencing new ventures are different from those which impact established firms and thus research has yet to identify the industry structural variables that are most important in the new venture environment.
> 3. Industry structure does not have a significant direct impact on firm performance, as hypothesized by scholars in the three fields of study. Instead, the impact of industry structure is strongly mitigated by other factors, including the strategy selected for entry.[22]

---

[22] S. W. Kunkel and C. W. Hofer, "The Impact of Industry Structure on New Venture Performance," *Frontiers of Entrepreneurship Research: 1993* (Babson Park, MA: Babson College, 1993).

Economics

Profits after Tax.
High and durable gross margins usually translate into strong and durable after-tax profits. Attractive opportunities have potential for durable profits of at least 10 percent to 15 percent and often 20 percent or more. Those generating after-tax profits of less than 5 percent are quite fragile.

Time to Breakeven and Positive Cash Flow.
As mentioned previously, breakeven and positive cash flow for attractive companies are possible within two years. Once the time to breakeven and positive cash flow is greater than three years, the attractiveness of the opportunity diminishes accordingly.

ROI Potential.
An important corollary to forgiving economics is reward. Very attractive opportunities have the potential to yield a return on investment of 25 percent or more per year. During the 1980s, many venture capital funds achieved only single-digit returns on investment. High and durable gross margins and high and durable after-tax profits usually yield high earnings per share and high return on stockholders' equity, thus generating a satisfactory harvest price for a company. This is most likely true whether the company is sold through an initial public offering or privately, or whether it is acquired. Given the risk typically involved, a return on investment potential of less than 15 percent to 20 percent per year is unattractive.

Capital Requirements.
Ventures that can be funded and have capital requirements that are low to moderate are attractive. Realistically, most higher-potential businesses need significant amounts of cash—several hundred thousand dollars and up—to get started. Businesses that can be started with little or no capital are rare, but they do exist. One such venture was launched in Boston in 1971 with $7,500 of the founder's capital and grew to over $30 million in sales by 1989. In today's venture capital market, the first round of financing is typically $1 million to $2 million or more for a start-up.[23] Some higher-potential ventures, such as those in the service sector or "cash sales" businesses, have lower capital requirements than do high-technology manufacturing firms with large research and development expenditures.

If the venture needs too much money or cannot be funded, it is unattractive. An extreme example is a venture that a team of students recently proposed to repair satellites. The students believed that the required start-up capital was in the $50 million to $200 million range. Projects of this magnitude are in the domain of the government and the very large corporation, rather than that of the entrepreneur and the venture capitalist.

Internal Rate of Return Potential.
Is the risk–reward relationship attractive enough? The response to this question can be quite personal, but the most attractive opportunities often have the promise of—and deliver on—a very substantial upside of 5 to 10 times the original investment in 5 to 10 years. Of course, the extraordinary successes can yield 50 to 100 times or more, but these are exceptions. A 25 percent or more annual compound rate of return is considered very healthy. In the early 1990s, those investments considered basically risk free had yields of 3 percent to 8 percent.

Free Cash Flow Characteristics.
Free cash flow is a way of understanding a number of crucial financial dimensions of any business: the robustness of its economics; its capital requirements, both working and fixed assets; its capacity to service external debt and equity claims; and its capacity to sustain growth.[24] We define unleveraged free cash flow (FCF) as earnings before interest but after taxes (EBIAT) *plus* amortization (A) and depreciation (D) *less* spontaneous working capital requirements (WC) *less* capital expenditures (CAPex), or FCF = EBIAT + [A+D] − [+ or − WC] − CAPex. EBIAT is driven by sales, profitability, and asset intensity. Low-asset-intensive, high-margin businesses generate the highest profits and sustainable growth.[25] We will explore this in detail in Chapter 13, Entrepreneurial Finance.

Gross Margins.
The potential for high and durable gross margins (i.e., the unit selling price less all direct and variable costs) is important. Gross margins exceeding 40 percent to 50 percent provide a tremendous built-in cushion that allows for more error and more flexibility to learn from mistakes than do gross margins of 20 percent or less. High and durable gross margins, in turn, mean that a venture can reach breakeven earlier, preferably within the first two years. Thus, for example, if gross margins are just 20 percent, for every $1 increase in fixed costs (e.g., insurance, salaries, rent, and utilities), sales need to increase $5 just to stay even. If gross margins are 75 percent, however, a $1 increase in fixed costs requires a sales increase of just $1.33. One entrepreneur, who built the international division of an emerging software company to $17 million in highly profitable sales in just five years (when he was 25 years old),

---

[23] J. A. Timmons, W. Bygrave, and N. Fast, "The Flow of Venture Capital to Highly Innovative Technology Ventures," a study for the National Science Foundation, reported in *Frontiers of Entrepreneurship Research: 1984* (Babson Park, MA: Babson College, 1984).

[24] For a more detailed description of free cash flow, see "Note on Free Cash Flow Valuation Models" by W. Sahlman, HBS 9-288-023, Harvard Business School, 1987.

[25] W. A. Sahlman, "Sustainable Growth Analysis," HBS 9-284-059, Harvard Business School, 1984.

offers an example of the cushion provided by high and durable gross margins. He stresses there is simply no substitute for outrageous gross margins by saying, "It allows you to make all kinds of mistakes that would kill a normal company. And we made them all. But our high gross margins covered all the learning tuition and still left a good profit."[26] Gross margins of less than 20 percent, particularly if they are fragile, are unattractive.

Time to Breakeven—Cash Flow and Profit and Loss (P&L).
New businesses that can quickly achieve a positive cash flow and become self-sustaining are highly desirable. It is often the second year before this is possible, but the sooner the better. Obviously, simply having a longer window does not mean the business will be lousy. Two great companies illustrate that a higher-potential business can have a longer window. Pilkington Brothers, an English firm that developed plate glass technology, ran huge losses for over 2½ years before it was regarded as a great company. Similarly, Federal Express went through an early period of enormous negative cash flows of $1 million a month.

Harvest Issues

Value-Added Potential.
New ventures that are based on strategic value in an industry, such as valuable technology, are attractive, while those with low or no strategic value are less attractive. For example, most observers contend that a product technology of compelling strategic value to Xerox was owned, in the mid-1980s, by a small company with about $10 million in sales and showing a prior-year loss of $1.5 million. Xerox purchased the company for $56 million. Opportunities with extremely large capital commitments, whose value on exit can be severely eroded by unanticipated circumstances, are less attractive. Nuclear power is a good example.

Thus one characteristic of businesses that command a premium price is that they have high value-added strategic importance to their acquirer, such as distribution, customer base, geographic coverage, proprietary technology, contractual rights, and the like. Such companies might be valued at four, five, or even six times (or more) last year's *sales*, whereas perhaps 60 percent to 80 percent of companies might be purchased at .75 to 1.25 times sales.

Valuation Multiples and Comparables.
Consistent with the previous point, there is a large spread in the value the capital markets place on private and public companies. Part of your analysis is to identify some historical boundaries for valuations

placed on companies in the market/industry/technology area you intend to pursue. The rules outlined in Exhibit 4.8 are variable and should be thought of as a boundary and a point of departure.

Exit Mechanism and Strategy.
Businesses that are eventually sold—privately or to the public—or acquired, usually are started and grown with a harvest objective in mind. Attractive companies that realize capital gains from the sale of their businesses have, or envision, a harvest or exit mechanism. Unattractive opportunities do not have an exit mechanism in mind. Planning is critical because, as is often said, it is much harder to get out of a business than to get into it. Giving some serious thought to the options and likelihood that the company can eventually be harvested is an important initial and ongoing aspect of the entrepreneurial process.

Capital Market Context.
The context in which the sale or acquisition of the company occurs is largely driven by the capital markets at that particular time. Timing can be a critical component of the exit mechanism because, as one study indicated, since World War II, the average bull market on Wall Street has lasted just six months. For a keener appreciation of the critical difference the capital markets can make, one only has to recall the stock market crash of October 19, 1987, the bank credit crunches of 1990–1992 and 2007, or the bear market of 2001–2003. By the end of 1987, the valuation of the Venture Capital 100 index dropped 43 percent, and private company valuations followed. Initial public offerings are especially vulnerable to the vicissitudes of the capital markets; here the timing is vital. Some of the most successful companies seem to have been launched when debt and equity capital were most available and relatively cheap.

Competitive Advantages Issues

Variable and Fixed Costs.
An attractive opportunity has the potential for being the lowest-cost producer and for having the lowest marketing and distribution costs. For example, Bowmar was unable to remain competitive in the market for electronic calculators after the producers of large-scale integrated circuits, such as Hewlett-Packard, entered the business. Being unable to achieve and sustain a position as a low-cost producer shortens the life expectancy of a new venture.

Degree of Control.
Attractive opportunities have potential for moderate to strong control over prices, costs, and channels of distribution. Fragmented

---

[26] R. D. Kahn, president, Interactive Images, Inc., speaking at Babson College about his experiences as international marketing director at McCormack & Dodge from 1978 through 1983.

markets where there is no dominant competitor—no IBM—have this potential. These markets usually have a market leader with a 20 percent market share *or less*. For example, sole control of the source of supply of a critical component for a product or of channels of distribution can give a new venture market dominance even if other areas are weak.

Lack of control over such factors as product development and component prices can make an opportunity unattractive. For example, in the case of Viatron, its suppliers were unable to produce several of the semiconductors the company needed at low enough prices to permit Viatron to make the inexpensive computer terminal that it had publicized extensively.

A market where a major competitor has a market share of 40 percent or more usually implies a market where power and influence over suppliers, customers, and pricing create a serious barrier and risk for a new firm. Such a firm will have few degrees of freedom. However, if a dominant competitor is at full capacity, is slow to innovate or to add capacity in a large and growing market, or routinely ignores or abuses the customer (remember "Ma Bell"), there may be an entry opportunity. But entrepreneurs usually do not find such sleepy competition in dynamic, emerging industries dense with opportunity.

Entry Barriers.   Having a favorable window of opportunity is important. Having or being able to gain proprietary protection, regulatory advantage, or other legal or contractual advantage, such as exclusive rights to a market or with a distributor, is attractive. Having or being able to gain an advantage in response/lead times is important because these can create barriers to entry or expansion by others. For example, advantages in response/lead times in technology, product innovation, market innovation, people, location, resources, or capacity make an opportunity attractive. Possession of well-developed, high-quality, accessible contacts that are the product of years of building a top-notch reputation and that cannot be acquired quickly is also advantageous. Sometimes this competitive advantage may be so strong as to provide dominance in the marketplace, even though many of the other factors are weak or average. An example of how quickly the joys of start-up may fade if others cannot be kept out is the experience of firms in the hard disk industry that were unable to erect entry barriers into the U.S. markets in the early to mid-1980s. By the end of 1983, some 90 hard disk drive companies were launched, and severe price competition led to a major industry shakeout.

If a firm cannot keep others out or if it faces already existing entry barriers, it is unattractive. An easily overlooked issue is a firm's capacity to gain distribution of its product. As simple as it may sound, even

venture-capital-backed companies fall victim to this market issue. Air Florida apparently assembled all the right ingredients, including substantial financing, yet was unable to secure sufficient gate space for its airplanes. Even though it sold passenger seats, it had no place to pick the passengers up or drop them off.

Management Team Issues

Entrepreneurial Team.   Attractive opportunities have existing teams that are strong and contain industry superstars. The team has proven profit and loss experience in the same technology, market, and service area, and members have complementary and compatible skills. An unattractive opportunity does not have such a team in place or has no team.

Industry and Technical Experience.   A management track record of significant accomplishment in the industry, with the technology, and in the market area, with a proven profit and lots of achievements where the venture will compete is highly desirable. A top-notch management team can become the most important strategic competitive advantage in an industry. Imagine relocating the Chicago Bulls or the Phoenix Suns to Halifax, Nova Scotia. Do you think you would have a winning competitor in the National Basketball Association?

Integrity.   Trust and integrity are the oil and glue that make economic interdependence possible. Having an unquestioned reputation in this regard is a major long-term advantage for entrepreneurs and should be sought in all personnel and backers. A shady past or record of questionable integrity is for B team players only.

Intellectual Honesty.   There is a fundamental issue of whether the founders know what they do and do not know, as well as whether they know what to do about shortcomings or gaps in the team and the enterprise.

Fatal Flaw Issues.   Basically, attractive ventures have no fatal flaws; an opportunity is rendered unattractive if it suffers from one or more fatal flaws. Usually these relate to one of the previous criteria, and examples abound of markets that are too small, that have overpowering competition, where the cost of entry is too high, where an entrant is unable to produce at a competitive price, and so on. An example of a fatal flaw entry barrier was Air Florida's inability to get flights listed on reservation computers.

Personal Criteria

Goals and Fit.   Is there a good match between the requirements of business and what the founders want out of it? Dorothy Stevenson pinpointed the crux of it with this powerful insight: "Success is *getting* what you want. Happiness is *wanting* what you get."

Upside/Downside Issues.   An attractive opportunity does not have excessive downside risk. The upside and the downside of pursuing an opportunity are not linear, nor are they on the same continuum. The upside is easy, and it has been said that success has a thousand sires. The downside is another matter: It has also been said that failure is an orphan. An entrepreneur needs to be able to absorb the financial downside in such a way that he or she can rebound without becoming indentured to debt obligations. If an entrepreneur's financial exposure in launching the venture is greater than his or her net worth—the resources he or she can reasonably draw upon, and his or her alternative disposable earnings stream if it does not work out—the deal may be too big. While today's bankruptcy laws are generous, the psychological burdens of living through such an ordeal are infinitely more painful than the financial consequences. An existing business needs to consider if a failure will be too demeaning to the firm's reputation and future credibility, aside from the obvious financial consequences.[27]

Opportunity Cost.   In pursuing any venture opportunity, there are also opportunity costs. An entrepreneur who is skilled enough to grow a successful, multimillion-dollar venture has talents that are highly valued by medium- to large-sized firms as well. While assessing benefits that may accrue in pursuing an opportunity, an entrepreneur needs to heed other alternatives, including potential "golden handcuffs," and account honestly for any cut in salary that may be involved in pursuing a certain opportunity.

Further, pursuing an opportunity can shape an entrepreneur in ways that are hard to imagine. An entrepreneur will probably have time to execute between two and four multimillion-dollar ventures between the ages of 25 and 50. Each of these experiences will position him or her, *for better or for worse*, for the next opportunity. Because an entrepreneur in the early years needs to gain relevant management experience and because building a venture (either one that works or one that does not) takes more time than is commonly believed, it is important to consider alternatives while assessing an opportunity.

Desirability.   A good opportunity is not only attractive but also desirable (i.e., good opportunity fits). An intensely personal criterion would be the desire for a certain lifestyle. This desire may preclude pursuing certain opportunities that may be excellent for someone else. The founder of a major high-technology

venture in the Boston area was asked why he located the headquarters of his firm in downtown Boston, while those of other such firms were located on the famous Route 128 outside the city. His reply was that he wanted to live in Boston because he loved the city and wanted to be able to walk to work. He said, "The rest did not matter."

Risk/Reward Tolerance.   Successful entrepreneurs take calculated risks or avoid risks they do not need to take; as a country western song puts it, "You have to know when to hold 'em, know when to fold 'em, know when to walk away, and know when to run." This is not to suggest that all entrepreneurs are gamblers or have the same risk tolerance; some are quite conservative while others actually seem to get a kick out of the inherent danger and thrill in higher-risk and higher-stake games. The real issue is fit— recognizing that gamblers and overly risk-averse entrepreneurs are unlikely to sustain any long-term successes.

Stress Tolerance.   Another important dimension of the fit concept is the stressful requirements of a fast-growth high-stakes venture. Or as President Harry Truman said so well, "If you can't stand the heat, get out of the kitchen."

Strategic Differentiation

Degree of Fit.   To what extent is there a good fit among the driving forces (founders and team, opportunity, and resource requirements) and the timing given the external environment?

Team.   There is no substitute for an absolutely top-quality team. The execution of and the ability to adapt and to devise constantly new strategies are vital to survival and success. A team is nearly unstoppable if it can inculcate into the venture a philosophy and culture of superior learning, as well as teaching skills, an ethic of high standards, delivery of results, and constant improvement. Are they free agents—clear of employment, noncompete, proprietary rights, and trade secret agreements—who are able to pursue the opportunity?

Service Management.   Several years ago, the Forum Corporation of Boston conducted research across a wide range of industries with several hundred companies to determine why customers stopped buying these companies' products. The results were surprising: 15 percent of the customers defected because of quality and 70 percent stopped using a product or service because of bad customer service. Having a "turbo-service" concept that can be delivered

---

[27] This point was made by J. Willard Marriott, Jr., at Founder's Day at Babson College, 1988.

consistently can be a major competitive weapon against small and large competitors alike. Home Depot, in the home supply business, and Lexus, in the auto industry, have set an entirely new standard of service for their respective industries.

Timing.   From business to historic military battles to political campaigns, timing is often the one element that can make a significant difference. Time can be an enemy or a friend; being too early or too late can be fatal. The key is to row with the tide, not against it. Strategically, ignoring this principle is perilous.

Technology.   A breakthrough, proprietary product is no guarantee of success, but it creates a formidable competitive advantage.

Flexibility.   Maintaining the capacity to commit and uncommit quickly, to adapt, and to abandon if necessary is a major strategic weapon, particularly when competing with larger organizations. Larger firms can typically take 6 years or more to change basic strategy and 10 to 20 years or more to change their culture.

Opportunity Orientation.   To what extent is there a constant alertness to the marketplace? A continual search for opportunities? As one insightful entrepreneur put it, "Any opportunity that just comes in the door to us, we do not consider an opportunity. And we do not have a strategy until we are saying no to lots of opportunities."

Pricing.   One common mistake of new companies with high-value-added products or services in a growing market is to underprice. A price slightly below to as much as 20 percent below competitors is rationalized as necessary to gain market entry. In a 30 percent gross margin business, a 10 percent price increase results in a 20 percent to 36 percent increase in gross margin and will lower the break-even sales level for a company with $900,000 in fixed costs to $2.5 million from $3 million. At the $3 million sales level, the company would realize an extra $180,000 in pretax profits.

Distribution Channels.   Having access to the distribution channels is sometimes overlooked or taken for granted. New channels of distribution can leapfrog and demolish traditional channels—for example, direct mail, home shopping networks, infomercials, and the coming revolution in interactive television in your own home.

Room for Error.   How forgiving is the business and the financial strategy? How wrong can the team be in estimates of revenue costs, cash flow, timing, and capital requirements? How bad can things get with the firm still able to survive? If some single-engine planes are more prone to accidents by 10 or more times, which plane do you want to fly in? High leverage, lower gross margins, and lower operating margins are the signals in a small company of flights destined for fatality.

Gathering Information

Finding Ideas

Factors suggest that finding a potential opportunity is most often a matter of being the right person, in the right place, at the right time. How can you increase your chances of being the next Anita Roddick of The Body Shop? Numerous sources of information can help generate ideas.

Existing Businesses   Purchasing an ongoing business is an excellent way to find a new business idea. Such a route to a new venture can save time and money and can reduce risk as well. Investment bankers and business brokers are knowledgeable about businesses for sale, as are trust officers. However, brokers do not advertise the very best private businesses for sale, and the real gems are usually bought by the individuals or firms closest to them, such as management, directors, customers, suppliers, or financial backers. Bankruptcy judges have a continual flow of ventures in serious trouble. Excellent opportunities may be buried beneath all the financial debris of a bankrupt firm.

Franchises   Franchising is another way to enter an industry, by either starting a franchise operation or becoming a franchisee. This is a fertile area. The number of franchisors nationally stands at more than 4,000, according to the International Franchise Association and the Department of Commerce, and franchisors account for well over $600 billion in sales annually and nearly one-third of all retail sales.[28] See Chapter 11 for a fuller discussion of franchises, including resource information.

Patents   Patent brokers specialize in marketing patents that are owned by individual inventors, corporations, universities, or other research organizations to those seeking new commercially viable products. Some brokers specialize in international product licensing, and occasionally a patent broker will purchase an invention and then resell it.

---

[28] See also "Economic Impact of Franchised Businesses," International Franchise Association, IFA Educational Foundation, 2004.

Although, over the years, a few unscrupulous brokers have tarnished the patent broker's image, acquisitions effected by reputable brokers have resulted in significant new products. Notable among these was Bausch & Lomb's acquisition, through National Patent Development Corporation, of the U.S. right to hydron, a material used in contact lenses. Some patent brokers are

- MGA Technology, Chicago.
- New Product Development Services, Kansas City, Missouri.
- University Patents, Chicago.
- Research Corporation, New York.
- Pegasus Corporation, New York.
- National Patent Development Corporation, New York.

Product Licensing   A good way to obtain exposure to many product ideas available from universities, corporations, and independent investors is to subscribe to information services such as the *American Bulletin of International Technology, Selected Business Ventures* (published by General Electric), *Technology Mart, Patent Licensing Gazette*, and the National Technical Information Service. In addition, corporations, not-for-profit research institutions, and universities are sources of ideas.

Corporations.   Corporations engaged in research and development often develop inventions or services that they do not exploit commercially. These inventions either do not fit existing product lines or marketing programs or do not represent sufficiently large markets to be interesting to large corporations. A good number of corporations license these kinds of inventions, either through patent brokers, product-licensing information services, or their own patent marketing efforts. Directly contacting a corporation with a licensing program may prove fruitful. Among the major corporations known to have active internal patent marketing efforts are the following:

- Gulf and Western Invention Development Corporation.
- Kraft Corporation, Research and Development.
- Pillsbury Company, Research and Development Laboratories.
- Union Carbide Corporation, Nuclear Division.
- RCA Corporation, Domestic Licensing.
- TRW Corporation, System Group.
- Lockheed Corporation, Patent Licensing.

Not-for-Profit Research Institutes.   These nonprofit organizations do research and development under contract to the government and private

industry as well as some internally sponsored research and development of new products and processes that can be licensed to private corporations for further development, manufacturing, and marketing. One example of how this works is Battelle Memorial Institute's participation in the development of xerography and the subsequent license of the technology to the Haloid Corporation, now Xerox Corporation. Some nonprofit research institutes with active licensing programs are

- Battelle Memorial Institute.
- ITT Research Institute.
- Stanford Research Institute.
- Southwest Research Institute.

Universities.   A number of universities are active in research in the physical sciences and seek to license inventions that result from this research either directly or through an associated research foundation that administers a patent program. Massachusetts Institute of Technology and the California Institute of Technology publish periodic reports containing abstracts of inventions they own that are available for licensing. In addition, because a number of very good ideas developed in universities never reach formal licensing outlets, another way to find these ideas is to become familiar with the work of researchers in your area of interest. Among universities that have active licensing programs are

- Massachusetts Institute of Technology.
- California Institute of Technology.
- University of Wisconsin.
- Iowa State University.
- Purdue University.
- University of California.
- University of Oregon.

Industry and Trade Contacts

Trade Shows and Association Meetings.   Trade shows and association meetings in a number of industries can be an excellent way to examine the products of many potential competitors, meet distributors and sales representatives, learn about product and market trends, and identify potential products. The American Electronics Association is a good example of an association that holds such seminars and meetings.

Customers.   Contacting potential customers of a certain type of product can identify a need and where existing products might be deficient or inadequate. Discussions with doctors who head medical services at hospitals might lead to product ideas in the biomedical equipment business.

Distributors and Wholesalers. Contacting people who distribute a certain type of product can yield extensive information about the strengths and weaknesses of existing products and the kinds of product improvements and new products that are needed by customers.

Competitors. Examining products offered by companies competing in an industry can show whether an existing design is protected by patent and whether it can be improved or imitated.

Former Employers. A number of businesses are started with products or services, or both, based on technology and ideas developed by entrepreneurs while others employed them. In some cases, research laboratories were not interested in commercial exploitation of technology, or the previous employer was not interested in the ideas for new products, and the rights were given up or sold. In others, the ideas were developed under government contract and were in the public domain. In addition, some companies will help entrepreneurs set up companies in return for equity.

Professional Contact. Ideas can also be found by contacting such professionals as patent attorneys, accountants, commercial bankers, and venture capitalists who come into contact with those seeking to license patents or to start a business using patented products or processes.

Consulting. A method for obtaining ideas that has been successful for technically trained entrepreneurs is to provide consulting and one-of-a-kind engineering designs for people in fields of interest. For example, an entrepreneur wanting to establish a medical equipment company can do consulting or can design experimental equipment for medical researchers. These kinds of activities often lead to prototypes that can be turned into products needed by a number of researchers. For example, this approach was used in establishing a company to produce psychological testing equipment that evolved from consulting done at the Massachusetts General Hospital and, again, in a company to design and manufacture oceanographic instruments that were developed from consulting done for an oceanographic institute.

Networking. Networks can be a stimulant and source of new ideas, as well as a source of valuable contacts with people. Much of this requires personal initiative on an informal basis; but around the country, organized networks can facilitate and accelerate the process of making contacts and finding new business ideas. Near Boston, a high-density area of exceptional entrepreneurial activity, several networks have emerged, including the Babson Entrepreneurial Exchange, the Smaller Business Association of New England (SBANE), the MIT Enterprise Forum, the 128 Venture Group, and the Boston Computer Society. Similar organizations can be found across the United States. A sampling includes the American Women's Economic Development Corporation in New York City; the Association of Women Entrepreneurs; the Entrepreneur's Roundtable of the UCLA Graduate Student Association; and the Association of Collegiate Entrepreneurs at Wichita State University.

Shaping Your Opportunity

You will need to invest in thorough research to shape your idea into an opportunity. *Data available about market characteristics, competitors, and so on are frequently inversely related to the real potential of an opportunity;* that is, if market data are readily available and if the data clearly show significant potential, then a large number of competitors will enter the market and the opportunity will diminish.

The good news: Most data will be incomplete, inaccurate, and contradictory, and their meaning will be ambiguous. For entrepreneurs, gathering the necessary information and seeing possibilities and making linkages where others see only chaos are essential.

Leonard Fuld defined competitor intelligence as highly specific and timely information about a corporation.[29] Finding out about competitors' sales plans, key elements of their corporate strategies, the capacity of their plants and the technology used in them, who their principal suppliers and customers are, and what new products rivals have under development is difficult, but not impossible, even in emerging industries, when talking to intelligence sources.[30]

Using published resources is one source of such information. Interviewing people and analyzing data are also critical. Fuld believes that because business transactions generate information, which flows into the public domain, one can locate intelligence sources by understanding the transaction and how intelligence behaves and flows.[31]

This can be done legally and ethically. There are, of course, less than ethical (not to mention illegal) tactics, which include conducting phony job interviews, getting customers to put out phony bid requests, and lying, cheating, and stealing. Entrepreneurs need to

---

[29] L. M. Fuld, *Competitor Intelligence: How to Get It: How to Use It* (New York: John Wiley & Sons, 1985), p. 9.

[30] Ibid. See also "How to Snoop on Your Competitors," *Fortune,* May 14, 1984, pp. 28–33; and also information published by accounting firms such as *Sources of Industry Data,* published by Ernst & Young.

[31] Fuld, *Competitor Intelligence,* pp. 12–17.

be careful to avoid such practices and are advised to consult legal counsel when in doubt.

The information sources given next are just a small start. Much creativity, work, and analysis will be involved to find intelligence and to extend the information obtained into useful form. For example, a competitor's income statement and balance sheet will rarely be handed out. Rather, this information must be derived from information in public filings or news articles or from credit reports, financial ratios, and interviews.[32]

Published Sources

The first step is a complete search of materials in libraries and on the Internet. You can find a huge amount of published information, databases, and other sources about industries, markets, competitors, and personnel. Some of this information will have been uncovered when you search for ideas. Listed here are additional sources that should help get you started.

Guides and Company Information

Valuable information is available in special issues and the Web sites of *BusinessWeek, Forbes, INC., The Economist, Fast Company,* and *Fortune* and online, in the following:

- Hoovers.com.
- ProQuest.com.
- Bloomberg.com.
- Harrisinfo.com.

Additional Internet Sites

- *Fast Company* (http://www.fastcompany.com).
- Ernst & Young (http://www.ey.com).
- Entrepreneur.com & magazine (http://www.entrepreneur.com).
- EDGAR database (http://www.sec.gov). Note that subscription sources, such as ThomsonResearch (http://www.thomsonfinancial.com), provide images of other filings as well.
- Venture Economics (http://www.ventureeconomics.com).

Journal Articles via Computerized Indexes

- Factiva with Dow Jones, *Reuters, The Wall Street Journal.*
- EBSCOhost.

- FirstSearch.
- Ethnic News Watch.
- LEXIS/NEXIS.
- *New York Times.*
- InfoTrac from Gale Group.
- ABI/Inform and other ProQuest databases.
- RDS Business Reference Suite.
- *The Wall Street Journal.*

Statistics

- Stat-USA (http://www.stat-usa.gov)—U.S. government subscription site for economic, trade and business data, and market research.
- U.S. Census Bureau (http://www.census.gov)—the source of many statistical data including
- Statistical Abstract of the United States.
- American FactFinder—population data.
- Economic Programs (http://www.census.gov/econ/www/index.html)—data by sector.
- County business patterns.
- Zip code business patterns.
- Knight Ridder . . . CRB Commodity Year Book.
- Manufacturing USA, Service Industries USA, and other sector compilations from Gale Group.
- Economic Statistics Briefing Room (http://www.whitehouse.gov/fsbr/esbr.html).
- Federal Reserve Bulletin.
- Survey of Current Business.
- FedStats (http://www.fedstats.gov/).
- Global Insight (http://www.globalinsight.com).
- International Financial Statistics—International Monetary Fund.
- World Development Indicators—World Bank.
- Bloomberg Database.

Consumer Expenditures

- New Strategist Publications.
- Consumer Expenditure Survey.
- Euromonitor.

Projections and Forecasts

- ProQuest.
- InfoTech Trends.
- Guide to Special Issues and Indexes to Periodicals (*Grey House Directory of Special Issues*).

---

[32] Ibid., p. 325.

- RDS Business Reference Suite.
- Value Line Investment Survey.

Market Studies

- LifeStyle Market Analyst.
- MarketResearch.com.
- Scarborough Research.
- Simmons Market Research Bureau.

Other Sources

- Wall Street Transcript.
- Brokerage house reports from Investext, Multex, etc.
- Company annual reports and Web sites.

Other Intelligence

Everything entrepreneurs need to know will not be found in libraries because this information needs to be highly specific and current. This information is most likely available from people—industry experts, suppliers, and the like (see box). Summarized next are some useful sources of intelligence.

Trade Associations   Trade associations, especially the editors of their publications and information officers, are good sources of information.[33] Trade shows and conferences are prime places to discover the latest activities of competitors.

Employees   Employees who have left a competitor's company often can provide information about the competitor, especially if the employee departed on bad terms. Also, a firm can hire people away from a competitor. While consideration of ethics in this situation is important, the number of experienced people in any industry is limited, and competitors must prove that a company hired a person intentionally to get specific trade secrets in order to challenge any hiring legally. Students who have worked for competitors are another source of information.

Consulting Firms   Consulting firms frequently conduct industry studies and then make this information available. Frequently, in such fields as computers or software, competitors use the same design consultants, and these consultants can be sources of information.

Market Research Firms   Firms doing market studies, such as those listed under published sources above, can be sources of intelligence.

Key Customers, Manufacturers, Suppliers, Distributors, and Buyers   These groups are often a prime source of information.

Public Filings   Federal, state, and local filings, such as filings with the Securities and Exchange Commission (SEC), Patent and Trademark Office, or Freedom of Information Act filings, can reveal a surprising amount of information. There are companies that process inquiries of this type.

Reverse Engineering   Reverse engineering can be used to determine costs of production and sometimes even manufacturing methods. An example of this practice is the experience of Advanced Energy Technology of Boulder, Colorado, which learned firsthand about such tactics. No sooner had it announced a new product, which was patented, when it received 50 orders, half of which were from competitors asking for only one or two of the items.

---

[33] Ibid., pp. 46, 48.

Internet Impact: Research

The Internet has become *the* resource for entrepreneurial research and opportunity exploration. The rapid growth of data sources, Web sites, sophisticated search engines, and consumer response forums allows for up-to-date investigations of business ideas, competitive environments, and value chain resources.

Google is currently the top search engine in the world. One of the reasons for Google's success is its increasingly deep and wide platform of tools. In 2007 Google offered the means to view, for example, the text of U.S. patents and scholarly papers, archives of news stories, and blogs on hundreds of subjects.

As virtual communities of people who share a common interest or passion, blogs can be a tremendously valuable resource of insights and perspectives on potential opportunities. Proactive, low- or no-cost research can also be conducted with e-mailed questionnaires or by directing potential subjects to a basic Web site set up to collect responses. In addition, the Internet provides entrepreneurs and other proactive searchers with the extraordinary capability to tap wisdom and advice from experts on virtually anything—anywhere in the world.

Networks   The networks mentioned in Chapter 3 as sources of new venture ideas also can be sources of competitor intelligence.

Other   Classified ads, buyers guides, labor unions, real estate agents, courts, local reporters, and so on, can all provide clues.[34]

---

[34] Fuld, *Competitor Intelligence,* pp. 369–418.

Chapter Summary

- Ideas are a dime a dozen. Perhaps one out of a hundred becomes a truly great business, and one in 10 to 15 becomes a higher-potential business. The complex transformation of an idea into a true opportunity is akin to a caterpillar becoming a butterfly.

- High-potential opportunities invariably solve an important problem, want, or need that someone is willing to pay for now. In renowned venture capitalist Arthur Rock's words, "I look for ideas that will change the way people live and work."

- There are decided patterns in superior opportunities, and recognizing these patterns is an entrepreneurial skill aspiring entrepreneurs need to develop.

- Rapid changes and disruptions in technology, regulation, information flows, and the like cause opportunity creation. The journey from idea to high-potential opportunity requires navigating an undulating, constantly changing, three-dimensional relief map while inventing the vehicle and road map along the way.

- Some of the best opportunities actually require some of the least amounts of capital, especially via the Internet.

- The best opportunities often don't start out that way. They are crafted, shaped, molded, and reinvented in real time and market space. Fit with the entrepreneur and resources, the timing, and the balance of risk and reward govern the ultimate potential.

- The highest-potential ventures are found in high-growth markets, with high gross margins, and robust free cash flow characteristics, because their underlying products or services add significantly greater value to the customer, compared with the next best alternatives.

- Trial and error, or learning by doing alone, is not enough for developing breakthrough ventures, which require experience, creativity, and conceptualizing.

Study Questions

1. What is the difference between an idea and a good opportunity?
2. Why is it said that ideas are a dime a dozen?
3. What role does experience play in the opportunity creation process, and where do most good opportunities come from? Why is trial-and-error learning not good enough?
4. List the sources of ideas that are most relevant to your personal interests, and conduct a search using the Internet.
5. What conditions and changes that may occur in society and the economy spawn and drive future opportunities? List as many as you can think of as you consider the next 10 years.
6. Evaluate your best idea against the summary criteria in Exhibit 5.8. What appears to be its potential? What has to happen to convert it into a high-potential business?
7. Draw a value chain and free cash flow chain for an existing business dominated by a few large players. How can you use the Internet, personal computer, and other information technology to capture (save) a significant portion of the margins and free cash flows?

Internet Resources for Chapter 5

www.ideafinder.com *This unique site celebrates innovative products and services. Includes History, Facts & Myths, Idea Showcase, and Future Ideas that may stimulate ideas for your own business.*

www.emc.score.org *Service Corps of Retired Executives. A nonprofit organization and a resource partner with the* U.S. *Small Business Administration with 11,500 volunteer members and 389 chapters throughout the United States.*

www.enterpriseforum.mit.edu/ *The MIT Enterprise Forum, Inc., builds connections to technology entrepreneurs and to the communities in which they reside*

MIND STRETCHERS

Have You Considered?

1. Steve Jobs, founder of Apple Computer, was 10 years old when he built his first computer. Colonel Sanders was 65 years old when he started Kentucky Fried Chicken. What is an opportunity for whom?

2. Most successful existing businesses are totally preoccupied with their most important, existing customers and therefore lack the peripheral opportunity vision to spot new products and services. How is this happening where you work? Is this an opportunity for you?

3. The most successful ventures have leadership and people as their most important competitive advantage. How does this change the way you think about opportunities?

4. Whom can you work with during the next few years to learn a business and have the chance to spot new opportunities outside the weak peripheral vision of an established business?

5. Barriers to entry can create opportunities for those with the right knowledge and experience. Why is this so? Can you find some examples?

Case

Burt's Bees

The biggest businesses have revolutionized civilization, changed the way we live. That's my aspiration: to change the world for the better through my company.

Roxanne Quimby

Introduction

By April 1997 Burt's Bees had 20 employees and was on track to make between $6 million and $8 million in sales for the year. Burt's Bees' margins were, on average, 35 percent of sales. A container of Burt's Bees lip balm, which cost 23 cents to make (including overhead), sold for $2.25–$2.50 in stores. The company distributed to every state in the country, could be found in more than 3,000 stores nationwide, and had just entered the European and Japanese markets. Burt's Bees products had also entered such conventional retailers' inventories as Eckerds, the Drug Emporium, and Fred Meyer. Roxanne Quimby, the president and founder of Burt's Bees, explained,

> It's not a lot of fun to go into these stores—it's a chore. They realize this and so they're looking for creative new products to liven things up, make shopping a more pleasant experience. We're starting to get a lot of inquiries from mainstream stores. They don't have an artistic inclination for merchandising, though, so we give them premade floor stands and displays to help with the backdrop and give meaning to the products for the consumer.

Pruning the Product Line

Burt's Bees' success was hard won through 18 to 24 months of pruning after the company's move from Guilford, Maine, in 1994. Production was extremely labor-intensive in Maine due to the large supply of low-paid unskilled labor. Burt's Bees had to automate production in North Carolina, though, to minimize the cost of its highly paid skilled labor. From 1994 to 1996, Roxanne Quimby cut products "like crazy." In 1994 alone, she took out $1.5 million in products including beeswax candles, the company's first and best-selling item. Every product Quimby cut was replaced with a skin care product since Burt's Bees had invested heavily in cosmetics manufacturing equipment, and the manufacturing processes involved in skin care were relatively straightforward. Quimby stated,

> We kept the lip balm, moisturizer, and baby powder, but that's it. There's not a single thing we made in 1987

that we still make today. We had to make more "goop" once we bought the blending and filling equipment. By the time we opened as a fully operational facility in North Carolina in 1994, we were still at $3 million but had totally different products. In terms of the marketing spin, that was predetermined by our environmental ethic (see Exhibit A for the company's mission statement). We draw the line at chemical preservatives. Our products had to be all-natural. If we ever step over that line, we have a whole lot of competition. As long as we're in the all-natural niche, we're the only one who doesn't add stuff like petroleum-synthesized fillers or artificial preservatives.

Burt's Bees' corporate attorney, Lanny Hiday, added, "We just went through a long trademarking process so we had to compile product lists from 1987 on. It was amazing to see how different our products are now. Sometimes we joke that we'll be making diesel engines in five years." By January 1997, Burt's Bees had over 70 "Earth Friendly, Natural Personal Care Products" (see Exhibit B).

Despite Burt's Bees' success as a manufacturer of personal care products, the company faced yet another dilemma: Should it enter the retail market? Walking through any mall in America today, you notice the market for retail personal care products is hardly vacant. How could Burt's Bees enter the retail market with the same success it had realized as a manufacturer only?

A Retail Experiment

In late 1996 Roxanne Quimby began what she called a "retail experiment." She opened a Burt's Bees retail store in Carrboro, North Carolina. While Burt's Bees had two other company-owned stores in Burlington, Vermont, and Ithaca, New York, the Carrboro store was established so that Quimby could develop a large-scale retail concept for the company. Quimby laughed,

> I worked at the Carrboro store for 10 hours the other day and sold only $400 worth of products while our vice president of marketing and sales sold something like $30,000 worth of products in 15 minutes on QVC. But I'm testing a very valuable concept. I'm interested in controlling the whole chain from manufacturing to retail. I don't like being separated from the end user. Our ultimate customers—the retailers—aren't interested in how the product works out for the person who takes it home.

© Copyright Jeffry A. Timmons, 1997, Rebecca Voomes, wrote this case under the direction of Jeffry A. Timmons, Franklin W. Olin Distinguished Professor of Entrepreneurship, Babson College Funding provided by the Ewing Marien Kauffman Foundation. All rights reserved.

EXHIBIT A

Burt's Bees' Mission Statement

Who We Are	What We Believe	What's In It?	What's It In?
We are Burt's Bees, a manufacturer of all-natural, Earth-friendly personal care products including: *herbal soaps* *aromatherapy bath oils* *powders* *bath salts* *salves* *balms* We make these products in our facility in North Carolina, and sell them through more than 3,000 stores across the country, including three company-owned stores in Burlington, VT; Carrboro, NC; and Ithaca, NY.	We believe that work is a creative, sustaining and fulfilling expression of the Inner Being. We believe that what is right is not always popular and what is popular is not always right. We believe that no one can do everything but everyone can do something. We believe that the most complicated and difficult problems we face as a civilization have the simplest solutions. We believe that Mother Nature has the answers and She teaches by example. We believe that by imitating Her economy, emulating Her generosity and appreciating Her graciousness, we will realize our rightful legacy on the magnificent Planet Earth.	Our ingredients are the best that Mother Nature has to offer: herbs, flowers, botanical oils, beeswax, essential oils and clay. Safe effective ingredients that have withstood the test of time. **What's Not In It?** We leave out the petroleum-synthesized fillers like mineral oil and propylene glycol. We don't use artificial preservatives such a methyl paraben or diazolidinyl urea. Take a closer look and read the label. We Deliver What Others Only Promise!	Bottles, jars, tubes, caps, closures, bags, dispensers, containers, "convenient" throwaway plastic. Our planet is awash in trash! How does Burt's Bees Reduce, Reuse, and Recycle? **We Reduce.** You'll find very little plastic here. We're exploring the use of simple, safe, effective and time-tested materials made of cotton, paper, metal and glass. **We Reuse.** Many of our containers can be used again and again. Use our cotton bags to hold jewelry or other small items. Try our tins for pins, pills, tacks, clips, nails, screws, and nuts and bolts. Our canisters make attractive pencil holders and our glass jars will safely store your herbs and spices. **We Recycle.** Bring back your empties. What we can't reuse we will recycle at our engineering recycling system at our plant in Raleigh, North Carolina.

WE LOOK DIFFERENT & WE ARE DIFFERENT

To me, the decision to buy is crucial. I like to just be in the store so I can observe customers and how they evaluate and respond to the products. I don't know whether we would open lots of company stores or start franchising or what, but that's what I'm trying to figure out.

The Market and Competition

Sales in the skin care and bath products industry demonstrated a distinct upward trend. Bath gels, washes, and scrubs, for example, increased 114 percent in dollar volume between 1994 and 1995—the largest category growth in the health and beauty market—while dollar volume of the entire health and beauty industry[1] increased only 64 percent in the same year.[2] Increased sales were partly aided by a virtual cut in half of prices. While the average bath gel debuted at around $10 in 1994, it cost $3.90 in 1996.[3] Skin care and bath products had developed into a major market niche over the past couple of years, accounting for $1.8 billion of the

health and beauty market's $14.2 billion in sales for 1995.[4] Even though competition was fierce, the size of the pie had increased dramatically—sales had doubled between 1993 and 1995.

Market entrants were quick to try to capitalize on this growth. Companies such as The Body Shop, Bath & Body Works, Garden Botanika, and Origins were aggressively battling for market dominance. Most new skin care and bath products claimed to be "all natural"

---

[1] Bath Gels, Washes, and Scrubs is a subset of the Bath Sundries product category, which is a subset of the overall Health & Beauty market. The Bath Sundries product category grew 32 percent in dollar volume between 1994 and 1995. The Health & Beauty category includes products such as meal supplements, tooth whiteners, thermometers, antacids, mouthwashes, razors, feminine hygiene, deodorant, acne preparations, and analgesics.

[2] "A Sofi Year for HBC," *Progressive Grocer*, May 1996, pp. 263–64.

[3] "Skincare: New Body Washes Make a Splash," *Progressive Grocer*, May 1996, p. 270.

[4] Ibid.

EXHIBIT B

Burt's Bees 1997 Product List

Product Collection	Product Name	Suggested Retail Price
Burt's Beeswax Collection	Beeswax Lip Balm (tin or tube)	$2.25–2.50
	Beeswax Face Soap 1.9 oz	$5.00
	Beeswax Moisturizing Creme 1 oz	$6.00
	Beeswax Moisturizing Creme 2 oz	$10.00
	Beeswax Pollen Night Creme 0.5 oz	$8.00
	Beeswax Royal Jelly Eye Creme 0.25 oz	$8.00
Wise Woman Collection	Comfrey Comfort Salve 1 oz	$4.00
	Calendula Massage Oil 4 fl oz	$8.00
	Mugwort & Yarrow Massage Oil 4 fl oz	$8.00
	Bladderwrack Massage Oil 4 fl oz	$8.00
	Comfrey Massage Oil 4 fl oz	$8.00
	Comfrey or Calendula Massage Oil 8 fl oz	$11.00
Ocean Potion Collection	Dusting Powder 5 oz	$14.00
	Dusting Powder Canister 3.5 oz	$6.00
	Emollient Bath & Body Oil 4 fl oz	$8.00
	Seaweed Soap 3.5 oz	$5.00
	Detox Dulse Bath 2 oz	$2.00
	Dead Sea Salts 25 oz	$12.00
	Sea Clay Mud Pack 6 oz	$10.00
Green Goddess Collection	Bath Salts 25 oz	$10.00
	Clay Mask 3 oz	$6.00
	Cleansing Gelee 4 oz	$8.00
	Beauty Bar 3.5 oz	$5.00
	Moisturizing Creme 2 oz	$10.00
	Dusting Powder 5 oz	$12.00
	Emollient Milk Bath 1 oz	$2.50
	Circulation Bath 1 oz	$2.50
	Foot Freshening Powder 3 oz	$8.00
	Flaxseed Eye Rest	$9.00
Farmer's Market Collection	Orange Essence Cleansing Creme 4 oz	$8.00
	Coconut Foot Creme 4 oz	$8.00
	Carrot Nutritive Creme 4 oz	$14.00
	Lemon Butter Cuticle Crème 1 oz	$5.00
	Citrus Facial Scrub 2 oz	$6.00
	Apple Cider Vinegar Toner 4 fl oz	$5.00
	Sunflower-Oatmeal Body Soak 1 oz	$2.50
	Avocado Hair Treatment 4 oz	$8.00
	Wheat Germ Bath & Body Oil 4 fl oz	$6.00
	Fruit Flavored Lip Gloss .25 oz	$3.50
Baby Dee Collection	Dusting Powder 5 oz	$12.00
	Dusting Powder Canister 2.5 oz	$8.00
	Skin Creme 2 oz	$10.00
	Buttermilk Soap 3.5 oz	$5.00
	Buttermilk Bath 1 oz	$3.00
	Apricot Baby Oil 4 fl oz	$6.00
	Apricot Baby Oil 8 fl oz	$10.00
Farmer's Friend Collection	Garden Soap 6 oz	$5.00
	Hand Salve 3 oz	$6.50

(continued)

EXHIBIT B   (concluded)

Product Collection	Product Name	Suggested Retail Price
	Hand Salve .30 oz	$2.00
	Lemon Grass Insect Lotion 2 fl oz	$5.00
Furry Friends Collection	Oat Straw Pet Soap 3.5 oz	$6.00
	Rosemary & Nettles Coat Conditioner 4 oz	$8.00
	Lemon Oil Dry Shampoo 1.5 oz	$4.00
	Tea Tree Pest Powder 3 oz	$6.50
	Calendula Hot Spot Ointment 1.5 oz	$6.00
	Burt's Bones 5.5 oz	$5.00
	Wheat Grass Seeds 1 oz	$3.00
	Cat Nip Toy	TBD
Kitchen Cupboard Collection	Kitchen Soap 6 oz	$6.00
	Kitchen Crème 2 oz	$6.50
	Lemon Oil Cuticle & Nail Soak 1 oz	$3.00
Bay Rum Collection	Exfoliating Soap 3.5 oz	$5.00
	Shaving Soap 3 oz	$5.00
	Cologne 3.25 fl oz	$16.00
	Shave Brush	$6.50
	Razor	$5.00
Sugar Body Scrubs Collection	Lavender Sugar Body Scrub 1 oz	$3.00
	Rose Sugar Body Scrub 1 oz	$3.00
	Vanilla Sugar Body Scrub 1 oz	$3.00
Rebound Collection	Deodorizing Body Powder 3 oz	$6.00
	Invigorating Foot Bath 1 oz	$2.50
	Stimulating Massage Oil 4 fl oz	$8.00
	Therapeutic Bath Crystals 1 lb	$8.00

and appealed primarily to young women who didn't purchase traditional personal care products found in mainstream department stores. Donald A. David, the editor of *Drug and Cosmetic Industry* journal, wrote in late 1996,

> There is a "market glut" in the soaps and scents business stimulated by the competition between The Body Shop and Bath & Body Works. Indeed, the retail outlets out there under the banners of these two companies (and their hard-charging competitors Garden Botanika, Crabtree & Evelyn, Aveda, Nature's Elements, and H₂O Plus) now number over 1,400 in the U.S. alone, a staggering number even if it isn't added to the ranks of scent-purveying store chains such as Victoria's Secret, Frederick's of Hollywood, The Gap, Banana Republic, and dozens more. . . . A shakeout seems inevitable. For example, when last heard from, Nature's Element was in Chapter 11, Garden Botanika's stock price plunged two-thirds in value three months after an initial public offering, and The Body Shop and H₂O Plus have been plagued by lagging profits. . . . Without having to deal with everyday product sales figures, this market watcher believes that the glut does not augur well for soaps and bath lines, wherever they are sold (see Exhibit C).[5]

EXHIBIT C

Retail Statistics for Cosmetic and Toiletry Sales (% of Total Sales by Retail Outlet)

Retail Outlet	1990	1994
Food stores	27%	25%
Drugstores	26%	23%
Mass merchandisers	16%	20%
Department stores	16%	17%
Direct sales	7%	8%
All other	8%	8%

Source: "Retail Statistics," *Stores*, October 1996, pp. 108–10. Courtesy of Stores Magazine/Deloitte.

Even if Burt's Bees stayed out of the retail market, competition was also fierce in manufacturing. The largest health and beauty products manufacturers (see Exhibits D and E), including Gillette, Lever Brothers, Chesebrough-Pond's, Jergens, Freeman, and St. Ives,

[5]D. A. David, "Glut Indeed," *Drug and Cosmetic Industry*, November 1996, p. 22.

EXHIBIT D

50 Largest Manufacturers in the Toilet Preparations Industry (SIC 2844), 1996

Rank	Company Name	Sales ($ million)	Employees (000)
1	Johnson & Johnson	15,734	81.5
2	Colgate-Palmolive	7,588	28.0
3	Amway	4,500	10.0
4	Helene Curtis Industries Inc.	1,266	3.4
5	Alberto-Culver Co.	1,216	8.5
6	Cosmair Inc.	1,000	0.4
7	Forever Living Products International	939	0.9
8	Perrigo Co.	669	3.9
9	Clairol Inc.	350	2.0
10	Freedom Chemical Co.	300	1.0
11	Neutrogena Corp.	282	0.8
12	Benckiser Consumer Products	230	1.5
13	John Paul Mitchell Systems	190	< 0.1
14	Del Laboratories Inc.	167	1.1
15	Johnson Co.	140	0.9
16	Dep Corp.	138	0.4
17	Kolmar Laboratories	130	0.8
18	Guest Supply Inc.	116	0.7
19	Redmond Products Inc.	115	0.2
20	Cosmolab Inc.	110	0.7
21	Accra Pac Group Inc.	100	0.8
22	Sebastian International Inc.	100	0.4
23	Andrew Jergens Co.	97	0.6
24	Houbigant Inc.	97	0.6
25	Cumberland-Swan Inc.	80	0.8
26	Combe Inc.	70	0.4
27	BeautiControl Cosmetics Inc.	64	0.3
28	Shiseido Cosmetics	60	0.2
29	Jean Phillipe Fragrances Inc.	59	< 0.1
30	NutraMax Products Inc.	56	0.5
31	Arthur Matney Company Inc.	55	0.5
32	Aramis Inc.	53	0.3
33	Luster Products Co.	53	0.3
34	Ranir Corp.	53	0.3
35	Aveda Corp.	50	0.3
36	DeMer and Dougherty Inc.	50	0.2
37	Russ Kalvin Inc.	49	0.3
38	Scott Chemical Co.	48	0.3
39	CCA Industries Inc.	48	0.1
40	Image Laboratories Inc.	47	0.3
41	Cosmyl Inc.	44	0.3
42	Pavion Ltd.	40	0.5
43	MEM Company Inc.	38	0.3
44	Pro-Line Corp.	38	0.3
45	Belcam Inc.	35	0.3
46	Penthouse Manufacturing	35	0.2

(continued)

EXHIBIT D   (concluded)

50 Largest Manufacturers in the Toilet Preparations Industry (SIC 2844), 1996

Rank	Company Name	Sales ($ million)	Employees (000)
47	Cosmar Corp.	33	< 0.1
48	Megas Beauty Care Inc.	32	0.3
49	American International Industries	31	0.2
50	Aminco Inc.	31	0.2

Source: A. J. Damay, ed., *Manufacturing USA: Industry Analyses, Statistics, and Leading Companies*, 5th ed (Farmington, MI: Gale Research, 1996), p. 834.

EXHIBIT E

1995 Top 9 Hand and Body Lotions

Rank	Brand	1995 Sales ($ million)	1995 Market Share (%)	Manufacturer
1	Intensive Care	149.9	18.6	Chesebrough-Pond's
2	Jergens	89.9	11.2	Andrew Jergens
3	Lubriderm	77.9	9.7	Warner-Wellcome
4	Nivea	44.1	5.5	Beiersdorf
5	Suave	43.0	5.3	Helene Curits
6	Eucerin	41.1	5.1	Beiersdorf
7	Curel	36.8	4.6	Bausch & Lomb
8	Neutrogena	34.5	4.3	Neutrogena
9	St. Ives	34.4	4.3	St. Ives

had been introducing their own "natural" skin care and bath products to ensure their continued market dominance.

Conclusion

Roxanne Quimby had always planned on selling Burt's Bees at some point, but she believed that no buyer would consider the company for purchase until it reached at least $25 million in sales. Quimby couldn't decide what the best route to $25 million was, though. Was it retail? If so, how could Burt's Bees establish a presence in such a crowded market? If retail wasn't a good move for the company, where did Burt's Bees' future lie? If Burt's Bees remained a manufacturer and direct seller, how could the company expand its product reach and close the gap between $6–$8 million and $25 million?

The devastating tsunami in Asia in late December 2004 was a sobering reminder of the massive, life-changing impact that such an event can have. The "sea change" metaphor is one we have used in earlier editions to urge aspiring entrepreneurs to research, brainstorm, and envision future quantum changes in technology and society. As we have seen, such sea changes as electricity, the airplane, the integrated circuit (Moore's law), and wireless communications have been the wellheads of new major industries. What will be the likely technology and societal changes during the next 20 to 30 years that will spawn the next generation of new industries? Entrepreneurs and innovators who anticipate the answers to this complex question will become the Gates, Jobs, Blank, and Stemberg of the next generation.

Purpose

The purpose of this exercise is to provide a pathway for exploring this question. We hope to broaden your horizon of technological literacy and enrich your vision of the next quarter century—the window of your life when you have the best chance of creating and seizing the mega-opportunities that lie ahead.

We ask you to do some research and thinking about the future directions of technology and how scientific inquiries which are under way today can lead to knowledge breakthroughs. This new scientific knowledge will, in turn, lead to innovations. When fueled, ignited, and driven by entrepreneurship, some of these innovations will become commercialized and in the process create entirely new industries.

The following steps will assist you in this research task, but you should not confine your efforts to these steps alone. You also need to pursue as many other sources as possible using Google and other resources. Be sure to "follow the data and your gut instinct." If you find an area of science and technology that excites you—or which you instinctively believe can change the way people will live, work, learn, or relax—then pursue it.

STEP 1

Go to the National Science Foundation summary of the 50 discoveries that the NSF believes have had the most impact on every American's life (www.nsf.gov/about/history/nifty50/index.jsp). You will find such breakthrough discoveries as bar codes, CAD/CAM, genomics, speech recognition, computer visualization techniques, and Web browsers. All of these are examples of sea changes—the spawners and drivers of new industries that we discussed in this chapter and in Chapter 3.

STEP 2

Select one or two of the nifty 50 that interest you the most. Now examine number 10 on the list: "computer visualiza-

tion techniques." Note the 11 industries and fields that have been significantly impacted by this basic discovery. Out of these 11 pick one or two you know the least about but for which you have the most passion. Conduct some keyword searches on Google and the like to identify products, companies, or market segments that are driven by the entrepreneurs behind these innovations. Repeat this process for all of the major discoveries you are attracted to. Once you have a good sense of how these linkages exist, go to Step 3.

STEP 3

Meet with two to five of your classmates over breakfast, lunch, dinner, and share what you have learned, your observations and insights about how industries are born, and what potential new fields might arise.

- What patterns and common characteristics did you find? What are the lead times and early indicators?

- What technologies have the most future potential impact on the way people live, work, learn?

- Who are the entrepreneurs who create the technology-based firms that utilize these discoveries? What are their background, preparation, skills, experience, and so forth? Any common denominators?

- Have any of your ideas, assumptions, and beliefs been altered about where and when the next biggest opportunities will emerge?

STEP 4

Visit the NSF home page (www.nsf.gov) and find the list of 11 different program areas, including geosciences, environmental research, and engineering. Select one that interests you the most and you know the least about. Go into the Web site and identify the research grants awarded to this topic over the past few years.

- What topics and problems are attracting the most money and activity? Why is this so?

- What new scientific knowledge and/or breakthroughs might be expected, and what are some of the potential sea change impacts?

- What potential commercial applications can be envisioned from these new technologies?

- What existing technologies, products, and services are most likely to be disrupted and replaced by these innovations?

- What societal trends can be combined with these future technologies to create entire new industries?

STEP 5

In class, or in informal groups, discuss and explore the implications of your findings from the exercise.

- What are two or three future sea changes you anticipate?

- What other exploration do you need to do?

- How can you better prepare yourself to be able to recognize and seize these future opportunities now, in 10 years, and in 15 years?

- What implications do you see for your personal entrepreneurial strategy, which you began to develop in Chapter 2—especially with regard to projects to work on, next education and work experience, and brain trust and mentor additions?

Opportunity-Creating Concepts and the Quest for Breakthrough Ideas

After you have fully digested the discussions in this chapter, you should aim to prepare an industry analysis utilizing the criteria listed in Exhibit 5.8. This should be a first cut analysis, not an overly exhaustive effort. Your value chain should be mapped out on one to two pages maximum, with the other questions/issues answered in bullet points on one to two pages maximum. Rather than an exhaustive effort, this exercise is designed to get you to a specific way of thinking.

Your task is to complete a *simple, clear, and articulate value chain analysis* of an industry that is of interest to you. Analyze the value chain as it *currently exists*. Next complete an *information flow analysis* of that value chain, overlaying an analysis of the flow of information through the various stages of the value chain. Then broaden your thinking to *create a value cluster* of that industry. Make sure you are thinking multidimensionally, not just linearly. Describe or visually depict the impact of these multiple dimensions on the flow of both goods/services *and* information. Explain how this value cluster expansion adds or intensifies value for that industry, as compared to the linear chain. Finally, provide a *succinct analysis of the margins in this value cluster*, with particular emphasis on the extremes (highs/lows).

Also consider the following:

- What are the deconstructors and reconstructors that drive the value chain and opportunity in this industry?

- What is your best estimate of the composition of the free cash flow, profit, and value chains in a business in this industry?

- What prevailing industry practices, conventions, wisdom in marketing, distribution, outsourcing customer services, IT, and capital investment are significant in this business?

- What new practices, conventions, and so forth are now in place, and what are their half-lives?

- What are the growth segments?

- Where do the pundits (Forrester, IDG, Research Sources, and other Wall Street analysts) think the next growth market will be?

- What are the parameters and characteristics of that market?

If you are planning to bring a high-tech product to market, you might want to consider the framework discussed in *Crossing the Chasm: Marketing and Selling High-Tech Products to Mainstream Customers* by Geoffrey Moore and Regis McKenna and look at the value chain and the specific industry segment(s) you plan to focus on. You should also consider reviewing Clayton M. Christensen's writings on disruptive innovation in, among others, *The Innovator's Dilemma*.

Exercise 3

Creative Squares

STEP 1

Divide Your Group by (a) Separating into a Number of Groups of Three or More People Each and (b) Having at Least Five Individuals Work Alone.

STEP 2

Show the Following Figure to Everyone and Ask the Groups and the Individuals to Count the Total Number of Squares in the Figure. Assume that the figure is a square box on a single flat plane. In counting, angles of any square must be right angles, and the sides must be of equal length.

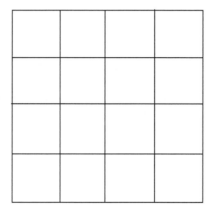

STEP 3

Discuss the Creative Processes by Which the Groups and the Individuals Reached Their Answers.

Idea Generation Guide

Before beginning the process of generating ideas for new ventures, it is useful to reflect on an old German proverb that says, "Every beginning is hard." If you allow yourself to think creatively, you will be surprised at the number of interesting ideas you can generate once you begin.

This idea generation guide is an exercise in generating ideas. The aim is for you to generate as many interesting ideas as possible. *While generating your ideas, do not evaluate them or worry about their implementation.* Discussion and exercises in the rest of the book will allow you to evaluate these ideas to see if they are opportunities and to consider your own personal entrepreneurial strategy.

And remember—in any creative endeavor there are no right answers.

Name:

Date:

STEP 1

Generate a List of as Many New Venture Ideas as Possible. As a consumer or paid user, think of the biggest, most frustrating, and painful task or situation you continually must take, and one which would be worth a lot to eliminate or minimize. These are often the seeds of real opportunities. Thinking about any unmet or poorly filled customer needs you know of that have resulted from regulatory changes, technological changes, knowledge and information gaps, lags, asymmetries, inconsistencies, and so forth will help you generate such a list. Also think about various products and services (and their substitutes) and the providers of these products or services. If you know of any weaknesses or vulnerabilities, you may discover new venture ideas.

STEP 2

Expand Your List if Possible. Think about your personal interests, your desired lifestyle, your values, what you feel you are likely to do very well, and contributions you would like to make.

STEP 3

Ask at Least Three People Who Know You Well to Look at Your List, and Revise Your List to Reflect Any New Ideas Emerging from This Exchange. See the discussion about getting feedback in Chapter 2.

STEP 4

Jot Down Insights, Observations, and Conclusions That Have Emerged about Your Business Ideas or Your Personal Preferences. Which ones solve the greatest pain point/aggravation/frustration for which you (and others you have spoken with) would pay a significant premium to eliminate?

Chapter Six

Screening Venture Opportunities

Entrepreneurs need to think big. You are going to end up exhausted in building a company. So you might as well end up exhausted and rich!

Patricia Cloherty
First Woman President of the National Venture Capital Association

Results Expected

At the conclusion of this chapter, you will be able to

1. Effectively utilize two screening methodologies—QuickScreen and the Venture Opportunity Screening Exercises (VOSE)—that can help you determine whether your ideas are potential opportunities.
2. Apply the opportunity criteria from Chapter 5 to your ideas and begin to assess the probable fit with you, your team, your resources, and the balance of risk and reward.
3. Articulate with more creativity and depth what you need to do to improve both the fit and the risk and reward relationship.
4. Determine whether your best idea at this time has sufficient potential to pursue the development of a thorough business plan.
5. Assess whether you believe you can sufficiently alter the idea and your strategy to create a good fit and an attractive risk–reward balance for you and your investors.
6. Discuss and share ideas about and analysis of the Globant case.

Screening Venture Opportunities

Time is the ultimate ally and enemy of the entrepreneur. The harsh reality is that you will not have enough time in a quarter, a year, or a decade to pursue all the ideas for businesses you and your team can think of. Perhaps the cruelest part of the paradox is that you have to find and make the time for the good ones. To complicate the paradox, *you do not have a strategy until you are saying no to lots of opportunities!* This demand is part of the both punishing and rewarding Darwinian aspect of entrepreneurship: Many will try, many will fail, some will succeed, and a few will excel. While the number of new enterprises launched in the United States can vary widely from year to year, only 10 to 15 percent of those will ever prove to be opportunities that achieve sales of $1 million or more.

This chapter will put you in the trenches, engaging in the first of many titanic struggles to determine whether your good idea is truly a good opportunity. Ideas that turn into superior businesses are not accidents; they are consistent with the model portrayed in Chapter 3 and with these four anchors we introduced in Chapter 5:

1. They create or add significant value to a customer or end user.
2. They do so by solving a significant problem, removing a serious pain point, or meeting a significant want or need—for which someone is willing to pay a premium.

3. They have robust market, margin, and money-making characteristics that will allow the entrepreneur to estimate and communicate sustainable value to potential stakeholders: large enough ($50 million +), high growth (20 percent +), high gross margins (40 percent +), strong and early free cash flow (recurring revenue, low assets, and working capital), high profit potential (10 to 15 percent + after tax), and attractive realizable returns for investors (25 to 30 percent + IRR).

4. They are a good *fit* with the founder(s) and management team at the time and marketplace—along with an attractive *risk–reward* balance.

QuickScreen

If most sophisticated private equity investors and venture capitalists invest in only 2 to 3 out of 100 ideas, then we can see how important it is to focus on a few superior ideas. The ability to quickly and efficiently reject ideas is a very important entrepreneurial mind-set. Saying no to lots of ideas directly conflicts with your passion and commitment for a particular idea. To make the struggle more manageable, this chapter provides two methodologies. The first, QuickScreen, should enable you to conduct a preliminary review and evaluation of an idea in an hour. Unless the idea has been, or you are confident it can be, molded and shaped so that it has the four anchors, you will waste a lot of time on a lower-potential idea. The QuickScreen exercise can be reproduced for your own use.

Venture Opportunity Screening Exercises (VOSE)

The Venture Opportunity Screening Exercises are designed to segment the screening of ideas into manageable pieces. The QuickScreen provides a broad overview of an idea's potential. In a team effort, each member of the team should complete the exercise separately and then meet as a team to merge the results. After each VOSE, you should revisit the QuickScreen and reevaluate your scoring. When you are satisfied that all the exercises are complete, the combined documents will provide the substance needed to complete your business plan. They also provide an audit trail of your opportunity-shaping activity. Not only does this help you memorialize your thinking, but it provides excellent articulation when explaining your thought process to sophisticated investors—many of whom will be asking probing questions to test your depth of knowledge.

Whether or not an entrepreneur plans to seek venture capital or an outside private investor to pursue an opportunity, it is vital to have a realistic view of the vulnerabilities and realities, as well as the opportunity's compelling strengths. Often the iterative process of carefully examining different ideas through many eyes, within and outside your team, often *triggers creative ideas and insights about how the initial business concept and strategy can be altered and molded to significantly enhance the value chain, free cash flow characteristics, and risk–reward relationships and thus the fit.* This process is central to value creation and the development of higher-potential ventures, but it is far from cut and dried.

This early seed stage is also a marvelous time for a "trial marriage" with prospective team members. This work can be detailed, tedious, and downright boring. Finding out now who can deliver what; who has the work ethic, consistency, and reliability; and whether you can work together will save a lot of money and headaches later. Ultimately the *fit* issue boils down to this: Do the opportunity, the resources required (and their cost), the other team members (if any), the timing, and balance of risk and reward *work for me?*

Internet Sources for Chapter 6

www.start-a-business.com *The web site offers advice and tools for starting a business; how-to guides including tax guides and incorporation services; and domain name registrations.*

Exercise 1

QuickScreen

I. Market and Margin-Related Issues

Criterion	Higher Potential	Lower Potential
Need/want/problem/pain point	Identified	Unfocused
Customers	Reachable and receptive	Unreachable/loyal to others
Payback to users	Less than one year	More than three years
Value added or created	IRR 40%+	IRR less than 20%
Market size	$50 million–$100 million	Less than $10 million or $1+ billion
Market growth rate	More than 20%	Less than 20%, contracting
Gross margin	More than 40% and durable	Less than 20% and fragile

Overall Potential:

1. Market   Higher _____ Average _____ Lower

2. Margins   Higher _____ Average _____ Lower

II. Competitive Advantages: Relative to the Current and Evolving Set of Competitors

	Higher Potential	Lower Potential
Fixed and variable costs	Lowest	Highest
Degree of control	Stronger	Weaker
Prices and cost		
Channels of supply and distribution		
Barriers to competitors' entry	Can create	Weak/None
Proprietary advantage	Defensible	None
Lead time advantage (product, technology, people, resources, location)	Slow competition	None
Service chain	Strong edge	No edge
Contractual advantage	Exclusive	None
Contacts and networks	Key access	Limited

Overall potential

1. Costs   Higher _____ Average _____ Lower

2. Channel   Higher _____ Average _____ Lower

3. Barriers to entry Higher _____ Average _____ Lower

4. Timing   Higher _____ Average _____ Lower

III. Value Creation and Realization Issues

	Higher Potential	Lower Potential
Profit after tax	10–15% or more and durable	Less than 5%; fragile
Time to breakeven	Less than 2 years	More than 3 years
Time to positive cash flow	Less than 2 years	More than 3 years
ROI potential	40%–70% +, durable	Less than 20%, fragile
Value	High strategic value[1]	Low strategic value
Capitalization requirements	Low–moderate; fundable	Very high; difficult to fund
Exit mechanism	IPO, acquisition	Undefined; illiquid investment

Overall value creation potential

1. Timing   Higher _____ Average _____ Lower

2. Profit/free cash flow Higher _____ Average _____ Lower

3. Exit/liquidity   Higher _____ Average _____ Lower

(continued)

---

[1] *Strategic value* can have many meanings. In the context of opportunity recognition, strategic value exists when a company in the value chain you would enter could substantively benefit from the launch of your business.

IV. Overall Potential

	Go	No Go	Go, if . . .
1. Margins and markets			
2. Competitive advantages			
3. Value creation and realization			
4. Fit: "O" + "R" + "T"			
5. Risk–reward balance			
6. Timing			
7. Other compelling issues: must know or likely to fail			
a.			
b.			
c.			
d.			
e.			

Venture Opportunity Screening Exercises

The new venture creation process requires due diligence. We recommend that the components of these exercises be used to channel your thought and data collection efforts toward creating the foundation for development of the complete business plan. Allow for dynamic processing of each component and thereby shaping of the opportunity and a plan to execute it. It is okay to be initially broad in your perspective and then become more focused in later iterations.

The VOSE is based on the criteria discussed in Chapter 5. At the end of each exercise, you should have a clearer idea of the relative attractiveness of your opportunity. Rarely is it simply cut and dried. Most of the time there will be considerable uncertainty and numerous unknowns and risks. Completing these exercises can, however, help you understand those uncertainties and risks as you make a decision about the idea. The process will help you devise ways to make these uncertainties and risks more acceptable for you; if not, then you know you need to keep searching.

Every venture is unique. Operations, marketing, cash flow cycles, and so forth vary a good bit from company to company, from industry to industry, from region to region, and from country to country. As a result, you may find that not every issue is pertinent to your venture, and perhaps some questions are irrelevant. Here and there you may need to add to these exercises or further tailor them to your circumstances.

Working through these exercises is a lengthy process. This is a map of how to think about the tough, dull legwork of good due diligence that should be done before launching into a venture. Completing these exercises will help you determine if your opportunity is attractive enough vis-à-vis the four anchors to develop a complete business plan. As you work through these exercises, you will find that much of the work of writing a business plan comes from your answers in the exercises. While you may decide to delay work on some of these exercises, eventually you will need to ask yourself and your team these questions.

Ideally each member of your team will complete these exercises.

As with other exercises in this text, feel free to make as many copies of the VOSE as needed.

Opportunity Concept and Strategy Statement

Briefly describe your vision, the opportunity concept, and your strategy. What is your vision for the business? What is the value creation proposition? What is the significant problem, want, or need that it will solve? Why is this problem/bottleneck/pain point/aggravation/joy important enough that a customer or end user will pay an above-average to premium price for it? Why does this opportunity exist, now, for you? Can you describe the concept and your entry strategy in 25 or fewer words?

Exercise 3

The Venture Opportunity Profile

Fill in this profile by indicating for each criterion where your venture is located on the *potential* continuum. Check off your best estimate of where your idea stacks up, being as specific as possible. If you are having trouble, information can be found in magazines and newsletters, from other entrepreneurs, from trade shows and fairs, or from online resources.

Venture Opportunity Profile

Criterion	Highest Potential	Lowest Potential
	Changes how people live and work	Incremental changes
Industry and Market		
Market: Need	Market driven; identified; recurring revenue niche	Unfocused; onetime revenue
Customers	Reachable; purchase orders	Loyal to others or unreachable
User benefits	Less than one year payback	Three years plus payback
Value added	High; advance payments	Low; minimal impact on market
Product life	Durable	Perishable
Market structure	Imperfect, fragmented competition or emerging industry	Highly concentrated or mature or declining industry
Market size	$100+ million to $1 billion sales potential	Unknown, less than $20 million or multibillion sales
Growth rate	Growth at 30% to 50% or more	Contracting or less than 10%
Market capacity	At or near full capacity	Under capacity
Market share attainable (Year 5)	20% or more; leader	Less than 5%
Cost structure	Low-cost provider; cost advantages	Declining cost

Criterion	Highest Potential	Lowest Potential
	Changes how people live and work	*Incremental changes*
Economics		
Profits after tax	10% to 15% or more; durable	Less than 15%; fragile
ROI potential	25% or more; high value	Less than 15% to 20%; low value
Capital requirements	Low to moderate; fundable	Very high; unfundable
Internal rate of return potential	25% or more per year	Less than 15% per year
Free cash flow characteristics:	Favorable; sustainable; 20 to 30 + % of sales	Less than 10% of sales
Sales growth	Moderate to high (15+ % to 20+ %)	Less than 10%
Asset intensity	Low/sales $	High/sales $
Spontaneous working capital	Low, incremental requirements	High requirements
R&D/capital expenditures	Low requirements	High requirements
Gross margins	Exceeding 40% and durable	Under 20%
Time to breakeven—cash flow	Less than 2 years; breakeven not creeping	Greater than 4 years; breakeven creeping up
Time to breakeven—P&L	Less than 2 years; breakeven not creeping	Greater than 4 years; breakeven creeping up
Harvest Issues		
Value-added potential	High strategic value	Low strategic value
Valuation multiples and comparables	p/e = 20 + ×; 8–10 + × EBIT; 1.5–2 + × revenue free cash flow 8–10 + ×	p/e = 5 ×, EBIT = 3–4×; revenue = .4
Exit mechanism and strategy	Present or envisioned options	Undefined; illiquid investment
Capital market context	Favorable valuations, timing, capital available; realizable liquidity	Unfavorable; credit crunch
Competitive Advantage Issues		
Fixed and variable costs	Lowest; high operating leverage	Highest
Control over costs, prices, and distribution	Moderate to strong	Weak

Criterion	Highest Potential	Lowest Potential
	Changes how people live and work	*Incremental changes*
Barriers to entry:		
Proprietary protection	Have or can gain	None
Response/lead time	Competition slow; napping	Unable to gain edge
Legal, contractual advantage	Proprietary or exclusivity	None
Contacts and networks	Well-developed; accessible	Crude; limited
Key people	Top talent; an A team	B or C team
Management Team		
Entrepreneurial team	All-star combination; free agents	Weak or solo entrepreneur
Industry and technical experience	Top of the field; super track record	Underdeveloped
Integrity	Highest standards	Questionable
Intellectual honesty	Know what they do not know	Do not want to know what they do not know
Fatal Flaw Issue		
	Nonexistent	One or more
Personal Criteria		
Goals and fit	Getting what you want; but wanting what you get	Surprises
Upside/downside issues	Attainable success/limited risks	Linear; on same continuum
Opportunity costs	Acceptable cuts in salary, etc.	Comfortable with status quo
Desirability	Fits with lifestyle	Simply pursuing big money
Risk/reward tolerance	Calculated risk; low R/R ratio	Risk averse or gambler
Stress tolerance	Thrives under pressure	Cracks under pressure
Strategic Differentiation		
Degree of fit	High	Low
Team	Best in class; excellent free agents	B team; no free agents

Criterion	Highest Potential	Lowest Potential
	Changes how people live and work	Incremental changes
Service management	Superior service concept	Perceived as unimportant
Timing	Rowing with the tide	Rowing against the tide
Technology	Groundbreaking; one-of-a-kind	Many substitutes or competitors
Flexibility	Able to adapt; commit and decommit quickly	Slow; stubborn
Opportunity orientation	Always searching for opportunities	Operating in a vacuum; napping
Pricing	At or near leader	Undercut competitor; low prices
Distribution channels	Accessible; networks in place	Unknown; inaccessible
Room for error	Forgiving strategy	Unforgiving, rigid strategy

Assess the external environment surrounding your venture opportunity, including the following:

- An assessment of the characteristics of the opportunity window, including its perishability:

- A statement of what entry strategy suits the opportunity, and why:

- A statement of evidence of and/or reasoning behind your belief that the external environment and the forces creating your opportunity, as described in Exercise 2 and the profile you just completed, fit:

- A statement of your exit strategy and an assessment of the prospects that this strategy can be met, including a consideration of whether the risks, rewards, and trade-offs are acceptable:

Checkpoint

Before you proceed to further exercises, be sure the opportunity you have outlined is compelling and you can answer the question, "Why does the opportunity exist now?" It is possible you ought to abandon or alter the product or service idea behind your venture at this point. The amount of money and time needed to get the product or service to market, and to be open for business, may be beyond your limits. Beware the opportunity for which the potential rewards are too large compared to the risks and vulnerabilities to obsolescence and competition.

Exercise 4

Opportunity-Shaping
Research and Exercise

Articulate the reasons that make you believe your idea is an opportunity. This will likely affect or "shape" your opportunity. We have listed some important questions that you should address, but you might also want to add additional perspectives. The principal objective of this exercise is to focus the lens on the major components of your opportunity.

Assess the attractiveness of your venture opportunity by applying screening criteria. Include the following:

- What is the critical problem, want, or need your product or service will solve?

- Why is this a critical problem or serious pain point/aggravation that demands removal?

- Who will pay a premium price, compared with alternatives, if you can address this problem or want?

- What is the underlying value creation proposition: How and why will it pay for itself, yield major benefits/advantages, and so on?

- A brief description of the market(s) or market niche(s) you want to enter:

- An exact description of the product(s) or service(s) to be sold and, if a product, its eventual end use(s). (If your product(s) or service(s) are already commercially available or exist as prototypes, attach specifications, photographs, samples of work, etc.)

- An estimate of how perishable the product(s) or service(s) are, including if it is likely to become obsolete and when:

- An assessment of whether there are substitutes for the product(s) or service(s):

- An assessment of the status of development and an estimate of how much time and money will be required to complete development, test the product(s) or service(s), and then introduce the product(s) or service(s) to the market:

Development Tasks		
Development Task	**Dollars Required**	**Months to Complete**

- An assessment of any major difficulties in manufacturing the product(s) or delivering the service(s) and how much time and money will be required to resolve them:

- An assessment of your primary customer group:

  —A description of the main reasons why your primary group of customers will buy your product or service, including whether customers in this group are reachable and receptive and how your product or service will add or create value, and what this means for your entry or expansion strategy:

- A description of the necessary customer support, such as warranty service, repair service, and training of technicians, salespeople, service people, or others:

- An assessment of the strengths and weaknesses, relative to the competition, of the product(s) or service(s) in meeting customer needs, including a description of payback of and value added by the product(s) or service(s):

—A list of 5 to 10 crucial questions you need to have answered and other information you need to know to identify good customer prospects:

—An indication of how customers buy products or services (e.g., from direct sales, either wholesale or retail; through manufacturers' representatives or brokers; through catalogs; via direct mail; on the Web):

—A description of the purchasing process (i.e., where it occurs and who is ultimately responsible for approving expenditures; what and who influence the sale; how long it takes from first contact to close, to delivery, and to cash receipt; and your conclusions about the competitive advantages you can achieve and how your product or service can add or create value):

- An assessment of the market potential for your venture's product or service, the competition, and what is required to bring and sell the product or service to the customer. (Such an analysis need not be precise or comprehensive but should eliminate from further consideration those ventures that have obvious market difficulties.) Include the following information:

  —An estimate, for the past, present, and future, of the *approximate* size of the *total* potential market, as measured in units and in dollars or number of customers. In making your estimates, use available market data to estimate *ranges* of values and to identify the area (country, region, locality, etc.) and data for each segment if the market is segmented:

Total Market Size				
Year				
20_ _	20_ _	20_ _	20_ _	20_ _

Sales of Units/
Number of Customers

Sales in Dollars

Sources of Data:

Researcher:

Confidence in Data:

—An assessment of the type of market in terms of price, quality, and service; degree of control; and so on; and your conclusions about what approaches are necessary to enter, survive, and win:

- What good news or information will arrive (or can you cause to arrive) that will enhance your opportunity?

- What are the odds for *(a)* implementation success or *(b)* sufficient magnitude of the new venture?

- What can you alter or add to enhance the opportunity?

- What can you do or learn to make *you* the most *knowledgeable* competitor in this industry?

- Other compelling issues:

Customer Contact Research and Exercise

Entrepreneurship is a full-contact activity. That contact is first and foremost with potentially revenue-generating customers. It is *essential* that you communicate with customers and document their responses. Attempt to reconcile customer reactions in this section to the opportunity-shaping research and exercise (Exercise 4). Please provide the following:

- An assessment, based on a survey of customers, of how your customers do business and what investigative steps are needed next:

	Customer Survey Customer		
	---	---	---
	No. 1	**No. 2**	**No. 3**
Nature of Customers			
Business or Role			
Reactions: Positive Negative Questions			

Specific Needs/Uses

Acceptable Terms—Price, Support, etc.

Basis of Purchase Decisions:

   Time Frame

   Who Makes Decision

   Dollar Limits

Substitutes/Competitive Products
or Services Used

Names of Competitors

Competitive Products

Substitute Products

Customers Surveyed	
No.	**Name**

Exercise 6

Mining the Value Chain—Defining the "White Space"[2]

Your opportunity must be placed in the context of both a competitive environment and an existing value chain that you believe can be improved upon and altered in a way that creates value. In addition to tracing the movement of physical goods, you should also map the flow of information and the resultant margins that flow to channel players. Please provide the following:

■ An assessment of how your product or service will be positioned in the market, including the following:

—A statement of any proprietary protection, such as patents, copyrights, or trade secrets, and what this means in the way of competitive advantage:

—An assessment of any competitive advantages you can achieve in the level of quality, service, and so forth, including an objective description of any strengths (and weaknesses) of the product or service:

---

[2] *White space* refers to the gaps in an industry or market into which your opportunity falls. When you complete the value chain exercise—looking at the flow of physical, informational, and financial margins—you will be able to see the market anomalies (positive or negative) that create space for your opportunity.

—An assessment of your pricing strategy versus those of competitors:

	Pricing Strategy[3]		
	Highest Price	**Average Price**	**Lowest Price**
Retail			
Wholesale			
Distributor			
Internet			
Manufacturing			
Other Channel			

---

[3] Consider the opportunity recognition process that led to the rotary electric toothbrush venture described in the previous chapter.

—An assessment of the competitors in your industry or market niche in terms of price versus performance/benefits/value added:[4]

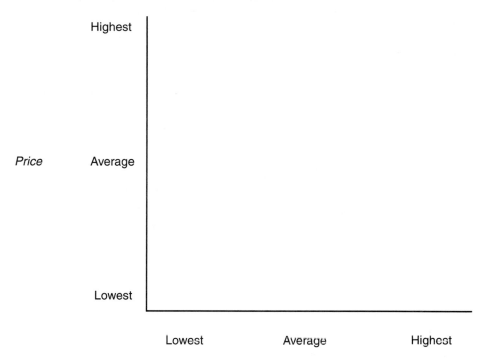

—An indication of how you plan to distribute and sell your product or services (e.g., through direct sales, mail order, manufacturers' representatives) and the likely sales, marketing, and advertising/trade promotion costs:

—A distribution plan for your product(s) or service(s), including any special requirements, such as refrigeration, and how much distribution costs will be as a percentage of sales and of total costs:

---

[4] Note: If there is a 10 to 30 times (or more) spread among competitive products, there is an opportunity lurking.

■ Complete this chart of the three flows (physical, informational, and margin) to find the value chain for your product or service. Following the physical flow, map how your product or service will get to the end user or consumer, the portion of the final selling price realized in each step, and the dollar and percentage markup and the dollar and percentage gross margin per unit. This exercise will help you identify the market anomalies (positive and negative) that can identify spaces in which you can create your opportunity. The value chain formed from these flows is constructed for a generalized consumer product and needs to be modified for your particular product, service, industry, or region.

Mining the Value Chain

Physical Flow	Components Materials and Labor Raw Materials	Manufacturer or Service Provider	Distributor	Wholesaler	End User or Customer
Margin Flow	Price/unit: Dollars Percent	Price/unit: Dollars Percent	Price/unit: Dollars Percent	Price/unit: Dollars Percent	Price/unit: Dollars Percent
	Markup/unit: Dollars Percent	Markup/unit: Dollars Percent	Markup/unit: Dollars Percent	Markup/unit: Dollars Percent	Markup/unit: Dollars Percent
	Gross margin: Dollars Percent	Gross margin: Dollars Percent	Gross margin: Dollars Percent	Gross margin: Dollars Percent	Gross margin: Dollars Percent
Informational Flow	Key data	Key data	Key data	Key data	Key data
	Mean of data transfer	Mean of data transfer	Mean of data transfer	Mean of data transfer	Mean of data transfer

Exercise 7

Economics of the Business—How Do You Make Money in the White Space?

Your mining of the value chain (Exercise 6) should present a view of the "white space" for your business. In this section we ask you to begin to *quantify* the space and to estimate the time and resources it will take to fill that space. These preliminary assessments will provide the foundation for the development of your financial statements, including income statement, balance sheet, cash flow, and break-even point. Please provide the following:

- A realistic estimate of approximate sales and market share for your product or service in the market area that your venture can attain in each of your first five years:

Product/Service Sales and Market Share

	Year				
	1	**2**	**3**	**4**	**5**

Total Market:
  Units
  Dollars					

Estimate Sales:
  Units
  Dollars					

Estimate Market Share (Percent):					

Estimate Market Growth:
  Units
  Dollars					

Source of Data:

Researcher:

Confidence in Data:

Checkpoint

Consider whether you suffer from *mousetrap myopia* or whether you lack enough experience to tackle the venture at this stage. It is possible that if your venture does not stand up to this evaluation, you may simply not be as far along as you had thought. Remember: The single largest factor contributing to stillborn ventures and to those who will ripen as lemons is lack of opportunity focus. If you were unable to fill in the chart on Product/Service Sales and Market Share on the previous page, or do not have much of an idea of how to answer it, it is possible that you need to do more work before proceeding with this venture.

■ An assessment of the costs and profitability of your product or service:

Product/Service Costs and Profitability

Product/service:

Sales price:

Sales level:

	Dollars/Unit	Percentage of Sales Price/Unit
Production Costs (e.g., labor and material costs) or Purchase Costs		
Gross Margin		
Fixed Costs		
Profit before Taxes		
Profit after Taxes		

■ An assessment of the minimum resources required to "get the doors open and revenue coming in"—the costs, dates required, alternative means of gaining control of (but not necessarily owning) these, and what this information tells you:

Resource Needs

	Minimum Needed	Cost ($)	Date Required	Probable Source
Plant, Equipment, and Facilities (remember, you only have to control the asset, not own it)				
Product/Service Development (include raw materials and other inventory)				
Market Research				
Setup of Sales and Distribution (e.g., brochures, demos, and mailers)				
One-Time Expenditures (e.g., legal costs)				
Lease Deposits and Other Prepayments (e.g., utilities)				

Overhead (e.g., salaries, rent, and insurance)

Sales Costs (e.g., trips to trade shows)

Other Start-Up Costs

TOTAL

COMMENTS

- A rough estimate of requirements for manufacturing and/or staff, operations, facilities, including the following:

    —An assessment of the major difficulties for such items as equipment, labor skills and training, and quality standards in the manufacture of your product(s) or the delivery of your service(s):

—An estimate of the number of people who will be required to launch the business and the key tasks they will perform:

—An assessment of how you will deal with these difficulties and your estimate of the time and money needed to resolve them and begin scalable production:

- An identification of the cash flow and cash conversion cycle for your business over the first 15 months (including a consideration of leads/lags in getting sales, producing your product or service, delivering your product or service, and billing and collecting cash). Show as a bar chart the timing and duration of each activity here:

Cash Flow, Conversion Cycle, and Timing of Key Operational Activities

Development of
forecasts

Manufacturing

Sales orders

Billing:

   Invoice

   Collect

Selling season

     1   2   3   4   5   6   7   8   9   10   11   12   13   14   15

Months

- A preliminary, estimated cash flow statement for the first year, including considerations of resources needed for start-up and your cash conversion cycle:

- Estimates of (1) the total amount of asset and working capital needed in peak months and (2) the amount of money needed to reach positive cash flow, the amount of money needed to reach breakeven, and an indication of the months when each will occur:

- Create a break-even chart similar to the following:

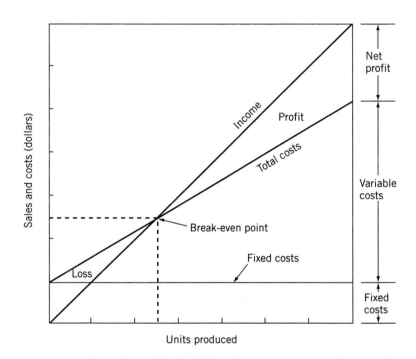

Units produced

To calculate the number of units required to breakeven: $ Selling price − Variable cost = $ Contribution margin/Unit fixed costs/$ Contribution margin = Units to breakeven

- An estimate of the capital required for asset additions and operating needs (and the months in which these will occur) to attain the sales level projected in five years:

Capital and Harvest— How Will You Realize Dollars from the Venture?

The amount and nature of capital requirements for launching a new venture must be articulated in the context of the needs of the resource provider(s). In this section you should purposefully link capital needs with the requirements of that provider(s). Specifically, the investor usually reaps a reward at harvest. The realistic timing and nature of the harvest will help define the logical investor or investors.

After reviewing both Chapter 5 and Chapter 14, think about your opportunity in the context of the capital markets food chain. Ask yourself the following questions:

Who is this opportunity for, and not for?

Who will, and will not, invest in this venture?

Who *should* invest?

Please provide the following:

- A statement of how you intend to raise capital, including all types (e.g., venture capital, financing raised through asset lenders, financing against inventory, receivables, equipment, and real estate), when, and from whom:

- A statement of whether you intend to harvest your venture, how and when this might occur, and the prospects. (If you do not intend to harvest the venture, include instead a statement of the prospects that profits will be both durable and large enough to be attractive.)

- An assessment of the sources of value, such as strategic, to another firm already in the market or one contemplating entry and an indication if there is a logical buyer(s) of your venture:

  —What do businesses similar to yours sell for as a multiple of sales, EBIT, cash flow, profits after taxes, and other metrics?

  —Who can help you find these answers?

- An assessment of how much it would take to liquidate the venture if you decided to exit and whether this is high:

Checkpoint

Reconsider if your venture opportunity is attractive. Beware of compromising on whether your opportunity has forgiving and rewarding economics. For example, are you convinced that the amount you need to raise is reasonable with respect to the venture's potential and risk? Are others convinced? If they are not, what do you know that they do not (and vice versa)? Most start-ups run out of cash before they secure enough profitable customers to sustain a positive cash flow. Your preliminary estimates of financial requirements need to be within the amount that an angel investor, venture capitalist, or other lender is willing to commit to a single venture or that you can personally raise. Even if your idea is not a candidate for venture capital financing, it is worth looking at your venture in this way.

Competitive Landscape—
Your Strategic Analysis

Every company has a competitor or substitute! Your customers were putting their money somewhere before you created your business. Look at both direct and indirect competitors. Who is the most knowledgeable person or competitor in this market? How does this affect you, your team, and your venture opportunity? Who can/should do this other than you? How do you become that person?

You may have acquired competitive information when you talked to potential customers in the customer contact research exercise (Exercise 5). Estimates and relative positions of the competitors are appropriate. When you have a relative understanding of the competitors, you should assess *your* position among these firms in terms of sustainable competitive advantages.

Please provide the following:

- An assessment of competitors in the market, including those selling substitute products:

Competitor No.	Name	Products/Services That Compete Directly	Substitutes

- A profile of the competition:

Competitor Profile

	Competitor No.			
	1	2	3	4
Estimated Sales/Year ($)				
Estimated Market Share (%)				
Description of Sales Force				

Marketing Tactics:

    Selling Terms

    Advertising/Promotion

    Distribution Channel

    Service/Training/Support

    Pricing

Major Strengths

Major Weaknesses

- A ranking of major competitors by market share:

No.	Competitor	Estimated Market Share

- A Robert Morris Associates statement study:

RMA Study

RMA Data for Period Ending	Estimates for Proposed Venture				
Asset Size	Under $250M	$250M to Less Than $1MM	$1MM to Less Than $10MM	$10MM to Less Than $50MM	All Sizes
Number of statements					
Assets	%	%	%	%	%
Cash					
Marketable securities					
Receivables net					
Inventory net					
All other current					
Total current					
Fixed assets net					
All other noncurrent					
Total					
Liabilities					
Due to banks—short-term					
Due to trade					
Income taxes					
Current maturities long-term debt					
All other current					
Total current debt					
Noncurrent debt, unsubordinated					
Total unsubordinated debt					
Subordinated debt					
Tangible net worth					
Total					
Income Data					
Net sales					
Cost of sales					
Gross profit					
All other expense net					
Profit before taxes					
Ratios					
Quick					
Current					
Fixed/worth					
Debt/worth					
Unsubordinated debt/capital funds					
Sales/receivables					
Cost sales/inventory					
Sales/working capital					
Sales/worth					
Percentage profit before taxes/worth					
Percentage profit before taxes/total assets					
Net sales/total asset					

M = thousand.
MM = million.

- An assessment of whether there are economies of scale in production and/or cost advantages in marketing and distribution:

- An assessment, for *each* competitor's product or service, of its costs and profitability:

Product/Service

Competitor Costs and Profitability			

Sales Price

Sales Level

For each:

	Dollars/Unit	Percentage of Sales Price/Unit
Production Costs (i.e., labor and material costs) or Purchase Costs		
Gross Margin		
Fixed Costs		
Profit before Taxes		
Profit after Taxes		

■ An assessment of the history and projections of competitors' profits and industry averages:

	Competitor Profits—Historical and Projected				
		Competitor			
	Industry Average	1	2	3	4
Profits (percentages of sales)					
Past Two Years					
Current Year					
Projected Next Two Years					
Sales/Employee					
Profits/Employee					

■ A ranking of competitors in terms of cost:

No.	Competitor

■ A profile for the current year of your competitors in terms of price and quality and of market share and profitability. Place competitors (using small circles identified by names) in the appropriate locations in the boxes here:

Array of Competitors

Highest

Price

Lowest

Last   *Quality*   Leader

Largest

Market Share

Smallest

Lowest   *Profitability*   Highest

- An assessment of the degree of control in the market (including that over prices, costs, and channels of distribution and by suppliers, buyers, etc.) and the extent to which you can influence these or will be subject to influence by others:

- An assessment of current lead times for changes in technology, capacity, product and market innovation, and so forth:

- An assessment of whether your venture will enjoy cost advantages or disadvantages in production and in marketing and distribution, and an indication of whether your venture will have the lowest, average, or highest costs of production, marketing, and distribution:

- An assessment of other competitive advantages that you have or can gain, how you would secure these, and what time and money are required, including the following:

  —An indication of whether your product or service will benefit from, or be subject to, any regulations and of the status of any copyrights, trade secrets, or patents or licenses and distribution or franchise agreements:

—An indication if you enjoy advantages in response and lead times for technology, capacity changes, product and market innovation, and so forth:

—An indication if you enjoy other unfair advantage, such as a strategic advantage, people advantage, resource advantage, location advantage, and so on:

—An assessment of whether you think you can be price competitive and make a profit, or other ways, such as product differentiation, in which you can compete:

- A ranking of your venture in terms of price and quality and of market share and profitability relative to your competitors. Add your venture to the Array of Competitors shown earlier:

- An assessment of whether any competitors enjoy competitive advantages, such as legal or contractual advantages:

- An assessment of whether any competitors are vulnerable, the time period of this vulnerability, and the impact on market structure of their succumbing to vulnerabilities:

Checkpoint

Do you have sufficient competitive advantage? Remember: A successful company sells to a market that is large and growing, where capturing a small market share can bring significant sales volume, where it does not face significant barriers to entry, and where its competition is profitable but not so strong as to be overwhelming. Further, a successful company has a product or service that solves significant problems that customers have with competitive products, such as poor quality, poor service, poor delivery, and the like, and a sales price that will enable it to penetrate the market.

Exercise 10
Founders' Commitment

For the team to conclude that the idea is truly an opportunity, the founders must assess the commitment of their partners. There are many aspects of commitment, including but not limited to trust, an understanding of and belief in responsibilities, financial contribution and extraction, and the overall belief in the team. Please provide the following:

- An assessment of your partners and/or management team:

  —An evaluation of whether the founders and/or the management team are sufficiently committed to the opportunity and how much they are personally willing to sacrifice, to invest in time, money, personal guarantees, and so forth:

  —An assessment of whether the founders and/or the management team possess the industry knowledge, experience, know-how, and skills required for the venture's success; if additional personnel are necessary and if these can be attracted to the venture; and if anyone on the team has managed previously what you are trying to undertake:

  —An assessment of whether the founders and/or management team have the necessary vision and entrepreneurial zest and whether they will be able to inspire this in others:

—An assessment of the level of trust felt among the founders and/or management team:

—A statement about who will do what—roles, responsibilities, and tasks:

—A statement about the contributions each founder and team member is expected to make:

—A statement about who will get what salary, what benefits, and what ownership share:

Checkpoint

Can do? Remember, the team is a primary force driving successful entrepreneurial ventures. It is important to question the assumptions on which your team has been shaped; for example, equal salaries and stock ownership can indicate that assumptions about tasks, roles, and responsibilities are naive. Someone on your team needs to be experienced and competent in the areas of team dynamics and management, or the team needs to be able to attract someone who is.

If you have completed Exercises 1 through 10 and reviewed each checkpoint, you should have a fairly good handle on whether your idea is an opportunity, and you will have completed most of the due diligence required to write a business plan. Completing the next two exercises will be very helpful as you build a strategy to launch time.

Flaws, Assumptions, and Downside Consequences—Risk Reconsidered

Assess whether your venture opportunity has any fatal flaws.

- List significant assumptions (assumptions about customer orders, sales projections, etc.), including the following:

  —A consideration of significant trade-offs that you have made:

  —A consideration of the major risks (unreliability of customer orders; overly optimistic sales projections; inability to achieve cost and time estimates; underestimating the magnitude, intensity, and vindictiveness of competitors' responses; etc.):

  —How far wrong can your revenue, cost, capital requirements, and time estimates be and still support a good business model?

- Rank assumptions according to importance:

- Evaluate the downside consequences, if any, when your assumptions are proved invalid; how severe the impact would be; and if and how these can be minimized, including the cost and consequences of (1) lost growth opportunities and (2) liquidation or bankruptcy to the company, to you, and to other stakeholders:

- Rate the risk of the venture as high, medium, or low:

Action Steps—Setting a Week-by-Week Schedule

List chronologically the 10 to 15 most critical actions you need to take during the next six months and the hurdles that need to be overcome to convert your idea into a real opportunity. It is a good idea to have another person review what you have listed and adjust the list, if warranted.

Date	Action

Make a week-by-week schedule of key tasks to be performed, when they are to be performed, and by whom. Break larger tasks into their smallest possible components. Be alert for conflicts.

Week No.	Task	Date Completed	Person Responsible

Checkpoint

It is important to take a hard look at the assumptions you have made, both implicit and explicit, and to assess the risk of the venture. Time and again, first-time entrepreneurs overestimate sales and delivery dates and underestimate costs, effort, and time required to execute the opportunity and to reach a positive cash flow. Also, while each new business has its risks and problems, as well as its opportunities, difficulties need to be identified as soon as possible so they can be avoided or eliminated or their impact minimized.

Four Anchors Revisited

Revisit Exercises 2 and 3.

A FINAL CHECKPOINT: Your responses to the VOSE will help you determine whether you want to continue with your venture and develop a completed business plan. If your venture has passed, a crucial question to consider before proceeding is, What do I want to get out of the business? You will want to think twice about whether the venture provides a strong fit with your personal goals, values, and needs; is what gives you energy; and leads you down the path you want to be on and to further and even better opportunities. Remember: You are what you do. If you have been able to complete all the exercises, you are satisfied that most of the results are positive, and the answers to the personal issues are yes (see the *Personal Entrepreneural Strategy* exercise in Chapter 2), then go for it!

After completing all the previous exercises, you should have a much sharper sense of the extent to which your good idea exhibits the four anchors described at the beginning of the chapter. Also ask yourself, Who are the one or two *best* people on the planet to answer the following questions, and what is their effect on me, my team, and this opportunity?

As you continue to work on your business you need to constantly consider the following questions because creative insights that can make a significant difference can occur at any time:

1. How can the value proposition be enhanced and improved?
2. What can be changed, added, modified, or eliminated to improve the *fit?*
3. What can be done to improve the value chain and the free cash flow characteristics?
4. What can be done to enhance the risk–reward balance?

Case

Globant

Preparation Questions

1. Discuss the nature of the challenge the team faces as they seek to build a global company. What are the strengths and weaknesses of their model?

2. Describe the sales cycle in offshore IT services. What differentiating factors should the Globant team focus on?

3. What industry segment(s) present the best opportunity for the Globant team, and why?

Martin Migoya set aside his copy of *La Nación*, a popular newspaper in Buenos Aires. Globant, a growing enterprise that he cofounded with CTO Guibert Engleibenne four years earlier, was now making business headlines as the largest independent information technology (IT) outsourcer in Argentina.

Migoya looked out over the vast Rio de la Plata shimmering in the morning sun. It was nice to be home, even if only for a short while. As CEO, it seemed he was always somewhere else or on the way there: London, Boston, Dallas, Dubai, Madrid. . . . Since the beginning, he and his partners had fueled sales by tapping their personal networks and by successfully following up on every lead and referral that had come their way. Those efforts had certainly paid off. With 600 employees and monthly revenue approaching $1 million, Globant appeared to be well on its way to becoming a world-class brand in a huge and growing market. That was the good news.

The downside was that by late 2007, Globant's sustained push for wins had produced a broadly diversified portfolio of clients and service offerings. This presented a significant challenge; increasingly tier one prospects were choosing IT service partners that could demonstrate a deep and wide understanding of their particular industries. In addition, the Argentina advantage—an educated talent pool, competitive wage economics, and time zone favorability for serving Europe and the Americas—had begun to attract a host of foreign competitors.

It was now clear that unless Globant developed a more focused and tactical approach to business development, it would become at best a marginalized player. Migoya was determined to avoid that fate. He glanced at his watch, then spun around to power off his laptop. He had a plane to catch.

We are most grateful to Professor Silvia Torres Carbonell, at IAE Business School, Universidad Austral in Buenos Aires, Argentina, for contributing this case—originally developed by four MIT Sloan School MBA candidates doing a study abroad session at IAE in 2006. They are Shingo Murakami, Roger Premo, Ina Trantcheva, and Erik Yeager. The case has been revised and updated by both Professor Carbonelli and Carl Hedberg.

Global Philosophy, Local Talent

Globant was founded in 2003 by four engineers (see Exhibit 1) who took note of the astonishing growth of the IT outsourcing industry in India. Inspired, they left their jobs at multinationals to start their own enterprise based on a simple strategy: Recruit the best local talent and deliver high-quality solutions while ensuring superb customer service.

In 2004, their suspicions were confirmed in a *Wall Street Journal* article about IT outsourcing:

> *Latin America comes out ahead of India and China in the offshoring equation when factors like labor quality, labor supply, and time zone differences are taken into account.*

One early challenge they faced was that there seemed to be a general lack of knowledge about their country among many potential clients. In addition, fears of criminal activity and political instability (realities of the past) often required a bit of explaining.

The partners sought to offer a portfolio of services that encompassed three phases of a software product's life cycle: software development services (from conception to final quality assurance); 24/7 infrastructure management; and globalization, including Internet marketing and design (see Exhibit 2). Globant COO Martin Umaran explained another important aspect of Globant's differentiation tactics:

> We place an emphasis on supporting and contributing to open source technologies for NET and Java applications and by utilizing agile development methodologies.[1] This working structure simplifies the implementation of solutions because it gives us the ability to be in constant contact with our clients anywhere in the world, and to stay alert to their changing needs and requirements.

By offering talented workers the chance to grow professionally without moving abroad or joining a multinational, Globant became a magnet for the best and brightest from all over the country, who thrived on the global aspects of the assignments.[2] From the beginning, the Globant culture was very close-knit and informal, and the company enjoyed a below industry average employee turnover rate of about 8 percent. Umaran said that he and his partners

---

[1] *Agile software development* was a conceptual framework for software engineering that promoted development iterations throughout the life cycle of the project.

[2] One recruiting advantage for the best local talent was that the company had received awards and recognitions from prestigious institutions, including *Global Services* magazine, *Endeavor* (Globant founders were selected as Endeavor Entrepreneurs in 2005), ExportAr, and the local journal *La Nación*.

EXHIBIT 1

Management Team Biographies

Martin Migoya, CEO

Martin has extensive experience in business management, sales, and marketing. As Globant's CEO, his focus is to drive revenue, objectives, and profitability. He oversees the company's long-term objectives, planning, and analysis. Prior to cofounding Globant, Martin was director of business development and Latin America's regional business manager at a large consulting and technology services company, developing the IT and Enterprise Resource Planning (ERP) markets in Brazil and Argentina. He was instrumental in managing and developing high-technology businesses related to SAP and the Internet, with customers like Procter & Gamble, Renault, and Roemmers Laboratories. Previously Martín worked as project manager for REPSOL–YPF, Argentina's largest oil and gas company. Martin has lived and worked in Argentina, Brazil, Mexico, and the U.K. He holds a degree in electronic engineering from La Plata University and a masters degree in business administration from CEMA University.

Guibert Englebienne, CTO

Guibert has extensive experience in the information technology and communication industries. As Globant's CTO, Guibert is in charge of the software production process and the creation and management of strategic company technology partnerships. Prior to cofounding Globant, Guibert was a scientific researcher at IBM and later the CTO for CallNow.com Inc., a telecommunications company based in New York providing international callback services through the Internet. He also conceived and developed a U.S.-patented technology powering a service named 2Speak, using the Internet to anonymously connect two parties through phone lines. Guibert was responsible for the phone chat implementation in Chinadotcom Co., owner of the biggest Asian Internet portals. He has also worked as an IT development manager outlining and developing software for tax collection through Internet governmental portals. Guibert has lived and worked in Argentina, the United States, Venezuela, and the U.K. He holds a degree in computer science and software engineering from UNICEN University.

Martin Umaran, COO

Martin has extensive experience in executive and business management for technology industries. As Globant's COO, Martin is responsible for the delivery of products and professional services and is actively involved in capacity growth and process initiatives. Prior to cofounding Globant, Martin was CEO for Neuwagen, a company focused on selling cars to Caja de Ahorro y Seguro's customers (Argentina's largest insurance company). He also worked at several technology companies as senior business manager. At Santander Bank he was responsible for Customer Relationship Management (CRM) implementation. He also negotiated, implemented, and operated a state-of-the-art tax collection system in several Venezuelan cities. At YPF Ecuador Martin worked as a manager of facilities automation and maintenance. He also worked at Roman Logistics, where he managed several projects for the Argentinean offices of Ford, GM, and Unilever. Martin has lived and worked in Argentina, Ecuador, Venezuela, and the U.K. He holds a degree in mechanical engineering from La Plata University and a masters in business administration from IDEA University.

Nestor Nocetti, VP of Corporate Services

Nestor has a considerable amount of experience in the information technology industry, in both operational and advisory roles. As Globant's VP of corporate services, Nestor is in charge of determining the structure for business consolidation and expansion, aligned with the corporate objectives and vision. Prior to cofounding Globant, Nestor worked as Internet manager in an Argentinean information technology company, where he specialized in Internet marketing and Web portals localization with customers like EMC, a world leader in information storage, and Techint, an engineering and procurement services provider. He also worked on several projects related to geographic information systems for Light Rio de Janeiro, electricity provider in Brazil, and UTE, a public electricity provider in Uruguay. He worked as a consultant on issues related to IT development, strategy, and operations in the oil and gas market for ENAP Chile and YPF Argentina. Nestor has lived and worked in Argentina, Chile, and Brazil. He holds a degree in electronic engineering from La Plata University and a degree in business direction from IAE University.

---

believed that the way to obtain excellent results as a company was with a perfect mix of hard work and fun:

> For us to rise as the best choice, for both our clients and employees, we have instituted some creative ideas. All of our development centers are built to be an enjoyable place of work that stimulates creativity. We have chill-out rooms, different games, brainstorming rooms, and excellent food.

To maintain this culture, human resources focused on three distinct areas. *People care* was oriented toward implementing programs to maximize personnel benefits and improve the work environment, including massages, yoga lessons, personal trainers, sports tournaments, and a gym. *Career and talent development* took care of employees' professional growth by offering training plans, courses, and mentoring programs. *Staffing and recruiting* focused on locating and bringing in new talent.

To overcome language barriers, Globant required every employee to master a business level of English proficiency—and offered free English lessons to help them get there. Globant hired a wide variety of backgrounds and technological skill sets, and employees' knowledge domains differed across platforms (Linux, Unix, and Windows), technologies (such as Java, NET, LAMP, and Oracle), system administration experience, and application design work. COO Umaran commented on the advantages of being able to provide any skill set a client might

EXHIBIT 2

Globant's Service Offerings

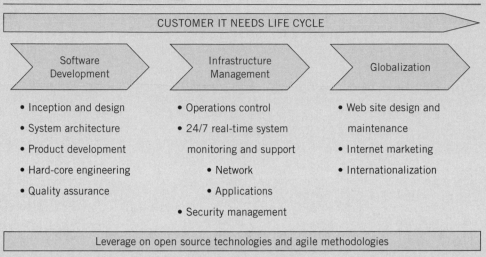

CUSTOMER IT NEEDS LIFE CYCLE

Software Development	Infrastructure Management	Globalization
• Inception and design	• Operations control	• Web site design and
• System architecture	• 24/7 real-time system	maintenance
• Product development	monitoring and support	• Internet marketing
• Hard-core engineering	• Network	• Internationalization
• Quality assurance	• Applications	
	• Security management	

Leverage on open source technologies and agile methodologies

request, as well as being able to attract talent with industry-specific expertise:

> Having the technical skills in-house helps us ensure a consistent quality of fulfillment, and we believe that superior service is the ultimate determinant of success with our clients. To increase awareness with potential customers, we're leveraging our growing reputation with an effective word-of-mouth marketing and referral campaign. When we get referrals from satisfied customers, they typically mention ease of communication, high levels of service, and our strong management ethic.

In addition, the team knew that direct contact with clients would be the most effective means of conveying their professional spirit, dedication, and philosophy to potential clients.

The IT Outsourcing Industry

IT outsourcing began in the early 1990s with the advent of the Internet and the vastly improved forms of communication that came with it. Initially companies were motivated by the desire to build commercially viable portals and by the need to prepare their IT systems for the Y2K changeover at the start of the new century. Since few U.S. companies had the internal capabilities to effectively address either of these issues, many began to outsource to a growing pool of domestic firms created specifically to provide these services.

Seeing this rise of domestic IT outsourcing in the United States, the Indian government seized the opportunity. Leveraging its already robust telecom infrastructure, and tapping into a growing dual base of technology professionals and low-cost labor, India was able to quickly establish a leadership position in the field of IT outsourcing.

EXHIBIT 3

U.S. IT and IT Outsourcing Spending

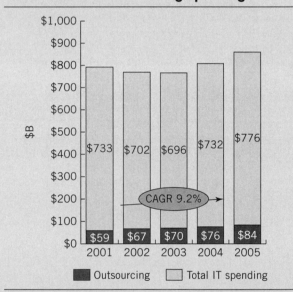

Source: Forrester Research.

Although IT spending had fluctuated over the years, by 2005 the IT outsourcing market in the United States had grown to $84 billion (see Exhibit 3). Many industries were now using offshore IT partners, including U.S. software and IT services firms. That segment was expected to increase its offshore spending to nearly $40 billion in five years (see Exhibit 4).

There were a number of reasons why firms chose to establish outsourcing relationships (see Exhibit 5). The three most critical were cost and time savings, access to expertise not available internally, and the ability to refocus on core business functions. Developing countries

EXHIBIT 4

U.S. Software and IT Services Offshore Spending

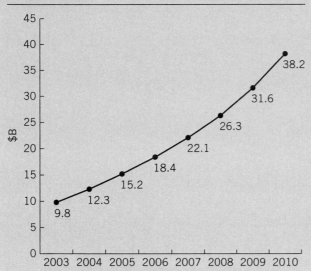

$B

38.2
31.6
26.3
22.1
18.4
15.2
12.3
9.8

2003 2004 2005 2006 2007 2008 2009 2010

Source: Global Insight.

offered the best opportunity for cost and time savings due to their low cost of labor; although depending on the scope and complexity of the undertaking, specialized skills and expertise could be found in the United States and nearby in Canada and Mexico, as well as overseas. Overall, firms were looking to offload areas

EXHIBIT 5

Reasons Firms Gave for Outsourcing Their IT Needs

Most Important

- Cost savings
- Access to outside expertise
- Improve focus on company's core business

Important

- Improve service
- Access to better technology
- Time savings

Somewhat Important

- Share risks
- Make capital funds available
- Cash infusion

of work that were not central to their business models. This allowed them to maximize their efforts in areas where they could best differentiate themselves.

The three most important of many factors that companies considered when evaluating outsourcing vendors were overall capabilities, total cost, and ease of communication (see Exhibit 6). Referrals were often a critical aspect of the due diligence done to evaluate potential outsourcing partners.

EXHIBIT 6

Selection Criteria for Choosing an Outsourcing Vendor

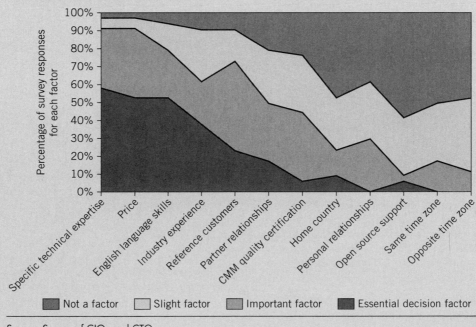

Percentage of survey responses for each factor

Specific technical expertise, Price, English language skills, Industry experience, Reference customers, Partner relationships, CMM quality certification, Home country, Personal relationships, Open source support, Same time zone, Opposite time zone

■ Not a factor   □ Slight factor   ▨ Important factor   ■ Essential decision factor

Source: Survey of CIOs and CTOs.

EXHIBIT 7

Reasons for IT Outsourcing Project Success and Failure

Importance	Success Factors	Challenges
High	• Ongoing management • Well-defined processes • Contract with clear goals and metrics	• Problems managing remote vendor team • Loss of control • Vendor team performance
Medium	• Work closely with vendor • Proper vendor selection • Communication	• Language and cultural barriers • Poor planning • Unclear contracts
Low	• Identify the details • Many releases • Simplicity	• Provider turnover • Accountability • Unforeseen expenses

The Competitive Challenge

The IT outsourcing industry had matured by 2006; and because the majority of companies reported having at least some experience managing outsourcing relationships, there was a catalog of knowledge about success factors and challenges with outsourcing projects (see Exhibit 7). Outsourcing vendors needed to prove that they were equipped to work closely with their clients and had a strong process in place to manage those projects. Migoya noted that the competition was fierce and growing across all sectors:

> There are many thousands of IT outsourcing companies in the world. In the United States there are giants like IBM and EDS, and in India it's firms like Infosys and WiPro. There are lots of smaller, regional companies that compete on various attributes [such as] cost, speed, size, geographic proximity, cultural fit, industry expertise, and functional expertise. Differentiation is very difficult given the sheer size of the industry and because there are usually several similar companies for any particular specialty or segment.

Firms seeking IT outsource vendors often looked first at the region (see Exhibit 8). As one of the oldest and most popular outsourcing destinations, India had built a strong reputation and had the most experience and largest number of existing relationships and reference customers. However, by the mid-2000s India had begun to experience staffing limitations. China and Southeast Asia had the lowest labor costs and large, growing labor pools, but these countires found it difficult to provide a cultural fit with Western companies. Migoya said that Latin America was in a better competitive position:

> We can offer low costs, geographic proximity, and cultural ties to the United States. Eastern Europe has low costs, but they are a better fit with Western Europe than

EXHIBIT 8

Representative Salaries and Hourly Rates for IT Outsourcers across the Globe

Country	Programmer Annual Salary	Hourly Rates
Ireland	$23,000–$36,000	$40–$80
Canada	$20,000–$40,000	$40–$80
Singapore	$9,000–$20,000	$30–$60
Mexico	$7,000–$12,000	$20–$35
Russia	$5,000–$9,000	$20–$40
India	$5,000–$9,000	$20–$40
Philippines	$5,000–$9,000	$20–$40
Vietnam	$3,000–$6,000	$15–$25
China	$3,000–$7,000	$15–$25

Source: Meta Group.

with the United States. Business culture and language skills are important to American firms. Sometimes they outsource to Canada or to the lower-cost Midwestern states. The cost benefits in these regions aren't as high as going overseas, but the business fit is ideal.

Globant faced a number of direct competitors, many with North American sales offices in the vicinity of Globant's office in Massachusetts (see Exhibit 9). CTO Englebienne described a few entrenched competitors they could expect to go up against:

> Tata Consulting Services [TCS] in Mumbai [India] was founded in 1968. They are the largest outsourcer in India, and they service all types of businesses. Last year [2006], 60 percent of their $4.3 billion in total revenues come from the U.S. market. TCS went public on the Bombay stock exchange in 2004, and they've got over 90,000 employees. With global development centers in

EXHIBIT 9

Descriptions of Various IT Outsourcing Companies

Company	Location(s)	Estimated Staff (Onshore–Offshore) Revenue	Services	Model	Client Types
StarSoft	San Francisco, CA St. Petersburg, Russian Federation Dnepopetrovsk, Ukraine	400 (NA–NA) $10.5M (2005)	Custom, maintenance, R&D, internationalization	Heavy offshore, ODC*	Corp. IT, IT services, ISVs**
SoftServe	Fort Myers, FL Lviv, Ukraine	450 (7–443) $6.5M est. (2005)	R&D, QA, maintenance, minimal corp. IT	Heavy offshore	ISVs, small to midsize
Lohika	San Bruno, CA Lviv, Ukraine Odessa, Ukraine	120 (15–105) $3.5M est. (2005)	ISV, R&D, including embedded SW	Hybrid, U.S.: system architects	ISVs, hardware/ device
Virtusa	West borough, MA U.K. Chennai, India Sri Lanka	1,800 (200–1,600 est.) $50–100m est.	Corp. IT, ISVs, maintenance, QA	Hybrid, leveraging offshore resources onsite (50+ H1s!)	Fortune 1,000, small->midsize ISVs, technology cos.
Patni Cambridge, MA	24 sales offices 8 offshore locations	11,000 $326M (2004)	IT, IT management, BPO***, R&D	Full IT services, hybrid model	Corporate IT, technology cos.
Sonata Software	7 sales offices 4 offshore locations in India	1,100 $77M	ISV, enterprise/corp. IT, embedded	Full IT services, hybrid model	Corp. IT, ISVs
E5 Systems	Reston, VA China India	NA	IT outsourcing	Heavy offshore	Corp. IT
Foliage	Burlington, MA India (partners)	150 (150–?) $30M est.	Consulting, systems development	Heavy onshore— "offshore ready"	Corp. clients, embedded systems
Array Software	Agawam, MA Partners: India, Russia, Ukraine	150 (20–130) $15M est.	Software maintenance	Hybrid, with offshore partners subcontracted	Technology cos.

*ODC: offshore development center.
**ISV: independent software vendor.
***BPO: business process outsourcing.
Source: Mark Kapij, MIT Sloan Fellow.

both Uruguay and Brazil, they are definitely someone we're watching closely.

Infosys was founded by a group of software professionals in Pune, India [in 1981]. The company is based in Bangalore and listed on the NASDAQ stock exchange. They've won many awards as the top IT firm in India. They have 80,000 employees and over $3 billion in revenues; they're about the same size as TCS, but considered to be a slightly more upscale firm. As with TCS, Infosys preferred to offer IT solutions across all industries. Infosys has no presence in Latin America [in 2007].

Luxoft in Eastern Europe is Russia's largest IT services firm. They started up in 2000, and they have about 1,400 employees and revenues of about $37 million. They're privately held, and they focus on four industries: IT/telecom, discrete manufacturing, financial services,

and software/product development. The company doesn't appear to have any plans to enter Latin America anytime soon, but they do a good job in the European marketplace.

Accenture [formerly Anderson Consulting] was formed in 1989. They're based in Chicago and have revenues of $19.7 billion and over 170,000 employees. Accenture dwarfs pretty much every one of its international competitors, especially because they often sell their IT outsourcing services together with their management consulting services. That is something that would be difficult for companies in developing countries to provide. They cover many industries, and they have offices all across Latin America, but they are considerably higher-priced than most other offshore vendors.

In addition to the challenge of competing on the basis of talent and proximity, Globant VP of North America Sales and Operations Daniel Kuperstein[3] noted that Globant also faced deep-rooted competitors:

Many of the most lucrative prospects out there already have long-standing [5- to 7-year] relationships with offshore partners. Those relationships represent a good deal of invested time and resources and can be an extremely difficult barrier to sales. Their current outsourcers are privy to confidential information and are usually engaged in important ongoing projects. A CTO of a Northeastern telco told me, "I've been working with my vendor for eight years. They satisfy our needs; I'm sorry, but I'm not looking for a new partner."

That said, a former VP of sales for an Eastern European outsourcing firm observed, "Many outsourcing relationships with multinationals have problems—find a way to identify and alleviate those problems, and you're starting out on common ground." In addition, many large firms that already had partners were looking to diversify their geopolitical risk by "multisourcing" in different geographic regions.

While small-to midsized businesses represented a very large and available pool of prospects, the individual contracts were smaller, and the relationships were typically not as valuable long-term as ones established with large global businesses.

Selecting a Target Market

As Globant entered a period of rapid growth in numerous segments, the team became concerned that the company could end up spreading itself too thin (see Exhibit 10). Geographically, they decided to focus on U.S. markets where Globant had established a base of existing customers. The plan was to begin on the East and West coasts and in Texas, using references to expand from there. A market size analysis indicated that the total addressable market

EXHIBIT 10

Sample List of Customers

High-Tech	EMC, Dell, Accenture, Sun
Telecom	Arbinet, 2speak
Travel	lastminute.com, Travelocity, Sabre, OAG
Financial Services	Citibank, Grupo Santander
Media	Google, Scottish TV, Sky

[3]Hired in 2006, Daniel was the former director of globalization for EMC, the largest information storage and management firm in the world. One of his key people in North America was Guillermo Marsicovetere, a former sales and clients solutions director for Sun Microsystems UK, who took up the position of Globant's VP for business development units.

within that targeted geography—focused on companies with annual revenues of $100 million to $1 billion—was approximately $2.6 billion (see Exhibit 11).

Agreeing that they needed to target specific industries as well as geographic regions, the management team selected four industries based on past experience, current clients, and their project expertise: high-tech, travel, telecom, and financial services. A more difficult task would be understanding the needs of each industry they were targeting.

Industry Review: High-Tech

With Globant's first and most consistent client being EMC, the high-tech sector appeared to be an obvious industry to target. Geographically, Globant understood that California represented about 30 percent of the high-tech market and contained many of the big-name companies that would provide the most value as reference customers. In terms of segments, high-tech manufacturing and computer peripheral companies were the most product-focused, followed by prepackaged software, data processing and preparation, and IT service companies themselves (see Exhibit 12).

High-tech manufacturing was concerned with squeezing every penny possible out of its operations. Because this included IT spending, firms in this subsegment were very willing to explore low-cost IT outsourcing relationships. Their largest areas of IT spending occurred around data analysis, IT cost containment, compliance, and manufacturing operations. Due to economies of scale, there were relatively few small to midsized manufacturing firms. For most of the larger firms the greatest outsourcing need was for customization expertise in packaged software such as SAP and Oracle.

Prepackaged software was unique in its IT outsourcing needs because not only would firms in this subsegment outsource their IT functions but approximately 80 percent of these companies outsourced pieces of their application and product development as well. Among all high-tech subsegments, prepackaged software had the most interest in large-scale outsourcing arrangements. The segment also had a strong interest in using open source technologies. Areas of focus included implementing service-oriented architecture (SOA), software as a service (SaaS), application development, and specialized IT services.

Data processing and preparation firms spent the largest percentage of their revenue on IT, averaging between 6 and 20 percent. However, due to sensitive data and proprietary software, these firms were often hesitant to outsource and were even more reluctant to engage offshore firms. When they did outsource, projects were usually discrete and short-term. The most common areas of outsourcing in this subsegment were quality assurance for applications,

EXHIBIT 11

Potential Market Size (East Coast and Texas)

	Number of target companies	Total sales amount	Market for outsourcing
Travel/leisure	174	$51,850M	$149M
Telecom	229	$66,782M	$493M
High-tech	343	$94,843M	$387M
Retail	766	$210,759M	$286M
Finance	747	$222,921M	$1,348M
			Total $2,663M

U.S. Market Segmentation by Number of Subsidiary Companies

	East Coast	Texas	Rest of United States
High-Tech	295 (40%)	48 (6%)	396 (54%)
Telecom	195 (55%)	33 (9%)	125 (35%)
Financial Services	636 (44%)	111 (8%)	705 (49%)
Travel	151 (43%)	23 (7%)	186 (53%)

U.S. Market for Outsourcing (in Millions)

	East Coast	Texas
High-Tech	$372	$56
Telecom	$471	$77
Financial Services	$1,227	$202
Travel	$139	$25

IT support, data collection and analysis, and large mainframe applications.

IT service companies were found to be the least likely to outsource, spending less than 2 percent of their budget on IT. They were known to engage another outsourcing company to serve as a "body shop" partner for low-cost labor or as a way of making their own consultants more productive with arrangements involving voice over IP (VOIP) and security solutions for mobility.

Industry Review: Travel

Globant had built up considerable knowledge in the travel industry working with two of its largest clients, OAG and lastminute.com. CTO Englebienne observed that the travel industry had undergone a tremendous shift in recent years toward online commerce:

For travel research and booking, the Internet customers value the convenience, speed, and easy access to competitive pricing and itinerary choices. [By 2005], 78 percent of all travelers had gone online for trip planning; that's up from 65 percent in 2004. This segment has an 11 percent growth rate, and by 2009 the online travel market is forecast to become a $91 billion industry [from $51 billion in 2004].

Travel is now the leading and fastest-growing category of e-commerce [accounting for over 45 percent of all online sales]. Although offshoring is still a relatively new idea in the travel industry, most lead players have already had successful experiences with it.

The industry structure consisted of suppliers (such as the airlines, hotels, and car rentals), agents and global distribution system (GDS) operators (such as Amadeus, Sabre, Expedia.com, and lastminute.com), and Web portals (such as Yahoo! and AOL) (see Exhibit 13). Although

EXHIBIT 12

Outsourcing Trends in the High-Tech Industries

Subsegment	IT Focus
High-tech manufacturing	• Better utilization and analysis of data • IT cost containment • Compliance • Lean manufacturing processes
Prepackaged software	• Building in SOA to all applications • Specific IT services requiring specialized knowledge (e.g., firewall maintenance) • Application development • SaaS for noncore activities—HR/payroll, recruiting, professional services automation • Further refine business process IT • Infrastructure support (including help desk) • Business analytics (how to evaluate implementations of software packages)
Data processing and preparation	• QA for applications • IT development and support • Further refine automation for data collection and analysis • Upgrade and retire legacy applications • 24/7 data collection and analysis • Large mainframe applications
IT services	• Web development • VOIP and other "distance-killing" applications for mobile workers • Infrastructure management • Mainly sales and HR applications • Security for mobile workers • Programming services during projects—low rates, body shop

EXHIBIT 13

Travel Industry Structure: Major Players

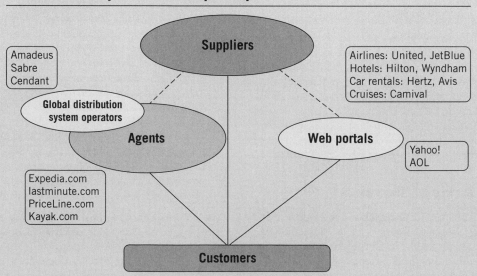

suppliers had traditionally relied on their agents and GDS operators to reach end users, airlines were now competing with agents, GDS operators, and Web portals for market share based on Web site features and user content. Fueling interest in outsourcing was the growing need for travel Web sites to cut costs and differentiate themselves through innovative technologies, breadth of functionality, and international capabilities.

The most common services being outsourced in 2007 were business processes, Web hosting, and technology solutions that included custom product development, online booking engines, pricing tools, back office automation, and 24/7 operations and support. Internet marketing was also yielding important benefits by reducing distribution costs and by enabling ongoing targeted dialog that improved customer loyalty.

Industry Review: Telecom

Having worked as an executive for a New York–based telecommunications company, CTO Englebienne had extensive experience in this sector. He offered this:

> Until recently, global telecoms were internally focused on reducing the huge debt burden they had built up in the 1990s with acquisitions, mergers, and infrastructure investments. As the winners get back into profitability, they are revamping their existing systems and evaluating their IT needs. Over the next five years, the offshoring growth rate in this sector is expected to be between 32 and 50 percent.

Historically Indian outsourcers had been the most popular offshoring destination for telecoms, and by 2007 large companies such as Wipro and Infosys had accrued a significant amount of knowledge and expertise in this field. There were also a lot of smaller but very experienced outsourcing firms competing for the offshore business of small and midsized companies that were under the radar of these big Indian outsourcers. A CIO of a midsized teleco offered this comment:

> Given the large number of outsourcers out there, expertise in both telecom and the specific technology we are using is a strong prerequisite for selecting an outsourcing vendor. Anyone lacking both pieces would not even be considered as a potential partner.

Industry Review: Financial Services

Because COO Umaran had experience overseeing managed IT implementation products in the financial services (FS) industry, the team was also looking at this sector. This industry was a leading consumer of IT services: 90 percent of firms were outsourcing to some degree, and a well-known research group estimated that spending on outsourcing would grow 4.2 percent CAGR through 2009.

The midsized market included retail bankers, brokerage firms, mortgage bankers, and investment advisory businesses. Retail banking, which included credit unions and regional and local banks, was by far the most numerous subsegment. Competition in this segment was fierce; customer acquisition and retention were driven by new offerings and innovations. Retail banks also sought to offer new products to their customers as a means of gaining a greater share of the banking spend (wallet share). Many of the new products, such as online banking, mobile banking, and electronic billing, were technology-based; and there was great heterogeneity in the degree to which retail banks used outsourcing, the types of technologies they deployed, and the types of customer needs they sought to address.

Umaran described some areas of interest:

> Data security is a huge issue. For competitive, regulatory, and operational reasons, it is essential to maintain system and data integrity. This has often been a hindrance to offshore infrastructure management, but not necessarily to application development. Also, some firms have come up with sophisticated means of maintaining their required level of security within the framework of outsourced relationships.
>
> Legacy systems are a big issue as well. Some of the core banking and trading applications for [financial services] customers are over 30 years old. The process of transitioning these archaic systems onto a modern platform is a complex, risky, and expensive undertaking. Expertise in both the legacy systems code [normally COBOL] and modern platforms [J2EE, for example] is needed, as well as understanding the business drivers for the new systems.

The build versus buy decision was more pertinent in the midsized segment. While larger firms had the scale to build their own applications, many smaller FS firms were purchasing third-party software to handle core banking, trading, online presence, and other functions. Although the use of commercial software was known to be widespread, the actual penetration was unknown.

Making the Sale

The selection of IT outsourcing vendors involved either an RFP (Request for Proposal) sent to several potential vendors or a direct request for a proposal based on a previous working relationship, reputation, or a referral. The vetting process would typically include live demonstrations, reference checks, and pilot engagements. Migoya described Globant's current strategy:

> From the beginning, we've pursued new contracts by networking, and we haven't faced a lot of competitive bidding situations. For instance, our European client

lastminute.com came to us by way of one of their previous clients. We continue to benefit greatly from consistently excellent referrals and informal networking like that, but we do recognize the need to develop a more systematic approach to selling.

There were two types of businesses that differed in their use of technology—technology creators (companies that used technology as a competitive advantage) and technology consumers. Given Globant's software development expertise, the team felt that companies defined as the technology creators would benefit more from Globant's services. They also saw their expertise with open source architecture as another strong technology differentiator. Other possible targets included multinationals with offices in Argentina and companies that were advertising online to hire IT engineers.

As the CIO of a software company noted, in the outsourcing business, cold calling was not an effective tactic:

I receive about 10 cold calls a day from various IT outsourcers. If the vendor can't give me some differentiating offer—specific technology or industry expertise—and be able to articulate that within five seconds, I hang up the phone. New entrants need to come up with better ways of connecting with potential customers and expanding their visibility.

Setting the Best Course

As his plane banked a slow turn due north, Migoya was given an expansive view of his vibrant home city. He looked out in the direction of the Globant offices. Their company was one of the fastest-growing independent offshore companies in Latin America, and the largest in Argentina. Revenues were projected to exceed $22 million in 2007, and their client base now spanned across the United States and Western Europe and included five different industries.

As he sat back for the long flight, Migoya recalled what he'd told a colleague earlier that morning:

Major competitors are now moving to set up satellites in Argentina, and sustaining momentum like we have is going to require more than skilled workers, an excellent service record, great referrals, and a favorable home base.

Right now we need to narrow down and prioritize the potential pool of clients out there and develop a more structured approach to business development. We've already taken steps to professionalize our selling efforts with training programs and key hires—especially in North America—and we've hired additional talent to establish the makings of a solid sales organization. What we need now is a focused plan.

Chapter Seven

Opportunities for Social Entrepreneurship

Social entrepreneurs are not content just to give a fish, or teach how to fish. They will not rest until they have revolutionized the fishing industry.

Bill Drayton, CEO and
founder of Ashoka
(http://ashoka.org)

Results Expected

After reading this chapter, you will be able to

1. Explain how social entrepreneurship is both similar to and different from traditional entrepreneurship.
2. Offer a definition of social entrepreneurship that encompasses social ventures and enterprising nonprofits.
3. Apply the Timmons Model of entrepreneurship to the social entrepreneurship context.
4. Discuss how the concept of adding value relates to socially focused organizations.
5. Evaluate and discuss the Northwest Community Ventures case.

What Is Social Entrepreneurship?

Social entrepreneurship has become a global movement —a movement with a goal to effect positive social change. On the surface we know social entrepreneurship is a good thing, but on further study it becomes quite apparent that social entrepreneurship is a complicated phenomenon and difficult to define. This leads to a perception of nebulous boundaries. Such ill-defined boundaries have led some to argue that *all* entrepreneurship is social, or any differences between social and the more traditional commercial entrepreneurship are neither well articulated nor understood. Some view social entrepreneurship purely as a form of entrepreneurship in nonprofit sectors. For example, a pundit in a large foundation questioned whether social entrepreneurs can even become economic entrepreneurs.[1] Such either/or thinking creates false boundaries and a perception that entrepreneurs have to choose between social and economic impact. As you will see from examples in this chapter, the reality is that social entrepreneurs can do both. Social entrepreneurship encompasses for-profit and not-for-profit ventures.

We are extremely grateful to Professor Heidi Neck of Babson College for this pioneering contribution to the edition, as well as David Boss, Heidi's able MBA research assistant, for his data collection efforts. Heidi's research and curriculum development in this area have advanced much of our thinking at Babson and for the book.

[1] http://www.philanthropy.com/free/update/2007/04/2007042301.htm.

EXHIBIT 7.1

Popular Definitions of Social Entrepreneurship (or Social Entrepreneur)

Definition	Author
Social entrepreneurs play the role of change agents in the social sector by (1) adopting a mission to create and sustain social value (not just private value); (2) recognizing and relentlessly pursuing new opportunities to serve that mission; (3) engaging in a process of continuous innovation, adaptation, and learning; (4) acting boldly without being limited by resources currently in hand; and (5) exhibiting heightened accountability to the constituencies served and for the outcomes created.	Greg Dees, 1998[a]
[Social entrepreneurship is] a process involving the innovative use and combination of resources to pursue opportunities to catalyze social change and/or address social needs.	Johanna Mair and Ignasi Marti, 2006[b]
Innovative, social value–creating activity that can occur within or across the nonprofit, business, or government sectors.	James Austin, Howard Stevenson, and Jane Wei-Skillern, 2006[c]
A process that includes the identification of a specific social problem and a specific solution (or set of solutions) to address it; the evaluation of the social impact, the business model, and the sustainability of the venture; and the creation of a social mission–oriented for-profit or a business-oriented nonprofit entity that pursues the double (or triple) bottom line.	Jeffrey Robinson, 2006[d]
Social entrepreneurship is (1) about applying practical, innovative, and sustainable approaches to benefit society in general, with an emphasis on those who are marginalized and poor; (2) a term that captures a unique approach to economic and social problems—an approach that cuts across sectors and disciplines; (3) grounded in certain value and processes that are common to each social entrepreneur.	The Schwab Foundation for Social Entrepreneurship[e]

[a]"The Meaning of Social Entrepreneurship," p. 4; http://www.caseatduke.org/documents/dees_SE.pdf.

[b]"Social Entrepreneurship Research: A Source of Explanation, Prediction, and Delight," *Journal of World Business* 41, p. 37.

[c]"Social and Commercial Entrepreneurship: Same, Different, Both?" *Entrepreneurship Theory & Practice*, January 2006, p. 2.

[d]"Navigating Social and Institutional Barriers to Market: How Social Entrepreneurs Identify and Evaluate Opportunities," in J. Mair, J. Robinson, and K. Hockerts (eds.), *Social Entrepreneurship*, p. 95.

[e]http://www.schwabfound.org/whatis.htm.

As with any emerging area of intellectual and practical significance, it is important to have a guiding definition for the purpose of shared understanding and discussion. A guiding definition does not, however, imply a unifying definition. Social entrepreneurship, in theory and in practice, does not have a unifying, agreed-upon definition. Exhibit 7.1 offers a few of its most popular definitions. These definitions share a common theme: Their method and execution are entrepreneurial in thinking and action, while their mission and purpose are driven by social need and benefit.

Recently I was speaking to an audience of approximately 50 academics, consultants, and PhD students, all interested in social entrepreneurship education. I asked each participant to write his or her definition of social entrepreneurship on an index card. Naturally I received 50 unique definitions, but there were identifiable patterns or commonalities across all the submitted definitions. Participants wrote about identifying opportunities, creating systemic social change, developing sustainable solutions to social problems, and generating economic and social returns. A personal favorite referred to social entrepreneurship as using principles of entrepreneurship to create economically sustainable social value. Jeff Stamp, an assistant professor at the University of North Dakota, offered a thought-provoking perspective: "All ventures require investment; all ventures require return. The social question is who pays and what is the return horizon. The decision is a social value decision." This question of value for what purpose and to whom resonates in this chapter—and indeed throughout this book.

The entrepreneurial process (Chapter 3) talks about entrepreneurship resulting in the "creation, enhancement, realization, and renewal of value." The result of social entrepreneurship is no different, but it helps clarify the concept of value. Specifically, social value is derived from entrepreneurial activities that seek to address problems related to people and problems related to the planet—regardless of profit orientation. In other words, social entrepreneurship seeks creative and valuable solutions to such issues as education, poverty, health care, global warming, global water shortages, and energy.

A single, definitive view of social entrepreneurship is not necessarily important. What is most important is understanding the key differentiating factors between social entrepreneurship and traditional entrepreneurship while also realizing that there is not just one type of social entrepreneurship.

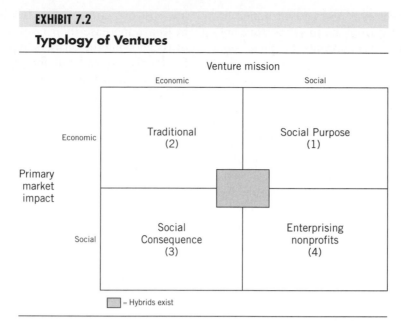

EXHIBIT 7.2

Typology of Ventures

Source: H. Neck, C. Brush, and E. Allen, "Exploring Social Entrepreneurship Activity in the United States: For-Profit Ventures Generating Social and Economic Value," Working Paper, Babson College.

Types of Social Entrepreneurship

The shaded area of Exhibit 7.2 depicts the territory of social entrepreneurship. The primary difference between traditional entrepreneurship and social entrepreneurship is the intended mission. Social entrepreneurs develop ventures with a mission to solve a pressing social problem. Social problems are most typically associated with such sectors as health care, education, poverty, environment, waste, water, and energy. We will address these opportunity sectors shortly. First let's acquire an understanding of the language, territory, and definitions of social entrepreneurship.

Social Purpose Ventures

Social purpose ventures (Exhibit 7.2, quadrant 1) are founded on the premise that a social problem will be solved, yet the venture is for profit and the impact on the market is typically seen as economic. Remember the Jim Poss case study in Chapter 4? This is a great example of a social entrepreneur starting a social venture like this. Poss founded Seahorse Power Company with the aim of building an enterprise that would help the environment. At the same time, the economic impact of his Big Belly solar trash compactor is driving sales and the growth of his company. According to Poss,

The problem at large is that there are 180,000 garbage trucks in the United States that burn over a billion gallons of diesel fuel every year. These are heavy particulates—cancer-causing, asthma-causing pollutants. Obviously greenhouse gases are being emitted. Those 180,000 garbage trucks also cost about $50 billion a year. So [waste companies] are pouring a lot of money into a system that is incredibly inefficient. The [trash] pickup frequency is driven by the container—the receptacle. So when it's full you have to make a garbage truck trip. We use technology [in the receptacle] to reduce the pickup frequency by about a factor of 5.[2]

Poss considers himself a social entrepreneur. He started studying the environment in 1992, and he found the problems and potential consequences of human action alarming. In Poss's eyes, starting a business was the best way to tackle some of the world's environmental problems. Social ventures like this one are mission-driven and economically sustainable. Remember, Poss's mission is social—to help the environment—but he recognizes the importance of sustainable business economics: "If you have a business that can sustain itself economically and do something environmentally beneficial, then it can be on its own growth path without the need for fund-raising every year to sustain."[3]

Enterprising Nonprofits

Exacerbating the confusion about social entrepreneurship is a preconceived notion that all entrepreneurship

---

[2] Interview with Jim Poss at Babson College on November 28, 2007.
[3] Ibid.

taking place in social sectors is reserved for nonprofit organizations. As we know from the Jim Poss story, not all social entrepreneurs start nonprofits. Furthermore, not all nonprofits are entrepreneurial. This is why the term "enterprising nonprofits" is used in quadrant 2 in Exhibit 7.2.

We might argue that any nonprofit start-up is entrepreneurial. However, consistent with the focus of this book and research in entrepreneurship, the scaling and sustainability of new ventures are incredibly important to the economy (as with for-profit ventures) and to systemic change (as with nonprofit organizations). It is not enough, from both an economic and social perspective, to simply start a venture; it must be scalable and sustainable. With longevity, innovation, and an eye toward growth, significant impact can be made.

There are two types of enterprising nonprofits. The first type utilizes earned-income activities, a form of venturing, to generate all or a portion of total revenue. In many ways enterprising nonprofits apply the principles of entrepreneurship to generate revenue to sustain their mission-driven organizations. The second type has a focus on growth and economic sustainability. Such an enterprising nonprofit may incorporate outside investment, in the form of venture philanthropy, to significantly scale the organization for better impact toward systemic social change. Just as a social venture may receive value-added venture capital or angel investment, an enterprising nonprofit may receive venture philanthropy funding, which is different from grant funding or donations. Venture philanthropy is a blend of financial assistance with a high level of professional engagement by the funder. This funding concept will be addressed later in this chapter.

Regardless of type, enterprising nonprofits represent a form of social entrepreneurship. In addition to their social mission, their impact on the market is social because the profit motive exists only to channel operating funds to the organization. Whereas social ventures may distribute profit to owners, enterprising nonprofits by law may not.

KickStart International is an example of an enterprising nonprofit using earned-income activities and venture philanthropy. Martin Fisher and Nick Moon founded KickStart in 1991 with a mission to end poverty in sub-Saharan Africa. They started in Kenya and today have offices in Tanzania and Mali. Though Fisher and Moon have introduced many technologies related to irrigation, oil processing, and building, their greatest success to date is with their micro-irrigation pump known as the MoneyMaker. This low-cost irrigation system has helped rural farmers in Kenya increase their crop production by a factor of 10, allowing the farmers to produce crops not only for family survival but for profitable return. Their metrics supporting success are inspiring. By early 2008 KickStart featured the following statistics on its Web site:[4]

- 45,000 pumps are in use by poor farmers.
- 29,000 new jobs have been created.
- The pumps generate $37 million per year in new profits and wages.
- More than 50 percent of the pumps are managed by women entrepreneurs.
- Four manufacturers produce the pumps.
- Over 400 retailers are selling the pumps throughout Kenya, Tanzania, and Mali.

Winner of the *Fast Company* social capitalist awards for 2007 and 2008, KickStart and its enterprising ways are making great strides in their mission of fighting poverty.

A study was conducted by the Yale School of Management and the Goldman Sachs Foundation Partnership on Nonprofit Ventures to better understand how and why enterprising nonprofits pursue earned-income activities.[5] Of the 519 nonprofit organizations participating in the study, 42 percent were operating earned-income ventures, 5 percent had tried but with little success, and 53 percent had never tried to pursue any type of revenue-generating activity beyond fund-raising, grant writing, and other activities. Some of the study's key findings were interesting. Nonprofits pursuing earned-income activities[6]

- Have more employees. Fifty-five percent of the enterprising nonprofits had 100+ employees compared to 36 percent that had never participated in any type of venturing activity.
- Believe they are more entrepreneurial. Seventy-seven percent of the enterprising nonprofits characterized themselves as entrepreneurs compared to 46 percent that had never participated in any type of venturing activity.
- Typically do not wait for complete financing before starting a business.
- Have budgets of $5 million to $25 million. This is an important figure because the majority of nonprofits in the United States never exceed a budget of $1 million.
- Do so to fund other programs (66 percent), become self-sustaining (52 percent), or diversify

[4] http://www.kickstart.org/tech/technologies/micro-irrigation.html.
[5] C. W. Massarsky and S. L. Beinhecker, "Enterprising Nonprofits: Revenue Generation in the Nonprofit Sector," 2002.
[6] Ibid., pp. 5–12.

revenue streams (51 percent). Other reasons include job creation and building community.

- Have a strong desire to see their ventures grow and replicate—but only 55 percent had actually written a business plan. However, 56 percent said they would find help writing a business plan valuable.

Hybrid Models of Social Entrepreneurship

Many types of ventures within the domain of social entrepreneurship do not fit nicely into quadrants 1 or 4 in Exhibit 7.2. In fact there are probably more hybrid arrangements than social ventures and enterprising nonprofits combined. In a recent survey 2,000 entrepreneurs were asked about the primary goals of their business.[7] Entrepreneurs chose one from the following four options:

- For profit—primarily achieving economic goals.
- For profit—primarily achieving social goals.
- For profit—equally emphasizing social and economic goals.
- Not for profit, serving a social mission.

How do you think 2,000 random entrepreneurs in the United States, not necessarily classified as social entrepreneurs, responded to this question?

As you might expect, the majority of the entrepreneurs (49 percent) were traditional enterprisers (quadrant 1). They identified themselves as having a for-profit venture with purely economic goals. Another 9 percent classified their ventures as for profit with a pure social purpose—similar to Jim Poss and his Big Belly solar trash compactor. Only 8 percent of the surveyed entrepreneurs identified themselves as not for profit. Most interesting were the 31 percent of entrepreneurs that claimed to be for profit with social and economic goals. These findings show that new ways of organizing are emerging: dual-purpose organizations with missions that equally emphasize economic and social goals.

Scojo Vision, an eyewear company, is an example of a hybrid model. Founded in New York by two entrepreneurs, Scott Berrie and Jordon Kassalow, the company mission addresses economic and social needs. In addition to stylish lines of eyewear, they have created a program that brings eye care and affordable reading glasses to rural areas of Latin America and India. The program, run by the Scojo Foundation, trains women entrepreneurs to build businesses by selling inexpensive reading glasses to workers that depend on their vision for their livelihood, such as tailors, textile workers, and weavers.[8]

Recently a new classification of organization has emerged called "for benefit." A growing army of volunteers and interested social entrepreneurs are participating in a community called the Fourth Sector Project.[9] The fourth sector emerges from a rather unchanged historical classification of businesses that have served either the private or public sector but not both. There are for-profit entities, nonprofit (nongovernmental) social organizations, and government. The Fourth Sector Project seeks to recognize a new model, the for-benefit model, as sectors begin to blur.

Hybrid models are *not* examples of corporate social responsibility—a term that is growing in popularity both in theory and in practice. Corporate social responsibility (CSR) emphasizes doing good and serving communities while still making a profit. You may be saying, "Well, this certainly sounds like a hybrid model of social entrepreneurship!" Revisit Exhibit 7.2 and recall that the primary difference between social entrepreneurship and the more traditional, commercial views of entrepreneurship is the intended mission. The primary mission of both social ventures and enterprising nonprofits is social regardless of market impact. The hybrid model *equally* emphasizes social and economic goals.

Corporations with CSR practices impact communities in which they operate and other stakeholders in many ways, but CSR is not the core component of their business models. For example, Dow Chemical donates Styrofoam to Habitat for Humanity for new home insulation. Starbucks builds relationships with local farmers, pays fair market prices, and extends credit so local farmers can grow their coffee bean businesses. Anheuser-Busch commercials encourage consumers to drink responsibly to prevent alcohol abuse and drunk driving. In 2005 Wal-Mart announced lofty long-term goals to show support for the environment. These goals stated that Wal-Mart would work to be supplied by 100 percent renewable energy, create zero waste, and sell environmentally friendly products.

Such CSR examples are numerous and growing, and many large corporations are making a positive impact on the world. Some companies have created CSR job functions. For example, The Walt Disney Company has a corporate responsibility department led by a

[7] Questions related to social entrepreneurship were included in the Global Entrepreneurship Monitor survey for the United States sponsored by Babson College. Social entrepreneurship results are included in H. Neck, C. Brush, and E. Allen, "Exploring Social Entrepreneurship Activity in the United States: For-Profit Ventures Generating Social and Economic Value," Working Paper, Babson College.
[8] http://www.scojo.com/eyewear.aspx.
[9] See http://www.fourthsector.net/ for more information.

senior manager of corporate responsibility. Similar positions can be found at other companies such as The Gap and American Express. But CSR is a support function. These companies were not founded on missions to solve the world's most pressing social problems. CSR activities benefit many but are not considered part of the domain of social entrepreneurship. CSR activities align best with Social Consequence ventures as seen in quadrant three of Exhibit 2.

The Timmons Model Interpreted for Social Entrepreneurship

Chapter 3 introduced the Timmons Model of the entrepreneurial process. The three major components of the Timmons Model—opportunity, resources, and team—certainly apply to social entrepreneurship; but the model requires a few contextual changes. Social opportunities, for example, are driven not only by markets but also by mission and social need. The brain trust aspect of the team—the external stakeholders—are especially important here because collaboration across boundaries is paramount in social entrepreneurship. Similar to traditional start-ups, the art of bootstrapping is a necessary method of resource acquisition. Yet capital markets exist for social entrepreneurs, and available funds are increasing in both the for-profit and not-for-profit sectors. The concepts of fit and balance remain because sustainability and growth are the essence of *any* entrepreneurial endeavor. Without longevity and value creation, impact is limited. This is particularly relevant to mission-driven social entrepreneurs.

Wicked Problems and Opportunity Spaces

Opportunities in social sectors, including environmental issues, are driven by large, complex problems. Perhaps we can be so bold as to call social problems "wicked problems." In the early 1970s the notion of wicked problems emerged out of the complexity of resolving issues related to urban and governmental planning; wicked problems were contrasted with tame problems.[10] In other words, the linear and traditional approaches to solving tame problems were being used on social issues with little success. Further observation indicated that the problems were ill-defined; so the perception of the actual problem was the symptom of another problem. As such, wicked problems became characterized as malign, viscious, tricky, and aggressive.[11] An examination of the characteristics of a wicked problem (Exhibit 7.3) reveals the considerable challenges facing social entrepreneurs.

We can use the aging of the U.S. population as an excellent example of a wicked problem; this is a significant social problem we are facing and will continue to face as the baby boomers retire. Between 2010 and 2020 we will see, for the first time in history, people over 65 outnumbering children under 5.[12] Given advances in health care, specifically disease control, humans are living longer. In 1903, for example, 15 percent of white females lived to the age of approximately 80; but today close to 70 percent of white females live to be 80 years old.[13]

This aging population creates significant challenges for society. Pensions and retirement incomes will need to last longer. Health care costs are likely to increase. The service economy will capture an

---

EXHIBIT 7.3

Wicked versus Tame Problems

Characteristics of Wicked Problems	Characteristics of Tame Problems
1. You don't understand the problem until you have developed a solution.	Have well-defined and stable problem statements.
2. Wicked problems have no stopping rule.	Have definite stopping points—when a solution is reached.
3. Solutions to wicked problems are not right or wrong.	Have solutions that can be objectively evaluated as right or wrong.
4. Every wicked problem is unique and novel.	Belong to a class of similar problems that are all solved in a similar way.
5. Every solution to a wicked problem is a "one-shot operation."	Have solutions that can be easily tried and abandoned.
6. Wicked problems have no given alternative solutions—infinite set.	Come with a limited set of alternative solutions.

Source: J. Conklin, *Dialogue Mapping: Building Shared Understanding of Wicked Problems*, chapter 1.

---

[10] H. Rittel and M. Webber, "Dilemmas in a General Theory of Planning," *Policy Sciences* 4 (1973), pp. 155–69.
[11] Ibid., p. 160.
[12] www.state.gov/g/oes/rls/or/81537.htm.
[13] Ibid.

increasing percentage of GDP as the elderly require more help from services as opposed to products. Also consider that the workforce pays for many social benefits of the elderly. As the population ages, there are fewer taxpayers supporting the growing number of nonworking retirees. But in addition to these tangible issues are the intangibles such as the emotional and physical sides of aging. The aging of the population creates challenges socially and economically, yet there are also issues related to human rights:

> Young people burn countertops with hot pans, forget appointments, and write overdrafts on their checking accounts. But when the old do these same things, they experience double jeopardy. Their mistakes are viewed not as accidents but rather as loss of functioning. Such mistakes have implications for their freedom.[14]

As with many such issues, this massive societal challenge represents a growing opportunity space for alert social entrepreneurs. Let's consider one aspect of this issue using the characteristics of wicked problems as the backdrop. Most elderly people want to maintain their independence as long as possible, so for many moving to an assisted living facility or nursing home is the last and least desired option. Furthermore, as the population ages and baby boomers enter their declining years, the availability of such assisted living facilities will decrease. A solution may be to create the next generation of smart homes that allow the elderly to stay in their own homes yet reap the benefits and security of assisted living. Let's assume the technology is in place and retrofitting existing homes is possible. Is this a good solution? On the surface yes, but consider other challenges:

- The elderly are not universally comfortable with technology.
- Older people may not earn money to pay for the smart features.
- Elderly people staying in their own homes may require assistance to reach hospitals in cases of emergency; so more elderly at home may stretch the 911 emergency response system.
- Cities and towns may be expected to create services for a larger elderly population, and these services may be funded by additional property taxes.

The list could go on, but the point is that sometimes we do not understand a whole problem until a solution is developed (#1). But let's continue with the idea of smart homes for the elderly. How much independence should be built into the homes? What are the trade-offs of being able to use both floors of a two-story home versus just the bottom floor? Does the entire home need to be smart? Wicked problems do not have a predetermined stopping rule (#2), so the social entrepreneur is forced to make rational choices based on a rigorous evaluation of trade-offs. The social entrepreneur must accept that a wicked problem is never fully solved and the solution is not likely to meet all expectations; this is also known as *satisficing* behavior. As characteristic #3 states, there are no right or wrong solutions. If smart homes are built, there will be criticism of the choices made or not made.

Independent living for the elderly is a unique social problem (#4), and interpretation of the dilemma is in the eye of the beholder. The problem in this example affects not only older people but also many other stakeholders. Potential solutions to wicked problems are known to have consequences over an extended period. A smart home may be a good idea for an old person wanting to maintain her independence, but consider the amount of work involved in retrofitting a home. What systems need to be installed? What changes to the home structure are anticipated? Finally how difficult will it be to sell an "elder smart" home on the market, and would it be easy or desirable to take the "smartness" out of the home after the death of the independent elder? Perhaps there are many other consequences of making a home smart in this context, but for a wicked problem only time will tell. Elderly independence is just one aspect of the social problem we will encounter as the population ages. There are innumerable possibilities, and wicked problem theory tells us that there is not a finite solution set (#6). Perhaps some see this as a limitation; but social entrepreneurs see an ocean of possibilities and opportunities.

The aging of the population (nationally and internationally) is just one of many wicked problems that are being addressed by social entrepreneurs. To get a better understanding of the social challenges facing the planet, the United Nations' Millennium Development Goals are a good starting point. The goals were developed in 2000 in a historically significant event when world leaders came together to address the world's most pressing social issues. The collaboration resulted in the inspiring United Nations Millennium Declaration. According to then Secretary-General Kofi Annan, the eight goals (Exhibit 7.4) with a target achievement date of 2015

> form a blueprint agreed by all the world's countries and all the world's leading development institutions—a set of simple but powerful objectives that every man and woman in the street, from New York to Nairobi to New Delhi, can easily support and understand. Since their adoption, the Goals have galvanized unprecedented efforts to meet the needs of the world's poorest.[15]

[14] M. Pipher, "Society Fears the Aging Process." in *The Aging of the Population*, Ed. L. Egendorft (1999), p. 53.
[15] The Millennium Development Goals Report 2005, p. 3 (http://www.un.org/millenniumgoals/background.html).

United Nations Millennium Development Goals

1. Eradicate extreme poverty and hunger.
2. Achieve universal primary education.
3. Promote gender equality and empower women.
4. Reduce child mortality.
5. Improve maternal health.
6. Combat HIV/AIDS, malaria, and other diseases.
7. Ensure environmental sustainability.
8. Develop a global partnership for development.

Source: The Millennium Development Goals Report 2005
(http://www.un.org/millenniumgoals/background.html).

Though these goals represent the UN's view of our most pressing social problems, the opportunity spaces for social entrepreneurs (in for-profit and non-profit areas) are vast and promising. The simplicity of entrepreneurship applied to wicked problems creates a powerful force for humankind. An opportunity is merely the positive view of a problem or challenge. We know from previous chapters that entrepreneurs think differently and identify opportunities that others cannot see. What opportunities can you identify in these spaces?

Resources

Not unlike the traditional entrepreneurial ventures discussed throughout this text, resource acquisition is critical to the success of social ventures, enterprising nonprofits, and even hybrid forms. Most social entrepreneurs will admit that access to capital is a burgeoning challenge as more and more social ventures emerge, especially with high growth aspirations and visions of international scalability. Bootstrapping is prevalent among passionate social entrepreneurs, who are often quiet in their approach as they struggle to build sustainable business models. Two sources of capital have emerged for social entrepreneurs.

Social venture capital (SVC) is subset of the traditional venture capital market. SVCs seek to invest in for-profit ventures not only for financial return but also for social and environmental return; this is also known as the *double bottom line* or *triple bottom line*. Research at Columbia University estimated that $2.6 billion is under management in the double bottom line private equity market.[16]

Within the social venture capital territory are three types of funds. First there is the "focused" fund. For example, Expansion Capital Partners with offices in San Francisco and New York invests solely in expansion-stage clean technology businesses related to energy, water, transportation, and manufacturing. Similarly, Commons Capital, operating outside Boston, invests in early-stage companies operating in one of four areas of social concern: education, health care, energy, and the environment. Both companies explicitly promote the environmental and social focus of their funds. The second type of fund is the "community" fund; its purpose is typically economic development and job creation in impoverished areas. CEI Ventures, headquartered in Portland, Maine, invests in businesses operating in underserved markets. Each company in the CEI portfolio is required to hire employees with low-income backgrounds from the community in which the business is operating. The case at the end of the chapter is an example of this type of SVC. The third type of fund is what has been referred to as "VC with a conscience."[17] These funds stipulate that a certain percentage will be invested in socially responsible businesses related to their target investment areas. For example, Solstice Capital operates offices in Boston, Massachusetts, and Tucson, Arizona. It invests 50 percent of its fund in information technology and the remaining 50 percent in socially responsible companies. According to its Web site, "Socially responsive investments can generate superior venture capital returns and make a positive contribution to the natural and social environments."[18]

Venture philanthropy provides value-added funding for nonprofit organizations to increase their potential for social impact. Though the origin of venture philanthropy has been attributed to John D. Rockefeller III in 1969 as he spoke before Congress in support of tax reform, the modern version looks more like venture capital but with a social return on investment.[19] There are various definitions of venture philanthropy, and the European Venture Philanthropy Association (EVPA) has adopted several tenets of venture philanthropy that are similar across all definitions of venture philanthropy—in both Europe and the United States, where the venture philanthropy concept is gaining unprecedented popularity (Exhibit 7.5).

New Profit Inc., based in Cambridge, Massachusetts, exemplifies venture philanthropy using venture capital methodology. With 25 full-time employees, New Profit has a venture fund that as of 2007 had

16 C. Clark, "RISE Capital Market Report: The Double Bottom Line Private Equity Landscape in 2002–2003," Columbia Business School, 2003.
17 Ibid.
18 http://www.solcap.com/objective.html.
19 R. John, "Venture Philanthropy: The Evolution of High-Engagement Philanthropy in Europe," Working Paper, Oxford Said Business School, Skoll Center for Entrepreneurship, 2006.

EXHIBIT 7.5

Accepted Principles of Venture Philanthropy from the European Venture Philanthropy Association

Characteristic	Description
High engagement	Venture philanthropists have a close, hands-on relationship with the social entrepreneurs and ventures they support, driving innovative and scalable models of social change. Some may take board places in these organizations, and all are far more intimately involved at strategic and operational levels than are traditional nonprofit funders.
Multiyear support	Venture philanthropists provide substantial and sustained financial support to a limited number of organizations. Support typically lasts at least three to five years, with an objective of helping the organization to become financially self-sustaining by the end of the funding period.
Tailored financing	As in venture capital, venture philanthropists take an investment approach to determine the most appropriate financing for each organization. Depending on their own missions and the ventures they choose to support, venture philanthropists can operate across the spectrum of investment returns.
Organizational capacity building	Venture philanthropists focus on building the operational capacity and long-term viability of the organizations in their portfolios, rather than funding individual projects or programs. They recognize the importance of funding core operating costs to help these organizations achieve greater social impact and operational efficiency.
Nonfinancial support	In addition to financial support, venture philanthropists provide value-added services such as strategic planning, marketing and communications, executive coaching, human resource advice, and access to other networks and potential funders.
Performance measurement	Venture philanthropy investment is performance-based, placing emphasis on good business planning, measurable outcomes, achievement of milestones, and high levels of financial accountability and management competence.

Source: R. John, "Venture Philanthropy: The Evaluation of High-Engagement Philanthropy in Europe," Working Paper, Oxford Said Business School, Skoll Center for Entrepreneurship, 2006.

invested in 20 nonprofit organizations, with plans to grow its total portfolio to 50 organizations by 2012. The average investment in each organization has been $1 million over a four-year period. However, New Profit tends to stay with organizations longer than four years to achieve sustainability and desired scale. In addition to providing growth capital financing, portfolio organizations receive strategic support from a New Profit portfolio manager and New Profit's signature partner, Monitor Group—a global advisory and financial services firm. Monitor Group, through a collaborative and unprecedented partnership, provides New Profit portfolio organizations with pro bono consulting as well as giving New Profit additional operating resources. It is estimated that since 1999 Monitor Group has provided New Profit and its portfolio organizations more than $30 million in pro bono services. Given the value-added investment capability of New Profit, this venture philanthropy organization is able to double the impact of each investment dollar from donors as illustrated in Exhibit 7.6. Thus donors (or investors) of New Profit know that for every $1 they invest, the nonprofit portfolio organization actually receives $1.98 due to services, support, and intellectual capital delivered by the New Profit team in conjunction with Monitor Group.

EXHIBIT 7.6

New Profit Doubles a $1 Investment

$1.00	Financial capital donated to New Profit portfolio organization
−0.00	New Profit expense or management fee (overhead and operating costs are covered by New Profit's board of directors)
+0.48	Value of New Profit portfolio manager
+0.50	Value of Monitor Group services donated
$1.98	Total investment to New Profit portfolio organization

Source: New Profit collateral materials, 2008.

New Profit has significantly increased the social impact of many nonprofit organizations across various sectors, including education, workforce development, and health care. To date (1997–2007) the New Profit portfolio as a whole boasts an impressive 44 percent compound annual growth rate for revenue and a 49 percent compound annual growth in lives touched. In 1999 New Profit portfolio organizations touched approximately 3,000 lives; by 2007 this number jumped to more than 700,000.[20] The innovative approach of venture philanthropists such as New Profit illustrates the power of entrepreneurial principles to scale nonprofit organizations to achieve unparalleled social reach.

[20] http://www.newprofit.com/impact_results.asp.

Social Entrepreneur Wins Nobel Peace Prize in 2006

This is not charity. This is business: business with a social objective, which is to help people get out of poverty.

Muhammad Yunus

Muhammad Yunus is the banker to the poor. He revolutionized the banking industry in the late 1970s when he started offering microloans with no collateral to the poorest of the poor in Bangladesh. Over 25 years later he and his Grameen Bank were introduced to the mainstream as recipients of the Nobel Peace Prize for their contributions to social and economic development by breaking the cycle of poverty through microcredit.

The idea is simple yet powerful. Borrowers are organized into groups of five, but not all members can borrow at once. Two borrowers may receive a microloan at one time; but not until these two borrowers begin to pay back the principal plus interest can the other members become eligible for their own loans. The average interest rate is 16 percent, and the repayment rate is an unprecedented 98 percent, which is attributed to group pressure, empowerment, and motivation. The loans are tiny—typically enough to buy a goat, tools, or a small piece of machinery that can be used to produce new sources of income.

The Grameen Bank was founded by Yunus with the following objectives:

- Extend banking facilities to poor men and women.
- Eliminate the exploitation of the poor by money lenders.
- Create opportunities for self-employment for the vast multitude of unemployed people in rural Bangladesh.
- Bring the disadvantaged, mostly women from the poorest households, within the fold of an organizational format they can understand and manage by themselves.
- Change the age-old vicious circle of low income, low savings, and low investment into the virtuous circle of low income, injection of credit, investment, more income, more savings, more investment, and more income.

As of October 2007 the Grameen Bank had served 7.34 million borrowers, of whom 97 percent were women. The bank operates 2,468 branches and employs 24,703 people. Since 1983 the Grameen Bank has disbursed $6.55 billion to the poor and has been profitable every year except 1983, 1991, and 1992.

The Importance of the Brain Trust in Social Entrepreneurship

The third component of the Timmons Model of the Entrepreneurial Process is the team. As we've discussed, social entrepreneurship seeks to solve wicked problems, and such problems cannot be solved alone or even with a small start-up team. The environment to solve social problems requires a spirit of collaboration; and therefore in the social entrepreneurship context the brain trust is particularly important.

The brain trust in social entrepreneurship can include the community, investors, the government, customers, suppliers, manufacturers, or in the case of the Grameen Bank, villagers. The list is endless in many respects and depends on the venture. The current momentum around social entrepreneurship is exciting, but the sustainability of doing good can be achieved only if it delivers some type of value for those most involved. In other words, social ventures must deliver value for key stakeholders. What the value is and to whom will vary, but it is important that the social entrepreneur understand the interactions among brain trust stakeholders as well as the potential value derived from being associated with the venture.

Think back to the Jim Poss example at the beginning of the chapter. Poss must understand the value proposition for each stakeholder. In a municipality, for example, the company responsible for waste management needs to see money saved by reducing the frequency of trash pickups. Poss must show the mayor of the city that the Big Belly supports green initiatives. For city planners, Poss can address space-saving and aesthetic features. But what about labor unions? What if reducing the number of trash pickups cuts the number of trucks and drivers needed? Every social innovation likely has a downside; the social entrepreneur needs to consider not only the value added but also the value loss to various stakeholder groups and assess consequences. A primary question underlying stakeholder theory is what is at stake and for whom. This is an important point. Even social entrepreneurs must assess the risk inherent in their new ventures.

The social entrepreneur can build his or her brain trust further by recognizing and participating in the powerful networks surrounding social entrepreneurship activities. There is something unique about like-minded entrepreneurs and investors coming together to address world problems and understanding that their solutions, or a lack thereof, will change the world forever. But communities are emerging everywhere to share best practices, learn, create, and collaborate to build and grow ventures for a better world. Social Venture Network, Investors Circle, Echoing Green, Ashoka, Net Impact, Social Enterprise Alliance, and University Network are just a few places to start building and participating in social entrepreneurship networks. Bill Drayton, founder of Ashoka, believes, "The inertia of our experience pulls us into conventional directions. We must engage in group entrepreneurship to collaborate and become far more than the sum of the parts."

Concluding Thoughts: Change Agent Now or Later?

Bank of America recently commissioned a report on philanthropy that found that entrepreneurs, on average, give 25 percent more to charitable causes than do other types of wealthy donors.[21] Of course this spirit of giving among entrepreneurs should be recognized and applauded; but is such giving sufficient? The story of a successful entrepreneur building a company, creating personal wealth, and *then* making significant charitable contributions is common. Social entrepreneurs, however, do not wait to give. Social entrepreneurs build businesses where economic value and societal contribution are two sides of the same coin. They identify opportunities to solve problems related to education, health care, poverty, energy, water, and the environment—to name a few. They are cause fighters and change agents using the fundamental principles of entrepreneurship to promote positive change and permanent impact. Social entrepreneurs are creating the future.

---

[21] C. Preston, "Entrepreneurs Are among Most Generous Wealthy, Report Finds," *Chronicle of Philanthropy* 20, no. 5 (December 13, 2007).

Chapter Summary

- The primary difference between traditional entrepreneurship and social entrepreneurship is the intended mission.
- There are two types of enterprising nonprofits. The first type utilizes earned-income activities, while the second has a focus on growth and economic sustainability.
- The primary mission of both social ventures and enterprising nonprofits is social regardless of market impact. The hybrid model equally emphasizes social and economic goals.

- Social opportunities are driven not only by markets but also by mission and social need.
- With social entrepreneurship, the team in the Timmons Model is expanded to include stakeholders external to the venture.
- As more social ventures emerge, access to capital becomes a greater challenge.
- Social venture capitalists seek to invest in for-profit ventures for financial return as well as for social and environmental return.

Study Questions

1. What are the differences among socially responsible ventures, social ventures, and enterprising nonprofits?
2. Why are corporate social responsibility (CSR) activities not considered to be part of the domain of social entrepreneurship?
3. What are three characteristics of wicked problems?

4. What is meant by the concept of double bottom line with regard to socially focused investing?
5. What is an example of a wicked problem facing humanity, and what types of opportunities might arise for social entrepreneurs in that space?

Internet Resources for Chapter 7

http://www.netimpact.org *Net Impact is a global network of leaders who are changing the world through business.*

http://www.echoinggreen.org *Since 1987, Echoing Green has provided seed funding and support to nearly 450 social entrepreneurs with bold ideas for social change in order to launch groundbreaking organizations around the world.*

http://www.se-alliance.org *An increasing number of organizations are working toward sustainable social innovation by applying the power of market-based strategies to advance social change. The Social Enterprise Alliance serves as a single point of reference and support and a source of education and networking lenders, investors, grant makers, consultants, researchers, and educators who recognize the increasing impact of social enterprise.*

http://www.svn.org *Founded in 1987 by Josh Mailman and Wayne Silby, Social Venture Network (SVN) is a nonprofit network committed to building a just and sustainable world through business.*

www.skollfoundation.org *The Skoll Foundation's mission is to advance systemic change to benefit communities around the world by investing in, connecting, and celebrating social entrepreneurs. Social entrepreneurs are proven leaders whose approaches and solutions to social problems are helping to better the lives and circumstances of countless underserved or disadvantaged individuals.*

MIND STRETCHERS

Have You Considered?

1. Identify three social ventures in your community, define the stakeholders, and ask them how they receive value from their social venture.

2. For the same three social ventures, define the nature of risk.

3. How would you advise Jim Poss to deal with the potential labor union problems described in this chapter?

4. What do you think your generation's most wicked problem will be?

Case
Northwest Community Ventures Fund

Preparation Questions

1. Discuss the fit for GBI of this particular for-profit avenue Eileen O'Brien has chosen.

2. When is it OK to forgo economic profit in order to increase social returns? How can social returns be measured? Can you put a monetary value on the social and the environmental benefits?

3. What is the upside for Michelle Foster if NCV succeeds? What are the professional risks she faces?

4. How should Foster position herself and her team prior to raising a follow-on fund?

Michelle Foster glanced at the unclaimed nametags on the front table. Unusually stormy weather in the Northwest had kept many people away from her conference on funding alternatives for growing businesses. The event was sponsored in part by Foster's equity fund, Northwest Community Ventures (NCV). Following its mandate to invest in rural communities in Oregon and Washington State, Foster's group depended on outreach venues such as this one to attract and build trust with rural entrepreneurs who worked far from the world of traditional venture capital.

In early 2005 NCV had just over 8 years remaining on its 10-year charter. Nevertheless Foster was already thinking about how to best position herself for raising a follow-on fund in Year 3. As with any venture fund, she'd be out looking for investors long before performance results were in on her current effort. Her concern was whether institutional investors could be attracted to NCV's brand of socially responsible venture capital—especially if better returns were available elsewhere at lower risk.

Her primary challenge, however, was Eileen O'Brien, the passionate founder of NCV's high-profile, nonprofit parent organization. At first their vastly different business philosophies had been a source of respect, philosophical curiosity, and even amusement. Increasingly, though, that relationship had become strained by the pressures that both women were facing to satisfy their respective—and highly disparate—goals and obligations.

Grassroots Business Initiatives, Inc.

Eileen O'Brien had grown up during the tail end of the turbulent sixties in America. As a young woman, she had traveled extensively to bring her energy (and fair

complexion) to civil rights rallies and marches throughout the United States. The violence, injustice, and social disparity that she witnessed in this "land of the free" steeled her resolve to make a real difference. When she arrived on the Oregon coast in the late 1970s, she knew she had found a place to begin a new sort of journey.

What she had discovered was a rural coastal community in dire straits. The farming, fishing, and forestry industries were vibrant, but the majority of the hardworking business owners—and almost all of their workers—were living at or below the national poverty line. The tall, self-assured redhead soon became a force in the state as she searched for ways to improve lives while maintaining the waters, farms, and forests that supported the rural communities. In 1979 she founded Grassroots Business Initiatives (GBI), a community development corporation (CDC) set up to make investments in small businesses, foster employment opportunities, and develop the state's natural resource industries.

Although O'Brien had no formal business training, she was a quick study and particularly adept at finance. She explained that for nearly 25 years, she and her like-minded team[1] had done well by being creative:

> As part of our effort to strengthen GBI financially, we began to develop innovative programs around economic development that could supplement and diversify our income stream. These programs were subsidized by federal and state agencies, as well as foundations. We made our loans conditional on things like improved wage rates, benefits, and working conditions. We generated income from the "spread" between our cost of capital—1 percent was typical for 10-year foundation money—and the rate at which we could lend it out.

Lending money to business organizations not only helped to foster economic development initiatives; it gave GBI a powerful voice to effect change within the business community. By 2000 the organization had increased its assets under management to nearly $75 million. That

---

[1] By 2005 GBI employed 75 individuals dedicated to O'Brien and her mission. Ironically, because GBI generally attracted liberal-minded social progressives, the organization had become a highly effective community development corporation whose workers collectively exhibited strong antibusiness sentiments. This culture was reinforced during the late 1990s as scandals on Wall Street and corporate America became headline news. GBI's board of directors had been chosen by O'Brien for their commitment to the values she embraced. Though some of the banks who supported her organization sat on her board, conservative business individuals were the exception.

This case was prepared by Carl Hedberg under the direction of Professor Natalie Taylor. Copyright Babson College, 2005. Funding provided by the F.W. Olin Graduate School and a gift from the class of 2003. All rights reserved.

was around the time that O'Brien had begun to sense a sea change on the funding horizon:

> The Bush administration was making it clear that in addition to tax cuts for the wealthy, they were going to cut back or dismantle government programs that we have always relied on. Also, Congress was saying that it might support changes in the Community Reinvestment Act.[2] I've been to Washington many times to meet with senior officials and politicians. But it's like global warming; they just don't get it.

O'Brien knew that numerous nonprofits were pursuing social entrepreneurship to sustain, and even drive, their efforts.[3] To the detractors that felt nonprofits had no business being in enterprise, O'Brien would say,

> If we lose government funding, there is no way that private sector donations, along with our lending practices, could come close to covering our expenses. And if we were forced to become aggressive fund-raisers, those efforts would severely distract us from our community development objectives. For us, it made total sense to close that gap with a for-profit investment fund.

Community Development Venture Capital

Back in the early 1990s, O'Brien and a few of her community development peers recognized that while conditional loans could advance modest social initiatives, the role of a lender in that relationship was too arm's length to afford true influence in their local markets. They also noted an absence of equity capital to support growth in rural markets. Using grant money from foundations, this loose coalition of creative lenders developed a structure for a socially progressive equity fund. Their concept, community development venture capital (CDVC), was one of several of types of community development

---

[2] The Community Reinvestment Act (CRA), enacted by Congress in 1977, was intended to encourage depository institutions to help meet the credit needs of the communities in which they operated—including channeling some of their investment funds into CDCs and similar entities. Banks with less than $250 million in assets could qualify for certain CRA exemptions. In 2005 a controversial FDIC proposal was advanced to exempt many more banks by raising that minimum threshold to $1 billion in assets.

[3] Social entrepreneurship—nonprofits raising money through businesslike arrangements to support a social mission—was a growing trend, but not entirely new. Goodwill Industries had long raised money through businesses to support its core mission, sometimes using its clients to help operate those businesses. At the heart of social entrepreneurship was the notion that many nonprofits had marketable assets that could be tapped to generate revenue to support and promote their missions. These assets included expertise, services, products, logos, volunteer networks, and even their reputation or standing in the community. Children's Television Workshop, for example, licensed *Sesame Street* characters for books, toys, and other products. By the early 2000s Girl Scouts of America was selling more than $200 million in cookies each year to support the organization. (Source: *Developments* newsletter, University of Pittsburgh, 2002.)

EXHIBIT 1

Community Development Financial Institutions (CDFI)

In 2005 community development corporations in the United States were operating 800–1,000 CDFIs, including

- 500 community development loan funds.
- 80 venture capital funds.
- 275 community development credit unions.
- 50 community development banks.

There were five generally recognized types of CDFIs:

- *Community development banks* provide capital to rebuild economically distressed communities through targeted lending and investment.
- *Community development credit unions* promote ownership of assets and savings and provide affordable credit and retail financial services to low-income people with special outreach to minority communities.
- *Community development loan funds* aggregate capital from individual and institutional social investors at below-market rates and lend this money primarily to nonprofit housing and business developers in economically distressed urban and rural communities.
- *Community development venture capital funds* provide equity and debt with equity features for community real estate and medium-sized business projects. The typical target internal rate of return (IRR) for these funds was between 10 and 12 percent, as opposed to a mainstream venture IRR goal of between 25 and 35 percent. Given the nascent stage of its development, the CDVC industry had not yet seen a full 10-year investment cycle played out, and was therefore unable to verify this return profile.
- *Microenterprise development loan funds* foster social and business development through loans and technical assistance to low-income people who were involved in very small businesses or self-employed and unable to access conventional credit.

---

financial institutions (CDFIs) that CDCs were using to advance rural reinvestment objectives (see Exhibit 1).

Like traditional venture capital (see Appendix A), CDVCs aimed to invest in companies that had solid business models, outstanding management teams, and excellent growth potential. However, this subset of the venture investment industry differed from mainstream venture capital in a number of ways (see Exhibit 2), with the most striking difference being that CDVCs sought both practical and altruistic returns—referred to by those within the community development arena as a double bottom line. This dual goal was to realize not only a financial return on an investment, but also a return to the local community in the form of such things as job creation for low-income workers, inner-city property revitalization, and opportunities for women and minorities.[4] In

---

[4] CDVC funds also tended to invest in more diverse industry sectors than traditional venture funds, which often focused their investments in technology or biotechnology—two sectors that did not provide many jobs for entry-level workers. By 2000 manufacturing had made up 49 percent of all CDVC investments, with services, retail trade, and software development following at 17, 7, and 6 percent, respectively.

EXHIBIT 2

Community Development Venture Capital versus Traditional Venture Capital

Aspect	CDVC Funds*	VC Funds
Total capital under management	About $300 million	About $134 billion
Average investment size per round	$186,000	$13.2 million
Typical time frame before exit	Five to eight years	Three to five years
Typical IRR goal range	10% to 12%	25% to 35%
Funding sources	Government, foundations, banks	Pension funds, trusts and foundations, university endowments, wealthy individuals

*Further distinctions:

Socially responsible venture capital (SRVC) typically encompassed the following additional criteria:

- *Diversity:* Women/minority-owned/founded businesses, diversity among suppliers, employees, partners, etc.
- *Workforce:* Benefits, profit sharing, employee ownership, quality of work environment.
- *Environmental:* Beneficial products/services, pollution prevention, recycling, alternative energy, building design.
- *Products:* Socially beneficial, quality, innovative, safe. Socially responsible investing also avoided supporting certain industries such as tobacco, adult entertainment, gambling, and firearms.

addition, the lower seed investment threshold of as little as $100,000 meant that these community development groups could be a potential resource for talented entrepreneurs working in rural America.

A New Model for Economic Development

Taking the CDVC concept a step further, in 2000 O'Brien began work on setting up an early-stage, triple bottom line[5] fund. Less than a year later O'Brien was able to persuade her board of directors to support the creation of a $10 million socially responsible venture capital fund. Her Northwest Community Ventures (NCV) fund laid out a specific set of criteria designed to focus equity investments in areas that could have the most positive impact (see Exhibit 3). Given her experience with lending, and having worked with a range of small businesses, O'Brien felt sure this fund would be a good fit:

GBI has been built on the strength of our talent to guide and nurture rural businesses, and this is an opportunity

to give us a voice in the boardrooms of high-potential ventures that can have a real impact in these communities. As a limited partner in the fund, we'd participate in long-term capital gains that would likely be far above what our lending programs can provide.

When a banker on her board emphasized the importance of bringing in an experienced individual to manage the fund, O'Brien agreed and set out to recruit a top venture capital professional willing to make some trade-offs.

Michelle Foster

Michelle Foster was born in southern California as the daughter of liberal-minded parents who had grown up in the sixties. Although she had always embraced those values, Foster chose a decidedly different track for her career. After earning her MBA at Babson College in Wellesley, Massachusetts, Foster landed a position at a prestigious venture capital fund in Boston. She worked her way up from analyst to associate to partner. She loved the job; it was diverse, exciting, and extremely rewarding both financially and intellectually.

Still, Foster was finding that the exclusive financial orientation of the deal maker's life left something to be desired. Seeking a better balance, she began searching online for opportunities closer to her native California. In the fall of 2001 she spotted an unusual offering in

[5] The term "triple bottom line" was a notion popularized by best-selling author and green-business guru John Elkington. In his book *Cannibals with Forks* Elkington argued that future market success would often depend on a company's ability to satisfy the three-pronged fork of profitability, environmental quality, and social justice. One issue supporters of this concept were trying to address was how to weigh and measure returns within each category and relative to each other.

EXHIBIT 3

NCV Investment Criteria

In traditional VC markets, criteria used to evaluate companies include the following:

- *Management:* Experienced within domain, able to understand demands of growth, receptive to working with VC investor as partner, realistic about own skills/experience and willing to change roles if needed; management team should be complete.
- *Market:* Large, fast-growing markets; identified pain point of customers.
- *Barrier to entry:* Typically intellectual property protection to defend product/service against competitors.
- *Financial:* Capital requirements appropriate to venture finance (e.g., not too capital intensive); strong profitability (gross margins).
- *Business model:* Scalable, consistent with current market conditions.

Within more rural markets, opportunities that meet most of these criteria can be found but have the following differences:

- *Management:* Management possesses strong domain experience but may not have worked with VCs before and may need education; management teams often are incomplete.
- *Market:* Unlike technology markets (denominated in $billions), markets served by more rural markets tend to be smaller in scale (denominated in $hundred millions) with less dramatic overall market growth (low–mid double-digit rather than the triple-digit growth of technology markets).
- *Barriers to entry:* For mid- and later-stage companies not operating in technology markets, barriers tend to be existing brands and current scale of business.

Portland, Oregon. Foster recalled that she and the founder hit it off immediately:

> Eileen's background and sensibilities were very similar to what my parents were all about. She joked that in person I was not nearly as scary as my résumé made me out to be. So she was getting a VC with a soul, and I saw this as a fabulous opportunity to bring my deep experience to a position that involved a lot more than just meeting financial objectives. This seemed like a match made in heaven.

O'Brien agreed:

> I could see that Michelle was a seasoned businessperson, but she was also a good listener. Not only that, she totally got what we were trying to accomplish with this innovative fund.

After a similarly positive meeting with the GBI board, Foster accepted the position in November 2001—at less than half the salary she'd been earning in Boston. She commented on the risks and trade-offs:

> The Portland area is so beautiful, and the pace of life is a pleasant change from what I had been doing on the

East Coast. But this was also a serious career decision. While I knew that NCV had a very challenging rural investment mission, I also saw it as an enormous opportunity to do something interesting and innovative—beyond what the CDVC industry had done to date. This looked like an excellent opportunity to prove that venture capital investments could realize a return and make a real difference in underserved markets.

> At the same time, I was aware that since no one at GBI had venture investment experience, I would have to set the tone and would probably spend a good deal of time explaining my decisions. But that was what I was being hired for—to be the expert. I was also a bit uncertain about what it would mean to be part of the unique nonprofit culture that existed at GBI.

With the recession in full swing following the 9/11 terrorist attacks, mainstream venture capitalists had been virtually shut down with regard to raising new funds from traditional sources like pension funds.[6] In the case of NCV, limited partner funding came primarily from foundations and banks with socially progressive mandates that were less sensitive to market conditions—job creation, affordable housing, tax credit programs,[7] and the like. Nevertheless, it took Foster 18 months to close the $10 million fund.

The economic slowdown was also having a deleterious effect on the parent company—especially with regard to cash flow. GBI clients and portfolio companies were struggling, deal flow had dried up, and recession-fighting interest rate cuts had dramatically reduced CDC income from lending activities.

The Investing Staff

In early 2003, when it appeared certain that NCV would achieve full funding, Foster hired Janet Lawson to administer the operation.[8] All the while Foster had been looking for an associate with venture experience and a similar willingness to put lifestyle choices ahead of monetary

---

[6] For groups seeking to raise private equity, there were two adverse consequences of the precipitous fall in the equity markets in 2001. The first was that because the IPO market had dried up virtually overnight, the harvest horizon had become highly uncertain. The second consequence of falling share prices was that as the aggregate portfolios of pension fund managers shrank, the denominator (which defined the percentage of total investments allocated to venture capital and private equity) also shrank. This resulted in a considerable overallocation for that asset class. Consequently pension fund managers had simply stopped investing their money in venture capital until the allocation percentage was back within a range set by their investing policies. (Source: Jeffry Timmons, Forte Ventures case, 2004.)

[7] Contributors or investors could obtain state tax credits based on 50 percent of their investments or contributions in a preapproved CDC. The CDC would then make equity investments or loans to a specific project within the designated redevelopment area.

[8] Previously Lawson had managed the operational affairs at Marshall Venture Partners, a Portland-based early-stage venture capital firm focusing on information technology and biotechnology investments.

rewards. In February 2004 she found what she was looking for in John Coolidge. Coolidge had an MBA from Stanford and some early nonprofit experience and had spent the last three years working for an international consulting firm. He explained that although he had loved that job, he recognized that he needed to make a change:

> I was always working with two clients simultaneously over a broad range of functional areas like growth strategy, marketing effectiveness, organizational strategy, and lean manufacturing. Within a short time I had gained a large breadth of experience across several sectors.
>
> It was a fantastic experience, but on the negative side, there were many weeks where I worked 70–80 hours while traveling two or three days. My wife and I had had our son while I was in business school, and it became a struggle to balance home life and my career. When our daughter was born in November 2003, I knew I had to make a change. After taking four weeks off for paternity leave, I went back and gave notice. I felt it was time to find a way to merge the social purpose and business sides of my career track.

When a lucrative job offer came through from a financial services firm in San Francisco, however, Coolidge once again found himself eyeing the fast lane. He explained that it was a wee-hours heart-to-heart that turned the tide:

> I was really close to accepting that Citibank job. The kids had finally nodded off at around one in the morning, so for the first time my wife and I had a chance to really talk. When she asked me if I was going to be excited to go to work on my first day, I just sort of froze. When I said no, she said, "Well, that settles it; you're not going to take that job." Given our suburban San Francisco mortgage, and having two young children, it didn't seem like such a straightforward decision. But I did turn down that position. Soon after, I was on the Internet and found the listing for what sounded like the perfect job up north in Oregon.

Coolidge was even more intrigued after his interview with Foster. Although the NCV job as an associate would represent a significant cut in pay, he found the social mission and the core business model very attractive. Coolidge and his wife also loved the area:

> The quality of life is fantastic here. We were able to get a house that would have been way out of our price range in San Francisco. I can ride my bike to work, and we live in a great town with good schools. I look out the window at the fishing boats and the harbor seals, and realize how much the consulting business had conditioned me to believe that there wasn't any other way to live besides working long hours and making lots of money.

For her part, Foster saw enough in the candidate's enthusiasm and background to overlook the fact that Coolidge had no venture capital experience:

> What's great about John's background is he made certain decisions that were based on quality of family life and a desire to integrate his values into his work. So there were enough linkages with where I was coming from, and John was obviously motivated and smart. I needed someone whose motivations were not purely financial—someone willing to adapt. I felt that John's nonprofit policy background would keep him from running shrieking from the boardroom when those for-profit versus nonprofit cultural issues flared up.

Developing Deal Flow

Together Foster and Coolidge handled the responsibilities of the investing team at the fund (see Exhibit 4). Although most mainstream venture capital firms were able to foster deal flow without a heavy reliance on

EXHIBIT 4
Investing Staff (President, Associate) Responsibilities

Deal sourcing: Through various means, identify, qualify, and secure interest from companies who are seeking capital.

Due diligence: Research the market, management, product/service, and financial forecasts to understand the risk, opportunity, and viability of the deal.

Negotiation (pricing, terms): Negotiate investment terms (price, security, and key legal/financial terms) with company owners and managers.

Decision making:
- Management decision—weigh risks and opportunities, chemistry with management, and other factors to arrive at go or no-go decision within the investment team.
- Board review—present investment recommendation to board of directors for vote.

Corporate governance and stakeholder management: With seat on board of directors, help govern the company, balancing interests of various stakeholders—investors/shareholders, management/staff, and community/environment.

Operational assistance: Assist company by providing both personal and professional efforts to help reach targets in the business plan; facilitate and deliver operational assistance services.

Return management: Work with management to keep financial and social objectives in view and within the timeframe agreed between investors and management; facilitate exit opportunities that maximize these returns.

Reporting: Prepare periodic fund and management reports:
- Board: Every six to eight weeks, report to board on fund operations and fund/portfolio performance.
- SBA: File and report to SBA as required by law and as is appropriate for this special investor.
- LPs: Report quarterly and annually to investors (limited partners or LPs) on fund operation's portfolio performance (financial, social).

Fund-raising: Prepare fund-raising documents for successor fund (typically three to five years after start of existing fund); identify and present to prospective investors to secure fund commitments.

marketing,[9] the NCV team was actively promoting its fund to a variety of groups across the region. Leads were generated through economic development organizations, other venture capital funds, and banks.

NCV also utilized business directories, chamber of commerce listings, and local and regional newspapers to identify and attract a range of prospects—from those actively seeking expansion capital, to promising rural enterprises that had never considered venture capital as a funding option. From these sources the team was able to identify the rough universe of companies that fit their broad investment criteria with regard to business sector, size, and key personnel.[10]

One of NCV's important outreach efforts was their educational seminar. Cosponsored by banks and service providers, and hosted and marketed by local economic development groups, these conferences presented a broad view of the growth and funding strategies available to promising businesses. Foster felt that this forum—which targeted rural entrepreneurs—was fairly unique in the venture investment industry:

> The format at VC symposium events is pretty standard across the country. Some have VCs on a panel, talking about second- and third-order issues such as "the latest trend in deal structuring," "evaluating term sheets," and so on; and some have entrepreneurs presenting their business plans to a group of angels and venture capitalists—with some time for networking afterward. These types of events are great for a knowledgeable audience but are of little value to someone who has no previous experience with outside investors.
>
> Our programs provide content that generally doesn't get covered in other forums; we are very transparent in everything we do. People will ask, "What is your valuation expectation?" or "What return do you expect?" Or sometimes they do not quite understand how venture capital works. We explain how we do not lend money like a bank, but that we price deals to target a high IRR because of the typical loss rates in venture capital. By *assuming* the risk—whereas banks mitigate risk—we share in the upside because we're sharing in the downside. Once they see the challenges of our work, they begin to understand why we usually require a substantial equity piece.

---

[9] Venture capitalists attended industry networking forums such as *The Venture Forum*, purchased listings in publications such as *Galante's Guide to Venture Capital*, and participated in panel sessions and in business plan competitions.

[10] The databases and publication on hand listed approximately 20,000 companies in the rural markets in Washington State and in Oregon. Assuming that the list spanned 80 percent of the potential companies, NCV estimated the total size of the business market to be 25,000. If 20 percent of this market (5,000) represented companies with VC characteristics and an estimated 20 percent of this subset (1,000) could fulfill progressive investment goals, then NCV had to find and invest in 152 companies out of an eligible market of 1,000—that is, NCV had to find and invest in approximately 1 in 66 companies (1,000 companies divided by 15 investments).

Cool Winds

Foster and her team worked on the second floor of a red brick, harborside shipping warehouse that O'Brien had long ago refurbished as her base of GBI operations. Even during a coastal storm the view was beautiful—and often more tranquil than what the team was experiencing inside the old building. Foster offered her take on the chilly reception that was now in its third year:

> Even though I had agreed to a huge cut in salary to do this, I am still making $5,000 more than Eileen. She's always been fine with that, but there is definitely resentment from some of her senior staff since they have been with her for many years, and their salaries are maybe only 65 percent of my base, and none of them have the potential upside that I do with carried interest.[11] But hey—we're talking two completely different models here: nonprofit versus a venture capital operation.

Because their previous jobs had often involved all manner of middle-management power struggles, Foster and Coolidge were able to carry on undeterred. Of more concern was that O'Brien had begun pushing for a significant level of input on funding decisions. It soon became clear that O'Brien was expecting NCV to accept her suggestions without resistance. Foster, who was sensitive to the top-down culture that O'Brien had established, had found tactful ways of deflecting these attempts at direct oversight. This had worked with moderate success until O'Brien decided to take a firm stand.

Turbulence

By the end of 2003 NCV had logged 187 investment investigations. Seven were under active consideration, 163 had been turned down, and 15 were considered dormant (not working but not turned down). Two firms had received equity investments. NCV's first investment was in the Portland Baking Company (PBC), a women-owned and -managed manufacturer of all-natural cakes and confections. The business had been operating for five years when founder Mary Bishop decided to set up an online store to sell high-margin gift packages. When sales doubled to $600,000 in eight months, the company began to seek funding to exploit its most lucrative online channel: corporate gift gifting to satisfied customers. PBC received $400,000 from NCV, as well as a $200,000 economic development loan set up through GBI. The company would use the money to hire

---

[11] Carried interest is the share of residual capital gains from a venture capital fund, minus expenses and allocations to limited partners. Carried interest payments were designed to create a significant economic incentive for venture capital fund managers to achieve capital gains. The term originated in the early days of VC, when general partners put up nothing in return for 20 percent of the profits; thus the limited partners "carried the interest" of the general partners.

additional employees and to install an automated packaging system.

The fund's second investment was extended to Sostenga, Inc., a catalog/e-commerce business that marketed sustainable energy systems for farms and off-the-grid residences. The company, founded by Manuel Gracioso and his brother Ricardo in 1996, had been growing quickly due to a resurgence of interest in alternative energy solutions in the United States. Sostenga had received $350,000 from NCV to support working capital for inventory purchases and for marketing expenditures related to catalog, Internet, and retail activities.

When Foster and Coolidge had begun conducting due diligence on Sostenga, O'Brien paid Foster a visit to express her reservations about the investment. While she favored the minority and environmental aspects of the deal, she was concerned that this "warehouse deal" could grow for quite a while without additional labor. As an alternative, O'Brien suggested that Foster revisit a call center (offering lower-income jobs) that had been rejected weeks before. Foster felt that it was time to push back:

> Ever since we started, Eileen has been floating in and out of my office to "check up" on progress with deals she has become fond of, or to promote opportunities that fit her progressive social agenda. I finally told her, "Look, you hired me because of my experience. The quid pro quo for me agreeing to work for a lower salary is that GBI needs to give me the benefit of the doubt on deal-related decision making."
>
> After all, GBI has no material real-world experience in this business, either directly or on their board. How can I be expected to take direction from a group that doesn't know what financial success looks like?

O'Brien, who was casting about for cash flow to mitigate her first loss in 20 years,[12] noted that management fees at the venture fund she herself had chartered were more than covering expenses.[13] Foster explained that she remained committed to running the fund in a manner that was commensurate with industry standards:

> How we spend our management fees is discretionary. As fund managers we decide what equipment we need, what conferences we want to attend, and what newsletters and news services we buy. Sure, in theory, we could operate very leanly and have excess cash that could flow

upward to the parent, but our job is to use those fees to find and close good deals . . . not to subsidize the parent.
>
> When I said to Eileen that our investors didn't invest so that she could fund a loss with our fees, she brought up the whole moral issue of supporting her nonprofit side of this business. But what about the ethical issue with regard to our fiduciary responsibility to other NCV limited partners?

Another difficult situation arose when Foster and Coolidge considered making an investment offer in an organic products manufacturer contingent on replacing the founder with a more experienced CEO. O'Brien had known the man for years, and GBI was planning to participate in the loan portion of the investment package. Foster explained that despite pressure from her board of directors—of which O'Brien was chair—she refused to back down:

> I didn't see it as a problem. We've got such challenging mandates already; we can't shy away from the best course of action just because it makes people uncomfortable. Sure, I liked the guy too; he just wasn't the one to take that business to the next level.
>
> As tension-creating as this all became, this would have been a fairly clear issue for traditional VCs. That happens a lot around here: A solution that to me seems basically straightforward can become a big crisis for the parent and this board.
>
> As it turned out, that particular investment wasn't going to happen. But practically speaking, if we could have structured the deal, then I probably would have suffered whatever wrath there would have been and gone ahead and replaced the guy.

Getting to Scale

As with any investment offering, whether or not socially responsible VC models like NCV would be successful long-term was dependent on their performance relative to the needs and expectations of investors. In the early 2000s CDVCs were still very much dependent on public sector funds and socially progressive foundations (see Exhibit 5). Referring to their 10-year financial expectations (see Exhibit 6), Foster emphasized that the success of CDVCs like hers could open the door to a whole new class of rural investment vehicles targeting communities in underserved regions of the country—but only if the industry could attract a more traditional base of limited partners:

> Should we expect mainstream institutional investors to subsidize socially responsible ventures in perpetuity? A 10 to 12 percent return might be reasonable from the point of view of GBI and mission-driven foundations, but if you can't get a pension fund or a bank to make a significant contribution, the market is telling you it's not the appropriate risk–reward.

[12] Although deficits were not uncommon for nonprofits in general and CDCs in particular, GBI had been one of the few in the country that had consistently been able to cover expenses.

[13] Annual management fees of 2 percent of the capital under management covered salaries, office expenses and other overhead, and all costs associated with locating, reviewing, and consummating investment opportunities. Money left over at the end of the year in traditional venture funds was typically disbursed as bonuses to the fund managers. Foster was anticipating little or no remaining capital at the end of the year.

EXHIBIT 5
Funding Sources for CDVCs

Banks and financial institutions	31%
Federal government	25%
Foundations and family trusts	17%
State and local government	11%
Individuals	6%
Corporations and partnerships	6%
Parent entities	3%
Other	1%
	100%

Source: J. B. Rubin, "CDVC; Double Bottom-Line
Approach to Poverty Alleviation," Harvard
Business School, 2001.

I tend to think that an IRR in that range is not sustainable long-term for the risk level that an early-stage fund like this takes on. Our theory is that if we target a materially higher IRR in the range of 15 to 22 percent, we'd be able attract the sort of limited partners that could fund a $50 million to $100 million CDVC effort.

Sustaining Momentum

With regard to the structure of the follow-on fund she was planning to raise, Foster felt that spinning off from GBI would offer more flexibility to craft and replicate the model—especially if this economic development vision of addressing underserved regions and sectors caught on. The question was how to present the idea to O'Brien as a win for GBI. And if O'Brien refused to have GBI step back into the role of a passive limited partner, how could the current working structure be improved?

At a recent CDVC peer group meeting in San Diego, Foster found that her colleagues—many of whom had no previous venture capital experience—were struggling as well:

It's hard enough to do venture investing without a VC background, and focusing on rural regions as a strategy certainly compounds the general execution risk. So it's not surprising that a lot of these managers are finding this to be a real challenge. The overall perception of CDVCs right now seems to be that we are minor-league players who value our social agenda over market-rate returns. That will change only if we can demonstrate that our focus on underserved communities and underserved sectors can be a market advantage—and even a lucrative source of proprietary deal flow.

By the time Foster started heading back from the NCV seminar in Eugene, the storm had long since given way to clear skies. The conference had not been fully attended, but nevertheless it had yielded a couple of interesting leads. While she was confident that NCV could source the deals they needed from their challenging geographic base, Foster needed to determine how she should best position herself and her team for the future.

EXHIBIT 6

NCV 10–Year Projections

	Year 1	Year 2	Year 3	Year 4	Year 5	Year 6	Year 7	Year 8	Year 9	Year 10
Capital Calls	$1,000,000	$3,000,000	$4,000,000	$2,000,000						
Management Fees*	300,000	300,000	300,000	300,000	$ 300,000	$ 300,000	$ 300,000	$ 300,000	$ 300,000	$ 300,000
Investments		600,000	2,800,000	4,000,000	1,900,000	700,000				
Divestments				575,000	1,800,000	5,500,000	6,400,000	8,500,000	7,200,000	5,500,000
Distributions to Investors				275,000	1,500,000	5,200,000	5,460,000	7,350,000	6,180,000	4,650,000
Carried Interest							940,000	1,150,000	1,020,000	850,000

*Annual management fees include president, $90,000; associate, $70,000; administrative assistant, $40,000.

265

Appendix A
Note on the Venture Capital Investing Process

Venture capitalists and entrepreneurs engage in a process whereby they assume and manage the risks associated with investing in compelling new business opportunities. Their aim is long-term value creation for themselves, their companies, their communities, and other stakeholders. The process begins with the conceptualization of an investment opportunity. A prospectus is then written to articulate the strategy and outline the qualifications and track record of the investment team. Raising the money is a networking and sales undertaking that typically gains momentum only after an institutional investment advisor—known as a gatekeeper—has committed capital to the fund.[14]

DIAGRAM A

Classic Venture Capital Investing Process

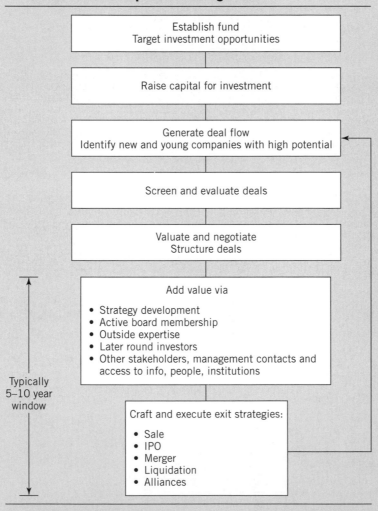

Note: This diagram and additional discussion of venture funding may be found in Chapter 14 of this text.

[14] Institutional investors such as corporations, foundations, and pension funds invest as limited partners in hundreds of venture capital and buyout funds. Many of these investors, having neither the resources nor the expertise to evaluate and manage fund investments, delegate these duties to investment advisors with expertise in the venture capital industry. These advisors pool the assets of their various clients and invest those proceeds on behalf of their limited partners into a venture or buyout fund currently raising capital. For this service, the advisors collect a fee of 1 percent of committed capital per annum. Because these investment experts exert a tremendous amount of influence over the allocation of capital to new and existing venture teams and funds, they are referred to as "gatekeepers."

Once the money is raised, the venture capital firm seeks to add value in many ways: identifying and evaluating business opportunities, negotiating and closing investments, tracking and coaching companies, providing technical and management assistance, and attracting additional capital, directors, management, suppliers, and other key resources (see Diagram A). Given the fortuitous convergence of factors (e.g., management talent, market timing, strategic vision) required for a start-up to reach a profitable harvest event such as an acquisition or an initial public offering (IPO), home runs are rare. In fact, historical data indicate that only about 1 out of every 15 of these investments ever realize a return of 10 times or more on invested capital.

The dominant legal structure for private venture capital funds has been the limited partnership for a specific term of years, with the venture capitalists assuming the role of general partners and the investors as limited partners (see Diagram B). The general partners act as organizers and investment managers of the fund, while the limited partners enjoy a passive role in fund management as well as limited liability for any fund activity. As compensation for their direct participation and risk exposure, general partners can reap substantial capital gains—known as carried interest—as successful portfolio ventures are harvested.

Between 1980 and the early 2000s, there were two recessions (in 1981–1982 and in 1990–1992) and a stock market panic in late 1987 that sent share prices plummeting 22 percent in a single day in October that year. Nevertheless, according to Venture Economics—a private equity database compiler—venture investments during that time yielded a 19.3 percent average annual return after fees and expenses. Over the same period, the S&P 500 and the Russell 2000 index of small companies generated average annual returns, respectively, of 15.7 percent and 13.3 percent.

Equity funds are typically conceived, invested, and exited on an 8- to 12-year cycle, with preparation for follow-on funds beginning in Years 3 and 4. To a large degree, that time frame is driven by the reality that, on average, it takes five to seven years to build and harvest a successful portfolio investment.

Successful funds yield a significant financial upside. In the early 2000s the average total pay packages (salary plus bonus) for managing general partners and senior partners were $1.24 million and $1.04 million, respectively. Carried interest distributions to a general partner of a top firm averaged $2.5 million over the life of the fund.

DIAGRAM B
Flows of Venture Capital

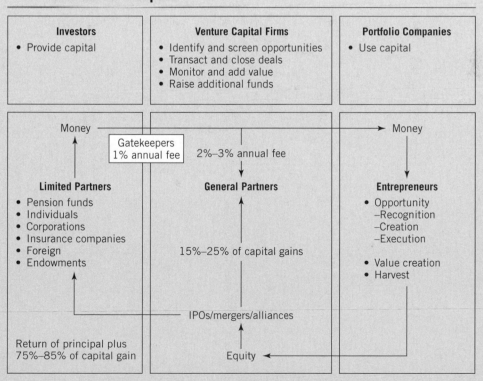

Note: This diagram and additional discussion of venture funding may be found in Chapter 14 of this text.

Chapter Eight

The Business Plan

Wanna make God laugh? Have a plan!

The late George Burns,
Hollywood and TV comedian

Results Expected

Upon completion of this chapter, you will be able to

1. Utilize a model of a proven business plan—refined over nearly 40 years of actual use.

2. Determine what needs to be included in the plan, why, and for whom.

3. Identify some pitfalls in the business plan preparation process and understand how to avoid them.

4. Articulate what has to be done to develop and complete a business plan for your proposed venture, and understand the level of commitment required to turn that vision into a written document.

5. Explain how a well-articulated business plan is an important part of the entrepreneurial process, not an end in itself.

6. Discuss and share ideas about the Newland Medical Technologies case study, and assess the business plan developed by that young entrepreneur to raise capital for her medical device venture.

Why Do a Business Plan?

The book *Undaunted Courage* tells the story of the extraordinary journey of the Lewis and Clark expedition to explore the new Louisiana Purchase and reach the Pacific Ocean. The two leaders of this incredibly ambitious trip invested two years to prepare an extremely thorough plan. Yet day after day during the journey—from 1804 to 1806—they ventured into uncharted territory, without good maps, or anyone on the original crew who knew the rivers and trails. Thus on numerous occasions the expedition would lose its way for long stretches and have to backtrack for miles. Encounters with grizzly bears were terrifying. And without the help of Native American tribes along the way, they all would have

perished. All the planning and preparation in the world could not have foreseen the unknowns they faced or prepared them with strategies and tactics to deal with each new situation.

This epic adventure has many things in common with most start-ups—especially for young entrepreneurs taking such a journey for the first time, as many of you are. It is an unmapped course; and as we discussed in Chapter 3, its dynamic and chaotic properties create many risks, surprises, and pitfalls, as well as rewards. Also, a first-time traveler has little or no experience to fall back on as a guide and reality check. Finally, for a first-time entrepreneur, grizzly bears are out there—you just don't know where, when you'll happen upon them, or how many will try to eat you. To embark on a perilous start-up journey without some serious planning defies sensibility. Particularly for a first-timer, a plan has numerous benefits:

- It is a great way for you and your current and/or prospective partners to learn about the business and to gain critical insights into each other's style, strengths and weaknesses, and how you will work together.
- It will give you intimate knowledge of the "four anchors" noted earlier, including key ingredients such as the opportunity, the buyer and user, the market and competition, the economics and financial characteristics of the business, and the likely entry strategy.
- It is a great tool with which to communicate and to persuade stakeholders, including potential backers, team members, key new hires, directors, brain trust prospects, and strategic partners.
- It will prevent (or at least minimize) any temptation to jump ahead prematurely, as well as limit sloppiness with regard to the hard thinking, the necessary research, and creative problem solving.
- It will test your commitment and prevent your heart from getting too far ahead of your head (falling in love with your idea and losing your objectivity).
- It will save you time, help you avoid common mistakes, and help create order out of what is fundamentally a chaotic and, in many respects, unpredictable and unplannable event—a core paradox of the entrepreneurial process—as suggested in the opening quotation by George Burns.
- It will help you create the best—but not perfect—road map and blueprint for you and your team to move ahead. And it *can* be changed.
- It is a medium for discussion with prospective investors, and it can reveal who among them is most knowledgeable, creative, suited for, and likely to add significant value to your venture.

Why would you *not* want to acquire these benefits?

When Is a Business Plan Not Needed?

Needless to say, not all new businesses have start-up business plans. Back-of-the envelope business plans that turn into legendary businesses defy convention. As a result, some people argue that business plans are not necessary at all—and even that they get in the way of action. Yet most of these legendary exceptions are from either genius-type entrepreneurs

(such as Bill Gates or the Google founders) or very experienced ones. Entrepreneurs who have previously made investors wealthy with their last ventures typically can raise capital for their next ventures without exhaustive start-up plans. Often two or three PowerPoint slides will suffice. There are opportunities that may simply be moving too fast, and the best tactic may be what we call a "dehydrated business plan." Before you reach your own conclusion, consider the ideas, tips, and issues we will share in the next few pages.

Developing the Business Plan

The business plan itself is the culmination of a usually lengthy, arduous, creative, and iterative process that, as we explored in Chapters 5 and 6, can transform the caterpillar of a raw idea into the magnificent butterfly of an opportunity. The plan will carefully articulate the merits, requirements, risks, and potential rewards of the opportunity and how it will be seized. It will demonstrate how the anchors noted here (and in Chapter 5) reveal themselves to the founders and investors by converting all the research, careful thought, and creative problem solving from the Venture Opportunity Screening Exercises into a thorough plan. The business plan for a high-potential venture reveals the business's ability to

- Create or add significant value to a customer or end user.
- Solve a significant problem, or meet a significant want or need for which someone will pay a premium.
- Have robust market, margin, and moneymaking characteristics: large enough ($50+ million), high growth (20-plus percent), high margins (40+ percent), strong and early free cash flow (recurring revenue, low assets, and working capital), high profit potential (10 to 15 percent after tax), and attractive realizable returns for investors (25 to 30 percent IRR).
- *Fit* well with the founder(s) and management team at the time, in the marketplace, and with the risk–reward balance.
- Scale with an eye toward sustainability and impacts.

The plan becomes the point of departure for prospective investors to begin their due diligence to ascertain potential and various risks of the venture: technology risks, market risks, management risks, competitive and strategic risks, and financial risks. Even if you do not intend to raise outside capital, this homework is vital. The collisions between founders and investors that occur during meetings, discussions,

Going beyond Green

Everyone is going green. Every day brings a new announcement of a company embracing environmental issues. Those ahead of the pack have grasped that the environment is a growing source of strategic opportunity for companies. A revolution is under way in business as forward-thinking companies gain competitive advantage by reorienting products and processes to take environmental issues into account.

We are hard-pressed to point to an industry or manufacturer able to ignore the trends. Company brand names and stock prices are increasingly influenced by environmental records. Growing numbers of firms working in areas as diverse as building construction, furnishings, food, energy, transportation, and materials design—to name a few—are bringing new green designs to market. But green gestures will not be enough if the competition understands a deeper dimension to the issues and builds its strategy accordingly.

Businesses now experience increased global regulatory pressure, demand for heightened transparency, and growing public concern about the environment and health. Government procurement and business buyers increasingly use environmental criteria in purchasing. Markets in and taxes on carbon emissions now factor into corporate strategy. Companies also face environmental performance pressures from the investment sector, including stockholder petitions and unprecedented growth in screened investment funds that rank corporate behavior on environmental issues. These forces have created a much more complex and challenging business climate, as well as numerous opportunities for proactive and creative new ventures.

Source: Adapted from *Going beyond "Green": Business Strategy at the Headwaters*, prospectus, A. Larson and K. P. O'Brien, March 2007.

---

and investigations reveal a great deal to all parties and begin to set the mood for their relationship and negotiations. Getting to know each other much more closely is a crucial part of the evaluation process. Everyone will be thinking, Are these intelligent people? Can we work well with them during thick but especially thin times? Are they creative? Do they listen? Can they add value to the venture? Is this the right management? Do I want them as business partners? Are they honest? Are we having fun yet?

The investors who can bring the most insight, know-how, and contacts to the venture, and thus add the greatest value, will reveal themselves as well. The most valuable investors will see weaknesses, even flaws, in how the market is viewed, the technology or service, the strategies, the proposed size and structure of the financing, and the team—and will propose strategies and people to correct these. If it is the right investor, it can make the difference between an average and a good or great venture.

The Plan Is Obsolete at the Printer

The authors have argued for three decades that the plan is obsolete the instant it emerges from the printer. In today's fast-paced climate, it is obsolete before it goes into the printer! The pace of technological and information-age change, and the dynamism of the global marketplace, shorten the already brief life expectancy of any business plan. It is nearly impossible to find a year-old venture today that is identical in strategy, market focus, products or services, and team as the original business plan described.

Work in Progress—Bent Knees Required

In such a rapidly changing environment, flexibility and responsiveness become critical survival skills. Developing an idea into a business, and articulating how this will be done via a business plan, requires an open mind and "bent knees," along with clear focus, commitment, and determination.

The business plan should be thought of as a work in progress. Though it must be completed if you are trying to raise outside capital, attract key advisors, directors, team members, or the like, it can never be finished. Like a cross-country flight plan, many unexpected changes can occur along the way: a thunderstorm, smoke-impaired visibility, fog, or powerful winds can develop. You have to be prepared to continually adjust course to minimize risk and ensure successful completion of the journey. Such risk–reward management is inherent in the business planning process.

The Plan Is Not the Business

Developing the business plan is one of the best ways to define the blueprint, strategy, resource, and people requirements for a new venture. This document focuses and communicates the founder's vision. The vast majority of *INC.*'s 500 fastest-growing companies had business plans at the outset. Without a business plan, it is exceedingly difficult to raise capital from informal or formal investors.

Too often first-time entrepreneurs jump to a simplistic conclusion: All that is needed is a fat, polished,

Do's and Don'ts for Preparing a Business Plan

Do

Involve all of the management team in the preparation of the business plan.

Make the plan logical, comprehensive, readable, and as short as possible.

Demonstrate commitment to the venture by investing a significant amount of time and some money in preparing the plan.

Articulate what the critical risks and assumptions are and how and why these are tolerable.

Disclose and discuss any current or potential problems in the venture.

Identify several alternative sources of financing.

Spell out the proposed deal—how much for what ownership share—and how investors will win.

Be creative in gaining the attention and interest of potential investors.

Remember that the plan is not the business and that an ounce of can-do implementation is worth two pounds of planning.

Accept orders and customers that will generate a positive cash flow, even if it means you have to postpone writing the plan.

Know your targeted investor groups (e.g., venture capitalist, angel investor, bank, or leasing company) and what they really want and what they dislike, and tailor your plan accordingly.

Let realistic market and sales projections drive the assumptions underlying the financial spreadsheets, rather than the reverse.

Don't

Have unnamed, mysterious people on the management team (e.g., a "Mr. G" who is currently a financial vice president with another firm and who will join you later).

Make ambiguous, vague, or unsubstantiated statements, such as estimating sales on the basis of what the team would like to produce.

Describe technical products or manufacturing processes using jargon or in a way that only an expert can understand, because this limits the usefulness of the plan.

Spend money on developing fancy brochures, elaborate PowerPoint and Flash presentations, and other "sizzle"; instead show the "steak."

Waste time writing a plan when you could be closing sales and collecting cash.

Assume you have a done deal when you have a handshake or verbal commitment but no money in the bank. (The deal is done when the check clears!)

---

and enticing business plan and the business will automatically be successful. They confuse the plan with building the business. Some of the most impressive business plans never become great businesses. And some of the weakest plans lead to extraordinary businesses. Mitch Kapor's original business plan for Lotus Development Corporation, creator of the 1-2-3 spreadsheet, was a brief letter, some descriptions of the personal computer market, a description of nearly 10 separate products, a one-year monthly start-up budget, and a five-year goal of $30 million in revenue, which would require about $200,000 to $300,000 in capital. Venture capital backers Sevin-Rosen basically discarded the plan, the strategy, the product mix, the capital requirements, the launch plan, and the vision for the venture's first five years. These venture capitalists concluded the opportunity was much bigger, that $1 million of start-up capital was required, that the company would either be several hundred million in revenue in five years or would not be in business, even at $30 million in sales. The first-mover advantage of a warp-speed

launch strategy was vital, and the rocket needed to be lit. The rest is history. Lotus Development reached $500 million in revenue in the first five years.

The message here is two-edged. The odds can be shaped in your favor through the development of a business plan. But just because you have a plan does not mean the business will be an automatic success. Unless the fundamental opportunity is there, along with the requisite resources and team needed to pursue it, the best plan in the world won't make much difference. Some helpful tips in preparing a business plan are summarized in Exhibit 8.1.

Some Tips from the Trenches

The most valuable lessons about preparing a business plan and raising venture capital come from entrepreneurs who have succeeded in these endeavors. Tom Huseby[1] is founder and head of SeaPoint Ventures outside Seattle, a venture capital firm allied with Venrock Venture Capital, Oak Venture Partners, and Sevin-Rosen Venture Partners. An engineering

---

[1] The authors are extremely grateful to Tom Huseby, a longtime friend, fellow fly fisherman, and wilderness explorer, for sharing his extraordinary wit and insights over the years in classes at Babson College, Harvard Business School, and with the Kauffman Fellows Program, and for his contribution here.

graduate of Columbia University and a Stanford MBA, Huseby spent 18 years with Raychem Corporation of California, first working in sales, then developing and managing new businesses, and eventually running Raychem's businesses in several countries. Tom is a remarkable entrepreneur who has raised more than $80 million of venture capital as CEO of two telecommunications start-up companies in the early and mid-1990s that subsequently became publicly traded companies: Innova Corporation (NASDAQ: INNV) and Metawave Corporation (NASDAQ: MWAV). Consider the following wisdom Tom gleaned from his own experience on both sides of the negotiating table: entrepreneur/CEO and venture capitalist.

RE: Venture Capitalists

- There are a lot of venture capitalists. Once you meet one you could end up meeting all 700-plus of them.

- Getting a no from venture capitalists is as hard as getting a yes; qualify your targets and force others to say no.

- Be vague about what other venture capitalists you are talking to.

- Don't ever meet with an associate or junior member twice without also meeting with a partner in that venture capital firm.

RE: The Plan

- Stress your business concept in the executive summary.

- The numbers don't matter; but the economics (e.g., value proposition and business model) really matter.

- Make the business plan look and feel good.

- Prepare lots of copies of published articles, contracts, market studies, purchase orders, and the like.

- Prepare very detailed résumés and reference lists of key players in the venture.

- If you can't do the details, make sure you hire someone who can.

RE: The Deal

- Make sure your current investors are as desperate as you are.

- Create a market for your venture.

- Never say no to an offer price.

- Use a lawyer who is experienced at closing venture deals.

- Don't stop selling until the money is in the bank.

- Make it a challenge.

- Never lie.

RE: The Fund-Raising Process

- It is much harder than you ever thought it could be.

- You can last much longer than you ever thought you could.

- The venture capitalists have done this before and have to do this for the rest of their lives!

This is particularly valuable advice for any entrepreneur seeking outside capital and anticipating dealing with investors.[2]

How to Determine If Investors Can Add Value

One of the most frequently missed opportunities in the entire process of developing a business plan and trying to convince outside investors to part with their cash is a consequence of sell-sell-sell! myopia by the founders. Selling ability is one of the most common denominators among successful entrepreneurs.

Too often, however, entrepreneurs—typically out of cash, or nearly so—become so obsessed with selling to prospective investors that they fail to ask great questions and do little serious listening. As a result, these founders learn little from these prospects, even though they probably know a great deal about the technology, market, and competitors. After all, that is the investor's business.

Entrepreneurs who not only succeed at developing a great business concept but also attract the right investors who can add a great deal of value to the venture through their experience, wisdom, and networks are usually very savvy listeners. They use the opportunity, beyond presenting their plan and selling themselves, to carefully query prospective investors: You've seen our concept, our story, and our strategies; what have we missed? Where are we vulnerable? How would you knock us off? Who will knock us off? How would you modify our strategy? What would you do differently? Whom do we need with us to make this succeed? What do you believe has to happen to make this highly successful? Be as blunt as you wish.

Two powerful forces are unleashed in this process. First, as a founder, you will begin to discern just how smart, knowledgeable, and, most important, creative the investors are about the proposed business. Do they have creative ideas, insights, and alternative ways of thinking about the opportunity and strategy

---

[2] See also W. A. Sahlman, "How to Write a Great Business Plan," *Harvard Business Review*, July–August 1997, pp. 98–108, for an excellent article about business plans.

that you and your team may not have thought of? This enables you, the founder, to ascertain just what value the investors might add to the venture and whether their approach to telling you and your team that you are "all wet" on certain things is acceptable. Would the relationship be likely to wear you out over time and demoralize you? In the process you will learn a great deal about your plan and the investors.

The second powerful force is the message implicitly sent to the investors when you make such genuine queries and listen, rather than become argumentative and defensive (which they may try to get you to do): We have given this our best shot. We are highly committed to our concept and believe we have the right strategy, but our minds are open. We listen; we learn; we have bent knees; we adapt and change when the evidence and ideas are compelling; we are not granite heads. Investors are much more likely to conclude that you are a founder and a team that they can work with.

The Dehydrated Business Plan

A dehydrated business plan usually runs from 4 to10 pages, but rarely more. It covers key points, such as those suggested for the executive summary in the business planning guide that follows. Essentially, such a plan documents the analysis of and information about the heart of the business opportunity, competitive advantages the company will enjoy, and creative insights that an entrepreneur often has.

Because it can usually be prepared in a few hours, it is preferred by entrepreneurs who find it difficult to find enough slack time while operating a business to write a complete plan. In many instances, investors prefer a dehydrated plan in the initial screening phase.

A dehydrated plan is not intended to be used exclusively in the process of raising or borrowing money; it can be a valuable compass to keep you on track. Consider it a map of the main battleground ahead, but remember that it will not provide the necessary details and tactical plans necessary to conduct the battle.

Who Develops the Business Plan?

Consideration often is given to hiring an outside professional to prepare the business plan so the management team can use its time to obtain financing and start the business.

There are two good reasons it is *not* a good idea to hire outside professionals. First, in the process of planning and of writing the business plan, the consequences of different strategies and tactics and the human and financial requirements for launching and building the venture can be examined before it is too late. For example, one entrepreneur discovered, while preparing his business plan, that the major market for his biomedical product was in nursing homes rather than in hospital emergency rooms, as he and his physician partner had previously assumed. This realization changed the focus of the marketing effort. Had he left the preparation to an outsider, this might not have been discovered or, at the very least, it is unlikely he would have had the same sense of confidence and commitment to the new strategy.

A Closer Look at the What

The Relationship between Goals and Actions

Consider a team that is enthusiastic about an idea for a new business and has done a considerable amount of thinking and initial work evaluating the opportunity (such as thoroughly working through the Venture Opportunity Screening Exercises in Chapter 6). Team members believe the business they are considering has excellent market prospects and fits well with the skills, experience, personal goals, values, and aspirations of the lead entrepreneur and the management team. They now need to ask about the most significant risks and problems involved in launching the enterprise, the long-term profit prospects, and the future financing and cash flow requirements. The team must determine the demands of operating lead times, seasonality, facility location, marketing and pricing strategy needs, and so forth, so they can take action.

These questions now need to be answered convincingly with the evidence for them shown *in writing*. The planning and the development of such a business plan is neither quick nor easy. In fact, effective planning is a difficult process that demands time, discipline, commitment, dedication, and practice. However, it also can be stimulating and fun as innovative solutions and strategies to solve nagging problems are found.

The skills to write a business plan are not necessarily the ones needed to make a venture successful (although some of these skills are certainly useful). The best single point of departure for, and an anchor during, the planning process is the motto on a small plaque in the office of Paul J. Tobin, past president of Cellular One, a company that was a pioneer in the cellular phone business in America. The motto says "Can Do" and is an apt one for planning and for making sure that a plan serves the practical purpose for which it is intended.

Further, if a venture intends to use the business plan to raise capital, it is important for the team to do the planning and write the plan itself. Investors attach great importance to the quality of the management team *and* to their complete understanding of the business they are preparing to enter. Thus investors want to be sure that what they see is what they get—that is, the team's analysis and understanding of the venture opportunity and its commitment to it. Investors usually correlate a team's ability to communicate the vision with their ability to make it a reality. They are going to invest in a team and a leader, not in a consultant. Nothing less will do, and anything less is usually obvious.

Segmenting and Integrating Information

When planning and writing a business plan, it is necessary to organize information in a way that it can be managed and that is useful.

An effective way to organize information with the idea of developing a business plan is to segment the information into sections, such as the target market, the industry, the competition, the financial plan, and so on, and then integrate the information into a business plan.

This process works best if sections are discrete and the information within them digestible. Then the order in which sections are developed can vary, and different sections can be developed simultaneously. For example, because the heart and soul of a plan lie in the analysis of the market opportunity, of the competition, and of a resultant competitive strategy that can win, it is a good idea to start with these sections and integrate information along the way. Because the financial and operations aspects of the venture will be driven by the rate of growth and the magnitude and the specific substance of the market revenue plans, these can be developed later.

The information is then further integrated into the business plan. The executive summary is prepared last.

Establishing Action Steps

The following steps, centered around actions to be taken, outline the process by which a business plan is written. These action steps are presented in the Business Plan Guide exercise at the end of this chapter.

- *Segmenting information.* An overall plan for the project, by section, needs to be devised and needs to include priorities—who is responsible for each section, the due date of a first draft, and the due date of a final draft.
- *Creating an overall schedule.* Next create a more specific list of tasks; identify priorities and who is responsible for them. Determine when they will be started and when they will be completed. This list needs to be as specific and detailed as possible. Tasks need to be broken down into the smallest possible components (e.g., a series of phone calls may be necessary before a

trip). The list then needs to be examined for conflicts and lack of reality in time estimates. Peers and business associates can be asked to review the list for realism, timing, and priorities.

- *Creating an action calendar.* Tasks on the *do* list then need to be placed on a calendar. When the calendar is complete, the calendar needs to be reexamined for conflicts or lack of realism.
- *Doing the work and writing the plan.* The necessary work needs to be done and the plan written. Adjustments need to be made to the *do* list and the calendar, as necessary. As part of this process, it is important to have a plan reviewed by an attorney to make sure it contains no misleading statements, unnecessary information, and caveats. The plan also needs to be reviewed by an objective outsider, such as an entrepreneurially minded executive who has significant profit and loss responsibility, or a venture capitalist who would not be a potential investor. No matter how good the lead entrepreneur and his or her team are in planning, there will be issues that they will overlook and certain aspects of the presentation that are inadequate or less than clear. A good reviewer also can act as a sounding board in the process of developing alternative solutions to problems and answers to questions investors are likely to ask.

Preparing a Business Plan

A Complete Business Plan

It may seem to an entrepreneur who has completed the exercises in Chapter 6 and who has spent hours informally thinking and planning that jotting down a few things is all that needs to be done. *However, there is a great difference between screening an opportunity and developing a business plan.*

There are two important differences in the way these issues need to be addressed. First, a business plan can have two uses: (1) inducing someone to part with $500,000 to $10 million or more, and (2) guiding the policies and actions of the firm over a number of years. Therefore, strategies and statements need to be well thought out, unambiguous, and capable of being supported.

Another difference is that more detail is needed. (The exception to this is the dehydrated business plan discussed earlier in this chapter.) This means the team needs to spend more time gathering detailed data, interpreting them, and presenting them clearly. For example, for the purpose of screening an opportunity, it may be all right to note (if you cannot do any better) that the target market for a product is in the $30 million to $60 million range and the market is growing over 10 percent per year. For planning an actual launch, this level of detail is not sufficient. The size range would need to be narrowed considerably; if it were not narrowed, those reading or using the plan would have little confidence in this critical number. And saying the target market is growing at over 10 percent is too vague. Does that mean the market grew at the stated rate between last year and the year before, or does it mean that the market grew on average by this amount over the past three years? Also, a statement phrased in terms of "over 10 percent" smacks of imprecision. The actual growth rate needs to be known and stated. Whether the rate will or will not remain the same, and why, must also be explained.

Preparing an effective business plan for a start-up can easily take 200 to 300 hours. Squeezing that amount of time into evenings and weekends can make the process stretch over 3 to 12 months.

A plan for a business expansion or for a situation such as a leveraged buyout typically takes half this effort because more is known about the business, including the market, its competition, financial and accounting information, and so on.

Exhibit 8.2 is a sample table of contents for a business plan. The information shown is included in most

---

EXHIBIT 8.2

Business Plan Table of Contents

I. EXECUTIVE SUMMARY
Description of the Business Concept and the Business Opportunity and Strategy.
Target Market and Projections.
Competitive Advantages.
The Team.
The Offering.

II. THE INDUSTRY AND THE COMPANY AND ITS PRODUCT(S) OR SERVICE(S)
The Industry.
The Company and the Concept.
The Product(s) or Service(s).
Entry and Growth Strategy.

III. MARKET RESEARCH AND ANALYSIS
Customers.
Market Size and Trends.
Competition and Competitive Edges.
Estimated Market Share and Sales.
Ongoing Market Evaluation.

IV. THE ECONOMICS OF THE BUSINESS
Gross and Operating Margins.
Profit Potential and Durability.
Fixed, Variable, and Semivariable Costs.
Months to Breakeven.
Months to Reach Positive Cash Flow.

V. MARKETING PLAN
Overall Marketing Strategy.
Pricing.
Sales Tactics.
Service and Warranty Policies.
Advertising and Promotion.
Distribution.

VI. DESIGN AND DEVELOPMENT PLANS
Development Status and Tasks.
Difficulties and Risks.
Product Improvement and New Products.
Costs.
Proprietary Issues.

VII. MANUFACTURING AND OPERATIONS PLAN
Operating Cycle.
Geographical Location.
Facilities and Improvements.
Strategy and Plans.
Regulatory and Legal Issues.

VIII. MANAGEMENT TEAM
Organization.
Key Management Personnel.
Management Compensation and Ownership.
Other Investors.
Employment and Other Agreements and Stock Option and Bonus Plans.
Board of Directors.
Other Shareholders, Rights, and Restrictions.
Supporting Professional Advisors and Services.

IX. SUSTAINABILITY AND IMPACT
Issues of Sustainability of the Venture.
Impact on the Environment.
Impact on the Community and Nation.

X. OVERALL SCHEDULE

XI. CRITICAL RISKS, PROBLEMS, AND ASSUMPTIONS

XII. THE FINANCIAL PLAN
Actual Income Statements and Balance Sheets.
Pro Forma Income Statements.
Pro Forma Balance Sheets.
Pro Forma Cash Flow Analysis.
Break-Even Chart and Calculation.
Cost Control.
Highlights.

XIII. PROPOSED COMPANY OFFERING
Desired Financing.
Offering.
Capitalization.
Use of Funds.
Investor's Return.

XIV. APPENDIXES

A Final Checklist*

This list will help you allocate your time and maintain your focus!
These points will also be important as you prepare for an
oral presentation of your business plan.

Make Your Point Quickly and Give Hierarchy to Your Data—The Details Matter!

✓ Hook the readers, especially in the executive summary, by having a compelling opportunity where you can:

- Identify a need or opportunity in a large and growing market.
- Conceptualize a business that will fill that need or take advantage of that opportunity.
- Demonstrate that you have the know-how and the team to effectively build a profitable and sustainable business (or identify how you will create such a team).

✓ Prioritize the points you are making into three categories:

- Essential—without this the plan makes no sense.
- Good to know—directly supports and gives context to your essential points.
- Interesting—provides a higher level of understanding of market dynamics, industry, and so on but may not relate directly to the nuts and bolts of your business plan. Interesting information should be relegated to the appendix so it doesn't get in the way of the reader.

✓ Articulate the size of your market: who are your customers, why they will purchase your product or service, how much they will buy at what price.

✓ Include evidence of customers—this will increase your credibility.

✓ Discuss the competition, and why the customer will buy your product or service versus the alternatives.

✓ Articulate your marketing strategy. How will customers become aware of your product and service, and how will you communicate the benefits?

✓ Be specific when discussing your team. Articulate what relevant experience each brings to the business. If you can't identify key managers, you should outline the type of experience you want and a plan for recruiting that person.

✓ Edit for the details—clarity and typos—a sloppy presentation says a lot!

° The authors are grateful to Greg White of Chicago Venture Partners, who developed this list, and to longtime friend and entrepreneur Frederic Alper for sharing this with us. They use this approach in their work with the Denali Initiative, a national program that teaches entrepreneurship to leaders of nonprofit organizations from many parts of the country, and use *New Venture Creation* in its curriculum.

effective business plans and is a good framework to follow. Organizing the material into sections makes dealing with the information more manageable. Also, while the amount of detail and the order of presentation may vary for a particular venture according to its circumstances, most effective business plans contain this information in some form. (The amount of detail and the order in which information is presented is important. These can vary for each particular situation and will depend on the purpose of the plan and the age and stage of the venture, among other factors.)

Chapter Summary

- The business plan is more of a process and work in progress than an end in itself.
- Given today's pace of change in all areas affecting an enterprise, the plan is obsolete the moment it emerges from the printer.
- The business plan is a blueprint and flight plan for a journey that converts ideas into opportunities, articulates and manages risks and rewards, and articulates the likely flight and timing for a venture.
- The numbers in a business plan don't matter, but the economics of the business model and value proposition matter enormously.

- The plan is not the business; some of the most successful ventures were launched without a formal business plan or with one that would be considered weak or flawed.
- Preparing and presenting the plan to prospective investors is one of the best ways for the team to have a trial marriage, to learn about the venture strategy, and to determine who can add the greatest value.
- The dehydrated business plan can be a valuable shortcut in the process of creating, shaping, and molding an idea into a business.

Study Questions

1. What is a business plan, for whom is it prepared, and why?
2. What should a complete business plan include?
3. Who should prepare the business plan?
4. How is the plan used by potential investors, and what are the four anchors they are attempting to validate?
5. What is a dehydrated business plan, and when and why can it be an effective tool?

6. Explain the expression, The numbers in the plan don't matter.
7. How can entrepreneurs use the business plan process to identify the best team members, directors, and value-added investors?
8. Prepare an outline of a business plan tailored to the specific venture you have in mind.

Internet Resources for Chapter 8

http://www.sba.gov/starting_business *Features a "Business Plan Road Map of Success" tutorial.*

http://www.businessplans.org *Helpful resources c/o Business Resource Software.*

MIND STRETCHERS

Have You Considered?

1. You have sell-sell-sell mind-set myopia, but it has to be tempered with listening, inquiry, and learning. Can you think of a time when you have oversold? What did you learn from that experience?
2. Under what conditions and circumstances is it not to your advantage to prepare a business plan?
3. Identify three businesses that exceed $10 million in sales, are profitable, and did not have a business plan at launch. Why, and what did you learn from this?

4. Some of the most valuable critiques and inputs on your venture will come from outside your team. Who else should review your plan? Who knows the industry/market/technology/competitors?
5. A good friend offers you a look at a business plan. You are a director of a company that is a potential competitor of the venture proposed in the plan. What would you do?

The Business Plan Guide

An Exercise and Framework

This Business Plan Guide follows the order of presentation outlined in Exhibit 8.2. Based on a guide originally developed at Venture Founders Corporation by Leonard E. Smollen and the late Brian Haslett, and on more than 30 years of observing and working with entrepreneurs and actually preparing and evaluating hundreds of plans, it is intended to make this challenging task easier.

There is no single best way to write a business plan; the task will evolve in a way that suits you and your situation. While there are many ways to approach the preparation for and writing of a business plan, it is recommended that you begin with the market research and analysis sections. In writing your plan, you should remember that although one of the important functions of a business plan is to influence investors, rather than preparing a fancy presentation, you and your team need to prove to yourselves and others that your opportunity is worth pursuing and to construct the means by which you will do it. Gathering information, making hard decisions, and developing plans come first.

The Business Plan Guide shows how to present information succinctly and in a format acceptable to investors. Although it is useful to keep in mind who your audience is and that information not clearly presented will most likely not be used, it also is important not to be concerned just with format. The Business Plan Guide indicates specific issues and shows you what needs to be included in a business plan and why.

You may feel as though you have seen much of this before. You should. The guide is based on the analytical framework described in the book and builds upon the Venture Opportunity Screening Exercises in Chapter 6. If you have not completed the Opportunity Screening Exercises, it is helpful to do so before proceeding. The Business Plan Guide will allow you to draw on data and analysis developed in the Venture Opportunity Screening Exercises as you prepare your business plan.

As you proceed through the Business Plan Guide, remember that statements need to be supported with data whenever possible. Note also that it is sometimes easier to present data in graphic, visual form. Include the source of all data, the methods and/or assumptions used, and the credentials of people doing research. If data on which a statement is based are available elsewhere in the plan, be sure to reference where.

Remember that the Business Plan Guide is just that—a guide. It is intended to be applicable to a wide range of product and service businesses. Certain critical issues are unique to any industry or market. In the chemical industry, for example, some special issues of significance currently exist, such as increasingly strict regulations at all levels of government concerning the use of chemical products and the operation of processes, diminishing viability of the high capital cost, special-purpose chemical processing plants serving a narrow market, and long delivery times of processing equipment. In the electronics industry, the special issues may be the future availability and price of new kinds of large-scale integrated circuits. Common sense should rule in applying the guide to your specific venture.

The Guide

Name:

Venture:

Date:

STEP 1

Segment Information into Key Sections.

Establish priorities for each section, including individual responsibilities and due dates for drafts and the final version. When you segment your information, it is vital to keep in mind that the plan needs to be logically integrated and that information should be consistent. Because the market opportunity section is the heart and soul of the plan, it may be the most difficult section to write; but it is best to assign it a high priority and to begin working there first. Remember to include such tasks as printing in the list.

Section or Task	Priority	Person(s) Responsible	Date to Begin	First Draft Due Date	Date Completed or Final Version Due Date

STEP 2

List Tasks That Need to Be Completed.

Devise an overall schedule for preparing the plan by assigning priorities, persons responsible, and due dates to each task necessary to complete the plan. It is helpful to break larger items (fieldwork to gather customer and competitor intelligence, trade show visits, etc.) into small, more manageable components (such as phone calls required before a trip can be taken) and to include the components as a task. *Be as specific as possible.*

Task	Priority	Person Responsible	Date to Begin	Date of Completion

STEP 3
Combine the List of Segments and the List of Tasks to Create a Calendar.
In combining your lists, consider if anything has been omitted and whether you have been realistic in what people can do, when they can do it, what needs to be done, and so forth. To create your calendar, place an X in the week when the task is to be started and an X in the week it is to be completed and then connect the Xs. When you have placed all tasks on the calendar, look carefully again for conflicts or lack of realism. In particular, evaluate whether team members are overscheduled.

Task	Week														
	1	2	3	4	5	6	7	8	9	10	11	12	13	14	15

STEP 4

A Framework to Develop and Write a Business Plan.

As has been discussed, the framework here follows the order of presentation of the table of contents shown in Exhibit 8.2. While preparing your own plan, you will most likely want to consider sections in a different order from the one presented in this exhibit. (Also, when you integrate your sections into your final plan, you may choose to present material somewhat differently.)

Cover

The cover page includes the name of the company, its address, its telephone number, the date, and the securities offered. Usually the name, address, telephone number, and the date are centered at the top of the page and the securities offered are listed at the bottom. Also suggested on the cover page at the bottom is the following text:

> This business plan has been submitted on a confidential basis solely for the benefit of selected, highly qualified investors in connection with the private placement of the above securities and is not for use by any other persons. Neither may it be reproduced, stored, or copied in any form. By accepting delivery of this plan, the recipient agrees to return this copy to the corporation at the address listed above if the recipient does not undertake to subscribe to the offering. Do not copy, fax, reproduce, or distribute without permission.

Table of Contents

Included in the table of contents is a list of the sections, subsections, and any appendixes, and the pages on which they can be found. (See Exhibit 8.2.)

I. Executive Summary   The first section in the body of the business plan is usually an executive summary. The summary is usually short and concise (one or two pages). The summary articulates what the opportunity conditions are and why they exist, who will execute the opportunity and why they are capable of doing so, and how the firm will gain entry and market penetration—it answers the questions we asked in Chapter 5: "For *what* reason does this venture exist and for *whom?*"

Essentially the summary for your venture needs to mirror the criteria shown in Exhibit 5.8 and the Venture Opportunity Screening Exercises in Chapter 6. This is your chance to clearly articulate how your business is durable and timely, and how it will create or add value to the buyer or end user.

The summary is usually prepared after the other sections of the business plan are completed. As the other sections are drafted, it is helpful to note one or two key sentences and some key facts and numbers from each.

The summary is important for those ventures trying to raise or borrow money. Many investors, bankers, managers, and other readers use the summary to determine quickly whether they find the venture of interest. Therefore, unless the summary is appealing and compelling, it may be the only section read, and you may never get the chance to make a presentation or discuss your business in person.

Leave plenty of time to prepare the summary. (Successful public speakers have been known to spend an hour of preparation for each minute of their speech.)

The executive summary usually contains a paragraph or two covering each of the following:

A. *Description of the business concept and the business.* Describe the business concept for the business you are or will be in. Be sure the description of your concept explains how your product or service will fundamentally change the way customers currently do certain things. For example, Arthur Rock, the lead investor in Apple Computer and Intel, has stated that he focuses on concepts that will change the way people live and/or work. You need to identify when the company was formed, what it will do, what is special or proprietary about its product, service, or technology, and so forth. Include summary information about any proprietary technology, trade secrets, or unique capabilities that give you an edge in the marketplace. If the company has existed for a few years, a brief summary of its size and progress is in order. Try to make your description use 25 or fewer words, and briefly describe the specific product or service.

B. *The opportunity and strategy.* Summarize what the opportunity is, why it is compelling, and the entry strategy planned to exploit it. Clearly state the main point or benefit you are addressing. This information may be presented as an outline of the key facts, conditions, competitors' vulnerabilities ("sleepiness," sluggishness, poor service, etc.), industry trends (is it fragmented or emerging?), and other evidence and logic that define the opportunity. Note plans for growth and expansion beyond the entry products or services and into other market segments (such as international markets) as appropriate.

C. *The target market and projections.* Identify and briefly explain the industry and market, who the primary customer groups are, how the product(s) or service(s) will be positioned, and how you plan to reach and service these groups. Include information about the structure of the market, the size and growth rate for the market segments or niches you are seeking, your unit and dollar sales estimates, your anticipated market share, the payback period for your customers, and your pricing strategy (including price versus performance/value/ benefits considerations).

D. *The competitive advantages.* Indicate the significant competitive edges you enjoy or can create as a result of your innovative product, service, and strategy; advantages in lead time or barriers to entry; competitors' weaknesses and vulnerabilities; and other industry conditions.

E. *The team.* Summarize the relevant knowledge, experience, know-how, and skills of the lead entrepreneur and any team members, noting previous accomplishments, especially those involving profit and loss responsibility and general management and people management experience. Include significant information, such as the size of a division, project, or prior business with which the lead entrepreneur or a team member was the driving force.

F. *The offering.* Briefly indicate the dollar amount of equity and/or debt financing needed, how much of the company you are prepared to offer for that financing, what principal use will be made of the capital, and how the investor, lender, or strategic partner will achieve its desired rate of return. Remember, your targeted resource provider has a well-defined appetite, and you must understand the "Circle of Venture Capital Ecstasy" (Exhibit 5.1).

II. The Industry and the Company and Its Product(s) or Service(s)
A major area of consideration is the company, its concept for its product(s) and service(s), and its interface with the industry in which it will be competing. This is the context into which the marketing information, for example, fits. Information needs to include a description of the industry, a description of the concept, a description of your company, and a description of the product(s) or service(s) you will offer, the proprietary position of these product(s) or service(s), their potential advantages, and entry and growth strategy for the product(s) or service(s).

A. *The industry.*

- Present the current status and prospects for the industry in which the proposed business will operate. Be sure to consider industry structure.

- Discuss briefly market size, growth trends, and competitors.

- Discuss any new products or developments, new markets and customers, new requirements, new entrants and exits, and any other national or economic trends and factors that could affect the venture's business positively or negatively.

- Discuss the environmental profile of the industry. Consider energy requirements, supply chain factors, waste generation, and recycling capabilities. Outline any new green technologies or trends that may have an impact on this opportunity.

B. *The company and the concept.*

- Describe generally the concept of the business, what business your company is in or intends to enter, what product(s) or service(s) it will offer, and who are or will be its principal customers.

- By way of background, give the date your venture was incorporated and describe the identification and development of its products and the involvement of the company's principals in that development.

- If your company has been in business for several years and is seeking expansion financing, review its history and cite its prior sales and profit performance. If your company has had setbacks or losses in prior years, discuss these and emphasize

current and future efforts to prevent a recurrence of these difficulties and to improve your company's performance.

C. *The product(s) or service(s).*

- Describe in some detail each product or service to be sold.

- Discuss the application of the product or service and describe the primary end use as well as any significant secondary applications. Articulate how you will solve a problem, relieve pain, or provide a benefit or needed service.

- Describe the service or product delivery system.

- Emphasize any unique features of the product or service and how these will create or add significant value; also, highlight any differences between what is currently on the market and what you will offer that will account for your market penetration. Be sure to describe how value will be added and the payback period to the customer—that is, discuss how many months it will take for the customer to cover the initial purchase price of the product or service as a result of its time, cost, or productivity improvements.

- Include a description of any possible drawbacks (including problems with obsolescence) of the product or service.

- Define the present state of development of the product or service and how much time and money will be required to fully develop, test, and introduce the product or service. Provide a summary of the functional specifications and photographs, if available, of the product.

- Discuss any head start you might have that would enable you to achieve a favored or entrenched position in the industry.

- Describe any features of the product or service that give it an "unfair" advantage over the competition. Describe any patents, trade secrets, or other proprietary features of the product or service.

- Discuss any opportunities for the expansion of the product line or the development of related products or services. (Emphasize opportunities and explain how you will take advantage of them.)

D. *Entry and growth strategy.*

- Indicate key success variables in your marketing plan (e.g., an innovative product, timing advantage, or marketing approach) and your pricing, channel(s) of distribution, advertising, and promotion plans.

- Summarize how fast you intend to grow and to what size during the first five years and your plans for growth beyond your initial product or service.

- Show how the entry and growth strategy is derived from the opportunity and value-added or other competitive advantages, such as the weakness of competitors.

- Discuss the overall environmental and social sustainability of your growth plan. Consider the effect on the community if the growth strategy involves offshore manufacturing or outsourced labor.

III. Market Research and Analysis

Information in this section needs to support the assertion that the venture can capture a substantial market in a growing industry and stand up to competition. Because of the importance of market analysis and the critical dependence of other parts of the plan on this information, you are advised to prepare this section of the business plan before any other. Take enough time to do this section very well and to check alternative sources of market data.

This section of the business plan is one of the most difficult to prepare, yet it is one of the most important. Other sections of the business plan depend on the market research and analysis presented here. For example, the predicted sales levels directly influence such factors as the size of the manufacturing operation, the marketing plan, and the amount of debt and equity capital you will require. Most entrepreneurs seem to have great difficulty preparing and presenting market research and analyses that show that their ventures' sales estimates are sound and attainable.

A. *Customers.*

- Discuss who the customers for the product(s) or service(s) are or will be. Note that potential customers need to be classified by relatively homogeneous groups having common, identifiable characteristics (e.g., by major market segment). For example, an automotive part might be sold to manufacturers and to parts distributors supplying the replacement market, so the discussion needs to reflect two market segments.

- Show who and where the major purchasers for the product(s) or service(s) are in each market segment. Include national regions and foreign countries, as appropriate.

- Indicate whether customers are easily reached and receptive, how customers buy (wholesale, through manufacturers' representatives, etc.), where in their organizations buying decisions are made, and how long decisions take. Describe customers' purchasing processes, including the bases on which they make purchase decisions (e.g., price, quality, timing, delivery, training, service, personal contacts, or political pressures) and why they might change current purchasing decisions.

- List any orders, contracts, or letters of commitment that you have in hand. These are the most powerful data you can provide. List also any potential customers who have expressed an interest in the product(s) or service(s) and indicate why. Also list any potential customers who have shown no interest in the proposed product or service, and explain why they are not interested and explain what you will do to overcome negative customer reaction. Indicate

how fast you believe your product or service will be accepted in the market.

- If you have an existing business, list your principal current customers and discuss the trends in your sales to them.

B. *Market size and trends.*

- Show for five years the size of the current total market and the share you will have, by market segment, and/or region, and/or country, for the product or service you will offer, in units, dollars, and potential profitability.

- Describe also the potential annual growth for at least three years of the total market for your product(s) or service(s) for each major customer group, region, or country, as appropriate.

- Discuss the major factors affecting market growth (e.g., industry trends, socioeconomic trends, government policy, environmental impacts, and population shifts) and review previous trends in the market. Any differences between past and projected annual growth rates need to be explained.

C. *Competition and competitive edges.*

- Make a realistic assessment of the strengths and weaknesses of competitors. Assess the substitute and/or alternative products and services and list the companies that supply them, both domestic and foreign, as appropriate.

- Compare competing and substitute products or services on the basis of market share, quality, price, performance, delivery, timing, service, warranties, and other pertinent features.

- Compare the fundamental value that is added or created by your product or service, in terms of economic benefits to the customer and to your competitors.

- Discuss the current advantages and disadvantages of these products and services and say why they are not meeting customer needs.

- Indicate any knowledge of competitors' actions that could lead you to new or improved products and an advantageous position. For example, discuss whether competitors are simply sluggish or nonresponsive or are asleep at the switch.

- Identify the strengths and weaknesses of the competing companies and determine and discuss each competitor's market share, sales, distribution methods, and production capabilities.

- Review the financial position, resources, costs, and profitability of the competition and their profit trends. Note that you can utilize Robert Morris Associates data for comparison.

- Indicate who are the service, pricing, performance, cost, and quality leaders. Discuss why any companies have entered or dropped out of the market in recent years.

- Discuss the three or four key competitors and why customers buy from them, and determine and discuss why customers leave them. Relate this to the basis for the purchase decision examined in IIIA.

- From what you know about the competitors' operations, explain why you think they are vulnerable and you can capture a share of their business. Discuss what makes you think it will be easy or difficult to compete with them. Discuss, in particular, your competitive advantages gained through such "unfair" advantage as patents.

D. *Estimated market share and sales.*

- Summarize what it is about your product(s) or service(s) that will make it salable in the face of current and potential competition. Mention, especially, the fundamental value added or created by the product(s) or service(s).

- Identify any major customers (including international customers) who are willing to make, or who have already made, purchase commitments. Indicate the extent of those commitments, and why they were made. Discuss which customers could be major purchasers in future years and why.

- Based on your assessment of the advantages of your product or service, the market size and trends, customers, competition and their products, and the trends of sales in prior years, estimate the share of the market and the sales in units and dollars that you will acquire in each of the next three years. Remember to show assumptions used.

- Show how the growth of the company sales in units and its estimated market share are related to the growth of the industry, the customers, and the strengths and weaknesses of competitors. Remember, the assumptions used to estimate market share and sales need to be clearly stated.

- If yours is an existing business, also indicate the total market, your market share, and sales for two prior years.

E. *Ongoing market evaluation.*

- Explain how you will continue to evaluate your target markets; assess customer needs and service; guide product improvement, pricing, and new product programs; plan for expansions of your production facility; and guide product/service pricing.

IV. The Economics of the Business   The economic and financial characteristics, including the apparent magnitude and durability of margins and profits generated, need to support the fundamental attractiveness of the opportunity. The underlying operating and cash conversion

cycle of the business, the value chain, and so forth need to make sense in terms of the opportunity and strategies planned.

A. *Gross and operating margins.*

- Describe the magnitude of the gross margins (i.e., selling price less variable costs) and the operating margins for each of the product(s) and/or service(s) you are selling in the market niche(s) you plan to attack. Include results of your contribution analysis.

B. *Profit potential and durability.*

- Describe the magnitude and expected durability of the profit stream the business will generate—before and after taxes—and reference appropriate industry benchmarks, other competitive intelligence, or your own relevant experience.

- Address the issue of how perishable or durable the profit stream appears to be. Provide reasons why your profit stream is perishable or durable, such as barriers to entry you can create, your technological and market lead time, and environmental sustainability, which in some cases can be a driver for cost reduction.

C. *Fixed, variable, and semivariable costs.*

- Provide a detailed summary of fixed, variable, and semivariable costs, in dollars and as percentages of total cost as appropriate, for the product or service you offer and the volume of purchases and sales upon which these are based.

- Show relevant industry benchmarks.

D. *Months to breakeven.*

- Given your entry strategy, marketing plan, and proposed financing, show how long it will take to reach a unit break-even sales level.

- Note any significant stepwise changes in your breakeven that will occur as you grow and add substantial capacity.

E. *Months to reach positive cash flow.*

- Given the above strategy and assumptions, show when the venture will attain a positive cash flow.

- Show if and when you will run out of cash. Note where the detailed assumptions can be found.

- Note any significant stepwise changes in cash flow that will occur as you grow and add capacity.

V. Marketing Plan   The marketing plan describes how the sales projections will be attained. The marketing plan needs to detail the overall marketing strategy that will exploit the opportunity and your competitive advantages. Include a discussion of sales and service policies; pricing, distribution, promotion, and advertising strategies; and

sales projections. The marketing plan needs to describe *what is* to be done, *how* it will be done, *when* it will be done, and *who* will do it.

A. *Overall marketing strategy.*

- Describe the specific marketing philosophy and strategy of the company, given the value chain and channels of distribution in the market niche(s) you are pursuing. Include, for example, a discussion of the kinds of customer groups that you already have orders from or that will be targeted for initial intensive selling effort and those targeted for later selling efforts; how specific potential customers in these groups will be identified and how they will be contacted; what features of the product or service, such as service, quality, price, delivery, warranty, or training, will be emphasized to generate sales; if any innovative or unusual marketing concepts will enhance customer acceptance, such as leasing where only sales were previously attempted; and so forth.

- Indicate whether the product(s) or service(s) will initially be introduced internationally, nationally, or regionally; explain why; and if appropriate, indicate any plans for extending sales later.

- Discuss any seasonal trends that underlie the cash conversion cycle in the industry and what can be done to promote sales out of season.

- Describe any plans to obtain government contracts as a means of supporting product development costs and overhead.

B. *Pricing.*

- Discuss pricing strategy, including the prices to be charged for your product and service, and compare your pricing policy with those of your major competitors, including a brief discussion of payback (in months) to the customer.

- Discuss the gross profit margin between manufacturing and ultimate sales costs, and indicate whether this margin is large enough to allow for distribution and sales, warranty, training, service, amortization of development and equipment costs, price competition, and so forth, and still allow a profit.

- Explain how the price you set will enable you to (1) get the product or service accepted, (2) maintain and increase your market share in the face of competition, and (3) produce profits.

- Justify your pricing strategy and differences between your prices and those for competitive or substitute products or services in terms of economic payback to the customer and value added through newness, quality, warranty, timing, performance, service, cost savings, efficiency, and the like.

- If your product is to be priced lower than those of the competition, explain how you will do this and maintain profitability (e.g., through greater value added via effectiveness in manufacturing and distribution, lower labor costs, lower material costs, lower overhead, or other cost component).

- Discuss your pricing policy, including a discussion of the relationship of price, market share, and profits.

C. *Sales tactics.*

- Describe the methods (e.g., own sales force, sales representatives, ready-made manufacturers' sales organizations, direct mail, or distributors) that will be used to make sales and distribute the product or service and both the initial plans and longer-range plans for a sales force. Include a discussion of any special requirements (e.g., refrigeration).

- Discuss the value chain and the resulting margins to be given to retailers, distributors, wholesalers, and salespeople and any special policies regarding discounts, exclusive distribution rights, and so on given to distributors or sales representatives, and compare these to those given by your competition. (See the Venture Opportunity Screening Guide Exercises.)

- Describe how distributors or sales representatives, if they are used, will be selected, when they will start to represent you, the areas they will cover and the head count of dealers and representatives by month, and the expected sales to be made by each.

- If a direct sales force is to be used, indicate how it will be structured and at what rate (a head count) it will be built up; indicate if it is to replace a dealer or representative organization and, if so, when and how.

- If direct mail, magazine, newspaper, or other media, telemarketing, or catalog sales are to be used, indicate the specific channels or vehicles, costs (per 1,000), expected response rates, and so on. Discuss how these will be built up.

- Show the sales expected per salesperson per year and what commission, incentive, and/or salary they are slated to receive, and compare these figures to the average for your industry.

- Present a selling schedule and a sales budget that includes all marketing promotion and service costs.

D. *Service and warranty policies.*

- If your company will offer a product that will require service, warranties, or training, indicate the importance of these to the customers' purchasing decisions and discuss your method of handling service problems.

- Describe the kind and term of any warranties to be offered, whether service will be handled by company service people, agencies, dealers and distributors, or returns to the factory.

- Indicate the proposed charge for service calls and whether service will be a profitable or break-even operation.
- Compare your service, warranty, and customer training policies and practices to those of your principal competitors.

E. *Advertising and promotion.*

- Describe the approaches the company will use to bring its product or service to the attention of prospective purchasers.
- For original equipment manufacturers and for manufacturers of industrial products, indicate the plans for trade show participation, trade magazine advertisements, direct mailings, the preparation of product sheets and promotional literature, and use of advertising agencies.
- For consumer products, indicate what kind of advertising and promotional campaign will introduce the product, including sales aids to dealers, trade shows, and so forth.
- Present a schedule and approximate costs of promotion and advertising (direct mail, telemarketing, catalogs, etc.), and discuss how these costs will be incurred.

F. *Distribution.*

- Describe the methods and channels of distribution you will employ. Discuss the availability and capacity of these channels.
- Indicate the sensitivity of shipping cost as a percentage of the selling price.
- Note any special issues or problems that need to be resolved or present potential vulnerabilities.
- If international sales are involved, note how these sales will be handled, including distribution, shipping, insurance, credit, and collections.

VI. Design and Development Plans

The nature and extent of any design and development work and the time and money required before a product or service is marketable need to be considered in detail. (Note that design and development costs are often underestimated.) Design and development might be the engineering work necessary to convert a laboratory prototype to a finished product; the design of special tooling; the work of an industrial designer to make a product more attractive and salable; or the identification and organization of employees, equipment, and special techniques, such as equipment, new computer software, and skills required for computerized credit checking, to implement a service business.

A. *Development status and tasks.*

- Describe the current status of each product or service and explain what remains to be done to make it marketable.

- Describe briefly the competence or expertise that your company has or will require to complete this development.
- List any customers or end users who are participating in the development, design, and/or testing of the product or service. Indicate results to date or when results are expected.

B. *Difficulties and risks.*

- Identify any major anticipated design and development problems and define approaches to their solution.
- Discuss the possible effect on the cost of design and development, on the time to market introduction, and so forth, of such problems.

C. *Product improvement and new products.*

- In addition to describing the development of the initial products, discuss any ongoing design and development work that is planned to keep the product(s) or service(s) that can be sold to the same group of customers. Discuss customers who have participated in these efforts and their reactions, and include any evidence that you may have.
- With regard to ongoing product development, outline any compliance issues relating to new, pending, or potential environmental legislation.

D. *Costs.*

- Present and discuss the design and development budget, including costs of labor, materials, consulting fees, and so on.
- Discuss the impact on cash flow projections of underestimating this budget, including the impact of a 15 percent to 30 percent contingency.

E. *Proprietary issues.*

- Describe any patent, trademark, copyright, or intellectual property rights you own or are seeking.
- Describe any contractual rights or agreements that give you exclusivity or proprietary rights.
- Discuss the impact of any unresolved issues or existing or possible actions pending, such as disputed rights of ownership, relating to proprietary rights on timing and on any competitive edge you have assumed.

VII. Manufacturing and Operations Plan

The manufacturing and operations plan needs to include such factors as plant location, the type of facilities needed, space requirements, capital equipment requirements, and labor force (both full- and part-time) requirements. For a manufacturing business, the manufacturing and operations plan needs to include policies on inventory control, purchasing, production control, and which parts of the product will be purchased and which operations will be performed by your workforce (called make-or-buy decisions). A service business may require particular attention to location (proximity to customers is generally a must), minimizing overhead, and obtaining competitive productivity from a labor force.

A. *Operating cycle.*

- Describe the lead/lag times that characterize the fundamental operating cycle in your business. (Include a graph similar to the one found in the Venture Opportunity Screening Exercises.)

- Explain how any seasonal production loads will be handled without severe dislocation (e.g., by building to inventory or using part-time help in peak periods).

B. *Geographical location.*

- Describe the planned geographical location of the business. Include any location analysis, and so on, that you have done.

- Discuss any advantages or disadvantages of the site location in terms of labor (including labor availability, whether workers are unionized, wage rates, and outsourcing), closeness to customers and/or suppliers, access to transportation, state and local taxes and laws (including zoning and environmental impact regulations), access to utilities (energy use and sustainability), and so forth.

C. *Facilities and improvements.*

- For an existing business, describe the facilities, including plant and office space, storage and land areas, special tooling, machinery, and other capital equipment currently used to conduct the company's business, and discuss whether these facilities are adequate and in compliance with health, safety, and environmental regulations. Discuss any economies of scale.

- For a start-up, describe how and when the necessary facilities to start production will be acquired.

- Discuss whether equipment and space will be leased or acquired (new or used) and indicate the costs and timing of such actions and how much of the proposed financing will be devoted to plant and equipment.

- Explain future equipment needs in the next three years.

- For start-ups expecting to outsource manufacturing, indicate the location and size of the firm, and discuss the advantages, risks, and monitoring regime.

- Discuss how and when, in the next three years, plant space and equipment will be expanded and capacities required by future sales projections and any plans to improve or add existing plant space. Discuss any environmental impacts related to those expansion requirements. If there are any plans to move the facility, outsource labor, or move production overseas, discuss the impact on the local community. Indicate the timing and cost of such acquisitions.

D. *Strategy and plans.*

- Describe the manufacturing processes involved in production of your product(s) and any decisions with respect to subcontracting of component parts, rather than complete in-house manufacture.

- Justify your proposed make-or-buy policy in terms of inventory financing, available labor skills, and other nontechnical questions, as well as production, cost, and capability issues.

- Discuss who potential subcontractors and/or suppliers are likely to be and any information about, or any surveys that have been made of, these subcontractors and suppliers.

- Present a production plan that shows cost/volume/inventory level information at various sales levels of operation with breakdowns of applicable material, labor, purchased components, and factory overhead.

- Describe your approach to quality control, production control, and inventory control; explain what quality control and inspection procedures the company will use to minimize service problems and associated customer dissatisfaction.

E. *Regulatory and legal issues.*

- Discuss any relevant state, federal, or foreign regulatory requirements unique to your product, process, or service such as licenses, zoning permits, health permits, and environmental approvals necessary to begin operation.

- Note any pending regulatory changes that can affect the nature of your opportunity and its timing.

- Discuss any legal or contractual obligations that are pertinent as well.

VIII. Management Team   This section of the business plan includes a description of the functions that will need to be filled, a description of the key management personnel and their primary duties, an outline of the organizational structure for the venture, a description of the board of directors, a description of the ownership position of any other investors, and so forth. You need to present indications of commitment, such as the willingness of team members to initially accept modest salaries, and of the existence of the proper balance of technical, managerial, and business skills and experience in doing what is proposed.

A. *Organization.*

- Present the key management roles in the company and the individuals who will fill each position. (If the company is established and of sufficient size, an organization chart needs to be appended.)

- If it is not possible to fill each executive role with a full-time person without adding excessive overhead, indicate how these functions will be performed (e.g., using part-time specialists or consultants to perform some functions), who will perform them, and when they will be replaced by a full-time staff member.

- If any key individuals will not be on board at the start of the venture, indicate when they will join the company.

- Discuss any current or past situations where key management people have worked together that could indicate how their skills complement each other and result in an effective management team.

B. *Key management personnel.*

- For each key person, describe in detail career highlights, particularly relevant know-how, skills, and track record of accomplishments, that demonstrate his or her ability to perform the assigned role. Include in your description sales and profitability achievements (budget size, number of subordinates, new product introductions, etc.) and other prior entrepreneurial or general management results.

- Describe the exact duties and responsibilities of each of the key members of the management team.

- Complete résumés for each key management member need to be included here or as an exhibit and need to stress relevant training, experience, and concrete accomplishments, such as profit and sales improvement, labor management success, manufacturing or technical achievements, and meeting budgets and schedules.

C. *Management compensation and ownership.*

- State the salary to be paid, the stock ownership planned, and the amount of equity investment (if any) of each key member of the management team.

- Compare the compensation of each key member to the salary he or she received at his or her last independent job.

D. *Other investors.*

- Describe here any other investors in your venture, the number and percentage of outstanding shares they own, when they were acquired, and at what price.

E. *Employment and other agreements and stock option and bonus plans.*

- Describe any existing or contemplated employment or other agreements with key members.

- Indicate any restrictions on stock and investing that affect ownership and disposition of stock.

- Describe any performance-dependent stock option or bonus plans.

- Summarize any incentive stock option or other stock ownership plans planned or in effect for key people and employees.

F. *Board of directors.*

- Discuss the company's philosophy about the size and composition of the board.

- Identify any proposed board members and include a one- or two-sentence statement of each member's background that shows what he or she can bring to the company.

G. *Other shareholders, rights, and restrictions.*

- Indicate any other shareholders in your company and any rights, restrictions, or obligations, such as notes or guarantees, associated with these. (If they have all been accounted for previously, simply note that there are no others.)

H. *Supporting professional advisors and services.*

- Indicate the supporting services that will be required.

- Indicate the names and affiliations of the legal, accounting, advertising, consulting, and banking advisors selected for your venture and the services each will provide.

IX. Sustainability and Impact

This section should address the social, economic, and environmental sustainability of your business model. Because customers (and investors) are increasingly interested in supporting companies that are proactive with regard to these issues, building a sustainable, socially responsible venture from the start can have competitive as well as economic advantages.

- Outline any environmental issues related to your business with regard to resources, waste generation, and legislative compliance.

- Discuss the nature of any opportunities for green impact, such as carbon reduction, recycling, and any green technologies or production capabilities that could enhance sustainability.

- Describe the nature of subcontractors and suppliers you plan to do business with.

- Describe any sustainability advantages you have or can develop, and how these might relate to building customer loyalty and community support for your product(s) or service(s).

- Summarize the employment opportunities that your business is likely to create, and describe any plans for outsourcing or using offshore labor and how that might impact the community and your labor pool.

- Examine the potential environmental impact of your business as it grows.

X. Overall Schedule

A schedule that shows the timing and interrelationship of the major events necessary to launch the venture and realize its objectives is an essential part of a business plan. The underlying cash conversion and operating cycle of the business will provide key inputs for the schedule. In addition to being a planning aid, by showing deadlines critical to a venture's success, a well-presented schedule can be extremely valuable in convincing potential investors that the management team is able to plan for venture growth in a way that recognizes obstacles and minimizes investor risk. Because the time to do things tends to be underestimated in most business plans, it is important to demonstrate that you have correctly estimated these amounts in determining the schedule. Create your schedule as follows:

1. Lay out (use a bar chart) the cash conversion cycle of the business for each product or service expected, the lead and elapsed times from an order to the purchase of raw materials, or inventory to shipping and collection.

2. Prepare a month-by-month schedule that shows the timing of product development, market planning, sales programs, production, and operations, and that includes sufficient detail to show the timing of the primary tasks required to accomplish an activity.

3. Show on the schedule the deadlines or milestones critical to the venture's success, such as these:
   - Incorporation of the venture.
   - Completion of design and development.
   - Completion of prototypes.
   - Obtaining sales representatives.
   - Obtaining product display at trade shows.
   - Signing distributors and dealers.
   - Ordering materials in production quantities.
   - Starting production or operation.
   - Receipt of first orders.
   - Delivery on first sale.
   - Receiving the first payment on accounts receivable.

4. Show on the schedule the "ramp-up" of the number of management personnel, the number of production and operations personnel, and plant or equipment and their relation to the development of the business.

5. Discuss in a general way the activities most likely to cause a schedule slippage, what steps will be taken to correct such slippages, and the impact of schedule slippages on the venture's operation, especially its potential viability and capital needs.

XI. Critical Risks, Problems, and Assumptions
The development of a business has risks and problems, and the business plan invariably contains some implicit assumptions about them. You need to include a description of the risks and the consequences of adverse outcomes relating to your industry, your company and its personnel, your product's market appeal, and the timing and financing of your startup. Be sure to discuss assumptions concerning sales projections, customer orders, and so forth. If the venture has anything that could be considered a fatal flaw, discuss why it is not. The discovery of any unstated negative factors by potential investors can undermine the credibility of the venture and endanger its financ-

ing. Be aware that most investors will read the section describing the management team first and then this section.

Do not omit this section. If you do, the reader will most likely come to one or more of the following conclusions:

1. You think he or she is incredibly naive or stupid, or both.
2. You hope to pull the wool over his or her eyes.
3. You do not have enough objectivity to recognize and deal with assumptions and problems.

Identifying and discussing the risks in your venture demonstrate your skills as a manager and increase the credibility of you and your venture with a venture capital investor or a private investor. Taking the initiative on the identification and discussion of risks helps you to demonstrate to the investor that you have thought about them and can handle them. Risks then tend not to loom as large black clouds in the investor's thinking about your venture.

1. Discuss the assumptions and risks implicit in your plan.
2. Identify and discuss any major problems and other risks, such as these:
   - Running out of cash *before* orders are secured.
   - Potential price cutting by competitors.
   - Any potentially unfavorable industry trends.
   - Design or manufacturing costs in excess of estimates.
   - Sales projections not achieved.
   - An unmet product development schedule.
   - Difficulties or long lead times encountered in the procurement of parts or raw materials.
   - Difficulties encountered in obtaining needed bank credit.
   - Larger-than-expected innovation and development costs.
   - Running out of cash *after* orders pour in.
3. Indicate what assumptions or potential problems and risks are most critical to the success of the venture, and describe your plans for minimizing the impact of unfavorable developments in each case.

XII. The Financial Plan
The financial plan is basic to the evaluation of an investment opportunity and needs to represent your best estimates of financial requirements. The purpose of the financial plan is to indicate the venture's potential and to present a timetable for financial viability. It also can serve as an operating plan for financial management using financial benchmarks. In preparing the financial plan, you need to look creatively at your venture and consider alternative ways of launching or financing it.

As part of the financial plan, financial exhibits need to be prepared. To estimate cash flow needs, use cash-based, rather than accrual-based, accounting (i.e., use a real-time cash flow analysis of expected receipts and disbursements). This analysis needs to cover three years, including current- and prior-year income statements and balance sheets, if applicable; profit and loss forecasts for three years; pro forma income statements and balance sheets;

and a break-even chart. On the appropriate exhibits, or in an attachment, specify assumptions behind such items as sales levels and growth, collections and payables periods, inventory requirements, cash balances, and cost of goods. Your analysis of the operating and cash conversion cycle in the business will enable you to identify these critical assumptions.

Pro forma income statements are the plan-for-profit part of financial management and can indicate the potential financial feasibility of a new venture. Because usually the level of profits, particularly during the start-up years of a venture, will not be sufficient to finance operating asset needs, and because actual cash inflows do not always match the actual cash outflows on a short-term basis, a cash flow forecast indicating these conditions and enabling management to plan cash needs is recommended. Further, pro forma balance sheets are used to detail the assets required to support the projected level of operations and, through liabilities, to show how these assets are to be financed. The projected balance sheets can indicate if debt-to-equity ratios, working capital, current ratios, inventory turnover, and the like are within the acceptable limits required to justify future financings that are projected for the venture. Finally, a break-even chart showing the level of sales and production that will cover all costs, including those costs that vary with production level and those that do not, is very useful.

A. *Actual income statements and balance sheets.* For an existing business, prepare income statements and balance sheets for the current year and for the prior two years.

B. *Pro forma income statements.*

- Using sales forecasts and the accompanying production or operations costs, prepare pro forma income statements for at least the first three years.

- Fully discuss assumptions (e.g., the amount allowed for bad debts and discounts, or any assumptions made with respect to sales expenses or general and administrative costs being a fixed percentage of costs or sales) made in preparing the pro forma income statement and document them.

- Draw on Section XI of the business plan and highlight any major risks, such as the effect of a 20 percent reduction in sales from those projected or the adverse impact of having to climb a learning curve on the level of productivity over time, that could prevent the venture's sales and profit goals from being attained, plus the sensitivity of profits to these risks.

C. *Pro forma balance sheets.* Prepare pro forma balance sheets semiannually in the first year and at the end of each of the first three years of operation.

D. *Pro forma cash flow analysis.*

- Project cash flows monthly for the first year of operation and quarterly for at least the next two years. Detail the amount and timing of expected cash inflows and outflows. Determine the need for and timing of additional financing and indicate peak requirements for working capital. Indicate how necessary additional financing is to be obtained, such as through equity financing, bank loans, or short-term lines of credit from banks, on what terms, and how it is to be repaid. Remember that these numbers are based on cash, not accrual, accounting.

- Discuss assumptions, such as those made on the timing of collection of receivables, trade discounts given, terms of payments to vendors, planned salary and wage increases, anticipated increases in any operating expenses, seasonality characteristics of the business as they affect inventory requirements, inventory turnovers per year, capital equipment purchases, and so forth. Again, these are real time (i.e., cash), not accruals.

- Discuss cash flow sensitivity to a variety of assumptions about business factors (e.g., possible changes in such crucial assumptions as an increase in the receivable collection period or a sales level lower than that forecast).

E. *Break-even chart.*

- Calculate breakeven and prepare a chart that shows when breakeven will be reached and any stepwise changes in breakeven that may occur.

- Discuss the breakeven shown for your venture and whether it will be easy or difficult to attain, including a discussion of the size of break-even sales volume relative to projected total sales, the size of gross margins and price sensitivity, and how the break-even point might be lowered in case the venture falls short of sales projections.

F. *Cost control.* Describe how you will obtain information about report costs and how often, who will be responsible for the control of various cost elements, and how you will take action on budget overruns.

G. *Highlights.* Highlight the important conclusions, including the maximum amount and timing of cash required, the amount of debt and equity needed, how fast any debts can be repaid, and so forth.

XIII. Proposed Company Offering

The purpose of this section of the plan is to indicate the amount of money that is being sought, the nature and amount of the securities offered to investors, a brief description of the uses that will be made of the capital raised, and a summary of how the investor is expected to achieve its targeted rate of return. It is recommended that you read the discussion about financing in Part IV.

The terms for financing your company that you propose here are the first steps in the negotiation process with those interested in investing, and it is very possible that your financing will involve different kinds of securities than originally proposed.

A. *Desired financing.* Based on your real-time cash flow projections and your estimate of how much money is required over the next three years to carry out the development and/or expansion of your business as described, indicate how much of this capital requirement will be obtained by this offering and how much will be obtained via term loans and lines of credit.

B. *Offering.*

- Describe the type (e.g., common stock, convertible debentures, debt with warrants, debt plus stock), unit price, and total amount of securities to be sold in this offering. If securities are not just common stock, indicate by type, interest, maturity, and conversion conditions.

- Show the percentage of the company that the investors of this offering will hold after it is completed or after exercise of any stock conversion or purchase rights in the case of convertible debentures or warrants.

- Securities sold through a private placement and that therefore are exempt from SEC registration should include the following statement in this part of the plan:

  The shares being sold pursuant to this offering are restricted securities and may not be resold readily. The prospective investor should recognize that such securities might be restricted as to resale for an indefinite period of time. Each purchaser will be required to execute a Nondistribution Agreement satisfactory in form to corporate counsel.

C. *Capitalization.*

- Present in tabular form the current and proposed (postoffering) number of outstanding shares of common stock. Indicate any shares offered by key management people and show the number of shares that they will hold after completion of the proposed financing.

- Indicate how many shares of your company's common stock will remain authorized but unissued after

the offering and how many of these will be reserved for stock options for future key employees.

D. *Use of funds.* Investors like to know how their money is going to be spent. Provide a brief description of how the capital raised will be used. Summarize as specifically as possible what amount will be used for such things as product design and development, capital equipment, marketing, and general working capital needs.

E. *Investors' return.* Indicate how your valuation and proposed ownership shares will result in the desired rate of return for the investors you have targeted and what the likely harvest or exit mechanism (IPO, outright sale, merger, MBO, etc.) will be.

XIV. Appendixes Include pertinent information here that is too extensive for the body of the business plan but that is necessary (product specs or photos; lists of references, suppliers of critical components; special location factors, facilities, or technical analyses; reports from consultants or technical experts; and copies of any critical regulatory approval, licenses, etc.).

STEP 5
Integrate Sections.
Integrate the discrete sections you have created into a coherent business plan that can be used for the purpose for which it was created.

STEP 6
Get Feedback.
Once written, it is recommended that you get the plan reviewed. No matter how good you and your team are, you will most likely overlook issues and treat aspects of your venture in a manner that is less than clear. A good reviewer can give you the benefit of an outside objective evaluation. Your attorney can make sure that there are no misleading statements in your plan and that it contains all the caveats and the like.

The Virtual Brain Trust

Finding the right date or partner for life is a daunting challenge. Everyone agrees that certain chemistry can make or break a relationship. This is certainly true in new ventures. Today all the various social networking Web sites and the worldwide connectivity of the Internet have opened up vast new opportunities to identify and build the most important part of the external team—the venture's brain trust. As you have seen (and will continue to see) in the text, cases, and discussions, ventures rarely succeed in isolation. Invariably there are one or a few external mentors, advisors (who are often also investors), coaches, and sources of great knowledge, insights, and contacts the venture desperately needs but does not have. Members of your brain trust must be direct and honest and have your best interests at heart. These can be very valuable individuals.

Consider the following example. In 1994 Gary Mueller and his brother George, both still in graduate school and in their 20s, were developing a business plan to launch a company they would call Internet Securities, Inc. (www.internetsecurities.com). Begun as a course project, their venture sought to develop a subscription service to provide financial, stock and bond market, economic, and related information—first from Poland and Russia and later from other emerging markets—all delivered over the Internet. The talented, motivated, and very entrepreneurial brothers had some good contacts, but this was their first serious venture, and there were many things they knew they didn't know. One basic issue was how to package, price, and sell this new service to clients such as investment banks, commercial banks, financial service firms, large accounting firms, and the like. The core question they asked was this: Who knows more about this than anyone in the world?

That is the key question to ask as you begin your search for potential members of your own brain trust. In the case of the Muellers, Professor Timmons knew the founder of what became First Call: Jeff Parker, who had created a new venture in the early 1980s that put the first desktop computer (an Apple II) on the desks of bond traders on Wall Street. This highly successful company led to other new ventures and a wealth of knowledge, networks, and experience in this market. Connecting the Muellers with Parker made a number of key results occur. For one thing, Parker agreed to invest $1 million and become chairman of the board. This was a great asset for the company because of the know-how and credibility he brought to the venture. It also meant that the Muellers were able to conserve equity by not having to raise venture capital. A venture capitalist wanted to invest more money, but for a controlling interest of the venture; Parker asked for 25 percent. This seasoned entrepreneur also knew the best people in the business from a sales perspective and was able to recruit his former national sales manager to ISI. This made a huge difference—early on with pricing and selling strategies, and later in achieving early revenue targets.

You can see here the potential and importance of the external brain trust. This exercise will help you to begin to identify and connect with potential brain trust advisors who can become invaluable to your venture's success.

STEP 1

Identify and List the Gaps at This Stage of the Venture.

Applying the Timmons Model to your opportunity and potential venture has put a zoom lens on each critical aspect of your venture—the opportunity, the resources, and the team (internal and external)—and has revealed important gaps and the extent of the fit in the venture. Remember, many gaps are uncovered by an honest assessment of the confidence you have in the critical assumptions you've made in your plan; the weaker your confidence, the greater the need for brain trust support. These missing pieces in the puzzle will point to the facts, people, information, access, insights, and the like that your venture needs and that no team members currently possess; without these pieces, the venture will likely fail; with them, the odds for success rise. Make a list of these critical gaps and needs.

STEP 2

Think: Who Knows What We Don't?

This step will draw on your personal networks. With the Internet you can articulate carefully what expertise/knowledge/experience you are looking for, and then start asking the people you know, who can eventually lead you to a source. Networking sites such as Facebook, MySpace, and LinkedIn can be especially fruitful search platforms. Match this list of potential brain trust members to the list of critical gaps and needs.

STEP 3

Revisit Step 1 as the Venture Develops.

During the course, as you work on your business plan, you can apply this method to various aspects of your zoom lens. Dive into the nuances of the opportunity, the team, and the minimal required resources you need to improve the fit by filling the gaps and managing risk and reward. Much will change as your idea evolves into a bona fide opportunity and then into a live venture: attracting key team members, valuing the business, raising capital, structuring and negotiating the deal, and other key negotiations with key hires and suppliers. Trying to learn all the things necessary to succeed the first time by doing it all yourself is a high-risk, high-tuition path that will delight your competitors! Reaching out to connect with people who can help you the most makes a huge difference—and is clearly one of the most vital entrepreneurial competencies.

A Cautionary Word: Scammers and Predators

Unfortunately the Internet has its share of scammers and predators. Be vigilant and thorough in checking out potential contacts! Ewing M. Kauffman always advised that "you should trust people" rather than assume they are all out to cheat you, lie to you, scam you, or steal from you. It's certainly true that at least 95 percent of the people you will encounter in your journey can be trusted. Just keep in mind the old adage: Trust everyone, but always cut the deck!

Case

Newland Medical Technologies

Preparation Questions

1. Discuss the process that Sarah Foster and her partners have gone through to bring to market their medical device. How might they have avoided some of the pitfalls they have encountered?

2. Examine Newland's strategy in light of the special circumstances in this industry. What is your recommendation for moving the company forward?

3. In light of your strategic plan for Newland Medical, how can Foster achieve a balance between her personal and professional objectives and commitments?

It had all seemed like a perfect plan. With two assertive angel investors guiding her medical device company on what seemed to be an acquisition fast track, Foster Foster and her husband decided that the time was right to start a family. However, by the fall of 2005 (the middle of her first trimester), everything had changed.

Foster, cofounder and president of Newland Medical Technologies, was now compelled to seriously reconsider the course she'd set for her company. In doing so, she was going to have to make some tough choices to strike a balance between motherhood and her professional passions.

Opportunity Recognition

Sarah Foster had been working with hip implant designs for Johnson & Johnson in Massachusetts for two years when the corporate office announced they were moving her division out west to Iowa. Foster loved the work, but she and her husband, a professor at a local college, also loved living in the Boston area. She passed on the offer and instead leveraged her engineering degrees from MIT and Stanford to secure employment close to home (see Exhibit 1). Still, the bright engineer never lost sight of her primary career objective:

I had been looking for a medical device opportunity ever since I left Johnson & Johnson. Then a friend of mine—a urologist at the Brigham and Women's Hospital in Boston—told me how there was a need for better stents[1] in urology, since most of the industry focus has been in cardiac work. He pointed out that even though it was commonly known that the ureter naturally dilates in the presence of a foreign body, no stent products had

This case was prepared by Carl Hedberg under the direction of Professor Stephen Spinelli. © Copyright Babson College, 2005.

taken full advantage of this fact. We felt that gently stimulating a wider dilation would improve urine flow and might even help pass kidney stones.

Kidney stones, or ureteral stones, were a debilitating malady that affected nearly 10 percent of the U.S. population. The pain of stone disease was most severe when the stone lodged in the ureter and obstructed urine flow.

A patient arriving with kidney stones was usually treated as an emergency. The emergency room physician would administer pain medication and almost always consult a urologist. The immediate and near-term treatment had to be safe and effective and keep the patient's options open for later procedures.

By the late 1990s, most urologists were meeting these needs with the "Double-J"—a standard polyurethane stent inserted into the ureter to relieve pain by allowing urine to flow around the stone. With the Double-J, stones often remained in the ureter; the choice of procedure to remove such stones was related to the size and location of the stone, as well as access to sophisticated equipment.

Patients with stones smaller than 5 mm typically waited in pain a few days or up to several weeks for the stone to pass. Larger stones were broken up using ultrasound and laser technologies—leaving fragments too small to retrieve but plenty big enough to ensure a painful passing. Basketing was a secondary procedure that was very effective in removing individual stone fragments, but it required a skilled surgeon and an extended operating time (see Exhibit 2).

In the winter of 1999, Foster and Dr. Grainer began brainstorming a sheath-covered stent that could be deployed in the same manner and with the same materials as the Double-J. Once inside the ureter, the sheath would be removed, and their stent would enlarge the passageway with a series of expansion bulbs along its length (see Exhibit 3). While their aim was to relieve urine flow to a greater degree than competitive products, during their initial trials on pigs they noticed that as the device was slowly withdrawn from the ureter, stones became trapped in the basket-like bulbs. Direct and atraumatic removal of stones from the ureter had never been done before; now they had their product.

[1] A medical stent was an expandable wire mesh or polyurethane tube that was inserted into a hollow structure of the body to keep it open or to provide strength. Stents were used on diverse structures such as coronary arteries, other blood vessels, the common bile duct, the esophagus, the trachea, and the ureter—the tract that conducts urine flow from the kidney to the bladder.

EXHIBIT 1

Résumé: Sarah Choi Foster

Education

2002–2004   **F.W. OLIN BUSINESS SCHOOL AT BABSON COLLEGE**   **Wellesley. MA**

M.B.A., May 2003, cum laude, Babson Fellow.
- Consulted with Boston Scientific, Inc.; competitive analysis and e-commerce initiatives.
- Entrepreneurship Intensity Track program, Hatchery company.

1996–1997   **STANFORD UNIVERSITY**   **Stanford, CA**

M.S. degree in Mechanical Engineering, Design, June 1997.
Concentration: Mechatronics (Mechanical Electronics) & Design for Manufacturability.
- Design projects: 3M-sponsored portable overhead projector, smart tag–playing robot, automated 3-D foam facsimile machine, automated paper palm-tree maker.

1992–1996   **MASSACHUSETTS INSTITUTE OF TECHNOLOGY**   **Cambridge, MA**

B.S. degree in Mechanical Engineering, May 1996. Minor in Music.
- UTAP Full Scholarship

Experience

2003–present   **NEWLAND MEDICAL TECHNOLOGIES, INC.**   **Boston, MA**

President and Founder
- Raised $600K to bring an FDA-approved patented product to market.
- Built team and running the business.

2002   **PERCEPTION ROBOTICS, INC.**   **Waltham, MA**

Kauffman Intern, Product Manager Intern
- Analyzed potential e-commerce partners for an interactive retail software system.
- Helped develop new product value proposition for Web cameras.

1999–2002   **THE GILLETTE COMPANY**   **Boston, MA**

Design Engineer, Shaving and Technology Lab
- Managed design process and testing of high-volume plastic packaging for various toiletries.
- Designed Economy Gel antiperspirant container from market requirement to mold production.

1998–1999   **JOHNSON & JOHNSON PROFESSIONAL, INC.**   **Raynham, MA**

Project Engineer, Hip R&D
- Served as lead engineer to design hip implant products; two patents granted, three pending.
- Launched the Bipolar and Calcar Hip instrumentation systems, developed with customers.
- Worked with team of Japanese surgeons to design custom implants for Asian population.
- Analyzed structural integrity of various hip prostheses by Finite Element Analysis.

1997–1998   **DEFENSE INTELLIGENCE AGENCY / PENTAGON**   **Washington, DC**

Analyst, Strategic Industries Branch
- Researched new technological developments in foreign countries, briefed division heads.
- Wrote articles in specialty field for internal publication to decision makers.

1995   **MISSILE & SPACE INTELLIGENCE CENTER**   **Huntsville, AL**

Intern, Surface to Air Missile Division
- Researched modifications to a foreign missile and resulting impact on U.S. defense strategies.
- Served as co-liaison to White Sands Testing Range and Sandia National Lab for testing.

Other:

Unigraphics, ProENGINEER, SolidWorks ANSYS, C, working knowledge of Korean and German.
Interests include symphony playing, triathlons, downhill skiing, cycling, and woodworking.

EXHIBIT 2

Anatomy and Stone Removal Procedures

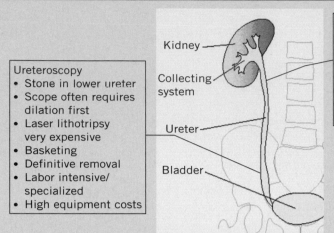

Kidney

Collecting system

Ureter

Bladder

Ureteroscopy
- Stone in lower ureter
- Scope often requires dilation first
- Laser lithotripsy very expensive
- Basketing
- Definitive removal
- Labor intensive/ specialized
- High equipment costs

ESWL (Shockwave)
- Stone in upper ureter or kidney
- Least invasive
- Equipment expensive (only 7% of hospitals have them)
- Shattered fragments created must be passed

EXHIBIT 3

The SRS: Insertion and Expanded Forms

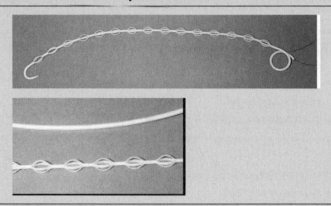

The SRS

To emphasize what they now saw as the *primary* attribute, Foster and Grainer named their device the Stone Removal Stent (SRS). A new series of animal trials led to the following procedure outline:

1. The ureter was located within the bladder using a cystoscope, and a guide wire was inserted up the ureter.
2. The SRS was slipped over the guide wire and pushed into place.
3. The sheath around the SRS was removed to open the baskets.
4. In one to two days, the SRS caused the ureter to passively dilate and enlarge the passageway.
5. The SRS was slowly withdrawn, whereby stones were either trapped in the baskets, fell into the baskets upon removal, or were merely swept alongside.

Throughout 2000 and into 2001, Foster took charge of the effort as Grainer returned to his full-time practice. She raised money from friends and family to secure a patent on the unique-application stent. At the same time, she continued to examine various aspects of the opportunity in order to assemble the business plan she would need to attract professional investors.

Target Market

Foster determined that the target market included kidney stones that received primary ureteroscopy and extracorporeal shock-wave lithotripsy (ESWL) therapy (the two most common procedures), as well as stenting to relieve urine flow. The price of ESWL machines ranged from $500,000 to $1.5 million, a prohibitive cost to all but the largest medical centers. Although these prices were coming down, there were only 400 units in the United

EXHIBIT 4

Procedure Market Tree

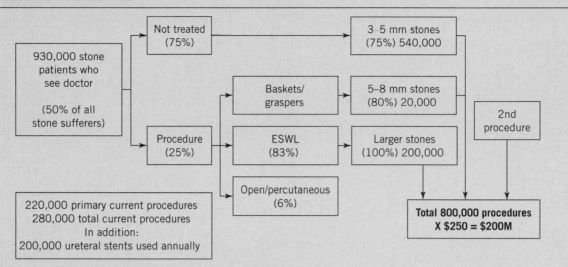

States, about 7 percent of all hospitals. Over $2 billion was spent every year on treating kidney stones. The average per patient annual expenditure was in the range of $7,000, excluding pharmaceuticals.

Foster found that in the early 2000s there were approximately 260,000 primary and secondary procedures each year in the United States. Because the SRS had proven effective in capturing smaller stones that were currently left painfully untreated, she added in 75 percent of those for a total U.S. market of 800,000 target procedures (see Exhibit 4). At a price of $250 each, the SRS represented a $200 million opportunity.

Customers

The two main customers for this stent would be urologists and medical centers. The urologist determined the procedure and decided which device would be used. The actual buyer would be the hospital, where purchasing administrators kept an eagle eye on the costs and were often strongly influenced by reimbursement procedure policies set by the Center for Medicare and by Medicaid Services. One method hospitals used to cut costs was to order aggregated packages of devices and services from highly diversified suppliers such as Johnson & Johnson.

Urologists were well educated, risk averse, and generally not keen on trying brand new devices and procedures. A physician's chief concerns would include patient comfort and safety, risk, and reimbursement. A decision to try an innovative device was most often prompted by a visit from a trusted sales representative. In making that decision, the urologist would be most influenced by endorsements from academically respected colleagues and from sound technical data from clinical studies. In 2001 there were just over 7,100 licensed

urologists in the United States, with most treating stones. A typical urologist cared for a large patient population, averaging 140 stone patients per year.

In the Internet age, patients were becoming more educated about options and could therefore be strong influencers. Patient concerns included relieving immediate pain, avoiding invasive procedures, and the definitive removal of the stone. Kidney stone patients were most often Caucasians between the ages of 20 and 40. Eighty percent were likely to have a recurrence.

Attracting the Competition

The main competitors were those who had a leading market share in basket retrieval and ureteral stent devices (see Exhibit 5). Stents like the Double-J were simple devices, produced by many manufacturers, and were not purchased on the basis of any technological superiority.

Revenue leader Boston Scientific had made many acquisitions. This suggested to Foster that their internal R&D structure did not provide the company with sufficient numbers of new innovations. Unit leader ACMI was undergoing a restructuring and a change of leadership that seemed indicative of a lull in new innovations. Neither company had a presence in the ESWL market.

Makers of the ESWL machines and laser lithotripsers were also suppliers of ESWL accessories such as water bags and fluids. Foster reasoned that large sellers like Dornier MedTech and Siemens Medical Systems might have an early-stage interest in a product like the SRS because it worked in conjunction with ESWL. In a sense, though, every stent competitor in the space was a potential distributor—or a research and development partner or parent. Major players in the industry, with their established and credible sales and marketing capabilities,

EXHIBIT 5

Competitor Profiles

	Location	Employees	Revenues	Products	Price Points	Perception
Cook Urological (private)	Spencer, IN	300, incl mnf (4,000 all Cook)	$25.1M	Stents, baskets, wires, and other lithotripsers	Medium	Good products and innovative—strong company (#1 in biliary market)
BARD (urological)	Covington, GA	8,100 (all BARD)	$95M w/out Foleys ($360M total) 1999	Stents, baskets, laser, and other lithotripsers	Low-end	Slow, no innovation
Microvasive (Boston Scientific)	Natick, MA	14,400 (all BSC)	$143M $133M (stones) 1999	Stents, baskets, laser, and other lithotripsers	High-end	Innovative (with acquisitions), good sales force, good products
Surgitek (ACMI) (private)	Southboro, MA (HQ); Racine, WI (Urology)		$17M stents	Stents, baskets, scopes, lasers	Low-end	Based on quantity, but no innovation, hungry for new products
Applied Medical	Rancho Santa Margarita, CA	375, incl mnf	$31M (all three divisions) 2001	Various dilators and specialty items	High-end	Interesting, good, clever products, not full product line

could significantly affect the speed of adoption of new devices.

Unlike most ventures, the strategy would not be to go up against top competitors, and investors would have little interest in closely monitoring the usual metrics such as sales revenues, gross margins, and projected net income. The objective would be to establish a following among the best medical practitioners in the world—even if that meant giving away the stents for free. Foster felt that once the SRS had proven market demand, the company would then have an excellent chance of being acquired.

Start-Up

Working part-time, Foster completed the business plan in the late summer of 2001. Because an acquisition harvest could not be accurately timed or priced, financial projections for the company she had named Newland Medical Technologies followed a standard scenario of steady growth (see Exhibit 6). By the spring of the following year, she had raised just over $600,000 in seed capital from friends, family, Grainer, and her own savings. When she began to discuss assembling a cohesive venture team, Foster was surprised to learn that Grainer had been assuming all along that she would serve as president and CEO. While she was very excited about the opportunity, she also knew what she didn't know:

To do it the right way, I was going to need some practical business education. In the fall of 2002, I was accepted into the MBA program at the F.W. Olin Graduate School of Business [at Babson College in Wellesley, Massachusetts]. I then switched jobs, to a position with a well-defined, short-range end point.

Patent work—mostly legal—took nearly a year and drained a third of the capital she had raised. After completing some additional R&D work on the stent, Foster applied for Food and Drug Administration (FDA) approval. Given her past experience with Johnson & Johnson, and some good advice from an expert at Babson College, no one was surprised when the SRS sailed through the usually tough FDA process in just under three months. Foster recalled the strategy:

Professor Boulnois[2] had come up with the idea of taking a two-tiered approach. First we got the SRS approved as a basic drainage stent—no problem there. When we filed our follow-on application with a different indication—stone removal—we got lucky because we had the same reviewer for both applications. She saw that it was the identical device that she had just approved, with a new indication, and because of that, we received that next approval in less than 30 days. And because stents are an established category of medical devices, we got our

[2] Dr. Jean-Luc Boulnois, an adjunct professor at Babson College, was founder and president of Interactive Consulting, Inc., a management consulting firm specializing in business development for European early-stage medical technology companies entering the U.S. market.

EXHIBIT 6

Newland Pro Forma Income Statement

	2004	2005	2006	2007	2008
Net Revenues	0	721,000	8,380,000	22,327,000	34,811,625
Total Cost of Goods Sold (see below)	0	335,160	2,692,135	6,620,487	9,434,219
Percentage of Revenues		46.5%	32.1%	29.7%	27.1%
Gross Profit	0	385,840	5,687,865	15,706,513	25,377,406
Percentage of Revenues		53.5%	67.9%	70.3%	72.9%
Operating Expenses					
Sales & Marketing	166,200	939,900	1,573,016	2,379,059	2,858,596
Research & Development	225,240	448,795	600,140	947,216	1,105,338
General & Administrative	153,800	315,700	680,055	1,057,531	1,398,100
Total Operating Expenses	545,240	1,704,395	2,853,211	4,383,806	5,362,034
Net Earnings before Taxes	(545,240)	(1,318,555)	2,834,654	11,322,707	20,015,372
Taxes	0	0	498,899	4,529,083	8,006,149
Net Earnings	(545,240)	(1,318,555)	2,335,755	6,793,624	12,009,223

Cost of Goods Sold Breakdown (e.g., 2005)

Direct Costs

Average Material Cost per Unit	8
Average Labor Cost per Unit	14
Sterilizing and Packaging per Unit	8
Manufacturer per Unit Markup (20%)	6
Total per Unit Direct Costs	36
Direct Costs: 6,200 Units (2005)	223,200

Indirect Costs

Salaries and Benefits	84,750
Facility; Shipping	7,210
Depreciation	20,000
Total Indirect Costs	111,960
Cost of Goods & Services	335,160

reimbursement codes in far less time than it would normally take a company with a brand new technology.[3]

[3] By the early 2000s, the Centers for Medicare & Medicaid Services (CMS) had become a bottleneck challenge for many ventures seeking to commercialize a medical device product. The CMS was charged with the subjective task of evaluating the costs and benefits of particular technologies—an evolving field with plenty of room for debate. Reimbursement issues could be so complex and complicated that receiving payment for new products had become the greatest stumbling block for early entrants—and CMS was only one piece of the coverage approval puzzle. To achieve reimbursement coverage and payment throughout the country for a new technology, medical device ventures were required to weave their way through a maze of several hundred payers. Moreover, new products had to struggle to get assigned a unique code that would distinguish them from existing technologies. Even after that code was assigned, it might take several years for Medicare to recognize that device as a new cost. Since health care facilities wouldn't use products that had not received proper payment approvals, it was not unusual for reimbursement gaps to derail the implementation of viable, FDA approved medical device innovations.

While attending the Olin School, Foster spent much of her time looking for the $1.7 million in venture funding she estimated Newland would need to commercialize the SRS device. After pitching her plan to numerous investors, angel groups, and business plan forums in the Boston area, Foster came across a business development foundation in Rhode Island. They agreed to put up $65,000—as long as 20 percent was spent directly in Rhode Island. As a result, Foster began working with a company in that state to produce prototypes in a manner that would satisfy the stringent FDA production and quality requirements. The company was also offering a total solution under one roof—from extrusion to packaging.

By the time she had graduated in January 2004, Foster had attracted two additional team members—an engineer she had met at a previous job and a business development talent who had approached her at a business plan forum. Because she had no money to pay them, in both cases she offered to "back pay" their earned salaries from the next round of funding she expected to raise.

Even though the economy had substantially recovered following the 2001 recession, investors were still very cautious. Ever since they had received FDA approval, Foster had been meeting with and receiving helpful feedback and additional contacts from numerous venture capitalists. She finally concluded, however, that Newland was at too early a stage for that type of investor.

At a business plan competition in spring 2004, a fellow Babson graduate recommended that she speak with his uncle, a local philanthropist and retired venture investor. Foster recalled that at first the lead appeared to be yet another dead end:

> Peter Cunningham is in his seventies, and he had told his nephew Bill that he wasn't doing any more investments. But Bill said, "You've got to meet this woman and see what she is doing." So I met him in November, and soon after, he became our first angel investor.

Cunningham invested $250,000 and attracted two other local angels, who each invested $75,000. The capital was a long way from full funding, but it provided sustaining salaries for the team and a one-room incubator space in Boston's south end—halfway between two major medical research centers. Their proximity to those research labs would prove immediately critical.

Setbacks

By getting to know the researchers at the animal testing facilities at New England Medical, Foster noted that they were able to further Newland's research at almost no cost:

> The labs were doing their cardio work on pigs in the morning and working with the urinary tract system most every afternoon. They were curious about the SRS capabilities and were willing to add our stent to their work with the ureters. It was great; we didn't have to hang around for it, and we could just walk over to discuss what sorts of indications and challenges they had identified.

While pre-FDA approval trials had confirmed that the SRS would perform as expected once the device was placed in the ureter, these latest tests brought to light some serious design flaws. Foster explained,

> Back when we started, the first five stents we designed wouldn't fit in the ureter. So our focus became making the baskets small enough to fit inside a sheath. We made a bunch, and when 15 in a row deployed successfully and worked as expected, I imme-

diately began to move forward on developing the business plan. Then when we got FDA approval and the reimbursement codes, I figured we were ready to go out into the market.

> The problem was Dr. Grainer and I hadn't talked to enough doctors early on when we were still in that design stage. For example, we chose an insertion guide wire that was larger than the standard—but one that an advisor said ought to be fine. We had created a device that worked—it could stay in the body, it dilated the ureter, patients didn't feel any pain, and it caught stones—but because our design was far more difficult to place than a standard stent, we had failed to create a salable product. When it became clear that this was never going to take off as a commercial venture, we went back to the drawing board.

Significantly compounding this challenge was that her chosen manufacturer had turned out to be not even remotely capable of being a one-stop shop. As a result, the team was compelled to assemble a supply chain of specialists: an extruder, a fine-tooling shop, a coating company, a sterilization expert, and a medical packager. Although Foster was pleased that this arrangement gave them more control over quality at each level of production, she understood that the need to pass off work-in-process between several companies would extend lead times and increase the possibility of communication challenges. From a strategy perspective, she explained that developing a single-site manufacturing capability may not have been the way to go anyway:

> I have found no consensus on whether medical device companies like ours should spend time and money perfecting a manufacturing capability. Some investors feel that having a production capacity would boost our appeal as an acquisition. Other investors feel just the opposite, that a big company like Boston Scientific would acquire Newland for the value of its patented devices, and would probably prefer to develop their own manufacturing systems.

Rebirth and Conception

In late 2004 the team—bolstered by 60 successful patient trials and very positive feedback from a range of physicians—began their full-scale effort to build a critical mass of advocates and attract at least one major distributor. They got a significant boost in March 2005, when Boston-based Taylor Medical Supply (TMS) agreed to test Newland's stent in a few of their major markets in the United States.

Meanwhile, Foster focused on raising funds to restore coffers depleted from the struggle to get back to the point where they had thought they had been months earlier. At an angel investor breakfast in late May, she met a pair of harvested entrepreneurs looking for investment opportunities. Chris Fallon had made his money when his single-product banking software venture was acquired by a major financial corporation in New York. Claudia Grimes was the cofounder of an adventure sports vacation portal that was snapped up by a multinational travel agency—just eight months after her venture had proven sales and profitability.

Both investors expressed interest in Newland, particularly because they felt that the company was at an excellent point for a lucrative early-stage acquisition. Foster explained,

> There are a few times when you can sell a medical device company like ours: after a product development milestone like proof of concept on animals, after FDA approval, after a series of successful clinical trials, and after your first million or so in sales.
>
> Chris and Claudia were certain that since we had a patented product that had FDA approval and payment codes, it was an excellent time for us to sell. They could see we were ready for market, and they were talking about putting up at least $200,000 apiece—as long as we pursued an acquisition strategy. Although an early-stage acquisition (pre-sales) was never in our plan, the more we thought about it, the more it sounded like an attractive option.

One constituent that was not pleased with what they saw as an abrupt shift in strategy was Taylor Medical Supply. Foster thought that their displeasure was particularly acute because of the way they learned about the change:

> Things had started to move very fast. We chose an investment banker whose initial task was to act as an intermediary between Newland and potential buyers. He called TMS to let them know we were pursing an acquisition, and to ask if they wanted in on it. They were definitely taken aback. They told the investment banker that from their perspective we'd been moving toward a distribution deal. That was news to me; they had never seemed more than lukewarm about taking on our device. Not only did they decline to put in an offer, but they suspended their test marketing of the SRS. Still, they did indicate that initial feedback from their clients had been very positive.

With endorsements from two prominent medical centers, and a few promising acquisition prospects considering the possibilities, it seemed that momentum was building for a speedy harvest. Encouraged by Newland's progress, that summer, Foster and her husband ran the numbers—with an allowance for misconceptions—and estimated that it was an excellent time to start a family. On paper, their planned parenthood coincided well with the harvest schedule that Newland's newest investors were espousing. The couple was a bit shocked, but thoroughly delighted, when Foster became pregnant that very month. Well, she mused, maybe the acquisition strategy would continue to charge down a similar fast track. It didn't.

A Fork in the Road with a Baby on Board

Despite assurances that all was going according to their plan, by the fall Foster was having a hard time dealing with the aggressive angels she'd brought on. The nature of the relationship provided them with a good deal of latitude with regard to setting the pace and direction of the acquisition strategy that Foster and her original investors had signed off on, and it wasn't long before Fallon and Grimes began to demand changes in the deal structure that would provide them with better returns.

In mid-October 2005 their investment banker brought an offer to the table from a middle-tier medical supply distributor based in Florida. The $9.5 million term sheet provided a generous five-year earn-out for Foster and her team—provided they stayed on in Boston to develop a line of innovative stents. The terms also required that Foster serve as president, and it was contingent upon FDA approval of Newland's latest innovation—now in early trials.[4] The offer provided no funds to make that happen, and when Fallon and Grimes said that any further capital would have to come with additional equity, Foster finally decided to confide in her original investors:

> I had kept Chris Cunningham and his group apprised of our decision to seek an acquisition, and they had agreed with that. But these two entrepreneur angels were so difficult to work with, and neither of them had any experience in the medical industry. Maybe that's not a crucial requirement, but overall, they just didn't seem to get what we were about. Mr. Cunningham looked at me and said, "Well, if what has been stopping you from tossing these two aside was the money, you should have come to me earlier."

But for Foster this wasn't just about the money, the equity split, or the harvest: it was about developing new and exciting medical products that could make a difference. Nevertheless, as president she felt that if Newland could strike a deal with a large company that would give current investors a decent return and provide

---

[4] Newland Medical was working on a line of stents designed to hold the ureter open against, for example, external compression from a tumor. Newland's ureteral structural stents would be significantly more resistant to compression than any product that was currently on the market. These devices would allow patients with locally and regionally invasive tumors (typically end-stage and terminal) to survive longer with healthy kidney function. Taking into account national occurrence rates for diseases that tended to exert pressure on urinary passageways, the team estimated that this represented a $25 million market opportunity.

Newland with a base of resources to further new product development, then that was the path she ought to pursue. On the other hand, staying the course and building a line of innovative products would significantly increase their acquisition value.

If not for her pregnancy, Foster wouldn't hesitate for a moment; she'd return to their original strategy—and to her passion for building an innovative medical device enterprise. To pursue that course now, however, she would be facing the prospect of being a new mother *and* running a growing business. With an offer on the table and funds running short, she swallowed hard against a particularly acute bout of morning sickness. It was time to make some tough decisions.

PART THREE

The Founder and Team

Entrepreneurial founders must take a personal role in attracting, motivating, inspiring, and retaining an effective team of both specialists and generalists. The quality of that team has never been more fundamental and important than it is now. The new millennium has ushered in a wave of new opportunities that will require nimble and creative teams. Some pundits have characterized this time as the communication era, characterized by galloping innovation—fueled by the ability of inventive engineers and creative entrepreneurs to instantly access and share information worldwide. Stung by the dot-com fallout and the recession that followed, private and venture capital investors have a renewed appreciation for the time-tested wisdom that successful new ventures are often all about the team. In this section we will look at the leadership issues inherent in building a company from scratch—and the significant recruiting, sales, and management skills the founder(s) must bring to bear as the enterprise grows through various stages.

Entrepreneurship titles now dominate the business sections at major booksellers like Barnes & Noble, and a growing number of students and professionals are seeking career opportunities in the entrepreneurial sector. While this has created a significant pool of talent to support the development of new ventures, one of the most critical aspects of entrepreneuring is in being able to attract the *right* people: team players whose skills and know-how are critical to the success of the enterprise. Ambiguity, risk, and the need to collectively turn on a dime in the face of shifting competitive landscapes require that entrepreneurial teams be greater than the sum of their parts. Like marriage, forming and building that team can be a rather unscientific, occasionally unpredictable, and frequently surprising experience. We will also be putting a zoom lens on the "people" portion of the Timmons Model.

The solo entrepreneur may make a living, but it is the team builder who develops an organization and a company with sustainable value and attractive harvest options. The vision of what these founders are trying to accomplish provides the unwritten ground rules that become the fabric, character, and purpose behind the venture. Effective lead entrepreneurs are able to build a culture around the business mission and the brand by rewarding success, supporting honest failure, sharing the wealth with those who helped to create it, and setting high ethical standards of conduct. Chapter 10—Ethical Decision Making and the Entrepreneur—addresses the complex and thorny issues of ethics and integrity for the entrepreneur, and how those decisions and choices can have a significant impact on future success.

Chapter Nine

The Entrepreneurial Leader and the Team

"People don't want to be managed. They want to be led!"

Ewing Marion Kauffman, Founder, Marion
Labs and the Ewing Marion Kauffman
Foundation, Kansas City, MO

Results Expected

Upon completion of this chapter, you will be able to

1. Explain the difference between an entrepreneurial leader and an administrator or manager, and discuss why the team is so important.
2. Identify stages of growth that firms experience, and the competencies and skills that are relevant for leading a venture through these turbulent waters.
3. Articulate the skills, competencies, and philosophies entrepreneurial-thinking founders apply as they form, build, and lead a new venture team, and discuss the critical issues and hurdles they face.
4. Analyze issues of rewards and equity ownership in a new venture, and develop a pro forma approach for your own venture.
5. Analyze and discuss the Maclean Palmer case.

The Entrepreneurial Leader

The quote we begin this chapter with says it all: People want to be *led*—not managed, manipulated, or forced to do things only because they need a paycheck. This is the reason why, for the past two decades in America, and now around the world, the battle for mind share and talent, time and again, is being won by entrepreneurial leaders. Young people today are attracted to the exciting, energetic, and compassionate workplaces created by a new generation of entrepreneurs.

Do you love where you work and whom you work for? Would you recommend it to your best friends and family? Why? There is a familiar ring to the answers; they boil down to the entrepreneurial lead-ership and the team culture that are created and built by the company's founders. They create energy and excitement and transform ideas and dreams into tangible visions that people believe they can achieve. At the extreme are Microsoft and Bill Gates, one of the most successful start-ups and entrepreneurial leaders of the last century. A less known but similarly stunning example is Matt Coffin, who graduated from Babson College in 1999. He built LowerMyBills.com from scratch to 250+ employees, and in May 2005 he sold it to Experian for $330 million. He stayed on for two years to run the company as a dynamic and motivating leader before deciding it was time to start something new. The entrepreneurial leadership skills he developed propelled the company into and through rapid and successful growth. It is the ability to lead a high-potential firm through the stages of growth that defines the entrepreneur in the 21st century.

Entrepreneurial leaders such as Gates and Coffin epitomize the entrepreneurial ways of reasoning, attitudes, values, and beliefs that we discussed in detail in Chapter 2. Their leadership approach manifests itself in actions and behaviors that attract and keep the best talent. What about them is so compelling? For one thing, they lead by deeds, not words, and set an example with a high work ethic, integrity and honesty, and fairness. They often have a keen sense of humor and spontaneity that engenders trust, as well as confidence: What you see is what you get. Their creativity and innovativeness, especially in the opportunity creation process with new product or service ideas, or in solving a tricky personnel or organization problem, invariably win confidence and enthusiastic followers. They are quick to give credit and recognize good performance, and they always accept more than their share of the blame when things don't work out. They are team builders, make heroes out of others, and do not have to be the center of attention and recognition.

This is vital in new ventures because the key to their success, as we have demonstrated previously, is the talent and quality of the lead entrepreneur and founding team. There is little time or priority in a start-up for coaching, training, mentoring, and development of new hires. *Every new hire has to think and act like an owner* and perform without much guidance and direction.

People Know Leaders When They Experience Them

For years, research has shown that peers are more accurate in identifying and ranking leaders than are outside observers, researchers, and experts. Whether it is a high school sports team, a club, or some other organization, people have an uncanny, intuitive sense of who are and will be the best leaders. They know when someone is truly committed rather than just saying the words and going through the motions. They distinguish the exceptionally creative and inventive entrepreneur with a nose for opportunity. They know when people truly care and show respect for others. A recent conversation, for example, with the head of a medical clinic of more than 30 professionals revealed that although the boss is considered a decent manager, he clearly is no leader. "He just doesn't seem to care who I am or what I do. I've been here over a year now and he has never asked about my two boys, my wife, or any of my personal interests." Understandably, this talented midcareer doctor plans to move on as soon as he can.

Think of some of the colloquial terms that describe many managers and administrators who are not leaders: control freak, compliance, custodial, policies and procedures, bureaucrat, dominating or dictatorial, nitpicker, blamer, manipulator, self-centered, and so on. It is no wonder entrepreneurial leaders are winning the race to attract and keep the best talent.

The Importance of the Team

The Connection to Success

Evidence suggests that a management team can make all the difference in venture success. There is a strong connection between the growth potential of a new venture (and its ability to attract capital beyond the founder's resources from private and venture capital backers) and the quality of its management team.

The existence of a quality management team is one of the major differences between a firm that provides its founder simply a job substitute, and the ability to employ perhaps a few family members and others, and a higher-potential venture. The lone-wolf entrepreneur may make a living, but the team builder creates an organization and a company with substantial value and harvest options.

Ventures that do not have teams are not necessarily predestined for the new venture graveyard. Yet building a higher-potential venture without a team is extremely difficult. Some entrepreneurs have acquired a distaste for partners, and some lead entrepreneurs can be happy only if they are in complete control; that is, they want employees, not partners, either internally or as outside investors. Take, for instance, an entrepreneur who founded a high-technology firm that grew steadily, but slowly, over 10 years to nearly $2 million in sales. As new patterns and technological advances in fiber optics drew much interest from venture capitalists, he had more than one offer of up to $5 million of funding, which he turned down because the investors wanted to own 51 percent or more of his venture. Plainly and simply, he said, "I do not want to give up control of what I have worked so long and hard to create." While clearly the exception to the rule, this entrepreneur has managed to grow his business to more than $20 million in sales.

Since the 1970s, numerous studies have pointed to the importance of a team approach to new venture creation. Solid teams are far more likely to attract venture capital; team-led start-ups have a greater chance of survival; and those enterprises often realize higher overall returns than ventures run by solo entrepreneurs.

Not only is the existence of a team important, but so too is the quality of that team. Because of this, venture capital investors are often very active in helping to shape—and reshape—management teams. A study in the late 1990s demonstrated the increasing importance of team formation, teamwork history, and cooperation between new venture teams and venture capitalists.[1] This is especially true today with highly technical ventures in areas such as biotechnology, nanotechnology, and photonics.

There is, then, a valuable role that the right partner(s) can play in a venture. In addition, mounting evidence suggests that entrepreneurs face loneliness, stress, and other pressures. At the very least, finding the right partner can mitigate these pressures.[2] The key is identifying and working with the right partner or partners. Getting the right partners and working with them successfully usually involve anticipating and dealing with some critical issues and hurdles when it is neither too early nor too late.

Stages of Growth

A Theoretical View

You can quickly see the implications and importance of the team concept when you think about what Matt Coffin did in growing a company to over 250 employees in a short time. Unique challenges you have not faced previously can occur as a company grows and goes through different stages, much like going from childhood to adolescence to adulthood.

Clearly entrepreneurship is not static. Exhibit 9.1 represents a *theoretical* view of the process of gestation and growth of new ventures and the transitions that occur at different boundaries in this process. Ventures are sown; they sprout, grow, and are harvested. Even those successful ventures that are not grown to harvest (i.e., those that have been defined as "attractive") go through stages of growth. This smooth, S-shape curve in the exhibit is rarely replicated

EXHIBIT 9.1

Stages of Venture Growth, Crucial Transitions, and Core Management Mode

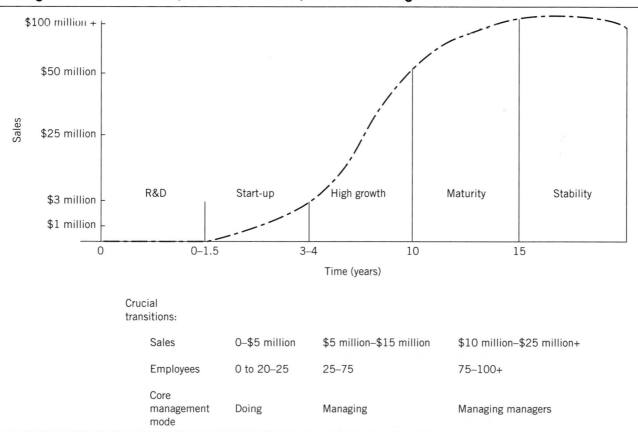

Crucial transitions:			
Sales	0–$5 million	$5 million–$15 million	$10 million–$25 million+
Employees	0 to 20–25	25–75	75–100+
Core management mode	Doing	Managing	Managing managers

---

[1] For another useful view of the stages of development of a firm and required management capabilities, see C. V. Kroeger, "Management Development and the Small Firm," *California Management Review* 17, no. 1 (Fall 1974), pp. 41–47.

[2] L. A. Griener, "Evolution and Revolution as Organizations Grow," in *Trials and Rewards of the Entrepreneur* (Boston: Harvard Business Review, 1977), pp. 47–56; and H. N. Woodward, "Management Strategies for Small Companies," in *Trials and Rewards of the Entrepreneur* (Boston: Harvard Business Review Press, 1981), pp. 57–66.

in the real world. If we actually tracked the progress of most emerging companies, the curve would be a ragged and jagged line with many ups and downs; these companies would experience some periods of rapid progress followed by setbacks and accompanying crises.

For illustration, venture stages are shown in terms of time, sales, and number of employees. It is at the boundaries between stages that new ventures seem to experience transitions. Several researchers have noted that a new venture invariably goes through transition and will face certain issues. Thus the exhibit shows the crucial transitions during growth and the key management tasks of the chief executive officer or founders. Most important and most challenging for the founding entrepreneur or a chief executive officer is coping with crucial transitions and the change in leadership focus—going from leading to leading managers—as a firm grows to roughly 30 employees, to 50, to 75, and then up.

The *research and development stage*, sometimes referred to as the nascent stage, is characterized by a single aspiring entrepreneur, or small team, doing the investigation and due diligence for their business idea. The nascent stage can be as short as a few months or can last years. Research indicates that if an idea is not turned into a going concern within 18 months, the chances of a start-up fall dramatically. Nascent entrepreneurs have many fits and starts, and the business model can change often in the process.

The *start-up stage* usually covers the first two or three years but perhaps as many as seven, is by far the most perilous stage and is characterized by the direct and exhaustive drive, energy, and entrepreneurial talent of a lead entrepreneur and a key team member or two. Here the critical mass of people, market and financial results, and competitive resilience are established, while investor, banker, and customer confidence is earned. The level of sales reached varies widely but typically ranges between $2 million and $20 million.

A new company then begins its *high-growth stage*—characterized by a continually increasing rate of growth or the slope of the revenue curve. The exact point at which this occurs can rarely be identified by a date on the calendar until well after the fact. It is in this stage that new ventures exhibit a failure rate exceeding 60 percent; that is, it is in this stage that the lemons ripen.

As with the other stages, the length of time it takes to go through the high-growth stage, as well as the magnitude of change occurring during the period, varies greatly. Probably the most difficult challenge for the founding entrepreneur occurs during the high-growth stage, when he or she finds it is necessary to let go of power and control (through veto) over key decisions that he or she has always had, and when key responsibilities need to be delegated without abdicating ultimate leadership and responsibility for results. But the challenges do not end there. For example, sales of Litton's microwave oven division had reached $13 million, and it had 275 employees. The long-range plan called for building sales volume to $100 million in five to seven years (i.e., growing at 40 percent per year, compounded). The head of the division said, "Having studied the market for the previous two years, I was convinced that the only limit on our growth was our organization's inability to grow as rapidly as the market opportunities."[3]

From the high-growth stage, a company then moves to what is called the *maturity stage*. In this stage, the key issue for the company is no longer survival; rather, it is one of steady, profitable growth. The *stability stage* usually follows.

Managing for Rapid Growth

The transition from rapid growth to maturity and stability is even less recognizable and less assured in the 21st century. Increased rates of new technology adoption and the reduced importance of asset density to gain business model scale make the maturity and stability stages less enduring. Entrepreneurship has become a required core competency of the modern firm.

Managing for rapid growth involves a leadership orientation not found in mature and stable environments. (This topic will be addressed again in Chapter 17.) For one thing, the tenet that one's responsibility must equal one's authority is often counterproductive in a rapid-growth venture. Instead results usually require close collaboration of a manager with people other than his or her subordinates, and managers invariably have responsibilities far exceeding their authority. Politics and personal power can be a way of life in many larger and stagnant institutions, as managers jockey for influence and a piece of a shrinking pie in a zero-sum game; but in rapid-growth firms, power and control are delegated and leadership is shared. Everyone is committed to making the pie larger, and power and influence are derived not only from achieving one's own goals but also from contributing to the achievements of others. Influence also is derived from keeping the overall goals in mind, from resolving differences, and from developing a reputation as a person who gets results, can lead others, and can build leadership talent as well.

Thus among successful entrepreneurs and entrepreneurial leaders, there is a well-developed capacity to exert influence *without* formal power. These

---

[3] W. W. George, "Task Teams for Rapid Growth," *Harvard Business Review*, March–April 1977.

people are adept at conflict resolution. They know when to use logic and when to persuade, when to make a concession and when to exact one. To run a successful venture, an entrepreneur learns to get along with many different constituencies, often with conflicting aims—the customer, the supplier, the financial backer, and the creditor, as well as the partners and others on the inside. Similarly, an entrepreneurial leader must operate in a world that is increasingly interdependent. Attempting to advise managers on how to exert "influence without authority," David L. Bradford and Allan R. Cohen asserted that as a leader, "you not only need to exercise influence skills with your peers and your own boss, but also to help the people who work for you learn to be effective influencers—even of you—since that will free you to spend more of your time seeking new opportunities and working the organization above and around you."[4]

Whereas successful entrepreneurs are interpersonally supporting and nurturing—not interpersonally competitive—successful entrepreneurial leaders understand their interdependencies and have learned to incorporate mutual respect, openness, trust, and benefit into their leadership style. Fundamental to this progressive style is the awareness and practice of reciprocity for mutual gain.[5] When a strong need to control, influence, and gain power over others characterizes the lead entrepreneur, or when he or she has an insatiable appetite for putting an associate down, more often than not the venture gets into trouble. A dictatorial, adversarial, and dominating management style makes it difficult to attract and keep people who thirst for achievement, responsibility, and results. Compliant partners and managers are often chosen. Destructive conflicts often erupt over who has the final say, who is right, and whose prerogatives are what.

In the corporate setting, the "hero-making" ability is identified as an essential attribute of successful entrepreneurial leaders.[6] These hero makers try to make the pie bigger and better, rather than jealously clutching and hoarding a tiny pie that is all theirs. They have a capacity for objective interpersonal relationships as well, which enables them to smooth out individual differences of opinion by keeping attention focused on the common goal to be achieved.[7]

Exhibit 9.2 characterizes probable crises that growing ventures will face, including erosion of creativity by founders and team members; confusion or resentment, or both, over ambiguous roles, responsibilities, and goals; failure to clone founders; specialization and eroding of collaboration; desire for autonomy and control; need for operating mechanisms and controls; and conflict and divorce among founders and members of the team. The exhibit further delineates issues that confront entrepreneurial leaders.

Compounding of Time and Change   In the high-growth stage, change, ambiguity, and uncertainty seem to be the only things that remain constant. Change creates higher levels of uncertainty,

---

EXHIBIT 9.2

Entrepreneurial Transitions

Modes/Stages	Planning	Doing	Leading	Leading Managers
Sales	$0	0–$5 million	$5 million–$15 million	$10 million or more
Employees	0–5	0–30	30–75	75 and up
Transitions	Characteristics:	Characteristics:	Probable crises:	Probable crises:
	Founder-driven	Founder-driven creativity	Erosion of creativity of founders	Failure to clone founders
	Wrenching changes	Constant change, ambiguity, and uncertainty	Confusion over ambiguous roles, responsibilities, and goals	Specialization/eroding of collaboration versus practice of power, information, and influence
	Highly influential informal advisor	Time compression	Desire for delegation versus autonomy and control	Need for operating controls and mechanisms
	Resource desperation	Informal communications	Need for organization and operating policies	Conflict among founders
	Very quick or very slow decision making	Counterintuitive decision making and structure		
		Relative inexperience		

---

[4] D. L. Bradford and A. R. Cohen, *Influence without Authority* (New York: John Wiley & Sons, 1990).

[5] Ibid.

[6] D. L. Bradford and A. R. Cohen, *Power Up: Transforming Organizations through Shared Leadership* (New York: John Wiley & Sons, 1998).

[7] C. Churchill, "Entrepreneurs and Their Enterprises: A Stage Model," in *Frontiers of Entrepreneurship Research: 1983*, ed J. A. Hornaday et al. (Babson Park, MA: Babson College, 1983), pp. 1–22.

ambiguity, and risk, which, in turn, compound to shrink time, an already precious commodity. One result of change is a series of shock waves rolling through a new and growing venture by way of new customers, new technologies, new competitors, new markets, and new people. In industries characterized by galloping technological change, with relatively minuscule lead and lag times in bringing new products to market and in weathering the storms of rapid obsolescence, the effects of change and time are extreme. For example, the president of a rapidly growing, small computer company said, "In our business it takes 6 to 12 months to develop a new computer, ready to bring to the market, and product technology obsolescence is running about 9 to 12 months." This time compression has been seen in such industries as electronics and aerospace in the 1960s; small computers, integrated circuits, and silicon chips in the 1970s; microcomputers in the 1980s; telecommunications, the Internet, and biotechnology in the 1990s; and nanotechnology in the 2000s.

Nonlinear and Nonparametric Events
Entrepreneurial leadership is characterized by nonlinear and nonparametric events. Just as the television did not come about by a succession of improvements in the radio, and the jet plane did not emerge from engineers and scientists attempting to develop a better piston engine plane, so too events do not follow straight lines, progress arithmetically, or even appear related within firms. Rather, they occur in bunches and in stepwise leaps. For example, a firm may double its sales force in 15 months, rather than over eight years, while another may triple its manufacturing capacity and adopt a new materials resource planning system immediately, rather than utilizing existing capacity by increasing overtime, then adding a third shift nine months later, and finally adding a new plant three years hence.

Relative Inexperience   The management team may be relatively inexperienced. The explosive birth and growth of these firms are usually unique events that cannot be replicated, and most of the pieces in the puzzle—technology, applications, customers, people, the firm itself—are usually new.

Rapid Growth and Disruptive Technology
Any new technology that is significantly cheaper, is much higher-performing, has greater functionality, or is more convenient to use will revolutionize worldwide markets by superseding existing technologies. "Paradigm shifting" is a well-worn connotation. Although the term may sound negative to some, it is in fact neutral. It is negative only to organizations that are unprepared for change and fail to adapt. The results are not just *evolutionary*, they are *revolutionary*. Companies will continue to go out of business as new products and processes emerge—just as the advent of the zipper eradicated some of the button industry, the vacuum cleaner decimated the broom industry, and the PC wiped out the typewriter.

Counterintuitive, Unconventional Decision Making   Yet another characteristic of rapidly growing ventures in the entrepreneurial domain is counterintuitive, unconventional patterns of decision making. For example, a computer firm needed to decide what approach to take in developing and introducing three new products in an uncertain, risky marketplace. Each proposed new product appeared to be aimed at the same end user market, and the person heading each project was similarly enthusiastic, confident, and determined about succeeding. A traditional approach to such a problem would have been to determine the size and growth rates of each market segment; evaluate the probable estimates of future revenue costs and capital requirements for their accuracy; compare the discounted, present value cash flow that would emerge from each project; and select the project with the highest yield versus the required internal rate of return. Such an analysis sometimes overlooks the fact that most rapid growth companies have many excellent alternatives; more commonly, the newness of technology, the immaturity of the marketplace, and the rapid discovery of further applications make it virtually impossible to know which of any product proposals is best. The computer firm decided to support all three new products at once, and a significant new business was built around each one. New market niches were discovered simultaneously, and the unconventional approach paid off.

Fluid Structures and Procedures   Most rapid growth ventures also defy conventional organizational patterns and structures. It is common to find a firm that has grown $25 million, $50 million, or even $150 million per year in sales and that still has no formal organizational chart. If an organizational chart does exist, it usually has three distinguishing features: First, it is inevitably out of date. Second, it changes frequently. For example, one firm had eight major reorganizations in its first five years as it grew to $5 million. Third, the organizational structure is usually flat (i.e., it has few management layers), and there is easy accessibility to the top decision makers. But the informality and fluidity of organization structures and procedures do not mean casualness or sloppiness when it comes to goals, standards, or clarity of direction and purpose. Rather, they translate into responsiveness and readiness to absorb and assimilate rapid changes while maintaining financial and operational cohesion.

Entrepreneurial Culture   There exists in growing new ventures a common value system, which is difficult to articulate, is even more elusive to measure, and is evident in behavior and attitudes. There are a belief in and commitment to growth, achievement, improvement, and success and a sense among members of the team that they are "in this thing together." Goals and the market determine priorities, rather than whose territory or whose prerogatives are being challenged. Managers appear unconcerned about status, power, and personal control. They are more concerned about making sure that tasks, goals, and roles are clear than whether the organizational chart is current or whether their offices and rugs reflect their current status. Likewise, they are more concerned about the evidence, competence, knowledge, and logic of arguments affecting a decision than the status given by a title or the formal position of the individual doing the arguing. Contrast this with a multibillion-dollar, but stagnant, firm in England. Reportedly 29 different makes and models of automobiles are used in the firm to signify one's position.

An entrepreneurial climate, or culture can exist in larger firms also. Such a climate attracts and encourages entrepreneurial achievers, and it helps perpetuate the intensity and pace so characteristic of high-growth firms. Exhibit 9.3 shows how five companies studied by Rosabeth Moss Kanter range from most to least entrepreneurial. Kanter, who has been studying "intrapreneurship" since the 1980s, asserts that the global economy was experiencing the postentrepreneurial revolution, which "takes entrepreneurship a step further, applying entrepreneurial principles to the traditional corporation, creating a marriage between entrepreneurial creativity and corporate discipline, cooperation, and teamwork."[8] This revolution has not made managing any easier; in fact, Kanter suggests, "This constitutes the ultimate corporate balancing act. Cut back and grow. Trim down and build. Accomplish more, and do it in new areas, with fewer resources."[9] Clearly some corporations will embrace these challenges with more success than others; the following section will shed some light on how "giants learn to dance."[10]

What Entrepreneurial Leaders Need to Know

Much of business education traditionally has emphasized and prepared students for life in administration. There is nothing wrong with that, but education preparing students to start and lead vibrant, growing new ventures cannot afford to emphasize administrative efficiency, maintenance tasks, resource ownership, and institutional formalization. Rather, such a program needs to emphasize skills necessary for life in entrepreneurship. For example, effective entrepreneurial leaders need to be especially skillful at managing conflict, resolving differences, balancing multiple viewpoints and demands, and building teamwork and consensus. These skills are particularly difficult when working with others outside one's immediate formal chain of command.

In talking about larger firms, Kanter identifies as necessary power and persuasion skills, skill in managing problems accompanying team and employee participation, and skill in understanding how change is designed and constructed in an organization. Kanter notes,

> In short, individuals do not have to be doing "big things" in order to have their cumulative accomplishments eventually result in big performance for the company. . . . They are only rarely the inventors of the "breakthrough" system. They are only rarely doing something that is totally unique or that no one, in any organization, ever thought of before. Instead, they are often applying ideas that have proved themselves elsewhere, or they are rearranging parts to create a better result, or they are noting a potential problem before it turns into a catastrophe and mobilizing the actions to anticipate and solve it.[11]

A study of midsized growth companies having sales between $25 million and $1 billion and a sales or profit growth of more than 15 percent annually over five years confirms the importance of many of these same fundamentals of entrepreneurial management.[12] For one thing, these companies practiced opportunity-driven management. According to the study, they achieved their first success with a unique product or distinctive way of doing business and often became leaders in market niches by delivering superior value to customers, rather than through low prices. They are highly committed to serving customers and pay close attention to them. For another thing, these firms emphasize financial control and managing every element of the business.

In a book that follows up on the implementation issues of how one gets middle managers to pursue and practice entrepreneurial excellence (first made famous in *In Search of Excellence* by Tom Peters and Bob Waterman), two authors note that some of the important fundamentals practiced by team-builder

---

[8] R. M. Kanter, *When Giants Learn to Dance* (New York: Simon & Schuster, 1989), pp. 9–10.
[9] Ibid., p. 31.
[10] Ibid.
[11] R. M. Kanter, *The Change Masters* (New York: Simon & Schuster, 1983), pp. 354–55.
[12] The study was done by McKinsey & Company. See "How Growth Companies Succeed," reported in *Small Business Report*, July 1984, p. 9.

EXHIBIT 9.3

Characteristics of Five Companies, Ranging from Most to Least Entrepreneurial

	Companies Studied				
	Chipco	**Radco**	**Medco**	**Finco**	**Utico**
Percentage of Effective Managers with Entrepreneurial Accomplishments	71%	69%	67%	47%	33%
Economic Trend	Steadily up.	Trend up but now down.	Upward trend.	Mixed.	Downward trend.
Change Issues	Change normal; constant change in product generation; proliferating staff and units.	Change normal in products, technologies; changeover to second management generation with new focus.	Reorganized 2–3 years ago to install matrix; normal product and technology changes.	Change a shock; new top management group from outside reorganizing and trying to add competitive market posture.	Change a shock; undergoing reorganization to install matrix and add competitive market posture and reducing staff.
Organization Structure	Matrix.	Matrix in some areas; product lines act as quasi divisions.	Matrix in some areas.	Divisional; unitary hierarchy within division; some central officers.	Functional organization; currently overlaying matrix of regions and markets.
Information Flow	Decentralized.	Mixed.	Mixed.	Centralized.	Centralized.
Communication Emphasis	Free, horizontal.	Free, horizontal.	Moderately free, horizontal.	Constricted, vertical.	Constricted, vertical.
Culture	Clear, consistent; favors individual initiative.	Clear, though in transition from invention emphasis to routinization and systems.	Clear; pride in company; belief that talent will be rewarded.	Idiosyncratic; depends on boss and area.	Clear but undergoing changes; favors security, maintenance, and protection.
Emotional Climate	Pride in company, team feeling, some burnout.	Uncertainty regarding changes.	Pride in company; team feeling.	Low trust; high uncertainty.	High uncertainty, confusion.
Rewards	Abundant; visibility, chance to do more challenging work in the future, and get bigger budget projects.	Abundant; visibility, chance to do more challenging work in the future, and get bigger budget projects.	Moderately abundant; conventional.	Scarce; primarily monetary.	Scarce; promotion and salary freeze; recognition by peers grudging.

Source: Reprinted by permission of *Harvard Business Review*. From "Middle Managers as Innovators" by R. M. Kanter, July–August 1982, p. 103. Copyright © 1982 by the Harvard Business School Publishing Corporation; all rights reserved.

entrepreneurs—who are more intent on getting results than just getting their own way—also are emulated by effective middle managers.[13] Or as John Sculley, of Apple Computer, explained,

The heroic style—the lone cowboy on horseback—is not the figure we worship anymore at Apple. In the new corporation, heroes won't personify any single set of achievements. Instead, they personify the process. They might be thought of as gatekeepers, information carriers, and teams. Originally heroes at Apple were the hackers and engineers who created the products. Now, more teams are heroes.[14]

The ability to shape and guide a cohesive team is particularly critical in high-tech firms where the competitive landscape can shift dramatically in the face of disruptive technologies. In his book *The Innovator's Dilemma*, Clayton Christensen finds that even aggressive, innovative, and customer-driven organizations can been rendered nearly obsolete if they fail to

[13] D. L. Bradford and A. R. Cohen, *Managing for Excellence* (New York: John Wiley & Sons, 1984), pp. 3–4.
[14] J. Sculley with J. Byrne, *Odyssey: Pepsi to Apple . . . A Journey of Adventures, Ides, and the Future* (New York: HarperCollins, 1987), p. 321.

EXHIBIT 9.4

Management Factors and Stages

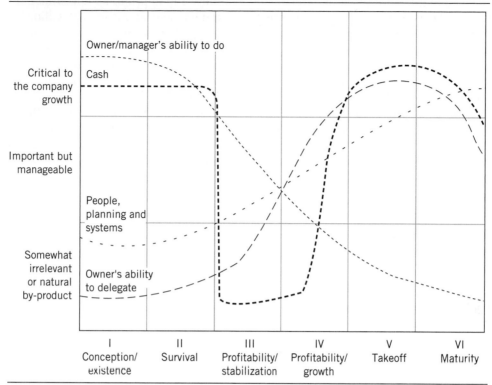

take decisive, and at times radical, actions to stay competitive.[15] The point of greatest peril in the development of a high-tech market, writes Geoffrey Moore in his book *Crossing the Chasm,* lies in making the transition from an early market, dominated by a few visionary customers, to a mainstream market that is dominated by a large block of customers who are predominantly pragmatists in orientation.[16] In Exhibit 9.4, Ed Marram, director of the Arthur M. Blank Center for Entrepreneurship at Babson College, depicts the aspects of leadership as a company grows to maturity.

Lead entrepreneurs whose companies successfully break into the mass market must then find a way to manage the hypergrowth and gigantic revenues that can result from an international surge in demand.[17] Several entrepreneurial managers who have skillfully negotiated these high-tech waters are as well-known as the companies they founded: think Dell, Gates, Jobs, and Ellison. What sort of skills and personality are required to achieve such high levels of performance in a dynamic and uncertain marketplace? As portrayed in Stephen Covey's classic work, *The 7 Habits of Highly Effective People,* these indi-

viduals are curious, proactive team builders who have a passion for continuous improvement and renewal in their lives and in their ventures. Maybe most important in this context: These leaders have "the ability to envision, to see the potential, to create with their minds what they cannot at present see with their eyes . . . "[18]

Competencies and Skills

Entrepreneurs who build substantial companies that grow to more than $10 million in sales and 75 to 100 employees are good entrepreneurs *and* good managers. Typically they will have developed a solid base and a wide breadth of skills and know-how over a number of years working in different areas (e.g., sales, marketing, manufacturing, and finance). It would be unusual for any single entrepreneur to be outstanding in all areas. More likely, a single entrepreneur will have strengths in one area, such as strong people management, conceptual and creative problem-solving skills, and marketing know-how, as well as some significant weaknesses. While it is risky

[15] C. M. Christensen, *The Innovator's Dilemma* (Harvard Business School Press, 1997).
[16] G. Moore, *Crossing the Chasm* (New York: HarperCollins, 2002).
[17] G. Moore, *Inside the Tornado: Marketing Strategies from Silicon Valley's Cutting Edge* (New York: HarperCollins, 1999).
[18] S. R. Covey, *The 7 Habits of Highly Effective People* (New York: Simon & Schuster, 1989).

to generalize, often entrepreneurs whose background is technical are weak in marketing, finance, and general management. Entrepreneurs who do not have a technical background are, as you might expect, often weakest in the technical or engineering aspects.

Throughout this book, the concept of fit has been stressed. Having a management team whose skills are complementary is important—not the possession by an individual of a single, absolute set of skills or a profile. The art and craft of entrepreneuring involves recognizing the skills and know-how needed to succeed in a venture, knowing what each team member does or does not know, and then compensating for shortcomings, either by getting key people on board to fill voids or by an individual accumulating the additional "chunks" before he or she takes the plunge. After all, the venture and the people are works in process.

Skills in Building Entrepreneurial Culture

Leaders of entrepreneurial firms need to recognize and cope with innovation, taking risks, and responding quickly, as well as with absorbing major setbacks. The most effective leaders seem to thrive on the hectic, and at times chaotic, pace and find it challenging and stimulating, rather than frustrating or overwhelming. They use a consensus approach to build a motivated and committed team, they balance conflicting demands and priorities, and they manage conflicts adroitly.

These leaders thus need interpersonal/teamwork skills that involve (1) the ability to create, through leadership a climate and spirit conducive to high performance, including pressing for performance while rewarding work well done and encouraging innovation, initiative, and calculated risk taking; (2) the ability to understand the relationships among tasks and between the leader and followers; and (3) the ability to lead in those situations where it is appropriate, including a willingness to manage actively and supervise and control activities of others through directions, suggestions, and the like.

These interpersonal skills can be called entrepreneurial influence skills because they have a great deal to do with the way these leaders exert influence over others.

Leadership, Vision, and Influence   These leaders are skillful in creating clarity out of confusion, ambiguity, and uncertainty. These entrepreneurial leaders are able to define adroitly and gain agreement on who has what responsibility and authority. Further, they do this in a way that builds motivation and commitment to cross-departmental and corporate goals, not just parochial interests. But this is not perceived by other managers as an effort to jealously carve out and guard personal turf and prerogatives. Rather, it is seen as a genuine effort to clarify roles, tasks, and responsibilities, and to make sure there are accountability and appropriate approvals. This does not work unless the leader is seen as willing to relinquish his or her priorities and power in the interest of an overall goal. It also requires skill in making sure the appropriate people are included in setting cross-functional or cross-departmental goals and in making decisions. When things do not go as smoothly as was hoped, the most effective leaders work them through to an agreement. Managers who are accustomed to traditional line/staff or functional chains of command are often baffled and frustrated in their new role. While some may be quite effective in dealing with their own subordinates, it is a new task to manage and work with peers, the subordinates of others, and even superiors outside one's chain of command.

Helping, Coaching, and Conflict Management   The most effective leaders are creative and skillful in handling conflicts, generating consensus decisions, and sharing their power and information. They are able to get people to open up instead of clamming up; they get problems out on the table instead of under the rug; and they do not become defensive when others disagree with their views. They seem to know that high-quality decisions require a rapid flow of information in all directions and that knowledge, competence, logic, and evidence need to prevail over official status or formal rank in the organization. The way they resolve conflicts is intriguing. They can get potential adversaries to be creative and to collaborate by seeking a reconciliation of viewpoints. Rather than emphasizing differences and playing the role of hard-nosed negotiator or devil's advocate to force their own solution, they blend ideas. They are more willing to risk personal vulnerability in this process—often by giving up their own power and resources—than are their less effective counterparts. They insist on fairness and integrity in the short and long term, rather than short-term gain. The trade-offs are not easy: At the outset, such an approach involves more people, takes more time, often appears to yield few immediate results, and seems like a more painful way to work. Later, however, the gains from the motivation, commitment, and teamwork anchored in consensus are striking. For one thing, swift and decisive actions and follow-through occur because the negotiating, compromising, and accepting of priorities are history. For another, new disagreements that emerge do not generally bring progress to a halt due to the high clarity and broad acceptance of the overall goals and underlying priorities. Without this consensus, each new problem or disagreement often necessitates a time-consuming and painful confrontation and renegotiation simply because these were not done initially.

Teamwork and Influence   Another form of entrepreneurial influence has to do with encouraging creativity and innovation and with taking calculated risks. Entrepreneurial leaders build confidence by encouraging innovation and calculated risk taking, rather than by punishing or criticizing whatever is less than perfect. They breed independent, entrepreneurial thinking by expecting and encouraging others to find and correct their own errors and to solve their own problems. This does not mean they follow a throw-them-to-the-wolves approach. Rather, they are perceived by their peers and other managers as accessible and willing to help when needed, and they provide the necessary resources to enable others to do the job. When it is appropriate, they go to bat for their peers and subordinates, even when they know they cannot always win. An ability to make heroes out of other team members and contributors and to make sure others are in the limelight, rather than accept these things oneself, is another critical skill.

The capacity to generate trust—the glue that binds an organization or relationship together—is critical. The most effective leaders are perceived as trustworthy; they behave in ways that create trust. They do this by being straightforward. They do what they say they are going to do. They are not the corporate rumor carriers. They are open and spontaneous, rather than guarded and cautious with each word. And they are perceived as being honest and direct. They treat their associates with respect, as they would want to be treated. They share the wealth with those who help create it by their high performance. Also, it is easy to envision the kind of track record and reputation these entrepreneurial leaders build for themselves. They have a reputation of getting results because they understand that the task of managing in a rapid-growth company usually goes well beyond one's immediate chain of command. They become known as the creative problem solvers who have a knack for blending and balancing multiple views and demands. Their calculated risk taking works out more often than it fails. And they have a reputation for developing human capital (i.e., they groom other effective team leaders by their example and their mentoring, and they reward achievers both financially and culturally; *they create heros*).

Other Leadership Competencies

Entrepreneurial leaders need a sound foundation in what are considered traditional management skills. Interestingly, in the study of practicing entrepreneurs mentioned earlier, no one assigned much importance to capital asset pricing models, beta coefficients, linear programming, and so forth—the prevailing and highly touted "new management techniques."[19]

The following list is divided into two cross-functional areas (administration and law and taxation) and four key functional areas (marketing, operations/production, finance, entrepreneurial leadership, law and taxes, and information technology). Technical skills unique to each venture are also necessary.

Marketing

- *Market research and evaluation.* Ability to analyze and interpret market research study results, including knowing how to design and conduct studies and to find and interpret industry and competitor information, and a familiarity with questionnaire design and sampling techniques. One successful entrepreneur stated that what is vital "is knowing where the competitive threats are and where the opportunities are and an ability to see the customers' needs."

- *Customer relations.* A drive to build a relationship with customers and react to changing demand.

- *Marketing planning.* Skill in planning overall sales, advertising, and promotion programs and in deciding on effective distributor or sales representative systems and setting them up.

- *Product pricing.* Ability to determine competitive pricing and margin structures and to position products in terms of price; and ability to develop pricing policies that maximize profits.

- *Sales management.* Ability to organize, supervise, and motivate a direct sales force, and the ability to analyze territory and account sales potential and to lead a sales force to obtain maximum share of market.

- *Direct selling.* Skills in identifying, meeting, and developing new customers and in closing sales. Without orders for a product or service, a company does not have a business.

- *Service management.* Ability to perceive service needs of particular products and to determine service and spare-part requirements, handle customer complaints, and create and lead an effective service organization.

- *Distribution management.* Ability to organize and manage the flow of product from manufacturing through distribution channels to ultimate customer, including familiarity with shipping costs, and scheduling techniques.

---

[19] J. A. Timmons and H. H. Stevenson, "Entrepreneurship Education in the 80s: What Entrepreneurs Say," in *Entrepreneurship: What It Is and How to Teach It*, ed. J. Kao and H. H. Stevenson (Boston: Harvard Business School Press, 1985), pp. 115–34.

- *Profit management.* Ability to recognize the flow of margin that follows the flow of goods.
- *Product management.* Ability to integrate market information, perceived needs, research and development, and advertising into a rational product plan, and the ability to understand market penetration and breakeven.
- *New product planning.* Skills in introducing new products, including market testing, prototype testing, and development of price/sales/merchandising and distribution plans for new products.

Operations/Production

- *Manufacturing management.* Knowledge of the production process, machines, personnel, and space required to produce a product and the skill in managing production to produce products within time, cost, and quality constraints.
- *Inventory control.* Familiarity with techniques of controlling in-process and finished goods inventories of materials.
- *Cost analysis and control.* Ability to calculate labor and materials costs, develop standard cost systems, conduct variance analyses, calculate overtime labor needs, and manage/control costs.
- *Quality control.* Ability to set up inspection systems and standards for effective control of quality of incoming, in-process, and finished materials; ability to benchmark continuous improvement.
- *Production scheduling and flow.* Ability to analyze work flow and to plan and manage production processes, to manage work flow, and to calculate schedules and flows for rising sales levels.
- *Purchasing.* Ability to identify appropriate sources of supply, to negotiate supplier contracts, and to manage the incoming flow of material into inventory, and familiarity with order quantities and discount advantages.
- *Job evaluation.* Ability to analyze worker productivity and needs for additional help, and the ability to calculate cost-saving aspects of temporary versus permanent help.

Finance

- *Raising capital.* Ability to decide how best to acquire funds for start-up and growth; ability to forecast funds needs and to prepare budgets; and familiarity with formal and informal sources and vehicles of short- and long-term financing.
- *Managing cash flow.* Ability to project cash requirements, set up cash controls, and manage the firm's cash position, and the ability to iden-

tify how much capital is needed, when and where cash will run out, and when breakeven will occur.

- *Credit and collection management.* Ability to develop credit policies and screening criteria and to age receivables and payables, and an understanding of the use of collection agencies and when to start legal action.
- *Short-term financing alternatives.* Understanding of payables management and the use of interim financing, such as bank loans, factoring of receivables, pledging and selling notes and contracts, bills of lading, and bank acceptance; and familiarity with financial statements and budgeting/profit planning.
- *Public and private offerings.* Ability to develop a business plan and an offering memo that can be used to raise capital, familiarity with the legal requirements of public and private stock offerings, and the ability to manage shareholder relations and to negotiate with financial sources.
- *Bookkeeping, accounting, and control.* Ability to determine appropriate bookkeeping and accounting systems as the company starts and grows, including various ledgers and accounts and possible insurance needs.
- *Other specific skills.* Ability to read and prepare an income statement and balance sheet, and the ability to do cash flow analysis and planning, including break-even analysis, contribution analysis, profit and loss analysis, and balance sheet management.

Entrepreneurial Leadership

- *Stakeholder management.* Ability to accurately define the value of varying stakeholder groups and manage the company to deliver value.
- *Problem solving.* Ability to anticipate potential problems; ability to gather facts about problems, analyze them for real causes, and plan effective action to solve them; and ability to be thorough in dealing with details of particular problems and to follow through.
- *Communications.* Ability to communicate effectively and clearly—orally and in writing—to media, public, customers, peers, and subordinates.
- *Planning.* Ability to set realistic and attainable goals, identify obstacles to achieving the goals, and develop detailed action plans to achieve those goals, and the ability to schedule personal time systematically.
- *Decision making.* Ability to make decisions on the best analysis of incomplete data, when the decisions need to be made.

- *Project management.* Skills in organizing project teams, setting project goals, defining project tasks, and monitoring task completion in the face of problems and cost/quality constraints.
- *Negotiating.* Ability to work effectively in negotiations, and the ability to balance quickly value given and value received, recognizing onetime versus ongoing relationships.
- *Managing outside professionals.* Ability to identify, manage, and guide appropriate legal, financial, banking, accounting, consulting, and other necessary outside advisors.
- *Personnel administration.* Ability to set up payroll, hiring, compensation, and training functions.

Law and Taxes

- *Corporate and securities law.* Familiarity with the Uniform Commercial Code, including forms of organization and the rights and obligations of officers, shareholders, and directors; and familiarity with Security and Exchange Commission, state, and other regulations concerning the securities of the firm, both registered and unregistered, and the advantages and disadvantages of different instruments.
- *Contract law.* Familiarity with contract procedures and requirements of government and commercial contracts, licenses, leases, and other agreements, particularly employment agreements and agreements governing the vesting rights of shareholders and founders.
- *Law relating to patent and proprietary rights.* Skills in preparation and revision of patent applications, and the ability to recognize strong patent, trademark, copyright, and privileged information claims, including familiarity with claim requirements, such as intellectual property.
- *Tax law.* Familiarity with state and federal reporting requirements, including specific requirements of a particular form of organization, of profit and other pension plans, and the like.
- *Real estate law.* Familiarity with leases, purchase offers, purchase and sale agreements, and so on, necessary for the rental or purchase and sale of property.
- *Bankruptcy law.* Knowledge of bankruptcy law, options, and the forgivable and nonforgivable liabilities of founders, officers, and directors.

Information Technology

- Information and management systems tools from laptop to Internet: sales, supply chain, inventory, payroll, and so on.

- Business to business, business to consumer, and business to government via the Internet.
- Sales, marketing, manufacturing, and merchandising tools.
- Financial, accounting, and risk analysis and management tools (e.g., Microsoft's Office platform).
- Telecommunications and wireless solutions for corporate information, data, and process management.

As has been said before, not all entrepreneurs will find they are greatly skilled in all of these areas; and if they are not, they will most likely need to acquire these skills through apprenticeship, through partners, or through the use of advisors. However, while many outstanding advisors, such as lawyers and accountants, are of enormous benefit to entrepreneurs, these people are not always businesspeople, and they often cannot make the best business judgments for those they are advising. For example, lawyers' judgments, in many cases, are so contaminated by a desire to provide perfect or fail-safe protection that they are totally risk averse.

Forming and Building Teams

Anchoring the Vision in Team Philosophy and Attitudes

The most successful entrepreneurs seem to anchor their vision of the future in certain entrepreneurial philosophies and attitudes (i.e., attitudes about what a team is, what its mission is, and how it will be rewarded). The soul of this vision concerns what the founder or founders are trying to accomplish and the unwritten ground rules that become the fabric, character, and purpose guiding how a team will work together, succeed and make mistakes together, and realize a harvest together. The rewards, compensation, and incentive structures rest on this philosophy and attitudes.

This fundamental mind-set is often evident in later success. The anchoring of this vision goes beyond all the critical nuts-and-bolts issues covered in the chapters and cases on the opportunity, the business plan, financing, and so forth. Each of these issues is vital, but each by itself may not lead to success. A single factor rarely, if ever, does.

The capacity of the lead entrepreneur to craft a vision and then to lead, inspire, persuade, and cajole key people to sign up for and deliver the dream makes an enormous difference between success and failure, between loss and profit, and between substantial harvest and "turning over the keys" to get out from under large personal guarantees of debt. Instilling a vision, and the passion to win, occurs very early, often during informal discussions, and seems to trigger a series of self-fulfilling prophecies that lead to success rather than to "almosts" or to failure. In a study to determine the actual existence of lead entrepreneurs in INC. 500 firms, it was found that among macro-entrepreneurial teams, lead entrepreneurs do exist and they have stronger entrepreneurial vision and greater self-efficacy or self-confidence to act on their vision and make it real.[20]

Thus lead entrepreneurs and team members who understand team building and teamwork have a secret weapon. Many with outstanding technical or other relevant skills, educational credentials, and so on will be at once prisoners and victims of the highly individualistic competitiveness that got them to where they are. They may be fantastic lone achievers, and some may even "talk a good team game." But when it comes to how they behave and perform, their egos can rarely fit inside an airplane hangar. They simply do not have the team mentality.

What are these team philosophies and attitudes that the best entrepreneurs have and are able to identify or instill in prospective partners and team members? These can be traced to the entrepreneurial mind-set discussed in Chapter 2—a mind-set that can be seen actively at work around the team-building challenge. While there are innumerable blends and variations, most likely the teams of those firms that succeed in growing up big will share many of the following:

- *Cohesion.* Members of a team believe they are all in this together, and if the company wins, everyone wins. Members believe that no one can win unless everyone wins and, conversely, if anyone loses, everyone loses. Rewards, compensation, and incentive structures rest on building company value and return on capital invested, no matter how small or sizable.

- *Teamwork.* A team that works as a team, rather than one where individual heroes are created, may be the single most distinguishing feature of the higher-potential company. Thus, on these teams, efforts are made to make others' jobs easier, to make heroes out of partners and key people, and to motivate people by celebrating their successes. As Harold J. Seigle, the highly successful, now retired, president and chief executive officer of the Sunmark Companies, has often said, "High performance breeds strong friendships!"

- *Integrity.* Hard choices and trade-offs are made regarding what is good for the customer, the

company, and value creation, rather than being based on purely utilitarian or Machiavellian ethics or narrow personal or departmental needs and concerns. There is a belief in and commitment to the notion of getting the job done without sacrificing quality, health, or personal standards.

- *Commitment to the long haul.* Like most organizations, new ventures thrive or wither according to the level of commitment of their teams. Members of a committed team believe they are playing for the long haul and that the venture is not a get-rich-quick drill. Rather, the venture is viewed as a delayed-gratification game in which it can take 5, 7, or even 10 or more years to realize a harvest. *No one gets a windfall profit by signing up now but bailing out early or when the going gets tough.* Stock vesting agreements reflect this commitment. For example, stock will usually be vested over five or seven years so that anyone who leaves early, for whatever reasons, can keep stock earned to date, but he or she is required to sell the remaining shares back to the company at the price originally paid. Of course, such a vesting agreement usually provides that if the company is unexpectedly sold or if a public offering is made long before the five- or seven-year vesting period is up, then stock is 100 percent vested automatically with that event.

- *Harvest mind-set.* A successful harvest is the name of the game. This means that eventual capital gain is viewed as the scorecard, rather than the size of a monthly paycheck, the location and size of an office, a certain car, or the like.

- *Commitment to value creation.* Team members are committed to value creation—making the pie bigger for everyone, including adding value for customers, enabling suppliers to win as the team succeeds, and making money for the team's constituencies and various stakeholders.

- *Equal inequality.* In successful emerging companies, democracy and blind equality generally do not work well, and diligent efforts are made to determine who has what responsibility for the key tasks. The president is the one to set the ground rules and to shape the climate and culture of the venture. Bill Foster, founder and president of Stratus Computer, was asked if he and his partners were all equal. He said, "Yes, we are, except I get paid the most and I own the most stock."[21] For example, stock is usually

[20] J. W. Carland and J. C. Carland, "Investigating the Existence of the Lead Entrepreneur," *Journal of Small Business Management* 38, no. 4 (2000), pp. 59–77.
[21] Remarks made at Babson College Venture Capital Conference, June 1985.

not divided equally among the founders and key managers. In one company of four key people, stock was split as follows: 34 percent for the president, 23 percent each for the marketing and technical vice presidents, and 6 percent for the controller. The remainder went to outside directors and advisors. In another company, seven founders split the company as follows: 22 percent for the president, 15 percent for each of the four vice presidents, and 9 percent for each of the two other contributors. An example of how failure to differentiate in terms of ownership impacts a business is seen in a third firm, where four owners each had equal share. Yet two of the owners contributed virtually everything, while the other two actually detracted from the business. Because of this unresolved problem, the company could not attract venture capital and never was able to grow dramatically.

- *Fairness.* Rewards for key employees and stock ownership are based on contribution, performance, and results over time. Because these can only be roughly estimated in advance, and because there will invariably be surprises and inequities, both positive and negative, as time goes on, adjustments are made. One good example is a company that achieved spectacular results in just two years in the cellular phone business. When the company was sold, it was evident that two of the six team members had contributed more than was reflected in their stock ownership position. To remedy this, another team member gave one of the two team members stock worth several hundred thousand dollars. Because the team was involved in another venture, the president made adjustments in the various ownership positions in the new venture, with each member's concurrence, to adjust for past inequities. In addition, it was decided to set aside 10 percent of the next venture to provide some discretion in making future adjustments for unanticipated contributions to ultimate success.

- *Sharing of the harvest.* This sense of fairness and justness seems to be extended by the more successful entrepreneurs to the harvest of a company, even when there is no legal or ethical obligation to do so. For example, as much as 10 percent to 20 percent of the "winnings" is frequently set aside to distribute to key employees. In one such recent harvest, employees were startled and awash with glee when informed they would each receive a year's salary after the company was sold. However, this is not always the case. In another firm, 90 percent of which was owned by an entrepreneur and his family, the president, who was the single person most responsible for the firm's success and spectacular valuation, needed to expend considerable effort to get the owners to agree to give bonuses to other key employees of around $3 million, an amount just over 1 percent of the $250 million sale price. (It is worth considering how this sense of fairness, or lack of it, affects future flows of quality people and opportunities from which these entrepreneurs can choose new ventures.)

A Process of Evolution

An entrepreneur considering issues of team formation will rarely discover black-and-white, bulletproof answers that hold up over time. Nor is it being suggested that an entrepreneur needs answers to all questions concerning what the opportunity requires, and when, before moving ahead. Emphasis on the importance of new venture teams also does not mean every new venture must start with a full team that plunges into the business. It may take some time for the team to come together as a firm grows, and there will also always be some doubt, a hope for more than a prospective partner can deliver, and a constant recalibration. Again, creative acts, such as running a marathon or entrepreneuring, will be full of unknowns, new ground, and surprises. Preparation is an insurance policy, and thinking through these team issues and team-building concepts in advance is inexpensive insurance.

The combination of the right team of people and a right venture opportunity can be very powerful. The whole is, in such instances, greater than the sum of the parts. However, the odds for highly successful venture teams are rather thin. Even if a venture survives, the turnover among team members during the early years probably exceeds the national divorce rate. Studies of new venture teams seeking venture capital show that many never get off the ground. These usually exhaust their own resources and commitment before raising the venture capital necessary to launch their ventures. Of those that are funded, about 1 in 20 becomes very successful in three to five years, in that it will return in excess of five times the original investment in realizable capital gains.

The formation and development of new venture team seem to be idiosyncratic, and there seem to be a multitude of ways in which venture partners come together. Some teams form by accidents of geography, common interest, or working together. Perhaps the common interest is simply that the team members want to start a business, whereas in other cases the interest is an idea that members believe responds to a market need. Others form teams by virtue of past friendships. For example, roommate arrangements or close friendships in college or graduate school frequently lead to business partnerships. This was the case with two of Jeff Timmons's classmates in the MBA program at the Harvard Business School. Concluding that they would eventually go into business together after rooming together for a week, Leslie Charm and Carl Youngman have been partners for over 32 years as owners of three national franchise companies, an entrepreneurial advisory and troubled business management company, and a venture capital company, AIGIS Ventures, LLC. Jiffy Lube was founded by college football coach Jim Hindman and some of his coaches and players—including Steve Spinelli.

In the evolution of venture teams, two distinct patterns are identifiable. In the first, one person has an idea (or simply wants to start a business), and then three or four associates join the team over the next one to three years as the venture takes form. Alternatively, an entire team forms at the outset based on such factors as a shared idea, a friendship, an experience, and so forth.

Filling the Gaps

There is no simple cookbook solution to team formation; rather, there are as many approaches to forming teams as there are ventures with multiple founders (see the "Internet Impact" box on this page).

Successful entrepreneurs search out people and form and build a team based on what the opportunity requires, and when.[22] Team members will contribute high value to a venture if they complement and balance the lead entrepreneur—and each other. Yet ironically, while a substantial amount of thought usually accompanies the decision of people to go into business together, an overabundance of the thinking, particularly among the less experienced, can focus on less critical issues, such as titles, corporate name, letterhead, or what kind of lawyer or accountant is needed. Thus teams are often ill-conceived from the outset and can easily plunge headlong into unanticipated and unplanned responses to crises, conflicts, and changes.

A team starts with a lead entrepreneur. In a start-up situation, the lead entrepreneur usually wears many hats. Beyond that, comparison of the nature and demands of the venture and the capabilities, motivations, and interests of the lead entrepreneur will sig-

Internet Impact: Virtual Teams and Collaboration

The ever-expanding number of devices designed to exploit Internet accessibility is having a profound impact on team building and collaboration. As a pervasive global network, the Internet provides a means for geographically dispersed parties to work from the same system, using the same information, in a real-time environment.

Using Web-based communications, organizations can now quickly and effectively keep value chain participants in the loop—from concept through design and delivery—without ever meeting in the same physical space. This includes the ability to utilize external systems such as cooperative research databases, property databases, road databases that include information relevant to routing, and demographic databases for marketing purposes.

The Internet also has become an effective tool for collaborative design, development, and data maintenance. Internet-based collaboration not only can nullify a development team's physical separation, enhance productivity, and shorten design cycles, but also opens up the talent base to include special application freelancers, as well as engineers under the employ of consultants, vendors, clients, and business partners.

nal gaps that exist and that need to be filled by other team members or by accessing other outside resources, such as a board of directors, consultants, lawyers, accountants, and so on.

Thus, for example, if the strengths of the lead entrepreneur or a team member are technical, other team members, or outside resources, need to fill voids in marketing, finance, and such. Realistically, there will be an overlapping and sharing of responsibilities; but team members need to complement, not duplicate, the lead entrepreneur's capabilities and those of other team members.

Note that a by-product of forming a team may be alteration of an entry strategy if a critical gap cannot be filled. For example, a firm may find that it simply cannot assault a certain market because it cannot hire the right marketing person. But it may find it could attract a top-notch person to exploit another niche with a modified product or service.

Most important, the process of evaluating and deciding who is needed, and when, is dynamic and not a onetime event. What know-how, skills, and expertise are required? What key tasks and action steps

---

[22] See J. A. Timmons, "The Entrepreneurial Team," *Journal of Small Business Management*, October 1975, pp. 36–37.

need to be taken? What are the requisites for success? What is the firm's distinctive competence? What external contacts are required? How extensive and how critical are the gaps? How much can the venture afford to pay? Will the venture gain access to the expertise it needs through additions to its board of directors or outside consultants? Questions such as these determine when and how these needs could be filled. And answers to such questions will change over time.

The following, organized around the analytical framework introduced in Chapter 3, can guide the formation of new venture teams.

The Founder   What kind of team is needed depends on the nature of the opportunity and what the lead entrepreneur brings to the game. One key step in forming a team is for the lead entrepreneur to assess his or her entrepreneurial strategy. (The personal entrepreneurial strategy exercise in Chapter 2 is a valuable input in approaching these issues.) Thus the lead entrepreneur needs to first consider whether the team is desirable or necessary and whether he or she wants to grow a higher-potential company. He or she then needs to assess what talents, know-how, skills, track record, contacts, and resources are being brought to the table—that is, what "chunks" have been acquired. (See the managerial skills and know-how assessment at the end of this chapter.) Once this is determined, the lead entrepreneur needs to consider what the venture has to have to succeed, who is needed to complement him or her, and when. The best entrepreneurs are optimistic realists and have a real desire to improve their performance. They work at knowing what they do and do not know and are honest with themselves. The lead entrepreneur needs to consider issues such as these:

- What relevant industry, market, and technological know-how and experience are needed to win, and do I bring these to the venture? Do I know the revenue and cost model better than anyone?
- Are my personal and business strengths in those specific areas critical to success in the proposed business?
- Do I have the contacts and networks needed (and will the ones I have make a competitive difference), or do I look to partners in this area?
- Can I attract a "first team" of all-star partners inside and externally, and can I manage these people and other team members effectively?
- Why did I decide to pursue this particular opportunity now, and what do I want out of the business (i.e., what are my goals and my income and harvest aspirations)?
- Do I know what the sacrifices and commitment will be, and am I prepared to make these?
- What are the risks and rewards involved, am I comfortable with them, and do I look for someone with a different risk-taking orientation?

Often a student going through this process will conclude that a more experienced person will be needed to lead the venture.

The Opportunity   The need for team members is something an entrepreneur constantly thinks about, especially in the idea stage before start-up. What is needed in the way of a team depends on the match between the lead entrepreneur and the opportunity, and how fast and aggressively he or she plans to proceed. (See the Venture Opportunity Screening Exercises in Chapter 6.) Although most new ventures plan to bootstrap it and bring on additional team members only as the company can afford them, the catch is that if a venture is looking for venture capital or serious private investors, having an established team will yield higher valuation and a smaller ownership share that will have to be parted with. Here are some questions that need to be considered:

- Have I clearly defined the value added and the economics of the business? Have I considered how (and with whom) the venture can make money in this business? For instance, whether a company is selling razors or razor blades makes a difference in the need for different team members.
- What are the critical success variables in the business I want to start, and what (or who) is needed to influence these variables positively?
- Do I have, or have access to, the critical external relationships with investors, lawyers, bankers, customers, suppliers, regulatory agencies, and so forth, that are necessary to pursue my opportunity? Do I need help in this area?
- What competitive advantage and strategy should I focus on? What people are necessary to pursue this strategy or advantage?

Outside Resources   The Sarbanes-Oxley law in the United States makes governance issues important, even with start-up enterprises.[23] Gaps can be filled by accessing outside resources, such as boards of directors, accountants, lawyers, consultants, and so forth.[24] Usually tax and legal expertise can best be

---

[23] Jay Lorsch, professor of Human Relations at Harvard Business School.
[24] See W. A. Sahlman and H. H. Stevenson, "Choosing Small Company Advisors," *Harvard Business Review*, March–April 1987.

obtained initially on a part-time basis. Other expertise (e.g., expertise required to design an inventory control system) is specialized and needed only once. Generally, if the resource is a onetime or periodic effort, or if the need is peripheral to the key tasks, goals, and activities required by the business, then an alternative such as using consultants makes sense. However, if the expertise is a must for the venture at the outset and the lead entrepreneur cannot provide it or learn it quickly, then one or more people will have to be acquired. Some questions to consider are these:

- Is the need for specialized, onetime, or part-time expertise peripheral or on the critical path?
- Will trade secrets be compromised if I obtain this expertise externally?

The Brain Trust   Throughout the book you will see references to the brain trust, and in Chapter 10 you will complete an exercise that will help to advance your thinking and your networking to develop your own. This is an important concept and tool for the entrepreneur and an integral part of the team that is external to the company. The brain trust can make the difference between success and failure in a company's fund-raising, marketing, and attracting key talent and directors. For instance, a first-time entrepreneur wanted to start an Internet-based financial and economic information service covering emerging markets. By introducing him to the right potential investor and director, one of his professors saved him months of work by connecting him to the perfect lead investor: an entrepreneur whose first start-up put the first desktop computers on Wall Street for bond traders in the early 1980s. This new member of his brain trust become chair of the board and helped the company raise nearly $15 million of venture capital and eventually sell the company for $55 million when it had just $10 million in sales.

In another case the CEO of a rapidly growing telecommunications company was contemplating taking his company public or selling it. Although he had sold another company, this was a quite different situation because he had no IPO experience. One member of his brain trust was able to connect him with a lead entrepreneur who had had a very successful IPO during similar capital market conditions and gave him valuable advice on how to select an underwriter, pitfalls to watch for, tips for doing a road show, and the like.

As you will see in the Chapter 10 exercise, your aim is to think beyond the internal team to the critical tasks and challenges ahead and identify the *external* people who know far more than you or any of your team members. These will become mentors, advisors, often directors, and valuable resources for

you. If you treat them like gold, they will help you far more than you can ever pay them in cash or stock—which you should do, as well as thank them personally and often when they help you. A word of caution: Don't just send an e-mail message of thanks. Instead send a personalized thank-you note or a creative gift.

The $50+ Million Mistake   Some years ago Professor Timmons connected a student to an old friend who we will call Fred. Fred was one of the leading people in the country who understood products sold through supermarkets, He had years of successful experience building a small family food brokerage firm into a 450-person integrated marketing services firm. For instance, his company had a computerized data bank that constantly monitored products in certain food categories on virtually every supermarket shelf in New England. He spent hours with the student providing valuable insights and advice on his business plan and strategy, as well as introductions to key CEOs and buyers in the food business. The student's start-up became quite successful and was sold.

A few years later the former student was launching another food-related business and had lost Fred's number. He called the author and got the number. A month later, when the author saw Fred, he asked him if he had heard from the former student. "Yes," he said. "How is he doing and what is he up to now?" His reply was brief: "I never returned the call." It turns out the student had never sent Fred a thank-you note, called him, given him an update, or anything of the sort. Our estimate is that this unprofessional behavior cost the former student somewhere between $50 million and $100 million! The venture he was trying to start would have been a perfect match to have Fred as a lead investor, director, and advisor. He never did get the venture off the ground.

This is a lesson we hope you will never forget. Both authors have shared and taught this story and lesson to our students for years.

Additional Considerations

Forming and building a team is, like marriage, a rather unscientific, occasionally unpredictable, and frequently surprising exercise—no matter how hard we may try to make it otherwise! The analogy of marriage and family, with all the accompanying complexities and consequences, is a particularly useful one. Forming a team has many of the characteristics of the courtship and marriage ritual, involving decisions based in part on emotion. There may be a certain infatuation among team members and an aura of admiration, respect, and often fierce loyalty. Similarly, the complex psychological joys, frustrations, and uncertainties that accompany the birth and raising of children (the product or service) are experienced in entrepreneurial teams as well.

Thus the following additional issues need to be considered:

- *Values, goals, and commitment.* It is critical that a team be well anchored in terms of values and goals. In any new venture, the participants establish psychological contracts and climates. Although these are most often set when the lead entrepreneur encourages standards of excellence and respect for team members' contributions, selection of team members whose goals and values agree can greatly facilitate establishment of a psychological contract and an entrepreneurial climate. In successful companies, the personal goals and values of team members align well, and the goals of the company are championed by team members as well. Although this alignment may be less exact in large publicly owned corporations and greatest in small, closely held firms, significant overlapping of a team member's goals with those of other team members and the overlap of corporate goals and team members' goals are desirable. Practically speaking, these evaluations of team members are some of the most difficult to make.

- *Definition of roles.* A diligent effort needs to be made to determine who is comfortable with and who has what responsibility for the key tasks so duplication of capabilities or responsibilities is minimized. Roles cannot be pinned down precisely for all tasks because some key tasks and problems simply cannot be anticipated, and contributions are not always made by the people originally expected to make them. Maintaining a loose, flexible, flat structure with shared responsibility and information is desirable for utilizing individual strengths, flexibility, rapid learning, and responsive decision making.

- *Peer groups.* The support and approval of family, friends, and coworkers can be helpful, especially when adversity strikes. Reference group approval can be a significant source of positive reinforcement for a person's career choice and, thus, his or her entire self-image and identity.[25] Ideally, peer group support for each team member should be there. (If it is not, the lead entrepreneur may have to accept the additional burden of encouragement and support in hard times, a burden that can be sizable.) Therefore, questions of whether a prospective team member's spouse is solidly in favor of his or her decision to pursue an entrepreneurial career and the sweat equity required and of whether the team member's close friends will be a source of support and encouragement or of detraction or negativism need to be considered.

Common Pitfalls

There can be difficulties in the practical implementation of these philosophies and attitudes, irrespective of the venture opportunity and the people involved. The company may come unglued before it gets started, may experience early mortality, or may live perpetually immersed in nasty divisive conflicts and power struggles that will cripple its potential, even if they do not kill the company.

Often a team lacks skill and experience in dealing with such difficult start-up issues, does not take the time to go through an extended "mating dance" among potential partners during the moonlighting phase before actually launching the venture, or does not seek the advice of competent advisors. As a result, a team may be unable to deal with such sensitive issues as who gets how much ownership, who will commit what time and money or other resources, how disagreements will be resolved, and how a team member can leave or be let go. Thus crucial early discussions among team members sometimes lead to a premature disbanding of promising teams with sound business ideas. Or in the rush to get going, or because the funds to pay for help in these areas are lacking, a team may stay together but not work through, even in a rough way, many of these issues. Such teams do not take advantage of the moonlighting phase to test the commitment and contribution made by team members. For example, to build a substantial business, a partner needs to be totally committed to the venture. The success of the venture is the partner's most important goal, and other priorities, including his or her family, come second.[26] Another advantage of using such a shakedown period effectively is that the risks inherent in such factors as premature commitment to permanent decisions regarding salary and stock are lower.

The common approach to forming a new venture team also can be a common pitfall for new venture teams. Here two to four entrepreneurs, usually friends or work acquaintances, decide to demonstrate their equality with such democratic trimmings as equal stock ownership, equal salaries, equal office space and cars, and other items symbolizing their peer status. Left unanswered are questions of who is in

---

[25] Reference groups—groups consisting of individuals with whom there is frequent interaction (such as family, friends, and coworkers), with whom values and interests are shared, and from whom support and approval for activities are derived—have long been known for their influence on behavior. See J. W. Thibault and H. H. Kelley, *The Social Psychology of Groups* (New York: John Wiley & Sons, 1966).

[26] This has been shown, for example, by E. H. Schein's research about entrepreneurs, general managers, and technical managers who are MIT alumni. See the Proceedings of the Eastern Academy of Management meeting, May 1972, Boston.

charge, who makes the final decisions, and how real differences of opinion are resolved. Although some overlapping of roles and a sharing in and negotiating of decisions are desirable in new venture teams, too much looseness is debilitating. Even sophisticated buy–sell agreements among partners often fail to resolve the conflicts.

Another pitfall is a belief that there are no deficiencies in the lead entrepreneur or the management team. Or a team is overly fascinated with or overcommitted to a product idea. For example, a lead entrepreneur who is unwilling or unable to identify his or her own deficiencies and weaknesses and to add appropriate team members to compensate for these, and who further lacks an understanding of what is really needed to make a new venture grow into a successful business, has fallen into this pitfall.[27]

Failing to recognize that creating and building a new venture is a dynamic process is a problem for some teams. Therefore, such teams fail to realize that initial agreements are likely not to reflect actual contributions of team members over time, regardless of how much time they devote to team-building tasks and regardless of the agreements team members make before start-up. In addition, they fail to consider that teams are likely to change in composition over time. The late Richard Testa, a leading attorney whose firm has dealt with such ventures as Lotus Development Corporation and with numerous venture capital firms, recently startled those attending a seminar on raising venture capital by saying,

> The only thing that I can tell you with great certainty about this start-up business has to do with you and your partners. I can virtually guarantee you, based on our decade plus of experience, that five years from now at least one of the founders will have left every company represented here today.[28]

Such a team, therefore, fails to put in place mechanisms that will facilitate and help structure graceful divorces and that will provide for the internal adjustments required as the venture grows.

Destructive motivations in investors, prospective team members, or the lead entrepreneur spell trouble. Teams suffer if they are not alert to signs of potentially destructive motivations, such as an early concern for power and control by a team member. In this context, it has been argued that conflict management is a central task for members of teams. A study of self-empowered teams found that how team members manage their conflicts could affect their self-efficacy, as well as overall team performance. Team

members in this study were most effective when they recognized they wanted to resolve the conflict for mutual benefit and that the goal is to help each other get what each other really needs and values, and not to try to win or to outdo each other.[29]

Finally, new venture teams may take trust for granted. Integrity is important in long-term business success, and the world is full of high-quality, ethical people; yet the real world also is inhabited by predators, crooks, sharks, frauds, and imposters. Chapter 10 contains a detailed discussion of the importance of integrity in entrepreneurial pursuits. It is paradoxical that an entrepreneur cannot succeed without trust, but he or she probably cannot succeed with blind trust either. Trust is something that is earned, usually slowly; it requires a lot of patience and a lot of testing in the real world. This is undoubtedly a major reason why investors prefer to see teams that have worked closely together. In the area of trust, a little cynicism goes a long way, and teams that do not pay attention to detail, such as performing due diligence with respect to a person or firm, fall into this pit.

Rewards and Incentives

Slicing the Founder's Pie

One of the most frequently asked questions from start-up entrepreneurs is, How much stock ownership should go to whom? (Chapter 13 examines the various methodologies used by venture capitalists and investors to determine what share of the company is required by the investor at different rounds of investment.) Consider the recent discussions with Jed, a former student, who secured substantial early-stage funding from John Doerr of Kleiner, Perkins, Caufield & Byers. The advice for Jed and all others is the same.

First, start with a philosophy and set of values that boil down to Ewing Marion Kauffman's great principle: Share the wealth with those who help to create the value and thus the wealth. Once over that hurdle, you are less likely to get hung up on the percentage of ownership issue. After all, 51 percent of nothing is nothing. The key is making the pie as large as possible. Second, the ultimate goal of any venture capital–backed company is to realize a harvest at a price at least 5 to 10 times the original investment. Thus the company will be sold either via an initial public offering (IPO) or to a larger company. It is useful to work backward from the capital structure at the time of the IPO to envision and define what will happen and who will get what.

[27] J. A. Timmons presented a discussion of these entrepreneurial characteristics at the First International Conference on Entrepreneurship. See "Entrepreneurial Behavior," Proceedings, First International Conference on Entrepreneurship, Center for Entrepreneurial Studies, Toronto, November 1973.
[28] The seminar, held at Babson College, was called "Raising Venture Capital," and was cosponsored by Venture Capital Journal and Coopers & Lybrand, 1985.
[29] S. Alper, D. Tjosvold, and K. S. Law, "Conflict Management, Efficacy, and Performance in Organizational Teams," Personnel Psychology 53, no. 3 (2000) pp. 625–42.

Most venture capital–backed, smaller company IPOs during the robust capital markets of the late 1990s would have 12 million to 15 million shares of stock outstanding after the IPO. In most situations 2.5 million to 4 million shares are sold to the public (mostly to institutional investors) at $12 to $15 per share, depending on the perceived quality of the company and the robustness of the appetite for IPOs at the time. The number could be halved or doubled. Typically the founder/CEO will own 1 million to 3 million shares after the IPO, worth somewhere between $12 million and $45 million. Put in this perspective, it is much easier to see why finding a great opportunity, building a great team, and sharing the wealth with widespread ownership in the team is far more important than what percentage of the company is owned.

Finally, especially for young entrepreneurs in their 20s or 30s, this will not be their last venture. The single most important thing is that it succeeds. Make this happen, and the future opportunities will be boundless. All this can be ruined if the founder/CEO simply gets greedy and overcontrolling, keeping most of the company to himself or herself, rather than creating a huge, shared pie.

An Approach to Rewards and Equity

There are five fundamental realities with nearly any new venture:

1. Cash is king, and there is never enough.
2. You will be out of cash much sooner than you think.
3. Sales are what count most.
4. Talent is the key to success.
5. Equity creation and realization determine the payoff.

Therefore, thinking through how the founders will compensate themselves and the team, new talent, and the brain trust is an essential early task of the founders. Keeping in mind some worthwhile principles can guide this effort and create a blueprint and expectations for the future.

Principle #1: Share the wealth with the high performers who contribute to its creation. This implies wider than normal stock ownership and a healthy stock option or comparable performance unit pool. Investors typically like to see a future pool of 10 to 20 percent of the fully diluted company set aside for attracting future talent and creating incentives and rewards for high performance. At the end of this chapter is an exercise "Slicing the Equity Pie," in which we provide some guidelines and suggest you work through the likely capital structure and ownership of the venture, recognizing that this will

take time, and that a 5- to 7-year vesting schedule will help remediate any hiring mistakes.

Principle #2: The fairness concept—treat other people as you would want to be treated. Is this equity and compensation a deal you would consider fair and reasonable if you were in the other person's situation? This does not imply that everyone should have equal ownership. This is where the brain trust can be valuable in helping to guide the numbers that represent the marketplace for talent in your area, whether it is marketing, financial, or technical. Imagine what these numbers would be like in Silicon Valley for a highly talented technical person versus a rural, small city in the upper Midwest or northern New England. If you can't get a good view of the range in the marketplace, you don't have the right brain trust yet for advice and have not done enough homework.

Principle #3: Reward results, and especially those who create revenue, and attract and grow key talent. This may seem obvious; but is it amazing to us how other criteria can creep in the way. For example, a smart, articulate, and strong-minded technical genius who is the first-time founder of a company can suffer the delusion that his or her technical contribution alone will drive the success of the company and thus should command 15 to 25 percent or more of the company's equity. An ownership structure like that will make it virtually impossible to raise venture capital and attract key talent to the company. This principle also implies a vesting schedule, usually of at least five and sometimes seven years or more, whereby the stock is restricted and earned by one's performance. Key people who don't work out earn only the stock they are entitled to, and the rest is still available to the company to reward and motivate others.

Principle #4: Sweat equity matters—a lot! The early stages of a company require very hard work and many sacrifices. Jae Chang, founding software and IT genius for the Internet-based information service company noted earlier, lived on $695 a month in Boston in the mid-1990s, including rent. He took stock in the company in lieu of salary because the founders had raised just over $100,000 of seed money and could not afford to pay salaries. The founding brothers shared a small apartment, and one slept on the couch for the first year. Thus a good test for founders is the will of prospective team members to sacrifice, tempered by the realities of the competition you face to attract talent.

Principle # 5: Chemistry–chemistry–chemistry. The most brilliant talent, the most creative product or service, and the most well-developed and financed business plan on the planet will not succeed unless there is strong chemistry among the founding team that is then embedded into the company's culture. The abilities to respect one another and to work well together, especially when the road is the bumpiest and steepest and darkest, are crucial.

As you and prospective team members begin to talk seriously about doing a venture together, it can be useful to agree on some governing principles. You may have others to add, but these will serve the process well. Without these underlying principles the process often bogs down into endless negotiations and a stillborn venture. These will not guarantee you will agree on an ownership structure, but they can certainly help.

Considerations of Value

The contributions of team members will vary in nature, extent, and timing. In developing the reward system, particularly the distribution of stock, contributions in certain areas are of particular value to a venture:

- *Idea.* In this area, the originator of the idea, particularly if trade secrets or special technology for a prototype was developed or if product or market research was done, needs to be considered.
- *Business plan preparation.* Preparing an acceptable business plan, in terms of dollars and hours expended, needs to be considered.
- *Commitment and risk.* A team member may invest a large percentage of his or her net worth in the company, be at risk if the company fails, have to make personal sacrifices, put in long hours and major effort, risk his or her reputation, accept reduced salary, or already have spent a large amount of time on behalf of the venture. This commitment and risk need to be considered.

- *Skills, experience, track record, or contacts.* A team member may bring to the venture skills, experience, track record, or contacts in such areas as marketing, finance, and technology. If these are of critical importance to the new venture and are not readily available, these need to be considered.
- *Responsibility.* The importance of a team member's role to the success of the venture needs to be considered.

Being the originator of the idea or expending a great amount of time or money in preparing the business plan is frequently overvalued. If these factors are evaluated in terms of the real success of the venture down the road, it is difficult to justify much more than 15 percent to 20 percent of equity for them. Commitment and risk, skills, experience, and responsibility contribute much more to producing success of a venture.

The previous list is valuable in attempting to weigh fairly the relative contributions of each team member. Contributions in each of these areas have some value; it is up to a team to agree on how to assign value to contributions and, further, to leave enough flexibility to allow for changes.

Compensation and Incentives in High-Potential Ventures

A useful technical note covering the important tax and accounting issues for stock options, incentive stock options, bonuses, phantom stock, and the like was developed by the author. "Compensation Incentives in High-Potential Ventures" (HBS 9-392-035) is available through Harvard Business School Publishing, Soldiers Field Road, Boston. An excellent CD-ROM has been developed on rewards and compensation in high-growth companies by the Ewing Marion Kauffman Foundation in Kansas City (800/489-4900).

Chapter Summary

- The growing enterprise requires that the founder and team develop competencies as entrepreneurial leaders.
- Founders who succeed in growing their firms beyond $10 million in sales learn to adapt and grow quickly themselves as leaders, or they do not survive.
- Founders of rapidly growing firms defy the conventional wisdom that entrepreneurs cannot manage growing beyond the start-up.
- A strong team is usually the difference between a great success and a marginal or failed company.
- Ventures go through stages of growth from start-up, through rapid growth, to maturity, to decline and renewal.

- Core philosophies, values, and attitudes—particularly sharing the wealth and ownership with those who create it—are key to team building.
- The fit concept is central to anticipating management gaps and building the team.
- The faster the rate of growth, the more difficult and challenging are the issues, and the more flexible, adaptive, and quick-learning the organization must be.
- Numerous pitfalls await the entrepreneur in team building and need to be avoided.
- Entrepreneurs create and invent new and unique approaches to organizing and leading teams.
- As ventures grow, the core competencies need to be covered by the team.

■   Compensating and rewarding team members
     requires both a philosophy and technical know-how

and can have enormous impact on the odds of
success.

Study Questions

1. What are the differences between an entrepreneurial leader and an administrator or manager?

2. How do founders grow their ventures beyond $10 million in sales, and why is the team so important?

3. Define the stages that most companies experience as they grow, and explain the leadership issues and requirements anticipated at each stage.

4. Describe what is meant by team philosophy and attitudes. Why are these important?

5. What are the most critical questions a lead entrepreneur needs to consider in thinking through the team issue? Why? What are some common pitfalls in team building?

6. What are the critical rewards, compensation, and incentive issues in putting a team together? Why are these so crucial and difficult to manage?

7. How does the lead entrepreneur allocate stock ownership and options in the new venture? Who should get what ownership, and why?

8. Can you compare and describe the principal differences in leadership, management, and organization between the best growing companies of which you are aware and large, established companies? Why are there differences?

9. What drives the extent of complexity and difficulty of issues in a growing company?

10. What would be your strategy for changing and creating an entrepreneurial culture in a large, nonentrepreneurial firm? Is it possible? Why or why not?

Internet Resources for Chapter 9

http://entrepreneurialleadership.org *This study, sponsored by the Society of Industrial and Organizational Psychologists (siop.org) and Fast Company magazine, examines the different styles of leadership exhibited by entrepreneurs and how those styles affect organizational culture.*

http://www.managementhelp.org *The Free Management Library offers comprehensive resources regarding the leadership and management of yourself, other individuals, groups, and organizations. Its content is relevant to the vast majority of people, whether they are in large or small for-profit or nonprofit organizations.*

http://fed.org *As a private foundation, the Foundation for Enterprise Development seeks to foster the advancement of entrepreneurial scientific and technology enterprises.*

http://www.eonetwork.org/ *The Entrepreneurs' Organization (EO) is a membership organization designed to engage leading entrepreneurs to learn and grow. We are a global community of business owners, all of whom run companies that exceed $1M (US) in revenue.*

MIND STRETCHERS

Have You Considered?

1. It is often said, "You cannot hire an entrepreneur." What are the implications for large companies today?

2. How would you characterize the attitudes, behaviors, and mind-sets of the most effective leaders and managers you have worked for? The worst? What accounts for the differences?

3. Think about a team in which you have been a member or a captain. What leadership and coaching principles characterized the most and least successful teams?

4. What is a team? What is its antithesis? A team may not be for everyone. How do you see the fit between you and the team concept?

5. One expert insists that the only guarantee he can make to a start-up team is that in five years, at least one or two members will leave or be terminated. What causes this? Why might your team be different?

6. Ask five people who have worked with you in a team to give you feedback about your team-building skills.

7. Read recent issues of *Fast Company* magazine and *Business 2.0:* What is happening in corporate America?

8. What should the president, the Congress, and governors do to encourage and accelerate entrepreneurship in America?

Leadership Skills and Know-How Assessment

Name:

Venture:

Date:

Part I—Management Competency Inventory

Part I of the exercise involves filling out the Management Competency Inventory and evaluating how critical certain management competencies are either (1) for the venture or (2) personally over the next one to three years. *How you rank the importance of management competencies, therefore, will depend on the purpose of your managerial assessment.*

STEP 1

Complete the Management Competency Inventory on the following pages. For each management competency, place a check in the column that best describes your knowledge and experience. Note that a section is at the end of the inventory for *unique skills* required by your venture; for example, if it is a service or franchise business, there will be some skills and know-how that are unique. Then rank from 1 to 3 particular management competencies as follows:

1 = Critical

2 = Very desirable

3 = Not necessary

	Competency Inventory			
Rank	**Thorough Knowledge and Experience (Done Well)**	**Some Knowledge and Experience (So–So)**	**No Knowledge or Experience (New Ground)**	**Importance (1–3 Years)**

Marketing

Market Research and Evaluation

Finding and interpreting industry and competitor information; designing and conducting market research studies; analyzing and interpreting market research data; etc.

		Competency Inventory			
	Rank	Thorough Knowledge and Experience (Done Well)	Some Knowledge and Experience (So–So)	No Knowledge or Experience (New Ground)	Importance (1–3 Years)
Market Planning *Planning overall sales, advertising, and promotion programs; planning and setting up effective distributor or sales representative systems; etc.*					
Product Pricing *Determining competitive pricing and margin structures and break-even analysis; positioning products in terms of price; etc.*					
Customer Relations Management (CRM)					
Customer Service *Determining customer service needs and spare-part requirements; managing a service organization and warranties; training; technical backup, telecom and Internet systems and tools; etc.*					
Sales Management *Organizing, recruiting, supervising, compensating, and motivating a direct sales force; analyzing territory and account sales potential; managing sales force; etc.*					
Direct Selling *Identifying, meeting, and developing new customers, suppliers, investors, brain trust and team; closing sales; etc.*					

	Rank	Competency Inventory			
		Thorough Knowledge and Experience (Done Well)	Some Knowledge and Experience (So–So)	No Knowledge or Experience (New Ground)	Importance (1–3 Years)
Direct Mail/ Catalog Selling *Identifying and developing appropriate direct mail and cata- log sales and related distribution; etc.*					
Electronic and Telemarketing *Identifying, planning, and implementing appropriate telemarketing programs; Internet-based programs; etc.*					

Supply Chain Management

	Rank				
Distribution Management *Organizing and managing the flow of product from manufacturing through distribution, channels to customers; knowing the margins throughout the value chain; etc.*					
Product Management *Integrating market information, perceived needs, research and development, and advertising into a rational product plan; etc.*					
New Product Planning *Planning the introduction of new products, including market testing, prototype testing, and development of price, sales, merchandising, and distribution plans; etc.*					

		Competency Inventory			
	Rank	Thorough Knowledge and Experience (Done Well)	Some Knowledge and Experience (So–So)	No Knowledge or Experience (New Ground)	Importance (1–3 Years)

Operations/ Production

Manufacturing Management

Managing production to produce products within time, cost, and quality constraints; knowledge of manufacturing resource planning; etc.

Inventory Control

Using techniques of controlling in-process and finished goods inventories, etc.

Cost Analysis and Control

Calculating labor and materials costs; developing standard cost systems; conducting variance analyses; calculating overtime labor needs; managing and controlling costs; etc.

Quality Control

Setting up inspection systems and standards for effective control of quality in incoming, in-process, and finished goods; etc.

Production Scheduling and Flow

Analyzing work flow; planning and managing production processes; managing work flow; calculating schedules and flows for rising sales levels; etc.

Purchasing

Identifying appropriate sources of supply; negotiating supplier contracts; managing the incoming flow of material into inventory; etc.

		Competency Inventory			
	Rank	**Thorough Knowledge and Experience (Done Well)**	**Some Knowledge and Experience (So–So)**	**No Knowledge or Experience (New Ground)**	**Importance (1–3 Years)**
Job Evaluation *Analyzing worker productivity and needs for additional help; calculating cost-saving aspects of temporary versus permanent help; etc.*					

Finance

Accounting *Determining appropriate bookkeeping and accounting systems; preparing and using income statements and balance sheets; analyzing cash flow, breakeven, contribution, and profit and loss; etc.*					
Capital Budgeting *Preparing budgets; deciding how best to acquire funds for start-up and growth; forecasting funds needs; etc.*					
Cash Flow Management *Managing cash position, including projecting cash requirements; etc.*					
Credit and Collection Management *Developing credit policies and screening criteria, etc.*					
Short-Term Financing *Managing payables and receivables; using interim financing alternatives; managing bank and creditor relations; etc.*					

	Rank	Competency Inventory			
		Thorough Knowledge and Experience (Done Well)	Some Knowledge and Experience (So–So)	No Knowledge or Experience (New Ground)	Importance (1–3 Years)
Public and Private Offering Skills *Developing a business plan and offering memo; managing shareholder relations; negotiating with financial sources; deal structuring and valuation; etc.*					

Entrepreneurial Leadership

	Rank	Thorough Knowledge and Experience (Done Well)	Some Knowledge and Experience (So–So)	No Knowledge or Experience (New Ground)	Importance (1–3 Years)
Problem Solving *Anticipating problems and planning to avoid them; analyzing and solving problems; etc.*					
Culture and Communications *Communicating effectively and clearly, both orally and in writing, to customers, peers, subordinates, and outsiders; treating others as you would be treated, sharing the wealth, giving back; etc.*					
Planning *Ability to set realistic and attainable goals, identify obstacles to achieving the goals, and develop detailed action plans to achieve those goals.*					
Decision Making *Making decisions based on the analysis of incomplete data; etc.*					
Ethical Competency *Ability to define and give life to an organization's guiding values; to create an environment that supports ethically sound behavior; and to instill a sense of shared accountability among employees.*					

	Competency Inventory				
	Rank	**Thorough Knowledge and Experience (Done Well)**	**Some Knowledge and Experience (So–So)**	**No Knowledge or Experience (New Ground)**	**Importance (1–3 Years)**
Project Management *Organizing project teams; setting project goals; defining project tasks; monitoring task completion in the face of problems and cost/ quality constraints; etc.*					
Negotiating *Working effectively in negotiations; etc.*					
Personnel Administration *Setting up payroll, hiring, compensation, and training functions; identifying, managing, and guiding appropriate outside advisors; etc.*					
Management Information Systems *Knowledge of relevant management information systems available and appropriate for growth plans; etc.*					
Information Technology and the Internet *Using spreadsheet, word processing, and other relevant software; using e-mail, management tools, and other appropriate systems.*					

	Rank	Thorough Knowledge and Experience (Done Well)	Some Knowledge and Experience (So–So)	No Knowledge or Experience (New Ground)	Importance (1–3 Years)
Competency Inventory					

Interpersonal Team

Entrepreneurial Leadership/Vision/ Influence
Actively leading, instilling vision and passion in others, and managing activities of others; creating a climate and spirit conducive to high performance; etc.

Helping
Determining when assistance is warranted and asking for or providing such assistance.

Feedback
Providing effective feedback or receiving it; etc.

Conflict Management
Confronting differences openly and obtaining resolution; using evidence and logic; etc.

Teamwork and Influence
Working with others to achieve common goals; delegating responsibility and coaching subordinates, etc.

Building a Brain Trust
Connecting with experts and seeking advice and value.

	Competency Inventory				
	Rank	**Thorough Knowledge and Experience (Done Well)**	**Some Knowledge and Experience (So–So)**	**No Knowledge or Experience (New Ground)**	**Importance (1–3 Years)**

Law

Corporations

Understanding the Uniform Commercial Code, including forms of organization and the rights and obligations of officers, shareholders, and directors; etc.

Contracts

Understanding the requirements of government and commercial contracts, licenses, leases, and other agreements; etc.

Taxes

Understanding state and federal reporting requirements; understanding tax shelters, estate planning, fringe benefits, and so forth; etc.

Securities

Understanding regulations of the Security and Exchange Commission and state agencies concerning the securities, both registered and unregistered; etc.

Patents and Proprietary Rights

Understanding the preparation and revision of patent applications; recognizing strong patent, trademark, copyright, and privileged information claims; etc.

Real Estate

Understanding agreements necessary for the rental or purchase and sale of property; etc.

	Rank	Competency Inventory			
		Thorough Knowledge and Experience (Done Well)	Some Knowledge and Experience (So–So)	No Knowledge or Experience (New Ground)	Importance (1–3 Years)
Bankruptcy *Understanding options and the forgivable and nonforgivable liabilities of founders, officers, directors, and so forth; etc.*					
Unique Skills *List unique competencies required:* *1.* *2.* *3.*					

Part II—Competency Assessment

Part II involves assessing management strengths and weaknesses, deciding which areas of competence are most critical, and developing a plan to overcome or compensate for any weaknesses and to capitalize on management strengths.

STEP 1

Assess competency strengths and weaknesses:

- Which skills are particularly strong?

- Which skills are particularly weak?

- What gaps are evident? When?

- Who in your team can overcome or compensate for each critical weakness?

- How can you leverage your critical strengths?

- What are the time implications of these actions? For you? For the team?

- How will you attract people to fill the critical gaps in your weaknesses?

STEP 2

Circle the areas of competence most critical to the success of the venture, and cross out those that are irrelevant.

STEP 3

Consider the implications for you and for developing the venture management team:

- What are the implications of this particular constellation of strengths and weaknesses?

STEP 4

Obtain feedback. If you are evaluating your management competencies as part of the development of a personal entrepreneurial strategy and planning your apprenticeship, refer back to the Crafting a Personal Entrepreneurial Strategy Exercise in Chapter 2. Complete this exercise if you have not done so already.

Slicing the Equity Pie

After considering the issues and criteria discussed in this chapter, in this exercise the lead entrepreneur will begin to think through the tricky and delicate compensation and equity allocations. Once the company or limited liability corporation (LLC) is ready to be legally formed, these decisions need to be made.

First, we urge you to anchor these deliberations in several principles and realities:

- The best companies share their wealth with the high performers that create and build it via creative incentives and rewards.

- Fairness is a prime consideration.

- When it comes to founders' salaries, less is more.

- The value-added contributions of the key players will drive ownership.

Second, it is useful to think about the capital structure and ownership of the company at an eventual IPO—even if you never go this route. As we saw in the capital markets food chain in Chapter 5, post-IPO the ownership will be roughly 50 percent in the hands of outside investors (angels, family, venture capitalists, etc.) and 20–25 percent in the hands of the public; the rest (25–30 percent) will be owned by the founders, management, and directors/advisors, including the option pool. It would also be common for a company to have 15–20 million shares of stock outstanding, post-IPO on a fully diluted basis. Thus the ownership in shares might approximate the following:

Public investors	=	4–5 million shares
Private investors	=	7.5–10 million shares
Founders:		
CEO	=	1–2 million shares
Marketing VP	=	500K–1 million shares
CFO	=	200–400K shares
Rest	=	1.5–2 million shares

Advisors and directors may have .25–1 percent, or roughly 10K to 200K shares, depending on their perceived value and the negotiation.

The Founder's Assignment

STEP 1

Draft a one-page summary of what you believe at this initial point the salaries and stock ownership (members' ownership in an LLC) will look like at the launch of your venture. Be specific about dollars, number of shares, and percentages for each.

STEP 2

Discuss your draft with at least three members of your brain trust who have been founders/principals in, or legal advisors to, a company that has gone public. This is to test your thinking, assumptions, and assessment of the potential contributions of the team.

STEP 3

After digesting their reactions and suggestions, make appropriate revisions.

STEP 4

Ask each founding team member (if you have any at this point) to do the same. Then share each draft and attempt to reach a consensus.

Be sure to avoid the temptation, as pointed out in this chapter, to simply make everyone equal. Although this can and does work, it often does not, and it is a way of avoiding the reality that not everyone will have equal responsibility, risk, and contributions.

Case

Maclean Palmer

Preparation Questions

1. Evaluate Maclean Palmer's decision to create a new venture capital fund in 2000 and his progress to date.
2. What is your evaluation of the team?
3. Outline the major risks you see, the due diligence questions you would focus on, and whom you would contact as a pension fund analyst or prospective limited in the fund.
4. Prepare a detailed outline of what you would include in a private placement memorandum to market the fund to potential investors.
5. Who should invest in a venture capital fund?

Maclean Palmer

Maclean Palmer strode out onto a Martha's Vineyard beach to enjoy the warm sun as it set on what had proved to be a pivotal day in his quest to start up a $200 million private equity fund. That August afternoon in 2000, Palmer and his four chosen partners had made a collective decision that would, for better or worse, change their lives forever.

In less than two months, the partners would quit their jobs, sell their homes, and move their families to Boston to begin crafting an offering memorandum for a private equity fund that they were certain would attract a differentiated and lucrative deal flow. With 2000 shaping up to be the largest venture fund-raising year in history, it seemed that they could not have picked a better time to strike out on their own.

The Venture Capital Investing Process

Venture capitalists and entrepreneurs engaged in a process whereby they assumed and managed the risks associated with investing in compelling new business opportunities. Their aim was long-term value creation for themselves, their companies, their communities, and other stakeholders. The process began with the conceptualization of an investment opportunity. A prospectus would then be written to articulate the strategy and outline the qualifications and track record of the investment team. Raising the money was a networking and sales undertaking that typically gained momentum only after an institutional investment advisor—known as a gatekeeper (see box)—had committed capital to the fund.

Once the money had been raised, the venture capital firm sought to add value in many ways: identifying and evaluating business opportunities, negotiating and closing the investment, tracking and coaching the company, providing technical and management assistance, and attracting additional capital, directors, management, suppliers, and other key resources (see Exhibit 1). Given the fortuitous convergence of factors (e.g., management talent, market timing, strategic vision) required for a start-up to reach a profitable harvest event such as an acquisition or an IPO, home runs were rare. In fact, historical data indicated that only about 1 out of every 15 of these investments ever realized a return of 10 times or more on invested capital. The venture capital process occurred in the context of mostly private, imperfect capital markets for new, emerging, and middle-market companies (i.e., those with $20 million to $150 million in sales).[1]

The dominant legal structure for private venture capital funds was the limited partnership, with the venture capitalists assuming the role of general partners and the investors as limited partners (see Exhibit 2). The general partners acted as organizers and investment managers of the fund, while the limited partners enjoyed a passive

The Gatekeepers

Institutional investors such as corporations, foundations, and pension funds invested as limited partners in hundreds of venture capital and buyout funds. Many of these investors, having neither the resources nor the expertise to evaluate and manage fund investments, delegated these duties to investment advisors with expertise in the venture capital industry. These advisors would pool the assets of their various clients and invest those proceeds on behalf of their limited partners into a venture or buyout fund currently raising capital. For this service, the advisors collected a fee of 1 percent of committed capital per annum. Because these investment experts exerted a tremendous amount of influence over the allocation of capital to new and existing venture teams and funds, they were referred to as gatekeepers.

[1] W. D. Bygrave and J. A. Timmons, *Venture Capital at the Crossroads* (Boston: Harvard School Press, 1992). Note: middle-market company figures reflect the range in the early 2000s.

This case was prepared by Carl Hedberg under the direction of Professor Jeffry Timmons, the Franklin W. Olin Distinguished Professor of Entrepreneurship at the Arthur M. Blank Center for Entrepreneurship, Babson College. © Copyright Babson College, 2004. Funding provided by the Franklin W. Olin Foundation. All rights reserved.

EXHIBIT 1

Classic VC Investing Process

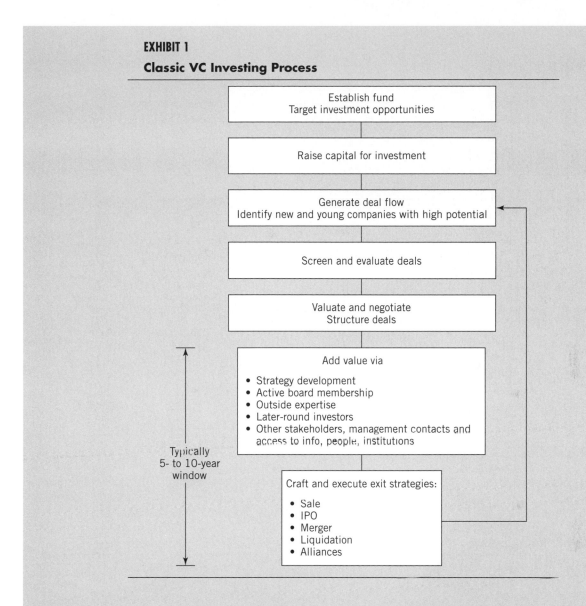

Establish fund
Target investment opportunities

Raise capital for investment

Generate deal flow
Identify new and young companies with high potential

Screen and evaluate deals

Valuate and negotiate
Structure deals

Add value via
- Strategy development
- Active board membership
- Outside expertise
- Later-round investors
- Other stakeholders, management contacts and access to info, people, institutions

Typically 5- to 10-year window

Craft and execute exit strategies:
- Sale
- IPO
- Merger
- Liquidation
- Alliances

role in fund management as well as limited liability for any fund activity. As compensation for their direct participation and risk exposure, general partners stood to reap substantial gains in the form of carried interest on successful portfolio companies.

This partnership structure stipulated a specific term of years for the fund. Extending that life span required the consent of the general partners and two-thirds of the limited partners. The fee structure between the general and limited partners was considerably varied and, as a result, affected the level of attraction of the fund.[2]

Between 1980 and mid-2000, there were two recessions (in 1981–1982 and in 1990–1992) and a stock market panic in late 1987 that sent share prices plummeting 22 percent in a single day in October that year. Nevertheless, according to Venture Economics (a private equity database compiler) venture investments during that time had yielded a 19.3 percent average annual return

after fees and expenses. Over the same period, the S&P 500 and the Russell 2000 index of small companies generated average annual returns, respectively, of 15.7 percent and 13.3 percent. The latest five-year trends showed venture returns far ahead of lackluster buyout performance and falling U.S. blue chip prices. Fueled by these figures and the high-profile Internet boom, year 2000 was shaping up to be a record-breaking period for venture fund-raising (see Exhibit 3).

Historically, equity funds had been conceived, invested, and exited on an 8- to 12-year cycle, with preparation for follow-on funds beginning in years three and four. To a large degree, that time frame had been driven by the reality that, on average, it took five to seven years to build and harvest a successful portfolio investment.

By the late 1990s, however, the throughput time for harvesting high-flyers had been slashed to the point where some companies were skipping from a first round of venture financing into a successful IPO—all in the

[2] Ibid.

EXHIBIT 2

Flows of VC

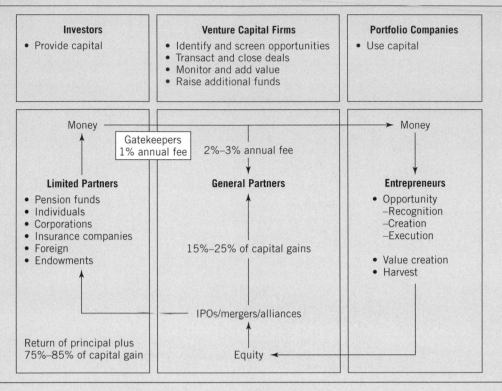

Note: These exhibits are discussed further in Chapter 14, Obtaining Venture and Growth Capital.

EXHIBIT 3

Funds, Fund Commitments, and Average Fund Size

	Venture Capital				Buyout and Mezzanine			
Year/Qtr	First-Time Funds	Total Funds	Average Fund Size ($mil)	Total Raised ($billions)	First-Time Funds	Total Funds	Average Fund Size ($mil)	Total Raised ($billions)
1994	25	138	56.5	7.8	31	103	202.9	20.9
1995	36	155	63.9	9.9	32	105	253.3	26.6
1996	54	163	74.2	12.1	38	112	300.9	33.7
1997	79	232	76.3	17.7	39	140	355.7	49.8
1998	82	277	109.7	30.4	42	166	386.1	64.1
1999	146	424	139.5	59.2	44	157	410.8	64.5
Q1 2000	45	165	132.1	21.8	9	42	300	12.6
Q2 2000	51	183	168.3	30.8	10	50	212	10.6

Source: National Venture Capital Association (http://www.nvca.org/nvca2_11_02.html).

space of a year or less, and typically in less than two years. While not all portfolio gems were cut loose this quickly, this new landscape had radically altered the frequency and capitalization of follow-on venture capital funds. For example, between 1994 and 2000, Spectrum Equity Investors (Boston/Menlo Park) had been able to close on four funds totaling just over $3 billion. Between 1998 and 2001, over $200 billion had been raised by venture groups—more than the total of the previous 40 years.

Concepting

With five years of direct investing experience in this heady private equity space as a principal at Point West Partners in San Francisco—along with 17 years of operating experience—venture capitalist Maclean Palmer, 40, decided in 1999 that the time was right to develop his own fund:

> As an ethnic minority, I had always been committed to minority business development, and I knew that there was a large pool of talented minority executives out there that traditional VCs weren't calling on to run portfolio companies. These executives have a tremendous amount of operating experience, and I figured there should be a way to build significant postinvestment value by bridging that operating experience with a solid investing strategy. I began to ask, "What should be the profile and experience of the team that could exploit that opportunity?"

In seeking advice, one of his first calls was to Wanda Felton, a director of private equity investments at Credit Suisse First Boston. During the early 1990s, Felton had honed her due diligence skills while working at Hamilton Lane, a Philadelphia-based gatekeeper with an interest in first-time funds in the minority space. She and Palmer had initially met as judges for a Wharton business plan competition, and later they worked together when she had assisted the Point West group in raising their fourth fund.

Outlining what she felt were important criteria for assessing first-time private equity offerings (see Exhibit 4), Felton recalled that while Palmer had some hurdles to clear, she sensed that he had come up with a salable concept:

> For a limited partner, putting money into a first-time fund has all the risks associated with a typical start-up investment. On top of that, this type of deal is a 10-year-plus commitment with no ability to get out. LPs, therefore, look for groups that can demonstrate that they have worked successfully together in the past, will stay together, and have a common view of how they'll run their portfolio businesses. Since Maclean was talking about developing a new team, this collective experience was of course something his fund would not have.

> Still, Maclean was describing a focused, "management-centric" concept—meaning that his core strategy would be to identify and recruit top-level ethnic minority managers from Fortune 1,000 companies to run—and add value to—his fund's investments. The other elements of the strategy included a focus on being company builders with an operating orientation, and the ability to leverage their combined operating and investing expertise to add value to their portfolio companies. This was intriguing, and it certainly differentiated him from the majority of private equity firms.

EXHIBIT 4

Due Diligence on New Funds

The Business

What is the overall strategy?

Is there a market opportunity, and can it be executed in the current market environment and during the expected commitment period?

Has the team articulated a strategic and operating business strategy for portfolio companies?

Do they have a viable exit plan?

Probably most crucial: How has the general partner group demonstrated that they will be able to add investment value to their portfolio companies?

The Team

Do the general partner and the team have the requisite private equity investing experience and resources to execute the strategy?

Will the team have access to deal flow within the stated strategy?

Is the team stable?

Has the team worked together before?

Do they have a common view as to how they will run the businesses?

Do they have a meaningful track record in the stated strategy?

Next Palmer contacted Grove Street Advisors (GSA) partner David Mazza, an expert in the venture executive search field and an outspoken champion of first-time funds.

The Advocates

Back in 1997 Dave Mazza had introduced Babson MBA Palmer—then a Kauffman Fellow (see box) at Advent International in Boston—to the venture group at Point West Partners. When Palmer (see Appendix A: Team Profiles) contacted Mazza in 1999 with an idea for developing a fund that would proactively seek out talented ethnic minority executives to back in mainstream ventures, the seasoned advisor was immediately drawn to the possibilities:

> I'm being told by the chairman of General Motors that if we could start three or four well-run ethnic-minority-owned supplier businesses, we could build them to $300 million to $400 million companies over the next four to five years—easily and profitably. That's an opportunity you don't always hear—and it's because of the minority aspect. In the automotive industry, 10 percent of all supplier contracts have to be set aside for minority businesses—that's life, and traditional venture capital firms like Kleiner, Bessemer and Sequoia can't effectively go after that market; but someone like Palmer could.

The Kauffman Fellowship

In 1993 the Ewing Marion Kauffman Foundation (www.emkf.org) established the Kauffman Fellows Program (www.kauffmanfellows.org), a program designed to educate and train emerging leaders in the venture capital process. The curriculum provided a rigorous yet flexible educational experience, enabling fellows to combine the theory and best practice of venture creation, while utilizing their position in venture capital as a learning laboratory. Like a medical residency, the fellowship was an apprenticeship program that featured a structured educational curriculum, an individual learning plan, facilitated mentoring, peer learning and networking, and leadership development in specific areas of interest.

Kauffman Fellows were students of the Center for Venture Education and could serve as either temporary or permanent full-time associates of the venture firm during the time of the fellowship. As associates, their salaries, benefits, and expenses were the responsibility of, and determined by, the firm.

Mazza added that the capabilities of nontraditional funds were something that gatekeepers like Hamilton Lane and GSA had been advocating for years:

Traditional institutional investors always look for the same things. They think that the guys who made money before are going to make it again; that's wrong—it's a different world now. The reality is that white boys aren't the only people who know how to make money. Sure, there are still going to be the guys making money in biotech and in semiconductors, but more and more we are seeing women entrepreneurs, African American entrepreneurs, Hispanic entrepreneurs. The trouble is, there has been no money going in that direction except for government funding programs—and those are not set up to provide critical post-money support.

GSA cofounder Clint Harris referred to his firm's detailed evaluation model (see Exhibit 5)

EXHIBIT 5
GSA Evaluation Process

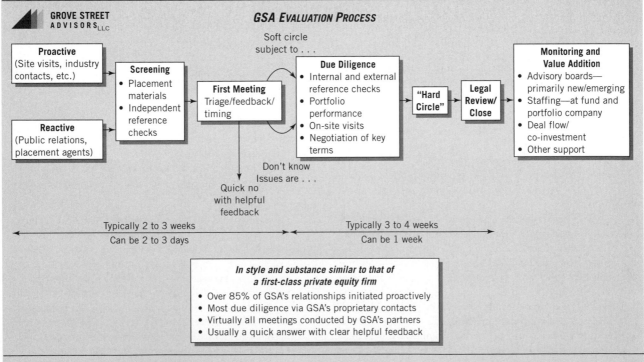

Source: Used by permission of Grove Street Advisors, LLC.

as he explained that identifying and supporting emerging talent was similar to the work of assessing new venture opportunities:

> As with start-ups and entrepreneurs, the difference between the average investment manager and the top performers is huge. And just like with successful venture investing, we look at a lot of offerings and meet with a lot of teams. We tend to say no quickly; when we do spot talent, we start small, help them along. As they gain experience and credibility as successful investors, we write bigger and bigger checks.

Although the GSA partners felt that Palmer had the background, the drive, and the personality to lead the charge, the influential player was adamant about the need to achieve critical mass by bringing in known, experienced players. Mazza elaborated:

> I told Maclean that what he really needed to do was create an effort that became so prominent that if you were a top entrepreneur, a CEO, an Oprah, or a Steadman Graham—and you weren't part of it—you'd feel like you were out of it. That's the ideal.
>
> This would have to be a very high-profile group with private equity expertise and some buyout experience. I wanted to see some names that people could immediately identify with—either on the advisory board or in the partnership ranks.

Palmer, however, felt that far too much emphasis was being placed on the minority aspect of what he was trying to develop; and he also had his own vision about the sort of partners he needed to attract:

> GSA made it clear that if they were going to make any kind of substantial investment in my concept, then they would prefer that I focused on finding partners with lots of deal experience. That was, of course, one thing I had to look at, but I don't think that prior experience working together is necessarily the most important consideration in building a team of people who I expect to be partners with for 20 or 30 years. Although experience and track record are key, who my partners are as people is much more important to me than what they have accomplished up until now.

Recruiting an "American" Lineup

Driven by his strategy to develop a compelling investment team that would reflect the focus of the fund they would manage, Palmer tirelessly networked and thoroughly investigated dozens of potential minority candidates. His due diligence gave him a good sense of not only their investment preferences, management abilities, and track records, but their personal styles as well. When asked about his first two choices, Wharton MBA

Clark Pierce,[3] 38, and Harvard MBA Andrew Simon, 30, Palmer referred to their respective résumés (see Appendix A: Team Profiles), adding,

> Clark was a principal with Ninos Capital with seven years of mezzanine experience. What attracted me most about him was that we knew each other well and had complementary skill sets. He had come up through the financial side, and I had come up through the venture operating side, so the things that he liked and was most experienced and skilled with, I was less inclined toward. Andrew had excellent fundamentals and I liked the way he thought. I could sense that even though he was a young guy, he definitely had what it took.

In the spring of 1999, Wanda Felton introduced Palmer to 61-year-old Ray Turner—a newly retired senior executive at a Fortune 50 heavy industry corporation who had thus far turned down seven CEO jobs and 38 offers to serve on boards of directors. Turner recalled his first meeting with the nascent group:

> The four of us met on a Saturday morning at Logan Airport, and we spent a lot of time talking beyond just intellect. It was about character. I told them that if this was all about excellence, then I would consider playing—but if not, I didn't want to touch it. These were young, bright guys, and I was energized by how committed they were.

Felton explained that while Turner's sterling credentials (see Appendix A: Team Profiles) would help raise the profile of the group, it was his understanding of operations and his ability to connect with and evaluate senior-level managers that would add the most value to the team:

> The pool of ethnic minority business talent—people with 20 or 30 years of experience—is something we haven't had in this country until very recently. Although there is now a huge cadre of senior managers—minority men and women who have risen to real positions of authority—they are not altogether visible because they have their heads down and they are doing their jobs. As a member of organizations like the Executive Leadership Council,[4] Ray has the ability to tap into that group.
>
> In most equity funds there are people executing the deals and there are people who are there because of whom they know, and because of their wisdom, vision, and experience. The marriage of younger, hungry investors like Maclean and Clark with Ray's Rolodex and experience would be seen as a big plus for the effort.

For the position of vice president, Palmer recruited Harvard MBA Dario Cardenas, 31, a young man whose

---

[3] Palmer and Pierce had first met in 1995. Seeing that they shared many of the same values and aspirations, they had kept in touch professionally and socially.

[4] The Executive Leadership Council was an independent, nonpartisan, nonprofit corporation founded in 1986 to provide African-American executives with a network and leadership forum designed to add perspective and direction to the achievement of excellence in business, economic, and public policies for the African-American community, corporate America, and the public.

name had come up on everyone's short list of the most talented Hispanic candidates in the country. Cardenas had earned that reputation in part because of his service—at just 23 years old—as the youngest elected mayor of a major U.S. city (see Appendix A: Team Profiles). Palmer explained that there was an advantage to bringing together people who were previously unknown to each other:

> One way to think about a private equity firm is that it is only as good as the combined talents and networks of its team members. For this reason, I wanted to set up a group that could bring to the table a diverse set of skills, contacts, and perspectives. What we wound up with was 57 years of operating and 25 years of private equity experience, leading deals of over $200 million, with $100 million returned on just four of 16 investments.

Clint Harris was impressed with the capable team that Palmer had recruited that year. Nevertheless, he remained concerned about their ability to evaluate and add significant value to opportunities that came their way:

> These guys had a good track record—which we verified with calls to their former colleagues, people at companies that they had invested in, and members of boards that they had served on. We could see that these were very bright and talented junior partner guys—as talented as any general partners that we had worked with—and Ray Turner was a real plus. In fact, a single half-hour call to my former suite mate at HBS—now CEO of General Motors—was all the due diligence I needed to learn that Ray would be a tremendous asset to the team, that he was totally committed, and that these young guys were top notch.
>
> That said, it takes time and investing results for anyone to learn the equity investment business, and to calibrate on their judgment and skills. These guys didn't have much of a track record, and in that respect they were on the thin edge of what we like to see.

Grove Street Advisors—Gatekeeper

Back in 1997 Clint Harris, a founder and former managing director of the Boston venture capital firm Advent International Corp., and Catherine Crocket, founder of the Gazelle Group, a state investment program advisor, moved to parlay their extensive venture capital relationships into a unique investment management practice for institutional clients.

Harris explained that the seemingly risk-averse approach of traditional fee-for-service investment advisors had served to, over time, shut their clients out of participating in top-tier funds (see Exhibits 6–8):

> Gatekeepers generally view first-time funds as too risky and therefore imprudent investments. With teams now raising new funds before they have proven track records, it becomes very difficult to evaluate a team based on their investments. By the time these teams do

EXHIBIT 6

Life Cycle of Private Equity Managers

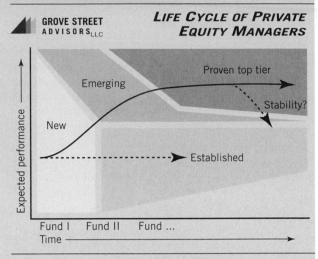

Source: Used by permission of Grove Street Advisors, LLC.

EXHIBIT 7

Gatekeeper Dilemma

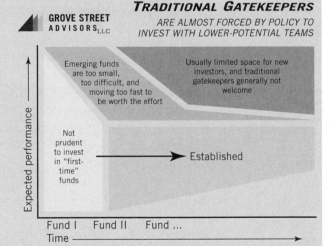

Source: Used by permission of Grove Street Advisors, LLC.

emerge as top-tier players, their funds are often closed to all but the people who have been supporting them all along. As an advisor and a fund of funds, the only way that we can hope to be on top 10 years from now is to identify and nurture the best new and emerging investment managers out there.

The other big issue is that the gatekeepers and their large pension fund clients are not set up to make small investments. It takes much more effort and personnel on a per-dollar basis to evaluate a large number of emerging teams, negotiate 10, $10 million commitments, and then monitor those relationships than it does to put $100 million into a single large, established fund. As a result,

EXHIBIT 8

Critical Issues and Development Stage

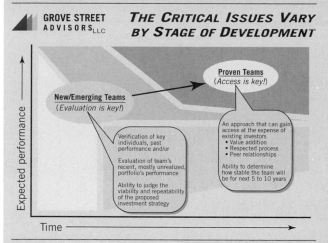

Source: Used by permission of Grove Street Advisors, LLC.

the truly top-tier private equity funds, as well as small funds in general, are not represented or are significantly underweighted in the portfolios of most of the major state pension funds.

Our idea was to offer these institutional investors a vehicle that could effectively identify, evaluate, and invest in a portfolio of very high-quality new and emerging fund managers. Over time, these relationships would translate into a far higher-quality core of funds in their private equity portfolios.

As a new organization with no track record, Harris and Crocket had assumed that they would start with a small client before going after a big state pension fund opportunity. Then, in the spring of 1998, the Grove Street pair met with Barry Gonder, senior investment officer for the California Public Employees Retirement System (CalPERS). After filling out their team with the addition of Dave Mazza—founder of the largest and best-known executive search practice serving the venture capital industry—and proposing the creation of a dedicated fund of funds they would call California Emerging Ventures I (CEV I), GSA succeeded in beating out several other firms for the $350 million account.

Almost immediately, GSA began opening venture capital doors for their sole client. By early 2001, CalPERS had increased their GSA capital stake to $750 million, and the advisor group had placed CEV I money with nearly 45 top venture capital firms. Harris explained that with a third of the total investment pool earmarked for new and emerging teams, his group was naturally drawn to nontraditional niche opportunities:

The paradox with demanding that mainstream investment standards are met is that those standards severely limit deal flow. We had our antennae up for minority and women investment opportunities, not for social reasons, but because we had the conviction that if we were

able to find a strong enough team, they would attract a proprietary deal flow by way of their demographic network. We also knew that there were a lot of pension fund managers out there that were very interested in minority funding opportunities—opportunities that were being ignored by the mainstream.

At the heart of GSA's effectiveness was a broad base of business and venture capital industry contacts that enabled them to consistently conduct a level of due diligence on private equity managers that had not been seen before. Some particularly critical observers of the industry felt that quite often, institutional investors were inclined to follow lead investors, rather than conduct extensive investigations on their own.

As they had done when they were venture capitalists, GSA interviewed, reviewed, and assessed hundreds of potential new fund managers and concepts—and passed on all but a few. Three funds received backing early on: the Audax Group, a firm led by two former Bain Capital partners, Geoffrey Rehnert and Marc Wolpow; New Mountain Capital, the brainchild of ex-Forstmann Little partner Steven Klinsky; and Solera Capital, headed by Molly Ashby, a former buyout and growth financing specialist at J.P. Morgan Capital Corporation.

Although Palmer had not recruited a senior partner with a proven return performance of "50 IRR over 20 years," the GSA group remained solidly behind his efforts. Now that the young venture capitalist had assembled a talented team that was demographically similar to the underserved and potentially lucrative entrepreneurial slice of America he aimed to target, Palmer knew that his next step was to foster a cohesive group dynamic.

Bonding the Team

Over the next few months, Palmer juggled the busy schedules of his potential partners in order to organize a number of in-depth strategy and bonding sessions (see Exhibit 9). He recalled that while these gatherings addressed issues related to the investment business that they would come together to create, the main focus was on building rapport and understanding:

At our first get-together each of us told our whole personal and professional story. Once we had a collective sense of who we were, then we began to talk in general terms about what we wanted to build. It had to be something we all believed in—something that would last over the long term—and be able to survive economic down cycles. Then we asked, "Does the market want what we envision, and do we have the collective talent to succeed?"

In the summer of 2000, Palmer took his wife and two young children to Martha's Vineyard for his first two-week

EXHIBIT 9

Meeting Notes

Agenda—Introduction and Strategy Session

All connected to the same Rope.

Date:	July 21, 2000

Vilma Martinez — Roy's Contact

9:00 a.m.   Introduction
- Progress to date — *Team / Research / LPs /*
- Team introductions — *Detailed / Worst trouble…*

10:30 a.m.   Discussion of fund strategy — *Broaden MKT → Serve, Employ, Located / Basket for General MKT Deals*
- Fund size — *$150M (→ $200M 7/16/00)*
- Deal stages — *Growth Equity → Buyouts*
- Industries — *focus on Ind w/ strong # prospects*
- Geography — *Midwest presence - access to deal flow*
- *MKT* • Deal flow — *Growth equity → Buyouts*
- Portfolio company management - *style / 2 per BOD*
- Side fund - *Charles Tribbett / Use of executives / Operating Affiliates → Second side fund*

11:30 a.m.   Firm operating philosophy — *End product → View of the firm and internal culture*
- Management philosophy — *open / all-hands, all-eyes / veto / No mng partner*
- Roles - *1-2 Admin / AN-LA, CMS, books, etc / All. PR resp.* *Fund*
- Decision making — *consensus*
- Due diligence — *set parameters / evolve over time*
- Partner meetings — *format*
- Portfolio management - *1 lead, 1 backup*

12:30 p.m.   Review draft budget — *startup*   `Timing`

12:45 p.m.   Discussion of fund-raising strategy
- First close goals —
- LP targets and amount for first close — *who / $ amounts*
- Placement agent? — *see notes from Wanda*

1:30 p.m.   Open issues for the team — *How do we get to a decision on whether to do this - timing / concerns / additional info needed*

2:00 p.m.   Next steps
Strategic Partner —
- Decision on doing it with or without Wind Point = *Financial + startup capital / Continuity and timing of close / don't pay for what you don't use*
- Timing for other decisions
- PPM draft—need team resumes and track record info
- Side fund—executive recruitment
- Pick counsel—for mgmt company, GP&LP documents
- Negotiate economics — *F/u w/ each individual and come back w/ proposal to*
- Start-up logistics— *who / when / the group / location / steps*
- Firm name? — *Input…*

---

vacation in 15 years. He used part of that time to further bond the team:

I invited everyone—partners and their families—to visit with us on the island for three days. I explained to their wives why I was asking their spouses to do this. I felt that I needed to look them in the eye and tell them that there were no guarantees, that there would be hard, lean times, and that we'd be working harder than we ever had before.

The team was experienced enough to understand that success with this venture would yield a financial upside that was commensurate with the risks and challenges they would be taking on. At that time, the average total pay package—salary plus bonus—for managing general partners and senior-level partners was $1.24 million and $1.04 million, respectively. In addition, effective equity investors stood to reap even greater rewards in the form of carried interest distributions as their investments matured; managing general partners were bringing home an average of $2.5 million in carry, compared with $1.0 million by senior-level partners.[5]

Palmer's wife Emily, a patent attorney with her own practice, recalled that from the beginning, the spouses were behind the idea:

> Our husbands had outlined for us a certain timetable, and we understood that this thing was probably going to take a lot of patience and fortitude. With regard to my career, I needed to figure out whether I would try to maintain my firm, reopen something in Boston, or do something different altogether. Still, I was very excited about the venture because they had a team that could make this a success.

The team estimated that their start-up expenses for one year of fund-raising would be just under $400,000 (see Exhibit 10)—funded out of pocket or through personal loans. They felt that if they could articulate an opportunity that leveraged their collective skill set (and resonated with potential investors), they could cut their fund-raising time and be in business by late fall of 2001.

The Opportunity

The fund that Palmer and his team were setting up would execute buyout investments in a broad range of profitable, small- to middle-market private companies that served or operated in the minority marketplace. When these portfolio companies needed to recruit or partner with talented managers, their primary strategy would be to marshal their contacts and tap into the "hidden" pool of experienced ethnic minority executives.

While they planned to pursue and evaluate investment opportunities in the manner of any professional private equity group, the team understood that many prospective limiteds would, consciously or otherwise, align them with previous minority-focused investment efforts that had been set up and managed by groups with little or no private equity experience. Clint Harris noted that many of those funds had lost sight of what should have been their main objective:

> Minority funds in the past were often driven by political and social agendas; money got wasted and didn't do

[5] Venture Capital Journal, November 1, 2000; The Compensation Game: While Opportunities Abound, Firms Entice Partner-Level VCs to Stick Around. Data was according to a compensation survey of over 100 private equity firms, conducted by William M. Mercer Inc. Performance & Rewards Consulting.

EXHIBIT 10
Start-Up Estimates

October 2000 to October 2001	
Variable Expenses	
Salaries	90,000[1]
Legal	44,000
Travel	20,000
Rent	62,500[2]
Phone	10,000
Postage and printing	14,000
Meals	10,000
Entertainment	20,000
	$270,500
Fixed Expenses	
Computers/networking/printers	40,000
Phone system	20,000
Office supplies	5,000
Office furniture	50,000
	$115,000
Total start-up expenses	$385,500

[1] Salaries: Three partners @ $40,000 each. Half salary for six months.

[2] Rent: 2,500 square feet @ $25/sf.

any good—and burned investors have very long memories. When this happens, it's not just the failure of the team and the fund; it's the failure of the good intentions to do social investing for the wrong reasons. Some succeeded in making money, but most of them failed to achieve investment returns that were robust enough to attract mainstream investors.

The team frequently encountered a tendency by some limited partner prospects to pigeonhole the fund as one that would, as prior funds had done, invest exclusively in existing minority enterprises. For instance, Judith Elsea, who was at that time the chief investment officer for the Ewing Marion Kauffman Foundation, noted that the challenge for some prospective limited partners would be in conducting due diligence:

> This team is proposing something different by addressing markets that are not as heavily trafficked by private equity groups. But while those markets are arguably underserved, they are also in areas where a lot of institutional investors don't have a lot of experience—or big networks where people would be easy to check out.

Palmer felt that the entire discussion was missing the point:

> I'm not worrying about what other minority firms are doing or have done, but I know that as soon as we sit down with potential investors, they are going to think we are investing exclusively in minority ventures. We are going to have to craft our presentation in a way that gets people

to stop thinking about that and instead see what we are doing as a generic way to go make money, a solid private equity strategy—no mirrors or hidden agendas. We're going to do it the old-fashioned way: back great managers, invest in fundamentally sound businesses, and then put our heads down and execute a value creation strategy over four to six years.

Wanda Felton agreed:

It is important to understand that this group was being set up to build and add value to a company, and then be able to sell that business to anybody. Sure, the minority angle might provide a competitive advantage on the margin in terms of proprietary deal flow, but the team needs to communicate that their business proposition will not necessarily rely on minority ownership or set-aside programs.

Since they were anticipating that much of their deal flow would involve established and later-stage opportunities, David Mazza cautioned against being too quick to initiate operations:

I told them that a $50 million buyout fund was only going to get them into trouble. We like to see a bare minimum of $100 million, and prefer $200 million to $250 million. You can certainly have a first closing at $100 million, but you want to end up with something that has critical mass.

The Beginning

Now that he had secured a unified commitment from the team to move to Boston by the end of the summer, Palmer decided that when his partners and their families arrived in September, he'd welcome them all with a van tour of the city. Then—all assembled and all on the same page—the team would take up the challenge of crafting the offering prospectus and raising the fund.

Appendix A: Team Profiles

Maclean Palmer, Jr.

Maclean Palmer, Jr. (41) has over 5 years of *direct* private equity experience and over 17 years of operating experience. Prior to joining Forte, he was a managing director with Point West Partners from 1997 to 2000 in their San Francisco office. While at Point West, Palmer was responsible for deal origination, transaction execution, and portfolio company management and focused on growth equity and buyout investments in the telecommunications, business-to-business services, industrial manufacturing, and auto sectors. Palmer led Point West investments in three competitive local exchange carriers

(CLECs): Cobalt Telecommunications, MBCS Telecommunications, and Concept Telephone. He continues to represent Point West on the board of directors of both MBCS and Concept Telephone.

From 1995 to 1997, Palmer was a vice president in the Boston office of Advent International. While at Advent, he focused on industrial and technology investments and led Advent's investment in ISI, a financial and business information services provider. From 1986 to 1995, Palmer worked in various management and engineering positions for three start-up companies—UltraVision Inc., Surglaze Inc., and DTech Corporation—that were all financed by private equity investors. During his start-up career, Palmer was involved in the development and successful market introduction of 12 new products. In addition, Palmer held engineering positions with Borg Warner Corporation from 1984 to 1986 and with the diesel division of a major automotive firm from 1983 to 1984.

Palmer sits on the board of JT Technologies, a minority-owned firm that develops battery and ultra-capacitor technology. He also sits on the board of the Cooper Enterprise Fund, a minority-focused fund based in New York; the Community Preparatory School, a private inner-city school focused on preparing middle school students for college preparatory high schools; and the Zell Laurie Entrepreneurial Institute at the University of Michigan Business School.

Palmer holds a BSME from the Automotive Institute and an MBA cum laude from Babson College, and was awarded a Kauffman Fellowship, graduating with the program's inaugural class.

Ray S. Turner

Ray S. Turner (61) has had a long and distinguished career as an operating executive at Fortune 50 companies. From October 1998 to March 2000, he was group vice president, North America Sales, Service, and Marketing for a multinational heavy-industry manufacturer. From 1990 to 1998, Turner also served as vice president and general manager for North America Sales and Manufacturing at that company.

From 1988 to 1990, he served as vice president for manufacturing operations. From 1977 to 1988, Turner served in senior manufacturing management and plant manager roles for a number of assembly and manufacturing operations for the company. Prior to his career at that corporation, Turner spent several years serving in a variety of positions in engineering, materials management, manufacturing, sales, personnel, and labor relations. He serves on the board of directors of two Fortune 100 corporations.

Turner received a bachelor's degree in business administration from Western Michigan University. He also completed the Executive Development Program at Harvard Business School and an Advanced International General Management Program in Switzerland.

Clark T. Pierce

Clark T. Pierce (38) has over seven years of mezzanine and private equity experience and over four years of corporate finance experience. Most recently he was a principal with Ninos Capital, a publicly traded mezzanine investment fund. While at Ninos he was responsible for leading all aspects of the investment process, including deal origination and evaluation, due diligence, deal, execution, and portfolio company management. Pierce has closed numerous transactions in various industries, including business services, distribution, manufacturing, and financial services.

From 1993 to 1995, Pierce managed Ninos Capital's Specialized Small Business Investment Company ("SSBIC"). This SSBIC was a $45 million investment vehicle directed toward minority owned and controlled companies. Prior to Ninos Capital, Pierce spent one year with Freeman Securities as a vice president in the Corporate Finance Group, where he advised bondholders and companies involved in the restructuring process. From 1989 to 1991, Pierce was an associate with Chase Manhattan Bank, N.A., in the Corporate Finance Group.

Pierce served on the board of directors of Sidewalks, Inc., a social services organization for troubled teenagers, and the Orphan Foundation of America, a nonprofit agency focusing on adoption of older children.

Pierce received a BA from Morehouse College, a JD from George Washington University, and an MBA from the Wharton Business School at the University of Pennsylvania.

Andrew L. Simon

Andrew L. Simon (30) has four years of direct private equity experience, as well as three years of strategy consulting experience. During his career, Simon has worked on private equity investments in numerous industry sectors including contract manufacturing, industrial products, health care, financial services, and direct marketing. Most recently he was a senior associate in the New York office at McCown De Leeuw & Co., Inc. ("MDC"), where he focused on growth and leveraged equity investments, including recapitalization and buy-

and-build acquisitions. While at MDC, Simon played a lead role in identifying potential investments, negotiating with sellers, and structuring and arranging debt financing, as well as supervising the legal documentation and closing of transactions. Post-acquisition, he played an active role in the financing and strategic direction of MDC portfolio companies and participated at board meetings.

From 1995 to 1997, Simon was an associate in the Boston office of Trident Partners ("Trident"). At Trident Simon was responsible for evaluating, prioritizing, and analyzing potential new acquisition opportunities, as well as supporting deal teams with business and analytical due diligence. From 1992 to 1995, Simon was a senior analyst at Marakon Associates, where he was responsible for valuation analysis, industry research, and strategy development. In addition, Simon has worked for Littlejohn & Co., an LBO firm focused on restructuring, Physicians Quality Care, a venture-backed health care services company, and Lotus Development.

Simon earned an AB degree from Princeton University's Woodrow Wilson School and earned his MBA, with honors, from Harvard Business School, where he was a Toigo Fellow.

Dario A. Cardenas

Most recently Dario A. Cardenas (31) was a managing director with MTG Ventures from 1999 to 2000. At MTG, a private equity firm focused on acquiring and operating manufacturing and service companies, Cardenas was responsible for deal origination, transaction execution, and portfolio company management. Prior to his role at MTG Ventures, Cardenas was a principal with MTG Advisors from 1992 to 1997, where he focused on strategy consulting and executive coaching. Concurrent with MTG Advisors, Cardenas was elected to two terms as mayor of Sunny Park, California, becoming, at 23, the mayor of that city. He has also served as assistant deputy mayor for public safety for the City of Los Angeles and as an analyst for McKinsey and Company.

Cardenas received a BA in political science from Harvard, cum laude, and his MBA from Harvard Business School.

Chapter Ten

Ethical Decision Making
and the Entrepreneur

If you gain financial success at the expense of your integrity, you are not a success at all.

John Cullinane
Founder of Cullinet, Inc., and a 1984 Inductee, Babson Academy of Distinguished Entrepreneurs

Results Expected

The fine line between success and failure in many a venture often boils down to the ethics and integrity of the founders and team. Careers and ventures have blossomed and crumbled because of the stellar or pitiful ethical decisions of founders. No subject in this entire book is more important, or more difficult to master, than this one.

Upon completion of this chapter, you will be able to

1. Discuss some of the history, philosophy, and research about the nature of business ethics and the context for thinking about ethical behavior.

2. Relate to the importance of ethical awareness and high standards in an entrepreneurial career.

3. Examine decisions involving ethical issues and your own decisions and reasoning in ethical situations.

4. Discuss with others the ethical implications of the decisions you made, and identify how they might affect you, your partners, your customers, and your competitors in the contexts described.

5. Describe some practical guidelines, tips, and advice for confronting and making sound ethical decisions.

The authors are most grateful to Professors James Klingler and William Bregman, Center for Entrepreneurship at Villanova University, Villanova, PA, for their contributions to our thinking on this challenging and important subject. We have included their insightful and practical work throughout this revised chapter. Their work has influenced how we now think about and present this material.

Overview of Ethics

The vast majority of successful entrepreneurs believe that high ethical standards and integrity are exceptionally important to long-term success. For example, Jeffry Timmons and his colleague Howard H. Stevenson conducted a study among 128 presidents/founders attending the Harvard Business School's Owner/President Management (OPM) program in 1983.[1] Their firms typically had sales of $40 million, and sales ranged from $5 million to $200 million. These entrepreneurs were also very experienced, with their average age in the mid-40s, and about half had founded their companies. They were asked to name the most critical concepts, skills, and know-how for success at their companies at the time and what they would be in five years. The answer to this question was startling enough that the Sunday *New York Times* reported the findings: 72 percent of the presidents responding stated that high ethical standards were the single most important factor in long-term success.[2] A May 2003 study by the Aspen Institute found that MBA students are concerned that their schools are not doing enough to prepare them for ethical dilemmas they may face in the business world. Seventeen hundred MBA students from the United States, Canada, and Britain were surveyed, and the results, plus student reactions, are addressed in the May 21, 2003, issue of *Chronicle of Higher Education*. Their concern and awareness are not surprising given the recent spate of corporate scandals. Ethical lapses like those of Enron executives, for example, erode the confidence in business activity at all levels. The trial ended in May 2006 with guilty verdicts for former top executives Kenneth Lay and Jeffrey Skilling.

Conventional ethical disciplines have been accused of dealing with the business realm by narrowly defining the scope of inquiry so as to be able to offer a definitive answer. What is ethical is not always obvious; rather, situations involving ethical issues are often ambiguous. Today, as throughout much of the last century, students, businesspeople, and others have received many conflicting signals, as "first artists and intellectuals, then broader segments of the society, challenged every convention, every prohibition, every regulation that cramped the human spirit or blocked its appetites and ambitions."[3]

This discussion has also generated much controversy. For example, a provocative and controversial article published in the *Harvard Business Review* asserted that the ethics of business were not those of society but rather those of the poker game.[4] The author of the article argued, "Most businessmen are not indifferent to ethics in their private lives, everyone will agree. My point is that in their office lives they cease to be private citizens; they become game players who must be guided by a somewhat different set of ethical standards." The author further argued that personal ethics and business ethics are often not in harmony, and by either negotiation or compromise, a resolution must be reached. The article provoked a storm of response. The question remains: How are businesspeople supposed to operate in this capitalist system?

In addition, the law, which you might expect to be black and white, is full of thorny issues. Laws have not only authority but also limitations. Laws are made with forethought and with the deliberate purpose of ensuring justice. They are, therefore, ethical in intent and deserve respect. However, laws are made in legislatures, not in heaven. They do not anticipate new conditions; they do not always have the effect they were intended to have; they sometimes conflict with one another; and they are, as they stand, incapable of making judgments where multiple ethical considerations hang in the balance or seem actually to war with one another. Thus, from the beginnings of recorded history in Egypt and the Middle East, a code of laws was always accompanied by a human interpreter of laws, a judge, to decide when breaking the letter of the law did not violate the spirit or situation that the law was intended to cover. Great moments in history, religion, philosophy, and literature focus on the legal/ethical dilemma, and debating teams would wither away if the dilemma were to disappear.

Ethical Stereotypes

Now, as in the past, the United States is viewed as providing an inviting and nurturing climate for those wishing to start their own enterprises and reap the rewards. To some extent, this is because the federal government has encouraged, to a greater degree than in most other countries, an atmosphere under which free market forces, private initiative, and individual responsibility and freedom can flourish.

---

[1] J. A. Timmons and H. H. Stevenson, "Entrepreneurship Education in the 1980s," presented at the 75th Anniversary Entrepreneurship Symposium, Harvard Business School, Boston, 1983. *Proceedings*, pp. 115–34.

[2] For an overview of the philosophical underpinnings of ethics and a decision-making framework, see "A Framework for Ethical Decision Making," J. L. Livingstone et al., Babson College Case Development Center, 2003.

[3] D. Bok, "Ethics, the University, & Society," *Harvard Magazine*, May–June 1988, p. 39.

[4] Reprinted by permission of *Harvard Business Review*. An excerpt from "Is Business Bluffing Ethical?" by A. Z. Carr, January–February 1968, pp. 145–52. Copyright © 1967 by the President and Fellows of Harvard College.

These laws, enacted in response to society's changing perceptions of what constitutes ethical business practices, have had the equally desirable effect of encouraging those in many industries to develop codes of ethics—in large part because they wished to have the freedom to set their own rules rather than to have rules imposed on them by legislatures.

As the ethical climate of business has changed, so has the image of the entrepreneur. Horatio Alger personifies the good stereotype. Entrepreneurs doing business in the unfettered economic climate of the 19th century—the era of the robber barons, where acts of industrial sabotage were common—represent the ruthless stereotype. The battles of James Hill and Edward Harriman over the rights of railroads, the alleged sabotage by John D. Rockefeller of his competitors' oil refineries, the exploitation of child labor in New England's textile mills and of black labor in the Southern cotton plantations, and the promoting of "snake oil" and Lydia Pinkham's tonics leave an unsavory aftertaste for today's more ethically conscious entrepreneurs.

Yet thoughtful historians of American entrepreneurship will also recall that regardless of the standards by which they are judged or of the motivations attributed to them, certain American entrepreneurs gave back to society such institutions as the Morgan Library and the Rockefeller Foundation. The extraordinary legacy of Andrew Carnegie is another example. (Scholars are much more inclined to examine and dissect the ethical behavior of the business sector, rather than that of the clergy, or even of academia itself. In many comparisons, the behavior of the business sector would look quite pure.)

Carnegie's case is also interesting because he described the total change of attitude that came over him after he had amassed his fortune. Carnegie, the son of a Scottish weaver, created a personal fortune of $300 million in the production of crude steel between 1873 and 1901. (That's $130 billion in today's dollars!) Carnegie believed that competition "insures the survival of the fittest in every department." Carnegie also felt that "the fact that this talent for organization and management is rare among men is proved by the fact that it invariably secures enormous rewards for its possessor."[5] So apparently satisfied was Carnegie with the correctness of his view, he did not try to reconcile it with the fact that British steel rails were effectively excluded by a protective tariff equaling over half the production price of each ton of steel rails.[6] That Carnegie's mind was not easy over

his fortune, however, is evident from his statement, "I would as soon give my son a curse as the almighty dollar."[7] After 1901, when he sold Carnegie Steel to United States Steel under pressure from a group headed by J. P. Morgan, Carnegie personally supervised donations in the United States and Great Britain of more than $300 million. Among his gifts to humanity were over 2,800 libraries, an Endowment for International Peace, and the Carnegie Institute of Pittsburgh.

From today's perspective, these entrepreneurs might be described as acting in enlightened self-interest. However, when the same sort of entrepreneurial generosity is demonstrated today by such people as Armand Hammer of Occidental Petroleum, Ted Turner of CNN fame, and Bill Gates of Microsoft, we are more likely to speak of their acts as philanthropy than as fulfilling their social contract.

A touch of suspicion still tinges entrepreneurial activity, and the word *entrepreneur* may still connote to some a person who belongs to a ruthless, scheming group located a good deal lower than the angels. In 1975 *Time* suggested that a businessman might make the best-qualified candidate for U.S. president but noted the "deep-rooted American suspicion of businessmen's motives."[8] Quoting John T. Conner, chair of Allied Chemical and former head of Merck and Company, *Time*'s editors added, "Anyone with previous business experience becomes immediately suspect. Certain segments think he can't make a decision in the public interest."[9] However, in 1988 the prophecy of *Time* was fulfilled when George Bush, an oil entrepreneur, was elected president of the United States. By the turn of the century, proven entrepreneurs like New York's Mayor Michael Bloomberg were seen as innovators who could bring a fresh new style of leadership to government.

Should Ethics Be Taught?

Just as the 1990s ushered in a new era of worldwide entrepreneurship, Andrew Stark asserts that the world of business ethics has redefined itself:

> Advocates of the new business ethics can be identified by their acceptance of two fundamental principles. While they agree with their colleagues that ethics and interest can conflict, they take that observation as the starting point, not the ending point, of an ethicist's analytical

---

[5] "Introduction to Contemporary Civilization in the West," *The Gospel of Wealth* (New York: Century, 1900), p. 620.
[6] W. E. Woodward, *A New American History* (Garden City, NY: Garden City Publishing, 1938), p. 704.
[7] Ibid., p. 622.
[8] "Time Essay: New Places to Look for Presidents," *Time,* December 15, 1975, p. 19.
[9] Ibid.

task.... Second, the new perspective reflects an awareness and acceptance of the messy work of mixed motives.[10]

The challenge facing this new group of business ethicists is to bridge the gap between the moral philosophers and the managers. The business ethicists talk of "moderation, pragmatism, minimalism"[11] in their attempt to "converse with real managers in a language relevant to the world they inhabit and the problems they face."[12] With this focus on the practical side of decision making, courses on ethics can be useful to entrepreneurs and all managers.

Ethics Can and Should Be Taught

In an article that examines the ancient tradition of moral education, the decline of moral instruction beginning in the 19th century, and the renaissance of interest in ethics in the 1960s, Derek Bok, former president of Harvard University, argues that ethics can and should be taught by educational institutions and that this teaching is both necessary and of value:

> Precisely because its community is so diverse, set in a society so divided and confused over its values, a university that pays little attention to moral development may find that many of its students grow bewildered, convinced that ethical dilemmas are simply matters of personal opinion beyond external judgment or careful analysis.
>
> Nothing could be more unfortunate or more unnecessary. Although moral issues sometimes lack convincing answers, that is often not the case. Besides, universities should be the last institutions to discourage belief in the value of reasoned argument and carefully considered evidence in analyzing even the hardest of human problems.[13]

John Shad, a former chairman of the New York Stock Exchange, gave more than $20 million to the Harvard Business School to help develop a way to include ethics in the MBA curriculum. Since the fall of 1988, first-year students at the Harvard Business School have been required to attend a three-week, nongraded ethics module called "Decision Making and Ethical Values." The cases discussed range from insider trading at Salomon Brothers to discrimination in employee promotions to locating a U.S. manufacturing unit in Mexico. Thomas R. Piper, associate dean, emphasizes that the role of the course is "not converting sinners . . . but we're taking young people who have a sense of integrity and trying to get

them to connect ethics with business decisions."[14] J. Gregory Dees, another ethics professor at Harvard, now at Duke University, stresses that the "primary objective of the course is to get people thinking about issues that are easy to avoid. . . . What we want people to leave DMEV with is a commitment to raising these issues in other settings, other courses, and on the job, with [an acceptable] comfort level in doing so."[15]

Since John Shad made his contribution, three second-year electives ("Moral Dilemmas of Management," "Managing Information in a Competitive Context," and "Profits, Markets, and Values") have been added to Harvard's ethics program. The Wharton School has a similar course required of first-year MBA students. "Leadership Skills" is a yearlong, graded course with a four-week ethics module. The Wharton faculty hope to introduce the core literature of business ethics and corporate responsibility, to expose students to discussions, and to stimulate the students to address these moral issues in their other courses. These two programs are part of a larger effort to incorporate ethics:

> Over 500 business-ethics courses are currently taught on American campuses; fully 90 percent of the nation's business schools now provide some kind of training in the area. There are more than 25 textbooks in the field and three academic journals dedicated to the topic. At least 16 business-ethics research centers are now in operation, and endowed chairs in business ethics have been established at Georgetown, Virginia, Minnesota, and a number of other prominent business schools.[16]

In addition, we are now seeing the emergence of numerous courses on socially responsible business and entrepreneurship, and on environmentally sustainable and responsible businesses.

The Entrepreneur's Competitive Edge: The Art of Self-Assessment

"It ain't what you don't know that hurts you.
It's what you know that ain't true!"

Mark Twain

As we saw in Chapters 2 and 9, one of the core principles of this book is the importance of self-assessment and self-awareness. We are more persuaded than ever that entrepreneurs who truly know themselves make the best decisions. This manifests itself in a number of

---

[10] A. Stark, "What's the Matter with Business Ethics?" *Harvard Business Review,* May–June 1993, p. 46.
[11] Ibid., p. 48.
[12] Ibid.
[13] D. Bok, "Is Dishonesty Good for Business?" *Business & Society Review,* Summer 1979, p. 50.
[14] J. A. Byrne, "Can Ethics Be Taught? Harvard Gives It the Old College Try," *BusinessWeek,* April 6, 1992, p. 34.
[15] C. Nayak, "Why Ethics DMEV Is under the Microscope," *The Harbus,* 1989.
[16] A. Stark, "What's the Matter with Business Ethics?" *Harvard Business Review,* May–June 1993, p. 38.

ways. They do a better job of knowing what they do and don't know—and thus who should be added to their team and brain trust. And their honesty and forthrightness about their own capabilities and short-comings instill trust and confidence; people see that they are not full of puffery and exaggeration. In addition, they must be acutely aware of the environment in which their decisions are made. Often in entrepreneurship, particularly in the launch and growth stages of a new venture, the environment is chaotic, unpredictable, and frequently unforgiving.

Despite this uncertainty, new venture decisions must be made whether or not the correct solution is evident. Plans must go forward. Serious mistakes, especially ethical ones, are rarely made during quiet and orderly times. Successful entrepreneurs make better decisions under pressure and in chaotic environments than those who fail. We believe that the odds of making the right choices under pressure will be greatly enhanced if you keep in mind that business decisions, even ethical ones, need to be made on a conscious level with your head, not your heart.

Take Time to Reflect   Forewarned is forearmed. To make good decisions you must identify and understand yourself and the scope and the effects of your own self-interest. Knowing your biases and weaknesses offers an opportunity for personal development or to proactively compensate for them. Failing to recognize these can result in poor choices.

The time to work on this is not when you face a tough decision in the midst of chaos, but in periods of calm reflection. During these times you can consider your stakeholders, your personal motivations, and the impact those can have on your decision making. Because your judgment will be less clouded prior to launch, the planning process for your new venture should include a good bit of introspection.

Recognize Self-Interest   Our perceptions are filtered by who we are: our experiences, our knowledge, our biases, our beliefs—all the things that make us unique. Our self-interest, which compels us to seek pleasure and benefit and avoid pain and loss, influences and colors our perceptions. When someone says, "You're kidding yourself," that ought to be a red flag that your self-interest may be clouding your perception of reality.

Henry Brooks Adams, a historian and author as well as the great-great-grandson of John Adams and the grandson of John Quincy Adams, summed up the

peril faced by a person who overwhelmingly pursues his or her own self-interest when he wrote, "Never esteem anything as of advantage to you that will make you break your word or lose your self-respect." The pursuit of self-interest without the realization of the pitfalls it presents can be costly and even dangerous. Here are some major influencers to consider:

Emotion: What you love, hate, or fear will influence your perception and therefore your decisions. The people whom you feel most strongly about can have a tremendous influence on your decisions. Like divorces, partnership breakups can become so emotionally charged with self-interest that decisions made have no relation to the best outcome for anyone involved.

Motivation: As we've noted in earlier chapters, contemplating a new venture involves an honest assessment of the motivating factors driving the decision. Entrepreneur and investor Khalil Tuzman, in his "Entrepreneur's Survival Kit," lists five individual motivators: to attain wealth, to achieve recognition or fame, to feel courageous, to be healthy, and to find contentment. If the motivation is to win at any cost, for example, fair play and ethics will have far less influence over your decisions than they should.

Stakeholders: Who will be affected by your decisions and how? Recognize that the closer they are to you, the more effect they will have on your decision making. If an entrepreneur's family welfare is at stake because she can't pay the mortgage, she may be tempted to pursue unethical solutions.

The Usefulness of Academic Ethics

The study of ethics does seem to make students more aware of the pervasiveness of ethical situations in business settings, bring perspective to ethical situations from a distance, and provide a framework for understanding ethical problems when they arise. Further, the study of ethics has been shown to affect, to some degree, both beliefs and behavior. For example, in a study of whether ethics courses affect student values, value changes in business school students who had taken a course in business ethics and those who did not were examined closely and were plotted across the multiple stages.[17]

The study used a sequence of stages, called the Kohlberg construct, developed by Kohlberg in 1967.[18] These stages are presented in Exhibit 10.1. In

---

[17] D. P. Boyd, "Enhancing Ethical Development by an Intervention Program," unpublished manuscript, Northeastern University, 1980.

[18] Lawrence Kohlberg was a professor at Harvard University. He became famous for his work there as a developmental psychologist and then moved to the field of moral education. His work was based on theories that human beings develop philosophically and psychologically in a progressive fashion. Kohlberg believed and demonstrated in several published studies that people progressed in their moral reasoning (i.e., in their bases for ethical behavior) through a series of six identifiable stages.

Copyright © The McGraw-Hill Companies, Inc.

EXHIBIT 10.1

Classification of Moral Judgment into Stages of Development

Stage	Orientation	Theme
1	Punishment and obedience	Morality of obedience
2	Instrumental relativism	Simple exchange
3	Interpersonal concordance	Reciprocal role taking
4	Law and order	Formal justice
5	Legitimate social contract	Procedural justice
6	Universal ethical principle	Individual conscience

Source: Adapted from Kohlberg (1967).

the Kohlberg construct, being moral in Stage 1 is synonymous with being obedient, and the motivation is to avoid condemnation. In Stage 2, the individual seeks advantage. Gain is the primary purpose, and interaction does not result in binding personal relationships. The orientation of Stage 3 is toward pleasing others and winning approval. Proper roles are defined by stereotyped images of majority behavior. Such reciprocity is confined to primary group relations. In Stage 4, cooperation is viewed in the context of society as a whole. External laws coordinate moral schemes, and the individual feels committed to the social order. We thus subscribe to formal punishment by police or the courts. In Stage 5, there is acknowledgment that reciprocity can be inequitable. New laws and social arrangements now may be invoked as corrective mechanisms. All citizens are assured of fundamental safety and equality. Cognitive structures at the Stage 6 level automatically reject credos and actions that the individual considers morally reprehensible, and the referent is a person's own moral framework, rather than stereotyped group behavior. Because most people endorse a law does not guarantee its moral validity. When confronting social dilemmas, the individual is guided by internal principles that may transcend the legal system. Although these convictions are personal, they are also universal because they have worth and utility apart from the individual espousing them. Kohlberg's final stage thus represents more than mere conformity with state, teacher, or institutional criteria. Rather, it indicates one's capacity for decision making and problem solving in the context of personal ethical standards. In the study, those who took a course in business ethics showed a progression up the ethical scale, while those who had not taken a course did not progress.

Foundations for Ethical Decision Making

Some may find it surprising to learn that there is no perfect approach to dealing with ethically charged situations. In fact, people who subscribe to a "one best" approach can find themselves making decisions that, after the fact, others view as unethical. Similarly, lacking an understanding of the different approaches may lead to missteps because the decision maker fails to recognize the ethical implications of a particular situation.

When considering what to do in a situation with ethical overtones, it is useful to be familiar with different approaches to ethics. These varied approaches become ethical screens—similar to the opportunity screens presented in Chapter 6. Taking a multifaceted approach can prevent someone from unknowingly making an ethical mistake. We will briefly consider three widely used approaches.

Aristotle, the Greek philosopher, provided one of the oldest approaches to ethics. To him it seemed that the aim of each person should be to perfect his or her inherent human nature, and if successful, become a person of virtue. The question then becomes, "What is virtuous, and how does one learn what a virtuous person would do in a given situation?" By striving to be virtuous, and by emulating what people who are widely considered to be virtuous do in similar situations, we can, over time, develop habits of virtue. In modern terms, this is akin to choosing to observe and emulate exemplary role models.

Two issues arising from this approach can lead an entrepreneur to make poor decisions. The first is choosing the wrong person to emulate. An entrepreneur imitating Jeff Skilling, the once-applauded Enron CEO now serving a 25-year prison sentence for fraud and abuse of his corporate power, could act in ways that would be widely viewed as unethical. The second is that neither the actions actually taken nor the consequences of the actions are directly addressed—only that the "court of opinion" holds the actions to have been virtuous.

A second approach to ethics focuses on the consequences or outcomes of actions. This approach is called utilitarianism, and its most often cited proponent is John Stewart Mill, a 19th-century English philosopher. It holds that the ethical person will always choose actions that will provide for the greatest good (or least bad) for the greatest number of people. When considering what action to take, an ethical entrepreneur acting from a utilitarian perspective would mentally calculate the impact of the action on each stakeholder. Therefore, it is not the action that is being judged as ethical or unethical, but rather the collective impact of that action. A familiar way of expressing this is the saying that "the ends (consequences) justify the means (actions taken)."

This is probably one of the most widely used approaches in business and is the only system many people consider. It is also known as Machiavellianism after the author of the famous book *The Prince*. The challenge with this approach is that you can hit a wall when conflicts and your own self-interest collide. For example, what is the ethical decision in this situation. A person comes to your door armed with a gun. He asks for your spouse and announces that he has come to kill that person. In all civilized societies, it would be illegal, immoral, and unethical for you to kill this person outside your home with no provocation other than his words. So what do you do?

A number of issues can make the utilitarian approach difficult to adhere to or can lead entrepreneurs to take actions that may be considered unethical. First, it permits decisions that may hurt some stakeholders, as long as the majority benefits from the action. Second, a narrow view of who the stakeholders are may lead to unethical decisions because we may fail to consider a stakeholder such as the environment. Third, the proximity of stakeholders, or the degree to which they demand attention, may cause the decision maker to ignore (or forget) them. Fourth, there is a thin line between seeking the greatest good for the greatest number and seeking the greatest good for yourself. Self-interest can justify many deplorable actions because they maximize personal outcomes to the exclusion of all else. The last important issue stems from the fact that people are judged as ethical or unethical based on the actions they take, not by how they calculate the utility of the outcomes. We must have a means of considering the action apart from the outcomes. That leads into our third approach, deontology.

Deontology means duty—one's duty to act. According to Immanuel Kant, the 18th-century German philosopher, deontology focuses on the precepts that should determine action. This approach is pursued without concern for the outcomes of actions, but according to whether the action is something that an ethical person would do. Actions, then, are undertaken because they are right in themselves, whether or not the outcomes benefit or harm the person taking the actions. People therefore should act in ways that one would hope would become the universal laws of society. In situations where one's duty to society conflicts with one's self-interest, one must act in accordance with the duty to society regardless of the consequences. For example, if lying is not what you would want to have as a universal law in society, then you should never lie, even if lying would benefit you personally or benefit your stakeholders.

There are difficulties with blind adherence to a deontological viewpoint. First, it is difficult for a person to take actions that violate self-interest— even when the person taking the action is not an egoist and is trying to truly do the greatest good for the greatest number. Second, unlike the virtue approach, the court of public opinion is not considered; one takes the action based on principle, not according to what others think. Third, deontology does not deal well with conflicts between actions that are each considered ethical. For example, consider the quandary of an entrepreneur caught between the desire to be with her ailing parents and the desire to go to Africa and build a venture that could bring potable water to thousands of villages.

Applying the Foundations

So how can we use these approaches? We suggest that you use them as decision-making screens to view the outcome and impact of any action you might take. A good place to start would be the most widely used approach, utilitarianism. Carefully enumerate the stakeholders, being sure to include everyone, not just the convenient ones or the ones making the most noise. When you have decided on an action, apply the Aristotelian approach by asking, "What would a really ethical entrepreneur in this situation do?" You might ask people in your network and brain trust to tell you what they have done in similar situations. Finally, look at the action you are taking alone—separate from the consequences. Is this action pure? That is, is it something that you would be proud to have as the headline your mother reads when she Googles you?

We also urge you to consider one of Ewing Marion Kauffman's key principles: Treat other people as you would want to be treated. This simple but powerful addition to your decision making can be a valuable aid. How many people do you know who would want to be cheated, lied to, deceived, or stolen from?

Will using these screens guarantee an ethical decision? Certainly not! But considering different approaches to the same issue will help prevent ethical myopia—a narrowly defined ethical perspective that can lead to trouble. Finally, consider how a given stakeholder might accuse you of taking an unethical action. Remember: Entrepreneurship involves risk and making tough calls—often ethically charged ones—on the fly. It is always best to approach those challenges knowingly, with your ethical eyes wide open.

Integrity as Governing Ethic

Harvard Business School Professor Lynn Paine distinguishes among avoiding legal sanctions, compliance, and the more robust standard of integrity:

From the perspective of integrity, the task of ethics management is to define and give life to an organization's

EXHIBIT 10.2

Ethical Decisions Matrix

	Possible Consequences of Each Alternative on Stakeholders				
Stakeholders	Decision Alternative 1	Decision Alternative 2	Decision Alternative 3	Decision Alternative 4	Decision Alternative 5
1.					
2.					
3.					
4.					
5.					
6.					
7.					
8.					

Source: J. L. Livingstone et al., *Framework for Ethical Decision Making,* Babson College, 2003.

guiding values, to create an environment that supports ethically sound behavior, and to instill a sense of shared accountability among employees.[19]

Paine goes on to characterize the hallmarks of an effective integrity strategy (see Exhibit 10.2) and the strategies for ethics management (see Exhibit 10.3). Clearly the call for ethical strategies and practices, first made in our original 1977 edition—which was the first text to do so—is being heard. That is good news for our society, our economy, and you!

EXHIBIT 10.3

Strategies for Ethics Management

Characteristics of Compliance Strategy

Ethos	Conformity with externally imposed standards
Objective	Prevent criminal misconduct
Leadership	Lawyer driven
Methods	Education, reduced discretion, auditing and controls, penalties
Behavioral Assumptions	Autonomous beings guided by material self-interest

Characteristics of Integrity Strategy

Ethos	Self-governance according to chosen standards
Objective	Stable responsible conduct
Leadership	Management driven with aid of lawyers, HR, others
Methods	Education, leadership, accountability, organizational systems and decision processes, auditing and controls, penalties
Behavioral Assumptions	Social beings guided by material self-interest, values, ideals, peers

Implementation of Compliance Strategy

Standards	Criminal and regulatory law
Staffing	Lawyers
Activities	Develop compliance standards, train, and communicate
Education	Compliance standards and system

Implementation of Integrity Strategy

Standards	Company values and aspirations, social obligations, including law
Staffing	Executives and managers with lawyers, others
Activities	Lead development of company values and standards
	Train and communicate
	Integrate into company systems
	Provide guidance and consultation
	Assess values performance
	Identify and resolve problems
	Oversee compliance activities
Education	Decision making and values
	Compliance standards and system

Source: Reprinted by permission of *Harvard Business Review.* From "Managing for Organizational Integrity," by L. S. Paine, March–April 1994, p. 113. Copyright ©1994 by the Harvard Business School Publishing Corporation; all rights reserved.

[19] L. S. Paine, "Managing for Organizational Integrity," *Harvard Business Review,* March–April 1994, pp. 105–17.

Entrepreneurs' Perspectives

Most entrepreneurs also believe ethics should be taught. In the research project previously mentioned, entrepreneurs and chief executive officers attending the Owner/President Management (OPM) program at the Harvard Business School were asked, Is there a role for ethics in business education for entrepreneurs? Of those responding, 72 percent said ethics can and should be taught as part of the curriculum. (Only 20 percent said it should not, and two respondents were not sure.)

The most prominently cited reason for including ethics was that ethical behavior is at the core of long-term business success because it provides the glue that binds enduring successful business and personal relationships together. In addition, the responses reflected a serious and thoughtful awareness of the fragile but vital role of ethics in entrepreneurial attainment and of the long-term consequences of ethical behavior for a business. Typical comments were these:

- If the free enterprise system is to survive, the business schools better start paying attention to teaching ethics. They should know that business is built on trust, which depends on honesty and sincerity. In a small company, lack of integrity is quickly exposed.

- If our society is going to move forward, it won't be based on how much money is accumulated in any one person or group. Our society will move forward when all people are treated fairly—that's my simple definition of ethics. I know of several managers, presidents, and the like with whom you would not want to get between them and their wallets or ambitions.

- In my experience the business world is by and large the most ethical and law-abiding part of our society.

- Ethics should be addressed, considered, and thoroughly examined; it should be an inherent part of each class and course . . .; instead of crusading with ethics, it is much more effective to make high ethics an inherent part of business—and it is.

However, these views were not universally held. One entrepreneur who helped to found a large company with international operations warned, "For God's sake, don't forget that 90 percent of the businessman's efforts consist of just plain hard work."

There is also some cynicism. The 40-year-old head of a real estate and construction firm in the Northeast with 300 employees and $75 million in annual sales said, "There is so much hypocrisy in today's world that even totally ethical behavior is questioned since many people think it is some new negotiating technique."

It would be unfortunate if the entrepreneur did not realize his or her potential for combining action with ethical purpose because of the suspicion that the two are unrelated or inimical. There is no reason they need be considered generically opposed. Nevertheless, in analyzing ethics, the individual can expect no substitute for his or her own effort and intelligence.

The Fog of War and Entrepreneurship: A Unique Context

The environment around a new venture is often chaotic. Lessons can be learned from an even more chaotic environment: combat. There is a concept called "the fog of war" that goes back to the 19th century, when Prussian general Carl von Clausewitz wrote,

> War is the realm of uncertainty; three-quarters of the factors on which action is based are wrapped in a fog of greater or lesser uncertainty.

When bullets are flying and lives are at stake, critical decisions must be made on the fly—without the benefit of a perfect understanding of the whole picture. In the same way, the fog of the start-up battle that a typical entrepreneur faces could include intense pressures from outside influences like the following:

- Your spouse says you're not home enough.
- Your Aunt Tillie, your father, and your mother-in-law have each put in $50,000 . . . which is gone.
- Everything takes too long and costs too much.
- Your business isn't working as it was supposed to.
- You are doing nothing but damage control.
- You have slowed down payments to creditors, who are now screaming and making threats.
- You have maxed out your refinanced line of credit and your credit cards, and you have discounted receivables and inventories to get the cash in sooner. Still, you figure you have just 18 business days of cash left.
- Investors will put in money, but they want two more seats on the board and a much larger percentage of ownership.
- The bank reminds you that you and your spouse have signed personal guarantees.
- The 80-ton dinosaur in your industry just moved into your market.
- The malcontent troublemaker you fired is suing you.

Now, in the midst of these sorts of pressures, make a decision that might have serious financial and ethical consequences that could follow you the rest of your life!

Action under Pressure

An entrepreneur will have to act on issues under pressure of time and when struggling for survival. In addition, the entrepreneur will most likely decide ethical questions that involve obligations on many fronts—to customers, employees, stockholders, family, partners, self, or a combination of these. As you will see in the ethically charged situations presented at the end of the chapter, walking the tightrope and balancing common sense with an ethical framework can be precarious.

To cope with the inevitable conflicts, an entrepreneur should develop an awareness of his or her own explicit and implicit ethical beliefs, those of his or her team and investors, and those of the milieu within which the company competes for survival. As the successful entrepreneurs quoted earlier believe, in the long run, succumbing to the temptations of situational ethics will, in all likelihood, result in a tumble into the quicksand, not a safety net—just ask Steve Madden or executives at Enron, Tyco, and Arthur Anderson.

An appreciation of this state of affairs is succinctly stated by Fred T. Allen, chairman and president of Pitney-Bowes:

> As businessmen we must learn to weigh short-term interests against long-term possibilities. We must learn to sacrifice what is immediate, what is expedient, if the moral price is too high. What we stand to gain is precious little compared to what we can ultimately lose.[20]

Advice and Tips from the Trenches

Many of the lessons learned in the military and on the battlefield can be instructive to entrepreneurs struggling with the chaos and uncertainties that go with the territory. Consider the following.

Experience Is Critical   Military troops are not sent into combat on the day they enlist. They receive relevant training and engage in stressful and chaotic simulations that are as close as possible to the real

EXHIBIT 10.4

Selected Ethical Dilemmas of Entrepreneurial Management

Dilemma: Elements	Issues That May Arise
Promoter:	What does honesty mean when promoting an innovation?
Entrepreneurial euphoria	Does it require complete disclosure of the risks and uncertainties?
Impression management	Does it require a dispassionate analysis of the situation, with equal time given to the downside as well as the upside?
Pragmatic versus moral considerations	What sorts of influence tactics cross the line from encouragement and inducement to manipulation and coercion?
Relationship:	Tension between perceived obligations and moral expectations.
Conflicts of interest and roles	Changes in roles and relationships: pre- versus post-venture status.
Transactional ethics	Decisions based on affiliative concerns rather than on task-based concerns.
Guerrilla tactics	Transition from a trust-based work environment to one that is more controlled.
Innovator:	Side effects and negative externalities force a social reconsideration of norms and values.
"Frankenstein's problem"	Heightened concern about the future impact of unknown harms.
New types of ethical problems	Who is responsible for the assessment of risk? Inventor? Government? Market?
Ethic of change	Breaking down traditions and creating new models.
Other dilemmas:	Is there a fair way to divide profits when they are the result of cooperative efforts?
Finders–keepers ethic	Should the entrepreneur take all the gains that are not explicitly contracted away?
Conflict between personal values and business goals	Managing an intimate connection between personal choices and professional decisions.
Unsavory business practices	Coping with ethical pressures with creative solutions and integrity.
	Seeking industry recognition while not giving in to peer pressure to conform.

Source: Adapted from J. G. Dees and J. A. Starr, "Entrepreneurship through an Ethical Lens," in *The State of the Art of Entrepreneurship*, ed. D. L. Sexton and J. D. Kasarda (Boston: PWS-Kent, 1992), p. 96.

[20] "Letter to Editor," *The Wall Street Journal*, October 17, 1975.

thing. In a new venture, an entrepreneur who has done it before has experience to help with chaos. In areas where they lack direct experience, entrepreneurs can compensate with a key hire, team member, mentor, consultant, board member, or professional.

Have a Plan B   Although designing "what if" scenarios is most often associated with the quantitative side of running a proactive business (costs, pricing, margins, and the like), thinking through contingency plans, particularly during the launch and growth stages, is an excellent way to avoid rash or ethically questionable decisions in the heat of a challenge. One technique to facilitate scenario dialog and planning is to have a brown-bag lunch with your partners and pose some tough ethical dilemmas you may face; what would each of you do?

Develop and Use Objective Standards
When faced with decisions on the fly—especially ones involving ethical issues—it can be helpful to have a clear and objective means to assess the situation. For example, at Everon IT, a remote IT services venture in based in Boston, critical metrics for incoming, outgoing, and ongoing calls are projected large on the facing wall of the service area. Other walls feature motivational posters, challenge goals, employee accolades, and descriptions of goal-related rewards ranging from dinners for all to lavish vacation retreats. With everyone pulling together to meet and beat well-defined milestones, the office is charged with a sense of mission and purpose.

Find a Pessimist You Can Trust   Every lead entrepreneur should have a trusted, no-nonsense advisor in the brain trust who can provide brutally honest assessments when things seem to be off base. When these cautious, somewhat pessimistic advisors express their approval of a given decision or strategy, that validation can be a real confidence booster.

Don't Forget the Mirror and Those Internet Headlines   Looking in the mirror can be a powerful, challenging exercise. You've just read the morning headlines all over the Internet that describe in intimate detail all of your actions and behaviors concerning a recent decision that—most unexpectedly—became highly visible and public. Is this the person you want to be known as? Is this a person the people you love and respect the most would admire and support? Is this a person you want your best friends and your family to know about? If you aren't fully comfortable with your answers to these questions and what you see in the mirror as a result of an ethical decision you have to make, then you don't have an acceptable answer yet. Don't give up—but clean it up!

Thorny Issues for Entrepreneurs

Although the majority of entrepreneurs take ethics seriously, researchers in this area are still responding to David McClelland's call for inquiry: "We do not know at the present time what makes an entrepreneur more or less ethical in his dealings, but obviously there are few problems of greater importance for future research."[21] One article outlined the topics for research (see Exhibit 10.4). Clearly an opportunity for further research still exists.

Different Views

Different reactions to what is ethical may explain why some aspects of venture creation go wrong, both during start-up and in the heat of the battle, for no apparent reason. Innumerable examples can be cited to illustrate that broken partnerships often can be traced to apparent differences in the personal ethics among the members of a management team. So too with investors. While the experienced venture capital investor seeks entrepreneurs with a reputation for integrity, honesty, and ethical behavior, the definition is necessarily subjective and depends in part on the beliefs of the investor and in part on the prevailing ethical climate in the industry sector in which the venture is involved.

Problems of Law

For entrepreneurs, situations where one law directly conflicts with another are increasingly frequent. For example, a small-business investment company in New York City got in serious financial trouble. The Small Business Administration stated the company should begin to liquidate its investments because it would otherwise be in defiance of its agreement with the SBA. However, the Securities and Exchange Commission stated that this liquidation would constitute unfair treatment of stockholders, due to resulting imbalance in their portfolios. After a year and a half of agonizing negotiation, the company was able to satisfy all the parties, but compromises had to be made on both sides.

Another example of conflicting legal demands involves conflicts between procedures of the civil service commission code and the Fair Employment Practice Acts (dating from FDR). The code states that hiring will include adherence to certain standards, a principle that was introduced in the 20th century to curb the patronage abuses in public service. Recently, however, the problem of encouraging and aiding minorities has led to the Civil Service Commission Fair Employment Practice Acts, which require the same public agencies that are guided by CSC standards to hire without prejudice, and without the requirement that a given test

---

[21] D. McClelland, *Achieving Society* (New York: Van Nostrand, 1961), p. 331.

shall serve as the criterion of selection. Both these laws are based on valid ethical intent, but the resolution of such conflicts is no simple matter.

Further, unlike the international laws governing commercial airline transportation, there is no international code of business ethics. When doing business abroad, entrepreneurs may find that those with whom they do business have little in common with them—no common language, no common historical context for conducting business, and no common set of ethical beliefs about right and wrong and everything in between. For example, in the United States, bribing a high official to obtain a favor is considered both ethically and legally unacceptable; in parts of the Middle East, it is the only way to get things done. What we see as a bribe, those in parts of the Middle East see as a tip, like what you might give the headwaiter at a fancy restaurant in New York for a good table.

"When in Rome" is one approach to this problem. Consulting a lawyer with expertise in international business before doing anything is another. Assuming that the object of an entrepreneur's international business venture is to make money, he or she needs to figure out some way that is legally tolerable under the laws that do apply and that is ethically tolerable personally.

Examples of the Ends-and-Means Issue

A central question in any ethical discussion concerns the extent to which a noble end may justify ignoble means—or whether using unethical means for assumed ethical ends may subvert the aim in some way. As an example of a noble end, consider the case of a university agricultural extension service whose goal was to help small farmers increase their crop productivity. The end was economically constructive and profit oriented only in the sense that the farmers might prosper from better crop yields. However, to continue being funded, the extension service was required to predict the annual increases in crop yield it could achieve—estimates it could not provide at the required level of specificity. Further, unless it could show substantial increases in crop yields, its funding might be heavily reduced. In this case, the extension service decided, if need be, to fudge the figures because it was felt that even though the presentation of overly optimistic predictions was unethical, the objectives of those running the organization were highly ethical and even the unethical aspects could be condoned within the context of the inability of the various groups involved to speak each other's language clearly. The funding source finally backed down in its demand, ameliorating the immediate problem. But if it had not, the danger existed that the individuals in this organization, altruistic though their intentions were, would begin to think that falsification was the norm

and would forget that actions that run contrary to ethical feelings gradually build a debilitating cynicism.

Another example is given in the case of a merger of a small rental service business with a midsize conglomerate, where a law's intent was in direct opposition to what would occur if the law was literally enforced. In this case, a partner in the rental firm became involved in a severe automobile accident and suffered multiple injuries shortly before the merger and was seemingly unable to return to work. The partner also knew that the outlook for his health in the immediate future was unpredictable. For the sake of his family, he was eager to seek some of the stock acquired in the merger and make a large portion of his assets liquid. However, federal law does not allow quick profit taking from mergers and therefore did not allow such a sale. The partner consulted the president and officers of the larger company, and they acquiesced in his plans to sell portions of his stock and stated their conviction that no adverse effect on the stock would result. Still unsure, the partner then checked with his lawyer and found that the federal law in question had almost never been prosecuted. Having ascertained the risk and having probed the rationale of the law as it applied to his case, the partner sold some of the stock acquired in the merger to provide security for his family in the possible event of his incapacitation or death. Although he subsequently recovered completely, this could not have been foreseen.

In this instance, the partner decided that a consideration of the intrinsic purpose of the law allowed him to act as he did. In addition, he made as thorough a check as possible of the risks involved in his action. He was not satisfied with the decision he made, but he believed it was the best he could do at the time. We can see in this example the enormous ethical tugs-of-war that go with the territory of entrepreneurship.

An Example of Integrity

The complicated nature of entrepreneurial decisions also is illustrated in the following example. At age 27, an entrepreneur joined a new computer software firm with sales of $1.5 million as vice president of international marketing of a new division. His principal goal was to establish profitable distribution for the company's products in the major industrialized nations. Stock incentives and a highly leveraged bonus plan placed clear emphasis on profitability rather than on volume. In one European country, the choice of distributors was narrowed to 1 from a field of more than 20. The potential distributor was a top firm, with an excellent track record and management, and the chemistry was right. In fact, the distributor was so eager to do business with the entrepreneur's company that it was willing to accept a 10 percent commission rather than the normal 15 percent royalty. The other terms of the deal were acceptable to both parties. In this actual case, the young vice president decided to give the distributor the full 15 percent commission, even though it would have settled for less. This approach was apparently quite successful because, in five years, this international division grew from zero to $18 million in very profitable sales, and a large firm acquired the venture for $80 million. In describing his reasoning, the entrepreneur said his main goal

was to create a sense of long-term integrity. He said further,

I knew what it would take for them to succeed in gaining the kind of market penetration we were after. I also knew that the economics of their business definitely needed the larger margins from the 15 percent, rather than the smaller royalty. So I figured that if I offered them the full royalty, they would realize I was on their side, and that would create such goodwill that when we

Code of Ethical Responsibility

Ethical Performance: Everyone's Responsibility

As an employee or independent contractor of The MENTOR Network, you have an obligation to be honest in all of your dealings with the individuals we serve, their families, fellow employees, independent contractors, vendors, and third parties. You must know and comply with applicable laws, regulations, licensing requirements, contractual obligations, and all company policies and procedures. Maintaining ethical standards is everyone's responsibility. If you know of a problem, you cannot remain silent. Step forward and be part of the solution.

For those employees and independent contractors involved in the coordination of services for individuals in care, the company expects you to

- Conduct yourself according to professional and ethical standards.
- Take responsibility for identifying, developing, and fully utilizing knowledge and abilities for professional practice.
- Obtain training/education and supervision to assure competent services.
- Not misrepresent professional qualifications, education, experience, or affiliations, and maintain the credentials required in order to deliver the type and intensity of services provided.
- Be aware of your own values and their implications for practice.
- Solicit collaborative participation by professionals, the individuals served, and family and community members to share responsibility for consumer outcomes.
- Work to increase public awareness and education of the human service industry.
- Advocate for adequate resources.
- Work to ensure the efficiency and effectiveness of services provided.
- Maintain boundaries between professional and personal relationships with individuals served.
- Report ethical violations to appropriate parties.

Ethical Performance: Leadership/Supervisory Responsibility

Leadership requires setting a personal example of high ethical standards in the performance of your job. Managers set the tone for the company. Managers are responsible for making sure that all employees, independent contractors, and vendors receive a copy of the code and assisting them in applying the code's ethical standards.

Conclusion

The company depends on everyone we work with to safeguard our standards and ethics. Although ethical requirements are sometimes unclear, the following questions will provide a good guideline for those in doubt about their conduct:

- Will my actions be ethical in every respect?
- Will my actions fully comply with the law and company standards?
- Will my actions be questioned by supervisors, associates, family, or the general public?
- How would I feel if my actions were reported in the newspaper?
- How would I feel if another employee, contractor, customer, or vendor acted in the same way?
- Will my actions have the appearance of impropriety?

Source: The MENTOR Network (www.TheMentorNetwork.com). Founded in 1980, The MENTOR Network is a national network of local human services providers offering an array of quality, community-based services to adults and children with developmental disabilities or acquired brain injury; to children and adolescents with emotional, behavioral, and medically complex challenges; and to elders in need of home care.

did have some serious problems down the road—and you always have them—then we would be able to work together to solve them. And that's exactly what happened. If I had exploited their eagerness to be our distributor, then it only would have come back to haunt me later on.

Ethics Exercise Revisited

The following statements are often made, even by practicing entrepreneurs: How can we think about ethics when we haven't enough time even to think about running our venture? Entrepreneurs are doers, not thinkers—and ethics is too abstract a concept to have any bearing on business realities. When you're struggling to survive, you're not worried about the means you use—you're fighting for one thing: survival.

However, the contemplation of ethical behavior is not unlike poetry—emotion recollected in tranquility. This chapter is intended to provide one such tranquil opportunity.

Through the decisions actually made, or not made, an individual could become more aware of his or her own value system and how making ethical decisions can be affected by the climate in which these decisions are made. We urge you to fully engage in the Ethical Decisions exercise. These three vignettes pose practical and not infrequent ethical dilemmas based on actual occurrences. One excellent way to do this is to take two or three friends to lunch—particularly those you imagine might make excellent venture partners. Over lunch, discuss in detail each of the vignettes—what you would and should do. Try to apply the ideas from the chapter. At the end, see if you can reach conclusions about what you have learned and what you plan to do differently.

Exercise 1

Ethics

In this exercise, decisions will be made in ethically ambiguous situations and then analyzed. As in the real world, all the background information on each situation will not be available, and assumptions will need to be made.

It is recommended that the exercise be completed before reading the following material, and then revisited after you have completed the chapter.

Name:

Date:

Part I

STEP 1
Make decisions in the following situations.

You will not have all the background information about each situation; instead you should make whatever assumptions you feel you would make if you were actually confronted with the decision choices described. Select the decision choice that most closely represents the decision you feel you would make personally. You should choose decision choices even though you can envision other creative solutions that were not included in the exercise.

Situation 1. You are taking a very difficult chemistry course, which you must pass to maintain your scholarship and to avoid damaging your application for graduate school. Chemistry is not your strong suit, and because of a just-below-failing average in the course, you must receive a grade of 90 or better on the final exam, which is two days away. A janitor who is aware of your plight informs you that he found the master copy of the chemistry final in a trash barrel and saved it. He will make it available to you for a price, which is high but which you could afford. What would you do?

_____ (a) I would tell the janitor thanks, but no thanks.

_____ (b) I would report the janitor to the proper officials.

_____ (c) I would buy the exam and keep it to myself.

_____ (d) I would not buy the exam myself, but I would let some of my friends, who are also flunking the course, know that it is available.

Situation 2. You have been working on some complex analytical data for two days now. It seems that each time you think you have them completed, your boss shows up with a new assumption or another what-if question. If you only had a copy of a new software program for your personal computer, you could plug in the new assumptions and revise the estimates with ease. Then a colleague offers to let you make a copy of some software that is copyrighted. What would you do?

_____ (a) I would readily accept my friend's generous offer and make a copy of the software.

_____ (b) I would decline to copy it and plug away manually on the numbers.

_____ (c) I would decide to go buy a copy of the software myself for $300 and hope I would be reimbursed by the company in a month or two.

_____ (d) I would request another extension on an already overdue project date.

Situation 3. Your small manufacturing company is in serious financial difficulty. A large order of your products is ready to be delivered to a key customer, when you discover that the product is simply not right. It will not meet all performance specifications, will cause problems for your customer, and will require rework in the field; but this, you know, will not become evident until after the customer has received and paid for the order. If you do not ship the order and receive the payment as expected, your business may be forced into bankruptcy. And if you delay the shipment or inform the customer of these problems, you may lose the order and also go bankrupt. What would you do?

_____ (a) I would not ship the order and place my firm in voluntary bankruptcy.

_____ (b) I would inform the customer and declare voluntary bankruptcy.

_____ (c) I would ship the order and inform the customer after I received payment.

_____ (d) I would ship the order and not inform the customer.

Situation 4. You are the cofounder and president of a new venture, manufacturing products for the recreational market. Five months after launching the business, one of your suppliers informs you it can no longer supply you with a critical raw material because you are not a large-quantity user. Without the raw material your business cannot continue. What would you do?

_____ (a) I would grossly overstate my requirements to another supplier to make the supplier think I am a much larger potential customer in order to secure the raw material from that supplier, even though this would mean the supplier will no longer be able to supply another, noncompeting small manufacturer who may thus be forced out of business.

_____ (b) I would steal raw material from another firm (noncompeting) where I am aware of a sizable stockpile.

_____ (c) I would pay off the supplier because I have reason to believe that the supplier could be persuaded to meet my needs with a sizable under-the-table payoff that my company could afford.

_____ *(d)* I would declare voluntary bankruptcy.

Situation 5. You are on a marketing trip for your new venture, calling on the purchasing agent of a major prospective client. Your company is manufacturing an electronic system that you hope the purchasing agent will buy. During your conversation, you notice on the cluttered desk of the purchasing agent several copies of a cost proposal for a system from one of your direct competitors. This purchasing agent has previously reported mislaying several of your own company's proposals and has asked for addi-

tional copies. The purchasing agent leaves the room momentarily to get you a cup of coffee, leaving you alone with your competitor's proposals less than an arm's length away. What would you do?

_____ *(a)* I would do nothing but await the man's return.

_____ *(b)* I would sneak a quick peek at the proposal, looking for bottom-line numbers.

_____ *(c)* I would put the copy of the proposal in my briefcase.

_____ *(d)* I would wait until the man returns and ask his permission to see the copy.

Part II

STEP 1

Based on the criteria you used, place your answers to each of the situations just described along the continuum of behavior shown here:

	Duty	Contractual	Utilitarian	Situational
Situation 1				
Situation 2				
Situation 3				
Situation 4				
Situation 5				

STEP 2

After separating into teams of five to six people, record the answers made by each individual member of your team on the form here. Record the answers of each team member in each box and the team's solution in the column on the far right:

Member Name:						Team Answer
Situation 1						
Situation 2						
Situation 3						
Situation 4						
Situation 5						

STEP 3

Reach a consensus decision in each situation (if possible) and record the consensus that your team has reached in the previous chart. Allow 20 to 30 minutes.

STEP 4

Report to the entire group your team's conclusions and discuss with them how the consensus, if any, was reached. The discussion should focus on the following questions:

- Was a consensus reached by the group?

- Was this consensus difficult or easy to achieve? Why?

- What kinds of ethical issues emerged?

- How were conflicts, if any, resolved? Or were they left unresolved?

- What creative solutions did you find to solve the difficult problems without compromising your integrity?

STEP 5

Discuss with the group the following issues:

- What role do ethical issues play? How important are they in the formation of a new venture management team?

- What role do ethical issues play and how important are they in obtaining venture capital? That is, how do investors feel about ethics and how important are they to them?

- What feelings bother participants most about the discussion and consensus reached? For example, if a participant believes that his or her own conduct was considered ethically less than perfect, does he or she feel a loss of self-respect or a sense of inferiority? Does he or she fear others' judgment, and so on?

- What does it mean to do the right thing?

STEP 6

Define each group member's general ethical position and note whether his or her ethical position is similar to or different from yours:

Member	Position	Different/Similar

STEP 7

Decide whom you would and would not want as business partners based on their ethical positions:

Would Want	Would Not Want

Ethical Decisions—What Would You Do?

Here are three interesting real-life ethical decision situations for your consideration.

Rim Job

Jeremy, a successful entrepreneur in the automotive industry, is a certified car fanatic who is passionate about having the latest, hottest look for his street rod. A line of new wheel rims is all the rage, and after checking the prices ($1,500 each), he decides to contact the manufacturer directly and see if he can make a better deal. He is told that they are sold only through speed shops and custom shops, and that his area does not have a sales representative. If he would agree to become a representative and get $10,000 worth of wholesale orders, the manufacturer would sell him a set of the rims at cost, in addition to paying him his commission. Jeremy agrees. Now he knows how he'll get his new rims.

First Jeremy goes to the biggest and best speed shop nearby and asks for the rims by name. The owner says he has never heard of them. Jeremy, after telling the owner that they are really a popular product and that he is the sales rep, leaves some literature and says he will call again. Meanwhile he hires four male students from a local college to each go into the shop once in the next two weeks and to ask for the rims by name. They are to indicate that they would buy them if they were available. For this he pays each student $100. He then returns after three weeks, and the owner reports that the rims must be as hot as Jeremy says—kids have been asking for them. He orders $15,000 worth of rims to be delivered over six months. Jeremy is able to buy a set of rims from the manufacturer for $335 each and receives a $380 sales commission on the total sale. The speed shop owner sells $30,000 worth of the rims and reorders after four months. Jeremy remains the sales representative collecting commissions, but he does not actively promote the rims.

Were Jeremy's actions ethical? Why or why not? What should he have done?

Empty Suits

Fred was excited to make his pitch to some angel investors; but he felt a bit uneasy because although he'd used the terms *team* and *we* throughout his business plan, he was the only one involved in his venture. He had not yet been able to attract any members to his team, but he had had several conversations with prospects. His personal contact in the angel group told him that his venture was likely to be funded, but there would be considerable focus on his team; a lot was riding on the meeting. For the presentation to the group he had four of his best friends, not at all connected to the business, dress in their best business suits, accompany him to the presentation, take seats in the back of the room, and say nothing. He hoped to make the impression that he had a team. He did a great job in the meeting, and his "team" filed out after him.

Was Fred being ethical? Why or why not? How should he have handled the situation?

A Moving Disclosure

Susan has been wrestling with moving her patio furniture manufacturing plant to Georgia from upstate Michigan, where her mother and father founded the company 58 years ago. Everything about her business will be easier there: closer to her markets, lower labor costs, lower raw materials costs, lower shipping costs, no problems with weather, and access to a labor pool that better fits her business. She finally makes the decision to move, but the site she has chosen will not be available for six months. Even though her company is a public company (she owns 35 percent) and her board is pushing her to maintain high production levels in Michigan as long as possible, she decides that in deference to her parents and their legacy in the community, she must tell her employees. Four days after signing the lease for the new site in Georgia, she holds a meeting on the shop floor and tells her employees. That afternoon she holds a press conference.

Was Susan ethical? Why or why not?

What are the implications and lessons from your discussion of the three cases? What role do ethical issues play in forming a team, selecting advisors and investors, and other entrepreneurial activities?

Chapter Summary

- The vast majority of CEOs, investors, and entrepreneurs believe that a high ethical standard is the single most important factor in long-term success.
- Historically, ethical stereotypes of businesspeople ranged widely, and today the old perceptions have given way to a more aware and accepting notion of the messy work of ethical decisions.
- Ethical issues and discussion are now a part of curricula at many of the top business school programs in the United States and abroad.

- Entrepreneurs can rarely, if ever, finish a day without facing at least one or two ethical issues.
- To make effective and ethical decisions you must understand yourself and be able to identify the scope and effects of your self-interest.
- Numerous ethical dilemmas challenge entrepreneurs at the most crucial moments of survival, like a precarious walk on a tightrope.

Study Questions

1. What conclusions and insights emerged from the ethics exercise?
2. Why have ethical stereotypes emerged, and how have they changed?
3. Why is ethics so important to entrepreneurial and other success?
4. Why do many entrepreneurs and CEOs believe ethics can and should be taught?

5. What are the most thorny ethical dilemmas that entrepreneurs face, and why?
6. Describe an actual example of how and why taking a high ethical ground results in a good decision for business.

Internet Resources for Chapter 10

http://www.managementhelp.org/ethics/ethics.htm *A range of papers and articles on ethics from the Free Management Library.*

http://www.pdcnet.org/beq.html Business Ethics Quarterly *publishes scholarly articles from a variety of disciplinary orientations that focus on the general subject of the application of ethics to the international business community.*

http://www.business-ethics.org *An international institute fostering global business practices to promote equitable economic development, resource sustainability, and just forms of government.*

http://www.business-ethics.com/ Business Ethics *is an online publication that offers information, opinion, and analysis of critical issues in the field of corporate responsibility.*

MIND STRETCHERS

Have You Considered?

1. How would you define your own ethics?
2. What was the toughest ethical decision you have faced? How did you handle it, and why? What did you learn?
3. How do you personally determine whether someone is ethical?

4. How would you describe the ethics of the president of the United States? Why? Would these ethics be acceptable to you in an investor, a partner, or a spouse?
5. When you look in the mirror, do you see someone with a commitment to pursuing high ethical standards? Are there limits to those standards?

PART FOUR

Financing Entrepreneurial Ventures

A financing strategy should be driven by corporate and personal goals, by resulting financial requirements, and ultimately by the available alternatives. In the final analysis, these alternatives are governed by the entrepreneur's relative bargaining power and skill in managing and orchestrating the fund-raising moves. In turn, that bargaining power is governed to a large extent by the cruelty of real time. It is governed by when the company will run out of cash given its current cash burn rate.

More numerous alternatives for financing a company exist now than ever before. Many contend that money remains plentiful for well-managed emerging firms with the promise of profitable growth. Savvy entrepreneurs should remain vigilant for the warnings noted here to avoid the myopic temptation to "take the money and run." The cost of money can vary considerably.

Although some of these alternatives look distinct and separate, a financing strategy probably will encompass a combination of both debt and equity capital. In considering which financial alternatives are best for a venture at any particular stage of growth, it is important to draw on the experience of other entrepreneurs, professional investors, lenders, accountants, and other professionals.

In the search for either debt or equity capital, entrepreneurs must take a professional approach to selecting and presenting their ventures to investors and lenders.

Chapter Eleven

Resource Requirements

When it comes to control of resources... all I need from a source is the ability to use the resources. There are people who describe the ideal business as a post office box to which people send cash.

Howard H. Stevenson
Harvard Business School

Results Expected

Upon completion of this chapter, you will be able to

1. Describe the successful entrepreneur's unique attitudes about and approaches to resources—people, capital, and other assets.
2. Identify the important issues in the selection and effective utilization of outside professionals, such as members of a board of directors, lawyers, accountants, and consultants.
3. Articulate decisions about financial resources.
4. Analyze and discuss the Quick Lube Franchise corporation case study.
5. Create simple cash flow and income statements and a balance sheet.
6. Describe the ways in which entrepreneurs turn less into more.

The Entrepreneurial Approach to Resources

Resources include (1) people, such as the management team, the board of directors, lawyers, accountants, and consultants; (2) financial resources; (3) assets, such as plant and equipment; and (4) business plan. Successful entrepreneurs view the need for and the ownership and management of these resources in the pursuit of opportunities differently than managers in many large organizations view them. This different way of looking at resources is reflected in a definition of entrepreneurship given in Chapters 1 and 2—the process of creating or seizing an opportunity *and pursuing it regardless of the resources currently controlled.*[1]

Howard H. Stevenson has contributed to understanding the unique approach to resources of successful entrepreneurs. The decisions on what resources are needed, when they are needed, and how to acquire them are strategic decisions that fit with the other driving forces of entrepreneurship. Furthermore, Stevenson has pointed out that entrepreneurs seek to use the minimum possible amount of all types of resources at each stage in their ventures' growth. Rather than own the resources they need, entrepreneurs seek to control resources.

---

[1] This definition was developed by Howard H. Stevenson and colleagues at the Harvard Business School. His work on a paradigm for entrepreneurial management has contributed greatly to this area of entrepreneurship. See H. H. Stevenson, "A New Paradigm for Entrepreneurial Management," in *Proceedings from the 7th Anniversary Symposium on Entrepreneurship, July 1983* (Boston: Harvard Business School Press, 1984).

Entrepreneurs with this approach reduce some of the risk in pursuing opportunities:

- *Less capital.* The amount of capital required is simply smaller due to the quest for parsimony. The financial exposure is therefore reduced, as is the dilution of the founder's equity.

- *Staged capital commitments.* Capital infusions are staged to match critical milestones that will signal whether it is prudent to keep going, and infuse additional capital, or abort the venture. Both the founder's and investor's financial exposure, and dilution of equity ownership, are thereby reduced.

- *More flexibility.* Entrepreneurs who do not own a resource are in a better position to commit and decommit quickly.[2] One price of resource ownership is an inherent inflexibility. With the rapidly fluctuating conditions and uncertainty with which most entrepreneurial ventures contend, inflexibility can be a curse. Response times must be short if a firm is to be competitive. Decision windows are usually small and elusive. Furthermore, it is extremely difficult to accurately predict the resources needed to exploit the opportunity. In addition, the entrepreneurial approach to resources permits iterations and strategic experiments in the venture process. That is, ideas can be tried and tested without committing to asset and resource ownership, to rapidly changing markets and technology, and so forth. For example, Howard Head says that if he had raised all the money he needed at the outset of his business, he would have failed by spending the funds too early on the wrong version of his metal ski. Consider also the inflexibility of a company that permanently commits to a certain technology, software, or management system.

- *Low sunk cost.* In addition, sunk costs are lower if the firm exercises its option to abort the venture at any point. Consider, in contrast, the enormous upfront capital commitment of a nuclear power plant and the cost of abandoning such a project.

- *Lower costs.* Fixed costs are lowered, thus favorably affecting breakeven. Of course, the other side of the coin is that variable costs may rise. If the entrepreneur has found an opportunity with forgiving and rewarding economics, then there will most likely still be ample gross margins in the venture to absorb this increase.

- *Reduced risk.* In addition to reducing total exposure, other risks, such as the risk of resource obsolescence, are also lower. For example, venture leasing has been used by biotechnology companies to supplement sources of equity financing.

Although some might scoff at the practice, erroneously assuming that the firm cannot afford to buy a resource, not owning a resource can provide advantages and options. Resource decisions are often extremely complex, involving consideration of such details as tax implications of leasing versus buying, and so forth.

Bootstrapping Strategies: Marshaling and Minimizing Resources

Minimizing resources is colloquially referred to as bootstrapping or, more formally, as a lack of resource intensity. *Bootstrapping* is defined as a multistage commitment of resources with a minimum commitment at each stage or decision point.[3] When discussing his philosophy on bootstrapping, Greg Gianforte (who retired at the age of 33 after he and his partners sold their software business, Brightwork Development Inc., to McAfee Associates for more than $10 million) stated, "A lot of entrepreneurs think they need money . . . when actually they haven't figured out the business equation."[4] According to Gianforte, lack of money, employees, and equipment—even lack of product—is actually a huge advantage because it forces the bootstrapper to concentrate on selling to bring cash into the business. Thus, to persevere, entrepreneurs ask at every step how they can accomplish a little more with a little less in order to pursue the opportunity.

The opposite attitude is often evident in large institutions, which are usually characterized by a trustee or custodial viewpoint. Managers in these larger institutions seek not only to have enough committed resources for the task at hand, but also to have a cushion against tough times.

Building Your Brain Trust

At Babson College, we have created a yearlong Entrepreneurship Intensity Track (EIT) tailored for second-year MBA candidates who have serious venture opportunities they want to launch. A central part of the EIT is the Babson Brain Trust (BBT). The example of Kirk Poss illustrates how this works, and why

---

[2] H. H. Stevenson, M. J. Roberts, and H. I. Grousbeck, *New Business Ventures and the Entrepreneur* (Homewood, IL: Richard D. Irwin, 1985).
[3] Ibid.
[4] E. Barker, "Start with Nothing," *INC.*, February 2002.

building a brain trust for your venture is a huge part of improving the "fit" vis-à-vis the Timmons Model.

Originally Kirk planned to go to medical school, so he found a job at Massachusetts General Hospital in Boston, one of the world's premier medical centers. While working on an imaging research project, he gained the respect of the distinguished doctor leading the project. The new imaging technology showed great promise. Mass General was willing to license the technology to a new company that Kirk and the doctor would create. In the meantime, Kirk decided to go back to Babson for an MBA. There he enrolled in the EIT to start the venture more quickly, more wisely, and more cost-effectively. Enter Professor Timmons, who created the Babson Brain Trust around his personal networks and trustees, faculty, and friends at Babson. After gaining an understanding of the opportunity and Kirk's background through a basic "gap analysis" and applying the Timmons Model to the venture, it became clear that two members of the BBT could add enormous value during the creation, launch, and building of the company. Mike Herman, a member of the BBT, spent more than 20 years helping Ewing Marion Kauffman build Marion Labs into a $1 billion pharmaceutical firm as chief financial officer, and was later a president of the Kauffman Foundation. As a private investor and director, he had extensive experience working with young medical industry start-ups. Another member of the BBT, Bob Compton, was the original venture capitalist who helped launch Sofamor-Danele. Later he became its chief operating officer, building it into the world's leading specialist in spinal and neck injury implants and corrective devices. Medtronic acquired the company for more than $3 billion in 1999.

Kirk's introduction to these two people allowed him access to their brains, their relevant and extensive experience, and their contacts with other talent pools and capital. It was up to Kirk, through his entrepreneurial energy, promise, and salesmanship, to capture their interest, gain their confidence, and tap into their talent. Happily, all this came together. Herman and Compton saw considerable opportunity in the technology, Kirk, and the potential—enough so that they became seed-round investors and directors. Note their decision process. They recognized high potential and that each could personally make a large impact on the odds of success *because* they knew what and how they could add value to this specific venture. The company has raised over $10 million and has surpassed every projected milestone significantly ahead of schedule. More important, the com-

pany recently closed on a valuable drug development deal. The "Build Your Brain Trust" exercise at the end of the chapter will walk you through the issues and tasks necessary to assemble a brain trust that can add maximum value to your venture.

As this example shows, the right advisors and brain trust members are very important. They can provide critical value to your venture. The most successful entrepreneurs think this through *before* they launch. They know what they need to fill in the gaps that exist on the team, and they ask themselves what they don't know. They focus on identifying individuals with know-how, experience, and networks and those who have access to critical talent, experience, and resources that can make the difference between success and failure.

Using Other People's Resources (OPR)

Use of other people's resources, particularly in the start-up and early growth stages of a venture, is an important approach for entrepreneurs. In contrast, large firms assume that virtually all resources have to be owned to control their use, and decisions revolve around how these resources will be acquired and financed; not so with entrepreneurs.

Having the use of a resource and being able to control or influence the deployment of a resource are critical. The quote at the beginning of the chapter illustrates this mind-set perfectly.

Other people's resources include, for example, money invested or lent by friends, relatives, business associates, or other investors. Resources such as people, space, equipment, or other material lent, provided inexpensively or free by customers or suppliers, or secured by bartering future services, opportunities, and the like can also be included. In fact, using other people's resources can be as simple as reading free booklets and pamphlets, such as those published by many of the old Big Six accounting firms, or using low-cost educational programs or government-funded management assistance programs. Extending accounts payable is one of the primary sources of working capital for many start-ups and growing firms.

How can you as an entrepreneur begin to tap into these resources? Howard H. Stevenson and William H. Sahlman suggest that you have to do "two seemingly contradictory things: seek out the best advisors—specialists if you have to—and involve them more thoroughly, and at an earlier stage, than you have in the past. At the same time, be more skeptical of their credentials and their advice."[5] A recent study found

---

[5] H. H. Stevenson and W. H. Sahlman, "How Small Companies Should Handle Advisors," in *The Entrepreneurial Venture* (Boston: Harvard Business School Press, 1992), p. 296. See also a *Harvard Business Review* reprint series called "Boards of Directors: Part I" and "Board of Directors: Part II" (Boston: Harvard Business Review, 1976).

EXHIBIT 11.1

Hypotheses Concerning Networks and Entrepreneurial Effectiveness

Effective entrepreneurs are more likely than others to systematically plan and monitor network activities.

- Effective entrepreneurs are able to *chart their present network* and to discriminate between production and symbolic ties.
- Effective entrepreneurs are able to *view effective networks as a crucial aspect for ensuring the success of their company.*
- Effective entrepreneurs are able to *stabilize and maintain networks* to increase their effectiveness and their efficiency.

Effective entrepreneurs are more likely than others to undertake actions toward increasing their network density and diversity.

- Effective entrepreneurs set aside time for purely random activities—things done with no specific problem in mind.
- Effective entrepreneurs are able to *check network density,* so as to avoid too many overlaps (because they affect network efficiency) while still attaining solidarity and cohesiveness.
- Effective entrepreneurs multiply, through extending the reachability of their networks, the stimuli for better and faster adaptation to change.

Source: Adapted from P. Dubini and H. Aldrich, "Executive Forum: Personal and Extended Networks Are Central to the Entrepreneurial Process," *Journal of Business Venturing* 6, no. 5 (September 1991), pp. 310–12. Copyright 1991, with permission from Elsevier.

that social capital, including having an established business network and encouragement from friends and family, is strongly associated with entrepreneurial activity.[6] In addition to networking with family, friends, classmates, and advisors, Stevenson and Sahlman suggest that the human touch enhances the relationship between the entrepreneur and the venture's advisors.[7] Accuracy in social perception, skill at impression management, skill at persuasion and influence, and a high level of social adaptability may be relevant to the activities necessary for successful new ventures.[8] Paola Dubini and Howard Aldrich have contributed to the growing body of knowledge about how these "social assets" may benefit the bottom line of a new venture; see Exhibit 11.1 for the strategic principles they have identified. However, a handful of studies have failed to demonstrate the influence networking activities have on venture performance.[9]

There are many examples of controlling people resources, rather than owning them. In real estate, even the largest firms do not employ top architects full-time but, rather, secure them on a per project basis. Most small firms do not employ lawyers; instead they obtain legal assistance as needed. Technical consultants, design engineers, and programmers are other examples of professionals who may be used on an as-needed basis. An example of this approach is a company that grew to $20 million in sales in about 10 years with $7,500 cash, liberal use of credit cards, reduced income for the founders, hard work and long hours. This company has not had to raise any additional equity capital.

An example of the opposite point of view is illustrated by a proposed new venture in the minicomputer software industry. The business plan called for about $300,000, an amount that would pay only for the development of the first products. The first priority in the deployment of the company's financial resources as outlined in the business plan was to buy outright a computer costing approximately $150,000. The founders refused to consider other options, such as leasing the computer or leasing computer time. The company was unable to attract venture capital, despite having an otherwise excellent business plan. The $150,000 raised from informal private investors was not enough money to pursue the opportunity, and the founders decided to return the funds and abandon the venture. A more entrepreneurial team would have found a way to keep going under these circumstances.

Outside People Resources

Board of Directors

Initial work in evaluating the need for people resources is done when forming a new venture team (see Chapter 9). Once resource needs have been determined and a team has been selected, obtaining additional outside resources will usually be necessary in the start-up stage as well as during other stages of growth.

[6] B. Honig and P. Davidsson, "The Role of Social and Human Capital among Nascent Entrepreneurs," *Academy of Management Proceedings,* 2001, pp. 1–7.
[7] Ibid., p. 301.
[8] R. A. Baron and G. D. Markman, "Beyond Social Capital: How Social Skills Can Enhance Entrepreneurs' Success," *Academy of Management Executive* 14 no. 1 (2000), pp. 106–17.
[9] O. O. Sawyerr and J. E. McGee, "The Impact of Personal Network Characteristics on Perceived Environmental Uncertainty: An Examination of Owners/Managers of New High Technology Firms," http://www.babson.edu/entrep/fer/papers99, 1999.

The decision of whether to have a board of directors and, if so, defining the process of choosing and finding the people who will sit on the board are troublesome for new ventures.[10]

The Decision   The decision of whether to have a board of directors is first influenced by the form of organization chosen for the entrepreneurial team. If the new venture is organized as a corporation, it must have a board of directors, which must be elected by shareholders. There is more flexibility with other forms of organization.

In addition, certain investors will require a board of directors. Venture capitalists almost always require boards of directors and representation on these boards.

Beyond that, deciding whether to involve outsiders merits careful thought. This decision making starts by identifying missing relevant experience, know-how, and networks, and determining if the venture has current needs that can be addressed by outside directors. Their probable contributions can be weighed against the greater external disclosure of operating and financing plans. Also, because one responsibility of a board of directors is to elect officers for the firm, the decision whether to have a board also is tied to financing decisions and ownership of the voting shares in the company.

> The flood of Internet IPOs over the past years raises concerns because their boards are dominated by company executives and venture capitalists.[11] According to the authors of this article, at least half of a board's members should be outside directors in order to provide independent, outside viewpoints.

When Art Spinner of Hambro International was interviewed by *INC.*, he explained,

> Entrepreneurs worry about the wrong thing . . . that the boards are going to steal their companies or take them over. Though entrepreneurs have many reasons to worry, that's not one of them. It almost never happens. In truth, boards don't even have much power. They are less well equipped to police entrepreneurs than to advise them.[12]

As Spinner suggests, the expertise that members of a board can bring to a venture, at an affordable price, can far outweigh any of the negative factors mentioned earlier. David Gumpert cites the crucial roles of the advisory board recruited by his partner

and him for what was originally NetMarquee, an online direct marketing agency. He describes the importance of intentionally choosing a board by focusing on "holes" that need to be filled, while also being mindful of financial constraints. According to Gumpert, "The board continually challenged us—in terms of tactics, strategy, and overall business philosophy." These challenges benefited their company by (1) preventing dumb mistakes, (2) keeping management focused on what really mattered, and (3) stopping management from getting gloomy.[13]

Selection Criteria: Add Value with Know-How and Contacts   Once the decision to have a board of directors has been made, finding the appropriate people for the board is a challenge. It is important to be objective and to select trustworthy people. Most ventures typically look to personal acquaintances of the lead entrepreneur or the team or to their lawyers, bankers, accountants, or consultants for their first outside directors. While such a choice might be the right one for a venture, the process also involves finding the right people to fill the gaps discovered in the process of forming the management team.

This issue of filling in the gaps relates to one criterion of a successful management team: intellectual honesty—that is, knowing what you know and what you need to know. In a study of boards and specifically venture capitalists' contribution to them, entrepreneurs seemed to value operating experience over financial expertise.[14] In addition, the study reported, "Those CEOs with a top-20 venture capital firm as the lead investor, on average, did rate the value of the advice from their venture capital board members significantly higher—but not outstandingly higher—than the advice from other outside board members."[15]

Defining expectations and minimum requirements for board members might be a good way to get the most out of a board of directors.

A top-notch outside director usually spends *at least* 9 to 10 days per year on his or her responsibilities. Four days per year are spent for quarterly meetings, a day of preparation for each meeting, a day for another meeting to cope with an unanticipated issue, plus up to a day or more for various phone calls. Yearly fees are usually paid for such a commitment.

Quality directors become involved for the learning and professional development opportunities rather

[10] The authors are indebted to Howard H. Stevenson of the Harvard Business School, and to Leslie Charm and Carl Youngman, formerly of Doktor Pet Centers and Command Performance hair salons, respectively, for insights into and knowledge of boards of directors.
[11] J. W. Lorsch, A. S. Zelleke, and K. Pick, "Unbalanced Boards," *Harvard Business Review*, February 1, 2001, p. 28.
[12] "Confessions of a Director: Hambro International's Art Spinner Says Most CEOs Don't Know How to Make Good Use of Boards. Here He Tells You How," *INC.*, April 1991, p. 119.
[13] D. E. Gumpert, "Tough Love: What You Really Want from Your Advisory Board," http://www.entreworld.org/content/entrebyline, 2001.
[14] J. Rosenstein, A. V. Bruno, W. D. Bygrave, and N. T. Taylor, "The CEO, Venture Capitalist, and the Board," *Journal of Business Venturing*, 1988, pp. 99–113.
[15] Ibid., pp. 99–100.

than for the money. Compensation to board members varies widely. Fees can range from as little as $500 to $1,000 for a half- or full-day meeting to $10,000 to $30,000 per year for four to six full-day to day-and-a-half meetings, plus accessibility on a continuous basis. Directors are also usually reimbursed for their expenses incurred in preparing for and attending meetings. Stock in a start-up company, often 2 to 5 percent, or options for 5,000 to 50,000 shares, are common incentives to attract and reward directors.

As a director of 11 companies and an advisor to two other companies, Art Spinner suggests the following as a simple set of rules to guide you toward a productive relationship with your board:

- Treat your directors as individual resources.
- Always be honest with your directors.
- Set up a compensation committee.
- Set up an audit committee.
- Never set up an executive committee.[16]

New ventures are finding that, for a variety of reasons, people who could be potential board members are increasingly cautious about getting involved.

Liability   Motivated by an apparent wave of corporate fraud scandals in the United States that many felt could lead to a crisis of confidence in the capital marketplace, Congress passed the Sarbanes-Oxley Act (SOX) in 2002. SOX requires companies to file paperwork with the Securities and Exchange Commission faster, create a more transparent means of collecting and posting financial data, maintain volumes of data, and test their procedures for posting accurate, timely information. The potential consequences of running afoul of this law are ominous. They include prison time and huge fines for the company's chief officers.

Although start-ups are usually not subject to the technical requirements of the act, the spirit of the law and emerging case law create higher disclosure standards for even small and growing firms. Audit committees sitting on start-up boards, for example, could have real SOX-like exposure.

As well, directors of a company can be held personally liable for its actions and those of its officers. A climate of litigation exists in many areas. Some specific grounds for liability of a director have included voting a dividend that renders the corporation insolvent, voting to authorize a loan out of corporate assets to a director or an officer who ultimately defaults,

and signing a false corporate document or report. Courts have held that if a director acts in good faith, he or she can be excused from liability. However, it can be difficult for a director to *prove* that he or she has acted in good faith, especially in a start-up situation. This proof is complicated by several factors, including possibly an inexperienced management team, the financial weaknesses and cash crises that occur and demand solution, and the lack of good and complete information and records, which are necessary as the basis for action. In recent years, many states have passed what is known as the "Dumb Director Law." In effect, the law allows that directors are normal human beings who can make mistakes and misjudgments. The law goes a long way toward taking the sting out of potential lawsuits that may be urged by ambulance chasers.

One solution to liability concerns is for the firm to purchase indemnity insurance for its directors. Unfortunately, such insurance is expensive. Despite the liability problems just noted, one survey found that just 11 percent of the respondents reported difficulty in recruiting board members.[17] In dealing with this issue, new ventures will want to examine a possible director's attitude toward risk and evaluate whether this is the type of attitude the team needs to have represented.

Harassment   Outside stockholders, who may have acquired stock through a private placement or through the over-the-counter market, can have unrealistic expectations about the risk involved in a new venture, the speed with which a return can be realized, and the size of the return. Such stockholders are a source of continual annoyance for boards and for their companies.

Time and Risk   Experienced directors know that it often takes more time and intense involvement to work with an early-stage venture with sales of $10 million or less than with a company having sales of $25 million or more, and that the former is riskier.

Paying the Board   The Mellon Financial Corporation's annual Board of Directors Compensation and Governance Practices Survey[18] found that new governance practices are reshaping the boardroom of corporate America, with significant increases in director pay, responsibility, and accountability. The survey results reflect the compensation practices of more

16 "Confessions of a Director," *INC.*, April 1991, p. 119. Reprinted with permission. © 1991 by Goldbirsh Group, Inc., 38 Commercial Wharf, Boston, MA 02110.
17 "The *Venture* Survey: Who Sits on Your Board?" *Venture*, April 1984, p. 32.
18 The Mellon Financial Corporation, *Board of Directors Compensation and Governance Practices Survey*, February 16, 2005.

than 200 U.S.-based companies. Analysis provides information on both cash- and equity-based compensation, retainers, meeting fees, and board or committee-based leadership differentials. Key findings include these:

- The median board retainer was $39,500, up 17.2 percent from the previous year.

- The median total cash compensation, including retainers and meeting fees, was up 13.1 percent to $54,385.

- Equity awards represent approximately 59 percent of total direct compensation in 2004.

- Thirty-eight percent of survey respondents require directors to own company stock.

- Twenty-three percent of companies have a nonexecutive chairman of the board; a further 48 percent have a lead director. More than 83 percent conduct meetings without corporate management present.

- Thirty-six percent of boards now conduct formal evaluations of their own members—more than double the findings in 2003.

Alternatives to a Formal Board

Advisors and quasi-boards can be a useful alternative to having a formal board of directors.[19] A board of advisors is designed to dispense advice, rather than make decisions, and therefore advisors are not exposed to personal liability. A firm can solicit objective observations and feedback from these advisors. Such informal boards can bring needed expertise without the legal entanglements and formalities of a regular board. Also, the possible embarrassment of having to remove someone who is not serving a useful role can be avoided. Informal advisors are usually much less expensive, with honorariums of $500 to $1,000 per meeting common. Remember, however, that the level of involvement of these advisors probably will be less than that of formal board members. The firm also does not enjoy the protection of law, which defines the obligations and responsibilities of members of a formal board.

An informal group of advisors can also be a good mechanism through which a new venture can observe a number of people in action and select one or two as regular directors. The entrepreneur gains the advantages of counsel and advice from outsiders without being legally bound by their decisions.

Attorneys

The Decision   Nearly all companies need and use the services of attorneys—entrepreneurial ventures perhaps more than most.[20] Because it is critical that entrepreneurs fully understand the legal aspects of any decisions and agreements they make, they should never outsource that knowledge to their attorney. Babson College Adjunct Professor Leslie Charm put it this way: "You must understand the meaning of any document you're considering as well as your attorneys because at the end of the day, when you close that deal, you are the one who has to live with it, not your lawyers." In addition, Charm noted that attorneys should be viewed as teachers and advisors; use them to explain legalese and articulate risk and ramifications; and in negotiations, use them to push to close the deal.

Various authors describe the importance of choosing and managing legal counsel. By following some legal basics and acquiring appropriate legal services, companies can achieve better legal health, including fewer problems and lower costs over the long term.[21] According to FindLaw, Inc., some of the legal work can be done by entrepreneurs who do not have law degrees by using self-help legal guides and preprinted forms. However, one should not rely exclusively on these materials. According to this organization, the factors to consider in choosing an attorney include availability, comfort level with the attorney, experience level and appropriateness to case, cost, and whether the lawyer knows the industry and has connections to investors and venture capital.[22]

How attorneys are used by entrepreneurial ventures depends on the needs of the venture at its particular stage. Size is also a factor. As company size increases, so does the need for advice in such areas as liability, mergers, and benefit plans. Contracts and agreements are almost uniformly the predominant use, regardless of the venture's size.

Entrepreneurs will most likely need to get assistance with the following legal areas:

- *Incorporation.* Issues such as the forgivable and nonforgivable liabilities of founders, officers, and directors or the form of organization chosen for a new venture are important. As tax laws and other circumstances change, they are important for more established firms as well. How important this area can be is illustrated by the case of a founder who nearly lost control of his company as a result of the legal maneuvering of the clerk and another shareholder. The clerk

---

[19] C. O. White and G. Gallop-Goodman, "Tap into Expert Input," *Black Enterprise* 30, no. 12 (2000), p. 47.
[20] The author wishes to acknowledge the input provided by Gerald Feigen of the Center for Entrepreneurial Studies, University of Maryland, from a course on entrepreneurship and the law he has developed and teaches at George Washington University Law School, and John Van Slyke of Alta Research.
[21] J. Adamec, "A Business Owner's Guide to Preventive Law," http://www.inc.com, 1997.
[22] FindLaw, Inc., "Selecting an Attorney," http://www.findlaw.com, 2000.

and the shareholder controlled votes on the board of directors, while the founder had controlling interest in the stock of the company. The shareholder tried to call a directors' meeting and not reelect the founder president. The founder found out about the plot and adroitly managed to call a stockholders' meeting to remove the directors first.

- *Franchising and licensing.* Innumerable issues concerning future rights, obligations, and ramifications in the event of nonperformance by either a franchisee or lessee or a franchisor or lessor require specialized legal advice.
- *Contracts and agreements.* Firms need assistance with contracts, licenses, leases, and other agreements such as noncompete employment agreements and those governing the vesting rights of shareholders.
- *Formal litigation, liability protection, and so on.* In today's litigious climate, sooner or later most entrepreneurs will find themselves as defendants in lawsuits and require counsel.
- *Real estate, insurance, and other matters.* It is hard to imagine an entrepreneur who, at one time or another, will not be involved in various kinds of real estate transactions, from rentals to the purchase and sale of property, that require the services of an attorney.
- *Copyrights, trademarks, patents, and intellectual property protection.* Products are hard to protect. Pushing ahead with product development before ample protection from the law is provided can be expedient in the short term but disastrous in the long term. For example, an entrepreneur—facing the cancellation of a $2.5 million sale of his business and uncollected fees of over $200,000 if his software was not protected—obtained an expert on the sale, leasing, and licensing of software products. The lawyer devised subtle but powerful protections, such as internal clocks in the software that shut down the software if they were not changed.
- *Employee plans.* Benefit and stock ownership plans have become complicated to administer and use effectively. The special know-how of lawyers can help avoid common pitfalls.
- *Tax planning and review.* Too frequently the tail of the accountant's tax avoidance advice wags the dog of good business sense. Entrepreneurs who can worry more about finding good opportunities, as opposed to tax shelters, are infinitely better off.

- *Federal, state, and other regulations and reports.* Understanding the impact of and complying with regulations is often not easy. Violations of federal, state, and other regulations can often have serious consequences.
- *Mergers and acquisitions.* Specialized legal knowledge is required when buying or selling a company. Unless an entrepreneur is highly experienced and has highly qualified legal advisors in these transactions, he or she can either lose the deal or end up having to live with costly legal obligations.
- *Bankruptcy.* Many people have heard tales of entrepreneurs who did not make deposits to pay various federal and state taxes in order to use that cash in their business. These entrepreneurs perhaps falsely assumed that if their companies went bankrupt, the government was out of luck, just like the banks and other creditors. They were wrong. The owners, officers, and often the directors are held personally liable for those obligations.
- *Other matters.* These matters can range from assistance with collecting delinquent accounts to labor relations.
- *Personal needs.* As entrepreneurs accumulate net worth (i.e., property and other assets), legal advice in estate, tax, and financial planning is important.

Selection Criteria: Add Value with Know-How and Contacts
In a survey of the factors that enter into the selection of a law firm or an attorney, 54 percent of respondents said personal contact with a member of the firm was the main factor.[23] Reputation was a factor for 40 percent, and a prior relationship with the firm was important for 26 percent of the respondents. Equally revealing was the fact that fees were mentioned by only 3 percent of respondents.

Many areas of the country have attorneys who specialize in new ventures and in firms with high growth potential. The best place to start in selecting an attorney is with acquaintances of the lead entrepreneur, of members of the management team, or of directors. Recommendations from accountants, bankers, and associates also are useful. Other sources are partners in venture capital firms, partners of a leading accounting firm (those who have privately owned and emerging company groups), a bar association, or the *Martindale-Hubbell Law Directory* (a listing of lawyers). To be effective, an attorney needs to have

---
[23] B. W. Ketchum, Jr., "You and Your Attorney," *INC.*, June 1982, p. 52.

the experience and expertise to deal with specific issues facing a venture. Stevenson and Sahlman state that hooking up with the vast resources of a large law firm or national accounting firm may be the best course, but we do not necessarily advise that strategy. You can usually get reasonable tax or estate-planning advice from a big law firm merely by picking up a telephone. The trade-off is that, if you are a small company and they have a dozen General Electrics as clients, you may get short shrift. One- or two-person firms can have an excellent referral network of specialists for problems outside their bailiwick. Use the specialist when you have to.[24]

As with members of the management team, directors, and investors, the chemistry also is important. Finally, advice to be highly selective and to expect to get what you pay for is sound. It is also important to realize that lawyers are not businesspeople and that they do not usually make *business* judgments. Rather, they seek to provide perfect or fail-safe protection.

Most attorneys are paid on an hourly basis. Retainers and flat fees are sometimes paid, usually by larger ventures. The amount a venture pays for legal services rises expectedly as the firm grows. Many law firms will agree to defer charges or initially to provide services at a lower than normal rate to obtain a firm's business. According to the *Massachusetts Lawyers Weekly,* legal fees fall into the following ranges: partners' hourly rates, from $195 to $400; associates' hourly rates, from $80 to $245; and paralegals' rates, between $45 and $165.

Bankers and Other Lenders

The Decision Deciding whether to have a banker or another lender usually involves decisions about how to finance certain needs. Most companies will need the services of a banker or other lender in this respect at some time. The decision also can involve how a banker or other lender can serve as an advisor.

As with other advisors, the banker or other lender needs to be a partner, not a difficult minority shareholder. First and foremost, therefore, an entrepreneur should carefully pick the *right banker or lender* rather than picking just a bank or a financial institution, although picking the bank or institution is also important. Different bankers and lenders have reputations ranging from "excellent" to "just OK" to "not OK" in how well they work with entrepreneurial companies. Their institutions also have reputations for how well they work with entrepreneurial companies. Ideally an entrepreneur needs an excellent

banker or lender with an excellent financial institution, although an excellent banker or lender with a just OK institution is preferable to a just OK banker or lender with an excellent institution.

As a starting point, an entrepreneur should know clearly what he or she needs from a lender. Some will have needs that are asset-based, such as money for equipment, facilities, or inventory. Others may need working capital to fund short-term operations.

Having a business plan is valuable preparation for selecting and working with a lender. Also, because a banker or other lender is a partner, it is important to invite him or her to see the company in operation, to avoid late financial statements (as well as late payments and overdrafts), and to be honest and straightforward in sharing information.

Selection Criteria: Add Value with Know-How and Contracts Bankers and other lenders are known to other entrepreneurs, lawyers, venture capitalists, and accountants that provide general business advisory services. Starting with their recommendations is ideal. From among four to seven or so possibilities, an entrepreneur will find the right lender and the right institution.

Today's banking and financial services marketplace is more competitive than it was in the past. There are more choices, and it is worth the time and effort to shop around.

Accountants

The Decision The accounting profession has come a long way from the "green eyeshades" stereotype one hears reference to occasionally. Today virtually all the larger accounting firms have discovered the enormous client potential of new and entrepreneurial ventures. A significant part of their business strategy is to cater specifically to these firms. In the Boston area, for instance, leading accounting firms from the former Big Six located offices for their small business groups on Route 128 in the heart of entrepreneurs' country.

Accountants often are unfairly maligned, especially after the fallout of the Enron/Arthur Andersen case. The activities that accountants engage in have grown and no longer consist of solely adding numbers.[25] Accountants who are experienced as advisors to emerging companies can provide valuable services in addition to audits and taxation advice. An experienced general business advisor can be valuable in helping to evaluate strategy, raising debt and equity capital, facilitating mergers and acquisitions, locating

---

[24] Stevenson and Sahlman, "How Small Companies Should Handle Advisors," p. 297.
[25] J. Andresky Fraser, "How Many Accountants Does It Take to Change an Industry?" http://www.inc.com, April 1, 1997.

directors, and even balancing business decisions with important personal needs and goals.

Selection Criteria: Add Value with Know-How and Contacts

In selecting accountants, the first step is for the venture to decide whether to go with a smaller local firm, a regional firm, or one of the major accounting firms. Although each company should make its own decision, in an informal survey of companies with sales between $4 million and $20 million, "more than 85 percent of the CEOs preferred working with smaller regional accounting firms, rather than the Big Six, because of lower costs and what they perceived as better personal attention."[26] In making this decision, you will need to address several factors:[27]

- *Service.* Levels of service offered and the attention likely to be provided need to be evaluated. Chances are, for most start-ups, both will be higher in a small firm than a large one. But if an entrepreneur of a higher-potential firm seeking venture capital or a strategic partner has aspirations to go public, a national firm is a good place to start.
- *Needs.* Needs, both current and future, have to be weighed against the capabilities of the firm. Larger firms are more equipped to handle highly complex or technical problems, while smaller firms may be preferable for general management advice and assistance because the principals are more likely to be involved in handling the account. In most instances, companies in the early stages of planning or that do not plan to go public do not require a top-tier accounting firm. However, one exception to this might be start-ups that are able to attract formal venture capital funds from day one.[28]
- *Cost.* Most major firms will offer very cost-competitive services to start-ups with significant growth and profit potential. That doesn't mean you'll be talking to a partner. If a venture needs the attention of a partner in a larger firm, services of the larger firm are more expensive. However, if the firm requires extensive technical knowledge, a larger firm may have more experience and therefore be cheaper. Many early-growth phase companies are not able to afford to hire a leading national accounting

firm, and therefore a small local firm is best. According to Tim McCorry of McCorry Group Inc., these firms should tell you when you are ready to move on to a larger firm that provides more extensive services.[29]

- *Chemistry.* Chemistry always is an important consideration.

The recent trend in the accounting market has led to increased competition, spiraling capital costs, declining profit margins, and an increase in lawsuits.[30] Entrepreneurs should shop around in such a buyer's market for competent accountants who provide the most suitable and appropriate services. Sources of reference for good attorneys are also sources of reference for accountants. Trade groups are also valuable sources.

Once a firm has reached significant size, it will have many choices. The founders of one firm, which had grown to about $5 million in sales and had a strong potential to reach $20 million in sales in the next five years and eventually go public, put together a brief summary of the firm, including its background and track record, and a statement of needs for both banking and accounting services. The founders were startled by the aggressive response they received from several banks and major accounting firms.

The accounting profession is straightforward enough. Whether the accounting firm is small or large, it sells time, usually by the hour. Today the hourly partner rates range from $250–$600 for Big Four firms to $150–$300 for a small, local firm.

Consultants

The Decision[31]

Consultants are hired to solve particular problems and to fill gaps not filled by the management team. There are many skilled consultants who can give valuable assistance. They are a great source of "other people's resources." The advice needed by the entrepreneur can be quite technical and specific or general and far-ranging. Problems and needs also vary widely, depending on whether the venture is just starting or is an existing business, among other things.

Start-ups usually require help with critical one-time tasks and decisions that will have lasting impact on the business. In a study of how consultants are used and their impact on venture formation,

---

[26] S. Greco and C. Caggiano, "Advisors: How Do You Use Your CPA?" *INC.*, September 1991.
[27] N. C. Churchill and L. A. Werbaneth, Jr., "Choosing and Evaluating Your Accountant," in *Growing Concerns*, ed. D. E. Gumpert (New York: John Wiley & Sons and *Harvard Business Review*, 1984), p. 265.
[28] J. A. Fraser, "Do I Need a Top-Tier Accounting Firm?" http://www.inc.com/incmagazine, June 1, 1998.
[29] Ibid., p. 2.
[30] A. Fraser, "How Many Accountants Does It Take To Change an Industry?"
[31] The following is excerpted in part from D. E. Gumpert and J. A. Timmons, *The Encyclopedia of Small Business Resources* (New York: Harper & Row, 1984), pp. 48–51.

Karl Bayer, of Germany's Institute for Systems and Innovation Research of the Fraunhofer-Society, interviewed 315 firms. He found that 96 used consultants and that consultants are employed by start-ups for the following reasons:

1. To compensate for a lower level of professional experience.

2. To target a wide market segment (possibly to do market research for a consumer goods firm).

3. To undertake projects that require a large start-up investment in equipment.[32]

These tasks and decisions might include assessing business sites, evaluating lease and rental agreements, setting up record and bookkeeping systems, finding business partners, obtaining start-up capital, and formulating initial marketing plans.

Existing businesses face ongoing issues resulting from growth. Many of these issues are so specialized that this expertise is rarely available on the management team. Issues of obtaining market research, evaluating when and how to go about computerizing business tasks, deciding whether to lease or buy major pieces of equipment, and determining whether to change inventory valuation methods can be involved.

While it is not always possible to pinpoint the exact nature of a problem, sometimes a fresh outside view helps when a new venture tries to determine the broad nature of its concern. Examples may include concerns such as personnel problems, manufacturing problems, or marketing problems. Mie-Yun Lee of BuyerZone.com offers helpful hints for establishing an effective consultation relationship: (1) Define, define, define—invest whatever time is necessary to define and communicate the expected outcome of the project; (2) when choosing a consultant, expect a long-term relationship because it takes time to get the consultant up to speed on your business; and (3) outsourcing is not a magic bullet that relieves you of work; communication is critical to success.[33]

Bayer reported that the use of consultants had a negative effect on sales three to five years later. Additionally, his surveys overwhelmingly reported (two-thirds of the 96) that "the work delivered by the consultants . . . [was] inadequate for the task."[34] Bayer suggests that the entrepreneur can adequately prepare a consultant so that gaps are filled and the firm benefits in the long run, but it takes diligence.

Selection Criteria: Add Value with Know-How and Contacts

Unfortunately, nowhere are the options as numerous, the quality as variable, and the costs as unpredictable as in the area of consulting. The number of people calling themselves management consultants is large and growing steadily. By 2006 there were an estimated 80,000 to 85,000 private management consultants around the country. An estimated 2,000 or more are added annually. More than half of the consultants were found to work on their own, while the remainder work for firms. In addition, government agencies (primarily the Small Business Administration) employ consultants to work with businesses. Various private and nonprofit organizations provide management assistance to help entrepreneurs; and others, such as professors, engineers, and so forth, provide consulting services part-time. Such assistance also may be provided by other professionals, such as accountants and bankers.

Again, the right chemistry is critical in selecting consultants. One company president who was asked what he had learned from talking to clients of the consultant he finally hired said, "They couldn't really pinpoint one thing, but they all said they would not consider starting and growing a company without him!"

As unwieldy and risky as the consulting situation might appear, there are ways to limit the choices. Consultants tend to have specialties. While some consultants claim wide expertise, most will indicate the types of situations with which they feel most comfortable and skillful. In seeking a consultant, consider the following:[35]

- Good consultants are not geographically bound; they will travel and can work via electronic sources.

- The best referral system is word of mouth. This point cannot be stressed enough.

- Always check references carefully. It is important to look at the solutions consultants have utilized in the past.

- People skills are essential and therefore should be assessed when interviewing a consultant.

- Ask about professional affiliations and verify that the consultant is in good standing with the affiliation.

Three or more potential consultants should be interviewed about their expertise and approach. Be sure to check their references. Candidates who pass this

[32] K. Bayer, "The Impact of Using Consultants during Venture Formation on Venture Performance," in *Frontiers of Entrepreneurship Research: 1991*, ed. N. H. Churchill et al. (Babson Park, MA: Babson College, 1991), pp. 298–99.

[33] M. Lee, "Finding the Right Consultant," http://www.inc.buyerzone.com, February 2, 2000.

[34] Bayer, "The Impact of Using Consultants," p. 301.

[35] J. Finnegan, "The Fine Art of Finding a Consultant," http://www.inc.com.incmagazine, July 1, 1997.

initial screening then can be asked to prepare specific proposals.

A written agreement, specifying the consultant's responsibilities, the assignment's objectives, the length of time the project will take, and the type and amount of compensation, is highly recommended. Some consultants work on an hourly basis, some on a fixed-fee basis, and some on a retainer-fee basis. Huge variations in consulting costs exist for similar services. At one end of the spectrum is the Small Business Administration, which provides consultants to small businesses free of charge. At the other end of the spectrum are well-known consulting firms that may charge large amounts for minimal marketing or technical feasibility studies.

While the quality of many products roughly correlates with their price, this is not so with consulting services. It is difficult to judge consultants solely on the basis of their fees.

Financial Resources

Analyzing Financial Requirements

Once the opportunity has been assessed, once a new venture team has been formed, and once all resource needs have been identified, it is time for an entrepreneur to evaluate the type, quantity, and timing of financial resources.

As has been noted previously, there is a temptation to place the cart before the horse. Entrepreneurs are tempted to begin their evaluation of business opportunities—particularly their thinking about formal business plans—by analyzing spreadsheets, rather than first focusing on defining the opportunity, deciding how to seize it, and preparing financial requirement estimates.

However, when the time comes to analyze financial requirements, it is important to realize that cash is the lifeblood of a venture. As James Stancill, Professor of Finance at the University of Southern California's Marshall School of Business has said, "Any company, no matter how big or small, moves on cash, not profits. You can't pay bills with profits, only cash. You can't pay employees with profits, only cash."[36] Financial resources are almost always limited, and important and significant trade-offs need to be made in evaluating a company's needs and the timing of those needs.

Spreadsheets   Computers and spreadsheet programs are tools that save time and increase productivity and creativity enormously. Spreadsheets are nothing more than pieces of accounting paper adapted for use with a computer.

The origins of the first spreadsheet program, VisiCalc, reveal its relevance for entrepreneurs. It was devised by MBA student Dan Bricklin while he was attending Harvard Business School. The student was faced with analyzing pro forma income statements and balance sheets, cash flows, and breakeven for his cases. The question "*What if* you assumed such and such?" was inevitably asked.

The major advantage provided by spreadsheets to analyze capital requirements is the ability to answer what-if questions. As Stancill points out, this takes on particular relevance also when one considers the following:

> Usual measures of cash flow—net income plus depreciation (NIPD) or earnings before interest and taxes (EBIT)—give a realistic indication of a company's cash position only during a period of steady sales.[37]

Take cash flow projections. An entrepreneur could answer a question such as, What if sales grow at just 5 percent, instead of 15 percent, and what if only 50 percent, instead of 65 percent, of amounts billed are paid in 30 days? The impact on cash flow of changes in these projections can be seen.

The same what-if process also can be applied to pro forma income statements and balance sheets, budgeting, and break-even calculations. To illustrate, by altering assumptions about revenues and costs such that cash reaches zero, breakeven can be analyzed. For example, RMA assumptions could be used as comparative boundaries for testing assumptions about a venture.

An example of how computer-based analysis can be enormously valuable is the experience of a colleague who was seriously considering starting a new publishing venture. His analysis of the opportunity was encouraging, and important factors such as relevant experience and commitment by the lead entrepreneur were there. Assumptions about fixed and variable costs, market estimates, and probable start-up resource requirements had also been assembled. The next task was to generate detailed monthly cash flows in order to more precisely determine the economic character of the venture, including the impact of the seasonal nature of the business. This analysis would enable the entrepreneur to determine the amount of money needed to launch the business and the amount and timing of potential rewards. In less than three hours, the assumptions about revenues and expenditures associated with the start-up were

---

[36] Reprinted by permission of *Harvard Business Review*. An excerpt from "When Is There Cash in Cash Flow?" by J. M. Stancill, March–April 1987, p. 38. Copyright © 1987 by the President and Fellows *of* Harvard College.
[37] Stancill, "When Is There Cash in Cash Flow?" p. 38.

entered into a computer model. Within another two hours, he was able to see what the venture would look like financially over the first 18 months and to see the impact of several different what-if scenarios. The net result was that the new venture idea was abandoned because the amount of money required appeared to outweigh the reward potential.

The strength of computer-based analysis is also a source of problems for entrepreneurs who place the "druther" before the fact. With so many moving parts, analysis that is not grounded in sound perceptions about an opportunity is likely to be inaccurate.

Internet Impact: Resources

Fund-Raising for Nonprofits

A dynamic online service model has emerged that is changing the way nonprofits conduct their fund-raising auctions. Charity auctions, which in 2004 accounted for $18 billion in charitable giving in the United States, often attract high-income individuals and freely donated, high-quality items. But coordinating and staffing those venues has always been a challenge,

particularly because volunteer turnover requires the retraining of a majority of the workforce each time an auction is held. In addition, physical auctions are typically catered affairs that are attended by only a small percentage of an organization's support base.

cMarket, Inc., a venture-funded start-up based in Cambridge, Massachusetts, has developed an online service model that allows nonprofits to promote their causes, build their donor base, provide value to corporate sponsors, and improve the results of their fund-raising programs. Jon Carson, president of the organization, noted, "Now any nonprofit—without training or in-house technical people—can hold a fund-raising event that reaches the inbox of its entire constituency."

In 2004, the company's first full year of operations, cMarket signed over 400 clients. Then in May 2005 the company announced a partnership with Network for Good. Founded in 2001 by the Time Warner Foundation and AOL, the Cisco Foundation and Cisco Systems, and Yahoo! Network for Good is an independent, nonprofit organization that works to advance nonprofit adoption of the Internet as a tool for fund-raising, volunteer recruitment, and community engagement.

Chapter Summary

- Successful entrepreneurs use ingenious bootstrapping approaches to marshal and minimize resources.
- Control of resources rather than ownership of resources is the key to a "less is more" resource strategy.
- Entrepreneurs are also creative in identifying other people's money and resources, thereby spreading and sharing the risks.

- Selecting outside advisors, directors, and other professionals boils down to one key criterion: Do they add value through their know-how and networks?
- Today access to financial and nonfinancial resources is greater than ever before and is increasing because of the Internet.
- Building a brain trust of the right mentors, advisors, and coaches is one of the entrepreneur's most valuable "secret weapons."

Study Questions

1. Entrepreneurs think and act ingeniously when it comes to resources. What does this mean, and why is it so important?
2. Describe at least two creative bootstrapping resources.

3. Why will the Internet become an increasingly important gateway to controlling resources?
4. In selecting outside advisors, a board, consultants, and the like, what are the most important criteria, and why?

Internet Resources for Chapter 11

http://www.gmarketing.com/ *Guerilla Marketing offers creative marketing tips to help you outsmart the competition.*

http://online.wsj.com/small-business *Small business resources from The Wall Street Journal.*

http://www.score.org *SCORE, "Counselors to America's Small Business," is a popular source of free*

and confidential small business advice for entrepreneurs.

http://smallbusiness.findlaw.com *This site provides comprehensive access to small-business lawyers and legal information..*

MIND STRETCHERS

Have You Considered?

1. Many successful entrepreneurs and private investors say it is just as bad to start out with too much money as it is too little. Why is this so? Can you find some examples?

2. It is said that money is the least important part of the resource equation and of the entrepreneurial process. Why is this so?

3. What bootstrapping strategies do you need to devise?

Exercise 1
Build Your Brain Trust

Building a cadre of mentors, advisors, coaches, and directors can be the difference between success and failure of a venture. Building this brain trust will require professionalism, thoroughness, salesmanship, and tenacity. You gain the trust and confidence of these mentors through your performance and integrity.

This exercise is intended to provide a framework for, and key steps in thinking through, your requirements and developing a brain trust for your ventures.

Part I: Gap and Fit Analysis vis-à-vis the Timmons Model

1. At each phase of development of a venture, different know-how and access to experience, expertise, and judgment external to the founding team are often required. A key risk–reward management tool is the gap and fit analysis using the model.

   ✓ Who has access to key know-how and resources that we do not?

   ✓ What is missing that we need in order to obtain a very good chance?

   ✓ Who can add the most value/insights/solid experience to the venture now and in the next two years, and how?

   ✓ Who are the smartest, most insightful people given what we are trying to do?

   ✓ Who has the most valuable perspective and networks that could help the venture in an area that you know least about?

2. Break down the Timmons Model to focus on each dimension:

   ▪ *Core opportunity.* If they are not on your team now, who are the people who know more than anyone else on the planet about the revenue and cost model and underlying drivers and assumptions? How to price, get sales, marketing, customer service, and distribution? IT and e-business? The competition? The free cash flow characteristics and economics of the business?

   ▪ *Resources.* Who can help you get the necessary knowledge of and access to people, networks, money, and key talent?

   ▪ *Team.* Who has 10 to 20 years more experience than you do in building a venture from ground zero?

   ▪ *Context.* Who understands the context, changes, and timing of the venture in terms of the capital markets, any key regulatory requirements, and the internal drivers of the industry/technology/market?

3. Conclusions: What and who can make the biggest difference in the venture? Usually just one to three key people or resources can make a huge difference.

Part II: Identify and Build the Brain Trust

1. Once you've figured out what and who can make the greatest difference, you need to arrange for introductions. Faculty, family friends, roommates, and the like are good places to start.

2. If you can't get the introductions, then you have to go with your wits and creativity to get a personal meeting.

   ✓ Be highly prepared and articulate.

   ✓ Send an executive summary and advance agenda.

   ✓ Know the reasons and benefits that will be most appealing to this person.

   ✓ Follow up and follow through—send a handwritten note, not just another e-mail message.

3. Ask for blunt and direct feedback to such questions
    as these:

    ✓ What have we missed here? What flaws do you
      see in our team, our marketing plan, our financial
      requirements, our strategy, and so forth?

    ✓ Are there competitors we don't know about?

    ✓ How would you compete with me?

    ✓ Who would reject and accept us for an investment?
      Why?

    ✓ Who have we missed?

    ✓ Whom else should we talk with?

You will gain significant insight into yourself and your
venture, as well as how knowledgeable and insightful
the potential brain trust member is about your business, from the questions he or she asks, and from your
own. You will soon know whether the person is interested and can add value.

4. Grow the brain trust to grow the venture. Think two
    years ahead and add to the brain trust people who
    have already navigated the difficult waters you ex-
    pect to travel.

How Entrepreneurs Turn Less into More

Entrepreneurs are often creative and ingenious in bootstrapping their ventures and in getting a great deal out of limited resources. This assignment can be done alone, in pairs, or in trios. Identify at least two or three entrepreneurs whose companies exceed $3 million in sales and are less than 10 years old and who have started their companies with less than $25,000 to $50,000 of initial seed capital. Interview them with a focus on their strategies and tactics that minimize and control (not necessarily own) the necessary resources:

1. What methods, sources, and techniques did they devise to acquire resources?

2. Why were they able to do so much with so little?

3. What assumptions, attitudes, and mind-sets seemed to enable them to think and function in this manner?

4. What patterns, similarities, and differences exist among the entrepreneurs you interviewed?

5. What impact did these minimizing bootstrapping approaches have on their abilities to conserve cash and equity and to create future options or choices to pursue other opportunities?

6. How did they devise unique incentive structures in the deals and arrangements with their people, suppliers, and other resource providers (their first office space or facility, brochures, etc.)?

7. In lieu of money, what other forms of currency did they use, such as bartering for space, equipment, or people or giving an extra day off or an extra week's vacation?

8. Can they think of examples of how they acquired (gained control of) a resource they could afford to pay for with real money and did not?

9. Many experienced entrepreneurs say that for first-time entrepreneurs it can be worse to start with too much money rather than too little. How do you see this, and why?

10. Some of the strongest new companies are started during an economic recession, among tight credit and capital markets. It is valuable to develop a lean-and-mean, make-do, less-is-more philosophy and sense of frugality and budgetary discipline. Can you think of any examples of this? Do you agree or disagree? Can you think of opposite examples, such as companies started at or near the peak of the 1990s economic boom with more capital and credit than they needed?

You will find as background reading the feature articles on bootstrapping in *INC.* magazine, *Success* magazine, *Fast Company,* and others to be very useful.

Case

Quick Lube Franchise Corporation (QLFC)

Preparation Questions

1. What grounds might QLFC have for filing a lawsuit against Huston?
2. Why do you think Huston has asked for a meeting with Herget?
3. What advice would you give Herget as he considers Huston's request for a meeting with QLFC?
4. As part of that advice, how much is QLFC worth?
5. Does your answer to Question 4 depend on how QLFC is harvested?

It had been a year since Huston, a major oil company, had bought 80 percent of Super Lube, Inc., the number one franchisor of quick lubrication and oil change service centers in the United States with 1,000 outlets. As a result of that takeover, Super Lube's largest franchisee, Quick Lube Franchise Corporation (QLFC), found itself in the position where its principal supplier, lead financing vehicle, and franchisor were the same entity. Was this an opportunity or a disaster? In April 1991 Frank Herget, founder, chairman, and CEO of QLFC was faced with one of the most important decisions of his life.

Historical Background

Super Lube was the innovator of the quick lube concept, servicing the lube, motor oil, and filter needs of motorists in a specialized building with highly refined procedures. It was founded in March 1979 by Jeff Martin. Frank Herget was one of the four founding members of Martin's team. After a few years, Herget became frustrated with life at the franchisor's headquarters in Dallas. He believed that the future of Super Lube was in operating service centers. That put him at odds with founder, chairman, and CEO Jeff Martin, who was passionately committed to franchising service centers as fast as possible. Martin and Herget had known each other for a long time, so they sought a mutually acceptable way to resolve their differences. Their discussions quickly resulted in the decision that Herget would buy a company-owned service center in northern California by swapping his Super Lube founder's stock valued at $64,000, which he had purchased originally for $13,000. Quick Lube Franchise Corporation was founded.

Early Success and Growth

Success in his first service center inspired growth. Eventually QLFC controlled service center development and operating rights to a geographic area covering parts of California and Washington with the potential for over 90 service centers. Herget's long-term goal was to build QLFC into a big chain of Super Lube service centers that would have a public stock offering or merge with a larger company (Exhibits A and B).

Herget financed QLFC's growth with both equity and debt (Exhibits C and D). Most of the additional equity came from former Super Lube employees who left the franchisor to join QLFC in senior management positions. They purchased stock in QLFC with cash realized by selling their stock in Super Lube. A key member of Herget's team was Mark Roberts, who had been Super Lube's CFO until 1986. He brought much needed financial sophistication to QLFC.

The primary debt requirement was for financing new service centers. In 1991 the average cost of land acquisition and construction had risen to $750,000 per service center from about $350,000 10 years earlier.

Growth was originally achieved through off-balance-sheet real estate partnerships. An Oregon bank lent about $4 million, and a Texas bank lent almost $3 million. However, rapid growth wasn't possible until QLFC struck a deal with Huston Oil for $6.5 million of subordinated debt. The Huston debt was 8 percent interest—only for 5 years and then amortized on a straight-line basis in years 6 through 10. The real estate developed with the Huston financing was kept in the company. QLFC was contractually committed to purchasing Huston products.

This case was prepared by Professors Stephen Spinelli and William By-grave. © Copyright Babson College, 1991. All rights reserved.

EXHIBIT A

QLFC Growth

	82	83	84	85	86	87	88	89	90	91
Service Centers	2	3	4	7	16	25	34	44	46	47
Sales ($ million)	.5	1.6	2.1	3.8	8.5	15.5	19	27	28	30

EXHIBIT B

Quick Lube Franchise Corp.: FY 1991 Budget Worksheet*

	Apr	May	Jun	Jul	Aug	Sep	Oct	Nov	Dec	Jan	Feb	Mar	Total
Sales	2,424,718	2,444,629	2,756,829	2,816,765	2,872,074	2,358,273	2,619,415	2,435,022	2,494,696	2,733,469	2,464,172	2,795,804	31,215,866
Cost of sales	544,689	549,348	613,728	626,809	639,126	529,542	588,628	547,137	573,063	627,574	565,836	642,144	7,047,624
Variable expenses†	805,251	826,956	894,782	914,080	943,260	790,276	893,236	819,709	844,626	911,313	826,811	949,576	10,419,876
Fixed expenses	358,640	349,858	351,828	363,917	371,498	366,260	371,988	391,686	378,485	388,381	399,375	393,974	4,485,890
Real estate cost	320,377	337,372	340,652	341,353	352,053	352,053	372,030	372,030	392,337	392,452	392,452	410,552	4,375,713
Store operating income	395,761	381,095	555,839	570,606	566,137	320,142	393,533	304,460	306,185	413,749	279,698	399,558	4,886,763
Overhead	255,515	261,573	245,083	241,089	263,458	278,333	258,655	274,724	277,974	269,551	279,819	275,440	3,181,214
Operating income	140,246	119,522	310,756	329,517	302,679	41,809	134,878	29,736	28,211	144,198	(121)	124,118	1,705,549
Other income	7,392	7,392	7,392	7,392	7,392	7,392	7,392	7,392	7,392	7,392	7,392	7,392	88,704
Dropped site expense	(8,333)	(8,333)	(8,333)	(8,333)	(8,333)	(8,333)	(8,333)	(8,333)	(8,333)	(8,333)	(8,333)	(8,333)	(99,996)
Minority interest	686	613	(2,610)	(3,254)	(3,145)	2,065	511	4,529	4,346	1,290	6,564	2,459	14,054
Interest expense	(5,495)	(5,495)	(5,495)	(5,495)	(5,495)	(5,495)	(5,495)	(5,495)	(5,495)	(5,495)	(5,495)	(5,495)	(65,940)
Taxable income	134,496	113,699	301,710	319,827	293,098	37,438	128,953	27,829	26,121	139,052	7	120,141	1,642,371
Income tax expense	54,921	47,253	119,971	126,613	115,680	17,885	53,211	17,790	16,727	58,652	6,880	51,779	687,362
Net income	79,575	66,446	181,739	193,214	177,418	19,553	75,742	10,039	9,394	80,400	(6,873)	68,362	955,009

* Budget revised March 21, 1990.
† Royalties to the franchisor equal 7% of gross sales.

EXHIBIT C

Quick Lube Franchise Corp.: Consolidated Balance Sheets

	Year Ended March 31	
	1991	**1990**
Assets		
Current assets		
Cash	$ 740,551	$ 665,106
Accounts receivable, net doubtful accounts of $61,000 in 1991 and $44,000 in 1990	518,116	309,427
Construction advances receivable	508,168	137,412
Due from government agency		407,678
Inventory	1,093,241	1,074,513
Prepaid expenses other	407,578	401,562
Total current assets	3,267,654	2,995,698
Property and equipment		
Land	351,772	351,772
Buildings	3,171,950	2,519,845
Furniture, fixtures, and equipment	2,988,073	2,644,801
Leasehold improvements	242,434	183,635
Property under capital leases	703,778	703,778
Construction in progress	68,138	531,594
	7,526,145	6,935,425
Less accumulated depreciation and amortization	(1,290,565)	(854,473)
	6,235,580	6,080,952
Other assets		
Area development and license agreements, net of accumulated amortization	923,970	988,314
Other intangibles, net accumulated amortization	273,737	316,960
Other	151,604	208,898
	$10,852,545	$10,590,822
Liabilities and Shareholders' Equity		
Current liabilities		
Accounts payable and accrued expenses	$ 3,085,318	$ 3,198,694
Income taxes payable	37,224	256,293
Note payable		250,000
Current portion—LTD	203,629	174,134
Current portion of capital lease	19,655	17,178
Total current liabilities	3,345,826	3,896,299
Long-term debt, less current	2,848,573	3,052,597
Capital lease obligations, less current	628,199	648,552
Other long-term liabilities	731,783	483,534
Minority interest	2,602	13,821
Total long-term liabilities	4,211,157	4,198,504
Shareholders' equity		
Common stock, par value $.01/share authorized 10,000,000 shares; issued 1,080,000 shares	10,800	10,800
Additional paid-in capital	1,041,170	774,267
Retained earnings	2,243,592	1,710,952
	3,295,562	2,496,019
	$10,852,545	$10,590,822

EXHIBIT D

Quick Lube Franchise Corp.: Consolidated Cash Flow

	Year Ended March 31		
Operating Activities	1991	1990	1989
Net income	$ 532,640	$ 764,794	$ 524,211
Adjustments to reconcile net income to net cash provided by operating activities:			
Depreciation and amortization	612,063	526,750	414,971
Provision for losses on accounts receivable	16,615	30,510	5,559
Provision for deferred income taxes	(15,045)	12,519	50,388
Minority interest in losses of subsidiaries	(11,217)	(129,589)	(83,726)
Loss (gain) on disposition of property and equipment	33,301	(420)	N/A
Changes in operating assets and liabilities:			
Accounts receivable	(225,304)	(58,700)	(135,585)
Inventory	(18,728)	(273,559)	(286,037)
Prepaid expenses and other	(6,016)	(102,117)	(34,334)
Accounts payable and accrued expenses	(113,376)	559,456	1,409,042
Income taxes payable	(219,069)	404,068	(620,434)
Due from shareholders and affiliates	N/A	N/A	(43,742)
Other long-term liabilities	263,294	167,501	84,697
Net cash provided by operating activities	849,158	1,901,213	1,285,010
Investing Activities			
Purchases of property and equipment	(599,327)	(1,922,892)	(1,922,852)
Proceeds from sale of property and equipment	374,592	8,523	782,519
Acquisition of license agreements	(44,000)	(127,000)	(117,000)
Acquisition of other intangibles	(2,615)	(327,549)	(2,500)
Change in construction advance receivable	(370,756)	593,017	(601,525)
Change in other assets	43,894	(138,816)	11,908
Net cash used in investing activities	(598,212)	(1,914,717)	(1,849,450)
Financing Activities			
Proceeds from long-term borrowings and revolving line of credit	4,940,000	4,026,441	2,448,071
Proceeds from borrowings from related parties	N/A	N/A	19,600
Principal payments on long-term borrowings	(5,364,529)	(3,463,693)	(2,658,534)
Principal payments on borrowings from related parties		(19,600)	(7,216)
Principal payments on capital lease obligations	(17,876)	(38,048)	N/A
Proceeds from sale of common stock and capital contributions	266,903	97,201	19,600
Net cash provided by (used in) financing activities	(175,502)	602,301	(178,479)
Increase (decrease) in cash	75,444	588,797	(742,919)
Cash at beginning of year	665,106	76,309	819,228

Super Lube's Relationship with Its Franchisees

Despite bridge financing of $10 million at the end of 1985 followed by a successful initial public offering, Super Lube's growth continued to outpace its ability to finance it. At the end of the 1980s, Super Lube was in technical default to its debt holders. Huston struck a deal to acquire 80 percent of the company in a debt restruc-turing scheme. However, during the time of Super Lube's mounting financial problems and the subsequent Huston deal, franchisees grew increasingly discontented.

A franchise relationship is governed by a contract called a license agreement. As a "business format" franchise, a franchisor offers a franchisee the rights to engage in a business system by using the franchisor's trade name, trademark, service marks, know-how, and method of doing business. The franchisee is contractu-ally bound to a system of operation and to pay the franchisor a royalty in the form of a percentage of top-line sales.

The Super Lube license agreement called for the franchisor to perform product development and quality assurance tasks. Super Lube had made a strategic decision early in its existence to sell franchises on the basis of area development agreements. These franchisees had grown to become a group of sophisticated, fully integrated companies. As the franchisees grew with multiple outlets and became increasingly self-reliant, the royalty became difficult to justify. When the franchisor failed to perform its contractually obligated tasks as its financial problems grew more and more burdensome toward the end of the 1980s, a franchisee revolt began to surface.

The Huston Era Begins

The new owners, Huston Oil, quickly moved to replace virtually the entire management team at Super Lube. The new CEO was previously a long-term employee of a Kmart subsidiary. He took a hard-line position on how the franchise system would operate and that Huston motor oil would be an important part of it. The first national convention after the Huston takeover was a disaster. The franchisees, already frustrated, were dismayed by the focus of the franchisor on motor oil sales instead of service center–level profitability.

Herget decided to make a thorough analysis of the historical relationship between Quick Lube Franchise Corporation and Super Lube. Three months of research and documentation led to Quick Lube Franchise Corpo-

ration calling for a meeting with Huston to review the findings and address concerns.

The meeting was held at the franchisor's offices with Herget and the franchisor's CEO and executive vice president. Herget described the meeting:

> The session amounted to a three-hour monologue by me followed by Super Lube's rejection of the past as relevant to the relationship. I was politely asked to trust that the future performance of the franchisor would be better and to treat the past as sunk cost. In response to my concern that Huston might have a conflict of interest in selling me product as well as being the franchisor and having an obligation to promote service center profitability, they answered that Huston bailed Super Lube out of a mess and the franchisees should be grateful, not combative.

Litigation

The QLFC board of directors received Herget's report and told him to select a law firm and to pursue litigation against Huston. QLFC's three months of research was supplied to the law firm. A suit against Huston was filed three months after the failed QLFC/Huston "summit."

Huston denied the charges and filed a countersuit. Document search, depositions, and general legal maneuvering had been going on for about three months when QLFC's attorneys received a call from Huston requesting a meeting. Herget immediately called a board meeting and prepared to make a recommendation for QLFC's strategic plan.

Chapter Twelve

Franchising

When you understand that the franchisees and the franchisor are partners, you create an almost unlimited opportunity for growth.

Bob Rosenberg
Founder and former CEO
Dunkin' Donuts

Results Expected

Upon completion of this chapter, you will be able to

1. Explain what franchising is, and discuss the nature of the roles of franchisors and franchisees.
2. Discuss the criteria for becoming a franchisee of an existing system, as well as for becoming a franchisor.
3. Describe a basic screening method for evaluating franchises with higher success probabilities.
4. Analyze the franchise relationship model and its use as a guide for developing a high-potential franchise venture.
5. Analyze and discuss the franchise growth strategy of a young start-up company, Bagelz, and the career decisions of one of its founders, Mike Bellobuono.

Introduction

In this chapter we will explore franchising and how well it fits the Timmons Model definition of entrepreneurship. We will consider the scope of franchising and examine the criteria for determining a franchise's stature, from the perspective of both prospective franchisee and an existing or prospective franchisor. We will present several templates and models that will be helpful in conducting due diligence on a franchise opportunity.

Let us consider how well franchising fits our definition of entrepreneurship from Chapters 2 and 3. You may recall that the focus of our definition of entrepreneurship is opportunity recognition for the purpose of wealth creation. The focus of franchising

is exactly the same. Franchising offers a thoughtful system for reshaping and executing a delivery system designed to extract maximum value from the opportunity. Just as opportunity, thought, and action are essential elements of an entrepreneurial venture, so too are they important components of a franchise opportunity. Franchising also fulfills our definition of entrepreneurship because each partner understands the wealth expectations of the other, and they work together toward these goals; their "bond" is sealed as partners in the franchise entrepreneurial alliance.

As eloquently described by Bob Rosenberg in the chapter's introduction, franchising is, at its core, an entrepreneurial alliance between two organizations, the franchisor and the franchisee. The successful franchise relationship defines and exploits an opportunity as a team. The franchisor is the concept innovator who grows by seeking partners or franchisees to operate the concept in local markets. A franchisor can be born when at least one company store exists and the opportunity has been beta tested. Once the concept is proven, the franchisor and the franchisee enter an agreement to grow the concept based on a belief that there are mutual advantages to the alliance. The nature of these advantages is defined by the ability of the partners to exploit particular aspects of the opportunity for which each is respectively better suited than the other. The heart of franchising is entrepreneurship—the pursuit of and intent to gain wealth by exploiting the given opportunity. A unique aspect of franchising is that it brings together two parties, both of which have individual intentions of wealth creation through opportunity exploitation, but who choose to achieve their goals by working together. Because franchising aligns the different skill sets and capabilities of the franchisor and franchisee, the whole of a franchise opportunity is greater than the sum of its parts.

At its most fundamental level, franchising is a large-scale growth opportunity based on a partnership rather than solely on individual effort. Once a business is operating successfully, according to the Timmons Model, it is appropriate to think about franchising as a growth tool. The sum of the activities between the partners is coalescent in a trademark or brand. The mission of the entrepreneurial alliance is to maintain and build the brand. The brand signals a price–value relationship in the minds of customers. Revenue is driven higher because the marketplace responds to the brand with more purchases or purchases at higher prices relative to the competition.

Job Creation versus Wealth Creation

As a franchise entrepreneur, we can control the growth of our franchise opportunity. For those whose life goal is to own a pizza restaurant and earn a comfortable income, the opportunity is there. Franchising allows us to do this, but it also allows us to build 30 pizza restaurants and to participate fully in the wealth creation process. A major strength of franchising is that it provides many options for individuals to meet their financial goals and business visions, however conservative or grandiose.

The ability to create wealth in any venture starts with the initial opportunity assessment. For example,

a franchise company may decide to limit its number of stores per geographic territory. Therefore, the expansion market is limited from the start for potential franchisees. Even if franchisees work hard and follow proven systems, they may be buying a job rather than creating wealth.

Some companies are designed to reward successful franchisees with the opportunity to buy more stores in a particular market or region. Franchisees who achieve prosperity with single units are rewarded with additional stores. The entrepreneurial process is encouraged, and wealth is created.

Much of the goal of *New Venture Creation* is to increase the odds of success and the scope of a new venture. Franchising can be an excellent vehicle for growth.

Franchising: A History of Entrepreneurship

The franchise entrepreneurial spirit in the United States has never been more alive than today. More than 4,500 franchise businesses with 600,000 outlets populate the marketplace; these businesses make up 36 percent of all retail sales nationwide. Internationally, franchising generates as much as 10 percent of retailing in the United Kingdom, France, and Australia. The International Franchise Association expects that franchise businesses will continue to thrive and prosper, accounting for 40 percent of U.S. retail sales by 2008.[1] The belief that franchising can be an exciting entrepreneurial venture is supported by the continued success of established franchise systems, the proliferation of new franchises, and the profitability reported by franchisees and franchisors.[2] These statistics hint at the scope and richness that franchising has achieved in a relatively short period of time. The process of wealth creation through franchising continues to evolve as we witness an increase in not only the number of multiple-outlet franchisors,[3] but also in the number of franchisees that operate multiple outlets in different franchise systems.

Evidence of the success of franchising as an entrepreneurial opportunity-exploiting and wealth-creating vehicle comes from one of the largest franchisors in the world—the U.K. conglomerate Allied Domecq, which owns Dunkin' Donuts, Baskin-Robbins, and Togo's restaurants. Bob Rosenberg,[4] son of Dunkin' Donuts founder Bill Rosenberg, grew the Dunkin' system from a few hundred to more than 3,000

---

[1] *Franchising Guide to Policy Making*, IFA, 2003.
[2] S. Spinelli, Jr., B. Leleux, and S. Birley, "An Analysis of Shareholder Return in Public Franchisors," Society of Franchising presentation, 2001.
[3] S. Shane, "Hybrid Organizational Arrangements and Their Implications for Firm Growth and Survival: A Study of New Franchisors," *Academy of Management Journal* 39 (1996), pp. 216–34.
[4] Bob Rosenberg is now an adjunct professor at Babson College and teaches in the entrepreneurship division. The authors have consulted with Professor Rosenberg on a number of issues in entrepreneurship, including franchising.

EXHIBIT 12.1

Franchise Facts about Some of the Largest U.S. Franchisors*

Franchise system age	21 years
Number of outlets per franchisor	2,652
Annual revenue	$871 million
Franchise fee	$28,559
Royalty rate	5.58%
Advertising rate	2.89%
License agreement term	14 years

*The average for 91 firms is used for all categories.

outlets before selling to Allied Domecq. Bob continued to operate Allied Domecq's North American retail operation for 10 years, doubling its size, until he retired in 1998. Bob believes, "Allied Domecq's franchise operation can double again in the United States, and the potential in Europe and Asia is exponential." Clearly franchising can be a global business model that is adaptable to most locales.

Another company that signaled the prevalence of franchising in contemporary business is Jiffy Lube International. Although most franchisors tend to think in terms of national scale, the team that grew Jiffy Lube purchased the then-small mom-and-pop company based in Ogden, Utah, and immediately added *International* to the company's name, sensing that globalization of the business model and service offering could be successful outside the United States.

When people hear the names Ray Kroc and Anita Roddick, most people certainly identify the founders of McDonald's and The Body Shop as entrepreneurs and their trademarks and brands as some of the most successful in the world. Exhibit 12.1 reveals several aspects of contemporary franchises.

Anyone exploring entrepreneurial opportunities should give serious consideration to the franchising option. As franchisor or franchisee, this option can be a viable way to share risk and reward, create and grow an opportunity, and raise human and financial capital.

Franchising: Assembling the Opportunity

As we saw in earlier chapters, the Timmons Model identifies the three components of opportunity as market demand, market size and structure, and margin analysis (the 3Ms). The franchise organization must understand the nature of demand as it resides both in the individual consumer and in the society. At the most fundamental level, the primary target audience (PTA) is the defining quality of the opportunity

recognition process. Without a customer, there is no opportunity; without an opportunity, there is no venture; without a sustainable opportunity, there can be no franchise.

As we discussed earlier in this chapter, our goal is to look at franchising because it presents opportunities for both franchisees and franchisors. We will now investigate several aspects of franchise opportunity recognition: PTA identification; service concept; service delivery system (SDS) design; training and operational support; field support, marketing, advertising, and promotion; and product purchase provision. Prospective franchisees should understand the nature and quality of each of these franchise components. Existing franchisors might study their offerings in light of this information. Those considering growth through franchising must pay attention to the details of their systems' offerings.

Primary Target Audience

Defining the target customer is essential because it dictates many diverse functions of the business. Most important, it measures primary demand. Once the primary target audience is defined, secondary targets may be identified. The degree of market penetration in the secondary target is less than that of the primary target. Although measuring market demand is not an exact science, a franchisor must continually collect data about its customers. Even after buying a franchise, the franchisee compares local market demographics with national profiles to estimate the potential of the local market in terms of the number of outlets that can be developed. Revenue projections are made from the identification of the target audiences and the degree of market penetration that can be expected based on historical information. Three major areas of data collection can be integral to refining the PTA.

Demographic Profiles   A demographic profile is a compilation of personal characteristics that enables the company to define the "average" customer. Most franchisors perform market research as a central function, developing customer profiles and disseminating this information to franchisees. Such research may include current user and nonuser profiles. Typically a demographic analysis includes age, gender, income, home address (driving or walking distance from the store), working address (driving or walking distance from the store), marital status, family status (number and ages of children), occupation, race and ethnicity, religion, and nationality. Demographics must be put into context by looking at concept-specific data such as average number of automobiles for a Midas franchise or percentage of disposable income spent on clothes for a Gap franchise.

Psychographic Profiles

Psychographic Profiles Psychographic profiles segment potential customers based on social class, lifestyle, and personality traits. Economic classes in the United States are generally divided into seven categories:

1. Upper uppers   1 percent
2. Lower uppers   2 percent
3. Upper middles   12 percent
4. Middle class   32 percent
5. Working class   38 percent
6. Upper lowers   9 percent
7. Lower lowers   7 percent

Lifestyle addresses such issues as health consciousness, fashion orientation, or being a "car freak." Personality variables such as confidence, conservation, and independence are used to segment markets.

Behavioral variables segment potential customers by their knowledge, attitude, and use of products in order to project usage of the product or service. By articulating detailed understanding of the target market, specifically why these consumers will buy the product or service, you gain great insight into the competitive landscape. Why will a consumer spend money with us rather than with a competitor?

Geographic Profiles The scope of a franchise concept can be local, regional, national, or international. The U.S. national market is typically divided into nine regions: Pacific, Mountain, West North Central, West South Central, East North Central, East South Central, South Atlantic, Middle Atlantic, and New England. Regions are further divided by population density and described as urban, suburban, or rural.

The smart franchise uses the ever-growing system of franchisees and company outlets to continuously gather data about customers. This helps dynamically shape the vision and therefore the strategic exploitation of the opportunity. The analysis of system data must include a link to the vision of the concept and to the vision's possibilities. For example, if we launched an earring company 10 years ago, we could have defined the target market as women ages 21 to 40, and the size of the market as the number of women within this age group in the United States. But perhaps looking beyond the existing data and anticipating the larger market that now exists can shape our vision. The target market for earrings could be defined as women and men ages 12 to 32, with an average of three earrings per individual, not two. The identification of the target market requires that we combine demographic data with our own unique vision for the venture.

The focus on PTA development as the core to franchise opportunity recognition is essential to estimating

---

Theory into Practice: Market Demand—Radio Shack's Moving Target Market

Target markets are dynamic, often metamorphosing very quickly. Radio Shack had to change its business to reflect the shift in its target market. In the 1970s and 1980s Radio Shack grew by addressing the needs of technophiles—young men with penchants for shortwave radios, stereo systems, walkie-talkies, and the like. The national retail chain supplied this audience with the latest gadgets and did very well.

Then, starting in the early 1990s, technology became more sophisticated. Personal electronic equipment began to include cell phones, handheld computers, and electronic organizers. The market for these products was expanding from a smaller group of technophiles to a larger group of middle-aged males who loved gadgets and who had more disposable income. Yet Radio Shack remained Radio Shack. Its audience dwindled while the personal electronics market boomed.

In the early 1990s Radio Shack refocused its business to target this new demographic. Its advertising addressed the needs of the 44-year-old upper-middle-class male versus the 29-year-old technophile. That 29-year-old who formerly shopped at Radio Shack was now 44! He was not going to make a radio, but he would buy a cell phone. Radio Shack made dramatic changes in its marketing and inventory. As a result, it has made dramatic changes in its profitability.

---

the consumer appeal of a franchise and to establish validity of the opportunity. We will consider a set of criteria that will help define the due diligence process in assessing how a franchise has exploited the opportunity. This discussion holds value for an overall understanding of franchising for existing franchisors and potential franchisors and franchisees alike.

Evaluating a Franchise: Initial Due Diligence

Before looking at the details of a franchise offering, the prospective franchisee must sift through the offerings of the 4,500 franchises in the United States. Although the next section is most appropriate for prospective franchisees, the savvy franchisor will use this information to better craft a franchise offering for potential franchisees.

EXHIBIT 12.2

Franchise Risk Profile Template

Criteria	Low Risk/Average Market Return 15–20%	Acceptable Risk/ Incremental 30% Return	High Risk/Marginal 40–50% Return	Extreme Risk/Large Return 60–100%
Multiple Market Presence	National	Regional	State	Local
Outlet Pro Forma Disclosed or Discerned	Yes, 90%+ apparently profitable	Yes, 80%+ apparently profitable	Yes, 70%+ apparently profitable	No, less than 70% profitable
Market Share	No. 1 and dominant	No. 1 or 2 with a strong competitor	Lower than No. 2	Lower than No. 3 with a dominant player
National Marketing Program	Historically successful creative process, national media buys in place	Creative plus regional media buys	Creative plus local media buys	Local media buys only
National Purchasing Program	More than 3%+ gross margin advantage in national purchasing contract	1–3% gross margin advantage versus independent operators	Regional gross margin advantages only	No discernible gross margin advantages
Margin Characteristics	50%+ gross margin 18%+ net outlet margin	40–50% gross margin 12–17% net outlet margin	30–40% gross margin less than 12% net outlet margin	Declining gross margin detected, erratic net outlet margin
Business Format	Sophisticated training, documented operations manual, identifiable feedback mechanism with franchisees	Initial training and dynamically documented operations manual, some field support	Training and operations but weak field support	Questionable training and field support and static operations
Term of the License Agreement	20 years with automatic renewal	15 years with renewal	Less than 15 years or no renewal	Less than 10 years
Site Development	Quantifiable criteria clearly documented and tied to market specifics	Markets prioritized with general site development criteria	General market development criteria outlined	Business format not tied to identifiable market segment(s)
Capital Required per Unit	$15,000–$25,000 working capital	Working capital plus $50,000–$100,000 machinery and equipment	Working capital plus machinery and equipment plus $500,000–$1,000,000 real estate	Erratic, highly variable, or ill-defined
Franchise Fee and Royalties	PDV* of the fees is less than the demonstrated economic advantages (reduced costs or increased revenue) of the franchise versus stand-alone		PDV of the fees is projected to be less than the expected economic advantages (reduced costs or increased revenue) of the franchise versus stand-alone	PDV of the fees is not discernibly less than the expected value of the franchise

*PDV is an abbreviation for present discounted value. If franchising is a risk reduction strategy, then the discount of future revenue should be less. Concurrently, the economies of scale in marketing should increase the amount of revenue a franchise can generate versus a stand-alone operation.

Exhibit 12.2 provides a franchise screening template designed to make a preliminary assessment of the key variables that constitute a franchise offering. The exercise is crafted to help map the risk profile of the franchise and highlight areas that will most likely need further investigation. If the following criteria are important to the potential franchisee, then they also provide a map of the growth and market positioning objectives a stable franchisor should pursue.

This exercise is not designed to yield a "go or no go" decision. Rather, prospective franchisees should use it to help evaluate if a franchise meets their personal risk/return profile. Franchisors should also review the exercise to examine the risk signals they may be sending to prospective franchisees. It is especially important to understand this risk profile in the context of the alternative investments available to a prospective franchisee.

Franchisor as the High-Potential Venture

As Ray Kroc and Anita Roddick demonstrate, becoming a franchisor can be a high-potential endeavor. Growth and scale are the essence of the franchise mentality. Throughout this chapter we have viewed franchising as entrepreneurship for both the franchisee and franchisor. In this section we focus principally on franchisors and their rewards. In a study of *publicly traded franchisors*, the size and scope of the firms that achieved public capital is impressive. The capital marketplace has rewarded many franchisors that have met the criteria for a high-potential venture franchise. They, in turn, have performed well in return to shareholders. Exhibit 12.3 illustrates the performance of public franchisors compared with the

Standard and Poor's 500. This analysis of total return to shareholders (dividends and stock price appreciation) demonstrates that while the S&P index was hit hard by the economic downturn after 2001, the public franchisor index was not. Although the stock market slide following the period of irrational exuberance in the late 1990s was precipitated by excessively high dot-com valuations, the correction tended to depress share prices across the board—even of blue chip stocks. The relative buoyancy of the franchisor index can be attributed to the index being heavily weighted in the food category. During a recession, when household budgets are tight, consumers seek out dining establishments that offer the best value—the primary driver of many food-based franchise organizations.

Even more interesting are those exceptional performers among high-achieving franchisors. Take, for example, the quintessential franchise, McDonald's Corporation. McDonald's is the world's largest food service organization with more than 30,000 restaurants in 122 countries as of May 2007. Its global infrastructure includes a network of suppliers and

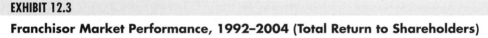

EXHIBIT 12.3

Franchisor Market Performance, 1992–2004 (Total Return to Shareholders)

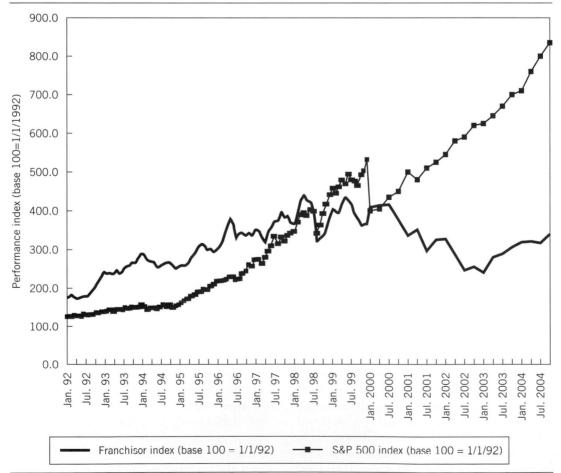

resources that allows it to achieve economies of scale and to offer great value to customers. In 2006 systemwide sales reached $21.6 billion, operating income was $4.6 billion, and earnings per share increased 3.3 percent. A local management team runs each market.

Allied Domecq's unique complementary day-part strategy combines two or three brand concepts in a single operation, attempting to optimize return on investment through more efficient use of resources. Launched in 1950, Dunkin' Donuts, now the world's largest chain of coffee and donut shops, has grown to more than 7,000 locations throughout the United States and 70 countries. Founded in 1971, Togo's is California's fastest-growing chain of sandwich eateries and is now spreading across the country. Baskin-Robbins' 31 flavors of sweet creamy treats are offered in more than 5,500 locations from California to Moscow.

Key Components of a Franchise Offering

In this section we describe the major aspects of delivering a franchise system. It is excellence in both concept and delivery that has created wealth for the franchisors in publicly traded companies. We have analyzed the features that propel the high-performance franchisor to exceptional returns. The excellent franchisor supports its franchisees, and the symbiotic nature of the relationship leverages return for both partners. After prospective franchisees narrow their search for a franchise (by using the screening guide among other activities), they should begin detailed analyses of the exact nature of a franchise. Franchisors should note the following in terms of how they might construct their offerings, knowing that prospective franchisees will conduct a detailed due diligence about these franchise components.

Service Delivery System

The road map for marshaling resources for the franchise comes from establishing the service delivery system (SDS). The opportunity dictates that we perform certain tasks to meet consumer demand. The assets put into place to meet these demands are largely the resources needed to launch the concept. In the franchise entrepreneurial alliance, the franchisor develops a method for delivering the product or service that fills customer demand. In essence, the service delivery system is the way in which resources are arrayed so that market demand can be captured. This service delivery system has to be well defined, documented, and tested by the company or prototype operation. The end result of the organization, execution, and transfer of the service delivery system is the creation of the firm's competitive advantage.

The Timmons Model first looks at opportunity assessment, which demands clear understanding of the target market and customer. Next it looks at resource marshaling or, in franchising, the establishment of the service delivery system. The SDS is the fundamental means by which customers will be served, and the fashion, often proprietary in design, in which the service delivery resources are arrayed to create competitive advantage in the marketplace. In franchising, this aspect is sometimes called the *business format*. A successful SDS's form and function will reflect the specific needs of the target customer. Highly successful and visible examples of business format innovations are the drive-through in fast-food restaurants and the bilevel facilities in quick oil change facilities. Every franchise has a well-defined SDS, however overt or transparent it may seem to an outside observer.

Because the SDS is truly the essence of the successful franchise, the detailed attention given to it should not be underestimated. For the concept innovator, the common phrase, "the devil is in the details," never takes on more meaning than when designing the SDS for the franchise. Steve Spinelli can corroborate this fact from experiences while expanding the Jiffy Lube franchise. One particular component of Jiffy Lube's expansion plans paints a vivid picture of the intricacy of the development of the SDS and reveals what a great benefit this design paid over time.

Jiffy Lube franchises must meet specific location criteria: high-volume car traffic, side of the street located for inbound or outbound traffic, high-profile retail area, and the far corner of any given street or block, among other requirements. Through trial and error, Jiffy Lube has determined the optimal location of the structure on any given property. Once these aspects are met, the building specifications follow. Structural specifications regarding the angle of the building and the width, depth, and angle of the entrance allow the optimal number of cars to stack in line waiting for the car in front to complete the service. On several occasions, facilities that met location criteria were failing to perform as expected. Analysis of the situation determined that the bend in the driveway was too sharp, preventing customers from driving their cars completely into the line and giving the inaccurate impression that the lot was full. Driveways were adjusted to accommodate an increased number of cars waiting for service.

This same level of refinement and detail orientation is encouraged for concept innovators when looking at their conceptual and actual SDS. Unless examined under a microscope, essential components of the SDS will be missed, deteriorating the value of the franchise. Jiffy Lube's experience also reinforces the benefits of a beta site, providing a real-world laboratory that can be adjusted and modified until the outlet reaches optimal performance.

Another part of the complete Jiffy Lube SDS was the design of the maintenance bay. Considering the limitations inherent in the use of hydraulic lifts, Jiffy Lube faced the dilemma of providing 30 minutes of labor in only 10 minutes. To deliver this 10-minute service, three technicians would need to work on a car at once without the use of a lift. This quandary led to the design of having cars drive into the bay and stop above an opening in the floor. This allowed one technician to service the car from below, another to service the car underneath the hood, and a third to service the car's interior. Without developing such a disruptive system,[5] Jiffy Lube would not have been able to succeed as it did.

The soundness of the decision to use the drive-through/bilevel system was confirmed when competitors, gas stations and car dealers, failed to deliver on offering a "quick lube" using hydraulic lifts and traditional bays. The sum of Jiffy Lube's intricately designed parts created the value of the SDS. Such is the level of detail needed for an SDS to deliver value to the customer and cost efficiencies to the operator. In much the same way, the accompanying box about Wendy's highlights the specific design components of the SDS that create value.

Training and Operational Support

Formal franchisor training programs transfer knowledge of the SDS to the franchisee's managers and line workers. Continuous knowledge gathering and transfer are important both before launch and on an ongoing basis. The license agreement must define the specific manner in which this franchisor responsibility will be performed. It should extend significantly beyond a manual and the classroom. Training will vary with the specifics of the franchise, but should include organized and monitored on-the-job experience in the existing system for the new franchisee and as many of the new staff members as the franchisor will allow. Established and stable franchise systems such as Jiffy Lube and Dunkin' Donuts require such operational experience in the existing system for as long as a year before the purchase of the franchise. However, this level of dedication to the franchisee's success is not the norm. Once the franchise is operational, the franchisee may be expected to do much or all of the

Theory into Practice: The Service Delivery System (SDS)—How Wendy's Used Its Business Format to Enter a "Saturated" Market

In 1972 Dave Thomas entered what many experts called a crowded hamburger fast-food market. His concept was to offer a "Cadillac hamburger" that was hot, fresh, and delivered more quickly than the competitions'. To execute Thomas's mission, Wendy's introduced the first drive-through in a national fast-food chain. Because Wendy's menu offered double and triple patties in addition to the traditional single-patty hamburger, its kitchens were designed to mass-produce hamburgers and deliver them to the front counter or drive-through window with minimal effort. To ensure a cooked just-in-time hamburger, each Wendy's restaurant included a large front window that enabled grill cooks (who were placed in clear view of the customer, not in a rear kitchen) to observe the flow of customers onto the premises.

Notwithstanding the huge market share owned by McDonald's and Burger King, Wendy's was able to successfully enter the fray because of the manner in which it arranged its resources to create a competitive advantage. In Wendy's, the sum of the intricacies—the drive-through window, the position of the cooks and kitchen, and the double and triple patties—has allowed the chain to compete and prosper in the fast-food hamburger market.

Dave Thomas's vision and personal impact on the fast-food industry were significant. When he passed away in January 2002, Wendy's received thousands of e-mail messages from customers expressing condolences.

on-site training of new hires. Still, as we will discuss in the next section, field support from the franchisor is often a signal of franchise stability and a reflection of the strength of the franchise partnership. Manuals, testing, training aids such as videos, and certification processes are often provided by the franchisor as part of this ongoing field support.

As discussed previously, the trade name and trademark are the most valuable assets in a franchise system. A franchisee's success rests soundly on the sales of products that are based on the brand equity and strength of the franchisor. As important as a sound service delivery system design is to the concept's foundation for success, the prospective training regimen is equally important. Without appropriately

---

[5] A disruptive business system is one that fundamentally changes the value proposition. McDonald's and Dairy Queen created the fast-food concept. Midas, Aamco, and Jiffy Lube pioneered targetd specialization in automotive service.

instructed individuals, an exceptional product will never reach the consumer's hands. As such, a poor training program will inevitably dilute the standardized, consistent delivery of the product and eventually erode the brand's value.

Field Support

Akin to the training program just mentioned is ongoing field support. This will take at least two forms: A franchisor's representative will visit the franchisee's location in person, and the franchisor will retain resident experts at corporate headquarters in each of the essential managerial disciplines that are available for consultation. Ideally the license agreement will provide for scheduled visits by the franchisor's agents to the franchisee's outlet with prescribed objectives, such as performance review, field training, facilities inspection, local marketing review, and operations audit. Unfortunately some franchisors use their field role as a diplomatic or pejorative exercise rather than for training and support. The greater the substance of the field functions, the easier it is for the franchisee to justify the royalty cost. Additionally, in the litigious environment in which we presently live, a well-documented field support program will mute franchisee claims of a lack of franchisor support.

One means of understanding the franchisor's field support motivation is to investigate the manner in which the field support personnel are compensated. If field staff members are paid commensurately with franchisee performance and ultimate profitability, then politics will play a diminished role. Key warning signs in this regard come when bonuses are paid for growth in the number of stores versus individual store growth, or for product usage (supplied by franchisor) by franchisee. Clearly, as with the training program prescribed by the franchisor and agreed to by the franchisee, a quality field support program is another integral success factor. A poor support program will eventually become problematic.

Marketing, Advertising, and Promotion

Marketing activities are certainly some of the most sensitive areas in the ongoing franchise relationship because they imprint the trade name and trademark in the mind of the consumer to gain awareness—the most important commodity of the franchise. If the

delivery of the product validates the marketing message, then the value of the franchise is enhanced; but if it is not congruent, there can be a detrimental effect at both the local and national levels. As the number of outlets grows, marketing budgets increase and spread across the growing organization, thereby optimizing the marketing program.

Generally marketing programs are funded and implemented at three different levels: national, regional, and local. A national advertising budget is typically controlled by the franchisor, and each franchisee contributes a percentage of top-line sales to the advertising fund. The franchisor then produces materials (television, radio, and newspaper advertisements; direct-mail pieces; and point-of-sale materials) for use by the franchisees and, depending on the size of the fund, also buys media time or space on behalf of the franchisees. Because it is impossible to allocate these services equally between franchisees of different sizes across different markets, the license agreement will specify the use of "best efforts" to approximate equal treatment between franchisees. Although "best efforts" will invariably leave some franchisees with more advertising exposure and some with less, over time this situation should balance itself. This is one area of marketing that requires careful monitoring by both parties.

Regional marketing, advertising, and promotion are structured on the basis of an area of dominant influence (ADI). All the stores in a given ADI (e.g., Greater Hartford, Connecticut) should contribute a percentage of their top-lines sales to the ADI advertising cooperative.[6] The cooperative's primary function is usually to buy media using franchisor-supplied or -approved advertising and to coordinate regional site promotions. If the franchise has a regional advertising cooperative requirement in the license agreement, it should also have standardized ADI cooperative bylaws. These bylaws will outline voting rights and expenditure parameters, among other things. Often a single-store franchisee can be disadvantaged in a poorly organized cooperative, whereas a major contributor to the cooperative may find his voting rights disproportionately low in any given cooperative.

The third and final scenario for marketing is typically dubbed local advertising or local store marketing. At this level, the franchisee is contractually obligated to make direct advertising expenditures. There is often a wide spectrum of permissible advertising expenditures, depending on the franchisor guidelines in the license agreement. Unfortunately, the license agreement will probably not be specific. Franchisors

---

[6] Advertising cooperatives in franchising are common. A cooperative is a contractual agreement whereby franchisees in a geographic area are bound to contribute a percentage of their revenue to a fund that executes a marketing plan, usually including media purchases. The cooperative is typically governed by the participating franchisees and sometimes includes representation from the franchisor and advertising agency.

will try to maintain discretion on this issue for maximum flexibility in the marketplace, while franchisees will vie for control of this area. Company-owned stores should have advertising requirements equal to those for the franchised units to avoid a franchisor having a free ride; in this regard, historical behavior is the best gauge of reasonableness.

The franchisor should monitor and enforce marketing expenditures. For example, the customer of a franchisee leaving one ADI and entering another will have been affected by the advertising of adjacent regions. Additionally, advertising expenditures not made are marketing impressions lost to the system. When this happens, the marketing leverage inherent in franchising is not optimized.

Supply

In most franchise systems, major benefits include bulk purchasing and inventory control. In the license agreement, there are several ways to account for this economy of scale advantage. Because of changing markets, competitors and U.S. antitrust law make it impossible for the franchisor to be bound to best-price requirements. The franchise should employ a standard of best efforts and good faith to acquire both national and regional supply contracts.

Depending on the nature of the product or service, regional deals might make more sense than national deals. Regional contact may provide greater advantages to the franchisee because of shipping weight and cost or service requirements. The savvy franchisor will recognize this and implement a flexible purchase plan. When local advantages exist and the franchisor does not act appropriately, the franchisees will fill the void. The monthly area of dominant influence (ADI) meeting then becomes an expanded forum for franchisees to voice their appreciations and concerns. The results of such ad hoc organizations can be reduced control of quality and expansion of franchisee association outside the confines of the license agreement. Advanced activity of this nature can often fractionalize a franchise system and even render the franchisor obsolete. In some cases, the franchisor and franchisee-operated buying cooperatives peaceably coexist, acting as competitors and lowering the costs to the operator. However, the dual buying co-ops usually reduce economies of scale and dilute system resources. They also provide fertile ground for conflict within the franchise alliance.

For quality control purposes, the franchisor will reserve the right to publish a product specifications list. The list will clearly establish the quality standards of raw materials or goods used in the operation. From those specifications, a subsequent list of approved suppliers is generated. This list can evolve into a franchise "tying agreement," which occurs when the business format franchise license agreement binds the franchisee to the purchase of a specifically branded product. This varies from the product specification list because brand, not product content, is the qualifying specification. The important question here is, Does the tying arrangement of franchise and product create an enhancement for the franchisee in the marketplace? If so, then are arm's-length controls in place to ensure that pricing, netted from the enhanced value, will yield positive results? Unfortunately this is impossible to precisely quantify. However, if the tying agreement is specified in the license agreement, then the prospective franchise owner is advised to make a judgment before purchasing the franchise. With this sort of decision at hand, the franchisor should prove the value of the tying agreement or abandon it.

Another subtle form of tying agreements occurs when the license agreement specifies an approved suppliers list that ultimately includes only one supplier. If adding suppliers to the list is nearly impossible, there is a de facto tying arrangement. Additionally, another tying arrangement can occur when the product specification is written so that only one brand can qualify. A franchisor should disclose any remuneration gained by the franchisor or its officers, directly or indirectly, from product purchase in the franchise system. In this case, the franchisor's market value enhancement test is again proof of a credible arrangement.

Franchise Relationship Model

Now that we have established the nature and components of the franchise relationship, we can connect these principles to the franchise relationship model (FRM), which we have developed over the past eight years (see Exhibit 12.4). The FRM connects the entrepreneurial framework provided by the Timmons Model to the specific processes that are unique to franchising. We have argued that franchising is a powerful entrepreneurial method because it fits the Timmons Model and because it creates wealth. The FRM illustrates both how a concept innovator (i.e., potential franchisor) can most efficiently construct a franchising company and how a concept implementer (i.e., potential franchisee) can determine which company to join. The FRM further helps to distinguish between those tasks best executed under a corporate

EXHIBIT 12.4

Franchise Relationship Model

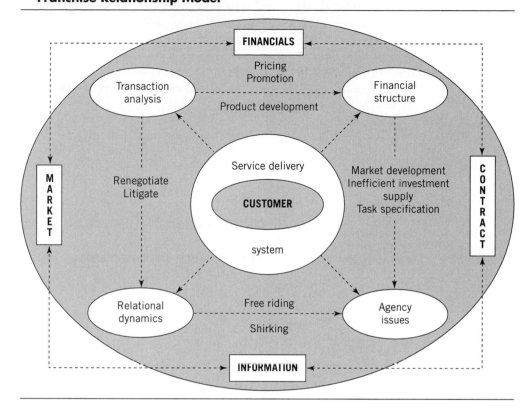

umbrella and those best done by the individual franchisee. Just as franchising is itself a risk-ameliorating tool for the entrepreneur, the franchise relationship model is also a tool that both franchisors and franchisees can use to judge the efficiency or success potential of a franchise opportunity. By overlaying the FRM template onto any given franchise, we can forecast to a great extent where bottlenecks will impede success or where improvements can be made that will offer a competitive advantage.

The FRM is a puzzle, a series of franchise principles, each of which fits into the others to form a powerful interlocking business concept that solidifies itself as the linkages are implemented more efficiently. Although the process starts in the center with the customer, moves to the service delivery system and follows from there, the outer perimeter of means and mechanisms drives the competitive advantage of a franchise system. The major areas of concern other than the customer and the SDS are transaction analy-

sis, financial structure, agency issues, and relational dynamics.

Transaction analysis considers which transactions are better served at a national level by the franchisor and which should be served at the local level by the franchisee.[7] Typically franchisor functions are centered on economies of scale. Franchisee functions include those that require on-site entrepreneurial capacity such as hiring and local promotion. The financial structure flows from pro forma analysis of customer demand and the cost associated with development and execution of the service delivery system. Agency issues concern delegating responsibility to a partner.[8] No franchisor can know absolutely that the franchisee is "doing the right thing" at the store level. Franchisees cannot possibly know that the franchisor is always acting in their best interest. Relational dynamics is the area that allows the partnership between franchisor and franchisee to continuously change and develop as the business continues to expand.[9] Any partnership

---

[7] O. E. Williamson, "Comparative Economic Organizations: The Analysis of Discrete Structural Alternatives," *Administrative Science Quarterly* (June 1991), pp. 269–288.

[8] F. Lafontaine, "Agency Theory and Franchising; Some Empirical Results," *RAND Journal of Economics* 23 (1992), pp. 263–68.

[9] I. R. Mcneil, "Economic Analysis of Contractual Relations: Its Shortfalls and Need for a 'Rich Classification Apparatus,'" *Northwestern University Law Review*, February 1980, pp. 1018–63.

that strictly adheres to a contract will end in litigation.

The franchise relationship model (Exhibit 12.4) is dynamic: As events affect one aspect of the model, all other aspects must be reviewed in an iterative process. For example, if renegotiation of the license agreement were to result in a reduced royalty, the financial model would be altered. A change in royalty could dictate a change in the services that the franchisor provides. Any change creates a cascading effect throughout the system—a reconstruction of the puzzle.

The franchise relationship model begins with opportunity recognition and shaping (customer) and then articulates the competitive advantages and costs of the service delivery system that will extract the demand (SDS) and create a return on investment. The competitive sustainability of the franchise is embedded in the delineation of responsibilities between franchisor and franchisee and in the conscious design of the service delivery system. The franchisor's tasks are centrally executed and focus on economies of scale; the franchisee concentrates on those responsibilities that require local on-site entrepreneurial intensity (transaction analysis). The emergent financial structure is the manifestation of the interaction between the primary target customer and the service delivery system. By sharing the burden of the service delivery system and the potential for return on investment, the franchise entrepreneurial alliance is formed.

Central to the long-term stability of the franchise system is the proper selection of partners and monitoring of key partner responsibilities (agency issues). However, even in the most stable relationship, a dynamic business environment dictates adjustments in the relationship to ensure continued competitive advantage. Understanding the partner's tolerance zone in performance and reacting to market changes can be standardized by formal review programs and kept unstructured by informal negotiations (relational dynamics). Failure to recognize the need for dynamic management of the relationship can often result in litigation, as noted.

The franchise relationship model illustrates how a concept innovator can construct a franchising company and the pathway for implementing it in the most entrepreneurial way. The model also eliminates those ideas that are best developed using another growth strategy, such as distributorships, licensing, or corporate-owned outlets.

We now understand that franchising is entrepreneurial, and we understand the unique components of franchising that enable this entrepreneurial alliance.

Internet Impact: Resources

The Network Enhanced

The essence of franchising is the creation of value in a trademark. Efficiently sharing information is a key to leveraging the experiences of each franchisee for the betterment of all franchisees. Because franchising is governed (primarily) by a long-term contract, the players in the system are motivated to share knowledge because enhanced performance builds the commonly held trademark.

Franchises have been pioneers in monitoring systems and feedback loops. Most franchising organizations have invested significantly in Internet and extranet systems. Originally (well before the Internet), these systems were primarily "policing" devices established to make sure franchisees followed the prescribed business format and then paid their royalties. Today these systems go far beyond the original control function.

McDonald's recently began testing an outsourcing of its restaurant drive-through ordering systems. A McDonald's franchisee created this system and now shares it with 300 other franchisees in a beta test. Early results show a significant increase in both speed of delivery and order accuracy.

Chapter Summary

Franchising is an inherently entrepreneurial endeavor. In this chapter we argue that opportunity, scale, and growth are at the heart of the franchise experience. The success of franchising is demonstrated by the fact that it accounts for more than one-third of all U.S. retailing. Equally important is the demonstrated performance of the top franchise companies, which consistantly outperform the Standard & Poor's 500. Franchising shares profits, risk, and strategic implementation between the franchisor and the franchisee. Unique aspects of

franchising as entrepreneurship are the wide spectrum of opportunity that exists and the matching of scale to appetite for a broad spectrum of entrepreneurs. Two tools have been provided in this chapter to help the entrepreneur. For those interested in creating a franchise, the franchise relationship model articulates the dynamic construction of the franchisor–franchisee alliance. For the prospective franchisee, the franchise risk profile helps the budding entrepreneur assess the risk–return scenario for any given franchise opportunity.

Study Questions

1. Can you describe the difference between the franchisor and the franchisee? How are these differences strategically aligned to create a competitive advantage?

2. We describe franchising as a "pathway to entrepreneurship" that provides a spectrum of entrepreneurial opportunities. What does this mean to you?

3. What are the most important factors in determining whether franchising is an appropriate method of rapidly growing a concept?

4. What are the five components of the franchise relationship model? Can you describe the interactive nature of these components?

5. Why do you think the public franchisors consistently outperform the S&P 500?

6. What would be the most attractive aspects of franchising to you? What is the least attractive part of franchising?

Internet Resources for Chapter 12

http://bison1.com/ *Our favorite site for franchising information.*

http://www.businessfranchisedirectory.com/ *A searchable database of franchise information and opportunities.*

http://www.franchisehelp.com/ *Help for those looking into a franchise: how it works and when to invest.*

http://www.aafd.org/ *The AAFD is a national nonprofit trade association focused on market-driven solutions to improve the franchising community.*

http://www.franchise.org/ *The International Franchise Association (IFA).*

MIND STRETCHERS

Have You Considered?

1. In what ways do you think entrepreneurs have created wealth because of franchising but *not* as a franchisor or franchisee?

2. The International Franchise Association reports that 90 percent of franchises succeed. Some academic research shows failure rates to be much higher. What differences in analysis could show such variation?

3. How would you choose a company from which to buy a franchise?

4. Can you list the top 10 franchises in the world? What criteria would you use to make your judgment?

5. Do you know anyone who owns a franchise? Do you think they work more or less hard than a "stand-alone" entrepreneur?

6. Who is franchising for and not for?

Case

Mike Bellobuono

Mike Bellobuono knew he had a lot to consider. It was a very exciting time for the bagel industry. Industry-wide sales had exploded, and his company, Bagelz, a Connecticut-based bagel chain, had established seven retail locations in three years. There was tremendous opportunity for growth, but Bellobuono knew that the company needed to achieve growth quickly or risk an inability to compete against larger players.

The company was at the point where the four-member management team had to decide whether to begin selling franchises or to remain as a fully company-owned operation. There was a lot at stake in this decision for President Joe Amodio, Vice President Wes Becher, Territory Development Manager Jamie Whalen, and Director of Operations Mike Bellobuono. Originally they had planned on remaining as a fully company-owned operation but then had met Fred DeLuca, who suggested franchising and offered financing. DeLuca, founder of Subway, a multimillion-dollar sandwich franchise, had the potential to be a tremendous asset for Bagelz. He had access to large amounts of capital, an array of resources such as advertising and legal support, and most of all experience: His company had more locations in the United States than any other franchiser. However, Bellobuono knew that Amodio and the team didn't want Bagelz to simply become an extension of DeLuca's empire. The four were used to operating as members of a small, closely knit team and weren't sure if partnering with DeLuca would result in their losing control of the whole operation.

If they decided to franchise, Bellobuono wondered if they would be able to find franchisees that had the finances, motivation, and ability to successfully run a Bagelz store. He had also heard many stories about conflicts arising out of franchiser–franchisee relationships. True, some of these conflicts were preventable, but inevitably there would be difficulties, probably ending in legal challenges. This greatly concerned him; he knew that disgruntled franchisees would poorly represent the company, and he wasn't sure if accelerated growth was worth the headaches and the possibility that unhappy franchisees would damage the company's reputation. He was also worried about maintaining the high standard of operations in franchisees' stores that Bagelz had put into place in its seven company-owned stores. He knew how difficult it was to build a name and how one bad incident could destroy it beyond repair. He thought about what happened to Jack-in-the-Box, another large fast-food franchise company. In January 1993 a customer had gotten sick and died from bacteria in an undercooked hamburger. Following this incident, the company hired independent inspectors to review every single franchise and ensure that all complied with the Board of Health's regulated cooking process.

Not one additional violation was found in any of the hundreds of locations; but nonetheless, following this incident, franchisees experienced declines in revenues of up to 35 percent.[1]

On the other hand, if they decided not to franchise they risked being locked out of certain geographical areas by the competition. Bruegger's Bagels was opening units all over New England (Exhibit A), and Manhattan Bagel, a new industry player, had gone public, giving the company access to large amounts of capital for expansion. Operating as a chain store, as Bagelz was currently doing, constrained the company's potential growth rate. If the company decided against franchising, the team wondered if Bagelz would be able to withstand the onslaught of competition that was sure to occur. They wanted to make the right decision, but there was much to consider, and the offer to partner with DeLuca would not stay on the table for long. The bagel wars were heating up, and Bellobuono knew that they had to develop a superior growth strategy.

Mike Bellobuono's Background

Bellobuono graduated from Babson College with a BS in May of 1991. He was working for a lawn service, but he and his college friend Jamie Whalen were looking to find a career in a hot market. Specifically, the two were looking at bagel and chicken franchises. Although neither of them had any previous food franchise experience, as part of a class project during Bellobuono's senior year, they had done an in-depth study of the food service industry (Exhibit B). Based on this research, they believed that the industry would experience continued growth, and that bagels and chicken would be the next high-growth segments.

It was then that Bellobuono first met Wes Becher and Joe Amodio. The two had opened a bagel store one year earlier by the name of Bagelz, and business had gone so well that they had opened a second store and set their sights on developing additional locations in the near future. (See Exhibit C for Bagelz's income statement.) Bellobuono was very impressed with Bagelz's operations and the possibility of getting in on a ground-floor opportunity. After considering alternatives such as Cajun Joe's, Boston Chicken, and Manhattan Bagel, he

This case was prepared by Andrea Alyse with assistance from Dan D'Heilly under the direction of Professor Stephen Spinelli. © Copyright Babson College, 1996. Funding provided by the Ewing Marion Kauffman Foundation. All rights reserved.

[1] "E-Coli Scare Deals Blow to Seattle Burger Sales," *Restaurant Business*, March 20, 1993; and "Fallout of E-Coli Episode Still Troubles Foodmarket," *Nation's Restaurant News*, March 20, 1995.

EXHIBIT A

Bruegger's Bagels Growth Statistics

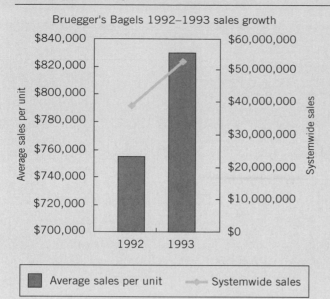

Bruegger's Bagels 1992–1993 sales growth

Bruegger's Bagels 1992–1993 unit growth

EXHIBIT B

Food Service Industry Growth

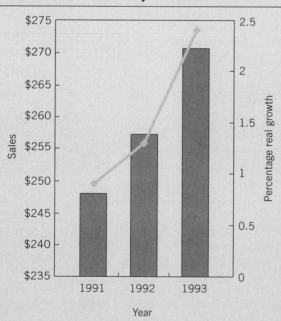

they could both remember. Through the years, the elder Whalen and Bellobuono had become so close that Bellobuono thought of him as his second father, and Mr. Whalen looked at Bellobuono as the perfect business partner for his son. He eagerly endorsed Bellobuono's idea and even felt that Whalen should leave school one year early to do this. Bellobuono's father, however, was somewhat less than enthused at first:

> My father wanted me to go to law school or work for Aetna, where I had a job offer, but to me, working for someone else was never an option. When I told him about Bagelz he said, "Bagels? You went to business school and now you're going to sell bagels?" He wasn't exactly convinced that I was making the right decision, but he supported my decision anyway.

Due Diligence

Bellobuono first approached Bruegger's about opening bagel stores in Connecticut, but the company believed that there was no market potential there. He then considered Manhattan Bagel. He liked its analysis of the bagel market, and the company also agreed that Connecticut was a viable market. However, in the end Bellobuono decided to invest in Bagelz because he felt that Bagelz had several distinct competitive advantages. First there was Irving Stearns. Stearns, Bagelz's chief bagel maker, had been in the business for more than 20 years and knew everything there was to know about bagels. He baked a product that tasted better than any Bellobuono had ever eaten, and he could quickly

decided he liked both the company and the taste of Bagelz bagels.

Whalen's father, who had originally approached Bellobuono about the possibility of Bellobuono becoming a partner with Whalen, was extremely supportive of the decision. Bellobuono and Whalen had grown up in the same neighborhood and been friends as far back as

EXHIBIT C

Bagelz Per Store Earning Claims 1993*

	Weekly	Annually	Percentage of Total Revenue per Store
Total revenue per store	$8,000.00	$416,000.00	100%
Cost of goods sold			
Salaries and wages	2,000.00	104,000.00	25%
Food	1,680.00	87,360.00	21%
Beverages	800.00	41,600.00	10%
Paper supplies	320.00	16,640.00	4%
Total COGS	$4,800.00	$249,600.00	60%
Gross profit on sales	$3,200.00	$166,400.00	40%
Operating expenses			
Payroll tax	136.00	7,072.00	1.70%
Payroll service	20.00	1,040.00	0.25%
Rent	480.00	24,960.00	6.00%
Connecticut Light & Power	200.00	10,400.00	2.50%
Connecticut Natural Gas	120.00	6,240.00	1.50%
Telephone	24.00	1,248.00	0.30%
Advertising	200.00	10,400.00	2.50%
Local advertising	80.00	4,160.00	1.00%
Insurance	80.00	4,160.00	1.00%
Linen and laundry	16.00	832.00	0.20%
Repairs and maintenance	80.00	4,160.00	1.00%
Rubbish removal	40.00	2,080.00	0.50%
Office supplies	40.00	2,080.00	0.50%
Uniforms	16.00	832.00	0.20%
Professional fees	40.00	2,080.00	0.50%
Miscellaneous	20.00	1,040.00	0.25%
Total operating expenses	$1,592.00	$82,784.00	19.90%
Total income from operations	$1,608.00	$83,616.00	20.10%

*All figures have been estimated based on industry data and do not necessarily represent the actual financial performance of a Bagelz store operation.

develop new products. There simply wasn't anyone else like Stearns. Bellobuono also liked the flexibility of Bagelz's management. They were quick to spot and react to new market trends and directions. For example, Bagelz offered customers five different kinds of flavored coffees before flavored coffees became popular—at a time when all their competitors offered only regular and decaffeinated. Finally, with Bagelz, he was on the ground floor.

Bagelz

Bellobuono and Whalen contacted Amodio and Becher about buying a franchise. They soon found out that companies that franchised were required to adhere to the U.S. Federal Trade Commission (FTC) Disclosure Rule. The rule stated that franchisers must disclose certain specified information to all prospective franchisees, in a format approved by the FTC (Exhibit D). Most franchisers used a Uniform Franchise Offering Circular (UFOC) format to comply with FTC regulations. A UFOC document contained information including a description of the business, estimated development costs, fee schedules, franchisee and franchiser obligations, other businesses affiliated with the franchise, and pending lawsuits. Additionally, 13 states required franchisers to file a UFOC prior to selling franchises. Producing this document was an expensive and time-consuming process; but without complying with the FTC's disclosure rule, Amodio and Becher weren't legally permitted to sell franchises. However, Bellobuono and Whalen persisted until Amodio and

EXHIBIT D

U.S. Federal Trade Commission Disclosure Rule

I. Rule Overview

A. Basic Requirement: Franchisors must furnish potential franchisees with written disclosures providing important information about the franchisor, the franchised business and the franchise relationship, and give them at least 10 business days to review it before investing.

B. Disclosure Option: Franchisors may make the required disclosures by following either the Rule's disclosure format or the Uniform Franchise Offering Circular Guidelines prepared by state franchise law officials.

C. Coverage: The Rule primarily covers business-format franchises, product franchises, and vending machine or display rack business opportunity ventures.

D. No Filing: The Rule requires disclosure only. Unlike state disclosure laws, no registration, filing, review or approval of any disclosures, advertising or agreements by the FTC is required.

E. Remedies: The Rule is a trade regulation rule with the full force and effect of federal law. The courts have held it may only be enforced by the FTC, not private parties. The FTC may seek injunctions, civil penalties and consumer redress for violations.

F. Purpose: The Rule is designed to enable potential franchisees to protect themselves before investing by providing them with information essential to an assessment of the potential risks and benefits, to meaningful comparisons with other investments, and to further investigation of the franchise opportunity.

G. Effective Date: The Rule, formally titled "Disclosure Requirements and Prohibitions Concerning Franchising and Business Opportunity Ventures," took effect on October 21, 1979, and appears at 16 C.F.R. Part 436.

II. Rule Requirements

A. General: The Rule imposes six different requirements in connection with the "advertising, offering, licensing, contracting, sale or other promotion" of a franchise in or affecting commerce:

1. Basic Disclosures: The Rule requires franchisors to give potential investors a basic disclosure document at the earlier of the first face-to-face meeting or 10 business days before any money is paid or an agreement is signed in connection with the investment (Part 436.1(a)).

2. Earnings Claims: If a franchisor makes earnings claims, whether historical or forecast, they must have a reasonable basis, and prescribed substantiating disclosures must be given to a potential investor in writing at the same time as the basic disclosures (Parts 436.1(b)–(d)).

3. Advertised Claims: The Rule affects only ads that include an earnings claim. Such ads must disclose the number and percentage of existing franchisees who have achieved the claimed results, along with cautionary language. Their use triggers required compliance with the Rule's earnings claim disclosure requirements (Part 436.1(e)).

4. Franchise Agreements: The franchisor must give investors a copy of its standard-form franchise and related agreements at the same time as the basic disclosures, and final copies intended to be executed at least 5 business days before signing (Part 436.1(g)).

5. Refunds: The Rule requires franchisors to make refunds of deposits and initial payments to potential investors, subject to any conditions on refundability stated in the disclosure document (Part 436.1(h)).

6. Contradictory Claims: While franchisors are free to provide investors with any promotional or other materials they wish, no written or oral claims may contradict information provided in the required disclosure document (Part 436.1(f)).

B. Liability: Failure to comply with any of the six requirements is a violation of the Franchise Rule. "Franchisors" and "franchise brokers" are jointly and severally liable for Rule violations.

1. A "franchisor" is defined as any person who sells a "franchise" covered by the Rule (Part 436.2(c)).

2. A "franchise broker" is defined as any person who "sells, offers for sale, or arranges for the sale" of a covered franchise (Part 436.2(j)), and includes not only independent sales agents, but also subfranchisors that grant subfranchises (44 FR 49963).

III. Business Relationships Covered

A. Alternate Definitions: The Rule employs parallel coverage definitions of the term "franchise" to reach two types of continuing commercial relationships: traditional franchises and business opportunities.

B. "Traditional Franchises": There are three definitional prerequisites to coverage of a business-format or product franchise (Parts 436.2(a)(1)(i) and (2)):

1. Trademark: The franchisor offers the right to distribute goods or services that bear the franchisor's trademark, service mark, trade name, advertising or other commercial symbol.

2. Significant Control or Assistance: The franchisor exercises significant control over, or offers significant assistance in, the franchisee's method of operation.

3. Required Payment: The franchisee is required to make any payment to the franchisor or an affiliate, or a commitment to make a payment, as a condition of obtaining the franchise or commencing operations. (NOTE: There is an exemption from coverage for required payments of less than $500 within six months of the commencement of the franchise (Part 436.2(a)(3)(iii))).

(continued)

EXHIBIT D   (continued)

C. Business Opportunities: There are also three basic prerequisites to the Rule's coverage of a business opportunity venture (Parts 436.2(a)(1)(ii) and (2)):

1. No Trademark: The seller simply offers the right to sell goods or services supplied by the seller, its affiliate, or a supplier with which the seller requires the franchisee to do business.

2. Location Assistance: The seller offers to secure retail outlets or accounts for the goods or services to be sold, to secure locations or sites for vending machines or rack displays, or to provide the services of someone who can do so.

3. Required Payment: The same as for franchises.

D. Coverage Exemptions/Exclusions: The Rule also exempts or excludes some relationships that would otherwise meet the coverage prerequisites (Parts 436.2(a)(3) and (4)):

1. Minimum Investment: This exemption applies if all payments to the franchisor or an affiliate until six months after the franchise commences operation are $500 or less (Part 436.2(a)(iii)).

2. Fractional Franchises: Relationships adding a new product or service to an established distributor's existing products or services, are exempt if (i) the franchisee or any of its current directors or executive officers has been in the same type of business for at least two years, and (ii) both parties anticipated, or should have, that sales from the franchise would represent no more than 20 percent of the franchisees sales in dollar volume (Parts 436.2(a)(3)(i) and 436.2(h)).

3. Single Trademark Licenses: The Rule language excludes a "single license to license a [mark]" where it "is the only one of its general nature and type to be granted by the licenser with respect to that [mark]" (Part 436.2(a)(4)(iv)). The Rule's Statement of Basis and Purpose indicates it also applies to "collateral" licenses [e.g., logo on sweatshirt, mug] and licenses granted to settle trademark infringement litigation (43 FR 59707–08).

4. Employment and Partnership Relationships: The Rule excludes pure employer–employee and general partnership arrangements. Limited partnerships do not qualify for the exemption (Part 436.2(a)(4)(i)).

5. Oral Agreements: This exemption, which is narrowly construed, applies only if no material term of the relationship is in writing (Part 436.2(a)(3)(iv)).

6. Cooperative Associations: Only agricultural co-ops and retailer-owned cooperatives "operated 'by and for' retailers on a cooperative basis," and in which control and ownership is substantially equal are excluded from coverage (Part 436.2(a)(4)(ii)).

7. Certification/Testing Services: Organizations that authorize use of a certification mark to any business selling products or services meeting their standards are excluded from coverage (e.g., Underwriters Laboratories) (Part 436.2(a)(4)(iii)).

8. Leased Departments: Relationships in which the franchisee simply leases space in the premises of another retailer and is not required or advised to buy the goods or services it sells from the retailer or an affiliate of the retailer are exempt (Part 436.2(a)(3)(ii)).

E. Statutory Exemptions: Section 18(g) of the FTC Act authorizes "any person" to petition the Commission for an exemption from a rule where coverage is "not necessary to prevent the acts or practices" that the rule prohibits (15 U.S.C. § 57a(g)). Franchise Rule exemptions have been granted for service station franchises (45 FR 51765), many automobile dealership franchises (45 FR 51763; 49 FR 13677; 52 FR 6612; 54 FR 1446), and wholesaler-sponsored voluntary chains in the grocery industry (48 FR 10040).

IV. Disclosure Options

A. Alternatives: Franchisors have a choice of formats for making the disclosures required by the Rule. They may use either the format provided by the Rule or the Uniform Franchise Offering Circular ("UFOC") format prescribed by the North American Securities Administrators' Association ("NASAA").

B. FTC Format: Franchisors may comply by following the Rule's requirements for preparing a basic disclosure document (Parts 436.1(a)(1)-(24)), and if they make earnings claims, for a separate earnings claim disclosure document (Parts 436.1(b)(3), (c)(3), and (d)). The Rule's Final Interpretive Guides provide detailed instructions and sample disclosures (44 FR 49966).

C. UFOC Format: The Uniform Franchise Offering Circular format may also be used for compliance in any state.

1. Guidelines: Effective January 1, 1996, franchisors using the UFOC disclosure format must comply with the UFOC Guidelines, as amended by NASAA on April 25, 1993. (44 FR 49970; 60 FR 51895).

2. Cover Page: The FTC cover page must be furnished to each potential franchisee, either in lieu of the UFOC cover page in nonregistration states or along with the UFOC (Part 436.1(a)(21); 44 FR 49970–71).

3. Adaptation: If the UFOC is registered or used in one state, but will be used in another without a franchise registration law, answers to state-specific questions must be changed to refer to the law of the state in which the UFOC is used.

4. Updating: If the UFOC is registered in a state, it must be updated as required by the state's franchise law. If the same UFOC is also adapted for use in a nonregistration state, updating must occur as required by the law of the state where the UFOC is registered. If the UFOC is not registered in a state with a franchise registration law, it must be revised annually and updated quarterly as required by the Rule.

5. Presumption: The Commission will presume the sufficiency, adequacy and accuracy of a UFOC that is registered by a state, when it is used in that state.

EXHIBIT D   (concluded)

D. UFOC vs. Rule: Many franchisors have adopted the UFOC disclosure format because roughly half of the 13 states with franchise registration requirements will not accept the Rule document for filing. When a format is chosen, all disclosure must conform to its requirements. Franchisors may not pick and choose provisions from each format when making disclosures (44 FR 49970).

E. Rule Primacy: If the UFOC is used, several key Rule provisions will still apply:

1. Scope: Disclosure will be required in all cases required by the Rule, regardless of whether it would be required by state law.

2. Coverage: The Rule will determine who is obligated to comply, regardless of whether they would be required to make disclosures under state law.

3. Disclosure Timing: When disclosures must be made will be governed by the Rule, unless state law requires even earlier disclosure.

4. Other Material: No information may appear in a disclosure document not required by the Rule or by nonpreempted state law, regardless of the format used, and no representations may be made that contradict a disclosure.

5. Contracts: Failure to provide potential franchisees with final agreements at least 5 days before signing will be a Rule violation regardless of the disclosure format used.

6. Refunds: Failure to make promised refunds also will be a Rule violation regardless of which document is used.

V. Potential Liability for Violations

A. FTC Action: Rule violations may subject franchisors, franchise brokers, their officers and agents to significant liabilities in FTC enforcement actions.

1. Remedies: The FTC Act provides the Commission with a broad range of remedies for Rule violations:

a. Injunctions: Section 13(b) of the Act authorizes preliminary and permanent injunctions against Rule violations (15 U.S.C. § 53(b)). Rule cases routinely have sought and obtained injunctions against Rule violations and misrepresentations in the offer or sale of any business venture, whether or not covered by the Rule.

b. Asset Freezes: Acting under their inherent equity powers, the courts have routinely granted preliminary asset freezes in appropriate Rule cases. The assets frozen have included both corporate assets and the personal assets, including real and personal property, of key officers and directors.

c. Civil Penalties: Section 5(m)(1)(A) of the Act authorizes civil penalties of up to $10,000 for each violation of the Rule (15 U.S.C. § 45(m)(1)(A)). The courts have granted civil penalties of as much as $870,000 in a Rule case to date.

d. Monetary Redress: Section 19(b) of the Act authorizes the Commission to seek monetary redress on behalf of investors injured economically by a Rule violation (15 U.S.C. § 57b). The courts have granted consumer redress of as much as $4.9 million in a Rule case to date.

e. Other Redress: Section 19(b) of the Act also authorizes such other forms of redress as the court finds necessary to redress injury to consumers from a Rule violation, including rescission or reformation of contracts, the return of property and public notice of the Rule violation. Courts may also grant similar relief under their inherent equity powers.

2. Personal Liability: Individuals who formulate, direct and control the franchisor's activities can expect to be named individually for violations committed in the franchisor's name, together with the franchisor entity, and held personally liable for civil penalties and consumer redress.

3. Liability for Others: Franchisors and their key officers and executives are responsible for violations by persons acting in their behalf, including independent franchise brokers, subfranchisors, and the franchisor's own sales personnel.

B. Private Actions: The courts have held that the FTC Act generally may not be enforced by private lawsuits.

1. Rule Claims: The Commission expressed its view when the Rule was issued that private actions should be permitted by the courts for Rule violations (43 FR 59723; 44 FR 49971). To date, no federal court has permitted a private action for Rule violations.

2. State Disclosure Law Claims: Each of the franchise laws in the 15 states with franchise registration and/or disclosure requirements authorizes private actions for state franchise law violations.

3. State FTC Act Claims: The courts in some states have interpreted state deceptive practices laws ("little FTC Acts") as permitting private actions for Rule violations.

VI. Legal Resources

A. Text of Rule: 16 C.F.R. Part 436.

B. Statement of Basis and Purpose: 43 FR 59614–59733 (Dec. 21, 1978) (discusses the evidentiary basis for promulgation of the Rule, and shows Commission intent and interpretation of its provisions—particularly helpful in resolving coverage questions).

C. Final Interpretive Guides: 44 FR 49966–49992 (Aug. 24, 1979) (final statement of policy and interpretation of each of the Rule's requirements—important discussions of coverage issues, use of the UFOC and requirements for basic and earnings claims disclosures in the Rule's disclosure format).

D. Staff Advisory Opinions: Business Franchise Guide (CCH) 6380 et seq. (interpretive opinions issued in response to requests for interpretation of coverage questions and disclosure requirements pursuant to 16 C.F.R. §§ 1.2–1.4).

Becher agreed to sell them a store as a limited partnership:

> I looked at a partnership as giving me greater control over my own destiny. If we didn't form a partnership, and I just opened up stores for them, I would have no control over any changes they decided to make; having this control was extremely important to me.

Bellobuono and Whalen opened the Manchester store in December of 1991. Then Becher, impressed by Bellobuono and Whalen's dedication, approached the two about becoming full partners in the company. Becher explained to Bellobuono that although he had several prospective investors, he was interested in offering the two a partnership because he and Amodio were looking for investors who would work for the company, not simply finance it. To buy into the company, Whalen and Bellobuono arranged financing through their fathers, and the two became full partners the next year. Bellobuono, Becher, Whalen, and Amodio handled all aspects of the partnership. Each store was visited by one of the four members of the team daily to ensure that operations were running smoothly and to solve any difficulties that arose. Becher, Whalen, and Bellobuono focused on the day-to-day operations, and Amodio on growing the company:

> Joe was the leader and a fly-by-the-seat-of-the-pants type of guy. Joe would point in a direction, and we three would make it happen. Joe had an incredible talent for salesmanship, a kind of way about him that enabled him to achieve the seemingly impossible. One Christmas we were in New York City, and we were in this restaurant. The owner was depressed because the restaurant was empty. Joe said he could fill the restaurant if the owner sat him by the window. He proceeded to put on quite a show, performing in the window, carrying on, gesturing, and waving, which drove people in who wanted to see what all the excitement was about. And you know what? He filled the restaurant in under an hour. But Joe wasn't finished yet. He then got the entire place to sing "The Twelve Days of Christmas," and when people forgot the words of a section of the song, he had them running out into the street asking people if they knew the words and could help out—I mean strangers, in the middle of New York City. It was unbelievable! Even the ending was like a fairy tale: As the crowd got to the twelfth day of Christmas, Joe was tipping his hat at the door and making his exit. To this day whenever he goes into that restaurant his dinner is free; the owner never forgot what Joe did for him.

By 1993 Bagelz had seven stores with the goal of saturating the entire state of Connecticut by the year 2000. Bruegger's wasn't there yet, and Manhattan had only a few locations, but Bellobuono knew they were coming:

> We were Bagelz, and we wanted to make Connecticut our turf, so that you knew that if you were going to go into Connecticut, you would have to fight us.

The Bagel Industry

Although the exact origin of the bagel is not fully known, legend maintains that the first bagel was created for the king of Poland, as celebration bread, when the king's army repelled a 1683 Turkish invasion. Jewish immigrants introduced the bagel in the United States, and for decades bagels were perceived as a strictly ethnic food with limited mass-market appeal.

Traditionally bagels were made from water, flour, yeast, and salt, combined and formed into a ring shape. These rings were boiled in water to create the crust and shiny appearance, and then baked in brick ovens to produce a crispy outside and a soft, chewy inside, considerably denser than most breads. As bagels gained mass-market acceptance across the country, the industry grew at an accelerating rate. Modern bakers often use machine-formed bagels and large stainless-steel ovens, complete with rotating racks for faster, more uniform baking. As competition between bagel shops has increased in the United States, the traditional bagel recipe has been adapted to increase the variety of flavors (e.g., egg, salt, garlic, onion, poppy seed, sesame seed, blueberry, chocolate chip, corn, and cheddar cheese).

Lender's, now a division of Kraft General Foods, first successfully marketed a mass-produced, frozen, supermarket bagel in 1962. Before this time, bagels had been sold only as fresh. By 1991 Lender's had grown to sales of $203 million, and Sara Lee, Lender's closest competitor, who had entered the frozen bagel market in 1985, had sales of $22.4 million.

In the 1980s Lender's and Bagel Nosh opened bagel shops nationally; but both companies failed, never able to attract enough customers. By the early 1990s bagels were gaining mass-market acceptance across the country. However, the industry was growing most notably on the East Coast where, as of mid-1992, more than half of all bagel sales in the United States (51 percent) came from 15 East Coast cities. Frozen supermarket bagels achieved sales of $211.9 million in 1992, an increase of 4 percent over the previous year; but fresh bagels, the most rapidly growing segment, increased sales to $95 million, up 28 percent from 1991. For 1993 sales of frozen bagels were projected to increase 6 percent to $224.4 million, and sales of fresh bagels were projected to increase 17 percent to $111 million. Consumer awareness and consumption of bagels had increased steadily, but most dramatically throughout the past six years (Exhibit E illustrates the increase in per capita bagel consumption for 1988 to 1993). Breakfast accounted for 65 percent of all bagel sales, and with the trend toward increased consumer health awareness, bagels had become a natural, low-fat, high-carbohydrate alternative to other menu items such as doughnuts and muffins.

EXHIBIT E
Bagel Consumption

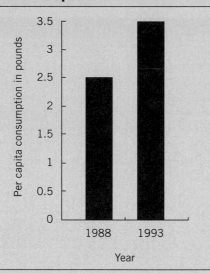

Fred DeLuca

In the spring of 1993 Fred DeLuca, founder of Subway, a large sandwich franchise, contacted the Bagelz team. A vendor that sold luncheon meat slicers to both Bagelz and Subway had told DeLuca about Bagelz's operation, and DeLuca decided that he wanted to tour the plant and meet the team. DeLuca was well known in the franchise industry. While still in college, he had opened his first Subway location in 1965. Nine years later he began franchising, and by 1995 Subway had grown to more than 10,000 locations. In addition, *Entrepreneur Magazine* rated Subway the No. 1 franchise in its annual franchising 500 six times between 1988 and 1994:

> We never thought that he wanted to do business with us. We were just excited to meet him. When we realized he was interested in making a deal, we were astonished.

It was then that the team first seriously considered franchising.

To Franchise or Not to Franchise?

DeLuca had offered to buy into Bagelz and turn it into a world-class franchise, but first he wanted to be sure that the bagel team was fully aware of, and ready to meet, all potential difficulties involved with franchising:

> Fred wanted to know why we wanted to franchise. He said, "Do you know what you are getting yourself into? Are you sure you really want to deal with all the problems that arise from franchising?"

The team weighed both the pros and cons of becoming a franchiser. They evaluated two basic strategies: either to grow rapidly throughout Connecticut as a chain, or to franchise and grow nationally. How many stores were the right number for Connecticut? Did they have the management talent, the money, and the time?

They were afraid of losing control if they franchised, but knew it would be difficult to grow quickly without franchising. They were also afraid they wouldn't be able to lock out the competition: Manhattan Bagel planned to expand into Connecticut, and Bruegger's had been named one of the 50 fastest-growing U.S. restaurants (Exhibit F). Last, Bellobuono and the team feared that DeLuca would lose interest. After all, they had already been negotiating for six months and hadn't reached an agreement. Then Subway began receiving increasing amounts of negative publicity regarding the company's support of its franchisees. One particularly disturbing article appeared in *The Wall Street Journal,*[2] and Bellobuono and the team began to wonder if aligning with DeLuca could ultimately have a negative effect on Bagelz. They knew, however, that time was running out and they needed to decide the best future direction for Bagelz.

[2] B. Welch, "Franchise Realities: Sandwich-Shop Chain Surges, But to Run One Can Take Heroic Effort," *The Wall Street Journal,* September 16, 1992, p. A1.

EXHIBIT F

50 Fastest-Growing Restaurants, 1992–1993

Name of Restaurant	City and State	Type of Restaurant	Does the Company Franchise?	Projected 1992–1993 % Change in Systemwide Sales	Projected 1992–1993 % Change in Units	Projected 1992–1993 % Change in Average Unit Sales
1 Boston Chicken	Naperville, IL	Fast food	Y	261.0%	161.4%	9.2%
2 Lone Star Steakhouse & Saloon	Wichita, KN	Casual steakhouse	Y	136.3	95.7	3.6
3 Italian Oven	Latrobe, PA	Casual Italian dinnerhouse	Y	126.2	60.0	11.7
4 Romano's Macaroni Grill	Dallas	Casual Italian dinnerhouse	N	107.7	86.7	0.2
5 Hooters	Atlanta	Casual dinnerhouse	Y	87.2	16.0	25.0
6 Papa John's	Louisville	Delivery/take-out pizza	Y	80.4	81.8	8.7
7 Outback Steakhouse	Tampa	Casual steakhouse	Y	77.9	71.8	6.7
8 Checkers Drive-In	Clearwater, FL	Drive-through hamburgers	Y	68.1	81.2	5.2
9 Taco Cabana	San Antonio, TX	Patio-style Mexican	Y	65.1	87.7	-4.2
10 Hot 'n Now	Irvine, CA	Drive-through hamburgers	N	64.0	80.9	3.6
11 Wall Street Deli	Memphis	Self-serve deli and buffet	N	56.2	26.4	5.0
12 Mick's	Atlanta	Casual dinnerhouse	N	53.8	50.0	1.5
13 Applebee's	Kansas City, MO	Casual dinnerhouse	Y	50.5	44.4	5.3
14 Starbucks	Seattle	Coffee specialist	N	50.0	63.7	6.7
15 Grady's American Grill	Dallas	Casual dinnerhouse	N	45.1	52.6	1.2
16 Bertucci's Brick Oven Pizza	Woburn, MA	Casual Italian dinnerhouse	N	45.0	42.9	5.9
17 Fresh Choice	Santa Clara, CA	Self-serve buffet	N	44.4	63.6	4.9
18 Miami Subs Grill	Fort Lauderdale, FL	Fast food	Y	42.9	23.2	3.5
19 Stacey's Buffet	Largo, FL	Self-serve buffet	Y	39.0	50.0	-5.3
20 Longhorn Steaks	Atlanta	Casual steakhouse	Y	37.4	32.5	-2.8
21 Panda Express	South Pasadena, CA	Fast-food Oriental	N	36.8	40.0	2.9
22 Bruegger's Bagel Bakery	Burlington, VT	Fast food	Y	36.5	44.8	9.5
23 California Pizza Kitchen	Los Angeles	Casual dinnerhouse	N	26.4	51.7	5.6
24 Old Country Buffet	Eden Prairie, MN	Self-serve buffet	N	33.7	28.6	4.3
25 Sfuzzi	Dallas	Casual Italian dinnerhouse	N	33.3	25.0	3.0
26 Claim Jumper	Irvine, CA	Dinnerhouse	N	33.3	30.0	4.3
27 Nathan's Famous	Westbury, NY	Fast food	Y	31.4	20.3	-4.0
28 Morton's of Chicago	Chicago	Upscale steakhouse	N	31.1	20.0	9.2
29 The Cheesecake Factory	Redondo Beach, CA	Casual dinnerhouse	N	29.9	60.0	1.2
30 Au Bon Pain	Boston	Bakery café	Y	28.8	11.0	5.5
31 Ruby Tuesday	Mobile, AL	Casual dinnerhouse	N	28.2	25.6	6.2

(continued)

Name of Restaurant	City and State	Type of Restaurant	Does the Company Franchise?	Projected 1992–1993 % Change in Systemwide Sales	Projected 1992–1993 % Change in Units	Projected 1992–1993 % Change in Average Unit Sales
32 Schlotzsky's Deli	Austin, TX	Fast food	Y	27.0	17.7	2.9
33 Blimpie	New York	Fast food	Y	26.6	27.9	0.0
34 Cracker Barrel	Lebanon, TN	Family restaurant	N	25.1	20.7	3.7
35 The Cooker Bar & Grille	Columbus, OH	Casual dinnerhouse	N	24.5	45.0	0.0
36 Subway	Milford, CN	Fast food	Y	22.7	13.9	6.0
37 The Spaghetti Warehouse	Garland, TX	Casual Italian dinnerhouse	N	21.7	37.0	11.5
38 Dunkin' Donuts	Randolph, MA	Fast food	Y	21.3	16.6	4.5
39 Sirloin Stockade	Hutchinson, KN	Budget steakhouse	Y	21.3	7.6	15.0
40 Cinnabon	Seattle	Fast food	Y	21.2	8.6	5.2
41 T.G.I. Friday's	Dallas	Casual dinnerhouse	Y	20.2	18.3	0.0
42 Don Pablo's	Bedford, TX	Casual Mexican dinnerhouse	N	19.8	47.4	2.7
43 Rally's	Louisville	Drive-through hamburgers	Y	19.6	20.0	-4.5
44 Chili's	Dallas	Casual dinnerhouse	Y	19.0	15.5	3.2
45 Damon's—The Place for Ribs	Columbus, OH	Casual dinnerhouse	Y	18.3	4.0	2.9
46 Red Robin	Irvine, CA	Casual dinnerhouse	Y	18.1	19.0	-3.5
47 Bain's Deli	King of Prussia, PA	Fast food	Y	17.9	8.0	10.3
48 On the Border Cafe	Dallas	Casual Mexican dinnerhouse	Y	17.9	46.7	0.0
49 Bojangles	Charlotte, NC	Fast food	Y	17.2	20.3	5.7
50 Ruth's Chris Steak House	New Orleans	Upscale steakhouse	Y	17.1	8.8	4.8

Source: *Restaurant Business*, July 20, 1994.

Chapter Thirteen

Entrepreneurial Finance

Happiness to an entrepreneur is a positive cash flow.

Fred Adler
Venture capitalist

Results Expected

Upon completion of this chapter, you will be able to

1. Describe critical issues in financing new ventures.

2. Discuss the difference between entrepreneurial finance and conventional administrative or corporate finance.

3. Describe the process of crafting financial and fund-raising strategies and the critical variables involved, including identifying the financial life cycles of new ventures, a financial strategy framework, and investor preferences.

4. Critically evaluate the Midwest Lighting case study.

Venture Financing: The Entrepreneur's Achilles' Heel[1]

There are three core principles of entrepreneurial finance: (1) More cash is preferred to less cash, (2) cash sooner is preferred to cash later, and (3) less risky cash is preferred to more risky cash. Although these principles seem simple enough, entrepreneurs, chief executive officers, and division managers often seem to ignore them. To these individuals, financial analysis seems intimidating, regardless of the size of the company. Even management teams, comfortable with the financial issues, may not be adept at linking strategic and financial decisions to their companies' challenges and choices. Take, for example, the following predicaments:

- Reviewing the year-end results just handed to you by your chief financial officer, you see no surprises—except that the company loss is even larger than you had projected three months earlier. Therefore, for the fourth year in a row, you will have to walk into the boardroom and deliver bad news. A family-owned business since 1945, the company has survived and prospered with average annual sales growth of 17 percent. In fact, the company's market share has actually increased during recent years despite the losses. With the annual growth rate in the industry averaging less than 5 percent, your mature markets offer few opportunities for sustaining higher growth. How can this be happening? Where do you and your company go from here? How do you explain to the board that for four years you have increased sales and market share but produced losses? How will you propose to turn the situation around?

- During the past 20 years, your cable television company has experienced rapid growth

---

[1] This section was drawn from J. A. Timmons, "Financial Management Breakthrough for Entrepreneurs."

through the expansion of existing properties and numerous acquisitions. Your net worth reached $25 million. The next decade of expansion was fueled by the high leverage common in the cable industry, and valuations soared. Ten years later your company had a market value in the $500 million range. You had a mere $300 million in debt, and you owned 100 percent of the company. Just two years later, your $200 million net worth is an astonishing zero! Additionally, you now face the personally exhausting and financially punishing restructuring battle to survive; personal bankruptcy is a very real possibility. How could this happen? Can the company be salvaged?[2]

- At mid-decade your company was the industry leader, meeting as well as exceeding your business plan targets for annual sales, profitability, and new stores. Exceeding these targets while doubling sales and profitability each year has propelled your stock price from $15 at the initial public offering to the mid $30s. Meanwhile you still own a large chunk of the company. Then the shocker—at decade's end your company loses $78 million on just over $90 million in sales! The value of your stock plummets. A brutal restructuring follows in which the stock is stripped from the original management team, including you, and you are ousted from the company you founded and loved. Why did the company spin out of control? Why couldn't you as the founder have anticipated its demise? Could you have saved the company in time?

- As the chair of a rapidly growing telecommunications firm, you are convening your first board meeting after a successful public stock offering. As you think about the agenda, your plans are to grow the company to $25 million in sales in the next three years, which is comfortable given the $18 million in sales last year, the $4 million of cash in the bank, and no debt on the balance sheet. Early in the meeting, one of the two outside directors asks the controller and the chief financial officer his favorite question: "When will you run out of cash?" The chief financial officer is puzzled at first; then he is indignant, if not outraged, by what he considers an irrelevant question. After all, he reasons, our company has plenty of cash and we don't need a bank line. However, 16 months later, without warning from the chief financial officer, the company is out of

cash and has overdrawn its $1 million credit line by $700,000, and the hemorrhaging may get worse. The board fires the president, the chief financial officer, and the senior audit partner from a major accounting firm. The chairman has to take over the helm and must personally invest half a million dollars in the collapsing company to keep it afloat. At this point it's the bank that is indignant and outraged. You have to devise an emergency battle plan to get on top of the financial crisis. How can this be done?

Financial Management Myopia: It Can't Happen to Me

All of these situations have three things in common. First, they are real companies and these are actual events.[3] Second, each of these companies was led by successful entrepreneurs who knew enough to prepare audited financial statements. Third, in each example, the problems stemmed from financial management myopia—a combination of self-delusion and just plain not understanding the complex dynamics and interplay between financial management and business strategy. Why is this so?

Getting Beyond "Collect Early, Pay Late"

During our nearly 40 years as educators, authors, directors, founders, and investors in entrepreneurial companies, we have met a few thousand entrepreneurs and managers, including executives participating in an executive MBA program, MBA students, Kauffman Fellows, company founders, presidents, members of the Young Presidents Organization, and the chief executive officers of middle-market companies. By their own admission, they felt uniformly uncomfortable, if not downright intimidated and terrified, by their lack of expertise in financial analysis and its relationship to management and strategy. The vast majority of entrepreneurs and nonfinancial managers are disadvantaged. Beyond "collect early, pay late," there is precious little sophistication and an enormous level of discomfort when it comes to these complex and dynamic financial interrelationships. Even good managers who are reveling in major sales increases and profit increases often fail to realize until it's too late the impact increased sales have on the cash flow required to finance the increased receivables and inventory.

---

[2] For more detail, see B. C. Hurlock and W. A. Sahlman, "Star Cablevision Group: Harvesting in a Bull Market," HBS Case 293-036, Harvard Business School Publishing.
[3] Their outcomes have ranged from demise to moderate success to radical downsizing followed by dramatic recovery.

EXHIBIT 13.1

The Crux of It: Anticipation and Financial Vigilance

To avoid some of the great tar pits like the ones described earlier, entrepreneurs need answers to questions that link strategic business decisions to financial plans and choices. The crux of it is anticipation: *What is most likely to happen? When? What can go right along the way? What can go wrong? What has to happen to achieve our business objectives and to increase or to preserve our options?* Financially savvy entrepreneurs know that such questions trigger a process that can lead to creative solutions to their financial challenges and problems. At a practical level, financially astute entrepreneurs and managers maintain vigilance over numerous key strategic and financial questions:

- What are the financial consequences and implications of crucial business decisions such as pricing, volume, and policy changes affecting the balance sheet, income statement, and cash flow? How will these change over time?
- How can we measure and monitor changes in our financial strategy and structure from a management, not just a GAAP, perspective?
- Do we have clear and accurate metrics to define our cash conversion cycle, especially the timing of cash commitments in advance of sales receipts?
- What does it mean to grow too fast in our industry? How fast can we grow without requiring outside debt or equity? How much capital is required if we increase or decrease our growth by X percent?
- What will happen to our cash flow, profitability, return on assets, and shareholder equity if we grow faster or slower by X percent?
- How much capital will this require? How much can be financed internally, and how much will have to come from external sources? What is a reasonable mix of debt and equity?
- What if we are 20% less profitable than our plan calls for? Or 20% more profitable?
- What should be our focus and priorities? What are the cash flow and net income break-even points for each of our product lines? For our company? For our business unit?
- What about our pricing, our volume, and our costs? How sensitive are our cash flow and net income to increases or decreases in price, variable costs, or volume? What price/volume mix will enable us to achieve the same cash flow and net income?
- How will these changes in pricing, costs, and volume affect our key financial ratios, and how will we stack up against others in our industry? How will our lenders view this?
- At each stage—start-up, rapidly growing, stagnating, or mature company—how should we be thinking about these questions and issues?

The Spreadsheet Mirage It is hard to imagine any entrepreneur who would not want ready answers to many financial vigilance questions, such as in Exhibit 13.1. Until now, however, getting the answers to these questions was a rarity. If the capacity and information are there to do the necessary analysis (and all too often they are not), it can take up to several weeks to get a response. In this era of spreadsheet mania, more often than not, the answers will come in the form of a lengthy report with innumerable scenarios, pages of numbers, backup exhibits, and possibly a presentation by a staff financial analyst, controller, or chief financial officer.

Too often the barrage of spreadsheet exhibits is really a mirage. What is missing? Traditional spreadsheets can only report and manipulate the data. The numbers may be there, the trends may be identified, but the connections and interdependencies between financial structure and business decisions inherent in key financial questions may be missed. As a result, gaining true insights and getting to creative alternatives and new solutions may be painfully slow, if not interminable. By themselves, spreadsheets cannot model the more complex financial and strategic interrelationships that entrepreneurs need to grasp. And for the board of directors, failure to get this information would be fatal, and any delay would mean too little and too late. Such a weakness in financial know-how becomes life-threatening for entrepreneurs such as those noted earlier, when it comes to anticipating the financial and risk–reward consequences of their business decisions. During a financial crisis, such a weakness can make an already dismal situation worse.

Time and again, the financially fluent and skillful entrepreneurs push what would otherwise be an average company toward and even beyond the brink of greatness. Clearly, financially knowledgeable CEOs enjoy a secret competitive weapon that can yield a decisive edge over less financially skilled entrepreneurs.

Critical Financing Issues

Exhibit 13.2 illustrates the central issues in entrepreneurial finance. These include the creation of value, the slicing and dividing of the value pie among those who have a stake or have participated in the venture, and the handling of the risks inherent in the venture. Developing financing and fundraising strategies, knowing what alternatives are available, and obtaining funding are tasks vital to the survival and success of most higher-potential ventures.

EXHIBIT 13.2

Central Issues in Entrepreneurial Finance

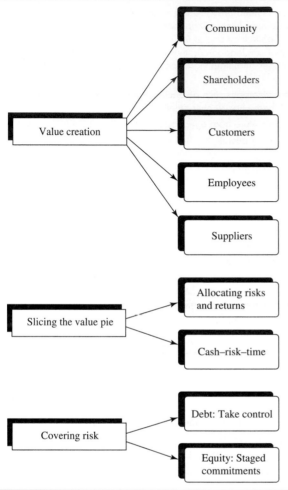

As a result, entrepreneurs face certain critical issues and problems that bear on the financing of entrepreneurial ventures, such as these:

- *Creating value.* Who are the constituencies for whom value must be created or added to achieve a positive cash flow and to develop harvest options? Answer this question starting with broad categories, and then get specific—even to include individuals.

- *Slicing the value pie.* How are deals, both for start-ups and for the purchases of existing ventures, structured and valued, and what are the critical tax consequences of different venture structures? What is the legal process, and what are the key issues involved in raising outside risk capital?

- *Covering risk.* How much money is needed to start, acquire, or expand the business, and when, where, and how can it be obtained on acceptable terms? What sources of risk and venture capital financing—equity, debt, and other innovative types—are available, and how is appropriate financing negotiated and obtained?

The entrepreneur will need to determine what financial contacts and networks will need to be accessed and developed. To sell the idea to financing and other sources, entrepreneurs must be able to make effective presentations of their business plans. These presentations should include a description of some of the nastier pitfalls, minefields, and hazards that need to be anticipated and prepared for, and express how critical and sensitive the timing is in each of these areas. In addition, they should be prepared to discuss whether a staged approach to resource acquisition could mitigate risk and increase return.

A clear understanding of the financing requirements is especially vital for new and emerging companies because new ventures go through financial straits compared to existing firms, both smaller and larger, that have a customer base and revenue stream. In the early going, new firms are gluttons for capital, yet are usually not very debt-worthy. To make matters worse, the faster they grow, the more gluttonous is their appetite for cash.

This phenomenon is best illustrated in Exhibit 13.3 where loss as a percentage of initial equity is plotted against time.[4] The shaded area represents the cumulative cash flow of 157 companies from their inception. For these firms, it took 30 months to achieve operating breakeven and 75 months (or going into the *seventh* year) to recover the initial equity. As can be seen from the illustration, *cash goes out for a long time before it starts to come in.* This phenomenon is at the heart of the financing challenges facing new and emerging companies.

Entrepreneurial Finance: The Owner's Perspective

If an entrepreneur who has had responsibility for financing in a large established company and in a private emerging firm is asked whether there are differences between the two, the person asking will get an earful. While there is some common ground, there are both stark and subtle differences, both in theory and in practice, between entrepreneurial finance as practiced in higher-potential ventures and

---

[4] Special appreciation is due to Bert Twaalfhoven, founder and chairman of Indivers, the Dutch firm that compiled this summary and that owns the firm on which the chart is based. Mr. Twaalfhoven is also a key figure in the promotion of entrepreneurship in Europe.

EXHIBIT 13.3

Initial Losses by Small New Ventures

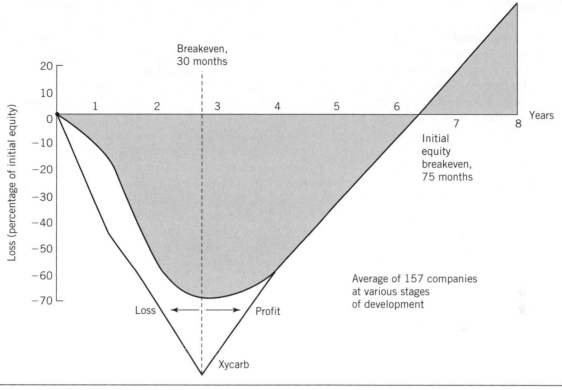

Source: Indivers.

corporate or administrative finance, which usually occurs in larger, publicly traded companies. Further, there are important limits to some financial theories as applied to new ventures.

Students and practitioners of entrepreneurial finance have always been dubious about the reliability and relevance of much of so-called modern finance theory, including the capital asset pricing model (CAPM), beta, and so on.[5] Apparently this skepticism is gaining support from a most surprising source: corporate finance theorists. As reported in a *Harvard Business Review* article,

> One of the strongest attacks is coming from a man who helped launch modern finance, University of Chicago Professor Eugene Fama. His research has cast doubt on the validity of a widely used measure of stock volatility: beta. A second group of critics is looking for a new financial paradigm; they believe it will emerge from the study of nonlinear dynamics and chaos theory. A third group, however, eschews the scientific approach altogether, arguing that investors aren't always rational and that managers' constant focus on the markets is ruining

corporate America. In their view, the highly fragmented U.S. financial markets do a poor job of allocating capital and keeping tabs on management.[6]

Challenging further the basic assumptions of corporate finance, the author continued, "These three concepts, the efficient market hypothesis, portfolio theory, and CAPM, have had a profound impact on how the financial markets relate to the companies they seek to value. . . . They have derailed and blessed countless investment projects."[7] Nancy Nichols concluded that "despite tidy theories, there may be no single answer in a global economy."[8]

It is especially noteworthy that even the most prestigious of modern finance theorists, prominent Nobel laureate Robert Merton of Harvard University, may have a lot to learn. His works and theories of finance were the basis for Long Term Capital Management, Inc. The total collapse of that firm in the late 1990s threatened to topple the entire financial system.

Acquiring knowledge of the limits of financial theories, of differences in the domain of entrepreneurial

---

[5] See P. A. Gompers and W. A. Sahlman, *Entrepreneurial Finance* (New York: John Wiley & Sons, 2002).
[6] N. A. Nichols, "In Question: Efficient? Chaotic? What's the New Finance?" *Harvard Business Review*, March–April 1993, p. 50.
[7] Ibid., p. 52.
[8] Ibid., p. 60.

finance, and of the implications is a core task for entrepreneurs. To begin to appreciate the character and flavor of these limits and differences, consider the following sampling.

Cash Flow and Cash   Cash flow and cash are the king and queen of entrepreneurial finance. Accrual-based accounting, earnings per share, or creative and aggressive use of the tax codes and rules of the Securities and Exchange Commission are not. Enron has become an infamous example of financial shenanigans like this.

Time and Timing   Financing alternatives for the financial health of an enterprise are often more sensitive to, or vulnerable to, the time dimension. In entrepreneurial finance, time for critical financing moves often is shorter and more compressed, the optimum timing of these moves changes more rapidly, and financing moves are subject to wider, more volatile swings from lows to highs and back.

Capital Markets   Capital markets for more than 95 percent of the financing of private entrepreneurial ventures are relatively imperfect in that they are frequently inaccessible, unorganized, and often invisible. Virtually all the underlying characteristics and assumptions that dominate such popular financial theories and models as the capital asset pricing model simply do not apply, even up to the point of a public offering for a small company. In reality, there are so many and such significant information, knowledge, and market gaps and asymmetries that the rational, perfect market models suffer enormous limitations.

Emphasis   Capital is one of the least important factors in the success of higher-potential ventures. Rather, higher-potential entrepreneurs seek not only the best deal but also the backer who will provide the most value in terms of know-how, wisdom, counsel, and help. In addition, higher-potential entrepreneurs invariably opt for the value added (beyond money), rather than just the best deal or share price.

Strategies for Raising Capital   Strategies that optimize or maximize the amount of money raised can actually increase risk in new and emerging companies, rather than lower it. Thus the concept of "staged capital commitments," whereby money is committed for a 3- to 18-month phase and is followed by subsequent commitments based on results and promise, is a prevalent practice among venture capitalists and other investors in higher-potential ventures. Similarly, wise entrepreneurs may refuse excess capital when the valuation is less attractive and when they believe that valuation will rise substantially.

Downside Consequences   Consequences of financial strategies and decisions are eminently more personal and emotional for the owners of new and emerging ventures than for the managements of large companies. The downside consequences for such entrepreneurs of running out of cash or failing are monumental and relatively catastrophic because personal guarantees of bank or other loans are common. Contrast these situations with that of Robert Nardelli, who became CEO of The Home Depot in December 2000 despite having no retail experience. The company's stagnating share price and Nardelli's blunt, critical, and autocratic management style turned off employees, and his $240 million compensation eventually earned the ire of investors. In 2006, as questions about his leadership mounted, Nardelli directed the board to skip the company's annual meeting and forbid shareholders from speaking more than a minute (they used large digital timers just to make sure). Criticism about his behavior at the meeting and the showdown over his compensation package caused the board to oust him in January 2007. His severance package was estimated at $210 million. In August 2007 Nardelli became chairman and CEO of the newly privatized Chrysler, with a current annual salary of one dollar (other compensation was not disclosed).

Risk–Reward Relationships   While the high-risk/high-reward and low-risk/low-reward relationship (a so-called law of economics and finance) works fairly well in efficient, mature, and relatively perfect capital markets (e.g., those with money market accounts, deposits in savings and loan institutions, widely held and traded stocks and bonds, and certificates of deposit), the opposite occurs too often in entrepreneurial finance to permit much comfort with this law. Some of the most profitable, highest-return venture investments have been quite low-risk propositions from the outset. Many leveraged buyouts using extreme leverage are probably much more risky than many start-ups. Yet the way the capital markets price these deals is just the reverse. The reasons are anchored in the second and third points just noted— timing and the asymmetries and imperfections of the capital markets for deals. Entrepreneurs or investors who create or recognize lower-risk/very high-yield business propositions, before others jump on the Brink's truck, will defy the laws of economics and finance. The recent bankruptcies of Kmart and Enron illustrate this point.

Valuation Methods   Established company valuation methods, such as those based on discounted cash flow models used in Wall Street megadeals, seem to favor the seller, rather than the buyer, of private emerging entrepreneurial companies. A seller loves to see a recent MBA or investment banking firm alumnus or alumna show up with an HP calculator or the latest laptop and then proceed to develop "the 10-year discounted cash flow stream." The assumptions normally made and the mind-set behind them are irrelevant or grossly misleading for valuation of smaller private firms because of dynamic and erratic historical and prospective growth curves.

Conventional Financial Ratios   Current financial ratios are misleading when applied to most private entrepreneurial companies. For one thing, entrepreneurs often own more than one company at once and move cash and assets from one to another. For example, an entrepreneur may own real estate and equipment in one entity and lease it to another company. Use of different fiscal years compounds the difficulty of interpreting what the balance sheet really means and the possibilities for aggressive tax avoidance. Further, many of the most important value and equity builders in the business are off the balance sheet or are hidden assets: the excellent management team; the best scientist, technician, or designer; know-how and business relationships that cannot be bought or sold, let alone valued for the balance sheet.

Goals   Creating value over the long term, rather than maximizing quarterly earnings, is a prevalent mind-set and strategy among highly successful entrepreneurs. Because profit is more than just the bottom line, financial strategies are geared to build value, often at the expense of short-term earnings. The growth required to build value often is heavily self-financed, thereby eroding possible accounting earnings.

Determining Capital Requirements

How much money does my venture need? When is it needed? How long will it last? Where and from whom can it be raised? How should this process be orchestrated and managed? These are vital questions to any entrepreneur at any stage in the development of a company. These questions are answered in the next two sections.

Financial Strategy Framework

The financial strategy framework shown in Exhibit 13.4 is a way to begin crafting financial and fundraising strategies.[9] The exhibit provides a flow and

---

[9] This framework was developed for the Financing Entrepreneurial Ventures course at Babson College and has been used in the Entrepreneurial Finance course at the Harvard Business School.

EXHIBIT 13.4

Financial Strategy Framework

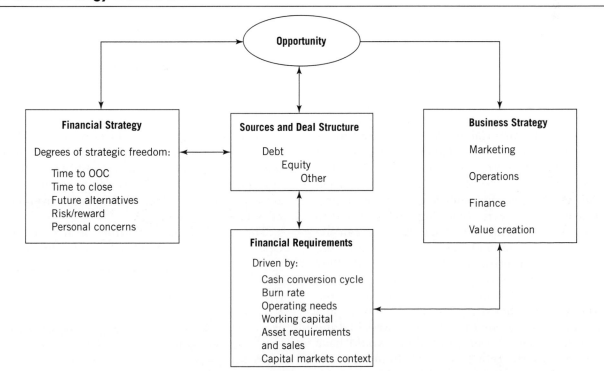

logic with which an otherwise confusing task can be attacked. *The opportunity leads and drives the business strategy, which in turn drives the financial requirements, the sources and deal structures, and the financial strategy.* (Again, until this part of the exercise is well defined, developing spreadsheets and "playing with the numbers" is just that—playing.)

Once an entrepreneur has defined the core of the market opportunity and the strategy for seizing it (of course, these may change, even dramatically), he or she can begin to examine the financial requirements in terms of (1) asset needs (for start-up or for expansion facilities, equipment, research and development, and other apparently onetime expenditures) and (2) operating needs (i.e., working capital for operations based on the cash conversion cycle). This framework leaves ample room for crafting a financial strategy, for creatively identifying sources, for devising a fund-raising plan, and for structuring deals.

Each *fund-raising strategy,* along with its accompanying deal structure, commits the company to actions that incur actual and real-time costs and may enhance or inhibit future financing options. Similarly, each *source* has particular requirements and costs—both apparent and hidden—that carry implications for both financial strategy and financial requirements. The premise is that successful entrepreneurs are aware of potentially punishing situations, and that they are careful to "sweat the details" and proceed with a certain degree of wariness as they evaluate, select, negotiate, and craft business relationships with potential funding sources. In doing so, they are more likely to find the right sources, at the right time, and on the right terms and conditions. They are also more likely to avoid potential mismatches, costly sidetracking for the wrong sources, and the disastrous marriage to these sources that might follow.

Certain changes in the financial climate, such as the aftershocks felt after October 1987 and March 2000, and in the second half of 2007, can cause repercussions across financial markets and institutions serving smaller companies. These take the form of greater caution by both lenders and investors as they seek to increase their protection against risk. When the financial climate becomes harsher, an entrepreneur's capacity to devise financing strategies and to effectively deal with financing sources can be stretched to the limit and beyond. For example, the subprime credit crisis in the summer of 2007 caused mayhem across the capital markets. Take, for instance, a 400-unit residential complex in the Southeast. Built between 2003 and 2004, a purchase and sale agreement was executed in June 2007. The price of over $40 million would have meant a superb return to the founders and investors. The deal was expected to close by mid-September, but unfortunately the buyer's financing

fell through—a victim of much tighter and less liquid credit markets.

Also, certain lures of cash that come in unsuspecting ways turn out to be a punch in the wallet. (The next chapter covers some of these potentially fatal lures and some of the issues and considerations needed to recognize and avoid these traps while devising a fund-raising strategy and evaluating and negotiating with different sources.)

Free Cash Flow: Burn Rate, OOC, and TTC

The core concept in determining the external financing requirements of the venture is free cash flow. Three vital corollaries are the burn rate (projected or actual), time to OOC (when will the company be out of cash), and TTC (or the time to close the financing and have the check clear). These have a major impact on the entrepreneur's choices and relative bargaining power with various sources of equity and debt capital, which is represented in Exhibit 13.5. Chapter 15 addresses the details of deal structuring, terms, conditions, and covenants.

The message is clear: If you are out of cash in 90 days or less, you are at a major disadvantage. OOC even in six months is perilously soon. But if you have a year or more, the options, terms, price, and covenants that you will be able to negotiate will improve dramatically. The implication is obvious: Ideally, raise money when you do not need it.

The cash flow generated by a company or project is defined as follows:

	Earnings before interest and taxes (EBIT)
Less	Tax exposure (tax rate times EBIT)
Plus	Depreciation, amortization, and other noncash charges
Less	Increase in operating working capital
Less	Capital expenditures

Economists call this result *free cash flow.* The definition takes into account the benefits of investing, the income generated, *and* the cost of investing, the amount of investment in working capital and plant and equipment required to generate a given level of sales and net income.

The definition can fruitfully be refined further. Operating working capital is defined as follows:

	Transactions cash balances
Plus	Accounts receivable
Plus	Inventory
Plus	Other operating current assets (e.g., prepaid expenses)
Less	Accounts payable
Less	Taxes payable
Less	Other operating current liabilities (e.g., accrued expenses)

EXHIBIT 13.5

Entrepreneur's Bargaining Power Based on Time to OOC

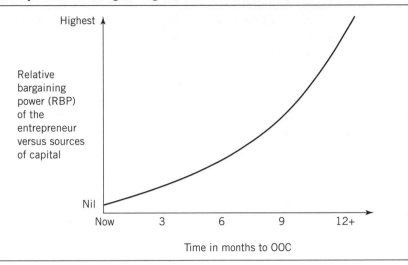

Finally, this expanded definition can be collapsed into a simpler one:[10]

	Earnings before interest but after taxes (EBIAT)
Less	Increase in net total operating capital (FA + WC)

where the increase in net total operating capital is defined as follows:

	Increase in operating working capital
Plus	Increase in net fixed assets

Crafting Financial and Fund-Raising Strategies

Critical Variables

When financing is needed, a number of factors affect the availability of the various types of financing and their suitability and cost:

- Accomplishments and performance to date.
- Investor's perceived risk.
- Industry and technology.
- Venture upside potential and anticipated exit timing.
- Venture anticipated growth rate.
- Venture age and stage of development.
- Investor's required rate of return or internal rate of return.

- Amount of capital required and prior valuations of the venture.
- Founders' goals regarding growth, control, liquidity, and harvesting.
- Relative bargaining positions.
- Investor's required terms and covenants.

Numerous other factors, especially an investor's or lender's view of the quality of a business opportunity and the management team, will also play a part in a decision to invest in or lend to a firm.

Generally a company's operations can be financed through debt and some form of equity financing.[11] Moreover, it is generally believed that a new or existing business needs to obtain both equity and debt financing if it is to have a sound financial foundation for growth without excessive dilution of the entrepreneur's equity.

Short-term debt (i.e., debt incurred for one year or less) usually is used by a business for working capital and is repaid out of the proceeds of its sales. Longer-term borrowings (i.e., term loans of one to five years or long-term loans maturing in more than five years) are used for working capital and/or to finance the purchase of property or equipment that serves as collateral for the loan. Equity financing is used to fill the nonbankable gaps, preserve ownership, and lower the risk of loan defaults.

However, a new venture just starting operations will have difficulty obtaining either short-term or longer-term bank debt without a substantial cushion of equity financing or long-term debt that is subordinated or

---

[10] This section is drawn directly from "Note on Free Cash Flow Valuation Models," HBS 288-023, pp. 2–3.
[11] In addition to the purchase of common stock, equity financing is meant to include the purchase of both stock and subordinated debt, or subordinated debt with stock conversion features or warrants to purchase stock.

junior to all bank debt.[12] As far as a lender is concerned, a start-up has little proven capability to generate sales, profits, and cash to pay off short-term debt and even less ability to sustain profitable operations over a number of years and retire long-term debt. Even the underlying protection provided by a venture's assets used as loan collateral may be insufficient to obtain bank loans. Asset values can erode with time; in the absence of adequate equity capital and good management, they may provide little real loan security to a bank.[13]

A bank may lend money to a start-up to some maximum debt-to-equity ratio. As a rough rule, a start-up may be able to obtain debt for working capital purposes that is equal to its equity and subordinated debt. A start-up can also obtain loans through such avenues as the Small Business Administration, manufacturers and suppliers, or leasing.

An existing business seeking expansion capital or funds for a temporary use has a much easier job obtaining both debt and equity. Sources such as banks, professional investors, and leasing and finance companies often will seek out such companies and regard them as important customers for secured and unsecured short-term loans or as good investment prospects. Furthermore, an existing and expanding business will find it easier to raise equity capital from private or institutional sources and to raise it on better terms than the start-up.

Awareness of criteria used by various sources of financing, whether for debt, equity, or some combination of the two, that are available for a particular situation is central to devise a time-effective and cost-effective search for capital.

Financial Life Cycles

One useful way to begin identifying equity financing alternatives, and when and if certain alternatives are available, is to consider what can be called the financial life cycle of firms. Exhibit 13.6 shows the types of capital available over time for different types of firms at different stages of development (i.e., as indicated by different sales levels).[14] It also summarizes, at different stages of development (research and development, start-up, early growth, rapid growth, and exit), the principal sources of risk capital and costs of risk capital.

As can be seen in the exhibit, sources have different preferences and practices, including how much money they will provide, when in a company's life cycle they

will invest, and the cost of the capital or expected annual rate of return they are seeking. The available sources of capital change dramatically for companies at different stages and rates of growth, and there will be variations in different parts of the country.

Many of the sources of equity are not available until a company progresses beyond the earlier stages of its growth. Some sources available to early-stage companies, especially personal sources, friends, and other informal investors or angels, will be insufficient to meet the financing requirements generated in later stages if the company continues to grow successfully.

Another key factor affecting the availability of financing is the upside potential of a company. Of the 3 million-plus new businesses of all kinds expected to be launched in the United States in 2008, probably 5 percent or fewer will achieve the growth and sales levels of high-potential firms. Foundation firms will total about 8 percent to 12 percent of all new firms, which will grow more slowly but exceed $1 million in sales and may grow to $20 million with 50 to 500 employees. Remaining are the traditional, stable lifestyle firms. High-potential firms (those that grow rapidly and are likely to exceed $20 million to $25 million or more in sales) are strong prospects for a public offering and have the widest array of financing alternatives, including combinations of debt and equity and other alternatives (which are noted later), while foundation firms have fewer, and lifestyle firms are limited to the personal resources of their founders and whatever net worth or collateral they can accumulate.

In general, investors believe the younger the company, the more risky the investment. This is a variation of the old saying in the venture capital business: The lemons ripen in two-and-a-half years, but the plums take seven or eight.

While the time line and dollar limits shown are only guidelines, they reflect how these money sources view the riskiness, and thus the required rate of return, of companies at various stages of development.

Internet Impact: Opportunity

International Finance and Trade

Like the global supply chains it has already fostered, the Internet has dramatically improved the facilitation and movement of financial instruments and

---

[12] For lending purposes, commercial banks regard such subordinated debt as equity. Venture capital investors normally subordinate their business loans to the loans provided by the bank or other financial institutions.

[13] The bank loan defaults by the real estate investment trusts (REITs) in 1975 and 1989–91 are examples of the failure of assets to provide protection in the absence of sound management and adequate equity capital.

[14] W. H. Wetzel, Jr., of the University of New Hampshire originally showed the different types of equity capital that are available to three types of companies. The exhibit is based on a chart by Wetzel, which the authors have updated and modified. See W. H. Wetzel, Jr., "The Cost of Availability of Credit and Risk Capital in New England," in *A Region's Struggling Savior: Small Business in New England*, ed. J. A. Timmons and D. E. Gumpert (Waltham, MA: Small Business Foundation of America, 1979).

EXHIBIT 13.6

Financing Life Cycles

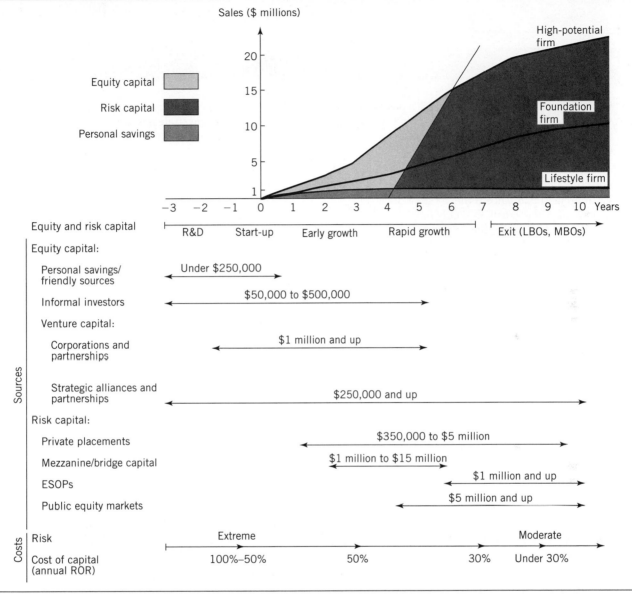

Source: Adapted and updated for 2008 from W. H. Wetzel, Jr., "The Cost of Availability of Credit and Risk Capital in New England," in *A Region's Struggling Savior: Small Business in New England,* ed. J. A. Timmons, D. E. Gumpert (Waltham, MA: Small Business Foundation of America, 1979), p. 175.

trade documents. The result has been an acceleration of transactions and collections that has strengthened cash flow, boosted investment income, and bolstered balance sheets.

Major financial institutions now offer sophisticated trade portals that support document creation and transmission, making it possible for all parties to a transaction (exporter, importer, bank, freight forwarder, ocean carrier, cargo insurer) to exchange information through the same secure site. Letters of credit (L/Cs), for example, frequently carry discrep-

ancies such as misspelled names, inaccurate descriptions of products, and faulty dates. Amending those errors has typically meant additional bank fees and higher port charges (to cover delays), slower movement through overseas customs, and the possibility of failing to perform within the legal timetable of the L/C. Electronic trade documentation helps avoid discrepancies in the first place and supports quick and easy corrections when needed.

In a similar way, the U.S. Export–Import Bank has leveraged the speed and ease of the Internet to structure stand-alone deals between its approved exporters and large finance companies that in the past worked only with regular clients. This is giving first-time and early-stage trade ventures that meet Ex-Im Bank's credit standards access to major suppliers of trade credit and insurance.

Chapter Summary

- Cash is king and queen. Happiness is a positive cash flow. More cash is preferred to less cash. Cash sooner is preferred to cash later. Less risky cash is preferred to more risky cash.
- Financial know-how, issues, and analysis are often the entrepreneurs' Achilles' heels.
- Entrepreneurial finance is the art and science of quantifying value creation, slicing the value pie, and managing and covering financial risk.

- Determining capital requirements, crafting financial and fund-raising strategies, and managing and orchestrating the financial process are critical to new venture success.
- Harvest strategies are as important to the entrepreneurial process as value creation itself. Value that is unrealized may have no value.

Study Questions

1. Define the following and explain why they are important: burn rate, free cash flow, OOC, TTC, financial management myopia, spreadsheet mirage.
2. Why is entrepreneurial finance simultaneously both the least and most important part of the entrepreneurial process? Explain this paradox.
3. What factors affect the availability, suitability, and cost of various types of financing? Why are these factors critical?

4. What is meant by *free cash flow*, and why do entrepreneurs need to understand this?
5. Why do financially savvy entrepreneurs ask the financial and strategic questions in Exhibit 13.1? Can you answer these questions for your venture?

Internet Resources for Chapter 13

http://www.businessfinance.com/ *Funding sources for small businesses.*

http://www.exim.gov/ *The Export–Import Bank supports the financing of U.S. goods and services.*

MIND STRETCHERS

Have You Considered?

1. To what extent might you be suffering from financial myopia and spreadsheet mirage?
2. People who believe that you first have to have money, in large amounts, to make money are naive and ignorant. Why is this so? Do you agree?

3. Whom do you need to get to know well to strengthen the entrepreneurial finance know-how on your team?
4. Can you talk with someone who had a financial setback due to the Summer 2007 credit crunch?

Midwest Lighting, Inc.

Preparation Questions

1. Evaluate the company. How much do you believe the company is worth? Bring to class a written bid showing how much you would pay for it if you were Scott and Peterson.

2. What should they do to resolve the ownership situation?

3. How would you finance the purchase of the company?

4. Assume you do purchase the company: What specific actions would you plan to take on the first day? By the end of the first week? By the end of six months? Explain how and why.

Jack Peterson was discouraged by the continuing conflicts with his partner, David Scott, and had sought advice on how to remedy the situation from friends and associates as early as 1996. By 2005 Jack had begun to believe that he and Scott had just grown too far apart to continue together. Peterson had to find a mutually agreeable way to accomplish a separation. One alternative was for one partner to buy the other out, but they would first have to agree on this and find an acceptable method. Scott seemed to have no interest in such an arrangement.

Throughout 2004 the differences between the partners had grown. The vacillations in leadership were disruptive to the operation and made the employees uncomfortable.

By early 2005 the situation was growing unbearable. Peterson recalled the executive committee's annual planning meeting in January:

> It was a total disaster. There were loud arguments and violent disagreements. It was so bad that no one wanted to ever participate in another meeting. We were all miserable.
>
> What was so difficult was that each of us truly thought he was right. On various occasions other people in the company would support each of our positions. These were normally honest differences of opinion, but politics also started to enter in.

Company Description

Midwest Lighting, Inc. (MLI), manufactured custom-engineered fluorescent lighting fixtures used for commercial and institutional applications. Sales in 2005 were approximately $5.5 million with profits of just over $144,000.

Most sales were for standard items within the nine major lines of products designed and offered by the company. Ten percent of sales were completely custom-designed or custom-built fixtures, and 15 percent of orders were for slightly modified versions of a standard product. In 2005 MLI shipped 82,500 fixtures. Although individual orders ranged from one unit to over 2,000 units, the average order size was approximately 15–20 fixtures. Modified and custom-designed fixtures averaged about 25 per order. Jack Peterson, MLI president, described their market position:

> Our product-marketing strategy is to try to solve lighting problems for architects and engineers. We design products which are architecturally styled for specific types of building constructions. If an architect has an unusual lighting problem, we design a special fixture to fit his needs. Or if he designs a lighting fixture, we build it to his specifications. We try to find products that satisfy particular lighting needs that are not filled by the giant fixture manufacturers. We look for niches in the marketplace.
>
> Having the right product to fit the architect's particular needs is the most important thing to our customer. Second is the relationship that the architect, the consulting engineer, or the lighting designer has with the people who are representing us. The construction business is such that the architect, engineer, contractor, distributor, and manufacturer all have to work as a team together on a specified project to ensure its successful completion. The architect makes a lot of mistakes in every building he designs, unless he just designs the same one over and over. Consequently, there's a lot of trading that goes on during the construction of a building, and everybody's got to give and take a little to get the job done. Then the owner usually gets a satisfactory job and the contractors and manufacturers make a fair profit. It requires a cooperative effort.
>
> Most of our bids for orders are probably compared with bids from half a dozen other firms across the country. Since a higher percentage of our orders are for premium-priced products, we are not as price sensitive as producers of more commonplace lighting fixtures. It is difficult for a small firm to compete in that market. As many as 30 companies might bid on one standard fixture job.

MLI owned its own modern manufacturing facility, located outside Pontiac, Michigan. Production consisted of stamping, cutting, and forming sheet metal; painting; and assembling the fixture with the electrical components that were purchased from outside suppliers. The company employed a total of 130 workers, with 42 people in sales, engineering, and administration and another 88 in production and assembly.

The company sold nationwide through regional distributors to contractors and architects for new buildings and renovations. Prior to 2003, MLI sold primarily to a regional market. At that time marketing activities were

EXHIBIT A

Historical Performance

Year	Net Sales	Profit after Tax	No. of Fixtures Shipped	Total Employees	Hourly Employees
2005	$5,515,239	$144,011	82,500	130	88
2004	4,466,974	126,266	72,500	118	73
2003	3,717,225	133,160	65,000	103	65
2002	3,669,651	79,270	67,500	103	63

broadened geographically. This was the primary reason that sales had been increasing over the last few years—even during a weak construction market. (See Exhibit A for historical sales, earnings, unit sales, and employment.)

Background

Midwest Lighting, Inc., was formed in Flint, Michigan, in 1956 by Daniel Peterson and Julian Walters. Each owned half of the company. Peterson was responsible for finance and engineering and Walters for sales and design. They subcontracted all manufacturing for the lighting systems they sold.

After several years, differences in personal work habits led Peterson to buy out Walters's interest. Daniel Peterson then brought in Richard Scott as his new partner. Scott had been one of his sheet metal subcontractors. Richard Scott became president and Daniel Peterson treasurer. Ownership was split so that Peterson retained a few shares more than half and all voting control because of his prior experience with the company.

In 1960 MLI began manufacturing and moved its operations to a multifloor 50,000-square-foot plant also located in Flint. The company grew and was quite profitable over the next decade. Peterson and Scott were satisfied with the earnings they had amassed during this period and were content to let the company remain at a steady level of about $1.2 million in sales and about $18,000 in profit after taxes.

Daniel Peterson's son, Jack, joined MLI as a salesman in 1983 after graduating from MIT and then Colorado Business School. Richard Scott's son, David, who was a graduate of Trinity College, became an MLI salesman in 1984 when he was discharged from the service. The two sons were acquaintances from occasional gatherings as they were growing up but had not been close friends.

In 1986 Daniel Peterson had a heart attack and withdrew from management of the business. Although he remained an interested observer and sometime advisor to his son, Daniel was inactive in company affairs after this time. Richard Scott assumed overall responsibility for the management of the company.

Jack Peterson moved inside to learn about other parts of the company in 1987. His first work assignments were in manufacturing and sales service. David Scott joined his father in the manufacturing area a year later. Jack Peterson became sales manager, David Scott became manufacturing manager, and, at Richard Scott's suggestion, another person was added as financial manager. These three shared responsibility for running the company and worked well together, but major decisions were still reserved for Richard Scott, who spent less and less time in the office.

As the new group began revitalizing the company, a number of employees who had not been productive and were not responding to change were given early retirement or asked to leave. When the man who had been Richard Scott's chief aide could not work with the three younger managers, they ultimately decided he had to be discharged. Richard Scott became so angry that he rarely entered the plant again.

For several years the three managers guided the company as a team. However, there were some spirited discussions over the basic strategic view of the company. As sales manager, Jack Peterson pressed for responding to special customer needs. This, he felt, would be their strongest market niche. David Scott argued for smooth production flows and less disruption. He felt they could compete well in the "semistandard" market.

In 1988 Jack Peterson began to work with an individual in forming a company in the computer field. The company rented extra space from MLI, and MLI provided management and administrative support, helping the new company with bidding and keeping track of contracts. Although David Scott was not active in this company, Jack split his partial ownership in this new company with Scott because they were partners and because Peterson was spending time away from MLI with the computer company.

In 1989 the fathers moved to restructure the company's ownership to reflect the de facto changes in management. The fathers converted their ownership to nonvoting class A stock, and then each transferred 44 percent of their nonvoting stock to their sons. Daniel Peterson decided to relinquish his voting control at that time in an effort to help things work as the new generation took over.

Accordingly, Jack Peterson and David Scott were each issued 50 percent of the class B voting shares.

Due to the demands associated with the start-up of the computer company, this new effort began to weaken the relationship between Peterson and Scott. At the same time Scott and the financial manager began to have strong disagreements. These seemed to arise primarily from errors in cost analysis, which led the financial manager to question some of Scott's decisions. There were also differences of opinion over relations with the workforce and consistency of policy. Scott preferred to control the manufacturing operation in his own way. Peterson felt Scott could be more consistent, less arbitrary, and more supportive of the workforce. When the computer company was sold in 1995, the financial manager joined it as treasurer and resigned from MLI.

Growing Conflict

The departure of the financial manager led to a worsening of the relationship between Peterson and Scott. Peterson had been made company president in 1990. Peterson recalled the decision:

> Richard Scott had resigned as president and the three of us were sitting around talking about who should be president. David Scott finally said, "I think you should be it." And I said, "Okay."

Yet even after Peterson became president, the three managers had really operated together as a team for major decisions. Now Peterson was upset that they had lost an excellent financial manager, someone critical to the operation (partially due, in his opinion, to the disagreements with Scott). Also, there was no longer a third opinion to help resolve conflicts. Although the financial manager was replaced with an old classmate of Scott's, the new manager became one of several middle-level managers who had been hired as the company grew.

The pressure of growth created more strains between Peterson and Scott. Sales had reached $2.3 million and had begun to tax MLI's manufacturing capacity. Peterson felt that some of the problems could be alleviated if Scott would change methods that had been acceptable during slacker periods but hindered intense production efforts. Scott had different views. Both, however, agreed to look for additional space.

The transition to a new factory outside Pontiac, Michigan, in 1997 eased the stresses between the partners. A major corporation had purchased an indirect competitor to obtain its product lines and sold MLI the 135,000-square-foot plant. MLI also entered into an agreement to manufacture some of the other company's light fixtures as a subcontractor. The plant was in poor condition, and David Scott took over the project of renovating it and continuing production of the other company's lines. That was also the year that Richard Scott died. Although he had remained chairman of the board, he had generally been inactive in the company since 1988. Daniel and Jack Peterson and David Scott were now the only directors.

Jack Peterson remained in Flint running the MLI operation alone until such time as it became possible to consolidate the entire operation in Pontiac. Peterson described this interlude:

> The next year was a sort of cooling-off period. David was immersed in the project with the new factory and I was busy with the continuing operation. David had always enjoyed projects of this sort and was quite satisfied with this arrangement.
>
> Then, in 1998, we hired a plant manager to run the Pontiac plant and David came back to work in Flint. By that time, of course, a lot of things had changed. All of Flint had been reporting to me. I had somewhat reshaped the operation and the people had gotten used to my management style, which was different from David's.
>
> David's reaction was to work primarily with the design and engineering people, but he really wasn't involved very much with the daily manufacturing anymore. He developed a lot of outside interests, business and recreation, that took up much of his time.
>
> I was very happy with the arrangement because it lessened the number of conflicts. But when he did come back, the disagreements that did rise would be worse. I guess I resented his attempts to change things when he only spent a small amount of his time in the company.
>
> Then, in 2000, we made the decision to sell the Flint plant and put the whole company in Pontiac. We were both involved in that. Most of the key people went with us. David and I were very active in pulling together the two groups and in integrating the operations.
>
> That began a fairly good time. I was spending my time with the sales manager trying to change the company from a regional company to a national one and was helping to find new representatives all over the country. David Scott spent his time in the engineering, design, and manufacturing areas. There was plenty of extra capacity in the new plant, so things went quite smoothly. In particular, David did an excellent job in upgrading the quality standards of the production force we had acquired with the plant. This was critical for our line of products and our quality reputation.
>
> This move really absorbed us for almost two years. It just took us a long time to get people working together and to produce at the quality level and rate we wanted. We had purchased the plant for an excellent price with a lot of new equipment and had started deleting marginal product lines as we expanded nationally. The company became much more profitable.

During the company's expansion, a group of six people formed the operating team. Scott concentrated on applications engineering for custom fixtures and new product design. In addition, there were a sales manager, financial manager, engineering manager, the plant manufacturing manager, and Peterson. Disagreements began again. Peterson recounted the problems:

> Our operating group would meet on a weekly or biweekly basis, whatever was necessary. Then we would have monthly executive committee meetings for broader planning issues. These became a disaster. Scott had reached the point where he didn't like much of anything that was going on in the company and was becoming very critical. I disagreed with him, as did the other managers on most occasions. Tempers often flared, and Scott became more and more isolated.
>
> He and I also began to disagree over which topics we should discuss with the group. I felt that some areas were best discussed between the two of us, particularly matters concerning personnel, and that other matters should be left for stockholders meetings. The committee meetings were becoming real battles.

Search for a Solution

When Peterson returned from a summer vacation in August 2005, he was greeted by a string of complaints from several of MLI's sales agents and also from some managers. Peterson decided that the problem had to be resolved. Peterson sought an intermediary:

> I knew that Scott and I weren't communicating and that I had to find a mediator Scott trusted. I had discussed this before with Allen Burke, our accountant. He was actually far more than our accountant. Allen is a partner with a Big Six accounting firm and is active in working with smaller companies. Allen was a boyhood friend who had grown up with Scott. I felt he had very high integrity and was very smart. Scott trusted him totally and Allen was probably one of Scott's major advisors about things.
>
> When I first talked to Burke in March, he basically said, "Well, you have problems in a marriage and you make it work. Go make it work, Peterson." He wasn't going to listen much.
>
> Then in early September, I went back to say that it wasn't going to work anymore. I asked him for his help. Allen said that Scott had also seen him to complain about the problems, so Allen knew that the situation had become intolerable.

Both directly and through Burke, Peterson pressured Scott to agree to a meeting to resolve the situation. Although Scott was also unhappy about their conflicts, he was hesitant to meet until he had thought through his options.

Peterson felt that there were several principal reasons for Scott's reluctance to meet. Since they couldn't seem to solve their differences, the alternative of having one of them leave the company or become a silent partner glared as a possibility. Peterson knew that Scott's only work experience was with MLI and was limited primarily to managing manufacturing operations he had known for years. Second, Peterson thought that Scott was very uncertain about financial analysis, in which he had little training. Because he had not been directly involved in the financial operations, he was not aware of all the financial implications of his decisions. Peterson felt that this made Scott's task of weighing the pros and cons of alternative courses of action much more difficult. Finally, there was the emotional tie to the company and the desire to avoid such a momentous decision.

As discussion began to result in the possibility that the partners would sell the company, Scott's reluctance waxed and waned. Just before Thanksgiving, Scott called Peterson, who was sick at home, and said he had decided to fire the financial manager and become the treasurer of the company. Scott wanted to look at the figures for a year or so, and then he would be able to make a better decision. Peterson felt that the financial manager was essential and could not be discharged. He thought that this was really more of an attempt to buy time. After some discussion, Peterson convinced Scott that the financial manager should be retained.

After another month of give and take, Peterson and Scott realized that they had no estimate of the value of the company if it were to be sold. Both felt that this might alter the attractiveness of the alternatives that each was considering.

Valuing the Company

Before making his decision, Peterson reviewed the thinking he had done since first considering the idea of buying or selling the company. He began with the company's current position. With the serious discussions going on about the buyout agreement, preparation of the financial statements for 2005 had been accelerated and they were already completed. (These are shown, together with the results of 2004 and 2003, as Exhibits B and C.)

Peterson had also begun developing the bank support he might need to fund a buyout. The company's banker indicated that he would lend Peterson funds secured by his other personal assets if Peterson was the buyer, but that since he had not worked with Scott, the bank would decline to finance an acquisition with Scott as the buyer. In addition, the bank would continue the company's existing line of credit, which was secured by MLI's cash and accounts receivable. The maximum that could be borrowed with this line was an amount equal to 100 percent of cash plus 75 percent of receivables. Both types of borrowing would be at 1 percent over the prime rate (then about 6 percent).

Peterson worked with the financial manager to develop financial projections and valuation assessments. To be conservative, Peterson had made the sales projections about 10 percent lower each year than he really thought they would achieve. Because fixed costs would not rise appreciably with modest increases in sales, any improvements in sales volume would directly increase profits. He felt he should consider how these various changes would impact his financing requirements and his assessment.

EXHIBIT B

Statement of Earnings

	Year Ended December 31		
	2005	**2004**	**2003**
Net sales	$5,515,239	$4,466,974	$3,717,225
Cost of goods sold:			
Inventories at beginning of year	928,634	741,481	520,640
Purchases	1,999,283	1,594,581	1,387,226
Freight in	24,400	33,244	26,208
Direct labor	537,693	450,710	410,609
Manufacturing expenses	1,221,536	1,002,715	842,054
	4,711,545	3,822,731	3,186,736
Inventories at end of year	1,032,785	928,634	741,481
	3,678,760	2,894,098	2,445,255
Gross profit	1,836,479	1,572,876	1,271,970
Product development expenses	164,683	161,011	127,874
Selling and administrative expenses	1,390,678	1,143,925	926,001
	1,555,360	1,304,936	1,053,875
Operating income	281,119	267,940	218,095
Other expense (income):			
Interest expense	70,324	47,238	40,520
Payments to retired employee	12,500	12,500	25,000
Miscellaneous	(1,154)	(1,939)	(7,741)
	81,570	57,799	57,779
Earnings before income taxes	199,449	210,141	160,316
Provision for income taxes	55,438	83,875	61,250
Earnings before extraordinary income	144,011	126,266	99,066
Extraordinary income—life insurance proceeds in excess of cash surrender value			34,094
Net earnings	$ 144,011	$ 126,266	$ 133,160
Earnings per share of common stock	$ 23.94	$ 20.99	$ 16.46

(continued)

EXHIBIT B (continued)

Statement of Earnings

	Year Ended December 31		
	2005	**2004**	**2003**
Assets			
Current assets:			
Cash	$ 64,060	$ 4,723	$ 88,150
Accounts receivable:			
Customers	750,451	538,438	397,945
Refundable income taxes	28,751		
Other		2,845	6,611
	779,203	541,283	404,556
Less allowance for doubtful receivables	4,375	4,375	4,375
	774,828	536,908	400,181
Inventories			
Raw materials	364,738	324,438	346,340
Work in progress	668,048	604,196	395,141
	1,032,785	928,634	741,481
Prepaid insurance and other	17,760	25,168	32,588
Total current assets	1,889,433	1,495,431	1,262,400
Property, plant, and equipment:			
Buildings and improvements	426,783	407,108	368,913
Machinery and equipment	263,116	216,341	169,274
Motor vehicles	40,723	40,723	36,776
Office equipment	53,583	54,881	46,186
	784,204	719,053	621,149
Less accumulated depreciation	341,605	291,805	231,519
	442,599	427,248	389,630
Land	13,876	13,876	13,876
	456,475	441,124	403,506
Other assets:			
Cash surrender value of life insurance policies (less loans of $24,348 in 2004, $24,488 in 2003, and $24,290 in 2002)	102,473	96,519	90,711
Total assets	$2,448,380	$2,033,074	$1,756,618

EXHIBIT B (continued)

Statement of Earnings

	Year Ended December 31		
	2005	**2004**	**2003**
Liabilities and Stockholders' Equity			
Current liabilities			
Current maturities of long-term debt	15,230	13,198	11,250
Note payable: bank	406,250	250,000	
Note payable: officer	37,500	37,500	48,750
Accounts payable	486,978	369,010	391,504
Amount due for purchase of treasury stock			93,750
Accrued liabilities	193,238	145,168	111,196
Total current liabilities	1,101,695	814,875	656,450
Long-term debt	220,653	236,403	244,638
Stockholders' Equity			
Contributed capital:			
6% cumulative preferred stock; authorized 10,000 shares of $12.50 par value: issued 2,000 shares	25,000	25,000	25,000
Common stock:			
Class A (nonvoting)			
Authorized 15,000 shares of $12.50 par value: issued 8,305 shares	103,813	103,813	103,813
Class B (voting)			
Authorized 5,000 shares of $12.50 par value: issued and outstanding 20 shares	250	250	250
	129,063	129,063	129,063
Retained earnings	1,115,495	971,484	845,218
	1,244,558	1,100,546	974,280
less shares reacquired and held in treasury, at cost: 2,000 shares 6% cumulative preferred stock	25,000	25,000	25,000
2,308 shares Class A common stock	93,750	93,750	93,750
	118,750	118,750	118,750
	1,125,808	981,796	855,530
Total liabilities and stockholders' equity	$2,448,155	$2,033,074	$1,756,618

(continued)

EXHIBIT B (continued)

Statement of Earnings

	Year Ended December 31		
	2005	**2004**	**2003**
Statement of Changes in Financial Position			
Working capital provided:			
From operations:			
Earnings before extraordinary income	144,011	126,266	99,066
Add depreciation not requiring outlay of working capital	69,973	63,323	55,334
Working capital provided from operation	213,984	189,589	154,400
Extraordinary income from life insurance proceeds		6,619	34,094
Capitalized equipment lease obligation			64,846
Proceeds from cash surrender value of life insurance policies	213,984	196,208	253,340
Total working capital provided			
Working capital applied:			
Additions to property, plant, and equipment	85,324	100,940	58,884
Increase in cash surrender value of life insurance policies; net of loans	5,954	5,808	7,443
Reduction of long-term debt	15,750	14,854	11,244
Purchase of 2,308 shares of nonvoting Class A stock			93,750
Total working capital applied	107,028	121,601	171,320
	106,956	74,606	82,020
Increase in working capital			
Net change in working capital consists of:			
Increase (decrease) in current assets:			
Cash	59,338	(83,428)	81,068
Accounts receivable: net	237,920	136,726	(4,435)
Inventories	104,151	187,153	220,841
Prepaid expenses	(7,633)	(7,420)	(6,225)
	393,776	233,031	291,249

EXHIBIT B (continued)

Statement of Earnings

	Year Ended December 31		
	2005	2004	2003
Increase (decrease) in current liabilities:			
Current portion of long-term debt	2,033	1,948	625
Note payable to bank	156,253	250,000	
Note payable to officer	(37,500)	(11,250)	
Accounts payable	117,968	(22,494)	130,104
Amount due for purchase of treasury stock		(93,750)	93,750
Contribution to profit-sharing trust			(25,000)
Accrued liabilities	48,070	33,971	9,751
Total	286,820	158,425	209,230
Increase in working capital	106,956	74,606	82,019
Working capital at beginning of year	680,556	605,950	523,931
Working capital at end of year	787,513	680,556	605,950

EXHIBIT C

Pro Forma Financial Statements

Historical Percentages			Projected Percentages		
2003	2004	2005	2006	2007	2008
100.00	100.00	100.00	100.0	100.0	100.0
65.80	64.79	66.70	67.0	67.0	67.0
34.22	35.21	33.30	33.0	33.0	33.0
28.61	29.28	28.25	28*	28.0	28.0
5.61	5.93	5.05	5.0	5.0	5.0
38.20	39.90	27.80	39†	39.0	39.0

	Thousands of Dollars		
	2006	2007	2008
Net sales	$6,000	$6,375	$6,750
Cost of goods sold	4,020	4,271	4,523
Gross income	1,980	2,104	2,228
Operating, general, and admin.	1,680	1,785	1,890
Profit before taxes	300	319	338
Taxes†	121	124	131
Net earnings	$ 179	$ 195	$ 206

*Projected percentages reflect an assumption that one partner will leave the company, and include a $30,000 cost reduction for the reduced salary requirements of a replacement.

†Effective tax rate.

Source: income statement projections (prepared by Jack Peterson).

Peterson also had sought out common valuation techniques. By looking through business periodicals and talking to friends, he found that these methods were not necessarily precise. Private manufacturing companies were most often valued at between 5 and 10 times after-tax earnings. Book net asset value also helped establish business worth, but it was often adjusted to reflect differences between the market value of assets and the carrying values shown on balance sheets. For MLI, this was significant because it had obtained the new plant at an excellent price. Peterson felt that it alone was probably worth $250,000 more than the stated book value.

To Peterson, the variations in worth suggested by these different methods not only reflected the uncertainty of financial valuation techniques but also showed that a business had different values to different people. His estimate would have to incorporate other, more personal and subjective elements.

Personal Financial Considerations

One important consideration was what amount of personal resources each could and should put at risk. Both Peterson and Scott were financially very conservative. Neither of them had ever had any personal long-term debt—even for a house. Peterson could gather a maximum of $815,000 of assets outside of MLI that could be pledged to secure borrowing. His bank had already confirmed that he could borrow against those assets. However, for him to put his entire worth at risk to purchase Scott's share of the company, he would want to be very comfortable that the price was a reasonable one. Peterson described his feelings: "You get very protective about what you have outside the company. The problem you always have with a small company is that most of your worth is tied up in it and you may have very little to fall back on if something goes sour. We both have never been big leverage buyers or anything like that."

Besides the element of increased financial risk, several other considerations tempered Peterson's willingness to pay a very high price. Since they had moved to the plant in Pontiac, the one-hour commute to work had been a bit burdensome. It would be nice not to have that drive. Peterson also felt that he had good experience in the overall management of a business, and his engineering undergraduate degree and MBA gave him a certain amount of flexibility in the job market. This was important because, for both financial and personal reasons, he felt he would still have to work if he was no longer associated with MLI.

On the other hand, some factors encouraged Peterson to be aggressive. His father cautioned him to be reasonable, but Peterson knew his father would be very disappointed if he lost the company, and Peterson himself had strong emotional ties to MLI. Peterson also developed a point of view that in some ways he was buying the entire company, rather than just half: "I'm sitting here with a company that I have no control over because of our disagreements. If I buy the other half share, I'm buying the whole company—I'm buying peace of mind, I could do what I want, I wouldn't have to argue. So I'd buy a 'whole peace of mind' if I bought the other half of the company."

Finally, Peterson considered his competitive position versus Scott. Although Scott had not accumulated the personal resources that Peterson had, he had a brother-in-law with a private company that Peterson knew had the ability to match Peterson's resources and might be willing to back Scott financially. The brother-in-law would also be giving Scott financial advice in evaluating his alternatives and setting a value for the company. Scott also probably had fewer job prospects if he sold out. His undergraduate study was in liberal arts, and his entire experience was within MLI. Peterson also thought Scott might have some doubts about his ability to manage the company on his own.

The Meeting

After another conversation with Allen Burke, Scott called Peterson at home one evening: "Peterson, I realize that you're right—I can't live in this tense environment any longer. I've spoken with Allen, and he has agreed to meet with both of us to discuss our situation, and to attempt to identify some possible solutions. Would Friday at 9:00 be convenient for you?"

Chapter Fourteen

Obtaining Venture and Growth Capital

Money is like a sixth sense without which you cannot make a complete use of the other five.

W. Somerset Maugham
Of Human Bondage

Results Expected

At the conclusion of this chapter, you will be able to

1. Discuss the capital markets food chain and its implications.
2. Identify informal and formal investment sources of equity capital.
3. Locate, contact, and deal with equity investors.
4. Describe how venture capital investors make decisions.
5. Provide comment and insights on Forte Ventures, a case about an entrepreneur's fund-raising strategies to launch and grow a new private equity business at the worst possible time in the history of the U.S. venture capital industry.

The Capital Markets Food Chain

Consider the capital markets for equity as a "food chain," whose participants have increasing appetites in terms of the deal size they want to acquire (Exhibit 14.1). This framework can help entrepreneurs identify and appreciate the various sources of equity capital at various stages of the venture's development, the amount of capital they typically provide, and the portion of the company and share price one might expect should the company eventually have an initial public offering (IPO) or trade sale.

The bottom row in Exhibit 14.1 shows this ultimate progression from R&D stage to IPO, where the capital markets are typically willing to pay $12 to $18 per share for new issues of small companies. Obviously these prices are lower when the so-called IPO window is tight or closed, as in 2001. Prices for the few offerings that do exist (1 to 3 per week versus more than 50 per week in June 1996) are $5 to $9 per share. In

hot IPO periods, 1999 for instance, offering prices reached as high as $20 per share and more. Since the last edition, the IPO markets suffered a severe decline and were basically shut down in 2001 to mid-2003.

In 2004 a modest revival began in the initial public offering markets with 91 venture capital–backed offerings, the largest since the boom of 1999 and 2000 according to the National Venture Capital Association. This trend continued into 2006 and became very robust in 2007. To illustrate, according to *The Wall Street Journal* (October 1, 2007), in the third quarter of 2007 there were 248 IPOs issued by U.S. firms worldwide. Of these, 69 were in Europe and 21 were in Latin America, 85 percent of which were in Brazil. Many of the deals were in solar energy, software, and finance. At this writing the fourth quarter of 2007 IPO activity was also expected to weather the credit crisis and economic tremors. Note the strong international activity. This was far and away the most robust quarter since the Internet boom in the late 1990s.

EXHIBIT 14.1

The Capital Markets Food Chain for Entrepreneurial Ventures

Stage of Venture	R&D	Seed	Launch	High Growth
Company Enterprise Value at Stage	Less than $1 million	$1 million–$5 million	More than $1 million–$50 million-plus	More than $100 million
Sources	Founders High net worth individuals FFF SBIR	FFF* Angel funds Seed funds SBIR	Venture capital series A, B, C . . . Strategic partners Very high net worth individuals Private equity	IPOs Strategic acquires Private equity
Amount of Capital Invested	Less than $50,000–$200,000	$10,000–$500,000	$500,000–$20 million	$10 million–$50 million-plus
% Company Owned at IPO	10–25%	5–15%	40–60% by prior investors	15–25% by public
Share Price and Number†	$.01–$.50 1–5 million	$.50–$1.00 1–3 million	$1.00–$8.00 +/–5–10 million	$12–$18 + 3–5 million

*Friends, families, and fools.

†At post-IPO.

The private equity capital markets for mergers and acquisitions, as one would expect, suffered severely from the July–August credit meltdown in 2007. In 2006, for example, worldwide deals matched the 1999 and 2000 peaks of $4 trillion worldwide, and April 2007 saw $695 billion in deals closed, again according to *The Wall Street Journal* and Dealogic. In August this amount plummeted to $222 billion—a direct casualty of the credit and capital markets meltdown that began in mid-July.

We can see just how quickly the tides of the capital markets can change. Because it often takes 6 to 12 months during robust capital markets to raise money for a new venture or to acquire a company, you can easily get blindsided in the midst of your fund-raising. Nevertheless, high-quality deals will still get done.

One of the toughest decisions for founders is whether to give up equity, and implicitly control, to have a run at creating very significant value. The row "% company owned at IPO" shows that by the time a company goes public, the founders may have sold 70 percent to 80 percent or more of their equity. As long as the market capitalization of the company is at least $100 million or more, the founders have created significant value for investors and themselves. During the peak of the dot-com mania in the late 1990s, companies went public with market capitalizations of $1 billion to $2 billion and more. Founders' shares on paper were at least initially worth $200 million to

EXHIBIT 14.2

The Venture Capital Food Chain for Entrepreneurial Ventures

Venture capital series A, B, C, . . . (Average size of round):
Example of three staged rounds

Round*
- "A" @ $1–$4 million: start-up
- "B" @ $6–$10 million: product development
- "C"[1] @ $10–$15 million: shipping product

*Valuations vary markedly by industry.

+Valuations vary by region and venture capital cycle.

$400 million and more. These were truly staggering, unprecedented valuations, which were not sustainable. Take Sycamore Networks for example. From start-up to IPO in less than 24 months, founders Desh Deshpanda and Don Smith achieved paper value in the billions each.[1] By late 2004 the founders had lost more than 90 percent of the paper value of their stock.

In the remainder of the chapter, we will discuss these various equity sources and how to identify and deal with them. Exhibit 14.2 summarizes the recent venture capital food chain. In the first three rounds, series A, B, C, we can see that on average, the amount of capital invested was quite substantial: $1–$4 million, $6–$10 million, and $10–$15 million.

---

[1] A. Pham, "MassFirm Takes $14B Rocket Ride" *The Boston Globe* 10/23/1999.

Cover Your Equity

One of the toughest trade-offs for any young company is to balance the need for start-up and growth capital with preservation of equity. Holding on to as much as you can for as long as you can is generally good advice for entrepreneurs. As was evident in Exhibit 13.6, the earlier the capital enters, regardless of the source, the more costly it is. Creative bootstrapping strategies can be great preservers of equity, as long as such parsimony does not slow the venture's progress so much that the opportunity weakens or disappears.

Three central issues should be considered when beginning to think about obtaining risk capital: (1) Does the venture need outside equity capital? (2) Do the founders want outside equity capital? and finally, (3) Who should invest? While these three issues are at the center of the management team's thinking, it is also important to remember that a smaller percentage of a larger pie is preferred to a larger percentage of a smaller pie. Or as one entrepreneur stated, "I would rather have a piece of a watermelon than a whole raisin."[2]

After reviewing the Venture Opportunity Screening Exercises in Chapter 6, the business plan you prepared in Chapter 8, and the free cash flow equations (including OOC, TTC, and breakeven) from Chapter 13, it may be easier to assess the need for additional capital. Deciding whether the capital infusion will be debt or equity is situation specific, and it may be helpful to be aware of the trade-offs involved; see Chapter 16 for an introduction to debt capital. In the majority of the high-technology start-ups and early-stage companies, some equity investment is normally needed to fund research and development, prototype development and product marketing, launch, and early losses.

Once the need for additional capital has been identified and quantified, the management team must consider the desirability of an equity investment. As was mentioned in Chapter 11, bootstrapping continues to be an attractive source of financing. For instance, *INC.* magazine suggested that entrepreneurs in certain industries tap vendors by getting them to extend credit.[3]

Other entrepreneurs interviewed by *INC.* suggested getting customers to pay quickly.[4] For instance, one entrepreneur, Rebecca McKenna, built a software firm that did $8 million in sales in 2001 with customers in the health care industry. The robustness of economic benefits to her customers justified a 25 percent advance payment with each signed contract.

This upfront cash has been a major source for her bootstrap financing. These options, and others, exist if the management team members believe that a loss of equity would adversely affect the company and their ability to manage it effectively. An equity investment requires that the management team firmly believe that investors can and will add value to the venture. With this belief, the team can begin to identify investors who bring expertise to the venture. Cash flow versus high rate of return required is an important aspect of the "equity versus other" financing decision.

Deciding *who* should invest is a process more than a decision. The management team has a number of sources to consider. There are informal and formal investors, private and public markets. The single most important criterion for selecting investors is what they can contribute to the value of the venture—beyond just funding. Angels or wealthy individuals are often sought because the amount needed may be less than the minimum investment required by formal investors (i.e., venture capitalists and private placements). Whether a venture capitalist would be interested in investing can be determined by the amount needed and the required rate of return.

Yet entrepreneurs should be cautioned that "only 30 percent to 40 percent of the companies seeking private equity actually wind up getting it at the end of the process."[5] Additionally, the fees due the investment bankers and attorneys involved in writing up the prospectus and other legal documents must be paid whether or not the company raises capital.

Timing

There are two times for a young company to raise money: when there is lots of hope, or lots of results, but never in between.

Georges Doriot

Timing is also critical. A venture should not wait to look for capital until it has a serious cash shortage. For a start-up, especially one with no experience or success in raising money, it is unwise to delay seeking capital because it is likely to take six months or more to raise money. In addition to the problems with cash flow, the lack of planning implicit in waiting until there is a cash shortage can undermine the credibility of a venture's management team and negatively impact its ability to negotiate with investors.

But if a venture tries to obtain equity capital too early, the equity position of the founders may be

[2] Taken from a lecture on March 4, 1993, at the Harvard Business School, given by Paul A. Maeder and Robert F. Higgins of Highland Capital Partners, a Boston venture capital firm.
[3] R. A. Mamis, "The Secrets of Bootstrapping," *INC.*, September 1992, p. 72.
[4] Ibid., p. 76.
[5] Ibid.

unnecessarily diluted and the discipline instilled by financial leanness may be eroded inadvertently.

Angels and Informal Investors

Who They Are

The greatest source of seed and start-up capital comes from successful entrepreneurs and executives who have achieved wealth from their gains on stock options in midsize and large companies. In 2006, according to the Center for Angel Investing at the University of New Hampshire, there were 234,000 active angels in the United States. In terms of the number of deals they finance, angels absolutely dwarf the venture capital industry. In 2006, for instance, angels funded 51,000 companies compared to just 3,522 for the entire U.S. venture capital industry. The total amount of capital they invested was $26.1 billion, about the same as the venture capital investments that year. By 2007 there were an estimated 207 angel groups around the country (go to wikipedia.com: Angel Investors).

New Hampshire's Bill Wetzel has found that these angels are mainly American self-made entrepreneur millionaires. They have made it on their own, have substantial business and financial experience, and are likely to be in their 40s or 50s. They are also well educated: 95 percent hold college degrees from four-year colleges, and 51 percent have graduate degrees. Of the graduate degrees, 44 percent are in a technical field and 35 percent are in business or economics. According to Scott Peters, cofounder and co-CEO of AngelSociety, 96 percent of angels are men. One growing effort to involve female entrepreneurs is Chicago-based Springboard Enterprises. By 2007 Springboard had become a leading forum for women entrepreneurs seeking start-up and growth capital (see springboardenterprises.org). Seventeen forums have been held since its inception in 2000 that have hosted 350+ companies and over 3,500 women entrepreneurs. A total of $4 billion in capital has been accessed from over 4,000 investors and financiers around the nation. To date, six companies from Springboard have had initial public offerings.

Since the typical informal investor will invest from $10,000 to $250,000 in any one deal, informal investors are particularly appropriate for the following:[6]

- Ventures with capital requirements of between $50,000 and $500,000.
- Ventures with sales potential of between $2 million and $20 million within 5 to 10 years.

- Small, established, privately held ventures with sales and profit growth of 10 percent to 20 percent per year, a rate that is not rapid enough to be attractive to a professional investor such as a venture capital firm.
- Special situations, such as very early financing of high-technology inventors who have not developed a prototype.
- Companies that project high levels of free cash flow within three to five years.

These investors may invest alone or in syndication with other wealthy individuals, may demand considerable equity for their interests, or may try to dominate ventures. They also can get very impatient when sales and profits do not grow as they expected.

Usually these informal investors will be knowledgeable and experienced in the market and technology areas in which they invest. If the right angel is found, he or she will add a lot more to a business than just money. As an advisor or director, his or her savvy, know-how, and contacts that come from having "made it" can be far more valuable than the $10,000 to $250,000 invested. Generally the evaluations of potential investments by such wealthy investors tend to be less thorough than those undertaken by organized venture capital groups, and such noneconomic factors as the desire to be involved with entrepreneurship may be important to their investment decisions. There is a clear geographic bias of working within a one-hour driving radius of the investors' base. For example, a successful entrepreneur may want to help other entrepreneurs get started, or a wealthy individual may want to help build new businesses in his or her community.

Finding Informal Investors

Finding these backers is not easy. One expert noted, "Informal investors, essentially individuals of means and successful entrepreneurs, are a diverse and dispersed group with a preference for anonymity. Creative techniques are required to identify and reach them."[7] The Internet has provided entrepreneurs with an effective method of locating such investors. Formal sources such as GarageTechnology Ventures (garage.com) and Business Partners (businesspartners.com) provide valuable advice, assistance, and information regarding potential investors and help forge the link between investors and entrepreneurs seeking capital. Specialized assistance for women includes womenangels.net (womenangels.net), the Center for Women & Enterprise (cweboston.org),

---

[6] R. Harrison and C. Mason, *Informal Venture Capital: Evaluating the Impact of Business Introduction Services*, Hemel Hempstead, Woodhead Faulkner, 1996.

[7] W. H. Wetzel, Jr., "Informal Investors—When and Where to Look," in *Pratt's Guide to Venture Capital Sources*, 6th ed., ed. S. E. Pratt (Wellesley Hills, MA: Capital Publishing, 1982), p. 22.

and the previously mentioned Springboard Enterprises (springboardenterprises.org)

Invariably financial backers are also found by tapping an entrepreneur's own network of business associates and other contacts. Other successful entrepreneurs know them, as do many tax attorneys, accountants, bankers, and other professionals. Apart from serendipity, the best way to find informal investors is to seek referrals from attorneys, accountants, business associates, university faculty, and entrepreneurs who deal with new ventures and are likely to know such people. Because such investors learn of investment opportunities from their business associates, fellow entrepreneurs, and friends, and because many informal investors invest together in a number of new venture situations, one informal investor contact can lead the entrepreneur to contacts with others.

In most larger cities, there are law firms and private placement firms that syndicate investment packages as Regulation D offerings to networks of private investors. They may raise from several hundred thousand dollars to several million. Directories of these firms are published annually by *Venture* magazine and are written about in magazines such as *INC*. Articles about angel investors can also be found in *Forbes, Fortune, The Wall Street Journal (WSJ Startup.com), BusinessWeek, Red Herring, Wired,* and their respective Web sites.

Contacting Investors

If an entrepreneur has obtained a referral, he or she needs to get permission to use the name of the person making a referral when the investor is contacted. A meeting with the potential investor then can be arranged. At this meeting, the entrepreneur needs to make a concise presentation of the key features of the proposed venture by answering the following questions:

- What is the market opportunity?
- Why is it compelling?
- How will/does the business make money?
- How soon can the business reach positive cash flow?
- Why is this the right team at the right time?
- How does an investor exit the investment?

Ever since the dot-com crash, investors throughout the capital markets food chain have been returning to these fundamental basics for evaluating potential deals.

Entrepreneurs need to avoid meeting with more than one informal investor at the same time. Meeting with more than one investor often results in any negative viewpoints raised by one investor being reinforced by another. It is also easier to deal with negative reactions and questions from only one investor at a time. Like a wolf on the hunt, if an entrepreneur isolates one target "prey" and then concentrates on closure, he or she will increase the odds of success.

Whether or not the outcome of such a meeting is continued investment interest, the entrepreneur needs to try to obtain the names of other potential investors from this meeting. If this can be done, the entrepreneur will develop a growing list of potential investors and will find his or her way into one or more networks of informal investors. If the outcome is positive, often the participation of one investor who is knowledgeable about the product and its market will trigger the participation of other investors.

Evaluation Process

An informal investor will want to review a business plan, meet the full management team, see any product prototype or design that may exist, and so forth. The investor will conduct background checks on the venture team and its product potential, usually through someone he or she knows who knows the entrepreneur and the product. The process is not dissimilar to the due diligence of professional investors but may be less formal and structured. The new venture entrepreneur, if given a choice, would be wise to select an informal investor who can add knowledge, wisdom, and networks as an advisor and whose objectives are consistent with those of the entrepreneur.

The Decision

If the investor decides to invest, he or she will have an investment agreement drafted by an attorney. This agreement may be somewhat simpler than those used by professional investors, such as venture capital firms. All the cautions and advice about investors and investment agreements that are discussed later in the chapter apply here as well.

Most likely, the investment agreement with an informal investor will include some form of a "put," whereby the investor has the right to require the venture to repurchase his or her stock after a specified number of years at a specified price. If the venture is not harvested, this put will provide an investor with a cash return.

For access to important documents for venture agreements, please see the Web site for this textbook for downloadable sample term sheets.[8]

---

[8] To access New Venture Creation online, go to http://highered.mcgraw-hill.com/sites/0072498404/information_center_view0/.

Venture Capital: Gold Mines and Tar Pits

There are only two classes of investors in new and young private companies: value-added investors and all the rest. If all you receive from an investor, especially a venture capitalist or a substantial private investor, is money, then you may not be getting a bargain. One of the keys to raising risk capital is to seek investors who will truly add value to the venture well beyond the money. Research and practice show that investors may add or detract value in a young company. Therefore, carefully screening potential investors to determine how they might fill some gaps in the founders' know-how and networks can yield significant results. Adding key management, new customers, or suppliers, or referring additional investment, are basic ways to add value.

A young founder of an international telecommunications venture landed a private investor who also served as an advisor. The following are examples of how this private investor provided critical assistance: introduced the founder to other private investors, to foreign executives (who became investors and helped in a strategic alliance), and to the appropriate legal and accounting firms; served as a sounding board in crafting and negotiating early rounds of investments; and identified potential directors and other advisors familiar with the technology and relationships with foreign investors and cross-cultural strategic alliances.

Numerous other examples exist of venture capitalists being instrumental in opening doors to key accounts and vendors that otherwise might not take a new company seriously. Venture capitalists may also provide valuable help in such tasks as negotiating original equipment manufacturer (OEM) agreements or licensing or royalty agreements, making key contacts with banks and leasing companies, finding key people to build the team and helping to revise or to craft a strategy. Norwest Venture Partners brought in Ashley Stephenson to run a portfolio company and then backed him in a second venture. "Most venture capitalists have a short list of first-class players. Those are the horses you back," says Norwest partner Ernie Parizeau.

It is always tempting for an entrepreneur desperately in need of cash to go after the money that is available, rather than wait for the value-added investor. These quick solutions to the cash problem usually come back to haunt the venture.

What Is Venture Capital?[9]

The word *venture* suggests that this type of capital involves a degree of risk and even something of a gamble. Specifically, "The venture capital industry supplies capital and other resources to entrepreneurs in business with high growth potential in hopes of achieving a high rate of return on invested funds."[10] The whole investing process involves many stages, which are represented in Exhibit 14.3. Throughout the investing process, venture capital firms seek to add value in several ways: identifying and evaluating business opportunities, including management, entry, or growth strategies; negotiating and closing the investment; tracking and coaching the company; providing technical and management assistance; and attracting additional capital, directors, management, suppliers, and other key stakeholders and resources. The process begins with the conception of a target investment opportunity or class of opportunities, which leads to a written proposal or prospectus to raise a venture capital fund. Once the money is raised, the value creation process moves from generating deals to crafting and executing harvest strategies and back to raising another fund. The process usually takes up to 10 years to unfold, but exceptions in both directions often occur.

The Venture Capital Industry

Although the roots of venture capital can be traced from investments made by wealthy families in the 1920s and 1930s, most industry observers credit Ralph E. Flanders, then president of the Federal Reserve Bank of Boston, with the idea. In 1946 Flanders joined a top-ranked team to found American Research and Development Corporation—the first firm, as opposed to individuals, to provide risk capital for new and rapidly growing firms, most of which were manufacturing and technology oriented.

Despite the success of American Research and Development, the venture capital industry did not experience a growth spurt until the 1980s, when the industry went ballistic. Before 1980, venture capital investing activities could be called dormant; just $460 million was invested in 375 companies in 1979. By the late 1980s, the industry had ballooned to more than 700 venture capital firms, which invested $3.94 billion in 1,729 portfolio companies. The sleepy cottage industry of the 1970s was transformed into

[9] Unless otherwise noted, this section is drawn from W. D. Bygrave and J. A. Timmons, *Venture Capital at the Crossroads* (Boston: Harvard Business School Press, 1992), pp. 13–14. Copyright 1992 by William D. Bygrave and Jeffry A. Timmons.
[10] "Note on the Venture Capital Industry (1981)," HBS Case 285–096, Harvard Business School, 1982, p. 1.

EXHIBIT 14.3

Classic Venture Capital Investing Process

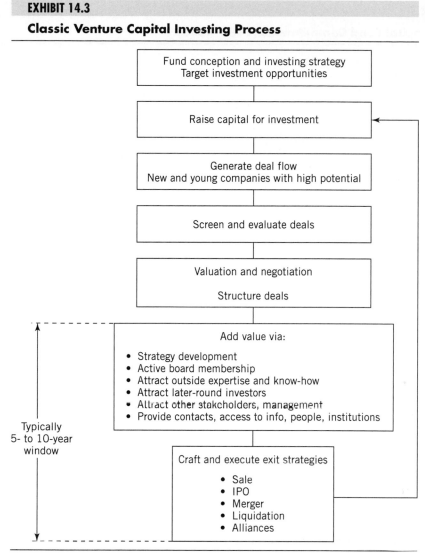

Source: Reprinted by permission of Harvard Business School Press. From *Venture Capital at the Crossroads* by W. D. Bygrave, J. A. Timmons. Boston, MA 1992. Copyright © 1992 by the Harvard Business School Publishing Corporation; all rights reserved.

a vibrant, at times frenetic, occasionally myopic, and dynamic market for private risk and equity capital.

The Booming 1990s

As we can see in Exhibits 14.4 and 14.5, the industry experienced an eightfold increase in the 1990s. While the absolute dollars committed and invested by 2000 were huge, the rate of increase in the 1980s was much greater, from $1 billion in 1979 to $31 billion in 1989.

By the early 2000s, not only had the commitments changed, but also a new structure was emerging, increasingly specialized and focused. Exhibit 14.6 summarizes some of the important

changes in the industry, which have implications for entrepreneurs seeking money and for those investing it. The major structural trends that emerged at the end of the 1980s continued through the 1990s:

1. The average fund size grew larger and larger, and these megafunds of more than $500 million accounted for nearly 80 percent of all capital under management. High-performing funds like Spectrum Equity Partners and Weston-Presidio, whose first fund just seven years earlier was in the $100 million to $200 million range, closed funds in 2000 well over $1 billion.

2. The average size of investments correspondingly grew much larger as well. Unheard of

EXHIBIT 14.4

Venture Capital Fund Commitments (1980–2006)

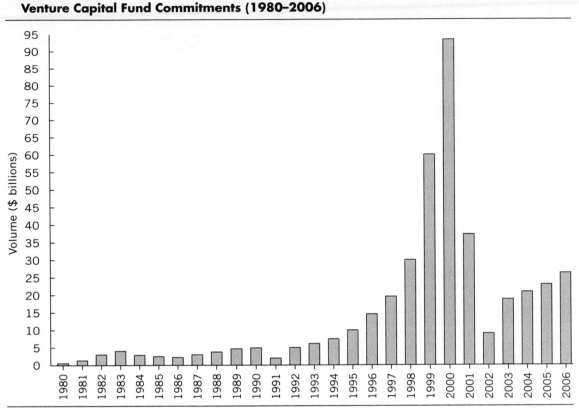

Source: 2006 *National Venture Capital Association Yearbook.*

EXHIBIT 14.5

Total Venture Capital under Management (1979–2006)

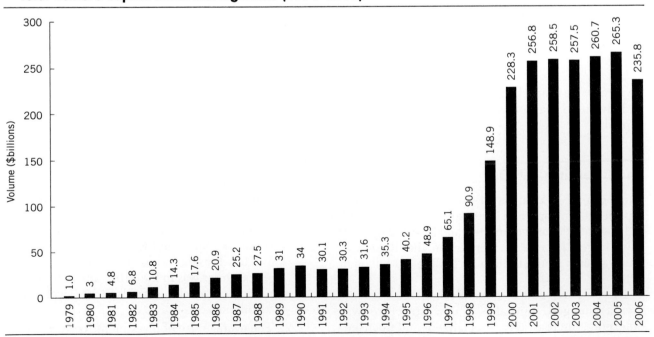

Source: 2006 *National Venture Capital Association Yearbook.*

EXHIBIT 14.6

New Heterogeneous Structure of the Venture Capital Industry

	Megafunds	Mainstream	Second Tier	Specialists and Niche Funds	Corporate Financial and Corporate Industrial
Estimated Number and Type (2005)	106 Predominantly private, independent funds	76 Predominantly private and independent; some large institutional SBICs and corporate funds	455 Mostly SBICs; some private independent funds	87 Private, independent	114
Size of Funds under Management	More than $500 million	$250–$499 million	Less than $250 million	$50–$100 million	$50–$100 million plus
Typical Investment	Series B, C, . . . $5–$25 million plus	Series A, B, C . . . $1–$10 million	Series A, B $500,000–$5 million	Series A, B $500,000–$2 million	Series A, B, C . . . $1–$25 million
Stage of Investment	Later expansion, LBOs, start-ups	Later expansion, LBOs, some Start-ups; mezzanine	Later stages; few start-ups; specialized areas	Seed and start-up; technology or market focus	Later
Strategic Focus	Technology; national and international markets; capital gains; broad focus	Technology and manufacturing; national and regional markets; capital gains; more specialized focus	Eclectic—more regional than national; capital gains, current income; service business	High-technology national and international links; "feeder funds," capital gains	Windows on technology; direct investment in new markets and suppliers; diversification; strategic partners; capital gains
Balance of Equity and Debt	Predominantly equity	Predominantly equity; convertible preferred	Predominantly debt; about 91 SBICs do equity principally	Predominantly equity	Mixed
Principal Sources of Capital	Mature national and international institutions; own funds; insurance company and pension funds; institutions and wealthy individuals; foreign corporation and person funds; universities	Mature national and international institutions; own funds; insurance company and pension funds; institutions and wealthy individuals: foreign corporation and pension funds; universities	Wealthy individuals; some smaller institutions	Institutions and foreign companies; wealthy individuals	Internal funds
Main Investing Role	Active lead or colead; frequent syndications; board seat	Less investing with some solo investing	Initial or lead investor; outreach; shirtsleeves involvement	Later stages, rarely start-ups; direct investor in funds and portfolio companies	Later stages, rarely start-ups; direct investment in new markets and suppliers; diversification; strategic partners; capital gains

Note: Target rates of return vary considerably, depending on stage and market conditions. Seed and start-up investors may seek compounded after-tax rates of return in excess of 50 to 100 percent; in mature, later-stage investments they may seek returns in the 30–40 percent range. The rule of thumb of realizing gains of 5 to 10 times the original investment in 5 to 10 years is a common investor expectation.

Source: 2001 *National Venture Capital Association Yearbook.* Revised and updated for 2008.

previously, start-up and early rounds of $20 million, $40 million, even $80 million were common in the dot-com and telecom feeding frenzy of the late 1990s.

3. The specialization pattern, which began in the 1980s, expanded to mainstream and megafunds. Oak Venture Partners, for instance, abandoned its longtime health care investing for information technology, along with many others.

The one significant trend that was reversed in the 1990s is especially good news for start-up entrepreneurs. By 1990, as funds grew larger and larger, investing in start-up and early-stage ventures had performed a disappearing act. During the 1990s, start-up and early-stage funds experienced a major rebirth as opportunities in the Internet, software, information technology and telecommunications, and networking exploded.

Beyond the Crash of 2000: The Venture Capital Cycle Repeats Itself

The crash of the NASDAQ began in March 2000, resulting in more than a 60 percent drop in value by late summer 2001. This major crash in equity values began a shakeout and downturn in the private equity and public stock markets. The repercussions and consequences were still being felt in 2005. Many high-flying companies went public in 1998 and 1999 at high prices, saw their values soar beyond $150 to $200 per share, then came plummeting down to low single-digit prices. For example, Sycamore Networks went public in October 1999 at $38 per share, soared to nearly $200 per share in the first week, and was trading around $3.50 per share by the summer of 2005. The list of dot-coms that went bankrupt is significant.

Similarly, beginning in the late summer of 2000, many young telecommunications companies saw their stocks begin to decline rapidly, losing 90 percent or more of their value in less than a year. These downdrafts swept the entire venture capital and private equity markets. By mid-2001 the amount of money being invested had dropped by half from the record highs of 2000, and valuations plummeted. Down rounds—investing at a lower price than the previous round—were very common. Not since the periods 1969–1974 and 1989–1993 have entrepreneurs experienced such a downturn.

To illustrate the consequences for entrepreneurs and investors alike, in 2001 as companies burned

through their invested capital and faced follow-on rounds of financing, the valuations were sagging painfully. Even companies performing on plan were seeing share prices 15 to 30 percent below the previous round a year or 18 months earlier. Where performance lagged milestones in the business plan, the down round could be 50 percent or more below the previous financing valuation. To make matters worse for entrepreneurs, the investing pace slowed significantly. Due diligence on companies was completed in 45 days or less during the binge of 1998–1999. By 2002 investors reported a six- to eight-month due diligence phase, which would be very close to the historical norm experienced before the feeding frenzy.[11]

The stark reality of all this is that the venture capital cycle—much like real estate—seems to repeat itself. Scarcity of capital leads to high returns, which attract an overabundance of new capital, which drives returns down. The new millennium welcomed the real "Y2K" problem. The meltdown side of the venture capital and private equity markets repeated the 1969–1974 and 1988–1992 pattern.

The Sine Curve Lives Circa 2005

Historically the venture capital cycle of ups and downs has had the shape of a sine curve; an "S" on its side. Fortunately, after a period of painful losses, too much time spent working on troubled portfolio companies, and too few exits in 2002–2003, the industry began to rebound in 2004, when, for instance, the total number of companies invested in rose for the first time since the 2000 bubble: from 2,825 to 2,873. Referring back to Exhibits 14.4 and 14.5, we see that the industry has been making steady gains. Fund commitments in 2006 were up to $26.3 billion, and total venture capital under management, while down slightly, exceeded $235 billion. Exhibit 14.7, which captures a bit more granularity on the nature of venture investments since 1990, shows that total investments increased from $18.95 billion in 2003 to $26.3 billion in 2006. The average deal size likewise increased from $6.65 million to $7.4 million.[12]

As we discussed earlier in this chapter, anytime there is a robust IPO market such as in 2007, the returns on venture capital invariably get much better, and mega–home runs like Google and YouTube arouse a new frenzy of investing activity. Institutional investors, such as pension funds, foundations, and others, are anxious to get in on the party, so more money pours into the industry. This occurred in the extreme in 2000, as shown in Exhibit 14.7. With

---

[11] The resurgence of dot-coms, especially with regard to user-generated content and collaboration and social networking sites such as MySpace, is often referred to as Web 2.0. This term also refers generally to this next generation of online companies and software.
[12] *Venture Capital Journal*, February 2005, pp. 29–30.

EXHIBIT 14.7

U.S. Venture Capital Investment by Year (1990–2006)

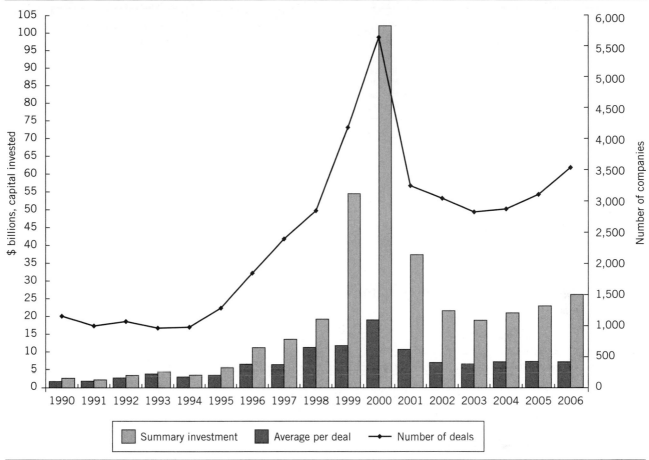

Source: PricewaterhouseCoopers/Venture Economics/National Venture Capital Association/Money Tree™ Report. Updated August 2007. Used by permission of PricewaterhouseCoopers.

annual investing of $25–$30 billion, the industry appears to have reached somewhat of an equilibrium—an oxymoron in this tumultuous world of entrepreneurship. The net impact for high-potential entrepreneurs is positive as the availability of capital remains robust.

Venture Capital Investing Is Global

Venture capital has existed in Europe since the late 1970s and began to take root in other parts of the world in the 1980s and 1990s. In many countries, such as Germany and France, banks would often be the first to create funds. In England private firms, often with U.S. associations, were launched. By the early 1980s even Sweden had begun a private venture industry. In the old Soviet Union, venture capital firms were usually formed by Americans working with local business and financial connections. One good example is Delta Capital, formed and led by

Patricia Cloherty, the first female president of the U.S. National Venture Capital Association, and past president of Patricoff and Company, a leading New York venture and private equity firm.

In the new century explosive growth of emerging economies has led to similar venture fund creation in Latin America, China, India, and even Vietnam. Leading U.S. venture capital firms such as Kleiner Perkins, Caufield & Byers, IDG Venture Capital, and Venrock have launched country-dedicated funds. IDG, for instance, has been active in China since 1992. Several new funds are being formed in India and China, and some spectacular returns have been achieved from investments such as Baidu, China's equivalent of Google. This is all very good news for American entrepreneurs because investors will now welcome business plans for enterprises that pursue these global markets.

Exhibit 14.8 represents the core activities of the venture capital process. At the heart of this dynamic flow is the collision of entrepreneurs, opportunities,

EXHIBIT 14.8

Flows of Venture Capital

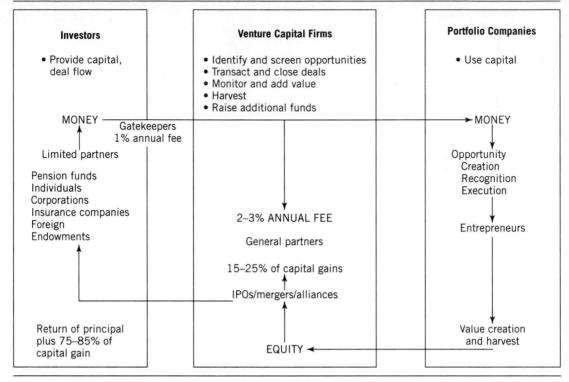

Source: Reprinted by permission of Harvard Business School Press. From *Venture Capital at the Crossroads* by W. D. Bygrave and J. A. Timmons. Boston, MA, 1992. Copyright © 1992 by the Harvard Business School Publishing Corporation; all rights reserved.

investors, and capital.[13] Because the venture capitalist brings, in addition to money, experience, networks, and industry contacts, a professional venture capitalist can be very attractive to a new venture. Moreover, a venture capital firm has deep pockets and contacts with other groups that can facilitate the raising of money as the venture develops.

The venture capital process occurs in the context of mostly private, quite imperfect capital markets for new, emerging, and middle-market companies (i.e., those companies with $5 million to $200 million in sales). The availability and cost of this capital depend on a number of factors:

- Perceived risk, in view of the quality of the management team and the opportunity.
- Industry, market, attractiveness of the technology, and fit.
- Upside potential and downside exposure.
- Anticipated growth rate.
- Age and stage of development.
- Amount of capital required.

- Founders' goals for growth, control, liquidity, and harvest.
- Fit with investors' goals and strategy.
- Relative bargaining positions of investors and founders given the capital markets at the time.

However, no more than 2 percent to 4 percent of those contacting venture capital firms receive financing from them. Despite the increase in funds in the recent boom years, observers comment that the repeat fund-raisers "stay away from seed and early-stage investments largely because those deals tend to require relatively small amounts of capital, and the megafunds, with $500 million-plus to invest, like to make larger commitments."[14] Further, an entrepreneur may give up 15 percent to 75 percent of his or her equity for seed/start-up financing. Thus after several rounds of venture financing have been completed, an entrepreneur may own no more than 10 percent to 20 percent of the venture.

The venture capitalists' stringent criteria for their investments limit the number of companies receiving venture capital money. Venture capital investors look

---

[13] Bygrave and Timmons, *Venture Capital at the Crossroads,* p. 11.
[14] Vachon, "Venture Capital Reborn," p. 35.

EXHIBIT 14.9

Characteristics of the Classic Superdeal from the Investor's Perspective

Mission

- Build a highly profitable and industry-dominant market leading company.
- Go public or merge within four to seven years at a high price–earnings (P/E) multiple.

Complete Management Team

- Led by industry "superstar."
- Possess proven entrepreneurial, general management, and P&L experience in the business.
- Have leading innovator or technologies/marketing head.
- Possess complementary and compatible skills.
- Have unusual tenacity, imagination, and commitment.
- Possess reputation for high integrity.

Proprietary Product or Service

- Has significant competitive lead and "unfair" and sustainable or defensible advantages.
- Has product or service with high value-added properties resulting in early payback to user.
- Has or can gain exclusive contractual or legal rights.

Large, Robust, and Sustainable Market

- Will accommodate a $100 million entrant in five years.
- Has sales of $200 million or more, is growing at 25% per year, and has a billion-dollar potential.
- Has no dominant competitor now.
- Has clearly identified customers and distribution channels.
- Possesses forgiving and rewarding economics, such as
  —Gross margins of 40% to 50% or more.
  — 10% or more profit after tax.
  —Early positive cash flow and break-even sales.

Deal Valuation and ROR

- Has "digestible" first-round capital requirements (i.e., greater than $1 million and less than $10 million).
- Able to return 10 times original investment in five years at P/E of 15 times or more and a market cap of $200–$300 million.
- Has possibility of additional rounds of financing at substantial markup.
- Has antidilution and IPO subscription rights and other identifiable harvest/liquidity options.

Source: Reprinted by permission of Harvard Business School Press. From *Venture Capital at the Crossroads* by W. D. Bygrave and J. A. Timmons. Boston, MA, 1992. Copyright © 1992 by the Harvard Business School Publishing Corporation; all rights reserved. Revised and updated for

for ventures with very high growth potential where they can quintuple their investment in five years; they place a premium on the quality of management in a venture; and they like to see a management team with complementary business skills headed by someone who has previous entrepreneurial or profit-and-loss (P&L) management experience. In fact, these investors are searching for the "superdeal." Superdeals meet the investment criteria outlined in Exhibit 14.9.

Identifying Venture Capital Investors

Venture capital corporations or partners have an established capital base and professional management. Their investment policies cover a range of preferences in investment size and the maturity, location, and industry of a venture. Capital for these investments can be provided by one or more wealthy families, one or more financial institutions (e.g., insurance companies or pension funds), and wealthy individu-

als. Most are organized as limited partnerships, in which the fund managers are the general partners and the investors are the limited partners. Today most of these funds prefer to invest from $2 million to $5 million or more. Although some of the smaller funds will invest less, most of their investments are in the range of $500,000 to $1.5 million. Some of the so-called megafunds with more than $500 million to invest do not consider investments of less than $5 million to $10 million. The investigation and evaluation of potential investments by venture capital corporations and partnerships are thorough and professional. Most of their investments are in high-technology businesses, but many will consider investments in other areas.

Sources and Guides   If an entrepreneur is searching for a venture capital investor, a good place to start is with *Pratt's Guide to Venture Capital Sources,* published by Venture Economics, as well as the ventureone Web site (ventureone.com), two of several directories of venture capital firms. Entrepreneurs also can seek referrals from accountants, lawyers, investment and commercial bankers, and businesspeople who are knowledgeable about professional investors. Especially good sources of information are other entrepreneurs who have recently tried, successfully or unsuccessfully, to raise money.

Sometimes professional investors find entrepreneurs. Rather than wait for a deal to come to them, a venture capital investor may decide on a product or technology it wishes to commercialize and then put its own deal together. Kleiner Perkins used this approach to launch Genentech and Tandem Computer Corporation, as did Greylock and J. H. Whitney in starting MassComp.

What to Look For

Entrepreneurs are well advised to screen prospective investors to determine the appetites of such investors for the stage, industry, technology, and capital requirements proposed. It is also useful to determine which investors have money to invest, which are actively seeking deals, and which have the time and people to investigate new deals. Depending on its size and investment strategy, a fund that is a year or two old will generally be in an active investing mode.

Early-stage entrepreneurs need to seek investors who (1) are considering new financing proposals and can provide the required level of capital; (2) are interested in companies at the particular stage of growth; (3) understand and have a preference for investments in the particular industry (i.e., market, product, technology, or service focus); (4) can provide good business advice, moral support, and contacts in the business and financial community; (5) are reputable, fair, and ethical people with whom the entrepreneur gets along; and (6) have successful track records of 10 years or more advising and building smaller companies.[15]

Entrepreneurs can expect a number of value-added services from an investor. Ideally the investor should define his or her role as a coach—thoroughly involved, but not a player. In terms of support, investors should have both patience and bravery. The entrepreneur should be able to go to the investor when he or she needs a sounding board, counseling, or an objective, detached perspective. Investors should be helpful with future negotiations, financing, and private and public offerings, as well as in relationship building with key contacts.

What to Look Out For

There are also some things to be wary of in finding investors. These warning signs are worth avoiding unless an entrepreneur is so desperate that he or she has no real alternatives:

- *Attitude.* Entrepreneurs need to be wary if they cannot get through to a general partner in an investment firm and keep getting handed off to a junior associate, or if the investor thinks he or she can run the business better than the lead entrepreneur or the management team.
- *Overcommitment.* Entrepreneurs need to be wary of lead investors who indicate they will be active directors but who also sit on the boards of six to eight other start-up and early-stage companies or are in the midst of raising money for a new fund.
- *Inexperience.* Entrepreneurs need to be wary of dealing with venture capitalists who have an MBA; are under 30 years of age; have worked only on Wall Street or as a consultant; have no operating, hands-on experience in new and growing companies; and have a predominantly financial focus.
- *Unfavorable reputation.* Entrepreneurs need to be wary of funds that have a reputation for early and frequent replacement of the founders or those where more than one-fourth of the portfolio companies are in trouble or failing to meet projections in their business plans.
- *Predatory pricing.* During adverse capital markets (e.g., 1969–1974, 1988–1992, 2000–2003), investors who unduly exploit these conditions by forcing large share price decreases in the new firms and punishing terms on prior investors do not make the best long-term financial partners.

How to Find Out

How does the entrepreneur learn about the reputation of the venture capital firm? The best source is the CEO/founders of prior investments. Besides the successful deals, ask for the names and phone numbers of CEOs the firm invested in whose results were only moderate to poor, and where the portfolio company had to cope with significant adversity. Talking with these CEOs will reveal the underlying fairness, character, values, ethics, and potential of the venture capital firm as a financial partner, as well as how it practices its investing philosophies. It is always interesting to probe regarding the behavior at pricing meetings.

[15] For more specifics, see H. A. Sapienza and J. A. Timmons, "Launching and Building Entrepreneurial Companies: Do the Venture Capitalists Build Value?" in *Proceedings of the Babson Entrepreneurship Research Conference,* May 1989, Babson Park, MA. See also J. A. Timmons, "Venture Capital: More Than Money," in *Pratt's Guide to Venture Capital Sources.* 13th ed., ed. J. Morris (Needham, MA: Venture Economics, 1989), p. 71.

Dealing with Venture Capitalists[16]

Don't forget that venture capitalists see lots of business plans and proposals, sometimes 100 or more a month. Typically they invest in only one to three of these. The following suggestions may be helpful in working with them.

If possible, obtain a personal introduction from someone that is well-known to the investors (a director or founder of one of their portfolio companies, a limited partner in their fund, a lawyer or accountant who has worked with them on deals) and who knows you well. After identifying the best targets, you should create a market for your company by marketing it. Have several prospects. Be vague about whom else you are talking with. You can end up with a rejection from everyone if the other firms know who was the first firm that turned you down. It is also much harder to get a yes than to get a no. You can waste an enormous amount of time before getting there.

When pushed by the investors to indicate what other firms/angels you are talking to, simply put it this way: "All our advisors believe that information is highly confidential to the company, and our team agrees. We are talking to other high-quality investors like yourselves. The ones with the right chemistry who can make the biggest difference in our company and are prepared to invest first will be our partner. Once we have a term sheet and deal on the table, if you also want co-investors we are more than happy to share these other investors' names." Failing to take such a tack usually puts you in an adverse negotiating position.

Most investors who have serious interest will have some clear ideas about how to improve your strategy, product line, positioning, and a variety of other areas. This is one of the ways they can add value—if they are right. Consequently, you need to be prepared for them to take apart your business plan and to put it back together. They are likely to have their own format and their own financial models. Working with them on this is a good way to get to know them.

Never lie. As one entrepreneur put it, "You have to market the truth, but do not lie." Do not stop selling until the money is in the bank. Let the facts speak for themselves. Be able to deliver on the claims, statements, and promises you make or imply in your business plan and presentations. Tom Huseby adds some final wisdom: "It's much harder than you ever thought it could be. You can last much longer than you ever thought you could. They have to do this for the rest of their lives!" Finally, never say no to an offer price. There is an old saying that your first offer may be your best offer.

Questions the Entrepreneur Can Ask

The presentation to investors when seeking venture capital is demanding and pressing, which is appropriate for this high-stakes game. Venture capitalists have an enormous legal and fiduciary responsibility to their limited partners, not to mention their powerful self-interest. Therefore, they are thorough in their due diligence and questioning to assess the intelligence, integrity, nimbleness, and creativity of the entrepreneurial mind in action. (See Chapter 2.)

Once the presentation and question–answer session is complete, the founders can learn a great deal about the investors and enhance their own credibility by asking a few simple questions:

- Tell us what you think of our strategy, how we size up the competition, and our game plan. What have we missed? Whom have we missed?
- Are there competitors we have overlooked? How are we vulnerable and how do we compete?
- How would you change the way we are thinking about the business and planning to seize the opportunity?
- Is our team as strong as you would like? How would you improve this and when?
- Give us a sense of what you feel would be a fair range of value for our company if you invested $\_\_\_\_\_$?

Their answers will reveal how much they have done and how knowledgeable they are about your industry, technology, competitors, and the like. This will provide robust insight as to whether and how they can truly add value to the venture. At the same time, you will get a better sense of their forthrightness and integrity: Are they direct, straightforward, but not oblivious to the impact of their answers? Finally, these questions can send a favorable message to investors: Here are entrepreneurs who are intelligent, open-minded, receptive, and self-confident enough to solicit our feedback and opinions even though we may have opposing views.

Due Diligence: A Two-Way Street

It can take several weeks or even months to complete the due diligence on a start-up, although if the investors know the entrepreneurs, it can go much more quickly. The verification of facts, backgrounds, and reputations of key people, market estimates, technical capabilities of the product, proprietary rights, and the like is a painstaking investigation for investors. They will want to talk with your directors, advisors, former bosses, and

---

[16] The authors express appreciation to Thomas Huseby of SeaPoint Ventures in Washington for his valuable insights in the following two sections.

previous partners. Make it as easy as possible for them by having very detailed résumés and lists of 10 to 20 references (with phone numbers and addresses) such as former customers, bankers, vendors, and so on who can attest to your accomplishments. Prepare extra copies of published articles, reports, studies, market research, contracts or purchase orders, technical specifications, and the like that can support your claims.

One recent research project examined how 86 venture capital firms nationwide conducted their intensive due diligence. To evaluate the opportunity, the management, the risks, and the competition, and to weigh the upside against the downside, firms spent from 40 to 400 hours, with the typical firm spending 120 hours. That is nearly three weeks of full-time effort. At the extreme, some firms engaged in twice as much due diligence.[17] Central to this investigation were careful checks of the management's references and verification of track record and capabilities.

While all this is going on, do your own due diligence on the venture fund. Ask for the names and phone numbers of some of their successful deals and some that did not work out, and the names of any presidents they ended up replacing. Who are their legal and accounting advisors? What footprints have they left in the sand regarding their quality, reputation, and record in truly adding value to the companies in which they invest? Finally, the chemistry between the management team and the general partner that will have responsibility for the investment and, in all likelihood, a board seat is crucial. If you do not have a financial partner you respect and can work closely with, then you are likely to regret ever having accepted the money.

Other Equity Sources

Small Business Administration's 7(a) Guaranteed Business Loan Program

The Small Business Administration (sba.gov) has a wide variety of programs and assistance for aspiring entrepreneurs, including the 7(A) loan program. For ventures that are not candidates for venture capital, such as all lifestyle and foundation firms, it would be useful to explore their Web site. Descriptions and links to training, resources, and other assistance programs for women, minorities, Native Americans, and most aspiring small businesses are available here.

Promoting small businesses by guaranteeing long-term loans, the Small Business Administration's 7(a) Guaranteed Business Loan Program has been supporting start-up and high-potential ventures since 1953.[18] The 7(a) loan program provides 40,000 loans annually. The 7(a) program is almost exclusively a guarantee program, but under this program the Small Business Administration also makes direct loans to women, veterans of the armed forces, and minorities, as well as other small businesses. The program entails banks and certain nonbank lenders making loans that are then guaranteed by SBA for between 50 percent and 90 percent of each loan, with a maximum of $1 million. Eligible activities under 7(a) include acquisition of borrower-occupied real estate, fixed assets such as machinery and equipment, and working capital for items such as inventory or meeting cash flow needs.[19]

SBA programs have a noteworthy effect on the economy and entrepreneurship. The $1 million guarantees, the largest of all the SBA programs, have helped many entrepreneurs start, stay in, expand, or purchase businesses. According to the SBA, in 2000, 541,539 jobs were created by SBA borrowers, and the SBA helped create 2.3 million jobs or about 15 percent of all jobs created by small businesses between 1993 and 1998.

Small Business Investment Companies

SBICs (small business investment companies) are licensed by the SBA and can obtain from it debt capital—$4 in loans for each $1 of private equity.[20] The impact of SBICs is evidenced by the many major U.S. companies that received early financing from SBICs, including Intel, Apple Computer, Staples, Federal Express, Sun Microsystems, Sybase, Inc., Callaway Golf, and Outback Steakhouse.[21] The SBIC program was established in 1958 to address the need for venture capital by small emerging enterprises and to improve opportunities for growth.[22] An SBIC's equity capital is generally supplied by one or more commercial banks, wealthy individuals, and the investing public. The benefit of the SBIC program is twofold: (1) Small businesses that qualify for assistance from the SBIC program may receive equity capital, long-term loans, and expert management assistance, and (2) venture capitalists participating in the SBIC program can supplement their own private investment capital with funds borrowed at favorable rates

[17] G. H. Smart, "Management Assessment Methods in Venture Capital," unpublished doctoral dissertation, 1998 (Claremont, CA: Claremont Graduate University), p. 109.

[18] Data were compiled from the Small Business Administration, http://www.sba.gov.

[19] D. R. Gamer, R. R. Owen, and R. P. Conway, *The Ernst & Young Guide to Raising Capital* (New York: John Wiley & Sons, 1991), pp. 165–66.

[20] This section was drawn from J. A. Timmons, *Planning and Financing the New Venture* (Acton, MA: Brick House Publishing, 1990), pp. 49–50.

[21] The National Association of Small Business Investment Companies (NASBIC), http://www.nasbic.org.

[22] Small Business Administration, http://www.sba.gov.

through the federal government. According to the National Association of Small Business Investment Companies, as of December 2000 there were 404 operating SBICs with more than $16 billion under management. Since 1958 the SBIC program has provided approximately $27 billion of long-term debt and equity capital to nearly 90,000 small U.S. companies.

SBICs are limited by law to taking minority shareholder positions and can invest no more than 20 percent of their equity capital in any one situation. Because SBICs borrow much of their capital from the SBA and must service this debt, they prefer to make some form of interest-bearing investment. Four common forms of financing are long-term loans with options to buy stock, convertible debentures, straight loans, and, in some cases, preferred stock. In 2000 the average financing by bank SBICs was $4 million. The median for all SBICs was $250,000.[23] Due to their SBA debt, SBICs tend not to finance start-ups and early-stage companies but to make investments in more mature companies.

In 2005, 2,299 companies benefited from SBIC financings totaling $2.9 billion.

Small Business Innovation Research

The risk and expense of conducting serious research and development are often beyond the means of start-ups and small businesses. The Small Business Innovation Research (SBIR) is a federal government program designed to strengthen the role of small businesses in federally funded R&D and to help develop a stronger national base for technical innovation (http://www.sba.gov/sbir).

The SBIR program provides R&D capital for innovative projects that meet specific needs of any one of 11 federal government agencies, including the Departments of Agriculture, Commerce, Education, Energy, and Homeland Security; the Environmental Protection Agency; and the National Science Foundation. SBIR is a highly competitive, three-phase process. Phase I provides funds to determine the feasibility of the technology. During Phase II, the necessary R&D is undertaken to produce a well-defined product or process. Phase III involves the commercialization of the technology using non-SBIR funds.

An SBIR small business is defined as an independently owned and operated, for-profit organization with no more than 500 employees. In addition, the small business must be at least 51 percent owned by U.S. citizens or lawfully admitted resident aliens, not be dominant in the field of operation in which it is proposing, and have its principal place of business in the United States.

Corporate Venture Capital

During the Internet boom in the late 1990s, corporate investors were very active. In 2000 alone, large corporations invested $17 billion in small and midsize opportunities. When the bubble burst, many of these funds scaled back or shut down entirely. But as we have seen, business investing is highly cyclical. In 2006 corporate-based venture capitalists were back, investing $1.9 billion in 671 deals.

While corporate venture capitalists are similar to traditional VCs in that they look for promising young companies on the verge of a spike in sales, corporations tend to be more risk-averse and specialized. Because investing in a relevant technology can reduce the costs of their own research and development, fit is usually an important aspect of the funding decision. When working with corporate funding sources, make sure you consider the corporations' philosophy and culture, as well as their investment track record with small businesses, before agreeing to any deal.

Mezzanine Capital

At the point where the company has overcome many of the early-stage risks, it may be ready for mezzanine capital.[24] The term *mezzanine financing* refers to capital that is between senior debt financing and common stock. In some cases it takes the form of redeemable preferred stock, but in most cases it is subordinated debt that carries an equity "kicker" consisting of warrants or a conversion feature into common stock. This subordinated-debt capital has many characteristics of debt but also can serve as equity to underpin senior debt. It is generally unsecured, with a fixed coupon and maturity of 5 to 10 years. A number of variables are involved in structuring such a loan: the interest rate, the amount and form of the equity, exercise/conversion price, maturity, call features, sinking fund, covenants, and put/call options. These variables provide a wide range of possible structures to suit the needs of both the issuer and the investor.

Offsetting these advantages are a few disadvantages to mezzanine capital compared to equity capital. As debt, the interest is payable on a regular basis, and the principal must be repaid, if not converted into equity. This is a large claim against cash and can be burdensome if the expected growth and/or profitability does not materialize and cash becomes tight.

---

[23] The National Association of Small Business Investment Companies (NASBIC), http://www.nasbic.org.
[24] This section was drawn from D. P. Remey, "Mezzanine Financing: A Flexible Source of Growth Capital," in *Pratt's Guide to Venture Capital Sources,* ed. D. Schutt (New York: Venture Economics Publishing, 1993). pp. 84–86.

In addition, the subordinated debt often contains covenants relating to net worth, debt, and dividends.

Mezzanine investors generally look for companies that have a demonstrated performance record, with revenues approaching $10 million or more. Because the financing will involve paying interest, the investor will carefully examine existing and future cash flow and projections.

Mezzanine financing is utilized in a wide variety of industries, ranging from basic manufacturing to high technology. As the name implies, however, it focuses more on the broad middle spectrum of business rather than on high-tech, high-growth companies. Specialty retailing, broadcasting, communications, environmental services, distributors, and consumer or business service industries are more attractive to mezzanine investors.

Private Placements

Private placements are an attractive source of equity capital for a private company that for whatever reason has ruled out the possibility of going public. If the goal of the company is to raise a specific amount of capital in a short time, this equity source may be the answer. In this transaction, the company offers stock to a few private investors rather than to the public as in a public offering. A private placement requires little paperwork compared to a public offering.

If the company's management team knows of enough investors, then the private placement could be distributed among a small group of friends, family, relatives, or acquaintances. Or the company may decide to have a broker circulate the proposal among a few investors who have expressed an interest in small companies. The following four groups of investors might be interested in a private placement:[25]

1. Let us say you manufacture a product and sell to dealers, franchisors, or wholesalers. These are the people who know and respect your company. Moreover, they depend on you to supply the product they sell. They might consider it to be in their interest to buy your stock if they believe it will help assure continuation of product supply, and perhaps give them favored treatment if you bring out a new product or product improvement. One problem is when one dealer invests and another does not: Can you treat both fairly in the future? Another problem is that a customer who invests might ask for exclusive rights to market your product in a particular geographical area, and you might find it hard to refuse.

2. A second group of prospective buyers for your stock are professional investors who are always on the lookout to buy a good, small company in its formative years and ride it to success. Very often these sophisticated investors choose an industry and a particular product or service in that industry they believe will become hot and then focus 99 percent of their attention on the caliber of the management. If your management, or one key individual, has earned a high reputation as a star in management, technology, or marketing, these risk-minded investors tend to flock to that person. (The high-tech industry is an obvious example.) Whether your operation meets their tests for stardom as a hot field may determine whether they find your private placement a risk to their liking.

3. Other investors are searching for opportunities to buy shares of smaller growth companies in the expectation that the company will soon go public and they will benefit as new investors bid the price up, as often happens. For such investors, news of a private placement is a tip-off that a company is on the move and worth investigating, always with an eye on the possibility of its going public.

4. Private placements also often attract venture capitalists who hope to benefit when the company goes public or when the company is sold. To help ensure that happy development, these investors get seriously active at the level of the board of directors, where their skill and experience can help the company reach its potential.

Initial Public Stock Offerings

Commonly referred to as an IPO, an initial public offering raises capital through federally registered and underwritten sales of the company's shares. Numerous federal and state securities laws and regulations govern these offerings; thus it is important that management consult with lawyers and accountants who are familiar with the current regulations.

In the past, such as during the strong bull market for new issues that occurred in 1983, 1986, 1992, 1996, and 1999, it was possible to raise money for an early-growth venture or even for a start-up. These boom markets are easy to identify because the number of new issues jumped from 78 in 1980 to an astounding 523 in 1983, representing a sharp increase from about $1 billion in 1980 to about 12 times that figure in 1983 (see Exhibit 14.10). Another boom came three years later in 1986, when the number of new issues reached

---

[25] The following examples are drawn directly from Garner, Owen, and Conway, *The Ernst & Young Guide to Raising Capital*, pp. 51–52.

EXHIBIT 14.10

Initial Public Offerings (1980–2003)

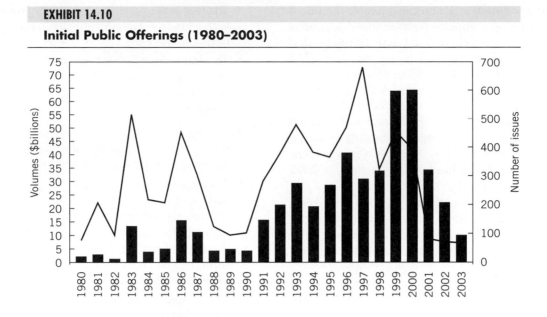

Source: The Security Industry and Financial Markets Association (SIFMA) Factbook 2007.

464. Although in 1992 the number of new issues (396) did not exceed the 1986 record, a record $22.2 billion was raised in IPOs. Accounting for this reduction in the number of new issues and the increase in the amounts raised, one observer commented, "The average size of each 1983 deal was a quarter of the $70 million average for the deals done in 1992."[26] In other, more difficult financial environments, such as following the 2001 recession, the new-issues market became very quiet for entrepreneurial companies, especially compared to the hot market of 1999. As a result, exit opportunities were limited. In addition, it was very difficult to raise money for early-growth or even more mature companies from the public market. Consider the following situations that resulted from the stock market crash on October 19, 1987:

An entrepreneur spent a dozen years building a firm in the industrial mowing equipment business from scratch to $50 million in sales. The firm had a solid record of profitable growth in recent years. Although the firm is still small by Fortune 500 standards, it was the dominant firm in the business in mid-1987. Given the firm's plans for continued growth, the entrepreneur, the backers, and the directors decided the timing was right for an IPO, and the underwriters agreed. By early 1987, everything was on schedule and the "road show," which was to

present the company to the various offices of the underwriter, was scheduled to begin in November. The rest is history. Nearly two years later, the IPO was still on hold.

In 1991, as the IPO market began to heat up, a Cambridge-based biotech firm was convinced by its investors and investment bankers to take the company public. In the spring the IPO window opened as medical and biotechnology stocks were the best performing of all industry groups. By May they had the book together; in June, the road show started in Japan, went through Europe, and ended in the United States in July. As the scheduled IPO date approached, so did the United Nations deadline for Saddam Hussein. After U.S. involvement, the new issues market turned downward, as the management of the biotech company watched their share price decline from $14 to $9 per share.[27]

A classic recent example occurred in 2000 as the NASDAQ collapsed and the IPO market shut down. A company we will call NetComm had raised more than $200 million in private equity and debt, was on track to exceed $50 million in revenue, and was 18 months away from positive cash flow. It would require another $125 million in capital to reach this point. The company had completed registration and was ready for an IPO in May 2000, but it was too late. Not only was the IPO canceled, but also subsequent efforts to merge the company failed; the company

[26] T. N. Cochran, "IPOs Everywhere: New Issues Hit a Record in the First Quarter," *Barron's*, April 19, 1993, p. 14. Though softened in 1997, the IPO market by any prior standard remains robust.
[27] "Rational Drug Design Corporation," HBS Case 293-102. Copyright © 1992 Harvard Business School. Used by permission of Harvard Business School; all rights reserved.

was liquidated for 20 cents on the dollar in the fall of 2000! Dozens of companies experienced a similar fate during this period. In 2004 activity rebounded significantly. The number of issues nearly tripled from the previous year; from 85 to 247. In 2006, 207 IPOs generated gross proceeds of $45.9 billion. As shown in Exhibit 14.11, 2002 ended with just 22 venture-backed IPOs from U.S. companies for a total offer size of $1.9 billion, down significantly from the 2000 record of $19.3 billion. A recovery was evident in 2004, although there has been less activity in 2005 and 2006.

The more mature a company is when it makes a public offering, the better the terms of the offering. A higher valuation can be placed on the company, and less equity will be given up by the founders for the required capital.

There are a number of reasons an entrepreneurial company would want to go public. The following are some of the advantages:

- To raise more capital with less dilution than occurs with private placements or venture capital.
- To improve the balance sheet and/or to reduce or to eliminate debt, thereby enhancing the company's net worth.
- To obtain cash for pursuing opportunities that would otherwise be unaffordable.
- To access other suppliers of capital and to increase bargaining power, as the company pursues additional capital when it needs it least.
- To improve credibility with customers, vendors, key people, and prospects. To give the impression: "You're in the big leagues now."
- To achieve liquidity for owners and investors.

- To create options to acquire other companies with a tax-free exchange of stock, rather than having to use cash.
- To create equity incentives for new and existing employees.

However, IPOs can be disadvantageous for a number of reasons:

- The legal, accounting, and administrative costs of raising money via a public offering are more disadvantageous than other ways of raising money.
- A large amount of management effort, time, and expense are required to comply with SEC regulations and reporting requirements and to maintain the status of a public company. This diversion of management's time and energy from the tasks of running the company can hurt its performance and growth.
- Management can become more interested in maintaining the price of the company's stock and computing capital gains than in running the company. Short-term activities to maintain or increase a current year's earnings can take precedence over longer-term programs to build the company and increase its earnings.
- The liquidity of a company's stock achieved through a public offering may be more apparent than real. Without a sufficient number of shares outstanding and a strong "market maker," there may be no real market for the stock and thus no liquidity.
- The investment banking firms willing to take a new or unseasoned company public may not be the ones with whom the company would like to do business and establish a long-term relationship.

EXHIBIT 14.11

Analysis of Recent IPO History

Year	Number of U.S. IPOs	Number of U.S. Venture-Backed IPOs	Total Venture-Backed Offer Size ($million)	Average Venture-Backed Offer Size ($million)	Total Venture-Backed Post-Offer Value ($million)	Average Venture-Backed Post-Offer Value ($million)
1996	771	268	11,605.6	43.1	56,123.0	208.6
1997	529	131	4,501.4	35.9	20,838.8	159.1
1998	301	75	3,515.4	48.3	16,837.4	224.5
1999	461	223	18,355.5	76.4	114,864.6	493.0
2000	340	226	19,343.0	93.3	106,324.3	470.5
2001	81	37	3,088.2	87.3	15,078.5	407.5
2002	71	22	1,908.5	86.8	8,219.6	373.6
2003	82	29	2,022.7	75.6	8,257.5	273.0
2004	246	93	11,014.9	131.5	61,087.6	699.6
2005	168	56	3,366.5	60.1	13,260.3	236.8
2006	168	57	4,284.1	75.2	17,724.9	311.0

Source: Thomson Venture Economics and National Venture Capital Association, June 12, 2007.

Private Placement after Going Public[28]

Sometimes a company goes public and then, for any number of reasons that add up to bad luck, the high expectations that attracted lots of investors early on turn sour. Your financial picture worsens; there is a cash crisis; down goes the price of your stock in the public marketplace. You find that you need new funds to work your way out of difficulties, but public investors are disillusioned and not likely to cooperate if you bring out a new issue.

Still, other investors are sophisticated enough to see beyond today's problems; they know the company's fundamentals are sound. Although the public has turned its back on you, these investors may be receptive if you offer a private placement to tide you over. In such circumstances you may use a wide variety of securities—common stock, convertible preferred stock, convertible debentures. There are several types of exempt offerings, usually described by reference to the securities regulation that applies to them.

Regulation D is the result of the first cooperative effort by the SEC and the state securities associations to develop a uniform exemption from registration for small issuers. A significant number of states allow for qualification under state law in coordination with the qualification under Regulation D. Heavily regulated states, such as California, are notable exceptions. However, even in California, the applicable exemption is fairly consistent with the Regulation D concept.

Although Regulation D outlines procedures for exempt offerings, there is a requirement to file certain information (Form D) with the SEC. Form D is a relatively short form that asks for certain general information about the issuer and the securities being issued, as well as some specific data about the expenses of the offering and the intended use of the proceeds.

Regulation D provides exemptions from registration when securities are being sold in certain circumstances. The various circumstances are commonly referred to by the applicable Regulation D rule number. The rules and their application are as follows:

Rule 504. Issuers that are not subject to the reporting obligations of the Securities Exchange Act of 1934 (nonpublic companies) and that are not investment companies may sell up to $1 million worth of securities over a 12-month period to an unlimited number of investors.

Rule 505. Issuers that are not investment companies may sell up to $5 million worth of securities over a 12-month period to no more than 35 nonaccredited purchasers and to an unlimited number of accredited investors. Such issuers may be eligible for this exemption even though they are public companies (subject to the reporting requirements of the 1934 Act).

Rule 506. Issuers may sell an unlimited number of securities to no more than 35 unaccredited but sophisticated purchasers and to an unlimited number of accredited purchasers. Public companies may be eligible for this exemption.

Employee Stock Ownership Plans (ESOPs)

ESOPs are another potential source of funding used by existing companies that have high confidence in the stability of their future earnings and cash flow. An ESOP is a program in which the employees become investors in the company, thereby creating an internal source of funding. An ESOP is a tax-qualified retirement benefit plan. In essence, an ESOP borrows money, usually from a bank or insurance company, and uses the cash proceeds to buy the company's stock (usually from the owners or the treasury). The stock then becomes collateral for the bank note, while the owners or treasury have cash that can be used for a variety of purposes. For the lender, 50 percent of the interest earned on the loan to the ESOP is tax exempt. The company makes annual tax-deductible contributions—of both interest and principal—to the ESOP in an amount needed to service the bank loan. "The combination of being able to invest in employer stock and to benefit from its many tax advantages makes the ESOP an attractive tool."[29]

Keeping Current about Capital Markets

One picture is vivid from all this: Capital markets, especially for closely held, private companies right through the initial public offering, are very dynamic, volatile, asymmetrical, and imperfect. Keeping abreast of what is happening in the capital markets in the 6 to 12 months before a major capital infusion can save valuable time and hundreds of thousands and occasionally millions of dollars. Here are some of the best sources currently available to keep you informed:

The European Private Equity and Venture Capital Association (www.evca.com).

The Angel Capital Association (www.angelcapitalassociation.org).

BusinessWeek magazine (www.businessweek.com).

INC. magazine (www.inc.com).

Red Herring magazine (www.redherring.com).

Business 2.0 magazine (www.money.cnn.com).

Private Equity Analyst (www.privateequity.dowjones.com).

[28] Garner, Owen, and Conway, *The Ernst & Young Guide to Raising Capital*, pp. 52–54.
[29] Ibid., p. 281.

Chapter Summary

- Appreciating the capital markets as a food chain looking for companies to invest in is key to understanding motivations and requirements.
- Entrepreneurs have to determine the need for outside investors, whether they want outside investors, and if so whom.
- America's unique capital markets include a wide array of private investors, from "angels" to venture capitalists.
- The search for capital can be very time-consuming, and whom you obtain money from is more important than how much.

- It is said that the only thing that is harder to get from a venture capitalist than a "yes" is a "no."
- Fortunately for entrepreneurs, the modest revival of the venture capital industry has raised the valuations and the sources available. Entrepreneurs who know what and whom to look for—and look out for—increase their odds for success.

Study Questions

1. What is meant by the following, and why are these important: cover your equity; angels; venture capital; valuation; due diligence; IPO; mezzanine; SBIC; private placement; Regulation D; Rules 504, 505, and 506; and ESOP?
2. What does one look for in an investor, and why?
3. How can founders prepare for the due diligence and evaluation process?
4. Describe the venture capital investing process and its implications for fund-raising.
5. Most venture capitalists say there is too much money chasing too few deals. Why is this so? When does this happen? Why and when will it reoccur?
6. What other sources of capital are available, and how are these accessed?
7. Explain the capital markets food chain and its implications for entrepreneurs and investors.

Internet Resources for Chapter 14

http://www.businesspartners.com *Business Partners is a global Internet-based service that connects entrepreneurs, early-stage companies, and established corporations with angel investors, venture capital, corporate investors, potential partners, and target data on mergers and acquisitions.*

http://www.nvca.org *The National Venture Capital Association.*

http://www.vcjnews.com/ *The online version of Venture Capital Journal.*

http://www.ventureone.com/ *One of the world's leading venture capital research firms.*

http://www.sba.gov/index.html *Small business resources and funding information from the Small Business Administration (SBA).*

http:/initial-public-offerings.com/ *Compilation of IPO-related Web sites. Find information relating to initial public offerings, SEC filings, and upcoming IPOs.*

Wiki–Google Search

Try these keywords and phrases:
venture capital
private equity

growth capital
angle capital
risk capital

MIND STRETCHERS

Have You Considered?

1. Some entrepreneurs say you shouldn't raise venture capital unless you have no other alternative. Do you agree or disagree, and why?

2. Identify a founder/CEO who has raised outside capital, and was later fired by the board of directors. What are the lessons here?

3. How do venture capitalists make money? What are the economics of venture capital as a business?

Preparation Questions

1. Evaluate the situation facing the Forte founders in April 2001 and the Private Placement Memorandum (PPM) (Appendix A) prepared to convince institutional investors to invest.
2. What should Maclean Palmer and his partners do, and why?
3. What are the economics of the venture capital business? Assume that Forte is a "top quartile" fund in terms of performance. What will the cumulative paychecks and distributions to the limited partners and the general partners be over 10 years?

Forte Ventures

Bite off more than you can chew, then chew it.

Roger Babson, Speech to the
Empire Club of Canada, 1922

Maclean Palmer hung up the phone and took another quick glance at an article from the Web site of the Boston-based firm of Hale & Dorr:

> ### April 6, 2001: Bear Market Drives IPOs into Hibernation
> *Further deterioration in the capital markets amidst growing concern about the health of the U.S. and global economy resulted in a dismal start to the 2001 IPO market. There has also been a reduction in the number of companies in registration as withdrawals continue to exceed new filings. Completed IPOs trailed the number of withdrawals every week during the first quarter . . .*

Roger Babson's urging was now haunting Palmer as he wondered whether he had bitten off more than he could chew in seeking to raise a first-time $200 million venture fund. Was a precipitous collapse of the venture capital and private equity markets coming at the worst possible time? Would it be best to shut down, minimize losses, and revisit the fund-raising when the markets revived? Or should they press on? As he tapped in the number for the next moneyed prospect on his list, Palmer smiled ruefully to himself.

What a difference a year makes . . .

Last winter, when he had begun to pull together a talented young private equity team from around the country, venture investments in new funds had been at an all-time high, and the capital markets were still riding the Internet wave. His partners had made the leap with him in September; they quit their jobs, sold their homes, and moved their families to Boston.

Convincing institutional investors to allocate a portion of their risk capital to a long-term, illiquid, nonrecourse investment with an unproven team was the challenge faced by all new venture groups as they set out to raise money. By the spring of 2001, however, a weakening economy had significantly increased that level of difficulty.

With IPOs in decline, and early-stage venture money being diverted to prop up existing portfolio investments, institutional investors had severely tightened their criteria as to what constituted a worthy new fund opportunity. In addition, the Forte group was encountering objections related to the very strategy that they felt gave them a distinctive edge. Dave Mazza, a partner at Grove Street Advisors (GSA), explained:

> The backdrop to all of this is that there have been a lot of African American–led funds; they've been predominantly SBICs, and few of them have come close to the top quartile performance that we have come to expect from private equity investors. We didn't have any question about what this team's motives were, but in the minds of some limited partners, they are always going to equate the two.

Despite the harsh environment, the news wasn't all bad. The GSA group—which had been early supporters of Palmer's concept—had recently committed $10 million to Forte, with a pledge of $15 million more once the team had garnered commitments of $50 million.

Now that the influential gatekeeper had given an official nod to the Forte group, a number of state pension funds had begun to take a closer look. Still, Palmer and his partners, who were bootstrapping this effort from their savings, understood that their targeted first closing of $100 million was likely to be a long way off.

The Offering

The team had spent the last quarter of 2000 developing their offering memorandum for a $200 million venture fund (see Appendix A). As private equity fund managers, Palmer and his partners would receive both management fees and performance-based incentives. The typical management fee was in the range of 1.5 to 2.5 percent of the total assets under management. The incentive was generally 20 percent of the investment returns in excess of a predetermined baseline—known as the preferred, or hurdle, rate.

While the plan articulated a clear preference for backing ethnic minority managers and opportunities, the team emphasized that their core mission was wealth creation. Palmer summarized their concept:

> We have put a new spin on a very successful private equity strategy that we believe has been proven successful in good and bad markets—a fundamental long-term

investing approach using a management-centric strategy. And since virtually no one is out there recruiting these seasoned ethnic minority managers, that gives us a unique advantage.

We will then partner with these managers and go out to buy a small middle-market company—but not necessarily an existing ethnic minority–owned business or even an ethnic minority marketplace. At the end of the day, we're going to do exactly what a firm like Point West does; it's just that we'll be tapping a different network.

What was most distinct about the Forte undertaking, though, was that unlike the venture funds of the late 1990s, this group would be working to raise capital in the midst of an increasingly tenuous environment.

The Venture Capital Climate in 2001

By early April 2001 the Internet bubble had clearly burst. Despite three federal funds rate cuts designed to stimulate the slowing (or contracting) economy, all major equity indexes remained in negative territory for the first three months of the year. As a result of this slowdown, many companies had pre-announced revenue and/or earnings shortfalls, declared that "future visibility was low," and issued cautious outlooks for the coming months. The year 2001 was looking to be a dismal period for venture fund-raising and for five-year private equity fund performance as well (see Exhibits 1 and 2).

As a result of all this negative news and outlook, the equity markets had an extremely difficult first quarter as the NASDAQ, S&P 500, and S&P Technology Sector were down 12.1 percent, 25.5 percent, and 24.8 percent, respectively. There were two adverse consequences of this precipitous fall in the equity markets. The first was that the IPO market had dried up virtually overnight. Consider that while the first quarter of 2000 had produced a solid record of 142 IPOs with gross

proceeds of $32.15 billion, the first three months of 2001 had generated just 20 IPOs with gross proceeds of $8.21 billion—85 percent of which had come from three offerings.

The second consequence of falling share prices was that as the aggregate portfolios of pension fund managers shrank, the denominator (which defined the percentage of total investments allocated to venture capital and private equity) also shrank. This resulted in a considerable over-allocation for that asset class. Consequently, pension fund managers had simply stopped investing their money in venture capital until the allocation percentage was back within a range set by their investing policies.

As Palmer and his partners struggled for footing in an increasingly soft market, they also needed to contend with an additional negative dynamic—unrelated to their experience but entirely related to who they were.

Fund-Raising: Perceptions and Realities

Because the Forte Ventures team had begun courting investors just as the capital markets had begun to weaken, it was hardly a revelation when pension fund managers and other prospective limited partners explained that in those increasingly uncertain times, they were unwilling to place a bet on an untested team. Palmer and his partners could appreciate why many limited partner prospects had almost no incentive to take a chance with a new fund: Profitable allocations were considered part of that job, and backing what in hindsight appeared to have been a long shot could get a pension fund manager fired. Palmer said that their fund-raising pitch emphasized the team and their commitment to success:

We were selling on the fact that we had put a lot of thought into deciding whom we wanted to be partners with. We all bet on ourselves and on each other. If we were willing to do it—literally burn all the boats and

EXHIBIT 1

Funds, Fund Commitments, and Average Fund Size

	Venture Capital				Buyout and Mezzanine			
Year/Quarter	First-Time Funds	Total Funds	Commitments ($billions)	Average Fund Size ($mil)	First-Time Funds	Total Funds	Commitments ($billions)	Average Fund Size ($mil)
Q1 1999	32	86	9.1	106	16	48	10	208
Q2 1999	27	92	9.5	103	10	40	12.9	323
Q3 1999	38	103	11.4	111	10	41	13.9	339
Q4 1999	59	194	29.6	153	12	62	25.5	411
Q1 2000	33	150	21.7	145	6	35	14.3	409
Q2 2000	56	167	29.2	175	13	42	22.8	543
Q3 2000	37	113	26.6	235	7	32	12.8	400
Q4 2000	51	147	23.8	162	8	34	20.6	606
Q1 2001	29	95	16.1	169	7	33	8.9	270

EXHIBIT 2

Five-Year Performance Trends

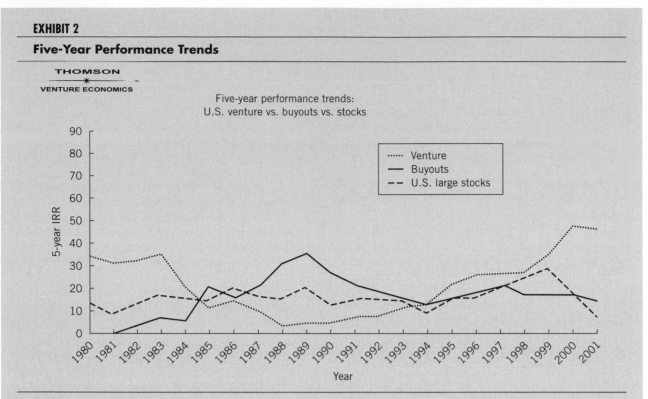

Five-year performance trends:
U.S. venture vs. buyouts vs. stocks

Source: Thomson Venture Economics/NVCA. Used by permission.

move to Boston before we ever raised a dime—we figured that ought to say something about our level of confidence and dedication.

Judith Elsea, at the time the chief investment officer with the Ewing Marion Kauffman Foundation, discussed her response to their prospectus:

What made Forte different from many minority-centric funds of the past was that they had a good deal of operating experience, so once they got the deals, they'd know what to do with them. The challenge was that many limiteds saw the team as a group whose investment activities would be outside of their sphere of contacts.

Even with the material support from GSA—as well as ongoing advice and referrals—by the spring of 2001 the team was making little headway with prospects who were watching the value of their investment portfolios decline with the falling capital markets. Mazza commented on the deteriorating fund-raising environment:

The limited partner excuses are coming in a few flavors: The market is terrible, Forte doesn't have a senior star equity player, and we are tapped out. They are all in real bad moods because they're losing a lot of money, and even though this fund is a good bet—and certainly doesn't have anything to do with their market losses—it is just about the worst time in the world to be raising a fund.

GSA founder Clint Harris reiterated that the ability of new funds to attract investors was unfortunately closely related to market conditions:

The bar has gone way up. If a new group like Forte had come to us a year earlier, we probably could have gotten them a check for half of the $200 million they're looking for.

The Worsening Storm

As Palmer hung up from yet another prospect that was planning to hold off on new investments for the time being, he had a hard time diverting his gaze from a tally of first-quarter market indices:

Index	1Q 2001
PVCI*	−31.4%
Dow Jones	−8.02%
S&P 400	−12.42%
S&P 500	−11.85
S&P 600	−6.57%
NASDAQ	−25.51%
Russell 1000	−12.56%
Russell 2000	−6.51%
Russell 3000	−12.51%

*The Warburg Pincus/Venture Economics Post-Venture Capital Index (PVCI) is a market cap weighted index of the stock performance of all venture backed companies taken public over the previous 10-year period.

Appendix A

FORTE VENTURES, L.P.: PRIVATE PLACEMENT MEMORANDUM (PPM)

I. Executive Summary

Introduction

Forte Ventures, L.P. (the "Fund" or the "Partnership"), is being formed principally to make equity investments in a broad range of profitable, small to middle-market private companies that are owned or managed by ethnic minorities. The Fund will also invest in businesses that serve or operate in the minority marketplace. Forte's core investment principles are to support or recruit high-quality management teams who are focused on wealth creation and to invest in businesses that, because of their strategic position, have attractive growth prospects. Forte's overriding investment thesis is to leverage its investment and operating expertise, as well as its extensive contacts and knowledge of the minority marketplace, in order to allocate capital to fundamentally sound businesses in an underserved market. Forte believes that it is uniquely positioned to execute this investment thesis and provide attractive returns to the Fund's Limited Partners.

Forte is currently offering limited partnership interests in Forte Ventures, L.P., to institutional investors and a limited number of qualified individuals with the objective of raising $200 million. The Fund will be managed by Maclean E. Palmer, Jr., Ray S. Turner, Clark T. Pierce, and Andrew L. Simon (the "Principals").

Forte's private equity transactions will take several forms, including recapitalizations, leveraged buyouts, industry consolidations/buildups, and growth equity investments. Forte will seek investments opportunistically with particular focus on industry sectors in which the Firm's Principals have substantial prior experience. These sectors currently include auto, auto aftermarket, business-to-business services, growth manufacturing, branded consumer products, OEM industrial products, health care, information technology services, and telecommunications.

Forte's Success Factors

Forte believes the Partnership represents an attractive investment opportunity for the following reasons:

- *Experienced team of investment professionals.* Messrs. Palmer, Pierce, and Simon have over 17 years of *direct* private equity experience. At their previous firms—Advent International, Point West Partners, Ninos Capital, Trident Partners, and McCown De Leeuw—

Palmer, Pierce, and Simon executed all aspects of private equity transactions. They have led investments in a variety of industries and have considerable experience in manufacturing, business services and outsourcing, health care, consumer products, financial services, and telecommunications. In addition, Palmer and Pierce led 13 transactions for their prior firms and were co-lead on three others, investing over $169 million.

- *Operating experience of principals.* Forte's team brings a combined 57 years of operating experience to the firm in addition to their investing expertise. The Principals have found that this experience and insight are invaluable in assessing investment opportunities, recruiting management teams, and adding value to portfolio companies postinvestment. The Principals will continue to leverage their operating experience through active involvement with portfolio management teams to develop and implement value creation strategies that will drive growth and deliver superior returns.

- *Proven investment track record.* As highlighted in the following table, Palmer has fully exited three of six equity transactions returning $75.2 million on $16.4 million invested, yielding a cash on cash return of 4.7× and an internal rate of return (IRR) of 113 percent. Pierce has fully exited one of ten mezzanine transactions returning $10.6 million on $5.3 million invested, yielding a cash on cash return of 2.0x and an IRR of 23 percent. For another three transactions where values have been established but are as yet unrealized, Palmer and Pierce have collectively generated $46.1 million on investments of $24 million for an imputed cash on cash return of 1.9×. The Principals believe there is substantial remaining value to be realized from these three unrealized investments, as well as the remaining nine unrealized investments.

- *Implementation of a proven and successful strategy.* Forte will implement a proven and effective two-part strategy that has been utilized by the Principals to generate excellent investment returns:

  - Support or recruit high-quality management teams with demonstrated records of success who are focused on creating shareholder value.

  - Invest in fundamentally sound businesses that, because of their strategic position, have sustainable margins and attractive growth prospects.

Summary Investment Track Record

	Number of Deals	Invested Capital ($m)	Value Realized ($m)	Value Unrealized ($m)	IRR (%)	Cash on Cash
Equity Investments						
Valuation Status						
Realized*	3	$16.4	$75.2		113%	4.7x
Established but unrealized	1	$8.0		$19.1	109%	2.4x
Unrealized*	2	$50.0		$50.0		1.0x
Total	**6**	**$74.4**	**$75.2**	**$69.1**	**112%**	**1.9x**
Mezzanine Investments						
Valuation Status						
Realized	1	$ 5.3	$ 10.6		23%	2.0x
Established but unrealized	2	$16.0	$ 10.5	$16.5	29%	1.7x
Unrealized*	7	$73.5		$68.4		0.9x
Total	**10**	**$94.8**	**$21.1**	**$84.9**	**26%**	**1.1x**

*Includes one investment each for which Palmer or Pierce had significant, but not full, responsibility.

The Principals believe that the ongoing refinement of this strategy in the target marketplace will contribute to the success of the Fund's investments. In addition, Forte's strategy will utilize, where appropriate, the minority status of the firms it invests in as a means to accelerate growth. However, it should be noted that because Forte intends to invest in fundamentally sound businesses, the minority status of its portfolio companies will not influence or be a substitute for the goal of building world-class operational capabilities in each portfolio company.

- *Attractiveness of minority companies and the minority marketplace.* Minority-managed or -controlled companies and the minority marketplace represent attractive investment opportunities for the following reasons:

  - The number of seasoned minority managers with significant P&L experience has grown appreciably over the past 15 years and provides a sizable pool from which Forte can recruit.[1,2]

  - The number of minority-controlled companies with revenues in excess of $10 million has increased dramatically over the past 15 years, and these companies need equity capital to continue their impressive growth rates.[3,4]

  - Rapid growth in the purchasing power of minority consumers, currently estimated at over $1.1 trillion of retail purchasing power and growing at seven times the rate of the overall U.S. population, presents an attractive investment opportunity for companies serving the minority marketplace.[5]

  - Numerous corporations have initiatives in place to increase their purchasing from minority suppliers; however, these corporations are being forced to reduce their supplier bases to remain competitive. Minority-controlled companies that serve these corporations need significant equity capital to support the growth rates demanded by their customers. Without this capital infusion, minority suppliers will be unable to remain competitive in an environment of supplier rationalization, and corporations will be unable to reach the targets they have set for their minority purchasing.[6]

  - The minority marketplace is overlooked and underserved by private equity investors. Despite the numerous investment opportunities, Forte estimates that less than 1 percent of the $250 billion in private equity capital is targeted at the minority marketplace.

- *Access to multiple sources of proprietary deal flow.* Over their years in private equity and operating positions, the Principals have developed an extensive network for sourcing and developing potential transactions and identifying and recruiting management teams. Forte expects the majority of its opportunities will be negotiated or initiated transactions developed from the following sources:

  - Proprietary investment ideas generated by the Principals involving world-class minority management talent.

  - Growth-stage opportunities led by minority management teams or companies serving the minority marketplace.

  - Traditional buyouts and corporate divestitures to minority-led management teams or companies serving the minority marketplace.

[1] July 2000 interview with senior Russell Reynolds & Associates executives.
[2] "What Minorities Really Want," *Fortune magazine*, vol. 142, no. 2 (July 10, 2000).
[3] U.S. Census Bureau, the Survey of Minority Owned Businesses, 1997.
[4] National Minority Supplier Development Council Survey, 1999.
[5] SBA Office of Advocacy, 1997 Economic Census.
[6] National Minority Supplier Development Council Survey, 1999.

- The existing pool of minority-controlled enterprises.

- Corporations seeking to increase their minority purchasing.

- Proactive calling efforts to generate proprietary deal flow that leverages the relationships of the Principals.

- Investment banks and other financial intermediaries.

- *Principals' extensive knowledge of the minority marketplace.* The Principals have direct experience sourcing and executing deals in the target marketplace through their involvement in two minority-focused funds. In addition, the Principals believe that the combination of their in-depth knowledge of the target marketplace, their operating experience, and their ability to identify and recruit exceptional management teams affords Forte a distinct competitive advantage.

II. Investment Strategy

Overview

The combined experience of Forte's Principals has helped them evolve a two-fold investment strategy:

- To support or recruit high-quality management teams with demonstrated records of success and provide them the opportunity for significant equity ownership in order to align their interests with the Fund.

- To acquire or invest in fundamentally sound companies in the minority marketplace that, because of their strategic positions, have sustainable margins and attractive growth prospects.

In executing this strategy during both the pre- and post-investment stages of a transaction, Forte's Principals will consistently take the following steps:

- Maintain a disciplined approach to valuation and structuring.

- Conduct a thorough due diligence examination to identify the stress points in the business model.

- Obtain controlling equity positions, possibly with co-investors, or significant equity positions with certain supermajority rights.

- Implement focused value creation plans and performance monitoring metrics.

- Align companies with strategic and corporate partners to control costs and accelerate growth and thus value creation.

- Exercise value-added operating leadership by supporting management in the development and achievement of business goals.

- Create liquidity through carefully timed and executed transactions.

Forte has developed an investment strategy that builds on the strengths of the Principals' prior experiences. It is also a strategy that has produced excellent results. The Principals expect the Fund's capital to be invested in approximately three to four years from the date of the first close. Forte will primarily seek to invest in established companies generally ranging in value from $25 million to $75 million and will typically invest $10 million to $35 million in any given investment.

Investment Focus

Forte will seek investments opportunistically with particular focus on industry sectors in which the Firm's Principals have substantial prior experience. These sectors currently include auto, auto aftermarket, business-to-business services, growth manufacturing, branded consumer products, OEM industrial products, health care, information technology services, and telecommunications. The Principals' depth of industry knowledge has led to a substantial flow of potential investments and an ability to rapidly and thoroughly evaluate proposed opportunities. It has also provided numerous industry contacts to call upon for assistance in due diligence and has been helpful in supporting management plans for growth and development. Furthermore, the Principals' industry expertise will enable Forte to be an attractive participant in corporate partnerships.

Forte's specific industry knowledge has evolved over time, and new industries will be added as the firm opportunistically explores new areas for potential investment. It is expected that Forte will leverage its analytical skills and network of contacts to continue developing logical extensions of its current preferences as well as new areas of focus in which high rates of growth and outstanding management are present. The following charts are representative of the Principals' prior allocation of investment dollars by stage and industry sector as well as Forte's expected allocations for the Fund.

Types of Investment Opportunities

Forte believes that the most attractive investments generally share several important characteristics:

- A proven and highly motivated management team that owns or wishes to acquire a significant equity interest in the company.

- A strong competitive market position or the ability to build one.

- Presence in an industry with attractive dynamics and an investment structure that supports sustainable earnings growth.

- An established track record of solid financial performance and resistance to earnings downturns during economic or industry cycles.

- The potential to increase operating earnings through focused value creation efforts.

Prior Allocations by Forte Principals ($ weighted)

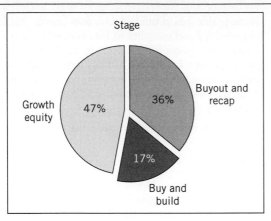

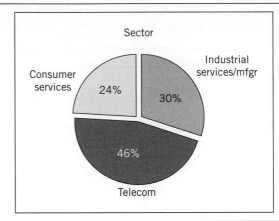

Projected Allocations in Forte Ventures ($ weighted)

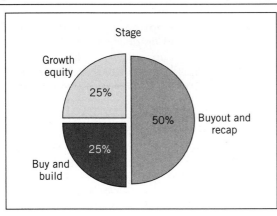

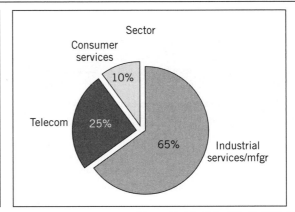

Because Forte's priorities start with the capability of the management team and a company's growth prospects, the actual form of a transaction is often secondary. Forte will seek to participate in the following types of transactions:

- *Leveraged buyouts:* Forte will initiate LBOs and participate in buyouts organized by management and other investment partners.

- *Recapitalizations:* Forte will assist in organizing recapitalizations of businesses in which management retains significant ownership. Forte will participate as either a majority or minority partner.

- *Growth capital investments:* Forte will provide capital to companies in need of equity to support attractive growth opportunities.

- *Industry consolidations/buildups:* Forte will support management teams that seek to build significant companies through acquisition within fragmented industries.

The Principals' prior transactions are indicative of the mix of transactions that will be pursued. Five of these prior transactions were LBOs, two were recapitalizations, three were consolidations/buildups, and five were growth capital investments.

III. Selected Investment Summaries

Cobalt Telecommunications

The Company Cobalt Telecommunications (Cobalt or the "Company") provides small to medium-sized businesses a resold package of local, long-distance, Internet, paging, and cellular telecommunications services from a variety of providers. The Company added value by aggregating the charges onto one customized bill, as well as providing one source for all customer support.

The Investment While at Point West Partners, Palmer became the lead investor in Cobalt in December 1997 with an investment of $2 million. In October 1998 he led another $2 million investment in the Company.

The Situation Cobalt was formed to capitalize on the deregulation of the local telecom marketplace. The Company's vision was to provide a higher level of customer service and a full suite of voice and data products to a neglected, but very profitable, customer segment. The Company needed financing to build its customer support and service-provisioning infrastructure, as well as recruit and support an agent-based sales channel.

Role of Forte Principal   Mr. Palmer worked with Cobalt management to develop the Company's strategy of concentrating its sales activity within a focused geography in the western Boston suburbs. Palmer also identified a low-cost, yet robust, billing and customer support platform that proved to be the key component of the Company's low-cost and efficient back office. Palmer recruited the Company's CFO prior to the investment, and he played a key role in the Company's acquisition efforts. He also worked with the Company to initiate price increases and cost reductions to improve gross margins. After recognizing weaknesses in the existing Sales VP, Palmer also identified and recruited a new VP of Sales and Marketing and worked with him to accelerate the performance of the Company's sales channels, as well as introduce a new telemarketing channel. The new sales focus enabled Cobalt to increase its sales by over 600 percent in one year.

Liquidity Event   In the summer of 1999 Palmer led the effort to identify potential strategic acquirers for the Company after it was determined that an attractive purchase price could be achieved. After an intense three-month process, the Company received and accepted an offer to be acquired by Macklin USA (NASDAQ: MLD). Palmer led the negotiations with Macklin and achieved, to Forte's knowledge, the highest multiple that has been paid to date for a pure reseller of telecom services. The transaction closed in December 1999 with a return to Point West Partners valued at 4.2× cash on cash and an 83 percent IRR.

MBCS Telecommunications

The Company   MBCS Telecommunications (MBCS or the "Company") is a switch-based provider of local, long-distance, Internet, data, and high-speed access services to small to medium-sized businesses. The Company has offices in five markets in the Ameritech region and is expanding its switch network in each of these markets.

The Investment   Palmer led Point West Partners' initial $3 million investment in MBCS in July 1998, and made a follow-on investment of $5 million in March 2000.

The Situation   MBCS had received a first-round investment in July 1997, which was used to finance the Company's growth in long-distance services and to recruit additional management. In 1998 the Company was seeking investors with telecom expertise to aid in the transition into local voice and data services.

Role of Forte Principal   Palmer worked with the Company to identify and select a low-cost, yet robust, billing and customer support platform that saved over $1 million in potential capital expenditures. This system has proven to be a key component in supporting MBCS's growth from 20,000 to over 70,000 customers. Palmer also played a key role in recruiting senior management team members, and advised and assisted management in two of the Company's three acquisitions. Most recently,

Palmer has been a leader in the Company's fund-raising efforts, introducing the Company to senior lenders and investment bankers and guiding the management team through the selection and approval process.

Valuation Events   In March 2000 MBCS received a third round of financing that was led by a new investor at a valuation that represented a 2.6× step up over the previous round (on a fully diluted basis). In September 2000 MBCS acquired a data services and high-speed access provider in a stock-for-stock transaction that valued LDM at a 1.6× step up over the third round.

X-Spanish Radio

The Company   X-Spanish Radio Networks, Inc. (X-Spanish or the "Company"), was built by acquiring radio stations in California, Arizona, Texas, and Illinois. These stations form a Spanish language radio network. The programming is satellite delivered from the Company's main studio located in Sacramento, California.

The Investment   Mr. Pierce led Ninos Capital's $5.25 million initial investment in X-Spanish in November 1994.

The Situation   X-Spanish's overall strategy was to acquire radio stations at attractive prices in desirable markets and keep operating costs low by delivering the programming via satellite to the entire network. To execute the strategy the Company needed capital to purchase additional stations. Over a four-year period X-Spanish was able to acquire 15 radio stations and build a loyal audience, which led to increasing advertising revenues.

Role of Forte Principal   Pierce sourced, structured, priced, and underwrote Ninos's investment in X-Spanish. He also performed a complete due diligence review of the Company, the management team, and the Company's competitive position in each of its target markets. Pierce's due diligence review included the technical performance of the stations, the demand for advertising in the target markets, and the "stick" value of the radio stations. In his board observer role, he monitored the Company's strategic plan, operating performance, and acquisition opportunities and was involved in the strategic decisions of the Company, including potential acquisitions and capital raising.

Liquidity Event   X-Spanish was sold to a financial buyer in November 1998, and this investment resulted in a 23 percent IRR to Ninos Capital.

Krieder Enterprises

The Company   Krieder Enterprises, Inc. (Krieder or the "Company"), is the largest manufacturer of nail enamel in bulk in the United States. Krieder is a leading supplier of enamel to the world's leading cosmetics companies.

The Investment   Pierce led Ninos Capital's $4 million initial investment in Krieder in April 1995 to finance a buyout.

The Situation   To gain market share and improve its competitive position, the Company needed to build infrastructure, upgrade and improve its manufacturing facilities, strengthen its laboratory and technical capabilities, increase the level of customer service, and build an organization that could support the planned growth. The buyout allowed the Company to evolve from an entrepreneurial managed company to a professionally managed one.

Role of Forte Principal   Mr. Pierce sourced, structured, priced, and underwrote Ninos's investment in Krieder. He also performed a complete due diligence review of the equity sponsor, the Company, the management team, and the Company's competitive position within its industry. In his board observer role, he evaluated and analyzed the Company's growth plans, acquisition candidates and deal structures, expansion of the manufacturing facilities, and the implementation of an MIS system.

Liquidity Event   For the three-year period 1997 to 1999, the Company's revenues and EBITDA grew at CAGRs of 20 percent and 33 percent, respectively. In January 1999 Ninos's investment was repaid along with an additional $1 million distribution. Ninos's warrant position is currently valued in excess of $3.5 million. The combination of the repayment and the warrant value yield a 29 percent IRR on this investment.

Cidran Food Service

The Company   Cidran Food Services II, L.P. (Cidran or the "Company"), owned and operated 130 Burger King restaurants in Louisiana, Arkansas, and Mississippi. Cidran owned and operated over 80 percent of the Burger King restaurants in Louisiana.

The Investment   Pierce led Ninos Capital's $12 million investment in Cidran in December 1998 to complete a recapitalization of the company and provide growth capital.

The Situation   The Company was recapitalized to repurchase the equity interests of several minority shareholders and to allow the Company to continue execution of its strategic plan. This plan required continuously upgrading and improving restaurants, aggressively opening new restaurants, and selectively pursuing acquisitions.

Role of Forte Principal   Pierce sourced, structured, priced, and underwrote Ninos's investment in Cidran. He performed a complete due diligence review of the Company, the management team, and the Company's competitive position in its markets. Through active participation in investor meetings, he evaluated and reviewed the Company's strategic planning and budgeting process, the

operating performance at the store-level, various advertising and marketing initiatives, new store-level development, and acquisition opportunities.

Liquidity Event   In June 2000 Pierce led Ninos's voluntary reinvestment in a combination of all the Cidran sister companies. The new company is called Cidran Services LLC ("Cidran Services"). As part of the reinvestment, Ninos sold its 5 percent warrant position back to Cidran in June 2000, which resulted in an IRR of 28 percent.

IV. Investment Process

Sourcing Investment Opportunities

The majority of the Principals' prior investments were originated by the Principals themselves. The Principals have developed sources and techniques for accessing quality investment opportunities, and the Principals' deal flow ability represents an important asset. Investment opportunities for the Fund are expected to emerge from a broad range of categories:

- Operating executives, entrepreneurs, board members, and other investment professionals with whom the Principals have forged relationships. The Principals have developed relationships with hundreds of potential partners and referral sources that understand the Principals' investment approach.

- Original concepts developed and implemented by the Principals.

- Service professionals (e.g., attorneys, accountants, and consultants).

- Professional financial community contacts and relationships (major investment banks, small and regional investment banks, and business brokers).

This network is maintained and developed by a combination of personal visits and telephone calls, as well as frequent mailings.

Evaluation of Investment Opportunities

The Principals possess strong analytical skills and seasoned judgment, reflecting over 17 years of collective investing experience and over 57 years of operating experience. The Principals will leverage this experience in selecting attractive investment opportunities. When considering investment opportunities, a team of Forte professionals will be assembled to conduct a thorough due diligence investigation of the target company, including its history, management, operations, markets, competition, and prospects. The deal team works closely with the target company's management to develop a thorough understanding of their individual goals and objectives as well as their capabilities. Each Forte managing director will also spend considerable time interacting with the CEO. The deal team will also spend considerable time conducting extensive reference checks on the senior team, especially the CEO. If the Principals determine that the management team requires strengthening, professional searches will be initiated during due diligence.

The deal team will independently assess the market by studying available research reports, attending industry trade conferences, conducting competitive interviews, and performing original market and industry research. The deal team will also conduct customer interviews and, in most cases, participate in sales calls, both with and without company personnel. Forte will augment the efforts of the deal team with outside resources such as attorneys, accountants, and function-specific consultants as appropriate. Market research consultants may also be engaged to validate management's market forecasts.

The Principals, because of their operating experience, work with all levels of an organization to understand the capabilities of each manager as well as the internal dynamics of the organization. In the considerable amount of time devoted to the management team, the deal team develops knowledge of each manager's objectives to ensure that they can be aligned in a common strategy to maximize growth and shareholder value.

Transaction Structuring

While engaged in due diligence, the deal team simultaneously structures the transaction, which includes valuing the company, negotiating with the seller, securing the financing, and arranging management's equity participation. As in the past, the Principals will price transactions based on conservative operating assumptions and capital structures. Forte will risk-adjust target rates of return for various investments based on general industry and financial risk, as well as specific operating characteristics of individual investments. Using these risk adjustment factors, the deal team will model a variety of possible operating results and exit outcomes.

Forte considers only investments where multiple exit alternatives are clearly identified at the time of the transaction. The Principals' years of transaction experience enhance their ability to successfully negotiate outcomes that satisfy Forte's investment goals. Generally the management team will invest its own funds on the same terms as Forte and participate in a performance-based option plan to augment their ownership interests. The management team's ownership will be carefully structured to ensure that the objectives of all the participants are aligned to the ultimate goal of maximizing the return on the investment.

Development and Implementation of a Focused Value Creation Plan

Prior to closing a transaction, Forte's Principals will work in partnership with the management team to develop a three- to five-year value creation plan. These plans will usually be anchored by systemic growth, which is most often achieved through management team development and operating and systems improvements that enhance the company's ability to serve its customers, as well as sales force development, new customer recruitment, and new product development.

Developing and Monitoring Investments

The Principals' posttransaction activities will involve extensive interaction with each portfolio company and its management, with the value creation plan serving as the blueprint for increasing shareholder value. Forte believes that its strategy of investing in small to middle-market companies with growth potential necessitates the dedication of Forte management resources to a significantly greater extent than might be required if Forte were investing in larger or slower-growing enterprises. The Principals' involvement will include regular communications with management, typically in the form of weekly flash reports, informal meetings and conversations, monthly or quarterly board meetings, and annual budgeting review sessions. The Principals also actively participate in strategic planning sessions and industry trade conferences. In addition, the Firm will assist each portfolio company on a project or functional basis as required. Forte will hold weekly staff meetings where each portfolio company is reviewed at least monthly to ensure full communication and input from all Forte professionals. Objectives for developing each company will be developed by Forte, and management will be encouraged to pursue activities to enhance investment value. Semiannual comprehensive reviews of the entire portfolio will also be conducted to ensure that prior objectives have been met and adequate progress has been targeted for the upcoming period. The Principals will also assist portfolio companies in addressing strategic issues through the creation and effective use of a strong board of directors. Two Forte Principals will generally sit on each portfolio company board, and the Principals will augment these boards through the recruitment of outside industry-specific directors, often from the group of successful executives with whom the Principals have previously worked.

Achieving Investment Liquidity

Forte's investment strategy focuses heavily on the ultimate exit strategy at the time each investment is made. Forte will regularly consider opportunities for investor liquidity as part of its formal semiannual portfolio company planning process or as specific circumstances arise.

The Principals have successfully led the exit of four investments and achieved significant realizations from two others. The four exited investments were strategic sales, and the Principals also have direct involvement in companies that have gone public or been acquired by other equity sponsors.

Internal Planning

At the end of each year, Forte will undertake an annual planning process during which it will evaluate its investment strategy and the financial and human resources needed to execute that strategy. Several days will be set aside by the Principals to set priorities and the targets for the coming year, as well as to give consideration to longer-term trends affecting Forte's business. The output of this planning process will provide a formal agenda for a second meeting of all Forte professionals. Forte believes that an emphasis on internal planning and evaluation will result in continued refinement of its investment strategy and identification and development of new partners to provide for the Firm's long-term continuity.

V. Investment Team

Forte Ventures, L.P., will be managed by the General Partner. The Principals of the General Partner are Maclean E. Palmer, Jr., Ray S. Turner, Clark T. Pierce, and Andrew L. Simon. Two of the Principals have known each other for over five years and developed a working relationship through their prior firms' co-investment in two deals. These two Principals have demonstrated the ability to generate superior returns for investors and have experience initiating investment opportunities, structuring and negotiating investments, and actively working with portfolio company management teams to maximize returns. Two members of Forte's team also bring over 57 years of operating experience covering a broad range of industry sectors including auto and other heavy industries, high-tech electronics, and health care. The team's operating experience was garnered from Fortune 100 companies as well as start-up and fast-growth companies financed by private equity investors.

Managing Directors

Maclean E. Palmer, Jr.
Maclean Palmer, Jr. (41), has over 5 years of direct private equity experience and over 17 years of operating experience. Prior to joining Forte, he was a managing director with Point West Partners from 1997 to 2000 in their San Francisco office. While at Point West, Palmer was responsible for deal origination, transaction execution, and portfolio company management, and focused on growth equity and buyout investments in the telecommunications, business-to-business services, industrial manufacturing, and auto sectors. Palmer led Point West investments in three competitive local exchange carriers (CLECs): Cobalt Telecommunications, MBCS Telecommunications, and Concept Telephone. He continues to represent Point West on the board of directors of both MBCS and Concept Telephone.

From 1995 to 1997 Palmer was a vice president in the Boston office of Advent International. While at Advent, he focused on industrial and technology investments and led Advent's investment in ISI, a financial and business information services provider. From 1986 to 1995 Palmer worked in various management and engineering positions for three start-up companies, UltraVision Inc., Surglaze Inc., and DTech Corporation, which were all financed by private equity investors. During his start-up career, Palmer was involved in the development and successful market introduction of 12 new products. In addition, Palmer held engineering positions with Borg Warner Corporation from 1984 to 1986 and with the diesel division of a major automotive firm from 1983 to 1984.

Palmer sits on the board of JT Technologies, a minority-owned firm that develops battery and ultracapacitor technology. He also sits on the board of the Cooper Enterprise Fund, a minority-focused fund based in New York; the Community Preparatory School, a private inner-city school focused on preparing middle school students for college preparatory high schools; and the Zell Laurie Entrepreneurial Institute at the University of Michigan Business School.

Palmer holds a BSME from the Automotive Institute and an MBA cum laude from Babson College and was awarded a Kauffman Fellowship, graduating with the program's inaugural class.

Ray S. Turner
Ray S. Turner (61) has had a long and distinguished career as an operating executive at Fortune 50 companies. From October 1998 to March 2000 he was group vice president, North America Sales, Service, and Marketing for a multinational heavy-industry manufacturer. From 1990 to 1998 Turner also served as vice president and general manager for North America Sales and Manufacturing at that company.

From 1988 to 1990 he served as vice president for manufacturing operations. From 1977 to 1988 Turner served in senior manufacturing management and plant manager roles for a number of assembly and manufacturing operations for the company. Prior to his career at that corporation, Turner spent several years serving in a variety of positions in engineering, materials management, manufacturing, sales, personnel, and labor relations.

Turner serves on the board of directors of two Fortune 100 corporations.

Turner received a bachelor's degree in business administration from Western Michigan University. He also completed the Executive Development Program at Harvard Business School and an Advanced International General Management Program in Switzerland.

Clark T. Pierce
Clark T. Pierce (38) has over 7 years of mezzanine and private equity experience and over 4 years of corporate finance experience. Most recently he was a principal with Ninos Capital, a publicly traded mezzanine investment fund. While at Ninos he was responsible for leading all aspects of the investment process, including deal origination and evaluation, due diligence, deal execution, and portfolio company management. Pierce has closed numerous transactions in various industries, including business services, distribution, manufacturing, and financial services.

From 1993 to 1995 Pierce managed Ninos Capital's Specialized Small Business Investment Company ("SSBIC"). This SSBIC was a $45 million investment vehicle directed toward minority-owned and controlled companies. Prior to Ninos Capital, Pierce spent one year with Freeman Securities as a vice president in the Corporate Finance Group, where he advised bondholders and companies involved in the restructuring process. From 1989 to 1991 Pierce was an associate with Chase Manhattan Bank, N.A., in the Corporate Finance Group.

Pierce served on the board of directors of Sidewalks, Inc., a social services organization for troubled teenagers, and The Orphan Foundation of America, a nonprofit agency focusing on adoption of older children.

Pierce received a BA from Morehouse College, a JD from George Washington University, and an MBA from the Wharton Business School at the University of Pennsylvania.

Andrew L. Simon Andrew L. Simon (30) has 4 years of direct private equity experience, as well as 3 years of strategy consulting experience. During his career Simon has worked on private equity investments in numerous industry sectors, including contract manufacturing, industrial products, health care, financial services, and direct marketing. Most recently he was a senior associate in the New York office at McCown De Leeuw & Co., Inc. ("MDC"), where he focused on growth and leveraged equity investments, including recapitalization and buy-and-build acquisitions. While at MDC, Simon played a lead role in identifying potential investments, negotiating with sellers, and structuring and arranging debt financing, as well as supervising the legal documentation and closing of transactions. Postacquisition he played an active role in the financing and strategic direction of MDC portfolio companies and participated at board meetings.

From 1995 to 1997 Simon was an associate in the Boston office of Trident Partners ("Trident"). At Trident Simon was responsible for evaluating, prioritizing, and analyzing potential new acquisition opportunities, as well as supporting deal teams with business and analytical due diligence. From 1992 to 1995 Simon was a senior analyst at Marakon Associates, where he was responsible for valuation analysis, industry research, and strategy development. In addition, Simon has worked for Littlejohn & Co., an LBO firm focused on restructuring; Physicians Quality Care, a venture-backed health care services company; and Lotus Development.

Simon earned an AB degree from Princeton University's Woodrow Wilson School and earned his MBA, with honors, from Harvard Business School, where he was a Toigo Fellow.

Vice President

Fidel A. Cardenas Most recently Fidel A. Cardenas (31) was a managing director with MTG Ventures from 1999 to 2000. At MTG, a private equity firm focused on acquiring and operating manufacturing and service companies, Cardenas was responsible for deal origination, transaction execution, and portfolio company management. Prior to his role at MTG Ventures, Cardenas was a principal with MTG Advisors from 1992 to 1997, where he focused on strategy consulting and executive coaching. Concurrent with MTG Advisors, Cardenas was elected to two terms as mayor of Sunny Park, California, becoming, at 23, the mayor of that city. He has also served as assistant deputy mayor for public safety for the City of Los Angeles and as an analyst for McKinsey and Company.

Cardenas received a BA in political science from Harvard, cum laude, and his MBA from Harvard Business School.

VI. Summary of Principal Terms

The following is a Summary of Terms relating to the formation of Forte Ventures, L.P. (the "Partnership"), a Delaware limited partnership. This Summary of Terms is by its nature incomplete and subject to the terms and conditions contained in the definitive limited partnership agreement of the Partnership (the "Partnership Agreement") and certain other documents. In the event that the description of terms in this Summary of Terms or elsewhere in this Memorandum is inconsistent with or contrary to the description in, or terms of, the Partnership Agreement or related documents, the terms of the Partnership Agreement and the related documents shall control.

Purpose

The principal purpose of the Partnership is to produce long-term capital appreciation for its partners through equity and equity-related investments in companies that are owned or managed by ethnic minorities or serve or operate in the minority marketplace.

Partnership Capital

The Partnership will have a target size of $200 million (together with the General Partner Commitment) of capital commitments. Commitments in excess of this amount may be accepted at the discretion of the General Partner.

General Partner

The general partner (the "General Partner") of the Partnership will be Forte Ventures, LLC, a Delaware limited liability company formed under the laws of the State of Delaware. Maclean E. Palmer, Jr., Clark T. Pierce, Ray S. Turner, and Andrew L. Simon will be the initial members of the General Partner. The General Partner will control the business and affairs of the Partnership.

Management Company

The management company (the "Management Company") will be Forte Equity Investors, LLC, a Delaware limited liability company. The Management Company will act as investment advisor to the Partnership pursuant to the terms of the Management Agreement.

The Management Company will be responsible for identifying investment opportunities, structuring and negotiating the terms and conditions of each acquisition, arranging for all necessary financing, and, after consummation, monitoring the progress of, and arranging for the disposition of, its interest in each portfolio company. The Management Company may, at its discretion, retain other professionals, including but not limited to accountants, lawyers, and consultants, to assist in rendering any services described herein. In addition, the Management Company may provide services directly to portfolio companies.

General Partner's Capital Contribution

The General Partner shall contribute an amount equal to the greater of $2 million or 1 percent of the total contributions of the Partners, at the same time and in the same manner as the Limited Partners.

Partnership Term

The Partnership term shall be 10 years from the First Closing unless extended by the General Partner for up to a maximum of three additional one-year periods to provide for the orderly liquidation of the Partnership.

Investment Period

The General Partner will generally not be permitted to make any capital calls for the purpose of making investments after the termination of the period (the "Investment Period") commencing on the First Closing and ending on the fifth anniversary thereof, other than commitments to make investments that were committed to prior to such fifth anniversary, and Follow-On Investments (occurring after the Investment Period) that will not exceed 15 percent of the committed capital of the Partnership.

Side Fund

The General Partner may establish an investment fund (the "Side Fund") for individual investors who will be assisting and/or advising the Management Company in connection with originating investment opportunities, recruiting senior management candidates, conducting due diligence, and analyzing selective industry opportunities. The aggregate capital commitments of the Side Fund shall not exceed $5 million. The Side Fund will have terms similar to the Partnership, *provided however* that the individual investors in the Side Fund will only be required to pay a nominal management fee, and the profits from investments made by the Side Fund will not be subject to a Carried interest. The Side Fund will invest alongside the Partnership in each Investment of the Partnership on a pro rata basis. A percentage of each Investment equal to the Capital Commitments of the Side Fund divided by the total Capital Commitments of the Side Fund, the Partnership, or any Parallel Regulatory Vehicle shall be reserved for co-investment by the Side Fund.

Investment Limits

The Partnership will not make investments (excluding Bridge Financings as noted next) in any single or group of related portfolio companies that exceed 25 percent of committed capital, or 35 percent of committed capital when combined with Bridge Financings, of such portfolio companies. With the consent of the Limited Partners, such investment limits may be increased by up to 10 percent with respect to one portfolio company or group of related companies.

Without the approval of the Limited Partners, the investments shall not include:

(i) any investment in an entity that provides for "Carried interests" or management fees to any persons other than the management of a portfolio company or the General Partner or the Management Company unless the General Partner waives its right to receive "Carried interest" distributions with respect to such investment or the General Partner makes a good faith determination that such investment is expected to (a) yield returns on investments within the range of returns expected to be provided by the equity and equity-related securities in which the Partnership was organized to invest (taking into account any management fee or Carried interest relating thereto), and (b) foster a strategic relationship with a potential source of deal flow for the Partnership, *provided however* that such investments shall not exceed 15 percent of the committed capital of the Partnership;

(ii) acquisition of control of businesses through a tender offer (or similar means) if such acquisition is opposed by a majority of the members of such business's board of directors or similar governing body;

(iii) any investment in an entity the principal business of which is the exploration for or development of oil and gas or development of real property;

(iv) investments in uncovered hedges or derivative securities; or

(v) any investment in marketable securities unless immediately after giving effect to such investment the total amount of the Partnership's investments in marketable securities does not exceed 15 percent of aggregate capital commitments of all Partners (other than an investment in marketable securities of an issuer which the General Partner intends to engage in a going private transaction on the date of such investment or in which the General Partner expects to obtain management rights).

The Partnership will not invest more than 20 percent of its committed capital in businesses that have their principal place of business outside of the United States. The Partnership will not invest in securities of entities formed outside of the United States unless it has first obtained comfort that Limited Partners of the Partnership will be subject to limited liability in such jurisdiction that is no less favorable than the limited liability they are entitled to under the laws of Delaware. The Partnership will use its reasonable efforts to ensure that Limited Partners are not subject to taxation in such jurisdiction(s) other than with respect to the income of the Partnership. The Partnership will not guarantee the obligations of the portfolio companies in an amount in excess of 10 percent of capital commitments to the Partnership at any time. The Partnership may borrow money only to pay reasonable expenses of the Partnership or to provide interim financings to the extent necessary to consummate the purchase of a portfolio company prior to receipt of capital contributions.

Bridge Financings

The Partnership may provide temporary financings with respect to any portfolio company ("Bridge Financings"). Any Bridge Financing repaid within 18 months will be restored to unpaid capital commitments.

Any Bridge Financing that is not repaid within 18 months shall no longer constitute Bridge Financing and will be a permanent investment in the portfolio company in accordance with the terms of the Partnership. Bridge Financings may not be incurred if, after giving *pro forma* effect to such incurrence, the aggregate principal amount of Bridge Financings outstanding is in excess of 10 percent (or up to 20 percent with the approval of the Limited Partners) of the Partnership's aggregate capital commitments.

Distributions

Distributions from the Partnership may be made at any time as determined by the General Partner. All distributions of current income from investments, proceeds from the disposition of investments (other than Bridge Financings and proceeds permitted to be reinvested), and any other income from assets of the Partnership (the "Investment Proceeds") from or with respect to each investment initially shall be apportioned among each partner (including the General Partner) in accordance with such Partner's Percentage Interest in respect of such investment. Notwithstanding the previous sentence, each Limited Partner's share of such distribution of Investment Proceeds shall be allocated between such Limited Partner, on the one hand, and the General Partner, on the other hand, and distributed as follows:

   i. *Return of Capital and Partnership Expenses:* First, 100 percent to such Limited Partner until such Limited Partner has received distributions equal to (A) such Limited Partner's capital contributions for all Realized Investments and such Limited Partner's pro-rata share of any unrealized losses on write-downs (net of write-ups) of the Partnership's other portfolio company investments and (B) such Limited Partner's capital contributions for all Organizational Expenses and Partnership Expenses allocated to Realized Investments and write-downs of the Partnership's other portfolio company investments (the amounts discussed in clauses (A) and (B) are referred to collectively as the "Realized Capital Costs");

   ii. *8 Percent Preferred Return:* 100 percent to such Limited Partner until cumulative distributions to such Limited Partner from Realized Investments represent an 8 percent compound annual rate of return on such Limited Partner's Realized Capital Costs;

   iii. *General Partner Catch-Up to 20 Percent:* 100 percent to the General Partner until cumulative distributions of Investment Proceeds under this clause (iii) equal 20 percent of the total amounts distributed pursuant to clauses (ii) and (iii); and

   iv. *80/20 Split:* Thereafter, 80 percent to such Limited Partner and 20 percent to the General Partner (the distributions to the General Partner pursuant to this clause (iv) and clause (iii) above are referred to collectively as the "Carried Interest Distributions").

The rate of return regarding each distribution relating to an investment shall be calculated from the date the capital contributions relating to such investment were used to make such investment to the date that the funds or the property being distributed to each Limited Partner have been received by the Partnership.

Proceeds from cash equivalent investments will be distributed to the Partners in proportion to their respective interests in Partnership assets producing such proceeds, as determined by the General Partner. Proceeds of Bridge Financings will be distributed in accordance with contributions to such Bridge Financings.

Subject, in each case, to the availability of cash after paying Partnership Expenses, as defined below, and setting aside appropriate reserves for reasonably anticipated liabilities, obligations, and commitments of the Partnership, current income earned (net of operating expenses) will be distributed at least annually, and the net proceeds from the disposition of securities of portfolio companies, other than proceeds permitted to be reinvested, shall be distributed as soon as practicable.

The General Partner may make distributions from the Partnership, as cash advances against regular distributions, to the Partners to the extent of available cash in amounts necessary to satisfy their tax liability (or the tax liability of the partners of the General Partner) with respect to their proportion of the Partnership taxable net income.

The Partnership will use its best efforts not to distribute securities in kind unless they are marketable securities or such distribution is in connection with the liquidation of the Partnership. If the receipt of such securities by a Limited Partner will violate law or if a Limited Partner does not wish to receive distributions in kind, the General Partner will make alternative arrangements with respect to such distribution.

Allocations of Profits and Losses

Profits and losses of the Partnership will be allocated among Partners in a manner consistent with the foregoing distribution provisions and the requirements of the Internal Revenue Code.

Clawback

If, following the dissolution of the Partnership, the General Partner shall have received Carried Interest Distributions with respect to a Limited Partner greater than 20 percent of the cumulative net profits (calculated as if all the profits and losses realized by the Partnership with respect to such Limited Partner had occurred simultaneously), then the General Partner shall pay over to such Limited Partner the lesser of (i) the amount of such excess or (ii) the amount of distributions received by the General Partner with respect to such Limited Partner reduced by the taxes payable by the General Partner with respect to such excess and increased by the amount of any tax benefits utilized by the General Partner as a result of such payment in the year of payment.

Management Fees

The Partnership will pay to the Management Company an annual management fee (the "Management Fee") equal to, during the Investment Period, 2 percent of the Partners' total capital committed to the Partnership and, during the period thereafter, 2 percent of the total capital contributions that were used to fund the cost of, and remain invested in, investments, which amount shall be increased quarterly by any capital contributions made during such period and decreased quarterly by amounts distributed to partners as a return of capital. The Management Fee will be payable in advance on a semiannual basis, with the first payment being made on the First Closing Date and each semiannual payment thereafter occurring on the first business day of each calendar semiannual period.

Management Fees may be paid out of monies otherwise available for distribution or out of capital calls. The payments by Additional Limited Partners with respect to the Management Fee and interest thereon will be paid to the Management Company.

Other Fees

The General Partner, the Management Company, and their affiliates may from time to time receive monitoring fees, directors' fees, and transaction fees from portfolio companies or proposed portfolio companies. All such fees will be first applied to reimburse the Partnership for all expenses incurred in connection with Broken Deal Expenses (as defined below) and 50 percent of any excess of such fees will be applied to reduce the Management Fees payable to the Management Company by the Partnership.

"Break-Up Fees" shall mean any fees received by the General Partner, Management Company, or their affiliates in connection with such proposed investment in a portfolio company that is not consummated, reduced by all out-of-pocket expenses incurred by the Partnership, the General Partner, the Management Company, or their affiliates in connection with such proposed investment in the portfolio company.

Partnership Expenses

The Partnership will be responsible for all Organizational Expenses and Operational Expenses (collectively, the "Partnership Expenses").

"Organizational Expenses" shall mean third-party and out-of-pocket expenses, including, without limitation, attorneys' fees, auditors' fees, capital raising, consulting and structuring fees, and other start-up expenses incurred by either of the Partnership, the General Partner, or Management Company, or any affiliates thereof in connection with the organization of the Partnership.

"Operational Expenses" shall mean with respect to the Partnership, to the extent not reimbursed by a prospective or actual portfolio company, if any, all expenses of operation of the Partnership, including, without limitation, legal, consulting, and accounting expenses (including expenses associated with the preparation of Partnership financial statements, tax returns, and K-1s); Management Fees; any taxes imposed on the Partnership; commitment fees payable in connection with credit facilities, accounting fees, third-party fees and expenses, attorney's fees, due diligence, and any other costs or fees related to the acquisition or disposition of securities or investment, whether or

not the transaction is consummated; expenses associated with the Limited Partners and other advisory councils and investment committees of the Partnership; insurance and the costs and expenses of any litigation involving the Partnership; and the amount of any judgments or settlements paid in connection therewith.

"Broken Deal Expenses" mean with respect to each investment, to the extent not reimbursed by a prospective or actual portfolio company, all third-party expenses incurred in connection with a proposed investment that is not ultimately made or a proposed disposition of an investment which is not actually consummated, including, without limitation, (i) commitment fees that become payable in connection with a proposed investment that is not ultimately made; (ii) legal, consulting, and accounting fees and expenses; (iii) printing expenses; and (iv) expenses incurred in connection with the completion of due diligence concerning the prospective portfolio company.

Limited Partner Advisory Committee

The General Partner shall establish a Limited Partner Advisory Committee (the "Advisory Committee") that will consist of between three and nine representatives of the Limited Partners selected by the General Partner.

VII. Risk Factors

An investment in Forte Ventures involves a high degree of risk. There can be no assurance that Forte Ventures' investment objectives will be achieved, or that a Limited Partner will receive a return of its capital. In addition, there will be occasions when the General Partner and its affiliates may encounter potential conflicts of interest in connection with Forte Ventures. The following considerations should be carefully evaluated before making an investment in Forte Ventures. Risk factors include

- Illiquid and long-term investments.
- General portfolio company risk.
- Reliance on the principals.
- Past performance not being indicative of future investment results.
- Lack of operating history.
- Lack of transferability of the limited partnership interests.
- Potential of contingent liabilities on dispositions of portfolio company investments.
- No separate counsel for limited partners.
- Uncertain nature of investments.
- Use of leverage increasing exposure to adverse economic factors.

Chapter Fifteen

The Deal: Valuation, Structure, and Negotiation

Always assume the deal will not close and keep several alternatives alive.

James Hindman
Founder, CEO, and chairman, Jiffy Lube International

Results Expected

Upon completion of this chapter, you will be able to

1. Describe methodologies used by venture capitalists and professional investors to estimate the value of a company.
2. Discuss how and why equity proportions are allocated to investors.
3. Describe how deals are structured, including critical terms, conditions, and covenants.
4. Discuss key aspects of negotiating and closing deals.
5. Characterize good versus bad deals and identify some of the sand traps entrepreneurs face in venture financing.
6. Analyze and discuss the Lightwave Technology case.

The Art and Craft of Valuation

The entrepreneur's and private investor's world of finance is very different from the corporate finance arena where public companies jostle and compete in well-established capital markets. The private company and private capital world of entrepreneurial finance is more volatile, more imperfect, and less accessible than corporate capital markets. The sources of capital differ. The companies are much younger and more dynamic, and the environments more rapidly changing and uncertain. The consequences, for entrepreneurs and investors alike, of this markedly different context are profound. Cash is king, and beta coefficients and elegant corporate financial theories are irrelevant. Also, liquidity and timing are everything, and there are innumerable, unavoidable conflicts between users and suppliers of capital. Finally, the determination of a company's value is elusive and more art than science.

What Is a Company Worth?

The answer: It all depends! Unlike the market for public companies, where millions of shares are traded daily and the firm's market capitalization (total shares outstanding times the price per share) is readily determined, the market for private companies is quite imperfect.

Determinants of Value

The criteria and methods applied in corporate finance to value companies traded publicly in the capital markets, when cavalierly applied to entrepreneurial companies, have severe limitations. The ingredients to the entrepreneurial valuation are cash, time, and risk. In Chapter 13 you determined the burn rate, OOC, and the TTC for your venture, so it is not hard to infer that the amount of cash available and the cash generated will play an important role in valuation. Similarly, Exhibit 13.5 showed that time also plays an influential role. Finally, risk or perception of risk contributes to the determination of value. The old adage, "The greater the risk, the greater the reward," plays a considerable role in how investors size up the venture.

Long-Term Value Creation versus Quarterly Earnings

The core mission of the entrepreneur is to build the best company possible and, if possible, to create a great company. This is the single surest way of generating long-term value for all the stakeholders and society. Such a mission has different strategic imperatives than one aimed solely at maximizing quarterly earnings to attain the highest share price possible given price/earnings ratios at the time. More will be said about this in Chapter 19.

Psychological Factors Determining Value

Time after time companies are valued at preposterous multiples of any sane price/earnings or sales ratios. In the best years, such as the 1982–1983 bull market, the New York Stock Exchange Index was trading at nearly 20 times earnings; it sank to around 8 after the stock market crash of October 1987. Even 12 to 15 would be considered good in many years. By 1998 to late 2001, the S&P 500 was above a P/E of 30. In contrast, consider a late 1990s survey of the top 100 public companies in Massachusetts. The stocks of many of these companies were being traded at 50 or more times earnings, and several were at 95 to 100 times earnings and 6 to 7 times sales! Even more extreme valuations were seen during the peak of the so-called dot-com bubble from 1998 to early 2000. Some companies were valued at 100 times revenue and more during this classic frenzy. In late 2007 the S&P 500 was trading at 16 times earnings.

Often behind extraordinarily high valuations is a psychological wave—a combination of euphoric enthusiasm for a fine company, exacerbated by greed and fear of missing the run-up. The same psychology can also drive prices to undreamed of heights in private companies. In the late 1960s, for instance, Xerox bought Scientific Data Systems, then at $100 million in sales and earning $10 million after taxes, for $1 billion: 10 times sales and 100 times earnings! Value is also in the eye of the beholder: In late 2007 Google was trading near $650 per share with a P/E of 50.

A Theoretical Perspective

Establishing Boundaries and Ranges Rather Than Calculating a Number   Valuation is much more than science, as can be seen from the examples just noted. There are at least a dozen different ways of estimating the value of a private company (real value occurs on sale of equity and is time dependent). A lot of assumptions and a lot of judgment calls are made in every valuation exercise. In one case, for example, the entrepreneur consulted 13 experts to determine how much he should bid for the other half of a $10 million in sales company. The answer ranged from $1 million to $6 million. He subsequently acquired the other half for $3.5 million.

It can be a serious mistake, therefore, to approach the valuation task in hopes of arriving at a single number or even a narrow range. All you can realistically expect is a range of values with boundaries driven by different methods and underlying assumptions for each. Within that range, the buyer and the seller need to determine the comfort zone of each. At what point are you basically indifferent to buying and selling? Determining your point of indifference can be a valuable aid in preparing you for negotiations to buy or sell.

Investor's Required Rate of Return (IRR)[1]

Various investors will require a different rate of return (ROR) for investments in different stages of development and will expect holding periods of various lengths. For example, Exhibit 15.1 summarizes, as ranges, the annual rates of return that venture capital investors seek on investments by stage of development and how long they expect to hold these investments. Several factors underlie the required ROR on a venture capital investment, including premiums for systemic risk, illiquidity, and value added. Of course, these can be expected to vary regionally and from time to time as market conditions change, because the investments are in what are decidedly imperfect capital market niches to begin with.

Investor's Required Share of Ownership

The rate of return required by the investor determines the investor's required share of the ownership,

---

[1] IRR is a synonym for internal rate of return, calculated annually.

EXHIBIT 15.1

Rate of Return Sought by Venture Capital Investors

Stage	Annual ROR%	Typical Expected Holding Period (Years)
Seed and start-up	50–100% or more	More than 10
First stage	40–60	5–10
Second stage	30–40	4–7
Expansion	20–30	3–5
Bridge and mezzanine	20–30	1–3
LBOs	30–50	3–5
Turnarounds	50+	3–5

EXHIBIT 15.2

Investor's Required Share of Ownership under Various ROR Objectives

Assumptions:
Amount of initial start-up investment = $1 million   Year 5 after-tax profit = $1 million
Holding period = 5 years   Year 5 price/earnings ratio = 15
Required rate of return = 50%
Calculating the required share of ownership: $\frac{\text{FV of investment}}{\text{FV of company}}$ = % ownership required

Price/Earnings Ratio	Investor's Return Objective (Percent/Year Compounded)			
	30%	40%	50%	60%
10×	37%	54%	76%	106%
15×	25	36	51	70
20×	19	27	38	52
25×	15	22	30	42

as Exhibit 15.2 illustrates. The future value of a $1 million investment at 50 percent compounded is $1 million $\times (1.5)^5$ = $1 million $\times$ 7.59 = $7.59 million. The future value of the company in Year 5 is profit after tax $\times$ price/earnings ratio = $1 million $\times$ 15 = $15 million. Thus the share of ownership required in Year 5 is

$$\frac{\text{Future value of the investment} = \$7.59 \text{ million}}{\text{Future value of the company} = \$15.00 \text{ million}} = 51\%$$

We can readily see that changing any of the key variables will change the results accordingly.

If the venture capitalists require the RORs mentioned earlier, the ownership they also require is determined as follows: In the start-up stage, 25 to 75 percent for investing all of the required funds; beyond the start-up stage, 10 to 40 percent, depending on the amount invested, maturity, and track record of the venture; in a seasoned venture in the later rounds of investment, 10 to 30 percent to supply the additional funds needed to sustain its growth.

The Theory of Company Pricing

In Chapter 14, we introduced the concept of the capital markets food chain, which we have included here as Exhibit 15.3. This chart depicts the evolution of a company from its idea stage through an initial public offering (IPO). The appetite of the various sources of capital—from family, friends, and angels, to venture capitalists, strategic partners, and the public markets—varies by company size, stage, and amount of money invested. We argue that entrepreneurs who understand these appetites and the food chain are better prepared to focus their fund-raising strategies on more realistic sources, amounts, and valuations.

The Theory of Company Pricing is simplistically depicted in Exhibit 15.4. In the ideal scenario, a venture capital investor envisions two to three rounds, starting at a $1.00 per share equivalent, then a 3 to 5 times markup to Series B, followed by a double markup to Series C, and then doubling that $8.00 round at an IPO. This generic pattern

EXHIBIT 15.3

The Capital Markets Food Chain for Entrepreneurial Ventures

	Stage of Venture			
	R&D	**Seed**	**Launch**	**High Growth**
Company Enterprise Value at Stage	Less than $1 million	$1 million–$5 million	$1 million–$50 million-plus	More than $100 million
Sources	Founders High net worth individuals FFF* SBIR	FFF* Angel funds Seed funds SBIR	Venture capital series A, B, C. . .† Strategic partners Very high net worth individuals Private equity	IPOs Strategic acquirers Private equity
Amount of Capital Invested	Less than $50,000–$200,000	$10,000–$500,000	$500,000–$20 million	$10 million–$50 million-plus
% Company Owned at IPO	10–25%	5–15%	40–60% by prior investors	15–25% by public
Share Price and Number‡	$.01–$.50 1–5 million	$.50–$1.00 1–3 million	$1.00–$8.00 +/– 5–10 million	$12–$18+ 3–5 million

*Friends, families, and fools.

†Venture capital series A, B, C, . . .(average size of round)

Round
$\begin{cases} \text{"A" @ \$3–\$5 million: start-up} \\ \text{"B" @ \$5–\$10 million: product development} \\ \text{"C"+ @ \$10 million: shipping product} \end{cases}$

Valuations vary markedly by industry.

Valuations vary by region and VC cycle.

‡ At post–IPO.

EXHIBIT 15.4

Theory of Company Pricing

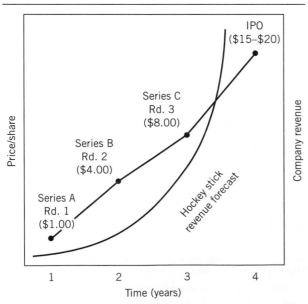

would characterize the majority of deals that succeeded to an IPO, but there are many variations to this central tendency. In truth, many factors can affect this theory.

The Reality

The past 25 years have seen the venture capital industry explode from investing only $50 million to $100 million per year to nearly $100 billion in 2000. Exhibit 15.5 shows how the many realities of the capital marketplace are at work, and how current market conditions, deal flow, and relative bargaining power influence the actual deal struck. Exhibit 15.6 shows how the dot-com explosion and the plummeting of the capital markets led to much lower values for private companies. The NASDAQ index fell from over 5000 to less than 2000, a 63 percent collapse in about nine months by year-end 2000. By 2005, the NASDAQ was barely above 2000, and by the fall of 2007 it had exceeded 2,600.

EXHIBIT 15.5

The Reality

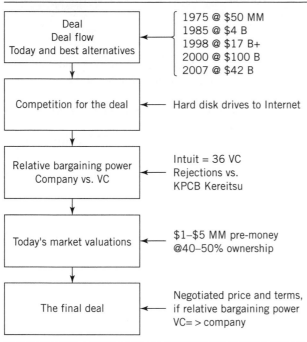

Deal / Deal flow / Today and best alternatives	1975 @ $50 MM / 1985 @ $4 B / 1998 @ $17 B+ / 2000 @ $100 B / 2007 @ $42 B
Competition for the deal	Hard disk drives to Internet
Relative bargaining power Company vs. VC	Intuit = 36 VC Rejections vs. KPCB Kereitsu
Today's market valuations	$1–$5 MM pre-money @40–50% ownership
The final deal	Negotiated price and terms, if relative bargaining power VC= > company

EXHIBIT 15.6

The Reality: The Down Round

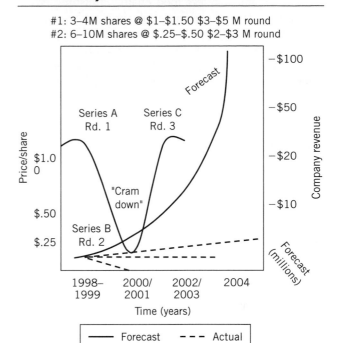

#1: 3–4M shares @ $1–$1.50 $3–$5 M round
#2: 6–10M shares @ $.25–$.50 $2–$3 M round

NASDAQ: peaked above 5000 in March 2000.
Dropped 63 percent by 12/31/2000.

The Down Round or Cram-Down circa 2003

In this environment, which also existed after the October 1987 stock market crash, entrepreneurs face rude shocks in the second or third round of financing. Instead of a substantial four or even five times increase in the valuation from Series A to B, or B to C, they are jolted with what is called a "cram-down" round: The price is typically one-fourth to two-thirds of the last round, as shown in Exhibit 15.6. This severely dilutes the founders' ownership, as investors are normally protected against dilution. Founder dilution as a result of failing to perform is one thing, but dilution because the NASDAQ and IPO markets collapsed seems unfair. But that is part of the reality of valuation.

Take, for example, two excellent young companies, one launched in 1998 and one in 1999. By the fall of 2001 the first had secured two rounds of venture financing, was on target to exceed $20 million in revenue, and was seeking a $25 million round of private equity. The previous round was at $4.50 per share. The Series C round was priced at $2.88 per share, a 36 percent discount from the prior round. The second company met or exceeded all its business plan targets and was expected to achieve $25 million of EBITDA in 2001. Its prior Series B round was priced at $8.50 per share. The new Series C was set at $6.50 per share: nearly a 24 percent discount.

In many financings in 2001 and 2002, onerous additional conditions were imposed, such as a three to five

times return to the Series C investors *before* Series A or B investors received a dime! Both the founders and early-round investors are severely punished by such cram-down financings. The principle of the last money in governing the deal terms still prevails.

We can sense just how vulnerable and volatile the valuation of a company can be in these imperfect markets when external events, such as the collapse of the NASDAQ, trigger a downward spiral. We also gains a new perspective on how critically important timing is. Even these two strongly performing companies were crammed down. Imagine those companies that didn't meet their plans: They were pummeled, if financed at all. What a startling reversal from the dot-com boom in 1998–1999, when companies at *concept stage* (with no product, no identifiable or defensible model of how they would make money or even break even, and no management team with proven experience) raised $20, $50, $70 million, and more *and* had an IPO with multibillion valuations. History asks, What is wrong with this picture? History also offers the answer: Happiness is still a positive cash flow!

Improved Valuations by 2008

As we saw in the previous chapter, both the flows of venture capital and the IPO market continued their strong rebound in 2007. IPOs establish the high-water mark for valuations, and that affects valuations throughout the capital markets food chain. Punishing cramdown rounds and preferential return covenants—common just a few years earlier—had disappeared. For entrepreneurs, higher valuations were a refreshing contrast to the post–Internet bubble bashing. Overall, looking ahead to 2008, the capital climate and valuations were once again showing vigor.

Valuation Methods

The Venture Capital Method[2]

This method is appropriate for investments in a company with negative cash flows at the time of the investment, but which in a number of years is projected to generate significant earnings. As discussed in Chapter 14, venture capitalists are the most likely professional investors to partake in this type of an investment—thus the reference to the venture capital method. The steps involved in this method are as follows:

1. Estimate the company's *net income* in a number of years, at which time the investor plans on harvesting. This estimate will be based on sales and margin projections presented by the entrepreneur in his or her business plan

2. Determine the appropriate *price-to-earnings ratio,* or P/E ratio. The appropriate P/E ratio can be determined by studying current multiples for companies with similar economic characteristics.

3. Calculate the projected *terminal value* by multiplying net income and the P/E ratio.

4. The terminal value can then be discounted to find the *present value* of the investment. Venture capitalists use discount rates ranging from 35 percent to 80 percent because of the risk involved in these types of investments.

5. To determine the investors' *required percentage of ownership,* based on their initial investment, the initial investment is divided by the estimated present value.

To summarize these steps, the following formula can be used:

$$\text{Final ownership required} = \frac{\text{Required future value (investment)}}{\text{Total terminal value}}$$

$$= \frac{(1 + \text{IRR})^{\text{years}} \text{ (investment)}}{\text{P/E ratio (terminal net income)}}$$

6. Finally, the number of shares and the share price must be calculated with the following formula:

$$\text{New shares} = \frac{\text{Percentage of ownership required by the investor}}{1 - \text{Percentage ownership required by the investor} \times \text{old shares}}$$

By definition, the share price equals the price paid divided by the number of shares.

This method is commonly used by venture capitalists because they make equity investments in industries often requiring a large initial investment with significant projected revenues; in addition, the percentage of ownership is a key issue in the negotiations.

The Fundamental Method

This method is simply the present value of the future earnings stream (see Exhibit 15.7).

The First Chicago Method[3]

Another alternative valuation method, developed at First Chicago Corporation's venture capital group, employs a lower discount rate but applies it to an *expected* cash flow. That expected cash flow is the average of three possible scenarios, with each scenario weighted according to its perceived probability. The equation to determine the investor's required final ownership is this:

$$\text{Required final ownership} = \frac{\text{Future value of investment} - \text{Future value of non-IPO cash flow}}{\text{Probability (success)} \text{ (Forecast terminal value)}}$$

This formula[4] differs from the original basic venture capital formula in two ways: (1) The basic formula assumes there are no cash flows between the investment and the harvest in Year 5; the future value of the immediate cash flows is subtracted from the future value of the investment because the difference between them is what must be made up for out of the terminal value; and (2) the basic formula does not distinguish between the *forecast* terminal value and the *expected* terminal value. The traditional method uses the forecast terminal value, which is adjusted through the use of a high discount rate. The formula

---

[2] The venture capital method of valuation is adapted from W. A. Sahlman, "A Method for Valuing High-Risk, Long-Term Investment: The 'Venture Capital Method,'" Note 9-288-006, Harvard Business School 1988, pp. 2–4. Copyright © 1988 by the President and Fellows of Harvard College.
[3] This paragraph is adapted from Sahlman, "A Method for Valuing High-Risk, Long-Term Investments," p. 56.
[4] Ibid., pp. 58–59.

EXHIBIT 15.7

Example of the Fundamental Method

Hitech, Inc.

Year	Percentage Growth of Revenue	Revenue (millions)	After-Tax Margin	After-Tax Profit (millions)	Present Value Factor	PV of Each Year's Earnings ($ millions)
1	50%	$3.00	–0–	–0–	1.400	–0–
2	50	4.50	4.0%	$ 0.18	1.960	$0.09
3	50	6.75	7.0	0.47	2.744	0.17
4	50	10.13	9.0	0.91	3.842	0.24
5	50	15.19	11.0	1.67	5.378	0.31
6	40	21.26	11.5	2.45	7.530	0.33
7	30	27.64	12.0	3.32	10.541	0.32
8	20	33.17	12.0	3.98	14.758	0.27
9	15	38.15	12.0	4.58	20.661	0.22
10	10	41.96	12.0	5.03	28.926	0.17
Total present value of earnings in the supergrowth period						2.12
Residual future value of earnings stream				$63.00	28.926	2.18
Total present value of company						4.30

EXHIBIT 15.8

Example of the First Chicago Method

	Success	Sideways Survival	Failure
1. Revenue growth rate (from base of $2 million)	60%	15%	0%
2. Revenue level after 3 years	$8.19 million	$3.04 million (liquidation)	$ 2 million
3. Revenue level after 5 years	$20.97 million (IPO)	$4.02 million	
4. Revenue level after 7 years		$5.32 million (acquisition)	
5. After-tax profit margin and earnings at liquidity	15%; $3.15 million	7%; $ .37 million	
6. Price/earnings ratio at liquidity	17	7	
7. Value of company liquidity	$53.55 million	$2.61 million	$ .69 million
8. Present value of company using discount rate of 40%	$9.96 million	$.25 million	$ .25 million
9. Probability of each scenario	.4	.4	.2
10. Expected present value of the company under each scenario	$3.98 million	$.10 million	$ .05 million
11. Expected present value of the company		$4.13 million	
12. Percentage ownership required to invest $2.5 million		60.5%	

employs the expected value of the terminal value. Exhibit 15.8 is an example of using this method.

Ownership Dilution[5]

The previous example is unrealistic because in most cases, several rounds of investments are necessary to finance a high-potential venture. Take, for instance, the pricing worksheet presented in Exhibit 15.9, in which three financing rounds are expected. In addition to estimating the appropriate discount rate for the current round, the first-round venture capitalist must now estimate the discount rates that are most likely to be applied in the following rounds, which are projected for Years 2 and 4. Although a 50 percent rate is still appropriate for Year 0, it is estimated that investors in Hitech, Inc., will demand a 40 percent return in Year 2 and a 25 percent return in Year 4.

[5] Ibid., p. 24.

EXHIBIT 15.9

Example of a Three-Stage Financing

Hitech, Inc. (000)						
	Year 0	Year 1	Year 2	Year 3	Year 4	Year 5
Revenues	500	1,250	2,500	5,000	81,000	12,800
New income	(250)	(62)	250	750	1,360	2,500
Working capital at 20%	100	250	500	1,000	1,600	2,560
Fixed assets at 40%	200	500	1,000	2,000	3,200	5,120
Free cash flow	(550)	(512)	(500)	(750)	(440)	(380)
Cumulative external financial need	500	1,653	1,543	2,313	2,753	3,133
Equity issues	1,500	0	1,000	0	1,000	0
Equity outstanding	1,500	1,500	2,500	2,500	3,500	3,500
Cash balance	950	436	938	188	748	368
Assume: long-term IRR required each round by investors	50%	45%	40%	30%	25%	20%

Source: From "A Method for Valuing High-Risk, Long-Term Investments," by W. A. Sahlman, Harvard Business School Note 9-288-006, p. 45. Reprinted by permission of Harvard Business School; all rights reserved. Revised and updated for 2008.

The final ownership that each investor must be left with, given a terminal price/earnings ratio of 15, can be calculated using the basic valuation formula:

Round 1:

$$\frac{\text{Future value (investment)}}{\text{Terminal value (company)}} = \frac{1.50^5 \times \$1.5 \text{ million}}{15. \times \$2.5 \text{ million}} = 30.4\% \text{ ownership}$$

Round 2:

$$(1.40^3 \times \$1 \text{ million}) / (15 \times \$2.5 \text{ million}) = 7.3\%$$

Round 3:

$$(1.25^1 \times \$1 \text{ million}) / (15 \times \$1.5 \text{ million}) = 3.3\%$$

Discounted Cash Flow

In a simple discounted cash flow method, three time periods are defined: (1) Years 1–5; (2) Years 6–10; and (3) Year 11 to infinity.[6] The necessary operating assumptions for each period are initial sales, growth rates, EBIAT/sales, and (net fixed assets + operating working capital)/ sales. While using this method, we should also note relationships and trade-offs. With these assumptions, the discount rate can be applied to the weighted average cost of capital (WACC).[7] Then the value for free cash flow (Years 1–10) is

added to the terminal value. This terminal value is the growth perpetuity.

Other Rule-of-Thumb Valuation Methods

Several other valuation methods are also employed to estimate the value of a company. Many of these are based on similar, most recent transactions of similar firms, established by a sale of the company or a prior investment. Such comparables may look at several different multiples, such as earnings, free cash flow, revenue, EBIT, EBITDA, and book value. Knowledgeable investment bankers and venture capitalists make it their business to know the activity in the current marketplace for private capital and how deals are being priced. These methods are used most often to value an existing company, rather than a start-up, because there are so many more knowns about the company and its financial performance.

Tar Pits Facing Entrepreneurs

There are several inherent conflicts between entrepreneurs or the users of capital and investors or the suppliers of capital.[8] While the entrepreneur wants to have as much time as possible for the financing, the investors want to supply capital just in time or to

[6] J. A. Timmons, "Valuation Methods and Raising Capital," lecture, Babson College, 2006.
[7] Note that it is WACC, not free cash flow, because of the tax factor.
[8] J. A. Timmons, "Deals and Deal Structuring," lecture, Babson College, 2006.

invest only when the company needs the money. Entrepreneurs should be thinking of raising money when they do not need it, while preserving the option to find another source of capital.

Similarly, users of capital want to raise as much money as possible, whereas the investors want to supply just enough capital in staged capital commitments. The investors, such as venture capitalists, use staged capital commitments to manage their risk exposure over 6- to 12-month increments of investing.

In the negotiations of a deal, the entrepreneur sometimes becomes attracted to a high valuation with the sentiment "My price, your terms." The investors will generally attempt to change this opinion because it is their capital. The investors will thus focus on a low valuation with the sentiment, "My price *and* my terms."

This tension applies not only to financial transactions but also to the styles of the users versus the styles of the suppliers of capital. The users value their independence and treasure the flexibility their own venture has brought them. However, the investors are hoping to preserve their options as well. These options usually include both reinvesting and abandoning the venture.

These points of view also clash in the composition of the board of directors, where the entrepreneur seeks control and independence, and the investors want the right to control the board if the company does not perform as well as was expected. This sense of control is an emotional issue for most entrepreneurs, who want to be in charge of their own destiny. Prizing their autonomy and self-determination, many of these users of capital would agree with the passion Walt Disney conveyed in this statement: "I don't make movies to make money. I make *money* to make movies." The investors may believe in the passions of these users of capital, but they still want to protect themselves with first refusals, initial public offering rights, and various other exit options.

The long-term goals of the users and suppliers of capital may also be contradictory. The entrepreneurs may be content with the progress of their venture and happy with a single or double. It is their venture, their baby; if it is moderately successful, many entrepreneurs believe they have accomplished a lot. The investors will not be quite as content with moderate success, but instead want their capital to produce extraordinary returns—they want a home run from the entrepreneur. Thus the pressures put on the entrepreneur may seem unwarranted to the entrepreneur, yet necessary for the investor.

These strategies contradict each other when they are manifest in the management styles of the users and providers of capital. While the entrepreneur is willing to take a calculated risk or is working to minimize or avoid unnecessary risks, the investor has bet on the art of the exceptional and thus is willing to bet the farm every day.

Entrepreneurs possess the ability to see opportunities and, more important, to seize those opportunities. They possess an instinctual desire to change, to adapt, or to decommit in order to seize new opportunities. Yet the investors are looking for clear steady progress, as projected in the business plan, which leaves little room for surprises.

Finally, the ultimate goals may differ. The entrepreneur who continues to build his or her company may find operating a company enjoyable. At this point, the definition of success both personally and for the company may involve long-term company building, such that a sustainable institution is created. But the investors will want to cash out in two to five years, so that they can reinvest their capital in another venture.

Staged Capital Commitments[9]

Venture capitalists rarely, if ever, invest all the external capital that a company will require to accomplish its business plan; instead they invest in companies at distinct stages in their development. As a result, each company begins life knowing that it has only enough capital to reach the next stage. By staging capital, the venture capitalists preserve the right to abandon a project whose prospects look dim. The right to abandon is essential because an entrepreneur will almost never stop investing in a failing project as long as others are providing capital.

Staging the capital also provides incentives to the entrepreneurial team. Capital is a scarce and expensive resource for individual ventures. Misuse of capital is very costly to venture capitalists but not necessarily to management. To encourage managers to conserve capital, venture capital firms apply strong sanctions if it is misused. These sanctions ordinarily take two basic forms. First, increased capital requirements invariably dilute management's equity share at an increasingly punitive rate. Second, the staged investment process enables venture capital firms to shut down operations. The credible threat to abandon a venture, even when the firm might be economically viable, is the key to the relationship between the entrepreneur and the venture capitalists. By denying capital, the venture capitalist also signals other capital suppliers that the company in question is a bad investment risk.

[9] W. A. Sahlman, "Structure of Venture Capital Organizations," *Journal of Financial Economics* 27 (1990), pp. 506–7. Reprinted with the permission of Elsevier.

Short of denying the company capital, venture capitalists can discipline wayward managers by firing or demoting them. Other elements of the stock purchase agreement then come into play. For example, the company typically has the right to repurchase shares from departing managers, often at prices below market value; and vesting schedules limit the number of shares employees are entitled to if they leave prematurely. Finally, noncompete clauses can impose strong penalties on those who leave, particularly if their human capital is closely linked to the industry in which the venture is active.

Entrepreneurs accept the staged capital process because they usually have great confidence in their own abilities to meet targets. They understand that if they meet those goals, they will end up owning a significantly larger share of the company than if they had insisted on receiving all of the capital up front.

Structuring the Deal

What Is a Deal?[10]

Deals are defined as economic agreements between at least two parties. In the context of entrepreneurial finance, most deals involve the allocation of cash flow streams (with respect to both amount and timing), the allocation of risk, and hence the allocation of value between different groups. For example, deals can be made between suppliers and users of capital, or between management and employees of a venture.

A Way of Thinking about Deals over Time

To assess and to design long-lived deals, Professor William A. Sahlman from Harvard Business School suggests the following series of questions as a guide for deal makers in structuring and in understanding how deals evolve:[11]

- Who are the players?
- What are their goals and objectives?
- What risks do they perceive and how have these risks been managed?
- What problems do they perceive?
- How much do they have invested, both in absolute terms and relative terms, at cost and at market value?
- What is the context surrounding the current decision?

- What is the form of their current investment or claim on the company?
- What power do they have to act? To precipitate change?
- What real options do they have? How long does it take them to act?
- What credible threats do they have?
- How and from whom do they get information?
- How credible is the source of information?
- What will be the value of their claims under different scenarios?
- How can they get value for their claims?
- To what degree can they appropriate value from another party?
- How much uncertainty characterizes the situation?
- What are the rules of the game (e.g., tax, legislative)?
- What is the context (e.g., state of economy, capital markets, industry specifics) at the current time? How is the context expected to change?

The Characteristics of Successful Deals[12]

While deal making is ultimately a combination of art and science, it is possible to describe some of the characteristics of deals that have proven successful over time:

- They are simple.
- They are robust (they do not fall apart when there are minor deviations from projections).
- They are organic (they are not immutable).
- They take into account the incentives of each party to the deal under a variety of circumstances.
- They provide mechanisms for communications and interpretation.
- They are based primarily on trust rather than on legalese.
- They are not patently unfair.
- They do not make it too difficult to raise additional capital.
- They match the needs of the user of capital with the needs of the supplier.
- They reveal information about each party (e.g., their faith in their ability to deliver on the promises).
- They allow for the arrival of new information before financing is required.

---

[10] From "Note on Financial Contracting Deals," by W. A. Sahlman, Harvard Business School Note 99-288-014, 1988, p. 1. Copyright © 1988 Harvard Business School Publishing; all rights reserved.

[11] Ibid., pp. 35–36.

[12] Ibid., p. 43.

- They do not preserve discontinuities (e.g., boundary conditions that will evoke dysfunctional behavior on the part of the agents of principals).
- They consider the fact that it takes time to raise money.
- They improve the chances of success for the venture.

The Generic Elements of Deals   A number of terms govern value distribution, as well as basic definitions, assumptions, performance incentives, rights, and obligations. The deal should also cover the basic mechanisms for transmitting timely, credible information. Representations and warranties, plus negative and positive covenants, will also be part of the deal structure. Additionally, default clauses and remedial action clauses are appropriate in most deals.

Tools for Managing Risk/Reward   In a deal, the claims on cash and equity are prioritized by the players. Some of the tools available to the players are common stock, partnerships, preferred stock (dividend and liquidation preference), debt (secured, unsecured, personally guaranteed, or convertible), performance conditional pricing (ratchets or positive incentives), puts and calls, warrants, and cash. Some of the critical aspects of a deal go beyond just the money:[13]

- Number, type, and mix of stocks (and perhaps of stock and debt) and various features that may go with them (such as puts) that affect the investor's rate of return.
- The amounts and timing of takedowns, conversions, and the like.
- Interest rates on debt or preferred shares.
- The number of seats, and who actually will represent investors, on the board of directors.
- Possible changes in the management team and in the composition of the board.
- Registration rights for investor's stock (in the case of a registered public offering).
- Right of first refusal granted to the investor on subsequent private placements or an IPO.
- Employment, noncompete, and proprietary rights agreements.
- The payment of legal, accounting, consulting, or other fees connected with putting the deal together.

- Specific performance targets for revenues, expenses, market penetration, and the like by certain target dates.

Understanding the Bets

Deals, because they are based on cash, risk, and time, are subject to interpretation. The players' perceptions of each of these factors contribute to the overall valuation of the venture and the subsequent proposed deal. As was described earlier, there are a number of different ways to value a venture, and these various valuation methods contribute to the complexity of deals. Consider, for instance, the following term sheets:[14]

- A venture capital firm proposes to raise $150 million to $200 million to acquire and build RSA Cellular Phone Properties. The venture capital firm will commit between $15 million and $30 million in equity and will lead in raising senior and subordinated debt to buy licenses. Licensees will have to claim about 30 percent of the future equity value in the new company; the venture capital firm will claim 60 percent (subordinated debt claim is estimated at 10 percent); and management will get 5 to 10 percent of the future equity, but only after all prior return targets have been achieved. The venture capital firm's worst-case scenario will result in 33 percent ROR to the firm, 9 percent ROR to licensees, and 0 percent for management. The noncompete agreements extend for 12 years, in addition to the vesting.
- An entrepreneur must decide between two deals:

    Deal A: A venture capital firm will lead a $3 million investment and requires management to invest $1 million. Future gains are to be split 50–50 after the venture capital firm has achieved a 25 percent ROR on the investment. Other common investment provisions also apply (vesting, employment agreements, etc.). The venture capital firm has the right of first refusal on all future rounds and other deals management may find.

    Deal B: Another venture capital firm will lead a $4 million investment. Management will invest nothing. The future gains are to be split 75 percent for the venture capital firm and 25 percent for management on a side-by-side basis. Until the venture achieves positive

[13] Timmons, Spinelli, and Zacharakis, "How to Raise Capital," McGraw-Hill, 2004.
[14] Timmons, "Deals and Deal Structuring" lecture, Babson College, 2006.

cash flow, this venture capital firm has the right of first refusal on future financing and deals management may find.

- A group of very talented money managers is given $40 million in capital to manage. The contract calls for the managers to receive 20 percent of the excess return on the portfolio over the Treasury bond return. The contract runs for five years. The managers cannot take out any of their share of the gains until the last day of the contracts (except to pay taxes).

While reading and considering these deals, try to identify the underlying assumptions, motivations, and beliefs of the individuals proposing the deals. Following are some questions that may help in identifying the players' bets:

- What is the bet?
- Whom is it for?
- Who is taking the risk? Who receives the rewards?
- Who should be making these bets?
- What will happen if the entrepreneurs exceed the venture capitalists' expectations? What if they fall short?
- What are the incentives for the money managers? What are the consequences of their success or failure to perform?
- How will the money managers behave? What will be their investing strategy?

Some of the Lessons Learned: The Dog in the Suitcase

A few years ago a friend, living in a New York City high-rise, called in great distress. Her beloved barkless dog had died in the middle of the night. She wanted a decent burial for the dog, but because it was the dead of winter, she did not know what to do. It was suggested that she contact a pet cemetery on Long Island and take the dog there. It would be frozen until spring, at which time it would be properly buried.

She gathered her courage, placed the dog in a suitcase, and headed down the elevator to the outdoors. As she struggled toward the nearest intersection to catch a cab, a young man noticed her struggle and offered to help. Puffing by now, she sized up the young man quickly and accepted his offer to carry the bag. In no time, she turned to find the young

man sprinting down the street with her suitcase. Imagine the look on the faces of the young man and his buddies when they opened the suitcase and discovered the loot!

The moral of this story is that raising capital can have all the surprises of a dog in the suitcase for the entrepreneur. The following tips may help to minimize many of these surprises:

- Raise money when you do not need it.
- Learn as much about the process and how to manage it as you can.
- Know your relative bargaining position.
- If all you get is money, you are not getting much.
- Assume the deal will never close.
- Always have a backup source of capital.
- The legal and other experts can blow it—sweat the details yourself!
- Users of capital are invariably at a disadvantage in dealing with the suppliers of capital.
- If you are out of cash when you seek to raise capital, suppliers of capital will eat you for lunch.
- Start-up entrepreneurs are raising capital for the first time; suppliers of capital have done it many times for a daily living.

Negotiations

Negotiations have been defined by many experts in a variety of ways, as the following examples demonstrate. Herb Cohen, the author of *You Can Negotiate Anything*, defines negotiations as "a field of knowledge and endeavor that focuses on gaining the favor of people from whom we want things"[15] or similarly, as "the use of information and power to affect behavior within a 'web of tension.'"[16] Other experts in the field of negotiations, Roger Fisher and William Ury, assert that negotiations are a "back-and-forth communication designed to reach an agreement when you and the other side have some interests that are shared and others that are opposed."[17]

What Is Negotiable?

Far more is negotiable than entrepreneurs think.[18] For instance, a normal ploy of the attorney representing the investors is to insist, matter-of-factly, that "this

---

[15] H. Cohen, *You Can Negotiate Anything* (New York: Bantam Books, 1982), p. 15.
[16] Ibid., p. 16.
[17] R. Fisher and W. Ury, *Getting to Yes* (New York: Penguin Books, 1991), p. xvii.
[18] See, for example, H. M. Hoffman and J. Blakey, "You Can Negotiate with Venture Capitalists," *Harvard Business Review*, March–April 1987, pp. 16–24.

is our boilerplate" and that the entrepreneur should take it or leave it. It is possible for an entrepreneur to negotiate and craft an agreement that represents his or her needs.

During the negotiation, the investors will be evaluating the negotiating skills, intelligence, and maturity of the entrepreneur. The entrepreneur has precisely the same opportunity to size up the investor. If the investors see anything that shakes their confidence or trust, they probably will withdraw from the deal. Similarly, if an investor turns out to be arrogant, hot-tempered, or unwilling to see the other side's needs and to compromise, or seems bent on getting every last ounce out of the deal by locking an entrepreneur into as many of the "burdensome clauses" as is possible, the entrepreneur might want to withdraw.

Throughout the negotiations, entrepreneurs need to bear in mind that a successful negotiation is one in which both sides believe they have made a fair deal. The best deals are those in which neither party wins and neither loses, and such deals are possible to negotiate. This approach is further articulated in the works of Fisher and Ury, who have focused neither on soft nor hard negotiation tactics, but rather on principled negotiation, a method developed at the Harvard Negotiation Project. This method asserts that the purpose of negotiations is "to decide issues on their merits rather than through a haggling process focused on what each side says it will and won't do. It suggests that you look for mutual gains wherever possible, and that where your interests conflict, you should insist that the result be based on some fair standards independent of the will of either side."[19] They continue to describe principled negotiations in the following four points:

People: Separate the people from the problem.

Interests: Focus on interests, not positions.

Options: Generate a variety of possibilities before deciding what to do.

Criteria: Insist that the result be based on some objective standard.

Others have spoken of this method of principled negotiation. For example, Bob Woolf of Bob Woolf Associates, a Boston-based firm that has represented everyone from Larry Bird to Gene Shalit, states simply, "You want the other side to be reasonable, not defensive—to work *with* you. You'll have a better chance of getting what you want. Treat someone the way that you would like to be treated, and you'll be successful most of the time."[20]

The Specific Issues Entrepreneurs Typically Face[21]

Whatever method you choose in your negotiations, the primary focus is likely to be on how much the entrepreneur's equity is worth and how much is to be purchased by the investor's investment. Even so, numerous other issues involving legal and financial control of the company and the rights and obligations of various investors and the entrepreneur in various situations may be as important as valuation and ownership share. Not the least of these is the value behind the money—such as contacts and helpful expertise, additional financing when and if required, and patience and interest in the long-term development of the company—that a particular investor can bring to the venture. The following are some of the most critical aspects of a deal that go beyond "just the money":

- Number, type, and mix of stocks (and perhaps of stock and debt) and various features that may go with them (such as puts) that affect the investor's rate of return.
- The amounts and timing of takedowns, conversions, and the like.
- Interest rate in debt or preferred shares.
- The number of seats, and who actually will represent investors, on the board of directors.
- Possible changes in the management team and in the composition of the board of directors.
- Registration rights for investor's stock (in case of a registered public offering).
- Right of first refusal granted to the investor on subsequent private or initial public stock offerings.
- Stock vesting schedule and agreements.
- The payment of legal, accounting, consulting, or other fees connected with putting the deal together.

Entrepreneurs may find some subtle but highly significant issues negotiated. If they, or their attorneys, are not familiar with these, they may be missed as just boilerplate when in fact they have crucial future implications for the ownership, control, and financing of the business. Here are some issues that can be burdensome for entrepreneurs:

- *Co-sale provision.* This is a provision by which investors can tender their shares of stock before an initial public offering. It protects the first-round investors but can cause conflicts with

---

[19] Fisher and Ury, *Getting to Yes*, p. xviii.
[20] Quoted in P. B. Brown and M. S. Hopkins, "How to Negotiate Practically Anything." Reprinted with permission *INC.* magazine (February 1989), p. 35. Copyright © 1989 by Goldhirsh Group, Inc., 38 Commercial Wharf, Boston, MA 02110.
[21] J. A. Timmons, "Deals and Deal Structuring" lecture, Babson College, 2006.

investors in later rounds and can inhibit an entrepreneur's ability to cash out.

- *Ratchet antidilution protection.* This enables the lead investors to get for free additional common stock if subsequent shares are ever sold at a price lower than originally paid. This protection allows first-round investors to prevent the company from raising additional necessary funds during a period of adversity for the company. While nice from the investor's perspective, it ignores the reality that, in distress situations, the last money calls the shots on price and deal structure.

- *Washout financing.* This is a strategy of last resort that wipes out all previously issued stock when existing preferred shareholders will not commit additional funds, thus diluting everyone.

- *Forced buyout.* Under this provision, if management does not find a buyer or cannot take the company public by a certain date, then the investors can find a buyer at terms they agree upon.

- *Demand registration rights.* Here investors can demand at least one IPO in three to five years. In reality, such clauses are hard to invoke because the market for new public stock issues, rather than the terms of an agreement, ultimately governs the timing of such events.

- *Piggyback registration rights.* These grant to the investors (and to the entrepreneur, if he or she insists) rights to sell stock at the IPO. Because the underwriters usually make this decision, the clause normally is not enforceable.

- *Key-person insurance.* This requires the company to obtain life insurance on key people. The named beneficiary of the insurance can be either the company or the preferred shareholders.

The Term Sheet

Regardless of whether you secure capital from angels or venture capitalists, you will want to be informed and knowledgeable about the terms and conditions that govern the deal you sign. Many experienced entrepreneurs will argue that the terms and who your investor is are more important than the valuation. Today the technical sophistication in deal structures creates an imperative for entrepreneurs and their legal counsel: If you don't know the details you will get what you deserve—not what you want.

To illustrate this point, consider the choice among four common instruments: (1) fully participating preferred stock, (2) partially participating preferred stock (4 times return), (3) common preference ($1.00/share to common), and (4) nonparticipating preferred stock. Then consider a $200 million harvest realized through either an IPO or an acquisition by another company. Why does any of this matter? Aren't these details better left to the legal experts?

Consider the economic consequences of each of these deal instruments under the two harvest scenarios in Exhibit 15.10. The graph shows there can be up to a $24 million difference in the payout received, even though, in the example, there are equal numbers of shares of common stock, typically owned by the founders, and preferred stock, owned by investors. The acquisition exit is more favorable to investors, especially because periodically the IPO market is closed to new companies.

Sand Traps[22]

Strategic Circumference

Each fund-raising strategy sets in motion some actions and commitments by management that will eventually scribe a strategic circumference around the company in terms of its current and future financing choices. These future choices will permit varying degrees of freedom as a result of the previous actions. Those who fail to think through the consequences of a fund-raising strategy and the effect on their degrees of freedom fall into this trap.

Although it is impossible to avoid strategic circumference completely, and while in some cases scribing a strategic circumference is clearly intentional, others may be unintended and, unfortunately, unexpected. For example, a company that plans to remain private or plans to maintain a 1.5 to 1.0 debt-to-equity ratio has intentionally created a strategic circumference.

Legal Circumference

Many people have an aversion to becoming involved in legal or accounting minutiae. Many believe that because they pay sizable professional fees, their advisors should and will pay attention to the details.

Legal documentation spells out the terms, conditions, responsibilities, and rights of the parties to a transaction. Because different sources have different ways of structuring deals, and because these legal and contractual details come at the *end* of the

---

[22] Copyright © 1990 by Jeffry A. Timmons.

EXHIBIT 15.10

Considering the Economics: $200 Million IPO or Acquisition?

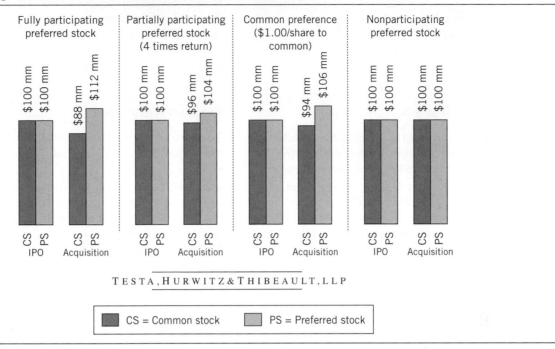

Source: Testa, Hurwitz & Thibeault, LLP, from a presentation by Heather M. Stone and Brian D. Goldstein at Babson College, October 3, 2001.

fund-raising process, an entrepreneur may arrive at a point of no return, facing some onerous conditions and covenants that not only are difficult to live with but also create tight limitations and constraints— legal circumference—on future choices that are potentially disastrous. Entrepreneurs cannot rely on attorneys and advisors to protect them in this vital matter.

To avoid this trap, entrepreneurs need to have a fundamental precept: "The devil is in the details." It is risky for an entrepreneur *not* to carefully read final documents and risky to use a lawyer who is *not* experienced and competent. It also is helpful to keep a few options alive and to conserve cash. This also can keep the other side of the table more conciliatory and flexible.

Attraction to Status and Size

It seems there is a cultural attraction to higher status and larger size, even when it comes to raising capital. Simply targeting the largest or the best known or most prestigious firms is a trap entrepreneurs often fall into. These firms are often most visible because of their size and investing activity and because they have been around a long time. Yet because the venture capital industry has become more heterogeneous, as well as for other reasons, such firms may or may not be a good fit.

Take, for example, an entrepreneur who had a patented, innovative device that was ready for use by manufacturers of semiconductors. He was running out of cash from an earlier round of venture capital investment and needed more money for his device to be placed in test sites and then, presumably, into production. Although lab tests had been successful, his prior backers would not invest further because he was nearly two years behind schedule in his business plan. For a year, he concentrated his efforts on many of the largest and most well-known firms and celebrities in the venture capital business, but to no avail. With the help of outside advice, he then decided to pursue an alternative fund-raising strategy. First he listed firms that were most likely prospects as customers for the device. Next he sought to identify investors who already had investments in this potential customer base; it was thought that these would be the most likely potential backers because they would be the most informed about his technology, its potential value-added properties, and any potential competitive advantages the company could achieve. Fewer than a dozen venture capital firms were identified (from among a pool of over 700 at the time), yet none had been contacted previously by this entrepreneur. In fact, many were virtually unknown to him, even though they were very active investors in the industry. In less than three months, offers were on the table from three of these, and the financing was closed.

It is best to avoid this trap by focusing your efforts toward financial backers, whether debt or equity, who have intimate knowledge and first-hand experience with the technology, marketplace, and networks of expertise in the competitive arena. Focus on those firms with relevant know-how that would be characterized as a good match.

Unknown Territory

Venturing into unknown territory is another problem. Entrepreneurs need to know the terrain in sufficient detail, particularly the requirements and alternatives of various equity sources. If they do not, they may make critical strategic blunders and waste time.

For example, a venture that is not a "mainstream venture capital deal" may be overvalued and directed to investors who are not a realistic match, rather than being realistically valued and directed to small and more specialized funds, private investors, or potential strategic partners. The preceding example is a real one. The founders went through nearly $100,000 of their own funds, strained their relationship to the limit, and nearly had to abandon the project.

Another illustration of a fund-raising strategy that was ill conceived and, effectively, a lottery—rather than a well-thought-out and focused search—is a company in the fiber optics industry we'll call Opti-Com.[23] Opti-Com was a spin-off as a start-up from a well-known public company in the industry. The management team was entirely credible, but its members were not considered superstars. The business plan suggested the company could achieve the magical $50 million in sales in five years, which the entrepreneurs were told by an outside advisor was the minimum size that venture capital investors would consider. The plan proposed to raise $750,000 for about 10 percent of the common stock of the company. Realistically, because the firm was a custom supplier for special applications rather than a provider of a new technology with a significant proprietary advantage, a sales estimate of $10 million to $15 million in five years would have been more plausible. The same advisor urged that their business plan be submitted to 16 blue-ribbon mainstream venture capital firms in the Boston area. Four months later they had received 16 rejections. The entrepreneurs then were told to "go see the same quality of venture capital firms in New York." A year later the founders were nearly out of money and had been unsuccessful in their search for capital. When redirected away from mainstream venture capitalists to a more suitable source, a small fund specifically created in Mass-

achusetts to provide risk capital for emerging firms that might not be robust enough to attract conventional venture capital but would be a welcome addition to the economic renewal of the state, the fit was right. Opti-Com raised the necessary capital, but at a valuation much more in line with the market for start-up deals.

Opportunity Cost

The lure of money often leads to a common trap—the opportunity cost trap. An entrepreneur's optimism leads him or her to the conclusion that with good people and products (or services), there has to be a lot of money out there with "our name on it!" In the process, entrepreneurs tend to grossly underestimate the real costs of getting the cash in the bank. Further, entrepreneurs also underestimate the real time, effort, and creative energy required. Indeed, the degree of effort fund-raising requires is perhaps the least appreciated aspect of obtaining capital. In both these cases, there are opportunity costs in expending these resources in a particular direction when both the clock and the calendar are moving.

In a start-up company, for instance, founders can devote nearly all their available time for months to seeking out investors and telling their story. It may take six months or more to get a yes and up to a year for a no. In the meantime, a considerable amount of cash and human capital has been flowing out rather than in, and this cash and capital might have been better spent elsewhere.

One such start-up began its search for venture capital in 2006. A year later the founders had exhausted $200,000 of their own seed money and had quit their jobs to devote themselves full-time to the effort. Yet they were unsuccessful after approaching more than 35 sources of capital. The opportunity costs are clear.

There are opportunity costs, too, in existing emerging companies. In terms of human capital, it is common for top management to devote as much as half of its time trying to raise a major amount of outside capital. Again, this requires a tremendous amount of emotional and physical energy as well, of which there is a finite amount to devote to the daily operating demands of the enterprise. The effect on near-term performance is invariably negative. In addition, if expectations of a successful fund-raising effort are followed by a failure to raise the money, morale can deteriorate and key people can be lost.

Significant opportunity costs are also incurred in forgone business and market opportunities that could

---

[23] This is a fictional name for an actual company.

have been pursued. Take, for example, the start-up firm just noted. When asked what level of sales the company would have achieved in the year had it spent the $200,000 of the founders' seed money on generating customers and business, the founder answered without hesitation, "We'd be at $1 million sales by now, and would probably be making a small profit."

Underestimation of Other Costs

Entrepreneurs tend to underestimate the out-of-pocket costs associated with both raising the money and living with it. There are incremental costs after a firm becomes a public company. The Securities and Exchange Commission requires regular audited financial statements and various reports, there are outside directors' fees and liability insurance premiums, there are legal fees associated with more extensive reporting requirements, and so on. These can add up quickly, often to $500,000 or more annually.

Another cost that can be easily overlooked is of the disclosure that may be necessary to convince a financial backer to part with his or her money. An entrepreneur may have to reveal much more about the company and his other personal finances than he or she ever imagined. Thus company weaknesses, ownership and compensation arrangements, personal and corporate financial statements, marketing plans and competitive strategies, and so forth may need to be revealed to people whom the entrepreneur does not really know and trust, and with whom he or she may eventually not do business. In addition, the ability to control access to the information is lost.

Greed

The entrepreneur—especially one who is out of cash or nearly so—may find the money irresistible. One of the most exhilarating experiences for an entrepreneur is the prospect of raising that first major slug of outside capital, or obtaining that substantial bank line needed for expansion. If the fundamentals of the company are sound, however, then there is money out there.

Being Too Anxious

Usually, after months of hard work finding the right source and negotiating the deal, another trap awaits the hungry but unwary entrepreneur, and all too often the temptation is overwhelming. It is the trap of believing that the deal is done and terminating discussions with others too soon. Entrepreneurs fall into this trap because they want to believe the deal is done with a handshake (or perhaps with an accompanying letter of intent or an executed term sheet).

A masterful handling of such a situation occurred when an entrepreneur and a key vice president of a company with $30 million in sales had been negotiating with several venture capitalists, three major strategic partners, and a mezzanine source for nearly six months. The company was down to 60 days' worth of cash, and the mezzanine investors knew it. They offered the entrepreneur $10 million as a take-it-or-leave-it proposition. The vice president, in summarizing the company's relative bargaining position, said, "It was the only alternative we had left; everything else had come to rest by late last month, and the negotiations with the three major companies had not reached serious stages. We felt like they were asking too much, but we needed the money." Yet the two had managed to keep this weakness from being apparent to the mezzanine. Each time negotiations had been scheduled, the entrepreneur had made sure he also had scheduled a meeting with one of the other larger companies for later that afternoon (a two-hour plane ride away). In effect, he was able to create the illusion that these discussions with other investors were far more serious than they actually were. The deal was closed on terms agreeable to both. The company went public six months later and is still highly successful today.

Impatience

Another trap is being impatient when an investor does not understand quickly, and not realizing each deal has velocity and momentum.

The efforts of one management group to acquire a firm in the cell phone business being sold by their employers provide an example. As members of the management team, they were the first to know in May that the company was going to be sold by its owners. By early July the investment bankers representing the sellers were expected to have the offering memorandum ready for the open market. To attempt to buy the company privately would require the team to raise commitments for approximately $150 million in three to four weeks—hardly enough time to put together even a crude business plan, let alone raise such a substantial sum. The train was moving at 140 miles per hour and gaining speed each day. The founders identified five top-notch, interested venture capital and leveraged buyout firms and sat down with representatives of each to walk through the summary of the business plan and the proposed financing. One excellent firm sent an otherwise very experienced and capable partner, but his questioning indicated how little he knew about this business. The team knew they had to look elsewhere.

Had the group been too impatient simply because the train was moving so quickly, they would have exposed themselves to additional risk. That potential investor lacked elementary knowledge of the industry and the business model and had not done his homework. If they had waited for this investor to become knowledgeable about the business, it would have been too late.

Take-the-Money-and-Run Myopia

A final trap in raising money for a company is a take-the-money-and-run myopia that invariably prevents an entrepreneur from evaluating one of the most critical longer-term issues: To what extent can the investor add value to the company beyond the money? Into this trap falls the entrepreneur who does not possess a clear sense that his or her prospective financial partner has the relevant experience and know-how in the market and industry area, the contacts the entrepreneur needs but does not have, the savvy and the reputation that add value in the relationship with the investor—and yet takes the money.

As has been said before, the successful development of a company can be critically affected by the interaction of the management team and the financial partners. If an effective relationship can be established, the value-added synergy can be a powerful stimulant for success. Many founders overlook the high value-added contributions tha t some investors are accustomed to making and erroneously opt for a "better deal."

Internet Impact: Resources

Real Estate Marketing and Sales

The Internet enables buyers and sellers of real estate to bypass agents whose function has been to collect data from many sources and make it available to end users. In that way, online resources are quickly changing the basis for competing and creating value in the real estate industry. Gone are the days where local agents—armed with the latest proprietary Multiple Listing Service (MLS) data—were the gatekeepers and purveyors of up-to-date information on available properties, community aspects, and comparative pricing.

Instead of spending weekends with a broker—or driving around town looking for sale signs and open houses—buyers can now conduct detailed searches on MLS portals like www.realtor.com, and on sale-by-owner sites like www.isoldmyhouse.com. For buyers looking to relocate or purchase secondary properties far from their current home, the Internet has become a powerful resource.

Despite many dire predictions in the early days of the Internet, it is unlikely that these online capabilities will ever do away with the need for professional intermediaries in the complex—and often emotional—purchase of real estate. However, as their commissions shrink along with the scope of the services they are being expected to provide, the success factor for real estate agents will be in taking on a value-added consultative role in the overall process.

Chapter Summary

- There is rarely a "fair fight" between users (entrepreneurs) and suppliers of capital (investors). Entrepreneurs need to be prepared by learning how the capital markets determine valuation risk.

- Several valuation methods are used to arrive at value for a company, the venture capital method being the most common.

- Investors prefer to stage their capital commitments, thereby managing and containing the risk and preserving their options to invest further or cease.

- Numerous potential conflicts exist between users and suppliers of capital, and these require appreciation

and managing. The economic consequences can be worth millions to founders.

- Successful deals are characterized by careful thought and sensitive balance among a range of important issues.

- Deal structure can make or break an otherwise sound venture, and the devil is always in the details.

- Negotiating the deal is both art and science, and also can make or break the relationship.

- The entrepreneur encounters numerous strategic, legal, and other "sand traps" during the fund-raising cycle and needs awareness and skill in coping with them.

Study Questions

1. Why can there be such wide variations in the valuations investors and founders place on companies?

2. What are the determinants of value?

3. Define and explain why the following are important: long-term value creation, IRR, investor's required

share of ownership, DCF, deal structure, and sand traps in fund-raising.

4. Explain five prevalent methods used in valuing a company and their strengths and weaknesses, given their underlying assumptions.

5. What is a staged capital commitment, and why is it important?

6. What is a company worth? Explain the theory and the reality of valuation.

7. What is a "cram-down" round?

8. What are some of the inherent conflicts between investors and entrepreneurs, and how and why can these affect a venture's odds for success?

9. What are the most important questions and issues to consider in structuring a deal? Why?

10. What issues can be negotiated in a venture investment, and why are these important?

11. What are the pitfalls and sand traps in fund-raising, and why do entrepreneurs sometimes fail to avoid them?

Internet Resources for Chapter 15

http://www.valuationresources.com/ *Valuation Resources is a free resource guide to business valuation resources, industry and company information, economic data, and more.*

http://www.nacva.com/ *The National Association of Certified Valuation Analysts.*

Wiki–Google Search

Try these keywords and phrases:
valuation methods
deal structure
terms sheet

negotiating deals
venture capital
dilution

MIND STRETCHERS

Have You Considered?

1. Who should and should not have outside investors in their companies?

2. It is said that a good deal structure cannot turn a bad business into a good one, but many a good business has been killed by a bad deal structure. Why is this so? Find an example of each.

3. What beliefs and assumptions are revealed by the bets made in different deals?

4. What is a good deal? Why?

5. You can negotiate anything. Why?

Case
Lightwave Technology, Inc.

Preparation Questions

1. In anticipation of an IPO, should the cofounders move forward with an additional round of bridge financing? Why or why not?

2. How would you structure and price this round, and why?

3. What should Kinson and Weiss do to grow their company?

4. How should the company evaluate and decide on whether to pursue an IPO at this time? How do they go about planning and managing that process?

The success of light-emitting diodes (LEDs) lies in their longevity (LEDs outlast incandescent lamps by a factor of 10), energy efficiency, durability, low maintenance cost, and compact size. Replacing conventional lamps with LEDs in the United States alone will bring energy benefits of up to $100 billion by 2025, saving up to 120 gigawatts of electricity annually.

Light-Emitting Diodes 2002;
Strategic Summit for LEDs in
Illumination

In the summer of 2003, seasoned entrepreneurs George Kinson and Dr. Schyler Weiss were evaluating, once again, whether to pursue an initial public offering (IPO) for their young and dynamic illumination company, Lightwave Technology.

The first time they had considered such a path was back in 2001, just before the Internet bubble burst. In the months following that dramatic reversal in the capital markets, the partners were instead forced to implement a restructuring plan to reorganize their operations. In addition to a painful write-off, the ensuing economic downturn thwarted the company's efforts to take full advantage of its leadership position in this emerging market. Nevertheless, its turnaround was successful—in large part due to Lightwave's unique and proprietary capabilities. Within just a couple of years, the company was back on track.

Because the IPO market in 2003 was still quite soft—and nobody would hazard a guess as to when it might recover—Kinson had to wonder whether it would be better to remain private until they had achieved even better numbers, as well as a greater dominance in a number of key illumination market segments. On the other hand, a successful IPO would provide capital and the high profile in the industry that could have a significant impact on their ability to do just that.

This case was prepared by Carl Hedberg under the direction of Professor Jeffry A. Timmons. © Copyright Jeffry A. Timmons, 2005. All rights reserved.

Traditional Illumination Products

The lightbulb was one of the most important inventions of the late 19th century. It revolutionized the way people lived, worked, and conducted business. Several improvements to Thomas Edison's original invention, including ductile tungsten filaments and fluorescent tubes, had modified the lighting industry, but the standard screw-in lightbulb remained the focus. The lighting market was divided into two segments: lamps (the bulbs and tubes) and fixtures (the plastic, metal, and glass housings for the lamps). In 2001 the illumination industry represented a $79 billion market: $17 billion in lamps and $62 billion in fixtures.[1] More than one-third of that market involved indoor lighting, with lamps and outdoor lighting being the next largest segments. In 2001 the United States represented 26 percent of the world market.

The illumination industry was dominated by a small group of very large, established multinationals. The major players in commercial lighting included General Electric Lighting, Philips Lighting, and OSRAM Sylvania, Inc., which together controlled 90 percent or more of the U.S. lamp market share and supplied 60 percent of the world lamp market.[2] Each major lighting manufacturer had a wide range of products for residential and commercial applications and was involved in the research and development of new products modified from existing traditional lighting technology.

Solid-State Lighting

Light-emitting diodes (LEDs)—small semiconductors encased in an epoxy material that gave off light when electrically charged—had been around since the 1960s. By varying the structure of the semiconductor, or the bandgap, the energy level of the LED changed to produce a colored light, typically either a red or a green (Exhibit 1). The first practical lighting applications of these LEDs were blinking clocks and indicators on such appliances as VCRs, microwaves, and stereos.

As solid-state lighting (SSL), LEDs exhibited theoretical quantum efficiencies (i.e., volume of light generated per unit of electrical input) of 60 to 70 percent. Legacy incandescent and fluorescent lamps had topped out at around 5 percent and 20 percent, respectively.[3] The

---

[1] Freedonia Group, Inc., www.freedoniagroup.com.
[2] P. Thurk, "Solid State Lighting: The Case for Reinventing the Light Bulb," in fulfillment of the requirements of a Kauffman Fellows Program grant, July 2002, p. 7.
[3] P. Thurk, "Solid State Lighting: The Case for Reinventing the Light Bulb," research paper in fulfillment of the requirements of a Kauffman Fellows Program, July 2002, pp. 4–5.

EXHIBIT 1

How an LED Emits Colored Light

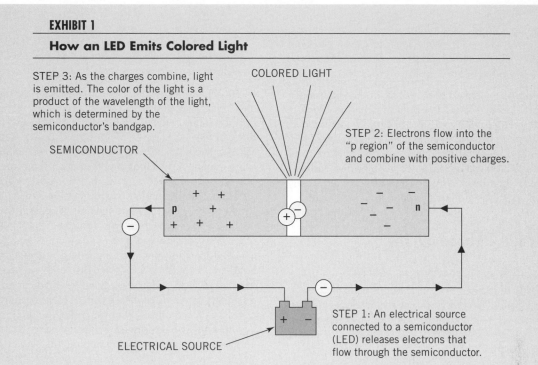

STEP 3: As the charges combine, light is emitted. The color of the light is a product of the wavelength of the light, which is determined by the semiconductor's bandgap.

COLORED LIGHT

SEMICONDUCTOR

STEP 2: Electrons flow into the "p region" of the semiconductor and combine with positive charges.

ELECTRICAL SOURCE

STEP 1: An electrical source connected to a semiconductor (LED) releases electrons that flow through the semiconductor.

balance of electricity used by typical lightbulbs was converted to heat, which limited the useful life by degrading the active elements of the light source. SSL energy efficiencies were particularly acute with respect to colorized lighting. Unlike traditional fixtures where light passed through a colored filter, SSL generated colors directly—from the emission itself. Color filters could tax the luminous output of standard lamps by as much as 70 to 80 percent.

Ultraviolet (UV) radiation from regular lights could damage or discolor many products and materials and had been shown to cause skin and eye conditions in humans. LEDs used for illumination emitted all of their light in the visible part of the color spectrum and therefore produced virtually no UV radiation.

Rather than burn out like incandescent bulbs, SSL faded over time. This attribute—in addition to long lifetimes, flexible form factors, low UV output, and strong color contrast—had begun to stimulate creative design across a range of industrial, architectural, and retail businesses. For example, the low heat, fast turn-on times, and small feature sizes of SSL had attracted automobile manufacturers, who were using the technology for their brake, accent, and console illumination.

Disruptive Ideas

George Kinson and Dr. Schyler Weiss had met while they were attending Carnegie Mellon University in the early 1990s. Kinson—outspoken and assertive—was a research engineer at the Field Robotics Center at the

university and attended classes in their Graduate School of Industrial Administration. As an undergraduate in 1993, he earned a dual major in electrical and computer engineering, with a minor in fine art.

Weiss was the more reserved half of the pair. He received his undergraduate, master's, and PhD degrees in electrical and computer engineering from Carnegie Mellon. His PhD thesis involved low-power digital circuitry. In the early 1990s Weiss and Kinson tinkered a lot with LEDs as a hobby—enough to conclude that the technology was the future of illumination. Specifically, they were anticipating the advent of a blue LED—a color they knew could be digitally "blended" with existing red and green hues to create a full spectrum of colors.

By 1994 the pair had diverged; Kinson had cofounded what would become a successful online securities portal, and Weiss had started up Weiz Solutions, developer of a mass spectrometry data acquisition software package. Despite their separate pursuits, when a Japanese group announced in 1996 that they had come up with the coveted blue LED, Kinson recalled that he and his friend were more than ready to charge ahead:

We had always figured that the development of a blue light-emitting diode would change the way that people used LEDs. It just so happened that the one they created was a very bright blue LED, and that brought about tremendous change very quickly. We realized that this new, high-intensity technology was perfect for illumination, and we had done enough research on this boring, old, complacent industry to know how slowly they would react to any sort of disruptive technology.[4] They were offering a commodity—brass, glass, and gas—not really technology at all. Even though we felt we had a pretty big window of opportunity, we wanted to move fast.

The engineers immediately got to work to develop a digital palette to "blend" the primaries. In the process, they pioneered a new industry: intelligent semiconductor illumination technologies. In the spring of 1997, Kinson left his position at his online information company and, with Weiss's help, began developing the business model, writing a business plan, and perfecting their initial prototypes for what was to be their new venture.

Lightwave Technology, Inc.

During the summer of 1997 Kinson used his savings and credit cards to finance the initial business development. After racking up $44,000 in credit card debt and seeing his savings account shrivel to $16, he incorporated Lightwave in the summer of 1997 and filed for patent protection on their color mixer.

By linking red, green, and blue LEDs to a microprocessor that controlled the combination and intensity of those primaries, Lightwave could, with a very small device, tremendously expand the color-producing capabilities of conventional lighting. In fact, each string of LEDs linked to a microprocessor could generate up to 24-bit color (16.7 million colors) and numerous dramatic effects, such as color washing and strobe lighting. They used the first successful prototype to secure more funding and build additional prototypes.

Believing that their business would grow up around the demands and imagination of a range of clients in industries from architecture to entertainment, they decided to take the bold move of demonstrating their new capabilities at one of the top lighting forums in the world.

Affirmation

The International Lighting Exposition in Las Vegas was where many lighting companies debuted their new lighting products. The small Lightwave team secured a booth and immediately became the talk of the show—as much for their innovative, colorful products as for their flashy, youthful personalities. Kinson said that the show was an affirmation that they had discovered a means to reinvent the illumination market:

> Schyler and I, accompanied by four MIT Sloan School students, flew out to this trade show with two backpacks full of prototypes. This was the first time we had shown

these in public, and then we win Architectural Lighting Product of the Year—the top award. That's a pretty good statement from the industry that intelligent semiconductor illumination technology was a significant opportunity.

As the entrepreneurs had suspected, Lightwave's new lighting capabilities had immediate appeal—particularly in the retailing markets. Output and coloration adaptability had far-reaching applications because a tiny Lightwave microprocessor system could replace existing lighting setups that often required numerous color-filtered bulbs, as well as large mechanical controls.

Besides an expanded range of color and aesthetics, Lightwave's technology had functional benefits over conventional lighting technology. The lower heat and lack of UV emissions generated by LEDs meant that SSL could be used in many applications where conventional hot lights could not, such as in retail displays and near clothing and artwork. Because Lightwave products could be designed to complement existing technologies, they could be used alongside conventional lighting products.

The team also envisioned significant economic and environmental benefit from expanding LED technologies. While conventional color lighting products had an average life of hundreds or thousands of hours, the source life of LEDs was estimated to be around 100,000 hours (equivalent to 24 hours a day for just over 11 years). Because lighting was a large user of energy (approximately 20 percent of the estimated $1 trillion spent annually on electricity[5]), SSL had the potential to produce significant savings. It was thought that for general bright white illumination for residences, hospitals, businesses, and the like, the gains from moving to SSL would lead to global annual savings of over $100 billion in electricity costs and to a reduction in carbon emissions of 200 million tons. In addition, the gains would alleviate the need for an estimated $50 billion in new electrical plant construction.[6]

The efficiency of the technology was attracting institutional users as well. California, for instance, had begun offering subsidies of up to 50 percent of the purchase price to municipalities that converted traffic signals to SSL alternatives. The state was also offering subsidy packages that could total up to 100 percent of the purchase price for businesses that switched their signage from neon to SSL.

Although the SSL segment was a small portion of the overall illumination market, the total LED segment had increased at a rate of 11 percent over the previous seven years to almost $2.3 billion in 1999. Signage lighting—which included a host of applications such as full-color outdoor displays, highway signs, and traffic signals—accounted for the largest sector of the LED market at 23 percent, or about $530 million. More narrowly, the

---

[4] Disruptive technology was an idea developed by Clayton Christensen of the Harvard Business School. In his book, *The Innovator's Dilemma*, Christensen defined a disruptive technology as an innovation that disrupted performance trajectories and resulted in the failure of the industry's leading firms.

[5] Bergh, Craford, Duggal, and Haitz, "The Promise and Challenge of Solid-State Lighting," *Physics Today*, December 2001, pp. 42–47.

[6] Tsao, Nelson, Haitz, Kish (Hewlett-Packard), "The Case for a National Research Program on Semiconductor Lighting," presented at the 1999 Optoelectronics Industry Development Association forum in Washington DC, October 6, 1999.

EXHIBIT 2

Haitz's Law: LED Light Output Increasing/Cost Decreasing

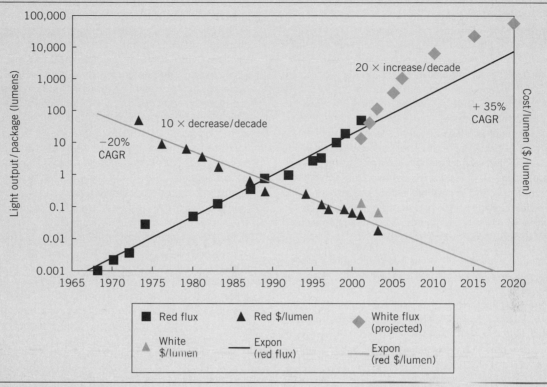

Source: Roland Haitz & Lumileds.

market for full-color LED outdoor display sign lighting grew at almost 78 percent per year from 1995 to about $150 million in 1999.

Display applications on communications equipment were the second largest sector at 22 percent of the market, closely followed by displays for computers and office equipment at 21 percent. The remainder of the market was divided among consumer applications with 15 percent of the market, automotive displays and lighting with 11 percent, and industrial instrumentation with 8 percent.[7] Of this total LED market, high-brightness LEDs—crucial to the illumination industry—had a market size of $680 million in 1999 (a nearly 500 percent growth from 1995 when the market size was $120 million). This number was projected to continue to grow to almost $1.75 billion by 2004.[8]

Despite all the proof and research and development progress that was being made at the turn of the century, illumination industry experts were very slow to embrace the use of LEDs for professional applications. Kinson explained that while there were still hurdles to overcome, he was sure that advances in SSL technology would

eventually force lighting companies to redefine the way they did business:

Similar to other disruptive technologies, LEDs are hitting an incumbent market by surprise and therefore are frequently discredited due to the traditional metrics that apply to the old market—in our case, illumination intensity and price. But what's fascinating is that while traditional "brass, gas, and glass" technology is not seeing dramatic growth, Haitz's Law (see Exhibit 2) shows that LEDs are exhibiting dramatic increases in intensity and longevity while the cost of making them is rapidly decreasing. Sure, low price and brightness are still not there for the white light market, but that will come. So everybody who works with or uses lighting in their business needs to look at what is going on here; if they don't change, they're going to be left behind.

Pioneering

Following the success at the lighting convention, Kinson finished out a financing round of $842,347 from angel investors. It had been no easy task, however. To close the round, Kinson had spoken with over 150 prospective investors and called the head of a leading lighting manufacturer 35 times before getting a response. Kinson noted, "You need to have persistence, and don't

---

[7] Strategies Unlimited, *High-Brightness LED Market Overview and Forecast*, February 2000.

[8] Ibid.

take 'No' for an answer; just keep 'smiling and dialing.' Raising money is an art."

The partners rented space across the hall from Kinson's apartment. Bootstrapping every step of the way, Kinson built the company's first computer server on a desktop computer using a Linux platform. The mail server, Web site, domain name, and office network all ran through a single desktop computer—accessed through a dial-up connection. In January 1998 they hired their first outside employee, Daniel Murdock, as vice president of finance.

As a pioneer in full-spectrum SSL technology intent on gaining a sizable lead on established players in the industry, Lightwave aggressively patented its technology and applications. The partners believed their revolutionary technology and strong intellectual property portfolio had wide-ranging market and licensing opportunities in a number of markets (see Exhibit 3). Kinson commented on this aspect of their mission:

> One of our primary strategies is to file for all the intellectual property that we can, because we realize this will be a huge market in the future. We plan to have a war chest of patents to protect our interest in the market—and quite a few of those patents will be applicable in the emerging white light segment. Our intellectual property portfolio is probably going to be the strongest asset in our company.

Lightwave shipped its first order in September 1998. The company managed a huge growth surge during the next two years, moving to a large office space in downtown Boston and expanding to over 75 employees. They continued to develop new products and applications for various markets at a frenetic pace.

In May 2000 the company opened a European sales office in London, England, and in December of that year Lightwave established a joint venture Japanese distributor in Tokyo. The venture's selling channel partners included lighting product distributors, manufacturers' representatives, and original equipment manufacturers (OEMs). Marketing efforts involved industry analyst updates, industry conferences, trade shows, Web promotions, news articles, electronic newsletters, print advertising, and speaking engagements. The marketing department also provided a variety of customer requirements, pricing, and positioning analysis for existing and new product offerings. In addition, they produced extensive material for distribution to potential customers, including presentation materials, customer profiles, product books, data sheets, product user guides, white papers, and press releases.

Determined to stay flexible and lean, the company outsourced all of its manufacturing and had no plans to develop a production capability in the future. The team developed supply agreements with a number of LED manufacturers, which allowed them to procure LEDs at favorable pricing with short lead times. Finished products and control systems were manufactured by companies in the United States and China, with the latter sup-

EXHIBIT 3

Target Markets (Excerpted from the Lightwave Offering Memorandum)

The markets for our lighting systems include the traditional markets for color-changing lighting such as theater and entertainment venues. However, many applications for this technology exist in numerous additional markets. Our lighting systems have been installed in thousands of end-user sites worldwide, in applications such as the following:

Commercial and Civic Architecture Our lighting systems are used to differentiate and accentuate architectural elements in a wide variety of corporate offices, public spaces, bridges, monuments, fountains, government facilities, churches, schools, universities, and hospitals.

Hospitality Hotels, casinos, cruise ships, restaurants, bars, and nightclubs add entertainment elements to their properties to attract and retain patrons. Dynamic lighting is an effective tool because much of this industry's business comes alive in the evening hours.

Retail and Merchandising Retailers competing for customer attention add entertainment value to the shopping experience by using dynamic lighting in their overall store design, in visual merchandising programs, and in store window displays.

Entertainment, Events, and Theatrical Production Theaters, concert halls, amusement parks, themed environments, and producers of live performances and events make extensive use of dramatic theatrical lighting and appreciate the enhanced dynamic that lighting adds to set design, stage lighting, and themed displays.

TV Production Studio-based television news programs, game shows, and talk shows use dynamic lighting to add excitement, glamour, and identity to show set designs and fill lighting.

Electronic Signage and Corporate Identity Signage and point-of-purchase designers and fabricators use dynamic lighting in projects such as backlit and uplit displays, glass signs, interior or exterior signs, and channel letters.

Residential Architecture Specialty and accent lighting are used in residential projects for applications such as cove, cabinet, undercounter, and landscape lighting, and home theaters.

Exhibits, Display, and Museums Dynamic lighting is used in trade show booths and museum displays to highlight featured areas or to add impact and entertainment value to the overall display.

plying the high-volume, low-priced items. Kinson had never stopped raising investment capital to support these efforts, and by early 2001 Lightwave had secured just over $31 million in four rounds of investment funding.[9]

Their success had certainly not gone unnoticed in the industry. Major lighting industry players had clearly begun to reevaluate the possibilities of LED technology. Since 1999 several ventures had been created between large traditional illumination companies and young, technologically advanced LED companies. Philips Lighting had joined up with Agilent Technologies to form a solid-state lighting venture called LumiLeds. Similarly, GE Lighting formed GELcore with the semiconductor company EMCORE, and OSRAM was working with LEDs in a subsidiary of Siemens in Germany. In addition, researchers from Agilent and Sandia National Laboratories in Albuquerque, New Mexico, were pressing the federal government for a $500 million, 10-year national research program on semiconductor lighting.

Kinson and his team felt that in light of these competitive tactics by multinational players, an IPO was their best strategy. They reasoned that going public would enhance their international exposure and would provide

[9] Series A—$842,347 for 1,020,285 shares; Series B—$4,354,994 for 3,956,208 shares; Series C—$13,020,880 for 3,355,897 shares; and Series D—$12,944,178 for 2,725,377 shares.

them with a significant base of capital to support rapid adoption of their products across a wide range of industries. Certain that the timing was right, they planned their public offering for the summer of 2001.

Pulling Back

Even before the terrorist attacks in September 2001, it had become painfully evident that the capital markets were softening. The Internet-driven boom had ended, and Lightwave, like many other companies, had to put on hold indefinitely its aspirations for an IPO. In the months following 9/11, the company struggled against a precipitous drop in orders and a recession-driven lack of interest by potential customers to pursue new and innovative projects. The company was forced to terminate 11 employees and abandon a large portion of a non-cancelable operating lease at their new facility in Boston.

Despite a restructuring charge of nearly $3.9 million that year, and their dashed hopes for a public offering, Lightwave continued to make progress in their core markets of architecture and entertainment. By the summer of 2003 the company had stabilized, and it appeared that Lightwave would achieve cash flow breakeven in the coming year (see Exhibits 4–6).

EXHIBIT 4

Income Statements

	2000	2001	2002	Internal Company Projections	
				2003	2004
Revenues					
Lighting systems	15,080,547	18,037,552	26,197,034	34,435,012	47,040,012
OEM and licensing	1,485,653	2,128,806	2,651,466	5,714,988	5,714,988
Total Revenues	16,566,200	20,166,358	28,848,500	40,150,000	52,755,000
Cost of Revenues					
Lighting systems	10,556,540	11,224,786	13,285,688	16,777,212	23,012,000
OEM and licensing	1,013,804	1,448,029	1,489,807	3,072,788	3,138,000
Total Cost of Revenues	11,570,344	12,672,815	14,775,495	19,850,000	26,150,000
Gross Profit	4,995,856	7,493,543	14,073,005	20,300,000	26,605,000
Operating Expenses					
Selling and marketing	9,345,322	7,847,764	7,615,145	8,515,000	11,191,000
Research and development	2,810,842	2,826,032	2,465,599	3,510,000	3,510,000
General and administrative	3,706,739	4,494,364	4,607,946	6,750,000	6,750,000
Restructuring	3,887,865		161,413		
Total Operating Expenses	19,750,768	15,168,160	14,850,103	18,775,000	21,451,000
Operating income (loss)	(14,754,912)	(7,674,617)	(777,098)	1,525,000	5,154,000
Interest income (expense), net	48,283	124,922	46,782	518,000	680,000
Equity in earnings of joint venture (Japan)	24,415	85,232	3,350	300,000	395,000
Net income (loss)	(14,682,214)	(7,464,463)	(726,966)	2,343,000	6,229,000

A Pivotal Time

With the recession apparently winding down, the air at Lightwave Technology was charged with possibility and mission. As pioneers of a clearly disruptive technology, Kinson, Weiss, and their team were in position to influence the course of the entire lighting industry into the next century. The question was how best to position their company for the next big push forward.

EXHIBIT 5

Cash Flow Statements

	2000	2001	2002
Cash Flows from Operating Activities			
Net loss	(14,682,214)	(7,464,463)	(726,966)
Adjustment to reconcile net loss to cash from operating activities:			
Depreciation and amortization	863,874	828,083	873,138
Stock-based compensation	150,000		76,449
Write-off of leasehold improvements in connection with restructuring	592,200		
Equity in earnings of joint venture (Japan)	(24,415)	(85,232)	(3,350)
Changes in current assets and liabilities			
Accounts receivable	329,027	443,049	(899,192)
Inventory	(1,588,379)	2,834,707	(1,502,304)
Prepaid expenses and other current assets	(44,526)	(62,983)	(113,144)
Restricted cash	480,848	(612,017)	676,436
Accounts payable	(675,949)	(475,901)	(41,502)
Accrued expenses	1,158,172	(757,473)	465,226
Deferred revenue	86,728	91,582	180,832
Accrued restructuring	1,956,152	(111,145)	(385,491)
Cash Flows from Operating Activities	(11,398,482)	(5,371,793)	(1,399,868)
Cash Flows from Investing Activities			
Investment in joint venture (Japan)	(165,260)		
Purchase of property and equipment	(1,085,427)	(467,181)	(519,197)
Cash Flows from Investing Activities	(1,250,687)	(467,181)	(519,197)
Cash Flows from Financing Activities			
Payments under equipment note payable and line of credit	(359,958)	(1,669,999)	(100,000)
Borrowings under line of credit	1,650,000		
Proceeds from the exercise of stock options	11,345	20,940	13,055
Proceeds from issuance of redeemable convertible preferred; net of issuance costs	17,095,382	6,883,266	
Cash Flows from Financing Activities	18,396,769	5,234,207	(86,945)
Effect of exchange rate changes on cash			3,719
Increase (Decrease) in Cash and Equivalents	5,747,600	(604,767)	(2,002,291)
Cash and equivalents: beginning of year	2,545,908	8,293,508	7,688,741
Cash and equivalents: end of year	8,293,508	7,688,741	5,686,450

EXHIBIT 6

Balance Sheets

Assets	2001	2002
Current Assets		
Cash and equivalents	7,688,741	5,686,450
Restricted cash	1,055,748	479,312
Accounts receivable	3,450,919	4,284,529
Allowance for doubtful accounts	(469,000)	(270,000)
Accounts receivable from related parties	163,217	29,799
Inventory	3,522,002	5,024,306
Prepaid expenses and other current assets	315,304	428,448
Total Current Assets	15,726,931	15,662,844
Property and Equipment: at Cost		
Computer equipment	1,334,784	1,503,046
Furniture and fixtures	640,105	624,899
Tooling	541,899	873,961
Leasehold improvements	996,882	996,882
Less: accumulated depreciation and amortization	(2,094,333)	(2,933,392)
Property and Equipment: Net	1,419,337	1,065,396
Investment in joint venture	285,082	288,432
Restricted cash: long-term portion	1,200,000	1,100,000
Total Assets	18,631,350	18,116,672

Liabilities and Stockholders' Equity (Deficiency)

	2001	2002
Current Liabilities		
Current portion of equipment note payable	100,000	
Accounts payable	1,546,392	1,483,324
Accounts payable to related party		21,566
Accrued expenses	911,956	811,970
Accrued compensation	760,567	1,471,202
Accrued restructuring	434,135	425,692
Accrued warranty	549,014	403,591
Deferred revenue	205,831	386,663
Total Current Liabilities	4,507,895	5,004,008
Accrued restructuring	1,410,872	1,033,824
Redeemable convertible preferred stock	41,115,602	41,115,602
Stockholders' Equity (Deficiency)		
Common stock, $0.001 par value; authorized 34,000,000 shares; issued and outstanding 2,781,419 and 2,804,325 shares in 2001 and 2002, respectively (12,130,979 shares pro forma)	2,781	2,804
Additional paid-in capital	214,869	304,350
Accumulated other comprehensive income	10,177	13,896
Accumulated deficit	(28,630,846)	(29,357,812)
Total Stockholders' Equity (Deficiency)	(28,403,019)	(29,036,762)
Liabilities and Stockholders' Equity	**18,631,350**	**18,116,672**

Chapter Sixteen

Obtaining Debt Capital

Leveraging a company is like driving your car with a sharp stick pointed at your heart through the steering wheel. As long as the road is smooth it works fine. But hit one bump in the road and you may be dead.

Warren Buffet

Results Expected

Capital markets can and do impact emerging companies, as we have seen. Because most new companies are heavy on equity and sweat equity, and by necessity short on or downright ineligible for debt financing, the debt credit markets aren't directly relevant for start-ups. Yet once a venture achieves some traction and a positive cash flow, bank credit is often an important part of the growing firm's financial strategy. Twice in this decade we have seen credit crises and a harsher lending environment: after the 2000 equity markets meltdown and with the subprime lending crisis in summer of 2007. This chapter aims at preparing you to cope better with such realities in the debt capital markets. But even as debt markets improve, lessons learned here will provide important competitive advantages.

Upon completion of this chapter, you will be able to

1. Identify sources of debt and explain how to access them in today's capital markets.
2. Describe the lender's perspective and criteria in making loans, how to prepare a loan proposal, and how to negotiate a loan.
3. Describe key aspects of managing and orchestrating the acquisition of debt capital.
4. Discuss how lenders estimate the debt capacity of a company.
5. Describe some tar pits entrepreneurs need to avoid in considering debt.
6. Provide ideas about and analysis of the Bank Documents case study.

2007: Subprime Loans Submerge Credit Markets

Just when the economy and outlook seem rosiest, trouble often seems to follow. Such was the unexpected story of the summer of 2007. The economy was experiencing the longest economic expansion in history without at least a 10 percent equity market correction—71 months by October 2007, which was 12 months longer than the previous record in 1982–1987 of 64 months. The real estate boom of the post-2000 stock market meltdown and post-9/11/01 economic rebound was in its finale. Risky subprime loans had fueled a new version of "irrational exuberance" that drove lending and residential real estate prices to unsustainable levels. In a few short days beginning in mid-July the party was over, with major

The authors wish to thank Babson College colleague and longtime friend Mr. Leslie Charm for his significant contributions to the revisions on this chapter.

repercussions throughout the credit and banking system. A liquidity crisis ensued; banks simply did not have enough cash to meet their obligations. As it did in 1987, the Federal Reserve stepped in to lend money to the banking system in order to avert a deepening crisis. In September 2007 it lowered the Federal Reserve discount rate a surprising 50 basis points for the first time in over four years, and more reductions were expected by early 2008. The Fed's aim was to soften the housing recession and to prevent a wider economic recession in the United States.

A Cyclical Pattern: Shades of 1990–1993

Any time such a credit crisis occurs, it takes a toll throughout the economy. For one thing, cash-strapped consumers and loan defaults evaporate spending on consumption, which is 70 percent of the entire economy. For another, banks stop lending; and when they do lend, their equity requirements jump significantly—from 10 to 25 percent in most cases.

For entrepreneurs and their investors, the punishing credit crunch and stagnant equity markets of 1990–1993 gave way to the most robust capital markets in U.S. history as we approached the end of the millennium. Interest rates reached historical lows, and the credit environment was much friendlier, mimicking the heady days of pre-crash 1987. The availability of bank loans and competition among banks increased dramatically from the dormant days of the early 1990s.

The improved credit environment led to lenders' greater awareness of growth companies' potential in the new entrepreneurial economy. Bank presidents and loan officers were aggressively seeking entrepreneurial companies as prospective clients. They worked with local universities and entrepreneurial associations to sponsor seminars, workshops, and business fairs, all to cultivate entrepreneurial customers. This was a welcome change in the credit climate for entrepreneurs. A less severe credit crunch, even with extremely low interest rates, began in 2000 and increased into 2002. By 2004 banks had become more aggressive, and throughout 2006 and into 2007 the pace of lending for real estate and private equity deals was at an all-time high. The stage was thus set for the subprime collapse and subsequent collapse of lending for these other deals. Even July's merger and acquisition activity dropped to a third of the April 2007 high. Many deals were postponed or canceled altogether. Remember though, the availability of credit is cyclical, and the fundamentals of credit don't change that much.

A Word of Caution

History suggests a favorable credit environment can and will change sometimes suddenly. When a credit climate reverses itself, personal guarantees come back. Even the most creditworthy companies with enviable records for timely repayment of interest and principal could be asked to provide personal guarantees by the owners. In addition, there could be a phenomenon viewed as a perversion of the debt capital markets. As a credit crunch becomes more severe, banks face their own illiquidity and insolvency problems, which might result in the failure of more banks as happened in the 1990s. To cope with their own balance sheet dissipation, banks can and might call the best loans first. Thousands of high-quality smaller companies can be stunned and debilitated by such actions. Also, as competition among banks lessens, pricing and terms can become more onerous as the economy continues in a period of credit tightening. Debt reduction could then become a dominant financial strategy of small and large companies alike.

The Lender's Perspective

Lenders have always been wary capital providers. Because banks may earn as little as a 1 percent net profit on total assets, they are especially sensitive to the possibility of a loss. If a bank writes off a $1 million loan to a small company, it must then be repaid an incremental $100 million in profitable loans to recover that loss.

Yet lending institutions are businesses and seek to grow and improve profitability as well. They can do this only if they find and bet on successful, young, growing companies. Historically, points and fees charged for making a loan have been a major contributor to bank profitability. During parts of the credit cycle, banks may seek various sweeteners to make loans. Take, for instance, a lending proposal for a company seeking a $15 million five-year loan. In addition to the up-front origination fees and points, the bank further proposed a YES, or yield enhancement security, as part of the loan. This additional requirement would entitle the bank to receive an additional $3 million payment from the company once its sales exceeded $10 million and it was profitable, or if it was sold, merged, or taken public. While this practice hasn't happened frequently in the current economic climate, it could be revived, depending on the cycle.

Sources of Debt Capital[1]

The principal sources of borrowed capital for new and young businesses are trade credit, commercial banks, finance companies, factors, and leasing companies.[2]

---

[1] J. A. Timmons, *Financing and Planning the New Venture* (Acton, MA: Brick House Publishing, 1990).
[2] Ibid., p. 68.

EXHIBIT 16.1

Debt Financing Sources for Types of Business

Source	Start-Up Company	Existing Company
Trade credit	Yes	Yes
Finance companies	Occasionally, with strong equity	Yes
Commercial banks	Rare (if assets are available)	Yes
Factors	Depends on nature of the customers	Yes
Leasing companies	Difficult, except for start-ups with venture capital	Yes
Mutual savings banks, savings and loans	Depends on strength of personal guarantee	Real estate and asset-based companies
Insurance companies	Rare, except alongside venture capital	Yes, depending on size
Private investors	Yes	Sometimes

Source: J. A. Timmons, *Financing and Planning the New Venture* (Acton, MA: Brick House Publishing, 1990), p. 34.

Start-ups have more difficulty borrowing money than existing businesses because they don't have assets or a track record of profitability and/or a positive cash flow. Nevertheless, start-ups managed by an entrepreneur with a track record and with significant equity in the business who can present a sound business plan can borrow money from one or more sources. Still, if little equity or collateral exists, the start-up won't have much success with banks.

The availability of such debt for high-tech start-ups can sometimes depend on where a business is located. Debt and leases as well as equity capital can be more available to start up companies in such hotbeds of entrepreneurial activity as eastern Massachusetts and Silicon Valley in California than, say, in the Midwest. The hotbed areas also feature close contact between venture capital firms and the high-technology-focused lending officers of banks. This contact tends to make it easier for start-ups and early-stage companies to borrow money, although banks rarely lend to new ventures. But even in these hotbeds, very few banks are active in this start-up environment.

The advantages and disadvantages of these sources, summarized in Exhibit 16.1, are basically determined by such obvious dimensions as the interest rate or cost of capital, the key terms, the conditions and covenants, and the fit with the owner's situation and the company's needs at the time.[3] How good a deal you can strike is a function of your relative bargaining position and the competitiveness among the alternatives.

Ultimately, most important is the person with whom you will be dealing, rather than the amount, terms, or institution. You will be better off seeking the right banker (or other provider of capital) than just the right bank. Once again, the industry and market characteristics, and the stage and health of the firm in terms of cash flow, debt coverage, and collateral, are central to the evaluation process. Exhibit 16.2 summarizes the term of financing available from these different sources. Note the difficulty in finding sources for more than one year of financing.

Finally, an enduring question entrepreneurs ask is, What is bankable? How much money can I expect to

[3] Ibid., p. 33.

EXHIBIT 16.2

Debt Financing Sources by Term of Financing

Source	Term of Financing		
	Short	**Medium**	**Long**
Trade credit	Yes	Yes	Possible
Commercial banks	Most frequently	Yes (asset-based)	Rare (depends on cash flow predictability)
Factors	Most frequently	Rare	No
Leasing companies	No	Most frequently	Some
Mutual savings banks, savings and loans	Yes	Yes	Real estate and other asset-based companies
Insurance companies	Rare	Rare	Most frequently
Private investors	Most frequently*	Yes	Rare

Source: J. A. Timmons, *Financing and Planning the New Venture* (Acton, MA: Brick House Publishing, 1990), p. 34.
*Usually as a convertible with equity or with warrants.

EXHIBIT 16.3

What Is Bankable? Specific Lending Criteria

Security	Credit Capacity
Accounts receivable	70–85% of those less than 90 days of acceptable receivables
Inventory	20–70% depending on obsolescence risk and salability
Equipment	70–80% of market value (less if specialized)
Chattel mortgage*	80% or more of auction appraisal value
Conditional sales contract	60–70% or more of purchase price
Plant improvement loan	60–80% of appraised value or cost

Source: J. A. Timmons, *Financing and Planning the New Venture* (Acton, MA: Brick House Publishing, 1990), p. 33, table 1.

*A lien on assets other than real estate breaking a loan.

---

borrow based on my balance sheet? Exhibit 16.3 summarizes some general guidelines in answer to this question. Because most loans and lines of credit are asset-based loans, knowing the lenders' guidelines is very important. The percentages of key balance sheet assets that are often allowable as collateral are only ranges and will vary from region to region, for different types of businesses, and for stages in the business cycle. For instance, nonperishable consumer goods versus technical products that may have considerable risk of obsolescence would be treated very differently in making a loan collateral computation. If the company already has significant debt and has pledged all its assets, there may not be much room for negotiations. A bank with full collateral in hand for a company having cash flow problems is unlikely to give up such a position to enable the company to attract another lender, even though the collateral is more than enough to meet these guidelines.

Trade Credit[4]

Trade credit is a major source of short-term funds for small businesses. Trade credit represents 30 percent to 40 percent of the current liabilities of nonfinancial companies, with generally higher percentages in smaller companies. It is reflected on the balance sheets as accounts payable, or sales payable—trade.

If a small business is able to buy goods and services and be given, or take, 30, 60, or 90 days to pay for them, that business has essentially obtained a loan of 30 to 90 days. Many small and new businesses are able to obtain such trade credit when no other form of debt financing is available to them. Suppliers offer trade credit as a way to get new customers, and often build the bad debt risk into their prices. Additionally, channel partners who supply trade credit often do so

with more industry-specific knowledge than can be obtained by commercial banks.[5]

The ability of a new business to obtain trade credit depends on the quality and reputation of its management and the relationships it establishes with its suppliers. Continued late payment or nonpayment may cause suppliers to cut off shipments or ship only on a COD basis. A key to keeping trade credit open is to continually pay some amount, even if it is not the full amount. Also, the real cost of using trade credit can be very high—for example, the loss of discounts for prompt payment. Because the cost of trade credit is seldom expressed as an annual amount, it should be analyzed carefully, and a new business should shop for the best terms.

Trade credit may take some of the following forms: extended credit terms; special or seasonal datings, where a supplier ships goods in advance of the purchaser's peak selling season and accepts payment 90 to 120 days later during the season; inventory on consignment, not requiring payment until sold; and loan or lease of equipment.

Commercial Bank Financing

Commercial banks prefer to lend to existing businesses that have a track record of sales, profits, and satisfied customers, and a current backlog. Their concern about the high failure rates in new businesses can make banks less than enthusiastic about making loans to such firms. They like to be lower-risk lenders, which is consistent with their profit margins. For their protection, they look first to positive cash flow and then to collateral, and in new and young businesses (depending on the credit environment) they are likely to require personal guarantees of the owners. Like equity investors, commercial

---

[4] Ibid., pp. 68–80.
[5] N. Jain, "Monitoring Costs and Trade Credit," *Quarterly Review of Economics and Finance* 41 (2001), pp. 89–111.

banks place great weight on the quality of the management team.

Notwithstanding these factors, certain banks do (rarely) make loans to start-ups or young businesses that have strong equity financings from venture capital firms. This has been especially true in such centers of entrepreneurial and venture capital activity as Silicon Valley, Boston, Los Angeles, Austin, Texas, and New York City.

Commercial banks are the primary source of debt capital for existing (not new) businesses. Small business loans may be handled by a bank's small business loan department or through credit scoring (where credit approval is done "by the numbers"). Your personal credit history will also impact the credit scoring matrix. Larger loans may require the approval of a loan committee. If a loan exceeds the limits of a local bank, part or the entire loan amount will be offered to "correspondent" banks in neighboring communities and nearby financial centers. This correspondent network enables the smaller banks in rural areas to handle loans that otherwise could not be made.

Most of the loans made by commercial banks are for one year or less. Some of these loans are unsecured, whereas receivables, inventories, or other assets secure others. Commercial banks also make a large number of intermediate term loans (or term loans) with a maturity of one to five years. On about 90 percent of these term loans, the banks require collateral, generally consisting of stocks, machinery, equipment, and real estate. Most term loans are retired by systematic, but not necessarily equal, payments over the life of the loan. Apart from real estate mortgages and loans guaranteed by the SBA or a similar organization, commercial banks make few loans with maturities greater than five years.

Banks also offer a number of services to the small business, such as computerized payroll preparation, letters of credit, international services, lease financing, and money market accounts.

There are now over 7,401 commercial banks in the United States—a 5 percent reduction in three years. A complete listing of banks can be found, arranged by states, in the *American Bank Directory* (McFadden Business Publications), published semiannually.

Line of Credit Loans

A line of credit is a formal or informal agreement between a bank and a borrower concerning the maximum loan a bank will allow the borrower for a one-year period. Often the bank will charge a fee of a certain percentage of the line of credit for a definite commitment to make the loan when requested.

Line of credit funds are used for such seasonal financings as inventory buildup and receivable financing. These two items are often the largest and most financeable items on a venture's balance sheet. It is general practice to repay these loans from the sales and reduction of short-term assets that they financed. Lines of credit can be unsecured, or the bank may require a pledge of inventory, receivables, equipment, or other acceptable assets. Unsecured lines of credit have no lien on any asset of the borrower and no priority over any trade creditor, but the banks may require that all debt to the principals and stockholders of the company be subordinated to the line of credit debt.

The line of credit is executed through a series of renewable 90-day notes. The renewable 90-day note is the more common practice, and the bank will expect the borrower to pay off his or her open loan within a year and to hold a zero loan balance for one to two months. This is known as "resting the line" or "cleaning up." Commercial banks may also generally require that a borrower maintain a checking account at the bank with a minimum ("compensating") balance of 5 percent to 10 percent of the outstanding loan.

For a large, financially sound company, the interest rates for a "prime risk" line of credit will be quoted at the prime rate or at a premium over LIBOR. (LIBOR stands for "London Interbank Offered Rate." Eurodollars—U.S. dollars held outside the United States—are most actively traded here, and banks use Eurodollars as the "last" dollars to balance the funding of their loan portfolios. Thus LIBOR represents the marginal cost of funds for a bank.) A small firm may be required to pay a higher rate. The true interest calculations should also reflect the multiple fees that may be added to the loan. Any compensating-balance or resting-the-line requirements or other fees will also increase effective interest rates.

Time-Sales Finance

Many dealers or manufacturers who offer installment payment terms to purchasers of their equipment cannot themselves finance installment or conditional sales contracts. In such situations, they sell and assign the installment contract to a bank or sales finance company. (Some very large manufacturers do their own financing through captive finance companies—such as the Ford Motor Company and Ford Credit. Most very small retailers merely refer their customer installment contracts to sales finance companies, which provide much of this financing, and on more flexible terms.)

From the manufacturer or dealer's point of view, time-sales finance is a way of obtaining short-term financing from long-term installment accounts receivable. From the purchaser's point of view, it is a way of financing the purchase of new equipment.

Under time-sales financing, the bank purchases installment contracts at a discount from their full value and takes as security an assignment of the manufacturer/dealer's interest in the conditional sales contract. In addition, the bank's financing of installment note receivables includes recourse to the seller in the event of loan default by the purchaser. Thus the bank has the payment obligation of the equipment purchaser, the manufacturer/dealer's security interest in the equipment purchased, and recourse to the manufacturer/dealer in the event of default. The bank also withholds a portion of the payment (5 percent or more) as a dealer reserve until the note is paid. Because the reserve becomes an increasing percentage of the note as the contract is paid off, an arrangement is often made when multiple contracts are financed to ensure that the reserve against all contracts will not exceed 20 percent or so.

The purchase price of equipment under a sales financing arrangement includes a "time-sales price differential" (e.g., an increase to cover the discount, typically 6 percent to 10 percent) taken by the bank that does the financing. Collection of the installments may be made directly by the bank or indirectly through the manufacturer/dealer.

Term Loans

Bank term loans are generally made for periods of one to five years, and may be unsecured or secured. Most of the basic features of bank term loans are the same for secured and unsecured loans.

Term loans provide needed growth capital to companies. They are also a substitute for a series of short-term loans made with the hope of renewal by the borrower. Banks make these generally on the basis of predictability of positive cash flow.

Term loans have three distinguishing features: Banks make them for periods of up to five years (and occasionally more); periodic repayment is required; and agreements are designed to fit the special needs and requirements of the borrower (e.g., payments can be smaller at the beginning of a loan term and larger at the end).

Because term loans do not mature for a number of years, during which time the borrower's situation and fortunes could change significantly, the bank must carefully evaluate the prospects and management of the borrowing company. Even the protection afforded by initially strong assets can be wiped out by several years of heavy losses. Term lenders stress the entrepreneurial and managerial abilities of the borrowing company. The bank will also carefully consider such things as the long-range prospects of the company and its industry, its present and projected profitability, and its ability to generate the cash required to meet the loan payments, as shown by past performance. Pricing for a term loan may be higher, reflecting a perceived higher risk from the longer term.

To lessen the risks involved in term loans, a bank will require some restrictive covenants in the loan agreement. These covenants might prohibit additional borrowing, merger of the company, payment of dividends, sales of assets, increased salaries to the owners, and the like. Also, the bank will probably require financial covenants to provide early warning of deterioration of the business, like debt to equity and cash flow to interest coverage.

Chattel Mortgages and Equipment Loans

Assigning an appropriate possession (chattel) as security is a common way of making secured term loans. The chattel is any machinery, equipment, or business property that is made the collateral of a loan in the same way as a mortgage on real estate. The chattel remains with the borrower unless there is default, in which case the chattel goes to the bank. Generally, credit against machinery and equipment is restricted primarily to new or highly serviceable and salable used items.

It should be noted that in many states, loans that used to be chattel mortgages are now executed through the security agreement forms of the Uniform Commercial Code (UCC). However, chattel mortgages are still used in many places and are still used for moving vehicles (i.e., tractors or cranes); and from custom, many lenders continue to use that term even though the loans are executed through the UCC's security agreements. The term chattel mortgage is typically from one to five years; some are longer.

Conditional Sales Contracts

Conditional sales contracts are used to finance a substantial portion of the new equipment purchased by businesses. Under a sales contract, the buyer agrees to purchase a piece of equipment, makes a nominal down payment, and pays the balance in installments over a period of from one to five years. Until the payment is complete, the seller holds title to the equipment. Hence the sale is conditional upon the buyer's completing the payments.

A sales contract is financed by a bank that has recourse to the seller should the purchaser default on the loan. This makes it difficult to finance a purchase of a good piece of used equipment at an auction. No recourse to the seller is available if the equipment is purchased at an auction; the bank would have to sell the equipment if the loan goes bad. Occasionally a firm seeking financing on existing and new equipment will sell some of its equipment to a dealer and repurchase it, together with new equipment, in order to get a conditional sales contract financed by a bank.

The effective rate of interest on a conditional sales contract is high, running to as much as 15 percent to 18 percent if the effect of installment features is considered. The purchaser/borrower should make sure the interest payment is covered by increased productivity and profitability resulting from the new equipment.

Plant Improvement Loans

Loans made to finance improvements to business properties and plants are called plant improvement loans. They can be intermediate or long-term and are generally secured by a first or second mortgage on the part of the property or plant that is being improved.

Commercial Finance Companies

The commercial bank is generally the lender of choice for a business. But when the bank says no, commercial finance companies, which aggressively seek borrowers, are a good option. They frequently lend money to companies that do not have positive cash flow, although commercial finance companies will not make loans to companies unless they consider them viable risks. In tighter credit economies, finance companies are generally more accepting of risk than are banks.

The primary factors in a bank's loan decision are the continuing successful operation of a business and its generation of more than enough cash to repay a loan. By contrast, commercial finance companies lend against the liquidation value of assets (receivables, inventory, equipment) that it understands and knows how and where to sell, and whose liquidation value is sufficient to repay the loan. Banks today own many of the leading finance companies. As a borrower gains financial strength and a track record, transfer to more attractive bank financing can be easier.

In the case of inventories or equipment, liquidation value is the amount that could be realized from an auction or quick sale. Finance companies will generally not lend against receivables more than 90 days old, federal or state government agency receivables (against which it is very difficult to perfect a lien and payment is slow), or any receivables whose collection is contingent on the performance of a delivered product.

Because of the liquidation criteria, finance companies prefer readily salable inventory items such as

electronic components or metal in such commodity forms as billets or standard shapes. Generally a finance company will not accept inventory as collateral unless it also has receivables. Equipment loans are made only by certain finance companies and against such standard equipment as lathes, milling machines, and the like. Finance companies, like people, have items with which they are more comfortable and therefore will extend more credit against certain kinds of collateral.

How much of the collateral value will a finance company lend? Generally 70 percent to 90 percent of acceptable receivables under 90 days old, 20 percent to 70 percent of the liquidation value of raw materials and/or finished goods inventory that are not obsolete or damaged, and 60 percent to 80 percent of the liquidation value of equipment, as determined by an appraiser, are acceptable. Receivables and inventory loans are for one year, whereas equipment loans are for three to seven years.

All these loans have tough prepayment penalties: Finance companies do not want to be immediately replaced by banks when a borrower has improved its credit image. Generally finance companies require a three-year commitment to do business with them, with prepayment fees if this provision is not met.

The data required for a loan from a finance company includes all that would be provided to a bank, plus additional details for the assets being used as collateral. For receivables financing, this includes detailed aging of receivables (and payables) and historical data on sales, returns, or deductions (all known as dilution), and collections.

For inventory financing, it includes details on the items in inventory, how long they have been there, and their rate of turnover. Requests for equipment loans should be accompanied by details on the date of purchase, cost of each equipment item, and appraisals, which are generally always required. These appraisals must be made by acceptable (to the lender) outside appraisers.

The advantage of dealing with a commercial finance company is that it will make loans that banks will not, and it can be flexible in lending arrangements. The price a finance company exacts for this is an interest rate anywhere from 0 to 6 percent over that charged by a bank, prepayment penalties, and, in the case of receivables loans, recourse to the borrower for unpaid collateralized receivables.

Because of their greater risk taking and asset-based lending, finance companies usually place a larger reporting and monitoring burden on the borrowing firm to stay on top of the receivables and inventory serving as loan collateral. Personal guarantees will generally be required from the principals of the business. A finance company or bank will generally reserve the right to reduce the percentage of the value lent against receivables or inventory if it gets nervous about the borrower's survivability.

Factoring

Factoring is a form of accounts receivable financing. However, instead of borrowing and using receivables as collateral, the receivables are sold, at a discounted value, to a factor. Factoring is accomplished on a discounted value of the receivables pledged. Invoices that do not meet the factor's credit standard will not be accepted as collateral. (Receivables more than 90 days old are not normally accepted.) A bank may inform the purchaser of goods that the account has been assigned to the bank, and payments are made directly to the bank, which credits them to the borrower's account. This is called a notification plan. Alternatively, the borrower may collect the accounts as usual and pay off the bank loan; this is a nonnotification plan.

Factoring can make it possible for a company to secure a loan that it might not otherwise get. The loan can be increased as sales and receivables grow. However, factoring can have drawbacks. It can be expensive, and trade creditors sometimes regard factoring as evidence of a company in financial difficulty, except in certain industries.

In a standard factoring arrangement, the factor buys the client's receivables outright, without recourse, as soon as the client creates them by shipment of goods to customers. Although the factor has recourse to the borrowers for returns, errors in pricing, and so on, the factor assumes the risk of bad debt losses that develop from receivables it approves and purchases. Many factors, however, provide factoring only on a recourse basis.

Cash is made available to the client as soon as proof is provided (old-line factoring) or on the average due date of the invoices (maturity factoring). With maturity factoring, the company can often obtain a loan of about 90 percent of the money a factor has agreed to pay on a maturity date. Most factoring arrangements are for one year.

Factoring can also be on a recourse basis. In this circumstance, the borrower must replace unpaid receivables after 90 days with new current receivables to allow the borrowings to remain at the same level.

Factoring fits some businesses better than others. For a business that has annual sales volume in excess of $300,000 and a net worth over $50,000 that sells on normal credit terms to a customer base that is 75 percent credit rated, factoring is a real option. Factoring has become almost traditional in such industries as textiles, furniture manufacturing, clothing manufacturing, toys, shoes, and plastics.

The same data required from a business for a receivable loan from a bank are required by a factor. Because a factor is buying receivables with no recourse, it will analyze the quality and value of a prospective client's receivables. It will want a detailed aging of receivables plus historical data on bad debts, return, and allowances. It will also investigate the credit history of customers to whom its client sells and establish credit limits for each customer. The business client can receive factoring of customer receivables only up to the limits so set.

The cost of financing receivables through factoring is higher than that of borrowing from a bank or a finance company. The factor is assuming the credit risk, doing credit investigations and collections, and advancing funds. A factor generally charges up to 2 percent of the total sales factored as a service charge.

There is also an interest charge for money advanced to a business, usually 2 percent to 6 percent above prime. A larger, established business borrowing large sums would command a better interest rate than the small borrower with a onetime, short-term need. Finally, factors withhold a reserve of 5 percent to 10 percent of the receivables purchased.

Factoring is not the cheapest way to obtain capital, but it does quickly turn receivables into cash. Moreover, although more expensive than accounts receivable financing, factoring saves its users credit agency fees, salaries of credit and collection personnel, and maybe bad debt write-offs. Factoring also provides credit information on collection services that may be better than the borrower's.

Leasing Companies

The leasing industry has grown substantially in recent years, and lease financing has become an important source of medium-term financing for businesses. There are about 700 to 800 leasing companies in the United States. In addition, many commercial banks and finance companies have leasing departments. Some leasing companies handle a wide variety of equipment, while others specialize in certain types of equipment—machine tools, electronic test equipment, and the like.

Common and readily resalable items such as automobiles, trucks, typewriters, and office furniture can be leased by both new and existing businesses. However, the start-up will find it difficult to lease other kinds of industrial, computer, or business equipment without providing a letter of credit or a certificate of deposit to secure the lease, or personal guarantees from the founders or from a wealthy third party.

An exception to this condition is high-technology start-ups that have received substantial venture capital. Some of these ventures have received large amounts of lease financing for special equipment from equity-oriented lessors, who receive some form of stock purchase rights in return for providing the start-up's lease line. Equate (of Oakland, California, with offices in Boston, New York, and Dallas) and Intertec (of Mill Valley, California) are two examples of companies doing this sort of venture leasing. Like many financing options, availability of venture leasing may be reduced significantly in tight money markets.

Generally industrial equipment leases have a term of three to five years but in some cases may run longer. There can also be lease renewal options for 3 percent to 5 percent per year of the original equipment value. Leases are usually structured to return the entire cost of the leased equipment plus finance charges to the lessor, although some so-called operating leases do not, over their term, produce revenues equal to or greater than the price of the leased equipment.

Typically an up-front payment is required of about 10 percent of the value of the item being leased. The interest rate on equipment leasing may be more or less than other forms of financing, depending on the equipment leased, the credit of the lessee, and the time of year.

Leasing credit criteria are similar to the criteria used by commercial banks for equipment loans. Primary considerations are the value of the equipment leased, the justification of the lease, and the lessee's projected cash flow over the lease term.

Should a business lease equipment? Leasing has certain advantages. It enables a young or growing company to conserve cash and can reduce its requirements for equity capital. Leasing can also be a tax advantage because payments can be deducted over a shorter period than can depreciation.

Finally, leasing provides the flexibility of returning equipment after the lease period if it is no longer needed or if it has become technologically obsolete. This can be a particular advantage to high-technology companies.

Leasing may or may not improve a company's balance sheet because accounting practice currently requires that the value of the equipment acquired in a capital lease be reflected on the balance sheet. Operating leases, however, do not appear on the balance sheet. Generally this is an issue of economic ownership rather than legal ownership. If the economic risk is primarily with the lessee, it must be capitalized and it therefore goes on the balance sheet along with the corresponding debt. Depreciation also follows the risk, along with the corresponding tax benefits. Start-ups that don't need such tax relief should be able to acquire more favorable terms with an operating lease.

Before the Loan Decision

Much of the following discussion of lending practices and decisions applies to commercial finance company lenders as well as to banks. A good lender relationship can sometimes mean the difference between the life and death of a business during difficult times. There have been cases where one bank has called its loans to a struggling business, causing it to go under, and another bank has stayed with its loans and helped a business to survive and prosper.

Banks that will not make loans to start-ups and early-stage ventures generally cite the lack of an operating track record as the primary reason for turning down a loan. Lenders that make such loans usually do so for previously successful entrepreneurs of means or for firms backed by investors with whom they have had prior relationships and whose judgment they trust (e.g., established venture capital firms when they believe that the venture capital company will invest in the next round).

In centers of high technology and venture capital, the main officers of the major banks will have one or more high-technology lending officers who specialize in making loans to early-stage, high-technology ventures. Through much experience, these bankers have come to understand the market and operating idiosyncrasies, problems, and opportunities of such ventures. They generally have close ties to venture capital firms and will refer entrepreneurs to such firms for possible equity financing. The venture capital firms, in turn, will refer their portfolio ventures to the bankers for debt financing.

What should an entrepreneur consider in choosing a lender? What is important in a lending decision? How should entrepreneurs relate to their lenders on an ongoing basis? In many ways the lender's decision is similar to that of the venture capitalist. The goal is to make money for his or her company through interest earned on good loans; the lender fears losing money by making bad loans to companies that default on their loans. To this end, he or she avoids risk by building in every conceivable safeguard. The lender is concerned with the client company's loan coverage, its ability to repay, and the collateral it can offer. Finally, but most important, he or she must judge the character and quality of the key managers of the company to whom the loan is being made.

Babson College Adjunct Professor Leslie Charm offers the following advice to entrepreneurs seeking to develop a constructive banking relationship:

Industry experience is critical. Choose a banker who understands your particular industry. He or she will have other clients in the same industry

EXHIBIT 16.4

Key Steps in Obtaining a Loan

Before choosing and approaching a banker or other lender, the entrepreneur and his or her management team should prepare by taking the following steps:

- Decide how much growth they want, and how fast they want to grow, observing the dictum that financing follows strategy.
- Determine how much money they require, when they need it, and when they can pay it back. To this end, they must
  —Develop a schedule of operating and asset needs.
  —Prepare a real-time cash flow projection.
  —Decide how much capital they need.
  —Specify how they will use the funds they borrow.
- Revise and update the "corporate profile" in their business plan. This should consist of
  —The core ingredients of the plan in the form of an executive summary.
  —A history of the firm (as appropriate).
  —Summaries of the financial results of the past three years.
  —Succinct descriptions of their markets and products.
  —A description of their operations.
  —Statements of cash flow and financial requirements.
  —Descriptions of the key managers, owners, and directors.
  —A rundown of the key strategies, facts, and logic that guide them in growing the corporation.
- Identify potential sources for the type of debt they seek, and the amount, rate, terms, and conditions they seek.
- Select a bank or other lending institution, solicit interest, and prepare a presentation.
- Prepare a written loan request.
- Present their case, negotiate, and then close the deal.

After the loan is granted, borrowers should maintain an effective relationship with the lending officer.

Source: J. A. Timmons, *Financing and Planning the New Venture* (Acton, MA: Brick Housing Publishing, 1990), pp. 82–83.

and may serve as a valuable resource for networking and service professionals with relevant experience. In addition, a bank that understands your industry will be more tolerant of problems and better able to help you exploit your opportunities. In the case of funding requests, bankers with industry knowledge are more apt to make a quick and reasoned determination.

Understand their business model. Every bank has different criteria with regard to working with new ventures, and their lending decisions are largely based on quantitative credit scoring metrics. The entrepreneur needs to understand how a particular bank works and determine whether that model is a fit with his or her venture.

Understand whom you're dealing with. Bankers are relationship managers whose job is to support their clients—including expediting the approval of loans and credit lines that fit with their bank's lending criteria. Like a lot of good vendors, the best of them have specialized knowledge and excellent contacts, and will take a genuine interest in your business.

Exhibit 16.4 outlines the key steps in obtaining a loan. Because of the importance of a banking relationship, an entrepreneur should shop around before making a choice. As Leslie Charm pointed out, the criteria for selecting a bank should be based on a lot more than just loan interest rates. Equally important, entrepreneurs should not wait until they have a dire need for funds to try to establish a banking relationship. When an entrepreneur faces a near-term financial crisis, the venture's financial statements are at their worst, and the banker has good cause to wonder about management's financial and planning skills—all to the detriment of the entrepreneur's chance of getting a loan.

G. B. Baty and J. M. Stancill describe some factors that are especially important to an entrepreneur in selecting a bank. First, the entrepreneur should consult accountants, attorneys, and other entrepreneurs who have had dealings with the bank.[6] The advice of entrepreneurs who have dealt with a bank through good and bad times can be especially useful. Second, the entrepreneur should meet with loan officers at several banks and systematically explore their attitudes and approaches to their business borrowers.

---

[6] G. B. Baty, *Entrepreneurship: Playing to Win* (Reston, VA: Reston Publishing, 1974), and J. M. Stancill, "Getting the Most from Your Banking Relationship," *Harvard Business Review*, March–April 1980.

Who meets with you, for how long, and with how many interruptions can be useful measures of a bank's interest in your account. Finally, ask for small business references from their list of borrowers and talk to the entrepreneurs of those firms. Throughout all of these contacts and discussions, check out particular loan officers as well as the viability of the bank itself; they are a major determinant of how the bank will deal with you and your venture.

The bank selected should be big enough to service your venture's foreseeable loans but not so large as to be relatively indifferent to your business. Banks differ greatly in their desire and capacity to work with small firms. Some banks have special small business loan officers and regard new and early-stage ventures as the seeds of very large future accounts. Other banks see such new venture loans as merely bad risks. Does the bank tend to call or reduce its loans to small businesses that have problems? When it has less capital to lend, will it cut back on small business loans and favor older, more solid customers? Is the bank imaginative, creative, and helpful when a venture has a problem or when things get tough? Or do they start looking in the small print for a quick exit? (See the accompanying box.) To quote Baty, "Do they just look at your balance sheet and faint, or do they try to suggest constructive financial alternatives?"

Approaching and Meeting the Banker

Obtaining a loan is, among other things, a sales job. Many borrowers tend to forget this. An entrepreneur with an early-stage venture must sell himself or herself as well as the viability and potential of the business to the banker. This is much the same situation that the early-stage entrepreneur faces with a venture capitalist.

The initial contact with a lender will likely be by telephone. The entrepreneur should be prepared to describe quickly the nature, age, and prospects of the venture; the amount of equity financing and who provided it; the prior financial performance of the business; the entrepreneur's experience and background; and the sort of bank financing desired. A referral from a venture capital firm, a lawyer or accountant, or other business associate who knows the banker can be very helpful.

If the loan officer agrees to a meeting, he or she may ask that a summary loan proposal, description of the business, and financial statements be sent ahead

Small Print, Big Problems

Matt Coffin, founder of LowerMyBills.com, was less than two years into his venture when the markets began to soften during the summer of 2001. Matt had just received a term sheet from a respected venture capitalist and a most unwelcome call from his bank:

> In the late 990s we had established a million-dollar line through a big bank in Silicon Valley— which at the time was giving out credit lines like candy. We had drawn down that line and now our cash balance was $750,000—less than what we owed them.
>
> So they sent over what they call an *adverse change notice*. At the time I had signed the documents I didn't even know what that meant; yeah sure, just give me the million dollars.
>
> Now I realize that an adverse change notice is a small print clause that allows the bank to demand immediate repayment of the outstanding balance—pretty much at any time they felt like it. If you can't do that, they can take all the cash on hand and begin calling in assets. So now, instead of running my business and raising money, I was meeting with lawyers and fighting with my bank just to stay alive. Over time, it became clear that they were basically trying to squeeze me for more—that is, warrant coverage as a percentage of the loan.

Seeing how dire the situation was becoming at LowerMyBills.com—and how close the venture had been to turning the corner—original investors came forward to help out. Investor Brett Markinson said that they all understood that Matt was the type of individual to support in a down market:

> Everyone, including myself, had gotten sucked into the idea of raising as much money as you could and spending it on making noise. Matt had focused on raising as little as possible; he just kept his head down and concerned himself with driving value.
>
> Since Matt hadn't raised too much money and had maintained a lean infrastructure, he was in a good position to really take advantage of the circumstances. While everyone else was cutting back or going out of business, Matt was able to rent space at a great price and hire excellent talent at a great price.

With a couple of investors putting in their own money, LowerMyBills.com was able to pay off the bank and secure the round. In the last quarter of that year, LowerMyBills.com posted its first profit, and in May 2005 Matt harvested the company for $330 million.

Source: Adapted from the "Matt Coffin" teaching case, Babson College, 2005.

of time. A well-prepared proposal and a request for a reasonable amount of equity financing should pique a banker's interest.

The first meeting with a loan officer will likely be at the venture's place of business. The banker will be interested in meeting the management team, seeing how team members relate to the entrepreneur, and getting a sense of the financial controls and reporting used and how well things seem to be run. The banker may also want to meet one or more of the venture's equity investors. Most of all, the banker is using this meeting to evaluate the integrity and business acumen of those who will ultimately be responsible for the repayment of the loan.

Throughout meetings with potential bankers, the entrepreneur must convey an air of self-confidence and knowledge. If the banker is favorably impressed by what has been seen and read, he or she will ask for further documents and references and begin to discuss the amount and timing of funds that the bank might lend to the business.

What the Banker Wants to Know[7]

You first need to describe the business and its industry. Exhibit 16.5 suggests how a banker "sees a company" from what the entrepreneur might say. What are you going to do with the money? Does the use of the loan make business sense? Should some or all of the money required be equity capital rather than debt? For new and young businesses, lenders do not like to see total debt-to-equity ratios greater than 1. The answers to these questions will also determine the type of loan (e.g., line of credit or term):

1. How much do you need? You must be prepared to justify the amount requested and describe how the debt fits into an overall plan for financing and developing the business. Further, the amount of the loan should have enough cushion to allow for unexpected developments (see Exhibit 16.6).

2. When and how will you pay it back? This is an important question. Short-term loans for seasonal inventory buildups or for financing receivables are easier to obtain than long-term loans, especially for early-stage businesses. How the loan will be repaid is the bottom-line question. Presumably you are borrowing money to finance activity that will generate enough cash to repay the loan. What is your contingency plan if things go wrong? Can you describe such risks and indicate how you will deal with them?

3. What is the secondary source of repayment? Are there assets or a guarantor of means?

EXHIBIT 16.5

How Your Banker Interprets the Income Statement

Sales	What do you sell?
	Whom do you sell to?
Cost of goods	How do you buy?
	What do you buy?
	Whom do you buy from?
Gross margin	Are you a supermarket or a boutique?
Selling	How do you sell and distribute the product?
G&A: general and administration	How much overhead and support are needed to operate?
R&D	How much is reinvested in the product?
Operating margins	Dollars available before financing costs?
Interest expense	How big is this fixed nut?
Profit before taxes	Do you make money?
Taxes	Corporation or LLC?
Profit after taxes	
Dividends/withdrawals	How much and to whom?
	How much money is left in the company?

Source: This exhibit was created by Kathie S. Stevens and Leslie Charm as part of a class discussion in the Entrepreneurial Finance course at Babson College, and is part of a presentation titled "Cash Is King, Assets Are Queen, and Everybody Is Looking for an Ace in the Hole." Ms. Stevens is former chief lending officer and member of the credit committee for a Boston bank.

---

[7] This section is drawn from Timmons, *Financing and Planning the New Venture* (Action, MA: Brick House Publishing, 1990), p. 85–88.

EXHIBIT 16.6

Sample of a Summary Loan Proposal

Date of request:	May 30, 2008	
Borrower:	Curtis-Palmer & Company, Inc.	
Amount:	$4,200,000	
Use of proceeds:	A/R, up to	$1,600,000
	Inventory, up to	824,000
	WIP, up to	525,000
	Marketing, up to	255,000
	Ski show specials	105,000
	Contingencies	50,000
	Officer loans due	841,000
		$4,200,000
Type of loan:	Seasonal revolving line of credit	
Closing date:	June 15, 2008	
Term:	One year	
Rate:	Prime plus ½ percent, no compensating balances, no points or origination fees	
Takedown:	$500,000 at closing	
	$1,500,000 on August 1, 2008	
	$1,500,000 on October 1, 2008	
	$700,000 on November 1, 2010	
Collateral:	70 percent of acceptable A/R under 90 days	
	50 percent of current inventory	
Guarantees:	None	
Repayment schedule:	$4,200,000 or balance on anniversary of note	
Source of funds for repayment:	a. Excess cash from operations (see cash flow)	
	b. Renewable and increase of line if growth is profitable	
	c. Conversion to three-year note	
Contingency source:	a. Sale and leaseback of equipment	
	b. Officer's loans (with a request for a personal guarantee)	

Source: Updated and adapted from J. A. Timmons, *Financing and Planning the New Venture* (Acton, MA: Brick House Publishing, 1990), p. 86.

4. When do you need the money? If you need the money tomorrow, forget it. You are a poor planner and manager. On the other hand, if you need the money next month or the month after, you have demonstrated an ability to plan ahead, and you have given the banker time to investigate and process a loan application. Typically it is difficult to get a lending decision in less than three weeks (some smaller banks still have once-a-month credit meetings).

One of the best ways for all entrepreneurs to answer these questions is from a well-prepared business plan. This plan should contain projections of cash flow, profit and loss, and balance sheets that will demonstrate the need for a loan and how it can be repaid. Particular attention will be given by the lender to the value of the assets and the cash flow of the business, and to such financial ratios as current assets to current liabilities, gross margins, net worth to debt, accounts receivable and payable periods, inventory turns, and net profit to sales. The ratios for the borrower's venture will be compared to averages for competing firms to see how the potential borrower measures up to them.

For an existing business, the lender will want to review financial statements from prior years prepared or audited by a CPA, a list of aged receivables and payables, the turnover of inventory, and lists of key customers and creditors. The lender will also want to know that all tax payments are current. Finally, he or she will need to know details of fixed assets and any liens on receivables, inventory, or fixed assets.

The entrepreneur–borrower should regard his or her contacts with the bank as a sales mission and provide required data promptly and in a form that can be readily understood. The better the material entrepreneurs can supply to demonstrate their business credibility, the easier and faster it will be to obtain a positive lending decision. The entrepreneur should also ask, early on, to meet with the banker's boss. This can go a long way to help obtain financing. Remember that you need to build a relationship with a bank—not just a banker.

The Lending Decision

One of the significant changes in today's lending environment is the centralized lending decision. Traditionally loan officers might have had up to several million dollars of lending authority and could make loans to small companies. Besides the company's creditworthiness as determined by analysis of its past results via the balance sheet, income statement, cash flow, and collateral, the lender's assessment of the character and reputation of the entrepreneur was central to the decision. Because loan decisions are made increasingly by loan committees or credit scoring, this face-to-face part of the decision process has given way to deeper analysis of the company's business plan, cash flow drivers and dissipaters, competitive environment, and the cushion for loan recovery given the firm's game plan and financial structure.

The implication for entrepreneurs is a demanding one: You can no longer rely on your salesmanship and good relationship with your loan officer alone to continue to get favorable lending decisions. You, or the key team member, need to be able to prepare the necessary analysis and documentation to convince people (you may never meet) that the loan will be repaid. You also need to know the financial ratios and criteria used to compare your loan request with industry norms and to defend the analysis. Such a presentation can make it easier and faster to obtain approval of a loan because it gives your relationship manager the ammunition to defend your loan request.

Lending Criteria

First and foremost, as with equity investors, the quality and track record of the management team will be a major factor. Historical financial statements, which show three to five years of profitability, are also essential. Well-developed business projections that articulate the company's sales estimates, market niche, cash flow, profit projections, working capital, capital expenditure, uses of proceeds, and evidence of competent accounting and control systems are essential.

In its simplest form, what is needed is analysis of the available collateral, based on guidelines such as those shown in Exhibit 16.3, and of debt capacity determined by analysis of the coverage ratio once the new loan is in place. Interest coverage is calculated as earnings before interest and taxes divided by interest (EBIT/interest). A business with steady, predictable cash flow and earnings would require a lower coverage ratio (say, in the range of 2) than would a company with a volatile, unpredictable cash flow stream—for example, a high-technology company with risk of competition and obsolescence (which might require a coverage ratio of 5 or more). The bottom line, of course, is the ability of the company to repay both interest and principal on time.

Loan Restrictions[8]

A loan agreement defines the terms and conditions under which a lender provides capital. With it, lenders do two things: try to assure repayment of the loan as agreed and try to protect their position as creditor. Within the loan agreement (as in investment agreements) there are negative and positive covenants. Negative covenants are restrictions on the borrower: for example, no further additions to the borrower's total debt, no pledge to others of assets of the borrower, and no payment of dividends or limitation on owners' salaries.

Positive covenants define what the borrower must do. Some examples are maintenance of some minimum net worth or working capital, prompt payment of all federal and state taxes, adequate insurance on key people and property, repayment of the loan and interest according to the terms of the agreement, and provision to the lender of periodic financial statements and reports.

Some of these restrictions can hinder a company's growth, such as a flat restriction on further borrowing. Such a borrowing limit is often based on the borrower's assets at the time of the loan. However, rather than stipulating an initially fixed limit, the loan agreement should recognize that as a business grows and increases its total assets and net worth, it will need and be able to carry the additional debt required to sustain its growth; but banks (especially in tighter credit periods) will still put maximums after allowed credit because this gives them another opportunity to recheck the loan. Similarly, covenants that require certain minimums on working capital or current ratios may be difficult for a highly seasonal business, for example, to maintain at all times of the year. Only analysis of past financial monthly statements can indicate whether such a covenant can be met.

Covenants to Look For

Before borrowing money, an entrepreneur should decide what sorts of restrictions or covenants are acceptable. Attorneys and accountants of the company should be consulted before any loan papers are signed. Some covenants are negotiable (this changes with the overall credit economy), and an entrepreneur

---

[8] Ibid., pp. 90–94.

should negotiate to get terms that the venture can live with next year as well as today. Once loan terms are agreed upon and the loan is made, the entrepreneur and the venture will be bound by them. Beware if the bank says, "Yes, but . . ."

- Wants to put constraints on your permissible financial ratios.
- Stops any new borrowing.
- Wants a veto on any new management.
- Disallows new products or new directions.
- Prevents acquiring or selling any assets.
- Forbids any new investment or new equipment.

What follows are some practical guidelines about personal guarantees: when to expect them, how to avoid them, and how to eliminate them.

Personal Guarantees and the Loan

Personal guarantees may be required of the lead entrepreneur or, more likely, shareholders of significance (more than 10 percent) who are also members of the senior management team. Also, personal guarantees are often "joint and severable"—meaning that each guarantor is liable for the total amount of the guarantee.

When to Expect Them

- If you are undercollateralized.
- If there are shareholder loans or lots of "due to" and "due from" officer accounts.
- If you have had a poor or erratic performance.
- If you have management problems.
- If your relationship with your banker is strained.
- If you have a new loan officer.
- If there is turbulence in the credit markets.
- If there has been a wave of bad loans made by the lending institution, and a crackdown is in force.
- If there is less understanding of your market.

How to Avoid Them

- Good to spectacular performance.
- Conservative financial management.
- Positive cash flow over a sustained period.
- Adequate collateral.
- Careful management of the balance sheet.
- If they are required in the deal, negotiate elimination *upfront* when you have some bargaining chips, based on certain performance criteria.

How to Eliminate Them (If You Already Have Them)

- See "How to Avoid Them."
- Develop a financial plan with performance targets and a timetable.
- Stay active in the search for backup sources of funds.

Building a Relationship

After obtaining a loan, entrepreneurs should cultivate a close working relationship with their bankers. Too many businesspeople do not see their lending officers until they need a loan. The astute entrepreneur will take a much more active role in keeping a banker informed about the business, thereby improving the chances of obtaining larger loans for expansion and cooperation from the bank in troubled times.

Some of the things that should be done to build such a relationship are fairly simple.[9] In addition to monthly and annual financial statements, bankers should be sent product news releases and any trade articles about the business or its products. The entrepreneur should invite the banker to the venture's facility, review product development plans and the prospects for the business, and establish a personal relationship with him or her. If this is done, when a new loan is requested, the lending officer will feel better about recommending its approval.

What about bad news? Never surprise a banker with bad news; make sure he or she sees it coming as soon as you do. Unpleasant surprises are a sign that an entrepreneur is not being candid with the banker or that management does not have the business under the proper control. Either conclusion by a banker is damaging to the relationship.

If a future loan payment cannot be met, entrepreneurs should not panic and avoid their bankers. On the contrary, they should visit their banks and explain why the loan payment cannot be made and say when it will be made. If this is done before the payment due date and the entrepreneur–banker relationship is good, the banker may go along. What else can he or she do? If an entrepreneur has convinced a banker of the viability and future growth of a business, the banker really does not want to call a loan and lose a customer to a competitor or cause bankruptcy. The real key to communicating with a banker is candidly to inform but not to scare. In other words, entrepreneurs must indicate that they are aware of adverse events and have a plan for dealing with them.

To build credibility with bankers further, entrepreneurs should borrow before they need to and then

---

[9] Baty, *Entrepreneurship: Playing to Win.*

repay the loan. This will establish a track record of borrowing and reliable repayment. Entrepreneurs should also make every effort to meet the financial targets they set for themselves and have discussed with their banker. If this cannot be done, the credibility of the entrepreneur will erode, even if the business is growing.

Bankers have a right to expect an entrepreneur to continue to use them as the business grows and prospers, and not to go shopping for a better interest rate. In return, entrepreneurs have the right to expect that their bank will continue to provide them with needed loans, particularly during difficult times when a vacillating loan policy could be dangerous for business survival.

The TLC of a Banker or Other Lender

1. Your banker is your partner, not a difficult minority shareholder.
2. Be honest and straightforward in sharing information.
3. Invite the banker to see your business in operation.
4. Always avoid overdrafts, late payments, and late financial statements.
5. Answer questions frankly and honestly. *Tell the truth.* Lying is illegal and undoubtedly violates loan covenants.
6. Understand the business of banking.
7. Have an "ace in the hole."

What to Do When the Bank Says No

What do you do if the bank turns you down for a loan? Regroup, and review the following questions.

1. Does the company really need to borrow now? Can cash be generated elsewhere? Tighten the belt. Are some expenditures unnecessary? Sharpen the financial pencil: Be lean and mean.
2. What does the balance sheet say? Are you growing too fast? Compare yourself to published industry ratios to see if you are on target.
3. Does the bank have a clear and comprehensive understanding of your needs? Did you really get to know your loan officer? Did you do enough homework on the bank's criteria and its likes and dislikes? Was your loan officer too busy to give your borrowing package proper consideration? A loan officer may have 50 to as many as 200 accounts. Is your relationship with the bank on a proper track?

4. Was your written loan proposal realistic? Was it a normal request, or something that differed from the types of proposals the bank usually sees? Did you make a verbal request for a loan without presenting any written backup?
5. Do you need a new loan officer or a new bank? If your answers to the previous questions put you in the clear, and your written proposal was realistic, call the head of the commercial loan department and arrange a meeting. Sit down and discuss the history of your loan effort, the facts, and the bank's reasons for turning you down.
6. Who else might provide this financing (ask the banker who turned you down)?

You should be seeing multiple lenders at the same time so you don't run out of time or money.

Tar Pits: Entrepreneurs Beware

Modern corporate financial theory has preached the virtues of zero cash balances and the use of leverage to enhance return on equity. When applied to closely held companies whose dream is to last forever, such thinking can be extremely destructive. If you judge by the 1980s, the excessive leverage used by so many larger companies was apparently simply not worth the risk: Two-thirds of the LBOs done in the 1980s have ended up in serious trouble. The serious erosion of IBM began about the same time that the company acquired debt on its balance sheet for the very first time, in the early 1980s. This problem was manifest in the acquisition binges of the early 1990s and in the high-technology feeding frenzy of the late 1990s. Following the 2000–2003 downturn, LBOs once again emerged as a popular growth vehicle.

Beware of Leverage: The ROE Mirage

According to the theory, one can significantly improve return on equity (ROE) by utilizing debt. Thus the present value of a company would also increase significantly as the company went from a zero debt-to-equity ratio to 100 percent, as shown in Exhibit 16.7. On closer examination, however, such an increase in debt improves the present value, given the 2 percent to 8 percent growth rates shown, by only 17 percent to 26 percent. If the company gets into any trouble—and the odds of that happening sooner or later are very high—its options and flexibility become seriously constrained by the covenants of the senior lenders. Leverage creates an unforgiving capital structure, and the potential additional ROI often is not worth the risk. If the upside is worth

EXHIBIT 16.7

Total Present Value

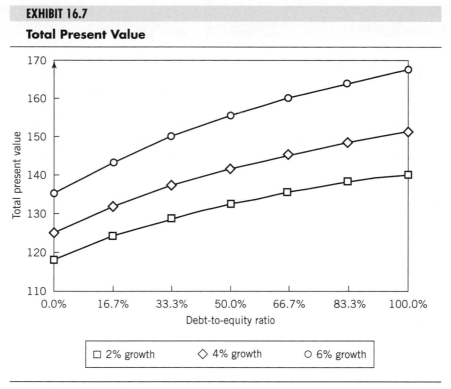

Source: W. A. Sahlman, "Note on Free Cash Flow Valuation Models," HBS Note 288-023, figure 5.

risking the loss of the entire company should adversity strike, then go ahead. This is easier said than survived, however.

Ask any entrepreneur who has had to deal with the workout specialists in a bank and you will get a sobering, if not frightening, message: It is hell and you will not want to do it again.

IRS: Time Bomb for Personal Disaster

There is a much lesser known tar pit that entrepreneurs need to be aware of when considering leveraging their companies. Once the company gets into serious financial trouble, a subsequent restructuring of debt is often part of the survival and recovery plan. In such a restructuring, the problem becomes that the principal and interest due to lenders may be forgiven in exchange for warrants, direct equity, or other considerations. Such forgiven debt becomes *taxable income* for the entrepreneur who owns the company and who has personally had to guarantee the loans. *Beware:* In one restructuring of a midwestern cable television company, the founder at one point faced a possible $12 million personal tax liability, which would have forced him into personal bankruptcy or possibly worse. In this case, fortunately, the creative deal restructuring enabled him to avoid such a calamitous outcome; but many other overleveraged entrepreneurs have not fared as well.

Neither a Lender nor a Borrower Be, But If You Must . . .

In Garrison Keillor's radio program *A Prairie Home Companion,* he describes the mythical town of Lake Wobegon, Minnesota. Inscribed in granite over the entrance to the Bank of Lake Wobegon is the motto "Neither a Lender nor a Borrower Be," which is actually very good advice for early-stage entrepreneurs. Thus the following may serve as useful tips if you must borrow:

1. Borrow when you do not need it (which is the surest way to accomplish No. 2).
2. Avoid personal guarantees. Put caps and time limits on the amounts based on performance milestones, such as achieving certain cash flow, working capital, and equity levels. Also, don't be afraid in many markets to offer your guarantee and then negotiate ways to get it back in whole or in part!
3. The devil is in the details. Read each loan covenant and requirement carefully—only the owner can truly appreciate their consequences.
4. Try to avoid or modify so-called hair-trigger covenants, such as this: "If there is any change or event of any kind that can have any material adverse effect on the future of the company, the loan shall become due and payable."
5. Be conservative and prudent.

Chapter Summary

- Business cycles impact lending cycles, with more or less restrictive behavior.
- Start-ups are generally not candidates for bank credit, but numerous sources of debt capital are available once profitability and a decent balance sheet are established.
- Managing and orchestrating the banking relationship before and after the loan decision are key task is for entrepreneurs.
- Knowing the key steps in obtaining a loan and selecting a banker—not a bank—who can add value can improve your odds.
- Loan covenants can have a profound impact on how you can and cannot run the business. The devil is in the details of the loan agreement.

- For the vast majority of small companies, leverage works only during the most favorable economic booms of credit availability. Leverage is a disaster if business turns sour.
- The IRS also places a time bomb for personal disaster with every entrepreneur who borrows money: If your bank debt is forgiven in a restructuring, it becomes taxable income to the borrower!
- When the bank says no to a loan request, several key questions need to be addressed in an effort to reverse the decision; or you need to seek sources of credit other than banks.

Study Questions

1. Define and explain the following and why they are important: sources of debt financing, trade credit, line of credit, accounts receivable financing, time-sales factoring, commercial finance company.
2. What security can be used for a loan, and what percentage of its value do banks typically lend?
3. What are the things to look for in evaluating a lender, and why are these important?
4. What does "value-added banker" mean, and how and why is this crucial?
5. What criteria do lenders use to evaluate a loan application, and what can be done before and after the loan decision to facilitate a loan request?

6. What restrictions and covenants might a lender require, and how and why should these be avoided whenever possible?
7. What issues need to be addressed to deal with a loan request rejection?
8. Why do entrepreneurs in smaller companies need to be especially wary of leverage?
9. Why is there an IRS time bomb anytime one borrows money?
10. When should a company borrow money?

Internet Resources for Chapter 16

http://www.aba.com/default.htm *American Bankers Association.*

http://federalreserve.gov/ *Board of Governors of the Federal Reserve System.*

http://research.kauffman.org *The research portal of the Ewing Marion Kauffman Foundation.*

Wiki–Google Search

Try these keywords and phrases:
leverage
factoring
sources of debt: short-term, long-term
banking relationship

personal guarantee
lending decision
loan covenants
loan rejection
obtaining a loan

MIND STRETCHERS

Have You Considered?

1. You have been married nearly 30 years and love your spouse and family. A credit crunch leads you to default on your loans, and the lenders forgive $50 million of debt. The IRS tells you that you owe them $15 million. Your lawyers say you should get divorced to protect other assets. What would you do?

2. Why is Warren Buffet so wary about leverage?

3. Can you calculate the debt capacity of your proposed venture three to four years hence if it achieves positive cash flow and profitability?

4. Can you predict the next credit crunch after the 2007 subprime chaos? What signs might you look for?

Case

Bank Documents: "The Devil Is in the Details"

Preparation Questions

1. Outline the transactions. Include the flow of funds among the individuals and the corporations.
2. What specific risks was the bank trying to protect itself against? Which specific terms were intended to provide the protection?
3. What does "subordination" and "personal guarantee" mean to the respective parties?
4. What in the numbers indicate why the bank took the position it did?

The Parent Company ("TPC") had been in existence for six to seven years under the control of a group of venture capitalists. The Parent Company was publicly held, two-thirds of which was held by the venture capitalists and the operating manager. It was in the business of manufacturing, under an overseas license, a product that was distributed throughout the United States. The Parent Company was running at an annual rate of $3 million to $4 million in sales, and substantially all of its assets were secured under a loan agreement to Union Trust ("The Bank"). The company had a negative net worth and had not made profits during the last five years.

This company determined it needed to expand the business by acquisition. It went into a substantially different industry to accomplish this tactic. It found through investment bankers a chain of retail stores. At the same time it was doing its due diligence on The Retail Company ("TRC"), it opened discussions with the major supplier of The Retail Company, The Distribution Company ("TDC"). The Distribution Company distributed products, all of which were manufactured by others, throughout the United States to 300 customers. It distributed its products from two warehouse locations: one on the East Coast and one on the West Coast. The products sold to retailers who did a great deal of their business during the Christmas season.

The Distribution Company was the largest in its industry and was a privately held company with sales of approximately $25 million and an irregular earnings history (see Exhibit 1, The Distribution Company's audited financial statements, and Exhibit 2, the bank's analysis of the financial statements).

In November 2000 The Parent Company purchased all the stock of The Retail Company for $2.5 million in cash and $500,000 in a Noncompetition Agreement for the owner and chief operating officer, who left the business after the acquisition. This money was raised from the existing investors. The Retail Company had locations in Massachusetts, New York, and Connecticut. The Retail Company had revenues of approximately $6 million and earnings before taxes of approximately $500,000.

In August 2001 The Parent Company merged with The Distribution Company by giving the owners of The Distribution Company 20 percent of the stock of The Parent Company. In addition, The Parent Company raised approximately $3.2 million from its venture capitalists to infuse needed working capital into The Distribution Company.

In addition to receiving 20 percent of the stock of The Parent Company, the owners of The Distribution Company received a consulting contract and a Noncompetition Agreement calling for monthly payments and continuing lease payments on certain equipment used by The Distribution Company. Both the consulting contract and the lease contract called for monthly payments that would be lowered if wholesale sales decreased by more than 10 percent or if certain specific extraordinary demands of The Distribution Company's cash flow occurred. In addition, the sellers had a secured note outstanding from The Distribution Company that was put on a full payout schedule. The owners and chief operating officer of The Distribution Company were not active in the business from the time of the merger.

Because of the financial markets at the time, The Parent Company needed to retain the existing bank that was lending money to The Distribution Company.

The bank was asked to finance both The Distribution Company and The Retail Company, and signed the Credit Facilities Modification Agreement (see Exhibit 3). The bank also required The Parent Company and the selling shareholders to guarantee the line of credit. The bank also required the selling shareholders to pledge their 20 percent interest in The Parent Company as additional security for the loan. In addition, the sellers' secured loan was subordinated to the bank.

This case was prepared by Babson Professor Leslie Charm. Funding provided by Ewing Marion Kauffman Foundation. © Copyright Babson College, 2002. All rights reserved.

EXHIBIT 1

Consolidated Balance Sheets of The Distribution Company

September 30, 1999, 1998, 1997			
	1999	1998	1997
Assets			
Current assets			
Cash and cash equivalents	$ 638,899	$ 1,149,730	$ 836,841
Accounts and notes receivable, net of allowance for doubtful accounts and notes (1994, $204,000; 1993, $510,000; 1992, $511,000)			
(Notes 2 and 7)*	5,081,489	3,279,823	2,674,876
Merchandise inventories			
(Notes 1 and 3)	3,831,577	3,969,947	4,180,428
Refundable income taxes	—	—	21,232
Other current assets			
(Notes 1 and 7)	82,251	306,775	757,031
Total current assets	9,634,216	8,706,275	8,470,408
Notes and receivable and other assets, noncurrent, net of allowance for doubtful notes (1994, $165,000; 1993, $640,000; 1992, $186,000) (Notes 1 and 2)	698,450	800,885	615,070
Investment in unconsolidated subsidiary, at cost, plus equity in undistributed earnings (Note 4)	669,652	641,521	601,512
Equipment and leasehold improvements at cost:			
Equipment	404,948	403,589	385,581
Leasehold improvements	123,040	213,978	192,530
	527,988	617,567	578,111
Less accumulated depreciation and amortization	(324,995)	(312,822)	(344,152)
	202,993	304,745	233,959
Total assets (Note 5)	$11,205,311	$10,453,426	$9,920,949
Liabilities and Shareholders' Equity			
Current liabilities			
Notes payable (Notes 5 and 7)*	$4,695,000	$3,251,000	$3,010,000
Current portion of long-term debt (Note 5)	345,595	349,344	353,156
Franchise deposits	75,835	49,000	67,000
Accounts payable and accrued expenses:			
Merchandise	1,723,836	2,397,287	2,723,878
Other (Note 7)	2,415,479	2,278,073	2,154,200
Income taxes payable	—	29,271	—
Deferred income taxes	356,537	265,083	282,448
Total current liabilities	9,612,282	8,619,058	8,590,682

*The accompanying notes are an integral part of the consolidated financial statements.

(continued)

EXHIBIT 1 (*continued*)

September 30, 1999, 1998, 1997

	1999	1998	1997
Liabilities and Shareholders' Equity			
Long-term debt, net of current portion (Note 5)	646,534	1,116,524	776,573
Deferred income taxes	132,000	34,600	25,670
Commitments and contingencies (Notes 6 and 7)			
Shareholders' equity			
Common stock, $.01 par value; authorized 300,000 shares; issued and outstanding 4,275 shares	43	43	43
Additional paid-in capital	940,679	940,679	940,679
Accumulated deficit	(126,227)	(257,478)	(412,698)
Total shareholder's equity	814,495	683,244	528,024
Total liabilities and shareholders' equity (Note 5)	$11,205,311	$10,453,426	$9,920,949

Consolidated Statements of Operations of The Distribution Company

For the years ending September 30, 1999, 1998, 1997

	1999	1998	1997
Revenues			
Merchandise sales	$19,172,938	$17,675,839	$16,050,887
Retail sales by company-owned stores	306,721	1,702,280	5,326,783
Franchise royalties and other income	5,818,428	5,356,993	4,691,235
Initial franchise and related fees	155,000	145,485	178,500
	25,453,087	24,880,597	26,247,405
Costs and expenses (Notes 6 and 7)*			
Cost of merchandise sold and distribution expenses	17,030,024	15,151,470	13,711,089
Cost of retail sales and direct operating expenses of company owned stores	317,345	1,721,405	4,972,098
Selling, general, and administrative expenses	7,915,565	7,915,053	7,360,408
Net (gain) loss from store sales	(48,391)	(244,394)	25,599
	25,214,543	24,543,534	26,069,194
Income from operations	238,544	337,063	178,211
Interest expense, net (Note 5)	425,293	176,043	149,956
Income (loss) before income taxes and cumulative effect of accounting change	(186,749)	161,020	28,255
Income tax expense (benefit) (Note 8)	(18,000)	5,800	19,000
Income (loss) before cumulative effect of accounting change	(168,749)	155,220	9,255
Cumulative effect to October 1, 1987, of change in method of accounting for inventory costs, net of tax (Note 1)	300,000	—	—
Net income	$ 131,251	$ 155,220	$ 9,255

*The accompanying notes are an integral part of the consolidated financial statements.

EXHIBIT 2

Comparative Statement of Financial Condition of The Distribution Company Prepared by The Bank

The Distribution Company
COMPARATIVE STATEMENT OF FINANCIAL CONDITION
Business: Wholesale Supply   SIC Code: 5199
In: $000s

Date:	9/30/98 UNQUAL		9/30/99 UNQUAL		9/30/00 UNQUAL		8/10/01 UNQUAL	(7)	8/11/01 BEG. B.S.	(8)
1. Current assets	8,167		8,858		9,384		4,838		4,723	
2. Current liabilities	8,219		9,447		11,463		9,318		9,858	
3. Working capital	(52)		(589)		(2,079)		(4,480)		(5,135)	
4. Total long-term debt	1,552		1,241		321		1,744		4,157	
5. Tangible net worth	579		815		(473)		(3,600)		(3,590)	
6. Net sales	24,881		25,341		25,757		19,817		0	
7. Net profits	155		132		(1,288)		(3,127)		0	
8. Cash generation	280		174		(1,227)		(3,089)		0	
9. Cash	1,150	11%	678	5.9%	793	7%	5	0.1%	5	0.0%
10. Marketable securities										
11. Receivables—net	2,907	27.8%	4,266	37.1%	4,123	36.5%	1,524	20.4%	1,063	5.8%
12. Inventory (FIFO) (1)	3,970	38%	3,832	33.3%	4,324	38.2%	3,010	40.3%	3,356	18.4%
13.										
14.										
15.										
16. Other current assets	140	1.3%	82	0.7%	44	1.3%	299	4%	299	1.6%
17. Prepaid expenses										
18. Total current assets	8,167	78.1%	8,858	77%	9,384	83%	4,838	64.8%	4,723	25.9%
19.										
20. Net fixed assets	305	2.9%	203	1.8%	180	1.6%	174	2.3%	1,187	6.5%
21. Due from affiliates	58	.6%	25	.2%	45	.4%	75	1%	75	.4%
22. Other receivables	43	.4%	376	3.3%	295	2.6%	207	2.8%	512	2.8%
23.										
24. Notes receivable	1,073	10.3%	2,041	17.7%	1,407	12.4%	2,168	29.1%	1,789	9.8%
25. Stores held for resale	63	.6%								
26. Inv. in unconsol. subs	641	6.1%								
27. Noncompetitive agreement									1,564	8.6%
28. Option agreement									575	3.2%
29.										

(continued)

533

Date:	9/30/98 UNQUAL		9/30/99 UNQUAL		9/30/00 UNQUAL		8/10/01 UNQUAL	(7)	8/11/01 BEG. B.S.	(8)
30. Intangibles (4)	104	1.0%							7,777	2.7%
31. TOTAL ASSETS	10,454	100%	11,503	100%	11,311	100%	7,462	100%	18,202	100%
32. Notes payable	2,851	27.3%	3,645	31.7%	2,800	24.8%	2,236	30%	2,236	2.3%
33. Notes payable	166	1.6%	598	5.2%	598	5.3%	588	7.9%	588	3.2%
34. Accounts payable—trade	2,397	22.9%	1,724	15%	3,261	28.8%	2,939	39.4%	2,939	6.1%
35. Accruals and payables (other)	2,351	22.5%	2,231	19.4%	2,864	25.3%	3,427	45.9%	3,803	0.9%
36. Current maturities LTD	349	3.3%	390	3.4%	146	1.3%	75	1.0%	239	1.3%
37. Franchise deposits	49	.5%	76	.7%	61	.5%	52	.7%	52	.3%
38. A/P affiliate			233	2%	383	3.4%	1	0%	1	0%
39. N/P affiliate	56	5%	550	4.8%	1,350	11.9%				
40.										
41.										
42. Total current liabilities	8,219	78.6%	9,447	82.1%	11,463	101.3%	9,318	124.9%	9,858	54.2%
43. LTD	442	4.2%	191	1.7%	71	.6%	155	2.1%	1,004	5.5%
44.										
45. Noncompetitive agreement									1,564	8.6%
46. Deferred items	35	.3%								
47. Subordinated LTD	1,075	10.3%	1,050	9.1%	250	2.2%	1,589	21.3%	1,589	8.7%
48. Total liabil and reserves	9,771	93.5%	10,688	92.9%	11,784	104.2%	11,062	148.2%	14,015	77%
49. Preferred stock										
50. Common stock										
51. Capital surplus	941	9%	941	8.2%	941	8.3%	941	12.6%	4,187	23%
52. Earned surplus	(258)	-2.5%	(126)	-1.1%	(1,414)	-12.5%	(4,541)	-60.9%		
53. Treasury stock										
54. TOTAL NET WORTH	683	6.5%	815	7.1%	(473)	-4.2%	(3,600)	-48.3%	4,187	23%
55. TOTAL LIABIL AND NET WORTH	10,454	100%	11,503	100%	11,311	100%	7,462	100%	18,202	100%
56. Annual lease rental	2,413	9.7%	2,444	9.6%	2,501	9.7%	2,371	12%	2,371	0%
57. Contingent liabilities (5)	1,142	10.9%	1,174	10.2%	991	8.8%	579	7.8%	579	3.2%
58. Fin goods										
59. INVENTORY Work process										
60. Raw material										
61. Land										
62. Buildings										
63. Leaseholds	214	34.6%	123	23.3%	134	23.7%	146	24.4%	96	8.1%
64. Furn. and fixt										
65. FIXED ASSETS Mach. and equip	404	65.4%	405	76.7%	432	76.3%	452	75.6%	1,091	100%

#	Date:	9/30/98 UNQUAL	9/30/99 UNQUAL	9/30/00 UNQUAL	8/10/01 UNQUAL	(7)	8/11/01 BEG. B.S.	(8)
66.	Gross F A	618 100%	528 100%	566 100%	598	100%	1,187	100%
67.	Depreciation	313 50.6%	325 61.6%	386 68.2%	424	70.9%		
68.	Spread done by:	MVD	HEW	CMS	CHV	CHV		
69.	Date spread done by:	1/21/99	2/23/00	2/22/01	2/22/02	2/22/02		
70.	Net sales	24,881 100%	25,341 100%	25,757 100%		19,817		100%
71.	Cost of merch sold/distr	15,152 60.9%	17,030 67.2%	17,779 69%		12,928		65.2%
72.	Cost of retail sales	1,721 6.9%	317 1.3%	0		14		.1%
73.	Gross profit	8,008 32.3%	7,994 31.5%	7,978 31%		6,875		34.7%
74.	General and admin expense	7,915 31.8%	7,838 30.9%	8,827 34.3%		9,750		49.2%
75.								
76.	Operating profit	93 .4%	156 .6%	(849) -3.3%		(2,875)		-14.5%
77.	Other income							
78.	Other expense							
79.	Earnings pre int and tax	473 1.9%	357 1.4%	(690) -2.7%		(2,640)		-13.3%
80.	Interest	312 1.3%	532 2.1%	598 2.3%		487		2.5%
81.	Profit before income tax	161 .6%	(175) -.7%	(1,288) -5%		(3,127)		-15.8%
82.	Income taxes	6 0%	(7) 0%					
83.	Extraordinary items (7)		300 1.2%					
84.	Net profit after tax	155 .6%	132 .5%	(1,288) -5%		(3,127)		-15.8%
85.	BEGINNING NET WORTH	528	683	815		(427)		
86.	Net income/loss	155	132	(1,288)		(3,127)		
87.	New equity							
88.								
89.								
90.								
91.	Dividends/withdrawals							
92.	Inc treasury stock							
93.	ENDING NET WORTH	683	815	(473)		(3,600)		
94.	Change in net worth	155	132	(1,288)		(3,127)		
95.	Officers salaries							
96.	Net profit after taxes	155	132	(1,288)		(3,127)		
97.	Depreciation	116	77	61		38		
98.	Amortization							
99.	Deferred items	9	(35)	0		0		
100.	SUBTOTAL CASH GENERATION	280	174	(1,227)		(3,089)		

(continued)

Date:	9/30/98 UNQUAL	9/30/99 UNQUAL	9/30/00 UNQUAL	8/10/01 UNQUAL (7)	8/11/01 BEG. B.S. (8)
101. New long-term debt	0	0	0	84	
102. New equity	0	0	0	0	
103. Decrease intangibles	96	104	0	0	
104. Due from affiliates	292	33	0	0	
105. Decrease other noncurren	0	0	715	0	
106. Inc in on—current liabs	0	0	0	0	
107. Inc subordinated debt	1,075	0	0	1,339	
108. Dec in fixed assets	0	25	0	0	
109.					
110. TOTAL SOURCES	1,743	336	(512)	(1,666)	
111.					
112.					
113.					
114. Repayment of LTD	335	251	120	0	
115. Capital expenditures	187	0	38	32	
116. Dividends/withdrawals	0	0	0	0	
117. Increase intangibles	0	0	0	0	
118. Due from affiliates	0	0	20	30	
119. Inc other noncurrent ass	139	597	0	673	
120. Dec subordinated debt	0	25	800	0	
121. Dec in noncurrent liabs	0	0	0	0	
122. Decrease in equity	0	0	0	0	
123.					
124.					
125.					
126. TOTAL APPLICATIONS	661	873	978	735	
127. CHANGE NET WORKING CAPITAL	1,082	(537)	(1,490)	(2,401)	
128. Current ratio	0.99	0.94	0.82	0.52	0.48
129. Quick ratio	0.49	0.52	0.43	0.16	0.11
130. Sales/receivables (days)	42	61	58	25	
131. Cost of sales/inven (days)	94	81	88	77	
132. Total debt/tang net worth	16.88	13.11	−24.91	−3.07	−3.9
133. Unsub debt/tang cap fnds	5.26	5.17	−51.72	−4.71	6.21
134. Net profit as % net worth	22.69%	16.2%	272.3%	94.76%	
135. Sales/working capital	−478.48	−43.02	−12.39	−4.83	
136. Sales/net worth	36.43	31.09	−54.45	6.01	
137. COGS/payables (days)	57	36	66	75	

536

EXHIBIT 2 (continued)

Cash Flow Summary of The Distribution Company Prepared by The Bank

Date:	9/30/98 UNQUAL	9/30/99 UNQUAL	9/30/00 UNQUAL	8/10/01 UNQUAL
GROSS CASH FLOW				
1. Net income (loss)	155	132	(1,288)	(3,127)
2. Depreciation	116	77	61	38
3. Amortization	0	0	0	0
4. Deferred items	9	(35)	0	0
5.				
6. TOTAL GROSS CASH FLOW	280	174	(1,227)	(3,089)
7. FLOWS FROM (FOR) WORKING ACCTS				
8. Receivables—net	(559)	(1,359)	143	2,599
9. Inventory (FIFO) (1)	210	138	(492)	1,314
10. Accounts payable—trade	(327)	(673)	1,537	(322)
11. Accruals and payables—other	790	(120)	633	563
12. Income taxes	0	0	0	0
13. Other current assets	(49)	58	(62)	(155)
14. Marketable securities	0	0	0	0
15. CASH GENER FROM OPER.	345	(1,782)	532	910
16. FLOWS FROM (FOR) NONCUR ACCTS				
17. Net fixed assets	(187)	25	(38)	(32)
18. Due from affiliates	292	33	(20)	(30)
19. Other noncurrent assets	(139)	(597)	715	(673)
20. Intangibles (4)	96	104	0	0
21. CASH AVAIL FOR EXT	407	(2,217)	1,189	175
22. REQUIRED PMTS AND RETIREMENTS				
23. Other cur liab	(837)	754	935	(1,741)
24. Other noncurrent liabs	0	0	0	0
25. Dividends/withdrawals	0	0	0	0
26. Current maturities LTD	(4)	41	(244)	(71)
27. INTERNAL CASH FLOW	(434)	(1,422)	1,880	(1,637)
28. FINANCING				
29. Notes payable—UST	(159)	794	(845)	(564)

(continued)

537

Date:	9/30/98 UNQUAL	9/30/99 UNQUAL	9/30/00 UNQUAL	8/10/01 UNQUAL
30. Notes payable—bank fiveq	166	432	0	(10)
31. Long-term debt	(335)	(251)	(120)	84
32. Subordinated LTD	1,075	(25)	(800)	1,339
33. Equity financing	0	0	0	0
34. INCREASE/DECREASE IN CA	313	(472)	115	(788)

Footnotes:

1. As of 10/1/98, the company changed its method of accounting for inventory to include overhead costs, which had previously been charged to expense.
   As of 8/11/01, the company changed the method of inventory valuation from LIFO to FIFO.
2. Consolidation up to and including FYE '99 did not include the finance company subsidiary. FYE 2000 financials include this subsidiary as a wholly owned subsidiary.
3. Previous to 8/10/01, the company's auditors were Cooper's & Lybrand.
4. In FYE '98, intangibles consist of unrecognized costs.
   At 8/11/97, intangibles consisted of goodwill, a noncompete agreement, and an option agreement.
5. Contingent liabilities consist of the company's guarantee on obligations of some franchisees, letters of credit with the bank, and various lawsuits about normal business.
6. Extraordinary item at FYE 2000 is the cumulative effect of the change in the method of accounting for inventory costs, net of tax effects.
7. Deloitte & Touche feels that there is substantial doubt whether the company will continue as a going concern due to historical losses and a deficiency in capital.
8. On August 11, 2001, The Parent Company acquired all the outstanding shares of The Distribution Company. Accordingly, the company's historical balance sheet at August 10, 2001, has been revalued to fair market value on the opening balance sheet of the company as of August 11, 2001.

538

EXHIBIT 3

Credit Facilities Modification Agreement

This is a Credit Facilities Modification Agreement made and entered into as of this 8th day of August 2001 by and among The Distribution Company, a Massachusetts corporation having a principal place of business at 385 Appleton Street, North Andover, Massachusetts ("TDC" "Borrower"); The Parent Company ("TPC"), a Delaware corporation with a principal place of business at 222 Benchley Avenue, Hartford, Connecticut; and The Retail Company ("TRC"), a Delaware corporation with principal place of business at 18 Holland Street, Hartford, Connecticut 06874; and the Bank ("Bank"), a Massachusetts banking corporation having an address at Boston, Massachusetts 02108.

Preamble

WHEREAS, on December 3, 1995, the Borrower entered into a $4,000,000.00 revolving loan facility with the Bank, as evidenced by two notes in the amounts of $1,500,000 and $2,500,000, respectively, secured by a security agreement covering all assets of the Borrower and further secured by an assignment of certain promissory notes payable to the Borrower (the Assignment); and

WHEREAS, on April 8, 1997, the Borrower executed a further "Security Agreement—Inventory, Accounts, Equipment and other Property" ("Security Agreement") securing all liabilities of the Borrower to the Bank (a true copy of which is attached hereto as Exhibit A-1); and

WHEREAS, on October 1, 1999, the Borrower executed a "Commercial Demand Note" in the amount of Three Million Five Hundred Thousand Dollars ($3,500,000.00), which Commercial Demand Note superseded the two notes dated as of December 3, 1995, and is secured by the Security Agreement (a true copy of which is attached hereto as Exhibit A-2); and

WHEREAS, on November 18, 1999, Sellers 1, 2, and 3 (S123) ("Individual Guarantors") each executed a "Limited Guaranty" of the liabilities of the Borrower (true copies of which are attached hereto as Exhibit A-3, A-4, and A-5); and

WHEREAS, on November 18, 1999, Seller, an affiliate of the Borrower, executed a Subordination Agreement in favor of the Bank in which certain notes of the Borrower held by Seller were subordinated to the Borrower's indebtedness to the Bank ("Subordination Agreement") (a true copy of which is attached hereto as Exhibit A-6); and

WHEREAS, the Individual Guarantors own all of the issued and outstanding common stock of the Borrower; and

WHEREAS, pursuant to an Agreement and Plan of Merger dated as of August 2001 ("Merger Agreement"), TDC has been merged into the Borrower so that the Borrower is now a wholly owned subsidiary of TPC and the Individual Guarantors have received Series E Preferred Stock of TPC in lieu of the common stock of the Borrower; and

WHEREAS, TRC is a wholly owned subsidiary of TPC which operates approximately nine TRCs in Massachusetts, Connecticut, and New York; and

WHEREAS, TPC, TRC, and the Borrower have requested that the existing credit facility from the Bank to the Borrower be continued and amended for the benefit of TPC and TRC, and in consideration thereof TPC and TRC have agreed to guaranty loans, the parties now wish to restate and amend the terms and conditions of the credit facility;

NOW, THEREFORE, for good and valuable consideration, the parties do hereby agree as follows:

Section 1. Definitions

Section 1.1. Acceptable Inventory. Acceptable Inventory shall mean such of the Borrower's new, unopened salable inventory shelf for sale to others (but excluding raw materials, work in progress, and materials used or consumed in the Borrower's business) as the Bank in its sole discretion deems eligible for borrowing.

Section 1.2. Acceptable Accounts. Acceptable Accounts shall mean accounts under sixty (60) days old measured from the date of the invoice, which arose from *bona fide* outright sales of merchandise to a Person which is not a subsidiary or affiliate of the Borrower, TPC, or TRC.

Section 1.3. Accounts. "Accounts" and "Accounts Receivable" include, without limitation, "accounts" as defined in the UCC, and also all accounts, accounts receivable, notes, drafts, acceptances, and other forms of obligations and receivables and rights to payment for credit extended and for goods sold or leased, or services rendered, whether or not yet earned by performance; all inventory which gave rise thereto, and all rights associated with such inventory, including the right of stoppage in transit; all reclaimed, returned, rejected, or repossessed inventory (if any) the sale of which gave rise to any Account.

Section 1.4. Bank. The Bank, a Massachusetts banking Corporation.

Section 1.5. Base Lending Rate. The rate of interest published internally and designated by the Bank from time to time, as its Base Lending Rate.

Section 1.6. Collateral. All assets of the Borrower, tangible and intangible, as described in the Security Agreement and in the Assignment, as amended herein.

Section 1.7. Corporate Guarantors. TPC and TRC.

Section 1.8 Credit Facilities Modification Agreement. This agreement and any and all subsequent amendments thereto.

EXHIBIT 3 (continued)

Section 1.9. Credit Facility.   The Loans granted to or for the benefit of the Borrower pursuant to the Loan Documents.

Section 1.10. Event of Default.   Any event described in Section 8 hereto.

Section 1.11. Guarantors.   The Corporate Guarantors, the Individual Guarantors, and Sellers.

Section 1.12. Individual Guarantors.   Sellers 1, 2, 3.

Section 1.13. Loan Documents.   This term shall refer, collectively, to (i) the Commercial Demand Note, (ii) the Security Agreement, (iii) the Assignment, (iv) all UCC Financial Statements, (v) the Subordination Agreement, (vi) the Individual Guarantees, (vii) TPC Guaranty, (viii) TRC Guaranty, (ix) the Sellers Guaranty, (x) the Sellers Pledge and Security Agreement, (xi) TPC Pledge of Stock of Borrower and TRC, (xii) TPC Subordination Agreement, (xiii) the Individual Guarantor's Pledge of Preferred Stock of TPC, (xiv) TRC Security Agreement, (xv) this Credit Facilities Modification Agreement, and all amendments, modifications, and extensions thereof, and any other document or agreement pursuant to which the Bank is granted a lien or other interest as security for the Borrower's obligations to it.

Section 1.14. Loan(s).   Loans or advances by the Bank to the Borrower pursuant to the Loan Documents. The Loan shall consist of a Revolving Loan of up to $2,800,000.00 as provided for in Sections 2.1 through 2.5 hereof, including any letters of credit issued by the Bank for the account of the Borrower as provided in Section 2.4 hereof. The Borrower and the Lender acknowledge that as of August 2001, the outstanding balance of the Revolving Loans was $_____.

Section 1.15. Loan Review Date.   July 31, 2002, or such later date to which the Loan may be extended pursuant to Section 2.5 hereof.

Section 1.16. Note.   The $3,500,000.00 Commercial Demand Note dated October 1, 1999.

Section 1.17. Obligations.   Those obligations described in Section 2 hereof.

Section 1.18. Person.   A corporation, association, partnership, trust, organization, business, individual or government, or any governmental agency or political subdivision thereof.

Section 1.19. Sellers Debt.   All loans from Sellers to the Borrower whether now existing or hereafter arising.

Section 1.20. Revolving Loan or Revolving Credit.   The revolving working capital loan evidenced by the Commercial Demand Note as described in this Agreement.

Section 1.21. Subordinated Debt.   The Sellers Debt and TPC Debt.

Section 1.22. Subsidiary.   Means any entity that is directly or indirectly controlled by the Borrower or TPC.

Section 1.23.   Capitalized terms not otherwise defined herein shall have the meanings ascribed thereto in the Loan Documents.

Section 2. Loans, Revision of Terms, Confirmation of Security Documents; Additional Security

Section 2.1   (a) *Amount of Availability of Revolving Credit.* The Bank has established a discretionary revolving line of credit in the Borrower's favor in the amount of the Borrower's Availability (as defined below), as determined by the Bank from time to time hereafter. All loans made by the Bank under this Agreement, and all of the Borrower's other liabilities to the Bank under or pursuant to this Agreement, are payable ON DEMAND.

As used herein, the term "Availability" refers at any time to the lesser of (i) or (ii) below:

(i) up to (A) Two Million Eight Hundred Thousand Dollars ($2,800,000.00) (or such other amount as the Bank may set from time to time, in the Bank's discretion),

minus . . .

(B) the aggregate amounts then undrawn on all outstanding letters of credit issued by the Bank for the account of the Borrower.

(ii) up to (A) seventy percent (70%) (or such revised percentage as the Bank may set from time to time, in the Bank's discretion) of the face amount (determined by the Bank in the Bank's sole discretion) of each of the Acceptable Accounts,

Plus . . .

(B) thirty percent (30%) (or such revised percentage as the Bank may set from time to time, in the Bank's discretion) of the value of the Acceptable Inventory (Acceptable Inventory being valued at the lower cost or market after deducting all transportation, processing, handling charges, and all other costs and expenses affecting the value thereof, all as determined by the Bank in its sole discretion) but not to exceed $1,200,000.

minus . . .

(C) the aggregate amounts then undrawn on all outstanding letters of credit issued by the Bank for the account of the Borrower (the "Formula Amount").

The Revolving Credit is not a committed line of financing. The borrowing formula described in this Section 2.1 is intended solely for monitoring purposes.

(b) *Advances.* Advances may consist of direct advances to the Borrower payable ON DEMAND, or letters of credit issued on behalf of the Borrower. The Borrower may borrow, repay, and re-borrow Revolving Loans under this Agreement by written notice

EXHIBIT 3 (continued)

given to the Bank at least two business days prior to the date of the requested advance. Each request for an advance shall be in an integral multiple of $50,000.00 and shall be subject to approval by the Bank, which approval may be granted, denied, or granted conditionally in the Bank's sole discretion.

(c) *Mandatory Reduction.* The Borrower shall reduce the outstanding balance of the Revolving Loan to $600,000.00 or less (exclusive of letters of credit) for a period of thirty (30) consecutive days between December 1, 2001, and January 31, 2002.

(d) *Availability—Overadvances.* The Borrower's Availability shall not exceed the Formula Amount (as set forth in Section 2.1 (a) (ii)), provided that the Borrower may borrow $700,000.00 in excess of the Formula Amount prior to September 30, 2001, and $300,000.00 in excess of the Formula Amount between February 28, 2002, and July 31, 2002, provided further that in no event shall outstanding advances ever exceed $2,800,000.00.

(e) *Approval of Accounts and Inventory:*

(i) *Accounts.* All account debtors shall be subject to the approval of the Bank in its sole discretion, and the Bank's eligibility determinations shall be final and conclusive. The determination by the Bank that a particular account from a particular account debtor is eligible for borrowing shall not obligate the Bank to deem subsequent accounts from the same account debtor to be eligible for borrowing, nor to continue to deem that account to be so eligible. All collateral not considered eligible for borrowing nevertheless secures the prompt, punctual, and faithful performance of the Borrower's Obligations. The determination that a given account of the Borrower is eligible for borrowing shall not be deemed a determination by the Bank relative to the actual value of the account in question. All risks concerning the creditworthiness of all accounts are and remain upon the Borrower.

(ii) *Inventory.* The Bank's determinations that certain inventory is, or is not, eligible for borrowing shall be final and conclusive. No sale of inventory shall be on consignment, approval, or under any other circumstances such that such inventory may be returned to the Borrower without the consent of the Bank, except for transactions in the normal course of business. None of the inventory will be stored or processed with a bailee or other third party without the prior written consent of the Bank.

(f) *Borrowing Certificate.* Each request for an advance shall be accomplished by a borrowing certificate, in form acceptable to the Bank, which shall be signed by such person whom the Bank reasonably believes to be authorized to act in this regard on behalf of the Borrower, and shall certify that as of the date of the subject certificate, (i) there has been no material adverse change in the Borrower's and Corporate Guarantors' respective financial conditions taken as a whole from the information previously furnished the Bank; (ii) the Borrower and TPC are in compliance with, and have not breached any of, the covenants contained herein; and (iii) no event has occurred or failed to occur which occurrence or failure is, or with the passage of time or giving of notice (or both) would constitute, an Event of Default (as described herein) whether or not the Bank has exercised any of its rights upon such occurrence.

(g) *Loan Account.*

(i) An account (hereinafter, the "Loan Account") has been opened on the books of the Bank in which account a record has been, and shall be, kept of all loans made by the Bank to the Borrower under or pursuant to this Loan and of all payments thereon.

(ii) The Bank may also keep a record (either in the Loan Account or elsewhere, as the Bank may from time to time elect) of all interest, service charges, costs, expenses, and other debits owed the Bank on account of the loan arrangement contemplated hereby and of all credits against such amounts so owed.

(iii) All credits against the Borrower's indebtedness indicated in the Loan Account shall be conditional upon final payment to the Bank of the items giving rise to such credits. The amount of any item credited against the Loan Account which is charged back against the Bank for any reason or is not so paid may be added to the Loan Account, or charged against any account maintained by the Borrower with the Bank (at the Bank's discretion and without notice, in each instance), and shall be Liability, in each instance whether or not the item so charged back or not so paid is returned.

(iv) Any statement rendered by the Bank to the Borrower shall be considered correct and accepted by the Borrower and shall be conclusively binding upon the Borrower unless the Borrower provides the Bank with written objection thereto within twenty (20) days from the mailing of such statement, which such written objection shall indicate with particularly the reason for such objection. The Loan Account and the Bank's books and records concerning the loan arrangement contemplated herein shall be prima facie evidence and proof of the items described therein.

Section 2.2. Note. The Borrower has executed and delivered the Note to the Bank. The Note evidences each advance under the Loan. The Note is on a DEMAND basis and is payable as to interest in arrears on the first day of each calendar month. The Note may be prepaid at any time, in whole or in part, without penalty. Except as modified herein, the Borrower hereby ratifies and confirms the Note in every respect.

Section 2.3. Interest and Fees

(a) *Interest.* The Loans (except the letters of credit) shall bear interest at a rate which, until the Loan may be due and payable, shall be the Base Lending Rate plus one percent (1%). The rate of interest shall vary from time to time as the Base Lending Rate varies, and any change in the rate of interest shall become effective on the date of the change in the Base Lending Rate. Interest shall be computed and adjusted on a daily basis using a 360-day year. Overdue principal and interest shall bear interest at the rate of two percent (2%) per annum above the Base Lending Rate.

(b) *Balances.* The Borrower shall maintain a balance (exclusive of balances necessary to cover service charges) at all times of at least ten percent (10%) of the outstanding balance of the Revolving Loan. For each day that the Borrower shall fail to maintain

EXHIBIT 3 (*continued*)

such balances, the Borrower shall pay to the Bank on the first day of the following month a fee to compensate the Bank for the lack of use of such funds during the previous month.

(c) *Alternative Pricing.*   At its election, the Bank may transfer the Revolving Credit from the commercial lending division to the asset-based lending division in which event the interest rate may be changed to the Base Lending Rate plus one and one-half percent (1 1/2%), with two business days' clearance. In addition the Borrower shall provide such further reports and information as is customarily required of Borrowers serviced by such division.

Section 2.4. Letters of Credit.   From time to time, the Bank has made loans to the Borrower in the form of letters of credit, as evidenced by the Applications for Commercial Credit as attached hereto as Exhibit B. The borrower may request that the Bank make additional loans in the form of further letters of credit provided that the total amount of Documentary Letters of Credit outstanding at any time shall not exceed $550,000.00 and the total amount of Standby Letters of Credit outstanding at any time shall not exceed $72,000.00. Each such request for the issuance of a letter of credit shall be made at least five (5) business days in advance and shall be accompanied by the Bank's standard form of "Application for Commercial Credit" and "Commercial Letter of Credit Agreement" duly executed by the Borrower. The Bank shall have the right, at its option, to limit the term of any letter of credit to the Loan Review Date. In the event the Bank elects to issue a Standby Letter of Credit, the Borrower shall pay the Bank a fee of one percent (1%) per annum of the face amount of such Standby Letter of Credit, and one-half of one percent (.5%) of the face amount of a Documentary Letter of Credit or, if different, the then standard or customary fee for the type and amount of letter of credit requested, in lieu of the interest otherwise required on the Loan. All drafts drawn on a letter of credit shall be immediately repayable in full by the Borrower without need for notice or demand, together with interest thereon at the rate of three percent (3%) above the Base Rate for each day that such draft remains outstanding.

Section 2.5. Review of Loan.   Without derogating from the DEMAND nature of the Revolving Loan, the Revolving Credit facility will be subject to review on July 31, 2002. There is no obligation on the Bank to renew the Revolving Credit or to extend it beyond July 31, 2002.

Section 2.6. Subordination of Sellers Debt.   Sellers, a Massachusetts general partnership controlled by the Individual Guarantors, acknowledge that the Subordination Agreement remains in full force and effect, that the Loans constitute Senior Debt under the Subordination Agreement, and that the Sellers Debt in the amount of $1,800,000.00 as evidenced by a Term Promissory Note in said amount dated as of August 8, 2001, remains subject and subordinate to the Loans as provided in the Subordination Agreement. The Term Promissory Note evidencing the Sellers Debt has this day been delivered to the Bank duly endorsed.

Section 2.7. Assignment.   The Borrower hereby ratifies and confirms the Assignment, and acknowledges that the Assignment secures the Loans. A current Schedule A to the Assignment is attached hereto as Exhibit C. The notes secured by the Assignment have this day been delivered to the Bank duly endorsed. Upon payment in full of any of the assigned notes by the makers thereof and the deposit of such funds in the Borrower's account at the Bank, the Bank shall redeliver the paid note(s) to the Borrower. From time to time, the Borrower may renegotiate the terms of such notes with the makers thereof on commercially reasonable terms and conditions in the Borrower's reasonable judgment. All such amendments or renegotiated notes shall be delivered to the Bank against delivery to the Borrower of the original notes, if required by it, and shall be included in the Assignment.

Section 2.8. Guaranty; Security.   (a) *Individual Guarantors.*   The Individual Guarantors hereby ratify and confirm their respective Limited Guarantees in all respects and further confirm that such Limited Guarantees apply to the Loan, including, without limitations to, the various letters of credit. To secure such guarantees, the Individual Guarantors have this day pledged to the Bank their Series E Preferred Stock of TPC as set forth in the respective Pledge Agreements attached hereto as Exhibit D. The Individual Guarantors may convert their Series E Preferred Stock into common stock of TPC, in which event all shares received as a result of such conversion shall be similarly pledged to the Bank as collateral for their respective Limited Guarantees.

(b) *Corporate Guarantors.*   TPC and TRC have this day guaranteed all of the Borrower's obligations to the Bank by the execution of "TPC Guaranty" and "TRC Guaranty" attached hereto as Exhibit E and F, respectively. TPC has secured TPC Guaranty by pledging to the Bank all of the Borrower's and TRC shares as set forth in the Pledge Agreement attached hereto as Exhibit G. TRC has further secured TRC Guaranty by executing and delivering to the Bank a Security Agreement on all of its assets as set forth on Exhibit H attached hereto. TRC has deposited $250,000.00 in an account at the Bank which amount may be used by TRC for working capital purposes.

(c) *Seller Associates.*   Seller has this day executed a limited guaranty of the Borrower's obligations to the Bank by the execution of the "Seller's Guaranty" attached hereto as Exhibit I. Seller has secured its guaranty by the execution and delivery to the Bank of a pledge and assignment of various payments due Seller from the Borrower under (i) the Consulting and Noncompetition Agreement, and (ii) the Seller's Debt, all as set forth in the "Seller's Pledge and Security Agreement" attached hereto as Exhibit J. Except as set forth in the Seller's Pledge and Security Agreement, all payments and proceeds received by Seller pursuant to the Consulting and Noncompetition Agreement and the Seller Debt shall be immediately deposited in a separate account with the Bank and pledged to the Bank as further security for the Guarantee. Except as set forth in the Seller's Pledge and Security Agreement, no funds may be withdrawn from such account until Loan has been paid in full and the Bank has no further obligation to advance funds hereunder. In the event that the Bank shall apply any funds received by Seller under Sections 3(a), 3(c), and 3(d) of the Consulting and Noncompetition Agreement (but not the Seller debt) against the Loan, the Individual Guarantors shall receive credit against their respective Limited Guarantees for the amount so applied by the Bank.

EXHIBIT 3 (*continued*)

Section 2.9. Security Agreement.   As the security for the prompt satisfaction of all its Obligations to the Bank, the Borrower has executed and delivered the Security Agreement. The Borrower hereby ratifies and confirms the Security Agreement and acknowledges that the Security Agreement remains in full force and effect and constitutes a first and exclusive lien on the Collateral. The Collateral, together with all other property of the Borrower of any kind held by the Bank, shall stand as one general continuing collateral security for all Obligations and may be retained by the Bank until all Obligations are paid in full.

Section 2.10. TPC Debt.   As of the date hereof, TPC has agreed to loan to the Borrower the sum of $2,750,000.00 ("TPC Loan") to be used as additional working capital. Of this sum, $575,000 will be advanced to Realty Trust to be applied toward the third mortgage on the property at 385 Appleton Street, North Andover, Massachusetts, and approximately $400,000 has been or will be advanced to pay (i) costs of a certain litigation settlement and (ii) accounting fees, legal fees, and closing costs incurred by the Borrower in connection with the Merger Agreement and this Loan. TPC has this day deposited the balance of TPC Loan, approximately $1,775,000, in an account to the Bank as security for the Loan as set forth in the "Pledge and Security Agreement— Cash Collateral Account" attached hereto as Exhibit K. At such time as TPC shall have restructured its loan with Union Bank & Trust as provided in Section 2.11 hereof (or otherwise restructured such debt in a manner reasonably satisfactory to the Bank), TPC may withdraw $250,000 from the Cash Collateral Account and may use such funds for its own corporate purposes. From time to time, and so long as there is not Event of Default hereunder, TPC may withdraw funds from the cash collateral account at the Bank and advance such funds to the Borrower by depositing such funds in the Borrower's account at the Bank for the purpose of implementing TPC Debt. At such time as TPC advances funds to the Borrower pursuant to TPC Debt, the Borrower shall execute one or more promissory notes to evidence TPC Debt and such note(s) shall be endorsed in favor of and delivered to the Bank. TPC Debt shall be fully subject and subordinate to the Loan, and the Bank and TPC have this day executed "TPC Subordination Agreement" in the form attached hereto as Exhibit L to evidence such subordination.

Section 2.11. Restructuring of Union Trust Debt.   TPC shall restructure its existing indebtedness with Union Trust Company as follows: (a) the line of credit shall not exceed $1,000,000; (b) the maturity date thereof shall be no earlier than July 31, 2002; and (c) Union Trust shall not have received any security interest in the assets of the Borrower or TPC Loan (or the proceeds thereof). TPC shall provide written evidence of such debt restructuring in form satisfactory to the Bank on or before August 30, 2001.

Section 2.12. Confirmation of Subsidiary Debt.   As of the date hereof, the Borrower shall provide written confirmation to the Bank, in form satisfactory to the Bank, that TDC debt to the Boston Five Cents Savings Bank has been extended on a term basis for not less than one year, that such debt does not exceed $598,000, that the Borrower has guaranteed the interest but not the principal thereof, and that the collateral securing the loan is set forth on a schedule submitted to and approved by the Bank.

Section 3. Use of Proceeds and Payments

Section 3.1. Use of Proceeds.   The Borrower has used and shall continue to use the proceeds of the Revolving Loan for its general working capital purposes.

Section 3.2. Payment.   All payments of commitment fees, fees for letters of credit, service fees, activity charges, and all payments and prepayments of principal and all payments of interest shall be made by the Borrower to the Bank in immediately available funds at the head office of the Bank in Boston, Massachusetts 02108. The Borrower hereby authorizes the Bank, without any further notice, to charge any account the Borrower maintains at the Bank for each payment due hereunder or under the Note (for interest, fees, service charges, activity charges, principal, or otherwise) on the due date thereof, provided that the Bank shall not charge any account in which the Borrower is acting as agent or trustee for any other person.

Section 3.3. Regular Activity Charges.   The Borrower shall pay to the Bank, on a monthly basis, the Bank's usual activity charges for banking services which such charges may be payable by maintaining adequate balances or by payment of a deficiency fee.

Section 4. Representations and Warranties of the Borrower

The Borrower represents and warrants that:

Section 4.1. Corporate Authority.

(a) *Incorporation; Good Standing.*   The Borrower is a corporation duly organized, validly existing, and in good standing under the laws of the Commonwealth of Massachusetts, and has all requisite corporate power to own its property and conduct its business as now conducted and as presently contemplated.

(b) *Authorization.*   The execution, delivery, and performance of this Agreement, the Note, the Security Agreement, the Assignment, and the transactions contemplated hereby and thereby (i) are within the authority of the Borrower; (ii) have been authorized by the Board of Directors of the Borrower; and (iii) will not contravene any provision of law, or the Borrower's Articles of Organization, By-Laws, or any other agreement, instrument, or undertaking binding upon the Borrower;

Section 4.2. Governmental and Other Approvals.   The execution, delivery, and performance of this Agreement, the Note, the Security Agreement, the Assignment, and the transactions contemplated hereby and thereby by the Borrower (a) do not require any approval or consent of, or filling with, any governmental agency or authority in the United States of America or otherwise which has not been obtained and which is not in full force and effect as of the date hereof; and (b) do not require any approval or consent of any security holder of the Borrower.

EXHIBIT 3 (*continued*)

Section 4.3. Title to Properties; Absence of Liens.   The Borrower has good and valid title to all of the Collateral free from all defects, liens, charges, and encumbrances.

Section 4.4. No Default.   The Borrower is not in default in any material respect under provision of its Articles of Organization, or any provisions of any material contract, agreement, or obligation, exclusive of leases (whether related to the Loans or otherwise), which default could result in a significant impairment of the ability of the Borrower to fulfill its obligations hereunder or under the Note or the Loan Documents or a significant impairment of the financial position or business of the Borrower.

Section 4.5. Margin Regulations.   The Borrower is not in the business of extending credit for the purpose of purchasing or carrying margin stock (within the meaning of Regulation G or Regulation U of the Board of Governors of the Federal Reserve System), and no portion of any Loan made to the Borrower hereunder has been or will be used, directly or indirectly, by the Borrower to purchase or carry or to extend credit to others for the purpose of purchasing or carrying any margin stock.

Section 4.6. Financial Statements.   The Borrower has furnished to the Bank an audited balance sheet and statement of income and changes in financial position of the Borrower for the period ended September 30, 2000 (the September 2000 Report), and an internally prepared income statement for the interim period ending May, 31 2001 (May 2001 Report), which has been certified to be true, accurate, and complete by the chief financial officer of the Borrower. The balance sheets, income statements, and statements of changes in financial position set forth in the "September 2000 Report" and the "May 2001 Report" present fairly the financial position of the Borrower as at the date thereof.

Section 4.7. Changes.   To the best of the Borrower's knowledge, since the September 2000 Report and the May 2001 Report, there has been no material change in the assets, liabilities, financial condition, or business of the Borrower which taken together would have a material, adverse effect on the net worth therein reported.

Section 4.8. Taxes   Except as set forth in Schedule ___ of the Merger Agreement, the Borrower has filed all United States Federal and State income tax returns and all other state, federal, or local tax returns required to be filed, and the Borrower and its Subsidiaries have paid or made adequate provision for the payment of all taxes, assessments, and other governmental charges due. The Borrower knows of no basis for any material additional assessment with respect to any fiscal year for which adequate reserves have not been established.

Section 4.9. Litigation.   Except as set forth in Exhibit 3.18 of the Merger Agreement, there is no material litigation pending or, to the knowledge of its officers, threatened against the Borrower, or any of the Individual Guarantors.

Section 5. Representation and Warranties of TPC and TRC

Each of the Corporate Guarantors warrants and represents as to itself as follows:

Section 5.1. Corporate Authority.

(a) *Incorporation; Good Standing.*   Each corporation is a corporation duly organized, validly existing, and in good standing under the law of Delaware and has all requisite corporate power to own its property and conduct its business as now conducted and as presently contemplated.

(b) *Authorization.*   The execution, delivery, and performance of this Agreement, and the transactions contemplated hereby and thereby, (i) are within the authority of such corporation; (ii) have been authorized by the Board of such corporation; and (iii) will not contravene any provision of law, or Articles of Organization, By-Laws, or any other agreement, instrument, or undertaking binding upon such corporation.

Section 5.2. Governmental and Other Approvals.   The execution, delivery, and performance of this Agreement, and the transactions contemplated hereby and thereby by the Corporate Guarantors, (a) do not require any approval or consent of, or filing with, any governmental agency or authority in the United States of America or otherwise which has not been obtained and which is not in full force and effect as of the date hereof; and (b) do not require any approval or consent of any security holder of such corporations.

Section 5.3. Title to Properties; Absence of Liens.   TRC has good and valid title to all of the collateral described in the TRC Security Agreement free from all defects, liens, charges, and encumbrances. TPC has good and valid title to the shares of the Borrower described in the TPC Pledge of Stock Agreement.

Section 5.4. No Default.   Such corporation is not in default in any material respect under any provision of its Articles of Organization, or any provisions of any material contract, agreement, or obligation (whether related to the Loans or otherwise), which default could result in a significant impairment of the ability of such corporation to fulfill its obligations hereunder or any of the Loan Documents or a significant impairment of the financial position or business of such corporation.

Section 5.5. Financial Statements.   TPC has furnished to the Bank a copy of its audited Consolidated Balance Sheet and Consolidated Statement of Operations for the period ended December 31, 2000 (the December 2000 Report), and for the interim period ending March 31, 2001 (March 2001 Report), which have been certified to be true, accurate, and complete by the chief financial officer of the Borrower. The Consolidated Balance Sheets, and Consolidated Statement of Operations set forth in the December 2000 Report and the March 2002 Report, present fairly the financial position of TPC as at the dates thereof.

EXHIBIT 3 (continued)

Section 5.6. Changes. Since the December 2000 Report and the March 2001 Report there has been no material change in the assets, liabilities, financial condition, or business of TPC which taken together would have a material, adverse effect on the net worth therein reported except as previously reported to the Bank in the May 31, 2001, interim Report.

Section 5.7. Taxes. TRC and its Subsidiaries have filed all United States Federal and State income tax returns and all other state, federal, or local tax returns required to be filed, and TPC and its Subsidiaries have paid or made adequate provision for the payment of all taxes, assessments, and other governmental charges due. TPC knows of no basis for any material additional assessment with respect to any fiscal year for which adequate reserves have not been established.

Section 5.8. Litigation. Except as set forth in TPC Form 10K dated as of December 31, 2000, there is no material litigation pending or, to the knowledge of its officers, threatened against either of the Corporate Guarantors.

Section 6. Conditions Precedent to Loans

Section 6.1. Conditions Precedent to Each Advance. The obligation of the Bank to continue to make future Revolving Loan advances and to issue additional letters of credit shall be subject to the performance by the Borrower of all its agreements heretofore to be performed by it and to the satisfaction, prior to or at the time of making each such advances, of the following conditions ("Conditions Precedent"):

(a) *First Advance.* Prior to the Bank's making the first advance after the date hereof, the Borrower shall provide to the Bank and the Bank shall have approved (i) evidence of compliance with the provisions of Section 2.10 and 2.12 hereof; (ii) internally prepared financial statements of TPC and TRC as of May 31, 2001, certified as accurate by the chief financial officer of such corporation; (iii) copies of all documents executed in connection with the Merger Agreement, including all exhibits and schedules thereto; (iv) copies of all documents by which TPC has generated or raised the amount of TPC Debt; (v) fully executed Loan Documents; (vi) certified or original copies of all corporate votes, consents, and authorizations necessary to implement this Agreement; and (vii) such other documents, certificates, instruments, and opinions as the Bank may reasonably require.

(b) *Authorized Signatures.* The Borrower shall have certified to the Bank the name and a specimen signature of each officer of the Borrower, authorized to sign requests for loan advances, borrowing certificates, or applications for letters of credit. The Bank may rely conclusively on such certification until it receives notice in writing to the contrary from the Borrower.

(c) *Corporate Action.* The Bank shall have received duly certified copies of all votes passed or other corporate action taken by the Board of Directors of the Borrower with respect to the Loan.

(d) *No Adverse Development.* Neither the consolidated financial position nor the business as a whole of the Borrower or the Corporate Guarantors, nor any substantial portion of the properties and assets of the Borrower or the Corporate Guarantors, shall have been materially adversely affected between the date of application and the date of any advanced hereunder as a result of any legislative or regulatory change or of any fire, explosion, tidal wave, flood, windstorm, earthquake, landslide, accident, condemnation, or governmental intervention, order of any court or governmental agency or commission, invalidity or expiration of any patent or patent license, act of God or of the public enemy or of armed forces, rebellion, strike, labor disturbance or embargo, or otherwise, whether or not insured against, which might impair materially the ability of the Borrower or Corporate Guarantors to fulfill punctually their obligations under this Agreement, the Note, the Loan Documents, and the Guarantee executed in connection herewith.

(e) *Legality.* The making of such Loans shall not contravene any law or rule or regulations thereunder or any Presidential Executive Order binding on the Borrower.

(f) *Representatives True; No Default or Event of Default and Compliance with Covenants.* The representations and warranties in Section 4 and 5 hereof and all other representations in writing made by or on behalf of the Borrower or the Corporate Guarantors in connection with the transactions contemplated by this Agreement shall be true in all material respects as of the date on which they were made and shall also be true in all material respects at and as of the time of the making of such Loans with the same effect as if made at and as of the time of the making of such Loans; no Event of Default or condition which with notice or the passage of time or both would constitute an Event of Default shall exist; and each covenant set forth in this Agreement shall be fully compiled.

(g) *Fees and Expenses Paid.* Any expenses and other amounts due and payable in connection with the Loan prior to or on the date of such advance shall have been paid.

(h) *No Other Debt.* Except for the Subordinated Debt and trade debt incurred in the normal course of business, the Borrower shall not have incurred any additional debt.

(i) *Delivery of Assigned Notes.* All of the notes secured by the Assignment shall have been delivered to the Bank, duly endorsed, and the Borrower and the Bank shall not have been notified of any claims, offsets, or defenses to the enforceability of the notes asserted by the respective makers thereof.

(j) *Miscellaneous.* The Borrower shall have submitted to the Bank such other agreements, documents, and certificates, in form and substance satisfactory to the Bank, as the Bank in its sole discretion deems appropriate or necessary.

Section 7. Covenants

The Borrower covenants and agrees that from the date hereof and as long as the Bank has any obligation to make Loans or any indebtedness to the Bank is outstanding hereunder:

Section 7.1. Notices. It will promptly notify the Bank in writing of the occurrence of any act, event, or condition which constitutes or which after notice or lapse of time, or both, would constitute a failure to satisfy any Condition Precedent set forth in Section 6 or a breach of any Warranty or Representation contained in Section 4 or 5.

EXHIBIT 3 (continued)

Section 7.2. Accuracy of Accounts.   The amount of each Account shown on the books, records, and invoices of the Borrower represented as owing or to be owing by each account debtor is and will be the correct amount actually owing or to be owing by such Account Debtor. The Borrower has no knowledge of any impairment of the validity or collectibility of any of the Accounts and shall notify the Bank of any such fact immediately after the Borrower becomes aware of any such impairment.

Section 7.3. Receipt of Proceeds of Accounts

(a) All accounts receivable and all proceeds and collections therefrom received by the Borrower shall be held in trust by the Borrower for the Bank and shall not be commingled with any of the Borrower's other funds or deposited in any bank account of the Borrower other than the Loan Account.

(b) At such time as any advances made by the Bank pursuant hereto or any letters of credit are outstanding, the Borrower shall deliver to the Bank as and when received by the Borrower, and in the same form as so received, all checks, drafts, and other items which represent the Accounts and any proceeds and collections therefrom, each of which checks, drafts, and other items shall be endorsed to the Bank or as the Bank may otherwise specify from time to time and which shall be accompanied by remittance reports in form satisfactory to the Bank. In addition, the Borrower shall cause any wire or other electronic transfer of funds which constitutes the Accounts or proceeds therefrom to be directed to the Bank. The Bank may apply the proceeds thereof to the Obligations in such manner as the Bank may determine, in its direction.

(c) At the Bank's request, in the Bank's discretion, so long as any Loans are then outstanding, or so long as the Bank has any obligation to make future advances hereunder, the Borrower shall cause all checks, drafts, and other items which represent the Account and any proceeds and collections therefrom to be delivered by the Borrower's account debtors directly to a lockbox, blocked account, or similar recipient over which the Bank has sole access and control. The Bank may apply the proceeds and collections so delivered to the Obligations in such manner as the Bank may determine, in its discretion.

Section 7.4. Status and Reports with Respect to Accounts Receivable and Inventory.   At the Bank's request, either daily or weekly as determined by the Bank, the Borrower shall provide the Bank with a detailed report (in such form as the Bank may specify from time to time) of any of the following, and within two business days prior to the date on which such report is so provided: (i) a listing of the name and amounts of all Accounts and the aging thereof; (ii) a schedule of all inventory and the location thereof; (iii) all allowances, adjustments, returns, and repossessions concerning the Accounts, account receivables, or inventory; (iv) any downgrading in the quality of any of the inventory or occurrence of any event which has an adverse effect upon such inventory's merchantability.

Section 7.5. Monthly Receivables and Inventory Reports.   Monthly, within fifteen (15) days following the end of the previous month (unless the Bank shall request such reports on a more frequent basis), the Borrower shall provide the Bank with:

(a) A listing and aging of the Borrower's Accounts as of the end of the subject month;

(b) A reconciliation of the Accounts with payments received as of the end of the month;

(c) A certificate listing the Borrower's inventory, in such form as the Bank may specify from time to time, as of the end of such month.

Section 7.6. Schedule of Collateral.   At such intervals as the Bank may indicate from time to time by written notice given the Borrower, the Borrower shall provide the Bank with a schedule (in such form as the Bank may specify from time to time) of all Collateral which has come into existence since the date of the last such schedule.

Section 7.7. Financial Statements.   It will furnish, or cause to be furnished, to the Bank:

(a) Within ninety (90) days after the end of each fiscal year, the consolidating balance sheet of the Borrower, TPC, and TRC as at the end of, and the related consolidated and consolidating statement of operations and consolidated and consolidating statement of changes in financial position for, such year certified by independent certified public accountants satisfactory to the Bank, together with a written statement by the accountants certifying such financial statements to the effect that in the course of the audit upon which their certification of such financial statements was based, they obtained knowledge of no condition or event relating to financial matters which constitutes or which with notice or the passage of time, or both, would constitute an Event of Default under this Agreement, or, if such accountants shall have obtained in the course of such audit knowledge of any such condition or event, they shall disclose in such written statement the nature and period of existence thereof, provided that the consolidating statements need not be audited and may be internally prepared and certified as accurate by the chief financial officer of TPC.

(b) Within twenty (20) days after the end of each month, the balance sheet of the Borrower, TPC, and TRC as at the end of such month, and the related statements of operations for the portion of the Borrower's, TPC's, and TRC's fiscal years then elapsed, in each case certified by the principal financial officer of the Borrower, TPC, and TRC as constituting a fair presentation of the Borrower's, TPC's, and TRC's respective financial positions as of such date.

(c) By June 30th of each year, personal financial statements of the Individual Guarantors and Seller, prepared as of May 31st of such year, satisfactory to the Bank and certified as accurate by the Individual Guarantors and by a partner of Seller.

(d) Within a reasonable period of time, and from time to time, such other financial data and information (including accountant's management letters) as the Bank may reasonably request provided that the Borrower, TPC, and TRC shall not be required to furnish any further financial data in audited form unless such materials have been prepared in audited form apart from the Lender's request thereof.

The Bank shall use reasonable care to treat such information as being confidential, but the Bank shall have the unrestricted right to use such information in all ways in the enforcement of the Bank's rights against the Borrower or TPC.

EXHIBIT 3 (continued)

The financial statements referred to above in this Section shall be prepared in accordance with generally accepted accounting principles in force at the time of the preparation thereof.

Section 7.8. Legal Existence; Maintenance of Properties; Ownership of Assets.   The Borrower and Corporate Guarantors will do or cause to be done all things necessary to preserve and keep in full force and effect their legal existence, rights, and franchises. The Borrower will cause all of its properties used or useful in the conduct of its business to be maintained and kept in good condition, repair, and working order and supplied with all necessary equipment and will cause to be made all necessary repairs, renewals, replacements, betterments, and improvements thereof, all as may be reasonably necessary so that the business carried on in connection therewith may be properly and advantageously conducted at all times.

Section 7.9. Conduct of Business Etc.   The Borrower will continue to engage solely in the businesses now conducted by it and in businesses directly related thereto.

Section 7.10. Use of Revolver.   Advances under the Revolving Loan shall be used for general working capital purposes of the Borrower, but in no event shall such advances be used to acquire Subsidiaries, to purchase new stores, or to open new company owned stores, it being expressly understood that any new stores shall be financed with additional equity; provided, however, that upon the prior written approval of the Bank which shall not be unreasonably withheld or delayed, the Borrower may use a portion of the Loan, not to exceed $25,000 per store, to purchase or repurchase existing TDC stores, up to a maximum of four stores.

Section 7.11. Deposit Account.   In order to perfect the Bank's security interest in the Borrower's assets, the Borrower shall maintain its principal depository and checking accounts at the Bank, including, without limitation, the account representing the proceeds of TPC Debt, when implemented.

Section 7.12. Compliance with Franchise Agreements.   The Borrower shall comply with all of the terms and conditions of its various franchise agreements.

Section 7.13. Books and Records.   The Borrower shall keep true records and books of account in which full, true, and correct entries will be made of all dealings or transactions in relation to its business and affairs in accordance with generally accepted accounting principals.

Section 7.14. Negative Covenants.   The Borrower does hereby covenant and agree with the Bank that, so long as any of the Obligations remain unsatisfied or any commitments hereunder remain outstanding, it will comply, and it will cause its Subsidiaries to comply, at all times with the following negative covenants, unless the Bank shall otherwise have agreed in writing:

(a) The Borrower will not change its name, enter into any merger, consolidation, reorganization, or recapitalization, or reclassify its capital stock, provided that nothing herein shall preclude the Borrower from changing the name of any of its product lines.

(b) The Borrower will not sell, transfer, lease, or otherwise dispose of all or (except in the ordinary course of business and except for obsolete or useless assets) any material part of its assets.

(c) The Borrower will not sell, lease, transfer, assign, or otherwise dispose of any of the Collateral except in the ordinary course of business (and except for obsolete or useless assets), provided that nothing herein shall preclude the Borrower from terminating unproductive or defaulting franchisees so long as the Borrower gives the Bank prior written notice of such intended action.

(d) The Borrower will not sell or otherwise dispose of, or for any reason cease operating, any of its divisions, franchises, or lines of business.

(e) The Borrower will not mortgage, pledge, grant, or permit to exist a security interest in, or a lien upon, any of its assets of any kind, now owned or hereafter acquired, except for those existing on the date hereof.

(f) The Borrower will not become liable, directly or indirectly, as guarantor or otherwise for any obligation of any other Person, except for the endorsement of commercial paper for deposit or collection in the ordinary course of business and except for guarantees of franchisees' leases in the normal course of business.

(g) The Borrower will not incur, create, assume, or permit to exist any Indebtedness except (1) the Loan; (2) the Subordinated Debt; (3) trade indebtedness incurred in the ordinary course of business (provided, however, that the Borrower may not acquire inventory other than for cash or on open account except as expressly approved in writing and in advance by the Bank).

(h) The Borrower will not declare or pay any dividends, or make any other payment or distribution on account of its capital stock, or make any assignment or transfer of accounts, or other than in the ordinary course of business or inventory.

(i) The Borrower will not form any subsidiary, make any investment in (including any assignment of inventory or other property), or make any loan in the nature of an investment to any Person, provided that nothing herein shall prohibit the Borrower from converting franchisees' accounts receivable into term notes, in which event such notes shall be endorsed in favor of and delivered to the Bank as additional Collateral hereunder.

(j) The Borrower will not make any loan or advance to any officer, shareholder, director, or employee of the Borrower, except for business travel and similar temporary advances in the ordinary course of business.

(k) The Borrower will not issue, redeem, purchase, or retire any of its capital stock or grant or issue, or purchase or retire for any consideration, any warrant, right, or option pertaining thereto or other security convertible into any of the foregoing, or permit any transfer, sale, redemption, retirement, or other change in the ownership of the outstanding capital stock of the Borrower.

EXHIBIT 3 (continued)

(l) Except as permitted in the Subordination Agreement, the Borrower will not prepay any Subordinated Debt or indebtedness for borrowed money (except the Loan) or enter into or modify any agreement as a result of which the terms of payment of any of the foregoing Indebtedness are waived or modified.

(m) The Borrower will not acquire or agree to acquire any stock, in all or substantially all of the assets, of any Person.

(n) The Borrower will not amend its lease of the premises at 385 Appleton Street, North Andover, Massachusetts, in such a way as to increase the rent or other monetary obligations due thereunder.

(o) The Borrower will not furnish the Bank any certificate or other document that will contain any untrue statement of material fact or that will omit to state a material fact necessary to make it not misleading in light of the circumstances under which it was furnished.

Section 7.15. TPC Covenants. So long as the Loan shall remain outstanding or Bank shall have any obligation to make future advances, TPC shall not (i) transfer, convey, sell, assign, hypothecate, grant a security interest in, or pledge any of the shares of the Borrower or all, or substantially all, of the assets of the Borrower; (ii) cause the Borrower to pay any dividends otherwise distribute cash or other assets to TPC, provided that TPC may cause the Borrower to distribute not more than $250,000 in the aggregate in any twelve month period by way of dividends, distributions, or salary to TPC and/or its officers and employees; or (iii) permit any transactions involving the stock of TPC which individually or in the aggregate shall cause a change of control or of management of TPC.

Section 8. Events of Default

Without derogating from the DEMAND nature of the Note and the Credit Facility, if any of the following events shall occur:

Section 8.1. If the Borrower shall fail to pay an installment of interest or of principal on the Note due hereunder on or before the due date thereof, if the Borrower shall fail to reduce the outstanding principal balance of the Loan as provided in Section 2.1 hereof, or if the full principal balance of the Note is not paid on the Loan Review Date (or such earlier date upon which such balance may become due and payable following an Event of Default) or on the making of demand by the Bank.

Section 8.2. If the Borrower shall fail in any material respect to perform within ten (10) days following written notice from the Bank any term, covenant, or agreement contained in Section 7 hereof, provided, however, that if such default is susceptible of cure but may not be cured within ten days, the Borrower shall commence to cure such default within ten days after notice thereof and shall proceed continuously and diligently to complete such cure but in any event within thirty (30) days of the date of such notice.

Section 8.3. If any representation or warranty of the Borrower in Section 4 or of the Corporate Guarantors in Section 5 hereof or in any certificate delivered hereunder shall prove to have been false in any material respect upon the date when made;

Section 8.4. If the Borrower shall fail to perform any other term, covenant, or agreement herein contained or contained in any Loan Documents, as amended, for ten (10) days after written notice of such failure has been given to the Borrower by the Bank, provided, however, that if such default is susceptible of cure but may not be cured within ten (10) days, the Borrower shall commence to cure such default with ten (10) days after notice thereof and shall proceed continuously and diligently to complete such cure but in any event within thirty (30) days of the date of such notice.

Section 8.5. If the Borrower, or any Guarantor, shall (i) apply for or consent to the appointment of, or the taking of possession by, a receiver, custodian, trustee, or liquidator of itself or of all or a substantial part of its property; (ii) admit in writing his or its inability, or generally unable, to pay his or its debts as such debts become due; (iii) make a general assignment for the benefit of its creditors; (iv) commence a voluntary case under the Federal Bankruptcy Code (as now or hereafter in effect); (v) file a petition seeking to take advantage of any other law relating to bankruptcy, insolvency, reorganization, winding-up, or composition or adjustment of debts; (vi) with respect to any Individual Guarantor, die, or become legally incompetent or incapacitated; (vii) with respect to any Corporate Guarantor dissolve or liquidate; (viii) fail to convert in a timely or appropriate manner, or acquiesce in writing to, any petition filed against the Borrower or any Corporate Guarantor in an involuntary case under such Bankruptcy Code; or (ix) take any corporate action for the purpose of effecting any of the foregoing.

Section 8.6. If a proceeding or case shall be commenced without the application or consent of the Borrower in any court of competent jurisdiction seeking (i) the liquidation, reorganization, dissolution, winding-up, or composition or readjustment of debts, of the Borrower or any Corporate Guarantor; (ii) the appointment of a trustee, receiver, custodian, liquidator, or the like of the Borrower or any Corporate Guarantor or of all or any substantial part of its assets; (iii) similar relief in respect of the Borrower or any Corporate Guarantor under any law relating to bankruptcy, insolvency, reorganization, winding-up, or composition or adjustment of debts, and such proceeding or case shall continue undismissed, or an order, judgment, or decree approving or ordering any of the foregoing shall be entered or an order of relief against the Borrower or any Corporate Guarantor shall be entered in an involuntary case under such Bankruptcy Code;

Then, and in every such event (an "Event of Default"): the Commitments of the Banks hereunder (if then outstanding) shall forthwith terminate, and the principal of and interest on the Loans (if any are then outstanding) shall be and become forthwith due and payable in each case all without presentment or demand for payment, notice of nonpayment, protest, or further notice or demand of any kind, all of which are expressly waived by the Borrower. No remedy herein conferred upon the holder of the Note is intended to be exclusive of any other remedy, and each and every remedy shall be cumulative and shall be in addition to every other remedy given hereunder or under any other agreement or now or hereafter existing at law or in equity or by statute or any other provision of law.

EXHIBIT 3 (concluded)

Section 9. Miscellaneous

Section 9.1. Notices.   Any notice or other communication in connection with this Agreement shall be deemed to be delivered if in writing (or in the form of a telegram) addressed as provided below and if either (a) actually delivered at said address or (b) in the case of a letter, three business days shall have elapsed after the same shall have been deposited in the United States mails, postage prepaid and registered or certified:

and in any case at such other address as the addressee shall have specified by written notice. All periods of notice shall be measured from the date of delivery thereof.

Section 9.2. Costs, Expenses, and Taxes.   The Borrower agrees to pay, whether or not any of the transactions contemplated hereby are consummated, the reasonable out-of-pocket costs and expenses of the Bank in connection with the preparation, execution, delivery, and enforcement of this Agreement, and any amendments, waivers, or consents with respect to any of the foregoing.

Section 9.3. Lien; Set-Off.   The Borrower grants to the Bank a direct and continuing lien and continuing security interest, as security for the performance of its obligations hereunder, in and upon all deposits, balances, and other sums credited by or due from the Bank to the Borrower. Regardless of the adequacy of any other collateral, if a demand has been made for the payment of the Note and has not been withdrawn, or if the Loan has otherwise become due and payable, any such deposits, balances, or other sums credited by or due from the Bank to the Borrower may at any time or from time to time, without notice to the Borrower or compliance with any other condition precedent now or hereafter imposed by statute, rule of law, or otherwise (all of which are hereafter expressly waived), be set off, appropriated, and applied by the Bank against any or all such obligation in such manner as the Bank in its discretion may determine; and, in addition, the Bank shall have the rights of a secured party under the Uniform Commercial Code with respect thereto.

Section 9.4. Cumulative Rights; Nonwaiver.   All of the rights of the Bank hereunder and under the Note, the Loan Documents, and each other agreement now or hereafter executed in connection herewith, therewith, or otherwise, shall be cumulative and may be exercised singly, together, or in such combination as the Bank may determine in its sole judgment. No waiver or condonation of a breach on any one occasion shall be deemed to be a waiver or condonation in other instance.

Section 9.5. Governing Law.   This Agreement and the rights and obligations of the parties hereunder and under the Loans shall be construed, interpreted, and determined in accordance with laws of the Commonwealth of Massachusetts.

Section 9.6. Successors and Assigns.   This Agreement shall be binding upon the Borrower and its successors and assigns and shall be binding upon and inure to the benefit of the Bank and its successors and assigns; provided, however, that that Borrower may not assign any of its rights hereunder.

Section 9.7. Table of Contents; Title and Headings.   Any table of contents, the titles of the Articles, and the headings of the Sections are not parts of this Agreement and shall not be deemed to affect the meaning or construction of any of its provisions.

Section 9.8. Counterparts.   This Agreement may be executed in several counterparts, each of which when executed and delivered is an original, but all of which together shall constitute one instrument. In making proof of this Agreement, it shall not be necessary to produce or account for more than one such counterpart.

Section 9.9. Indemnification.   The Borrower hereby agrees to indemnify the Bank and hold it harmless against any and all liabilities, obligations, loans, damages, penalties, actions, judgments, costs, or expenses of any kind whatsoever (including without limitation, reasonable attorney fees and disbursements) that may be imposed on or incurred by or asserted against the Bank in any way relating to or arising out of or in connection with any of the transactions contemplated herein.

Section 9.10. Venue; Jury Trial.   The Borrower and the Guarantors hereby agree that any action or proceeding involving this Agreement or any other agreement or document referred to herein, including the Note, may be brought in, and hereby expressly submit to the jurisdiction of, all state courts located in the Commonwealth of Massachusetts. To the extent permitted by applicable law, the Borrower and the Guarantors hereby waive trial by jury in any action on or with respect to this Agreement, the Note, or any other agreement with the Bank.

Section 9.11. Conflicting Provisions.   In the event that any provision, term, and condition of any of the Loan Documents shall conflict with any of the provisions, terms, and conditions of this Agreement, the provisions, terms, and conditions set forth herein shall prevail.

IN WITNESS WHEREOF, the parties hereto have executed this Agreement as of the 8th day of August, 2001, by their respective officers hereunto duly authorized.

PART FIVE

Startup and Beyond

Under conditions of rapid growth, entrepreneurs face unusual paradoxes and challenges as their companies grow and the management modes required by these companies change.

Whether they have the adaptability and resilience in the face of swift developments to grow fast enough as managers and whether they have enough courage, wisdom, and discipline to balance controlled growth with growing fast enough to keep pace with the competition and industry turbulence will become crystal clear.

Entrepreneurs face enormous pressures and physical and emotional wear and tear during the rapid growth of their companies. It goes with the territory. Entrepreneurs after start-up find that "it" has to be done now, that there is no room to falter, and that there are no "runners-up." Those who have a personal entrepreneurial strategy, who are healthy, who have

their lives in order, and who know what they are signing up for fare better than those who do not.

Among all the stimulating and exceedingly difficult challenges entrepreneurs face—and can meet successfully—none is more liberating and exhilarating than a successful harvest. Perhaps the point is made besting one of the final lines of the musical *Oliver:* "In the end, all that counts is in the bank, in large amounts!"

Obviously money is not the only thing, or everything. But money can ensure both independence and autonomy to do what you want to do, mostly on your terms, and can significantly increase the options and opportunities at your discretion. Although value creation was the goal, the measure of success is wealth creation and how one chooses to distribute and use that wealth. In effect, for entrepreneurs, net worth is the final scorecard of the value creation process and for one's potential for philanthropy.

551

Chapter Seventeen

Leading Rapid Growth, Crises, and Recovery

Bite off more than you can chew, and then chew it!

Roger Babson
Founder, Babson College

Results Expected

Upon completion of the chapter, you will be able to

1. Discuss how higher-potential, rapidly growing ventures have invented new organizational paradigms to replace brontosaurus capitalism.

2. Describe how higher-potential ventures "grow up big" and the special problems, organization, and leadership requirements of rapid growth.

3. Discuss concepts of organizational culture and climate, and how entrepreneurial leaders foster favorable cultures.

4. Identify specific signals and clues that can alert entrepreneurial managers to impeding crises, and describe both quantitative and qualitative symptoms of trouble.

5. Describe the principal diagnostic methods used to devise intervention and turnaround plans, and identify remedial actions for dealing with lenders, creditors, and employees.

6. Analyze and discuss the Telephony Translations, Inc., case study.

Inventing New Organizational Paradigms

At the beginning of this text we examined how nimble and fleet-footed entrepreneurial firms have supplanted aging corporate giants with new leadership approaches, a passion for value creation, and an obsession with opportunity that have been unbeatable in the marketplace for talent and ideas. These entrepreneurial ventures have experienced rapid to explosive growth and have become the investments of choice of the U.S. venture capital community.

Because of their innovative nature and competitive breakthroughs, entrepreneurial ventures have demonstrated a remarkable capacity to invent new paradigms of organization and management. They have abandoned the organizational practices and structures typical of the industrial giants from the post–World War II era to the 1990s. We could characterize those approaches thus: What they lacked in creativity and flexibility to deal with ambiguity and rapid change, they made up for with rules, structure, hierarchy, and quantitative analysis.

Special thanks to Ed Marram, entrepreneur, educator, and friend, for his lifelong commitment to studying and leading growing businesses and sharing his knowledge with the authors. Ed is past director of the Arthur M. Blank Center for Entrepreneurship at Babson College.

The epitome of this pattern is the Hay System, which by the 1980s became the leading method of defining and grading management jobs in large companies. Scoring high with "Hay points" was the key to more pay, a higher position in the hierarchy, and greater power. The criteria for Hay points include number of people who are direct reports, value of assets under management, sales volume, number of products, square feet of facilities, total size of operating and capital budget, and the like. We can easily see who gets ahead in such a system: Be bureaucratic, have the most people and largest budget, increase head count and levels under your control, and think up the largest capital projects. Missing in the criteria are all the basic components of entrepreneurship we have seen in this book: value creating, opportunity creating and seizing, frugality with resources, bootstrapping strategies, staged capital commitments, team building, achieving better fits, and juggling paradoxes.

Contrast the multilayered, hierarchical, military-like levels of control and command that characterize traditional capitalism with the common patterns among entrepreneurial firms: They are flat—often only one or two layers deep—adaptive, and flexible; they look like interlocking circles rather than ladders; they are integrative around customers and critical missions; they are learning- and influence-based rather than rank- and power-based. People lead more through influence and persuasion, which are derived from knowledge and performance rather than through formal rank, position, or seniority. They create a perpetual learning culture. They value people and share the wealth with people who help create it.

Take, for example, a 2003 IT start-up in Argentina whose founder took a radically different organizational approach to human resource management and issues. Instead of having a human resources department, he created what he called the "People Care Department." Its charter and message went far beyond the realm of traditional human resources management (custodial care for health benefits and pensions, vacation and sick days, wage and compensation structures, and the like). This highly innovative department developed a number of services that sent a powerful message about how much he cared about his people and how important they were. Measures included special play areas and day care for associates with children, and special days off to devote extra attention to important family events. These progressive practices have enabled the firm to attract and keep the best talent in the area.

Entrepreneurial Leaders Are Not Administrators or Managers

In the growing business, owner–entrepreneurs focus on recognizing and choosing opportunities, allocating re-

sources, motivating employees, and maintaining control— while encouraging the innovative actions that cause a business to grow. In a new venture the entrepreneur's immediate challenge is to learn how to dance with elephants without being trampled to death! Once beyond the start-up phase, the ultimate challenge of the owner–entrepreneur is to develop the firm to the point where it is able to lead the elephants on the dance floor.

Consider the following quotes from two distinguished business leaders, based on their experiences with holders of MBAs in the 1960s–1980s. Fred Smith, founder, chairman, and CEO of Federal Express: "MBAs are people in Fortune 500 companies who make careers out of saying no!" And according to General George Doriot, father of American venture capital and for years a professor at Harvard Business School, "There isn't any business that a Harvard MBA cannot analyze out of existence!"

Those are profound statements, given the sources. These perceptions also help to explain the stagnancy and eventual demise of brontosaurus capitalism. Legions of MBAs in the 1950s, 1960s, 1970s, and early 1980s were taught the old style of management. Until the 1980s virtually all the cases, problems, and lectures in MBA programs were about large, established companies.

Consider the comparison of key underlying assumptions and orientations of what can be thought of as the tradition of general management versus what we call entrepreneurial leadership and the entrepreneurial organization, as noted in the box on next page.

Ask yourself, Which set of characteristics is most compelling for me? It is not hard to see why entrepreneurial leaders and their innovative and refreshing approaches to organization have won over the hearts and minds of today's young people. Such underlying beliefs have translated into practices that liberate talent and encourage higher performance. It is no wonder that these approaches are here to stay and that so many large companies worldwide are seeking to reinvent their obsolete general management approach to people. In terms of competitive advantages, these creative ways of organizing and leading are not capital intensive at all; they are leadership intensive. What an exciting way to live and an inexpensive way to win! The spirit and principles of Ewing Marion Kauffman live!

Breakthrough Strategy: Babson's F.W. Olin Graduate School

The first MBA program in the world to break the lockstep of the prior 50 years was the Franklin W. Olin Graduate School of Business at Babson College. In 1992, practicing what they taught, faculty members discarded the traditional, functional approach to an MBA education, consisting of individual courses

Traditional General Management	Entrepreneurial Leadership and Organization
▪ Pyramidal/hierarchical.	▪ Flat, flexible, think/act like an owner.
▪ Incremental improvement.	▪ Stepwise and disruptive change.
▪ Risk avoidance/embrace stability.	▪ Fearless, relentless experimentation.
▪ Avoid and punish failure.	▪ Specialize in new mistakes.
▪ Resource allocation, budget driven.	▪ Opportunity obsessed.
▪ Central command and control.	▪ Front-line, customer driven.
▪ Resource optimization.	▪ Creativity = capital.
▪ Cost oriented.	▪ Resource frugality and parsimony.
▪ Linear, sequential.	▪ Systems and nonlinear.
▪ Local focus.	▪ Global perspective.
▪ Compensate and reward.	▪ Create and share the wealth.
▪ Manage and control.	▪ People want to be led, not managed.
▪ Zero defects/error free.	▪ Manage risk: reward and fit.

in accounting, marketing, finance, information technology, operations, and human resources in stand-alone sequence, with too many lectures.

A revolutionary curriculum for the first year of the MBA took its place: An entirely new and team-taught curriculum in a series of highly integrative modules anchored conceptually in the model of the entrepreneurial process from *New Venture Creation*.[1] MBAs now experience a unique learning curve that immerses them for the first year in cases, assignments, and content that has immediate and relevant applicability to the entrepreneurial process. Emerging entrepreneurial companies are the focal points for most case studies, while larger, established companies seeking to recapture their entrepreneurial spirit and management approach are examined in others. After more than five years, students, employers, and faculty have characterized the program as a resounding success. (See the Babson College Web site: www.babson.edu.)

Leading Practices of High-Growth Companies[1]

In Chapter 3 we examined a summary of research conducted on fast-growth companies to determine the leading practices of these firms. Now this research will likely take on new meaning to you. As we examine each of these four practice areas—marketing, finance, management, and planning—we can see the practical side of how fast-growth entrepreneurs pursue opportunities; devise, manage, and orchestrate their financial strategies; build a team with collaborative decision making; and plan with vision, clarity, and flexibility. Clearly, rapid growth is a different game, requiring an entrepreneurial mind-set and skills.

Growing Up Big

Stages of Growth Revisited

Higher-potential ventures do not stay small for long. Although an entrepreneur may have done a good job of assessing an opportunity, forming a new venture team, marshaling resources, planning, and so forth, managing and growing such a venture is a different leadership game.

Ventures in the high-growth stage face the problems discussed in Chapter 9. These include forces that limit the creativities of the founders and team; that cause confusion and resentment over roles, responsibilities, and goals; that call for specialization and therefore erode collaboration; that require operating mechanisms and controls; and more.

Recall also that founders of rapidly growing ventures are usually relatively inexperienced in launching a new venture and yet face situations where time and change are compounded and where events are nonlinear and nonparametric. Usually structures, procedures, and patterns are fluid, and decision making needs to follow counterintuitive and unconventional patterns.

Chapter 9 discussed the stages or phases companies experience during their growth. Recall that generally the first three years before start-up are called the research and development (R&D) stage; the first three years after launch, the start-up stage; years 4 through 10, the early-growth stage; the 10th year through the 15th or so, maturity; and after the 15th year, the stability stage. These time estimates are approximate and may vary.

Various models, and our previous discussion, depicted the life cycle of a growing firm as a smooth curve with rapidly ascending sales and profits and a

[1] Special appreciation is given to Ernst & Young LLP and the Kauffman Center for Entrepreneurial Leadership for permission to include the summary of their research here.

leveling off toward the peak and then dipping toward extended decline.

In truth, however, very few, if any, new and growing firms experience such smooth and linear phases of growth. If the actual growth curves of new companies are plotted over their first 10 years, the curves will look far more like the ups and downs of a rollercoaster ride than the smooth progressions usually depicted. Over the life of a typical growing firm, there are periods of jerks, bumps, hiccups, indigestion, and renewal interspersed with periods of smooth sailing. Sometimes there is continual upward progress through all this, but other firms occasionally seem near collapse or at least in considerable peril. Ed Marram characterizes the five stages of a firm as Wonder, Blunder, Thunder, Plunder, and Asunder (see Exhibit 17.1). Wonder is the period that is filled with uncertainty about survival. Blunder is a growth stage when many firms stumble and fail. The Thunder stage occurs when growth is robust and the entrepreneur has built a solid management team. Cash flow is robust during Plunder, but in Asunder the firm needs to renew or will decline.

Core Leadership Mode

As was noted earlier, changes in several critical variables determine just how frantic or easy transitions from one stage to the next will be. As a result, it is possible to make some generalizations about the main leadership challenges and transitions that will be encountered as a company grows. The core leadership mode is influenced by the number of employees a firm has, which is in turn related to its dollar sales.[2]

Recall, as shown in Exhibit 9.1, that until sales reach approximately $5 million and employees number about 25, the core leadership mode is one of *doing.* Between $5 million and $15 million in sales and 25 to 75 employees, the core leadership mode is *managing.* When sales exceed $10 million and employees number over 75, the core leadership mode is *leading team leaders.* Obviously these revenue and employment figures are broad generalities. The number of people is an indicator of the complexity of the leadership task and suggests a new wall to be scaled, rather than a precise point.

To illustrate how widely sales per employee (SPE) can vary among established firms, consider Exhibit 17.2. Netflix, by virtue of an online model and an effective home delivery management system, is generating over $907,000 in SPE, whereas a heavily retail-based business in the same industry—Blockbuster—is generating in the range of $163,000 in SPE.

These numbers are boundaries, constantly moving as a result of inflation and competitive dynamics. Sales per employee can illustrate how a company stacks up in its industry, but remember that the number is a relative measurement; SPEs can vary tremendously across industries and firm size. Consider, for example, that retailer Wal-Mart with 2007 sales of $370.5 billion had SPE of $195,000, while biotechnology firm

EXHIBIT 17.1

Growth Stages

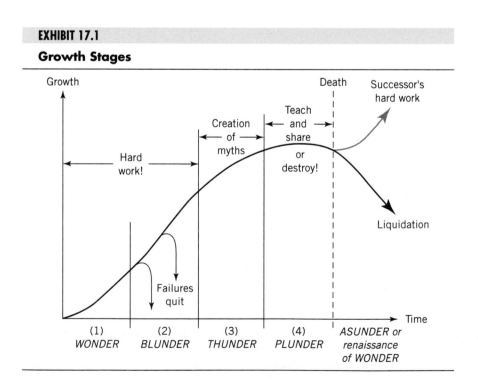

[2] Harvey "Chet" Krentzman described this phenomenon to the authors many years ago. The principle still applies.

EXHIBIT 17.2

2007 Sales per Employee

Company	(005)
Genentech	1,089.0
Costco	943.7
Google	940.6
Netflix	907.7
Dell	715.6
Microsoft	684.4
Cisco	589.7
Nike	572.8
Biogen	560.0
Time Warner	504.0
Sony Corporation	490.7
Monsanto	485.1
Juniper Networks	462.8
Bristol-Myers Squibb	434.2
Sun Microsystems	406.4
Home Depot	359.2
Delta Airlines	333.7
Bank of America	330.8
Raytheon	300.2
IBM	262.4
Timberland	234.9
Wal-Mart	195.0
Yum Brands Restaurants	191.2
Blockbuster	162.8
Intercontinental Hotel Group	150.1
Sonesta International Hotels	77.4
McDonald's	49.8

Source: Yahoo! Finance.

Genentech (2007 sales of $11.5 billion) was generating SPE of over a million. Interestingly, another big-box retailer, Costco, with 2007 sales of $66 billion, is near the top of our list with SPE of just under $974,000.

During each growth stage of a firm, there are entrepreneurial crises, or hurdles, that most firms will confront. Exhibit 17.3 and the following discussion consider by stage some indications of crisis.[3] As the exhibit shows, for each fundamental driving force of entrepreneurship, a number of signals indicate that crises are imminent. While the list is long, these are not the only indicators of crises—only the most common. Each of these signals does not necessarily indicate that particular crises will happen to every company at each stage, but when the signals are there, serious difficulties cannot be too far behind.

The Problem in Rate of Growth

Difficulties in recognizing crisis signals and developing management approaches are compounded by rate of growth itself. The faster the rate of growth, the greater the potential for difficulty; this is because of the various pressures, chaos, confusion, and loss of control. It is not an exaggeration to say that these pressures and demands increase geometrically, rather than in a linear way (see the discussion in Chapter 9).

Growth rates affect all aspects of a business. Thus as sales increase, as more people are hired, and as inventory increases, sales outpace manufacturing capacity. Facilities are then increased, people are moved between buildings, accounting systems and controls cannot keep up, and so on. The cash burn rate accelerates. As such acceleration continues, learning curves do the same. Worst of all, cash collections lag behind, as shown in Exhibit 17.4.

Distinctive issues caused by rapid growth were considered at seminars at Babson College with the founders and presidents of rapidly growing companies—companies with sales of at least $1 million and growing in excess of 30 percent per year.[4] These founders and presidents pointed to the following:

- *Opportunity overload:* Rather than lacking enough sales or new market opportunities (a classic concern in mature companies), these firms faced an abundance. Choosing from among these was a problem.

- *Abundance of capital:* Whereas most stable or established small or medium-sized firms often have difficulties obtaining equity and debt financing, most of the rapidly growing firms were not constrained by this. The problem was, rather, how to evaluate investors as partners and the terms of the deals with which they were presented.

- *Misalignment of cash burn and collection rates:* These firms all pointed to problems of cash burn rates racing ahead of collections. They found that unless effective integrated accounting, inventory, purchasing, shipping, and invoicing systems and controls are in place, this misalignment can lead to chaos and collapse. One firm, for example, had tripled its sales in three years from $5 million to $16 million. Suddenly its president resigned, insisting that, with the systems that were in

---

[3] The crises discussed here are the ones the authors consider particularly critical. Usually, failure to overcome even a few can imperil a venture at a given stage. There are, however, many more, but a complete treatment of all of them is outside the scope of this book.

[4] These seminars were held at Babson College near Boston in 1985 and 1999. A good number of the firms represented had sales over $1 million, and many were growing at greater than 100 percent per year.

EXHIBIT 17.3

Crises and Symptoms

Pre–Start-Up (Years −3 to −0)

Entrepreneurs

- *Focus:* Is the founder really an entrepreneur, bent on building a company, or an inventor, technical dilettante, or the like?
- *Selling:* Does the team have the necessary selling and closing skills to bring in the business and make the plan—on time?
- *Management:* Does the team have the necessary management skills and relevant experience, or is it overloaded in one or two areas (e.g., the financial or technical areas)?
- *Ownership:* Have the critical decisions about ownership and equity splits been resolved, and are the members committed to these?

Opportunity

- *Focus:* Is the business really user-, customer-, and market-driven (by a need/pain point), or is it driven by an invention or a desire to create?
- *Customers:* Have customers been identified with specific names, addresses, and phone numbers, and have purchase levels been estimated, or is the business still only at the concept stage?
- *Supply:* Are costs, margins, and lead times to acquire supplies, components, and key people known?
- *Strategy:* Is the entry plan a shotgun and cherry-picking strategy, or is it a rifle shot at a well-focused niche?

Resources

- *Resources:* Have the required capital resources been identified?
- *Cash:* Are the founders already out of cash (OOC) and their own resources?
- *Business plan:* Is there a business plan, or is the team "hoofing it"?
- *Creativity-capital:* Are bootstrapping and sweat equity being used creatively? Is the brain trust being built?

Start-Up and Survival (Years 0 to 3)

Entrepreneurs

- *Leadership:* Has a top leader been accepted, or are founders vying for the decision role or insisting on equality in all decisions?
- *Goals:* Do the founders share and have compatible goals and work styles, or are these starting to conflict and diverge once the enterprise is under way and pressures mount?
- *Leadership:* Are the founders anticipating and preparing for a shift from doing to managing and letting go—of decisions and control—that will be required to make the plan on time?
- *Courage and ethics:* Can the founders stand the heat and maintain their integrity?

Opportunity

- *Economics:* Are the economic benefits and payback to the customer actually being achieved on time?
- *Strategy:* Is the company a one-product company with no encore in sight?
- *Competition:* Have previously unknown competitors or substitutes appeared in the marketplace? Are revenue targets met?
- *Distribution:* Are there surprises and difficulties in actually achieving planned channels of distribution on time?

Resources

- *Cash:* Is the company facing a cash crunch early as a result of not having a business plan (and a financial plan)? That is, is it facing a crunch because no one is asking, When will we run out of cash? Are the owners' pocketbooks exhausted?
- *Schedule:* Is the company experiencing serious deviations from projections and time estimates in the business plan? Is the company able to marshall resources according to plan and on time?
- *Creativity-capital:* Is this practiced and rewarded?

Early Growth (Years 4 to 10)

Entrepreneurs

- *Doing or leading:* Are the founders still just *doing,* or are they building and leading the team for results by a plan? Have the founders begun to delegate and let go of critical decisions, or do they maintain veto power over all significant decisions?
- *Focus:* Is the mind-set of the founders operational only, or is serious strategic thinking going on as well?
- *E-culture:* Are the founders building an entrepreneurial organization?

Opportunity

- *Market:* Are repeat sales and sales to new customers being achieved on time, according to plan, and because of interaction with customers, or are these coming from the engineering, R&D, or planning group? Is the company shifting to a marketing orientation without losing its killer instinct for closing sales?
- *Competition:* Are price and quality being blamed for loss of customers or for an inability to achieve targets in the sales plan, while customer service is rarely mentioned?
- *Economics:* Are gross margins beginning to erode?

(continued)

EXHIBIT 17.3   (concluded)
Crises and Symptoms

Resources

- *Financial control:* Are accounting and information systems and control (purchasing orders, inventory, billing, collections, cost and profit analysis, cash management, etc.) keeping pace with growth and being there when they are needed?
- *Cash:* Is the company always out of cash or nearly OOC, and is no one asking when it will run out, or is sure why or what to do about it?
- *Contacts:* Has the company developed the outside networks (directors, contacts, etc.) it needs to continue growth?

Maturity (Years 10 to 15 plus)

Entrepreneurs

- *Goals:* Are the partners in conflict over control, goals, or underlying ethics or values?
- *Health:* Are there signs that the founders' marriages, health, or emotional stability are coming apart (i.e., are there extramarital affairs, drug and/or alcohol abuse, or fights and temper tantrums with partners or spouses)?
- *Teamwork:* Is there a sense of team building for a "greater purpose," with the founders now managing managers, or is there conflict over control of the company and disintegration?

Opportunity

- *Economics/competition:* Are the products and/or services that have gotten the company this far experiencing unforgiving economics as a result of perishability, competitor blind sides, new technology, or offshore competition, and is there a plan to respond?
- *Product encore:* Has a major new product introduction been a failure?
- *Strategy:* Has the company continued to cherry-pick in fast-growth markets, with a resulting lack of strategic definition (which opportunities to say no to)?

Resources

- *Cash:* Is the firm OOC again? Does it use cash rather than accrual budgeting?
- *Development/information:* Has growth gotten out of control, with systems, training, and development of new managers failing to keep pace?
- *Financial control:* Have systems continued to lag behind sales?

Harvest/Stability (Years 15 to 20 plus)

Entrepreneurs

- *Succession/ownership:* Are there mechanisms in place to provide for management succession and the handling of very tricky ownership issues (especially family)?
- *Goals:* Have the partners' personal and financial goals and priorities begun to conflict and diverge? Are any of the founders simply bored or burned out, and are they seeking a change of view and activities?
- *Entrepreneurial passion:* Has there been an erosion of the passion for creating value through the recognition and pursuit of opportunity, or are turf-building, acquiring status and power symbols, and gaining control favored?

Opportunity

- *Strategy:* Is there a spirit of innovation and renewal in the firm (e.g., a goal that half the company's sales come from products or services less than five years old), or has lethargy set in?
- *Economics:* Have the core economics and durability of the opportunity eroded so far that profitability and return on investment are nearly as low as that for the Fortune 500?

Resources

- *Cash:* Has OOC been solved by increasing bank debt and leverage because the founders do not want—or cannot agree—to give up equity?
- *Accounting:* Have accounting and legal issues, especially their relevance for wealth building and estate and tax planning, been anticipated and addressed? Has a harvest concept been part of the long-range planning process?

place, the company would be able to grow to $100 million. However, the computer system was disastrously inadequate, which compounded other management weaknesses. It was impossible to generate any believable financial and accounting information for many months. Losses of more than $1 million annually mounted, and the company's lenders panicked. To make matters worse, the auditors failed to stay on top of the situation until it was too late and were replaced. While the company has survived, it has had to restructure its business and has shrunk to $6 million in sales to pay off bank debt and to avoid bankruptcy. Fortunately it is recovering.

- *Decision making:* Many of the firms succeeded because they executed functional day-to-day and week-to-week decisions, rather than strategizing. Strategy had to take a back seat. Many

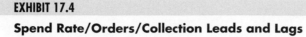

EXHIBIT 17.4

Spend Rate/Orders/Collection Leads and Lags

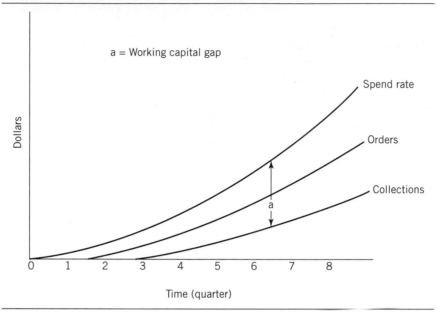

of the representatives of these firms argued that in conditions of rapid growth, strategy was only about 10 percent of the story.

- *Expanding facilities and space. . . and surprises:* Expansion of space or facilities is a problem and one of the most disrupting events during the early explosive growth of a company. Managers of many of these firms were not prepared for the surprises, delays, organizational difficulties, and system interruptions that are spawned by such expansion.

Chaos Happens

On a recent trip to Venezuela to work with entrepreneurship educators from several countries in the region, we heard some remarkable stories about the realities of being an entrepreneur there today. One entrepreneur put it this way: "They change the rules every two days in ways that affect everything in our business—from employment, to contracts, to ownership, to taxes and regulations. And you cannot predict what or when they will change." Another told us about a Venezuelan who rose through the ranks to become worldwide chair of the Swiss multinational Nestlé. When asked how a Venezuelan who had worked for only three years in this country of 26 million people could rise to such a position, the response was, "You have to realize that in those three years, we had a coup d'état and change of government, two devaluations of the currency, high inflation and unemployment,

general economic chaos, and major political and social unrest. In Switzerland it would take five generations of Swiss managers to accumulate that much experience!"

There is a profound lesson here: Environments of high uncertainty are wonderful learning grounds for entrepreneurs. There is no better way to see if you can hit a fast ball than to swing at one!

Challenges and chaotic environments are of course not unique to Venezuela. Industry turbulence is common in new and uncharted territories, where often the best opportunities lie. Firms with higher growth rates are usually found in industries that are developing rapidly. These industries are often characterized by many new entrants with competing products or services and with substitutes.

The turbulence in the semiconductor industry in the 1980s is a good example. From June 1984 to June 1985, the price to original equipment manufacturers (OEMs) of 64K memory chips fell from $2.50 each to 50 cents. The price to OEMs of 256K chips fell from $15 to $3. The same devastating industry effect manifested in the years 2000–2002 when cellular airtime pricing plunged by more than 50 percent. Imagine the disruption this caused in marketing and sales projections, in financial planning and cash forecasting, and the like for firms in these industries. Often, too, there are rapid shifts in cost and experience curves. The consequences of missed steps in growing business are profound. Consider the examples of Polaroid and Xerox shown in Exhibit 17.5.

EXHIBIT 17.5

How the Mighty Have Fallen

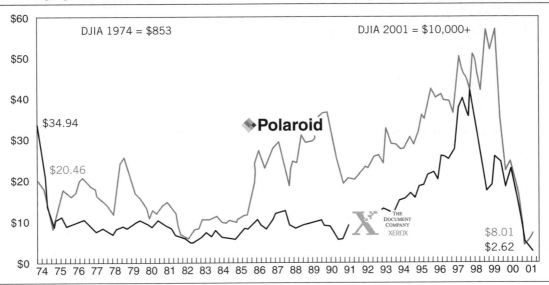

DJIA 1974 = $853

DJIA 2001 = $10,000+

Polaroid

$34.94

$20.46

THE DOCUMENT COMPANY XEROX

$8.01

$2.62

74 75 76 77 78 79 80 81 82 83 84 85 86 87 88 89 90 91 92 93 94 95 96 97 98 99 00 01

Source: The authors wish to thank Ed Marram for sharing this analysis.

When the Bloom Is Off the Rose

There is a saying among horseback riders that the person who has never been thrown from a horse probably has never ridden one. Jim Hindman, founder of Jiffy Lube, is fond of saying, "Ultimately it is not how many touchdowns you score but how fast and often you get up after being tackled." These insights capture the essence of the ups and downs that can occur during the growth and development of a new venture.

Getting Into Trouble—The Causes

Trouble can be caused by external forces not under the control of management. Among the most frequently mentioned are recession, interest rate changes, changes in government policy, inflation, the entry of new competition, and industry/product obsolescence.

Experts who manage turnarounds say that although such circumstances define the environment to which a troubled company needs to adjust, they are rarely the principal reason for a company failure. External shocks impact all companies in an industry, and only some of them fail. Others survive and prosper.

Most causes of failure can be found within company management. Although there are many causes of trouble, the most frequently cited fall into three broad areas: inattention to strategic issues, general management problems, and poor financial/accounting systems and practices. There is striking similarity between these causes of trouble and the causes of failure for start-ups given in Chapter 3.

Strategic Issues

- *Misunderstood market niche:* The first of these issues is a failure to understand the company's market niche and to focus on growth without considering profitability. Instead of developing a strategy, these firms take on low-margin business and add capacity in an effort to grow. They then run out of cash.

- *Mismanaged relationships with suppliers and customers:* Related to the issue of not understanding market niche is the failure to understand the economics of relationships with suppliers and customers. For example, some firms allow practices in the industry to dictate payment terms, when they may be in a position to dictate their own terms. In other cases, firms are slow to collect receivables for fear of offending valued new customers.

Special credit is due to Robert Bateman, Scott Douglas, and Ann Morgan for contributing material in this chapter. The material is the result of research and interviews with turnaround specialists and was submitted in a paper as a requirement for the author's Financing Entrepreneurial Ventures course in the MBA program at Babson College.

The authors are especially grateful to two specialists, Leslie B. Charm and Carl Youngman, who together have owned three national franchise companies, an entrepreneurial advisory and troubled business management company, and a venture capital company, AIGIS Ventures, LLC; and Leland Goldberg of Coopers & Lybrand, Boston, who contributed enormously to the efforts of Bateman, Douglas, and Morgan and to the material.

- *Diversification into an unrelated business area:* A common failing of cash-rich firms that suffer from the growth syndrome is diversification into unrelated business areas. These firms use the cash flow generated in one business to start another without good reason. As one turnaround consultant said, "I couldn't believe it. There was no synergy at all. They added to their overhead but not to their contribution. No common sense!"

- *Mousetrap myopia:* Related to the problem of starting a firm around an idea, rather than an opportunity, is the problem of firms that have "great products" and are looking for other markets where they can be sold. This is done without analyzing the firm's opportunities.

- *The big project:* The company gears up for a big project without looking at the cash flow implications. Cash is expended by adding capacity and hiring personnel. When sales do not materialize, or take longer than expected to materialize, there is trouble. Sometimes the big project is required by the nature of the business opportunity. An example of this would be the high-technology start-up that needs to capitalize on a first-mover advantage. The company needs to prove the product's "right to life" and grow quickly to the point where it can achieve a public market or become an attractive acquisition candidate for a larger company. This ensures that a larger company cannot use its advantages in scale and existing distribution channels, after copying the technology, to achieve dominance over the start-up.

- *Lack of contingency planning:* As has been stated over and over, the path to growth is not a smooth curve upward. Firms need to be geared to think about what happens if things go sour, sales fall, or collections slow. There need to be plans in place for layoffs and capacity reduction.

Leadership Issues

- *Lack of leadership skills, experience, and know-how:* While companies grow, founders need to change their leadership mode from doing to leading teams to leading team leaders.

- *Weak finance function:* Often, in a new and emerging company, the finance function is nothing more than a bookkeeper. One company was five years old, with $20 million in sales, before the founders hired a financial professional.

- *Turnover in key management personnel:* Although turnover of key management personnel can be difficult in any firm, it is a critical concern in businesses that deal in specialized or proprietary knowledge. For example, one firm lost a bookkeeper who was the only person who really understood what was happening in the business.

- *Big-company influence in accounting:* A mistake that some companies often make is to focus on accruals rather than cash.

Poor Planning, Financial/Accounting Systems, Practices, and Controls

- *Poor pricing, overextension of credit, and excessive leverage:* These causes of trouble are not surprising and need not be elaborated. Some of the reasons for excess use of leverage are interesting. Use of excess leverage can result from growth outstripping the company's internal financing capabilities. The company then relies increasingly on short-term notes until a cash flow problem develops. Another reason a company becomes overleveraged is by using guaranteed loans in place of equity for either start-up or expansion financing. One entrepreneur remarked, "[The guaranteed loan] looked just like equity when we started, but when trouble came it looked more and more like debt."

- *Lack of cash management:* This is a most frequently cited cause of trouble. In small companies, cash budgets/projections are often not done. In addition, lack of viability often stems from management failing to base their decisions on cash flow impacts; paying the trade faster than collecting accounts receivable; using working capital financing to fund capital equipment; and in general, using short-term financing for any long-term need.

- *Poor management reporting:* While some firms have good financial reporting, they suffer from poor management reporting. As one turnaround consultant stated, "[The financial statement] just tells where the company has been. It doesn't help *manage* the business. If you look at the important management reports—inventory analysis, receivables aging, sales analysis—they're usually late or not produced at all. The same goes for billing procedures. Lots of emerging companies don't get their bills out on time."

- *Lack of standard costing:* Poor management reporting extends to issues of costing, too. Many emerging businesses have no standard costs against which they can compare the actual costs of manufacturing products. The result is they have no variance reporting. The company cannot identify problems in process and take corrective action. The company will know only after the fact how profitable a product is.

Even when standard costs are used, it is not uncommon to find that engineering, manufacturing, and accounting each has its own version of the bill of material. The product is designed one way, manufactured a second way, and costed a third.

- *Poorly understood cost behavior:* Companies often do not understand the relationship between fixed and variable costs. For example, one manufacturing company thought it was saving money by closing on Saturday. In this way, management felt it would save paying overtime. It had to be pointed out to the lead entrepreneur by a turnaround consultant that, "He had a lot of high-margin product in his manufacturing backlog that more than justified the overtime."

It is also important for entrepreneurs to understand the difference between theory and practice in this area. The turnaround consultant just mentioned said, "Accounting theory says that all costs are variable in the long run. In practice, almost all costs are fixed. The only truly variable cost is a sales commission."

Getting Out of Trouble

The major protection against and the biggest help in getting out of these troubled waters is to have a set of advisors and directors who have been through this in the past. They possess skills that aren't taught in school or in most corporate training programs. An outside vision is critical. The speed of action has to be different; control systems have to be different; and organization generally needs to be different.

Troubled companies face a situation similar to that described by Winston Churchill in *While England Slept:* "Descending constantly, fecklessly, the stairway which leads to dark gulf. It is a fine broad stairway at the beginning, but after a bit the carpet ends, a little farther on there are only flagstones, and a little farther on still these break beneath your feet."

Although uncontrollable external factors such as new government regulations do arise, an opportunity-driven firm's crisis is usually the result of management error. Within these management errors can often be found part of the solution to the troubled company's problems. It is pleasing to see that many companies—even companies that are insolvent or have negative net worth or both—can be rescued and restored to profitability.

Predicting Trouble

Crises develop over time and typically result from an accumulation of fundamental errors. Can a crisis be predicted? The obvious benefit of being able to predict crisis is that the entrepreneur, employees, and significant outsiders, such as investors, lenders, trade creditors—and even customers—can see trouble brewing in time to take corrective actions.

There have been several attempts to develop predictive models. Two presented here have been selected because each is easy to calculate and uses information available in common financial reports. Because management reporting in emerging companies is often inadequate, the predictive model needs to use information available in common financial reports.

Each of these two approaches uses easily obtained financial data to predict the onset of crisis as much as two years in advance. For the smaller public company, these models can be used by all interested observers. With private companies, they are useful only to those privy to the information and are probably of benefit only to such nonmanagement outsiders as lenders and boards of directors.

The most frequently used denominator in all these ratios is the figure for total assets. This figure often is distorted by creative accounting, with expenses occasionally improperly capitalized and carried on the balance sheet or by substantial differences between tangible book value and book value (i.e., overvalued or undervalued assets).

Net-Liquid-Balance-to-Total-Assets Ratio

The model shown in Exhibit 17.6 was developed by Joel Shulman, a Babson College professor, to predict loan defaults. Shulman found that his ratio can predict loan defaults with significant reliability as much as two years in advance.

EXHIBIT 17.6

Net-Liquid-Balance-to-Total-Assets Ratio

Net-liquid-balance-to-total-assets ratio = NLB/Total assets
where
NLB = (Cash + Marketable securities) − (Notes payable + Contractual obligations)

Source: J. Shulman, "Primary Rule for Detecting Bankruptcy: Watch the Cash," *Financial Analyst Journal,* September 1988.

Shulman's approach is noteworthy because it explicitly recognizes the importance of cash. Among current accounts, Shulman distinguishes between operating assets (such as inventory and accounts receivable) and financial assets (such as cash and marketable securities). The same distinction is made among liabilities, where notes payable and contractual obligations are financial liabilities and accounts payable are operating liabilities.

Shulman then subtracts financial liabilities from financial assets to obtain a figure known as the net liquid balance (NLB). NLB can be thought of as "uncommitted cash," cash the firm has available to meet contingencies. Because it is the short-term margin for error should sales change, collections slow, or interest rates change, it is a true measure of liquidity. The NLB is then divided by total assets to form the predictive ratio.

Nonquantative Signals

Earlier we discussed patterns and actions that could lead to trouble, indications of common trouble by growth stage, and critical variables that can be monitored.

Turnaround specialists also use some nonquantitative signals as indicators of possible trouble. As with the signals we outlined, the presence of a single one of these does not necessarily imply an immediate crisis. However, once any of these surfaces and if the others follow, then trouble is likely to mount:

- Inability to produce financial statements on time.
- Changes in behavior of the lead entrepreneur (such as avoiding phone calls or coming in later than usual).
- Change in management or advisors, such as directors, accountants, or other professional advisors.
- Accountant's opinion that is qualified and not certified.
- New competition.
- Launching of a big project.
- Lower research and development expenditures.
- Special write-offs of assets and/or addition of new liabilities.
- Reduction of credit line.

The Gestation Period of Crisis

Crisis rarely develops overnight. The time between the initial cause of trouble and the point of intervention can run from 18 months to five years. What happens to a company during the gestation period has implications for the later turnaround of the company. Thus how management reacts to crisis and what happens to morale determine what will need to happen in the intervention. Usually a demoralized and unproductive organization develops when its members think only of survival, not turnaround, and its entrepreneur has lost credibility. Further, the company has lost valuable time.

In looking backward, the graph of a company's key statistics shows trouble. We can see the sales growth rate (and the gross margin) have slowed considerably. This is followed by an increasing rise in expenses as the company assumes that growth will continue. When the growth doesn't continue, the company still allows the growth rate of expenses to remain high so it can "get back on track."

The Paradox of Optimism

In a typical scenario for a troubled company, the first signs of trouble (such as declining margins, customer returns, or falling liquidity) go unnoticed or are written off as teething problems of a new project or as the ordinary vicissitudes of business. For example, one entrepreneur saw increases in inventory and receivables as a good sign because sales were up and the current ratio had improved. However, although sales were up, margins were down, and he did not realize he had a liquidity problem until cash shortages developed.

Although management may miss the first signs, outsiders usually do not. When banks, board members, suppliers, and customers see trouble brewing, they wonder why management isn't responding. Credibility begins to erode.

Soon management has to admit that trouble exists, but valuable time has been lost. Furthermore, requisite actions to meet the situation are anathema. The lead entrepreneur is emotionally committed to people, to projects, or to business areas. Cutting back in any of these areas goes against instinct because the company will need these resources when the good times return.

The company continues its downward fall, and the situation becomes stressful. Turnaround specialists mention that stress can cause avoidance on the part of an entrepreneur. Others have likened the entrepreneur in a troubled company to a deer caught in a car's headlights. The entrepreneur is frozen and can take no action. Avoidance has a basis in human psychology. One organizational behavior consultant who has worked on turnarounds said, "When a person under stress does not understand the problem and does not have the sense to deal with it, the person will tend to replace the unpleasant reality with fantasy." The consultant went on to say, "The outward manifestation of this fantasy is avoidance." This consultant noted it is common for an entrepreneur to deal with pleasant and well-understood tasks, such as selling to customers, rather than dealing with the trouble. The result is that credibility is lost with bankers, creditors, and so forth. (These are the very people whose cooperation needs to be secured if the company is to be turned around.)

Often the decisions the entrepreneur does make during this time are poor and accelerate the company on its downward course. The accountant or the controller may be fired, resulting in a company that is then flying blind. One entrepreneur, for example, running a company that manufactured a high-margin product, announced across-the-board cuts in expenditures, including advertising, without stopping to think that cutting advertising on such a product only added to the cash flow problem.

Finally, the entrepreneur may make statements that are untrue or may make promises that cannot be kept. This is the death knell of his or her credibility.

The Bloom Is Off the Rose—Now What?

Generally when an organization is in trouble some telltale trends appear:

- Outside advice is ignored.
- The worst is yet to come.
- People (including and especially the entrepreneur) have stopped making decisions and also have stopped answering the phone.
- Nobody in authority has talked to the employees.
- Rumors are flying.
- Inventory is out of balance. That is, it does not reflect historical trends.
- Accounts receivable aging is increasing.
- Customers are becoming afraid of new commitments.
- A general malaise has settled in while a still high-stressed environment exists (an unusual combination).

Decline in Organizational Morale

Among those who notice trouble developing are the employees. They deal with customer returns, calls from creditors, and the like, and they wonder why management does not respond. They begin to lose confidence in management.

Despite troubled times, the lead entrepreneur talks and behaves optimistically or hides in the office declining to communicate with employees, customers, or vendors. Employees hear of trouble from each other and from other outsiders. They lose confidence in the formal communications of the company.

The grapevine, which is always exaggerated, takes on increased credibility. Company turnover starts to increase. Morale is eroding.

It is obvious there is a problem and that it is not being dealt with. Employees wonder what will happen, whether they will be laid off, and whether the firm will go into bankruptcy. With their security threatened, employees lapse into survival mode. As an organizational behavior consultant explains,

> The human organism can tolerate anything except *uncertainty*. It causes so much stress that people are no longer capable of thinking in a cognitive, creative manner. They focus on survival. That's why in turnarounds you see so much uncooperative, finger-pointing behavior. The only issue people understand is directing the blame elsewhere [or in doing nothing].

Crisis can force intervention. The occasion is usually forced by the board of directors, lender, or a lawsuit. For example, the bank may call a loan, or the firm may be put on cash terms by its suppliers. Perhaps creditors try to put the firm into involuntary bankruptcy. Or something from the outside world fundamentally changes the business environment.

The Threat of Bankruptcy

Debtor control within the bankruptcy arena characterized the period of the 1970s through the early 1990s. During this time the courts gave the troubled company the flexibility to make disbursements to creditors for the benefit of the company. Having such control over cash often gave the debtor control over the outcome of the case.

Over the past several years, however, there has been a dramatic shift to creditor-controlled proceedings. Debtors are now instructed that once they are in the vicinity of bankruptcy, they have to pay attention to all creditor groups. Although this creditor control model has been weakened with recent court decisions, the fact remains that the right side of the balance sheet now has a far greater influence, and in many cases control, over the cash. To further help control cash, lenders often demand that the company hire workout specialists to guide the debtor through the process—to the benefit of the creditors.

In addition, the majority of bankruptcy cases today result in a change of ownership. Bidding for companies in bankruptcy has become a big business, and this makes bankruptcy a treacherous journey for any entrepreneur. This trend will likely continue because there are now well-capitalized groups that specialize in acquiring companies and technology in this fashion.

Voluntary Bankruptcy

When bankruptcy is granted to a business under bankruptcy law (often referred to as Chapter 11), the firm is given immediate protection from creditors. Payment of interest or principal is suspended, and creditors must wait for their money. Generally the current management (a debtor in possession) is allowed to run the company, but sometimes an outsider, a trustee, is named to operate the company, and creditor committees are formed to watch over the operations and to negotiate with the company.

The greatest benefit of Chapter 11 is that it buys time for the firm. The firm has 120 days to come up with a reorganization plan and 60 days to obtain acceptance of that plan by creditors. Under a reorganization plan, debt can be extended. Debt also can be restructured (composed). Interest rates can be increased, and convertible provisions can be introduced to compensate debt holders for any increase in their risk as a result of the restructuring. Occasionally debt holders need to take part of their claims in the form of equity. Trade creditors can be asked to take equity as payment, and they occasionally need to accept partial payment. If liquidation is the result of the reorganization plan, partial payment is the rule, with the typical payment ranging from zero to 30 cents on the dollar, depending on the priority of the claim.

In April 2005 President George Bush signed legislation making it more difficult for Americans with large credit card and medical bills to erase their obligations. The bill, representing the most significant change to the nation's bankruptcy laws in 25 years, makes it harder for individuals to file Chapter 7 bankruptcy, which eliminates most debts. Individuals whose earnings exceed their state's median income are required to file Chapter 13, which sets up a court-ordered repayment plan.

Involuntary Bankruptcy

In involuntary bankruptcy, creditors force a troubled company into bankruptcy. Although this is regarded as a rare occurrence, it is important for an entrepreneur to know the conditions under which creditors can force a firm into bankruptcy.

A firm can be forced into bankruptcy by any three creditors whose total claim exceeds the value of assets held as security by $5,000, and by any single creditor who meets this standard when the total number of creditors is less than 12.

Bargaining Power

For creditors, having a firm go into bankruptcy is not particularly attractive. *Bankruptcy, therefore, is a tremendous source of bargaining power for the troubled company.* Bankruptcy is not attractive to creditors because once protection is granted to a firm, creditors must wait for their money. Further, they are no longer dealing with the troubled company but with the judicial system, as well as with other creditors. Even if creditors are willing to wait for their money, they may not get full payment and may have to accept payment in some unattractive form. Last, the legal and administrative costs of bankruptcy, which can be substantial, are paid before any payments are made to creditors.

Faced with these prospects, many creditors conclude that their interests are better served by negotiating with the firm. Because the law defines the priority of creditors' claims, an entrepreneur can use it to determine who might be willing to negotiate.

For example, because trade debt has the lowest claim (except for owners), these creditors are often the most willing to negotiate. The worse the situation, the more willing they may be. If the firm has negative net worth but is generating some cash flow, trade debt creditors should be willing to negotiate extended terms or partial payment, or both, unless there is no trust in current management.

However, secured creditors, with their higher-priority claims, may be less willing to negotiate. Many factors affect the willingness of secured creditors to negotiate. Two of the most important are the strength of their collateral and their confidence in management. Bankruptcy is still something they wish to avoid for the reasons cited.

Bankruptcy can free a firm from obligations under executory contracts. This has caused some firms to file for bankruptcy as a way out of union contracts. Because bankruptcy law in this case conflicts with the National Labor Relations Act, the law has been updated and a good-faith test has been added. The firm must be able to demonstrate that a contract prevents it from carrying on its business. It is also possible for the firm to initiate other executory contracts such as leases, executive contracts, and equipment leases. If a company has gradually added to its overhead in a noneconomic fashion, it may be able to reduce its overhead significantly using bankruptcy as a tool.

Intervention

A company in trouble usually will want to use the services of an outside advisor who specializes in turnarounds.

The situation the outside advisor usually finds at intervention is not encouraging. The company is often technically insolvent or has negative net worth. It already may have been put on a cash basis by its suppliers. It may be in default on loans, or if not, it is probably in violation of loan covenants. Call provisions may be exercised. At this point, as the situation deteriorates more, creditors may be trying to force the company into bankruptcy, and the organization is demoralized.

The critical task is to quickly diagnose the situation, develop an understanding of the company's bargaining position with its many creditors, and produce a detailed cash flow business plan for the turnaround of the organization. To this end, a turnaround advisor usually quickly signals that change is coming. He or she will elevate the finance function, putting the "cash person" (often the consultant) in charge of the business. Some payments may be put on hold until problems can be diagnosed and remedial actions decided upon.

Diagnosis

Diagnosis can be complicated by the mixture of strategic and financial errors. For example, in a company with large receivables, questions need to be answered about whether receivables are bloated because of poor credit policy or because the company is in a business where liberal credit terms are required to compete.

Diagnosis occurs in three areas: the appropriate strategic posture of the business, the analysis of management, and "the numbers."

Strategic Analysis This analysis in a turnaround tries to identify the markets in which the company is capable of competing and decide on a competitive strategy. With small companies, turnaround experts state that most strategic errors relate to the involvement of firms in unprofitable product lines, customers, and geographic areas. It is outside the scope of this book to cover strategic analysis in detail. (See the many texts in the area.)

Analysis of Management Analysis of management consists of interviewing members of the management team and coming to a subjective judgment of who belongs and who does not. Turnaround consultants can give no formula for how this is done except that it is the result of judgment that comes from experience.

The Numbers Involved in "the numbers" is a detailed cash flow analysis, which will reveal areas for remedial action. The task is to identify and quantify the profitable core of the business.

- *Determine available cash:* The first task is to determine how much cash the firm has available in the near term. This is accomplished by looking at bank balances, receivables (those not being used as security), and the confirmed order backlog.

- *Determine where money is going:* This is a more complex task than it appears to be. A common technique is called subaccount analysis, where every account that posts to cash is found and accounts are arranged in descending order of cash outlays. Accounts then are scrutinized for patterns. These patterns can indicate the functional areas where problems exist. For example, one company had its corporate address on its bills, rather than the lockbox address at which checks were processed, adding two days to its dollar days outstanding.

- *Calculate percentage-of-sales ratios for different areas of a business and then analyze trends in costs:* Typically several trends will show flex points where relative costs have changed. For example, for one company that had undertaken a big project, an increase in cost of sales, which coincided with an increase in capacity and in the advertising budget, was noticed. Further analysis revealed this project was not producing enough in dollar contribution to justify its existence. Once the project was eliminated, excess capacity could be reduced to lower the firm's break-even point.

- *Reconstruct the business:* After determining where the cash is coming from and where it is going, the next step is to compare the business as it should be to the business as it is. This involves reconstructing the business from the ground up. For example, a cash budgeting exercise can be undertaken and collections, payments, and so forth determined for a given sales volume. Or the problem can be approached by determining labor, materials, and other direct costs and the overhead required to drive a given sales volume. Essentially a cash flow business plan is created.

- *Determine differences:* Finally the cash flow business plan is tied into pro forma balance sheets and income statements. The ideal cash flow plan and financial statements are compared to the business's current financial statements. For example, the pro forma income statements can be compared to existing statements to see where expenses can be reduced. The differences between the projected and actual financial statements form the basis of the turnaround plan and remedial actions.

The most commonly found areas for potential cuts/improvements are these: (1) working capital management, from order processing and billing to receivables, inventory control, and, of course, cash management; (2) payroll; and (3) overcapacity and underutilized assets. More than 80 percent of potential reduction in expenses can usually be found in workforce reduction.

The Turnaround Plan

The industry standard for turnarounds is the 13-week cash flow plan that is based on a longer-term cash flow model. In his practice as a turnaround expert, Carl Youngman requires the following:

- A 12-month cash flow model.
- A rolling 13-week cash flow plan, updated weekly.
- A rolling 30-day daily cash flow projection.

The turnaround plan not only defines remedial actions but, because it is a detailed set of projections, also provides a means to monitor and control turnaround activity. Further, if the assumptions about unit sales volume, prices, collections, and negotiating success are varied, it can provide a means by which worst-case scenarios—complete with contingency plans—can be constructed.

Because short-term measures may not solve the cash crunch, a turnaround plan gives a firm enough credibility to buy time to put other remedial actions in place. For example, one firm's consultant could approach its bank to buy time with the following: By reducing payroll and discounting receivables, we can improve cash flow to the point where the firm can be current in five months. If we are successful in negotiating extended terms with trade creditors, then the firm can be current in three months. If the firm can sell some underutilized assets at 50 percent off, it can become current immediately.

The turnaround plan helps address organizational issues. The plan replaces uncertainty with a clearly defined set of actions and responsibilities. Because it signals to the organization that action is being taken, it helps get employees out of their survival mode. An effective plan breaks tasks into the smallest achievable units, so successful completion of these simple tasks soon follows and the organization begins to experience success. Soon the downward spiral of organizational morale is broken.

Finally, the turnaround plan is an important source of bargaining power. By identifying problems and providing for remedial actions, the turnaround plan enables the firm's advisors to approach creditors and tell them in very detailed fashion how and when they will be paid. If the turnaround plan proves that creditors are better off working with the company as a going concern, rather than liquidating it, they will most likely be willing to negotiate their claims and terms of payment. Payment schedules can then be worked out that can keep the company afloat until the crisis is over.

Quick Cash Ideally the turnaround plan establishes enough creditor confidence to buy the turnaround consultant time to raise additional capital and turn underutilized assets into cash. It is imperative, however, to raise cash quickly. The result of the actions described next should be an improvement in cash flow. The solution is far from complete, however, because suppliers need to be satisfied.

For the purpose of quick cash, the working capital accounts hold the most promise.

Accounts receivable is the most liquid noncash asset. Receivables can be factored, but negotiating such arrangements takes time. The best route to cash is discounting receivables. How much receivables can be discounted depends on whether they are securing a loan. For example, a typical bank will lend up to 80 percent of the value of receivables that are under 90 days. As receivables age past 90 days, the bank needs to be paid. New funds are advanced as new receivables are established as long as the 80 percent and under-90-day criteria are met. Receivables under 90 days old can be discounted no more than 20 percent if the bank obligation is to be met. Receivables over 90 days old can be discounted as much as is needed to collect them because they are not securing bank financing. One needs to use judgment in deciding exactly how large a discount to offer. A common method is to offer a generous discount with a time limit on it, after which the discount is no longer valid. This provides an incentive for the customer to pay immediately.

Consultants agree it is better to offer too large a discount than too small a one. If the discount is too small and needs to be followed by further discounts, customers may hold off paying in the hope that another round of discounts will follow. Generally it is the slow payers that cause the problems, and discounting may not help. By getting on the squeaky-wheel list of a particular slow-paying customer, you might get attention. A possible solution is to put on a note with the objective of having the customer start paying you on a regular basis; also, adding a small additional amount to every new order helps to work down the balance.

Inventory is not as liquid as receivables but still can be liquidated to generate quick cash. An inventory "fire sale" gets mixed reviews from turnaround

We are most appreciative to Carl Youngman for his insightful review of and additions to this chapter.

experts. The most common objection is that excess inventory is often obsolete. The second objection is that because much inventory is work in process, it is not in salable form and requires money to put in salable form. The third is that discounting finished-goods inventory may generate cash but is liable to create customer resistance to restored margins after the company is turned around. The sale of raw materials inventory to competitors is generally considered the best route. Another option is to try to sell inventory at discounted prices to new channels of distribution. In these channels, the discounted prices might not affect the next sale.

One interesting option for the company with a lot of work-in-process inventory is to ease credit terms. It often is possible to borrow more against receivables than against inventory. By easing credit terms, the company can increase its borrowing capacity perhaps enough to get cash to finish work in process. This option may be difficult to implement because, by the time of intervention, the firm's lenders are likely following the company very closely and may veto the arrangements.

Also relevant to generating quick cash is the policy regarding current sales activity. Guiding criteria for this need to include increasing the total dollar value of margin, generating cash quickly, and keeping working capital in its most liquid form. Prices and cash discounts need to be increased and credit terms eased. Easing credit terms, however, can conflict with the receivables policy just described. Obviously care needs to be taken to maintain consistent policy. Easing credit is really an "excess inventory" policy. The overall idea is to leverage policy in favor of cash first, receivables second, and inventory third.

Putting all accounts payable on hold is the next option. Clearly this eases the cash flow burden in the near term. Although some arrangement to pay suppliers needs to be made, the most important uses of cash at this stage are meeting payroll and paying lenders. Lenders are important, but if you do not get suppliers to ship goods you are out of business. Getting suppliers to ship is critical. A company with negative cash flow simply needs to prioritize its use of cash. Suppliers are the least likely to force the company into bankruptcy because, under the law, they have a low priority claim.

Dealing with Lenders   The next step in the turnaround is to negotiate with lenders. To continue to do business with the company, lenders need to be satisfied that there is a workable long-term solution.

However, at the point of intervention, the company is most likely in default on its payments. Or if payments are current, the financial situation has probably deteriorated to the point where the company is in violation of loan covenants. It also is likely that many of the firm's assets have been pledged as collateral. To make matters worse, it is likely that the troubled entrepreneur has been avoiding his or her lenders during the gestation period and has demonstrated that he or she is not in control of the situation. Credibility has been lost.

It is important for a firm to know that it is not the first ever to default on a loan, that the lender is usually willing to work things out, and that it is still in a position to bargain.

Strategically, there are two sources of bargaining power. The first is that bankruptcy is an unattractive result to a lender, despite its senior claims. A low-margin business cannot absorb large losses easily. (Recall that banks typically earn 0.5 percent to 1.0 percent total return on assets.)

The second is credibility. The firm that, through its turnaround specialist, has diagnosed the problem and produced a detailed turnaround plan with best-case/worst-case scenarios, the aim of which is to prove to the lender that the company is capable of paying, is in a better bargaining position. The plan details specific actions (layoffs, assets plays, changes in credit policy, etc.) that will be undertaken, and this plan must be met to regain credibility.

There are also two tactical sources of bargaining power. First, there is the strength of the lender's collateral. The second is the bank's inferior knowledge of aftermarkets and the entrepreneur's superior ability to sell.

The following example illustrates that when the lender's collateral is poor, it has little choice but to look to the entrepreneur for a way out without incurring a loss. It also shows that the entrepreneur's superior knowledge of his or her business and ability to sell can get both the firm and the lender out of trouble. One company in turnaround in the leather business overbought inventory one year; at the same time, a competitor announced a new product that made his inventory almost obsolete. Because the entrepreneur went to the lender with the problem, the lender was willing to work with him. The entrepreneur had plans to sell the inventory at reduced prices and also to enter a new market that looked attractive. The trouble was that he needed more money to do it, and he was already over his credit limit. The lender was faced with the certainty of losing 80 percent of its money and putting its customer out of business or the possibility of losing money by throwing good money after bad. The lender decided to work with the entrepreneur. It got a higher interest rate and put the entrepreneur on a "full following mechanism," which meant that all payments were sent to a lockbox. The lender processed the checks and reduced its exposure before it put money in his account.

Another example illustrates the existence of bargaining power with a lender that is undercollateralized and stands to take a large loss. A company was importing look-alike Cabbage Patch dolls from Europe. This was financed with a letter of credit. However, when the dolls arrived in this country, the company could not sell the dolls because the Cabbage Patch doll craze was over. The dolls, and the bank's collateral, were worthless. The company found that the doll heads could be replaced, and with the new heads, the dolls did not look like Cabbage Patch dolls. It found also that one doll buyer would buy the entire inventory. The company needed $30,000 to buy the new heads and have them put on, so it went back to the bank. The bank said that if the company wanted the money, key members of management had to give liens on their houses. When this was refused, the banker was astounded. But what was he going to do? The company had found a way for him to get his money, so it got the $30,000.

Lenders are often willing to advance money for a company to meet its payroll. This is largely a public relations consideration. Also, if a company does not meet its payroll, a crisis may be precipitated before the lender can consider its options.

When the situation starts to improve, a lender may call the loan. Such a move will solve the lender's problem but may put the company under. Although many bankers will deny this ever happens, some will concede that such an occurrence depends on the loan officer.

Dealing with Trade Creditors   In dealing with trade creditors, the first step is to understand the strength of the company's bargaining position. Trade creditors have the lowest-priority claims should a company file for bankruptcy and, therefore, are often the most willing to deal. In bankruptcy, trade creditors often receive just a few cents on the dollar.

Another bargaining power boost with trade creditors is the existence of a turnaround plan. As long as a company demonstrates that it can offer a trade creditor a better result as a going concern than it can in bankruptcy proceedings, the trade creditor should be willing to negotiate. It is generally good to make sure that trade creditors are getting a little money on a frequent basis. Remember trade creditors have a higher gross margin than a bank, so their getting paid pays down their "risk" money faster. This is especially true if the creditor can ship new goods and get paid for that, and also get some money toward the old receivables.

Also, trade creditors have to deal with the customer relations issue. Trade creditors will work with a troubled company if they see it as a way to preserve a market.

The relative weakness in the position of trade creditors has allowed some turnaround consultants to negotiate impressive deals. For example, one company got trade creditors to agree to a 24-month payment schedule for all outstanding accounts. In return, the firm pledged to keep all new payables current. The entrepreneur was able to keep the company from dealing on a cash basis with many of its creditors and to convert short-term payables into what amounted to long-term debt. The effect on current cash flow was very favorable.

The second step is to prioritize trade creditors according to their importance to the turnaround. The company then needs to take care of those creditors that are most important. For example, one entrepreneur told his controller never to make a commitment he could not keep. The controller was told that if the company was going to miss a commitment, he was to get on the phone and call. The most important suppliers were told that if something happened and they needed payment sooner than had been agreed, they were to let the company know and it would do its best to come up with the cash.

The third step in dealing with trade creditors is to switch vendors if necessary. The lower-priority suppliers will put the company on cash terms or refuse to do business. The troubled company needs to be able to switch suppliers, and its relationship with its priority suppliers will help it to do this because they can give credit references. One firm said, "We asked our best suppliers to be as liberal with credit references as possible. I don't know if we could have established new relationships without them."

The fourth step in dealing with trade creditors is to communicate effectively. "Dealing with the trade is as simple as telling the truth," one consultant said. If a company is honest, at least a creditor can plan.

Workforce Reductions   With workforce reduction representing 80 percent of the potential expense reduction, layoffs are inevitable in a turnaround situation.

A number of turnaround specialists recommend that layoffs be announced to an organization as a one-time reduction in the workforce and be done all at once. They recommend further that layoffs be accomplished as soon as possible because employees will never regain their productivity until they feel some measure of security. Finally, they suggest that a firm cut deeper than seems necessary to compensate for other remedial actions that may be difficult to implement. For example, it is one thing to set out to reduce capacity by half and quite another thing to sell or sublet half a plant.

Longer-Term Remedial Actions

If the turnaround plan has created enough credibility and has bought the firm time, longer-term remedial actions can be implemented.

These actions will usually fall into three categories:

- *Systems and procedures:* Systems and procedures that contributed to the problem can be improved, or others can be implemented.

- *Asset plays:* Assets that could not be liquidated in a shorter time frame can be liquidated. For example, real estate can be sold. Many smaller companies, particularly older ones, carry real estate on their balance sheets at far below market value. This can be sold and leased back or can be borrowed against to generate cash.

- *Creative solutions:* Creative solutions need to be found. For example, one firm had a large amount of inventory that was useless in its current business. However, it found that if the inventory could be assembled into parts, there would be a market for it. The company shipped the inventory to Jamaica, where labor rates were low, for assembly, and it was able to sell very profitably the entire inventory.

Many companies—even companies that are insolvent or have negative net worth or both—can be rescued and restored to profitability. It is perhaps helpful to recall another quote from Winston Churchill: "I have nothing to offer but blood, toil, tears, and sweat."

The Importance of Culture and Organizational Climate

Six Dimensions

The organizational culture and climate, either of a new venture or of an existing firm, are critical in how well the organization will deal with growth and crises. Studies of performance in large businesses that used the concept of organizational climate (i.e., the perceptions of people about the kind of place it is to work) have led to two general conclusions.[5] First, the climate of an organization can have a significant impact on performance. Further, climate is created both by the expectations people bring to the organization and by the practices and attitudes of the key managers.

The climate notion has relevance for new ventures, as well as for entrepreneurial efforts in large organizations. An entrepreneur's style and priorities—particularly how he or she manages tasks and people—are well known by the people being managed and affect performance. Recall the entrepreneurial climate described by Roger Enrico of Pepsi, where the critical factors included setting high performance standards by developing short-run objectives that would not sacrifice long-run results, providing responsive personal leadership, encouraging individual initiative, helping others to succeed, developing individual networks for success, and so forth. Or listen to the tale of Gerald H. Langeler, the president of the systems group of Mentor Graphics Corporation, who explained what "the vision trap" was.[6] Langeler described the vision of his company's entrepreneurial climate as simply to "build something people will buy."[7] The culture of Mentor Graphics was definitely shaped by the founders' styles because "there were perhaps 15 of us at the time—we could not only share information very quickly, we could also create a sense of urgency and purpose without the help of an articulated vision."[8]

Evidence suggests that superior teams function differently than inferior teams in setting priorities, in resolving leadership issues, in what and how roles are performed by team members, in attitudes toward listening and participation, and in dealing with disagreements. Further, evidence suggests that specific approaches to management can affect the climate of a growing organization. For example, gains from motivation, commitment, and teamwork, which are anchored in a consensus approach to management, while not immediately apparent, are striking later. At that time, there are swiftness and decisiveness in actions and in follow-through because the negotiating, compromising, and accepting of priorities are history. Also, new disagreements that emerge generally do not bring progress to a halt because there are both high clarity and broad acceptance of overall goals and underlying priorities. Without this consensus, each new problem or disagreement often necessitates a time-consuming and painful confrontation and renegotiation simply because this was not done initially.

Organizational climate can be described along six basic dimensions:

- *Clarity:* The degree of organizational clarity in terms of being well organized, concise, and efficient in the way that tasks, procedures, and assignments are made and accomplished.

- *Standards:* The degree to which management expects and puts pressure on employees for high standards and excellent performance.

- *Commitment:* The extent to which employees feel committed to the goals and objectives of the organization.

---

[5] See J. A. Timmons, "The Entrepreneurial Team: Formation and Development," paper presented at the Academy of Management annual meeting, Boston, August 1973.
[6] G. H. Langeler, "The Vision Trap," *Harvard Business Review,* March–April 1992, reprint 92204.
[7] Ibid., p. 4.
[8] Ibid., p. 5.

- *Responsibility:* The extent to which members of the organization feel responsibility for accomplishing their goals without being constantly monitored and second-guessed.
- *Recognition:* The extent to which employees feel they are recognized and rewarded (nonmonetarily) for a job well done, instead of only being punished for mistakes or errors.
- *Esprit de corps:* The extent to which employees feel a sense of cohesion and team spirit—of working well together.

Approaches to E-Leadership

In achieving the entrepreneurial culture and climate just described, certain approaches to management (also discussed in Chapter 9) are common across core management modes.

E-Leadership No single leadership pattern seems to characterize successful ventures. Leadership may be shared or informal, or a natural leader may guide a task. What is common, however, is a manager who defines and gains agreements on who has what responsibility and authority and who does what with and to whom. Roles, tasks, responsibilities, accountabilities, and appropriate approvals are defined.

There is no competition for leadership in these organizations, and leadership is based on expertise, not authority. Emphasis is placed on performing task-oriented roles, but someone invariably provides for "maintenance" and group cohesion by good humor and wit. Further, the leader does not force his or her own solution on the team or exclude the involvement of potential resources. Instead the leader understands the relationships among tasks and between the leader and his or her followers and is able to lead in those situations where it is appropriate, including managing actively the activities of others through directions, suggestions, and so forth.

This approach is in direct contrast to the commune approach, where two to four entrepreneurs, usually friends or work acquaintances, leave unanswered such questions as who is in charge, who makes the final decisions, and how real differences of opinion are resolved. While some overlapping of roles and a sharing in and negotiating of decisions are desirable in a new venture, too much looseness is debilitating.

This approach also contrasts with situations where a self-appointed leader takes over, where there is competition for leadership, or where one task takes precedence over other tasks.

Consensus Building Leaders of most successful new ventures define authority and responsibility in a way that builds motivation and commitment to cross-departmental and corporate goals. Using a consensus approach to management requires managing and working with peers and with the subordinates of others (or with superiors) outside formal chains of command and balancing multiple viewpoints and demands.

In the consensus approach, the manager is seen as willing to relinquish his or her priorities and power in the interests of an overall goal, and the appropriate people are included in setting cross-functional or cross-departmental goals and in making decisions. Participation and listening are emphasized.

In addition, the most effective managers are committed to dealing with problems and working problems through to agreement by seeking a reconciliation of viewpoints, rather than emphasizing differences, and by blending ideas, rather than playing the role of hard-nosed negotiator or devil's advocate to force their own solutions. There are open confrontation of differences of opinion and a willingness to talk out differences, assumptions, reasons, and inferences. Logic and reason tend to prevail, and there is a willingness to change opinions based on consensus.

Communication The most effective leaders share information and are willing to alter individual views. Listening and participation are facilitated by such methods as circular seating arrangements, few interruptions or side conversations, and calm discussion versus many interruptions, loud or separate conversations, and so forth, in meetings.

Encouragement Successful leaders build confidence by encouraging innovation and calculated risk taking, rather than by punishing or criticizing what is less than perfect, and by expecting and encouraging others to find and correct their own errors and to solve their own problems. Their peers and others perceive them as accessible and willing to help when needed, and they provide the necessary resources to enable others to do the job. When it is appropriate, they go to bat for their peers and subordinates, even when they know they cannot always win. Further, differences are recognized and performance is rewarded.

Trust The most effective leaders are perceived as trustworthy and straightforward. They do what they say they are going to do; they are not the corporate rumor carriers; they are more open and spontaneous, rather than guarded and cautious with each word; and they are perceived as being honest and direct. They have a reputation of getting results and become known as the creative problem solvers who have a knack for blending and balancing multiple views and demands.

Development Effective leaders have a reputation for developing human capital (i.e., they groom and grow other effective managers by their example and their mentoring). As noted in Chapter 9, Bradford and Cohen distinguish between the heroic manager, whose need to be in control in many instances actually may stifle cooperation, and the post-heroic manager, a developer who actually brings about excellence in organizations by developing entrepreneurial middle management. If a company puts off developing middle management until price competition appears and its margins erode, the organization may come unraveled. Linking a plan to grow human capital at the middle management and the supervisory levels with the business strategy is an essential first step.

Entrepreneurial Leadership for the 21st Century: Three Breakthroughs

Three extraordinary companies have been built or revolutionized in the past two decades: Marion Labs, Inc., of Kansas City; Johnsonville Sausage of Cheboygan, Wisconsin; and Springfield Remanufacturing Corporation of Springfield, Missouri. Independently and unbeknown to each other, these companies created "high standard, perpetual learning cultures," which create and foster a "chain of greatness." The lessons from these three great companies provide a blueprint for entrepreneurial leadership in the 21st century. They set the standard and provide a tangible vision of what is possible. Not surprisingly, the most exciting, faster-growing, and profitable companies in America today have striking similarities to these firms.

Ewing Marion Kauffman and Marion Labs

As described in Chapter 1, Marion Laboratories, founded in Ewing Marion Kauffman's garage in 1950, had reached $2.5 billion in sales by the time it merged with Merrill Dow in 1989. Its market capitalization was $6.5 billion. Over 300 millionaires and 13 foundations, including the Ewing Marion Kauffman Foundation, were created from the builders of the company. In sharp contrast, RJR Nabisco, about 10 times larger than Marion Labs at the time of the KKR leveraged buyout, generated only 20 millionaires. Clearly these were very different companies. Central to Marion Labs' phenomenal success story was the combination of a high-potential opportunity with management execution based on core values and an entrepreneurial leadership philosophy ahead of its time. These principles are simple enough, but difficult to inculcate and sustain through good times and bad:

1. Treat everyone as you would want to be treated.
2. Share the wealth with those who have created it.

3. Pursue the highest standards of performance and ethics.

As noted earlier, the company had no organizational chart, referred to all its people as associates, not employees, and had widespread profit-sharing and stock participation plans. Having worked for a few years now with Mr. K and the top management that built Marion Labs and then ran the foundation, the authors can say that they are genuine and serious about these principles. They also have fun while succeeding, but they are highly dedicated to the practice of these core philosophies and values.

Jack Stack and Springfield Remanufacturing Corporation

The truly remarkable sage of this revolution in entrepreneurial leadership is Jack Stack; his book, *The Great Game of Business*, should be read by all entrepreneurs. In 1983 Stack and a dozen colleagues acquired a tractor engine remanufacturing plant from the failing International Harvester Corporation. With an 89-to-1 debt-to-equity ratio and 21 percent interest, they acquired the company for 10 cents a share. In 1993 the company's shares were valued near $20 for the employee stock ownership plan, and the company had completely turned around with sales approaching $100 million. What happened?

Like Ewing Marion Kauffman, Jack Stack created and implemented some management approaches and values radically opposite to the top-down, hierarchical, custodial management commonly found in large manufacturing enterprises. At the heart of his leadership was creating a vision called *The Big Picture: Think and act like owners, be the best we can be, and be perpetual learners. Build teamwork as the key by learning from each other, open the books to everyone, and educate everyone so they can become responsible and accountable for the numbers, both short and long term.* Stack puts it this way:

We try to take ignorance out of the workplace and force people to get involved, not with threats and intimidation but with education. In the process, we are trying to close the biggest gap in American business—the gap between workers and managers. We're developing a system that allows everyone to get together and work toward the same goals. To do that, you have to knock down the barriers that separate people, that keep people from coming together as a team.[9]

At Springfield Remanufacturing Corporation, everyone learns to read and interpret all the financial statements, including an income statement, balance

[9] J. Stack, *The Great Game of Business* (New York: Currency/Doubleday Books, 1991), p. 5.

sheet, and cash flow, and how his or her job affects each line item. This open-book leadership style is linked with pushing responsibility downward and outward, and to understanding both wealth creation (i.e., shareholder value) and wealth sharing through short-term bonuses and long-term equity participation. Stack describes the value of this approach thus: "The payoff comes from getting the people who create the numbers to understand the numbers. When that happens, the communication between the bottom and the top of the organization is just phenomenal."[10] The results he achieved in 10 years are astounding. Even more amazing is that he has found the time to share this approach with others. More than 150 companies have participated in seminars that have enabled them to adopt this approach.

Ralph Stayer and Johnsonville Sausage Company[11]

In 1975 Johnsonville Sausage was a small company with about $5 million in sales and a fairly traditional, hierarchical, and somewhat custodial management. In just a few years Ralph Stayer, the owner's son, radically transformed the company through a leadership revolution whose values, culture, and philosophy are remarkably similar to the principles of Ewing Marion Kauffman and Jack Stack.

The results are astonishing: By 1980 the company had reached $15 million in sales; by 1985, $50 million; and by 1990, $150 million. At the heart of the changes he created was the concept of a *total learning culture: Everyone is a learner, seeking to improve constantly, finding better ways. High performance standards accompanied by an investment in training, and performance measures that made it possible to reward fairly both short- and long-term results were critical to the transition.* Responsibility and accountability were spread downward and outward. For example, instead of forwarding complaint letters to the marketing department, where they are filed and the standard response is sent, they go directly to the front-line sausage stuffer responsible for the product's taste. The sausage stuffers are the ones who respond to customer complaints now. Another example is the interviewing, hiring, and training process for new people. A newly hired woman pointed out numerous shortcomings with the existing process and proposed ways to improve it. As a result, the entire responsibility was

shifted from the traditional human resources/personnel group to the front line, with superb results.

As one might guess, such radical changes do not come easily. Consider Stayer's insight:

> In 1980 I began looking for a recipe for change. I started by searching for a book that would tell me how to get people to care about their jobs and their company. Not surprisingly, the search was fruitless. No one could tell me how to wake up my own workforce; I would have to figure it out for myself. . . . The most important question any manager can ask is, "In the best of all possible worlds what would I really want to happen?"[12]

Even having taken such a giant step, Stayer was ready to take the next, equally perilous steps:

> Acting on instinct, I ordered a change. "From now on," I announced to my management team, "you're all responsible for making your own decisions.". . . I went from authoritarian control to authoritarian abdication. No one had asked for more responsibility; I had forced it down their throats.[13]

Further insight into just how challenging it is to transform a company like Johnsonville Sausage is revealed in another Stayer quote:

> I spent those two years pursuing another mirage of well-detailed strategic and tactical plans that would realize my goals of Johnsonville as the world's greatest sausage maker. We tried to plan organizational structure two to three years before it would be needed. . . . Later I realized that these structural changes had to grow from day-to-day working realities; no one could dictate them from above, and certainly not in advance.[14]

Exhibit 17.7 summarizes the key steps in the transformation of Johnsonville Sausage over several years. Such a picture undoubtedly oversimplifies the process and understates the extraordinary commitment and effort required to pull it off, but it does show how the central elements weave together.

The Chain of Greatness

As we reflect on these three great companies, we can see that there is clearly a pattern here, with some common denominators in both the ingredients and the process. This chain of greatness becomes reinforcing and perpetuating (see Exhibit 17.8). Leadership that instills across the company a vision of greatness and an owner's mentality is a common beginning. A philosophy of perpetual learning

---

[10] Ibid., p. 93.

[11] For an excellent discussion of this transformation, see "The Johnsonville Sausage Company," HBS case 387-103, rev. June 27, 1990. Copyright © 1990 by the President and Fellows of Harvard College. See also R. Stayer, "How I Learned to Let My Workers Lead," *Harvard Business Review,* November–December 1990. Copyright © 1990 by the President and Fellows of Harvard College.

[12] Stayer, "How I Learned to Let My Workers Lead," p. 1.

[13] Ibid., pp. 3–4.

[14] Ibid., p. 4.

EXHIBIT 17.7

Summary of the Johnsonville Sausage Company

The critical aspects of the transition:

1. Started at the top: Ralph Stayer recognized that he was the heart of the problem and recognized the need to change—the most difficult step.
2. Vision was anchored in human resource management and in a particular idea of the company's culture:
   - Continuous learning organization.
   - Team concept—change players.
   - New model of jobs (Ralph Stayer's role and decision making).
   - Performance- and results-based compensation and rewards.
3. Stayer decided to push responsibility and accountability downward to the front-line decision makers:
   - Front-liners are closest to the customer and the problem.
   - Define the whole task.
   - Invest in training and selection.
   - Job criteria and feedback = development tool.
4. Controls and mechanisms make it work:
   - Measure performance, not behavior, activities, and the like.
   - Emphasize learning and development, not allocation of blame.
   - Customize to you and the company.
   - Decentralize and minimize staff.

EXHIBIT 17.8

The Chain of Greatness

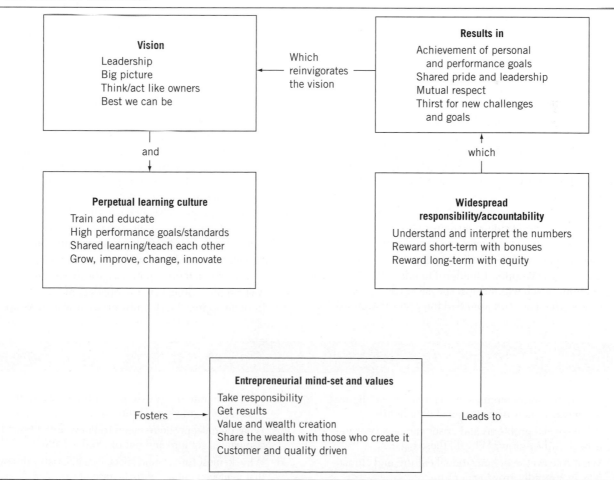

throughout the organization accompanied by high standards of performance is key to the value-creating entrepreneurial cultures at the three firms. A culture that teaches and rewards teamwork, improvement, and respect for each other provides the oil and glue to make things work. Finally, a fair and generous short- and long-term reward system, as well as the necessary education to make sure that everyone knows and can use the numbers, creates a mechanism for sharing the wealth with those who contributed to it. The results speak for themselves: extraordinary levels of personal, professional, and financial achievement.

Internet Impact: Opportunity

Consumer Power

The Internet has begun to profoundly after the relationship between buyers, vendors, and producers. Online consumers expect convenience, speed, straightforward comparative information, best prices, and around-the-clock service.

Empowered with blocking software and the click of a mouse, customers are increasingly able to select and control the commercial content they view. Tolerance for hype is therefore low. Flashy ads, flagrant pop-ups, and banal messages are eschewed in favor of hard content like independent reviews, vendor-specific information, and community forums where customers can garner feedback from people who have no vested interest in the product or service in question.

The Internet is fostering the creation of a real-time, global marketplace where transactions are coordinated, consummated, and fulfilled 24/7. Using sophisticated service platforms, e-vendors such as Amazon.com, Expedia.com, Drugstore.com, and Campmor have been able to partner with a wide variety of producers whose product data, fulfillment processes, and finances are linked together behind the scenes of customer-friendly portals.

What customers get is the ability to create a personal account with stored billing, payment, purchase history, and preference data. From there they can browse merchandise, order products, and choose shipping and other fulfillment options. From hotel rooms to camping supplies, online vendors must fight for market share the old-fashioned way: by offering their customers excellent service and value.

Chapter Summary

- The demands of rapid growth have led to the invention of new organizational and leadership paradigms by entrepreneurs.

- The entrepreneurial organization today is flatter, faster, and more flexible and responsive, and copes readily with ambiguity and change. It is the opposite of the hierarchy, layers of management, and more-is-better syndrome prevalent in brontosaurus capitalism.

- Entrepreneurs in high-growth firms distinguish themselves with leading entrepreneurial practices in marketing, finance, management, and planning.

- As high-potential firms "grow up big" they experience stages (Wonder, Blunder, Thunder, Plunder, and Asunder), each with its own special challenges and crises, which are compounded the faster the growth.

- Numerous signals of impending trouble—strategic issues, poor planning and financial controls, and running out of cash—invariably point to a core cause: top management.

- Crises don't develop overnight. Both quantitative and qualitative signals can predict patterns and actions that could lead to trouble. Often it takes 18 months to five years before a company is sick enough to trigger a turnaround intervention.

- Turnaround specialists begin with a diagnosis of the numbers—cash, strategic market issues, and management—and develop a turnaround plan.

- Establishing a culture and climate conducive to entrepreneurship is a core task for the venture.

- A chain of greatness characterizes some breakthrough approaches to entrepreneurial leadership.

Study Questions

1. Why have old hierarchical management paradigms given way to new organizational paradigms?

2. What special problems and crises can new ventures expect as they grow? Why do these occur?

3. What role do the organizational culture and climate play in a rapidly growing venture?

4. Why is the rate of growth the central driver of the challenges a growing venture faces?

5. What do entrepreneurs need to know about how companies get into and out of trouble? Why?

6. Why do most turnaround specialists invariably discover that management is the root cause of trouble?

7. Why is it difficult for existing management to detect and to act early on signals of trouble?

8. What are some key predictors and signals that warn of impending trouble?

9. What diagnosis is done to detect problems, and why and how does cash play the central role?

10. What are the main components of a turnaround plan, and why are these so important?

11. What is the chain of greatness, and how can entrepreneurs benefit from this concept?

Internet Resources for Chapter 17

http://www.churchillclub.org *The Churchill Club is Silicon Valley's premier business and technology forum. The 5,000-member, nonprofit organization has built a reputation for dynamic, in-the-news programs featuring Silicon Valley CEOs, up-and-coming executives, and national business leaders.*

www.finance.yahoo.com *Stock market news and research engine.*

www.findlaw.com *An extensive guide to legal resources.*

http://www.law.cornell.edu/wex/index.php/Bankruptcy *Bankruptcy information and legal resources from the law school at Cornell University.*

www.turnaround.org *The Turnaround Management Association.*

http://www.export.gov/ *Trade resources and one-on-one assistance for new and established international ventures.*

MIND STRETCHERS

Have You Considered?

1. Many large organizations are now attempting to reinvent themselves. What will be the biggest challenge in this process, and why?

2. How fast should a company grow? How fast is too fast, organizationally and financially?

3. In the 1970s IBM had more cash on its balance sheet than the total sales of the rest of the computer industry. Why, and how, did IBM get into so much trouble 10 years later?

4. Talk in person to an entrepreneur who has personal loan guarantees and has been through bankruptcy. What lessons were learned?

5. Could Google become a troubled company? When, and why?

6. In your ideal world, how would you describe what it is like to live and work within the perfect entrepreneurial organization?

Telephony Translations, Inc. (A)

Preparation Questions

1. Evaluate Dave Santolli's entrepreneurial thinking and leadership at Faxtech and at TTI.

2. What lessons and insights are most important for you here?

3. Evaluate the progress and situation facing TTI in 2006. What should the company do? What should the investors/directors do?

Dave Santolli's entrepreneurial career had long embodied the notion that life is about the journey rather than the destination. At 42 he'd experienced both the glow of venture success and the sting of business failure. He'd stood up to the dreadful shock of learning that his wife Terry was facing an uphill battle with cancer, and felt waves of relief when she pulled through.

In early 2005 it was beginning to seem as if all that had been but a preseason practice for the current swarm of challenges. His last venture—a stunning reversal of fortune—was still haunting him in the form of an investor suit, and legal defense fees had ripped through their personal resources to the extent that Dave and Terry were now living without a safety net.

How does a young company with a global footprint, $50 million in revenue, 650 employees, and over $280 million in capitalization get forced into total liquidation via a Chapter 7 bankruptcy overnight?

Dave's new venture, Telephony Translations, Inc. (TTI), was still not turning a profit after five years. Although Dave had always insisted that such losses could be expected, his investors had replaced him as CEO in order to provide a second opinion and perspective on that. While the business seemed to be on the right track with a complex technology solution developed well ahead of a predicted demand, this was an enormously critical time in the development of the opportunity.

And yet here was Dave, informing his stunned staff that he had a particularly vicious form of cancer that would sideline him for months in a state of discomfort that would make it impossible for him to offer the slightest guidance or leadership. He assured the group that he'd be back and that their company would turn the corner very soon. What else could he say?

This case was prepared by Carl Hedberg under the direction of Professor Jeffry Timmons. © Copyright Jeffry Timmons, 2007. All rights reserved.

A Passion for Enterprise

While majoring in industrial engineering at Cornell University, Dave Santolli developed a publication for students living on campus. Under his direction, *Student Life* magazine grew to a controlled circulation of 1.2 million. In 1987, four years after graduating from Cornell, he sold his venture to Time, Inc., for nearly $1 million and moved to New York City as part of an attractive earn-out agreement with the publisher. Although he enjoyed his work in the city, it wasn't long before Dave was longing for the edgy, frenetic life he'd known as a start-up entrepreneur.

The following year Dave entered Harvard Business School (HBS), intent on having his next enterprise ready for launch by graduation. Dave was unconcerned that his search for a compelling opportunity would take him outside his immediate universe of understanding:

> Conventional wisdom says you ought to start a venture in an industry where you have some previous experience, but given the fast pace of growth in information technologies, that's where I wanted to be. I had an engineering background, so I wasn't intimidated by technology. I was sure that I could start a successful venture in an area in which I had no experience—provided of course that I was willing to thoroughly research the industry and the idea.

Throughout his second year in the program, Dave methodically devised, reviewed, and ultimately rejected eight distinct business concepts. His final investigation, which developed into a comprehensive independent research project during his final semester, reached a similar conclusion: intriguing but not revolutionary.

Dave graduated in 1990 as an HBS Baker Scholar—a high-distinction honor given to the top 5 percent of the graduating class. Not surprisingly, a prominent consulting firm approached him with a lucrative employment offer. Although Dave was as determined as ever to launch a new venture, he was also prepared to be practical:

> I let them know that I would spend the summer trying to spot a viable opportunity, and if I hadn't found anything by September, I'd take the job. They were very supportive—especially since they probably figured that my chances of success were minimal. After all, I'd already been looking at ideas for nearly two years.

In mid-July a write-up in an AT&T technology journal caught his attention:

> This article was describing the various types of information that people were sending over phone lines. The

phone companies had no way of knowing whether an open line was being used for voice or data. It also said that data travels seven times more efficiently than voice, meaning a fax transmission was utilizing only one-seventh of the capacity of a given line.

I called the author of the article to confirm the fundamental viability of the idea that with the right equipment, a company could send many times the volume of data than a basic fax machine transmitting over the switched-voice networks of companies like AT&T, Sprint, and MCI. I wasn't about to jump in without a lot more research, but I was pretty certain that this was the opportunity I'd been searching for.

Post-MBA Sweet Spot: Faxtech International

By the end of the summer of 1990, Dave had respectfully declined the consulting position in favor of developing Faxtech International, a business that would offer vastly superior facsimile transmission service between the United States and major international cities like Tokyo, London, Paris, and Dubai. His first hire quickly became his first fire:

I knew I needed a director of engineering, and searched for three months before I found someone. He lasted a month before I made the difficult decision to let him go. In February [of 1991] I met John Tyler.

At age 52 John had spent most of his adult life in either engineering project management or product development, including 12 years at AT&T Bell Labs and four years at GTE. When their paths crossed, John was making a good living as an engineering management consultant. So good, in fact, that Dave was compelled to give up more of the business than he had originally intended:

John was pretty firm about what he needed to come on board, and this became a very difficult decision for me. I needed his expertise, we seemed to have a shared vision of what sort of company this could be, and I sensed that we would get along well. I concluded that it just doesn't pay to be greedy. Sure, I might have fought harder and held onto a few more shares, but a few extra percent of nothing is still nothing. I needed to focus on getting the job done, and John was a good man at the right time.

For his part, John recalled that his attraction to the opportunity went beyond what he saw in the plan for Faxtech:

Virtually every company I consulted for had asked me to join them full-time. Dave's offer was the first one I even considered. My interest had to do with how I felt about Dave and his philosophy for treating people. I believe there is an enormous gulf in our society between what is known about how people should be treated, and the

way most managers actually treat people in practice. Dave and I saw eye-to-eye on the importance of treating and rewarding people fairly.

Even after John's arrival, it would be another six months before the company had filled out the engineering team, found suitable headquarters, and begun serious development on their technology. Dave smiled:

It's funny; when I first thought of this idea, I actually believed I could get a working prototype up by the end of 1990. As it turned out, it wasn't until the summer of 1991 before I felt knowledgeable enough about what I was doing even to sit down and write the plan. . . . No matter how closely you try to calculate a timetable, it always takes longer than you think. There are just too many unknowns.

Clearing the Hurdles

Their research indicated that the key to customer adoption would be a user-friendly, bug-free system that required little or no change in how a fax was transmitted. John's technology team designed a plug-in redialer that scanned every outgoing call.[1] This linking device would reroute calls destined for a foreign city. Those fax transmissions would travel via regular phone lines to a Faxtech node in the states, where they would be bundled with other transmissions bound for the same foreign city. Once overseas, the faxes would reach their local destinations over regular phone lines.

Their proprietary system would provide customers with a 50 percent savings over current rates and generate gross margins of nearly 60 percent. Profitability, however, would require not only substantial margins but an enormous base of call volume. For that reason, Dave understood that this was to be a long ramp involving the establishment of Faxtech centers all over the world.

Based on an analysis of market size, growth rate, cost of entry, cost of customer acquisition, and short- and long-term profit potential, Faxtech's initial objective was to establish a leadership position in the United States-to-Tokyo market, followed by a Tokyo-to-United States operation. Once that loop was secure, the company would set up operations in Paris and London.

Having saved most of the money he'd received in the harvest of his publishing venture, Dave was in a good

[1] A redialer was a simple device, smaller than a cigar box, that physically sat between a fax machine and the wall. Its sole purpose was to grab fax traffic before it reached the private branch exchange (PBX) switch or, at smaller organizations, the public switched telephone network (PSTN), then redirect it to a fax service bureau or ISP that would send the fax and bill the faxer. The Faxtech redialer was a highly sophisticated machine that could differentiate between all types of calls, block 900 numbers, and not reroute 800 numbers. The proprietary system, which was entirely and remotely programmable, recognized alternative fax numbers along with local holidays and business hours at the destination point, and, in the event of a busy signal, rerouted the documents and rescheduled delivery.

position to fund the initial IP development and early-stage operations of this new enterprise. Nevertheless, he was determined to use no more than half of his nest egg:

> It was important to raise money from outside sources because if I couldn't convince people to invest, then there was probably something wrong with the idea or how we were presenting it. At first I tried the approach I'd heard at HBS: Raise as much as you can up front. I soon discovered that venture capitalists who were willing to invest at this early stage insisted on taking a majority of the company. Private investors, on the other hand, were unwilling to take a risk at the idea stage.

He ultimately concluded that the best source of start-up funding was his management team. Following an internal seed round of $335,000, Dave devised a milestone approach to attract outside investors:

> I decided to lay out our start-up process as a series of distinct hurdles—such as a completed prototype or a government approval. As we moved forward and met our goals, the project gained credibility, and we were gradually able to find investors to share the risk.
>
> People are as afraid of missing an opportunity to make money as they are of losing money. Once you've delivered on your promises and convinced them that the odds are reasonably good that the idea is viable, raising money becomes much less of a challenge.

In February 1992 the company brought total funding to $1 million with the close of a round with private investors. To cover a monthly burn rate of $175,000,[2] they managed to close a second round of $1 million by late spring.

Their technology was testing well, and Faxtech was planning to go live in March. In addition to operating from a base of flawless technology, Dave believed that the success of their concept would critically depend on developing a highly effective and responsive service department. To head up that effort, Dave hired an individual he'd worked with before—Terry Carson, his wife:

> Terry had worked closely with me at Cornell on my first business. Not only did I find that she was extremely capable, but we didn't experience any of the problems that many couples seem to encounter in similar situations. With respect to Faxtech, I knew we might have to search months to find someone as qualified as she was for the position,[3] and even then it would take months

more before that hire understood the business or our vision the way Terry already did.

> Having Terry in the business gave us the added advantage of better communication with the other employees. No matter how open I try to be with everyone here, there would always be things that employees might be reluctant to tell their boss. Terry was very close with everyone. They all knew that if something was bothering them, they could share it with her and that it would get back to me right away. This was very helpful in terms of maintaining a culture of open communication and understanding.

Despite severe cash flow challenges and sporadic, systemwide shutdowns, the proprietary Faxtech systems worked as expected, and the company grew quickly. In late 1992, even though his U.S. operations were far from stable, Dave felt it was time to pursue the next phase of his vision.

Going Global before Globalization: Faxtech–Japan

From the beginning, Dave believed that one key to success would be opening up a two-way communications channel between the United States and Japan. Because that would utilize established Faxtech connections, the new network would be capable of carrying traffic at a very low variable cost. Succeeding in Japan would also represent Faxtech's go-ahead to open offices around the world.

After considering a number of strategies,[4] Dave decided to work with Japanese companies as partners while maintaining a majority ownership. His first and most important contact was Sachio Moto, cofounder and senior vice president of a major telecommunications firm in Japan. Although the initial introduction had come from Dave's former professor of entrepreneurial finance at HBS, the seasoned executive recalled that it was Dave's enthusiasm that had drawn his attention:

> Dave had faxed me a request for a meeting: to get feedback from me as a successful entrepreneur who was also very familiar with the Japanese telecommunications business. He had wanted to meet me in Japan, but since I was due to be in Atlanta later that week, I suggested that he could meet me there. I was sure the short notice and his desire to meet in Tokyo would be disincentive enough. But I also knew that if he had a good passion for this business, he would come.
>
> When he arrived in Atlanta, I knew he had the type of enthusiasm one must have as an entrepreneur to take advantage of every opportunity that arises. I would also

---

[2] The burn rate included salaries ($60K), asset expenses ($16K), office operating expenses ($15K), expenses in Japan ($20K), fixed communication expenses ($25K), and miscellaneous start-up expenses (lawyers, network installation, equipment, travel: $39K).

[3] Terry graduated from Cornell with a BS in mechanical engineering in 1986 and then entered the U.S. Air Force as an officer. Terry left the Air Force in 1991 as a captain and enrolled in graduate school at Harvard to pursue a master's degree in U.S. history. After completing all of her coursework at Harvard, in 1992 Terry made the difficult decision to put her thesis on hold to take the position of vice president of service at Faxtech International. After a six-year diversion at Faxtech International, Terry finally returned to Harvard to complete her thesis and received her MS degree in 2001.

[4] Strategic possibilities for setting up FIJ included financing the start-up through a franchise system, allowing a local partner to own a large part of the operation, and setting up Faxtech as a holding company for the Japanese operation.

add that if Dave had not come to Atlanta, we would never have met.

In addition to being impressed with the man behind Faxtech–Japan, Mr. Moto was also intrigued by Dave's clearly defined concept. He agreed to help the younger entrepreneur enter the Japanese telecommunications market. As meetings got under way in 1993, Mr. Moto continued to be pleased with Dave's drive and commitment:

> Dave would spend whole days at the hotel analyzing changed conditions [from follow-up meetings]. He was patient and tremendously flexible. He'd come to Japan without specific return dates, which was very unusual for an American businessman. That way he had the slack to cope with last-moment changes in previously agreed-upon conditions. Dave also paid very good attention to each personal detail, like greeting others properly. Dave has the hearty collaboration and the personal, human touch that a good chief executive needs.

Throughout 1993 Dave struggled to secure solid commitments from Japanese businessmen who "never intended to say yes, but who were not prepared to say no." Dave explained that making matters more difficult was the fact that all the time and money he was spending to break into the Japanese market had become a destabilizing force on his U.S. operations:

> By the way, just in case you think everything was going smoothly with the base business during this period, it wasn't at all. The sales organization that had been so successful in the first six months [of 1993] absolutely fell apart in July. Morale was at an all-time low; they had no strategy and no confidence in the existing sales director.

Replacing the director of sales got them back on track, but Dave noted that the economics were a primary concern:

> Faxtech was eating up more and more capital as our growth accelerated, and our breakeven was still out of reach and getting further away all the time.[5] I don't believe that we ever had more than two months of cash in the bank at any point in time that year. This might sound either impossible or extremely strange, but it was our reality. While I was trying to negotiate from strength in Japan, we were constantly involved in the process of raising money to keep the U.S. operations in business.

As negotiations in Japan dragged on into 1994, Dave could see that he and his team were locked in a delicate and fragile balancing act:

> We can either be a small U.S.-based operation, or we can be a worldwide telecommunications company; we can't exist somewhere in between. . . . The staff that is needed to grow the business worldwide is way too big to support without setting up operations in multiple countries—and quickly.
>
> Our goal is not to be profitable at this point in time; our goal is to grow as fast as possible while trying to raise money at higher and higher share prices so that we pro-

tect [our base of] investors. There is a constant struggle going on between the desire that people have to see profits and the desire that people have to see growth. The real trick lies in balancing these two needs within the real limitation of constantly running out of cash as you try to grow.

When Faxtech–Japan finally went live in late 1994, it ushered in the opportunity for global expansion Dave had long envisioned. In 1995, however, the business would suddenly seem totally secondary to a far more critical challenge.

A Frightful Reality

By 1995 Terry was managing a service department of over 200 people. With Faxtech doing well and their future looking bright, Dave and Terry decided it would be a good time to start a family. Terry recalled that during a routine pregnancy exam, her physician made a shocking discovery:

> It was October of 1995, right when the company was really beginning to take off. Basically they told me I wasn't going to make it. It was a bad thing; they called it ALL—short for acute lymphocytic leukemia—*I had it ALL*—stage-four over my whole body. They were saying Even though you're only 30, it is very unlikely you'll be able to make it through this. But if you don't start treatment in a week, you'll be dead within a month.

Terry lost the baby but made it through the first month of treatment, and then the next. Unable to do much for his dear wife and partner as she battled for her life at a Boston-area hospital, Dave focused his energy on their growing business. In addition to his own duties as CEO, he would now oversee the service department until Terry returned.

Against all medical odds, Terry would endure the severe pain and rigors of a massively invasive chemotherapy regime for two years—and ultimately beat the cancer. The downside to this wonderful news was a heart-wrenching prognosis: Terry would be unable to ever have children.

At the same time, after a long, lean, and difficult struggle, Faxtech had finally achieved the critical mass it required to survive and prosper.

Excellence and Execution

By 1997 Faxtech employed 650 people in 18 offices throughout the world, including Australia, Canada, Japan, Korea, and the United States. Annual growth had

---

[5] By mid-1993 their aggressive growth strategy in the United States had boosted the net monthly revenue of Faxtech to just under $350,000, but the negative cash flow rate had grown to $250,000/month. The monthly break-even point grew at an equally aggressive pace of approximately $502,000.

averaged 180 percent since 1992, and in 1997 the company was listed as number 20 on the *INC. 500* list of fastest-growing private companies in the United States. By that time Faxtech had raised total funding of $105 million from a wide range of sources including friends, family, angels, and corporations like ORIX and Singapore Airlines.

Dave and his team felt certain that the time was right to establish a dominant position in the marketplace with a massive effort that would include development of enhanced fax and delivery services and the expansion of their international communications network to 27 countries, including Belgium, Italy, Switzerland, and Indonesia. Well aware of the technology threat posed by the emerging Internet space, the Faxtech team was actively developing an online portal that would allow their customers to place service orders and track their faxes on the Internet, just as FedEx was doing with packages.

Dave said they were also preparing to deal with another major challenge on the horizon:

> Deregulation in our industry was a reality that we were preparing for. The world knew it was coming, and as a company we were investing in new products that anticipated that change. We said, All right, given that those changes are clearly going to hurt our core value proposition, how do we transition and still make this happen?

To support their push for market dominance, the company needed to raise an additional $175 million.[6] The typical avenue for attracting such funds might have been a public offering; instead the team opted for a bond offering of high-yield (14 percent) debt securities—an equity preservation strategy made feasible by Faxtech's growing global reputation for excellence and execution.

With the bond issue closed, total debt and equity funding stood at just over $260 million (see Exhibit 1).

[6] At the time of the closing, the company had less than $1 million on hand—and a monthly burn rate of over $3 million. Had the bond offering not closed in January 1997, Faxtech would have been forced to begin shutting down operations within weeks.

The company was approaching breakeven on annual sales of about $50 million; Faxtech had finally become a major, seemingly unstoppable force in the telecommunications sector.

Free Fall

In early 1997 the World Trade Organization (WTO) reached an agreement with over 200 countries to fully deregulate international communications. In less than a year, the average price per minute for international calls in every market where Faxtech was operating dropped from 75 cents per minute to 25 cents. Dave explained how this new environment stripped the wings off his company:

> Our incremental cost per minute was about 15 cents. We entered 1997 charging 50 cents a minute on international fax calls—a cost savings to the customer of 33 percent over the average price of 80 cents a minute. By the end of the year we were forced to drop our price down to the new market price of 25 cents per minute. Although we still had positive margin at this rate, we no longer had an exciting sales model.
>
> Prior to deregulation, we could hire salespeople off the street and they would sell 15 customers a month—and those customers would all stay. With the new pricing, they were selling maybe three customers a month, but the churn within the customer base exceeded their ability to add.
>
> The core model of our existing business was just totally broken. We realized that we had essentially gotten in at the tail end [of an industry cycle]; there was a huge market and tons of money sitting there. The downside, of course, was that the opportunity could disappear pretty quickly. The financial structure of the business has to be aligned with the duration of the opportunity, and with Faxtech, we had placed a long-term financial model on a short-term opportunity.

EXHIBIT 1

Faxtech Capitalization

Timing	Round and Source	Debt @	Rate	Convertible Preferred @	Share Price	Total $ Raised
Fall 1990	Founder and seed financing	200,000	12%			300,000
Fall 1991	Series A: private investors @ $25,000 each	500,000	12%	500,000	$1.00	1,000,000
Fall 1992	Series B: several large angel investors			2,500,000	$1.00	2,500,000
Spring 1994	Faxtect–Japan financing; partners owned 49% of subsidiary					10,000,000
Spring 1994	Series C: several large international private equity funds			3,000,000	$3.50	3,000,000
Spring 1995	Malasia Telecom Investment	30,000,000	12%	40,000,000	$3.50	70,000,000
Spring 1997	Public high-yield debt offering	175,000,000	14%			175,000,000
	Total funding					**261,500,000**

Having recently closed their debt round of high-interest bonds, Faxtech was flush with cash—enough, Dave felt, to fund a transition strategy his team had been conceptualizing for months. Dave said that the bondholders, however, wanted out:

> Our current investors were telling us, Look, we put the money in for the right reason, the world changed dramatically in a way you couldn't have anticipated, and so we need to shut the company down and return their money. They wanted to restructure by shutting it down; we wanted to restructure by bringing in new investors and by paying the bondholders some appropriate fee to bring them into an equity position. We had no legal obligation to return the funds, and we believed, of course, that we could produce a much bigger result if they let us finish the strategy. The early investors, whose money was already spent, were willing to let us try.

The ongoing debate over how best to move forward on the fly, the crashing market conditions, and having to let go hundreds of loyal and excellent employees was putting a tremendous strain on management and on the board of directors. By early 1998 Dave had replaced his CFO, COO, and vice president of development with executives who he felt would be more likely to succeed in moving the company through a very difficult transition:

> I asked the new COO and CFO to work together to drive a process of systematically reducing our sales staff by 50 percent in order to help conserve cash—without closing any of our international sales offices completely.[7] While my executive team focused on scaling back and completing the development of our new products, I shifted my full attention to finding a way to restructure and convert our high-interest bondholders to some form of partial equity.

In March 1998 all the outside directors resigned from the board—ostensibly over issues involving a struggling branch office in France, but more as a final vote of no confidence. Dave described another particularly stark indicator of how fast they were falling:

> At the end of 1997 I owned approximately 15 percent of the company. At the same time the directors were leaving, I was purchasing all of the stock owned by Malasia Telecom in order to facilitate MalTel's exit from the business. MalTel originally invested $70 million ($30 million equity plus $40 million debt). In order to give MalTel a simple exit from their stock position, I agreed to purchase their shares for $10,000. At the end of this transaction I owned more than 50 percent of the stock of the outstanding shares of the company, but obviously the stock wasn't worth anything at that point since we had a public high-yield debt overhang of $175 million.

Clark Thomas, the tax director in Faxtech's finance group, recalled that even in the face of numerous stark realities, most employees remained hopeful that Dave would find a way:

> We had a common goal as to where we were going as a company, and things seemed to have been going along very well. One of Dave's best attributes is being able to keep people moving forward and believing. I think a lot of people felt as though something would be done to save the company—maybe in a scaled-back version. These were dedicated, hardworking people who had a lot of invested time in the company. The hardest thing was the recognition that it may be ending.

Clark added that although the customers were largely unaware of the turmoil at the company, the investors were very unhappy:

> When something like this comes to light, they certainly ask why, and of course they believe something has gone wrong internally. But to some degree there were some real, rational reasons in the industry why this was happening. Some investors were able to grasp that, and others were quite bitter about the prospect that the investment they made would not be returning something to them.

At the behest of an early investor, turnaround expert Steve Oldman came on the scene to see what could be done to stabilize the business. Steve said that he encountered a hopeless situation:

> I met with Dave, [CFO] Tom Basinger, [tax director] Clark Thomas, and a couple of other key guys. I built a model and explained they'd be bankrupt in 90 days. The best I could do at that point was to make a series of recommendations and restructure their forecasts to give them 9 to 10 months rather than 90 days.
>
> How could this have happened? Faxtech had identified an exciting niche in the huge global communications industry, developed a product that was well received by customers in the market, and succeeded in raising an enormous amount of money to expand the service around the world in an attempt to secure a first-mover advantage.
>
> First-mover, by the way, is a term that was almost never used before the mid-1990s with some early technology companies. Historically, the first one into the space figures out it's a business but then dies because they typically haven't raised enough capital to support the change in the market. The second entrant gets it a little better, and then the third one in generally wins because they can see the pitfalls and avoid them. Faxtech had raised plenty of money, but they just hadn't anticipated how quickly institutional regulators were prepared to move in order to assert their authority over the system.

Steve added that Dave's state of mind was common for someone in that situation:

> Dave is a very logical thinker. He wasn't emotional; he had the ability to convince people, through logic, that he was right. So he got great allegiance to his visions by

---

[7] By the fall of 1998 Faxtech would cut its global staff from 750 to fewer than 400.

the managers and the people around him. They wanted to follow that bright star.

When I got there, he was in deep trouble, and personally in denial: This couldn't happen to me, I've always been successful, I've always been right, the brightest, the best. It was an interesting time in his life—to discover that he could actually fail at something.

Clark noted that some loyal employees were struggling with reality as well:

The realization had now hit that we were not going to turn this thing around. There was still hope, and talk about some deals in the works to try to sell the company. There was certainly a core group that thought that might happen, that their jobs would still exist, and they could go on in some sort of buy-out fashion.

The bondholders had now grown angry. Knowing they couldn't force Dave to throw in the towel, they assured him that if he failed and lost their money, they would most certainly take legal action against him. Dave recalled that he didn't fully appreciate the situation:

I have to say that I didn't understand the risk posed by their threat to sue me if we failed. I'd been in business for a long time already; this was my second venture. I had a lot of experience, and we had a lot of sophisticated people around us. But nobody was able to articulate the downside of the risk I was taking.

The team struggled for many more months to regain the footing they had lost; but by November they realized that they were not going to be able to transition to a new suite of products before the money ran out. It was all over.

The bankruptcy court quickly initiated proceedings to force Faxtech into complete liquidation for less than one cent per dollar invested. Before the last snow that winter, this company, which had raised hundreds of millions in capital from seasoned investors and had employed at its peak 650 dedicated individuals, would be closed forever.

Convergence of Opportunities

Back in the mid-1990s, Dave had spotted what he felt was going to be a fundamental disconnect in the telecom sector:

Faxtech was all about the early stage of bridging the telephone network—a circuit-switched network—with the Internet, which is a packet-switched network. A circuit switch is a physical communication system—like a tin can and a string—more sophisticated than that, but that's the idea. On the Internet, every bit of communication is broken down into little packets and routed through a general network—that's why router companies like Cisco have been pretty successful. There are no circuits anymore—just routes through a global electronic network.

That core transition from circuit-switched to packet-switched started in the telecom world in the early 1990s, and we were participating in it at Faxtech. I started to realize that when the transition really got going, a telephone number—the routable address in a circuit-switched network—would have no meaning on the Internet.

To many young and tech-savvy Internet investors, entrepreneurs, and industry observers, this seemed like a nonissue; telephone numbers would simply become a thing of the past, like slide rules, floppy disks, and cassette tapes. Dave disagreed:

People who grow up in [the world of technology] almost always overstate their position; it's growing, it's exciting, it's new, it's the hip thing, it's the IN thing.... They get confused into thinking that everything they're doing will make sense to everyone. But yet there were a good 50 years or so of pretty impressive work that went into building the global communications network that we know today.

I'm thinking that with 6 billion people on the planet—all trained over the years to dial telephone numbers—I'm thinking that the telephone number is going to survive—that this was going to be convergence, not a takeover. We filed a patent around the concept that giving meaning to telephone numbers in this new network was going to require a complex translation function inside that network.

At the time there was no standard, no names for what we were describing. So we made up our own phrasing to describe what we were doing, like this: The telephone number was going to have to be *queried* against the database to *discover* Internet service addresses for different services associated with that number. . . . The title of our core patent in this area explained the service as follows: *Method and apparatus for correlating a unique identifier, such as a PSTN telephone number, to an Internet address to enable communications over the Internet . . .*

With Faxtech headed for bankruptcy, Dave was spending more and more time looking at this convergent opportunity. It wasn't long before he got some pointed advice from back home:

My mother called me and said, Just tell me you're not going to do that again; *get a job*. And that led to this real heart-to-heart with Terry about my career options. She asked about what I was willing to consider: Corporate work, consulting? I had the education and experience to do virtually anything. And we walked down the list: Would you consider this, that, this?

Ultimately it came down to deciding what I wanted to do with my life—independent of all the stuff that I couldn't control. That stuff is going to happen no matter what—I could only control how I was going to spend my life. . . . The only thing I'm really interested in doing is starting a business that's going to have an objective of revolutionizing an industry—or participating in that revolutionizing process. The answer was obvious: I had to start this new venture, and Terry was totally supportive of that.

With regard to the looming lawsuit, Dave added,

> There was no way to mitigate that personal risk. The reality was that if the creditors from Faxtech sued me and won, they could come after all my assets, including stock in a new business. But what am I going to do, not start?

The Phoenix Rises: Telephony Translations, Inc.

By the time proceedings to dispose of the assets of Faxtech got under way in June 1999, Dave had walked turnaround specialist Steve Oldman through the details of the intellectual property (IP) that was going up for bid. Dave described the situation:

> I laid out for Steve the Faxtech IP that I felt could become the foundation for a new company in the converged telephone number addressing space. My wife Terry and I decided to risk $26,000 to acquire that technology at the auction. That was pennies on the dollar of the actual value, and our assumption was that the bankruptcy trustee and the audience at the auction would not be aware of the years of work embodied in some key patent applications—and hence would be unwilling to bid up the price of those assets.

After his lengthy discussions with Dave about this IP portfolio, Steve realized that he knew exactly how to approach, manage, and orchestrate a solution where they could execute the purchase within a completely legal and ethical framework:

> Because Dave was explicitly excluded from participating in the auction process under direction from the bankruptcy trustee, we recruited his old friend John Tyler [the original vice president of engineering at Faxtech]. John Tyler agreed to join the auction and bid on the patents, with the understanding that he would then sell the patents back to Dave and Terry in return for a stock position in their new company.

Dave said it worked beautifully:

> Although several people showed up to bid on the patent applications, John, who was armed with a briefcase full of cash, was successful in purchasing all of the patents we needed (see Exhibit 2).

With his core patents secured and with a base of loyal and highly skilled Faxtech employees readily available for a new challenge, Dave said that his next enterprise rose seamlessly from the ashes of the previous one:

> We hit the ground running with Telephony Translations (TTI). It was the benefit of having people from the original team, and this being my third time around; I mean, you do get better at this, right? It was so fast; six months from writing the first plan to having 20 people in an office writing code.

EXHIBIT 2

TTI Intellectual Property

TTI's patents and pending applications include hundreds of claims covering processes and implementation concepts relating to the use of a shared directory in IP-based communications. Outlined below is a brief summary of TTI's three areas of patent activity.

Method and apparatus for correlating a unique identifier, such as a PSTN Telephone number, to an Internet address to enable communications over the Internet

This series of issued patents (U.S. Patent 6,539,077, U.S. Patent 6,748,057, European Patent 1142286) and pending applications initially filed in December 1999 describe the use of a shared "Directory Service" (DS) to convert a PSTN telephone number into Internet address information. Such information will allow the creation of a communication link over a data network between two unrelated communications platforms using only standard telephone numbers for addressing. The application contains claims specifically relating to the use of a shared directory to allow real-time voice, voice messaging, remote printing, and unified messaging applications over the Internet using standard telephone numbers for addressing.

Method and apparatus for identifying and replying to a caller

This set of issued patents (U.S. Patent 6,292,799, Chinese Patent ZL 99807952.9, Australian Patent 748758) initially filed in June 1998 apply a shared Internet directory to global voice messaging services. Specifically, the patent describes the use of a shared directory enabling end users to utilize an IP network to "reply for free" to voicemail messages. The directory converts a return telephone number into a reply address for any Internet-enabled voicemail, e-mail, or unified-messaging system. The patent was granted with multiple claims covering various aspects of Internet voice messaging and directory services.

Method and apparatus for accessing a network computer to establish a push-to-talk session

This patent application (continuation-in-part of U.S. 6,539,077, 6,748,057, 6,292,799) describes a communications architecture where a wireless phone user registered for push-to-talk (PTT) services desires a PTT session with a party on a network computer accessible via a public data network that is not registered with any PTT service. The wireless phone user initiates a session by entering a unique identifier as a destination address for the network computer. The wireless operator's PTT server queries a Directory Service, available on the public data network, to obtain a PTT address for the destination computer, thus enabling the PTT server to discover any number of push-to-talk enabled PCs available on the public data network.

Source: www.TTI.com.

To fund the effort, Dave knew he needed to bring in new blood:

> One of the real pains of Faxtech not making it was that I lost so many great financial contacts. I had raised money all over the world—the problem was I lost money all over the world. As much as those investors like to say they bet for the right reason, that I worked really hard, and they liked everything I did, the truth is, I lost their money.

Dave's father, a retired AT&T executive, reached out into his network and found a friend who had a friend in the venture capital business: Bob Cooper of Signit Ventures. Bob recalled his first impressions:

> Several things struck me at the time. Faxtech had clearly been a time-windowed opportunity that Dave hadn't understood. He had tried to grow it to the moon at a time when he should have been looking for a buyer. What I saw in Dave was a guy who was a brilliant thinker and strategist, but maybe not a skilled operator. He was also a guy that had the courage to stand up again even after the horrendous problems he went through.
>
> Dave's best skill, as is the case with all of us, can also be a liability. He believes in himself so strongly, and he is so bright, he can go into a closet by himself and think through the 40 zillion different combinations of the strategy and come out and say, "I know the answer and that's it." That process dredges out a better depth than anyone else, and once aligned to the right direction, Dave can contribute better on a new idea, and communicate it to a community and to the rest of the team in a way that they can build a product around it, better than any person I've ever seen.
>
> The downside, of course, is that his certainty makes Dave as stubborn as he can be. That is the good and bad news about an entrepreneur: They rarely see the market not aligned with that strategy they have settled on.
>
> I would also tell you that I saw Dave as the chief marketing officer and never anticipated that Dave would be the CEO of that company long-term. I shared with him that I would watch him for a while as CEO, but I would only do the deal if I had the choice as to when we needed to bring in a CEO to be his partner, not to replace him.

Dave was excited to have found a new supporter:

> So I was hot on the heels of having lost many millions of dollars, and yet Bob and his group were willing to listen. Signit is to be credited for having the foresight and the willingness to accept that experience often comes with setbacks and failures. If you're really going to be in the game and you're really going to push hard, everything isn't going to work out.
>
> Positive (and negative) outcomes are the result of a combination of many factors—only a few of which you control—and so, if you value yourself based purely on the outcome, you're not really being honest. The assessment should really be based on the quality of your work over that long period of that time—independent of the outcome. Bob understood that.

Dave added that Signit was very intrigued by his vision that at some point in the future, the telecommunications industry was going to come looking for a technical bridge to transition the old physical structures into the digital age:

> Phone numbers are going to need to survive because that's how people are accustomed to placing a call, but they don't have any real meaning on the digital network. To bridge the two, there has to be a highly complex solution in the middle. When the big telcos realize they need this bridge, they are going to buy that solution from someone. As a new entrant, the only way to have any chance of participating is to build [the technology] when nobody wants it—so when they do want it, you've actually got it. Alternatively, if you're not there when they want it, they are going to contact proven names like Ericsson, Lucent, Siemens, or Nortel, and they are going to pay one of them to develop it.
>
> Those big-name guys aren't building it right now because nobody's willing to pay them to do it. So we have to go spend venture money to build this technology, and it's going to take years. And I don't know when it's going to happen. But when it happens, it's going to be a great business for 30 years because people don't make these transitions very quickly. Customers need stability. The industry needs stability. But the problem is, how do you know when they're going to need it? I don't know. If it turns out they need it in six months, we're screwed because we can't build it in six months. If it turns out they won't need it for 10 years, we're also screwed because we can't wait around that along.

Signit agreed to invest $10 million for 40 percent of the business (fully diluted)—in monthly allocations in order to mitigate the risk of the dark legal cloud that was hanging over the lead entrepreneur in the deal. In June 2000, just three days before the statute deadline, that legal action thundered down. Although Dave had been preparing himself for this eventuality, the documents still took his breath away.

Trust—but Verify

A group of creditors led by the bankruptcy trustee filed an $80 million creditor lawsuit against the directors and officers of the company. Although Dave and the other officers did not have sufficient assets to warrant the attention of the creditors, the Faxtech lawsuit was born out of a desire by creditors to gain access to a $10 million directors and officers (D&O) insurance policy carried by the company. The entire board was named in the suit, but Dave could see that he was the one who'd have to fight it. When Dave referred the action to his insurance carrier, the news was not good:

> The first thing that happened is the insurance company says, That's not a valid claim,[8] so we're not going to cover it. I'm trying to build TTI, and at the same time, I'm putting pressure on the insurance company—while I dig and scrape and sell assets to pay for my own defense. By the time the insurance company agreed to pick it up, I had already paid $140,000—after tax—in legal fees.

Dave recalled that the legal attack itself was far more painful than the money worries it caused:

> The actual act of getting sued is so much worse than I had been prepared for. I didn't think I did anything wrong, but that didn't stop them from suing me, and it didn't stop them from writing really long papers that described me as absolute scum; he's bad for this reason, he's really bad for this reason, and just imagine how bad he must be for these other reasons. I had to say to the [TTI] board, Look, I'm sorry, I'm being sued for $80 million for breach of fiduciary responsibility. That just sounds so bad: *breach of fiduciary responsibility!*
>
> And of course that destabilizes the board. All of a sudden the board isn't sure about anything: Are you sure about this direction [for TTI]? Do you think we should do it this way? Maybe we should do it another way.
>
> Remember: These are really good people who bet on me for all the right reasons. Nonetheless, having that outside force sending thick documents that say I'm a terrible person and a crooked manager is an understandable cause for investor concern.

The board believed, as the insurance company ultimately did, that the lawsuit against Dave would be dismissed or settled before it ever reached a jury. Nevertheless, the whole awful affair had heightened investor concerns about what a central figure Dave was in their TTI investment. Dave recalled one particularly stressful meeting:

> They said, Look, you're the largest stockholder. You invented all the technology; you're the holder of all the patents; you've brought in the whole team; and that team is committed to you and would leave anytime you told them to. You raised all the money. You're the founder and the CEO, and you're the only one we can talk to. How do we know you're right? We're supposed to be the board, but what exactly would we say? How do we actually have a debate?

That was really an interesting and valid point. There was no way for there to be a balance of power. What is their power? All they could do was say, I don't know . . . I don't know if what you told me is right.

Dave said that the board was also concerned that even the technology plan (see Exhibit 3) had to be taken largely on faith:

> What we do is so geeky. I'm not kidding—there are not 50 people on the planet who understand what we do well enough to evaluate our potential. I don't even bother to explain it. Just trust me: Phone numbers don't work on the Internet, the world is going to demand phone numbers, so somehow you have to achieve that transition. Our technology solution is the special sauce that performs that function.

New CEO

Dave swallowed hard when the board presented what seemed like a harsh solution for mitigating their risk:

> Their answer was, Hire someone they know and trust to be CEO of TTI, and I just have to accept that. And then they'll have someone here who can assure them that I know what I'm doing, and that I can do what I say. So George Marsh will be coming in to *replace me (!)* as CEO.[9] His job will be to run the business side: pricing, sales, contracts, fulfillment. As the founder, I will be in charge of strategy and product development.

Bob Turner wasn't surprised that Dave had been very confident that a new CEO would not be necessary:

> This happened about a year into the process, so it didn't take that long. I say the same thing to all the entrepreneurs that I start with: that I will take you as far as I can, I'll surround you with all the skills that I think will make you better and be able to last as long as you can. If at some point in time I see the mix not being right, then we will quickly add the right people with the right skills. They are almost always shocked by the speed of change once we make that decision.

Bob explained his reasoning for making the change:

> Dave's skill is his great ability to conceptualize a business that hasn't yet been formed where there are no rules. But to be successful someone like that needs someone who can balance his strong intellect and brilliant mind with his absolute devotion to his brilliant mind. He

---

[8] Faxtech had maintained a $10 million directors and officers (D&O) insurance policy. From Dave's perspective, the policy covered the board members against all external claims. The policy, however, had an exclusion for claims brought by the company against its own members. This "insured vs. insured" exclusion was the clause the insurance cited when they refused to cover the directors against a lawsuit that was brought by the bankruptcy trustee on behalf of the company's creditors. The insurance company claimed that the bankruptcy trustee was acting "on behalf of the company" and hence this triggered the "insured vs. insured" exclusion.

[9] Prior to joining TTI, George was the chief executive officer, president, and cochair of a public video processing technology company. He was formerly president and CEO of a provider of wireless messaging services with 9 million subscribers. Earlier George served as vice chair of a leading worldwide provider of credit card transaction processing, health care claims processing, and document management/imaging services with revenues exceeding $3 billion.

EXHIBIT 3

Multiapplication Addressing Architecture

The TITAN™ platform is a highly flexible, carrier-grade, multiprotocol, next-generation addressing infrastructure that service providers and interconnect carriers license to support multiple IP and SS7/C7 address resolution services. Addressing applications supported on TITAN include among others: Carrier-ENUM, Number-Portability, Calling-Name, SPID, and GTT.

Query protocols supported on the platform include ENUM, SIP, DNS, SOAP/XML, and multiple SS7/C7 protocols (AIN 0.2, PCS-1900, IS-41, GSM/MAP) via SIGTRAN or low-speed link.

This platform is licensed to carriers as a software package that can be configured or customized to support multiple address resolution services on a variety of high-performance, off-the-shelf hardware platforms and operating systems.

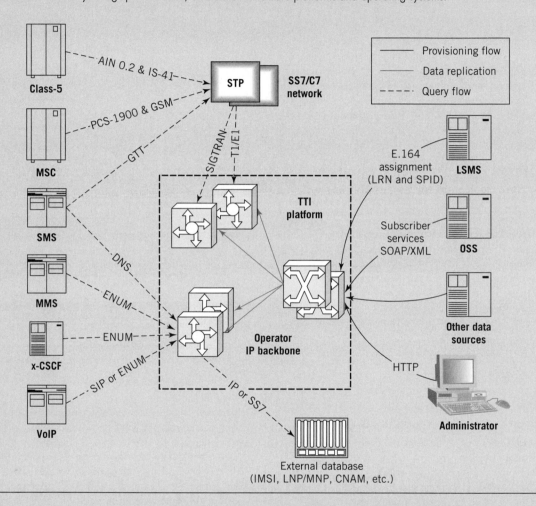

needs someone to say no, to say no not now, and someone to argue points with him.

George is one of my senior guys, my best strategist, and one of my best business executors. He ran four or five of my businesses for me—from tens of millions to billions. I trusted George implicitly, but I said to them both, Neither can proceed unless you can both agree. I respect you both greatly, and this is an area that is going to take some judgment, some perceptualizing on how an industry might be formed, and a terrific bond to each other to make it happen.

The board's decision was not open for discussion, and in that respect Dave felt the situation was handled badly.

Dave recalled that it wasn't long, however, before he had wholeheartedly embraced the arrangement:

George was an excellent choice: smart and flexible. The two of us were thrown into this, and it's worked out really well. His ability to be CEO is totally dependent on his ability to maintain a tie with me, and my ability to continue being the entrepreneur and driver of this business is completely dependent on my ability to maintain a relationship with him.

You know, it takes two people to have a great relationship, and we both work at it every day. It's not like it's painful, it's like anything—you've got to keep working at it. I have total respect for his area, he has total respect for my area, and we spend plenty of time staying in synch with each other and with Sam Walker,[10] the head of our development team. And it works.

As the TTI team successfully adjusted to the new management dynamic, a telco giant in Europe was coming to the realization that their 21st-century digital network was going to require a complex software link that would preserve the "meaningless" telephone number.

Success in Trying

By early 2000 Terry was looking and feeling very much recovered from her long illness. Although they still wanted to start a family, Terry recalled that no one believed that would be possible:

> The doctors were saying that after going through two years of intense chemotherapy, there was no way I could possibly have a baby. We went to fertility clinics that turned us away the moment they learned about my cancer treatments—they wouldn't even consider us because all we'd do is mess up their [success rate] statistics.

The couple refused to give up hope. Against all odds, in January 2001 Terry gave birth to their first daughter. A year and a half later they would be a family of four with two healthy little girls.

In April 2001 TTI formed a strategic partnership with Indica Software, a Los Angeles–based Internet infrastructure company, to "facilitate the deployment of wholly transparent, network access numbering technologies." In August the venture closed a $15 million round with participation from a venture capital subsidiary of Science International Corp. and by VeriSign, an Internet security firm. A vice president from each company was given a seat on TTI's board of directors.

Dave recalled that the tragic events of 9/11 threw everything off schedule:

> We are about a year into [the venture], and all of a sudden the world goes through this total telecom meltdown. Nobody was buying anything. Lucent let go 40,000 people! It was an unbelievable disaster . . . and it was happening all over the world. Fortunately our partnership with Indigo enabled us to grab onto an existing niche and apply our technology to deliver that service more efficiently. That was just a better mousetrap, but it gave us some money while we waited for the industry to recover.

In early 2002 the team offered former Faxtech manager Clark Thomas the post of vice president of finance and administration. Clark, who had been building a successful

practice as a tax and finance consultant to high-tech startups, took a hard look before saying yes:

> I think Dave has a lot of skills to run a company and to rally people and focus people on a particular direction. He is a great dynamic leader, he is a very good visionary, but I thought there were some things he needed to learn from [the Faxtech] experience.
>
> I thought a couple of things he was lacking at Faxtech were a real strong board of directors and some real strong dissenting opinions on his executive team. I saw that with TTI Dave recognized those weaknesses, and this time he is very open to taking advice from other people to make it work.

At around the same time, Dave began to have some interesting conversations about the future:

> In February I flew out to meet with one of British Telecom's [BT] R&D groups outside London. I felt that I had achieved a real meeting of the minds with Ned Saxon, a young guy in the group. BT was still years away from needing the TTI solution, and we were still in the middle of building it, but I could see how it might all come together.
>
> Ned did a great job of finding the right group within BT. This group was designing the "21st-Century Network"—a $20 billion project to make the transition away from circuit-switched technologies. Ned succeeded in getting me a meeting with the design group despite their reluctance to meet with a small company from Massachusetts. During the initial meeting, we reviewed the complete problem space and explored how our technology could solve their routing problems. I explained to them why the [big players] in the industry can't do this, and why what we are building is in fact the answer they will be looking for.
>
> At the end of the meeting, they said that's an outstanding story, but we simply are not knowledgeable enough to know whether it's right or wrong. The head of the group says, I can tell you for sure it's an impressive story, but I can also tell you we don't buy things from 30-person organizations in Massachusetts.

Dave thanked them for their time. He was determined they'd meet again:

> BT was the only tier-one carrier on the planet planning such a complete transition. I knew one thing: We had to win that contract. In fact, the whole reason we are here is to win that contract. And if we don't win it, we're not going to get the learning. And if we don't get it, that learning will go to someone named Siemens or Ericsson—firms with infinite resources. If we lose out to one of them, we're all done.

In early 2004 Dave had another meeting with the British Telecom group:

> They seemed a bit exasperated. They said, "The way this is supposed to work is BT goes to a big company—like Ericsson—and Ericsson is supposed to find you. You don't come to us." Then they say that Ericsson has

---

[10] Sam was TTI's chief technical officer and vice president of development and operations. At Faxtech Sam had served as of architecture and technology.

assured them that they have the technology. And I shake my head and say, Okay, I understand that you guys can't possibly know whether I'm telling you the truth, or whether this is just a total story. I get that.

So I hand them my card and say, In some amount of time in the future you're going to find out that Ericsson can't do this, and it's going to be painful, because they're going to stretch you out, and it's going to be at the last minute, and they're going to have to finally fess up that they can't do it. And when that happens, you call me.

As a confident group inside Ericsson got down to work to devise their own version of this intricate solution, TTI began fielding offers from other players in the industry who were interested in betting on what could be a lucrative capability. Dave and the team felt it was far too early to consider a harvest:

> We won't be interested in selling until we feel that someone is way overvaluing the business, or the dynamics change and our real competitive advantage has been narrowed. We believe that even if [a competitor] is working really hard right now, they're still several years behind us. We'll eventually sell to someone who is planning to run with it for 30 years. But first we want to build value by getting our solution into the marketplace.

A Sudden Leave of Absence

In December 2004, with his company right in the middle of its most critical phase of development, Dave's world took a nasty turn:

They called it head and neck cancer, stage three. They believed it originated somewhere in my throat region—sinuses, tongue, throat, somewhere in there—and then it moved to my lymph system. But because they couldn't find the exact origin, the doctors were going to have to treat the cancer by applying maximum radiation to everything from my upper chest to the bridge of my nose.

At this point the problem wasn't the cancer—I seemed to be getting along just fine with my cancer! I knew from watching what Terry had gone through that the cancer treatments are the problem. I was in for a horrible period of many months of radiation treatment and recovery, and I just knew I was going to have to disappear for a while.

The initial shock wave was followed closely with great sorrow because statistics showed that the five-year survival rate for Dave's type of cancer was just 40 percent. Clark said that the news was a huge blow to the company but that Dave handled it well:

> He has that unique characteristic of being able to put a positive spin on almost anything. He was totally upfront about what he was facing. He had a meeting and explained in great detail what he was going to have to go through, and he explained his whole treatment process of aggressively attacking the cancer. His openness, and his willingness to let people know what he was facing, helped people to deal with it in the best way possible.

With the company still in the development phase and with revenues still an undetermined way out, the team needed to assess the impact of this terrible news and decide how best to move forward.

Chapter Eighteen

The Family as Entrepreneur

Whoever thought that safeguarding the brands, assets, and customers that made your company a success would constitute risky behavior? But these days it is—if it is all your company is doing. By conserving resources and honing operational efficiencies, established companies try to guarantee that there is never an unexpected downside. In so doing they often miss out on the real action in today's economy—capitalizing on the upside potential of new ideas.

Gary Hamel[1]

Results Expected

Upon the completion of this chapter, you be able to

1. Describe the significant economic and entrepreneurial contribution families make to communities and countries worldwide.
2. Discuss the different roles families play as part of the entrepreneurial process.
3. Provide a definition of family enterprising and transgenerational entrepreneurship.
4. Assess your family on the mind-set and methods continua for family enterprising and identify key issues for family dialogue.
5. Explore key questions on the six dimensions for family enterprising.
6. Plot your family's resources and capabilities on the "familiness f + f − assessment continuum" and understand their advantages and constraints.
7. Analyze and discuss the Indulgence Spa Products case study.

Families, Entrepreneurship, and the Timmons Model

The tension among generations in families can often revolve around the aggressive younger executives seeking to explore new and exciting deals and the older executive who seeks to march forward on the pathway that created the family's fortune. The purpose of this chapter is to help families (and those working with families) understand that opportunity recognition and balance in the Timmons Model helps guide the family's decision-making process. By encouraging the discussion toward the model, we ask, "What is the richest opportunity?" and "Are the opportunity, team, and resources well balanced?" Families have special knowledge, experience, and often resources that bring competitive advantages. We aspire to leverage these special factors to create a "familiness" advantage that creates value.

The concepts and models presented in this chapter are based on the research and writing of Timothy Habbershon and colleagues, including T. G. Habbershon and M L. Williams, "A Resource Based Framework for Assessing the Strategic Advantages of Family Firms," *Family Business Review* 12, 1999, pp. 1–25; T. G. Habbershon, M. Williams, and I. C. MacMillan, "A Unified Systems Perspective of Family Firm Performance," *Journal of Business Venturing* 18(4), 2003, pp. 451–65; and T. G. Habbershon and J. Pistrui, "Enterprising Families Domain: Family-Influenced Ownership Groups in Pursuit of Transgenerational Wealth," *Family Business Review* 15(1), 2002, pp. 223–37.

[1] G. Hamel, "Bringing Silicon Valley Inside," *Harvard Business Review* 77, no. 5 (September–October 1999), p. 70.

Building Entrepreneurial Family Legacies[2]

When we hear the phrase *family business,* images of high-flying, harvesting entrepreneurs are not usually the first thoughts that come to our mind. We more often think of small mom-and-pop businesses or the large business family fights that hold the potential for reality TV. It is fair to say that family businesses do not always look and act entrepreneurially. They can focus on serving local markets, sustaining the family's lifestyle, or providing jobs to family members. They are often conflicted due to family dynamics, constrained by nepotism, or limited by their conservative risk profile.

But these realities should be held in tension with the corresponding truth that families comprise the dominant form of business organization worldwide and provide more resources for the entrepreneurial economy than any other source. We must be careful that we do not form mental caricatures about either family businesses or entrepreneurs that might keep us from exploring the link between entrepreneurship and family or, more important, keep us from understanding the significance the linkage holds for social and economic wealth creation in our communities and countries worldwide.

The purpose of this chapter is to deepen our understanding of entrepreneurship in the family context. We will explore the entrepreneurial commitments, capabilities, and contributions of families and their businesses. To describe families who leverage the entrepreneurial process in the family context we use the phrase *family enterprising.* As enterprise refers to economic activity, enterprising is the action of generating economic activity. Consistent with earlier definitions of entrepreneurship, families who are enterprising generate new economic activity and build long-term value across generations. We refer to this outcome as *transgenerational entrepreneurship and wealth creation,* and it is how to build entrepreneurial family legacies. This chapter will provide families with three sets of assessment and strategy tools to assist them in knowing how to become enterprising and build their family legacy.

Large Company Family Legacies

We must first begin by understanding the economic and entrepreneurial significance of families. It is difficult to walk into a Marriot Hotel, see the father and son picture of J. Willard Marriott Jr. and Sr., and not think about entrepreneurial family legacies. From a small root beer concession stand, who would have expected the emergence of a $10 billion and 133,000-employee company? The Marriotts are now operating in their third generation of family leadership and are just one example of the many U.S. companies and branded products that are synonymous with family names and legacies.

Ford Motor Company celebrated 100 years of making cars in 2003. Henry Ford's original company is in its fifth generation with fourth-generation leader William (Bill) Clay Ford, Jr., as the chairman and CEO. The Ford family still controls about 40 percent of the voting shares in the $170 billion-plus company, and board member Edsel B. Ford II said that they are interested in creating a new generation of entrepreneurs.

Walgreen Co. began when Chicago pharmacist and entrepreneur Charles Walgreen borrowed $2,000 from his father for a down payment on his first drugstore in 1901. Today the company is in its fourth generation of Walgreen family involvement with Charles R. Walgreen III as the chairman emeritus of the board of directors and his son Kevin Walgreen as a vice president. It has grown through the generations to over 4,800 stores with $37.5 billion in annual revenue. It has fewer stores than its rival CVS but still beats them in annual sales.

Cargill is the largest privately held corporation in the United States, generating more than $62 billion in annual revenues across a diversified group of food, agricultural, and risk management businesses around the globe. One hundred and forty years after its inception, the founding Cargill and MacMillan families still own 85 percent of the company.

Although it is often assumed that family companies cannot play in the technology and telecommunications arena, father and son team Ralph and Brian Roberts have grown the Comcast cable company into the largest in the United States. Even with a $54 billion takeover of AT&T Broadband in 2002, the Roberts family still maintains 33 percent of the voting shares and top leadership positions.[3]

Families also dominate many of the leading financial services and banking institutions worldwide. In Boston, Fidelity and the Johnson family are a leading business family. The Johnsons control 49 percent of the largest mutual fund company in the world. They have more than $1 trillion under management. Ned Johnson continues to lead the company as CEO and chairman, while his daughter is president of the fastest-growing Retirement Services Unit.

Many of the popular branded product companies are controlled by families, including Tyson Foods, an

---

[2] Primary financial, performance, and ownership data from Hoovers Online.
[3] "A New Cable Giant," *BusinessWeek,* November 18, 2002, p. 108.

Arkansas-based $26 billion company in which the family controls 80 percent and the grandson of the founder is the current chairman and CEO. Mars is still 100 percent family owned, and the $20 billion company has multiple generations of family members at all levels of top leadership. Cosmetic, fragrance, and skin care products company Estee Lauder generates nearly $6 billion in revenues with the founding family controlling approximately 88 percent of its voting shares and six members in top management bearing the Lauder name. Wrigleys gum, a $3.6 billion company currently run by the founder's great-grandson, William Wrigley Jr., far outperforms its rivals with a 20.3 percent return on assets. Smucker's Jam—"With a name like Smucker's, it has to be good"—has sales of over $2 billion with brothers Tim and Richard continuing to grow the 100-year-old company.

Another interesting category of entrepreneurial family involvement is the investment-holding company. Warren Buffet may be one of the most famous examples. Buffet's company, Berkshire Hathaway, owns many recognizable companies such as GEICO Insurance, Fruit of the Loom, and Dairy Queen. For over 37 years, Buffet's investments in companies have provided an average annual return of 22.6 percent and have increased the value of Berkshire by over 195,000 percent since 1965. His 38 percent stake in the $74 billion Berkshire gives him an estimated net worth of $41 billion and makes him the second richest person in the world, behind only Bill Gates.[4] Warren's son, Howard G. Buffet, is a director at several Berkshire subsidiaries and currently sits on the board at Berkshire. Although succession planning at Berkshire is highly secretive, it is anticipated that Howard Buffet will take over as chairman of the board.

Minnesota-based Carlson Companies is a less well-known company. In 1998 Marilyn Carlson Nelson took over as CEO of her family holding company. By 2007 she had grown the business nearly 70 percent to $37.1 billion in revenues. The 100 percent family-owned company is predominantly in hospitality and travel, owning companies such as the TGI Friday's restaurant chain, Radisson, Regent International Hotels, and Park Plaza Hotels & Resorts.

There are many smaller family investment-holding companies such as the Berwind Group in Philadelphia, Pennsylvania, that fly under the radar in our cities. The multibillion-dollar fifth-generation family company invested more than $900 million in acquisi-

tions during their most recent three-year planning cycle, including the acquisition of Elmer's Products.

In keeping with this picture of family legacy contributions, in 2006 over a third of Fortune 500 companies were controlled or managed by families. These family-influenced companies consistently outperform nonfamily businesses on annual shareholder return, return on assets, and both annual revenue and income growth.[5] But these large family companies only begin to tell the story of the entrepreneurial and economic contribution made by business families. (See Exhibit 18.1.)

Wal-Mart: A Growth-Oriented Family Enterprise

Whether one loves or hates Wal-Mart, the Walton family tops the list of family wealth creation legacies. The family still controls nearly 40 percent of the largest company in the world with $288 billion in annual revenue. The family fortune totals $100 billion—more than Bill Gates and Warren Buffet combined, or more than the GDP of Singapore. There are five Walton family members[6] in the top 10 of the list of richest Americans,[7] and they contributed more than $700 million in charitable giving with 80 percent of their donations to education since 1998. The visible link between the company and the family is Wal-Mart Chairman Rob Walton, who is commended by *Fortune* magazine as one of "the most knowledgeable non-executive chairmen in American business." Rob's father, Sam Walton, had a vision to allow ordinary folks to buy what only rich people could once buy. This aspiration was translated into the company slogan "everyday low prices." Chairman Rob Walton makes clear that the Walton vision is alive and well, proclaiming that "Wal-Mart is still a growth company."[8]

Smaller and Midsized Family Legacies

In many regards, the real heart and often overlooked segment of the U.S. economy and entrepreneurial activity is the smaller and midsize companies. This segment is substantively controlled by families, and they are not all your typical mom-and-pop operations.

Cardone Manufacturing in Philadelphia, Pennsylvania, is a prime example. Founded by a father and son team in 1970, it is the largest nongovernment employer in the city and the largest privately held remanufacturer of car parts in the United States. The founding

4 "Forbes 400 List," September 24, 2004, *Forbes,* http://www.forbes.com/400richest/.

5 J. Weber et al., "Family Inc.," *BusinessWeek,* November 10, 2003.

6 On June 27, 2005, John Walton, son of Sam Walton, tragically died in a crash of his ultralight plane near Jackson Hole, Wyoming. John was tied for fourth richest person according to *Forbes* with a net worth of $18 billion. It is still unsure what will be done with his remaining fortune.

7 "Forbes 400 List," September 24, 2004, *Forbes,* http://www.forbes.com/400richest/.

8 A. Serwer et al., "The Waltons: Inside America's Richest Family," *Fortune* 150, no. 10 (November 15, 2004), p. 86.

EXHIBIT 18.1

Performance Comparison

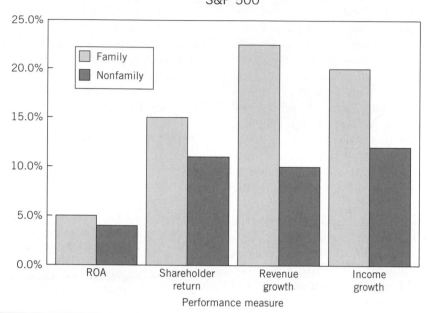

Family vs. Nonfamily Firm Performance in the S&P 500

Source: "Family Inc.," *BusinessWeek,* November 10, 2003. Used by permission of the McGraw-Hill Companies, Inc.

son, Michael Cardone, and his third-generation children are continuing their entrepreneurial legacy by expanding the multi-hundred-million-dollar company into Europe and China, while moving into the new car parts arena.

The largest privately held hair salon chain in the United States was founded by a husband and wife. The Ratner Company has a strong top leadership team and is training its second generation of family members. They outperform their larger public rival, Regis, and continue to act entrepreneurially. With nearly 1,000 company stores in their largest brand, Hair Cuttery, they are moving into franchising, expanding their upscale brands, and establishing strategic partnerships to continue their global expansion. Although cofounder Dennis Ratner could be resting on his accomplishments, he is committed to family enterprising, telling his children, "You either eat or get eaten."

Many family companies may not have brand names consumers recognize, but they are dominant in their industries because they play in the supply chains of large multinationals. Bloomer Chocolates in Chicago, Illinois, is known as the company that makes Chicago smell like chocolate. The third-generation multi-hundred-million-dollar company is the largest roaster of chocolate beans in the United States. They have taken a low-margin commodities business that large chocolate companies have outsourced and created a profitable niche. Many of the chocolate products from companies such as Hershey's and Nestlé are made from chocolate produced by Bloomer.

The list of these "everyday" family entrepreneurs is endless. In Boston, Gentle Giant is the largest regional moving company. The entrepreneurial vision of this $20 million company sets the standard for the moving industry, and they plan to replicate it in other cities. The largest distributor of IAMS pet food on the East Coast has a third generation of entrepreneurs at the helm. Having recently bought the business from their father, two brothers are next-generation entrepreneurs, growing Pet Food Experts and diversifying it to lessen the risk of being a dedicated distributor. In the ski industry, dominated by large public resort companies, Tim and Diane Mueller stand out as successful family entrepreneurs. Since 1982 they have grown the run-down Vermont ski resort they purchased to a $100 million company and have acquired a resort in Denver. CarSense is a new concept car dealership that has grown to $100 million in sales in seven years after the second-generation entrepreneur sold the families' traditional car dealerships to innovate for the future. Majestic Athletic, a sports apparel company in eastern Pennsylvania, run by the Capobianco family, makes the uniforms for all of major league baseball. Many critics felt major league baseball was crazy to choose a small family-run company

EXHIBIT 18.2

Family Businesses' Economic Contribution

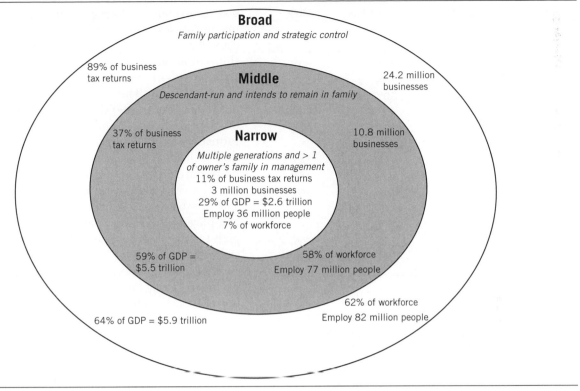

Broad
Family participation and strategic control

89% of business tax returns

24.2 million businesses

Middle
Descendant-run and intends to remain in family

37% of business tax returns

10.8 million businesses

Narrow
Multiple generations and > 1 of owner's family in management
11% of business tax returns
3 million businesses
29% of GDP = $2.6 trillion
Employ 36 million people
7% of workforce

59% of GDP = $5.5 trillion

58% of workforce
Employ 77 million people

62% of workforce
Employ 82 million people

64% of GDP = $5.9 trillion

Source: J. H. Astrachan and M. C. Shanker, "Family Businesses' Contribution to the U.S. Economy: A Closer Look," *Family Business Review* 16, no. 3 (September 2003), p. 211. Copyright 2003 Blackwell Publishing. Used by permission.

instead of a large apparel maker, but the hands-on quality approach of the family has been a big hit for the company and the league.

In this montage of families we have not even mentioned the nascent entrepreneurs and smaller companies that will become the next-generation Marriott, Smucker, or Ratner family companies. Nor have we considered the children in existing family firms who will become nascent entrepreneurs. In a recent undergraduate class on family entrepreneurship at Babson College, more than 80 percent of the students said that they wanted to start *their own company* as an extension of their family company. They were not just looking to run their family company. Students like Toby Donath created a business plan to move his mother's business, Backerhaus Veit, from manufacturing and wholesaling to retailing and branded products. Brothers Colby and Drew West are starting a technology company with their parents as "support investors" based on a new technology developed by Drew. Student Jonathan Gelpey has a plan to commercialize a product for which his grandfather holds

the patent. All of these young entrepreneurs fulfill our vision for next-generation entrepreneurship and family enterprising.

The Family Contribution and Roles

It is clear from our descriptions of family companies that families still dominate the U.S. economy and even more fully the economies of other countries worldwide. The most recent economic impact study in the United States reported that 89 percent of all business tax returns and 60 percent of all public companies had family participation and strategic control. That is more than 24 million businesses and represents nearly $6 trillion in gross domestic product (64 percent of GDP) and 82 million jobs (62 percent of the workforce).[9] Worldwide, the economic numbers are similar to those in countries like Italy, reporting that 93 percent of their businesses are family controlled, and Brazil, 90 percent.[10] (See Exhibits 18.2 and 18.3.)

Once we acknowledge the economic relevance of families, we can better understand the significant

[9] J. H. Astrachan and M. C. Shanker, "Family Businesses' Contribution to the U.S. Economy: A Closer Look," *Family Business Review* 16, no. 3 (September 2003), p. 211.
[10] "IFERA. Family Businesses Dominate," *Family Business Review* 16, no. 4 (December 2003), p. 235.

EXHIBIT 18.3

Worldwide Highlights of Family Businesses

Country	Definition	% of FBs	GNP
Brazil	Middle	90%	63%
Chile	Broad	75%	50–70%
USA	Broad	96%	40%
Belgium	Narrow	70%	55%
Finland	Narrow	80%	40–45%
France	Broad	> 60%	> 60%
Germany	Middle	60%	55%
Italy	Broad	93%	
Netherlands	Narrow	74%	54%
Poland	Broad	Up to 80%	35%
Portugal	Broad	70%	60%
Spain	Narrow	79%	
UK	Middle	70%	
Australia	Narrow	75%	50%
India	Broad		65%

pool of resources and potential they represent for entrepreneurial activity. There was a day when "business" meant "family" because the family was understood to be foundational to all socioeconomic progress.[11] Today, however, we must more intentionally categorize the roles families play economically and entrepreneurially. Exhibit 18.4 presents five different roles families can play in the entrepreneurial process and distinguishes between a formal and informal application of these roles.

In this regard the categories are both descriptive and prescriptive. They describe what roles families play and how they play them, but also hint at a prescription for a more formal approach to entrepreneurship in the family context. By "formal" we mean establishing individual and organizational disciplines and structure of the entrepreneurial process. We do not mean "bureaucratic." Many family entrepreneurs, particularly senior-generation entrepreneurs, embrace the myth that any formalization will constrain their entrepreneurial behavior. Nothing could be further from the truth. With informed intuition, disciplined processes, clear financial benchmarks, and organizational accountability, family teams can generate higher-potential ventures and get the odds in their favor for transgenerational entrepreneurship and wealth creation.

The first and dominant role families play is what we call *family-influenced start-ups*. Data from the

GEM report indicated that there were 25 million "new family firms" started in 2002 worldwide.[12] Because families are driven by social forces of survival, wealth creation, and progeny, it is natural that start-up businesses think family first. Family-influenced start-ups are new businesses where the family ownership vision and/or leadership influence impacts the strategic intent, decision making, and financial goals of the company. They may have family involvement in the beginning, intend to have family involvement, or end up having family involvement during the formative stages of the company. Some families begin their collective entrepreneurship experience with a more formal vision and planning process that delineates how the family will capture a new opportunity. This approach often clarifies the role family members will play in the start-up and puts them on a faster path for successfully meeting their family and financial goals.

The *family corporate venturing* category occurs when an existing family company or group starts new businesses. Families are often, and quite naturally, portfolio entrepreneurs who build numerous businesses under a family umbrella. Although they may not always grow each of the businesses to their fullest potential, the new businesses are often synergistic, create jobs for a community, and grow the net worth of the family. Often they are started so that family members have their own businesses to run. The more formal approach to family corporate venturing makes the new business process part of an overall strategic plan for growing family wealth while leveraging the resources and capabilities of family members.

Family corporate renewal occurs where the family's entrepreneurial activity is focused on creating new streams of value within the business or group through innovation and transformational change activities. Companies that launch new products or services, enter new markets, or establish new business models are renewing their strategies for the future. This type of strategic or structural renewal is particularly prevalent during family generational transitions or when a family realizes their legacy business can no longer compete. A more formal approach to corporate renewal is proactive, continuous, and institutionalized versus waiting for transitions or competitive triggers to start the renewal processes.

One of the primary roles families play is to provide *family private cash* to family members who want to

---

[11] H. E. Aldrich and J. E. Cliff, "The Pervasive Effects of Family on Entrepreneurship: Toward a Family Embeddedness Perspective," *Journal of Business Venturing* 18, no. 5 (September 2003), p. 573.

[12] GEM 2002, Special Report on Family Sponsored New Ventures.

EXHIBIT 18.4

Roles Families Play in the Entrepreneurial Process

	Family-Influenced Start-Ups	Family Corporate Venturing	Family Corporate Renewal	Family Private Cash	Family Investment Funds
Formal	An entrepreneur with no legacy assets/existing business, but who formally launches a new business with family and/or intending to involve family.	Family holding companies or businesses that have formal new venture creation and/or acquisition strategies, plans, departments, or capabilities.	Family-controlled companies with a formal strategic growth plan for creating new streams of value through change in business strategy, model, or structure.	Start-up money from family member or business with a formal written agreement for market-based ROI and or repayment.	Stand-alone professional private equity or venture capital fund controlled by family and/or using family-generated capital.
Informal	An entrepreneur with no legacy assets/existing business who happens to start a new business out of necessity and it begins to involve family members.	Family holding companies or businesses that grow through more informal, intuitive, and opportunistic business start-up and acquisitions.	Intuitive growth initiatives that result in a change in business strategy, model, or structure and new streams of value for the family company.	Start-up money or gift from family member or business with no agreement or conversation about ROI or repayment.	Internal capital and/or funds used by family owners to invest in real estate or passive partnerships or seed new businesses.

EXHIBIT 18.5

Distribution of Businesses with Family Venture Backing

	Planning Stage Start-Ups	New Firms	Established Firms
Number of Cases	1,425	1,594	3,743
Family-Sponsored Ventures	63%	76%	85%

Source: *Family Sponsored Ventures.* J. H. Astrachan, S. A. Zahra, and P. Sharma. Publication for The Entrepreneurial Advantage of Nationals: First Annual Global Entrepreneurship Symposium, United Nations Headquarters. April 29, 2003; based on findings from the Global Entrepreneurship Monitor 2002 sponsored by Babson College, London Business School and the Kauffman Foundation.

start a business. More than 63 percent of businesses in the planning stage and up to 85 percent of existing new ventures used family funding. Between 30 percent and 80 percent of all informal (non–venture capital) funding comes from family. In the United States this amounts to nearly .05 percent of GDP and as high as 3 percent of GDP in South Korea.[13] Most often the family cash is given based on altruistic family sentiments rather than having more formal investment criteria. While providing seed capital, whether formal or informal, is clearly a significant role in the entrepreneurial process, having some formal investment criteria can avoid future confusion or conflict among family members. It also creates more discipline and accountability for family entrepreneurs. (See Exhibit 18.5.)

Family investment funds are pools of family capital that families use for entrepreneurial activities. These family funds, both formal and informal, are becoming increasingly more common as families find themselves flush with cash. Most often the formal family investment funds are created after a family has liquidated all or part of their family group. These funds are generally formed in conjunction with a family office. Informal family investment funds are pools of money, generally from cash flows, that family leaders invest in entrepreneurial activities as a way to diversify their family portfolios and/or have fun. They often invest within their network of peers, and the investments are usually nonoperating investments in businesses or real estate deals. These investments are often significant portions of their total wealth.

When we catalog the wide range of informal and formal roles families can play in the entrepreneurial process, we see the contribution they are capable of making to the entrepreneurial economy. We believe business families who are interested in transgenerational entrepreneurship and wealth creation must cultivate the more formal approach to entrepreneurship. The remainder of this chapter assists families in formalizing their entrepreneurship roles. We present three strategy frames that are based on the Timmons Model introduced in Chapter 3. The frames focus on the controllable components of the entrepreneurial processes that can be assessed, influenced, and altered.

[13] Ibid.

Frame One: The Mind-Set and Method for Family Enterprising

Families who are enterprising are a particular type of family and *not* just a family who is in business. Enterprising families understand that today's dynamic and hypercompetitive marketplace requires families to act entrepreneurially. That is, they must generate new economic activity if they intend to survive and prosper over long periods of time. The Timmons Model shows us that at the heart of the entrepreneurial process is the opportunity. Families who intend to act entrepreneurially must be opportunity focused. Consistent with this focus, enterprising is seen as the decision that leaders and organizations make to investigate opportunity and seek growth "when expansion is neither pressing nor particularly obvious."[14] The enterprising decision to search for opportunity precedes the economic decision to capture the opportunity. It is when families are faced with a decision (knowingly or unknowingly) to continue along their existing path, versus to expend effort and commit resources to investigate whether there are higher-potential opportunities that are not yet obvious, that the "spirit of enterprising" is evidenced. We thus define enterprising as the proactive and continuous search for opportunistic growth.

Twelve Challenges to Family Enterprising

Like the gravitational pull that keeps us bound to the earth, families face a number of inherent challenges that may keep them bound to past strategies rather than pursuing new opportunities.

1. Families assume that their past success will guarantee their future success.
2. Family members attribute "legacy value" to their businesses or assets, but that value does not translate into a market value or advantage.
3. Families want a "legacy pass" in the market—"We are 50 years old and we deserve another 50 years since we have been such good citizens."
4. Leaders try to balance the risk profile (risk and reward expectations) of their shareholders with the risk and investment demands of the marketplace.
5. Senior and successor generations have different risk profiles and goals for how the business should grow in the future.

6. Families find it hard to pass the entrepreneurial commitments and capabilities from the senior generation to a less "hungry" successor generation.
7. Families build their first-generation businesses on the founder's intuition, but the business never establishes more intentional entrepreneurial processes to keep the entrepreneurial contributions alive.
8. Families will not use many of the financial strategies that entrepreneurs use to grow businesses: debt, equity capital, strategic alliances, and partnerships.
9. Families do not shed unproductive assets and underperforming businesses to reallocate resources to more productive places.
10. Successor generation family members feel entitled to get a business rather than seek next-generation entrepreneurial opportunity.
11. Senior leaders communicate to the next generation that business planning and entrepreneurial analysis are a waste of time.
12. Family members are given a business to run as part of their legacy, and that is viewed as entrepreneurship in the family.

Enterprising families institutionalize the opportunity-seeking processes in the mind-set and methods of both their family ownership group and their business organizations. Those families who simply try to maintain their local advantage, safeguard their brands, assets, and customers, or hone their operational efficiencies put themselves at a competitive risk in the shorter run. In the longer run, if their strategic planning is mainly focused on how to pass their business from one generation to the next, rather than developing people and strategies for creating new streams of value, their future may be limited. We would certainly not describe these types of families as enterprising or assume that they are transgenerational.

Enterprising Mind-Set and Methods

The first assessment and strategy frame for family enterprising is the mind-set and methods model (Exhibit 18.6). The model shows that family enterprising is the combination of a financial ownership mind-set and entrepreneurial strategic methods. The purpose of the model is to ensure that families talk about both the ownership *and* management requirements for carrying out the entrepreneurial process in their family and business. The mind-set and methods

---

[14] J. E. Penrose, *The Theory of the Growth of the Firm,* 3rd ed. (New York: Oxford University Press, 1995).

EXHIBIT 18.6

Mind-Set and Methods Enterprising Model

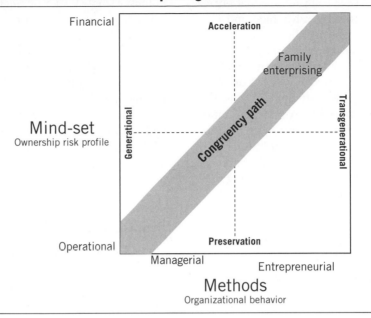

Source: © Habbershon and Pistrui.

assessment instruments[15] at the back of this chapter will enable families to determine their level of congruence on the two dimensions. It will also allow them to have a strategic conversation about where they currently are and how they might need to change in order to become more enterprising.

What Enterprising Is Not

It is often useful in defining a concept to understand *what it is not*. Judith Penrose takes this approach by contrasting the concept of enterprising with three categories of firms that are not necessarily enterprising.*

"Just grew firms": The "just grew" category are those that were in the right place at the right time. They were on the wave of an expanding market, and they had to expand to keep up with demand. The decision to grow was automatic, and because they were able to capitalize on the circumstances, they grew. The situation may continue for a long time, but because markets do not expand indefinitely and competitors fill the opportunity gap, firm growth and the firm will come to an end.

"Comfort firms": This category is often referred to as lifestyle firms. There are firms who refrain from taking full advantage of opportunities for expansion because it would increase their effort and risk. Firms that are comfortable with their income and position have no incentive to grow beyond their acceptable level of profits. These are firms where the goals of the owners to be comfortable are closely aligned with the goals of the firm. Like "just grew firms," comfort firms may continue for decades, but in the end meeting the comfort needs of the owners is not a driver for advantage or renewal.

"Competently managed firms": Many firms are competently managed and consequently are able to find normal returns for relatively long periods by maintaining their operational efficiencies. Competently managed firms are often striving to sustain the entrepreneurial efforts of a founder. They may be competing in more traditional, less dynamic circumstances, have a distinctive market niche, or maintain a regional advantage as a favored business. Although these are exploitable strategies, they are not inherently sustainable and may quickly disappear.

* J. E. Penrose, *The Theory of the Growth of the Firm*, 3rd ed. (New York: Oxford University Press, 1995).

---

[15] The content and questions from the mind-set and methods inventories are based on the following literature:

J. G. Covin and D. P. Slevin, "Strategic Management in Small Firms in Hostile and Benign Environments," *Strategic Management Journal* 10, no. 1 (1989), pp. 75–87.

R. G. McGrath and I. MacMillan, *The Entrepreneurial Mindset: Strategies for Continuously Creating Opportunity in an Age of Uncertainty* (Boston: Harvard Business School Press, 2000).

D. L. Mconaughy, C. H. Matthews, and A. S. Fialko, "Founding Family Controlled Firms: Performance, Risk, and Value," *Journal of Small Business Management* 39, no. 1 (January 2001), p. 31.

D. Miller, "The Correlates of Entrepreneurship in Three Types of Firms," *Management Science* 29, no. 7 (1983), p. 770.

D. Miller and P. H. Friesen, "Innovation in Conservative and Entrepreneurial Firms: Two Models of Strategic Momentum," *Strategic Management Journal* 3, no. 1 (January–March 1982), p. 1.

S. Zahra, "Entrepreneurial Risk Taking in Family Firms," *Family Business Review* 18, no. 1 (March 2005), p. 23.

The *mind-set continuum* is primarily a measure of the financial risk profile of the family owners–shareholders. In general, it reflects the financial premise that entrepreneurial leaders gain strategic advantage and find above-normal rents by deploying their resources to points of highest return and by developing strategies that exploit new opportunity. Family leaders who have an operational mind-set predominantly focus on management strategies, operational efficiencies, and the perpetuity of a *particular* business. A financial mind-set moves beyond the operational focus to an investor focus with a view toward the overall capital strategy of the family, creating new streams of value and finding a return on the *totality* of assets. While the operational mind-set is a requirement for running an efficient business, the financial focus is a requirement for transgenerational entrepreneurship and wealth creation.

The financial mind-set for enterprising includes the following characteristics[16]

- A proclivity for higher risk and above-normal returns.
- A willingness to sell and redeploy assets to seek higher returns.
- A desire to grow by creating new revenue streams with higher returns.
- A commitment to generating next-generation entrepreneurship.
- A willingness to continuously revisit the existing business model.
- An assumption that a percentage of the business will become obsolete.
- A willingness to leverage the business to grow and find higher returns.
- A desire to reinvest versus distribute capital.
- A willingness to enter into partnerships and alliances to grow.
- A strategy to manage the family's wealth for a total return.
- A commitment to innovation in business strategies and structures.
- A belief that bold, wide-ranging acts are necessary to achieve investment objectives in today's environment.

The *methods continuum* is a measure of the entrepreneurial orientation and actions in business organizations. It assumes that enterprising organizations are taking bold, innovative, market-leading actions to seek a competitive advantage and generate new streams of value. It also reflects the premise that to be enterprising (proactively and continuously seeking new opportunities for growth), organizations must have a collection of individuals who act like an entrepreneur and not just a single leader or small group of family leaders. A single leader acting entrepreneurially might generate entrepreneurial actions in the business during his or her generation but will not create a transgenerational family business or group. Enterprising organizations move beyond managerial methods that focus on maintaining the existing and implementing incremental change. They are seeking and creating "the new" and establishing entrepreneurial renewal processes. Although entrepreneurial methods do not replace the need for managerial actions, managerial actions are not sufficient conditions for enterprising and transgenerational wealth creation.

The entrepreneurial methods for enterprising include the following characteristics:[17]

- Allocating disproportionate resources to new business opportunities.
- Systematically searching for and capturing new investment opportunities.
- Seeking new opportunities beyond the core (legacy) business.
- Creating a core competency in innovation at the business unit level.
- Making significant changes in products, services, markets, and customers.
- Initiating competitive change to lead the market.
- Investing early to develop or adopt new technology and processes.
- Typically adopting an "undo the competitor" market posture.
- Having institutionalized the entrepreneurial process in the organization.
- Having formal routines for gathering and disseminating market intelligence.
- Having people at every level in the organization think like competitors.
- Typically adopting a bold, aggressive posture to maximize the probability of exploiting potential investment opportunities.

Creating the Dialogue for Congruence

The mind-set and methods model helps families fulfill key process conditions for family enterprising and transgenerational wealth creation:

Creating a healthy *dialogue* in the family ownership group and organization around the mind-set and methods issues.

[16] J. G. Covin and D. P. Slevin, "Strategic Management in Small Firms in Hostile and Benign Environments," *Strategic Management Journal* 10, no. 1 (1989), p. 75.
[17] Ibid.

EXHIBIT 18.7

Backerhaus Veit Analysis

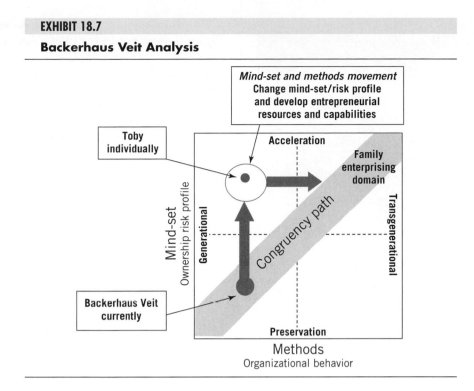

Establishing *congruence* between the mind-set of the owner–shareholder group and the methods of the business organization(s).

One of the major differences between family enterprising and entrepreneurship as it is normally envisioned is that by definition the team includes the family. Family entrepreneurs are either currently working with family members or planning to work with family members; they either are multigenerational teams or hope to be a multigenerational team; they either have multiple family member shareholders and stakeholders or will have them as they go through time. This inherent familial condition requires families to cultivate effective communication skills to build relationship capital for family enterprising. Families know that it takes financial capital for entrepreneurial activity, but they do not always know that it also requires relationship capital. Relationship capital allows families to have healthy dialogue and find congruence around the mind-set and methods for enterprising.

Sabine Veit, founder of Backerhaus Veit in Toronto, Canada, realized the importance of dialogue and congruence when her son came home from college toting a business plan for aggressive growth. She had built her artisan bread manufacturing company into a $20 million (U.S.) force in the industry. When her son Toby won Babson's business planning competition she was definitely proud, but she also knew she was in trouble. The

plan was to grow *her* business. Sabine loved the thought of working with Toby, and he definitely shared her passion for artisan breads. In fact, during college Toby took every class with the artisan bread industry in mind. How could a parent hope for anything more?

But Toby didn't want to just run her company someday. He wanted to move the business beyond manufacturing and wholesaling into branded products and retailing, and he wanted to do it now. On the mind-set and methods model (Exhibit 18.7), Backerhaus Veit was on the congruency path as an operationally focused, managerially sound business. Sabine had a self-defined lifestyle firm that was competitive in her niche with a clear harvest strategy. But Toby was committed to family enterprising and wanted to be a growth firm. This meant moving beyond their current niche and lifestyle expectations. Clearly Toby had a mind-set for much higher risk than Sabine.

On the methods continuum, Backerhaus Veit did not have the entrepreneurial methods to exploit Toby's plan. Sabine individually had the capabilities and Toby believed he did, but the entrepreneurial team and organization would have to be built. There was clearly significant incongruence as a family and business. The challenge for Sabine and Toby was to establish a plan and process for aligning their mind-set and methods if they wanted to capture the new opportunity and become an enterprising family.

Successful Next-Generation Entrepreneurship

The challenge for multigenerational family teams like Toby and Sabine is to "keep it in dialogue" rather than letting it turn into a debate or disconnect. Debates become personal, and disconnect cuts off opportunity. When family members turn the situation into right and wrong, good and bad, winning or losing, there is very little listening, give-and-take, or changing one's position. In contrast, the word *dialogue* actually means "talking through" an issue. It assumes the ability to challenge each other's assumptions, to keep an open mind, and to test different options. It looks at the big picture, considers the long-term perspective, and discusses the process for getting there. Most important, dialogue does not follow hierarchical roles like parent–child, boss–employee, or the one who owns the business versus the one who does not. The goal of dialogue is to find solutions that are not constrained by the boundaries of either of the original positions.

There are a number of things Toby and Sabine needed to do to ensure they were an enterprising family. First, they needed to develop communication skills to have an effective dialogue. Most families assume they are able to carry on a dialogue simply because they are a family. In actuality the familiarity of a family can make it very difficult to challenge assumptions and talk about differing views. Often families need a facilitator to help them develop communication skill and have a dialogue.

Second, they needed to make sure their views of the future were the same. Families often have a vague notion of "working together," and they assume that they will figure the details out over time. This is a clear formula for future discontent and conflict. In reality, Toby and Sabine had very different visions for their futures. Sabine's vision was to enjoy her passion for breads while balancing growth with her lifestyle interests. Toby's vision was to exploit his passion for breads by building new businesses on the family's reputation and skills.

Third, Toby and Sabine had very different risk profiles. What Sabine was willing to risk for future returns was very different from what Toby was willing to risk and the returns he desired. It is not surprising that the successor generation is willing to risk more than the senior generation. The key is to keep talking until you understand each other's perspective. Once you understand each other you can create a business model and structures that accommodate the risk profiles of both generations. Locking into one generational perspective or the other undermines the collective strengths of a multigenerational team.

Fourth, remember that timing is everything. Usually for the successors the time is *now* and for the seniors the time is *someday*. Chances are that both generations will end up out of their comfort zones a little. Toby and Sabine realized that timing was really a strategy question of how they would proceed, not just if or when they would proceed.

Fifth, get creative. You can be sure that the final outcome will not look exactly as either of you envisioned. Through dialogue it became clear to Toby and Sabine that the range of options was fairly extensive. We often tell family members to "remember their algebra" when it comes to dialogue. Just because "a equals b" it doesn't mean that "a" might not equal "c, d, or even e, f, and g." The point is that once you start a true dialogue, you may find many more options than you originally envisioned.

Frame Two: The Six Dimensions for Family Enterprising

The second assessment and strategy frame for family enterprising addresses the team component of the Timmons Model. In family enterprising "team" is a much broader and complex concept. It encompasses the family ownership group and the family and nonfamily entrepreneurial capabilities. The entrepreneurial process cannot occur unless there is alignment in the team's ownership mind-set and entrepreneurial methods as just described. When the entrepreneurial leader is a family member, there is potentially another layer of team complexity around issues such as parent–child relationships, altruistic versus entrepreneurial decision making, nepotism and competency, family versus personal equity and compensation, and success measures. In essence, the family as team can create more perfect balance in the Timmons Model or can cause imbalance. One key is to stay focused on the opportunity and stress that the team is in support of exploiting that opportunity.

The six dimensions for family enterprising provide family teams with six areas that they can address to assist them in aligning their mind-set and methods and moving up the congruency path toward the enterprising domain. The six dimensions and the corresponding strategic questions apply key entrepreneurial considerations to the family context. As family owners and leaders answer the questions, they are creating unity within the team for entrepreneurial action. The six dimensions are as follows:

Leadership

Relationship

Vision

Strategy

Governance

Performance

There are an internal logic and order to the six dimensions. We begin with the *leadership dimension* because leaders are the catalyst for organizational behavior and have the responsibility for creating the team. Leaders also set the tone for the relationship commitments and culture in the family and organization. The *vision and relationship dimension* is often overlooked, but it is the foundation for organizational effectiveness and health, especially in family teams and enterprising. The *vision and strategy dimensions* flow out of the leadership and relationship dimensions. At the end of the day, strategy and planning are simply extended organizational conversations. Organizational strategy is only as effective as the leadership and relationships in the family and organization. Governance structures and policies simply enable organizations to carry out their strategies. The *governance dimension* must, therefore, follow both ownership and business strategy formulation. In an interesting way, the *performance dimension* is the last dimension because it is an organizational outcome, but it is also feedback that leaders use to frame their leadership actions.

Leadership Dimension: Does Your Leadership Create a Sense of Shared Urgency for Enterprising and Transgenerational Wealth Creation?

Entrepreneurial leaders create a sense of shared urgency in the organization. The goal is to have everyone, from the owners to those carrying out tasks, thinking and acting like competitors.[18] Families are traditionally and systemically hierarchical in nature—parent–child, older–younger siblings, male–female—and their family organizations often embody these hierarchies in their leadership models. A transgenerational commitment requires families to move beyond the "great leader" model to the "great group."[19] Family leaders who strive to turn their families into a team based on the great group philosophy overcome many of the negative caricatures often associated with family business leadership and empower the family and organization to be enterprising.

Leadership Dimension Diagnostic Questions

Do family leaders understand the requirements to be transgenerational?

Do they develop next-generation leadership?

Do they move the family beyond the "great leader" model?

Do they promote a sense of openness and mutuality?

Do they encourage participation by family members at all levels in the family and organization?

Do they lead others to think and act like entrepreneurs?

Do they help the family grow beyond a hierarchical model of leadership to become the "great group"?

Relationship Dimension: Does Your Family Have the Relationship Capital to Sustain Their Transgenerational Commitments?

Effective teams are built on healthy relationships. We describe healthy relationships as those that build relationship capital and allow efficient interpersonal interactions in the team. Relationship capital is the reserve of attributes such as trust, loyalty, positive feelings, benefit of the doubt, goodwill, forgiveness, commitment, and altruistic motives. Relationship capital is a necessary condition for long-lasting teams and transgenerational families. Now here are two opposite but simultaneously true statements: Families have the natural potential to build relationship capital better than other social groups *and* families have the natural potential to destroy relationship capital more ruthlessly than any other social group. Is this good news or bad news for family enterprising? It depends. Those families who intentionally gain the skills and strive to build relationship capital leverage the natural advantage of family teams. But those families who assume they will always have relationship capital or take their relationships for granted open themselves up to potentially destructive tendencies of families. Families who have relationship capital reserves are more likely to create the dialogue that moves them up the congruence path to the family enterprising domain.

Relationship Dimension Diagnostic Questions

Is your family intentionally building relationship capital?

---

[18] R. G. McGrath and I. MacMillan, *The Entrepreneurial Mindset: Strategies for Continuously Creating Opportunity in an Age of Uncertainty* (Boston: Harvard Business School Press, 2000).

[19] D. R. Ireland and M. A. Hitt, "Achieving and Maintaining Strategic Competitiveness in the 21st Century: The Role of Strategic Leadership," *The Academy of Management Executive* 13, no. 1 (February 1999), p. 43.

Are you investing in the communication and relationship building skills you need to build relationship capital?

Are there healthy relationships among family siblings and branches and across generations?

Does your family have formal family meetings to discuss family ownership and relationship issues?

Do you experience synergy in your family relationships?

Do you have a positive vision for working together as a family?

Do family members see relationship health as part of their competitive advantage?

Vision Dimension: Does Your Family Have a Compelling Multigenerational Vision That Energizes People at Every Level?

A compelling vision is what creates the shared urgency for family enterprising and mobilizes people to carry out the vision. By "compelling" we mean that it makes sense to people in light of tomorrow's marketplace realities. Often a vision might make sense for the moment, but it does not make sense for the future. For enterprising families, the vision must describe how the family will collectively create new streams of wealth that allow them to be transgenerational. It also has to be multigenerational. It is easy for the different generations to craft their personal visions for the future. Transgenerational families must craft a vision that is compelling to all generations and in a sense transcends generational perspectives. This multigenerational necessity also underscores the importance of establishing participatory leadership and building relationship capital.

Vision Dimension Diagnostic Questions

Does your family have a vision that makes sense for tomorrow's marketplace?

Would all generations describe the vision as compelling?

Was the vision developed by everyone in the family?

Does the vision have relevance for your decision making and lives?

Does your family regularly review and test the vision as an ownership group?

Is the vision transgenerational?

Is the vision larger than the personal interests of the family?

Does the vision mobilize others to create new streams of value?

Do all family members share in the rewards from the vision?

Strategy Dimension: Does Your Family Have an Intentional Strategy for Finding Their Competitive Advantage as a Family?

We have already said that there is a more intentional and formal application of the entrepreneurial process within the family context. Part of that formal approach is developing strategies for both cultivating and capturing new business opportunities. But for families it means much more. The family's strategic thinking and planning should be based on determining how to exploit their unique family-based resources and capabilities to find advantages in enterprising. Although we will address this more specifically in the next section, it includes things like finding synergies with current assets, leveraging networks of personal relationships, cultivating next-generation entrepreneurs, and extending the power of the family reputation. Because families tend to take their family-influenced resources and capabilities for granted, they often fail to see the opportunities they represent for providing them with a long-term advantage for enterprising.

Strategy Dimension Diagnostic Questions

How does your family provide you with an advantage in entrepreneurial wealth creation?

What resources and capabilities are unique to your family?

Does your family have a formal planning process to direct their enterprising?

Does your organization have formal systems for cultivating and capturing new opportunities?

Does your family mentor next-generation family members to become entrepreneurs?

Do your strategic thinking and planning empower your family to fulfill their transgenerational vision?

What role does your family play in the strategy process?

Governance Dimension: Does Your Family Have Structures and Policies That Stimulate Change and Growth in the Family and Organization?

Few family leaders would consider that governance structures and policies could actually stimulate growth and change. Most would equate the word *governance* with bureaucracies and, at best, acknowledge that structures and policies are a necessary evil to be tolerated and minimized. But we offer two different perspectives. First, the lack of effective governance structures and policies creates significant ambiguity in families and constrains enterprising. Second, when entrepreneurial processes are institutionalized through the governance structures and policies, this promotes growth and change activities. For example, when ownership, equity, or value realization is unclear or undiscussable, it discourages family entrepreneurs. But when financial conversations are part of the professional culture and there are transparent ownership structures, family entrepreneurs are clear on the rules of the game. Governance structures are thus critical to transgenerational entrepreneurship and wealth creation.

Governance Dimension Diagnostic Questions

Does your family view governance as a positive part of their family and business lives?

Are your governance structures static or fluid?

Do your structures and policies promote family unity?

Do your governance structures and policies give an appropriate voice to family members?

Do your governance structures and policies assist you in finding your family advantage?

Do you have formal processes that institutionalize the entrepreneurial process in your family and businesses?

Do your governance structures and policies promote next-generation involvement and entrepreneurship?

Performance Dimension: Does Your Performance Meet the Requirements for Transgenerational Entrepreneurship and Wealth Creation?

The performance dimension is where families clarify whether or not they are really committed to family enterprising. Families who are enterprising are market driven and seek to accelerate their wealth creation through their opportunistic entrepreneurial actions. They have clear financial benchmarks and information for assessing their performance against the market. Lifestyle firms often assume that they are performing well because they are sustaining their lifestyles. Enterprising also implies a process of matching the organization's core competencies with external opportunities in order to create new streams of value. Enterprising families do not rely on past performance as an indicator that they will perform well in the future; nor do they define success by the

preservation of an asset. Their success measures are their abilities to fulfill their transgenerational vision for social and economic wealth creation.

Performance Dimension Diagnostic Questions

Does your family talk openly about financial performance issues, or are finances secretive?

Are you in lifestyle or enterprising mode?

Are your strategies driven by a clear market orientation?

Do family owners agree on their risk and return expectations?

Are performance expectations clear to next-generation entrepreneurs?

Are there clear transparency and accountability structures in relation to meeting performance expectations?

Is there family dialogue about performance expectations—growth, dividends, reinvestment, ROE?

Frame Three: The Familiness Advantage for Family Enterprising

All entrepreneurial success and the opportunity to capture above-average returns are premised upon finding an advantage over your competitors. Correspondingly, the potential for finding an advantage is rooted in the distinctive resources and capabilities that an organization possesses. The "resources" aspect of the Timmons Model is where enterprising can get exciting for families. Because every family is unique, they can generate very idiosyncratic bundles of resources and capabilities that can give them an advantage in the entrepreneurial process if they know how to identify and leverage them. We refer to this idiosyncratic bundle of resources and capabilities as their *familiness*.

The family systems model in Exhibit 18.8 shows how the familiness bundle of resources and capabilities is generated. As the vision, history, and capabilities of the collective family interact with the goals, skills, and commitments of the individual family members, and they in turn interact with the organizational history, culture, and resources of the business entities, it creates this familiness effect or the "f factor" of resources$_f$ and capabilities$_f$. If we think of the four resource categories—people, financial, assets, and plan—we can explore how the systemic family influence impacts, changes, or somehow reconfigures the properties of the resource. We identify familiness resources and capabilities with a subscript "f"

EXHIBIT 18.8

Familiness Systems Model

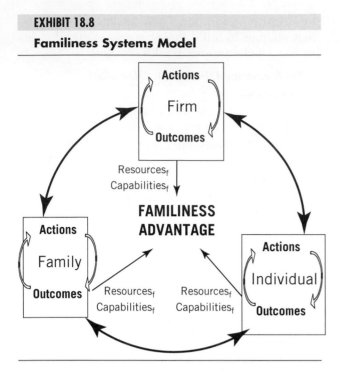

such as capital$_f$, leadership$_f$, networking$_f$, knowledge$_f$, reputation$_f$.

The familiness assessment frame helps families become realists. What we mean is the assessment process leads families to realistically evaluate where their family influence might be positive and where it might be negative. One of the key insights from this model is the understanding that family cannot be characterized as either good or bad. Rather, family influence must be viewed as one of the inputs that entrepreneurs need to intentionally manage. As family leaders manage the actions and outcomes within the subsystems—family unit, individuals, and business entities—and between the subsystems, they are managing their bundle of resources$_f$ and capabilities$_f$.

When these familiness resources$_f$ and capabilities$_f$ lead to a competitive advantage for the family, we refer to them as "distinctive familiness" or an "f+." When they constrain the competitive enterprising ability of the family, we refer to them as "constrictive familiness" or "f−." Exhibit 18.9 allows families to place their resources and capabilities on an assessment continuum. The job of families who desire to be enterprising is to determine how to generate and exploit their distinctive familiness and to minimize or shed their constrictive familiness. When families begin assessing and planning based on their distinctive and constrictive familiness, they move from an intuitive and informal to the intentional and formal mode of family enterprising.

To better understand familiness, let's return to the family enterprising decision that Toby and Sabine have to make in regard to Backerhaus Veit (BV). If we analyze the distinctive (f+) and constrictive (f−) familiness in their situation, we can bring significant focus to the dialogue and move them along the mindset and methods congruence path.

Exhibit 18.10 is their familiness resource and capabilities continuum as it relates to the new venture opportunity. When you see the f+ f− assessment, it is a comprehensive and revealing picture of their individual and organizational contribution to the new venture. But it is not only the final picture that is useful to families. The conversation to identify the resources and capabilities and to determine where they should be placed is the real learning outcome.

First, you will notice that there are clear resources and capabilities specifically associated with the senior and successor generations and others that are mixed. While Toby's successor drive is an f+, his business capabilities and lack of experience are an f−. Sabine readily admits that without Toby's drive she would never consider this opportunity. But Sabine's advisors are concerned that Toby may

EXHIBIT 18.9

f+ f− Familiness Advantage

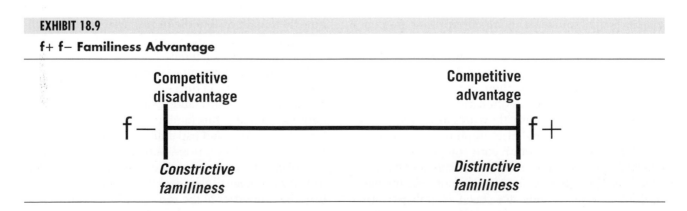

EXHIBIT 18.10

Backerhaus Veit f+ f− Analysis

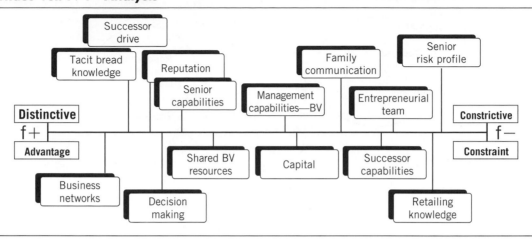

overestimate his capabilities and contribution. This discussion is very natural in next-generation entrepreneurship, and families should "normalize" it and not allow it to become personal. Conversely, Sabine's senior capabilities, business networks, and reputation are an f+ for Toby's new venture. Toby readily admits that Sabine's role makes his business plan a much higher-potential venture. On the other hand, Sabine's risk profile and lifestyle goals are a significant f− and constraint to enterprising. But we need to remember that they fit very well for her current strategy.

Second, there are resources and capabilities associated with BV. Toby's business plan calls for BV to provide valuable shared resources such as wholesale bread supply, bookkeeping, used equipment, repair services, and the like. This opportunity creates a very significant resource advantage that we would call "plan$_{f+}$" because only family members with existing businesses could incorporate these into their plan. The existing management team capabilities are also an f+, but because the existing team is not entrepreneurial (in fact, they see the new venture as a drain on the existing business), we have to give an f− to entrepreneurial team.

Third, certain resources are associated with both Sabine and Toby. Most important is the f+ for tacit bread knowledge. They both know bread making, but the particularly interesting point is to see how advanced Toby is as a young person because he grew up in the bread industry. Correspondingly, the f− for retailing is significant. While Sabine grew up in the retail bread industry (her family has 70 retail bakeries in Germany), she does not know the casual dining bread industry (like Panera Bread Company), and

this is the target for Toby's plan. While decision making is an f+, family communication is an f−. The family has great relationships, but in the business setting, they sometimes communicate like mother and son rather than business peers.

The f+ f− continuum makes Toby's and Sabine's "prelaunch" work very clear. Managing the f+ and f− continuum is how families build their resources and capabilities bundle as part of formalizing the entrepreneurial process. It is a critical step in getting the odds more in their favor. Toby and Sabine now need to create a work plan for each of the constraining resources in order to move them to a point of neutrality or advantage.

An additional realization from this analysis is to see the potential synergy between the successor and senior generations for family enterprising. Four things are immediately clear from the analysis. First, as we already noted, Sabine would never explore or capture this opportunity if it were not for Toby driving the process. Second, Toby does not have the synergistic familiness resources and capabilities if he tries to do the business on his own. Third, while there are positive reasons to do it together, there are also constraints that must be addressed. Fourth, family enterprising will occur when they decide to do it together as a family, rather than not doing it, or Toby doing it on his own. That is not to say that one way is right or wrong, but simply that doing it together is a family enterprising approach.

We will provide a final assessment of Sabine and Toby using the Timmons Model to discuss fit and balance. Clearly the opportunity for Backerhaus Veit to move into the retail fast-casual-eating market is very large and growing. In fact, the opportunity is probably

EXHIBIT 18.11

Timmons Model for Backerhaus Veit

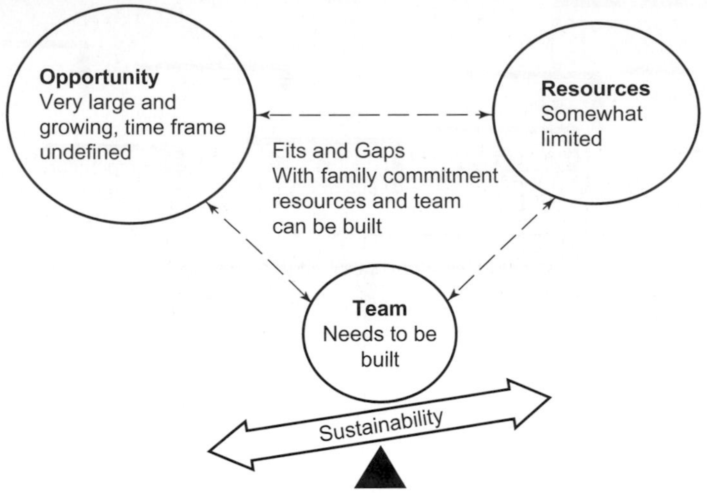

greater than the current resources and capabilities of BV, Toby, and Sabine to meet them without outside resources. Currently the weakest link in the model is the team. While Toby and Sabine have great bread knowledge, they do not have the entrepreneurial team for the retailing initiative. Further, the BV leaders and advisors are strongly committed to managing their current assets rather than launching an entrepreneurial business. Exhibit 18.11 shows that the model is "out of balance" and reaffirms the conclusions from our previous assessment that there is significant prelaunch work to be done to ensure a fit. If they do this prelaunch work and can get the Timmons Model into balance, however, they have a great high-potential venture for the family.

Conclusion

For business families who would like to act more entrepreneurially and become intentional enterprising families that have multiple generations seeking higher-potential opportunities, we suggest that four strategic shifts may need to occur:

- From a lifestyle firm that has the goal of personal comfort to an enterprising family committed to transgenerational entrepreneurship and wealth creation.
- From an intuitive family business that "kicks around" (as one family entrepreneur described it) to see what new opportunities turn up to an intentional entrepreneurial process that seeks to generate and capture new opportunities.
- From a senior-generation entrepreneur who does it to a successor-generation entrepreneurial process and team that create opportunities for others to do it.
- From a low-potential entrepreneurial family that creates one-off businesses as they can to a higher-potential entrepreneurial family that mobilizes resources to create transgenerational wealth.

Chapter Summary

- We began by demonstrating the significant contributions families make to the economy and entrepreneurial process. It is often overlooked that the majority of the businesses worldwide are controlled and managed by families, including many of the very largest businesses that we normally do not associate with family.

- Families play a diverse number of formal and informal roles in the entrepreneurial process. We described them as (a) the family-influenced start-up, (b) family corporate venturing, (c) family corporate renewal, (d) family private cash, and (e) family investment funds.

- Family enterprising was defined as the proactive and continuous search for opportunistic growth when expansion is neither pressing nor particularly obvious. The outcome of family enterprising is transgenerational entrepreneurship and wealth creation through balance in the Timmons Model.

- The mind-set continuum assesses the family's risk profile, and those interested in enterprising move from an operational to a financial investor strategy. The methods continuum assesses the organizational behavior of leaders and organizations and requires a move from managerial to entrepreneurial strategies for enterprising.

- There are six dimensions for family enterprising that were described as antecedents from the entrepreneurship literature: leadership, relationship, vision, strategy, governance, and performance. The chapter presented key questions for each dimension to assist families in becoming more enterprising.

- We defined the familiness of an organization as the unique bundle of resources and capabilities that result from the interaction of the family and individual family members with the business entities. Families can have positive and negative family influence, which we described as an f+ or f−.

Study Questions

1. What are the entrepreneurial implications of not appreciating or understanding the role and contribution of families to the economies of our communities and countries?

2. Describe the advantages of a more formal approach for each of the roles families play in the entrepreneurial process. Give a few contrasting examples from a family firm with which you are familiar.

3. Define family enterprising, familiness, and relationship capital and relate each of them to the Timmons Model of the entrepreneurial process.

4. Choose a family firm with which you are familiar and plot them on the mind-set and methods model. Describe the firm in light of the mind-set and method definition. Make six recommendations for what they could do to become more enterprising.

5. How do the six dimensions for family enterprising relate to one another? How do they enhance family

enterprising? Describe how the six dimensions can be used to stimulate positive family dialogue.

6. If a family is trying to find their competitive advantage, how can the familiness assessment approach help them? How is the familiness approach a more formal application of the entrepreneurial process? How can the familiness approach change the family dialogue?

7. Given the familiness assessment of Backerhaus Veit in the chapter, describe why Sabine should or should not partner with Toby to implement his business plan. Describe the familiness action steps that they should take if you say they should launch the business. Describe the familiness reasons for why they possibly should not launch the business.

8. Assess a family firm with which you are familiar on the familiness resource and capabilities continuum. Describe what action steps they need to take to enhance their competitive advantage as a family organization.

Internet Resources for Chapter 18

http://www.fbn-i.org/ *The Family Business Network is the world's leading network of business-owning families.*

http://familybusinessmagazine.com/ *The Family Business library is a searchable archive covering a wide array of topics on family business.*

http://www.ffi.org/ *The Family Firm Institute (FFI) is an international professional membership organization*

dedicated to providing interdisciplinary education and networking opportunities for family business and family wealth advisors, consultants, educators, and researchers and to increasing public awareness about trends and developments in the family business and family wealth fields.

MIND STRETCHERS

Have You Considered?

1. Like a bumblebee that should not be able to fly, it is said that family businesses should not be able to compete. Why might this be a true statement? Why are families so economically dominant worldwide if they are like the bumblebee?

2. How can a lifestyle firm be both a fine choice for a family and a dangerous choice for a family at the same time?

3. Give 10 reasons why dialogue can be harder for families than nonfamilies even though families are supposed to have closer relationships.

4. If you were a Marriott successor-generation family member, what expectations would you have about your future?

5. Watch the DVD *Born Rich* by Jamie Johnson (HBO documentary). What did you learn about wealth and entrepreneurship?
(*Resource note:* The DVD *Born Rich* by Jamie Johnson can be purchased on Amazon.com. Additional questions to consider for *Born Rich:* Are wealthy families the same as entrepreneurial families? Is Jamie Johnson entrepreneurial? Is Paris Hilton entrepreneurial? Is this the same as family enterprising? What are their family legacies?)

Exercises

Determine where your family is on the mind-set and methods continuum and what familiness advantage you might have for enterprising. Fill out the assessment surveys, plot your family group on the family enterprising model, and fill out the resources and capabilities continuum.

Mind-Set Continuum

The mind-set continuum establishes the family's financial risk and return expectations and their competitive posture in relation to the marketplace. There are no right and wrong answers. The point of the assessment is to surface family members' beliefs and fuel the family dialogue.

Using the assessment continua, have the family member shareholders and future shareholders answer the questions on the mind-set continuum listed here. Circle the number between the two statements that best reflects the strength of your belief about the family as a shareholder group. Total scores are between 12 and 84, reflecting views from the most traditional to the most enterprising.

In general, family member shareholders...

Have a strong proclivity for low-risk businesses and investment opportunities (with normal and certain returns).	1 2 3 4 5 6 7	Have a strong proclivity for high-risk business and investment opportunities (with chances for high returns).
Would sacrifice a higher return to preserve the family's legacy business.	1 2 3 4 5 6 7	Are willing to sell and redeploy assets to find a higher return in the market.
Tend to think about cultivating our current businesses for current returns.	1 2 3 4 5 6 7	Desire to grow by creating new revenue streams with higher possibilities for returns.
Have a commitment to operating the business and providing job opportunities for family.	1 2 3 4 5 6 7	Have a commitment to mentoring next-generation entrepreneurs to create new streams of value.
Feel we have a good business model that will take us into the future.	1 2 3 4 5 6 7	Feel we should continuously revisit the assumptions of our business model.
Feel that our current businesses and products will serve us well in the future.	1 2 3 4 5 6 7	Assume that a significant percentage of our businesses will become obsolete.
Desire to avoid debt and grow with internally generated cash as we can.	1 2 3 4 5 6 7	Are willing to leverage the businesses to grow and find higher returns in the market.
Desire to increase our financial ability to provide distributions and/or liquidity.	1 2 3 4 5 6 7	Desire to reinvest more aggressively for faster growth and higher returns.

Desire to grow within our current financial and equity structures in order to ensure control over our destiny.	1 2 3 4 5 6 7	Are willing to use alliances and partnerships, share equity, or dilute share positions in order to grow.
Would describe ourselves more as a conservative company meeting our family's financial and personal goals.	1 2 3 4 5 6 7	Would describe ourselves as a risk-taking group seeking higher total returns for the family as investment group.
Would describe our business models and strategy as making us steady rather than opportunistic.	1 2 3 4 5 6 7	Are willing to be innovative in our business models and structures in order to be opportunistic.
Believe that a steady and consistent approach will allow us to fulfill our family's vision and goals for the future.	1 2 3 4 5 6 7	Believe that bold, wide-ranging acts are necessary to achieve our family investment objectives in today's environment.

TOTAL:

Methods Continuum

The methods continuum establishes the organization's entrepreneurial orientation and actions. It reflects the beliefs of the shareholders and stakeholders on how the leaders incite entrepreneurship in the organization.

Using the assessment contiua, have the family member shareholders and future shareholders answer the questions on the methods continuum listed here. Circle the number between the two statements that best reflects the strength of your belief about the family as a shareholder group. Total scores are between 12 and 84, reflecting views from the most traditional to the most enterprising.

In general, senior leaders in our family organization(s) . . .

Spend their time nurturing the existing businesses.	1 2 3 4 5 6 7	Pay a disproportionate amount of attention to new business opportunities.
Place a strong emphasis on pursuing returns by reinvesting in tried and true businesses.	1 2 3 4 5 6 7	Place a strong emphasis on searching for and capturing new business investment opportunities.
Have pursued no new investment opportunities outside of our core operating arena (in the last five years).	1 2 3 4 5 6 7	Have pursued many new investment opportunities beyond our core operating arena (in the last five years).
Believe our core competency is in managing efficient businesses.	1 2 3 4 5 6 7	Believe our core competency is in innovating for opportunistic growth.
Have made minor changes in our businesses, products, services, markets, or business units during the current generation of leaders.	1 2 3 4 5 6 7	Have made significant changes in our products, services, markets, or business units as the market required it.
Typically respond to actions that competitors or the market initiates.	1 2 3 4 5 6 7	Typically initiate actions and competitive change to lead the market and competitors.
Are generally moderate to slow in adopting new technologies and technological processes in our industry.	1 2 3 4 5 6 7	Are often early in investing to develop or adopt new technologies and technological processes in our industry.
Tend to avoid competitive clashes, preferring friendly "live and let live" competition.	1 2 3 4 5 6 7	Typically adopt a competitive "undo-the-competitor" posture when making investment decisions.
Are more intuitive and informal in how the organization thinks about seeking or capturing new opportunities.	1 2 3 4 5 6 7	Have established formal structures and policies to institutionalize the entrepreneurial process in the organization.
Rely on family leaders to know the markets and customers and get the information to the organization.	1 2 3 4 5 6 7	Have more formal plans and approaches to how they gather and disseminate market intelligence.
Rely on family leaders to set the tone and ensure that the organization is competitive through time.	1 2 3 4 5 6 7	Encourage and empower people at every level of the organization to think and act like competitors.
Typically adopt a cautious "wait and see" posture to minimize the probability of making costly investment decisions.	1 2 3 4 5 6 7	Typically adopt a bold, aggressive posture to maximize the probability of exploiting potential investment opportunities.

TOTAL

Family Enterprising Model

Plot your score totals from the mind-set and methods assessment surveys. The lowest possible score is a 12 and the highest possible score is an 84. Plotting the scores provides you with a visual basis for your family dialogue. Does the plotted score rightly describe your family? Is your family on the "congruence path"? Does everyone agree on where your family is on the model? Develop strategies to move your family on the model if necessary.

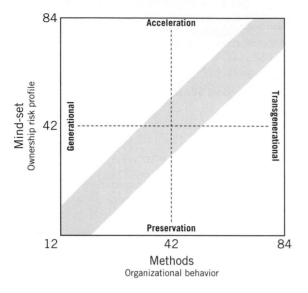

Familiness f+ f− Continuum

Identify where the family influences on your resources and capabilities are part of a competitive advantage (f+) and a competitive constraint (f−). You can conduct this analysis on many levels. The "meta" analysis would be of the larger family group as a whole, while the "micro" analysis would be of a particular business unit, or in relation to a specific innovation or new venture (such as the Backerhaus Veit example in the chapter). Identify the unit of analysis you are assessing and list the f+ and f− resources and capabilities.

Identify Unit of Analysis	
Resources and Capabilities (f+)	**Resources and Capabilities (f−)**

Plot the f+ and f− resources and capabilities from the chart on the following continuum. Place them in position relative to one another so that you see a picture of how the resources and capabilities are related.

Here is a list of potential resources and capabilities to choose from:

Successor leadership	Experienced leadership	Entrepreneurial processes	Team
Land	Treatment of employees	Firm-specific knowledge	Patient capital
Location	Conflict resolution	Firm-specific skills	Debt structure
Cash	Effective communication	Leadership development	Strategic alliances
Access to capital	Decision making	Managerial talent	Compensation
Distribution systems	Learning environment	Employee productivity	Strategy making and planning
Intellectual property	Openness to ideas	Network of relationships	Information flow
Raw materials	Cross-functional communication	Employee commitment	Organizational culture
Contracts/alliances	Reputation of company	Personal values	Unified beliefs and goals
Manufacturing processes	Market intelligence gathering	Flexible work practices	Time horizons
Innovation processes	Reporting structures	Trustworthiness	Brand name
Reputation of company	Coordination and control	Training	Governance structure

Case
Indulgence Spa Products

Preparation Questions

1. Are this family and case about "family business" or "family enterprising"? How would you delineate the differences? Why does this distinction matter for understanding the case?

2. Assess the Dawson business/family using the mind-set and methods model for family enterprising.

3. How well is Jimella prepared to successfully grow Indulgence Spa? What are her strengths and weaknesses? Identify what resources and capabilities she represents to the family group and to her start-up business.

4. What are the differences in market demand that Indulgence will face versus the Dawson Products target market? How will these differences affect the Indulgence business model? Does the new target market change the resource and capabilities requirements?

5. Craft a series of recommendations to Jimella for how she can grow her entrepreneurial business while advancing a family enterprising strategy. Are the two mutually exclusive? How do your recommendations address the succession and family legacy issues in the case?

Jimella, the youngest of the Dawson children, smiled as she peeked into her mother's office.

"Good morning, Mom! Do you have a minute?"

"Sure, come in. I'm just preparing for a meeting. You're early this morning, Jimella. I thought I was the only one here."

Ulissa wasn't really surprised to see her daughter. Jimella, age 32, liked to work hard. Jimella had learned every aspect of the family personal care products business—from filling and capping containers on the line to working with markets, spas, and salons. She had started selling products door-to-door when she was 11. After completing her undergraduate degree at Wharton and receiving her MBA from Duke, she was now Dawson's chief marketing officer. Soon after taking that position, she orchestrated a clean sweep of the department—a bold move that required the transfer of a well-liked 45-year-old worker and the firing of a number of employees that she determined had lazy and unproductive work habits. Until then, the company had developed a reputation for being a nurturing, family-oriented place where workers—even unproductive ones—could feel confident of long-term employment. Not only did Jimella's aggressive new management style send a wake-up call to marginal employees, but her initiative cut the marketing budget by a third and doubled profits—just as her spreadsheets had said they would.

Ulissa had come to expect this type of proactive, exceptional performance from her daughters (Angela, 39, was Dawson's COO). Now that her husband and cofounder, Robert Dawson, had begun spending much of his time speaking and teaching throughout the country about the need for African Americans to become economically self-sufficient, Jimella and Angela had become key figures in the growth trajectory of their family enterprise. And here her youngest was again, looking as if she was preparing to take another bold step. Ulissa was intrigued.

"What's on your mind, Jimella?"

"I'm going in some new directions with my plans for Indulgence Spa Products, and I'd like your opinion."

"Sure."

"First of all, I'm changing my marketing strategy. My target market will be all women—not just women of color. These products are outstanding, and Indulgence is limiting its growth by not positioning itself as a company that creates luxury spa products for all women."

"Sounds interesting, Jimella. But how do you plan to do this?"

Jimella's pause increased her mother's curiosity.

"My main marketing method will be direct sales—the same basic strategy that we have recently begun using at Dawson's Cosmetics. I'm going to build a national team of independent beauty advisors who will sell primarily through home calls and Indulgence house parties."

This time Jimella's pause had Ulissa more concerned than curious.

"And?"

"And to do that right, I'll need to make Indulgence a separate company from Dawson Products.

"Mom," Jimella added as gently as she could, "I've decided to go off on my own."

A Family Enterprise

In 1959 Robert Dawson invested $10 in a Fuller Products sales kit and began selling that line of personal care products door-to-door in Brooklyn, New York. Three years later he met Ulissa Moser, who was selling the same line of products to earn money for college tuition. They fell in love and were married in 1963. A few years later the couple opened a Fuller Products distributorship in Chicago, Illinois. The branch quickly became the top producing distributorship of Fuller Products. In 1971, when their mentor S. B. Fuller was hit hard by a national boycott (see Appendix A), the Dawsons moved quickly

This case was prepared by Sandra Sowell-Scott. © Copyright Babson College, 2005.

to establish their own manufacturing capabilities—initially out of their kitchen. They packaged their products in used containers they obtained from local hairdressers and supplemented with whatever they could find, including old jelly and mayonnaise jars.

By 1978 the company had expanded to include the Dawson Beauty School and a chain of beauty supply stores throughout the Midwest. Robert Dawson served as president, and Ulissa assumed a significant role in the administrative and manufacturing areas. From an early age, their two girls had participated in the business and learned how to sell door-to-door by developing their own small businesses selling products such as popcorn, baked goods, fruit, and even panty hose.

Robert and Ulissa very much wanted their children and the employees to understand that building and running a business was about hard work and discipline. They regularly brought Angela and Jimella to the office after school, and the girls were given specific tasks to perform. This not only helped instill a powerful work ethic but also provided a common mission that brought the family together.

In 1988 they opened a 37,000-square-foot corporate headquarters and manufacturing facility south of Chicago. The children continued to learn all aspects of the business from sales and marketing to manufacturing. In 1991 they opened the Dawson Cosmetology Center (DDC) at the site. The DDC became an important facility for training employees interested in working for the Dawson Beauty Schools. In 1997 Dawson's corporate and manufacturing divisions moved nearby into an 80,000-square-foot state-of-the-art facility.

By the new millennium, the company manufactured and marketed a line of over 400 professional and retail hair care and personal care products designed primarily for African American consumers.[1] The Dawson campus included a travel agency, a hotel, and a convention center. Their overall goal continued to be to empower people and aid in their education and provide opportunities for self-sufficiency and economic development. In 2004 revenues were just over $32 million, and Dawson employed a total workforce of nearly 500 people, most of whom were outside sales representatives.

The Cosmetics Division

In 1993, after she had completed Harvard Law School, Jimella's older sister Angela had officially joined the family business as legal counsel. A year later the company acquired a cosmetics manufacturing firm as a means of building a Dawson Cosmetics line. Angela developed the business and became president of the division, as well as Dawson's chief operating officer. As with all Dawson products, the cosmetic line was not sold in retail stores. Rather, their products were sold through salon owners, who subsequently sold them to customers. This gave salon owners the opportunity to make money on a proprietary brand product without having to compete directly with retail stores. Although Dawson sales representatives (those who contacted and sold products to the salon owners) occasionally sold door-to-door in the manner of the Fuller business model, this represented a very small portion of total sales.

Jimella came on board as marketing director in 1998. Her reorganization initiatives caused a stir among rank-and-file employees, but the resounding support from her parents quelled those rumblings. In 2000 she launched a new product development strategy within the cosmetics division. This line of luxury spa products—named Indulgence—was initially sold alongside other Dawson products. As demand for the line grew,[2] however, Jimella began formulating a plan to more effectively capitalize on that popularity.

In the spring of 2003 Jimella instituted a major redesign of the work and compensation structure for the cosmetology division. Instead of using salaried sales representatives, Dawson Cosmetics would be sold using a multilevel marketing sales model, also known as direct selling. Sales representatives would now be independent distributors whose purpose was to sell the product and to recruit and mentor new representatives.[3] Companies such as Mary Kay, The Pampered Chef, and Tupperware had used this "party plan" method to build successful businesses. Jimella felt that direct selling strongly supported the company mission of creating economic self-sufficiency within the African American community.

---

[1] Many African American hair products were specially formulated. For example, Caucasian hair products took oil out, while African American products put oil in. Dawson offered different products based on hair texture and style. (Examples of styles were Naturals, Dreads, Straight styles, and all of the preceding including color.)

[2] There was an explosion of personal care/spa products in the United States. Many consumers who had difficulty justifying spa treatments were instead turning to comparable products that they could self-administer in the home. In fact, as quality personal care products continued to proliferate, spas were having an increasingly difficult task creating a significantly value-added experience. (Source: The ISPA 2004 Consumer Trends Report—Executive Summary.)

[3] The multilevel compensation plan paid representatives/distributors based not only on their personal production but on the product sales of their "downline"—the people they had brought into the business. In turn, as those downline representatives established their own network, a portion of their commissions would flow back up to the original sponsor. This multitiered commission structure was most appropriate with proprietary, premium-priced, consumable products. In 2003 there were approximately 13.3 million people involved in direct selling—90 percent operated their business part-time. Products were sold primarily through in-home product demonstrations, parties, and one-on-one selling. The Direct Selling Association (www.dsa.org) estimated that more than 55 percent of the American public had purchased goods or services through direct selling.

Parental Support

Until that morning, Ulissa had been assuming that Jimella would follow in her sister's path and become one of the directors of Dawson Products. Along with that, she had assumed that the new Indulgence line would remain in the division. Ulissa got up from her mahogany desk and walked to the window. From her office, she had an excellent view of a good portion of the Dawson complex—now the city's third largest employer. She looked out at the "Dawson University Inn" and the Manors Convention Center and Dawson Cosmetology University. She thought about how hard they had worked to create this enterprise. Like a proud mother, Ulissa had loved watching this special child develop and grow. Although she and her husband were not nearly ready to relinquish control, this move of Jimella's would upset a succession plan that they had been taking for granted.

"With a dad like Robert Dawson," she mused to herself, "the world's greatest salesman and entrepreneur— we've raised them to dream big and not take the easy path." They had taught their daughters to be self-sufficient when they were young, and now they were bright, energetic, and independent. It seemed that instilling them with that entrepreneurial spirit and drive had led directly to this situation. So how could she not support Jimella in her quest to strike out on her own?

At that moment Jimella walked in. Ulissa turned to face her youngest.

"Jimella, are you sure this is what you want? Running a business is tough, you know."

"Yes, I'm confident that I can make it work—you and Dad prepared me for challenges like this. I'm used to working long hours, and I can make tough choices. When we were growing up and working in the business, you taught us to expect at least one problem a week. Learning to anticipate challenges and planning for the unexpected has helped me tremendously. I guess I just have good genes. I know I'm ready."

"How do you plan to finance this move?"

"I've been saving for several years and I have enough to make a reasonable start."

"That's good."

Ulissa smiled. She had tried to teach her children the importance of saving. Jimella had always been frugal. By the time she was ready to attend undergraduate school, she had saved $25,000 to put toward her first-year tuition.

"However, I am going to need some additional working capital."

Ulissa wasn't surprised. She knew her daughter.

"I could go to a bank," Jimella continued, "but before I do that I wanted to discuss this with you and Dad. I'd like to see if we could make an arrangement to have Dawson Products help fund Indulgence."

"That sounds reasonable to me, and I'm sure your father will be willing to listen."

Jimella walked around the desk and hugged her mother. Ulissa, normally very perky, responded slowly. Jimella sensed that her mom was not really excited about the idea. Her parents had raised her and her sister to run the family business, not to go out on their own. Jimella didn't want to hurt them or Dawson Products, but she needed her independence. She wanted to think for herself and make her own decisions. She knew that as long as she was at Dawson, her parents would continue to make all of the important decisions for her. Her father had made this clear one day when she was suggesting a change in policy. "I don't pay you to think," he had said teasingly. He had always admired her assertiveness, but he wanted her to be clear who the boss was. She had found this so frustrating that she knew she had to be out on her own. Nothing would change as long as her parents were running the business. Jimella realized that although her parents were past retirement age, they were not even close to being ready to slow down.

"Thanks, Mom. I've got to run. I have a staff meeting. I'll speak with you and Dad together later this week when he gets back."

Jimella's "Indulgence"

It took three weeks and many hours of conversation to develop a plan that provided Jimella with the capital support and independence she sought—without putting a strain on the parent company. The arrangement was that Jimella would continue to work at Dawson and handle special projects. In return for her contributions to the family business, Dawson would lend Indulgence Spa Products $250,000 and allow Jimella to use the Dawson business infrastructure to support her venture and manufacture most of her products.

One of Jimella's responsibilities was to manage the company hotel. Realizing that her continued support for Indulgence would be related to her performance at Dawson, she worked hard. She increased Dawson Hotel's profitability by raising prices (they were well below market rates) and by increasing the number of outside events.

Jimella had tried to use every resource available to assist her in her Indulgence project. She became active with the Direct Selling Association.[4] Her parents were sustaining members, so she took advantage of its educational programs and used it to develop helpful contacts and mentors. She met the leaders of Mary Kay, Avon, and other companies with door-to-door operations. She toured the Avon facility and received some top-level advice.

She began to create competitive marketing strategies. She determined that her major direct competitor was The Body Shop at Home—a new division of The Body Shop.

---

[4] The Direct Selling Association (DSA) was the national trade association of the leading firms that manufactured and distributed goods and services sold directly to consumers. In the early 2000s more than 150 companies were members of the association, including many well-known brand names. DSA provided educational opportunities for direct selling professionals and worked with Congress, numerous government agencies, consumer protection organizations, and others on behalf of its member companies.

She believed her other direct competitor to be Warm Spirits, which was a new venture owned by a white male chemist and a black female. She didn't consider the other large health and beauty care companies to be competitors because they did not specialize in spa products.

Jimella designed a product guide that featured women of all races using the spa products. On its opening page, the product guide stated that "the company was founded on the belief that women can be better friends, mothers, and wives when they take a moment to refresh and rejuvenate their inner spirit." She also expanded the product line to include luxury linens and a monthly flower club.

Jimella traveled and presented her products at numerous holiday bazaars, trade shows, and other events. As Jimella talked with prospective distributors and customers, some people openly questioned her age, while others were polite and moved on when they learned that she owned the company.

She advertised in national publications and was slowly developing a national group of independent beauty advisors. Laura Michaels—a top producer—had joined the company after responding to one of the ads. As a middle-aged white woman with lots of experience in direct sales, Laura represented the precise demographic that Jimella was certain Indulgence needed to appeal to. Laura's enthusiasm and capability had been a real boost to the enterprise, but despite that distributor's success in building a base of white clients, most Indulgence recruits were African American.

Jimella had set aggressive growth goals for her venture. She planned to attract 100 beauty advisors, $100,000 in monthly sales, and profitability by the end of fiscal year 2006 (see Exhibit 1). She was off to a good start. After just seven weeks in business, she had contracted with 28 beauty consultants and had reached $15,000 in monthly sales.

EXHIBIT 1

Pro Forma Profit and Loss, FY 2005–2009

	2005	2006	2007	2008	2009
Sales	**$585,271**	**$869,755**	**$1,561,976**	**$2,829,716**	**$5,158,227**
Direct costs of goods	$169,831	$195,417	$340,731	$603,346	$1,081,017
Fulfillment payroll	$0	$12,500	$12,500	$75,000	$100,000
Fulfillment	$18,729	$27,832	$49,983	$90,551	$165,063
Cost of goods sold	**$188,560**	**$235,749**	**$403,214**	**$768,897**	**$1,346,080**
Gross margin	**$396,712**	**$634,006**	**$1,158,762**	**$2,060,819**	**$3,812,147**
Operating expenses					
Sales and marketing expenses:					
Sales and marketing payroll	$52,000	$75,000	$165,000	$240,000	$280,000
Advertising/promotion	$15,000	$26,093	$62,479	$141,486	$257,911
National trade shows and distributor rallies	$50,000	$75,000	$100,000	$125,000	$150,000
Total sales and marketing expenses	**$117,000**	**$176,093**	**$327,479**	**$506,486**	**$687,911**
General and administrative expenses					
General and administrative payroll	$73,000	$90,000	$120,000	$152,500	$180,000
Commissions and overrides	$92,000	$156,556	$281,156	$622,538	$392,721
Depreciation	$24,123	$36,720	$45,580	$63,328	$79,992
Rent	$7,500	$12,000	$25,000	$35,000	$50,000
Utilities	$3,000	$3,600	$3,600	$3,600	$5,000
Insurance	$16,749	$21,756	$27,599	$44,039	$58,075
Payroll taxes	$21,900	$26,625	$44,625	$70,125	$84,000
Legal fees	$8,000	$14,000	$35,000	$50,000	$75,000
Total general and administrative expenses	**$246,272**	**$361,256**	**$582,560**	**$1,041,130**	**$1,924,788**
Purchase of Indulgence assets	$75,000	$0	$0	$0	$0
Total operating expenses	**$438,272**	**$537,349**	**$910,039**	**$1,547,616**	**$2,612,699**
Profit before interest and taxes	($41,560)	$96,657	$248,723	$513,204	$1,199,447
Interest expense	$12,924	$12,373	$10,392	$8,288	$6,054
Taxes incurred	$0	$31,185	$88,183	$186,819	$441,556
Net profit	**($54,484)**	**$53,099**	**$150,149**	**$318,097**	**$751,838**
Net profit/sales	**−9.31%**	**6.11%**	**9.61%**	**11.24%**	**14.58%**

Parent Company Concerns

By the spring of 2005, Ulissa noted that Jimella was appearing quite satisfied with the arrangement with Dawson Products and with the progress of the Indulgence venture. Still, Ulissa felt pulled in two directions: She truly hoped that Jimella succeeded, but she also wanted to make sure that Dawson Products could remain a successful, growing family business. Earlier that week, she had confided to a close friend:

> What makes Dawson Products so successful is not the bottles or jars that contain our products. It's not even the products themselves because many of our competitors have similar things. It's our spirit that makes us number one. We have always known how to take what we've got and make what we want of it.
>
> In time Robert and I will start focusing on leaving this business to our daughters, but now we might have to re-craft our succession strategy. If Jimella leaves and Angela is in charge, we'll certainly have to hire an executive support staff. Even if most of those hires come from within the company, I wonder whether or not the employees would have the same loyalty to Angela as they have had toward us all these years. Would old-timers be constantly questioning new ideas and procedures?
>
> Robert and I feel strongly that Dawson products must always remain a family business. We treat all of our employees like family. Many have several children and family members that work for Dawson. We will always try to take care of them—they believe in us and our mission.

Ulissa and Robert had another, more global, reason for wanting to keep the company private. Dawson was one of a very few African American personal care businesses that had managed to avoid a spate of corporate buyouts by white-controlled multinationals (see Appendix B). One particularly painful sale had involved their close friends, the Johnsons.

Johnsons Products had been a premier African American–owned hair care company. In the early 1990s George and Joan Johnson had gotten divorced after 35 years of marriage. Looking to avoid a messy court battle, George had transferred all of his stock to his wife. Their son, Eric, became president and began to grow the company. Under his able control, profits rose 50 percent. Unfortunately Eric deeply offended his sister Joanie by offering her a position in the family business that she felt was beneath her. Joanie retaliated and convinced her mother, who was chair of the board, to oust Eric. Soon after, things began to fall apart. When Eric resigned in 1993, the company was sold to IVAC, a majority-owned Florida-based generic drug company, for $61 million.[5]

[5] K. Springer and L. Reibstein, "So Much for Family Ties," *Newsweek* 119, no. 12 (March 23, 1992), p. 49.

Ulissa certainly understood why the Johnson saga had caused such a controversy within the African American community. Although she and her husband had been approached to sell on several occasions, they had always refused. They were dedicated to keeping Dawson Products an African American family-owned business—a role model for the community and a driving force in helping African Americans become "job makers" instead of "job takers."

Ulissa looked at her watch. Curiously, Jimella was late for their usual lunch date.

A Hard Truth

Although Jimella had continued to work aggressively, charging full speed ahead, Indulgence sales for fiscal year 2005 had fallen short of expectations (see Exhibit 2). As she set these actuals against her pro formas, she realized that to stay on track, she would have to increase sales dramatically in the coming weeks (see Exhibits 3 and 4).

Just as Jimella rose from her desk to head over for lunch with her mom, she was compelled to sit down with a phone call from Laura Michaels, her perpetually upbeat, enthusiastic, and talented Indulgence representative.

"Jimella, I don't understand what happened."

"Laura, what are you talking about?"

"My cousin Patricia was ready to sign up, and then she called back and told me she had changed her mind. I had been so excited about her potential—she has a lot of friends who would love these products. She would have been an excellent distributor—with a lucrative downline in the white market."

Jimella paused. She knew that building a base of white customers would be tough, but she hadn't anticipated that it would be this difficult. It wasn't that she hadn't been warned. When she had presented her business idea at a local university, the graduate students questioned whether a black female could be successful in a white-dominated, competitive market. And white bias wasn't the only problem. Jimella also knew that many blacks resented the fact that she was using the Spa Indulgence line to "cross over" into the white market. This group included many employees of Dawson Products.

"It will be okay; things like this always happen in direct sales," Jimella said, trying hard but failing to sound encouraging.

Laura had caught the faltering tone.

"You know, I'm usually really good at spotting potential distributors. I hate to say it, Jimella, but my cousin's attitude changed when I told her that a young black female owned the company. Lately, I'm sensing that kind of attitude more and more. I really don't understand it. How can people be so narrow-minded?"

"I don't know, Laura. Or maybe it's just that I don't want to know."

EXHIBIT 2

Actuals, FY 2005

	Jun	Jul	Aug	Sep	Oct	Nov	Dec	Jan	Feb	Mar	Apr	May	2005
	$5,500	$6,750	$10,000	$15,000	$25,000	$50,000	$60,000	$70,000	$75,000	$80,000	$90,000	$100,000	$587,250
Sales	$5,500	$6,750	$9,813	$14,961	$24,665	$46,020	$34,199	$36,172	$46,195	$55,330	$62,293	$67,383	$409,281
Direct costs of goods	$1,670	$2,055	$2,836	$4,359	$6,999	$12,398	$9,807	$10,459	$13,441	$16,084	$18,431	$20,223	$118,763
Fulfillment payroll	$0	$0	$0	$0	$0	$C	$0	$0	$0	$0	$0	$0	$0
Fulfillment	$176	$216	$314	$479	$789	$1,473	$1,094	$1,158	$1,478	$1,771	$1,993	$2,156	$13,097
Cost of goods sold	$1,846	$2,271	$3,150	$4,837	$7,788	$13,870	$10,902	$11,617	$14,920	$17,854	$20,425	$22,380	$131,860
Gross margin	$3,654	$4,479	$6,662	$10,124	$16,877	$32,150	$23,297	$24,556	$31,276	$37,475	$41,868	$45,003	$277,421
Operating expenses:													
Sales and marketing expenses:													
Sales and marketing payroll	$3,500	$3,500	$3,500	$3,500	$3,500	$3,500	$3,500	$5,000	$5,000	$5,000	$5,000	$5,000	$49,500
Advertising/promotion	$165	$230	$294	$449	$740	$1,381	$1,026	$1,085	$1,386	$1,660	$1,869	$2,021	$12,278
National trade shows	$0	$0	$15,000	$10,000	$0	$0	$0	$15,000	$0	$0	$3,500	$3,500	$47,000
Total sales and marketing expenses	$3,665	$3,703	$18,794	$13,949	$4,240	$4,881	$4,526	$21,085	$6,386	$6,660	$10,369	$10,521	$108,778
General and administrative expenses:													
General and administrative payroll	$5,666	$5,666	$5,666	$5,666	$5,666	$5,666	$5,666	$5,666	$5,666	$5,666	$5,666	$5,670	$67,996
Commissions and overrides	$990	$1,215	$1,766	$2,693	$4,440	$8,284	$6,156	$6,511	$8,315	$9,959	$11,213	$12,129	$73,671
Depreciation	$1,271	$1,271	$1,271	$1,757	$1,757	$1,757	$2,507	$2,507	$2,507	$2,507	$2,507	$2,507	$24,123
Rent	$0	$0	$750	$750	$750	$750	$750	$750	$750	$750	$750	$750	$7,500
Utilities	$0	$0	$300	$300	$300	$300	$300	$300	$300	$300	$300	$300	$3,000
Insurance	$642	$645	$1,550	$1,259	$690	$729	$708	$1,701	$819	$1,797	$2,560	$3,649	$16,749
Payroll taxes	$1,375	$1,375	$1,375	$1,375	$1,375	$1,375	$1,375	$1,600	$1,600	$1,600	$1,600	$1,601	$17,624
Legal fees	$0	$2,500	$2,500	$0	$0	$0	$0	$1,000	$0	$1,000	$0	$1,000	$8,000
Total general and administrative expenses	$9,945	$12,672	$15,180	$13,801	$14,978	$18,860	$17,461	$20,035	$19,957	$23,579	$24,595	$27,605	$218,664
Purchase of Indulgence assets	$0	$75,000	$0	$0	$0	$0	$0	$0	$0	$0	$0	$0	$75,000
Total other expenses	$9,944	$12,671	$15,178	$13,800	$14,978	$18,860	$17,461	$20,035	$19,957	$23,579	$24,595	$27,605	$218,664
Total operating expenses	$13,609	$91,374	$33,972	$27,749	$19,218	$23,741	$21,987	$41,120	$26,343	$30,239	$34,964	$38,127	$402,442
Profit before interest and taxes	($9,955)	($86,895)	($27,310)	($17,625)	($2,341)	$8,409	$1,310	($16,564)	$4,933	$7,236	$6,905	$6,876	($125,021)
Interest expense	$0	$1,238	$1,225	$1,213	$1,200	$1,138	$1,175	$1,163	$1,150	$1,137	$1,124	$1,111	$12,924
Taxes incurred	$0	$0	$0	$0	$0	$0	$0	$0	$0	$0	$0	$0	$0
Net profit	($9,955)	($88,132)	($28,535)	($18,838)	($3,541)	$7,221	$135	($17,727)	$3,783	$6,099	$5,781	$5,765	($137,945)
Net profit/sales	181.01%	1305.67%	290.81%	125.91%	14.36%	15.69%	0.39%	49.01%	8.19%	11.02%	9.28%	8.56%	33.20%

EXHIBIT 3

Indulgence Actual and Projected Cash Flows

Cash Received	2005	2006	2007	2008	2009
			Actual Fiscal Year		
Cash from operations:					
Cash sales	$409,281	$869,755	$1,561,976	$2,829,716	$5,158,227
Cash from receivables	$0	$0	$0	$0	$0
Subtotal cash from operations	**$409,281**	**$869,755**	**$1,561,976**	**$2,829,716**	**$5,158,227**
Additional cash received					
Sales tax, VAT, HST/GST received	$30,696	$65,232	$117,148	$212,229	$386,867
Dawson loan proceeds	$250,000	$0	$0	$0	$0
Sales of long-term assets	$689,977	$934,987	$1,679,124	$3,041,945	$5,545,094
Subtotal cash received					
Expenditures	2005	2006	2007	2008	2009
Expenditures from operations:					
Cash spending	$117,496	$177,500	$297,500	$467,500	$560,000
Payment of accounts payable	$336,763	$547,641	$973,793	$1,836,107	$3,462,894
Subtotal spent on operations	**$454,260**	**$725,141**	**$1,271,293**	**$2,303,607**	**$4,022,894**
Additional cash spent					
Sales tax, VAT, HST/GST paid out	$25,905	$65,232	$117,148	$212,229	$386,867
Principal repayment of Dawson loan	$27,776	$32,027	$34,008	$36,112	$38,346
Purchase long-term assets	$40,950	$75,000	$85,000	$125,000	$150,000
Subtotal cash spent	**$548,891**	**$897,400**	**$1,507,450**	**$2,676,948**	**$4,598,107**
Net cash flow	**$141,086**	**$37,586**	**$171,674**	**$364,997**	**$946,987**
Cash balance	**$161,086**	**$198,672**	**$370,346**	**$735,344**	**$1,682,331**

EXHIBIT 4

Indulgence Actual and Projected Balance Sheets

Assets		Actual Fiscal Year			
	2005	2006	2007	2008	2009
Current assets					
Cash	$161,086	$198,672	$370,346	$735,344	$1,682,331
Accounts receivable	$0	$0	$0	$0	$0
Inventory	$75,000	$100,000	$125,000	$200,000	$300,000
Other current assets	$0	$0	$0	$0	$0
Total current assets	**$236,086**	**$298,672**	**$495,346**	**$935,344**	**$1,982,331**
Long-term assets					
Long-term assets	$65,950	$140,950	$225,950	$350,950	$500,950
Accumulated depreciation	$0	$60,843	$106,423	$169,751	$249,743
Total long-term assets	**$65,950**	**$80,107**	**$119,527**	**$181,199**	**$251,207**
Total assets	**$302,036**	**$378,779**	**$614,873**	**$1,116,542**	**$2,233,538**

Liabilities and Capital	2005	2006	2007	2008	2009
Accounts payable	$70,924	$150,718	$270,672	$490,356	$893,860
Dawson loan balance	$222,224	$190,196	$156,188	$120,076	$81,730
Other current liabilities	$4,791	$4,791	$4,791	$4,791	$4,791
Subtotal current liabilities	**$297,938**	**$345,706**	**$431,651**	**$615,223**	**$980,381**
Long-term liabilities	$0	$0	$0	$0	$0
Total liabilities	**$297,938**	**$345,706**	**$431,651**	**$615,223**	**$980,381**
Paid-in capital	$0	$0	$0	$0	$0
Retained earnings	$138,000	$55	$53,154	$203,303	$521,400
Earnings	($119,404)	$53,099	$150,149	$318,097	$751,838
Total capital	**$18,596**	**$53,154**	**$203,303**	**$521,400**	**$1,273,238**
Total liabilities and capital	**$316,534**	**$398,860**	**$634,954**	**$1,136,624**	**$2,253,619**
Net worth	**$4,097**	**$33,073**	**$183,222**	**$501,319**	**$1,253,157**

Appendix A

S. B. FULLER (1905–1988)

It is contrary to the laws of nature for man to stand still; he must move forward, or the eternal march of progress will force him backward. This the Negro has failed to understand; he believes that the lack of civil rights legislation, and the lack of integration have kept him back. But this is not true....

S. B. Fuller

Samuel B. Fuller was one of the wealthiest and most successful black entrepreneurs in mid-20th-century America. His Chicago-based business empire included Fuller Products, which manufactured health and beauty aids and cleaning products; a $3 million ownership in real estate, including the famous Regal Theater, comparable to Harlem's Apollo Theater; the South Center (later changed to Fuller) Department Store and Office Building; a New York real estate trust, the Fuller Guaranty Corporation; the *Pittsburgh Courier,* the largest black newspaper chain; and the Fuller Philco Home Appliance Center; as well as farm and livestock operations.

Fuller was born into rural poverty in Ouachita Parish, Louisiana, in 1905. From an early age, he gained a reputation for reliability and resourcefulness. After coming to Chicago in 1920, he worked in a wide range of menial jobs, eventually rising to become manager of a coal yard. Although he had a secure job during the Depression, he struck out on his own, preferring freedom to security. Starting with $25, he founded Fuller Products in 1934.

By 1960, at the height of his business success, with sales of $10 million, there were 85 branches of his Fuller Products Company in 38 states. His employees, black and white, included 5,000 salespeople and some 600 workers in his office and factory, who produced and sold the 300 different products manufactured by Fuller. In 1947 Fuller secretly purchased Boyer International Laboratories, a white cosmetic manufactory, which opened a southern white consumer-based market. Fuller also held interest in the Patricia Stevens Cosmetic Company and J. C. McBrady and Company.

Fuller Products gave training to many future entrepreneurs and other leaders. Post–World War II black millionaires John H. Johnson, publisher, George Johnson, hair products manufacturer, and Robert Dawson, hair products manufacturer, have all acknowledged Fuller as their role model. He had little patience for race baiters, black or white. "It doesn't make any difference," he declared, "about the color of an individual's skin. No one cares whether a cow is black, red, yellow, or brown. They want to know how much milk it can produce."

Fuller was a leading black Republican, although he always had an independent streak. He promoted civil rights and briefly headed the Chicago South Side NAACP. Along with black Birmingham businessman A. G. Gaston, he tried to organize a cooperative effort to purchase the segregated bus company during the Montgomery bus boycott. He told Martin Luther King, Jr., "The bus company is losing money and is willing to sell. We should buy it." King was skeptical of the idea, and not enough blacks came forward to raise the money. Despite his belief in civil rights, however, Fuller's emphasis had always been on the need for blacks to go into business. In 1958 he blasted the federal government for undermining free enterprise and fostering socialism. He feared that it was "doing the same thing today as was done in the days of Caesar—destroying incentive and initiative." He argued that wherever "there is capitalism, there is freedom."

In the early 1960s Fuller's financial empire collapsed. Southern whites discovered his ownership in Boyer International Laboratories. A 100 percent white boycott of the company's products resulted in an abrupt drop of 60 percent of the Fuller Product Line. In addition, Fuller Products suffered severe reverses after S. B. Fuller gave a controversial speech to the National Association of Manufacturers in 1963. In his speech, Fuller charged that too many blacks were using their lack of civil rights as an excuse for failure. Many of his comments were reported out of context. Major national black leaders reacted angrily and called for a boycott of Fuller Products.

Despite a record of remarkable business success, Fuller was unable to raise professional capital to offset losses. Attempts to generate funds by selling stock in Fuller Products failed. In 1964 the Securities and Exchange Commission charged Fuller with sale of unregistered securities. He was forced to pay $1.5 million to his creditors, including black salespeople who also filed claims. Fullers sold off various enterprises to meet his debts.

After bankruptcy, but with six-figure financial support in gifts and loans from leading Chicago black business people, Fuller Products was reorganized in 1972 but never recovered as a major black business. Fuller continued manufacturing a line of cleaning products and cosmetics, with sales through distributorship franchises: $1,000 for Fuller Products valued at $26,000. In 1975 Fuller showed sales of almost $1 million. S. B. Fuller died in 1988.

Source: J. E. K. Walker and S. B. Fuller, *Encyclopedia of African American Business History* (Westport, CT: Greenwood Press, 1999).

Appendix B
THE ETHNIC HEALTH AND BEAUTY CARE INDUSTRY

Overview

The ethnic health and beauty care industry (HBC) consisted of hair and skin products and cosmetics, designed for and sold to minority groups. The three largest minority groups in the United States were African Americans, Hispanics, and Asians. Of these three minority groups, African Americans were by far the biggest purchasers of ethnic HBC products. For this reason, the vast majority of ethnic HBC products were directed toward African American consumers. This lucrative and fertile industry was once the domain of African American companies. When major manufacturers realized the potential of the ethnic HBC industry, they moved in rapidly and eventually captured all but a small fraction of the market.

In 2004 the combined retail market for ethnic hair care, color cosmetic, and skin care products was valued at $1.6 billion and was estimated to grow to $1.9 billion by 2006. The largest HBC category was hair care, 72 percent of the total at $1.124 billion, then cosmetics at $327 million or 20 percent, and skin care at $110 million or 7 percent. Products not sold through traditional retail chains (such as products used by professional stylists, Indulgence Spa and Dawson Products) are not reflected in these retail figures.

African Americans Are the Largest Consumers of HBC Products

Various studies indicated that African Americans spent three to five times more on HBC products than the general population. According to AHBAI (American Health and Beauty Aids Institute), a trade group representing African American hair care manufacturers, African Americans buy 19 percent of all health and beauty aids and 34 percent of all hair care products while accounting for approximately 12 percent of the overall population. In 2005 the purchasing power of the African American population exceeded $688 billion.

The Growth and Development of the Ethnic Health and Beauty Care Industry

African Americans founded and built what we today call the ethnic health and beauty care industry. The founding pioneers of the ethnic industry, Madame C. J. Walker, S. B. Fuller, and George E. Johnson, were among the first to see the great potential in creating businesses catering to the hair and skin care needs of African American men and women.

During their time, there were virtually no hair and skin care products designed for African Americans; and for a very long period ethnic industry was ignored by mainstream manufacturers who did not see the value in producing ethnic products. Up until the late 19th century, the ethnic market consisted mainly of products manufactured by African Americans, for African Americans.

Madame C. J. Walker, America's first black self-made female millionaire, set the pace with the development, manufacturing, and selling of hair care products she created herself. She also developed innovations to the pressing comb, which gave rise to an entire industry. Following in her footsteps was S. B. Fuller (see Appendix A). One of Fuller's many disciples, George E. Johnson, heeded the call and pioneered the modern ethnic health and beauty care industry. Johnson Products was a company that established many firsts in the industry. From their legacy came Dawson Products, Bronner Brothers, Pro-Line, Soft Sheen, Luster, and many others.

The Role African American Hair Companies Played in the African American Community

The handful of African American health and beauty care companies existing during Madame C. J. Walker's time would grow to nearly 20 over the next three decades. As the industry developed, thousands of jobs were created within the African American community.

During the segregation period in America there was much turmoil and unrest among African Americans who had grown weary of the unequal treatment they were receiving from white society. Many African Americans felt that developing strong businesses in the African American community was the only way to achieve freedom, justice, and equality. For that reason, African American entrepreneurs were hailed as heroes, leaders, and examples in their communities. They represented black success, and their presence in the community fostered racial pride and self-esteem among African Americans.

Following desegregation, many black-owned businesses began losing market share to white companies. Black-owned banks, hotels, and corner stores soon disappeared. The only black businesses making big profits serving blacks were black hair care companies, and by the 1970s they began to face serious challenges by mainstream corporations.

The Movement of Non–African American Companies into the Ethnic Health and Beauty Care Industry

In the early 1970s mainstream companies began to see abundant opportunities in the ethnic market. Prior to that, the handful of African American hair companies in existence at the time were growing and thriving. In the late 1970s the ethnic market received a tremendous boost with the enormous popularity of the Jheri Curl—one of the hottest styles of the time. Many companies experienced skyrocketing profits—some exceeding 40 percent.

The Jheri Curl was a product of the International Playtex Corporation—a white-owned company. Customer demand for the Jheri Curl was fueled when celebrities like Michael Jackson began sporting the glossy curls. An ample number of products were needed to achieve and maintain the Jheri Curl look, and many African American hair care companies reaped tremendous revenues from it. According to a 1986 *Newsweek* article, the Jheri Curl "spurred industry growth at a 32 percent rate."

The soaring profits reaped by African American hair care companies from this popular style did not go unnoticed by mainstream manufacturers. Corporate giants like Alberto-Culver and Revlon entered the market. Following in their footsteps, Gillette entered the market in the middle 1980s with the purchase of Lustrasilk.

How the Changes in Ownership Affected African Americans' Companies

Many African American health and beauty care companies, not having the capital to compete with these billion-dollar corporations, sold, merged, or went bankrupt. Black-owned companies that did survive lost significant market share.

The shake-up shifted the balance of power to non–African American companies. For example, Johnson Products, the modern industry pioneer, controlled 80 percent of the relaxer market in 1976. In 1977 the FTC ordered Johnson Products to put warning labels on its lye-based relaxer. This action gave Johnson Products a negative public image, and it cost the company customers. Revlon, a corporate giant, avoided a similar FTC ruling for almost two years. Eventually Revlon complied, but not until it had captured a significant portion of the relaxer market through its Realistic and Fabulaxer products. Carson Products, makers of Dark & Lovely Relaxers, cornered the market in the late 1970s when it introduced its no-lye relaxer product. Atlanta-based M&M, Inc., maker of Sta-Sof-Fro, sold over $47 million of products in 1983 but was out of

business by 1990. Johnson Products later acquired the assets of M&M.

By the 1980s African American health and beauty care companies were in serious trouble. Once controlling 80 percent of the total market, their share was estimated by industry analysts to be as low as 48 percent.

The Founding of the American Health and Beauty Aids Institute

In response to competition in the industry, the American Health and Beauty Aids Institute (AHBAI) was formed in 1981. AHBAI is a national nonprofit organization of black-owned companies that produce hair care and cosmetic products specifically for black consumers. AHBAI created the "Proud Lady" logo (a black woman in silhouette featuring three layers of hair). The logo was stamped on the back of all manufacturing members' products, printed materials, and packing and promotional materials. The mission of AHBAI was to make consumers aware of products that were manufactured by African American-owned companies.

The Revlon Pronouncement

While African American hair care companies were facing dwindling revenues and threats of corporate acquisitions, mergers, and takeovers, Irving Bottner, a high-ranking Revlon official, was quoted in the October 1986 issue of *Newsweek* magazine as having said, "In the next couple of years, the black-owned businesses will disappear. They'll all be sold to the white companies."

In the same article, Bottner went on to criticize AHBAI, the trade organization representing black manufacturers, saying that AHBAI's campaign to encourage black consumers to purchase products from black companies was unfair to white business: "They're making a social issue out of a business issue. When you produce what the consumer wants, loyalties disappear."

Bottner also stated that black companies tend to offer "poorer grade" products: "We are accused of taking business away from the black companies, but black consumers buy quality products—too often their black brothers didn't do them any good." In response, Jesse Jackson launched a boycott against Revlon, demanding that Revlon divest in South African operations, hire more black managers, and use more black suppliers. Black publications such as *Essence, Ebony,* and *Jet* temporarily stopped carrying Revlon advertisements. In response, Revlon sponsored a $3 million advertising campaign, announcing that money spent with black businesses supports the black community.

The situation escalated in the 1990s. Company by company, mergers and acquisitions dismantled black-owned health and beauty care businesses. In 1993 majority-owned IVAX, a Florida-based generic drug company, acquired Johnson Products Co., the maker of Afro-Sheen and Ultra-Sheen. IVAX also purchased Flori Roberts Cosmetics, a majority-owned line of cosmetics for women of color. In 1998 L'Oreal bought Soft Sheen. Ownership of Johnson Products changed hands that same year from IVAX to Carson Inc., a mainstream company based in Savannah, Georgia. In March 2000 Alberto-Culver, a $1.6 billion personal care products manufacturing company in Melrose Park, Illinois, bought Pro-Line, the third largest black-owned manufacturer, for an undisclosed amount.

In 2000 L'Oreal acquired Carson. As a result, the top two black-owned hair care companies (Johnson Products and Soft Sheen) were joined under the L'Oreal umbrella. Based in France, L'Oreal was now the world's dominant manufacturer of ethnic health and beauty care products, with Soft Sheen/Carson brands such as Dark & Lovely and Optimum Care as its top sellers. Soft Sheen/Carson was the name L'Oreal had given to the newly merged Soft Sheen Products and Carson Products businesses.

Lafayette Jones, president and CEO of Segmented Marketing Services, estimated that the 2004 sales of L'Oreal's ethnic market divisions were in the range of $1 billion, and those of Alberto-Culver were around $100 million. Jones is also publisher of *Urban Call,* a trade magazine for urban retailers and businesses, and *Shades of Beauty,* a magazine for multicultural salons. Alfred Washington, chairman of the American Health and Beauty Aids Institute, said in 2004, "The combination of L'Oreal's massive marketing power plus the acquired brands of Soft Sheen and Carson will work to squeeze black manufacturers from the retail shelf."

For a better understanding of the impact of the sales of many prominent African American–owned HBC product manufacturers, see "Bad Hair Days" in *Black Enterprise Magazine* (November 2000).

Chapter Nineteen

The Harvest and Beyond

And don't forget: Burial shrouds have no pockets.

The Late Sidney Rabb
Chairman emeritus, Stop & Shop, Boston

"I made all my money by selling too early!"

Bernard Baruch

Results Expected

The old saying "Life is a journey, not a destination" is never more true than in the entrepreneurial arena. The exhilarations and disappointments are legendary, and you have studied and encountered these over the semester. This chapter poses the challenges of the future, the joy of the harvest, and its paradox: So what, and then what?

Upon completion of this chapter, you will be able to

1. Discuss the importance of first building a great company and thereby creating harvest options.

2. Explain why harvesting is an essential element of the entrepreneurial process and does not necessarily mean abandoning the company.

3. Identify the principal harvest options, including trade sale, going public, and cash flow (which we call a cash cow).

4. Discuss the importance of creating a longer-term legacy from personal and family wealth by pursuing philanthropic activities and contributing to community renewal.

5. Provide insights for and analysis of the Optitech case study.

A Journey, Not a Destination

A common sentiment among successful entrepreneurs is that the challenge and exhilaration of the journey give them the greatest energy and fulfillment. Perhaps Walt Disney said it best: "I don't make movies to make money. I make money to make movies." It is the thrill of the chase that counts.

These entrepreneurs also talk of the venture's insatiable appetite for not only cash but also time, attention, and energy. Some say it is an addiction. Most say it is far more demanding and difficult than they ever imagined. Most, however, plan not to retire and would do it again—usually sooner rather than later. They also say it is more fun and satisfying than any other career they have had.

For the vast majority of entrepreneurs, it takes 10, 15, even 20 years or more to build a significant net worth. According to the popular press and government statistics, there are more millionaires than ever in the United States, and in 2007 there were nearly 10 million millionaires in the world. Sadly, a million dollars is not really all that much money today as a result of inflation, and whereas lottery and sweepstakes winners become instant millionaires, entrepreneurs do not. The number of years it usually takes to accumulate such a net worth is a far cry from the instant millionaire, the get-rich-quick impression associated with lottery winners or fantasy or "reality" TV shows.

Wealth in Families

This is the title of a wonderful book by Charles W. Collier, senior philanthropic advisor at Harvard University. The book is a must-read: full of wisdom, lessons, and practical advice on the delicate, contradictory, and often perplexing subject of handling wealth in families. In nearly every culture there is an equivalent version of the proverb "Shirtsleeves to shirtsleeves in three generations." In China, for example, it is "Rice paddy to rice paddy in three generations." Around the world the global entrepreneurial revolution is creating unprecedented family wealth. As the proverbs reveal, this wealth can become a curse or a vehicle for renewal.

Collier's book shares many stories of how wealthy families handle wealth—how they teach the next generation a deeper meaning of wealth, instill a passion for work, and express their financial well-being through philanthropy, not just consumption. These case studies illustrate how families use wealth for personal renewal, to create a sense of social responsibility among the next generation, and to create a legacy of societal renewal through giving back. Time and again this philanthropy is a shared family activity that expresses deep family and personal values and creates significant family legacies. *Wealth in Families* is also an excellent resource book with a rich bibliography of Web sites and sources of information. Read it and share it with your family.

The Journey Can Be Addictive

The total immersion required, the huge workload, the many sacrifices for a family, and the burnout often experienced by an entrepreneur are real. Maintaining the energy, enthusiasm, and drive to get across the finish line, to achieve a harvest, may be exceptionally difficult. For instance, one entrepreneur in the computer software business, after working alone for several years, developed highly sophisticated software. Yet he insisted he could not stand the computer business for another day. Imagine trying to position a company for sale effectively and to negotiate a deal for a premium price after such a long battle.

Some entrepreneurs wonder if the price of victory is too high. One very successful entrepreneur put it this way:

> What difference does it make if you win, have $20 million in the bank—I know several who do—and you are a basket case, your family has been washed out, and your kids are a wreck?

The opening quote of the chapter is a sobering reminder, and its message is clear: Unless an entrepreneur enjoys the journey and thinks it is worthy, he or she may end up on the wrong train to the wrong destination.

First Build a Great Company

One of the simplest but most difficult principles for nonentrepreneurs to grasp is that wealth and liquidity are results—not causes—of building a great company. They fail to recognize the difference between making money and spending money. Most successful entrepreneurs possess a clear understanding of this distinction; they get their kicks from growing the company. They know the payoff will take care of itself if they concentrate on proving and building a sustainable venture for the founders, the investors, and other stakeholders—with a watchful eye for future generations.

Create Harvest Options and Capture the Value

Here is yet another great paradox in the entrepreneurial process: Build a great company but do not forget to harvest. This apparent contradiction is difficult to reconcile, especially among entrepreneurs with several generations in a family-owned enterprise. Perhaps a better way to frame this apparent contradiction is to keep harvest options open and to think of harvesting as a vehicle for reducing risk and for creating future entrepreneurial choices and options, not simply selling the business and heading for the golf course or the beach, although these options may appeal to a few entrepreneurs. To appreciate the importance of this perspective, consider the following actual situations.

An entrepreneur in his 50s, Nigel reached an agreement with Brian, a young entrepreneur in his 30s, to join the company as marketing vice president. Their agreement also included an option for Brian to acquire the company in the next five years for $1.5 million. At the time the firm, a small biscuit maker, had revenues of $500,000 per year. By the end of the third year, Brian had built the company to $5 million in sales and substantially improved profitability. He notified Nigel of his intention to exercise his option to buy the company. Nigel immediately fired Brian, who had no other source of income and had a family and a $400,000 mortgage on a house whose fair market value had dropped to $275,000. Brian learned that Nigel had also received an offer from a company for $6 million. Thus Nigel wanted to renege on his original agreement with Brian. Unable to muster the legal resources, Brian settled out of court for less than $100,000. When the other potential buyer learned how Nigel had treated Brian, the $6 million offer was withdrawn. Then there were no buyers. Within two years Nigel drove the company into bankruptcy. At that point he called Brian and asked if he would now be interested in buying the company. Brian used colorful language to decline the offer.

In a quite different case, a buyer was willing to purchase a 100-year-old family business for $100 million, a premium valuation by any standard. The family insisted that it would never sell the business under any circumstances. Two years later, market conditions changed and the credit crunch transformed slow-paying customers into nonpaying customers. The business was forced into bankruptcy, which wiped out 100 years of family equity.

It is not difficult to think of a number of alternative outcomes for these two firms and many others like them, who have erroneously assumed that the business will go on forever. By stubbornly and steadfastly refusing to explore harvest options and exiting as a natural part of the entrepreneurial process, owners may actually increase their overall risk and deprive themselves of future options. Innumerable examples exist whereby entrepreneurs sold or merged their companies and then went on to acquire or start another company and pursued new dreams:

- Robin Wolaner founded *Parenting* magazine in the mid-1980s and sold it to Time-Life.[1] Wolaner then joined Time and built a highly successful career there, and in July 1992 she became the head of Time's Sunset Publishing Corporation.[2]
- Right after graduate school, brothers George and Gary Mueller launched a company George had started as an MBA student. That company grew rapidly and was sold in early 2000 for more than $50 million. About three years into the start-up, younger brother Gary decided he would pursue his own start-up. He left Securities Online on the best of terms and created ColorKinetics, Inc., in Boston. That company, by early 2003, had raised over $48 million of venture capital and would soon exceed $30 million in sales as the leading firm in LED lighting technology. These will not be either George or Gary's last start-ups, we predict.
- Craig Benson founded Cabletron in the 1980s, which became a highly successful company. Eventually he brought in a new CEO and became involved as a trustee of Babson College, and then began teaching entrepreneurship classes with a focus on information technology and the Internet. He was later elected governor of New Hampshire as another way of giving back to society and to pursue his new dreams.
- While in his early 20s, Steve Spinelli was recruited by his former college football coach, Jim Hindman (see the Jiffy Lube case series), to help start and build Jiffy Lube International. As a captain of the team, Steve had exhibited the qualities of leadership, tenacity, and competitive will to win that Hindman knew were needed to create a new company. Steve later built the largest franchise in America, and after selling his 49 stores to Pennzoil in 1993, he returned to his MBA alma mater to teach. So invigorated by this new challenge, he even went back to earn his doctorate. Steve then became director of the Arthur M. Blank Center for Entrepreneurship at Babson, first division chair of the very first full-fledged entrepreneurship division at any American university, and then vice provost. Steve is now president of Philadelphia University.
- After creating and building the ninth largest pharmaceutical company in the United States, Marion Laboratories, Ewing Marion Kauffman led an extraordinary life as a philanthropist and sportsman. His Kauffman Foundation and its Center for Entrepreneurial Leadership became the first and premier foundation in the nation dedicated to accelerating entrepreneurship. He brought the Kansas City Royals baseball team to that city and made sure it would stay there by giving the team to the city with the stipulation that it stay there when the team was sold. The $75 million proceeds of the sale were also donated to charitable causes in Kansas City.

---

[1] This example is drawn from "Parenting Magazine," Harvard Business School case 291–015.
[2] L. M. Fisher, "The Entrepreneur Employee," *New York Times*, August 2, 1992, p. 10.

- Jeff Parker built and sold two companies, including Technical Data Corporation,[3] by the time he was 40. His substantial gain from these ventures has led to a new career as a private investor who works closely with young entrepreneurs to help them build their companies.
- In mid-1987 George Knight, founder and president of Knight Publications,[4] was actively pursuing acquisitions to grow his company into a major force. Stunned by what he believed to be exceptionally high valuations for small companies in the industry, he concluded that this was the time to be a seller rather than a buyer. Therefore, in 1988 he sold Knight Publications to a larger firm, within which he could realize his ambition of contributing as a chief executive officer to the growth of a major company. Having turned around the troubled divisions of this major company, he is currently seeking a small company to acquire and to grow into a large company.

These are a tiny representation of the tens of thousands of entrepreneurs that build on their platforms of entrepreneurial success to pursue highly meaningful lives in philanthropy, public service, and community leadership. By realizing a harvest, such options become possible, yet the vast majority of entrepreneurs make these contributions to society while continuing to build their companies. This is one of the best-kept secrets in American culture: The public has little awareness and appreciation of just how common this pattern of generosity is of time, leadership, and money. One could fill a book with numerous other examples. The entrepreneurial process is endless.

A Harvest Goal: Value Realization

Having a harvest goal and crafting a strategy to achieve it are what separate successful entrepreneurs from the rest of the pack. Many entrepreneurs seek only to create a job and a living for themselves. It is quite different to grow a business that creates a living for many others, including employees and investors, by creating value that can result in a capital gain.

Setting a harvest goal achieves many purposes, not the least of which is helping an entrepreneur get after-tax cash out of an enterprise and enhancing substantially his or her net worth. Such a goal can also create high standards and a serious commitment to excellence over the course of developing the

business. It can provide, in addition, a motivating force and a strategic focus that does not sacrifice customers, employees, and value-added products and services just to maximize quarterly earnings.

There are other good reasons to set a harvest goal. The workload demanded by a harvest-oriented venture versus one in a venture that cannot achieve a harvest may actually be less and is probably no greater. Such a business may be less stressful than managing a business that is not oriented to harvest. Imagine the plight of the 46-year-old entrepreneur, with three children in college, whose business is overleveraged and on the brink of collapse. Contrast that frightful pressure with the position of the founder and major stockholder of another venture who, at the same age, sold his venture for $15 million. Further, the options open to the harvest-oriented entrepreneur seem to rise geometrically as investors, other entrepreneurs, bankers, and the marketplace respond. Remember the cliché that "success breeds success."

There is a very significant societal reason as well for seeking and building a venture worthy of a harvest. These are the ventures that provide enormous impact and value added in a variety of ways. These are the companies that contribute most disproportionately to technological and other innovations, to new jobs, to returns for investors, and to economic vibrancy.

Also, within the harvest process, the seeds of renewal and reinvestment are sown. Such a recycling of entrepreneurial talent and capital is at the very heart of our system of private responsibility for economic renewal and individual initiative. Entrepreneurial companies organize and manage for the long haul in ways to perpetuate the opportunity creation and recognition process and thereby to ensure economic regeneration, innovation, and renewal.

Thus a harvest goal is not just a goal of selling and leaving the company. Rather, it is a long-term goal to create real value added in a business. (It is true, however, that if real value added is not created, the business simply will not be worth much in the marketplace.)

Crafting a Harvest Strategy: Timing Is Vital

Consistently entrepreneurs avoid thinking about harvest issues. In a survey of the computer software industry between 1983 and 1986, Steven Holmberg found that 80 percent of the 100 companies surveyed had only an informal plan for harvesting. The rest of

[3] For TDC's business plan, see "Technical Data Corporation Business Plan," Harvard Business School case 283–973. Revised November 1987. For more about TDC's progress and harvest strategy, see "Technical Data Corporation," Harvard Business School case 283–072. Revised December 1987.
[4] For a detailed description of this process, see Harvard Business School case 289–027, revised February 1989.

the sample confirmed the avoidance of harvest plans by entrepreneurs—only 15 percent of the companies had a formal written strategy for harvest in their business plans, and the remaining 5 percent had a formal harvest plan written after the business plan.[5] When a company is launched, then struggles for survival and finally begins its ascent, the furthest thing from its founder's mind usually is selling out. Selling is often viewed by the entrepreneur as the equivalent of complete abandonment of his or her very own "baby."

Too often a founder does not consider selling until terror, in the form of the possibility of losing the whole company, is experienced. Usually this possibility comes unexpectedly: New technology threatens to leapfrog the current product line, a large competitor suddenly appears in a small market, or a major account is lost. A sense of panic then grips the founders and shareholders of the closely held firm, and the company is suddenly for sale—at the wrong time, for the wrong reasons, and thus for the wrong price. Selling at the right time, willingly, involves hitting one of the many strategic windows that entrepreneurs face.

Entrepreneurs find that harvesting is a nonissue until something begins to sprout, and again there is a vast distance between creating an existing revenue stream of an ongoing business and ground zero. Most entrepreneurs agree that securing customers and generating continuing sales revenue are much harder and take much longer than they could have imagined. Further, the ease with which those revenue estimates can be cast and manipulated on a spreadsheet belies the time and effort necessary to turn those projections into cash.

At some point, with a higher-potential venture, it becomes possible to realize the harvest. It is wiser to be selling as the strategic window is opening than as it is closing. Bernard Baruch's wisdom is as good as it gets on this matter. He has said, "I made all my money by selling too early." For example, a private candy company with $150 million in sales was not considering selling. After contemplating advice to sell early, the founders recognized a unique opportunity to harvest and sold the firm for 19 times earnings, an extremely high valuation. Another example is that of a cellular phone company that was launched and built from scratch and began operations in late 1987. Only 18 months after purchasing the original rights to build and operate the system, the founders decided to sell the company, even though the future looked extremely bright. They sold because the sellers' market they faced at the time had resulted in a premium valuation—30 percent higher on a per capita basis (the industry valuation norm) than that for any previous

cellular transaction to date. The harvest returned over 25 times the original capital in a year and a half. (The founders had not invested a dime of their own money.)

If the window is missed, disaster can strike. For example, at the same time as the harvests described previously were unfolding, another entrepreneur saw his real estate holdings rapidly appreciate to nearly $20 million, resulting in a personal net worth, on paper, of nearly $7 million. The entrepreneur used this equity to refinance and leverage existing properties (to more than 100 percent in some cases) to seize what he perceived as further prime opportunities. Following a change in federal tax law in 1986 and the stock market crash of 1987, there was a major softening of the real estate market in 1988. As a result, by early 1989, half of the entrepreneur's holdings were in bankruptcy, and the rest were in a highly precarious and vulnerable position. The prior equity in the properties had evaporated, leaving no collateral as increasing vacancies and lower rents per square foot turned a positive cash flow into a negative one.

This same pattern happened again in 2000–2003 after the dot-com bubble burst and the NASDAQ began to crash, losing 63 percent of its value from its high of over 5,000 to under 1,100. California's Silicon Valley was particularly hard hit by the rapid downturn. Technology and Internet entrepreneurs who had exercised their stock options when their company's stock was soaring in the $80 to $100 range, on the hope that such escalation would continue for a long time, faced a rude awakening. As the stock plummeted to single-digit prices, they still faced a huge capital gains tax on the difference between the cost of their options and the price at which their stock was acquired.

Shaping a harvest strategy is an enormously complicated and difficult task. Thus crafting such a strategy cannot begin too early. In 1989–1991 banking policies that curtailed credit and lending severely exacerbated the downturn following the October 1987 stock market crash. One casualty of this was a company we will call Cable TV. The value of the company in early 1989 exceeded $200 million. By mid-1990 this had dropped to below zero! The heavy debt overwhelmed the company. It took over five years of sweat, blood, tears, and rapid aging of the founder to eventually sell the company. The price: about one-quarter of the peak value of 1989.

This same pattern was common again in 2001 and 2002 as major companies declared bankruptcy in the wake of the dot-com and stock market crash, including luminaries such an Enron, Kmart, Global Crossing, and dozens of lesser known but larger telecommunications and networking-related companies. This

[5] S. R. Holmberg, "Value Creation and Capture: Entrepreneurship Harvest and IPO Strategies," in *Frontiers of Entrepreneurship Research: 1991*, ed. N. Churchill et al. (Babson Park, MA: Babson College, 1991), pp. 191–205.

is one history lesson that seems to repeat itself. While building a company is the ultimate goal, failure to preserve the harvest option, and utilize it when it is available, can be deadly.

In shaping a harvest strategy, some guidelines and cautions can help:

- *Patience:* As has been shown, several years are required to launch and build most successful companies; therefore patience can be valuable. A harvest strategy is more sensible if it allows for a time frame of at least 3 to 5 years and as long as 7 to 10 years. The other side of the patience coin is not to panic as a result of sudden events. Selling under duress is usually the worst of all worlds.

- *Realistic valuation:* If impatience is the enemy of an attractive harvest, then greed is its executioner. For example, an excellent small firm in New England, which was nearly 80 years old and run by the third generation of a line of successful family leaders, had attracted a number of prospective buyers and had obtained a bona fide offer for more than $25 million. The owners, however, had become convinced that this "great little company" was worth considerably more, and they held out. Before long there were no buyers, and market circumstances changed unfavorably. In addition, interest rates skyrocketed. Soon thereafter the company collapsed financially, ending up in bankruptcy. Greed was the executioner.

- *Outside advice:* It is difficult but worthwhile to find an advisor who can help craft a harvest strategy while the business is growing and, at the same time, maintain objectivity about its value and have the patience and skill to maximize it. A major problem seems to be that people who sell businesses, such as investment bankers or business brokers, are performing the same economic role and function as real estate brokers; in essence, their incentive is their commissions during a short time frame, usually a matter of months. However, an advisor who works with a lead entrepreneur for five years or more can help shape and implement a strategy for the whole business so that it is positioned to spot and respond to harvest opportunities when they appear.

Harvest Options

There are seven principal avenues by which a company can realize a harvest from the value it has created. Described on the next pages, these most commonly seem to occur in the order in which they are listed. No attempt is made here to do more than briefly describe each avenue because there are entire books written about each of these, including their legal, tax, and accounting intricacies.

Capital Cow

A "capital cow" is to the entrepreneur what a "cash cow" is to a large corporation. In essence, the high-margin profitable venture (the cow) throws off more cash for personal use (the milk) than most entrepreneurs have the time and uses or inclinations for spending. The result is a capital-rich and cash-rich company with enormous capacity for debt and reinvestment. Take, for instance, a health care–related venture that was started in the early 1970s that realized early success and went public. Several years later the founders decided to buy the company back from the public shareholders and to return it to its closely held status. Today the company has sales in excess of $100 million and generates extra capital of several million dollars each year. This capital cow has enabled its entrepreneurs to form entities to invest in several other higher-potential ventures, which included participation in the leveraged buyout of a $150 million sales division of a larger firm and in some venture capital deals. Sometimes the creation of a capital cow results in substantial real estate holdings by the entrepreneur, off the books of the original firm. This allows for greater flexibility in the distribution of cash flow and the later allocation of the wealth.

Employee Stock Ownership Plan

Employee stock ownership plans have become very popular among closely held companies as a valuation mechanism for stock for which there is no formal market. They are also vehicles through which founders can realize some liquidity from their stock by sales to the plan and other employees. And because an ESOP usually creates widespread ownership of stock among employees, it is viewed as a positive motivational device as well.

Management Buyout

Another avenue, called a management buyout (MBO), is one in which a founder can realize a gain from a business by selling it to existing partners or to other key managers in the business. If the business has both assets and a healthy cash flow, the financing can be arranged via banks, insurance companies, and financial institutions that do leveraged buyouts

(LBOs) and MBOs. Even if assets are thin, a healthy cash flow that can service the debt to fund the purchase price can convince lenders to do the MBO.

Usually the problem is that the managers who want to buy out the owners and remain to run the company do not have the capital. Unless the buyer has the cash up front—and this is rarely the case—such a sale can be very fragile, and full realization of a gain is questionable. MBOs typically require the seller to take a limited amount of cash up front and a note for the balance of the purchase price over several years. If the purchase price is linked to the future profitability of the business, the seller is totally dependent on the ability and integrity of the buyer. Further, the management, under such an arrangement, can lower the price by growing the business as fast as possible, spending on new products and people, and showing little profit along the way. In these cases it is often seen that after the marginally profitable business is sold at a bargain price, it is well positioned with excellent earnings in the next two or three years. The seller will end up on the short end of this type of deal.

Merger, Acquisition, and Strategic Alliance

Merging with a firm is still another way for a founder to realize a gain. For example, two founders who had developed high-quality training programs for the rapidly emerging personal computer industry consummated a merger with another company. These entrepreneurs had backgrounds in computers, rather than in marketing or general management, and the results of the company's first five years reflected this gap. Sales were under $500,000, based on custom programs and no marketing, and they had been unable to attract venture capital, even during the market of 2001–2002. The firm with which they merged was a $15 million company that had an excellent reputation for its management training programs, had a Fortune 1000 customer base, had repeat sales of 70 percent, and had requests from the field sales force for programs to train managers in the use of personal computers. The buyer obtained 80 percent of the shares of the smaller firm to consolidate the revenues and earnings from the merged company into its own financial statements, and the two founders of the smaller firm retained a 20 percent ownership in their firm. The two founders also obtained employment contracts, and the buyer provided nearly $1.5 million

of capital advances during the first year of the new business. Under a put arrangement, the founders will be able to realize a gain on their 20 percent of the company, depending on performance of the venture over the next few years.[6] The two founders now are reporting to the president of the parent firm, and one founder of the parent firm has taken a key executive position with the smaller company, an approach common for mergers between closely held firms.

In a strategic alliance, founders can attract badly needed capital, in substantial amounts, from a large company interested in their technologies. Such arrangements often can lead to complete buyouts of the founders downstream.

Outright Sale

Most advisors view outright sale as the ideal route to go because up-front cash is preferred over most stock, even though the latter can result in a tax-free exchange.[7] In a stock-for-stock exchange, the problem is the volatility and unpredictability of the stock price of the purchasing company. Many entrepreneurs have been left with a fraction of the original purchase price when the stock price of the buyer's company declined steadily. Often the acquiring company wants to lock key management into employment contracts for up to several years. Whether this makes sense depends on the goals and circumstances of the individual entrepreneur.

Public Offering

Probably the most sacred business cow of them all—other than the capital cow—is the notion of taking a company public.[8] The vision or fantasy of having one's venture listed on a stock exchange arouses passions of greed, glory, and greatness. For many would-be entrepreneurs, this aspiration is unquestioned and enormously appealing. Yet for all but a chosen few, taking a company public, and then living with it, may be far more time and trouble—and expense—than it is worth.

After the stock market crash of October 1987, the market for new issues of stock shrank to a fraction of the robust IPO market of 1986 and a fraction of those of 1983 and 1985, as well. The number of new issues and the volume of IPOs did not rebound; instead they declined between 1988 and 1991. Then in 1992 and into the beginning of 1993 the IPO window opened again. During this IPO frenzy, "small companies with

---

[6] This is an arrangement whereby the two founders can force (the put) the acquirer to purchase their 20 percent at a predetermined and negotiated price.

[7] See several relevant articles on selling a company in *Growing Concerns*, ed. D. E. Gumpert (New York: John Wiley & Sons, 1984), pp. 332–98.

[8] The Big Five accounting firms, such as Ernst & Young, publish information on deciding to take a firm public, as does NASDAQ. See also R. Salomon, "Second Thoughts on Going Live with Wall Street," *Harvard Business Review*, reprint no. 91309.

total assets under $500,000 issued more than 68 percent of all IPOs."[9] Previously small companies had not been as active in the IPO market. (Companies such as Lotus, Compaq, and Apple Computer do get unprecedented attention and fanfare, but these firms were truly exceptions.)[10] The SEC tried "to reduce issuing costs and registration and reporting burdens on small companies, and began by simplifying the registration process by adopting Form S-18, which applies to offerings of less than $7,500,000, and reduced disclosure requirements."[11] Similarly, Regulation D created exemptions from registration of up to $500,000 over a 12-month period.[12]

This cyclical pattern repeated itself again during the mid-1990s into 2002. As the dot-com, telecommunications, and networking explosion accelerated from 1995 to 2000, the IPO markets exploded as well. In June 1996, for instance, nearly 200 small companies had initial public offerings, and the pace remained very strong through 1999, even into the first two months of 2000. Once the NASDAQ began its collapse in March 2000, the IPO window virtually shut. In 2001 there were months when not a single IPO occurred, and for the year it was well under 100! Few signs of recovery were evident in 2002. The lesson is clear: Depending on the IPO market for a harvest is a highly cyclical strategy, which can cause both great joy and disappointment. Such is the reality of the stock markets. Exhibits 19.1 and 19.2 show this pattern vividly.

EXHIBIT 19.1

Number of Recent IPOs

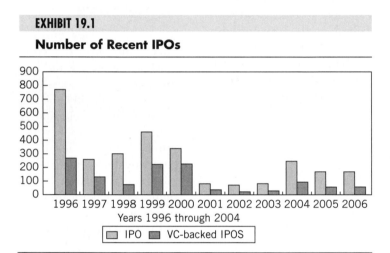

Source: Thomson Venture Economics/NVCA. Used by permission.

EXHIBIT 19.2

Recent IPOs ($millions)

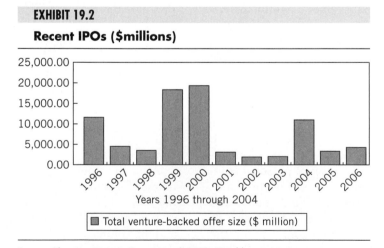

Source: Thomson Venture Economics/NVCA. Used by permission.

---

[9] S. Jones, M. B. Cohen, and V. V. Coppola, "Going Public," in *The Entrepreneurial Venture*, ed. W. A. Sahlman and H. H. Stevenson (Boston: Harvard Business School Publishing, 1992), p. 394.

[10] For an updated discussion of these issues, see C. Bagley and C. Dauchy, "Going Public," in *The Entrepreneurial Venture*, 2nd ed., ed. W. A. Sahlman and H. H. Stevenson (Boston: Harvard Business School Publishing, 1999), pp. 404–40.

[11] Jones et al., p. 395.

[12] Ibid.

There are several advantages to going public, many of which relate to the ability of the company to fund its rapid growth. Public equity markets provide access to long-term capital while also meeting subsequent capital needs. Companies may use the proceeds of an IPO to expand the business in the existing market or to move into a related market. The founders and initial investors might be seeking liquidity, but SEC restrictions limiting the timing and the amount of stock that the officers, directors, and insiders can dispose of in the public market are increasingly severe. As a result, it can take several years after an IPO before a liquid gain is possible. Additionally, as Jim Hindman (of Jiffy Lube) believed, a public offering not only increases public awareness of the company but also contributes to the marketability of the products, including franchises.

However, there are also some disadvantages to being a public company. For example, 50 percent of the computer software companies surveyed by Holmberg agreed that the focus on short-term profits and performance results was a negative attribute of being a public company.[13] Also, because of the disclosure requirements, public companies lose some of their operating confidentiality, not to mention having to support the ongoing costs of public disclosure, audits, and tax filings. With public shareholders, the management of the company has to be careful about the flow of information because of the risk of insider trading. Thus it is easy to see why companies need to think about the positive and negative attributes of being a public company.

Wealth-Building Vehicles

The 1986 Tax Reform Act severely limited the generous options previously available to build wealth within a private company through large deductible contributions to a retirement plan. To make matters worse, the administrative costs and paperwork necessary to comply with federal laws have become a nightmare. Nonetheless, there are still mechanisms that can enable an owner to contribute up to 25 percent of his or her salary to a retirement plan each year, an amount that is deductible to the company and grows tax free. Entrepreneurs who can contribute such amounts for just a short time will build significant wealth.

Beyond the Harvest

A majority of highly successful entrepreneurs seem to accept a responsibility to renew and perpetuate the system that has treated them so well. They are keenly aware that our unique American system of opportunity and mobility depends in large part on a self-renewal process.

There are many ways in which this happens. Some of the following data often surprise people:

- *College endowments:* Entrepreneurs are the most generous regarding larger gifts and the most frequent contributors to college endowments, scholarship funds, and the like. At Babson College, for example, one study showed that eight times as many entrepreneurs, compared to all other graduates, made large gifts to their colleges.[14] On college and university campuses across America, a huge number of dorms, classroom buildings, arts centers, and athletic facilities are named for contributors. In virtually every case, these contributors are entrepreneurs whose highly successful companies enabled them to make major gifts of stock to their alma mater. Earlier at MIT, more than half of the endowment was from gifts of founders' stock. Today that figure is probably even higher.

- *Community activities:* Entrepreneurs who have harvested their ventures often reinvest their leadership skills and money in such community activities as symphony orchestras, museums, and local colleges and universities. These entrepreneurs lead fund-raising campaigns, serve on boards of directors, and devote many hours to other volunteer work. One Swedish couple, after spending six months working with venture capital firms in Silicon Valley and New York, was "astounded at the extent to which these entrepreneurs and venture capitalists engage in such voluntary, civic activities." The couple found this pattern in sharp contrast to the Swedish pattern, where paid government employees perform many of the same services as part of their jobs.

- *Investing in new companies:* Postharvest entrepreneurs also reinvest their efforts and resources in the next generation of entrepreneurs and their opportunities. Successful entrepreneurs

---

[13] Holmberg, "Value Creation and Capture," p. 203.

[14] J. A. Hornaday, "Patterns of Annual Giving," in *Frontiers of Entrepreneurship Research: 1984,* ed. J. A. Hornaday et al. (Babson Park, MA: Babson College, 1984).

behave this way because they seem to know that perpetuating the system is far too important, and too fragile, to be left to anyone else. They have learned the hard lessons. As angel investors, experienced entrepreneurs are the key source of capital for start-up firms.

Innovation, job creation, and economic renewal and vibrancy are all results of the entrepreneurial process. Government does not cause this complicated and little understood process, though it facilitates and/or impedes it. It is not caused by the stroke of a legislative pen, though it can be ended by such a stroke. Rather, entrepreneurs, investors, and hardworking people in pursuit of opportunities create it.

Fortunately entrepreneurs seem to accept a disproportionate share of the responsibility to make sure the process is renewed. And judging by the new wave of entrepreneurship in the United States, both the marketplace and society once again are prepared to allocate rewards to entrepreneurs that are commensurate with their acceptance of responsibility and delivery of results.

The Road Ahead: Devise a Personal Entrepreneurial Strategy

Goals Matter—A Lot!

Of all the anchors one can think of in the entrepreneurial process, three loom above all the rest:

1. A passion for achieving goals.
2. A relentless competitive spirit and desire to win, and the will to never give up.
3. A high standard of personal ethics and integrity.

These three habits drive the quest for learning, personal growth, continuous improvement, and all other development. Without these good habits, most quests will fall short. Chapter 2 includes an exercise on Crafting a Personal Entrepreneurial Strategy. Completing this lengthy exercise will help you develop these good habits.

Values and Principles Matter—A Lot!

We have demonstrated, in numerous places throughout the book, that values and principles matter a great deal. We have encouraged you to consider those of Ewing M. Kauffman and to develop your own anchors. This is a vital part of your leadership approach, and who and what you are:

- Treat others as you would want to be treated.

- Share the wealth with the high performers who help you create it.
- Give back to the community and society.

We would add a fourth principle in the Native American spirit of considering every action with the seventh-generational impact foremost in mind:

- Be a guardian and a steward of the air, land, water, and environment.

One major legacy of the coming generations of entrepreneurial leaders can be the sustainability of our economic activities. It is possible to combine a passion for entrepreneurship with love of the land and the environment. The work of such organizations as the Conservation Fund of Arlington, Virginia, the Nature Conservancy, the Trust for Public Land, the Henry's Fork Foundation, the Monadnock Conservancy in New Hampshire, and dozens of others is financially made possible by the contributions of money, time, and leadership from highly successful entrepreneurs. It is also one of the most durable ways to give back. Practicing what he preaches, Professor Timmons and his wife recently made a permanent gift of nearly 500 acres of their New Hampshire farm to a conservation easement. Other neighbors joined in for a combined total of over 1,000 acres of land preserved forever, never to be developed. This has led to a regional movement that involves landowners from a dozen surrounding towns.

Seven Secrets of Success

The following seven secrets of success are included for your contemplation and amusement:

1. Happiness is a positive cash flow.
2. There are no secrets. Understanding and practicing the fundamentals discussed here, along with hard work, will get results.
3. As soon as there is a secret, everyone else knows about it, too. Searching for secrets is a pointless exercise.
4. If you teach a person to work for others, you feed him or her for a year; but if you teach a person to be an entrepreneur, you feed him or her, and others, for a lifetime.
5. Do not run out of cash.
6. Entrepreneurship is fundamentally a human process, rather than a financial or technological process. You can make an enormous difference.
7. Happiness is a positive cash flow.

Chapter Summary

- Entrepreneurs thrive on the challenges and satisfactions of the game: It is a journey, not a destination.
- First and foremost, successful entrepreneurs strive to build a great company: wealth follows that process.
- Harvest options mean more than simply selling the company, and these options are an important part of the entrepreneur's know-how.

- Entrepreneurs know that to perpetuate the system for future generations, they must give back to their communities and invest time and capital in the next entrepreneurial generation.

Study Questions

1. Why did Walt Disney say, "I don't make movies to make money. I make money to make movies"?
2. Why is it essential to focus first on building a great company, rather than on just getting rich?
3. Why is a harvest goal so crucial for entrepreneurs and the economy?
4. Define the principal harvest options, the pros and cons of each, and why each is valuable.
5. Beyond the harvest, what do entrepreneurs do to give back, and why is this so important to their communities and the nation?

Internet Resources for Chapter 19

http://www.main-usa.com *Minority Angel Investor Network (MAIN) is a network of accredited investors with an interest and commitment to invest in high-growth, minority-owned, or minority-led companies.*

http://www.investopedia.com *Articles, resources, and definitions for investors.*

http://www.philanthropyroundtable.org *The Philanthropy Roundtable is a national association of individual donors, foundation trustees and staff, and corporate giving officers.*

Books of Interest

Tom Ashbrook, *The Leap*
Randy Komisar, *The Monk and the Riddle*

Jerry Kaplan, *Startup*
Joel Shulman, *Getting Bigger by Growing Smaller*

MIND STRETCHERS

Have You Considered?

1. The Outdoor Scene company became the largest independent tent manufacturer in North America but eventually went out of business. The founder never realized a dime of capital gain. Why?
2. When Steve Pond sold his company in the late 1980s, he wrote checks for hundreds of thousands of dollars to several people who had left the company up to several years previously but who had been real contributors to the early success of the company. What are the future implications for Steve? For you?
3. Dorothy Stevenson, the first woman to earn a ham radio license in Utah, said, "Success is getting what you want. Happiness is wanting what you get." What does this mean? Why should you care?

Tear Out And Keep A Copy For Yourself

"Wisdom from the Harvest"

An Interview with a Harvested Entrepreneur

"Success is getting what you want. Happiness is wanting what you get!"
Dorothy Stevenson

At the beginning of the book we asked you to interview an entrepreneur who had built a company in the past 10 years or so into sales of $10 million or more. Now, in the spirit of Dorothy Stevenson's wisdom here, we suggest there is much to learn from engaging an entrepreneur at the other end of the life cycle of value creation and realization.

Tim Russert, the famed national journalist, in his recent book *Wisdom of Our Fathers*, captured wonderfully insightful and heartrending stories about relationships between children and their fathers. The book is based on tens of thousands of letters he received from these kids—now in their 30s to 50s—after they read his book *Big Russ and Me*, a chronicle about the love and wisdom gained from his own father. A third must-read book is Charlie Collier's *Wealth in Families*, noted earlier in this chapter. We highly recommend these books in general, and they will provide an excellent foundation for this exercise and interview as well.

Find a founder, aged 45 to 60+, who has a very substantial net worth realized from building and harvesting his or her company. As a guideline, if the company exceeded $50 million to $100 million in revenue, the odds are the firm would have been valued for a similar amount or more. Further, determine whether this entrepreneur has any intention of retiring; in all likelihood, he or she is involved in another venture, or even two or three, as a founder, cofounder, or angel investor who also serves as an advisor or director.

We find this pattern the rule rather than the exception. Take, for example, John Connolly. He founded Course Technology in Boston in the early 1990s. His company later achieved an IPO and became one of the first very successful learning technology companies. Then, in his mid-40s John acquired another company, MainSpring, for about $20 million; he turned it around, built it up, and sold it for over $600 million. Now 54 years old and financially able to retire and never work again, he made it clear in a recent conversation that this is the furthest thing from his mind. He put it this way: "I love building and starting companies and being a CEO. I don't think I'll ever retire!"

There are precious insights and lessons to gain from spending an hour or more over a cup of coffee or lunch with harvested entrepreneurs like John. Here are some questions to guide your conversation and for sharing what you have learned with classmates, friends, and family. We

urge you to pursue many such interviews along your own entrepreneurial journey.

1. Tell me about your company, your decision to sell/merge or take it public, and what you have been doing since, and why.

2. What were the most difficult conflicts, ethical dilemmas, and decisions you had to make along the way and in deciding to harvest?

3. What were the most challenging and rewarding aspects of balancing your marriage, family life, and the welfare of your associates and investors?

4. Were there any experiences and tribulations along the way that you were glad you did not know about in advance, or you might never have tried to start a company? How might that advice translate for me?

5. Some very ambitious entrepreneurs (perhaps blindly) are so consumed by winning and financial success that they abandon their personal integrity and reputation for ethical dealing. They seem to be able to rationalize their behavior, believing all the way to prison or the grave that they did nothing wrong—as we saw with Koslowski at Tyco and with Skilling and Delay at Enron. What advice and insights do you have from your observations of entrepreneurs who have maintained their reputation for integrity—and those who did not?

6. When you became very successful financially, how old were your children? How aware were they of your family's elite financial status? Did you talk about your family's wealth, family values, and philanthropy? What impact did this have on their beliefs and values, their expectations (cars, vacations, material things, etc.), and their motivation to work hard?

7. Were there any specific things you said or did with your children in their formative years to enable them to remain grounded, to give them a sense of frugality and a work ethic, and to leave them a legacy of ambition and giving back?

8. What have you seen as the best and the worst in how other successful entrepreneurs have handled these issues with their kids, and the outcomes? What did they—and you—want to preserve besides financial assets?

9. Tell me about the most inspiring and the most depressing wealthy families you know of (you don't

have to reveal any names) in dealing with the visibility, peer pressures, and circumstances the family faced growing up. What does each consider to be the family's true assets?

10. For someone like me who aspires to have my own venture(s) and become very successful, what are the most important advice, insights, and lessons you have for me?

11. Some entrepreneurs seem to achieve balance in their lives, have meaningful marriages, contribute to the community, and have children who are valuable additions to the family and the community. Others tell horror stories about wealthy entrepreneurs that include alcoholism and drug abuse (by the parents and eventually the children), affairs leading to failed marriages, little community involvement, and other sad tales that seem to negate most sensible notions of success. What have you seen in this regard, and what, in your experience, is the difference between these outcomes? What can a young entrepreneur do to emulate the former rather than the latter?

12. What made you decide *not* to retire and to continue to pursue more ventures? Tell me about the personal and psychological rewards this entails for you.

13. How wealthy do you want your kids and grandchildren to be, and why?

14. Are there any other things you'd like to share with me in the way of observations and advice that we have not talked about?

Finally, add any other questions you'd like here.

_____

_____

_____

_____

Summation and Sharing

Put together a one- to two-page summary of what you have found, the lessons and insights that you believe are most important, and any way you feel this will change your own goals and thinking. Share your results with classmates.

You will likely want to revisit these topics along the way in your own entrepreneurial career.

A Final Thought: What If the Money Is Gone?

What will your legacy be? What do you want to preserve besides financial assets? How do you want to be able to answer these questions when you are 50 or so, and what do you need to do about that now and in the future? (*Tip:* Read *Wealth in Families*.)

Case

Optitech

Preparation Questions

1. What strategic path should Jim Harris choose? What are the major issues influencing your opinion?
2. Discuss the process and methods used to value a privately held company.
3. Discuss the dilemmas, decisions, and future strategic choices Harris faces.
4. Evaluate the analysis presented by Shields and Company in Exhibits 1–7. What criteria would you use to evaluate and select an investment banker?

January 2008. Heading back up to Denver, Jim Harris taxied his Lear 35 out onto the small, dusty airstrip due east of Tucson. His other jet, a Lear 55, was earning its keep in Harris's new side business, aircraft charters, and it felt good to be back at the controls of this classic aircraft.

As he waited for clearance, Harris thought about Optitech, a business he'd been building for nearly 14 years—and one that had given him the means to pursue his love of flying. He was just as passionate about his company, and here he was in talks that could result in the sale of that venture. As lucrative as that move could be, Harris wanted to be sure that postharvest life would be as filled with fun and challenge as it was this moment.

Competitive Urges

Jim Harris attended the University of Colorado at Boulder, not too far from where he grew up in Denver. Like Mark Twain, he didn't let his classwork get in the way of his schooling; in Harris's case, that meant athletics. His father Bill, an accomplished businessman, was a bit concerned about his son's grade point average but not too worried about Jim's long-term prospects:

> Jim has always been supercompetitive, and athletics were a major factor in his background. When he was 18, he won the state championship in cross-country against guys who probably should have beaten him. But Jim was getting up at five in the morning to train and working out twice a day. He ended up blowing the field away. It was pretty clear that whatever he got into he was going to give it 110 percent.

When Harris graduated in 1993 with a history and political science degree, he followed his girlfriend Karen to San Diego. She had a job, and he had a plan:

> I wanted to try to make a living as a professional triathlete. It didn't take long for me to realize that that wasn't

going to happen. I was out of money, so I decided to move back home to Denver. Karen stayed in San Diego, but we stayed in touch.

Before long Harris found work in sales with a supplier of remanufactured laser jet toner cartridges. He enjoyed the challenge; but after just three months, the New York–based company closed its Denver office. His boss offered him a position in a similar start-up, but Harris was keen to lead his own charge:

> I was living at home, with few bills other than my car and gas. My parents lent me $8,500, and I started selling remanufactured toner cartridges out of my car. I had no clue at all about what I was doing. This wasn't something I gave too much thought to; I just went out and did it. I just don't analyze things too much; if I get a gut feel, I just go with it. I figured that if it didn't work out, I'd go do something else. But this was definitely a business I thought I could make some money at.

Getting in the Game

In 1994 the $2.2 billion aftermarket for printer cartridges was dominated by nearly 6,000 small, local sales and fulfillment operations. The proliferation of printer designs and toner cartridge configurations was under way, and remanufacturers were competing largely on the basis of product compatibility and functionality. Harris explained that by the time he started up his company, Optitech, a doctrine had begun to take hold regarding the proper way to refurbish a laser jet toner cartridge:[1]

> The heart of the cartridge, the photo-optic drum, has to be replaced, along with the silicone wiper blade and the developer roller and magnetic roller sleeve. The primary corona wire (which is the heat source) would either be replaced or professionally cleaned, and the waste toner bin had to be vacuumed out. A high-density toner mixture was then poured into the toner hopper, and the unit was sealed and packaged for resale. This process took around 30 minutes per cartridge, and it gave customers the same quality and number of prints as first-run cartridges but at a much lower price.

As was the case with many other start-up vendors of remanufactured cartridges, Harris sourced ready-for-sale inventory and set up shop in his garage. To bring his business to life, Harris opened up the telephone

[1] An early method of remanufacturing involved refilling units through a hole drilled in the side. These "drill and fill" operations could turn around units quickly, but their products often failed when low-grade toner mixed with shards of plastic left from the drilling.

book and applied a telemarketing formula he'd learned on the job:

> I was targeting area businesses that were likely to have a high print volume, like hospitals and legal and accounting firms. These were not huge companies, and at the time there was not a lot of competition for their business. From working at the other company I knew this was a numbers game; if I set 15 appointments a week, I could expect to sell one out of three of those. It took a lot of discipline and hundreds of calls just to get started. I was on the phone several hours a day, five days a week—mostly seven days.
>
> One of the main challenges in this industry that never goes away is that most big companies bundle their office supply purchases and order everything from one vendor. Trying to convince purchasing managers that it is worth it to pull the toner out of that one-stop-shop order is often a tough sell. It means more work on their part because they need to create a separate order category. . . . Even getting them to calculate what they are currently paying for toners can be difficult.
>
> I will say that all the rejection was awful, and I tried to use my discipline from triathlons to block that negativity out of my mind. I also felt that when some of the better prospects didn't actually say no, that represented a light at the end of the tunnel. If I could just get one or two of those accounts to come on board, I knew it was going to get a lot easier.

Jim's mom Charlotte commented on those early days:

> Jim was at it for months. We're a family that connects over dinner, and we talked a lot about how hard this business was to get off the ground. The problem was that although he was making what seemed like lots of sales, these were mostly smaller businesses that just weren't using that many printer cartridges.

Harris knew that the only way he was going to build a sustainable base of recurring revenue was to land a few large accounts. Organizations like that, he learned, had deep and wide bureaucracies that could take up to two years to make a decision—and required big account references Harris wouldn't have until he landed a few. On the plus side, due to margins in the range of 25 to 30 percent (and low overhead), Harris was able to turn a small profit almost from day one. By the summer Harris had built monthly revenues to around $12,000. Still, he knew he'd have to do a lot better than that if he was going to grow out of his parents' garage.

Just when he'd begun to explore the idea of factoring his meager receivables as a way to free up some additional capital, he scored:

> I had been talking to a VA hospital here in Denver for a long time. Hospitals place large orders at the end of every fiscal year, and in September they gave me a purchase order for $118,000. That was huge in two ways. It gave me a base of working capital, and that sale got me a foot in the door to the health care industry.

Relentless Dissatisfaction

To capture more value, in late 1995 Harris set up his own remanufacturing operation using empty cartridges (blanks) sourced from third parties.[2] Over the next couple of years, Optitech built up a wide range of end user clients—from sole proprietorships to large-volume firms—and began to earn a reputation for quality products and highly responsive customer service.

Unlike many of his competitors, Harris maintained a flat, simple structure as his business grew. His accountant was "a local guy" who worked out of his home; the Optitech plant was a no-frills space in a low-rent section of town. Harris noted that his drive to keep costs down did not include his most important asset:

> By running a lean operation, we are able to treat our employees very well. Their pay and benefit packages have always been among the best in the industry. That has given us a very low turnover and a culture that goes the extra mile to service our customers.

In 1996 Karen had moved back from California and found similar work in Denver. The following spring she and Jim were married. Karen recalled that settling into that life took some doing:

> Sometimes it seemed crazy how many hours Jim was putting into the business. Sure, it's about building a great company, but for Jim it's always been more than that. Most people out there will go in, do their job, and go home. That's not Jim. He just has this relentless dissatisfaction with the way things are. That's all great, but I have to say that being married to an entrepreneur like Jim can be pretty tough at times.

By the late 1990s Optitech had monthly sales of approximately $800,000. Jim's father, who had continued to offer advice and encouragement from the sidelines, commented on Jim's path to profits:

> One of the things that helped Jim out a lot was that he concentrated on selling to end users. All of Optitech's biggest competitors are wholesalers because in many ways selling and managing retail accounts as Jim does is a more difficult business to build and operate. But that high-service business has given Jim an extra layer of margin to work with relative to the competition.
>
> I thought it was great that he was building a lean and profitable organization, but I was starting to feel that the company could use a bit more structure. Jim was accustomed to doing whatever it took to get and keep accounts, so he didn't have much in the way of an executive-level team. He had hired some really good workers, but this was still very much Jim's operation.

---

[2] Remanufacturers generally considered empties management to be a noncore and nondifferentiating activity. Therefore, many large-scale remanufacturing companies relied on vendors to collect, inspect, sort, and store their empty cartridges, buying only those cartridges required for production demand.

Big Win

By the early 2000s office supply superstores had begun to stock remanufactured toner cartridges. In February 2004 Harris learned that All Office Supply (AOS), a national superstore, was taking bids from toner remanufacturers. He approached with caution:

> At first I wasn't excited about the idea. All Office Supply had a reputation for being a tough company to work with; the last two private-brand sellers that had signed up with AOS had gone bankrupt. Wholesale is a low-margin, volume business, which is completely different than what we were doing. But one thing led to another, and we ended up being one of 12 companies that AOS decided to consider.

With annual sales of $15 million, Optitech was by far the smallest company in the running. Harris and his managers put together a proposal and made some presentations at the AOS offices in Dallas. After AOS executives toured the modest but well-run plant in Denver, Harris got word that they'd made the final cut. With the prize in sight, Harris's competitive nature kicked in:

> Nobody was going to offer consignment because the slim margins didn't allow any room for error. So I took a chance by offering that on a few models. It wasn't a very good deal for us at all. I was just trying to get our foot in the door—and after that I would figure out how to maneuver where we could make money at it.

After 15 months of meetings and presentations as far away as Munich, Optitech was awarded a five-year contract with a three-year renewal option. In May 2005 Optitech purchased a 55,000-square-foot wholesale facility in Tucson, Arizona, a city where he and Karen had a home for long weekends and getaways.[3] The new operation started up with a manager and eight employees who, like Harris, were willing to do whatever it took to keep and build the AOS account. Harris recalled that it was even more difficult than he'd imagined it would be:

> We had made a good deal of money going into this deal, so I thought we'd have a pretty good buffer. Equipment-wise we put in about $2.5 million, which was a lot for us. We were used to getting paid in 20 days. When we

started shipping product [in November 2005] AOS was stretching us to 140 days. By early 2006 we were holding over $12 million in receivables out for AOS alone.

> It was a huge and risky undertaking, and there were times when we were in bad shape. We had to pull a line of credit out of Merrill Lynch, and we put all of the cash we were making from the retail side into supporting this deal. Two years earlier we wouldn't have had enough money to pull it off, and as it was, there were at least six months where it was really uncertain whether we would continue to do it. Building the retail side was a piece of cake compared to this, and that was a lot of hard work. It's been the best learning experience I've ever had in my life.

Optitech persevered, and by early summer AOS was paying in 70 days (standard with superstores) and accepting product without consignment.[4] Within a year the Optitech plant in Tucson was operating at full capacity with 40 employees. Seeing an area where he could add significant value, Bill Harris joined his son's company to help source Asian suppliers:

> Going to China for parts and finished product requires substantial volume to get the kind of prices that they can offer. We knew the AOS deal would give us the means to attract some highly credible suppliers, but we were also aware of some of the horror stories about getting into China, including quality that was nothing like the level of the samples they would send, complicated paperwork, delivered inventory counts that were way off, and shipments often delayed for weeks. It said to us, If we do this, we have to approach it in the right way.

> We knew we had to have somebody on site in China who could check on quality and shipments. We didn't have anybody in mind, but my brother-in-law suggested a gentleman in Taiwan whom he'd done business with off and on for 25 years. His name is Vincent Ma: very honest and hardworking—sleeps maybe three or four hours a night . . .

Vincent accompanied the Optitech team to a major industry trade show in Taiwan. He helped with translations, took copious notes, and followed up with potential suppliers. After Vincent was satisfied with five suppliers, the team toured those plants and, again with Vincent's help, negotiated contracts with the owners. For a 1.42 percent commission on all the products Optitech ordered from China, Vincent Ma would handle the stringent export documentation and inspect every shipment for quality and inventory counts. Although this complex supply chain wasn't perfect, Bill Harris said that going offshore had been a significant win for the entire company:

> The quality has been excellent. Most of the owners of these plants are young and entrepreneurial—in their middle to late 40s. We have been bowled over by how good and responsive they are. When we've had a problem, they've

---

[3] As an experienced pilot and owner of a pair of Learjets for both business and pleasure, Harris almost never used commercial airlines when traveling within the continental United States. Harris discussed the economics: "I paid $1.8 million for the first plane and put $300K into it, and I have about $3.5 million into the second jet. Using a charter service, I generate $80,000 a month in revenue, plus a 20 percent depreciation write-off on the $5.7 million for both planes. So now I can fly about 20 hours a month at no cost because the charter program and write-off are covering those expenses. Not only is it working out as a good investment, but I can get to a bunch of locations quickly. For example, on Tuesday I'm going on a two-day trip to visit current and potential customers in Birmingham (AL), Dallas, Oakland, Los Angeles, Las Vegas, and Tucson. Can you imagine trying to do that using commercial airlines?"

[4] By mid-2006 Optitech had worked out a deal with a bank in Denver that effectively cut the AOS payment terms to 25 days, minus a small discount.

jumped on it right away. Right now we are dealing with shipping delays of as much as three weeks, but that is being addressed. The key is having an honest and intelligent and hardworking individual in Taiwan who is there for us.

This has helped us tremendously with AOS, and the cost advantages have spilled over to the retail side of the business. Big-box stores are getting more and more powerful, so we are planning retail stores that will help us continue to go direct to big end users. . . . If we don't, eventually we will get cut out of that business.

By mid-2006 annual sales to AOS were approaching $30 million.[5] Optitech was now a well-positioned company with industry-leading levels of profitability. The enterprise had 200 employees, production facilities in Tucson and Denver, and regional sales offices in Denver, Kansas City, and Los Angeles. Although the Tucson plant and Chinese supply chain put Optitech in a good position to close its original remanufacturing operation in Denver, Harris wasn't about to do that:

> The Denver factory is pieced together and not very well laid out. It should all be in Tucson. I could shut it down and literally save $300,000 a year. At the end of the day, it's about being loyal to the people who have taken care of me over the years.

OEMs on the Offense

As the industry matured, original equipment manufacturers (OEMs) began to look for ways to interrupt the flow of their branded empties to "profiteering" remanufacturers. One tactic involved the use of smart chips, also known as killer chips. Touted as an end user feature that tracked printer functions and prints remaining, chip-enabled cartridges were useless as blanks because the imbedded chips couldn't be reset. For a while this disruptive technology made life difficult for consumers who refilled their own cartridges, and it posed a significant challenge for recyclers and remanufacturers. Although compatible replacement chips were soon widely available in the remanufacturing sector, these added to the cost of the finished product.

Seeking a more sustainable pushback, OEMs, including Canon, Epson, HP, Lexmark, Ricoh, and Xerox, had begun to sue remanufacturers for patent infringement.[6] Harris said that this was the beginning of what could become a major struggle:

> These big players have a lot of money, and they are making billions of dollars a year from this product as a

consumable. The aftermarket business accounts for 20 to 25 percent market share. . . . That's a ton of money in what is now an $80 billion industry.

Epson just got a ruling for a general exclusion for products in violation of their patents. That's pretty much all of the compatible Epsons that we sell. It's not a huge percentage of our sales—less than $2 million of $45 million, but it is a profitable part of our business.

The ruling does not cover older-model blanks, and we already have an inside line with a major broker in the United States to tie up and ship 150,000 Epson empties to China for remanufacturing. Dozens of third-party supplier firms have been named in infringement suits like this; so far we've been under the radar.

Harris and his team took some comfort in the idea that because Epson did a significant volume of sales with AOS, they might not push too hard—even if Optitech did appear on their radar. George Arnold, Harris's longtime broker at Merrill Lynch, noted that the OEMs weren't the only challenge Optitech was facing:

> Things have changed a lot since Jim started, and in many ways it's a lot tougher space to be in. In the last couple of years, 30 percent of the competition has gone out of business because they weren't doing the quantities to stay price competitive.
>
> Staples is now into remanufacturing, and Cartridge World is offering a refill program.[7] All of this is pushing prices down further, increasing the competition for blanks, and giving Optitech's best retail clients more options for buying toner cartridges.

Because Harris very much enjoyed the business he was building, and the people he had hired to grow with him, it took a few calls from Arnold before Harris warmed to the idea of engaging the services of an investment banking firm that Arnold felt was well suited to the task.

Assessing the Possibilities

Founded in 1991, Boston-based Shields and Company provided investment banking services to private and public companies.[8] Harris's broker had sensed a particularly good match because Shields and Company had worked extensively with entrepreneurs and closely held ventures. There was also an experience factor: When Managing Director Timothy White had worked in the technology group for Barclays Global Investors banking division, he

[5] Remanufactured toner cartridges were a $120 million category for All Office Supply. A second supplier made up the difference.
[6] Intellectual property (IP) cases were being heard in high-level courts around the world. The U.S. Supreme Court ruled against Independent Ink; an IP case reached the High Court, Japan; and Epson and HP fielded complaints with the U.S. International Trade Commission as well as in U.S. federal courts.
[7] Harris said it was unlikely that All Office Supply would be going direct anytime soon: Four years ago AOS tried to do business in China and fell flat on its face. It is not easy to do if you are a big company. You need to be fairly quick on your feet, and it takes some learning.
[8] Investment banking services included exclusive sale and acquisition assignments; debt and equity capital raising; recapitalizations and other financial transactions; fairness opinions; and business, intangible assets, and securities valuations.

EXHIBIT 1

Industry Overview

The industry has been in a constant state of change for the past several years.

- Market is mature and increasingly aware of remanufacturing as an option.
- Educated end users continue to change the marketplace.
- Trends toward global sourcing are continuing.
- Uncertainty of availability of supplies (blanks) is a continuing issue.
- Increasingly complex links and quality demands.
- Cartridge World and retailers offering refill programs are a concern.

Larger, vertically integrated OEMs are getting increasingly aggressive.

- Xerox selling drums and bulk toner.
- Pitney Bowes penetrating the market through acquisition.
- Most OEMs have been involved in one or more lawsuits.

New OEM strategies, tactics, and tends are emerging.

- Smart chips (examples: Canon's *war chip* and Lexmark's *killer chip*).
- Mechanical vs. chemical solutions.
- Licensing remanufactures: Is this the future?

The investment community is showing more aggressive interest in the consumables market.

- PE friendly business model; low CapEx, scalable, fragmented.
- Public markets have been less favorable, due in part to weaker performance of several players, such as Adsero, American Toner Serve, and Danka.
- Global Imaging Systems has been rewarded by the markets for its consolidation strategy.

Source: Shields and Company, Boston, Massachusetts.

EXHIBIT 2

Income Statement and Forecast

($ in thousands)	Fiscal Year Ended December 31,				Shields Forecast Fiscal
	2003	**2004**	**2005**	**2006**	**2007**
Revenue	$11,960	$13,816	$20,471	$33,699	$50,000
Cost of sales	8,248	9,582	15,066	25,173	37,500
Gross profit	3,712	4,234	5,405	8,526	12,500
Officers' compensation	195	219	200	200	200
Operating expense	1,874	1,394	1,788	2,958	4,000
Depreciation	3	–	–	–	–
Operating income	$1,640	$2,621	$3,417	$5,368	$8,300
Calculation of EBITDA:					
Operating income	$1,640	$2,621	$3,417	$5,368	$8,300
Plus: Depreciation and amortization	3	–	–	–	–
EBITDA	$1,643	$2,621	$3,417	$5,368	$8,300
Sales growth	NA	15.5%	48.2%	NA	144.2%
As a percentage of revenue:					
Gross profit	31.0%	30.6%	26.4%	25.3%	25.0%
Operating expense	15.7%	10.1%	8.7%	8.8%	8.0%
EBITDA	13.7%	19.0%	16.7%	15.9%	16.6%

Source: Optitech management and Shields and Company.

EXHIBIT 3

Balance Sheet: June 2007

($ in thousands)	As of June 30, 2007		
Assets		**Liabilities and Stockholder's Equity**	
Current assets:		Current liabilities:	
Cash and cash equivalents	$ 191	Line of credit	$ 655
Accounts receivable, net	9,768	Accounts payable–trade	7,311
Inventory	730	Accounts payable—other	8
Deposits	2	*Total current liabilities*	7,974
Total current assets	10,691	Long-term liabilities	—
Fixed assets, net	641	*Total liabilities*	7,974
Other assets	—	Stockholder's equity	3,358
Total assets	**$11,332**	**Total liabilities and stockholder's equity**	**$11,332**

Source: Optitech management.

had been involved in IBM's spinoff of Lexmark, now an industry heavyweight.

In early 2007 White and two associates met with Harris in Denver.[9] They toured the Optitech facility and collected additional data that would assist them in developing an assessment of the possibilities. They offered their assessment of the industry (see Exhibit 1) and worked up a financial snapshot that included an estimated fiscal 2007 EBITDA of $8.3 million on sales of $50 million (see Exhibits 2 and 3). Although the Shields team was very impressed with Optitech's performance and profitability, White noted that Harris's rather loose approach to building Optitech had created some issues:

Jim has built a great enterprise, but it lacks structure. They've got to hire a national sales manager and a quality engineer to manage and develop documentation on that side of the operation. Our biggest frustration was with the finance and accounting; they were going to have to get a better handle on the numbers.

Our other major concern was their heavy dependence on AOS, especially because there are three or four good-sized competitors that would love to get that business. They are constantly knocking on All Office Supply's door, and Optitech is doing somersaults to keep AOS happy.

Two weeks after a follow-up visit to the Tucson plant, the Shields team presented their assessment of the

opportunity, including strengths and risks (see Exhibit 4), and a discussion of the four strategic alternatives they saw for Optitech: status quo, acquisitions, strategic sale, and equity recapitalization (see Exhibit 5). Harris felt that two of the four were worth pursuing:

Status quo wasn't going to work because in this industry if you're not growing you're shrinking. We didn't have much interest in going public or bringing in minority interests for an equity recapitalization. That was a way to get some money off the table, but I was already making plenty of money, and I didn't really want additional shareholders.

Based on their valuation methods (see Exhibit 6) and comparables (see Exhibit 7), Shields and Company came up with a potential value of around $60 million. That was a big surprise, and it got me thinking a lot about the other two options they talked about—especially using our profitable base to grow by acquisition.

Such a strategy was in line with Harris's goal to aggressively build up the retail side of the business to balance out the wholesale account with AOS. He explained how he'd do that:

I've talked with Shields and Company about maybe doing some B2B [business to business] acquisitions of remanufacturers with retail sales of around $5 million—not nearly enough volume to buy direct from China. If we rolled four or five of those up into our business, we could build a $150 million business and increase our overall margin a good 20 percent. We think we'd get our money back [from those investments] in 18 to 24 months and have a very profitable and balanced company.

In the midst of planning to take the company in this direction, Shields and Company suddenly came up with a new possibility.

[9] Engaging the services of investment bankers began with meetings and due diligence to determine whether there was a mutual interest in moving forward. The investment banker would produce a prospectus outlining the nature of the challenges and opportunities facing the client, as well as scenarios and valuations based on a range of methodologies. In this case, Shields and Company would charge a retainer fee of $84,000, paid monthly. That fee was absorbed by their fee upon sale: 2 percent up to $50 million plus 1 percent of anything over $50 million.

EXHIBIT 4

Preliminary Discussion of Investment Considerations

Positive Factors	Risks That Need to Be Mitigated
Remarkable revenue growth trend.	Industry is becoming increasingly competitive. Hardware OEMs are litigious, and imports are a threat. How will Optitech drive continued growth at current levels?
Industry-leading levels of profitability.	Growth in big-box channel and imports create pressure on margins. Higher-margin customer programs need to be protected.
Strong balance sheet with capacity to support organic or external growth.	Growth with All Office Supply and larger entities will place pressure on working capital. Need to understand and position management's ability to operate in a leveraged environment.
Young but experienced management.	Lean organization supported by Harris's energy and experience. Could current infrastructure support the company under a range of future scenarios?
Opportunities for continued organic or external expansion.	Organic growth will require investment in sales and marketing infrastructure. Growth through acquisition will require investment in management and financial infrastructure.
Favorable trends in consumables usage.	Although more cartridges are being used, the current lawsuits will be a negative factor with banks and/or investors. Need to watch pending rulings with Lexmark carefully.
Consistant investment in R&D and technology.	Although it is clear that Optitech has made substantial investments in capacity, "smart chip" technologies appear to be here to stay, and technology spend will only be increasing.
Excellent customer reputation.	Increased retail competition (Cartridge World, Staples) could disrupt relationships. More educated consumers help remanufactures but create more price sensitivity.
Low capital requirements.	Ongoing growth can be supported through imports from Asia requiring little capital expenditure; but this also lowers competitive barriers to entry.

Source: Shields and Company.

The Exit Option

Harris and his team had been in contact with Shields and Company for about seven months when the investment banker came across a $2 billion private equity firm in St. Louis that was showing interest in the toner industry. In the previous year, Talcott Equity Partners had done some acquisitions in that space, and Shields spotted an opportunity. Harris was intrigued:

> Andrew Fields is a guy who used to work for the largest aftermarket supply company in the world, which is where we bought all of our toner drums. So we had a good relationship with them for a long time, and Andrew was real familiar with us. Andrew's job [at Talcott] was to go out and find companies to buy [in the industry].

Andrew Fields explained what he had in mind:

> We are looking at building a business to $400 million revenue from about four to five acquisitions: a roll-up strategy to an IPO that will max out the value. Optitech is a strategic buy because they are selling B2B retail as well as to superstores. The All Office Supply percentage of their business is fine with us because the roll-up will dilute that dependence. They've also got some minor issues like outmoded facilities, especially in Denver, and some challenges on the accounting end.

Harris discussed the conversation:

> In the roll-up, everything we have in the way of accounting and financial reports will have to comply with Sarbanes-Oxley.[10] We've had a firm working on that for the last four months. And it is pretty accurate from what they are telling us.
>
> Talcott would definitely shut down the Denver facility and put it all into one. There would be a lot of job loss. I have some key people in this company, and it has to be a good deal for everyone involved. There are people who really helped me get to this point, and I obviously want to make sure they are taken care of. It sounds like a good fit, though.
>
> They're talking between $40 million and $50 million, but because we'd have no control over the stock, we're going to push for at least 75 percent up front in cash. There are not a lot of companies out there our size making this kind of money, so I think we are in a good [bargaining] position for that.

As the early-stage talks progressed, Talcott indicated that they would present two separate deal structures based on whether Harris would be willing to stay at the helm of his acquired company—and for how long. Harris, realizing he'd never worked for anyone before, had a lot to consider.

[10] Due to the requirements of the Sarbanes-Oxley Act, companies required more control of what they were outsourcing, and senior management had to be more closely and directly involved in making sure their company conformed to expected standards of care and good practices, many of which had been codified in industry or regulatory papers.

EXHIBIT 5

Strategic Alternatives

Key Scenario Considerations

- Liquidity goals and risk/return profiles of shareholders.
- Projected company performance and corresponding business risk associated with projections.
- Ongoing roles and involvement of current management.
- Transaction due diligence consideration, including litigation, environmental, management.
- Market timing: current M&A and capital market conditions and corresponding market risk in future periods.
- Size and growth potential of toner cartridge manufacturing industry.

Option A: Status Quo—Maintain Private Company Structure

Benefits	Disadvantages
Maintain control of operations.	Lack of significant liquidity for shareholders.
Continuity for management.	Increased liability exposure for officers.
Ability to dividend funds to shareholders.	Competition from large growing companies.
Pursue continued growth strategy.	Potential capital constraints for growth.
	Management succession issues.

Option B: Growth through Acquisition Strategy

Benefits	Disadvantages
Provides immediate growth.	Integration risk.
Increased market share.	Realization of synergies.
Greater purchasing power and other synergies.	Finding the right target(s) at the right price.
Could generate substantial future value.	Managing additional leverage.
	More eggs in the same basket.

Option C: Strategic Sale of the Company

Benefits	Disadvantages
Significant liquidity to all shareholders.	Few large industry players.
Potentially partnering with larger entity.	Lack of control to manage and run company.
Capitalizing on current strength in the M&A and capital markets.	Management and employees may or may not stay on following the transaction.
Potential synergies may increase sale value.	Exposure to industry competition from sharing confidential information. Limited ability to benefit from future growth in the business.

Source: Shields and Company.

Life Choices

As he dipped one wing of his sleek jet toward the desert below in a graceful arc that set him on course for the Rocky Mountains, Harris recalled what he'd told his parents last week over dinner:

> If I sell the company, I'll have the money to do whatever I want to do; but what would I do? I've been enjoying this for 13 years. Part of me would love to keep it all together and grow by acquisition; but then I think, How much energy do I really have to get this to $150 million in sales?

At 36 Harris was at a fruitful fork in the road. With a recession looming in the wake of the falling dollar and the subprime mortgage mess, he knew it would be all the more difficult to grow his business exponentially. Still, Harris had spent all but a few months since college building this great enterprise—a success he was quick to attribute to family support and his loyal and hardworking employees. As the deal with the private equity firm moved into the go/no go phase, Harris knew it was time to make some major life decisions.

EXHIBIT 6

Methodologies and Valuation

Methodology	Description
Guideline company analysis	Publicly traded guideline companies whose operations are similar to those of the subject company demonstrate relative minority interest positions being accorded by the investing public to earnings, book values, and revenues of such businesses.
Precedent transaction analysis	Publicly disclosed data from arm's-length transactions involving similar companies demonstrate relationships or value measures between the price paid for target company and the underlying financial performance of that company.
Specific company accretion/dilution analysis	Maximum value that a specifically identified buyer can pay for a target without having the aquisition be dilutive to its unadjusted pro forma earnings per share.
Discounted cash flow/leveraged buyout analysis	The fair market value of the subject company is derived by assuming returns on invested equity based on Optitech's future cash flows and the availability of debt capital.

Preliminary Valuation Analysis

	Median Multiples	Optitech Estimated Financials	Implied Enterprise Value	Less: Debt Net of Cash	Implied Equity Value
Comparable company analysis					
Enterprise value / 2006 net sales	0.8x	$50,000	$40,000	—	$40,000
Enterprise value / 2006 EBITDA	8.7x	$8,300	$72,210	—	$72,210
Recent M&A transaction analysis					
Enterprise value / 2006 net sales	1.0x	$50,000	$50,000	—	$50,000
Enterprise value / 2006 EBITDA	7.5x	$8,300	$62,250	—	$62,250
Shields and Company recent private equity recapitalizations					
Enterprise value / 2006 EBITDA	8.0x	$8,300	$66,400	—	$66,400

Source: Based on Shields and Company financial estimates and recapitalization processes.

EXHIBIT 7

Valuation Multiples

($ in millions)

Consumables Industry Participants	Ticker Symbol	Total Enterprise Value	Revenue	Gross Profit	EBITDA	EBIT	LTM Revenue	LTM EBITDA	Book Value	Net Income
			Latest 12 Months as of March 21, 2007				Total Enterprise Value		Market Cap	
Adsero Corp.	OTCPK: ADSO	$19.9	$27.3	$4.1	($4.6)	($6.7)	0.7x	NM*	NM	NM
American Toner-Serv Corp.	OTCBB: SSVP	$9.6	$0.4	$0.2	($0.4)	($0.4)	23.8x	NM	NM	NM
Astro-Med Inc.	NasdaqNM: ALOT	$58.3	$64.0	$26.6	$5.2	$3.9	0.9x	11.2x	1.8x	13.0x
Color Imaging Inc.	OTCPK: CHG	$9.1	$20.9	$6.0	$1.0	$0.4	0.4x	8.7x	0.6x	30.9x
Danka Business Systems plc	NasdaqSC: DANK.Y	$638.8	$1,017.4	$323.0	$2.2	($1.8)	0.6x	28.8x	5.5x	NM
Global Imaging Systems Inc.	NasdaqNM: GISX	$1,182.0	$1,096.8	$429.2	$142.1	$123.6	1.1x	8.3x	1.9x	14.7x
Ingram Micro Inc.	NYSE: IM	$3,477.2	$31,357.5	$1,685.3	$510.8	$449.6	0.1x	6.8x	1.1x	12.4x
Jadi Imaging Holdings Bhd	KLSE: JADI	$42.1	$15.5	$5.7	$5.1	$4.1	2.7x	8.2x	2.4x	13.9x
Media Sciences International	NasdaqSC: MSII	$56.5	$23.1	$13.2	$4.8	$3.9	2.4x	11.9x	5.0x	24.4x
Turbon AG	DUSE: TUR	$58.6	$160.3	$30.1	$6.7	$4.1	0.4x	8.7x	0.9x	NM
						Median	**0.8x**	**8.7x**	**1.8x**	**14.3x**
						Mean	3.3x	11.6x	2.4x	18.2x
						High	23.8x	28.8x	5.5x	30.9x
						Low	0.1x	6.8x	0.6x	12.4x
Industry Giants										
Hewlett-Packard Co.	NYSE: HPQ	$102,798.4	$93,748.0	$23,050.0	$10,161.0	$7,728.0	1.1x	10.1x	2.8x	16.5x
Lexmark International	NYSE: LXK	$5,293.1	$5,108.1	$1,694.1	$811.8	$610.9	1.0x	6.5x	5.5x	16.8x
Pitney Bowes Inc.	NYSE: PBI	$14,592.7	$5,004.9	$3,093.5	$1,541.5	$1,187.4	2.9x	9.5x	14.5x	96.3x
Xerox Corp.	NYSE: XRX	$22,434.6	$15,055.0	$6,459.0	$2,279.0	$1,643.0	1.5x	9.8x	2.3x	13.4x
						Median	1.3x	9.7x	4.2x	16.7x

Source: Capital IQ c/o Shields and Company.

*Not meaningful.

INDEX

Page numbers followed by n indicate material found in notes.

C

G

H

I

The Teacher's Calendar

School Year 2000-2001

The Day-by-Day
Directory to Holidays,
Historic Events,
Birthdays and Special Days,
Weeks and Months

Compiled by Sandy Whiteley
With Kim Summers and Sally M. Walker

CB
CONTEMPORARY BOOKS

☆ *The Teacher's Calendar, 2000–2001* ☆

NTC/CONTEMPORARY PUBLISHING GROUP, INC.
A TRIBUNE EDUCATION COMPANY
4255 WEST TOUHY AVENUE
LINCOLNWOOD, ILLINOIS 60712-1975
FAX: (847) 679-2595
PHONE: (847) 679-5500

Printed in USA

— NOTICE —

Events listed herein are not necessarily endorsed by the editors or publisher. Every effort has been made to assure the correctness of all entries, but neither the authors nor the publisher can warrant their accuracy. IT IS IMPERATIVE, IF FINANCIAL PLANS ARE TO BE MADE IN CONNECTION WITH DATES OR EVENTS LISTED HEREIN, THAT PRINCIPALS BE CONSULTED FOR FINAL INFORMATION.

GRAPHIC IMAGES

The interior illustrations were created for this book by Dan Krovatin.

Library of Congress Cataloging-in-Publication Data

Whiteley, Sandra, 1943–
    The teacher's calendar, 2000–2001 : the day-by-day directory to holidays, special days, weeks and months, festivals, historic events, and birthdays / compiled by Sandy Whiteley with Kim Summers and Sally Walker.
       p.   cm.
    Includes bibliographical references and index.
    ISBN 0-8092-2521-2
    1. Holidays.   2. Birthdays.   3. Anniversaries.   4. Festivals.
5. Schedules, School.   I. Summers, Kim (Kim A.)   II. Walker, Sally M.   III. Title.   IV. Title: Teacher's calendar.
LB3525.W55   2000
371.2′3—dc21   99-13240
                                          CIP

☆ *The Teacher's Calendar, 2000–2001* ☆

TABLE OF CONTENTS

★ in text indicates Presidential Proclamations

☆ *The Teacher's Calendar, 2000–2001* ☆

WELCOME TO *THE TEACHER'S CALENDAR*

Welcome to The Teacher's Calendar

This edition of *The Teacher's Calendar* contains more than 4,200 events that you can use in planning the school calendar, creating bulletin boards and developing lesson plans. Some of the entries were taken from the 2000 edition of *Chase's Calendar of Events*, a reference book which for 43 years has provided librarians and the media with events arranged day-by-day. Hundreds of entries were written especially for *The Teacher's Calendar*. For example, among the Birthdays Today entries are birthdays for hundreds of authors of children's books. We've also added the dates of national professional meetings for teachers, children's book conferences and other events of interest to professional educators.

Types of Events

Presidential Proclamations: We have included in the day-by-day chronology proclamations that have continuing authority with a formula for calculating the dates of observance and those that have been issued consistently since 1995. The president issues proclamations only a few days before the actual event so it is possible that some dates may vary slightly for 2000–2001. The most recent proclamations can be found on the World Wide Web at the Federal Register Online: www.access.gpo.gov.

National holidays and State Days: Public holidays of other nations are gleaned from United Nations documents and from information from tourism agencies. Technically, the United States has no national holidays. Those holidays proclaimed by the president apply only to federal employees and to the District of Columbia. Governors of the states proclaim holidays for their states. In practice, federal holidays are usually proclaimed as state holidays as well. Some governors also proclaim holidays unique to their state but not all state holidays are commemorated with the closing of schools and offices.

Religious Observances: Principal observances of the Christian, Jewish and Muslim faiths are presented with background information from their respective calendars. We use anticipated dates for Muslim holidays. There is no single Hindu calendar and different Hindu sects define the Hindu lunar month differently. There is no single lunar calendar that serves as a model for all Buddhists either. Therefore, we are able to provide only a limited number of religious holidays for these faiths.

Historic Events and Birth Anniversaries: Dates for these entries have been gathered from a wide range of reference books. Most birthdays here are for people who are deceased. Birthdays of living people are usually listed under Birthdays Today.

Astronomical Phenomena: Information about eclipses, equinoxes and solstices, and moon phases is calculated from the annual publication, *Astronomical Phenomena*, from the US Naval Observatory. Dates for these events in *Astronomical Phenomena* are given in Universal Time (i.e., Greenwich Mean Time). We convert these dates and times into Eastern Standard or Eastern Daylight Time.

Sponsored Events: We obtain information on these events directly from their sponsors and provide contact information for the sponsoring organization.

Other Special Days, Weeks and Months: Information on these events is also obtained from their sponsors.

Process for Declaring Special Observances

How do special days, weeks and months get created? The president of the United States has the authority to declare a commemorative event by proclamation, but this is done infrequently. In 1999, for example, the president issued about 100 proclamations. Many of these, such as Mother's Day and Bill of Rights Week, were proclamations for which there was legislation giving continuing authority for a proclamation to be issued each year.

Until 1995, Congress was active in seeing that special observances were commemorated. Members of the Senate and House could introduce legislation for a special observance to commemorate people, events and other activities they thought worthy of national recognition. Because these bills took up a lot of time on the part of members of Congress, when Congress met in January 1995 to reform its rules and procedures, it was decided to discontinue this practice. Today, the Senate passes resolutions commemorating special days, weeks and months but these resolutions do not have the force of law.

It is not necessary to have the president or a senator declare a special day, week or month; many of the events in *The Teacher's Calendar* have been declared only by their sponsoring organizations.

Websites

Web addresses have been provided when relevant. These URLs were checked the first week in December 1999. Although we have tried to select sites maintained by the government, universities and other stable organizations, some of these sites undoubtedly will have disappeared by the time you try and look at them.

Curriculum Connections

These sidebars were written by Sally M. Walker, an author of children's books and a children's literature consultant, to give teachers ideas for integrating some of the events in *The Teacher's Calendar* into the classroom.

Acknowledgements

Thanks to the staff at the Evanston and Skokie public libraries who helped in the process of compiling *The Teacher's Calendar*. Special thanks to our colleagues at NTC/Contemporary Publishing: Martha Best, Denise Duffy-Fieldman, Gigi Grajdura, Richard Spears, Terry Stone and Jeanette Wojtyla. And now Associate Editor Kim Summers and I invite you to join us in the celebration of the coming school year.

January 2000   Sandy Whiteley, MLS, Editor

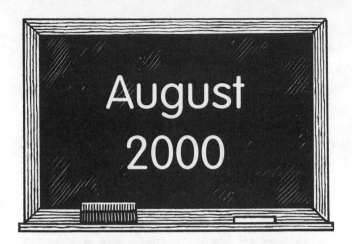

AUGUST 1 — TUESDAY

Day 214 — 152 Remaining

AMERICAN HISTORY ESSAY CONTEST. Aug 1–Dec 15. American History Committee activities are promoted throughout the year with the essay contest conducted in grades 5–8 beginning in August. Essays are submitted for judging by Dec 15, with the winners announced in April at the Daughters of the American Revolution Continental Congress. Events vary, but include programs, displays, spot announcements and recognition of essay writers. Essay topic can be obtained from DAR Headquarters. For info: Natl Soc Daughters of the American Revolution, Office of the Historian-General, Admin Bldg, 1776 D St NW, Washington, DC 20006-5392. Phone: (202) 628-1776.

BENIN, PEOPLE'S REPUBLIC OF: NATIONAL DAY: 40th ANNIVERSARY. Aug 1. Public holiday. Commemorates independence from France in 1960. Benin at that time was known as Dahomey.

BURK, MARTHA (CALAMITY JANE): DEATH ANNIVERSARY. Aug 1, 1903. Known as a frontierswoman and companion to Wild Bill Hickock, Calamity Jane Burk was born Martha Jane Canary at Princeton, MO, in May 1852. As a young girl living in Montana, she became an excellent markswoman. She went to the Black Hills of South Dakota as a scout for a geological expedition in 1875. Several opposing traditions account for her nickname, one springing from her kindness to the less fortunate, while another attributes it to the harsh warnings she would give men who offended her. She died Aug 1, 1903, at Terry, SD, and was buried at Deadwood, SD, next to Wild Bill Hickock.

CHILDREN'S VISION AND LEARNING MONTH. Aug 1–31. A monthlong campaign encouraging parents to have their children's vision examined by an eye-care professional prior to the start of the new school year. For info: Mike Smith, Exec Dir, American Foundation for Vision Awareness (AFVA), 243 N Lindbergh Blvd, St. Louis, MO 63141. Phone: (800) 927-AFVA. Fax: (314) 991-4101. E-mail: afva@aol.com.

COLORADO: ADMISSION DAY: ANNIVERSARY. Aug 1, 1876. Colorado became the 38th state. Observed on the first Monday in August in Colorado (Aug 7 in 2000).

AUGUST 1–31
NATIONAL INVENTORS MONTH

What is an "invention"? Depending on who you ask, you may receive answers such as a gadget, a device, a creation or a new discovery. Explore National Inventors Month by letting small groups of students brainstorm about what they think defines an invention. Questions that will stimulate their ideas and help them decide about definitions might include: "Does a pencil qualify as an invention? If so, why?" "Does a poem qualify as an invention? Why or why not?"

Each group can also list 10 inventions they think make a difference in their lives. Compare and contrast the different groups' definitions and choices. An additional small group task might be to answer the question "What kind of person can be an inventor?" Emphasize the need for perseverance. An inventor's motto is often the cliché, "If at first you don't succeed, try, try again."

Some inventions have been around for thousands of years. These include simple machines such as the wedge, wheels and axles, inclined planes and levers. Flint tools and the plow are other examples. A creative writing project might revolve around scripting a play that tells a story of how prehistoric peoples may have "discovered" these machines. Posters advertising the newfangled machines could complement the performances, which would be effective in a Reader's Theater format. It might be fun to create a poster display featuring landmark inventions. Compare early inventions with the very complex inventions we have today. Notice how many modern inventions rely on electrical power.

In October 1999, the Arts & Entertainment TV cable channel polled a number of people in an effort to determine the most influential people of the millennium. Johannes Gutenberg, the inventor of the printing press, was number one. Another writing project might be a fantasy of what life today would be like if the printing press had not been invented.

Introduce books written by Jules Verne and H.G. Wells to middle school and junior high school students. These early science fiction writers envisioned many futuristic inventions, some of which are now realities. An art project might involve asking students to forecast the future and to design and draw an invention they feel would be beneficial to future societies.

Additional topics for older students could include researching public response to new inventions and how attitudes change over time. One example is early photography. Some people were (and are) extremely superstitious about having their image captured on a piece of paper.

Choose a long-standing invention like the refrigerator or the telephone and examine how it has changed from decade to decade. Include shape and design, efficiency, marketing slogans and price changes.

There are many fine biographies of famous inventors for young readers. Feature an Inventor of the Week and see how many interesting facts about that person students can find. Perhaps parents or grandparents recall an anecdote about one of them. My father remembers being out on a walk with his parents one day and meeting Albert Einstein. Einstein was eating an ice cream cone. Grandparents' memories might include getting their first TV set.

Related books that students will enjoy are: *The Kids' Invention Book*, by Arlene Erlbach (Lerner, 0-8225-9844-2, $9.95 Gr. 3–6); *The Lightbulb*, by Joseph Wallace (Simon & Schuster, 0-689-82816-0, $17.95 Gr. 4 & up); *The Telephone*, by Sarah Gearhart (Simon & Schuster, 0-689-82815-2, $17.95 Gr. 4 & up).

DIARY OF ANNE FRANK: THE LAST ENTRY: ANNIVERSARY. Aug 1, 1944. To escape deportation to concentration camps, the Jewish family of Otto Frank hid for two years in the warehouse of his food products business at Amsterdam. Gentile friends smuggled in food and other supplies during their confinement. Thirteen-year-old Anne Frank, who kept a journal during the time of their hiding, penned her last entry in the diary Aug 1, 1944: "[I] keep on trying to find a way of becoming what I would like to be, and what I could be, if . . . there weren't any other people living in the world." Three days later (Aug 4, 1944) Grüne Polizei raided the "Secret Annex" where the Frank family was hidden. Anne and her sister were sent to Bergen-Belsen concentration camp where Anne died at age 15, two months before the liberation of Holland. Young Anne's diary, later found in the family's hiding place, has been translated into 30 languages and has become a symbol of the indomitable strength of the human spirit. See also: "Frank, Anne: Birth Anniversary" (June 12). For more info: www.annefrank.com.

EMANCIPATION OF 500: ANNIVERSARY. Aug 1, 1791. Virginia planter Robert Carter III confounded his family and friends by filing a deed of emancipation for his 500 slaves. One of the wealthiest men in the state, Carter owned 60,000 acres over 18 plantations. The deed included the following words: "I have for some time past been convinced that to retain them in Slavery is contrary to the true principles of Religion and Justice and therefore it is my duty to manumit them." The document established a schedule by which 15 slaves would be freed each Jan 1, over a 21-year period, plus slave children would be freed at age 18 for females and 21 for males. It is believed this was the largest act of emancipation in US history and predated the Emancipation Proclamation by 70 years.

FIRST US CENSUS: ANNIVERSARY. Aug 1, 1790. The first census revealed that there were 3,939,326 citizens in the 16 states and the Ohio Territory. The US has taken a census every 10 years since 1790. The most recent one was taken in April 2000. For the exact population of the US today, calculated to the minute, go to www.census.gov/main/www/popclock.html.

HOLY YEAR 2000. Dec 25, 1999–Jan 6, 2001. An estimated 13 million people will travel to Rome to celebrate the Great Jubilee of the Incarnation of Christ. A World Youth Day, Aug 19–20, is expected to attract two million young people. For info: Great Jubilee 2000, Vatican City, 00120. Web: www.vatican.va/.

KEY, FRANCIS SCOTT: BIRTH ANNIVERSARY. Aug 1, 1779. American attorney, social worker, poet and author of the US national anthem. While on a legal mission during the War of 1812, Key was detained on shipboard off Baltimore, during the British bombardment of Fort McHenry on the night of Sept 13–14, 1814. Thrilled to see the American flag still flying over the fort at daybreak, Key wrote the poem "The Star Spangled Banner." Printed in the *Baltimore American* Sept 21, 1814, it was soon popularly sung to the music of an old English tune, "Anacreon in Heaven." It did not become the official US national anthem until 117 years later when, Mar 3, 1931, President Herbert Hoover signed into law an act for that purpose. Key was born at Frederick County, MD, and died at Baltimore, MD, Jan 11, 1843.

MITCHELL, MARIA: BIRTH ANNIVERSARY. Aug 1, 1818. An interest in her father's hobby and an ability for mathematics resulted in Maria Mitchell's becoming the first female professional astronomer. In 1847, while assisting her father in a survey of the sky for the US Coast Guard, Mitchell discovered a new comet and determined its orbit. She received many honors because of this, including being elected to the American Academy of Arts and Sciences—its first woman. Mitchell joined the staff at Vassar Female College in 1865—the first US female professor of astronomy—and in 1873 was a cofounder of the Association for the Advancement of Women. Born at Nantucket, MA, Mitchell died June 28, 1889, at Lynn, MA.

NATIONAL BACK-TO-SCHOOL MONTH. Aug 1–31. Grassroots community activities such as free shopping sprees for kids to help impoverished children prepare mentally, emotionally and physically for the upcoming school year. A key component of the Back-To-School program is insuring that children have the proper clothes and supplies they need to feel good about going to school. To find out activities happening in your community call: Donna Strout, Operation Blessings Intl, 977 Centerville Turnpike, Virginia Beach, VA 23463. Phone: (757) 226-2443. Fax: (757) 226-6183. E-mail: donna.strout@OB.ORG.

NATIONAL INVENTORS' MONTH. Aug 1–31. To educate the American public about the value of creativity and inventiveness and the importance of inventions and inventors to the quality of our lives. This will be accomplished through the placement of media stories about living inventors in most of the top national, local and trade publications, as well as through the electronic media. Sponsored by the United Inventors Association of the USA (UIA-USA), the Academy of Applied Science and *Inventors' Digest*. *See* Curriculum Connection. For info: Julia Schopick. Phone: (708) 848-4788. Fax: (708) 848-4769 or Joanne Hayes-Rines, Inventors' Digest. Phone: (617) 367-4540. Fax: (617) 723-6988. Web: www.inventorsdigest.com.

NATIONAL NIGHT OUT. Aug 1. Designed to heighten crime prevention awareness and to promote police-community partnerships. Annually, the first Tuesday in August. For info: Matt A. Peskin, Dir, Natl Assn of Town Watch, PO Box 303, Wynnewood, PA 19096. Phone: (610) 649-7055 or (800) 648-3688. Web: www.natw.org.

OAK RIDGE ATOMIC PLANT BEGUN: ANNIVERSARY. Aug 1, 1943. Ground was broken at Oak Ridge, TN, for the first plant built to manufacture the uranium 235 needed to build an atomic bomb. The plant was largely completed by July of 1944 at a final cost of $280 million. By August 1945 the total cost for development of the A-bomb ran to $1 billion.

PRESIDENT'S ENVIRONMENTAL YOUTH AWARD NATIONAL COMPETITION. Aug 1–July 31, 2001. Young people in all 50 states are invited to participate in the President's Environmental Youth Awards program, which offers them, individually and collectively, an opportunity to be recognized for environmental efforts in their community. The program encourages individuals, school classes, schools, summer camps and youth organizations to promote local environmental awareness and positive community involvement. *See* Curriculum Connection. For

		S	M	T	W	T	F	S
August				1	2	3	4	5
2000		6	7	8	9	10	11	12
		13	14	15	16	17	18	19
		20	21	22	23	24	25	26
		27	28	29	30	31		

AUGUST 1–JULY 31
PRESIDENT'S ENVIRONMENTAL YOUTH AWARD NATIONAL COMPETITION

This annual competition encourages young people to become environmentally active by informing members of their community about environmental issues and initiating programs that foster community participation. Because this is a yearlong competition and the Environmental Protection Agency is interested in ongoing efforts, students should be informed about this early in the academic year so they have adequate time for program planning, preparation and implementation. Interested students can obtain information and competition guidelines in the main text entry under Aug 1.

Young people can and do make a positive difference in their environments. There are many ways they can participate. Students can look around the school building to see what kinds of environment-friendly projects are already in place. Does the school have a paper and can recycling program? Are there opportunities for a school garden? If so, perhaps it could center around a curriculum unit such as a butterfly or prairie garden. Students may consider forming a cleanup patrol to tidy the playground and school walkways. One of their activities might be writing and presenting "Clean Playground" skits to younger students. Older students might organize a mentoring program for younger students and involve them in a "Proud to Be Part of a Healthy Environment" campaign. *Taking Care of the Earth: Kids in Action*, by Laurence Pringle (Boyds Mills, 1-56397-634-X, $7.95 Gr. 3–8) is an excellent resource for stimulating student creativity and ideas, as well as a good place to begin a quest for an environmental project.

Students may want to become involved with community projects like river cleanups and town park beautification efforts. If an environmental "problem area" exists—an unsightly empty lot, for example—students from several schools could work with the town to develop a community garden plan. In conjunction with other schools in the area, students might organize letter-writing campaigns to area businesses about local environmental concerns.

Other literature connections: *To Save the Earth: The American Environmental Movement*, by Jules Archer (Viking, 0-670-87121-4, $17.99 Gr. 5 & up) is a good overview of early pioneers in environmental fields and how they became involved. *A River Ran Wild*, by Lynne Cherry (Harcourt, 0-15-200542-0, $16 Gr. K–3) depicts the story of a polluted New Hampshire river and how people worked to restore its health.

See River of Words Environmental Poetry and Art Contest (Feb 15) for another environmental competition for students.

info: Doris Gillispie, Environmental Education Coord, US Environmental Protection Agency, 401 M St, #1707, Washington, DC 20460. Phone: (202) 260-8749. Fax: (202) 260-0790.

SOUTH DAKOTA STATE FAIR. Aug 1–6. Huron, SD. Grandstand entertainment nightly, 10 free stages with multiple shows daily, hundreds of commercial exhibits and thousands of livestock exhibits. One of the largest agricultural fairs in the US. Est attendance: 250,000. For info: Jewel Tschetter, Mgr, South Dakota State Fair, PO Box 1275, Huron, SD 57350-1275. Phone: (605) 353-7340. Fax: (605) 353-7348.

SWITZERLAND: NATIONAL DAY. Aug 1. Anniversary of the founding of the Swiss Confederation. Commemorates a pact made in 1291. Parades, patriotic gatherings, bonfires and fireworks. Young citizens' coming-of-age ceremonies. Observed since 600th anniversary of Swiss Confederation was celebrated in 1891.

TRINIDAD AND TOBAGO: EMANCIPATION DAY. Aug 1. Public holiday.

US GIRLS' JUNIOR (GOLF) CHAMPIONSHIP. Aug 1–5. Pumpkin Ridge Golf Club, Plains, OR. For info: US Golf Assn, Golf House, Championship Dept, Far Hills, NJ 07931. Phone: (908) 234-2300. Fax: (908) 234-9687. E-mail: usga@ix.netcom.com. Web: www.usga.org.

WORLD WIDE WEB: 10th ANNIVERSARY. Aug 1, 1990. The creation of what would become the World Wide Web was suggested this month by Tim Berners-Lee and Robert Cailliau at CERN, the European Laboratory for Particle Physics at Switzerland. By October, they had designed a prototype Web browser. By early 1993, there were 50 Web servers worldwide.

BIRTHDAYS TODAY

Gail Gibbons, 56, author and illustrator (*Fire! Fire!*), born Oak Park, IL, Aug 1, 1944.

AUGUST 2 — WEDNESDAY
Day 215 — 151 Remaining

ALBERT EINSTEIN'S ATOMIC BOMB LETTER: ANNIVERSARY. Aug 2, 1939. Albert Einstein, world-famous scientist, a refugee from Nazi Germany, wrote a letter to US President Franklin D. Roosevelt, first mentioning a possible "new phenomenon . . . chain reactions . . . vast amounts of power" and "the construction of bombs." "A single bomb of this type," he wrote, "carried by boat and exploded in a port, might very well destroy the whole port together with some of the surrounding territory." An historic letter that marked the beginning of atomic weaponry. Six years and four days later, Aug 6, 1945, the Japanese port of Hiroshima was destroyed by the first atomic bombing of a populated place.

DECLARATION OF INDEPENDENCE: OFFICIAL SIGNING ANNIVERSARY. Aug 2, 1776. Contrary to widespread misconceptions, the 56 signers did not sign as a group and did not do so July 4, 1776. John Hancock and Charles Thompson signed only draft copies that day, the official day the Declaration was adopted by Congress. The signing of the official declaration occurred Aug 2, 1776, when 50 men probably took part. George Washington, Patrick Henry and several others were not in Philadelphia and thus were unable to sign. Later that year, five more signed separately and one added his name in a subsequent year. (From "Signers of the Declaration . . ." US Dept of the Interior, 1975.) See also: "Declaration of Independence" (July 4).

DISABILITY DAY IN KENTUCKY. Aug 2.

L'ENFANT, PIERRE CHARLES: BIRTH ANNIVERSARY. Aug 2, 1754. The architect, engineer and Revolutionary War officer who designed the plan for the city of Washington, DC, Pierre Charles L'Enfant was born at Paris, France. He died at Prince Georges County, MD, June 14, 1825.

MACEDONIA, FORMER YUGOSLAV REPUBLIC OF: NATIONAL DAY. Aug 2. Commemorates the nationalist uprising against the Ottoman Empire in 1903. Also known as St. Elias Day, the most sacred and celebrated day of the Macedonian people.

NATIONAL COUNCIL FOR GEOGRAPHIC EDUCATION MEETING. Aug 2–5. The Hotel Intercontinental, Chicago, IL. For info: Natl Council for Geographic Education, 16A Leonard Hall, Indiana Univ of PA, Indiana, PA 15705. Phone: (412) 357-6290. Web: www.ncge.org.

SCOTLAND: ABERDEEN INTERNATIONAL YOUTH FESTIVAL. Aug 2–12. Aberdeen, Scotland. Talented young people from all areas of the performing arts come from around the world to participate in this festival. Est attendance: 30,000. For info: Nicola Wallis, 3 Nuborn House, Clifton Rd, London, England SW19 4QT. Phone: (44) (181) 946-2995. Fax: (44) (181) 944-6507.

James Howe, 54, author (the Bunnicula series), born Oneida, NY, Aug 2, 1946.

AUGUST 3 — THURSDAY
Day 216 — 150 Remaining

COLUMBUS SAILS FOR THE NEW WORLD: ANNIVERSARY. Aug 3, 1492. Christopher Columbus, "Admiral of the Ocean Sea," set sail half an hour before sunrise from Palos, Spain. With three ships, the *Niña*, the *Pinta* and the *Santa Maria*, and a crew of 90, he sailed "for Cathay" but found instead a New World of the Americas, first landing at Guanahani (San Salvador Island in the Bahamas) Oct 12. See also: "Columbus Day (Traditional)" (Oct 12).

GUINEA-BISSAU: COLONIZATION MARTYR'S DAY. Aug 3. National holiday is observed.

NEW JERSEY STATE FAIR. Aug 3–13 (tentative). Cherry Hill, NJ. Reithoffer Shows, book fair, various types of music entertainment, circus, food booths and sports events. Est attendance: 206,000. For info: New Jersey State Fair, 406 Richard Rd, Rockledge, FL 32955. Phone: (407) 633-4028. Fax: (407) 633-6930.

NIGER: INDEPENDENCE DAY: 40th ANNIVERSARY. Aug 3. Commemorates the independence of this West African nation from France on this date in 1960.

SCOPES, JOHN T.: 100th BIRTH ANNIVERSARY. Aug 3, 1900. Central figure in a cause célèbre (the "Scopes Trial" or the "Monkey Trial"), John Thomas Scopes was born at Paducah, KY. An obscure 24-year-old schoolteacher at the Dayton, TN, high school in 1925, he became the focus of world attention. Scopes never uttered a word at his trial, which was a contest between two

	S	M	T	W	T	F	S
August			1	2	3	4	5
2000	6	7	8	9	10	11	12
	13	14	15	16	17	18	19
	20	21	22	23	24	25	26
	27	28	29	30	31		

of America's best-known lawyers (William Jennings Bryan and Clarence Darrow). The trial, July 10–21, 1925, resulted in Scopes's conviction "for teaching evolution" in Tennessee. He was fined $100. The verdict was upset on a technicality and the statute he was accused of breaching was repealed in 1967. Scopes died at Shreveport, LA, Oct 21, 1970. For more info: www.law.umkc.edu/faculty/projects/ftrials/ftrials.htm.

WISCONSIN STATE FAIR. Aug 3–13. State Fair Park, Milwaukee, WI. Wisconsin celebrates its rural heritage at the state's most popular and most historic annual event. Features giant midway, concessions, livestock, food and flower judging and top-name entertainment. [Call 24-hour recorded information line at (414) 266-7188 for performance times and dates.] Est attendance: 930,000. For info: PR Dept, Wisconsin State Fair Park, PO Box 14990, West Allis, WI 53214-0990. Phone: (414) 266-7060. Fax: (414) 266-7007. E-mail: wsfp@mail.state.wi.us. Web: www.wsfp.state.wi.us.

Mary Calhoun, 74, author (*High-Wire Henry*), born Keokuk, IA, Aug 3, 1926.

AUGUST 4 — FRIDAY
Day 217 — 149 Remaining

COAST GUARD DAY. Aug 4. Celebrates anniversary of founding of the US Coast Guard in 1790.

MANDELA, NELSON: ARREST ANNIVERSARY. Aug 4, 1962. Nelson Rolihlahla Mandela, charismatic black South African leader, was born in 1918, the son of the Tembu tribal chief, at Umtata, Transkei territory of South Africa. A lawyer and political activist, Mandela, who in 1952 established the first black law partnership in South Africa, had been in conflict with the white government there much of his life. Acquitted of a treason charge after a trial that lasted from 1956 to 1961, he was apprehended again by security police, Aug 4, 1962. The subsequent trial, widely viewed as an indictment of white domination, resulted in Mandela's being sentenced to five years in prison. In 1963 he was taken from the Pretoria prison to face a new trial—for sabotage, high treason and conspiracy to overthrow the government—and in June 1964 he was sentenced to life in prison. See also: "Mandela, Nelson: Prison Release: Anniversary" (Feb 11).

OHIO STATE FAIR. Aug 4–20. Columbus, OH. Family fun, amusement rides, games, food booths, parades, entertainment, rodeos, circus, auto thrill show and tractor pulls. Est attendance: 900,000. For info: Ohio State Fair, 717 E 17th Ave, Columbus, OH 43211. Phone: (614) 644-4000. Fax: (614) 644-4031.

SCHUMAN, WILLIAM HOWARD: 90th BIRTH ANNIVERSARY. Aug 4, 1910. American composer who won the first Pulitzer Prize for composition and founded the Juilliard School of Music, was born at New York. His compositions include *American Festival Overture*, the baseball opera *The Mighty Casey* and *On Freedom's Ground*, written for the centennial of the Statue of Liberty in 1986. He was instrumental in the conception of the Lincoln Center for the Performing Arts and served as its first president. In 1985 he was awarded a special Pulitzer Prize. He also received a National Medal of Arts in 1985 and a Kennedy Center Honor in 1989. Schuman died at New York City, Feb 15, 1992.

Yasser Arafat, 71, president of the Palestinian National Authority, born Jerusalem, Aug 4, 1929.

Roger Clemens, 38, baseball player, born Dayton, OH, Aug 4, 1962.
Jeff Gordon, 29, race car driver, born Pittsboro, IN, Aug 4, 1971.

AUGUST 5 — SATURDAY
Day 218 — 148 Remaining

BATTLE OF MOBILE BAY: ANNIVERSARY. Aug 5, 1864. A Union fleet under Admiral David Farragut attempted to run past three Confederate forts into Mobile Bay, AL. After coming under fire, the Union fleet headed into a maze of underwater mines, known at that time as torpedoes. The ironclad *Tecumseh* was sunk by a torpedo, after which Farragut is said to have exclaimed, "Damn the torpedoes, full steam ahead." The Union fleet was successful and Mobile Bay was secured.

BURKINA FASO: REPUBLIC DAY: 40th ANNIVERSARY. Aug 5. Burkina Faso (formerly Upper Volta) gained autonomy from France in 1960.

ELIOT, JOHN: BIRTH ANNIVERSARY. Aug 5, 1604. American "Apostle to the Indians," translator of the Bible into an Indian tongue (the first Bible to be printed in America), was born at Hertfordshire, England. He died at Roxbury, MA, May 21, 1690.

FIRST ENGLISH COLONY IN NORTH AMERICA: FOUNDING ANNIVERSARY. Aug 5, 1583. Sir Humphrey Gilbert, English navigator and explorer, aboard his sailing ship, the *Squirrel*, sighted the Newfoundland coast and took possession of the area around St. John's harbor in the name of the Queen, thus establishing the first English colony in North America. Gilbert was lost at sea, in a storm off the Azores, on his return trip to England.

LYNCH, THOMAS: BIRTH ANNIVERSARY. Aug 5, 1749. Signer, Declaration of Independence, born Prince George's Parish, SC. Died 1779 (lost at sea, exact date of death unknown).

NATIONAL MUSTARD DAY. Aug 5. Mustard lovers across the nation pay tribute to the king of condiments by slathering their favorite mustard on hot dogs, pretzels, licorice and even ice cream (an acquired taste)! The Mount Horeb Mustard Museum contains the world's largest collection of prepared mustards and mustard memorabilia. Celebration festivities include free hot dogs, mustard games and mustard squirting. Annually, the first Saturday in August. Est attendance: 1,000. For info: Barry M. Levenson, Curator, The Mount Horeb Mustard Museum, 109 E Main St, Mount Horeb, WI 53572. Phone: (608) 437-3986. Fax: (608) 437-4018. E-mail: curator@mustardweb.com. Web: www.mustardweb.com.

WALLENBERG, RAOUL: BIRTH ANNIVERSARY. Aug 5, 1912. Swedish architect Raoul Gustaf Wallenberg was born at Stockholm, Sweden. He was the second person in history (Winston Churchill was the first) to be voted honorary American citizenship (US House of Representatives 396–2, Sept 22, 1981). He is credited with saving 100,000 Hungarian Jews from almost certain death at the hands of the Nazis during WWII. Wallenberg was arrested by Soviet troops at Budapest, Hungary, Jan 17, 1945, and, according to the official Soviet press agency Tass, died in prison at Moscow, July 17, 1947.

BIRTHDAYS TODAY

Neil Alden Armstrong, 70, former astronaut (first man to walk on moon), born Wapakoneta, OH, Aug 5, 1930.
Brendon Ryan Barrett, 14, actor (*Casper*), born Roseville, CA, Aug 5, 1986.
Patrick Aloysius Ewing, 38, basketball player, born Kingston, Jamaica, Aug 5, 1962.

AUGUST 6 — SUNDAY
Day 219 — 147 Remaining

AMERICAN FAMILY DAY IN ARIZONA. Aug 6. Commemorated on the first Sunday in August.

ATOMIC BOMB DROPPED ON HIROSHIMA: 55th ANNIVERSARY. Aug 6, 1945. At 8:15 AM, local time, an American B-29 bomber, the *Enola Gay*, dropped an atomic bomb named "Little Boy" over the center of the city of Hiroshima, Japan. The bomb exploded about 1,800 ft above the ground, killing more than 105,000 civilians and destroying the city. It is estimated that another 100,000 persons were injured and died subsequently as a direct result of the bomb and the radiation it produced. This was the first time in history that such a devastating weapon had been used by any nation.

BOLIVIA: INDEPENDENCE DAY: 175th ANNIVERSARY. Aug 6. National holiday. Gained freedom from Spain in 1825. Named after Simon Bolivar.

FIRST WOMAN SWIMS THE ENGLISH CHANNEL: ANNIVERSARY. Aug 6, 1926. The first woman to swim the English Channel was 19-year-old Gertrude Ederle of New York, NY. Her swim was completed in 14 hours and 31 minutes.

FLEMING, ALEXANDER: BIRTH ANNIVERSARY. Aug 6, 1881. Sir Alexander Fleming, Scottish bacteriologist, discoverer of penicillin and 1954 Nobel Prize recipient, was born at Lochfield, Scotland. He died at London, England, Mar 11, 1955.

"GREAT DEBATE": ANNIVERSARY. Aug 6–Sept 10, 1787. The Constitutional Convention engaged in the "Great Debate" over the draft constitution, during which it determined that Congress should have the right to regulate foreign trade and interstate commerce, established a four-year term of office for the president and appointed a five-man committee to prepare a final draft of the Constitution.

HALFWAY POINT OF SUMMER. Aug 6. On this day, 47 days will have elapsed and the equivalent will remain before Sept 22, 2000, the autumnal equinox and the beginning of autumn.

HIROSHIMA DAY: 55th ANNIVERSARY. Aug 6. There are memorial observances in many places for victims of the first atomic bombing of a populated place, which occurred at Hiroshima, Japan, in 1945, when an American B-29 bomber dropped an atomic bomb over the center of the city. More than 205,000 civilians died either immediately in the explosion or subsequently of radiation. A peace festival is held annually at Peace Memorial Park at Hiroshima in memory of the victims of the bombing.

INTERNATIONAL ASSOCIATION OF SCHOOL LIBRARIANS CONFERENCE. Aug 6–10. Malmo, Sweden. For info: Intl Assn of School Librarians, Box 34069, Seattle, WA 98124-1069. Fax: (604) 925-0566. E-mail: iasl@rockland.com. Web: www.hi.is/~anne/iasl.html.

JAMAICA: INDEPENDENCE ACHIEVED: ANNIVERSARY. Aug 6, 1962. Jamaica attained its independence this date after centuries of British rule. Independence Day is observed on the first Monday in August (Aug 7 in 2000).

MOON PHASE: FIRST QUARTER. Aug 6. Moon enters First Quarter phase at 9:02 PM, EDT.

ROOSEVELT, EDITH KERMIT CAROW: BIRTH ANNIVERSARY. Aug 6, 1861. Second wife of Theodore Roosevelt, 26th president of the US, whom she married in 1886. Born at Norwich, CT, she died at Long Island, NY, Sept 30, 1948.

SISTERS' DAY. Aug 6. Celebrating the spirit of sisterhood— sisters nationwide show appreciation and give recognition to one another for the special relationship they share. Send a card, make a phone call, share memories, photos, flowers, candy, etc. Sisters may include biological sisters, sisterly friends, etc. Annually, the first Sunday in August each year. For info: Tricia Eleogram, 666 Hawthorne, Memphis, TN 38107. Phone: (901) 725-5190 or (901) 755-0751. Fax: (901) 754-9923. E-mail: sistersday@aol.com.

VOTING RIGHTS ACT OF 1965 SIGNED: 35th ANNIVERSARY. Aug 6, 1965. Signed into law by President Lyndon Johnson, the Voting Rights Act of 1965 was designed to thwart attempts to discriminate against minorities at the polls. The act suspended literacy and other disqualifying tests, authorized appointment of federal voting examiners and provided for judicial relief on the federal level to bar discriminatory poll taxes. Congress voted to extend the Act in 1975, 1984 and 1991.

BIRTHDAYS TODAY

Frank Asch, 54, author and illustrator (*Mooncake*), born Somerville, NJ, Aug 6, 1946.

Barbara Cooney, 83, illustrator and author (Caldecott for *The Ox-Cart Man, Miss Rumphius*), born Brooklyn, NY, Aug 6, 1917.

Catherine Hicks, 49, actress ("7th Heaven"), born Scottsdale, AZ, Aug 6, 1951.

David Robinson, 35, basketball player, born Key West, FL, Aug 6, 1965.

AUGUST 7 — MONDAY

Day 220 — 146 Remaining

ANTIGUA AND BARBUDA: AUGUST MONDAY. Aug 7–8. The first Monday in August and the day following form the August Monday public holiday in this Caribbean nation.

AUSTRALIA: PICNIC DAY. Aug 7. The first Monday in August is a bank holiday in New South Wales and Picnic Day in Northern Territory, Australia.

BAHAMAS: EMANCIPATION DAY. Aug 7. Public holiday in Bahamas. Annually, the first Monday in August. Commemorates the emancipation of slaves by the British in 1834.

BUNCHE, RALPH JOHNSON: BIRTH ANNIVERSARY. Aug 7, 1904. American statesman, UN official, Nobel Peace Prize recipient (the first black to win the award), born at Detroit, MI. Died Dec 9, 1971, at New York, NY.

CANADA: CIVIC HOLIDAY. Aug 7. The first Monday in August is observed as a holiday in seven of Canada's 10 provinces. Civic Holiday in Manitoba, Northwest Territories, Ontario and Saskatchewan, British Columbia Day in British Columbia, New Brunswick Day in New Brunswick, Natal Day in Nova Scotia and Heritage Day in Alberta.

August *2000*	S	M	T	W	T	F	S
			1	2	3	4	5
	6	7	8	9	10	11	12
	13	14	15	16	17	18	19
	20	21	22	23	24	25	26
	27	28	29	30	31		

COLORADO: ADMISSION DAY: OBSERVED. Aug 7. Colorado. Annually, the first Monday in August. Commemorates Admission Day when Colorado became the 38th state, Aug 1, 1876.

COTE D'IVOIRE: NATIONAL DAY: 40th ANNIVERSARY. Aug 7. Commemorates the independence of the Ivory Coast from France in 1960.

DESERT SHIELD: 10th ANNIVERSARY. Aug 7, 1990. Five days after the Iraqi invasion of Kuwait, US President George Bush ordered the military buildup that would become known as Desert Shield, to prevent further Iraqi advances. In January 1991, this would lead to the Persian Gulf War or Desert Storm.

FIRST PICTURE OF EARTH FROM SPACE: ANNIVERSARY. Aug 7, 1959. US satellite *Explorer VI* transmitted the first picture of Earth from space. For the first time we had a likeness of our planet based on more than projections and conjectures. For a current view of Earth from a satellite, visit Earth Viewer: www.fourmilab.to/earthview.

GRENADA: EMANCIPATION DAY. Aug 7. Grenada observes public holiday annually on the first Monday in August. Commemorates the emancipation of slaves by the British in 1834.

ICELAND: SHOP AND OFFICE WORKERS' HOLIDAY. Aug 7. In Iceland an annual holiday for shop and office workers is observed on the first Monday in August.

JAMAICA: INDEPENDENCE DAY OBSERVED. Aug 7. National holiday observing achievement of Jamaican independence from Britain Aug 6, 1962. Annually, the first Monday in August.

PURPLE HEART: ANNIVERSARY. Aug 7, 1782. At Newburgh, NY, General George Washington ordered the creation of a Badge of Military Merit. The badge consisted of a purple cloth heart with silver braided edge. Only three are known to have been awarded during the Revolutionary War. The award was reinstituted on the bicentennial of Washington's birth, Feb 22, 1932, and recognizes those wounded in action.

US WAR DEPARTMENT ESTABLISHED: ANNIVERSARY. Aug 7, 1789. The second presidential cabinet department, the War Department, was established by Congress.

ZAMBIA: YOUTH DAY. Aug 7. National holiday. Focal point is Lusaka's Independence Stadium. Annually, the first Monday in August.

BIRTHDAYS TODAY

Betsy Byars, 72, author (*The Summer of the Swans*, the Bingo Brown series), born Charlotte, NC, Aug 7, 1928.

Maia Wojciechowska, 73, author (*Shadow of a Bull*), born Warsaw, Poland, Aug 7, 1927.

AUGUST 8 — TUESDAY

Day 221 — 145 Remaining

BHUTAN: NATIONAL DAY. Aug 8. National holiday observed commemorating independence from India in 1949.

BONZA BOTTLER DAY™. Aug 8. To celebrate when the number of the day is the same as the number of the month. Bonza Bottler Day™ is an excuse to have a party at least once a month. For info: Gail M. Berger, 109 Matthew Ave, Poca, WV 25159. Phone: (304) 776-7746. E-mail: gberger5@aol.com.

HENSON, MATTHEW A.: BIRTH ANNIVERSARY. Aug 8, 1866. American black explorer, born at Charles County, MD. He met Robert E. Peary while working in a Washington, DC, store in 1888 and was hired to be Peary's valet. He accompanied Peary on his seven subsequent Arctic expeditions. During the successful 1908–09 expedition to the North Pole, Henson and two of the four Eskimo guides reached their destination on Apr 6, 1909. Peary arrived minutes later and verified the location. Henson's account of the expedition, *A Negro Explorer at the North Pole*, was published in 1912. In addition to the Congressional medal awarded all members of the North Pole expedition, Henson received the Gold Medal of the Geographical Society of Chicago and, at 81, was made an honorary member of the Explorers Club at New York, NY. Died Mar 9, 1955, at New York, NY.

ODIE: BIRTHDAY. Aug 8, 1978. Commemorates the birthday of Odie, Garfield's sidekick, who first appeared in the Garfield comic strip in 1978. For info: Kim Campbell, Paws, Inc, 5440 E Co Rd, 450 N, Albany, IN 47320. Web: www.garfield.com.

RAWLINGS, MARJORIE KINNAN: BIRTH ANNIVERSARY. Aug 8, 1896. American short-story writer and novelist (*The Yearling*), born at Washington, DC. Rawlings died at St. Augustine, FL, Dec 14, 1953.

BIRTHDAYS TODAY

JC Chasez, 24, singer ('N Sync), born Joshua Scott, Washington, DC, Aug 8, 1976.

Jane Dee Hull, 65, Governor of Arizona (R), born Kansas City, MO, Aug 8, 1935.

Edward T. Schafer, 54, Governor of North Dakota (R), born Bismarck, ND, Aug 8, 1946.

AUGUST 9 — WEDNESDAY

Day 222 — 144 Remaining

ATOMIC BOMB DROPPED ON NAGASAKI: 55th ANNIVERSARY. Aug 9, 1945. Three days after the atomic bombing of Hiroshima, an American B-29 bomber named *Bock's Car* left its base on Tinian Island carrying a plutonium bomb nicknamed "Fat Man." Its target was the Japanese city of Kokura, but because of clouds and poor visibility the bomber headed for a secondary target, Nagasaki, where at 11:02 AM, local time, it dropped the bomb, killing an estimated 70,000 persons and destroying about half the city. The next day the Japanese government surrendered, bringing WWII to an end.

COCHRAN, JACQUELINE: 20th DEATH ANNIVERSARY. Aug 9, 1980. American pilot Jacqueline Cochran was born at Pensacola, FL, in 1910. She began flying in 1932 and by the time of her death she had set more distance, speed and altitude records than any other pilot, male or female. She was founder and head of the WASPs (Women's Air Force Service Pilots) during WWII. She also won the Distinguished Service Medal in 1945 and the US Air Force Distinguished Flying Cross in 1969. She died at Indio, CA.

INDIANA STATE FAIR. Aug 9–20. Indiana State Fairgrounds Event Center, Indianapolis, IN. Top-rated livestock exhibition, world-class harness racing, top country music, giant midway and Pioneer Village. Est attendance: 725,000. For info: Jeff Fites, Media Relations Dir, Indiana State Fair, 1202 E 38th St, Indianapolis, IN 46205-2869. Phone: (317) 927-7500. Fax: (317) 927-7578. Web: www.state.in.us/statefair.

NIXON RESIGNS: ANNIVERSARY. Aug 9, 1974. Richard Milhous Nixon's resignation from the presidency of the US, which he had announced in a speech to the American people on Thursday evening, Aug 8, became effective at noon. Nixon, under threat of impeachment as a result of the Watergate scandal, became the first person to resign the presidency. He was succeeded by Vice President Gerald Rudolph Ford, the first person to serve as vice president and president without having been elected to either office. Ford granted Nixon a "full, free and absolute pardon" Sept 8, 1974. Although Nixon was the first US president to resign, two vice presidents had resigned: John C. Calhoun, Dec 18, 1832, and Spiro T. Agnew, Oct 10, 1973.

PIAGET, JEAN: BIRTH ANNIVERSARY. Aug 9, 1896. Born at Neuchatel, Switzerland, Piaget is the major figure in developmental psychology. His theory of cognitive development still influences educators today. Piaget died at Geneva, Switzerland, Sept 16, 1980.

PERSEID METEOR SHOWERS. Aug 9–13. Among the best-known and most spectacular meteor showers are the Perseids, peaking about Aug 10–12. As many as 50–100 may be seen in a single night. Wish upon a "falling star"!

SINGAPORE: INDEPENDENCE DAY: 35th ANNIVERSARY. Aug 9, 1965. Most festivals in Singapore are Chinese, Indian or Malay, but celebration of national day is shared by all to commemorate the withdrawal of Singapore from Malaysia and its becoming an independent state in 1965. Music, parades, dancing.

SOUTH AFRICA: NATIONAL WOMEN'S DAY. Aug 9. National holiday. Commemorates the march of women in Pretoria to protest the pass laws in 1956.

TRAVERS, P. L.: BIRTH ANNIVERSARY. Aug 9, 1899. Famous for her Mary Poppins series, P.L. Travers was born at Maryborough, Queensland, Australia. *Mary Poppins* was made into a movie by Disney in 1964. Travers died at London, England, Apr 23, 1996.

UNITED NATIONS: INTERNATIONAL DAY OF THE WORLD'S INDIGENOUS PEOPLE. Aug 9. On Dec 23, 1994, the General Assembly decided that the International Day of the World's Indigenous People shall be observed every year during the International Decade of the World's Indigenous People (1994–2004) (Res 49/214). The date marks the anniversary of the first day of the meeting in 1992 of the Working Group on Indigenous Populations of the Subcommission on Prevention of Discrimination and Protection of Minorities. For info: United Nations, Dept of Public Info, Public Inquiries Unit, RM GA-57, New York, NY 10017. Phone: (212) 963-4475. Fax: (212) 963-0071. E-mail: inquiries@un.org.

VEEP DAY. Aug 9. Commemorates the day in 1974 when Richard Nixon's resignation let Gerald Ford succeed to the presidency of the US. This was the first time the new Constitutional provisions for presidential succession in the Twenty-fifth Amendment of 1967 were used. For info: c/o Bob Birch, The Puns Corps, PO Box 2364, Falls Church, VA 22042-0364. Phone: (703) 533-3668.

WEBSTER-ASHBURTON TREATY SIGNED: ANNIVERSARY. Aug 9, 1842. The treaty delimiting the eastern section of the Canadian-American border was negotiated by the US Secretary of State, Daniel Webster, and Alexander Baring, president of the British Board of Trade. The treaty established the boundaries between the St. Croix and Connecticut rivers, between Lake Superior and the Lake of the Woods and between Lakes Huron and Superior. The treaty was signed at Washington, DC.

BIRTHDAYS TODAY

William Daley, 52, US Secretary of Commerce (Clinton administration), born Chicago, IL, Aug 9, 1948.

Chamique Holdsclaw, 23, basketball player, born Flushing, NY, Aug 9, 1977.

Whitney Houston, 37, singer ("And I Will Always Love You"), actress (*Waiting to Exhale*), born Newark, NJ, Aug 9, 1963.

Brett Hull, 36, hockey player, born Belleville, Ontario, Canada, Aug 9, 1964.

Hazel Hutchins, 48, author (*One Duck*), born Calgary, Alberta, Canada, Aug 9, 1952.

Ashley Johnson, 17, actress ("Growing Pains," voice of Gretchen on "Recess"), born Camarillo, CA, Aug 9, 1983.

Patricia McKissack, 56, author, with her husband Fredrick (*Christmas in the Big House*), born Nashville, TN, Aug 9, 1944.

Deion Sanders, 33, football and baseball player, born Ft Meyers, FL, Aug 9, 1967.

Seymour Simon, 69, author (*Earthquakes, The Universe*), born New York, NY, Aug 9, 1931.

AUGUST 10 — THURSDAY

Day 223 — 143 Remaining

ECUADOR: INDEPENDENCE DAY. Aug 10. National holiday. Celebrates declaration of independence in 1809. Freedom from Spain attained May 24, 1822.

HOOVER, HERBERT CLARK: BIRTH ANNIVERSARY. Aug 10, 1874. The 31st president of the US was born at West Branch, IA. Hoover was the first president born west of the Mississippi River and the first to have a telephone on his desk (installed Mar 27, 1929). "Older men declare war. But it is youth that must fight and die," he said at Chicago, IL, at the Republican National Convention, June 27, 1944. Hoover died at New York, NY, Oct 20, 1964. The Sunday nearest Aug 10th is observed in Iowa as Herbert Hoover Day (Aug 13 in 2000).

IOWA STATE FAIR. Aug 10–20. Iowa State Fairgrounds, Des Moines, IA. One of America's oldest and largest state fairs with one of the world's largest livestock shows. Ten-acre carnival, superstar grandstand stage shows, track events, spectacular free entertainment. 160-acre campgrounds. Est attendance: 900,000. For info: Kathie Swift, Mktg Dir, Iowa State Fair, Statehouse, 400 E 14th St, Des Moines, IA 50319. Phone: (515) 262-3111. Fax: (515) 262-6906. Web: iowastatefair.org.

JAPAN'S UNCONDITIONAL SURRENDER: 55th ANNIVERSARY. Aug 10, 1945. A gathering to discuss surrender terms took place in Emperor Hirohito's bomb shelter; the participants were stalemated. Hirohito settled the question, believing continuation of the war would only result in further loss of Japanese lives. A message was transmitted to Japanese ambassadors in Switzerland and Sweden to accept the terms issued at Potsdam July 26, 1945, except that the Japanese emperor's sovereignty must be maintained. The Allies devised a plan under which the emperor and the Japanese government would administer under the rule of the Supreme Commander of the Allied Powers and the Japanese surrendered.

MISSOURI: ADMISSION DAY: ANNIVERSARY. Aug 10. Became 24th state in 1821.

MISSOURI STATE FAIR. Aug 10–20. Sedalia, MO. Livestock shows, commercial and competitive exhibits, horse show, car races, tractor pulls, carnival and headline musical entertainment. Economical family entertainment. Est attendance: 350,000. For info: Kimberly Allen, PR Dir, Missouri State Fair, 2503 W 16th, Sedalia, MO 65301. Phone: (816) 530-5600. Fax: (816) 530-5609. Web: www.mostatefair.com.

SMITHSONIAN INSTITUTION FOUNDED: ANNIVERSARY. Aug 10, 1846. Founding of the Smithsonian Institution at Washington, DC, designed to hold the many scientific, historical and cultural collections that belong to the US. The National Museum of Natural History, the National Zoo, the National Museum of American Art, the National Air and Space Museum and the National Gallery of Art are among the museums in the Smithsonian Institution. For info for teachers from the Smithsonian: educate.si.edu. For info: Smithsonian Institution, 900 Jefferson Dr SW, Washington, DC 20560. Phone: (202) 357-2700.

BIRTHDAYS TODAY

Thomas J. Dygard, 69, author of sports books (*Game Plan*), born Little Rock, AR, Aug 10, 1931.

AUGUST 11 — FRIDAY

Day 224 — 142 Remaining

ATCHISON, DAVID R.: BIRTH ANNIVERSARY. Aug 11, 1807. Missouri legislator who was president of the US for one day. Born at Frogtown, KY, Atchison's strong pro-slavery opinions made his name prominent in legislative debates. He served as president pro tempore of the Senate a number of times, and he became president of the US for one day—Sunday, Mar 4, 1849—pending the swearing in of President-elect Zachary Taylor, Mar 5, 1849. The city of Atchison, KS, and the county of Atchison, MO, are named for him. He died at Gower, MO, Jan 26, 1886.

CHAD: INDEPENDENCE DAY: 40th ANNIVERSARY. Aug 11. National holiday. Commemorates independence from France in 1960.

FREDERICK DOUGLASS SPEAKS: ANNIVERSARY. Aug 11, 1841. Having escaped from slavery only three years earlier, Frederick Douglass was legally a fugitive when he first spoke before an audience. At an antislavery convention on Nantucket Island, Douglass spoke simply but eloquently about his life as a slave. His words were so moving that he was asked to become a full-time lecturer for the Massachusetts Anti-Slavery Society. Douglass became a brilliant orator, writer and abolitionist who championed the rights of blacks as well as the rights of all humankind.

August *2000*	S	M	T	W	T	F	S
			1	2	3	4	5
	6	7	8	9	10	11	12
	13	14	15	16	17	18	19
	20	21	22	23	24	25	26
	27	28	29	30	31		

FREEMAN, DON: BIRTH ANNIVERSARY. Aug 11, 1908. Author and illustrator (*Corduroy*), born at San Diego, CA. Died Feb 1, 1978.

HALEY, ALEX PALMER: BIRTH ANNIVERSARY. Aug 11, 1921. Born at Ithaca, NY, Alex Haley was raised by his grandmother at Henning, TN. In 1939 he entered the US Coast Guard and served as a cook, but eventually he became a writer and college professor. His first book, *The Autobiography of Malcolm X*, sold six million copies and was translated into eight languages. *Roots*, his Pulitzer Prize-winning book published in 1976, sold millions, was translated into 37 languages and was made into an eight-part TV miniseries in 1977. The story generated an enormous interest in family ancestry. Haley died at Seattle, WA, Feb 13, 1992.

"RUGRATS" TV PREMIERE: ANNIVERSARY. Aug 11, 1991. This animated cartoon features the toddler children of a trio of suburban families. One-year-old Tommy Pickles and his dog Spike play with 15-month-old twins Phil and Lil DeVille. Other characters include Tommy's three-year-old cousin Angelica, two-year-old Chuckie and Tommy's new brother Dil. Created by the animators of "The Simpsons." *The Rugrats Movie* was released in 1998.

SAINT CLARE OF ASSISI: FEAST DAY. Aug 11, 1253. Chiara Favorone di Offreduccio, a religious leader inspired by St. Francis of Assisi, was the first woman to write her own religious order rule. Born at Assisi, Italy, July 16, 1194, she died there Aug 11, 1253. A "Privilege of Poverty" freed her order from any constraint to accept material security, making the "Poor Clares" totally dependent on God.

BIRTHDAYS TODAY

Joanna Cole, 56, author (The Magic School Bus series), born Newark, NJ, Aug 11, 1944.

Will Friedle, 24, actor ("Boy Meets World"), born Hartford, CT, Aug 11, 1976.

Hulk Hogan, 47, wrestler, actor, born Terry Gene Bollea, Augusta, GA, Aug 11, 1953.

Tim Hutchinson, 51, US Senator (R, Arkansas), born Gravette, AR, Aug 11, 1949.

Stephen Wozniak, 50, Apple computer cofounder, born Sunnyvale, CA, Aug 11, 1950.

AUGUST 12 — SATURDAY
Day 225 — 141 Remaining

BUD BILLIKEN PARADE. Aug 12. Chicago, IL. A parade especially for children begun in 1929 by Robert S. Abbott. The second largest parade in the US, it features bands, floats, drill teams and celebrities. Annually, the second Saturday in August. For info: Michael Brown, PR Dir, Chicago Defender Charities, 2400 S Michigan, Chicago, IL 60616. Phone: (312) 225-2400. Fax: (312) 255-9231.

KING PHILIP ASSASSINATION: ANNIVERSARY. Aug 12, 1676. Philip, son of Massasoit, chief of the Wampanog tribe, was killed near Mt Hope, RI, by a renegade Indian of his own tribe, bringing to an end the first and bloodiest war between American Indians and white settlers of New England, a war that had raged for nearly two years and was known as King Philip's War.

MONTANAFAIR. Aug 12–14. MetraPark, Billings, MT. Montana's biggest event featuring exhibits, livestock events, carnival, rodeo and entertainment. Est attendance: 240,000. For info: MetraPark, PO Box 2514, Billings, MT 59103. Phone: (406) 256-2400.

SPACE MILESTONE: *ECHO I* (US): 40th ANNIVERSARY. Aug 12, 1960. First successful communications satellite in Earth's orbit launched, used to relay voice and TV signals from one ground station to another.

THAILAND: BIRTHDAY OF THE QUEEN. Aug 12. The entire kingdom of Thailand celebrates the birthday of Queen Sirikit.

BIRTHDAYS TODAY

Mary Ann Hoberman, 70, author (*One of Each*), born Stamford, CT, Aug 12, 1930.

Ann Martin, 45, author (The Baby-Sitters Club series), born Princeton, NJ, Aug 12, 1955.

Fredrick McKissack, 61, author, with his wife Patricia (*Christmas in the Big House*), born Nashville, TN, Aug 12, 1939.

Walter Dean Myers, 63, author (*Slam!, Harlem: A Poem*), born Martinsburg, WV, Aug 12, 1937.

Kyla Pratt, 12, actress (*Dr. Dolittle*, "The Baby-Sitters Club"), born North Kansas City, MO, Aug 12, 1988.

Pete Sampras, 29, tennis player, born Washington, DC, Aug 12, 1971.

Antoine Walker, 24, basketball player, born Chicago, IL, Aug 12, 1976.

AUGUST 13 — SUNDAY
Day 226 — 140 Remaining

BERLIN WALL ERECTED: ANNIVERSARY. Aug 13, 1961. Early in the morning, the East German government closed the border between the east and west sectors of Berlin with barbed wire fence to discourage further population movement to the west. Telephone and postal services were interrupted, and, later in the week, a concrete wall was built to strengthen the barrier between official crossing points. The dismantling of the wall began Nov 9, 1989. See also: "Berlin Wall Opened: Anniversary" (Nov 9).

CAXTON, WILLIAM: BIRTH ANNIVERSARY. Aug 13, 1422. First English printer, born at Kent, England. Died at London, England, 1491. Caxton produced the first book printed in English (while working for a printer at Bruges, Belgium), the *Recuyell of the Histories of Troy*, in 1476, and in the autumn of 1476 set up a print shop at Westminster, becoming the first printer in England.

CENTRAL AFRICAN REPUBLIC: INDEPENDENCE DAY: 40th ANNIVERSARY. Aug 13. Commemorates Proclamation of Independence from France of the Central African Republic in 1960.

DON'T WAIT—CELEBRATE! WEEK. Aug 13–19. To encourage frequent festivities acknowledging small but significant accomplishments such as team wins, good grades, completed projects, new neighbors, braces off, balanced checkbooks. Gathering for these minigalas will enhance and nurture relationships while raising the self-esteem of the honorees. Annually, the second full week in August. For info: Patty Sachs, Celebration Creations, 4520 Excelsior Blvd, Minneapolis, MN 55416. Phone: (612) 879-4592. E-mail: partysachs@internetmci.com. Web: www.geocities.com /~partyexpert/Dontwait.html.

INTERNATIONAL LEFT-HANDERS DAY. Aug 13. To recognize the needs and frustrations of left-handers and celebrate the good life of left-handedness. *See* Curriculum Connection. For info: Lefthanders Intl, Box 8249, Topeka, KS 66608. Phone: (913) 234-2177. Fax: (913) 232-3999.

INTERNATIONAL FEDERATION OF LIBRARY ASSOCIATIONS ANNUAL CONFERENCE. Aug 13–18. Jerusalem, Israel. For info: Intl Federation of Library Associations, The Royal Library, PO Box 95312, 2509 The Hague, Netherlands. Web: www.ifla.org.

OAKLEY, ANNIE: BIRTH ANNIVERSARY. Aug 13, 1860. Annie Oakley was born at Darke County, OH. She developed an eye as a markswoman early as a child, becoming so proficient that she was able to pay off the mortgage on her family farm by selling the game she killed. A few years after defeating vaudeville marksman Frank Butler in a shooting match, she married him and they toured as a team until joining Buffalo Bill's Wild West Show in 1885. She was one of the star attractions for 17 years. She died Nov 3, 1926, at Greenville, OH.

STONE, LUCY: BIRTH ANNIVERSARY. Aug 13, 1818. American women's rights pioneer, born near West Brookfield, MA, Lucy Stone dedicated her life to the abolition of slavery and the emancipation of women. A graduate of Oberlin College, she had to finance her education by teaching for nine years because her father did not favor college education for women. An eloquent speaker for her causes, she headed the list of 89 men and women who signed the call to the first national Woman's Rights Convention, held at Worcester, MA, October 1850. On May 1, 1855, she married Henry Blackwell. She and her husband aided in the founding of the American Suffrage Association, taking part in numerous referendum campaigns to win suffrage amendments to state constitutions. She died Oct 18, 1893, at Dorchester, MA.

TAIWAN: CHENG CHENG KUNG BIRTH ANNIVERSARY. Aug 13. Joyous celebration of birth of Cheng Cheng Kung (Koxinga), born at Hirado, Japan, the Ming Dynasty loyalist who ousted the Dutch colonists from Taiwan in 1661. Dutch landing is commemorated annually Apr 29, but Cheng's birthday is honored on the 14th day of the seventh moon according to the Chinese lunar calendar. Cheng Cheng Kung died June 23, 1662, at Taiwan. See also: "Taiwan: Cheng Cheng Kung Landing Day" (Apr 29).

August
2000

S	M	T	W	T	F	S
		1	2	3	4	5
6	7	8	9	10	11	12
13	14	15	16	17	18	19
20	21	22	23	24	25	26
27	28	29	30	31		

AUGUST 13
INTERNATIONAL LEFT-HANDER'S DAY

Put yourself in another person's place. Today, all left- and right-handers should swap handedness for short periods of time. This can be a real classroom challenge, as well as an opportunity for children to learn to tolerate differences.

At recess, set up a row of trash cans. Divide students into squads. Have a relay race where students toss balls to land one in the can nearest their line. All balls must be thrown with the "new" hand. Once the ball is in the can, the student can retrieve it and pass it to the next person in line. Don't make the distance too far; it's a lot harder than it sounds. Remember to open the door with your other hand on the way back inside.

During writing, announce, "Pencils down, switch hands. The next three sentences (five words for primary students) must be written with your other hand." Point out how difficult it is to see the written words as the students are writing. Right-handers don't cover the words with their hand as they write; left-handers are forced to. Afterward, ask students to identify letters that were easy and hard to make. Let them rewrite the same words using their "normal" hand and compare them.

In science, talk about the brain and which area determines left- and right-handedness. As a math assignment, count how many students are really left-handed. Compare the percentage in your class with that estimated for the general population (about 10 percent).

Point out small differences that we don't normally consider, such as using right- and left-handed scissors. Turning screws may be difficult for lefties. Have right-handed students button their clothing with their left hand. Is it harder? Poll left-handed students and see how many have adapted and use their right hand for things like opening doors or picking up food with a fork. Many people are left- or right-eyed as well. Ask students which eye they look through a camera or telescope with. Is it on the same side as the hand they write with?

Above all, encourage students to notice that when they use the "other" hand, they often have to slow down and be more patient. Getting angry and frustrated doesn't make the job easier. That's a helpful observation for all students to note and remember, especially when working with younger siblings or people who may not have the same ability levels they do.

For more information about left-handedness, special products for left-handers, famous lefties and fun stuff, visit Rosemary West's Left-Handed Page at www.rosemarywest.com/left.

TUNISIA: WOMEN'S DAY. Aug 13. General holiday. Celebration of independence of women.

BIRTHDAYS TODAY

Fidel Castro, 73, President of Cuba, born Mayari, Cuba, Aug 13, 1927.

AUGUST 14 — MONDAY
Day 227 — 139 Remaining

ATLANTIC CHARTER SIGNING: ANNIVERSARY. Aug 14, 1941. The charter grew out of a three-day conference aboard ship in the Atlantic Ocean, off the Newfoundland coast, and stated policies and goals for the postwar world. The eight-point agreement was signed by US President Franklin D. Roosevelt and British Prime Minister Winston S. Churchill.

CANADA: YUKON DISCOVERY DAY. Aug 14. In the Klondike region of the Yukon, at Bonanza Creek (formerly known as Rabbit Creek), George Washington Carmack discovered gold Aug 16 or 17, 1896. During the following year more than 30,000 people joined the gold rush to the area. Anniversary is celebrated as a holiday (Discovery Day) in the Yukon, on nearest Monday.

CHINA: FESTIVAL OF HUNGRY GHOSTS. Aug 14. Important Chinese festival, also known as Ghosts Month. According to Chinese legend, during the 7th lunar month the souls of the dead are released from purgatory to roam the Earth. Joss sticks are burnt in homes; prayers, food and "ghost money" are offered to appease the ghosts. Market stallholders combine to hold celebrations to ensure that their businesses will prosper in the coming year. Wayang (Chinese street opera) and puppet shows are performed, and fruit and Chinese delicacies are offered to the spirits of the dead. Chung Yuan (All Souls' Day) is observed on the 15th day of the 7th lunar month.

SOCIAL SECURITY ACT: 65TH ANNIVERSARY. Aug 14, 1935. The Congress approved the Social Security Act, which contained provisions for the establishment of a Social Security Board to administer federal old-age and survivors' insurance in the US. By signing the bill into law, President Franklin D. Roosevelt was fulfilling a 1932 campaign promise.

V-J (VICTORY IN JAPAN) DAY: 55th ANNIVERSARY. Aug 14, 1945. Anniversary of President Truman's announcement that Japan had surrendered to the Allies, setting off celebrations across the nation. Official ratification of surrender occurred aboard the USS *Missouri* at Tokyo Bay, Sept 2 (Far Eastern time).

BIRTHDAYS TODAY

Earvin ("Magic") Johnson, Jr, 41, former basketball player, born Lansing, MI, Aug 14, 1959.

Gary Larson, 50, cartoonist ("The Far Side"), born Tacoma, WA, Aug 14, 1950.

Alice Provensen, 82, author and illustrator, with her husband Martin (Caldecott for *The Glorious Flight: Across the Channel with Louis Bleriot*), born Chicago, IL, Aug 14, 1918.

AUGUST 15 — TUESDAY

Day 228 — 138 Remaining

ASSUMPTION OF THE VIRGIN MARY. Aug 15. Greek and Roman Catholic churches celebrate Mary's ascent to Heaven.

BONAPARTE, NAPOLEON: BIRTH ANNIVERSARY. Aug 15, 1769. Anniversary of birth of French emperor Napoleon Bonaparte on the island of Corsica. He died in exile May 5, 1821, on the island of St. Helena. Public holiday at Corsica, France.

CHAUVIN DAY. Aug 15. A day named for Nicholas Chauvin, French soldier from Rochefort, France, who idolized Napoleon and who eventually became a subject of ridicule because of his blind loyalty and dedication to anything French. Originally referring to bellicose patriotism, chauvinism has come to mean blind or absurdly intense attachment to any cause. Observed on Napoleon's birth anniversary because Chauvin's birth date is unknown.

CONGO (BRAZZAVILLE): NATIONAL HOLIDAY: 40th ANNIVERSARY. Aug 15. National day of the People's Republic of the Congo. Commemorates independence from France in 1960.

HARDING, FLORENCE KLING DeWOLFE: BIRTH ANNIVERSARY. Aug 15. Wife of Warren Gamaliel Harding, 29th president of the US, born at Marion, OH, Aug 15, 1860. Died at Marion, OH, Nov 21, 1924.

INDIA: INDEPENDENCE DAY. Aug 15. National holiday. Anniversary of Indian independence from Britain in 1947.

KOREA, REPUBLIC OF: LIBERATION DAY: 55th ANNIVERSARY. Aug 15. National holiday commemorates acceptance by Japan of Allied terms of surrender in 1945, thereby freeing Korea from 36 years of Japanese domination. Also marks formal proclamation of the Republic of Korea in 1948. Military parades and ceremonies throughout country.

LIECHTENSTEIN: NATIONAL DAY. Aug 15. Public holiday.

MOON PHASE: FULL MOON. Aug 15. Moon enters Full Moon phase at 1:13 AM, EDT.

TRANSCONTINENTAL US RAILWAY COMPLETION: ANNIVERSARY. Aug 15, 1870. The Golden Spike ceremony at Promontory Point, UT, May 10, 1869, was long regarded as the final link in a transcontinental railroad track reaching from an Atlantic port to a Pacific port. In fact, that link occurred unceremoniously on another date in another state. Diaries of engineers working at the site establish "the completion of a transcontinental track at a point 928 feet east of today's milepost 602, or 3,812 feet east of the present Union Pacific depot building at Strasburg (formerly Comanche)," CO. The final link was made at 2:53 PM, Aug 15, 1870. Annual celebration at Strasburg, CO, on a weekend in August. See also: "Golden Spike Driving: Anniversary" (May 10).

BIRTHDAYS TODAY

Ben Affleck, 28, actor (*Good Will Hunting*), born Berkeley, CA, Aug 15, 1972.

Stephen G. Breyer, 62, Associate Justice of the Supreme Court, born San Francisco, CA, Aug 15, 1938.

Linda Ellerbee, 56, journalist, host of "Nick News," born Bryan, TX, Aug 15, 1944.

AUGUST 16 — WEDNESDAY

Day 229 — 137 Remaining

BENNINGTON BATTLE DAY: ANNIVERSARY. Aug 16, 1777. Anniversary of this Revolutionary War battle is a legal holiday in Vermont.

DOMINICAN REPUBLIC: RESTORATION OF THE REPUBLIC. Aug 16. The anniversary of the Restoration of the Republic in 1863 is celebrated as an official public holiday.

LAWRENCE (OF ARABIA), T. E.: BIRTH ANNIVERSARY. Aug 16, 1888. British soldier, archaeologist and writer, born at Tremadoc, North Wales. During WWI, led the Arab revolt against the Turks and served as a spy for the British. His book, *Seven Pillars of Wisdom*, is a personal account of the Arab revolt. He was killed in a motorcycle accident at Dorset, England, May 19, 1935.

Matt Christopher, 83, author of sports books (*On the Court With . . . Michael Jordan*), born Bath, PA, Aug 16, 1917.

Diana Wynne Jones, 66, author (*Dark Lord of Derkholm*), born London, England, Aug 16, 1934.

LL Cool J, 32, rap singer, born James Todd Smith, Queens, NY, Aug 16, 1968.

Reginald VelJohnson, 48, actor ("Family Matters"), born Raleigh, NC, Aug 16, 1952.

AUGUST 17 — THURSDAY

Day 230 — 136 Remaining

BALLOON CROSSING OF ATLANTIC OCEAN: ANNIVERSARY. Aug 17, 1978. Three Americans—Maxie Anderson, 44, Ben Abruzzo, 48, and Larry Newman, 31—all of Albuquerque, NM, became the first people to complete a transatlantic trip in a balloon. Starting from Presque Isle, ME, Aug 11, they traveled some 3,200 miles in 137 hours, 18 minutes, landing at Miserey, France (about 60 miles west of Paris), in their craft, named the *Double Eagle II*.

CROCKETT, DAVID "DAVY": BIRTH ANNIVERSARY. Aug 17, 1786. American frontiersman, adventurer and soldier, born at Hawkins County, TN. Died during final heroic defense of the Alamo, Mar 6, 1836, at San Antonio, TX. In his *Autobiography* (1834), Crockett wrote, "I leave this rule for others when I'm dead, Be always sure you're right—then go ahead."

FORT SUMTER SHELLED BY NORTHERN FORCES: ANNIVERSARY. Aug 17, 1863. In what would become a long siege, Union forces began shelling Fort Sumter at Charleston, SC. The site of the first shots fired during the Civil War, Sumter endured the siege for a year and a half before being returned to Union hands.

FULTON SAILS STEAMBOAT: ANNIVERSARY. Aug 17, 1807. Robert Fulton began the first American steamboat trip between Albany and New York, NY, on a boat later called the *Clermont*. After years of promoting submarine warfare, Fulton engaged in a partnership with Robert R. Livingston, the US minister to France, allowing Fulton to design and construct a steamboat. His first success came in August 1803 when he launched a steam-powered vessel on the Seine. That same year the US Congress granted Livingston and Fulton exclusive rights to operate steamboats on New York waters during the next 20 years. The first Albany-to-New York trip took 32 hours to travel the 150-mile course. Although his efforts were labeled "Fulton's Folly" by his detractors, his success allowed the partnership to begin commercial service the next year, Sept 4, 1808.

GABON: NATIONAL DAY: 40th ANNIVERSARY. Aug 17. National holiday. Commemorates independence from France in 1960.

INDONESIA: INDEPENDENCE DAY: 55th ANNIVERSARY. Aug 17. National holiday. Republic proclaimed in 1945. It was only after several years of fighting, however, that Indonesia was formally granted its independence by the Netherlands, Dec 27, 1949.

KENTUCKY STATE FAIR (WITH WORLD CHAMPIONSHIP HORSE SHOW). Aug 17–27. Kentucky Fair and Expo Center, Louisville, KY. Midway, concerts by nationally known artists and the World's Championship Horse Show. Est attendance: 700,000. For info: Harold Workman, KY Fair and Expo Center, Box 37130, Louisville, KY 40233. Phone: (502) 367-5000.

TURKISH EARTHQUAKE: ANNIVERSARY. Aug 17, 1999. An earthquake with a magnitude of 7.4 struck northwestern Turkey where 45 percent of the population lives. More than 15,000 people were killed and thousands more were missing, in many cases because of the shoddy construction of the apartment buildings in which they lived. Later that year there were earthquakes in Greece (139 dead) and Taiwan (2,200 dead).

Christian Laettner, 31, NBA forward, member of the Dream team in the 1992 Olympics, born Angola, NY, Aug 17, 1969.

Myra Cohn Livingston, 74, poet (*Sky Songs, Space Songs*), born Omaha, NE, Aug 17, 1926.

AUGUST 18 — FRIDAY

Day 231 — 135 Remaining

CALIFORNIA STATE FAIR. Aug 18–Sept 4. Sacramento, CA. Top-name entertainment, fireworks, California counties exhibits, livestock nursery, culinary delights, carnival rides, demolition derbies and award-winning wines and microbrews. For info: Cal Expo, PO Box 15649, Sacramento, CA 95852. Phone: (916) 263-3000. E-mail: SallyCSF@aol.com.

CLEMENTE, ROBERTO: BIRTH ANNIVERSARY. Aug 18, 1934. National League baseball player, born at Carolina, Puerto Rico. Drafted by the Pittsburgh Pirates in 1954, he played his entire major league career with them. Clemente died in a plane crash Dec 31, 1972, while on a mission of mercy to Nicaragua to deliver supplies he had collected for survivors of an earthquake. He was elected to the Baseball Hall of Fame in 1973.

DARE, VIRGINIA: BIRTH ANNIVERSARY. Aug 18, 1587. Virginia Dare, the first child of English parents to be born in the New World, was born to Ellinor and Ananias Dare, at Roanoke Island, NC. When a ship arrived to replenish their supplies in 1591, the settlers (including Virginia Dare) had vanished, without leaving a trace of the settlement.

GINZA HOLIDAY: JAPANESE CULTURAL FESTIVAL. Aug 18–20. Midwest Buddhist Temple, Chicago, IL. Experience the Waza (National Treasures tradition) by viewing 300 years of Edo craft tradition and seeing it come alive as master craftsmen from

		S	M	T	W	T	F	S
August				1	2	3	4	5
2000		6	7	8	9	10	11	12
		13	14	15	16	17	18	19
		20	21	22	23	24	25	26
		27	28	29	30	31		

AUGUST 18
MERIWETHER LEWIS'S BIRTHDAY

Meriwether Lewis was an American explorer born in 1774. He and William Clark were commissioned by Thomas Jefferson to lead an expedition to explore routes to the west that would lead to the Pacific Ocean.

They began their trek in May 1804 by traveling up the Missouri River. They spent the winter of 1804–1805 in what is now North Dakota. The following spring and summer their party crossed the Rocky Mountains. They canoed across several river systems, finally paddling down the Columbia River and reaching the Pacific Coast in November 1805. Native Americans helped the explorers survive the harsh winter that followed. They arrived back in St. Louis in September 1806, after traveling more than 8,000 miles.

Lewis served as the expedition's naturalist. His journal recorded descriptions and drawings of the many rock formations, plants and animals he saw.

In science, have students read excerpts from Lewis's journal (look for copies in the public library or on the website noted here) that described the natural surroundings. Go on an expedition outside the school building. Ask students to pretend they are naturalists from another planet. Have them describe the plants, animals and other things they see as reports that will be transmitted back to their home planet.

Also for science, have students compare and contrast the kinds of rock, flora and fauna that Lewis encountered in two ways. First, how did they change as Lewis and Clark made their way across the territory. Second, how did what Lewis saw differ from the flora and fauna in the area where you live.

For geography, chart the course of Lewis and Clark's trip, labeling the major rivers, mountains and other physical boundaries they encountered, including weather phenomena.

Language arts projects may include writing a narrative poem that chronicles the expedition. Divide students into groups, then have each group write a stanza that represents a specific leg of the trip.

Foray into the musical arts and write a song (set to the tune of a song everyone knows) about the voyage. Present the song at a school assembly.

Literature connections include: *How We Crossed the West: The Adventures of Lewis & Clark*, by Rosalyn Schanzer (National Geographic, 0-79-223738-2, $18 Gr. 3–7). *My Name Is York*, by Elizabeth Van Steenwyk (Northland, 0-87358-650-6, $14.95 Gr. 2–4) is an account of the expedition told through the eyes of York, a slave who accompanied them. Sacagawea was a young Shoshone Indian woman who served as interpreter for Lewis and Clark. Biographies about her are available for every reading level. Some examples: the novel *Streams to the River, River to the Sea*, by Scott O'Dell (Houghton Mifflin, 0-395-40430-4, $16 Gr. 8–12); *Girl of the Shining Mountains: Sacagawea's Story*, by Peter Roop and Connie Roop (Hyperion, 0-786-80492-0, $14.99 Gr. 5–8); and *A Picture Book of Sacagawea*, by David A. Adler (Holiday House, 0-823-41485-X, $16.95 All ages). *Seaman: The Dog Who Explored the West with Lewis & Clark*, by Gail Karwoski (Peachtree, 1-56145-190-8, $8.95 Gr. 4–8) is a novel that dramatizes the story of Seaman, the Newfoundland dog that joined the expedition.

The website for the PBS television program "Lewis and Clark: The Corps of Discovery" has classroom resources at www.pbs.org/lewisandclark.

Tokyo demonstrate their arts. Japanese folk and classical dancing, martial arts, taiko (drums), flower arrangements and cultural displays. Chicken teriyaki, sushi, udon, shaved ice, corn on the cob and refreshments. Annually, the third weekend in August. Est attendance: 5,000. For info: Office Secretary, Midwest Buddhist Temple, 435 W Menomonee St, Chicago, IL 60614. Phone: (312) 943-7801. Fax: (312) 943-8069.

LEWIS, MERIWETHER: BIRTH ANNIVERSARY. Aug 18, 1774. American explorer (of Lewis and Clark expedition), born at Albemarle County, VA. Died Oct 11, 1809, near Nashville, TN. *See* Curriculum Connection.

MAIL-ORDER CATALOG: ANNIVERSARY. Aug 18, 1872. The first mail-order catalog was published by Montgomery Ward. It was only a single sheet of paper. By 1904, the Montgomery Ward catalog weighed four pounds.

NINETEENTH AMENDMENT TO US CONSTITUTION RATIFIED: 80th ANNIVERSARY. Aug 18, 1920. The 19th Amendment extended the right to vote to women.

BIRTHDAYS TODAY

Rosalynn (Eleanor) Smith Carter, 73, former First Lady, wife of President Jimmy Carter, 39th president of the US, born Plains, GA, Aug 18, 1927.

Paula Danziger, 56, author (*The Cat Ate My Gymsuit, Amber Brown Is Not a Crayon*), born Washington, DC, Aug 18, 1944.

Mike Johanns, 50, Governor of Nebraska (R), born Osage, IA, Aug 18, 1950.

Martin Mull, 57, actor ("Sabrina, the Teenage Witch"), born Chicago, IL, Aug 18, 1943.

AUGUST 19 — SATURDAY
Day 232 — 134 Remaining

AFGHANISTAN: INDEPENDENCE DAY. Aug 19. National day. Commemorates independence from British control over foreign affairs in 1919.

CLINTON, WILLIAM JEFFERSON (BILL): BIRTHDAY. Aug 19, 1946. The 42nd president of the US, born at Hope, AR. Reelected to a second term in 1996.

COLORADO STATE FAIR. Aug 19–Sept 4. State Fairgrounds, Pueblo, CO. One of the nation's oldest western fairs, it is also Colorado's largest single event, drawing more than a million visitors. Family fun, top-name entertainment, lots of food and festivities. For info: Colorado State Fair, Jerry Robbe, Pres/General Mgr, Pueblo, CO 81004. Phone: (719) 561-8484.

★**NATIONAL AVIATION DAY.** Aug 19. Presidential Proclamation 2343, of July 25, 1939, covers all succeeding years. Always Aug 19 of each year since 1939. Observed annually on anniversary of birth of Orville Wright, who piloted "first self-powered flight in history," Dec 17, 1903. First proclaimed by President Franklin D. Roosevelt.

SPACE MILESTONE: *SPUTNIK 5* (USSR): 40th ANNIVERSARY. Aug 19, 1960. Space menagerie satellite with dogs Belka and Strelka, mice, rats, houseflies and plants launched. These passengers became first living organisms recovered from orbit when the satellite returned safely to Earth the next day.

WRIGHT, ORVILLE: BIRTH ANNIVERSARY. Aug 19, 1871. Aviation pioneer (with his brother Wilbur), born at Dayton, OH, Aug 19, 1871, and died there Jan 30, 1948.

WYOMING STATE FAIR. Aug 19–26. Douglas, WY. Recognizing the products, achievements and cultural heritage of the people of Wyoming. Bringing together rural and urban citizens for an inexpensive, entertaining and educational experience. Features Livestock show for beef, swine, sheep and horses, Junior Livestock show for beef, swine, sheep, horses, dogs and rabbits, competitions and displays for culinary arts, needlework, visual arts and floriculture, 4-H and FFA County Chapters State qualifications competitions, Youth Talent Show, Demo Derby, live entertainment, midway, PRCA Rodeo and an All Girl Rodeo (rough stock). Est attendance: 82,000. For info: Wyoming State Fair, Drawer 10, Douglas, WY 82633. Phone: (307) 358-2398. Fax: (307) 358-6030. E-mail: wystfair@coffey.com.

BIRTHDAYS TODAY

Victor Ambrus, 65, author (*The Three Poor Tailors*), born Budapest, Aug 19, 1935.

William Jefferson (Bill) Clinton, 54, 42nd president of the US, born Hope, AR, Aug 19, 1946.

Tipper Gore, 52, Second Lady, wife of Al Gore, 45th vice president of the US, born Mary Elizabeth Aitcheson, Washington, DC, Aug 19, 1948.

John Stamos, 37, actor ("Full House"), born Cypress, CA, Aug 19, 1963.

Fred Thompson, 58, US Senator (R, Tennessee), actor (*In the Line of Fire*), born Sheffield, AL, Aug 19, 1942.

AUGUST 20 — SUNDAY
Day 233 — 133 Remaining

HARRISON, BENJAMIN: BIRTH ANNIVERSARY. Aug 20, 1833. The 23rd president of the US, born at North Bend, OH. He was the grandson of William Henry Harrison, 9th president of the US. His term of office, Mar 4, 1889–Mar 3, 1893, was preceded and followed by the presidential terms of Grover Cleveland (who thus became the 22nd and 24th president of the US). Harrison died at Indianapolis, IN, Mar 13, 1901.

HUNGARY: ST. STEPHEN'S DAY. Aug 20. National holiday. Commemorates the canonization of St. Stephen in 1083. Under the Communists celebrated as Constitution Day.

O'HIGGINS, BERNARDO: BIRTH ANNIVERSARY. Aug 20, 1778. First ruler of Chile after its declaration of independence. Called the "Liberator of Chile." Born at Chillan, Chile. Died at Lima, Peru, Oct 24, 1842.

PERRY, OLIVER HAZARD: BIRTH ANNIVERSARY. Aug 20, 1785. American naval hero, born at South Kingston, RI. Died Aug 23, 1819, at sea. Best remembered is his announcement of victory at the Battle of Lake Erie, Sept 10, 1813 during the War of 1812: "We have met the enemy, and they are ours."

	S	M	T	W	T	F	S
August			1	2	3	4	5
2000	6	7	8	9	10	11	12
	13	14	15	16	17	18	19
	20	21	22	23	24	25	26
	27	28	29	30	31		

SPACE MILESTONE: *VOYAGER 2* (US). Aug 20, 1977. This unmanned spacecraft journeyed past Jupiter in 1979, Saturn in 1981, Uranus in 1986 and Neptune in 1989, sending photographs and data back to scientists on Earth.

BIRTHDAYS TODAY

Al Roker, 46, TV meteorologist ("Today Show"), born Brooklyn, NY, Aug 20, 1954.

AUGUST 21 — MONDAY
Day 234 — 132 Remaining

HAWAII: ADMISSION DAY: ANNIVERSARY. Aug 21, 1959. President Dwight Eisenhower signed a proclamation admitting Hawaii to the Union. The statehood bill had passed the previous March with a stipulation that statehood should be approved by a vote of Hawaiian residents. The referendum passed by a huge margin in June and Eisenhower proclaimed Hawaii the 50th state Aug 21. The third Friday in August is observed as a state holiday in Hawaii, commemorating statehood (Aug 18 in 2000).

LITTLE LEAGUE BASEBALL WORLD SERIES. Aug 21–27. Williamsport, PA. Eight teams from the US and foreign countries compete for the World Championship. Est attendance: 100,000. For info: Little League Baseball HQ, Box 3485, Williamsport, PA 17701. Phone: (570) 326-1921. Web: www.littleleague.org.

SWEDISH LANGUAGE AND CULTURE DAY CAMP. Aug 21–25. West Riverside Historic Site, Cambridge, MN. Children learn to speak Swedish and understand Swedish culture through songs, games, language classes and craft classes. Families see what their children have learned at a program at the end of the week. Annually, the last full week in August. For info: Valerie Arrowsmith, Isanti County Historical Soc, PO Box 525, Cambridge, MN 55008. Phone: (612) 689-4229. Fax: (612) 689-5134.

BIRTHDAYS TODAY

Steve Case, 42, president, America Online, born Honolulu, HI, Aug 21, 1958.

Akili Smith, 25, football player, born San Diego, CA, Aug 21, 1975.

Arthur Yorinks, 47, author (*Hey, Al*), born Roslyn, NY, Aug 21, 1953.

AUGUST 22 — TUESDAY
Day 235 — 131 Remaining

BE AN ANGEL DAY. Aug 22. A day to do "one small act of service for someone. Be a blessing in someone's life." Annually, Aug 22. For info: Angel Heights Healing Center, Rev Jayne M. Howard, PO Box 95, Upperco, MD 21155. Phone: (410) 833-6912. Fax: (410) 429-4077. E-mail: blessing@erols.com. Web: drwnet.com/angel.

CAMEROON: VOLCANIC ERUPTION: ANNIVERSARY. Aug 22, 1986. Deadly fumes from a presumed volcanic eruption under Lake Nios at Cameroon killed more than 1,500 persons. A similar occurrence two years earlier had killed 37 persons. For more info visit Volcano World: volcano.und.nodak.edu.

DEBUSSY, CLAUDE: BIRTH ANNIVERSARY. Aug 22, 1862. (Achille) Claude Debussy, French musician and composer, especially remembered for his impressionistic "tone poems," was born at St. Germain-en-Laye, France. He died at Paris, France, Mar 25, 1918.

MICHIGAN STATE FAIR. Aug 22–Sept 4. State Fairgrounds, Detroit, MI. Est attendance: 400,000. For info: State of Michigan, Dept of Agriculture, 1120 W State Fair Ave, Detroit, MI 48203. Phone: (313) 369-8250.

MOON PHASE: LAST QUARTER. Aug 22. Moon enters Last Quarter phase at 2:51 PM, EDT.

VIETNAM CONFLICT BEGINS: 55th ANNIVERSARY. Aug 22, 1945. Less than a week after the Japanese surrender ended WWII, a team of Free French parachuted into southern Indochina in response to a successful coup by a Communist guerrilla named Ho Chi Minh in the French colony.

BIRTHDAYS TODAY

Ray Bradbury, 80, author (*The Toynbee Convector, Fahrenheit 451*), born Waukegan, IL, Aug 22, 1920.

Howie Dorough, 27, singer (Backstreet Boys), born Orlando, FL, Aug 22, 1973.

Paul Molitor, 44, baseball player, born St. Paul, MN, Aug 22, 1956.

AUGUST 23 — WEDNESDAY
Day 236 — 130 Remaining

FIRST MAN-POWERED FLIGHT: ANNIVERSARY. Aug 23, 1977. At Schafter, CA, Bryan Allen pedaled the 70-lb *Gossamer Condor* for a mile at a "minimal altitude of two pylons" in a flight certified by the Royal Aeronautical Society of Britain, winning a £50,000 prize offered by British industrialist Henry Kremer.

NEVADA STATE FAIR. Aug 23–27. Reno Livestock Events Center, Reno, NV. State entertainment and carnival, with home arts, agriculture and commercial exhibits. Est attendance: 73,000. For info: Gary Lubra, CEO, Nevada State Fair, 1350-A N Wells Ave, Reno, NV 89512. Phone: (775) 688 5767. Fax: (775) 688-5763. E-mail: nvstatefair@inetworld.com. Web: www.nevadastatefair.org.

VIRGO, THE VIRGIN. Aug 23–Sept 22. In the astronomical/astrological zodiac, which divides the sun's apparent orbit into 12 segments, the period Aug 23–Sept 22 is identified, traditionally, as the sun sign of Virgo, the Virgin. The ruling planet is Mercury.

BIRTHDAYS TODAY

Kobe Bryant, 22, basketball player, born Philadelphia, PA, Aug 23, 1978.

Rik Smits, 34, basketball player, born Eindhoven, The Netherlands, Aug 23, 1966.

AUGUST 24 — THURSDAY
Day 237 — 129 Remaining

ITALY: VESUVIUS DAY. Aug 24, AD 79. Anniversary of the eruption of Vesuvius, an active volcano in southern Italy, which destroyed the cities of Pompeii, Stabiae and Herculaneum. For more info: *In Search of Pompeii* (Peter Bedrick, 0-87226-545-5, $18.95 Gr. 5 & up) or visit Volcano World: volcano.und .nodak.edu.

MINNESOTA STATE FAIR. Aug 24–Sept 4. St. Paul, MN. Major entertainers, agricultural displays, arts, crafts, food, carnival rides, animal judging and performances. Est attendance: 1,700,000. For info: Minnesota State Fair, 1265 Snelling Ave N, St. Paul, MN 55108-3099. Phone: (651) 642-2200. E-mail: fairinfo@statefair .gen.mn.us.

NEW YORK STATE FAIR. Aug 24–Sept 4. Empire Expo Center, Syracuse, NY. Agricultural and livestock competitions, top-name entertainment, the International Horse Show, business and industrial exhibits, the midway and ethnic presentations. Est attendance: 900,000. For info: Joseph LaGuardia, Dir of Mktg, NY State Fair, Empire Expo Center, Syracuse, NY 13209. Phone: (315) 487-7711. Fax: (315) 487-9260.

OREGON STATE FAIR. Aug 24–Sept 4. Salem, OR. Exhibits, products and displays illustrate Oregon's role as one of the nation's major agricultural and recreational states. Floral gardens, carnival, big-name entertainment, horse show and food. Annually, 12 days ending on Labor Day. Est attendance: 730,000. For info: Oregon State Fair, 2330 17th St NE, Salem, OR 97303-3201. Phone: (503) 378-3247.

UKRAINE: INDEPENDENCE DAY. Aug 24. National day. Commemorates independence from the former Soviet Union in 1991.

WARNER WEATHER QUOTATION: ANNIVERSARY. Aug 24, 1897. Charles Dudley Warner, American newspaper editor for the *Hartford Courant*, published this now-famous and oft-quoted sentence, "Everybody talks about the weather, but nobody does anything about it." The quotation is often mistakenly attributed to his friend and colleague Mark Twain. Warner and Twain were part of the most notable American literary circle during the late 19th century. Warner was a journalist, essayist, novelist, biographer and author who collaborated with Mark Twain in writing *The Gilded Age* in 1873.

WASHINGTON, DC: INVASION ANNIVERSARY. Aug 24–25, 1814. During the War of 1812, British forces briefly invaded and raided Washington, DC, burning the Capitol, the president's house and most other public buildings. President James Madison and other high US government officials fled to safety until British troops (not knowing the strength of their position) departed the city two days later.

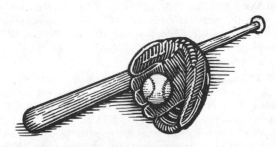

BIRTHDAYS TODAY

Max Cleland, 58, US Senator (D, Georgia), born Atlanta, GA, Aug 24, 1942.

Mike Huckabee, 45, Governor of Arkansas (R), born Hope, AR, Aug 24, 1955.

Reginald (Reggie) Miller, 35, basketball player, born Riverside, CA, Aug 24, 1965.

Kenny Quinn, 64, Governor of Nevada (R), born Garland, AR, Aug 24, 1936.

Calvin Edward (Cal) Ripken, Jr, 40, baseball player, born Havre de Grace, MD, Aug 24, 1960.

Merlin Tuttle, 59, scientist who works with bats, author (*Bats for Kids*), born Honolulu, HI, Aug 24, 1941.

AUGUST 25 — FRIDAY
Day 238 — 128 Remaining

ALASKA STATE FAIR 2000. Aug 25–Sept 4. Palmer, AK. Cows and critters, music and dancing, rides, excitement and family fun at the state's largest summer extravaganza. See 100 lb cabbages, native art and more than 500 events including demonstrations, high-caliber entertainment, rodeos, horse shows, crafts and agricultural exhibits. Est attendance: 280,000. For info: Alaska State Fair, Inc, 2075 Glenn Hwy, Palmer, AK 99645. Phone: (907) 745-4827 or (800) 850-FAIR. Fax: (907) 746-2699. Web: www .akstatefair.org.

BE KIND TO HUMANKIND WEEK. Aug 25–31. All of the negative news that you read about in the paper each day and hear on your local news station is disheartening—but the truth is the "positive" stories outweigh the negative stories by a long shot! We just don't hear about them as often. Take heart . . .most people are caring individuals. Show you care by being kind. For info: Lorraine Jara, PO Box 586, Island Heights, NJ 08732-0586.

BERNSTEIN, LEONARD: BIRTH ANNIVERSARY. Aug 25, 1918. American conductor and composer, born at Lawrence, MA. One of the greatest conductors in American music history, he first conducted the New York Philharmonic Orchestra at age 25 and was its director from 1959 to 1969. His musicals include *West Side Story* and *On the Town*, and his operas and operettas include *Candide*. He died five days after his retirement Oct 14, 1990, at New York, NY.

KELLY, WALT: BIRTH ANNIVERSARY. Aug 25, 1913. American cartoonist and creator of the comic strip "Pogo" was born at Philadelphia, PA. It was Kelly's character Pogo who paraphrased Oliver Hazard Perry to say, "We has met the enemy, and it is us." Kelly died at Hollywood, CA, Oct 18, 1973. See also: "Perry, Oliver Hazard: Birth Anniversary" (Aug 23).

MARYLAND STATE FAIR. Aug 25–Sept 4. Timonium, MD. Home arts, agricultural and livestock presentations, midway rides, live entertainment and thoroughbred horse racing. Est attendance: 500,000. For info: Max Mosner, State Fairgrounds, PO Box 188, Timonium, MD 21094. Phone: (410) 252-0200.

NEBRASKA STATE FAIR. Aug 25–Sept 4. Lincoln, NE. Book fair, food booths, variety of entertainment, rodeos, amusement rides and tractor pulls. For info: Nebraska State Fair, PO Box 81223, Lincoln, NE 68501. Phone: (402) 473-4110. Fax: (402) 473-4114. E-mail: nestatefair@statefair.org.

PARIS LIBERATED: ANNIVERSARY. Aug 25, 1944. As dawn broke, the men of the 2nd French Armored Division entered Paris, ending the long German occupation of the City of Light. That afternoon General Charles de Gaulle led a parade down the Champs Elysées. Though Hitler had ordered the destruction of Paris, German occupying-officer General Dietrich von Choltitz refused that order and instead surrendered to French Major General Jacques Le Clerc.

SMITH, SAMANTHA: 15th DEATH ANNIVERSARY. Aug 25, 1985. American schoolgirl whose interest in world peace drew praise and affection from people around the world. In 1982, the 10-year-old wrote a letter to Soviet leader Yuri Andropov asking him, "Why do you want to conquer the whole world, or at least our country?" The letter was widely publicized in the USSR and Andropov replied personally to her. Samantha Smith was invited to visit and tour the Soviet Union. On Aug 25, 1985, the airplane on which she was riding crashed at Maine, killing all aboard, including Samantha and her father. In 1986, minor planet No 3147, an asteroid between Mars and Jupiter, was named Samantha Smith in her memory.

URUGUAY: INDEPENDENCE DAY. Aug 25. National holiday. Gained independence from Brazil in 1828.

***THE WIZARD OF OZ* FIRST RELEASED: ANNIVERSARY.** Aug 25, 1939. This motion-picture classic featured Dorothy and her dog Toto. The two were swept into a tornado and landed in a fictional place called Munchkinland. To get home she must go and see the Wizard of Oz and on the way meets the Scarecrow, the Tin Man and the Cowardly Lion. The cast included Judy Garland as Dorothy, Frank Morgan as the Wizard, Ray Bolger as Scarecrow, Bert Lahr as the Lion, Jack Haley as Tin Man and Margaret Hamilton as the Wicked Witch of the West.

BIRTHDAYS TODAY

Albert Belle, 34, baseball player, born Shreveport, LA, Aug 25, 1966.
Tim Burton, 42, producer (*The Nightmare Before Christmas*), born Burbank, CA, Aug 25, 1958.
Sean Connery, 70, actor (James Bond movies; *The Man Who Would Be King*), born Edinburgh, Scotland, Aug 25, 1930.
Kel Mitchell, 22, actor ("All That," "Kenan & Kel"), born Chicago, IL, Aug 25, 1978.

AUGUST 26 — SATURDAY
Day 239 — 127 Remaining

CHILDREN'S DAY. Aug 26. Woodstock, VT. Traditional farm activities from corn shelling to sawing firewood—19th-century games, traditional spelling bee, ice cream and butter making, wagon rides. Children ages 12 and under and accompanied by an adult are admitted free. For info: Deborah Bulissa, Exec Asst, Billings Farm Museum, PO Box 489, Woodstock, VT 05091. Phone: (802) 457-2355. Fax: (802) 457-4663. E-mail: billings.farm @valley.net.

De FOREST, LEE: BIRTH ANNIVERSARY. Aug 26, 1873. American inventor of the electron tube, radio knife for surgery and the photoelectric cell and a pioneer in the creation of talking pictures and television. Born at Council Bluffs, IA, De Forest was holder of hundreds of patents but perhaps best remembered by the moniker he gave himself in the title of his autobiography, *Father of Radio*, published in 1950. So unbelievable was the idea of wireless radio broadcasting that De Forest was accused of fraud and arrested for selling stock to underwrite the invention that later was to become an essential part of daily life. De Forest died at Hollywood, CA, June 30, 1961.

FIRST BASEBALL GAMES TELEVISED: ANNIVERSARY. Aug 26, 1939. WXBS television, at New York City, broadcast the first major league baseball games—a doubleheader between the Cincinnati Reds and the Brooklyn Dodgers at Ebbets Field. Announcer Red Barber interviewed Leo Durocher, manager of the Dodgers, and William McKechnie, manager of the Reds, between games.

August 2000	S	M	T	W	T	F	S
			1	2	3	4	5
	6	7	8	9	10	11	12
	13	14	15	16	17	18	19
	20	21	22	23	24	25	26
	27	28	29	30	31		

KRAKATOA ERUPTION: ANNIVERSARY. Aug 26, 1883. Anniversary of the biggest explosion in historic times. The eruption of the Indonesian volcanic island, Krakatoa (Krakatau) was heard 3,000 miles away, created tidal waves 120 ft high (killing 36,000 persons), hurled five cubic miles of earth fragments into the air (some to a height of 50 miles) and affected the oceans and the atmosphere for years.

LOS ANGELES LATINO BOOK AND FAMILY FESTIVAL. Aug 26–27. Los Angeles Convention Center. To expose children and adults to a wide range of English and Spanish-language books. Author readings, arts and crafts, health, career and travel information, entertainment. Est attendance: 26,000. For info: Los Angeles Latino Book and Family Festival, 3445 Catalina Dr, Carlsbad, CA 92008-2856. E-mail: kathy@latinofestivals.com. Web: www.latinofestivals.com.

MONTGOLFIER, JOSEPH MICHEL: BIRTH ANNIVERSARY. Aug 26, 1740. French merchant and inventor, born at Vidalonlez-Annonay, France, who, with his brother Jacques Etienne in November 1782, conducted experiments with paper and fabric bags filled with smoke and hot air which led to the invention of the hot-air balloon and man's first flight. Died at Balarucles-Bains, France, June 26, 1810. See also: "Montgolfier, Jacques Etienne: Birth Anniversary" (Jan 7), "First Balloon Flight: Anniversary" (June 5) and "Aviation History Month" (Nov 1).

SABIN, ALBERT BRUCE: BIRTH ANNIVERSARY. Aug 26, 1906. American medical researcher, born at Bialystok, Poland. He is most noted for his oral vaccine for polio, which replaced Jonas Salk's injected vaccine because Sabin's provided lifetime protection. He was awarded the US National Medal of Science in 1971. Sabin died Mar 3, 1993, at Washington, DC.

★**WOMEN'S EQUALITY DAY.** Aug 26. Presidential Proclamation issued in 1973 and 1974 at request and since 1975 without request.

WOMEN'S EQUALITY DAY. Aug 26. Anniversary of certification as part of US Constitution, in 1920, of the 19th Amendment, prohibiting discrimination on the basis of sex with regard to voting. Congresswoman Bella Abzug's bill to designate Aug 26 of each year as "Women's Equality Day" in August 1974 became Public Law 93–382.

BIRTHDAYS TODAY

Patricia Beatty, 78, author (*Charley Skedaddle*), born Portland, OR, Aug 26, 1922.

Macaulay Culkin, 20, actor (*Home Alone, My Girl*), born New York, NY, Aug 26, 1980.

Thomas J. Ridge, 55, Governor of Pennsylvania (R), born Munhall, PA, Aug 26, 1945.

Robert G. Torricelli, 49, US Senator (D, New Jersey), born Paterson, NJ, Aug 26, 1951.

AUGUST 27 — SUNDAY

Day 240 — 126 Remaining

★**AMERICA GOES BACK TO SCHOOL.** Aug 27–Sept 9.

BELGIUM: WEDDING OF THE GIANTS. Aug 27. Traditional cultural observance. Annually, the fourth Sunday in August.

DAWES, CHARLES GATES: BIRTH ANNIVERSARY. Aug 27, 1865. The 30th vice president of the US (1925–1929), born at Marietta, OH. Won the Nobel Peace Prize in 1925 for the "Dawes Plan" for German reparations. Died at Evanston, IL, Apr 23, 1951.

FIRST COMMERCIAL OIL WELL: ANNIVERSARY. Aug 27, 1859. W.A. "Uncle Billy" Smith discovered oil in a shaft being sunk by Colonel E.L. Drake at Titusville, in western Pennsylvania. Drilling had reached 69 feet, 6 inches when Smith saw a dark film floating on the water below the derrick floor. Soon 20 barrels of crude were being pumped each day. At first, oil was refined into kerosene and used for lighting, in place of whale oil. Only later was it refined into gasoline for cars. The first gas station opened in 1907.

FIRST PLAY PRESENTED IN NORTH AMERICAN COLONIES: ANNIVERSARY. Aug 27, 1655. Acomac, VA, was the site of the first play presented in the North American colonies. The play was *Ye Bare and Ye Cubb*, by Phillip Alexander Bruce. Three local residents were arrested and fined for acting in the play. At the time, most colonies had laws prohibiting public performances; Virginia, however, had no such ordinance.

HAMLIN, HANNIBAL: BIRTH ANNIVERSARY. Aug 27, 1809. The 15th vice president of the US (1861–1865), born at Paris, ME. Died at Bangor, ME, July 4, 1891.

JOHNSON, LYNDON BAINES: BIRTH ANNIVERSARY. Aug 27, 1908. The 36th president of the US succeeded to the presidency following the assassination of John F. Kennedy. Johnson's term of office: Nov 22, 1963–Jan 20, 1969. In 1964, he said: "The challenge of the next half-century is whether we have the wisdom to use [our] wealth to enrich and elevate our national life—and to advance the quality of American civilization." Johnson was born near Stonewall, TX, and died at San Antonio, TX, Jan 22, 1973. His birthday is observed as a holiday in Texas.

MOLDOVA: INDEPENDENCE DAY. Aug 27. Republic of Moldova declared its independence from the Soviet Union in 1991.

MOTHER TERESA: 90th BIRTH ANNIVERSARY. Aug 27, 1910. Albanian Roman Catholic nun, born Agnes Gonxha Bojaxhiu at Skopje, Macedonia. She founded the Order of the Missionaries of Charity, which cared for the destitute of Calcutta, India. She won the Nobel Peace Prize in 1979. She died at Calcutta, Sept 5, 1997.

BIRTHDAYS TODAY

Suzanne Fisher, 55, author (*Shabanu, Daughter of the Wind*), born Philadelphia, PA, Aug 27, 1945.

J. Robert Kerrey, 57, US Senator (D, Nebraska), born Lincoln, NE, Aug 27, 1943.

Suzy Kline, 57, author (the Horrible Harry series), born Berkeley, CA, Aug 27, 1943.

Carlos Moya, 24, tennis player, born Palma de Mallorca, Aug 27, 1976.

Paul Rubens (Pee-Wee Herman), 48, actor, writer ("Pee-Wee's Playhouse," *Pee-Wee's Big Adventure*), born Peekskill, NY, Aug 27, 1952.

AUGUST 28 — MONDAY

Day 241 — 125 Remaining

FEAST OF SAINT AUGUSTINE. Aug 28. Bishop of Hippo, author of *Confessions* and *The City of God*, born Nov 13, 354, at Tagaste, in what is now Algeria. Died Aug 28, 430, at Hippo, also in North Africa.

HAYES, LUCY WARE WEBB: BIRTH ANNIVERSARY. Aug 28, 1831. Wife of Rutherford Birchard Hayes, 19th president of the US, born at Chillicothe, OH. Died at Fremont, OH, June 25, 1889. She was nicknamed "Lemonade Lucy" because she and the president, both abstainers, served no alcoholic beverages at White House receptions.

HONG KONG: LIBERATION DAY. Aug 28. Public holiday to celebrate liberation from the Japanese in 1945. Annually, the last Monday in August.

MARCH ON WASHINGTON: ANNIVERSARY. Aug 28, 1963. More than 250,000 people attended this Civil Rights rally at Washington, DC, at which Reverend Dr. Martin Luther King, Jr made his famous "I have a dream" speech. For the text of his speech: *I Have a Dream*, by Dr. Martin Luther King, Jr (Scholastic, 0-590-20516-1, $16.95 All ages).

PETERSON, ROGER TORY: BIRTH ANNIVERSARY. Aug 28, 1908. Naturalist, author of *A Field Guide to Birds*, born at Jamestown, NY. Peterson died at Old Lyme, CT, July 28, 1996.

RADIO COMMERCIALS: ANNIVERSARY. Aug 28, 1922. Broadcasters realized radio could earn profits from the sale of advertising time. WEAF in New York ran a commercial "spot," which was sponsored by the Queensboro Realty Corporation of Jackson Heights to promote Hawthorne Court, a group of apartment buildings at Queens. The commercial rate was $100 for 10 minutes.

SETON, ELIZABETH ANN BAYLEY: BIRTH ANNIVERSARY. Aug 28, 1774. First American-born saint was born at New York, NY. Seton died Jan 4, 1821, at Emmitsburg, MD. The founder of the American Sisters of Charity, the first American order of Roman Catholic nuns, she was canonized in 1975.

SPACE MILESTONE: *MIR* ABANDONED (USSR). Aug 28, 1999. The last crew left the *Mir* space station, launched in 1986. *Mir's* core component had been aloft for close to 5,000 days and orbited Earth more than 77,000 times. Nearly 100 people, 7 of them American, had spent some time on *Mir*. See also: "Space Milestone: *Mir* Space Station (USSR)" (Feb 20).

BIRTHDAYS TODAY

William S. Cohen, 60, US Secretary of Defense (Clinton administration), born Bangor, ME, Aug 28, 1940.

Michael Galeota, 16, actor (*Can't Be Heaven, Clubhouse Detectives*), born Long Island, NY, Aug 28, 1984.

Scott Hamilton, 42, Olympic gold medal figure skater, born Toledo, OH, Aug 28, 1958.

J. Brian Pinkney, 39, illustrator (*Duke Ellington: The Piano Prince and His Orchestra*), born Boston, MA, Aug 28, 1961.

LeAnn Rimes, 18, singer, born Jackson, MS, Aug 28, 1982.

Allen Say, 63, illustrator and author (Caldecott for *Grandfather's Journey*), born Yokohama, Japan, Aug 28, 1937.

AUGUST 29 — TUESDAY

Day 242 — 124 Remaining

"ACCORDING TO HOYLE" DAY (EDMOND HOYLE DEATH ANNIVERSARY). Aug 29, 1769. A day to remember Edmond Hoyle and a day for fun and games *according to the rules*. He is believed to have studied law. For many years he lived at London, England, and gave instructions in the playing of games. His "Short Treatise" on the game of whist (published in 1742) became a model guide to the rules of the game. Hoyle's name became synonymous with the idea of correct play according to the rules, and

		S	M	T	W	T	F	S
August				1	2	3	4	5
2000		6	7	8	9	10	11	12
		13	14	15	16	17	18	19
		20	21	22	23	24	25	26
		27	28	29	30	31		

the phrase "according to Hoyle" became a part of the English language. Hoyle was born about 1672, at London and died there.

AMISTAD SEIZED: ANNIVERSARY. Aug 29, 1839. In January 1839, 53 Africans were seized near modern-day Sierra Leone, taken to Cuba and sold as slaves. While being transferred to another part of the island on the ship *Amistad*, led by the African, Cinque, they seized control of the ship, telling the crew to take them back to Africa. However, the crew secretly changed course and the ship landed at Long Island, NY, where it and its "cargo" were seized as salvage. The *Amistad* was towed to New Haven, CT where the Africans were imprisoned and a lengthy legal battle began to determine if they were property to be returned to Cuba or free men. John Quincy Adams took their case all the way to the Supreme Court, where on Mar 9, 1841 it was determined that they were free and could return to Africa. A replica of the *Amistad* is being built at the Mystic Seaport Museum, Mystic, CT. For more info: amistad.mysticseaport.org and www.law.umkc.edu/faculty/projects/ftrials/ftrials.htm.

MOON PHASE: NEW MOON. Aug 29. Moon enters New Moon phase at 6:19 AM, EDT.

SHAYS REBELLION: ANNIVERSARY. Aug 29, 1786. Daniel Shays, veteran of the battles of Lexington, Bunker Hill, Ticonderoga and Saratoga, was one of the leaders of more than 1,000 rebels who sought redress of grievances during the depression days of 1786–87. They prevented general court sessions and they prevented Supreme Court sessions at Springfield, MA, Sept 26. On Jan 25, 1787, they attacked the federal arsenal at Springfield; Feb 2, Shays's troops were routed and fled. Shays was sentenced to death but pardoned June 13, 1788. Later he received a small pension for services in the American Revolution.

SOVIET COMMUNIST PARTY SUSPENDED: ANNIVERSARY. Aug 29, 1991. The Supreme Soviet, the parliament of the USSR, suspended all activities of the Communist Party, seizing its property and bringing to an end the institution that ruled the Soviet Union for nearly 75 years. The action followed an unsuccessful coup Aug 19–21 that sought to overthrow the government of Soviet President Mikhail Gorbachev but instead prompted a sweeping wave of democratic change. Gorbachev quit as party leader Aug 24.

BIRTHDAYS TODAY

Karen Hesse, 48, author (Newbery for *Out of the Dust*), born Baltimore, MD, Aug 29, 1952.

Michael Jackson, 42, singer, songwriter ("We Are the World," *Bad, Thriller, Beat It*), born Gary, IN, Aug 29, 1958.

John Sidney McCain III, 64, US Senator (R, Arizona), born Panama Canal Zone, Aug 29, 1936.

AUGUST 30 — WEDNESDAY

Day 243 — 123 Remaining

ARTHUR, ELLEN LEWIS HERNDON: BIRTH ANNIVERSARY. Aug 30, 1837. Wife of Chester Alan Arthur, 21st president of the US, born at Fredericksburg, VA. Died at New York, NY, Jan 12, 1880.

BURTON, VIRGINIA LEE: BIRTH ANNIVERSARY. Aug 30, 1909. Author and illustrator, born at Newton Centre, MA. Her book *The Little House* won the Caldecott Medal in 1942. Other works include *Choo, Choo* and *Mike Mulligan and His Steam Shovel*. Burton died at Boston, MA, Oct 15, 1968.

FIRST WHITE HOUSE PRESIDENTIAL BABY: BIRTH ANNIVERSARY. Aug 30, 1893. Frances Folsom Cleveland (Mrs Grover Cleveland) was the first presidential wife to have a baby at the White House when she gave birth to a baby girl (Esther). The first child ever born in the White House was a granddaughter to Thomas Jefferson in 1806.

MacMURRAY, FRED: BIRTH ANNIVERSARY. Aug 30, 1908. Born at Kankakee, IL, MacMurray's film and television career included a wide variety of roles, ranging from comedy (*The Absent-Minded Professor, Son of Flubber, The Shaggy Dog*) to serious drama (*The Caine Mutiny, Double Indemnity*). During 1960–72 he portrayed the father on "My Three Sons," which was second only to "Ozzie and Harriet" as network TV's longest running family sitcom. He died Nov 5, 1991, at Santa Monica, CA.

PERU: SAINT ROSE OF LIMA DAY. Aug 30. Saint Rose of Lima was the first saint of the western hemisphere. She lived at the time of the colonization by Spain in the 16th century. Patron saint of the Americas and the Philippines. Public holiday in Peru.

RUTHERFORD, ERNEST: BIRTH ANNIVERSARY. Aug 30, 1871. Physicist, born at Nelson, New Zealand. He established the nuclear nature of the atom, the electrical structure of matter and achieved the transmutation of elements, research which later resulted in the atomic bomb. Rutherford died at Cambridge, England, Oct 19, 1937.

SHELLEY, MARY WOLLSTONECRAFT: BIRTH ANNIVERSARY. Aug 30, 1797. English novelist Mary Shelley, daughter of the philosopher William Godwin and the feminist Mary Wollstonecraft and wife of the poet Percy Bysshe Shelley, was born at London and died there Feb 1, 1851. In addition to being the author of the famous novel *Frankenstein*, Shelley is important in literary history for her work in the editing and publishing of her husband's unpublished work after his early death.

SPACE MILESTONE: *DISCOVERY* (US). Aug 30, 1984. Space shuttle *Discovery* was launched from Kennedy Space Center, FL, for its maiden flight with a six-member crew. During the flight the crew deployed three satellites and used a robot arm before landing at Edwards Air Force Base, CA, Sept 5.

TURKEY: VICTORY DAY. Aug 30. Commemorates victory in War of Independence in 1922. Military parades, performing of the Mehtar band (the world's oldest military band), fireworks.

WILKINS, ROY: BIRTH ANNIVERSARY. Aug 30, 1901. Roy Wilkins, grandson of a Mississippi slave, civil rights leader, active in the National Association for the Advancement of Colored People (NAACP), retired as its executive director in 1977. Born at St. Louis, MO, he died at New York, NY, Sept 8, 1981.

BIRTHDAYS TODAY

Donald Crews, 62, author, illustrator (*Bigmama's, Freight Train*), born Newark, NJ, Aug 30, 1938.
Ted Williams, 82, Baseball Hall of Fame outfielder, born San Diego, CA, Aug 30, 1918.

AUGUST 31 — THURSDAY
Day 244 — 122 Remaining

CANADA: KLONDIKE ELDORADO GOLD DISCOVERY: ANNIVERSARY. Aug 31, 1896. Two weeks after the Rabbit/Bonanza Creek claim was filed, gold was discovered on Eldorado Creek, a tributary of Bonanza. More than $30 million worth of gold (worth some $600–$700 million in today's dollars) was mined from the Eldorado Claim in 1896.

KYRGYZSTAN: INDEPENDENCE DAY. Aug 31. National holiday. Commemorates independence from the former Soviet Union in 1991.

MALAYSIA: NATIONAL DAY. Aug 31. National holiday. Commemorates independence from Britain in 1957.

MONTESSORI, MARIA: BIRTH ANNIVERSARY. Aug 31, 1870. Italian physician and educator, born at Chiaraville, Italy. Founder of the Montessori method of teaching children. She believed that children need to work at tasks that interest them and if given the right materials and tasks, they learn best through individual attention. Montessori died at Noordwijk, Holland, May 6, 1952.

POLAND: SOLIDARITY FOUNDED: 20th ANNIVERSARY. Aug 31, 1980. The Polish trade union Solidarity was formed at the Baltic Sea port of Gdansk, Poland. Outlawed by the government, many of its leaders were arrested. Led by Lech Walesa, Solidarity persisted in its opposition to the Communist-controlled government, and on Aug 19, 1989, Polish president Wojcieck Jaruzelski astonished the world by nominating for the post of prime minister Tadeusz Mazowiecki, a deputy in the Polish Assembly, 1961–72, and editor-in-chief of Solidarity's weekly newspaper, bringing to an end 42 years of Communist Party domination.

TRINIDAD AND TOBAGO: INDEPENDENCE DAY. Aug 31. National holiday. Became Commonwealth nation in 1962.

BIRTHDAYS TODAY

Jennifer Azzi, 32, basketball player, born Oak Ridge, TN, Aug 31, 1968.
Edwin Corley Moses, 45, Olympic gold medal track athlete, born Dayton, OH, Aug 31, 1955.
Hideo Nomo, 32, baseball player, born Osaka, Japan, Aug 31, 1968.

SEPTEMBER 1 — FRIDAY

Day 245 — 121 Remaining

BABY SAFETY MONTH. Sept 1–30. The Juvenile Products Manufacturers Association, Inc (JPMA), a national trade organization of juvenile product manufacturers devoted to helping parents keep baby safe, is disseminating information to parents, grandparents and other child caregivers about baby safety. The information from JPMA pertains to safe selection of juvenile products through the Association's Safety Certification Program and tips on correct use of products such as cribs, car seats, infant carriers and decorative accessories. For a free copy of JPMA's brochure "Safe and Sound for Baby," write to the address below and mark ATTN: JPMA Safety Brochure. Enclose a self-addressed stamped envelope and specify whether you want the brochure in English or Spanish. For info: JPMA, PR Dept, 236 Rte 38-W, Ste 100, Moorestown, NJ 08057.

BRAZIL: INDEPENDENCE WEEK. Sept 1–7. The independence of Brazil from Portugal in 1822 is commemorated with civic and cultural ceremonies promoted by federal, state and municipal authorities. On Sept 7, a grand military parade takes place and the National Defense League organizes the Running Race in Honor of the Symbolic Torch of the Brazilian Nation.

BURROUGHS, EDGAR RICE: 125th BIRTH ANNIVERSARY. Sept 1, 1875. US novelist (*Tarzan of the Apes*), born at Chicago, IL. Correspondent for the *Los Angeles Times*, he died at Encino, CA, Mar 19, 1950.

CARTIER, JACQUES: DEATH ANNIVERSARY. Sept 1, 1557. French navigator and explorer who sailed from St. Malo, France, Apr 20, 1534, in search of a northwest passage to the Orient. Instead, he discovered the St. Lawrence River, explored Canada's coastal regions and took possession of the country for France. Cartier was born at St. Malo, about 1491 (exact date unknown) and died there.

CHILDREN'S EYE HEALTH AND SAFETY MONTH. Sept 1–30. Prevent Blindness America® directs its educational efforts to common causes of eye injuries and common eye problems among children. Materials that can easily be posted or distributed to the community will be provided. For info: Prevent Blindness America®, 500 E Remington Rd, Schaumburg, IL 60173. Phone: (800) 331-2020. Fax: (847) 843-8458. Web: www.prevent-blindness.org.

CHILDREN'S GOOD MANNERS MONTH. Sept 1–30. Starts the school year with a national program of teachers and parents encouraging good manners in children. The yearlong program includes monthly objectives that work in conjunction with a reinforcing home program. *See* Curriculum Connection. For info: "Dr. Manners," Fleming Allaire, PhD, 35 Eastfield St, Manchester, CT 06040. Phone: (860) 643-0051.

CHILE: NATIONAL MONTH. Sept 1–30. A month of special significance in Chile: arrival of spring, Independence of Chile anniversary (proclaimed Sept 18, 1810), anniversary of the armed forces rising of Sept 11, 1973, to overthrow the government and celebration of the 1980 Constitution and Army Day, Sept 19.

D.A.R.E. LAUNCHED: ANNIVERSARY. Sept 1, 1983. D.A.R.E. (Drug Abuse Resistance Education) is a police officer-led series of classroom lessons that teaches students how to resist peer pressure and lead productive drug- and violence-free lives. The program, which was developed jointly by the Los Angeles Police Department and the Los Angeles Unified School District, initially focused on elementary school children but has now been expanded to include middle and high school students. D.A.R.E. has been implemented in 75 percent of US school districts and in 44 other countries. For info: D.A.R.E. America, PO Box 512090, Los Angeles, CA 90051-0090. Phone: (800) 223-DARE. Web: www.dare-america.com.

EMMA M. NUTT DAY. Sept 1. A day to honor the first woman telephone operator, Emma M. Nutt, who reportedly began her professional career at Boston, MA, Sept 1, 1878, and continued working as a telephone operator for some 33 years.

LIBRARY CARD SIGN-UP MONTH. Sept 1–30. National effort to sign up every child for a library card. Annually, the month of September. For info: Linda Wallace, American Library Assn, Public Information Office, 50 E Huron St, Chicago, IL 60611. Phone: (312) 280-5043 or (312) 280-5042. E-mail: pio@ala.org. Web: www.ala.org.

LIBYA: REVOLUTION DAY. Sept 1. Commemorates the revolution in 1969 when King Idris I was overthrown by Colonel Qaddafi. National holiday.

NATIONAL CHILDHOOD INJURY PREVENTION WEEK. Sept 1–7. To stress the importance of community involvement in protecting the nation's children from harm. Safety By Design® sponsors this week, providing a full week of opportunities to raise awareness of the problem of unintentional injury to children and highlight the roles members of the community play in reducing injury rates. Information and materials are available. For info: Safety By Design® Ltd, PO Box 4312, Great Neck, NY 11023. Phone and Fax: (516) 482-1475.

NATIONAL FOOD EDUCATION SAFETY MONTH. Sept 1–30. An initiative sponsored by the International Food Safety Council, a coalition of the restaurant and food service industry dedicated to food safety education. The goals are to encourage food safety training among all food service workers, to heighten awareness about the importance of food safety education and to build public understanding of the food service industry's expertise in food safety and its commitment to serving safe food. For info: Cindy Wilson, Intl Food Safety Council, 250 S Wacker Dr, Ste 1400, Chicago, IL 60606-5834. Phone: (312) 715-6770. Fax: (312) 715-0807. E-mail: cwilson@foodtrain.com.

NATIONAL HISTORY DAY. Sept 1, 2000–June 2001. This yearlong project begins in September when curriculum and contest

		S	M	T	W	T	F	S
September							1	2
2000		3	4	5	6	7	8	9
		10	11	12	13	14	15	16
		17	18	19	20	21	22	23
		24	25	26	27	28	29	30

SEPTEMBER 1–30
CHILDREN'S GOOD MANNERS MONTH

In the hustle and bustle of today's society, we sometimes forget to practice the common courtesy of good manners. The Golden Rule is often left by the wayside in our haste to get there on time, be first in line or snatch the biggest piece of cake. Letters in the Ann Landers and Dear Abby columns frequently lament ungracious behavior. Good manners demonstrate a person's consideration of and respect for others. Students will find that a hidden plus of practicing good manners is an increase in self-awareness and self-esteem.

A good way to start the school year is with a discussion of the kind of manners that are suitable for the classroom and school. A zany, but accurate, look at inappropriate behavior can be found in *David Goes to School*, by David Shannon (Scholastic, 0-590-48087-1, $14.95 Gr. PreS–2). School situations that call for good manners include: waiting in line (a frequent pastime), lunchroom practices, playground courtesy and behavior during assemblies or while someone is talking. One way to illustrate how good manners can affect waiting time is by surreptitiously using a timer to record the length of time spent organizing students in a line to go out for recess without good manners and cooperation. Use your normal pattern of waiting for students to pay attention, get quiet, put away books, etc. When students come inside, let them know how long it took. Retime the procedure the next day, practicing good manners and see if they can "beat the clock." Time saved means a longer recess.

Catch student interest with the formation of a classroom Good Citizen Club. Place a small box in the front of the room and label it "Good Citizen Points." Keep a stack of recycled paper cut into squares next to it. Announce to students that when you see an example of good manners you will jot it down and add it to the box. Students can do this as an observance of another child's good manners *or* as a record of using an instance of good manners on their own. Model the procedure by choosing an example and writing it down. Examples of good manners might be "Susie held the door open for John," "Tom waited quietly in line," "Mary picked up a piece of trash and put it in the trash can without being asked." Set a goal of attaining a certain number of Good Citizen Points by a specific date. Reward accomplishing the goal with an extra 10 minutes of recess or silent reading time, a classroom game or other nonmaterial pleasure students will find fun.

Create a simple poster depicting a Good Manners Thermometer and call it "We're Hot on Good Manners." As students demonstrate using good manners, they can color the mercury up one degree. Try to reach the top and burst the mercury bulb.

Discuss good manners for assemblies. Let students list things that annoy them or make them unhappy during assemblies (not counting boring speakers). Getting stepped on, someone pushing, someone talking or being unable to see the front are frequent complaints. Ask what they do in those situations. Sometimes their initial response may aggravate the situation. Talk about how good manners can diffuse the situation. Put on classroom skits or write stories about good and bad manners in various school settings and the results attained by each. (By the way, it wouldn't hurt to offer some suggestions on how you conduct yourself when confronted with a boring speaker.)

Create a classroom "insiders" good manners joke. Make up an imaginary creature that exhibits rude behavior. Give it a name and list its rude manners. The name can be used as a good-manners-needed-here "flag" when a student needs a reminder.

materials are distributed to coordinators and teachers around the country. District History Day contests are usually held in February or March and state contests in late April or early May. The national contest is held in June at the University of Maryland. There are two divisions of the competition: junior (Gr. 6–8) and senior (Gr. 9–12). Students can enter the contest with a paper, an individual or group exhibit, an individual or group performance or individual or group media, The theme for the 2000–2001 school year is "Turning Points in History: People, Ideas, Events." For info: Natl History Day, 0119 Cecil Hall, Univ of Maryland, College Park, MD 20742. Phone: (301) 314-9739. E-mail: hstryday@aol.com.

NATIONAL HONEY MONTH. Sept 1–30. To honor the US's 211,600 beekeepers and 2.63 million colonies of honey bees, which produce more than 220 million pounds of honey each year. For info: Gretchen Lichtenwalner, Natl Honey Board, 390 Lashley St, Longmont, CO 80501-6045. Phone: (303) 776-2337. Web: www.honey.com.

NATIONAL PEDICULOSIS PREVENTION MONTH. Sept 1–30. To promote awareness of how to prevent pediculosis (lice). For info: Natl Pediculosis Assn, PO Box 610189, Newton, MA 02161. Phone: (781) 449-NITS. Fax: (781) 449-8129. Web: www.headlice.org or www.licemeister.org.

NATIONAL PIANO MONTH. Sept 1–30. Recognizes America's most popular instrument and its more than 20 million players; also encourages piano study by people of all ages. For info: Donald W. Dillon, Exec Dir, Natl Piano Foundation, 4020 McEwen, Ste 105, Dallas, TX 75244-5019. Phone: (972) 233-9107. Fax: (972) 490-4219. E-mail: don@dondillon.com. Web: www.pianonet.com.

NATIONAL SCHOOL SUCCESS MONTH. Sept 1–30. Today's young people have many distractions from school and are sometimes overwhelmed when it comes to academics. Parents are often unskilled at effectively redirecting the attention of their children, especially their teenagers. This observance is to recognize parents who want to support and encourage their children to succeed in school and to explore ways to do that. Annually, the month of September. For info send SASE to: Teresa Langston, Dir, Parenting Without Pressure, 1330 Boyer St, Longwood, FL 32750-6311. Phone: (407) 767-2524.

PTA MEMBERSHIP ENROLLMENT MONTH IN TEXAS. Sept 1–30. Texas PTA is the largest child-advocacy organization in Texas with more than 750,000 members. National PTA is the largest child-advocacy organization in the nation with nearly 6.5 million members. For info: Joann Thurman, Texas PTA, 408 W 11th St, Austin, TX 78701-2199. Phone: (512) 476-6769 or (800) TALK-PTA. Fax: (512) 476-8152. E-mail: info@txpta.org. Web: www.txpta.org.

SEA CADET MONTH. Sept 1–30. Nationwide year-round youth program for boys and girls 11–17 teaches leadership and self-discipline with emphasis on nautically-oriented training without military obligation. Est attendance: 9,000. For info: US Naval Sea Cadet Corps, 2300 Wilson Blvd, Arlington, VA 22201. Phone: (703) 243-6910. Fax: (703) 243-3985. E-mail: mford @NAVYLEAGUE.org. Web: www.seacadets.org.

SLOVAKIA: NATIONAL DAY. Sept 1. Anniversary of the adoption of the Constitution of the Slovak Republic in 1992.

UZBEKISTAN: INDEPENDENCE DAY. Sept 1. National holiday. Commemorates independence from the Soviet Union in 1991.

VERMONT STATE FAIR. Sept 1–10. Fairgrounds, Rutland, VT. Annually, the Friday before Labor Day to the weekend after Labor Day. Est attendance: 100,000. For info: Vermont State Fair, 175 S Main St, Rutland, VT 05701. Phone: (802) 775-5200. Web: vtlife.intervis.com/travelvt/.

BIRTHDAYS TODAY

Jim Arnosky, 54, author and illustrator (*Watching Water Birds*), born New York, NY, Sept 1, 1946.

Rosa Guy, 72, author (*Billy the Great*), born Trinidad, West Indies, Sept 1, 1928.

Tim Hardaway, 34, basketball player, born Chicago, IL, Sept 1, 1966.

SEPTEMBER 2 — SATURDAY
Day 246 — 120 Remaining

CALENDAR ADJUSTMENT DAY: ANNIVERSARY. Sept 2. Pursuant to the British Calendar Act of 1751, Britain (and the American colonies) made the "Gregorian Correction" in 1752. The Act proclaimed that the day following Wednesday, Sept 2, should become Thursday, Sept 14, 1752. There was rioting in the streets by those who felt cheated and who demanded the eleven days back. The Act also provided that New Year's Day (and the change of year number) should fall Jan 1 (instead of Mar 25) in 1752 and every year thereafter. See also: "Gregorian Calendar Adjustment: Anniversary" (Feb 24, Oct 4).

DAYS OF MARATHON: ANNIVERSARY. Sept 2–9, 490 BC. Anniversary of the event during the Persian Wars from which the marathon race is derived. Phidippides, "an Athenian and by profession and practice a trained runner," according to Herodotus, was dispatched from Marathon to Sparta (26 miles), Sept 2 to seek help in repelling the invading Persian army. Help being unavailable by religious law until after the next full moon, Phidippides ran the 26 miles back to Marathon Sept 4. Without Spartan aid, the Athenians defeated the Persians at the Battle of Marathon Sept 9. According to legend Phidippides carried the news of the battle to Athens and died as he spoke the words, "Rejoice, we are victorious." The marathon race was revived at the 1896 Olympic Games in Athens. Course distance, since 1924, is 26 miles, 385 yards.

ENGLAND: GREAT FIRE OF LONDON: ANNIVERSARY. Sept 2–5, 1666. The fire generally credited with bringing about our system of fire insurance started Sept 2, 1666, in the wooden house of a baker named Farryner, at London's Pudding Lane, near the Tower. During the ensuing three days more than 13,000 houses were destroyed, though it is believed that only six lives were lost in the fire.

FORTEN, JAMES: BIRTH ANNIVERSARY. Sept 2, 1766. James Forten was born of free black parents at Philadelphia, PA. As a powder boy on an American Revolutionary warship, he escaped being sold as a slave when his ship was captured due to the intervention of the son of the British commander. While in England he became involved with abolitionists. On his return to Philadelphia, he became an apprentice to a sailmaker and eventually purchased the company for which he worked. He was active in the abolition movement, and in 1816, his support was sought by the American Colonization Society for the plan to settle American blacks at Liberia. He rejected their ideas and their plans to make him the ruler of the colony. From the large profits of his successful sailmaking company, he contributed heavily to the abolitionist movement and was a supporter of William Lloyd Garrison's anti-slavery journal, *The Liberator*. Died at Philadelphia, PA, Mar 4, 1842.

McAULIFFE, CHRISTA: BIRTH ANNIVERSARY. Sept 2, 1948. Christa McAuliffe, a 37-year-old Concord, NH, high school teacher, was to have been the first "ordinary citizen" in space. Born Sharon Christa Corrigan at Boston, MA, she perished with six crew members in the Space Shuttle *Challenger* explosion Jan 28, 1986. See also: "*Challenger* Space Shuttle Explosion: Anniversary" (Jan 28).

NATIONAL STORYTELLER OF THE YEAR CONTEST. Sept 2. Millersport, OH. Official Storyteller of the Year named at this event. Sponsored by the Creative Arts Institute, Inc, *Adventures in Storytelling* magazine and the Ohio Arts Council. Annually, the Saturday before Labor Day. Est attendance: 500. For info: Donna Foster, Creative Arts, 8021 Kennedy Rd, Blacklick, OH 43004. Phone: (614) 759-9407. Fax: (614) 759-8480. E-mail: dfoster @freenet.columbus.oh.us.

SHERMAN ENTERS ATLANTA: ANNIVERSARY. Sept 2, 1864. After a four-week siege, Union General William Tecumseh Sherman entered Atlanta, GA. The city had been evacuated on the previous day by Confederate troops under General John B. Hood. Hood had mistakenly assumed Sherman was ending the siege Aug 27, when actually Sherman was beginning the final stages of his attack. Hood then sent troops to attack the Union forces at Jonesboro. Hood's troops were defeated, opening the way for the capture of Atlanta.

US TREASURY DEPARTMENT: ANNIVERSARY. Sept 2, 1789. The third presidential cabinet department, the Treasury Department, was established by Congress.

V-J (VICTORY IN JAPAN) DAY: 55th ANNIVERSARY. Sept 2, 1945. Official ratification of Japanese surrender to the Allies occurred aboard the USS *Missouri* at Tokyo Bay Sept 2 (Far Eastern time) in 1945, thus prompting President Truman's declaration of this day as Victory-over-Japan Day. Japan's initial, informal agreement of surrender was announced by Truman and celebrated in the US Aug 14.

VIETNAM: INDEPENDENCE DAY: 55th ANNIVERSARY. Sept 2. Ho Chi Minh formally proclaimed the independence of Vietnam from France and the establishment of the Democratic Republic of Vietnam in 1945. National holiday.

BIRTHDAYS TODAY

John Bierhorst, 64, author (*The Woman Who Fell from the Sky*), born Boston, MA, Sept 2, 1936.

Demi, 58, author (*One Grain of Rice*), born Charlotte Dumaresque Hunt, Cambridge, MA, Sept 2, 1942.

Barbara Dillon, 73, author (*The Teddy Bear Tree*), born Montclair, NJ, Sept 2, 1927.

Bernard Most, 63, author and illustrator (*Where to Look for a Dinosaur*), born New York, NY, Sept 2, 1937.

Carlos Valderrama, 39, soccer player, born Santa Marta, Colombia, Sept 2, 1961.

September 2000

S	M	T	W	T	F	S
					1	2
3	4	5	6	7	8	9
10	11	12	13	14	15	16
17	18	19	20	21	22	23
24	25	26	27	28	29	30

SEPTEMBER 3 — SUNDAY

Day 247 — 119 Remaining

DOUGLASS ESCAPES TO FREEDOM: ANNIVERSARY. Sept 3, 1838. Dressed as a sailor and carrying identification papers borrowed from a retired merchant seaman, Frederick Douglass boarded a train at Baltimore, MD, a slave state, and rode to Wilmington, DE, where he caught a steamboat to the free city of Philadelphia. He then transferred to a train headed for New York City where he entered the protection of the Underground Railway network. Douglass later became a great orator and one of the leaders of the antislavery struggle.

ITALY: HISTORICAL REGATTA. Sept 3. Venice. Traditional competition among two-oar racing gondolas, preceded by a procession of Venetian ceremonial boats of the epoch of the Venetian Republic. Annually, the first Sunday in September.

ITALY SURRENDERS: ANNIVERSARY. Sept 3, 1943. General Giuseppe Castellano signed three copies of the "short armistice," effectively surrendering unconditionally for the Italian government in World War II. That same day the British Eighth Army, commanded by General Bernard Montgomery, invaded the Italian mainland.

QATAR: INDEPENDENCE DAY. Sept 3. National holiday. Commemorates the severing in 1971 of the treaty with Britain which had handled Qatar's foreign relations.

SAN MARINO: NATIONAL DAY. Sept 3. Public holiday. Honors St. Marinus, the traditional founder of San Marino.

TREATY OF PARIS ENDS AMERICAN REVOLUTION: ANNIVERSARY. Sept 3, 1783. Treaty between Britain and the US, ending the Revolutionary War, signed at Paris, France. American signatories: John Adams, Benjamin Franklin and John Jay.

BIRTHDAYS TODAY

Aliki, 71, Aliki Liacouras Brandenberg, author and illustrator (*Three Gold Pieces*), born Wildwood Crest, NJ, Sept 3, 1929.

Damon Stoudamire, 27, basketball player, born Portland, OR, Sept 3, 1973.

SEPTEMBER 4 — MONDAY

Day 248 — 118 Remaining

CANADA: LABOR DAY. Sept 4. Annually, the first Monday in September.

LABOR DAY. Sept 4. Legal public holiday. Public Law 90–363 sets Labor Day on the first Monday in September. Observed in all states. First observance believed to have been a parade at 10 AM, Tuesday, Sept 5, 1882, at New York, NY, probably organized by Peter J. McGuire, a Carpenters and Joiners Union secretary. In 1883, a union resolution declared "the first Monday in September of each year a Labor Day." By 1893, more than half of the states were observing Labor Day on one or another day and a bill to establish Labor Day as a federal holiday was introduced in Congress. On June 28, 1894, President Grover Cleveland signed into law an act making the first Monday in September a legal holiday for federal employees and the District of Columbia. Canada also celebrates Labor Day on the first Monday in September. In most other countries, Labor Day is observed May 1. For links to Labor Day websites, go to: deil.lang.uiuc.edu/web.pages/holidays/labor.html.

LOS ANGELES, CALIFORNIA FOUNDED: ANNIVERSARY. Sept 4, 1781. Los Angeles founded by decree and called "El Pueblo de Nuestra Senora La Reina de Los Angeles de Porciuncula."

NEWSPAPER CARRIER DAY. Sept 4. Anniversary of the hiring of the first "newsboy" in the US, 10-year-old Barney Flaherty, who is said to have answered the following classified advertisement which appeared in *The New York Sun*, in 1833: "To the Unemployed—a number of steady men can find employment by vending this paper. A liberal discount is allowed to those who buy to sell again."

POLK, SARAH CHILDRESS: BIRTH ANNIVERSARY. Sept 4, 1803. Wife of James Knox Polk, 11th president of the US. Born at Murfreesboro, TN, and died at Nashville, TN, Aug 14, 1891.

BIRTHDAYS TODAY

Joan Aiken, 76, author (the Mortimer series), born Rye, Sussex, England, Sept 4, 1924.

Jason David Frank, 27, actor (*Turbo: A Power Rangers Movie*, "Power Rangers Turbo"), born Covina, CA, Sept 4, 1973.

Syd Hoff, 88, author (*Corn Is Maize: The Gift of the Indians*), born New York, NY, Sept 4, 1912.

Mike Piazza, 32, baseball player, born Norristown, PA, Sept 4, 1968.

SEPTEMBER 5 — TUESDAY

Day 249 — 117 Remaining

BE LATE FOR SOMETHING DAY. Sept 5. To create a release from the stresses and strains resulting from a consistent need to be on time. For info: Les Waas, Pres, Procrastinators' Club of America, Inc, Box 712, Bryn Athyn, PA 19009. Phone: (215) 947-9020. Fax: (215) 947-7007.

FIRST CONTINENTAL CONGRESS ASSEMBLY: ANNIVERSARY. Sept 5, 1774. The first assembly of this forerunner of the US Congress took place at Philadelphia, PA. All 13 colonies were represented except Georgia. Peyton Randolph, delegate from Virginia, was elected president. The second Continental Congress met beginning May 10, 1775, also at Philadelphia.

JAMES, JESSE: BIRTH ANNIVERSARY. Sept 5, 1847. Western legend and bandit Jesse Woodson James was born at Centerville (now Kearney), MO. His criminal exploits were glorified and romanticized by writers for Eastern readers looking for stories of Western adventure and heroism. After the Civil War, James and his brother, Frank, formed a group of eight outlaws who robbed banks, stagecoaches and stores. In 1873, the James gang began holding up trains. The original James gang was put out of business Sept 7, 1876, while attempting to rob a bank at Northfield, MN. Every member of the gang except for the James brothers was killed or captured. The brothers formed a new gang and resumed their criminal careers in 1879. Two years later, the governor of Missouri offered a $10,000 reward for their capture, dead or alive. On Apr 3, 1882 at St. Joseph, MO, Robert Ford, a member of the gang, shot 34-year-old Jesse in the back of the head and claimed the reward.

MOON PHASE: FIRST QUARTER. Sept 5. Moon enters First Quarter phase at 12:27 PM, EDT.

NIELSEN, ARTHUR CHARLES: BIRTH ANNIVERSARY. Sept 5, 1897. Marketing research engineer, founder of A.C. Nielsen Company, in 1923, known for radio and TV audience surveys and ratings, was born at Chicago, IL, and died there June 1, 1980.

SPACE MILESTONE: *VOYAGER 1* (US). Sept 5, 1977. Twin of *Voyager 2* which was launched Aug 20. On Feb 18, 1998, *Voyager 1* set a new distance record when after more than 20 years in space it reached 6.5 billion miles from Earth.

UNITED NATIONS: INTERNATIONAL DAY OF PEACE/OPENING DAY OF GENERAL ASSEMBLY. Sept 5. The United Nations General Assembly, Nov 30, 1981, declared "the opening day of the regular sessions of the General Assembly shall be officially proclaimed and observed as International Day of Peace and shall be devoted to commemorating and strengthening the ideals of peace both within and among all nations and peoples." The UN has declared this the Millennium Assembly. For more info: www.un.org/millennium. See also: "United Nations: Millennium Summit" (Sept 6).

BIRTHDAYS TODAY

Paul Fleischman, 48, author, poet (Newbery for *Joyful Noise: Poems for Two Voices*), born Monterey, CA, Sept 5, 1952.

Roxie Munro, 55, author (*The Inside-Outside Book of Libraries*), born Mineral Wells, TX, Sept 5, 1945.

SEPTEMBER 6 — WEDNESDAY
Day 250 — 116 Remaining

ADDAMS, JANE: BIRTH ANNIVERSARY. Sept 6, 1860. American worker for peace, social welfare and the rights of women. The founder of Chicago's Hull House settlement house, she was co-winner of the Nobel Peace Prize in 1931. Born at Cedarville, IL, she died May 21, 1935, at Chicago, IL.

BALTIC STATES' INDEPENDENCE RECOGNIZED: ANNIVERSARY. Sept 6, 1991. The Soviet government recognized the independence of the Baltic states—Latvia, Estonia and Lithuania. The action came 51 years after the Baltic states were annexed by the Soviet Union. All three Baltic states had earlier declared their independence, and many nations had already recognized them diplomatically, including the US, Sept 2, 1991.

LAFAYETTE, MARQUIS DE: BIRTH ANNIVERSARY. Sept 6, 1757. French general and aristocrat, Lafayette, whose full name was Marie-Joseph-Paul-Yves-Roch-Gilbert du Motier, came to America to assist in the revolutionary cause. He was awarded a major-generalship and began a lasting friendship with the American commander-in-chief, George Washington. After an alliance was signed with France, he returned to his native country and persuaded Louis XVI to send a 6,000-man force to assist the Americans. On his return, he was given command of an army at Virginia and was instrumental in forcing the surrender of Lord Cornwallis at Yorktown, leading to the end of the war and American independence. He was hailed as "The Hero of Two Worlds" and was appointed a brigadier general on his return to France in 1782. He

became a leader of the liberal aristocrats during the early days of the French revolution, presenting to the National Assembly his draft of "A Declaration of the Rights of Man and of the Citizen." As the commander of the newly formed national guard of Paris, he rescued Louis XVI and Marie-Antoinette from a crowd that stormed Versailles Oct 6, 1789, returning them to Paris where they became hostages of the revolution. His popularity waned after his guards opened fire on angry demonstrators demanding abdication of the king in 1791. He fled to Austria with the overthrow of the monarchy in 1792, returning when Napoleon Bonaparte came to power. Born at Chavaniac, he died at Paris, May 20, 1834. For more info: *Why Not, Lafayette?*, by Jean Fritz (Putnam, 0-399-23411-X, $16.99 Gr. 3–7).

SAINT PETERSBURG NAME RESTORED: ANNIVERSARY. Sept 6, 1991. Russian legislators voted to restore the name Saint Petersburg to the nation's second largest city. The city had been known as Leningrad for 67 years in honor of the Soviet Union's founder, Vladimir I. Lenin. The city, founded in 1703 by Peter the Great, has had three names in the 20th century with Russian leaders changing its German-sounding name to Petrograd at the beginning of WWI in 1914 and Soviet Communist leaders changing its name to Leningrad in 1924 following their leader's death.

SWAZILAND: INDEPENDENCE DAY. Sept 6. Commemorates attainment of independence from Britain in 1968. National holiday.

UNITED NATIONS: MILLENNIUM SUMMIT. Sept 6. The UN General Assembly has decided that the turn of the century constitutes a unique and symbolically compelling moment for the membership of the UN to articulate and affirm an animating vision for the UN in the new era. When the heads of state and/or government of the member states of the UN convene at UN headquarters in New York City on this day, it will be the largest single gathering of such leaders in the history of the world. For more info: www.un.org/millennium.

BIRTHDAYS TODAY

Chad Scott, 26, football player, born Washington, DC, Sept 6, 1974.

SEPTEMBER 7 — THURSDAY
Day 251 — 115 Remaining

BRAZIL: INDEPENDENCE DAY. Sept 7. Declared independence from Portugal in 1822. National holiday.

ELIZABETH I: BIRTH ANNIVERSARY. Sept 7, 1533. Queen of England, after whom the "Elizabethan Age" was named, born at Greenwich Palace, daughter of Henry VIII and Anne Boleyn. She succeeded to the throne in 1558 and ruled England until her death on May 24, 1603. Her reign was one of the most dynamic in English history and she was held in great affection by her people. The British defeated the Spanish Armada and England became a world power during her reign. For more info: *Good Queen Bess: The Story of Elizabeth I of England*, by Diane Stanley and Peter Vennema (Morrow, out-of-print).

GRANDMA MOSES DAY. Sept 7. Anna Mary Robertson Moses, modern primitive American painter, born at Greenwich, NY, Sept 7, 1860. She started painting at the age of 78. Her 100th birthday was proclaimed Grandma Moses Day in New York state. Died at Hoosick Falls, NY, Dec 13, 1961. *See* Curriculum Connection.

NEITHER SNOW NOR RAIN DAY. Sept 7. Anniversary of the opening to the public, on Labor Day, 1914, of the New York Post Office Building at Eighth Avenue between 31st and 33rd Streets. On the front of this building was an inscription supplied by

	S	M	T	W	T	F	S
September						1	2
2000	3	4	5	6	7	8	9
	10	11	12	13	14	15	16
	17	18	19	20	21	22	23
	24	25	26	27	28	29	30

SEPTEMBER 7
GRANDMA MOSES DAY

Anna Mary Robertson was born on Sept 7, 1860, in Washington County, New York. Anna married Thomas Moses, a farmer, when she was 17. They had ten children; five died in infancy. She did not start painting until 1938, when she was 78 years old. Grandma Moses never had an art lesson and was completely self-taught. She used to embroider pictures on canvas. She turned to painting when her fingers, crippled by arthritis, made holding embroidery needles too difficult. Although embroidery was her first artistic medium, she proved to be a talented painter as well. She is known for the clean, simple lines of her artwork, which displays scenes she remembered from daily life in the rural setting where she grew up. Her work is very popular and can often be found reprinted on calendars and note cards. Examples of her art can be found on the Web at artcyclopedia.com/artists/moses_grandma.html. Grandma Moses died on Dec 13, 1961. She was 101 years old.

Clementine (pronounced Cle-men-teen) Hunter was also a folk artist. She was the first self-taught African American artist to receive nationwide attention in the media. Called Tebé by her family and friends, Hunter was born near the southern end of Louisiana's Cane River in 1886 (actual date unknown). Her life story reflects a rich cultural diversity. One of her grandmothers was a black Indian. Some of her family were Creoles. Hunter spoke French and didn't learn English until she married her husband Emmanuel in 1924. She had seven children; two died as babies. She lived on Melrose Plantation for more than 75 years, where she and her family worked as manual laborers. Her jobs included picking cotton and pecans. Hunter began painting in the 1930s. Like Grandma Moses, Clementine Hunter enjoyed needlework. She also liked sketching. Hunter used bright colors to depict life as she experienced it in the rural south. Her simple, folk art style brims with life as it reflects the daily routine and rituals she saw. Clementine Hunter died on Jan 1, 1988. She was 101 years old.

Introduce both artists to your students. Talk about how their lives may have been similar and different. Discuss how their paintings are alike and how they differ. Although both women began painting later in life, it's likely they were artistically inclined as children. Have students paint a scene depicting their own lives. Hang all the art in a celebration of Grandma Moses and Clementine Hunter.

Literature connections: *The Grandma Moses Night Before Christmas*, by Clement Moore, illustrated by Grandma Moses (Random House, 0-679-91526-5, $15.99 All ages); *Grandma Moses*, by Zibby O'Neal (Puffin, 0-14-032220-5, $4.99 Gr. 4–8); *Talking With Tebé: Clementine Hunter, Memory Artist*, edited by Mary Lyons (Houghton Mifflin, 0-395-72031-1, $16 Gr. 4–8). There are adult books about Moses and one on Hunter as well, and both artists are included in several folk art books.

William M. Kendall of the architectural firm that planned the building. The inscription, a free translation from Herodotus, reads: "Neither snow nor rain nor heat nor gloom of night stays these couriers from the swift completion of their appointed rounds." This has long been believed to be the motto of the US Post Office and Postal Service. They have, in fact, no motto . . . but the legend remains. [Info from: New York Post Office, Public Info Office and US Postal Service.]

UTAH STATE FAIR. Sept 7–17. Salt Lake City, UT. Est attendance: 360,000. For info: Utah State Fair Park, 155 N 1000 W, Salt Lake City, UT 84116. Phone: (801) 538-8440. Fax: (801) 538-8455. E-mail: donna@fiber.net.

BIRTHDAYS TODAY

Alexandra Day, 59, author and illustrator (*The Teddy Bears' Picnic*), born Cincinnati, OH, Sept 7, 1941.
Daniel Ken Inouye, 76, US Senator (D, Hawaii), born Honolulu, HI, Sept 7, 1924.

SEPTEMBER 8 — FRIDAY
Day 252 — 114 Remaining

ANDORRA: NATIONAL HOLIDAY. Sept 8. Honors our Lady of Meritxell.

GALVESTON HURRICANE: 100th ANNIVERSARY. Sept 8, 1900. The worst national disaster in US history in terms of lives lost. More than 6,000 people were killed when a hurricane struck Galveston, TX.

INTERNATIONAL LITERACY DAY. Sept 8. Celebrated worldwide to promote reading and its benefits. Various events, programs and workshops occur throughout the United States and other countries. For info: Exec Office, Intl Reading Assn, 800 Barksdale Rd, PO Box 8139, Newark, DE 19714-8139. Phone: (302) 731-1600. Fax: (302) 731-1057. E-mail: acutts@reading.org. Web: www.reading.org.

KANSAS STATE FAIR. Sept 8–17. Hutchinson, KS. Commercial and competitive exhibits, entertainment, carnival, car racing and other special attractions. Annually, beginning the first Friday after Labor Day. Est attendance: 400,000. For info: Bill Ogg, Gen Mgr, Kansas State Fair, 2000 N Poplar, Hutchinson, KS 67502. Phone: (316) 669-3600.

McGWIRE HITS 62nd HOME RUN: ANNIVERSARY. Sept 8, 1998. Mark McGwire of the St. Louis Cardinals hit his 62nd home run, breaking Roger Maris's 1961 record for the most home runs in a single season. McGwire hit his homer against pitcher Steve Trachsel of the Chicago Cubs at Busch Stadium at St. Louis as the Cardinals won, 6–3. A few days later, Sept 13, 1998, Sammy Sosa of the Chicago Cubs hit his 62nd homer. McGwire ended the season with a total of 70 home runs; Sosa with a total of 66.

NEW MEXICO STATE FAIR. Sept 8–24. Albuquerque, NM. Fireworks, blues, country, gospel, pop and rock entertainment. Rodeos, circus, auto thrill show, tractor pulls, horse racing and free grandstand shows. For info: New Mexico State Fair, Po Box 8546, Albuquerque, NM 87198. Phone: (505) 265-1791. Fax: (505) 266-7784.

NORTHERN PACIFIC RAILROAD COMPLETED: ANNIVERSARY. Sept 8, 1883. After 19 years of construction, the Northern Pacific Railroad became the second railroad to link the two coasts. The Union Pacific and Central Pacific lines met at Utah in 1869.

"STAR TREK" TV PREMIERE: ANNIVERSARY. Sept 8, 1966. The first of 79 episodes of the TV series "Star Trek" was aired on the NBC network. Although the science fiction show set in the future only lasted a few seasons, it has remained enormously popular through syndication reruns. It has been given new life through six motion pictures, a cartoon TV series and the very popular TV series "Star Trek: The Next Generation," "Star Trek: Deep Space Nine" and "Star Trek: Voyager." It has consistently ranked among the biggest titles in the motion picture, television, home video and licensing divisions of Paramount Pictures.

TENNESSEE STATE FAIR. Sept 8–17. Nashville, TN. A huge variety of exhibits, carnival midway, animal and variety shows, live stage presentations, livestock, agricultural and craft competitions and food and game booths. Est attendance: 350,000. For info: Tennessee Fair Office, PO Box 40208, Melrose Station, Nashville, TN 37204. Phone: (615) 862-8980. Fax: (615) 862-8992. Web: www.nashville.org/tsf.

UNITED NATIONS: INTERNATIONAL LITERACY DAY. Sept 8. An international day observed by the organizations of the United Nations system. Info from: United Nations, Dept of Public Info, New York, NY 10017.

BIRTHDAYS TODAY

Jack Prelutsky, 60, poet (*The New Kid on the Block*), born Brooklyn, NY, Sept 8, 1940.
Jon Scieszka, 46, author (*The Stinky Cheese Man and Other Fairly Stupid Tales, Math Curse*), born Flint, MI, Sept 8, 1954.
Latrell Sprewell, 30, basketball player, born Milwaukee, WI, Sept 8, 1970.
Jonathan Taylor Thomas, 19, actor ("Home Improvement," voice of Simba in *The Lion King*), born Bethlehem, PA, Sept 8, 1981.

SEPTEMBER 9 — SATURDAY
Day 253 — 113 Remaining

BONZA BOTTLER DAY™. Sept 9. To celebrate when the number of the day is the same as the number of the month. Bonza Bottler Day™ is an excuse to have a party at least once a month. For info: Gail M. Berger, 109 Matthew Ave, Poca, WV 25159. Phone: (304) 776-7746. E-mail: gberger5@aol.com.

CALIFORNIA: ADMISSION DAY: 150th ANNIVERSARY. Sept 9. Became 31st state in 1850.

September 2000	S	M	T	W	T	F	S
						1	2
	3	4	5	6	7	8	9
	10	11	12	13	14	15	16
	17	18	19	20	21	22	23
	24	25	26	27	28	29	30

COLONIES BECOME UNITED STATES: ANNIVERSARY. Sept 9, 1776. The Continental Congress resolved that the name United States was to replace United Colonies.

"FAT ALBERT AND THE COSBY KIDS" TV PREMIERE: ANNIVERSARY. Sept 9, 1972. This cartoon series was hosted by Bill Cosby, with characters based on his childhood friends at Philadelphia. Its central characters—Fat Albert, Weird Harold, Mush Mouth and Donald—were weird-looking but very human. The show sent messages of tolerance and harmony. In 1979 the show was renamed "The New Fat Albert Show."

★**FEDERAL LANDS CLEANUP DAY.** Sept 9. Presidential Proclamation 5521, of Sept 5, 1986, covers all succeeding years. The first Saturday after Labor Day. (PL99–402 of Aug 27, 1986.)

KID'RIFIC. Sept 9–10. Hartford, CT. A two-day children's festival on Constitution Plaza in downtown Hartford, produced by the Hartford Downtown Council. Kid'rific will feature hands-on art and science activities, storytelling, master teaching artists' workshops, continuous stage entertainment, a petting zoo with a 13' tall giraffe and lots more. Annually, the first weekend after Labor Day. Est attendance: 50,000. For info: Steven A. Lazaroff, Dir for Events Programming, Hartford Downtown Council, 250 Constitution Plaza, Hartford, CT 06103. Phone: (860) 728-3089. Fax: (860) 527-9696. Web: www.hartford-hdc.com.

KOREA, DEMOCRATIC PEOPLE'S REPUBLIC OF: NATIONAL DAY. Sept 9. National holiday in the Democratic People's Republic of [North] Korea.

LUXEMBOURG: ANNIVERSARY LIBERATION CEREMONY. Sept 9. Petange. Commemoration of liberation of Grand-Duchy by the Allied forces in 1944. Ceremony at monument of the American soldier.

PUBLIC LANDS DAY. Sept 9. To involve citizen volunteers in cleaning and maintaining public lands. Annually, the Saturday after Labor Day. Est attendance: 1,000,000. For info: Keep America Beautiful, Inc, Washington Square, 1010 Washington Blvd, Stamford, CT 06901. E-mail: keepamerbe@aol.com.

TAJIKISTAN: INDEPENDENCE DAY. Sept 9. National holiday commemorating independence from the Soviet Union in 1991.

WILLIAM, THE CONQUEROR: DEATH ANNIVERSARY. Sept 9, 1087. William I, The Conqueror, King of England and Duke of Normandy, whose image is portrayed in the Bayeux Tapestry, was born about 1028 at Falaise, Normandy. Victorious over Harold at the Battle of Hastings (the Norman Conquest) in 1066, William was crowned King of England at Westminster Abbey on Christmas Day of that year. Later, while waging war in France, William met his death at Rouen, Sept 9, 1087.

BIRTHDAYS TODAY

Benjamin Roy ("BJ") Armstrong, 33, basketball player, born Detroit, MI, Sept 9, 1967.
Kimberly Willis Holt, 40, author (*When Zachary Beaver Came to Town*) born Pensacola, FL, Sept 9, 1960.
Adam Sandler, 34, actor (*The Waterboy, Billy Madison*), born Brooklyn, NY, Sept 9, 1966.
Mildred Pitts Walter, 78, author (*Justin and the Best Biscuits in the World*), born De Ridder, LA, Sept 9, 1922.

SEPTEMBER 10 — SUNDAY
Day 254 — 112 Remaining

BELIZE: SAINT GEORGE'S CAYE DAY. Sept 10. Public holiday celebrated in honor of the battle between the European Baymen Settlers and the Spaniards for the territory of Belize.

BRAXTON, CARTER: BIRTH ANNIVERSARY. Sept 10, 1736. American revolutionary statesman and signer of the Declaration of Independence. Born at Newington, VA, he died Oct 10, 1797, at Richmond, VA.

ENGLAND: BATTLE OF BRITAIN WEEK. Sept 10–16. Annually, the third week of September—the week containing Battle of Britain Day (Sept 15).

KEIKO RETURNS TO ICELAND: ANNIVERSARY. Sept 10, 1998. Keiko, the killer whale or orca who starred in the 1993 film *Free Willy*, was returned to his home in waters off Iceland after spending 19 years in captivity. Keiko was to be kept in a specially-built cage in the ocean until it was determined if he can return to the wild.

MARIS, ROGER: BIRTH ANNIVERSARY. Sept 10, 1934. Baseball player, born Roger Eugene Maras at Hibbing, MN. In 1961, Maris broke one of baseball's sacred records, hitting 61 home runs to surpass the mark set by Babe Ruth in 1927. This record wasn't broken until 1998. He won the American League MVP award in 1960 and 1961 and finished his career with the St. Louis Cardinals. Died at Houston, TX, Dec 14, 1985.

NATIONAL 5-A-DAY WEEK. Sept 10–16. To encourage all Americans to increase the amount of fruits and vegetables they eat to five or more servings per day, to better their health and reduce their risk of cancer and other chronic diseases. For info: Produce for Better Health Foundation, 5301 Limestone Rd, Ste 101, Wilmington, DE 19808. Web: www.5aday.com.

★**NATIONAL GRANDPARENTS' DAY.** Sept 10. Presidential Proclamation 4679, of Sept 6, 1979, covers all succeeding years. First Sunday in September following Labor Day (PL96–62 of Sept 6, 1979). First issued in 1978 (Proc 4580 of Aug 3, 1978), requested by Public Law 325 of July 28, 1978.

SUBSTITUTE TEACHER APPRECIATION WEEK. Sept 10–16. Although substitute teachers get no sick days or respect, they teach when the regular teacher cannot and continually adjust to different classroom situations. Annually, the second week of September. For info: Dorothy Zjawin, 61 W Colfax Ave, Roselle Park, NJ 07204. Phone: (908) 241-6241. Fax: (908) 241-6241.

BIRTHDAYS TODAY

Matt Geiger, 31, baseball player, born Salem, MA, Sept 10, 1969.
Randy Johnson, 37, baseball player, born Walnut Creek, CA, Sept 10, 1963.

SEPTEMBER 11 — MONDAY
Day 255 — 111 Remaining

BATTLE OF BRANDYWINE: ANNIVERSARY. Sept 11, 1777. The largest engagement of the American Revolution, between the Continental Army led by General George Washington and British forces led by General William Howe. Howe was marching to take Philadelphia when Washington chose an area on the Brandywine Creek near Chadds Ford, PA to stop the advance. The American forces were defeated here and the British went on to take Philadelphia Sept 26. They spent the winter in the city while Washington's troops suffered in their encampment at Valley Forge, PA. For more info, visit the Independence Hall Association website at www.ushistory.org/brandywine/index.html.

ETHIOPIA: NEW YEAR'S DAY. Sept 11. Public holiday. This day in 2000 begins the year 1994 on the Ethiopian calendar. This is also the beginning of the year 1717 on the Coptic calendar.

"LITTLE HOUSE ON THE PRAIRIE" TV PREMIERE: ANNIVERSARY. Sept 11, 1974. This hour-long family drama was based on the books by Laura Ingalls Wilder. It focused on the Ingalls family and their neighbors living at Walnut Grove, MN: Michael Landon as Charles (Pa), Karen Grassle as Caroline (Ma), Melissa Sue Anderson as daughter Mary, Melissa Gilbert as daughter Laura, from whose point of view the stories were told, Lindsay and Sidney Greenbush as daughter Carrie and Wendi and Brenda Turnbaugh as daughter Grace. The series spent one season at Winoka, Dakota. In its last season (1982), the show's name was changed to "Little House: A New Beginning." Landon appeared less often and the show centered around Laura and her husband.

911 DAY. Sept 11. To foster the implementation of a universal emergency telephone number system. For info: Sonya Carius, Publications Mgr, Natl Emergency Number Assn, 47849 Papermill Rd, Coshocton, OH 43812. Phone: (614) 622-8911. Fax: (614) 622-2090. Web: www.nena9-1-1.org.

PAKISTAN: FOUNDER'S DEATH ANNIVERSARY. Sept 11. Pakistan observes the death anniversary in 1948 of Quaid-i-Azam Mohammed Ali Jinnah (founder of Pakistan) as a national holiday.

SPACE MILESTONE: *MARS GLOBAL SURVEYOR* (US). Sept 11, 1997. Launched Nov 7, 1996, this unmanned vehicle was put in orbit around Mars. It is designed to compile global maps of Mars by taking high resolution photos. This mission inaugurated a new series of Mars expeditions in which NASA will launch pairs of orbiters and landers to Mars every 26 months into the next decade. *Mars Global Surveyor* was paired with the lander *Mars Pathfinder*. See also: "Space Milestone: *Mars Pathfinder*" (July 4).

BIRTHDAYS TODAY

Daniel Akaka, 76, US Senator (D, Hawaii), born Honolulu, HI, Sept 11, 1924.
Anthony Browne, 54, author (*Voices in the Park*), born Sheffield, England, Sept 11, 1946.

SEPTEMBER 12 — TUESDAY
Day 256 — 110 Remaining

CHINA: MID-AUTUMN FESTIVAL. Sept 12. To worship the moon god. According to folk legend this day is also the birthday of the earth god T'u-ti Kung. The festival indicates the year's hard work in the fields will soon end with the harvest. People express gratitude to heaven as represented by the moon and earth as symbolized by the earth god for all good things from the preceding year. 15th day of eighth month of Chinese lunar calendar.

ETHIOPIA: NATIONAL REVOLUTION DAY. Sept 12. Observed as a national holiday. Commemorates the overthrow of Haile Selassie in 1974.

"FRAGGLE ROCK" TV PREMIERE: ANNIVERSARY. Sept 12, 1987. This children's show was a cartoon version of the live Jim Henson puppet production on HBO. It was set in the rock underneath a scientist's house and featured characters such as the Fraggles, the Doozers and the Gorgs.

KOREA: CHUSOK. Sept 12. Gala celebration by Koreans everywhere. Autumn harvest thanksgiving moon festival. Observed on 15th day of eighth lunar month (eighth full moon of lunar calendar) each year. Koreans pay homage to ancestors and express gratitude to guarding spirits for another year of rich crops. A time to visit tombs, leave food and prepare for coming winter season. Traditional food is "moon cake," made on eve of Chusok, with rice, chestnuts and jujube fruits. Games, dancing and gift exchanges. Observed since Silla Dynasty (beginning of first millennium).

☆ *The Teacher's Calendar, 2000–2001* ☆

"LASSIE" TV PREMIERE: ANNIVERSARY. Sept 12, 1954. This long-running series was originally about a boy and his courageous and intelligent dog, Lassie (played by more than six different dogs, all male). For the first few seasons, Lassie lived on the Miller farm and had lots of adventures. The family included Jeff (Tommy Rettig), his widowed mother Ellen (Jan Clayton) and George Cleveland as Gramps. Throughout the years there were many format and cast changes, as Lassie was exchanged from one family to another in order to have a variety of new perils and escapades. Other featured performers over the years include Cloris Leachman, June Lockhart and Larry Wilcox.

MARYLAND: DEFENDERS DAY. Sept 12. Maryland. Annual reenactment of bombardment of Fort McHenry in 1814 which inspired Francis Scott Key to write the "Star-Spangled Banner."

MOON FESTIVAL or MID-AUTUMN FESTIVAL. Sept 12. This festival, observed on the 15th day of the eighth moon of the lunar calendar year, is called by different names in different places, but is widely recognized throughout the Far East, including People's Republic of China, Taiwan, Korea, Singapore and Hong Kong. An important harvest festival at the time the moon is brightest, it is also a time for homage to ancestors. Special harvest foods are eaten, especially "moon cakes."

OWENS, JESSE: BIRTH ANNIVERSARY. Sept 12, 1913. James Cleveland (Jesse) Owens, American athlete, winner of four gold medals at the 1936 Olympic Games at Berlin, Germany, was born at Oakville, AL. Owens set 11 world records in track and field. During one track meet, at Ann Arbor, MI, May 23, 1935, Owens, representing Ohio State University, broke five world records and tied a sixth in the space of 45 minutes. Died at Tucson, AZ, Mar 31, 1980.

SPACE MILESTONE: *LUNA 2* (USSR). Sept 12, 1959. First spacecraft to land on moon was launched.

VIDEO GAMES DAY. Sept 12. A day for kids who love video games to celebrate the fun they have playing them and to thank their parents for all the cartridges and quarters they have provided to indulge this hobby.

September 2000

S	M	T	W	T	F	S
					1	2
3	4	5	6	7	8	9
10	11	12	13	14	15	16
17	18	19	20	21	22	23
24	25	26	27	28	29	30

BIRTHDAYS TODAY

Sam Brownback, 44, US Senator (R, Kansas), born Garnett, KS, Sept 12, 1956.
Peter Scolari, 46, actor ("Honey I Shrunk the Kids: The TV Show"), born Rochelle, IL, Sept 12, 1954.

SEPTEMBER 13 — WEDNESDAY

Day 257 — 109 Remaining

BARRY, JOHN: DEATH ANNIVERSARY. Sept 13, 1803. Revolutionary War hero John Barry, first American to hold the rank of commodore, died at Philadelphia, PA. He was born at Tacumshane, County Wexford, Ireland, in 1745. He has been called the "Father of the American Navy."

DAHL, ROALD: BIRTH ANNIVERSARY. Sept 13, 1916. Author (*Charlie and the Chocolate Factory, James and the Giant Peach, Matilda*), born at Llandaff, South Wales, Great Britain. Died Nov 23, 1990, at Oxford, England.

HARVEST MOON. Sept 13. So called because the full moon nearest the autumnal equinox extends the hours of light into the evening and helps the harvester with his long day's work. Moon enters Full Moon phase at 3:37 PM, EDT.

MOON PHASE: FULL MOON. Sept 13. Moon enters Full Moon phase at 3:37 PM, EDT.

"THE MUPPET SHOW" TV PREMIERE: ANNIVERSARY. Sept 13, 1976. This comedy variety show was hosted by Kermit the Frog from "Sesame Street." Other Jim Henson puppet characters included Miss Piggy, Fozzie the Bear and The Great Gonzo. Many celebrities made guest appearances on the show, which was broadcast in more than 100 countries. "Muppet Babies" was a Saturday morning cartoon spin-off that aired from 1984 to 1992. *The Muppet Movie* (1979) was the first of five films based on "The Muppet Show."

REED, WALTER: BIRTH ANNIVERSARY. Sept 13, 1851. American army physician especially known for his Yellow Fever research. Born at Gloucester County, VA, he served as an army surgeon for more than 20 years and as a professor at the Army Medical College. He died at Washington, DC, Nov 22, 1902. The US Army's general hospital at Washington, DC, is named in his honor.

SCHUMANN, CLARA: BIRTH ANNIVERSARY. Sept 13, 1819. Pianist and composer, wife of composer Robert Schumann. Born at Leipzig, Germany, she died May 20, 1896, at Frankfurt, Germany. *See* Curriculum Connection.

"STAR-SPANGLED BANNER" INSPIRED: ANNIVERSARY. Sept 13–14, 1814. During the War of 1812, on the night of Sept 13, Francis Scott Key was aboard a ship that was delayed in Baltimore harbor by the British attack there on Fort Henry. Key had no choice but to anxiously watch the battle. That experience and seeing the American flag still flying over the fort the next morning inspired him to pen the verses that, coupled with the tune of a popular drinking song, became our official national anthem in 1931, 117 years after the words were written.

SEPTEMBER 13
BIRTHDAY OF CLARA SCHUMANN

Clara, born in 1819, was the daughter of Marianne and Frederick Wieck (pronounced Veek). Frederick was well-known in the German music community as a teacher and the owner of a piano store. Quiet, shy Clara seldom spoke when she was a very young child. In fact, she did not speak at all until she was four years old. As a result, some people believed she was deaf or possible mentally handicapped.

Clara always loved to watch her father play the piano. She often imitated the movement of his hands as he played. Her father decided she could begin lessons when she was five years old. Clara quickly demonstrated that she possessed an innate musical ability and was highly talented. Frederick decided he would raise Clara to be a musical virtuoso. An apt pupil, Clara was eager to please her demanding father. Once she began playing the piano, she also began speaking, although hesitantly.

By the time Clara was nine years old she had debuted as a piano prodigy. At 11, she made her first European concert tour. This was highly unusual for a woman, let alone a girl. At that time women were not encouraged to perform in public or become professionals.

Clara's brilliance as a concert pianist stunned audiences. In 1840, she married Robert Schumann, a composer and long-time friend. Clara also began composing music for the piano, voice and other instruments. She continued performing and composing, even as she raised her eight children. Robert had a history of mental illness, which gradually worsened. He died in 1856, and Clara became the sole provider for her family.

As an adult, Clara had many friends in the music world. She was particularly close to Johannes Brahms. Together, they published and made famous some of Robert Schumann's compositions.

Until recently, Clara's work has not received widespread attention. In the past few years, however, greater attention is being paid to her compositions and her pieces are beginning to be published and performed publicly.

Introduce your students to the joy of classical music and this extraordinary woman. Use her music, and that of her contemporaries, as a soft backdrop during quiet reading time, art class, writing periods or whenever the mood strikes.

Although we have no recordings of her brilliant playing, recordings of music she composed are widely available, as are recordings of music composed by Robert Schumann and Johannes Brahms. Look in your library's collection.

Two excellent biographies for young readers are: *Clara Schumann: Piano Virtuoso*, by Susanna Reich (Clarion, 0-395-89119-1, $18 Gr. 5 & up) and *Her Piano Sang: A Story About Clara Schumann*, by Barbara Allman (Carolrhoda, 1-57505-012-9, $15.95 Gr. 3–6).

US CAPITAL ESTABLISHED AT NEW YORK CITY: ANNIVERSARY. Sept 13, 1789. Congress picked New York, NY, as the location of the new US government in place of Philadelphia, which had served as the capital up until this time. In 1790 the capital moved back to Philadelphia, and in 1800 moved permanently to Washington, DC.

BIRTHDAYS TODAY

William Janklow, 61, Governor of South Dakota (R), born Chicago, IL, Sept 13, 1939.

Else Holmelund Minarik, 80, author (the Little Bear series), born Aarhus, Denmark, Sept 13, 1920.

Ben Savage, 20, actor ("Boy Meets World"), born Chicago, IL, Sept 13, 1980.

Mildred Taylor, 57, author (Newbery for *Roll of Thunder, Hear My Cry*), born Jackson, MS, Sept 13, 1943.

SEPTEMBER 14 — THURSDAY
Day 258 — 108 Remaining

ARMSTRONG, WILLIAM H.: BIRTH ANNIVERSARY. Sept 14, 1914. Newbery Award-winning author (*Sounder*). Born at Lexington, VA, he died Apr 11, 1999, at Kent, CT.

CORN ISLAND STORYTELLING FESTIVAL—ON NATIVE GROUND. Sept 14–16. Louisville, KY. More than 50 storytellers. Festival includes an "olio," mixture of tales, "Fest of Storytelling" and "ghost tales" told at Long Run Park. 25th anniversary will feature all Native American tellers and Native American stories. Est attendance: 16,000. For info: Joy Pennington, Intl Order of EARS, Inc, 12019 Donohue Ave, Louisville, KY 40243. Phone: (502) 245-0643. Fax: (502) 254-7542.

SOLO TRANSATLANTIC BALLOON CROSSING: ANNIVERSARY. Sept 14–18, 1984. Joe W. Kittinger, 56-year-old balloonist, left Caribou, ME, in a 10-story-tall helium-filled balloon named *Rosie O'Grady's Balloon of Peace* Sept 14, 1984, crossed the Atlantic Ocean and reached the French coast, above the town of Capbreton, in bad weather Sept 17 at 4:29 PM, EDT. He crash-landed amid wind and rain near Savone, Italy, at 8:08 AM, EDT, Sept 18. His nearly 84-hour flight, covering about 3,535 miles, was the first solo balloon crossing of the Atlantic Ocean.

"THE WALTONS" TV PREMIERE: ANNIVERSARY. Sept 14, 1972. This epitome of the family drama spawned nearly a dozen knock-offs during its nine-year run on CBS. The drama was based on creator/writer Earl Hamner, Jr's experiences growing up during the Depression in rural Virginia. It began as the TV movie "The Homecoming," which was so well-received that it was turned into a weekly series covering the years 1933–43. The cast went through numerous changes through the years; the principals were: Michael Learned as Olivia Walton, mother of the clan, Ralph Waite as John Walton, father, Richard Thomas as John-Boy, eldest son, Jon Walmsley as son Jason, Judy Norton-Taylor as daughter Mary Ellen, Eric Scott as son Ben, Mary Elizabeth McDonough as daughter Erin, David W. Harper as son Jim-Bob and Kami Cotler as daughter Elizabeth. The Walton grandparents were played by Ellen Corby (Esther) and Will Geer (Zeb).

WILSON, JAMES: BIRTH ANNIVERSARY. Sept 14, 1742. Signer of the Declaration of Independence and one of the first associate justices of the US Supreme Court. Born at Fifeshire, Scotland, he died Aug 21, 1798, at Edenton, NC.

BIRTHDAYS TODAY

John Steptoe, 50, author and illustrator (*Mufaro's Beautiful Daughters: An African Tale*), born Brooklyn, NY, Sept 14, 1950.

Elizabeth Winthrop, 52, author (*Belinda's Hurricane*), born Washington, DC, Sept 14, 1948.

SEPTEMBER 15 — FRIDAY
Day 259 — 107 Remaining

AUSTRALIA: SUMMER OLYMPICS OPENING CEREMONY. Sept 15. Sydney, Australia. More than 10,000 athletes from 198 nations will participate in 28 sports in the XXVII Olympiad. Because of the 14-hour time difference between Australia and the US, the Opening Ceremony will take place on Sept 14 US time. Closing ceremonies are Oct 1 (Sept 30 US time).

THE BIG E. Sept 15–Oct 1. West Springfield, MA. New England's fall classic and one of the nation's largest fairs. Each September, The Big E features all free entertainment including top-name talent, a big-top circus and horse show. Also children's attractions, daily parade, historic village, Avenue of States, Better Living Center and much more. Annually, beginning the second Friday after Labor Day. Est attendance: 1,200,000. For info: Eastern States Exposition, 1305 Memorial Ave, West Springfield, MA 01089. Phone: (413) 737-2443. Ticket info: (800) 334-2443. Fax: (413) 787-0127. E-mail: sales@thebige.com. Web: www.thebige.com.

COOPER, JAMES FENIMORE: BIRTH ANNIVERSARY. Sept 15, 1789. American novelist, historian and social critic, born at Burlington, NJ, Cooper was one of the earliest American writers to develop a native American literary tradition. His most popular works are the five novels comprising *The Leatherstocking Tales,* featuring the exploits of one of the truly unique American fictional characters, Natty Bumppo. These novels, *The Deerslayer, The Last of the Mohicans, The Pathfinder, The Pioneers* and *The Prairie,* chronicle Natty Bumppo's continuing flight away from the rapid settlement of America. Cooper died Sept 14, 1851, at Cooperstown, NY, the town founded by his father.

COSTA RICA: INDEPENDENCE DAY. Sept 15. National holiday. Gained independence from Spain in 1821.

EL SALVADOR: INDEPENDENCE DAY. Sept 15. National holiday. Gained independence from Spain in 1821.

ENGLAND: BATTLE OF BRITAIN DAY. Sept 15. Commemorates end of biggest daylight bombing raid of Britain by German Luftwaffe, in 1940. Said to have been the turning point against Hitler's siege of Britain in WWII.

FIRST NATIONAL CONVENTION FOR BLACKS: ANNIVERSARY. Sept 15, 1830. The first national convention for blacks was held at Bethel Church, Philadelphia, PA. The convention was called to find ways to better the condition of black people and was attended by delegates from seven states. Bishop Richard Allen was elected as the first convention president.

GUATEMALA: INDEPENDENCE DAY. Sept 15. National holiday. Gained independence from Spain in 1821.

HONDURAS: INDEPENDENCE DAY. Sept 15. National holiday. Gained independence from Spain in 1821.

JAPAN: OLD PEOPLE'S DAY OR RESPECT FOR THE AGED DAY. Sept 15. National holiday.

KIRSTEN, SAMANTHA AND MOLLY DEBUT: ANNIVERSARY. Sept 15, 1986. The first three American Girl dolls representing different historical periods debuted. They were joined in later years by Addy, Felicity and Josefina. More than 4 million dolls and 48 million books about them have been sold. For more info: www.americangirl.com.

LIONS CLUBS INTERNATIONAL PEACE POSTER CONTEST. Sept 15. Contest for children ages 11–13. All entries must be sponsored by a local Lions Club. Today is the deadline for sponsorship requests by schools and youth groups. Posters due to sponsoring Lions Club by Nov 30, 2000. Finalist judging held at Chicago in March 2001. For info: Public Relations Dept, Intl Assn of Lions Clubs, 300 22nd St, Oak Brook, IL 60523-8842. Phone: (630) 571-5466. Web: www.lionsclub.org.

September *2000*	S	M	T	W	T	F	S
						1	2
	3	4	5	6	7	8	9
	10	11	12	13	14	15	16
	17	18	19	20	21	22	23
	24	25	26	27	28	29	30

"THE LONE RANGER" TV PREMIERE: ANNIVERSARY. Sept 15, 1949. This character was created for a radio serial in 1933 by George W. Trendle. The famous masked man was the alter ego of John Reid, a Texas Ranger who was the only survivor of an ambush. He was nursed back to health by his Native American friend, Tonto. Both men traveled around the West on their trusty steeds, Silver and Scout, fighting injustice. On TV Clayton Moore played the Lone Ranger/John Reid and Jay Silverheels costarred as Tonto. The theme music was Rossini's "William Tell Overture."

$$\begin{array}{r} 105 \\ \times\ 3 \\ \hline 315 \end{array}$$

MATHCOUNTS. Sept 15. A national math coaching and competition program for 7th and 8th grade students. At the beginning of each year, the MATHCOUNTS Foundation distributes its free school handbook. Teachers and volunteers use these materials to coach "mathletes." Participating schools select four students to compete individually and as a team in written and oral competitions in one of more than 500 local meets in February. Winners progress to state contests in March. State winners go to the national finals in Washington, DC in May. Est attendance: 500,000. For info: MATHCOUNTS Foundation, 1420 King St, Alexandria, VA 22314. Phone: (703) 684-2828. E-mail: mathcounts@nspe.org. Web: www.mathcounts.org.

★ **NATIONAL HISPANIC HERITAGE MONTH.** Sept 15–Oct 15. Presidential Proclamation. Beginning in 1989, always issued for Sept 15–Oct 15 of each year (PL 100–402 of Aug 17, 1988). Previously issued each year for the week including Sept 15 and 16 since 1968 at request (PL90–498 of Sept 17, 1968). *See* Curriculum Connection.

NATIVE AMERICAN DAY IN MASSACHUSETTS. Sept 15. Proclaimed annually by the governor for the third Friday in September.

NICARAGUA: INDEPENDENCE DAY. Sept 15. National holiday. Gained independence from Spain in 1821.

PIPER, WATTY: BIRTH ANNIVERSARY. Sept 15, 1870. Born Mabel Caroline Bragg at Milford, MA. Piper is best-known for her classic tale *The Little Engine That Could.* She died Apr 25, 1945.

STATE FAIR OF OKLAHOMA. Sept 15–Oct 1. Fairgrounds, Oklahoma City, Oklahoma. Third largest fair in North America includes seven buildings of commercial exhibits; Walt Disney's World on Ice, the State Fair Super Circus, PRCA championship rodeo, livestock competitions, top-name concerts and motorsports events. Annually, second Friday after Labor Day. Est attendance: 1,300,000. For info: State Fair of Oklahoma, PO Box 74943, Oklahoma City, OK 73107. Phone: (405) 948-6700. Fax: (405) 948-6828. E-mail: oklafair@oklafair.org.

TAFT, WILLIAM HOWARD: BIRTH ANNIVERSARY. Sept 15, 1857. The 27th president of the US was born at Cincinnati, OH. His term of office was Mar 4, 1909–Mar 3, 1913. Following his presidency he became a law professor at Yale University until his appointment as Chief Justice of the US Supreme Court in

SEPTEMBER 15–OCTOBER 15
NATIONAL HISPANIC HERITAGE MONTH

Celebrate the many Hispanic cultures that have enriched the United States. In some regions, differing Hispanic heritages have given birth to the community's roots. Variations include descendants of and/or immigrants from Mexico, Cuba, Puerto Rico, Central and South America and Spain.

Books that contain information about some of these Hispanic cultures include: *The Cuban American Family Album* (Oxford University Press, 0-19-510340-8 $19.95 All ages); *I Am Mexican American*, by Isobel Seymour (out of print); *Puerto Rico: Hello, USA*, by Joyce Johnston (Lerner, 0-8225-9721-7, $5.95 Gr. 3–6); *Big Spanish Heritage Activity Book*, by Walter Yoder (Sunstone Press, 0-86534-239-3, $8.95 Gr. 3–9); and *The Other Side, How Kids Live in a California Latino Neighborhood*, by Kathleen Krull (Penguin, 0-14-036521-4, $16.99 Gr. 2–6).

Invite parents and relatives of Hispanic students to visit the classroom and share any family traditions that have roots in their Hispanic heritage. Traditions may include the celebration of holidays such as the Day of the Dead or Cinco de Mayo. Some holiday menus feature traditional food. Hold an evening fiesta and serve holiday fare. Ask parents to participate by helping children prepare the special dishes. If the families are recent immigrants, they may be willing to share the process of immigration with the class.

Music and the arts have a rich Hispanic tradition. Pablo Casals played the cello and Andres Segovia played the guitar; both were world-famous musicians. Many people enjoy Placido Domingo's resounding operatic singing and the popular songs sung by Ricky Martin and Gloria Estefan. Check your local library for recordings. The paintings of Diego Rivera and Frieda Kahlo, Hispanic artists who painted during the first half of the 20th century, hang in many museums and private collections. There are a number of biographies about them available for children and adults.

Don't forget to feature the important discoveries made by Spanish explorers. Hernando de Soto led the first European expedition to the Mississippi. He also defeated the Incan empire. Francisco Vasquez de Coronado explored the American southwest. Hernando Cortés conquered the Aztecs in what is now central and south Mexico. Juan Ponce de León claimed Florida for Spain and also searched for the "fountain of youth." Students can trace their voyages on a map and write postcards to "the folks back home" from each port of call. They can discuss the dangers-both real and imaginary-faced by these people as they arrived in a new territory.

While looking at Spanish settlers, you might also delve into the cultures they conquered. Many Central and Southern Americans and Mexicans have roots that stem from the indigenous peoples from these regions. *Lost Temple of the Aztecs*, by Shelley Tanaka (Hyperion, 0-7868-0441-6, $16.95 Gr. 3–6); *Lost Treasure of the Inca*, by Peter Lourie (Boyds Mills, 1-56397-743-5, $18.95 Gr. 3–6); and *Mayeros: A Yucatec Maya Family*, by George Ancona (Lothrop, 0-688-13465-3 $16 Gr. 1 & up).

Several new literature connections feature plays in Spanish and English. *25 Spanish Plays for Emergent Readers*, by Carol Pugliano-Martin (Scholastic, 0-439-10546-3, $10.95 Gr. K–1), although intended for children who already speak Spanish, includes short plays that would be great fun in beginning Spanish language classes. They connect to many areas of the curriculum. *You're On! Seven Plays in English and Spanish*, edited by Lori Carlson (Morrow, 0-688-16237-1, $17 Gr. 3–7) contains seven plays by noted Hispanic authors. They are well suited for Reader's Theater productions.

1921. Died at Washington, DC, Mar 8, 1930, and was buried at Arlington National Cemetery.

BIRTHDAYS TODAY

Tomie DePaola, 66, illustrator and author (*Strega Nona*), born Thomas DePaola, Meriden, CT, Sept 15, 1934.

Prince Harry, 16, Henry Charles Albert David, son of Prince Charles and Princess Diana, born London, England, Sept 15, 1984.

Robert McCloskey, 86, illustrator and author (Caldecott for *Time of Wonder, Make Way for Ducklings*), born Hamilton, OH, Sept 15, 1914.

SEPTEMBER 16 — SATURDAY
Day 260 — 106 Remaining

CHEROKEE STRIP DAY: ANNIVERSARY. Sept 16, 1893. Optional holiday, Oklahoma. Greatest "run" for Oklahoma land in 1893.

GENERAL MOTORS: FOUNDING ANNIVERSARY. Sept 16, 1908. The giant automobile manufacturing company was founded by William Crapo "Billy" Durant, a Flint, MI, entrepreneur.

LAURA INGALLS WILDER FESTIVAL. Sept 16–17. Pepin, WI. 9th annual. Experience life in the mid-1800s with demonstrations of blacksmithing, woodworking, ironworking, weaving, quilting and wool-spinning by individuals dressed in period costumes. Stories and songs cited in Little House books are also performed and there's a Laura Ingalls look-alike contest. Additional attractions include a traveling exhibit of Wilder's written materials, sanctioned horse-pull, Civil War encampment, children's games from the period, parade, crafts and antiques at Laura Ingalls Wilder Memorial Park. For info: Wisconsin Dept of Tourism, Laura Ingalls Festival, PO Box 7976, Madison, WI 53707. Phone: (715) 442-2461 or (715) 442-2147. E-mail: tourinfo@tourism.state.wi.us. Web: travelwisconsin.com.

MAYFLOWER DAY: ANNIVERSARY. Sept 16, 1620. Anniversary of the departure of the *Mayflower* from Plymouth, England with 102 passengers and a small crew. Vicious storms were encountered en route which caused serious doubt about the wisdom of continuing, but she reached Provincetown, MA, Nov 21, and discharged the Pilgrims at Plymouth, MA, Dec 26, 1620.

MEXICO: INDEPENDENCE DAY. Sept 16. National Day. The official celebration begins at 11 PM, Sept 15 and continues through Sept 16. On the night of the 15th, the President of Mexico steps onto the balcony of the National Palace at Mexico City and voices the same "El Grito" (Cry for Freedom) that Father Hidalgo gave on the night of Sept 15, 1810, which began Mexico's rebellion from Spain.

NATIONAL KIDSDAY®. Sept 16. A national holiday to recognize the value, dignity and inherent worth of children everywhere (also known as National Children's Day™). Supervised and licensed by KidsPeace®, The National Center for Kids Overcoming Crisis, a private, not-for-profit organization that has been providing hope and healing to kids in crisis since 1882. KidsPeace offers the country's widest array of children's critical care services available under a "single roof" and crisis education to families across the US. Annually, the third Saturday in September. For info: Paula Knouse, KidsPeace, 5300 KidsPeace Dr, Orefield, PA 18069-9101. Phone: (610) 799-8325. Web: www.kidsday.net.

NATIONAL PLAY-DOH® DAY. Sept 16. To commemorate the introduction of Play-Doh. Joe McVicker of Cincinnati sent some non-toxic wallpaper cleaner to his sister-in-law, a nursery school teacher. She found it to be an excellent replacement for modeling clay. In 1955, McVicker took the product to an educational convention and by 1956 Play-Doh was being sold commercially.

PAPUA NEW GUINEA: INDEPENDENCE DAY: 25th ANNIVERSARY. Sept 16. National holiday. Commemorates independence from Australian administration in 1975.

REY, H.A.: BIRTH ANNIVERSARY. Sept 16, 1898. Born Hans Augusto Rey at Hamburg, Germany. Rey illustrated the Curious George series, while his wife, Margaret Rey, wrote the stories. He died at Cambridge, MA, Aug 26, 1977.

UNITED NATIONS: INTERNATIONAL DAY FOR THE PRESERVATION OF THE OZONE LAYER. Sept 16. On Dec 19, 1994, the General Assembly proclaimed this day to commemorate the date in 1987 on which Montreal Protocol on Substances that Deplete the Ozone Layer was signed (Res 49/114). States are invited to devote the Day to promote, at the national level, activities in accordance with the objectives of the Protocol. The ozone layer filters sunlight and prevents the adverse effects of ultraviolet radiation from reaching the Earth's surface, thereby preserving life on the planet. For info: United Nations, Dept of Public Info, Public Inquiries Unit, Rm GA-57, New York, NY 10017. Phone: (212) 963-4475. Fax: (212) 963-0071. E-mail: inquiries@un.org.

BIRTHDAYS TODAY

David Copperfield, 44, magician, illusionist, born Metuchen, NJ, Sept 16, 1956.

Robin Yount, 45, Baseball Hall of Fame player, born Danville, IL, Sept 16, 1955.

SEPTEMBER 17 — SUNDAY

Day 261 — 105 Remaining

BATTLE OF ANTIETAM: ANNIVERSARY. Sept 17, 1862. This date has been called America's bloodiest day in recognition of the high casualties suffered in the Civil War battle between General Robert E. Lee's Confederate forces and General George McClellan's Union army. Estimates vary, but more than 25,000 Union and Confederate soldiers were killed or wounded in this battle on the banks of the Potomac River at Maryland.

BURGER, WARREN E.: BIRTH ANNIVERSARY. Sept 17, 1907. Former Chief Justice of the US, Warren E. Burger was born at St. Paul, MN. A conservative on criminal matters, but a pro-

		S	M	T	W	T	F	S
September							1	2
2000		3	4	5	6	7	8	9
		10	11	12	13	14	15	16
		17	18	19	20	21	22	23
		24	25	26	27	28	29	30

gressive on social issues, he had the longest tenure (1969–86) of any chief justice in this century. Appointed by President Nixon, he voted in the majority on *Roe v Wade* (1973), which upheld a woman's right to an abortion, and on *US v Nixon* (1974), which forced Nixon to surrender audio tapes to the Watergate special prosecutor. He died June 25, 1995, at Washington, DC.

★**CITIZENSHIP DAY.** Sept 17. Presidential Proclamation always issued for Sept 17 at request (PL82–261 of Feb 29, 1952). Customarily issued as "Citizenship Day and Constitution Week." Replaces Constitution Day.

CONSTITUTION OF THE US: ANNIVERSARY. Sept 17, 1787. Delegations from 12 states at the Constitutional Convention at Philadelphia, PA, voted unanimously to approve the proposed document. Thirty-nine of the 42 delegates present signed it and the Convention adjourned, after drafting a letter of transmittal to the Congress. The proposed constitution stipulated that it would take effect when ratified by nine states. This day is a legal holiday in Arizona and Florida. For activities and lesson plans on the Constitution, visit the National Archives website at www.nara .gov/education/teaching/constitution/home.html.

★**CONSTITUTION WEEK.** Sept 17–23. Presidential Proclamation always issued for the period of Sept 17–23 each year since 1955 (PL 84–915 of Aug 2, 1956).

FOSTER, ANDREW "RUBE": BIRTH ANNIVERSARY. Sept 17, 1879. Rube Foster's efforts in baseball earned him the title of "The Father of Negro Baseball." He was a manager and star pitcher, pitching 51 victories in one year. In 1919, he called a meeting of black baseball owners and organized the first black baseball league, the Negro National League. He served as its president until his death in 1930. Foster was born at Calvert, TX, the son of a minister. He died Dec 9, 1930, at Kankakee, IL.

HENDRICKS, THOMAS ANDREWS: BIRTH ANNIVERSARY. Sept 17, 1819. The 21st vice president of the US (1885), born at Muskingum County, OH. Died at Indianapolis, IN, Nov 25, 1885.

"HOME IMPROVEMENT" TV PREMIERE: ANNIVERSARY. Sept 17, 1991. This comedy centered around the Taylors. Tim Taylor, played by Tim Allen, was a TV host on the popular fix-it show "Tool Time." Jill, played by Patricia Richardson, was a housewife and mother going back to school to get a degree in psychology. The couple's three sons were played by Zachery Ty Bryan, Jonathan Taylor Thomas and Taran Noah Smith. Other cast members included Richard Karn, Earl Hindman, Debbe Dunning and Pamela Anderson. The last episode aired May 25, 1999.

NATIONAL CONSTITUTION CENTER CONSTITUTION WEEK. Sept 17–23. To celebrate and commemorate the signing of the US Constitution Sept 17, 1787, the National Constitution Center sponsors ceremonial signings of the Constitution nationwide. Everyone is invited to participate and receive educational materials about the world's oldest working Constitution. For info: Natl Constitution Center, The Bourse, 111 S Independence Mall East, Ste 560, Philadelphia, PA 19106. Phone: (215) 923-0004. Fax: (215) 923-1749. Web: www.constitutioncenter.org.

NATIONAL CONSTITUTION CENTER GROUNDBREAKING: ANNIVERSARY. Sept 17, 2000. Established by an act of Congress, the National Constitution Center is being constructed on Independence Mall at Philadelphia. It will open in 2002. It was established to increase awareness and understanding of the US Constitution, its history and relevance to our daily lives. For more info, including teacher resources: www.constitutioncenter.org.

NATIONAL FARM ANIMALS AWARENESS WEEK. Sept 17–23. A week to promote awareness of farm animals and their natural behaviors. Each day of the week is dedicated to learning about a specific group of farm animals and to appreciating their many interesting and unique qualities. Annually, the third full week in September. For info: David Kuemmerle, Program Mgr, The Humane Soc of the US, Farm Animal Section, 2100 L St NW, Washington, DC 20037. Phone: (202) 452-1100. E-mail: davehsus @ix.netcom.com.

★**NATIONAL FARM SAFETY AND HEALTH WEEK.** Sept 17–23. Presidential Proclamation issued since 1982 for the third week in September. Previously, from 1944, for one of the last two weeks in July.

NATIONAL FOOTBALL LEAGUE FORMED: 80th ANNIVERSARY. Sept 17, 1920. The National Football League was formed at Canton, OH.

★**NATIONAL HISTORICALLY BLACK COLLEGES AND UNIVERSITIES WEEK.** Sept 17–23.

SPACE MILESTONE: *PEGASUS 1* (US). Sept 17, 1978. This 23,000-pound research satellite broke up over Africa and fell to Earth. Major pieces are believed to have fallen into Atlantic Ocean off the coast of Angola. The satellite had been orbiting Earth for more than 13 years since being launched Feb 16, 1965.

VIRGINIA CHILDREN'S FESTIVAL. Sept 17. Town Point Park, Norfolk, VA. An all-day family program hosted by nationally famous children's entertainers, costumed characters and five stages of entertainment. Also, magic, giant puppets, creative dance and many other activities for a day of fantasy and fun. Est attendance: 45,000. For info: Norfolk Festevents, Ltd, 120 W Main St, Norfolk, VA 23510. Phone: (757) 441-2345. Fax: (757) 441-5198.

VON STEUBEN, BARON FRIEDRICH: BIRTH ANNIVERSARY. Sept 17, 1730. Prussian-born general, born at Magdeburg, Prussia, who served in the American Revolution. He died at Remsen, NY, Nov 28, 1794.

BIRTHDAYS TODAY

Bjorn Berg, 77, illustrator (*Old Mrs Pepperpot*), born Munich, Germany, Sept 17, 1923.

Paul Goble, 67, author and illustrator (Caldecott for *The Girl Who Loved Wild Horses*), born Surrey, England, Sept 17, 1933.

Charles Ernest Grassley, 67, US Senator (R, Iowa), born New Hartford, IA, Sept 17, 1933.

Philip D. (Phil) Jackson, 55, basketball coach, former player, born Deer Lodge, MT, Sept 17, 1945.

Gail Carson Levine, 53, author (*Ella Enchanted*), born New York, NY, Sept 17, 1947.

David H. Souter, 61, Associate Justice of the US Supreme Court, born Melrose, MA, Sept 17, 1939.

SEPTEMBER 18 — MONDAY
Day 262 — 104 Remaining

"THE ADDAMS FAMILY" TV PREMIERE: ANNIVERSARY. Sept 18, 1964. Charles Addams' quirky *New Yorker* cartoon creations were brought to life in this ABC sitcom about a family full of oddballs. John Astin played lawyer Gomez Addams, with Carolyn Jones as his morbid wife Morticia, Ken Weatherwax as son Pugsley, Lisa Loring as daughter Wednesday, Jackie Coogan as Uncle Fester, Ted Cassidy as both Lurch, the butler, and Thing, a disembodied hand, Blossom Rock as Grandmama and Felix Silla as Cousin Itt. *The Addams Family* movie was released in 1991, starring Angelica Huston as Morticia, Raul Julia as Gomez, Christopher Lloyd as Uncle Fester, Jimmy Workman as Pugsley and Christina Ricci as Wednesday. *Addams Family Values* was released in 1993.

CHILE: INDEPENDENCE DAY. Sept 18. National holiday. Gained independence from Spain in 1810.

DIEFENBAKER, JOHN: BIRTH ANNIVERSARY. Sept 18, 1895. Canadian lawyer, statesman and Conservative prime minister (1957–63). Born at Normandy Township, Ontario, Canada, he died at Ottawa, Ontario, Aug 16, 1979. Diefenbaker was a member of the Canadian Parliament from 1940 until his death.

IRON HORSE OUTRACED BY HORSE: ANNIVERSARY. Sept 18, 1830. In a widely celebrated race, the first locomotive built in America, the Tom Thumb, lost to a horse. Mechanical difficulties plagued the steam engine over the nine-mile course between Riley's Tavern and Baltimore, MD, and a boiler leak prevented the locomotive from finishing the race. In the early days of trains, engines were nicknamed "Iron Horses."

READ, GEORGE: BIRTH ANNIVERSARY. Sept 18, 1733. Lawyer and signer of the Declaration of Independence, born at Cecil County, MD. Died Sept 21, 1798, at New Castle, DE.

STORY, JOSEPH: BIRTH ANNIVERSARY. Sept 18, 1779. Associate justice of the US Supreme Court (1811–45) was born at Marblehead, MA. "It is astonishing," he wrote a few months before his death, "how easily men satisfy themselves that the Constitution is exactly what they wish it to be." Story died Sept 10, 1845, at Cambridge, MA, having served 33 years on the Supreme Court bench.

US AIR FORCE ESTABLISHED: ANNIVERSARY. Sept 18, 1947. Although its heritage dates back to 1907 when the Army first established military aviation, the US Air Force became a separate military service on this date.

US CAPITOL CORNERSTONE LAID: ANNIVERSARY. Sept 18, 1793. President George Washington laid the Capitol cornerstone at Washington, DC, in a Masonic ceremony. That event was the first and last recorded occasion at which the stone with its engraved silver plate was seen. In 1958, during the extension of the east front of the Capitol, an unsuccessful effort was made to find it.

BIRTHDAYS TODAY

Lance Armstrong, 29, cyclist, born Plano, TX, Sept 18, 1971.

Robert F. Bennett, 67, US Senator (R, Utah), born Salt Lake City, UT, Sept 18, 1933.

SEPTEMBER 19 — TUESDAY
Day 263 — 103 Remaining

CARROLL, CHARLES: BIRTH ANNIVERSARY. Sept 19, 1737. American Revolutionary leader and signer of the Declaration of Independence, born at Annapolis, MD. The last surviving signer of the Declaration, he died Nov 14, 1832, at Baltimore, MD.

MEXICO CITY EARTHQUAKE: 15th ANNIVERSARY. Sept 19–20, 1985. Nearly 10,000 persons perished in the earthquakes (8.1 and 7.5 respectively, on the Richter Scale) that devastated Mexico City. Damage to buildings was estimated at more than $1 billion, and 100,000 homes were destroyed or severely damaged.

NETHERLANDS: PRINSJESDAG. Sept 19. Official opening of parliament at The Hague. The queen of the Netherlands, by tradition, rides in a golden coach to the hall of knights for the annual opening of parliament. Annually, on the third Tuesday in September.

POWELL, LEWIS F., JR: BIRTH ANNIVERSARY. Sept 19, 1907. Former associate justice of the Supreme Court of the US, nominated by President Nixon Oct 21, 1971. (Took office Jan 7, 1972.) Justice Powell was born at Suffolk, VA. In 1987, he announced his retirement from the Court. He died Aug 25, 1998, at Richmond, VA.

SAINT CHRISTOPHER (SAINT KITTS) AND NEVIS: INDEPENDENCE DAY. Sept 19. National holiday. Commemorates the independence of these Caribbean islands from Britain in 1983.

SAINT JANUARIUS (GENNARO): FEAST DAY. Sept 19. Fourth-century bishop of Benevento, martyred near Naples, Italy, whose relics in the Naples Cathedral are particularly famous because on his feast days the blood in a glass vial is said to liquefy in response to prayers of the faithful. This phenomenon is said to occur also on the first Saturday in May (May 5 in 2001).

BIRTHDAYS TODAY

James Haskins, 59, author (*Bayard Rustin: Behind the Scenes of the Civil Rights Movement*), born Montgomery, AL, Sept 19, 1941.

Kevin Zegers, 16, actor (*Air Bud*), born St. Mary's, Ontario, Canada, Sept 19, 1984.

SEPTEMBER 20 — WEDNESDAY
Day 264 — 102 Remaining

"THE COSBY SHOW" TV PREMIERE: ANNIVERSARY. Sept 20, 1984. Comedian Bill Cosby starred as Dr. Cliff Huxtable in this sitcom about an upper-middle class black family living in Brooklyn. Phylicia Rashad played his wife Claire, an attorney. Their five children were played by Sabrina LeBeauf, Lisa Bonet, Malcolm-Jamal Warner, Tempestt Bledsoe and Keshia Knight Pulliam. "A Different World" was a spin-off, with daughter Denise (Lisa Bonet) attending her parents' alma mater, Hillman College.

MOON PHASE: LAST QUARTER. Sept 20. Moon enters Last Quarter phase at 9:28 PM, EDT.

September 2000	S	M	T	W	T	F	S
						1	2
	3	4	5	6	7	8	9
	10	11	12	13	14	15	16
	17	18	19	20	21	22	23
	24	25	26	27	28	29	30

BIRTHDAYS TODAY

Arthur Geisert, 59, author and illustrator (*Roman Numerals I to M*), born Dallas, TX, Sept 20, 1941.

SEPTEMBER 21 — THURSDAY
Day 265 — 101 Remaining

ARMENIA: NATIONAL DAY. Sept 21. Public holiday. Commemorates independence from the Soviet Union in 1991.

BELIZE: INDEPENDENCE DAY. Sept 21. National holiday. Commemorates independence of the former British Honduras from Britain in 1981.

HOPKINSON, FRANCIS: BIRTH ANNIVERSARY. Sept 21, 1737. Signer of the Declaration of Independence. Born at Philadelphia, PA, he died there May 9, 1791.

HURRICANE HUGO HITS AMERICAN COAST: ANNIVERSARY. Sept 21, 1989. After ravaging the Virgin Islands, Hurricane Hugo hit the American coast at Charleston, SC. In its wake, Hugo left destruction totaling at least $8 billion.

JOSEPH, CHIEF: DEATH ANNIVERSARY. Sept 21, 1904. Nez Percé chief, whose Indian name was In-Mut-Too-Yah-Lat-Lat, was born about 1840 at Wallowa Valley, Oregon Territory, and died on the Colville Reservation at Washington State. Faced with war or resettlement to a reservation, Chief Joseph led a dramatic attempt to escape to Canada. After three months and more than 1,000 miles, he and his people were surrounded 40 miles from Canada and sent to a reservation at Oklahoma. Though the few survivors were later allowed to relocate to another reservation at Washington, they never regained their ancestral lands.

MALTA: INDEPENDENCE DAY: ANNIVERSARY. Sept 21. National Day. Commemorates independence from Britain in 1964.

NATIONAL STUDENT DAY™. Sept 21. Created to recognize all students from preschool through postgraduate, this is the perfect day to show the students in our lives how proud we are of them, to recognize their hard work and to show support for their efforts. For info: Ralph E. Williams, Exec Dir, Natl Assn of College Students, 8695 College Pkwy, Ste 300, Ft Myers, FL 33919. Phone: (800) 500-4255 or (941) 489-1530. Fax: (941) 489-1142. E-mail: nacs@collegeknowledge.com. Web: www.collegeknowledge.com.

NORTHERN APPALACHIAN STORYTELLING FESTIVAL. Sept 21–24. Straughn Hall, Mansfield University, Mansfield, PA. Showcases the talent of the nation's top storytellers who share through their performances a sense of roots and cultural diversity. There are performances Saturday afternoon and Friday and Saturday evening, plus a ghost story session late Friday night. In addition, there are storytelling master classes Saturday morning and a workshop on Thursday and Friday. Est attendance: 3,000. For info: Dr. Priscilla M Travis, N Appalachian Storytelling Fest, PO Box 434, Mansfield, PA 16933. Phone: (717) 662-4785. Fax: (717) 662-4112. E-mail: ptravis@mnsfld.edu. Web: wso.net /storyfest.

STATE FAIR OF VIRGINIA ON STRAWBERRY HILL. Sept 21–Oct 1. Richmond, VA. The pride of Virginia's industry of agriculture can be seen in more than 3,000 exhibitions, competitions and shows. Virginia's greatest annual educational and entertainment event. Est attendance: 600,000. For info: Keith T. Hessey, General Mgr, 600 E Laburnum Ave, Richmond, VA 23222. Phone: (804) 228-3200. Fax: (804) 228-3252. Web: www.statefair.com.

TAYLOR, MARGARET SMITH: BIRTH ANNIVERSARY. Sept 21, 1788. Wife of Zachary Taylor, 12th president of the US, born at Calvert County, MD. Died Aug 18, 1852.

BIRTHDAYS TODAY

Stephen King, 53, author (*Pet Sematary, The Shining, Misery*), born Portland, ME, Sept 21, 1947.

Bill Murray, 50, comedian ("Saturday Night Live"), actor (*Ghostbusters, Groundhog Day*), born Evanston, IL, Sept 21, 1950.

SEPTEMBER 22 — FRIDAY
Day 266 — 100 Remaining

AUTUMN. Sept 22–Dec 21. In the Northern Hemisphere, autumn begins today with the autumnal equinox, at 1:27 PM, EDT. Note that in the Southern Hemisphere today is the beginning of spring. Everywhere on Earth (except near the poles) the sun rises due east and sets due west and daylight length is nearly identical—about 12 hours, 8 minutes.

ELEPHANT APPRECIATION DAY. Sept 22. Celebrate the earth's largest, most interesting and most noble endangered land animal. Free info kit from: Wayne Hepburn, Wild Heart Productions, PO Box 3588, Sarasota, FL 34230-3588. Phone: (941) 955-2950. Fax: (941) 955-5723. E-mail: mail@wildheart.com. Web: www.wildheart.com.

EMANCIPATION PROCLAMATION: ANNIVERSARY. Sept 22, 1862. One of the most important presidential proclamations of American history is that of Sept 22, 1862, in which Abraham Lincoln, by executive proclamation, freed the slaves in the rebelling states. (Four slave states had not seceded from the Union.) "That on . . . [Jan 1, 1863] . . . all persons held as slaves within any state or designated part of a state, the people whereof shall then be in rebellion against the United States, shall be then, thenceforward, and forever, free. . . ." See also: "13th Amendment: Anniversary" (Dec 18) for abolition of slavery in all states.

ICE CREAM CONE: BIRTHDAY. Sept 22, 1903. Italo Marchiony emigrated from Italy in the late 1800s and soon thereafter went into business at New York, NY, with a pushcart dispensing lemon ice. Success soon led to a small fleet of pushcarts, and the inventive Marchiony was inspired to develop a cone, first made of paper, later of pastry, to hold the tasty delicacy. On Sept 22, 1903, his application for a patent for his new mold was filed, and US Patent No 746971 was issued to him Dec 15, 1903.

MALI: INDEPENDENCE DAY: 40th ANNIVERSARY. Sept 22. National holiday commemorating independence from France in 1960. Mali, in West Africa, was known as the French Sudan while a colony.

US POSTMASTER GENERAL ESTABLISHED: ANNIVERSARY. Sept 22, 1789. Congress established the office of postmaster general, following the departments of state, war and treasury.

BIRTHDAYS TODAY

Bonnie Hunt, 36, actress (*Beethoven, Beethoven's 2*), born Chicago, IL, Sept 22, 1964.

Ronaldo, 24, Brazilian soccer star, born Ronaldo Luiz Nazario de Lima, Rio de Janeiro, Brazil, Sept 22, 1976.

Esphyr Slobodkina, 92, author and illustrator (*Caps for Sale: A Tale of a Peddler, Some Monkeys and Their Monkey Business*), born Cheliabinsk, Siberia, Sept 22, 1908.

SEPTEMBER 23 — SATURDAY
Day 267 — 99 Remaining

BANNED BOOKS WEEK—CELEBRATING THE FREEDOM TO READ. Sept 23–30. Brings to the attention of the general public the importance of the freedom to read and the harm censorship causes to our society. Sponsors: American Library Association, American Booksellers Association, American Booksellers Association for Free Expression, American Society of Journalists and Authors, Association of American Publishers, National Association of College Stores. For lists of frequently challenged books, visit the following websites: www.ala.org/bbooks/index.html and www.cs.cmu.edu/People/spok/most-banned.html. For info: Judith F. Krug, American Library Assn, Office for Intellectual Freedom, 50 E Huron St, Chicago, IL 60611. Phone: (312) 280-4223. Fax: (312) 280-4227. E-mail: oif@ala.org.

"THE JETSONS" TV PREMIERE: ANNIVERSARY. Sept 23, 1962. "Meet George Jetson. His boy Elroy. Daughter Judy. Jane, his wife. . . . " These words introduced us to the Jetsons, a cartoon family living in the twenty-first century, the Flintstones of the Space Age. We followed the exploits of George and his family, as well as his unstable work relationship with his greedy, ruthless boss Cosmo Spacely. Voices were provided by George O'Hanlon as George, Penny Singleton as Jane, Janet Waldo as Judy, Daws Butler as Elroy, Don Messick as Astro, the family dog and Mel Blanc as Spacely. New episodes were created in 1985 which introduced a new pet, Orbity.

KIWANIS KIDS' DAY. Sept 23. To honor and assist youth—our greatest resource. Annually, the fourth Saturday in September. For info: Kiwanis Intl, Program Dvmt Dept, 3636 Woodview Trace, Indianapolis, IN 46268. E-mail: kiwanismail@kiwanis.org. Web: www.kiwanis.org.

LIBRA, THE BALANCE. Sept 23–Oct 22. In the astronomical/astrological zodiac that divides the sun's apparent orbit into 12 segments, the period Sept 23–Oct 22 is identified traditionally as the sun sign of Libra, the Balance. The ruling planet is Venus.

"LITTLE ROCK NINE": ANNIVERSARY. Sept 23, 1957. Nine African American students entered Central High School in Little Rock, AR. They had tried to begin school Sept 4 but were denied entrance by National Guard troops called out by Governor Orval Faubus to resist integration. President Dwight Eisenhower responded by sending federal troops to protect the students. Eight of the nine students completed the school year, showing America that black students could endure the hatred directed at them.

McGUFFEY, WILLIAM HOLMES: 200th BIRTH ANNIVERSARY. Sept 23, 1800. American educator and author of the famous *McGuffey Readers*, born at Washington County, PA. Probably no other textbooks have had a greater influence on American life. More than 120 million copies were sold. McGuffey died at Charlottesville, VA, May 4, 1873.

★**NATIONAL HUNTING AND FISHING DAY.** Sept 23. Presidential Proclamation 4682, of Sept 11, 1979, covers all succeeding years. Annually, the fourth Saturday of September.

PLANET NEPTUNE DISCOVERY: ANNIVERSARY. Sept 23, 1846. Neptune is 2,796,700,000 miles from the sun (about 30 times as far from the sun as Earth). Eighth planet from the sun, Neptune takes 164.8 years to revolve around the sun. Diameter is about 31,000 miles compared to Earth at 7,927 miles. Discovered by German astronomer Johann Galle. For more info, go to Nine Planets: Multimedia Tour of the Solar System at www.seds.org/billa/tnp.

SAUDI ARABIA: ANNIVERSARY KINGDOM UNIFICATION. Sept 23. National holiday. Commemorates unification in 1932.

Bruce Brooks, 50, author (*What Hearts, The Moves Make the Man*), born Washington, DC, Sept 23, 1950.

Eric Scott Montross, 29, basketball player, born Indianapolis, IN, Sept 23, 1971.

SEPTEMBER 24 — SUNDAY
Day 268 — 98 Remaining

BEHN, HARRY: BIRTH ANNIVERSARY. Sept 24, 1898. Author, best remembered for his children's books, *Trees* and *Crickets and Bullfrogs and Whispers of Thunder*. Born at McCabe, CT, Behn died Sept 5, 1973.

DEAF AWARENESS WEEK. Sept 24–30. Nationwide celebration to promote deaf culture, American Sign Language and deaf heritage. Activities include library displays, interpreted story hours, Open Houses in residential schools and mainstream programs, exhibit booths in shopping malls with "Five Minute Sign Language Lessons," material distribution. For info: Natl Assn for the Deaf, 814 Thayer Ave, Silver Spring, MD 20910-4500. Fax: (301) 587-1791. E-mail: nadinfo@nad.org. Web: www.nad.org.

★ **GOLD STAR MOTHER'S DAY.** Sept 24. Presidential Proclamation always for last Sunday of each September since 1936. Proclamation 2424 of Sept 14, 1940, covers all succeeding years.

GUINEA-BISSAU: INDEPENDENCE DAY: ANNIVERSARY. Sept 24. National holiday. Commemorates independence from Portugal in 1974.

HENSON, JIM: BIRTH ANNIVERSARY. Sept 24, 1936. Puppeteer, born at Greenville, MS. Jim Henson created a unique brand of puppetry known as the Muppets. Kermit the Frog, Big Bird, Rowlf, Bert and Ernie, Gonzo, Animal, Miss Piggy and Oscar the Grouch are a few of the puppets that captured the hearts of children and adults alike in television and film productions including "Sesame Street," "The Jimmy Dean Show," "The Muppet Show," *The Muppet Movie, The Muppets Take Manhattan, The Great Muppet Caper* and *The Dark Crystal*. Henson began his career in 1954 as producer of the TV show "Sam and Friends" at Washington, DC. He introduced the Muppets in 1956. His creativity was rewarded with 18 Emmy Awards, seven Grammy Awards, four Peabody Awards and five ACE Awards from the National Cable Television Association. Henson died unexpectedly May 16, 1990, at New York, NY.

HONG KONG: BIRTHDAY OF CONFUCIUS. Sept 24. Religious observances are held by the Confucian Society at Confucius Temple at Causeway Bay. Observed on 27th day of 8th lunar month.

MARSHALL, JOHN: BIRTH ANNIVERSARY. Sept 24, 1755. Fourth Chief Justice of Supreme Court, born at Germantown, VA. Served in House of Representatives and as secretary of state under John Adams. Appointed by President Adams to the position of chief justice in January 1801, he became known as "The Great Chief Justice." Marshall's court was largely responsible for defining the role of the Supreme Court and basic organizing principles of government in the early years after adoption of the Constitution in such cases as *Marbury v Madison, McCulloch v Maryland, Cohens v Virginia* and *Gibbons v Ogden*. He died at Philadelphia, PA, July 6, 1835.

NATIONAL DOG WEEK. Sept 24–30. To promote the relationship of dogs to mankind and emphasize the need for the proper care and treatment of dogs. Annually, the last full week in September. For info: Morris Raskin, Secy, Dogs on Stamps Study Unit (DOSSU), 202 A Newport Rd, Cranbury, NJ 08512. Phone: (609) 655-7411.

RAWLS, WILSON: BIRTH ANNIVERSARY. Sept 24, 1913. Author (*Where the Red Fern Grows*), born at Scraper, OK. Died Dec 16, 1984.

SOUTH AFRICA: HERITAGE DAY. Sept 24. A celebration of South African nationhood, commemorating the multicultural heritage of this rainbow nation.

Kevin Sorbo, 42, actor ("Hercules"), born Mound, MN, Sept 24, 1958.

SEPTEMBER 25 — MONDAY
Day 269 — 97 Remaining

FIRST AMERICAN NEWSPAPER PUBLISHED: ANNIVERSARY. Sept 25, 1690. The first (and only) edition of *Publick Occurrences Both Foreign and Domestick* was published by Benjamin Harris, at the London-Coffee-House, Boston, MA. Authorities considered this first newspaper published in the US offensive and ordered immediate suppression.

FIRST WOMAN SUPREME COURT JUSTICE: ANNIVERSARY. Sept 25, 1981. Sandra Day O'Connor was sworn in as the first woman associate justice of the US Supreme Court on this date. She had been nominated by President Ronald Reagan in July 1981.

GREENWICH MEAN TIME BEGINS: ANNIVERSARY. Sept 25, 1676. On this day two very accurate clocks were set in motion at the Royal Observatory at Greenwich, England. Greenwich Mean Time (now called Universal Time) became standard for England; in 1884 it became standard for the world.

MAJOR LEAGUE BASEBALL'S FIRST DOUBLE HEADER: ANNIVERSARY. Sept 25, 1882. The first major league baseball double header was played between the Providence, RI and Worcester, MA teams.

September 2000	S	M	T	W	T	F	S
						1	2
	3	4	5	6	7	8	9
	10	11	12	13	14	15	16
	17	18	19	20	21	22	23
	24	25	26	27	28	29	30

PACIFIC OCEAN DISCOVERED: ANNIVERSARY. Sept 25, 1513. Vasco Núñez de Balboa, a Spanish conquistador, stood high atop a peak in the Darien, in present-day Panama, becoming the first European to look upon the Pacific Ocean, claiming it as the South Sea in the name of the King of Spain.

"THE PARTRIDGE FAMILY" TV PREMIERE: ANNIVERSARY. Sept 25, 1970. A fatherless family of five kids form a rock band with their mother Shirley (played by Shirley Jones), and go on the road. Son Keith was played by David Cassidy (who became a real-life rock star), daughter Laurie was played by Susan Dey, Danny Bonaduce played son Danny, youngest son Chris was played by Jeremy Gelbwaks and Brian Forster and youngest daughter Tracy by Suzanne Crough. Reuben Kincaid, the family's agent, was played by Dave Madden. The TV family recorded several albums and songs such as "I Think I Love You" and "Cherish" went on to be hits.

SEQUOIA NATIONAL PARK ESTABLISHED: ANNIVERSARY. Sept 25, 1890. Area in central California established as a national park. For more park info: Sequoia Natl Park, Three Rivers, CA 93271. Web: www.nps.gov/sequ.

BIRTHDAYS TODAY

Jim Murphy, 53, author of nonfiction (*The Great Fire*), born Newark, NJ, Sept 25, 1947.

Scottie Pippen, 35, basketball player, born Hamburg, AR, Sept 25, 1965.

James Ransome, 39, illustrator (*Sweet Clara and the Freedom Quilt*), born Rich Square, NC, Sept 25, 1961.

Christopher Reeve, 48, actor (*Superman*), born New York, NY, Sept 25, 1952.

Will Smith, 32, rapper, actor ("The Fresh Prince of Bel Air," *Men in Black*), born Philadelphia, PA, Sept 25, 1968.

Barbara Walters, 69, journalist, interviewer, TV host ("20/20"), born Boston, MA, Sept 25, 1931.

SEPTEMBER 26 — TUESDAY

Day 270 — 96 Remaining

APPLESEED, JOHNNY: BIRTH ANNIVERSARY. Sept 26, 1774. John Chapman, better known as Johnny Appleseed, believed to have been born at Leominster, MA. Died at Allen County, IN, Mar 11, 1845. Planter of orchards and friend of wild animals, he was regarded as a great medicine man by the Indians.

"THE BRADY BUNCH" TV PREMIERE: ANNIVERSARY. Sept 26, 1969. This sitcom, which spawned a whole industry, starred Robert Reed as widower Mike Brady, who has three sons and is married to Carol (played by Florence Henderson), who has three daughters. Nutty housekeeper Alice was played by Ann B. Davis. Sons Greg (Barry Williams), Peter (Christopher Knight) and Bobby (Mike Lookinland) and daughters Marcia (Maureen McCormick), Jan (Eve Plumb) and Cindy (Susan Olsen) experienced the typical crises of youth. The show steered clear of social issues, portraying childhood as a time of innocence. This is probably why it has remained popular in reruns in the after-school time slot. "The Brady Kids" (1972–74) was a Sunday morning cartoon show. On "The Brady Bunch Hour" (1976–77) the family hosted a variety show. "The Brady Brides" (1981) was a sitcom about the two older girls adjusting to marriage. *A Very Brady Christmas* (1988) was CBS's highest-rated special for the season. *The Brady Bunch Movie*, released in 1995, appealed to fans who had watched the show 25 years before.

FIRST TELEVISED PRESIDENTIAL DEBATE: 40th ANNIVERSARY. Sept 26, 1960. The debate between presidential candidates John F. Kennedy and Richard Nixon was televised from a Chicago TV studio.

GERSHWIN, GEORGE: BIRTH ANNIVERSARY. Sept 26, 1898. American composer remembered for his many enduring songs and melodies, including "The Man I Love," "Strike Up the Band," "Funny Face," "I Got Rhythm" and the opera *Porgy and Bess*. Many of his works were in collaboration with his brother, Ira. Born at Brooklyn, NY, he died of a brain tumor at Beverly Hills, CA, July 11, 1937. See also: "Gershwin, Ira: Birth Anniversary" (Dec 6).

POPE PAUL VI: BIRTH ANNIVERSARY. Sept 26, 1897. Giovanni Battista Montini, 262nd pope of the Roman Catholic Church, born at Concesio, Italy. Elected pope June 21, 1963. Died at Castel Gandolfo, near Rome, Italy, Aug 6, 1978.

SHAMU'S BIRTHDAY: 15th ANNIVERSARY. Sept 26. Shamu was born at Sea World at Orlando, FL, Sept 26, 1985, and is the first killer whale born in captivity to survive. Shamu is now living at Sea World's Texas park. For more info: www.seaworld.org /killer_whale/killerwhales.html.

BIRTHDAYS TODAY

Christine T. Whitman, 54, Governor of New Jersey (R), born New York, NY, Sept 26, 1946.

Serena Williams, 19, tennis player, born Saginaw, MI, Sept 26, 1981.

SEPTEMBER 27 — WEDNESDAY

Day 271 — 95 Remaining

ADAMS, SAMUEL: BIRTH ANNIVERSARY. Sept 27, 1722. Revolutionary leader and Massachusetts state politician Samuel Adams, cousin to President John Adams, was born at Boston. He died there Oct 2, 1803. As a delegate to the First and Second Continental Congresses, Adams urged a vigorous stand against England. He signed the Declaration of Independence and the Articles of Confederation and supported the war for independence. Adams served as lieutenant governor of Massachusetts under John Hancock from 1789 to 1793 and then as governor until 1797.

ANCESTOR APPRECIATION DAY. Sept 27. A day to learn about and appreciate one's forebears. For info: W.D. Chase, A.A.D. Assn, PO Box 3, Montague, MI 49437-0003.

McGWIRE HITS 70th HOME RUN: ANNIVERSARY. Sept 27, 1998. Mark McGwire of the St. Louis Cardinals made baseball history by hitting his 70th home run of the season. On Sept 8, 1998, he had broken the previous record of 61 homers set by Roger Maris in 1961. *See* Curriculum Connection.

MOON PHASE: NEW MOON. Sept 27. Moon enters New Moon phase at 3:53 PM, EDT.

SAINT VINCENT DE PAUL: FEAST DAY. Sept 27. French priest, patron of charitable organizations, and founder of the Vincentian Order and cofounder of the Sisters of Charity. Canonized 1737 (lived 1581?–1660).

SEPTEMBER 27
HOORAY FOR MARK MCGWIRE'S 70 HOME RUNS!!

On Sept 27, 1998, Mark McGwire, first baseman for the St. Louis Cardinals, made baseball history by hitting 70 home runs in a season. Sammy Sosa, right fielder for the Chicago Cubs, ran a close second with 66 home runs. McGwire's 70 slammers broke the previous record of 61 home runs in a season, a record held by Roger Maris, an outfielder for the New York Yankees.

Students can have math fun with McGwire's accomplishment in many ways. If you plan ahead and are doing a unit on estimation and prediction, have students predict how many home runs they think specific players will hit by the end of the season. Choose professional baseball players whose club plays near your community or solicit names of favorites from your students. Ask them to estimate how many total home runs are hit by a team during a typical season. Post the student estimations. Let several students research how many were actually hit by that team each year for the past three or four years. Ask the students to present their findings to the class. Revise and record new predictions based on the students' research.

Older students who are learning percent and ratios may have fun figuring out what percent of all McGwire's hits were home runs. What percent of his "at bats" were home runs? How does the number of home runs compare with the number of singles, doubles, etc?

Upper elementary students can create 10 different addition problems, each with two 2-digit addends, whose total equals 70. Compare problems and see how many students used the same numbers. Challenge them to invent new problems that haven't already been used. Play with sums involving students' ages. Can they combine ages of several students to equal 70?

First and second grade students can draw flash card problems that illustrate groups of numbers. For example, have them draw 14 groups of 5 baseballs; or draw 7 groups of 10 baseballs. Students can help each other reinforce their oral counting skills by fives, tens, etc.

Students learning graphing skills can graph the gradual monthly rise in McGwire's season. They also can create a bar graph that compares the total number of home runs hit by each professional team. This type of exercise can be modified to fit seasonal sports records from other athletic games.

September 2000

S	M	T	W	T	F	S
					1	2
3	4	5	6	7	8	9
10	11	12	13	14	15	16
17	18	19	20	21	22	23
24	25	26	27	28	29	30

BIRTHDAYS TODAY

Martin Handford, 44, author and illustrator (*Where's Waldo?*), born London, England, Sept 27, 1956.

Stephen Douglas (Steve) Kerr, 35, basketball player, born Beirut, Lebanon, Sept 27, 1965.

Mike Schmidt, 51, Baseball Hall of Fame third baseman, born Dayton, OH, Sept 27, 1949.

Gerhard Schröder, 50, Chancellor of Germany, born Mossenberg, Germany, Sept 27, 1950.

Bernard Waber, 76, author (*Ira Sleeps Over*), born Philadelphia, PA, Sept 27, 1924.

SEPTEMBER 28 — THURSDAY
Day 272 — 94 Remaining

CABRILLO DAY: ANNIVERSARY OF DISCOVERY OF CALIFORNIA. Sept 28, 1542. California. Commemorates discovery of California by Portuguese navigator Juan Rodriguez Cabrillo who reached San Diego Bay. Cabrillo died at San Miguel Island, CA, Jan 3, 1543. His birth date is unknown. The Cabrillo National Monument marks his landfall and Cabrillo Day is still observed in California (in some areas on the Saturday nearest Sept 28, Sept 30 in 2000).

POKÉMON DEBUTS: ANNIVERSARY. Sept 28, 1998. This wildly popular Game Boy game, featuring Mewtwo, Pikachu, Meowth and Giovanni, first debuted in Japan on Feb 27, 1996. The goal of the game is to find, capture and train all 151 Pokémons (pocket monsters). Trading cards also proved popular with US kids. The Pokémon animated TV show debuted in 1998 and *Pokémon the First Movie: Mewtwo Strikes Back* was released Nov 10, 1999.

TAIWAN: CONFUCIUS'S BIRTHDAY AND TEACHERS' DAY. Sept 28. National holiday, designated as Teachers' Day. Confucius is the Latinized name of Kung-futzu, born at Shantung province on the 27th day of the tenth moon (lunar calendar) in the 22nd year of Kuke Hsiang of Lu (551 BC). He died at age 72, having spent some 40 years as a teacher. Teachers' Day is observed annually on Sept 28.

WIGGIN, KATE DOUGLAS: BIRTH ANNIVERSARY. Sept 28, 1856. Kate Wiggin was born Kate Douglas Smith at Philadelphia, PA. She helped organize the first free kindergarten on the West Coast in 1878 at San Francisco and in 1880 she and her sister established the California Kindergarten Training School. After moving back to the East Coast she devoted herself to writing, producing a number of children's books including *The Birds' Christmas Carol*, *Polly Oliver's Problem* and *Rebecca of Sunnybrook Farm*. She died at Harrow, England, Aug 24, 1923.

WILLARD, FRANCES ELIZABETH CAROLINE: BIRTH ANNIVERSARY. Sept 28, 1839. American educator and reformer, president of the Women's Christian Temperance Union, 1879–98 and women's suffrage leader, born at Churchville, NY. Died at New York, NY, Feb 18, 1898.

BIRTHDAYS TODAY

Se Ri Pak, 23, golfer, born Daejeon, South Korea, Sept 28, 1977.
Gwyneth Paltrow, 27, actress (*Hook, Emma*), born Los Angeles, CA, Sept 28, 1973.

SEPTEMBER 29 — FRIDAY
Day 273 — 93 Remaining

ENGLAND: SCOTLAND YARD: FIRST APPEARANCE ANNIVERSARY. Sept 29, 1829. The first public appearance of Greater London's Metropolitan Police occurred amid jeering and abuse from disapproving political opponents. Public sentiment turned to confidence and respect in the ensuing years. The Metropolitan Police had been established by an act of Parliament in June 1829, at the request of Home Secretary Sir Robert Peel, after whom the London police officers became more affectionately known as "bobbies." Scotland Yard, the site of their first headquarters near Charing Cross, soon became the official name of the force.

FERMI, ENRICO: BIRTH ANNIVERSARY. Sept 29, 1901. Nuclear physicist, born at Rome, Italy. Played a prominent role in the splitting of the atom and in the construction of the first American nuclear reactor. Died at Chicago, IL, Nov 16, 1954.

MICHAELMAS. Sept 29. The feast of St. Michael and All Angels in the Greek and Roman Catholic Churches.

ROSH HASHANAH BEGINS AT SUNDOWN. Sept 29. Jewish New Year. See "Rosh Hashanah" (Sept 30).

SPACE MILESTONE: *DISCOVERY* (US). Sept 29, 1988. Space Shuttle *Discovery*, after numerous reschedulings, launched from Kennedy Space Center, FL, with a five-member crew on board, and landed Oct 3 at Edwards Air Force Base, CA. It marked the first American manned flight since the Challenger tragedy in 1986. See also: "*Challenger* Space Shuttle Explosion: Anniversary" (Jan 28).

STATE FAIR OF TEXAS. Sept 29–Oct 22. Fair Park, Dallas, TX. Features a Broadway musical, college football games, new car show, concerts, livestock shows and traditional events and entertainment including exhibits, creative arts and parades. Est attendance: 3,200,000. For info: Nancy Wiley, State Fair of Texas, PO Box 150009, Dallas, TX 75315. Phone: (214) 421-8716. Fax: (214) 421-8710. E-mail: pr@greatstatefair.com. Web: www.bigtex.com.

BIRTHDAYS TODAY

Stan Berenstain, 77, author and illustrator, with his wife Jan (the Berenstain Bears series), born Philadelphia, PA, Sept 29, 1923.
Bryant Gumbel, 52, TV host ("Today," "The Public Eye"), sportscaster, born New Orleans, LA, Sept 29, 1948.

Donald Hall, 72, poet and author (*The Ox-Cart Man, When Willard Met Babe Ruth*), born New Haven, CT, Sept 29, 1928.
Lech Walesa, 57, Poland labor leader, Solidarity founder, born Popowo, Poland, Sept 29, 1943.

SEPTEMBER 30 — SATURDAY
Day 274 — 92 Remaining

BABE SETS HOME RUN RECORD: ANNIVERSARY. Sept 30, 1927. George Herman "Babe" Ruth hit his 60th home run of the season off Tom Zachary of the Washington Senators. Ruth's record for the most homers in a single season stood for 34 years—until Roger Maris hit 61 in 1961. Maris's record was broken in 1998, first by Mark McGwire of the St. Louis Cardinals and then by Sammy Sosa of the Chicago Cubs.

BOTSWANA: INDEPENDENCE DAY. Sept 30. National holiday. The former Bechuanaland Protectorate (British Colony) became the independent Republic of Botswana in 1966.

D'AULAIRE, EDGAR PARIN: BIRTH ANNIVERSARY. Sept 30, 1898. Author, with his wife Ingri (*Norse Gods and Giants*), born at Munich, Germany. Died May 1, 1986.

FEAST OF SAINT JEROME. Sept 30. Patron saint of scholars and librarians.

"THE FLINTSTONES" TV PREMIERE: ANNIVERSARY. Sept 30, 1960. This Hanna Barbera cartoon comedy was set in prehistoric times. Characters included two Stone Age families, Fred and Wilma Flintstone and their neighbors Barney and Betty Rubble. In 1994 *The Flintstones* film was released, starring John Goodman, Rick Moranis, Elizabeth Perkins and Rosie O'Donnell.

MEREDITH ENROLLS AT OLE MISS: ANNIVERSARY. Sept 30, 1962. Rioting broke out when James Meredith became the first black to enroll in the all-white University of Mississippi. President Kennedy sent US troops to the area to force compliance with the law. Three people died in the fighting and 50 were injured. On June 6, 1966, Meredith was shot while participating in a civil rights march at Mississippi. On June 25 Meredith, barely recovered, rejoined the marchers near Jackson, MS.

ROSH HASHANAH or JEWISH NEW YEAR. Sept 30–Oct 1. Jewish holy day; observed on following day also. Hebrew calendar date: Tishri 1, 5761. Rosh Hashanah (literally "Head of the Year") is the beginning of 10 days of repentance and spiritual renewal. (Began at sundown of previous day.)

BIRTHDAYS TODAY

Mike Damus, 21, actor ("Teen Angel"), born New York, NY, Sept 30, 1979.
Carol Fenner, 71, author (*Yolonda's Genius*), born New York, NY, Sept 30, 1929.
Martina Hingis, 20, tennis player, born Kosice, Slovakia, Sept 30, 1980.
Blanche Lambert Lincoln, 40, US Senator (D, Arkansas), born Helena, MT, Sept 30, 1960.
Dominique Moceanu, 19, gymnast, born Hollywood, CA, Sept 30, 1981.

OCTOBER 1 — SUNDAY
Day 275 — 91 Remaining

ADOPT-A-SHELTER DOG MONTH. Oct 1–31. To promote the adoption of dogs from local shelters, the ASPCA sponsors this important observance. For info: ASPCA Public Affairs Dept, 424 E 92nd St, New York, NY 10128. Phone: (212) 876-7700. E-mail: press@aspca.org. Web: www.aspca.org.

AUSTRALIA: SUMMER OLYMPICS CLOSING CEREMONY. Oct 1. Sydney, Australia. Closing of the XXVII Olympiad. Because of the 14-hour time difference, this will occur Sept 30 US time.

BOOK IT! READING INCENTIVE PROGRAM. Oct 1, 2000–Mar 31, 2001. This is a five-month program for students in grades K–8 sponsored by Pizza Hut. Teachers set monthly reading goals for students. When a monthly reading goal is met, the child receives a certificate for a free pizza. If the whole class meets its goal, a pizza party is provided for the class. For info: Book It!, PO Box 2999, Wichita, KS 67201. Phone: (800) 4-BOOK IT. Fax: (316) 687-8937. Web: www.bookitprogram.com.

CD PLAYER DEBUTS: ANNIVERSARY. Oct 1, 1982. The first compact disc player, jointly developed by Sony, Philips and Polygram, went on sale. It cost $625 (more than $1,000 in current dollars).

CHILD HEALTH MONTH. Oct 1–31. For info: American Academy of Pediatrics, 141 Northwest Point Blvd, Elk Grove Village, IL 60007. Phone: (847) 228-5005.

CHINA, PEOPLE'S REPUBLIC OF: NATIONAL DAY: ANNIVERSARY. Oct 1. Commemorates the founding of the People's Republic of China in 1949.

COMPUTER LEARNING MONTH. Oct 1–31. A monthlong focus of events and activities for learning new uses of computers and software, sharing ideas and helping others gain the benefits of computers and software. Numerous national contests are held to recognize students, educators and parents for their innovative ideas; computers and software are awarded to winning entries. Annually, the month of October. For info: Computer Learning Foundation, Dept CHS, PO Box 60007, Palo Alto, CA

94306-0007. Phone: (408) 720-8898. Fax: (408) 720-8777. E-mail: clf@computerlearning.org. Web: www.computerlearning.org.

CYPRUS: INDEPENDENCE DAY: 40th ANNIVERSARY. Oct 1. National holiday. Commemorates independence from Britain in 1960.

DISNEY WORLD OPENED: ANNIVERSARY. Oct 1, 1971. Disney's second theme park opened at Orlando, FL. See also "Disneyland Opened: Anniversary" (July 17).

DIVERSITY AWARENESS MONTH. Oct 1–31. Celebrating, promoting and appreciating the diversity of our society. Also, a month to foster and further our understanding of the inherent value of all races, genders, nationalities, age groups, religions, sexual orientations, classes and disabilities. Annually, in October. For info: Carole Copeland Thomas, C. Thomas & Assoc, 400 W Cummings Park, Ste 1725-154, Woburn, MA 01801. Phone: (800) 801-6599. Fax: (617) 361-1355.

DOMESTIC VIOLENCE AWARENESS MONTH. Oct 1–31. Commemorated since 1987, this month attempts to raise awareness of efforts to end violence against women and their children. The Domestic Violence Awareness Month Project is a collaborative effort of the National Resource Center on Domestic Violence, Family Violence Prevention Fund, National Coalition Against Domestic Violence, National Domestic Violence Hotline and the National Network to End Domestic Violence. For info: Natl Resource Center on Domestic Violence, 6400 Flank Dr, Ste 1300, Harrisburg, PA 17112-2778. Phone: (800) 537-2238.

FAMILY HEALTH MONTH. Oct 1–31. For info: American Academy of Family Physicians, 8880 Ward Pkwy, Kansas City, MO 64114-2797. Phone: (800) 274-2237 or (816) 333-9700.

FAMILY HISTORY MONTH. Oct 1–31. To celebrate and publicize family history: the challenge of the research, the fascination of gathering family stories, customs and traditions, the fun of involving family members, its importance as an academic discipline and the value of passing it on to our children. Annually, the month of October. For info: Nancy O. Heydt, Monmouth County Genealogy Soc, PO Box 5, Lincroft, NJ 07738-0005. E-mail: jheydt@monmouth.com.

FIREPUP'S BIRTHDAY. Oct 1. Firepup spends his time teaching fire safety awareness to children in a fun-filled and nonthreatening manner. The US Fire Administration's site at www.usfa.fema.gov/kids/ has materials to help kids learn fire safety. For info: Natl Fire Safety Council, Inc, PO Box 378, Michigan Center, MI 49254-0378. Phone: (517) 764-2811.

GET ORGANIZED WEEK. Oct 1–7. This is an opportunity to streamline your life, create more time, lower your stress and increase your profit. Simplify your situation and make it more manageable by taking advantage of this time to get organized. Annually, the first week in October. For info: Stephanie Denton, Natl Assn of Professional Organizers, 1033 LaPosada Dr, Ste 220, Austin, TX 78752-3880. Phone: (513) 871-8807. E-mail: 104340.14@compuserve.com.

HARRISON, CAROLINE LAVINIA SCOTT: BIRTH ANNIVERSARY. Oct 1, 1832. First wife of Benjamin Harrison, 23rd president of the US, born at Oxford, OH. Died at Washington, DC, Oct 25, 1892. She was the second first lady to die in the White House.

INTERNATIONAL DINOSAUR MONTH. Oct 1–31. Devoted to the study of dinosaurs and the protection and preservation of their fossils. Also in appreciation of the contributions to human knowledge of paleontologists, dino-artists and dino-educators. *See* Curriculum Connection. For info: Dinosaurs Intl, Planetarium

	S	M	T	W	T	F	S
October	1	2	3	4	5	6	7
2000	8	9	10	11	12	13	14
	15	16	17	18	19	20	21
	22	23	24	24	26	27	28
	29	30	31				

Station, Box 502 IDM00, New York, NY 10024-0502. Web: www
.dinosaur.org.

JAPAN: NEWSPAPER WEEK. Oct 1–7. During this week newspapers make an extensive effort to acquaint the public with their functions and the role of a newspaper in a free society. Annually, the first week in October.

MARIS HITS 61st HOME RUN: ANNIVERSARY. Oct 1, 1961. Roger Maris of the New York Yankees hit his 61st home run, breaking Babe Ruth's record for the most home runs in a season. Maris hit his homer against pitcher Tracy Stallard of the Boston Red Sox as the Yankees won, 1–0. Controversy over the record arose because the American League had adopted a 162-game schedule in 1961, and Maris played in 161 games. In 1927, when Ruth set his record, the schedule called for 154 games, and Ruth played in 151. On Sept 8, 1998, Mark McGwire of the St. Louis Cardinals hit his 62nd home run, breaking Maris's record, and a few days later, Sept 13, 1998, Sammy Sosa of the Chicago Cubs also hit his 62nd.

★ **MINORITY ENTERPRISE DEVELOPMENT WEEK.** Oct 1–7. Presidential Proclamation issued without request since 1983 for the first full week in October except in 1991 when issued for Sept 22–28, in 1992 for Sept 27–Oct 3, to coincide with the National Conference and in 1997 for Sept 21-27.

MONTH OF THE YOUNG ADOLESCENT. Oct 1–31. Youth between the ages of 10–15 undergo more extensive physical, mental, social and emotional changes than at any other time of life, with the exception of infancy. Initiated by the National Middle School Association and endorsed by 29 other national organizations focusing on youth, this month is designed to bring attention to the importance of this age in a person's development. For info: Natl Middle School Assn, 2600 Corporate Exchange Dr, Ste 370, Columbus, OH 43231. Phone: (800) 528-NMSA. Web: www.nmsa.org.

MONTH OF THE DINOSAUR. Oct 1–31. Promoting scientific awareness and educating everyone about our environment both present and past. Special on-line forums and activities as well as educational materials available to educators. *See* Curriculum Connection. For info: Ellen Sue Blakey, Big Horn Basin Foundation, PO Box 71, Thermopolis, WY 82443.

NATIONAL CAMPAIGN FOR HEALTHIER BABIES MONTH. Oct 1–31. For info: March of Dimes Birth Defects Foundation, 1275 Mamaroneck Ave, White Plains, NY 10605. Phone: (914) 997-4600.

NATIONAL CARAMEL MONTH. Oct 1–31. A monthlong celebration of one of America's favorite treats, the caramel. First created in "sweet home" Chicago in 1875, Americans now consume more than 10 million pounds of the chewy, gooey sweets each year—as snacks as well as ingredients in favorite baked goods including brownies, bars, cookies, pies and cakes. Sponsored by Favorite Brands International, the makers of Farley's Original Chewy Caramels. From traditional caramel apples to haunting party recipes for Halloween gatherings, Caramel Month is a great excuse to go caramel crazy. For info send SASE: Favorite Brands Intl, Dept C, 25 Tri State International, Ste 400, Lincolnshire, IL 60069.

OCTOBER 1–31
INTERNATIONAL DINOSAUR MONTH

The word "dinosaur" means terrible lizard, and indeed many dinosaur species looked ferocious. Whether fearsome or placid, dinosaurs intrigue adults and enthrall elementary school children. Bring dinosaurs into your classroom and take advantage of this high-interest topic.

Dinosaurs first appeared on the Earth about 230 million years ago. Different dinosaur species lived at different times. You can use dinosaurs to introduce students to the concept of geologic time periods. For example, *Stegosaurus* lived during the early Jurassic period, *Allosaurus* during the late Jurassic, *Plateosaurs* during the late Triassic, *Iguanodons* during the early Cretaceous and *Velociraptors* during the late Cretaceous. Try making a timeline across one wall of your room. If you construct it proportionately, starting with the Mesozoic era and working up to the Cenozoic era (the present), children gain a better understanding of how long dinosaurs lived on the Earth in comparison to the relatively short time people have.

Primary students can begin learning the principles of scientific classification by sorting dinosaurs. First ask them to divide dinosaurs into two-legged and four-legged species. Then sort meat-eaters and plant-eaters. Other criteria could include horned, big and little, water and land creatures and so on. Students should understand why each dinosaur is a member of its group. Have them label each category with a topic sentence such as: "[Dinosaur name] belongs in this group because it [characteristic]." Here is an opportunity to introduce terms such as "like" and "unlike" and "similar" and "different."

As a science project, middle school students can compare the anatomy of the two major divisions of dinosaurs: the ornithischians (bird-hipped) and saurischians (lizard-hipped). New research indicates that some birds and dinosaurs may be related. Students can compare and contrast the structure and physiology of modern birds, transitional birds and possible dinosaur ancestors.

Dinosaur poetry is always fun. *Dinosaur Rap* (Rock n' Learn, 1-878489-59-3, $9.95 audio cassette and book) has catchy rhythms, and *Bone Poems*, by Jeffrey Moss (Workman, 0-7611-0884-X, $14.95 Gr. 2–6) has several funny dinosaur poems that will stimulate creative thought.

Studying fossils and how they are made is an offshoot of dinosaur units. Create your own fossil "dig" with a large box, plaster of Paris, a few bones from the supermarket, some leaves and some soil. You can make dinosaur footprints or leaf prints in the same manner as molds of student handprints are often done as classroom art projects. For a more layered "rock" approach, have students mix the plaster of Paris and, while it's still soft, put several bones on the surface. Position some of the bones upright. When the mixture dries, cover the bones with a second layer of plaster of Paris and top with a layer of soil. Using small chisels or dental instruments, conduct a classroom dig. If students follow proper scientific techniques, they should remove the plaster in layered increments, diagram the location of bones and measure the bone positions in relation to the whole plaster unit.

Literature connections include: *Dinosaur Babies*, by Kathleen Weidner Zoehfeld (Harper, 0-06-445162-3, $4.95 Gr. K–3); *A Dinosaur Named Sue*, by Fay Robinson (Scholastic, 0-439-09983-8, $3.99 Gr. 2–4); and *Did Dinosaurs Live in Your Backyard?* by Melvin and Gilda Berger (Scholastic, 0-439-08568-3, $5.95 Gr. 1–4).

The skeleton of Sue, the largest and most complete Tyrannosaurus Rex ever discovered, is now on display at Chicago's Field Museum (see May 17). *Jobaria* is another recent dinosaur find (see Nov 13).

NATIONAL CRIME PREVENTION MONTH. Oct 1–31. During Crime Prevention Month, individuals can commit to working on at least one of three levels—family, neighborhood or community—to drive violence and drugs from our world. It is also a time to honor individuals who have accepted personal responsibility for their neighborhoods and groups who work for the community's common good. Annually, every October. For info: Natl Crime Prevention Council, 1700 K St, Second Floor, Washington, DC, 2006-1356. Phone: (202) 466-6272. Fax: (202) 296-1356. Web: www.weprevent.org or www.ncpc.org.

★**NATIONAL DAY OF CONCERN ABOUT YOUNG PEOPLE AND GUN VIOLENCE.** Oct 1. Students are asked to voluntarily sign a "Student Pledge Against Gun Violence," a promise never to bring a gun to school, never to use a gun to settle a dispute and to discourage their friends from using guns.

NATIONAL DENTAL HYGIENE MONTH. Oct 1–31. To increase public awareness of the importance of preventive oral health care and the dental hygienist's role as the preventive professional. Annually, during the month of October. For info: Public Relations, American Dental Hygienists' Assn, 444 N Michigan Ave, Ste 3400, Chicago, IL 60611. Phone: (312) 440-8900. Fax: (312) 440-6780. Web: www.adha.org.

★**NATIONAL DISABILITY EMPLOYMENT AWARENESS MONTH.** Oct 1–31. Presidential Proclamation issued for the month of October (PL100–630, Title III, Sec 301a of Nov 7, 1988). Previously issued as "National Employ the Handicapped Week" for a week beginning during the first week in October since 1945.

★**NATIONAL DOMESTIC VIOLENCE AWARENESS MONTH.** Oct 1–31.

NATIONAL FAMILY SEXUALITY EDUCATION MONTH. Oct 1–31. A national coalition effort to support parents as the first and primary sexuality educators of their children by providing information for parents and young people. For info: Planned Parenthood Federation of America, Education Dept, 810 Seventh Ave, New York, NY 10019. Phone: (800) 829-7732. Fax: (212) 247-6269. E-mail: education@ppfa.org. Web: www .plannedparenthood.org.

NATIONAL ORTHODONTIC HEALTH MONTH. Oct 1–31. A beautiful, healthy smile is only the most obvious benefit of orthodontic treatment. National Orthodontic Health Month spotlights the important role of orthodontic care in overall physical health and emotional well-being. The observance is sponsored by the American Association of Orthodontists (AAO), which supports research and education leading to quality patient care and promotes increased public awareness of the need for and bene-

fits of orthodontic treatment. For info: Bill Beggs, Media Relations Mgr, The Hughes Group, 130 S Bemiston, St. Louis, MO 63105.

NATIONAL PASTA MONTH. Oct 1–31. To promote the nutritional value of pasta while educating the public about healthy, easy ways to prepare it. Annually, the month of October. For info: Emily A. Holt or Robert Davis. Phone: (703) 841-0818. Web: www .ilovepasta.org.

NATIONAL POPCORN POPPIN' MONTH. Oct 1–31. To celebrate the wholesome, economical, natural food value of popcorn, America's native snack. *See* Curriculum Connection. For info: The Popcorn Board, 401 N Michigan Ave, Chicago, IL 60611-4267. Phone: (312) 644-6610. Fax: (312) 245-1083. Web: www.popcorn.org.

NATIONAL ROLLER SKATING MONTH. Oct 1–31. A month-long celebration recognizing the health benefits and recreational enjoyment of this long-loved pastime. Also includes in-line skating and an emphasis on Safe Skating. For info: Roller Skating Assn, 6905 Corporate Dr, Indianapolis, IN 46278. Phone: (317) 347-2626. Fax: (317) 347-2636. E-mail: RSA@oninternet.com. Web: www.rollerskating.com.

NATIONAL STAMP COLLECTING MONTH. Oct 1–31. Sponsored by the US Postal Service, which also sponsors STAMPERS, a program to introduce a new generation to the exciting world of stamp collecting. By calling the toll-free number 1-888-STAMP-FUN, children can receive free mailings which include magazines, posters and other educational items to help them start their own stamp collection. For info: Stamp Services, US Postal Service, 475 L'Enfant Plaza SW, Rm 4474-EB, Washington, DC 20260.

NIGERIA: INDEPENDENCE DAY: 40th ANNIVERSARY. Oct 1. National holiday. This West African nation became independent of Great Britain in 1960 and a republic in 1963.

PEDIATRIC CANCER AWARENESS MONTH. Oct 1–31. Cancer is the chief cause of death by disease in children. More than 1,000 children in the US die of cancer every year. For info: Bear Necessities Pediatric Cancer Foundation, 85 W Algonquin Rd, Ste 165, Arlington Heights, IL 60005. Phone: (847) 952-9164.

POLISH AMERICAN HERITAGE MONTH. Oct 1–31. A national celebration of Polish history, culture and pride, in cooperation with the Polish American Congress and Polonia Across America. For info: Michael Blichasz, Chair, Polish American Cultural Center, Natl HQ, 308 Walnut St, Philadelphia, PA 19106. Phone: (215) 922-1700. Fax: (215) 922-1518. Web: www.polishamericancenter.org.

STOCKTON, RICHARD: BIRTH ANNIVERSARY. Oct 1, 1730. Lawyer and signer of the Declaration of Independence, born at Princeton, NJ. Died there, Feb 8, 1781.

SUPER MARIO BROTHERS RELEASED: ANNIVERSARY. Oct 1, 1985. In 1985 the Nintendo Entertainment System (NES) for home use was introduced and the popular game for the NES, Super Mario Brothers, was released on this date. In 1989 Nintendo introduced Game Boy, the first hand-held game system with interchangeable game paks. For more info: www.nintendo.com.

TUVALU: NATIONAL HOLIDAY. Oct 1. Commemorates independence from Great Britain in 1978.

UNITED NATIONS: INTERNATIONAL DAY OF OLDER PERSONS. Oct 1. On Dec 14, 1990, the General Assembly designated Oct 1 as the International Day for the Elderly. It appealed for contributions to the Trust Fund for Aging (which supports projects in developing countries in implementation of the Vienna International Plan of Action on Aging adopted at the 1982 World Assembly on Aging) and endorsed an action program on aging

October 2000	S	M	T	W	T	F	S
	1	2	3	4	5	6	7
	8	9	10	11	12	13	14
	15	16	17	18	19	20	21
	22	23	24	24	26	27	28
	29	30	31				

OCTOBER 1–31
NATIONAL POPCORN POPPIN' MONTH

We are a nation of popcorn eaters. After buying tickets in a movie theater, the next stop is usually a visit to the popcorn vendor. Supermarket snack aisles display a wide variety of flavored popcorn, microwave popcorn and plain, old-fashioned, bottled kernels. CrackerJack, the caramel-coated popcorn treat with a prize in each box, was once a baseball game staple.

Europeans first encountered popcorn when they reached the New World. They were introduced to it by native North and Central Americans, who had known about popcorn for more than a thousand years. Indians ate popcorn and also used it for decoration and in ritual ceremonies.

Popcorn kernels are usually smaller than seed corn kernels. A popcorn kernel's soft, moist interior is protected by a hard outer covering. But it's the moisture inside that drives the "pop." When a kernel is heated, the moisture inside expands as a gas. When it does, the kernel explodes and becomes a piece of fluffy, white popcorn.

Children can have lots of fun with popcorn. Art projects may include unpopped kernel mosaics. Use different colored corn seed (or other dried seeds) for contrast. Mention how many Christmas trees in the past were hung with strings of popped corn. It's a great family activity that can be done easily while sitting around talking or watching TV. With care, the strands will last for years. The strands can also be hung outside for birds and other backyard wildlife.

In language arts, students can have fun writing poems about popcorn. Focus on their experiences with it and their eating habits. Mention alliteration. The explosive *p* is satisfying and appropriate to the subject.

In math, unpopped kernels can be used for simple counting tasks and for estimation purposes. Fill different sized containers and let students estimate what the quantity might be. Encourage them to first measure a certain number of kernels. Add the measurements and then divide to find the average kernel size. Or, fill a known area—one cubic inch, for example—with kernels and count the number of kernels inside. Estimate from that number how many kernels are in a much larger container. They will have to calculate the volume of the larger container.

Play with popcorn volume, too. Again, measure out small amounts of kernels—perhaps a teaspoon, a tablespoon and a quarter cup. Have students predict how much space the same kernels will fill after they have been popped. Use a hot air popper to avoid oily spills, and caution students about proper, safe use of the popper.

In science, several experiments can be carried out in a short span of time. Corn germinates in about a week. Plan ahead and have available a few different kinds of corn seed. Have each student "plant" one kernel on moist paper and five other seeds in dirt. Mark the location of each seed with a toothpick. At three-day intervals, uncover and observe how the seeds have changed. Replant if the students want to keep the seeds growing.

In social studies, students can research how Native Americans (North and Central) used maize. Their planting techniques were varied and interesting. For geography, students might shade areas on a U.S. map to reflect the states that are major corn producers.

Related literature includes: *Popcorn at the Palace*, by Emily McCully (Harcourt, 0-15-277699-0, $16 Gr. K–3); *Popcorn: Poems*, by James Stevenson (Morrow, 0-688-15261-9, $15. Gr. 3 & up); *Four Seasons of Corn: A Winnebago Tradition*, by Sally Hunter (Lerner, 0-8225-9741-1, $6.95 Gr. 3–6); *Popcorn Plants*, by Kathleen V. Kudlinski (Lerner, 0-8225-3014-7, $16.95 Gr. 2–3).

for 1992 and beyond as outlined by the Secretary-General. (Res 45/106.) On Dec 21, 1995, the Assembly changed the name from "for the Elderly" to "of Older Persons" to conform with the 1991 UN Principles for Older Persons. Info from: United Nations, Dept of Public Info, Public Inquiries Unit, Rm GA-57, New York, NY 10017. Phone: (212) 963-4475. Fax: (212) 963-0071. E-mail: inquiries@un.org.

UNIVERSAL CHILDREN'S WEEK. Oct 1–7. To disseminate throughout the world info on the needs of children and to distribute copies of the Declaration of the Rights of the Child. For complete info, send $4 to cover expense of printing, handling and postage. Annually, the first seven days of October. For info: Dr. Stanley Drake, Pres, Intl Soc of Friendship and Good Will, 40139 Palmetto Dr, Palmdale, CA 93551-3557.

UNMASKING HALLOWEEN DANGERS. Oct 1–31. Children should be encouraged to use makeup instead of masks, which obscure vision. Costume props should be carefully selected so that Halloween will be fun and safe. For info: Prevent Blindness America®, 500 E Remington Rd, Schaumburg, IL 60173. Phone: (800) 331-2020. Fax: (847) 843-8458. Web: www.preventblindness.org.

US 2001 FEDERAL FISCAL YEAR BEGINS. Oct 1, 2000–Sept 30, 2001.

VEGETARIAN AWARENESS MONTH. Oct 1–31. This educational event advances awareness of the many surprising ethical, environmental, economic, health, humanitarian and other benefits of the increasingly popular vegetarian lifestyle. Each year in the US about one million more people become vegetarians. This event promotes personal and planetary healing with respect for all life. For info: Vegetarian Awareness Network, Communications Center, PO Box 321, Knoxville, TN 37901-0321. Phone: (800) EAT-VEGE.

WORLD COMMUNION SUNDAY. Oct 1. Communion is celebrated by Christians all over the world. Annually, the first Sunday in October.

WORLD VEGETARIAN DAY. Oct 1. Celebration of vegetarianism's benefits to humans, animals and our planet. In addition to individuals, participants include libraries, schools, colleges, restaurants, food services, health-care centers, health food stores, workplaces and many more. For info: North American Vegetarian Soc, Box 72, Dolgeville, NY 13329. Phone: (518) 568-7970. Fax: (518) 568-7979. E-mail: navs@telenet.net. Web: www.navs-online.org.

YOSEMITE NATIONAL PARK ESTABLISHED: ANNIVERSARY. Oct 1, 1890. Yosemite Valley and Mariposa Big Tree Grove, granted to the State of California June 30, 1864, were combined and established as a national park. For more park info: Yosemite Natl Park, PO Box 577, Yosemite Natl Park, CA 95389. Web: www.nps.gov/yose.

BIRTHDAYS TODAY

Jimmy Carter, 76, 39th president of the US, born James Earl Carter, Jr, Plains, GA, Oct 1, 1924.

Stephen Collins, 53, actor ("7th Heaven"), born Des Moines, IA, Oct 1, 1947.

Mark McGwire, 37, baseball player, born Pomona, CA, Oct 1, 1963.

Elizabeth Partridge, 49, author (*Restless Spirit: The Life and Work of Dorothea Lange*), born Berkeley, CA, Oct 1, 1951.

William Hubbs Rehnquist, 76, Chief Justice of the US Supreme Court, born Milwaukee, WI, Oct 1, 1924.

OCTOBER 2 — MONDAY
Day 276 — 90 Remaining

★**CHILD HEALTH DAY.** Oct 2. Presidential Proclamation always issued for the first Monday of October. Proclamation has been issued since 1928. In 1959 Congress changed celebration day from May 1 to the present observance (Pub Res No. 46 of May 18, 1928, and PL86–352 of Sept 22, 1959).

FAST OF GEDALYA. Oct 2. Jewish holiday. Hebrew calendar date: Tishri 3, 5761. Tzom Gedalya begins at first light of day and commemorates the 6th-century BC assassination of Gedalya Ben Achikam.

GANDHI, MOHANDAS KARAMCHAND (MAHATMA): BIRTH ANNIVERSARY. Oct 2, 1869. Indian political and spiritual leader who achieved world honor and fame for his advocacy of nonviolent resistance as a weapon against tyranny was born at Porbandar, India. He was assassinated in the garden of his home at New Delhi, Jan 30, 1948. On the anniversary of Gandhi's birth (Gandhi Jayanti) thousands gather at the park on the Jumna River at Delhi where Gandhi's body was cremated. Hymns are sung, verses from the Gita, the Koran and the Bible are recited and cotton thread is spun on small spinning wheels (one of Gandhi's favorite activities). Other observances held at his birthplace and throughout India on this public holiday.

GUINEA: INDEPENDENCE DAY. Oct 2. National Day. Guinea gained independence from France in 1958.

NATIONAL CUSTODIAL WORKERS DAY. Oct 2. A day to honor custodial workers—those who clean up after us. For info: Bette Tadajewski, Saint John the Baptist Church, 2425 Frederick, Alpena, MI 49707. Phone: (517) 354-3019.

NATIONAL WALK OUR CHILDREN TO SCHOOL WEEK. Oct 2–6. Parents and other caregivers are encouraged to walk children to school to demonstrate the healthful effects of walking, to teach children safe pedestrian behaviors and to help select safe routes to school. For info: Walking Magazine, 45 Bromfield St, 8th Floor, Boston, MA 02108. Phone: (617) 574-0076. Fax: (617) 338-7433.

***PEANUTS* DEBUTS: 50th ANNIVERSARY.** Oct 2, 1950. This comic strip by Charles M. Schulz featured Charlie Brown, his sister Sally, Lucy, Linus and Charlie's dog Snoopy. The last daily *Peanuts* strip was published Jan 3, 2000 and the last Sunday strip was published Feb 13, 2000.

REDWOOD NATIONAL PARK ESTABLISHED: ANNIVERSARY. Oct 2, 1968. California's Redwood National Park was established. For more park info: Redwood Natl Park, 1111 Second St, Crescent City, CA 95531. Web: www.nps.gov/redw.

SUPREME COURT 2000–2001 TERM BEGINS. Oct 2. Traditionally, the Supreme Court's annual term begins on the first Monday in October and continues with seven two-week sessions of oral arguments. Between the sessions are six recesses during which the opinions are written by the Justices. Ordinarily, all cases are decided by the following June or July. For a database of cases, biographies of the justices past and present and a virtual tour of the Supreme Court Building on the Web: oyez.nwu.edu.

UNITED NATIONS: WORLD HABITAT DAY. Oct 2. The United Nations General Assembly, by a resolution of Dec 17, 1985, has designated the first Monday of October each year as World Habitat Day. The first observance of this day, Oct 5, 1986, marked the 10th anniversary of the first international conference on the subject. (Habitat: United Nations Conference on Human Settlements, Vancouver, Canada, 1976.) Info from: United Nations, Dept of Public Info, Public Inquiries Unit, Rm GA-57, New York, NY 10017. Phone: (212) 963-4475. Fax: (212) 963-0071. E-mail: inquiries@un.org.

BIRTHDAYS TODAY

Jennifer Owings Dewey, 59, author (*Stories on Stone*), born Chicago, IL, Oct 2, 1941.

Thomas Muster, 33, tennis player, born Leibnitz, Austria, Oct 2, 1967.

OCTOBER 3 — TUESDAY
Day 277 — 89 Remaining

"THE ANDY GRIFFITH SHOW" TV PREMIERE: 40th ANNIVERSARY. Oct 3, 1960. Marks the airing of the first episode of this popular show set at Mayberry, NC. Andy Griffith starred as Sheriff Andy Taylor, Ron Howard was his son Opie, Frances Bavier was Aunt Bee Taylor and Don Knotts played Deputy Barney Fife. The 12,000+ members of "The Andy Griffith Show" Rerun Watchers Club and others celebrate this day with festivities every year.

"CAPTAIN KANGAROO" TV PREMIERE: ANNIVERSARY. Oct 3, 1955. On the air until 1985, this was the longest-running children's TV show until it was surpassed by "Sesame Street." Starring Bob Keeshan as Captain Kangaroo, it was broadcast on CBS and PBS. Other characters included Mr Green Jeans, Grandfather Clock, Bunny Rabbit, Mr Moose and Dancing Bear. Keeshan was an advocate for excellence in children's programming and even supervised which commercials would appear on the program. In 1997 "The All New Captain Kangaroo" debuted, starring John McDonough.

GERMAN REUNIFICATION: 10th ANNIVERSARY. Oct 3, 1990. After 45 years of division, East and West Germany reunited, just four days short of East Germany's 41st founding anniversary (Oct 7, 1949). The new united Germany took the name the Federal Republic of Germany, the formal name of the former West

October 2000	S	M	T	W	T	F	S
		1	2	3	4	5	6	7
	8	9	10	11	12	13	14
	15	16	17	18	19	20	21
	22	23	24	24	26	27	28
	29	30	31				

Germany and adopted the constitution of the former West Germany. Today is a national holiday in Germany.

HONDURAS: FRANCISCO MORAZAN HOLIDAY. Oct 3. Public holiday in honor of Francisco Morazan, national hero, who was born in 1799.

KOREA: NATIONAL FOUNDATION DAY. Oct 3. National holiday also called Tangun Day, as it commemorates day when legendary founder of the Korean nation, Tangun, established his kingdom of Chosun in 2333 BC.

"MICKEY MOUSE CLUB" TV PREMIERE: 45th ANNIVERSARY. Oct 3, 1955. This afternoon show for children was on ABC. Among its young cast members were Mouseketeers Annette Funicello and Shelley Fabares. The show was revived in 1977 and 1989. Christina Aguilera, Keri Russell and Britney Spears were cast members.

ROBINSON NAMED BASEBALL'S FIRST BLACK MAJOR LEAGUE MANAGER: ANNIVERSARY. Oct 3, 1974. The only major league player selected most valuable player in both the American and National Leagues, Frank Robinson was hired by the Cleveland Indians as baseball's first black major league manager. During his playing career Robinson represented the American League in four World Series playing for the Baltimore Orioles, led the Cincinnati Reds to a National League pennant and hit 586 home runs in 21 years of play.

BIRTHDAYS TODAY

Jeff Bingaman, 57, US Senator (D, New Mexico), born El Paso, TX, Oct 3, 1943.

Kevin Richardson, 28, singer (Backstreet Boys), born Lexington, KY, Oct 3, 1972.

OCTOBER 4 — WEDNESDAY

Day 278 — 88 Remaining

"THE ALVIN SHOW" TV PREMIERE: ANNIVERSARY. Oct 4, 1961. This prime-time cartoon was based on Ross Bagdasarian's novelty group called The Chipmunks, which had begun as recordings with speeded-up vocals. In the series, the three chipmunks, Alvin, Simon and Theodore, sang and had adventures along with their songwriter-manager David Seville. Bagdasarian supplied the voices. Part of the show featured the adventures of inventor Clyde Crashcup. "Alvin" was more successful as a Saturday morning cartoon. It returned in reruns in 1979 and also prompted a sequel, called "Alvin and the Chipmunks," in 1983.

GREGORIAN CALENDAR ADJUSTMENT: ANNIVERSARY. Oct 4, 1582. Pope Gregory XIII issued a bulletin that decreed that the day following Thursday, Oct 4, 1582, should be Friday, Oct 15, 1582, thus correcting the Julian Calendar, then 10 days out of date relative to the seasons. This reform was effective in most Catholic countries, though the Julian Calendar continued in use in Britain and the American colonies until 1752, in Japan until 1873, in China until 1912, in Russia until 1918, in Greece until 1923 and in Turkey until 1927. See also: "Gregorian Calendar Day: Anniversary" (Feb 24) and "Calendar Adjustment Day: Anniversary" (Sept 2).

HAYES, RUTHERFORD BIRCHARD: BIRTH ANNIVERSARY. Oct 4, 1822. The 19th president of the US (Mar 4, 1877–Mar 3, 1881), born at Delaware, OH. In his inaugural address, Hayes said: "He serves his party best who serves the country best." He died at Fremont, OH, Jan 17, 1893.

JOHNSON, ELIZA McCARDLE: BIRTH ANNIVERSARY. Oct 4, 1810. Wife of Andrew Johnson, 17th president of the US, born at Leesburg, TN. Died at Greeneville, TN, Jan 15, 1876.

"LEAVE IT TO BEAVER" TV PREMIERE: ANNIVERSARY. Oct 4, 1957. This family sitcom was a stereotypical portrayal of American family life. It focused on Theodore "Beaver" Cleaver (Jerry Mathers), his misadventures and his family: his patient, understanding, all-knowing and firm father, Ward (Hugh Beaumont), impeccably dressed housewife and mother June (Barbara Billingsley) and Wally (Tony Dow), Beaver's good-natured all-American brother. The "perfectness" of the Cleaver family was balanced by other, less than perfect characters. "Leave It to Beaver" remained popular in reruns.

LESOTHO: NATIONAL DAY. Oct 4. National holiday. Commemorates independence from Britain in 1966.

MISSISSIPPI STATE FAIR. Oct 4–15. Jackson, MS. Features nightly professional entertainment, livestock show, midway carnival, domestic art exhibits. Est attendance: 620,000. For info: Mississippi Fair Commission, PO Box 892, Jackson, MS 39205. Phone: (601) 961-4000. Fax: (601) 354-6545.

NATIONAL WALK OUR CHILDREN TO SCHOOL DAY. Oct 4. This day was established to encourage adults and children to walk together to raise awareness about three things: the exercise value of walking, the importance of teaching children safe walking behaviors and the need for more walkable communities. In 1998 children from 775 elementary schools in 27 states and 5 Canadian provinces took part. Sponsored by the Partnership for a Walkable America, a national alliance of public and private organizations committed to making walking safer, easier and more enjoyable. Annually, the Wednesday of the first full week in October. For info: Natl Walk Our Children to School Day, Natl Safety Council, 1121 Spring Lake Dr, Itasca, IL 60143-3201. Phone: (800) 621-7615, ext 2383. Fax: (630) 775-2185. E-mail: thompsoh@nsc.org.

SAINT FRANCIS OF ASSISI: FEAST DAY. Oct 4. Giovanni Francesco Bernardone, religious leader, founder of the Friars Minor (Franciscan Order), born at Assisi, Umbria, Italy, in 1181. Died at Porziuncula, Oct 3, 1226. One of the best-loved saints of all time.

SPACE MILESTONE: *SPUTNIK* (USSR). Oct 4, 1957. Anniversary of launching of first successful man-made earth satellite. *Sputnik I* ("satellite") weighing 184 lbs was fired into orbit from the USSR's Tyuratam launch site. Transmitted radio signal for 21 days, decayed Jan 4, 1958. The beginning of the Space Age and man's exploration beyond Earth. This first-in-space triumph by the Soviets resulted in a stepped-up emphasis on the teaching of science in American classrooms.

STRATEMEYER, EDWARD L.: BIRTH ANNIVERSARY. Oct 4, 1862. American author of children's books, Stratemeyer was born at Elizabeth, NJ. He created numerous series of popular children's books including The Bobbsey Twins, The Hardy Boys, Nancy Drew and Tom Swift. He and his Stratemeyer Syndicate, using 60 or more pen names, produced more than 800 books. More than four million copies were in print in 1987. Stratemeyer died at Newark, NJ, May 10, 1930.

Rachel Leigh Cook, 21, actress (*She's All That*, "The Baby-Sitters Club"), born Minneapolis, MN, Oct 4, 1979.

Karen Cushman, 59, author (*Catherine, Called Birdy*, Newbery for *The Midwife's Apprentice*), born Chicago, IL, Oct 4, 1941.

Chuck Hagel, 54, US Senator (R, Nebraska), born North Platte, NE, Oct 4, 1946.

Alicia Silverstone, 24, actress (*Batman & Robin*), born San Francisco, CA, Oct 4, 1976.

Donald Sobol, 76, author (Encyclopedia Brown series), born New York, NY, Oct 4, 1924.

OCTOBER 5 — THURSDAY
Day 279 — 87 Remaining

ARTHUR, CHESTER ALAN: BIRTH ANNIVERSARY. Oct 5, 1829. The 21st president of the US, born at Fairfield, VT, succeeded to the presidency following the death of James A. Garfield. Term of office: Sept 20, 1881–Mar 3, 1885. Arthur was not successful in obtaining the Republican party's nomination for the following term. He died at New York, NY, Nov 18, 1886.

CHIEF JOSEPH SURRENDER: ANNIVERSARY. Oct 5, 1877. After a 1,700-mile retreat, Chief Joseph and the Nez Perce Indians surrendered to US Cavalry troops at Bear's Paw near Chinook, MT, Oct 5, 1877. Chief Joseph made his famous speech of surrender, "From where the sun now stands, I will fight no more forever."

FITZHUGH, LOUISE: BIRTH ANNIVERSARY. Oct 5, 1928. Author (*Harriet the Spy*), born at Memphis, TN. Died Nov 19, 1974.

GODDARD, ROBERT HUTCHINGS: BIRTH ANNIVERSARY. Oct 5, 1882. The "father of the Space Age," born at Worcester, MA. Largely ignored or ridiculed during his lifetime because of his dreams of rocket travel, including travel to other planets. Launched a liquid-fuel-powered rocket Mar 16, 1926, at Auburn, MA. Died Aug 10, 1945, at Baltimore, MD. See also: "Goddard Day" (Mar 16).

MOON PHASE: FIRST QUARTER. Oct 5. Moon enters First Quarter phase at 6:59 AM, EST.

SOUTH CAROLINA STATE FAIR. Oct 5–15. Columbia, SC. Conklin Shows, rides, musical entertainment, food booths and children's activities. Est attendance: 576,000. For info: South Carolina

October 2000	S	M	T	W	T	F	S
	1	2	3	4	5	6	7
	8	9	10	11	12	13	14
	15	16	17	18	19	20	21
	22	23	24	24	26	27	28
	29	30	31				

State Fair, PO Box 393, Columbia, SC 29202. Phone: (803) 799-3387. Fax: (803) 799-1760. E-mail: geninfo@scsn.net.

STONE, THOMAS: DEATH ANNIVERSARY. Oct 5, 1787. Signer of the Declaration of Independence, born 1743 (exact date unknown) at Charles County, MD. Died at Alexandria, VA.

TECUMSEH: DEATH ANNIVERSARY. Oct 5, 1813. Shawnee Indian chief and orator, born at Old Piqua near Springfield, OH, in March 1768. Tecumseh is regarded as one of the greatest of American Indians. He came to prominence between the years 1799 and 1804 as a powerful orator, defending his people against whites. He denounced as invalid all treaties by which Indians ceded their lands and condemned the chieftains who had entered into such agreements. With his brother Tenskwatawa, the Prophet, he established a town on the Tippecanoe River near Lafayette, IN, and then embarked on a mission to organize an Indian confederation to stop white encroachment. Although he advocated peaceful methods and negotiation, he did not rule out war as a last resort as he visited tribes throughout the country. While he was away, William Henry Harrison defeated the Prophet at the Battle of Tippecanoe Nov 7, 1811, and burned the town. Tecumseh organized a large force of Indian warriors and assisted the British in the War of 1812. Tecumseh was defeated and killed at the Battle of the Thames, Oct 5, 1813.

ZION, GENE: BIRTH ANNIVERSARY. Oct 5, 1913. Author, best known for *Harry the Dirty Dog*, born at New York, NY. Zion died Dec 5, 1975.

Grant Hill, 28, basketball player, born Dallas, TX, Oct 5, 1972.

Bil Keane, 78, cartoonist ("Family Circus"), born Philadelphia, PA, Oct 5, 1922.

Mario Lemieux, 35, Hall of Fame hockey player, born Montreal, Quebec, Canada, Oct 5, 1965.

Patrick Roy, 35, hockey player, born Quebec City, Quebec, Canada, Oct 5, 1965.

David Shannon, 41, author and illustrator (*No, David!*), born Washington, DC, Oct 5, 1959.

Kate Winslet, 25, actress (*Titanic*), born Reading, England, Oct 5, 1975.

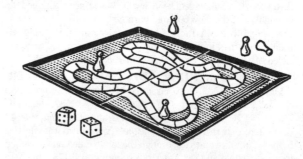

OCTOBER 6 — FRIDAY
Day 280 — 86 Remaining

ALABAMA NATIONAL FAIR. Oct 6–14. Garrett Coliseum/Fairgrounds, Montgomery, AL. A midway filled with exciting rides and games, arts and crafts, exhibits, livestock shows, racing pigs, a circus, a petting zoo, food and entertainment. Est attendance: 227,000. For info: Hazel Ashmore, PO Box 3304, Montgomery, AL 36109-0304. Phone: (334) 272-6831. Fax: (334) 272-6835.

ARKANSAS STATE FAIR AND LIVESTOCK SHOW. Oct 6–15. Barton Coliseum and State Fairground, Little Rock, AR. Est attendance: 400,000. For info: Arkansas State Fair, PO Box

166660, Little Rock, AR 72216. Phone: (501) 372-8341. Fax: (501) 372-4197. Web: www.arkfairgrounds.com.

EGYPT: ARMED FORCES DAY. Oct 6. The Egyptian Army celebrates crossing into Sinai in 1973. For info: Egyptian Tourist Authority, 645 N Michigan Ave, Ste 829, Chicago, IL 60611. Phone: (312) 280-4666. Fax: (312) 280-4788.

GEORGIA NATIONAL FAIR. Oct 6–15. Georgia National Fairgrounds, Perry, GA. Traditional state agricultural fair features thousands of entries in horse, livestock, horticultural, youth, home and fine arts categories. Family entertainment, education and fun. Sponsored by the State of Georgia. Annually, beginning the fifth Friday after Labor Day. Est attendance: 352,000. For info: John P. Webb, Jr, CFE, Georgia Natl Fair, PO Box 1367, 401 Larry Walker Pkwy, Perry, GA 31069. Phone: (912) 987-3247. Fax: (912) 987-7218. E-mail: webb1@alltell.net. Web: www.gnfa.com.

HONG KONG: CHUNG YEUNG FESTIVAL. Oct 6. This festival relates to the old story of the Han Dynasty, when a soothsayer advised a man to take his family to a high place on the ninth day of the ninth moon for 24 hours in order to avoid disaster. The man obeyed and found, on returning home, that all living things had died a sudden death in his absence. Part of the celebration is climbing to high places.

★**NATIONAL GERMAN-AMERICAN DAY.** Oct 6. Celebration of German heritage and contributions German Americans have made to the building of the nation. A Presidential Proclamation has been issued each year since 1987. Annually, Oct 6.

NATIONAL STORYTELLING FESTIVAL. Oct 6–8. Jonesborough, TN. Tennessee's oldest town plays host to the most dynamic storytelling event dedicated to the oral tradition. This three-day celebration showcases storytellers, stories and traditions from across America and around the world. Annually, the first full weekend in October. Est attendance: 10,000. For info: Storytelling Foundation Intl (SFI), 116 W Main, Jonesborough, TN 37659. Phone: (800) 952-8392. Fax: (423) 913-8219. Web: www.storytellingfestival.net.

VINING, ELIZABETH GRAY: BIRTH ANNIVERSARY. Oct 6, 1902. Author of *Adam of the Road* under the name Elizabeth Gray, born at Philadelphia, PA. Won Newbery Medal (1943). Died Nov 27, 1999, at Kennett Square, PA.

YOM KIPPUR WAR: ANNIVERSARY. Oct 6–25, 1973. A surprise attack by Egypt and Syria pushed Israeli forces several miles behind the 1967 cease-fire lines. Israel was caught off guard, partly because the attack came on the holiest Jewish religious day. After 18 days of fighting, hostilities were halted by the UN Oct 25. Israel partially recovered from the initial setback but failed to regain all the land lost in the fighting.

BIRTHDAYS TODAY

James Gilmore III, 51, Governor of Virginia (R), born Richmond, VA, Oct 6, 1949.

Betsy Hearne, 58, author (*Seven Brave Women*), born Wilsonville, AL, Oct 6, 1942.
Rebecca Lobo, 27, basketball player, born Southwick, MA, Oct 6, 1973.
Jeanette Winter, 61, author and illustrator (*My Name Is Georgia*), born Chicago, IL, Oct 6, 1939.

OCTOBER 7 — SATURDAY
Day 281 — 85 Remaining

"ARTHUR" TV PREMIERE: ANNIVERSARY. Oct 7, 1996. This animated show, based on Marc Brown's popular series of books, features the aardvark Arthur, his sister D.W. and a host of friends from their elementary school.

BASKETBALL HALL OF FAME ENSHRINEMENT CEREMONIES. Oct 7 (tentative). Springfield, MA. New electees are enshrined into the Basketball Hall of Fame. Est attendance: 1,500. For info: Public Relations & Publishing, Basketball Hall of Fame, 1150 W Columbus Ave, PO Box 179, Springfield, MA 01101-0179. Phone: (413) 781-6500.

CABBAGE PATCH® KIDS DEBUTED: ANNIVERSARY. Oct 7, 1983. These popular dolls come with their own birth certificates and adoption papers. More than 3 million of the dolls were sold for the holiday season in 1983. Today, there are several varieties of Cabbage Patch® Kids.

NATIONAL FRUGAL FUN DAY. Oct 7. A day to celebrate that having fun doesn't have to be costly. Do at least one fun thing for yourself and/or your family that is free of cost or under $5 a person: a concert or play, a hike, a meal out, a picnic, an art gallery or museum tour, a day trip, a boat ride. Annually, the first Saturday in October. For info: Shel Horowitz, PO Box 1164, Northampton, MA 01061-1164. Phone: (413) 586-2388. Fax: (617) 249-0153. E-mail: info@frugalfun.com. Web: www.frugalfun.com.

RODNEY, CAESAR: BIRTH ANNIVERSARY. Oct 7, 1728. Signer of the Declaration of Independence who cast a tie-breaking vote. Born near Dover, DE, he died at Dover, June 29, 1784.

WALLACE, HENRY AGARD: BIRTH ANNIVERSARY. Oct 7, 1888. The 33rd vice president of the US (1941–45), born at Adair County, IA. Died at Danbury, CT, Nov 18, 1965.

BIRTHDAYS TODAY

Diane Ackerman, 52, author (*The Moon of Light*), born Waukegan, IL, Oct 7, 1948.
Desmond Tutu, 69, South African archbishop, Nobel Peace Prize winner, born Klerksdrop, South Africa, Oct 7, 1931.

OCTOBER 8 — SUNDAY
Day 282 — 84 Remaining

AMERICAN SAMOA: WHITE SUNDAY. Oct 8. Second Sunday in October is "children's day" on the island. Children demonstrate skits, prayers, songs and special presentations for parents, friends and relatives. A feast is prepared by the parents and served to the children.

FIRE PREVENTION WEEK. Oct 8–14. To increase awareness of the dangers of fire and to educate the public on how to stay safe from fire. The theme this year is "Fire Drills: The Great Escape!" *See* Curriculum Connection. For info: Public Affairs Office, Natl Fire Protection Assn, One Batterymarch Park, Quincy, MA 02269. Phone: (617) 770-3000. Web: www.nfpa.org.

★ **FIRE PREVENTION WEEK.** Oct 8–14. Presidential Proclamation issued annually for the first or second week in October since 1925. For many years prior to 1925, National Fire Prevention Day was observed in October. Annually, the Sunday through Saturday period during which Oct 9 falls.

GRANDMOTHER'S DAY IN FLORIDA AND KENTUCKY. Oct 8. A ceremonial day on the second Sunday in October.

GREAT CHICAGO FIRE: ANNIVERSARY. Oct 8, 1871. Great fire of Chicago began, according to legend, when Mrs O'Leary's cow kicked over the lantern in her barn on DeKoven Street. The fire leveled 3½ sq miles, destroying 17,450 buildings and leaving 98,500 people homeless and about 250 people dead. Financially, the loss was $200 million. On the same day a fire destroyed the entire town of Peshtigo, WI, killing more than 1,100 people.

★ **NATIONAL CHILDREN'S DAY.** Oct 8.

NATIONAL METRIC WEEK. Oct 8–14. To maintain an awareness of the importance of the metric system as the primary system of measurement for the US. Annually, the week of the tenth month containing the tenth day of the month. For info: Natl Council of Teachers of Mathematics, 1906 Association Dr, Reston, VA 20191-1593. Phone: (703) 620-9840. Fax: (703) 476-2970. E-mail: infocentral@nctm.org. Web: www.nctm.org.

NATIONAL SCHOOL LUNCH WEEK. Oct 8–14. To celebrate good nutrition and healthy, low-cost school lunches. Annually, the second full week in October. For info: Communications Dept, American School Food Service Assn, 1600 Duke St, 7th Fl, Alexandria, VA 22314-3436. Phone: (703) 739-3900 x133.

★ **NATIONAL SCHOOL LUNCH WEEK.** Oct 8–14. Presidential Proclamation issued for the week beginning with the second Sunday in October since 1962 (PL87–780 of Oct 9, 1962). Note: Not issued in 1981.

PERU: DAY OF THE NAVY. Oct 8. Public holiday in Peru, commemorating Combat of Angamos.

PESHTIGO FOREST FIRE: ANNIVERSARY. Oct 8, 1871. One of the most disastrous forest fires in history began at Peshtigo, WI, the same day the Great Chicago Fire began. The Wisconsin fire burned across six counties, killing more than 1,100 persons.

SAMOA: WHITE SUNDAY. Oct 8. The second Sunday in October. For the children of Samoa, this is the biggest day of the year. Traditional roles are reversed, as children lead church services, are served special foods and receive gifts of new church clothes and other special items. All the children dress in white. The following Monday is an official holiday.

October 2000	S	M	T	W	T	F	S
	1	2	3	4	5	6	7
	8	9	10	11	12	13	14
	15	16	17	18	19	20	21
	22	23	24	24	26	27	28
	29	30	31				

OCTOBER 8–14
FIRE PREVENTION WEEK

Each year, fires in the home are responsible for the loss of life and property. Many of these fires and the accompanying heartbreak could have been prevented.

All children should be educated in fire prevention and what to do in case of fire. Panic during a fire can lead to tragic results. That's why school fire drills are so important. An orderly evacuation plan saves lives. Unfortunately, many homeowners never take the time to plan ahead. That's where you can help.

Fire departments across the nation are observing Fire Prevention Week. Call your local unit and request a fire prevention assembly. Visits to the fire station may be possible. If not, your local unit may be able to bring an engine to the school. One of the things to point out to children is the importance of leaving fire hydrants clear. In today's crowded cities, people seem to ignore parking laws and forget to park well away from hydrants.

During science, it's important to discuss the mechanics of fire. A fire cannot burn unless oxygen is present. A simple experiment can illustrate this. Bring in a small birthday cake candle. Light it and let it drip onto a saucer. Blow out the candle and fix it upright in the wax drop on the saucer. Light the candle. Explain how the candle's flame burns as long as oxygen can reach it. Cover the candle with a drinking glass. After a few seconds, as the flame uses up the oxygen available under the glass, the flame will dim and then go out. That's why children are taught to "Stop, Drop and Roll" if their clothing should catch fire.

When you speak with firefighters about a visit, ask if they have a video (or experiment) that shows the danger of smoke. It's easy to tell kids smoke rises and to stay low, but if you can visually demonstrate it for them, they will remember better.

Talk with students about safety measures the school building has: smoke alarms, sprinklers, etc. Ask each student to talk with their parents about fire safety in their homes. List and graph the kinds of preventive devices the class as a whole has in their homes. Create a "My Home is Safe—We Have a Fire Plan" classroom goal. At the very least, every child should be able to articulate an escape plan. Encourage them to draw a map of ways they could escape from their home if a fire started.

Discuss 911 and how it operates. Children can work in pairs and act out 911 call scenarios. It could save the life of someone they love. Stress the serious nature of using 911 and that it is never acceptable to call it for fun. See if you can get a 911 call receiver to visit your classroom. He or she will help reinforce the message.

Fire prevention in parklands is also important. Younger students can become acquainted with Smokey the Bear. While the symbol was created in 1944 by the National Forest Service, in 1950, a real Smokey Bear was found in New Mexico's Lincoln National Forest. For more information, go to www.smokeybear .com.

Have a poster campaign to illustrate the danger of fire and its prevention. Display all the posters in the school hallways and find out if the municipal building or the public library would be willing to display them as well. If you have a shopping area, merchants might be willing to participate and hang the posters in their store windows. It's worth a try, and makes for good public relations.

The National Fire Protection Association website has lesson plans for elementary and middle grades at www.nfpa.org. Their Sparky the Fire Dog site (www.sparky.org) has information for kids.

YOM KIPPUR BEGINS AT SUNDOWN. Oct 8. Jewish Day of Atonement. See "Yom Kippur" (Oct 9).

BIRTHDAYS TODAY

Chevy Chase, 57, comedian, actor (*Christmas Vacation, Vegas Vacation*), born Cornelius Crane, New York, NY, Oct 8, 1943.

Matt Damon, 30, actor (*Saving Private Ryan*), born Cambridge, MA, Oct 8, 1970.

Barthe DeClements, 80, author (*Nothing's Fair in Fifth Grade*), born Seattle, WA, Oct 8, 1920.

Jesse Jackson, 59, clergyman, civil rights leader ("I am somebody," "Keep hope alive"), born Greenville, NC, Oct 8, 1941.

Faith Ringgold, 70, artist, author (*Tar Beach, My Dream of Martin Luther King*), born New York, NY, Oct 8, 1930.

Rashaan Salaam, 26, football player, born San Diego, CA, Oct 8, 1974.

R.L. Stine, 57, author (the Goosebumps series), born Columbus, OH, Oct 8, 1943.

OCTOBER 9 — MONDAY

Day 283 — 83 Remaining

CANADA: THANKSGIVING DAY. Oct 9. Observed on second Monday in October each year.

COLUMBUS DAY OBSERVANCE. Oct 9. Public Law 90–363 sets observance of Columbus Day on the second Monday in October. Applicable to federal employees and to the District of Columbia, but observed also in most states. Commemorates the landfall of Columbus in the New World, Oct 12, 1492. See also: "Columbus Day (Traditional)" (Oct 12). For links to Columbus Day websites, go to: deil.lang.uiuc.edu/web.pages/holidays/columbus.html.

★**COLUMBUS DAY.** Oct 9. Presidential Proclamation always the second Monday in October. Observed Oct 12 from 1934 to 1970 (Pub Res No 21 of Apr 30, 1934). PL90–363 of June 28, 1968, required that beginning in 1971 it would be observed on the second Monday in October.

ICELAND: LEIF ERIKSON DAY. Oct 9. Celebrates discovery of North America in the year 1000 by Norse explorer.

JAPAN: HEALTH-SPORTS DAY ANNIVERSARY. Oct 10. National holiday to encourage physical activity for building sound body and mind. Created in 1966 to commemorate the day of the opening of the 18th Olympic Games at Tokyo, Oct 10, 1964.

KOREA: ALPHABET DAY (HANGUL): ANNIVERSARY. Oct 9. Celebrates anniversary of promulgation of Hangul (24-letter phonetic alphabet) by King Sejong of the Yi Dynasty, in 1446.

★**LEIF ERIKSON DAY.** Oct 9. Presidential Proclamation always issued for Oct 9 since 1964 (PL88–566 of Sept 2, 1964) at request. Honors the Norse explorer who is widely believed to have been the first European to visit the American continent. For information on the 1,000-year anniversary of this event to take place in 2000, visit the Leif Ericson Millennium Celebration website at www.leif.2000.

NATIONAL PET PEEVE WEEK. Oct 9–13. A chance for people to make others aware of all the little things in life they find so annoying, in the hope of changing some of them. Annually, the second full week of October. When requesting info, please send SASE. For info: Ad-America, Pine Tree Center Indust Park, 2215 29th St SE, Ste B-7, Grand Rapids, MI 49508. Phone: (616) 247-3797. Fax: (616) 247-3798. E-mail: adamerica@aol.com.

NATIVE AMERICANS' DAY IN SOUTH DAKOTA. Oct 9. Observed as a legal holiday, dedicated to the remembrance of the great Native American leaders who contributed so much to the history of South Dakota. Annually, the second Monday in October.

PLANET FRIENDS' CIRCLE WEEK. Oct 9–15. Today's technology has moved young people out of their neighborhoods and on to a large multicultural playground called Planet Earth. The Planet Friends' Circle encourages children and teens to think globally, experience new cultures and create a circle of friends spanning the planet. For info: Planet Friends' Circle, PO Box 10929, Pittsburgh, PA 15236.

UGANDA: INDEPENDENCE DAY. Oct 9. National holiday commemorating achievement of autonomy from Britain in 1962.

UNITED NATIONS: WORLD POST DAY. Oct 9. An annual special observance of Postal Administrations of the Universal Postal Union (UPU). For info: United Nations, Dept of Public Info, Public Inquiries Unit, Rm GA-57, New York, NY 10017. Phone: (212) 963-4475. Fax: (212) 963-0071. E-mail: inquiries@un.org.

VIRGIN ISLANDS–PUERTO RICO FRIENDSHIP DAY. Oct 9. Columbus Day (second Monday in October) also celebrates historical friendship between peoples of Virgin Islands and Puerto Rico.

"WISHBONE" TV PREMIERE: ANNIVERSARY. Oct 9, 1995. The first episode of this popular series that retells classic stories with a dog named Wishbone who imagines himself as a character in signature scenes premiered on PBS. It was the first of a two-part series titled "Tail in Twain," based on Mark Twain's *The Adventures of Tom Sawyer*. Other episodes have been based on stories by Ovid, Goethe, Jane Austen, Washington Irving, Edgar Allen Poe and others.

YOM KIPPUR OR DAY OF ATONEMENT. Oct 9. Holiest Jewish observance. A day for fasting, repentance and seeking forgiveness. Hebrew calendar date: Tishri 10, 5761.

YORKTOWN VICTORY DAY. Oct 9. Observed as a holiday in Virginia. Annually, the second Monday in October. See "Yorktown Day: Anniversary" (Oct 19).

BIRTHDAYS TODAY

Zachery Ty Bryan, 19, actor ("Home Improvement"), born Aurora, CO, Oct 9, 1981.

Steven Burns, 27, TV host ("Blue's Clues"), born Boyertown, PA, Oct 9, 1973.

Johanna Hurwitz, 63, author (*Busybody Nora*), born New York, NY, Oct 9, 1937.

Trent Lott, 59, US Senator (R, Mississippi), born Duck Hill, MS, Oct 9, 1941.

Mike Singletary, 42, Hall of Fame football player, born Houston, TX, Oct 9, 1958.

Annika Sorenstam, 30, golfer, born Stockholm, Sweden, Oct 9, 1970.

OCTOBER 10 — TUESDAY

Day 284 — 82 Remaining

BONZA BOTTLER DAY™. Oct 10. To celebrate when the number of the day is the same as the number of the month. Bonza Bottler Day™ is an excuse to have a party at least once a month. For info: Gail M. Berger, 109 Matthew Ave, Poca, WV 25159. Phone: (304) 776-7746. E-mail: gberger5@aol.com.

DOUBLE TENTH DAY: ANNIVERSARY. Oct 10. Tenth day of 10th month, Double Tenth Day, is observed by many Chinese as the anniversary of the outbreak of the revolution against the imperial Manchu dynasty, Oct 10, 1911. Sun Yat-Sen and Huan Hsing were among the revolutionary leaders.

FIJI: INDEPENDENCE DAY: 30th ANNIVERSARY. Oct 10. National holiday. Commemorates independence from Britain in 1970.

LITERATURE FESTIVAL. Oct 10. University of Kansas Union, Lawrence, KS. Festival of children's literature. For info: The Writing Conference, Inc, PO Box 664, Ottawa, KS 66067. Fax: (785) 242-0407. E-mail: jbushman@writingconference.com. Web: www.writingconference.com.

MARSHALL, JAMES: BIRTH ANNIVERSARY. Oct 10, 1942. Illustrator, born at San Antonio, TX. Marshall is best known for his George and Martha series of books. He illustrated more than 70 children's books including *The Owl and the Pussycat*. Died at New York, NY, Oct 13, 1992.

★ **NATIONAL WILDLIFE WEEK.** Oct 10–16. A time for all Americans to learn about and celebrate the magnificent collection of lands set aside for wildlife and for the American spirit. This is a time for renewed awareness and commitment to wildlife conservation.

BIRTHDAYS TODAY

Nancy Carlson, 47, author (*Arnie and the New Kid*), born Minneapolis, MN, Oct 10, 1953.

Brett Favre, 31, quarterback, born Gulfport, MS, Oct 10, 1969.

Mario Lopez, 27, actor ("Saved by the Bell," "Pacific Blue"), born San Diego, CA, Oct 10, 1973.

Robert D. San Souci, 54, author (*Cendrillon: A Caribbean Cinderella*), born San Francisco, CA, Oct 10, 1946.

OCTOBER 11 — WEDNESDAY
Day 285 — 81 Remaining

★ **GENERAL PULASKI MEMORIAL DAY.** Oct 11. Presidential Proclamation always issued for Oct 11 since 1929. Requested by Congressional Resolution each year from 1929–1946. (Since 1947 has been issued by custom.) Note: Proclamation 4869, of Oct 5, 1981, covers all succeeding years.

ROBINSON, ROSCOE, JR: BIRTH ANNIVERSARY. Oct 11, 1928. The first black American to achieve the Army rank of four-star general. Born at St. Louis, MO, and died at Washington, DC, July 22, 1993.

ROOSEVELT, ANNA ELEANOR: BIRTH ANNIVERSARY. Oct 11, 1884. Wife of Franklin Delano Roosevelt, 32nd president of the US, was born at New York, NY. She led an active and independent life and was the first wife of a president to give her own news conference in the White House (1933). Widely known throughout the world, she was affectionately called "the first lady of the world." She served as US delegate to the United Nations General Assembly for a number of years before her death at New York, NY, Nov 7, 1962. A prolific writer, she wrote in *This Is My Story*, "No one can make you feel inferior without your consent."

STONE, HARLAN FISKE: BIRTH ANNIVERSARY. Oct 11, 1872. Former associate justice and later chief justice of the US Supreme Court who wrote more than 600 opinions and dissents for that court, Stone was born at Chesterfield, NH. He served on the Supreme Court from 1925 until his death, at Washington, DC, Apr 22, 1946.

October *2000*	S	M	T	W	T	F	S
	1	2	3	4	5	6	7
	8	9	10	11	12	13	14
	15	16	17	18	19	20	21
	22	23	24	24	26	27	28
	29	30	31				

UNITED NATIONS: INTERNATIONAL DAY FOR NATURAL DISASTER REDUCTION. Oct 11. The General Assembly made this designation for the second Wednesday of October each year as part of its efforts to foster international cooperation in reducing the loss of life, property damage and social and economic disruption caused by natural disasters. For info: United Nations, Dept of Public Info, New York, NY 10017.

VATICAN COUNCIL II: ANNIVERSARY. Oct 11, 1962. The 21st ecumenical council of the Roman Catholic Church was convened by Pope John XXIII. It met in four annual sessions, concluding Dec 8, 1965. It dealt with the renewal of the Church and introduced sweeping changes, such as the use of the vernacular rather than Latin in the Mass.

BIRTHDAYS TODAY

Russell Freedman, 71, author (Newbery for *Lincoln: A Photobiography*), born San Francisco, CA, Oct 11, 1929.

Orlando Hernandez, 31, baseball player, known as "El Duque," born Villa Clara, Cuba, Oct 11, 1969.

Patty Murray, 50, US Senator (D, Washington), born Seattle, WA, Oct 11, 1950.

Michelle Trachtenberg, 15, actress (*Harriet the Spy, Inspector Gadget*), born New York, NY, Oct 11, 1985.

Jon Steven "Steve" Young, 39, football player, born Salt Lake City, UT, Oct 11, 1961.

OCTOBER 12 — THURSDAY
Day 286 — 80 Remaining

ARIZONA STATE FAIR. Oct 12–29. Phoenix, AZ. Festival, concerts, flea markets, entertainment and food. For info: Mktg Dept, Arizona State Fair, PO Box 6728, Phoenix, AZ 85005. Phone: (602) 252-6771. Fax: (602) 495-1302.

BAHAMAS: DISCOVERY DAY. Oct 12. Commemorates the landing of Columbus in the Bahamas in 1492.

BOER WAR: ANNIVERSARY. Oct 12, 1899. The Boers of the Transvaal and Orange Free State in southern Africa declared war on the British. The Boer states were annexed by Britain in 1900 but guerrilla warfare on the part of the Boers caused the war to drag on. It was finally ended May 31, 1902 by the Treaty of Vereeniging.

CHICAGO INTERNATIONAL CHILDREN'S FILM FESTIVAL. Oct 12–22 (tentative). Cannes for Kids! Children's films from around the world plus workshops with directors, animators and movie makeup artists. For info: Chicago Intl Children's Film Festival, Facets Multimedia, 1517 W Fullerton Ave, Chicago, IL 60614. Phone: (773) 281-9075. E-mail: kidsfest@facets.org.

COLUMBUS DAY (TRADITIONAL). Oct 12. Public holiday in most countries in the Americas and in most Spanish-speaking countries. Observed under different names (Dia de la Raza or Day of the Race) and on different dates (most often, as in US, on the second Monday in October). Anniversary of Christopher Columbus's arrival, Oct 12, 1492, after a dangerous voyage across "shoreless Seas," at the Bahamas (probably the island of Guanahani), which he renamed El Salvador and claimed in the name of the Spanish crown. In his *Journal*, he wrote: "As I saw that they (the natives) were friendly to us, and perceived that they could be much more easily converted to our holy faith by gentle means than by force, I presented them with some red caps, and strings of beads to wear upon the neck, and many other trifles of small value, wherewith they were much delighted, and becamed wonderfully attached to us." See also: "Columbus Day Observance" (Oct 9).

DAY OF THE SIX BILLION: ANNIVERSARY. Oct 12, 1999. According to the United Nations, the population of the world reached six billion on this date. More than one-third of the world's people live in China and India. It wasn't until 1804 that the world's population reached one billion; now a billion people are added to the population about every 12 years. See also: "Day of the Five Billion: Anniversary" (July 11).

EQUATORIAL GUINEA: INDEPENDENCE DAY. Oct 12. National holiday. The former Spanish Guinea gained independence from Spain in 1968.

MEXICO: DIA DE LA RAZA. Oct 12. Columbus Day is observed as the "Day of the Race," a fiesta time to commemorate the discovery of America as well as the common interests and cultural heritage of the Spanish and Indian peoples and the Hispanic nations.

SPAIN: NATIONAL HOLIDAY. Oct 12.

BIRTHDAYS TODAY

Kirk Cameron, 30, actor ("Growing Pains"), born Panorama City, CA, Oct 12, 1970.

Alice Childress, 80, author (*A Hero Ain't Nothin' But a Sandwich*), born Charlestown, SC, Oct 12, 1920.

John Engler, 52, Governor of Michigan (R), born Mt Pleasant, MI, Oct 12, 1948.

Marion Jones, 25, track runner, born Los Angeles, CA, Oct 12, 1975.

OCTOBER 13 — FRIDAY

Day 287 — 79 Remaining

BROWN, JESSE LEROY: BIRTH ANNIVERSARY. Oct 13, 1926. Jesse Leroy Brown was the first black American naval aviator and also the first black naval officer to lose his life in combat when he was shot down over Korea, Dec 4, 1950. On Mar 18, 1972, USS *Jesse L. Brown* was launched as the first ship to be named in honor of a black naval officer. Brown was born at Hattiesburg, MS.

FRIDAY THE THIRTEENTH. Oct 13. Variously believed to be a lucky or unlucky day. Every year has at least one Friday the 13th, but never more than three. One Friday in 2000 falls on the 13th day, in October. Two Fridays in 2001 fall on the 13th, in April and July. Fear of the number 13 is known as triskaidekaphobia.

HUNTER'S MOON. Oct 13. The full moon following Harvest Moon. So called because the moon's light in evening extends day's length for hunters. Moon enters Full Moon phase at 4:53 AM, EDT.

MOON PHASE: FULL MOON. Oct 13. Moon enters Full Moon phase at 4:53 AM, EDT.

NATIONAL SCHOOL CELEBRATION. Oct 13. "Pledge Across America"—a synchronized recitation of the Pledge of Allegiance coast to coast, 8 AM Hawaiian time to 2 PM Eastern time. The National School Celebration will provide a high-profile celebration uniting our nation's youth during regular school hours for a patriotic observance. Every school in the nation is invited to participate. This event perpetuates the original spirit of the 1892 National School Celebration declared by President Benjamin Harrison, for which the first Pledge of Allegiance was written. Free resources available from Farmers Insurance and Celebration USA, including a CD with musical renditions of the Pledge, Constitution, Bill of Rights and other selections. Annually, the second Friday in October. For info: Paula Burton, Pres, Celebration USA, 17853 Santiago Blvd, Ste 107, Villa Park, CA 92667. Phone: (714) 283-1892. Web: www.americanpromise.com.

PITCHER, MOLLY: BIRTH ANNIVERSARY. Oct 13, 1754. "Molly Pitcher," heroine of the American Revolution, was a water carrier at the Battle of Monmouth (Sunday, June 28, 1778) where she distinguished herself by loading and firing a cannon after her husband, John Hays, was wounded. Affectionately known as "Sergeant Molly" after General Washington issued her a warrant as a noncommissioned officer. Her real name was Mary Hays McCauley (née Ludwig). Born near Trenton, NJ, she died at Carlisle, PA, Jan 22, 1832.

RICHTER, CONRAD: BIRTH ANNIVERSARY. Oct 13, 1890. Author of books for children and adults, born at Pine Grove, PA. His book *The Light in the Forest* was made into a Disney film in 1958. *The Fields* won the Pulitzer Prize for fiction in 1951. Other works include *The Trees* and *The Town*. Richter died at Pottsville, PA, Oct 30, 1968.

SOUTHERN FESTIVAL OF BOOKS: A CELEBRATION OF THE WRITTEN WORD. Oct 13–15. War Memorial Plaza, Nashville, TN. To promote reading, writing, the literary arts and a broader understanding of the language and culture of the South, this annual festival will feature readings, talks and panel discussions by more than 200 authors, exhibit booths of publishing companies and bookstores, autographing sessions, a comprehensive children's program and the Cafe Stage, which is a performance corner for authors, storytellers and musicians. Est attendance: 30,000. For info: Galyn Martin, Coord, Southern Festival of Books, Tennessee Humanities Council, 1003 18th Ave S, Nashville, TN 37212. Phone: (615) 320-7001 ext 15. Fax: (615) 321-4586. E-mail: galyn@tn-humanities.org.

SUKKOT BEGINS AT SUNDOWN. Oct 13. Jewish Feast of Tabernacles. See "Sukkot" (Oct 14).

US NAVY: 225th AUTHORIZATION ANNIVERSARY. Oct 13, 1775. Commemorates legislation passed by Second Continental Congress authorizing the acquisition of ships and establishment of a navy.

WHITE HOUSE CORNERSTONE LAID: ANNIVERSARY. Oct 13, 1792. The cornerstone for the presidential residence at 1600 Pennsylvania Ave NW, Washington, DC, designed by James Hoban, was laid. The first presidential family to occupy it was that of John Adams, in November 1800. With three stories and more than 100 rooms, the White House is the oldest building at Washington. First described as the "presidential palace," it acquired the name "White House" about 10 years after construction was completed. Burned by British troops in 1814, it was reconstructed, refurbished and reoccupied by 1817. Take a virtual tour of the White House at www.whitehouse.gov. Young children can visit the White House for Kids site at www.whitehouse.gov /WH/kids/html/home.html.

BIRTHDAYS TODAY

Jerry Rice, 38, football player, born Starkville, MS, Oct 13, 1962.

Summer Sanders, 28, Olympic gold medal swimmer, host ("Figure It Out"), born Roseville, CA, Oct 13, 1972.

Paul Simon, 59, singer/songwriter, born Newark, NJ, Oct 13, 1941.

OCTOBER 14 — SATURDAY

Day 288 — 78 Remaining

ALASKA DAY CELEBRATION. Oct 14–18. Sitka, AK. Celebration of the transfer ceremony in which the Russian flag was lowered and the Stars and Stripes raised, formally transferring the ownership of Alaska to the US, Oct 18, 1867. Annually, Oct 14–18. For info: Sitka Conv and Visitors Bureau, Box 1226, Sitka, AK 99835. Phone: (907) 747-5940.

BELIZE: COLUMBUS DAY. Oct 14. Public holiday.

EISENHOWER, DWIGHT DAVID: BIRTH ANNIVERSARY. Oct 14, 1890. The 34th president of the US, born at Denison, TX. Served two terms as president, Jan 20, 1953–Jan 20, 1961. Nicknamed "Ike," he held the rank of five-star general of the army (resigned in 1952, and restored by act of Congress in 1961). He served as supreme commander of the Allied forces in western Europe during WWII. In his Farewell Address (Jan 17, 1961), speaking about the "conjunction of an immense military establishment and a large arms industry," he warned: "In the councils of government, we must guard against the acquisition of unwarranted influence, whether sought or unsought, by the military-industrial complex. The potential of the disastrous rise of misplaced power exists and will persist." An American hero, Eisenhower died at Washington, DC, Mar 28, 1969.

KING WINS NOBEL PEACE PRIZE: ANNIVERSARY. Oct 14, 1964. Martin Luther King, Jr, became the youngest recipient of the Nobel Peace Prize when awarded the honor. Dr. King donated the entire $54,000 prize money to furthering the causes of the civil rights movement.

LEE, FRANCIS LIGHTFOOT: BIRTH ANNIVERSARY. Oct 14, 1734. Signer of the Declaration of Independence. Born at Westmoreland County, VA, he died Jan 11, 1797, at Richmond County, VA.

LENSKI, LOIS: BIRTH ANNIVERSARY. Oct 14, 1893. Children's author and illustrator, born at Springfield, OH. She wrote *Cotton In My Sack* and *Strawberry Girl*, which was awarded the Newbery Medal in 1946. Lenski died at Tarpon Springs, FL, Sept 11, 1974.

PENN, WILLIAM: BIRTH ANNIVERSARY. Oct 14, 1644. Founder of Pennsylvania, born at London, England. Penn died July 30, 1718, at Buckinghamshire, England. Presidential Proclamation 5284 of Nov 28, 1984, conferred honorary citizenship of the USA upon William Penn and his second wife, Hannah Callowhill Penn. They were the third and fourth persons to receive honorary US citizenship (following Winston Churchill and Raoul Wallenberg).

SOUND BARRIER BROKEN: ANNIVERSARY. Oct 14, 1947. Flying a Bell X-1 at Muroc Dry Lake Bed, CA, Air Force pilot Chuck Yeager flew faster than the speed of sound, ushering in the era of supersonic flight.

SUKKOT, SUCCOTH or FEAST OF TABERNACLES, FIRST DAY. Oct 14. Hebrew calendar date: Tishri 15, 5761, begins nine-day festival in commemoration of Jewish people's 40 years of wandering in the desert and thanksgiving for the fall harvest. This high holiday season closes with Shemini Atzeret (see entry on Oct 21) and Simchat Torah (see entry on Oct 22).

BIRTHDAYS TODAY

Jordan Brower, 19, actor ("Teen Angel"), born Vandenberg, CA, Oct 14, 1981.

Elisa Kleven, 42, author (*The Puddle Pail*), born Los Angeles, CA, Oct 14, 1958.

OCTOBER 15 — SUNDAY

Day 289 — 77 Remaining

AMERICA'S SAFE SCHOOLS WEEK. Oct 15–21. To motivate key education and law enforcement policymakers, as well as parents, students and community residents, to vigorously advocate schools that are safe and free of violence, weapons and drugs. Annually, the third week in October, from Sunday–Saturday. For info: Natl School Safety Center, 141 Duesenberg Dr, Ste 11, Westlake Village, CA 91362. Phone: (805) 373-9977. Web: www .nssc1.org.

CROW RESERVATION OPENED FOR SETTLEMENT: ANNIVERSARY. Oct 15, 1892. By Presidential Proclamation 1.8 million acres of Crow Indian reservation were opened to settlers. The government had induced the Crow to give up a portion of their land in the mountainous western area in the state of Montana, for which they received 50 cents per acre.

FIRST MANNED FLIGHT: ANNIVERSARY. Oct 15, 1783. Jean Francois Pilatre de Rozier and Francois Laurent, Marquis d'Arlandes became the first people to fly when they ascended in a Montgolfier hot-air balloon at Paris, France, less than three months after the first public balloon flight demonstration (June 5, 1783), and only a year after the first experiments with small paper and fabric balloons by the Montgolfier brothers, Joseph and Jacques, in November 1782. The first manned free flight lasted about 4 minutes and carried the passengers at a height of about 84 feet. On Nov 21, 1783, they soared 3,000 feet over Paris for 25 minutes.

"I LOVE LUCY" TV PREMIERE: ANNIVERSARY. Oct 15, 1951. This enormously popular sitcom, TV's first smash hit, starred the real-life husband and wife team of Cuban actor/bandleader Desi Arnaz and talented redheaded actress/comedienne Lucille Ball. They played Ricky and Lucy Ricardo, a New York bandleader and his aspiring actress/homemaker wife who was always scheming to get on stage. Costarring were William Frawley and Vivian Vance as Fred and Ethel Mertz, the Ricardos' landlords and good friends. This was the first sitcom to be filmed live before a studio audience and it did extremely well in the ratings both the first time around and in reruns.

MY MOM IS A STUDENT DAY. Oct 15. Kids can show their support to their moms by treating them with new pens, paper clips and other little school supplies. They can also fix mom a school

October 2000	S	M	T	W	T	F	S
	1	2	3	4	5	6	7
	8	9	10	11	12	13	14
	15	16	17	18	19	20	21
	22	23	24	24	26	27	28
	29	30	31				

lunch with a supportive note inside. Annually, Oct 15. For info: Patti Veld, c/o Davenport College Library, 8200 Georgia St, Merrillville, IN 46410.

★**NATIONAL CHARACTER COUNTS WEEK.** Oct 15–21. One of the greatest building blocks of character is citizen service. The future belongs to those who have the strength of character to live a life of service to others.

★**NATIONAL FOREST PRODUCTS WEEK.** Oct 15–21. Presidential Proclamation always issued for the week beginning with the third Sunday in October since 1960 (PL86–753 of Sept 13, 1960).

NATIONAL GROUCH DAY. Oct 15. Honor a grouch. All grouches deserve a day to be recognized. Annually, Oct 15. For info: Alan R. Miller, Carter Middle School, 300 Upland Dr, Room 207, Clio, MI 48420. Phone: (810) 591-0503.

NATIONAL SCHOOL BUS SAFETY WEEK. Oct 15–21. This week is set aside to focus attention on school bus safety—from the standpoint of the bus drivers, students and the motoring public. Annually, the third full week of October, starting on Sunday. For info: Natl School Bus Safety Week Committee, PO Box 2639, Springfield, VA 22152.

SPACE MILESTONE: *CASSINI* (US). Oct 15, 1997. This plutonium-powered spacecraft is to arrive at Saturn in July 2004. It will orbit the planet, take pictures of its 18 known moons and dispatch a probe to Titan, the largest of these moons.

TEEN READ WEEK. Oct 15–21. The teen years are a time when many kids reject reading as being just another dreary assignment. The goal of Teen Read Week is to encourage young adults to read for sheer pleasure as well as learning. Also to remind parents, teachers and others that reading for fun is important for teens as well as young children and to increase awareness of the resources available at libraries. For info: Young Adult Library Services Assn, American Library Assn, 50 E Huron St, Chicago, IL 60611. Phone: (800) 545-2433, ext 4390. E-mail: yalsa@ala.org. Web: www.ala .org/teenread.

★**WHITE CANE SAFETY DAY.** Oct 15. Presidential Proclamation always issued for Oct 15 since 1964 (PL88–628 of Oct 6, 1964).

WILSON, EDITH BOLLING GALT: BIRTH ANNIVERSARY. Oct 15, 1872. Second wife of Woodrow Wilson, 28th president of the US, born at Wytheville, VA. She died at Washington, DC, Dec 28, 1961.

BIRTHDAYS TODAY

Barry Moser, 60, illustrator (*The Bird House*), born Chattanooga, TN, Oct 15, 1940.

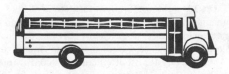

OCTOBER 16 — MONDAY

Day 290 — 76 Remaining

AMERICA'S FIRST DEPARTMENT STORE: ANNIVERSARY. Oct 16, 1868. Salt Lake City, UT. America's first department store, "ZCMI" (Zion's Co-Operative Mercantile Institution), is still operating at Salt Lake City. It was founded under the direction of Brigham Young. For info: Museum of Church History and Art, 45 North West Temple, Salt Lake City, UT 84150. Phone: (801) 240-4604.

BEN-GURION, DAVID: BIRTH ANNIVERSARY. Oct 16, 1886. First prime minister of the state of Israel. Born at Plonsk, Poland, he died at Tel Aviv, Israel, Dec 1, 1973.

DICTIONARY DAY. Oct 16. The birthday of Noah Webster, American teacher and lexicographer, is occasion to encourage every person to acquire at least one dictionary—and to use it regularly.

DOUGLAS, WILLIAM ORVILLE: BIRTH ANNIVERSARY. Oct 16, 1898. American jurist, world traveler, conservationist, outdoorsman and author. Born at Maine, MN, he served as justice of the US Supreme Court longer than any other justice (36 years). Died at Washington, DC, Jan 19, 1980.

GRANT PUT IN CHARGE OF THE MISSISSIPPI REGION: ANNIVERSARY. Oct 16, 1863. After his impressive success taking Vicksburg, MS, Ulysses S. Grant, a brigadier general of the militia, was appointed a general in the regular army and, with the subsequent reorganization of the departments of war at Ohio, Cumberland and Tennessee, was placed in charge of the newly formed Military Division of the Mississippi. Grant's first priority was to save the besieged and starving Union troops at Chattanooga, TN.

JAMAICA: NATIONAL HEROES DAY. Oct 16. National holiday established in 1969. Always observed on third Monday of October.

JOHN BROWN'S RAID: ANNIVERSARY. Oct 16, 1859. Abolitionist John Brown, with a band of about 20 men, seized the US Arsenal at Harpers Ferry, WV. Brown was captured and the insurrection put down by Oct 19. Brown was hanged at Charles Town, VA (now WV), Dec 2, 1859.

MILLION MAN MARCH: ANNIVERSARY. Oct 16, 1995. Hundreds of thousands of black men met at Washington, DC, for a "holy day of atonement and reconciliation" organized by Louis Farrakhan, leader of the Nation of Islam. Marchers pledged to take responsibility for themselves, their families and their communities.

NATIONAL HEALTH EDUCATION WEEK. Oct 16–22. Annually, the third week in October. For info: Lynne Whitt, Natl Center for Health Education, 72 Spring St, Ste 208, New York, NY 10012. Phone: (212) 334-9470.

UNITED NATIONS: WORLD FOOD DAY. Oct 16. Annual observance to heighten public awareness of the world food problem and to strengthen solidarity in the struggle against hunger, malnutrition and poverty. Date of observance is anniversary of the founding of the Food and Agriculture Organization (FAO), Oct 16, 1945, at Quebec, Canada. For info: United Nations, Dept of Public Info, New York, NY 10017.

VIRGIN ISLANDS: HURRICANE THANKSGIVING DAY. Oct 16. Third Monday of October is a legal holiday celebrating the end of hurricane season.

WEBSTER, NOAH: BIRTH ANNIVERSARY. Oct 16, 1758. American teacher and journalist whose name became synonymous with the word "dictionary" after his compilations of the earliest American dictionaries of the English language. Born at West Hartford, CT, he died at New Haven, CT, May 28, 1843.

WORLD FOOD DAY. Oct 16. To increase awareness, understanding and informed action on hunger. Annually, on the founding date of the UN Food and Agriculture Organization. For info: Patricia Young, US Natl Committee for World Food Day, 2175 K St NW, Washington, DC 20437. Phone: (202) 653-2404. Web: www.gsu.edu/~wwwwfd.

Joseph Bruchac, 58, author (*The Boy Who Lived with Bears and Other Iroquois Stories*), born Saratoga Springs, NY, Oct 16, 1942.

Paul Kariya, 26, hockey player, born Vancouver, British Columbia, Canada, Oct 16, 1974.

Kordell Stewart, 28, football player, born New Orleans, LA, Oct 16, 1972.

OCTOBER 17 — TUESDAY
Day 291 — 75 Remaining

BLACK POETRY DAY. Oct 17 (tentative). To recognize the contribution of black poets to American life and culture and to honor Jupiter Hammon, the first black in America to publish his own verse. Jupiter Hammon of Huntington, Long Island, NY, was born Oct 17, 1711. For info: Alexis Levitin, Black Poetry Day Committee, Dept of English, SUNY-Plattsburgh, Plattsburgh, NY 12901-2681. Phone: (518) 564-2426. Fax: (518) 564-2140. E-mail: levitia @splava.cc.plattsburgh.edu.

HAMMON, JUPITER: BIRTH ANNIVERSARY. Oct 17, 1711. America's first published black poet, whose birth anniversary is celebrated annually as Black Poetry Day, was born into slavery, probably at Long Island, NY. He was taught to read, however, and as a trusted servant was allowed to use his master's library. "With the publication on Christmas Day, 1760, of the 88-line broadside poem 'An Evening Thought,' Jupiter Hammon, then 49, became the first black in America to publish poetry." Hammon died in 1790. The exact date and place of his death are unknown.

JOHNSON, RICHARD MENTOR: BIRTH ANNIVERSARY. Oct 17, 1780. Ninth vice president of the US (1837–41). Born at Floyd's Station, KY, he died at Frankfort, KY, Nov 19, 1850.

POPE JOHN PAUL I: BIRTH ANNIVERSARY. Oct 17, 1912. Albino Luciani, 263rd pope of the Roman Catholic Church. Born at Forno di Canale, Italy, he was elected pope Aug 26, 1978. Died at Rome, 34 days after his election, Sept 28, 1978. Shortest papacy since Pope Leo XI (Apr 1–27, 1605).

SAN FRANCISCO 1989 EARTHQUAKE: ANNIVERSARY. Oct 17, 1989. The San Francisco Bay area was rocked by an earthquake registering 7.1 on the Richter scale at 5:04 PM, EDT, just as the nation's baseball fans settled in to watch the 1989 World Series. A large audience was tuned in to the pregame coverage when the quake hit and knocked the broadcast off the air. The quake caused damage estimated at $10 billion and killed 67 people, many of whom were caught in the collapse of the double-decked Interstate 80, at Oakland, CA.

UNITED NATIONS: INTERNATIONAL DAY FOR THE ERADICATION OF POVERTY. Oct 17. The General Assembly proclaimed this observance (Res 47/196) to promote public awareness of the need to eradicate poverty and destitution in all countries, particularly the developing nations. For more info, go to the UN's website for children at www.un.org/Pubs/Cyber-SchoolBus/.

Brandon Call, 24, actor ("Step By Step"), born Torrance, CA, Oct 17, 1976.

		S	M	T	W	T	F	S
October		1	2	3	4	5	6	7
2000		8	9	10	11	12	13	14
		15	16	17	18	19	20	21
		22	23	24	24	26	27	28
		29	30	31				

Judith Caseley, 49, author (*When Grandpa Came to Stay*), born Rahway, NJ, Oct 17, 1951.

Alan Garner, 66, author (*The Stone Book*), born Congleton, England, Oct 17, 1934.

Mae Jemison, 44, scientist, astronaut, host ("Susan B. Anthony Slept Here"), born Decatur, AL, Oct 17, 1956.

Chris Kirkpatrick, 29, singer ('N Sync), born Pittsburgh, PA, Oct 17, 1971.

OCTOBER 18 — WEDNESDAY
Day 292 — 74 Remaining

ALASKA DAY. Oct 18. Alaska. Anniversary of transfer of Alaska from Russia to the US which became official on Sitka's Castle Hill in 1867. This is a holiday in Alaska; when it falls on a weekend it is observed on the following Monday.

MISSOURI DAY. Oct 18. Observed by teachers and pupils of schools with appropriate exercises throughout the state of Missouri. Annually, the third Wednesday of October.

SAINT LUKE: FEAST DAY. Oct 18. Patron saint of doctors and artists, himself a physician and painter, authorship of the third Gospel and Acts of the Apostles is attributed to him. Died about AD 68. Legend says that he painted portraits of Mary and Jesus.

SILVERSTEIN, SHEL: BIRTH ANNIVERSARY. Oct 18, 1932. Cartoonist and children's author, best remembered for his poetry that included *A Light in the Attic* and *The Giving Tree*. Silverstein won the Michigan Young Reader's Award for *Where The Sidewalk Ends*. Also a songwriter, he wrote "The Unicorn Song" and "A Boy Named Sue" for Johnny Cash. Born at Chicago, IL, he died at Key West, FL, May 9, 1999.

WATER POLLUTION CONTROL ACT: ANNIVERSARY. Oct 18, 1972. Overriding President Nixon's veto, Congress passed a $25 billion Water Pollution Control Act.

Joyce Hansen, 58, author (*I Thought My Soul Would Rise and Fly: The Diary of Patsy, a Freed Girl*), born New York, NY, Oct 18, 1942.

Jesse Helms, 79, US Senator (R, North Carolina), born Monroe, NC, Oct 18, 1921.

OCTOBER 19 — THURSDAY
Day 293 — 73 Remaining

JEFFERSON, MARTHA WAYLES SKELTON: BIRTH ANNIVERSARY. Oct 19, 1748. Wife of Thomas Jefferson, third president of the US. Born at Charles City County, VA, she died at Monticello, VA, Sept 6, 1782.

YORKTOWN DAY: "AMERICA'S REAL INDEPENDENCE DAY." Oct 19. Yorktown, VA. Representatives of the US, France and other nations involved in the American Revolution gather to celebrate the anniversary of the victory (Oct 19, 1781) that assured American independence. Parade and commemorative ceremonies. Annually, Oct 19. Est attendance: 2,000. For info: Public Affairs Officer, Colonial National Historical Park, Box 210, Yorktown, VA 23690. Phone: (757) 898-3400. Web: www.nps.gov /colo.

YORKTOWN DAY: ANNIVERSARY. Oct 19, 1781. More than 7,000 English and Hessian troops, led by British General Lord Cornwallis, surrendered to General George Washington at Yorktown, VA, effectively ending the war between Britain and her American colonies. There were no more major battles, but the provisional treaty of peace was not signed until Nov 30, 1782, and the final Treaty of Paris, Sept 3, 1783.

BIRTHDAYS TODAY

Philip Pullman, 54, author (*The Subtle Knife, His Dark Materials*), born Norwich, England, Oct 19, 1946.

OCTOBER 20 — FRIDAY
Day 294 — 72 Remaining

DEWEY, JOHN: BIRTH ANNIVERSARY. Oct 20, 1859. Philosopher of education, born near Burlington, VT. A professor at the University of Chicago and Columbia University, Dewey was committed to child-centered education, learning by doing and integrating schools with the outside world. He died at New York, NY, June 2, 1952.

GUATEMALA: REVOLUTION DAY. Oct 20. Public holiday in Guatemala.

JOHNSON, CROCKETT: BIRTH ANNIVERSARY. Oct 20, 1906. Author (*Harold and the Purple Crayon*), born David Leisk at New York, NY. Died July 11, 1975.

KENYA: KENYATTA DAY. Oct 20. Observed as a public holiday. Honors Jomo Kenyatta, first president of Kenya.

MacARTHUR RETURNS TO THE PHILIPPINES: ANNIVERSARY. Oct 20, 1944. In mid-September of 1944 American military leaders made the decision to begin the invasion of the Philippines on Leyte, a small island north of the Surigao Strait. With General Douglas MacArthur in overall command, US aircraft dropped hundreds of tons of bombs in the area of Dulag. Four divisions landed on the east coast, and after a few hours General MacArthur set foot on Philippine soil for the first time since he was ordered to Australia Mar 11, 1942, thus fulfilling his promise, "I shall return."

MANTLE, MICKEY: BIRTH ANNIVERSARY. Oct 20, 1931. Baseball Hall of Famer, born at Spavinaw, OK. Died Aug 13, 1995, at Dallas, TX.

MOON PHASE: LAST QUARTER. Oct 20. Moon enters Last Quarter phase at 3:59 AM, EDT.

BIRTHDAYS TODAY

Peter Fitzgerald, 40, US Senator (R, Illinois), born Elgin, IL, Oct 20, 1960.

Nikki Grimes, 50, poet and author (*Meet Danitra Brown*), also writes as Naomi McMillen, born New York, NY, Oct 20, 1950.

Eddie Jones, 29, basketball player, born Pompano Beach, FL, Oct 20, 1971.

OCTOBER 21 — SATURDAY
Day 295 — 71 Remaining

THE DAY OF NATIONAL CONCERN ABOUT YOUNG PEOPLE AND GUN VIOLENCE. Oct 21. Students are encouraged on this day to sign a pledge that they will never carry a gun to school or resolve a dispute with a gun and they will urge their friends to do the same. More than 1,000,000 middle and high school students have signed the Pledge Against Gun Violence. For info: Student Pledge Against Gun Violence, 112 Nevada St, Northfield, MN 55057. Phone: (507) 645-5378. Web: www.pledge.org.

FILLMORE, CAROLINE CARMICHAEL McINTOSH: BIRTH ANNIVERSARY. Oct 21, 1813. Second wife of Millard Fillmore, 13th president of the US, born at Morristown, NJ. Died at New York, NY, Aug 11, 1881.

INCANDESCENT LAMP DEMONSTRATED: ANNIVERSARY. Oct 21, 1879. Thomas A. Edison demonstrated the first incandescent lamp that could be used economically for domestic purposes. This prototype, developed at his Menlo Park, NJ, laboratory, could burn for 13-½ hours.

NOBEL, ALFRED BERNHARD: BIRTH ANNIVERSARY. Oct 21, 1833. Swedish chemist and engineer who invented dynamite was born at Stockholm, Sweden, and died at San Remo, Italy, Dec 10, 1896. His will established the Nobel Prize. See also "Nobel Prize Awards Ceremonies" (Dec 10). For more info: www.nobel.se.

SHEMINI ATZERET. Oct 21. Hebrew calendar date: Tishri 22, 5761. The eighth day of Solemn Assembly, part of the Sukkot Festival (see entry on Oct 14), with memorial services and cycle of Biblical readings in the synagogue.

SOMALIA DEMOCRATIC REPUBLIC: NATIONAL DAY. Oct 21. National holiday. Anniversary of the revolution.

TAIWAN: OVERSEAS CHINESE DAY. Oct 21. Thousands of overseas Chinese come to Taiwan for this and other occasions that make October a particularly memorable month.

WORLD RAINFOREST WEEK. Oct 21–29. Rainforest activists from 140 worldwide action groups will sponsor events to increase public awareness of rainforest destruction and motivate people to protect the Earth's rainforest and support the rights of their inhabitants. The global rate of destruction of rainforests is 2.4 acres per second—equivalent to two US football fields. For info: M. Holmgren, Grassroots Coord, Rainforest Action Network, 221 Pine St, 5th Floor, San Francisco, CA 94104. Phone: (415) 398-4404. E-mail: rags@ran.org. Web: www.ran.org.

BIRTHDAYS TODAY

Janet Ahlberg, 56, illustrator (*The Jolly Postman*), born Croydon, England, Oct 21, 1944.

Nakia Burrise, 26, actress (*Turbo: A Power Rangers Movie*, "Power Rangers Turbo"), born San Diego, CA, Oct 21, 1974.

Ann Cameron, 57, author (*The Most Beautiful Place in the World*), born Rice Lake, WI, Oct 21, 1943.

Ursula K. Le Guin, 71, author of science fiction (*The Tombs of Atuan*), born Berkeley, CA, Oct 21, 1929.

Jeremy Miller, 24, actor ("Growing Pains"), born West Covina, CA, Oct 21, 1976.

OCTOBER 22 — SUNDAY
Day 296 — 70 Remaining

FOXX, JIMMIE: BIRTH ANNIVERSARY. Oct 22, 1907. Baseball Hall of Fame first baseman, born at Sudlersville, MD. Died at Miami, FL, July 21, 1967.

HOLY SEE: NATIONAL HOLIDAY. Oct 22. The state of Vatican City and the Holy See observe Oct 22 as a national holiday.

LISZT, FRANZ: BIRTH ANNIVERSARY. Oct 22, 1811. Hungarian pianist and composer (*Hungarian Rhapsodies*). Born at Raiding, Hungary, he died July 31, 1886, at Bayreuth, Germany.

RANDOLPH, PEYTON: 225th DEATH ANNIVERSARY. Oct 22, 1775. First president of the Continental Congress, died at Philadelphia, PA. Born about 1721 (exact date unknown), at Williamsburg, VA.

SIMCHAT TORAH. Oct 22. Hebrew calendar date: Tishri 23, 5761. Rejoicing in the Torah concludes the nine-day Sukkot Festival (see entry on Oct 14). Public reading of the Pentateuch is completed and begun again, symbolizing the need for ever-continuing study.

BIRTHDAYS TODAY

Brian Anthony Boitano, 37, Olympic gold medal figure skater, born Mountain View, CA, Oct 22, 1963.

Jeff Goldblum, 48, actor (*The Lost World: Jurassic Park*), born Pittsburgh, PA, Oct 22, 1952.

Zachary Walker Hanson, 15, singer (Hanson), born Arlington, VA, Oct 22, 1985.

Bill Owens, 50, Governor of Colorado (R), born Fort Worth, TX, Oct 22, 1950.

OCTOBER 23 — MONDAY
Day 297 — 69 Remaining

APPERT, NICOLAS: BIRTH ANNIVERSARY. Oct 23, 1752. Also known as "Canning Day," this is the anniversary of the birth of French chef, chemist, confectioner, inventor and author Nicolas Appert, at Chalons-Sur-Marne. Appert, who also invented the bouillon tablet, is best remembered for devising a system of heating foods and sealing them in airtight containers. Known as the "father of canning," Appert won a prize of 12,000 francs from the French government in 1809, and the title "Benefactor of Humanity" in 1812, for his inventions which revolutionized our previously seasonal diet. Appert died at Massy, France, June 3, 1841.

HUNGARY: ANNIVERSARY OF 1956 REVOLUTION. Oct 23. National holiday.

HUNGARY DECLARED INDEPENDENT: ANNIVERSARY. Oct 23, 1989. Hungary declared itself an independent republic, 33 years after Russian troops crushed a popular revolt against Soviet rule. The announcement followed a week-long purge by Parliament of the Stalinist elements from Hungary's 1949 constitution, which defined the country as a socialist people's republic. Acting head of state Matyas Szuros made the declaration in front of tens of thousands of Hungarians at Parliament Square, speaking from the same balcony from which Imre Nagy addressed rebels 33 years earlier. Nagy was hanged for treason after Soviet intervention. Free elections held in March 1990 removed the Communist party to the ranks of the opposition for the first time in four decades.

October 2000	S	M	T	W	T	F	S
	1	2	3	4	5	6	7
	8	9	10	11	12	13	14
	15	16	17	18	19	20	21
	22	23	24	24	26	27	28
	29	30	31				

SCORPIO, THE SCORPION. Oct 23–Nov 22. In the astronomical/astrological zodiac that divides the sun's apparent orbit into 12 segments, the period Oct 23–Nov 22 is identified, traditionally, as the sun sign of Scorpio, the Scorpion. The ruling planet is Pluto or Mars.

STEVENSON, ADLAI EWING: BIRTH ANNIVERSARY. Oct 23, 1835. The 23rd vice president of the US (1893–97), born at Christian County, KY. Died at Chicago, IL, June 14, 1914. He was grandfather of Adlai E. Stevenson, the Democratic candidate for president in 1952 and 1956.

THAILAND: CHULALONGKORN DAY. Oct 23. Annual commemoration of the death of King Chulalongkorn the Great, who died Oct 23, 1910, after a 42-year reign. King Chulalongkorn abolished slavery in Thailand. Special ceremonies with floral tributes and incense at the foot of his equestrian statue in front of Bangkok's National Assembly Hall.

BIRTHDAYS TODAY

Laurie Halse Anderson, 39, author (*Speak*), born Potsdam, NY, Oct 23, 1961.

Jim Bunning, 69, US Senator (R, Kentucky), born Southgate, KY, Oct 23, 1931.

Pele, 60, former soccer player, born Edson Arantes do Nascimento, Tres Coracoes, Brazil, Oct 23, 1940.

Keith Van Horn, 25, basketball player, born Fullerton, CA, Oct 23, 1975.

"Weird Al" Yankovic, 41, singer, satirist ("The Weird Al Show"), born Lynwood, CA, Oct 23, 1959.

OCTOBER 24 — TUESDAY
Day 298 — 68 Remaining

SHERMAN, JAMES SCHOOLCRAFT: BIRTH ANNIVERSARY. Oct 24, 1855. The 27th vice president of the US (1909–12), born at Utica, NY. Died there Oct 30, 1912.

★**UNITED NATIONS DAY.** Oct 24. Presidential Proclamation. Always issued for Oct 24 since 1948. (By unanimous request of the UN General Assembly.)

UNITED NATIONS DAY: 55th ANNIVERSARY OF FOUNDING. Oct 24, 1945. Official United Nations holiday commemorates founding of the United Nations and effective date of the United Nations Charter. In 1971 the General Assembly recommended this day be observed as a public holiday by UN Member States (Res 2782/xxvi). For more info, visit the UN's website for children at www.un.org/Pubs/CyberSchoolBus/.

UNITED NATIONS: DISARMAMENT WEEK. Oct 24–30. In 1978, the General Assembly called on member states to highlight the danger of the arms race, propagate the need for its cessation and increase public understanding of the urgent task of disarmament. Observed annually, beginning on the anniversary of the founding of the UN.

UNITED NATIONS: WORLD DEVELOPMENT INFORMATION DAY. Oct 24. Anniversary of adoption by United Nations General Assembly, in 1970, of the International Development Strategy for the Second United Nations Development Decade. Object is to "draw the attention of the world public opinion each year to development problems and the necessity of strengthening international cooperation to solve them." For info: United Nations, Dept of Public Info, New York, NY 10017.

ZAMBIA: INDEPENDENCE DAY: ANNIVERSARY. Oct 24. Zambia. National holiday commemorates independence of what was then Northern Rhodesia from Britain in 1964. Celebrations in all cities, but main parades of military, labor and youth organizations are at capital, Lusaka.

Kweisi Mfume, 52, NAACP president, born Baltimore, MD, Oct 24, 1948.

Monica, 20, singer, born Monica Arnold, Atlanta, GA, Oct 24, 1980.

Catherine Sutherland, 26, actress (*Turbo: A Power Rangers Movie*, "Power Rangers Turbo"), born Sydney, Australia, Oct 24, 1974.

OCTOBER 25 — WEDNESDAY

Day 299 — 67 Remaining

ISRA AL MI'RAJ: ASCENT OF THE PROPHET MUHAMMAD. Oct 25. Islamic calendar date: Rajab 27, 1421. Commemorates the journey of the Prophet Muhammad from Mecca to Jerusalem, his ascension into the Seven Heavens and his return on the same night. Muslims believe that on that night Muhammad prayed together with Abraham, Moses and Jesus in the area of the Al-Aqsa Mosque at Jerusalem. The rock from which he is believed to have ascended to heaven to speak with God is the one inside The Dome of the Rock. Different methods for "anticipating" the visibility of the new moon crescent at Mecca are used by different Muslim groups. US date may vary.

NATIONAL FFA CONVENTION. Oct 25–28. Kentucky Fair & Exposition Center, Louisville, KY. This 73rd annual convention is an opportunity for recognition, business, elections and celebration. Delegates from each state discuss topics affecting the national agriculture education organization and elect a new team of national officers. Students compete in final rounds of leadership and career events and learn about education and career opportunities in a 300-exhibitor career show. Est attendance: 45,000. For info: Natl FFA Organization, 1410 King St, Ste 400, Alexandria, VA 22314. Phone: (800) 772-0939 or (703) 838-5889. E-mail: aboutffa@ffa.org. Web: www.ffa.org.

PICASSO, PABLO RUIZ: BIRTH ANNIVERSARY. Oct 25, 1881. Called by many the greatest artist of the 20th century, Pablo Picasso excelled as a painter, sculptor and engraver. He is said to have commented once: "I am only a public entertainer who has understood his time." Born at Malaga, Spain, he died Apr 9, 1973, at Mougins, France. For more info: *Picasso*, by Stefano Loria (Peter Bedrick, 0-87226-318-5, $22.50 Gr. 4–7).

STATE CONSTITUTION DAY IN MASSACHUSETTS. Oct 25. Proclaimed annually by the governor to commemorate the adoption of the state constitution in 1780.

TAIWAN: RETROCESSION DAY: 55th ANNIVERSARY. Oct 25. Commemorates restoration of Taiwan to Chinese rule in 1945, after half a century of Japanese occupation.

TECHNOLOGY + LEARNING CONFERENCE. Oct 25–28. Denver, CO. The 14th annual conference will bring together 3,000 K–12 educators to see what's new, share experiences and find out what's working in every area of education technology. Sponsored by the National School Board Association and cosponsored by 25 education organizations. Workshops, roundtables, exhibits and more. For info: Natl School Boards Assn, 1680 Duke St, Alexandria, VA 22314. Phone: (703) 838-6722. E-mail: info@nsba.org. Web: www.nsba.org.

Brad Gilchrist, 41, cartoonist ("Nancy"), works with his brother Guy Gilchrist, born Torrington, CT, Oct 25, 1959.

Benjamin Gould, 20, actor ("Saved By the Bell: The New Class"), born Sacramento, CA, Oct 25, 1980.

Pedro Martinez, 29, baseball player, born Manoguyabo, Dominican Republic, Oct 25, 1971.

Midori, 29, violinist, born Osaka, Japan, Oct 25, 1971.

OCTOBER 26 — THURSDAY

Day 300 — 66 Remaining

AUSTRIA: NATIONAL DAY. Oct 26. National holiday observed.

ERIE CANAL: 175th ANNIVERSARY. Oct 26, 1825. The Erie Canal, first US major man-made waterway, was opened, providing a water route from Lake Erie to the Hudson River. Construction started July 4, 1817, and the canal cost $7,602,000. Cannons fired and celebrations were held all along the route for the opening. For more info: *The Amazing, Impossible Erie Canal*, by Cheryl Harness (S&S, 0-02-742641-6, $16 Gr. 3–8) or the New York State Canal System's website at www.canals.state.ny.us/.

INDIA: DIWALI (DEEPAVALI). Oct 26. Diwali (or Divali), the five-day festival of lights, is the prettiest of all Indian festivals. It celebrates the victory of Lord Rama over the demon king Ravana. Thousands of flickering lights illuminate houses and transform the drab urban landscape of cities and towns while fireworks add color and noise. The goddess of wealth, Lakshmi, is worshipped in Hindu homes on Diwali. Houses are white-washed and cleaned and elaborate designs drawn on thresholds with colored powder to welcome the fastidious goddess. Because there is no one universally accepted Hindu calendar, this holiday may be celebrated on a different date in some parts of India but it always falls in the months of October or November. For more info: *Divali*, by Dilip Kadodwala (Raintree, 0-8172-4616-9, $22.11 Gr. 4–6).

MULE DAY. Oct 26. Anniversary of the first importation of Spanish jacks to the US, a gift from King Charles III of Spain. Mules are said to have been bred first in this country by George Washington from a pair delivered at Boston, Oct 26, 1785.

STATE FAIR OF LOUISIANA. Oct 26–Nov 5. Fairgrounds, Shreveport, LA. Educational, agricultural, commercial exhibits, entertainment. Est attendance: 250,000. For info: Sam Giordano, Pres/General Mgr, Louisiana State Fairgrounds, PO Box 38327, Shreveport, LA 71133. Phone: (318) 635-1361. Fax: (318) 631-4909.

Hillary Rodham Clinton, 53, First Lady, wife of Bill Clinton, 42nd president of the US, born Park Ridge, IL, Oct 26, 1947.

Steven Kellogg, 59, author and illustrator (*Can I Keep Him?*, *Chicken Little*), born Norwalk, CT, Oct 26, 1941.

Natalie Merchant, 37, singer, born Jamestown, NY, Oct 26, 1963.

OCTOBER 27 — FRIDAY

Day 301 — 65 Remaining

BAGNOLD, ENID: BIRTH ANNIVERSARY. Oct 27, 1889. Novelist and playwright (*National Velvet*), born at Rochester, Kent, England. She died at London, England, Mar 31, 1981.

COOK, JAMES: BIRTH ANNIVERSARY. Oct 27, 1728. English sea captain and explorer who discovered the Hawaiian Islands and brought Australia and New Zealand into the British Empire. Born at Marton-in-Cleveland, Yorkshire, England and was killed Feb 14, 1779, at Hawaii.

HURRICANE MITCH: ANNIVERSARY. Oct 27, 1998. More than 6,000 people were killed in Honduras by flooding caused by Hurricane Mitch. Several thousand more were killed in other Central American countries, especially Nicaragua. On Sept 21, 1974, more than 8,000 people had been killed in Honduras by flooding caused by a hurricane.

MOON PHASE: NEW MOON. Oct 27. Moon enters New Moon phase at 3:58 AM, EDT.

NAVY DAY. Oct 27. Observed since 1922.

NEW YORK CITY SUBWAY: ANNIVERSARY. Oct 27, 1904. Running from City Hall to West 145th Street, the New York City subway began operation. It was privately operated by the Interborough Rapid Transit Company and later became part of the system operated by the New York City Transit Authority.

ROOSEVELT, THEODORE: BIRTH ANNIVERSARY. Oct 27, 1858. The 26th president of the US, succeeded to the presidency on the assassination of William McKinley. He was the youngest man to have ever served as president of the US. His term of office: Sept 14, 1901–Mar 3, 1909. Roosevelt was the first president to ride in an automobile (1902), to submerge in a submarine (1905) and to fly in an airplane (1910). Although his best remembered quote is, "Speak softly and carry a big stick," he also said, "The first requisite of a good citizen in this Republic of ours is that he shall be able and willing to pull his weight." Born at New York, NY, Roosevelt died at Oyster Bay, NY, Jan 6, 1919. For more info: *Bully for You, Teddy Roosevelt!*, by Jean Fritz (Putnam, 0-399-21769-X, $15.99, Gr. 7–9). *See* Curriculum Connection.

SAINT VINCENT AND THE GRENADINES: INDEPENDENCE DAY. Oct 27. National Day.

TURKMENISTAN: INDEPENDENCE DAY. Oct 27. National holiday. Commemorates independence from the Soviet Union in 1991.

October 2000

S	M	T	W	T	F	S
1	2	3	4	5	6	7
8	9	10	11	12	13	14
15	16	17	18	19	20	21
22	23	24	24	26	27	28
29	30	31				

OCTOBER 27
THEODORE ROOSEVELT'S BIRTHDAY

Theodore "Teddy" Roosevelt, born in 1858, was one of the four children of Theodore and Martha Roosevelt. As a child Teddy was somewhat frail, very nearsighted and suffered from asthma. He was an avid reader and liked learning about nature and being outdoors. Indoors, he maintained a large collection of dead animals that he had brought to his room for nature study. By the time he reached his teen years, Teddy had become a fitness devotee and frequently exercised in the family's home gym. His workouts helped him to overcome his asthma and enabled him to pursue boxing, hiking and hunting.

After graduating from Harvard University, Teddy served in the New York State Assembly for several years. He left politics after his wife and his mother died in 1884 and he "retired" to the Dakota Territory, where he ran two cattle ranches. Two years later, he was back in New York and had remarried.

During the Spanish-American War, Teddy organized and commanded the cavalry unit known as the Rough Riders. The regiment's success during the war made Teddy a national hero. He was elected governor of New York. In 1900, he was elected vice president of the United States. He became president in 1901, when President McKinley was assassinated.

Teddy was an avid hunter, but he was also concerned about preserving natural areas. He established the first federal wildlife refuge and added more than 100 million acres to the nation's forest reserve areas.

Students will enjoy meeting Teddy Roosevelt. One way to celebrate his birthday is with a Teddy Bear School Visit Day. The toy bears were named after Roosevelt. Students might have fun researching that story and the political cartoon that gave rise to the name. Roosevelt was also well-known for "Bully!," his energetic shout of approval. Language arts fun could involve writing stories to explain how the phrase came about.

Roosevelt approved a treaty with Panama that granted the United States control over a narrow strip of land in that country. That led to the construction of the Panama Canal, which Teddy considered one of his greatest achievements. Older students can investigate and discuss the importance of the canal to shipping and trade and the hand-over of its control to Panama at the end of 1999.

The Roosevelt children were a rowdy bunch. A bit of research will turn up amusing stories about their many White House adventures.

Teddy Roosevelt was the first U.S. president to have much of his life chronicled on film. Recently, more than 100 films in the Library of Congress's film collection were made available on the Web. Students can get a firsthand glimpse of this energetic man at www.loc.gov/ammem/trfh.tml.

Literature connections include: *Young Teddy Roosevelt*, by Cheryl Harness (National Geographic, 0-7922-7094-0, $17.95 Gr. 2–5); and *Bully for You, Teddy Roosevelt*, by Jean Fritz (Paperstar, 0-698-11609-7, $5.95 Gr. 5–8).

"WALT DISNEY" TV PREMIERE: ANNIVERSARY. Oct 27, 1954. This highly successful and long-running show appeared on different networks under different names but was essentially the same show. It was the first ABC series to break the Nielsen's Top Twenty and the first prime-time anthology series for kids. "Walt Disney" was originally titled "Disneyland" to promote the park and upcoming Disney releases. Later the title was changed to "Walt Disney Presents." When it switched networks, it was called "Walt Disney's Wonderful World of Color" to highlight its being broadcast in color. Future titles included "The Wonderful World of Disney," "Disney's Wonderful World," "The Disney Sunday Movie" and "The Magical World of Disney." Presentations included edited versions of previously released Disney films and original productions (including natural history documentaries, behind-the-scenes at Disney shows and dramatic shows, including the popular Davy Crockett segments that were the first TV miniseries). The show went off the air in December 1980 after 25 years, making it the longest-running series in prime-time TV history.

BIRTHDAYS TODAY

Brad Radke, 28, baseball player, born Eau Claire, WI, Oct 27, 1972.

OCTOBER 28 — SATURDAY
Day 302 — 64 Remaining

CHILDREN'S LITERATURE FESTIVAL. Oct 28. Keene State College, Keene, NH. To promote the reading, studying and use of children's literature. Speakers for the festival include Phyllis Reynolds Naylor, P.J. Lynch, Mark Teague, Janet Stevens and Denise Fleming. For info: Dr. David E. White, Festival Dir, Keene State College, 229 Main St, Keene, NH 03435. Phone: (603) 358-2302. E-mail: dwhite@keene.edu. Web: www.keene.edu/clf/clfnews.htm.

CZECH REPUBLIC: FOUNDATION OF THE REPUBLIC: ANNIVERSARY. Oct 28, 1918. National Day, anniversary of the bloodless revolution in Prague, after which the Czechs and Slovaks united to form Czechoslovakia (a union they dissolved without bloodshed in 1993).

GREECE: "OHI DAY": 60th ANNIVERSARY. Oct 28. National holiday commemorating Greek resistance and refusal to open her borders when Mussolini's Italian troops attacked Greece in 1940. "Ohi" means no! Celebrated with military parades, especially at Athens and Thessaloniki.

MAKE A DIFFERENCE DAY. Oct 28. This national day of community service is sponsored by *USA WEEKEND* (a Sunday magazine delivered in more than 500 newspapers). Volunteer projects completed are judged by well-known celebrities. More than $2.5 million in donations are awarded to charity. Key projects are honored in April during National Volunteer Week at a special Make A Difference Day awards luncheon and at the White House. The Points of Light Foundation is a partner. Nearly two million people nationwide participate. For info: Make a Difference Day, *USA WEEKEND*, 1000 Wilson Blvd, Arlington, VA 22229-0012. Phone: (800) 416-3824 or (703) 276-4531. Web: www.usaweekend.com (keyword: diffday).

SAINT JUDE'S DAY. Oct 28. St. Jude, the saint of hopeless causes, was martyred along with St. Simon at Persia, and their feast is celebrated jointly. St. Jude was supposedly the brother of Jesus, and, like his brother, a carpenter by trade. He is most popular with those who attempt the impossible and with students, who often ask for his help on exams.

SALK, JONAS: BIRTH ANNIVERSARY. Oct 28, 1914. Dr. Jonas Salk, developer of the Salk polio vaccine, was born at New York, NY. Salk announced his development of a successful vaccine in 1953, the year after a polio epidemic claimed some 3,300 lives in the US. Polio deaths were reduced by 95 percent after the introduction of the vaccine. Salk spent the last 10 years of his life doing AIDS research. He died June 23, 1995, at La Jolla, CA.

SPACE MILESTONE: INTERNATIONAL SPACE RESCUE AGREEMENT: 30th ANNIVERSARY. Oct 28, 1970. US and USSR officials agreed upon space rescue cooperation.

STATUE OF LIBERTY: DEDICATION ANNIVERSARY. Oct 28, 1886. Frederic Auguste Bartholdi's famous sculpture, the statue of *Liberty Enlightening the World*, on Bedloe's Island at New York Harbor, was dedicated. Ground breaking for the structure was in April 1883. A sonnet by Emma Lazarus, inside the pedestal of the statue, contains the words: "Give me your tired, your poor, your huddled masses yearning to breathe free, the wretched refuse of your teeming shore. Send these, the homeless, tempest-tost to me, I lift my lamp beside the golden door!" For more info, visit the National Parks Service website at www.nps.gov/stli/mainmenu.htm.

BIRTHDAYS TODAY

Terrell Davis, 28, football player, born San Diego, CA, Oct 28, 1972.
Bill Gates, 45, computer software executive (Microsoft), born Seattle, WA, Oct 28, 1955.

OCTOBER 29 — SUNDAY
Day 303 — 63 Remaining

DAYLIGHT SAVING TIME ENDS; STANDARD TIME RESUMES. Oct 29–Apr 1, 2001. Standard Time resumes at 2 AM on the last Sunday in October in each time zone, as provided by the Uniform Time Act of 1966 (as amended in 1986 by Public Law 99–359). Many use the popular rule: "spring forward, fall back" to remember which way to turn their clocks.

EMMETT, DANIEL DECATUR: BIRTH ANNIVERSARY. Oct 29, 1815. Creator of words and music for the song "Dixie," which became a fighting song for Confederate troops and the unofficial "national anthem" of the South. Emmett was born at Mount Vernon, OH, and died there June 28, 1904.

INTERNET CREATED: ANNIVERSARY. Oct 29, 1969. The first connection on what would become the Internet was made on this day when bits of data flowed between computers at UCLA and the Stanford Research Institute. This was the beginning of Arpanet, the precursor to the Internet developed by the Department of Defense. By the end of 1969, four sites were connected: UCLA, the Stanford Research Institute, the University of California, Santa Barbara and the University of Utah. By the next year there were 10 sites and soon there were applications like e-mail and file transfer utilities. The @ symbol was adopted in 1972 and a year later 75 percent of Arpanet traffic was e-mail.

SPACE MILESTONE: *DISCOVERY* (US): OLDEST MAN IN SPACE. Oct 29, 1998. Former astronaut and senator John Glenn became the oldest man in space when he traveled on the shuttle *Discovery* at the age of 77. In 1962 on *Friendship 7* he had been the first American to orbit Earth. See "Space Milestone: *Friendship 7*" (Feb 20).

STOCK MARKET CRASH: ANNIVERSARY. Oct 29, 1929. Prices on the New York Stock Exchange plummeted and virtually collapsed four days after President Herbert Hoover had declared, "The fundamental business of the country . . . is on a sound and prosperous basis." More than 16 million shares were dumped and billions of dollars were lost. The boom was over and the nation faced nearly a decade of depression. Some analysts had warned that the buying spree, with prices 15 to 150 times above earnings, had to stop at some point. Frightened investors ordered their brokers to sell at whatever price. The resulting Great Depression, which lasted till about 1939, involved North America, Europe and other industrialized countries. In 1932 one out of four US workers was unemployed.

TURKEY: REPUBLIC DAY. Oct 29. Anniversary of the founding of the republic in 1923.

BIRTHDAYS TODAY

Rhonda Gowler Greene, 45, author (*Barnyard Song*), born Salem, IL, Oct 29, 1955.

Dirk Kempthorne, 49, Governor of Idaho (R), born San Diego, CA, Oct 29, 1951.

Connie Mack III, 60, US Senator (R, Florida), born Philadelphia, PA, Oct 29, 1940.

OCTOBER 30 — MONDAY
Day 304 — 62 Remaining

ADAMS, JOHN: BIRTH ANNIVERSARY. Oct 30, 1735. Second president of the US (Mar 4, 1797–Mar 3, 1801), born at Braintree, MA. Adams had been George Washington's vice president. He once wrote in a letter to Thomas Jefferson: "You and I ought not to die before we have explained ourselves to each other." John Adams and Thomas Jefferson died on the same day, July 4, 1826, the 50th anniversary of adoption of the Declaration of Independence. Adams's last words: "Thomas Jefferson still survives." Jefferson's last words: "Is it the fourth?" Adams was the father of John Quincy Adams (sixth president of the US).

DEVIL'S NIGHT. Oct 30. Formerly a "Mischief Night" on the evening before Halloween and an occasion for harmless pranks, chiefly observed by children. However, in some areas of the US, the destruction of property and endangering of lives has led to the imposition of dusk-to-dawn curfews during the last two or three days of October. Not to be confused with "Trick or Treat" or "Beggar's Night," usually observed on Halloween. See also: "Hallowe'en" (Oct 31).

POST, EMILY: BIRTH ANNIVERSARY. Oct 30, 1872. Emily Post was born at Baltimore, MD. Published in 1922, her book *Etiquette: The Blue Book of Social Usage* instantly became the American bible of manners and social behavior and established Post as the household name in matters of etiquette. It was in its 10th edition at the time of her death Sept 25, 1960, at New York, NY. *Etiquette* inspired a great many letters asking Post for advice on manners in specific situations. She used these letters as the basis for her radio show and for her syndicated newspaper column, which eventually appeared in more than 200 papers.

October *2000*	S	M	T	W	T	F	S
	1	2	3	4	5	6	7
	8	9	10	11	12	13	14
	15	16	17	18	19	20	21
	22	23	24	24	26	27	28
	29	30	31				

BIRTHDAYS TODAY

Diego Maradona, 40, former soccer player, born Lanus, Argentina, Oct 30, 1960.

Henry Winkler, 55, producer, actor ("The Fonz" on "Happy Days"), born New York, NY, Oct 30, 1945.

OCTOBER 31 — TUESDAY
Day 305 — 61 Remaining

FIRST BLACK PLAYS IN NBA GAME: 50th ANNIVERSARY. Oct 31, 1950. Earl Lloyd became the first black ever to play in an NBA game when he took the floor for the Washington Capitols at Rochester, NY. Lloyd was actually one of three blacks to become NBA players in the 1950 season, the others being Nat "Sweetwater" Clifton, who was signed by the New York Knicks, and Chuck Cooper, who was drafted by the Boston Celtics (and debuted the night after Lloyd).

HALLOWE'EN or ALL HALLOW'S EVE. Oct 31. An ancient celebration combining Druid autumn festival and Christian customs. Hallowe'en (All Hallow's Eve) is the beginning of Hallowtide, a season that embraces the Feast of All Saints (Nov 1) and the Feast of All Souls (Nov 2). The observance, dating from the sixth or seventh centuries, has long been associated with thoughts of the dead, spirits, witches, ghosts and devils. In fact, the ancient Celtic Feast of Samhain, the festival that marked the beginning of winter and of the New Year, was observed Nov 1. See also: "Trick or Treat or Beggar's Night" (Oct 31). For more info: *Halloween Program Sourcebook*, edited by Sue Ellen Thompson (Omnigraphics, 0-7808-0388-4, $48 All ages). For links to sites about Halloween on the web go to: deil.lang.uiuc.edu/web.pages /holidays/halloween.html.

LOW, JULIET GORDON: BIRTH ANNIVERSARY. Oct 31, 1860. Founded Girl Scouts of the USA Mar 12, 1912, at Savannah, GA. Born at Savannah, she died there Jan 17, 1927.

MOUNT RUSHMORE COMPLETION: ANNIVERSARY. Oct 31, 1941. The Mount Rushmore National Memorial was completed after 14 years of work. First suggested by Jonah Robinson of the South Dakota State Historical Society, the memorial was dedicated in 1925, and work began in 1927. The memorial contains sculptures of the heads of Presidents George Washington, Thomas Jefferson, Abraham Lincoln and Theodore Roosevelt. The 60-foot-tall sculptures represent, respectively, the nation's founding, political philosophy, preservation, expansion and conservation. For more info: www.nps.gov/moru.

NATIONAL MAGIC DAY. Oct 31. Traditionally observed on the anniversary of the death of Harry Houdini in 1926.

★**NATIONAL UNICEF DAY.** Oct 31. Presidential Proclamation 3817, of Oct 27, 1967, covers all succeeding years. Annually, Oct 31. For more info: www.unicef.org.

NEVADA: ADMISSION DAY: ANNIVERSARY. Oct 31. Became 36th state in 1864. Observed as a holiday in Nevada.

PACA, WILLIAM: BIRTH ANNIVERSARY. Oct 31, 1740. Signer of the Declaration of Independence. Born at Abingdon, MD, he died Oct 13, 1799, at Talbot County, MD.

REFORMATION DAY: ANNIVERSARY. Oct 31, 1517. Anniversary on which Martin Luther nailed his 95 theses to the door of Wittenberg's Palace church, denouncing the selling of papal indulgences—the beginning of the Reformation in Germany. Observed by many Protestant churches as Reformation Sunday, on this day if it is a Sunday or on the Sunday before Oct 31 (Oct 29 in 2000).

TAIWAN: CHIANG KAI-SHEK DAY: ANNIVERSARY. Oct 31. National holiday to honor memory of Generalissimo Chiang Kai-Shek, the first constitutional president of the Republic of China, born in 1887.

TAYLOR, SYDNEY: BIRTH ANNIVERSARY. Oct 31, 1904. Author (*All-of-a-Kind Family*), born at New York, NY. Died Feb 12, 1978.

TRICK OR TREAT or BEGGAR'S NIGHT. Oct 31. A popular custom on Hallowe'en, in which children wearing costumes visit neighbors' homes, calling out "Trick or Treat" and "begging" for candies or gifts to place in their beggars' bags. Some children Trick or Treat for UNICEF, collecting money for this organization. For more info, go to www.unicef.org. In recent years there has been increased participation by adults, often parading in elaborate or outrageous costumes and also requesting candy.

BIRTHDAYS TODAY

Katherine Paterson, 68, author (Newbery for *The Bridge to Terabithia, Jacob Have I Loved*), born Qing Jiang, China, Oct 31, 1932.

Jane Pauley, 50, TV journalist ("Dateline"), born Indianapolis, IN, Oct 31, 1950.

Dan Rather, 69, journalist (coanchor "CBS Evening News"), born Wharton, TX, Oct 31, 1931.

Adrienne Richard, 79, author (*Pistol*), born Evanston, IL, Oct 31, 1921.

November 2000

NOVEMBER 1 — WEDNESDAY
Day 306 — 60 Remaining

ALGERIA: REVOLUTION ANNIVERSARY. Nov 1. National holiday commemorating the revolution against France in 1954.

ALL HALLOWS or ALL SAINTS' DAY. Nov 1. Roman Catholic Holy Day of Obligation. Commemorates the blessed, especially those who have no special feast days. Observed Nov 1 since Pope Gregory IV set the date of recognition in 835. All Saints' Day is a legal holiday in Louisiana. Halloween is the evening before All Hallows Day.

ANTIGUA AND BARBUDA: NATIONAL HOLIDAY. Nov 1. Commemorates independence from Britain in 1981.

AVIATION HISTORY MONTH. Nov 1–30. Anniversary of aeronautical experiments in November 1782 (exact dates unknown), by Joseph Michel Montgolfier and Jacques Etienne Montgolfier, brothers living at Annonay, France. Inspired by Joseph Priestley's book *Experiments Relating to the Different Kinds of Air*, the brothers experimented with filling paper and fabric bags with smoke and hot air, leading to the invention of the hot-air balloon, man's first flight and the entire science of aviation and flight. *See* Curriculum Connection.

GUATEMALA: KITE FESTIVAL OF SANTIAGO SACATE-PEQUEZ. Nov 1. Long ago, when evil spirits disturbed the good spirits in the local cemetery, a magician told the townspeople a secret way to get rid of the evil spirits—by flying kites (because the evil spirits were frightened by the noise of wind against paper). Since then, the kite festival has been held at the cemetery each year Nov 1 or Nov 2, and it is said that "to this day no one knows of bad spirits roaming the streets or the cemetery of Santiago Sacatepequez," a village about 20 miles from Guatemala City. Nowadays, the youth of the village work for many weeks to make the elaborate and giant kites to fly on All Saints' Day (Nov 1) or All Souls' Day (Nov 2).

HOCKEY MASK INVENTED: ANNIVERSARY. Nov 1, 1959. Tired of stopping hockey pucks with his face, Montreal Canadiens goalie Jacques Plante, having received another wound, reemerged from the locker room with seven new stitches—and a

	S	M	T	W	T	F	S
November				1	2	3	4
2000	5	6	7	8	9	10	11
	12	13	14	15	16	17	18
	19	20	21	22	23	24	25
	26	27	28	29	30		

NOVEMBER 1–30
AVIATION HISTORY MONTH

Today we board an airplane and minutes or hours later arrive at a destination which a century ago would have been impossible to reach in such a short time. It has been less than 100 years since Wilbur and Orville Wright's first powered flight took place on Dec 17, 1903. However, people have been fascinated by the idea of flight for many hundreds of years. Indeed, most people have dreamed at least once of being able to fly. A classroom observance of Aviation History Month can be a rich and rewarding experience.

In ancient Greek mythology, Daedulus fashioned wings made of feathers and wax so he and his son Icarus could escape from Crete. There are many published versions of this myth and also that of Pegasus, the flying horse. Students can illustrate their own versions of these myths.

Leonardo da Vinci drew a prototype for a flying machine with flapping wings in about AD 1500. A picture of this machine can be found in *Leonardo Da Vinci*, by Diane Stanley (Morrow, 0-688-10437-1, $16 Gr. 2 & up). Many people experimented with variations of da Vinci's machine in the 1800s. Students might research and compare them with da Vinci's.

The hot-air balloon, first flown in France in 1783, was used for spy missions during the American Civil War. Hot-air balloonists have circled the globe. Students can compare modern-day balloons with older models. Perhaps a balloon enthusiast could pay a visit to your school. There are many children's books featuring hot-air balloons, including: *Full of Hot Air: Launching, Floating High, and Landing*, by Gary Paulsen (Delacorte, 0-385-30887-6, $14.95 Gr. 4 & up); and *Spy in the Sky*, by Kathleen Karr (Hyperion, 0-7868-1165-X, $3.95 Gr. 2–5).

There are many ways to bring the history of engine-powered flight into the classroom. Videos about Charles Lindbergh, Amelia Earhart and other early aviators, and film clips of early flying machines are available. Check your local library and the Internet for sources. An antique airplane enthusiast might be available in your area. Call small, local airports to ask about clubs. Many children build and fly model airplanes. See if students in your school can organize a schoolwide exhibition.

Children's literature abounds with books on aviation "firsts." To get started, look at: *Fly, Bessie, Fly!*, by Lynn Joseph (Simon & Schuster, 0-689-81339-2, $16 Gr. 1–4); *One Giant Leap: The Story of Neil Armstrong*, by Don Brown (Houghton, 0-395-88401-2, $16 Gr. 1–4); *The Glorious Flight: Across the Channel with Louis Bleriot*, by Alice and Martin Provensen (Puffin, 0-14-050729-9, $5.99 Gr. 3–6); and *First on the Moon*, by Barbara Henner (Hyperion, 0-7868-0489-0, $16.99 Gr. 3–7). For easy readers and novels try: *First Flight*, by George Shea (Harper, 0-06-444215-2, $3.95 Gr. K–3) and *Airfield*, by Jeanette Ingold (Harcourt, 0-15-202053-5, $17 Gr. 6–10).

plastic face mask he had made from fiberglass and resin. Although Cliff Benedict had tried a leather mask back in the '20s, the idea didn't catch on but after Plante wore his, goalies throughout the NHL began wearing protective plastic face shields.

INTERNATIONAL DRUM MONTH. Nov 1–30. To celebrate the worldwide popularity of all types of drums. Annually, the month of November. For info: David Levine, Full Circle Management, Percussion Mktg Council, 12665 Kling St, Studio City, CA

91604. Phone: (818) 753-1310. Fax: (818) 753-1313. E-mail: DLEVINE360@aol.com.

MEDICAL SCHOOL FOR WOMEN OPENED AT BOSTON: ANNIVERSARY. Nov 1, 1848. Founded by Samuel Gregory, a pioneer in medical education for women, the Boston Female Medical School opened as the first medical school exclusively for women. The original enrollment was 12 students. In 1874, the school merged with the Boston University School of Medicine and formed one of the first coed medical schools in the world.

MERLIN'S SNUG HUGS FOR KIDS. Nov 1–Dec 13. Nationwide. Each community is encouraged to provide new winter outerwear for foster and needy children. Event runs for six weeks, and includes Kids Helping Kids, scout participation and the Crochet and Knit-A-Thon and on the final day (Dec 13) Merlin's caravan collects the new winter clothes and delivers them to Children's Home & Aid Society. Sponsor: Merlin's Muffler & Brake. Annually, the first week of November through the third week of December. For info: Kathleen Quinn, ProQuest Communications, 626 Carraiage Hill Dr, Glenview, IL 60025-5401. Phone: (847) 998-9950. Fax: (847) 998-9945. E-mail: proquest@aol.com. Web: www.merlins.com.

MEXICO: DAY OF THE DEAD. Nov 1–2. Observance begins during last days of October when "Dead Men's Bread" is sold in bakeries—round loaves, decorated with sugar skulls. Departed souls are remembered not with mourning but with a spirit of friendliness and good humor. Cemeteries are visited and graves are decorated.

★**NATIONAL ADOPTION MONTH.** Nov 1–30.

★**NATIONAL AMERICAN INDIAN HERITAGE MONTH.** Nov 1–30.

NATIONAL ASSOCIATION FOR GIFTED CHILDREN CONVENTION. Nov 1–5. Atlanta, GA. Educational sessions for administrators, counselors, coordinators, teachers and parents. Est attendance: 3,000. For info: Natl Assn for Gifted Children, 1707 L St NW, Ste 550, Washington, DC 20036. Phone: (202) 785-4268.

NATIONAL AUTHORS' DAY. Nov 1. This observance was adopted by the General Federation of Women's Clubs in 1929 and in 1949 was given a place on the list of special days, weeks and months prepared by the US Dept of Commerce. The resolution states: "by celebrating an Authors' Day as a nation, we would not only show patriotism, loyalty, and appreciation of the men and women who have made American literature possible, but would also encourage and inspire others to give of themselves in making a better America. . . ." It was also resolved "that we commemorate an Authors' Day to be observed on November First each year." *See* Curriculum Connection.

NATIONAL FAMILY LITERACY DAY®. Nov 1. Celebrated all over the country with special activities and events that showcase the importance of family literacy programs. Family literacy programs bring parents and children together in the classroom to learn and support each other in efforts to further their education and improve their life skills. Sponsored by the National Center for Family Literacy and Toyota. Annually, Nov 1. *See* Curriculum Connection. For info: Natl Center for Family Literacy, 325 W Main St, Ste 200, Louisville, KY 40202. Phone: (502) 584-1133. Fax: (502) 584-0172. E-mail: ncfl@famlit.org. Web: www.famlit.org.

NATIONAL HEALTHY SKIN MONTH. Nov 1–30. For info: American Academy of Dermatology, PO Box 681069, Schaumburg, IL 60168. Phone: (847) 330-0230.

PEANUT BUTTER LOVERS' MONTH. Nov 1–30. Celebration of America's favorite food and #1 sandwich. For info: Peanut Advi-

NOVEMBER 1
NATIONAL AUTHORS DAY/NATIONAL FAMILY LITERACY DAY

Try a new slant while celebrating these two days. Some children, particularly boys and reluctant readers, find nonfiction books more interesting and entertaining than fiction. Other children may have trouble writing and developing a story line in fiction. All children can write nonfiction, yet we seldom encourage them to do this when observing young author days. If you celebrate Authors Day and Family Literacy Day by asking your students to be authors of nonfiction, every student should be able to achieve success. And by sharing their work with their families, both will be working toward achieving the goal of family literacy. Focus on nonfiction in several ways.

A *short* research project can be assigned two weeks or so in advance. Ask each student to choose a topic that especially interests him or her. Start them thinking by posing the general statement and question: "We're going to brainstorm. What kinds of things interest you?" There is, of course, no right or wrong answer. List 10–15 topics on the blackboard. Then, ask each student to list five things he or she is interested in on a sheet of paper. Students will choose their research topics from their short list. Topics are likely to range widely from dinosaurs, to sports, to music, to animals, etc. Students should spend the time between choosing their topic and National Authors Day/National Family Literacy Day doing the necessary research and writing per your regular policies and guidelines regarding report writing. The emphasis should be on producing a literary work that *informs* a reader about the writer's topic *while conveying the writer's love of that topic.*

Prior to Nov 1, arrange with the learning center director to flood your classroom with nonfiction books on a wide variety of topics. Encourage students to browse and discuss them during regularly scheduled reading time.

Let students develop a "Family Response Sheet." On it, they might ask for family input regarding their topic, editing of drafts, word choice and how family members have noticed student interest in the topic in the past (belonging to a sports team, caring for a pet, etc.). Ask family members to write their responses to the student's work.

On Nov 1, use regularly scheduled reading time to let students share their work in small groups. Provide a place where the work can be read by others during the following week. Emphasize the fact that the students are now successful authors, like the authors of the nonfiction books that have surrounded them for the past weeks.

Literature connections include: *Creative Nonfiction: How to Live It & Write It,* by Lee Gutkind (Chicago Review Press, 1-55652-266-5, $14.95); *Writing Science Research Papers: An Introductory Step by Step Approach to A's,* by David B. Williams (Biotech Publishing, 1-880319-17-9, $14.95 Gr. 7 & up); and *How to Write Nonfiction,* by Jo E. Moore (Evan Moor, 1-55799-285-1, $5.95 Gr. 3–6).

sory Board, 500 Sugar Mill Rd, Ste 105A, Atlanta, GA 30350. Web: www.peanutbutterlovers.com.

PRESIDENT FIRST OCCUPIES THE WHITE HOUSE: 200th ANNIVERSARY. Nov 1, 1800. The federal government had been located at Philadelphia from 1790 until 1800. On Nov 1, 1800, President John Adams and his family moved into the newly-completed White House at Washington, DC, the nation's new capital. To take a virtual tour of the White House, go to: www.whitehouse.gov.

PRIME MERIDIAN SET: ANNIVERSARY. Nov 1, 1884. Delegates from 25 nations met in October 1884, at Washington, DC at the International Meridian Conference to set up time zones for the world. On this day the treaty adopted by the Conference took effect, making Greenwich, England the Prime Meridian (i.e., zero longitude) and setting the International Date Line at 180° longitude in the Pacific. Every 15° of longitude equals one hour and there are 24 meridians. While some countries do not strictly observe this system (for example, while China stretches over five time zones, it is the same time everywhere in China), it has brought predictability and logic to time throughout the world.

VIRGIN ISLANDS: LIBERTY DAY. Nov 1. Officially "D. Hamilton Jackson Memorial Day," commemorating establishment of the first press in the Virgin Islands in 1915.

WORLD COMMUNICATION WEEK. Nov 1–7. To stress the importance of communication among the more than five billion human beings in the world who speak more than 3,000 languages and to promote communication by means of the international language Esperanto. For complete info, send $4 to cover expense of printing, handling and postage. Annually, the first seven days of November. For info: Dr. Stanley Drake, Pres, Intl Soc of Friendship and Goodwill, 412 Cherry Hills Dr, Bakersfield, CA 93309-7902.

BIRTHDAYS TODAY

Hilary Knight, 74, illustrator (Eloise series), born Hempstead, Long Island, NY, Nov 1, 1926.

Fernando Anguamea Valenzuela, 40, baseball player, born Navojoa, Sonora, Mexico, Nov 1, 1960.

NOVEMBER 2 — THURSDAY
Day 307 — 59 Remaining

ALL SOULS' DAY. Nov 2. Commemorates the faithful departed. Catholic observance.

BOONE, DANIEL: BIRTH ANNIVERSARY. Nov 2, 1734. American frontiersman, explorer and militia officer, born at Berks County, near Reading, PA. In February 1778, he was captured at Blue Licks, KY, by Shawnee Indians, under Chief Blackfish, who adopted Boone when he was inducted into the tribe as "Big Turtle." Boone escaped after five months, and in 1781 was captured briefly by the British. He experienced a series of personal and financial disasters during his life but continued a rugged existence, hunting until his 80s. Boone died at St. Charles County, MO, Sept 26, 1820. The bodies of Daniel Boone and his wife, Rebecca, were moved to Frankfort, KY, in 1845.

	S	M	T	W	T	F	S
November				1	2	3	4
2000	5	6	7	8	9	10	11
	12	13	14	15	16	17	18
	19	20	21	22	23	24	25
	26	27	28	29	30		

FIRST SCHEDULED RADIO BROADCAST: 80th ANNIVERSARY. Nov 2, 1920. Station KDKA at Pittsburgh, PA broadcast the results of the presidential election. The station received its license to broadcast Nov 7, 1921. By 1922 there were about 400 licensed radio stations in the US.

HARDING, WARREN GAMALIEL: BIRTH ANNIVERSARY. Nov 2, 1865. The 29th president of the US was born at Corsica, OH. His term of office: Mar 4, 1921–Aug 2, 1923 (died in office). His undistinguished administration was tainted by the Teapot Dome scandal, and his sudden death while on a western speaking tour (San Francisco, CA, Aug 2, 1923) prompted many rumors.

NATIONAL MIDDLE SCHOOL ASSOCIATION ANNUAL CONFERENCE. Nov 2–5. St. Louis, MO. For info: Natl Middle School Assn, 2600 Corporate Exchange Dr, Ste 370, Columbus, OH 43231. Phone: (614) 895-4730 or (800) 528-NMSA. Web: www.nmsa.org.

NORTH DAKOTA: ADMISSION DAY: ANNIVERSARY. Nov 2. Became 39th state in 1889.

POLK, JAMES KNOX: BIRTH ANNIVERSARY. Nov 2, 1795. The 11th president of the US (Mar 4, 1845–Mar 3, 1849) was born at Mecklenburg County, NC. A compromise candidate at the 1844 Democratic Party convention, Polk was awarded the nomination on the ninth ballot. He declined to be a candidate for a second term and declared himself to be "exceedingly relieved" at the completion of his presidency. He died shortly thereafter at Nashville, TN, June 15, 1849.

SOUTH DAKOTA: ADMISSION DAY: ANNIVERSARY. Nov 2. Became 40th state in 1889.

BIRTHDAYS TODAY

Jeannie Baker, 50, author and illustrator (*Where the Forest Meets the Sea*), born Nov 2, 1950.

Danny Cooksey, 25, actor ("Pepper Ann," *The Little Mermaid*), born Moore, OK, Nov 2, 1975.

Adam Luke Springfield, 18, actor ("Wishbone"), born Santa Barbara, CA, Nov 2, 1982.

NOVEMBER 3 — FRIDAY
Day 308 — 58 Remaining

AUSTIN, STEPHEN FULLER: BIRTH ANNIVERSARY. Nov 3, 1793. A principal founder of Texas, for whom its capital city was named, Austin was born at Wythe County, VA. He first visited Texas in 1821 and established a settlement there the following year, continuing a colonization project started by his father, Moses Austin. Thrown in prison when he advocated formation of a separate state (Texas still belonged to Mexico), he was freed in 1835, lost a campaign for the presidency (of the Republic of Texas) to Sam Houston (q.v.) in 1836, and died (while serving as Texas secretary of state) at Austin, TX, Dec 27, 1836.

DOMINICA: NATIONAL DAY. Nov 3. National holiday. Commemorates the independence of this Caribbean island from Britain on this day in 1978.

JAPAN: CULTURE DAY. Nov 3. National holiday.

MICRONESIA, FEDERATED STATES OF: INDEPENDENCE DAY. Nov 3. National holiday commemorating independence from the US in 1986.

PANAMA: INDEPENDENCE DAY. Nov 3. Panama declared itself independent of Colombia in 1903.

PUBLIC TELEVISION DEBUTS: ANNIVERSARY. Nov 3, 1969. A string of local educational TV channels united on this day under the Public Broadcasting System banner. Today there are 348 PBS stations.

SANDWICH DAY: BIRTH ANNIVERSARY OF JOHN MONTAGUE. Nov 3, 1718. A day to recognize the inventor of the sandwich, John Montague, Fourth Earl of Sandwich, born at London, England. He was England's first lord of the admiralty, secretary of state for the northern department, postmaster general and the man after whom Captain Cook named the Sandwich Islands in 1778. A rake and a gambler, he is said to have invented the sandwich as a time-saving nourishment while engaged in a 24-hour-long gambling session in 1762. He died at London, England, Apr 30, 1792.

SPACE MILESTONE: *SPUTNIK 2* (USSR). Nov 3, 1957. A dog named Laika became the first animal sent into space. Total weight of craft and dog was 1,121 lbs. The satellite was not capable of returning the dog to Earth and she died when her air supply was gone. Nicknamed "Muttnik" by the American press.

WHITE, EDWARD DOUGLASS: BIRTH ANNIVERSARY. Nov 3, 1845. Ninth Chief Justice of the Supreme Court, born at La Fourche Parish, LA. During the Civil War, he served in the Confederate Army after which he returned to New Orleans to practice law. Elected to the US Senate in 1891, he was appointed to the Supreme Court by Grover Cleveland in 1894. He became Chief Justice under President William Taft in 1910 and served until 1921. He died at Washington, DC, May 19, 1921.

BIRTHDAYS TODAY

Brent Ashabranner, 79, author (*Our Beckoning Borders: Illegal Immigration to America*), born Shawnee, OK, Nov 3, 1921.

Roseanne, 47, comedienne, actress ("Roseanne," *She-Devil*), born Roseanne Barr, Salt Lake City, UT, Nov 3, 1953.

NOVEMBER 4 — SATURDAY
Day 309 — 57 Remaining

FESTIVAL OF BOOKS FOR YOUNG PEOPLE. Nov 4. Iowa Memorial Union, Iowa City, IA. Annual festival will feature talks by children's authors, booktalk sessions and exhibits of new books for young people. For info: School of Library and Information Science, Univ of Iowa, Iowa City, IA 52242-1420. Phone: (319) 335-5707. E-mail: ethel-bloesch@uiowa.edu.

ITALY: VICTORY DAY. Nov 4. Commemorates the signing of a WWI treaty by Austria in 1918 which resulted in the transfer of Trentino and Trieste from Austria to Italy.

JEWISH BOOK MONTH. Nov 4–Dec 4. To promote interest in Jewish books. For info: Carolyn Starman Hessel, Jewish Book Council, 15 E 26th St, New York, NY 10010. Phone: (212) 532-4949. Fax: (212) 481-4174. E-mail: JBC@jewishbooks.org. Web: www.avotaynu.com/jbc.html.

KING TUT TOMB DISCOVERY: ANNIVERSARY. Nov 4, 1922. In 1922, one of the most important archaeological discoveries of modern times occurred at Luxor, Egypt. It was the tomb of Egypt's child-king, Tutankhamen, who became pharaoh at the age of nine and died, probably in the year 1352 BC, when he was 19. Perhaps the only ancient Egyptian royal tomb to have escaped plundering by grave robbers, it was discovered more than 3,000 years after Tutankhamen's death by English archaeologist Howard Carter, leader of an expedition financed by Lord Carnarvon. The priceless relics yielded by King Tut's tomb were placed in Egypt's National Museum at Cairo.

MISCHIEF NIGHT. Nov 4. Observed in England, Australia and New Zealand. Nov 4, the eve of Guy Fawkes Day, is occasion for bonfires and firecrackers to commemorate failure of the plot to blow up the Houses of Parliament Nov 5, 1605. See also: "England: Guy Fawkes Day" (Nov 5).

MOON PHASE: FIRST QUARTER. Nov 4. Moon enters First Quarter phase at 2:27 AM, EST.

NORTH, STERLING: BIRTH ANNIVERSARY. Nov 4, 1906. Author (*Rascal*), born at Edgerton, WI. Died Dec 21, 1974.

PANAMA: FLAG DAY. Nov 4. Public holiday.

SADIE HAWKINS DAY. Nov 4. Widely observed in US, usually on the first Saturday in November. Tradition established in "Li'l Abner" comic strip in 1930s by cartoonist Al Capp. A popular occasion when women and girls are encouraged to take the initiative in inviting the man or boy of their choice for a date. A similar tradition is associated with Feb 29 in leap years.

SWEDEN: ALL SAINTS' DAY. Nov 4. Honors the memory of deceased friends and relatives. Annually, the Saturday following Oct 30.

UNESCO: ANNIVERSARY. Nov 4, 1946. The United Nations Educational, Scientific and Cultural Organization was formed.

BIRTHDAYS TODAY

Gail E. Haley, 61, author and illustrator (Caldecott for *A Story, A Story*), born Charlotte, NC, Nov 4, 1939.

Ralph Macchio, 38, actor ("Eight Is Enough," *The Karate Kid*), born Huntington, NY, Nov 4, 1962.

Andrea McArdle, 37, singer, actress (Broadway's *Annie*), born Philadelphia, PA, Nov 4, 1963.

NOVEMBER 5 — SUNDAY
Day 310 — 56 Remaining

CIRCLE K INTERNATIONAL SERVICE WEEK. Nov 5–11. This week is set aside for all Circle K clubs worldwide to perform a campus and community service project to benefit children ages 6–13. Circle K is a college student service organization sponsored by Kiwanis. For info: Circle K Intl, 3636 Woodview Trace, Indianapolis, IN 46268-3196. Phone: (317) 875-8755 or (317) 875-8755. Fax: (317) 879-0204. E-mail: cki@kiwanis.org. Web: www.kiwanis.org.

ENGLAND: GUY FAWKES DAY. Nov 5. United Kingdom. Anniversary of the "Gunpowder Plot." Conspirators planned to blow up the Houses of Parliament and King James I in 1605. Twenty barrels of gunpowder, which they had secreted in a cellar under Parliament, were discovered on the night of Nov 4, the very eve of the intended explosion, and the conspirators were arrested. They were tried and convicted, and Jan 31, 1606, eight (including Guy Fawkes) were beheaded and their heads displayed on pikes at London Bridge. Though there were at least 11 conspirators, Guy Fawkes is most remembered. In 1606, the Parliament, which was to have been annihilated, enacted a law establishing Nov 5 as a day of public thanksgiving. It is still observed, and on the night of Nov 5, the whole country lights up with bonfires and celebration. "Guys" are burned in effigy and the old verses repeated: "Remember, remember the fifth of November,/Gunpowder treason and plot;/I see no reason why Gunpowder Treason/Should ever be forgot."

NATIONAL CHEMISTRY WEEK. Nov 5–11. To celebrate the contributions of chemistry to modern life and to help the public understand that chemistry affects every part of our lives. Activities include an array of outreach programs such as open houses, contests, workshops, exhibits and classroom visits. 10 million participants nationwide. For info: Natl Chemistry Week Office, American Chemical Soc, 1155 16th St NW, Washington, DC 20036. Phone: (202) 872-6078. Fax: (202) 833-7722. E-mail: ncw@acs.org. Web: www.chemcenter.org.

NATIONAL SPLIT PEA SOUP WEEK. Nov 5–11. To promote the use of split peas in split pea soup. For info: Peter Mundt, USA Dry Pea and Lentil Council, 5071 Highway 8 W, Moscow, ID 83843-4023. Phone: (208) 882-3023. Fax: (208) 882-6406. E-mail: pulse@pea-lentil.com.

ROGERS, ROY: BIRTH ANNIVERSARY. Nov 5, 1912. Known as the "King of the Cowboys," Rogers was born Leonard Slye at Cincinnati, OH. His many songs included "Don't Fence Me In" and "Happy Trails to You." He made his acting debut in *Under Western Stars* in 1935 and later hosted his own show, "The Roy Rogers Show," in 1951. Rogers died at Apple Valley, CA, July 6, 1998. See also: "The Roy Rogers Show" TV Premiere: Anniversary (Dec 30).

BIRTHDAYS TODAY

Tatum O'Neal, 37, actress (Oscar for *Paper Moon*; *Bad News Bears*), born Los Angeles, CA, Nov 5, 1963.

Marcia Sewall, 65, author (*The Pilgrims of Plimoth*), born Providence, RI, Nov 5, 1935.

Jerry Stackhouse, 26, basketball player, born Kinston, NC, Nov 5, 1974.

NOVEMBER 6 — MONDAY

Day 311 — 55 Remaining

AUSTRALIA: RECREATION DAY. Nov 6. The first Monday in November is observed as Recreation Day at Northern Tasmania, Australia.

"GOOD MORNING AMERICA" TV PREMIERE: 25th ANNIVERSARY. Nov 6, 1975. This ABC morning program, set in a living room, is a mixture of news reports, features and interviews with newsmakers and people of interest. It was the first program to compete with NBC's "Today" show and initially aired as "A.M. America." Hosts have included David Hartman, Nancy Dussault, Sandy Hill, Charles Gibson, Joan Lunden, Lisa McRee and Kevin Newman.

HALFWAY POINT OF AUTUMN. Nov 6. On this day, 45 days of autumn will have elapsed and the equivalent will remain before Dec 21, which is the winter solstice and the beginning of winter.

KIDS' GOALS EDUCATION WEEK. Nov 6–10. Encourage parents to foster goal-setting habits in their children's lives so that their children can make their dreams come true. *See* Curriculum Connection. For info: Gary Ryan Blair, The GoalsGuy, 911 East Klosterman Rd, Tarpon Springs, FL 34689. Phone: (877) GOALS-GUY. Fax: (800) 731-GOALS. E-mail: kgew@goalsguy.com. Web: www.goalsguy.com.

	S	M	T	W	T	F	S
November				1	2	3	4
2000	5	6	7	8	9	10	11
	12	13	14	15	16	17	18
	19	20	21	22	23	24	25
	26	27	28	29	30		

NOVEMBER 6–10
KIDS' GOALS EDUCATION WEEK

Kids' Goals Education Week provides a good theme week opportunity to get parents involved in their children's education. Many school districts hold parent-teacher conferences during the first week in November, so teachers can inform parents about this week then.

Prior to conferences, make a simple handout that can be given to parents during the conference. Use a heading such as "Go for the Goal." The text of the handout might read: "[Student's name] has already achieved one goal this year. He/she has worked hard and can [accomplishment]. [Student's name] and I have talked. We think a worthwhile new goal is [goal], and you can help [student's name] achieve it. Nov 6–10 is Kids' Goals Education Week. As a class we are committed to achieving our goals. Please give [student's name] the gift of your time and work with him/her to achieve the goal he/she has set."

Talk about setting personal goals with your students. Mention goals you have set for yourself. Ask them to discuss goal setting with their parents. What have been some of the goals their parents have set? Stress that even small goals can be stepping stones to a successful day. Brainstorm with students and create a blackboard list of goals they might want to choose. Suggest addition and subtraction, handwriting, reading, spelling or sitting quietly while attendance is being taken. Guide students who may have difficulty attaining certain goals into choosing appropriate goals that will challenge but not frustrate them. Successful achievement is important for encouraging goal-setting habits.

NAISMITH, JAMES: BIRTH ANNIVERSARY. Nov 6, 1861. Inventor of the game of basketball was born at Almonte, Ontario, Canada. Died at Lawrence, KS, Nov 28, 1939. Basketball became an Olympic sport in 1936.

RANDOM ACTS OF KINDNESS WEEK. Nov 6–12. The 6th annual RAK week has been changed from its usual February time frame to November to coincide with the 1st annual World Kindness Day, Nov 13. RAK Week is a global grass roots awareness campaign and celebration of the power of Random Acts of Kindness as a counterbalance to random acts of violence. Anyone can join in during this week and the Random Acts of Kindness can help you with ideas on how to promote this wonderful celebration! Call for a Community Coordinator Kit or a Teacher's Kit. For info: Random Acts of Kindness Foundation. Phone: (800) 660-2811. Web: www.actsofkindness.org.

SAXOPHONE DAY (ADOLPHE SAX BIRTH ANNIVERSARY). Nov 6. A day to recognize the birth anniversary of Adolphe Sax, Belgian musician and inventor of the saxophone and the saxotromba. Born at Dinant, Belgium in 1814, Antoine Joseph Sax, later known as Adolphe, was the eldest of 11 children of a musical instrument builder. Sax contributed an entire family of brass wind instruments for band and orchestra use. He was accorded fame and great wealth, but business misfortunes led to bankruptcy. Sax died in poverty at Paris, Feb 7, 1894.

SOUSA, JOHN PHILIP: BIRTH ANNIVERSARY. Nov 6, 1854. American composer and band conductor, remembered for stirring marches such as "The Stars and Stripes Forever," "Semper Fidelis," "El Capitan," born at Washington, DC. Died at Reading, PA, Mar 6, 1932. See also: "The Stars and Stripes Forever: Anniversary" (May 14).

SWEDEN: GUSTAVUS ADOLPHUS DAY. Nov 6. Honors Sweden's King and military leader killed in 1632.

Sally Field, 54, actress (Oscars for *Norma Rae, Places in the Heart; Mrs Doubtfire*), born Pasadena, CA, Nov 6, 1946.

Ethan Hawke, 30, actor (*Dead Poets Society, Reality Bites*), born Austin, TX, Nov 6, 1970.

Maria Shriver, 45, broadcast journalist ("Today"), author (*What's Heaven?*), born Chicago, IL, Nov 6, 1955.

NOVEMBER 7 — TUESDAY
Day 312 — 54 Remaining

CANADIAN PACIFIC RAILWAY: TRANSCONTINENTAL COMPLETION ANNIVERSARY. Nov 7, 1885. At 9:30 AM the last spike was driven at Craigellachie, British Columbia, completing the Canadian Pacific Railway's 2,980-mile transcontinental railroad track between Montreal, Quebec, in the east and Port Moody, British Columbia, in the west.

CURIE, MARIE SKLODOWSKA: BIRTH ANNIVERSARY. Nov 7, 1867. Polish chemist and physicist, born at Warsaw, Poland. In 1903 she was awarded, with her husband Pierre, the Nobel Prize for physics for their discovery of the element radium. Died near Sallanches, France, July 4, 1934. For more info: *Marie Curie*, by Leonard Everett Fisher (Macmillan, 0-02-735375-3, $14.95 Gr. 3–6).

ELECTION DAY. Nov 7. Annually, the first Tuesday after the first Monday in November. Many state and local government elections are held on this day, as well as presidential and congressional elections. All US House seats and one-third of US Senate seats are up for election in even-numbered years. Presidential elections are held in even-numbered years that can be divided by four. This day is a holiday in 12 states.

FIRST BLACK GOVERNOR ELECTED: ANNIVERSARY. Nov 7, 1989. L. Douglas Wilder was elected governor of Virginia, becoming the first elected black governor in US history. Wilder had previously served as lieutenant governor of Virginia.

GREAT OCTOBER SOCIALIST REVOLUTION: ANNIVERSARY. Nov 7, 1917. This holiday in the old Soviet Union was observed for two days with parades, military displays and appearances by Soviet leaders. According to the old Russian calendar, the revolution took place Oct 25, 1917. Soviet calendar reform causes observance to fall Nov 7 (Gregorian). The Bolshevik Revolution began at Petrograd, Russia, on the evening of Nov 6 (Gregorian), 1917. A new government headed by Nikolai Lenin took office the following day under the name Council of People's Commissars. Leon Trotsky was commissar for foreign affairs and Josef Stalin became commissar of national minorities. In the mid-1990s, President Yeltsin issued a decree renaming this holiday the "Day of National Reconciliation and Agreement."

REPUBLICAN SYMBOL: ANNIVERSARY. Nov 7, 1874. Thomas Nast used an elephant to represent the Republican Party in a satirical cartoon in *Harper's Weekly*. Today the elephant is still a well-recognized symbol for the Republican Party in political cartoons.

ROOSEVELT ELECTED TO FOURTH TERM: ANNIVERSARY. Nov 7, 1944. Defeating Thomas Dewey, Franklin D. Roosevelt became the first, and only, person elected to four terms as President of the US. Roosevelt was inaugurated the following Jan 20 but died in office Apr 12, 1945, serving only 53 days of the fourth term.

RUSSIA: OCTOBER REVOLUTION. Nov 7. National holiday in Russia and Ukraine. Commemorates the Great Socialist Revolution which occurred in October 1917 under the Old Style calendar. In the mid-1990s, President Yeltsin issued a decree renaming the holiday the "Day of National Reconciliation and Agreement."

Mary Travers, 63, composer, singer (Peter, Paul and Mary, "Puff, the Magic Dragon"), born Louisville, KY, Nov 7, 1937.

NOVEMBER 8 — WEDNESDAY
Day 313 — 53 Remaining

CORTÉS CONQUERS MEXICO: ANNIVERSARY. Nov 8, 1519. After landing on the Yucatan peninsula in April, Spaniard Hernan Cortés and his troops marched into the interior of Mexico to the Aztec capital and took the Aztec emperor Montezuma hostage.

HALLEY, EDMUND: BIRTH ANNIVERSARY. Nov 8, 1656. Astronomer and mathematician, born at London, England. Astronomer Royal, 1721–42. Died at Greenwich, England, Jan 14, 1742. He observed the great comet of 1682 (now named for him), first conceived its periodicity and wrote in his *Synopsis of Comet Astronomy*: " . . . I may venture to foretell that this Comet will return again in the year 1758." It did, and Edmund Halley's memory is kept alive by the once-every-generation appearance of Halley's Comet. There have been 28 recorded appearances of this comet since 240 BC. Average time between appearances is 76 years. Halley's Comet is next expected to be visible in 2061.

MONTANA: ADMISSION DAY: ANNIVERSARY. Nov 8. Became 41st state in 1889.

NATIONAL YOUNG READER'S DAY. Nov 8. Pizza Hut and the Center for the Book in the Library of Congress established National Young Reader's Day to remind Americans of the joys and importance of reading for young people. Schools, libraries, families and communities nationwide use this day to celebrate youth reading in a variety of creative and educational ways. Ideas on ways you can celebrate this special day available. For info: Shelley Morehead, The BOOK IT! Program, PO Box 2999, Wichita, KS 67201. Phone: (800) 426-6548. Fax: (316) 685-0977. E-mail: read@bookitprogram.com. Web: www.bookitprogram.com.

NATIONAL ASSOCIATION FOR THE EDUCATION OF YOUNG CHILDREN CONFERENCE. Nov 8–11. Atlanta, GA. For info: Natl Assn for the Education of Young Children, 1509 16th St NW, Washington, DC 20036. Phone: (202) 232-8777. Fax: (202) 328-1846. E-mail: naeyc@naeyc.org. Web: www.naeyc.org.

X-RAY DISCOVERY DAY: ANNIVERSARY. Nov 8, 1895. Physicist Wilhelm Conrad Röntgen discovered X-rays, beginning a new era in physics and medicine. Although X-rays had been observed previously, it was Röntgen, a professor at the University of Wurzburg (Germany), who successfully repeated X-ray experimentation and who is credited with the discovery. For more info: *The Mysterious Rays of Dr. Röntgen*, by Beverly Gherman (Atheneum, 0-689-31839-1, $14.95 Gr. 2–5).

BIRTHDAYS TODAY

Alfre Woodard, 47, actress (*Cross Creek, Miss Evers' Boys*), born Tulsa, OK, Nov 8, 1953.

NOVEMBER 9 — THURSDAY
Day 314 — 52 Remaining

AGNEW, SPIRO THEODORE: BIRTH ANNIVERSARY. Nov 9, 1918. The 39th vice president of the US, born at Baltimore, MD. Twice elected vice president (1968 and 1972), Agnew, Oct 10, 1973, became the second person to resign that office. Agnew entered a plea of no contest to a charge of income tax evasion (on contract kickbacks received while he was governor of Maryland and after he became vice president). He died Sept 17, 1996, at Berlin, MD. See also: "Calhoun, John Caldwell: Birth Anniversary" (Mar 18).

BANNEKER, BENJAMIN: BIRTH ANNIVERSARY. Nov 9, 1731. American astronomer, mathematician, clockmaker, surveyor and almanac author, called "first black man of science." Took part in original survey of city of Washington. Banneker's *Almanac* was published 1792–97. Born at Elliott's Mills, MD, he died at Baltimore, MD, Oct 9, 1806. A fire that started during his funeral destroyed his home, library, notebooks, almanac calculations, clocks and virtually all belongings and documents related to his life. For more info: *Dear Benjamin Banneker*, by Andrea Davis Pinkney (Harcourt, 0-15-200417-3, $14.95 Gr. 2–4). *See* Curriculum Connection.

BERLIN WALL OPENED: ANNIVERSARY. Nov 9, 1989. After 28 years as a symbol of the Cold War, the Berlin Wall was opened. East Germany opened checkpoints along its border with West Germany after a troubled month that saw many citizens flee to the West through other countries. Coming amidst the celebration of East Germany's 40-year anniversary, the pro-democracy demonstrations led to the resignation of Erich Honecker, East Germany's head of state and party chief, who had supervised the construction of the Wall. He was replaced by Egon Krenz, who promised open political debate and a lessening of restrictions on travel in attempts to stem the flow of East Germans to the West. By opening the Berlin Wall, East Germany began a course that led to the de facto reunification of the two Germanys by summer 1990. The Berlin Wall was constructed Aug 13, 1961. Berlin was at the center of a superpower crisis as US President Kennedy increased troop strength in response to the blockade of West Berlin by the Soviets. Honecker started construction, with Soviet leader Krushchev's blessing, of the 27.9-mile wall across the city. Many attempts to scale or breech the wall ensued throughout the years. But on the evening of Nov 9, 1989, citizens of both sides

	S	**M**	**T**	**W**	**T**	**F**	**S**
November				1	2	3	4
2000	5	6	7	8	9	10	11
	12	13	14	15	16	17	18
	19	20	21	22	23	24	25
	26	27	28	29	30		

NOVEMBER 9
BENJAMIN BANNEKER'S BIRTHDAY

Considered to be the "first black man of science," Benjamin Banneker was born Nov 9, 1731. He was the grandson of Bannaky, an African slave, and Molly Walsh, an indentured servant from England. Benjamin's family lived on a tobacco farm. Benjamin taught himself astronomy and higher mathematics. He wrote an almanac, first published in 1802, which provided information that helped farmers and travelers. He was a member of the surveying team that designed and planned Washington, DC. Banneker also carved wooden clockworks and built the first clock that was completely made in America.

One way you might celebrate Benjamin Banneker's contribution to history is by looking at the building and design of our nation's capital. Prior to the city's completion, the land was swampy and often mosquito infested. Named after George Washington, it was considered the most elaborately planned American city of its time. As Washington celebrates its bicentennial in 2000, Banneker's contributions to the construction of this city should be highlighted.

You might also have students research Banneker's almanac and compare the kinds of information it contained with that of modern almanacs.

For biographies about Banneker and his family see: *Molly Bannaky*, by Alice McGill (Houghton Mifflin, 0-395-72287-X, $16 All ages), *Dear Benjamin Banneker*, by Andrea Davis Pinkney (Gulliver, 0-15-200417-3, $16 Gr. K–3) and *What Are You Figuring Now?*, by Jeri Ferris (Lerner, 0-87614-521-7, $5.95 Gr. 3–6). Several websites feature Benjamin Banneker; for example, web.mit.edu/invent/www/inventorsA-H/Banneker.html.

walked freely through the barrier as others danced atop the structure to celebrate the end of an era.

CAMBODIA: INDEPENDENCE DAY. Nov 9. National Day. Commemorates independence from France in 1949.

EAST COAST BLACKOUT: 35th ANNIVERSARY. Nov 9, 1965. Massive electric power failure starting in western New York state at 5:16 PM, cut electric power to much of northeastern US and Ontario and Quebec in Canada. More than 30 million persons in an area of 80,000 square miles were affected. The experience provoked studies of the vulnerability of 20th-century technology.

KRISTALLNACHT (CRYSTAL NIGHT): ANNIVERSARY. Nov 9–10, 1938. During the evening of Nov 9 and into the morning of Nov 10, 1938, mobs in Germany destroyed thousands of shops and homes carrying out a pogrom against Jews. Synagogues were burned down or demolished. There were bonfires in every Jewish neighborhood, fueled by Jewish prayer books, Torah scrolls and volumes of philosophy, history and poetry. More than 30,000 Jews were arrested and 91 killed. The night got its name from the smashing of glass store windows.

NATIONAL CHILD SAFETY COUNCIL: 45th FOUNDING ANNIVERSARY. Nov 9, 1955. National Child Safety Council (NCSC) at Jackson, MI. NCSC is the oldest and largest nonprofit organization in the US dedicated solely to the personal safety and well-being of young children. For info: Barbara Handley Huggett, Dir Research and Development, NCSC, Box 1368, Jackson, MI 49204-1368. Phone: (517) 764-6070.

THOMPSON, KAY: BIRTH ANNIVERSARY. Nov 9, 1908. Born at St. Louis, MO, Thompson wrote the Eloise series of children's books. Eloise is a spoiled, mischievous six-year-old who lives in New York's Plaza Hotel. Books include *Eloise in Paris, Eloise in Moscow* and *The Absolutely Essential Eloise*. In 1999, Simon and Schuster released a new version of *Eloise*. Thompson died at New York, NY, July 2, 1998.

BIRTHDAYS TODAY

Pat Cummings, 50, author (*Talking with Adventurers*), born Chicago, IL, Nov 9, 1950.

Lois Ehlert, 66, author and illustrator (*Hands, Nuts to You*), born Beaver Dam, WI, Nov 9, 1934.

Lou Ferrigno, 49, actor (*Pumping Iron*, "The Incredible Hulk"), former bodybuilder, born Brooklyn, NY, Nov 9, 1951.

Robert Graham, 64, US Senator (D, Florida), born Dade County, FL, Nov 9, 1936.

Lynn Hall, 63, author (the Dragon series), born Lombard, IL, Nov 9, 1937.

NOVEMBER 10 — FRIDAY
Day 315 — 51 Remaining

EDMUND FITZGERALD SINKING: 25th ANNIVERSARY. Nov 10, 1975. The ore carrier *Edmund Fitzgerald* broke in two during a heavy storm in Lake Superior (near Whitefish Point). There were no survivors of this, the worst Great Lakes ship disaster of the decade, which took the lives of 29 crew members.

MARINE CORPS BIRTHDAY: 225th ANNIVERSARY. Nov 10. Commemorates the Marine Corps' establishment in 1775. Originally part of the navy, it became a separate unit July 11, 1789.

MICROSOFT RELEASES WINDOWS: ANNIVERSARY. Nov 10, 1983. In 1980, Microsoft signed a contract with IBM to design an operating system, MS-DOS, for a personal computer that IBM was developing. On this date Microsoft released Windows, an extension of MS-DOS with a graphical user interface.

"SESAME STREET" TV PREMIERE: ANNIVERSARY. Nov 10, 1969. An important, successful long-running children's show, "Sesame Street" educates children while they have fun. It takes place along a city street, featuring a diverse cast of humans and puppets. Through singing, puppetry, film clips and skits, kids are taught letters, numbers, concepts and other lessons. Shows are "sponsored" by letters and numbers. Human cast members have included: Loretta Long, Matt Robinson, Roscoe Orman, Bob McGrath, Linda Bove, Buffy Sainte-Marie, Ruth Buzzi, Will Lee, Northern J. Calloway, Emilio Delgado and Sonia Manzano. Favorite Jim Henson Muppets include Ernie, Bert, Grover, Oscar the Grouch, Kermit the Frog, Cookie Monster, life-sized Big Bird and Mr Snuffleupagus. Variations on "Sesame Street" are aired in 78 countries.

SPACE MILESTONE: *LUNA 17* (USSR): 30th ANNIVERSARY. Nov 10, 1970. This unmanned spacecraft landed and released *Lunakhod 1* (8-wheel, radio-controlled vehicle) on Moon's Sea of Rains Nov 17, which explored lunar surface, sending data back to Earth.

TEXAS BOOK FESTIVAL. Nov 10–12. Austin, TX. For info: Texas Book Festival, PO Box 13143, Austin, TX 78711. Phone: (512) 477-4055. Fax: (512) 322-0722. Web: www.austin360.com/texas-bookfestival.

BIRTHDAYS TODAY

Sal Barracca, 53, author, with wife Debra (*The Adventures of Taxi Dog*), born Brooklyn, NY, Nov 10, 1947.

Sinbad, 44, actor (*Unnecessary Roughness*, "A Different World"), born David Adkins, Benton Harbor, MI, Nov 10, 1956.

NOVEMBER 11 — SATURDAY
Day 316 — 50 Remaining

ANGOLA: INDEPENDENCE DAY: 25th ANNIVERSARY. Nov 11, 1975. National holiday. The West African state of Angola gained its independence from Portugal.

BONZA BOTTLER DAY™. Nov 11. To celebrate when the number of the day is the same as the number of the month. Bonza Bottler Day™ is an excuse to have a party at least once a month. For info: Gail M. Berger, 109 Matthew Ave, Poca, WV 25159. Phone: (304) 776-7746. E-mail: gberger5@aol.com.

CANADA: REMEMBRANCE DAY. Nov 11. Public holiday.

FRENCH WEST INDIES: CONCORDIA DAY. Nov 11. St. Martin. Public holiday. Parades and joint ceremony by French and Dutch officials at the obelisk Border Monument commemorating the long-standing peaceful coexistence of both countries. For info: Ms Michel Coutosiev, Mktg Challenges Intl, 10 E 21st St, New York, NY 10010. Phone: (212) 529-9069.

"GOD BLESS AMERICA" FIRST PERFORMED: ANNIVERSARY. Nov 11, 1938. Irving Berlin wrote this song especially for Kate Smith. She first sang it during her regular radio broadcast. It quickly became a great patriotic favorite of the nation and one of Smith's most requested songs.

MARTINMAS. Nov 11. The Feast Day of St. Martin of Tours, who lived about AD 316–397. A bishop, he became one of the most popular saints of the Middle Ages. The period of warm weather often occurring about the time of his feast day is sometimes called St. Martin's Summer (especially in England).

MOON PHASE: FULL MOON. Nov 11. Moon enters Full Moon phase at 4:15 PM, EST.

POLAND: INDEPENDENCE DAY. Nov 11. Poland regained independence in 1918, after having been partitioned among Austria, Prussia and Russia for more than 120 years.

SPACE MILESTONE: *GEMINI 12* (US). Nov 11, 1966. Last Project Gemini manned Earth orbit launched. Buzz Aldrin spent five hours on a space walk, setting a new record.

SWEDEN: SAINT MARTIN'S DAY. Nov 11. Originally in memory of St. Martin of Tours; also associated with Martin Luther, who is celebrated the day before. Marks the end of the autumn's work and the beginning of winter activities.

VETERANS DAY. Nov 11. Veterans Day was observed Nov 11 from 1919 through 1970. Public Law 90–363, the "Monday Holiday Law," provided that, beginning in 1971, Veterans Day would be observed on "the fourth Monday in October." This movable observance date, which separated Veterans Day from the Nov 11 anniversary of WWI Armistice, proved unpopular. State after state moved its observance back to the traditional Nov 11 date, and finally Public Law 94–97 of Sept 18, 1975, required that, effective Jan 1, 1978, the observance of Veterans Day revert to Nov 11. See also: "Armistice Day" (Nov 11). For more info about Veterans Day, go to the website of the Veterans of Foreign Wars at www.vfw.org/amesm/origins.shtml.

★**VETERANS DAY.** Nov 11. Presidential Proclamation. Formerly called "Armistice Day" and proclaimed each year since 1926 for Nov 11. PL83–380 of June 1, 1954, changed the name to "Veterans Day." PL90–363 of June 28, 1968, required that beginning in 1971 it would be observed the fourth Monday in October. PL 94–97 of Sept 18, 1975, required that effective Jan 1, 1978, the observance would revert to Nov 11.

WASHINGTON: ADMISSION DAY: ANNIVERSARY. Nov 11. Became 42nd state in 1889.

WORLD WAR I ARMISTICE: ANNIVERSARY. Nov 11, 1918. Anniversary of armistice between Allied and Central Powers ending WWI, signed at 5 AM, Nov 11, 1918, in Marshal Foch's railway car in the Forest of Compiegne, France. Hostilities ceased at 11 AM. Recognized in many countries as Armistice Day, Remembrance Day, Veterans Day, Victory Day or World War I Memorial Day. Many places observe a silent memorial at the 11th hour of the 11th day of the 11th month each year. See also: "Veterans Day" (Nov 11).

BIRTHDAYS TODAY

Barbara Boxer, 60, US Senator (D, California), born Brooklyn, NY, Nov 11, 1940.

Leonardo DiCaprio, 25, actor (*Parenthood, Titanic*), born Ridgewood, NJ, Nov 11, 1975.

Peg Kehret, 64, author (*Horror at the Haunted House*), born LaCrosse, WI, Nov 11, 1936.

Kurt Vonnegut, Jr, 78, novelist (*Slaughterhouse Five, Cat's Cradle*), born Indianapolis, IN, Nov 11, 1922.

NOVEMBER 12 — SUNDAY

Day 317 — 49 Remaining

★**AMERICAN EDUCATION WEEK.** Nov 12–18. Presidential Proclamation 5403, of Oct 30, 1985, covers all succeeding years. Always the first full week preceding the fourth Thursday in November. Issued from 1921–25 and in 1936, sometimes for a week in December and sometimes as National Education Week. After an absence of a number of years, this proclamation was issued each year from 1955–82 (issued in 1955 as a prelude to the White House Conference on Education). Previously, Proclamation 4967, of Sept 13, 1982, covered all succeeding years as the second week in November.

AMERICAN EDUCATION WEEK. Nov 12–18. Focuses attention on the importance of education and all that it stands for. Annually, the week preceding the week of Thanksgiving. For info: Natl Education Assn (NEA), 1201 16th St NW, Washington, DC 20036. Phone: (202) 833-4000. Web: www.nea.org.

BLACKMUN, HARRY A.: BIRTH ANNIVERSARY. Nov 12, 1908. Former associate justice of the Supreme Court of the US, nominated by President Nixon Apr 14, 1970. Justice Blackmun was born at Nashville, IL, Nov 12, 1908. He retired from the Court Aug 3, 1994, and died Mar 4, 1999, at Arlington, VA.

NATIONAL GEOGRAPHY AWARENESS WEEK. Nov 12–18. Focus public awareness on the importance of the knowledge of geography. To be on the mailing list for information on obtaining a Geography Awareness Week packet of teaching materials, send your name and mailing address to Geography Education Program, Natl Geographic Soc, PO Box 98190, Washington, DC 20090-8190. *See* Curriculum Connection. For additional information, visit the Society's website at www.nationalgeographic .com.

STANTON, ELIZABETH CADY: BIRTH ANNIVERSARY. Nov 12, 1815. American woman suffragist and reformer, Elizabeth Cady Stanton was born at Johnstown, NY. "We hold these truths to be self-evident," she said at the first Women's Rights

		S	M	T	W	T	F	S
November					1	2	3	4
2000		5	6	7	8	9	10	11
		12	13	14	15	16	17	18
		19	20	21	22	23	24	25
		26	27	28	29	30		

NOVEMBER 12–18
NATIONAL GEOGRAPHY AWARENESS WEEK

Geographical awareness is important in our world of instantaneous global communication. An event that occurs in a town halfway across the world is reported on TV and radio within minutes of its happening. It's a good idea to know, at least in general, where momentous events have taken place. Keep a map of the world displayed in your classroom. Ask students to search the first section of the newspaper or listen to the evening news for the locations of leading stories. Make arrow-shaped cutouts large enough to write an event, town and country location on. Pin the labeled arrow with its tip pointing to the geographical location on the world map. Change cutouts weekly, or when the need arises. You can coordinate events with the curriculum. Feature the locations of hurricanes, tornadoes or earthquakes on your map and connect them with weather units, and so on.

Map skills are crucial. One way to help students understand maps is by making a map relevant to their own lives. Have students pin stars on the map to show where they were born and where their parents or grandparents have lived. Label each star with the name of the relative, his or her classroom connection and the town's name. In the case of ancestors who immigrated, feature a boat with names listed on it in the appropriate ocean. The same can be done for present-day relatives who may have arrived by airplane.

To develop further map reading skills, students can plan a trip to locations accessible by car. Using a road atlas, they can trace and write out the route they would travel if they were to make a visit to a relative's home or another place they would like to go. On a local scale, have students map the streets they use while traveling from home to school.

Older students may want to participate in *National Geographic* magazine's Geography Bee. Information about school participation in the nationwide bee can be found at www.nationalgeographic.com/geographybee. This involves a series of tests at the school level. Winners are then tested at the state and national levels.

Maps have been used as navigation tools for many years. *Mapping the World*, by Sylvia Johnson (Simon & Schuster, 0-689-81813-0, $16 Gr. 4–8) gives an overview of how maps drawn throughout history reflect people's perception of the world.

Convention, in 1848, "that all men and women are created equal." She died at New York, NY, Oct 26, 1902. For more info: *You Want Women to Vote, Lizzie Stanton?*, by Jean Fritz (Putnam, 0-399-22786-5, $16.99 Gr. 5–9) or www.nps.gov/wori/ecs.htm.

SUN YAT-SEN: BIRTH ANNIVERSARY (TRADITIONAL). Nov 12. Although his actual birth date in 1866 is not known, Dr. Sun Yat-Sen's traditional birthday commemoration is held Nov 12. Heroic leader of China's 1911 revolution, he died at Peking, Mar 12, 1925. The death anniversary is also widely observed. See also: "Sun Yat-Sen: Death Anniversary" (Mar 12).

TYLER, LETITIA CHRISTIAN: BIRTH ANNIVERSARY. Nov 12, 1790. First wife of John Tyler, 10th president of the US, born at New Kent County, VA. Died at Washington, DC, Sept 10, 1842.

BIRTHDAYS TODAY

Jack Reed, 51, US Senator (D, Rhode Island), born Providence, RI, Nov 12, 1949.

Sammy Sosa, 32, baseball player, born San Pedro de Macoris, Dominican Republic, Nov 12, 1968.

NOVEMBER 13 — MONDAY
Day 318 — 48 Remaining

BRANDEIS, LOUIS DEMBITZ: BIRTH ANNIVERSARY. Nov 13, 1856. American jurist, associate justice of US Supreme Court (1916–39), born at Louisville, KY. Died at Washington, DC, Oct 5, 1941.

JOBARIA EXHIBITED: ANNIVERSARY. Nov 13, 1999. The dinosaur *Jobaria tiguidensis* was first exhibited at the National Geographic Society at Washington, DC on this date. The 135-million-year-old sauropod was discovered in the African country of Niger in 1997. It is 15 feet high at the hip and 70 feet long. A mold of the plant-eating dinosaur is being exhibited since the actual skeleton is too heavy. The original skeleton is being returned to Niger. For more info: www.jobaria.org.

NATIONAL CHILDREN'S BOOK WEEK. Nov 13–19. To encourage the enjoyment of reading for young people. Each year, the week has a theme. For the 81st annual celebration, the theme is "Fuel Your Mind." Posters and a suggested activity brochure are available from the sponsor. For info: The Children's Book Council, Inc, 568 Broadway, Ste 404, New York, NY 10012. Phone: (212) 966-1990. Fax: (212) 966-2073. E-mail: staff@cbcbooks.org. Web: www.cbcbooks.org.

STEVENSON, ROBERT LOUIS: 150th BIRTH ANNIVERSARY. Nov 13, 1850. Scottish author, born at Edinburgh, Scotland, known for his *Child's Garden of Verses* and novels such as *Treasure Island* and *Kidnapped*. Died at Samoa, Dec 3, 1894.

STOKES BECOMES FIRST BLACK MAYOR IN US: ANNIVERSARY. Nov 13, 1967. Carl Burton Stokes became the first black in the US elected mayor when he won the Cleveland, OH, mayoral election. Died Apr 3, 1996.

YOUTH APPRECIATION WEEK. Nov 13–19. Annually, the second full week of November, Monday–Sunday. For info: Optimist Intl, 4494 Lindell Blvd, St. Louis, MO 63108. Phone: (314) 371-6000 or your local Optimist club.

BIRTHDAYS TODAY

Jez Alborough, 41, author and illustrator (*Where's My Teddy?*), born Surrey, England, Nov 13, 1959.

Whoopi Goldberg, 51, comedienne, actress (*Ghost, Sister Act, The Color Purple*), born New York, NY, Nov 13, 1949.

Vincent (Vinny) Testaverde, 37, football player, born New York, NY, Nov 13, 1963.

NOVEMBER 14 — TUESDAY
Day 319 — 47 Remaining

AROUND THE WORLD IN 72 DAYS: ANNIVERSARY. Nov 14, 1889. Newspaper reporter Nellie Bly (pen name used by Elizabeth Cochrane Seaman) set off in 1889, to attempt to break Jules Verne's imaginary hero Phileas Fogg's record of voyaging around the world in 80 days. She did beat Fogg's record, taking 72 days, 6 hours, 11 minutes and 14 seconds to make the trip.

BLOOD TRANSFUSION: ANNIVERSARY. Nov 14, 1666. Samuel Pepys, diarist and Fellow of the Royal Society, wrote in his diary for Nov 14, 1666: "Dr. Croone told me. . .there was a pretty experiment of the blood of one dog let out, till he died, into the body of another on one side, while all his own run out on the other side. The first died upon the place, and the other very well and likely to do well. This did give occasion to many pretty wishes, as of the blood of a Quaker to be let into an Archbishop, and such like; but, as Dr. Croone says, may, if it takes, be of mighty use to man's health, for the amending of bad blood by borrowing from a better body."

COPLAND, AARON: 100th BIRTH ANNIVERSARY. Nov 14, 1900. American composer, born at Brooklyn, NY. Incorporating American folk music, he strove to create an American music style that was both popular and artistic. He composed ballets, film scores and orchestral works, including *Fanfare for the Common Man* (1942), *Appalachian Spring* (1944) (for which he won the Pulitzer Prize) and the score for *The Heiress* (1948) (for which he won an Oscar). He died Dec 2, 1990, at North Tarrytown, NY.

EISENHOWER, MAMIE DOUD: BIRTH ANNIVERSARY. Nov 14, 1896. Wife of Dwight David Eisenhower, 34th president of the US, born at Boone, IA. Died Nov 1, 1979, at Gettysburg, PA.

GUINEA-BISSAU: RE-ADJUSTMENT MOVEMENT'S DAY. Nov 14. National holiday.

INDIA: CHILDREN'S DAY. Nov 14. Holiday observed throughout India.

JORDAN: KING HUSSEIN: BIRTH ANNIVERSARY. Nov 14. H.M. King Hussein is honored each year on the anniversary of his birth in 1935 at Amman, Jordan. He died there Feb 7, 1999.

MILES, MISKA: BIRTH ANNIVERSARY. Nov 14, 1899. Author (*Annie and the Old One*), whose real name was Patricia Miles Martin, born at Cherokee, KS. Died Jan 1, 1986.

MONET, CLAUDE: BIRTH ANNIVERSARY. Nov 14, 1840. French Impressionist painter (*Water Lillies*), born at Paris. Died at Giverny, France, Dec 5, 1926.

NATIONAL AMERICAN TEDDY BEAR DAY. Nov 14. The Vermont Teddy Bear Company® annually celebrates the birth of America's most beloved companion, the Teddy bear. The legend goes that President Theodore Roosevelt spared the life of a bear cub while on a big game hunt in Mississippi in 1902. Clifford Berryman, political cartoonist, recorded the incident. Thus America's love affair with the Teddy bear began. For info: The Vermont Teddy Bear Company®, 6655 Shelburne Rd, Shelburne, VT 05482. Web: VermontTeddyBear.com.

NATIONAL COMMUNITY EDUCATION DAY. Nov 14. To recognize and promote strong relationships between public schools and the communities they serve and to help schools develop new relationships with parents, community members, local organizations and agencies. Annually, the Tuesday of American Education Week. For info: Natl Community Education Assn, 3929 Old Lee Hwy, Ste 91-A, Fairfax, VA 22030-2401. Phone: (703) 359-8973. Fax: (703) 359-0972. E-mail: ncea@ncea.com. Web: www.ncea.com.

NEHRU, JAWAHARLAL: BIRTH ANNIVERSARY. Nov 14, 1889. Indian leader and first prime minister after independence. Born at Allahabad, India, he died May 27, 1964, at New Delhi.

BIRTHDAYS TODAY

Ben Cayetano, 61, Governor of Hawaii (D), born Honolulu, HI, Nov 14, 1939.

Prince Charles, 52, Prince of Wales, heir to the British throne, born London, England, Nov 14, 1948.

Astrid Lindgren, 93, children's author (*Pippi Longstocking, The Brothers Lionheart*), born Vimmerby, Sweden, Nov 14, 1907.

Curt Schilling, 34, baseball player, born Anchorage, AK, Nov 14, 1966.

William Steig, 93, cartoonist, illustrator and author (*Pete's a Pizza*, Caldecott for *Sylvester and the Magic Pebble*), born New York, NY, Nov 14, 1907.

NOVEMBER 15 — WEDNESDAY
Day 320 — 46 Remaining

BRAZIL: REPUBLIC DAY. Nov 15. Commemorates the Proclamation of the Republic in 1889.

JAPAN: SHICHI-GO-SAN. Nov 15. Annual children's festival. The *Shichi-Go-San* (Seven-Five-Three) rite, observed Nov 15, is "the most picturesque event in the autumn season." Parents take their three-year-old children of either sex, five-year-old boys and seven-year-old girls to the parish shrines dressed in their best clothes. There the guardian spirits are thanked for the healthy growth of the children and prayers are offered for their further development.

NATIONAL EDUCATIONAL SUPPORT PERSONNEL DAY. Nov 15. A mandate of the delegates to the 1987 National Education Association Representative Assembly called for a special day during American Education Week to honor the contributions of school support employees. Local associations and school districts salute support staff on this 13th annual observance, the Wednesday of American Education Week. For info: Connie Morris, Natl Education Assn (NEA), 1201 16th St NW, Washington, DC 20036. Phone: (202) 822-7262. Fax: (202) 822-7292. Web: www.nea.org.

O'KEEFFE, GEORGIA: BIRTH ANNIVERSARY. Nov 15, 1887. Described as one of the greatest American artists of the 20th century, O'Keeffe painted desert landscapes and flower studies. Born at Sun Prairie, WI, she was married to the famous photographer Alfred Stieglitz. She died at Santa Fe, NM, Mar 6, 1986. For more info: *My Name is Georgia: A Portrait*, by Jeanette Winter (Harcourt, 0-15-201649-X, $16 Gr. 2–4).

November 2000	S	M	T	W	T	F	S
				1	2	3	4
	5	6	7	8	9	10	11
	12	13	14	15	16	17	18
	19	20	21	22	23	24	25
	26	27	28	29	30		

BIRTHDAYS TODAY

Daniel Pinkwater, 59, author (*Smarkout Boys and the Avocado of Death*), born Memphis, TN, Nov 15, 1941.

NOVEMBER 16 — THURSDAY
Day 321 — 45 Remaining

AMERICAN SPEECH–LANGUAGE–HEARING ASSOCIATION CONVENTION. Nov 16–19. Washington Convention Center, Washington, DC. Scientific sessions held on language, speech disorders, hearing science and hearing disorders and matters of professional interest to speech-language pathologists and audiologists. Est attendance: 10,000. For info: Cheryl Russell, Conv Dir, American Speech–Language–Hearing Assn, 10801 Rockville Pike, Rockville, MD 20852-3279. Phone: (301) 897-5700. Web: www.asha.org.

GREAT AMERICAN SMOKEOUT. Nov 16. A day observed annually to celebrate smoke-free environments. Annually, the third Thursday in November. For info: PR Dept, American Cancer Soc, 1599 Clifton Rd NE, Atlanta, GA 30329. Phone: (404) 329-5735. Web: www.cancer.org/gasp/index.html.

NATIONAL COUNCIL OF TEACHERS OF ENGLISH ANNUAL CONVENTION. Nov 16–19. Milwaukee, WI. For info: Natl Council of Teachers of English, 1111 W Kenyon Rd, Urbana, IL 61801-1096. Phone: (800) 369-6283 or (217) 328-3870. Web: www.ncte.org.

OKLAHOMA: ADMISSION DAY: ANNIVERSARY. Nov 16. Became 46th state in 1907.

RIEL, LOUIS: HANGING ANNIVERSARY. Nov 16, 1885. Born at St. Boniface, Manitoba, Canada, Oct 23, 1844, Louis Riel, leader of the Metis (French/Indian mixed ancestry), was elected to Canada's House of Commons in 1873 and 1874, but never seated. Confined to asylums for madness (feigned or falsely charged, some said), Riel became a US citizen in 1883. In 1885 he returned to western Canada to lead the North West Rebellion. Defeated, he surrendered and was tried for treason, convicted and hanged, at Regina, Northwest Territory, Canada. Seen as a patriot and protector of French culture in Canada, Riel's life and death became a legend and a symbol of the problems between French and English Canadians.

ROMAN CATHOLICS ISSUE NEW CATECHISM: ANNIVERSARY. Nov 16, 1992. For the first time since 1563, the Roman Catholic Church issued a new universal catechism, which addressed modern-day issues.

SAINT EUSTATIUS, WEST INDIES: STATIA AND AMERICA DAY: ANNIVERSARY. Nov 16. St. Eustatius, Leeward Islands. To commemorate the first salute to an American flag by a foreign government, from Fort Oranje in 1776. Festivities include sports events and dancing. During the American Revolution St. Eustatius was an important trading center and a supply base for the colonies.

SPACE MILESTONE: *VENERA 3* (USSR). Nov 16, 1965. This unmanned space probe crashed into Venus, Mar 1, 1966. First manmade object on another planet.

UNITED NATIONS: INTERNATIONAL DAY FOR TOLERANCE. Nov 16. On Dec 12, 1996, the General Assembly established the International Day for Tolerance, to commemorate the adoption by UNESCO member states of the Declaration of Principles on Tolerance Nov 16, 1995. For info: United Nations, Dept of Public Info, New York, NY 10017.

Oksana Baiul, 23, Olympic figure skater, born Dniepropetrovsk, Ukraine, Nov 16, 1977.

Victoria Chess, 61, illustrator (*King Long Shanks*), born Chicago, IL, Nov 16, 1939.

Jean Fritz, 85, author (Laura Ingalls Wilder Medal for *The Cabin Faced West*), born Hankow, China, Nov 16, 1915.

Dwight Eugene Gooden, 36, baseball player, born Tampa, FL, Nov 16, 1964.

Robin McKinley, 48, author (Newbery for *The Hero and the Crown*), born Jennifer Carolyn Robin McKinley, Warren, OH, Nov 16, 1952.

NOVEMBER 17 — FRIDAY

Day 322 — 44 Remaining

AMERICAN COUNCIL ON THE TEACHING OF FOREIGN LANGUAGES ANNUAL CONFERENCE. Nov 17–19. Boston, MA. For info: American Council on the Teaching of Foreign Languages, 6 Executive Plaza, Yonkers, NY 10701-6801. Phone: (914) 963-8830. Web: www.actfl.org.

NATIONAL COUNCIL FOR THE SOCIAL STUDIES ANNUAL MEETING. Nov 17–19. San Antonio, TX. 80th annual. For info: Natl Council for the Social Studies, 3501 Newark St NW, Washington, DC 20016. Phone: (202) 966-7840. Web: www.ncss.org.

★ **NATIONAL FARM-CITY WEEK.** Nov 17–23. Presidential Proclamation issued for a week in November since 1956, customarily for the week ending with Thanksgiving Day. Requested by congressional resolutions from 1956–1958; since 1959 issued annually without request.

TEXAS PTA CONVENTION. Nov 17–19. Anatole, Dallas, TX. The annual business meeting of the Texas PTA. General business meeting includes adoption of legislative positions and resolutions. More than 40 workshops are presented on parenting and parent involvement issues. Est attendance: 2,000. For info: Joan Thurman, Texas PTA, 408 W 11th St, Austin, TX 78701-2199. Phone: (512) 476-6769 or (800) TALK-PTA. Fax: (512) 476-8152. E-mail: info@txpta.org. Web: www.txpta.org.

WORLD PEACE DAY. Nov 17. World Peace Day was created to give the common person a way to demonstrate their desire for peace. To do this, people pray for peace all day, drive with their headlights on, wear a white ribbon for peace (everyday) and sign our petition for peace (available on our web page) or print our petition for peace and have 20 people sign it. Annually, Nov 17. For info: Don Morris, PO Box 565245, Miami, FL 33256-5245. Phone: (305) 270-8890. E-mail: peaceguy@peaceday.org. Web: www.peaceday.org.

Justin Cooper, 12, actor (*Liar, Liar*, "Brother's Keeper"), born Los Angeles, CA, Nov 17, 1988.

Howard Dean, 52, Governor of Vermont (D), born East Hampton, NY, Nov 17, 1948.

Danny DeVito, 56, actor (*Twins*, *Matilda*), born Neptune, NJ, Nov 17, 1944.

(Clarke) Isaac Hanson, 20, singer (Hanson), born Tulsa, OK, Nov 17, 1980.

James M. Inhofe, 66, US Senator (R, Oklahoma), born Des Moines, IA, Nov 17, 1934.

NOVEMBER 18 — SATURDAY

Day 323 — 43 Remaining

DAGUERRE, LOUIS JACQUES MANDE: BIRTH ANNIVERSARY. Nov 18, 1789. French tax collector, theater scene-painter, physicist and inventor, was born at Cormeilles-en-Parisis, France. He is remembered for his invention of the daguerreotype photographic process—one of the earliest to permit a photographic image to be chemically fixed to provide a permanent picture. The process was presented to the French Academy of Science Jan 7, 1839. Daguerre died near Paris, France, July 10, 1851.

LATVIA: INDEPENDENCE DAY. Nov 18. National holiday. Commemorates the declaration of an independent Latvia in 1918.

MICKEY MOUSE'S BIRTHDAY. Nov 18. The comical activities of squeaky-voiced Mickey Mouse first appeared in 1928, on the screen of the Colony Theatre at New York City. The film, Walt Disney's *Steamboat Willie*, was the first animated cartoon talking picture. For more info: disney.go.com.

MOON PHASE: LAST QUARTER. Nov 18. Moon enters Last Quarter phase at 10:24 AM, EST.

OMAN: NATIONAL HOLIDAY. Nov 18. Sultanate of Oman celebrates its national day.

SHEPARD, ALAN: BIRTH ANNIVERSARY. Nov 18, 1923. Astronaut, born at East Derry, NH. Shepard was the first American in space when he flew *Freedom 7* in 1961, just 23 days after Russian Yuri Gargarin was the first person in space. Shepard died July 21, 1998, near Monterey, CA.

SOUTH AFRICA ADOPTS NEW CONSTITUTION: ANNIVERSARY. Nov 18, 1993. After more than 300 years of white majority rule, basic civil rights were finally granted to blacks in South Africa. The constitution providing such rights was approved by representatives of the ruling party, as well as members of 20 other political parties.

THAILAND: ELEPHANT ROUND-UP AT SURIN. Nov 18. Elephant demonstrations in morning, elephant races and tug-of-war between 100 men and one elephant. Observed since 1961 on third Saturday in November. Special trains from Bangkok on previous day.

US UNIFORM TIME ZONE PLAN: ANNIVERSARY. Nov 18, 1883. Charles Ferdinand Dowd, a Connecticut school teacher and one of the early advocates of uniform time, proposed a time zone plan of the US (four zones of 15 degrees), which he and others persuaded the railroads to adopt and place in operation. Info from National Bureau of Standards Monograph 155. See also: "US Standard Time Act: Anniversary" (Mar 19).

Dante Bichette, 37, baseball player, born West Palm Beach, FL, Nov 18, 1963.

Wilma Mankiller, 55, Chief of the Cherokee Nation 1985–95, born Tahlequah, OK, Nov 18, 1945.

Warren Moon, 44, football player, born Los Angeles, CA, Nov 18, 1956.

Ted Stevens, 77, US Senator (R, Alaska), born Indianapolis, IN, Nov 18, 1923.

Nancy Van Laan, 61, author (*So Say the Little Monkeys*), born Baton Rouge, LA, Nov 18, 1939.

NOVEMBER 19 — SUNDAY
Day 324 — 42 Remaining

BELIZE: GARIFUNA DAY. Nov 19. Public holiday celebrating the first arrival of Black Caribs from St. Vincent and Rotan to Southern Belize.

CAMPANELLA, ROY: BIRTH ANNIVERSARY. Nov 19, 1921. Baseball Hall of Fame catcher, born at Philadelphia, PA. Died at Woodland Hills, CA, June 26, 1993.

COLD WAR FORMALLY ENDED: 10th ANNIVERSARY. Nov 19–21, 1990. A summit was held at Paris with the leaders of the Conference on Security and Cooperation in Europe (CSCE) Nov 19–21, 1990. The highlight of the summit was the signing of a treaty to dramatically reduce conventional weapons in Europe, thereby ending the Cold War.

FIRST AUTOMATIC TOLL COLLECTION MACHINE: ANNIVERSARY. Nov 19, 1954. At the Union Toll Plaza on New Jersey's Garden State Parkway motorists dropped 25¢ into a wire mesh hopper and a green light would flash. The first modern toll road was the Pennsylvania Turnpike which opened in 1940.

GARFIELD, JAMES ABRAM: BIRTH ANNIVERSARY. Nov 19, 1831. The 20th president of the US (Mar 4–Sept 19, 1881) was born at Orange, OH and was the first left-handed president. Term of office: Mar 4–Sept 19, 1881. While walking into the Washington, DC, railway station on the morning of July 2, 1881, Garfield was shot by disappointed office seeker Charles J. Guiteau. He survived, in very weak condition, until Sept 19, 1881, when he succumbed to blood poisoning at Elberon, NJ (where he had been taken for recuperation). Guiteau was tried, convicted and hanged at the jail at Washington, June 30, 1882.

GERMANY: VOLKSTRAUERTAG. Nov 19. Memorial Day and national day of mourning in all German states. Observed on the Sunday before Totensonntag.

LINCOLN'S GETTYSBURG ADDRESS: ANNIVERSARY. Nov 19, 1863. Seventeen acres of the Civil War battlefield at Gettysburg, PA, were dedicated as a national cemetery. Noted orator Edward Everett spoke for two hours; the address that Lincoln delivered in less than two minutes was later recognized as one of the most eloquent of the English language. Five manuscript copies in Lincoln's hand survive, including the rough draft begun in ink at the executive mansion at Washington and concluded in pencil at Gettysburg on the morning of the dedication (kept at the Library of Congress). For more info: *The Gettysburg Address* (Houghton Mifflin, 0-395-69824-3, $14.95 Gr. 3–5).

	S	M	T	W	T	F	S
November				1	2	3	4
2000	5	6	7	8	9	10	11
	12	13	14	15	16	17	18
	19	20	21	22	23	24	25
	26	27	28	29	30		

MONACO: NATIONAL HOLIDAY. Nov 19.

NATIONAL ADOPTION WEEK. Nov 19–25. To commemorate the success of three kinds of adoption—infant, special needs and intercountry—through a variety of special events. Annually, the week of Thanksgiving. Est attendance: 15,000. For info: Natl Council for Adoption, 1930 17th St NW, Washington, DC 20009-6207. Phone: (202) 328-1200. Fax: (202) 332-0935.

NATIONAL BIBLE WEEK. Nov 19–26. An interfaith campaign to promote reading and study of the Bible. Resource packets available. Governors and mayors across the country proclaim National Bible Week observance in their constituencies. Annually, from the Sunday preceding Thanksgiving to the following Sunday. For info: Thomas R. May, Exec Dir, Natl Bible Assn, 1865 Broadway, 7th Floor, New York, NY 10023. Phone: (212) 408-1390.

★**NATIONAL FAMILY WEEK.** Nov 19–25.

NATIONAL GAME AND PUZZLE WEEK. Nov 19–25. To increase appreciation of games and puzzles while conserving the tradition of investing time with family and friends. Annually, the last week in November. For info: Frank Beres, Patch Products, PO Box 268, Beloit, WI 53512-0268. Phone: (608) 362-6896. Fax: (608) 362-8178. E-mail: patch@patchproducts.com. Web: www.patchproducts.com.

PUERTO RICO: DISCOVERY DAY. Nov 19. Public holiday. Columbus discovered Puerto Rico in 1493 on his second voyage to the New World.

RETIRED TEACHER'S DAY IN FLORIDA. Nov 19. A ceremonial day to honor the retired teachers of the state.

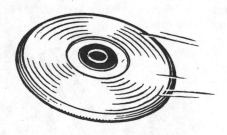

"ROCKY AND HIS FRIENDS" TV PREMIERE: ANNIVERSARY. Nov 19, 1959. This popular cartoon featured the adventures of a talking squirrel, Rocky (Rocket J. Squirrel), and his friend Bullwinkle, a flaky moose. The tongue-in-cheek dialogue contrasted with the simple plots in which Rocky and Bullwinkle tangled with Russian bad guys Boris Badenov and Natasha (who worked for Mr Big). Other popular segments on the show included the adventures of Sherman and Mr Peabody (an intelligent talking dog). In 1961 the show was renamed "The Bullwinkle Show," but the cast of characters remained the same.

SCHAEFER, JACK: BIRTH ANNIVERSARY. Nov 19, 1907. Author of the bestseller *Shane*, which was later made into an award-winning film. Born at Cleveland, OH, Schaefer died Jan 24, 1991, at Santa Fe, NM.

Eileen Collins, 44, first female shuttle commander, Lieutenant Colonel USAF, born Elmira, NY, Nov 19, 1956.

Gail Devers, 34, Olympic gold medal sprinter, born Seattle, WA, Nov 19, 1966.

Jodie Foster, 38, actress (*Little Man Tate, Nell*), director (*Home for the Holidays*), born Los Angeles, CA, Nov 19, 1962.

Thomas R. Harkin, 61, US Senator (D, Iowa), born Cumming, IA, Nov 19, 1939.

Jim Hodges, 44, Governor of South Carolina (D), born Lancaster, SC, Nov 19, 1956.

Ahmad Rashad, 51, sportscaster, former football player, born Bobby Moore, Portland, OR, Nov 19, 1949.

Meg Ryan, 39, actress (*Sleepless in Seattle*), born Fairfield, CT, Nov 19, 1961.

Kerri Strug, 23, Olympic gymnast, born Tucson, AZ, Nov 19, 1977.

Tommy G. Thompson, 59, Governor of Wisconsin (R), born Elroy, WI, Nov 19, 1941.

Ted Turner, 62, baseball, basketball and cable TV executive, born Cincinnati, OH, Nov 19, 1938.

NOVEMBER 20 — MONDAY
Day 325 — 41 Remaining

BILL OF RIGHTS: ANNIVERSARY OF FIRST STATE RATIFICATION. Nov 20, 1789. New Jersey became the first state to ratify 10 of the 12 amendments to the US Constitution proposed by Congress Sept 25. These 10 amendments came to be known as the Bill of Rights.

FINLAND: INTERNATIONAL CHILDREN'S FILM FESTIVAL. Nov 20–26. Oulu. This one-week event gives festival visitors an opportunity to view several dozen feature-length films. Est attendance: 10,000. For info: Finnish Tourist Board, 655 Third Ave, New York, NY 10017. Phone: (212) 885-9700 or (358) (8) 881-1293. Fax: (358) (8) 8811290. Web: www.ouka.fi/oek/.

KENNEDY, ROBERT FRANCIS: 75th BIRTH ANNIVERSARY. Nov 20, 1925. US Senator and younger brother of John F. Kennedy (35th president), born at Brookline, MA. An assassin shot him at Los Angeles, CA, June 5, 1968, while he was campaigning for the presidential nomination. He died the next day. Sirhan Sirhan was convicted of his murder.

LAURIER, SIR WILFRED: BIRTH ANNIVERSARY. Nov 20, 1841. Canadian statesman (premier, 1896–1911), born at St. Lin, Quebec. Died Feb 17, 1919, at Ottawa, Ontario.

MEXICO: REVOLUTION: 90th ANNIVERSARY. Nov 20. Anniversary of the social revolution launched by Francisco I. Madero in 1910. National holiday.

UNITED NATIONS: UNIVERSAL CHILDREN'S DAY. Nov 20. Designated by the United Nations General Assembly as Universal Children's Day. First observance was in 1953. A time to honor children with special ceremonies and festivals and to make children's needs known to governments. Observed on different days in more than 120 nations; Nov 20 marks the day in 1959 when the General Assembly adopted the Declaration of the Rights of the Child.

WOLCOTT, OLIVER: BIRTH ANNIVERSARY. Nov 20, 1726. Signer of the Declaration of Independence, Governor of Connecticut, born at Windsor, CT. Died Dec 1, 1797, at Litchfield, CT.

BIRTHDAYS TODAY

Marion Dane Bauer, 62, author (*On My Honor*), born Oglesby, IL, Nov 20, 1938.

Joseph Robinette Biden, Jr, 58, US Senator (D, Delaware), born Scranton, PA, Nov 20, 1942.

Robert C. Byrd, 83, US Senator (D, West Virginia), born North Wilkesboro, NC, Nov 20, 1917.

NOVEMBER 21 — TUESDAY
Day 326 — 40 Remaining

CONGRESS FIRST MEETS IN WASHINGTON: 200th ANNIVERSARY. Nov 21, 1800. Congress met at Philadelphia from 1790 to 1800, when the north wing of the new Capitol at Washington, DC was completed. The House and Senate were scheduled to meet in the new building Nov 17, 1800 but a quorum wasn't achieved until Nov 21. To take a virtual tour of the Capitol, go to: www.senate.gov/vtour.

NORTH CAROLINA RATIFIES CONSTITUTION: ANNIVERSARY. Nov 21. Became 12th state to ratify Constitution in 1789.

SPEARE, ELIZABETH GEORGE: BIRTH ANNIVERSARY. Nov 21, 1908. Author (Newbery for *The Bronze Bow*, *The Witch of Blackbird Pond*), born at Melrose, MA. Died at Tucson, AZ, Nov 15, 1994.

UNITED NATIONS: WORLD TELEVISION DAY. Nov 21. On Dec 17, 1996, the General Assembly proclaimed this day as World Television Day, commemorating the date in 1996 on which the first World Television Forum was held at the UN. Info from: United Nations, Dept of Public Info, New York, NY 10017.

WORLD HELLO DAY. Nov 21. Everyone who participates greets 10 people. People in 180 countries have participated in this annual activity for advancing peace through personal communication. Heads of state of 114 countries have expressed approval of the event. 28th annual observance. For info: Michael McCormack, The McCormack Brothers, Box 993, Omaha, NE 68101. Web: www.worldhelloday.org.

BIRTHDAYS TODAY

Troy Aikman, 34, football player, born West Covina, CA, Nov 21, 1966.

Richard J. Durbin, 56, US Senator (D, Illinois), born East St. Louis, IL, Nov 21, 1944.

George Kenneth (Ken) Griffey, Jr, 31, baseball player, born Donora, PA, Nov 21, 1969.

Stanley ("Stan the Man") Musial, 80, Baseball Hall of Fame outfielder and first baseman, born Donora, PA, Nov 21, 1920.

Harold Ramis, 56, actor (*Ghostbusters*, *Ghostbusters II*), born Chicago, IL, Nov 21, 1944.

Marlo Thomas, 62, actress ("That Girl"), author (*Free to Be . . . You and Me*), born Detroit, MI, Nov 21, 1938.

Megan Whalen Turner, 35, author (*The Thief*), born Fort Sill, OK, Nov 21, 1965.

NOVEMBER 22 — WEDNESDAY
Day 327 — 39 Remaining

ADAMS, ABIGAIL SMITH: BIRTH ANNIVERSARY. Nov 22, 1744. Wife of John Adams, second president of the US, born at Weymouth, MA. Died Oct 28, 1818, at Quincy, MA.

GARNER, JOHN NANCE: BIRTH ANNIVERSARY. Nov 22, 1868. The 32nd vice president of US (1933–41) born at Red River County, TX. Died at Uvalde, TX, Nov 7, 1967.

GERMANY: BUSS UND BETTAG. Nov 22. Buss und Bettag (Repentance Day) is observed on the Wednesday before the last Sunday of the church year. A legal public holiday in all German states except Bavaria (where it is observed only in communities with predominantly Protestant populations).

LEBANON: INDEPENDENCE DAY. Nov 22. National Day. Gained independence from France in 1943.

NATIONAL STOP THE VIOLENCE DAY. Nov 22. Radio and television stations across the nation are encouraged to promote "Peace on the Streets" and help put an end to gang (and other) violence through Stop the Violence Day. Participating stations unite to call for a one-day cease fire, the idea being, "If we can stop the violence for one day, we can stop the violence everyday, one day at a time." Stations also encourage listeners/viewers to wear and display white ribbons that day and drive with their headlights on as a show of peace. Many stations hold peace rallies with local community leaders and also conduct a moment of silence on the air in honor of the year's victims of violence. Begun in 1990. Annually, on the anniversary of President John F. Kennedy's assassination. For info: Cliff Berkowitz, Pres, Lost Coast Communications, Inc, PO Box 25, Ferndale, CA 95536. Phone: (707) 786-5104. Fax: (707) 786-5100.

"WHAT DO YOU LOVE ABOUT AMERICA" DAY. Nov 22. One day to talk about what's great about our country and its people. In the midst of cynicism, let's talk to each other about what we love. Annually, the day before Thanksgiving. For info: Chuck Sutherland, 6906 Waggoner Pl, Dallas, TX 75230. Phone: (214) 696-9214. Fax: (214) 696-6742. E-mail: sutherla@swbell.net.

BIRTHDAYS TODAY

Boris Becker, 33, tennis player, born Leimen, Germany, Nov 22, 1967.
Guion S. Bluford, Jr, 58, first black astronaut in space, born Philadelphia, PA, Nov 22, 1942.
Jamie Lee Curtis, 42, actress, author (*Today I Feel Silly and Other Moods That Make My Day*), born Los Angeles, CA, Nov 22, 1958.

NOVEMBER 23 — THURSDAY
Day 328 — 38 Remaining

AMERICA'S THANKSGIVING PARADE. Nov 23. Woodward Ave, Detroit, MI. The annual parade kicks off the holiday season with nearly 100 units marching. Annually, on Thanksgiving morning. Est attendance: 1,300,000. For info: Dennis Carnovale, The Parade Co, 9600 Mt Elliott, Detroit, MI 48211. Phone: (313) 923-7400. Fax: (313) 923-2920.

JAPAN: LABOR THANKSGIVING DAY. Nov 23. National holiday.

MACY'S THANKSGIVING DAY PARADE. Nov 23. New York, NY. Starts at 9 AM, EST, in Central Park West. A part of everyone's Thanksgiving, the parade grows bigger and better each year. Featuring floats, giant balloons, marching bands and famous stars, the parade is televised for the whole country. 72nd annual parade. For info: New York CVB, 810 Seventh Ave, New York, NY 10019. Phone: (212) 484-1222. Web: www.nycvisit.com.

PIERCE, FRANKLIN: BIRTH ANNIVERSARY. Nov 23, 1804. The 14th president of the US (Mar 4, 1853–Mar 3, 1857) was born at Hillsboro, NH. Not nominated until the 49th ballot at the Democratic party convention in 1852, he was refused his party's nomination in 1856 for a second term. Pierce died at Concord, NH, Oct 8, 1869.

RUTLEDGE, EDWARD: BIRTH ANNIVERSARY. Nov 23, 1749. Signer of the Declaration of Independence, governor of South Carolina, born at Charleston, SC. Died there Jan 23, 1800.

November 2000	S	M	T	W	T	F	S
				1	2	3	4
	5	6	7	8	9	10	11
	12	13	14	15	16	17	18
	19	20	21	22	23	24	25
	26	27	28	29	30		

SAGITTARIUS, THE ARCHER. Nov 23–Dec 21. In the astronomical/astrological zodiac that divides the sun's apparent orbit into 12 segments, the period Nov 22–Dec 21 is identified, traditionally, as the sun-sign of Sagittarius, the Archer. The ruling planet is Jupiter.

★**THANKSGIVING DAY.** Nov 23. Presidential Proclamation. Always issued for the fourth Thursday in November. See also: "First US Holiday by Presidential Proclamation: Anniversary" (Nov 26).

THANKSGIVING DAY. Nov 23. Legal public holiday. (Public Law 90–363 sets Thanksgiving Day on the fourth Thursday in November). Observed in all states. In most states, the Friday after Thanksgiving is also a holiday; in Nevada it is called Family Day. For links to sites about Thanksgiving on the web, go to: deil.lang.uiuc.edu /web.pages/holidays/thanksgiving.html.

BIRTHDAYS TODAY

Vin Baker, 29, basketball player, born Lake Wales, FL, Nov 23, 1971.
Mary L. Landrieu, 45, US Senator (D, Louisiana), born Arlington, VA, Nov 23, 1955.
Charles E. Schumer, 50, US Senator (D, New York), born Brooklyn, NY, Nov 23, 1950.

NOVEMBER 24 — FRIDAY
Day 329 — 37 Remaining

BARKLEY, ALBEN WILLIAM: BIRTH ANNIVERSARY. Nov 24, 1877. The 35th vice president of the US (1949–53), born at Graves County, KY. Died at Lexington, VA, Apr 30, 1956.

BLACK FRIDAY. Nov 24. The traditional beginning of the Christmas shopping season on the Friday after Thanksgiving.

BURNETT, FRANCES HODGSON: BIRTH ANNIVERSARY. Nov 24, 1849. Children's author, noted for the classics *Little Lord Fauntleroy*, *The Secret Garden* and *A Little Princess*. Born at Manchester, England, she died at Long Island, NY, Oct 29, 1924.

BUY NOTHING DAY. Nov 24. A 24-hour moratorium on consumer spending, a celebration of simplicity, about getting our runaway consumer culture back onto a sustainable path. Annually, on the first shopping day after Thanksgiving. For info: The Media Foundation, 1243 W 7th Ave, Vancouver, BC, Canada V6H 1B7. Phone: (800) 663-1243. Fax: (604) 737-6021. E-mail: buynothingday@adbusters.org.

FAMILY DAY IN NEVADA. Nov 24. Observed annually on the Friday following the fourth Thursday in November.

TAYLOR, ZACHARY: BIRTH ANNIVERSARY. Nov 24, 1784. The soldier who became 12th president of the US (Mar 4, 1849–July 9, 1850) was born at Orange County, VA. He was nominated at the Whig party convention in 1848, but, the story goes, he did not accept the letter notifying him of his nomination because it had postage due. He cast his first vote in 1846, when he was 62 years old. Becoming ill July 4, 1850, he died at the White House, July 9.

UCHIDA, YOSHIKO: BIRTH ANNIVERSARY. Nov 24, 1921. Author (*Journey to Topaz: A Story of the Japanese-American Evacuation*), born at Alameda, CA. Died 1992.

BIRTHDAYS TODAY

Sylvia Louise Engdahl, 67, author (*Enchantress from the Stars*), born Los Angeles, CA, Nov 24, 1933.

Mordicai Gerstein, 65, author (*The Wild Boy*), born Los Angeles, CA, Nov 24, 1935.

Dan Glickman, 56, US Secretary of Agriculture, born Wichita, KS, Nov 24, 1944.

Meredith Henderson, 17, actress ("The Adventures of Shirley Holmes: Detective"), born Ottawa, Ontario, Canada, Nov 24, 1983.

NOVEMBER 25 — SATURDAY
Day 330 — 36 Remaining

AUTOMOBILE SPEED REDUCTION: ANNIVERSARY. Nov 25, 1973. Anniversary of the presidential order requiring a cutback from the 70 mph speed limit due to the energy crisis. The 55 mph National Maximum Speed Limit (NMSL) was established by Congress in January 1974. The National Highway Traffic Administration reported that "the 55 mph NMSL forestalled 48,310 fatalities through 1980. There were also reductions in crash-related injuries and property damage." Motor fuel savings were estimated at 2.4 billion gallons per year. Notwithstanding, in 1987 Congress permitted states to increase speed limits on rural interstate highways to 65 mph.

CARNEGIE, ANDREW: BIRTH ANNIVERSARY. Nov 25, 1835. American financier, philanthropist and benefactor of more than 2,500 libraries, was born at Dunfermline, Scotland. Carnegie Hall, Carnegie Foundation and the Carnegie Endowment for International Peace are among his gifts. Carnegie wrote in 1889, "Surplus wealth is a sacred trust which its possessor is bound to administer in his lifetime for the good of the community. . . . The man who dies . . . rich dies disgraced." Carnegie died at his summer estate, "Shadowbrook," MA, Aug 11, 1919.

DiMAGGIO, JOSEPH PAUL (JOE): BIRTH ANNIVERSARY. Nov 25, 1914. Baseball Hall of Fame outfielder, born at Martinez, CA. In 1941 he was on "the streak," getting a hit in 56 consecutive games. He was the American League MVP for three years, was the batting champion in 1939 and led the league in RBIs in both 1941 and 1948. DiMaggio died at Harbour Island, FL, Mar 8, 1999.

EASTMAN, P.D.: BIRTH ANNIVERSARY. Nov 25, 1909. Philip Dey Eastman was born at Amherst, MA. His *Are You My Mother?* and *Go, Dog, Go!* rank among the best-selling children's books of all time. He died Jan 7, 1986.

MEXICO: GUADALAJARA INTERNATIONAL BOOK FAIR. Nov 25–Dec 3. Mexico's largest book fair with exhibitors from all over the Spanish-speaking world. Est attendance: 275,000. For info: David Unger, Guadalajara Book Fair–US Office, Div of Hum, NAC 6293, City College, New York, NY 10031. Phone: (212) 650-7925. Fax: (212) 650-7912. E-mail: daucc@cunyvm.cuny.edu.

MOON PHASE: NEW MOON. Nov 25. Moon enters New Moon phase at 6:11 PM, EST.

POPE JOHN XXIII: BIRTH ANNIVERSARY. Nov 25, 1881. Angelo Roncalli, 261st pope of the Roman Catholic Church, born at Sotte il Monte, Italy. Elected pope, Oct 28, 1958. Died June 3, 1963, at Rome, Italy.

SHOPPING REMINDER DAY. Nov 25. One month before Christmas, a reminder to shoppers that there are only 24 more shopping days (excluding Sundays, Thanksgiving and Christmas Eve) after today until Christmas, and that one month from today a new countdown will begin for Christmas 2001.

SURINAME: INDEPENDENCE DAY: 25th ANNIVERSARY. Nov 25. Holiday. Gained independence from the Netherlands in 1975.

BIRTHDAYS TODAY

Marc Brown, 54, author and illustrator (the Arthur series), born Erie, PA, Nov 25, 1946.

Crescent Dragonwagon, 48, author (*Half a Moon and One Whole Star*), born Ellen Zolotow, New York, NY, Nov 25, 1952.

Donovan McNabb, 24, football player, born Dolton, IL, Nov 25, 1976.

NOVEMBER 26 — SUNDAY
Day 331 — 35 Remaining

CUSTER BATTLEFIELD BECOMES LITTLE BIGHORN BATTLEFIELD: ANNIVERSARY. Nov 26, 1991. The US Congress approved a bill renaming Custer Battlefield National Monument as Little Bighorn Battlefield National Monument. The bill also authorized the construction of a memorial to the Native Americans who fought and died at the battle known as Custer's Last Stand. Introduced by then Representative Ben Nighthorse Campbell, the only Native American in Congress, the bill was signed into law by President George Bush.

FIRST US HOLIDAY BY PRESIDENTIAL PROCLAMATION: ANNIVERSARY. Nov 26, 1789. President George Washington proclaimed Nov 26, 1789, to be Thanksgiving Day. Both Houses of Congress, by their joint committee, had requested him to recommend a day of public thanksgiving and prayer, to be observed by acknowledging with grateful hearts the many and signal favors of Almighty God, especially by affording them an opportunity to peaceably establish a form of government for their safety and happiness. Proclamation issued Oct 3, 1789.

JOHN F. KENNEDY DAY IN MASSACHUSETTS. Nov 26. Proclaimed annually by the governor for the last Sunday in November.

PASADENA DOO DAH PARADE. Nov 26. Pasadena, CA. No theme, no judging, no prizes, no order of march, no motorized vehicles and no animals. Annually, the Sunday following Thanksgiving Day.

SCHULZ, CHARLES: BIRTH ANNIVERSARY. Nov 26, 1922. Cartoonist ("Peanuts"), born at Minneapolis, MN. Died Feb 12, 2000, at Santa Rosa, CA.

SLINKY® INTRODUCED: ANNIVERSARY. Nov 26, 1945. In 1943 engineer Richard James was working in a Philadelphia shipyard trying to find a way to stabilize a piece of equipment on a ship in heavy seas. One idea was to suspend it on springs. One day a spring tumbled off his desk, giving him the idea for a toy. The accidental plaything was introduced by James and his wife in a Philadelphia department store during the 1945 Christmas season. Today more than 250,000,000 Slinkys have been sold. For more info: www.poof-toys.com.

TRUTH, SOJOURNER: DEATH ANNIVERSARY. Nov 26, 1883. A former slave who had been sold four different times, Sojourner Truth became an evangelist who argued for abolition and women's rights. After a troubled early life, she began her evangelical career in 1843, traveling through New England until she discovered the utopian colony called the Northampton Association of Education and Industry. It was there she was exposed to, and became an advocate for, the cause of abolition, working with Frederick Douglass, Wendall Phillips, William Lloyd Garrison and others. In 1850 she befriended Lucretia Mott, Elizabeth Cady Stanton and other feminist leaders and actively began supporting calls for women's rights. In 1870 she attempted to petition Congress to create a "Negro State" on public lands in the West. Born at Ulster County, NY, about 1790, she died Nov 26, 1883, at Battle Creek, MI. For more info: www.sojournertruth.org.

BIRTHDAYS TODAY

Jessica Bowman, 20, actress ("Dr. Quinn, Medicine Woman"), born Walnut Creek, CA, Nov 26, 1980.
Shannon Dunn, 28, Olympic snowboarder, born Arlington Heights, IL, Nov 26, 1972.
Shawn Kemp, 31, NBA forward, member of Dream Team II, born Elkhart, IN, Nov 26, 1969.
Laurence Pringle, 65, science writer (*An Extraordinary Life: The Story of a Monarch Butterfly*), born Rochester, NY, Nov 26, 1935.

NOVEMBER 27 — MONDAY

Day 332 — 34 Remaining

LIVINGSTON, ROBERT R.: BIRTH ANNIVERSARY. Nov 27, 1746. Member of the Continental Congress, farmer, diplomat and jurist, born at New York, NY. It was Livingston who administered the oath of office to President George Washington in 1789. He died at Clermont, NY, Feb 26, 1813.

RAMADAN: THE ISLAMIC MONTH OF FASTING. Nov 27–Dec 26. Begins on Islamic lunar calendar date Ramadan 1, 1421. Ramadan, the ninth month of the Islamic calendar, is holy because it was during this month that the Holy Qur'an [Koran] was revealed. All adults of sound body and mind fast from dawn (before sunrise) until sunset to achieve spiritual and physical

	S	M	T	W	T	F	S
November				1	2	3	4
2000	5	6	7	8	9	10	11
	12	13	14	15	16	17	18
	19	20	21	22	23	24	25
	·26	27	28	29	30		

purification and self-discipline, abstaining from food, drink and intimate relations. It is a time for feeling a common bond with the poor and needy, a time of piety and prayer. Different methods for "anticipating" the visibility of the new moon crescent at Mecca are used by different Muslim groups. US date may vary. For links to Ramadan sites on the web, go to: deil.lang.uiuc.edu /web.pages/holidays/ramadan.html or holidays.net/ramadan/.

WEIZMANN, CHAIM: BIRTH ANNIVERSARY. Nov 27, 1874. Israeli statesman, born near Pinsk, Byelorussia. He played an important role in bringing about the British government's Balfour Declaration, calling for the establishment of a national home for Jews at Palestine. He died at Tel Aviv, Israel, Nov 9, 1952.

BIRTHDAYS TODAY

Kevin Henkes, 40, author and illustrator (*Lilly's Purple Plastic Purse*), born Racine, WI, Nov 27, 1960.
Bill Nye, 45, host ("Bill Nye, the Science Guy"), born Washington, DC, Nov 27, 1955.
Nick Van Exel, 29, basketball player, born Kenosha, WI, Nov 27, 1971.
Jaleel White, 24, actor ("Family Matters"), born Los Angeles, CA, Nov 27, 1976.

NOVEMBER 28 — TUESDAY

Day 333 — 33 Remaining

ALBANIA: INDEPENDENCE DAY. Nov 28. National holiday. Commemorates independence from the Ottoman Empire in 1912.

MAURITANIA: INDEPENDENCE DAY: 40th ANNIVERSARY. Nov 28. National holiday. This country in the northwest part of Africa attained sovereignty from France on this day in 1960.

PANAMA: INDEPENDENCE FROM SPAIN. Nov 28. Public holiday. Commemorates the independence of Panama (which at the time was part of Colombia) from Spain in 1821.

BIRTHDAYS TODAY

Ed Harris, 50, actor (*The Right Stuff*), born Englewood, NJ, Nov 28, 1950.
Mary Lyons, 53, author of biographies (*Catching the Fire: Philip Simmons, Blacksmith*), born Macon, GA, Nov 28, 1947.
Ed Young, 69, author and illustrator (Caldecott for *Lon Po Po: A Red Riding Hood Story from China*), born Tientsin, China, Nov 28, 1931.

NOVEMBER 29 — WEDNESDAY

Day 334 — 32 Remaining

ALCOTT, LOUISA MAY: BIRTH ANNIVERSARY. Nov 29, 1832. American author, born at Philadelphia, PA. Died at Boston, MA, Mar 6, 1888. Her most famous novel was *Little Women*, the classic story of Meg, Jo, Beth and Amy.

CZECHOSLOVAKIA ENDS COMMUNIST RULE: ANNIVERSARY. Nov 29, 1989. Czechoslovakia ended 41 years of one-party communist rule when the Czechoslovak parliament voted unanimously to repeal the constitutional clauses giving the Communist Party a guaranteed leading role in the country and promoting Marxism-Leninism as the state ideology. The vote came at the end of a 12-day revolution sparked by the beating of protestors Nov 17. Although the Communist party remained in power, the tide of reform led to its ouster by the Civic Forum, headed by playwright Vaclav Havel. The Civic Forum demanded free elections with equal rights for all parties, a mixed economy and support for foreign investment. In the first free elections in Czechoslovakia since WWII, Vaclav Havel was elected president.

"KUKLA, FRAN AND OLLIE" TV PREMIERE: ANNIVERSARY. Nov 29, 1948. This popular children's show featured puppets created and handled by Burr Tillstrom and was equally popular with adults. Fran Allison was the only human on the show. Tillstrom's lively and eclectic cast of characters, called the "Kuklapolitans," included the bald, high-voiced Kukla, the big-toothed Oliver J. Dragon (Ollie), Fletcher Rabbit, Cecil Bill, Beulah the Witch, Colonel Crackie, Madame Ooglepuss and Dolores Dragon. Most shows were performed without scripts.

LEWIS, C.S. (CLIVE STAPLES): BIRTH ANNIVERSARY. Nov 29, 1898. British scholar, novelist and author (*The Screwtape Letters, Chronicles of Narnia*), born at Belfast, Ireland. *The Lion, the Witch and the Wardrobe*, the first volume in the seven-volume Chronicles of Narnia series, was published in 1950. Died at Oxford, England, Nov 22, 1963.

NATIONAL COMMUNITY EDUCATION ASSOCIATION CONFERENCE. Nov 29–Dec 2. The Nugget, Reno, NV. 35th annual. Largest national gathering for community educators and others interested in promoting parent-community involvement in education, forming community partnerships to address community needs and expanding lifelong learning opportunities for all community residents. Est attendance: 700. For info: Ursula Ellis, Dir of Communications, Natl Community Education Assn, 3929 Old Lee Hwy, Ste 91-A, Fairfax, VA 22030-2401. Phone: (703) 359-8973. Fax: (703) 359-0972. E-mail: ncea@ncea.com. Web: www.ncea.com.

WAITE, MORRISON R.: BIRTH ANNIVERSARY. Nov 29, 1816. Seventh Chief Justice of the Supreme Court, born at Lyme, CT. Appointed Chief Justice by President Ulysses S. Grant Jan 19, 1874. The Waite Court is remembered for its controversial rulings that did much to rehabilitate the idea of states' rights after the Civil War and early Reconstruction years. Waite died at Washington, DC, Mar 23, 1888.

BIRTHDAYS TODAY

Helga Aichinger, 63, illustrator (*The Shepherd*), born Traun, Austria, Nov 29, 1937.

Eric Beddows, 49, illustrator (*Joyful Noise*), born Ontario, Canada, Nov 29, 1951.

Jacques Rene Chirac, 68, French President, born Paris, France, Nov 29, 1932.

Madeleine L'Engle, 82, author (Newbery for *A Wrinkle in Time, The Time Quartet*), born New York, NY, Nov 29, 1918.

Howie Mandel, 45, actor, producer ("Bobby's World"), born Toronto, Ontario, Canada, Nov 29, 1955.

Andrew McCarthy, 38, actor (*Pretty in Pink, Weekend at Bernie's*), born Westfield, NJ, Nov 29, 1962.

Mariano Rivera, 31, baseball player, born Panama City, Panama, Nov 29, 1969.

Adam Zolotin, 17, actor (*Jack*), born Long Island, NY, Nov 29, 1983.

NOVEMBER 30 — THURSDAY
Day 335 — 31 Remaining

BARBADOS: INDEPENDENCE DAY. Nov 30. National holiday. Gained independence from Great Britain in 1966.

MONTGOMERY, LUCY MAUD: BIRTH ANNIVERSARY. Nov 30, 1874. Author, known for her classic Anne of Green Gables series of books. Her first, *Anne of Green Gables*, was published in 1908. Born at New London, Prince Edward Island, Canada, Montgomery died at Toronto, Canada, Apr 24, 1952.

NATIONAL GEOGRAPHY BEE, SCHOOL LEVEL. Nov 27, 2000–Jan 12, 2001. Principals must register their schools by Oct 15, 2000. Nationwide contest involving millions of students at the school level. The Bee is designed to encourage the teaching and study of geography. There are three levels of competition. A student must win school-level Bee in order to win the right to take a written exam. The written test determines the top 100 students in each state who are eligible to go on to the state level. National Geographic brings the state winner and his/her teacher to Washington for the national level in May. Alex Trebek moderates the national level. For info: Natl Geography Bee, Natl Geographic Soc, 1145 17th St NW, Washington, DC 20036. Phone: (202) 857-7001. Web: www.nationalgeographic.com.

PHILIPPINES: BONIFACIO DAY. Nov 30. Also known as National Heroes' Day. Commemorates birth in 1863 of Andres Bonifacio, leader of the 1896 revolt against Spain.

SAINT ANDREW'S DAY. Nov 30. Feast day of the apostle and martyr, Andrew, who died about AD 60. Patron saint of Scotland.

TWAIN, MARK: BIRTH ANNIVERSARY. Nov 30, 1835. Celebrated American author, born Samuel Langhorne Clemens, whose books include: *The Adventures of Tom Sawyer, The Adventures of Huckleberry Finn* and *The Prince and the Pauper*. Born at Florida, MO, Twain is quoted as saying, "I came in with Halley's Comet in 1835. It is coming again next year, and I expect to go out with it." He did. Twain died at Redding, CT, Apr 21, 1910 (just one day after Halley's Comet perihelion).

ZEMACH, MARGOT: BIRTH ANNIVERSARY. Nov 30, 1931. Illustrator (Caldecott for *Duffy and the Devil*), born at Los Angeles, CA. Died May 21, 1989.

BIRTHDAYS TODAY

Joan Ganz Cooney, 71, founder of the Children's Television Workshop and developer of "Sesame Street," born Nov 30, 1929.

Des'ree, 30, singer (*I Ain't Movin'*), born London, England, Nov 30, 1970.

Mandy Patinkin, 48, actor (Tony for *Evita; Sunday in the Park with George*, "Chicago Hope"), born Chicago, IL, Nov 30, 1952.

Ivan Rodriguez, 29, baseball player, born Vega Baja, Puerto Rico, Nov 30, 1971.

Paul Stookey, 63, singer, songwriter (Peter, Paul and Mary), born Baltimore, MD, Nov 30, 1937.

Lawrence Summers, 46, US Secretary of the Treasury (Clinton administration), born New Haven, CT, Nov 30, 1954.

Natalie Williams, 30, basketball player, born Long Beach, CA, Nov 30, 1970.

December 2000

DECEMBER 1 — FRIDAY
Day 336 — 30 Remaining

ANTARCTICA MADE A SCIENTIFIC PRESERVE: ANNIVERSARY. Dec 1, 1959. Representatives of 12 nations, including the US and the Soviet Union, signed a treaty at Washington, DC, setting aside Antarctica as a scientific preserve, free from military activity. Antarctica is equal in area to the US and Europe combined. For more info: quest.arc.nasa.gov/antarctica2/main/s_index.html.

BASKETBALL CREATED: ANNIVERSARY. Dec 1, 1891. James Naismith was a teacher of physical education at the International YMCA Training College at Springfield, MA. In order to create an indoor sport that could be played during the winter months, he nailed up peach baskets at opposite ends of the gym and gave students soccer balls to toss into them. Thus was born the game of basketball.

CHRISTMAS TREE AT ROCKEFELLER CENTER. Dec 1. (Date approximate.) New York, NY. Lighting of the huge Christmas tree in Rockefeller Plaza signals the opening of the holiday season at New York City. Date is usually a weekday during the first week of December.

HUG-A-WEEK FOR THE HEARING IMPAIRED. Dec 1–31. Give a hug to someone who doesn't hear so well, each week until the end of the year. As we approach the holiday season, start with a weekly hug and find out how you might proactively include people with hearing loss in the season's festivities. A little extra time and a few special moments may help someone who can't hear so well be included and more able to share throughout the season. Annually, the month of December. For info: Carol MacKenzie, Communicate with Care, 12 Kayla Cir, Plymouth, MA 02362. Phone: (508) 224-3640. E-mail: commwcare@aol.com.

PORTUGAL: INDEPENDENCE DAY. Dec 1. Public holiday. Became independent of Spain in 1640.

ROMANIA: NATIONAL DAY. Dec 1. National holiday. Commemorates unification of Romania and Transylvania in 1918.

ROSA PARKS DAY: 45th ANNIVERSARY OF ARREST. Dec 1, 1955. Anniversary of the arrest of Rosa Parks, at Montgomery, AL, for refusing to give up her seat and move to the back of a municipal bus. Her arrest triggered a yearlong boycott of the city bus system and led to legal actions which ended racial segregation on municipal buses throughout the southern US. The event has been called the birth of the modern civil rights movement. Rosa McCauley Parks was born at Tuskegee, AL, Feb 4, 1913. For more info: *If a Bus Could Talk: The Story of Rosa Parks*, by Faith Ringgold (S&S, 0-68-981892-0, $16 Gr. K–3).

SAFE TOYS AND GIFTS MONTH. Dec 1–31. What are the top 10 dangerous toys to children's eyesight? Prevent Blindness America® issues a list of toys hazardous to eyesight. Tips on how to choose age-appropriate toys will be distributed. For info: Prevent Blindness America®, 500 E Remington Rd, Schaumburg, IL 60173. Phone: (800) 331-2020. Fax: (847) 843-8458. Web: www.prevent-blindness.org.

UNITED NATIONS: WORLD AIDS DAY. Dec 1. In 1988 the World Health Organization of the United Nations declared Dec 1 as World AIDS Day, an international day of awareness and education about AIDS. The WHO is the leader in global direction and coordination of AIDS prevention, control, research and education. A program called UN-AIDS was created to bring together the skills and expertise of the World Bank, UNDP, UNESCO, UNICEF, UNFPA and the WHO to strengthen and expand national capacities to respond to the pandemic. Also see the World AIDS Day entry (Dec 1) for information address in US.

UNIVERSAL HUMAN RIGHTS MONTH. Dec 1–31. To disseminate throughout the world information about human rights and distribute copies of the Universal Declaration of Human Rights in English and other languages. Please send $4 to cover expense of printing, handling and postage. Annually, the month of December. For info: Dr. Stanley Drake, Pres, Intl Soc of Friendship & Good Will, 40139 Palmetto Dr, Palmdale, CA 93551-3557.

WORLD AIDS DAY. Dec 1. US observance of UN day to focus world attention on the fight against HIV/AIDS. For info: American Assn for World Health, World AIDS Day, 1825 K St NW, Ste 1208, Washington, DC 20006. Phone: (202) 466-5883. Fax: (202) 466-5896. E-mail: aawhstaff@aol.com. Web: www.aawhworld-health.org.

BIRTHDAYS TODAY

Jan Brett, 51, author and illustrator (*Trouble with Trolls, The Mitten*), born Hingham, MA, Dec 1, 1949.

Larry Walker, 34, baseball player, born Maple Ridge, British Columbia, Canada, Dec 1, 1966.

Tisha Waller, 30, track and field athlete, born Atlanta, GA, Dec 1, 1970.

December 2000	S	M	T	W	T	F	S
						1	2
	3	4	5	6	7	8	9
	10	11	12	13	14	15	16
	17	18	19	20	21	22	23
	24	25	26	27	28	29	30
	31						

DECEMBER 2 — SATURDAY
Day 337 — 29 Remaining

ARTIFICIAL HEART TRANSPLANT: ANNIVERSARY. Dec 2, 1982. Barney C. Clark, 61, became the first recipient of a permanent artificial heart. The operation was performed at the University of Utah Medical Center at Salt Lake City. Near death at the time of the operation, Clark survived almost 112 days after the implantation. He died Mar 23, 1983.

FIRST SELF-SUSTAINING NUCLEAR CHAIN REACTION: ANNIVERSARY. Dec 2, 1942. Physicist Enrico Fermi led a team of scientists at the University of Chicago in producing the first controlled, self-sustaining nuclear chain reaction. As part of the "Manhattan Project," their first simple nuclear reactor was built under the stands of the University's football stadium. This work led to the development of the atomic bomb, first tested on July 16, 1945, at Alamogordo, NM.

LAOS: NATIONAL DAY: 25th ANNIVERSARY. Dec 2. National holiday commemorating proclamation of Lao People's Democratic Republic in 1975.

MONROE DOCTRINE: ANNIVERSARY. Dec 2, 1823. President James Monroe, in his annual message to Congress, enunciated the doctrine that bears his name and that was long hailed as a statement of US policy." . . . In the wars of the European powers in matters relating to themselves we have never taken any part . . . we should consider any attempt on their part to extend their system to any portion of this hemisphere as dangerous to our peace and safety. . . ."

★ **PAN AMERICAN HEALTH DAY.** Dec 2. Presidential Proclamation 2447, of Nov 23, 1940, covers all succeeding years. Annually, Dec 2. The 1940 Pan American Conference of National Directors of Health adopted a resolution recommending that a "Health Day" be held annually in the countries of the Pan American Union.

SEURAT, GEORGES: BIRTH ANNIVERSARY. Dec 2, 1859. French Neo-Impressionist painter, born at Paris, France. Died there Mar 29, 1891. Seurat is known for his style of painting with small dots of color called "pointillism."

UNITED ARAB EMIRATES: NATIONAL DAY: ANNIVERSARY OF INDEPENDENCE. Dec 2. Anniversary of the day in 1971 when a federation of seven sheikdoms declared independence and became known as the United Arab Emirates.

BIRTHDAYS TODAY

Wayne Allard, 57, US Senator (R, Colorado), born Fort Collins, CO, Dec 2, 1943.

Randy Gardner, 42, figure skater, born Marina del Rey, CA, Dec 2, 1958.

David Macaulay, 54, illustrator and author (*The New Way Things Work*, Caldecott for *Black and White*), born Burton-on-Trent, England, Dec 2, 1946.

Stone Phillips, 46, anchor ("Dateline," "20/20"), born Texas City, TX, Dec 2, 1954.

Harry Reid, 61, US Senator (D, Nevada), born Searchlight, NV, Dec 2, 1939.

Monica Seles, 27, tennis player, born Novi Sad, Yugoslavia, Dec 2, 1973.

Britney Spears, 19, singer, born Kentwood, LA, Dec 2, 1981.

William Wegman, 57, artist/photographer (of dogs), born Holyoke, MA, Dec 2, 1943.

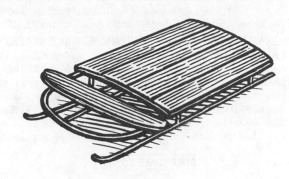

DECEMBER 3 — SUNDAY
Day 338 — 28 Remaining

ADVENT, FIRST SUNDAY. Dec 3. Advent includes the four Sundays before Christmas: Dec 3, Dec 10, Dec 17 and Dec 24 in 2000.

CLERC-GALLAUDET WEEK. Dec 3–9. Week in which to celebrate the birth anniversaries of Laurent Clerc (Dec 26, 1785) and Thomas Hopkins Gallaudet (Dec 10, 1787). Clerc and Gallaudet pioneered education for the deaf in the US. Library activities will include a lecture on Clerc and Gallaudet, storytelling for all ages and a display of books, videotapes, magazines, newspapers and posters. Library Kit available for $15 postpaid. For info: Library for Deaf Action, 2930 Craiglawn Rd, Silver Spring, MD 20904-1816. Phone: (301) 572-5168 (TTY). Fax: (301) 572-4134. E-mail: alhagemeyer@juno.com.

ILLINOIS: ADMISSION DAY: ANNIVERSARY. Dec 3. Became 21st state in 1818.

MOON PHASE: FIRST QUARTER. Dec 3. Moon enters First Quarter phase at 10:55 PM, EST.

UNITED NATIONS: INTERNATIONAL DAY OF DISABLED PERSONS. Dec 3. On Oct 14, 1992 (Res 47/3), at the end of the Decade of Disabled Persons, the General Assembly proclaimed Dec 3 to be an annual observance to promote the continuation of integrating the disabled into general society.

BIRTHDAYS TODAY

Francesca Lia Block, 38, author (*Weetzie Bat, Violet & Claire*), born Los Angeles, CA, Dec 3, 1962.

Brian Bonsall, 19, actor (*Blank Check*, "Family Ties"), born Torrance, CA, Dec 3, 1981.

Anna Chlumsky, 20, actress (*My Girl, My Girl 2*), born Chicago, IL, Dec 3, 1980.

Sheree Fitch, 44, author (*Toes in My Nose, Sleeping Dragons All Around*), born Ottawa, Ontario, Canada, Dec 3, 1956.

Brendan Fraser, 32, actor (*George of the Jungle*), born Indianapolis, IN, Dec 3, 1968.

Katarina Witt, 35, Olympic figure skater, born Karl-Marx-Stadt, East Germany, Dec 3, 1965.

DECEMBER 4 — MONDAY
Day 339 — 27 Remaining

CENTRAL AFRICAN REPUBLIC: NATIONAL DAY OBSERVED. Dec 4. Commemorates Proclamation of the Republic Dec 1, 1958. On this date, the country called Ubangi-Shari changed its name to Central African Republic. In 1960 it gained its independence from France. Usually observed on the first Monday in December.

LEAF, MUNRO: BIRTH ANNIVERSARY. Dec 4, 1905. Born at Hamilton, MD. Leaf authored and illustrated the children's book *The Story of Ferdinand*. He died at Garrett Park, MD, Dec 21, 1976.

SPACE MILESTONE: INTERNATIONAL SPACE STATION LAUNCH (US). Dec 4, 1998. The shuttle *Endeavour* took a US component of the space station named *Unity* into orbit 220 miles from Earth where spacewalking astronauts fastened it to a component launched by the Russians on Nov 20, 1998. It will take a total of 45 US and Russian launches over the next five years before the space station is complete. When completed, it will be 356 feet across and 290 feet long and will support a crew of up to seven.

BIRTHDAYS TODAY

George Ancona, 71, author (*Pablo Remembers: The Fiesta of the Day of the Dead*), born New York, NY, Dec 4, 1929.

Tyra Banks, 27, model, author (*Tyra's Beauty Inside & Out*), born Los Angeles, CA, Dec 4, 1973.

Jeff Blake, 30, football player, born Sanford, FL, Dec 4, 1970.

DECEMBER 5 — TUESDAY
Day 340 — 26 Remaining

"THE ABBOTT AND COSTELLO SHOW" TV PREMIERE: ANNIVERSARY. Dec 5, 1952. Bud Abbott and Lou Costello made 52 half-hour films for television incorporating many of their best burlesque routines. The show ran for two seasons, until 1954. In 1966 Hanna-Barbera Productions produced an animated cartoon based on the characters of Abbott and Costello. Abbott supplied his own voice while Stan Irwin imitated Costello. Bud Abbott was born at Asbury Park, NJ, Oct 2, 1895 and died at Woodland Hills, CA, Apr 24, 1974. Lou Costello was born at Paterson, NJ, Mar 6, 1906 and died at East Los Angeles, CA, Mar 3, 1959.

AFL-CIO FOUNDED: 45th ANNIVERSARY. Dec 5. The American Federation of Labor and the Congress of Industrial Organizations joined together in 1955, following 20 years of rivalry, to become the nation's leading advocate for trade unions.

DISNEY, WALT: BIRTH ANNIVERSARY. Dec 5, 1901. Animator, filmmaker, born at Chicago, IL. Disney died at Los Angeles, CA, Dec 15, 1966.

HAITI: DISCOVERY DAY: ANNIVERSARY. Dec 5. Commemorates the discovery of Haiti by Christopher Columbus in 1492. Public holiday.

MONTGOMERY BUS BOYCOTT BEGINS: 45th ANNIVERSARY. Dec 5, 1955. Rosa Parks was arrested at Montgomery, AL, Dec 1, 1955, for refusing to give up her seat on a bus to a white man. In support of Parks, and to protest the arrest, the black community of Montgomery organized a boycott of the bus system. The boycott lasted from Dec 5, 1955, to Dec 20, 1956, when a US Supreme Court ruling was implemented at Montgomery, integrating the public transportation system.

NETHERLANDS: SINTERKLAAS. Dec 5. Traditionally on the eve of St. Nicholas Day (Dec 6), Sinterklaas brings gifts to Dutch children, accompanied by his Moorish helper, "Black Pete." However, the number of people celebrating this holiday has dropped, as more Dutch families exchange gifts on Dec 25 instead.

	S	M	T	W	T	F	S
December						1	2
2000	3	4	5	6	7	8	9
	10	11	12	13	14	15	16
	17	18	19	20	21	22	23
	24	25	26	27	28	29	30
	31						

THAILAND: KING'S BIRTHDAY AND NATIONAL DAY. Dec 5. Celebrated throughout the kingdom with colorful pageantry. Stores and houses decorated with spectacular illuminations at night. Public holiday.

TWENTY-FIRST AMENDMENT TO THE US CONSTITUTION RATIFIED: ANNIVERSARY. Dec 5, 1933. Prohibition ended with the repeal of the Eighteenth Amendment by the Twenty-First Amendment.

UNITED NATIONS: INTERNATIONAL VOLUNTEER DAY FOR ECONOMIC AND SOCIAL DEVELOPMENT. Dec 5. In a resolution of Dec 17, 1985, the United Nations General Assembly recognized the desirability of encouraging the work of all volunteers. It invited governments to observe, annually Dec 5, the "International Volunteer Day for Economic and Social Development, urging them to take measures to heighten awareness of the important contribution of volunteer service." A day commemorating the establishment in December 1970 of the UN Volunteers program and inviting world recognition of volunteerism in the international development movement. For info: United Nations, Dept of Public Info, Public Inquiries Unit, Rm GA-57, New York, NY 10017. Phone: (212) 963-4475. Fax: (212) 963-0071. E-mail: inquiries@un.org.

VAN BUREN, MARTIN: BIRTH ANNIVERSARY. Dec 5, 1782. The eighth president of the US (Mar 4, 1837–Mar 3, 1841), Van Buren was the first to have been born a citizen of the US. He had served as vice-president under Andrew Jackson. He was a widower for nearly two decades before he entered the White House. His daughter-in-law, Angelica, served as White House hostess during an administration troubled by bank and business failures, depression and unemployment. Van Buren was born at Kinderhook, NY, and died there July 24, 1862.

WHEATLEY, PHILLIS: DEATH ANNIVERSARY. Dec 5, 1784. Born at Senegal, West Africa about 1753, Phillis Wheatley was brought to the US in 1761 and purchased as a slave by a Boston tailor named John Wheatley. She was allotted unusual privileges for a slave, including being allowed to learn to read and write. She wrote her first poetry at age 14, and her first work was published in 1770. Wheatley's fame as a poet spread throughout Europe as well as the US after her *Poems on Various Subjects, Religious and Moral* was published at England in 1773. She was invited to visit George Washington's army headquarters after he read a poem she had written about him in 1776. Phillis Wheatley died at about age 30 at Boston, MA.

BIRTHDAYS TODAY

Strom Thurmond, 98, US Senator (R, South Carolina), born Edgefield, SC, Dec 5, 1902.

DECEMBER 6 — WEDNESDAY
Day 341 — 25 Remaining

ECUADOR: DAY OF QUITO. Dec 6. Commemorates founding of city of Quito by Spaniards in 1534.

FINLAND: INDEPENDENCE DAY. Dec 6. National holiday. Declaration of independence from Russia in 1917.

GERALD FORD SWEARING-IN AS VICE PRESIDENT: ANNIVERSARY. Dec 6, 1973. Gerald Ford was sworn in as vice president under Richard Nixon, following the resignation of Spiro Agnew who pled no contest to a charge of income tax evasion. See also "Agnew, Spiro Theodore: Birth Anniversary" (Nov 9).

GERSHWIN, IRA: BIRTH ANNIVERSARY. Dec 6, 1896. Pulitzer Prize–winning American lyricist and author who collaborated with his brother, George, and with many other composers.

Among his Broadway successes: *Lady Be Good, Funny Face, Strike Up the Band* and such songs as "The Man I Love," "Someone to Watch Over Me," "I Got Rhythm" and hundreds of others. Born at New York, NY, he died at Beverly Hills, CA, Aug 17, 1983. See also: "Gershwin, George: Birth Anniversary" (Sept 26).

HALIFAX, NOVA SCOTIA, DESTROYED: ANNIVERSARY. Dec 6, 1917. More than 1,650 people were killed at Halifax when the Norwegian ship *Imo* plowed into the French munitions ship *Mont Blanc. Mont Blanc* was loaded with 4,000 tons of TNT, 2,300 tons of picric acid, 61 tons of other explosives and a deck of highly flammable benzene, which ignited and touched off an explosion. In addition to those killed, 1,028 were injured. A tidal wave, caused by the explosion, washed much of the city out to sea.

MISSOURI EARTHQUAKES: ANNIVERSARY. Dec 6, 1811. The most violent and prolonged series of earthquakes in US history occurred not in California, but in the Midwest at New Madrid, MO. They lasted until Feb 12, 1812. There were few deaths because of the sparse population.

SAINT NICHOLAS DAY. Dec 6. One of the most venerated saints of both eastern and western Christian churches, of whose life little is known, except that he was Bishop of Myra in what is now Turkey in the fourth century, and that from early times he has been one of the most often pictured saints, especially noted for his charity. Santa Claus and the presentation of gifts is said to derive from Saint Nicholas.

THIRTEENTH AMENDMENT TO THE US CONSTITUTION RATIFIED: ANNIVERSARY. Dec 6, 1865. The Thirteenth Amendment to the Constitution was ratified, abolishing slavery in the US. "Neither slavery nor involuntary servitude, save as a punishment for crime whereof the party shall have been duly convicted, shall exist within the United States, or any place subject to their jurisdiction." This amendment was proclaimed Dec 18, 1865. The Thirteenth, Fourteenth and Fifteenth amendments are considered the Civil War Amendments. See also: "Emancipation Proclamation: Anniversary" (Jan 1) for Lincoln's proclamation freeing slaves in the rebelling states.

BIRTHDAYS TODAY

Andrew Cuomo, 43, US Secretary of Housing and Urban Development (Clinton administration), born Queens, NY, Dec 6, 1957.

John Reynolds Gardiner, 56, author (*Stone Fox, Top Secret*), born Los Angeles, CA, Dec 6, 1944.

Don Nickles, 52, US Senator (R, Oklahoma), born Ponca City, OK, Dec 6, 1948.

DECEMBER 7 — THURSDAY

Day 342 — 24 Remaining

DELAWARE RATIFIES CONSTITUTION: ANNIVERSARY. Dec 7, 1787. Delaware became the first state to ratify the proposed Constitution. It did so by unanimous vote.

PEARL HARBOR DAY: ANNIVERSARY. Dec 7, 1941. At 7:55 AM (local time), "a date that will live in infamy," nearly 200 Japanese aircraft attacked Pearl Harbor, HI, long considered the US "Gibraltar of the Pacific." The raid, which lasted little more than one hour, left nearly 3,000 dead. Nearly the entire US Pacific Fleet was at anchor there, and few ships escaped damage. Several were sunk or disabled, while 200 US aircraft on the ground were destroyed. The attack on Pearl Harbor brought about immediate US entry into WWII, a Declaration of War being requested by President Franklin D. Roosevelt and approved by the Congress Dec 8, 1941.

SPACE MILESTONE: *GALILEO* (US): 5th ANNIVERSARY. Dec 7, 1995. Launched Oct 18, 1989 by the space shuttle *Atlantis*, the spacecraft *Galileo* entered the orbit of Jupiter on this date after a six-year journey. It orbited Jupiter for two years, sending out probes to study three of its moons. Organic compounds, the ingredients of life, were found on them. For more info: www.jpl .nasa.gov/galileo/index.htm.

TUNIS, JOHN: BIRTH ANNIVERSARY. Dec 7, 1889. Author of sports books (*The Kid Comes Back, Iron Duke*), born at Boston, MA. Died Feb 4, 1975.

UNITED NATIONS: INTERNATIONAL CIVIL AVIATION DAY. Dec 7. On Dec 6, 1996, the General Assembly proclaimed Dec 7 as International Civil Aviation Day. On Dec 7, 1944, the convention on International Civil Aviation, which established the International Civil Aviation Organization, was signed. Info from: United Nations, Dept of Public Info, New York, NY 10017.

BIRTHDAYS TODAY

Larry Bird, 44, basketball coach, former player, born West Baden, IN, Dec 7, 1956.

Aaron Carter, 13, singer ("Shake It"), born Tampa, FL, Dec 7, 1987.

Thad Cochran, 63, US Senator (R, Mississippi), born Pontotoc, MS, Dec 7, 1937.

Susan M. Collins, 48, US Senator (R, Maine), born Caribou, ME, Dec 7, 1952.

Anne Fine, 53, author (*The Tulip Touch, Alias Madame Doubtfire*), born County Durham, England, Dec 7, 1947.

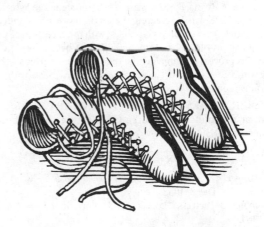

DECEMBER 8 — FRIDAY

Day 343 — 23 Remaining

AMERICAN FEDERATION OF LABOR (AFL) FOUNDED: ANNIVERSARY. Dec 8, 1886. Originally founded at Pittsburgh, PA, as the Federation of Organized Trades and Labor Unions of the United States and Canada in 1881, the union was reorganized in 1886 under the name American Federation of Labor (AFL). The AFL was dissolved as a separate entity in 1955 when it merged with the Congress of Industrial Organizations to form the AFL-CIO. See also: "AFL-CIO Founded: Anniversary (Dec 5)."

CHINESE NATIONALISTS MOVE TO FORMOSA: ANNIVERSARY. Dec 8, 1949. The government of Chiang Kai–Shek moved to Formosa (Taiwan) after being driven out of mainland China by the Communists led by Mao Tse–Tung.

CIVIL RIGHTS WEEK IN MASSACHUSETTS. Dec 8–14. Proclaimed annually by the governor.

FEAST OF THE IMMACULATE CONCEPTION. Dec 8. Roman Catholic Holy Day of Obligation.

FIRST STEP TOWARD A NUCLEAR-FREE WORLD: ANNIVERSARY. Dec 8, 1987. The former Soviet Union and the US signed a treaty at Washington eliminating medium-range and shorter-range missiles. This was the first treaty completely doing away with two entire classes of nuclear arms. These missiles, with a range of 500 to 5,500 kilometers, were to be scrapped under strict supervision within three years of the signing.

GUAM: LADY OF CAMARIN DAY HOLIDAY: ANNIVERSARY. Dec 8. Declared a legal holiday by Guam legislature, Mar 2, 1971.

NAFTA SIGNED: ANNIVERSARY. Dec 8, 1993. President Clinton signed the North American Free Trade Agreement which cut tariffs and eliminated other trade barriers between the US, Canada and Mexico. The Agreement went into effect Jan 1, 1994.

SEGAR, ELZIE CRISLER: BIRTH ANNIVERSARY. Dec 8, 1894. Creator of *Thimble Theater*, the comic strip that came to be known as *Popeye*. Centered on the Oyl family, especially daughter Olive, the strip introduced a new central character in 1929. A one-eyed sailor with bulging muscles, Popeye became the strip's star attraction almost immediately. Popeye made it to the silver screen in animated form and in 1980 became a movie with Robin Williams playing the lead. Segar was born at Chester, IL. He died Oct 13, 1938, at Santa Monica, CA.

SOVIET UNION DISSOLVED: ANNIVERSARY. Dec 8, 1991. The Union of Soviet Socialist Republics ceased to exist, as the republics of Russia, Byelorussia and Ukraine signed an agreement at Minsk, Byelorussia, creating the Commonwealth of Independent States. The remaining republics, with the exception of Georgia, joined in the new Commonwealth as it began the slow and arduous process of removing the yoke of Communism and dealing with strong separatist and nationalistic movements within the various republics.

THURBER, JAMES: BIRTH ANNIVERSARY. Dec 8, 1894. Author for adults and children (*The Thirteen Clocks*), born at Columbus, OH. Died at New York, NY, Nov 2, 1961.

<u>*BIRTHDAYS TODAY*</u>

Kim Basinger, 47, actress (*Batman*, *My Stepmother Is an Alien*), born Athens, GA, Dec 8, 1953.

Teri Hatcher, 36, actress ("Lois & Clark"), born Sunnyvale, CA, Dec 8, 1964.

DECEMBER 9 — SATURDAY
Day 344 — 22 Remaining

BIRDSEYE, CLARENCE: BIRTH ANNIVERSARY. Dec 9, 1886. American industrialist who developed a way of deep-freezing foods. He was marketing frozen fish by 1925 and was one of the founders of General Foods Corporation. Born at Brooklyn, NY, he died at New York, NY, Oct 7, 1956.

BRUNHOFF, JEAN DE: BIRTH ANNIVERSARY. Dec 9, 1899. Author and illustrator of *The Story of Babar* and *The Little Elephant*. Born at Paris, France, Brunhoff died at Switzerland, Oct 16, 1937. In later years, the Babar series was continued by his son Laurent.

COMPUTER MOUSE DEVELOPED: ANNIVERSARY. Dec 9, 1968. Designed as a pointing device to help users interact with their computers, the mouse was first developed in 1968 but its use didn't become widespread until 1984 when Apple attached it to its Macintosh computer.

HARRIS, JOEL CHANDLER: BIRTH ANNIVERSARY. Dec 9, 1848. American author, creator of the Uncle Remus stories, born at Eatonton, GA. Died July 3, 1908, at Atlanta, GA.

TANZANIA: INDEPENDENCE AND REPUBLIC DAY. Dec 9. Tanganyika became independent of Britain in 1961. The republics of Tanganyika and Zanzibar joined to become one state (Apr 27, 1964) renamed (Oct 29, 1964) the United Republic of Tanzania.

<u>*BIRTHDAYS TODAY*</u>

Joan W. Blos, 72, author (Newbery for *A Gathering of Days: A New England Girl's Journal, 1830–1832*), born New York, NY, Dec 9, 1928.

Thomas Andrew Daschle, 53, US Senator (D, South Dakota), born Aberdeen, SD, Dec 9, 1947.

Mary Downing Hahn, 63, author (*The Doll in the Garden: A Ghost Story*), born Washington, DC, Dec 9, 1937.

Eloise McGraw, 85, author (*The Moorchild*), born Houston, TX, Dec 9, 1915.

Donny Osmond, 43, actor, singer ("Donny and Marie;" stage: *Joseph and the Amazing Technicolor Dreamcoat*), born Ogden, UT, Dec 9, 1957.

DECEMBER 10 — SUNDAY
Day 345 — 21 Remaining

DEWEY, MELVIL: BIRTH ANNIVERSARY. Dec 10, 1851. American librarian and inventor of the Dewey decimal book classification system was born at Adams Center, NY. Born Melville Louis Kossuth Dewey, he was an advocate of spelling reform, urged use of the metric system and was interested in many other education reforms. Dewey died at Highlands County, FL, Dec 26, 1931.

DICKINSON, EMILY: BIRTH ANNIVERSARY. Dec 10, 1830. One of America's greatest poets, Emily Dickinson was born at Amherst, MA. She was reclusive and frail in health. She died May 15, 1886, at Amherst. Seven of her poems were published during her life, but after her death her sister, Lavinia, discovered almost 2,000 more poems locked in her bureau. They were published gradually, over 50 years, beginning in 1890. The little-known Emily Dickinson who was born, lived and died at Amherst is now recognized as one of the most original poets of the English-speaking world.

December 2000	S	M	T	W	T	F	S
						1	2
	3	4	5	6	7	8	9
	10	11	12	13	14	15	16
	17	18	19	20	21	22	23
	24	25	26	27	28	29	30
	31						

FIRST US SCIENTIST RECEIVES NOBEL PRIZE: ANNIVERSARY. Dec 10, 1907. University of Chicago professor Albert Michelson, eminent physicist known for his research on the speed of light and optics, became the first US scientist to receive the Nobel Prize.

GALLAUDET, THOMAS HOPKINS: BIRTH ANNIVERSARY. Dec 10, 1787. A hearing educator who, with Laurent Clerc, founded the first public school for deaf people, Connecticut Asylum for the Education and Instruction of Deaf and Dumb Persons (now the American School for the Deaf), at Hartford, CT, Apr 15, 1817. Gallaudet was born at Philadelphia, PA, and died Sept 9, 1851, at Hartford, CT.

GODDEN, RUMER: BIRTH ANNIVERSARY. Dec 10, 1907. Author of the popular children's tales *The Mousewife* and *The Story of Holly & Ivy*. Born at Sussex, England, Godden died at Thornhill, Scotland, Nov 8, 1998.

★**HUMAN RIGHTS DAY.** Dec 10. Presidential Proclamation 2866, of Dec 6, 1949, covers all succeeding years. Customarily issued as "Bill of Rights Day, Human Rights Day and Week." *See* Curriculum Connection.

★**HUMAN RIGHTS WEEK.** Dec 10–16. Presidential Proclamation issued since 1958 for the week of Dec 10–16, except in 1986. See also: "Human Rights Day" (Dec 10) and "Bill of Rights Day" (Dec 15). *See* Curriculum Connection.

INTERNATIONAL CHILDREN'S DAY OF BROADCASTING. Dec 10. A celebration of the enormous energy and creative potential of children. More than 2,000 broadcasters around the world produce special programs for and about children. Annually, the second Sunday in December. For more info: UNICEF, United Nations, New York, NY 10017. Web: www.unicef.org/icdb.

INTERNATIONAL SHAREWARE DAY. Dec 10. A day to take the time to reward the efforts of thousands of computer programmers who trust that if we try their programs and like them, we will pay for them. Unfortunately, very few payments are received, thus stifling the programmers' efforts. This observance is meant to prompt each of us to inventory our PCs and Macs, see if we are using any shareware, and then take the time in the holiday spirit to write payment checks to the authors. Hopefully this will keep shareware coming. Annually, the second Sunday in December. For info: David Lawrence, Host, Online Today, c/o Noblestar, PO Box 32320, Baltimore, MD 21282. Phone: (703) 237-2498. E-mail: david@online-today.com. Web: online-today.com.

"THE MIGHTY MOUSE PLAYHOUSE" TV PREMIERE: 45th ANNIVERSARY. Dec 10, 1955. An all-time favorite of the Saturday-morning crowd (including adults). CBS had a hit with their pint-sized cartoon character Mighty Mouse, who was a tongue-in-cheek version of Superman. The show had other feature cartoons such as "The Adventures of Gandy Goose" and "Heckle and Jeckle."

MISSISSIPPI: ADMISSION DAY: ANNIVERSARY. Dec 10. Became 20th state in 1817.

NATIONAL CHILDREN'S MEMORIAL DAY. Dec 10. A day to remember the more than 79,000 young people who die in the US every year. Annually, the second Sunday in December. For info: The Compassionate Friends, Inc, PO Box 3696, Oak Brook, IL 60522-3696. Phone: (630) 990-0010. E-mail: tcf_national @prodigy.com. Web: www.compassionatefriends.com.

NOBEL PRIZE AWARDS CEREMONIES. Dec 10. Oslo, Norway and Stockholm, Sweden. Alfred Nobel, Swedish chemist and inventor of dynamite who died in 1896, provided in his will that income from his $9 million estate should be used for annual prizes

---

DECEMBER 10–17
HUMAN RIGHTS WEEK, HUMAN RIGHTS DAY (DEC 10), AND BILL OF RIGHTS DAY (DEC 15)

Often, when we feel vexed at the outcome of a disagreement, we say in a frustrated tone, "But I have the *right*. . ." There is sometimes confusion about the difference between a "right" and a "privilege." A right is a protection that our government (or individuals) must grant to its citizens (or other human beings). A privilege is a benefit that is given but is not mandatory, like a driver's license.

All students can list what they feel are their rights. As a class, discuss the items listed and work at sorting out the "rights" from the "privileges." (This is almost an adjunct list to a description of "needs" and "wants," which you might want to discuss first. It helps clarify the topic for younger students.)

Begin the discussion with basic human rights: dignity, respect, love, etc. Guide students to talk about ways that people infringe upon those rights on a national scale. Gradually turn the discussion to ways that human rights are infringed upon around them. Focus on a classroom and peer level. Many students do not perceive that their actions and comments can actually infringe upon others' rights. Ask students for their suggestions on small things each of them can do to protect the rights of others, which in turn protects their own rights. Perhaps these suggestions could be announced over the PA system during the week.

Students can research and write about groups that seek to demean, harm or take away the rights of others. Media attention has been focused on what actions constitute hate crimes. Students can discuss the motivating emotions (fear and low self-esteem are two) behind these harmful behaviors.

Children also can talk about what rights they have as students. The American Civil Liberties Union has a website at www.aclu.org.

Talk about the rights we are entitled to under our form of government and why those rights were included as part of our Constitution. Have students make Bill of Rights signs. Each one might feature a specific amendment and an example of what it guarantees as it relates to us today.

Also, students can be encouraged to research the way children are treated in various countries, including the United States. All children are not given education, nor are they protected from abuses in the workplace. Many consumer goods and sports products we use regularly are produced by child labor.

Literature connections include: *A Kid's Guide to America's Bill of Rights*, by Kathleen Krull (Avon, 0-380-97497-5, $16 Gr. 5 & up); *Living the Bill of Rights*, by Nat Hentoff (Harper, 0-06-019010-8, $25 Gr. 8 & up); *Human Rights*, edited by Mary Williams (Greenhaven, 1-56510-796-9, $16.20 Gr. 5–12); and the five titles in the *What Do We Mean By Human Rights?* series (Franklin Watts, call 1-800-621-1115 for prices and individual titles, Gr. 4–8).

---

to be awarded to people who are judged to have made the most valuable contributions to the good of humanity. The Nobel Peace Prize is awarded by a committee of the Norwegian parliament and the presentation is made at the Oslo City Hall. Five other prizes, for physics, chemistry, medicine, literature and economics, are presented in a ceremony at Stockholm, Sweden. Both ceremonies traditionally are held on the anniversary of the death of Alfred Nobel. The current value of each prize is about $1,000,000. See also "Nobel, Alfred Bernhard: Birth Anniversary" (Oct 21). For more info: www.nobel.se.

NORTON, MARY: BIRTH ANNIVERSARY. Dec 10, 1903. British children's writer known for The Borrowers series, for which she received the Carnegie Medal. Her book *Bed-Knob and Broomstick* was made into a movie by Disney in 1971. Born at London, England, she died at Hartland, Devon, England, Aug 29, 1992.

RALPH BUNCHE AWARDED NOBEL PEACE PRIZE: 50th ANNIVERSARY. Dec 10, 1950. Dr. Ralph Johnson Bunche became the first black man awarded the Nobel Peace Prize. Bunche was awarded the prize for his efforts in mediation between Israel and neighboring Arab states in 1949.

RED CLOUD: DEATH ANNIVERSARY. Dec 10, 1909. Sioux Indian chief Red Cloud was born in 1822 (exact date unknown), near North Platte, NE. A courageous leader and defender of Indian rights, Red Cloud was the son of Lone Man and Walks as She Thinks. His unrelenting determination caused US abandonment of the Bozeman trail and of three forts that interfered with Indian hunting grounds. Red Cloud died at Pine Ridge, SD.

THAILAND: CONSTITUTION DAY. Dec 10. A public holiday throughout Thailand.

TREATY OF PARIS ENDS SPANISH-AMERICAN WAR: ANNIVERSARY. Dec 10, 1898. Following the conclusion of the Spanish-American War in 1898, American and Spanish ambassadors met at Paris, France, to negotiate a treaty. Under the terms of this treaty, Spain granted the US the Philippine Islands and the islands of Guam and Puerto Rico, and agreed to withdraw from Cuba. Senatorial debate over the treaty centered on the US's move toward imperialism by acquiring the Philippines. A vote was taken Feb 6, 1899 and the treaty passed by a one-vote margin. President William McKinley signed the treaty Feb 10, 1899.

UNITED NATIONS: HUMAN RIGHTS DAY: ANNIVERSARY. Dec 10. Official United Nations observance day. Date is the anniversary of adoption of the "Universal Declaration of Human Rights" in 1948. The Declaration sets forth basic rights and fundamental freedoms to which all men and women everywhere in the world are entitled. For more info, go to the UN's website for children at www.un.org/Pubs/CyberSchoolBus/.

UNITED NATIONS: THIRD DECADE TO COMBAT RACISM AND RACIAL DISCRIMINATION: YEAR SEVEN. Dec 10. In 1973 the United Nations General Assembly proclaimed the years 1973–83, beginning Dec 10, UN Human Rights Day, as the Decade to Combat Racism and Racial Discrimination. Renewing its efforts, the UN designated the years 1983–93 as the Second Decade to Combat Racism and Racial Discrimination. The adopted Program of Action states the decade's goals and outlines the measures to be taken at the regional, national and international levels to achieve them. In Res 47/77 of Dec 16, 1992, the Assembly called upon the international community to provide resources for the program to be carried out during a third decade (1993–2003), particularly for the monitoring of the transition from apartheid in South Africa. Info from: United Nations, Dept of Public Info, New York, NY 10017.

BIRTHDAYS TODAY

Raven Symone, 15, actress ("The Cosby Show," *Doctor Dolittle*), born Atlanta, GA, Dec 10, 1985.

	S	M	T	W	T	F	S
December						1	2
2000	3	4	5	6	7	8	9
	10	11	12	13	14	15	16
	17	18	19	20	21	22	23
	24	25	26	27	28	29	30
	31						

DECEMBER 11 — MONDAY
Day 346 — 20 Remaining

BURKINA FASO: NATIONAL DAY. Dec 11.

INDIANA: ADMISSION DAY: ANNIVERSARY. Dec 11. Became 19th state in 1816.

MOON PHASE: FULL MOON. Dec 11. Moon enters Full Moon phase at 4:03 AM, EST.

SPACE MILESTONE: *MARS CLIMATE ORBITER* (US). Dec 11, 1998. This unmanned rocket was to track the movement of water vapor over Mars which it was scheduled to reach in September 1999. However, it flew too close to Mars and is presumed destroyed. On Jan 3, 1999 *Mars Polar Lander* was launched. It was to burrow into the ground and analyze the soil of Mars. However, on Dec 3, 1999, as it was landing, communications with the robot craft were lost.

UNITED NATIONS: UNICEF ANNIVERSARY. Dec 11, 1946. Anniversary of the establishment by the United Nations General Assembly of the United Nations International Children's Emergency Fund (UNICEF). For info: United Nations, Dept of Public Info, New York, NY 10017. Web: www.unicef.org.

BIRTHDAYS TODAY

Max Baucus, 59, US Senator (D, Montana), born Helena, MT, Dec 11, 1941.

Jermaine Jackson, 46, singer, musician (Jackson 5, "Daddy's Home," "Let's Get Serious"), born Gary, IN, Dec 11, 1954.

William Joyce, 43, author and illustrator (*Bently and Egg*), born Shreveport, LA, Dec 11, 1957.

John F. Kerry, 57, US Senator (D, Massachusetts), born Denver, CO, Dec 11, 1943.

Rider Strong, 21, actor ("Boy Meets World"), born San Francisco, CA, Dec 11, 1979.

DECEMBER 12 — TUESDAY
Day 347 — 19 Remaining

BONZA BOTTLER DAY™. Dec 12. To celebrate when the number of the day is the same as the number of the month. Bonza Bottler Day™ is an excuse to have a party at least once a month. For info: Gail M. Berger, 109 Matthew Ave, Poca, WV 25159. Phone: (304) 776-7746. E-mail: gberger5@aol.com.

DAY OF OUR LADY OF GUADALUPE. Dec 12. The legend of Guadalupe tells how in December 1531, an Indian, Juan Diego, saw the Virgin Mother on a hill near Mexico City, who instructed him to go to the bishop and have him build a shrine to her on the site of the vision. After his request was initially rebuffed, the Virgin Mother appeared to Juan Diego three days later. She instructed him to pick roses growing on a stony and barren hillside nearby and take them to the bishop as proof. Although flowers do not normally bloom in December, Juan Diego found the roses and took them to the bishop. As he opened his mantle to drop the roses on the floor, an image of the Virgin Mary appeared among them. The bishop built the sanctuary as instructed. Our Lady of Guadalupe became the patroness of Mexico City and by 1746 was the patron saint of all New Spain and by 1910 of all Latin America.

FIRST BLACK SERVES IN US HOUSE OF REPRESENTATIVES: ANNIVERSARY. Dec 12, 1870. Joseph Hayne Rainey of Georgetown, SC, was sworn in as the first black to serve in the US House of Representatives. Rainey filled the seat of Benjamin Franklin Whittemore, which had been declared vacant by the House. He served until Mar 3, 1879.

JAY, JOHN: BIRTH ANNIVERSARY. Dec 12, 1745. American statesman, diplomat and first chief justice of the US Supreme Court (1789–95), coauthor (with Alexander Hamilton and James Madison) of the influential *Federalist* papers, was born at New York, NY. Jay died at Bedford, NY, May 17, 1829.

KENYA: JAMHURI DAY. Dec 12. Jamhuri Day (Independence Day) is Kenya's official National Day, commemorating proclamation of the republic and independence from the UK in 1963.

MEXICO: GUADALUPE DAY. Dec 12. One of Mexico's major celebrations. Honors the "Dark Virgin of Guadalupe," the republic's patron saint. Parties and pilgrimages, with special ceremonies at the Shrine of Our Lady of Guadalupe, at Mexico City.

PENNSYLVANIA RATIFIES CONSTITUTION: ANNIVERSARY. Dec 12, 1787. Pennsylvania became the second state to ratify the US Constitution, by a vote of 46 to 23.

POINSETTIA DAY (JOEL ROBERTS POINSETT: DEATH ANNIVERSARY). Dec 12. A day to enjoy poinsettias and to honor Dr. Joel Roberts Poinsett, the American diplomat who introduced the Central American plant which is named for him into the US. Poinsett was born at Charleston, SC, Mar 2, 1799. He also served as a member of Congress and as secretary of war. He died near Statesburg, SC, Dec 12, 1851. The poinsettia has become a favorite Christmas season plant.

RUSSIA: CONSTITUTION DAY. Dec 12. National holiday commemorating adoption of new constitution in 1993.

Tracy Austin, 38, former tennis player, born Rolling Hills Estates, CA, Dec 12, 1962.

Mayim Bialik, 25, actress ("Blossom"), born San Diego, CA, Dec 12, 1975.

DECEMBER 13 — WEDNESDAY
Day 348 — 18 Remaining

LINCOLN, MARY TODD: BIRTH ANNIVERSARY. Dec 13, 1818. Wife of Abraham Lincoln, 16th president of the US, born at Lexington, KY. Died at Springfield, IL, July 16, 1882.

MALTA: REPUBLIC DAY. Dec 13. National holiday. Malta became a republic in 1974.

NEW ZEALAND FIRST SIGHTED BY EUROPEANS: ANNIVERSARY. Dec 13, 1642. Captain Abel Tasman of the Dutch East India Company first sighted New Zealand but was kept from landing by Maori warriors. In 1769 Captain James Cook landed and claimed formal possession for Great Britain.

NORTH AND SOUTH KOREA END WAR: ANNIVERSARY. Dec 13, 1991. North and South Korea signed a treaty of reconciliation and nonaggression, formally ending the Korean War—38 years after fighting ceased in 1953. This agreement was not hailed as a peace treaty, and the armistice that was signed July 27, 1953, between the UN and North Korea, was to remain in effect until it could be transformed into a formal peace.

SWEDEN: SANTA LUCIA DAY. Dec 13. Nationwide celebration of festival of light, honoring St. Lucia. Many hotels have their own Lucia, a young girl attired in a long, flowing white gown with a wreath of candles in her hair, who serves guests coffee and lussekatter (saffron buns) in the early morning.

Sergei Federov, 31, hockey player, born Pskov, Russia, Dec 13, 1969.

Johan Reinhard, 57, author (*Discovering the Inca Ice Maiden, My Adventures on Ampato*), born Joliet, IL, Dec 13, 1943.

Dick Van Dyke, 75, actor, comedian (*Mary Poppins*, "The Dick Van Dyke Show"), born West Plains, MO, Dec 13, 1925.

Tom Vilsack, 50, Governor of Iowa (D), born Pittsburgh, PA, Dec 13, 1950.

DECEMBER 14 — THURSDAY
Day 349 — 17 Remaining

ALABAMA: ADMISSION DAY: ANNIVERSARY. Dec 14. Became the 22nd state in 1819.

HALCYON DAYS. Dec 14–28. Traditionally, the seven days before and the seven days after the winter solstice. To the ancients a time when fabled bird (called the halcyon–pronounced hal-cee-on) calmed the wind and waves—a time of calm and tranquility.

SOUTH POLE DISCOVERY: ANNIVERSARY. Dec 14, 1911. The elusive object of many expeditions dating from the 7th century, the South Pole was located and visited by Roald Amundsen with four companions and 52 sled dogs. All five men and 12 of the dogs returned to base camp safely. Next to visit the South Pole, Jan 17, 1912, was a party of five led by Captain Robert F. Scott, all of whom perished during the return trip. A search party found their frozen bodies 11 months later. See also: "Amundsen, Roald: Birth Anniversary" (July 16).

SUTCLIFFE, ROSEMARY: BIRTH ANNIVERSARY. Dec 14, 1920. Author of historical novels for children (*The Mark of the Horse Lord*), born at East Clanden, England. Died July 23, 1992.

Craig Biggio, 35, baseball player, born Smithtown, NY, Dec 14, 1965.

Rhoda Blumberg, 83, author (*Full Steam Ahead: The Race to Build a Transcontinental Railroad*), born New York, NY, Dec 14, 1917.

Patty Duke, 54, actress (Oscar for *The Miracle Worker*; Emmy for *My Sweet Charlie*), born New York, NY, Dec 14, 1946.

DECEMBER 15 — FRIDAY
Day 350 — 16 Remaining

★**BILL OF RIGHTS DAY.** Dec 15. Presidential Proclamation. Has been proclaimed each year since 1962, but was omitted in 1967 and 1968. (Issued in 1941 and 1946 at Congressional request and in 1947 without request.) Since 1968 has been included in Human Rights Day and Week Proclamation.

BILL OF RIGHTS: ANNIVERSARY. Dec 15, 1791. The first 10 amendments to the US Constitution, known as the Bill of Rights, became effective following ratification by Virginia. The anniversary of ratification and of effect is observed as Bill of Rights Day and is proclaimed annually by the President. For more info: *A Kids' Guide to America's Bill of Rights: Curfews, Censorship, and the 100-Pound Giant*, by Kathleen Krull (Avon/Camelot, 0-380-97497-5, $16 Gr. 5–8).

CURACAO: KINGDOM DAY AND ANTILLEAN FLAG DAY. Dec 15. This day commemorates the Charter of Kingdom, signed at the Knight's Hall at The Hague in 1954, granting the Netherlands Antilles complete autonomy. The Antillean Flag was hoisted for the first time Dec 15, 1959.

"DAVY CROCKETT" TV PREMIERE: ANNIVERSARY. Dec 15, 1954. This show, a series of five segments, can be considered TV's first miniseries. Shown on Walt Disney's "Disneyland" show, it starred Fess Parker as American western hero Davy Crockett and was immensely popular. The show spawned Crockett paraphernalia, including the famous coonskin cap (even after we found out that Boone never wore a coonskin cap).

EIFFEL, ALEXANDRE GUSTAVE: BIRTH ANNIVERSARY. Dec 15, 1832. Eiffel, the French engineer who designed the 1,000 ft-high, million-dollar, open-lattice wrought iron Eiffel Tower, and who participated in designing the Statue of Liberty, was born at Dijon, France. The Eiffel Tower, weighing more than 7,000 tons, was built for the Paris International Exposition of 1889. Eiffel died at Paris, France, Dec 23, 1923.

PUERTO RICO: NAVIDADES. Dec 15–Jan 6. Traditional Christmas season begins mid-December and ends on Three Kings Day. Elaborate nativity scenes, carolers, special Christmas foods and trees from Canada and US. Gifts on Christmas Day and on Three Kings Day.

SITTING BULL: DEATH ANNIVERSARY. Dec 15, 1890. Famous Sioux Indian leader, medicine man and warrior of the Hunkpapa Teton band. Known also by his native name, Tatankayatanka, Sitting Bull was born on the Grand River, SD. He first accompanied his father on the warpath at the age of 14 against the Crow and thereafter rapidly gained influence within his tribe. In 1886 he led a raid on Fort Buford. His steadfast refusal to go to a reservation led General Phillip Sheridan to initiate a campaign against him which led to the massacre of Lieutenant Colonel George Custer's men at Little Bighorn, after which Sitting Bull fled to Canada, remaining there until 1881. Although many in his tribe surrendered on their return, Sitting Bull remained hostile until his death in a skirmish with the US soldiers along the Grand River.

SMITH, BETTY: BIRTH ANNIVERSARY. Dec 15, 1904. Author, born at New York, NY. Her books include *A Tree Grows in Brooklyn, Tomorrow Will be Better* and *Joy In the Morning*. Smith died at Shelton, CT, Jan 17, 1972.

UNDERDOG DAY. Dec 15. To salute, before the year's end, all of the underdogs and unsung heroes—the Number Two people who contribute so much to the Number One people we read about. (Sherlock Holmes's Dr. Watson and Robinson Crusoe's Friday are examples.) Observed annually on the third Friday in December since its founding in 1976 by the late Peter Moeller, THE Chief Underdog. For info: A. Moeller, Box 71, Clio, MI 48420-1042.

BIRTHDAYS TODAY

Alexandra Stevenson, 20, tennis player, born San Diego, CA, Dec 15, 1980.

Garrett Wang, 32, actor ("Star Trek: Voyager"), born Riverside, CA, Dec 15, 1968.

December 2000	S	M	T	W	T	F	S
						1	2
	3	4	5	6	7	8	9
	10	11	12	13	14	15	16
	17	18	19	20	21	22	23
	24	25	26	27	28	29	30
	31						

DECEMBER 16 — SATURDAY
Day 351 — 15 Remaining

BAHRAIN: INDEPENDENCE DAY. Dec 16. National holiday. Commemorates independence from British protection in 1971.

BANGLADESH: VICTORY DAY. Dec 16. National holiday. Commemorates victory over Pakistan in 1971. The former East Pakistan became Bangladesh.

BATTLE OF THE BULGE: ANNIVERSARY. Dec 16, 1944. By late 1944 the German Army was in retreat and Allied forces were on German soil. But a surprise German offensive was launched in the Belgian Ardennes Forest on this date. The Nazi commanders, hoping to minimize any aerial counterattack by the Allies, chose a time when foggy, rainy weather prevailed and the initial attack by eight armored divisions along a 75-mile front took the Allies by surprise, the 5th Panzer Army penetrating to within 20 miles of crossings on the Meuse River. US troops were able to hold fast at bottlenecks in the Ardennes, but by the end of December the German push had penetrated 65 miles into the Allied lines (though their line had narrowed from the initial 75 miles to 20 miles). By that time the Allies began to respond and the Germans were stopped by Montgomery on the Meuse and by Patton at Bastogne. The weather cleared and Allied aircraft began to bomb the German forces and supply lines by Dec 26. The German Army withdrew from the Ardennes, Jan 21, 1945, having lost 120,000 men.

BEETHOVEN, LUDWIG VAN: BIRTH ANNIVERSARY. Dec 16, 1770. Regarded by many as the greatest orchestral composer of all time, Ludwig van Beethoven was born at Bonn, Germany. Impairment of his hearing began before he was 30, but even total deafness did not halt his composing and conducting. His last appearance on the concert stage was to conduct the premiere of his *Ninth Symphony*, at Vienna, May 7, 1824. He was unable to hear either the orchestra or the applause. Of a stormy temperament, he is said to have died during a violent thunderstorm Mar 26, 1827, at Vienna.

BOSTON TEA PARTY: ANNIVERSARY. Dec 16, 1773. Anniversary of Boston patriots' boarding of British vessel at anchor at Boston Harbor. Contents of nearly 350 chests of tea were dumped into the harbor to protest the British monopoly on tea imports. This was one of several events leading to the American Revolution. *See* Curriculum Connection.

KAZAKHSTAN, REPUBLIC OF: REPUBLIC DAY. Dec 16. National Day. Commemorates independence from the Soviet Union in 1991.

MEXICO: POSADAS. Dec 16–24. A nine-day annual celebration throughout Mexico. Processions of "pilgrims" knock at doors asking for posada (shelter), commemorating the search by Joseph and Mary for a shelter in which the infant Jesus might be born. Pilgrims are invited inside, and fun and merrymaking ensue with blindfolded guests trying to break a "piñata" (papier mache decorated earthenware utensil filled with gifts and goodies) suspended from the ceiling. Once the piñata is broken, the gifts are distributed and celebration continues.

PHILIPPINES: SIMBANG GABI. Dec 16–25. Nationwide. A nine-day novena of predawn masses, also called "Misa de Gallo." One of the traditional Filipino celebrations of the holiday season.

SOUTH AFRICA: RECONCILIATION DAY. Dec 16. National holiday. Celebrates the spirit of reconciliation, national unity and peace amongst all citizens.

DECEMBER 16
BOSTON TEA PARTY

On Dec 16, 1773, colonists angered at the East India Company's monopoly of the tea market tossed 342 chests of tea into Boston Harbor. They feared the monopoly could put American merchants out of business. They also resented the imposition of British laws on American people.

Students can research a number of details about this event. How many people participated in the protest? Did they represent the way most people in the community felt? Had they presented their grievances to the authorities in any other way first? Middle school students can write letters to King George protesting the British policies. They can also use American ingenuity to come up with advertising campaigns for a new drink alternative to tea. Support the new drink with posters that advocate turning away from British-supplied tea. Have them write flyers that urge a boycott against the East India Tea Company.

Another research project might include investigating the York Tea Party, which occurred in York, Maine, in 1774, when a group of Maine patriots burned tea in a warehouse. Compare and contrast it with Boston's Tea Party.

Today, an action like the Boston Tea Party might be regarded as vandalism. Britain's response was to impose more taxes, some of which the colonists regarded as harsher than the original ones. Middle school and junior high students can research how our government would be likely to respond to these actions now. Have them write a letter to an elected official and ask for his or her perspective on how the government would respond. They can also research other protests involving the destruction of property and see how frequently violent acts invoke violent responses. Have them look into possible nonviolent alternatives to the Tea Party. They might want to have more modern figures (like Gandhi, or Martin Luther King, Jr.) agree to "meet" with the Tea Party members and present their cases for other means of protest. Ask them to script some of the alternatives and present them for the class.

Among the many books about this historical event are *The Boston Tea Party*, by Laurie O'Neill (Millbrook, 0-761-30006-6, $23.90 Gr. 3–6); and *The Boston Tea Party*, by Steven Kroll (Holiday, 0-823-41316-0, $16.95 Gr. 3–6).

BIRTHDAYS TODAY

Bill Brittain, 70, author (*The Wish Giver: Three Tales of Coven Tree*), born Rochester, NY, Dec 16, 1930.

Peter Dickinson, 73, author (*The Lion Tamer's Daughter: And Other Stories*), born Livingston, Zambia, Dec 16, 1927.

DECEMBER 17 — SUNDAY
Day 352 — 14 Remaining

AZTEC CALENDAR STONE DISCOVERY: ANNIVERSARY. Dec 17, 1790. One of the wonders of the western hemisphere—the Aztec Calendar or Solar Stone—was found beneath the ground by workmen repairing Mexico City's Central Plaza. The intricately carved stone, 11 feet, 8 inches in diameter and weighing nearly 25 tons, proved to be a highly developed calendar monument to the sun. Believed to have been carved in the year 1479, this extraordinary time-counting basalt tablet originally stood in the Great Temple of the Aztecs. Buried along with other Aztec idols, soon after the Spanish conquest in 1521, it remained hidden until 1790. Its 52-year cycle had regulated many Aztec ceremonies, including human sacrifices to save the world from destruction by the gods.

CLEAN AIR ACT PASSED BY CONGRESS: ANNIVERSARY. Dec 17, 1967. A sweeping set of laws to protect us from air pollution was passed this day. This was the first legislation to place pollution controls on the automobile industry.

FLOYD, WILLIAM: BIRTH ANNIVERSARY. Dec 17, 1734. Signer of the Declaration of Independence, member of Congress, born at Brookhaven, NY. Died at Westernville, NY, Aug 4, 1821.

KING, W.L. MACKENZIE: BIRTH ANNIVERSARY. Dec 17, 1874. Former Canadian prime minister, born at Berlin, Ontario. Served 21 years, the longest term of any prime minister in the English-speaking world. Died at Kingsmere, Canada, July 22, 1950.

LAILAT UL QADR: THE NIGHT OF POWER. Dec 17 (also Dec 19, 21, 23 or 25). "The Night of Power" falls on one of the last 10 days of Ramadan on an odd-numbered day (Islamic calendar dates: Ramadan 21, 23, 25, 27 or 29, 1421). The Holy Qur'an states that praying on this night is better than praying 1,000 months. Since it is not known which day it is, Muslims feel it is best to pray on each of the possible nights. Different methods for "anticipating" the visibility of the new moon crescent at Mecca are used by different Muslim sects or groups. US date may vary.

MOON PHASE: LAST QUARTER. Dec 17. Moon enters Last Quarter phase at 7:41 PM, EST.

★**PAN AMERICAN AVIATION DAY.** Dec 17. Presidential Proclamation 2446, of Nov 18, 1940, covers all succeeding years (Pub Res No. 105 of Oct 10, 1940).

REENACTMENT OF THE BOSTON TEA PARTY. Dec 17. Congress Street Bridge, Boston, MA. Reenactment of "Boston's most notorious protest, the single most important event leading to the American Revolution." Annually, the Sunday closest to Dec 16. Starts at Old South Meeting House 5:30 PM. Est attendance: 1,000. For info: Boston Tea Party Ship, Congress Street Bridge, Boston, MA 02210. Phone: (617) 338-1773. Fax: (617) 338-1974.

TELL SOMEONE THEY'RE DOING A GOOD JOB WEEK. Dec 17–23. Every day this week tell someone "you're doing a good job." *See* Curriculum Connection. For info: Joe Hoppel, Radio Station WCMS, 900 Commonwealth Place, Virginia Beach, VA 23464. Phone: (757) 424-1050. Fax: (804) 424-3479. E-mail: wcms @norfolk.infi.net. Web: www.wcms.com.

★**WRIGHT BROTHERS DAY.** Dec 17. Presidential Proclamation always issued for Dec 17 since 1963 (PL88–209 of Dec 17, 1963). Issued twice earlier at Congressional request in 1959 and 1961.

DECEMBER 17–23
TELL SOMEONE THEY'RE DOING A GOOD JOB WEEK

Have fun while students encourage each other to "do a good job." There's nothing like a pat on the back to brighten up a person's day. Talk with your students about how you feel when someone lets you know your work has been appreciated. Ask them how they feel when they are told that something they did was good. Explain that you and they are going to spread those kinds of feelings around the school this week.

Let the students design a short form along these lines: "The students in Mr./Mrs./Ms. _____ class noticed that _____ did a good job _____. We really appreciated it and want to give you a round of applause and a great big THANK-YOU."

Encourage students to notice the kinds of jobs people around them are doing well. For example, how clean the school halls are in the morning, that lunch was ready for them in the cafeteria, library books were on the shelves, Ms. _____'s class was quiet and well behaved during assembly or the bus driver drove carefully. Students will likely come up with additional examples. Fill in the "Good Job" doer's name and job and deliver the note via school mailbox, or let two or three students hand deliver them along with a verbal thank-you.

In the classroom, students can help each other do a good job in many ways. They might work in pairs or threes and help each other with math facts. They can listen to each other read aloud in pairs. They can read and make positive and constructive comments on each other's writing.

You might set up a "Good Job" list on the blackboard. Have categories like Lining Up, Walking Quietly in the Hall, Good Behavior at Assembly and Tidy Room at the End of the Day. Reward each class's good job with a star. Set a goal of five stars per category. No extrinsic awards for "winning"—just the satisfaction of a job well done.

Remind students that they can compliment family members on their good jobs, too. Mom and Dad appreciate compliments now and then!

WRIGHT BROTHERS FIRST POWERED FLIGHT: ANNIVERSARY. Dec 17, 1903. Orville and Wilbur Wright, brothers, bicycle shop operators, inventors and aviation pioneers, after three years of experimentation with kites and gliders, achieved the first documented successful powered and controlled flights of an airplane. The flights, near Kitty Hawk, NC, piloted first by Orville then by Wilbur Wright, were sustained for less than one minute but represented man's first powered airplane flight and the beginning of a new form of transportation. Orville Wright was born at Dayton, OH, Aug 19, 1871, and died there Jan 30, 1948. Wilbur Wright was born at Millville, IN, Apr 16, 1867, and died at Dayton, OH, May 30, 1912. For more info: *The Wright Brothers: How They Invented the Airplane*, by Russell Freedman (Holiday, 0-8234-0875-2, $18.95 Gr. 4–6).

BIRTHDAYS TODAY

Ernie Hudson, 55, actor (*Ghostbusters, Ghostbusters II*), born Benton Harbor, MI, Dec 17, 1945.

	S	M	T	W	T	F	S
December						1	2
2000	3	4	5	6	7	8	9
	10	11	12	13	14	15	16
	17	18	19	20	21	22	23
	24	25	26	27	28	29	30
	31						

David Kherdian, 69, author (*The Road from Home: The Story of an Armenian Girl*), born Racine, WI, Dec 17, 1931.

DECEMBER 18 — MONDAY
Day 353 — 13 Remaining

COBB, TY: BIRTH ANNIVERSARY. Dec 18, 1886. Tyrus (Ty) Cobb, Baseball Hall of Fame outfielder, born at Narrows, GA. He played 24 years and got more hits than any other player, until Pete Rose. Inducted into the Hall of Fame in 1936. Died at Atlanta, GA, July 17, 1961. For more info: www.cmgww.com/baseball /cobb/index2.html.

MEETING OF THE ELECTORS. Dec 18. On the Monday following the second Wednesday in December in presidential election years, the Electors of the Electoral College formally cast their ballots for president and vice president of the US, meeting in their respective state capitals. The Electors' ballots are transmitted "to the Seat of Government of the United States, directed to the President of the Senate," who "in the presence of the Senate and the House of Representatives," at 1 PM on Jan 6 following the election, officially counts the electoral votes and announces the result, legally completing the election process if any candidate has received a majority of the electoral votes.

NEW JERSEY RATIFIES CONSTITUTION: ANNIVERSARY. Dec 18, 1787. New Jersey became the third state to ratify the Constitution (following Delaware and Pennsylvania). It did so unanimously.

NIGER: REPUBLIC DAY. Dec 18. National holiday. This West African nation gained autonomy within the French community on this day in 1958.

BIRTHDAYS TODAY

Christina Aguilera, 20, singer, born Staten Island, NY, Dec 18, 1980.

Brad Pitt, 36, actor (*Interview with a Vampire, A River Runs Through It*), born Shawnee, OK, Dec 18, 1964.

Marilyn Sachs, 73, author (the Veronica Ganz series), born The Bronx, NY, Dec 18, 1927.

Steven Spielberg, 53, producer, director (*E.T.: The Extra-Terrestrial, Indiana Jones, Close Encounters of the Third Kind, Jurassic Park*), born Cincinnati, OH, Dec 18, 1947.

Kiefer Sutherland, 34, actor (*Flatliners, A Few Good Men*), born Los Angeles, CA, Dec 18, 1966.

DECEMBER 19 — TUESDAY
Day 354 — 12 Remaining

CHRISTMAS GREETINGS FROM SPACE: ANNIVERSARY. Dec 19, 1958. At 3:15 PM, EST, the US Earth satellite *Atlas* transmitted the first radio voice broadcast from space, a 58-word recorded Christmas greeting from President Dwight D. Eisenhower: "to all mankind America's wish for peace on earth and good will toward men everywhere." The satellite had been launched from Cape Canaveral Dec 18.

LA FARGE, OLIVER: BIRTH ANNIVERSARY. Dec 19, 1901. American author and anthropologist, born at New York, NY. La Farge wrote the children's book *Laughing Boy*. He died at Albuquerque, NM, Aug 2, 1963.

WOODSON, CARTER GODWIN: 125th BIRTH ANNIVERSARY. Dec 19, 1875. Historian who introduced black studies to colleges and universities, born at New Canton, VA. His scholarly works included *The Negro in Our History, The Education of the Negro Prior to 1861*. Known as the father of Black history, he inaugurated Negro History Week. Woodson was working on a six-volume *Encyclopaedia Africana* when he died at Washington, DC, Apr 3, 1950.

BIRTHDAYS TODAY

Eve Bunting, 72, author (*Sixth-Grade Sleepover, Smoky Night*), born Anne Evelyn Bolton, Maghera, Ireland, Dec 19, 1928.

Alyssa Milano, 28, actress ("Who's the Boss," "Melrose Place"), born Brooklyn, NY, Dec 19, 1972.

Warren Sapp, 28, football player, born Plymouth, FL, Dec 19, 1972.

Reggie White, 39, football player, born Chattanooga, TN, Dec 19, 1961.

DECEMBER 20 — WEDNESDAY

Day 355 — 11 Remaining

AMERICAN POET LAUREATE ESTABLISHMENT: 15th ANNIVERSARY. Dec 20, 1985. A bill empowering the Librarian of Congress to annually name a Poet Laureate/Consultant in Poetry was signed into law by President Ronald Reagan. In return for a $10,000 stipend as Poet Laureate and a salary (about $35,000) as the Consultant in Poetry, the person named will present at least one major work of poetry and will appear at selected national ceremonies. The first Poet Laureate of the US was Robert Penn Warren, appointed to that position by the Librarian of Congress, Feb 26, 1986.

CLINTON IMPEACHMENT PROCEEDINGS: ANNIVERSARY. Dec 20, 1998. President Bill Clinton was impeached by a House of Representatives that was divided along party lines. He was charged with perjury and obstruction of justice stemming from a relationship with a White House intern. He was then tried by the Senate in January 1999. On Feb 12, 1999, he was acquitted on both charges. Clinton was only the second US president to undergo impeachment proceedings. Andrew Johnson was impeached by the House in 1867 but the Senate voted against impeachment and he finished his term of office. See also: "Johnson Impeachment Proceedings: Anniversary" (Feb 24).

LOUISIANA PURCHASE DAY. Dec 20, 1803. One of the greatest real estate deals in history, when more than a million square miles of the Louisiana Territory were turned over to the US by France, for a price of about $20 per square mile. It nearly doubled the size of the US, extending the western border to the Rocky Mountains.

MACAU: REVERTS TO CHINESE CONTROL: ANNIVERSARY. Dec 20, 1999. Macau, a tiny province on the southeast coast of China, reverted to Chinese rule on this day. It had been a Portuguese colony since 1557. With the return of Hong Kong in 1997 and the return of Macau, no part of mainland China is occupied by a foreign power.

SACAGAWEA: DEATH ANNIVERSARY. Dec 20, 1812. As a young Shoshone Indian woman, Sacagawea in 1805 (with her two-month-old boy strapped to her back) traveled with the Lewis and Clark Expedition, serving as an interpreter. It is said that the expedition could not have succeeded without her aid. She was born about 1787 and died at Fort Manuel on the Missouri River. Few other women have been so often honored. There are statues, fountains and memorials of her, and her name has been given to a mountain peak. In 2000 the US Mint is issuing a $1 coin with Sacagawea's picture on it.

SAMUEL SLATER DAY IN MASSACHUSETTS. Dec 20. Proclaimed annually by the governor, this day commemorates Samuel Slater, the founder of the American factory system. He came to America from England and built a cotton mill at Rhode Island in 1790. He directed many New England mills until his death in 1835.

SOUTH CAROLINA: SECESSION ANNIVERSARY. Dec 20, 1860. South Carolina's legislature voted to secede from the US, the first state to do so. By Feb 1, 1861, 10 more states had seceded and formed the Confederate States of America (Alabama, Arkansas, Florida, Georgia, Louisiana, Mississippi, North Carolina, South Carolina, Tennessee, Texas and Virginia) .

VIRGINIA COMPANY EXPEDITION TO AMERICA: ANNIVERSARY. Dec 20, 1606. Three small ships, the *Susan Constant*, the *Godspeed* and the *Discovery*, commanded by Captain Christopher Newport, departed London, England, bound for America, where the royally chartered Virginia Company's approximately 120 persons established the first permanent English settlement in what is now the US at Jamestown, VA, May 14, 1607.

BIRTHDAYS TODAY

Lulu Delacre, 43, author (*Arroz Con Leche: Popular Songs and Rhymes from Latin America*), born Rio Piedras, Puerto Rico, Dec 20, 1957.

Uri Geller, 54, psychic, clairvoyant, born Tel Aviv, Israel, Dec 20, 1946.

DECEMBER 21 — THURSDAY

Day 356 — 10 Remaining

FIRST CROSSWORD PUZZLE: ANNIVERSARY. Dec 21, 1913. The first crossword puzzle was compiled by Arthur Wynne and published in a supplement to the *New York World*. *See* Curriculum Connection.

HUMBUG DAY. Dec 21. Allows all those preparing for Christmas to vent their frustrations. Twelve "humbugs" allowed. [© 1999 by WH] For info: Tom or Ruth Roy, Wellcat Holidays, PO Box 774, Lebanon, PA 17042-0774. Phone: (717) 279-0184. E-mail: wellcat@supernet.com. Web: www.wellcat.com.

PILGRIM LANDING: ANNIVERSARY. Dec 21, 1620. According to Governor William Bradford's *History of Plymouth Plantation*, "On Munday," [Dec 21, 1620, New Style] the Pilgrims, aboard the *Mayflower*, reached Plymouth, MA, "sounded ye harbor, and founde it fitt for shipping; and marched into ye land, & founde diverse cornfields, and ye best they could find, and ye season & their presente necessitie made them glad to accepte of it. . . . And after wards tooke better view of ye place, and resolved wher to pitch their dwelling; and them and their goods." Plymouth Rock, the legendary place of landing since it first was "identified" in 1769, nearly 150 years after the landing, has been a historic shrine since. The landing anniversary is observed in much of New England as Forefathers' Day.

SPACE MILESTONE: *APOLLO 8* (US). Dec 21, 1968. First moon voyage launched, manned by Colonel Frank Borman, Captain James A. Lovell, Jr and Major William A. Anders. Orbited moon Dec 24, returned to Earth Dec 27. First men to orbit the moon and see the side of the moon away from Earth.

WINTER. Dec 21–Mar 20, 2001. In the Northern Hemisphere winter begins today with the winter solstice, at 8:37 AM, EST. Note that in the Southern Hemisphere today is the beginning of summer. Between Equator and Arctic Circle the sunrise and sunset points on the horizon are farthest south for the year and daylight length is minimum (ranging from 12 hours, 8 minutes, at the equator to zero at the Arctic Circle).

YALDA. Dec 21. Yalda, the longest night of the year, is celebrated by Iranians. The ceremony has an Indo-Iranian origin, where Light and Good were considered to struggle against Darkness and Evil. With fires burning and lights lit, family and friends gather to stay up through the night helping the sun in its battle against darkness. They recite poetry, tell stories and eat special fruits and nuts until the sun, triumphant, reappears in the morning. For info: Yassaman Djalali, Librarian, West Valley Branch Library, 1243 San Tomas Aquino Rd, San Jose, CA 95117. Phone: (408) 244-4766.

DECEMBER 21, 1913
CROSSWORD PUZZLES FIRST PUBLISHED

Chances are likely that students are getting excited about the approaching school vacation. Attention spans are shortening and their minds (yours, too?) may not be totally focused on academic matters. Why not have some crossword fun and celebrate the 87th anniversary of the first publication of crossword puzzles? If you plan ahead, you can ask the school secretary to save paper targeted for recycling and use the backs of those sheets for copying.

During first period, divide the students into groups of four or five. Arrange groups so that each one includes a couple of students who can be relied upon to keep the process moving along. Assign each group a subject: science, math, reading, gym, etc. The group should brainstorm a list of words they are currently using in that part of the curriculum. Limit the list to 10 so they don't get bogged down trying to think of terms. Unrelated words can be used to fill other squares.

Give the students a blank grid with 10 boxes across and 10 down. (For copying purposes, make them small enough to fit two grids per sheet.) They can lightly pencil in their words, blended together crossword style. While one student is doing this, the others should be writing clues for each word across and down. Blacken the boxes where no letters appear. Number the boxes *after* unused boxes are colored in, so students can number the clues consecutively. Students should number the clues according to the box where the word begins. Erase lightly penciled letters from the grid. Hopefully, the creation of the puzzles will not exceed two class periods.

When the crossword puzzles are finished, copy them and give them to students to fill out that afternoon or to take home for fun during vacation.

	S	M	T	W	T	F	S
December						1	2
2000	3	4	5	6	7	8	9
	10	11	12	13	14	15	16
	17	18	19	20	21	22	23
	24	25	26	27	28	29	30
	31						

BIRTHDAYS TODAY

Chris Evert Lloyd, 46, broadcaster and former tennis player, born Ft Lauderdale, FL, Dec 21, 1954.

DECEMBER 22 — FRIDAY
Day 357 — 9 Remaining

CAPRICORN, THE GOAT. Dec 22–Jan 19. In the astronomical and astrological zodiac that divides the sun's apparent orbit into 12 segments, the period Dec 22–Jan 19 is identified, traditionally, as the sun-sign of Capricorn, the Goat. The ruling planet is Saturn.

CHANUKAH. Dec 22–29. Feast of Lights or Feast of Dedication. This festival lasting eight days commemorates the victory of Maccabees over Syrians (165 BC) and rededication of the Temple of Jerusalem. Begins on Hebrew calendar date Kislev 25, 5761. For more info: *A Hanukkah Treasury*, edited by Eric A. Kimmel (Holt, 0-8050-5293-3, $19.95 All ages).

"DING DONG SCHOOL" TV PREMIERE: ANNIVERSARY. Dec 22, 1952. Named by a three-year-old after watching a test broadcast of the opening sequence (a hand ringing a bell), "Ding Dong School" was one of the first children's educational series. Miss Frances (Dr. Frances Horwich, head of Roosevelt College's education department at Chicago) was the host of this weekday show. The show aired until 1956.

FIRST GORILLA BORN IN CAPTIVITY: BIRTH ANNIVERSARY. Dec 22, 1956. "Colo" was born at the Columbus, OH, zoo, weighing in at $3\frac{1}{4}$ pounds, the first gorilla born in captivity.

OGLETHORPE, JAMES EDWARD: BIRTH ANNIVERSARY. Dec 22, 1696. English general, author and colonizer of Georgia. Founder of the city of Savannah. Oglethorpe was born at London. He died June 30, 1785, at Cranham Hall, Essex, England.

BIRTHDAYS TODAY

Hector Elizondo, 64, actor (*Pretty Woman*, "Chicago Hope"), born New York, NY, Dec 22, 1936.

Claudia Alta "Lady Bird" Johnson, 88, former First Lady, widow of Lyndon Johnson, the 36th president of the US, born Karnack, TX, Dec 22, 1912.

Jerry Pinkney, 61, illustrator (*John Henry*), born Philadelphia, PA, Dec 22, 1939.

Diane K. Sawyer, 54, journalist ("60 Minutes," "Prime Time Live"), born Glasgow, KY, Dec 22, 1946.

DECEMBER 23 — SATURDAY
Day 358 — 8 Remaining

FIRST NONSTOP FLIGHT AROUND THE WORLD WITHOUT REFUELING: ANNIVERSARY. Dec 23, 1987. Dick Rutan and Jeana Yeager set a new world record of 216 hours of continuous flight, breaking their own record of 111 hours set July 15, 1986. The aircraft *Voyager* departed from Edwards Air Force Base at California Dec 14, 1987, and landed Dec 23, 1987. The journey covered 24,986 miles at an official speed of 115 miles per hour.

JAPAN: BIRTHDAY OF THE EMPEROR. Dec 23. National Day. Holiday honoring Emperor Akihito, born in 1933.

METRIC CONVERSION ACT: 25th ANNIVERSARY. Dec 23, 1975. The Congress of the US passed Public Law 94–168, known as the Metric Conversion Act of 1975. This act declares that the SI (International System of Units) will be this country's basic system of measurement and establishes the United States Metric Board which is responsible for the planning, coordination and implementation of the nation's voluntary conversion to SI. (Congress had authorized the metric system as a legal system of measurement in the US by an act passed July 28, 1866. In 1875, the US became one of the original signers of the Treaty of the Metre, which established an international metric system.)

MEXICO: FEAST OF THE RADISHES. Dec 23. Oaxaca. Figurines of people and animals cleverly carved out of radishes are sold during festivities.

TRANSISTOR INVENTED: ANNIVERSARY. Dec 23, 1947. John Bardeen, Walter Brattain and William Shockley of Bell Laboratories shared the Nobel Prize for their invention of the transistor, which led to a revolution in communications and electronics.

BIRTHDAYS TODAY

Akihito, 67, Emperor of Japan, born Tokyo, Japan, Dec 23, 1933.

Avi, 63, author (*The True Confessions of Charlotte Doyle*), born Avi Wortis, New York, NY, Dec 23, 1937.

Corey Haim, 28, actor (*Murphy's Romance, The Lost Boys*), born Toronto, Ontario, Canada, Dec 23, 1972.

Martin Kratt, 35, zoologist, cohost with his brother Chris ("Kratts' Creatures"), born Summit, NJ, Dec 23, 1965.

DECEMBER 24 — SUNDAY

Day 359 — 7 Remaining

AUSTRIA: "SILENT NIGHT, HOLY NIGHT" CELEBRATIONS. Dec 24. Oberndorf, Hallein and Wagrain, Salzburg, Austria. Commemorating the creation of the Christmas carol here in 1818.

CARSON, CHRISTOPHER "KIT": BIRTH ANNIVERSARY. Dec 24, 1809. American frontiersman, soldier, trapper, guide and Indian agent best known as Kit Carson. Born at Madison County, KY, he died at Fort Lyon, CO, May 23, 1868.

CHRISTMAS EVE. Dec 24. Family gift-giving occasion in many Christian countries.

GRUELLE, JOHNNY: BIRTH ANNIVERSARY. Dec 24, 1880. Author of the Raggedy Ann and Raggedy Andy books, born at Arcola, IL. Died Jan 9, 1938.

LIBYA: INDEPENDENCE DAY. Dec 24. Libya gained its independence from Italy in 1951.

BIRTHDAYS TODAY

Debra Barracca, 47, author, with husband Sal (*The Adventures of Taxi Dog*), born New York, NY, Dec 24, 1953.

Eddie Pope, 27, soccer player, born Greensboro, NC, Dec 24, 1973.

Jeff Sessions, 54, US Senator (R, Alabama), born Hybart, AL, Dec 24, 1946.

DECEMBER 25 — MONDAY

Day 360 — 6 Remaining

BARTON, CLARA: BIRTH ANNIVERSARY. Dec 25, 1821. Clarissa Harlowe Barton, American nurse and philanthropist, founder of the American Red Cross, was born at Oxford, MA. In 1881, she became first president of the American Red Cross (founded May 21, 1881). She died at Glen Echo, MD, Apr 12, 1912.

CHRISTMAS. Dec 25. Christian festival commemorating the birth of Jesus of Nazareth. Most popular of Christian observances, Christmas as a Feast of the Nativity dates from the 4th century. Although Jesus's birth date is not known, the Western church selected Dec 25 for the feast, possibly to counteract the non-Christian festivals of that approximate date. Many customs from non-Christian festivals (Roman Saturnalia, Mithraic sun's birthday, Teutonic yule, Druidic and other winter solstice rites) have been adopted as part of the Christmas celebration (lights, mistletoe, holly and ivy, holiday tree, wassailing and gift giving, for example). Some Orthodox Churches celebrate Christmas Jan 7 based on the "old calendar" (Julian). Theophany (recognition of the divinity of Jesus) is observed Dec 25 and also Jan 6, especially by the Eastern Orthodox Church. For links to sites about Christmas on the web, go to: deil.lang.uiuc.edu/web.pages/holidays/christmas.html.

MOON PHASE: NEW MOON. Dec 25. Moon enters New Moon phase at 12:22 PM, EST.

SOLAR ECLIPSE. Dec 25. Partial eclipse of the sun. Eclipse begins at 10:26 AM, EST, reaches greatest eclipse at 12:34 PM and ends at 2:43 PM. Visible in Mexico, West Indies, North America except Northwest, west Atlantic Ocean, South Greenland.

BIRTHDAYS TODAY

Rickey Henderson, 42, baseball player, born Chicago, IL, Dec 25, 1958.

Sissy (Mary Elizabeth) Spacek, 51, actress (Oscar for *Coal Miner's Daughter; Missing*), born Quitman, TX, Dec 25, 1949.

DECEMBER 26 — TUESDAY

Day 361 — 5 Remaining

BAHAMAS: JUNKANOO. Dec 26. Kaleidoscope of sound and spectacle combining a bit of Mardi Gras, mummer's parade and ancient African tribal rituals. Revelers in colorful costumes parade through the streets to sounds of cowbells, goat skin drums and many other homemade instruments. Annually, on Boxing Day.

BOXING DAY. Dec 26. Ordinarily observed on the first day after Christmas. A legal holiday in Canada, the United Kingdom and many other countries. Formerly a day when Christmas gift boxes were expected by a postman, the lamplighter, the trash man and others who render services to the public at large. When Boxing Day falls on a Saturday or Sunday, the Monday or Tuesday immediately following may be proclaimed or observed as a bank or public holiday.

CLERC, LAURENT: BIRTH ANNIVERSARY. Dec 26, 1785. The first deaf teacher in America, Laurent Clerc assisted Thomas Hopkins Gallaudet in establishing the first public school for the deaf, Connecticut Asylum for the Education and Instruction of Deaf and Dumb Persons (now the American School for the Deaf), at Hartford, CT, in 1817. For 41 years Clerc trained new teachers in the use of sign language and in methods of teaching the deaf. Clerc was born at LaBalme, France, and died July 18, 1869.

KIDS AFTER CHRISTMAS. Dec 26–Jan 31. Mystic, CT. Everyone pays the youth admission and enjoys a full day of crafts, entertainment and the lore of the sea. Est attendance: 3,000. For info: Mystic Seaport, 75 Greenmanville Ave, Box 6000, Mystic, CT 06355. Phone: (860) 572-5315 or (888) 9SEAPORT. Web: www.mysticseaport.org.

KWANZAA. Dec 26–Jan 1, 2001. American black family observance created in 1966 by Dr. Maulana Karenga in recognition of traditional African harvest festivals. This seven-day festival stresses self-reliance and unity of the black family, with a harvest feast (karamu) on the next to the last day and a day of meditation on the final one. Each day is dedicated to a principle that African Americans should live by— Day 1: Unity; Day 2: Self-determination; Day 3: Collective work and responsibility; Day 4: Cooperative economics; Day 5: Purpose; Day 6: Creativity; Day 7: Faith. Kwanzaa means "first fruit" in Swahili. For more info: *The Children's Book of Kwanzaa: A Guide to Celebrating the Holiday*, by Dolores Johnson (Atheneum, 0-68-980864-X, $16 Gr. 4–6).

MAO TSE-TUNG: BIRTH ANNIVERSARY. Dec 26, 1893. Chinese librarian, teacher, communist revolutionist and "founding father" of the People's Republic of China, born at Hunan Province, China. Died at Beijing, Sept 9, 1976.

NATIONAL WHINER'S DAY™. Dec 26. A day dedicated to whiners, especially those who return Christmas gifts and need lots of attention. People are encouraged to be happy about what they do have, rather than unhappy about what they don't have. The most famous whiner(s) of the year will be announced. Nominations accepted through Dec 15. For more info, please send SASE to: Rev Kevin C. Zaborney, 4900 Campau Dr, Midland, MI 48640. Phone: (517) 631-5740. E-mail: kzaborney@aol.com.

NELSON, THOMAS: BIRTH ANNIVERSARY. Dec 26, 1738. Merchant and signer of the Declaration of Independence, born at Yorktown, VA. Died at Hanover County, VA, Jan 4, 1789.

RADIUM DISCOVERED: ANNIVERSARY. Dec 26, 1898. French scientists Pierre and Marie Curie discovered the element radium, for which they later won the Nobel Prize for Physics.

SAINT STEPHEN'S DAY. Dec 26. One of the seven deacons named by the apostles to distribute alms. Died during 1st century. Feast Day is observed as a public holiday in Austria.

SECOND DAY OF CHRISTMAS. Dec 26. Observed as holiday in many countries.

SOUTH AFRICA: DAY OF GOODWILL. Dec 26. National holiday. Replaces Boxing Day.

BIRTHDAYS TODAY

Evan Bayh, 45, US Senator (D, Indiana), born Shirkieville, IN, Dec 26, 1955.
Susan Butcher, 46, sled dog racer, born Cambridge, MA, Dec 26, 1954.

December 2000	S	M	T	W	T	F	S
						1	2
	3	4	5	6	7	8	9
	10	11	12	13	14	15	16
	17	18	19	20	21	22	23
	24	25	26	27	28	29	30
	31						

Gray Davis, 58, Governor of California (D), born The Bronx, NY, Dec 26, 1942.

DECEMBER 27 — WEDNESDAY
Day 362 — 4 Remaining

CHRISTMAS AT THE TOP MUSEUM. Dec 27–28. Spinning Top Museum, Burlington, WI. Enjoy the traditional, universal toys of tops and top games, well-loved Christmas gifts around the world in the 2-hour museum program: 35 hands-on games and experiments, two videos, view the exhibit of 2,000 items, plus a live show by top collector. Reservations required. For info: Spinning Top Museum, 533 Milwaukee Ave (Hwy 36), Burlington, WI 53105. Phone: (262) 763-3946.

D'AULAIRE, INGRI: BIRTH ANNIVERSARY. Dec 27, 1904. Author, with her husband Edgar (*Norse Gods and Giants*), born at Kongsberg, Norway. Died Oct 24, 1980.

EID-AL-FITR: CELEBRATING THE FAST. Dec 27. Islamic calendar date: Shawwal 1, 1421. This feast/festival celebrates having completed the Ramadan fasting (which began Nov 27) and usually lasts for several days. Everyone wears new clothes; children receive gifts from parents and relatives; games, folktales, plays, puppet shows, trips to amusement parks; children allowed to stay up late. Different methods for "anticipating" the visibility of the new moon crescent at Mecca are used by different Muslim groups. US date may vary.

"HOWDY DOODY" TV PREMIERE: ANNIVERSARY. Dec 27, 1947. The first popular children's show was brought to TV by Bob Smith and was one of the first regular NBC shows to be shown in color. The show was set in the circus town of Doodyville, populated by people and puppets. Children sat in the bleachers' "Peanut Gallery" and participated in activities such as songs and stories. Human characters were Buffalo Bob (Bob Smith), the silent clown Clarabell (Bob Keeshan, Bobby Nicholson and Lew Anderson), storekeeper Cornelius Cobb (Nicholson), Chief Thunderthud (Bill LeCornec), Princess Summerfall Winterspring (Judy Tyler and Linda Marsh), Bison Bill (Ted Brown) and wrestler Ugly Sam (Dayton Allen). Puppet costars included Howdy Doody, Phineas T. Bluster, Dilly Dally, Flub-a-Dub, Captain Scuttlebutt, Double Doody and Heidi Doody. The filmed adventures of Gumby were also featured. In the final episode, Clarabell broke his long silence to say, "Goodbye, kids."

PASTEUR, LOUIS: BIRTH ANNIVERSARY. Dec 27, 1822. French chemist-bacteriologist, born at Dole, Jura, France. Died at Villeneuve l'Etang, France, Sept 28, 1895. Among his contributions to the germ theory of disease, he was the discoverer of prophylactic inoculation against rabies. He also proved that the spoilage of perishable food products could be prevented by the technique of heat treatment. This process, pasteurization, was named for him.

SAINT JOHN, APOSTLE-EVANGELIST: FEAST DAY. Dec 27. Son of Zebedee, Galilean fisherman, and Salome. Died about AD 100. Roman Rite Feast Day is Dec 27. (Observed May 8 by Byzantine Rite.)

BIRTHDAYS TODAY

Lisa Jakub, 20, actress (*Mrs Doubtfire*, *A Pig's Tale*), born Toronto, Ontario, Canada, Dec 27, 1980.
Diane Stanley, 57, author and illustrator (*Peter the Great*), born Abilene, TX, Dec 27, 1943.
Ernesto Zedillo Ponce de Leon, 49, president of Mexico, born Mexico City, Mexico, Dec 27, 1951.

DECEMBER 28 — THURSDAY

Day 363 — 3 Remaining

AUSTRALIA: PROCLAMATION DAY. Dec 28. Observed in South Australia.

BRINK, CAROL RYRIE: BIRTH ANNIVERSARY. Dec 28, 1895. Author (*Caddie Woodlawn*), born at Moscow, ID. Died Aug 15, 1981.

HOLY INNOCENTS DAY (CHILDERMAS). Dec 28. Commemoration of the massacre of children at Bethlehem, ordered by King Herod who wanted to destroy, among them, the infant Savior. Early and medieval accounts claimed as many as 144,000 victims, but more recent writers, noting that Bethlehem was a very small town, have revised the estimates of the number of children killed to between six and 20.

IOWA: ADMISSION DAY: ANNIVERSARY. Dec 28. Became 29th state in 1846.

PLEDGE OF ALLEGIANCE RECOGNIZED: 55th ANNIVERSARY. Dec 28, 1945. The US Congress officially recognized the Pledge of Allegiance and urged its frequent recitation in America's schools. The pledge was composed in 1892 by Francis Bellamy, a Baptist minister. At the time, Bellamy was chairman of a committee of state school superintendents of education, and several public schools adopted his pledge as part of the Columbus Day quadricentennial celebration that year. In 1955, the Knights of Columbus persuaded Congress to add the words "under God" to the pledge.

POOR RICHARD'S ALMANACK: ANNIVERSARY. Dec 28, 1732. The *Pennsylvania Gazette* carried the first known advertisement for the first issue of *Poor Richard's Almanack* by Richard Saunders (Benjamin Franklin) for the year 1733. The advertisement promised "many pleasant and witty verses, jests and sayings . . ." America's most famous almanac, *Poor Richard's* was published through the year 1758 and has been imitated many times since. From *The Autobiography of Benjamin Franklin*: "In 1732 I first publish'd my Almanack, under the name of *Richard Saunders*; it was continu'd by me about twenty-five years, commonly call'd *Poor Richard's Almanack*. I endeavor'd to make it both entertaining and useful, and it accordingly came to be in such demand, that I reap'd considerable profit from it, vending annually near ten thousand. And observing that it was generally read, scarce any neighborhood in the province being without it, I consider'd it as a proper vehicle for conveying instruction among the common people, who bought scarcely any other books; I therefore filled all the little spaces that occurr'd between the remarkable days in the calendar with proverbial sentences, chiefly such as inculcated industry and frugality, as the means of procuring wealth, and thereby securing virtue; it being more difficult for a man in want, to act always honestly, as, to use here one of those proverbs, *it is hard for an empty sack to stand upright*."

WILSON, WOODROW: BIRTH ANNIVERSARY. Dec 28, 1856. The 28th president of the US was born Thomas Woodrow Wilson at Staunton, VA. Twice elected president (1912 and 1916), it was Wilson who said, "The world must be made safe for democracy," as he asked the Congress to declare war on Germany, Apr 2, 1917. His first wife, Ellen, died Aug 6, 1914, and he married Edith Bolling Galt, Dec 18, 1915. He suffered a paralytic stroke Sept 16, 1919, never regaining his health. There were many speculations about who (possibly Mrs Wilson?) was running the government during his illness. His second term of office ended Mar 3, 1921, and he died at Washington, DC, Feb 3, 1924.

BIRTHDAYS TODAY

Cynthia DeFelice, 49, author (*The Apprenticeship of Lucas Whitaker*), born Philadelphia, PA, Dec 28, 1951.

Elizabeth Fitzgerald Howard, 73, author (*Aunt Flossie's Hats, Chita's Christmas Tree*), born Boston, MA, Dec 28, 1927.

Tim Johnson, 54, US Senator (D, South Dakota), born Canton, SD, Dec 28, 1946.

Patrick Rafter, 28, tennis player, born Mount Isa, Queensland, Australia, Dec 28, 1972.

Todd Richards, 31, Olympic snowboarder, born Worcester, MA, Dec 28, 1969.

MacKenzie Rosman, 11, actress ("7th Heaven"), born Charleston, SC, Dec 28, 1989.

Denzel Washington, 46, actor ("St. Elsewhere," *Glory, Malcolm X*), born Mt Vernon, NY, Dec 28, 1954.

DECEMBER 29 — FRIDAY

Day 364 — 2 Remaining

ATWATER, RICHARD: BIRTH ANNIVERSARY. Dec 29, 1892. Author, with his wife Florence, of the Newbery Award winner *Mr Popper's Penguins*. Born at Chicago, IL, he died Aug 21, 1948.

JOHNSON, ANDREW: BIRTH ANNIVERSARY. Dec 29, 1808. The 17th president of the US (Apr 15, 1865–Mar 3, 1869), Andrew Johnson was born at Raleigh, NC. Upon Abraham Lincoln's assassination Johnson became president. He was the only US president to be impeached, and he was acquitted Mar 26, 1868. After his term as president he made several unsuccessful attempts to win public office. Finally he was elected to the US Senate from Tennessee and served in the Senate from Mar 4, 1875, until his death, at Carter's Station, TN, July 31, 1875.

NEPAL: BIRTHDAY OF HIS MAJESTY THE KING. Dec 29. National holiday of Nepal commemorating birth of King in 1945. Three-day celebration with huge public rally at Tundikkel, gay pageantry, musical bands and illumination in the towns at night.

TEXAS: ADMISSION DAY: ANNIVERSARY. Dec 29. Became 28th state in 1845.

UNITED NATIONS: INTERNATIONAL DAY FOR BIOLOGICAL DIVERSITY. Dec 29. On Dec 19, 1994, the General Assembly proclaimed this observance for Dec 29, the date of entry into force of the Convention on Biological Diversity (Res 49/119). Designation of the Day had been recommended by the Conference of the Parties to the Convention, held at Nassau Nov 28–Dec 9, 1994. For info: United Nations, Dept of Public Info, New York, NY 10017.

WOUNDED KNEE MASSACRE: ANNIVERSARY. Dec 29, 1890. Anniversary of the massacre of more than 200 Native American men, women and children by the US 7th Cavalry at Wounded Knee Creek, SD. Government efforts to suppress a ceremonial religious practice, the Ghost Dance (which called for a messiah who would restore the bison to the plains, make the white men disappear and bring back the old Native American way of life), had resulted in the death of Sitting Bull Dec 15, 1890, which further inflamed the disgruntled Native Americans and culminated in the slaughter at Wounded Knee Dec 29. For more info: *Wounded Knee, 1890: The End of the Plains Indian Wars*, by Tom Streissguth (Facts on File, 0-8160-3600-4, $19.95 Gr. 7–12).

YMCA ORGANIZED: ANNIVERSARY. Dec 29, 1851. The first US branch of the Young Men's Christian Association was organized at Boston. It was modeled on an organization begun at London in 1844.

BIRTHDAYS TODAY

Molly Garrett Bang, 57, author and illustrator (*The Paper Crane, Ten, Nine, Eight*), born Princeton, NJ, Dec 29, 1943.

Irene Brady, 57, author and illustrator (*Wild Mouse*), born Ontario, OR, Dec 29, 1943.

Ted Danson, 53, actor ("Cheers," *Three Men and a Baby*), born San Diego, CA, Dec 29, 1947.

Jan Greenberg, 58, author (*Chuck Close, Up Close*), born St. Louis, MO, Dec 29, 1942.

DECEMBER 30 — SATURDAY

Day 365 — 1 Remaining

KIPLING, RUDYARD: BIRTH ANNIVERSARY. Dec 30, 1865. English poet, novelist and short story writer, Nobel prize laureate, Kipling was born at Bombay, India. After working as a journalist at India, he traveled around the world. He married an American and lived at Vermont for several years. Kipling is best known for his children's stories, such as the *Jungle Book* and *Just So Stories* and poems such as "The Ballad of East and West" and "If." He died at London, England, Jan 18, 1936.

MADAGASCAR: NATIONAL HOLIDAY. Dec 30. Anniversary of the change of the name Malagasy Republic to the Democratic Republic of Madagascar in 1975.

PHILIPPINES: RIZAL DAY: ANNIVERSARY. Dec 30. Commemorates martyrdom of Dr. Jose Rizal in 1896.

"THE ROY ROGERS SHOW" TV PREMIERE: ANNIVERSARY. Dec 30, 1951. This very popular TV western starred Roy Rogers and his wife, Dale Evans, as themselves. It also featured Pat Brady as Rogers's sidekick who rode a jeep named Nellybelle, the singing group Sons of the Pioneers, Rogers's horse Trigger, Evans's horse Buttermilk and a German shepherd named Bullet. This half-hour show was especially popular with young viewers.

BIRTHDAYS TODAY

Jane Langton, 78, author (*The Fledgling*), born Boston, MA, Dec 30, 1922.

Matt Lauer, 43, news anchor ("Today"), born New York, NY, Dec 30, 1957.

Mercer Mayer, 57, author and illustrator (*East of the Sun, West of the Moon*), born Little Rock, AR, Dec 30, 1943.

Julianne Moore, 40, actress (*The Lost World: Jurassic Park*), born Fayetteville, NC, Dec 30, 1960.

Tracey Ullman, 41, actress, singer ("The Tracey Ullman Show," *I Love You to Death*), born Buckinghamshire, England, Dec 30, 1959.

Tiger (Eldrick) Woods, 25, golfer, born Cypress, CA, Dec 30, 1975.

DECEMBER 31 — SUNDAY

Day 366 — 0 Remaining

FIRST BANK OPENS IN US: ANNIVERSARY. Dec 31, 1781. The first modern bank in the US, the Bank of North America, was organized by Robert Morris and received its charter from the Confederation Congress in 1781. It began operations Jan 7, 1782, at Philadelphia.

December 2000	S	M	T	W	T	F	S
						1	2
	3	4	5	6	7	8	9
	10	11	12	13	14	15	16
	17	18	19	20	21	22	23
	24	25	26	27	28	29	30
	31						

LEAP SECOND ADJUSTMENT TIME. Dec 31. One of the times that have been favored for the addition or subtraction of a second from clock time (to coordinate atomic and astronomical time). The determination to adjust is made by the Central Bureau of the International Earth Rotation Service at Paris.

MAKE UP YOUR MIND DAY. Dec 31. A day for all those people who have a hard time making up their minds. Make a decision today and follow through with it! Annually, Dec 31. For info: A.C. Moeller and M.A. Dufour, Box 71, Clio, MI 48420-1042.

MATISSE, HENRI: BIRTH ANNIVERSARY. Dec 31, 1869. Painter, born at Le Cateau, France. Matisse also designed textiles and stained glass windows. Died at Nice, France, Nov 3, 1954. For more info: *Matisse from A to Z*, by Marie Sellier (Peter Bedrick, 0-87226-475-0, $14.95 All ages).

NEW YEAR'S EVE. Dec 31. The last evening of the Gregorian calendar year, traditionally a night for merrymaking to welcome in the new year. This year is a special one, as we welcome a new millennium. *See* Curriculum Connection.

ORANGE BOWL PARADE. Dec 31. Miami, FL. Annual New Year's Eve parade for the past 63 years. Nationally televised, parade moves 2.2 miles along downtown Miami's Biscayne Boulevard by the bay. Est attendance: 500,000. For info: John Shaffer, Orange Bowl Committee, 601 Brickell Key Dr, Ste 206, Miami, FL 33131. Phone: (305) 371-4600.

PANAMA: ASSUMES CONTROL OF CANAL: ANNIVERSARY. Dec 31, 1999. With the expiration of the Panama Canal Treaty of 1979 at noon, the Republic of Panama assumed full responsibility for the canal and the US Panama Canal Commission ceased to exist.

BIRTHDAYS TODAY

Anthony Hopkins, 63, actor (*Amistad*), born Port Talbot, Wales, Great Britain, Dec 31, 1937.

Val Kilmer, 41, actor (*Batman Forever*), born Los Angeles, CA, Dec 31, 1959.

DECEMBER 31
THE END OF A MILLENNIUM!

Though there was a great deal of celebrating at the end of 1999, technically today is the end of the second millennium. A millennium is a period of 1,000 years. Our era is divided into two periods, BC (before Christ) and AD (anno Domini, which means "in the year of our Lord"). However, in the eighth century when this system started to be widely used, Arabic numerals were not yet known in Europe. The Roman numerals then in use did not have a symbol for zero so the first year of the first millennium was not AD 0 but AD 1 and the year 1,000 was the 1,000th year. That means that Jan 1, 1001 was the first day of the second millennium and Jan 1, 2001 will be the first day of the third millennium.

For more info: *The Story of Clocks and Calendars: Marking a Millennium*, by Betsy Maestro (Lathrop, 0-688-14549-3, $15.93 Gr. 1 & up) and *The Greenwich Guide to Time and the Millennium*, by Jeff Edwards (Heinemann, 1-57572-802-8, $16.95 Gr. 4–7). Visit the Greenwich Royal Observatory website in the UK at www.rog.nmm.ac.uk/leaflets/new_mill.html.

JANUARY 1 — MONDAY

Day 1 — 364 Remaining

MONDAY, JANUARY ONE, 2001. Jan 1. First day of the first month of the Gregorian calendar year, Anno Domini 2001, a Common Year, and (until July 4th) the 225th year of American independence. This is the first day of the third millennium. New Year's Day is a public holiday in the US and in many other countries. Traditionally, it is a time for personal stocktaking and for making resolutions for the coming year. Financial accounting begins anew for businesses and individuals whose fiscal year is the calendar year. Jan 1 has been observed as the beginning of the year in most English-speaking countries since the British Calendar Act of 1751, prior to which the New Year began Mar 25 (approximating the vernal equinox). Earth begins another orbit of the sun, during which it, and we, will travel some 583,416,000 miles in 365.24219 days. New Year's Day has been called "Everyman's Birthday," and in some countries a year is added to everyone's age Jan 1 rather than on the anniversary of each person's birth.

AUSTRALIA: COMMONWEALTH FORMED: 100th ANNIVERSARY. Jan 1, 1901. The six colonies of Victoria, New South Wales, Queensland, South Australia, Western Australia and Northern Territory were united into one nation. The British Parliament had passed the Commonwealth Constitution Bill in the spring of 1900 and Queen Victoria signed the document Sept 17, 1900. Australia will celebrate its centennial as a nation in 2001.

BEANIE BABIES® INTRODUCED: ANNIVERSARY. Jan 1, 1994. During this month the first nine Beanie Babies were introduced. Since then, more than 135 models of the plush animals were released. For more info: www.ty.com.

BONZA BOTTLER DAY™. Jan 1. (Also Feb 2, Mar 3, Apr 4, May 5, June 6, July 7, Aug 8, Sept 9, Oct 10, Nov 11 and Dec 12.) To celebrate when the number of the day is the same as the number of the month. Bonza Bottler Day™ is an excuse to have a party at least once a month. For info: Gail M. Berger, 109 Matthew Ave, Poca, WV 25159. Phone: (304) 776-7746. E-mail: gberger5 @aol.com.

CUBA: ANNIVERSARY OF THE REVOLUTION. Jan 1. National holiday celebrating the overthrow of the government of Fulgencio Batista in 1959 by the revolutionary forces of Fidel Castro, which had begun a civil war in 1956.

CUBA: LIBERATION DAY: ANNIVERSARY. Jan 1. A national holiday that celebrates the end of Spanish rule in 1899. Cuba, the largest island of the West Indies, was a Spanish possession from its discovery by Columbus (Oct 27, 1492) until 1899. Under US military control 1899–1902 and 1906–09, a republican government took over Jan 28, 1909 and controlled the island until overthrown Jan 1, 1959, by Fidel Castro's revolutionary movement.

CZECH-SLOVAK DIVORCE: ANNIVERSARY. Jan 1, 1993. As Dec 31, 1992, gave way to Jan 1, 1993, the 74-year-old state of Czechoslovakia separated into two nations—the Czech and Slovak Republics. The Slovaks held a celebration through the night in the streets of Bratislava amid fireworks, bell ringing, singing of the new country's national anthem and the raising of the Slovak flag. In the new Czech Republic no official festivities took place, but later in the day the Czechs celebrated with a solemn oath by their parliament. The nation of Czechoslovakia ended peacefully though polls showed that most Slovaks and Czechs would have preferred that Czechoslovakia survive. Before the split Czech Prime Minister Vaclav Klaus and Slovak Prime Minister Vladimir Meciar reached an agreement on dividing everything from army troops and gold reserves to the art on government building walls.

ELLIS ISLAND OPENED: ANNIVERSARY. Jan 1, 1892. Ellis Island was opened on New Year's Day in 1892. Over the years more than 20 million individuals were processed through the immigration station. The island was used as a point of deportation as well; in 1932 alone, 20,000 people were deported from Ellis Island. When the US entered WWII in 1941, Ellis Island became a Coast Guard Station. It closed Nov 12, 1954, and was declared a national park in 1956. After years of disuse it was restored and was reopened as a museum in 1990. For more info: www.nps.gov/stli/serv02.htm.

EURO INTRODUCED: ANNIVERSARY. Jan 1, 1999. The euro, the common currency of 11 members of the European Union, was introduced for use by banks. The value of the currencies of Austria, Belgium, Finland, France, Germany, Ireland, Italy, Luxembourg, the Netherlands, Portugal and Spain are locked in at a permanent conversion rate to the euro. On Jan 1, 2002, euro bills and coins will begin circulating and other currencies will be phased out.

HAITI: INDEPENDENCE DAY. Jan 1. A national holiday commemorating the proclamation of independence in 1804. Haiti, occupying the western third of the island Hispaniola (second largest of the West Indies), was a Spanish colony from the time of its discovery by Columbus in 1492 until 1697, then a French colony until the proclamation of independence in 1804.

IT'S OKAY TO BE DIFFERENT!. Jan 1–31. A month dedicated to teaching children to be tolerant and accepting of different races, cultures and religions. Author Ramona Winner published a children's picture book with English/Spanish text exquisitely celebrating the uniqueness of each individual. Endorsed by educators and loved by children. For info: BrainStorm 3000, PO Box 42246, Santa Barbara, CA 93140. Phone: (805) 961-9810.

JAPANESE ERA NEW YEAR. Jan 1–3. Celebration of the beginning of the year Heisei Thirteen, the 13th year of Emperor Akihito's reign.

KLIBAN, B(ERNARD): BIRTH ANNIVERSARY. Jan 1, 1935. Cartoonist B. Kliban was born at Norwalk, CT. He was known for his satirical drawings of cats engaged in human pursuits, which appeared in the books *Cat* (1975), *Never Eat Anything Bigger than Your Head & Other Drawings* (1976) and *Whack Your Porcupine* (1977). His drawings appeared on T-shirts, greeting cards, calendars, bedsheets and other merchandise, creating a $50 million industry before his death at San Francisco, CA, Aug 12, 1990.

MARCH OF DIMES BIRTH DEFECTS PREVENTION MONTH. Jan 1–31. To heighten awareness of birth defects and how they may be prevented, to inform the public about the work of the March of Dimes and to offer opportunities to new volunteers for service in the prevention of birth defects. For info: March of Dimes Birth Defects Foundation, 1275 Mamaroneck Ave, White Plains, NY 10605. Phone: (914) 997-4600.

MEXICO: ZAPATISTA REBELLION: ANNIVERSARY. Jan 1, 1994. Declaring war against the government of President Carlos Salinas de Gortari, the Zapatista National Liberation Army seized four towns in the state of Chiapas in southern Mexico. The rebel group, which took its name from the early 20th-century Mexican revolutionary Emiliano Zapata, issued a declaration stating that they were protesting discrimination against the Indian population of the region and against their severe poverty.

MUMMERS PARADE. Jan 1. Philadelphia, PA. World famous New Year's Day parade of 20,000 spectacularly costumed Mummers in a colorful parade that goes on all day. Est attendance: 100,000. For info: Mummers Parade, 1100 S 2nd St, Philadelphia, PA 19147. Phone: (215) 636-1666. E-mail: mummersmus@aol.com. Web: www.mummers.com.

NATIONAL BATH SAFETY MONTH. Jan 1–31. To raise awareness of the potential of hazards that exist and encourage people to conduct a bathroom safety audit. For info: Homecare America, 5 Wellwood Ave, Farmingdale, NY 11735. Phone: (516) 454-6664. Fax: (516) 454-8572. E-mail: richards@homecareamerica.com. Web: www.homecareamerica.com.

NATIONAL BOOK MONTH. Jan 1–31. When the world demands more and more of our time, National Book Month invites everyone in America to take time out to treat themselves to a unique pleasure: reading a good book. Readers participate in National Book Month annually through literary events held at schools, bookstores, libraries, community centers and arts organizations. The organization also sponsors the annual National Book Awards, which include an award for a children's book. For info: Natl Book Foundation, 260 Fifth Ave, Rm 904, New York, NY 10001. Phone: (212) 685-0261. Fax: (212) 235-6570. E-mail: NatBkFdn@mindspring.com. Web: www.publishersweekly.com /NBF/docs/nbf.html.

NATIONAL ENVIRONMENTAL POLICY ACT: ANNIVERSARY. Jan 1, 1970. The National Environmental Policy Act of 1969 established the Council on Environmental Quality and made it federal government policy to protect the environment.

NATIONAL EYE CARE MONTH. Jan 1–31. Sponsored by the American Academy of Ophthalmology, this month promotes awareness of eye health, importance of medical eye care and prevention to avoid eye injuries and disease. A free kit of materials is available to businesses and organizations to increase awareness at local and community levels. Fax a copy of your mailing label with your request. For info: American Academy of Ophthalmology–NECM, PO Box 7424, San Francisco, CA 94140-7424. Fax: (415) 561-8567. E-mail: PIMR@aao.org. Web: www.eyenet.org.

NATIONAL HOT TEA MONTH. Jan 1–31. To celebrate one of nature's most popular, soothing and relaxing beverages; the only beverage in America commonly served hot or iced, anytime, anywhere, for any occasion. For info: Joseph P. Simrany, Pres, The Tea Council of the USA, 420 Lexington Ave, Ste 825, New York, NY 10170. Phone: (212) 986-6998. Fax: (212) 697-8658.

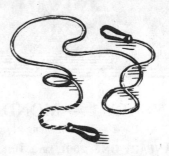

NATIONAL PERSONAL SELF-DEFENSE AWARENESS MONTH. Jan 1–31. To educate Americans about realistic self-defense options, tactics and techniques in an increasingly aggressive world. Seminars and related events nationally focus on issues of awareness, prevention, risk reduction, confrontation avoidance and physical self-defense techniques to encourage individuals to take a pro-active role in their self-defense and in building self-confidence. For info: Natl Self-Defense Institute, Inc, 1521 Alton Rd, Box 131, Miami Beach, FL 33139. Phone: (305) 868-NSDI. Fax: (305) 577-8213.

NEW YEAR'S DAY. Jan 1. Legal holiday in all states and territories of the US and in most other countries. The world's most widely celebrated holiday.

NEW YEAR'S DISHONOR LIST. Jan 1. Since 1976, America's dishonor list of words banished from the Queen's English. Overworked words and phrases (e.g., *uniquely unique, first time ever, safe sex*). Send nominations to the following address: For info: PR Office, Lake Superior State Univ, Sault Ste. Marie, MI 49783. Phone: (906) 635-2315. Fax: (906) 635-2623. Web: www.lssu.edu.

OATMEAL MONTH. Jan 1–31. "Celebrate oatmeal, a low-fat, sodium-free, whole grain that when eaten daily as a part of a diet that's low in saturated fat and cholesterol may help reduce the risk of heart disease. Delicious recipes, helpful hints and tips from Quaker® Oats, The Oat Expert, will make enjoying the heart health benefits oatmeal has to offer easy, convenient and, above all, delicious." For info: The Oat Expert, 225 W Washington, Ste 1440, Chicago, IL 60606. Phone: (312) 629-1234.

REVERE, PAUL: BIRTH ANNIVERSARY. Jan 1, 1735. American patriot, silversmith and engraver, maker of false teeth, eyeglasses, picture frames and surgical instruments. Best remembered for his famous ride Apr 18, 1775, to warn patriots that the British were coming, celebrated in Longfellow's poem, "The Midnight Ride of Paul Revere." Born at Boston, MA, died there May 10, 1818. See also: "Paul Revere's Ride: Anniversary" (Apr 18).

ROSE BOWL GAME. Jan 1. Pasadena, CA. Football conference champions from Big Ten and Pac-10 meet in the Rose Bowl game. Tournament of Roses has been an annual New Year's Day event since 1890; Rose Bowl football game since 1902. Michigan defeated Stanford 49–0 in what was the first postseason football

January 2001	S	M	T	W	T	F	S
		1	2	3	4	5	6
	7	8	9	10	11	12	13
	14	15	16	17	18	19	20
	21	22	23	24	25	26	27
	28	29	30	31			

game. Called the Rose Bowl since 1923, it is preceded each year by the Tournament of Roses Parade. Est attendance: 100,000. For info: Bridget Schinnerer, Program Coord, Rose Bowl Stadium, 1001 Rose Bowl Drive, Pasadena, CA 91103. Phone: (626) 449-4100. Fax: (626) 449-9066. Web: www.tournamentofroses.com.

ROSS, BETSY: BIRTH ANNIVERSARY. Jan 1, 1752. According to legend based largely on her grandson's revelations in 1870, needleworker Betsy Ross created the first stars-and-stripes flag in 1775, under instructions from George Washington. Her sewing and her making of flags were well known, but there is little corroborative evidence of her role in making the first stars-and-stripes. The account is generally accepted, however, in the absence of any documented claims to the contrary. She was born Elizabeth Griscom at Philadelphia, PA, and died there Jan 30, 1836.

RUSSIA: NEW YEAR'S DAY OBSERVANCE. Jan 1–2. National holiday. Modern tradition calls for setting up New Year's trees in homes, halls, clubs, palaces of culture and the hall of the Kremlin Palace. Children's parties with Granddad Frost and his granddaughter, Snow Girl. Games, songs, dancing, special foods, family gatherings and exchanges of gifts and New Year's cards.

SAINT BASIL'S DAY. Jan 1. St. Basil's or St. Vasily's feast day observed by Eastern Orthodox churches. Special traditions for the day include serving St. Basil cakes, each of which contains a coin. Feast day observed Jan 14 by those churches using the Julian calendar.

SOLEMNITY OF MARY, MOTHER OF GOD. Jan 1. Holy Day of Obligation in Roman Catholic Church since calendar reorganization of 1969, replacing the Feast of the Circumcision, which had been recognized for more than 14 centuries.

SUDAN: INDEPENDENCE DAY. Jan 1. National holiday. Sudan was proclaimed a sovereign independent republic Jan 1, 1956, ending its status as an Anglo-Egyptian condominium (since 1899).

TOURNAMENT OF ROSES PARADE. Jan 1. Pasadena, CA. 112th annual parade. Rose Parade starting at 8 AM, EST, includes floats, bands and equestrians. Est attendance: 1,000,000. For info: Pasadena Tournament of Roses Assn, 391 S Orange Grove Blvd, Pasadena, CA 91184. Phone: (626) 449-4100. Fax: (626) 449-9066. Web: www.tournamentofroses.com.

UNITED NATIONS: DECADE FOR HUMAN RIGHTS EDUCATION: YEAR SEVEN. Jan 1–Dec 31. On Dec 23, 1994, the General Assembly proclaimed this decade to begin in 1995, and welcomed the Plan of Action for the Decade submitted by the Secretary-General (Res 49/184). The Assembly expressed its conviction that human rights education should constitute a lifelong process, by which people learn respect for the dignity of others. Info from: United Nations, Dept of Public Info, New York, NY 10017.

UNITED NATIONS: DECADE FOR THE ERADICATION OF POVERTY: YEAR FIVE. Jan 1–Dec 31. General Assembly, Dec 20, 1995 (Res 50/107 II), proclaimed 1997–2006 (the decade following the International Year for the Eradication of Poverty—1996) to be a time for governments and organizations to pursue implementation of the recommendations of the major UN conferences on this issue, particularly the World Summit for Social Development held in Copenhagen in March 1995. Info from: United Nations, Dept of Public Info, New York, NY 10017.

UNITED NATIONS: INTERNATIONAL DECADE OF THE WORLD'S INDIGENOUS PEOPLE: YEAR EIGHT. Jan 1–Dec 9. Proclaimed by the General Assembly, Dec 21, 1993 (Res 48/163), this decade (1994–2003) focuses international attention and cooperation on the problems of indigenous people in a range of areas, such as human rights, health, education, development and environment. Governments are encouraged to include representatives of these people in planning and executing goals and activities for the decade. Info from: United Nations, Dept of Public Info, New York, NY 10017.

UNITED NATIONS: INTERNATIONAL DECADE FOR A CULTURE OF PEACE AND NON-VIOLENCE FOR THE CHILDREN OF THE WORLD: YEAR ONE. Jan 1–Dec 31. The General Assembly (Res 53/25) invites religious bodies, educational institutions, artists and the media to support this decade for the benefit of every child of the world. Member states are invited to ensure that the practice of peace and non-violence is taught at all levels in their societies, including in educational institutions.

UNITED NATIONS: INTERNATIONAL YEAR OF VOLUNTEERS. Jan 1–Dec 31. A year to enhance the recognition, facilitation, networking and promotion of volunteer service in order to encourage service from an expanded number of individuals. The United Nations Volunteer Program is the focal point for the year. Info from: United Nations, Dept of Public Info, New York, NY 10017.

UNITED NATIONS: YEAR OF DIALOGUE AMONG CIVILIZATIONS. Jan 1–Dec 31. The General Assembly (Res 53/22) invites governments, international organizations and non-governmental organizations to implement cultural, educational and social programs to promote the concept of dialogue among civilizations, including organizing conferences and seminars and disseminating information on the subject. For more info: United Nations, Dept of Public Info, New York, NY 10017.

WAYNE, "MAD ANTHONY": BIRTH ANNIVERSARY. Jan 1, 1745. American Revolutionary War general whose daring, sometimes reckless, conduct earned him the nickname "Mad Anthony" Wayne. His courage and shrewdness as a soldier made him a key figure in the capture of Stony Point, NY (1779), preventing Benedict Arnold's delivery of West Point to the British, and in subduing hostile Indians of the Northwest Territory (1794). He was born at Waynesboro, PA and died at Presque Isle, PA, Dec 15, 1796.

Z DAY. Jan 1. To give recognition on the first day of the year to all persons and places whose names begin with the letter "Z" and who are always listed or thought of last in any alphabetized list. For info: Tom Zager, 4545 Kirkwood Dr, Sterling Heights, MI 48310.

BIRTHDAYS TODAY

Ernest F. Hollings, 79, US Senator (D, South Carolina), born Charleston, SC, Jan 1, 1922.

Gary Johnson, 48, Governor of New Mexico (R), born Minot, ND, Jan 1, 1953.

Tony Knowles, 58, Governor of Alaska (D), born Tulsa, OK, Jan 1, 1943.

JANUARY 2 — TUESDAY

Day 2 — 363 Remaining

ASIMOV, ISAAC: BIRTH ANNIVERSARY. Jan 2, 1920. Although Isaac Asimov was one of the world's best-known writers of science fiction, his almost 500 books dealt with subjects as diverse as the Bible, works for preschoolers, college textbooks, mysteries, chemistry, biology, limericks, Shakespeare, Gilbert and Sullivan and modern history. During his prolific career he helped to elevate science fiction from pulp magazines to a more intellectual level. Some of his works include the *Foundation Trilogy, The Robots of Dawn, Robots and Empire, Nemesis, Murder at the A.B.A.* (in which he himself was a character), *The Gods Themselves* and *I, Robot*, in which he posited the famous Three Laws of Robotics. *The Clock We Live On* is a book for children on the origins of calendars. Asimov was born near Smolensk, Russia, and died at New York, NY, Apr 6, 1992.

55-MPH SPEED LIMIT: ANNIVERSARY. Jan 2, 1974. President Richard Nixon signed a bill requiring states to limit highway speeds to a maximum of 55 mph. This measure was meant to conserve energy during the crisis precipitated by the embargo imposed by the Arab oil-producing countries. A plan, used by some states, limited sale of gasoline on odd-numbered days for cars whose plates ended in odd numbers and even-numbered days for even-numbered plates. Some states limited purchases to $2–$3 per auto and lines as long as six miles resulted in some locations. See also: "Arab Oil Embargo Lifted: Anniversary" (Mar 13).

GEORGIA RATIFIES CONSTITUTION: ANNIVERSARY. Jan 2, 1788. By unanimous vote, Georgia became the fourth state to ratify the Constitution.

HAITI: ANCESTORS' DAY. Jan 2. Commemoration of the ancestors. Also known as Hero's Day. Public holiday.

JAPAN: KAKIZOME. Jan 2. Traditional Japanese festival gets under way when the first strokes of the year are made on paper with the traditional brushes.

MOON PHASE: FIRST QUARTER. Jan 2. Moon enters First Quarter phase at 5:31 PM, EST.

RUSSIA: PASSPORT PRESENTATION. Jan 2. A ceremony for 16-year-olds, who are recognized as citizens of the country. Always on the first working day of the New Year.

	S	M	T	W	T	F	S
January		1	2	3	4	5	6
2001	7	8	9	10	11	12	13
	14	15	16	17	18	19	20
	21	22	23	24	25	26	27
	28	29	30	31			

SPACE MILESTONE: *LUNA 1* (USSR). Jan 2, 1959. Launch of robotic moon probe that missed the moon and became the first spacecraft from Earth to orbit the sun.

SPAIN CAPTURES GRANADA: ANNIVERSARY. Jan 2, 1492. Spaniards took the city of Granada from the Moors, ending seven centuries of Muslim rule in Spain.

TAFT, HELEN HERRON: BIRTH ANNIVERSARY. Jan 2, 1861. Wife of William Howard Taft, 27th president of the US, born at Cincinnati, OH. Died at Washington, DC, May 22, 1943.

WOLFE, JAMES: BIRTH ANNIVERSARY. Jan 2, 1727. English general who commanded the British army's victory over Montcalm's French forces on the Plains of Abraham at Quebec City in 1759. As a result, France surrendered Canada to England. Wolfe was born at Westerham, Kent, England. He died at the Plains of Abraham of battle wounds, Sept 13, 1759.

BIRTHDAYS TODAY

David Cone, 38, baseball player, born Kansas City, MO, Jan 2, 1963.
Dennis Hastert, 59, Speaker of the House of Representatives, born Aurora, IL, Jan 2, 1942.
Richard Riley, 68, US Secretary of Education, born Greenville, SC, Jan 2, 1933.

JANUARY 3 — WEDNESDAY

Day 3 — 362 Remaining

ALASKA: ADMISSION DAY: ANNIVERSARY. Jan 3. Alaska, which had been purchased from Russia in 1867, became the 49th state in 1959. The area of Alaska is nearly one-fifth the size of the rest of the US.

CONGRESS ASSEMBLES. Jan 3. The Constitution provides that "the Congress shall assemble at least once in every year. . . ." and the 20th Amendment specifies "and such meeting shall begin at noon on the 3rd day of January, unless they shall by law appoint a different day."

COOLIDGE, GRACE ANNA GOODHUE: BIRTH ANNIVERSARY. Jan 3, 1879. Wife of Calvin Coolidge, 30th president of the US, born at Burlington, VT. Died at Northampton, MA, July 8, 1957.

DRINKING STRAW PATENTED: ANNIVERSARY. Jan 3, 1888. A drinking straw made out of paraffin-covered paper was patented by Marvin Stone of Washington, DC. It replaced natural rye straws.

MOTT, LUCRETIA (COFFIN): BIRTH ANNIVERSARY. Jan 3, 1793. American teacher, minister, antislavery leader and (with Elizabeth Cady Stanton) one of the founders of the women's rights movement in the US. Born at Nantucket, MA, she died near Philadelphia, PA, Nov 11, 1880.

TOLKIEN, J[OHN] R[ONALD] R[EUEL]: BIRTH ANNIVERSARY. Jan 3, 1892. Author of *The Hobbitt* (1937) and the trilogy *The Lord of the Rings*. Though best known for his fantasies, Tolkien was also a serious philologist. Born at Bloemfontein, South Africa, he died at Bournemouth, England, Sept 2, 1973.

BIRTHDAYS TODAY

Alma Flor Ada, 63, author (*Yours Truly, Goldilocks*), born Camaguey, Cuba, Jan 3, 1938.
Joan Walsh Anglund, 75, author and illustrator (*Crocus in the Snow, Bedtime Book*), born Hinsdale, IL, Jan 3, 1926.
Mel Gibson, 45, actor (*Lethal Weapon*, voice of John Smith in *Pocahontas*), born New York, NY, Jan 3, 1956.

Robert (Bobby) Hull, 62, Hockey Hall of Fame left wing, born Point Anne, Ontario, Canada, Jan 3, 1939.

Alex Linz, 12, actor (*Home Alone 3*), born Santa Barbara, CA, Jan 3, 1989.

Jason Marsden, 26, actor ("Step By Step"), born Providence, RI, Jan 3, 1975.

JANUARY 4 — THURSDAY
Day 4 — 361 Remaining

BRAILLE, LOUIS: BIRTH ANNIVERSARY. Jan 4, 1809. The inventor of a widely used touch system of reading and writing for the blind was born at Coupvray, France. Permanently blinded at the age of three by a leatherworking awl in his father's saddle-making shop, Braille developed a system of writing that used, ironically, an awl-like stylus to punch marks in paper that could be felt and interpreted by the blind. The system was largely ignored until after Braille died in poverty, suffering from tuberculosis, at Paris, Jan 6, 1852. *See* Curriculum Connection.

EARTH AT PERIHELION. Jan 4. At approximately 4 AM, EST, planet Earth will reach Perihelion, that point in its orbit when it is closest to the sun (about 91,400,000 miles). The Earth's mean distance from the sun (mean radius of its orbit) is reached early in the months of April and October. Note that Earth is closest to the sun during Northern Hemisphere winter. See also: "Earth at Aphelion" (July 4).

GENERAL TOM THUMB: BIRTH ANNIVERSARY. Jan 4, 1838. Charles Sherwood Stratton, perhaps the most famous midget in history, was born at Bridgeport, CT. His growth almost stopped during his first year, but he eventually reached a height of three feet, four inches and a weight of 70 pounds. "Discovered" by P.T. Barnum in 1842, Stratton, as "General Tom Thumb," became an internationally known entertainer and on tour performed before Queen Victoria and other heads of state. On Feb 10, 1863, he married another midget, Lavinia Warren. Stratton died at Middleborough, MA, July 15, 1883.

GRIMM, JACOB: BIRTH ANNIVERSARY. Jan 4, 1785. Librarian, mythologist and philologist, born at Hanau, Germany. Most remembered for *Grimm's Fairy Tales* (in collaboration with his brother Wilhelm). Died at Berlin, Germany, Sept 20, 1863. See also: "Grimm, Wilhelm Carl: Birth Anniversary (Feb 24).

MYANMAR: INDEPENDENCE DAY. Jan 4. National Day. The British controlled the country from 1826 until 1948 when it was granted independence. Formerly Burma, the country's name was changed to the Union of Myanmar in 1989 to reflect that the population is made up not just of the Burmese but of many other ethnic groups as well.

NEWTON, SIR ISAAC: BIRTH ANNIVERSARY. Jan 4, 1643. Sir Isaac Newton was the chief figure of the scientific revolution of the 17th century, a physicist and mathematician who laid the foundations of calculus, studied the mechanics of planetary motion and discovered the law of gravitation. Born at Woolsthorpe, England, he died at London, England, Mar 20, 1727. Newton was born before Great Britain adopted the Gregorian calendar. His Julian (Old Style) birth date is Dec 25, 1642.

JANUARY 4
LOUIS BRAILLE'S BIRTHDAY

Louis Braille was born near Paris, France in 1809. At the age of three, he injured his eye in his father's shop. Infection set in and resulted in the loss of sight. When he got older, he attended Paris's Royal Institution for Blind Youths. Louis was a boy who enjoyed learning, and he desperately wanted to learn how to read. While at the Royal Institution, he heard about a military code used to send messages to soldiers at night. The message system used a series of dots punched into cardboard. Louis adapted the code to make raised letters that blind people could read with their fingers.

Students can learn the Braille alphabet and punch their names in Braille. They can experiment with simple words and learning to read them. If your school district has a Learning about Disabilities program, arrange for the coordinator or one of the program's representatives to visit your room and discuss blindness. He or she may be able to bring in a Braille book, a cane or a video about guide dogs.

Blind people depend on their other senses to interpret the world around them. To get students into the spirit of seeing with their other senses, place an assortment of objects your students are unlikely to be familiar with in a covered box or bag. After they feel the object inside, have them describe what they found in writing or orally. Students also can try "seeing" with their ears. Record a series of sounds—a car starting, a door opening or closing, footsteps, a sneeze, etc. See how many sounds they can identify correctly.

January is also Eye Care Month. In conjunction with this, an eye care professional might be willing to visit and talk about eye exams and working in the eye care professions. Try inviting a local optometrist to speak with your class. He or she could talk about how glasses and contact lenses are made.

Will your school district be conducting eye screening this month? If so (or even if not), it's a good time to talk about wearing glasses. Extol the virtues of seeing clearly and underscore that needing to wear glasses is not something to fear or be sad about. (By the way, keep your eyes on the alert for student "squinters" and refer them for eye testing.) Talk about teasing and how unkind it is. Harken back to your celebration of Good Manners Month (see Sept 1).

Have the school nurse visit your class and talk with the children about eye safety. He or she might mention the danger snowballs present, since winter vacation has just ended and in some areas the ground may be snow-covered. The nurse can also stress the importance of wearing safety glasses while working with certain tools and chemicals.

Two biographies about Braille that students will enjoy are: *Louis Braille: The Blind Boy Who Wanted to Read*, by Dennis Fradin (Silver, 0-614-29054-6, $6.95 Gr. K–5); and *Out of Darkness: The Story of Louis Braille*, by Russell Freedman (Houghton, 0-395-77516-7, $15.95 Gr. 5 & up). Other books about being blind and how eyes work that will interest students are: *Do You Remember the Color Blue?*, by Sally Alexander (Simon & Schuster, 0-6708-8043-4, $15.99 Gr. 4–9); *T.J.'s Story*, by Arlene Schulman (Lerner, 0-8225-2586-0, $15.95 Gr.2–4); *How Do Our Eyes See?*, by Carol Ballard (Raintree, 0-8172-4736-X, $22.83, Gr. 2–5); and *What Do You See?*, by Patricia Lauber (Crown, 0-517-59390-4, $17 Gr. 3–7).

For a guide to websites about Braille the man and the technology, go to www.nyise.org/braille.htm.

POLISH-AMERICAN IN THE HOUSE: ANNIVERSARY. Jan 4, 1977. Maryland Democrat Barbara Mikulski took her seat in the US House of Representatives, the first Polish-American ever to do so. An able voice for female as well as working class Baltimore constituents of the 3rd District, Mikulski went on to be elected to the US Senate.

POP MUSIC CHART INTRODUCED: 65th ANNIVERSARY. Jan 4, 1936. *Billboard* magazine published the first list of best-selling pop records, covering the week that ended Dec 30, 1935. On the list were recordings by the Tommy Dorsey and the Ozzie Nelson orchestras.

TRIVIA DAY. Jan 4. In celebration of those who know all sorts of facts and/or have doctorates in uselessology. For info: Robert L. Birch, Puns Corps, Box 2364, Falls Church, VA 22042-0364. Phone: (703) 533-3668.

UTAH: ADMISSION DAY: ANNIVERSARY. Jan 4. Became the 45th state in 1896.

BIRTHDAYS TODAY

Robert Burleigh, 65, poet (*Hoops*), born Chicago, IL, Jan 4, 1936.
Etienne Delessert, 60, author and illustrator (*How the Mouse Was Hit on the Head With a Stone and So Discovered the World*), born Lausanne, Switzerland, Jan 4, 1941.
Phyllis Reynolds Naylor, 68, author (Newbery for *Shiloh*), born Anderson, IN, Jan 4, 1933.

JANUARY 5 — FRIDAY

Day 5 — 360 Remaining

AILEY, ALVIN: 70th BIRTH ANNIVERSARY. Jan 5, 1931. Born at Rogers, TX, Alvin Ailey began his career as a choreographer in the late 1950s after a successful career as a dancer. He founded the Alvin Ailey American Dance Theater, drawing from classical ballet, jazz, Afro-Caribbean and modern dance idioms to create the 79 ballets of the company's repertoire. He and his work played a central part in establishing a role for blacks in the world of modern dance. Ailey died Dec 1, 1989, at New York, NY.

ASARAH B'TEVET. Jan 5. Hebrew calendar date: Tevet 10, 5761. The Fast of the 10th of Tevet begins at first morning light and commemorates the beginning of the Babylonian siege of Jerusalem in the 6th century BC.

CARVER, GEORGE WASHINGTON: DEATH ANNIVERSARY. Jan 5, 1943. Black American agricultural scientist, author, inventor and teacher. Born into slavery at Diamond Grove, MO, probably in 1864. His research led to the creation of synthetic products made from peanuts, potatoes and wood. Carver died at Tuskegee, AL. His birthplace became a national monument in 1953. For more info: *George Washington Carver: Nature's Trailblazer*, by Theresa Rogers (Twenty First Century, 0-8050-2115-9, $14.95 Gr. 5–7).

DECATUR, STEPHEN: BIRTH ANNIVERSARY. Jan 5, 1779. American naval officer (whose father and grandfather, both also named Stephen Decatur, were also seafaring men) born at Sinepuxent, MD. In a toast at a dinner in Norfolk in 1815, Decatur spoke his most famous words: "Our country! In her intercourse with foreign nations may she always be in the right; but our country, right or wrong." Mortally wounded in a duel with Commodore James Barron, at Bladensburg, MD, on the morning of Mar 22, 1820, Decatur was carried to his home at Washington where he died a few hours later.

ITALY: EPIPHANY FAIR. Jan 5. Piazza Navona, Rome, Italy. On the eve of Epiphany a fair of toys, sweets and presents takes place among the beautiful Bernini Fountains.

PICCARD, JEANNETTE RIDLON: BIRTH ANNIVERSARY. Jan 5, 1895. First American woman to qualify as a free balloon pilot (1934). One of the first women to be ordained an Episcopal priest (1976). Pilot for record-setting balloon ascent into stratosphere (57,579 ft) from Dearborn, MI, Oct 23, 1934, with her husband, Jean Felix Piccard. She was an identical twin married to an identical twin. Born at Chicago, IL, she died at Minneapolis, MN, May 17, 1981. See also: "Piccard, Jean Felix: Birth Anniversary" (Jan 28) and "Piccard, Auguste: Birth Anniversary" (Jan 28).

TWELFTH NIGHT. Jan 5. Evening before Epiphany. Twelfth Night marks the end of medieval Christmas festivities and the end of Twelfthtide (the 12-day season after Christmas ending with Epiphany). Also called Twelfth Day Eve.

WYOMING INAUGURATES FIRST WOMAN GOVERNOR IN US: ANNIVERSARY. Jan 5, 1925. Nellie Tayloe (Mrs William B.) Ross became the first woman to serve as governor upon her inauguration as governor of Wyoming. She had previously finished out the term of her husband, who had died in office. In 1974 Ella Grasso of Connecticut became the first woman to be elected governor in her own right.

BIRTHDAYS TODAY

Mike DeWine, 54, US Senator (R, Ohio), born Springfield, OH, Jan 5, 1947.
Warrick Dunn, 26, football player, born Baton Rouge, LA, Jan 5, 1975.
Walter Frederick "Fritz" Mondale, 73, 42nd vice president of the US and candidate for president in 1984, born Ceylon, MN, Jan 5, 1928.

JANUARY 6 — SATURDAY

Day 6 — 359 Remaining

ARMENIAN CHRISTMAS. Jan 6. Christmas is observed in the Armenian Church, the oldest national Christian church.

CARNIVAL SEASON. Jan 6–Feb 27. A secular festival preceding Lent. A time of merrymaking and feasting before the austere days of Lenten fasting and penitence (40 weekdays between Ash Wednesday and Easter Sunday). The word *carnival* probably is derived from the Latin *carnem levare*, meaning "to remove meat." Depending on local custom, the carnival season may start any

January 2001	S	M	T	W	T	F	S
		1	2	3	4	5	6
	7	8	9	10	11	12	13
	14	15	16	17	18	19	20
	21	22	23	24	25	26	27
	28	29	30	31			

time between Nov 11 and Shrove Tuesday. Conclusion of the season is much less variable, being the close of Shrove Tuesday in most places. Celebrations vary considerably, but the festival often includes many theatrical aspects (masks, costumes and songs) and has given its name (in the US) to traveling amusement shows that may be seen throughout the year. Observed traditionally in Roman Catholic countries from Epiphany through Shrove Tuesday.

EPIPHANY or TWELFTH DAY. Jan 6. Known also as Old Christmas Day and Twelfthtide. On the twelfth day after Christmas, Christians celebrate the visit of the Magi or Wise Men to the baby Jesus. In many countries, this is the day children receive gifts, rather than Christmas day. Epiphany of Our Lord, one of the oldest Christian feasts, is observed in Roman Catholic churches in the US on a Sunday between Jan 2 and 8. Theophany of the Eastern Orthodox Church is observed on this day in churches using the Gregorian calendar and Jan 19 in those churches using the Julian calendar and celebrates the manifestation of the divinity of Jesus at the time of his baptism in the Jordan River by John the Baptist.

ITALY: LA BEFANA. Jan 6. Epiphany festival in which the "Befana," a kindly witch, bestows gifts on children—toys and candy for those who have been good, but a lump of coal or a pebble for those who have been naughty. The festival begins on the night of Jan 5 with much noise and merrymaking (when the Befana is supposed to come down the chimneys on her broom, leaving gifts in children's stockings) and continues with fairs, parades and other activities.

JOAN OF ARC: BIRTH ANNIVERSARY. Jan 6, 1412. Born at the village of Domremy, in the Meuse River valley of France. At this time there was civil war in France, with one faction being aided by the English. As a teenager, Joan led an army to drive the English out of northern France. Captured, she was burned at the stake as a witch and a heretic on May 30, 1431. Her martyrdom inspired the unification of the French people, who drove the English out of France. Joan was made a saint in 1920. For more info: *Joan of Arc*, by Diane Stanley (Morrow, 0-688-14330-X, $15.95 Gr. 4–8). See also: "Saint Joan of Arc: Feast Day" (May 30).

NATIONAL SMITH DAY. Jan 6. The commonest surname in the English-speaking world is Smith. There are an estimated 2,382,500 Smiths in the US. This special day honors the birthday in 1580 of Captain John Smith, the leader of the English colonists who settled at Jamestown, VA, in 1607, thus making him one of the first American Smiths. On this special day, all derivatives, such as Goldsmith, are invited to participate. For info: Adrienne Sioux Koopersmith, 1437 W Rosemont, 1W, Chicago, IL 60660-1319. Phone: (773) 743-5341. Fax: (773) 743-5395. E-mail: kooper @interaccess.com.

NEW MEXICO: ADMISSION DAY: ANNIVERSARY. Jan 6. Became 47th state in 1912.

PAN AM CIRCLES EARTH: ANNIVERSARY. Jan 6, 1942. A Pan American Airways plane arrived in New York to complete the first around-the-world trip by a commercial aircraft.

SANDBURG, CARL: BIRTH ANNIVERSARY. Jan 6, 1878. American poet ("Fog," "Chicago"), biographer of Lincoln, historian and folklorist, born at Galesburg, IL. Died at Flat Rock, NC, July 22, 1967. For more info: *Carl Sandburg: A Biography*, by Milton Meltzer (Millbrook, 0-7613-1364-8, $29.90 Gr. 5–10). *See* Curriculum Connection.

SMITH, JEDEDIAH STRONG: BIRTH ANNIVERSARY. Jan 6, 1799. Mountain man, fur trader and one of the first explorers of the American West, Smith helped develop the Oregon Trail.

JANUARY 6
CARL SANDBURG'S BIRTHDAY

Carl Sandburg was born Jan 6, 1878, in Galesburg, Illinois. Although Sandburg never completed high school or college, he loved literature and writing. He worked a number of odd jobs and even spent several years living as a hobo! From 1912 until the 1920s, Sandburg worked as a newspaper writer and he gained fame for his poetry. He garnered literary acclaim, receiving the Pulitzer Prize for history in 1940, in recognition of his four-volume biography *Abraham Lincoln: The War Years*. In 1951, he received the Pulitzer Prize for poetry for his collection of poems titled *Complete Poems*, published in 1950. Children, however, are most likely to know Sandburg through his humorous stories, published as the *Rootabaga Stories*.

Sandburg's use of language, sense of the absurd and ability to convey the sense of "folks chatting amongst themselves" make his stories delightful to read aloud. *The Rootabaga Stories*, (Harcourt, 0-15-269062-X, $19.95 Gr. K & up), illustrated by Michael Hague, is a lovely collection. *The Huckabuck Family* (Farrar, 0-374-33511-7, $16 All ages) is a "don't miss" single Rootabaga story, illustrated as a picture book by David Small.

Students can make up lists of favorite turns of phrase or silly names used by Sandburg. They also can hunt for literary devices such as alliteration.

Sandburg's poetry appeals to many age groups. Older students can read and discuss his poems relating to war, cruelty and greed. He attacks these topics with a very hard-hitting style. Younger students will enjoy *Grassroots*, Sandburg poems illustrated by Wendell Minor (Harcourt, 0-15-200082-8, $18 All ages), and the humor and visual nonsense found in *Poems for Children Nowhere Near Old Enough to Vote*, illustrated by Istvan Banyai (Knopf, 0-679-88990-0, $16.99 Gr. 3 & up). Look for a copy of Sandburg's well-known "Fog." Examine the imagery and words chosen to depict fog. Students can have fun writing their own weather poems patterned on the poetic devices used by Sandburg.

He was the first American to reach California by land and first to travel by land from San Diego, up the West Coast to the Canadian border. Smith was born at Jericho (now Bainbridge), NY, and was killed by Comanche Indians along the Santa Fe Trail in what is now Kansas, May 27, 1831.

SPACE MILESTONE: *LUNAR EXPLORER* (US). Jan 6, 1998. NASA headed back to the moon for the first time since the *Apollo 17* flight 25 years before. This unmanned probe searches for evidence of frozen water on the moon.

THREE KINGS DAY. Jan 6. Major festival of Christian Church observed in many parts of the world with gifts, feasting, last lighting of Christmas lights and burning of Christmas greens. In many European countries children get their Christmas presents on Three Kings Day. Twelfth and last day of the Feast of the Nativity. Commemorates visit of the Three Wise Men (Kings or Magi) to Bethlehem.

UNIVERSAL LETTER-WRITING WEEK. Jan 6–13. The purpose of this week is for people all over the world to get the new year off to a good start by sending letters and cards to friends and acquaintances not only in their own country but to people throughout the world. For complete information and suggestions about writing good letters, send $4 to cover expense of printing, handling and postage. *See* Curriculum Connection. For info: Dr. Stanley Drake, Pres, Intl Soc of Friendship and Goodwill, 40139 Palmetto Dr, Palmdale, CA 93551-3557.

JANUARY 6–13
UNIVERSAL LETTER WRITING WEEK

Expressing ourselves clearly in writing gives us an advantage in our personal lives and in the business world. There are many different styles of written correspondence. A well-written business letter may lead to a lucrative position. Faithful correspondence helps maintain friendships when people are separated by distance. Letters may be mementos that chronicle an important event or accomplishment in someone's life. Students can celebrate Universal Letter Writing Week by writing a different style of letter each day.

On Monday, students can focus on a business letter. Ask them to write a letter to a business, complimenting the firm for good customer service. Then ask students to write a letter to the same firm stating dissatisfaction with a product and asking for a refund. Be sure to provide examples of correct headings and forms of address.

On Tuesday, students again focus on the business community by writing a letter to a company, this time as a job applicant. They should mention the specific title of the job they are interested in and why they are qualified for the position. The letter could be to a real or imaginary company.

Wednesday, switch to a personal letter. Students can write a newsy, chatty and informal letter to a friend. It doesn't have to be long. If it's a classmate or another student in the school and you want to avoid postage, set up a cardboard "mailbox," and designate a student to be the official mail carrier. The envelope should have the addressee's name, teacher and classroom number on it. If the letter is to a friend or relative outside the school setting, encourage students to bring in a stamped envelope so the letter gets mailed and doesn't become just a classroom exercise. Have a supply of stamps on hand so forgetful students can purchase one from you.

Thursday is invitation and thank-you day. Students can invite someone to a party that celebrates a significant occasion in their lives. Since many holidays have recently ended, chances are excellent that many students owe thank-you notes. Let them write one or two in class, and you will earn the gratitude of many a grandparent or other gift-giver.

Designate Friday as E-mail day. With the help of the learning center director, it should be possible to establish at least a temporary E-mail site from which students can send a short note via the Internet to a student in another classroom in your school or in another building within the district.

A historical approach to Universal Letter Writing Week could focus on how mail has been delivered in the past. The Pony Express is an example.

BIRTHDAYS TODAY

Johnny Yong Bosch, 25, actor (*Turbo: A Power Rangers Movie*, "Power Rangers Turbo"), born Topeka, KS, Jan 6, 1976.

Ina R. Friedman, 75, author (*How My Parents Learned to Eat*), born Chester, PA, Jan 6, 1926.

Gabrielle Reece, 31, pro volleyball player, born La Jolla, CA, Jan 6, 1970.

January 2001

S	M	T	W	T	F	S
	1	2	3	4	5	6
7	8	9	10	11	12	13
14	15	16	17	18	19	20
21	22	23	24	25	26	27
28	29	30	31			

JANUARY 7 — SUNDAY
Day 7 — 358 Remaining

FILLMORE, MILLARD: BIRTH ANNIVERSARY. Jan 7, 1800. The 13th president of the US (July 10, 1850–Mar 3, 1853), Fillmore succeeded to the presidency upon the death of Zachary Taylor, but he did not get the hoped-for nomination from his party in 1852. He ran for president unsuccessfully in 1856 as candidate of the "Know-Nothing Party," whose platform demanded, among other things, that every government employee (federal, state and local) should be a native-born citizen. Fillmore was born at Locke, NY, and died at Buffalo, NY, Mar 8, 1874.

FIRST BALLOON FLIGHT ACROSS ENGLISH CHANNEL: ANNIVERSARY. Jan 7, 1785. Dr. John Jeffries, a Boston physician, and Jean-Pierre Blanchard, French aeronaut, crossed the English Channel from Dover, England, to Calais, France, landing in a forest after being forced to throw overboard all ballast, equipment and even most of their clothing to avoid a forced landing in the icy waters of the English Channel. Blanchard's trousers are said to have been the last article thrown overboard.

GERMANY: MUNICH FASCHING CARNIVAL. Jan 7–Feb 27. Munich. From Jan 7 through Shrove Tuesday is Munich's famous carnival season. Costume balls are popular throughout carnival. High points on Fasching Sunday (Feb 25) and Shrove Tuesday (Feb 27) with great carnival outside at the Viktualienmarkt and on Pedestrian Mall.

JAPAN: NANAKUSA. Jan 7. Festival dates back to the 7th century and recalls the seven plants served to the emperor that are believed to have great medicinal value—shepherd's purse, chickweed, parsley, cottonweed, radish, hotoke-no-za and aona.

JAPAN: USOKAE (BULLFINCH EXCHANGE FESTIVAL). Jan 7. Dazaifu, Fukuoka Prefecture. "Good Luck" gilded wood bullfinches, mixed among many plain ones, are sought after by the throngs as priests of the Dazaifu Shrine pass them out in the dim light of a small bonfire.

MONTGOLFIER, JACQUES ETIENNE: BIRTH ANNIVERSARY. Jan 7, 1745. Merchant and inventor, born at Vidalon-lez Annonay, Ardèche, France. With his older brother, Joseph Michel, in November 1782, conducted experiments with paper and fabric bags filled with smoke and hot air, which led to invention of the hot-air balloon and human's first flight. Died at Serrieres, France, Aug 2, 1799. See also: "First Balloon Flight: Anniversary" (June 5); "Montgolfier, Joseph Michel: Birth Anniversary" and "Aviation History Month" (Nov 1).

OLD CALENDAR ORTHODOX CHRISTMAS. Jan 7. Some Orthodox Churches celebrate Christmas which is the "Old" (Julian) calendar date.

RUSSIA: CHRISTMAS OBSERVANCE. Jan 7. National holiday.

TRANSATLANTIC PHONING: ANNIVERSARY. Jan 7, 1927. Commercial transatlantic telephone service between New York and London was inaugurated. There were 31 calls made the first day.

BIRTHDAYS TODAY

Kay Chorao, 64, author and illustrator (*A Magic Eye for Ida*), born Elkhart, IN, Jan 7, 1937.

Katie Couric, 44, cohost, "Today Show," born Arlington, VA, Jan 7, 1957.

Minfong Ho, 50, author (*Hush!: A Thai Lullaby*), born Rangoon, Burma, Jan 7, 1951.

JANUARY 8 — MONDAY
Day 8 — 357 Remaining

AT&T DIVESTITURE: ANNIVERSARY. Jan 8, 1982. In the most significant antitrust suit since the breakup of Standard Oil in 1911, American Telephone and Telegraph agreed to give up its 22 local Bell System companies ("Baby Bells"). These companies represented 80 percent of AT&T's assets. This ended the corporation's virtual monopoly of US telephone service.

BATTLE OF NEW ORLEANS: ANNIVERSARY. Jan 8, 1815. British forces suffered crushing losses (more than 2,000 casualties) in an attack on New Orleans, LA. Defending US troops were led by General Andrew Jackson, who became a popular hero as a result of the victory. Neither side knew that the War of 1812 had ended two weeks previously with the signing of the Treaty of Ghent, Dec 24, 1814. Battle of New Orleans Day is observed in Louisiana.

CHOU EN-LAI: 25th DEATH ANNIVERSARY. Jan 8, 1976. Anniversary of the death of Chou En-Lai, premier of the State Council of the People's Republic of China. He was born in 1898 (exact date unknown).

EARTH'S ROTATION PROVED: 150th ANNIVERSARY. Jan 8, 1851. Using a device now known as Foucault's pendulum in his Paris home, physicist Jean Foucault demonstrated that the Earth rotates on its axis.

ENGLAND: PLOUGH MONDAY. Jan 8. Always the Monday after Twelfth Day. Work on the farm is resumed after the festivities of the 12 days of Christmas. On preceding Sunday ploughs may be blessed in churches. Celebrated with dances and plays.

GREECE: MIDWIFE'S DAY or WOMEN'S DAY. Jan 8. Midwife's Day or Women's Day is celebrated Jan 8 each year to honor midwives and all women. "On this day women stop their housework and spend their time in cafés, while the men do all the housework chores and look after the children." In some villages, men caught outside "will be stripped . . . and drenched with cold water."

JAPAN: COMING-OF-AGE DAY. Jan 8. National holiday for youth of the country who have reached adulthood during the preceding year. Annually, the second Monday in January.

NATIONAL CLEAN-OFF-YOUR-DESK DAY. Jan 8. To provide one day early each year for every desk worker to see the top of the desk and prepare for the following year's paperwork. Annually, the second Monday in January. For info: A.C. Moeller, Box 71, Clio, MI 48420-1042.

NATIONAL JOYGERM DAY. Jan 8. Joygerm junkies invade and pervade the earth with merriment and mirth, joy and cheer, kindness and courtesy, silliness and sacredness and happiness and humor. Festivities include smile check-up clinics, chuckling, chortling and grinning and winning over gruff and grumpy grouches to the Joygerm Generation. For info: Joygerm Joan E. White, Founder, Joygerms Unlimited, PO Box 219, Eastwood Station, Syracuse, NY 13206-0219. Phone: (315) 472-2779.

NATIONAL THANK GOD IT'S MONDAY! DAY. Jan 8. Besides holidays, such as President's Day, being celebrated on Mondays, people everywhere start new jobs, have birthdays, celebrate promotions and begin vacations on Mondays. A day in recognition of this first day of the week. Annually, the second Monday in January. For info: Dorothy Zjawin, 61 W Colfax Ave, Roselle Park, NJ 07204. Phone: (908) 241-6241. Fax: (908) 241-6241.

PRESLEY, ELVIS AARON: BIRTH ANNIVERSARY. Jan 8, 1935. Popular American rock singer, born at Tupelo, MS. Although his middle name was spelled incorrectly as "Aron" on his birth certificate, Elvis had it legally changed to "Aaron," which is how it is spelled on his gravestone. Died at Memphis, TN, Aug 16, 1977.

WAR ON POVERTY: ANNIVERSARY. Jan 8, 1964. President Lyndon Johnson declared a War on Poverty in his State of the Union address. He stressed improved education as one of the cornerstones of the program. The following Aug 20, he signed a $947.5 million anti-poverty bill designed to assist more than 30 million citizens.

BIRTHDAYS TODAY

Nancy Bond, 56, author (*A String on the Harp*), born Bethesda, MD, Jan 8, 1945.

Slade Gorton, 73, US Senator (R, Washington), born Chicago, IL, Jan 8, 1928.

Lauren Hewett, 20, actress ("Spellbinder: Land of the Dragon Lord"), born Sydney, Australia, Jan 8, 1981.

Bob Taft, 59, Governor of Ohio (R), born Boston, MA, Jan 8, 1942.

JANUARY 9 — TUESDAY
Day 9 — 356 Remaining

AVIATION IN AMERICA: ANNIVERSARY. Jan 9, 1793. A Frenchman, Jean-Pierre Francois Blanchard, made the first manned free-balloon flight in America's history at Philadelphia, PA. The event was watched by President George Washington and many other high government officials. The hydrogen-filled balloon rose to a height of about 5,800 feet, traveled some 15 miles and landed 46 minutes later in New Jersey. Reportedly Blanchard had one passenger on the flight—a little black dog.

CATT, CARRIE LANE CHAPMAN: BIRTH ANNIVERSARY. Jan 9, 1859. American women's rights leader, founder (in 1919) of the National League of Women Voters. Born at Ripon, WI, she died at New Rochelle, NY, Mar 9, 1947.

CONNECTICUT RATIFIES CONSTITUTION: ANNIVERSARY. Jan 9, 1788. By a vote of 128 to 40, Connecticut became the fifth state to ratify the Constitution.

LUNAR ECLIPSE. Jan 9. Total eclipse of the moon. Moon enters penumbra at approximately 12:43 PM, EST, reaches middle of eclipse at 3:20 PM and leaves penumbra at 5:57 PM. The beginning visible in northern region of Canada, most of Alaska, Greenland, Arctic, Europe, most of Africa, Australia, western Micronesia, Asia, Queen Mary coast of Antarctica, northeastern North Atlantic Ocean, eastern South Atlantic Ocean, Indian Ocean and western Pacific Ocean; the end visible in northeastern North America, Greenland, Arctic, northeastern South America, Europe, Africa, coast of Antarctica near Cape Ann, Asia, Atlantic Ocean, Indian Ocean and western Philippine Sea.

MOON PHASE: FULL MOON. Jan 9. Moon enters Full Moon phase at 3:24 PM, EST.

NIXON, RICHARD MILHOUS: BIRTH ANNIVERSARY. Jan 9, 1913. Richard Nixon served as the 36th vice president of the US (under President Dwight D. Eisenhower) Jan 20, 1953 to Jan 20, 1961. He was the 37th president of the US, serving Jan 20, 1969, to Aug 9, 1974, when he resigned the presidency while under threat of impeachment. First US president to resign that office. He was born at Yorba Linda, CA, and died at New York, NY, Apr 22, 1994.

PANAMA: MARTYRS' DAY. Jan 9. Public holiday.

PERIGEAN SPRING TIDES. Jan 9. Spring tides, the highest possible tides, occur when New Moon or Full Moon takes place within 24 hours of the moment the Moon is nearest Earth (perigee) in its monthly orbit, at 3 PM, EST. The word spring refers not to the season but comes from the German word *springen*, "to rise up."

PHILIPPINES: FEAST OF THE BLACK NAZARENE. Jan 9. Culmination of a nine-day fiesta. Manila's largest procession takes place in the afternoon of Jan 9, in honor of the Black Nazarene, whose shrine is at the Quiapo Church.

BIRTHDAYS TODAY

Clyde Robert Bulla, 87, author (*The Chalk Box Kid*), born King City, MO, Jan 9, 1914.

Sergio Garcia, 21, golfer, born Borriol, Spain, Jan 9, 1980.

Bill Graves, 48, Governor of Kansas (R), born Salina, KS, Jan 9, 1953.

A.J. McLean, 23, singer (Backstreet Boys), born West Palm Beach, FL, Jan 9, 1978.

Joely Richardson, 36, actress (*101 Dalmatians*), born London, England, Jan 9, 1965.

JANUARY 10 — WEDNESDAY

Day 10 — 355 Remaining

LEAGUE OF NATIONS: ANNIVERSARY. Jan 10, 1920. Through the Treaty of Versailles, the League of Nations came into existence. Fifty nations entered into a covenant designed to avoid war. The US never joined the League of Nations, which was dissolved Apr 18, 1946.

UNITED NATIONS GENERAL ASSEMBLY: 55th ANNIVERSARY. Jan 10, 1946. On the 26th anniversary of the establishment of the unsuccessful League of Nations, delegates from 51 nations met at London, England, for the first meeting of the UN General Assembly.

WOMEN'S SUFFRAGE AMENDMENT INTRODUCED IN CONGRESS: ANNIVERSARY. Jan 10, 1878. Senator A.A. Sargent of California, a close friend of Susan B. Anthony, introduced into the US Senate a women's suffrage amendment known as the Susan B. Anthony Amendment. It wasn't until Aug 26, 1920, 42 years later, that the amendment was signed into law.

BIRTHDAYS TODAY

Lloyd Bloom, 54, illustrator (*Like Jake and Me*), born New York, NY, Jan 10, 1947.

Remy Charlip, 72, author and illustrator (*Hooray for Me!*), born Jan 10, 1929.

Glenn Robinson, 28, basketball player, member of 1996 Dream Team, born Gary, IN, Jan 10, 1973.

January 2001	S	M	T	W	T	F	S
		1	2	3	4	5	6
	7	8	9	10	11	12	13
	14	15	16	17	18	19	20
	21	22	23	24	25	26	27
	28	29	30	31			

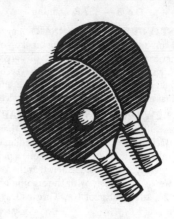

JANUARY 11 — THURSDAY

Day 11 — 354 Remaining

CUCKOO DANCING WEEK. Jan 11–17. To honor the memory of Laurel and Hardy, whose theme, "The Dancing Cuckoos," shall be heard throughout the land as their movies are seen and their antics greeted by laughter by old and new fans of these unique masters of comedy. [Originated by the late William T. Rabe of Sault Ste. Marie, MI.]

"DESIGNATED HITTER" RULE ADOPTED: ANNIVERSARY. Jan 11, 1973. American League adopted the "designated hitter" rule, whereby an additional player is used to bat for the pitcher.

FIRST BLACK SOUTHERN LIEUTENANT GOVERNOR: 15th ANNIVERSARY. Jan 11, 1986. L. Douglas Wilder was sworn in as lieutenant governor of Virginia. He was the first black elected to statewide office in the South since Reconstruction. He later served as governor of Virginia.

HOSTOS, EUGENIO MARIA: BIRTH ANNIVERSARY. Jan 11, 1839. Puerto Rican patriot, scholar and author of more than 50 books. Born at Rio Canas, Puerto Rico, he died at Santo Domingo, Dominican Republic, Aug 11, 1903. The anniversary of his birth is observed as a public holiday in Puerto Rico.

LEOPOLD, ALDO: BIRTH ANNIVERSARY. Jan 11, 1886. Naturalist and author who made a profound contribution to the American environmental movement. Born at Burlington, IA, he died Apr 21, 1948, at Sauk County, WI. *See* Curriculum Connection.

MacDONALD, JOHN A.: BIRTH ANNIVERSARY. Jan 11, 1815. Canadian statesman, first prime minister of Canada. Born at Glasgow, Scotland, he died June 6, 1891, at Ottawa, Canada.

NEPAL: NATIONAL UNITY DAY. Jan 11. Celebration paying homage to King Prithvinarayan Shah (1723–75), founder of the present house of rulers of Nepal and creator of the unified Nepal of today.

O'BRIEN, ROBERT C.: BIRTH ANNIVERSARY. Jan 11, 1918. Author (Newbery for *Mrs Frisby and the Rats of NIMH*), born Robert Conly at Brooklyn, NY. Died at Washington, DC, Mar 5, 1973.

US SURGEON GENERAL DECLARES CIGARETTES HAZARDOUS: ANNIVERSARY. Jan 11, 1964. US Surgeon General Luther Terry issued the first government report saying that smoking may be hazardous to one's health.

JANUARY 11
ALDO LEOPOLD'S BIRTHDAY

Aldo Leopold, the author of *A Sand County Almanac and Sketches Here and There*, helped redefine how biologists and conservationists regarded the natural world. Although his name does not command the immediate recognition of Rachel Carson or John Muir, you don't have to look far to find his influence on the modern environmental movement. Leopold's early commitment to establishing wilderness areas ensured that large tracts of natural areas were left undeveloped for future generations to enjoy. He recognized the need for land stewardship, wilderness preservation and the importance of predators to the wildlife's natural balance. Conservation efforts to restore wolves to their historic habitats were fueled by Leopold's writings. He practically founded the field of wildlife ecology.

Leopold's appreciation of the natural world and its creatures is superbly conveyed with humor, a gentle poetic touch and a storyteller's voice in *A Sand County Almanac and Sketches Here and There*. Since it was first published in 1949, the slim volume has sold almost 2.5 million copies. Last year, the book celebrated the 50th anniversary of its publication. Today's students continue to savor Leopold's use of language and sensitivity in describing the world around us.

Junior and senior high school students can read the book in its entirety. They can compare its 22 essays (which follow the months of the year) with Rachel Carson's *Silent Spring*. Both were regarded as ahead of their time for their view of people and their relationship to the natural world. Students could begin their own school-year almanac, writing their observations of the natural world as they see it change month by month around them.

City children may have to focus on what remnants of nature they can find, such as the changes in weather and how it affects them. If you really want to get students motivated, find a school in your state with a rural setting—either via a Chamber of Commerce or an Internet website—and see what kinds of bridges your students can build by sharing their observations with children who live in a completely different setting.

All students can become familiar with at least portions of *A Sand County Almanac*. They can read "From Thinking Like a Mountain" and write a companion piece to describe the hunt of the last great predators from your area. "January Thaw" imagines what a skunk's story is by following its tracks. Use Jim Arnosky's *Animal Tracker's Journal* (Random House, 0-679-86717-1, $7.99), or other animal track guides and let students choose a set of tracks. They can write their own imaginings on what that animal's day might have been like, based on their own fictional "track" record.

For a look at plant life, read "Good Oak," an 80-year time trip that describes events that occurred during each year of the growth rings found in a section of tree cut for firewood. Students can choose a tree in the neighborhood (get help from a naturalist, or the person who planted the tree, on age estimation without harming the tree) and write about the events that occurred in your town during the tree's life.

BIRTHDAYS TODAY

Jean Chretien, 67, 20th prime minister of Canada, born Shawinigan, Quebec, Jan 11, 1934.

JANUARY 12 — FRIDAY
Day 12 — 353 Remaining

"BATMAN" TV PREMIERE: 35th ANNIVERSARY. Jan 12, 1966. ABC's crime-fighting show gained a place in Nielsen's top 10 ratings in its first season. The series was based on the DC Comic characters created by Bob Kane in 1939. Adam West starred as millionaire Bruce Wayne and superhero alter ego, Batman. Burt Ward costarred as Dick Grayson/Robin, the Boy Wonder. A colorful assortment of villains guest-starring each week included: Cesar Romero as the Joker, Eartha Kitt and Julie Newmar as Catwoman, Burgess Meredith as the Penguin and Frank Gorshin as the Riddler. Some other stars making memorable appearances included Liberace, Vincent Price, Milton Berle, Tallulah Bankhead and Ethel Merman. The series played up its comic-strip roots with innovative and sharply skewed camera angles, bright bold colors and wild graphics. "Batman's" memorable theme song, composed by Neal Hefti, can be heard today with some 120 episodes in syndication. Many Batman movies have been made, the first in 1943. The most recent was *Batman & Robin*, released in 1997 and starring George Clooney and Chris O'Donnell.

HANCOCK, JOHN: BIRTH ANNIVERSARY. Jan 12, 1737. American patriot and statesman, first signer of the Declaration of Independence. Born at Braintree, MA, he died at Quincy, MA, Oct 8, 1793. Because his signature was the most conspicuous one on the Declaration, Hancock's name has become part of the American language, referring to any handwritten signature, as in "Put your John Hancock on that!"

HAYES, IRA HAMILTON: BIRTH ANNIVERSARY. Jan 12, 1922. Ira Hayes was one of six US Marines who raised the American flag on Iwo Jima's Mount Suribachi, Feb 23, 1945, following a US assault on the Japanese stronghold. The event was immortalized by AP photographer Joe Rosenthal's famous photo and later by a Marine War Memorial monument at Arlington, VA. Hayes was born on a Pima Indian Reservation at Arizona. He returned home after WWII a much celebrated hero but Hayes was unable to cope with fame. He was found dead of "exposure to freezing weather and over-consumption of alcohol" on the Sacaton Indian Reservation at Arizona, Jan 24, 1955.

LONDON, JACK: 125th BIRTH ANNIVERSARY. Jan 12, 1876. American author of more than 50 books: short stories, novels and travel stories of the sea and of the far north, many marked by brutal realism. His most widely known work is *The Call of the Wild*, the great dog story published in 1903. London was born at San Francisco, CA. He died by suicide Nov 22, 1916, near Santa Rosa, CA.

NATIONAL HANDWRITING DAY. Jan 12. Popularly observed on the birthday of John Hancock to encourage more legible handwriting.

PESTALOZZI, JOHANN HEINRICH: BIRTH ANNIVERSARY. Jan 12, 1746. Swiss educational reformer, born at Zurich. His theories laid the groundwork for modern elementary education. He died Feb 17, 1827, at Brugg, Switzerland.

TANZANIA: ZANZIBAR REVOLUTION DAY. Jan 12. National day. Zanzibar became independent in December 1963, under a sultan.

BIRTHDAYS TODAY

Kirstie Alley, 46, actress (*Look Who's Talking*), born Wichita, KS, Jan 12, 1955.

Andrew Lawrence, 13, actor ("Brotherly Love," *Prince for a Day*), born Philadelphia, PA, Jan 12, 1988.

JANUARY 13 — SATURDAY

Day 13 — 352 Remaining

ALGER, HORATIO, JR: BIRTH ANNIVERSARY. Jan 13, 1834. American clergyman and author of more than 100 popular books for boys (some 20 million copies sold). Honesty, frugality and hard work assured that the heroes of his books would find success, wealth and fame. Born at Revere, MA, he died at Natick, MA, July 18, 1899.

FRISBEE INTRODUCED: ANNIVERSARY. Jan 13, 1957. Legend has it that in the 1920s New England college students tossed pie tins from the Frisbie Baking Company of Bridgeport, CT. The first plastic flying disc was released by the Wham-O Company on this date as the Pluto Platter, for its resemblance to a UFO. In 1958 it was re-named the Frisbee. More than 100 million Frisbees have been sold and there are numerous Frisbee tournaments across America every year.

MINORITY SCIENTISTS SHOWCASE. Jan 13–15. St. Louis, MO. Open new doors to future science careers and interests during Martin Luther King, Jr weekend with hands-on activities and information available as part of a free program. Meet and talk with African Americans working in science-related fields throughout the St. Louis area. Annually, Martin Luther King, Jr weekend. Est attendance: 2,000. For info: Bev Pfeifer-Harms, St. Louis Science Center, 5050 Oakland Ave, St. Louis, MO 63110. Phone: (314) 289-4419. Fax: (314) 533-8687. E-mail: bpharms@slsc.org. Web: www.slsc.org.

RADIO BROADCASTING: ANNIVERSARY. Jan 13, 1910. Radio pioneer and electron tube inventor Lee De Forest arranged the world's first radio broadcast to the public at New York, NY. He succeeded in broadcasting the voice of Enrico Caruso along with other stars of the Metropolitan Opera to several receiving locations in the city where listeners with earphones marveled at wireless music from the air. Though only a few were equipped to listen, it was the first broadcast to reach the public and the beginning of a new era in which wireless radio communication became almost universal. See also: "First Scheduled Radio Broadcast: Anniversary" (Nov 2). *See* Curriculum Connection.

★**STEPHEN FOSTER MEMORIAL DAY.** Jan 13. Presidential Proclamation 2957 of Dec 13, 1951 (designating Jan 13, 1952), covers all succeeding years. (PL82–225 of Oct 27, 1951.) Observed

		S	M	T	W	T	F	S
January			1	2	3	4	5	6
2001		7	8	9	10	11	12	13
		14	15	16	17	18	19	20
		21	22	23	24	25	26	27
		28	29	30	31			

JANUARY 13
FIRST RADIO BROADCAST

When Lee De Forest aired the first radio broadcast to a select group of people in New York City in 1910, he set the wheels in motion for a communication revolution. Bring the excitement of the momentous accomplishment into your classroom.

A visit to the public library is in order for several supplies. Find a recording of Enrico Caruso singing the role of Radames in *Aida*, if you can. (It has kid appeal because of the Egyptian setting.) If it isn't available, another Caruso recording will do. During the library visit, look for a book that shows pictures of early radios. In the audiocassette section, many libraries have reissued recordings of historic radio shows. Look for Sherlock Holmes, "The Shadow" or Orson Welles's "War of the Worlds," a 1938 Halloween "treat" that caused major panic.

In school, tell your students that together you are going to create a very important moment in history. Ask them to close their eyes and listen. Play the Caruso recording. When the aria ends, let them think for a few moments and then ask them to try to describe Caruso's voice. You may need to come up with some prompts. Talk about how they imagine the singer looks. Tell students that Lee De Forest, the electron tube inventor, chose the voice of Caruso and the Metropolitan Opera as the first radio broadcast. Discuss the manner of radio reception of the broadcast (see Jan 13). Show them a picture of Caruso and tell them about his opera career. Show students how the size and shape of the radio has changed since its early days. Share radio memories you may have. Perhaps you listened to baseball games through an ear plug while in bed late at night. Maybe you hung out at the beach or around the community pool in the summer where broadcasts were aired over the PA system. Did you ever laugh with Jean Shepherd?

Talk about how families gathered to listen to radio shows the way we gather and watch TV. If you found a recording, play one of the old radio shows. Ask students what kinds of things had to be done differently to produce a radio show as opposed to a TV show: sound effects, clear voices, no relying on body language, etc.

Have students write and air their own radio broadcast. If you have PA system capabilities or the technical apparatus to broadcast from a separate room, that's great. But it's no problem if you don't. Create your own broadcasting booth with a setup of table and chairs. Cardboard rolls from paper towels or toilet paper can be microphones. Just anchor a tennis ball to the roll. Cover the ball with aluminum foil and the roll with black construction paper. Add a wire to the bottom, if you wish.

Divide the students into groups of four or five. To complement all areas of the curriculum feature segments like New Developments in Science (what's your current topic?), An Interview with a Star (a student), Restaurant Report (cafeteria offerings), a short dramatic production (adapt a selection from language arts) and Sports (from recess and gym). Someone will need to provide sound effects for dramatic presentations.

If you locate a Caruso recording of *Aida*, you may find the book *Aida: A Picture Book for All Ages*, as told by Leontyne Price (Harcourt, 0-15-200405-X, $16.95 Gr. K & up), helpful for understanding the story line.

on the anniversary of Foster's death, Jan 13, 1864, at New York, NY. See also: "Foster, Stephen: Birth Anniversary" (July 4).

TOGO: LIBERATION DAY. Jan 13. National holiday. Commemorates 1963 uprising.

Michael Bond, 75, author (*A Bear Called Paddington, Paddington At Work*), born Newbury, Berkshire, England, Jan 13, 1926.

JANUARY 14 — SUNDAY
Day 14 — 351 Remaining

ARNOLD, BENEDICT: BIRTH ANNIVERSARY. Jan 14, 1741. American officer who deserted to the British during the Revolutionary War and whose name has since become synonymous with treachery. Born at Norwich, CT, he died June 14, 1801, at London, England.

INTERNATIONAL PRINTING WEEK. Jan 14–20. To develop public awareness of the printing/graphic arts industry. Annually, the week including Ben Franklin's birthday, Jan 17. For info: Kevin P. Keane, Exec Dir, Intl Assn of Printing House Craftsmen, 7042 Brooklyn Blvd, Minneapolis, MN 55429-1370. Phone: (612) 560-1620. Web: www.iaphc.org.

LOFTING, HUGH: BIRTH ANNIVERSARY. Jan 14, 1886. Author and illustrator, known for the Doctor Dolittle series. In his books the famous Dr. Dolittle has the ability to talk with animals. *The Voyages of Dr. Dolittle* won the Newbery Medal in 1923. Born at Maidenhead, England, Lofting died at Santa Monica, CA, Sept 26, 1947.

RATIFICATION DAY. Jan 14, 1784. Anniversary of the act that officially ended the American Revolution and established the US as a sovereign power. On Jan 14, 1784, the Continental Congress, meeting at Annapolis, MD, ratified the Treaty of Paris, thus fulfilling the Declaration of Independence of July 4, 1776.

SECRET PAL DAY. Jan 14. A day for secret pals to remember and do something special for each other. Annually, the second Sunday in January. For info: Eagles Lodge #4080, PO Box 1319, Hayden Lake, ID 83835. Phone: (208) 772-4901 or (208) 772-0687.

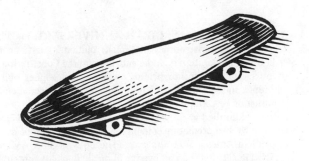

"THE SIMPSONS" TV PREMIERE: ANNIVERSARY. Jan 14, 1990. FOX TV's hottest animated family, "The Simpsons," premiered as a half-hour weekly sitcom. The originator of Homer, Marge, Bart, Lisa and Maggie is cartoonist Matt Groening.

SPACE MILESTONE: *SOYUZ 4* (USSR). Jan 14, 1969. First docking of two manned spacecraft (with *Soyuz 5*) and first interchange of spaceship personnel in orbit by means of space walks.

SWITZERLAND: MEITLISUNNTIG. Jan 14. On Meitlisunntig, the second Sunday in January, the girls of Meisterschwanden and Fahrwangen, in the Seetal district of Aargau, Switzerland, stage a procession in historical uniforms and a military parade before a female General Staff. According to tradition, the custom dates from the Villmergen War of 1712, when the women of both communes gave vital help that led to victory. Popular festival follows the procession.

WHIPPLE, WILLIAM: BIRTH ANNIVERSARY. Jan 14, 1730. American patriot and signer of the Declaration of Independence. Born at Kittery, ME, he died at Portsmouth, NH, Nov 10, 1785.

Shannon Lucid, 58, astronaut, holds the record for longest stay in space by an American, born Shanghai, China, Jan 14, 1943.

JANUARY 15 — MONDAY
Day 15 — 350 Remaining

DO SOMETHING: KINDNESS & JUSTICE CHALLENGE. Jan 15–26. More than two million students perform Acts of Kindness (helping others) and Justice (standing up for what is right) in honor of the Martin Luther King, Jr national holiday. For two weeks, starting on the Martin Luther King, Jr holiday, K–12 students write down the Acts of Kindness and Justice they perform and post their lists on the Internet. Each school that performs 1,000 or more acts will receive special recognition. A free guide with grade-appropriate curriculum is available for teachers. For info: Do Something, 423 W 55th St, 8th Floor, New York, NY 10019. Web: www.dosomething.org.

"HAPPY DAYS" TV PREMIERE: ANNIVERSARY. Jan 15, 1974. This nostalgic comedy was set in Milwaukee in the 1950s. Teenager Richie Cunningham was played by Ron Howard and his best friends "Potsie" Weber and Ralph Malph by Anson Williams and Don Most. Richie's parents were played by Tom Bosley and Marion Ross and his sister, Joanie, was played by Erin Moran. "The Fonz"—Arthur "Fonzie" Fonzarelli—was played by Henry Winkler. "Happy Days" aired until 1984 and has been in syndication ever since. "Laverne and Shirley" and "Mork & Mindy" were spin-offs of this popular program.

KING, MARTIN LUTHER, JR: BIRTH ANNIVERSARY. Jan 15, 1929. Black civil rights leader, minister, advocate of non-violence and recipient of the Nobel Peace Prize (1964). Born at Atlanta, GA, he was assassinated at Memphis, TN, Apr 4, 1968. After his death many states and territories observed his birthday as a holiday. In 1983 the Congress approved HR 3706, "A bill to amend Title 5, United States Code, to make the birthday of Martin Luther King, Jr, a legal public holiday." Signed by the president on Nov 2, 1983, it became Public Law 98–144. The law sets the third Monday in January for observance of King's birthday. First observance was Jan 20, 1986. See also: "King, Martin Luther, Jr: Birthday Observed" (Jan 15).

KING, MARTIN LUTHER, JR: BIRTHDAY OBSERVED. Jan 15. Public Law 98–144 designates the third Monday in January as an annual legal public holiday observing the birth of Martin Luther King, Jr. First observed in 1986. In New Hampshire, this day is designated Civil Rights Day. See also: "King, Martin Luther, Jr: Birth Anniversary" (Jan 15). For links to sites on the web about Dr. King, go to: deil.lang.uiuc.edu/web.pages/holidays/king.html.

LEE-JACKSON-KING DAY IN VIRGINIA. Jan 15. Annually, the third Monday in January.

LIVINGSTON, PHILIP: BIRTH ANNIVERSARY. Jan 15, 1716. Merchant and signer of the Declaration of Independence, born at Albany, NY. Died at York, PA, June 12, 1778.

★**MARTIN LUTHER KING, JR FEDERAL HOLIDAY.** Jan 15. Presidential Proclamation has been issued without request each year for the third Monday in January since 1986.

BIRTHDAYS TODAY

Andrea Martin, 54, actress (*Bogus, Anastasia*), born Portland, ME, Jan 15, 1947.

JANUARY 16 — TUESDAY
Day 16 — 349 Remaining

DEAN, DIZZY: 90th BIRTH ANNIVERSARY. Jan 16, 1911. Jay Hanna "Dizzy" Dean, major league pitcher (St. Louis Cardinals) and Baseball Hall of Fame member was born at Lucas, AR. Following his baseball career, Dean established himself as a radio and TV sports announcer and commentator, becoming famous for his innovative delivery. "He slud into third," reported Dizzy, who on another occasion explained that "Me and Paul [baseball player brother Paul "Daffy" Dean] . . . didn't get much education." Died at Reno, NV, July 17, 1974.

JAPAN: HARU-NO-YABUIRI. Jan 16. Employees and servants who have been working over the holidays are given a day off.

MOON PHASE: LAST QUARTER. Jan 16. Moon enters Last Quarter phase at 7:35 AM, EST.

NATIONAL NOTHING DAY. Jan 16. Anniversary of National Nothing Day, an event created by newspaperman Harold Pullman Coffin and first observed in 1973 "to provide Americans with one national day when they can just sit without celebrating, observing or honoring anything." Since 1975, though many other events have been listed on this day, lighthearted traditional observance of Coffin's idea has continued. Coffin, a native of Reno, NV, died at Capitola, CA, Sept 12, 1981.

PERSIAN GULF WAR BEGINS: 10th ANNIVERSARY. Jan 16, 1991. Allied forces launched a major air offensive against Iraq to begin the Gulf War. The strike was designed to destroy Iraqi air defenses, command, control and communication centers. As Desert Shield became Desert Storm, the world was able to see and hear for the first time an initial engagement of war as CNN broadcasters, stationed at Baghdad, broadcast the attack live.

PROHIBITION (EIGHTEENTH) AMENDMENT: ANNIVERSARY. Jan 16, 1919. Nebraska became the 36th state to ratify the prohibition amendment on this date, and the 18th Amendment became part of the US Constitution. One year later, Jan 16, 1920, the 18th Amendment took effect and the sale of alcoholic beverages became illegal in the US with the Volstead Act providing for enforcement. This was the first time that an amendment to the Constitution dealt with a social issue. The 21st Amendment, repealing the 18th, went into effect Dec 6, 1933.

RELIGIOUS FREEDOM DAY. Jan 16, 1786. The legislature of Virginia adopted a religious freedom statute that protected Virginians against any requirement to attend or support any church and against discrimination. This statute, which had been drafted by Thomas Jefferson and introduced by James Madison, later was the model for the First Amendment to the US Constitution.

January 2001	S	M	T	W	T	F	S
		1	2	3	4	5	6
	7	8	9	10	11	12	13
	14	15	16	17	18	19	20
	21	22	23	24	25	26	27
	28	29	30	31			

★**RELIGIOUS FREEDOM DAY.** Jan 16. On the day of the adoption in 1786 of a religious freedom statute by the Virginia legislature.

BIRTHDAYS TODAY

Kate McMullan, 54, author (the Dragon Slayers' Academy Series), born St. Louis, MO, Jan 16, 1947.

Martha Weston, 54, author and illustrator (*Bad Baby Brother*), born Asheville, NC, Jan 16, 1947.

JANUARY 17 — WEDNESDAY
Day 17 — 348 Remaining

FIRST NUCLEAR-POWERED SUBMARINE VOYAGE: ANNIVERSARY. Jan 17, 1955. The world's first nuclear-powered submarine, the *Nautilus*, now forms part of the *Nautilus* Memorial Submarine Force Library and Museum at the Naval Submarine Base New London at Groton, CT. At 11 AM, EST, her commanding officer, Commander Eugene P. Wilkerson, ordered all lines cast off and sent the historic message: "Under way on nuclear power." Highlights of the *Nautilus*: keel laid by President Harry S Truman June 14, 1952; christened and launched by Mrs Dwight D. Eisenhower Jan 21, 1954; commissioned to the US Navy Sept 30, 1954.

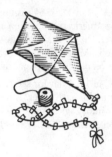

FRANKLIN, BENJAMIN: BIRTH ANNIVERSARY. Jan 17, 1706. "Elder statesman of the American Revolution," oldest signer of both the Declaration of Independence and the Constitution, scientist, diplomat, author, printer, publisher, philosopher, philanthropist and self-made, self-educated man. Author, printer and publisher of *Poor Richard's Almanack* (1733–58). Born at Boston, MA, Franklin died at Philadelphia, PA, Apr 17, 1790. In 1728 Franklin wrote a premature epitaph for himself. It first appeared in print in Ames's 1771 almanac: "The Body of BENJAMIN FRANKLIN/Printer/Like a Covering of an old Book/Its contents torn out/And stript of its Lettering and Gilding,/Lies here, Food for Worms;/But the work shall not be lost,/It will (as he believ'd) appear once more/In a New and more beautiful Edition/Corrected and amended/By the Author."

JAPAN SUFFERS MAJOR EARTHQUAKE: ANNIVERSARY. Jan 17, 1995. Japan suffered its second most deadly earthquake in the 20th century when a 20-second temblor left 5,500 dead and more than 21,600 people injured. The epicenter was six miles beneath Awaji Island at Osaka Bay. This was just 20 miles west of Kobe, Japan's sixth-largest city and a major port that accounted for 12 percent of the country's exports. Measuring 7.2 on the Richter scale, the quake collapsed or badly damaged more than 30,400 buildings and left 275,000 people homeless.

LEWIS, SHARI: BIRTH ANNIVERSARY. Jan 17, 1934. Puppeteer Shari Lewis, creator of Lamb Chop and Charlie Horse, was born Shari Hurwitz at New York, NY. She died Aug 3, 1998, at Los Angeles, CA.

MEXICO: BLESSING OF THE ANIMALS AT THE CATHE-DRAL. Jan 17. Church of San Antonio at Mexico City or Xochimilco provide best sights of chickens, cows and household pets gaily decorated with flowers. (Saint's day for San Antonio Abad, patron saint of domestic animals.)

SOUTHERN CALIFORNIA EARTHQUAKE: ANNIVERSARY. Jan 17, 1994. An earthquake measuring 6.6 on the Richter scale struck the Los Angeles area about 4:20 AM. The epicenter was at Northridge in the San Fernando Valley, about 20 miles northwest of downtown Los Angeles. A death toll of 51 was announced Jan 20. Sixteen of the dead were killed in the collapse of one apartment building. More than 25,000 people were made homeless by the quake and 680,000 lost electric power. Many buildings were destroyed and others made uninhabitable due to structural damage. A section of the Santa Monica Freeway, part of the Simi Valley Freeway and three major overpasses collapsed. Hundreds of aftershocks occurred in the following several weeks. Costs to repair the damages were estimated at 15–30 billion dollars.

BIRTHDAYS TODAY

Muhammad Ali, 59, former heavyweight champion boxer who changed his name after converting to Islam, born Cassius Marcellus Clay, Jr, Louisville, KY, Jan 17, 1942.

Jim Carrey, 39, actor (*Dumb and Dumber, Mask, Ace Ventura*), comedian, born Newmarket, Ontario, Canada, Jan 17, 1962.

Robert Cormier, 74, author (*The Chocolate War*), born Leominster, MA, Jan 17, 1927.

JANUARY 18 — THURSDAY
Day 18 — 347 Remaining

FIRST BLACK US CABINET MEMBER: 35th ANNIVERSARY. Jan 18, 1966. Robert Clifton Weaver was sworn in as Secretary of Housing and Urban Development, becoming the first black cabinet member in US history. He was nominated by President Lyndon Johnson. Born Dec 29, 1907 at Washington, DC, Weaver died at New York, NY, July 17, 1997.

POOH DAY: A.A. MILNE: BIRTH ANNIVERSARY. Jan 18, 1882. Anniversary of the birth of A(lan) A(lexander) Milne, English author, especially remembered for his children's stories: *Winnie the Pooh* and *The House at Pooh Corner*. Also the author of *Mr Pim Passes By, When We Were Very Young* and *Now We Are Six*. Born at London, England, he died at Hartfield, England, Jan 31, 1956. *See* Curriculum Connection.

RANSOME, ARTHUR: BIRTH ANNIVERSARY. Jan 18, 1884. Author, born at Leeds, Yorkshire, England. His children's books were based on his travels during his life and featured children whose parents could indulge them in long vacations. His works include *We Didn't Mean to Go to Sea, Secret Water* and *Swallows and Amazons*. He won the Carnegie Medal in 1936 for *The Pigeon Post*. Ransome died June 3, 1967.

ROGET, PETER MARK: BIRTH ANNIVERSARY. Jan 18, 1779. English physician, best known as author of Roget's *Thesaurus of English Words and Phrases*, first published in 1852. Roget was also the inventor of the "log-log" slide rule. Born at London, England, Roget died at West Malvern, Worcestershire, England, Sept 12, 1869.

BIRTHDAYS TODAY

Mark Messier, 40, hockey player, born Edmonton, Alberta, Canada, Jan 18, 1961.

Alan Schroeder, 40, author of biographies (*Ragtime Tumpie*), born Alameda, CA, Jan 18, 1961.

JANUARY 18
POOH DAY: A.A. MILNE'S BIRTHDAY

Lovable, pot-bellied Winnie the Pooh has enchanted young readers since he made his debut in 1926. Two years later, the success of *Winnie the Pooh* was followed by *The House at Pooh Corner*. Milne modeled the books on his son, Christopher Robin, and the stuffed toys he played with. The many humorous adventures embarked upon by Christopher Robin, Pooh, Tigger, Piglet and Eeyore took place in the Hundred Acre Wood. Many students are familiar with Pooh and his friends from Disney movies and spin-off books. Introduce them to the real thing. Begin a Winnie the Pooh read-aloud of the classic version.

Make a Pooh Day Classroom Honey Jar. Stuff it with poems written by A.A. Milne. See his books *Now We Are Six* and *When We Were Very Young* for his collected poems. Several times during the day, call a halt to class work and let a student reach into the Honey Jar and read a poem aloud.

Let groups of students write scripts from short dialogue selections from *Winnie the Pooh* and present them to the class as Reader's Theater. Encourage selections that focus on sensitively depicted emotional aspects of the novels: the friendship and caring among characters, helping Pooh cope with fear, the silliness of Tigger and droopy old Eeyore.

Ask very young children to draw a picture of themselves and a favorite toy. Older students can write about an imaginary adventure with one of their well-loved toys. Publish these as class books and celebrate by letting each child write an invitation to his toy protagonist, asking it to visit the classroom. The toys and students can celebrate Pooh Day with a Hundred Acre Wood afternoon tea. Serve honey on bread triangles. (Substitute apricot jelly for those who don't care for honey.)

Visit The Page at Pooh Corner website at chaos.trxinc.com /jmilne/Pooh.

JANUARY 19 — FRIDAY
Day 19 — 346 Remaining

ARBOR DAY IN FLORIDA. Jan 19. A ceremonial day on the third Friday in January.

CÉZANNE, PAUL: BIRTH ANNIVERSARY. Jan 19, 1839. French post-Impressionist painter known for his landscapes, born at Aix-en-Provence, France. He died at Aix, Oct 22, 1906. For more info: *Cézanne from A to Z*, by Marie Sellier (Peter Bedrick, 0-87226-476-9, $14.95 All ages).

CONFEDERATE HEROES DAY. Jan 19. Observed on anniversary of Robert E. Lee's birthday. Official holiday in Texas.

LEE, ROBERT E.: BIRTH ANNIVERSARY. Jan 19, 1807. Greatest military leader of the Confederacy, son of Revolutionary War General Henry (Light Horse Harry) Lee. His surrender Apr 9, 1865, to Union General Ulysses S. Grant brought an end to the Civil War. Born at Westmoreland County, VA, he died at Lexington, VA, Oct 12, 1870. His birthday is observed in Florida, Kentucky, Louisiana, South Carolina and Tennessee. Observed on third Monday in January in Alabama, Arkansas and Mississippi (Jan 15 in 2001).

POE, EDGAR ALLAN: BIRTH ANNIVERSARY. Jan 19, 1809. American poet and story writer, called "America's most famous man of letters." Born at Boston, MA, he was orphaned in dire poverty in 1811 and was raised by Virginia merchant John Allan. A magazine editor of note, he is best remembered for his poetry (especially "The Raven") and for his tales of suspense. Died at Baltimore, MD, Oct 7, 1849.

TIN CAN PATENT: ANNIVERSARY. Jan 19, 1825. Ezra Daggett and Thomas Kensett obtained a patent for a process for storing food in tin cans.

BIRTHDAYS TODAY

Nina Bawden, 76, author (*Carrie's War*), born London, England, Jan 19, 1925.

Jodie Sweetin, 19, actress ("Full House"), born Los Angeles, CA, Jan 19, 1982.

JANUARY 20 — SATURDAY
Day 20 — 345 Remaining

AQUARIUS, THE WATER CARRIER. Jan 20–Feb 19. In the astronomical/astrological zodiac, which divides the sun's apparent orbit into 12 segments, the period Jan 20–Feb 19 is identified, traditionally, as the sun-sign of Aquarius, the Water Carrier. The ruling planet is Uranus or Saturn.

BRAZIL: NOSSO SENHOR DO BONFIM FESTIVAL. Jan 20–30. Salvador, Bahia, Brazil. Our Lord of the Happy Ending Festival is one of Salvador's most colorful religious feasts. Climax comes with people carrying water to pour over church stairs and sidewalks to cleanse them of impurities.

CAMCORDER DEVELOPED: ANNIVERSARY. Jan 20, 1982. Five companies (Hitachi, JVC, Philips, Matsushita and Sony) agreed to cooperate on the construction of a camera with a built-in videocassette recorder.

GUINEA-BISSAU: NATIONAL HEROES DAY. Jan 20. National holiday.

INAUGURATION DAY. Jan 20. The 20th Amendment provides that "The terms of the President and Vice President shall end at noon on the 20th day of January . . . and the terms of their successors shall then begin . . ." A holiday in the District of Columbia. Occurs every four years.

LEE, RICHARD HENRY: BIRTH ANNIVERSARY. Jan 20, 1732. Signer of the Declaration of Independence. Born at Westmoreland County, VA, he died June 19, 1794, at his birthplace.

PHILIPPINES: ATI-ATIHAN FESTIVAL. Jan 20–21. Kalibo, Aklan. One of the most colorful celebrations in the Philippines, the Ati-Atihan Festival commemorates the peace pact between the Ati of Panay (pygmies) and the Malays, who were early migrants in the islands. The townspeople blacken their bodies with soot, don colorful and bizarre costumes and sing and dance in the streets. The festival also celebrates the Feast Day of Santo Niño (the infant Jesus). Annually, the third weekend in January.

US REVOLUTIONARY WAR: CESSATION OF HOSTILITIES: ANNIVERSARY. Jan 20, 1783. The British and US Commissioners signed a preliminary "Cessation of Hostilities," which was ratified by England's King George III Feb 14 and led to the Treaties of Paris and Versailles, Sept 3, 1783, ending the war.

BIRTHDAYS TODAY

Edwin "Buzz" Aldrin, 71, former astronaut, one of first three men on moon, born Montclair, NJ, Jan 20, 1930.

		S	M	T	W	T	F	S
January			1	2	3	4	5	6
2001		7	8	9	10	11	12	13
		14	15	16	17	18	19	20
		21	22	23	24	25	26	27
		28	29	30	31			

Paul D. Coverdell, 62, US Senator (R, Georgia), born Des Moines, IA, Jan 20, 1939.

JANUARY 21 — SUNDAY
Day 21 — 344 Remaining

ALLEN, ETHAN: BIRTH ANNIVERSARY. Jan 21, 1738. Revolutionary War hero and leader of the Vermont "Green Mountain Boys." Born at Litchfield, CT, he died at Burlington, VT, Feb 12, 1789.

BRECKINRIDGE, JOHN CABELL: BIRTH ANNIVERSARY. Jan 21, 1821. The 14th vice president of the US (1857–61), serving under President James Buchanan. Born at Lexington, KY, he died there May 17, 1875.

FIRST CONCORDE FLIGHT: 25th ANNIVERSARY. Jan 21, 1976. The supersonic Concorde airplane was put into service by Britain and France.

JACKSON, THOMAS JONATHAN "STONEWALL": BIRTH ANNIVERSARY. Jan 21, 1824. Confederate general and one of the most famous soldiers of the American Civil War, best known as "Stonewall" Jackson. Born at Clarksburg, VA (now WV), Jackson died of wounds received in battle near Chancellorsville, VA, May 10, 1863.

WORLD RELIGION DAY. Jan 21. To proclaim the oneness of religion and the belief that world religion will unify the peoples of the earth. Baha'i-sponsored observance established in 1950. Annually, the third Sunday in January. For info: Office of Public Information, Baha'is of the US, 866 UN Plaza, Ste 120, New York, NY 10017-1822. Phone: (212) 803-2500. Fax: (212) 803-2573. E-mail: usopi-ny@bic.org. Web: www.us.bahai.org.

BIRTHDAYS TODAY

Hakeem Abdul Olajuwon, 38, basketball player, born Lagos, Nigeria, Jan 21, 1963.

JANUARY 22 — MONDAY
Day 22 — 343 Remaining

ANSWER YOUR CAT'S QUESTION DAY. Jan 22. If you will stop what you are doing and take a look at your cat, you will observe that the cat is looking at you with a serious question. Meditate upon it, then answer the question! Annually, Jan 22. [© 1999 by WH] For info: Tom or Ruth Roy, Wellcat Holidays, PO Box 774, Lebanon, PA 17042-0774. Phone: (717) 279-0184. E-mail: wellcat @supernet.com. Web: www.wellcat.com.

VINSON, FRED M.: BIRTH ANNIVERSARY. Jan 22, 1890. The 13th Chief Justice of the US Supreme Court, born at Louisa, KY. Served in the House of Representatives, appointed Director of War Mobilization during WWII and Secretary of the Treasury under Harry Truman. Nominated by Truman to succeed Harlan F. Stone as Chief Justice. Died at Washington, DC, Sept 8, 1953.

Sheila Gordon, 74, author (*Waiting for the Rain*), born Johannesburg, South Africa, Jan 22, 1927.

Blair Lent, 71, author and illustrator (*Tikki Tikki Tembo*), born Boston, MA, Jan 22, 1930.

Rafe Martin, 55, author (*The Boy Who Lived with the Seals*), born Rochester, NY, Jan 22, 1946.

Beverly Mitchell, 20, actress (*Mother of the Bride*, "7th Heaven"), born Arcadia, CA, Jan 22, 1981.

JANUARY 23 — TUESDAY
Day 23 — 342 Remaining

BLACKWELL, ELIZABETH, AWARDED MD: ANNIVERSARY. Jan 23, 1849. Dr. Elizabeth Blackwell became the first woman to receive an MD degree. The native of Bristol, England, was awarded her degree by the Medical Institution of Geneva, NY.

HEWES, JOSEPH: BIRTH ANNIVERSARY. Jan 23, 1730. Signer of the Declaration of Independence. Born at Princeton, NJ, he died Nov 10, 1779, at Philadelphia, PA.

MANET, ÉDOUARD: BIRTH ANNIVERSARY. Jan 23, 1832. French artist (*Déjeuner dur l'herbe, Olympia*), born at Paris, France. He died at Paris, Apr 30, 1883.

NATIONAL PIE DAY. Jan 23. To focus attention on pie as an American art form, culinary inheritance and taste delight through pie tastings, pie-making classes for adults and kids, pie recipe collections and competitions. For info: John Lehndorff, 512 Concord Ave, Boulder, CO 80304. Phone: (303) 449-0165. E-mail: nibbleman@aol.com.

STEWART, POTTER: BIRTH ANNIVERSARY. Jan 23, 1915. Associate Justice of the Supreme Court of the US, nominated by President Eisenhower, Jan 17, 1959. (Oath of office, May 15, 1959.) Born at Jackson, MI, he retired in July 1981 and died Dec 7, 1985, at Putney, VT. Buried at Arlington National Cemetery.

TWENTIETH AMENDMENT TO US CONSTITUTION RATIFIED: ANNIVERSARY. Jan 23, 1933. The 20th Amendment was ratified, fixing the date of the presidential inauguration at the current Jan 20 instead of the previous Mar 4. It also specified that were the president-elect to die before taking office, the vice president-elect would succeed to the presidency. In addition, it set Jan 3 as the official opening date of Congress each year.

TWENTY-FOURTH AMENDMENT TO US CONSTITUTION RATIFIED: ANNIVERSARY. Jan 23, 1964. Poll taxes and other taxes were eliminated as a prerequisite for voting in all federal elections by the 24th Amendment.

Frank R. Lautenberg, 77, US Senator (D, New Jersey), born Paterson, NJ, Jan 23, 1924.

JANUARY 24 — WEDNESDAY
Day 24 — 341 Remaining

BOLIVIA: ALACITIS FAIR. Jan 24–26. La Paz. Traditional annual celebration by Aymara Indians with prayers and offerings to god of prosperity.

CALIFORNIA GOLD DISCOVERY: ANNIVERSARY. Jan 24, 1848. James W. Marshal, an employee of John Sutter, accidentally discovered gold while building a sawmill near Coloma, CA. Efforts to keep the discovery secret failed, and the gold rush got under way in 1849. Had the Gold Rush not occurred, it might have taken California years to reach the population of 60,000 necessary for statehood, but the 49ers increased the population beyond that figure in one year and in 1850 California became a state.

CHINESE NEW YEAR. Jan 24. Traditional Chinese lunar year begins at sunset on the day of second New Moon following the winter solstice. The New Year can begin any time from Jan 10 through Feb 19. Begins year 4699 of the ancient Chinese calendar, designated as the Year of the Snake. Generally celebrated until the Lantern Festival 15 days later, but merchants usually reopen their stores and places of business on the fifth day of the first lunar month (Jan 28, 2001). See also: "China: Lantern Festival" (Feb 7). This holiday is celebrated as Tet in Vietnam. For more info: *Celebrating Chinese New Year*, by Diane Hoyt-Goldsmith (Holiday House, 0-8234-1393-4, $16.95 Gr. 3–5).

MACINTOSH COMPUTER RELEASED: ANNIVERSARY. Jan 24, 1984. Apple Computer released its new Macintosh model on this day, which eventually replaced the Apple II.

MOON PHASE: NEW MOON. Jan 24. Moon enters New Moon phase at 8:07 AM, EST.

NATIONAL COMPLIMENT DAY. Jan 24. This day is set aside to compliment at least five people. Not only are compliments appreciated by the receiver, they lift the spirit of the giver. Compliments provide a quick and easy way to connect positively with those you come in contact with. Giving compliments forges bonds, dispels loneliness and just plain feels good. Annually, the fourth Wednesday in January. For info: Deborah Hoffman, Positive Results Seminars, 12 Campion Circle, Concord, NH 03303-3410. Phone: (603) 225-0991. E-mail: prseminars@compuserve.com or Katherine Chamberlin, Heart to Heart Seminars, 724 Park Ave, Contoocook, NH 03229-3089. Phone: (603) 746-6227. E-mail: Kathiecham@aol.com.

NATIONAL SCHOOL NURSE DAY. Jan 24. A day to honor and recognize the school nurse, School Nurse Day has been established to foster a better understanding of the role of school nurses in the educational setting. Annually, the fourth Wednesday in January. Brochures available for purchase. For info: Judy Barker, Adm Asst, Natl Assn of School Nurses, Inc, PO Box 1300, Scarborough, ME 04070-1300. Phone: (207) 883-2117. Fax: (207) 883-2683. E-mail: nasnweb@aol.com.

Tatyana M. Ali, 22, actress ("Sesame Street," "The Fresh Prince of Bel Air"), born Long Island, NY, Jan 24, 1979.

Mary Lou Retton, 33, Olympic gold medal gymnast, born Fairmont, WV, Jan 24, 1968.

JANUARY 25 — THURSDAY
Day 25 — 340 Remaining

CHILDREN'S LITERATURE CONFERENCE. Jan 25–27. Hyatt Regency, Columbus, OH. For info: Roy Wilson, Ohio State Univ. Phone: (614) 292-7902. E-mail: wilson.418@osu.edu.

CURTIS, CHARLES: BIRTH ANNIVERSARY. Jan 25, 1860. The 31st vice president of the US (1929–33). Born at Topeka, KS, he died at Washington, DC, Feb 8, 1936.

FIRST SCHEDULED TRANSCONTINENTAL FLIGHT: ANNIVERSARY. Jan 25, 1959. American Airlines opened the jet age in the US with the first scheduled transcontinental flight on a Boeing 707 nonstop from California to New York.

Conrad Burns, 66, US Senator (R, Montana), born Gallatin, MO, Jan 25, 1935.

Chris Chelios, 39, hockey player, born Chicago, IL, Jan 25, 1962.

Christine Lakin, 22, actress ("Step By Step"), born Dallas, TX, Jan 25, 1979.

JANUARY 26 — FRIDAY

Day 26 — 339 Remaining

AUSTRALIA: AUSTRALIA DAY—FIRST BRITISH SETTLEMENT: ANNIVERSARY. Jan 26, 1788. A shipload of convicts arrived briefly at Botany Bay (which proved to be unsuitable) and then at Port Jackson (later the site of the city of Sydney). Establishment of an Australian prison colony was to relieve crowding of British prisons. Australia Day, formerly known as Foundation Day or Anniversary Day, has been observed since about 1817 and has been a public holiday since 1838. Observed Jan 26 if a Monday, otherwise on the first Monday thereafter (Jan 29 in 2001).

COLEMAN, BESSIE: BIRTH ANNIVERSARY. Jan 26, 1893. The first African American to receive a pilot's license, Coleman had to go to France to study flying, since she was denied admission to aviation schools in the US because of her race and sex. She took part in acrobatic air exhibitions where her stunt-flying and figure eights won her many admirers. Born at Atlanta, TX, she died in a plane crash at Jacksonville, FL, Apr 30, 1926.

DENTAL DRILL PATENT: ANNIVERSARY. Jan 26, 1875. George F. Green, of Kalamazoo, MI, patented the electric dental drill.

DODGE, MARY MAPES: BIRTH ANNIVERSARY. Jan 26, 1831. Children's author, known for her book *Hans Brinker or, The Silver Skates*. Born at New York, NY, she died at Ontenora Park, NY, Aug 21, 1905.

DOMINICAN REPUBLIC: NATIONAL HOLIDAY. Jan 26. An official public holiday celebrates the birth anniversary of Juan Pablo Duarte, one of the fathers of the republic.

FRANKLIN PREFERS TURKEY: ANNIVERSARY. Jan 26, 1784. In a letter to his daughter, Benjamin Franklin expressed his unhappiness over the choice of the eagle as the symbol of America. He preferred the turkey. "I wish the bald eagle had not been chosen as the representative of our country; he is a bird of bad moral character; like those among men who live by sharping and robbing; he is generally poor, and often very lousy. The turkey is a much more respectable bird, and withal a true original native of America."

GRANT, JULIA DENT: 175th BIRTH ANNIVERSARY. Jan 26, 1826. Wife of Ulysses Simpson Grant, 18th president of the US. Born at St. Louis, MO, died at Washington, DC, Dec 14, 1902.

INDIA: REPUBLIC DAY. Jan 26. National holiday. Anniversary of Proclamation of the Republic, Basant Panchmi. In 1929, Indian National Congress resolved to work for establishment of a sovereign republic, a goal that was realized Jan 26, 1950, when India became a democratic republic and its constitution went into effect.

		S	M	T	W	T	F	S
January			1	2	3	4	5	6
2001		7	8	9	10	11	12	13
		14	15	16	17	18	19	20
		21	22	23	24	25	26	27
		28	29	30	31			

MICHIGAN: ADMISSION DAY: ANNIVERSARY. Jan 26. Became 26th state in 1837.

Wayne Gretzky, 40, Hall of Fame hockey player, born Brantford, Ontario, Canada, Jan 26, 1961.

JANUARY 27 — SATURDAY

Day 27 — 338 Remaining

APOLLO I : SPACECRAFT FIRE: ANNIVERSARY. Jan 27, 1967. Three American astronauts, Virgil I. Grissom, Edward H. White and Roger B. Chaffee, died when fire suddenly broke out at 6:31 PM in *Apollo I* during a launching simulation test, as it stood on the ground at Cape Kennedy, FL, Jan 27, 1967. First launching in the Apollo program had been scheduled for Feb 27, 1967.

CARROLL, LEWIS: BIRTH ANNIVERSARY. Jan 27, 1832. Pseudonym of English mathematician and author, born Charles Lutwidge Dodgson at Cheshire, England. Best known for his children's classic, *Alice's Adventures in Wonderland*. *Alice* was written for Alice Liddell, daughter of a friend, and first published in 1886. *Through the Looking-Glass*, a sequel, and *The Hunting of the Snark* followed. Carroll's books for children proved equally enjoyable to adults, and they overshadowed his serious works on mathematics. He died at Guildford, Surrey, England, Jan 14, 1898.

MOZART, WOLFGANG AMADEUS: BIRTH ANNIVERSARY. Jan 27, 1756. One of the world's greatest music makers. Born at Salzburg, Austria, into a gifted musical family, Mozart began performing at age three and composing at age five. Some of the best known of his more than 600 compositions include the operas *Marriage of Figaro*, *Don Giovanni*, *Cosi fan tutte* and *The Magic Flute*, his unfinished Requiem Mass, his C major symphony known as the "Jupiter" and many quartets and piano concertos. He died at Vienna, Dec 5, 1791.

VIETNAM WAR ENDS: ANNIVERSARY. Jan 27, 1973. US and North Vietnam, along with South Vietnam and the Viet Cong, signed an "Agreement on ending the war and restoring peace in Vietnam." Signed at Paris, France, to take effect Jan 28 at 8 AM Saigon time, thus ending US combat role in a war that had involved American personnel stationed in Vietnam since defeated French forces had departed under terms of the Geneva Accords in 1954. Longest war in US history. More than one million combat deaths (US deaths: 46,079).

Harry Allard, 73, author, with James Marshall (*Miss Nelson Is Missing!*), born Evanston, IL, Jan 27, 1928.

James M. Deem, 51, author (*Bodies from the Bog*), born Wheeling, WV, Jan 27, 1950.

Julie Foudy, 30, soccer player, born San Diego, CA, Jan 27, 1971.

Laura McGee Kvasnosky, 50, author (*Zelda and Ivy*), born Sacramento, CA, Jan 27, 1951.

Julius B. Lester, 62, author (*To Be a Slave, Black Folktales*), born St. Louis, MO, Jan 27, 1939.

JANUARY 28 — SUNDAY

Day 28 — 337 Remaining

CATHOLIC SCHOOLS WEEK. Jan 28–Feb 3. Jointly sponsored by the National Catholic Educational Association and the US Catholic Conference. Annually, beginning on the last Sunday in January. For info: Natl Catholic Educational Assn, 1077 30th St NW,

Ste 100, Washington, DC 20007-3852. Phone: (202) 337-6232. E-mail: nceaadmin@ncea.org. Web: www.ncea.org.

CHALLENGER SPACE SHUTTLE EXPLOSION: 15th ANNIVERSARY. Jan 28, 1986. At 11:39 AM, EST, the Space Shuttle *Challenger STS-51L* exploded, 74 seconds into its flight and about 10 miles above the earth. Hundreds of millions around the world watched television replays of the horrifying event that killed seven people, destroyed the billion-dollar craft, suspended all shuttle flights and halted, at least temporarily, much of the US manned space flight program. Killed were teacher Christa McAuliffe (who was to have been the first ordinary citizen in space) and six crew members: Francis R. Scobee, Michael J. Smith, Judith A. Resnik, Ellison S. Onizuka, Ronald E. McNair and Gregory B. Jarvis.

MacKENZIE, ALEXANDER: BIRTH ANNIVERSARY. Jan 28, 1822. The man who became the first Liberal prime minister of Canada (1873–78) was born at Logierait, Perth, Scotland. He died at Toronto, Apr 17, 1892.

MARTÍ, JOSÉ JULIAN: BIRTH ANNIVERSARY. Jan 28, 1853. Cuban author and political activist, born at Havana, Cuba. Martí was exiled to Spain, where he studied law before coming to the US in 1890. He was killed in battle at Dos Rios, Cuba, May 19, 1895.

★**NATIONAL CONSUMER PROTECTION WEEK.** Jan 28–Feb 3.

PICCARD, AUGUSTE: BIRTH ANNIVERSARY. Jan 28, 1884. Scientist and explorer, born at Basel, Switzerland. Record-setting balloon ascents into stratosphere and ocean depth descents and explorations. Twin brother of Jean Felix Piccard. Died at Lausanne, Switzerland, Mar 24, 1962. See also: "Piccard, Jeannette Ridlon: Birth Anniversary" (Jan 5) and "Piccard, Auguste: Birth Anniversary" (Jan 28).

PICCARD, JEAN FELIX: BIRTH ANNIVERSARY. Jan 28, 1884. Scientist, engineer, explorer, born at Basel, Switzerland. Noted for cosmic-ray research and record-setting balloon ascensions into stratosphere. Reached 57,579 ft in sealed gondola piloted by his wife, Jeannette, in 1934. Twin brother of Auguste Piccard. Died at Minneapolis, MN, Jan 28, 1963. See also: "Piccard, Jeannette Ridlon: Birth Anniversary" (Jan 5) and "Piccard, Auguste: Birth Anniversary" (Jan 28).

SUPER BOWL XXXV. Jan 28. Tampa, FL. The battle between the NFC and AFC champions. Annually, the last Sunday in January. For info: PR Dept, The Natl Football League, 410 Park Ave, New York, NY 10022. Phone: (212) 758-1500. Web: www.nfl.com.

BIRTHDAYS TODAY

Nick Carter, 21, singer (Backstreet Boys), born Jamestown, NY, Jan 28, 1980.

Daunte Culpepper, 24, football player, born Ocala, FL, Jan 28, 1977.
Joey Fatone, 24, singer ('N Sync), born Brooklyn, NY, Jan 28, 1977.
Jeanne Shaheen, 54, Governor of New Hampshire (D), born St. Charles, MO, Jan 28, 1947.
Vera B. Williams, 74, author and illustrator (*A Chair for My Mother*), born Hollywood, CA, Jan 28, 1927.
Elijah Wood, 20, actor (*Flipper, Deep Impact*), born Cedar Rapids, IA, Jan 28, 1981.

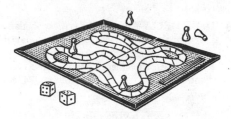

JANUARY 29 — MONDAY
Day 29 — 336 Remaining

KANSAS: ADMISSION DAY: ANNIVERSARY. Jan 29. Became the 34th state in 1861.

McKINLEY, WILLIAM: BIRTH ANNIVERSARY. Jan 29, 1843. The 25th president of the US, born at Niles, OH. Died in office, at Buffalo, NY, Sept 14, 1901, as the result of a gunshot wound by an anarchist assassin Sept 6, 1901, while he was attending the Pan-American Exposition.

NATIONAL PUZZLE DAY. Jan 29. To recognize puzzles and games and their creators. Call or write for free information on the origins and creators of puzzles and games. For info: Carol Handz, Jodi Jill Features, 1705 14th St, Ste 321, Boulder, CO 80302. Phone: (303) 786-9849. Fax: (303) 786-9401.

BIRTHDAYS TODAY

Christopher Collier, 71, author of historical fiction, with his brother James Lincoln Collier (*My Brother Sam Is Dead*), born New York, NY, Jan 29, 1930.
Dominik Hasek, 36, hockey player, born Pardubice, Czech Republic, Jan 29, 1965.
Andrew Keegan, 22, actor ("Party of Five"), born Shadow Hills, CA, Jan 29, 1979.
Ronald Stacey King, 34, basketball player, born Lawton, OK, Jan 29, 1967.
Bill Peet, 86, author and illustrator (*Whingdingdilly, The Wump World*), born Grandview, IN, Jan 29, 1915.
Jason James Richter, 21, actor (*Free Willy*), born Medford, OR, Jan 29, 1980.
Rosemary Wells, 58, author and illustrator (*Noisy Nora, Benjamin and Tulip*, The Max series), born New York, NY, Jan 29, 1943.
Oprah Winfrey, 47, TV talk show hostess (Emmys for "The Oprah Winfrey Show"), actress (*Beloved*), born Kosciusko, MS, Jan 29, 1954.

JANUARY 30 — TUESDAY
Day 30 — 335 Remaining

NATIONAL INANE ANSWERING MESSAGE DAY. Jan 30. Annually, the day set aside to change, shorten, replace or delete those ridiculous and/or annoying answering machine messages that waste the time of anyone who must listen to them. [© 1999 by WH]. For info: Thomas and Ruth Roy, Wellcat Holidays, PO Box 774, Lebanon, PA 17042-0774. Phone: (717) 279-0184. E-mail: wellcat@supernet.com. Web: www.wellcat.com.

ROOSEVELT, FRANKLIN DELANO: BIRTH ANNIVER-SARY. Jan 30, 1882. The 32nd president of the US, Roosevelt was the only president to serve more than two terms, FDR was elected four times. Term of office: Mar 4, 1933–Apr 12, 1945. He supported the Allies in WWII before the US entered the struggle by supplying them with war materials through the Lend-Lease Act; he became deeply involved in broad decision making after the Japanese attack on Pearl Harbor Dec 7, 1941. Born at Hyde Park, NY, he died a few months into his fourth term at Warm Springs, GA, Apr 12, 1945.

SCOTLAND: UP HELLY AA. Jan 30. Lerwick, Shetland Islands. Norse galley burned in impressive ceremony symbolizing sacrifice to the sun. Old Viking custom. Annually, the last Tuesday in January. Tourist Information Centre, Market Cross, Lerwick, Shetland, Scotland ZE1 0LU. Phone: (44) (1595) 693434. Fax: (44) (1595) 695807.

BIRTHDAYS TODAY

Lloyd Alexander, 77, author (*The Black Cauldron*, Newbery for *The High King*), born Philadelphia, PA, Jan 30, 1924.

Allan W. Eckert, 70, author (*Incident at Hawk's Hill*), born Buffalo, NY, Jan 30, 1931.

Guy Gilchrist, 44, author, illustrator, cartoonist (*Mudpie, Tiny Dinos*), with his brother Brad Gilchrist, born Winsted, CT, Jan 30, 1957.

Polly Horvath, 44, author (*The Trolls*), born Kalamazoo, MI, Jan 30, 1957.

Tony Johnston, 59, author (*The Magic Maguey*), born Los Angeles, CA, Jan 30, 1942.

Frank O'Bannon, 71, Governor of Indiana (D), born Louisville, KY, Jan 30, 1930.

JANUARY 31 — WEDNESDAY
Day 31 — 334 Remaining

McDONALD'S INVADES THE SOVIET UNION: ANNI-VERSARY. Jan 31, 1990. McDonald's Corporation opened its first fast-food restaurant in the Soviet Union.

MORRIS, ROBERT: BIRTH ANNIVERSARY. Jan 31, 1734. Signer of the Declaration of Independence, the Articles of Confederation and the Constitution. One of only two men to sign all three documents. Born at Liverpool, England, he died May 7, 1806, at Philadelphia, PA.

NAURU: NATIONAL HOLIDAY. Jan 31. Republic of Nauru. Commemorates independence in 1968 from a UN trusteeship administered by Australia, New Zealand and the UK.

ROBINSON, JACKIE: BIRTH ANNIVERSARY. Jan 31, 1919. Jack Roosevelt Robinson, athlete and business executive, first black to enter professional major league baseball (Brooklyn Dodgers, 1947–56). Voted National League's Most Valuable Player in 1949 and elected to the Baseball Hall of Fame in 1962. Born at Cairo, GA, Robinson died at Stamford, CT, Oct 24, 1972.

SPACE MILESTONE: *EXPLORER 1* (US). Jan 31, 1958. The first successful US satellite. Although launched four months later than the Soviet Union's *Sputnik*, *Explorer* reached a higher altitude and detected a zone of intense radiation inside Earth's magnetic field. This was later named the Van Allen radiation belts. More than 65 subsequent *Explorer* satellites were launched through 1984.

SPACE MILESTONE: PROJECT MERCURY TEST (US). Jan 31, 1961. A test of Project Mercury spacecraft accomplished the first US recovery of a large animal from space. Ham, the chimpanzee, successfully performed simple tasks in space.

BIRTHDAYS TODAY

Queen Beatrix, 63, Queen of the Netherlands, born Sostdijk, Netherlands, Jan 31, 1938.

Denise Fleming, 51, author (*In the Small, Small Pond*), born Toledo, OH, Jan 31, 1950.

Gerald McDermott, 60, illustrator and author (Caldecott for *Arrow to the Sun*), born Detroit, MI, Jan 31, 1941.

(Lynn) Nolan Ryan, 54, Baseball Hall of Fame player, born Refugio, TX, Jan 31, 1947.

Justin Timberlake, 20, singer ('N Sync), born Memphis, TN, Jan 31, 1981.

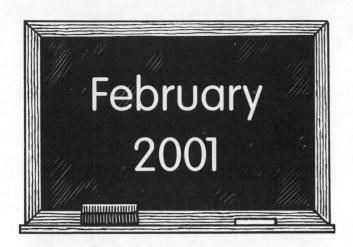

FEBRUARY 1 — THURSDAY
Day 32 — 333 Remaining

★**AMERICAN HEART MONTH.** Feb 1–28. Presidential Proclamation issued each year for February since 1964. (PL88–254 of Dec 30, 1963.)

AMERICAN HEART MONTH. Feb 1–28. Volunteers across the country spend one to four weeks canvassing neighborhoods and providing educational information about heart disease and stroke. For info: Cathy Yarbrough, News Media Relations, American Heart Assn, 7272 Greenville Ave, Dallas, TX 75231. Phone: (800) AHA-USA1. Fax: (214) 369-3685. Web: www.americanheart.org.

BLACK HISTORY MONTH. Feb 1–28. Traditionally the month containing Abraham Lincoln's birthday (Feb 12) and Frederick Douglass's presumed birthday (Feb 14). Observance of a special period to recognize achievements and contributions by African Americans dates from February 1926, when it was launched by Dr. Carter G. Woodson and others. Variously designated Negro History, Black History, Afro-American History, African-American History, Black Heritage and Black Expressions, the observance period was initially one week, but since 1976 has been the entire month of February. Each year Black History Month has a theme. Visit the website of the Association for African-American Life and History for the theme for the current year and information on a theme-related kit you can purchase from the Association. The price for the 2000 kit was $35. *Black History Month Resource Book* (2nd ed, Gale, 0-7876-1755-X, $47) includes both programmatic ideas and lists of resources in all media for all ages. *See* Curriculum Connection. For info: Assn for Afro-American Life and History, 1407 14th St NW, Washington, DC 20005-3704. Phone: (202) 667-2822. Fax: (202) 387-9802. Web: www.artnoir.com/asalh/.

BLACK MARIA STUDIO: ANNIVERSARY. Feb 1, 1893. The first moving picture studio was completed, built on Thomas Edison's laboratory compound at West Orange, NJ, at a cost of less than $700. The wooden structure of irregular oblong shape was covered with black tar paper. It had a sharply sloping roof hinged at one edge so that half of it could be raised to admit sunlight. Fifty feet in length, it was mounted on a pivot enabling it to be swung around to follow the changing position of the sun. There was a stage draped in black at one end of the single room. Though the structure was officially called a Kinetographic Theater, it was nicknamed the "Black Maria" because it resembled an old-fashioned police wagon. It was described as "hot and cramped" by "Gentleman" Jim Corbett, the pugilistic idol who was the subject of an early movie made in the studio.

FEBRUARY 1–28
BLACK HISTORY MONTH

African Americans in all walks of life have made many noteworthy contributions to the success and growth of the United States. Celebrate the rich heritage found in the African American tradition.

In language arts, older students will enjoy reading poetry and novels written by African Americans. Organize a literature study by choosing several different poets and novelists from different decades of American history. Compare thematic issues addressed in the novels and poetry. Novelists, newswriters and poets you might feature include: Jupiter Hammon (1760s), Phillis Wheatley (1770s), Samuel Cornish and John Russworm (1820s), Frederick Douglass (1840s–1860s), Ida B. Wells (1890s) and Paul Laurence Dunbar (late 1890s, early 1900s). Another literature focus might compare works by the writers of the Harlem Renaissance. During the 1920s, in the Harlem district of New York City, literature flourished in the black community. Langston Hughes, Countee Cullen, James Weldon Johnson, Jesse Fauset, Claude McKay, Alain Locke and Zora Neale Hurston were prominent writers of this movement. The strong voices in their novels and poems reflect the African American experience at the end of the 1800s and the first half of the 20th century. Activists and educators from this period include Booker T. Washington and Mary Church Terrell.

While it's informative to learn about famous leaders, it's valuable to learn about the contributions of regular citizens, too. Many African Americans fought in the Revolutionary War, the Civil War, both World Wars, Korea and Vietnam. Books about African American soldiers include: *Black, Grey, & Blue*, by James Haskins (Simon & Schuster, 0-689-80655-8, $16 Gr. 4 & up); *Buffalo Soldiers* (a title in Chelsea House's African American Achiever Series, 0-7910-2596-9, $8.95, Gr. 6 & up); *The Forgotten Heroes*, by Clinton Cox (Scholastic, out of print, but available in libraries); and the series *African-American Soldiers* (Twenty First Century Books). The novel *Fallen Angels*, by Walter Dean Myers (Scholastic, 0-590-40943-3, $4.99 Gr. 7 & up) is a riveting story about young men fighting in Vietnam.

Inventors and explorers you can feature include Matthew Henson, who accompanied Robert E. Peary to the North Pole in 1909. See his book *A Negro Explorer at the North Pole* for a firsthand account of the trip. Students can compare his voyage (supplies, temperatures, etc.) with that of Ernest Shackleton's ill-fated trip to the South Pole.

Many people know the story of Rosa Parks and the Montgomery Bus Boycott. Another civil rights story is the courage shown by six-year-old Ruby Bridges during the integration of schools in the South. Every unit on civil rights should have a copy of *Through My Eyes*, by Ruby Bridges (Scholastic, 0-590-18923-9, $16.95 Gr. 4 & up). The cruelty she faced is almost unimaginable. The photographs are well chosen and reveal both the charm of a little girl and the ugly face of racism.

Bring jazz, blues and swing into the classroom. Play recordings of music by Charlie Parker, Miles Davis, Billie Holiday, Thelonius Monk and Count Basie. Write response pieces to reflect the moods fostered by different artists.

There have been many famous African American sports figures. See *Satchel Paige*, by Lesa Cline-Ransome (Simon & Schuster, 0-689-81161-9, $16 Gr. 2 & up) for a gorgeously illustrated picture book biography told with a storyteller's voice.

Contact your learning center director and local public library for additional suggestions concerning African American contributions to music, fine arts, politics and sports.

CAR INSURANCE FIRST ISSUED: ANNIVERSARY. Feb 1, 1898. Travelers Insurance Company issued the first car insurance against accidents with horses.

EASY-BAKE® OVEN DEBUTS: ANNIVERSARY. Feb 1, 1964. This toy was officially introduced this month at the American Toy Fair. Later Easy-Bake brand snack mixes to be used with the ovens were introduced. More than 16 million ovens and more than 100 million mix sets have been sold.

FIRST SESSION OF THE SUPREME COURT: ANNIVERSARY. Feb 1, 1790. The Supreme Court of the United States met for the first time at New York City with Chief Justice John Jay presiding.

FREEDOM DAY: ANNIVERSARY. Feb 1. Anniversary of President Abraham Lincoln's approval, Feb 1, 1865, of the 13th Amendment to the US Constitution (abolishing slavery): "1. Neither slavery nor involuntary servitude, except as a punishment for crime whereof the party shall have been duly convicted, shall exist within the United States or any place subject to their jurisdiction. 2. Congress shall have power to enforce this article by appropriate legislation." The amendment had been proposed by the Congress Jan 31, 1865; ratification was completed Dec 18, 1865.

GREENSBORO SIT-IN: ANNIVERSARY. Feb 1, 1960. Commercial discrimination against blacks and other minorities provoked a nonviolent protest. At Greensboro, NC, four students from the Agricultural and Technical College at Greensboro (Ezell Blair, Jr, Franklin McCain, Joseph McNeill and David Richmond) sat down at a Woolworths store lunch counter and ordered coffee. Refused service, they remained all day. The following days similar sit-ins took place at the Woolworths lunch counter. Before the week was over they were joined by a few white students. The protest spread rapidly, especially in southern states. More than 1,600 persons were arrested before the year was over for participating in sit-ins. Civil rights for all became a cause for thousands of students and activists. In response, equal accommodation regardless of race became the rule at lunch counters, hotels and business establishments in thousands of places.

HUGHES, LANGSTON: BIRTH ANNIVERSARY. Feb 1, 1902. African American poet and author, born at Joplin, MO. Among his works are the poetry collection *Montage of a Dream Deferred*, plays, a novel and short stories. Hughes died May 22, 1967, at New York, NY.

LIBRARY LOVERS' MONTH. Feb 1–28. A monthlong celebration of school, public and private libraries of all types. This is a time for everyone, especially library support groups, to recognize the value of libraries and to work to assure that the nation's libraries will continue to serve. *See* Curriculum Connection. For info: Stephanie Stokes, 1980 Washington, No 107, San Francisco, CA 94109-2930. Phone: (415) 749-0130. Fax: (415) 749-0735. E-mail: librarylovers@calibraries.org. Web: www.calibraries.org/librarylovers.

MOON PHASE: FIRST QUARTER. Feb 1. Moon enters First Quarter phase at 9:02 AM, EST.

★ **NATIONAL AFRICAN AMERICAN HISTORY MONTH.** Feb 1–28.

		S	M	T	W	T	F	S
February						1	2	3
2001		4	5	6	7	8	9	10
		11	12	13	14	15	16	17
		18	19	20	21	22	23	24
		25	26	27	28			

FEBRUARY 1–28
LIBRARY LOVER'S MONTH

The library—be it public, school or private—should be one of a student's best friends. Whether students use their library as a source of research materials or pleasure reading, a quiet place to do homework while escaping from the noisy outside world or a combination of all three, the library is a place with doors open to everyone.

Celebrate Library Lover's Month by arranging a visit to the public library. It's shocking how many school-age children do not have public library cards. See that your students know where the library is and how to get there. No child should ever be disadvantaged because he or she has no books at home and doesn't know where to get information. If walking to the library is out of the question, look into PTA-funded school bus trips. Arrange with the children's librarian for a library tour and a story session. Budget time for the librarian to instruct older children on using the library's microfiche readers. Let the librarian know, in advance, about instruction on these "esoteric" materials. That way she or he has time to find a high-interest, old news story on microfiche. She or he might also instruct students how to use library Internet links, if they are available.

Ask the school media center director to visit your classroom. Tell him or her you would like a 5- to 10-minute presentation about the materials available in the school library. This should be a "get them excited preview." Then, during regularly scheduled class visits, ask the director to expand on each kind of material. For example, one visit could concentrate on encyclopedias and their use; another might focus on finding nonfiction materials; and a third could center on choosing a good picture book or novel. Create simple exercises that require finding specific material.

Feb 13 celebrates the date of the first magazine published in America (see Feb 13). Ask the media center director to feature magazines one day. *Ranger Rick, Cricket* and *Cobblestone* are three magazines many libraries have in their collections. They contain articles that are extremely useful and complement many areas of the curriculum. Check and see if the media center director has suggestions for you on how to tap into this wealth of material.

For other ideas to help commemorate this month, see *Library Celebrations*, by Cyndy Dingwall (Highsmith, 1-5797-0027-2, $16.95).

NATIONAL CHERRY MONTH. Feb 1–28. To publicize the colorful red tart cherry. Recipes, posters and table tents available. For info: Jane Baker, Mktg Dir, Cherry Marketing Institute, PO Box 30285, Lansing, MI 48909-7785. Phone: (517) 669-4264. Fax: (517) 669-3354. E-mail: jbaker@cherrymkt.org. Web: www.cherrymkt.org.

NATIONAL CHILDREN'S DENTAL HEALTH MONTH. Feb 1–28. To increase dental awareness and stress the importance of regular dental care. For info: American Dental Assn, 211 E Chicago Ave, Chicago, IL 60611. To purchase materials, phone in US: (800) 947-4746. Web: www.ada.org.

NATIONAL EDUCATION GOALS: ANNIVERSARY. Feb 1, 1990. In September 1989, President Bush and 50 governors met at an historic Education Summit to draft goals for American K–12 schools for the year 2000. In February 1990, the National Education Goals were announced by the president and adopted by the governors. In July 1990, the National Education Goals Panel was formed to assess and report state and national progress towards the goals. For more info: www.negp.gov.

★ **NATIONAL FREEDOM DAY.** Feb 1. Presidential Proclamation 2824, Jan 25, 1949, covers all succeeding years (PL80–842 of June 30, 1948).

NATIONAL SIGN UP FOR SUMMER CAMP MONTH. Feb 1–28. Every year more than nine million children continue a national tradition by attending day or resident camps. Building self-confidence, learning new skills and making memories that last a lifetime are just a few examples of what makes camp special and why camp does children a world of good. To find the right program, parents begin looking at summer camps during this month—and sign their children up while there are still vacancies. For info: Public Relations, American Camping Assn, 5000 State Rd 67N, Martinsville, IN 46151. Phone: (765) 342-8456. E-mail: jmccormick@aca-camps.org. Web: www.ACAcamps.org.

NATIONAL WILD BIRD FEEDING MONTH. Feb 1–28. To recognize that February is one of the most difficult winter months in much of the US for birds to survive in the wild and to encourage people to provide food, water and shelter to supplement the wild birds' natural diet of weed seeds and harmful insects. For info: Sue Wells, Exec Dir, Natl Bird-Feeding Soc, PO Box 23, Northbrook, IL 60065-0023. Phone: (847) 272-0135. E-mail: feedbirds@aol.com.

NORTH CAROLINA SWEETPOTATO MONTH. Feb 1–28. To educate the public about the nutritional benefits and versatility of sweet potatoes. North Carolina farmers want America to know that sweet potatoes aren't just for turkeys anymore. Available year-round, sweet potatoes are loaded with beta carotene and vitamin C. They can be boiled, baked, microwaved, grilled, broiled, fried, mashed, sauteed, candied or served raw. North Carolina produces more sweet potatoes than any other state. For info: Sue Johnson-Langdon, North Carolina SweetPotato Commission, 1327 N Brightleaf Blvd, Ste H, Smithfield, NC 27577. Phone: (919) 989-7323. Fax: (919) 989-3015. E-mail: ncsweetsue@aol.com. Web: www.ncsweetpotatoes.com.

RETURN SHOPPING CARTS TO THE SUPERMARKET MONTH. Feb 1–28. A monthlong opportunity to return stolen shopping carts, milk crates, bread trays and ice cream baskets to supermarkets and to avoid the increased food prices that these thefts cause. Annually, the month of February. Sponsor: Illinois Food Retailers Association. For info: Anthony A. Dinolfo, Grocer, Retired, 8148 S Homan Ave, Chicago, IL 60652. Phone: (773) 737-6540.

ROBINSON CRUSOE DAY. Feb 1. Anniversary of the rescue, Feb 1, 1709, of Alexander Selkirk, Scottish sailor who had been put ashore (in September 1704) on the uninhabited island, Juan Fer-

nandez, at his own request after a quarrel with his captain. His adventures formed the basis for Daniel Defoe's book *Robinson Crusoe*. A day to be adventurous and self-reliant.

ST. LAURENT, LOUIS STEPHEN: BIRTH ANNIVERSARY. Feb 1, 1882. Canadian lawyer and prime minister, born at Compton, Quebec. Died at Quebec City, July 25, 1973.

BIRTHDAYS TODAY

Michael B. Enzi, 57, US Senator (R, Wyoming), born Bremerton, WA, Feb 1, 1944.
Jerry Spinelli, 60, author (*Wringer*, Newbery for *Maniac Magee*), born Norristown, PA, Feb 1, 1941.
Boris Yeltsin, 70, former Russian president, born Sverdlovsk, Russia, Feb 1, 1931.

FEBRUARY 2 — FRIDAY
Day 33 — 332 Remaining

BABE VOTED INTO BASEBALL HALL OF FAME: 65th ANNIVERSARY. Feb 2, 1936. The five charter members of the brand-new Baseball Hall of Fame at Cooperstown, NY, were announced. Of 226 ballots cast, Ty Cobb was named on 222, Babe Ruth on 215, Honus Wagner on 215, Christy Mathewson on 205 and Walter Johnson on 189. A total of 170 votes were necessary to be elected to the Hall of Fame.

BAN ON AFRICAN NATIONAL CONGRESS LIFTED: ANNIVERSARY. Feb 2, 1990. The 30-year ban on the African National Congress was lifted by South African President F.W. de Klerk. De Klerk also vowed to free Nelson Mandela and lift restrictions on 33 other opposition groups.

BONZA BOTTLER DAY™. Feb 2. To celebrate when the number of the day is the same as the number of the month. Bonza Bottler Day™ is an excuse to have a party at least once a month. For info: Gail M. Berger, 109 Matthew Ave, Poca, WV 25159. Phone: (304) 776-7746. E-mail: gberger5@aol.com.

CALIFORNIA KIWIFRUIT DAY. Feb 2. National campaign to educate Americans about the nutritional benefits of kiwifruit, the most nutrient-dense fruit (they provide twice the vitamin C of oranges); ways to enjoy kiwifruit and kiwifruit's colorful history. Annually, Feb 2. For info: Laura Bachmann, Porter Novelli, 444 Market St, Ste 3000, San Francisco, CA 94111. Fax: (415) 733-1770.

CANDLEMAS DAY or PRESENTATION OF THE LORD. Feb 2. Observed in Roman Catholic and Eastern Orthodox Churches. Commemorates presentation of Jesus in the Temple and the purification of Mary 40 days after his birth. Candles have been blessed since the 11th century. Formerly called the Feast of Purification of the Blessed Virgin Mary. Old Scottish couplet proclaims: "If Candlemas is fair and clear/There'll be two winters in the year."

GROUNDHOG DAY. Feb 2. Old belief that if the sun shines on Candlemas Day, or if the groundhog sees his shadow when he emerges on this day, six weeks of winter will ensue. For links to websites about Groundhog Day, go to deil.lang.uiuc.edu/web.pages/holidays/groundhog.html.

GROUNDHOG DAY IN PUNXSUTAWNEY, PENNSYLVANIA. Feb 2. Widely observed traditional annual Candlemas Day event at which "Punxsutawney Phil, king of the weather prophets," is the object of a search. Tradition is said to have been established by early German settlers. The official trek (which began in 1887) is followed by a weather prediction for the next six weeks. Phil made his dramatic film debut with Bill Murray in *Groundhog Day*.

MEXICO: DIA DE LA CANDELARIA. Feb 2. All Mexico celebrates Candlemas Day with dances, processions, bullfights.

***THE RECORD OF A SNEEZE* : ANNIVERSARY.** Feb 2, 1893. One day after Thomas Edison's "Black Maria" studio was completed at West Orange, NJ, a studio cameraman took the first "close-up" in film history. *The Record of a Sneeze*, starring Edison's assistant Fred P. Ott, was also the first motion picture to receive a copyright (1894). See also: "Black Maria Studio: Anniversary" (Feb 1).

TREATY OF GUADALUPE HIDALGO: ANNIVERSARY. Feb 2, 1848. The war between Mexico and the US formally ended with the signing of the Treaty of Guadalupe Hidalgo, signed in the village for which it was named. The treaty provided for Mexico's cession to the US of the territory that became the states of California, Nevada, Utah, most of Arizona and parts of New Mexico, Colorado and Wyoming, in exchange for $15 million from the US. In addition, Mexico relinquished all rights to Texas north of the Rio Grande. The Senate ratified the treaty Mar 10, 1848.

WALTON, GEORGE: DEATH ANNIVERSARY. Feb 2, 1804. Signer of the Declaration of Independence. Born at Prince Edward County, VA, 1749 (exact date unknown). Died at Augusta, GA.

BIRTHDAYS TODAY

Judith Viorst, 70, author (*The Tenth Good Thing About Barney*), born Newark, NJ, Feb 2, 1931.

FEBRUARY 3 — SATURDAY

Day 34 — 331 Remaining

ENDANGERED SPECIES ACT: ANNIVERSARY. Feb 3, 1973. President Richard Nixon signed the Endangered Species Act into law.

FIFTEENTH AMENDMENT TO US CONSTITUTION RATIFIED: ANNIVERSARY. Feb 3, 1870. The 15th Amendment granted that the right of citizens to vote shall not be denied on account of race, color or previous condition of servitude.

HALFWAY POINT OF WINTER. Feb 3. On this date, 45 days of winter will have elapsed and the equivalent remain before Mar 20, 2001, which is the spring equinox and the beginning of spring.

INCOME TAX BIRTHDAY: SIXTEENTH AMENDMENT TO US CONSTITUTION: RATIFICATION ANNIVERSARY. Feb 3, 1913. The 16th Amendment granted Congress the authority to levy taxes on income. (Church bells did not ring throughout the land and no dancing in the streets was reported.)

JAPAN: BEAN-THROWING FESTIVAL (SETSUBUN). Feb 3. Setsubun marks the last day of winter according to the lunar calendar. Throngs at temple grounds throw beans to drive away imaginary devils.

LAURA INGALLS WILDER GINGERBREAD SOCIABLE. Feb 3. Pomona, CA. The 34th annual event commemorates the birthday (Feb 7, 1867) of the renowned author of the Little House books. The library has on permanent display the handwritten manuscript of *Little Town on the Prairie* and other Wilder memorabilia. Entertainment by fiddlers, craft displays, apple cider and gingerbread. Annually, the first Saturday in February. Est atten-

February 2001	S	M	T	W	T	F	S
					1	2	3
	4	5	6	7	8	9	10
	11	12	13	14	15	16	17
	18	19	20	21	22	23	24
	25	26	27	28			

dance: 300. For info: Marguerite F. Raybould, Friends of the Pomona Public Library, 625 S Garey Ave, Pomona, CA 91766. Phone: (909) 620-2017. Fax: (909) 620-3713.

NORTH AMERICA'S COLDEST RECORDED TEMPERATURE: ANNIVERSARY. Feb 3, 1947. At Snag, in Canada's Yukon Territory, a temperature of 81 degrees below zero (Fahrenheit) was recorded on this date, a record low for all of North America.

SPACE MILESTONE: *CHALLENGER STS-10* (US). Feb 3, 1984. Shuttle *Challenger* launched from Kennedy Space Center, FL, with a crew of five (Vance Brand, Robert Gibson, Ronald McNair, Bruce McCandless and Robert Stewart). On Feb 7 two astronauts became the first to fly freely in space (propelled by their backpack jets), untethered to any craft. Landed at Cape Canaveral, FL, Feb 11.

BIRTHDAYS TODAY

Joan Lowery Nixon, 74, author (the Orphan Train series), born Los Angeles, CA, Feb 3, 1927.

Paul S. Sarbanes, 68, US Senator (D, Maryland), born Salisbury, MD, Feb 3, 1933.

Maura Tierney, 36, actress (*Liar, Liar*), born Boston, MA, Feb 3, 1965.

FEBRUARY 4 — SUNDAY

Day 35 — 330 Remaining

AFRICAN AMERICAN READ-IN. Feb 4–5. Schools, libraries and community organizations are urged to make literacy a significant part of Black History Month by hosting Read-Ins in their communities. Report your results by submitting the 2001 African American Read-In Chain Report Card. This 12th national Read-In is sponsored by the Black Caucus of the National Council of Teachers of English. Annually, the first Sunday in February for communities and the first Monday in February for schools. For a Read-In Chain Packet: Dr. Sandra E. Gibbs, NCTE Special Programs, 1111 W Kenyon Rd, Urbana, IL 61801-1096. Phone: (217) 328-3870. E-mail: sgibbs@ncte.org. Web: www.ncte.org.

APACHE WARS BEGAN: ANNIVERSARY. Feb 4, 1861. The period of conflict known as the Apache Wars began at Apache Pass, AZ, when Army Lieutenant George Bascom arrested Apache Chief Cochise for raiding a ranch. Cochise escaped and declared war. The wars lasted 25 years under the leadership of Cochise and, later, Geronimo.

BOY SCOUTS OF AMERICA ANNIVERSARY WEEK. Feb 4–10. Commemorating the founding of the organization Feb 8, 1910. For info: Boy Scouts of America, 1325 W Walnut Hill Ln, Irving, TX 75015-2079. Phone: (214) 580-2263. Web: www.bsa.scouting.org.

LINDBERGH, CHARLES AUGUSTUS: BIRTH ANNIVERSARY. Feb 4, 1902. American aviator Charles "Lucky Lindy" Lindbergh was the first to fly solo and nonstop over the Atlantic Ocean, New York to Paris, May 20–21, 1927. Born at Detroit, MI, he died at Kipahula, Maui, HI, Aug 27, 1974. See also: "Lindbergh Flight: Anniversary" (May 20).

SRI LANKA: INDEPENDENCE DAY. Feb 4. Democratic Socialist Republic of Sri Lanka observes National Day. On Feb 4, 1948, Ceylon (as it was then known) obtained independence from Great Britain. The name Sri Lanka was adopted in 1972.

SWITZERLAND: HOMSTROM. Feb 4. Scuol. Burning of straw men on poles as a symbol of winter's imminent departure. Annually, the first Sunday in February.

BIRTHDAYS TODAY

Rod Grams, 53, US Senator (R, Minnesota), born Princeton, MN, Feb 4, 1948.

Russell Hoban, 76, author of books illustrated by his wife Lillian (*Bedtime for Frances*), born Lansdale, PA, Feb 4, 1925.

Rosa Lee Parks, 88, civil rights leader who refused to give up her seat on the bus, born Tuskegee, AL, Feb 4, 1913.

FEBRUARY 5 — MONDAY
Day 36 — 329 Remaining

FAMILY-LEAVE BILL: ANNIVERSARY. Feb 5, 1993. President William Clinton signed legislation requiring companies with 50 or more employees (and all government agencies) to allow employees to take up to 12 weeks unpaid leave in a 12-month period to deal with the birth or adoption of a child or to care for a relative with a serious health problem. The bill became effective Aug 5, 1993.

MEXICO: ANNIVERSARY OF THE CONSTITUTION. Feb 5. The present constitution, embracing major social reforms, was adopted in 1917.

NATIONAL GIRLS AND WOMEN IN SPORTS DAY. Feb 5. Celebrates and honors all girls and women participating in sports. Recognizes the passage of Title IX in 1972, the law that guarantees gender equity in federally-funded school programs, including athletics. Sponsored by Girls Inc, the Girl Scouts, the National Association for Girls and Women in Sports, the Women's Sports Foundation and the YWCA. For info: Women's Sports Foundation, Eisenhower Park, East Meadow, NY 11554. Phone: (516) 542-4700.

NATIONAL SCHOOL COUNSELING WEEK. Feb 5–9. Promotes counseling in the school and community. For info: American School Counselor Assn, 801 N Fairfax St, Ste 310, Alexandria, VA 22314. Phone: (800) 306-4722. Fax: (703) 683-1619. E-mail: asca@erols.com. Web: www.schoolcounselor.org.

WEATHERMAN'S [WEATHERPERSON'S] DAY. Feb 5. Commemorates the birth of one of America's first weathermen, John Jeffries, a Boston physician who kept detailed records of weather conditions, 1774–1816. Born at Boston, Feb 5, 1744, and died there Sept 16, 1819. See also: "First Balloon Flight Across English Channel: Anniversary" (Jan 7).

WITHERSPOON, JOHN: BIRTH ANNIVERSARY. Feb 5, 1723. Clergyman, signer of the Declaration of Independence and reputed coiner of the word *Americanism* (in 1781). Born near Edinburgh, Scotland. Died at Princeton, NJ, Nov 15, 1794.

BIRTHDAYS TODAY

Henry Louis (Hank) Aaron, 67, baseball executive, Baseball Hall of Fame outfielder, all-time home run leader, born Mobile, AL, Feb 5, 1934.

Roberto Alomar, 33, baseball player, born Ponce, Puerto Rico, Feb 5, 1968.

Patricia Lauber, 77, author (the Let's Read and Find Out science series, *Volcano: The Eruption and Healing of Mount St. Helens*), born New York, NY, Feb 5, 1924.

David Wiesner, 44, author and illustrator (Caldecott for *Tuesday*), born Bridgewater, NJ, Feb 5, 1957.

FEBRUARY 6 — TUESDAY
Day 37 — 328 Remaining

ACCESSION OF QUEEN ELIZABETH II: ANNIVERSARY. Feb 6, 1952. Princess Elizabeth Alexandra Mary succeeded to the British throne (becoming Elizabeth II, Queen of the United Kingdom of Great Britain and Northern Ireland and Head of the Commonwealth) upon the death of her father, King George VI, Feb 6, 1952. Her coronation took place June 2, 1953, at Westminster Abbey at London.

BURR, AARON: BIRTH ANNIVERSARY. Feb 6, 1756. Third vice president of the US (Mar 4, 1801–Mar 3, 1805). While vice president, Burr challenged political enemy Alexander Hamilton to a duel and mortally wounded him July 11, 1804, at Weehawken, NJ. Indicted for the challenge and for murder, he returned to Washington to complete his term of office (during which he presided over the impeachment trial of Supreme Court Justice Samuel Chase). In 1807 Burr was arrested, tried for treason (in an alleged scheme to invade Mexico and set up a new nation in the West) and acquitted. Born at Newark, NJ, he died at Staten Island, NY, Sept 14, 1836.

MASSACHUSETTS RATIFIES CONSTITUTION: ANNIVERSARY. Feb 6, 1788. By a vote of 187 to 168, Massachusetts became the sixth state to ratify the Constitution.

NEW ZEALAND: WAITANGI DAY. Feb 6. National Day. Commemorates signing of the Treaty of Waitangi in 1840 (at Waitangi, Chatham Islands, New Zealand). The treaty, between the native Maori and the European peoples, provided for development of New Zealand under the British Crown.

100th BILLIONTH CRAYOLA CRAYON® PRODUCED: ANNIVERSARY. Feb 6, 1996. On this date, the 100th billionth crayola was produced by Binney & Smith, Inc in New York. The first box of eight crayons was introduced in 1903 in the popular yellow and green box. Since 1903, crayons have come in boxes of 24, 48, 64 and 96. The word "crayola" means oily chalk.

RUTH, "BABE": BIRTH ANNIVERSARY. Feb 6, 1895. One of baseball's greatest heroes, George Herman "Babe" Ruth was born at Baltimore, MD. The left-handed pitcher—"the Sultan of Swat,"—hit 714 home runs in 22 major league seasons of play and played in 10 World Series. Died at New York, NY, Aug 16, 1948.

BIRTHDAYS TODAY

Ronald Reagan, 90, 40th president of the US, born Tampico, IL, Feb 6, 1911.

FEBRUARY 7 — WEDNESDAY
Day 38 — 327 Remaining

ASSOCIATION FOR EDUCATIONAL COMMUNICATION AND TECHNOLOGY CONFERENCE. Feb 7–11. Charlotte, NC. For info: Assn for Educational Communications & Technology, 1025 Vermont Ave NW, Ste 820, Washington, DC 20005-3516. Phone: (202) 347-7834. Fax: (202) 347-7839. Web: www.aect.org.

BALLET INTRODUCED TO THE US: ANNIVERSARY. Feb 7, 1827. Renowned French danseuse Madame Francisquy Hutin introduced ballet to the US with a performance of *The Deserter*, staged at the Bowery Theater, New York, NY. A minor scandal erupted when the ladies in the lower boxes left the theater upon viewing the light and scanty attire of Madame Hutin and her troupe.

CHINA: LANTERN FESTIVAL. Feb 7. Traditional Chinese festival falls on 15th day of first month of Chinese lunar calendar year. Lantern processions mark end of the Chinese New Year holiday season. See also: "Chinese New Year" (Jan 24).

DICKENS, CHARLES: BIRTH ANNIVERSARY. Feb 7, 1812. English social critic and novelist, born at Portsmouth, England. Among his most successful books: *Oliver Twist, The Posthumous Papers of the Pickwick Club, David Copperfield* and *A Christmas Carol*. Died at Gad's Hill, England, June 9, 1870, and was buried at Westminster Abbey. For more info: *Charles Dickens: The Man Who Had Great Expectations*, by Diane Stanley and Peter Vennema (Morrow, 0-688-09111-3, $14.93 Gr. 4–8).

ELEVENTH AMENDMENT TO US CONSTITUTION (SOVEREIGNTY OF THE STATES): RATIFICATION ANNIVERSARY. Feb 7, 1795. The 11th Amendment to the Constitution was ratified, curbing the powers of the federal judiciary in relation to the states. The amendment reaffirmed the sovereignty of the states by prohibiting suits against them.

GIPSON, FRED: BIRTH ANNIVERSARY. Feb 7, 1908. Born near Mason, TX. Gipson is known for such works as *Old Yeller, Savage Sam* and *Little Arliss*. In 1959, he won the William Allen White Children's Book Award and the First Sequoyah Award. Gipson died at Mason County, TX, Aug 17, 1973.

GRENADA: INDEPENDENCE DAY. Feb 7. National Day. Commemorates independence from Great Britain in 1974.

SPACE MILESTONE: *STARDUST* (US). Feb 7, 1999. *Stardust* began its 3 billion-mile journey to collect comet dust on this date. The unmanned mission will meet up with Comet Wild-2 in January 2004 and the comet samples will reach Earth in January 2006. This is the first US mission devoted solely to a comet. NASA plans three more over a four-year period.

TAIWAN: LANTERN FESTIVAL AND TOURISM DAY. Feb 7. Fifteenth day of the First Moon of the lunar calendar marks end of New Year holiday season. Lantern processions and contests.

WILDER, LAURA INGALLS: BIRTH ANNIVERSARY. Feb 7, 1867. Author of *The Little House on the Prairie* and its sequels. Born at Pepin, WI, Wilder died Feb 10, 1957, at Mansfield, MO.

For more info, go to the Little House on the Prairie home page at www.vvv.com/~jenslegg/index.htm.

BIRTHDAYS TODAY

Garth Brooks, 39, singer, born Tulsa, OK, Feb 7, 1962.
Juwan Howard, 28, basketball player, born Chicago, IL, Feb 7, 1973.
Herb Kohl, 66, US Senator (D, Wisconsin), born Milwaukee, WI, Feb 7, 1935.
Pete Postlethwaite, 56, actor (*The Lost World: Jurassic Park*), born London, England, Feb 7, 1945.

FEBRUARY 8 — THURSDAY
Day 39 — 326 Remaining

BOY SCOUTS OF AMERICA FOUNDED: ANNIVERSARY. Feb 8, 1910. The Boy Scouts of America was founded at Washington, DC, by William Boyce, based on the work of Sir Robert Baden-Powell with the British Boy Scout Association. For more info: www.bsa.scouting.org.

FLORIDA STATE FAIR. Feb 8–19 (tentative). Florida State Fair Grounds, Tampa, FL. The fair features the best arts, crafts, competitive exhibits, equestrian shows, livestock, entertainment and food found in Florida. Also not to be missed is "Cracker Country," where cultural and architectural history has been preserved. Annually, in February. Est attendance: 500,000. For info: Sherry Powell, Mktg & Advertising Mgr, Florida State Fair, PO Box 11766, Tampa, FL 33680. Phone: (813) 621-7821 or (813) 622-PARK. Web: www.fl-ag.com/statefair.

JAPAN: HA-RI-KU-YO (NEEDLE MASS). Feb 8. Ha-Ri-Ku-Yo, a Needle Mass, may be observed on either Feb 8 or Dec 8. Girls do no needlework; instead they gather old and broken needles, which they dedicate to the Awashima Shrine at Wakayama. Girls pray to Awashima Myozin (their protecting deity) that their needlework, symbolic of love and marriage, will be good. Participation in the Needle Mass hopefully leads to a happy marriage.

JAPAN: SNOW FESTIVAL. Feb 8–12. Sapporo, Hokkaido. Huge, elaborate snow and ice sculptures are erected on the Odori-Koen Promenade.

MOON PHASE: FULL MOON. Feb 8. Moon enters Full Moon phase at 2:12 AM, EST.

	S	M	T	W	T	F	S
February					1	2	3
2001	4	5	6	7	8	9	10
	11	12	13	14	15	16	17
	18	19	20	21	22	23	24
	25	26	27	28			

100th DAY OF SCHOOL. Feb 8. Use your own school calendar to compute this date for your students. This day can help you teach lower elementary students the concept of 100. For activities that will facilitate this, visit users.aol.com/a100thday/ideas.html. The following books will also be helpful: *100 Days of School*, by Trudy Harris (Millbrook, 0-7613-1271-4, $21.90 Gr. K–2) and *The 100th Day of School*, by Angela Shelf Medearis (Scholastic, 0-590-25944-X, $3.99 Gr. K–2). Also see the November 1999 issue of *Book Links* for "Celebrating the One Hundredth Day of School."

OPERA DEBUT IN THE COLONIES: ANNIVERSARY. Feb 8, 1735. The first opera produced in the colonies was performed at the Courtroom, at Charleston, SC. The opera was *Flora; or the Hob in the Well*, written by Colley Cibber.

PERIGEAN SPRING TIDES. Feb 8. Spring tides, the highest possible tides, which occur when New Moon or Full Moon takes place within 24 hours of the moment the Moon is nearest Earth (perigee) in its monthly orbit at 2 PM, EST. The word spring refers not to the season but comes from the German word *springen*, "to rise up."

SHERMAN, WILLIAM TECUMSEH: BIRTH ANNIVERSARY. Feb 8, 1820. Born at Lancaster, OH, General Sherman is especially remembered for his devastating march through Georgia during the Civil War and his statement "War is hell." Died at New York, NY, Feb 14, 1891.

SPACE MILESTONE: *ARABSAT-1*. Feb 8, 1985. League of Arab States communications satellite launched into geosynchronous orbit from Kourou, French Guiana, by European Space Agency.

TU B'SHVAT. Feb 8. Hebrew calendar date: Shebat 15, 5761. The 15th day of the month of Shebat in the Hebrew calendar year is set aside as Hamishah Asar (New Year of the Trees or Jewish Arbor Day), a time to show respect and appreciation for trees and plants.

VERNE, JULES: BIRTH ANNIVERSARY. Feb 8, 1828. French writer, sometimes called "the father of science fiction," born at Nantes, France. Author of *Around the World in Eighty Days, Twenty Thousand Leagues Under the Sea* and many other novels. Died at Amiens, France, Mar 24, 1905.

BIRTHDAYS TODAY

Alonzo Mourning, 31, basketball player, born Chesapeake, VA, Feb 8, 1970.

FEBRUARY 9 — FRIDAY
Day 40 — 325 Remaining

HARRISON, WILLIAM HENRY: BIRTH ANNIVERSARY. Feb 9, 1773. Ninth president of the US (Mar 4–Apr 4, 1841). His term of office was the shortest in our nation's history—32 days. He was the first president to die in office (of pneumonia contracted during inaugural ceremonies). Born at Berkeley, VA, he died at Washington, DC, Apr 4, 1841.

BIRTHDAYS TODAY

David Gallagher, 16, actor ("7th Heaven"), born College Point, NY, Feb 9, 1985.
Joe Pesci, 58, actor (*Home Alone, Home Alone 2*), born Newark, NJ, Feb 9, 1943.

FEBRUARY 10 — SATURDAY
Day 41 — 324 Remaining

MALTA: FEAST OF ST. PAUL'S SHIPWRECK. Feb 10. Valletta. Holy day of obligation. Commemorates shipwreck of St. Paul on the north coast of Malta in AD 60.

TWENTY-FIFTH AMENDMENT TO US CONSTITUTION RATIFIED (PRESIDENTIAL SUCCESSION, DISABILITY): ANNIVERSARY. Feb 10, 1967. Procedures for presidential succession were further clarified by the 25th Amendment, along with provisions for continuity of power in the event of a disability or illness of the president. The 25th Amendment was ratified Feb 10, 1967.

BIRTHDAYS TODAY

Frank Keating, 57, Governor of Oklahoma (R), born St. Louis, MO, Feb 10, 1944.
E.L. Konigsburg, 71, author (Newbery for *The View From Saturday, From the Mixed-up Files of Mrs Basil E. Frankweiler*), born Elaine Lobl, New York, NY, Feb 10, 1930.

FEBRUARY 11 — SUNDAY
Day 42 — 323 Remaining

CAMEROON: YOUTH DAY. Feb 11. Public holiday.

EDISON, THOMAS ALVA: BIRTH ANNIVERSARY. Feb 11, 1847. American inventive genius and holder of more than 1,200 patents (including the incandescent electric lamp, phonograph, electric dynamo and key parts of many now-familiar devices such as the movie camera, telephone transmitter, etc). Edison said, "Genius is 1 percent inspiration and 99 percent perspiration." His birthday is now widely observed as Inventor's Day. Born at Milan, OH, and died at Menlo Park, NJ, Oct 18, 1931.

FULLER, MELVILLE WESTON: BIRTH ANNIVERSARY. Feb 11, 1833. Eighth chief justice of the US Supreme Court. Born at Augusta, ME, he died at Sorrento, ME, July 4, 1910.

HOMES FOR BIRDS WEEK. Feb 11–17. A week to encourage people to clean out, fix up and put up homes for wild birds. Annually, the third week in February. For info: John F. Gardner, Pres, Wild Bird Marketplace, 1891 Santa Barbara Dr, Ste 106, Lancaster, PA 17601. Phone: (717) 581-5310. Fax: (717) 581-5312. E-mail: jfg @wildbird.com. Web: www.wm-bird.com.

IRAN, ISLAMIC REPUBLIC OF: NATIONAL DAY. Feb 11. National holiday. Commemorates the founding of the republic in 1979.

JAPAN: NATIONAL FOUNDATION DAY: ANNIVERSARY. Feb 11. Marks the founding of the Japanese nation. In 1872 the government officially set Feb 11, 660 BC, as the date of accession to the throne of the Emperor Jimmu (said to be Japan's first emperor) and designated the day a national holiday by the name of Empire Day. The holiday was abolished after WWII, but was revived as National Foundation Day in 1966. Ceremonies are held with Their Imperial Majesties the Emperor and Empress, the Prime Minister and other dignitaries attending. National holiday.

MANDELA, NELSON: PRISON RELEASE: ANNIVERSARY. Feb 11, 1990. After serving more than 27½ years of a life sentence (convicted, with eight others, of sabotage and conspiracy to overthrow the government), South Africa's Nelson Mandela, 71 years old, walked away from the Victor Verster prison farm at Paarl, South Africa, a free man. He had survived the governmental system of apartheid. Mandela greeted a cheering throng of well-wishers, along with hundreds of millions of television viewers worldwide, with demands for an intensification of the struggle for equality for blacks, who make up nearly 75 percent of South Africa's population. For more info: www.anc.org.za/people/mandela.html.

★ **NATIONAL CHILD PASSENGER SAFETY AWARENESS WEEK.** Feb 11–17. Always the week in February containing Valentine's Day. For info: Office of Occupant Protection, Natl Highway Safety Administration, 400 Seventh St SW, Washington, DC 20590. Phone: (202) 366-9550.

SPACE MILESTONE: *OSUMI* (JAPAN). Feb 11, 1970. First Japanese satellite launched. Japan became fourth nation to send a satellite into space.

VATICAN CITY: INDEPENDENCE ANNIVERSARY. Feb 11, 1929. The Lateran Treaty, signed by Pietro Cardinal Gasparri and Benito Mussolini, guaranteed the independence of the State of Vatican City and recognized the sovereignty of the Holy See over it. Area is about 109 acres.

BIRTHDAYS TODAY

Brandy (Norwood), 22, singer, actress ("Cinderella," "Moesha"), born Macomb, MS, Feb 11, 1979.

Jeb Bush, 48, Governor of Florida (R), born Midland, TX, Feb 11, 1953.

Mel Carnahan, 67, Governor of Missouri (D), born Birch Tree, MO, Feb 11, 1934.

Matthew Lawrence, 21, actor ("Brotherly Love," "Boy Meets World"), born Abington, PA, Feb 11, 1980.

Mike Leavitt, 50, Governor of Utah (R), born Cedar City, UT, Feb 11, 1951.

Jane Yolen, 62, author (*Owl Moon*), born New York, NY, Feb 11, 1939.

February *2001*	S	M	T	W	T	F	S
					1	2	3
	4	5	6	7	8	9	10
	11	12	13	14	15	16	17
	18	19	20	21	22	23	24
	25	26	27	28			

FEBRUARY 12 — MONDAY
Day 43 — 322 Remaining

ADAMS, LOUISA CATHERINE JOHNSON: BIRTH ANNIVERSARY. Feb 12, 1775. Wife of John Quincy Adams, sixth president of the US. Born at London, England, she died at Washington, DC, May 14, 1852.

DARWIN, CHARLES ROBERT: BIRTH ANNIVERSARY. Feb 12, 1809. Author and naturalist, born at Shrewsbury, England. Best remembered for his books *On the Origin of Species by Means of Natural Selection, or the Preservation of Favoured Races in the Struggle for Life* and *The Descent of Man and Selection in Relation to Sex.* Died at Down, Kent, England, Apr 19, 1882. For more info: *Charles Darwin: Revolutionary Biologist*, by J. Edward Evans (Lerner, 0-8225-4914-X, $21.50 Gr. 6–9).

KOSCIUSKO, THADDEUS: BIRTH ANNIVERSARY. Feb 12, 1746. Polish patriot and American Revolutionary War figure. Born at Lithuania, he died at Solothurn, Switzerland, Oct 15, 1817. The governor of Massachusetts proclaims the first Sunday in February as Kosciusko Day (Feb 4 in 2001).

LINCOLN, ABRAHAM: BIRTH ANNIVERSARY. Feb 12, 1809. The 16th president of the US (Mar 4, 1861–Apr 15, 1865) and the first to be assassinated (on Good Friday, Apr 14, 1865, at Ford's Theatre at Washington, DC). His presidency encompassed the tragic Civil War. Especially remembered are his Emancipation Proclamation (Jan 1, 1863) and his Gettysburg Address (Nov 19, 1863). Born at Hardin County, KY, he died at Washington, DC, Apr 15, 1865. Lincoln's birthday is observed as part of President's Day in most states, but is a legal holiday in Florida, Illinois and Kentucky and an optional bank holiday in Iowa, Maryland, Michigan, Pennsylvania, Washington and West Virginia. See also: "Presidents' Day," (Feb 21). For more info: *Lincoln: A Photobiography*, by Russell Freedman (Houghton Mifflin, 0-89-919380-3, $17 Gr. 4–6) and *Lincoln: In His Own Words*, edited by Milton Meltzer (Harcourt Brace, 0-15-245437-3, $22.95 Gr. 6–8). For links to Lincoln sites on the web, go to: deil.lang.uiuc.edu/web.pages/holidays/lincoln.html.

LOST PENNY DAY. Feb 12. Today is set aside to put all of those pennies stashed in candy dishes, bowls and jars back in circulation. Take those pennies and give them to a shelter or agency that assists the homeless or your local Humane Society. Annually, on President Abraham Lincoln's birthday, the man depicted on the copper penny. [©1995] For info: Adrienne Sioux Koopersmith, 1437 W Rosemont, #1W, Chicago, IL 60660-1319. Phone: (773) 743-5341. Fax: (773) 743-5395. E-mail: adrienet@earthlink.net.

LUXEMBOURG: BURGSONNDEG. Feb 12. Young people build a huge bonfire on a hill to celebrate the victorious sun, marking the end of winter. A tradition dating to pre-Christian times.

NAACP FOUNDED: ANNIVERSARY. Feb 12, 1909. The National Association for the Advancement of Colored People was founded by W.E.B. Dubois and Ida Wells-Barnett, among others, to wage a militant campaign against lynching and other forms of racial oppression. Its legal wing brought many lawsuits that successfully challenged segregation in the 1950s and 60s.

SAFETYPUP'S® BIRTHDAY. Feb 12. This year Safetypup®, created by the National Child Safety Council, joyously celebrates his birthday by bringing safety awareness/education messages to children in a positive, nonthreatening manner. Safetypup® has achieved a wonderful balance of safety sense, caution and childlike enthusiasm about life and helping kids "Stay Safe and Sound." For info: Barbara Handley Huggett, Dir, NCSC, Research and Development, Box 1368, Jackson, MI 49204-1368. Phone: (517) 764-6070.

Ann Atwood, 88, author and illustrator (*Haiku: The Mood of Earth*), born California, Feb 12, 1913.

Ehud Barak, 59, Israeli prime minister, born Mishmar, Hasharon, Israel, Feb 12, 1942.

Judy Blume, 63, author (*Blubber, Superfudge*), born Elizabeth, NJ, Feb 12, 1938.

Joanna Kerns, 48, actress ("Growing Pains"), born San Francisco, CA, Feb 12, 1953.

Josephine Poole, 68, author (*Joan of Arc*), born London, England, Feb 12, 1933.

Christina Ricci, 21, actress (*Casper, Addams Family Values*), born Santa Monica, CA, Feb 12, 1980.

Arlen Specter, 71, US Senator (R, Pennsylvania), born Wichita, KS, Feb 12, 1930.

Jacqueline Woodson, 37, author (*I Hadn't Meant to Tell You This*), born Columbus, OH, Feb 12, 1964.

FEBRUARY 13 — TUESDAY

Day 44 — 321 Remaining

FIRST MAGAZINE PUBLISHED IN AMERICA: ANNIVERSARY. Feb 13, 1741. Andrew Bradford published *The American Magazine* just three days ahead of Benjamin Franklin's *General Magazine*.

GET A DIFFERENT NAME DAY. Feb 13. If you dislike your name, or merely find it boring, today is the day to adopt the moniker of your choice. [© 1999 by WPL] For info: Thomas or Ruth Roy, Wellness Permission League, 2418 Long Ln, Lebanon, PA 17046. Phone: (230) 332-4886. Fax: (230) 332-4886. E-mail: wellcat@supernet.com. Web: www.wellcat.com.

TRUMAN, BESS (ELIZABETH) VIRGINIA WALLACE: BIRTH ANNIVERSARY. Feb 13, 1885. Wife of Harry S Truman, 33rd president of the US. Born at Independence, MO and died there Oct 18, 1982.

WOOD, GRANT: BIRTH ANNIVERSARY. Feb 13, 1892. American artist, especially noted for his powerful realism and satirical paintings of the American scene, was born near Anamosa, IA. He was a printer, sculptor, woodworker and high school and college teacher. Among his best-remembered works are *American Gothic, Fall Plowing* and *Stone City.* Died at Iowa City, IA, Feb 12, 1942.

Janet Taylor Lisle, 54, author (*Afternoon of the Elves*), born Englewood, NJ, Feb 13, 1947.

Ouida Sebestyen, 77, author (*Words by Heart*), born Vernon, TX, Feb 13, 1924.

William Sleator, 56, author (*The Boy Who Reversed Himself*), born Havre de Grace, MD, Feb 13, 1945.

Simms Taback, 69, author and illustrator (*There Was an Old Lady Who Swallowed a Fly*), born New York, NY, Feb 13, 1932.

Chuck Yeager, 78, pilot who broke the sound barrier, born Myra, WV, Feb 13, 1923.

FEBRUARY 14 — WEDNESDAY

Day 45 — 320 Remaining

ARIZONA: ADMISSION DAY: ANNIVERSARY. Feb 14. Became the 48th state in 1912.

FERRIS WHEEL DAY. Feb 14, 1859. Anniversary of the birth of George Washington Gale Ferris, American engineer and inventor, at Galesburg, IL. Among his many accomplishments as a civil engineer, Ferris is best remembered as the inventor of the Ferris wheel, which he developed for the World's Columbian Exposition at Chicago, IL, in 1893. Built on the Midway Plaisance, the 250-feet-in-diameter Ferris wheel (with 36 coaches, each capable of carrying 40 passengers), proved one of the greatest attractions of the fair. It was America's answer to the Eiffel Tower of the Paris International Exposition of 1889. Ferris died at Pittsburgh, PA, Nov 22, 1896.

FIRST PRESIDENTIAL PHOTOGRAPH: ANNIVERSARY. Feb 14, 1849. President James Polk became the first US president to be photographed while in office. The photographer was Mathew B. Brady, who would become famous for his photography during the American Civil War.

MOON PHASE: LAST QUARTER. Feb 14. Moon enters Last Quarter phase at 10:23 PM, EST.

OREGON: ADMISSION DAY: ANNIVERSARY. Feb 14. Became 33rd state in 1859.

RACE RELATIONS DAY. Feb 14. A day designated by some churches to recognize the importance of interracial relations. Formerly was observed on Abraham Lincoln's birthday or on the Sunday preceding it. Since 1970 observance has generally been Feb 14.

READ TO YOUR CHILD DAY. Feb 14. Motto: "Show your kids you love them: Read to them." To encourage parents, teachers and other caregivers to engage in the wonderfully beneficial and delightfully fun practice of reading to children. A packet of materials is available, including ideas for campaigns to promote literacy, plus reproducible flyers on classroom reading, family reading at home and sharing books with babies. Flyers describe the benefits of read-aloud sessions, give tips for oral reading and list books people can read for more information. Annually, on Valentine's Day. For packet send business-sized, stamped, self-addressed envelope plus two first class stamps tucked inside (to cover photocopy expenses) to Dee Anderson, 1023 25 St, #1, Moline, IL 61265.

VALENTINE'S DAY. Feb 14. St. Valentine's Day celebrates the feasts of two Christian martyrs of this name. One, a priest and physician, was beheaded at Rome, Italy, Feb 14, AD 269, during the reign of Emperor Claudius II. Another Valentine, the Bishop of Terni, is said to have been beheaded, also at Rome, Feb 14 (possibly in a later year). Both history and legend are vague and contradictory about details of the Valentines and some say that Feb 14 was selected for the celebration of Christian martyrs as a diversion from the ancient pagan observance of Lupercalia. An old legend has it that birds choose their mates on Valentine's Day. Now it is one of the most widely observed unofficial holidays. It is an occasion for the exchange of gifts (usually books, flowers or sweets) and greeting cards with affectionate or humorous messages. For links to Valentine's Day sites on the web go to: deil.lang.uiuc.edu/web.pages/holidays/valentine.html.

Drew Bledsoe, 29, football player, born Ellensburg, WA, Feb 14, 1972.

Odds Bodkin, 48, storyteller, author (*The Crane Wife*), born New York, NY, Feb 14, 1953.

Judd Gregg, 54, US Senator (R, New Hampshire), born Nashua, NH, Feb 14, 1947.

Jamake Highwater, 59, author (*Anpao: An American Indian Odyssey*), born Glacier County, MT, Feb 14, 1942.

Phyllis Root, 52, author (*What Baby Wants*), born Fort Wayne, IN, Feb 14, 1949.

Donna Shalala, 60, US Secretary of Health and Human Services (Clinton administration), born Cleveland, OH, Feb 14, 1941.

Paul O. Zelinsky, 48, illustrator (Caldecott for *Rapunzel*, *Rumpelstiltskin*), born Evanston, IL, Feb 14, 1953.

FEBRUARY 15 — THURSDAY

Day 46 — 319 Remaining

CLARK, ABRAHAM: 275th BIRTH ANNIVERSARY. Feb 15, 1726. Signer of the Declaration of Independence, farmer and lawyer. Born at Elizabethtown, NJ and died there Sept 15, 1794.

GALILEI, GALILEO: BIRTH ANNIVERSARY. Feb 15, 1564. Physicist and astronomer who helped overthrow medieval concepts of the world, born at Pisa, Italy. He proved the theory that all bodies, large and small, descend at equal speed and gathered evidence to support Copernicus's theory that the Earth and other planets revolve around the sun. Galileo died at Florence, Italy, Jan 8, 1642. For more info: *Starry Messenger*, by Peter Sis (Farrar, Straus, 0-374-37191-1, $16 Gr. 2–6).

RIVER OF WORDS ENVIRONMENTAL POETRY AND ART CONTEST. Feb 15. Deadline for submissions for this annual poetry and art contest on the theme of watersheds. Open to students K–12. Co-sponsored by the International Rivers Network and the Library of Congress Center for the Book. Teacher's Guide and teacher training workshops available. For entry form, contact the following: River of Words Project, PO Box 4000-J, Berkeley, CA 94704. Phone: (510) 433-7020. Fax: (510) 848-1008. E-mail: row@irn.org. Web: www.irn.org.

SUTTER, JOHN AUGUSTUS: BIRTH ANNIVERSARY. Feb 15, 1803. Born at Kandern, Germany, Sutter established the first white settlement on the site of Sacramento, CA, in 1839, and owned a large tract of land there, which he named New Helvetia. The first great gold strike in the US was on his property, at Sutter's Mill, Jan 24, 1848. His land was soon overrun by gold seekers who, he claimed, slaughtered his cattle and stole or destroyed his property. Sutter was bankrupt by 1852. Died at Washington, DC, June 18, 1880.

Norman Bridwell, 73, author and illustrator (*Clifford, the Big Red Dog*), born Kokomo, IN, Feb 15, 1928.

Matt Groening, 47, cartoonist ("The Simpsons"), born Portland, OR, Feb 15, 1954.

Doris Orgel, 72, author (*The Devil in Vienna*), born Vienna, Austria, Feb 15, 1929.

February 2001	S	M	T	W	T	F	S
					1	2	3
	4	5	6	7	8	9	10
	11	12	13	14	15	16	17
	18	19	20	21	22	23	24
	25	26	27	28			

FEBRUARY 16 — FRIDAY

Day 47 — 318 Remaining

HEART 2 HEART DAY. Feb 16. Confide something to your diary—start young and you'll write a whole book before you know it! Annually, two days after Valentine's Day. For info: Fine Print Publishing Co, PO Box 916401, Longwood, FL 32791-6401. Phone: (407) 814-7777. Fax: (407) 814-7677.

LITHUANIA: INDEPENDENCE DAY. Feb 16. National Day. The anniversary of Lithuania's declaration of independence in 1918 is observed as the Baltic state's Independence Day. In 1940, Lithuania became a part of the Soviet Union under an agreement between Joseph Stalin and Adolf Hitler. On Mar 11, 1990, Lithuania declared its independence from the Soviet Union, the first of the Soviet republics to do so. After demanding independence, Lithuania set up a border police force and aided young men in efforts to avoid the Soviet military draft, prompting then Soviet leader Mikhail Gorbachev to send tanks into the capital of Vilnius and impose oil and gas embargoes. In the wake of the failed coup attempt in Moscow, Aug 19, 1991, Lithuanian independence finally was recognized.

THE NATIONAL CONFERENCE ON EDUCATION. Feb 16–19. Orlando, FL. 133rd annual conference. For info: American Assn of School Administrators, 1801 N Moore St, Arlington, VA 22209. Phone: (703) 528-0700. Web: www.aasa.org.

WILSON, HENRY: BIRTH ANNIVERSARY. Feb 16, 1812. The 18th vice president of the US (1873–75). Born at Farmington, NH, died at Washington, DC, Nov 22, 1875.

Jerome Bettis, 29, football player, born Detroit, MI, Feb 16, 1972.

LeVar Burton, 44, actor, host ("Reading Rainbow"), born Landsthul, Germany, Feb 16, 1957.

FEBRUARY 17 — SATURDAY

Day 48 — 317 Remaining

GERONIMO: DEATH ANNIVERSARY. Feb 17, 1909. American Indian of the Chiricahua (Apache) tribe was born about 1829 in Arizona. He was the leader of a small band of warriors whose devastating raids in Arizona, New Mexico and Mexico caused the US Army to send 5,000 men to recapture him after his first escape. He was confined at Fort Sill, OK, where he died Feb 17, 1909, after dictating, for publication, the story of his life.

NATIONAL PTA FOUNDERS' DAY: ANNIVERSARY. Feb 17, 1897. Celebrates the PTA's founding by Phoebe Apperson Hearst and Alice McLellan Birney. For info: Natl PTA, 330 N Wabash, Ste 2100, Chicago, IL 60611. Phone: (312) 670-6782. Fax: (312) 670-6783. E-mail: info@pta.org. Web: www.pta.org.

Vanessa Atler, 19, gymnast, born Valencia, CA, Feb 17, 1982.

Joseph Gordon-Levitt, 20, actor ("3rd Rock from the Sun," *Halloween H20*), born Los Angeles, CA, Feb 17, 1981.

Michael Jeffrey Jordan, 38, former basketball player, former minor league baseball player, born Brooklyn, NY, Feb 17, 1963.

Robert Newton Peck, 73, author (the Soup series, *A Day No Pigs Would Die*), born Vermont, Feb 17, 1928.

Chaim Potok, 72, author (*Zebra and Other Stories*), born Brooklyn, NY, Feb 17, 1929.

Craig Thomas, 68, US Senator (R, Wyoming), born Cody, WY, Feb 17, 1933.

FEBRUARY 18 — SUNDAY
Day 49 — 316 Remaining

COW MILKED WHILE FLYING IN AN AIRPLANE: ANNIVERSARY. Feb 18, 1930. Elm Farm Ollie became the first cow to fly in an airplane. During the flight, which was attended by reporters, she was milked and the milk was sealed in paper containers and parachuted over St. Louis, MO.

DAVIS, JEFFERSON: INAUGURATION ANNIVERSARY. Feb 18, 1861. In the years before the Civil War, Jefferson Davis was the acknowledged leader of the Southern bloc in the US Senate and a champion of states' rights, but he had little to do with the secessionist movement until after his home state of Mississippi joined the Confederacy Jan 9, 1861. Davis withdrew from the Senate that same day. He was unanimously chosen as president of the Confederacy's provisional government and inaugurated at Montgomery, AL, Feb 18. Within the next year he was elected to a six-year term by popular vote and was inaugurated a second time Feb 22, 1862, at Richmond, VA.

GAMBIA: INDEPENDENCE DAY: ANNIVERSARY. Feb 18, 1965. National holiday. Independence from Britain granted. Referendum in April 1970 established Gambia as a republic within the Commonwealth.

NATIONAL ENGINEERS WEEK. Feb 18–24. This annual observance, cosponsored by 74 national engineering societies and 61 major national corporations, will feature classroom programs in elementary and secondary schools throughout the US, shopping mall exhibits, engineering workplace tours and other events. For more info: Natl Engineers Week Headquarters, 1420 King St, Alexandria, VA 22314. Phone: (703) 684-2852. E-mail: eweek @nspe.org. Web: www.eweek.org.

PLANET PLUTO DISCOVERY: ANNIVERSARY. Feb 18, 1930. Pluto, the ninth planet, was discovered by astronomer Clyde Tombaugh at the Lowell Observatory at Flagstaff, AZ. It was given the name of the Roman god of the underworld. For more info, go to Nine Planets: Multimedia Tour of the Solar System at www.seds.org/billa/tnp.

BIRTHDAYS TODAY

Barbara Joosse, 52, author (*Ghost Trap: A Wild Willie Mystery*), born Grafton, WI, Feb 18, 1949.

John William Warner, 74, US Senator (R, Virginia), born Washington, DC, Feb 18, 1927.

FEBRUARY 19 — MONDAY
Day 50 — 315 Remaining

BROTHERHOOD/SISTERHOOD WEEK. Feb 18–24. A kick-off period for programs emphasizing a commitment to brotherhood/sisterhood. The National Program Office develops educational materials for use during this period that can be used year round. Annually, the third full week in February. Sponsor: The National Conference for Community and Justice (founded as the National Conference of Christians and Jews). For info: The Natl Conference for Community and Justice, 475 Park Ave South, New York, NY 10016. Phone: (212) 545-1300.

COPERNICUS, NICOLAUS: BIRTH ANNIVERSARY. Feb 19, 1473. Polish astronomer and priest who revolutionized scientific thought with what came to be called the Copernican theory, that placed the sun instead of the Earth at the center of our planetary system. Born at Torun, Poland, died at East Prussia, May 24, 1543.

JAPANESE INTERNMENT: ANNIVERSARY. Feb 19, 1942. As a result of President Franklin Roosevelt's Executive Order 9066, some 110,000 Japanese-Americans living in coastal Pacific areas were placed in concentration camps in remote areas of Arizona, Arkansas, inland California, Colorado, Idaho, Utah and Wyoming. The interned Japanese-Americans (two-thirds were US citizens) lost an estimated $400 million in property. They were allowed to return to their homes Jan 2, 1945. For more info: *Life in a Japanese American Internment Camp*, by Diane Yancey (Lucent, 1-56006-345-9, $17.96 Gr. 6–12). *See* Curriculum Connection.

PRESIDENTS' DAY. Feb 19. Presidents' Day observes the birthdays of George Washington (Feb 22) and Abraham Lincoln (Feb 12). With the adoption of the Monday Holiday Law (which moved the observance of George Washington's birthday from Feb 22 each year to the third Monday in February), some of the specific significance of the event was lost and added impetus was given to the popular description of that holiday as Presidents' Day. Present usage often regards Presidents' Day as a day to honor all former presidents of the US. While the federal holiday still is George Washington's birthday, many states now declare Presidents' Day to be a holiday. Annually, the third Monday in February.

FEBRUARY 19
JAPANESE INTERNMENT

President Franklin D. Roosevelt signed Executive Order 9066 on this date in 1942. This order resulted in the internment of Japanese Americans who lived along the United States' western coast into concentration camps located in several western states (see Feb 19).

For many years, the subject was not discussed and was excluded from mention in history textbooks. In recent years, concerned people have worked to educate others about this period of our nation's history.

Classroom discussion could center around the political and social climates that provided the seeds that led to internment. Older students can debate what constitutes a government's reasonable right to protect its citizens from internal threat versus over-reaction and abrogation of a citizen's rights. They could compare concentration camps established at different times in history. Millions of people were imprisoned in the Soviet Gulags from the late 1920s up into the 1950s. In the 1990s, concentration camps were established by each of the warring factions in Bosnia-Herzegovina.

Junior high school students might do a literature comparison of World War II concentration camps. Compare and contrast: *The Devil's Arithmetic*, by Jane Yolen (Puffin, 0-14-034535-3, $4.99 Gr. 5–9); the biographical *Journey to Topaz*, by Yoshiko Uchida (Creative Arts, 0-916870-85-5, $9.95 Gr. 4–12); and *Beyond Paradise*, by Jane Hertenstein (Morrow, 0-688-16381-5, $16. Gr. 7–10) the story of an American girl imprisoned in a Japanese-run camp in the Philippines.

Students can research the United States' government's efforts to provide remuneration to those who were interned and their families.

Other literature connections include: *The Children of Topaz: The Story of a Japanese-American Internment Camp Based on a Classroom Diary*, by Michael O. Tunnell and George Chilcoat (Holiday House, 0-8234-1239-3, $16.95 Gr. 4–7); and the fictional *The Journal of Ben Uchida*, by Barry Denenberg (Scholastic, 0-590-48531-8, $10.95 Gr. 6–9).

WASHINGTON, GEORGE: BIRTHDAY OBSERVANCE (LEGAL HOLIDAY). Feb 19. Legal public holiday (Public Law 90–363 sets Washington's birthday observance on the third Monday in February each year—applicable to federal employees and to the District of Columbia). Observed on this day in all states. See also: "Washington, George: Birth Anniversary" (Feb 22). For links to websites about this holiday and George Washington, go to: deil.lang.uiuc.edu/web.pages/holidays/washington.html.

BIRTHDAYS TODAY

Jeff Daniels, 46, actor (*101 Dalmatians, Fly Away Home*), born Chelsea, MI, Feb 19, 1955.

Jill Krementz, 61, author and photographer (*A Very Young Dancer*, the How It Feels series), born New York, NY, Feb 19, 1940.

FEBRUARY 20 — TUESDAY
Day 51 — 314 Remaining

ADAMS, ANSEL: BIRTH ANNIVERSARY. Feb 20, 1902. American photographer, known for his photographs of Yosemite National Park, born at San Francisco, CA. Adams died at Monterey, CA, Apr 22, 1984.

DOUGLASS, FREDERICK: DEATH ANNIVERSARY. Feb 20, 1895. American journalist, orator and antislavery leader. Born at Tuckahoe, MD, probably in February 1817. Died at Anacostia Heights, Washington, DC. His original name before his escape from slavery was Frederick Augustus Washington Bailey.

NORTHERN HEMISPHERE HOODIE-HOO DAY. Feb 20. At high noon (local time) citizens are asked to go outdoors and yell "Hoodie-Hoo" to chase away winter and make ready for spring, one month away. [© 1999 by WH] For info: Tom or Ruth Roy, Wellcat Holidays, 2418 Long Ln, Lebanon, PA 17046. Phone: (230) 332-4886. E-mail: wellcat@supernet.com. Web: www.wellcat.com.

PISCES, THE FISH. Feb 20–Mar 20. In the astronomical/astrological zodiac, which divides the sun's apparent orbit into 12 segments, the period Feb 20–Mar 20 is identified, traditionally, as the sun sign of Pisces, the Fish. The ruling planet is Neptune.

SPACE MILESTONE: *FRIENDSHIP 7* (US): FIRST AMERICAN TO ORBIT EARTH. Feb 20, 1962. John Herschel Glenn, Jr, became the first American, and the third man, to orbit Earth. Aboard the capsule *Friendship 7*, he made three orbits of Earth. Spacecraft was *Mercury-Atlas 6*. In 1998 the 77-year-old Glenn went into space once again on the space shuttle *Discovery* to study the effects of aging.

SPACE MILESTONE: *MIR* SPACE STATION (USSR): 15th ANNIVERSARY. Feb 20, 1986. A "third-generation" orbiting space station, *Mir* (Peace), was launched without crew from the Baikonur space center at Leninsk, Kazakhstan. Believed to be 40 feet long, weigh 47 tons and have six docking ports. Russian and American crews used the station for 13 years. After many equipment failures in 1998, the Russians took Mir out of service in August 1999. See also: "Space Milestone: *Mir* Abandoned (USSR)" (Aug 28).

STUDENT VOLUNTEER DAY. Feb 20. To honor students who give of themselves and of their personal time to improve the lives of others and their communities. Annually, Feb 20. Est attendance: 250. For info: Susquehanna Univ, Center for Service Learning and Volunteer Programs, 514 University Ave, Selinsgrove, PA 17870-1001. Phone: (717) 372-4139. Fax: (717) 372-2745. E-mail: woodsd@susqu.edu.

BIRTHDAYS TODAY

Charles Barkley, 38, former basketball player, born Leeds, AL, Feb 20, 1963.

Rosemary Harris, 78, author (*The Moon in the Cloud*), born London, England, Feb 20, 1923.

Brian Littrell, 26, singer (Backstreet Boys), born Lexington, KY, Feb 20, 1975.

Mitch McConnell, 59, US Senator (R, Kentucky), born Colbert County, AL, Feb 20, 1942.

FEBRUARY 21 — WEDNESDAY
Day 52 — 313 Remaining

BANGLADESH: MARTYRS' DAY. Feb 21. National mourning day or Shaheed Day in memory of martyrs of the Bengali Language Movement in 1952.

BATTLE OF VERDUN: ANNIVERSARY. Feb 21–Dec 18, 1916. The German High Command launched an offensive on the Western Front at Verdun, France which became WWI's single longest battle. An estimated one million men were killed, decimating both the German and French armies.

FIRST WOMAN TO GRADUATE FROM DENTAL SCHOOL: ANNIVERSARY. Feb 21, 1866. Lucy Hobbs became the first woman to graduate from a dental school at Cincinnati, OH.

WASHINGTON MONUMENT DEDICATED: ANNIVERSARY. Feb 21, 1885. Monument to the first president was dedicated at Washington, DC.

BIRTHDAYS TODAY

Jim Aylesworth, 58, author (*The Gingerbread Man*), born Jacksonville, FL, Feb 21, 1943.

Patricia Hermes, 65, author (*When Snow Lay Soft on the Mountain*), born Brooklyn, NY, Feb 21, 1936.

Jennifer Love Hewitt, 22, actress (*I Know What You Did Last Summer*, "Party of Five"), born Waco, TX, Feb 21, 1979.

Victor Martinez, 47, author (National Book Award for *Parrot in the Oven: Mi Vida*), born Fresno, CA, Feb 21, 1954.

Olympia J. Snowe, 54, US Senator (R, Maine), born Augusta, ME, Feb 21, 1947.

FEBRUARY 22 — THURSDAY
Day 53 — 312 Remaining

BADEN-POWELL, ROBERT: BIRTH ANNIVERSARY. Feb 22, 1857. British army officer who founded the Boy Scouts and Girl Guides. Born at London, England, he died at Kenya, Africa, Jan 8, 1941.

MONTGOMERY BOYCOTT ARRESTS: 45th ANNIVERSARY. Feb 22, 1956. On Feb 20 white city leaders of Montgomery, AL, issued an ultimatum to black organizers of the three-month-old Montgomery bus boycott. They said if the boycott ended immediately there would be "no retaliation whatsoever." If it did not end, it was made clear they would begin arresting black leaders. Two days later, 80 well-known boycotters, including Rosa Parks, Martin Luther King, Jr and E.D. Nixon, marched to the sheriff's office in the county courthouse, where

	S	M	T	W	T	F	S
February					1	2	3
2001	4	5	6	7	8	9	10
	11	12	13	14	15	16	17
	18	19	20	21	22	23	24
	25	26	27	28			

they gave themselves up for arrest. They were booked, finger-printed and photographed. The next day the story was carried by newspapers all over the world.

SAINT LUCIA: INDEPENDENCE DAY: ANNIVERSARY. Feb 22. National holiday. Commemorates independence from Britain in 1979.

WADLOW, ROBERT PERSHING: BIRTH ANNIVERSARY. Feb 22, 1918. Tallest man in recorded history, born at Alton, IL. Though only 9 lbs at birth, by age 10 Wadlow already stood more than 6 feet tall and weighed 210 lbs. When Wadlow died at age 22, he was a remarkable 8 feet 11.1 inches tall, 490 lbs. His gentle, friendly manner in the face of constant public attention earned him the name "Gentle Giant." Wadlow died July 15, 1940, at Manistee, MI, of complications resulting from a foot infection.

WASHINGTON, GEORGE: BIRTH ANNIVERSARY. Feb 22, 1732. First president of the US ("First in war, first in peace and first in the hearts of his countrymen" in the words of Henry "Light-Horse Harry" Lee). Born at Westmoreland County, VA, Feb 22, 1732 (New Style). When he was born the colonies were still using the Julian (Old Style) calendar and the year began in March, so the date on the calendar when he was born was Feb 11, 1731. He died at Mount Vernon, VA, Dec 14, 1799. See also: "Washington, George: Birthday Observance (Legal Holiday)" (Feb 19 in 2001).

WOOLWORTHS FIRST OPENED: ANNIVERSARY. Feb 22, 1879. The first chain store, Woolworths, opened at Utica, NY. In 1997, the closing of the chain was announced.

BIRTHDAYS TODAY

Drew Barrymore, 26, actress (*E.T.: The Extra Terrestrial, The Wedding Singer*), born Los Angeles, CA, Feb 22, 1975.

Michael Te Pei Chang, 29, tennis player, born Hoboken, NJ, Feb 22, 1972.

Lisa Fernandez, 30, softball player, born Long Beach, CA, Feb 22, 1971.

William Frist, 49, US Senator (R, Tennessee), born Nashville, TN, Feb 22, 1952.

Edward Moore (Ted) Kennedy, 69, US Senator (D, Massachusetts), born Boston, MA, Feb 22, 1932.

Jayson Williams, 33, basketball player, born Ritter, SC, Feb 22, 1968.

FEBRUARY 23 — FRIDAY
Day 54 — 311 Remaining

BRUNEI DARUSSALAM: NATIONAL DAY. Feb 23. National holiday.

DUBOIS, W.E.B.: BIRTH ANNIVERSARY. Feb 23, 1868. William Edward Burghardt Dubois, American educator and leader of the movement for black equality. Born at Great Barrington, MA, he died at Accra, Ghana, Aug 27, 1963. "The cost of liberty," he wrote in 1909, "is less than the price of repression."

FIRST CLONING OF AN ADULT ANIMAL: ANNIVERSARY. Feb 23, 1997. Researchers in Scotland announced the first cloning of an adult animal, a lamb they named Dolly with a genetic makeup identical to that of her mother. This led to worldwide speculation about the possibility of human cloning. On Mar 4, President Clinton imposed a ban on the federal funding of human cloning research.

GUYANA: ANNIVERSARY OF REPUBLIC. Feb 23, 1970. National holiday.

HANDEL, GEORGE FREDERICK: BIRTH ANNIVERSARY. Feb 23, 1685. Born at Halle, Saxony, Germany, Handel and Bach, born the same year, were perhaps the greatest masters of Baroque music. Handel's most frequently performed work is the oratorio *Messiah*, which was first heard in 1742. He died at London, England, Apr 14, 1759. See also: "Bach, Johann Sebastian: Birth Anniversary" (Mar 21).

MOON PHASE: NEW MOON. Feb 23. Moon enters New Moon phase at 3:21 AM, EST.

TAYLOR, GEORGE: DEATH ANNIVERSARY. Feb 23, 1781. Signer of the Declaration of Independence. Born 1716 at British Isles (exact date unknown). Died at Easton, PA.

BIRTHDAYS TODAY

Laura Geringer, 53, author (the Myth Men series), born New York, NY, Feb 23, 1948.

Patricia Richardson, 49, actress ("Home Improvement"), born Bethesda, MD, Feb 23, 1952.

Rodney Slater, 46, US Secretary of Transportation (Clinton administration), born Tutwyler, MS, Feb 23, 1955.

FEBRUARY 24 — SATURDAY
Day 55 — 310 Remaining

BRAZIL: CARNIVAL. Feb 24–27. Especially in Rio de Janeiro, this carnival is one of the great folk festivals, and the big annual event in the life of Brazilians. Begins on Saturday night before Ash Wednesday and continues through Shrove Tuesday.

ESTONIA: INDEPENDENCE DAY. Feb 24. National holiday. Commemorates declaration of independence from the Soviet Union in 1918. However, independence was brief; Estonia was to be part of the Soviet Union until 1991.

FRENCH WEST INDIES: CARNIVAL. Feb 24–28. Martinique. For five days, business comes to a halt. Streets spill over with parties and parades. Carnival Queen is elected. For info: Ms Muriel Wiltord, Martinique Promo Bureau, 444 Madison Ave, 16th Floor, New York, NY 10022. Phone: (800) 391-4909. Fax: (212) 838-7855. E-mail: martinique@nyo.com. Web: www.martinique.org.

GREGORIAN CALENDAR DAY: ANNIVERSARY. Feb 24, 1582. Pope Gregory XIII, enlisting the expertise of distinguished astronomers and mathematicians, issued a bill correcting the Julian calendar that was then 10 days in error. The new calendar named for him, the Gregorian calendar, became effective Oct 4, 1582, in most Catholic countries, in 1752 in Britain and the American colonies, in 1918 in Russia and in 1923 in Greece. It is the most widely used calendar in the world today. See also: "Calendar Adjustment Day: Anniversary" (Sept 2) and "Gregorian Calendar Adjustment: Anniversary" (Oct 4).

GRIMM, WILHELM CARL: BIRTH ANNIVERSARY. Feb 24, 1786. Mythologist and author, born at Hanau, Germany. Best remembered for *Grimm's Fairy Tales*, in collaboration with his brother, Jacob. Died at Berlin, Germany, Dec 16, 1859. See also: "Grimm, Jacob: Birth Anniversary" (Jan 4).

JOHNSON IMPEACHMENT PROCEEDINGS: ANNIVERSARY. Feb 24, 1867. In a showdown over reconstruction policy following the Civil War, the House of Representatives voted to impeach President Andrew Johnson. During the two years following the end of the war, the Republican-controlled Congress had sought to severely punish the South. Congress passed the Reconstruction Act that divided the South into five military districts headed by officers who were to take their orders from General Grant, the head of the army, instead of from President Johnson. In addition, Congress passed the Tenure of Office Act, which required Senate approval before Johnson could remove any official whose appointment was originally approved by the Senate. Johnson vetoed this act but the veto was overridden by Congress. To test the constitutionality of the act, Johnson dismissed Secretary of War Edwin Stanton, triggering the impeachment vote. On Mar 5, 1868, the Senate convened as a court to hear the charges against President Johnson. The Senate vote of 35–19 fell one vote short of the two-thirds majority necessary for impeachment. For more info: www.law.umkc.edu/faculty/projects/ftrials /ftrials.htm.

WAGNER, HONUS: BIRTH ANNIVERSARY. Feb 24, 1874. American baseball great, born John Peter Wagner at Carnegie, PA. Nicknamed the "Flying Dutchman," Wagner was among the first five players elected to the Baseball Hall of Fame in 1936. Died at Carnegie, Dec 6, 1955.

BIRTHDAYS TODAY

Beth Broderick, 42, actress ("Sabrina, the Teenage Witch"), born Long Beach, CA, Feb 24, 1959.

Lleyton Hewitt, 20, tennis player, born Adelaide, Australia, Feb 24, 1981.

Steven Jobs, 46, founder of Apple computer company, born Los Altos, CA, Feb 24, 1955.

Joseph I. Lieberman, 59, US Senator (D, Connecticut), born Stamford, CT, Feb 24, 1942.

George Ryan, 67, Governor of Illinois (R), born Maquoketa, IA, Feb 24, 1934.

Don Siegelman, 55, Governor of Alabama (D), born Mobile, AL, Feb 24, 1946.

FEBRUARY 25 — SUNDAY

Day 56 — 309 Remaining

CLAY BECOMES HEAVYWEIGHT CHAMP: ANNIVERSARY. Feb 25, 1964. Twenty-two-year-old Cassius Clay (later Muhammad Ali) became world heavyweight boxing champion by defeating Sonny Liston. At the height of his athletic career Ali was well known for both his fighting ability and personal style. His most famous saying was, "I am the greatest!" In 1967 he was convicted of violating the Selective Service Act and was stripped of his title for refusing to be inducted into the armed services during the Vietnam War. Ali cited religious convictions as his reason

	February 2001	S	M	T	W	T	F	S
						1	2	3
		4	5	6	7	8	9	10
		11	12	13	14	15	16	17
		18	19	20	21	22	23	24
		25	26	27	28			

for refusal. In 1971 the Supreme Court reversed the conviction. Ali is the only fighter to win the heavyweight title three separate times. He defended that title nine times.

FASCHING SUNDAY. Feb 25. Germany and Austria. The last Sunday before Lent.

ITALY: CARNIVAL WEEK. Feb 25–Mar 3. Milan. Carnival week is held according to local tradition, with shows and festive events for children on Tuesday and Thursday. Parades of floats, figures in the costume of local folk characters Meneghin and Cecca, parties and more traditional events are held on Saturday. Annually, the Sunday–Saturday of Ash Wednesday week.

KUWAIT: NATIONAL DAY. Feb 25. National holiday.

NATIONAL BANK CHARTERED BY CONGRESS: ANNIVERSARY. Feb 25, 1791. The First Bank of the US at Philadelphia, PA, was chartered. Proposed as a national (or central) bank by Alexander Hamilton, it lost its charter in 1811. The Second Bank of the US received a charter in 1816 which expired in 1836. Since that time, the US has had no central bank. Central banking functions are carried out by the Federal Reserve System, established in 1913.

RENOIR, PIERRE AUGUSTE: BIRTH ANNIVERSARY. Feb 25, 1841. Impressionist painter, born at Limoges, France, Renoir's paintings are known for their joy and sensuousness as well as his use of light. In his later years he was crippled by arthritis and would paint with the brush strapped to his hand. He died at Cagnes-sur-Mer, Provence, France, Dec 17, 1919.

SHROVETIDE. Feb 25–27. The three days before Ash Wednesday: Shrove Sunday, Monday and Tuesday—a time for confession and for festivity before the beginning of Lent.

BIRTHDAYS TODAY

Cynthia Voigt, 59, author (Newbery for *Dicey's Song*), born Boston, MA, Feb 25, 1942.

FEBRUARY 26 — MONDAY

Day 57 — 308 Remaining

CARNIVAL. Feb 26–27. Period of festivities, feasts, foolishness and gaiety immediately before Lent begins on Ash Wednesday. Ordinarily Carnival includes only Fasching (the Feast of Fools), being the Monday and Tuesday immediately preceding Ash Wednesday. The period of Carnival may also be extended to include longer periods in some areas.

CODY, WILLIAM FREDERIC "BUFFALO BILL": BIRTH ANNIVERSARY. Feb 26, 1846. American frontiersman who claimed to have killed more than 4,000 buffaloes, born at Scott

County, IA. Subject of many heroic yarns, Cody became successful as a showman, taking his Wild West Show across the US and to Europe. Died Jan 10, 1917, at Denver, CO.

CYPRUS: GREEN MONDAY. Feb 26. Green, or Clean, Monday is the first Monday of Lent on the Orthodox calendar. Lunch in the fields, with bread, olives and uncooked vegetables and no meat or dairy products.

DENMARK: STREET URCHINS' CARNIVAL. Feb 26. Observed on Shrove Monday.

FASCHING. Feb 26–27. In Germany and Austria, Fasching, also called Fasnacht, Fasnet or Feast of Fools, is a Shrovetide festival with processions of masked figures, both beautiful and grotesque. Always the two days (Rose Monday and Shrove Tuesday) between Fasching Sunday and Ash Wednesday.

FEDERAL COMMUNICATIONS COMMISSION CREATED: ANNIVERSARY. Feb 26, 1934. President Franklin D. Roosevelt ordered the creation of a Communications Commission, which became the FCC. It was created by Congress June 19, 1934 to oversee communication by radio, wire or cable. TV and satellite communication later became part of its charge.

GRAND CANYON NATIONAL PARK ESTABLISHED: ANNIVERSARY. Feb 26, 1919. By an act of Congress, Grand Canyon National Park was established. An immense gorge cut through the high plateaus of northwest Arizona by the raging Colorado River and covering 1,218,375 acres, Grand Canyon National Park is considered one of the most spectacular natural phenomena in the world. For more info: www.nps.gov/grca.

ICELAND: BUN DAY. Feb 26. Children invade homes in the morning with colorful sticks and receive gifts of whipped cream buns (on the Monday before Shrove Tuesday).

ORTHODOX LENT. Feb 26–Apr 7. Great Lent or Easter Lent, observed by Eastern Orthodox Churches, lasts until Holy Week begins on Orthodox Palm Sunday (Apr 8).

SHROVE MONDAY. Feb 26. The Monday before Ash Wednesday. In Germany and Austria, this is called Rose Monday.

STRAUSS, LEVI: BIRTH ANNIVERSARY. Feb 26, 1829. Bavarian immigrant Levi Strauss created the world's first pair of jeans—Levi's 501 jeans—for California's gold miners in 1850. Born at Buttenheim, Bavaria, Germany, he died in 1902.

TRINIDAD: CARNIVAL. Feb 26–27. Port of Spain. Called by islanders "the mother of all carnivals," a special tradition that brings together people from all over the world in an incredible colorful setting that includes the world's most celebrated calypsonians, steel band players, costume designers and masqueraders. Annually, the two days before Ash Wednesday. For info: Natl Carnival Commission, Tourism and Industrial Development Co, Administration Bldg, Queen Park Savannah, Port of Spain, Trinidad and Tobago, West Indies. Phone: (809) 623-1932. Fax: (809) 623-3848.

BIRTHDAYS TODAY

Sarah Ezer, 20, actress ("The Adventures of Shirley Holmes: Detective"), born Vancouver, British Columbia, Canada, Feb 26, 1981.

Marshall Faulk, 28, football player, born New Orleans, LA, Feb 26, 1973.

Sharon Bell Mathis, 64, author (*The Hundred Penny Box*), born Atlantic City, NJ, Feb 26, 1937.

Jenny Thompson, 28, Olympic swimmer, born Dover, NH, Feb 26, 1973.

Bernard Wolf, 71, author (*HIV Positive*), born New York, NY, Feb 26, 1930.

FEBRUARY 27 — TUESDAY
Day 58 — 307 Remaining

DOMINICAN REPUBLIC: INDEPENDENCE DAY. Feb 27. National Day. Independence gained in 1844 with the withdrawal of Haitians, who had controlled the area for 22 years.

ICELAND: BURSTING DAY. Feb 27. Feasts with salted mutton and thick pea soup. (Shrove Tuesday.)

KUWAIT LIBERATED AND 100-HOUR WAR ENDS: 10th ANNIVERSARY. Feb 27, 1991. Allied troops entered Kuwait City, Kuwait, four days after launching a ground offensive. President George Bush declared Kuwait to be liberated and ceased all offensive military operations in the Gulf War. The end of military operations at midnight EST came 100 hours after the beginning of the land attack.

LONGFELLOW, HENRY WADSWORTH: BIRTH ANNIVERSARY. Feb 27, 1807. American poet and writer, born at Portland, ME. He is best remembered for his classic narrative poems, such as *The Song of Hiawatha*, *Paul Revere's Ride* and *The Wreck of the Hesperus*. Died at Cambridge, MA, Mar 24, 1882. For more info: *Henry Wadsworth Longfellow: America's Beloved Poet*, by Bonnie Lukes (Morgan Reynolds, 1-883846-31-5, $19.95 Gr. 6–12).

MARDI GRAS. Feb 27. Celebrated especially at New Orleans, LA, Mobile, AL, and certain Mississippi and Florida cities. Last feast before Lent. Although Mardi Gras (Fat Tuesday, literally) is properly limited to Shrove Tuesday, it has come to be popularly applied to the preceding two weeks of celebration.

NO BRAINER DAY. Feb 27. This is a day where you can slack off, play hookey or find the easy way out. If you are going to do anything at all, make it a no brainer, something you can do without any serious thought. A drop in heart attacks is found on days like this-just what the doctor ordered. You have the rest of the year for a hectic schedule. For info: Adrienne Sioux Koopersmith, 1437 W Rosemont, 1W, Chicago, IL 60660-1319. Phone: (773) 743-5341. Fax: (773) 743-5395. E-mail: kooper@interaccess.com.

SHROVE TUESDAY. Feb 27. Always the day before Ash Wednesday. Sometimes called Pancake Tuesday. A legal holiday in certain counties in Florida.

TESOL ANNUAL CONFERENCE. Feb 27–Mar 3. St. Louis, MO. Annual meeting of Teachers of English to Speakers of Other Languages. For info: TESOL, 700 S Washington St, Ste 200, Alexandria, VA 22314. Phone: (703) 836-0774. E-mail: conv@tesol.edu. Web: www.tesol.edu.

TWENTY-SECOND AMENDMENT TO US CONSTITUTION (TWO-TERM LIMIT): RATIFICATION ANNIVERSARY. Feb 27, 1950. After the four successive presidential terms of Franklin Roosevelt, the 22nd Amendment limited the tenure of presidential office to two terms.

BIRTHDAYS TODAY

Uri Shulevitz, 66, author and illustrator (*The Treasure*), born Warsaw, Poland, Feb 27, 1935.

FEBRUARY 28 — WEDNESDAY
Day 59 — 306 Remaining

ASH WEDNESDAY. Feb 28. Marks the beginning of Lent. Forty weekdays and six Sundays (Saturday considered a weekday) remain until Easter Sunday. Named for use of ashes in ceremonial penance.

LENT BEGINS. Feb 28–Apr 14. Most Christian churches observe period of fasting and penitence (40 weekdays and six Sundays— Saturday considered a weekday) beginning on Ash Wednesday and ending on the Saturday before Easter.

NATIONAL ASSOCIATION OF INDEPENDENT SCHOOLS ANNUAL CONFERENCE. Feb 28–Mar 3. Boston, MA. For info: Natl Assn of Independent Schools, 1620 L St NW, Ste 1100, Washington, DC 20036. Phone: (202) 973-9700. E-mail: confpreview@nais-schools.org. Web: www.nais.org.

TENNIEL, JOHN: BIRTH ANNIVERSARY. Feb 28, 1820. Illustrator and cartoonist, born at London, England. Best remembered for his illustrations for Lewis Carroll's *Alice's Adventures in Wonderland.* Died at London, Feb 25, 1914.

BIRTHDAYS TODAY

Eric Lindros, 28, hockey player, born London, Ontario, Canada, Feb 28, 1973.

Dean Smith, 70, basketball coach, born Emporia, KS, Feb 28, 1931.

MARCH 1 — THURSDAY

Day 60 — 305 Remaining

★**AMERICAN RED CROSS MONTH.** Mar 1–31. Presidential Proclamation for Red Cross Month issued each year for March since 1943. Issued as American Red Cross Month since 1987.

THE ARRIVAL OF MARTIN PINZON: ANNIVERSARY. Mar 1, 1493. Martin Alonzo Pinzon (1440–1493), Spanish shipbuilder and navigator (and co-owner of the *Niña* and the *Pinta*), accompanied Christopher Columbus on his first voyage, as commander of the *Pinta*. Storms separated the ships on their return voyage, and the *Pinta* first touched land at Bayona, Spain, where Pinzon gave Europe its first news of the discovery of the New World before Columbus's landing at Palos. Pinzon's brother, Vicente Yanez Pinzon, was commander of the third caravel of the expedition, the *Niña*.

ARTICLES OF CONFEDERATION RATIFIED: ANNIVERSARY. Mar 1, 1781. This compact made among the original 13 states had been adopted by the Continental Congress Nov 15, 1777, and submitted to the states for ratification Nov 17, 1777. Maryland was the last state to approve, Feb 27, 1781, but Congress named Mar 1, 1781, as the day of formal ratification. The Articles of Confederation remained the supreme law of the nation until Mar 4, 1789, when Congress first met under the Constitution.

BELGIUM: CAT FESTIVAL. Mar 1. Traditional cultural observance. Annually, on the second day of Lent.

BIBLE WOMEN AWARENESS MONTH. Mar 1–31. To help raise awareness of the women in the Bible and the stories of their lives which are role models for women today and the heritage of all who live in our Judeo-Christian society. For info: Web: www.christianwomen.com/ministries.

BOSNIA AND HERZEGOVINA: INDEPENDENCE DAY. Mar 1. Commemorates independence in 1991.

HEMOPHILIA MONTH. Mar 1–31. For info: Natl Hemophilia Foundation, 116 W 32nd St, 11th Floor, New York, NY 10001. Phone: (800) 42H-ANDI. Web: www.hemophilia.org.

★**IRISH-AMERICAN HERITAGE MONTH.** Mar 1–31. Presidential Proclamation called for by House Joint Resolution 401 (PL 103–379).

JAPAN: OMIZUTORI (WATER-DRAWING FESTIVAL). Mar 1–14. Todaiji, Nara. At midnight, a solemn rite is performed in the flickering light of pine torches. People rush for sparks from the torches, which are believed to have magic power against evil.

Most spectacular on the night of Mar 12. The ceremony of drawing water is observed at 2 AM Mar 13, to the accompaniment of ancient Japanese music.

KOREA: SAMILJOL or INDEPENDENCE MOVEMENT DAY. Mar 1. Koreans observe the anniversary of the independence movement against Japanese colonial rule in 1919.

MENTAL RETARDATION AWARENESS MONTH. Mar 1–31. To educate the public about the needs of this nation's more than seven million citizens with mental retardation and about ways to prevent retardation. The Arc is a national organization on mental retardation, formerly the Association for Retarded Citizens. For info: Liz Moore, The Arc, 500 E Border St, Ste 300, Arlington, TX 76010. Phone: (817) 261-6003. Fax: (817) 277-3491. Web: thearc.org/welcome.html.

MUSIC IN OUR SCHOOLS MONTH. Mar 1–31. To increase public awareness of the importance of music education as part of a balanced curriculum. Additional information and awareness items are available from MENC. For info: Deidre Healy, Mgr Special Programs, MENC: Music Educators Natl Conference, 1806 Robert Fulton Dr, Reston, VA 20191. Phone: (800) 336-3768. Web: www.menc.org.

NATIONAL CRAFT MONTH. Mar 1–31. Promoting the fun and creativity of hobbies and crafts. For info: Hobby Industry Assn, Natl Craft Month, Richartz and Fliss, 400 Morris Ave, Denville, NJ 07834. Phone: (973) 627-8180. Fax: (973) 672-8410. Web: www.i-craft.com. Info also available from: Assn of Crafts and Creative Industries, 1100-H Brandywine Blvd, PO Box 2188, Zanesville, OH 43702-2188. Phone: (614) 452-4541.

NATIONAL FROZEN FOOD MONTH. Mar 1–31. Promotes a national awareness of the economical and nutritional benefits of frozen foods. Annually, the month of March. For info: Lori B. Pohlman, VP Communications & New Media, Natl Frozen Food Assn, 4755 Linglestown Rd, Ste 300, Harrisburg, PA 17112. Phone: (717) 657-8601. Fax: (717) 657-9862. E-mail: nffm@nffa.org. Web: www.nffa.org.

NATIONAL MIDDLE LEVEL EDUCATION MONTH. Mar 1–31. To encourage middle level schools to schedule local events focusing on the educational needs of early adolescents. For info: Dir of Middle Level Services, Natl Assn of Secondary School Principals, 1904 Association Dr, Reston, VA 20190. Phone: (703) 860-7263.

NATIONAL NUTRITION MONTH®. Mar 1–31. To educate consumers about the importance of good nutrition by providing the latest practical information on how simple it can be to eat healthfully. For info: The American Dietetic Assn, Natl Center for Nutrition and Dietetics, 216 W Jackson Blvd, Chicago, IL 60606-6995. Phone: (312) 899-0040. Fax: (312) 899-4739. E-mail: nnm@eatright.org. Web: www.eatright.org.

NATIONAL PIG DAY. Mar 1. To accord to the pig its rightful, though generally unrecognized, place as one of man's most intelligent and useful domesticated animals. Annually, Mar 1. For more info send SASE to: Ellen Stanley, 7006 Miami, Lubbock, TX 79413.

NATIONAL TALK WITH YOUR TEEN ABOUT SEX MONTH. Mar 1–31. The importance of frank talk with teenagers about sex is emphasized. Parents are encouraged to provide their teenage children with current, accurate information and open lines for communication, as well as support their self-esteem, reduce misinformation and guide teenagers toward making responsible decisions regarding sex. Annually, the month of March. For info send SASE to: Teresa Langston, Dir, Parenting Without Pressure (PWOP), 1330 Boyer St, Longwood, FL 32750-6311. Phone: (407) 767-2524.

NATIONAL UMBRELLA MONTH. Mar 1–31. In honor of one of the most versatile and underrated inventions of the human race, this month is dedicated to the purchase, use of and conversation about umbrellas. Annually, the month of March. For info: Thomas Edward Knibb, 8819 Adventure Ave, Walkersville, MD 21793-7828. Phone: (301) 898-3009. E-mail: tomknibb@hotmail.com.

NATIONAL WOMEN'S HISTORY MONTH. Mar 1–31. A time for reexamining and celebrating the wide range of women's contributions and achievements that are too often overlooked in the telling of US history. A theme kit on Women's History Month for grades 5–12 is available each year from the National Women's History Project. *See* Curriculum Connection. For info: Natl Women's History Project, 7738 Bell Rd, Dept P, Windsor, CA 95492. Phone: (707) 838-6000. Fax: (707) 838-0478. E-mail: nwhp@aol.com. Web: www.nwhp.org.

NEBRASKA: ADMISSION DAY: ANNIVERSARY. Mar 1. Became 37th state in 1867.

NEWSCURRENTS STUDENT EDITORIAL CARTOON CONTEST DEADLINE. Mar 1. Students in grades K–12 can win US Savings Bonds and get their work published in a national book by entering the annual Newscurrents Student Editorial Cartoon Contest. Participants must submit original cartoons on any subject of nationwide interest. Complete rules available. For info: Jeff Robbins, Knowledge Unlimited, PO Box 52, Madison, WI 53701. Phone: (800) 356-2303. Fax: (800) 618-1570. E-mail: jrobbins@ku.com. Web: www.knowledgeunlimited.com.

OHIO: ADMISSION DAY: ANNIVERSARY. Mar 1. Became 17th state in 1803.

OPTIMISM MONTH. Mar 1–31. To encourage people to boost their optimism. Research proves optimists achieve more health, prosperity and happiness than pessimists. Use this monthlong celebration to practice optimism and turn optimism into a delightful, permanent habit. Free "Tip Sheets" available. For info: Dr. Michael Mercer & Dr. Maryann Troiani, The Mercer Group, Inc, 25597 Drake Rd, Barrington, IL 60010. Phone: (847) 382-0690. For media interviews, Victoria Sterling. Phone: (847) 382-6420.

PEACE CORPS FOUNDED: 40th ANNIVERSARY. Mar 1, 1961. Official establishment of the Peace Corps by President John F. Kennedy's signing of executive order. The Peace Corps has sent more than 150,000 volunteers to 132 developing countries to help people help themselves. The volunteers assist in projects such as health, education, water sanitation, agriculture, nutrition and forestry. For info: Peace Corps, 1990 K St, Washington, DC 20526.

	S	M	T	W	T	F	S
March					1	2	3
2001	4	5	6	7	8	9	10
	11	12	13	14	15	16	17
	18	19	20	21	22	23	24
	25	26	27	28	29	30	31

MARCH 1–31
NATIONAL WOMEN'S HISTORY MONTH

There are many excellent biographies about influential women who lived in the past. Call Women's History Month to your students' attention by borrowing a collection of biographies from your school's learning center or the public library. Let students decide how to group and arrange the books. They may sort them by historical era or by topic areas. Women you might consider including are: Mary Cassatt, Rosa Bonheur, Beatrix Potter, Laura Ingalls Wilder, Rachel Carson, Sojourner Truth, Marie Curie, Sandra Day O'Connor, Wilma Mankiller, Jane Addams and Florence Kelley. Have students develop a bulletin board timeline of women's history.

Encourage students to identify influential woman who have excelled in a subject area they find interesting. In small groups, students can "introduce" each other to the women they find. For example, a child who loves sharks could acquaint the others with Eugenie Clark, a marine biologist and pioneer in the study of sharks.

Middle school students can research and write "news flash" style headlines that announce women's historical "firsts." Suggestions might feature Valentina Tereshkova, the first woman astronaut, or Elizabeth Blackwell, the first American woman to receive a medical degree. An amusing project for small groups of older students is to write a classroom TV talk show (a lá "Oprah"), during which famous women confront their critics. Each group should have a host, an influential woman, a critic and two or three enthusiastic audience members who can ask questions and put in their two cents.

Develop a unit on "The Women in Our Lives." As a class, create a list of good interview questions. Have children interview older women in their families. Keep the focus on what life was like for the person being interviewed. Questions might include asking about favorite foods, the kinds of clothes they wore, fashion fads, household chores and jobs held in the past. Encourage the children to bring in family history stories about women from past generations. Invite parents to bring old photos and/or memorabilia pertaining to those women to the classroom. To prevent damage or loss, ask them to share the material with the students, answer student questions and then take the items home. Several parents could be scheduled concurrently to speak to small groups rather than the whole class. Each small group can jot down short notes during the meetings and later give a quick recap of the high points to the whole class.

Phone: (800) 424-8580 or (202) 606-3010. Fax: (202) 606-3110. Web: www.peacecorps.gov.

PLAY-THE-RECORDER MONTH. Mar 1–31. American Recorder Society members all over the continent will celebrate the organization's annual Play-the-Recorder Month by performing in public places such as libraries, bookstores, museums and shopping malls. Some will offer workshops on playing the recorder or demonstrations in schools. Founded in 1939, the ARS is the membership organization for all recorder players, including amateurs to leading professionals. Annually, the month of March. For info: American Recorder Soc, PO Box 631, Littleton, CO 80160-0631. Phone: (303) 347-1120. E-mail: recorder@compuserve.com. Web: ourworld.compuserve.com/homepages/recorder.

RED CROSS MONTH. Mar 1–31. To make the public aware of American Red Cross service in the community. There are some 1,300 Red Cross offices nationwide; each local office plans its own activities. For info on activities in your area, contact your local Red Cross office. For info: American Red Cross Natl HQ, Office of Public Inquiry, 1621 N Kent St, Arlington, VA 22209. Phone: (703) 248-4222. E-mail: info@usa.redcross.org. Web: www.red-cross.org.

RETURN THE BORROWED BOOKS WEEK. Mar 1–7. To remind you to make room for those precious old volumes that will be returned to you, by cleaning out all that worthless trash that your friends are waiting for. Annually, the first seven days of March. For info: Inter-Global Soc for Prevention of Cruelty to Cartoonists, Al Kaelin, Secy, 3119 Chadwick Dr, Los Angeles, CA 90032. Phone: (323) 221-7909.

SILLY PUTTY® DEBUTS: ANNIVERSARY. Mar 1, 1950. Sometime this month, Silly Putty was launched in Connecticut by Peter Hodgson. It had been discovered six years earlier by an engineer at General Electric who was trying to develop a synthetic rubber. He combined boric acid and silicone oil and got bouncing putty. No one at GE could figure out anything practical to do with it. Hodgson bought a batch of the stuff, put it in plastic eggs and it went on to become a very popular toy. In the late 1970s, Silly Putty was bought by Binney & Smith Inc, the company that makes Crayola crayons.

SLAYTON, DONALD "DEKE" K.: BIRTH ANNIVERSARY. Mar 1, 1924. "Deke" Slayton, longtime chief of flight operations at the Johnson Space Center, was born at Sparta, WI. Slayton was a member of Mercury Seven, the original group of young military aviators chosen to inaugurate America's sojourn into space. Unfortunately, a heart problem prevented him from participating in any of the Mercury flights. When in 1971 the heart condition mysteriously went away, Slayton flew on the last Apollo Mission. The July 1975 flight, involving a docking with a Soviet Soyuz spacecraft, symbolized a momentary thaw in relations between the two nations. During his years as chief of flight operations, Slayton directed astronaut training and selected the crews for nearly all missions. He died June 13, 1993, at League City, TX.

SWITZERLAND: CHALANDRA MARZ. Mar 1. Engadine. Springtime traditional event when costumed young people, ringing bells and cracking whips, drive away the demons of winter.

WALES: SAINT DAVID'S DAY. Mar 1. Celebrates patron saint of Wales. Welsh tradition calls for the wearing of a leek on this day.

★**WOMEN'S HISTORY MONTH.** Mar 1–31.

YELLOWSTONE NATIONAL PARK: ANNIVERSARY. Mar 1, 1872. The first area in the world to be designated a national park, most of Yellowstone is in Wyoming, with small sections in Montana and Idaho. It was established by an act of Congress. For more info: www.nps.gov/yell.

YOUTH ART MONTH. Mar 1–31. To emphasize the value and importance of participation of art in the development of all children and youth. For info: Council for Art Education, Inc, 128 Main St, PO Box 479, Hanson, MA 02341. Phone: (781) 293-4100. Fax: (781) 294-0808.

BIRTHDAYS TODAY

Barbara Helen Berger, 56, author (*A Lot of Otters*), born Lancaster, CA, Mar 1, 1945.

John B. Breaux, 57, US Senator (D, Louisiana), born Crowley, LA, Mar 1, 1944.

Mark-Paul Gosselaar, 27, actor ("Saved by the Bell," "She Cried No"), born Panorama City, CA, Mar 1, 1974.

Yolanda Griffith, 31, basketball player, born Chicago, IL, Mar 1, 1970.

Ron Howard, 47, actor ("Happy Days," "Andy Griffith Show"), producer (*Parenthood, Far and Away*), born Duncan, OK, Mar 1, 1954.

Alan Thicke, 54, actor ("Growing Pains"), born Kirkland Lake, Ontario, Canada, Mar 1, 1947.

MARCH 2 — FRIDAY

Day 61 — 304 Remaining

ETHIOPIA: ADWA DAY. Mar 2, 1896. Ethiopian forces under Menelik II inflicted a crushing defeat on the invading Italians at Adwa.

GEISEL, THEODOR "DR. SEUSS": BIRTH ANNIVERSARY. Mar 2, 1904. Theodor Seuss Geisel, the creator of *The Cat in the Hat* and *How the Grinch Stole Christmas*, was born at Springfield, MA. Known to children and parents as Dr. Seuss, his books have sold more than 200 million copies and have been translated into 20 languages. His career began with *And to Think That I Saw It on Mulberry Street*, which was turned down by 27 publishing houses before being published by Vanguard Press. His books included many messages, from environmental consciousness in *The Lorax* to the dangers of pacifism in *Horton Hatches the Egg* and *Yertel the Turtle*'s thinly veiled references to Hitler as the title character. He was awarded a Pulitzer Prize in 1984 "for his contribution over nearly half a century to the education and enjoyment of America's children and their parents." He died Sept 24, 1991, at La Jolla, CA.

HOUSTON, SAM: BIRTH ANNIVERSARY. Mar 2, 1793. American soldier and politician, born at Rockbridge County, VA, is remembered for his role in Texas history. Houston was a congressman (1823–27) and governor (1827–29) of Tennessee. He resigned his office as governor in 1829 and rejoined the Cherokee Indians (with whom he had lived for several years as a teenage runaway), who accepted him as a member of their tribe. Houston went to Texas in 1832 and became commander of the Texan army in the War for Texan Independence, which was secured when Houston routed the much larger Mexican forces led by Santa Ana, Apr 21, 1836, at the Battle of San Jacinto. After Texas's admission to the Union, Houston served as US senator and later as governor of the state. He was deposed in 1861 when he refused to swear allegiance to the Confederacy. Houston, the only person to have been elected governor of two different states, failed to serve his full term of office in either. The city of Houston, TX, was named for him. He died July 26, 1863, at Huntsville, TX.

MOON PHASE: FIRST QUARTER. Mar 2. Moon enters First Quarter phase at 9:03 PM, EST.

MOUNT RAINIER NATIONAL PARK ESTABLISHED: ANNIVERSARY. Mar 2, 1899. Located in the Cascade Range in north-central Washington state, this is the fourth oldest park in the national park system. For more info: www.nps.gov/mora.

READ ACROSS AMERICA DAY. Mar 2. A national reading campaign that advocates that all children read a book the evening of Mar 2. Celebrated on Dr. Seuss's birthday. For info: Natl Education Assn, 1201 16th St NW, Washington, DC, 20036. Phone: (202) 822-7830. Fax: (888) 747-READ. Web: www.nea.org/readacross.

SPACE MILESTONE: *PIONEER 10* (US). Mar 2, 1972. This unmanned probe began a journey on which it passed and photographed Jupiter and its moons, 620 million miles from Earth, in December 1973. It crossed the orbit of Pluto, and then in 1983 become the first known Earth object to leave our solar system. On Sept 22, 1987 *Pioneer 10* reached another space milestone at 4:19 PM, when it reached a distance 50 times farther from the sun than the sun is from Earth.

SPACE MILESTONE: *SOYUZ 28* (USSR). Mar 2, 1978. Cosmonauts Alexi Gubarev and Vladimir Remek linked with *Salyut 6* space station Mar 3, visiting crew of *Soyuz 26*. Returned to Earth Mar 10. Remek, from Czechoslovakia, was the first person in space from a country other than the US or USSR. Launched Mar 2, 1978.

TEXAS INDEPENDENCE DAY. Mar 2, 1836. Texas adopted Declaration of Independence from Mexico.

WORLD DAY OF PRAYER. Mar 2. An ecumenical event that reinforces bonds between peoples of the world as they join in a global circle of prayer. Annually, the first Friday in March. Sponsor: International Committee for World Day of Prayer. Church Women United is the National World Day of Prayer Committee for the US. For info: Mary Cline Detrick, Dir for Ecumenical Celebrations, Church Women United, 475 Riverside Dr, 5th Floor, New York, NY 10115. Phone: (212) 870-2347 or (800) 298-5551. Fax: (212) 870-2338.

BIRTHDAYS TODAY

Leo Dillon, 68, illustrator, with his wife Diane Dillon (Caldecotts for *Why Mosquitoes Buzz in People's Ears, Ashanti to Zulu: African Traditions*), born Brooklyn, NY, Mar 2, 1933.

Russell D. Feingold, 48, US Senator (D, Wisconsin), born Janesville, WI, Mar 2, 1953.

MARCH 3 — SATURDAY

Day 62 — 303 Remaining

BONZA BOTTLER DAY™. Mar 3. To celebrate when the number of the day is the same as the number of the month. Bonza Bottler Day™ is an excuse to have a party at least once a month. For info: Gail M. Berger, 109 Matthew Ave, Poca, WV 25159. Phone: (304) 776-7746. E-mail: gberger5@aol.com.

BULGARIA: LIBERATION DAY. Mar 3. Grateful tribute to the Russian, Romanian and Finnish soldiers and Bulgarian volunteers who, in the Russo-Turkish War, 1877–78, liberated Bulgaria from five centuries of Ottoman rule.

FLORIDA: ADMISSION DAY: ANNIVERSARY. Mar 3. Became 27th state in 1845.

I WANT YOU TO BE HAPPY DAY. Mar 3. A day dedicated to reminding people to be thoughtful of others by showing love and care and concern, even if things are not going well for them. For info: Harriette W. Grimes, Grandmother, PO Box 545, Winter Garden, FL 34777-0545. Phone: (407) 656-3830. Fax: (407) 656-2790.

JAPAN: HINAMATSURI (DOLL FESTIVAL). Mar 3. This special festival for girls is observed throughout Japan. Annually, Mar 3.

MALAWI: MARTYR'S DAY. Mar 3. Public holiday in Malawi.

NATIONAL ANTHEM DAY. Mar 3, 1931. The bill designating "The Star-Spangled Banner" as our national anthem was adopted by the US Senate and went to President Herbert Hoover for signature. The president signed it the same day. *See* Curriculum Connection.

		S	M	T	W	T	F	S
March						1	2	3
2001		4	5	6	7	8	9	10
		11	12	13	14	15	16	17
		18	19	20	21	22	23	24
		25	26	27	28	29	30	31

MARCH 3
NATIONAL ANTHEM DAY

The words to the "Star-Spangled Banner" were written by Francis Scott Key during the War of 1812. On Sept 13, 1814, while the British bombarded Fort McHenry, Key was detained overnight on a flag of truce ship in Baltimore Harbor. The next morning, the sight of the American flag flying over the fort inspired him to write several poetic verses about the flag. The anthem's melody is from an old English drinking song, popular in the late 1700s, which had also served as the melody for other patriotic songs of early America. In 1931, the US Congress officially approved the "Star-Spangled Banner" as the national anthem. President Herbert Hoover signed the bill the same day.

In addition to singing or playing a recording of the song, print out (or have students write) the four verses. Discuss the words and meaning of each verse. Elementary students are often confused about what the words to the first verse are. Reading them helps sort out the meaning.

Compare the "Star-Spangled Banner" with "America the Beautiful," by Katherine Lee Bates. Hold a class vote on which song the students like best and why they feel the way they do. A multicultural approach to North American national anthems makes a nice musical contrast. Play the national anthems of Canada ("O Canada") and Mexico ("Himno Nacional de Mexico"). Talk about the kinds of emotions different anthems evoke.

March is also Music In Our Schools Month. To further celebrate music, have some "state spirit" and find out if your state has an official state song (some do). If yours doesn't, your class could write the words for one. Start by brainstorming important features of your state. You might include some state symbols, such as the state bird, flower, etc.

For an even more relevant song, invite the high school band to pay a visit to your school. Chances are the town high school(s) has a school anthem. (But not the high school football fight song!) Encourage your students to appreciate the school spirit that such anthems inspire. Let the students write verses for a school song about your school. Middle and junior high students interested in music might try their hands at writing melodies; a music teacher might lend a hand.

Invite students to bring in selections of music they enjoy. Set guidelines as to what is appropriate for classroom use. Consult with the learning center director to see if the school owns some music collections. You could designate one week as Rock 'n' Roll, a second as Classical, a third as Children's Songs and a fourth as World Music. Use the music as background during silent reading periods or during attendance taking. Each week the students can vote on a "song of the week."

As always, try to encourage parents with musical expertise to visit the classroom and share their love of music. A daily music break gives all of us a few moments to relax, reflect and examine ourselves. Music provides an opportunity to slow down the hectic pace of today's life.

SPECIAL OLYMPICS WORLD WINTER GAMES. Mar 3–10. Anchorage, AK. The Special Olympics provide year-round sports training and athletic competition in a variety of Olympic-type sports for individuals with mental retardation by giving them continuing opportunities to develop physical fitness, demonstrate courage and experience joy with others. Est attendance: 70,000. For info: Special Olympics Intl, 1325 G St NW, Washington, DC,

20005-3104. Phone: (202) 628-3630. Fax: (202) 824-0200. E-mail: specialolympics@msn.com. Web: www.specialolympics.org.

TIME MAGAZINE FIRST PUBLISHED: ANNIVERSARY. Mar 3, 1923. The first issue of *Time* bore this date. The magazine was founded by Henry Luce and Briton Hadden.

BIRTHDAYS TODAY

Jessica Biel, 19, actress ("7th Heaven"), born Ely, MN, Mar 3, 1982.

Jacqueline (Jackie) Joyner-Kersee, 39, Olympic gold medal heptathlete, born East St. Louis, IL, Mar 3, 1962.

Patricia MacLachlan, 63, author (Newbery for *Sarah, Plain and Tall*), born Cheyenne, WY, Mar 3, 1938.

MARCH 4 — SUNDAY
Day 63 — 302 Remaining

ADAMS, JOHN QUINCY: RETURN TO CONGRESS ANNIVERSARY. Mar 4, 1830. John Quincy Adams returned to the House of Representatives to represent the district of Plymouth, MA. He was the first former president to do so and served for eight consecutive terms.

CONGRESS: ANNIVERSARY OF FIRST MEETING UNDER CONSTITUTION. Mar 4, 1789. The first Congress met at New York, NY. A quorum was obtained in the House on Apr 1, in the Senate Apr 5 and the first Congress was formally organized Apr 6. Electoral votes were counted, and George Washington was declared president (69 votes) and John Adams vice president (34 votes).

CONSERVE WATER/DETECT-A-LEAK WEEK. Mar 4–10. To help everyone learn why it is important to conserve our water and how to help accomplish this goal. Annually, the first full week in March. For info: American Leak Detection, 888 Research Dr, Ste 100, Palm Springs, CA 92262. Phone: (800) 755-6697. Fax: (760) 320-1288. E-mail: sbangs@leakbusters.com. Web: www.leakbusters.com.

GROVER CLEVELAND'S SECOND PRESIDENTIAL INAUGURATION: ANNIVERSARY. Mar 4, 1893. Grover Cleveland was inaugurated for a second but nonconsecutive term as president. In 1885 he had become 22nd President of the US and in 1893 the 24th. Originally a source of some controversy, the Congressional Directory for some time listed him only as the 22nd president. The Directory now lists him as both the 22nd and 24th presidents though some historians continue to argue that one person cannot be both. Benjamin Harrison served during the intervening term, defeating Cleveland in electoral votes, though not in the popular vote.

OLD INAUGURATION DAY. Mar 4. Anniversary of the date set for beginning the US presidential term of office, 1789–1933. Although the Continental Congress had set the first Wednesday of March 1789 as the date for the new government to convene, a quorum was not present to count the electoral votes until Apr 6. Though George Washington's term of office began Mar 4, he did not take the oath of office until Apr 30, 1789. All subsequent presidential terms (except successions following the death of an incumbent), until Franklin D. Roosevelt's second term, began Mar 4. The 20th Amendment (ratified Jan 23, 1933) provided that "the terms of the President and Vice President shall end at noon on the 20th day of January . . . and the terms of their successors shall then begin."

PENNSYLVANIA DEEDED TO WILLIAM PENN: ANNIVERSARY. Mar 4, 1681. To satisfy a debt of £16,000, King Charles II of England granted a royal charter, deed and governorship of Pennsylvania to William Penn.

PEOPLE MAGAZINE: ANNIVERSARY. Mar 4, 1974. This popular gossip magazine was officially launched with the Mar 4, 1974, issue featuring a cover photo of Mia Farrow.

PULASKI, CASIMIR: BIRTH ANNIVERSARY. Mar 4, 1747. American Revolutionary hero, General Kazimierz (Casimir) Pulaski, born at Winiary, Mazovia, Poland, the son of a count. He was a patriot and military leader in Poland's fight against Russia of 1770–71 and went into exile at the partition of Poland in 1772. He went to America in 1777 to join the Revolution, fighting with General Washington at Brandywine and also serving at Germantown and Valley Forge. He organized the Pulaski Legion to wage guerrilla warfare against the British. Mortally wounded in a heroic charge at the siege of Savannah, GA, he died aboard the warship *Wasp* Oct 11, 1779. Pulaski Day is celebrated Oct 11 in Massachusetts and on the first Monday of March in Illinois (Mar 5 in 2001).

ROCKNE, KNUTE: BIRTH ANNIVERSARY. Mar 4, 1888. Legendary Notre Dame football coach, born at Voss, Norway. Known for such sayings as "Win one for the Gipper," he died at Cottonwood Falls, KS, Mar 31, 1931.

SAVE YOUR VISION WEEK. Mar 4–10. To remind Americans that vision is one of the most vital of all human needs and its protection is of great significance to the health and welfare of every individual. Annually, the first full week in March. For info: American Optometric Assn, 243 N Lindbergh Blvd, St. Louis, MO 63141. Phone: (314) 991-4100. Fax: (314) 991-4101. E-mail: optinfo@aol.com. Web: www.aoanet.org.

★**SAVE YOUR VISION WEEK.** Mar 4–10. Presidential Proclamation issued for the first week of March since 1964, except 1971 and 1982 when issued for the second week of March. (PL88–1942, of Dec 30, 1963.)

SPACE MILESTONE: *OGO 5* (US). Mar 4, 1968. Orbiting Geophysical Observatory (OGO) collected data on sun's influence on Earth. Launched Mar 4, 1968. Six OGOs were launched in all.

TELEVISION ACADEMY HALL OF FAME: FIRST INDUCTEES ANNOUNCED: ANNIVERSARY. Mar 4, 1984. The Television Academy of Arts and Sciences announced the formation of the Television Academy Hall of Fame at Burbank, CA. The first inductees were Lucille Ball, Milton Berle, Paddy Chayefsky, Norman Lear, Edward R. Murrow, William S. Paley and David Sarnoff.

VERMONT: ADMISSION DAY: ANNIVERSARY. Mar 4. Became 14th state in 1791.

YAWM ARAFAT: THE STANDING AT ARAFAT. Mar 4. Islamic calendar date: Dhu-Hijjah 9, 1421. The day when people on the Hajj (pilgrimage to Mecca) assemble for "the Standing" at the plain of Arafat at Mina, Saudi Arabia, near Mecca. This gathering is a foreshadowing of the Day of Judgment. Different methods for "anticipating" the visibility of the new moon crescent at Mecca are used by different Muslim groups. US date may vary.

Peyton Manning, 25, football player, born New Orleans, LA, Mar 4, 1976.

Dav Pilkey, 35, author and illustrator (The Dumb Bunnies series, *The Paperboy*), born Cleveland, OH, Mar 4, 1966.

Peggy Rathmann, 48, author and illustrator (Caldecott for *Officer Buckle and Gloria*), born St. Paul, MN, Mar 4, 1953.

MARCH 5 — MONDAY
Day 64 — 301 Remaining

BOSTON MASSACRE: ANNIVERSARY. Mar 5, 1770. A skirmish between British troops and a crowd at Boston, MA, became widely publicized and contributed to the unpopularity of the British regime in America before the American Revolution. Five men were killed and six more were injured by British troops commanded by Captain Thomas Preston.

CRISPUS ATTUCKS DAY: DEATH ANNIVERSARY. Mar 5, 1770. Honors Crispus Attucks, possibly a runaway slave, who was the first to die in the Boston Massacre.

EID-AL-ADHA: FEAST OF THE SACRIFICE. Mar 5. Islamic calendar date: Dhu-Hijja 10, 1421. Commemorates Abraham's willingness to sacrifice his son Ishmael in obedience to God. It is part of the Hajj (pilgrimage to Mecca). The day begins with the sacrifice of an animal in remembrance of the Angel Gabriel's substitution of a lamb as Abraham's offering. One-third of the meat is given to the poor and the rest is shared with friends and family. Celebrated with gifts and general merrymaking, the festival usually continues for several days. It is celebrated as Tabaski in Benin, Burkina Faso, Guinea, Guinea-Bissau, Ivory Coast, Mali, Niger and Senegal and as Kurban Bayram in Turkey and Bosnia. Different methods for "anticipating" the visibility of the moon crescent at Mecca are used by different Muslim groups. US date may vary.

GUAM: DISCOVERY DAY or MAGELLAN DAY. Mar 5. Commemorates discovery of Guam in 1521. Annually, the first Monday in March.

MERCATOR, GERHARDUS: BIRTH ANNIVERSARY. Mar 5, 1512. Cartographer-geographer Mercator was born at Rupelmonde, Belgium. His Mercator projection for maps provided an accurate ratio of latitude to longitude and is still used today. He also introduced the term "atlas" for a collection of maps. He died at Duisberg, Germany, Dec 2, 1594.

NATIONAL SCHOOL BREAKFAST WEEK. Mar 5–9. To focus on the importance of a nutritious breakfast served in the schools, giving children a good start to their day. Annually, the first full week in March (weekdays). For info: American School Food Service Assn, 1600 Duke St, 7th Floor, Alexandria, VA 22314-3436. Phone: (703) 739-3900. E-mail: asfsa@asfsa.org. Web: www.asfsa .org.

NEWSPAPER IN EDUCATION WEEK. Mar 5–9. A weeklong celebration using newspapers in the classroom as living textbooks. More than 700 newspapers in the US and Canada participate in this event annually. Annually, the first full week in March (weekdays). *See* Curriculum Connection. For info: Mgr Education Programs, Newspaper Assn of America Foundation, 1921 Gallows

		S	M	T	W	T	F	S
March						1	2	3
2001		4	5	6	7	8	9	10
		11	12	13	14	15	16	17
		18	19	20	21	22	23	24
		25	26	27	28	29	30	31

MARCH 5–9
NEWSPAPER IN EDUCATION WEEK

Reading newspapers fosters literacy and stimulates interest in current events. The latest scientific research is usually first section news. Articles about health and space exploration are far more up-to-date than classroom textbooks and are important curriculum supplements. Coverage of political events can be used to stimulate interest in government. Voter apathy is becoming widespread; being aware and informed is one way to combat this trend.

Newspapers often feature interviews with people who are making the news. Children should be encouraged to analyze the kinds of questions that were asked to elicit the responses reported in each article. They can learn to formulate effective interviewing skills, which avoid yes or no answers. For example, asking "What kind of sports do you like?" versus "Do you like sports?" Let students pair off and interview each other. They also might want to try interviewing people in the community.

Bring in an article from a tabloid. Discuss what draws our attention to that kind of writing and why we read it. Ask students to dissect the article and search for unsupported statements and vague references. Ask them to cite the author's evidence. Alert students to the use of unspecific "they" references as a source of information. Elect a student moderator to conduct a classroom discussion on the difference between gossip and fact. Encourage them to explore how events in their lives get distorted and turned into harmful and painful gossip.

Play with the comics section during art class. Discuss the different kinds of comics depicted. Examine artistic technique and textual content. Some comics are very simple drawings, while others are much more detailed. The situations that occur in some strips reflect family life, while others explore social issues. Some are just plain silly. Talk about what makes a good comic strip. Contrast the comic section with editorial cartoons. Make collages of headlines, sporting events, financial news and other themes that interest students.

Ask students to research old newspaper issues on microfilm and see how the funny pages and editorial cartoons have changed over the years. At the same time, have them note top stories of the day and the prices of merchandise advertised in the paper. Compare and contrast them with today's stories and prices. Most public libraries have a microfilm reader, some with copying capabilities. Learning to use microfilm and microfiche readers allow students to expand and develop their research skills.

Call attention to the ratio of advertising and reported news. Some papers are heavily weighted one way or the other. Students can compare the quality of reporting in each case.

Students can clip stories from newspapers at home. At school, they can create and maintain a weekly or monthly bulletin board that feature stories voted on by the class as the craziest, scariest, saddest, best headline, etc. of the week or month.

Pick up copies of several newspapers and let your imagination run wild. There are lesson plan idea nuggets galore. The cost is minimal and the satisfaction immense.

Some newspapers have devoted a part of their websites to materials for the classroom. At The New York Times Learning Network, for example, there is a lesson plan every day suitable for grades 6 and up. Go to www.nytimes.com/learning/.

Rd, Ste 600, Vienna, VA 22182-3900. Phone: (703) 902-1730. E-mail: abboj@naa.org. Web: www.naa.org.

PYLE, HOWARD: BIRTH ANNIVERSARY. Mar 5, 1853. Illustrator and author, known for the children's books *Bearskin* and *The Merry Adventures of Robin Hood*. Born at Wilmington, DE, Pyle died at Florence, Italy, Nov 9, 1911.

SAINT PIRAN'S DAY. Mar 5. Celebrates the birthday of St. Piran, the patron saint of Cornish tinners. Cornish worldwide celebrate this day. For info: The Cornish American Heritage Soc, 2405 N Brookfield Rd, Brookfield, WI 53045. Phone: (414) 786-9358. E-mail: jjolliff@post.its.mcw.edu.

BIRTHDAYS TODAY

Merrion Frances (Mem) Fox, 55, author (*Possum Magic, Koala Lou*), born Australia, Mar 5, 1946.

John Kitzhaber, 54, Governor of Oregon (D), born Colfax, WA, Mar 5, 1947.

MARCH 6 — TUESDAY
Day 65 — 300 Remaining

BROWNING, ELIZABETH BARRETT: BIRTH ANNIVERSARY. Mar 6, 1806. English poet, author of *Sonnets from the Portuguese*, wife of poet Robert Browning and subject of the play *The Barretts of Wimpole Street*, was born near Durham, England. She died at Florence, Italy, June 29, 1861.

FALL OF THE ALAMO: ANNIVERSARY. Mar 6, 1836. Anniversary of the fall of the Texan fort, the Alamo, in what is now San Antonio, TX. The siege, led by Mexican general Santa Ana, began Feb 23 and reached its climax Mar 6, when the last of the defenders was slain. Texans, under General Sam Houston, rallied with the war cry "Remember the Alamo" and, at the Battle of San Jacinto, Apr 21, defeated and captured Santa Ana, who signed a treaty recognizing Texas's independence.

GHANA: INDEPENDENCE DAY. Mar 6. National holiday. Received independence from Great Britain in 1957.

MICHELANGELO: BIRTH ANNIVERSARY. Mar 6, 1475. Michelangelo Buonarroti, a prolific Renaissance painter, sculptor, architect and poet who had a profound effect on Western art, born at Caprese, Italy. Michelangelo's fresco painting on the ceiling of the Sistine Chapel at the Vatican in Rome and his statues *David* and *The Pieta* are among his best-known achievements. Appointed architect of St. Peter's in 1542, a post he held until his death Feb 18, 1564, at Rome. For more info: *Michelangelo*, by Gabriella Di Cagno (Peter Bedrick, 0-87226-319-3, $22.50 Gr. 4–7).

TOWN MEETING DAY IN VERMONT. Mar 6. The first Tuesday in March is an official state holiday in Vermont. Nearly every town elects officers, approves budget items and deals with a multitude of other items in a daylong public meeting of the voters.

BIRTHDAYS TODAY

Christopher Samuel Bond, 62, US Senator (R, Missouri), born St. Louis, MO, Mar 6, 1939.

Alan Greenspan, 75, economist, Chairman of the Federal Reserve Board, born New York, NY, Mar 6, 1926.

Shaquille Rashan O'Neal, 29, basketball player, born Newark, NJ, Mar 6, 1972.

MARCH 7 — WEDNESDAY
Day 66 — 299 Remaining

BURBANK, LUTHER: BIRTH ANNIVERSARY. Mar 7, 1849. American naturalist and author, creator and developer of many new varieties of flowers, fruits, vegetables and trees. Luther Bur-bank's birthday is observed by some as Bird and Arbor Day. Born at Lancaster, MA, he died at Santa Rosa, CA, Apr 11, 1926.

HOPKINS, STEPHEN: BIRTH ANNIVERSARY. Mar 7, 1707. Colonial governor (Rhode Island) and signer of the Declaration of Independence. Born at Providence, RI and died there July 13, 1785.

MONOPOLY INVENTED: ANNIVERSARY. Mar 7, 1933. Monopoly was mass marketed by Parker Brothers beginning in 1935.

BIRTHDAYS TODAY

Michael Eisner, 59, Disney executive, born Mount Kisco, NY, Mar 7, 1942.

MARCH 8 — THURSDAY
Day 67 — 298 Remaining

FIRST US INCOME TAX: ANNIVERSARY. Mar 8, 1913. The Internal Revenue Service began to levy and collect income taxes.

GRAHAME, KENNETH: BIRTH ANNIVERSARY. Mar 8, 1859. Scottish author, born at Edinburgh. His children's book, *The Wind in the Willows*, has as its main characters a mole, a rat, a badger and a toad. He died July 6, 1932, at Pangbourne, Berkshire.

INTERNATIONAL (WORKING) WOMEN'S DAY. Mar 8. A day to honor women, especially working women. Said to commemorate an 1857 march and demonstration at New York, NY, by female garment and textile workers. Believed to have been first proclaimed for this date at an international conference of women held at Helsinki, Finland, in 1910, "that henceforth Mar 8 should be declared International Women's Day." The 50th anniversary observance, at Peking, China, in 1960, cited Clara Zetkin (1857–1933) as "initiator of Women's Day on Mar 8." This is perhaps the most widely observed holiday of recent origin and is unusual among holidays originating in the US in having been widely adopted and observed in other nations, including socialist countries. In Russia it is a national holiday, and flowers or gifts are presented to women workers.

RUSSIA: INTERNATIONAL WOMEN'S DAY. Mar 8. National holiday.

SYRIAN ARAB REPUBLIC REVOLUTION DAY: ANNIVERSARY. Mar 8, 1963. Official public holiday commemorating assumption of power by Revolutionary National Council.

TA'ANIT ESTHER (FAST OF ESTHER). Mar 8. Hebrew calendar date: Adar 13, 5761. Commemorates Queen Esther's fast, in the 6th century BC, to save the Jews of ancient Persia. Ordinarily observed Adar 13, the Fast of Esther is observed on the previous Thursday (Adar 11) when Adar 13 is a Sabbath.

UNITED NATIONS: INTERNATIONAL WOMEN'S DAY. Mar 8. An international day observed by the organizations of the United Nations system. For more info, visit the UN's website for children at www.un.org/Pubs/CyberSchoolBus/.

VAN BUREN, HANNAH HOES: BIRTH ANNIVERSARY. Mar 8, 1783. Wife of Martin Van Buren, 8th president of the US. Born at Kinderhook, NY, she died at Albany, NY, Feb 5, 1819.

BIRTHDAYS TODAY

James Van Der Beek, 24, actor ("Dawson's Creek"), born Cheshire, CT, Mar 8, 1977.

MARCH 9 — FRIDAY
Day 68 — 297 Remaining

BARBIE DEBUTS: ANNIVERSARY. Mar 9, 1959. The popular doll debuted in stores. More than 800 million dolls have been sold. For more info: www.barbie.com.

BELIZE: BARON BLISS DAY. Mar 9. Official public holiday. Celebrated in honor of Sir Henry Edward Ernest Victor Bliss, a great benefactor of Belize.

GRANT COMMISSIONED COMMANDER OF ALL UNION ARMIES: ANNIVERSARY. Mar 9, 1864. In Washington, DC, Ulysses S. Grant accepted his commission as Lieutenant General, becoming the commander of all the Union armies.

MOON PHASE: FULL MOON. Mar 9. Moon enters Full Moon phase at 12:23 PM, EST.

PANIC DAY. Mar 9. Run around all day in a panic, telling others you can't handle it anymore. [© 1999 by WH] For info: Tom or Ruth Roy, Wellcat Holidays, 2418 Long Ln, Lebanon, PA 17046. Phone: (230)332-4886. E-mail: wellcat@supernet.com. Web: www.wellcat.com.

PURIM. Mar 9. Hebrew calendar date: Adar 14, 5761. Feasts, gifts, charity and the reading of the Book of Esther mark this joyous commemoration of Queen Esther's intervention, in the 6th century BC, to save the Jews of ancient Persia. Haman's plot to exterminate the Jews was thwarted, and he was hanged on the very day he had set for the execution of the Jews.

SHABBAT ACROSS AMERICA. Mar 9. More than 600 participating synagogues (Conservative, Orthodox, Reform and Reconstructionist) encourage Jews to observe the Sabbath on this Friday night. For info: Natl Jewish Outreach Program, 485 5th Ave, New York, NY 10017-6104. Phone: (888) SHA-BBAT or (212) 986-7450. Web: www.njop.org/saapage/saa2.htm.

VESPUCCI, AMERIGO: 550th BIRTH ANNIVERSARY. Mar 9, 1451. Italian navigator, merchant and explorer for whom the Americas were named. Born at Florence, Italy. He participated in at least two expeditions between 1499 and 1502 which took him to the coast of South America, where he discovered the Amazon and Plata rivers. Vespucci's expeditions were of great importance because he believed that he had discovered a new continent, not just a new route to the Orient. Neither Vespucci nor his exploits achieved the fame of Columbus, but the New World was to be named for Amerigo Vespucci, by an obscure German geographer and mapmaker, Martin Waldseemuller. Ironically, in his work as an outfitter of ships, Vespucci had been personally acquainted with Christopher Columbus. Vespucci died at Seville, Spain, Feb 22, 1512. See also: "Waldseemuller, Martin: Remembrance Day" (Apr 25).

BIRTHDAYS TODAY

Margot Apple, 55, illustrator (*Sheep in a Jeep*), born Detroit, MI, Mar 9, 1946.

Emmanuel Lewis, 30, actor ("Webster"), born Brooklyn, NY, Mar 9, 1971.

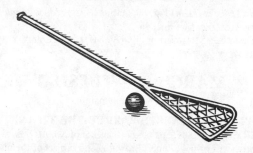

MARCH 10 — SATURDAY
Day 69 — 296 Remaining

SALVATION ARMY IN THE US: ANNIVERSARY. Mar 10, 1880. Commissioner George Scott Railton and seven women officers landed at New York to officially begin the work of the Salvation Army in the US.

TELEPHONE INVENTION: 125th ANNIVERSARY. Mar 10, 1876. Alexander Graham Bell transmitted the first telephone message to his assistant in the next room: "Mr Watson, come here, I want you," at Cambridge, MA. See also: "Bell, Alexander Graham: Birth Anniversary" (Mar 3).

TUBMAN, HARRIET: DEATH ANNIVERSARY. Mar 10, 1913. American abolitionist, Underground Railroad leader, born a slave at Bucktown, Dorchester County, MD, about 1820 or 1821. She escaped from a Maryland plantation in 1849 and later helped more than 300 slaves reach freedom. Died at Auburn, NY. For more info: *Minty: A Story of Young Harriet Tubman*, by Alan Schroeder (Dial, 0-8037-1889-6, $16.99 Gr. K–3). For more info on the Underground Railroad, visit www.undergroundrailroad.com.

US PAPER MONEY ISSUED: ANNIVERSARY. Mar 10, 1862. The first paper money was issued in the US on this date. The denominations were $5 (Hamilton), $10 (Lincoln) and $20 (Liberty). They were not legal tender when first issued but became so by Act of Mar 17, 1862.

BIRTHDAYS TODAY

Kim Campbell, 54, first woman prime minister of Canada, born Vancouver Island, British Columbia, Canada, Mar 10, 1947.

MARCH 11 — SUNDAY
Day 70 — 295 Remaining

BUREAU OF INDIAN AFFAIRS ESTABLISHED: ANNIVERSARY. Mar 11, 1824. The US War Department created the Bureau of Indian Affairs.

CHILDREN AND HEALTHCARE WEEK™. Mar 11–17. The goal of this observance is to increase awareness among families, schools, local communities and all health care professionals of

	S	M	T	W	T	F	S
March					1	2	3
2001	4	5	6	7	8	9	10
	11	12	13	14	15	16	17
	18	19	20	21	22	23	24
	25	26	27	28	29	30	31

the special needs of children and their families in health care settings. A comprehensive guide of planning materials is available for $10. For info: Assn for the Care of Children's Health, 19 Mantua Rd, Mt Royal, NJ 08061. Phone: (609) 224-1742. Fax: (609) 423-3420. E-mail: amk@smarthub.com. Web: www.look.net /acch.

FLU PANDEMIC OF 1918 HITS US: ANNIVERSARY. Mar 11, 1918. The first cases of the "Spanish" influenza were reported in the US when 107 soldiers became sick at Fort Riley, KS. By the end of 1920 nearly 25 percent of the US population had had it. As many as 500,000 civilians died from the virus, exceeding the number of US troops killed abroad in WWI. Worldwide, more than 1 percent of the global population, or 22 million people, had died by 1920. The origin of the virus was never determined absolutely, though it was probably somewhere in Asia. The name "Spanish" influenza came from the relatively high number of cases in that country early in the epidemic. Due to the panic, cancellation of public events was common and many public service workers wore masks on the job. Emergency tent hospitals were set up in some locations due to overcrowding.

GAG, WANDA: BIRTH ANNIVERSARY. Mar 11, 1893. Author and illustrator (*Millions of Cats*), born at New Ulm, MN. Died at Milford, NJ, June 27, 1946.

GIRL SCOUT WEEK. Mar 11–18. To observe the anniversary of the founding of the Girl Scouts of the USA, the largest voluntary organization for girls and women in the world, which began Mar 12, 1912. Special observances include: Girl Scout Sabbath, Mar 17, Girl Scout Sunday, Mar 18, when Girl Scouts gather to attend religious services together, and Girl Scout Birthday, Mar 12. For info: Media Services, Girl Scouts of the USA, 420 Fifth Ave, New York, NY 10018. Phone: (212) 852-8000. Fax: (212) 852-6514. Web: www.gsusa.org.

JOHNNY APPLESEED DAY (JOHN CHAPMAN DEATH ANNIVERSARY). Mar 11, 1845. Anniversary of the death of John Chapman, better known as Johnny Appleseed, believed to have been born at Leominster, MA, Sept 26, 1774. The planter of orchards and friend of wild animals was regarded by the Indians as a great medicine man. He died at Allen County, IN. See also: "Appleseed, Johnny: Birth Anniversary" (Sept 26).

KEATS, EZRA JACK: 85th BIRTH ANNIVERSARY. Mar 11, 1916. Author and illustrator (Caldecott for *The Snowy Day*), born at Brooklyn, NY. Died May 6, 1983, at New York, NY.

★**NATIONAL POISON PREVENTION WEEK.** Mar 11–17. Presidential Proclamation issued each year for the third week of March since 1962. (PL87–319 of Sept 26, 1961.)

PAINE, ROBERT TREAT: BIRTH ANNIVERSARY. Mar 11, 1731. Jurist and signer of the Declaration of Independence. Born at Boston, MA, died there May 11, 1814.

WORLD SUMMIT ON MEDIA FOR CHILDREN. Mar 11–15. Thessaloniki, Greece. Third annual conference. Sponsored by European Children's Television Centre, Greece. For more info: www.childrens-media.org.

BIRTHDAYS TODAY

Roy Barnes, 53, Governor of Georgia (D), born Mableton, GA, Mar 11, 1948.

Curtis Brown, Jr, 45, astronaut, commander of the 1998 shuttle *Discovery*, born Elizabethtown, NC, Mar 11, 1956.

Jonathan London, 54, author (the Froggy series), born Brooklyn, NY, Mar 11, 1947.

Antonin Scalia, 65, Associate Justice of the US Supreme Court, born Trenton, NJ, Mar 11, 1936.

MARCH 12 — MONDAY
Day 71 — 294 Remaining

BOYCOTT, CHARLES CUNNINGHAM: BIRTH ANNIVERSARY. Mar 12, 1832. Charles Cunningham Boycott, born at Norfolk, England, has been immortalized by having his name become part of the English language. In County Mayo, Ireland, the Tenants' "Land League" in 1880 asked Boycott, an estate agent, to reduce rents (because of poor harvest and dire economic conditions). Boycott responded by serving eviction notices on the tenants, who retaliated by refusing to have any dealings with him. Charles Stewart Parnell, then President of the National Land League and agrarian agitator, retaliated against Boycott by formulating and implementing the method of economic and social ostracism that came to be called a "boycott." Boycott died at Suffolk, England, June 19, 1897.

CAMP FIRE BOYS AND GIRLS BIRTHDAY WEEK. Mar 12–18. To celebrate the anniversary of Camp Fire Boys and Girls (founded in 1910 as Camp Fire Girls). For info: Camp Fire Boys and Girls, 4601 Madison Ave, Kansas City, MO 64112. Phone: (816) 756-1950. Fax: (816) 756-0258. E-mail: info@campfire.org. Web: www.campfire.org.

GIRL SCOUTS OF THE USA FOUNDING: ANNIVERSARY. Mar 12, 1912. Juliet Low founded the Girl Scouts of the USA at Savannah, GA. For more info: www.gsusa.org.

LESOTHO: MOSHOESHOE'S DAY. Mar 12. National holiday. Commemorates the great leader, Chief Moshoeshoe I, who unified the Basotho people, beginning in 1820.

MAURITIUS: INDEPENDENCE DAY. Mar 12. National holiday commemorates attainment of independent nationhood (within the British Commonwealth) by this island state in the western Indian Ocean on this day in 1968.

PIERCE, JANE MEANS APPLETON: BIRTH ANNIVERSARY. Mar 12, 1806. Wife of Franklin Pierce, 14th president of the US. Born at Hampton, NH, she died at Concord, NH, Dec 2, 1863.

SUN YAT-SEN: DEATH ANNIVERSARY. Mar 12, 1925. The heroic leader of China's 1911 revolution is remembered on the anniversary of his death at Peking, China. Observed as Arbor Day in Taiwan.

UNITED KINGDOM: COMMONWEALTH DAY. Mar 12. Replaces Empire Day observance recognized until 1958. Observed on second Monday in March. Also observed in the British Virgin Islands, Gibraltar and Newfoundland, Canada.

Kent Conrad, 53, US Senator (D, North Dakota), born Bismarck, ND, Mar 12, 1948.

Virginia Hamilton, 65, author (*The People Could Fly, M.C. Higgins the Great*), born Yellow Springs, OH, Mar 12, 1936 (some sources say 1933).

Darryl Strawberry, 39, baseball player, born Los Angeles, CA, Mar 12, 1962.

MARCH 13 — TUESDAY
Day 72 — 293 Remaining

ARAB OIL EMBARGO LIFTED: ANNIVERSARY. Mar 13, 1974. The oil-producing Arab countries agreed to lift their five-month embargo on petroleum sales to the US. During the embargo prices went up 300 percent and a ban was imposed on Sunday gasoline sales. The embargo was in retaliation for US support of Israel during the October 1973 Middle-East War.

DEAF HISTORY MONTH. Mar 13–Apr 15. Observance of three of the most important anniversaries for deaf Americans: Apr 15, 1817, establishment of the first public school for the deaf in America, later known as The American School for the Deaf; Apr 8, 1864, charter signed by President Lincoln authorizing the Board of Directors of the Columbia Institution (now Gallaudet University) to grant college degrees to deaf students; Mar 13, 1988, the victory of the Deaf President Now movement at Gallaudet. For info: FOLDA, Inc, 2930 Craiglawn Rd, Silver Spring, MD 20904-1816. Phone: (301) 572-5168. Fax: (301) 572-4134. E-mail: alhagemeyer@juno.com.

EARMUFFS PATENTED: ANNIVERSARY. Mar 13, 1887. Chester Greenwood of Maine received a patent for earmuffs.

FILLMORE, ABIGAIL POWERS: BIRTH ANNIVERSARY. Mar 13, 1798. First wife of Millard Fillmore, 13th president of the US. Born at Stillwater, NY. It is said that the White House was without any books until Abigail Fillmore, formerly a teacher, made a room on the second floor into a library. Within a year, Congress appropriated $250 for the president to spend on books for the White House. Died at Washington, DC, Mar 30, 1853.

NATIONAL OPEN AN UMBRELLA INDOORS DAY. Mar 13. The purpose of this day is for people to open umbrellas indoors and note whether they have any bad luck. Annually, Mar 13. For

March *2001*	S	M	T	W	T	F	S
					1	2	3
	4	5	6	7	8	9	10
	11	12	13	14	15	16	17
	18	19	20	21	22	23	24
	25	26	27	28	29	30	31

info: Thomas Edward Knibb, 8819 Adventure Ave, Walkersville, MD 21793-7828. Phone: (301) 898-3009. E-mail: tomknibb@juno.com.

PLANET URANUS DISCOVERY: ANNIVERSARY. Mar 13, 1781. German-born English astronomer Sir William Herschel discovered the seventh planet from the sun, Uranus. For more info, go to Nine Planets: Multimedia Tour of the Solar System at www.seds.org/billa/tnp.

PRIESTLY, JOSEPH: BIRTH ANNIVERSARY. Mar 13, 1733. English clergyman and scientist, discoverer of oxygen, born at Fieldhead, England. He and his family narrowly escaped an angry mob attacking their home because of his religious and political views. They moved to the US in 1794. Died at Northumberland, PA, Feb 6, 1804.

SAINT AUBIN, HELEN "CALLAGHAN" CANDAELE: BIRTH ANNIVERSARY. Mar 13, 1929. Helen Candaele St. Aubin, known as Helen Callaghan during her baseball days, was born at Vancouver, British Columbia, Canada. Saint Aubin and her sister, Margaret Maxwell, were recruited for the All-American Girls Professional Baseball League, which flourished in the 1940s when many major league players were off fighting WWII. She first played at age 15 for the Minneapolis Millerettes, an expansion team that moved to Indiana and became the Fort Wayne Daisies. For the 1945 season the left-handed outfielder led the league with a .299 average and 24 extra base hits. In 1946 she stole 114 bases in 111 games. Her son Kelly Candaele's documentary on the women's baseball league inspired the film *A League of Their Own*. Saint Aubin, who was known as the "Ted Williams of women's baseball," died Dec 8, 1992, at Santa Barbara, CA.

TAIWAN: BIRTHDAY OF KUAN YIN, GODDESS OF MERCY. Mar 13. Nineteenth day of Second Moon of the lunar calendar, celebrated at Taipei's Lungshan (Dragon Mountain) and other temples.

Diane Dillon, 68, illustrator, with her husband Leo Dillon (Caldecotts for *Why Mosquitoes Buzz in People's Ears, Ashanti to Zulu: African Traditions*), born Glendale, CA, Mar 13, 1933.

Ellen Raskin, 73, author (Newbery for *The Westing Game*), born Milwaukee, WI, Mar 13, 1928 (some sources say 1925).

MARCH 14 — WEDNESDAY
Day 73 — 292 Remaining

DE ANGELI, MARGUERITE: BIRTH ANNIVERSARY. Mar 14, 1889. Author and illustrator, born at Lampeer, MI. She won the Newbery Medal in 1950 for her classic *The Door in the Wall*. Her first book was *Ted & Nina Go to the Grocery Store* in 1935. She died at Detroit, MI, June 16, 1987.

EINSTEIN, ALBERT: BIRTH ANNIVERSARY. Mar 14, 1879. Theoretical physicist best known for his theory of relativity. Born at Ulm, Germany, he won the Nobel Prize in 1921. Died at Princeton, NJ, Apr 18, 1955. For more info: *Einstein, Visionary Scientist*, by John B. Severance (Clarion, 0-395-93100-2, $15 Gr. 5–8).

JONES, CASEY: BIRTH ANNIVERSARY. Mar 14, 1864. Railroad engineer and hero of ballad, whose real name was John Luther Jones. Born near Cayce, KY, he died in a railroad wreck near Vaughn, MS, Apr 30, 1900.

MARSHALL, THOMAS RILEY: BIRTH ANNIVERSARY. Mar 14, 1854. The 28th vice president of the US (1913–21). Born at North Manchester, IN, he died at Washington, DC, June 1, 1925.

MOTH-ER DAY. Mar 14. A day set aside to honor moth collectors and specialists. Celebrated in museums or libraries with moth collections. For info: Bob Birch, Puns Corps Grand Punscorpion, Box 2364, Falls Church, VA 22042-0364. Phone: (703) 533-3668.

NATIONAL ART EDUCATION ASSOCIATION ANNUAL CONVENTION. Mar 14–18. New York, NY. For info: Natl Art Education Assn, 1916 Association Dr, Reston, VA 20191-1590. Phone: (703) 860-8000. Web: www.naea-reston.org.

TAYLOR, LUCY HOBBS: BIRTH ANNIVERSARY. Mar 14, 1833. Lucy Beaman Hobbs, first woman in America to receive a degree in dentistry (Ohio College of Dental Surgery, 1866) and to be admitted to membership in a state dental association. Born at Franklin County, NY. In 1867 she married James M. Taylor, who also became a dentist (after she instructed him in the essentials). Active women's rights advocate. Died at Lawrence, KS, Oct 3, 1910.

BIRTHDAYS TODAY

Michael Caine, 68, actor (*The Muppet Christmas Carol*), born Bermondsey, London, England, Mar 14, 1933.

Jordan Taylor Hanson, 18, singer (Hanson), born Jenks, OK, Mar 14, 1983.

MARCH 15 — THURSDAY
Day 74 — 291 Remaining

ABSOLUTELY INCREDIBLE KID DAY. Mar 15. Camp Fire Boys and Girls, one of the nation's oldest and largest youth development organizations, holds this annual event to encourage adults to write a letter to a child in their life to tell children how special they are and how much they mean to them. Annually, the third Thursday in March. For info: Camp Fire Boys and Girls, 4601 Madison Ave, Kansas City, MO 64112. Phone: (816) 756-1950. Fax: (816) 756-0258. E-mail: kidday@yahoo.com. Web: www.campfire.org/.

BE KIND TO ANIMALS KIDS CONTEST DEADLINE. Mar 15. Application deadline for this contest. The national winner will receive a $5,000 scholarship. For info: American Humane Assn, 63 Inverness Dr East, Englewood, CO 80112. Phone: (303) 792-9900. Web: www.americanhumane.org.

IDES OF MARCH. Mar 15. On the Roman calendar, days were not numbered sequentially through a month. Instead, each month had three division days: kalendes, nones and ides. Days were then numbered around these divisions: e.g., III Kalendes or IV Nones.

The ides occurred on the 15th of the month (or on the 13th in months with less than 31 days). Julius Caesar was assassinated on this day in 44 BC. This system continued to be used in Europe through the Middle Ages. When Shakespeare wrote "Beware the ides of March" in his play *Julius Caesar*, his audience understood what this meant.

JACKSON, ANDREW: BIRTH ANNIVERSARY. Mar 15, 1767. Seventh president of the US (Mar 4, 1829–Mar 3, 1837) was born in a log cabin at Waxhaw, SC. Jackson was the first president since George Washington who had not attended college. He was a military hero in the War of 1812. His presidency reflected his democratic and egalitarian values. Died at Nashville, TN, June 8, 1845. His birthday is observed as a holiday in Tennessee.

MAINE: ADMISSION DAY: ANNIVERSARY. Mar 15. Became 23rd state in 1820. Prior to this date, Maine had been part of Massachusetts.

WASHINGTON'S ADDRESS TO CONTINENTAL ARMY OFFICERS: ANNIVERSARY. Mar 15, 1783. George Washington addressed a meeting at Newburgh, NY of Continental Army officers who were dissatisfied and rebellious for want of back pay, food, clothing and pensions. General Washington called for patience, opening his speech with the words: "I have grown grey in your service. . . ." Congress later acted to satisfy most of the demands.

"THE WONDER YEARS" TV PREMIERE: ANNIVERSARY. Mar 15, 1988. A coming-of-age tale set in suburbia in the 1960s and 1970s. This drama/comedy starred Fred Savage as Kevin Arnold, Josh Saviano as his best friend Paul and Danica McKellar as girlfriend Winnie. Kevin's dad was played by Dan Lauria, his homemaker mom by Alley Mills, his hippie sister by Olivia D'Abo and his bully brother by Jason Hervey. Narrator Daniel Stern was the voice of the grown-up Kevin. Though the series ended in 1993, it remains popular in reruns.

BIRTHDAYS TODAY

Ruth Bader Ginsburg, 68, Associate Justice of the US Supreme Court, born Brooklyn, NY, Mar 15, 1933.

Don Sundquist, 65, Governor of Tennessee (R), born Moline, IL, Mar 15, 1936.

Ruth White, 59, author (*Belle Prater's Boy*), born Whitewood, VA, Mar 15, 1942.

MARCH 16 — FRIDAY
Day 75 — 290 Remaining

BLACK PRESS DAY: ANNIVERSARY OF THE FIRST BLACK NEWSPAPER. Mar 16, 1827. Anniversary of the founding of the first black newspaper in the US, *Freedom's Journal*, on Varick Street at New York, NY.

CLYMER, GEORGE: BIRTH ANNIVERSARY. Mar 16, 1739. Signer of the Declaration of Independence and of the US Constitution. Born at Philadelphia, PA and died there Jan 24, 1813.

GODDARD DAY. Mar 16, 1926. Commemorates first liquid-fuel-powered rocket flight, devised by Robert Hutchings Goddard (1882–1945) at Auburn, MA.

"THE GUMBY SHOW" TV PREMIERE: ANNIVERSARY. Mar 16, 1957. This kids' show was a spin-off from "Howdy Doody," where the character of Gumby was first introduced in 1956. Gumby and his horse Pokey were clay figures whose adventures were filmed using the process of "claymation." "The Gumby Show," created by Art Clokey, was first hosted by Bobby Nicholson and later by Pinky Lee. It was syndicated in 1966 and again in 1988. In 1995 *Gumby: The Movie* was released.

MADISON, JAMES: 250th BIRTH ANNIVERSARY. Mar 16, 1751. Fourth president of the US (Mar 4, 1809–Mar 3, 1817), born at Port Conway, VA. He was president when British forces invaded Washington, DC, requiring Madison and other high officials to flee while the British burned the Capitol, the president's residence and most other public buildings (Aug 24–25, 1814). Died at Montpelier, VA, June 28, 1836. For more info: *The Great Little Madison*, by Jean Fritz (Putnam, 0-399-21768-1, $15.99, Gr. 7–9).

MOON PHASE: LAST QUARTER. Mar 16. Moon enters Last Quarter phase at 3:45 PM, EST.

NIXON, THELMA CATHERINE PATRICIA RYAN: BIRTH ANNIVERSARY. Mar 16, 1912. Wife of Richard Milhous Nixon, 37th president of the US. Born at Ely, NV, she died at Park Ridge, NJ, June 22, 1993.

BIRTHDAYS TODAY

Mary Chalmers, 74, author and illustrator (*Come for a Walk With Me*), born Camden, NJ, Mar 16, 1927.

Sid Fleischman, 81, author (Newbery for *The Whipping Boy*), born Albert Sidney Fleischman, Brooklyn, NY, Mar 16, 1920.

William Mayne, 73, author (*Lady Muck*), born Kingston-upon-Hull, England, Mar 16, 1928.

Daniel Patrick Moynihan, 74, US Senator (D, New York), born Tulsa, OK, Mar 16, 1927.

MARCH 17 — SATURDAY

Day 76 — 289 Remaining

ASSOCIATION FOR SUPERVISION AND CURRICULUM DEVELOPMENT CONFERENCE. Mar 17–19. Boston, MA. For info: Assn for Supervision and Curriculum Development, 1703 N Beauregard St, Alexandria, VA 22311-1714. Phone: (703) 578-9600. Fax: (703) 575-5400. Web: www.ascd.org.

CAMP FIRE BOYS AND GIRLS: ANNIVERSARY. Mar 17. To commemorate the anniversary of the founding of Camp Fire Boys and Girls and the service given to children and youth across the nation. Founded in 1910 as Camp Fire Girls. For info: Camp Fire Boys and Girls, 4601 Madison Ave, Kansas City, MO 64112. Phone: (816) 756-1950. Fax: (816) 756-0258. E-mail: info@campfire.org. Web: www.campfire.org.

EVACUATION DAY IN MASSACHUSETTS. Mar 17, 1776. Proclaimed annually by the governor, Evacuation Day commemorates the anniversary of the evacuation from Boston of British troops.

IRELAND: NATIONAL DAY. Mar 17. St. Patrick's Day is observed in the Republic of Ireland as a legal national holiday.

NORTHERN IRELAND: SAINT PATRICK'S DAY HOLIDAY. Mar 17. National Holiday.

RUSTIN, BAYARD: BIRTH ANNIVERSARY. Mar 17, 1910. Black pacifist and civil rights leader, Bayard Rustin was an organizer and participant in many of the great social protest marches—for jobs, freedom and nuclear disarmament. He was arrested and imprisoned more than 20 times for his civil rights and pacifist activities. Born at West Chester, PA, Rustin died at New York, NY, Aug 24, 1987.

	S	M	T	W	T	F	S
March					1	2	3
2001	4	5	6	7	8	9	10
	11	12	13	14	15	16	17
	18	19	20	21	22	23	24
	25	26	27	28	29	30	31

SAINT PATRICK'S DAY. Mar 17. Commemorates the patron saint of Ireland, Bishop Patrick (AD 389–461) who, about AD 432, left his home in the Severn Valley, England, and introduced Christianity into Ireland. Feast Day in the Roman Catholic Church. A national holiday in Ireland and Northern Ireland. For links to websites about St. Patrick's Day, go to: deil.lang.uiuc.edu/web.pages/holidays/stpatrick.html.

SAINT PATRICK'S DAY PARADE. Mar 17. Fifth Avenue, New York, NY. Held since 1762, the parade of 125,000 begins the two-mile march at 11:30 AM and lasts about six hours. Starts on 42nd Street and 5th Avenue and ends at 86th Street and First Avenue. Est attendance: 1,000,000. For info: NY CVB, 810 Seventh Ave, New York, NY 10019. Phone: (800) NYC-VISIT or (212) 484-1222.

SAVE THE FLORIDA PANTHER DAY. Mar 17. A ceremonial day on the third Saturday in March.

SOUTH AFRICAN WHITES VOTE TO END MINORITY RULE: ANNIVERSARY. Mar 17, 1992. A referendum proposing ending white minority rule through negotiations was supported by a whites-only ballot. The vote of 1,924,186 (68.6 percent) whites in support of President F.W. de Klerk's reform policies was greater than expected.

TANEY, ROGER B.: BIRTH ANNIVERSARY. Mar 17, 1777. Fifth Chief Justice of the Supreme Court, born at Calvert County, MD. Served as Attorney General under President Andrew Jackson. Nominated as Secretary of the Treasury, he became the first presidential nominee to be rejected by the Senate because of his strong stance against the Bank of the United States as a central bank. A year later, he was nominated to the Supreme Court as an associate justice by Jackson, but his nomination was stalled until the death of Chief Justice John Marshall July 6, 1835. Taney was nominated to fill Marshall's place on the bench and after much resistance he was sworn in as Chief Justice in March 1836. His tenure on the Supreme Court is most remembered for the Dred Scott decision. He died at Washington, DC, Oct 12, 1864.

BIRTHDAYS TODAY

Patrick Duffy, 52, actor ("Step By Step"), born Townsend, MT, Mar 17, 1949.

Penelope Lively, 68, author (*Moon Tiger*), born Cairo, Egypt, Mar 17, 1933.

MARCH 18 — SUNDAY

Day 77 — 288 Remaining

ARUBA: FLAG DAY. Mar 18. Aruba national holiday. Display of flags, national music and folkloric events.

CALHOUN, JOHN CALDWELL: BIRTH ANNIVERSARY. Mar 18, 1782. American statesman and first vice president of the US to resign that office (Dec 28, 1832). Born at Abbeville District, SC, he died at Washington, DC, Mar 31, 1850.

CAMP FIRE BOYS AND GIRLS BIRTHDAY SUNDAY. Mar 18. A day when Camp Fire Boys and Girls commemorate the organization's founding and worship together and participate in the services of their churches or temples. For info: Camp Fire Boys and Girls, 4601 Madison Ave, Kansas City, MO 64112. Phone: (816) 756-1950. Fax: (816) 756-0258. E-mail: info@campfire.org. Web: www.campfire.org.

CHILDREN'S LITERATURE FESTIVAL. Mar 18–20 (tentative). Central Missouri State University, Warrensburg, MO. Designed for teachers to introduce them to authors of children's and young adult literature. Est attendance: 7,000. For info: Pal V. Rao, Children's Literature Festival, Central Missouri State Univ, Warrensburg, MO 64093. Phone: (660) 543-4140. Fax: (660) 543-8001. E-mail: Pal@libserv.cmsu.edu. Web: library.cmsu.edu.

CLEVELAND, GROVER: BIRTH ANNIVERSARY. Mar 18, 1837. The 22nd (Mar 4, 1885–Mar 3, 1889) and 24th (Mar 4, 1893–Mar 3, 1897) president of the US was born Stephen Grover Cleveland at Caldwell, NJ. He ran for president for the intervening term and received a plurality of votes cast but failed to win electoral college victory for that term. Only president to serve two nonconsecutive terms. Also the only president to be married in the White House. He married 21-year-old Frances Folsom, his ward. Their daughter, Esther, was the first child of a president to be born in the White House. Died at Princeton, NJ, June 24, 1908.

JOBS FOR TEENS WEEK. Mar 18–24. To encourage young adults to better prepare themselves for their future career through practical experience in the workplace. Free information/resource kit available for teachers, librarians, counselors. Annually, during the week containing the first day of Spring. For info: Highsmith Press, PO Box 800, Ft Atkinson, WI 53538-0800. Phone: (800) 558-2110. Fax: (920) 563-4801. E-mail: hpress@highsmith.com. Web: www.hpress.highsmith.com.

JORDAN'S BACK!: ANNIVERSARY. Mar 18, 1995. Michael Jordan, considered one of the National Basketball Association's greatest all-time players, made history again when he announced that he was returning to professional play after a 17-month break. The 32-year-old star had retired just before the start of the 1993–94 season, following the murder of his father, James Jordan. Jordan, who averaged 32.3 points a game during regular season play, had led the Chicago Bulls to three successive NBA titles. While retired, he tried a baseball career, playing for the Chicago White Sox minor league team. After returning to the Bulls, he led them to three more NBA titles. He announced his retirement again Jan 13, 1999 after the six-month NBA lockout was resolved.

NATIONAL AGRICULTURE WEEK. Mar 18–24. To honor America's providers of food and fiber and to educate the general public about the US agricultural system. Annually, the week that includes the first day of spring. For info: Agriculture Council of America, 11020 King St, Ste 205, Overland Park, KS 66210. Phone: (913) 491-1895. Fax: (913) 491-6502. E-mail: info@agday.org. Web: www.agday.org.

NATIONAL POISON PREVENTION WEEK. Mar 18–24. To aid in encouraging the American people to learn of the dangers of accidental poisoning and to take preventive measures against it. Annually, the third full week in March. For info: Ken Giles, Secy, Poison Prevention Week Council, Box 1543, Washington, DC 20013. E-mail: kgiles@cpsc.gov. Web: www.cpsc.gov.

SPACE MILESTONE: *VOSKHOD 2* **(USSR).** Mar 18, 1965. Colonel Leonov stepped out of the capsule for 20 minutes in a special space suit, the first man to leave a spaceship. It was two months prior to the first US space walk. See also "Space Milestone: *Gemini 4* (US)" (June 3).

Bonnie Blair, 37, former Olympic gold medal speed skater, born Cornwall, NY, Mar 18, 1964.
Queen Latifah, 31, singer, actress ("Living Single"), born Dana Owens, East Orange, NJ, Mar 18, 1970.

MARCH 19 — MONDAY
Day 78 — 287 Remaining

AUSTRALIA: CANBERRA DAY. Mar 19. Australian Capital Territory. Public holiday the third Monday in March.

BRADFORD, WILLIAM: BIRTH ANNIVERSARY. Mar 19, 1589. Pilgrim father, governor of Plymouth Colony, born at Yorkshire, England, and baptized Mar 19, 1589. Sailed from Southampton, England, on the *Mayflower* in 1620. Died at Plymouth, MA, May 9, 1657. For more info: *William Bradford: Rock of Plymouth*, by Kieran Doherty (Twenty First Century, 0-7613-1304-4, $22.90 Gr. 6–10).

EARP, WYATT: BIRTH ANNIVERSARY. Mar 19, 1848. Born at Monmouth, IL, and died Jan 13, 1929, at Los Angeles, CA. A legendary figure of the Old West, Earp worked as a railroad hand, saloonkeeper, gambler, lawman, gunslinger, miner and real estate investor at various times. Best known for his involvement in the gunfight at the OK Corral Oct 26, 1881, at Tombstone, AZ.

McKEAN, THOMAS: BIRTH ANNIVERSARY. Mar 19, 1734. Signer of the Declaration of Independence. Born at Chester County, PA, he died June 24, 1817.

NATIONAL ENERGY EDUCATION WEEK. Mar 19–23. To make energy education part of the school curriculum. The week ending in the second to the last Friday in March. For info: Natl Energy Education Development Project, PO Box 2518, Reston, VA 20195. Phone: (800) 875-5029.

SWALLOWS RETURN TO SAN JUAN CAPISTRANO. Mar 19. Traditional date (St. Joseph's Day), since 1776, for swallows to return to old mission of San Juan Capistrano, CA.

US STANDARD TIME ACT: ANNIVERSARY. Mar 19, 1918. Anniversary of passage by the Congress of the Standard Time Act, which authorized the Interstate Commerce Commission to establish standard time zones for the US. The Act also established "Daylight Saving Time," to save fuel and to promote other economies in a country at war. Daylight-saving time first went into operation on Easter Sunday, Mar 31, 1918. The Uniform Time Act of 1966, as amended in 1986, by Public Law 99–359, now governs standard time in the US. See also: "US: Daylight Saving Time Begins" (Apr 1).

WARREN, EARL: BIRTH ANNIVERSARY. Mar 19, 1891. American jurist, 14th Chief Justice of the US Supreme Court. Born at Los Angeles, CA, died at Washington, DC, July 9, 1974.

BIRTHDAYS TODAY

Glenn Close, 54, actress (*101 Dalmatians*), born Greenwich, CT, Mar 19, 1947.

Hazel Dodge, 42, author (*The Ancient Life: Life in Classical Athens & Rome*), born Feltham, England, Mar 19, 1959.

Bruce Willis, 46, actor (*Die Hard*, voice in *Look Who's Talking 2*), born Penn's Grove, NJ, Mar 19, 1955.

MARCH 20 — TUESDAY
Day 79 — 286 Remaining

ANONYMOUS GIVING WEEK. Mar 20–26. A time to celebrate the true spirit of giving. Experience the joy in random acts of kindness. Leave a legacy of anonymous contribution. Perfect for a one-time or all-week adventure designed to share time, talent and treasure. Annually, beginning on the first day of Spring. For info: Janna Krammer, Legacy Institute, 42805 Blackhawk Rd, Harris, MN 55032. Phone: (612) 674-0227. Fax: (612) 674-0228. E-mail: info@legacyinsititute.com.

LEGOLAND OPENS: ANNIVERSARY. Mar 20, 1999. The Legoland theme park for children ages 2–12 opened on this day at Carlsbad, CA. It is the third Legoland park; the others are in Denmark and England. More than 30 million Lego pieces went into the construction of 40 rides and attractions. Since its beginnings in the 1950s, the Danish maker has manufactured more than 189 billion Lego blocks. Legos were introduced in the US in 1962. For info: Legoland, One Lego Dr, Carlsbad, CA 92008. Phone: (760) 918-LEGO. Web: lego.com.

NATIONAL AGRICULTURE DAY. Mar 20. A day to honor America's providers of food and fiber and to educate the general public about the US agricultural system. Week of celebration: Mar 19–25. Annually, the first day of spring. For info: Agriculture Council of America, 11020 King St, Ste 205, Overland Park, KS 66210. Phone: (913) 491-1895. Fax: (913) 491-6502. E-mail: aca @nama.org. Web: www.agday.org.

SPRING. Mar 20–June 21. In the Northern Hemisphere spring begins today with the vernal equinox, at 8:31 AM, EST. Note that in the Southern Hemisphere today is the beginning of autumn. Sun rises due east and sets due west everywhere on Earth (except

		S	M	T	W	T	F	S
March							1	2	3
2001		4	5	6	7	8	9	10
		11	12	13	14	15	16	17
		18	19	20	21	22	23	24
		25	26	27	28	29	30	31

near poles) and the daylight length (interval between sunrise and sunset) is virtually the same everywhere today: 12 hours, 8 minutes.

TUNISIA: INDEPENDENCE DAY. Mar 20. Commemorates treaty in 1956 by which France recognized Tunisian autonomy.

BIRTHDAYS TODAY

Mitsumasa Anno, 75, author and illustrator (*Topsy-Turvies, Anno's Alphabet*), born Tsuwano, Japan, Mar 20, 1926.

Ellen Conford, 59, author (*Hail, Hail Camp Timberwood*), born New York, NY, Mar 20, 1942.

Lois Lowry, 64, author (Newbery for *Number the Stars, The Giver*), born Honolulu, HI, Mar 20, 1937.

Patrick James (Pat) Riley, 56, basketball coach and former player, born Schenectady, NY, Mar 20, 1945.

Fred Rogers, 73, producer, TV personality ("Mr Rogers' Neighborhood"), born Latrobe, PA, Mar 20, 1928.

Louis Sachar, 47, author (National Book Award for *Holes*), born East Meadow, NY, Mar 20, 1954.

MARCH 21 — WEDNESDAY
Day 80 — 285 Remaining

ARIES, THE RAM. Mar 21–Apr 19. In the astronomical/astrological zodiac, which divides the sun's apparent orbit into 12 segments, the period Mar 21–Apr 19 is identified, traditionally, as the sun sign of Aries, the Ram. The ruling planet is Mars.

BACH, JOHANN SEBASTIAN: BIRTH ANNIVERSARY. Mar 21, 1685. Organist and composer, one of the most influential composers in musical history. Born at Eisenach, Germany, he died at Leipzig, Germany, July 28, 1750. For more info: *Sebastian: A Book about Bach*, by Jeanette Winter (Harcourt, 0-15-200629-X, $16 Gr. 2–4).

CHILDREN'S BOOK FESTIVAL. Mar 21–23 (tentative). Hattiesburg, MS. This three-day spring festival brings together children's authors and illustrators for workshops, question and answer sessions and storytelling. For info: Kalicia Henderson, Children's Book Festival, USM Continuing Education, Box 5055B, Hattiesburg, MS 39406. Phone: (601) 266-4186. Web: ocean.st .usm.edu/~mhamilto/.

FIRST ROUND-THE-WORLD BALLOON FLIGHT: ANNIVERSARY. Mar 21, 1999. Swiss psychiatrist Bertrand Piccard and British copilot Brian Jones landed in the Egyptian desert on this date, having flown 29,056 miles non-stop around the world in a hot-air balloon, the *Breitling Orbiter 3*. Leaving from Chateau d'Oex in the Swiss Alps on Mar 1, the trip took 19 days, 21 hours and 55 minutes. Piccard is the grandson of balloonist Auguste Piccard, who was the first to ascend into the stratosphere in a balloon. See also: "Piccard, Auguste: Birth Anniversary" (Jan 28).

IRANIAN NEW YEAR: NORUZ. Mar 21. National celebration for all Iranians, this is the traditional Persian New Year. (In Iran spring comes Mar 21.) It is a celebration of nature's rebirth. Every household spreads a special cover with symbols for the seven good angels on it. These symbols are sprouts, wheat germ, apples, hyacinth, fruit of the jujube, garlic and sumac heralding life, rebirth, health, happiness, prosperity, joy and beauty. A fish bowl is also customary, representing the end of the astrological year, and wild rue is burnt to drive away evil and bring about a happy New Year. This pre-Islamic holiday, a legacy of Zoroastrianism, is also celebrated as Navruz, Nau-Roz or Noo Roz in Afghanistan, Albania, Azerbaijan, Kazakhstan, Kyrgyzstan, Tajikistan and Turkmenistan. For info: Mahvash Tafreshi, Librarian, Farmingdale Public Library, 116 Merritts Rd, Farmingdale, NY 11735. Phone:

(516) 249-9090. Fax: (516) 694-9697 or Yassaman Djalali, Librarian, West Valley Branch Library, 1243 San Tomas Aquino Rd, San Jose, CA 95117. Phone: (408) 244-4766.

JAPAN: VERNAL EQUINOX DAY. Mar 21. A national holiday in Japan. When Mar 21 falls on a weekend, it is celebrated on the nearest weekday.

JUAREZ, BENITO: BIRTH ANNIVERSARY. Mar 21, 1806. A full-blooded Zapotec Indian, Benito Pablo Juarez was born at Oaxaca, Mexico and grew up to become the president of Mexico. He learned Spanish at age 12. Juarez became judge of the civil court in Oaxaca in 1842, a member of congress in 1846 and governor in 1847. In 1858, following a rebellion against the constitution, the presidency was passed to Juarez. He died at Mexico City, July 18, 1872. A symbol of liberation and of Mexican resistance to foreign intervention, his birthday is a public holiday in Mexico.

LEWIS, FRANCIS: BIRTH ANNIVERSARY. Mar 21, 1713. Signer of the Declaration of Independence, born at Wales. Died Dec 31, 1802, at Long Island, NY.

NAMIBIA: INDEPENDENCE DAY. Mar 21. National Day. Commemorates independence from South Africa in 1990.

NAW-RUZ. Mar 21. Baha'i New Year's Day. Astronomically fixed to commence the year. One of the nine days of the year when Baha'is suspend work. For info: Baha'is of the US, Office of Public Info, 866 UN Plaza, Ste 120, New York, NY 10017-1822. Phone: (212) 803-2500. Fax: (212) 803-2573. E-mail: usopi-ny@bic.org. Web: www.us.bahai.org.

POCAHONTAS (REBECCA ROLFE): DEATH ANNIVERSARY. Mar 21, 1617. Pocahontas, daughter of Powhatan, born about 1595, near Jamestown, VA, leader of the Indian union of Algonkin nations, helped to foster good will between the colonists of the Jamestown settlement and her people. Pocahontas converted to Christianity, was baptized with the name Rebecca and married John Rolfe Apr 5, 1614. In 1616, she accompanied Rolfe on a trip to his native England, where she was regarded as an overseas "ambassador." Pocahontas's stay in England drew so much attention to the Virginia Company's Jamestown settlement that lotteries were held to help support the colony. Shortly before she was scheduled to return to Jamestown, Pocahontas died at Gravesend, Kent, England, of either smallpox or pneumonia.

SINGLE PARENTS DAY. Mar 21. Dedicated to recognizing and heightening awareness of Americans to the issues related to single-parent households. In 1984, Congress established Mar 21 as Single Parents Day. Each year the Coalition for Single Parents gives out the Single Parent of the Year Award. 1998 recipient: Rosie O'Donnell. For info: Janice S. Moglen, PO Box 61014, Denver, CO 80206. Phone: (303) 899-4971. Fax: (303) 832-1667. E-mail: daymar21@privatei.com.

SOUTH AFRICA: HUMAN RIGHTS DAY. Mar 21. National holiday. Commemorates the massacre in 1960 at Sharpeville and all those who lost their lives in the struggle for equal rights as citizens of South Africa.

UNITED NATIONS: INTERNATIONAL DAY FOR THE ELIMINATION OF RACIAL DISCRIMINATION. Mar 21. Initiated by the United Nations General Assembly in 1966 to be observed annually Mar 21, the anniversary of the killing of 69 African demonstrators at Sharpeville, South Africa in 1960, as a day to remember "the victims of Sharpeville and those countless others in different parts of the world who have fallen victim to racial injustice" and to promote efforts to eradicate racial discrimination worldwide. Info from: United Nations, Dept of Public Info, New York, NY 10017.

BIRTHDAYS TODAY

Matthew Broderick, 39, actor (*Inspector Gadget*), born New York, NY, Mar 21, 1962.

Peter Catalanotto, 42, author and illustrator (*Dylan's Day Out*), born Long Island, NY, Mar 21, 1959.

Lisa Desimini, 37, author and illustrator (*My House*), born Brooklyn, NY, Mar 21, 1964.

Michael Foreman, 63, author and illustrator (*Seal Surfer*), born Pakefield, Suffolk, England, Mar 21, 1938.

Margaret Mahy, 65, author (*The Rattlebang Picnic*), born Whakatane, New Zealand, Mar 21, 1936.

Rosie O'Donnell, 39, talk show host, actress (*A League of Their Own, The Flintstones*), born Commack, NY, Mar 21, 1962.

David Wisniewski, 48, illustrator and author (Caldecott for *Golem*), born Middlesex, England, Mar 21, 1953.

MARCH 22 — THURSDAY
Day 81 — 284 Remaining

CALDECOTT, RANDOLPH: BIRTH ANNIVERSARY. Mar 22, 1846. Illustrator who brought greater beauty to children's books, born at Chester, England. He died at St. Augustine, FL, Feb 12, 1886. The Caldecott Medal given annually by the American Library Association for the most distinguished American picture book for children is named in his honor. *See* Curriculum Connection.

EQUAL RIGHTS AMENDMENT SENT TO STATES FOR RATIFICATION: ANNIVERSARY. Mar 22, 1972. The Senate passed the 27th Amendment, prohibiting discrimination on the basis of sex, sending it to the states for ratification. Hawaii led the way as the first state to ratify and by the end of the year 22 of the required states had ratified it. On Oct 6, 1978, the deadline for ratification was extended to June 30, 1982, by Congress. The amendment still lacked three of the required 38 states for ratification. This was the first extension granted since Congress set seven years as the limit for ratification. The amendment failed to achieve ratification as the deadline came and passed and no additional states ratified the measure.

FIRST WOMEN'S COLLEGIATE BASKETBALL GAME: ANNIVERSARY. Mar 22, 1893. The first women's collegiate basketball game was played at Smith College at Northampton, MA. Senda Berenson, then Smith's director of physical education and "mother of women's basketball," supervised the game, in which Smith's sophomore team beat the freshman team 5–4. For info: Dir of Media Relations, Smith College, Office of College Relations, Northampton, MA 01063. Phone: (413) 585-2190. Fax: (413) 585-2174. E-mail: lfenlason@colrel.smith.edu.

INTERNATIONAL GOOF-OFF DAY. Mar 22. A day of relaxation and a time to be oneself; a day for some good-humored fun and some good-natured silliness. Everyone needs one special day each year to goof off. For info: Monica A. Dufour, 471 S Vanburen Circle, Davison, MI 48423-8535. Phone: (810) 658-3147.

MARCH 22
RANDOLPH CALDECOTT'S BIRTHDAY

Randolph Caldecott was born in Chester, England on this date in 1846. He is remembered for his lively illustration of children's books. Caldecott's work drew the attention of the general public to the charm and value of illustrated children's books. During the 17th and 18th centuries, children were regarded as little adults. By the latter part of the 19th century, society's views had altered and childhood was starting to be accepted as a playing and learning time. Caldecott's artistic style was well suited to the new concept of children's literature as a pleasurable, rather than a didactic or an educational, experience. His humorous pictures held great appeal for young readers.

The Caldecott Medal is awarded in the United States by the American Library Association to the illustrator of the most distinguished picture book for children published in the preceding year. The award was named in recognition of Randolph Caldecott's contribution to the field of picture books and children's book illustration.

Caldecott's illustrations can be found in three books that contain his collected works, published by Frederick Warne. Although they are out of print, they should be available in public library collections. *Randolph Caldecott: The Children's Illustrator*, by Marguerite Lewis (Highsmith, 0-913853-22-4, $10.95 Gr. 2–7) is a biography.

March is also Youth Art Month. One way to celebrate this month and Caldecott's birthday is by focusing on children's book illustration. *What Do Illustrators Do?* by Eileen Christelow (Clarion, 0-395-90230-4, $15 Gr. 1–4) provides a nice overview of how illustrators work. Pat Cummings has edited a three-volume collection, published by Simon & Schuster, titled *Talking With Artists*. Barbara Elleman's *Tomie dePaola: His Art and His Stories* (Putnam, 0-399-23129-3, $35) is a retrospective study of the work of a popular children's book author and illustrator. *A Caldecott Celebration: Six Authors Share Their Paths to the Caldecott Medal*, by Leonard Marcus (Walker, 0-8027-8656-1, $18.95) focuses on how six children's illustrators created their award-winning books.

To begin your celebration of illustration, choose a selection of Caldecott Medal books from various years. Arrange them in chronological order around the front of the room. Ask students, as a class, to talk about the illustrations in each book, starting with the oldest example. Note their comments on the overhead or blackboard. One of the changes students will note is the development of the four-color printing process and how it altered the look of picture books. *Color*, by Ruth Heller (Putnam, 0-399-22815-2, $18.95 Gr. 2–6) will be helpful to explain the process.

Next, explore different artistic media and styles. Categorize a selection of books by medium: paint, pencil, collage, printmaking, photography and computer-generated art. Another way to categorize is by choosing a selection based on artistic style, including representations of realistic, cartoon, impressionistic and abstract illustrations. Let students create their own artwork by making classroom books to reflect each artistic style. Talk about representing emotion or physical movement in illustration and how the different styles may be used effectively. Above all, stress that art and illustration should engage readers and make them want to become involved in the reading/looking experience.

For a larger connection to the art world, students may compare artistic styles found in children's book illustration with famous works done by the grand masters of the art world at large.

LASER PATENTED: ANNIVERSARY. Mar 22, 1960. The first patent for a laser (Light Amplification by Stimulated Emission of Radiation) was granted to Arthur Schawlow and Charles Townes.

NATIONAL SCIENCE TEACHERS ASSOCIATION NATIONAL CONVENTION. Mar 22–25. St. Louis, MO. For info: Natl Science Teachers Assn, 1840 Wilson Blvd, Arlington, VA 22201-3000. Phone: (703) 243-7100. Web: www.nsta.org.

SPACE MILESTONE: RECORD TIME IN SPACE. Mar 22, 1995. A Russian cosmonaut returned to Earth after setting a record of 439 days in space aboard *Mir*. Previous records include three Soviet cosmonauts who spent 237 days in space at *Salyut 7* space station in 1984, a Soviet cosmonaut who spent 326 days aboard *Mir* in 1987 and two Soviets who spent 366 days aboard *Mir* in 1988. The longest stay in space by any US astronaut was Shannon Lucid's 188-day stay on *Mir* in 1996. This also set a record for women in space.

UNITED NATIONS: WORLD DAY FOR WATER. Mar 22. The General Assembly declared this observance (Res 47/193) to promote public awareness of how water resource development contributes to economic productivity and social well-being.

BIRTHDAYS TODAY

Shawn Bradley, 29, basketball player, born Landstuhl, West Germany, Mar 22, 1972.

Robert Quinlan (Bob) Costas, 49, sportscaster, born New York, NY, Mar 22, 1952.

Orrin Grant Hatch, 67, US Senator (R, Utah), born Pittsburgh, PA, Mar 22, 1934.

Cristen Powell, 22, race car driver, born Portland, OR, Mar 22, 1979.

William Shatner, 70, actor (Captain Kirk of "Star Trek"; "TJ Hooker"), author (*Tek* novels), born Montreal, Quebec, Canada, Mar 22, 1931.

Elvis Stojko, 29, skater, born Newmarket, Ontario, Canada, Mar 22, 1972.

MARCH 23 — FRIDAY
Day 82 — 283 Remaining

COLFAX, SCHUYLER: BIRTH ANNIVERSARY. Mar 23, 1823. The 17th vice president of the US (1869–73). Born at New York, NY. Died Jan 13, 1885, at Mankato, MN.

LIBERTY DAY: ANNIVERSARY. Mar 23, 1775. Anniversary of Patrick Henry's speech for arming the Virginia militia at St. Johns Church, Richmond, VA. "I know not what course others may take, but as for me, give me liberty or give me death."

NEAR MISS DAY. Mar 23, 1989. A mountain-sized asteroid passed within 500,000 miles of Earth, a very close call according to NASA. Impact would have equaled the strength of 40,000 hydrogen bombs, created a crater the size of the District of Columbia and devastated everything for 100 miles in all directions.

NEW ZEALAND: OTAGO AND SOUTHLAND PROVINCIAL ANNIVERSARY. Mar 23. In addition to the statutory public holidays of New Zealand, there is in each provincial district a holiday for the provincial anniversary. This is observed in Otago and Southland.

PAKISTAN: REPUBLIC DAY: ANNIVERSARY. Mar 23. National holiday. The All-India-Muslim League adopted a resolution calling for a Muslim homeland in 1940. On the same day in 1956 Pakistan declared itself a republic.

UNITED NATIONS: WORLD METEOROLOGICAL DAY. Mar 23. An international day observed by meteorological services throughout the world and by the organizations of the UN system. For info: United Nations, Dept of Public Info, New York, NY 10017.

BIRTHDAYS TODAY

Eleanor Cameron, 89, author (*The Court of the Stone Children*), born Winnipeg, Manitoba, Canada, Mar 23, 1912.

Jason Kidd, 28, basketball player, born San Francisco, CA, Mar 23, 1973.

Moses Eugene Malone, 47, former basketball player, born Petersburg, VA, Mar 23, 1954.

MARCH 24 — SATURDAY
Day 83 — 282 Remaining

EXXON VALDEZ OIL SPILL: ANNIVERSARY. Mar 24, 1989. The tanker *Exxon Valdez* ran aground at Prince William Sound, leaking 11 million gallons of oil into one of nature's richest habitats.

HOUDINI, HARRY: BIRTH ANNIVERSARY. Mar 24, 1874. Magician and escape artist, born at Budapest, Hungary. Lecturer, athlete, author, expert on history of magic, exposer of fraudulent mediums and motion picture actor. Was best known for his ability to escape from locked restraints (handcuffs, straitjackets, coffins, boxes and milk cans). He died at Detroit, MI, Oct 31, 1926. Anniversary of his death (Halloween) has been the occasion for meetings of magicians and attempts at communication by mediums.

MOON PHASE: NEW MOON. Mar 24. Moon enters New Moon phase at 8:21 PM, EST.

NATIONAL SCHOOL BOARDS ASSOCIATION ANNUAL CONFERENCE. Mar 24–27. San Diego, CA. For info: Natl School Boards Assn, 1680 Duke St, Alexandria, VA 22314. Phone: (703) 838-6722. Fax: (703) 683-7590. E-mail: info@nsba.org. Web: www.nsba.org.

PHILIPPINE INDEPENDENCE: ANNIVERSARY. Mar 24, 1934. President Franklin Roosevelt signed a bill granting independence to the Philippines. The bill, which took effect July 4, 1946, brought to a close almost half a century of US control of the islands.

RHODE ISLAND VOTERS REJECT CONSTITUTION: ANNIVERSARY. Mar 24, 1788. In a popular referendum, Rhode Island rejected the new Constitution by a vote of 2,708 to 237. The state later (May 29, 1790) ratified the Constitution and ratified the Bill of Rights, June 7, 1790.

TB BACILLUS DISCOVERED: ANNIVERSARY. Mar 24, 1882. The tuberculosis bacillus was discovered by German scientist Robert Koch.

BIRTHDAYS TODAY

Dr. Roger Bannister, 72, distance runner, broke the 4-minute-mile record in 1954, born Harrow, Middlesex, England, Mar 24, 1929.

MARCH 25 — SUNDAY
Day 84 — 281 Remaining

BORGLUM, GUTZON: BIRTH ANNIVERSARY. Mar 25, 1871. American sculptor who created the huge sculpture of four American presidents (Washington, Jefferson, Lincoln and Theodore Roosevelt) at Mount Rushmore National Memorial in the Black Hills of South Dakota. Born John Gutzon de la Mothe Borglum at Bear Lake, ID, the son of Mormon pioneers, he worked the last 14 years of his life on the Mount Rushmore sculpture. He died at Chicago, IL, Mar 6, 1941.

★**EDUCATION AND SHARING DAY.** Mar 25.

EUROPE: SUMMER DAYLIGHT SAVING TIME. Mar 25–Oct 28. Many European countries observe daylight-saving (summer) time from 2 AM on the last Sunday in March until 3 AM on the last Sunday in October.

FEAST OF ANNUNCIATION. Mar 25. Celebrated in the Roman Catholic Church in commemoration of the message of the Angel Gabriel to Mary that she was to be the Mother of Christ.

GREECE: INDEPENDENCE DAY. Mar 25. National holiday. Celebrates the beginning of the Greek revolt for independence from the Ottoman Empire in 1821. Greece attained independence in 1829.

★**GREEK INDEPENDENCE DAY: A NATIONAL DAY OF CELEBRATION OF GREEK AND AMERICAN DEMOCRACY.** Mar 25.

MARYLAND DAY. Mar 25. Commemorates arrival of Lord Baltimore's first settlers in Maryland in 1634.

NATO ATTACKS YUGOSLAVIA: ANNIVERSARY. Mar 25, 1999. After many weeks of unsuccessful negotiations with Yugoslav leader Slobodan Milosevic over the treatment of ethnic Albanians in the Kosovo Province by Serb forces, NATO forces began bombing Serbia and Kosovo. In retaliation, hundreds of thousands of Kosovo Albanians were driven from their homes into Albania, Macedonia and Montenegro. Peace talks began in June 1999.

PECAN DAY: ANNIVERSARY. Mar 25, 1775. Anniversary of the planting by George Washington, of pecan trees (some of which still survive) at Mount Vernon. The trees were a gift to Washington from Thomas Jefferson, who had planted a few pecan trees from the southern US at Monticello, VA. The pecan, native to southern North America, is sometimes called "America's own nut." First cultivated by American Indians, it has been transplanted to other continents but has failed to achieve wide use or popularity outside the US.

TRIANGLE SHIRTWAIST FIRE: 90th ANNIVERSARY. Mar 25, 1911. At about 4:30 PM, fire broke out at the Triangle Shirtwaist Company at New York, NY, minutes before the seamstresses were to go home. Some workers were fatally burned while others leaped to their deaths from the windows of the 10-story building. The fire lasted only 18 minutes but left 146 workers dead, most of them young immigrant women. It was found that some of the deaths were a direct result of workers being trapped on the ninth floor by a locked door. Labor law forbade locking factory doors while employees were at work, and owners of the company were indicted on charges of first- and second-degree manslaughter. The tragic fire became a turning point in labor history, bringing about reforms in health and safety laws.

UNITED KINGDOM: SUMMER TIME. Mar 26–Oct 28. "Summer Time" (one hour in advance of Standard Time), similar to daylight-saving time, is observed from 0100 hours on the day after the fourth Saturday in March until 0100 hours on the day after the fourth Saturday in October.

BIRTHDAYS TODAY

Cammi Granato, 30, Olympic ice hockey player, born Maywood, IL, Mar 25, 1971.

Elton John, 54, singer, songwriter, born Reginald Kenneth Dwight, Pinner, England, Mar 25, 1947.

Avery Johnson, 36, basketball player, born New Orleans, LA, Mar 25, 1965.

MARCH 26 — MONDAY

Day 85 — 280 Remaining

BANGLADESH: INDEPENDENCE DAY: 30th ANNIVERSARY. Mar 26. Commemorates East Pakistan's independence in 1971 as the state of Bangladesh. Celebrated with parades, youth festivals and symposia.

CAMP DAVID ACCORD SIGNED: ANNIVERSARY. Mar 26, 1979. Israeli Prime Minister Menachem Begin and Egyptian President Anwar Sadat signed the Camp David peace treaty, ending 30 years of war between their two countries. The agreement was fostered by President Jimmy Carter.

FROST, ROBERT LEE: BIRTH ANNIVERSARY. Mar 26, 1874. American poet who tried his hand at farming, teaching, shoemaking and editing before winning acclaim as a poet. Pulitzer Prize winner. Born at San Francisco, CA, he died at Boston, MA, Jan 29, 1963.

ISLAMIC NEW YEAR. Mar 26. Islamic calendar date: Muharram 1, 1422. The first day of the first month of the Islamic calendar. Different methods for "anticipating" the visibility of the new moon crescent at Mecca are used by different groups. US date may vary.

MAKE UP YOUR OWN HOLIDAY DAY. Mar 26. This day is a day you may name for whatever you wish. Reach for the stars! Make up a holiday! Annually, Mar 26. [© 1999 by WH] For info: Thomas and Ruth Roy, Wellcat Holidays, 2418 Long Ln, Lebanon, PA 17046. Phone: (230) 332-4886. E-mail: wellcat@supernet.com. Web: www.wellcat.com.

NATIONAL SLEEP AWARENESS WEEK. Mar 26–Apr 1. All Americans are urged to recognize the dangers of untreated sleep disorders and the importance of proper sleep to their health, safety and productivity. "8ZZZs, please!" Annually, the last Monday in March to the first Sunday in April. For info: Natl Sleep Foundation, 729 15th St NW, 4th Floor, Washington, DC 20005. Phone: (888) NSF-SLEEP.

PRINCE JONAH KUHIO KALANIANOLE DAY. Mar 26. Hawaii. Commemorates the man, who as Hawaii's delegate to the US Congress, introduced the first bill for statehood in 1919. Not until 1959 did Hawaii become a state.

SEWARD'S DAY: ANNIVERSARY OF THE ACQUISITION OF ALASKA. Mar 26. Observed in Alaska near anniversary of its acquisition from Russia in 1867. The treaty of purchase was signed between the Russians and the Americans Mar 30, 1867, and ratified by the Senate May 28, 1867. The territory was formally transferred Oct 18, 1867. Annually, the last Monday in March.

SOVIET COSMONAUT RETURNS TO NEW COUNTRY: ANNIVERSARY. Mar 26, 1992. After spending 313 days in space in the Soviet *Mir* space station, cosmonaut Serge Krikalev returned to Earth and to what was for him a new country. He left Earth May 18, 1991, a citizen of the Soviet Union, but during his stay aboard the space station, the Soviet Union crumbled and became the Commonwealth of Independent States. Originally scheduled to return in October 1991, Krikalev's return was delayed by five months due to his country's disintegration and the ensuing monetary problems.

BIRTHDAYS TODAY

Marcus Allen, 41, football player, born San Diego, CA, Mar 26, 1960.

Lincoln Chafee, 48, US Senator (R, Rhode Island), born Warwick, RI, Mar 26, 1953.

Sandra Day O'Connor, 71, Associate Justice of the US Supreme Court, born El Paso, TX, Mar 26, 1930.

John Houston Stockton, 39, basketball player, born Spokane, WA, Mar 26, 1962.

MARCH 27 — TUESDAY

Day 86 — 279 Remaining

AMERICAN ALLIANCE FOR HEALTH, PHYSICAL EDUCATION, RECREATION AND DANCE ANNUAL MEETING. Mar 27–31. Cincinnati, OH. For info: American Alliance for Health, Physical Education, Recreation & Dance, 1900 Association Dr, Reston, VA 20191-1599. Phone: (800) 213-7193 or (703) 476-3400. Web: www.aahperd.org.

AMERICAN DIABETES ALERT. Mar 27. A one-day "wake-up call" for those eight million Americans who have diabetes and don't even know it. During the Alert, local ADA affiliates use the diabetes risk test—a simple paper-and-pencil quiz—to communicate the risk factors and symptoms of the disease. For more info: call 1-800-DIABETES (342-2383). Annually, the fourth Tuesday in March. For info: (800) 232-3472.

EARTHQUAKE STRIKES ALASKA: ANNIVERSARY. Mar 27, 1964. The strongest earthquake in North American history (8.4 on the Richter scale) struck Alaska, east of Anchorage. 117 people were killed.

FUNKY WINKERBEAN: ANNIVERSARY. Mar 27, 1972. Anniversary of the nationally syndicated comic strip. For info: Tom Batiuk, Creator, 2750 Substation Rd, Medina, OH 44256. Phone: (330) 722-8755.

RÖNTGEN, WILHELM KONRAD: BIRTH ANNIVERSARY. Mar 27, 1845. German scientist who discovered x-rays (1895) and won a Nobel Prize in 1901. Born at Lennep, Prussia, he died at Munich, Germany, Feb 10, 1923. See also: "X-Ray Discovery Day: Anniversary" (Nov 8).

BIRTHDAYS TODAY

Mariah Carey, 31, singer, born New York, NY, Mar 27, 1970.

Randall Cunningham, 38, football player, born Santa Barbara, CA, Mar 27, 1963.

March *2001*	S	M	T	W	T	F	S
					1	2	3
	4	5	6	7	8	9	10
	11	12	13	14	15	16	17
	18	19	20	21	22	23	24
	25	26	27	28	29	30	31

MARCH 28 — WEDNESDAY
Day 87 — 278 Remaining

CHINA: QING MING FESTIVAL. Mar 28. This Confucian festival is celebrated on the fourth or fifth day of the third month. It is observed by the maintenance of ancestral graves, the presentation of food, wine and flowers as offerings and the burning of paper money at gravesides to help ancestors in the afterworld. People also picnic and gather for family meals. Also observed in Korea and Taiwan.

CZECH REPUBLIC: TEACHERS' DAY. Mar 28. Celebrates birth on this day of Jan Amos Komensky (Comenius), Moravian educational reformer (1592–1671).

"GREATEST SHOW ON EARTH" FORMED: ANNIVERSARY. Mar 28, 1881. P.T. Barnum and James A. Bailey merged their circuses to form the "Greatest Show on Earth."

SPACE MILESTONE: *NOAA 8* (US). Mar 28, 1983. Search and Rescue Satellite (SARSAT) launched from Vandenburg Air Force Base, CA, to aid in locating ships and aircraft in distress. *Kosmos 1383*, launched July 1, 1982, by the USSR, in a cooperative rescue effort, is credited with saving more than 20 lives.

THREE MILE ISLAND NUCLEAR POWER PLANT ACCIDENT: ANNIVERSARY. Mar 28, 1979. A series of accidents beginning at 4 AM, EST, at Three Mile Island on the Susquehanna River about 10 miles southeast of Harrisburg, PA, was responsible for extensive reevaluation of the safety of existing nuclear power generating operations. Equipment and other failures reportedly brought Three Mile Island close to a meltdown of the uranium core, threatening extensive radiation contamination.

BIRTHDAYS TODAY

Byrd Baylor, 77, author (*I'm In Charge of Celebrations*), born San Antonio, TX, Mar 28, 1924.

Frank Hughes Murkowski, 68, US Senator (R, Alaska), born Seattle, WA, Mar 28, 1933.

MARCH 29 — THURSDAY
Day 88 — 277 Remaining

"AMERICA'S SUBWAY" DAY: 25th ANNIVERSARY. Mar 29, 1976. The Washington (DC) Metropolitan Area Transit Authority ran its first Metrorail passenger train 25 years ago. The Metro system consisted of only five stations and 4.6 miles on the Red Line Route. In 1999 two more stations and three miles of track were added to the system. Metro now consists of 78 stations and 98 miles of service. Passengers make more than 500,000 trips each weekday in the nation's capital and the greater Washington area. Many of these are made by tourists from across the country and around the world — hence the moniker "America's Subway." For info: Cheryl Johnson, Washington Metropolitan Area Transit Authority, 600 Fifth St NW, Washington, DC 20001. Phone: (202) 962-1051. Fax: (202) 962-2897.

CANADA: BRITISH NORTH AMERICA ACT: ANNIVERSARY. Mar 29, 1867. This act of the British Parliament established the Dominion of Canada, uniting Ontario, Quebec, Nova Scotia and New Brunswick. Union was proclaimed July 1, 1867. The remaining colonies in Canada were still ruled directly by Great Britain until Manitoba joined the Dominion in 1870, British Columbia in 1871, Prince Edward Island in 1873, Alberta and Saskatchewan in 1905 and Newfoundland in 1949. See also: "Canada: Canada Day" (July 1).

HOOVER, LOU HENRY: BIRTH ANNIVERSARY. Mar 29, 1875. Wife of Herbert Clark Hoover, 31st president of the US. Born at Waterloo, IA, she died at Palo Alto, CA, Jan 7, 1944.

MADAGASCAR: COMMEMORATION DAY. Mar 29. Commemoration Day for the victims of the rebellion in 1947 against French colonization.

TAIWAN: YOUTH DAY. Mar 29.

TEXAS LOVE THE CHILDREN DAY. Mar 29. A day recognizing every child's right and need to be loved. Promoting the hope that one day all children will live in loving, safe environments and will be given proper health care and equal learning opportunities. Precedes the start of National Child Abuse Prevention Month (April). For info: Patty Murphy, 7713 Chasewood Dr, North Richland Hills, TX 76180. Phone: (817) 498-5840. E-mail: MURPH0@flash.net.

TWENTY-THIRD AMENDMENT TO US CONSTITUTION RATIFIED: 40th ANNIVERSARY. Mar 29, 1961. District of Columbia residents were given the right to vote in presidential elections under the 23rd Amendment.

TYLER, JOHN: BIRTH ANNIVERSARY. Mar 29, 1790. The 10th president of the US (Apr 6, 1841–Mar 3, 1845). Born at Greenway, VA, Tyler succeeded to the presidency upon the death of William Henry Harrison. Tyler's first wife died while he was president, and he remarried before the end of his term of office, becoming the first president to marry while in office. Fifteen children were born of the two marriages. In 1861 he was elected to the Congress of the Confederate States but died at Richmond, VA, Jan 18, 1862, before being seated. His death received no official tribute from the US government.

YOUNG, DENTON TRUE (CY): BIRTH ANNIVERSARY. Mar 29, 1867. Baseball Hall of Fame pitcher, born at Gilmore, OH. Young is baseball's all-time winningest pitcher, having accumulated 511 victories in his 22-year career. The Cy Young Award is given each year in his honor to major league's best pitcher. Inducted into the Hall of Fame in 1937. Died at Peoli, OH, Nov 4, 1955.

BIRTHDAYS TODAY

Lucy Lawless, 33, actress ("Xena"), born Mount Albert, Auckland, New Zealand, Mar 29, 1968.

MARCH 30 — FRIDAY
Day 89 — 276 Remaining

ANESTHETIC FIRST USED IN SURGERY: ANNIVERSARY. Mar 30, 1842. Dr. Crawford W. Long, having seen the use of nitrous oxide and sulfuric ether at "laughing gas" parties, observed that individuals under their influences felt no pain. On this date, he removed a tumor from the neck of a man who was under the influence of ether.

DOCTORS' DAY. Mar 30. Traditional annual observance since 1933 to honor America's physicians on anniversary of occasion when Dr. Crawford W. Long became the first physician to use ether as an anesthetic agent in a surgical technique, Mar 30, 1842. The red carnation has been designated the official flower of Doctors' Day.

NO HOMEWORK DAY. Mar 30. Teachers don't give students homework on this day. Annually, the last Friday in March. For info: Julia Levita Chase, 2681 Balmoral Ct, Baltimore, MD 48103. E-mail: batz_maru_99@yahoo.com.

PENCIL PATENTED: ANNIVERSARY. Mar 30, 1858. First pencil with the eraser top was patented by Hyman Lipman.

SEWELL, ANNA: BIRTH ANNIVERSARY. Mar 30, 1820. Born at Yarmouth, England, Anna Sewell is best known for her book *Black Beauty*. Published in 1877, her tale centers around the abuses and injustices to horses she saw while growing up. She died at Old Catton, Norfolk, England, Apr 25, 1878.

TRINIDAD AND TOBAGO: SPIRITUAL BAPTIST LIBERATION SHOUTER DAY. Mar 30. Public Holiday. For info: Information Dept, Tourism Div, Tourism and Industrial Development Co, 10-14 Phillips St, Port of Spain, Trinidad, West Indies.

VAN GOGH, VINCENT: BIRTH ANNIVERSARY. Mar 30, 1853. Dutch post-Impressionist painter, especially known for his bold and powerful use of color (*Sunflowers, The Starry Night*). Born at Groot Zundert, Netherlands, he died at Auvers-sur-Oise, France, July 29, 1890. For more info: *Vincent Van Gogh*, by Enrica Crispino (Peter Bedrick, 0-87226-525-0, $22.50 Gr. 4–7).

BIRTHDAYS TODAY

Robert C. Smith, 60, US Senator (R, New Hampshire), born Tuftonboro, NH, Mar 30, 1941.

MARCH 31 — SATURDAY
Day 90 — 275 Remaining

CHAVEZ, CESAR ESTRADA: BIRTH ANNIVERSARY. Mar 31, 1927. Labor leader who organized migrant farm workers in support of better working conditions. Chavez initiated the National Farm Workers Association in 1962, attracting attention to the migrant farm workers' plight by organizing boycotts of products including grapes and lettuce. He was born at Yuma, AZ, and died Apr 23, 1993, at San Luis, AZ. His birthday is a holiday in California.

CHESNUT, MARY BOYKIN MILLER: BIRTH ANNIVERSARY. Mar 31, 1823. Born at Pleasant Hill, SC, and died Nov 22, 1886, at Camden, SC. During the Civil War Chesnut accompanied her husband, a Confederate staff officer, on military missions. She kept a journal of her experiences and observations, which was published posthumously as *A Diary from Dixie*, a perceptive portrait of Confederate military and political leaders and an insightful view of Southern life during the Civil War.

EIFFEL TOWER: ANNIVERSARY. Mar 31, 1889. Built for the Paris Exhibition of 1889, the tower was named for its architect, Alexandre Gustave Eiffel, and is one of the world's best known landmarks.

JOHNSON, JOHN (JACK) ARTHUR: BIRTH ANNIVERSARY. Mar 31, 1878. In 1908 Jack Johnson became the first black to win the heavyweight boxing championship when he defeated Tommy Burns at Sydney, Australia. Unable to accept a black's triumph, the boxing world tried to find a white challenger. Jim Jeffries, former heavyweight title holder, was badgered out of retirement. On July 4, 1919, at Reno, NV, the "battle of the century" proved to be a farce when Johnson handily defeated Jeffries. Race riots swept the US and plans to exhibit the film of the fight were canceled. Johnson was born at Galveston, TX, and died in an automobile accident June 10, 1946, at Raleigh, NC. He was inducted into the Boxing Hall of Fame in 1990. The film *The Great White Hope* is based on his life.

NASA AMES SPACE SETTLEMENT CONTEST. Mar 31. Deadline for annual contest for 6–12th graders to design an orbital space settlement. For info: Al Globus, MS T27A-1, NASA Ames Research Center, Moffett Field, CA 94035. Web: www.nas .nasa.gov/Services/Education/SpaceSettlement.

US AIR FORCE ACADEMY ESTABLISHED: ANNIVERSARY. Mar 31, 1954. The US Air Force Academy was established at Colorado Springs, CO, to train officers for the Air Force.

VIRGIN ISLANDS: TRANSFER DAY. Mar 31. Commemorates transfer resulting from purchase of the Virgin Islands by the US from Denmark, Mar 31, 1917, for $25 million.

BIRTHDAYS TODAY

William Daniels, 74, actor ("Boy Meets World"), born Brooklyn, NY, Mar 31, 1927.

Al Gore, 53, 45th vice president of the US, born Albert Gore, Jr, Washington, DC, Mar 31, 1948.

Angus King, Jr, 57, Governor of Maine (I), born Alexandria, VA, Mar 31, 1944.

Patrick J. Leahy, 61, US Senator (D, Vermont), born Montpelier, VT, Mar 31, 1940.

Rhea Perlman, 53, actress (*Matilda*), born Brooklyn, NY, Mar 31, 1948.

Steve Smith, 32, basketball player, born Highland Park, MI, Mar 31, 1969.

APRIL 1 — SUNDAY
Day 91 — 274 Remaining

ALCOHOL AWARENESS MONTH. Apr 1–30. To help raise awareness among community prevention leaders and citizens about the problem of underage drinking. Concentrates on community grassroots activities. For info: Public Info Dept, Natl Council on Alcoholism and Drug Dependence, Inc, 12 W 21st St, New York, NY 10010. Phone: (212) 206-6770. Fax: (212) 645-1690. Web: www.ncadd.org.

APRIL FOOLS' or ALL FOOLS' DAY. Apr 1. "The joke of the day is to deceive persons by sending them upon frivolous and nonsensical errands; to pretend they are wanted when they are not, or, in fact, any way to betray them into some supposed ludicrous situation, so as to enable you to call them 'An April Fool.'"–Brady's *Clavis Calendaria*, 1812. For links to April Fools' Day sites on the web, go to: deil.lang.uiuc.edu/web.pages /holidays/aprilfool.html.

BULGARIA: SAINT LASARUS'S DAY. Apr 1. Ancient Slavic holiday of young girls, in honor of the goddess of spring and love.

CANADA: NUNAVUT INDEPENDENCE: ANNIVERSARY. Apr 1, 1999. Nunavut became Canada's third independent territory. This self-governing territory with an Inuit majority was created from the eastern half of the Northwest Territories. In 1992 Canada's Inuit people accepted a federal land-claim package granting them control over the new territory.

★CANCER CONTROL MONTH. Apr 1–30.

CHECK YOUR BATTERIES DAY. Apr 1. A day set aside for checking the batteries in your smoke detector, carbon monoxide detector, HVAC thermostat, audio/visual remote controls and other electronic devices. This could save your life! Annually, the first Sunday in April.

DAYLIGHT SAVING TIME BEGINS. Apr 1–Oct 28. Daylight Saving Time begins at 2 AM. The Uniform Time Act of 1966 (as amended in 1986 by Public Law 99–359), administered by the US Dept of Transportation, provides that Standard Time in each zone be advanced one hour from 2 AM on the first Sunday in April until 2 AM on the last Sunday in October (except where state legislatures provide exemption, as in Hawaii and parts of Arizona and Indiana). Many use the popular rule "spring forward, fall back," to remember which way to turn their clocks.

EXCHANGE CLUB CHILD ABUSE PREVENTION MONTH. Apr 1–30. Nationwide effort to raise awareness of child abuse and how to prevent it. For info: The Natl Exchange Club, Foundation for Prevention of Child Abuse, 3050 Central

Ave, Toledo, OH 43606-1700. Phone: (419) 535-3232 or (800) 760-3413. Fax: (419) 535-1989. E-mail: info@preventchildabuse.com. Web: www.preventchildabuse.com.

GOLDEN RULE WEEK. Apr 1–7. The purpose of this week is to remind everyone of the importance of the Golden Rule in making this a better world in which we all may live. For a copy of the Golden Rule of 10 religions, send $4 to cover printing and postage. For info: Dr. S.J. Drake, Pres, Intl Soc of Friendship and Goodwill, 40139 Palmetto Dr, Palmdale, CA 93551-3557.

GREECE: DUMB WEEK. Apr 1–7. The week preceding Holy Week on the Orthodox calendar is known as Dumb Week, as no services are held in churches throughout this period except on Friday, eve of the Saturday of Lazarus.

HARVEY, WILLIAM: BIRTH ANNIVERSARY. Apr 1, 1578. Physician, born at Folkestone, England. The first to discover the mechanics of the circulation of the blood. Died at Roehampton, England, June 3, 1657.

INTERNATIONAL AMATEUR RADIO MONTH. Apr 1–30. To disseminate information about the important part amateur radio operators or "hams" throughout the world are playing in promoting friendship, peace and good will. To obtain complete information about becoming an International Good Will Ambassador as well as a list of amateur radio operators in many countries, send $4 to cover expense of printing, handling and postage. Annually, the month of April. For info: Dr. Stanley Drake, Pres, Intl Soc of Friendship and Good Will, 40139 Palmetto Dr, Palmdale, CA 93551-3557.

KEEP AMERICA BEAUTIFUL MONTH. Apr 1–30. To educate Americans about their personal responsibility for litter prevention, proper waste disposal and environmental improvement through various community projects. Annually, the month of April. For info: Evan Jones, Dir of Communications, Keep America Beautiful, Inc, Washington Square, 1010 Washington Blvd, Stamford, CT 06901. Phone: (203) 323-8987. Fax: (203) 325-9199. E-mail: keepamerbe@aol.com.

$$
\begin{array}{r}
105 \\
\times\ 3 \\
\hline
315
\end{array}
$$

MATHEMATICS EDUCATION MONTH. Apr 1–30. An opportunity for students, teachers, parents and the community as a whole to focus on the importance of mathematics and the changes taking place in mathematics education. *See* Curriculum Connection. For info: Communications Mgr, Natl Council of Teachers of Mathematics, 1906 Association Dr, Reston, VA 20191-1593. Phone: (703) 620-9840. Fax: (703) 476-2970. E-mail: infocentral@nctm.org. Web: www.nctm.org.

MONTH OF THE YOUNG CHILD®. Apr 1–30. Michigan. To promote awareness of the importance of young children and their specific needs in today's society. Many communities celebrate with special events for children and families. For info: Michigan Assn for the Education of Young Children, Beacon Pl, Ste 1-D, 4572 S Hagadorn Road, East Lansing, MI 48823-5385. Phone: (800) 336-6424 or (517) 336-9700. Fax: (517) 336-9790. E-mail: moyc @miaeyc.com. Web: www.miaeyc.com.

APRIL 1–30
MATHEMATICS EDUCATION MONTH

Focus on incorporating fun math activities into the daily classroom routine. Primary students can create ongoing addition problems centered around the date. For example: Apr 1 = 1 + 0; Apr 2 = 1 + 1 or 2 + 0; Apr 14 = 7 + 7, 10 + 4, 8 + 6, etc. Challenge students to see how many different sums they can find for each day. The same exercise can be extended as multiplication problems for third and fourth grade students.

Explore numbering systems used by different cultures. The *History of Counting*, by Denise Schmandt-Besserat (Morrow, 0-688-14118-8, $17 Gr. 5–8) discusses and presents the history of several different counting systems. *How Tall, How Short, How Faraway?*, by David Adler (Holiday, 0-8234-1375-6, $15.95 Gr. 1–4) also looks at number systems, but is intended for a much younger audience. It encourages experimentation, measuring and calculation.

Talk about base two and binary counting and how computers use this system to encode information. Students might want to try converting familiar numbers—their age, weight or birth date, etc.—into base two numbers. Try keeping score in gym class in a new numbering system.

Huge numbers don't have to be intimidating. *On Beyond a Million*, by David Schwartz (Bantam, 0-385-32217-8, $15.95 Gr. 1–5) helps explain exponential notation and the importance of zero as a place holder. Older readers will find *G is for Googol*, by David Schwartz (Tricycle, 1-8836-7258-9, $16.95 Gr. 5 & up) contains many terms and definitions used in higher levels of math.

Playing games with numbers is a great way to cure "math block." *25 Super Cool Math Board Games*, by Loraine Egan (Scholastic, 0-590-37872-4, $12.95 Gr. 3–6); *Math Games for Middle Schoolers*, by Mario Salvadori (Chicago Review Press, 1-55652-288-6, $16.95 Gr. 6–9); *Math Games and Activities from Around the World*, by Claudia Zaslavsky (Chicago Review Press, 1-55652-287-8, $14.95 Gr. 3–7); *Logic Posters, Problems & Puzzles*, by Honi Bamberger (Scholastic, 0-590-64273-1, $12.95 Gr. 3–6); and *Counting Caterpillars & Other Math Poems*, by Betsy Franco (Scholastic, 0-590-64210-3, $9.95 Gr. K–2) are all books that incorporate different levels of the math curriculum and emphasize having fun with math.

MOON PHASE: FIRST QUARTER. Apr 1. Moon enters First Quarter phase at 6:49 AM, EDT.

NATIONAL AUTISM AWARENESS MONTH. Apr 1–30. A month filled with events such as poster contests, a state proclamation by the governor and family activities on autism. This is a national celebration. Annually, the month of April. For info: Jennifer Swenson, Coord of Mktg & PR, COSAC, 1450 Parkside Ave, Ste 22, Ewing, NJ 08638. Phone: (609) 883-8100. Fax: (609) 883-5509. E-mail: njautism@aol.com. Web: members.aol.com /njautism.

NATIONAL BLUE RIBBON WEEK. Apr 1–7. Wear a blue ribbon to show your concern about and objection to child abuse. Nationwide public awareness effort. Annually, the first full week

		S	M	T	W	T	F	S
April		1	2	3	4	5	6	7
2001		8	9	10	11	12	13	14
		15	16	17	18	19	20	21
		22	23	24	25	26	27	28
		29	30					

in April. For info: The Natl Exchange Club, 3050 Central Ave, Toledo, OH 43606-1700. Phone: (419) 535-3232 or (800) 924-2643. Fax: (419) 535-1989. E-mail: nechq@aol.com. Web: www .nationalexchangeclub.com.

★**NATIONAL CHILD ABUSE PREVENTION MONTH.** Apr 1–30.

NATIONAL HUMOR MONTH. Apr 1–30. Focuses on the joy and therapeutic value of laughter and how it can reduce stress, improve job performance and enrich the quality of life. For info: send SASE (55¢) to: Larry Wilde, Dir, The Carmel Institute of Humor, 25470 Canada Dr, Carmel, CA 93923-8926. E-mail: larrywilde@aol.com.

NATIONAL KNUCKLES DOWN MONTH. Apr 1–30. To recognize and revive the American tradition of playing and collecting marbles and keep it rolling along. Please send self-addressed, stamped envelope with inquiries. For info: Cathy C. Runyan-Svacina, The Marble Lady, 7812 NW Hampton Rd, Kansas City, MO 64152. Phone: (816) 587-8687. Fax: Same as Phone.

NATIONAL LIBRARY WEEK. Apr 1–7. A nationwide observance sponsored by the American Library Association. Celebrates libraries and librarians, the pleasures and importance of reading and invites library use and support. For programming ideas, see: *Library Celebrations*, by Cyndy Dingwall (Highsmith, 1-5795-0027-7, $16.95). Call the American Library Association at 1-800-545-2433 for a catalog of NLW materials. For info: American Library Assn, Public Info Office, 50 E Huron St, Chicago, IL 60611. Phone: (312) 280-5044. Fax: (312) 944-8520. E-mail: pio@ala.org. Web: www.ala.org.

NATIONAL POETRY MONTH. Apr 1–30. Annual observance to pay tribute to the great legacy and ongoing achievement of American poets and the vital place of poetry in American culture. In a proclamation issued in honor of the first observance, President Bill Clinton called it "a welcome opportunity to celebrate not only the unsurpassed body of literature produced by our poets in the past, but also the vitality and diversity of voices reflected in the works of today's American poets . . . Their creativity and wealth of language enrich our culture and inspire a new generation of Americans to learn the power of reading and writing at its best." Spearheaded by the Academy of American Poets, this is the largest and most extensive celebration of poetry in American history. *See* Curriculum Connection. For info: Academy of American Poets, 584 Broadway, Ste 1208, New York, NY 10012-3250. Phone: (212) 274-0343. Web: www.poets.org.

NATIONAL PUBLIC HEALTH WEEK. Apr 1–7. Annually, the first full week in April. For info: American Public Health Assn, 1015 15th St NW, Washington, DC, 20005. Phone: (202) 789-5600.

NATIONAL YOUTH SPORTS SAFETY MONTH. Apr 1–30. Bringing public attention to the prevalent problem of injuries in youth sports. This event promotes safety in sports activities and is supported by more than 60 national sports and medical organizations. For info: Michelle Glassman, Exec Dir, Natl Youth Sports Safety Fdtn, 333 Longwood Ave, Ste 202, Boston, MA 02115. Phone: (617) 277-1171. Fax: (617) 277-2278. E-mail: NYSSF @aol.com. Web: www.nyssf.org.

PASSION WEEK. Apr 1–7. The week beginning on the fifth Sunday in Lent; the week before Holy Week.

PASSIONTIDE. Apr 1–14. The last two weeks of Lent (Passion Week and Holy Week), beginning with the fifth Sunday of Lent (Passion Sunday) and continuing through the day before Easter (Holy Saturday).

APRIL 1–30
NATIONAL POETRY MONTH AND YOUNG PEOPLE'S POETRY WEEK

To have a monthlong celebration of poetry, categorize poetry into four thematic groups, one for each week. The first week, focus on the elements of poetry. Explore topics like meaning, rhythm, sound patterns, figurative language and sensory images. Robert Frost's "The Road Not Taken" is a thought-provoking poem for discussing meaning. Sound patterns include rhyme, onomatopoeia, alliteration and consonance. There are many examples of these scattered throughout poetry collections. Try David McCord's "Song of the Train" for a great example of a speeding train. Figurative language—the use of similes and metaphors, personification and hyperbole—and sensory images also are found in many collections. Read through several volumes of children's poetry; personal taste will help you find poems which best illustrate these elements for you.

The second week focus on story poems (long narratives that tell a story). Narrative poems students usually enjoy include "The Shooting of Dan McGrew" and "The Cremation of Sam McGee," by Robert Service; "The Highwayman," by Alfred Noyes and "The Raven," by Edgar Allan Poe. All of them are lovely for reading aloud or arranged as choral readings. *The Illiad* and *The Odyssey* are suitable for upper junior high and high school readers.

During the third week (Young People's Poetry Week, Apr 16–22), read humorous poetry. This light-hearted look at poetry ties in beautifully with Families Laughing Through Humor Week and Young People's Poetry Week, both celebrated this week. Shel Silverstein, Jack Prelutsky, Edward Lear, Bruce Lansky and David Harrison have written collections of humorous poetry for children. Share them with each other in the classroom. Talk about what makes them funny. Suggest students read them aloud with their families. In further conjunction with Families Laughing Through Humor Week, encourage students to recall humorous family moments and then write them up as a silly poem.

For the fourth week feature different kinds of poetry on successive days. Topics could include haiku, limericks, nursery rhymes and concrete poems. Or you might want to feature poems about different subjects—trees, flowers, math, animals, science, etc.

Several noteworthy new books of poetry for children are: *Relatively Speaking*, by Ralph Fletcher (Orchard, 0-531-33141-5, $14.95 Gr. 3–9); *Old Elm Speaks*, by Kristine O'Connell George (Clarion, 0-395-87611-7, $15 Gr. K–5); *Touch the Poem*, by Arnold Adoff (Scholastic, 0-590-47970-9, $16.95 Gr. 2–7); *Flicker Flash*, by Joan Graham (Houghton, 0-395-90501-X, $15 Gr. 1–4); and *Classic Poetry: An Illustrated Collection*, selected by Michael Rosen (Candlewick, 1-56402-890-9, $21.99 Gr. 5 & up).

PREVENTION OF ANIMAL CRUELTY MONTH. Apr 1–30. The ASPCA sponsors this crucial month which is designed to prevent cruelty to animals by focusing on public awareness, advocacy and public education campaigns. For info: ASPCA Public Affairs Dept, 424 E 92nd St, New York, NY 10128. Phone: (212) 876-7700. E-mail: press@aspca.org. Web: www.aspca.org.

SCHOOL LIBRARY MEDIA MONTH. Apr 1–30. Celebrates the work of school library media specialists in our nation's elementary and secondary schools. For info: American Assn of School Librarians, American Library Assn, 50 E Huron St, Chicago, IL 60611. Phone: (800) 545-2433. E-mail: AASL@ala.org. Web: www.ala.org/aasl.

SCHOOLTECH EXPO AND CONFERENCE. Apr 1–3. New York, NY. Sponsored by *Technology & Learning* magazine, the conference features training workshops and technology exhibits. Est attendance: 3,000. For info: Miller Freeman Inc, 600 Harrison St, San Francisco, CA 94109. Phone: (888) 857-6883. Web: www.schooltechexpo.com.

SPORTS EYE SAFETY MONTH. Apr 1–30. During this month's observance, Prevent Blindness America will encourage young athletes to wear eye/face protection when participating in sports. Materials that can easily be posted or distributed to the community will be provided. For info: Prevent Blindness America®, 500 E Remington Rd, Schaumburg, IL 60173. Phone: (800) 331-2020. Fax: (847) 843-8458. Web: www.preventblindness.org.

US HOUSE OF REPRESENTATIVES ACHIEVES A QUORUM: ANNIVERSARY. Apr 1, 1789. First session of Congress was held Mar 4, 1789, but not enough representatives arrived to achieve a quorum until Apr 1.

WEEK OF THE YOUNG CHILD. Apr 1–7. To focus on the importance of quality early childhood education. For info: Pat Spahr, Dir of Info Development, Natl Assn for the Educ of Young Children, 1509 16th St NW, Washington, DC 20036. Phone: (800) 424-2460. Fax: (202) 328-1846. E-mail: naeyc@naeyc.org. Web: www.naeyc.org.

ZAM! ZOO AND AQUARIUM MONTH. Apr 1–30. A national celebration to focus public attention on the role of zoos and aquariums in wildlife education and conservation. Held at 184 AZA member institutions in the US and Canada. Sponsor: American Zoo and Aquarium Association. For information, contact your local zoo or aquarium. For info: Zoo and Aquarium Assn, 7970 Old Georgetown Rd, Bethesda, MD 20814. Phone: (301) 907-7777. Fax: (301) 907-2980.

BIRTHDAYS TODAY

Anne McCaffrey, 75, author (*The Dragonriders of Pern*), born Cambridge, MA, Apr 1, 1926.

Karen Wallace, 50, author (*Imagine You Are a Crocodile*), born Ottawa, Ontario, Canada, Apr 1, 1951.

APRIL 2 — MONDAY
Day 92 — 273 Remaining

ANDERSEN, HANS CHRISTIAN: BIRTH ANNIVERSARY. Apr 2, 1805. Author chiefly remembered for his more than 150 fairy tales, many of which are regarded as classics of children's literature. Among his tales are "The Princess and the Pea," "The Snow Queen" and "The Ugly Duckling." Andersen was born at Odense, Denmark and died at Copenhagen, Denmark, Aug 4, 1875.

BARTHOLDI, FREDERIC AUGUSTE: BIRTH ANNIVERSARY. Apr 2, 1834. French sculptor who created *Liberty Enlightening the World* (better known as the Statue of Liberty), which stands in New York Harbor. Also remembered for the *Lion of Belfort* at Belfort, France. Born at Colman, Alsace, France, he died at Paris, France, Oct 4, 1904.

FIRST WHITE HOUSE EASTER EGG ROLL: ANNIVERSARY. Apr 2, 1877. The first White House Easter Egg Roll took place during the administration of Rutherford B. Hayes. The traditional event was discontinued by President Franklin D. Roosevelt in 1942 and reinstated Apr 6, 1953, by President Dwight D. Eisenhower.

INTERNATIONAL CHILDREN'S BOOK DAY. Apr 2. Commemorates the international aspects of children's literature and observes Hans Christian Andersen's birthday. Sponsor: International Board on Books for Young People, Nonnenweg 12, Postfach, CH-4003 Basel, Switzerland. For info: USBBY Secretariat, c/o Intl Reading Assn, Box 8139, Newark, DE 19714-8139.

NICKELODEON CHANNEL TV PREMIERE: ANNIVERSARY. Apr 2, 1979. Nickelodeon, the cable TV network for kids owned by MTV Networks, premiered. In 1985, Nick at Nite began offering classic TV programs in the evening hours.

PASCUA FLORIDA DAY. Apr 2. Also known as Florida State Day, this holiday commemorates the sighting of Florida by Ponce de Leon in 1513. He named the land Pascua Florida because of its discovery at Easter, the "Feast of the Flowers." Florida also commemorates Pascua Florida Week, Mar 27–Apr 2. When April 2 falls on a weekend, the Governor may declare the preceding Friday or the following Monday as State Day.

PONCE DE LEON DISCOVERS FLORIDA: ANNIVERSARY. Apr 2, 1513. Juan Ponce de Leon discovered Florida, landing at the site that became the city of St. Augustine. He claimed the land for the King of Spain.

US MINT: ANNIVERSARY. Apr 2, 1792. The first US Mint was established at Philadelphia, PA, as authorized by an act of Congress.

BIRTHDAYS TODAY

Ruth Heller, 77, science author and illustrator (the How to Hide . . . series), born Winnipeg, Manitoba, Canada, Apr 2, 1924.

Doug Wechsler, 50, author (*Bizarre Bugs*), born New York, NY, Apr 2, 1951.

APRIL 3 — TUESDAY
Day 93 — 272 Remaining

BLACKS RULED ELIGIBLE TO VOTE: ANNIVERSARY. Apr 3, 1944. The US Supreme Court, in an 8–1 ruling, declared that blacks could not be barred from voting in the Texas Democratic primaries. The high court repudiated the contention that political parties are private associations and held that discrimination against blacks violated the 15th Amendment.

BOSTON PUBLIC LIBRARY: ANNIVERSARY. Apr 3, 1848. The Massachusetts legislature passed legislation enabling Boston to levy a tax for a public library. This created the funding model for public libraries in the US. The Boston Public Library opened its doors in 1854.

IRVING, WASHINGTON: BIRTH ANNIVERSARY. Apr 3, 1783. American author, attorney and one time US Minister to Spain, Irving was born at New York, NY. Creator of *Rip Van Winkle* and *The Legend of Sleepy Hollow*, he was also the author of many historical and biographical works, including *A History of the Life and Voyages of Christopher Columbus* and the *Life of Washington*. Died at Tarrytown, NY, Nov 28, 1859.

MARSHALL PLAN: ANNIVERSARY. Apr 3, 1948. Suggested by Secretary of State George C. Marshall in a speech at Harvard, June 5, 1947, the legislation for the European Recovery Program,

popularly known as the Marshall Plan, was signed by President Truman on Apr 3, 1948. After distributing more than $12 billion in war-torn Europe, the program ended in 1952.

WOMAN PRESIDES OVER US SUPREME COURT: ANNIVERSARY. Apr 3, 1995. Supreme Court Justice Sandra Day O'Connor became the first woman to preside over the US high court when she sat in for Chief Justice William H. Rehnquist and second in seniority Justice John Paul Stevens when both were out of town.

BIRTHDAYS TODAY

Amanda Bynes, 15, actress ("All That," "The Amanda Show"), born Thousand Oaks, CA, Apr 3, 1986.

Jane Goodall, 67, biologist, author (*The Chimpanzee Family Book*), born London, England, Apr 3, 1934.

Eddie Murphy, 40, comedian, actor (*Doctor Dolittle*), born Brooklyn, NY, Apr 3, 1961.

Picabo Street, 30, Olympic skier, born Triumph, ID, Apr 3, 1971.

APRIL 4 — WEDNESDAY
Day 94 — 271 Remaining

ASHURA: TENTH DAY. Apr 4. Islamic calendar date: Muharram 10, 1422. Commemorates death of Muhammad's grandson and the Battle of Karbala. A time of fasting, reflection and meditation. Jews of Medina fasted on the tenth day in remembrance of their salvation from Pharoah. Different methods for "anticipating" the visibility of the new moon crescent at Mecca are used by different groups. US date may vary.

BONZA BOTTLER DAY™. Apr 4. To celebrate when the number of the day is the same as the number of the month. Bonza Bottler Day™ is an excuse to have a party at least once a month. For info: Gail M. Berger, 109 Matthew Ave, Poca, WV 25159. Phone: (304) 776-7746. E-mail: gberger5@aol.com.

DIX, DOROTHEA LYNDE: BIRTH ANNIVERSARY. Apr 4, 1802. American social reformer and author, born at Hampden, ME. She left home at age 10, was teaching at age 14 and founded a home for girls at Boston while still in her teens. In spite of frail health, she was a vigorous crusader for humane conditions in insane asylums, jails and almshouses and for the establishment of state-supported institutions to serve those needs. Named superintendent of women nurses during the Civil War. Died at Trenton, NJ, July 17, 1887.

FLAG ACT OF 1818: ANNIVERSARY. Apr 4, 1818. Congress approved the first flag of the US.

ITALY: BOLOGNA INTERNATIONAL CHILDREN'S BOOK FAIR. Apr 4–7 (tentative). Bologna Exhibition Centre, Bologna, Italy. Publishers from 79 countries exhibit their books to the trade. Est attendance: 25,000. For info: Bologna Children's Book Fair, Piazza Costituzione, Italy. Phone: 51-282-361. Fax: 51-282-333. E-mail: dir.com@bolognafiere.it. Web: www.bolognafiere.it/BookFair.

KING, MARTIN LUTHER, JR: ASSASSINATION ANNIVERSARY. Apr 4, 1968. The Reverend Dr. Martin Luther King, Jr, was shot at Memphis, TN. James Earl Ray was serving a 99-year sentence for the crime at the time of his death in 1998. See also: "King, Martin Luther, Jr: Birth Anniversary" (Jan 15).

KING OPPOSES VIETNAM WAR: ANNIVERSARY. Apr 4, 1967. Speaking before the Overseas Press Club at New York City, Reverend Dr. Martin Luther King, Jr, announced his opposition to the Vietnam War. That same day at the Riverside Church, King suggested that those who saw the war as dishonorable and unjust

April *2001*	S	M	T	W	T	F	S
	1	2	3	4	5	6	7
	8	9	10	11	12	13	14
	15	16	17	18	19	20	21
	22	23	24	25	26	27	28
	29	30					

should avoid military service. He proposed that the US take new initiatives to conclude the war.

NATIONAL READING A ROAD MAP WEEK. Apr 4–10. To promote map reading as an enjoyable pastime and as a survival skill for present and future drivers and all armchair travelers. Motto: Happiness is knowing how to read a road map. For info: RosaLind Schilder, 309 Florence Ave, #225N, Jenkintown, PA 19046. E-mail: mikenroz18@aol.com.

NORTH ATLANTIC TREATY RATIFIED: ANNIVERSARY. Apr 4, 1949. The North Atlantic Treaty Organization was created by this treaty, which was signed by 12 nations, including the US. (Other countries joined later.) The NATO member nations are united for common defense.

SALTER ELECTED FIRST WOMAN MAYOR IN US: ANNI-VERSARY. Apr 4, 1887. The first woman elected mayor in the US was Susanna Medora Salter, who was elected mayor of Argonia, KS. Her name had been submitted for election without her knowledge by the Woman's Christian Temperance Union, and she did not know she was a candidate until she went to the polls to vote. She received a two-thirds majority vote and served one year for the salary of $1.

SENEGAL: INDEPENDENCE DAY: ANNIVERSARY. Apr 4. National holiday. Commemorates independence from France in 1960.

VITAMIN C ISOLATED: ANNIVERSARY. Apr 4, 1932. Vitamin C was first isolated by C.C. King at the University of Pittsburgh.

BIRTHDAYS TODAY

Richard G. Lugar, 69, US Senator (R, Indiana), born Indianapolis, IN, Apr 4, 1932.

Johanna Reiss, 69, author (*The Upstairs Room*), born Winterswijk, Netherlands, Apr 4, 1932.

APRIL 5 — THURSDAY
Day 95 — 270 Remaining

LISTER, JOSEPH: BIRTH ANNIVERSARY. Apr 5, 1827. English physician who was the founder of aseptic surgery, born at Upton, Essex, England. Died at Walmer, England, Feb 10, 1912.

RESNIK, JUDITH A.: BIRTH ANNIVERSARY. Apr 5, 1949. Dr. Judith A. Resnik, the second American woman in space (1984), was born at Akron, OH. The 36-year-old electrical engineer was the mission specialist on the Space Shuttle *Challenger*. She perished with all others aboard when *Challenger* exploded Jan 28, 1986. See also: "*Challenger* Space Shuttle Explosion: Anniversary" (Jan 28).

TAIWAN: NATIONAL TOMB-SWEEPING DAY. Apr 5. National holiday since 1972. According to Chinese custom, the tombs of ancestors are swept "clear and bright" and rites honoring ancestors are held. Tomb-Sweeping Day is observed Apr 5, except in leap years, when it falls Apr 4.

WASHINGTON, BOOKER TALLAFERRO: BIRTH ANNI-VERSARY. Apr 5, 1856. Black educator and leader, born at Franklin County, VA. "No race can prosper," he wrote in *Up from Slavery*, "till it learns that there is as much dignity in tilling a field as in writing a poem." Died at Tuskegee, AL, Nov 14, 1915.

BIRTHDAYS TODAY

Richard Peck, 67, author (*Lost in Cyberspace*), born Decatur, IL, Apr 5, 1934.

Colin Powell, 64, general, former Chairman US Joint Chiefs of Staff, born New York, NY, Apr 5, 1937.

APRIL 6 — FRIDAY
Day 96 — 269 Remaining

"BARNEY & FRIENDS" TV PREMIERE: ANNIVERSARY. Apr 6, 1992. Although most adults find it saccharine, this PBS show is enormously popular with preschoolers. Purple dinosaur Barney, his dinosaur pals Baby Bop and B.J. and a multi-ethnic group of children sing, play games and learn simple lessons about getting along with one another. "Bedtime with Barney" was a 1994 prime-time special.

FIRST MODERN OLYMPICS: ANNIVERSARY. Apr 6, 1896. The first modern Olympics formally opened at Athens, Greece, after a 1,500-year hiatus.

NATIONAL GEOGRAPHY BEE, STATE LEVEL. Apr 6. Site is different in each state—many are in state capital. Winners of school-level competitions who scored in the top 100 in their state on a written test compete in the State Geography Bees. The winner of each state bee will go to Washington, DC, for the national level in May. Est attendance: 450. For info: Natl Geography Bee, Natl Geographic Soc, 1145 17th St NW, Washington, DC 20036. Phone: (202) 857-7001. Web: www.nationalgeographic.com.

NORTH POLE DISCOVERED: ANNIVERSARY. Apr 6, 1909. Robert E. Peary reached the North Pole after several failed attempts. The team consisted of Peary, leader of the expedition, Matthew A. Henson, a black man who had served with Peary since 1886 as ship's cook, carpenter and blacksmith, and then as Peary's co-explorer and valuable assistant and four Eskimo guides—Coquesh, Ootah, Eginwah and Seegloo. They sailed July 17, 1908, on the ship *Roosevelt*, wintering on Ellesmere Island. After a grueling trek with dwindling food supplies, Henson and two of the Eskimos were first to reach the Pole. An exhausted Peary arrived 45 minutes later and confirmed their location. Dr. Frederick A. Cook, surgeon on an earlier expedition with Peary, claimed to have reached the Pole first, but that could not be substantiated and the National Geographic Society credited the Peary expedition.

STUDENT GOVERNMENT DAY IN MASSACHUSETTS. Apr 6. Proclaimed annually by the governor for the first Friday in April.

TEFLON INVENTED: ANNIVERSARY. Apr 6, 1938. Polytetrafluoroethylene resin was invented by Roy J. Plunkett while he was employed by E.I. Du Pont de Nemours & Co. Commonly known as Teflon, it revolutionized the cookware industry. This substance or something similar coated three-quarters of the pots and pans in America at the time of Plunkett's death in 1994.

THAILAND: CHAKRI DAY. Apr 6. Commemorates foundation of present dynasty by King Rama I (1782–1809), who also established Bangkok as capital.

US ENTERS WORLD WAR I: ANNIVERSARY. Apr 6, 1917. After Congress approved a declaration of war against Germany, the US entered WWI, which had begun in 1914.

US SENATE ACHIEVES A QUORUM: ANNIVERSARY. Apr 6, 1789. The US Senate was formally organized after achieving a quorum.

BIRTHDAYS TODAY

Alice Bach, 59, author (*The Meat in the Sandwich*), born New York, NY, Apr 6, 1942.

Graeme Base, 43, author and illustrator (*The Worst Band in the Universe*), born Amersham, England, Apr 6, 1958.

Candace Cameron Bure, 25, actress ("Full House"), born Panorama City, CA, Apr 6, 1976.

APRIL 7 — SATURDAY
Day 97 — 268 Remaining

KING, WILLIAM RUFUS DEVANE: BIRTH ANNIVERSARY. Apr 7, 1786. The 13th vice president of the US who died on the 46th day after taking the Oath of Office, of tuberculosis, at Cahawba, AL, Apr 18, 1853. The Oath of Office had been administered to King Mar 4, 1853 at Havana, Cuba, as authorized by a special act of Congress (the only presidential or vice presidential oath to be administered outside the US). Born at Sampson County, NY, King was the only vice president of the US who had served in both the House of Representatives and the Senate.

METRIC SYSTEM: ANNIVERSARY. Apr 7, 1795. The metric system was adopted at France, where it had been developed.

MOON PHASE: FULL MOON. Apr 7. Moon enters Full Moon phase at 11:22 PM, EDT.

NATIONAL ASSOCIATION OF ELEMENTARY SCHOOL PRINCIPALS ANNUAL CONFERENCE. Apr 7–10. San Diego, CA. For info: Natl Assn of Elementary School Principals, 1615 Duke St, Alexandria, VA 22314. Phone: (703) 684-3345 or (800) 38-NAESP. Fax: (800) 39N-AESP. E-mail: naesp@naesp.org. Web: www.naesp.org.

NO HOUSEWORK DAY. Apr 7. No trash. No dishes. No making of beds or washing of laundry. And no guilt. Give it a rest. [© 1999 by WH] For info: Tom or Ruth Roy, Wellcat Holidays, 2418 Long Ln, Lebanon, PA 17046. Phone: (230) 332-4886. E-mail: wellcat@supernet.com. Web: www.wellcat.com.

PASSOVER BEGINS AT SUNDOWN. Apr 7. See "Pesach" (Apr 8).

UNITED NATIONS: WORLD HEALTH DAY. Apr 7. A United Nations observance commemorating the establishment of the World Health Organization in 1948. For more information, visit the UN's website for children at www.un.org/Pubs/CyberSchoolBus/.

WORLD HEALTH ORGANIZATION: ANNIVERSARY. Apr 7, 1948. This agency of the UN was founded to coordinate international health systems. It is headquartered at Geneva. Among its achievements is the elimination of smallpox.

WORLD HEALTH DAY. Apr 7. A complete planning kit available. For info: American Assn for World Health, World Health Day, 1825 K St NW, Ste 1208, Washington, DC 20006. Phone: (202) 466-5883. Fax: (202) 466-5896. E-mail: aawhstaff@aol.com. Web: www.aawhworldhealth.org.

BIRTHDAYS TODAY

Alan R. Carter, 54, author (*Up Country*), born Eau Claire, WI, Apr 7, 1947.

Jackie Chan, 47, actor, martial arts star, born Hong Kong, Apr 7, 1954.

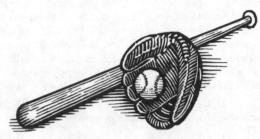

APRIL 8 — SUNDAY
Day 98 — 267 Remaining

BIRTHDAY OF THE BUDDHA: BIRTH ANNIVERSARY. Apr 8. Among Buddhist holidays, this is the most important as it commemorates the birthday of the Buddha. The founder of Buddhism had the given name Siddhartha, the family name Gautama and the clan name Shaka. He is commonly called the Buddha, meaning in Sanskrit "the enlightened one." He is thought to have lived in India from c. 563 BC to 483 BC.

BLACK SENATE PAGE APPOINTED: ANNIVERSARY. Apr 8, 1965. Sixteen-year-old Lawrence Bradford of New York City was the first black page appointed to the US Senate.

HOLY WEEK. Apr 8–14. Christian observance dating from the fourth century, known also as Great Week. The seven days beginning on the sixth and final Sunday in Lent (Palm Sunday), consisting of: Palm Sunday, Monday of Holy Week, Tuesday of Holy Week, Spy Wednesday (or Wednesday of Holy Week), Maundy Thursday, Good Friday and Holy Saturday (or Great Sabbath or Easter Even). A time of solemn devotion to and memorializing of the suffering (passion), death and burial of Christ. Formerly a time of strict fasting.

HOME RUN RECORD SET BY HANK AARON: ANNIVERSARY. Apr 8, 1974. Henry ("Hammerin' Hank") Aaron hit the 715th home run of his career, breaking the record set by Babe Ruth in 1935. Playing for the Atlanta Braves, Aaron broke the record at Atlanta in a game against the Los Angeles Dodgers. He finished his career in 1976 with a total of 755 home runs. This record remains unbroken. At the time of his retirement, Aaron also held records for first in RBIs, second in at-bats and runs scored and third in base hits.

JAPAN: FLOWER FESTIVAL (HANA MATSURI). Apr 8. Commemorates Buddha's birthday. Ceremonies in all temples.

MORRIS, LEWIS: 275th BIRTH ANNIVERSARY. Apr 8, 1726. Signer of the Declaration of Independence, born at Westchester County, NY. Died Jan 22, 1798, at the Morrisania manor at NY.

	S	M	T	W	T	F	S
April	1	2	3	4	5	6	7
	8	9	10	11	12	13	14
2001	15	16	17	18	19	20	21
	22	23	24	25	26	27	28
	29	30					

NATIONAL WEEK OF THE OCEAN. Apr 8–14. A week focusing on humanity's interdependence with the ocean, asking each of us to appreciate, protect and use the ocean wisely. Annually, the second full week in April. *See* Curriculum Connection. For info: Pres/Cofounder, Cynthia Hancock, Natl Week of the Ocean, Inc, PO Box 179, Ft Lauderdale, FL 33302. Phone: (954) 462-5573.

ORTHODOX PALM SUNDAY. Apr 8. Celebration of Christ's entry into Jerusalem, when His way was covered with palms by the multitudes. Beginning of Holy Week in the Orthodox Church. Most of the time Orthodox holidays associated with Easter fall on a later date than the same Western holidays, but in 2001 the Orthodox and Western church holidays are on the same date.

PALM SUNDAY. Apr 8. Commemorates Christ's last entry into Jerusalem, when His way was covered with palms by the multitudes. Beginning of Holy (or Great) Week in Western Christian churches.

★**PAN AMERICAN WEEK.** Apr 8–14. Presidential Proclamation customarily issued as "Pan American Day and Pan American Week." Always issued for the week including Apr 14, except in 1965, from 1946 through 1948, 1955 through 1977, and 1979.

PESACH or PASSOVER. Apr 8–15. Hebrew calendar dates: Nisan 15–22, 5761. Apr 8, the first day of Passover, begins an eight-day celebration of the delivery of the Jews from slavery in Egypt. Unleavened bread (matzoh) is eaten at this time.

SEVENTEENTH AMENDMENT TO US CONSTITUTION RATIFIED. Apr 8, 1913. Prior to the 17th Amendment, members of the Senate were elected by each state's respective legislature. The advent and popularity of primary elections during the last decade of the 19th century and the early 20th century and a string of senatorial scandals, most notably a scandal involving William Lorimer, an Illinois political boss in 1909, forced the Senate to end its resistance to a constitutional amendment requiring direct popular election of senators.

WHITE, RYAN: DEATH ANNIVERSARY. Apr 8, 1990. This young man, born Dec 6, 1971, at Kokomo, IN, put the face of a child on AIDS and helped promote greater understanding of the disease. Ryan, a hemophiliac, contracted AIDS from a blood transfusion. Banned from the public school system in Central Indiana in 1984 at the age of 10, he moved with his mother and sister to Cicero, IN, where he was accepted by students and faculty alike. Ryan once stated that he only wanted to be treated as a normal teenager, but that was not to be as media attention made him a celebrity. A few days after attending the Academy Awards in 1990, 18-year-old Ryan was hospitalized and lost his valiant fight, at Indianapolis, IN. His funeral was attended by many celebrities.

WILLIAMS, WILLIAM: BIRTH ANNIVERSARY. Apr 8, 1731. Signer of the Declaration of Independence, born at Lebanon, CT. Died there Aug 2, 1811.

BIRTHDAYS TODAY

Kofi Annan, 63, UN Secretary General, born Kumasi, Ghana, Apr 8, 1938.

Susan Bonners, 54, author and illustrator (*A Penguin Year*), born Chicago, IL, Apr 8, 1947.

Ruth Chew, 81, author and illustrator (*The Wednesday Witch*), born Minneapolis, MN, Apr 8, 1920.

Betty (Elizabeth) Ford, 83, former First Lady, wife of Gerald Ford, 38th president of the US, born Chicago, IL, Apr 8, 1918.

Trina Schart Hyman, 62, illustrator (Caldecott for *Saint George and the Dragon*), born Philadelphia, PA, Apr 8, 1939.

Taran Noah Smith, 17, actor ("Home Improvement"), born San Francisco, CA, Apr 8, 1984.

APRIL 8–14
NATIONAL WEEK OF THE OCEAN

If you have ever looked at pictures of the Earth taken from satellites or space vehicles, you may have been struck by how blue our planet looks. The waters of our five oceans—the Atlantic, Pacific, Indian, Arctic and Antarctic Oceans—are responsible for its stunning blue color. Oceans cover about 70 percent of our planet's surface and hold 97 percent of Earth's water.

The deep-sea floor of Earth's oceans are our last unexplored frontier. New technology now enables scientists to map and "visit" great depths via sounding devices. Small, specially equipped submarines transport scientists to depths close to 7,000 feet. Fascinating creatures, such as six-foot-long tube worms and giant clams, survive in dark water. Tiny microbial life teems in the waters near hydrothermal vents. Scientists now estimate that millions of species inhabit ocean waters deeper than 10,000 feet.

Ocean life is truly diverse. Curriculum units about oceans can easily center around several different ocean environments. Have students set up an ocean environments bulletin board. Microscopic phytoplankton are the base of the ocean's food chain. They convert sunlight into energy. Larger organisms gain that energy when they gobble the phytoplankton. Find pictures of phytoplankton, and let students observe and redraw them. Create a phytoplankton bulletin board to represent the view as it would be seen through a microscope. Reefs, beaches, tide pools, marine mammals, dark-water dwellers and frigid waters are other ocean environment bulletin board ideas. Cardboard-box ocean environment dioramas are a smaller scale and individualized alternative.

Create a classroom "ocean surround." Affix fish and seaweed cutouts to the windows and walls. Suspend ocean creatures on nylon thread from the ceiling. Some students may want to bring in and display shell collections. Protect them from poking fingers.

Get ready for Young People's Poetry Week (Apr 16–22) by writing ocean poems and collating them into a classroom book. Students might write from a fish or ocean mammal's perspective. Write concrete poems to represent shell or wave outlines.

The health of Earth's oceans is threatened in several ways, including over-fishing (removing too many fishes from a specific area), coastal development, underwater mining and pollution. Middle school and junior high students can investigate these topics and hold debates to explore the environmental and economic pros and cons for each. They can write letters to elected officials and ask what efforts the present congress and senate are making to ensure healthy oceans in the future.

Many excellent books are available about oceans and their inhabitants. Here are some that will get your students started. *The Oceans Atlas*, by Anita Ganeri (Dorling Kindersley, 1-56458-475-5, $19.95 Gr. 3–8); *Dive! My Adventures in the Deep Frontier*, by Sylvia A. Earle (National Geographic, 0-7922-7144-0, $18.95 Gr. 4–8); *Exploring the Deep, Dark Sea*, by Gail Gibbons (Little, Brown, 0-316-30945-1, $14.95 Gr. 2–4); *Sea Soup: Phytoplankton*, by Mary Cerullo (Tilbury House, 0-88448-208-1, $16.95 Gr. 3–6); and *Sea Soup Teacher's Guide*, by Betsy T. Stevens (0-88448-209-X); *Sea Horses*, by Sally M. Walker (Carolrhoda, 1-57505-317-9, $16.95 Gr. 3–8); and *Gentle Giant Octopus*, by Karen Wallace (Candlewick Press, 0-7636-0318-X, $15.99 Gr. K–2).

APRIL 9 — MONDAY

Day 99 — 266 Remaining

BLACK PAGE APPOINTED TO US HOUSE OF REPRESENTATIVES: ANNIVERSARY. Apr 9, 1965. Fifteen-year-old Frank Mitchell of Springfield, IL, was the first black appointed a page to the US House of Representatives.

CIVIL RIGHTS BILL OF 1866: ANNIVERSARY. Apr 9, 1866. The Civil Rights Bill of 1866, passed by Congress over the veto of President Andrew Johnson, granted blacks the rights and privileges of American citizenship and formed the basis for the Fourteenth Amendment to the US Constitution.

CIVIL WAR ENDING: ANNIVERSARY. Apr 9, 1865. At 1:30 PM, General Robert E. Lee, commander of the Army of Northern Virginia, surrendered to General Ulysses S. Grant, commander-in-chief of the Union Army, ending four years of civil war. The meeting took place in the house of Wilmer McLean at the village of Appomattox Court House, VA. Confederate soldiers were permitted to keep their horses and go free to their homes, while Confederate officers were allowed to retain their swords and side arms as well. Grant wrote the terms of surrender. Formal surrender took place at the Courthouse Apr 12. Death toll for the Civil War is estimated at 500,000 men.

ECKERT, J(OHN) PRESPER, JR: BIRTH ANNIVERSARY. Apr 9, 1919. Coinventor with John W. Mauchly of ENIAC (Electronic Numerical Integrator and Computer), which was first demonstrated at the Moore School of Electrical Engineering at the University of Pennsylvania at Philadelphia, Feb 14, 1946. This is generally considered the birth of the computer age. Originally designed to process artillery calculations for the Army, ENIAC was also used in the Manhattan Project. Eckert and Mauchly formed Electronic Control Company, which later became Unisys Corporation. Eckert was born at Philadelphia and died at Bryn Mawr, PA, June 3, 1995.

April 2001	S	M	T	W	T	F	S
	1	2	3	4	5	6	7
	8	9	10	11	12	13	14
	15	16	17	18	19	20	21
	22	23	24	25	26	27	28
	29	30					

KRUMGOLD, JOSEPH: BIRTH ANNIVERSARY. Apr 9, 1908. Author (Newbery for *Onion John* and . . . *And Now Miguel*), born at Jersey City, NJ. Died July 10, 1980.

PHILIPPINES: ARAW NG KAGITINGAN. Apr 9, 1942. National observance to commemorate the fall of Bataan. The infamous "Death March" is reenacted at the Mount Samat Shrine, the Dambana ng Kagitingan.

ROBESON, PAUL BUSTILL: BIRTH ANNIVERSARY. Apr 9, 1898. Paul Robeson, born at Princeton, NJ, was an All-American football player at Rutgers University and received his law degree from Columbia University in 1923. After being seen by Eugene O'Neill in an amateur stage production, he was offered a part in O'Neill's play, *The Emperor Jones*. His performance in that play with the Provincetown Players established him as an actor. Without ever having taken a voice lesson, he also became a popular singer. His stage credits include *Show Boat*, *Porgy and Bess*, *The Hairy Ape* and *Othello*, which enjoyed the longest Broadway run of a Shakespearean play. In 1950 he was denied a passport by the US for refusing to sign an affidavit stating whether he was or ever had been a member of the Communist Party. The action was overturned by the Supreme Court in 1958. His film credits include *Emperor Jones*, *Show Boat*, *King Solomon's Mines* and *Song of Freedom*. Robeson died at Philadelphia, PA, Jan 23, 1976.

TUNISIA: MARTYRS' DAY. Apr 9.

WINSTON CHURCHILL DAY. Apr 9. Anniversary of enactment of legislation in 1963 that made the late British statesman an honorary citizen of the US.

BIRTHDAYS TODAY

Jacques Villeneuve, 30, auto racer, born St. Jean d'Iberville, Quebec, Canada, Apr 9, 1971.

APRIL 10 — TUESDAY

Day 100 — 265 Remaining

CHILDREN'S DAY IN FLORIDA. Apr 10. A legal holiday on the second Tuesday in April.

COMMODORE PERRY DAY. Apr 10, 1794. Matthew Calbraith Perry, commodore in the US Navy, negotiator of first treaty between US and Japan (Mar 31, 1854). Born at South Kingston, RI, he died Mar 4, 1858, at New York, NY.

LIBERATION OF BUCHENWALD CONCENTRATION CAMP: ANNIVERSARY. Apr 10, 1945. Buchenwald, north of Weimar, Germany, was entered by Allied troops. It was the first of the Nazi concentration camps to be liberated. It had been established in 1937 and about 56,000 people died there.

PULITZER, JOSEPH: BIRTH ANNIVERSARY. Apr 10, 1847. American journalist and newspaper publisher, founder of the Pulitzer Prizes, born at Budapest, Hungary. Died at Charleston, SC, Oct 29, 1911. Pulitzer Prizes have been awarded annually since 1917.

ROBERT GRAY BECOMES FIRST AMERICAN TO CIRCUMNAVIGATE THE EARTH: ANNIVERSARY. Apr 10, 1790. When Robert Gray docked the *Columbia* at Boston Harbor, he became the first American to circumnavigate the earth. He sailed from Boston, MA, in September 1787, to trade with Indians of the Pacific Northwest. From there he sailed to China and then continued around the world. His 42,000-mile journey opened trade between New England and the Pacific Northwest and helped the US establish claims to the Oregon Territory.

SAFETY PIN PATENTED: ANNIVERSARY. Apr 10, 1849. Walter Hunt of New York patented the first safety pin.

SALVATION ARMY FOUNDER'S DAY. Apr 10, 1829. Birth anniversary of William Booth, a Methodist minister who began an evangelical ministry in the East End of London in 1865 and established mission stations to feed and house the poor. In 1878 he changed the name of the organization to the Salvation Army. Booth was born at Nottingham, England, he died at London, Aug 20, 1912.

BIRTHDAYS TODAY

David A. Adler, 54, author (Cam Jansen mystery series), born New York, NY, Apr 10, 1947.

Haley Joel Osment, 13, actor (*The Sixth Sense, Bogus*), born Los Angeles, CA, Apr 10, 1988.

APRIL 11 — WEDNESDAY
Day 101 — 264 Remaining

CIVIL RIGHTS ACT OF 1968: ANNIVERSARY. Apr 11, 1968. Exactly one week after the assassination of Martin Luther King, Jr, the Civil Rights Act of 1968 (protecting civil rights workers, expanding the rights of Native Americans and providing antidiscrimination measures in housing) was signed into law by President Lyndon B. Johnson, who said: "... the proudest moments of my presidency have been times such as this when I have signed into law the promises of a century."

EVERETT, EDWARD: BIRTH ANNIVERSARY. Apr 11, 1794. American statesman and orator, born at Dorcester, MA. It was Edward Everett who delivered the main address at the dedication of Gettysburg National Cemetery, Nov 19, 1863. President Abraham Lincoln also spoke at the dedication, and his brief speech (less than two minutes) has been called one of the most eloquent in the English language. Once a candidate for vice president of the US (1860), Everett died at Boston, MA, Jan 15, 1865.

HUGHES, CHARLES EVANS: BIRTH ANNIVERSARY. Apr 11, 1862. The 11th chief justice of the US Supreme Court. Born at Glens Falls, NY, he died at Osterville, MA, Aug 27, 1948.

SPACE MILESTONE: *APOLLO 13* (US). Apr 11, 1970. Astronauts Lovell, Haise and Swigert were endangered when an oxygen tank ruptured. The planned moon landing was cancelled. Details of the accident were made public and the world shared concern for the crew who splashed down successfully in the Pacific Apr 17. The film *Apollo 13*, starring Tom Hanks, accurately told this story.

THANK YOU SCHOOL LIBRARIAN DAY. Apr 11. Recognizes the unique contribution made by school librarians who are resource people extraordinaire, supporting the myriad educational needs of faculty, staff, students and parents *all year long*! Three cheers to all the public, private and parochial school infomaniacs whose true love of reading and lifelong learning make them great role models for kids of all ages. To help celebrate, take your school librarian to lunch, donate a book in his/her honor to the library, tell your librarian what a difference he/she has made in your life. Sponsor: "Carpe Libris" (Seize the Book), a loosely knit group of underappreciated librarians. Press packet available for $5. For info: Judyth Lessee, Organizer, Carpe Libris, PO Box 40503, Tucson, AZ 85717-0503. Phone: (520) 318-2954. E-mail: rinophyl@rtd.com.

UGANDA: LIBERATION DAY: ANNIVERSARY. Apr 11. Republic of Uganda celebrates anniversary of overthrow of Idi Amin's dictatorship in 1979.

BIRTHDAYS TODAY

Josh Server, 22, actor (Nickelodeon's "All That"), born Highland Park, IL, Apr 11, 1979.

APRIL 12 — THURSDAY
Day 102 — 263 Remaining

ANNIVERSARY OF THE BIG WIND. Apr 12, 1934. The highest-velocity natural wind ever recorded occurred in the morning at the Mount Washington, NH, Observatory. Three weather observers, Wendell Stephenson, Alexander McKenzie and Salvatore Pagliuca, observed and recorded the phenomenon in which gusts reached 231 miles per hour—"the strongest natural wind ever recorded on the earth's surface."

CLAY, HENRY: BIRTH ANNIVERSARY. Apr 12, 1777. Statesman, born at Hanover County, VA. Was the Speaker of the House of Representatives and later became the leader of the new Whig party. He was defeated for the presidency three times. Clay died at Washington, DC, June 29, 1852.

MAUNDY THURSDAY or HOLY THURSDAY. Apr 12. The Thursday before Easter, originally "dies mandate," celebrates Christ's injunction to love one another, "Mandatus novum do vobis. ..." ("A new commandment I give to you. ...")

NATIONAL COUNCIL OF TEACHERS OF MATHEMATICS ANNUAL MEETING. Apr 12–15. Chicago, IL. For info: Natl Council of Teachers of Mathematics, 1906 Association Dr, Reston, VA 20191-1593. Phone: (703) 620-9840. Fax: (703) 476-2970. E-mail: infocentral@nctm.org. Web: www.nctm.org.

★**NATIONAL D.A.R.E. DAY.** Apr 12. The Drug Abuse Resistance Education (D.A.R.E.) program helps children in grades K–12 learn the skills they need to avoid involvement in drugs, gangs and violence.

POLIO VACCINE: ANNIVERSARY. Apr 12, 1955. Anniversary of announcement that the polio vaccine developed by American physician Dr. Jonas E. Salk was "safe, potent and effective." Incidence of the dreaded infantile paralysis, or poliomyelitis, declined by 95 percent following introduction of preventive vaccines.

ROOSEVELT, FRANKLIN DELANO: DEATH ANNIVERSARY. Apr 12, 1945. With the end of WWII only months away, the nation and the world were stunned by the sudden death of the president shortly into his fourth term of office. Roosevelt, the 32nd president of the US (Mar 4, 1933–Apr 12, 1945), was the only president to serve more than two terms—he was elected to four consecutive terms. He died at Warm Springs, GA.

SPACE MILESTONE: *COLUMBIA STS 1* (US) FIRST SHUTTLE FLIGHT: 20th ANNIVERSARY. Apr 12, 1981. First flight of Shuttle *Columbia*. Two astronauts (John Young and Robert Crippen), on first manned US space mission since *Apollo-Soyuz* in July 1976, spent 54 hours in space (36 orbits of Earth) before landing at Edwards Air Force Base, CA, Apr 14.

SPACE MILESTONE: *VOSTOK I*, FIRST MAN IN SPACE: 40th ANNIVERSARY. Apr 12, 1961. Yuri Gagarin became the first man in space when he made a 108-minute voyage, orbiting Earth in a 10,395-lb vehicle, *Vostok I*, launched by the USSR.

TRUANCY LAW: ANNIVERSARY. Apr 12, 1853. The first truancy law was enacted at New York. A $50 fine was charged against parents whose children between the ages of five and 15 were absent from school.

BIRTHDAYS TODAY

Nicholas Brendon, 30, actor ("Buffy the Vampire Slayer"), born Los Angeles, CA, Apr 12, 1971.

Beverly Cleary, 85, author (Ramona series for children; winner of the Newbery Medal for *Dear Mr Henshaw*), born McMinnville, OR, Apr 12, 1916.

Gary Soto, 49, poet, author (*Neighborhood Odes, Too Many Tamales*), born Fresno, CA, Apr 12, 1952.

APRIL 13 — FRIDAY
Day 103 — 262 Remaining

BUTTS, ALFRED M.: BIRTH ANNIVERSARY. Apr 13, 1899. Alfred Butts was a jobless architect in the Depression when he invented the board game Scrabble. The game was just a fad for Butts's friends until a Macy's executive saw the game being played at a resort in 1952, and the world's largest store began carrying it. Manufacturing of the game was turned over to Selchow & Righter when 35 workers were producing 6,000 sets a week. Butts received three cents per set for years. He said, "One-third went to taxes. I gave one-third away, and the other third enabled me to have an enjoyable life." Butts was born at Poughkeepsie, NY. He died Apr 4, 1993, at Rhinebeck, NY.

GOOD FRIDAY. Apr 13. Observed in commemoration of the crucifixion. Oldest Christian celebration. Possible corruption of "God's Friday." Observed in some manner by most Christian sects and as a public holiday or part holiday in Delaware, Florida, Hawaii, Illinois, Indiana, Kentucky, New Jersey, North Carolina, Pennsylvania and Tennessee.

HENRY, MARGUERITE: BIRTH ANNIVERSARY. Apr 13, 1902. Born at Milwaukee, WI, Henry received the Newbery Medal in 1949 for her book *The King of the Wind*. She also authored *Misty of Chincoteague, Brighty of Grand Canyon* and other books about horses. Henry died at Rancho Santa Fe, CA, Nov 26, 1997.

INDIA: BAISAKHI. Apr 13. Sikh holiday that commemorates the founding of the brotherhood of Khalsa in 1699. A large fair is held at the Golden Temple at Amritsar, the central shrine of Sikhism.

JEFFERSON, THOMAS: BIRTH ANNIVERSARY. Apr 13, 1743. Third president of the US (Mar 4, 1801–Mar 3, 1809), born at Shadwell, VA. He had previously served as vice president under

John Adams. Jefferson, who died at Charlottesville, VA, July 4, 1826, wrote his own epitaph: "Here was buried Thomas Jefferson, author of the Declaration of American Independence, of the statute of Virginia for religious freedom, and father of the University of Virginia." A holiday in Alabama and Oklahoma.

★**JEFFERSON, THOMAS: BIRTH ANNIVERSARY.** Apr 13. Presidential Proclamation 2276, of Mar 21, 1938, covers all succeeding years. (Pub Res No. 60 of Aug 16, 1937.)

NATIONAL YOUTH SERVICE DAY. Apr 13–14. An annual public education and recruitment campaign, highlighting the efforts of young people to become involved in volunteering and promoting the benefits of youth service to the American people. More than two million people participate. For info: Youth Service America, 1101 15th St NW, Ste 200, Washington, DC 20005. Phone: (202) 296-2992. Web: www.ysa.org.

***SILENT SPRING* PUBLICATION: ANNIVERSARY.** Apr 13, 1962. Rachel Carson's *Silent Spring* warned humankind that for the first time in history every person is subjected to contact with dangerous chemicals from conception until death. Carson painted a vivid picture of how chemicals—used in many ways but particularly in pesticides—have upset the balance of nature, undermining the survival of countless species. This enormously popular and influential book was a soft-spoken battle cry to protect our natural surroundings. Its publication signaled the beginning of the environmental movement.

THAILAND: SONGKRAN FESTIVAL. Apr 13–15. Public holiday. Thai water festival. To welcome the new year the image of Buddha is bathed with holy or fragrant water and lustral water is sprinkled on celebrants. Joyous event, especially observed at Thai Buddhist temples. (Dates of observance subject to alteration.)

SRI LANKA: SINHALA AND TAMIL NEW YEAR. April 13–14. This New Year festival includes traditional games, the wearing of new clothes in auspicious colors and special foods. Public holiday.

BIRTHDAYS TODAY

Jonathan Brandis, 25, actor (*Outside Providence, Ladybugs*), born Danbury, CT, Apr 13, 1976.

Ben Nighthorse Campbell, 68, US Senator (R, Colorado), born Auburn, CA, Apr 13, 1933.

Erik Christian Haugaard, 78, author (*The Rider and His Horse*), born Frederiksberg, Denmark, Apr 13, 1923.

Lee Bennett Hopkins, 63, poet (*Blast Off!: Poems about Space*), born Scranton, PA, Apr 13, 1938.

APRIL 14 — SATURDAY
Day 104 — 261 Remaining

EASTER EVEN. Apr 14. The Saturday before Easter. Last day of Holy Week and of Lent.

FIRST AMERICAN ABOLITION SOCIETY FOUNDED: ANNIVERSARY. Apr 14, 1775. The first abolition organization

April 2001	S	M	T	W	T	F	S
	1	2	3	4	5	6	7
	8	9	10	11	12	13	14
	15	16	17	18	19	20	21
	22	23	24	25	26	27	28
	29	30					

formed in the US was The Society for the Relief of Free Negroes Unlawfully Held in Bondage, founded at Philadelphia, PA.

FIRST DICTIONARY OF AMERICAN ENGLISH PUBLISHED: ANNIVERSARY. Apr 14, 1828. Noah Webster published his *American Dictionary of the English Language*.

HONDURAS: DIA DE LAS AMERICAS. Apr 14. Honduras. Pan-American Day, a national holiday.

LINCOLN, ABRAHAM: ASSASSINATION ANNIVERSARY. Apr 14, 1865. President Abraham Lincoln was shot while watching a performance of *Our American Cousin* at Ford's Theatre, Washington, DC. He died the following day. Assassin was John Wilkes Booth, a young actor.

★ **PAN AMERICAN DAY.** Apr 14. Presidential Proclamation 1912, of May 28, 1930, covers every Apr 14 (required by Governing Board of Pan American Union). Proclamation issued each year since 1948.

PAN-AMERICAN DAY IN FLORIDA. Apr 14. A holiday to be observed in the public schools of Florida honoring the republics of Latin America. If Apr 14 should fall on a day that is not a school day, then Pan-American Day should be observed on the preceding school day.

SULLIVAN, ANNE: BIRTH ANNIVERSARY. Apr 14, 1866. Anne Sullivan, born at Feeding Hills, MA, became well known for "working miracles" with Helen Keller, who was blind and deaf. Nearly blind herself, Sullivan used a manual alphabet communicated by the sense of touch to teach Keller to read, write and speak and then to help her go on to higher education. Anne Sullivan died Oct 20, 1936, at Forest Hills, NY.

YMCA HEALTHY KIDS DAY. Apr 14. To promote the healthiness of children nationwide. Contact your local YMCA for events in your area. For info: YMCA of the USA, 101 N Wacker Dr, Chicago, IL 60606. Phone: (312) 269-1198 or (312) 977-9063. Web: www.ymca.net.

YO-YO DAYS. Apr 14–15 (tentative). Spinning Top Museum, Burlington, WI. Midwest yo-yo convention, Wisconsin State Yo-Yo Contest, classes, demonstrations, collections of yo-yos on exhibit and yo-yo shows for all generations. For info: Spinning Top Museum, 533 Milwaukee Ave (Hwy 36), Burlington, WI 53105. Phone: (414) 763-3946.

BIRTHDAYS TODAY

Cynthia Cooper, 38, basketball player, born Chicago, IL, Apr 14, 1963.
Sarah Michelle Gellar, 24, actress ("Buffy the Vampire Slayer"), born New York, NY, Apr 14, 1977.
Gregory Alan (Greg) Maddux, 35, baseball player, born San Angelo, TX, Apr 14, 1966.
Pete Rose, 60, former baseball manager and player, born Cincinnati, OH, Apr 14, 1941.

APRIL 15 — SUNDAY
Day 105 — 260 Remaining

EASTER SUNDAY. Apr 15. Commemorates the Resurrection of Christ. Most joyous festival of the Christian year. The date of Easter, a movable feast, is derived from the lunar calendar: the first Sunday following the first ecclesiastical full moon on or after Mar 21—always between Mar 22 and Apr 25. The Council of Nicaea (AD 325) prescribed that Easter be celebrated on the Sunday after Passover, as that feast's date had been established in Jesus' time. Orthodox Christians continue to use the Julian calendar, so that Easter can sometimes be as much as five weeks apart in the Western and Eastern churches but this year the Eastern and Western dates for Easter happen to coincide. Easter in 2002 will be Mar 31; in 2003 it will be Apr 20. Many other dates in the Christian year are derived from the date of Easter. See also: "Orthodox Easter Sunday or Pascha." For links to Easter websites, go to: deil.lang.uiuc.edu/web.pages/holidays/easter.html.

FIRST MCDONALD'S OPENS: ANNIVERSARY. Apr 15, 1955. The first franchised McDonald's was opened at Des Plaines, IL, by Ray Kroc, who had gotten the idea from a hamburger joint at San Bernardino, CA, run by the McDonald brothers. By the mid-1990s, there were more than 15,000 McDonald's in 70 countries.

FIRST SCHOOL FOR DEAF FOUNDED: ANNIVERSARY. Apr 15, 1817. Thomas Hopkins Gallaudet and Laurent Clerc founded the first US public school for the deaf, Connecticut Asylum for the Education and Instruction of Deaf and Dumb Persons (now the American School for the Deaf), at Hartford, CT.

MOON PHASE: LAST QUARTER. Apr 15. Moon enters Last Quarter phase at 11:31 AM, EDT.

NATIONAL COIN WEEK. Apr 15–21. To promote the history and lore of numismatics and the hobby of coin collecting. For info: James Taylor, Dir of Educ, American Numismatic Assn, 818 N Cascade Ave, Colorado Springs, CO 80903. Phone: (719) 632-2646 or (800) 367-9723. Fax: (719) 634-4085. E-mail: anaedu @money.org. Web: www.money.org.

NATIONAL ORGAN AND TISSUE DONOR AWARENESS WEEK. Apr 15–21. To encourage Americans to consider organ and tissue donation and to sign donor cards when getting a driver's license. For info: Natl Kidney Foundation, 30 E 33rd St, New York, NY 10016. Phone: (800) 622-9010 or (212) 889-2210. Web: www.kidney.org or www.organdonor.gov.

NATIONAL SCIENCE AND TECHNOLOGY WEEK. Apr 15–21. National Science and Technology Week is sponsored by the Office of Legislative and Public Affairs of the National Science Foundation to promote awareness of science and technology to the general public and especially to children. Annually, the third full week in April. For info: Mary Bullock, Natl Science Fdtn, 4201 Wilson Blvd, Arlington, VA 22230. E-mail: nstw@nsf.gov. Web: www.nsf.gov.

ORTHODOX EASTER SUNDAY OR PASCHA. Apr 15. Observed by Eastern Orthodox Churches. See also: "Easter Sunday."

REACH OUT & READ WEEK. Apr 15–21. This is a national campaign to promote the availability and use of libraries, radio reading services and special-information media services for the visually-disabled community. "ROAR Week" is now a part of Syracuse University "Living Book Project." For info: Dawn L. Jordan, Outreach Dir, Pediatric Library Services, Non-Profit Reading Service, 115 Brenton St, Richmond, VA 23222. Phone: (804) 321-2063.

SINKING OF THE *TITANIC*: ANNIVERSARY. Apr 15, 1912. The "unsinkable" luxury liner *Titanic* on its maiden voyage from Southampton, England, to New York, NY struck an iceberg just before midnight Apr 14, and sank at 2:27 AM, Apr 15. The *Titanic* had 2,224 persons aboard. Of these, more than 1,500 were lost. About 700 people were rescued from the icy waters off Newfoundland by the liner *Carpathia*, which reached the scene about two hours after the *Titanic* went down. The sunken *Titanic* was located and photographed in September 1985. In July 1986, an expedition aboard the *Atlantis II* descended to the deck of the *Titanic* in a submersible craft, *Alvin*, and guided a robot named Jason, Jr in a search of the ship. Two memorial bronze plaques were left on the deck of the ship. *See* Curriculum Connection.

APRIL 15
AN ICEBERG SINKS THE *TITANIC*

The tragic voyage of the *Titanic*, the famous ocean liner that struck an iceberg and sank, has fascinated people for decades. In 1985, when Robert Ballard found its wreckage and released pictures, renewed interest surged. The recent blockbuster movie created a near frenzy for information about the ship. There is no doubt that the subject captures a child's interest. But few people realize students can become equally engrossed in learning about icebergs. During the days leading up to the 15th, feature snow, ice and glaciers in your classroom. Let students know they will be setting the stage for one of history's most famous disasters.

Create a snowy atmosphere in your room. As an art project, let students cut out paper snowflakes and hang them from the ceiling and on the walls. (This will make your room stand out from others, which are most likely featuring tulips. That creates a mysterious air and raises the question "Why are they doing that?") Point out that in real life no two snowflakes are the same.

On Jan 15, 1885, Wilson Bentley, a 19-year-old man, took the first photograph of a single snowflake. He took thousands more after that. His original photographs have been published in a book. Caldecott Medal Winner *Snowflake Bentley*, by Jacqueline B. Martin (Clarion, 0-395-86162-4, $16 Gr. 1–5) is a lovely picture book biography about Bentley's work.

In science, investigate crystals and how snowflakes form. Discuss snow accumulation and how snowflake crystals change as they are subjected to pressure. In climates where the snow cannot melt each spring and summer, it continues to accumulate and eventually forms a glacier. *Icebergs & Glaciers*, by Seymour Simon (Morrow, 0-688-06186-9, $16 Gr. PreS–3) and *Glaciers: Ice on the Move*, by Sally M. Walker (Carolrhoda, 0-87614-373-7, $16.95 Gr. 3–6) both describe the process and contain photographs and diagrams.

After learning about how glaciers form and move, it's easy to turn the focus to icebergs. When a glacier flows into a body of water, large chunks of ice calve, or break, from the main body of ice and float away. They are called icebergs. Large icebergs pose threats to ships that travel through frigid waters (and one caused the *Titanic* to sink). Students can make mini-icebergs for a concrete understanding of the hidden danger an iceberg poses. All they need to do is plop a piece of ice in a glass of water. Ask them to observe the ice and draw how it appears above and below the water. Measure the ice and determine what percent sticks out of the water.

In geography, students can track the course of a gigantic present-day iceberg, called B-10A. This iceberg broke off from Antarctica in 1985 and began moving away from the continent in 1992. It broke in half in 1995. B-10A is the piece now drifting toward the southern Atlantic Ocean. Have your students look in newspapers and news magazines for articles about B-10A. (There was a wonderful front-page article about it in the Sunday, Oct 10, 1999, edition of the *Chicago Tribune*.) The National Oceanic and Atmospheric Administration's National Ice Center maintains a website with photos and the latest news about the iceberg at www.natice.noaa.gov.

April 2001

S	M	T	W	T	F	S
1	2	3	4	5	6	7
8	9	10	11	12	13	14
15	16	17	18	19	20	21
22	23	24	25	26	27	28
29	30					

Evelyn Ashford, 44, Olympic gold medal track athlete, born Shreveport, LA, Apr 15, 1957.
Jacqueline Briggs Martin, 56, author (*Snowflake Bentley*), born Lewiston, ME, Apr 15, 1945.
Emma Thompson, 42, actress (*Junior*), born Paddington, England, Apr 15, 1959.

APRIL 16 — MONDAY
Day 106 — 259 Remaining

DENMARK: QUEEN MARGRETHE'S BIRTHDAY. Apr 16. Thousands of children gather to cheer the queen at Amalienborg Palace and the Royal Guard wears scarlet gala uniforms.

DIEGO, JOSE de: BIRTH ANNIVERSARY. Apr 16, 1866. Puerto Rican patriot and political leader, Jose de Diego was born at Aguadilla, Puerto Rico. His birthday is a holiday in Puerto Rico. He died July 16, 1918, at New York, NY.

EASTER MONDAY. Apr 16. Holiday or bank holiday in many places, including England, Northern Ireland, Wales, Canada and North Carolina in the US.

EGG SALAD WEEK. Apr 16–22. Dedicated to the many delicious uses for all of the Easter eggs that have been cooked, colored, hidden and found. Annually, the full week after Easter. For info: Linda Braun, Consumer Serv Dir, American Egg Board, 1460 Renaissance Dr, Park Ridge, IL 60068. E-mail: aebnet@aol.com. Web: www.aeb.org.

FAMILIES LAUGHING THROUGH HUMOR WEEK. Apr 16–22. By Word of Mouth Storytelling Guild and Teachable Moments Publishing will be distributing educational information to family-oriented and storytelling agencies and organizations, teaching them how to encourage instruction that will enhance the telling of humorous family stories. This activity not only promotes the art of storytelling, but also leaves lasting, laughing memories for family participants. For info: Shirley Trout, Teachable Moments, PO Box 359, Waverly, NE 68462. Phone: (402) 786-3100. Fax: (402) 788-2131. E-mail: strout@teachablemoments.com. Web: www.teachablemoments.com.

INCOME TAX PAY DAY. Apr 16. A day all Americans need to know—the day by which taxpayers are supposed to make their accounting of the previous year and pay their share of the cost of government. Usually Apr 15, but since that date falls on a Sunday this year, taxpayers get an extension until Monday. The US Internal Revenue Service provides free forms.

MASIH, IQBAL: DEATH ANNIVERSARY. Apr 16, 1995. Twelve-year-old Iqbal Masih, born at Pakistan in 1982, who reportedly had received death threats after speaking out against Pakistan's child labor practices, was shot to death, at Muridke Village, Punjab Province. Masih, who was sold into labor as a carpet weaver at the age of four, spent the next six years of his life shackled to a loom. He began speaking out against child labor after escaping from servitude at the age of ten. In November of 1994 he spoke at an international labor conference in Sweden and he received a $15,000 Reebok Youth in Action Award a month later. There were reports after the shooting that Masih's death was arranged by a "carpet mafia." For more info: *Iqbal Masih and the Crusaders against Child Slavery*, by Susan Kuklin (Holt, 0-8050-5459-6, $16.95 Gr. 6–12).

MOMENT OF LAUGHTER DAY. Apr 16. Laughter is a potent and powerful way to deal with the difficulties of modern living. Since the physical, emotional and spiritual benefits of laughter are widely accepted, this day is set aside for everyone to take the necessary time to experience the power of laughter. For info: Izzy Gesell, Head Honcho of Wide Angle Humor, PO Box 962, Northampton, MA 01061. Phone: (413) 586-2634. Fax: (413) 585-0407. E-mail: izzy@izzyg.com. Web: www.izzyg.com.

★ **NATIONAL PARK WEEK.** Apr 16–22.

PATRIOT'S DAY IN MASSACHUSETTS AND MAINE. Apr 16. Commemorates Battles of Lexington and Concord, 1775. Annually, the third Monday in April.

SOUTH AFRICA: FAMILY DAY. Apr 16. National holiday. Annually, Easter Monday.

WHITE HOUSE EASTER EGG ROLL. Apr 16. Traditionally held on the south lawn of the executive mansion on Easter Monday. Custom is said to have started at the Capitol grounds about 1810. It was transferred to the White House Lawn in the 1870s.

WRIGHT, WILBUR: BIRTH ANNIVERSARY. Apr 16, 1867. Aviation pioneer (with his brother Orville), born at Millville, IN. Died at Dayton, OH, May 30, 1912.

YOUNG PEOPLES' POETRY WEEK. Apr 16–22. Annually, during National Poetry Month. An annual event, sponsored by The Children's Book Council, that highlights poetry for children and young adults and encourages everyone to celebrate poetry—read it, enjoy it, write it—in their homes, childcare centers, classrooms, libraries and bookstores. The CBC is coordinating its promotional efforts with the Academy of American Poets, the sponsor of National Poetry Month in April, and The Center for the Book in the Library of Congress. For info: Children's Book Council, 568 Broadway, Ste 404, New York, NY 10012. Phone: (212) 966-1990. Fax: (212) 966-2073. E-mail: staff@cbcbooks.org. Web: www.cbcbooks.org.

BIRTHDAYS TODAY

Kareem Abdul-Jabbar, 54, Basketball Hall of Fame center, born Lewis Ferdinand Alcindor, Jr, New York, NY, Apr 16, 1947.

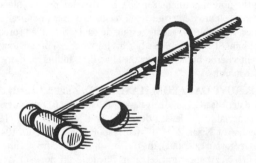

APRIL 17 — TUESDAY
Day 107 — 258 Remaining

AMERICAN SAMOA: FLAG DAY: ANNIVERSARY. Apr 17. National holiday commemorating first raising of American flag in what was formerly Eastern Samoa in 1900. Public holiday with singing, dancing, costumes and parades.

COUNCIL FOR EXCEPTIONAL CHILDREN ANNUAL CONVENTION. Apr 17–22. Kansas City, MO. For info: Council for Exceptional Children, 1920 Association Dr, Reston, VA 20191-1589. Phone: (888) CEC-SPED or (703) 620-3660. Fax: (703) 264-9494. Web: www.cec.sped.org.

NATIONAL CATHOLIC EDUCATIONAL ASSOCIATION CONVENTION AND EXPOSITION. Apr 17–21 (tentative). Milwaukee, WI. Annual meeting for NCEA members and anyone working in, or interested in, the welfare of Catholic education. Est attendance: 11,000. For info: Nancy Brewer, Conv Dir, Natl Catholic Educational Assn, 1077 30th St NW, Ste 100, Washington, DC 20007. Phone: (202) 337-6232. Fax: (202) 333-6706. E-mail: convasst@ncea.org. Web: www.ncea.org.

SPACE MILESTONE: *COLUMBIA NEUROLAB* **(US).** Apr 17, 1998. Seven astronauts and scientists were launched with 2,000 animals (crickets, mice, snails and fish) to study the nervous system in space.

SYRIAN ARAB REPUBLIC: INDEPENDENCE DAY. Apr 17. Official holiday. Proclaimed independence from France in 1946.

VERRAZANO DAY: ANNIVERSARY. Apr 17, 1524. Celebrates discovery of New York harbor by Giovanni Verrazano, Florentine navigator, 1485–1527.

BIRTHDAYS TODAY

Jane Kurtz, 49, author (*Pulling the Lion's Tale*), born Portland, OR, Apr 17, 1952.

APRIL 18 — WEDNESDAY
Day 108 — 257 Remaining

CANADA: CONSTITUTION ACT OF 1982: ANNIVERSARY. Apr 18, 1982. Replacing the British North America Act of 1867, the Canadian Constitution Act of 1982 provides Canada with a new set of fundamental laws and civil rights. Signed by Queen Elizabeth II, at Parliament Hill, Ottawa, Canada, it went into effect at 12:01 AM, Sunday, Apr 19, 1982.

THE HOUSE THAT RUTH BUILT: ANNIVERSARY. Apr 18, 1923. More than 74,000 fans attended Opening Day festivities as the New York Yankees inaugurated their new stadium. Babe Ruth christened it with a game-winning three-run homer into the right-field bleachers. In his coverage of the game for the *New York Evening Telegram* sportswriter Fred Lieb described Yankee Stadium as "The House That Ruth Built," and the name stuck.

PAUL REVERE'S RIDE: ANNIVERSARY. Apr 18, 1775. The "Midnight Ride" of Paul Revere and William Dawes started at about 10 PM, to warn American patriots between Boston, MA, and Concord, MA of the approaching British.

PET OWNERS INDEPENDENCE DAY. Apr 18. Dog and cat owners take day off from work and the pets go to work in their place, since most pets are jobless, sleep all day and do not even take out the trash. [© 1999 by WH] For info: Tom or Ruth Roy, Wellcat Holidays, 2418 Long Ln, Lebanon, PA 17046. Phone: (230) 332-4886. E-mail: wellcat@supernet.com. Web: www.wellcat.com.

SAN FRANCISCO 1906 EARTHQUAKE: 95th ANNIVERSARY. Apr 18, 1906. The business section of San Francisco, approximately 10,000 acres, was destroyed by earthquake. The first quake registered at 5:13 AM, followed by fire. Nearly 4,000 lives were lost during the quake.

"THIRD WORLD" DAY: ANNIVERSARY. Apr 18, 1955. Anniversary of the first use of the phrase "third world," which was used by Indonesia's President Sukarno in his opening speech at the Bandung Conference. Representatives of nearly 30 African and Asian countries (2,000 attendees) heard Sukarno praise the American war of independence, "the first successful anticolonial war in history." More than half the world's population, he said, was represented at this "first intercontinental conference of the so-called colored peoples, in the history of mankind." The phrase and the idea of a "third world" rapidly gained currency, generally signifying the aggregate of nonaligned peoples and nations—the nonwhite and underdeveloped portion of the world.

ZIMBABWE: INDEPENDENCE DAY: ANNIVERSARY. Apr 18. National holiday commemorates the recognition by Great Britain of Zimbabwean independence in 1980. Prior to this, the country had been the British colony of Southern Rhodesia.

BIRTHDAYS TODAY

Melissa Joan Hart, 25, actress ("Sabrina, the Teenage Witch"), born Long Island, NY, Apr 18, 1976.

Rick Moranis, 48, actor (*Honey, I Shrunk the Kids, Honey We Shrunk Ourselves*), born Toronto, Ontario, Canada, Apr 18, 1953.

APRIL 19 — THURSDAY
Day 109 — 256 Remaining

BATTLE OF LEXINGTON AND CONCORD: ANNIVERSARY. Apr 19, 1775. Massachusetts. Start of the American Revolution as the British fired the "shot heard 'round the world."

GARFIELD, LUCRETIA RUDOLPH: BIRTH ANNIVERSARY. Apr 19, 1832. Wife of James Abram Garfield, the 20th president of the US, born at Hiram, OH. Died at Pasadena, CA, Mar 14, 1918.

ICELAND: "FIRST DAY OF SUMMER." Apr 19. A national public holiday, *Sumardagurinn fyrsti*, with general festivities, processions and much street dancing, especially at Reykjavik, greets the coming of summer. Flags are flown on this day. Annually, the third Thursday in April.

OKLAHOMA CITY BOMBING: ANNIVERSARY. Apr 19, 1995. A car bomb exploded outside the Alfred P. Murrah Federal Building at Oklahoma City, OK, at 9:02 AM, killing 168 people, 19 of them children at a day-care center; a nurse died of head injuries sustained while helping in rescue efforts. The bomb, estimated to have weighed 5,000 pounds, had been placed in a rented truck. The blast ripped off the north face of the nine-story building, leaving a 20-foot-wide crater and debris two stories high. Cost of the damage was estimated at $500 million. Structurally unsound and increasingly dangerous, the bombed building was razed May 23. Timothy J. McVeigh, a decorated Gulf War army vet who is alleged to have been deeply angered by the Bureau of Alcohol, Tobacco and Firearms attack on the Branch Davidian compound at Waco, TX, exactly two years before, was convicted of the bombing. Terry L. Nicholls, an army buddy of McVeigh, was convicted of lesser charges.

April *2001*	S	M	T	W	T	F	S
	1	2	3	4	5	6	7
	8	9	10	11	12	13	14
	15	16	17	18	19	20	21
	22	23	24	25	26	27	28
	29	30					

PATRIOT'S DAY IN FLORIDA. Apr 19. A ceremonial day commemorating the first blood shed in the American Revolution at Lexington and Concord in 1775.

SHERMAN, ROGER: BIRTH ANNIVERSARY. Apr 19, 1721. American statesman, member of the Continental Congress (1774–81 and 1783–84), signer of the Declaration of Independence and of the Constitution, was born at Newton, MA. He also calculated astronomical and calendar information for an almanac. Sherman died at New Haven, CT, July 23, 1793.

SIERRA LEONE: NATIONAL HOLIDAY. Apr 19. Sierra Leone became a republic in 1971.

SPACE MILESTONE: *SALYUT* (USSR): 30th ANNIVERSARY. Apr 19, 1971. The Soviet Union launched *Salyut*, the first manned orbiting space laboratory. It was replaced in 1986 by *Mir*, a manned space station and laboratory.

BIRTHDAYS TODAY

Tim Curry, 55, actor (*Muppet Treasure Island, Home Alone 2*), born Cheshire, England, Apr 19, 1946.

APRIL 20 — FRIDAY
Day 110 — 255 Remaining

EGYPT: SHAM EL-NESSIM. Apr 20 (tentative date). Sporting Holiday. This feast has been celebrated by all Egyptians since pharaonic time; people go out and spend the day in parks and along the Nile's banks. For info: Egyptian Tourist Authority, 645 N Michigan Ave, Ste 829, Chicago, IL 60611. Phone: (312) 280-4666.

HITLER, ADOLF: BIRTH ANNIVERSARY. Apr 20, 1889. German dictator, frustrated artist, obsessed with superiority of the "Aryan race" and the evil of Marxism (which he saw as a Jewish plot). Hitler was born at Braunau am Inn, Austria. Turning to politics, despite a five-year prison sentence (writing *Mein Kampf* during the nine months he served), his rise was predictable and a German plebiscite vested sole executive power in Führer Adolf Hitler Aug 19, 1934. Facing certain defeat by the Allied Forces, he shot himself Apr 30, 1945 while his mistress, Eva Braun, took poison in a Berlin bunker where they had been hiding for more than three months.

HOLOCAUST DAY (YOM HASHOAH). Apr 20. Hebrew calendar date: Nisan 27, 5761. A day established by Israel's Knesset as a memorial to the Jewish dead of WWII. Anniversary in Jewish calendar of Nisan 27, 5705 (corresponding to Apr 10, 1945, in the Gregorian calendar), the day on which Allied troops liberated the first Nazi concentration camp, Buchenwald, north of Weimar, Germany, where about 56,000 prisoners, many of them Jewish, perished.

TAURUS, THE BULL. Apr 20–May 20. In the astronomical/astrological zodiac that divides the sun's apparent orbit into 12 segments, the period Apr 20–May 20 is identified, traditionally, as the sun sign of Taurus, the Bull. The ruling planet is Venus.

BIRTHDAYS TODAY

Mary Hoffman, 56, author (*Amazing Grace*), born Eastleigh, Hampshire, England, Apr 20, 1945.

Joey Lawrence, 25, actor ("Brotherly Love," "Blossom"), born Strawbridge, PA, Apr 20, 1976.

Pat Roberts, 65, US Senator (R, Kansas), born Topeka, KS, Apr 20, 1936.

John Paul Stevens, 81, Associate Justice of the US Supreme Court, born Chicago, IL, Apr 20, 1920.

APRIL 21 — SATURDAY
Day 111 — 254 Remaining

BRAZIL: TIRADENTES DAY. Apr 21. National holiday commemorating execution of national hero, dentist Jose da Silva Xavier, nicknamed Tiradentes (tooth-puller), a conspirator in revolt against the Portuguese in 1789.

FROEBEL, FRIEDRICH: BIRTH ANNIVERSARY. Apr 21, 1782. German educator and author Friedrich Froebel, who believed that play is an important part of a child's education, was born at Oberwiessbach, Thuringia. Froebel invented the kindergarten, founding the first one at Blankenburg, Germany, in 1837. Froebel also invented a series of toys which he intended to stimulate learning. (The American architect Frank Lloyd Wright as a child received these toys [maplewood blocks] from his mother and spoke throughout his life of their value.) Froebel's ideas about the role of directed play, toys and music in children's education had a profound influence in England and the US, where the nursery school became a further extension of his ideas. Froebel died at Marienthal, Germany, June 21, 1852.

INDONESIA: KARTINI DAY. Apr 21. Republic of Indonesia. Honors Raden Adjeng Kartini, pioneer in the emancipation of the women of Indonesia.

ITALY: BIRTHDAY OF ROME. Apr 21. Celebration of the founding of Rome, traditionally thought to be in 753 BC.

KINDERGARTEN DAY. Apr 21. A day to recognize the importance of play, games and "creative self-activity" in children's education and to note the history of the kindergarten. Observed on the anniversary of the birth of Friedrich Froebel (Apr 21, 1782) who established the first kindergarten in 1837. German immigrants brought Froebel's ideas to the US in the 1840s. The first kindergarten in a public school in the US was started in 1873, at St. Louis, MO.

SAN JACINTO DAY. Apr 21. Texas. Commemorates Battle of San Jacinto in which Texas won independence from Mexico. A 570-foot monument, dedicated on the 101st anniversary of the battle, marks the site on the banks of the San Jacinto River, about 20 miles from the present city of Houston, TX, where General Sam Houston's Texans decisively defeated the Mexican forces led by Santa Ana in the final battle between Texas and Mexico.

BIRTHDAYS TODAY

Queen Elizabeth II, 75, Queen of the United Kingdom, born London, England, Apr 21, 1926.

Charles Grodin, 66, actor (*Beethoven, Beethoven's 2*), born Pittsburgh, PA, Apr 21, 1935.

Barbara Park, 54, author (the Junie B. Jones series), born Mt Holly, NJ, Apr 21, 1947.

APRIL 22 — SUNDAY
Day 112 — 253 Remaining

BRAZIL: DISCOVERY OF BRAZIL DAY: ANNIVERSARY. Apr 22. Commemorates discovery by Pedro Alvarez Cabral in 1500.

COINS STAMPED "IN GOD WE TRUST": ANNIVERSARY. Apr 22, 1864. By Act of Congress, the phrase "In God We Trust" began to be stamped on all US coins.

EARTH DAY. Apr 22. Earth Day, first observed Apr 22, 1970, with the message "Give Earth a Chance" and attention to reclaiming the purity of the air, water and living environment. Earth Day 1990 was a global event with more than 200 million participating in 142 countries. Annually, Apr 22. Note: Earth Day activities are held by many groups on various dates, often on the weekend closest to Apr 22. The vernal equinox (i.e., the first day of Spring) has been chosen by some for this observance. For info: Earth Day Network, PO Box 9827, San Diego, CA 92169. Phone: (619) 272-0347. Fax: (619) 272-2933. E-mail: cdchase@znet.com. Web: www.sdearthtimes.com/edn.

FIRST SOLO TRIP TO NORTH POLE: ANNIVERSARY. Apr 22, 1994. Norwegian explorer Borge Ousland became the first person to make the trip to the North Pole alone. The trip took 52 days, during which he pulled a 265-pound sled. Departing from Cape Atkticheskiy at Siberia Mar 2, he averaged about 18 1/2 miles per day over the 630-mile journey. Ousland had traveled to the Pole on skis with Erling Kagge in 1990.

GRANGE WEEK. Apr 22–28. State and local recognition for Grange's contribution to rural/urban America. Celebrated at National Headquarters at Washington, DC, and in all states with local, county and state Granges. Begun in 1867, the National Grange is the oldest US rural community service, family-oriented organization with a special interest in agriculture. Annually, the last full week in April. For info: Kermit W. Richardson, Natl Master, The Natl Grange, 1616 H St NW, Washington, DC 20006. Phone: (202) 628-3507 or (888) 4-GRANGE. Fax: (202) 347-1091. Web: www.grange.org.

★**JEWISH HERITAGE WEEK.** Apr 22–29.

NATIONAL PTA EARTH WEEK. Apr 22–28. In 1990, the National PTA recognized the importance of the environment to the health and safety of our children and designated the week in which Earth Day falls (Apr 22) as Earth Week. During Earth Week, PTA members and others work to improve the environment in their homes, schools and communities. For info: Natl PTA Environmental Awareness Program, 330 N Wabash Ave, Ste 2100, Chicago, IL 60611-3690. Phone: (312) 670-6782. Fax: (312) 670-6783. E-mail: info@pta.org. Web: www.pta.org.

NATIONAL VOLUNTEER WEEK. Apr 22–28. National Volunteer Week honors those who reach out to others through volunteer community service and calls attention to the need for more community services for individuals, groups and families to help solve serious social problems that affect our communities. For info: Customer Information Center, Points of Light Foundation, 1737 H St NW, Washington, DC 20006. Phone: (202) 223-9186. Fax: (202) 223-9256. E-mail: volnet@aol.com. Web: www.pointsoflight.org.

NATIONAL YWCA WEEK. Apr 22–28. To promote the YWCA of the USA nationally. Annually, the last full week in April. For info: YWCA of the USA, Empire State Bldg, Ste 301, 350 Fifth Ave, New York, NY 10118. Phone: (212) 273-7800.

OKLAHOMA DAY. Apr 22. Oklahoma.

OKLAHOMA LAND RUSH: ANNIVERSARY. Apr 22, 1889. At noon a gun shot signaled the start of the Oklahoma land rush as thousands of settlers rushed into the territory to claim land. Under pressure from cattlemen, the federal government opened 1,900,000 acres of central Oklahoma that had been bought from the Creek and Seminole tribes.

READING IS FUN WEEK. Apr 22–28. To highlight the importance and fun of reading. Annually, the last full week of April. For info: Rachael Walker, Reading Is Fundamental, Inc, 600 Maryland Ave SW, Rm 600, Washington, DC 20024-2569. Phone: (202) 287-3371. Fax: (202) 287-3196. Web: www.rif.org.

SKY AWARENESS WEEK. Apr 22–28. A celebration of the sky and an opportunity to appreciate its natural beauty, to understand sky and weather processes and to work together to protect the sky as a natural resource (it's the only one we have). Events are held at schools, nature centers, etc, all across the US. For info: Barbara G. Levine, How The Weatherworks, 1522 Baylor Ave, Rockville, MD 20850. Phone: (301) 762-7669 or (301) 251-0242. Fax: (301) 762-7669. E-mail: skyweek@weatherworks.com. Web: www.weatherworks.com.

BIRTHDAYS TODAY

Paula Fox, 78, author (Newbery for *The Slave Dancer*), born New York, NY, Apr 22, 1923.

S.E. Hinton, 52, author (*The Outsiders, Tex*), born New York, NY, Apr 22, 1949.

APRIL 23 — MONDAY
Day 113 — 252 Remaining

ASTRONOMY WEEK. Apr 23–29. To take astronomy to the people. Astronomy Week is observed during the calendar week in which Astronomy Day falls. See also: "Astronomy Day" (Apr 28).

BERMUDA: PEPPERCORN CEREMONY: ANNIVERSARY. Apr 23. St. George. Commemorates the payment of one peppercorn in 1816 to the governor of Bermuda for rental of Old State House by the Masonic Lodge.

BUCHANAN, JAMES: BIRTH ANNIVERSARY. Apr 23, 1791. The 15th president of the US, born near Mercersburg, PA, was the only president who never married. He served one term in office, Mar 4, 1857–Mar 3, 1861, and died at Lancaster, PA, June 1, 1868.

CANADA: NEWFOUNDLAND: SAINT GEORGE'S DAY. Apr 23. Holiday observed in Newfoundland on Monday nearest Feast Day (Apr 23) of Saint George.

FIRST MOVIE THEATER OPENS: ANNIVERSARY. Apr 23, 1896. The first movie theater opened in Koster and Bial's Music Hall at New York City. Up until this time, people viewed movies individually by looking into a Kinetoscope, a box-like "peep show." The first Kinetoscope parlor opened at New York in 1894. But in 1896 Thomas Edison introduced the Vitascope which projected films on a screen. This was the first time in the US that an audience sat in a theater and viewed a movie together.

FIRST PUBLIC SCHOOL IN AMERICA: ANNIVERSARY. Apr 23, 1635. The Boston Latin School opened and is America's oldest public school.

MOON PHASE: NEW MOON. Apr 23. Moon enters New Moon phase at 11:26 AM, EDT.

NATIONAL PLAYGROUND SAFETY WEEK. Apr 23–27. An opportunity for families, community parks, schools and child-care facilities to focus on preventing public playground-related injuries. Sponsored by the National Program for Playground Safety (NPPS), this event helps educate the public about the more than 200,000 children (that's one child every 2 ½ minutes) that require emergency room treatment for playground-related injuries each year. For info: Natl Program for Playground Safety, School of HPELS, UNI, Cedar Falls, IA 50614-0618. Phone: (800) 554-PLAY. Fax: (319) 273-7308. Web: www.uni.edu/playground.

NATIONAL TV TURNOFF WEEK. Apr 23–29. For the eighth annual event, more than 7 million Americans will go without TV for 7 days. *See* Curriculum Connection. For info: TV-Free America, Dept P, Ste 3A, 1611 Connecticut Ave NW, Washington, DC 20009. Phone: (800) 939-6737. Web: www.tvfa.org.

★**NATIONAL VOLUNTEER WEEK.** Apr 23–29.

PEARSON, LESTER B.: BIRTH ANNIVERSARY. Apr 23, 1897. The 14th prime minister of Canada, born at Toronto, Canada. He was Canada's chief delegate at the San Francisco conference where the UN charter was drawn up and later served as president of the General Assembly. He wrote the proposal that resulted in the formation of the North Atlantic Treaty Organization (NATO). He was awarded the Nobel Peace Prize. Died at Rockcliffe, Canada, Dec 27, 1972.

PHYSICISTS DISCOVER TOP QUARK: ANNIVERSARY. Apr 23, 1994. Physicists at the Department of Energy's Fermi National Accelerator Laboratory found evidence for the existence of the subatomic particle called the top quark, the last undiscovered quark of the six predicted to exist by current scientific theory. The discovery provides strong support for the quark theory of the structure of matter. Quarks are subatomic particles that make up protons and neutrons found in the nuclei of atoms. The five other quark types that had already been proven to exist are the up quark, down quark, strange quark, charm quark and bottom quark. Further experimentation over many months confirmed the discovery, and it was publicly announced Mar 2, 1995.

SAINT GEORGE FEAST DAY. Apr 23. Martyr and patron saint of England, who died Apr 23, AD 303. Hero of the George and the dragon legend. The story says that his faith helped him slay a vicious dragon that demanded daily sacrifice after the king's daughter became the intended victim.

SHAKESPEARE, WILLIAM: BIRTH AND DEATH ANNIVERSARY. Apr 23. England's most famous and most revered poet and playwright. He was born at Stratford-on-Avon, England, Apr 23, 1564 (Old Style), baptized there three days later and died there on his birthday, Apr 23, 1616 (Old Style). Author of at least 36 plays and 154 sonnets, Shakespeare created the most influential and lasting body of work in the English language, an extraordinary exploration of human nature. His epitaph: "Good frend for Jesus sake forbeare, To digg the dust enclosed heare. Blese be ye man that spares thes stones, And curst be he that moves my bones." For more info: *Bard of Avon: The Story of William Shakespeare*, by Diane Stanley and Peter Vennema (Morrow, 0-688-09109-1, $15.93 Gr. K–3).

SPAIN: BOOK DAY AND LOVER'S DAY. Apr 23. Barcelona. Saint George's Day and the anniversary of the death of Spanish writer Miguel de Cervantes have been observed with special ceremonies in the Palacio de la Disputacion and throughout the city since 1714. Book stands are set up in the plazas and on street corners. This is Spain's equivalent of Valentine's Day. Women give books to men; men give roses to women.

TURKEY: NATIONAL SOVEREIGNTY AND CHILDREN'S DAY. Apr 23, 1923. Commemorates Grand National Assembly's inauguration.

April 2001	S	M	T	W	T	F	S
	1	2	3	4	5	6	7
	8	9	10	11	12	13	14
	15	16	17	18	19	20	21
	22	23	24	25	26	27	28
	29	30					

APRIL 23–29
NATIONAL TV TURNOFF WEEK

Before TV Turnoff Week, work with students to develop a list of TV alternatives. It's shocking, but many children literally have no idea what to do without TV. The class can make a game out of celebrating the week in a positive way. First, let students think up a number of slogans for the week. One suggestion is: Turn Off Your TV: Turn On Your Brain! This also acts as informal brainstorming for things to do while the TV is off. Make posters to hang in the school hallways that feature your slogans.

Students can designate a specific activity for each day of TV Turnoff Week. The evenings without TV might extend the curriculum: Monday evening can be a hands-on science-related activity, Tuesday a homonym night and so on. Activities also can be unrelated to the curriculum, but revolve around themes like Be Kind to Mom. Monday could be Help Cook Dinner Day; Tuesday could be Vacuum the Living Room Night. Other theme suggestions are Read to your sibling, Take time to daydream, What do I see when I look out the window, Learn a new card game, Read an exciting book, Write a note to a friend and Listen to a new song. Students also can do completely unrelated activities each night of the week. The important thing is to prompt creative thinking and reinforce the idea that people don't need TV to have fun. If you let the school and public librarians know about TV Turnoff Week, they may be able to feature books and recordings that will stimulate student interest.

Incorporate National TV Turnoff Week into the Math Month theme in several ways. Let students conduct polls and surveys for each day of the week (or weeks) prior to TV Turnoff Week. Surveys should include finding out what shows students watch, how many hours a day they spend watching TV, how often they turn on the TV out of boredom without a specific show in mind, whether families watch TV during meals and any other questions your students can think up. They can graph their answers and see what days are most popular TV days, etc. If they are really motivated, tie Math Month in again and create math goals such as "learn the seven times table" or "counting by fives" for turnoff nights.

During the week students can keep a record of how they spend former TV time. At the end of the week, they can evaluate new perceptions of time and TV.

UNITED NATIONS: WORLD BOOK AND COPYRIGHT DAY. Apr 23. Observed throughout the United Nations system.

BIRTHDAYS TODAY

Gabriel Damon, 25, actor (*Newsies*), born Reno, NV, Apr 23, 1976.
Barry Watson, 27, actor ("7th Heaven"), born Traverse City, MI, Apr 23, 1974.

APRIL 24 — TUESDAY
Day 114 — 251 Remaining

ARMENIA: ARMENIAN MARTYRS DAY: ANNIVERSARY. Apr 24. Commemorates the massacre of Armenians under the Ottoman Turks in 1915 and when deportations from Turkey began. Also called Armenian Genocide Memorial Day. Adolf Hitler, in a speech at Obersalzberg Aug 22, 1939, is reported to have said, "Who today remembers the Armenian extermination?" in an apparent justification of the Nazi's use of genocide.

IBM PERSONAL COMPUTER INTRODUCED: 20th ANNIVERSARY. Apr 24, 1981. Although IBM was one of the pioneers in making mainframe and other large computers, this was the company's first foray into the desktop computer market. Eventually, more IBM-compatible computers were manufactured by IBM's competitors than by IBM itself.

IRELAND: EASTER RISING. Apr 24, 1916. Irish nationalists seized key buildings in Dublin and proclaimed an Irish republic. The rebellion collapsed, however, and it wasn't until 1922 that the Irish Free State, the predecessor of the Republic of Ireland, was established.

LIBRARY OF CONGRESS: ANNIVERSARY. Apr 24, 1800. Congress approved an act providing "for the purchase of such books as may be necessary for the use of Congress . . . and for fitting up a suitable apartment for containing them." Thus began one of the world's greatest libraries. Originally housed in the Capitol, it moved to its own quarters in 1897. For more information about the Library, visit its website at lcweb.loc.gov.

NATIONAL TEACH CHILDREN TO SAVE DAY. Apr 24. Contact your local bank for materials for grades K–12. For info: American Bankers Assn Education Foundation, 1120 Connecticut Ave NW, Washington, DC 20036. Phone: (202) 663-5000. Web: www.aba.com.

NESS, EVALINE: 90th BIRTH ANNIVERSARY. Apr 24, 1911. Author and illustrator (Caldecott for *Sam, Bangs & Moonshine*), born at Union City, OH. Died Aug 12, 1986.

BIRTHDAYS TODAY

A. Paul Cellucci, 53, Governor of Massachusetts (R), born Hudson, MA, Apr 24, 1948.
Jim Geringer, 57, Governor of Wyoming (R), born Wheatland, WY, Apr 24, 1944.
Larry "Chipper" Jones, 29, baseball player, born DeLand, FL, Apr 24, 1972.

APRIL 25 — WEDNESDAY
Day 115 — 250 Remaining

ANZAC DAY: ANNIVERSARY. Apr 25. Australia, New Zealand and Samoa. Memorial day and veterans' observance, especially to mark WWI Anzac landing at Gallipoli, Turkey, in 1915 (ANZAC: Australia and New Zealand Army Corps).

EGYPT: SINAI DAY. Apr 25. National holiday celebrating the liberation of Sinai in 1982 after the peace treaty between Egypt and Israel. For info: Egyptian Tourist Authority, 645 N Michigan Ave, Ste 829, Chicago, IL 60611. Phone: (312) 280-4666. Fax: (312) 280-4788.

FIRST LICENSE PLATES: 100th ANNIVERSARY. Apr 25, 1901. New York began requiring license plates on automobiles, the first state to do so.

ITALY: LIBERATION DAY: ANNIVERSARY. Apr 25. National holiday. Commemorates the liberation of Italy from German troops in 1945.

LOVELACE, MAUD HART: BIRTH ANNIVERSARY. Apr 25, 1892. Author of the Betsy-Tacy books, born at Mankato, MN. Died at California, Mar 11, 1980.

MARCONI, GUGLIELMO: BIRTH ANNIVERSARY. Apr 25, 1874. Inventor of wireless telegraphy (1895) born at Bologna, Italy. Died at Rome, Italy, July 20, 1937.

PORTUGAL: LIBERTY DAY. Apr 25. Portugal. Public holiday. Anniversary of the 1974 revolution.

SPACE MILESTONE: HUBBLE SPACE TELESCOPE DEPLOYED (US). Apr 25, 1990. Deployed by *Discovery*, this telescope is the largest on-orbit observatory to date and is capable of imaging objects up to 14 billion light-years away. The resolution of images was expected to be seven to 10 times greater than images from Earth-based telescope's, since the Hubble Space Telescope is not hampered by Earth's atmospheric distortion. Launched Apr 12, 1990, from Kennedy Space Center, FL. Unfortunately, the telescope's lenses were defective so that the anticipated high quality of imaging was not possible. In 1993, however, the world watched as a shuttle crew successfully retrieved the Hubble from orbit, executed the needed repair and replacement work and released it into orbit once more. In December 1999, the space shuttle *Discovery* was launched to do major repairs on the telescope.

WALDSEEMULLER, MARTIN: REMEMBRANCE DAY. Apr 25, 1507. Little is known about the obscure scholar now called the "godfather of America," the German geographer and mapmaker Martin Waldseemuller, who gave America its name. In a book titled *Cosmographiae Introductio*, published Apr 25, 1507, Waldseemuller wrote: "Inasmuch as both Europe and Asia received their names from women, I see no reason why any one should justly object to calling this part Amerige, i.e., the land of Amerigo, or America, after Amerigo, its discoverer, a man of great ability." Believing it was the Italian navigator and merchant Amerigo Vespucci who had discovered the new continent, Waldseemuller sought to honor Vespucci by placing his name on his map of the world, published in 1507. First applied only to the South American continent, it soon was used for both the American continents. Waldseemuller did not learn about the voyage of Christopher Columbus until several years later. Of the thousand copies of his map that were printed, only one is known to have survived. Waldseemuller probably was born at Radolfzell, Germany, about 1470. He died at St. Die, France, about 1517–20. See also: "Vespucci, Amerigo: Birth Anniversary" (Mar 9).

BIRTHDAYS TODAY

Tim Duncan, 25, basketball player, born St. Croix, US Virgin Islands, Apr 25, 1976.
Jon Kyl, 59, US Senator (R, Arizona), born Oakland, NE, Apr 25, 1942.

April 2001	S	M	T	W	T	F	S
	1	2	3	4	5	6	7
	8	9	10	11	12	13	14
	15	16	17	18	19	20	21
	22	23	24	25	26	27	28
	29	30					

George Ella Lyon, 52, author (*Come a Tide, Dreamplace*), born Harlan, KY, Apr 25, 1949.

APRIL 26 — THURSDAY
Day 116 — 249 Remaining

AUDUBON, JOHN JAMES: BIRTH ANNIVERSARY. Apr 26, 1785. American artist and naturalist, best known for his *Birds of America*, born at Haiti. Died Jan 27, 1851, at New York, NY. For more info: *Capturing Nature: The Writings and Art of John James Audubon*, edited by Peter and Connie Roop (Walker, 0-8027-8205-1, $17.85 Gr. 4–6).

CHERNOBYL NUCLEAR REACTOR DISASTER: 15th ANNIVERSARY. Apr 26, 1986. At 1:23 AM, local time, an explosion occurred at the Chernobyl atomic power station at Pripyat in the Ukraine. The resulting fire burned for days, sending radioactive material into the atmosphere. More than 100,000 persons were evacuated from a 300-square-mile area around the plant. Three months later 31 people were reported to have died and thousands exposed to dangerous levels of radiation. Estimates projected an additional 1,000 cancer cases in nations downwind of the radioactive discharge. The plant was encased in a concrete tomb in an effort to prevent the still-hot reactor from overheating again and to minimize further release of radiation.

CONFEDERATE MEMORIAL DAY IN FLORIDA AND GEORGIA. Apr 26. See also: Confederate Memorial Day entries for Apr 30, May 10, May 28 and June 3.

NATIONAL PLAYGROUND SAFETY DAY. Apr 26. An opportunity for families, community parks, schools and childcare facilities to focus on preventing public playground-related injuries. Sponsored by the National Program for Playground Safety (NPPS), this event helps educate the public about the more than 200,000 children (that's one child every 2 1/2 minutes) that require emergency room treatment for playground-related injuries each year. Annually, the last Thursday in April. For info: Natl Program for Playground Safety, School of HPELS, UNI, Cedar Falls, IA 50614-0618. Phone: (800) 554-PLAY. Fax: (319) 273-7308. Web: www.uni.edu/playground.

RICHTER SCALE DAY. Apr 26. A day to recognize the importance of Charles Francis Richter's research and his work in development of the earthquake magnitude scale that is known as the Richter scale. Richter, an American author, physicist and seismologist, was born Apr 26, 1900, near Hamilton, OH. An Earthquake Awareness Week was observed in recognition of his work. Richter died at Pasadena, CA, Sept 30, 1985.

SOUTH AFRICAN MULTIRACIAL ELECTIONS: ANNIVERSARY. Apr 26–29, 1994. For the first time in the history of South Africa, the nation's approximately 18 million blacks voted in multiparty elections. This event marked the definitive end of apartheid, the system of racial separation that had kept blacks and other minorities out of the political process. The election resulted in Nelson Mandela of the African National Congress being elected president and F.W. de Klerk (incumbent president) of the National Party vice president.

TAKE OUR DAUGHTERS TO WORK DAY. Apr 26. A national public education campaign sponsored by the Ms Foundation for Women in which girls aged nine–15 go to work with adult hosts— parents, grandparents, cousins, aunts, uncles, friends. Take Our Daughters to Work Day has succeeded in mobilizing parents, educators, employers and other caring adults to take action to redress the inequalities in girls' lives and focus national attention on the concerns, hopes and dreams of girls. Annually, the fourth Thursday in April. For info: Lauren Wechsler, Natl Media Mgr, Take Our Daughters to Work Day, Ms Foundation for Women, 120 Wall St, 33rd Floor, New York, NY 10005. Phone: (800) 676-7780 or (212) 742-2300. Fax: (212) 742-1531. E-mail: todtwcom@ms .foundation.org. Web: www.ms.foundation.org.

TANZANIA: UNION DAY. Apr 26. Celebrates union between mainland Tanzania (formerly Tanganyika) and the islands of Zanzibar and Pemba, in 1964.

BIRTHDAYS TODAY

Patricia Reilly Giff, 66, author (*Lily's Crossing*), born Brooklyn, NY, Apr 26, 1935.

APRIL 27 — FRIDAY
Day 117 — 248 Remaining

BABE RUTH DAY: ANNIVERSARY. Apr 27, 1947. Babe Ruth Day was celebrated in every ballpark in organized baseball in the US as well as Japan. Mortally ill with throat cancer, Ruth appeared at Yankee Stadium to thank his former club for the honor.

BEMELMANS, LUDWIG: BIRTH ANNIVERSARY. Apr 27, 1898. Author, illustrator and artist, born at Austria. Ludwig Bemelmans created the Madeline series, including *Mad About Madeline: The Complete Series*. In 1998, a Madeline film was released. Bemelmans died at New York, NY, Oct 1, 1962. For more info: *Bemelmans: The Life & Art of Madeline's Creator*, by John Bemelmans Marciano (Viking, 0-670-88460-X, $40).

CONNECTICUT STORYTELLING FESTIVAL. Apr 27–29. Connecticut College, New London, CT. Annual festival features performances for families and adults, plus workshops and story-sharing by Connecticut and nationally renowned storytellers. Annually, the last full weekend in April. Est attendance: 300. For info: Annie Burnham, Adm, Connecticut Storytelling Center, Connecticut College Box 5295, 270 Mohegan Ave, New London, CT 06320. Phone: (860) 439-2764. Fax: (860) 439-2895. E-mail: csc @conncoll.edu.

GRANT, ULYSSES SIMPSON: BIRTH ANNIVERSARY. Apr 27, 1822. The 18th president of the US (Mar 4, 1869–Mar 3, 1877), born Hiram Ulysses Grant at Point Pleasant, OH. He graduated from the US Military Academy in 1843. President Lincoln promoted Grant to lieutenant general in command of all the Union armies Mar 9, 1864. On Apr 9, 1865, Grant received General Robert E. Lee's surrender, at Appomattox Court House, VA, which he announced to the Secretary of War as follows: "General Lee surrendered the Army of Northern Virginia this afternoon on terms proposed by myself. The accompanying additional correspondence will show the conditions fully." Nicknamed "Unconditional Surrender Grant," he died at Mount McGregor, NY, July 23, 1885, just four days after completing his memoirs. He was buried at Riverside Park, New York, NY, where Grant's Tomb was dedicated in 1897.

ISRAEL: YOM HA'ZIKKARON (REMEMBRANCE DAY). Apr 27. Hebrew date: Iyar 4, 5761. Honors the more than 20,000 Israeli soldiers killed in battle since the start of the nation's war for independence in 1947. Always the day before Israeli Independence Day.

LANTZ, WALTER: BIRTH ANNIVERSARY. Apr 27, 1900. Originator of Universal Studios' animated opening sequence for their first major musical film, *The King of Jazz*. Walter Lantz is best remembered as the creator of Woody Woodpecker, the bird with the wacky laugh and the taunting ways. Lantz received a lifetime achievement Academy Award for his animation in 1979. He was born at New Rochelle, NY, and died Mar 22, 1994, at Burbank, CA.

MAGELLAN, FERDINAND: DEATH ANNIVERSARY. Apr 27, 1521. Portuguese explorer Ferdinand Magellan was probably born near Oporto, Portugal, about 1480, but neither the place nor the date is certain. Usually thought of as the first man to circumnavigate the earth, he died before completing the voyage; thus his co-leader, Basque navigator Juan Sebastian de Elcano, became the world's circumnavigator. The westward, 'round-the-world expedition began Sept 20, 1519, with five ships and about 250 men. Magellan was killed by natives of the Philippine island of Mactan.

MORSE, SAMUEL FINLEY BREESE: BIRTH ANNIVERSARY. Apr 27, 1791. American artist and inventor, after whom the Morse code is named, was born at Charlestown, MA, and died at New York, NY, Apr 2, 1872. Graduating from Yale University in 1810, he went to the Royal Academy of London to study painting. After returning to America he achieved success as a portraitist. Morse conceived the idea of an electromagnetic telegraph while on shipboard, returning from art instruction in Europe in 1832, and he proceeded to develop his idea. With financial assistance approved by Congress, the first telegraph line in the US was constructed, between Washington, DC, and Baltimore, MD. The first message tapped out by Morse from the Supreme Court Chamber at the US Capitol building May 24, 1844, was: "What hath God wrought?"

NATIONAL ARBOR DAY. Apr 27. The Committee for National Arbor Day has as its goal the observance of Arbor Day in all states on the same day, the last Friday in April. This unified Arbor Day date would provide our citizenry with the opportunity to better learn the importance of trees to our way of life. This date is a good planting date for many states throughout the country. National Arbor Day has been observed in 1970, 1972, 1988, 1990, 1991 and 1993 by Presidential Proclamation. More than half the states now observe Arbor Day on the proposed April Friday. Sponsors include: International Society of Arboriculture, Society of Municipal Arborists, American Association of Nurserymen, National Arborist Association, National Recreation and Park Association and the Arborists Association of New Jersey. For info: Committee for Natl Arbor Day, 63 Fitzrandolph Rd, West Orange, NJ 07052. Phone: (201) 731-0840. Fax: (201) 731-6020.

SCHOOL PRINCIPALS' RECOGNITION DAY IN MASSACHUSETTS. Apr 27. Proclaimed annually by the governor.

SIERRA LEONE: INDEPENDENCE DAY. Apr 27. National Day. Commemorates independence from Britain in 1961.

SOUTH AFRICA: FREEDOM DAY. Apr 27. National holiday. Commemorates the day in 1994 when, for the first time, all South Africans had the opportunity to vote.

TOGO: INDEPENDENCE DAY: ANNIVERSARY. Apr 27. National holiday. Gained independence from France in 1960.

YUGOSLAVIA: NATIONAL DAY. Apr 27.

BIRTHDAYS TODAY

Coretta Scott King, 74, lecturer, writer, widow of Dr. Martin Luther King, Jr, born Marion, AL, Apr 27, 1927.

APRIL 28 — SATURDAY
Day 118 — 247 Remaining

ASTRONOMY DAY. Apr 28. To take astronomy to the people. International Astronomy Day is observed on a Saturday near the first quarter moon between mid-April and mid-May. Cosponsored by 15 astronomical organizations. See also: "Astronomy Week" (Apr 23). For info: Gary E. Tomlinson, Coord, Astronomy Day Headquarters, c/o Chaffee Planetarium, 272 Pearl NW, Grand Rapids, MI 49504. Phone: (616) 456-3532. E-mail: gtomlinson @triton.net. Web: www.astroleague.org.

BIOLOGICAL CLOCK GENE DISCOVERED: ANNIVERSARY. Apr 28, 1994. Northwestern University announced that the so-called biological clock, that gene governing the daily cycle of waking and sleeping called the circadian rhythm, had been found in mice. Never before pinpointed in a mammal, the biological clock gene was found on mouse chromosome #5.

ISRAEL: YOM HA'ATZMA'UT (INDEPENDENCE DAY). Apr 28. Hebrew calendar date: Iyar 5, 5761. Celebrates proclamation of independence from British mandatory rule by Palestinian Jews and establishment of the state of Israel and the provisional government May 14, 1948 (Hebrew calendar date: Iyar 5, 5708). Dates in the Hebrew calendar vary from their Gregorian equivalents from year to year, so, while Iyar 5 in 1948 was May 14, in 2001 it is Apr 28.

MARYLAND RATIFIES CONSTITUTION: ANNIVERSARY. Apr 28, 1788. Maryland became the seventh state to ratify the Constitution, by a vote of 63 to 11.

MONROE, JAMES: BIRTH ANNIVERSARY. Apr 28, 1758. The fifth president of the US was born at Westmoreland County, VA, and served two terms in that office (Mar 4, 1817–Mar 3, 1825). Monrovia, the capital city of Liberia, is named after him, as is the Monroe Doctrine, which he enunciated at Washington, DC, Dec 2, 1823. Last of three presidents to die on US Independence Day, Monroe died at New York, NY, July 4, 1831.

MUTINY ON THE *BOUNTY*: ANNIVERSARY. Apr 28, 1789. The most famous of all naval mutinies occurred on board HMS *Bounty*. Captain of the *Bounty* was Lieutenant William Bligh, a mean-tempered disciplinarian. The ship, with a load of breadfruit tree plants from Tahiti, was bound for Jamaica. Fletcher Christian, leader of the mutiny, put Bligh and 18 of his loyal followers adrift in a 23-foot open boat. Miraculously Bligh and all of his supporters survived a 47-day voyage of more than 3,600 miles, before landing on the island of Timor, June 14, 1789. In the

meantime, Christian had put all of the remaining crew (excepting eight men and himself) ashore at Tahiti where he picked up 18 Tahitians (six men and 12 women) and set sail again. Landing at Pitcairn Island in 1790 (probably uninhabited at the time), they burned the *Bounty* and remained undiscovered for 18 years, when an American whaler, the *Topaz*, called at the island (1808) and found only one member of the mutinous crew surviving. However, the little colony had thrived and, when counted by the British in 1856, numbered 194 persons.

NATIONAL CHILD CARE PROFESSIONALS DAY. Apr 28. A day of recognition for child care providers. A day to increase the visibility of the role child care providers play in our society and celebrate the partnership between parents and caregivers to help children develop to their full potential. Sponsored by Child Care Aware and Cheerios®. For info: Anne Nicolai, Child Care Aware, 2116 Campus Dr SE, Rochester, MN 55904. Phone: (800) 424-2246 or (612) 835-3335.

NATIONAL PUPPETRY DAY. Apr 28. A day to celebrate the lively art of puppetry through performances, seminars, lectures and parades. Sponsored by Puppeteers of America, Inc. Annually, the Saturday of the last full weekend in April. For info: Rick Morse, 3104 Vineyard Ln, Flushing, MI 48433. Phone: (810) 230-0105. E-mail: Rickpuppet@aol.com. Web: www.puppeteers .org.

BIRTHDAYS TODAY

Lois Duncan, 67, author (*The Circus Comes Home, I Know What You Did Last Summer*), born Philadelphia, PA, Apr 28, 1934.

Harper Lee, 75, author (*To Kill A Mockingbird*), 1961 Pulitzer Prize for fiction, born Monroeville, AL, Apr 28, 1926.

Jay Leno, 51, TV talk show host ("Tonight Show"), comedian, born New Rochelle, NY, Apr 28, 1950.

Catherine Reef, 50, writer of history and biography (*John Steinbeck*), born New York, NY, Apr 28, 1951.

Nate Richert, 23, actor ("Sabrina, the Teenage Witch"), born St. Paul, MN, Apr 28, 1978.

APRIL 29 — SUNDAY
Day 119 — 246 Remaining

ELLINGTON, "DUKE" (EDWARD KENNEDY): BIRTH ANNIVERSARY. Apr 29, 1899. "Duke" Ellington, one of the most influential individuals in jazz history, was born at Washington, DC. By 1923 he was leading a small group of musicians at the Kentucky Club at New York City who became the core of his big band. Ellington is credited with being one of the founders of big band jazz. He used his band as an instrument for composition and orchestration to create big band pieces, film scores,

April	S	M	T	W	T	F	S
2001	1	2	3	4	5	6	7
	8	9	10	11	12	13	14
	15	16	17	18	19	20	21
	22	23	24	25	26	27	28
	29	30					

operas, ballets, Broadway shows and religious music. Ellington was responsible for more than 1,000 musical pieces. He drew together instruments from different sections of the orchestra to develop unique and haunting sounds such as that of his famous "Mood Indigo." "Duke" Ellington died May 24, 1974, at New York City. For more info: *Duke Ellington: The Piano Prince and His Orchestra*, by Andrea Davis Pinkney (Hyperion, 0-7868-2150-7, $16.49 Gr. K–3).

ELLSWORTH, OLIVER: BIRTH ANNIVERSARY. Apr 29, 1745. Third chief justice of the US Supreme Court, born at Windsor, CT. Died there, Nov 26, 1807.

HIROHITO MICHI-NO-MIYA, EMPEROR: 100th BIRTH ANNIVERSARY. Apr 29, 1901. Former Emperor of Japan, born at Tokyo. Hirohito's death Jan 27, 1989, ended the reign of the world's longest ruling monarch. He became the 124th in a line of monarchs when he ascended to the Chrysanthemum Throne in 1926. Hirohito presided over perhaps the most eventful years in the 2,500 years of recorded Japanese history, including the attempted military conquest of Asia, the attack on the US that brought that country into WWII, leading to Japan's ultimate defeat after the US dropped atomic bombs on Hiroshima and Nagasaki and the amazing economic restoration following the war that led Japan to a preeminent position of economic strength. Although he opposed initiating hostilities with the US, he signed a declaration of war, allowing Japan's militarist Prime Minister, Hideki Tojo, to begin the fateful campaign. During the war's final days he overruled Tojo and advocated surrender. Hirohito broadcast a taped message to the Japanese people to stop fighting and "endure the unendurable." This radio message was the first time the emperor's voice had ever been heard outside the imperial household and inner circle of government. After the war, Hirohito was allowed to remain on his throne. He denounced his divinity in 1946, bestowed upon him by Japanese law, and became a "symbol of the state" in Japan's new parliamentary democracy. Hirohito turned his energies to his real passion, marine biology, becoming a recognized world authority in the field.

INTERNATIONAL READING ASSOCIATION ANNUAL CONVENTION. Apr 29–May 4. New Orleans, LA. 46th annual convention. For info: Intl Reading Assn, 800 Barksdale Rd, PO Box 8139, Newark, DE 19714-8139. Phone: (302) 731-1600. E-mail: conferences@reading.org. Web: www.reading.org.

MOTHER, FATHER DEAF DAY. Apr 29. A day to honor deaf parents and recognize the gifts of culture and language they give to their hearing children. Annually, the last Sunday of April. Sponsored by Children of Deaf Adults International Inc (CODA). For info: Trudy Schafer-Jeffers, CODA, PO Box 30715, Santa Barbara, CA, 93130-0715. Phone: (617) 789-3862 (TTY or Voice). Fax: (301) 572-4134.

TAIWAN: CHENG CHENG KUNG LANDING DAY. Apr 29. Commemorates landing in Taiwan in 1661 of Ming Dynasty loyalist Cheng Cheng Kung (Koxinga), who ousted Dutch colonists who had occupied Taiwan for 37 years. Main ceremonies held at Tainan, in south Taiwan, where Dutch had their headquarters and where Cheng is buried. Cheng's birthday is also joyously celebrated, but according to the lunar calendar—on the 14th day of the seventh moon, Sept 1, 2001.

ZIPPER PATENTED: ANNIVERSARY. Apr 29, 1913. Gideon Sundbach of Hoboken, NJ, received a patent for the zipper.

BIRTHDAYS TODAY

Andre Kirk Agassi, 31, tennis player, born Las Vegas, NV, Apr 29, 1970.

Kate Mulgrew, 46, actress ("Star Trek: Voyager"), born Dubuque, IA, Apr 29, 1955.

Jill Paton Walsh, 64, author (*Fireweed*), born London, England, Apr 29, 1937.

APRIL 30 — MONDAY
Day 120 — 245 Remaining

CONFEDERATE MEMORIAL DAY IN MISSISSIPPI. Apr 30. Annually, last Monday in April. Observed on other days in other states.

DÍA DE LOS NIÑOS/DÍA DE LOS LIBROS. Apr 30. A celebration of children and bilingual literacy. Cosponsored by REFORMA: The National Association to Promote Library Services to the Spanish Speaking and MANA: A National Latina Organization. Annually, Apr 30. For info: Natl Assn for Bilingual Education, 1220 L St NW, Ste 605, Washington, DC 20005-4018. Phone: (202) 898-1829. Web: www.nabe.org.

FIRST PRESIDENTIAL TELECAST: ANNIVERSARY. Apr 30, 1939. Franklin D. Roosevelt was the first president to appear on television in a telecast from the New York World's Fair. However, since scheduled programming had yet to begin, he was beamed to only 200 TV sets in a 40-mile radius. See also: "Regular TV Broadcasts Begin: Anniversary" (July 1).

HARRISON, MARY SCOTT LORD DIMMICK: BIRTH ANNIVERSARY. Apr 30, 1858. Second wife of Benjamin Harrison, 23rd president of the US, born at Honesdale, PA. Died at New York, NY, Jan 5, 1948.

INTERNATIONAL SCHOOL SPIRIT SEASON. Apr 30–Sept 30. To recognize everyone who has helped to make school spirit better and to provide time to plan improved spirit ideas for the coming school year. For info: Jim Hawkins, Chairman, Pepsters, Committee for More School Spirit, PO Box 122652, San Diego, CA 92112. Phone: (619) 280-0999.

LOUISIANA: ADMISSION DAY: ANNIVERSARY. Apr 30. Became 18th state in 1812.

MOON PHASE: FIRST QUARTER. Apr 30. Moon enters New Moon phase at 1:08 PM, EDT.

NATIONAL HONESTY DAY (WITH HONEST ABE AWARDS). Apr 30. To celebrate honesty and those who are honest and honorable in their dealings with others. Nominations accepted for most honest people and companies. Winners to be awarded "Honest Abe" awards and given "Abies" on National Honesty Day. Annually, Apr 30. For info: M. Hirsh Goldberg, Author of *The Book of Lies*, 3103 Szold Dr, Baltimore, MD 21208. Phone: (410) 486-4150.

NETHERLANDS: QUEEN'S BIRTHDAY. Apr 30. A public holiday in celebration of the Queen's birthday and the Dutch National Day. The whole country parties as young and old participate in festivities such as markets, theater, music and games.

ORGANIZATION OF AMERICAN STATES FOUNDED: ANNIVERSARY. Apr 30, 1948. This regional alliance was founded by 21 nations of the Americas at Bogota, Colombia. Its purpose is to further economic development and integration among nations of the Western hemisphere, to promote representative democracy and to help overcome poverty. The Pan-American Union, with offices at Washington, DC, serves as the General Secretariat for the OAS.

SPANK OUT DAY USA. Apr 30. A day on which all caretakers of children—parents, teachers and daycare workers—are asked not to use corporal punishment as discipline and to become aquainted with positive, effective disciplinary alternatives. For info: Nadine Block, EPOCH-USA, 155 W Main St, Ste 100-B, Columbus, OH 43215. Phone: (614) 221-8829. E-mail: nblock@infinet.com. Web: www.stophitting.com.

SWEDEN: FEAST OF VALBORG. Apr 30. An evening celebration in which Sweden "sings in the spring" by listening to traditional hymns to the spring, often around community bonfires. Also known as Walpurgis Night, the Feast of Valborg occurs annually, Apr 30.

THEATER IN NORTH AMERICA FIRST PERFORMANCE: ANNIVERSARY. Apr 30, 1598. On the banks of the Rio Grande, near present day El Paso, TX, the first North American theatrical performance was acted. The play was a Spanish commedia featuring an expedition of soldiers. On July 10 of the same year, the same group produced *Moros y Los Cristianos* (Moors and Christians), an anonymous play.

WASHINGTON, GEORGE: PRESIDENTIAL INAUGURATION ANNIVERSARY. Apr 30, 1789. George Washington was inaugurated as the first president of the US under the new Constitution at New York, NY. Robert R. Livingston administered the oath of office to Washington on the balcony of Federal Hall, at the corner of Wall and Broad Streets.

BIRTHDAYS TODAY

Dorothy Hinshaw Patent, 61, author (*Bold and Bright Black-and-White Animals*), born Rochester, MN, Apr 30, 1940.

MAY 1 — TUESDAY
Day 121 — 244 Remaining

★**ASIAN PACIFIC AMERICAN HERITAGE MONTH.** May 1–31. Presidential Proclamation issued honoring Asian Pacific Americans each year since 1979. Public Law 102-450 of Oct 28, 1992, designated the observance for the month of May each year.

FREEDOM SHRINE MONTH. May 1–31. To bring America's heritage of freedom to public attention through presentations or rededications of Freedom Shrine displays of historic American documents by Exchange Clubs. For info: The Natl Exchange Club, 3050 Central Ave, Toledo, OH 43606-1700. Phone: (419) 535-3232 or (800) 924-2643. Fax: (419) 535-1989. E-mail: nechq@aol.com. Web: www.nationalexchangeclub.com.

"FREEDOM RIDERS": 40th ANNIVERSARY. May 1, 1961. Militant students joined James Farmer of the Congress of Racial Equality (CORE) to conduct "freedom rides" on public transportation from Washington, DC, across the deep South to New Orleans. The trips were intended to test Supreme Court decisions and Interstate Commerce Commission regulations prohibiting discrimination in interstate travel. In several places riders were brutally beaten by local people and policemen. The rides were patterned after a similar challenge to segregation, the 1947 Journey of Reconciliation, which tested the US Supreme Court's June 3, 1946, ban against segregation in interstate bus travel.

GET CAUGHT READING MONTH. May 1–31. Celebrities appear in ads appealing to young people to remind them of the joys of reading. For info: Assn of American Publishers, 71 Fifth Ave, New York, NY 10003. Phone: (212) 255-0200. Web: www.publishers.org.

GREAT BRITAIN FORMED: ANNIVERSARY. May 1, 1707. A union between England and Scotland resulted in the formation of Great Britain. (Wales had been part of England since the 1500s.) Today's United Kingdom consists of Great Britain and Northern Ireland.

KEEP MASSACHUSETTS BEAUTIFUL MONTH. May 1–31. Proclaimed annually by the governor.

LABOR DAY. May 1. In 76 countries, May 1 is observed as a workers' holiday. When it falls on a Saturday or Sunday, the following Monday is observed as a holiday. Bermuda, Canada and the US are the only countries that observe Labor Day in September.

★**LAW DAY.** May 1. Presidential Proclamation issued each year for May 1 since 1958 at request. (PL87–20 of Apr 7, 1961.)

LAW ENFORCEMENT APPRECIATION MONTH IN FLORIDA. May 1–31. A ceremonial observance. May 15 is designated Law Enforcement Memorial Day.

LEI DAY. May 1. Hawaii. On this special day—the Hawaiian version of May Day—leis are made, worn, given, displayed and entered in lei-making contests. One of the most popular Lei Day celebrations takes place in Honolulu at Kapiolani Park at Waikiki. Includes the state's largest lei contest, the crowning of the Lei Day Queen, Hawaiian music, hula and flowers galore.

★**LOYALTY DAY.** May 1. Presidential Proclamation issued annually for May 1 since 1959 at request. (PL85–529 of July 18, 1958.) Note that an earlier proclamation was issued in 1955. .

MARSHALL ISLANDS, REPUBLIC OF THE: CONSTITUTION DAY. May 1. National holiday.

MAY DAY. May 1. The first day of May has been observed as a holiday since ancient times. Spring festivals, maypoles and may baskets are still common, but the political importance of May Day has grown since the 1880s, when it became a workers' day. Now widely observed as a workers' holiday or as Labor Day. In most European countries, when May Day falls on Saturday or Sunday, the Monday following is observed as a holiday, with bank and store closings, parades and other festivities.

MOTHER GOOSE DAY. May 1. To re-appreciate the old nursery rhymes. Motto is "Either alone or in sharing, read childhood nursery favorites and feel the warmth of Mother Goose's embrace." Annually, May 1. For info: Gloria T. Delamar, Founder, Mother Goose Soc, 7303 Sharpless Rd, Melrose Park, PA 19027. Phone: (215) 782-1059. E-mail: Mother.Goose.Society@juno.com. Web: www.gbalc.org/MotherGooseSociety.

NATIONAL ALLERGY/ASTHMA AWARENESS MONTH. May 1–31. Kit of materials available for $15 from this nonprofit organization. For info: Frederick S. Mayer, Pres, Pharmacist Planning Services, Inc, c/o Allergy Council of America (ACA), 101 Lucas Valley Rd, #210, San Rafael, CA 94903. Phone: (415) 479-8628. Fax: (415) 479-8608. E-mail: ppsi@aol.com.

NATIONAL BARBECUE MONTH. May 1–31. To encourage people to start enjoying barbecuing early in the season when Daylight Saving Time lengthens the day. Annually, the month of May. Sponsor: Barbecue Industry Association. For info: NBM, DHM Group, Inc, PO Box 767, Dept CC, Holmdel, NJ 07733-0767. Fax: (732) 946-3343.

NATIONAL BIKE MONTH. May 1–31. 44th annual celebration of bicycling for recreation and transportation. Local activities sponsored by bicycling organizations, environmental groups, PTAs, police departments, health organizations and civic groups. About five million participants nationwide. Annually, the month of May. For info: Donald Tighe, Program Dir, League of American Bicyclists, 1612 K St, Ste 401, Washington, DC 20006. Phone: (202) 822-1333. Fax: (202) 822-1334. E-mail: DWTLAW@aol.com. Web: www.bikeleague.org.

NATIONAL EGG MONTH. May 1–31. Dedicated to the versatility, convenience, economy and good nutrition of "the incredible edible egg." Annually, the month of May. *See* Curriculum Connection. For info: Linda Braun, Consumer Serv Dir, American Egg Board, 1460 Renaissance Dr, Park Ridge, IL 60068. E-mail: aeb@aeb.org. Web: www.aeb.org.

NATIONAL HAMBURGER MONTH. May 1–31. Sponsored by White Castle, the original fast-food hamburger chain, founded in 1921, to pay tribute to one of America's favorite foods. With or without condiments, on or off a bun or bread, hamburgers have grown in popularity since the early 1920s and are now an American meal mainstay. For info: White Castle System, Inc, Mktg Dept, 555 W Goodale St, Columbus, OH 43215-1171. Phone: (614) 228-5781. Fax: (614) 228-8841. Web: www.whitecastle.com.

NATIONAL HEPATITIS AWARENESS MONTH. May 1–31. For info: Hepatitis Foundation Intl, 30 Sunrise Terrace, Cedar Grove, NJ 07009. Phone: (800) 891-0707. E-mail: hfi@intac.com. Web: www.hepfi.org.

NATIONAL MENTAL HEALTH MONTH. May 1–31. For info: Natl Mental Health Assn, 1021 Prince St, Alexandria, VA 22314-2971. Phone: (800) 969-6642 or (703) 684-7722. E-mail: nmhainfo@aol.com. Web: www.nmha.org.

NATIONAL MOVING MONTH. May 1–31. Recognizing America's mobile roots and kicking off the busiest moving season of the year. Each year more than 21 million Americans move between Memorial Day and Labor Day, with the average American moving every seven years. During this month moving experts will be educating Americans on how to plan a successful move, to pack efficiently and handle the uncertainties and questions that moving children may have. For info: Allied Van Lines, PO Box 9569, Downers Grove, IL 60515. Phone: (630) 241-2538. Fax: (630) 241-4343. Web: www.alliedvan.com.

NATIONAL SALAD MONTH. May 1–31. Americans celebrate salads and their role in today's healthy lifestyle. Annually, the month of May. For info: The Assn for Dressings and Sauces, 5775 Peachtree-Dunwoody Rd, Ste 500-G, Atlanta, GA 30342. Phone: (404) 252-3663. Fax: (404) 252-0774. E-mail: ads@assnhq.com. Web: www.dressings-sauces.org.

NATIONAL SALSA MONTH. May 1–31. Recognizing salsa as America's favorite condiment, used more often than even ketchup as a topping, dip, marinade and to spice up countless recipes. National Salsa Month celebrates more than 50 years of picante sauce, a salsa created in 1947, and celebrates Cinco de Mayo, a major Mexican holiday now recognized across North America. For info: Mary Uhlig, VP, Dublin & Assoc, 111 Soledad, Ste 1600, San Antonio, TX 78205. Phone: (210) 227-0221. Fax: (210) 226-7097. Web: www.pacefoods.com.

NATIONAL TEACHING AND JOY MONTH. May 1–31. A month of celebrating the joy of great teaching and great learning. Thank a teacher for creating an atmosphere of joy. Notice those students who demonstrate a love of learning. Call or write someone who helped you learn an important life skill. For info: Dr. Jim Scott, Jackson Community College, 2111 Emmons Rd, Jackson, MI 49201. Phone: (517) 796-8488. Fax: (517) 796-8631. E-mail: jim_scott@jackson.cc.mi.us.

		S	M	T	W	T	F	S
May				1	2	3	4	5
2001		6	7	8	9	10	11	12
		13	14	15	16	17	18	19
		20	21	22	23	24	25	26
		27	28	29	30	31		

MAY 1–31
NATIONAL EGG MONTH

Have some "egg-cellent" fun turning your classroom into a giant incubator. First explain what an incubator is and how it works. Focus on its nurturing aspect. Talk about how a classroom is a place for incubating ideas. Put a giant construction paper egg on the bulletin board. Leave the top edge open so idea slips can be inserted. Solicit student ideas for creatively spelling words, solving math problems, finding out answers to questions. You might also include egg-related trivia facts such as the smallest, largest or heaviest eggs. Have students write ideas, facts or even egg poems on slips of paper and put them inside the egg pocket. Designate a time each day, perhaps 10:00 AM because it has three egg-shaped zeros in it, to pull one idea from the pocket and share with the class.

For silly egg fun, brainstorm with students on idioms that contain references to eggs. The term "goose egg" instead of zero, saving a "nest egg" and "don't put all your eggs in one basket" are a few examples. Write silly stories that offer explanations of how these phrases were invented. Have fun making egg puns by converting words with "ex" to "egg" (like "eggs-it") and drawing pictures to illustrate the pun.

See if you can get someone to donate ladybug or praying mantis egg cases to the classroom. Students can observe and record changes in appearance and length of hatching time. When the eggs hatch, let the insects go free in nearby gardens. *What About Ladybugs?*, by Celia Godkin (Sierra Club, 0-871-56549-8, $14.95 Gr. K–3) is a picture book story about how ladybugs are beneficial to gardeners. *The Backyard Hunter*, by Bianca Lavies (Puffin, 0-14-055494-7, $4.99 Gr. K–3), discusses the life cycle of praying mantises.

Sea turtles travel hundreds of miles to lay their eggs on specific beaches. *Into the Sea*, by Brenda Z. Guiberson (Holt, 0-8050-2263-5, $15.95 Gr. K–3) is a beautifully illustrated story of a sea turtle's life. Students can research how turtle, shark, frog and butterfly eggs differ from those of birds.

★**OLDER AMERICANS MONTH.** May 1–31. Presidential Proclamation; from 1963 through 1973 this was called "Senior Citizens Month." In May 1974 it became Older Americans Month. In 1980 the title included Senior Citizens Day, which was observed May 8, 1980. Always has been issued since 1963.

PEN-FRIENDS WEEK INTERNATIONAL. May 1–7. To encourage everyone to have one or more pen-friends not only in their own country but in other countries. For complete information on how to become a good pen-friend and information about how to write good letters, send $4 to cover expense of printing, handling and postage. Annually, May 1–7. For info: Dr. Stanley J. Drake, Pres, Intl Soc of Friendship and Good Will, 40139 Palmetto Dr, Palmdale, CA 93551-3557.

RUSSIA: INTERNATIONAL LABOR DAY. May 1–2. Public holiday in Russian Federation. "Official May Day demonstrations of working people."

SAVE THE RHINO DAY. May 1. May day! May day! Rhinos still in danger! Help save the world's remaining rhinos on the verge of extinction! Get involved with local, national and international conservation efforts to stop the senseless slaughter of these gentle pachyderms. Call your local zoo or write Really, Rhinos! for a $5 information packet. For info: Judyth Lessee, Founder, Really, Rhinos!, PO Box 40503, Tucson, AZ 85717-0503. Phone: (520) 327-9048. E-mail: rinophyl@rtd.com.

SCHOOL PRINCIPALS' DAY. May 1. A day of recognition for all elementary, middle and high school principals for their leadership and dedication to providing the best education possible for their students. Annually, May 1. For info: Janet Dellaria, 202 Bennett St, Geneva, IL 60134. Phone: (630) 232-0425.

VEGETARIAN RESOURCE GROUP'S ESSAY CONTEST FOR KIDS. May 1. Children ages 18 and under are encouraged to submit a two–three-page essay on topics related to vegetarianism. Essays accepted up to May 1. Winners announced Sept 15 and will receive a $50 savings bond. For info: The Vegetarian Resource Group, PO Box 1463, Baltimore, MD 21203. Phone: (410) 366-8343. Fax: (410) 366-8804. E-mail: vrg@vrg.org. Web: www.vrg.org.

WILLIAMS, ARCHIE: BIRTH ANNIVERSARY. May 1, 1915. Archie Williams, along with Jesse Owens and others, debunked Hitler's theory of the superiority of Aryan athletes at the 1936 Berlin Olympics. As a black member of the US team Williams won a gold medal by running the 400-meter in 46.5 seconds (.4 second slower than his own record of earlier that year). Williams, who was born at Oakland, CA, earned a degree in mechanical engineering from the University of California-Berkeley in 1939 but had to dig ditches for a time because they weren't hiring black engineers. In time Williams became an airplane pilot and for 22 years he trained Tuskegee Institute pilots including the black air corp of WWII. He joined the Army Air Corps in 1942. When asked during a 1981 interview about his treatment by the Nazis during the 1936 Olympics, he replied, "Well, over there at least we didn't have to ride in the back of the bus." Archie Williams died June 24, 1993, at Fairfax, CA.

BIRTHDAYS TODAY

Curtis Martin, 28, football player, born Pittsburgh, PA, May 1, 1973.
Elizabeth Marie Pope, 84, author (*The Perilous Gard*), born Washington, DC, May 1, 1917.

MAY 2 — WEDNESDAY
Day 122 — 243 Remaining

KING JAMES BIBLE PUBLISHED: ANNIVERSARY. May 2, 1611. King James I had appointed a committee of learned men to produce a new translation of the Bible in English which was published this day. This version, popularly called the King James Version, is known in England as the Authorized Version.

LEONARDO DA VINCI: DEATH ANNIVERSARY. May 2, 1519. Italian artist, scientist and inventor. Painter of the famed *Last Supper*, perhaps the first painting of the High Renaissance, and of the *Mona Lisa*. Inventor of the first parachute. Born at Vinci, Italy, in 1452 (exact date unknown), he died at Amboise, France. For more info: *Leonardo Da Vinci*, by Diane Stanley (Morrow, 0-688-10438-X, $15.93 Gr. K–3) or www.mos.org/sln/Leonardo/LeoHomePage.html.

PROJECT ACES DAY. May 2. Twelfth annual celebration of fitness when All Children Exercise Simultaneously. "The World's Largest Exercise Class" takes place the first Wednesday in May as schools in all 50 states and 50 different countries hold fitness classes, assemblies and other fitness education events involving millions of children, parents and teachers. Conducted in cooperation with the President's Council of Physical Fitness and Sports during National Physical Fitness and Sports Month. For info send SASE to: Dept C, Youth Fitness Coalition, PO Box 6452, Jersey City, NJ 07306-0452. Phone: (201) 433-8993. Fax: (201) 332-3060. E-mail: yfcprojectaces@excite.com.

ROBERT'S RULES DAY. May 2, 1837. Anniversary of the birth of Henry M. Robert (General, US Army), author of *Robert's Rules of Order*, a standard parliamentary guide. Born at Robertville, SC, he died at Hornell, NY, May 11, 1923.

SPOCK, BENJAMIN: BIRTH ANNIVERSARY. May 2, 1903. Pediatrician and author, born at New Haven, CT. His book on child-rearing, *Common Sense Book of Baby and Child Care* later called *Baby and Child Care*, has sold more than 30 million copies. In 1955 he became professor of child development at Western Reserve University at Cleveland, OH. He resigned from this position in 1967 to devote his time to the pacifism movement. Spock died at San Diego, CA, Mar 15, 1998.

BIRTHDAYS TODAY

Jenna Von Oy, 24, actress (voice on "Pepper Ann," "Blossom"), born Newtown, CT, May 2, 1977.

MAY 3 — THURSDAY
Day 123 — 242 Remaining

"CBS EVENING NEWS" TV PREMIERE: ANNIVERSARY. May 3, 1948. This news program began as a 15-minute telecast with Douglas Edwards as anchor. Walter Cronkite succeeded him in 1962 and expanded the show to 30 minutes; Eric Sevareid served as commentator. Dan Rather anchored the newscasts upon Cronkite's retirement in 1981. At one point, to boost sagging ratings, Connie Chung was added to the newscast as Rather's coanchor, but she left in 1995 in a well-publicized dispute. Rather remains solo, and, as Cronkite would say, " . . . that's the way it is."

JAPAN: CONSTITUTION MEMORIAL DAY. May 3. National holiday commemorating constitution of 1947.

MEXICO: DAY OF THE HOLY CROSS. May 3. Celebrated especially by construction workers and miners, a festive day during which anyone who is building must give a party for the workers. A flower-decorated cross is placed on every piece of new construction in the country.

★**NATIONAL DAY OF PRAYER.** May 3. Presidential Proclamation always issued for the first Thursday in May since 1981. (PL100–307 of May 5, 1988.) From 1957 to 1981, a day in October was designated, except in 1972 and 1975 through 1977.

NATIONAL PUBLIC RADIO FIRST BROADCAST: 30th ANNIVERSARY. May 3, 1971. National noncommercial radio network, financed by Corporation for Public Broadcasting, began programming.

POLAND: CONSTITUTION DAY (SWIETO TRZECIEGO MAJO). May 3. National Day. Celebrates ratification of Poland's first constitution, 1791.

UNITED NATIONS: WORLD PRESS FREEDOM DAY. May 3. A day to recognize that a free, pluralistic and independent press is an essential component of any democratic society and to promote press freedom in the world.

WHALE AWARENESS DAY IN MASSACHUSETTS. May 3. Proclaimed annually by the governor for the first Thursday in May.

BIRTHDAYS TODAY

Mavis Jukes, 54, author (*Like Jake and Me*), born Nyack, NY, May 3, 1947.

Pete Seeger, 82, author (*Abiyoyo*), born New York, NY, May 3, 1919.

Ron Wyden, 52, US Senator (D, Oregon), born Wichita, KS, May 3, 1949.

MAY 4 — FRIDAY
Day 124 — 241 Remaining

CHINA: YOUTH DAY. May 4. Annual public holiday "recalls the demonstration on May 4, 1919, by thousands of patriotic students in Beijing's Tiananmen Square to protest imperialist aggression in China."

CURACAO: MEMORIAL DAY. May 4. Victims of WWII are honored on this day. Military ceremonies at the War Monument. Not an official public holiday.

DISCOVERY OF JAMAICA BY CHRISTOPHER COLUMBUS: ANNIVERSARY. May 4, 1494. Christopher Columbus discovered Jamaica. The Arawak Indians were its first inhabitants.

FEMINIST BOOKSTORE WEEK. May 4–13. Visit your favorite feminist bookstore for author signings and other special events. Annually, the weekend before Mother's Day through Mother's Day. For info: Feminist Bookstore News, PO Box 882554, San Francisco, CA 94188. Phone: (415) 642-9993. Fax: (415) 642-9995. E-mail: carol@FemBkNews.com.

INTERNATIONAL TUBA DAY. May 4. To recognize tubists in musical organizations around the world who have to go through the hassle of handling a tuba in order to make beautiful music. Annually, the first Friday in May. Est attendance: 300. For info: Dr. Sy Brandon, Music Dept, Millersville Univ, PO Box 1002, Millersville, PA 17551-0302. Phone: (717) 872-3439. Fax: (717) 871-2304. E-mail: sbrandon@marander.millersv.edu.

MANN, HORACE: BIRTH ANNIVERSARY. May 4, 1796. American educator, author, public servant, known as the "father of public education in the US," was born at Franklin, MA. Founder of Westfield (MA) State College, president of Antioch College and editor of the influential *Common School Journal*. Mann died at Yellow Springs, OH, Aug 2, 1859.

NATIONAL WEATHER OBSERVER'S DAY. May 4. For those people, amateurs and professionals alike, who love to follow the everyday phenomenon known as weather. Annually, May 4. For info: Alan W. Brue, 2006 NW 55th Ave, #H-5, Gainesville, FL 32653. E-mail: afn05660@afn.org.

SCHOOL-TO-WORK LAUNCHED: ANNIVERSARY. May 4, 1994. President Clinton signed the School-to-Work Opportunities Act. It provides seed money to states and local partnerships to develop school-to-work systems of education reform, worker preparation and economic development to prepare youth for the high wage, high skill careers of the global economy. For info: Natl School-to-Work Learning & Information Center, 400 Virginia Ave, Rm 150, Washington, DC 20024. Phone: (800) 251-7236. Fax: (202) 401-6211. E-mail: stw-lc@ed.gov. Web: stw.ed.gov/general /general.htm.

SPACE MILESTONE: *ATLANTIS* (US). May 4, 1989. First American planetary expedition in 11 years. Space shuttle *Atlantis* was launched, its major objective to deploy the *Magellan* spacecraft on its way to Venus to map the planet's surface. The shuttle was on its 65th orbit when it landed May 8, mission accomplished.

TYLER, JULIA GARDINER: BIRTH ANNIVERSARY. May 4, 1820. Second wife of John Tyler, 10th president of the US, born at Gardiners Island, NY. Died at Richmond, VA, July 10, 1889.

BIRTHDAYS TODAY

Lance Bass, 22, musician ('N Sync), born Laurel, MS, May 4, 1979.

Ben Grieve, 25, baseball player, 1998 American League Rookie of the Year, born Arlington, TX, May 4, 1976.

Dawn Staley, 31, basketball player, born Philadelphia, PA, May 4, 1970.

Don Wood, 56, illustrator (*King Bidgood's in the Bathtub*), born Atwater, CA, May 4, 1945.

MAY 5 — SATURDAY
Day 125 — 240 Remaining

BASEBALL'S FIRST PERFECT GAME: ANNIVERSARY. May 5, 1904. Denton T. "Cy" Young pitched baseball's first perfect game, not allowing a single opposing player to reach first base. Young's outstanding performance led the Boston Americans in a 3–0 victory over Philadelphia in the American League. The Cy Young Award for pitching was named in his honor.

BLY, NELLIE: BIRTH ANNIVERSARY. May 5, 1867. Born at Cochran's Mills, PA, Nellie Bly was the pseudonym used by pioneering American journalist Elizabeth Cochrane Seaman. Like her namesake in a Stephen Foster song, Nellie Bly was a social reformer and human rights advocate. As a journalist, she is best known for her exposé of conditions in what were then known as "insane asylums," where she posed as an "inmate." As an adventurer, she is best known for her 1889–90 tour around-the-world in 72 days, in which she bettered the time of Jules Verne's fictional character Phileas Fogg by eight days. She died at New York, NY, Jan 27, 1922.

BONZA BOTTLER DAY™. May 5. To celebrate when the number of the day is the same as the number of the month. Bonza Bottler Day™ is an excuse to have a party at least once a month. For info: Gail M. Berger, 109 Matthew Ave, Poca, WV 25159. Phone: (304) 776-7746. E-mail: gberger5@aol.com.

HALFWAY POINT OF SPRING. May 5. On this date, 47 days of spring will have elapsed, and the equivalent will remain before June 21, which is the summer solstice and the beginning of summer.

JAPAN: CHILDREN'S DAY. May 5. National holiday. Observed on the fifth day of the fifth month each year.

KOREA: CHILDREN'S DAY. May 5. A time for families to take their children on excursions. Parks and children's centers throughout the country are packed with excited and colorfully dressed children. A national holiday since 1975.

LIONNI, LEO: BIRTH ANNIVERSARY. May 5, 1910. Author and illustrator, born at Amsterdam, Netherlands. Lionni wrote his first children's book *Little Blue and Little Yellow* in 1959. He wrote and illustrated more than 30 children's books including *Frederick* and *Swimmy*. He died at Chianti, Italy, Oct 11, 1999.

May 2001	S	M	T	W	T	F	S
			1	2	3	4	5
	6	7	8	9	10	11	12
	13	14	15	16	17	18	19
	20	21	22	23	24	25	26
	27	28	29	30	31		

MALTA: CARNIVAL. May 5–6. Valletta. Festival dates from 1535 when Knights of St. John introduced Carnival at Malta. Dancing, bands, decorated trucks and grotesque masks. Annually, the first weekend after May 1.

MEXICO: CINCO DE MAYO: ANNIVERSARY. May 5. Mexican national holiday recognizing the anniversary of the Battle of Puebla, May 5, 1862, in which Mexican troops under General Ignacio Zaragoza, outnumbered three to one, defeated invading French forces of Napoleon III. Anniversary is observed by Mexicans everywhere with parades, festivals, dances and speeches. For more info: www.latinobeat.net/info/html/cinco.htm.

NETHERLANDS: LIBERATION DAY: ANNIVERSARY. May 5. Marks liberation of the Netherlands from Nazi Germany in 1945.

RHODE ISLAND FESTIVAL OF CHILDREN'S BOOKS AND AUTHORS. May 5–6 (tentative). Lincoln School, Providence, RI. 12th annual. The festival provides an opportunity for readers of children's books to meet authors and illustrators. Kids can also enjoy performers, crafts, book-related videos and meeting popular book characters. For info: Development Office, Lincoln School, 301 Butler Ave, Providence, RI 02906-5545. Phone: (401) 331-9696.

SPACE MILESTONE: *FREEDOM 7* (US): 40th ANNIVERSARY. May 5, 1961. First US astronaut in space, second man in space, Alan Shepard, Jr, projected 115 miles into space in suborbital flight reaching a speed of more than 5,000 mph. This was the first piloted Mercury mission.

THAILAND: CORONATION DAY. May 5. Thailand.

BIRTHDAYS TODAY

Danielle Fishel, 20, actress ("Boy Meets World"), born Mesa, AZ, May 5, 1981.

MAY 6 — SUNDAY

Day 126 — 239 Remaining

BE KIND TO ANIMALS WEEK®. May 6–12. To promote kindness and humane care toward animals. Annually, the first full week of May. Features "Be Kind to Animals Kid Contest." For info: Joyce Briggs, American Humane Assn, 63 Inverness Dr E, Englewood, CO 80112. Phone: (800) 227-4645 or (303) 792-9900. Fax: (303) 792-5333. E-mail: joyceb@americanhumane.org. Web: www.americanhumane.org.

NATIONAL FAMILY WEEK. May 6–12. Traditionally the first Sunday and the first full week in May are observed as National Family Week in many Christian churches.

NATIONAL PET WEEK. May 6–12. To promote public awareness of veterinary medical service for animal health and care. Annually, the first full week in May. For info: The American Veterinary Medical Assn, 1931 N Meacham Rd, Schaumburg, IL 60173. Phone: (847) 925-8070. Fax: (847) 925-1329. Web: www.avma.org.

NATIONAL PTA TEACHER APPRECIATION WEEK. May 6–12. PTAs across the country conduct activities to strengthen respect and support for teachers and the teaching profession. Annually, the first full week in May. For info: Natl PTA, 330 N Wabash Ave, Ste 2100, Chicago, IL 60611. Phone: (312) 670-6782. Fax: (312) 670-6783. E-mail: info@pta.org. Web: www.pta.org.

NATIONAL TOURISM WEEK. May 6–12. To promote and enhance awareness of travel and tourism's importance to the economic, social and cultural well-being of the US. Annually, beginning the first Sunday in May. *See* Curriculum Connection. For info: Travel Industry Assn of America, 1100 New York Ave NW, Ste 450, Washington, DC 20005-3934. Phone: (202) 408-8422. E-mail: ckeefe@tia.org. Web: www.tia.org.

PEARY, ROBERT E.: BIRTH ANNIVERSARY. May 6, 1856. Born at Cresson, PA. Peary served as a cartographic draftsman in the US Coast and Geodetic Survey for two years, then joined the US Navy's Corps of Civil Engineers in 1881. He first worked as an explorer in tropical climates as he served as subchief of the Inter-Ocean Canal Survey in Nicaragua. After reading of the inland ice of Greenland, Peary became attracted to the Arctic. He organized and led eight Arctic expeditions and is credited with the verification of Greenland's island formation, proving that the polar ice cap extended beyond 82° north latitude, and the discovery of the Melville meteorite on Melville Bay, in addition to his famous discovery of the North Pole, Apr 6, 1909. Peary died Feb 20, 1920, at Washington, DC.

MAY 6–12
NATIONAL TOURISM WEEK

Although this week is to promote awareness of the importance tourism has on the social, economic and cultural well-being of the United States, each town contributes in its own way to the things to see and do in our country. Encourage students to take pride in the contributions of their community by advertising it to the world at large.

This week is also National Postcard Week (May 7–13). Have students cut paper into postcard-sized pieces. Have them address the card to "The Folks Back Home." Let students imagine they are first-time visitors to your town. Single out one aspect of the town each finds interesting and write a wish-you-were-here note about it. Sketch a picture on the other side of the card. Make several paper kites. Label them with your town's name and use the postcards fastened to string as the kites' tails. Or display the postcards from the ceiling as mobiles. You might want to ask town officials if they could be displayed in the town hall or the public library.

Let students make travel brochures about your town. They can include notable citizens, historic landmarks, public parks, etc. As part of geography class, students could draw a map of the downtown area. An additional geography project could be titled "Come Down and See Us!" Students could research the locations of area train and bus depots and also local airports. See if they can obtain train and bus schedules and decipher them correctly.

Learning which main roads connect your town to others is another geography project. As a math assignment, students can use an atlas to measure mileage from your town to others, maybe even to towns that share the same name but are located in other states. They can estimate travel times between cities.

On 8 1/2" X 11" paper students can design travel posters for town landmarks or businesses. Ask merchants in the downtown area to display the travel posters in store windows.

You might hold an essay contest titled "Five Things I Like About My Town." Declare everyone a winner and display all entries in a public area.

Many towns have websites. See if yours is on the Internet and if so, what information the site contains.

PENN, JOHN: BIRTH ANNIVERSARY. May 6, 1740. Signer of the Declaration of Independence, born at Caroline County, VA. Died Sept 14, 1788.

TEACHER APPRECIATION WEEK. May 6–12. A week for elementary through high school students to show appreciation to their teachers. Students are urged to thank their teachers for their care and concerned effort, to be extra cooperative with them. For info: Natl Education Assn, 1201 16th St NW, Washington, DC 20036. Phone: (202) 833-4000. Web: www.nea.org.

BIRTHDAYS TODAY

Tony Blair, 48, British prime minister, born Edinburgh, Scotland, May 6, 1953.

George Clooney, 40, actor ("ER," *Batman and Robin*), born Augusta, KY, May 6, 1961.

Kristine O'Connell George, 47, author (*The Great Frog Race: And Other Poems*), born Denver, CO, May 6, 1954.

Ted Lewin, 66, author and illustrator (*The Storytellers*), born Buffalo, NY, May 6, 1935.

Willie Mays, 70, Baseball Hall of Fame outfielder, born Westfield, AL, May 6, 1931.

Barbara McClintock, 46, author and illustrator (*The Fantastic Drawings of Danielle*), born Flemington, NJ, May 6, 1955.

Richard C. Shelby, 67, US Senator (D, Alabama), born Birmingham, AL, May 6, 1934.

MAY 7 — MONDAY

Day 127 — 238 Remaining

BARRIER AWARENESS DAY IN KENTUCKY. May 7.

BEAUFORT SCALE DAY: (FRANCIS BEAUFORT BIRTH ANNIVERSARY). May 7, 1774. A day to honor the British naval officer, Sir Francis Beaufort, who devised in 1805 a scale of wind force from 0 (calm) to 12 (hurricane) that was based on observation, not requiring any special instruments. The scale was adopted for international use in 1874 and has since been enlarged and refined. Beaufort was born at Flower Hill, Meath, Ireland, and died at Brighton, England, Dec 17, 1857.

BEETHOVEN'S *NINTH SYMPHONY* PREMIERE: ANNIVERSARY. May 7, 1824. Beethoven's *Ninth Symphony in D Minor* was performed for the first time at Vienna, Austria. Known as the *Choral* because of his use of voices in symphonic form for the first time, the Ninth was his musical interpretation of Schiller's *Ode to Joy*. Beethoven was completely deaf when he composed it, and it was said a soloist had to tug on his sleeve when the performance was over to get him to turn around and see the enthusiastic response he could not hear.

BROWNING, ROBERT: BIRTH ANNIVERSARY. May 7, 1812. English poet and husband of poet Elizabeth Barrett Browning, born at Camberwell, near London. Known for his dramatic monologues. Died at Venice, Italy, Dec 12, 1889.

DIEN BIEN PHU FALLS: ANNIVERSARY. May 7, 1954. Vietnam's victory over France at Dien Bien Phu ended the Indochina War. This battle is considered one of the greatest victories won by a former colony over a colonial power.

	S	M	T	W	T	F	S
May			1	2	3	4	5
2001	6	7	8	9	10	11	12
	13	14	15	16	17	18	19
	20	21	22	23	24	25	26
	27	28	29	30	31		

GERMANY'S FIRST SURRENDER: ANNIVERSARY. May 7, 1945. Russian, American, British and French ranking officers crowded into a second-floor recreation room of a small redbrick schoolhouse (which served as Eisenhower's headquarters) at Reims, Germany. Representing Germany, Field Marshall Alfred Jodl signed an unconditional surrender of all German fighting forces. After a signing that took almost 40 minutes, Jodl was ushered into Eisenhower's presence. The American general asked the German if he fully understood what he had signed and informed Jodl that he would be held personally responsible for any deviation from the terms of the surrender, including the requirement that German commanders sign a formal surrender to the USSR at a time and place determined by that government.

MOON PHASE: FULL MOON. May 7. Moon enters Full Moon phase at 9:52 AM, EDT.

NATIONAL ETIQUETTE WEEK. May 7–11. A national recognition of proper etiquette in all areas of American life (business, social, dining, international, wedding, computer, etc.). A self-assessment on the current status of civility in the US. Annually, the second week in May starting on Monday. For info: Sandra Morisset, Protocol Training Services, PO Box 4981, New York, NY 10185. Phone: (212) 802-9098.

PUBLIC SERVICE RECOGNITION WEEK. May 7–13. Take this opportunity to thank the "Unsung Heroes and Heroines" of the public work force who perform a range of vital services. Public employees are scientists and police officers, teachers and doctors, astronauts and zoologists, engineers and food inspectors, forest rangers and claims representatives, researchers and foreign service agents. Free resource materials to promote the celebration available. Annually, the first Monday–Sunday in May. For info: Nick Nolan, Exec Dir, Public Employees Roundtable, PO Box 44801, Washington, DC 20026-4801. Phone: (202) 401-4344. E-mail: permail@patriot.net. Web: www.theroundtable.org.

TCHAIKOVSKY, PETER ILICH: BIRTH ANNIVERSARY. May 7, 1840. Ranked among the outstanding composers of all time, Peter Ilich Tchaikovsky was born at Vatkinsk, Russia. His musical talent was not encouraged and he embarked upon a career in law, not studying music seriously until 1861. Among his famous works are the three-act ballet *Sleeping Beauty*, two-act ballet *The Nutcracker* and the symphony *Pathetique*. Mystery surrounds Tchaikovsky's death. It was believed he'd caught cholera from contaminated water, but 20th-century scholars believe he probably committed suicide to avoid his homosexuality being revealed. He died at St. Petersburg, Nov 6, 1893.

BIRTHDAYS TODAY

Pete V. Domenici, 69, US Senator (R, New Mexico), born Albuquerque, NM, May 7, 1932.

Nonny Hogrogian, 69, author and illustrator (Caldecott for *One Fine Day*), born New York, NY, May 7, 1932.

MAY 8 — TUESDAY

Day 128 — 237 Remaining

CHILDHOOD DEPRESSION AWARENESS DAY. May 8. Also known as Green Ribbon Day. Annually, the first Tuesday in the first full week in May. For info: Natl Mental Heath Assn, 1021 Prince St, Alexandria, VA 22314-2971. Phone: (800) 969-6642 or (703) 684-7722. Web: www.nmha.org.

CZECH REPUBLIC: LIBERATION DAY: ANNIVERSARY. May 8. Commemorates the liberation of Czechoslovakia from the Germans in 1945.

DUNANT, JEAN HENRI: BIRTH ANNIVERSARY. May 8, 1828. Author and philanthropist, founder of the Red Cross Society, was born at Geneva, Switzerland. Nobel prize winner in 1901. Died at Heiden, Switzerland, Oct 30, 1910.

FRANCE: ARMISTICE DAY: ANNIVERSARY. May 8. Commemorates the surrender of Germany to Allied forces and the cessation of hostilities in 1945.

GERMANY'S SECOND SURRENDER: ANNIVERSARY. May 8, 1945. Stalin refused to recognize the document of unconditional surrender signed at Reims the previous day, so a second signing was held at Berlin. The event was turned into an elaborate formal ceremony by the Soviets who had lost some 10 million lives during the war. As in the Reims document, the end of hostilities was set for 12:01 AM local time on May 9.

LAVOISIER, ANTOINE LAURENT: EXECUTION ANNIVERSARY. May 8, 1794. French chemist and the "father of modern chemistry." Especially noted for having first explained the real nature of combustion and for showing that matter is not destroyed in chemical reactions. Born at Paris, France Aug 26, 1743, Lavoisier was guillotined at the Place de la Revolution for his former position as a tax collector. The Revolutionary Tribunal is reported to have responded to a plea to spare his life with the statement: "We need no more scientists in France."

NATIONAL TEACHER DAY. May 8. To pay tribute to American educators, sponsored by the National Education Association, Teacher Day falls during the National PTA's Teacher Appreciation Week. Local communities and organizations are encouraged to use this opportunity to honor those who influence and inspire the next generation through their work. Annually, the Tuesday of the first full week in May. For info: Natl Education Assn (NEA), 1201 16th St NW, Washington, DC 20036. Phone: (202) 833-4000. Web: www.nea.org.

NO SOCKS DAY. May 8. If we give up wearing socks for one day, it will mean a little less laundry, thereby contributing to the betterment of the environment. Besides, we will all feel a bit freer, at least for one day. Annually, May 8. [© 1999 by WH] For info: Thomas and Ruth Roy, Wellcat Holidays, 2418 Long Ln, Lebanon, PA 17046. Phone: (230) 332-4886. E-mail: wellcat@supernet.com. Web: www.wellcat.com.

SLOVAK REPUBLIC: LIBERATION DAY: ANNIVERSARY. May 8. Commemorates the liberation of Czechoslovakia from the Germans in 1945.

TRUMAN, HARRY S: BIRTH ANNIVERSARY. May 8, 1884. The 33rd president of the US, succeeded to that office upon the death of Franklin D. Roosevelt, Apr 12, 1945, and served until Jan 20, 1953. Born at Lamar, MO, Truman was the last of nine US presidents who did not attend college. Affectionately nicknamed "Give 'em Hell Harry" by admirers. Truman died at Kansas City, MO, Dec 26, 1972. His birthday is a holiday in Missouri.

V-E DAY: ANNIVERSARY. May 8, 1945. Victory in Europe Day commemorates the unconditional surrender of Germany to Allied Forces. The surrender document was signed by German representatives at General Dwight D. Eisenhower's headquarters at Reims to become effective, and hostilities to end, at one minute past midnight on May 9, 1945, which was 9:01 PM, EDT on May 8 in the US. President Harry S Truman on May 8 declared May 9, 1945, to be "V-E Day," but it later came to be observed on May 8 in the US. A separate German surrender to the USSR was signed at Karlshorst, near Berlin, May 8. See also: "Russia: Victory Day: Anniversary" (May 9).

WORLD RED CROSS DAY. May 8. A day for commemorating the birth of Jean Henry Dunant, the Swiss founder of the International Red Cross Movement in 1863, and for recognizing the humanitarian work of the Red Cross around the world. For info on activities in your area, contact your local Red Cross chapter. For info: Darren Irby, Media Associate, American Red Cross Natl Headquarters, 1621 N Kent St, Arlington, VA 22209. Phone: (703) 248-4219. Fax: (703) 248-4256.

BIRTHDAYS TODAY

Peter Benchley, 61, author (*Jaws*), born New York, NY, May 8, 1940.

Peter Connolly, 66, author (*The Ancient City: Life in Classical Athens & Rome*), born Surrey, England, May 8, 1935.

Milton Meltzer, 86, author (*Langston Hughes: A Biography; Brother, Can You Spare a Dime: The Great Depression*), born Worcester, MA, May 8, 1915.

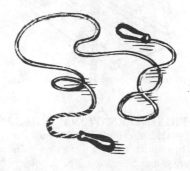

MAY 9 — WEDNESDAY

Day 129 — 236 Remaining

BARRIE, J.M.: BIRTH ANNIVERSARY. May 9, 1860. Author, born at Kirriemuir, Scotland. Wrote the popular children's tale *Peter Pan*, which first became a movie in 1924. Barrie died at London, England, June 19, 1937.

BROWN, JOHN: BIRTH ANNIVERSARY. May 9, 1800. Abolitionist leader, born at Torrington, CT, and hanged Dec 2, 1859, at Charles Town, WV. Leader of attack on Harpers Ferry, Oct 16, 1859, which was intended to give impetus to movement for escape and freedom for slaves. His aim was frustrated and in fact resulted in increased polarization and sectional animosity. Legendary martyr of the abolitionist movement.

THE DAY OF THE TEACHER (EL DIA DEL MAESTRO). May 9. California honors its teachers every year on the Day of the Teacher. Patterned after "El Dia Del Maestro" celebrated in Mexico, the Day of the Teacher was originated by the Association of Mexican-American Educators and the California Teachers Association and designated by the California legislature. A tribute to all teachers and their lasting influence on children's lives. Annually, the second Wednesday of May. For info: California Teachers Assn, PO Box 921, Burlingame, CA 94010. Phone: (650) 697-1400. Fax: (650) 697-0786. Web: www.cta.org.

DU BOIS, WILLIAM PENE: 85th BIRTH ANNIVERSARY. May 9, 1916. Illustrator and author of children's books, born at Nutley, NJ. Du Bois was the recipient of the Newbery Medal in 1948 for his book, *The Twenty-One Balloons*. He died at Nice, France, Feb 5, 1993.

ESTES, ELEANOR: BIRTH ANNIVERSARY. May 9, 1906. Author, born at West Haven, CT. Known for her book *The Hundred Dresses*, Estes won a Newbery Medal in 1952 for her children's book *Ginger Pye*. Died at Hamden, CT, July 15, 1988.

EUROPEAN UNION: ANNIVERSARY OBSERVANCE. May 9, 1950. Member countries of the European Union commemorate the announcement by French statesman Robert Schuman of the "Schuman Plan" for establishing a single authority for production of coal, iron and steel in France and Germany. This organization was a forerunner of the European Economic Community, founded in 1957, which later became the European Union.

PHILADELPHIA INTERNATIONAL CHILDREN'S FESTIVAL. May 9–13. Philadelphia, PA. 17th annual festival of theater and film. In addition to eight theater pieces from around the world, there will be free outdoor performances by musicians, singers and jugglers and craft activities. Est attendance: 20,000. For info: The Annenberg School, University of Pennsylvania, 3620 Walnut St, Philadelphia, PA 19104. Phone: (215) 898-3900.

RUSSIA: VICTORY DAY: ANNIVERSARY. May 9. National holiday observed annually to commemorate the 1945 Allied Forces defeat of Nazi Germany in WWII and to honor the 20 million Soviet people who died in that war. Hostilities ceased and the German surrender became effective at one minute after midnight May 9, 1945. See also: "V-E Day: Anniversary" (May 9).

"VAST WASTELAND" SPEECH: 40th ANNIVERSARY. May 9, 1961. Speaking before the bigwigs of network TV at the annual convention of the National Association of Broadcasters, Newton Minow, the new chairman of the Federal Communications Commission, exhorted those executives to sit through an entire day of their own programming. He suggested that they "will observe a vast wasteland." Further, he urged them to try for "imagination in programming, not sterility; creativity, not imitation; experimentation, not conformity; excellence, not mediocrity."

	S	M	T	W	T	F	S
May			1	2	3	4	5
2001	6	7	8	9	10	11	12
	13	14	15	16	17	18	19
	20	21	22	23	24	25	26
	27	28	29	30	31		

BIRTHDAYS TODAY

Richard Adams, 81, author (*Watership Down*), born Newbury, England, May 9, 1920.

John Ashcroft, 59, US Senator (R, Missouri), born Springfield, MO, May 9, 1942.

Candice Bergen, 55, actress ("Murphy Brown"), daughter of ventriloquist Edgar Bergen, born Beverly Hills, CA, May 9, 1946.

Tony Gwynn, 41, baseball player, born Los Angeles, CA, May 9, 1960.

MAY 10 — THURSDAY
Day 130 — 235 Remaining

CONFEDERATE MEMORIAL DAY IN SOUTH CAROLINA. May 10. See also Apr 26, Apr 30, May 28 and June 3 for Confederate Memorial Day observances in other southern states.

GOLDEN SPIKE DRIVING: ANNIVERSARY. May 10, 1869. Anniversary of the meeting of Union Pacific and Central Pacific railways, at Promontory Point, UT. On that day a golden spike was driven by Leland Stanford, president of the Central Pacific, to celebrate the linkage. The golden spike was promptly removed for preservation. Long called the final link in the ocean-to-ocean railroad, this event cannot be accurately described as completing the transcontinental railroad, but it did complete continuous rail tracks between Omaha and Sacramento. See also: "Transcontinental US Railway Completion: Anniversary" (Aug 15).

JEFFERSON DAVIS CAPTURED: ANNIVERSARY. May 10, 1865. Confederate President Jefferson Davis, his wife and cabinet officials were captured at Irwinville, GA, by the 4th Michigan Cavalry. The prisoners were taken to Nashville, TN, and later sent to Richmond, VA.

THE READ IN. May 10. A daylong reading project for students in grades K–12. During the 8th annual Read In, students will chat together online with 22 of the best children's and young adult literature authors. This day is a culmination of several weeks of online participation by teachers and students during which they share information about their schools and communities. Annually, the second Thursday in May. For info: Jane Coffey, Program Dir, The Read In Foundation, 6043 Channel Dr, Riverbank, CA 95367. Phone: (209) 869-0713. E-mail: Thereadin@aol.com.

ROSS, GEORGE: BIRTH ANNIVERSARY. May 10, 1730. Lawyer and signer of the Declaration of Independence, born at New Castle, DE. Died at Philadelphia, PA, July 14, 1779.

SINGAPORE: VESAK DAY. May 10. Public holiday. Monks commemorate their Lord Buddha's entry into Nirvana by chanting holy sutras and freeing captive birds.

TRUST YOUR INTUITION DAY. May 10. Today is the day we pay homage to the wonderful gift of sixth sense, "gut" feelings or that still small voice that is sometimes the only clue we have to go on in this ever-changing world. [©1994] For info: Adrienne Sioux Koopersmith, 1437 W Rosemont, #1W, Chicago, IL 60660-1319. Phone: (773) 743-5341. Fax: (773) 743-5395. E-mail: adrienet@earthlink.net.

BIRTHDAYS TODAY

Christopher Paul Curtis, 47, author (*The Watsons Go to Birmingham—1963*), born Flint, MI, May 10, 1954.

Bruce McMillan, 54, author and illustrator (*Jelly Beans for Sale*), born Boston, MA, May 10, 1947.

Rick Santorum, 43, US Senator (R, Pennsylvania), born Winchester, VA, May 10, 1949.

Kenan Thompson, 23, actor ("All That," "Kenan & Kel"), born Atlanta, GA, May 10, 1978.

MAY 11 — FRIDAY
Day 131 — 234 Remaining

DENMARK: COMMON PRAYER DAY. May 11. Public holiday. The fourth Friday after Easter, known as "Store Bededag," is a day for prayer and festivity.

EAT WHAT YOU WANT DAY. May 11. Here's a day you may actually enjoy yourself. Ignore all those on-again/off-again warnings. [© 1999 by WH] For info: Tom and Ruth Roy, Wellcat Holidays, 2418 Long Ln, Lebanon, PA 17046. Phone: (230) 332-4886. E-mail: wellcat@supernet.com. Web: www.wellcat.com.

FAIRBANKS, CHARLES WARREN: BIRTH ANNIVERSARY. May 11, 1852. The 26th vice president of the US (1905–09), born at Unionville Center, OH. Died at Indianapolis, IN, June 4, 1918.

GLACIER NATIONAL PARK ESTABLISHED: ANNIVERSARY. May 11, 1910. This national park is located in northwest Montana, on the Canadian border. In 1932 Glacier and Waterton Lakes National Park in Alberta were joined together by the governments of the US and Canada as Waterton-Glacier International Peace Park. For more info: www.nps.gov/glac.

GRAHAM, MARTHA: BIRTH ANNIVERSARY. May 11, 1894. Martha Graham was born at Allegheny, PA, and became one of the giants of the modern dance movement in the US. She began her dance career at the comparatively late age of 22 and joined the Greenwich Village Follies in 1923. Her new ideas began to surface in the late '20s and '30s, and by the mid-1930s she was incorporating the rituals of the southwestern American Indians in her work. She is credited with bringing a new psychological depth to modern dance by exploring primal emotions and ancient rituals in her work. She performed until the age of 75, and premiered in her 180th ballet, *The Maple Leaf Rag*, in the fall of 1990. Died Apr 1, 1991, at New York, NY. For more info: *Martha Graham: A Dancer's Life*, by Russell Freedman (Clarion, 0-395-74655-8, $18 Gr. 7–12).

HART, JOHN: DEATH ANNIVERSARY. May 11, 1779. Signer of the Declaration of Independence, farmer and legislator, born about 1711 (exact date unknown), at Stonington, CT, died at Hopewell, NJ.

JAPAN: CORMORANT FISHING FESTIVAL. May 11–Oct 15. Cormorant fishing on the Nagara River, Gifu. "This ancient method of catching Ayu, a troutlike fish, with trained cormorants, takes place nightly under the light of blazing torches."

LAG B'OMER. May 11. Hebrew calendar date: Iyar 18, 5761. Literally, the 33rd day of the omer (harvest time), the 33rd day after the beginning of Passover. Traditionally a joyous day for weddings, picnics and outdoor activities.

MINNESOTA: ADMISSION DAY: ANNIVERSARY. May 11. Became 32nd state in 1858.

SPACE DAY. May 11 (tentative). Previous Space Days have included a live broadcast over the Web in which astronauts and scientists answered questions from kids worldwide; a live satellite broadcast about space exploration, and local events in schools and communities. The Space Day website contains lesson plans for teachers and games and puzzles for kids. For info: www.spaceday.com.

BIRTHDAYS TODAY

James Jeffords, 67, US Senator (R, Vermont), born Rutland, VT, May 11, 1934.

Austin O'Brien, 20, actor ("The Baby-Sitters Club," *My Girl 2*), born Eugene, OR, May 11, 1981.

Natasha Richardson, 38, actress (*The Parent Trap*), born London, England, May 11, 1963.

Peter Sis, 52, illustrator and author (*The Starry Messenger*), born Prague, Czechoslovakia, May 11, 1949.

Zilpha Keatley Snyder, 74, author (*The Witches of Worm, The Headless Cupid*), born Lemoore, CA, May 11, 1927.

MAY 12 — SATURDAY
Day 132 — 233 Remaining

LEAR, EDWARD: BIRTH ANNIVERSARY. May 12, 1812. English artist and author, remembered for his children's book *The Owl and the Pussycat*. Born at Highgate, England, Lear died at San Remo, Italy, Jan 29, 1888.

LIMERICK DAY. May 12. Observed on the birthday of one of its champions, Edward Lear, who was born in 1812. The limerick, which dates from the early 18th century, has been described as the "only fixed verse form indigenous to the English language." It gained its greatest popularity following the publication of Edward Lear's *Book of Nonsense* (and its sequels). Write a limerick today! Example: There was a young poet named Lear/Who said, it is just as I fear/Five lines are enough/For this kind of stuff/Make a limerick each day of the year.

NETHERLANDS: NATIONAL WINDMILL DAY. May 12. About 950 windmills still survive and some 300 still are used occasionally and have been designated national monuments by the government. As many windmills as possible are in operation on National Windmill Day for the benefit of tourists. Annually, the second Saturday in May.

NIGHTINGALE, FLORENCE: BIRTH ANNIVERSARY. May 12, 1820. English nurse and public health activist who contributed perhaps more than any other single person to the development of modern nursing procedures and the dignity of nursing as a profession. During the Crimean War, she supervised nursing care in the British hospital at Scutari, Turkey, where she reduced the death rate dramatically. Returning to England, she reorganized the army medical service. She was the founder of the Nightingale training school for nurses and author of *Notes on Nursing*. Born at Florence, Italy, she died at London, England, Aug 13, 1910.

BIRTHDAYS TODAY

Jennifer Armstrong, 40, author (*Black-Eyed Susan, Mary Mehan Awake*), born Waltham, MA, May 12, 1961.

Yogi Berra, 76, former baseball manager and Baseball Hall of Fame catcher, born Lawrence Peter Berra, St. Louis, MO, May 12, 1925.

Tony Hawk, 32, skateboarder, born Carlsbad, CA, May 12, 1969.

Farley Mowat, 80, author (*Owls in the Family*), born Belleville, Ontario, Canada, May 12, 1921.

MAY 13 — SUNDAY
Day 133 — 232 Remaining

FAMILY AWARENESS MONTH. May 13–June 17. A time to reflect and re-establish family ties. A time to rekindle the ties that bind... Family love, family awareness, family remembrance, family celebrations. A time to gather together and remember the greatness of our nation which lies in the heart of each and every family in America. Annually, Mother's Day until Father's Day. For info: Judith Natale, CEO & Founder, Natl Children & Family Awareness of America, Administrative Headquarters, 3060 Rt 405 Hwy, Muncy, PA 17756-8808. Phone: (888) MAA-DESK. E-mail: ChildAware@aol.com or MaaJudith@aol.com.

GIRLS INCORPORATED WEEK. May 13–19. To focus national and local attention on the goals of Girls Incorporated as an organization for the rights and needs of girls. Begins the second Sunday in May. For info: Galia Schechter, Girls Inc, 30 East 33rd St, New York, NY 10016-5394. Phone: (212) 509-2000. E-mail: HN3580@handsnet.org. Web: www.girlsinc.org.

★**MOTHER'S DAY.** May 13. Presidential Proclamation always issued for the second Sunday in May. (Pub Res No. 2 of May 8, 1914.)

MOTHER'S DAY. May 13. Observed first in 1907 at the request of Anna Jarvis of Philadelphia, PA, who asked her church to hold service in memory of all mothers on the anniversary of her mother's death. Annually, the second Sunday in May. For links to Mother's Day sites on the web, go to: deil.lang.uiuc.edu/web .pages/holidays/mother.html.

NATIONAL ALCOHOL AND OTHER DRUG-RELATED BIRTH DEFECTS WEEK. May 13–19. For info: Natl Council on Alcoholism and Drug Dependence, 12 W 21st St, New York, NY 10010. Phone: (212) 206-6770.

NATIONAL EMERGENCY MEDICAL SERVICES (EMS) WEEK. May 13–19. Honoring EMS providers nationwide who provide life-saving care in a multitude of circumstances. Also a time for the public to learn about injury prevention, safety awareness and emergency preparedness. Annually, the third week in May. For info: American College of Emergency Physicians, PO Box 619911, Dallas, TX 75261-9911. Phone: (800) 748-1822. E-mail: emsweek@acep.org. Web: www.acep.org.

NATIONAL FAMILY MONTH®. May 13–June 17. A monthlong national observance to celebrate and promote strong, supportive families. Sponsored by KidsPeace®, a private, not-for-profit organization that has been helping kids overcome crisis since 1982. Annually, Mother's Day through Father's Day. For info: Paula Knouse, KidsPeace, 5300 Kidspeace Dr, Orefield, PA 18069. Phone: (610) 799-8325. Web: www.kidspeace.org.

May 2001	S	M	T	W	T	F	S
			1	2	3	4	5
	6	7	8	9	10	11	12
	13	14	15	16	17	18	19
	20	21	22	23	24	25	26
	27	28	29	30	31		

MAY 13–19
NATIONAL HISTORIC PRESERVATION WEEK

Last week's focus on tourism (May 6–12) is a perfect lead-in for National Historic Preservation Week. Those who have lived in one area for many years may be aware of their town's heritage, while others may be too busy to take notice. Many people in today's society do not live in the town where they grew up. Unlike generations before ours, who often remained in the same area for years, job opportunities sometimes carry us far from our roots. Regardless of where you come from, learning about the heritage of the town you live in makes you part of that community.

Children can become involved with historic landmarks in many ways. One way is to notice the architecture of the buildings that occupy the oldest part of town. Features like roof lines, cornices and building materials often provide clues to the period in which the building was constructed. Students could compile an architectural directory of the styles they see in different areas of town. A tour book format, with numbered "stops," makes a useful guide. Another possibility is a series of "Can you identify this building?" flash cards, each depicting a historic landmark.

The local history section of your public library should have information about the history of existing landmarks, as well as those that have been lost to progress. Each student can choose a building and research the people who built it and how the building's use may have changed over the years. Encourage students to raise their eyes and look for clues on buildings. For example, the original occupants sometimes had their names chiseled into stonework high on the facade; some buildings have old signs painted on the side.

If you live along a waterway, groups of students can research specific time periods and present to the class information about the boats that used the water during each era.

Many towns preserve old cemeteries. If possible, visit one and note the names of the people who are buried there. See how many names the students can connect to buildings they have researched. Tombstone inscriptions are often interesting and can tell stories of their own. Suggest students look for deaths during specific wars or multiple deaths during a short period of time that could be indicative of disease (the 1918 flu epidemic, for example). Students may want to try their hand at tombstone rubbings. Use thin paper and charcoal or chalk. Take care not to mar stones or nearby plantings in any way.

If possible, arrange for a class trip to famous local landmarks, especially living history displays or ongoing archeological digs. A wealth of fascinating cultural information may be close at hand. *Breaking Ground, Breaking Silence: The Story of New York's African Burial Ground*, by Joyce Hansen (Holt, 0-8050-5012-4, $17.95 Gr. 5–8) is a marvelous example of archeological investigation. Invite the town historian to visit your classroom and talk about historic buildings and settlement patterns. Check and see if landmarks from Native American, Spanish or French settlements existed in your area.

By preserving old buildings and getting to know the people who built them and lived in the area before we did, we become involved in our town's history. It forges a connection between us and our past and helps us become aware that we have a stake in the town's future.

NATIONAL HISTORIC PRESERVATION WEEK. May 13–19. To draw public attention to historic preservation including neighborhoods, districts, landmark buildings, open space and maritime heritage. Annually, the second full week in May. *See* Curriculum Connection. For info: Diana Onorio, Natl Trust for Historic Preservation, 1785 Massachusetts Ave NW, Washington, DC 20036. Phone: (202) 588-6141. Fax: (202) 588-6299. E-mail: pr @nthp.org. Web: www.nationaltrust.org.

NATIONAL POLICE WEEK. May 13–19. See also "Peace Officer Memorial Day" (May 15). For info: American Police Hall of Fame and Museum, 3801 Biscayne Blvd, Miami, FL 33137. Phone: (305) 573-0070.

★**NATIONAL TRANSPORTATION WEEK.** May 13–19. Presidential Proclamation issued for week including third Friday in May since 1960. (PL 86–475 of May 20, 1960, first requested; PL87–449 of May 14, 1962, requested an annual proclamation.)

★**POLICE WEEK.** May 13–19. Presidential Proclamation 3537 of May 4, 1963, covers all succeeding years. (PL87–726 of Oct 1, 1962.) Always the week including May 15 since 1962.

SPACE MILESTONE: *ENDEAVOUR* (US). May 13, 1992. Three astronauts from the shuttle *Endeavour* simultaneously walked in space for the first time.

★**WORLD TRADE WEEK.** May 13–19. Presidential Proclamation has been issued each year since 1948 for the third week of May with three exceptions: 1949, 1955 and 1966.

BIRTHDAYS TODAY

Francine Pascal, 63, author (the Sweet Valley High series), born New York, NY, May 13, 1938.

Dennis Keith ("Worm") Rodman, 40, former basketball player, born Trenton, NJ, May 13, 1961.

Stevie Wonder, 50, singer, musician (16 Grammy Awards; "I Just Called to Say I Love You"), born Steveland Morris Hardaway, Saginaw, MI, May 13, 1951.

MAY 14 — MONDAY

Day 134 — 231 Remaining

FAHRENHEIT, GABRIEL DANIEL: BIRTH ANNIVERSARY. May 14, 1686. German physicist whose name is attached to one of the major temperature measurement scales. He introduced the use of mercury in thermometers and greatly improved their accuracy. Born at Danzig, Germany, he died at Amsterdam, Holland, Sept 16, 1736.

FIRST FEMALE HOUSE PAGE APPOINTMENT: ANNIVERSARY. May 14, 1973. The House of Representatives received formal approval of the appointment of female pages in 1972. In the 93rd Congress, Felda Looper was appointed as the first female page with a regular term. Gene Cox had served as a female page for three hours 34 years earlier.

JAMESTOWN, VIRGINIA: FOUNDING ANNIVERSARY. May 14, 1607. The first permanent English settlement in what is now the US took place at Jamestown, VA (named for England's King James I), on this date. Captains John Smith and Christopher Newport were among the leaders of the group of royally chartered Virginia Company settlers who had traveled from Plymouth, England, in three small ships: *Susan Constant*, *Godspeed* and *Discovery*.

LEWIS AND CLARK EXPEDITION: ANNIVERSARY. May 14, 1804. Charged by President Thomas Jefferson with finding a route to the Pacific, Meriwether Lewis and Captain William Clark left St. Louis, MO, May 14, 1804. They arrived at the Pacific coast of Oregon in November 1805 and returned to St. Louis, Sept 23, 1806. For more info: www.pbs.org/lewisandclark.

NATIONAL EDUCATIONAL BOSSES WEEK. May 14–18. A special week to honor bosses in the field of education such as principals and school superintendents. Annually, the third week in May. For info: Natl Assn of Educational Office Personnel, PO Box 12619, Wichita, KS 67277. Fax: (316) 942-7100.

NORWAY: MIDNIGHT SUN AT NORTH CAPE. May 14–July 30. In the "Land of the Midnight Sun," this is the first day of the season with around-the-clock sunshine. At North Cape and parts of Russia, Alaska, Canada and Greenland surrounding the Arctic Ocean, the sun never dips below the horizon from May 14 to July 30, but the night is bright long before and after these dates. At the equator, on the other hand, the length of day and night never varies.

PARAGUAY: INDEPENDENCE DAY. May 14–15. Commemorates independence from Spain, attained 1811.

SEATTLE INTERNATIONAL CHILDREN'S FESTIVAL. May 14–19. Seattle, WA. The largest performing arts festival for families in the US. Artists from Europe, Asia, Africa, Australia and the Americas present theater, dance, music, puppets and acrobatics. Est attendance: 51,000. For info: Seattle Intl Children's Festival, 305 Harrison, Seattle, WA 98109-3944. Phone: (206) 684-7338. E-mail: kidsfest@kidsfest.seanet.com. Web: seattle2000 .com/festival/.

SMALLPOX VACCINE DISCOVERED: ANNIVERSARY. May 14, 1796. In the 18th century, smallpox was a widespread and often fatal disease. Edward Jenner, a physician in rural England, heard reports of dairy farmers who apparently became immune to smallpox as a result of exposure to cowpox, a related but milder disease. After two decades of studying the phenomenon, Jenner injected cowpox into a healthy eight-year-old boy, who subsequently developed cowpox. Six weeks later, Jenner inoculated the boy with smallpox. He remained healthy. Jenner called this new procedure *vaccination*, from *vaccinia*, another term for cowpox. Within 18 months, 12,000 people in England had been vaccinated and the number of smallpox deaths dropped by two-thirds.

SPACE MILESTONE: *SKYLAB* (US). May 14, 1973. The US launched *Skylab*, its first manned orbiting laboratory.

"THE STARS AND STRIPES FOREVER" DAY: ANNIVERSARY. May 14, 1897. Anniversary of the first public performance of John Philip Sousa's march, "The Stars and Stripes Forever," at Philadelphia, PA. The occasion was the unveiling of a statue of George Washington. President William McKinley was present.

WAAC: ANNIVERSARY. May 14, 1942. During WWII women became eligible to enlist for noncombat duties in the Women's Auxiliary Army Corps (WAAC) by an act of Congress. Women also served as Women Appointed for Voluntary Emergency Service (WAVES), Women's Auxiliary Ferrying Squadron (WAFS) and Coast Guard or Semper Paratus Always Ready Service (SPARS), the Women's Reserve of the Marine Corp.

Byron L. Dorgan, 59, US Senator (D, North Dakota), born Dickinson, ND, May 14, 1942.

George Lucas, 57, filmmaker (*The Empire Strikes Back, Star Wars*), born Modesto, CA, May 14, 1944.

George Selden, 72, author (*The Cricket in Times Square*), born George Selden Thompson, Hartford, CT, May 14, 1929.

Valerie Still, 40, basketball player, born Lexington, KY, May 14, 1961.

MAY 15 — TUESDAY
Day 135 — 230 Remaining

BAUM, L(YMAN) FRANK: BIRTH ANNIVERSARY. May 15, 1856. The American newspaperman who wrote the Wizard of Oz stories was born at Chittenango, NY. Although *The Wonderful Wizard of Oz* is the most famous, Baum also wrote many other books for children, including more than a dozen about Oz. He died at Hollywood, CA, May 6, 1919.

FIRST FLIGHT ATTENDANT: ANNIVERSARY. May 15, 1930. Ellen Church became the first airline stewardess (today's flight attendant), flying on a United Airlines flight from San Francisco to Cheyenne, WY.

GASOLINE RATIONING: ANNIVERSARY. May 15, 1942. Seventeen eastern states initiated gasoline rationing as part of the war effort. By Sept 25, rationing was nationwide. A limit of three gallons a week for nonessential purposes was set and a 35 mph speed limit was imposed.

JAPAN: AOI MATSURI (HOLLYHOCK FESTIVAL). May 15. Kyoto. The festival features a pageant reproducing imperial processions of ancient times that paid homage to the shrine of Shimogamo and Kamigamo.

MEXICO: SAN ISIDRO DAY. May 15. Day of San Isidro Labrador celebrated widely in farming regions to honor St. Isidore, the Plowman. Livestock is gaily decorated with flowers. Celebrations usually begin about May 13 and continue for about a week.

MOON PHASE: LAST QUARTER. May 15. Moon enters Last Quarter phase at 6:11 AM, EDT.

NATIONAL BIKE TO WORK DAY. May 15. At the state or local level, Bike to Work events are conducted by small and large businesses, city governments, bicycle clubs and environmental groups. About two million participants nationwide. Annually, the third Tuesday in May. For info: Donald Tighe, Program Dir, League of American Bicyclists, 1612 K St NW, Ste 401, Washington, DC 20006. Phone: (202) 822-1333. Fax: (202) 822-1334. E-mail: bikeleague@aol.com. Web: www.bikeleague.org.

NYLON STOCKINGS: ANNIVERSARY. May 15, 1940. Nylon hose went on sale at stores throughout the country. Competing producers bought their nylon yarn from E.J. du Pont de Nemours. W.H. Carothers of Du Pont developed nylon, called "Polymer 66," in 1935. It was the first totally man-made fiber and over time substituted for other materials and came to have widespread application.

★ **PEACE OFFICER MEMORIAL DAY.** May 15. Presidential Proclamation 3537, of May 4, 1963, covers all succeeding years.

May 2001	S	M	T	W	T	F	S
			1	2	3	4	5
	6	7	8	9	10	11	12
	13	14	15	16	17	18	19
	20	21	22	23	24	25	26
	27	28	29	30	31		

(PL87–726 of Oct 1, 1962.) Always May 15 of each year since 1963; however, first issued in 1962 for May 14.

PEACE OFFICER MEMORIAL DAY. May 15. An event honored by some 21,000 police departments nationwide. Memorial ceremonies at 10 AM in American Police Hall of Fame and Museum, Miami, FL. See also: "National Police Week" (May 13–19). Sponsor: National Association of Chiefs of Police. Est attendance: 1,000. For info: American Police Hall of Fame and Museum, 3801 Biscayne Blvd, Miami, FL 33137. Phone: (305) 573-0070. Web: www.aphf.org.

UNITED NATIONS: INTERNATIONAL DAY OF FAMILIES. May 15. The general assembly (Res 47/237) Sept 20, 1993, voted this as an annual observance beginning in 1994.

WILSON, ELLEN LOUISE AXSON: BIRTH ANNIVERSARY. May 15, 1860. First wife of Woodrow Wilson, 28th president of the US, born at Savannah, GA. She died at Washington, DC, Aug 6, 1914.

Madeleine Albright, 64, US Secretary of State (Clinton administration), born Prague, Czechoslovakia, May 15, 1937.

George Brett, 48, Baseball Hall of Fame player, born Glen Dale, WV, May 15, 1953.

Norma Fox Mazer, 70, author (*A Figure of Speech*), born New York, NY, May 15, 1931.

Leigh Ann Orsi, 20, actress ("Home Improvement," *Pet Shop*), born Los Angeles, CA, May 15, 1981.

Emmitt Smith, 32, football player, born Escambia, FL, May 15, 1969.

Paul Zindel, 65, author (*The Pigman*), born Staten Island, NY, May 15, 1936.

MAY 16 — WEDNESDAY
Day 136 — 229 Remaining

BIOGRAPHERS DAY. May 16, 1763. Anniversary of the meeting, at London, England, of James Boswell and Samuel Johnson, beginning history's most famous biographer-biographee relationship. Boswell's *Journal of a Tour to the Hebrides* (1785) and his *Life of Samuel Johnson* (1791) are regarded as models of biographical writing. Thus, this day is recommended as one on which to start reading or writing a biography.

FIRST ACADEMY AWARDS: ANNIVERSARY. May 16, 1929. About 270 people attended a dinner at the Hollywood Roosevelt Hotel at which the first Academy Awards were given in 12 categories for films made in 1928. The silent film *Wings* won Best Picture. A committee of only 20 members selected the winners that year. By the third year, the entire membership of the Academy voted. For links to Academy Awards sites on the web, go to: deil.lang.uiuc.edu/web.pages/holidays/oscars.html.

GWINNETT, BUTTON: DEATH ANNIVERSARY. May 16, 1777. Signer of the Declaration of Independence, born at Down Hatherley, Gloucestershire, England, about 1735 (exact date unknown). Died following a duel at St. Catherine's Island, off of Savannah, GA.

MORTON, LEVI PARSONS: BIRTH ANNIVERSARY. May 16, 1824. The 22nd vice president of the US (1889–93) was born at Shoreham, VT. Died at Rhinebeck, NY, May 16, 1920.

REY, MARGARET: 95th BIRTH ANNIVERSARY. May 16, 1906. Children's author, born at Hamburg, Germany. Together with her illustrator husband, H.A. Rey, she produced the Curious George series. Rey died at Cambridge, MA, Dec 21, 1996.

BIRTHDAYS TODAY

Caroline Arnold, 57, author (*Trapped in Tar*), born Minneapolis, MN, May 16, 1944.

David Boreanaz, 30, actor ("Buffy the Vampire Slayer"), born Philadelphia, PA, May 16, 1971.

Bruce Coville, 51, author (*Aliens Ate My Homework*), born Syracuse, NY, May 16, 1950.

Tracey Gold, 32, actress ("Growing Pains"), born New York, NY, May 16, 1969.

James B. Hunt, Jr, 64, Governor of North Carolina (D), born Greensboro, NC, May 16, 1937.

Gabriela Sabatini, 31, tennis player, born Buenos Aires, Argentina, May 16, 1970.

Joan (Benoit) Samuelson, 44, Olympic gold medal runner, born Cape Elizabeth, ME, May 16, 1957.

MAY 17 — THURSDAY
Day 137 — 228 Remaining

BROWN v BOARD OF EDUCATION DECISION: ANNIVERSARY. May 17, 1954. The US Supreme Court ruled unanimously that segregation of public schools "solely on the basis of race" denied black children "equal educational opportunity" even though "physical facilities and other 'tangible' factors may have been equal. Separate educational facilities are inherently unequal." The case was argued before the Court by Thurgood Marshall, who would go on to become the first black appointed to the Supreme Court.

JENNER, EDWARD: BIRTH ANNIVERSARY. May 17, 1749. English physician, born at Berkeley, England. He was the first to establish a scientific basis for vaccination with his work on smallpox. Jenner died at Berkeley, England, Jan 26, 1823.

NEW YORK STOCK EXCHANGE ESTABLISHED: ANNIVERSARY. May 17, 1792. Some two dozen merchants and brokers agreed to establish what is now known as the New York Stock Exchange. In fair weather they operated under a buttonwood tree on Wall Street, at New York, NY. In bad weather they moved to the shelter of a coffeehouse to conduct their business.

NORWAY: CONSTITUTION DAY OR INDEPENDENCE DAY. May 17. National holiday. The constitution was signed in 1814. Parades and children's festivities.

SUE EXHIBITED: ANNIVERSARY. May 17, 2000. Sue, the largest and most complete *Tyrannosaurus rex* ever discovered, went on exhibition this day at the Field Museum in Chicago. Sue's skeleton was discovered in South Dakota in 1990. The meat-eating dinosaur is 65 million years old. Sue is named after Susan Hendrickson, the fossil hunter who discovered the dinosaur. The Field Museum spent more than $8 million to purchase Sue in 1997. For info: Field Museum, Roosevelt Road at Lake Shore Drive, Chicago, IL 60605-2496. Phone: (312) 322-8859. Web: www.fmnh.org.

UNITED NATIONS: WORLD TELECOMMUNICATION DAY. May 17. A day to draw attention to the necessity and importance of further development of telecommunications in the global community. For more information, visit the UN's website for children at www.un.org/Pubs/CyberSchoolBus/.

BIRTHDAYS TODAY

Eloise Greenfield, 72, author (*Night on Neighborhood Street*), born Parmalee, NC, May 17, 1929.

Mia Hamm, 29, soccer player, born Selma, AL, May 17, 1972.

Gary Paulsen, 62, author (*The Hatchet*), born Minneapolis, MN, May 17, 1939.

Bob Saget, 45, actor ("Full House"), host ("America's Funniest Home Videos"), born Philadelphia, PA, May 17, 1956.

MAY 18 — FRIDAY
Day 138 — 227 Remaining

FONTEYN, MARGOT: BIRTH ANNIVERSARY. May 18, 1919. Born Margaret Hookman at Reigate, Surrey, England, Margot Fonteyn was a famed ballet dancer during the 30s and 40s. She died at Panama City, Panama, Feb 21, 1991.

HAITI: FLAG AND UNIVERSITY DAY. May 18. Public holiday.

INTERNATIONAL MUSEUM DAY. May 18. To pay tribute to museums of the world. "Museums are an important means of cultural exchange, enrichment of cultures and development of mutual understanding, cooperation and peace among people." Annually, May 18. Sponsor: International Council of Museums, Paris, France. For info: AAM/ICOM, 1575 Eye St NW, 4th Floor, Washington, DC 20005. Phone: (202) 289-1818. Fax: (202) 289-6578.

INTERNATIONAL PICKLE WEEK. May 18–28. To give national recognition to the world's most humorous vegetable. Sponsor: Pickle Packers International, Inc. For info: IPW, DHM Group, Inc, PO Box 767, Dept CC, Holmdel, NJ 07733-0767. Fax: (732) 946-3343.

MOUNT SAINT HELENS ERUPTION: ANNIVERSARY. May 18, 1980. A major eruption of Mount St. Helens volcano, in southwestern Washington, blew steam and ash more than 11 miles into the sky. This was the first major eruption of Mount St. Helens since 1857, though Mar 26, 1980, there had been a warning eruption of smaller magnitude. For more info visit Volcano World: volcano.und.nodak.edu.

★**NATIONAL DEFENSE TRANSPORTATION DAY.** May 18. Presidential Proclamation customarily issued as "National Defense Transportation Day and National Transportation Week." Issued each year for the third Friday in May since 1957. (PL85–32 of May 16, 1957.)

POPE JOHN PAUL II: BIRTHDAY. May 18, 1920. Karol Wojtyla, 264th pope of the Roman Catholic Church, born at Wadowice, Poland. Elected pope Oct 16, 1978. He was the first non-Italian to be elected pope in 456 years (since the election of Pope Adrian VI, in 1522) and the first Polish pope.

SCIENCE OLYMPIAD. May 18–19. University of Colorado, Colorado Springs, CO. A fun day for grades K–3 involves children in noncompetitive hands-on science experiences at the school or district level. For grades 4–6, teams compete at the district or regional level. For grades 6–9 and 9–12, competition takes place at the state and national level as well. For info: Science Olympiad, 5955 Little Pine Lane, Rochester, MI 48306. Phone: (248) 651-4013. Fax: (248) 651-7835.

TEACHER'S DAY IN FLORIDA. May 18. A ceremonial day on the third Friday in May.

VISIT YOUR RELATIVES DAY. May 18. A day to renew family ties and joys by visiting often-thought-of-seldom-seen relatives. Annually, May 18. For info: A.C. Moeller, Box 71, Clio, MI 48420-1042.

BIRTHDAYS TODAY

Karyn Bye, 30, Olympic ice hockey player, born River Falls, WI, May 18, 1971.

Debra (Debbie) Dadey, 42, author, with Marcia Thornton Jones (The Bailey School Kids series), born Morganfield, KY, May 18, 1959.

Irene Hunt, 94, author (*Across Five Aprils*), born Newton, IL, May 18, 1907.

Reginald Martinez (Reggie) Jackson, 55, Baseball Hall of Fame outfielder, born Wyncote, PA, May 18, 1946.

MAY 19 — SATURDAY
Day 139 — 226 Remaining

★**ARMED FORCES DAY.** May 19. Presidential Proclamation 5983, of May 17, 1989, covers the third Saturday in May in all succeeding years. Originally proclaimed as "Army Day" for Apr 6, beginning in 1936 (S.Con.Res. 30 of Apr 2, 1936). S.Con.Res. 5 of Mar 16, 1937, requested annual Apr 6 issuance, which was done through 1949. Always the third Saturday in May since 1950. Traditionally issued once by each Administration.

BOYS' CLUBS FOUNDED: 95th ANNIVERSARY. May 19, 1906. The Federated Boys' Clubs, which later became the Boys' Clubs of America, was founded.

MALCOLM X: BIRTH ANNIVERSARY. May 19, 1925. Black nationalist and civil rights activist Malcolm X was born Malcolm Little at Omaha, NE. While serving a prison term he resolved to transform his life. On his release in 1952 he changed his name to Malcolm X and worked for the Nation of Islam until he was suspended by Black Muslim leader Elijah Muhammed Dec 4, 1963. Malcolm X later made the pilgrimage to Mecca and became an orthodox Muslim. He was assassinated as he spoke to a meeting

	S	M	T	W	T	F	S
May			1	2	3	4	5
2001	6	7	8	9	10	11	12
	13	14	15	16	17	18	19
	20	21	22	23	24	25	26
	27	28	29	30	31		

at the Audubon Ballroom at New York, NY, Feb 21, 1965. For more info: *Malcolm X: By Any Means Necessary*, by Walter Dean Myers (Scholastic, 0-590-46484-1, $10.75 Gr. 6–9).

NATIONAL SAFE BOATING WEEK. May 19–25. Brings boating safety to the public's attention, decreases the number of boating fatalities and makes the waterways safer for all boaters. Sponsor: US Coast Guard. For info: Jo Calkin, Commandant (G-OPB-2), US Coast Guard, 2100 Second St SW, Washington, DC 20593. Phone: (800) 368-5647.

★**NATIONAL SAFE BOATING WEEK.** May 19–25. Presidential Proclamation during May since 1995. From 1958 through 1977, issued for a week including July 4 (PL85–445 of June 4, 1958). From 1981 through 1994, issued for the first week in June (PL96–376 of Oct 3, 1980). From 1995, issued for a seven-day period ending on the Friday before Memorial Day. Not issued from 1978 through 1980.

TURKEY: YOUTH AND SPORTS DAY. May 19. Public holiday commemorating the beginning of a national movement for independence in 1919, led by Mustafa Kemal Ataturk.

TWENTY-SEVENTH AMENDMENT RATIFIED: ANNIVERSARY. May 19, 1992. The 27th amendment to the Constitution was ratified, prohibiting Congress from giving itself immediate pay raises.

BIRTHDAYS TODAY

Sarah Ellis, 49, author (*Back of Beyond: Stories of the Supernatural*), born Vancouver, British Columbia, Canada, May 19, 1952.

Tom Feelings, 68, author (*The Middle Passage: White Ships, Black Cargo*), born Brooklyn, NY, May 19, 1933.

Kevin Garnett, 25, basketball player, born Mauldin, SC, May 19, 1976.

Eric Lloyd, 15, actor (*Dunston Checks In, The Santa Clause*), born Glendale, CA, May 19, 1986.

MAY 20 — SUNDAY
Day 140 — 225 Remaining

CAMEROON: NATIONAL HOLIDAY. May 20. Republic of Cameroon. Commemorates declaration of the United Republic of Cameroon May 20, 1972. Prior to this, the country had been a federal republic with two states, Eastern Cameroon and Western Cameroon.

COUNCIL OF NICAEA I: ANNIVERSARY. May 20–Aug 25, 325. The first ecumenical council of Christian Church, called by Constantine I, first Christian emperor of the Roman Empire. Nearly 300 bishops are said to have attended this first of 21 ecumenical councils (latest, Vatican II, began Sept 11, 1962), which was held at Nicaea, in Asia Minor (today's Turkey). The council condemned Arianism (which denied the divinity of Christ), formulated the Nicene Creed and fixed the day of Easter—always on a Sunday.

ELIZA DOOLITTLE DAY. May 20. To honor Miss Doolittle (heroine of Bernard Shaw's *Pygmalion*) for demonstrating the importance and the advantage of speaking one's native language properly. For info: H.M. Chase, Doolittle Day Committee, 2460 Devonshire Rd, Ann Arbor, MI 48104-2706.

HOMESTEAD ACT: ANNIVERSARY. May 20, 1862. President Lincoln signed the Homestead Act, opening millions of acres of government-owned land in the West to settlers or "homesteaders," who had to reside on the land and cultivate it for five years.

LINDBERGH FLIGHT: ANNIVERSARY. May 20–21, 1927. Anniversary of the first solo trans-Atlantic flight. Captain Charles

Augustus Lindbergh, 25-year-old aviator, departed from muddy Roosevelt Field, Long Island, NY, alone at 7:52 AM, May 20, 1927, in a Ryan monoplane named *Spirit of St. Louis*. He landed at Le Bourget airfield, Paris, at 10:24 PM Paris time (5:24 PM, NY time), May 21, winning a $25,000 prize offered by Raymond Orteig for the first nonstop flight between New York City and Paris, France (3,600 miles). The "flying fool" as he had been dubbed by some doubters became "Lucky Lindy," an instant world hero. See also: "Lindbergh, Charles Augustus: Birth Anniversary" (Feb 4).

MADISON, DOLLY (DOROTHEA) DANDRIDGE PAYNE TODD: BIRTH ANNIVERSARY. May 20, 1768. Wife of James Madison, 4th president of the US, born at Guilford County, NC. Died at Washington, DC, July 12, 1849.

RURAL LIFE SUNDAY OR SOIL STEWARDSHIP SUNDAY. May 20. With an increase in ecological and environmental concerns, Rural Life Sunday emphasizes the concept that Earth belongs to God, who has granted humanity the use of it, along with the responsibility of caring for it wisely. Rural Life Sunday was first observed in 1929. The day is observed annually by churches of many Christian denominations and includes pulpit exchanges by rural and urban pastors. Under the auspices of the National Association of Soil and Water Conservation Districts, the week beginning with Rural Life Sunday is now widely observed as Soil Stewardship Week, with the Sunday itself alternatively termed Soil Stewardship Sunday. Traditionally, Rural Life Sunday is Rogation Sunday, the Sunday preceding Ascension Day.

WEIGHTS AND MEASURES DAY: ANNIVERSARY. May 20. Anniversary of international treaty, signed May 20, 1875, providing for the establishment of an International Bureau of Weights and Measures. The bureau was founded on international territory at Sevres, France.

BIRTHDAYS TODAY

Michael Crapo, 50, US Senator (R, Idaho), born Idaho Falls, May 20, 1951.

Mary Pope Osborne, 52, author (*One World, Many Religions*), born Fort Sill, OK, May 20, 1949.

David Wells, 38, baseball player, born Torrance, CA, May 20, 1963.

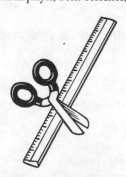

MAY 21 — MONDAY
Day 141 — 224 Remaining

AMERICAN RED CROSS: FOUNDING ANNIVERSARY. May 21, 1881. Commemorates the founding of the American Red Cross by Clara Barton, its first president. The Red Cross had been founded in Switzerland in 1864 by representatives from 16 European nations. The organization is a voluntary, not-for-profit organization governed and directed by volunteers and provides disaster relief at home and abroad. 1.1 million volunteers are involved in community services such as collecting and distributing donated blood and blood products, teaching health and safety classes and acting as a medium for emergency communication between Americans and their armed forces.

BUCKLE UP AMERICA! WEEK. May 21–28. An observance to remind Americans of the importance of wearing seat belts. For info: Office of Occupant Protection, Natl Highway Safety Administration, 400 Seventh St SW, Washington, DC 20590. Phone: (202) 366-9550.

CANADA: VICTORIA DAY. May 21. Commemorates the birth of Queen Victoria, May 24, 1819. Observed annually on the first Monday preceding May 25.

GEMINI, THE TWINS. May 21–June 20. In the astronomical/astrological zodiac, which divides the sun's apparent orbit into 12 segments, the period May 21–June 20 is traditionally identified as the sun sign period of Gemini, the Twins. The ruling planet is Mercury.

NATIONAL BACKYARD GAMES WEEK. May 21–28. Observance to celebrate the unofficial start of summer by fostering social interaction and family togetherness through backyard games. Get outside and be both physically and mentally stimulated, playing classic games of the past while discovering and creating new ways to be active and interact with neighbors and friends. For info: Frank Beres, Patch Products, PO Box 268, Beloit, WI 53511. Phone: (608) 362-6896. Fax: (608) 362-8178. E-mail: patch@patchproducts.com. Web: www.patchproducts.com.

SWITZERLAND: PACING THE BOUNDS. May 21. Liestal. Citizens set off at 8 AM and march along boundaries to the beating of drums and firing of pistols and muskets. Occasion for fetes. Annually, the Monday before Ascension Day.

BIRTHDAYS TODAY

Judge Reinhold, 45, actor (*The Santa Clause*), born Wilmington, DE, May 21, 1956.

Mr T, 49, actor (*Rocky III*, "The A-Team"), born Lawrence Tero or Tureaud, Chicago, IL, May 21, 1952.

MAY 22 — TUESDAY
Day 142 — 223 Remaining

LOBEL, ARNOLD: BIRTH ANNIVERSARY. May 22, 1933. Illustrator and author (the Frog and Toad series, Caldecott for *Fables*), born at Los Angeles, CA. Died Dec 4, 1987, at New York, NY.

"MISTER ROGERS' NEIGHBORHOOD" TV PREMIERE: ANNIVERSARY. May 22, 1967. Presbyterian minister Fred Rogers hosts this long-running PBS children's program. Puppets and human characters interact in the neighborhood of make-believe. Rogers plays the voices of many of the puppets and educates young viewers on a variety of important subjects. The human cast members include: Betty Aberlin, Joe Negri, David Newell, Don Brockett, Francois Clemmons, Audrey Roth, Elsie Neal and Yoshi Ito. More than 600 half-hour episodes of the program have aired.

MOON PHASE: NEW MOON. May 22. Moon enters New Moon phase at 10:46 PM, EDT.

NATIONAL GEOGRAPHY BEE: NATIONAL FINALS. May 22–23. National Geographic Society Headquarters, Washington, DC. The first place winner from each state-level competition, Apr 6, advances to the national level. Alex Trebek of "Jeopardy!" fame moderates the finals which are televised on PBS stations. Students compete for scholarships and prizes totaling more than $50,000. Est attendance: 400. For info: Natl Geography Bee, Natl Geographic Soc, 1145 17th St NW, Washington, DC 20036. Phone: (202) 857-7001. Web: www.nationalgeographic.com.

NATIONAL MARITIME DAY. May 22. Anniversary of departure for first steamship crossing of the Atlantic from Savannah, GA, to Liverpool, England, by the steamship *Savannah* in 1819.

★**NATIONAL MARITIME DAY.** May 22. Presidential Proclamation always issued for May 22 since 1933. (Pub Res No. 7 of May 20, 1933.)

SRI LANKA: NATIONAL HEROES DAY. May 22. Commemorates the struggle of the leaders of the National Independence Movement to liberate the country from colonial rule. Public holiday.

YEMEN: NATIONAL DAY: ANNIVERSARY. May 22. Public holiday. Commemorates the reunification of Yemen in 1990.

BIRTHDAYS TODAY

Ann Cusack, 40, actress (*A League of Their Own*, "The Jeff Foxworthy Show"), born Evanston, IL, May 22, 1961.

MAY 23 — WEDNESDAY
Day 143 — 222 Remaining

BROWN, MARGARET WISE: BIRTH ANNIVERSARY. May 23, 1910. Children's author, born at Brooklyn, NY. Brown wrote *Goodnight Moon* and *The Runaway Bunny*. She died at Nice, France, Nov 13, 1952.

DEBORAH SAMSON DAY IN MASSACHUSETTS. May 23. Proclaimed annually by the governor to commemorate Deborah Samson, a Massachusetts schoolteacher who outfitted herself in men's clothing and fought in the American Revolution.

MESMER, FRIEDRICH ANTON: BIRTH ANNIVERSARY. May 23, 1734. German physician after whom Mesmerism was named. Magnetism and hypnotism were used by him in treating disease. Born at Iznang, Swabia, Germany, he died Mar 5, 1815, at Meersburg, Swabia, Germany.

NEW YORK PUBLIC LIBRARY: ANNIVERSARY. May 23, 1895. New York's then-governor Samuel J. Tilden was the driving force that resulted in the combining of the private Astor and Lenox libraries with a $2 million endowment and 15,000 volumes from the Tilden Trust to become the New York Public Library.

O'DELL, SCOTT: BIRTH ANNIVERSARY. May 23, 1898. Born at Los Angeles, CA. Scott O'Dell won the Newbery Medal in 1961 for his book *Island of the Blue Dolphins*. He published more than 26 children's books, including *The Black Pearl*. In 1972, O'Dell was awarded the Hans Christian Andersen International Award for lifetime achievement. He died at Santa Monica, CA, Oct 15, 1989.

SOUTH CAROLINA RATIFIES CONSTITUTION: ANNIVERSARY. May 23, 1788. By a vote of 149 to 73, South Carolina became the eighth state to ratify the Constitution.

SWEDEN: LINNAEUS DAY. May 23. Stenbrohult. Commemorates the birth in 1707, of Carolus Linnaeus (Carl von Linne), Swedish naturalist who died at Uppsala, Sweden, Jan 10, 1778.

		S	M	T	W	T	F	S
May				1	2	3	4	5
2001		6	7	8	9	10	11	12
		13	14	15	16	17	18	19
		20	21	22	23	24	25	26
		27	28	29	30	31		

BIRTHDAYS TODAY

Susan Cooper, 66, author (Newbery for *The Grey King*), born Buckinghamshire, England, May 23, 1935.
Jewel, 27, singer, born Jewel Kilcher, Payson, UT, May 23, 1974.

MAY 24 — THURSDAY
Day 144 — 221 Remaining

ASCENSION DAY. May 24. Commemorates Christ's ascension into heaven. Observed since AD 68. Ascension Day is the 40th day after the Resurrection, counting Easter as the first day.

BASEBALL FIRST PLAYED UNDER LIGHTS: ANNIVERSARY. May 24, 1935. The Cincinnati Reds defeated the Philadelphia Phillies by a score of 2–1, as more than 20,000 fans enjoyed the first night baseball game in the major leagues. The game was played at Crosley Field, Cincinnati, OH.

BELIZE: COMMONWEALTH DAY. May 24. Public holiday.

BROOKLYN BRIDGE OPENED: ANNIVERSARY. May 24, 1883. Nearly 14 years in construction, the $16 million Brooklyn Bridge over the East River connecting Manhattan and Brooklyn opened. Designed by John A. Roebling, the steel suspension bridge has a span of 1,595 feet. For more info: *The Brooklyn Bridge*, by Elaine Pascoe (Blackbirch, 1-56711-173-4, $17.95 Gr. 4–6).

BULGARIA: ENLIGHTENMENT AND CULTURE DAY. May 24. National holiday celebrated by schoolchildren, students, people of science and art.

ERITREA: INDEPENDENCE DAY. May 24. National Day. Gained independence from Ethiopia in 1993 after 30-year civil war.

LEUTZE, EMANUEL: BIRTH ANNIVERSARY. May 24, 1816. Itinerant painter, born at Wurttemberg, Germany, who came to the US when he was nine years old and began painting by age 15. He painted some of the most famous of American works, such as *Washington Crossing the Delaware, Washington Rallying the Troops at Monmouth* and *Columbus Before the Queen*. Died July 18, 1868, at Washington, DC.

MORSE OPENS FIRST US TELEGRAPH LINE: ANNIVERSARY. May 24, 1844. The first US telegraph line was formally opened between Baltimore, MD, and Washington, DC. Samuel F.B. Morse sent the first officially telegraphed words "What hath God wrought?" from the Capitol building to Baltimore. Earlier messages had been sent along the historic line during testing, and one, sent May 1, contained the news that Henry Clay had been nominated as president by the Whig party, from a meeting in Baltimore. This message reached Washington one hour prior to a train carrying the same news.

ORTHODOX ASCENSION DAY. May 24. Observed by Eastern Orthodox Churches.

RABI'I: THE MONTH OF THE MIGRATION. May 24. Begins on Islamic calendar date Rabi'I 1, 1422. The month of the migration or Hegira of the Prophet Muhammad from Mecca to Medina in AD 622, the event that was used as the starting year of the

Islamic era. Different methods for "anticipating" the visibility of the new moon crescent at Mecca are used by different Muslim groups. US date may vary.

BIRTHDAYS TODAY

Diane DeGroat, 54, illustrator and author (*Happy Birthday to You, You Belong in the Zoo*), born Newton, NJ, May 24, 1947.

John Rowland, 44, Governor of Connecticut (R), born Waterbury, CT, May 24, 1957.

MAY 25 — FRIDAY
Day 145 — 220 Remaining

AFRICAN FREEDOM DAY: ANNIVERSARY. May 25. Public holiday in Chad, Zambia, Zimbabwe and some other African states. Members of the Organization for African Unity (formed May 25, 1963) commemorate their independence from colonial rule with sports contests, political rallies and tribal dances.

ARGENTINA: NATIONAL HOLIDAY. May 25. Commemoration of the declaration of independence of Argentina in 1810.

CONSTITUTIONAL CONVENTION: ANNIVERSARY. May 25, 1787. At Philadelphia, PA, the delegates from seven states, forming a quorum, opened the Constitutional Convention, which had been proposed by the Annapolis Convention Sept 11–14, 1786. Among those who were in attendance: George Washington, Benjamin Franklin, James Madison, Alexander Hamilton and Elbridge Gerry.

JORDAN: INDEPENDENCE DAY: 55th ANNIVERSARY. May 25. National holiday. Commemorates treaty in 1946, proclaiming autonomy (from Britain) and establishing monarchy.

NATIONAL MISSING CHILDREN'S DAY. May 25. To promote awareness of the problem of missing children, to offer a forum for change and to offer safety information for children in school and communities. Annually, May 25. For info: Child Find of America, Inc, PO Box 277, New Paltz, NY 12561-0277. Phone: (914) 255-1848. Natl toll-free hotline phone numbers: (800) I-AM-LOST or (800) A-WAY-OUT.

NATIONAL TAP DANCE DAY. May 25. To celebrate this unique American art form that represents a fusion of African and European cultures and to transmit tap to succeeding generations through documentation and archival and performance support. Held on the anniversary of the birth of Bill "Bojangles" Robinson to honor his outstanding contribution to the art of tap dancing on stage and in films through the unification of diverse stylistic and racial elements.

POETRY DAY IN FLORIDA. May 25. In 1947 the Legislature decreed this day to be Poetry Day in all the public schools of Florida.

ROBINSON, BILL "BOJANGLES": BIRTH ANNIVERSARY. May 25, 1878. Born at Richmond, VA, the grandson of a slave, Robinson is considered one of the greatest tap dancers. He is best known for a routine in which he tap-danced up and down a staircase with Shirley Temple. He taught Gene Kelly, Sammy Davis, Jr and others. He died at New York, NY, Nov 25, 1949.

BIRTHDAYS TODAY

Martha Alexander, 81, author and illustrator (*Nobody Asked Me If I Wanted a Baby Sister*), born Augusta, GA, May 25, 1920.

Ann McGovern, 71, author (*Too Much Noise*), born New York, NY, May 25, 1930.

Gordon Smith, 49, US Senator (R, Oregon), born Pendleton, OR, May 25, 1952.

Sheryl Swoopes, 30, basketball player, US Olympic Basketball Team, born Brownfield, TX, May 25, 1971.

Joyce Carol Thomas, 63, author (*Marked by Fire*), born Ponca City, OK, May 25, 1938.

MAY 26 — SATURDAY
Day 146 — 219 Remaining

GEORGIA: INDEPENDENCE RESTORATION DAY: 10th ANNIVERSARY. May 26. National Day. Commemorates independence from the Soviet Union in 1991.

BIRTHDAYS TODAY

Brent Musburger, 62, sportscaster, born Portland, OR, May 26, 1939.

Paul E. Patton, 64, Governor of Kentucky (D), born Fallsburg, KY, May 26, 1937.

Sally Kristen Ride, 50, one of the first seven women in the US astronaut program and the first American woman in space, born Encino, CA, May 26, 1951.

MAY 27 — SUNDAY
Day 147 — 218 Remaining

BLOOMER, AMELIA JENKS: BIRTH ANNIVERSARY. May 27, 1818. American social reformer and women's rights advocate, born at Homer, NY. Her name is remembered especially because of her work for more sensible dress for women and her recommendation of a costume that had been introduced about 1849 by Elizabeth Smith Miller but came to be known as the "Bloomer Costume" or "Bloomers." Amelia Bloomer died at Council Bluffs, IA, Dec 30, 1894. *See* Curriculum Connection.

CARSON, RACHEL (LOUISE): BIRTH ANNIVERSARY. May 27, 1907. American scientist and author, born at Springdale, PA. She was the author of *The Sea Around Us* and *Silent Spring* (1962), a book that provoked widespread controversy over the use of pesticides and contributed to the beginning of the environmental movement. She died Apr 14, 1964, at Silver Spring, MD. For more info: *Rachel Carson: A Wonder of Nature*, by Catherine Reef (Twenty First Century, 0-941477-38-X, $14.95 Gr. 2–5).

CELLOPHANE TAPE PATENTED: ANNIVERSARY. May 27, 1930. Richard Gurley Drew received a patent for his adhesive tape, later manufactured by 3M as Scotch tape.

DUNCAN, ISADORA: BIRTH ANNIVERSARY. May 27, 1878. American-born interpretive dancer who revolutionized the entire concept of dance. Bare-footed, freedom-loving, liberated woman and rebel against tradition, she experienced worldwide professional success and profound personal tragedy (her two children drowned, her marriage failed and she met a bizarre death when the long scarf she was wearing caught in a wheel of the open car in which she was riding, strangling her). Born at San Francisco, CA, she died at Nice, France, Sept 14, 1927.

GOLDEN GATE BRIDGE OPENED: ANNIVERSARY. May 27, 1937. More than 200,000 people crossed San Francisco's Golden Gate Bridge on its first day.

MAY 27
AMELIA JENKS BLOOMER'S BIRTHDAY

Amelia Jenks was born in Homer, New York, in 1818. An educated woman, she worked as a teacher before she married David Bloomer, a newspaper editor from Seneca Falls, New York. The couple moved to Seneca Falls, and several years later, Amelia altered the course of women's fashion.

Seneca Falls was the site of the 1848 Women's Rights Convention. Prominent spokeswoman Elizabeth Cady Stanton lived there. Stanton's quest for women's rights influenced Amelia's life. In 1848, when the Ladies' Temperance Society was formed, Amelia served as one of its officers. She began the journal *The Lily*, which was the first newspaper edited and run entirely by a woman. *The Lily* informed its readers on women's issues and the suffrage movement. Amelia believed in women's rights and served as the town's deputy postmaster to demonstrate that a woman had the right to fill any position as long as she could serve it capably.

While she worked tirelessly for suffrage, the issue that pushed Amelia into the public eye was an article she wrote about women's clothing. Amelia loved a "new" French outfit worn by a visiting cousin. A short skirt worn over baggy pantaloons offered women freedom from the heavy, constricting long dresses they normally wore. Amelia's article was an overnight sensation and the startling, new garment rocked the nation. Some women's rights advocates and women athletes began wearing the garment and received mixed public reaction. Because Amelia wore and publicly supported the outfit, people dubbed it "bloomers."

Students can observe Amelia's birthday in several ways. First, they can examine the issue of women's rights. In particular, focus on how a woman was discouraged from owning and operating certain businesses and how she was regarded as her husband's property. Discuss voting rights and the amendment that granted women the right to vote. Students can make time lines to chronicle the suffrage movement and its main spokespeople.

In a lighter vein, students can explore fashion and how it has changed over time. One exercise might be to imagine that bloomers (actually the pants that followed them) had not become an accepted mode of dress. How might the activities girls participate in today be different? Students could design and draw what they think future fashions will be like.

A look at "foreign" fashions is an interesting way to bring multiculturalism into the classroom. Many cultures have ceremonial dress that reflects a variety of artistic styles. Students may enjoy looking at unusual fashion trends and fads, too. Frequently these relate to the subject of beauty. Some suggestions are corsets, the 19th-century European custom of surgically removing a rib for slimmer waists, the custom of foot binding, the elaborate hairstyles of the 1700s, neck rings worn by certain African women, tattoos and the modern American fascination with body piercing.

Amelia's birthday might be designated as a classroom "dress crazy day."

Literature connections include: *You Forgot Your Skirt, Amelia Bloomer!*, by Shana Corey (Scholastic, 0-439-07819-9, $16.95 Gr. 3–6); *Bloomers!*, by Rhoda Blumberg (Simon & Schuster, 0-689-80455-5, $5.95 Gr. K–3); *Dressed for the Occasion: What Americans Wore 1620–1970*, by Brandon Miller (Lerner, 0-8225-1738-8, $16.95 Gr. 6–9); and *Ballot Box Battle*, by Emily McCully (Knopf, 0-679-87938-2, $17. Gr. 1–4). There are also many individual biographies about prominent leaders in the suffrage movement.

HICKOCK, WILD BILL: BIRTH ANNIVERSARY. May 27, 1837. American frontiersman, legendary marksman, lawman, army scout and gambler, he was born at Troy Grove, IL, and died Aug 2, 1876, at Deadwood, SD. Hickock's end came when he was shot dead at a poker table by a drunk in the Number Ten saloon.

HUMPHREY, HUBERT HORATIO: 90th BIRTH ANNIVERSARY. May 27, 1911. Born at Wallace, SD, he served as 38th vice president of the US and ran for president in 1968 but lost narrowly to Richard Nixon. Humphrey died at Waverly, MN, Jan 13, 1978.

ITALY: PALIO DEI BALESTRIERI. May 27. Gubbio. The last Sunday in May is set aside for a medieval crossbow contest between Gubbio and Sansepolcro; medieval costumes, arms.

ITALY: WEDDING OF THE SEA. May 27. Venice. The feast of the Ascension is the occasion of the ceremony recalling the "Wedding of the Sea" performed by Venice's Doge, who cast his ring into the sea from the ceremonial ship known as the *Bucintoro*, to symbolize eternal dominion. Annually, on the Sunday following Ascension.

BIRTHDAYS TODAY

Christopher J. Dodd, 57, US Senator (D, Connecticut), born Willimantic, CT, May 27, 1944.

Antonio Freeman, 29, football player, born Baltimore, MD, May 27, 1972.

Frank Thomas, 33, baseball player, born Columbus, GA, May 27, 1968.

MAY 28 — MONDAY
Day 148 — 217 Remaining

AZERBAIJAN: DAY OF THE REPUBLIC. May 28. Public holiday. Commemorates the declaration of the Azerbaijan Democratic Republic in 1918.

CONFEDERATE MEMORIAL DAY IN VIRGINIA. May 28. Annually, the last Monday in May. See also Apr 26, Apr 30, May 10 and June 3 for observations in other states.

FLEMING, IAN: BIRTH ANNIVERSARY. May 28, 1908. Author of *Chitty Chitty Bang Bang*, which was made into a popular movie for children, as well as the James Bond series of books. Born at London, England, he died at Canterbury, England, Aug 12, 1964.

MEMORIAL DAY. May 28. Legal public holiday. Also known as Decoration Day because of the tradition of decorating the graves of servicemen. An occasion for honoring those who have died in battle. Observance dates from Civil War years in US: first documented observance at Waterloo, NY, May 5, 1865. See also: "Confederate Memorial Day" (Apr 26, Apr 30, May 10, May 28 and June 3).

★**MEMORIAL DAY, PRAYER FOR PEACE.** May 28. Presidential Proclamation issued each year since 1948. PL81–512 of May 11, 1950, asks President to proclaim annually this day as a day of prayer for permanent peace. PL90–363 of June 28, 1968, requires that beginning in 1971 it will be observed the last Monday in May. Often titled "Prayer for Peace Memorial Day," and traditionally requests the flying of the flag at half-staff "for the customary forenoon period."

SHAVUOT or FEAST OF WEEKS. May 28. Jewish Pentecost holy day. Hebrew date, Sivan 6, 5761. Celebrates giving of Torah (the Law) to Moses on Mount Sinai.

SIERRA CLUB FOUNDED: ANNIVERSARY. May 28, 1892. Founded by famed naturalist John Muir, the Sierra Club promotes conservation of the natural environment by influencing public policy. It has been especially important in the founding of and protection of our national parks. For info: Sierra Club, 85 Second St, 2nd Floor, San Francisco, CA 94105-3441. Phone: (415) 977-5500.

THORPE, JAMES FRANCIS (JIM): BIRTH ANNIVERSARY. May 28, 1888. This distinguished Native American athlete was the winner of pentathlon and decathlon events at the 1912 Olympic Games and a professional baseball and football player. Born near Prague, OK, he died at Lomita, CA, Mar 28, 1953.

BIRTHDAYS TODAY

Glen Rice, 34, basketball player, born Flint, MI, May 28, 1967.

MAY 29 — TUESDAY
Day 149 — 216 Remaining

AMNESTY ISSUED FOR SOUTHERN REBELS: ANNIVERSARY. May 29, 1865. President Andrew Johnson issued a proclamation giving a general amnesty to all who participated in the rebellion against the US. High ranking members of the Confederate government and military and those who owned more than $20,000 worth of property were excepted and had to apply individually to the President for a pardon. Once an oath of allegiance was taken, all former property rights, except those in slaves, were returned to the former owners.

CONSTANTINOPLE FELL TO THE TURKS: ANNIVERSARY. May 29, 1453. The city of Constantinople was captured by the Turks, who renamed it Istanbul (although the name wasn't officially changed until 1930). This conquest marked the end of the Byzantine Empire; the city became the capital of the Ottoman Empire.

HENRY, PATRICK: BIRTH ANNIVERSARY. May 29, 1736. American revolutionary leader and orator, born at Studley, VA, and died near Brookneal, VA, June 6, 1799. Especially remembered for his speech (Mar 23, 1775) for arming the Virginia militia, at St. Johns Church, Richmond, VA, when he declared: "I know not what course others may take, but as for me, give me liberty or give me death."

KENNEDY, JOHN FITZGERALD: BIRTH ANNIVERSARY. May 29, 1917. The 35th president of the US, born at Brookline, MA. Kennedy was the youngest man ever elected to the presidency, the first Roman Catholic and the first president to have served in the US Navy. He was assassinated while riding in an open automobile, at Dallas, TX, Nov 22, 1963. (Accused assassin Lee Harvey Oswald was killed at the Dallas police station by a gunman, Jack Ruby, two days later.) He was the fourth US president to be killed by an assassin, and the second to be buried at Arlington National Cemetery (the first was William Howard Taft). For more info: www.cs.umb.edu/jfklibrary/index.htm.

MOON PHASE: FIRST QUARTER. May 29. Moon enters First Quarter phase at 6:09 PM, EDT.

MOUNT EVEREST SUMMIT REACHED: ANNIVERSARY. May 29, 1953. New Zealand explorer Sir Edmund Hillary and Tensing Norgay, a Sherpa guide, became the first team to reach the summit of Mount Everest, the world's highest mountain.

RHODE ISLAND RATIFIES CONSTITUTION: ANNIVERSARY. May 29. Became the 13th state to ratify the Constitution in 1790.

VIRGINIA PLAN PROPOSED: ANNIVERSARY. May 29, 1787. Just five days after the Constitutional Convention met at Philadelphia, PA, the "Virginia Plan" was proposed. It called for establishment of a government consisting of a legislature with two houses, an executive (chosen by the legislature) and a judicial branch.

WISCONSIN: ADMISSION DAY: ANNIVERSARY. May 29, 1848. Became 30th state in 1848.

BIRTHDAYS TODAY

Brock Cole, 63, author and illustrator (*Alpha and the Dirty Baby*), born Charlotte, MI, May 29, 1938.

Rupert Everett, 42, actor (*Inspector Gadget*), born Norfolk, England, May 29, 1959.

Blake Foster, 16, actor (*Turbo: A Power Rangers Movie*, "Power Rangers Turbo"), born Northridge, CA, May 29, 1985.

MAY 30 — WEDNESDAY
Day 150 — 215 Remaining

CROATIA: NATIONAL DAY. May 30. Public holiday commemorating statehood in 1990.

FIRST AMERICAN DAILY NEWSPAPER PUBLISHED: ANNIVERSARY. May 30, 1783. *The Pennsylvania Evening Post* became the first daily newspaper published in the US. The paper was published at Philadelphia, PA, by Benjamin Towne.

LINCOLN MEMORIAL DEDICATION: ANNIVERSARY. May 30, 1922. The memorial is made of marble from Colorado and Tennessee and limestone from Indiana. It stands in West Potomac Park at Washington, DC. The outside columns are Doric, the inside, Ionic. The Memorial was designed by architect Henry Bacon and its cornerstone was laid in 1915. A skylight lets light into the interiors where the compelling statue "Seated Lincoln," by sculptor Daniel Chester French, is situated.

NATIONAL SPELLING BEE FINALS. May 30–31. Washington, DC. Newspapers and other sponsors across the country send 245–255 youngsters to the finals at Washington, DC. Annually, Wednesday and Thursday of Memorial Day week. Est attendance: 1,000. For info: Dir, Natl Spelling Bee, Scripps-Howard, PO Box 5380, Cincinnati, OH 45201. Phone: (513) 977-3040.

SAINT JOAN OF ARC: FEAST DAY. May 30. French heroine and martyr, known as the Maid of Orleans, led the French against the English invading army. She was captured, found guilty of heresy and burned at the stake in 1431 (at age 19). Her innocence was declared in 1456 and she was canonized in 1920.

SPACE MILESTONE: *MARINER 9* (US): 30th ANNIVERSARY. May 30, 1971. Unmanned spacecraft was launched, entering Martian orbit the following Nov 13. The craft relayed temperature and gravitational fields and sent back spectacular photographs of both the surface of Mars and of her two moons. It was the first spacecraft to orbit another planet.

TRINIDAD: INDIAN ARRIVAL DAY. May 30. Port of Spain. Public holiday. About 40 percent of Trinidad's population is descended from immigrants who were brought from India by the British in the 1840s.

Blake Bashoff, 20, actor (*The New Swiss Family Robinson*), born Philadelphia, PA, May 30, 1981.

Omri Katz, 25, actor ("Eerie, Indiana"), born Los Angeles, CA, May 30, 1976.

Trey Parker, 29, director, creator ("South Park"), born Auburn, AL, May 30, 1972.

Manuel "Manny" Ramirez, 29, baseball player, born Santo Domingo, Dominican Republic, May 30, 1972.

MAY 31 — THURSDAY
Day 151 — 214 Remaining

COPYRIGHT LAW PASSED: ANNIVERSARY. May 31, 1790. President George Washington signed the first US copyright law. It gave protection for 14 years to books written by US citizens. In 1891, the law was extended to cover books by foreign authors as well.

JOHNSTOWN FLOOD: ANNIVERSARY. May 31, 1889. Heavy rains caused the Connemaugh River Dam to burst. At nearby Johnstown, PA, the resulting flood killed more than 2,300 persons and destroyed the homes of thousands more. Nearly 800 unidentified drowning victims were buried in a common grave at Johnstown's Grandview Cemetery. So devastating was the flood and so widespread the sorrow for its victims that "Johnstown Flood" entered the language as a phrase to describe a disastrous event. The valley city of Johnstown, in the Allegheny Mountains, has been damaged repeatedly by floods. Floods in 1936 (25 deaths) and 1977 (85 deaths) were the next most destructive.

WHITMAN, WALT: BIRTH ANNIVERSARY. May 31, 1819. Poet and journalist, born at West Hills, Long Island, NY. Whitman's best known work, *Leaves of Grass* (1855), is a classic of American poetry. His poems celebrated all of modern life, including subjects that were considered taboo at the time. He died Mar 26, 1892, at Camden, NJ.

WORLD NO-TOBACCO DAY. May 31. Intended to discourage tobacco users from consuming tobacco and to encourage governments, communities, groups and individuals to become aware of the challenge and to take action. Annually, May 31. For info: World No-Tobacco Day, American Assn for World Health, 1825 K St NW, Ste 1208, Washington, DC 20006. Phone: (202) 466-5883. Fax: (202) 466-5896. E-mail: aawhstaff@aol.com. Web: www.aawhworldhealth.org.

Clint Eastwood, 71, actor, director (Oscar for *Unforgiven*), born San Francisco, CA, May 31, 1930.

Kenny Lofton, 34, baseball player, born East Chicago, IN, May 31, 1967.

Harry Mazer, 76, author (*The Wild Kid*), born New York, NY, May 31, 1925.

JUNE 1 — FRIDAY

Day 152 — 213 Remaining

ATLANTIC, CARIBBEAN AND GULF HURRICANE SEA-SON. June 1–Nov 30. For info: US Dept of Commerce, Natl Oceanic and Atmospheric Admin, Rockville, MD 20852. Web: www.nws.noaa.gov.

BAHAMAS: LABOR DAY. June 1. Public holiday. First Friday in June celebrated with parades, displays and picnics.

CANADA: YUKON INTERNATIONAL STORYTELLING FESTIVAL. June 1–3. Whitehorse, Yukon. Storytellers from all over Canada and abroad. Est attendance: 5,000. For info: Yukon Intl Storytelling Fest, PO Box 5029, Whitehorse, Yukon, Canada Y1A 4S2. Phone: (867) 633-7550. E-mail: yukonstory@yknet.yk.ca. Web: www.yukonweb.com/special/storytelling/.

CANCER FROM THE SUN MONTH. June 1–30. To promote education and awareness of the dangers of skin cancer from too much exposure to the sun. Kit of materials available for $15 from this nonprofit organization. For info: Frederick Mayer, Pres, Pharmacy Council on Dermatology (PCD), 101 Lucas Valley Rd, #210, San Rafael, CA 94903. Phone: (415) 479-8628. Fax: (415) 479-8608. E-mail: ppsi@aol.com.

CHILDREN'S AWARENESS MONTH. June 1–30. A monthlong celebration of being aware of America's children in our everyday lives and communities while lovingly remembering all of America's children who we have lost through violence and violent deaths in our nation. These could have been our child or grandchild. We choose to remember the living during the month of June. For info: Judith Natale, CEO & Founder, Natl Children & Family Awareness of America, Administrative Headquarters, 3060 Rt 405 Hwy, Muncy, PA 17756-8808. Phone: (888) MAA-DESK. E-mail: MaaJudith@aol.com.

CHINA, PEOPLE'S REPUBLIC OF: INTERNATIONAL CHILDREN'S DAY. June 1. Shanghai.

CNN DEBUTED: ANNIVERSARY. June 1, 1980. The Cable News Network, TV's first all-news service, went on the air.

FIREWORKS SAFETY MONTH. June 1–July 4. Activities during this month are designed to warn and educate parents and children about the dangers of playing with fireworks. Prevent

JUNE 1–30
FIREWORKS SAFETY MONTH

June may seem a bit early for talking about this, but children need to start thinking about the dangers presented by improper use of fireworks. Too many avoidable accidents occur on the Fourth of July.

Fireworks get their explosive power from gunpowder. The colorful fireworks that we see on the Fourth of July and other special occasions are a combination of gunpowder and chemicals such as sodium, copper and barium and strontium compounds. When mixed, they produce the dazzling yellow, blue, green and red color bursts. As a science-related writing project, have students contact the organization in your town responsible for arranging fireworks displays. Ask for the name of the manufacturer. Students can write to the company for information on how the umbrella shapes, twirly patterns and sizzlers are controlled.

Invite one of the people responsible for igniting your town's fireworks to visit your classroom or school and give a demonstration of the safety practices they use while setting off the fireworks. He or she can also discuss firecracker and sparkler danger, and if appropriate to your area, the illegality of possessing explosive devices. *Follow My Leader*, by James Garfield (Puffin, 0-14-036485-4, $4.99 Gr. 3–7) is a novel about a boy blinded by a firecracker. His adjustment to blindness and the use of a guide dog are particularly appealing.

Fireworks have been used as part of celebrations for hundreds of years. *The Firework maker's Daughter*, by Philip Pullman (Scholastic, 0-590-18719-8, $15.95 Gr. 3–7), set in ancient times, is an entertaining novel about Lila, a headstrong heroine, determined to become a Firework-maker, a title traditionally bestowed only on men.

Children can have fun making their own fireworks art displays. Bring in picture books with scratchboard illustrations (Brian Pinkney has done many) to provide examples of finished products. Students can use crayons to cover paper with colors, scribble over the colorful pattern with black crayon and scratch fireworks display patterns into the black crayon with an unbent paper clip or scissors edge. Three-dimensional fireworks can be made with curly ribbon, metallic streamers and other items. Hang them from the ceiling.

Talk about fireworks music. The *1812 Overture*, by Peter Tchaikovsky, written to commemorate the withdrawal of Napoleon I and his troops from Moscow, is a stirring piece that resounds with fireworks-like booms. Look for a recording that includes cannons. Play the piece while students are creating their fireworks art displays.

Blindness America will offer suggestions for safer ways to celebrate the Fourth of July. Materials that can easily be posted or distributed to the community will be provided. *See* Curriculum Connection. For info: Prevent Blindness America®, 500 E Remington Rd, Schaumburg, IL 60173. Phone: (800) 331-2020. Fax: (847) 843-8458. Web: www.preventblindness.org.

INTERNATIONAL VOLUNTEERS WEEK. June 1–7. To honor men and women throughout the world who serve as volunteers, rendering valuable service without compensation to the communities in which they live and to honor nonprofit organizations dedicated to making the world a better place in which to live. For complete info, send $4 to cover expense of printing, handling and postage. Annually, the first seven days of June. *See* Curriculum Connection. For info: Dr. Stanley Drake, Pres, Intl Soc of Friendship and Good Will, 40139 Palmetto Dr, Palmdale, CA 93551-3557.

JUNE 1–7
INTERNATIONAL VOLUNTEER WEEK

There are many women and men in our lives who selflessly donate their time and energy to making the world a better place. Students should honor these people and show their appreciation for their kindness. The very best way to honor them is by following their example and volunteering to help others. Although in some areas this is the end of the school year, students can still get involved.

Junior high and middle school students can contact the local shelter for homeless people. They often need volunteers to provide an evening meal for the shelter. Students can circulate a sign-up list for dishes. Cooked dishes can be brought to the school, where the meal can be loaded in one or two vehicles. The parent drivers and several students deliver the meal to the shelter. Students should call the shelter to find out the usual procedure, meal requirements and date(s) a meal may be needed.

Students might organize a group of volunteers who are willing to give up their recess time once a week and read aloud to children in a lower grade. Some students could tutor younger children or peers in learning math facts or the alphabet or be one-on-one listening ears for students who are struggling to read. Often another child's enthusiasm for a subject will ignite a response in an area where a teacher has not been able to succeed.

Senior citizens are often delighted to welcome children into nursing homes. Some schools now sponsor programs where a student is paired with a "grandparent" who resides in the home. Short weekly or monthly visits offer an opportunity to exchange news, ideas and talents between old and young.

Students could also volunteer to set up a clothing drive to donate used garments to local chapters of Goodwill or the Salvation Army. Think ahead to the holiday season. Students can begin to plan a toy, book or mitten drive to be held when the new school year begins. Organizations such as the Salvation Army welcome volunteer bell-ringers during the holiday season.

Invite representatives from the American Red Cross, the American Cancer Society and local hospitals to visit your school and discuss how children can become volunteers in their organizations.

Local historical and art museums welcome volunteers. See if they have opportunities for student volunteers. If not, why not organize one?

Students can honor members of the PTA or PTO who have worked all year to make their school a better place for learning. Rather than give them gifts, why not invite them to an assembly where students can give choral response presentations of thank-you poems or songs they have written in honor of the week. Teachers should make students aware of the benefits they received from the volunteer efforts of parent groups. Many students don't have the faintest idea of what a PTO does.

The United Nations has declared 2001 the International Year of Volunteers. For more information, go to www.un.org.

Above all, students should be encouraged to appreciate that giving their time to others will make the world a better place and them happier people. Also see National Youth Service Day (Apr 13).

June 2001

S	M	T	W	T	F	S
					1	2
3	4	5	6	7	8	9
10	11	12	13	14	15	16
17	18	19	20	21	22	23
24	25	26	27	28	29	30

JUNE IS TURKEY LOVERS' MONTH. June 1–30. A monthlong campaign to promote awareness and increase turkey consumption at a nonholiday time. Annually, the month of June. For info: Natl Turkey Federation, 1225 New York Ave NW, Ste 400, Washington, DC 20005. Phone: (202) 898-0100. Fax: (202) 898-0203. E-mail: info@turkeyfed.org. Web: www.eatturkey.com.

KENTUCKY: ADMISSION DAY: ANNIVERSARY. June 1. Became 15th state in 1792.

KENYA: MADARAKA DAY. June 1. Madaraka Day (Self-Rule Day) is observed as a national public holiday.

MARQUETTE, JACQUES: BIRTH ANNIVERSARY. June 1, 1637. Father Jacques Marquette (Père Marquette), Jesuit missionary-explorer of the Great Lakes region. Born at Laon, France, he died at Ludington, MI, May 18, 1675.

NATIONAL ACCORDION AWARENESS MONTH. June 1–30. To increase public awareness of this multicultural instrument and its influence and popularity in today's music. For info: All Things Accordion, 3551 Pierce St, San Francisco, CA 94123. Phone: (415) 440-0800. E-mail: bellows@ladyofspain.com.

NATIONAL BLESS-A-CHILD MONTH. June 1–30. Grassroots community activities to increase public awareness of the challenges facing at-risk children and promote volunteer as well as community involvement in their lives. For info: Donna Strout, Operation Blessing Intl, 977 Centerville Turnpike, Virginia Beach, VA 23463. Phone: (757) 226-2443. Fax: (757) 226-6183. E-mail: donna.strout@OB.ORG.

NATIONAL CANDY MONTH. June 1–30. Sponsored by *Confectioner Magazine* and manufacturers, wholesalers and retailers to promote candy as a fun food and enhance consumer awareness of products available in the US. Consumer celebrations include chocolate festivals, contests and information on candy making, decorating with candy and the history of chocolate and chewing and bubble gum. *See* Curriculum Connection. For info: Lisbeth Echeandia, Confectioner Magazine, PO Box 388, Savoy, TX 75479. Phone: (800) 826-8586. E-mail: confectioner@texoma.net.

NATIONAL FROZEN YOGURT MONTH. June 1–30. To inform the public of the benefits and colorful history of frozen yogurt, one of America's new favorite desserts. Annually, the month of June. For info: Stacy Duckett, TCBY, 1200 TCBY Tower, 425 W Capitol Ave, Little Rock, AR 72201. Phone: (501) 688-8229.

NATIONAL ROSE MONTH. June 1–30. To recognize American grown roses, our national floral emblem. America's favorite flower is grown in all 50 states and more than 1.2 billion fresh cut roses are sold at retail each year. For info: Mktg Dir, Roses Inc, Box 99, Haslett, MI 48840. Phone: (517) 339-9544. Web: www.rosesinc.org.

NATIONAL SAFETY MONTH. June 1–30. For info: American Soc of Safety Engineers, 1800 E Oakton, Des Plaines, IL 60018-2187. Phone: (847) 699-2929.

SAMOA: NATIONAL DAY. June 1. Holiday in the country formerly known as Western Samoa.

STAND FOR CHILDREN DAY. June 1. Stand for Children is a national organization that encourages individuals to improve children's lives. Its mission is to identify, train and connect local children's activists engaging in advocacy, awareness-raising and service initiatives as part of Children's Action Teams. Annually, June 1. On this day each year a special issue, such as quality child care, is highlighted. For more info: *Stand for Children*, by Marian Wright Edelman (Hyperion, 0-7868-0365-7, $15.95 Gr. 5–8). For info: Children's Defense Fund, Stand for Children, 1834 Con-

JUNE 1–30
NATIONAL CANDY MONTH

Candy lovers stand up and be counted. Sweeten student attitudes with curriculum treats. The United States is a nation of candy lovers. We eat an average of 20 pounds of candy a year per person. The kinds of candy we eat vary widely from chocolate bars, to chewy treats, to brittle nutty nibbles. You can have classroom candy fun—without the calories or cavities—in lots of ways.

Sugar is the primary component in most candies. In science, older students can experiment with melting sugar crystals. Use candy thermometers to record melting points and how they vary according to the addition of other ingredients. Experiments for younger students, that don't require heat, are easy, too. Teach the concepts of solutions, saturation and supersaturated liquids by stirring varying amounts of sugar into water. To supersaturate, students will have to use hot tap water. Students can read about making gum in *Bubble Gum*, by Arlene Erlbach (Lerner, 0-8225-2391-4, $14.95 Gr. 2–5).

Math problems don't seem like work when students are graphing candy preferences. Conduct surveys to find out which types of candy are most popular. Make bar graphs to record results. Survey for monthly candy consumption. Ask students to estimate on a scale of 1 to 10 how much candy they eat in a given month. October, December and the month Easter occurs in are likely to approach 10. Use line graphs to reflect consumption. Take the fear out of word problems with *The Candy Counting Book*, by Lisa McCourt (Bridgewater, 0-8167-6329-1, $15.95 Gr. K–3), a yummy collection of word problems. After learning how to decipher and solve these problems, students can write their own candy word problems. Barbara McGrath has written several M&M math counting books (Charlesbridge).

Each student can invent his or her own candy. List ingredients, test-market names in the classroom and at home, design a wrapper and create an advertising poster or commercial.

Writing fun could include a prompt like "Eating [an onion] would be fun if it tasted like [a candy apple] because [_____]." Write concrete poems in the shape of a favorite candy. The poem should reflect what makes the candy appealing.

Find "candy" music and play it in the room. An example is the music for the "Dance of the Sugar Plum Fairies" from the *Nutcracker* ballet by Tchaikovsky. There are several silly chewing gum "pop" songs, too.

For social studies students can research candies that were popular when their parents and grandparents were little. Investigate biographies of famous candy makers such as Milton S. Hershey. Students can research prices and sizes of candy bars from the past and compare them to today's bars.

Encourage students to look into the favorite candies of children in different countries. Visiting students and recent immigrants may have fond memories of candy from their birth country. Ask them to share candy names and descriptions. The Internet may be a source for the names of candy manufacturers in foreign countries.

necticut Ave NW, Washington, DC 20009. Phone: (800) 663-4032. Fax: (202) 234-0217. E-mail: tellstand@stand.org. Web: www.stand.org.

TENNESSEE: ADMISSION DAY: ANNIVERSARY. June 1. Became 16th state in 1796. Observed as a holiday in Tennessee.

BIRTHDAYS TODAY

Alexi Lalas, 31, soccer player, born Detroit, MI, June 1, 1970.

JUNE 2 — SATURDAY
Day 153 — 212 Remaining

BULGARIA: HRISTO BOTEV DAY: 125th ANNIVERSARY. June 2. Poet and national hero Hristro Botev fell fighting Turks, 1876.

ITALY: REPUBLIC DAY. June 2. National holiday. Commemorates referendum in 1946 in which republic status was selected instead of return to monarchy.

UNITED KINGDOM: CORONATION DAY. June 2. Commemorates the crowning of Queen Elizabeth II in 1953.

YELL "FUDGE" AT THE COBRAS IN NORTH AMERICA DAY. June 2. Anywhere north of the Panama Canal. In order to keep poisonous cobra snakes out of North America, all citizens are asked to go outdoors at noon, local time, and yell "Fudge." Fudge makes cobras gag and the mere mention of it makes them skeedaddle. Annually, June 2. [© 1999 by WH] For info: Thomas or Ruth Roy, Wellcat Holidays, 2418 Long Lane, Lebanon, PA 17046. Phone: (230) 332-4886. E-mail: wellcat@supernet.com. Web: www.wellcat.com.

BIRTHDAYS TODAY

Dana Carvey, 46, comedian, actor (*Wayne's World*, "Saturday Night Live"), born Missoula, MT, June 2, 1955.
Paul Galdone, 87, author (*The Little Red Hen*), born Budapest, June 2, 1914.
Norton Juster, 72, author (*The Phantom Tollbooth*), born Brooklyn, NY, June 2, 1929.
Jerry Mathers, 53, actor ("Leave It to Beaver"), born Sioux City, IA, June 2, 1948.

JUNE 3 — SUNDAY
Day 154 — 211 Remaining

CHIMBORAZO DAY. June 3. To bring the shape of the earth into focus by publicizing the fact that Mount Chimborazo, Ecuador, near the equator, pokes farther out into space than any other mountain on earth, including Mount Everest. (The distance from sea level at the equator to the center of the earth is 13 miles greater than the radius to sea level at the north pole. This means that New Orleans is about six miles further from the center of the earth than is Lake Itasca at the headwaters of the Mississippi, so the Mississippi flows uphill.) For info: Robert L. Birch, Puns Corps, Box 2364, Falls Church, VA 22042-0364. Phone: (703) 533-3668.

CONFEDERATE MEMORIAL DAY/JEFFERSON DAVIS DAY IN KENTUCKY. June 3. Commemorated on the birthday of Jefferson Davis.

DAVIS, JEFFERSON: BIRTH ANNIVERSARY. June 3, 1808. American statesman, US senator, only president of the Confederate States of America. Imprisoned May 10, 1865–May 13, 1867, but never brought to trial, deprived of rights of citizenship after the Civil War. Davis was born at Todd County, KY, and died at New Orleans, LA, Dec 6, 1889. His citizenship was restored, posthumously, Oct 17, 1978, when President Carter signed an Amnesty Bill. This bill, he said, "officially completes the long process of reconciliation that has reunited our people following the tragic conflict between the states." Davis's birth anniversary is observed in Florida, Kentucky and South Carolina on this day, in Alabama on the first Monday in June and in Mississippi on the last Monday in May. Davis's birth anniversary is observed as Confederate Memorial Day in Kentucky and Tennessee.

DREW, CHARLES RICHARD: BIRTH ANNIVERSARY. June 3, 1904. African American physician who discovered how to store blood plasma and who organized the blood bank system in the US and UK during WWII. Born at Washington, DC, he was killed in an automobile accident near Burlington, NC, Apr 1, 1950. For more info: *Charles Drew: A Life-Saving Doctor*, by Miles Shapiro (Raintree, 0-8172-4403-4, $18.98 Gr. 5–12).

FIRST WOMAN RABBI IN US: ANNIVERSARY. June 3, 1972. Sally Jan Priesand was ordained the first woman rabbi in the US. She became assistant rabbi at the Stephen Wise Free Synagogue, New York City, Aug 1, 1972.

HOBART, GARRET AUGUSTUS: BIRTH ANNIVERSARY. June 3, 1844. The 24th vice president of the US (1897–99), born at Long Branch, NJ. Died at Paterson, NJ, Nov 21, 1899.

JAPAN: DAY OF THE RICE GOD. June 3. Chiyoda. Annual rice-transplanting festival observed on first Sunday in June. Centuries-old rural folk ritual revived in 1930s and celebrated with colorful costumes, parades, music, dancing and prayers to the Shinto rice god Wbai-sama.

ORTHODOX PENTECOST. June 3. Observed by Eastern Orthodox churches.

PENTECOST. June 3. The Christian feast of Pentecost commemorates descent of the Holy Spirit unto the Apostles, 50 days after Easter. Observed on the seventh Sunday after Easter. Recognized since the third century. See also: "Whitsunday" (June 3).

★ **SMALL BUSINESS WEEK.** June 3–9. To honor the 22 million small businesses in the US. Annually, the first full week in June. For info: Small Business Administration, Info Services, 409 3rd St SW, 7th Floor, Washington, DC 20416. Phone: (202) 205-6606 or (202) 205-6531. Web: www.sba.gov.

June 2001	S	M	T	W	T	F	S
						1	2
	3	4	5	6	7	8	9
	10	11	12	13	14	15	16
	17	18	19	20	21	22	23
	24	25	26	27	28	29	30

SPACE MILESTONE: *GEMINI 4* (US). June 3, 1965. James McDivitt and Edward White made 66 orbits of Earth. White took the first space walk by an American and maneuvered 20 minutes outside the capsule.

TEACHER'S DAY IN MASSACHUSETTS. June 3. Proclaimed annually by the governor for the first Sunday in June.

WHITSUNDAY. June 3. Whitsunday, the seventh Sunday after Easter, is a popular time for baptism. "White Sunday" is named for the white garments formerly worn by the candidates for baptism and occurs at the Christian feast of Pentecost. See also: "Pentecost" (June 3).

BIRTHDAYS TODAY

Margaret Cosgrove, 75, author and illustrator (*Wonders of the Tree World*), born Sylvania, OH, June 3, 1926.

Anita Lobel, 67, author and illustrator (*Away From Home*), born Krakow, Poland, June 3, 1934.

JUNE 4 — MONDAY
Day 155 — 210 Remaining

CHINA: TIANANMEN SQUARE MASSACRE: ANNIVERSARY. June 4, 1989. After almost a month and a half of student demonstrations for democracy, the Chinese government ordered its troops to open fire on the unarmed protestors at Tiananmen Square at Beijing. The demonstrations began Apr 18 as several thousand students marched to mourn the death of Hu Yaobang, a pro-reform leader within the Chinese government. A ban was imposed on such demonstrations; Apr 22, 100,000 gathered in Tiananmen Square in defiance of the ban. On May 13, 2,000 of the students began a hunger strike and May 20, the government imposed martial law and began to bring in troops. On June 2, the demonstrators turned back an advance of unarmed troops in the first clash with the People's Army. Under the cover of darkness, early June 4, troops opened fire on the assembled crowds and armored personnel carriers rolled into the square crushing many of the students as they lay sleeping in their tents. Although the government claimed that few died in the attack, estimates range from several hundred to several thousand casualties. In the following months thousands of demonstrators were rounded up and jailed.

FINLAND: FLAG DAY. June 4. Finland's armed forces honor the birth anniversary of Carl Gustaf Mannerheim, born in 1867.

GHANA: REVOLUTION DAY. June 4. National holiday.

MAWLID AL NABI: THE BIRTHDAY OF THE PROPHET MUHAMMAD. June 4. Mawlid al-Nabi (Birth of the Prophet Muhammad) is observed on Muslim calendar date Rabi al-Awal 12, 1422. Different methods for calculating the visibility of the new moon crescent at Mecca are used by different Muslim groups.

TONGA: EMANCIPATION DAY: ANNIVERSARY. June 4. National holiday. Commemorates independence from Britain in 1970.

UNITED NATIONS: INTERNATIONAL DAY OF INNOCENT CHILDREN VICTIMS OF AGGRESSION. June 4. On Aug 19, 1982, the General Assembly decided to commemorate June 4 of each year as the International Day of Innocent Children Victims of Aggression.

WHITMONDAY. June 4. The day after Whitsunday is observed as a public holiday in many European countries.

Andrea Jaeger, 36, former tennis player, born Chicago, IL, June 4, 1965.

Scott Wolf, 33, actor ("Party of Five"), born Boston, MA, June 4, 1968.

JUNE 5 — TUESDAY
Day 156 — 209 Remaining

APPLE II COMPUTER RELEASED: ANNIVERSARY. June 5, 1977. The Apple II computer, with 4K of memory, went on sale for $1,298. Its predecessor, the Apple I, was sold largely to electronic hobbyists the previous year. Apple released the Macintosh computer Jan 24, 1984.

DENMARK: CONSTITUTION DAY: ANNIVERSARY. June 5. National holiday. Commemorates Denmark's becoming a constitutional monarchy in 1849.

FIRST BALLOON FLIGHT: ANNIVERSARY. June 5, 1783. The first public demonstration of a hot-air balloon flight took place at Annonay, France, where the coinventor brothers, Joseph and Jacques Montgolfier, succeeded in launching their unmanned 33-foot-diameter *globe aerostatique*. It rose an estimated 1,500 feet and traveled, windborne, about 7,500 feet before landing after the 10-minute flight—the first sustained flight of any object achieved by man. The first manned flight was three months later. See also: "First Manned Flight: Anniversary" (Oct 15).

MOON PHASE: FULL MOON. June 5. Moon enters Full Moon phase at 9:39 PM, EDT.

SCARRY, RICHARD McCLURE: BIRTH ANNIVERSARY. June 5, 1919. Author and illustrator of children's books was born at Boston, MA. Two widely known books of the more than 250 Scarry authored are *Richard Scarry's Best Word Book Ever* (1965) and *Richard Scarry's Please & Thank You* (1973). The pages are crowded with small animal characters who live like humans. More than 100 million copies of his books sold worldwide. Died Apr 30, 1994, at Gstaad, Switzerland.

UNITED NATIONS: WORLD ENVIRONMENT DAY. June 5. Observed annually on the anniversary of the opening of the UN Conference on the Human Environment held in Stockholm in 1972, which led to establishment of UN Environment Programme, based in Nairobi. The General Assembly has urged marking the day with activities reaffirming concern for the preservation and enhancement of the environment. For more info, visit the UN's website for children at www.un.org/Pubs/Cyber-SchoolBus/.

Allan Ahlberg, 63, author (*The Jolly Postman*), born Croydon, England, June 5, 1938.

Joe Clark, 62, Canada's 16th prime minister, 1979–80, born High River, Alberta, Canada, June 5, 1939.

Mark Wahlberg, 30, singer (Marky Mark), host ("AIXN"), born Dorchester, MA, June 5, 1971.

JUNE 6 — WEDNESDAY
Day 157 — 208 Remaining

BONZA BOTTLER DAY™. June 6. To celebrate when the number of the day is the same as the number of the month. Bonza Bottler Day™ is an excuse to have a party at least once a month. For info: Gail M. Berger, 109 Matthew Ave, Poca, WV 25159. Phone: (304) 776-7746. E-mail: gberger5@aol.com.

D-DAY: ANNIVERSARY. June 6, 1944. In the early-morning hours Allied forces landed in Normandy on the north coast of France. In an operation that took months of planning, a fleet of 2,727 ships of every description converged from British ports from Wales to the North Sea. Operation *Overlord* involved 2,000,000 tons of war materials, including more than 50,000 tanks, armored cars, jeeps, trucks and half-tracks. The US alone sent 1,700,000 fighting men. The Germans believed the invasion would not take place under the adverse weather conditions of this early June day. But as the sun came up the village of Saint Mèere Eglise was liberated by American parachutists and by nightfall the landing of 155,000 Allies attested to the success of D-Day. The long-awaited second front of WWII had at last materialized.

HALE, NATHAN: BIRTH ANNIVERSARY. June 6, 1755. American patriot Nathan Hale was born at Coventry, CT. During the battles for New York in the American Revolution, he volunteered to seek military intelligence behind enemy lines and was captured on the night of Sept 21, 1776. In an audience before General William Howe, Hale admitted he was an American officer and was ordered hanged the following morning. Although some question them, his dying words, "I only regret that I have but one life to lose for my country," have become a symbol of American patriotism. He was hanged Sept 22, 1776, at Manhattan, NY.

KOREA: MEMORIAL DAY. June 6. Nation pays tribute to the war dead and memorial services are held at the National Cemetery at Seoul. Legally recognized Korean holiday.

SPACE MILESTONE: *SOYUZ 11* (USSR): 30th ANNIVERSARY. June 6, 1971. Launched with cosmonauts G.T. Dobrovolsky, V.N. Volkov and V.I. Patsayev, who died during the return landing June 30, 1971, after a 24-day space flight. *Soyuz 11* had docked at *Salyut* orbital space station June 7–29; the cosmonauts entered the space station for the first time and conducted scientific experiments. First humans to die in space.

SUSAN B. ANTHONY FINED FOR VOTING: ANNIVERSARY. June 6, 1872. Seeking to test for women the citizenship and voting rights extended to black males under the 14th and 15th Amendments, Susan B. Anthony led a group of women who registered and voted at a Rochester, NY, election. She was arrested, tried and sentenced to pay a fine. She refused to do so and was allowed to go free by a judge who feared she would appeal to a higher court.

SWEDEN: FLAG DAY. June 6. Commemorates the day upon which Gustavus I (Gustavus Vasa) ascended the throne of Sweden in 1523.

Verna Aardema, 90, author (*Anansi Does the Impossible: An Ashanti Tale*), born New Era, MI, June 6, 1911.

Dalai Lama, 66, Tibet's spiritual leader and Nobel Peace Prize winner, born Taktser, China, June 6, 1935.

Marian Wright Edelman, 62, president of Children's Defense Fund, civil rights activist, born Bennettsville, SC, June 6, 1939.

Staci Keanan, 26, actress ("Step By Step"), born Devon, PA, June 6, 1975.

Cynthia Rylant, 47, author (Newbery for *Missing May*), born Hopewell, VA, June 6, 1954.

Peter Spier, 74, illustrator and author (Caldecott for *Noah's Ark*), born Amsterdam, Netherlands, June 6, 1927.

JUNE 7 — THURSDAY
Day 158 — 207 Remaining

APGAR, VIRGINIA: BIRTH ANNIVERSARY. June 7, 1909. Dr. Apgar developed the simple assessment method that permits doctors and nurses to evaluate newborns while they are still in the delivery room to identify those in need of immediate medical care. The Apgar score was first published in 1953 and the Perinatal Section of the American Academy of Pediatrics is named for Dr. Apgar. Born at Westfield, NJ, Apgar died Aug 7, 1974, at New York, NY.

GAUGUIN, PAUL: BIRTH ANNIVERSARY. June 7, 1848. French painter, born at Paris. He became a painter in middle age and renounced his life at Paris and moved to Tahiti. He is remembered for his broad, flat tones and use of color. He died on the island of Hiva Oa in the Marquesas, May 8, 1903.

VCR INTRODUCED: ANNIVERSARY. June 7, 1975. The Sony Corporation released its videocassette recorder, the Betamax, which sold for $995. Eventually, another VCR format, VHS, proved more successful and Sony stopped making the Betamax.

Gwendolyn Brooks, 84, poet ("We Real Cool," Pulitzer for *Annie Allen*), born Topeka, KS, June 7, 1917.

Louise Erdrich, 47, author (*The Birchbark House, Tracks*), born Little Falls, MN, June 7, 1954.

Nikki Giovanni, 58, author (*Spin a Soft Black Song*), born Knoxville, TN, June 7, 1943.

Allen Iverson, 26, basketball player, born Hampton, VA, June 7, 1975.

Anna Kournikova, 20, tennis player, born Moscow, Russia, June 7, 1981.

Mike Modano, 31, hockey player, born Livonia, MI, June 7, 1970.

Larisa Oleynik, 20, actress ("The Secret World of Alex Mack"), born San Francisco, CA, June 7, 1981.

JUNE 8 — FRIDAY
Day 159 — 206 Remaining

BILL OF RIGHTS PROPOSED: ANNIVERSARY. June 8, 1789. The Bill of Rights, which led to the first 10 amendments to the US Constitution, was first proposed by James Madison.

June 2001	S	M	T	W	T	F	S
						1	2
	3	4	5	6	7	8	9
	10	11	12	13	14	15	16
	17	18	19	20	21	22	23
	24	25	26	27	28	29	30

COCHISE: DEATH ANNIVERSARY. June 8, 1874. Born around 1810 in the Chiricahua Mountains of Arizona, Cochise became a fierce and courageous leader of the Apache. After his arrest in 1861, he escaped and launched the Apache Wars, which lasted for 25 years. He died 13 years later near his stronghold in southeastern Arizona.

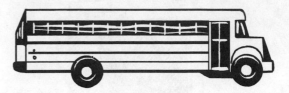

HOORAY FOR YEAR-ROUND SCHOOL DAY. June 8. To promote the benefits of a year-round school calendar which makes learning a continuous process and better suits the demanding educational needs of today's world. Annually, the second Friday in June. For more info, send 9½" SASE to: Hooray for Year-Round School Day, Horace Mann Choice School, 3530-38th Ave, Rock Island, IL 61201.

McKINLEY, IDA SAXTON: BIRTH ANNIVERSARY. June 8, 1847. Wife of William McKinley, 25th president of the US, born at Canton, OH. Died at Canton, May 26, 1907.

WHITE, BYRON RAYMOND: BIRTHDAY. June 8, 1917. Retired associate justice of the Supreme Court of the US, nominated by President Kennedy Apr 3, 1962. (Oath of office, Apr 16, 1962.) Justice White was born at Fort Collins, CO.

WRIGHT, FRANK LLOYD: BIRTH ANNIVERSARY. June 8, 1867. American architect, born at Richland Center, WI. In his autobiography Wright wrote: "No house should ever be *on* any hill or on anything. It should be *of* the hill, belonging to it, so hill and house could live together each the happier for the other." Wright died at Phoenix, AZ, Apr 9, 1959.

WYTHE, GEORGE: DEATH ANNIVERSARY. June 8, 1806. Signer of the Declaration of Independence. Born at Elizabeth County, VA, about 1726 (exact date unknown). Died at Richmond, VA.

Tim Berners-Lee, 46, inventor of the World Wide Web, born London, England, June 8, 1955.

Barbara Pierce Bush, 76, former First Lady, wife of George Bush, 41st president of the US, born Rye, NY, June 8, 1925.

Lindsay Davenport, 25, tennis player, born Palos Verdes, CA, June 8, 1976.

Judy Sierra, 56, author (*Nursery Tales Around the World, Counting Crocodiles*), born Washington, DC, June 8, 1945.

JUNE 9 — SATURDAY
Day 160 — 205 Remaining

DONALD DUCK: BIRTHDAY. June 9, 1934. Donald Duck was "born," introduced in the Disney short, *Orphans' Benefit*.

INTERNATIONAL YOUNG EAGLES DAY. June 9. The Young Eagles Program offers youth 8–17 an opportunity to fly in a private airplane with a qualified pilot. On the second Saturday in June each year local chapters celebrate International Young Eagles Day with special exhibits and unreserved flights. For info: Young Eagles Program, Experimental Aircraft Assn Aviation Foundation, PO Box 2683, Oshkosh, WI 54903-2683. Phone: (877) 806-8902. Web: www.youngeagles.org.

TAKE A KID FISHING WEEKEND. June 9–10 (tentative). St. Paul, MN. Resident adults may fish without a license on these days when fishing with a child under age 16. For info: Jack Skrypek, Fisheries Chief, DNR, Box 12, 500 Lafayette Rd, St. Paul, MN 55155. Phone: (612) 296-0792 or (612) 296-3325. Fax: (612) 297-4916. Web: www.dnr.state.mn.us.

UNITED KINGDOM: TROOPING THE COLOUR— QUEEN'S OFFICIAL BIRTHDAY PARADE. June 9 (tentative). National holiday in the United Kingdom. Horse Guards Parade, Whitehall, London. Colorful ceremony with music and pageantry during which Her Majesty The Queen takes the salute. Starts at 11 AM. When requesting info, send stamped, self-addressed envelope. [Final date not set at press time.] Trooping the Colour is always on a Saturday in June; the Queen's real birthday is Apr 21. Est attendance: 10,000. For info: The Ticket Office, HQ Household Division, 1 Chelsea Barracks, London, England SW1H 8RF. Phone: (44) (171) 414-2357.

BIRTHDAYS TODAY

Michael J. Fox, 40, actor ("Family Ties," *Back to the Future* films), born Edmonton, Alberta, Canada, June 9, 1961.

JUNE 10 — SUNDAY
Day 161 — 204 Remaining

BALL-POINT PEN PATENTED: ANNIVERSARY. June 10, 1943. Hungarian Laszlo Biro patented the ball-point pen, which he had been developing since the 1930s. He was living at Argentina, where he had gone to escape the Nazis. In many languages, the word for ball-point pen is "biro."

CHILDREN'S DAY IN MASSACHUSETTS. June 10. Annually, the second Sunday in June. The governor proclaims this day each year.

CHILDREN'S SUNDAY. June 10. Traditionally the second Sunday in June is observed as Children's Sunday in many Christian churches.

JORDAN: GREAT ARAB REVOLT AND ARMY DAY: 85th ANNIVERSARY. June 10. Commemorates the beginning of the Great Arab Revolt in 1916. National holiday.

★**NATIONAL FLAG WEEK.** June 10–16. Presidential Proclamation issued each year since 1966 for the week including June 14. (PL89–443 of June 9, 1966.) In addition, the president often calls upon the American people to participate in public ceremonies in which the Pledge of Allegiance is recited.

ORTHODOX FESTIVAL OF ALL SAINTS. June 10. Observed by Eastern Orthodox churches on the Sunday following Orthodox Pentecost (June 3 in 2001). Marks the end of the 18-week Triodion cycle.

PORTUGAL: DAY OF PORTUGAL. June 10, 1580. National holiday. Anniversary of the death of Portugal's national poet, Luis Vas de Camoes (Camoens), born in 1524 (exact date unknown) at either Lisbon or possibly Coimbra. Died at Lisbon, Portugal.

RACE UNITY DAY. June 10. Baha'i-sponsored observance promoting racial harmony and understanding and the essential unity of humanity. Annually, the second Sunday in June. For info: Office of Public Information, Baha'is of the US, 866 UN Plaza, Ste 120, New York, NY 10017-1822. Phone: (212) 803-2500. Fax: (212) 803-2573. E-mail: usopi-ny@bic.org. Web: www.us.bahai.org.

TRINITY SUNDAY. June 10. Christian Holy Day on the Sunday after Pentecost commemorates the Holy Trinity, the three divine persons—Father, Son and Holy Spirit—in one God. See also: "Pentecost" (June 3).

BIRTHDAYS TODAY

John Edwards, 48, US Senator (D, North Carolina), born Seneca, SC, June 10, 1953.

Tara Lipinski, 19, figure skater, born Philadelphia, PA, June 10, 1982.

Maurice Sendak, 73, author, illustrator (*Chicken Soup with Rice*, Caldecott for *Where the Wild Things Are*), born Brooklyn, NY, June 10, 1928. *See* Curriculum Connection.

Leelee Sobieski, 19, actress (*Deep Impact*), born Liliane Sobieski, New York, NY, June 10, 1982.

JUNE 10
MAURICE SENDAK'S BIRTHDAY

For decades children have thrilled to the adventures Max found after sailing in and out of a day "to where the wild things are." Max and his wolf suit, from the Caldecott Medal book *Where the Wild Things Are*, are instantly recognized by many children (adults, too). Celebrate the author/illustrator Sendak's birthday with a Sendak Fest.

Young children may want to dress as a favorite character from a Sendak story. Max, Pierre, the Wolf from *Swine Lake*, and Little Bear are a few possibilities. You can welcome parents to the classroom for the Fest. Let the children write and illustrate invitations to the party.

Max made mischief of "one kind or another." Have students look at the illustrations in the book and try to imagine what mischief Max might have done that would warrant being sent to his room. They can also write a story featuring themselves as Max and draw what they would do if they were King of the Wild Things.

Hold a Sendak Scavenger Hunt. Create a list of pictures, words and phrases from books illustrated by Sendak. You might use words like "rumpus," "kitchen," "Grisly-Beard," "rice" and "higglety." Divide students into teams and let them hunt through Sendak books in the learning center for the items. Older students could look for visual puns in Sendak books. *Swine Lake*, by James Marshall (Harper, 0-06-204171-7, $15.95 Gr. 2 & up) is loaded with slyly humorous illustrations.

Weston Woods Studios produced an excellent (and unusual) animated video of *Where the Wild Things Are* that students may enjoy. See if it is available in your learning center. Read *Swine Lake*, Marshall and Sendak's piggy parody of *Swan Lake*. Bring music and dance into the room with a recording of *Swan Lake*, by Peter Tchaikovsky. Students can address the book's theme: music tames the savage beast. Ask what music they would use to bring out the artist in themselves.

Some of Sendak's works have a more serious side. *We Are All in the Dumps With Jack and Guy* deals with homelessness. Both *Where the Wild Things Are* and *Outside Over There* represent how children handle their emotions. Middle school students might explore and compare these and other picture books, such as *Elizabeth Imagined An Iceberg*, by Chris Raschka (Orchard, 0-531-06817-X, $14.95), that feature children dealing with difficult topics.

JUNE 11 — MONDAY
Day 162 — 203 Remaining

COUSTEAU, JACQUES: BIRTH ANNIVERSARY. June 11, 1910. French undersea explorer, writer and filmmaker, born at St. Andre-de-Cubzac, France. He invented the Aqualung, which allowed him and his colleagues to produce more than 80 documentary films about undersea life, two of which won Oscars. This scientist and explorer was awarded the French Legion of Honor for his work in the Resistance in WWII. He died at Paris, France, June 25, 1997.

KING KAMEHAMEHA I DAY. June 11. Designated state holiday in Hawaii honors memory of Hawaiian monarch (1737–1819). Governor appoints state commission to plan annual celebration.

MOUNT PINATUBO ERUPTS IN PHILIPPINES: 10th ANNIVERSARY. June 11, 1991. Long-dormant volcano Mount Pinatubo erupted with a violent explosion, spewing ash and gases that could be seen for more than 60 miles, into the air. The surrounding areas were covered with ash and mud created by rainstorms. US military bases Clark and Subic Bay were also damaged. On July 6, 1992, Ellsworth Dutton of the National Oceanic and Atmospheric Administration's Climate Monitoring and Diagnostics Laboratory announced that a layer of sulfuric acid droplets released into the Earth's atmosphere by the eruption had cooled the planet's average temperature by about 1 degree Fahrenheit. The greatest difference was noted in the Northern Hemisphere with a drop of 1.5 degrees. Although the temperature drop was temporary, the climate trend made determining the effect of greenhouse warming on the Earth more difficult. For more info visit Volcano World: volcano.und.nodak.edu.

★**NATIONAL LITTLE LEAGUE BASEBALL WEEK.** June 11–17. Presidential Proclamation 3296, of June 4, 1959, covers all succeeding years. Always the week beginning with the second Monday in June. (H.Con.Res. 17 of June 1, 1959.)

RANKIN, JEANNETTE: BIRTH ANNIVERSARY. June 11, 1880. First woman elected to the US Congress, a reformer, feminist and pacifist, was born at Missoula, MT. She was the only member of Congress to vote against a declaration of war against Japan in December 1941. Died May 18, 1973, at Carmel, CA.

June 2001	S	M	T	W	T	F	S
						1	2
	3	4	5	6	7	8	9
	10	11	12	13	14	15	16
	17	18	19	20	21	22	23
	24	25	26	27	28	29	30

BIRTHDAYS TODAY

Parris Glendening, 59, Governor of Maryland (D), born The Bronx, NY, June 11, 1942.
Joe Montana, 45, former sportscaster and football player, born New Eagle, PA, June 11, 1956.
Robert Munsch, 56, author (*Love You Forever*), born Pittsburgh, PA, June 11, 1945.
Gene Wilder, 68, actor (*Willy Wonka & the Chocolate Factory*), born Milwaukee, WI, June 11, 1933.

JUNE 12 — TUESDAY
Day 163 — 202 Remaining

FRANK, ANNE: BIRTH ANNIVERSARY. June 12, 1929. Born at Frankfurt, Germany. Anne Frank moved with her family to Amsterdam to escape the Nazis but after Holland was invaded by Germany, they had to go into hiding. In 1942, Anne began to keep a diary. She died at Bergen-Belsen concentration camp in 1945. After the war, her father published her diary, on which a stage play and movie were later based. See also "Diary of Anne Frank: The Last Entry: Anniversary" (Aug 1). For more info: www.annefrank.com.

***LOVING v VIRGINIA* : ANNIVERSARY.** June 12, 1967. The US Supreme Court decision in *Loving v Virginia* swept away all 16 remaining state laws prohibiting interracial marriages.

NATIONAL BASEBALL HALL OF FAME: ANNIVERSARY. June 12, 1939. The National Baseball Hall of Fame and Museum, Inc, was dedicated at Cooperstown, NY. More than 200 individuals have been honored for their contributions to the game of baseball by induction into the Baseball Hall of Fame. The first players chosen for membership (1936) were Ty Cobb, Honus Wagner, Babe Ruth, Christy Mathewson and Walter Johnson. Relics and memorabilia from the history of baseball are housed at this shrine of America's national sport.

PHILIPPINES: INDEPENDENCE DAY. June 12. National holiday. Declared independence from Spain in 1898.

RUSSIA: INDEPENDENCE DAY: 10th ANNIVERSARY. June 12. National holiday. Commemorates the election in 1991 of the first popularly elected leader (Gorbachev) in the 1,000-year history of the Russian state.

BIRTHDAYS TODAY

Spencer Abraham, 49, US Senator (R, Michigan), born Lansing, MI, June 12, 1952.
George Herbert Walker Bush, 77, 41st president of the US, born Milton, MA, June 12, 1924.
Helen Lester, 65, author (*Hooway for Wodney Wat*), born Evanston, IL, June 12, 1936.
Hillary McKay, 42, author (*The Amber Cat*), born the Midlands, England, June 12, 1959.

JUNE 13 — WEDNESDAY
Day 164 — 201 Remaining

***MIRANDA* DECISION: 35th ANNIVERSARY.** June 13, 1966. The US Supreme Court rendered a 5–4 decision in the case of *Miranda v Arizona*, holding that the Fifth Amendment of the Constitution "required warnings before valid statements could be taken by police." The decision has been described as "providing basic legal protections to persons who might otherwise not be aware of their rights." Ernesto Miranda, the 23-year-old whose name became nationally known, was retried after the Miranda Decision, convicted and sent back to prison. Miranda was stabbed to death in a card game dispute at Phoenix, AZ, in 1976. A suspect in the killing was released by police after he had been read his "Miranda rights." Police procedures now routinely require the reading of a prisoner's constitutional rights ("Miranda") before questioning.

MOON PHASE: LAST QUARTER. June 13. Moon enters Last Quarter phase at 11:28 PM, EDT.

SCOTT, WINFIELD: BIRTH ANNIVERSARY. June 13, 1786. American army general, negotiator of peace treaties with the Indians and twice nominated for president (1848 and 1852). Leader of brilliant military campaign in Mexican War in 1847. Scott was born at Petersburg, VA and died at West Point, NY, May 29, 1866.

BIRTHDAYS TODAY

Tim Allen, 48, comedian, actor ("Home Improvement"), born Denver, CO, June 13, 1953.

Ashley Olsen, 14, actress ("Full House," "Two of a Kind"), born Los Angeles, CA, June 13, 1987.

Mary-Kate Olsen, 14, actress ("Full House," "Two of a Kind"), born Los Angeles, CA, June 13, 1987.

JUNE 14 — THURSDAY

Day 165 — 200 Remaining

AMERICAN LIBRARY ASSOCIATION ANNUAL CONFERENCE. June 14–20. San Francisco, CA. Est attendance: 20,000. For info: Public Information Office, American Library Assn, 50 E Huron St, Chicago, IL 60611. Phone: (312) 280-5044. Fax: (312) 944-8520. E-mail: pro@ala.org. Web: www.ala.org.

ARMY ESTABLISHED BY CONGRESS: ANNIVERSARY. June 14, 1775. Anniversary of Resolution of the Continental Congress establishing the army as the first US military service.

BARTLETT, JOHN: BIRTH ANNIVERSARY. June 14, 1820. American editor and compiler of Bartlett's *Familiar Quotations* [1855] was born at Plymouth, MA. Though he had little formal education, he created one of the most-used reference works of the English language. No quotation of his own is among the more than 22,000 listed today, but in the preface to the first edition he wrote that the object of this work "originally made without any view of publication" was to show "the obligation our language owes to various authors for numerous phrases and familiar quotations which have become 'household words.'" Bartlett died at Cambridge, MA, Dec 3, 1905. His book remains in print today in the 16th edition.

FIRST NONSTOP TRANSATLANTIC FLIGHT: ANNIVERSARY. June 14–15, 1919. Captain John Alcock and Lieutenant Arthur W. Brown flew a Vickers Vimy bomber 1,900 miles nonstop from St. Johns, Newfoundland, to Clifden, County Galway, Ireland. In spite of their crash landing in an Irish peat bog, their flight inspired public interest in aviation. See also: "Lindbergh Flight: Anniversary" (May 20).

★ **FLAG DAY.** June 14. Presidential Proclamation issued each year for June 14. Proclamation 1335, of May 30, 1916, covers all succeeding years. Has been issued annually since 1941. (PL 81–203 of Aug 3, 1949.) Customarily issued as "Flag Day and National Flag Week," as in 1986; the president usually mentions "a time to honor America," Flag Day to Independence Day (89 Stat. 211). See also: "National Flag Day USA: Pause for the Pledge" (this date).

FLAG DAY: ANNIVERSARY OF THE STARS AND STRIPES. June 14, 1777. John Adams introduced the following resolution before the Continental Congress, meeting at Philadelphia, PA: "Resolved, That the flag of the thirteen United States shall be thirteen stripes, alternate red and white; that the union be thirteen stars, white on a blue field, representing a new constellation." Legal holiday in Pennsylvania.

JAPAN: RICE PLANTING FESTIVAL. June 14. Osaka. Ceremonial transplanting of rice seedlings in paddy field at Sumiyashi Shrine, Osaka.

NATIONAL FLAG DAY USA: PAUSE FOR THE PLEDGE. June 14. Held simultaneously across the country at 7 PM, EDT. Public law 99–54 recognizes the Pause for the Pledge as part of National Flag Day ceremonies. The concept of the Pause for the Pledge of Allegiance was conceived as a way for all citizens to share a patriotic moment. National ceremony at Fort McHenry National Monument and Historic Shrine.

STOWE, HARRIET BEECHER: BIRTH ANNIVERSARY. June 14, 1811. American writer Harriet Beecher Stowe, daughter of the Reverend Lyman Beecher and sister of Henry Ward Beecher. Author of *Uncle Tom's Cabin*, an antislavery novel that provoked a storm of protest and resulted in fame for its author. Two characters in the novel attained such importance that their names became part of the English language—the Negro slave, Uncle Tom, and the villainous slaveowner, Simon Legree. The reaction to *Uncle Tom's Cabin* and its profound political impact are without parallel in American literature. It is said that during the Civil War, when Harriet Beecher Stowe was introduced to President Abraham Lincoln, his words to her were, "So you're the little woman who wrote the book that made this great war." Stowe was born at Litchfield, CT and died at Hartford, CT, July 1, 1896. For more info: *Harriet Beecher Stowe and the Beecher Preachers*, by Jean Fritz (Putnam, 0-399-22666-4, $15.99 Gr. 7–9).

UNIVAC COMPUTER: 50th ANNIVERSARY. June 14, 1951. Univac 1, the world's first commercial computer, designed for the US Bureau of the Census, was unveiled, demonstrated and dedicated at Philadelphia, PA. Though this milestone of the computer age was the first commercial electronic computer, it had been preceded by ENIAC (Electronic Numeric Integrator and Computer), completed under the supervision of J. Presper Eckert, Jr and John W. Mauchly, at the University of Pennsylvania, in 1946.

WARREN G. HARDING BECOMES FIRST PRESIDENT TO BROADCAST ON RADIO: ANNIVERSARY. June 14, 1922. Warren G. Harding became the first president to broadcast a message over the radio. The event was the dedication of the Francis Scott Key Memorial at Baltimore, MD. The first official government message was broadcast Dec 6, 1923.

BIRTHDAYS TODAY

Bruce Degen, 56, author and illustrator (*Jamberry*), born Brooklyn, NY, June 14, 1945.

Stephanie Maria (Steffi) Graf, 32, tennis player, born Bruhl, West Germany, June 14, 1969.

James Gurney, 43, author and illustrator (*Dinotopia*), born Glendale, CA, June 14, 1958.

Laurence Yep, 53, author (*Dragon's Gate*, *The Rainbow's People*), born San Francisco, CA, June 14, 1948.

JUNE 15 — FRIDAY

Day 166 — 199 Remaining

ARKANSAS: ADMISSION DAY: ANNIVERSARY. June 15. Became the 25th state in 1836.

JACKSON, RACHEL DONELSON ROBARDS: BIRTH ANNIVERSARY. June 15, 1767. Wife of Andrew Jackson, 7th president of the US, born at Halifax County, NC. Died at Nashville, TN, Dec 22, 1828.

MAGNA CARTA DAY: ANNIVERSARY. June 15. Anniversary of King John's sealing, in 1215, of the Magna Carta "in the meadow called Ronimed between Windsor and Staines on the fifteenth day of June in the seventeenth year of our reign." This document is regarded as the first charter of English liberties and one of the most important documents in the history of political and human freedom. Four original copies of the 1215 charter survive.

TWELFTH AMENDMENT TO US CONSTITUTION RATIFIED: ANNIVERSARY. June 15, 1804. The 12th Amendment to the Constitution was ratified. It changed the method of electing the president and vice president after a tie in the electoral college during the election of 1800. Rather than each elector voting for two candidates with the candidate receiving the most votes elected president and the second-place candidate elected vice president, each elector was now required to designate his choice for president and vice president, respectively.

BIRTHDAYS TODAY

Courteney Cox Arquette, 37, actress ("Friends," "Family Ties"), born Birmingham, AL, June 15, 1964.
Wade Boggs, 43, baseball player, born Omaha, NE, June 15, 1958.
Christopher Castile, 21, actor ("Step By Step," *Beethoven*), born Los Alamitos, CA, June 15, 1980.
Brian Jacques, 62, author (the Redwall series), born Liverpool, England, June 15, 1939.
Justin Leonard, 29, golfer, born Dallas, TX, June 15, 1972.
Betty Ren Wright, 74, author (*The Dollhouse Murders*), born Wakefield, MI, June 15, 1927.

JUNE 16 — SATURDAY
Day 167 — 198 Remaining

SOUTH AFRICA: YOUTH DAY. June 16, 1976. National holiday. Commemorates a student uprising in Soweto against "Bantu Education" and the enforced teaching of the Afrikaans language.

SPACE MILESTONE: FIRST WOMAN IN SPACE, *VOSTOK 6* (USSR). June 16, 1963. Valentina Tereshkova, 26, former cotton-mill worker, born on a collective farm near Yaroslavl, USSR, became the first woman in space when her spacecraft, *Vostok 6*, took off from the Tyuratam launch site. She manually controlled *Vostok 6* during the 70.8-hour flight through 48 orbits of Earth and landed by parachute (separate from her cabin) June 19, 1963. In November 1963 she married cosmonaut Andrian Nikolayev, who had piloted *Vostok 3* through 64 earth orbits, Aug 11–15, 1962. Their child Yelena (1964) was the first born to space-traveler parents.

WORLD JUGGLING DAY. June 16. Juggling clubs all over the world hold local festivals to demonstrate, teach and celebrate their art. For info: Intl Jugglers' Assn, PO Box 218, Montague, MA 01351. Phone: (413) 367-2401. Fax: (413) 367-0259. E-mail: IJugglersA@aol.com. Web: www.juggle.org/wjd/.

BIRTHDAYS TODAY

Lincoln Almond, 65, Governor of Rhode Island (R), born Central Falls, RI, June 16, 1936.

	S	M	T	W	T	F	S
June *2001*						1	2
	3	4	5	6	7	8	9
	10	11	12	13	14	15	16
	17	18	19	20	21	22	23
	24	25	26	27	28	29	30

Cobi Jones, 31, soccer player, played in 1994 World's Cup, born Westlake Village, CA, June 16, 1970.
Kerry Wood, 24, baseball player, born Irving, TX, June 16, 1977.

JUNE 17 — SUNDAY
Day 168 — 197 Remaining

BRANSCUM, ROBBIE: BIRTH ANNIVERSARY. June 17, 1937. Author best known for *The Adventures of Johnny May* and *Cameo Rose*. She won the Friends of American Writers Award in 1977 and the Edgar Allen Poe Award in 1983. Born near Big Flat, AR, Branscum died at Harrisonburg, VA, May 24, 1997.

BUNKER HILL DAY IN MASSACHUSETTS. June 17. Legal holiday in the county in commemoration of the Battle of Bunker Hill that took place in 1775. Proclaimed annually by the governor.

CORPUS CHRISTI (US OBSERVANCE). June 17. A movable Roman Catholic celebration commemorating the institution of the Holy Eucharist. The solemnity has been observed on the Thursday following Trinity Sunday since 1246, except in the US, where it is observed on the Sunday following Trinity Sunday.

★**FATHER'S DAY.** June 17. Presidential Proclamation issued for third Sunday in June in 1966 and annually since 1971. (PL 92–278 of Apr 24, 1972.)

FATHER'S DAY. June 17. Recognition of the third Sunday in June as Father's Day occurred first at the request of Mrs John B. Dodd of Spokane, WA, June 19, 1910. It was proclaimed for that date by the mayor of Spokane and recognized by the governor of Washington. The idea was publicly supported by President Calvin Coolidge in 1924, but not presidentially proclaimed until 1966. It was assured of annual recognition by Public Law 92–278 of April 1972.

HOOPER, WILLIAM: BIRTH ANNIVERSARY. June 17, 1742. Signer of the Declaration of Independence, born at Boston, MA. Died Oct 14, 1790, at Hillsboro, NC.

ICELAND: INDEPENDENCE DAY. June 17. Anniversary of founding of republic in 1944 and independence from Denmark is major festival, especially in Reykjavik. Parades, competitions, street dancing.

SOUTH AFRICA REPEALS LAST APARTHEID LAW: 10th ANNIVERSARY. June 17, 1991. The Parliament of South Africa repealed the Population Registration Act, removing the law that was the foundation of apartheid. The law, first enacted in 1950, required the classification by race of all South Africans at birth. It established four compulsory racial categories: white, mixed race, Asian and black. Although this marked the removal of the last of the apartheid laws, blacks in South Africa still could not vote.

UNITED NATIONS: WORLD DAY TO COMBAT DESERTIFICATION AND DROUGHT. June 17. Proclaimed by the General Assembly Dec 19, 1994 (Res 49/115). States were invited to devote the World Day to promoting public awareness of the need for international cooperation to combat desertification and the effects of drought and on the implementation of the UN Convention to Combat Desertification. For info: United Nations, Dept of Public Info, New York, NY 10017.

BIRTHDAYS TODAY

Leslie Baker, 52, author and illustrator (*The Third-Story Cat*), born Baltimore, MD, June 17, 1949.

Liza Ketchum, 55, author (*Orphan Journey Home, The Gold Rush*), born Albany, NY, June 17, 1946.

Venus Williams, 21, tennis player, born Lynwood, CA, June 17, 1980.

JUNE 18 — MONDAY
Day 169 — 196 Remaining

FIRST AMERICAN WOMAN IN SPACE: ANNIVERSARY. June 18, 1983. Dr. Sally Ride, 32-year-old physicist and pilot, functioned as a "mission specialist" and became the first American woman in space when she began a six-day mission aboard the space shuttle *Challenger*. The "near-perfect" mission was launched from Cape Canaveral, FL, and landed, June 24, 1983, at Edwards Air Force Base, CA.

NATIONAL SPLURGE DAY. June 18. Today is the day to go out and do something indulgent. Have fun! [©1994] For info: Adrienne Sioux Koopersmith, 1437 W Rosemont, #1W, Chicago, IL 60660-1319. Phone: (773) 743-5341. Fax: (773) 743-5395. E-mail: adrienet@earthlink.net.

SEYCHELLES: CONSTITUTION DAY. June 18. National holiday commemorating 1993 constitution.

SPACE MILESTONE: *CHALLENGER STS-7* (US). June 18, 1983. Shuttle *Challenger*, launched from Kennedy Space Center, FL, with crew of five, including Sally K. Ride (first American woman in space), Robert Crippen, Norman Thagard, John Fabian and Frederick Houck. Landed at Edwards Air Force Base, CA, June 24 after a near-perfect six-day mission.

VIRGIN ISLANDS: ORGANIC ACT DAY: ANNIVERSARY. June 18. Commemorates the enactment by the US Congress, July 22, 1954, of the Revised Organic Act, under which the government of the Virgin Islands is organized. Observed annually on the third Monday in June.

WAR OF 1812: DECLARATION ANNIVERSARY. June 18, 1812. After much debate in Congress between "hawks" such as Henry Clay and John Calhoun, and "doves" such as John Randolph, Congress issued a declaration of war on Great Britain. The action was prompted primarily by Britain's violation of America's rights on the high seas and British incitement of Indian warfare on the frontier. War was seen by some as a way to acquire Florida and Canada. The hostilities ended with the signing of the Treaty of Ghent, Dec 24, 1814, at Ghent, Belgium.

BIRTHDAYS TODAY

Pam Conrad, 54, author (*Prairie Songs*), born New York, NY, June 18, 1947.

Pat Hutchins, 59, author and illustrator (*Changes, Changes, The Wind Blew*), born Yorkshire, England, June 18, 1942.

Angela Johnson, 40, author (*Heaven*), born Tuskegee, AL, June 18, 1961.

Paul McCartney, 59, singer, songwriter (The Beatles), born Liverpool, England, June 18, 1942.

John D. Rockefeller IV, 64, US Senator (D, West Virginia), born New York, NY, June 18, 1937.

Chris Van Allsburg, 52, illustrator and author (Caldecott for *The Polar Express, Jumanji*), born Grand Rapids, MI, June 18, 1949.

JUNE 19 — TUESDAY
Day 170 — 195 Remaining

EMANCIPATION DAY IN TEXAS. June 19, 1865. In honor of the emancipation of the slaves in Texas.

FORTAS, ABE: BIRTH ANNIVERSARY. June 19, 1910. Abe Fortas was born at Memphis, TN. He was appointed to the Supreme Court by President Lyndon Johnson in 1965. Prior to his appointment he was known as a civil libertarian, having argued cases for government employees and other individuals accused by Senator Joe McCarthy of having communist affiliations. He argued the 1963 landmark Supreme Court case of *Gideon v Wainwright*, which established the right of indigent defendants to free legal aid in criminal prosecutions. In 1968, he was nominated by Johnson to succeed Chief Justice Earl Warren, but his nomination was withdrawn after much conservative opposition in the Senate. In 1969 Fortas became the first Supreme Court Justice to be forced to resign after revelations about questionable financial dealings were made public. He died Apr 5, 1982, at Washington, DC.

GARFIELD: BIRTHDAY. June 19, 1978. America's favorite lasagna-loving cat is 23. "Garfield," a modern classic comic strip created by Jim Davis, first appeared in 1978, and has brought laughter to millions. For info: Paws, Inc, Kim Campbell, 5440 E Co Rd 450 N, Albany, IN 47320. Web: www.garfield.com.

GEHRIG, LOU: BIRTH ANNIVERSARY. June 19, 1903. Henry Louis Gehrig, Baseball Hall of Fame first baseman, born Ludwig Heinrich Gehrig, at New York, NY. Gehrig, known as the "Iron Horse," played in 2,130 consecutive games, a record not surpassed until Cal Ripken did in 1995. He played 17 years with the Yankees, hit .340 and slugged 493 home runs, 23 of them grand slams. Gehrig retired in 1939 and was diagnosed with the degenerative muscle disease amyotrophic lateral sclerosis, later known as Lou Gehrig's disease. Died at New York, NY, June 2, 1941.

JUNETEENTH. June 19. Celebrated in Texas to commemorate the day when Union General Granger proclaimed the slaves of Texas free. This is also a ceremonial holiday in Florida, commemorating the day slaves in Florida were notified of the Emancipation Proclamation. Juneteenth has become a day for commemoration by African Americans in many parts of the US.

BIRTHDAYS TODAY

Andrew Lauer, 36, actor (*I'll Be Home for Christmas*), born Santa Monica, CA, June 19, 1965.

Brian McBride, 29, soccer player, born Arlington Heights, IL, June 19, 1972.

JUNE 20 — WEDNESDAY
Day 171 — 194 Remaining

CHESNUTT, CHARLES W.: BIRTH ANNIVERSARY. June 20, 1858. Born at Cleveland, OH, Chesnutt was considered by many as the first important black novelist. His collections of short stories included *The Conjure Woman* (1899) and *The Wife of His Youth and Other Stories of the Color Line* (1899). *The Colonel's Dream* (1905) dealt with the struggles of the freed slave. His work has been compared to later writers such as William Faulkner, Richard Wright and James Baldwin. He died Nov 15, 1932, at Cleveland.

CHICAGO BULLS WIN THIRD CONSECUTIVE NBA CHAMPIONSHIP: ANNIVERSARY. June 20, 1993. With a four-games-to-two victory over the Phoenix Suns in the National Basketball Association (NBA) finals the Chicago Bulls earned their third straight NBA title. The Bulls became the first team to win three in a row since 1966, when the Boston Celtics won their eighth in a row. In 1996 they won the NBA title for a fourth time, in 1997 for a fifth and in 1998 for a sixth, for another three-in-a-row sweep.

WEST VIRGINIA: ADMISSION DAY: ANNIVERSARY. June 20. Became 35th state in 1863. Observed as a holiday in West Virginia. The state of West Virginia is a product of the Civil War. Originally part of Virginia, West Virginia became a separate state when Virginia seceded from the Union.

BIRTHDAYS TODAY

John Goodman, 49, actor (*Arachnophobia, The Flintstones*), born Afton, MO, June 20, 1952.
Annette Curtis Klause, 48, author (*Blood and Chocolate*), born Bristol, England, June 20, 1953.

JUNE 21 — THURSDAY
Day 172 — 193 Remaining

CANCER, THE CRAB. June 21–July 22. In the astronomical/astrological zodiac, which divides the sun's apparent orbit into 12 segments, the period June 21–July 22 is identified, traditionally, as the sun sign of Cancer, the Crab. The ruling planet is the moon.

MOON PHASE: NEW MOON. June 21. Moon enters New Moon phase at 7:58 AM, EDT.

NEW HAMPSHIRE RATIFIES CONSTITUTION: ANNIVERSARY. June 21, 1788. By a vote of 57 to 47, New Hampshire became the ninth state to ratify the Constitution.

SOLAR ECLIPSE. June 21. Total eclipse of the sun. Eclipse begins at 5:32 AM, EDT, reaches greatest eclipse at 7:57 AM, and ends at 10:34 AM. Visible in South Atlantic Ocean, Angola, Zambia, Zimbabwe, Madagascar and Indian Ocean.

SUMMER. June 21–Sept 22. In the Northern Hemisphere summer begins today with the summer solstice, at 3:38 AM, EDT. Note that in the Southern Hemisphere today is the beginning of winter. Anywhere between the Equator and Arctic Circle, the sun rises and sets farthest north on the horizon for the year and length of daylight is maximum (12 hours, 8 minutes at equator, increasing to 24 hours at Arctic Circle).

TOMPKINS, DANIEL D.: BIRTH ANNIVERSARY. June 21, 1774. Sixth vice president of the US (1817–25), born at Fox Meadows, NY. Died at Staten Island, NY, June 11, 1825.

WASHINGTON, MARTHA DANDRIDGE CUSTIS: BIRTH ANNIVERSARY. June 21, 1731. Wife of George Washington,

		S	M	T	W	T	F	S
June							1	2
2001		3	4	5	6	7	8	9
		10	11	12	13	14	15	16
		17	18	19	20	21	22	23
		24	25	26	27	28	29	30

first president of the US, born at New Kent County, VA. Died at Mount Vernon, VA, May 22, 1802.

BIRTHDAYS TODAY

Berke Breathed, 44, cartoonist ("Bloom County"), born Croatia, June 21, 1957.
Robert Kraus, 76, author (*Leo the Late Bloomer*), born Milwaukee, WI, June 21, 1925.
Togo D. West, 59, US Secretary of Veterans Affairs (Clinton administration), born Winston-Salem, NC, June 21, 1942.
Prince William, 19, son of Prince Charles and Princess Diana, born London, England, June 21, 1982.

JUNE 22 — FRIDAY
Day 173 — 192 Remaining

SWITZERLAND: MORAT BATTLE ANNIVERSARY. June 22, 1476. The little, walled town of Morat played a decisive part in Swiss history. There, the Confederates were victorious over Charles the Bold of Burgundy, laying the basis for French-speaking areas to become Swiss. Now an annual children's festival.

US DEPARTMENT OF JUSTICE: ANNIVERSARY. June 22. Established by an act of Congress, the Department of Justice is headed by the attorney general. Prior to 1870, the attorney general (whose office had been created Sept 24, 1789) had been a member of the president's cabinet but had not been the head of a department.

BIRTHDAYS TODAY

Dianne Feinstein, 68, US Senator (D, California), born San Francisco, CA, June 22, 1933.
Lindsay Ridgeway, 16, actress ("Boy Meets World"), born Loma Linda, CA, June 22, 1985.

JUNE 23 — SATURDAY
Day 174 — 191 Remaining

DENMARK: MIDSUMMER EVE. June 23. Celebrated all over the country with bonfires and merrymaking.

FIRST TYPEWRITER: ANNIVERSARY. June 23, 1868. First US typewriter was patented by Luther Sholes.

LAURA INGALLS WILDER PAGEANT. June 29–July 1 (also July 6–8 and July 13–15). De Smet, SD. An outdoor pageant on the natural prairie stage depicting "Medley of Memories," historically based on Laura Ingalls Wilder's life. Est attendance: 10,000. For info: The Laura Ingalls Wilder Pageant, PO Box 154, De Smet, SD 57231. Phone: (605) 692-2108.

LUXEMBOURG: NATIONAL HOLIDAY. June 23. Commemorating birth of His Royal Highness Grand Duke Jean in 1921. Luxembourg's independence is also celebrated.

MIDSUMMER DAY/EVE CELEBRATIONS. June 23. Celebrates the beginning of summer with maypoles, music, dancing and bonfires. Observed mainly in northern Europe, including Finland, Latvia and Sweden. Day of observance is sometimes St. John's Day (June 24), with celebration on St. John's Eve (June 23) as well, or June 19. Time approximates the summer solstice. See also: "Summer" (June 21).

BIRTHDAYS TODAY

Theodore Taylor, 80, author (*The Cay*), born Statesville, NC, June 23, 1921.
Clarence Thomas, 53, Associate Justice of the Supreme Court, born Pinpoint, GA, June 23, 1948.

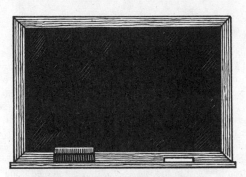

JUNE 24 — SUNDAY
Day 175 — 190 Remaining

AMERICA'S KIDS DAY. June 24. A day set aside to reach out and teach our children in America the value of life, liberty and the pursuit of happiness. A time to help our kids learn about the great nation that they live in and help by demonstrating what it means to be an American. A time to teach them the historical value of their heritage as America's kids. "America . . .They're not heavy . . . They're our children." Annually, the fourth Sunday in June. For info: Judith Natale, CEO & Founder, Natl Children & Family Awareness of America, Administrative Headquarters, 3060 Rt 405 Hwy, Muncy, PA 17756-8808. Phone: (888) MAA-DESK. E-mail: ChildAware@aol.com or MaaJudith@aol.com.

BERLIN AIRLIFT: ANNIVERSARY. June 24, 1948. In the early days of the Cold War the Soviet Union challenged the West's right of access to Berlin. The Soviets created a blockade and an airlift to supply some 2,250,000 people at West Berlin resulted. The airlift lasted a total of 321 days and brought into Berlin 1,592,787 tons of supplies. Joseph Stalin finally backed down and the blockade ended May 12, 1949.

CANADA: NEWFOUNDLAND DISCOVERY DAY. June 24. Commemorates the discovery of Newfoundland by John Cabot in 1497.

CANADA: QUEBEC FÊTE NATIONALE. June 24. Saint Jean Baptiste Day.

CIARDI, JOHN: 85th BIRTH ANNIVERSARY. June 24, 1916. Poet for adults and children (*You Read to Me, I'll Read to You*), born at Boston, MA. Died Mar 30, 1986, at Edison, NJ.

DEAF-BLINDNESS AWARENESS WEEK. June 24–30. A week to observe the birth anniversary of Helen Keller who was born June 27, 1880. Annually, the full week that includes Helen Keller's birthday. For info: Library for Deaf Action, 2930 Craiglawn Rd, Silver Spring, MD 20904-1816. Phone: (301) 572-5168 (TTY). Fax: (301) 572-4134. E-mail: alhagemeyer@juno.com.

JOHN CARVER DAY IN MASSACHUSETTS. June 24. Proclaimed annually by the governor on the fourth Sunday in June to commemorate the first governor of the Plymouth Colony, John Carver, who served from 1620 to 1621.

LATVIA: JOHN'S DAY (MIDSUMMER NIGHT DAY). June 24. The festival of Jani, which commemorates the summer solstice and the name day of (Janis) John, is one of Latvia's most ancient as well as joyous rituals. This festival is traditionally celebrated in the countryside, as it emphasizes fertility and the beginning of summer. Festivities begin June 23. For info: Embassy of Latvia, 4325 17th St NW, Washington, DC 20011. Phone: (202) 726-8213.

THORNTON, MATTHEW: DEATH ANNIVERSARY. June 24, 1803. Signer of the Declaration of Independence. Born at Ireland about 1714, he died at Newburyport, MA.

BIRTHDAYS TODAY

Kathryn Lasky, 57, author (*Sugaring Time*), born Indianapolis, IN, June 24, 1944.

Jean Marzollo, 59, author (*Happy Birthday, Martin Luther King*), born Manchester, CT, June 24, 1942.

George Pataki, 56, Governor of New York (R), born Peekskill, NY, June 24, 1945.

Predrag "Preki" Radosavljevic, 38, soccer player, born Belgrade, Yugoslavia, June 24, 1963.

JUNE 25 — MONDAY
Day 176 — 189 Remaining

BATTLE OF LITTLE BIGHORN: 125th ANNIVERSARY. June 25, 1876. Lieutenant Colonel George Armstrong Custer, leading military forces of more than 200 men, attacked an encampment of Sioux Indians led by Chiefs Sitting Bull and Crazy Horse near Little Bighorn River, MT. Custer and all men in his immediate command were killed in the brief battle (about two hours) of Little Bighorn. For more info: *It Is a Good Day to Die: Indian Eyewitnesses Tell the Story of the Battle of Little Bighorn*, by Herman Viola (Crown, 0-517-70913-9, $19.99 Gr. 5–8).

CBS SENDS FIRST COLOR TV BROADCAST OVER THE AIR: 50th ANNIVERSARY. June 25, 1951. Columbia Broadcast System broadcast the first color television program. The four-hour program was carried by stations in New York City, Baltimore, Philadelphia, Boston and Washington, DC, although no color sets were owned by the public. At the time CBS, itself, owned fewer than 40 color receivers.

CHINA: DRAGON BOAT FESTIVAL. June 25. An important Chinese observance, the Dragon Boat Festival commemorates a hero of ancient China, poet Qu Yuan, who drowned himself in protest against injustice and corruption. It is said that rice dumplings were cast into the water to lure fish away from the body of the martyr, and this is remembered by the eating of zhong zi, glutinous rice dumplings filled with meat and wrapped in bamboo leaves. Dragon boat races are held on rivers. The Dragon Boat Festival is observed in many countries by their Chinese populations. Also called Fifth Month Festival or Summer Festival. Annually, the fifth day of the fifth lunar month.

CIVIL WAR IN YUGOSLAVIA: 10th ANNIVERSARY. June 25, 1991. In an Eastern Europe freed from the iron rule of communism and the USSR, separatist and nationalist tensions suppressed for decades rose to a violent boiling point. The republics of Croatia and Slovenia declared their independence, sparking a fractious and bitter war that spread throughout what was formerly Yugoslavia. Ethnic rivalries between Serbians and Croatians began the military conflicts that spread to Slovenia, and in 1992 fighting began in Bosnia-Herzegovina between Serbians and ethnic Muslims. Although the new republics were recognized by the UN and sanctions passed to stop the fighting, it raged on through 1995 despite the efforts of UN peacekeeping forces.

KIM CAMPBELL SWORN IN AS CANADIAN PRIME MINISTER: ANNIVERSARY. June 25, 1993. After winning the June 13 election to the leadership of the ruling Progressive-Conservative Party, Kim Campbell became Canada's 19th prime minister and its first woman prime minister. However, in the general election held Oct 25, 1993, the Liberal Party routed the Progressive-Conservatives in the worst defeat for a governing political party in Canada's 126-year history, reducing the former government's seats in the House of Commons from 154 to 2. Campbell was among those who lost their seats.

KOREA: TANO DAY. June 25. Fifth day of fifth lunar month. Summer food offered at the household shrine of the ancestors. Also known as Swing Day, since girls, dressed in their prettiest clothes, often compete in swinging matches. The Tano Festival usually lasts from the third through eighth day of the fifth lunar month: June 23–28.

KOREAN WAR BEGAN: ANNIVERSARY. June 25, 1950. Forces from northern Korea invaded southern Korea, beginning a civil war. US ground forces entered the conflict June 30. An armistice was signed at Panmunjom July 27, 1953, formally dividing the country in two—North Korea and South Korea. For more info: korea50.army.mil/teachers.html. The Fall 1999 issue of *Cobblestone* (for students ages 9–14) is devoted to the Korean War.

LAST GREAT BUFFALO HUNT: ANNIVERSARY. June 25–27, 1882: By 1882 most of the estimated 60–75 million buffalo had been killed by white hide hunters, the meat left to rot. Buffalo numbered only about 50,000 when "The Last Great Buffalo Hunt" took place on Indian reservation lands near Hettinger, ND. Some 2,000 Teton Sioux Indians in full hunting regalia killed about 5,000 buffalo. The occasion is also referred to as "The Last Stand of the American Buffalo" as within 16 months the last of the free-ranging buffalo were gone. *See* Curriculum Connection. For info: Wendy Hehn, Dir Community Promotions, Box 1323, Hettinger, ND 58639. Phone: (701) 567-2531. Fax: (701) 567-2690. E-mail: adamsdv@hettinger.ctctel.com. Web: www.hettingernd.com.

MONTSERRAT: VOLCANO ERUPTS: ANNIVERSARY. June 25, 1997. After lying dormant for 400 years, the Soufriere Hills volcano began to come to life in July 1995. It erupted in 1997, covering Plymouth, Montserrat's capital city, and two-thirds of the rest of the lush Caribbean island with a heavy layer of ash. Two-thirds of the population relocated to other islands or to Great Britain. For more info visit Volcano World: volcano.und.nodak.edu.

MOZAMBIQUE: INDEPENDENCE DAY: ANNIVERSARY. June 25. National holiday. Commemorates independence from Portugal in 1975.

SLOVENIA: NATIONAL DAY: 10th ANNIVERSARY. June 25. Public holiday. Commemorates independence from the former Yugoslavia in 1991.

SUPREME COURT BANS OFFICIAL PRAYER: ANNIVERSARY. June 25, 1962. The US Supreme Court ruled that a prayer read aloud in public schools violated the 1st Amendment's separation of church and state. The court again struck down a law pertaining to the First Amendment when it disallowed an Alabama law that permitted a daily one-minute period of silent meditation or prayer in public schools June 1, 1985. (Vote 6–3.)

TWO YUGOSLAV REPUBLICS DECLARE INDEPENDENCE: 10th ANNIVERSARY. June 25, 1991. The republics of Slovenia and Croatia formally declared independence from Yugoslavia. The two northwestern republics did not, however, secede outright.

VIRGINIA RATIFIES CONSTITUTION: ANNIVERSARY. June 25. Became the 10th state to ratify the Constitution in 1788.

		S	M	T	W	T	F	S
June							1	2
2001		3	4	5	6	7	8	9
		10	11	12	13	14	15	16
		17	18	19	20	21	22	23
		24	25	26	27	28	29	30

JUNE 25–27
LAST GREAT BUFFALO HUNT

Although most Americans call this shaggy, hump-shouldered animal a buffalo, zoologists consider them bison. Bison differ from true buffalo in shape and in skeleton. Gigantic herds of bison once roamed the North American prairies. In the mid-1800s, as many as 20 million bison lived in America. Observers said the ground shook when the herds ran and the thundering of their hoofs could be heard more than a mile away.

Native Americans hunted bison and used all parts of the body for food, clothing, tools and shelter. When white settlers came from the east in the late 1800s, they conducted huge hunts, often removing only the head as a trophy. Carcasses were left to rot on the prairie. By 1890, fewer than 600 bison were found in a free-range head count. (See entry in main text for more information about the Last Great Buffalo Hunt.)

Social studies' units can focus on the Plains Indian cultures whose societies revolved around the buffalo hunt. Cultural connections could include researching preparations for the hunt, such as tribal buffalo dances. *The Song of the Buffalo*, by Joseph Bruchac (Harcourt, 0-150200044-5, $16 Gr. 1–4) and *Buffalo Jump*, by Peter Roop (Northland, 0-87358616-6, $14.95 Gr. K–3) are two picture books with a Native American perspective on the importance of the buffalo hunt. *Buffalo Hunt*, by Russell Freedman (Holiday House, 0-8234-0702-0, $19.95 Gr. 3–7) is a nonfiction examination of the history of buffalo hunting. *Buffalo Days*, by Diane Hoyt-Goldsmith (Holiday, 0-8234-1327-6, $16.95 Gr. 3–6) is a modern perspective on buffalo and the Crow Indians.

Students can research the home construction of Indians who hunted buffalo as a mainstay and compare it to the homes of more sedentary Indians. Discuss how mobility was an important factor in the lives of buffalo-hunting societies.

All parts of the buffalo were used by Indians. Students can investigate how meat and hides were preserved, the kind of clothing that was made and how bones and sinew were used to make tools.

A science aspect of buffalo/bison could focus around reports on the bison life cycle and conservation efforts to prevent the species from becoming extinct. *American Bison*, by Ruth Berman (Carolrhoda, 0-87614-697-3, $16.95 Gr. 2–5) is an excellent presentation of physical characteristics, life cycle, traditional history and conservation.

A language arts project might be to write newspaper articles describing two scenes: a Native American buffalo hunt and that of the white hunters, who sometimes rode trains to a buffalo herd, got off, hunted and then re-entered the train.

Art projects could include making a painted cottonball-covered buffalo constructed with three-dimensional materials like cardboard tubing and balloons.

BIRTHDAYS TODAY

Eric Carle, 72, author (*The Very Clumsy Click Beetle*), born Syracuse, NY, June 25, 1929.

Dikembe Mutombo, 35, basketball player, born Kinshasa, Zaire, June 25, 1966.

JUNE 26 — TUESDAY
Day 177 — 188 Remaining

BAR CODE INTRODUCED: ANNIVERSARY. June 26, 1974. A committee formed in 1970 by US grocers and food manufacturers recommended in 1973 a Universal Product Code (i.e., a bar code) for supermarket items that would allow electronic scanning of prices. On this day in 1974 a pack of Wrigley's gum was swiped across the first checkout scanner at a supermarket at Troy, OH. Today bar codes are used to keep track of everything from freight cars to cattle.

BORDEN, SIR ROBERT LAIRD: BIRTH ANNIVERSARY. June 26, 1854. Canadian statesman and prime minister, born at Grand Pre, Nova Scotia. Died at Ottawa, June 10, 1937.

BUCK, PEARL: BIRTH ANNIVERSARY. June 26, 1892. Author (*The Big Wave*), noted authority on China and humanitarian. Nobel Prize winner. Born at Hillsboro, WV. Died Mar 6, 1973, at Danby, VT.

CN TOWER: 25th OPENING ANNIVERSARY. June 26, 1976. Birthday of the world's tallest building and freestanding structure, the CN Tower, 1,815 feet, 5 inches high, at Toronto, Ontario, Canada. For info: CN Tower, 301 Front St W, Toronto, Ont, Canada M5V 2T6. Phone: (416) 360-8500. Fax: (416) 601-4713.

FARLEY, WALTER: BIRTH ANNIVERSARY. June 26, 1922. Children's author, born at New York, NY. He wrote the tale of the famous horse, *The Black Stallion* and later wrote the prequel, *The Young Black Stallion* with his son in 1989. Farley died at Sarasota, FL, Oct 16, 1989.

FLAG AMENDMENT DEFEATED: ANNIVERSARY. June 26, 1990. The Senate rejected a proposed constitutional amendment that would have permitted states to prosecute those who destroyed or desecrated American flags. Similar legislation continues to be considered by Congress.

MADAGASCAR: INDEPENDENCE DAY. June 26. National holiday. Commemorates independence from France in 1960.

MIDDLETON, ARTHUR: BIRTH ANNIVERSARY. June 26, 1742. American Revolutionary leader and signer of the Declaration of Independence, born near Charleston, SC. Died at Goose Creek, SC, Jan 1, 1787.

PIZARRO, FRANCESCO: DEATH ANNIVERSARY. June 26, 1541. Spanish conqueror of Peru, born at Extremadura, Spain, ca. 1471. Pizarro died at Lima, Peru.

SAINT LAWRENCE SEAWAY DEDICATION: ANNIVERSARY. June 26, 1959. President Dwight D. Eisenhower and Queen Elizabeth II jointly dedicated the St. Lawrence Seaway in formal ceremonies held at St. Lambert, Quebec, Canada. A project undertaken jointly by Canada and the US, the waterway (which provides access between the Atlantic Ocean and the Great Lakes) had been opened to traffic Apr 25, 1959.

UNITED NATIONS CHARTER SIGNED: ANNIVERSARY. June 26, 1945. The UN Charter was signed at San Francisco by 50 nations.

UNITED NATIONS: INTERNATIONAL DAY AGAINST DRUG ABUSE AND ILLICIT TRAFFICKING. June 26, 1987. Following a recommendation of the 1987 International Conference on Drug Abuse and Illicit Trafficking, the United Nations General Assembly (Res 42/112), expressed its determination to strengthen action and cooperation for an international society free of drug abuse and proclaimed June 26 as an annual observance to raise public awareness. For info: UN, Dept of Public Info, Public Inquiries Unit, RM GA-57, New York, NY 10017. Phone: (212) 963-4475. Fax: (212) 963-0071. E-mail: inquiries@un.org.

ZAHARIAS, MILDRED "BABE" DIDRIKSON: BIRTH ANNIVERSARY. June 26, 1914. Born Mildred Ella Didrikson at Port Arthur, TX, the great athlete was nicknamed "Babe" after legendary baseball player Babe Ruth. She was named to the women's All-America basketball team when she was 16. At the 1932 Olympic Games, she won two gold medals and also set world records in the javelin throw and the 80-meter high hurdles; only a technicality prevented her from obtaining the gold in the high jump. Didrikson married professional wrestler George Zaharias in 1938, six years after she began playing golf casually. In 1946 Babe won the US Women's Amateur tournament, and in 1947 she won 17 straight golf championships and became the first American winner of the British Ladies' Amateur Tournament. Turning professional in 1948, she won the US Women's Open in 1950 and 1954, the same year she won the All-American Open. Babe also excelled in softball, baseball, swimming, figure skating, billiards—even football. In a 1950 Associated Press poll she was named the woman athlete of the first half of the 20th century. She died of cancer, Sept 27, 1956, at Galveston, TX. For more info: *Babe Didrikson Zaharias: The Making of a Champion*, by Russell Freedman. (Clarion, 0-395-63367-2, $18 Gr. 5 & up).

BIRTHDAYS TODAY

Robert Burch, 76, author (*Christmas with Ida Early*), born Inman, GA, June 26, 1925.

Derek Jeter, 27, baseball player, born Pequannock, NJ, June 26, 1974.

Chris O'Donnell, 31, actor (*Dead Poet's Society, Batman & Robin*), born Winnetka, IL, June 26, 1970.

Charles Robb, 62, US Senator (D, Virginia), born Phoenix, AZ, June 26, 1939.

Jason Schwartzman, 21, actor (*Rushmore*), born Los Angeles, CA, June 26, 1980.

Nancy Willard, 65, author (Newbery for *A Visit to William Blake's Inn: Poems for Innocent and Experienced Travelers*), born Ann Arbor, MI, June 26, 1936.

Charlotte Zolotow, 86, author (*The Moon Was the Best, Peter and the Pigeons*), born Norfolk, VA, June 26, 1915.

JUNE 27 — WEDNESDAY
Day 178 — 187 Remaining

DJIBOUTI: INDEPENDENCE DAY. June 27. National day. Commemorates independence from France in 1977.

HAPPY BIRTHDAY TO "HAPPY BIRTHDAY TO YOU." June 27, 1859. The melody of probably the most often sung song in the world, "Happy Birthday to You," was composed by Mildred J. Hill, a schoolteacher, born at Louisville, KY. Her younger sister, Patty Smith Hill, was the author of the lyrics which were first published in 1893 as "Good Morning to All," a classroom greeting published in the book *Song Stories for the Sunday School*. The lyrics were amended in 1924 to include a stanza beginning "Happy Birthday to You." Now it is sung somewhere in the world every minute of the day. Although the authors are believed to have earned very little from the song, reportedly it later generated about $1 million a year for its copyright owner. The song is expected to enter public domain upon expiration of copyright in 2010. Mildred Hill died at Chicago, IL, June 5, 1916 without knowing that her melody would become the world's most popular song. Patty Hill, born Mar 27, 1868, at Louisville, KY, died at New York, NY, May 25, 1946.

KELLER, HELEN: BIRTH ANNIVERSARY. June 27, 1880. Born at Tuscumbia, AL, Helen Keller was left deaf and blind by a disease she contracted at 18 months of age. With the help of her teacher, Anne Sullivan, she graduated from college and had a career as an author and lecturer. She died June 1, 1968, at Westport, CT. For more info: *A Girl Named Helen Keller*, by Margo Lundell (Scholastic, 0-590-47963-6, $3.99 Gr. 1–3) or *Helen Keller*, by Johanna Hurwitz (Random House, 0-679-87705-3, $3.99 Gr. 2–4) or *Helen Keller*, by Lois Nicholson (Chelsea House, 0-7910-2086-X, $19.95 Gr. 4 & up).

MOON PHASE: FIRST QUARTER. June 27. Moon enters First Quarter phase at 11:19 PM, EDT.

BIRTHDAYS TODAY

Bruce Babbitt, 63, US Secretary of Interior (Clinton administration), born Los Angeles, CA, June 27, 1938.

Lucille Clifton, 65, author (*Everett Anderson's Goodbye*), born Depew, NY, June 27, 1936.

James Lincoln Collier, 73, author of historical fiction, with his brother Christopher Collier (*My Brother Sam Is Dead*), born New York, NY, June 27, 1928.

Captain Kangaroo (Bob Keeshan), 74, TV personality, born Lynbrook, NY, June 27, 1927.

JUNE 28 — THURSDAY
Day 179 — 186 Remaining

FORBES, ESTHER: BIRTH ANNIVERSARY. June 28, 1891. Author and illustrator, born at Westborough, MA. She won the Pulitzer Prize for history in 1943 for her book *Paul Revere and the World He Lived In*. Her children's book, *Johnny Tremain*, was awarded the 1944 Newbery Medal. Forbes died at Worcester, MA, Aug 12, 1967.

MONDAY HOLIDAY LAW: ANNIVERSARY. June 28, 1968. President Lyndon B. Johnson approved Public Law 90–363, which amended section 6103(a) of title 5, United States Code, establishing Monday observance of Washington's Birthday, Memorial Day, Labor Day, Columbus Day and Veterans Day. The new holiday law took effect Jan 1, 1971. Veterans Day observance subsequently reverted to its former observance date, Nov 11. See individual holidays for more details.

	S	M	T	W	T	F	S
June						1	2
2001	3	4	5	6	7	8	9
	10	11	12	13	14	15	16
	17	18	19	20	21	22	23
	24	25	26	27	28	29	30

TREATY OF VERSAILLES: ANNIVERSARY. June 28, 1919. The signing of the Treaty of Versailles at Versailles, France formally ended World War I.

BIRTHDAYS TODAY

John Elway, 41, former football player, born Port Angeles, WA, June 28, 1960.

Mark Grace, 37, baseball player, born Winston-Salem, NC, June 28, 1964.

Bette Greene, 67, author (*Philip Hall Likes Me, I Reckon Maybe*), born Memphis, TN, June 28, 1934.

Carl Levin, 67, US Senator (D, Michigan), born Detroit, MI, June 28, 1934.

JUNE 29 — FRIDAY
Day 180 — 185 Remaining

KEPES, JULIET A.: BIRTH ANNIVERSARY. June 29, 1919. Author and illustrator (Caldecott for *Five Little Monkeys*), born at London, England. Died Mar 11, 1999, at Cambridge, MA.

LATHROP, JULIA C.: BIRTH ANNIVERSARY. June 29, 1858. A pioneer in the battle to establish child-labor laws, Julia C. Lathrop was the first woman member of the Illinois State Board of Charities and in 1900 was instrumental in establishing the first juvenile court in the US. In 1912, President Taft named Lathrop chief of the newly created Children's Bureau, then part of the US Department of Commerce and Labor. In 1925 she became a member of the Child Welfare Committee of the League of Nations. Born at Rockford, IL, she died there Apr 15, 1932.

PETER AND PAUL DAY. June 29. Feast day for Saint Peter and Saint Paul. Commemorates dual martyrdom of Christian apostles Peter (by crucifixion) and Paul (by beheading) during persecution by Roman Emperor Nero. Observed since third century.

SAINT-EXUPERY, ANTOINE DE: BIRTH ANNIVERSARY. June 29, 1900. French aviator and children's author, born at Lyons, France. Saint-Exupery is best known for *The Little Prince*. Other books include *Wind, Sand and Stars* and *Night Flight*. Saint-Exupery died at sea, July 31, 1944.

BIRTHDAYS TODAY

Theo Fleury, 33, hockey player, born Oxbow, Saskatchewan, Canada, June 29, 1968.

JUNE 30 — SATURDAY
Day 181 — 184 Remaining

CHARLES BLONDIN'S CONQUEST OF NIAGARA FALLS: ANNIVERSARY. June 30, 1859. Charles Blondin, a French acrobat and aerialist (whose real name was Jean François Gravelet), in view of a crowd estimated at more than 25,000 persons, walked across Niagara Falls on a tightrope. The walk required only about five minutes. On separate occasions he crossed blindfolded, pushing a wheelbarrow, carrying a man on his back and even on stilts.

Blondin was born Feb 28, 1824, at St. Omer, France, and died at London, England, Feb 19, 1897.

COLONIAL CHILDREN'S FAIR. June 30–July 1 (tentative). Yorktown Victory Center, Yorktown, VA. 18th-century games and entertainment and crafts to make and take home are among a variety of activities planned for young people. Est attendance: 1,500. For info: Jamestown-Yorktown Foundation, PO Box 1607, Williamsburg, VA 23187. Phone: (757) 253-4838. Fax: (757) 253-5299. Web: www.historyisfun.org.

CONGO (KINSHASA): INDEPENDENCE DAY: ANNIVERSARY. June 30. National holiday. The Democratic Republic of Congo was previously known as Zaire. Commemorates independence from Belgium in 1960.

GUATEMALA: ARMED FORCES DAY. June 30. Guatemala observes public holiday.

LAST HURRAH FOR BRITISH HONG KONG: ANNIVERSARY. June 30, 1997. The crested flag of the British Crown Colony was officially lowered at midnight and replaced by a new flag (marked by the bauhinia flower) representing China's sovereignty over Hong Kong and the official transfer of power. Though Britain owned Hong Kong in perpetuity, the land areas surrounding the city were leased from China and the lease expired July 1, 1997. Rather than renegotiate a new lease, Britain ceded its claim to Hong Kong.

LEAP SECOND ADJUSTMENT TIME. June 30. June 30 is one of the times that has been favored for the addition or subtraction of a second from our clock time (to coordinate atomic and astronomical time). The determination to adjust is made by the Central Bureau of the International Earth Rotation Service, at Paris, France.

MONROE, ELIZABETH KORTRIGHT: BIRTH ANNIVERSARY. June 30, 1768. Wife of James Monroe, fifth president of the US, born at New York, NY. Died at their Oak Hill estate at Loudon County, VA, Sept 23, 1830.

NOW FOUNDED: 35th ANNIVERSARY. June 30, 1966. The National Organization for Women was founded at Washington, DC, by people attending the Third National Conference on the Commission on the Status of Women. NOW's purpose is to take action to take women into full partnership in the mainstream of American society, exercising all privileges and responsibilities in equal partnership with men. For info: Natl Organization for Women, 733 15th St NW, Washington, DC 20005. Phone: (202) 628-8NOW. Web: www.now.org.

TWENTY-SIXTH AMENDMENT RATIFIED: 30th ANNIVERSARY. June 30, 1971. The 26th Amendment to the Constitution granted the right to vote in all federal, state and local elections to all persons 18 years or older. On the date of ratification the US gained an additional 11 million voters. Up until this time, the minimum voting age was set by the states; in most states it was 21.

WHEELER, WILLIAM ALMON: BIRTH ANNIVERSARY. June 30, 1819. The 19th vice president of the US (1877–81), born at Malone, NY. Died there June 4, 1887.

BIRTHDAYS TODAY

Mollie Hunter, 79, author (*A Sound of Chariots*), born Longniddry, Scotland, June 30, 1922.

David McPhail, 61, author and illustrator (*Pigs Ahoy!*), born Newburyport, MA, June 30, 1940.

Mitchell "Mitch" Richmond, 36, basketball player, born Ft Lauderdale, FL, June 30, 1965.

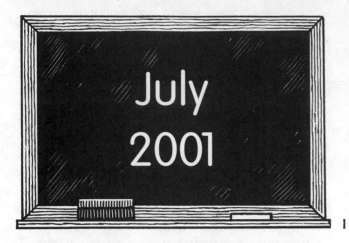

JULY 1 — SUNDAY
Day 182 — 183 Remaining

BATTLE OF GETTYSBURG: ANNIVERSARY. July 1, 1863. After the Southern success at Chancellorsville, VA, Confederate General Robert E. Lee led his forces on an invasion of the North, initially targeting Harrisburg, PA. As Union forces moved to counter the invasion, the battle lines were eventually formed at Gettysburg, PA, in one of the Civil War's most crucial battles, beginning July 1, 1863. On the climactic third day of the battle (July 3), Lee ordered an attack on the center of the Union line, later to be known as Pickett's Charge. The 15,000 rebels were repulsed, ending the Battle of Gettysburg. After the defeat, Lee's forces retreated back to Virginia, listing more than one-third of the troops as casualties in the failed invasion. Union General George Meade initially failed to pursue the retreating rebels, allowing Lee's army to escape across the rain-swollen Potomac River.

BURUNDI: INDEPENDENCE DAY. July 1. National holiday. Anniversary of establishment of independence in 1962. Had been under Belgian administration as part of Ruanda-Urundi.

CANADA: CANADA DAY. July 1. National holiday. Canada's national day, formerly known as Dominion Day. Observed on following day when July 1 is a Sunday (July 2 in 2001). Commemorates the confederation of Upper and Lower Canada and some of the Maritime Provinces into the Dominion of Canada in 1867.

DIANA, PRINCESS OF WALES: 40th BIRTH ANNIVERSARY. July 1, 1961. Former wife of Charles, Prince of Wales, and mother of Prince William and Prince Harry. Born Lady Diana Spencer at Sandringham, England, she died in an automobile accident at Paris, France, Aug 31, 1997.

DORSEY, THOMAS A.: BIRTH ANNIVERSARY. July 1, 1899. Thomas A. Dorsey, the father of gospel music, was born at Villa Rica, GA. Originally a blues composer, Dorsey eventually combined blues and sacred music to develop gospel music. It was Dorsey's composition "Take My Hand, Precious Lord" that Reverend Dr. Martin Luther King, Jr, had asked to have performed just moments before his assassination. Dorsey, who composed

	S	M	T	W	T	F	S
July		1	2	3	4	5	6	7
2001	8	9	10	11	12	13	14
	15	16	17	18	19	20	21
	22	23	24	25	26	27	28
	29	30	31				

more than 1,000 gospel songs and hundreds of blues songs in his lifetime, died Jan 23, 1993, at Chicago, IL.

FIRST ADHESIVE US POSTAGE STAMPS ISSUED: ANNIVERSARY. July 1, 1847. The first adhesive US postage stamps were issued by the US Postal Service.

FIRST US ZOO: ANNIVERSARY. July 1, 1874. The Philadelphia Zoological Society, the first US zoo, opened. Three thousand visitors traveled by foot, horse and carriage and steamboat to visit the exhibits. Price of admission was 25 cents for adults and 10 cents for children. There were 1,000 animals in the zoo on opening day.

GHANA: REPUBLIC DAY: ANNIVERSARY. July 1. National holiday. Commemorates the inauguration of the Republic in 1960.

NATIONAL BAKED BEAN MONTH. July 1–31. To pay tribute to one of America's favorite and most healthful and nutritious foods, baked beans, made with dry or canned beans. For info: Gwen DeVries, Bean Education & Awareness Network, 303 E Wacker Dr, Ste 440, Chicago, IL 60601. Phone: (312) 861-5200. Fax: (312) 861-5252.

NATIONAL EDUCATION ASSOCIATION MEETING. July 1–6 (tentative). Los Angeles, CA. More than 9,000 delegates from the local and state level debate issues and set NEA policy at the Representative Assembly. Est attendance: 10,000. For info: Natl Education Assn, 1201 16th St NW, Washington, DC 20036-3290. Phone: (202) 822-7769. Web: www.nea.org.

NATIONAL FOREIGN LANGUAGE MONTH. July 1–31. Start to learn a foreign language this month. *See* Curriculum Connection. For info: Jonathan Earling, 1264 Olde Farm Rd, Schaumburg, IL 60173. Phone: (847) 397-6601.

NATIONAL HOT DOG MONTH. July 1–31. Celebrates one of America's favorite hand–held foods with fun facts and new topping ideas. More than 16 billion hot dogs per year are sold in the US. For info: Natl Hot Dog & Sausage Council, 1700 N Moore St, Ste 1600, Arlington, VA 22209. Phone: (703) 841-2400. Web: www.hot-dog.org.

NATIONAL JULY BELONGS TO BLUEBERRIES MONTH. July 1–31. To make the public aware that this is the peak month for fresh blueberries. For info: North American Blueberry Council, 4995 Golden Foothill Parkway, Ste #2, El Dorado Hills, CA 95762.

NATIONAL RECREATION AND PARKS MONTH. July 1–31. To showcase and invite community participation in quality leisure activities for all segments of the population. For info: Natl Recreation and Park Assn, 22377 Belmont Ridge Rd, Ashburn, VA 20148. Phone: (703) 858-0784. Fax: (703) 858-0794. E-mail: info@nrpa.org. Web: www.activeparks.org.

NICK AT NITE TV PREMIERE: ANNIVERSARY. July 1, 1985. The first broadcast of Nick at Nite, the creation of the kids' network Nickelodeon. Owned and operated by MTV Networks, Nick at Nite presents many of the old classic television series, such as "Happy Days," "The Brady Bunch" and "My Three Sons." For more info visit www.nick-at-nite.com.

REGULAR TV BROADCASTS BEGIN: ANNIVERSARY. July 1, 1941. The Federal Communications Commission allowed 18 television stations to begin broadcasting this day. However, only two were ready: the New York stations owned by NBC and CBS.

RWANDESE REPUBLIC: INDEPENDENCE DAY. July 1. National holiday. Commemorates independence from Belgium in 1962.

JULY 1–31
NATIONAL FOREIGN LANGUAGE MONTH

The media frequently mention we now live in a "global community." What better way to acknowledge this than by starting to learn a foreign language?

Often children are afraid to try another language because they think classmates will laugh at them. Learning songs is a nonthreatening first step since everyone can sing together. *Spanish Children's Songs*, by Carole Flatau (Warner Brothers, 0-7692-1664-1, $6.95) and *French Songs*, by Anthony Marks and Sylvestre Balazard (EDC, 0-7460-2425-8, $6.95) are collections of songs in Spanish and French. Ask one of your district's music teachers for other suggestions or for names of community members who might be willing to visit the classroom and teach a song in a different language. There are many CD sources on the Internet that list world music collections for children.

It's also fun to learn the alphabet, especially if it looks different from the standard English alphabet. The Greek and Cyrillic alphabets are fairly easy to learn. Braille and American sign language are also different language alternatives.

See if any parents have expertise in a foreign language and would be willing to come in and share with the class. Fun things they could teach are commonly used idioms or phrases that students could use in place of "What's happening?," "That's okay" or "See you later, alligator." Compile a list of cognates in Spanish or French and English. Children enjoy discovering similarities between languages and cognates are easy to remember.

Have students make foreign language labels for objects in the classroom. Remember, English may be a second language in some students' homes. For a twist on labeling, students and their families could label objects in their home in English. It's a fun way to learn and foster literacy for both generations.

Try to learn the equivalents of "good morning," "good afternoon," "thank you" and other routine daily phrases. Organize the month into sections, depending on how many languages you want to introduce (and how many phrases you can gather). Perhaps choose four languages that would have applicability to ethnic heritages found in your school. Feature one language each week of the month. Middle school teachers might want to consider a FLEX (Foreign Language Exploratory Program) course. *Exploring Languages: A Complete Introduction for Foreign Language Students* teaches about languages in general, then English in particular, followed by exploratory units on 12 different languages, including Japanese, Swahili and Hebrew (NTC/Contemporary Publishing Group, 0-8442-9360-1, $21.88 Gr. 6–8).

Many publishing companies produce picture books that contain English text and another language, too. For example, *Mother Goose on the Rio Grande*, by Frances Alexander (2d ed, NTC/Contemporary Publishing Group, 0-8442-7642-1, $7.95 Gr. K–3) is filled with rhymes, songs, games, poems and riddles in Spanish and English. NTC/Contemporary Publishing Group also publishes a series of bilingual fables in Spanish and English. Call 1-800-323-4900 or e-mail ntcpub@tribune.com for a free copy of their elementary and middle school World Languages catalog.

Incorporate language fun into game sessions during recess. Simple games like Simon Says become more challenging when actions and commands are given in another language. Although not part of recess, out-loud recitation of simple addition, subtraction and multiplication problems is also fun. The mental translation of numbers into another language doubly reinforces the lesson in each problem.

SPACE MILESTONE: *KOSMOS 1383* (USSR). July 1, 1982. First search and rescue satellite—equipped to hear distress calls from aircraft and ships—launched in cooperative project with the US and France.

UNITED NATIONS: INTERNATIONAL DAY OF COOPERATIVES. July 7. On Dec 16, 1992, the General Assembly proclaimed this observance for the first Saturday of July 1995 (Res 47/60). On Dec 23, 1994, recognizing that cooperatives are becoming an indispensable factor of economic and social development, the Assembly invited governments, international organizations, specialized agencies and national and international cooperative organizations to observe this day annually (Res 49/155). For info: United Nations, Dept of Public Info, New York, NY 10017.

WALKMAN DEBUTS: ANNIVERSARY. July 1, 1979. This month Sony introduced the Walkman under the name Soundabout, selling for $200. It had been released in Japan six months earlier. More than 185 million have been sold.

ZIP CODES INAUGURATED: ANNIVERSARY. July 1, 1963. The US Postal Service introduced the five-digit zip code on this day.

BIRTHDAYS TODAY

Diane Hoyt-Goldsmith, 51, author (*Buffalo Days*), born Peoria, IL, July 1, 1950.

Carl Lewis, 40, Olympic gold medal sprinter and long jumper, born Birmingham, AL, July 1, 1961.

Emily Arnold McCully, 62, author and illustrator (Caldecott for *Mirette on the High Wire*), born Galesburg, IL, July 1, 1939.

JULY 2 — MONDAY
Day 183 — 182 Remaining

CARIBBEAN OR CARICOM DAY. July 2. The anniversary of the treaty establishing the Caribbean Community (also called the Treaty of Chaguaramas), signed by the prime ministers of Barbados, Guyana, Jamaica and Trinidad and Tobago July 4, 1973. Observed as a public holiday by the participating nations. Annually, the first Monday in July.

CIVIL RIGHTS ACT OF 1964: ANNIVERSARY. July 2, 1964. President Lyndon Johnson signed the Voting Rights Act of 1964 into law, prohibiting discrimination on the basis of race in public accommodations, in publicly owned or operated facilities, in employment and union membership and in the registration of voters. The bill included Title VI, which allowed for the cutoff of federal funding in areas where discrimination persisted.

CONSTITUTION OF THE US TAKES EFFECT: ANNIVERSARY. July 2, 1788. Cyrus Griffin of Virginia, the president of the Congress, announced that the Constitution had been ratified by the required nine states (the ninth being New Hampshire June 21, 1788), and a committee was appointed to make preparations for the change of government.

DECLARATION OF INDEPENDENCE RESOLUTION: 225th ANNIVERSARY. July 2, 1776. Anniversary of adoption by the Continental Congress, Philadelphia, PA, of a resolution introduced June 7, 1776, by Richard Henry Lee of Virginia: "Resolved, That these United Colonies are, and of right ought to be, free and independent States, that they are absolved from all allegiance to the British Crown, and that all political connection between them and the State of Great Britain is, and ought to be, totally dissolved. That it is expedient forthwith to take the most effectual measures for forming foreign Alliances. That a plan of confederation be prepared and transmitted to the respective Colonies for their consideration and approbation." This resolution prepared the way for adoption, July 4, 1776, of the Declaration of Independence. See also: "Declaration of Independence: Anniversary" (July 4).

HALFWAY POINT OF 2001. July 2. At noon on July 2, 2001, 182½ days of the year will have elapsed and 182½ will remain before Jan 1, 2002.

MARSHALL, THURGOOD: BIRTH ANNIVERSARY. July 2, 1908. Thurgood Marshall, the first African American on the US Supreme Court, was born at Baltimore, MD. For more than 20 years, he served as director-counsel of the NAACP Legal Defense and Educational Fund. He experienced his greatest legal victory May 17, 1954, when the Supreme Court decision on *Brown v Board of Education* declared an end to the "separate but equal" system of racial segregation in public schools in 21 states. Marshall argued 32 cases before the Supreme Court, winning 29 of them, before becoming a member of the high court himself. Nominated by President Lyndon Johnson, he began his 24-year career on the high court Oct 2, 1967, becoming a voice of dissent in an increasingly conservative court. Marshall announced his retirement June 27, 1991, and he died Jan 24, 1993, at Washington, DC.

VESEY, DENMARK: DEATH ANNIVERSARY. July 2, 1822. Planner of what would have been the biggest slave revolt in US history, Denmark Vesey was executed at Charleston, SC. He had been born around 1767, probably in the West Indies, where he was sold at around age 14 to Joseph Vesey, captain of a slave ship. He purchased his freedom in 1800. In 1818 Vesey and others began to plot an uprising; he held secret meetings, collected disguises and firearms and chose a date in June 1822. But authorities were warned, and police and the military were out in full force. Over the next two months 130 blacks were taken into custody; 35, including Vesey, were hanged and 31 were exiled. As a result of the plot Southern legislatures passed more rigorous slave codes.

ZAMBIA: HEROES DAY. July 2. First Monday in July is Zambian national holiday—memorial day for Zambians who died in the struggle for independence. Political rallies stress solidarity.

BIRTHDAYS TODAY

Jose Canseco, Jr, 37, baseball player, born Havana, Cuba, July 2, 1964.
Jack Gantos, 50, author (the Rotten Ralph series), born Mount Pleasant, PA, July 2, 1951.
Rita Golden Gelman, 64, author (*More Spaghetti, I Say!*), born Bridgeport, CT, July 2, 1937.
Jean Craighead George, 82, author (Newbery for *Julie of the Wolves*), born Washington, DC, July 2, 1919.

July 2001	S	M	T	W	T	F	S
	1	2	3	4	5	6	7
	8	9	10	11	12	13	14
	15	16	17	18	19	20	21
	22	23	24	25	26	27	28
	29	30	31				

Lindsay Lohan, 15, actress (*The Parent Trap*), born New York, NY, July 2, 1986.
Chris Lynch, 39, author (*Slot Machine*), born Boston, MA, July 2, 1962.

JULY 3 — TUESDAY
Day 184 — 181 Remaining

AIR CONDITIONING APPRECIATION DAYS. July 3–Aug 15. Northern Hemisphere. During Dog Days, the hottest time of the year in the Northern Hemisphere, to acknowledge the contribution of air conditioning to a better way of life. Annually, July 3–Aug 15. For info: Air-Conditioning and Refrig Institute, 4301 N Fairfax Dr, Ste 425, Arlington, VA 22203. Phone: (703) 524-8800. Fax: (703) 528-3816. E-mail: ari@ari.org. Web: www.ari.org.

BELARUS: INDEPENDENCE DAY: 10th ANNIVERSARY. July 3. National holiday. A former republic of the Soviet Union, it became independent in 1991.

BENNETT, RICHARD BEDFORD: BIRTH ANNIVERSARY. July 3, 1870. Former Canadian prime minister, born at Hopewell Hill, New Brunswick, Canada. Died at Mickelham, England, June 26, 1947.

CANADA: NEWFOUNDLAND MEMORIAL DAY. July 3.

DOG DAYS. July 3–Aug 15. Hottest days of the year in Northern Hemisphere. Usually about 40 days, but variously reckoned at 30–54 days. Popularly believed to be an evil time "when the sea boiled, wine turned sour, dogs grew mad, and all creatures became languid, causing to man burning fevers, hysterics and phrensies" (from Brady's *Clavis Calendarium*, 1813). Originally the days when Sirius, the Dog Star, rose just before or at about the same time as sunrise (no longer true owing to precession of the equinoxes). Ancients sacrificed a brown dog at beginning of Dog Days to appease the rage of Sirius, believing that star was the cause of the hot, sultry weather.

HUNTINGTON, SAMUEL: BIRTH ANNIVERSARY. July 3, 1731. President of the Continental Congress, Governor of Connecticut, signer of the Declaration of Independence, born at Windham, CT, died at Norwich, CT, Jan 5, 1796.

IDAHO: ADMISSION DAY: ANNIVERSARY. July 3. Became 43rd state in 1890.

STAY OUT OF THE SUN DAY. July 3. For health's sake, give your skin a break today. [© 1999 by WH] For info: Tom and Ruth Roy, Wellcat Holidays, 2418 Long Ln, Lebanon, PA 17046. Phone: (230) 332-4886. E-mail: wellcat@supernet.com. Web: www.wellcat.com.

TAIWAN: BIRTHDAY OF CHENG HUANG. July 3. Thirteenth day of fifth moon. Celebrated with a procession of actors on stilts doing dragon and lion dances.

VIRGIN ISLANDS: DANISH WEST INDIES EMANCIPATION DAY: ANNIVERSARY. July 3, 1848. Commemorates freeing of slaves in the Danish West Indies. Ceremony at Frederiksted, St. Croix, where actual proclamation was first read by Governor-General Peter Von Scholten.

ZAMBIA: UNITY DAY. July 3. Memorial day for Zambians who died in the struggle for independence. Political rallies stressing solidarity throughout country. Annually, the first Tuesday in July.

BIRTHDAYS TODAY

Moises Alou, 35, baseball player, born Atlanta, GA, July 3, 1966.

Franny Billingsley, 47, author (*Well Wished*), born Chicago, IL, July 3, 1954.

Tom Cruise, 39, actor (*Rain Man, Born on the Fourth of July*), born Syracuse, NY, July 3, 1962.

Teemu Selanne, 31, hockey player, born Helsinki, Finland, July 3, 1970.

JULY 4 — WEDNESDAY
Day 185 — 180 Remaining

"AMERICA THE BEAUTIFUL" PUBLISHED: ANNIVERSARY. July 4, 1895. The poem "America the Beautiful" by Katherine Lee Bates, a Wellesley College professor, was first published in the *Congregationalist*, a church publication. Later it was set to music. For more info: *Purple Mountain Majesties: The Story of Katherine Lee Bates and "America the Beautiful"*, by Barbara Younger (Dutton, 0-525-45653-8, $15.99 Gr. 3–5). In *America the Beautiful* 16 landscape paintings by Neil Waldman help bring the lyrics alive for children (0-689-31861-8, Atheneum, $16 All ages).

COOLIDGE, CALVIN: BIRTH ANNIVERSARY. July 4, 1872. The 30th president of the US was born John Calvin Coolidge at Plymouth, VT. He succeeded to the presidency Aug 3, 1923, following the death of Warren G. Harding. Coolidge was elected president once, in 1924, but did "not choose to run for president in 1928." Nicknamed Silent Cal, he is reported to have said, "If you don't say anything, you won't be called on to repeat it." Coolidge died at Northampton, MA, Jan 5, 1933.

DECLARATION OF INDEPENDENCE APPROVAL AND SIGNING: 225th ANNIVERSARY. July 4, 1776. The Declaration of Independence was approved by the Continental Congress: "Signed by Order and in Behalf of the Congress, John Hancock, President, Attest, Charles Thomson, Secretary." The official signing occurred Aug 2, 1776. The manuscript journals of the Congress for that date state: "The declaration of independence being engrossed and compared at the table was signed by the members."

EARTH AT APHELION. July 4. At approximately 10 AM, EDT, planet Earth will reach aphelion, that point in its orbit when it is farthest from the sun (about 94,510,000 miles). The Earth's mean distance from the sun (mean radius of its orbit) is reached early in the months of April and October. Note that Earth is farthest from the sun during Northern Hemisphere summer. See also: "Earth at Perihelion" (Jan 4).

FOSTER, STEPHEN: 175th BIRTH ANNIVERSARY. July 4, 1826. Stephen Collins Foster, one of America's most famous and best-loved songwriters, was born at Lawrenceville, PA. Among his nearly 200 songs: "Oh! Susanna," "Camptown Races," "Old Folks at Home" ("Swanee River"), "Jeanie with the Light Brown Hair," "Old Black Joe" and "Beautiful Dreamer." Foster died in poverty at Bellevue Hospital at New York, NY, Jan 13, 1864. The anniversary of his death has been observed as Stephen Foster Memorial Day by Presidential Proclamation since 1952.

INDEPENDENCE DAY (FOURTH OF JULY): 225th ANNIVERSARY. July 4, 1776. The US commemorates adoption of the Declaration of Independence by the Continental Congress. The nation's birthday. Legal holiday in all states and territories. For links to websites about the Fourth of July, go to: deil.lang.uiuc .edu/web.pages/holidays/fourth.html.

NATIONAL TOM SAWYER DAYS (WITH FENCE PAINTING CONTEST). July 4–7. Hannibal, MO. Frog jumping, mud volleyball, Tom and Becky Contest, parade, Tomboy Sawyer Contest, 10K run, arts & crafts show and fireworks launched from the banks of the Mississippi River. Highlight is the National Fence Painting Contest. Sponsor: Hannibal Jaycees. Est attendance: 100,000. For info: Hannibal Visitors Bureau, 505 N 3rd St, Hannibal, MO 63401. Phone: (573) 221-2477.

PHILIPPINES: FIL-AMERICAN FRIENDSHIP DAY. July 4. Formerly National Independence Day, when the Philippines were a colony of the US, now celebrated as Fil-American Friendship Day.

SPACE MILESTONE: *MARS PATHFINDER* (US). July 4, 1997. Unmanned spacecraft landed on Mars after a seven-month flight. Carried *Sojourner*, a roving robotic explorer that sent back photographs of the landscape. One of its missions was to find if life ever existed on Mars. See also: "Space Milestone: *Mars Global Surveyor*" (Sept 11). For more info: *The Adventures of Sojourner: The Mission to Mars that Thrilled the World*, by Susi Trautmann Wunsch (Firefly, 0-9650493-5-3, $22.95 Gr. 4–7).

SPACE MILESTONE: *NOZOMI* (JAPAN). July 4, 1998. Japan launched this mission to Mars, making it the third country (after the US and Russia) to try an interplanetary space mission. *Nozomi*, which means "Hope," will orbit 84 miles above Mars and beam images back to Earth.

BIRTHDAYS TODAY

BIRTHDAYS TODAY

Harvey Grant, 36, basketball player, born Augusta, GA, July 4, 1965.

Horace Grant, 36, basketball player, born Augusta, GA, July 4, 1965.

JULY 5 — THURSDAY
Day 186 — 179 Remaining

ALGERIA: INDEPENDENCE DAY. July 5. National holiday. Commemorates the day in 1962 when Algeria gained independence from France, after more than 100 years as a colony.

BARNUM, PHINEAS TAYLOR: BIRTH ANNIVERSARY. July 5, 1810. Promoter of the bizarre and unusual. Barnum's American Museum opened in 1842, promoting unusual acts including the Feejee Mermaid, Chang and Eng (the original Siamese Twins) and General Tom Thumb. In 1850 he began his promotion of Jenny Lind, "The Swedish Nightingale," and parlayed her singing talents into a major financial success. Barnum also cultivated a keen interest in politics. As a founder of the newspaper *Herald of Freedom*, his outspoken editorials resulted not only in lawsuits but also in at least one jail sentence. In 1852 he declined the Democratic nomination for governor of Connecticut but did serve two terms in the Connecticut legislature beginning in 1865. He was defeated in a bid for US Congress in 1866 but served as mayor of Bridgeport, CT, from 1875 to 1876. In 1871 "The Greatest Show on Earth" opened at Brooklyn, NY; Barnum merged with his rival J.A. Bailey in 1881 to form the Barnum and Bailey Circus. P.T. Barnum was born at Bethel, CT, and died at Bridgeport, CT, Apr 7, 1891.

CAPE VERDE: NATIONAL DAY: ANNIVERSARY. July 5. Commemorates independence from Portugal in 1975.

LUNAR ECLIPSE. July 5. Partial eclipse of the Moon. Moon enters penumbra 8:10 AM, EDT, middle of eclipse 10:55 AM, Moon leaves penumbra 1:39 PM. The beginning of the umbral phase is visible in Antarctica, Australia, New Zealand, eastern Asia except the far north, Aleutian Islands, Pacific Ocean except extreme east and the eastern Indian Ocean; the end visible in Australia, Antarctica, New Zealand, Asia except extreme northern part, eastern Africa, western Pacific Ocean and the Indian Ocean.

MICHIGAN STORYTELLERS FESTIVAL. July 5–7. Flint, MI. Storytelling performances, workshops and swaps come together for family fun and professional support at this 21st annual event. Annually, the weekend after July 4th. Est attendance: 1,500. For info: Cynthia Stilley, Flint Public Library, 1026 E Kearsley, Flint, MI 48502. Phone: (810) 232-7111. Fax: (810) 232-8360. E-mail: cstilley@flint.lib.mi.us.

MOON PHASE: FULL MOON. July 5. Moon enters Full Moon phase at 11:04 AM, EDT.

SLOVAKIA: SAINT CYRIL AND METHODIUS DAY. July 5. This day is dedicated to the Greek priests and scholars from Thessalonniki, who were invited by Prince Rastislav of Great Moravia to introduce Christianity and the first Slavic alphabet to the pagan people of the kingdom in AD 863.

VENEZUELA: INDEPENDENCE DAY. July 5. National holiday. Commemorates Proclamation of Independence from Spain in 1811. Independence achieved in 1821.

BIRTHDAYS TODAY

Janice Del Negro, 46, author (*Lucy Dove*), born The Bronx, NY, July 5, 1955.

Meredith Ann Pierce, 43, fantasy author (*The Darkangel*), born Seattle, WA, July 5, 1958.

JULY 6 — FRIDAY
Day 187 — 178 Remaining

COMOROS: INDEPENDENCE DAY: ANNIVERSARY. July 6. Federal and Islamic Republic of Comoros commemorates Declaration of Independence from France in 1975.

CZECH REPUBLIC: COMMEMORATION DAY OF BURNING OF JOHN HUS. July 6. In honor of Bohemian religious reformer John Hus, who was condemned as a heretic and burned at the stake in 1415.

FIRST SUCCESSFUL ANTIRABIES INOCULATION: ANNIVERSARY. July 6, 1885. Louis Pasteur gave the first successful antirabies inoculation to a boy who had been bitten by an infected dog.

GERMANY: CAPITAL RETURNS TO BERLIN: ANNIVERSARY. July 6, 1999. The monthlong process of moving the German government from Bonn to Berlin began, eight years after Parliament had voted to return to its prewar seat. Parliament reconvened at the newly restored Reichstag on Sept 7, 1999.

LUXEMBOURG: ETTELBRUCK REMEMBRANCE DAY. July 6. In honor of US General George Patton, Jr, liberator of the Grand-Duchy of Luxembourg in 1945, who is buried at the American Military Cemetery at Hamm, Germany, among 5,100 soldiers of his famous Third Army.

MAJOR LEAGUE BASEBALL HOLDS FIRST ALL-STAR GAME: ANNIVERSARY. July 6, 1933. The first midsummer All-Star Game was held at Comiskey Park, Chicago, IL. Babe Ruth led the American League with a home run, as they defeated the National League 4–2. Prior to the summer of 1933, All-Star contests consisted of pre- and postseason exhibitions that often found teams made up of a few stars playing beside journeymen and even minor leaguers.

MALAWI: REPUBLIC DAY. July 6. National holiday. Commemorates independence of the former Nyasaland from Britain in 1964 and Malawi's becoming a republic in 1966.

BIRTHDAYS TODAY

George W. Bush, 55, Governor of Texas (R), born Midland, TX, July 6, 1946.

Tamera Mowry, 23, actress ("Sister, Sister"), born West Germany, July 6, 1978.

	S	M	T	W	T	F	S
July 2001	1	2	3	4	5	6	7
	8	9	10	11	12	13	14
	15	16	17	18	19	20	21
	22	23	24	25	26	27	28
	29	30	31				

Tia Mowry, 23, actress ("Sister, Sister"), born West Germany, July 6, 1978.

Nancy Davis Reagan, 80, former First Lady, wife of Ronald Reagan, 40th president of the US, born New York, NY, July 6, 1921.

JULY 7 — SATURDAY

Day 188 — 177 Remaining

BONZA BOTTLER DAY™. July 7. To celebrate when the number of the day is the same as the number of the month. Bonza Bottler Day™ is an excuse to have a party at least once a month. For info: Gail M. Berger, 109 Matthew Ave, Poca, WV 25159. Phone: (304) 776-7746. E-mail: gberger5@aol.com.

FATHER-DAUGHTER TAKE A WALK TOGETHER DAY. July 7. A special time in the summer for fathers and daughters of all ages to spend time together in the beautiful weather. Annually, July 7. For info: Janet Dellaria, 202 N Bennett St, Geneva, IL 60134. Phone: (630) 232-0425.

HAWAII ANNEXED BY US: ANNIVERSARY. July 7, 1898. President William McKinley signed a resolution annexing Hawaii. No change in government took place until 1900, when Congress passed an act making Hawaii an "incorporated" territory of the US. This act remained in effect until Hawaii became a state in 1959.

JAPAN: TANABATA (STAR FESTIVAL). July 7. As an offering to the stars, children set up bamboo branches to which colorful strips of paper bearing poems are tied.

PAIGE, LEROY ROBERT (SATCHEL): 95th BIRTH ANNIVERSARY. July 7, 1906. Baseball Hall of Fame pitcher, born at Mobile, AL. Paige was the greatest attraction in the Negro Leagues and was also, at age 42, the first black pitcher in the American League. Inducted into the Hall of Fame in 1971. Died at Kansas City, MO, June 8, 1982. For more info: *Satchel Paige*, by Lesa Cline-Ransome (S&S, 0-689-81151-9, $16 Gr. 2–4).

SOLOMON ISLANDS: INDEPENDENCE DAY. July 7. National holiday. Commemorates independence from Britain in 1978.

TANZANIA: SABA SABA DAY. July 7. Tanzania's mainland ruling party, TANU, was formed in 1954.

BIRTHDAYS TODAY

Michelle Kwan, 21, figure skater, born Torrance, CA, July 7, 1980.

Joe Sakic, 32, hockey player, born Burnaby, British Columbia, Canada, July 7, 1969.

JULY 8 — SUNDAY

Day 189 — 176 Remaining

DECLARATION OF INDEPENDENCE FIRST PUBLIC READING: 225th ANNIVERSARY. July 8, 1776. Colonel John Nixon read the Declaration of Independence to the assembled residents at Philadelphia's Independence Square.

FAST OF TAMMUZ. July 8. Jewish holiday. Hebrew calendar date: Tammuz 17, 5761. Shiva Asar B'Tammuz begins at first light of day and commemorates the first-century Roman siege that breached the walls of Jerusalem. Begins a three-week time of mourning.

PUPPETEERS OF AMERICA NATIONAL FESTIVAL. July 8–14. Tampa, FL. Celebrate puppetry with an intense week of performances, workshops, panels and parties. *See* Curriculum Connection. For info: Puppeteers of America, #5 Cricklewood Path, Pasadena, CA 91107-1002. Web: www.puppeteers.org.

JULY 8–14
PUPPETEERS OF AMERICA NATIONAL FESTIVAL

Puppets have entertained and delighted audiences for hundreds of years. One of the most famous puppets is Punch, from the Punch and Judy shows that originated in the latter half of the 1600s. Today, almost everyone recognizes the faces of Miss Piggy and Kermit, Muppets created by Jim Henson.

Students can have lots of fun with puppets. Have them write their own short productions or adapt selections from favorite fairy tales or picture books. If your students are learning a new language, they could write simple puppets shows that use the language in several conversational settings.

Constructing a puppet theater doesn't have to be a major undertaking. The quickest puppet "stages" can be made by turning a table on its side or by tying a rope between two chairs and laying a sheet over the rope. Students may enjoy making a more elaborate stage from cardboard.

Preschoolers and kindergartners love to tell "puppet" stories with simple felt cutouts placed on felt-covered boards. Sometimes this is easier than using regular puppets since it doesn't require much manual dexterity.

Puppets are easy to make with a number of materials that can be found in the classroom or at home. Stick or rod puppets can be constructed with paper and a twig. Cut into fanciful shapes, they can be simple or quite elaborate. Put them behind a sheet and backlight them for shadow presentations and they are even more dramatic.

Use gloves or old socks to construct hand puppets. Attach string, yarn, buttons, paper and other materials to create facial features and clothing.

Marionettes take a bit more work, but older students enjoy constructing them and the challenge of operating them.

Literature connections include: *What's It Like to Be a Puppeteer?*, by Susan Poskanzer (Troll, 0-8167-1433-9, $3.95 Gr. 1–3); *Creative Paper Plate Puppetry*, by Elaine Cole and David Cole (Children's Outreach, 1-883426-18-9, $5 Gr. 1–12); and *Puppet Shows Made Easy*, by Nancy Renfro (Nancy Renfro Studios, 0-931044-13-8, $16.95 Gr. 2–12).

See the entry in the main text for information about the Puppeteers of America and ask your librarian if she can locate videos of multicultural puppetry.

ROCKEFELLER, NELSON ALDRICH: BIRTH ANNIVERSARY. July 8, 1908. The 41st vice president of the US (1974–77), born at Bar Harbor, ME. Rockefeller was nominated for vice president by President Ford when Ford assumed the presidency after the resignation of Richard Nixon. Rockefeller was the second person to have become vice president without being elected (Gerald Ford was the first). Rockefeller died Jan 26, 1979, at New York, NY.

BIRTHDAYS TODAY

Raffi Cavoukian, 53, children's singer and songwriter, born Cairo, Egypt, July 8, 1948.

James Cross Giblin, 68, author (*Chimney Sweep*), born Cleveland, OH, July 8, 1933.

Phil Gramm, 59, US Senator (R, Texas), born Fort Benning, GA, July 8, 1942.

JULY 9 — MONDAY
Day 190 — 175 Remaining

ARGENTINA: INDEPENDENCE DAY. July 9. Anniversary of establishment of independent republic, with the declaration of independence from Spain in 1816.

FOURTEENTH AMENDMENT TO US CONSTITUTION RATIFIED: ANNIVERSARY. July 9, 1868. The 14th Amendment defined US citizenship and provided that no State shall have the right to abridge the rights of any citizen without due process and equal protection under the law. Coming three years after the Civil War, the 14th Amendment also included provisions for barring individuals who assisted in any rebellion or insurrection against the US from holding public office and releasing federal and state governments from any financial liability incurred in the assistance of rebellion or insurrection against the US.

BIRTHDAYS TODAY

Nancy Farmer, 60, author (*A Girl Named Disaster, The Ear, the Eye and the Arm*), born Phoenix, AZ, July 9, 1941.

Tom Hanks, 45, actor (*Big, Sleepless in Seattle*; Oscars for *Philadelphia, Forrest Gump*), born Concord, CA, July 9, 1956.

Fred Savage, 25, actor ("The Wonder Years," *The Princess Bride*), born Highland Park, IL, July 9, 1976.

JULY 10 — TUESDAY
Day 191 — 174 Remaining

ASHE, ARTHUR: BIRTH ANNIVERSARY. July 10, 1943. Born at Richmond, VA, Arthur Ashe became a legend for his list of firsts as a black tennis player. He was chosen for the US Davis Cup team in 1963 and became captain in 1980. He won the US men's singles championship and US Open in 1968 and in 1975 the men's singles at Wimbledon. Ashe won a total of 33 career titles. In 1985 he was inducted into the International Tennis Hall of Fame. A social activist, Ashe worked to eliminate racism and stereotyping. He helped create inner-city tennis programs for youth and wrote the three-volume *A Hard Road to Glory: A History of the African-American Athlete*. Aware that *USA Today* intended to publish an article revealing that he was infected with the AIDS virus, Ashe announced Apr 8, 1992, that he probably contracted HIV through a transfusion during bypass surgery in 1983. He began a $5 mil-

July *2001*	S	M	T	W	T	F	S
	1	2	3	4	5	6	7
	8	9	10	11	12	13	14
	15	16	17	18	19	20	21
	22	23	24	25	26	27	28
	29	30	31				

lion fundraising effort on behalf of the Arthur Ashe Foundation for the Defeat of AIDS and during his last year campaigned for public awareness of the AIDS epidemic. He died at New York, NY, Feb 6, 1993.

BAHAMAS: INDEPENDENCE DAY. July 10. Public holiday. At 12:01 AM in 1973, the Bahamas gained their independence after 250 years as a British Crown Colony.

BORIS YELTSIN INAUGURATED AS RUSSIAN PRESIDENT: 10th ANNIVERSARY. July 10, 1991. Boris Yeltsin took the oath of office as the first popularly elected president in Russia's 1,000-year history. He defeated the Communist Party candidate resoundingly, establishing himself as a powerful political counterpoint to Mikhail Gorbachev, the president of the Soviet Union, of which Russia was the largest republic. Yeltsin had been dismissed from the Politburo in 1987 and resigned from the Communist Party in 1989. His popularity forced Gorbachev to make concessions to the republics in the new union treaty forming the Confederation of Independent States.

CLERIHEW DAY. July 10. A day recognized in remembrance of Edmund Clerihew Bentley, journalist and author of the celebrated detective thriller *Trent's Last Case* (1912), but perhaps best known for his invention of a popular humorous verse form, the clerihew, consisting of two rhymed couplets of unequal length:/Edmund's middle name was Clerihew/A name possessed by very few,/But verses by Mr Bentley/Succeeded eminently./ Bentley was born at London, July 10, 1875, and died there, Mar 30, 1956.

DALLAS, GEORGE MIFFLIN: BIRTH ANNIVERSARY. July 10, 1792. The 11th vice president of the US (1845–49), born at Philadelphia, PA. Died there, Dec 31, 1864.

DON'T STEP ON A BEE DAY. July 10. Ten-year-old Michael Roy of the Wellness Permission League reminds kids and grown-ups that now is the time of year when going barefoot can mean getting stung by a bee. If you get stung tell Mom. [© 1999 by WH] For info: Michael Roy, Wellcat Holidays, 2418 Long Ln, Lebanon, PA 17046. Phone: (230) 332-4886. E-mail: wellcat@supernet.com. Web: www.wellcat.com.

O'HARA, MARY: BIRTH ANNIVERSARY. July 10, 1885. Born at Cape May, NJ, Mary O'Hara Alsop wrote the children's horse tale *My Friend Flicka*. She died at Chevy Chase, MD, Oct 15, 1980.

SPACE MILESTONE: *TELSTAR* (US). July 10, 1962. First privately owned satellite (American Telephone and Telegraph Company) and first satellite to relay live TV pictures across the Atlantic was launched.

US LIFTS SANCTIONS AGAINST SOUTH AFRICA: 10th ANNIVERSARY. July 10, 1991. President George Bush lifted US trade and investment sanctions against South Africa. The sanctions had been imposed through the Comprehensive Anti-Apartheid Act of 1986, which Congress had passed to punish South Africa for policies of racial separation.

WYOMING: ADMISSION DAY: ANNIVERSARY. July 10. Became 44th state in 1890.

BIRTHDAYS TODAY

Candice F. Ransom, 49, author (*The Big Green Pocketbook*), born Washington, DC, July 10, 1952.

JULY 11 — WEDNESDAY
Day 192 — 173 Remaining

ADAMS, JOHN QUINCY: BIRTH ANNIVERSARY. July 11, 1767. Sixth president of the US and the son of the second president, John Quincy Adams was born at Braintree, MA. After his single term as president, he served 17 years as a member of Congress from Plymouth, MA. He died Feb 23, 1848, at the House of Representatives (in the same room in which he had taken the presidential Oath of Office Mar 4, 1825). John Quincy Adams was the only president whose father had also been president of the US.

DAY OF THE FIVE BILLION: ANNIVERSARY. July 11, 1987. An eight-pound baby boy, Matej Gaspar, born at 1:35 AM, EST, at Zagreb, Yugoslavia, was proclaimed the five billionth inhabitant of Earth. The United Nations Fund for Population Activities, hoping to draw attention to population growth, proclaimed July 11 as "Day of the Five Billion," noting that 150 babies are born each minute. See also: "Day of the Six Billion: Anniversary" (Oct 12).

MONGOLIA: NAADAM NATIONAL HOLIDAY. July 11. Public holiday. Commemorates overthrow of the feudal monarch in 1921.

SMITH, JAMES: DEATH ANNIVERSARY. July 11, 1806. Signer of the Declaration of Independence, born at Ireland about 1719 (exact date unknown). Died at York, PA.

SPACE MILESTONE: *SKYLAB* (US): FALLS TO EARTH. July 11, 1979. The 82-ton spacecraft launched May 14, 1973, re-entered Earth's atmosphere. Expectation was that 20–25 tons probably would survive to hit Earth, including one piece of about 5,000 pounds. This generated intense international public interest in where it would fall. The chance that some person would be hit by a piece of *Skylab* was calculated at one in 152. Targets were drawn and *Skylab* parties were held but *Skylab* broke up and fell to Earth in a shower of pieces over the Indian Ocean and Australia, with no known casualties.

UNITED NATIONS: WORLD POPULATION DAY. July 11. In June 1989, the Governing Council of the United Nations Development Programme recommended that July 11 be observed by the international community as World Population Day. An outgrowth of the Day of Five Billion (July 11, 1987), the Day seeks to focus public attention on the urgency and importance of population issues, particularly in the context of overall development plans and programs and the need to create solutions to these problems. For info: United Nations, Dept of Public Info, Public Inquiries Unit, RM GA-57, New York, NY 10017. Phone: (212) 963-4475. Fax: (212) 963-0071. E-mail: inquiries@un.org.

WHITE, E.B.: BIRTH ANNIVERSARY. July 11, 1899. Author of books for adults and children (*Charlotte's Web, Trumpet of the Swan, Stuart Little*) and *New Yorker* editor. Born at Mount Vernon, NY, White died at North Brooklyn, ME, Oct 1, 1985.

BIRTHDAYS TODAY

Helen Cresswell, 67, author (*The Night Watchmen*), born Nottinghamshire, England, July 11, 1934.

Mike Foster, 71, Governor of Louisiana (R), born Shreveport, LA, July 11, 1930.

Jane Gardam, 73, author (*A Long Way from Verona*), born Coatham, England, July 11, 1928.

Patricia Polacco, 57, author (*Chicken Sunday, Pink and Say*), born Lansing, MI, July 11, 1944.

James Stevenson, 72, author and illustrator (*I Meant to Tell You*), born New York, NY, July 11, 1929.

JULY 12 — THURSDAY
Day 193 — 172 Remaining

AMERICAN FEDERATION OF TEACHERS CONVENTION. July 12–14. Marriott Wardman Park, Washington, DC. For info: American Federation of Teachers, 555 New Jersey Ave NW, Washington, DC 20001. Phone: (202) 879-4587. Web: www.aft.org.

ETCH-A-SKETCH INTRODUCED: ANNIVERSARY. July 12, 1960. In 1958 a French garage mechanic named Arthur Granjean developed a drawing toy he called The Magic Screen. In 1959 he exhibited his toy at a toy fair at Nuremberg, West Germany where it was seen by a representative of the Ohio Art Company, a toy company at Bryan, OH. The rights were purchased and the product was renamed and released in 1960. More than 100 million have been sold.

KIRIBATI: INDEPENDENCE DAY. July 12. Republic of Kiribati attained independence from Britain in 1979. Formerly known as the Gilbert Islands.

NORTHERN IRELAND: ORANGEMEN'S DAY. July 12. National holiday commemorates Battle of Boyne, July 1 (Old Style), 1690, in which the forces of King William III of England, Prince of Orange, defeated those of James II, at Boyne River in Ireland. Ordinarily observed July 12. If July 12 is a Saturday or a Sunday the holiday observance is on the following Monday.

SAO TOME AND PRINCIPE: NATIONAL DAY: ANNIVERSARY. July 12. National holiday observed. Commemorates independence from Portugal in 1975.

SPYRI, JOHANNA: BIRTH ANNIVERSARY. July 12, 1827. Children's author, born at Hirzel, Switzerland. Her book *Heidi* is the story of an orphan girl who goes to live with her grandfather in the mountains. *Heidi* was made into a movie in 1920. Spyri wrote several other books, including *Heidi Grows Up* and *Heidi's Children*. She died at Zurich, Switzerland, July 7, 1901.

THOREAU, HENRY DAVID: BIRTH ANNIVERSARY. July 12, 1817. American author and philosopher, born at Concord, MA. Died there May 6, 1862. In *Walden* he wrote, "I frequently tramped eight or ten miles through the deepest snow to keep an appointment with a beechtree, or a yellow birch, or an old acquaintance among the pines." For more info: *Into the Deep Forest with Henry David Thoreau*, by Jim Murphy (Clarion, 0-395-60522-9, $14.95 Gr. 5–8).

BIRTHDAYS TODAY

Bill Cosby, 63, comedian, actor (Emmys for "I Spy," "The Cosby Show"), born Philadelphia, PA, July 12, 1938.

Kristi Yamaguchi, 30, Olympic gold medal figure skater, born Hayward, CA, July 12, 1971.

JULY 13 — FRIDAY
Day 194 — 171 Remaining

JAPAN: BON FESTIVAL (FEAST OF LANTERNS). July 13–15. Religious rites throughout Japan in memory of the dead, who, according to Buddhist belief, revisit Earth during this period. Lanterns are lighted for the souls. Spectacular bonfires in the shape of the character *dai* are burned on hillsides on the last day of the Bon or O-Bon Festival, bidding farewell to the spirits of the dead.

MOON PHASE: LAST QUARTER. July 13. Moon enters Last Quarter phase at 2:45 PM, EDT.

NORTHWEST ORDINANCE: ANNIVERSARY. July 13, 1787. The Northwest Ordinance, providing for government of the territory north of the Ohio River, became law. The ordinance guaranteed freedom of worship and the right to trial by jury, and it prohibited slavery.

WORLD CUP INAUGURATED: ANNIVERSARY. July 13, 1930. The first World Cup soccer competition was held at Montevideo, Uruguay, with 14 countries participating. The host country had the winning team. The next World Cup competition will be in Japan and Korea in 2002.

BIRTHDAYS TODAY

Marcia Brown, 83, illustrator and author (Caldecott for *Shadow, Once a Mouse, Cinderella*), born Rochester, NY, July 13, 1918.

Ashley Bryan, 78, author and illustrator (*Lion and the Ostrich: And Other African Folk Tales*), born The Bronx, NY, July 13, 1923.

Harrison Ford, 59, actor (*American Graffiti, Star Wars* and *Indiana Jones* films), born Chicago, IL, July 13, 1942.

Patrick Stewart, 61, actor ("Star Trek: The Next Generation," *Excalibur, LA Story*), born Mirfield, England, July 13, 1940.

JULY 14 — SATURDAY
Day 195 — 170 Remaining

CHILDREN'S PARTY AT GREEN ANIMALS. July 14. Green Animals Topiary Gardens, Portsmouth, RI. Annual party for children and adults at Green Animals, a delightful topiary garden and

July 2001	S	M	T	W	T	F	S
	1	2	3	4	5	6	7
	8	9	10	11	12	13	14
	15	16	17	18	19	20	21
	22	23	24	25	26	27	28
	29	30	31				

children's toy museum. Party includes pony rides, merry-go-round, games, clowns, refreshments, hot dogs, hamburgers and more. Annually, July 14. Est attendance: 200. For info: The Preservation Soc of Newport County, 424 Bellevue Ave, Newport, RI 02840. Phone: (401) 847-1000. Fax: (401) 847-1361. Web: www.NewportMansions.org.

FRANCE: BASTILLE DAY OR FETE NATIONAL. July 14. Public holiday commemorating the fall of the Bastille at the beginning of the French Revolution in 1789. Also celebrated or observed in many other countries. For more info: www.premier-ministre.gouv.fr/GB/HIST/FETNAT.HTM.

GARFIELD, LEON: 80th BIRTH ANNIVERSARY. July 14, 1921. Author of children's books (*Smith*), born at Brighton, England. Died at London, England, June 2, 1996.

GUTHRIE, WOODY: BIRTH ANNIVERSARY. July 14, 1912. Singer famous for the song *This Land Is Your Land*. Guthrie wrote more than 1,000 folk songs, ballads and children's songs. Born at Okemah, OK, Guthrie died at New York, NY, Oct 3, 1967.

SINGER, ISAAC BASHEVIS: BIRTH ANNIVERSARY. July 14, 1904. Author who wrote in Yiddish and won the Nobel Prize for literature in 1978. His books for children include *The Fearsome Inn, When Shlemiel Went to Warsaw and Other Stories* and *Zlateh the Goat and Other Stories*. Born at Radzymin, Poland, I.B. Singer died at Surfside, FL, July 24, 1991.

BIRTHDAYS TODAY

Gerald Rudolph Ford, 88, 38th president of the US, born Leslie King, Omaha, NE, July 14, 1913.

Matthew Fox, 35, actor ("Party of Five"), born Crowheart, WY, July 14, 1966.

Laura Joffe Numeroff, 48, author (*If You Give a Mouse a Cookie*), born Brooklyn, NY, July 14, 1953.

Peggy Parish, 74, author (the Amelia Bedelia series), born Manning, SC, July 14, 1927.

JULY 15 — SUNDAY
Day 196 — 169 Remaining

BATTLE OF THE MARNE: ANNIVERSARY. July 15, 1918. General Erich Ludendorff launched Germany's fifth, and last, offensive to break through the Chateau-Thierry salient during WWI. This all-out effort involved three armies branching out from Rheims to cross the Marne River. The Germans were successful in crossing the Marne near Chateau-Thierry before American, British and Italian divisions stopped their progress. On July 18 General Foch, Commander-in-Chief of the Allied troops, launched a massive counteroffensive that resulted in a German retreat that continued for four months until they sued for peace in November.

★**CAPTIVE NATIONS WEEK.** July 15–21. Presidential proclamation issued each year since 1959 for the third week of July. (PL86–90 of July 17, 1959.)

MAXWELL, GAVIN: BIRTH ANNIVERSARY. July 15, 1914. Born at Elrig, Scotland. Children's author and illustrator, known for *Ring of Bright Water* and *The Rocks Remain*. Maxwell died at Inverness, Scotland, Sept 6, 1969.

MOORE, CLEMENT CLARKE: BIRTH ANNIVERSARY. July 15, 1779. American author and teacher, best remembered for his popular verse, "A Visit from Saint Nicholas" (" 'Twas the Night Before Christmas"), which was first published anonymously and without Moore's knowledge in a newspaper, Dec 23, 1823. Moore was born at New York, NY, and died at Newport, RI, July 10, 1863.

NATIONAL FARRIER'S WEEK. July 15–21. A salute from horse owners to the men and women who keep their horses shod and equine feet and legs in top-notch condition. Annually, the third week in July. For info: Frank Lessiter, American Farriers Journal, PO Box 624, Brookfield, WI 53008-0624. Phone: (414) 782-4480. Fax: (414) 782-1252. E-mail: Lesspub@aol.com.

REMBRANDT: BIRTH ANNIVERSARY. July 15, 1606. Dutch painter and etcher, born at Leiden, Holland. Known for *The Night Watch* and many portraits and self-portraits, he died at Amsterdam, Holland, Oct 4, 1669. For more info: *Rembrandt and 17th Century Holland*, by Claudio Pescio (Peter Bedrick, 0-87226-317-7, $22.50 Gr. 4–7).

SAINT FRANCES XAVIER CABRINI: BIRTH ANNIVERSARY. July 15, 1850. First American saint, founder of schools, orphanages, convents and hospitals, born at Lombardy, Italy. Died of malaria at Chicago, IL, Dec 22, 1917. Canonized July 7, 1946.

SAINT SWITHIN'S DAY. July 15. Swithun (Swithin), Bishop of Winchester (AD 852–862), died July 2, 862. Little is known of his life, but his relics were transferred into Winchester Cathedral July 15, 971, a day on which there was a heavy rainfall. According to old English belief, it will rain for 40 days thereafter when it rains on this day. "St. Swithin's Day, if thou dost rain, for 40 days it will remain; St. Swithin's Day, if thou be fair, for 40 days, –will rain nea mair."

SPACE WEEK. July 15–21. The calendar week containing July 20 has been observed in a number of communities and states as Space Week, commemorating the July 20, 1969, landing on the moon by two US astronauts, Neil Alden Armstrong and Edwin Eugene Aldrin, Jr. See also: "Space Milestone: Moon Day" (July 20). *See* Curriculum Connection.

BIRTHDAYS TODAY

Marcia Thornton Jones, 43, author, with Debbie Dadey (the Bailey School Kids series), born Joliet, IL, July 15, 1958.
Jesse Ventura, 50, Governor of Minnesota (I), born Minneapolis, MN, July 15, 1951.
George V. Voinovich, 65, US Senator (R, Ohio), born Cleveland, OH, July 15, 1936.

JULY 15–21
SPACE WEEK

This special week includes the commemoration of the first moon landing on July 20, 1969. Millions of people, glued to their television sets, watched as Neil Armstrong stepped down from the lunar landing module and said, "That's one small step for a man, one giant leap for mankind." Celebrate Space Week by researching many space "firsts."

For language arts, bring in several pictures of Earth taken from space. Ask students to imagine they are astronauts leaving Earth for the first time. Have them write a poem about the sounds heard during a blastoff or write a letter to their families describing how they feel about the trip.

In science, look at the changes in technology regarding the shape and size of rockets, space shuttles and landing capsules. There have been many modifications over the years. Also, chart the path taken by rockets to the moon, including any earth orbits prior to heading for the moon. Students can research what life is like on a space station. The International Space Station, now under construction, will be finished in 2004. It is being funded jointly by 16 nations. The first astronauts moved in last year. For more information, visit the ISS website at spaceflight.nasa.gov/station/index.html.

Try to get videos of the moon landing. See your learning center director for help in locating them. There are also videos about space exploration.

Discuss the risks of space exploration, such as the tragic launch pad fire of the Apollo mission on Jan 27, 1967 and the *Challenger* space shuttle explosion on Jan 28, 1986. Many people were moved to write poems describing the *Challenger* disaster. The death of high school teacher Christa McAuliffe, a member of the crew, was particularly felt in the education community. Many classrooms had TV hookups that day to watch and celebrate the much anticipated liftoff.

Looking toward the future, compare the kinds of information probes we send out now to those of the past. Have students hypothesize about manned expeditions to Mars. How long would the trip take? What would they need to take along? Also, using newspapers and magazines, students could research the new investigations into possible life forms that may have existed on Mars.

There are many excellent books about space exploration. *First on the Moon*, by Barbara Henner (Hyperion, 0-7868-0489-0, $16.99 Gr. 3–7); *Spacebusters: The Race to the Moon*, by Philip Wilkinson (Dorling Kindersley, 0-7894-2961-6, $3.95 Gr. K–3); and *One Giant Leap: The Story of Neil Armstrong*, by Don Brown (Houghton Mifflin, 0-395-88401-2, $16 Gr. K–4) are all about moon exploration. *Close Encounters*, by Elaine Scott (Hyperion, 0-7868-0147-6 $16.95) is a good teacher resource space overview. *Space Exploration*, by Carole Stott (Knopf, 0-679-88563-3, $19 Gr. 3–7) contains interesting photos concerning all aspects of space exploration. *The History News: Space*, by Michael Johnstone (Candlewick, 0-7636-0490-9, $16.99 Gr. 3–7) offers a newspaper-style overview of space exploration. *Discover Mars*, by Gloria Skurzynski (National Geographic, 0-7922-7099-1, $17.95 Gr. 5–10); *Is There Life in Outer Space?*, by Franklyn Branley (Harper, 0-06-445192-5, $4.95 Gr. 2–4) and *Floating in Space*, by Franklyn Branley (Harper, 0-06-445142-9, $4.95 Gr. 2–4) all contain helpful material regarding the exploration of the universe and other planets. Also visit the NASA for Kids website at www.nasa.gov/kids.html.

JULY 16 — MONDAY

Day 197 — 168 Remaining

AMUNDSEN, ROALD: BIRTH ANNIVERSARY. July 16, 1872. Norwegian explorer, born near Oslo, Roald Amundsen was the first man to sail from the Atlantic to the Pacific Ocean via the Northwest Passage (1903–05). He discovered the South Pole (Dec 14, 1911) and flew over the North Pole in a dirigible in 1926. He flew, with five companions, from Norway, June 18, 1928, in a daring effort to rescue survivors of an Italian Arctic expedition. No trace of the rescue party or the airplane was ever located. See also: "South Pole Discovery: Anniversary" (Dec 14).

ATOMIC BOMB TESTED: ANNIVERSARY. July 16, 1945. In the New Mexican desert at Alamogordo Air Base, 125 miles southeast of Albuquerque, the experimental atomic bomb was set off at 5:30 AM. Dubbed "Fat Boy" by its creator, the plutonium bomb vaporized the steel scaffolding holding it as the immense fireball rose 8,000 feet in a fraction of a second—ultimately creating a mushroom cloud to a height of 41,000 feet. At ground zero the bomb emitted heat three times the temperature of the interior of the sun. All plant and animal life for a mile around ceased to exist. When informed by President Truman at Potsdam of the successful experiment, Winston Churchill responded, "It's the Second Coming in wrath!"

COMET CRASHES INTO JUPITER: ANNIVERSARY. July 16, 1994. The first fragment of the comet Shoemaker-Levy crashed into the planet Jupiter, beginning a series of spectacular collisions, each unleashing more energy than the combined effect of an explosion of all our world's nuclear arsenal. Video imagery from earthbound telescopes as well as the Hubble telescope provided vivid records of the explosions and their aftereffects. In 1993 the comet had shattered into a series of about a dozen large chunks that resembled "pearls on a string" after its orbit brought it within the gravitational effects of our solar system's largest planet.

DISTRICT OF COLUMBIA: ESTABLISHING LEGISLATION ANNIVERSARY. July 16, 1790. George Washington signed legislation that selected the District of Columbia as the permanent capital of the US. Boundaries of the district were established in 1792. Plans called for the government to remain housed at Philadelphia, PA, until 1800, when the new national capital would be ready for occupancy.

SPACE MILESTONE: *APOLLO 11* (US): MAN SENT TO THE MOON. July 16, 1969. This launch resulted in man's first moon landing, the first landing on any extraterrestrial body. See also: "Space Milestone: Moon Day" (July 20).

WELLS, IDA B.: BIRTH ANNIVERSARY. July 16, 1862. African American journalist and anti-lynching crusader Ida B. Wells was born the daughter of slaves at Holly Springs, MS and grew up as Jim Crow and lynching were becoming prevalent. Wells argued that lynchings occurred not to defend white women but because of whites' fear of economic competition from blacks. She traveled extensively, founding anti-lynching societies and black women's clubs. Wells's *Red Record* (1895) was one of the first accounts of lynchings in the South. She died Mar 25, 1931, at Chicago, IL.

		S	M	T	W	T	F	S
July			1	2	3	4	5	6	7
2001		8	9	10	11	12	13	14
		15	16	17	18	19	20	21
		22	23	24	25	26	27	28
		29	30	31				

JULY 17 — TUESDAY

Day 198 — 167 Remaining

DISNEYLAND OPENED: ANNIVERSARY. July 17, 1955. Disneyland, America's first theme park, opened at Anaheim, CA.

GERRY, ELBRIDGE: BIRTH ANNIVERSARY. July 17, 1744. Fifth vice president of the US (1813–14), born at Marblehead, MA. Died at Washington, DC, Nov 23, 1814. His name became part of the language (gerrymander) after he signed a redistricting bill while governor of Massachusetts in 1812.

IRAQ: NATIONAL DAY. July 17. National holiday commemorating the 1968 revolution.

KOREA: CONSTITUTION DAY. July 17. Legal national holiday. Commemorates the proclamation of the constitution of the republic of Korea in 1948. Ceremonies at Seoul's capitol plaza and all major cities.

PUERTO RICO: MUÑOZ-RIVERA DAY. July 17. Public holiday on the anniversary of the birth of Luis Muñoz-Rivera. The Puerto Rican patriot, poet and journalist was born at Barranquitas, Puerto Rico in 1859. He died at Santurce, a suburb of San Juan, Puerto Rico, Nov 15, 1916.

SPACE MILESTONE: *APOLLO-SOYUZ* LINKUP (US, USSR). July 17, 1975. After three years of planning, negotiation and preparation, the first US–USSR joint space project reached fruition with the linkup in space of *Apollo 18* (crew: T. Stafford, V. Brand, D. Slayton; landed in Pacific Ocean July 24, during 136th orbit) and *Soyuz 19* (crew: A.A. Leonov, V.N. Kubasov; landed July 21, after 96 orbits). *Apollo 18* and *Soyuz 19* were linked for 47 hours (July 17–19) while joint experiments and transfer of personnel and materials back and forth between craft took place. Launch date was July 15, 1975.

SPACE MILESTONE: *SOYUZ T-12* (USSR). July 17, 1984. Cosmonaut Svetlana Savitskaya became the first woman to walk in space (July 25) and the first woman to make more than one space voyage. With cosmonauts V. Dzhanibekov and I. Volk. Docked at *Salyut 7* July 18 and returned to Earth July 29.

Karla Kuskin, 69, author and illustrator (*The Philharmonic Gets Dressed, City Dog*), born New York, NY, July 17, 1932.

JULY 18 — WEDNESDAY

Day 199 — 166 Remaining

PRESIDENTIAL SUCCESSION ACT: ANNIVERSARY. July 18, 1947. President Harry S Truman signed an Executive Order determining the line of succession should the president be temporarily incapacitated or die in office. The speaker of the house and president pro tem of the senate are next in succession after the vice president. This line of succession became the 25th Amendment to the Constitution, which was ratified Feb 10, 1967.

RUTLEDGE, JOHN: DEATH ANNIVERSARY. July 18, 1800. American statesman, associate justice on the Supreme Court, born at Charleston, SC, in September 1739. Nominated second Chief Justice of the Supreme Court to succeed John Jay and served as Acting Chief Justice until his confirmation was denied because of his opposition to the Jay Treaty. He died at Charleston, SC.

BIRTHDAYS TODAY

John Glenn, 80, astronaut, first American to orbit Earth, former US Senator (D, Ohio), born Cambridge, OH, July 18, 1921.

Anfernee "Penny" Hardaway, 29, basketball player, born Memphis, TN, July 18, 1972.

Nelson Mandela, 83, former president of South Africa, born Transkei, South Africa, July 18, 1918.

Jerry Stanley, 60, author (*Children of the Dust Bowl*), born Highland Park, MI, July 18, 1941.

JULY 19 — THURSDAY

Day 200 — 165 Remaining

DEGAS, EDGAR: BIRTH ANNIVERSARY. July 19, 1834. French Impressionist painter, especially noted for his paintings of ballet dancers and horse races, was born at Paris, France. He died at Paris, Sept 26, 1917.

DELAWARE STATE FAIR. July 19–28. Harrington, DE. Fireworks, country, gospel and pop talent, rodeos, demolition derby, amusement rides and harness racing. Plenty of food and entertainment. Est attendance: 216,000. For info: Delaware State Fair, PO Box 28, Harrington, DE 19952. Phone: (302) 398-3269. Fax: (302) 398-5030. Web: www.delawarestatefair.com.

MERRIAM, EVE: BIRTH ANNIVERSARY. July 19, 1916. Poet, known for her children's books *You Be Good and I'll Be Night* and *A Gaggle of Geese*. Born at Philadelphia, PA, Merriam died Apr 11, 1992.

NEWBERY, JOHN: BIRTH ANNIVERSARY. July 19, 1713. The first bookseller and publisher to make a specialty of children's books. Born at Waltham St. Lawrence, England, he died Dec 22, 1767, at London, England. The American Library Association awards the Newbery Medal annually for the most distinguished contribution to American literature for children.

NICARAGUA: NATIONAL LIBERATION DAY. July 19. Following the National Day of Joy (July 17—anniversary of date in 1979 when dictator Anastasio Somoza Debayle fled Nicaragua) is annual July 19 observance of National Liberation Day, anniversary of day the National Liberation Army claimed victory over the Somoza dictatorship.

WOMEN'S RIGHTS CONVENTION AT SENECA FALLS: ANNIVERSARY. July 19, 1848. A convention concerning the rights of women, called by Lucretia Mott and Elizabeth Cady Stanton, was held at Seneca Falls, NY, July 19–20, 1848. The issues discussed included voting, property rights and divorce. The convention drafted a "Declaration of Sentiments" that paraphrased the Declaration of Independence, addressing man instead of King George, and called for women's "immediate admission to all the rights and privileges which belong to them as citizens of the United States." This convention was the beginning of an organized women's rights movement in the US. The most controversial issue was Stanton's demand for women's right to vote.

BIRTHDAYS TODAY

Teresa Edwards, 37, basketball player, born Cairo, GA, July 19, 1964.

Chris Kratt, 32, biologist, cohost with his brother Martin ("Kratts' Creatures"), born Summit, NJ, July 19, 1969.

JULY 20 — FRIDAY

Day 201 — 164 Remaining

COLOMBIA: INDEPENDENCE DAY. July 20. National holiday. Commemorates the beginning of the independence movement with an uprising against Spanish officials in 1810 at Bogota. Colombia gained independence from Spain in 1819 when Simon Bolivar decisively defeated the Spanish.

FIRST SPECIAL OLYMPICS: ANNIVERSARY. July 20, 1968. One thousand mentally retarded athletes from the US and Canada competed in the first Special Olympics at Soldier Field, Chicago, IL. Today more than one million athletes from 146 countries compete in local, national and international games.

MOON PHASE: NEW MOON. July 20. Moon enters New Moon phase at 3:44 PM, EDT.

NORTH DAKOTA STATE FAIR. July 20–28. Minot, ND. For nine days the State Fair features the best in big-name entertainment, farm and home exhibits, displays, the Midway and NPRA rodeo. Est attendance: 250,000. For info: North Dakota State Fair, Box 1796, Minot, ND 58702. Phone: (701) 857-7620. Fax: (701) 857-7622. E-mail: ndsf@minot.com.

PROVENSEN, MARTIN: 85th BIRTH ANNIVERSARY. July 20, 1916. Author and illustrator, with his wife Alice (Caldecott for *The Glorious Flight: Across the Channel with Louis Bleriot*), born at Chicago, IL. Died Mar 27, 1987, at New York, NY.

SPACE MILESTONE: MOON DAY. July 20, 1969. Anniversary of man's first landing on moon. Two US astronauts (Neil Alden Armstrong and Edwin Eugene Aldrin, Jr) landed lunar module *Eagle* at 4:17 PM, EDT and remained on lunar surface 21 hours, 36 minutes and 16 seconds. The landing was made from the *Apollo XI*'s orbiting command and service module, code named *Columbia*, whose pilot, Michael Collins, remained aboard. Armstrong was first to set foot on the moon. Armstrong and Aldrin were outside the spacecraft, walking on the moon's surface, approximately 2¼ hours. The astronauts returned to Earth July 24, bringing photograph and rock samples.

BIRTHDAYS TODAY

Larry E. Craig, 56, US Senator (R, Idaho), born Council, ID, July 20, 1945.

Peter Forsberg, 28, hockey player, born Ornskoldvik, Sweden, July 20, 1973.

Charles Johnson, Jr, 30, baseball player, born Ft Pierce, FL, July 20, 1971.

Barbara Ann Mikulski, 65, US Senator (D, Maryland), born Baltimore, MD, July 20, 1936.

JULY 21 — SATURDAY
Day 202 — 163 Remaining

BELGIUM: NATIONAL HOLIDAY. July 21. Marks accession of first Belgian king, Leopold I, in 1831 after independence from the Netherlands.

CLEVELAND, FRANCES FOLSOM: BIRTH ANNIVERSARY. July 21, 1864. Wife of Grover Cleveland, 22nd and 24th president of the US, born at Buffalo, NY. She was the youngest First Lady at age 22, and the first to marry a president in the White House. Died at Princeton, NJ, Oct 29, 1947.

GUAM: LIBERATION DAY. July 21. US forces returned to Guam in 1944.

BIRTHDAYS TODAY

Brandi Chastain, 33, soccer player (US Soccer Team), born San Jose, CA, July 21, 1968.

Hatty Jones, 13, actress (*Madeline*), born London, England, July 21, 1988.

Janet Reno, 63, US Attorney General (Clinton administration), born Miami, FL, July 21, 1938.

Paul D. Wellstone, 57, US Senator (D, Minnesota), born Washington, DC, July 21, 1944.

Robin Williams, 49, actor (*Patch Adams, Mrs Doubtfire*), born Chicago, IL, July 21, 1952.

JULY 22 — SUNDAY
Day 203 — 162 Remaining

BIANCO, MARGERY WILLIAMS: BIRTH ANNIVERSARY. July 22, 1881. Author of children's books (*The Velveteen Rabbit*, written under the name Margery Williams). Born at London, England, she died at New York, NY, Sept 4, 1944.

PIED PIPER OF HAMELIN: ANNIVERSARY—MAYBE. July 22, 1376. According to legend, the German town of Hamelin, plagued with rats, bargained with a piper who promised to, and did, pipe the rats out of town and into the Weser River. Refused payment for his work, the piper then piped the children out of town and into a hole in a hill, never to be seen again. More recent historians suggest that the event occurred in 1284 when young men of Hamelin left the city on colonizing adventures.

SPOONER'S DAY (*WILLIAM SPOONER BIRTH ANNIVERSARY*). July 22. A day named for the Reverend William Archibald Spooner (born at London, England, July 22, 1844), whose frequent slips of the tongue led to coinage of the term *spoonerism* to describe them. A day to remember the scholarly man whose accidental transpositions gave us blushing crow (for crushing blow), tons of soil (for sons of toil), queer old dean (for dear old queen),

swell foop (for fell swoop) and half-warmed fish (for half-formed wish). Warden of New College, Oxford, 1903–24, Spooner died at Oxford, England, Aug 29, 1930.

BIRTHDAYS TODAY

Tim Brown, 35, football player, born Dallas, TX, July 22, 1966.

Kay Bailey Hutchison, 58, US Senator (R, Texas), born Galveston, TX, July 22, 1943.

William V. Roth, 80, US Senator (R, Delaware), born Great Falls, MT, July 22, 1921.

JULY 23 — MONDAY
Day 204 — 161 Remaining

EGYPT, ARAB REPUBLIC OF: ANNIVERSARY NATIONAL DAY. July 23, 1952. Anniversary of the Revolution in 1952, which was launched by army officers and changed Egypt from a monarchy to a republic.

FIRST US SWIMMING SCHOOL: OPENING ANNIVERSARY. July 23, 1827. The first swimming school in the US opened at Boston, MA. Its pupils included John Quincy Adams and James Audubon.

LEO, THE LION. July 23–Aug 22. In the astronomical/astrological zodiac, which divides the sun's apparent orbit into 12 segments, the period July 23–Aug 22 is identified, traditionally, as the sun sign of Leo, the Lion. The ruling planet is the sun.

SPACE MILESTONE: *COLUMBIA*: FIRST FEMALE COMMANDER. July 23, 1999. Colonel Eileen Collins led a shuttle mission to deploy a $1.5 billion X-ray telescope, the Chandra Observatory, into space. It is a sister satellite to the Hubble Space Telescope. It is named after Nobel Prize winner Subrahmanyar Chandrasekhar.

SPACE MILESTONE: *SOYUZ 37* (USSR). July 23, 1980. Cosmonauts Viktor Gorbatko and, the first non-Caucasian in space, Lieutenant Colonel Pham Tuan (Vietnam), docked at *Salyut 6* July 24. Returned to Earth July 31.

VIRGIN ISLANDS: HURRICANE SUPPLICATION DAY. July 23. Legal holiday. Population attends churches to pray for protection from hurricanes. Annually, the fourth Monday in July.

BIRTHDAYS TODAY

Anthony M. Kennedy, 65, Supreme Court Justice, born Sacramento, CA, July 23, 1936.

Gary Payton, 33, basketball player, born Oakland, CA, July 23, 1968.

Robert Quackenbush, 72, author (the Miss Mallard series), born Hollywood, CA, July 23, 1929.

JULY 24 — TUESDAY
Day 205 — 160 Remaining

BOLIVAR, SIMON: BIRTH ANNIVERSARY. July 24, 1783. "The Liberator," born at Caracas, Venezuela. Commemorated in Venezuela and other Latin American countries. Died Dec 17, 1830, at Santa Marta, Colombia. Bolivia is named after him.

PIONEER DAY: ANNIVERSARY. July 24. Utah. Commemorates the first settlement in the Salt Lake Valley in 1847 by Brigham Young.

BIRTHDAYS TODAY

Barry Bonds, 37, baseball player, born Riverside, CA, July 24, 1964.

Karl Malone, 38, basketball player, born Summerfield, LA, July 24, 1963.

July 2001	S	M	T	W	T	F	S
	1	2	3	4	5	6	7
	8	9	10	11	12	13	14
	15	16	17	18	19	20	21
	22	23	24	25	26	27	28
	29	30	31				

Albert Marrin, 65, author of military history (*Commander in Chief Abraham Lincoln and the Civil War*), born New York, NY, July 24, 1936.

Anna Paquin, 19, actress (*Fly Away Home*), born Wellington, New Zealand, July 24, 1982.

Marc Racicot, 53, Governor of Montana (R), born Thompson Falls, MT, July 24, 1948.

Mara Wilson, 14, actress (*Mrs Doubtfire, Matilda*), born Burbank, CA, July 24, 1987.

JULY 25 — WEDNESDAY
Day 206 — 159 Remaining

CHINCOTEAGUE PONY PENNING. July 25–26. Chincoteague Island, VA. To round up the 150 wild ponies living on Assateague Island and swim them across the inlet to Chincoteague, where about 50–60 of them are sold. Annually, the last Wednesday and Thursday of July. Marguerite Henry's *Misty of Chincoteague* is an account of this event. Est attendance: 50,000. For info: Jacklyn Russell, Chamber of Commerce, Box 258, Chincoteague, VA 23336. Phone: (757) 336-6161. Fax: (757) 336-1242. E-mail: pony@shore.intercom.net. Web: www.chincoteague.com/ponya.html.

HARRISON, ANNA SYMMES: BIRTH ANNIVERSARY. July 25, 1775. Wife of William Henry Harrison, ninth president of the US, born at Morristown, NJ. Died at North Bend, IN, Feb 25, 1864.

PUERTO RICO: CONSTITUTION DAY ANNIVERSARY. July 25. Also called Commonwealth Day or Occupation Day. Commemorates proclamation of constitution in 1952.

TEST-TUBE BABY: BIRTHDAY. July 25, 1978. Anniversary of the birth of Louise Brown at Oldham, England. First documented birth of a baby conceived outside the body of a woman. Parents: Gilbert John and Lesley Brown, of Bristol, England. Physicians: Patrick Christopher Steptoe and Robert Geoffrey Edwards.

BIRTHDAYS TODAY

Ron Barrett, 64, illustrator (*Cloudy with a Chance of Meatballs*), born The Bronx, NY, July 25, 1937.

Clyde Watson, 54, author (*Applebet: An ABC*), born New York, NY, July 25, 1947.

JULY 26 — THURSDAY
Day 207 — 158 Remaining

AMERICANS WITH DISABILITIES ACT SIGNED: ANNIVERSARY. July 26, 1990. President Bush signed the Americans with Disabilities Act, which went into effect two years later. It required that public facilities be made accessible to the disabled.

CATLIN, GEORGE: BIRTH ANNIVERSARY. July 26, 1796. American artist known for his paintings of Native American life, born at Wilkes-Barre, PA. He toured the West, painting more than 500 portraits. He died Dec 23, 1872, at Jersey City, NJ.

CLINTON, GEORGE: BIRTH ANNIVERSARY. July 26, 1739. Fourth vice president of the US (1805–12), born at Little Britain, NY. Died at Washington, DC, Apr 20, 1812.

CUBA: NATIONAL HOLIDAY: ANNIVERSARY OF REVOLUTION. July 26. Anniversary of 1953 beginning of Fidel Castro's revolutionary "26th of July Movement."

CURACAO: CURACAO DAY. July 26. "Although not officially recognized by the government as a holiday, various social entities commemorate the fact that on this day Alonso de Ojeda, a companion of Christopher Columbus, discovered the Island of Curaçao in 1499, sailing into Santa Ana Bay, the entrance of the harbor of Willemstad."

LIBERIA: INDEPENDENCE DAY. July 26. National holiday. Became republic in 1847, under aegis of the US Societies for Repatriating Former Slaves in Africa.

MALDIVES: INDEPENDENCE DAY: ANNIVERSARY. July 26. National holiday. Commemorates the independence of this group of 200 islands in the Indian Ocean from Britain in 1965.

NEW YORK RATIFIES CONSTITUTION: ANNIVERSARY. July 26. Became 11th state to ratify the Constitution in 1788.

US ARMY FIRST DESEGREGATION: ANNIVERSARY. July 26, 1944. During WWII the US Army ordered desegregation of its training camp facilities. Later the same year black platoons were assigned to white companies in a tentative step toward integration of the battlefield. However, it was not until after the War—July 26, 1948—that President Harry Truman signed an order officially integrating the armed forces.

WHOLE LANGUAGE UMBRELLA CONFERENCE. July 26–29. Palmer House Hilton, Chicago, IL. Affiliated with the National Council of Teachers of English, this conference presents children's authors speaking about their books. For info: Olga Vaughn, Conference Chair. Phone: (716) 266-0991. E-mail: nev27@aol.com.

BIRTHDAYS TODAY

Jan Berenstain, 78, author and illustrator, with her husband Stan (the Berenstain Bears series), born Philadelphia, PA, July 26, 1923.

JULY 27 — FRIDAY
Day 208 — 157 Remaining

BARBOSA, JOSÉ CELSO: BIRTH ANNIVERSARY. July 27, 1857. Puerto Rican physician and patriot, born at Bayamon, Puerto Rico. His birthday is a holiday in Puerto Rico. He died at San Juan, Puerto Rico, Sept 21, 1921.

INSULIN FIRST ISOLATED: 80th ANNIVERSARY. July 27, 1921. Dr. Frederick Banting and his assistant at the University of Toronto Medical School, Charles Best, gave insulin to a dog whose pancreas had been removed. In 1922 insulin was first administered to a diabetic, a 14-year-old boy.

IOWA STORYTELLING FESTIVAL. July 27–28. City Park, Clear Lake, IA. This annual storytelling event is held in a scenic lakeside setting. Friday evening "Stories After Dark." Two performances Saturday plus story exchange for novice tellers. Annually, the last Friday and Saturday in July. Est attendance: 800. For info: Jean Casey, Dir, Clear Lake Public Library, 200 N 4th St, Clear Lake, IA 50428. Phone: (515) 357-6133. Fax: (515) 357-4645.

KOREAN WAR ARMISTICE: ANNIVERSARY. July 27, 1953. Armistice agreement ending war that had lasted three years and 32 days was signed at Panmunjom, Korea (July 26, US time), by US and North Korean delegates. Both sides claimed victory at conclusion of two years, 17 days of truce negotiations. For more info: korea50.army.mil/teachers.html. The Fall 1999 issue of *Cobblestone* (for ages 9–14) was devoted to the Korean War.

MOON PHASE: FIRST QUARTER. July 27. Moon enters First Quarter phase at 6:08 AM, EDT.

US DEPARTMENT OF STATE FOUNDED: ANNIVERSARY. July 27, 1789. The first presidential cabinet department, called the Department of Foreign Affairs, was established by the Congress. Later the name was changed to Department of State.

BIRTHDAYS TODAY

Paul Janeczko, 56, poet (*Home on the Range: Cowboy Poetry*), born Passaic, NJ, July 27, 1945.

Alex Rodriguez, 26, baseball player, born New York, NY, July 27, 1975.

JULY 28 — SATURDAY
Day 209 — 156 Remaining

ALLEGANY COUNTY INVITATIONAL DRUM AND BUGLE CORPS CHAMPIONSHIPS. July 28. Cumberland, MD. Eastern Regional Senior Drum and Bugle Corps Championship featuring 10 drum and bugle corps competing for top honors. Annually, the last Saturday in July. Est attendance: 7,000. For info: Drumfest, PO Box 3571, LaVale, MD 21504. Phone: (301) 777-8325.

HEYWARD, THOMAS: BIRTH ANNIVERSARY. July 28, 1746. American Revolutionary soldier, signer of the Declaration of Independence. Died Mar 6, 1809.

MONTANA STATE FAIR. July 28–Aug 5. Great Falls, MT. Horse racing, petting zoo, carnival, discount days, nightly entertainment and plenty of food. Est attendance: 200,000. For info: Kelly Michel, State Fair, Box 1888, Great Falls, MT 59403. Phone: (406) 727-8900. Fax: (406) 452-8955.

ONASSIS, JACQUELINE LEE BOUVIER KENNEDY: BIRTH ANNIVERSARY. July 28, 1929. Editor, widow of John Fitzgerald Kennedy (35th president of the US), born at Southampton, NY. Later married (Oct 20, 1968) Greek shipping magnate Aristotle Socrates Onassis, who died Mar 15, 1975. The widely admired and respected former First Lady died May 19, 1994, at New York, NY.

PERU: INDEPENDENCE DAY. July 28. San Martin declared independence in 1821. After the final defeat of Spanish troops by Simon Bolivar in 1824, Spanish rule ended.

POTTER, (HELEN) BEATRIX: BIRTH ANNIVERSARY. July 28, 1866. Author and illustrator of the Peter Rabbit stories for children, born at London, England. Died at Sawrey, Lancashire,

	S	M	T	W	T	F	S
July	1	2	3	4	5	6	7
2001	8	9	10	11	12	13	14
	15	16	17	18	19	20	21
	22	23	24	25	26	27	28
	29	30	31				

Dec 22, 1943. For more info: *Beatrix Potter*, by Alexandra Wallner (Holiday House, 0-8234-1181-8, $15.95 Gr. K–2).

WORLD WAR I BEGINS: ANNIVERSARY. July 28, 1914. Archduke Francis Ferdinand of Austria-Hungary and his wife were assassinated at Sarajevo, Bosnia, by a Serbian nationalist, touching off the conflict that became WWI. Austria-Hungary declared war on Serbia July 28, the formal beginning of the war. Within weeks, Germany entered the war on the side of Austria-Hungary and Russia, France and Great Britain on the side of Serbia.

BIRTHDAYS TODAY

Natalie Babbitt, 69, author and illustrator (*Tuck Everlasting*), born Dayton, OH, July 28, 1932.

Jim Davis, 56, creator ("Garfield"), born Marion, IN, July 28, 1945.

JULY 29 — SUNDAY
Day 210 — 155 Remaining

NASA ESTABLISHED: ANNIVERSARY. July 29, 1958. President Eisenhower signed a bill creating the National Aeronautics and Space Administration to direct US space policy.

★ **PARENTS' DAY.** July 29. To pay tribute to the millions of men and women whose devotion as parents strengthens our society and forms the foundation for a bright future for America. Public Law 103-362.

ROOSEVELT, ALICE HATHAWAY LEE: BIRTH ANNIVERSARY. July 29, 1861. First wife of Theodore Roosevelt, 26th President of the US, whom she married in 1880. Born at Chestnut Hill, MA, she died at New York, NY, Feb 14, 1884.

TISHA B'AV OR FAST OF AB. July 29. Hebrew calendar date: Ab 9, 5761. Commemorates and mourns the destruction of the first and second Temples in Jerusalem (586 BC and AD 70).

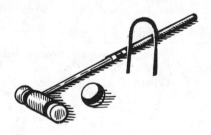

BIRTHDAYS TODAY

Debbie Black, 35, basketball player, born Philadelphia, PA, July 29, 1966.

Sharon Creech, 56, author (Newbery for *Walk Two Moons*), born Cleveland, OH, July 29, 1945.

Elizabeth Hanford Dole, 65, former president of American Red Cross, former secretary of transportation and secretary of labor, born Salisbury, NC, July 29, 1936.

Peter Jennings, 63, journalist (anchorman for "ABC Evening News"), born Toronto, Ontario, Canada, July 29, 1938.

Kathleen Krull, 49, author of nonfiction (*Wilma Unlimited: How Wilma Rudolph Became the World's Fastest Woman*), born Ft Leonard Wood, MO, July 29, 1952.

JULY 30 — MONDAY
Day 211 — 154 Remaining

PAPERBACK BOOKS INTRODUCED: ANNIVERSARY. July 30, 1935. Although books bound in soft covers were first introduced in 1841 at Leipzig, Germany, by Christian Bernhard Tauchnitz, the modern paperback revolution dates to the publication of the first Penguin paperback by Sir Allen Lane at London in 1935. Penguin Number 1 was *Ariel the Life of Shelley* by Andre Maurois.

VANUATU: INDEPENDENCE DAY: ANNIVERSARY. July 30. Vanuatu became an independent republic in 1980, breaking ties with France and the UK, and observes its national holiday.

BIRTHDAYS TODAY

Irene Ng, 27, actress ("Mystery Files of Shelby Woo"), born Malaysia, July 30, 1974.

Arnold Schwarzenegger, 54, bodybuilder, actor (*The Terminator, Twins, True Lies*), born Graz, Austria, July 30, 1947.

JULY 31 — TUESDAY
Day 212 — 153 Remaining

US PATENT OFFICE OPENS: ANNIVERSARY. July 31, 1790. The first US Patent Office opened its doors and the first US patent was issued to Samuel Hopkins of Vermont for a new method of making pearlash and potash. The patent was signed by George Washington and Thomas Jefferson.

BIRTHDAYS TODAY

Lynn Reid Banks, 72, author (*The Indian in the Cupboard*), born London, England, July 31, 1929.

Dean Cain, 35, actor ("Lois & Clark"), born Mt Clemens, MI, July 31, 1966.

J.K. Rowling, 36, author (the Harry Potter series), born Joanne Rowling, Bristol, England, July 31, 1965.

THE NATIONAL EDUCATION GOALS

1. By the year 2000, all children in America will start school ready to learn.
2. By the year 2000, the high school graduation rate will increase to at least 90 percent.
3. By the year 2000, American students will leave grades four, eight, and twelve having demonstrated competency in challenging subject matter including English, mathematics, science, foreign languages, civics and government, economics, art, history, and geography; and every school in America will insure that all students learn to use their minds well, so they may be prepared for responsible citizenship, further learning, and productive employment in our nations modern economy.
4. By the year 2000, the nation's teaching force will have access to programs for the continued improvement of their professional skills and the opportunity to acquire the knowledge and skills needed to instruct and prepare all American students for the next century.
5. By the year 2000, U.S. students will be first in the world in science and mathematics achievement.
6. By the year 2000, every adult American will be literate and will possess the knowledge and skills necessary to compete in a global economy and exercise the rights and responsibilities of citizenship.
7. By the year 2000, every school in America will be free of drugs, violence, and the unauthorized presence of firearms and alcohol and will offer a disciplined environment conducive to learning.
8. By the year 2000, every school will promote partnerships that will increase parental involvement and participation in promoting the social, emotional, and academic growth of children.

In September, 1989, President George Bush and the governors of the 50 states convened a historic Education Summit and agreed to set education goals for the nation. In February, 1990, the National Education Goals were announced by President Bush and adopted by governors. The National Education Goals Panel was created by President Bush and the 50 governors in July, 1990, to measure progress towards the goals. The Panel is an independent executive branch agency charged with a variety of responsibilities to support systemwide education reform. In March, 1994, President Clinton signed the "Goals 2000: Educate America Act" which codified the eight National Education Goals.

The Panel had issued many reports in the last ten years. For the most current information:

National Education Goals Panel
1255 22nd St NW, Ste 502
Washington, DC 20037
Phone: (202) 724-0015
Fax: (202) 632-0957
Web: www.negp.gov

CALENDAR INFORMATION FOR THE YEAR 2000

Time shown is Eastern Standard Time. All dates are given in terms of the Gregorian calendar.
(Based in part on information prepared by the Nautical Almanac Office, US Naval Observatory.)

ERAS

	YEAR	BEGINS
Jewish*	5761	Sept 29
Chinese (Year of the Dragon)	4698	Feb 5
Japanese (Heisei)	12	Jan 1
Indian (Saka)	1922	Mar 21
Islamic (Hegira)**	1421	Apr 6

*Year begins at sunset.   **Year begins at moon crescent.

RELIGIOUS CALENDARS—2000

Christian Holy Days

Epiphany	Jan 6
Shrove Tuesday	Mar 7
Ash Wednesday	Mar 8
Lent	Mar 8–Apr 22
Palm Sunday	Apr 16
Good Friday	Apr 21
Easter Day	Apr 23
Ascension Day	June 1
Whit Sunday (Pentecost)	June 11
Trinity Sunday	June 18
First Sunday in Advent	Dec 3
Christmas Day (Monday)	Dec 25

Eastern Orthodox Church Observances

Great Lent begins	Mar 13
Pascha (Easter)	Apr 30
Ascension	June 8
Pentecost	June 18

Jewish Holy Days

Purim	Mar 21
Passover (1st day)	Apr 20
Shavuot	June 9
Tisha B'av	Aug 10
Rosh Hashanah (New Year)	Sept 30–Oct 1
Yom Kippur	Oct 9
Succoth	Oct 14–22
Chanukah	Dec 22–29

Islamic Holy Days

Eid-Al-Fitr (1420)	Jan 8
Islamic New Year (1421)	Apr 6
First Day of Ramadan (1421)	Nov 27
Eid-Al-Fitr (1421)	Dec 27

CIVIL CALENDAR—USA—2000

New Year's Day	Jan 1
Martin Luther King's Birthday (obsvd)	Jan 17
Lincoln's Birthday	Feb 12
Washington's Birthday (obsvd)/Presidents' Day	Feb 21
Memorial Day (obsvd)	May 29
Independence Day	July 4
Labor Day	Sept 4
Columbus Day (obsvd)	Oct 9
General Election Day	Nov 7
Veterans Day	Nov 11
Thanksgiving Day	Nov 23

Other Days Widely Observed in US—2000

Groundhog Day (Candlemas)	Feb 2
St. Valentine's Day	Feb 14
St. Patrick's Day	Mar 17
Mother's Day	May 14
Flag Day	June 14
Father's Day	June 18
National Grandparents Day	Sept 10
Hallowe'en	Oct 31

CIVIL CALENDAR—CANADA—2000

Victoria Day	May 22
Canada Day	July 1
Labor Day	Sept 4
Thanksgiving Day	Oct 9
Remembrance Day	Nov 11
Boxing Day	Dec 26

CIVIL CALENDAR—MEXICO—2000

New Year's Day	Jan 1
Constitution Day	Feb 5
Benito Juarez Birthday	Mar 21
Labor Day	May 1
Battle of Puebla Day (Cinco de Mayo)	May 5
Independence Day*	Sept 16
Dia de La Raza	Oct 12
Mexican Revolution Day	Nov 20
Guadalupe Day	Dec 12

*Celebration begins Sept 15 at 11:00 P.M.

ECLIPSES—2000

Total eclipse of the Moon	Jan 21
Partial eclipse of the Sun	Feb 5
Partial eclipse of the Sun	July 1
Total eclipse of the Moon	July 16
Partial eclipse of the Sun	July 31
Partial eclipse of the Sun	Dec 25

SEASONS—2000

Spring (Vernal Equinox)	Mar 20, 2:35 AM, EST
Summer (Summer Solstice)	June 20, 9:48 PM, EDT
Autumn (Autumnal Equinox)	Sept 22, 1:27 PM, EDT
Winter (Winter Solstice)	Dec 21, 8:37 AM, EST

DAYLIGHT SAVING TIME SCHEDULE—2000

Sunday, Apr 2, 2:00 AM–Sunday, Oct 29, 2:00 AM—in all time zones.

CALENDAR INFORMATION FOR THE YEAR 2001

Time shown is Eastern Standard Time. All dates are given in terms of the Gregorian calendar.
(Based in part on information prepared by the Nautical Almanac Office, US Naval Observatory.)

ERAS

	YEAR	BEGINS
Jewish*	5762	Sept 18
Chinese (Year of the Snake)	4699	Jan 24
Japanese (Heisei)	13	Jan 1
Indian (Saka)	1923	Mar 20
Islamic (Hegira)**	1422	Mar 26

*Year begins at sunset.   **Year begins at moon crescent.

RELIGIOUS CALENDARS—2001

Christian Holy Days

Epiphany	Jan 6
Shrove Tuesday	Feb 27
Ash Wednesday	Feb 28
Lent	Feb 28–Apr 14
Palm Sunday	Apr 8
Good Friday	Apr 13
Easter Day	Apr 15
Ascension Day	May 24
Whit Sunday (Pentecost)	June 3
Trinity Sunday	June 10
First Sunday in Advent	Dec 2
Christmas Day (Tuesday)	Dec 25

Eastern Orthodox Church Observances

Great Lent begins	Feb 26
Pascha (Easter)	Apr 15
Ascension	May 24
Pentecost	June 3

Jewish Holy Days

Purim	Mar 9
Passover (1st day)	Apr 8
Shavuot	May 28
Tisha B'av	July 29
Rosh Hashanah (New Year)	Sept 18–19
Yom Kippur	Sept 27
Succoth	Oct 2–10
Chanukah	Dec 10–17

Islamic Holy Days

Islamic New Year (1422)	Mar 26
First Day of Ramadan (1422)	Nov 16
Eid-Al-Fitr (1422)	Dec 16

CIVIL CALENDAR—USA—2001

New Year's Day	Jan 1
Martin Luther King's Birthday (obsvd)	Jan 15
Lincoln's Birthday	Feb 12
Washington's Birthday (obsvd)/Presidents' Day	Feb 19
Memorial Day (obsvd)	May 28
Independence Day	July 4
Labor Day	Sept 3
Columbus Day (obsvd)	Oct 8
General Election Day	Nov 6
Veterans Day	Nov 11
Thanksgiving Day	Nov 22

Other Days Widely Observed in US—2001

Groundhog Day (Candlemas)	Feb 2
St. Valentine's Day	Feb 14
St. Patrick's Day	Mar 17
Mother's Day	May 13
Flag Day	June 14
Father's Day	June 17
National Grandparents Day	Sept 9
Hallowe'en	Oct 31

CIVIL CALENDAR—CANADA—2001

Victoria Day	May 21
Canada Day	July 2
Labor Day	Sept 3
Thanksgiving Day	Oct 8
Remembrance Day	Nov 11
Boxing Day	Dec 26

CIVIL CALENDAR—MEXICO—2001

New Year's Day	Jan 1
Constitution Day	Feb 5
Benito Juarez Birthday	Mar 21
Labor Day	May 1
Battle of Puebla Day (Cinco de Mayo)	May 5
Independence Day*	Sept 16
Dia de La Raza	Oct 12
Mexican Revolution Day	Nov 20
Guadalupe Day	Dec 12

*Celebration begins Sept 15 at 11:00 p.m.

ECLIPSES—1999

Penumbral eclipse of the Moon	Jan 31
Annular eclipse of the Sun	Feb 16
Partial eclipse of the Moon	July 28
Total eclipse of the Sun	Aug 11

SEASONS

Spring (Vernal Equinox)	Mar 20, 8:31 am, est
Summer (Summer Solstice)	June 21, 3:38 am, edt
Autumn (Autumnal Equinox)	Sept 22, 7:05 pm, edt
Winter (Winter Solstice)	Dec 21, 2:22 pm, est

DAYLIGHT SAVING TIME SCHEDULE—2001

Sunday, Apr 1, 2:00 am–Sunday, Oct 28, 2:00 am—in all time zones.

Perpetual Calendar, 1753–2100

A perpetual calendar lets you find the day of the week for any date in any year. Since January 1 may fall on any of the seven days of the week, and may be a leap or non-leap year, 14 different calendars are possible. The number next to each year corresponds to one of the 14 calendars. Calendar 6 will be used in 1999; calendar 14 will be used in 2000.

Year	No.	Year	No.	Year	No.	Year	No.	Year	No.	Year	No.	Year	No.	Year	No.	Year	No.
1753	2	1792	8	1831	7	1870	7	1909	6	1948	12	1987	5	2026	5	2065	5
1754	3	1793	3	1832	8	1871	1	1910	7	1949	7	1988	13	2027	6	2066	6
1755	4	1794	4	1833	3	1872	9	1911	1	1950	1	1989	1	2028	14	2067	7
1756	12	1795	5	1834	4	1873	4	1912	9	1951	2	1990	2	2029	2	2068	8
1757	7	1796	13	1835	5	1874	5	1913	4	1952	10	1991	3	2030	3	2069	3
1758	1	1797	1	1836	13	1875	6	1914	5	1953	5	1992	11	2031	4	2070	4
1759	2	1798	2	1837	1	1876	14	1915	6	1954	6	1993	6	2032	12	2071	5
1760	10	1799	3	1838	2	1877	2	1916	14	1955	7	1994	7	2033	7	2072	13
1761	5	1800	4	1839	3	1878	3	1917	2	1956	8	1995	1	2034	1	2073	1
1762	6	1801	5	1840	11	1879	4	1918	3	1957	3	1996	9	2035	2	2074	2
1763	7	1802	6	1841	6	1880	12	1919	4	1958	4	1997	4	2036	10	2075	3
1764	8	1803	7	1842	7	1881	7	1920	12	1959	5	1998	5	2037	5	2076	11
1765	3	1804	8	1843	1	1882	1	1921	7	1960	13	1999	6	2038	6	2077	6
1766	4	1805	3	1844	9	1883	2	1922	1	1961	1	2000	14	2039	7	2078	7
1767	5	1806	4	1845	4	1884	10	1923	2	1962	2	2001	2	2040	8	2079	1
1768	13	1807	5	1846	5	1885	5	1924	10	1963	3	2002	3	2041	3	2080	9
1769	1	1808	13	1847	6	1886	6	1925	5	1964	11	2003	4	2042	4	2081	4
1770	2	1809	1	1848	14	1887	7	1926	6	1965	6	2004	12	2043	5	2082	5
1771	3	1810	2	1849	2	1888	8	1927	7	1966	7	2005	7	2044	13	2083	6
1772	11	1811	3	1850	3	1889	3	1928	8	1967	1	2006	1	2045	1	2084	14
1773	6	1812	11	1851	4	1890	4	1929	3	1968	9	2007	2	2046	2	2085	2
1774	7	1813	6	1852	12	1891	5	1930	4	1969	4	2008	10	2047	3	2086	3
1775	1	1814	7	1853	7	1892	13	1931	5	1970	5	2009	5	2048	11	2087	4
1776	9	1815	1	1854	1	1893	1	1932	13	1971	6	2010	6	2049	6	2088	12
1777	4	1816	9	1855	2	1894	2	1933	1	1972	14	2011	7	2050	7	2089	7
1778	5	1817	4	1856	10	1895	3	1934	2	1973	2	2012	8	2051	1	2090	1
1779	6	1818	5	1857	5	1896	11	1935	3	1974	3	2013	3	2052	9	2091	2
1780	14	1819	6	1858	6	1897	6	1936	11	1975	4	2014	4	2053	4	2092	10
1781	2	1820	14	1859	7	1898	7	1937	6	1976	12	2015	5	2054	5	2093	5
1782	3	1821	2	1860	8	1899	1	1938	7	1977	7	2016	13	2055	6	2094	6
1783	4	1822	3	1861	3	1900	2	1939	1	1978	1	2017	1	2056	14	2095	7
1784	12	1823	4	1862	4	1901	3	1940	9	1979	2	2018	2	2057	2	2096	8
1785	7	1824	12	1863	5	1902	4	1941	4	1980	10	2019	3	2058	3	2097	3
1786	1	1825	7	1864	13	1903	5	1942	5	1981	5	2020	11	2059	4	2098	4
1787	2	1826	1	1865	1	1904	13	1943	6	1982	6	2021	6	2060	12	2099	5
1788	10	1827	2	1866	2	1905	1	1944	14	1983	7	2022	7	2061	7	2100	6
1789	5	1828	10	1867	3	1906	2	1945	2	1984	8	2023	1	2062	1		
1790	6	1829	5	1868	11	1907	3	1946	3	1985	3	2024	9	2063	2		
1791	7	1830	6	1869	6	1908	11	1947	4	1986	4	2025	4	2064	10		

Calendar 1

```
JAN                      APR                      JULY                     OCT
S  M  T  W  T  F  S       S  M  T  W  T  F  S       S  M  T  W  T  F  S       S  M  T  W  T  F  S
1  2  3  4  5  6  7                         1                         1       1  2  3  4  5  6  7
8  9 10 11 12 13 14       2  3  4  5  6  7  8       2  3  4  5  6  7  8       8  9 10 11 12 13 14
15 16 17 18 19 20 21      9 10 11 12 13 14 15       9 10 11 12 13 14 15      15 16 17 18 19 20 21
22 23 24 25 26 27 28     16 17 18 19 20 21 22      16 17 18 19 20 21 22      22 23 24 25 26 27 28
29 30 31                 23 24 25 26 27 28 29      23 24 25 26 27 28 29      29 30 31
                         30                        30 31

FEB                      MAY                      AUG                      NOV
S  M  T  W  T  F  S       S  M  T  W  T  F  S       S  M  T  W  T  F  S       S  M  T  W  T  F  S
         1  2  3  4             1  2  3  4  5  6          1  2  3  4  5                1  2  3  4
5  6  7  8  9 10 11       7  8  9 10 11 12 13       6  7  8  9 10 11 12       5  6  7  8  9 10 11
12 13 14 15 16 17 18     14 15 16 17 18 19 20      13 14 15 16 17 18 19      12 13 14 15 16 17 18
19 20 21 22 23 24 25     21 22 23 24 25 26 27      20 21 22 23 24 25 26      19 20 21 22 23 24 25
26 27 28                 28 29 30 31               27 28 29 30 31           26 27 28 29 30

MAR                      JUNE                     SEPT                     DEC
S  M  T  W  T  F  S       S  M  T  W  T  F  S       S  M  T  W  T  F  S       S  M  T  W  T  F  S
         1  2  3                   1  2  3                      1  2                      1  2
4  5  6  7  8  9 10       4  5  6  7  8  9 10       3  4  5  6  7  8  9       3  4  5  6  7  8  9
11 12 13 14 15 16 17     11 12 13 14 15 16 17      10 11 12 13 14 15 16      10 11 12 13 14 15 16
18 19 20 21 22 23 24     18 19 20 21 22 23 24      17 18 19 20 21 22 23      17 18 19 20 21 22 23
25 26 27 28 29 30 31     25 26 27 28 29 30         24 25 26 27 28 29 30      24 25 26 27 28 29 30
                                                                            31
```

Calendar 2

```
JAN                      APR                      JULY                     OCT
S  M  T  W  T  F  S       S  M  T  W  T  F  S       S  M  T  W  T  F  S       S  M  T  W  T  F  S
   1  2  3  4  5  6       1  2  3  4  5  6  7       1  2  3  4  5  6  7          1  2  3  4  5  6
7  8  9 10 11 12 13       8  9 10 11 12 13 14       8  9 10 11 12 13 14       7  8  9 10 11 12 13
14 15 16 17 18 19 20     15 16 17 18 19 20 21      15 16 17 18 19 20 21      14 15 16 17 18 19 20
21 22 23 24 25 26 27     22 23 24 25 26 27 28      22 23 24 25 26 27 28      21 22 23 24 25 26 27
28 29 30 31              29 30                     29 30 31                  28 29 30 31

FEB                      MAY                      AUG                      NOV
S  M  T  W  T  F  S       S  M  T  W  T  F  S       S  M  T  W  T  F  S       S  M  T  W  T  F  S
         1  2  3                1  2  3  4  5             1  2  3  4                1  2  3
4  5  6  7  8  9 10       6  7  8  9 10 11 12       5  6  7  8  9 10 11       4  5  6  7  8  9 10
11 12 13 14 15 16 17     13 14 15 16 17 18 19      12 13 14 15 16 17 18      11 12 13 14 15 16 17
18 19 20 21 22 23 24     20 21 22 23 24 25 26      19 20 21 22 23 24 25      18 19 20 21 22 23 24
25 26 27 28              27 28 29 30 31            26 27 28 29 30 31         25 26 27 28 29 30
```

2001

```
MAR                      JUNE                     SEPT                     DEC
S  M  T  W  T  F  S       S  M  T  W  T  F  S       S  M  T  W  T  F  S       S  M  T  W  T  F  S
         1  2  3                   1  2                      1                         1
4  5  6  7  8  9 10       3  4  5  6  7  8  9       2  3  4  5  6  7  8       2  3  4  5  6  7  8
11 12 13 14 15 16 17     10 11 12 13 14 15 16       9 10 11 12 13 14 15       9 10 11 12 13 14 15
18 19 20 21 22 23 24     17 18 19 20 21 22 23      16 17 18 19 20 21 22      16 17 18 19 20 21 22
25 26 27 28 29 30 31     24 25 26 27 28 29 30      23 24 25 26 27 28 29      23 24 25 26 27 28 29
                                                  30                        30 31
```

3 — 2002

JAN
```
 S  M  T  W  T  F  S
          1  2  3  4  5
 6  7  8  9 10 11 12
13 14 15 16 17 18 19
20 21 22 23 24 25 26
27 28 29 30 31
```

FEB
```
 S  M  T  W  T  F  S
                1  2
 3  4  5  6  7  8  9
10 11 12 13 14 15 16
17 18 19 20 21 22 23
24 25 26 27 28
```

MAR
```
 S  M  T  W  T  F  S
                1  2
 3  4  5  6  7  8  9
10 11 12 13 14 15 16
17 18 19 20 21 22 23
24 25 26 27 28 29 30
31
```

APR
```
 S  M  T  W  T  F  S
    1  2  3  4  5  6
 7  8  9 10 11 12 13
14 15 16 17 18 19 20
21 22 23 24 25 26 27
28 29 30
```

MAY
```
 S  M  T  W  T  F  S
          1  2  3  4
 5  6  7  8  9 10 11
12 13 14 15 16 17 18
19 20 21 22 23 24 25
26 27 28 29 30 31
```

JUNE
```
 S  M  T  W  T  F  S
                      1
 2  3  4  5  6  7  8
 9 10 11 12 13 14 15
16 17 18 19 20 21 22
23 24 25 26 27 28 29
30
```

JULY
```
 S  M  T  W  T  F  S
    1  2  3  4  5  6
 7  8  9 10 11 12 13
14 15 16 17 18 19 20
21 22 23 24 25 26 27
28 29 30 31
```

AUG
```
 S  M  T  W  T  F  S
                1  2  3
 4  5  6  7  8  9 10
11 12 13 14 15 16 17
18 19 20 21 22 23 24
25 26 27 28 29 30 31
```

SEPT
```
 S  M  T  W  T  F  S
 1  2  3  4  5  6  7
 8  9 10 11 12 13 14
15 16 17 18 19 20 21
22 23 24 25 26 27 28
29 30
```

OCT
```
 S  M  T  W  T  F  S
          1  2  3  4  5
 6  7  8  9 10 11 12
13 14 15 16 17 18 19
20 21 22 23 24 25 26
27 28 29 30 31
```

NOV
```
 S  M  T  W  T  F  S
                   1  2
 3  4  5  6  7  8  9
10 11 12 13 14 15 16
17 18 19 20 21 22 23
24 25 26 27 28 29 30
```

DEC
```
 S  M  T  W  T  F  S
 1  2  3  4  5  6  7
 8  9 10 11 12 13 14
15 16 17 18 19 20 21
22 23 24 25 26 27 28
29 30 31
```

4

JAN
```
 S  M  T  W  T  F  S
             1  2  3  4
 5  6  7  8  9 10 11
12 13 14 15 16 17 18
19 20 21 22 23 24 25
26 27 28 29 30 31
```

FEB
```
 S  M  T  W  T  F  S
                      1
 2  3  4  5  6  7  8
 9 10 11 12 13 14 15
16 17 18 19 20 21 22
23 24 25 26 27 28
```

MAR
```
 S  M  T  W  T  F  S
                      1
 2  3  4  5  6  7  8
 9 10 11 12 13 14 15
16 17 18 19 20 21 22
23 24 25 26 27 28 29
30 31
```

APR
```
 S  M  T  W  T  F  S
             1  2  3  4  5
 6  7  8  9 10 11 12
13 14 15 16 17 18 19
20 21 22 23 24 25 26
27 28 29 30
```

MAY
```
 S  M  T  W  T  F  S
                1  2  3
 4  5  6  7  8  9 10
11 12 13 14 15 16 17
18 19 20 21 22 23 24
25 26 27 28 29 30 31
```

JUNE
```
 S  M  T  W  T  F  S
 1  2  3  4  5  6  7
 8  9 10 11 12 13 14
15 16 17 18 19 20 21
22 23 24 25 26 27 28
29 30
```

JULY
```
 S  M  T  W  T  F  S
          1  2  3  4  5
 6  7  8  9 10 11 12
13 14 15 16 17 18 19
20 21 22 23 24 25 26
27 28 29 30 31
```

AUG
```
 S  M  T  W  T  F  S
                   1  2
 3  4  5  6  7  8  9
10 11 12 13 14 15 16
17 18 19 20 21 22 23
24 25 26 27 28 29 30
31
```

SEPT
```
 S  M  T  W  T  F  S
    1  2  3  4  5  6
 7  8  9 10 11 12 13
14 15 16 17 18 19 20
21 22 23 24 25 26 27
28 29 30
```

OCT
```
 S  M  T  W  T  F  S
             1  2  3  4
 5  6  7  8  9 10 11
12 13 14 15 16 17 18
19 20 21 22 23 24 25
26 27 28 29 30 31
```

NOV
```
 S  M  T  W  T  F  S
                      1
 2  3  4  5  6  7  8
 9 10 11 12 13 14 15
16 17 18 19 20 21 22
23 24 25 26 27 28 29
30
```

DEC
```
 S  M  T  W  T  F  S
    1  2  3  4  5  6
 7  8  9 10 11 12 13
14 15 16 17 18 19 20
21 22 23 24 25 26 27
28 29 30 31
```

5

JAN
```
 S  M  T  W  T  F  S
                1  2  3
 4  5  6  7  8  9 10
11 12 13 14 15 16 17
18 19 20 21 22 23 24
25 26 27 28 29 30 31
```

FEB
```
 S  M  T  W  T  F  S
 1  2  3  4  5  6  7
 8  9 10 11 12 13 14
15 16 17 18 19 20 21
22 23 24 25 26 27 28
```

MAR
```
 S  M  T  W  T  F  S
 1  2  3  4  5  6  7
 8  9 10 11 12 13 14
15 16 17 18 19 20 21
22 23 24 25 26 27 28
29 30 31
```

APR
```
 S  M  T  W  T  F  S
             1  2  3  4
 5  6  7  8  9 10 11
12 13 14 15 16 17 18
19 20 21 22 23 24 25
26 27 28 29 30
```

MAY
```
 S  M  T  W  T  F  S
                   1  2
 3  4  5  6  7  8  9
10 11 12 13 14 15 16
17 18 19 20 21 22 23
24 25 26 27 28 29 30
31
```

JUNE
```
 S  M  T  W  T  F  S
    1  2  3  4  5  6
 7  8  9 10 11 12 13
14 15 16 17 18 19 20
21 22 23 24 25 26 27
28 29 30
```

JULY
```
 S  M  T  W  T  F  S
             1  2  3  4
 5  6  7  8  9 10 11
12 13 14 15 16 17 18
19 20 21 22 23 24 25
26 27 28 29 30 31
```

AUG
```
 S  M  T  W  T  F  S
                      1
 2  3  4  5  6  7  8
 9 10 11 12 13 14 15
16 17 18 19 20 21 22
23 24 25 26 27 28 29
30 31
```

SEPT
```
 S  M  T  W  T  F  S
          1  2  3  4  5
 6  7  8  9 10 11 12
13 14 15 16 17 18 19
20 21 22 23 24 25 26
27 28 29 30
```

OCT
```
 S  M  T  W  T  F  S
             1  2  3
 4  5  6  7  8  9 10
11 12 13 14 15 16 17
18 19 20 21 22 23 24
25 26 27 28 29 30 31
```

NOV
```
 S  M  T  W  T  F  S
 1  2  3  4  5  6  7
 8  9 10 11 12 13 14
15 16 17 18 19 20 21
22 23 24 25 26 27 28
29 30
```

DEC
```
 S  M  T  W  T  F  S
          1  2  3  4  5
 6  7  8  9 10 11 12
13 14 15 16 17 18 19
20 21 22 23 24 25 26
27 28 29 30 31
```

6 — 1999

JAN
```
 S  M  T  W  T  F  S
                   1  2
 3  4  5  6  7  8  9
10 11 12 13 14 15 16
17 18 19 20 21 22 23
24 25 26 27 28 29 30
31
```

FEB
```
 S  M  T  W  T  F  S
    1  2  3  4  5  6
 7  8  9 10 11 12 13
14 15 16 17 18 19 20
21 22 23 24 25 26 27
28
```

MAR
```
 S  M  T  W  T  F  S
    1  2  3  4  5  6
 7  8  9 10 11 12 13
14 15 16 17 18 19 20
21 22 23 24 25 26 27
28 29 30 31
```

APR
```
 S  M  T  W  T  F  S
                1  2  3
 4  5  6  7  8  9 10
11 12 13 14 15 16 17
18 19 20 21 22 23 24
25 26 27 28 29 30
```

MAY
```
 S  M  T  W  T  F  S
                      1
 2  3  4  5  6  7  8
 9 10 11 12 13 14 15
16 17 18 19 20 21 22
23 24 25 26 27 28 29
30 31
```

JUNE
```
 S  M  T  W  T  F  S
          1  2  3  4  5
 6  7  8  9 10 11 12
13 14 15 16 17 18 19
20 21 22 23 24 25 26
27 28 29 30
```

JULY
```
 S  M  T  W  T  F  S
                1  2  3
 4  5  6  7  8  9 10
11 12 13 14 15 16 17
18 19 20 21 22 23 24
25 26 27 28 29 30 31
```

AUG
```
 S  M  T  W  T  F  S
 1  2  3  4  5  6  7
 8  9 10 11 12 13 14
15 16 17 18 19 20 21
22 23 24 25 26 27 28
29 30 31
```

SEPT
```
 S  M  T  W  T  F  S
             1  2  3  4
 5  6  7  8  9 10 11
12 13 14 15 16 17 18
19 20 21 22 23 24 25
26 27 28 29 30
```

OCT
```
 S  M  T  W  T  F  S
                   1  2
 3  4  5  6  7  8  9
10 11 12 13 14 15 16
17 18 19 20 21 22 23
24 25 26 27 28 29 30
31
```

NOV
```
 S  M  T  W  T  F  S
    1  2  3  4  5  6
 7  8  9 10 11 12 13
14 15 16 17 18 19 20
21 22 23 24 25 26 27
28 29 30
```

DEC
```
 S  M  T  W  T  F  S
          1  2  3  4
 5  6  7  8  9 10 11
12 13 14 15 16 17 18
19 20 21 22 23 24 25
26 27 28 29 30 31
```

Year 7

JAN

S	M	T	W	T	F	S
						1
2	3	4	5	6	7	8
9	10	11	12	13	14	15
16	17	18	19	20	21	22
23	24	25	26	27	28	29
30	31					

FEB

S	M	T	W	T	F	S
		1	2	3	4	5
6	7	8	9	10	11	12
13	14	15	16	17	18	19
20	21	22	23	24	25	26
27	28					

MAR

S	M	T	W	T	F	S
		1	2	3	4	5
6	7	8	9	10	11	12
13	14	15	16	17	18	19
20	21	22	23	24	25	26
27	28	29	30	31		

APR

S	M	T	W	T	F	S
					1	2
3	4	5	6	7	8	9
10	11	12	13	14	15	16
17	18	19	20	21	22	23
24	25	26	27	28	29	30

MAY

S	M	T	W	T	F	S
1	2	3	4	5	6	7
8	9	10	11	12	13	14
15	16	17	18	19	20	21
22	23	24	25	26	27	28
29	30	31				

JUNE

S	M	T	W	T	F	S
			1	2	3	4
5	6	7	8	9	10	11
12	13	14	15	16	17	18
19	20	21	22	23	24	25
26	27	28	29	30		

JULY

S	M	T	W	T	F	S
					1	2
3	4	5	6	7	8	9
10	11	12	13	14	15	16
17	18	19	20	21	22	23
24	25	26	27	28	29	30
31						

AUG

S	M	T	W	T	F	S
	1	2	3	4	5	6
7	8	9	10	11	12	13
14	15	16	17	18	19	20
21	22	23	24	25	26	27
28	29	30	31			

SEPT

S	M	T	W	T	F	S
				1	2	3
4	5	6	7	8	9	10
11	12	13	14	15	16	17
18	19	20	21	22	23	24
25	26	27	28	29	30	

OCT

S	M	T	W	T	F	S
						1
2	3	4	5	6	7	8
9	10	11	12	13	14	15
16	17	18	19	20	21	22
23	24	25	26	27	28	29
30	31					

NOV

S	M	T	W	T	F	S
		1	2	3	4	5
6	7	8	9	10	11	12
13	14	15	16	17	18	19
20	21	22	23	24	25	26
27	28	29	30			

DEC

S	M	T	W	T	F	S
				1	2	3
4	5	6	7	8	9	10
11	12	13	14	15	16	17
18	19	20	21	22	23	24
25	26	27	28	29	30	31

Year 8

JAN

S	M	T	W	T	F	S
1	2	3	4	5	6	7
8	9	10	11	12	13	14
15	16	17	18	19	20	21
22	23	24	25	26	27	28
29	30	31				

FEB

S	M	T	W	T	F	S
			1	2	3	4
5	6	7	8	9	10	11
12	13	14	15	16	17	18
19	20	21	22	23	24	25
26	27	28	29			

MAR

S	M	T	W	T	F	S
				1	2	3
4	5	6	7	8	9	10
11	12	13	14	15	16	17
18	19	20	21	22	23	24
25	26	27	28	29	30	31

APR

S	M	T	W	T	F	S
1	2	3	4	5	6	7
8	9	10	11	12	13	14
15	16	17	18	19	20	21
22	23	24	25	26	27	28
29	30					

MAY

S	M	T	W	T	F	S
		1	2	3	4	5
6	7	8	9	10	11	12
13	14	15	16	17	18	19
20	21	22	23	24	25	26
27	28	29	30	31		

JUNE

S	M	T	W	T	F	S
					1	2
3	4	5	6	7	8	9
10	11	12	13	14	15	16
17	18	19	20	21	22	23
24	25	26	27	28	29	30

JULY

S	M	T	W	T	F	S
1	2	3	4	5	6	7
8	9	10	11	12	13	14
15	16	17	18	19	20	21
22	23	24	25	26	27	28
29	30	31				

AUG

S	M	T	W	T	F	S
			1	2	3	4
5	6	7	8	9	10	11
12	13	14	15	16	17	18
19	20	21	22	23	24	25
26	27	28	29	30	31	

SEPT

S	M	T	W	T	F	S
					1	2
3	4	5	6	7	8	9
10	11	12	13	14	15	16
17	18	19	20	21	22	23
24	25	26	27	28	29	30

OCT

S	M	T	W	T	F	S
	1	2	3	4	5	6
7	8	9	10	11	12	13
14	15	16	17	18	19	20
21	22	23	24	25	26	27
28	29	30	31			

NOV

S	M	T	W	T	F	S
				1	2	3
4	5	6	7	8	9	10
11	12	13	14	15	16	17
18	19	20	21	22	23	24
25	26	27	28	29	30	

DEC

S	M	T	W	T	F	S
						1
2	3	4	5	6	7	8
9	10	11	12	13	14	15
16	17	18	19	20	21	22
23	24	25	26	27	28	29
30	31					

Year 9

JAN

S	M	T	W	T	F	S
	1	2	3	4	5	6
7	8	9	10	11	12	13
14	15	16	17	18	19	20
21	22	23	24	25	26	27
28	29	30	31			

FEB

S	M	T	W	T	F	S
				1	2	3
4	5	6	7	8	9	10
11	12	13	14	15	16	17
18	19	20	21	22	23	24
25	26	27	28	29		

MAR

S	M	T	W	T	F	S
					1	2
3	4	5	6	7	8	9
10	11	12	13	14	15	16
17	18	19	20	21	22	23
24	25	26	27	28	29	30
31						

APR

S	M	T	W	T	F	S
	1	2	3	4	5	6
7	8	9	10	11	12	13
14	15	16	17	18	19	20
21	22	23	24	25	26	27
28	29	30				

MAY

S	M	T	W	T	F	S
			1	2	3	4
5	6	7	8	9	10	11
12	13	14	15	16	17	18
19	20	21	22	23	24	25
26	27	28	29	30	31	

JUNE

S	M	T	W	T	F	S
						1
2	3	4	5	6	7	8
9	10	11	12	13	14	15
16	17	18	19	20	21	22
23	24	25	26	27	28	29
30						

JULY

S	M	T	W	T	F	S
	1	2	3	4	5	6
7	8	9	10	11	12	13
14	15	16	17	18	19	20
21	22	23	24	25	26	27
28	29	30	31			

AUG

S	M	T	W	T	F	S
				1	2	3
4	5	6	7	8	9	10
11	12	13	14	15	16	17
18	19	20	21	22	23	24
25	26	27	28	29	30	31

SEPT

S	M	T	W	T	F	S
1	2	3	4	5	6	7
8	9	10	11	12	13	14
15	16	17	18	19	20	21
22	23	24	25	26	27	28
29	30					

OCT

S	M	T	W	T	F	S
		1	2	3	4	5
6	7	8	9	10	11	12
13	14	15	16	17	18	19
20	21	22	23	24	25	26
27	28	29	30	31		

NOV

S	M	T	W	T	F	S
					1	2
3	4	5	6	7	8	9
10	11	12	13	14	15	16
17	18	19	20	21	22	23
24	25	26	27	28	29	30

DEC

S	M	T	W	T	F	S
1	2	3	4	5	6	7
8	9	10	11	12	13	14
15	16	17	18	19	20	21
22	23	24	25	26	27	28
29	30	31				

Year 10

JAN

S	M	T	W	T	F	S
		1	2	3	4	5
6	7	8	9	10	11	12
13	14	15	16	17	18	19
20	21	22	23	24	25	26
27	28	29	30	31		

FEB

S	M	T	W	T	F	S
					1	2
3	4	5	6	7	8	9
10	11	12	13	14	15	16
17	18	19	20	21	22	23
24	25	26	27	28	29	

MAR

S	M	T	W	T	F	S
						1
2	3	4	5	6	7	8
9	10	11	12	13	14	15
16	17	18	19	20	21	22
23	24	25	26	27	28	29
30	31					

APR

S	M	T	W	T	F	S
		1	2	3	4	5
6	7	8	9	10	11	12
13	14	15	16	17	18	19
20	21	22	23	24	25	26
27	28	29	30			

MAY

S	M	T	W	T	F	S
				1	2	3
4	5	6	7	8	9	10
11	12	13	14	15	16	17
18	19	20	21	22	23	24
25	26	27	28	29	30	31

JUNE

S	M	T	W	T	F	S
1	2	3	4	5	6	7
8	9	10	11	12	13	14
15	16	17	18	19	20	21
22	23	24	25	26	27	28
29	30					

JULY

S	M	T	W	T	F	S
		1	2	3	4	5
6	7	8	9	10	11	12
13	14	15	16	17	18	19
20	21	22	23	24	25	26
27	28	29	30	31		

AUG

S	M	T	W	T	F	S
					1	2
3	4	5	6	7	8	9
10	11	12	13	14	15	16
17	18	19	20	21	22	23
24	25	26	27	28	29	30
31						

SEPT

S	M	T	W	T	F	S
	1	2	3	4	5	6
7	8	9	10	11	12	13
14	15	16	17	18	19	20
21	22	23	24	25	26	27
28	29	30				

OCT

S	M	T	W	T	F	S
			1	2	3	4
5	6	7	8	9	10	11
12	13	14	15	16	17	18
19	20	21	22	23	24	25
26	27	28	29	30	31	

NOV

S	M	T	W	T	F	S
						1
2	3	4	5	6	7	8
9	10	11	12	13	14	15
16	17	18	19	20	21	22
23	24	25	26	27	28	29
30						

DEC

S	M	T	W	T	F	S
	1	2	3	4	5	6
7	8	9	10	11	12	13
14	15	16	17	18	19	20
21	22	23	24	25	26	27
28	29	30	31			

11

	S	M	T	W	T	F	S
JAN				1	2	3	4
	5	6	7	8	9	10	11
	12	13	14	15	16	17	18
	19	20	21	22	23	24	25
	26	27	28	29	30	31	
FEB							1
	2	3	4	5	6	7	8
	9	10	11	12	13	14	15
	16	17	18	19	20	21	22
	23	24	25	26	27	28	29
MAR	1	2	3	4	5	6	7
	8	9	10	11	12	13	14
	15	16	17	18	19	20	21
	22	23	24	25	26	27	28
	29	30	31				
APR				1	2	3	4
	5	6	7	8	9	10	11
	12	13	14	15	16	17	18
	19	20	21	22	23	24	25
	26	27	28	29	30		
MAY						1	2
	3	4	5	6	7	8	9
	10	11	12	13	14	15	16
	17	18	19	20	21	22	23
	24	25	26	27	28	29	30
	31						
JUNE		1	2	3	4	5	6
	7	8	9	10	11	12	13
	14	15	16	17	18	19	20
	21	22	23	24	25	26	27
	28	29	30				
JULY				1	2	3	4
	5	6	7	8	9	10	11
	12	13	14	15	16	17	18
	19	20	21	22	23	24	25
	26	27	28	29	30	31	
AUG							1
	2	3	4	5	6	7	8
	9	10	11	12	13	14	15
	16	17	18	19	20	21	22
	23	24	25	26	27	28	29
	30	31					
SEPT			1	2	3	4	5
	6	7	8	9	10	11	12
	13	14	15	16	17	18	19
	20	21	22	23	24	25	26
	27	28	29	30			
OCT					1	2	3
	4	5	6	7	8	9	10
	11	12	13	14	15	16	17
	18	19	20	21	22	23	24
	25	26	27	28	29	30	31
NOV	1	2	3	4	5	6	7
	8	9	10	11	12	13	14
	15	16	17	18	19	20	21
	22	23	24	25	26	27	28
	29	30					
DEC			1	2	3	4	5
	6	7	8	9	10	11	12
	13	14	15	16	17	18	19
	20	21	22	23	24	25	26
	27	28	29	30	31		

12

	S	M	T	W	T	F	S
JAN					1	2	3
	4	5	6	7	8	9	10
	11	12	13	14	15	16	17
	18	19	20	21	22	23	24
	25	26	27	28	29	30	31
FEB	1	2	3	4	5	6	7
	8	9	10	11	12	13	14
	15	16	17	18	19	20	21
	22	23	24	25	26	27	28
	29						
MAR		1	2	3	4	5	6
	7	8	9	10	11	12	13
	14	15	16	17	18	19	20
	21	22	23	24	25	26	27
	28	29	30	31			
APR					1	2	3
	4	5	6	7	8	9	10
	11	12	13	14	15	16	17
	18	19	20	21	22	23	24
	25	26	27	28	29	30	
MAY							1
	2	3	4	5	6	7	8
	9	10	11	12	13	14	15
	16	17	18	19	20	21	22
	23	24	25	26	27	28	29
	30	31					
JUNE			1	2	3	4	5
	6	7	8	9	10	11	12
	13	14	15	16	17	18	19
	20	21	22	23	24	25	26
	27	28	29	30			
JULY					1	2	3
	4	5	6	7	8	9	10
	11	12	13	14	15	16	17
	18	19	20	21	22	23	24
	25	26	27	28	29	30	31
AUG	1	2	3	4	5	6	7
	8	9	10	11	12	13	14
	15	16	17	18	19	20	21
	22	23	24	25	26	27	28
	29	30	31				
SEPT				1	2	3	4
	5	6	7	8	9	10	11
	12	13	14	15	16	17	18
	19	20	21	22	23	24	25
	26	27	28	29	30		
OCT						1	2
	3	4	5	6	7	8	9
	10	11	12	13	14	15	16
	17	18	19	20	21	22	23
	24	25	26	27	28	29	30
	31						
NOV		1	2	3	4	5	6
	7	8	9	10	11	12	13
	14	15	16	17	18	19	20
	21	22	23	24	25	26	27
	28	29	30				
DEC				1	2	3	4
	5	6	7	8	9	10	11
	12	13	14	15	16	17	18
	19	20	21	22	23	24	25
	26	27	28	29	30	31	

13

	S	M	T	W	T	F	S
JAN						1	2
	3	4	5	6	7	8	9
	10	11	12	13	14	15	16
	17	18	19	20	21	22	23
	24	25	26	27	28	29	30
	31						
FEB		1	2	3	4	5	6
	7	8	9	10	11	12	13
	14	15	16	17	18	19	20
	21	22	23	24	25	26	27
	28	29					
MAR			1	2	3	4	5
	6	7	8	9	10	11	12
	13	14	15	16	17	18	19
	20	21	22	23	24	25	26
	27	28	29	30	31		
APR						1	2
	3	4	5	6	7	8	9
	10	11	12	13	14	15	16
	17	18	19	20	21	22	23
	24	25	26	27	28	29	30
MAY	1	2	3	4	5	6	7
	8	9	10	11	12	13	14
	15	16	17	18	19	20	21
	22	23	24	25	26	27	28
	29	30	31				
JUNE				1	2	3	4
	5	6	7	8	9	10	11
	12	13	14	15	16	17	18
	19	20	21	22	23	24	25
	26	27	28	29	30		
JULY						1	2
	3	4	5	6	7	8	9
	10	11	12	13	14	15	16
	17	18	19	20	21	22	23
	24	25	26	27	28	29	30
	31						
AUG		1	2	3	4	5	6
	7	8	9	10	11	12	13
	14	15	16	17	18	19	20
	21	22	23	24	25	26	27
	28	29	30	31			
SEPT					1	2	3
	4	5	6	7	8	9	10
	11	12	13	14	15	16	17
	18	19	20	21	22	23	24
	25	26	27	28	29	30	
OCT							1
	2	3	4	5	6	7	8
	9	10	11	12	13	14	15
	16	17	18	19	20	21	22
	23	24	25	26	27	28	29
	30	31					
NOV			1	2	3	4	5
	6	7	8	9	10	11	12
	13	14	15	16	17	18	19
	20	21	22	23	24	25	26
	27	28	29	30			
DEC					1	2	3
	4	5	6	7	8	9	10
	11	12	13	14	15	16	17
	18	19	20	21	22	23	24
	25	26	27	28	29	30	31

14

2000

	S	M	T	W	T	F	S
JAN							1
	2	3	4	5	6	7	8
	9	10	11	12	13	14	15
	16	17	18	19	20	21	22
	23	24	25	26	27	28	29
	30	31					
FEB			1	2	3	4	5
	6	7	8	9	10	11	12
	13	14	15	16	17	18	19
	20	21	22	23	24	25	26
	27	28	29				
MAR				1	2	3	4
	5	6	7	8	9	10	11
	12	13	14	15	16	17	18
	19	20	21	22	23	24	25
	26	27	28	29	30	31	
APR							1
	2	3	4	5	6	7	8
	9	10	11	12	13	14	15
	16	17	18	19	20	21	22
	23	24	25	26	27	28	29
	30						
MAY		1	2	3	4	5	6
	7	8	9	10	11	12	13
	14	15	16	17	18	19	20
	21	22	23	24	25	26	27
	28	29	30	31			
JUNE					1	2	3
	4	5	6	7	8	9	10
	11	12	13	14	15	16	17
	18	19	20	21	22	23	24
	25	26	27	28	29	30	
JULY							1
	2	3	4	5	6	7	8
	9	10	11	12	13	14	15
	16	17	18	19	20	21	22
	23	24	25	26	27	28	29
	30	31					
AUG			1	2	3	4	5
	6	7	8	9	10	11	12
	13	14	15	16	17	18	19
	20	21	22	23	24	25	26
	27	28	29	30	31		
SEPT						1	2
	3	4	5	6	7	8	9
	10	11	12	13	14	15	16
	17	18	19	20	21	22	23
	24	25	26	27	28	29	30
OCT	1	2	3	4	5	6	7
	8	9	10	11	12	13	14
	15	16	17	18	19	20	21
	22	23	24	25	26	27	28
	29	30	31				
NOV				1	2	3	4
	5	6	7	8	9	10	11
	12	13	14	15	16	17	18
	19	20	21	22	23	24	25
	26	27	28	29	30		
DEC						1	2
	3	4	5	6	7	8	9
	10	11	12	13	14	15	16
	17	18	19	20	21	22	23
	24	25	26	27	28	29	30
	31						

☆ *The Teacher's Calendar, 2000–2001* ☆

SELECTED SPECIAL YEARS: 1965–2005

Intl Cooperation Year: 1965
Intl Book Year: 1972
World Population Year: 1974
Intl Women's Year: 1975
Intl Year of the Child: 1979
Intl Year for Disabled Persons: 1981
World Communications Year: 1983
Intl Youth Year: 1985
Intl Year of Peace: 1986
Intl Year of Shelter for the Homeless: 1987
Year of the Reader: 1987
Year of the Young Reader: 1989
Intl Literacy Year: 1990
US Decade of the Brain: 1990-99
Intl Space Year: 1992
Intl Year for World's Indigenous Peoples: 1993
Intl Year of the Family: 1994
Year for Tolerance: 1995
Intl Year for Eradication of Poverty: 1996
Intl Year of the Ocean: 1998
Intl Year of Older Persons: 1999
Intl Year for the Culture of Peace: 2000
Intl Year of Thanksgiving: 2000
Intl Year of Volunteers: 2001
Intl Year of Dialogue Among Civilizations: 2001
Intl Year of Mobilization Against Racism: 2001
Intl Year of Mountains: 2002
Intl Year of Ecotourism: 2002
Intl Year of Microcredit: 2005

CHINESE CALENDAR

The Chinese lunar year is divided into 12 months of 29 or 30 days. The calendar is adjusted to the length of the solar year by the addition of extra months at regular intervals. The years are arranged in major cycles of 60 years. Each successive year is named after one of 12 animals. These 12-year cycles are continuously repeated.

1996	Rat
1997	Ox
1998	Tiger
1999	Hare
2000	Dragon
2001	Snake
2002	Horse
2003	Sheep (Goat)
2004	Monkey
2005	Rooster
2006	Dog
2007	Pig

LOOKING FORWARD

2001
- 21st Century and Third Millennium of the Christian Era
- Centennial of Australian Federation
- James Madison's birth, 250th anniversary

2002
- Winter Olympics (Salt Lake City)

2003
- Ohio Statehood Bicentennial
- Wright Brothers' first flight, 100th anniversary

2004
- First successful newspaper in America, 300th anniversary
- US presidential election
- Summer Olympics (Athens, Greece)

2006
- Benjamin Franklin's birth, 300th anniversary
- Woodrow Wilson's birth, 150th anniversary
- Winter Olympics (Turin, Italy)

2007
- Oklahoma Statehood Centennial
- Jamestown Colony, 400th anniversary
- Sputnik launched by USSR, 50th anniversary
- William H. Taft's birth, 150th anniversary

2008
- James Monroe's birth, 250th anniversary
- Andrew Johnson's birth, 200th anniversary
- Theodore Roosevelt's birth, 150th anniversary
- Lyndon Johnson's birth, 100th anniversary
- US presidential election

2009
- Abraham Lincoln's birth, 200th anniversary

2010
- US population projected to be 298,000,000
- 23rd Decennial Census of the US

2011
- Ronald Reagan's birth, 100th anniversary

2012
- Arizona Statehood Centennial
- Louisiana Statehood Bicentennial
- New Mexico Statehood Centennial
- US presidential election

2013
- Richard Nixon's birth, 100th anniversary
- Gerald Ford's birth, 100th anniversary

2015
- US population projected to be 310,000,000

2016
- Indiana Statehood Bicentennial
- US presidential election

2017
- Mississippi Statehood Bicentennial
- John Q. Adams's birth, 250th anniversary
- Andrew Jackson's birth, 250th anniversary
- John F. Kennedy's birth, 100th anniversary

2018
- Illinois Statehood Bicentennial

2019
- Alabama Statehood Bicentennial
- Apollo 11 astronauts walk on moon, 50th anniversary

2020
- US population projected to be 323,000,000
- 24th Decennial Census of the US
- Maine State Bicentennial
- US presidential election

2050
- US population projected to be 394,000,000
- World population of 9 billion predicted

2061
- Halley's comet returns

SOME FACTS ABOUT THE STATES

State	Capital	Popular name	Area (sq. mi.)	State bird	State flower	State tree	Admitted to the Union	Order of Admission
Alabama	Montgomery	Cotton or Yellowhammer State; or Heart of Dixie	51,609	Yellowhammer	Camellia	Southern pine (Longleaf pine)	1819	22
Alaska	Juneau	Last Frontier	591,004	Willow ptarmigan	Forget-me-not	Sitka spruce	1959	49
Arizona	Phoenix	Grand Canyon State	114,000	Cactus wren	Saguaro (giant cactus)	Palo Verde	1912	48
Arkansas	Little Rock	The Natural State	53,187	Mockingbird	Apple blossom	Pine	1836	25
California	Sacramento	Golden State	158,706	California valley quail	Golden poppy	California redwood	1850	31
Colorado	Denver	Centennial State	104,091	Lark bunting	Rocky Mountain columbine	Blue spruce	1876	38
Connecticut	Hartford	Constitution State	5,018	Robin	Mountain laurel	White oak	1788	5
Delaware	Dover	First State	2,044	Blue hen chicken	Peach blossom	American holly	1787	1
Florida	Tallahassee	Sunshine State	58,664	Mockingbird	Orange blossom	Cabbage (sabal) palm	1845	27
Georgia	Atlanta	Empire State of the South	58,910	Brown thrasher	Cherokee rose	Live oak	1788	4
Hawaii	Honolulu	Aloha State	6,471	Nene (Hawaiian goose)	Hibiscus	Kukui	1959	50
Idaho	Boise	Gem State	83,564	Mountain bluebird	Syringa (mock orange)	Western white pine	1890	43
Illinois	Springfield	Prairie State	56,345	Cardinal	Native violet	White oak	1818	21
Indiana	Indianapolis	Hoosier State	36,185	Cardinal	Peony	Tulip tree or yellow poplar	1816	19
Iowa	Des Moines	Hawkeye State	56,275	Eastern goldfinch	Wild rose	Oak	1846	29
Kansas	Topeka	Sunflower State	82,277	Western meadowlark	Sunflower	Cottonwood	1861	34
Kentucky	Frankfort	Bluegrass State	40,409	Kentucky cardinal	Goldenrod	Kentucky coffeetree	1792	15
Louisiana	Baton Rouge	Pelican State	47,752	Pelican	Magnolia	Bald cypress	1812	18
Maine	Augusta	Pine Tree State	33,265	Chickadee	White pine cone and tassel	White pine	1820	23
Maryland	Annapolis	Old Line State	10,577	Baltimore oriole	Black-eyed Susan	White oak	1788	7
Massachusetts	Boston	Bay State	8,284	Chickadee	Mayflower	American elm	1788	6
Michigan	Lansing	Wolverine State	58,527	Robin	Apple blossom	White pine	1837	26
Minnesota	St. Paul	North Star State	84,402	Common loon	Pink and white lady's-slipper	Norway, or red, pine	1858	32
Mississippi	Jackson	Magnolia State	47,689	Mockingbird	Magnolia	Magnolia	1817	20
Missouri	Jefferson City	Show Me State	69,697	Bluebird	Hawthorn	Flowering dogwood	1821	24
Montana	Helena	Treasure State	147,046	Western meadowlark	Bitterroot	Ponderosa pine	1889	41
Nebraska	Lincoln	Cornhusker State	77,355	Western meadowlark	Goldenrod	Cottonwood	1867	37
Nevada	Carson City	Silver State	110,540	Mountain bluebird	Sagebrush	Single-leaf piñon	1864	36
New Hampshire	Concord	Granite State	9,304	Purple finch	Purple lilac	White birch	1788	9
New Jersey	Trenton	Garden State	7,787	Eastern goldfinch	Purple violet	Red oak	1787	3
New Mexico	Santa Fe	Land of Enchantment	121,593	Roadrunner	Yucca flower	Piñon, or nut pine	1912	47
New York	Albany	Empire State	49,108	Bluebird	Rose	Sugar maple	1788	11
North Carolina	Raleigh	Tar Heel State or Old North State	52,669	Cardinal	Dogwood	Pine	1789	12
North Dakota	Bismarck	Peace Garden State	70,702	Western meadowlark	Wild prairie rose	American elm	1889	39

State	Capital	Popular name	Area (sq. mi.)	State bird	State flower	State tree	Admitted to the Union	Order of Admission
Ohio	Columbus	Buckeye State	41,330	Cardinal	Scarlet carnation	Buckeye	1803	17
Oklahoma	Oklahoma City	Sooner State	69,956	Scissortail flycatcher	Mistletoe	Redbud	1907	46
Oregon	Salem	Beaver State	97,073	Western meadowlark	Oregon grape	Douglas fir	1859	33
Pennsylvania	Harrisburg	Keystone State	45,308	Ruffed grouse	Mountain laurel	Hemlock	1787	2
Rhode Island	Providence	Ocean State	1,212	Rhode Island Red	Violet	Red maple	1790	13
South Carolina	Columbia	Palmetto State	31,113	Carolina wren	Carolina jessamine	Palmetto	1788	8
South Dakota	Pierre	Sunshine State	77,116	Ring-necked pheasant	American pasqueflower	Black Hills spruce	1889	40
Tennessee	Nashville	Volunteer State	42,114	Mockingbird	Iris	Tulip poplar	1796	16
Texas	Austin	Lone Star State	266,807	Mockingbird	Bluebonnet	Pecan	1845	28
Utah	Salt Lake City	Beehive State	84,899	Sea Gull	Sego lily	Blue spruce	1896	45
Vermont	Montpelier	Green Mountain State	9,614	Hermit thrush	Red clover	Sugar maple	1791	14
Virginia	Richmond	Old Dominion	40,767	Cardinal	Dogwood	Dogwood	1788	10
Washington	Olympia	Evergreen State	68,139	Willow goldfinch	Coast rhododendron	Western hemlock	1889	42
West Virginia	Charleston	Mountain State	24,231	Cardinal	Rhododendron	Sugar maple	1863	35
Wisconsin	Madison	Badger State	56,153	Robin	Wood violet	Sugar maple	1848	30
Wyoming	Cheyenne	Equality State	97,809	Meadowlark	Indian paintbrush	Cottonwood	1890	44

STATE & TERRITORY ABBREVIATIONS: UNITED STATES

Alabama ... AL	Kentucky ... KY	Oklahoma ... OK
Alaska ... AK	Louisiana ... LA	Oregon ... OR
Arizona ... AZ	Maine ... ME	Pennsylvania ... PA
Arkansas ... AR	Maryland ... MD	Puerto Rico ... PR
American Samoa ... AS	Massachusetts ... MA	Rhode Island ... RI
California ... CA	Michigan ... MI	South Carolina ... SC
Colorado ... CO	Minnesota ... MN	South Dakota ... SD
Connecticut ... CT	Mississippi ... MS	Tennessee ... TN
Delaware ... DE	Missouri ... MO	Texas ... TX
District of Columbia ... DC	Montana ... MT	Utah ... UT
Florida ... FL	Nebraska ... NE	Vermont ... VT
Georgia ... GA	Nevada ... NV	Virginia ... VA
Guam ... GU	New Hampshire ... NH	Virgin Islands ... VI
Hawaii ... HI	New Jersey ... NJ	Washington ... WA
Idaho ... ID	New Mexico ... NM	West Virginia ... WV
Illinois ... IL	New York ... NY	Wisconsin ... WI
Indiana ... IN	North Carolina ... NC	Wyoming ... WY
Iowa ... IA	North Dakota ... ND	
Kansas ... KS	Ohio ... OH	

PROVINCE & TERRITORY ABBREVIATIONS: CANADA

Alberta ... AB	Newfoundland ... NF	Quebec ... QC
British Columbia ... BC	Nova Scotia ... NS	Saskatchewan ... SK
Manitoba ... MB	Ontario ... ON	Yukon Territory ... YT
New Brunswick ... NB	Prince Edward Island ... PE	Northwest Territories ... NT

SOME FACTS ABOUT CANADA

Province/Territory	Capital	Population*	Flower	Land/Fresh Water (sq. mi.)	Total Area
Alberta	Edmonton	2,774,512	Wild rose	400,423/10,437	410,860
British Columbia	Victoria	3,835,748	Pacific dogwood	578,230/11,227	589,458
Manitoba	Winnipeg	1,141,727	Prairie crocus	340,834/63,129	403,964
New Brunswick	Fredericton	761,873	Purple violet	44,797/835	45,633
Newfoundland	St. John's	571,192	Pitcher plant	230,219/21,147	251,367
Northwest Territories	Yellowknife	66,164	Mountain avens	2,017,306/82,829	2,100,136
Nova Scotia	Halifax	941,235	Mayflower	32,835/1,647	34,482
Ontario	Toronto	11,209,474	White trillium	553,788/110,229	664,012
Prince Edward Island	Charlottetown	137,316	Lady's-slipper	3,515/0	3,515
Quebec	Quebec City	7,366,883	White garden lily	843,109/114,269	957,379
Saskatchewan	Regina	1,020,138	Red lily	354,365/51,347	405,712
Yukon Territory	Whitehorse	31,107	Fireweed	297,050/2,784	299,835

*1996

SOME FACTS ABOUT THE PRESIDENTS

	Name	Birthdate, Place	Party	Tenure	Died	First Lady	Vice President
1.	George Washington	2/22/1732, Westmoreland Cnty, VA	Federalist	1789–1797	12/14/1799	Martha Dandridge Custis	John Adams
2.	John Adams	10/30/1735, Braintree (Quincy), MA	Federalist	1797–1801	7/4/1826	Abigail Smith	Thomas Jefferson
3.	Thomas Jefferson	4/13/1743, Shadwell, VA	Democratic-Republican	1801–1809	7/4/1826	Martha Wayles Skelton	Aaron Burr, 1801–05 George Clinton, 1805–09
4.	James Madison	3/16/1751, Port Conway, VA	Democratic-Republican	1809–1817	6/28/1836	Dolley Payne Todd	George Clinton, 1809–12 Elbridge Gerry, 1813–14(?)
5.	James Monroe	4/28/1758, Westmoreland Cnty, VA	Democratic-Republican	1817–1825	7/4/1831	Elizabeth Kortright	Daniel D. Tompkins
6.	John Q. Adams	7/11/1767, Braintree (Quincy), MA	Democratic-Republican	1825–1829	2/23/1848	Louisa Catherine Johnson	John C. Calhoun
7.	Andrew Jackson	3/15/1767, Waxhaw Settlement, SC	Democrat	1829–1837	6/8/1845	Mrs. Rachel Donelson Robards	John C. Calhoun, 1829–32 Martin Van Buren, 1833–37
8.	Martin Van Buren	12/5/1782, Kinderhook, NY	Democrat	1837–1841	7/24/1862	Hannah Hoes	Richard M. Johnson
9.	William H. Harrison	2/9/1773, Charles City Cnty, VA	Whig	1841	4/4/1841†	Anna Symmes	John Tyler
10.	John Tyler	3/29/1790, Charles City Cnty, VA	Whig	1841–1845	1/18/1862	Letitia Christian Julia Gardiner	
11.	James K. Polk	11/2/1795, near Pineville, NC	Democrat	1845–1849	6/15/1849	Sarah Childress	George M. Dallas
12.	Zachary Taylor	11/24/1784, Barboursville, VA	Whig	1849–1850	7/9/1850†	Margaret Mackall Smith	Millard Fillmore
13.	Millard Fillmore	1/7/1800, Locke, NY	Whig	1850–1853	3/8/1874	Abigail Powers Mrs. Caroline Carmichael McIntosh	
14.	Franklin Pierce	11/23/1804, Hillsboro, NH	Democrat	1853–1857	10/8/1869	Jane Means Appleton	William R. D. King
15.	James Buchanan	4/23/1791, near Mercersburg, PA	Democrat	1857–1861	6/1/1868		John C. Breckinridge

☆ *The Teacher's Calendar, 2000–2001* ☆

16.	Abraham Lincoln	2/12/1809, near Hodgenville, KY	Republican	1861–1865	4/15/1865*	Mary Todd	Hannibal Hamlin, 1861–65 Andrew Johnson, 1865
17.	Andrew Johnson	12/29/1808, Raleigh, NC	Democrat	1865–1869	7/31/1875	Eliza McCardle	
18.	Ulysses S. Grant	4/27/1822, Point Pleasant, OH	Republican	1869–1877	7/23/1885	Julia Boggs Dent	Schuyler Colfax, 1869–73 Henry Wilson, 1873–75
19.	Rutherford B. Hayes	10/4/1822, Delaware, OH	Republican	1877–1881	1/17/1893	Lucy Ware Webb	William A. Wheeler
20.	James A. Garfield	11/19/1831, Orange, OH	Republican	1881	9/19/1881*	Lucretia Rudolph	Chester A. Arthur
21.	Chester A. Arthur	10/5/1829, Fairfield, VT	Republican	1881–1885	11/18/1886	Ellen Lewis Herndon	
22.	Grover Cleveland	3/18/1837, Caldwell, NJ	Democrat	1885–1889	6/24/1908	Frances Folsom	Thomas A. Hendricks, 1885
23.	Benjamin Harrison	8/20/1833, North Bend, OH	Republican	1889–1893	3/13/1901	Caroline Lavinia Scott Mrs. Mary Dimmick	Levi P. Morton
24.	Grover Cleveland	3/18/1837, Caldwell, NJ	Democrat	1893–1897	6/24/1908	Frances Folsom	Adlai Stevenson, 1893–97
25.	William McKinley	1/29/1843, Niles, OH	Republican	1897–1901	9/14/1901*	Ida Saxton	Garret A. Hobart, 1897–99 Theodore Roosevelt, 1901
26.	Theodore Roosevelt	10/27/1858, New York, NY	Republican	1901–1909	1/6/1919	Alice Hathaway Lee Edith Kermit Carow	Charles W. Fairbanks
27.	William H. Taft	9/15/1857, Cincinnati, OH	Republican	1909–1913	3/8/1930	Helen Herron	James S. Sherman
28.	Woodrow Wilson	12/28/1856, Staunton, VA	Democrat	1913–1921	2/3/1924	Ellen Louise Axson Edith Bolling Galt	Thomas R. Marshall
29.	Warren G. Harding	11/2/1865, near Corsica, OH	Republican	1921–1923	8/2/1923†	Florence Kling DeWolfe	Calvin Coolidge
30.	Calvin Coolidge	7/4/1872, Plymouth Notch, VT	Republican	1923–1929	1/5/1933	Grace Anna Goodhue	Charles G. Dawes
31.	Herbert C. Hoover	8/10/1874, West Branch, IA	Republican	1929–1933	10/20/1964	Lou Henry	Charles Curtis
32.	Franklin D. Roosevelt	1/30/1882, Hyde Park, NY	Democrat	1933–1945	4/12/1945†	Eleanor Roosevelt	John N. Garner, 1933–41 Henry A. Wallace, 1941–45 Harry S. Truman, 1945
33.	Harry S. Truman	5/8/1884, Lamar, MO	Democrat	1945–1953	12/26/1972	Elizabeth Virginia (Bess) Wallace	Alben W. Barkley
34.	Dwight D. Eisenhower	10/14/1890, Denison, TX	Republican	1953–1961	3/28/1969	Mamie Geneva Doud	Richard M. Nixon
35.	John F. Kennedy	5/29/1917, Brookline, MA	Democrat	1961–1963	11/22/1963*	Jacqueline Lee Bouvier	Lyndon B. Johnson
36.	Lyndon B. Johnson	8/27/1908, near Stonewall, TX	Democrat	1963–1969	1/22/1973	Claudia Alta (Lady Bird) Taylor	Hubert H. Humphrey
37.	Richard M. Nixon	1/9/1913, Yorba Linda, CA	Republican	1969–1974**	4/22/1994	Thelma Catherine (Pat) Ryan	Spiro T. Agnew, 1969–73 Gerald R. Ford, 1973–74
38.	Gerald R. Ford	7/14/1913, Omaha, NE	Republican	1974–1977		Elizabeth (Betty) Bloomer	Nelson A. Rockefeller
39.	James E. Carter, Jr	10/1/1924, Plains, GA	Democrat	1977–1981		Rosalynn Smith	Walter F. Mondale
40.	Ronald W. Reagan	2/6/1911, Tampico, IL	Republican	1981–1989		Nancy Davis	George H. W. Bush
41.	George H. W. Bush	6/12/1924, Milton, MA	Republican	1989–1993		Barbara Pierce	J. Danforth Quayle
42.	William J. Clinton	8/19/1946, Hope, AR	Democrat	1993–2001		Hillary Rodham	Albert Gore, Jr.

* assassinated while in office
** resigned Aug 9, 1974
† died while in office—nonviolently

Sources: *World Book*, 1991 Edition; *Encyclopedia Americana*, 1990 Edition; *Collier's Encyclopedia*, 1994 Edition

2000 AMERICAN LIBRARY ASSOCIATION AWARDS FOR CHILDREN'S BOOKS

NEWBERY MEDAL

For most distinguished contribution to American literature for children published in 1999:

Christopher Paul Curtis, author, *Bud, Not Buddy* (Delacorte, 0-385-32306-9, $15.95 All Ages)

Honor Books

Audrey Couloumbis, author, *Getting Near to Baby* (Putnam, 0-39-923389-X, $17.99 Gr. 4–8)

Tomie dePaola, author and illustrator, *26 Fairmount Avenue* (Putnam, 0-39-923246-X, $13.99 Gr. 4–8)

Jennifer L. Holm, author, *Our Only May Amelia* (HarperCollins, 0-06-027822-6, $15.95 Gr. 4–8)

CALDECOTT MEDAL

For most distinguished American picture book for children published in 1999:

Simms Taback, illustrator, *Joseph Had a Little Overcoat* (Viking, 0-67-087855-3, $15.99 Gr. K–3)

Honor Books

David Wiesner, illustrator and author, *Sector 7* (Houghton Mifflin, 0-39-574656-6, $16 Gr. K–3)

Jerry Pinkney, illustrator, *The Ugly Duckling* (Morrow, 0-68-815932-X, $16 Gr. K–3)

Molly Bang, illustrator and author, *When Sophie Gets Angry–Really, Really Angry* (Scholastic, 0-590-18979-4, $15.95 Gr. K–3)

Trina Schart Hyman, illustrator, *A Child's Calendar* (Holiday House, 0-8234-1445-0, $16.95 Gr. K–3)

CORETTA SCOTT KING AWARD

For outstanding books by African American authors and illustrators:

Christopher Paul Curtis, author, *Bud, Not Buddy* (Delacorte, 0-385-32306-9, $15.95 All Ages)

Brian Pinkney, illustrator, *In the Time of the Drums* (Hyperion, 0-7868-0436-X, $15.99 Gr. K–3)

Honor Books-Authors

Karen English, *Francie* (Farrar, Straus, 0-374-32456-5, $16 Gr. 4–8)

Patricia C. and Frederick L. McKissack, *Black Hands, White Sails: The Story of African-American Whalers* (Scholastic, 0-590-48313-7, $15.95 Gr. 4–8)

Walter Dean Myers, *Monster* (HarperCollins, 0-06-028077-8, $15.95 Gr. 7 & up)

Honor Books-Illustrators

E.B. Lewis, *My Rows and Piles of Coins* (Clarion, 0-395-75186-1, $15 Gr. K–3)

Christopher Myers, *Black Cat* (Scholastic, 0-590-03375-1, $16.95 Gr. K–3)

MICHAEL L. PRINTZ AWARD

For excellence in writing literature for young adults:

Walter Dean Myers, *Monster* (HarperCollins, 0-06-028077-8, $15.95 Gr. 7 & up)

Honor Books

Ellen Wittlinger, *Hard Love* (Simon & Schuster, 0-68-982134-4, $16.95 Gr. 6 & up)

David Almond, *Skellig* (Delacorte, 0-385-32653-X, $15.95 Gr. 4–8)

Laurie Halse Anderson, *Speak* (Farrar, Straus, 0-374-37152-0, $16 Gr. 8 & up)

MARGARET A. EDWARDS AWARD

For lifetime achievement in writing books for young adults:

Chris Crutcher, recipient

PURA BELPRÉ AWARD

For Latino authors and illustrators whose work best portrays and celebrates Latino culture in a children's book:

Alma Flor Ada, author, *Under the Royal Palms: A Childhood in Cuba* (Atheneum, 0-689-80631-0, $15 Gr. 4–8)

Carmen Lomas Garza, *Making Magic Windows: Cut-paper Art and Stories* (Children's Book Press, 0-892-39159-6, $9.95 Gr. 4–8)

Honor Books-Author

Francisco X. Alarcón, *From the Bellybutton of the Moon and Other Summer Poems* (Children's Book Press, 0-892-39153-7, $15.95 Gr. K–4)

Juan Felipe Herrera, *Laughing Out Loud, I Fly: Poems in English and Spanish* (HarperCollins, 0-06-027604-5, $15.95 Gr. 5–8)

Honor Books-Illustrators

George Ancona, *Barrio: José's Neighborhood* (Harcourt, 0-15-201808-5, $9 Gr. 4–8)

Felipe Dávalos, *The Secret Stars* (Marshall Cavendish, 0-7614-5027-0, $15.95 Gr. K–3)

Amelia Lau Carling, *Mama & Papa Have a Store* (Dial, 0-8037-2044-0, $15.99 Gr. K–3)

MILDRED L. BATCHELDER AWARD

For the best children's book first published in a foreign language in a foreign country and subsequently translated into English for publication in the US:

Walker and Company, publisher, *The Baboon King* (0-8027-8711-8, $16.95 Gr. 7 & up)

Honor Books

R&S Books, *Vendela in Venice* (9-129-64559-X, $18 Gr. 4–8)

Farrar, Straus and Giroux, *The Collector of Moments* (0-374-31520-5, $18 Gr. 4–8)

Front Street, *Asphalt Angels* (1-886910-24-3, $15.95 Gr. 7 & up)

ANDREW CARNEGIE MEDAL FOR EXCELLENCE IN CHILDREN'S VIDEO

Paul R. Gagne, *Miss Nelson Has a Field Day* (Weston Woods, Gr. K–3)

SCOTT O'DELL AWARD FOR HISTORICAL FICTION

Miriam Bat-Ami, *Two Suns in the Sky* (Front Street, 0-812629-00-0, $15.95, Gr. 7 & up).

MAY HILL ARBUTHNOT LECTURE AWARD

Susan Cooper, recipient

RESOURCES

PROFESSIONAL READING

Financial Tips for Teachers, by Alan Jay Weiss and Larry Strauss. 7th edition. Lowell House, 0-7373-0302-6, $13.95.

The Teacher's Almanac: The Professional Teacher's Handbook, by Pat Woodward. 2nd edition. Lowell House, 0-7373-0025-6, $15.

Unbelievably Good Deals That You Absolutely Can't Get Unless You're a Teacher, by Barry Harrington and Beth Christensen. 2nd edition. Contemporary Books, 0-8092-2877-7, $12.95.

BIBLIOGRAPHIES

Literature Connection to American History, K-6: Resources to Enhance and Entice, by Lynda G. Adamson. Libraries Unlimited, 1-56308-502-X, $33.50.

A similar volume by Adamson covers books appropriate for grades 7-12.

Great Books for African American Children, by Pamela Toussaint. Plume, 0-45-228044-3, $12.95.

Great Books for Boys: More Than 600 Books for Boys 2 to 14, by Kathleen Odean. Ballantine, 0-34-542083-7, $12.95.

Great Books for Girls: More Than 600 Books to Inspire Today's Girls and Tomorrow's Women, by Katheleen Odean. Ballantine, 0-34-540484-X, $12.95.

Once Upon a Heroine: 450 Books for Girls to Love, by Alison Cooper-Mullin and Jennifer Marmaduke Coye. Contemporary Books, 0-8092-3020-8, $16.95.

ACTIVITY BOOKS

Library Celebrations, by Cyndy Dingwall. Highsmith, 1-5795-0027-7, $16.95.

Creative programs for Children's Book Week, National Library Week, author visits and other events that celebrate books and libraries.

PERIODICALS

Both these publications suggest books and electronic products related to specific themes for grades K–8.

Book Links: Connecting Books, Libraries, and Classrooms. 6/year at $24.95. American Library Association, 50 E Huron St, Chicago, IL 60611. Web: www.ala.org/BookLinks.

Online/Offline: Themes and Resources. 9/year at $66.50. Rock Hill Press, 14 Rock Hill Rd, Bala Cynwyd, PA 19004. Web: www.rockhillpress.com/products.htm.

WEBSITES

CIA World Factbook: www.odci.gov/cia/publications/factbook/index.html. Detailed information about every country of the world.

United Nations Infonation: www.un.org/Pubs/CyberSchoolBus/infonation/e_infonation.htm. Statistical information on 185 nations.

Fifty States and Capitals: www.50states.com. Information on US states and territories, plus many relevant links.

Consumer Information Center: www.pueblo.gsa.gov. Many helpful government pamphlets available online.

Libraries: sunsite.berkeley.edu/Libweb. Links to the catalogs of more than 2,000 libraries in 70 countries can be found here.

The American Memory Project at the Library of Congress: memory.loc.gov/ammen. Thousands of photographs and the text of documents and pamphlets suitable for upper elementary and middle school students.

Ask ERIC: www.askeric.org. The Virtual Library section of this site contains lesson plans, links to the companion study guides to

TV series and access to the journal literature and research reports in the ERIC (Education Resources Information Center) system.

Oyate Native American site: www.oyate.org. This site features evaluations of books and other materials for children that provide honest portrayals of Native Americans.

Center for the Study of Books in Spanish for Children and Adolescents site: www.csusm.edu/cwis/campus_centers/csb. Evaluations of more than 5,000 books for youth.

PBS site: www.pbs.org. This site has information on kids' favorite TV shows, such as "Arthur" and "Kratts' Creatures." "Reading Rainbow" is also found here. Bill Nye, the Science Guy has his own website at nyelabs.kcts.org.

CBC site: www.cbc4kids.ca This site from the Canadian Broadcasting Corporation has stuff for kids on both sides of the border.

How Stuff Works site: www.howstuffworks.com Simple explanations of how airplanes fly or refrigerators work.

Author sites

Many children's authors and illustrators have websites. Dav Pikey, Virginia Hamilton and Jan Brett, for example, have interesting ones. For links to these sites, go to the Children's Literature Web Guide at www.acs.ucalgary.ca/~dkbrown/authors.html or Kay Vandergrift's Learning about the Author and Illustrator Pages at www.scils.rutgers.edu/special.kay/author.html. For scheduled chats with authors, go to Scholastic's Authors Online site: teacher.scholastic.com/authorsandbooks/authors/index.htm.

Corporate websites.

These sites sometimes have useful information for teachers. For example, look at www.crayola.com.

ALPHABETICAL INDEX

Events are generally listed under key words; events that can be attended are also listed under the states or countries where they are to be held. Many broad categories have been created, including African American, Agriculture, Animals, Aviation, Books, Civil Rights, Civil War, Computer, Constitution, Disabled, Earthquakes, Education, Employment, Environment, Ethnic Observances, Fire, Food and Beverages, Health and Welfare, Human Relations, Library/Librarians, Literature, Music, Native American, Parades, Poetry, Reading, Revolution (American), Safety, Science/Technology, Space Milestones, Storytelling, Television, Time, United Nations, United States, World War I, World War II, Women, names of sports, etc. The index indicates only the initial date for each event. See the chronology for inclusive dates of events lasting more than one day.

Bluford, Guion S., Jr: Birth, Nov 22
Blumberg, Rhoda: Birth, Dec 14
Blume, Judy: Birth, Feb 12
Bly, Nellie: Around the World in 72 Days: Anniv, Nov 14
Bly, Nellie: Birth Anniv, May 5
Boats, Ships, Things That Float
  First American to Circumnavigate Earth: Anniv, Apr 10
  Fulton Sails Steamboat: Anniv, Aug 17
  Halifax, Nova Scotia, Destroyed: Anniv, Dec 6
  Historical Regatta (Italy), Sept 3
  Safe Boating Week, Natl, May 19
  Safe Boating Week, Natl (Pres Proc), May 19
Bodkin, Odds: Birth, Feb 14
Boer War: Anniv, Oct 12
Boggs, Wade: Birth, June 15
Boitano, Brian: Birth, Oct 22
Bolivar, Simon: Birth Anniv, July 24
Bolivia
  Alacitis Fair, Jan 24
  Independence Day, Aug 6
Bologna Intl Children's Book Fair (Italy), Apr 4
Bombing, Oklahoma City: Anniv, Apr 19
Bon Fest (Feast of Lanterns) (Japan), July 13
Bonaparte, Napoleon: Birth Anniv, Aug 15
Bond, Christopher Samuel: Birth, Mar 6
Bond, Michael: Birth, Jan 13
Bond, Nancy: Birth, Jan 8
Bonds, Barry: Birth, July 24
Bonners, Susan: Birth, Apr 8
Bonsall, Brian: Birth, Dec 3
Bonza Bottler Day, Jan 1
Bonza Bottler Day, Feb 2
Bonza Bottler Day, Mar 3
Bonza Bottler Day, Apr 4
Bonza Bottler Day, May 5
Bonza Bottler Day, June 6
Bonza Bottler Day, July 7
Bonza Bottler Day, Aug 8
Bonza Bottler Day, Sept 9
Bonza Bottler Day, Oct 10
Bonza Bottler Day, Nov 11
Bonza Bottler Day, Dec 12
Books. See also Library/Librarians
  African American Read-In, Feb 4
  Authors' Day, Natl, Nov 1
  Banned Books Week, Sept 23
  Bible Week, Natl, Nov 19
  Biographers Day, May 16
  Bologna Intl Children's Book Fair (Italy), Apr 4
  Book Day (Spain), Apr 23
  Book It! Reading Incentive Program, Oct 1
  Book Month, Natl, Jan 1
  Children's Book Day, Intl, Apr 2
  Children's Book Week, Natl, Nov 13
  Children's Literature Festival (Warrensburg, MO), Mar 18
  Copyright Law Passed: Anniv, May 31
  Dia de los Niños/Dia de los Libros, Apr 30
  Dictionary Day, Oct 16
  Fest of Books for Young People (Iowa City, IA), Nov 4
  First Dictionary of American English Published: Anniv, Apr 14
  Get Caught Reading Month, May 1
  Guadalajara Intl Book Fair, Nov 25
  Jewish Book Month, Nov 4
  Literacy Day, Intl, Sept 8
  Los Angeles Latino Book and Family Fest, Aug 26
  Paperback Books Introduced: Anniv, July 30
  Reach Out & Read Week, Apr 15
  Read Across America Day, Mar 2
  Read In, May 10
  Read to Your Child Day, Feb 14
  Reading Is Fun Week, Apr 22
  Return the Borrowed Books Week, Mar 1
  Southern Fest of Books (Nashville, TN), Oct 13
  Spotlight On Books (Alexandria, MN), Mar 1
  Teen Read Week, Oct 15
  World Book and Copyright Day (UN), Apr 23
  Young Reader's Day, Natl, Nov 8
Boone, Daniel: Birth Anniv, Nov 2
Borden, Sir Robert Laird: Birth Anniv, June 26
Boreanaz, David: Birth, May 16
Borglum, Gutzon: Birth Anniv, Mar 25
Bosch, Johnny Yong: Birth, Jan 6

Bosnia and Herzegovina
  Independence Day, Mar 1
Boston Massacre: Anniv, Mar 5
Boston Public Library: Anniv, Apr 3
Boston Tea Party, Reenactment of (Boston, MA), Dec 17
Boston Tea Party: Anniv, Dec 16
Botswana
  Independence Day, Sept 30
Bounty, Mutiny on the: Anniv, Apr 28
Bowman, Jessica: Birth, Nov 26
Boxer, Barbara: Birth, Nov 11
Boxing
  Clay Becomes Heavyweight Champ: Anniv, Feb 25
Boxing Day (United Kingdom), Dec 26
Boy Scouts: Baden-Powell, Robert: Birth Anniv, Feb 22
Boy Scouts of America Anniv Week, Feb 4
Boy Scouts of America Founded: Anniv, Feb 8
Boycott, Charles C.: Birth Anniv, Mar 12
Boys' Clubs Founded: Anniv, May 19
Bradbury, Ray: Birth, Aug 22
Bradford, William: Birth Anniv, Mar 19
Bradley, Shawn: Birth, Mar 22
Brady Bunch TV Premiere, The: Anniv, Sept 26
Brady, Irene: Birth, Dec 29
Brady, Mathew: First Presidential Photograph: Anniv, Feb 14
Braille, Louis: Birth Anniv, Jan 4
Brandeis, Louis D.: Birth Anniv, Nov 13
Brandis, Jonathan: Birth, Apr 13
Brandy (Norwood): Birth, Feb 11
Branscum, Robbie: Birth Anniv, June 17
Braxton, Carter: Birth Anniv, Sept 10
Brazil
  Carnival, Feb 24
  Discovery of Brazil Day, Apr 22
  Independence Day, Sept 7
  Independence Week, Sept 1
  Nosso Senhor Do Bonfim Fest, Jan 20
  Republic Day, Nov 15
  Tiradentes Day, Apr 21
Breathed, Berke. Birth, June 21
Breaux, John B.: Birth, Mar 1
Breckinridge, John Cabell: Birth Anniv, Jan 21
Brendon, Nicholas: Birth, Apr 12
Brett, George: Birth, May 15
Brett, Jan: Birth, Dec 1
Breyer, Stephen G.: Birth, Aug 15
Bridwell, Norman: Birth, Feb 15
Brink, Carol Ryrie: Birth Anniv, Dec 28
British North America Act: Anniv, Mar 29
Brittain, Bill: Birth, Dec 16
Broderick, Beth: Birth, Feb 24
Broderick, Matthew: Birth, Mar 21
Brooklyn Bridge Opened: Anniv, May 24
Brooks, Bruce: Birth, Sept 23
Brooks, Garth: Birth, Feb 7
Brooks, Gwendolyn: Birth, June 7
Brotherhood/Sisterhood Week, Feb 19
Brower, Jordan: Birth, Oct 14
Brown, Curtis, Jr: Birth, Mar 11
Brown, Jesse Leroy: Birth Anniv, Oct 13
Brown, John: Birth Anniv, May 9
Brown, John: Raid Anniv, Oct 16
Brown, Louise: First Test Tube Baby Birth, July 25
Brown, Marc: Birth, Nov 25
Brown, Marcia: Birth, July 13
Brown, Margaret Wise: Birth Anniv, May 23
Brown, Tim: Birth, July 22
Brownback, Sam: Birth, Sept 12
Browne, Anthony: Birth, Sept 11
Browning, Elizabeth Barrett: Birth Anniv, Mar 6
Browning, Robert: Birth Anniv, May 7
Bruchac, Joseph: Birth, Oct 16
Brunei
  National Day, Feb 23
Brunhoff, Jean de: Birth Anniv, Dec 9
Bryan, Ashley: Birth, July 13
Bryan, Richard H.: Birth, July 16
Bryan, Zachery Ty: Birth, Oct 9
Bryant, Kobe: Birth, Aug 23
Buchanan, James: Birth Anniv, Apr 23
Buck, Pearl: Birth Anniv, June 26

Buckle Up America! Week, May 21
Buddha: Birth Anniv, Apr 8
Buffalo Bill (William F. Cody): Birth Anniv, Feb 26
Buffalo Hunt, Last Great: Anniv, June 25
Bulgaria
  Enlightenment and Culture Day, May 24
  Hristo Botev Day, June 2
  Liberation Day, Mar 3
  Saint Lasarus's Day, Apr 1
Bulla, Clyde Robert: Birth, Jan 9
Bullfinch Exchange Fest (Japan), Jan 7
Bun Day (Iceland), Feb 26
Bunche, Ralph: Awarded Nobel Peace Prize: Anniv, Dec 10
Bunche, Ralph: Birth Anniv, Aug 7
Bunker Hill Day (MA), June 17
Bunning, Jim: Birth, Oct 23
Bunting, Eve: Birth, Dec 19
Buonarroti Simoni, Michelangelo: Birth Anniv, Mar 6
Burbank, Luther: Birth Anniv, Mar 7
Burch, Robert: Birth, June 26
Bure, Candace Cameron: Birth, Apr 6
Bureau of Indian Affairs Established, Mar 11
Burger, Warren E.: Birth Anniv, Sept 17
Burk, Martha (Calamity Jane): Death Anniv, Aug 1
Burkina Faso
  National Day, Dec 11
  Republic Day, Aug 5
Burleigh, Robert: Birth, Jan 4
Burnett, Frances Hodgson: Birth Anniv, Nov 24
Burns, Conrad: Birth, Jan 25
Burns, Steven: Birth, Oct 9
Burr, Aaron: Birth Anniv, Feb 6
Burrise, Nakia: Birth, Oct 21
Burroughs, Edgar Rice: Birth Anniv, Sept 1
Bursting Day (Iceland), Feb 27
Burton, LeVar: Birth, Feb 16
Burton, Tim: Birth, Aug 25
Burton, Virginia Lee: Birth Anniv, Aug 30
Burundi
  Independence Day, July 1
Bush, Barbara Pierce: Birth, June 8
Bush, George: Birth, June 12
Bush, George W.: Birth, July 6
Bush, Jeb: Birth, Feb 11
Business: AT&T Divestiture: Anniv, Jan 8
Business Week, Small (Pres Proc), June 3
Butcher, Susan: Birth, Dec 26
Butts, Alfred M.: Birth Anniv, Apr 13
Buy Nothing Day, Nov 24
Byars, Betsy: Birth, Aug 7
Bye, Karyn: Birth, May 18
Bynes, Amanda: Birth, Apr 3
Byrd, Robert C.: Birth, Nov 20
Cabbage Patch Dolls Debuted: Anniv, Oct 7
Cabrillo Day (CA), Sept 28
Cain, Dean: Birth, July 31
Caine, Michael: Birth, Mar 14
Calamity Jane (Martha Burk): Death Anniv, Aug 1
Caldecott, Randolph: Birth Anniv, Mar 22
Calendar Adjustment Day: Anniv, Sept 2
Calendar Day, Gregorian, Feb 24
Calendar Stone, Aztec, Discovery: Anniv, Dec 17
Calhoun, John C.: Birth Anniv, Mar 18
Calhoun, Mary: Birth, Aug 3
California
  Admission Day, Sept 9
  Cabrillo Day, Sept 28
  California Gold Discovery: Anniv, Jan 24
  California State Fair (Sacramento), Aug 18
  Cesar Chavez Day, Mar 31
  Disneyland Opened: Anniv, July 17
  Education Assn Mtg, Natl (Los Angeles), July 1
  Golden Gate Bridge Opened: Anniv, May 27
  Laura Ingalls Wilder Gingerbread Sociable (Pomona), Feb 3
  Los Angeles Founded: Anniv, Sept 4
  Los Angeles Latino Book and Family Fest, Aug 26
  Pasadena Doo Dah Parade (Pasadena), Nov 26
  Redwood Natl Park: Anniv, Oct 2
  Rose Bowl Game (Pasadena), Jan 1

Maryland Day, **Mar 25**
Ratification Day, **Apr 28**
State Fair (Timonium), **Aug 25**
Marzollo, Jean: Birth, June 24
Masih, Iqbal: Death Anniv, Apr 16
Massachusetts
American Council on Teaching of Foreign
Languages (Boston), **Nov 17**
Basketball Hall of Fame Enshrinement
(Springfield), **Oct 7**
Big E (West Springfield), **Sept 15**
Boston Public Library: Anniv, **Apr 3**
Bunker Hill Day, **June 17**
Children's Day, **June 10**
Civil Rights Week, **Dec 8**
Deborah Samson Day, **May 23**
Evacuation Day, **Mar 17**
First Women's Collegiate Basketball Game:
Anniv, **Mar 22**
John Carver Day, **June 24**
John F. Kennedy Day, **Nov 26**
Keep Massachusetts Beautiful Month, **May 1**
Native American Day, **Sept 15**
Patriot's Day, **Apr 16**
Ratification Day, **Feb 6**
Reenactment of Boston Tea Party (Boston),
Dec 17
Samuel Slater Day, **Dec 20**
School Principals' Recognition Day, **Apr 27**
State Constitution Day, **Oct 25**
Student Government Day, **Apr 6**
Supervision and Curriculum Development, Assn
for, Conf (Boston), **Mar 17**
Teacher's Day, **June 3**
Whale Awareness Day, **May 3**
MATHCOUNTS, Sept 15
Mathematics Education Month, Apr 1
**Mathematics, Natl Council of Teachers of,
Annual Mtg (Chicago, IL), Apr 12**
Mathers, Jerry: Birth, June 2
Mathis, Sharon Bell: Birth, Feb 26
Matisse, Henri: Birth Anniv, Dec 31
Maundy Thursday (Holy Thursday), Apr 12
Mauritania
Independence Day, **Nov 28**
Mauritius
Independence Day, **Mar 12**
**Mawlid al Nabi: Birthday of Prophet
Muhammad, June 4**
Maxwell, Gavin: Birth Anniv, July 15
May Day, May 1
Mayer, Mercer: Birth, Dec 30
Mayflower Day, Sept 16
Mayne, William: Birth, Mar 16
Mays, Willie: Birth, May 6
Mazer, Harry: Birth, May 31
Mazer, Norma Fox: Birth, May 15
**Mazowiecki, Tadeusz: Poland: Solidarity
Founded, Aug 31**
McArdle, Andrea: Birth, Nov 4
McAuliffe, Christa: Birth Anniv, Sept 2
McBride, Brian: Birth, June 19
McCaffrey, Anne: Birth, Apr 1
McCain, John Sidney, III: Birth, Aug 29
McCarthy, Andrew: Birth, Nov 29
McCartney, Paul: Birth, June 18
McClintock, Barbara: Birth, May 6
McCloskey, Robert: Birth, Sept 15
McConnell, Mitch: Birth, Feb 20
McCully, Emily Arnold: Birth, July 1
McDermott, Gerald: Birth, Jan 31
**McDonald's Invades the Soviet Union: Anniv,
Jan 31**
McGovern, Ann: Birth, May 25
McGraw, Eloise: Birth, Dec 9
McGuffey, William H.: Birth Anniv, Sept 23
McGwire Hits 62nd Home Run: Anniv, Sept 8
McGwire Hits 70th Home Run: Anniv, Sept 27
McGwire, Mark: Birth, Oct 1
McKay, Hillary: Birth, June 12
McKean, Thomas: Birth Anniv, Mar 19
McKinley, Ida Saxton: Birth Anniv, June 8
McKinley, Robin: Birth, Nov 16
McKinley, William: Birth Anniv, Jan 29
McKissack, Fredrick: Birth, Aug 12
McKissack, Patricia: Birth, Aug 9
McLean, A.J.: Birth, Jan 9
McMillan, Bruce: Birth, May 10
McMullan, Kate: Birth, Jan 16
McNabb, Donovan: Birth, Nov 25

McPhail, David: Birth, June 30
**Media: World Summit on Media for Children
(Thessaloniki, Greece), Mar 11**
**Medical School for Women Opened: Anniv,
Nov 1**
Mtg of the Electors, Dec 18
Meltzer, Milton: Birth, May 8
Memorial Day, Confederate (FL, GA), Apr 26
Memorial Day, Confederate (VA), May 28
Memorial Day (Observed), May 28
Memorial Day (Pres Proc), May 28
Mental Health Month, Natl, May 1
Mental Retardation Awareness Month, Mar 1
Mercator, Gerhardus: Birth Anniv, Mar 5
Merchant, Natalie: Birth, Oct 26
**Meredith (James) Enrolls at Ole Miss: Anniv,
Sept 30**
Merriam, Eve: Birth Anniv, July 19
Mesmer, Friedrich: Birth Anniv, May 23
Messier, Mark: Birth, Jan 18
Meteor Showers, Perseid, Aug 9
Meteorological Day, World (UN), Mar 23
Metric Conversion Act: Anniv, Dec 23
Metric System Developed: Anniv, Apr 7
Metric Week, Natl, Oct 8
**Mexican-American: Day of the Teacher (El Dia
Del Maestro), May 9**
Mexico
Anniv of Constitution, **Feb 5**
Aztec Calendar Stone Discovery: Anniv,
Dec 17
Blessing of Animals at the Cathedral, **Jan 17**
Cinco de Mayo, **May 5**
Cortes Conquers Mexico: Anniv, **Nov 8**
Day of the Dead, **Nov 1**
Day of the Holy Cross, **May 3**
Dia de la Candelaria, **Feb 2**
Dia de la Raza, **Oct 12**
Feast of the Radishes (Oaxaca), **Dec 23**
Guadalajara Intl Book Fair, **Nov 25**
Guadalupe Day, **Dec 12**
Independence Day, **Sept 16**
Juarez, Benito: Birth Anniv, **Mar 21**
Mexico City Earthquake: Anniv, **Sept 19**
Posadas, **Dec 16**
Revolution Anniv, **Nov 20**
San Isidro Day, **May 15**
Treaty of Guadalupe Hidalgo (with US): Anniv,
Feb 2
Zapatista Rebellion: Anniv, **Jan 1**
Mfume, Kweisi: Birth, Oct 24
Michigan
Admission Day, **Jan 26**
Michigan Storytellers Fest (Flint), **July 5**
Michigan Thanksgiving Parade (Detroit),
Nov 23
Month of the Young Child, **Apr 1**
State Fair (Detroit), **Aug 22**
Michaelmas, Sept 29
Michelangelo: Birth Anniv, Mar 6
**Michelson, Albert: First US Scientist Receives
Nobel: Anniv, Dec 10**
Mickey Mouse Club TV Premiere: Anniv, Oct 3
Mickey Mouse's Birthday, Nov 18
**Micronesia, Federated States of:
Independence Day, Nov 3**
Microsoft Releases Windows: Anniv, Nov 10
Middle Level Education Month, Natl, Mar 1
**Middle School Assn, Natl, Annual Conf (St.
Louis, MO), Nov 2**
Middleton, Arthur: Birth Anniv, June 26
Midori: Birth, Oct 25
Midsummer Day/Eve Celebrations, June 23
Midwife's Day (Greece), Jan 8
**Mighty Mouse Playhouse TV Premiere: Anniv,
Dec 10**
Mikulski, Barbara Ann: Birth, July 20
**Mikulski, Barbara: Polish-American in the
House: Anniv, Jan 4**
Milano, Alyssa: Birth, Dec 19
Miles, Miska: Birth Anniv, Nov 14
Millennium Summit: See UN, Sept 6
Miller, Jeremy: Birth, Oct 21
Miller, Reggie: Birth, Aug 24
Million Man March: Anniv, Oct 16
Milne, A.A.: Birth Anniv (Pooh Day), Jan 18
Minarik, Else Holmelund: Birth, Sept 13
Mind Day, Make Up Your, Dec 31
Minnesota
Admission Day, **May 11**

Spotlight On Books (Alexandria), **Mar 1**
State Fair (St. Paul), **Aug 24**
Take a Kid Fishing Weekend (St. Paul), **June 9**
**Minority Enterprise Development Week (Pres
Proc), Oct 1**
**Minow, Newton: Vast Wasteland Speech:
Anniv, May 9**
Mint, US: Anniv, Apr 2
Miranda Decision: Anniv, June 13
Mischief Night, Nov 4
Missing Children's Day, Natl, May 25
Mississippi
Admission Day, **Dec 10**
Children's Book Fest (Hattiesburg), **Mar 21**
Confederate Memorial Day, **Apr 30**
Meredith (James) Enrolls at Ole Miss: Anniv,
Sept 30
State Fair (Jackson), **Oct 4**
Missouri
Admission Day, **Aug 10**
Children's Literature Fest (Warrensburg),
Mar 18
Council for Exceptional Children Annual Conv
(Kansas City), **Apr 17**
Earthquakes: Anniv, **Dec 6**
Minority Scientists Showcase (St. Louis),
Jan 13
Missouri Day, **Oct 18**
Science Teachers Assn Conv, Natl (St. Louis),
Mar 22
State Fair (Sedalia), **Aug 10**
TESOL Annual Conf (St. Louis), **Feb 27**
Tom Sawyer Days, Natl (Hannibal), **July 4**
**Mister Rogers' Neighborhood TV Premiere:
Anniv, May 22**
Mitchell, Beverly: Birth, Jan 22
Mitchell, Kel: Birth, Aug 25
Mitchell, Maria: Birth Anniv, Aug 1
Moceanu, Dominique: Birth, Sept 30
Modano, Mike: Birth, June 7
Moldova
Independence Day, **Aug 27**
Molitor, Paul: Birth, Aug 22
Mom Is a Student Day, My, Oct 15
Moment of Laughter Day, Apr 16
Monaco
National Holiday, **Nov 19**
Mondale, Fritz: Birth, Jan 5
Monday Holiday Law: Anniv, June 28
Monet, Claude: Birth Anniv, Nov 14
Money, Paper, Issued: Anniv, Mar 10
Mongolia
National Holiday, **July 11**
Monica: Birth, Oct 24
**Monkey Trial: John T. Scopes Birth Anniv,
Aug 3**
Monopoly Invented: Anniv, Mar 7
Monroe Doctrine: Anniv, Dec 2
Monroe, Elizabeth K.: Birth Anniv, June 30
Monroe, James: Birth Anniv, Apr 28
Montana
Admission Day, **Nov 8**
Battle of Little Bighorn: Anniv, **June 25**
MontanaFair (Billings), **Aug 12**
State Fair (Great Falls), **July 28**
Montana, Joe: Birth, June 11
Montessori, Maria: Birth Anniv, Aug 31
Montgolfier, Jacques: Birth Anniv, Jan 7
Montgolfier, Joseph M.: Birth Anniv, Aug 26
Montgomery Boycott Arrests: Anniv, Feb 22
**Montgomery Bus Boycott Begins: Anniv,
Dec 5**
Montgomery, Lucy Maud: Birth Anniv, Nov 30
Month of the Dinosaur, Oct 1
Month of the Young Adolescent, Oct 1
Montross, Eric Scott: Birth, Sept 23
Montserrat: Volcano Erupts: Anniv, June 25
Moon Day (First Moon Landing), July 20
Moon Fest, Sept 12
Moon, Harvest, Sept 13
Moon, Hunter's, Oct 13
Moon, Warren: Birth, Nov 18
Moore, Clement: Birth Anniv, July 15
Moore, Julianne: Birth, Dec 30
Moranis, Rick: Birth, Apr 18
**Morazan, Francisco: Holiday (Honduras),
Oct 3**
Morris, Lewis: Birth Anniv, Apr 8
Morris, Robert: Birth Anniv, Jan 31
Morse, Samuel F.: Birth Anniv, Apr 27